The New Moulton's library
of literary criticism /

The

CHELSEA HOUSE LIBRARY
of LITERARY CRITICISM

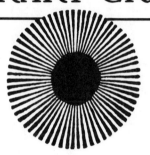

The

CHELSEA HOUSE LIBRARY
of LITERARY CRITICISM

The
NEW MOULTON'S
LIBRARY *of* LITERARY CRITICISM

Volume 8

Mid-Victorian

General Editor

HAROLD BLOOM

1989
CHELSEA HOUSE PUBLISHERS
NEW YORK
NEW HAVEN   PHILADELPHIA

MANAGING EDITOR
S. T. Joshi

ASSISTANT EDITOR
Jack Bishop

EDITORIAL COORDINATOR
Karyn Gullen Browne

COPY CHIEF
Richard Fumosa

EDITORIAL STAFF
Jacques L. Denis
Susanne E. Rosenberg

RESEARCH
Ann Bartunek
Anthony C. Coulter

PICTURE RESEARCH
Monica Gannon

DESIGN
Susan Lusk

3   5   7   9   8   6   4   2

Library of Congress Cataloging in Publication
Data

The New Moulton's library of literary criticism.
    (The Chelsea House library of literary criti-
    cism)
    Cover title: The New Moulton's.
    Rev. ed. of: Moulton's library of literary
    criticism.
    Contents: v. 1. Medieval—early Renaissance.
v. 8. Mid-Victorian.
    1. English literature—History and criticism—
Collected works. 2. American literature—
History and criticism—Collected works.
I. Bloom, Harold. II. Moulton's library of liter-
ary criticism
PR85.N39   1985   820'.9   84-27429
ISBN 0-87754-779-3 (v. 1)
      0-87754-786-6 (v. 8)

CONTENTS

The Index to this series, *The New Moulton's Library*, appears in Volume 11.

ILLUSTRATIONS

EDGAR ALLAN POE

1809–1849

Edgar Allan Poe was born Edgar Poe in Boston on January 19, 1809, the son of traveling actors. Shortly after his birth his father disappeared, and in 1811 his mother died. He was taken into the home of John Allan (from whom Poe derived his middle name), a wealthy merchant living in Richmond, Virginia. In 1815 the Allans took Poe to England, where he attended the Manor House School at Stoke Newington, later the setting for his story "William Wilson." Poe returned to Richmond with the Allans in 1820. In 1826 he became engaged to Elmira Royster, whose parents broke off the engagement. That fall he entered the University of Virginia. At first he excelled in his studies, but in December 1826 he was taken out of school by John Allan after accumulating considerable gambling debts which Allan refused to pay. Unable to honor these debts himself, Poe fled to Boston, where he enlisted in the army under the name of Edgar A. Perry.

Poe began his literary career with the anonymous publication of *Tamerlane and Other Poems* (1827) at his own expense. In 1829 he was honorably discharged from the army. Later that year he published a second collection of verse, *Al Aaraaf, Tamerlane, and Minor Poems*, containing revisions of poems from his first collection as well as new material. This volume was well received, leading to a tentative reconciliation with John Allan. In 1830 Poe entered West Point, but after another falling out with John Allan, who withdrew his financial support, Poe deliberately got himself expelled in 1831 through flagrant neglect of his duties. Nonetheless, he managed before leaving to gather enough cadet subscriptions to bring out his third collection of verse, *Poems* (1831). In 1833 Poe's final attempt at reconciliation was rejected by the ailing John Allan, who died in 1834 without mentioning Poe in his will.

In the meantime Poe's literary career was progressing satisfactorily. In 1833 he had won a prize from the *Baltimore Saturday Visitor* for one of his first short stories, "MS. Found in a Bottle," and in 1835 he was hired as editor of the recently established *Southern Literary Messenger*, which thrived under his direction. In 1836 Poe felt financially secure enough to marry Virginia Clemm, his fourteen-year-old cousin, but later that year he was fired from the *Messenger*, partly because of what appeared to be chronic alcoholism. In fact, Poe seems to have suffered from a physical ailment that rendered him so sensitive to alcohol that a single drink could induce a drunken state. Poe was later an editor of *Burton's Gentleman's Magazine* (1839–40), *Graham's Magazine* (1841–42), and the *Broadway Journal* (1845–46). In this capacity he wrote many important reviews—notably of Hawthorne, Dickens, and Macaulay—and occasionally gained notoriety for the severity and acerbity of his judgments. In particular he wrote a series of polemics against Henry Wadsworth Longfellow, whom he accused of plagiarism.

Meanwhile Poe continued to write fiction voluminously. His longest tale, *The Narrative of Arthur Gordon Pym* (apparently unfinished), appeared in 1838; *Tales of the Grotesque and Arabesque*, containing "The Fall of the House of Usher" and other important stories, was published in 1840; and *Tales* appeared in 1845. As a fiction writer Poe wrote not only tales of the macabre and the supernatural ("The Pit and the Pendulum," "The Black Cat," "The Tell-Tale Heart," "Ligeia") but also many humorous or parodic pieces ("King Pest," "Some Words with a Mummy"), prose poems ("Silence—a Fable," "Shadow—a Parable"), and what are generally considered the first true detective stories: "The Murders in the Rue Morgue" (1841), "The Gold-Bug" (1843), "The Purloined Letter" (1845), and others.

In 1844 Poe moved to New York, and in the following year achieved international fame with his poem "The Raven," published in *The Raven and Other Poems* (1845). In 1847 Poe's wife Virginia, who had been seriously ill since 1842, died, leaving Poe desolate. For the few remaining years of his life he helped support himself by delivering a series of public lectures, including "The Poetic Principle" (published posthumously in 1850). Among his publications were the philosophical treatise *Eureka: A Prose Poem* (1848) and the lyric "Annabel Lee" (1849). His *Marginalia* was published serially from 1844 to 1849. After his wife's death Poe had several romances, including an affair with the Rhode Island poet Sarah Helen Whitman, and in 1849 he became engaged for a second time to Elmira Royster (then Mrs. Shelton). Before they could be married, however, Poe died in Baltimore on October 7, 1849, under mysterious circumstances.

In spite of the fact that Poe's memory was damned by his posthumous editor Rufus Wilmot Griswold, who propagated many long-standing myths about his alcoholism and misanthropy, Poe was one of the first American authors to be widely appreciated in Europe. He had a great influence on the development of French Symbolism, much of his work being translated by Baudelaire and Mallarmé. In England he was greatly admired by such figures as Swinburne, Wilde, and Rossetti.

Personal

From childhood's hour I have not been
As others were—I have not seen
As others saw—I could not bring
My passions from a common spring—
From the same source I have not taken
My sorrow—I could not awaken
My heart to joy at the same tone—
And all I lov'd—*I* lov'd alone—
Then—in my childhood—in the dawn
Of a most stormy life—was drawn
From ev'ry depth of good and ill
The mystery which binds me still—
From the torrent, or the fountain—
From the red cliff of the mountain—
From the sun that 'round me roll'd
In its autumn tint of gold—
From the lightning in the sky
As it pass'd me flying by—
From the thunder, and the storm—
And the cloud that took the form
(When the rest of Heaven was blue)
Of a demon in my view—
—EDGAR ALLAN POE, "Alone," 1829

Edgar A. Poe (you know him by character, no doubt, if not personally), has become one of the strangest of our literati. He and I are old friends,—have known each other since boyhood, and it gives me inexpressible pain to notice the vagaries to which he has lately become subject. Poor fellow! he is not a teetotaller by any means, and I fear he is going headlong to destruction, moral, physical and intellectual.—L. A. WILMER, Letter to Mr. Tomlin (May 20, 1843), cited in *Passages from the Correspondence and Other Papers of Rufus W. Griswold*, ed. W. M. Griswold, 1898, p. 143

My Dear Heart, My dear Virginia! our Mother will explain to you why I stay away from you this night. I trust the interview I am promised, will result in some *substantial good* for me, for your dear sake, and hers—Keep up your heart in all hopefulness, and trust yet a little longer—In my last great disappointment, I should have lost my courage *but for you*—my little darling wife you are my *greatest* and *only* stimulus now. to battle with this uncongenial, unsatisfactory and ungrateful life—I shall be with you tomorrow P.M. and be assured until I see you, I will keep in *loving remembrance* your *last words* and your fervant prayer!—EDGAR ALLAN POE, Letter to Virginia Poe (June 12, 1846)

Edgar Allan Poe is dead. He died in Baltimore the day before yesterday. This announcement will startle many, but few will be grieved by it. The poet was well known personally or by reputation, in all this country; he had readers in England, and in several of the states of Continental Europe; but he had few or no friends; and the regrets for his death will be suggested principally by the consideration that in him literary art lost one of its most brilliant, but erratic stars. ⟨. . .⟩

The character of Mr. Poe we cannot attempt to describe in this very hastily written article. We can but allude to some of the more striking phases.

His conversation was at times almost supra-mortal in its eloquence. His voice was modulated with astonishing skill, and his large and variably expressive eyes looked repose or shot fiery tumult into theirs who listened, while his own face glowed or was changeless in pallor, as his imagination quickened his blood, or drew it back frozen to his heart. His imagery was from the worlds which no mortal can see but with the vision of genius. Suddenly starting from a proposition exactly and sharply defined in terms of utmost simplicity and clearness, he rejected the forms of customary logic, and in a crystalline process of accretion, built up his ocular demonstrations in forms of gloomiest and ghostliest grandeur, or in those of the most airy and delicious beauty, so minutely, and so distinctly, yet so rapidly, that the attention which was yielded to him was chained till it stood among his wonderful creations—till he himself dissolved the spell, and brought his hearers back to common and base existence, by vulgar fancies or by exhibitions of the ignoble passions.

He was at times a dreamer—dwelling in ideal realms—in heaven or hell, peopled with creations and the accidents of his brain. He walked the streets, in madness or melancholy, with lips moving in indistinct curses, or with eyes upturned in passionate prayers, (never for himself, for he felt, or professed to feel, that he was already damned but for their happiness who at that moment were objects of his idolatry); or with his glance introverted to a heart gnawed with anguish, and with a face shrouded in gloom, he would brave the wildest storms; and all night, with drenched garments and arms wildly beating the wind and rain, he would speak as if to spirits that at such times only could be evoked by him from that Aidenn close by whose portals his disturbed soul sought to forget the ills to which his constitution subjected him—close by that Aidenn where were those he loved—the Aidenn which he might never see but in fitful glimpses, as its gates opened to receive the less fiery and more happy natures whose listing to sin did not involve the doom of death. He seemed, except when some fitful pursuit subjected his will and engrossed his faculties, always to bear the memory of some controlling sorrow. The remarkable poem of "The Raven" was probably much more nearly than has been supposed, even by those who were very intimate with him, a reflection and an echo of his own history. He was the bird's

> unhappy master,
> Whom unmerciful disaster
> Followed fast and followed faster
> Till his song the burden bore—
> Melancholy burden bore
> Of "Nevermore," of "Nevermore."

Every genuine author in a greater or less degree leaves in his works, whatever their design, traces of his personal character; elements of his immortal being, in which the individual survives the person. While we read the pages of the "Fall of the House of Usher," or of "Mesmeric Revelation," we see in the solemn and stately gloom which invests one, and in the subtle metaphysical analysis of both, indications of the idiosyncracies,—of what was most peculiar—in the author's intellectual nature. But we see here only the better phases of this nature, only the symbols of his juster action, for his harsh experience had deprived him of all faith in man or woman.

He had made up his mind upon the numberless complexities of the social world, and the whole system was with him an imposture. This conviction gave a direction to his shrewd and naturally unamiable character. Still though he regarded society as composed of villains, the sharpness of his intellect was not of that kind which enabled him to cope with villainy, while it continually caused him overshots, to fail of the success of honesty. He was in many respects like Francis Vivian in Bulwer's novel of the *Caxtons*. Passion, in him, comprehended many of the worst emotions which militate against human happiness. You could not contradict him, but you raised quick choler; you could not speak of wealth, but his cheek paled with gnawing envy. The astonishing natural advantage of this poor boy—his beauty, his readiness, the daring spirit that breathed around him like a fiery atmosphere—had raised his constitutional self-confidence into an arrogance that turned his very claims to admiration into prejudice against him. Irascible, envious—bad enough, but not the worst, for these salient angles were all varnished over with a cold repellant cynicism while his passions vented themselves in sneers. There seemed to him no moral susceptibility; and what was more remarkable in a proud nature, little or nothing of the true point of honor. He had, to a morbid excess, that desire to rise which is vulgarly called ambition, but no wish for the esteem or the love of his species; only the hard wish to succeed—not shine, not serve—succeed, that he might have the right to despise a world which galled his self-conceit.—RUFUS WILMOT GRISWOLD, *New York Tribune*, Oct. 9, 1849

I am not deceived in you, you *still* wish your poor desolate friend to come to you. . . . I have written to poor Elmira, and have to wait for her answer. They are already making arrangements to publish the works of my *darling lost one*. I have been waited on by several gentlemen, and have finally arranged with Mr. Griswold to arrange and bring them out, and he wishes it done immediately. Mr. Willis is to share with him this labour of love. They say I am to have the *entire* proceeds, so you see, Annie, I will not be entirely destitute. I have had many letters of condolence, and one which has, indeed, comforted me. Neilson Poe, of Baltimore, has written to me, and says he died in the Washington Medical College, not the Hospital, and of congestion of the brain, and not of what the vile, vile papers accuse him. He had many kind friends with him, and was attended to the grave by the literati of Baltimore, and many friends. *Severe excitement* (and no doubt some imprudence) brought this on; he never had one interval of reason. I cannot tell you all now. . . . They now appreciate him and will do justice to his beloved memory. They propose to raise a monument to his memory. Some of the papers, indeed, nearly all, do him justice. I enclose this article from a Baltimore paper. But this, my dear Annie, will not restore him. Never, oh, never, will I see those dear lovely eyes. I feel *so desolate, so wretched, friendless, and alone.* . . . I have a beautiful letter from General Morris; he did, indeed, love him. He has many friends, but of what little consequence to him *now*.—MARIA CLEMM, Letter to "Annie" (Oct. 13, 1849), cited in John H. Ingram, *Edgar Allan Poe: His Life, Letters, and Opinions*, 1880, Vol. 2, pp. 239–40

Some four or five years since, when editing a daily paper in this city, Mr. Poe was employed by us, for several months, as critic and sub-editor. This was our first personal acquaintance with him. He resided with his wife and mother at Fordham, a few miles out of town, but was at his desk in the office from nine in the morning till the evening paper went to press. With the highest admiration for his genius, and a willingness to let it atone for more than ordinary irregularity, we were led by common report to expect a very capricious attention to his duties, and occasionally a scene of violence and difficulty. Time went on, however, and he was invariably punctual and industrious. With his pale, beautiful, and intellectual face as a reminder of what genius was in him, it was impossible, of course, not to treat him always with deferential courtesy, and to our occasional request that he would not probe too deep in a criticism, or that he would erase a passage colored too highly with his resentments against society and mankind, he readily and courteously assented,—far more yielding than most men, we thought, on points so excusably sensitive. With a prospect

of taking the lead in another periodical, he at last voluntarily gave up his employment with us, and through all this considerable period we had seen but one presentment of the man,—a quiet, patient, industrious, and most gentlemanly person, commanding the utmost respect and good feeling by his unvarying deportment and ability.

Residing as he did in the country, we never met Mr. Poe in hours of leisure; but he frequently called on us afterwards at our place of business, and we met him often in the street,—invariably the same sad-mannered, winning, and refined gentleman such as we had always known him. It was by rumor only, up to the day of his death, that we knew of any other development of manner or character. We heard, from one who knew him well (what should be stated in all mention of his lamentable irregularities), that, with a *single glass* of wine, his whole nature was reversed, the demon became uppermost, and, though none of the usual signs of intoxication were visible, his *will* was palpably insane. Possessing his reasoning faculties in excited activity at such times, and seeking his acquaintances with his wonted look and memory, he easily seemed personating only another phase of his natural character, and was accused, accordingly, of insulting arrogance and bad-heartedness. In this reversed character, we repeat, it was never our chance to see him. We know it from hearsay, and we mention it in connection with this sad infirmity of physical constitution, which puts it upon very nearly the ground of a temporary and almost irresponsible insanity.

The arrogance, vanity, and depravity of heart of which Mr. Poe was generally accused seem to us referable altogether to this reversed phase of his character. Under that degree of intoxication which only acted upon him by demonizing his sense of truth and right, he doubtless said and did much that was wholly irreconcilable with his better nature; but when himself, and as we knew him only, his modesty and unaffected humility, as to his own deservings, were a constant charm to his character.—N. P. WILLIS, "Death of Edgar A. Poe" (1849), cited in *The Complete Works of Edgar Allan Poe*, ed. James A. Harrison, 1902, Vol. 1, pp. 360–62

Literature with him was religion; and he, its high-priest, with a whip of scorpions scourged the money-changers from the temple. In all else he had the docility and kind-heartedness of a child. No man was more quickly touched by a kindness—none more prompt to atone for an injury. For three or four years I knew him intimately, and for eighteen months saw him almost daily; much of the time writing or conversing at the same desk; knowing all his hopes, his fears, and little annoyances of life, as well as his high-hearted struggle with adverse fate—yet he was always the same polished gentleman—the quiet, unobtrusive, thoughtful scholar—the devoted husband—frugal in his personal expenses—punctual and unwearied in his industry—*and the soul of honor*, in all his transactions. This, of course, was in his better days, and by them *we* judge the man. ⟨. . .⟩

I shall never forget how solicitous of the happiness of his wife and mother-in-law he was, whilst one of the editors of *Graham's Magazine*—his whole efforts seemed to be to procure the comfort and welfare of his home. Except for their happiness—and the natural ambition of having a magazine of his own—I never heard him deplore the want of wealth. The truth is, he cared little for money, and knew less of its value, for he seemed to have no personal expenses. What he received from me in regular monthly instalments, went directly into the hands of his mother-in-law for family comforts—and *twice* only, I remember his purchasing some rather expensive luxuries for his house, and then he was nervous to the degree of misery until he had, by extra articles, covered what he considered an imprudent indebtedness. His love for his wife was a sort of rapturous worship of the spirit of beauty which he felt was fading before his eyes. I have seen him hovering around her when she was ill, with all the fond fear and tender anxiety of a mother for her first-born—her slightest cough causing in him a shudder, a heart-chill that was visible. I rode out one summer evening with them, and the remembrance of his watchful eyes eagerly bent upon the slightest change of hue in that loved face, haunts me yet as the memory of a sad strain. It was this hourly *anticipation* of her loss, that made him a sad and thoughtful man, and lent a mournful melody to his undying song.

It is true that later in life Poe had much of those morbid feelings which a life of poverty and disappointment is so apt to engender in the heart of man—the sense of having been ill-used, misunderstood, and put aside by men of far less ability, and of none, which preys upon the heart and clouds the brain of many a child of song: A consciousness of the inequalities of life, and of the abundant power of mere wealth allied even to vulgarity, to over-ride all distinctions, and to thrust itself bedaubed with dirt and glittering with tinsel, into the high places of society, and the chief seats of the synagogue; whilst he, a worshiper of the beautiful and true, who listened to the voices of angels, and held delighted companionship with them as the cold throng swept disdainfully by him, and often in danger of being thrust out, houseless, homeless, beggared upon the world, with all his fine feelings strung to a tension of agony when he thought of his beautiful and delicate wife dying hourly before his eyes. What wonder, that he then poured out the vials of a long-treasured bitterness upon the injustice and hollowness of all society around him. ⟨. . .⟩

He was a worshiper of INTELLECT—longing to grasp the power of mind that moves the stars—to bathe his soul in the dreams of seraphs. He was himself all ethereal, of a fine essense, that moved in an atmosphere of spirits—of spiritual beauty overflowing and radiant—twin brother with the angels, feeling their flashing wings upon his heart, and almost clasping them in his embrace. Of them, and as an expectant archangel of that high order of intellect, stepping out of himself, as it were, and interpreting the time, he reveled in delicious luxury in a world beyond, with an audacity which we fear in madmen, but in genius worship as the inspiration of heaven. —GEORGE R. GRAHAM, "The Late Edgar Allan Poe" (letter to N. P. Willis, Feb. 2, 1850), *Graham's Magazine*, March 1850, pp. 225–26

We have been told by those who knew Mr. Poe well, that so weakly strung were all his nerves, that the smallest modicum of stimulant had an alarming effect upon him, and produced actions scarcely resolvable by sanity. It may be said that it is not the quantity of stimulant, but the effect produced, which constitutes the drunkard, and that Mr. Poe was as much to blame for the inebriation of a glass as of a bottle; but we would tell these cold-blooded fishes—for they are not men—that it is not given to the common-place men either to feel the raptures of poetical inspiration, or the despondency of prostrated energies. The masses are wisely, as Pope says,

Content to dwell in decencies for ever.

There is a homely verse in an old ballad which was made upon Shakespeare's masterpiece of human philosophy:

Hamlet loved a maid;
Calumny had passed her:

She never had played tricks—
Because nobody had asked her.

This rough and unconditional doggrel gives a graphic insight into the proprieties of the masses: they have neither had the impulse nor the opportunity to be indiscreet. Let our readers clearly understand we are not the apologists of Mr. Poe's errors—as Mark Antony says,

We come to bury Cæsar, not to praise him;

but, at the same time, we will not allow any undue deference to the opinion of the world.—THOMAS POWELL, "Edgar Allan Poe," *The Living Authors of America*, 1850, pp. 123–24

The peculiarities of Edgar Poe's organization and temperament doubtless exposed him to peculiar infirmities. We need not discuss them here. They have been already too elaborately and painfully illustrated elsewhere to need further comment. How fearfully he expiated them only those who best knew and loved him can ever know. We are told that ideas of right and wrong are wholly ignored by him—that "no recognitions of conscience or remorse are to be found on his pages." If not *there*, where, then, shall we look for them? In "William Wilson," in "The Man of the Crowd," and in "The Tell-Tale Heart," the retributions of conscience are portrayed with a terrible fidelity. In yet another of his stories, which we will not name, the fearful fatality of crime—the dreadful fascination consequent on the indulgence of a perverse will is portrayed with a relentless and awful reality. May none ever read it who do not need the fearful lesson which it brands on the memory in characters of fire! In the relation of this remarkable story we recognise the power of a genius like that which sustains us in traversing the lowest depths of Dante's *Inferno*. The rapid descent in crime which it delineates, and which becomes at last involuntary, reminds us of the subterranean staircase by which Vathek and Nouronihar reached the Hall of Eblis, where, as they descended, they felt their steps frightfully accelerated till they seemed falling from a precipice.

Poe's private letters to his friends offer abundant evidence that he was not insensible to the keenest pangs of remorse. Again and again did he say to the Demon that tracked his path, "Anathema Maranatha," but again and again did it return to torture and subdue. He saw the handwriting on the wall but had no power to avert the impending doom.

In relation to this, the fatal temptation of his life, he says, in a letter written within a year of his death, "The agonies which I have lately endured have passed my soul through fire. Henceforth I am strong. This those who love me shall know as well as those who have so relentlessly sought to ruin me. . . . I have absolutely *no* pleasure in the stimulants in which I sometimes so madly indulge. It has not been in the pursuit of pleasure that I have perilled life and reputation and reason. It has been in the desperate attempt to escape from torturing memories—memories of wrong and injustice and imputed dishonor—from a sense of insupportable loneliness and a dread of some strange impending doom." We believe these statements to have been sincerely uttered, and we would record here the testimony of a gentleman who, having for years known him intimately and having been near him in his states of utter mental desolation and insanity, assured us that he had never heard from his lips a word that would have disgraced his heart or brought reproach upon his honor.

Could we believe that any plea we may have urged in extenuation of Edgar Poe's infirmities and errors would make the fatal path he trod less abhorrent to others, such would never have been proffered. No human sympathy, no human charity could avert the penalties of the erring life. One clear glance into its mournful corridors—its "halls of tragedy and chambers of retribution," would appal the boldest heart.

Theodore Parker has nobly said that "every man of genius has to hew out for himself, from the hard marbles of life, the white statue of Tranquillity." Those who have best succeeded in this sublime work will best know how to look with pity and reverent awe upon the melancholy torso which alone remains to us of Edgar Poe's misguided efforts to achieve that beautiful and august statue of Peace.—SARAH HELEN WHITMAN, *Edgar Poe and His Critics*, 1860, pp. 82–85

A gushing youth once wrote me to this effect:—

> DEAR SIR: Among your literary treasures, you have doubtless preserved several autographs of our country's late lamented poet, Edgar A. Poe. If so, and you can spare one, please enclose it to me, and receive the thanks of yours truly.

I promptly responded, as follows:—

> DEAR SIR: Among my literary treasures, there happens to be exactly *one* autograph of our country's late lamented poet, Edgar A. Poe. It is his note of hand for fifty dollars, with my indorsement across the back. It cost me exactly $50.75 (including protest), and you may have it for half that amount. Yours, respectfully.

—HORACE GREELEY, *Recollections of a Busy Life*, 1868, pp. 196–97

Edgar A. Poe I remember seeing on a single occasion. He announced a lecture to be delivered at the Society Library building on Broadway, under the title of the "Universe." It was a stormy night, and there were not more than sixty persons present in the lecture-room. I have seen no portrait of Poe that does justice to his pale, delicate, intellectual face and magnificent eyes. His lecture was a rhapsody of the most intense brilliancy. He appeared inspired, and his inspiration affected the scant audience almost painfully. He wore his coat tightly buttoned across his slender chest; his eyes seemed to glow like those of his own raven, and he kept us entranced for two hours and a half. The late Mr. Putnam, the publisher, told me that the next day the wayward, luckless poet presented himself to him with the manuscript of the "Universe." He told Putnam that in it he solved the whole problem of life; that it would immortalize its publisher as well as its author; and, what was of less consequence, that it would bring to him the fortune which he had so long and so vainly been seeking. Mr. Putnam, while an admirer of genius, was also a cool, calculating man of business. As such, he could not see the matter in exactly the same light as the poet did, and the only result of the interview was that he lent Poe a shilling to take him home to Fordham, where he then resided.—MAUNSELL B. FIELD, *Memories of Many Men and Some Women*, 1873, pp. 224–25

The next number of the *Saturday Visitor* contained the "MS. Found in a Bottle," and announced the author. My office, in these days, was in the building still occupied by the Mechanics' Bank, and I was seated at my desk on the Monday following the publication of the tale, when a gentleman entered and introduced himself as the writer, saying that he came to thank me, as one of the committee, for the award in his favor. Of this interview, the only one I ever had with Mr. Poe, my recollection is very distinct indeed, and it requires but a small effort of imagination to place him before me now, as plainly almost as I see any one of my audience. He was, if anything, below the middle size, and yet could not be described as a small man. His

figure was remarkably good, and he carried himself erect and well, as one who had been trained to it. He was dressed in black, and his frock-coat was buttoned to the throat, where it met the black stock, then almost universally worn. Not a particle of white was visible. Coat, hat, boots and gloves had very evidently seen their best days, but so far as mending and brushing go, everything had been done, apparently, to make them presentable. On most men his clothes would have looked shabby and seedy, but there was something about this man that prevented one from criticising his garments, and the details I have mentioned were only recalled afterwards. The impression made, however, was that the award in Mr. Poe's favor was not inopportune. *Gentleman* was written all over him. His manner was easy and quiet, and although he came to return thanks for what he regarded as deserving them, there was nothing obsequious in what he said or did. His features I am unable to describe in detail. His forehead was high and remarkable for the great development at the temple. This was the characteristic of his head, which you noticed at once, and which I have never forgotten. The expression of his face was grave, almost sad, except when he was engaged in conversation, when it became animated and changeable. His voice, I remember, was very pleasing in its tone and well modulated, almost rhythmical, and his words were well chosen and unhesitating. Taking a seat, we conversed a while on ordinary topics, and he informed me that Mr. Kennedy, my colleague in the committee, on whom he had already called, had either given, or promised to give him, a letter to the *Southern Literary Messenger*, which he hoped would procure him employment. I asked him whether he was then occupied with any literary labor. He replied that he was engaged on a voyage to the moon, and at once went into a somewhat learned disquisition upon the laws of gravity, the height of the earth's atmosphere and the capacities of balloons, warming in his speech as he proceeded. Presently, speaking in the first person, he began the voyage, after describing the preliminary arrangements, as you will find them set forth in one of his tales, called "The Adventure of One Hans Pfaall," and leaving the earth, and becoming more and more animated, he described his sensation, as he ascended higher and higher, until, at last, he reached the point in space where the moon's attraction overcame that of the earth, when there was a sudden bouleversement of the car and a great confusion among its tenants. By this time the speaker had become so excited, spoke so rapidly, gesticulating much, that when the turn-up-side-down took place, and he clapped his hands and stamped with his foot by way of emphasis, I was carried along with him, and, for aught to the contrary that I now remember, may have fancied myself the companion of his aerial journey. The climax of the tale was the reversal I have mentioned. When he had finished his description he apologised for his excitability, which he laughed at himself. The conversation then turned upon other subjects, and soon afterward he took his leave. I never saw him more. Dr. Griswold's statement "that Mr. Kennedy accompanied him (Poe) to a clothing store and purchased for him a respectable suit, with a change of linen, and sent him to a bath," is a sheer fabrication.—JOHN H. B. LATROBE, "Reminiscences of Poe," *Edgar Allan Poe: A Memorial Volume*, ed. Sara Sigourney Rice, 1877, pp. 60–61

General

There comes Poe, with his raven, like Barnaby Rudge,
Three fifths of him genius and two fifths sheer fudge,
Who talks like a book of iambs and pentameters,
In a way to make people of common sense damn metres,

Who has written some things quite the best of their kind,
But the heart somehow seems all squeezed out by the mind.
—JAMES RUSSELL LOWELL, A *Fable for Critics*,
1848

Unquestionably he was a man of great genius. Among the *littérateurs* of his day he stands out distinctively as an original writer and thinker. In nothing did he conform to established custom. Conventionality he contemned. Thus his writings admit of no classification. And yet in his most eccentric vagaries he was always correct. The fastidious reader may look in vain, even among his earlier poems—where "wild words wander here and there"—for an offence against rhetorical propriety. He did not easily pardon solecisms in others; he committed none himself. It is remarkable too that a mind so prone to unrestrained imaginings should be capable of analytic investigation or studious research. Yet few excelled Mr. Poe in power of analysis or patient application. Such are the contradictions of the human intellect. He was an impersonated antithesis.—JOHN R. THOMPSON, "The Late Edgar A. Poe," *Southern Literary Messenger*, Nov. 1849, p. 694

It has been remarked of him that he united singularly the qualities of the Poet with the faculties of the Analyst. He wrote charming little ballads, and was a curious disentangler of evidence—criminal evidence, for instance—and fond of problems and cipher. The union is indubitable; but I scarcely think it should have been so much dwelt upon. Every man of fine intellect of the highest class includes a capacity more or less for all branches of inquiry. Carlyle was distinguished in arithmetic long before he became the Teacher which we hail him as, now. On the other hand, inventors in the regions of mechanics partake of something poetic in their inspiration. Brindley was as eccentric as Goldsmith. Watt would muse over a tea-kettle as Rousseau did over *la pervenche*, or over the lake into which he dropped sentimental tears. One very curious theory was hit upon by a solid critic a little while ago to explain Poe's two-handedness. He knew that Poe wrote fine poetry—he knew Poe made subtle calculations; and what was his inference? *Credite posteri!* He insisted that the calculating faculty was *the* fact, and that the poetry was calculation! I scarcely ever remember a more curious instance of the "cart being put before the horse"—by the ass! Nothing can be more clear, to be sure, than that Poe employed a great deal of ingenuity and calculation in the finishing of his Tales and polishing of his poems. But all this leaves the poetic inspiration pure at the bottom as the essential fact. Otherwise, if we are to make the calculating the predominant faculty, we may look out for a volume of Sonnets by Cocker! Poe has admitted us, in one of his essays, to the *genesis* of "The Raven," and has even told us which stanza he wrote first, and on what mechanical principles he managed the arrangement of the story. But surely all this presupposes the pure creative genius necessary to the conception?

Keeping the distinction in view, we shall easily see that all his Tales—analytic and other—resolve themselves into poems, instead of the poems resolving themselves into machinery. The "Gold Bug," for example, makes a most ingenious use of a cipher, but the cipher is only *materiel*. Without creative genius mere cipher is an affair for the Foreign Office—which still remains a very inferior place to Parnassus. The same remark applies to his other poetical exercises—for such they are—in Mesmerism, Physics, Circumstantial Evidence, &c. Far from being a narrow student of the details of these, he always has clearly an eye in using them to the poetic goal or result—JAMES HANNAY, "The Life and Genius of Edgar Allan Poe," *The Poetical Works of Edgar Allan Poe*, 1852, pp. xxv–xxvi

Poe's Art consisted mostly in classical imitation. Not that he exactly aped the finished refinement of Greek Art, but that, possessing the highest poetic sense—a sense made affluent by the most polished education—he essayed not exactly to create a New Epoch, but to teach a servile race of mannerists how to avoid that everlasting platitude which is the besetting sin of the Age. I do not mean, by this, that he did not possess the genius for high things; but that he chose rather to make use of already existing materials than to suffer the intellectual travail necessary to create new. I allude now more especially to the "Raven." When I say this I mean to be understood that America never produced a man—nor indeed, any other Country—who possessed a higher *sense* of the Poetic Art than he did—not that grotesqueness of abandon, any more than the bizarrerie of fantasqueness, constitutes the *true* Poetic Art. Had he lived, he would have redeemed the platitude of the Age not only from its wantonness of affection, but also from its insipid sentimentality. One of his greatest faults was, his want of profound meditation—or, what Balzac beautifully calls—*La patience Angelique du genie*.

He had the genius to conceive, but not the boldness to execute. His ideal was great, but he had not the audacity to realize it in any creation passionately tangible to the soul. It was the statue of Pygmalion without the immortal soul to animate it. He could conceive of the grandeur, invention and grace which characterized the immortal works of the Carracci family; but he wanted the passion of Claude to suffuse them with that roseate glow of vitality necessary to true Beauty. But what distinguished him above every one of his contemporaries, was, his ability to see the imperfections in which they reveled. But one of his unaccountable deficiencies was, his utter inability to see that any work, to be perfect—or even to *approach* perfection,—must be the result of an equal blending of Art and Passion—that is, the highest Passion united with the most exalted Art—the passion moulding the Art.

His Ideal of Art was Raffaelesque, as his forms were Michaelangelesque; but he wanted the Venetian vitality to give living warmth to his Picture. Like Lodovico Carracci, he possessed the power to mingle in one form all the forms of all the other Artists that had preceeded him but, being destitute of that very quality which gave him the power to create a New School—namely, Nature,—his work will not remain a Model for all.

His Art was nothing but Art, without a particle of Nature to enliven it—was wanting in the very essentials of true genius—that which makes all Art glorious—the true Shekinah of Inspiration, namely—*fortuitousness*. He was deficient in that very power which Bellari says was the peculiar characteristic of Domenichino, *delinea gli animi, colorisce la vita*—for he neither drew the soul, nor coloured the life. He possessed the grace of Albano, and the delicacy of Guido, without possessing those other vivifying qualities which made their faces look like people from Paradise.

He was rather an Ambrosial Eclecticist than the *Fons ingeniorum*, the En-Ador, or Fons Pythonis of his Age—for he lacked the *Festina lente* necessary to the *crystalline revelation of the Divine Idea*—that is, the utterable sigh of an unutterable love breathed from the depths of our souls—which is the revelation of true Poesy.

Perhaps I can better describe the nature of his mind by saying that it was *feminine* and lacked *manliness*. Nor do I mean by this that the female mind is not perfectly adapted for Poetic contemplation; but, that, where man's mind partakes of this nature, it argues an inability to achieve great things. This was not only the case with Poe, but he was the most *boyish* man that

I ever met. When I say this, I do not mean that a certain kind of *naiveté* is not necessary to Poetical composition, but that Poe did not possess it. But, what I mean by his femininness is, that he was wanting in *manly decision*. Nothing would have pleased him better than being considered the Hero of Dante's *Inferno* for he was always, in imagination, at least, making toilsome Pilgrimages through the dim Regions of Pluto.—THOMAS HOLLEY CHIVERS, *New Life of Edgar Allan Poe*, c. 1857

> Such as into Himself at last eternity changes
> him, the Poet stirs with a naked sword
> his century dismayed to have ingored
> that death still triumphed in this voice so strange!
>
> With a hydra-spasm, once hearing the angel endow
> with a sense more pure the words of the tribe,
> they loudly proclaimed the sortilege imbibed
> from the dishonorable flood of some black brew.
>
> Alas, from the warring heaven and earth, if
> our concept cannot carve a bas-relief
> with which to adorn Poe's dazzling sepulcher,
> calm block fallen down here from some dark
> disaster, let this granite forever mark
> bounds to dark flights of Blasphemy scarce in the future.
> —STEPHANE MALLARMÉ, "Le Tombeau d'Edgar Poe," 1876

Poe's place in purely imaginative prose-writing is as unquestionable as Hawthorne's. He even succeeded, which Hawthorne did not, in penetrating the artistic indifference of the French mind; and it was a substantial triumph, when we consider that Baudelaire put himself or his friends to the trouble of translating even the prolonged platitudes of *Eureka* and the wearisome narrative of *Arthur Gordon Pym*. Neither Poe nor Hawthorne has ever been fully recognized in England; and yet no Englishman of our time, not even De Quincey, has done any prose imaginative work to be named with theirs. But in comparing Poe with Hawthorne, we see that the genius of the latter has hands and feet as well as wings, so that all his work is solid as masonry, while Poe's is broken and disfigured by all sorts of inequalities and imitations; he not disdaining, for want of true integrity, to disguise and falsify, to claim knowledge that he did not possess, to invent quotations and references, and even, as Griswold showed, to manipulate and exaggerate puffs of himself. I remember the chagrin with which I looked through Tieck, in my student-days, to find the "Journey into the Blue Distance" to which Poe refers in the "House of Usher;" and how one of the poet's intimates laughed me to scorn for being deceived by any of Poe's citations, saying that he hardly knew a word of German.

But, making all possible deductions, how wonderful remains the power of Poe's imaginative tales, and how immense is the ingenuity of his puzzles and disentanglements! The conundrums of Wilkie Collins never renew their interest after the answer is known; but Poe's can be read again and again. It is where spiritual depths are to be touched, that he shows his weakness; where he attempts it, as in "William Wilson," it seems exceptional; where there is the greatest display of philosophic form, he is often most trivial, whereas Hawthorne is often profoundest when he has disarmed you by his simplicity. The truth is, that Poe lavished on things comparatively superficial those great intellectual resources which Hawthorne reverently husbanded and used. That there is something behind even genius to make or mar it, this is the lesson of the two lives.

Poe makes one of his heroes define another as "that *monstrum horrendum*, an unprincipled man of genius." It is in the malice and fury of his own critical work that his low moral tone most betrays itself. No atmosphere can be more belittling than that of his "New York Literati:" it is a mass of vehement dogmatism and petty personalities; opinions warped by private feeling, and varying from page to page. He seemed to have absolutely no fixed standard of critical judgment, though it is true that there was very little anywhere in America during those acrimonious days, when the most honorable head might be covered with insult or neglect, while any young poetess who smiled sweetly on Poe or Griswold or Willis might find herself placed among the Muses. Poe complimented and rather patronized Hawthorne, but found him only "peculiar and *not original*;" saying of him, "He has not half the material for the exclusiveness of literature that he has for its universality," whatever that may mean; and finally he tried to make it appear that Hawthorne had borrowed from himself. He returned again and again to the attack on Longfellow as a wilful plagiarist, denouncing the trivial resemblance between his "Midnight Mass for the Dying Year" and Tennyson's "Death of the Old Year," as "belonging to the most barbarous class of literary piracy." To make this attack was, as he boasted, "to throttle the guilty;" and while dealing thus ferociously with Longfellow, thus condescendingly with Hawthorne, he was claiming a foremost rank among American authors for obscurities now forgotten, such as Mrs. Amelia B. Welby and Estelle Anne Lewis. No one ever did more than Poe to lower the tone of literary criticism in this country; and the greater his talent the greater the mischief.

As a poet he held for a time the place earlier occupied by Byron, and later by Swinburne, as the patron saint of all wilful boys suspected of genius, and convicted at least of its infirmities. He belonged to the melancholy class of wasted men, like the German Hoffman, whom perhaps of all men of genius he most resembled. No doubt, if we are to apply any standard of moral weight or sanity to authors,—a proposal which Poe would doubtless have ridiculed,—it can only be in a very large and generous way. If a career has only a manly ring to it, we can forgive many errors—as in reading, for instance, the autobiography of Benvenuto Cellini, carrying always his life in his hand amid a brilliant and reckless society. But the existence of a poor Bohemian, besotted when he has money, angry and vindictive when the money is spent, this is a dismal tragedy, for which genius only makes the footlights burn with more lustre. There is a passage in Keats's letters, written from the haunts of Burns, in which he expresses himself as filled with pity for the poet's life: "he drank with blackguards, he was miserable; we can see horribly clear in the works of such a man his life, as if we were God's spies." Yet Burns's sins and miseries left his heart unspoiled, and this cannot be said of Poe. After all, the austere virtues—the virtues of Emerson, Hawthorne, Whittier—are the best soil for genius.—THOMAS WENTWORTH HIGGINSON, "Poe" (1879), *Short Studies of American Authors*, 1888, pp. 16–20

Better perhaps than anyone else, Poe possessed those intimate affinities that could satisfy the requirements of Des Esseintes' mind.

If Baudelaire had made out among the hieroglyphics of the soul the critical age of thought and feeling, it was Poe who, in the sphere of morbid psychology, had carried out the closest scrutiny of the will.

In literature he had been the first, under the emblematic title "The Imp of the Perverse," to study those irresistible impulses which the will submits to without fully understanding them, and which cerebral pathology can now explain with a fair degree of certainty; he had been the first again, if not to point out, at least to make known the depressing influence fear has on the will, which it affects in the same way as anaesthetics which paralyse the senses and curare which cripples the motory nerves. It was on this last subject, this lethargy of the will, that he had concentrated his studies, analysing the effects of this moral poison and indicating the symptoms of its progress— mental disturbances beginning with anxiety, developing into anguish, and finally culminating in a terror that stupefies the faculties of volition, yet without the intellect, however badly shaken it may be, giving way.

As for death, which the dramatists had so grossly abused, he had in a way given it a sharper edge, a new look, by introducing into it an algebraic and superhuman element; though to tell the truth, it was not so much the physical agony of the dying he described as the moral agony of the survivor, haunted beside the death-bed by the monstrous hallucinations engendered by grief and fatigue. With awful fascination he dwelt on the effects of terror, on the failures of will-power, and discussed them with clinical objectivity, making the reader's flesh creep, his throat contract, his mouth go dry at the recital of these mechanically devised nightmares of a fevered brain.

Convulsed by hereditary neuroses, maddened by moral choreas, his characters lived on their nerves; his women, his Morellas and Ligeias, possessed vast learning steeped in the mists of German philosophy and in the cabbalistic mysteries of the ancient East, and all of them had the inert, boyish breasts of angels, all were, so to speak, unsexed.—JORIS-KARL HUYSMANS, À *Rebours*, tr. Robert Baldick, 1884, Ch. 14

On American poets ⟨Tennyson said⟩: "I know several striking poems by American poets, but I think that Edgar Poe is (taking his poetry and prose together) the most original American genius." When asked to write an epitaph of one line for Poe's monument in Westminster Churchyard, Baltimore, he answered: "How can so strange and so fine a genius, and so sad a life, be exprest and comprest in one line?"—HALLAM TENNYSON, *Alfred Lord Tennyson: A Memoir*, 1897, Vol. 2, pp. 292–93

Works

POETRY

Never did a country need more than America such an influence as ⟨Whitman's⟩. We may understand and even approve his reproachful and scornful fear of the overweening "British element" when we see what it has hitherto signified in the literature of his country. Once as yet, and once only, has there sounded out of it all one pure note of original song— worth singing, and echoed from the singing of no other man; a note of song neither wide nor deep, but utterly true, rich, clear, and native to the singer; the short exquisite music, subtle and simple and sombre and sweet, of Edgar Poe. All the rest that is not of mocking-birds is of corncrakes, varied but at best for an instant by some scant-winded twitter of linnet or of wren.—ALGERNON CHARLES SWINBURNE, *Under the Microscope*, 1872

Almost without the first sign of moral principle, or of the concrete or its heroisms, or the simpler affections of the heart, Poe's verses illustrate an intense faculty for technical and abstract beauty, with the rhyming art to excess, an incorrigible propensity toward nocturnal themes, a demoniac undertone behind every page—and, by final judgment, probably belong among the electric lights of imaginative literature, brilliant and dazzling, but with no heat. There is an indescribable magne-

tism about the poet's life and reminiscences, as well as the poems. To one who could work out their subtle retracing and retrospect, the latter would make a close tally no doubt between the author's birth and antecedents, his childhood and youth, his physique, his so-call'd education, his studies and associates, the literary and social Baltimore, Richmond, Philadelphia and New York, of those times—not only the places and circumstances in themselves, but often, very often, in a strange spurning of, and reaction from them all.

⟨. . .⟩ By its popular poets the calibres of an age, the weak spots of its embankments, its sub-currents, (often more significant than the biggest surface ones,) are unerringly indicated. The lush and the weird that have taken such extraordinary possession of Nineteenth century verse-lovers—what mean they? The inevitable tendency of poetic culture to morbidity, abnormal beauty—the sickliness of all technical thought or refinement in itself—the abnegation of the perennial and democratic concretes at first hand, the body, the earth and sea, sex and the like—and the substitution of something for them at second or third hand—what bearings have they on current pathological study?—WALT WHITMAN, "Edgar Poe's Significance," *Critic*, June 3, 1882, p. 147

It is understood that Edgar Allan Poe is still unforgiven in New England. "Those singularly valueless verses of Poe," was the now celebrated *dictum* of a Boston prophet. It is true that, if "that most beguiling of all little divinities, Miss Walters of the *Transcript*," is to be implicitly believed, Edgar Poe was very rude and naughty at the Boston Lyceum in the spring of 1845. But surely bygones should be bygones, and Massachusetts might now pardon the *Al Aaraaf* incident. It is not difficult to understand that there were many sides on which Poe was likely to be long distasteful to Boston, Cambridge, and Concord. The intellectual weight of the man, though unduly minimised in New England, was inconsiderable by the side of that of Emerson. But in poetry, as one has to be always insisting, the battle is not to the strong; and apart from all faults, weaknesses, and shortcomings of Poe, we feel more and more clearly, or we ought to feel, the perennial charm of his verses. The posy of his still fresh and fragrant poems is larger than that of any other deceased American writer, although Emerson may have one or two single blossoms to show which are more brilliant than any of his. If the range of the Baltimore poet had been wider, if Poe had not harped so persistently on his one theme of remorseful passion for the irrecoverable dead, if he had employed his extraordinary, his unparalleled gifts of melodious invention, with equal skill, in illustrating a variety of human themes, he must have been with the greatest poets. For in Poe, in pieces like "The Haunted Palace," "The Conqueror Worm," "The City in the Sea," and "For Annie," we find two qualities which are as rare as they are invaluable, a new and haunting music, which constrains the hearer to follow and imitate and a command of evolution in lyrical work so absolute that the poet is able to do what hardly any other lyrist has dared to attempt, namely, as in "To One in Paradise," to take a normal stanzaic form, and play with it as a great pianist plays with an air.

So far as the first of these attributes is concerned, Poe has proved himself to be the Piper of Hamelin to all later English poets. From Tennyson to Austin Dobson there is hardly one whose verse-music does not show traces of Poe's influence. To impress the stamp of one's personality on a succeeding generation of artists, to be an almost (although not wholly) flawless technical artist one's self, to charm within a narrow circle to a degree that shows no sign, after forty years, of lessening, is this to prove a claim to rank with the Great Poets?

No, perhaps not quite; but at all events it is surely to have deserved great honour from the country of one's birthright. —EDMUND GOSSE, "Has America Produced a Poet?" (1889), *Questions at Issue*, 1893, pp. 88–90

Poe, like Swinburne, was a verbal poet merely; empty of thought, empty of sympathy, empty of love for any real thing: a graceful and nimble skater up and down over the deeps and shallows of life,—deep or shallow, it was all the same to him. Not one real thing did he make more dear to us by his matchless rhyme; not one throb of the universal heart, not one flash of the universal mind, did he seize and put in endearing form for his fellow men. Our band of New England poets have helped enrich and ennoble human life; the world is fairer, life is sweeter, because they lived and sang; character, heroism, truth, courage, devotion, count for more since Emerson and Longfellow and Whittier and Lowell were inspired by these themes. I am not complaining that Poe was not didactic: didacticism is death to poetry. I am complaining that he was not human and manly, and that he did not touch life in any helpful and liberating way. His poems do not lay hold of real things. I do not find the world a more enjoyable or beautiful place because he lived in it. I find myself turning to his poems, not for mental or spiritual food, as I do to Wordsworth or Emerson or Whitman, or for chivalrous human sentiments as in Tennyson, but to catch a glimpse of the weird, the fantastic, and, as it were, of the night-side or dream-side of things.

> You are not wrong who deem
> That my days have been a dream.

But the man whose days are a dream, no matter with what skill he portrays his dream, will never take deep hold upon men's hearts. Think of the difference, for instance, between Burns and Poe. We are drawn to Burns the man; he touches our most tender and human side; his art does not occupy our attention. With Poe it is quite the reverse: we care nothing for the man, nothing for the matter of his poems; his art alone seems important, and elicits our admiration. ⟨. . .⟩

I would not undervalue Poe. He was a unique genius. But I would account for his failure to deeply impress his own countrymen, outside the professional literary guild. His fund of love and sympathy was small. He was not broadly related to his fellows, as were Longfellow and Whittier and Whitman. His literary equipment was remarkable; his human equipment was not remarkable: hence his failure to reach the general fame of the New England poets.—JOHN BURROUGHS, "Mr. Gosse's Puzzle over Poe," *Dial*, Oct. 16, 1893, pp. 214–15

The brief story I have to tell about ⟨"The Raven"⟩ I got orally from an author who once had some vogue, but who is now nearly completely forgotten. His name was at one time in many of our best periodicals; and the old *Democratic Review* once had a considerable critique upon his poetic position and promise. He was likened by the writer of the review article to Shelley and Keats; and there were passages of his verse given which brought out, as I remember, a considerable of the suggested resemblance. Probably, though, his poem of "The Sword of Bunker Hill"—which was set to music—best typifies his prevailing poetic style, which was, in the main, noted for being eloquent and patriotic.

William Ross Wallace (for it is he to whom I refer) was not unlike Poe in both temperament and habits. He was not a little like him in physique—in brightness of the eye, and in a superb courtliness of manner. He had the same, or a similar, irresolute will; but he was a delightful companion to meet if you met him at the right time. He was, I believe, a Southerner by birth, as Poe was by acclimation.

Wallace told me (in the early war-time when I first met him) that he knew Poe tolerably well. They were, he said, on pleasant and familiar terms; and, it would seem (as Keats and Reynolds did), they read over to each other their not yet published poetical work. It was in obedience to this habit that Poe, on meeting Wallace one day, told him in some such words as these (I will be sponsor now only for their substance, and not for their form, or for the form of the colloquy between the known and the now-unknown poet):

"Wallace," said Poe, "I have just written the greatest poem that ever was written."

"Have you?" said Wallace. "That is a fine achievement."

"Would you like to hear it?" said Poe.

"Most certainly," said Wallace.

Thereupon Poe began to read the soon to-be famous verses in his best way—which I believe was always an impressive and captivating way. When he had finished he turned to Wallace for his approval of them—when Wallace said:

"Poe—they are fine; uncommonly fine."

"Fine?" said Poe, contemptuously. "Is that all you can say for this poem? I tell you it's the greatest poem that was ever written."

And then they separated—not, however, before Wallace had tried to placate, with somewhat more pronounced praise, the pettish poet.

And to-day there are critics who say—not knowing Poe's own opinion of "The Raven"—that it is "the greatest poem ever written." Whether it is or not, it bids fair to be the one that will be the most and the longest talked about.—JOEL BENTON, "Poe's Opinion of 'The Raven'" (1897), *In the Poe Circle*, 1899, pp. 57–60

TALES

You are mistaken in supposing that you are not "favorably known to me." On the contrary, all that I have read from your pen has inspired me with a high idea of your power; and I think you are destined to stand among the first romance-writers of the country, if such be your aim.—HENRY WADSWORTH LONGFELLOW, Letter to Edgar Allan Poe (May 19, 1841)

Mr. Poe's tales need no aid of newspaper comment to give them popularity; they have secured it. We are glad to see them given to the public in this neat form, so that thousands more may be entertained by them without injury to their eyesight.

No form of literary activity has so terribly degenerated among us as the tale. Now that everybody who wants a new hat or bonnet takes this way to earn one from the magazines or annuals, we are inundated with the very flimsiest fabrics ever spun by mortal brain. Almost every person of feeling or fancy could supply a few agreeable and natural narratives, but when instead of using their materials spontaneously they set to work with geography in hand to find unexplored nooks of wild scenery in which to locate their Indians or interesting farmers' daughters, or with some abridgment of history to hunt monarchs or heroes yet unused to become the subjects of their crude coloring, the sale-work produced is a sad affair indeed and "gluts the market" to the sorrow both of buyers and lookers-on.

In such a state of things the writings of Mr. Poe are a refreshment, for they are the fruit of genuine observations and experience, combined with an invention which is not "making up," as children call their way of contriving stories, but a penetration into the causes of things which leads to original but credible results. His narrative proceeds with vigor, his colors are applied with discrimination, and where the effects are fantastic they are not unmeaningly so.

The "Murders in the Rue Morgue" especially made a great impression upon those who did not know its author and were not familiar with his mode of treatment. Several of his stories make us wish he would enter the higher walk of the metaphysical novel and, taking a mind of the self-possessed and deeply marked sort that suits him, give us a deeper and longer acquaintance with its life and the springs of its life than is possible in the compass of these tales.

As Mr. Poe is a professed critic and of all the band the most unsparing to others, we are surprised to find some inaccuracies in the use of words, such as these: "he had with him many books, but rarely *employed* them."—"His results have, in truth, the *whole air* of intuition."

The degree of skill shown in the management of revolting or terrible circumstances makes the pieces that have such subjects more interesting than the others. Even the failures are those of an intellect of strong fiber and well-chosen aim. —MARGARET FULLER, "Poe's Tales," *New York Daily Tribune*, July 11, 1845

The tales themselves ⟨in *The Works of Edgar Allan Poe*, ed. John H. Ingram, Vols. 1 and 2⟩ are all before us in these two volumes; and though Mr. Ingram does not tell us whether they are there printed in chronological order, I fancy we shall not be mistaken in regarding some of the last stories in the second volume, as being also among the last he wrote. There is no trace, in these, of the brilliant and often solid workmanship of his better moments. The stories are ill-conceived and written carelessly. There is much laughter; but it is a very ghastly sort of laughter at best—the laughter of those, in his own words, "who laugh, but smile no more." He seems to have lost respect for himself, for his art, and for his audience. When he dealt before with horrible images, he dealt with them for some definite enough creative purpose, and with a certain measure and gravity suitable to the occasion; but he scatters them abroad in these last tales with an indescribable and sickening levity, with something of the ghoul or the furious lunatic that surpasses what one had imagined to oneself of Hell. There is a duty to the living more important than any charity to the dead; and it would be criminal in the reviewer to spare one harsh word in the expression of his own loathing and horror, lest, by its absence, another victim should be permitted to soil himself with the perusal of the infamous "King Pest." He who could write "King Pest" had ceased to be a human being. For his own sake, and out of an infinite compassion for so lost a spirit, one is glad to think of him as dead. But if it is pity that we feel towards Poe, it is certainly not pity that inspires us as we think of Baudelaire, who could sit down in cold blood, and dress out in suitable French this pointless farrago of horrors. There is a phase of contempt that, if indulged, transcends itself and becomes a phase of passionate self-satisfaction; so for the weal of our own spirits, it is better to think no more of Baudelaire or "King Pest."

It is not the fashion of Poe's earlier tales to be pointless, however it may be with these sorry ones of the end. Pointlessness is, indeed, the very last charge that could be brought reasonably against them. He has the true story-teller's instinct. He knows the little nothings that make stories, or mar them. He knows how to enhance the significance of any situation, and give colour and life with seemingly irrelevant particulars. Thus, the whole spirit of "The Cask of Amontillado" depends on Fortunato's carnival costume of cap and bells and motley. When

Poe had once hit upon this device of dressing the victim grotesquely, he had found the key of the story; and so he sends him with uneven steps along the catacombs of the Montresors, and the last sound we hear out of the walled-up recess is the jingling of the bells upon his cap. Admirable, also, is the use he makes of the striking clock at Prince Prospero's feast, in "The Mask of the Red Death." Each time the clock struck (the reader will remember), it struck so loudly that the music and the dancing must cease perforce until it had made an end; as the hours ran on towards midnight, these pauses grew naturally longer; the maskers had the more time to think and look at one another, and their thoughts were none the more pleasant. Thus, as each hour struck, there went a jar about the assemblage; until, as the reader will remember, the end comes suddenly. Now, this is quite legitimate; no one need be ashamed of being frightened or excited by such means; the rules of the game have been respected; only, by the true instinct of the story-teller he has told his story to the best advantage, and got full value for his imaginations. This is not so always, however; for sometimes he will take a high note falsetto; sometimes, by a sort of conjuring trick, get more out of his story than he has been able to put into it; and, while the whole garrison is really parading past us on the esplanade, continue to terrify us from the battlements with sham cannon and many fierce-looking shakos upon broom-sticks. For example, in "The Pit and the Pendulum," after having exhausted his bedevilled imagination in the conception of the pendulum and the red-hot collapsing walls, he finds he can figure forth nothing more horrible for the pit; and yet the pit was to be the crowning horror. This is how he affects his purpose (vol. i. p. 214):—

> Amid the thought of the fiery destruction that impended, the idea of the coolness of the well came over my soul like balm. I rushed to its deadly brink. I threw my straining vision below. The glare from the enkindled roof illumined its inmost recesses. Yet for a wild moment did my spirit refuse to comprehend the meaning of what I saw. At length it forced—it wrestled its way into my soul—it burned itself in upon my shuddering reason. O for a voice to speak! oh horror! oh, any horror but this!

And that is all. He knows no more about the pit than you or I do. It is a pure imposture, a piece of audacious, impudent thimble-rigging; and yet, even with such bugs as these he does manage to frighten us. You will find the same artifice repeated in "Hans Pfaal," about the mysteries of the moon; and again, though with a difference, in the abrupt conclusion of *Arthur Gordon Pym*. His imagination is a willing horse; but three times, as you see, he has killed it under him by over-riding, and come limping to the post on foot. With what a good grace does he not turn these failures to advantage, and make capital out of each imaginative bankruptcy! Even on a critical retrospect, it is hard to condemn him as he deserves; for he cheats with gusto.

After this knowledge of the stage, this cleverness at turning a story out, perhaps the most striking of Poe's peculiarities is an almost incredible insight into the debateable region between sanity and madness. The "Imp of the Perverse," for example, is an important contribution to morbid psychology; so, perhaps, is "The Man of the Crowd;" "Berenice," too, for as horrible as it is, touches a chord in one's own breast, though perhaps it is a chord that had better be left alone; and the same idea recurs in "The Tell-Tale Heart." Sometimes we can go with him the whole way with a good conscience; sometimes—instead of saying, yes, this is how I should be if I were just a little more mad than ever I was—we can say frankly, this is what I am. There is one passage of analysis in this more normal vein, in the story of "Ligeia," as to the expression of Ligeia's eyes. He tells us how he felt ever on the point of understanding their strange quality, and ever baffled at the last moment, just as "in our endeavours to recall to memory something long forgotten, we often find ourselves upon the very verge of remembrance, without being able in the end to remember;" and how, in streams of running water, in the ocean, in the falling of a meteor, in the glances of unusually aged people, in certain sounds from stringed instruments, in certain passages from books, in the commonest sights and sensations of the universe, he found ever and anon some vague inexplicable analogy to the expression and the power of these loved eyes. This, at least, or the like of it, we all know. But, in the general, his subtlety was more of a snare to him than anything else. "Nil sapientiae odiosius," he quotes himself from Seneca, "nil sapientiae odiosius acumine nimio." And though it is delightful enough in the C. Auguste Dupin trilogy—it was Baudelaire who called it a trilogy—yet one wearies in the long run of this strain of ingenuity; one begins to marvel at the absence of the good homespun motives and sentiments that do the business of the everyday world; although the demonstrator is clever, and the cases instructive and probably unique, one begins to weary of going round this madhouse, and long for the society of some plain harmless person, with business habits and a frock coat, and nerves not much more shattered than the majority of his plain and harmless contemporaries. Nor did this exaggerated insight make him wearisome only; it did worse than that—it sometimes led him astray. Thus, in "The Pit and the Pendulum," when the hero has been condemned, "the sound of the inquisitorial voices," he says, seemed merged in one dreamy indeterminate hum. "It conveyed to my soul the idea of *revolution*, perhaps from its association in fancy with the burr of a mill-wheel." Now, it wants but a moment's reflection to prove how much too clever Poe has been here, how far from true reason he has been carried by this *nimium acumen*. For— the man being giddy—the "idea of revolution" must have preceded the merging of the inquisitorial voices into an indeterminate hum, and most certainly could not have followed it as any fanciful deduction. Again, as before in the matter of effect, one cannot help fearing that some of the subtlety is fustian. To take an example of both sorts of imagination—the fustian and the sincere—form the same story *Arthur Gordon Pym*: the four survivors on board the brig *Grampus* have lashed themselves to the windlass, lest they should be swept away; one of them, having drawn his lashings too tight, is ready to yield up his spirit for a long while, is nearly cut in two, indeed, by the cord about his loins. "No sooner had we removed it, however," Poe goes on, "than he spoke and seemed to experience instant relief—being able to move with much greater ease than either Parker or myself" (two who had not tied themselves so closely). *"This was no doubt owing to the loss of blood."* Now, whether medically correct or not, this is, on the face of it, sincerely imagined. Whether correct or not in fact, it is correct in art. Poe evidently believed it true; evidently it appeared to him that thus, and not otherwise, the thing would fall out. Now, turn a page back, and we shall find (ii. 78), in the description of the visions that went before Pym while thus bound, something to be received very much more deliberately. "I now remember," he writes,

> that in all which passed before my mind's eye, *motion* was a predominant idea. Thus I never fancied any stationary object, such as a house, a mountain,

or anything of that kind; but windmills, ships, large birds, balloons, people on horseback, carriages driving furiously, and similar moving objects presented themselves in endless succession.

This may be true; it may be the result of great erudition in the thoughts of people in such sore straits; but the imagination does not adopt these details, they do not commend themselves to our acceptance, it is nowise apparent why stationary objects should *not* present themselves to the fancy of a man tied to the windlass of a dismasted brig; and, this being so, the whole passage, as art, stands condemned. If it be mere causeless fancy (as it seems), it is fustian of the most unpardonable sort; if it be erudition,—well then, it may be erudition, but never art. Things are fit for art so far only as they are both true and apparent. To make what I mean clear: Mr. Ruskin, in some one or other of his delightful books, quotes and approves a poet (I think it was Homer) who said of a brave man that he was as brave as a fly; and proceeds, in his usual happy manner, to justify the epithet. The fly, he tells us, is in very deed the most madly courageous of all created beings. And therefore the simile is good—excellent good. And yet the reader's instinct would tell him, I am sure, that the simile is a vile simile. Let him prefer his instinct before Mr. Ruskin's natural history. For, though it be based on what is true, this comparison is not based upon a truth that is apparent; it does not commend itself to our acceptance; it is not art.—ROBERT LOUIS STEVENSON, *Academy*, Jan. 2, 1875, pp. 1–2

Although it may be doubted whether the fiery and tumultuous rush of a volcano, which might be taken to typify Poe, is as powerful or impressive in the end as the calm and inevitable progression of a glacier, to which, for the purposes of this comparison only, we may liken Hawthorne, yet the weight and influence of Poe's work are indisputable. One might hazard the assertion that in all Latin countries he is the best known of American authors. Certainly no American writer has been so widely accepted in France. Nothing better of its kind has ever been done than the 'Pit and the Pendulum,' or than the 'Fall of the House of Usher' (which has been compared aptly with Browning's *Childe Roland to the Dark Tower Came* for its power of suggesting intellectual desolation). Nothing better of its kind has ever been done than the 'Gold Bug,' or than the 'Purloined Letter,' or than the 'Murders in the Rue Morgue.'

The 'Murders in the Rue Morgue' is indeed a story of the most marvellous skill: it was the first of its kind, and to this day it remains a model, not only unsurpassed, but unapproachable. It was the first of detective stories; and it has had thousands of imitations and no rival. The originality, the ingenuity, the verisimilitude of this tale and of its fellows are beyond all praise. Poe had a faculty which one may call imaginative ratiocination to a degree beyond all other writers of fiction. He did not at all times keep up to the high level, in one style, of the 'Fall of the House of Usher,' and, in another, of the 'Murders in the Rue Morgue,' and it was not to be expected that he should. Only too often did he sink to the grade of the ordinary 'Tale from *Blackwood*,' which he himself satirised in his usual savage vein of humour.

And yet there is no denying that even in his flimsiest and most tawdry tales we see the truth of Mr. Lowell's assertion that Poe had "two of the prime qualities of genius,—a faculty of vigorous yet minute analysis, and a wonderful fecundity of imagination." Mr. Lowell said also that Poe combined "in a very remarkable manner two faculties which are seldom found united,—a power of influencing the mind of the reader by the impalpable shadows of mystery, and a minuteness of detail which does not leave a pin or a button unnoticed. Both are, in truth, the natural results of the predominating quality of his mind, to which we have before alluded,—analysis." In Poe's hands, however, the enumeration of pins and buttons, the exact imitation of the prosaic facts of humdrum life in this workaday world, is not an end, but a means only, whereby he constructs and intensifies the shadow of mystery which broods over the things thus realistically portrayed.—BRANDER MATTHEWS, *The Philosophy of the Short-Story* (1885), 1901, pp. 44–48

It is a singular and not very creditable fact that (as we have recently experienced) the tales of Edgar Allan Poe should be difficult to procure in their entirety—apart from complete editions of his works. It is the more regrettable and singular because these creations of genius touch on two sides of the most popular modern schools of British fiction. Perhaps, indeed, this is the explanation of it: that the derivative has ousted the original. On the one side they have relation to the "detective" fiction of Dr. Conan Doyle, on the other they are in contact with the fantastic fiction of Mr. Wells. And between these two extremes is enthroned the very Poe—single, singular, with no predecessor and no authentic successor—unless it be the Stevenson of *Dr. Jekyll and Mr. Hyde*. That central and—artistically—supreme class of his tales is difficult to describe, for, indeed, to describe it is to describe Poe himself. It has been the tendency of the modern romantic school, and of modern poets in general, to make themselves the heroes of their own work. Chateaubriand, Byron, Shelley, are instances that come at once to one's mind, and Byron had strong influence on the early Poe. But not Byron, not even the author of *Epipsychidion* and *Alastor*, hardly the author of *Atala*, had such a peculiar gift for arabesquing their own lives, for transcendentalising themselves, their happenings, and environment. In nearly all these tales of idealistic terror or beauty, of which the "House of Usher" is an example, the hero is Poe himself; while they constantly revolve round situations suggested by his own history. To consider Poe is to consider these tales, to consider the tales is to consider Poe.

It is significant that his family was alleged to be descended from the Irish family of Le Poer—one of the English Pale, it is true, but thoroughly Irished by long residence and intermixture. The spirit of his work is Celtic, if the form of his poetry be not, indeed, of direct Celtic origin. It is at least possible that he should have seen some of Mangan's poems, and that unfortunate Irish poet anticipates Poe's peculiar form so strikingly that it is difficult to believe the resemblance can be accident alone. Yet, hardly less singular than such a coincidence would be, is the coincidence between the lives of the two men—identical in drudgery, misery, poverty, bondage to stimulants, and not far from identical in their deaths. It is the visionary and ethereal spirit of Celtic romance which informs the central group of tales no less than the poems. The Celtic temperament would go far to explain Poe's weakness and strength; his brilliant caprice, his pride and passion, his literary quarrels, his lack of robust moral stamina, his ready enslavement to alcohol. The Celtic visionariness, with its lack of hold on earth, is further accentuated in him by the love of strange ways in reading which he shared with Shelley. The trait is constantly appearing—implicit or explicit—in his heroes. The hero of the scarcely-sane "Ligeia" relates:

> With how vast a triumph, with how vivid a delight, with how much of all that is ethereal in hope did I feel—as she bent over me in studies but little sought, but less known—that delicious vista by slow

degrees expanding before me, down whose long, gorgeous, and all untrodden path I might at length pass onward to the goal of a wisdom too divinely precious not to be forbidden?

His quotations testify to the same thing. Glanville, Raymond Lully, Platonists like Henry King; by his citation of them he indicates the shadowy and mysterious authors whom he found congenial to his mind. But not to penetrate them, so far as we can see, with the zeal of the thinker. He loved, as he says himself, "those who feel rather than those who think." They give him dreams, suggest the stuff of tales or poetry; they are indeed, to him, in no disparaging sense, "such stuff as dreams are made on." When a mind thus exalted, and of such natural development in one supermundane direction applies itself to fiction, the result must needs be strange, almost monstrous. The pearl is an abnormality, the result of external irritation which provokes the precious excretion. These tales are no less precious and abnormal. One feels the reading of them as it were an unlawful pleasure, wrung from pain, disease, calamity, and the fruitage of delirium. The cost is too great, and the pleasure itself scarcely human. We said of "Ligeia" that it was hardly sane; we might have said thus of all the group to which we refer. Poe was conscious of this, and absolutely suggested—before Lombroso—a relation between madness and genius. For the hero of "Eleonora" surely speaks in the name of Poe:

> Men [he says] have called me mad, but the question is not yet settled whether madness is or is not the loftiest intelligence, whether much that is glorious, whether all that is profound, does not spring from disease of thought, from *moods* of mind exalted at the expense of the general intellect. They who dream by day are cognisant of many things which escape those who dream only by night. In their grey visions they obtain glimpses of eternity, and thrill, in waking, to find that they have been upon the verge of the great secret. In snatches they learn something of the wisdom which is of good and more of the mere knowledge which is of evil. They penetrate, however rudderless or compassless, into the vast ocean of the "light ineffable."

This perilous doctrine is at least not far from descriptive of Poe's own genius. There was something uncanny about the man which forbade intimacy, almost approach. Of the hero (there is virtually but one) who paces through these tales in Poe's image you feel that no woman could live with him without going mad—or dying. And death, accordingly, is Poe's gift to all his women. The tales are vital with a wrongful vitality. They are told by heroes whose sensitive nerves have the preternatural acuteness of initial insanity; colour, sound, scent—every detail of description in their rendering becomes morbidly distinct to us, like the ticking of a clock in the dark. In the "House of Usher" this feature becomes conscious of itself; the hero hears the beating of a woman's heart while she stands without the closed door. Beauty and terror are alike portentous, "larger than human," like figures in a mist. The landscapes are preterhuman, painted as with fire, and blinded with a light such as only streams from the fountains of the dreaming brain. The heroes live by choice in chambers out of nightmare, where curtains like molten silver fall in cataracts on carpets of burning gold, lighted by coloured flames which writhe from antique lamps, and perfumed from carven censers; on golden tapestries phantasmal figures waver in the rushing of a continuous wind. Amid such surroundings women of unearthly beauty, or the shadow of Poe's own child-wife, pass and die, and dying, give rise to tragedies of impermissible terror; the

Red Death incarnates itself among the fated revellers; or a man flies through life pursued by the visible presence of himself. Beauty which cannot separate itself from terror, terror haunted by beauty, are the powers which rule this world of an opium-dream.

It is the deliberate turning away of a man from the normal; it is the obsession by the desire for better bread than is made from wheat. When Poe theorises on landscape-gardening, he avows his preference for the artificial style, but must have a "spiritualised " artificiality, an artifice which suggests the more than mortal. Yet this world at which the human heart aches becomes real while we read—there is the genius. The art is admirable in its sureness and delicacy. The imagination has seized these things of beauty and terror with more than the closeness of a poet—with the closeness of a dream; and there is no closeness, either to terror or beauty, so appalling as that of a dream. The scope is strange and narrow, but the mastership is absolute.

Yet the same man who can thus handle ideal horror and loveliness with the touch and arts of a poet is also, on another side, and within the limits of romance, one of the most convincing of realists. The man who wrote "The Fall of the House of Usher" and "The Masque of the Red Death" wrote also *The Narrative of Arthur Gordon Pym* and "The Descent into the Maelström." For the dreamer was also a keen analyst and an amateur of science; and had his active days in youth. Mr. Wells himself has not combined romance and realism more startlingly than that feat is achieved in *Arthur Gordon Pym*. The seizure of the ship, and, above all, the whole episode of the storm and subsequent starvation, are done with amazing wealth and verisimilitude of imaginative detail. In reading the description of the escape from the Maelström, in the other tale we have mentioned, it is hard to realise that Poe, in all probability, never was in the neighbourhood of the Scandinavian seas. The little vivid touches seem the result of experience. ⟨. . .⟩

Finally, this wonderfully original artist has struck out and set the method for yet another class of tale—the "detective story" now represented by Dr. Conan Doyle. For, with Mr. Blatchford, we refuse to concede that the deductive method is undeveloped in Poe's tales of this class.

Certain applications of the deductive method Dr. Doyle has developed from his medical experience which are not to be found in Edgar Poe. But the deductive method itself is used by Poe with consummate skill. Dr. Doyle may also pride himself that in many cases he has trusted his mystery entirely to the ingenuity of the problem: whereas Poe holds back the essential clues the better to effect his surprise. But the merit of the tales lies deeper than their display of analysis. It is the finished art of construction and narrative, bringing out the ghastly element or the thrill of excitement with exact *crescendo* of effect; the beauty of the exposition; and, over all, the style of a master, which can endow with immortality a thing in its essence so ephemeral as this species has shown itself in other hands. Let it be, if you will, that the great Dupin was the bungling pretender which the great Holmes, we know, once declared him to be. Yet Poe makes us believe in his greatness—and that is *the* thing which matters in art. Perhaps the truth is that Dr. Doyle, too, is an artist, and knows the artistic value of "bounce" in the right place. From the artistic standpoint, however, these latter tales—"The Murders in the Rue Morgue" and their kind—though they were the first to make Poe's fame as a tale-writer, will be the last to keep it. It is on the two former classes that his fame must chiefly rest—and rest securely. —FRANCIS THOMPSON, "A Dreamer of Things Impossible"

(1901), *Literary Criticisms*, ed. Terence L. Connolly, 1948, pp. 317–22

CRITICISM

I presume the publishers will have sent you a copy of *Mosses from an Old Manse*—the latest (and probably the last) collection of my tales and sketches. I have read your occasional notices of my productions with great interest—not so much because your judgment was, upon the whole, favorable, as because it seemed to be given in earnest. I care for nothing but the truth; and shall always much more readily accept a harsh truth, in regard to my writings, than a sugared falsehood.

I confess, however, that I admire you rather as a writer of tales than as a critic upon them. I might often—and often do—dissent from your opinions in the latter capacity, but could never fail to recognize your force and originality in the former.—NATHANIEL HAWTHORNE, Letter to Edgar Allan Poe (June 17, 1846), cited in George E. Woodberry, "Poe in New York," *Century Magazine*, Oct. 1894, p. 860

As a critic, Poe was illiberal and perverse, burning incense before second-rate writers, and stinging the author he professed to admire. His article on Hawthorne, like Antony's oration, with its blasting phrase, "Yet Brutus was an honorable man," leaves an impression contrary and fatal to the frequent professions of high appreciation which make the refrain of his article. As a critic, Poe spent himself upon questions of detail, and, in all cases, belittled his subject. He did not exercise the most engaging faculties of his mind. He is brilliant, caustic, stinging, personal without geniality, expressing an irritated mind. Reading his criticisms, we think his literary being might be said to resemble a bush that blossoms into a few perfect flowers, but always has its thorns in thickest profusion. Poe was what may be called a *technical critic*. He delighted to involve his reader in the mechanism of poetry, and convict his victim of ignorance, while he used his knowledge as a means to be exquisitely insolent. He was like an art critic stuffed with the jargon of studios, talking an unknown language; careless about the elements of the subject which, properly, are the chief and only concern of the public. That Poe was acute, that he was exact, that he was original, no one can question; but he was not stimulating, and comprehensive, and generous, like the more sympathetic critics, as, for example, Diderot or Carlyle. It was his misfortune to have been called to pronounce upon the ephemera of literature, conscious that he was *expected* to think them fixed stars. His critical notices of American men of letters show the incessant struggle of a supreme scorn muffled and quieted from time to time in the acknowledgment of mitigating circumstances to excuse the literary criminals that he had assembled. When he wishes to be indulgent and generous, it is the indulgence and generosity of a cat stroking a mouse—the claw is *felt* by the breathless victim. He probably *tore* his subject more than any critic that ever lived. In his criticisms, the sentences are sharp, stinging, pointed, and sparkling; they are like so many surgical knives—they lay open the living subject, quivering and fainting, to the bone. Poe had no indulgence for literary offenders. He had the instincts of a mole slaking its thirst over its prey. Poe scratched almost every one of his literary contemporaries, and, in nine cases out of ten, he was right in his destructive work. But he was virulent, mocking, incensing, seeming to be animated with a personal animosity for his subject; he was like a literary pirate, sparing neither friend nor foe, always accusing other people of stealing, while his own hands were not pure.—EUGENE BENSON, "Poe and Hawthorne," *Galaxy*, Dec. 1868, pp. 747–48

There was but little literary criticism in the United States at the time Hawthorne's earlier works were published; but among the reviewers Edgar Poe perhaps held the scales the highest. He, at any rate, rattled them loudest, and pretended, more than any one else, to conduct the weighing-process on scientific principles. Very remarkable was this process of Edgar Poe's, and very extraordinary were his principles; but he had the advantage of being a man of genius, and his intelligence was frequently great. His collection of critical sketches of the American writers flourishing in what M. Taine would call his *milieu* and *moment*, is very curious and interesting reading, and it has one quality which ought to keep it from ever being completely forgotten. It is probably the most complete and exquisite specimen of *provincialism* ever prepared for the edification of men. Poe's judgments are pretentious, spiteful, vulgar; but they contain a great deal of sense and discrimination as well, and here and there, sometimes at frequent intervals, we find a phrase of happy insight imbedded in a patch of the most fatuous pedantry.—HENRY JAMES, *Hawthorne*, 1879, p. 62

His critical writings, collected in the sixth, seventh, and eighth volumes of Stedman and Woodberry's edition of his works, are the only ones in which he shows how he could deal with actual fact; and in dealing with actual fact he proved himself able. Though some of the facts he dealt with, however, were worthy of his pen,—he was among the first, for example, to recognise the merit of Tennyson and of Mrs. Browning,—most of them in the course of fifty years have proved of no human importance. For all this, they existed at the moment. Poe was a journalist, who had to write about what was in the air; and he wrote about it so well that in certain aspects this critical work seems his best. He dabbled a little in philosophy, of course, particularly on the æsthetic side; but he had neither the seriousness of nature—spiritual insight, one might call it,—which must underlie serious philosophising, nor yet the scholarly training which must precede lasting, solid thought. What he did possess to a rare degree was the temper of an enthusiastic artist, who genuinely enjoyed and welcomed whatever in his own art, of poetry, he found meritorious. No doubt he was more than willing to condemn faults; whoever remembers any of his critical activity, for example, will remember how vigorously he attacked Longfellow for plagiarism. We ought to recall with equal certainty how willingly Poe recognised in the same Longfellow those traits which he believed excellent. Poe's serious writing does not concern the eternities as did the elder range of American literature, nor yet does it touch on public matters. True or not, indeed, that grotesque story of his death typifies his relation to political affairs. His critical writing, all the same, deals with questions of fine art in a spirit which if sometimes narrow, often dogmatic, and never scholarly, is sincere, fearless, and generally eager in its impulsive recognition of merit.—BARRETT WENDELL, *A Literary History of America*, 1900, pp. 208–9

JAMES RUSSELL LOWELL
From "Edgar Allan Poe"

Graham's Magazine, February 1845, pp. 49–53

Mr. Poe is at once the most discriminating, philosophical, and fearless critic upon imaginative works who has written in America. It may be that we should qualify our remark a little, and say that he *might be*, rather than that he always *is*, for he seems sometimes to mistake his phial of prussic-acid for his inkstand. If we do not always agree with

him in his premises, we are, at least, satisfied that his deductions are logical, and that we are reading the thoughts of a man who thinks for himself, and says what he thinks, and knows well what he is talking about. His analytic power would furnish forth bravely some score of ordinary critics. We do not know him personally, but we suspect him for a man who has one or two pet prejudices on which he prides himself. These sometimes allure him out of the strict path of criticism, [1] but, where they do not interfere, we would put almost entire confidence in his judgments. Had Mr. Poe had the control of a magazine of his own, in which to display his critical abilities, he would have been as autocratic, ere this, in America, as Professor Wilson has been in England; and his criticisms, we are sure, would have been far more profound and philosophical than those of the Scotsman. As it is, he has squared out blocks enough to build an enduring pyramid, but has left them lying carelessly and unclaimed in many different quarries.

Remarkable experiences are usually confined to the inner life of imaginative men, but Mr. Poe's biography displays a vicissitude and peculiarity of interest such as is rarely met with. The offspring of a romantic marriage, and left an orphan at an early age, he was adopted by Mr. Allan, a wealthy Virginian, whose barren marriage-bed seemed the warranty of a large estate to the young poet. Having received a classical education in England, he returned home and entered the University of Virginia, where, after an extravagant course, followed by reformation at the last extremity, he was graduated with the highest honors of his class. Then came a boyish attempt to join the fortunes of the insurgent Greeks, which ended at St. Petersburg, where he got into difficulties through want of a passport, from which he was rescued by the American consul and sent home. He now entered the military academy at West Point, from which he obtained a dismissal on hearing of the birth of a son to his adopted father, by a second marriage, an event which cut off his expectations as an heir. The death of Mr. Allan, in whose will his name was not mentioned, soon after relieved him of all doubt in this regard, and he committed himself at once to authorship for a support. Previously to this, however, he had published (in 1827) a small volume of poems, which soon ran through three editions, and excited high expectations of its author's future distinction in the minds of many competent judges. ⟨. . .⟩

Mr. Poe's early productions show that he could see through the verse to the spirit beneath, and that he already had a feeling that all the life and grace of the one must depend on and be modulated by the will of the other. We call them the most remarkable boyish poems that we have ever read. We know of none that can compare with them for maturity of purpose, and a nice understanding of the effects of language and metre. Such pieces are only valuable when they display what we can only express by the contradictory phrase of *innate experience*. We copy one of the shorter poems written when the author was only *fourteen!* There is little dimness in the filling up, but the grace and symmetry of the outline are such as few poets ever attain. There is a smack of ambrosia about it.

TO HELEN

Helen, thy beauty is to me
  Like those Nicean barks of yore,
That gently, o'er a perfumed sea,
  The weary, way-worn wanderer bore
  To his own native shore.

On desperate seas long wont to roam,
  Thy hyacinth hair, thy classic face,
Thy Naiad airs have brought me home

> To the glory that was Greece
> And the grandeur that was Rome.
> Lo! in yon brilliant window-niche
> How statue-like I see thee stand!
> The agate lamp within thy hand,
> Ah! Psyche, from the regions which
> Are Holy Land!

It is the *tendency* of the young poet that impresses us. Here is no "withering scorn," no heart "blighted" ere it has safely got into its teens, none of the drawing-room sansculottism which Byron had brought into vogue. All is limpid and serene, with a pleasant dash of the Greek Helicon in it. The melody of the whole, too, is remarkable. It is not of that kind which can be demonstrated arithmetically upon the tips of the fingers. It is of that finer sort which the inner ear alone can estimate. It seems simple, like a Greek column, because of its perfection. In a poem named "Ligeia," under which title he intended to personify the music of nature, our boy-poet gives us the following exquisite picture:

> Ligeia! Ligeia!
>   My beautiful one,
> Whose harshest idea
>   Will to melody run,
> *Say, is it thy will*
>   *On the breezes to toss,*
> *Or, capriciously still,*
>   *Like the lone albatross,*
> *Incumbent on night,*
>   *As she on the air,*
> *To keep watch with delight*
>   *On the harmony there?*

John Neal, himself a man of genius, and whose lyre has been too long capriciously silent, appreciated the high merit of these and similar passages, and drew a proud horoscope for their author. The extracts which we shall presently make from Mr. Poe's later poems, fully justify his predictions.

Mr. Poe has that indescribable something which men have agreed to call *genius*. No man could ever tell us precisely what it is, and yet there is none who is not inevitably aware of its presence and its power. Let talent writhe and contort itself as it may, it has no such magnetism. Larger of bone and sinew it may be, but the wings are wanting. Talent sticks fast to earth, and its most perfect works have still one foot of clay. Genius claims kindred with the very workings of Nature herself, so that a sunset shall seem like a quotation from Dante or Milton, and if Shakespeare be read in the very presence of the sea itself, his verses shall but seem nobler for the sublime criticism of ocean. Talent may make friends for itself, but only genius can give to its creations the divine power of winning love and veneration. Enthusiasm cannot cling to what itself is unenthusiastic, nor will he ever have disciples who has not himself impulsive zeal enough to be a disciple. Great wits are allied to madness only inasmuch as they are possessed and carried away by their demon, while talent keeps him as Paracelsus did, securely prisoned in the pommel of its sword. To the eye of genius, the veil of the spiritual world is ever rent asunder, that it may perceive the ministers of good and evil who throng continually around it. No man of mere talent ever flung his inkstand at the devil.

When we say that Mr. Poe has genius, we do not mean to say that he has produced evidence of the highest. But to say that he possesses it at all is to say that he needs only zeal, industry, and a reverence for the trust reposed in him, to achieve the proudest triumphs and the greenest laurels. If we may believe the Longinuses and Aristotles of our newspapers, we have quite too many geniuses of the loftiest order to render a place among them at all desirable, whether for its hardness of attainment or its seclusion. The highest peak of our Parnassus is, according to these gentlemen, by far the most thickly settled portion of the country, a circumstance which must make it an uncomfortable residence for individuals of a poetical temperament, if love of solitude be, as immemorial tradition asserts, a necessary part of their idiosyncrasy. There is scarce a gentleman or lady of respectable moral character to whom these liberal dispensers of the laurel have not given a ticket to that once sacred privacy, where they may elbow Shakespeare and Milton at leisure. A transient visiter, such as a critic must necessarily be, sees these legitimate proprietors in common, parading their sacred enclosure as thick and buzzing as flies, each with "Entered according to act of Congress" labeled securely to his back. Formerly one Phœbus, a foreigner, we believe, had the monopoly of transporting all passengers thither, a service for which he provided no other conveyance than a vicious horse, named Pegasus, who could, of course, carry but one at a time, and even that but seldom, his back being a ticklish seat, and one fall proving generally enough to damp the ardor of the most zealous aspirant. The charges, however, were moderate, as the poet's pocket formerly occupied that position in regard to the rest of his outfit which is now more usually conceded to his head. But we must return from our little historical digression.

Mr. Poe has two of the prime qualities of genius, a faculty of vigorous yet minute analysis, and a wonderful fecundity of imagination. The first of these faculties is as needful to the artist in words, as a knowledge of anatomy is to the artist in colors or in stone. This enables him to conceive truly, to maintain a proper relation of parts, and to draw a correct outline, while the second groups, fills up, and colors. Both of these Mr. Poe has displayed with singular distinctness in his prose works, the last predominating in his earlier tales, and the first in his later ones. In judging of the merit of an author, and assigning him his niche among our household gods, we have a right to regard him from our own point of view, and to measure him by our own standard. But, in estimating his works, we must be governed by his own design, and, placing them by the side of his own ideal, find how much is wanting. We differ with Mr. Poe in his opinions of the objects of art. He esteems that object to be the creation of Beauty, and perhaps it is only in the definition of that word that we disagree with him. But in what we shall say of his writings we shall take his own standard as our guide. The temple of the god of song is equally accessible from every side, and there is room enough in it for all who bring offerings, or seek an oracle.

In his tales, Mr. Poe has chosen to exhibit his power chiefly in that dim region which stretches from the very utmost limits of the probable into the weird confines of superstition and unreality. He combines in a very remarkable manner two faculties which are seldom found united; a power of influencing the mind of the reader by the impalpable shadows of mystery, and a minuteness of detail which does not leave a pin or a button unnoticed. Both are, in truth, the natural results of the predominating quality of his mind, to which we have before alluded, analysis. It is this which distinguishes the artist. His mind at once reaches forward to the effect to be produced. Having resolved to bring about certain emotions in the reader, he makes all subordinate parts tend strictly to the common centre. Even his mystery is mathematical to his own mind. To him x is a known quantity all along. In any picture that he paints, he understands the chemical properties of all his colors.

However vague some of his figures may seem, however formless the shadows, to him the outline is as clear and distinct as that of a geometrical diagram. For this reason Mr. Poe has no sympathy with *Mysticism*. The Mystic dwells *in* the mystery, is enveloped with it, it colors all his thoughts; it effects his optic nerve especially, and the commonest things get a rainbow edging from it. Mr. Poe, on the other hand, is a spectator *ab extrà*. He analyzes, he dissects, he watches

> with an eye serene,
> The very pulse of the machine,

for such it practically is to him, with wheels and cogs and piston-rods all working to produce a certain end. It is this that makes him so good a critic. Nothing baulks him, or throws him off the scent, *except now and then a prejudice.*

This analyzing tendency of his mind balances the poetical, and, by giving him the patience to be minute, enables him to throw a wonderful reality into his most unreal fancies. A monomania he paints with great power. He loves to dissect these cancers of the mind, and to trace all the subtle ramifications of its roots. In raising images of horror, also, he has a strange success; conveying to us sometimes by a dusky hint some terrible *doubt* which is the secret of all horror. He leaves to imagination the task of finishing the picture, a task to which only she is competent.

> For much imaginary work was there;
> Conceit deceitful, so compact, so kind,
> That for Achilles' image stood his spear
> Grasped in an armed hand; himself behind
> Was left unseen, save to the eye of mind.

We have hitherto spoken chiefly of Mr. Poe's *collected* tales, as by them he is more widely known than by those published since in various magazines, and which we hope soon to see collected. In these he has more strikingly displayed his analytic propensity.

Beside the merit of conception, Mr. Poe's writings have also that of form. His style is highly finished, graceful and truly classical. It would be hard to find a living author who had displayed such varied powers. As an example of his style we would refer to one of his tales, "The House of Usher," in the first volume of his *Tales of the Grotesque and Arabesque*. It has a singular charm for us, and we think that no one could read it without being strongly moved by its serene and sombre beauty. Had its author written nothing else it would alone have been enough to stamp him as a man of genius, and the master of a classic style. ⟨. . .⟩

Beside his *Tales of the Grotesque and Arabesque*, and some works unacknowledged, Mr. Poe is the author of *Arthur Gordon Pym*, a romance, in two volumes, which has run through many editions in London; of a system of Conchology, of a digest and translation of Lemmonnier's *Natural History*, and has contributed to several reviews in France, in England, and in this country. He edited the *Southern Literary Messenger* during its novitiate, and by his own contributions gained it most of its success and reputation. He was also, for some time, the editor of this magazine, and our readers will bear testimony to his ability in that capacity.

Mr. Poe is still in the prime of life, being about thirty-two years of age, and has probably as yet given but an earnest of his powers. As a critic, he has shown so superior an ability that we cannot but hope that he will collect his essays of this kind and give them a more durable form. They would be a very valuable contribution to our literature, and would fully justify all we have said in his praise. We could refer to many others of his poems than those we have quoted, to prove that he is the possessor of a pure and original vein. His tales and essays have equally shown him a master in prose. It is not for us to assign him his definite rank among contemporary authors, but we may be allowed to say that we know of *none* who has displayed more varied and striking abilities.

Notes

1. We cannot but think that this was the case in his review of W. E. Channing's poems, in which we are sure that there is much which must otherwise have challenged Mr. Poe's hearty liking.

CHARLES BAUDELAIRE
From "Edgar Allan Poe: His Life and Works"
tr. Jean Alexander [1]

Revue de Paris, March–April 1852, pp. 90–110

Some destinies are fatal. In the literature of every country there are men who bear the word *unlucky* written with mysterious letters in the sinuous folds of their foreheads. Some time ago a wretch with the strange tattoo *no luck* on his forehead was led before the court. He carried the label of his life with him everywhere, as a book bears its title, and the questioning proved that his existence conformed to his advertisement. In literary history there are similar fates. One might say that the blind Angel of Expiation, seizing certain men, whips them with all his might for the edification of the others. Yet if we study their lives attentively we find they have talent, virtue and grace. Society pronounces a special anathema and condemns them for the very vices of character that its persecution has given them. What did Hoffman fail to do to disarm destiny? What did Balzac fail to do to exorcize fortune? Hoffmann was obliged to destroy himself at the very moment, so long desired, when he began to be safe from necessity, when bookstores fought over his tales, when at last he possessed his beloved library. Balzac had three dreams: a well-organized, complete edition of his works; the settling of his debts; and a marriage long savored in the depths of his heart. Thanks to an amount of labor which stuns the most ambitious and painstaking imagination the edition was made, the debts were paid and the marriage accomplished. Balzac was happy, no doubt. But malevolent destiny, having permitted him to put one foot on the promised land, wrenched it away at once. Balzac experienced a horrible agony worthy of his strength.

Is there a Providence preparing men for misfortune from the cradle? These men whose somber and desolate talent awes us have been cast *with premeditation* into a hostile milieu. A tender and delicate spirit, a Vauvenargues, slowly unfolds its frail leaves in the gross atmosphere of a garrison. A mind that loves the open air and adores free nature struggles for a long time behind the stifling wall of a seminary. This ironic and ultragrotesque comic talent, whose laugh sometimes resembles a gasp or a sob, has been imprisoned in vast offices with green boxes and men with gold spectacles. Are there then some souls dedicated to the altar, *sanctified*, so to speak, who must march to their death and glory through perpetual self-immolation? Will the nightmare of *Tenebrae* always envelop these chosen spirits? They defend themselves in vain, they take all precautions, they perfect prudence. Let us block all the exits, close the door with a double lock, stop up the chinks in the windows. Oh! we forgot the keyhole; the Devil has already entered.

> Leur chien même les mord et leur donne la rage.
> Un ami jurera qu'ils ont trahi le roi.

Alfred de Vigny has written a book demonstrating that the poet's place is in neither a republic, nor an absolute monarchy, nor a constitutional monarchy; and no one has answered him.

The life of Edgar Poe is a wretched tragedy, and the horror of its ending is increased by its triviality. The various documents that I have just read have persuaded me that the United States was a vast cage for Poe, a great accounting establishment. All his life he made grim efforts to escape the influence of that antipathetic atmosphere. One of his biographers says that if Poe had wanted to regularize his genius and apply his creative faculties in a way more appropriate to the American soil he could have been an author with money, *a making-money author*. He said that after all, the times were not so hard for a talented man; he always found enough to live on, provided that he behaved with order and economy and used material wealth with moderation. Elsewhere, a critic shamelessly declares that however fine the genius of Poe might be, it would have been better to have merely had talent because talent is more easily turned to cash than genius is. A note written by one of his friends states that Poe was difficult to employ on a magazine, and he had to be paid less than the others because he wrote in a style too far above the ordinary. All of that reminds me of the odious paternal proverb, *"Make money, my son, honestly, if you can, BUT MAKE MONEY." What a smell of department stores*, as J. de Maistre said concerning Locke.

If you talk to an American and speak to him of Poe, he will admit Poe's genius, willingly even; perhaps he will be proud, but he will end by saying, in his superior tone, "But I am a practical man." Then, with a sardonic air, he will speak to you of the great minds that cannot retain anything; he will speak to you of Poe's loose life—his alcoholic breath, which would have caught fire by a candle's flame, his nomadic habits. He will tell you that he was an erratic creature, a planet out of orbit, that he roved from New York to Philadelphia, from Boston to Baltimore, from Baltimore to Richmond. And if, your heart already moved by these signs of a calamitous existence, you remind him that Democracy certainly has its defects—in spite of its benevolent mask of liberty, it does not always permit, perhaps, the growth of individuality; it is often very difficult to think and write in a country where there are twenty or thirty million sovereigns; moreover, *you have heard it said* that there was a tyranny much more cruel and inexorable than that of a monarchy, in the United States (that of opinion)—then you will see his eyes open wide and cast off sparks. The froth of wounded patriotism mounts to his lips, and America, by his mouth, will heap insults on metaphysics and on Europe, its old mother. America is a practical creature, vain about its industrial power and a little jealous of the old continent. It does not have time to have compassion for a poet who could be maddened by pain and isolation. It is so proud of its young immensity, so naively trusting in the omnipotence of industry, so convinced that it will finally devour the Devil, that it has a certain pity for all these incoherent dreams. Onward it says; onward and ignore the dead. It would gladly walk over solitary, free spirits and trample them as lightheartedly as the immense railways overrun the leveled forests and the monster ships overrun the debris of a ship burned the previous evening. It is in a hurry to arrive. Time and money are everything.

Some time before Balzac descended into the final abyss while uttering the noble plaints of a hero who still has great things to do, Edgar Poe, who is similar to him in many ways, was stricken by a frightful death. France lost one of her greatest geniuses and America lost a novelist, critic and philosopher scarcely made for her. Many people here are ignorant of the death of Edgar Poe; many others believe that he was a rich young gentleman, writing little, producing his strange and terrible creations in the most agreeable leisure, and knowing literary life only through rare and striking successes. The reality was quite the opposite. ⟨. . .⟩

Poe's death caused real emotion in America. Authentic testimony of pain rose from various parts of the Union. Sometimes death causes many things to be forgiven. We are happy to mention a letter from Longfellow, which does him all the more honor because Poe had treated him badly: "What a melancholy end, that of Mr. Poe, a man so richly endowed with genius! I have never known him personally, but I have always had great esteem for his power as a prose writer and as a poet. His prose is remarkably vigorous and direct, yet copious, and his verse breathes a special melodious charm, an atmosphere of true poetry, which is all-pervasive. The harshness of his criticism I have never attributed to anything but the irritability of an overly sensitive nature, exasperated by all manifestations of falseness."

The prolix author of *Evangeline* is amusing when he talks of *copiousness*. Does he take Edgar Poe for a mirror?

Comparing the character of a great man with his works is a very great and rewarding pleasure. A very legitimate curiosity has always been stimulated by biographies, by notes on manners and habits and by the physical appearance of artists and writers. People seek Erasmus' acuity of style and precision of idea in the cut of his profile; we examine the heads of Diderot and Mercier, where a little swagger mingles with goodfellowship, to find the warmth and show of their work. Voltaire's battle face reveals his stubborn irony, and his horizon-searching eye reveals his power of command or of prophecy. The solid countenance of Joseph de Maistre is that of the eagle and the bull at the same time. And who has not cudgeled his brains to decipher the *Human Comedy* by means of the powerful and complex forehead and face of Balzac?

Edgar Poe was a little below average in stature, but his body was solidly built; his feet and hands were small. Before his health was undermined, he was capable of marvelous feats of strength. I believe that it has often been noticed that Nature makes life very hard for those of whom she expects great things. Although they appear frail sometimes, they are built like athletes, and are as good for pleasure as for suffering. Balzac corrected the proofs for his books while attending the rehearsals of the *Resources de Quinola* and directing and playing all the roles himself; he dined with the actors, and when everyone was exhausted and had retired to sleep, he returned to work with ease. Everyone knows that he committed great excesses of insomnia and sobriety. Edgar Poe, in his youth, distinguished himself in all exercises of skill and strength and—as is revealed in his work—calculations and problems. One day he made a bet that he could leave one of the Richmond docks, swim upstream seven miles in the James River, and return on foot the same day; and he did it. It was a boiling summer day, and he did not carry it off badly. Expression of face, gestures, gait posture of head—everything singled him out, in his good days, as a man of great distinction. He was *marked* by Nature as one of those who, in a social circle, at a cafe, or in the street, *compel* the eye of the observer and engross him. If ever the word *strange* (which has been much abused in modern descriptions) has been aptly applied to anything, it is certainly to Poe's type of beauty. His features were not large, but quite regular. His complexion was a light brunette, his expression sad, distraught, and, although neither angry nor insolent, somehow displeasing. His singularly fine eyes seemed at first glance to be dark grey, but on closer examination they appeared frosted with a light indefinable violet. His forehead was superb. It did not have the ridiculous proportions invented by bad artists when, in order to flatter a genius, they transform him into a hydrocephalic, but an overflowing inner force seemed to push forward the organs of reflection and construction. The parts to which phrenologists attribute the sense of the picturesque were not absent, however; they merely seemed disturbed, jostled by the haughty and usurping tyranny of comparison, construction and causation. The sense of ideality and absolute beauty, the esthetic sense par excellence, also reigned in this forehead with calm pride. In spite of all these qualities, the head did not present an agreeable and harmonious impression. Seen full-face, it was striking and commanded attention by the domineering and inquisitorial effect of the forehead, but the profile revealed certain lacks; there was an immense mass of brain in front and back, and a moderate amount in the middle. In short, there was enormous animal and intellectual power, but weakness in the area of veneration and the affections. The despairing echoes of melancholy running through the works of Poe have a penetrating tone, it is true, but one must also admit that it is a very solitary melancholy, uncongenial to the ordinary man. I cannot help laughing when I think of some lines that a writer highly esteemed in the United States wrote about Poe some time after his death. I quote from memory, but I will answer for the meaning. "I have just reread the works of the regrettable Poe. What an admirable poet! What an amazing storyteller! What a prodigious and superhuman mind! He was really the original mind of our country. Well, I would give all of his seventy mystic, analytic and grotesque tales, so brilliant and full of ideas, for the good little hearthside book, the family book, that he could have written with the marvelously pure style that gives him such superiority over us. How much greater Mr. Poe would be!" To ask a family book of Edgar Poe! It is true, then, that human folly is the same in all climates, and the critic always wants to tie gross vegetables to ornamental shrubs.

Poe had black hair, shot through with some white threads, and a bristling moustache which he neglected to trim and to comb properly. He dressed with good taste but was a little negligent, like a gentleman who has many other things to do. His manners were excellent, very polished and self-assured, but his conversation deserves special comment. The first time that I questioned an American about it, he answered me, laughing, "Oh! oh! His conversation was not at all coherent!" After some explanation, I understood that Mr. Poe took great leaps in the world of ideas, like a mathematician who demonstrates for very intelligent students, and that he often carried on monologs. In fact, it was an essentially meaty conversation. He was not a *fine talker.* Moreover, he had a horror of conventionality, in speaking as in writing, but his vast knowledge, acquaintance with several languages, profound studies and ideas gathered in several countries made his conversation an excellent instruction. In short, he was the proper man for people who measure friendship according to the spiritual profit that they can make. Yet it seems that Poe was very indiscriminate in his choice of listeners. He scarcely troubled to discover whether his hearers were capable of understanding his tenuous abstractions or admiring the glorious conceptions which constantly flashed through the somber sky of his mind. He sat in a tavern beside a sordid ruffian and gravely expounded the great lines of his terrible book *Eureka* with a relentless coolness, as though he were dictating to a secretary or disputing with Kepler, Bacon or Swedenborg. That is a special trait of his. No man has ever freed himself more completely from the rules of society, or troubled himself less about passersby; that is why, on certain

days, he was received in low class cafes but was refused entrance to the places where *respectable people* drink. No society has ever forgiven such things, still less an English or American society. Besides, Poe already had to be forgiven his genius. In the *Messenger* he had ferociously pursued mediocrity; his criticism had been hard and disciplinary, like that of a superior, solitary man who is interested only in ideas. A moment of disgust for all things human had arrived, when only metaphysics mattered to him. Dazzling his young, unformed country with his intelligence and shocking men who thought themselves his equals with his manners, Poe inevitably became one of the most unfortunate of writers. Hostility came in crowds; solitude surrounded him. In Paris or Germany he would have found friends to give him understanding and solace. In America he had to fight for his bread. In this way his intoxication and perpetual moving are explained. He traveled through life as though it were a Sahara, and he changed abodes like an Arab.

But there are other reasons—his deep domestic sorrows, for example. We have seen his precocious youth suddenly cast into the asperity of life. Poe was almost always alone; in addition, the terrible battle in his mind and the harshness of his work must have made him seek the delight of oblivion in wine and liquor. What fatigues others gave him solace. Finally, Poe escaped literary animosity, the vertigo of the infinite, domestic sorrows and the outrages of misery in the darkness of intoxication, like the darkness of the tomb. He did not drink like a glutton but like a barbarian. The alcohol had scarcely touched his lips before he rooted himself at the counter and drank glass after glass until his good Angel was drowned and his faculties were annihilated. It is a miraculous fact, verified by all who knew him, that neither the purity and perfection of his style, nor the precision of his thought, nor his eagerness for work and difficult study was disturbed by his terrible habit. The composition of most of the good pieces preceded or followed one of his attacks. After the appearance of *Eureka*, he gave himself over furiously to drink. The very morning when the *Whig Review* published "The Raven" and the name of Poe was on every tongue, with everyone discussing his poem, he crossed Broadway in New York, stumbling and staggering against the buildings.

Literary intoxication is one of the most common and lamentable phenomena of modern life, but perhaps there are many extenuating circumstances. In the time of Saint-Amant, Chapelle and Colletet, literature was also intoxicated, but joyfully, in the company of nobles who were highly literate and who had no fear of the cabaret. Even certain ladies would not have blushed to have a taste for wine, as is proved by the adventure of one whose servant found her with Chapelle, both of them weeping hot tears after supper because of the death of poor Pindar, dead through the fault of ignorant doctors. In the eighteenth century the tradition continues, a little impaired. The school of Retif drinks, but it is already a school of pariahs, a subterranean world. Mercier, very old, is found in Cor-Honore Street. Napoleon has conquered the eighteenth century; Mercier is a little drunk, and he says that *he no longer lives except by curiosity*. Today, literary drunkenness has assumed a somber and sinister character. Now there is no particularly literate class that does itself the honor of associating with men of letters. Their absorbing work and aversion for schools hinders their uniting. As for women, their formless education and political and literary incompetence keep many authors from seeing anything in them but household utensils or objects of lust. Once dinner is digested and the animal satisfied, the poet enters the vast solitude of his thought; sometimes he is exhausted by his craft. What then? His mind grows accustomed to the idea of its invincible strength, and he can no longer resist the hope of finding again in drink the serene or terrible visions which are already his old friends. The same transformation of customs that makes the literate world a class apart is also undoubtedly responsible for the immense consumption of tobacco in the new literature.

I shall try to give an idea of the general character of the works of Edgar Poe. Giving an analysis of each work would be impossible without writing a book, for this singular man, in spite of his disordered and diabolic life, produced a great deal.

When he was appointed editor of the *Southern Literary Messenger*, it was stipulated that he receive 2500 francs a year. In exchange for this paltry salary, he was responsible for reading and selecting pieces for each month's issue and composing the part called *editorial*—that is to say, he evaluated all the works that appeared and weighed all of the literary events. In addition, he very often contributed a novella or a bit of poetry. He plied this trade for nearly two years. Thanks to his active direction and the originality of his criticism, the *Literary Messenger* soon attracted all eyes. Before me I have the issues of those two years. The editorial part is considerable, and the articles are very long. In the same issue, we often find reviews of a novel, a book of poetry, a medical book and a book on physics or history. All the reviews are written with the greatest care and indicate a knowledge of various literatures and a scientific aptitude reminiscent of French writers of the eighteenth century. Apparently Poe had put his time to good use during his previous misfortunes, and had turned over many ideas. He wrote a remarkable quantity of critical reviews of the principal English and American authors, and often of French memoirs. The source of an idea, its origin and end, the school to which it belonged, the salutary or noxious method of the author—all of these were neatly, clearly and rapidly explained. Although Poe attracted much attention, he also made many enemies. Profoundly absorbed in his opinions, he waged tireless war on false reasoning, stupid pastiches, solecisms, barbarisms and all the literary crimes daily committed in books and newspapers. Yet he could not be reproached, for he preached by example. His style is pure; it is adequate to his ideas and renders their precise impression. Poe is always correct. It is very remarkable that a man of such roving and ambitious imagination should at the same time be so fond of rules and so capable of careful analysis and patient research. He could be called an antithesis made flesh. But his fame as a critic damaged his literary future a great deal. Many wanted to be avenged, and every possible reproach was cast in his face as the number of his works increased. Everyone knows the long, banal litany: immorality, lack of tenderness, absence of conclusions, extravagance, useless literature. French criticism has never forgiven Balzac for *Le grand homme de province à Paris*.

In poetry, Edgar Poe is a solitary spirit. Almost alone on the other side of the ocean he represents the Romantic movement. Properly speaking, he is the first American to make his style a tool. His profound and plaintive poetry is nevertheless finely wrought, pure, correct and brilliant as a crystal jewel. In spite of the amazing qualities which have made soft, tender spirits adore them, Alfred de Musset and Alphonse de Lamartine would obviously not have been his friends if he had lived here. They do not have enough will and self-mastery. Although Edgar Poe loved complicated rhythms, he shaped them in a profound harmony no matter how complicated they were. One of his short poems, "The Bells," is a veritable literary curiosity, but it is totally untranslatable. "The Raven" had a huge success. In the judgment of Longfellow and Emerson, it is a marvel. The content is slight; it is a pure work of art. 〈. . .〉

The tone is grave and almost supernatural, like insomniac thoughts; the lines fall one by one, like monotonous tears. In "Dreamland," he tried to portray the series of dreams and fantastic images besieging the soul when the body's eye is closed. Other poems, such as "Ulalume" and "Annabel Lee" enjoy equal fame. But the poetic stock of Edgar Poe is slight. His condensed and finely-worked poetry undoubtedly cost much effort, and he was often in need of money in order to surrender himself to that delightful and fruitless pain.

As a novelist and storyteller, Edgar Poe is unique in his field, just as Maturin, Balzac and Hoffmann were in theirs. The various pieces scattered throughout the magazines have been gathered into two sheaves, *Tales of the Grotesque and Arabesque* and *Edgar A. Poe's Tales* in the edition of Wiley and Putnam. There are approximately 72 pieces. Some are purely grotesque, some are preoccupied with magnetism, some are wild clownings, some are unleashed aspirations towards the infinite. The tiny volume of tales has had great success in Paris as well as in America because it contains stories that are highly dramatic, but dramatic in a special way.

I should like to characterize Poe's work very briefly and exactly, for it is a totally new creation. The qualities that essentially define it and distinguish it from others are (if I may be pardoned these strange words) conjecturism and probabilism. My assertions can be verified by examining some of his subjects.

"The Gold Bug": analysis of a succession of methods for deciphering a cryptogram which will help to disclose hidden treasure. I cannot help thinking regretfully that the unfortunate E. Poe must have dreamed more than once of means of discovering treasure. The explanation of this method, which becomes the odd literary specialty of certain police secretaries, is eminently logical and lucid. The description of the treasure is fine; what a good sense of warmth and dazzlement one has! For the treasure is found. *It was not a dream* as usually happens in novels—the author awakening us brutally after having aroused our spirits by whetting our hopes. This time it is a *real* treasure and the decipherer has truly won it. Here is the exact sum: in money, $450,000 (not an ounce of silver, but all gold and very ancient, enormous, weighty pieces with unreadable inscriptions), 110 diamonds, 18 rubies, 310 emeralds, 21 sapphires, one opal, 200 rings and massive earrings, some 30 chains, 83 crucifixes, 5 censors, an enormous punchbowl of gold with vine leaves and bacchantes, 2 sword-handles and 197 watches adorned with precious stones. The content of the coffer is first valued at a million and a half dollars, but the sale of the jewels brings the total above that. The description of this treasure makes one dizzy with largesse and ambitions of benevolence. The coffer hidden by the pirate Kidd contained enough, certainly, to ease many unknown desperations.

"The Maelstrom": Would it not be possible to descend into an abyss whose bottom has never been sounded, in studying the laws of gravity in a new way?

"The Murders in the Rue Morgue" could instruct prosecuting attorneys. A murder has been committed. How? By whom? This affair contains some inexplicable and contradictory facts, and the police have given up. A young man who is gathering evidence for the love of the art presents himself. Through extreme concentration of thought and successive analysis of all the phenomena of understanding, he happens upon the law of the generation of ideas. Between one word and the next, between two ideas which are apparently unrelated, he can establish a complete intermediary series before the dazzled eyes of the police, and fill in the lacuna of unexpressed and almost unconscious ideas. He has closely studied all the possibilities and all the probable associations. He has ascended from induction to induction until he succeeds in showing decisively that an ape has committed the crime.

"The Mesmeric Revelation": The author's point of departure has evidently been this question: With the help of the unknown power called magnetic fluid, could we discover the law that rules the ultimate worlds? The beginning is full of dignity and solemnity. The physician has put his patient to sleep simply to ease him. "What do you think about your illness?—I will die.—Will that cause you sorrow?—No." The patient complains that he is badly questioned. "Direct me, says the doctor.—Begin at the beginning.—What is the beginning?—(Very low) It is GOD.—Is God a spirit?—No.—Is he matter, then?—No." A vast theory of matter follows, of gradations of matter and the hierarchy of beings. I published this story in an issue of *Liberté de Penser* in 1848.

Elsewhere there is an account of a spirit that had lived on an extinguished planet. This was the point of departure: Can one, by means of induction and analysis, determine what physical and moral phenomena would occur among the inhabitants of a world approached by a murderous comet?

At other times we find the purely fantastic modeled on nature, without explanation, in the manner of Hoffman: "The Man of the Crowd" plunges endlessly into the heart of the crowd; he swims with delight in the human sea. When the shadowy twilight full of tremulous lights descends, he flies from the silenced districts and ardently seeks the places where human matter swarms busily. As the circle of light and life shrinks, he seeks the center uneasily. Like men in a flood, he clings desperately to the last culminating points of public movement. And that is all we know. Is he a criminal who has a horror of solitude? Is he an imbecile who cannot endure himself? ⟨. . .⟩

Poe usually suppresses the minor details or gives them a minimal value. Because of this harsh severity, the generating idea is more evident and the subject stands out vividly against the bare background. His method of narration is simple. He overuses the first person pronoun with cynical monotony. One might say that he is so sure of being interesting that he does not bother to vary his technique. His tales are nearly always the account or manuscript of the main character. As for his ardent exploration of the horrible, I have noticed it in various men, and it is often the result of a great unoccupied vital energy, of an obstinate chastity sometimes, and also of a profound sensibility which has been thwarted. The supernatural pleasure that a man can experience in seeing his own blood run—the brusque, useless movements, the cries almost involuntarily piercing the air—is a similar phenomenon. Pain is a release from pain, and action is a relaxation from repose.

Another peculiar trait of his work is that it is completely anti-feminine. Let me explain. Women write and write in a swift overflow; their hearts prattle by the ream. Generally, they know neither art, nor measure, nor logic. Their style trains and coils like their garments. In spite of her superiority, the very great and justly famous George Sand has not entirely escaped this law of temperament; she throws her masterpieces into the mail as though they were letters. It is said that she writes her books on letter paper.

In Poe's books the style is condensed, tightly linked. The ill will or laziness of the reader cannot slip through the mesh of this logically woven net. All ideas, like obedient arrows, fly to the same target.

I have followed a long trail of tales without finding one love story. This man is so intoxicating that I did not think about it until the end. Without claiming to extol the ascetic system of an ambitious mind absolutely, I think that such an austere literature would be a useful weapon against the invading fatuity of women, who are more and more stimulated by the disgusting idolatry of men. And I am very lenient toward Voltaire, who thought it well in the preface to his womanless tragedy, *La Mort de César*, to emphasize his glorious tour de force by feigning excuses for his impertinence.

In Edgar Poe there are no enervating whines, but always a tireless ardor for the ideal. Like Balzac, who died perhaps saddened because he was not a pure scholar, Poe is enchanted by science. He wrote a *Manual for the Conchologist*, which I have forgotten to mention. Like conquerors and philosophers, he has a compelling aspiration toward unity and he assimilates morality into physical things. It could be said that he attempts to apply the procedures of philosophy to literature, and the methods of algebra to philosophy. In the constant ascent toward the infinite, one loses his breath. In this literature the air is rarefied as in a laboratory. We endlessly contemplate the glorification of will applied to induction and analysis. Poe seems to intend to wrench language from the prophets and to monopolize rational explanation. Thus, the landscapes which sometimes serve as background for his feverish fictions are pale as ghosts. Poe scarcely shared the passions of other men; he sketched trees and clouds that seem to be the dream of clouds and trees, or strange characters shaken by a supernatural, galvanic shiver.

Once, however, he set himself to write a purely human book. *The Narrative of Arthur Gordon Pym*, which has had no great success, is a story of sailors who, after severe damage to the ship, have been becalmed in the South Seas. The author's genius delights in these terrible scenes and in the amazing sketches of tribes and islands which are not indicated on the maps. The style of this book is extremely simple and detailed. ⟨. . .⟩

Although *Eureka* was undoubtedly the long-cherished dream of Edgar Poe, I cannot write a precise account of it here, for it is a book that requires a special article. Whoever has read the "Mesmeric Revelation" knows the metaphysical tendencies of the author. *Eureka* attempts to develop the process and show the law by which the universe assumed its present visible form and organization. It shows that the same law which began creation will act to destroy the world and absorb it. One readily comprehends why I do not care to engage lightly in discussion of such an ambitious attempt. I would be afraid of erring and slandering an author for whom I have the deepest respect. Edgar Poe has already been accused of pantheism, and although I may be forced to agree that appearances lead to such a conclusion, I can assert that, like many other great men bewitched by logic, he sometimes contradicts himself. It is to his credit. Thus his pantheism is counteracted by his ideas on the hierarchy of beings and by many passages that obviously affirm the permanence of personality.

Edgar Poe was very proud of this book, which naturally did not have the same success as his tales. One must read it cautiously and verify his strange ideas by checking them against similar and opposite systems.

I had a friend who was also a metaphysician in his fashion, obsessed and absolute, with the air of a Saint Just. He often said to me, taking an example from the world and looking at me from the corner of his eye, "Every mystic has a hidden vice." And I continued his thought: Then he must be destroyed. But I laughed, because I did not understand. One day, as I was chatting with a well-known, busy bookseller whose specialty is to cater to the enthusiasms of all the mystical band and the obscure courtesans of occult sciences, I asked for information on his clientele. He said to me, "Remember that every mystic has a hidden vice, often a very material one—drunkenness, gormandizing, lewdness. One will be avaricious, the other cruel, etc."

Good Lord! I said to myself. Then what is the fatal law that binds us, dominates us, and avenges the violation of its insufferable despotism by degrading and sapping our moral being? The visionaries have been the greatest of men. Why must they be punished for their greatness? Hasn't their ambition been the most noble? Will man eternally be so limited that one of his faculties cannot expand except at the expense of the others? If wanting to know the truth at all costs is a great crime, or if it can lead to great error, if stupidity and indifference are virtues and guarantees of balance, I think we should be very forbearing towards these illustrious criminals, for we children of the eighteenth and nineteenth centuries can all be accused of the same vice.

I say this shamelessly, because I feel it comes from a profound feeling of pity and tenderness: Edgar Poe—drunkard, pauper, oppressed, pariah—pleases me more than do the calm and virtuous Goethe and W. Scott. I would readily say of him and of a particular class of men what the catechism says of our Lord: "He has suffered much for us."

We could write on his tomb, "All you who have passionately sought to discover the laws of your being, who have aspired to infinity, you whose rebuffed feelings have had to seek a frightful relief in the wine of debauchery, pray for him. His corporeal being, now purified, floats among the beings whose existence he glimpsed. Pray for him who sees and knows: he will intercede for you."

Notes

1. From Jean Alexander, *Affidavits of Genius: Edgar Allan Poe and the French Critics, 1847–1924* (Port Washington, NY: Kennikat Press, 1971), pp. 99–121. Reprinted with permission.

GEORGE GILFILLAN
From "Edgar Poe"
A Third Gallery of Portraits
1854, pp. 380–88

A case so strange as Poe's compels us into new and more searching forms of critical, as well as of moral analysis. Genius has very generally been ascribed to him; but some will resist and deny the ascription—proceeding partly upon peculiar notions of what genius is, and partly from a very natural reluctance to concede to a wretch so vile a gift so noble, and in a degree, too, so unusually large. Genius has often been defined as something inseparably connected with the *genial* nature. If this definition be correct, Poe was not a genius any more than Swift, for geniality neither he nor his writings possessed. But if genius mean a compound of imagination and inventiveness, original thought heated by passion, and accompanied by power of fancy, Poe was a man of great genius. In wanting geniality, however, he wanted all that makes genius lovely and beloved, at once beautiful and dear. A man of genius, without geniality, is a mountain clad in snow, companioned by tempests, and visited only by hardy explorers who love sublime nakedness, and to snatch a fearful joy from gazing down black precipices; a man whose genius is steeped in the genial nature, is an autumn landscape, suggesting not only images of beauty, and giving thrills of delight, but yielding peaceful and plenteous fruits, and in which the heart finds a rest and a home. From the one the timid, the weak, and the gentle retire in a terror which overpowers their admiration; but in the other the lowest and feeblest find shelter and repose. Even Dante and Milton, owing to the excess of their intellectual and imaginative powers over their genial feelings, are less loved than admired; while the vast supremacy of Shakspere is due, not merely to his universal genius, but to the predominance of geniality and heart in all his writings. Many envy and even hate Dante and Milton; and had Shakspere only written his loftier tragedies, many might have hated and envied him too; but who can entertain any such feelings for the author of the *Comedy of Errors* and *Twelfth Night*, the creator of Falstaff, Dogberry, and Verres? If genius be the sun, geniality is the atmosphere through which alone his beams can penetrate with power, or be seen with pleasure.

Poe is distinguished by many styles and many manners. He is the author of fictions as matter-of-fact in their construction and language as the stories of Defoe, and of tales as weird and wonderful as those of Hoffman; of amatory strains trembling, if not with heart, with passion, and suffused with the purple glow of love, and of poems, dirges either in form or in spirit, into which the genius of desolation has shed its dreariest essence; of verses, gay with apparent, but shallow joy, and of others dark with a misery which reminds us of the helpless, hopeless, infinite misery, which sometimes visits the soul in dreams. But, amid all this diversity of tone and of subject, the leading qualities of his mind are obvious. These consist of strong imagination—an imagination, however, more fertile in incidents, forms, and characters, than in images; keen power of analysis, rather than synthetic genius; immense inventiveness; hot passions, cooled down by the presence of art, till they resemble sculptured flame, or "lightning in the hand of a painted Jupiter;" knowledge rather *recherché* and varied, than strict, accurate, or profound; and an unlimited command of words, phrases, musical combinations of sound, and all the other materials of an intellectual workman. The direction of these powers was controlled principally by his habits and circumstances. These made him morbid; and his writings have all a certain morbidity about them. You say at once, cool and clear as most of them are, these are not the productions of a healthy or happy man. But surely never was there such a calm despair—such a fiery torment so cased in ice! When you compare the writings with the known facts of the author's history, they appear to be so like, and so unlike, his character. You seem looking at an inverted image. You have the features, but they are discovered at an unexpected angle. You see traces of the misery of a confirmed debauchee, but none of his disconnected ravings, or of the partial imbecility which often falls upon his powers. There is a strict, almost logical, method in his wildest productions. He tells us himself that he wrote "The Raven" as coolly as if he had been working out a mathematical problem. His frenzy, if that name must be given to the strange fire which was in him, is a conscious one; he feels his own pulse when it is at the wildest, and looks at his foaming lips in the looking-glass.

Poe was led by a singular attraction to all dark, dreadful, and disgusting objects and thoughts: maelstroms, mysteries, murders, mummies, premature burials, excursions to the moon, solitary mansions surrounded by mist and weighed down by mysterious dooms, lonely tarns, trembling to the winds of autumn, and begirt by the shivering ghosts of woods—

these are the materials which his wild imagination loves to work with, and out of them to weave the most fantastic and dismal of worlds. Yet there's "magic in the web." You often revolt at his subjects; but no sooner does he enter on them, than your attention is riveted, you lend him your ears—nay, that is a feeble word, you surrender your whole being to him for a season, although it be as you succumb, body and soul, to the dominion of a nightmare. What greatly increases the effect, as in *Gulliver's Travels*, is the circumstantiality with which he recounts the most amazing and incredible things. His tales, too, are generally cast into the autobiographical form, which adds much to their living vraisemblance and vivid power. It is Coleridge's "Old Mariner" over again. Strange, wild, terrible, is the tale he has to tell; haggard, wo-begone, unearthly, is the appearance of the narrator. Every one at first, like the wedding guest, is disposed to shrink and beat his breast; but he holds you with his glittering eye, he forces you to follow him into his own enchanted region, and once there, you forget everything, your home, your friends, your creed, your very personal identity, and become swallowed up like a straw in the maelstrom of his story, and forget to breathe till it is ended, and the mysterious tale-teller is gone. And during all the wild and whirling narrative, the same chilly glitter has continued to shine in his eye, his blood has never warmed, and he has never exalted his voice, above a thrilling whisper.

Poe's power may perhaps be said to be divisible into two parts: first, that of adding an air of circumstantial verity to incredibilities; and, secondly, that of throwing a weird lustre upon commonplace events. He tells fiction so minutely, and with such apparent simplicity and sincerity, that you almost believe it true; and he so combines and so recounts such incidents as you meet with every day in the newspapers, that you feel truth to be stranger far than fiction. Look, as a specimen of the first, to his "Descent into the Maelstrom," and to his "Hans Pfaal's Journey to the Moon." Both are impossible; the former as much so as the latter; but he tells them with such Dante-like directness, and such Defoe-like minuteness, holding his watch, and marking, as it were, every second in the progress of each stupendous lie, that you rub your eyes at the close, and ask the question, Might not all this actually have occurred? And then turn to the "Murders in the Rue St Morgue," or to the "Mystery of Marie Roget," and see how, by the disposition of the drapery he throws over little or ordinary incidents, connected, indeed, with an extraordinary catastrophe, he lends

> The light which never was on sea or shore

to streets of revelry and vulgar sin, and to streams whose sluggish waters are never disturbed save by the plash of murdered victims, or by the plunge of suicides desperately hurling their bodies to the fishes, and their souls to the flames.

In one point, Poe bears a striking resemblance to his own illustrious countryman, Brockden Brown—neither resort to agency absolutely supernatural, in order to produce their terrific effects. They despise to start a ghost from the grave—they look upon this as a cheap and *fade* expedient—they appeal to the "mightier might" of the human passions, or to those strange unsolved phenomena in the human mind, which the terms mesmerism and somnambulism serve rather to disguise than to discover, and sweat out from their native soil superstitions far more powerful than those of the past. Once only does Poe approach the brink of the purely preternatural—it is in that dreary tale, the "Fall of the House of Usher;" and yet, nothing so discovers the mastery of the writer, as the manner in which he avoids, while nearing, the gulf. There is really nothing,

after all, in the strange incidents of that story, but what natural principles can explain. But Poe so arranges and adjusts the singular circumstances to each other, and weaves around them such an artful mist, that they produce a most unearthly effect. Perhaps some may think that he has fairly crossed the line in that dialogue between Charmian and Iras, describing the conflagration of the world. But, even there, how admirably does he produce a certain feeling of probability, by the management of the natural causes which he brings in to produce the catastrophe. He burns his old witch-mother, the earth, scientifically! We must add that the above is the only respect in which Poe resembles Brown. Brown was a virtuous and amiable man, and his works, although darkened by unsettled religious views, breathe a fine spirit of humanity. Poe wonders at, and hates man; Brown wonders at, but at the same time pities, loves, and hopes in him. Brown mingled among men like a bewildered angel; Poe like a prying fiend.

We have already alluded to the singular power of analysis possessed by this strange being. This is chiefly conspicuous in those tales of his which turn upon circumstantial evidence. No lawyer or judge has ever equalled Poe in the power he manifests of sifting evidence—of balancing probabilities—of finding the *multum* of a large legal case in the *parvum* of some minute and well-nigh invisible point—and in constructing the real story out of a hundred dubious and conflicting incidents. What scales he carries with him! how fine and tremulous with essential justice! And with what a microscopic eye he watches every footprint! Letters thrown loose on the mantelpiece, bell-ropes, branches of trees, handkerchiefs, &c., become to him instinct with meaning, and point with silent finger to crime and to punishment. And to think of this subtle algebraic power, combined with such a strong ideality, and with such an utterly corrupted moral nature! Surely none of the hybrids which geology has dug out of the graves of chaos, and exhibited to our shuddering view, is half so strange a compound as was Edgar Poe. We have hitherto scarcely glanced at his poetry. It, although lying in a very short compass, is of various merit: it is an abridgment of the man in his strength and weakness. Its chief distinction, as a whole, from his prose, is its peculiar music. *That*, like all his powers, is fitful, changeful, varying; but not more so than to show the ever-varying moods of his mind, acting on a peculiar and indefinite theory of sound. The alpha and omega of that theory may be condensed in the word "reiteration." He knows the effect which can be produced by ringing changes on particular words. The strength of all his strains consequently lies in their chorus, or "oure turn," as we call it in Scotland. We do not think that he could have succeeded in sustaining the harmonies or keeping up the interest of a large poem. But his short flights are exceedingly beautiful, and some of his poems are miracles of melody. All our readers are familiar with "The Raven." It is a dark world in itself; it rises in your sky suddenly as the cloud like a man's hand rose in the heaven of Palestine, and covers all the horizon with the blackness of darkness. As usual in his writings, it is but a common event idealised; there is nothing supernatural or even extraordinary in the incident recounted; but the reiteration of the one dreary word "nevermore;" the effect produced by seating the solemn bird of yore upon the bust of Pallas; the manner in which the fowl with its fiery eyes becomes the evil conscience or memory of the lonely widower; and the management of the time, the season, and the circumstances—all unite in making the Raven in its flesh and blood a far more terrific apparition than ever from the shades made night hideous, while "revisiting the glimpses of the moon." The poem belongs to a singular class of poetic uniques, each of which is itself enough to make a reputation, such as Coleridge's *Rime of the Anciente Marinere*, or *Christabel*, and Aird's "Devil's Dream upon Mount Acksbeck"—poems in which some one new and generally dark idea is wrought out into a whole so strikingly complete and self-contained as to resemble creation, and in which thought, imagery, language, and music combine to produce a similar effect, and are made to chime together like bells. What entireness of effect, for instance, is produced in the "Devil's Dream," by the unearthly theme, the strange title, the austere and terrible figures, the singular verse, and the knotty and contorted language; and in the *Rime of the Anciente Marinere*, by the ghastly form of the narrator—the wild rhythm, the new mythology, and the exotic diction of the tale he tells! So Poe's "Raven" has the unity of a tree blasted, trunk, and twigs, and root, by a flash of lightning. Never did melancholy more thoroughly "mark for its own" any poem than this. All is in intense keeping. Short as the poem is, it has a beginning, middle, and end. Its commencement how abrupt and striking—the time a December midnight—the poet a solitary man, sitting, "weak and weary," poring in helpless fixity, but with no profit or pleasure, over a black-letter volume; the fire half expired, and the dying embers haunted by their own ghosts, and shivering above the hearth! The middle is attained, when the raven mounts the bust of Pallas, and is fascinating the solitary wretch by his black, glittering plumage, and his measured, melancholy croak. And the end closes as with the wings of night over the sorrow of the unfortunate, and these dark words conclude the tale:—

> And my soul from out that shadow that lies floating
> on the floor,
> Shall be lifted Nevermore.

You feel as if the poem might have been penned by the finger of one of the damned.

The same shadow of unutterable wo rests upon several of his smaller poems, and the effect is greatly enhanced by their gay and song-like rhythm. That madness or misery which *sings* out its terror or grief, is always the most desperate. It is like a burden of hell set to an air of heaven. "Ulalume" might have been written by Coleridge during the sad middle portion of his life. There is a sense of dreariness and desolation as of the last of earth's autumns, which we find nowhere else in such perfection. What a picture these words convey to the imagination:—

> The skies they were ashen and sober;
> The leaves they were crisped and sere—
> The leaves they were withering and sere,
> It was night in the lonesome October
> Of my most immemorial year.
> It was hard by the dim lake of Auber,
> In the misty mid-region of Weir—
> It was down by the dark tarn of Auber,
> In the ghoul-haunted woodland of Weir.

These to many will appear only words; but what wondrous words. What a spell they wield! Like a wasted haggard face, they have no bloom or beauty; but what a tale they tell! Weir—Auber—where are they? They exist not, except in the writer's imagination, and in yours, for the instant they are uttered, a misty picture, with a tarn, dark as a murderer's eye, below, and the last thin, yellow leaves of October fluttering above—exponents both of a misery which scorns the name of sorrow, and knows neither limit nor termination—is hung up in the chamber of your soul for ever. What power, too, there is in the "Haunted Palace," particularly in the last words, "They laugh, but smile no more!" Dante has nothing superior in all those

chilly yet fervent words of his, where "the ground burns frore, and cold performs the effect of fire."

We must now close our sketch of Poe; and we do so with feelings of wonder, pity, and awful sorrow, tempted to look up to heaven, and to cry, "Lord, why didst thou make this man in vain?" Yet perhaps there was even in him some latent spark of goodness, which may even now be developing itself under a kindlier sky. He has gone far away from the misty mid-region of Weir; his dreams of cosmogonies have been tested by the searching light of Eternity's truth; his errors have received the reward that was meet; and we cannot but say, ere we close, Peace even to the well-nigh putrid dust of Edgar Poe.

EDMUND CLARENCE STEDMAN
From "Edgar Allan Poe"
Poets of America
1885, pp. 225–28, 248–64

I

Upon the roll of American authors a few names are written apart from the many. With each of these is associated some accident of condition, some memory of original or eccentric genius, through which it arrests attention and claims our special wonder. The light of none among these few has been more fervid and recurrent than that of Edgar Allan Poe. But, as I in turn pronounce his name, and in my turn would estimate the man and his writings, I am at once confronted by the question, Is this poet, as now remembered, as now portrayed to us, the real Poe who lived and sang and suffered, and who died but little more than a quarter-century ago?

The great heart of the world throbs warmly over the struggles of our kind; the imagination of the world dwells upon and enlarges the glory and the shame of human action in the past. Year after year, the heart-beats are more warm, the conception grows more distinct with light and shade. The person that was is made the framework of an image to which the tender, the romantic, the thoughtful, the simple, and the wise add each his own folly or wisdom, his own joy and sorrow and uttermost yearning. Thus, not only true heroes and poets, but many who have been conspicuous through force of circumstances, become idealized as time goes by. The critic's first labor often is the task of distinguishing between men, as history and their works display them, and the ideals which one and another have conspired to urge upon his acceptance.

The difficulty is increased when, as in the case of Poe, a twofold ideal exists, of whose opposite sides many that have written upon him seem to observe but one. In the opinion of some people, even now, his life was not only pitiful, but odious, and his writings are false and insincere. They speak of his morbid genius, his unjust criticisms, his weakness and ingratitude, and scarcely can endure the mention of his name. Others recount his history as that of a sensitive, gifted being, most sorely beset and environed, who was tried beyond his strength and prematurely yielded, but still uttered not a few undying strains. As a new generation has arisen, and those of his own who knew him are passing away, the latter class of his reviewers seems to outnumber the former. A chorus of indiscriminate praise has grown so loud as really to be an ill omen for his fame; yet, on the whole, the wisest modern estimate of his character and writings has not lessened the interest long ago felt in them at home and abroad.

It seems to me that two things at least are certain. First, and although his life has been the subject of the research which is awarded only to strange and suggestive careers, he was, after all, a man of like passions with ourselves,—one who, if weaker in his weaknesses than many, and stronger in his strength, may not have been so bad, nor yet so good, as one and another have painted him. Thousands have gone as far toward both extremes, and the world never has heard of them. Only the gift of genius has made the temperament of Poe a common theme. And thus, I also think, we are sure, in once more calling up his shade, that we invoke the manes of a poet. Of his right to this much-abused title there can be little dispute, nor of the claim that, whatever he lacked in compass, he was unique among his fellows,—so different from any other writer that America has produced as really to stand alone. He must have had genius to furnish even the basis for an ideal which excites this persistent interest. Yes, we are on firm ground with relation to his genuineness as a poet. But his narrowness of range, and the slender body of his poetic remains, of themselves should make writers hesitate to pronounce him our greatest one. His verse is as conspicuous for what it shows he could not do as for that which he did. He is another of those poets, outside the New England school, of whom each has made his mark in a separate way,—among them all, none more decisively than Poe. So far as the judgment of a few rare spirits in foreign lands may be counted the verdict of "posterity," an estimate of him is not to be lightly and flippantly made. Nor is it long since a group of his contemporaries and successors, in his own country, spoke of him as a poet whose works are a lasting monument, and of his "imperishable" fame.

After every allowance, it seems difficult for one not utterly jaded to read his poetry and tales without yielding to their original and haunting spell. Even as we drive out of mind the popular conceptions of his nature, and look only at the portraits of him in the flesh, we needs must pause and contemplate, thoughtfully and with renewed feeling, one of the marked ideal faces that seem—like those of Byron, De Musset, Heine—to fulfil all the traditions of genius, of picturesqueness, of literary and romantic effect. ⟨. . .⟩

IV

Few and brief are ⟨the⟩ *reliquiæ* which determine his fame as a poet. What do they tell us of his lyrical genius and method? Clearly enough, that he possessed an exquisite faculty, which he exercised within definite bounds. It may be that within those bounds he would have done more if events had not hindered him, as he declared, "from making any serious effort" in the field of his choice. In boyhood he had decided views as to the province of song, and he never afterward changed them. The preface to his West Point edition, rambling and conceited as it is,—affording such a contrast to the proud humility of Keats's preface to *Endymion*,—gives us the gist of his creed, and shows that the instinct of the young poet was scarcely less delicate than that of his nobler kinsman. Poe thought the object of poetry was pleasure, not truth; the pleasure must not be definite, but subtile, and therefore poetry is opposed to romance; music is an *essential*, "since the comprehension of sweet sound is our most indefinite conception." Metaphysics in verse he hated, pronouncing the Lake theory a new form of didacticism that had injured even the tuneful Coleridge. For a neophyte this was not bad, and after certain reservations few will disagree with him. Eighteen years later, in his charming lecture, "The Poetic Principle," he offered simply an extension of these ideas, with reasons why a long poem "cannot exist." One is tempted to rejoin that the standard of length in a poem, as in a piece of music, is relative, depending upon the power of the

maker and the recipient to prolong their exalted moods. We might, also, quote Landor's "Pentameron," concerning the greatness of a poet, or even Beecher's saying that "pint measures are soon filled." The lecture justly denounces the "heresy of the didactic," and then declares poetry to be the child of Taste,—devoted solely to the Rhythmical Creation of Beauty, as it is in music that the soul most nearly attains the supernal end for which it struggles. In fine, Poe, with "the mad pride of intellectuality," refused to look beyond the scope of his own gift, and would restrict the poet to one method and even to a single theme. In his *ex post facto* analysis of "The Raven" he conceives the highest tone of beauty to be sadness, caused by the pathos of existence and our inability to grasp the unknown. Of all beauty that of a beautiful woman is the supremest, her death is the saddest loss—and therefore "the most poetical topic in the world." He would treat this musically by application of the refrain, increasing the sorrowful loveliness of his poem by contrast of something homely, fantastic, or quaint.

Poe's own range was quite within his theory. His juvenile versions of what afterward became poems were so very "indefinite" as to express almost nothing; they resembled those marvellous stanzas of Dr. Chivers, that sound magnificently, .—I have heard Bayard Taylor and Swinburne rehearse them with shouts of delight—and that have no meaning at all. Poe could not remain a Chivers, but sound always was his forte. We rarely find his highest imagination in his verse, or the creation of poetic phrases such as came to the lips of Keats without a summons. He lacked the dramatic power of combination, and produced no symphony in rhythm,—was strictly a melodist, who achieved wonders in a single strain. Neither Mrs. Browning nor any other poet had "applied" the refrain in Poe's fashion, nor so effectively. In "The Bells" its use is limited almost to one word, the only English word, perhaps, that could be repeated incessantly as the burden of such a poem. In "The Raven," "Lenore," and elsewhere, he employed the repetend also, and with still more novel results:—

> An anthem for the queenliest dead that ever died so young,
> A dirge for her, the doubly dead, in that she died so young.

> Our talk had been serious and sober,
> But our thoughts they were palsied and sere,
> Our memories were treacherous and sere.

One thing profitably may be noted by latter-day poets. Poe used none but elementary English measures, relying upon his music and atmosphere for their effect. This is true of those which seem most intricate, as in "The Bells" and "Ulalume." "Lenore" and "For Annie" are the simplest of ballad forms. I have a fancy that our Southern poet's ear caught the music of "Annabel Lee" and "Eulalie," if not their special quality, from the plaintive, melodious negro songs utilized by those early writers of "minstrelsy" who have been denominated the only composers of a genuine American school. This suggestion may be scouted, but an expert might suspect the one to be a patrician refinement upon the melody, feeling, and humble charm of the other.

Poe was not a single-poem poet, but the poet of a single mood. His materials were seemingly a small stock in trade, chiefly of Angels and Demons, with an attendance of Dreams, Echoes, Ghouls, Gnomes and Mimes, ready at hand. He selected or coined, for use and re-use, a number of what have been called "beautiful words,"—"albatross," "halcyon," "scintillant," "Ligeia," "Weir," "Yaanek," "Auber," "D'Elormie," and the like. Everything was subordinate to sound. But his poetry, as it places us under the spell of the senses, enables us to enter, through their reaction upon the spirit, his indefinable mood; nor should we forget that Coleridge owes his specific rank as a poet, not to his philosophic verse, but to melodious fragments, and greatly to the rhythm of *The Ancient Mariner* and of *Christabel*. Poe's melodies lure us to the point where we seem to hear angelic lutes and citherns, or elfin instruments that make music in "the land east of the sun and west of the moon." The enchantment may not be that of Israfel, nor of the harper who exorcised the evil genius of Saul, but it is at least that of some plumed being of the middle air, of a charmer charming so sweetly that his numbers are the burden of mystic dreams.

V

If Poe's standing depended chiefly upon these few poems, notable as they are, his name would be recalled less frequently. His intellectual strength and rarest imagination are to be found in his *Tales*. To them, and to literary criticism, his main labors were devoted.

The limits of this chapter constrain me to say less than I have in mind concerning his prose writings. As with his poems, so with the "Tales,"—their dates are of little importance. His irregular life forced him to alternate good work with bad, and some of his best stories were written early. He was an apostle of the art that refuses to take its color from a given time or country, and of the revolt against commonplace, and his inventions partook of the romantic and the wonderful. He added to a Greek perception of form the Oriental passion for decoration. All the materials of the wizard's craft were at his command. He was not a pupil of Beckford, Godwin, Maturin, Hoffman, or Fouqué; and yet if these writers were to be grouped we should think also of Poe, and give him no second place among them. "The young fellow is highly imaginative, and a little given to the terrific," said Kennedy, in his honest way. Poe could not have written a novel, as we term it, as well as the feeblest of Harper's or Roberts's yearlings. He vibrated between two points, the realistic and the mystic, and made no attempt to combine people or situations in ordinary life, though he knew how to lead up to a dramatic tableau or crisis. His studies of character were not made from observation, but from acquaintance with himself; and this subjectivity, or egoism, crippled his invention and made his "Tales" little better than prose poems. He could imagine a series of adventures—the experience of a single narrator—like *Arthur Gordon Pym*, and might have been, not Le Sage nor De Foe, but an eminent raconteur in his own field. His strength is unquestionable in those clever pieces of ratiocination, "The Murders in the Rue Morgue," "The Mystery of Marie Rogêt," "The Purloined Letter"; in some of a more fantastic type, "The Gold Bug" and "Hans Pfaall"; and especially in those with elements of terror and morbid psychology added, such as "The Descent into the Maelstrom," "The Black Cat," "The Tell-Tale Heart," and the mesmeric sketches. When composing these he delighted in the exercise of his dexterous intellect, like a workman testing his skill. No poet is of a low grade who possesses, besides an ear for rhythm, the resources of a brain so fine and active. Technical gifts being equal, the more intellectual of two poets is the greater. "Best bard, because the wisest."

His artistic contempt for metaphysics is seen even in those tales which appear most transcendental. They are charged with a feeling that in the realms of psychology we are dealing with something ethereal, which is none the less substance if we might but capture it. They are his resolute attempts to find a clew to the invisible world. Were he living now, how much he would make of our discoveries in light and sound, of the correlation of forces! He strove by a kind of divination to put his hand upon the links of mind and matter, and reach the hiding-places of the soul. It galled him that anything should lie outside the domain of human intelligence. His imperious intellect rebelled against the bounds that shut us in, and found passionate expression in works of which "Ligeia," "The Fall of the House of Usher," and "William Wilson" are the best types. The tales in which lyrics are introduced are full of complex beauty, the choicest products of his genius. They are the offspring of yearnings that lifted him so far above himself as to make us forget his failings and think of him only as a creative artist, a man of noble gifts.

In these short, purely ideal efforts—finished as an artist finishes a portrait, or a poet his poem—Poe had few equals in recent times. That he lacked sustained power of invention is proved, not by his failure to complete an extended work, but by his under-estimation of its value. Such a man measures everything by his personal ability, and finds plausible grounds for the resulting standard. Hawthorne had the growing power and the staying power that gave us *The Scarlet Letter* and *The House of the Seven Gables*. Poe and Hawthorne were the last of the romancers. Each was a master in his way, and that of Poe was the more obvious and material. He was expert in much that concerns the structure of works, and the modelling touches of the poet left beauty-marks upon his prose. Yet in spiritual meaning his tales were less poetic than those of Hawthorne. He relied upon his externals, making the utmost of their gorgeousness of color, their splendor and gloom of light and shade. Hawthorne found the secret meaning of common things, and knew how to capture, from the plainest aspects of life, an essence of evasive beauty which the senses of Poe often were unable to perceive. It was Hawthorne who heard the melodies too fine for mortal ear. Hawthorne was wholly masculine, with the great tenderness and gentleness which belong to virile souls. Poe had, with the delicacy, the sophistry and weakness of a nature more or less effeminate. He opposed to Hawthorne the fire, the richness, the instability of the tropics, as against the abiding strength and passion of the North. His own conceptions astonished him, and he often presents himself "with hair on end, at his own wonders." Of these two artists and seers, the New Englander had the profounder insight; the Southerner's magic was that of the necromancer who resorts to spells and devices, and, when some apparition by chance responds to his incantations, is bewildered by the phantom himself has raised.

Poe failed to see that the Puritanism by which Hawthorne's strength was tempered was also the source from which it sprang; and in his general criticism did not pay full tribute to a genius he must have felt. In some of his sketches, such as "The Man of the Crowd," he used Hawthorne's method, and with inferior results. His reviews of other authors and his occasional literary notes have been so carefully preserved as to show his nature by a mental and moral photograph. His *Marginalia*, scrappy and written for effect, are the notes of a thinking man of letters. The criticisms raised a hubbub in their day, and made Poe the bogy of his generation—the unruly censor whom weaklings not only had cause to fear, but often regarded with a sense of cruel injustice. I acknowledge their frequent dishonesty, vulgarity, prejudice, but do not, therefore, hold them to be worthless. Even a scourge, a pestilence, has its uses; before it the puny and frail go down, the fittest survive. And so it was in Poe's foray. Better that a time of unproductiveness should follow such a thinning out than that false and feeble things should continue. I suspect that *The Literati* made room for a new movement, sure though long delayed, in American authorship. Mr. Higginson, however, is entirely right when he intimates that Margaret Fuller, by her independent reviews in *The Tribune*, sustained her full and early part in the chase against "such small deer." The shafts of Dian were more surely sped, and much less vindictively, than the spear of her brother-huntsman. Poe's sketches are a prose Dunciad, waspish and unfair, yet not without touches of magnanimity. He had small respect for the feeling that it is well for a critic to discover beauties, since any one can point out faults. When, as in the cases of Tennyson, Mrs. Browning, Taylor, and others, he pronounced favorably upon the talents of a claimant, and was uninfluenced by personal motives, his judgments not seldom have been justified by the after-career. Besides, what a cartoon he drew of the writers of his time,—the corrective of Griswold's optimistic delineations! In the description of a man's personal appearance he had the art of placing the subject before us with a single touch. His tender mercies were cruel; he never forgot to prod the one sore spot of the author he most approved,—was especially intolerant of his own faults in others, and naturally detected these at once. When meting out punishment to a pretentious writer, he revelled in his task, and often made short work, as if the pleasure was too great to be endurable. The keenness of his satire, just or unjust, is mitigated by its obvious ferocity: one instinctively takes part with the victim. Nothing in journalistic criticism, even at that time, was more scathing and ludicrous than his conceit of a popular bookwright in the act of confabulation with the Universe. But he marred the work by coarseness, telling one man that he was by no means a fool, although he did write "De Vere," and heading a paper on the gentlest and most forbearing of poets—"Mr. Longfellow and Other Plagiarists." In short, he constantly dulled the edge and temper of his rapier, and resorted to the broad-axe, using the latter even in his deprecation of its use by Kit North. Perhaps it was needed in those salad days by offenders who could be put down in no other wise; but I hold it a sign of progress that criticism by force of arms would now be less effective.

VI

Some analysis of Poe's general equipment will not be out of place. Only in the most perfect tales can his English style be called excellent, however significant his thought. His mannerisms—constant employment of the *dash* for suggestiveness, and a habit of italicizing to make a point or strengthen an illusion—are wearisome, and betray a lack of confidence in his skill to use plain methods. While asserting the power of words to convey absolutely any idea of the human mind, he relied on sound, quaintness, surprise, and other artificial aids. His prose is inferior to Hawthorne's; but sometimes he excels Hawthorne in qualities of form and proportion which are specially at the service of authors who are also poets. The abrupt beginnings of his stories often are artistic:—

> We had now reached the summit of the loftiest crag. For some minutes the old man seemed too much exhausted to speak. ("Descent into the Maelstrom.")

> The thousand injuries of Fortunato I had borne as best I could; but when he ventured upon insult, I vowed revenge. ("The Cask of Amontillado.")

His endings were equally good, when he had a clear knowledge of his own purpose, and some of his conceptions terminate at a dramatic crisis. The tone, also, of his masterpieces is well sustained throughout. In "The Fall of the House of Usher,"

the approach to the fated spot, the air, the landscape, the tarn, the mansion itself, are a perfect study, equal to the ride of Childe Roland,—and here Poe excels Browning: we not only come with him to the dark tower, but we enter and partake its mystery, and alone know the secret of its accursed fate. The poet's analytic faculty has been compared to that of Balzac, but a parallel goes no farther than the material side. In condensation he surpassed either Balzac or Hawthorne.

His imagination was not of the highest order, for he never dared to trust to it implicitly; certainly not in his poetry, since he could do nothing with a measure like blank verse, which is barren in the hands of a mere songster, but the glory of English metrical forms when employed by one commanding the strength of diction, the beauty and grandeur of thought, and all the resources of a strongly imaginative poet. Neither in verse nor in prose did he cut loose from his minor devices, and for results of sublimity and awe he always depends upon that which is grotesque or out of nature. Beauty of the fantastic or grotesque is not the highest beauty. Art, like nature, must be fantastic, not in her frequent, but in her exceptional moods. The rarest ideal dwells in a realm beyond that which fascinates us by its strangeness or terror, and the votaries of the latter have masters above them as high as Raphael is above Doré.

In genuine humor Poe seemed utterly wanting. He also had little of the mother-wit that comes in flashes and at once; but his powers of irony and satire were so great as to make his frequent lapses into invective the more humiliating. The command of humor has distinguished men whose genius was both high and broad. If inessential to exalted poetic work, its absence is hurtful to the critical and polemic essay. Poe knew this as well as any one, but a measureless self-esteem would not acknowledge the flaw in his armor. Hence efforts which involved the delusion that humor may come by works and not by inborn gift. Humor is congenital and rare, the fruit of natural mellowness, of sensitiveness to the light and humane phases of life. It is, moreover, set in action by an unselfish heart. Such is the mirth of Thackeray, of Cervantes and Molière, and of the one master of English song. Poe's consciousness of his defect, and his refusal to believe it incurable, are manifest in trashy sketches for which he had a market, and which are humorous only to one who sees the ludicrous side of their failure. He analyzed mirth as the product of incongruity, and went to work upon a theory to produce it. The result is seen not only in the extravaganzas to which I refer,—and it is a pity that these should have been hunted up so laboriously,—but in the use of what he thought was humor to barb his criticisms, and as a contrast to the exciting passages of his analytical tales. One of his sketches, "The Duc de l'Omelette," after the lighter French manner, has grace and jaunty persiflage, but most of his whimsical "pot-boilers" are deplorably absurd. There is something akin to humor in the sub-handling of his favorite themes,—such as the awe and mystery of death, the terrors of pestilence, insanity, or remorse. The grotesque and nether side of these matters presents itself to him, and then his irony, with its repulsive fancies, is as near humor as he ever approaches. That is to say, it is grave-yard humor, the kind which sends a chill down our backs, and implies a contempt for our bodies and souls, for the perils, helplessness, and meanness of the stricken human race.

Poe is sometimes called a man of extraordinary learning. Upon a first acquaintance, one might receive the impression that his scholarship was not only varied, but thorough. A study of his works has satisfied me that he possessed literary resources and knew how to make the most of them. In this he resembled Bulwer, and, with far less abundant materials than the latter

4272

required, employed them as speciously. He easily threw a glamour of erudition about his work, by the use of phrases from old authors he had read, or among whose treatises he had foraged with special design. It was his knack to cull sentences which, taken by themselves, produce a weird or impressive effect, and to reframe them skilfully. This plan was clever, and resulted in something that could best be muttered "darkly, at dead of night"; but it partook of trickery, even in its art. He had little exact scholarship, nor needed it, dealing, as he did, not with the processes of learning, but with results that could subserve the play of his imagination. Shakespeare's anachronisms and illusions were made as he required them, and with a fine disdain. Poe resorted to them of malice aforethought, and under pretence of correctness. Still, the work of a romancer and poet is not that of a book-worm. What he needs is a good reference-knowledge, and this Poe had. His irregular school-boy training was not likely to give him the scholastic habit, nor would his impatient manhood otherwise have confirmed it. I am sure that we may consider that portion of his youth to have been of most worth which was devoted, as in the case of many a born writer, to the unconscious education obtained from the reading, for the mere love of it, of *all* books to which he had access. This training served him well. It enabled him to give his romance an alchemic air, by citation from writers like Chapman, Thomas More, Bishop King, etc., and from Latin and French authors in profusion. His French tendencies were natural, and he learned enough of the language to read much of its current literature and get hold of modes unknown to many of his fellow-writers. I have said that his stock in trade was narrow, but for the adroit display of it examine any of his tales and sketches,—for example, "Berenice," or "The Assignation."

In knowledge of what may be called the properties of his romance, he was more honestly grounded. He had the good fortune to utilize the Southern life and scenery which he knew in youth. It chanced, also, that during some years of his boyhood—that formative period whose impressions are indelible—he lived in a characteristic part of England. He had seen with his own eyes castles, abbeys, the hangings and tapestries and other by-gone trappings of ancient rooms, and remembered effects of decoration and color which always came to his aid. These he used as if he were born to them; never, certainly, with the surprise at their richness which vulgarizes Disraeli's *Lothair*. In some way, known to genius, he also caught the romance of France, of Italy, of the Orient, and one tale or another is transfused with their atmosphere; while the central figure, however disguised, is always the image of the romancer himself. His equipment, on the whole, was not a pedant's, much less that of a searcher after truth; it was that of a poet and a literary workman. Yet he had the hunger which animates the imaginative student, and, had he been led to devote himself to science, would have contributed to the sum of knowledge. In writing *Eureka* he was unquestionably sincere, and forgot himself more nearly than in any other act of his professional life. But here his inexact learning betrayed him. What was begun in conviction—a swift generalization from scientific theories of the universe—grew to be so far beyond the data at his command, or so inconsistent with them, that he finally saw he had written little else than a prose poem, and desired that it should be so regarded. Of all sciences, astronomy appeals most to the imagination. What is rational in *Eureka* mostly is a re-statement of accepted theories: otherwise the treatise is vague and nebulous,—a light dimmed by its own vapor. The work is curiously saturated with our modern Pantheism; and although in many portions it shows the author's weariness, yet it was a

notable production for a layman venturing within the precincts of the savant. The poetic instinct hits upon truths which the science of the future confirms; but as often, perhaps, it glorifies some error sprung from a too ardent generalization. Poe's inexactness was shown in frequent slips,—sometimes made unconsciously, sometimes in reliance upon the dulness of his rivals to save him from detection. He was on the alert for other people's errors; for his own facts, were he now alive, he could not call so lightly upon his imagination. Even our younger authors, here and abroad, now are so well equipped that their learning seems to handicap their winged steeds. Poe had, above all, the gift of poetic induction. He would have divined the nature of an unknown world from a specimen of its flora, a fragment of its art. He felt himself something more than a bookman. He was a creator of the beautiful, and hence the conscious struggle of his spirit for the sustenance it craved. Even when he was most in error, he labored as an artist, and it is idle criticism that judges him upon any other ground.

Accept him, then, whether as poet or romancer, as a pioneer of the art feeling in American literature. So far as he was devoted to art for art's sake, it was for her sake as the exponent of beauty. No man ever lived in whom the passion for loveliness more plainly governed the emotions and convictions. His service of the beautiful was idolatry, and he would have kneeled with Heine at the feet of Our Lady of Milo, and believed that she yearned to help him. This consecration to absolute beauty made him abhor the mixture of sentimentalism, metaphysics, and morals, in its presentation. It was a foregone conclusion that neither Longfellow, Emerson, Lowell, nor Hawthorne should wholly satisfy him. The question of "moral" tendency concerned him not in the least. He did not feel with Keats that "Beauty is truth, truth beauty," and that a divine perfection may be reached by either road. This deficiency narrowed his range both as a poet and as a critic. His sense of justice was a sense of the fitness of things, and—strange to say—when he put it aside he forgot that he was doing an unseemly thing. Otherwise, he represents, or was one of the first to lead, a rebellion against formalism, commonplace, the spirit of the bourgeois. In this movement Whitman is his countertype at the pole opposite from that of art; and hence they justly are picked out from the rest of us and associated in foreign minds. Taste was Poe's supreme faculty. Beauty, to him, was a definite and logical reality, and he would have scouted Véron's claim that it has no fixed objective laws, and exists only in the nature of the observer. Although the brakes of art were on his imagination, his taste was not wholly pure; he vacillated between the classic forms and those allied with color, splendor, Oriental decoration; between his love for the antique and his impressions of the mystical and grotesque. But he was almost without confraternity. An artist in an unartistic period, he had to grope his way, to contend with stupidity and coarseness. Again, his imagination, gloating upon the possibilities of taste, violated its simplicity. Poe longed for the lamp of Aladdin, for the riches of the Gnomes. Had unbounded wealth been his, he would have outvied Beckford, Landor, Dumas, in barbaric extravagance of architecture. His efforts to apply the laws of the beautiful to imaginary decoration, architecture, landscape, are very fascinating as seen in "The Philosophy of Furniture," "Landscape Gardening," and "Landor's Cottage." "The Domain of Arnheim" is a marvellous dream of an earthly paradise, and the close is a piece of word-painting as effective as the language contains. Regarding this sensitive artist, this original poet, it seems indeed a tragedy that a man so ideal in either realm, so unfit for contact with ugliness, dulness, brutality, should have come to eat husks with the swine, to be misused by their human counterparts, and to die the death of a drunkard, in the refuge which society offers to the most forlorn and hopeless of its castaways.

GEORGE E. WOODBERRY
From "The End of the Play"
Edgar Allan Poe
1885, p. 286–301

In the history of Poe's mental development, *Eureka*, the principal work of his last years, necessarily occupies an important place. The earliest indication that such topics occupied his mind occurs in the review of Macaulay's Essays: "That we know no more today of the nature of Deity—of its purposes—and thus of man himself—than we did even a dozen years ago—is a proposition disgracefully absurd; and of this any astronomer could assure Mr. Macaulay. Indeed, to our own mind, the *only* irrefutable argument in support of the soul's immortality—or, rather, the only conclusive proof of man's alternate dissolution and rejuvenescence *ad infinitum*—is to be found in analogies deduced from the modern established theory of the nebular cosmogony." Shortly after this utterance the metaphysical tales begin, but the speculations of Poe were not fully developed until the publication of *Eureka*. In the following criticism, which necessarily partakes somewhat of the abstract nature of its subject, only what is peculiar to Poe will be dwelt on; and it may as well be premised that the end in view is not the determination of abstract truth, but simply the illustration alike of Poe's genius and character by the light of his speculations.

Poe's hypothesis is as follows: The mind knows intuitively—by inductive or deductive processes which escape consciousness, elude reason, or defy expression—that the creative act of Deity must have been the simplest possible; or, to expand and define this statement, it must have consisted in willing into being a primordial particle, the germ of all things, existing without relations to aught, or, in the technical phrase, unconditioned. This particle, by virtue of the divine volition, radiated into space uniformly in all directions a shower of atoms of diverse form, irregularly arranged among themselves, but all, generally speaking, equally distant from their source; this operation was repeated at intervals, but with decreased energy in each new instance, so that the atoms were impelled less far. On the exhaustion of the radiating force, the universe was thus made up of a series of concentric hollow spheres, like a nest of boxes, the crusts of the several spheres being constituted of the atoms of the several discharges. The radiating force at each of its manifestations is measured by the number of atoms then thrown off; or, since the number of atoms in any particular case must have been directly proportional with the surface of the particular sphere they occupied, and since the surfaces of a series of concentric spheres are directly proportional with the squares of their distances from the centre, the radiating force in the several discharges was directly proportional with the squares of the distances to which the several atomic showers were driven.

On the consummation of this secondary creative act, as the diffusion may be called, there occurred, says Poe, a recoil, a striving of the atoms each to each in order to regain their primitive condition; and this tendency, which is now being satisfied, is expressed in gravitation, the mutual attraction of atoms with a force inversely proportional with the squares of

the distances. In other words, the law of gravitation is found to be the converse of the law of radiation, as would be the case if the former energy were the reaction of the latter as is claimed; furthermore, the distribution of the atoms in space is seen to be such as would result from the mode of diffusion described. The return of the atoms into their source, however, would take place too rapidly, adds Poe, and without accomplishing the Deity's design of developing out of the original homogeneous particle the utmost heterogeneity, were it not that God, in this case a true *Deus ex machina*, has interposed by introducing a repelling force which began to be generated at the very inception of the universal reaction, and ever becomes greater as the latter proceeds. Poe names this force electricity, while at the same time he suggests that light, heat, and magnetism are among its phases, and ascribes to it all vital and mental phenomena; but of the principle itself he makes a mystery, since he is intuitively convinced that it belongs to that spiritual essence which lies beyond the limits of human inquiry. In the grand reaction, then, the universe is through attraction becoming more condensed, and through repulsion more heterogeneous. Attraction and repulsion taken together constitute our notion of matter; the former is the physical element, the Body, the latter is the spiritual element, the Soul. Incidentally it should be remarked that since in a divine design, being perfect, no one part exists for the sake of others more than the others for its sake, it is indifferent whether repulsion be considered, as hitherto, an expedient to retard the attractive force, or, on the other hand, the attractive force as an expedient to develop repulsion; in other words, it is indifferent whether the physical be regarded as subordinate to the spiritual element, or *vice versa*. To return to the main thread, Poe affirms that repulsion will not increase indefinitely as the condensation of the mass proceeds, but when in the process of time it has fulfilled its purpose—the evolution of heterogeneity—it will cease, and the attractive force, being unresisted, will draw the atoms back into the primordial particle in which, as it has no parts, attraction will also cease; now, attraction and repulsion constituting our notion of matter, the cessation of these two forces is the same thing with the annihilation of matter, or in other words, the universe, at the end of the reaction which has been mentally followed out, will sink into the nihility out of which it arose. In conclusion Poe makes one last affirmation, to wit, that the diffusion and ingathering of the universe is the diffusion and ingathering of Deity itself, which has no existence apart from the constitution of things.

It is difficult to treat this hypothesis, taken as a metaphysical speculation, with respect. To examine it for the purpose of demolition would be a tedious, though an easy task; but fortunately there is no need to do more than point out a few of its confusions in order to illustrate the worthlessness of Poe's thought in this field, and to indicate the depth of the delusion under which he labored in believing himself a discoverer of new truth. For this purpose it will be best to take the most rudimentary metaphysical ideas involved. The primordial particle is declared to be unconditioned—"my particle proper is absolute Irrelation,"—or in other words it is the Absolute; but this is incompatible with its being willed into being by Deity, to which it would then necessarily stand related as an effect to its cause; on the contrary, it must itself, being the Absolute, be Deity with which Poe at last identifies it. In other words, when Poe has reached the conception of the primordial particle as first defined by him, he is just where he started, that is, at the conception of Deity, and at that point, as has been seen, he had to end. The difficulty which bars inquiry—the inconceivability of creation—remains as insuperable as ever, although

Poe may have cheated himself into believing it overcome by the legerdemain of a phrase from physics; in the attempt to describe the generation of the phenomenal universe out of the unknowable, he has been foiled by the old obstacles—the impossibility of making an equation between nothing and something, of effecting a transformation of the absolute into the conditioned. If the primordial particle be material, it is only the scientific equivalent of the old turtle of the Hindoos, on which the elephant stands to support the globe; if it be immaterial, it is the void beneath.

Such a criticism as the above belongs to the primer of thought in this science; but objections as obvious, brief, and fatal may be urged against every main point of the argument. Without entering on such a discussion it is sufficient to observe, as characteristic illustrations of the density of Poe's ignorance in this department of knowledge, that he regards space not as created but as given, explains the condensation of the universe as being a physical reaction upon the immaterial will of God (for the original radiating force cannot be discriminated from and is expressly identified with the divine volition, just as the primordial particle cannot be discriminated from and is expressly identified with the divine essence), and lastly so confuses such simple notions as final and efficient causes that he contradistinguishes the force of repulsion from that of attraction as arising and disappearing in obedience to the former instead of the later sort. In a word, Poe's theory belongs to the infancy of speculation, to the period before physics was separated from ontology; in this sense, and in no other, Kennedy's remark that Poe wrote like "an old Greek philosopher," was just.

What Poe himself most prized in this hypothesis was its pantheistic portion. The sentence of Baron Bielfeld,—"nous ne connaissons rien de la nature ou de l'essence de Dieu;—pour savoir ce qu'il est, il faut être Dieu même,"—had made a deep impression on his mind early in life; it is one of the half-dozen French quotations that he introduces at every opportunity into his compositions; in *Eureka* he translates it, "We know absolutely *nothing* of the nature or essence of God; in order to comprehend what he is, we should have to be God ourselves,"—and he immediately adds, "I nevertheless venture to demand if this our present ignorance of the Deity is an ignorance to which the soul is *everlastingly* condemned." Now after reflection he boldly took the only road to such knowledge that was left open by the apothegm, and affirmed that he was God, being persuaded thereto by his memories of an ante-natal and his aspiration for an immortal existence, and in particular by his pride. "My whole nature utterly *revolts*," he exclaimed, "at the idea that there is any Being in the Universe superior to *myself!*" On reading so violent an expression of belief one involuntarily examines the matter more closely and pushes home the question whether Poe did actually so fool himself to the top of his bent; and after some little investigation one finds that, if he was his own dupe, the reason is not far to seek. It is necessary here to summarize the speculations which were put forth elsewhere by Poe, especially in the metaphysical tales, and either led up to or supplemented the views of *Eureka*.

According to these other statements, the Universe is made up of gross matter sensibly perceived and of fine matter so minutely divided that the atoms coalesce (this is, of course, a contradiction in terms) and form an unparticled substance which permeates and impels all things. This unparticled substance or imperceptible coalescent matter is the universal mind (into such unintelligible phraseology is the keen analyst forced); its being is Deity; its motion, regarded on the material or energetic side, is the divine volition, or, regarded on the mental or conscious side, is the creative thought. Deity and its activity, being such in its universal existence, is individualized, by means of gross matter made for that end, into particular creatures, among which are men; the human being, in other words, is a specialization of the universal, or is God incarnate, as is every other creature whatsoever. It is superfluous to follow Poe in his fantastic conception of the universe as the abode of countless rudimentary incarnations of the Deity, each a divine thought and therefore irrevocable; the peculiar form of his pantheism would not be more defined thereby. At the first glance one sees that his theory is built out of Cartesian notions, crudely apprehended, and rendered ridiculous by the effort to yoke them with thoroughly materialistic ideas. In fact, Poe's scraps of speculative philosophy came from such opposite quarters that when his mind began to work on such contradictory information he could not well help falling into inextricable confusion. On the one hand he had derived, early in life, from obscure disciples of the French *philosophes*, the first truth that a materialist ever learns,—the origin of all knowledge in experience, and the consequent limitation of the mind to phenomena; on the other hand he had at a later period gleaned some of the conceptions of transcendentalism from Coleridge, Schlegel, and other secondary sources; from the union of such principles the issue was naturally monstrous, two-natured, like the Centaur. Essentially Poe was a materialist; whether, by gradually refining and subdividing matter, he reaches the unparticled substance, or by reversing the evolution of nature he arrives at the fiery mist and the primordial particle, he seeks to find out God by searching matter; and even in adopting the radically spiritual idea of pantheism, he is continually endeavoring to give it a materialistic form. He persuaded himself, as it is easy for ignorance to do; subtle as his mind was, well furnished for metaphysical thought both by his powers of abstraction and of reasoning, he wrote the jargon that belongs to the babbling days of philosophy because he did not take the pains to know the results of past inquiry and to train himself in modern methods. By his quick perception and adroit use of analogies, and especially by his tireless imagination, he gave his confused dogmatism the semblance of a reasoned system; but in fact his metaphysics exhibit only the shallowness of his scholarship and the degrading self-delusion of an arrogant and fatuous mind.

It is probable that few readers of *Eureka* ever seriously tried to understand its metaphysics. Its power—other than the fascination which some readers feel in whatever makes of their countenances "a foolish face of wonder"—lies in its exposition of Laplace's nebular theory and its vivid and popular presentation of astronomical phenomena. In this physical portion of the essay it has been fancied that Poe anticipated some of the results of later science; but this view cannot be sustained with candor. His own position that matter came from nihility and consisted of centres of force had been put forth as a scientific theory by Boscovich in 1758–59, had been widely discussed, and had found its way into American text-books. The same theory in a modified form had just been revived and brought to the notice of scientists by Faraday in his lecture in 1844. It has not, however, occupied the attention of first-class scientific men since that time. There may be, in the claim that "the recent progress of scientific thought runs in Poe's lines," some reference to Sir William Thomson's vortex theory of the constitution of atoms, but its resemblance to Poe's theory of vortices is only superficial, for what he puts forth was merely a revival of one of the earliest attempts to explain the Newtonian law, long since abandoned by science. It is true that in several particulars, such as the doctrine of the evolution of the universe from the simple to the complex, Poe's line of thought has now been followed out in detail; these suggestions, however, were not at the time peculiar to Poe, were not originated or developed by him, but on the contrary were common scientific property, for he appropriated ideas, just as he paraphrased statements of fact, from the books he read. He was no more a forerunner of Spencer, Faraday, and Darwin than scores of others, and he did nothing to make their investigations easier.

Poe's purely scientific speculations are mainly contained in the unpublished *addenda* to a report of his lecture on "The Universe" sent to a correspondent, and consist either of mathematical explanations of Kepler's first and third laws; or of statements, "that the sun was condensed at once (not gradually according to the supposition of Laplace) into his smallest size," and afterwards "sent into space his substance in the form of a vapor" from which Neptune was made; or of similar theories. They exhibit once more Poe's tenacity of mind, the sleuth-hound persistence of his intellectual pursuit; but, like his metaphysics, they represent a waste of power. They are, moreover, characterized by extraordinary errors. Some of the data are quite imaginary, it being impossible to determine what are the facts; some of them are quite wrong. The density of Jupiter, for example, in a long and important calculation, is constantly reckoned as two and one half, whereas it is only something more than one fifth, and the densities of the planets are described as being inversely as their rotary periods, whereas in any table of the elements of the solar system some wide departures from this rule are observable. Again, it is stated that Kepler's first and third laws "cannot be explained upon the principle of Newton's theory;" but, in fact, they follow mathematical deduction from it. Poe's own explanation of them is merely a play upon figures. A striking instance of fundamental ignorance of astronomical science is his statement at various places that the planets rotate (on their own axes) in elliptical orbits, and the reference he frequently makes to the *breadth* of their orbits (the breadth of their paths through space) agreeably to this supposition. Such a theory is incompatible with the Newtonian law of gravitation, according to which any revolution in an elliptical orbit implies a source of attraction at the focus of the ellipse. Examples of bodies which have breadth of orbit in Poe's sense are found in the satellites of all the planets, each of which, however, has its primary as a source of attraction to keep it in its elliptical orbit; the primary by its revolution round the sun gives then the satellite a breadth of orbit. But to make the proper rotation of the planets themselves take place about a focus, which would be merely a point moving in an elliptical orbit about the sun, would be to give them an arbitrary motion with no force to produce it.

So far was Poe from being a seer of science, that he was fundamentally in error with regard to the generalizations which were of prime importance to his speculations. The one grand assumption of his whole speculation is the universality of the law of inverse squares as applied to attraction and repulsion, whereas it has been known since the beginning of study regarding them that that law does not explain all the forces involved, as, for example, molecular forces; and for this Boscovich himself had provided. Again, to illustrate his scientific foresight, he reproaches Herschel for his reluctance to doubt the stability of the universe, and himself boldly affirms, consistently with his theory, that it is in a state of ever swifter collapse; than this nothing could be more at variance with the great law of the conservation of energy. Undoubtedly Poe had talents for scientific investigation, had he been willing to devote himself to such work; but, so far as appears from this essay, he had not advanced farther in science than the elements of physics, mathematics, and astronomy, as he had learned them at school or from popular works, such as Dr. Nichol's *Architecture of the Heavens*, or from generalizations, such as the less technical chapters of Auguste Comte's *La Philosophie positif*. Out of such a limited stock of knowledge Poe could not by mere reflection generate any Newtonian truth; that he thought he had done so, measures his folly. In a word, for this criticism must be brought to a close, *Eureka* affords one of the most striking instances in literature of a naturally strong intellect tempted by overweening pride to an Icarian flight and betrayed, notwithstanding its merely specious knowledge, into an ignoble exposure of its own presumption and ignorance. The facts are not to be obscured by the smooth profession of Poe that he wished this work to be looked on only as a poem; for, though he perceived that his argument was too fragmentary and involved to receive credence, he was himself profoundly convinced that he had revealed the secret of eternity. Nor, were *Eureka* to be judged as a poem, that is to say, as a fictitious cosmogony, would the decision be more favorable; even then so far as it is obscure to the reader it must be pronounced defective, so far as it is understood, involving as it does in its primary conceptions incessant contradictions of the necessary laws of thought, it must be pronounced meaningless. Poe believed himself to be that extinct being, a universal genius of the highest order; and he wrote this essay to prove his powers in philosophy and in science. To the correspondent to whom he sent the *addenda* he declared, "As to the lecture, I am very quiet about it—but if you have ever dealt with such topics, you will recognize the novelty and *moment* of my views. What I have propounded will (in good time) revolutionize the world of Physical and Metaphysical science. I say this calmly, but I say it." Poe succeeded only in showing how egregiously genius may mistake its realm.

CHARLES WHIBLEY
From "Edgar Allan Poe"
New Review, January 1896, pp. 617–25

His first success was achieved (in 1833) with "The MS. Found in a Bottle," which won a prize offered by *The Saturday Visitor*. Henceforth, with varying fortune, he earned his living by his pen. He wrote stories, satires, poems; his criticism became the terror of the incompetent; and though his Southern descent, his genius, his reasonable contempt, rendered him unpopular in the North, he was, many years before his death, the best hated and most highly respected of his class. The one constant ambition of his life—to start a magazine of his own—was disappointed; but alone of his contemporaries he captured a reputation in Europe, and neither ill-health nor misfortune shook for an instant his legitimate confidence in himself, his determination to set in their place the pigmies who surrounded him. Meanwhile, his strange marriage with Virginia Clemm, who, at the ceremony, was not yet fourteen, with his unfailing devotion to his fragile wife and her mother, disproved the boorish cruelty wherewith he was so complacently charged. On the other hand, the affection, required yet unsuccessful, which he cherished at the end for Mrs. Whitman, for "Annie," and for Mrs. Shelton, does not suggest the humour of one who had a strong, rational hold upon existence. But he lived his own life, as he died his own death, and it is for the Griswolds to hold their peace in the presence of genius.

At least his works remain to confute the blasphemer, and it is certain that no writer ever bequeathed so many examples to posterity. Although he went not beyond the tradition of his time, although he owed something to Maturin and Mrs. Radclyffe, something also, in decoration and decay, to the *romantiques* of 1830, he was essentially an inventor. He touched no kind of story without making it a type for all time. Even *The Narrative of Arthur Gordon Pym*, which you confess to be tiresome and elaborate, has been a stimulus to a whole generation of romance-mongers; and you feel, despite its faults, that it displays a greater verisimilitude, if not a greater knowledge, than the best of its successors. Before all things, Poe had the faculty of detaching himself from the present and of imagining unseen continents. With seamanship, science, erudition, mysticism, with all the branches of human knowledge he feigned an acquaintance. He tells you with pride that "The MS. Found in a Bottle" was written many years before he had seen the maps of Mercator; and you find yourself eagerly forgiving the amiable pedantry. But it is in *The Tales of the Grotesque and Arabesque* that Poe first revealed his personal imagination—an imagination rather of tone than of incident. "The House of Usher," "Ligeia," and the rest surpass all other stories in economy of method and suggestion. Death, catalepsy, and the supernatural are the material of them all. They know neither time nor place; they are enwrapped in an atmosphere only substantial enough to enclose phantoms; spectral castles frown upon sombre tarns, destined to engulph them; clouds, fantastically outlined, chase one another across an imagined sky; ancient families totter to their doom, overwhelmed in misery and disease; ruined halls are resplendent with red lanterns and perfumed with swinging censers; the heroine's hand is cold as marble, marble-cold also is her forehead, but she is learned in all the sciences, and the castle library contains the works of Cælius Secundus Curio and Tertullian. Everywhere there is a sombre splendour, a forbidding magnificence. No wonder that the dweller in an English abbey shudders at "the Bedlam patterns of the carpets of tufted gold." Naught save the names, which are of no country and of no age, heightens the colour of the monotone romance. Madeleine, Berenice, Ligeia, Morella, Eleonora—do they not sing in your ear, and by their beauty make more horrible the cold tragedy of their deaths? To analyse these fantasies closely is impossible; you must leave them to the low, dim-tinted atmosphere wherein Poe has enveloped them. They are vague, fleeting, mystical—a sensation of tapestry, wherein spectral figures wander hand in hand. Silence and horror are their cult, and there is not one of the ladies whose ever-approaching death would not be hastened by a breath of reality. Ligeia dwells in "a dim and decaying city by the Rhine," but who would seek to discover her habitation? It were as infamous as to discover beneath a tropical sun, "the Valley of the Many-coloured Grass," where pined the hapless Eleonora. The best of the fancies are rather poetry than prose, and already Poe had perfected his artifice of the refrain. The finest passage in "Eleonora" is repeated with the stateliest effect, and the horror of "Silence" is increased tenfold by the oft-recurring phrase: "And the man trembled in the solitude, but the night waned, and he sat upon the rock." In these grotesque imaginings even laughter becomes a terror. At Sparta, says the monster of "The Assignation," "the altar of Laughter survived all the others," and he chuckles at the very point of death. When, in "The Cask of Amontillado," the last stone is fitted to Fortunato's living tomb, "there came from out the niche a low laugh," which might well have sent Montresor's hair on end. Not even did Morella's lover meet his doom with tears. "I laughed with

a long and bitter laugh," he says, "as I found no trace of the first in the charnel where I laid the second—Morella." But, worst of all, the demon laughs when the whole world is cursed to silence: wherefrom you may deduce as sinister a theory of the ludicrous as you please.

And then he turned to another kind, and created at a breath M. Dupin, that master of insight, who proved that the complex was seldom profound, and who discovered by the natural transition from a colliding fruiterer, through street stones, stereotomy, Epicurus, Dr. Nicholls and Orion, that Chantilly was a very little fellow, and would do better for the Théâtre des Variétes. Now, Monsieur Charles A. Dupin was of good family—so much you are ready to believe; he was also young—a statement you decline to accept on the word of a creator, unless, indeed, he be the Wandering Jew. But whatever his age and breeding, he is a master of analysis, and plays at ratiocination as a boy plays with a peg-top. He knows by long experience that in pitting your intelligence against another's you are sure to win if you identify yourself with your adversary. And when once this principle is understood, it is as easy as a game of marbles, and more profitable. M. Dupin loves darkness better than light, not because his deeds are evil, but because, being a poet and a mathematician, he works better by lamplight. Hence it was his practice to live through the day by the glimmer of two flickering candles, and to walk abroad at night under the spell of the gas-lamps. When serious work was toward, or he was forced to interview the doltish Prefect of Police, then he sat in the dark, and silently puffed his meerschaum. The smallest indication was sufficient for him, and while the police fumbled over the murders in the Rue Morgue, arresting a harmless bank-clerk, he not only discovered the true culprit, but was convinced that the culprit's master was a sailor, belonging to a Maltese vessel. "How was it possible?" asked his incredulous accomplice, "that you should know the man to be a sailor, and belonging to a Maltese vessel?" "I do not *know* it," said Dupin. "I am not *sure* of it! Here, however, is a small piece of ribbon, which from its form, and from its greasy appearance, has evidently been used in tying the hair in one of those long *queues* of which sailors are so fond. Moreover, this knot is one which few besides sailors can tie, and is peculiar to the Maltese." Imagine the joy of happening upon this masterpiece of combined observation and analysis, in the days before the trick had not been vulgarised beyond recognition! And yet, despite this flash of genius, M. Dupin affected to despise ingenuity, which he regarded as the cheapest of human qualities; and he would persuade you that all his finest effects were produced by pure reason! His most daring deed was done in the Rue Morgue: the instant discovery of the inhuman murderer was adroitness itself; and the advertisement of the recovered Ourang-Outang was even more brilliant. Unhappily there is a touch of melodrama in the locked door, the pistol upon the table, and the extorted confession. But M. Dupin is seldom guilty of such an indiscretion, and you readily forgive him. A more subtle achievement was the recovery of the purloined letter, for in this exploit he opposed the great Minister D——, and proved the superior at all points. In brief, his shining qualities are as stars in the night, nor have they been dimmed by the unnumbered imitators, who to-day are mimicking the tone and the manner of the inimitable Dupin.

Though "The Gold Bug" is a masterpiece of another kind, it is nearly related to "The Purloined Letter." It displays the perfect logic, the complete lucidity, the mastery of analysis, which make M. Dupin immortal. No step in the adventure but is foreseen and inevitable. Never before nor since has use so admirable been made of ciphers and buried treasure. The material, maybe, was not new, but the treatment, as of a glorified problem in mathematics, was Poe's own invention. In his hands the slightest incident ceased to be curious, and became (so to say) a link in the chain of fate. Not only was he unrivalled in the art of construction, but he touched the simplest theme with a clairvoyant intelligence, which seemed at the same moment to combine and analyse the materials of his story. Thus, also, the best of his scientific parables convince the imagination, even if they leave the reason refractory. But the purpose of these is too obvious, their central truths too heavily weighted with pretended documents for immortality. It is upon the grotesque, the horrible, and the ingenious that Poe has established his reputation. And surely the author of "Ligeia," of "Silence," of "William Wilson," of the Dupin Cycle, of "The Gold Bug," and of "The Mask of the Red Death" need not defend his title to undying fame.

Though Poe was a maker of great stories, he was not a great writer. That he might have been is possible, for none ever showed in fragments a finer sense of words; that he was not is certain. Mr. Stedman attempts to excuse him upon the ground that he lived before Pater, Flaubert, and Arnold. Never was a more preposterous theory formulated. As though the art of prose were newly invented! The English tongue, accurate, noble, coloured, is centuries older than Pater; and even in Poe's own time there were models worth the following. He knew Coleridge from end to end, and did not profit by his example. So conscious is he of style in others, that he condemns the Latinity of Lamb, but he rarely knits his own sentences to perfection. The best he wraps round with coils of useless string, and he is not incapable of striking false notes upon the Early-Victorian drum. He shocks you, for instance, by telling you that William Wilson at Oxford "vied in profuseness of expenditure with the haughtiest heirs of the wealthiest earldoms in Great Britain"—a sentence equally infamous whether it appeal to the ear or to the brain. Egeaus, again, the ghoulish lover of Berenice, boasts with a pride which Mrs. Radclyffe might envy that "there are no towers in land more time-honoured than my gloomy, gray, hereditary halls." This is fustian, and you regret it the more because in construction, in idea, Poe was seldom at fault. The opening of his stories is commonly perfect. How could you better the first page of "The House of Usher," whose weird effect is attained throughout by the simplest means? Another writer would take five pages to explain what Poe has touched off in the first five lines of "The Oval Portrait"; and to how many writers has this rejection of all save the essential been a noble example? But Poe, writing on the impulse of a whim, let the style which he knew elude his grasp, and if his carelessness cast a shadow upon his true masterpieces, it reduces the several volumes of properly forgotten fantasies to the lower level of journalism.

The criticism of Poe inaugurated a new era, a new cult of taste and beauty. Whether in theory or in practice he was ahead not only of his time, but of all time. That same keen intelligence which created M. Dupin, tore to pieces the prevailing superstitions and disclosed in a few pages the true qualities of literature. Beauty is his cult; poetry for him is "the rhythmical creation of beauty." He is neither preacher nor historian. Being an artist, he esteems facts as lightly as morals. Art, he says, has "no concern whatever either with Duty or with Truth." A poem is written solely for the poem's sake. "Perseverance," again, 'is one thing, genius quite another," and the public has as little to do with the industry as with the inspiration of the artist. To us who have lived through the dark age of naturalism his passage upon Truth rings like a prophecy:

"The demands of Truth," he writes in "The Poetic Principle," "the demands of Truth are severe; she has no sympathy with the myrtles. All *that* which is so indispensable in Song, is precisely all *that* with which *she* has nothing whatever to do. It is but making her a flaunting paradox to wreath her in gems and flowers." Even more precise and bitter is his epigrammatic indictment of Realism. "The defenders of this pitiable stuff"— you will find the lines in *Marginalia*—"uphold it on the ground of its truthfulness. Taking the thesis into question, the truthfulness is the one overwhelming defect. An original idea that—to laud the accuracy with which the stone is hurled that knocks us in the head. A little less accuracy might have left us more brains. And here are critics absolutely commending the truthfulness with which only the disagreeable is conveyed! In my view, if an artist must paint decayed cheeses, his merit will lie in their looking as little like decayed cheeses as possible." And that was written twenty years before the advent of Zola!

In "The Philosophy of Composition," moreover, he explains, what should never have needed explanation, that a work of art is the result not of accident but of a reasoned artifice; and he illustrates his thesis by a whimsical, far-fetched analysis of his own "Raven." He treats the poem with the same impartial intelligence which M. Dupin would have brought to the detection of a murderer or the discovery of a missing trinket. In truth, Poe might be called the Dupin of Criticism. For he looked, with his keen eye and rapid brain, through the innumerable follies wherewith literature was obscured, and he rejected the false hypotheses as scornfully as M. Dupin set aside the Prefect's imbecilities. As a practical critic Poe was a fighter. His sense of honour knew neither civility nor favouritism. He alone among critics has come forth with a chivalrous defence of his craft, in which he took a fierce pride. He was no adulator ready-made to serve some Society of Authors: he was a judge, condemning the guilty with an honourable severity. "When we attend less to authority," he wrote, "and more to principles, when we look *less* at merit and *more* at demerit, we shall be better critics than we are." Is that not enough to make the Popular Novelist turn green with fury, especially since it is the deliberate utterance of a man, whose example has furnished forth a whole library of popular novels? Twice he quotes the parable of the critic who "presented to Apollo a severe censure upon an excellent poem. The god asked him for the beauties of the work. He replied that he only troubled himself about the errors. Apollo presented him with a sack of unwinnowed wheat, and bade him pick out the chaff for his pains." Now, this is the critic's severest condemnation, and yet Poe is honest enough to declare that he is not sure that the god was in the right.

Being a severe judge, he was generously misunderstood. Longfellow was magnanimous enough to attribute "the harshness of his criticism to the irritation of a sensitive nature, chafed by some indefinite sense of wrong." Thus the Illiterate Novelist is wont to ascribe the lightest censure to a critic's envy. And they do not see, neither Longfellow nor the Illiterate Novelist, that they are bringing superfluous charges of bad faith. Is it possible that Longfellow could not imagine the necessity of censure? Is it possible that he, like the bleating lambs of fiction, believed that criticism was written, not for its own sake, but for the voidance of gall? If such were his creed, if he, being a critic, would never have written a line, unblotted by hatred or irritation, it is fortunate that he never lapsed from his devotion to poetry. But Poe was not always harsh, and when he used the scourge, he used it in defence of literature. It was his misfortune to review his contemporaries; and they, though they resented his censure, have already justified his severity by crawling, one and all, into oblivion. A bolder editor, indeed, would have suppressed the two volumes of books reviewed—articles which served their turn at the moment, which are ill-written, and which dimly reflect the brilliant insight of *Marginalia*. But when Poe encountered a master, he was eager in appreciation. His praise of Alfred Tennyson was as generous as it was wise. "In perfect sincerity," he wrote, "I regard him as the noblest poet that ever lived." And, again, remembering that this was written in 1843, you recognise in Poe the gift of prophecy.

But to complete the cycle of his accomplishments he was also a poet, and it is as a poet that he wears the greener bays. Here his practice coincided accurately with his theory. He believed that a long poem was a contradiction in terms, and he only erred once against the light, when he called *Eureka*, a tedious treatise upon all things and nothing, "a prose poem." In his eyes the sole aim of poetry was beauty, and such beauty as should touch the ear rather than the brain. His musical art eludes analysis, and he esteemed it great in proportion as it receded from the hard shapes and harder truths of life. Of him it might be said truly that "he seemed to see with his ear." You do not question "Annabel Lee" and "Ulalume." You do not attempt to drag a common meaning from their gossamer loveliness. You listen to their refrains and repeated cadences; you delight in their rippling sound and subtle variations; and you are content to find yourself in the presence of an art, which, like music, does not represent, but merely presents, an emotion. And because Poe acknowledged the artifice of his poetry, some have denied him imagination. As though imagination did not most clearly manifest herself in artistic expression!

It is not surprising that Poe's multiform genius should have proved a dominant influence upon European literature. Not only was he a sombre light to the decadence, not only was he a guiding flame in the pathway of the mystics; but also he revived the novel of adventure and lost treasure, of the South Seas and of Captain Kidd. The atrocities which have been committed in the name of his Dupin are like the sands for number, and the detective of fact, as of romance, has attempted to model himself upon this miracle of intelligence. Thus he has been an example to both houses—to Huysmans, who has emulated his erudition, and to Gaboriau, who has cheapened his mystery. It is his unique distinction to have anticipated even the trivialities of life. His title, "The Man That Was Used Up," has let in upon us the legion of imbeciles who did or didn't, who would or wouldn't. And stranger still, he it was that imagined the philosopher, who, in the vanity of his heart, should spell his god with a little g! His influence came not from America but from France. No sooner was "The Murders in the Rue Morgue" published in America, than it appeared as a *feuilleton* in *Le Commerce*, and in 1846 was printed a volume of *Contes*, translated by Isabelle Meunier. Ten years later Baudelaire began the brilliant series of translations, which added the glory of Poe to French literature. That Poe gained in the transference there is no doubt: the looseness of his style—his most grievous fault—was tightened in the distinguished prose of Baudelaire; and henceforth Poe was free to shape the literary future of France. It was his example that moulded the *conte* to its ultimate completion. His talents of compression and facile exposition, his gift of building up a situation in a hundred words, were imitated by the army of writers, who first perfected the short story, and then sent it across the Channel. Nor is Baudelaire the only poet who has done Poe into French. M. Stéphane Mallarmé, also, has proved his sympathy with the author of "The Raven" in a set

of matchless translations. He has turned the verse of Poe into a rhythmical prose, and withal he has kept so close to the original, that the prose echoes not only the phrase but the cadence of the verse. And from France Poe penetrated every country in Europe. He is known and read in those remote corners which he described, yet never saw. He is as familiar in Spain as in Scandinavia, and but a year ago "The Raven" was translated "direct from English" in far-off Valparaiso.

And here is the final contrast of his life. The prophet of silence and seclusion is blown to the four winds of heaven. But he has conquered glory without stooping one inch from his proper attitude of aristocracy. He is still as exclusive and morose as his stories. Between him and his fantasies there is no discord. You imagine him always stern-faced and habited in black, with Virginia Clemm at his side, Virginia shadowy as Ligeia, amiable as the mild Eleonora in the Valley of the Many-coloured Grass. He dwelt in mid America, and he was yet in fairy-land. Though the squalor of penury and the magazines gave him neither "ancestral hall" nor "moss-grown abbey," he lived and died enclosed within the impregnable castle of his mind.

LEWIS E. GATES
From "Edgar Allan Poe"
Studies and Appreciations
1900, pp. 110–28

Poe is a better poet in his prose than in his poetry. A reader of Poe's poetry, if he be quick to take umbrage at artificiality and prone to cavil, feels, after a dozen poems, like attempting an inventory of Poe's literary workshop—the material Poe uses is so uniform and the objects he fashions are so few and inevitable. The inventory might run somewhat as follows: One plaster bust of Pallas slightly soiled; one many-wintered Raven croaking *Nevermore*; a parcel of decorative names—Auber, Yaanek, Zante, Israfel; a few robes of sorrow, a somewhat frayed funeral pall, and a coil of Conqueror Worms; finally, one beautiful lay figure whom the angels name indifferently Lenore, Ulalume, and Annabel Lee. Masterly as is Poe's use of this poetical outfit, subtle as are his cadences and his sequences of tone-colour, it is only rarely that he makes us forget the cleverness of his manipulation and wins us into accepting his moods and imagery with that unconscious and almost hypnotic subjection to his will which the true poet secures from his readers.

In the best of his visionary *Tales*, on the other hand, Poe is much more apt to have his way with us. He works with a far greater variety of appliances, which it is by no means easy to number and call by name; the effects he aims at are manifold and not readily noted and classified; and the details that his imagination elaborates come upon us with a tropical richness and apparent confusion that mimic well the splendid lawlessness and undesignedness of nature. Moreover, even if the artifice in these tales were more palpable than it is, it would be less offensive than in poetry, inasmuch as the standard of sincerity is in such performances confessedly less exacting. The likeness in aim and in effect between the tales and the poems, however, cannot be missed—between such tales as "Ligeia" and "Eleonora" and such poems as "The Raven" and "Ulalume." Mr. Leslie Stephen has somewhere spoken of De Quincey's impassioned prose as aiming to secure in unmeasured speech very many of the same effects that Keats's *Odes* produce in authentic verse. This holds true also of the best of Poe's romances; they are really prose-poems. And, indeed, Poe has himself recognized in his essay on Hawthorne the close kinship between tale and poem, assigning to the poem subjects in the treatment of which the creation of beauty is the ruling motive, and leaving to the prose tale the creation of all other single effects, such as horror, humour, and terror. Both poem and tale must be brief, absolutely unified, and must create a single overwhelming mood.

The world that Poe's genuinely fantastic tales take us into has the burnish, the glow, the visionary radiance of the world of Romantic poetry; it is as luxuriantly unreal, too, as phantasmagoric—though it lacks the palpitating, buoyant loveliness of the nature that such poets as Shelley reveal, and is somewhat enamelled or metallic in its finish. Its glow and burnish come largely from the concreteness of Poe's imagination, from his inveterate fondness for sensations, for colour, for light, for luxuriant vividness of detail. Poe had the tingling senses of the genuine poet, senses that vibrated like delicate silver wire to every impact. He was an amateur of sensations and loved to lose himself in the O *Altitudo* of a perfume or a musical note. He pored over his sensations and refined upon them, and felt to the core of his heart the peculiar thrill that darted from each. He had seventy times seven colours in his emotional rainbow, and was swift to fancy the evanescent hue of feeling that might spring from every sight or sound—from the brazen note, for example, of the clock in "The Masque of the Red Death," from "the slender stems" of the ebony and silver trees in "Eleonora," or from the "large and luminous orbs" of Ligeia's eyes. Out of the vast mass of these vivid sensations—"passion-wingèd ministers of thought"—Poe shaped and fashioned the world in which his romances confine us, a world that is, therefore, scintillating and burnished and vibrant, quite unlike the world in Hawthorne's tales, which is woven out of dusk and moonlight.

Yet, curiously enough, this intense brilliancy of surface does not tend to exorcise mystery, strangeness, terror from Poe's world, or to transfer his stories into the region of everyday fact. Poe is a conjurer who does not need to have the lights turned down. The effects that he is most prone to aim at are, of course, the shivers of awe, crispings of the nerves, shuddering thrills that come from a sudden, overwhelming sense of something uncanny, abnormal, ghastly, lurking in the heart of life. And these nervous perturbations are even more powerfully excited by those of his stories that, like "Eleonora" and "Ligeia," have a lustrous finish, than by sketches that, like "Shadow" and "Silence," deal with twilight lands and half-visualized regions. In "The Masque of the Red Death," in "The Fall of the House of Usher," and in "A Descent into the Maelström," the details of incident and background flash themselves on our imaginations with almost painful distinctness.

The terror in Poe's tales is not the terror of the child that cannot see in the dark, but the terror of diseased nerves and morbid imaginations, that see with dreadful visionary vividness and feel a mortal pang. Poe is a past master of the moods of diseased mental life, and in the interests of some one or other of these semi-hysterical moods many of his most uncannily prevailing romances are written. They are prose-poems that realize for us such half-frenetic glimpses of the world as madmen have; and *suggest* in us for the moment the breathless, haggard mood of the victim of hallucinations.

It must not, however, be forgotten that Poe wrote tales of ratiocination as well as romances of death. In his ability to turn out with equal skill stories bordering on madness and stories where intellectual analysis, shrewd induction, reasoning upon evidence, all the processes of typically sane mental life, are carried to the utmost pitch of precision and effectiveness, lies one of the apparent anomalies of Poe's genius and art. In "The Murders in the Rue Morgue," "The Mystery of Marie Rogêt," and "The Purloined Letter," Poe seems sanity incarnate, pure mental energy untouched by moods or passions, weaving and unweaving syllogisms and tracking out acutely the subtlest play of thought. What in these stories has become of Poe the fancy-monger, the mimic maniac, the specialist in moodiness and abnormality?

After all, the difficulty here suggested is only superficial and yields speedily to a little careful analysis. We have not really to deal with a puzzling case of double personality, with an author who at his pleasure plays at being Dr. Jekyll or Mr. Hyde. In all Poe's stories the same personality is at work, the same methods are followed, and the material used, though at first sight it may seem in the two classes of tales widely diverse, will also turn out to be quite the same, at any rate in its artificiality, in its remoteness from real complex human nature, and in its origin in the mind of the author. Certain instructions that in an essay on Hawthorne Poe has given to would-be writers of tales are delightfully serviceable to the anxious unraveller of the apparent contradictions in Poe's personality. ⟨. . .⟩

The shallowness of Poe's treatment of life and character is almost too obvious to need illustration. Not only does he disdain, as Hawthorne disdains, to treat any individual character with minute realistic detail, but he does not even portray typical characters in their large outlines, with a view to opening before us the permanent springs of human action or putting convincingly before us the radical elements of human nature. The actors in his stories are all one-idea'd creatures, monomaniac victims of passion, or grief, or of some perverse instinct, or of an insane desire to guess riddles. They are magniloquent *poseurs*, who dine off their hearts in public, or else morbidly ingenious intellects for the solving of complicated problems. The worthy Nietzsche declares somewhere that the actors in Wagner's music-dramas are always just a dozen steps from the mad-house. We may say the same of Poe's characters, with the exception of those that are merely Babbage calculating machines. Complex human characters, characters that are approximately true to the whole range of human motive and interest, Poe never gives us. He conceives of characters merely as means for securing his artificial effects on the nerves of his readers.

The world, too, into which Poe takes us, burnished as it is, vividly visualized as it is, is a counterfeit world, magnificently false like his characters. Sometimes it is a phantasmagoric world, full of romantic detail and sensuous splendour. Its bright meadows are luxuriant with asphodels, hyacinths, and acanthuses, are watered with limpid rivers of silence that lose themselves shimmeringly in blue Da Vinci distances, are lighted by tripletinted suns, and are finally shut in by the "golden walls of the universe." When not an exotic region of this sort, Poe's world is apt to be a dextrously contrived toy universe, full of trap-doors, unexpected passages, and clever mechanical devices of all sorts, fit to help the conjurer in securing his effects. Elaborately artificial in some fashion or other, Poe's world is sure to be, designed with nice malice to control the reader's imagination and put it at Poe's mercy. In short, in all that he does, in the material that he uses, in the characters that he conjures up to carry on the action of his stories, in his methods of weaving together incident and description and situation and action, Poe is radically artificial, a calculator of effects, a reckless scorner of fact and of literal truth.

And, indeed, it is just this successful artificiality that for many very modern temperaments constitutes Poe's special charm; he is thoroughly irresponsible; he whistles the commonplace down the wind and forgets everything but his dream, its harmony, its strenuous flight, its splendour and power. The devotees of art for art's sake have now for many years kept up a tradition of unstinted admiration for Poe. This has been specially true in France, where, indeed, men of all schools have joined in doing him honour. Barbey d'Aurevilly wrote an eulogistic essay on him as early as 1853, an essay to which he has since from time to time made various additions, the last in 1883. Baudelaire translated Poe's tales in several instalments between 1855 and 1865. Émile Hennequin published, a few years ago, an elaborate study and life of Poe; and Stéphane Mallarmé has of late conferred a new and perhaps somewhat dubious immortality upon the "Raven," through a translation into very symbolistic prose. In truth, Poe was a decadent before the days of decadence, and he has the distinction of having been one of the earliest defiant practisers of art for art's sake. In his essay on the "Poetic Principle," he expressly declared that a poem should be written solely "for the poem's sake,"—a phrase which almost anticipates the famous formula of modern æstheticism. The drift of this essay, Poe's opinion elsewhere recorded, and his practice as a story-teller, all agree in implying or urging that art is its own justification, that the sole aim of art is the creation of beauty, and that art and actual life need have nothing to do with one another. To be sure, Poe's comments on everyday life have not acquired quite the exquisite contempt and the epigrammatic finish characteristic of modern decadence; yet the root of the matter was in Poe—witness a letter in which he boasts of his insensibility to the charms of "temporal life," and of being "profoundly excited" solely "by music and by some poems."

Poe and his heroes curiously anticipate, in many respects, the morbid dreamers whom French novelists of the decadent school have of recent years repeatedly studied, and of whom Huysmans's Des Esseintes may be taken as a type. The hero in "The Fall of the House of Usher," with his "cadaverousness of complexion," his "eye large, liquid, and luminous beyond comparison," his "habitual trepidancy," his "hollow-sounding enunciation," "his morbid acuteness of the senses," and his suffering when exposed to the odours of certain flowers and to all sounds save those of a few stringed instruments, might be a preliminary study for Huysmans's memorable Des Esseintes. Usher has not the French hero's sophistication and self-consciousness; he suffers dumbly, and has not Des Esseintes's consolation in knowing himself a "special soul," supersensitive and delicate beyond the trite experience of nerves and senses prescribed by practical life. He does not carry on his morbid experimentations debonairly as does Des Esseintes, and he takes his diseases too seriously. But he nevertheless anticipates Des Esseintes astonishingly in looks, in nerves, in physique, and even in tricks of manner. Poe's heroes, too, are forerunners of modern decadents in their refinings upon sensation, in their fusion of the senses, and in their submergence in moods. As Herr Nordau says of the Symbolists, they have eyes in their ears; they see sounds; they smell colours. One of them hears rays of light that fall upon his retina. They are all extraordinarily alive to the "unconsidered trifles" of sensation. The man in the "Pit and the Pendulum" smells the odour of the sharp steel blade that swings past him. They detect with morbid delicacy of perception shades of feeling that give likeness to the most apparently diverse sensations. The lover in "Ligeia" feels

in his "intense scrutiny of Ligeia's eyes" the same sentiment that at other times overmasters him "in the survey of a rapidly growing vine, in the contemplation of a moth, a butterfly, . . . in the falling of a meteor, . . . in the glances of unusually aged people, . . ." and when listening to "certain sounds from stringed instruments." Moods become absorbing and monopolizing in the lives of these vibrating temperaments. "Men have called me mad," the lover in "Eleonora" ingratiatingly assures us; "but the question is not yet settled whether madness is or is not the loftiest intelligence; whether much that is glorious, whether all that is profound, does not spring from disease of thought—from moods of mind exalted at the expense of the general intellect." Finally, Poe's heroes anticipate the heroes of modern decadence in feeling the delicate artistic challenge of sin and of evil: they hardly reach the audacities of French Diabolism and Sadism; but at least they have the whim of doing or fancying moral evil that æsthetic good may come.

All these characteristics of Poe's work may be summed up by saying that his heroes are apt to be neuropaths or degenerates. And doubtless Poe himself was a degenerate, if one cares to use the somewhat outworn idiom of the evangelist of the Philistines. He had the ego-mania of the degenerate, a fact which shows itself strikingly in his art through his preoccupation with death. In his poetry and prose alike the fear of death as numbing the precious core of personality is an obsession with him, and such subjects as premature burial, metempsychosis, revivification after death, the sensations that may go with the change from mortality to immortality (see the "Colloquy of Monos and Una"), had an irresistible fascination for him. Moreover, throughout Poe's art there are signs of egomania in the almost entire lack of the social sympathies. Where in Poe's stories do we find portrayed the sweet and tender relationships and affections that make human life endurable? Where are friendship and frank comradeship and the love of brothers and sisters and of parents and children? Where are the somewhat trite but after all so necessary virtues of loyalty, patriotism, courage, pity, charity, self-sacrifice? Such old-fashioned qualities and capacities, the stuff out of which what is worth while in human nature has heretofore been wrought, are curiously unrecognized and unportrayed in Poe's fiction. They seem to have had no artistic meaning for him—these so obvious and commonplace elements in man and life. Perhaps they simply seemed to him not the stuff that dreams are made of.

When all is said, there is something a bit inhuman in Poe, which, while at times it may give a special tinge to our pleasure in his art, occasionally vitiates or destroys that pleasure. His taste is not immaculate; he will go any length in search of a shudder. Sometimes he is fairly repulsive because of his callous recital of loathsome physical details, for example in his description of the decimated Brigadier-General, in "The Man That Was Used Up." In "King Pest," "The Premature Burial," and "M. Valdemar," there is this same almost vulgar insensibility in the presence of the unclean and disgusting. At times, this callousness leads to artistic mischance, and causes a shudder of laughter where Poe wants a shiver of awe. Surely this is apt to be the case in "Berenice," the story where the hero is fascinated by the beautiful teeth of the heroine, turns amateur dentist after her death, and in a frenzy of professional enthusiasm breaks open her coffin, and extracts her incisors, bicuspids, and molars, thirty-two altogether—the set was complete.

When this inhumanity of Poe's does not lead to actual repulsiveness or to unintentional grotesqueness, it is nevertheless responsible for a certain aridity and intellectual cruelty that in the last analysis will be found pervading pretty much all he has written. This is what Barbey d'Aurevilly has in mind when he speaks of Poe's *sécheresse*, the terrible dryness of his art. And looking at the matter wholly apart from the question of ethics, this dryness is a most serious defect in Poe's work as an artist. His stories and characters have none of the buoyancy, the tender, elastic variableness, and the grace of living things; they are hard in finish, harsh in surface, mechanically inevitable in their working out. They seem calculated, the result of ingenious calculation, not because any particular detail impresses the reader as conspicuously false—Poe keeps his distance from life too skilfully and consistently for this—but because of their all-pervading lack of deeply human imagination and interest, because of that shallowness in Poe's hold upon life that has already been noted. The stories and the characters seem the work of pure intellect, of intellect divorced from heart; and for that very reason they do not wholly satisfy, when judged by the most exacting artistic standards. They seem the product of some ingenious mechanism for the manufacture of fiction, of some surpassing rival of Maelzel's chess-playing automaton. This faultily faultless accuracy and precision of movement may very likely be a penalty Poe has to submit to because of his devotion to art for art's sake. He is too much engrossed in treatment and manipulation; his dexterity of execution perhaps presupposes, at any rate goes along with, an almost exclusive interest in technical problems and in "effects," to the neglect of what is vital and human in the material he uses.

Closely akin to this dryness of treatment is a certain insincerity of tone or flourish of manner, that often interferes with our enjoyment of Poe. We become suddenly aware of the gleaming eye and complacent smile of the concealed manipulator in the writing-automaton. The author is too plainly lying in wait for us; or he is too ostentatiously exhibiting his cleverness and resource, his command of the tricks of the game. One of the worst things that can be said of Poe from this point of view is that he contains the promise and potency of Mr. Robert Hichens, and of other cheap English decadents. Poe himself is never quite a mere acrobat; but he suggests the possible coming of the acrobat, the clever tumbler with the ingenious grimace and the palm itching for coppers.

The same perfect mastery of technique that is characteristic of Poe's treatment of material is noticeable in his literary style. When one stops to consider it, Poe's style, particularly in his romances, is highly artificial, an exquisitely fabricated medium. Poe is fond of inversions and involutions in his sentence-structure, and of calculated rhythms that either throw into relief certain picturesque words, or symbolize in some reverberant fashion the mood of the moment. He seems to have felt very keenly the beauty of De Quincey's intricate and sophisiticated cadences, and more than once he actually echoes some of the most noteworthy of them in his own distribution of accents. Special instances of this might be pointed out in "Eleonora" and in "The Premature Burial." Poe's fondness for artificial musical effects is also seen in his emphatic reiteration of specially picturesque phrases, a trick of manner that every one associates with his poetry, and that is more than once found in his prose writings. "And, all at once, the moon arose through the thin ghastly mist, and was crimson

in color. And mine eyes fell upon a huge gray rock which stood by the shore of the river, and was lighted by the light of the moon. And the rock was gray, and ghastly, and tall—and the rock was gray." Echolalia, Herr Nordau would probably call this trick in Poe's verse and prose, and he would regard it as an incontestable proof of Poe's degeneracy. Nevertheless, the beauty of the effects to which this mannerism leads in Poe's more artificial narratives is very marked.

In Poe's critical essays his style takes on an altogether different tone and movement, and becomes analytical, rapid, incisive, almost acrid in its severity and intellectuality. The ornateness and the beauty of cadence and colour that are characteristic of his decorative prose disappear entirely. Significantly enough, Macaulay was his favourite literary critic. "The style and general conduct of Macaulay's critical papers," Poe assures his readers, "could scarcely be improved." A strange article of faith to find in the literary creed of a dreamer, an amateur of moods, an artistic epicure. Yet that Poe was sincere in this opinion is proved by the characteristics of his own literary essays. He emulates Macaulay in his briskness, in the downrightness of his assertions, in his challengingly demonstrative tone, and in his unsensitiveness to the artistic shade. Of course, he is far inferior to Macaulay in knowledge and in thoroughness of literary training, while he surpasses him in acuteness of analysis and in insight into technical problems.

Poe's admiration for Macaulay and his emulation of him in his critical writings are merely further illustrations of the peculiar intellectual aridity that has already been noted as characteristic of him. Demonic intellectual ingenuity is almost the last word for Poe's genius as far as regards his real personality, the quintessential vital energy of the man. His intellect was real; everything else about him was exquisite feigning. His passion, his human sympathy, his love of nature, all the emotions that go into his fiction, have a counterfeit unreality about them. Not that they are actually hypocritical, but that they seem unsubstantial, mimetic, not the expression of a genuine nature. There was something of the cherub in Poe, and he had to extract his feelings from his head. Much of the time a reader of Poe is cajoled into a delighted forgetfulness of all this unreality, Poe is so adroit a manipulator, such a master of technique. He adapts with unerring tact his manner to his matter and puts upon us the perfect spell of art. Moreover, even when a reader forces himself to take notice of Poe's artificiality, he may, if he be in the right temper, gain only an added delight, the sort of delight that comes from watching the exquisitely sure play of a painter's firm hand, adapting its action consciously to all the difficulties of its subject. Poe's precocious artistic sophistication is one of his rarest charms for the appreciative amateur. But if a reader be exorbitant and relentless and ask from Poe something more than intellectual resource and technical dexterity, he is pretty sure to be disappointed; Poe has little else to offer him. Doubtless it is Philistinish to ask for this something more; but people have always asked for it in the past, and seem likely to go on asking for it, even despite the fact that Herr Max Nordau has almost succeeded in reducing the request to an absurdity.

ANNE BRONTË

1820–1849

Anne Brontë, novelist, and younger sister of Charlotte and Emily Brontë, was born in Thornton, Yorkshire on January 17, 1820. She was educated largely at home, where she was particularly close to Emily, with whom she invented the imaginary country of Gondal in which many of their dramatic poems are set. Anne became governess to the Ingham family at Blake Hall in 1839, and from 1841 to 1845 she was governess to the Robinson family at Thorp Green Hall, near York. These experiences were the basis of her first novel, *Agnes Grey*, written during the winter of 1845–46 and published in December 1847 together with Emily Brontë's *Wuthering Heights*. The novel appeared under the pseudonym Acton Bell, as did a selection of her poems, published with those of her sisters as *Poems by Currer, Ellis, and Acton Bell* (1846). Her second novel, *The Tenant of Wildfell Hall* (1848), concerned a marriage ruined by the dissipation and extravagance of the husband.

Shortly after the deaths of her brother Branwell and her sister Emily, Anne herself became ill with tuberculosis, and died on May 28, 1849. Her *Complete Poems*, including verses discovered after her death, was edited by C. K. Shorter and published in 1920.

General

I hoped, that with the brave and strong,
　My portioned task might lie;
To toil amid the busy throng,
　With purpose pure and high.

But God has fixed another part,
　And He has fixed it well;
I said so with my bleeding heart,
　When first the anguish fell.

A dreadful darkness closes in
　On my bewildered mind;
Oh, let me suffer and not sin,
　Be tortured, yet resigned.

Shall I with joy thy blessings share
　And not endure their loss?
Or hope the martyr's crown to wear
　And cast away the cross?

Thou, God, hast taken our delight,
　Our treasured hope away;
Thou bidst us now weep through the night
　And sorrow through the day.

These weary hours will not be lost,
　These days of misery,
These nights of darkness, anguish-tost,
　Can I but turn to Thee.

Weak and weary though I lie,
　Crushed with sorrow, worn with pain,
I may lift to Heaven mine eye,
　And strive to labour not in vain;

That inward strife against the sins
　That ever wait on suffering
To strike whatever first begins:
　Each ill that would corruption bring;

That secret labour to sustain
　With humble patience every blow;
To gather fortitude from pain,
　And hope and holiness from woe.

Thus let me serve Thee from my heart,
　Whate'er may be my written fate:
Whether thus early to depart,
　Or yet a while to wait.

If thou shouldst bring me back to life,
　More humbled I should be;

More wise, more strengthened for the strife,
　More apt to lean on Thee.
Should death be standing at the gate,
　Thus should I keep my vow;
But, Lord! whatever be my fate,
　Oh, let me serve Thee now!
　　—ANNE BRONTË, "Last Lines," 1849

In looking over my sister Anne's papers, I find mournful evidence that religious feeling had been to her but too much like what it was to Cowper; I mean, of course, in a far milder form. Without rendering her a prey to those horrors that defy concealment, it subdued her mood and bearing to a perpetual pensiveness; the pillar of a cloud glided constantly before her eyes; she ever waited at the foot of a secret Sinai, listening in her heart to the voice of a trumpet sounding long and waxing louder. Some, perhaps, would rejoice over these tokens of sincere though sorrowing piety in a deceased relative: I own, to me they seem sad, as if her whole innocent life had been passed under the martyrdom of an unconfessed physical pain: their effect, indeed, would be too distressing, were it not combated by the certain knowledge that in her last moments this tyranny of a too tender conscience was overcome; this pomp of terrors broke up, and, passing away, left her dying hour unclouded. Her belief in God did not then bring to her dread, as of a stern Judge—but hope, as in a Creator and Saviour: and no faltering hope was it, but a sure and steadfast conviction, on which, in the rude passage from Time to Eternity, she threw the weight of her human weakness, and by which she was enabled to bear what was to be borne, patiently—serenely—victoriously.
—CHARLOTTE BRONTË, "Preface" (c. 1850) to *The Complete Poems of Anne Brontë*, ed. Clement K. Shorter, 1920

The Tenant of Wildfell Hall, by Acton Bell, had ⟨. . .⟩ an unfavourable reception. At this I cannot wonder. The choice of subject was an entire mistake. Nothing less congruous with the writer's nature could be conceived. The motives which dictated this choice were pure, but, I think, slightly morbid. She had, in the course of her life, been called on to contemplate, near at hand, and for a long time, the terrible effects of talents misused and faculties abused: hers was naturally a sensitive, reserved, and dejected nature; what she saw sank very deeply into her mind; it did her harm. She brooded over it till she believed it to be a duty to reproduce every detail (of course with fictitious characters, incidents, and situations,) as a warning to others. She hated her work, but would pursue it. When reasoned with on the subject, she regarded such reasonings as a temptation to self-indulgence. She must be honest; she must not varnish, soften, nor conceal. This well-meant resolution brought on her misconstruction, and some abuse, which she bore, as it was her custom to bear whatever was unpleasant, with mild, steady patience. She was a very sincere and practical Christian, but the tinge of religious melancholy communicated a sad shade to her brief, blameless life.

⟨. . .⟩ I have said that she was religious, and it was by leaning on those Christian doctrines in which she firmly believed, that she found support through her most painful journey. I witnessed their efficacy in her latest hour and greatest trial, and must bear my testimony to the calm triumph with which they brought her through. She died May 28, 1849. ⟨. . .⟩

Anne's character was milder and more subdued ⟨than Emily's⟩; she wanted the power, the fire, the originality of her sister, but was well endowed with quiet virtues of her own. Long-suffering, self-denying, reflective, and intelligent, a constitutional reserve and taciturnity placed and kept her in the shade, and covered her mind, and especially her feelings, with a sort of nun-like veil, which was rarely lifted. Neither Emily nor Anne was learned; they had no thought of filling their pitchers at the well-spring of other minds; they always wrote from the impulse of nature, the dictates of intuition, and from such stores of observation as their limited experience had enabled them to amass. I may sum up all by saying, that for strangers they were nothing, for superficial observers less than nothing; but for those who had known them all their lives in the intimacy of close relationship, they were genuinely good and truly great.—CHARLOTTE BRONTË, "Biographical Notice of Ellis and Acton Bell," *Wuthering Heights and Agnes Grey,* 1850

The gifts of Anne Brontë were those of the hymn-writer, whose object is rather to stir and set in motion well-defined pre-existing ideas of the readers than to introduce new ones. Anne Brontë's is a pathetic figure; much of her life was spent timidly, working hard amongst strangers; she never had the hard grip of either of her sisters; she was fitted only for gentle things, and yet she had, in the strongest measure, the literary cravings and aspirations of her family, and was called upon, like poor Ophelia, to take part in a tragedy. She was thus tried beyond her strength. Her two novels are failures, but her verses have a tender pathos of their own. Her last composition, having found its way into popular hymnbooks, is perhaps at this moment the widest-known work of the three sisters. I refer to the lines beginning—

> I hoped that with the brave and strong.
> —AUGUSTINE BIRRELL, *Life of Charlotte Brontë,*
> 1887, p. 92

It can scarcely be doubted that Anne Brontë's two novels, *Agnes Grey* and *The Tenant of Wildfell Hall,* would have long since fallen into oblivion but for the inevitable association with the romances of her two greater sisters. While this may be taken for granted, it is impossible not to feel, even at the distance of more than half a century, a sense of Anne's personal charm. Gentleness is a word always associated with her by those who knew her. When Mr. Nicholls saw what professed to be a portrait of Anne in a magazine article, he wrote: "What an awful caricature of the dear, gentle Anne Brontë!" Mr. Nicholls had a portrait of Anne in his possession, drawn by Charlotte, which he pronounced to be an admirable likeness,

and this does convey the impression of a sweet and gentle nature. ⟨. . .⟩

Apart from the correspondence we know little more than this—that Anne was the least assertive of the three sisters, and that she was more distinctly a general favourite. We have Charlotte's own word for it that at least one of the curates ventured upon "sheep's eyes" at Anne. We know all too little of her two experiences as governess, first at Blake Hall with Mrs. Ingham, and later at Thorp Green with Mrs. Robinson. The painful episode of Branwell's madness came to disturb her sojourn at the latter place, but long afterwards her old pupils, the Misses Robinson, called to see her at Haworth; and one of them, who became a Mrs. Clapham of Keighley, always retained the most kindly memories of her gentle governess.

With the exception of these two uncomfortable episodes as governess, Anne would seem to have had no experience of the larger world. Even before Anne's death, Charlotte had visited Brussels, London, and Hathersage (in Derbyshire). Anne never, but once, set foot out of her native country, although she was the only one of her family to die away from home. ⟨. . .⟩

Agnes Grey, as we have noted, was published by Newby, in one volume, in 1847. *The Tenant of Wildfell Hall* was issued by the same publisher, in three volumes, in 1848. It is not generally known that *The Tenant of Wildfell Hall* went into a second edition the same year; and I should have pronounced it incredible, were not a copy of the later issue in my possession, that Anne Brontë had actually written a preface to this edition. The fact is entirely ignored in the correspondence. The preface in question makes it quite clear, if any evidence of that were necessary, that Anne had her brother in mind in writing the book. "I could not be understood to suppose," she says, "that the proceedings of the unhappy scapegrace, with his few profligate companions I have here introduced, are a specimen of the common practices of society: the case is an extreme one, as I trusted none would fail to perceive; but I knew that such characters do exist, and if I have warned one rash youth from following in their steps, or prevented one thoughtless girl from falling into the very natural error of my heroine, the book has not been written in vain." "One word more and I have done," she continues. "Respecting the author's identity, I would have it to be distinctly understood that Acton Bell is neither Currer nor Ellis Bell, and, therefore, let not his faults be attributed to them. As to whether the name is real or fictitious, it cannot greatly signify to those who know him only by his works." —CLEMENT K. SHORTER, *Charlotte Brontë and Her Circle,* 1896, pp. 181–84

As for the gentle Anne, she remains—well, just the gentle Anne—pious, patient and trustful. Her talent was of that evangelical, pietistic type which never lacks a certain gracefulness and never rises above a certain intellectual level. Had she lived in our day her novels would have attracted little attention, and her poetry would hardly have found admission into any first-class magazine. It remains clear as ever that her immortality is due to her sisters. Upon those bright twin-stars many telescopes are turned, and then there swims into the beholder's view this third, mild-shining star of the tenth magnitude, which otherwise would have remained invisible. It follows that Anne will always have a place assigned her in the chart of the literary heavens. Nothing, however, is ever likely to occur either to heighten our estimate of her literary ability or to lessen the affection which her character inspires.—ANGUS M. MACKAY, *The Brontës: Fact and Fiction,* 1897, pp. 20–21

⟨. . .⟩ the work ⟨. . .⟩ of Anne Brontë may be speedily dismissed. She was a gentle, delicate creature both in mind and body; and but for her greater sisters her writings would now be forgotten. Her pleasing but commonplace tale of *Agnes Grey* was followed by *The Tenant of Wildfell Hall*, in which she attempted, without success, to depict a profligate.—HUGH WALKER, *The Age of Tennyson*, 1897, p. 102

Works

THE TENANT OF WILDFELL HALL

While I acknowledge the success of the present work ⟨*The Tenant of Wildfell Hall*⟩ to have been greater than I anticipated, and the praises it has elicited from a few kind critics to have been greater than it deserved, I must also admit that from some other quarters it has been censured with an asperity which I was as little prepared to expect, and which my judgment, as well as my feelings, assures me is more bitter than just. It is scarcely the province of an author to refute the arguments of his censors and vindicate his own productions; but I may be allowed to make here a few observations with which I would have prefaced the first edition, had I foreseen the necessity of such precautions against the misapprehensions of those who would read it with a prejudiced mind or be content to judge it by a hasty glance.

My object in writing the following pages was not simply to amuse the Reader; neither was it to gratify my own taste, nor yet to ingratiate myself with the Press and the Public: I wished to tell the truth, for truth always conveys its own moral to those who are able to receive it. But as the priceless treasure too frequently hides at the bottom of a well, it needs some courage to dive for it, especially as he that does so will be likely to incur more scorn and obloquy for the mud and water into which he has ventured to plunge, than thanks for the jewel he procures; as, in like manner, she who undertakes the cleansing of a careless bachelor's apartment will be liable to more abuse for the dust she raises than commendation for the clearance she effects. Let it not be imagined, however, that I consider myself competent to reform the errors and abuses of society, but only that I would fain contribute my humble quota towards so good an aim; and if I can gain the public ear at all, I would rather whisper a few wholesome truths therein than much soft nonsense.

As the story of *Agnes Grey* was accused of extravagant over-colouring in those very parts that were carefully copied from the life, with a most scrupulous avoidance of all exaggeration, so, in the present work, I find myself censured for depicting *con amore*, with 'a morbid love of the coarse, if not of the brutal,' those scenes which, I will venture to say, have not been more painful for the most fastidious of my critics to read than they were for me to describe. I may have gone too far; in which case I shall be careful not to trouble myself or my readers in the same way again; but when we have to do with vice and vicious characters, I maintain it is better to depict them as they really are than as they would wish to appear. To represent a bad thing in its least offensive light is, doubtless, the most agreeable course for a writer of fiction to pursue; but is it the most honest, or the safest? Is it better to reveal the snares and pitfalls of life to the young and thoughtless traveller, or to cover them with branches and flowers? Oh, reader! if there were less of this delicate concealment of facts—this whispering, 'Peace, peace,' when there is no peace, there would be less of sin and misery to the young of both sexes who are left to wring their bitter knowledge from experience.

I would not be understood to suppose that the proceedings of the unhappy scapegrace, with his few profligate companions I have here introduced, are a specimen of the common practices of society—the case is an extreme one, as I trusted none would fail to perceive; but I know that such characters do exist, and if I have warned one rash youth from following in their steps, or prevented one thoughtless girl from falling into the very natural error of my heroine, the book has not been written in vain. But, at the same time, if any honest reader shall have derived more pain than pleasure from its perusal, and have closed the last volume with a disagreeable impression on his mind, I humbly crave his pardon, for such was far from my intention; and I will endeavour to do better another time, for I love to give innocent pleasure. Yet, be it understood, I shall not limit my ambition to this—or even to producing 'a perfect work of art': time and talents so spent, I should consider wasted and misapplied. Such humble talents as God has given me I will endeavour to put to their greatest use; if I am able to amuse, I will try to benefit too; and when I feel it my duty to speak an unpalatable truth, with the help of God, I *will* speak it, though it be to the prejudice of my name and to the detriment of my reader's immediate pleasure as well as my own.

One word more, and I have done. Respecting the author's identity, I would have it to be distinctly understood that Acton Bell is neither Currer nor Ellis Bell, and therefore let not his faults be attributed to them. As to whether the name be real or fictitious, it cannot greatly signify to those who know him only by his works. As little, I should think, can it matter whether the writer so designated is a man, or a woman, as one or two of my critics profess to have discovered. I take the imputation in good part, as a compliment to the just delineation of my female characters; and though I am bound to attribute much of the severity of my censors to this suspicion, I make no effort to refute it, because, in my own mind, I am satisfied that if a book is a good one, it is so whatever the sex of the author may be. All novels are, or should be, written for both men and women to read, and I am at a loss to conceive how a man should permit himself to write anything that would be really disgraceful to a woman, or why a woman should be censured for writing anything that would be proper and becoming for a man. —ANNE BRONTË, "Preface" to *The Tenant of Wildfell Hall*, 1848

The three Bells ⟨. . .⟩ ring in a chime so harmonious as to prove that they have issued from the same mould. The resemblance borne by their novels to each other is curious. *The Tenant of Wildfell Hall* must not hope to gain the popularity of her elder sister *Jane Eyre*,—but the blood of the family is in her veins. ⟨. . .⟩

The reader is by this time curious to get a peep of "the tenant" of such a wild abode: being convinced that, since

Vague mystery hangs about these desert places,

she must be a Lady with "a history." But not a line or passage of this shall be divulged in the *Athenæum*,—however tempted to lengthen our lecture on family likeness. With regard to one point, however, we cannot remain silent:—The Bells must be warned against their fancy for dwelling upon what is disagreeable. The brutified estate of Mr. Huntingdon might have been displayed within a smaller compass in place of being elaborated with the fond minuteness of a Jan Steen. The position of the wife with regard to her husband's paramour is, on the other hand, treated with a sort of hard indifference,—natural enough, it may be, but not in harmony with the impressions of the Lady which we have been invited to entertain. Were the metal from this Bell foundry of baser quality than it is it would be lost time to point out flaws and take exceptions. As matters stand, our hints may not be without their use to future "castings:" nor will they be unpalatable, seeing that they are followed by our honest recommendation of *Wildfell Hall* as the most interesting novel which we have read for a month past. —HENRY F. CHORLEY, *Athenaeum*, July 8, 1848, pp. 670–71

The Tenant of Wildfell Hall is altogether a less unpleasing story than its immediate predecessor ⟨*Wuthering Heights*⟩, though it resembles it in the excessive clumsiness with which the plot is arranged, and the prominence given to the brutal element of human nature. The work seems a convincing proof, that there is nothing kindly or genial in the author's powerful mind, and that, if he continues to write novels, he will introduce into the land of romance a larger number of hateful men and women than any other writer of the day. Gilbert, the hero, seems to be a favorite with the author, and to be intended as a specimen of manly character; but he would serve as the ruffian of any other novelist. His nature is fierce, proud, moody, jealous, revengeful, and sometimes brutal. We can see nothing good in him except a certain rude honesty; and that quality is seen chiefly in his bursts of hatred and his insults to women. Helen, the heroine, is doubtless a strong-minded woman, and passes bravely through a great deal of suffering; but if there be any lovable or feminine virtues in her composition, the author has managed to conceal them. She marries a profligate, thinking to reform him; but the gentleman, with a full knowledge of her purpose, declines reformation, goes deeper and deeper into vice, and becomes at last as fiendlike as a very limited stock of brains will allow. This is a reversal of the process carried on in *Jane Eyre*; but it must be admitted that the profligate in *The Tenant of Wildfell Hall* is no Rochester. He is never virtuously inclined, except in those periods of illness and feebleness which his debaucheries have occasioned, thus illustrating the old proverb,—

When the devil was sick, the devil a monk would be,
When the devil was well, the devil a monk was he.

He has almost constantly by him a choice coterie of boon companions, ranging from the elegant libertine to the ferocious sensualist, and the reader is favored with exact accounts of their drunken orgies, and with numerous scraps of their profane conversation. All the characters are drawn with great power and precision of outline, and the scenes are as vivid as life itself. Everywhere is seen the tendency of the author to degrade passion into appetite, and to give prominence to the selfish and malignant elements of human nature; but while he succeeds in making profligacy disgusting, he fails in making virtue pleasing. His depravity is total depravity, and his hard and impudent debauchees seem to belong to that class of reprobates whom Dr. South considers "as not so much born as damned into the world." The reader of Acton Bell gains no enlarged view of mankind, giving a healthy action to his sympathies, but is confined to a narrow space of life, and held down, as it were, by main force, to witness the wolfish side of his nature literally and logically set forth. But the criminal courts are not the places in which to take a comprehensive view of humanity, and the novelist who confines his observation to them is not likely to produce any lasting impression, except of horror and disgust.—EDWIN P. WHIPPLE, "Novels of the Season," *North American Review*, Oct. 1848, pp. 359–60

Anne, the younger and more gentle sister, was of a different mould; yet some passages of her *Tenant of Wildfell Hall* would lead us to suppose that she was gentle chiefly through contrast with her Spartan sister, and that the savage elements about her

found an occasional echo from within. *Agnes Grey*, which appeared with *Wuthering Heights*, made little impression; her reputation rests upon her second and last work, *The Tenant of Wildfell Hall*. ⟨. . .⟩

It must be owned that she did not "varnish" the horrors which she painted, and which her first readers did not suspect of causing the artist so much suffering. We can now trace the quiverings of a sister's heart through the hateful details of a vicious manhood; and if the book fail somewhat in its attempt to become a warning, it may at least claim the merit of a well-meant effort.—MARGARET SWEAT, "Charlotte Brontë and the Brontë Novels," *North American Review*, Oct. 1857, pp. 328–29

⟨. . .⟩ Anne Brontë's second work, *The Tenant of Wildfell Hall*; which deserves perhaps a little more notice and recognition than it has ever received. It is ludicrously weak, palpably unreal, and apparently imitative, whenever it reminds the reader that it was written by a sister of Charlotte and Emily Brontë; but as a study of utterly flaccid and invertebrate immorality it bears signs of more faithful transcription from life than anything in *Jane Eyre* or *Wuthering Heights*.—ALGERNON CHARLES SWINBURNE, "Emily Brontë" (1883), *Miscellanies*, 1886, p. 264

CHARLES KINGSLEY
From "Recent Novels"

Fraser's Magazine, April 1849, pp. 423–26

It ⟨*The Tenant of Wildfell Hall*⟩ is, taken altogether, a powerful and an interesting book. Not that it is a pleasant book to read, nor, as we fancy, has it been a pleasant book to write; still less has it been a pleasant training which could teach an author such awful facts, or give courage to write them. The fault of the book is coarseness—not merely that coarseness of subject which will be the stumbling-block of most readers, and which makes it utterly unfit to be put into the hands of girls; of that we do not complain. There are foul and accursed undercurrents in plenty, in this same smug, respectable, whitewashed English society, which must be exposed now and then; and Society owes thanks, not sneers, to those who dare to shew her the image of her own ugly, hypocritical visage. We must not lay Juvenal's coarseness at Juvenal's door, but at that of the Roman world which he stereotyped in his fearful verses. But the world does not think so. It will revile Acton Bell for telling us, with painful circumstantiality, what the house of a profligate, uneducated country squire is like, perfectly careless whether or not the picture be true, only angry at having been disturbed from its own self-complacent doze—just as it has reviled gallant 'S. G. O.' for nasty-mindedness, and what not, because, having unluckily for himself a human heart and eyes, he dared to see what was under his nose in the bedrooms of Dorsetshire labourers.

It is true, satirists are apt to be unnecessarily coarse. Granted; but are they half as coarse, though, as the men whom they satirise? That gnat-straining, camel-swallowing Pharisee, the world, might, if it chose, recollect that a certain degree of coarse-naturedness, while men continue the one-sided beings which they are at present, may be necessary for all reformers, in order to enable them to look steadily and continuously at the very evils which they are removing. Shall we despise the surgeon because he does not faint in the dissecting-room? Our Chadwicks and Southwood Smiths would make but poor sanitary reformers if their senses could not bid defiance to sulphuretted hydrogen and ammonia. Whether their nostrils suffer or not, ours are saved by them: we have no cause to grumble. And even so with 'Acton Bell.'

But taking this book as a satire, and an exposure of evils, still all unnecessary coarseness is a defect,—a defect which injures the real usefulness and real worth of the book. The author introduces, for instance, a long diary, kept by the noble and unhappy wife of a profligate squire; and would that every man in England might read and lay to heart that horrible record. But what greater mistake, to use the mildest term, can there be than to fill such a diary with written oaths and curses, with details of drunken scenes which no wife, such as poor Helen is represented, would have the heart, not to say the common decency, to write down as they occurred? Dramatic probability and good feeling are equally outraged by such a method. The author, tempted naturally to indulge her full powers of artistic detail, seems to have forgotten that there are silences more pathetic than all words.

A cognate defect, too, struck us much; the splenetic and bitter tone in which certain personages in the novel are mentioned, when really, poor souls, no deeds of theirs are shewn which could warrant such wholesale appellations as 'brute' and 'demon.' One is inclined sometimes to suspect that they are caricatures from the life, against whom some private spite is being vented; though the author has a right to reply, that the whole novel being the autobiography of a young gentleman farmer, such ferocities are to be charged on him, not on her. True, but yet in his mouth as much as in any one's else they want cause for them to be shewn, according to all principles of fiction; and if none such exists on the face of the story, it only indicates a defect in the youth's character which makes his good fortune more improbable. For the book sets forth how the gallant Gilbert wins the heart, and after her husband's death, the hand of the rich squire's well-born and highly-cultivated wife.

Now we do not complain of the 'impossibility' of this. *Ne me dites jamais ce bête de mot*, as Mirabeau said. Impossible? Society is full of wonders; our worst complaint against fiction-mongers is, that they are so tame, so common-place, so shamefully afraid of wonders, of ninety-nine hundredths of what a man may see every day of the week by putting his head out of his own window. You old whited sepulchre of a world! there are dead men's bones enough inside you, of which you could give but an ugly account! It was but the other day, for instance, we heard a true story of piracy and parricide, of ill-gotten wealth, worse than heathen barbarity, and God's awful judgments, transacted among scenery of such romantic horror, physical and spiritual, as would make Mr. Ainsworth's fortune. We would offer now to sell him the story for twenty pounds, as the best investment he ever made in his life, were it not so fearfully true and recent, that its publication would wantonly wound the hearts of many innocent people now living. So much for improbabilities. But the novelist, especially when he invents a story, instead of merely giving dramatic life to one ready made, which is the Shakspearian, and, as we suspect, the higher path of art, must give some internal and spiritual probability to his outward miracles; and this, we think, Acton Bell has in this case failed to do. We cannot see any reason why Gilbert Markham, though no doubt highly attractive to young ladies of his own calibre, should excite such passionate love in Helen, with all her bitter experiences of life, her painting, and her poetry, her deep readings and deep thoughts—absolutely no reason at all, except the last one in the world, which either the author or she would have wished, namely, that there was no other man in

the way for her to fall in love with. We want to see this strange intellectual superiority of his to the general run of his class (for we must suppose some such); and all the characteristics we do find, beyond the general dashing, manful spirit of a young farmer, is a very passionate and somewhat brutal temper, and, to say the least, a wanton rejection of a girl to whom he has been giving most palpable and somewhat rough proofs of affection, and whom he afterwards hates bitterly, simply because she rallies him on having jilted her for a woman against whose character there was every possible ground for suspicion. This is not to be counterbalanced by an occasional vein of high-flown sentimentalism in the young gentleman (and that, too, not often) when he comes in contact with his lady-love. If the author had intended to work out the noble old Cymon and Iphigenia myths, she ought to have let us see the gradual growth of the clown's mind under the influence of the accomplished woman; and this is just what she has not done. Gilbert Markham is not one character oscillating between his old low standard and his higher new one, according as he comes in contact with his own countrified friends or his new lady-love, but two different men, with no single root-idea of character to unite and explain the two opposite poles of his conduct. For instance, Mr. Markham is one day talking to Helen in the following high-flown vein:—

> 'It gives me little consolation to think that I shall next behold you as a disembodied spirit, or an altered being, with a frame perfect and glorious, but not like this; and a heart, perhaps, entirely estranged from me.'
>
> 'No, Gilbert, there is perfect love in heaven.'
>
> 'So perfect, I suppose, that it soars above distinctions, and you will have no closer sympathy with me than with any one of the ten thousand thousand angels, and the innumerable multitude of happy spirits round us.'

And so on; very fine indeed. But, lo! the same evening he goes to call upon an old and intimate friend, whom, after having brutally knocked him down and left him in a ditch, careless whether he died or not, on the supposition that he was, like himself, a lover of Helen, he has suddenly discovered to be neither more or less than her brother; and after this fashion he makes his apology for having nearly killed him:—

> My task must be performed at once, however, in some fashion; and so I plunged into it at once, and floundered through it as I could.
>
> 'The truth is, Lawrence, I have not acted quite correctly to you of late, especially on this last occasion; and I am come to—in short, to express my regret for what I've done, and to beg your pardon. If you don't choose to grant it,' I added, hastily, not liking the aspect of his face, 'it's no matter; only I've done *my* duty, that's all.'

To which *amende honorable* the knight of the broken head answering more sensibly than gratefully:—

> 'I forgot to tell you that it was in consequence of a mistake,' muttered I. 'I should have made a very handsome apology, but you provoked me so confoundedly' (the young gentleman, like most characters in the book, is very fond of such expletives, and still stronger ones) 'with your —— Well, I suppose it's all my fault. The fact is, I didn't know that you were Mrs. Graham's brother,' &c. &c.

Quantum mutatus ab illo Hectore! To us, this and many other scenes seem as vulgar and improbable in conception, as they are weak and disgusting in execution. The puffs inform us that the book is very like *Jane Eyre*. To us it seems to have exaggerated all the faults of that remarkable book, and retained very few of its good points. The superior *religious* tone in which alone it surpasses *Jane Eyre* is, in our eyes, quite neutralised by the low *moral* tone which reigns throughout.

Altogether, as we said before, the book is painful. The dark side of every body and every thing is dilated on; we had almost said, revelled in. There are a very few quite perfect people in the book, but they are kept as far out of sight as possible; they are the 'accidentals,' the disagreeable people, the 'necessary' notes of the melody; and the 'timbre' of the notes themselves is harsh and rough. The author has not had the tact which enabled Mr. Thackeray, in *Vanity Fair*, to construct a pleasing whole out of most unpleasing materials, by a harmonious unity of parts, and, above all, by a tone of tender grace and solemn ironic indignation, in the midst of all his humour, spreading over and softening down the whole;—that true poetic instinct, which gives to even the coarsest of Fielding's novels and Shakspeare's comedies, considered as wholes, a really pure and lofty beauty. The author has not seen that though it is quite fair to write in a melancholy, or even harsh key, and to introduce accidental discords, or even sounds in themselves disagreeable, yet that this last must be done only to set off by contrast the background of harmony and melody, and that the key of the whole must be a correct and a palpable one; it must not be buried beneath innumerable occasional flats and sharps; above all, we must not, as in *The Tenant of Wildfell Hall*, with its snappish fierceness, be tortured by a defective chord, in which one false note is perpetually recurring; or provoked by a certain flippant, rough staccato movement throughout, without softness, without repose, and, therefore, without dignity. We advise the author, before the next novel is taken in hand, to study Shakspeare somewhat more carefully, and see if she[1] cannot discover the secret of the wonderful harmony with which he, like Raphael, transfigures the most painful, and, apparently, chaotic subjects.

Notes

1. We have spoken of the author in the feminine gender, because, of whatever sex the name 'Acton Bell' may be, a woman's pen seems to us indisputably discernible in every page. The very coarseness and vulgarity is just such as a woman, trying to write like a man, would invent,—second-hand and clumsy, and not such as men do use; the more honour to the writer's heart, if not to her taste.

MARY A. WARD
"Introduction"
The Tenant of Wildfell Hall
1900, pp. ix–xix

Anne Brontë serves a twofold purpose in the study of what the Brontës wrote and were. In the first place, her gentle and delicate presence, her sad, short story, her hard life and early death, enter deeply into the poetry and tragedy that have always been entwined with the memory of the Brontës, as women and as writers; in the second, the books and poems that she wrote serve as matter of comparison by which to test the greatness of her two sisters. She is the measure of their genius—like them, yet not with them.

Many years after Anne's death her brother-in-law protested against a supposed portrait of her, as giving a totally wrong impression of the 'dear, gentle, Anne Brontë.' 'Dear' and 'gentle' indeed she seems to have been through life, the

youngest and prettiest of the sisters, with a delicate complexion, a slender neck, and small, pleasant features. Notwithstanding, she possessed in full the Brontë seriousness, the Brontë strength of will. When her father asked her at four years old what a little child like her wanted most, the tiny creature replied—if it were not a Brontë it would be incredible!—'Age and experience.' When the three children started their *Island Plays* together in 1827, Anne, who was then eight, chose Guernsey for her imaginary island, and peopled it with 'Michael Sadler, Lord Bentinck, and Sir Henry Halford.' She and Emily were constant companions, and there is evidence that they shared a common world of fancy from very early days to mature womanhood. *The Gondal Chronicles* seem to have amused them for many years, and to have branched out into innumerable books, written in the 'tiny writing' of which Mr. Clement Shorter has given us facsimiles. 'I am now engaged in writing the fourth volume of Solala Vernon's Life,' says Anne at twenty-one. And four years later Emily says, 'The Gondals still flourish bright as ever. I am at present writing a work on the First War. Anne has been writing some articles on this and a book by Henry Sophona. We intend sticking firm by the rascals as long as they delight us, which I am glad to say they do at present.'

That the author of *Wildfell Hall* should ever have delighted in the Gondals, should ever have written the story of Solala Vernon or Henry Sophona, is pleasant to know. Then, for her too, as for her sisters there was a moment when the power of 'making out' could turn loneliness and disappointment into riches and content. For a time at least, and before a hard and degrading experience had broken the spring of her youth, and replaced the disinterested and spontaneous pleasure that is to be got from the life and play of imagination, by a sad sense of duty, and an inexorable consciousness of moral and religious mission, Anne Brontë wrote stories for her own amusement, and loved the 'rascals' she created.

But already in 1841, when we first hear of the Gondals and Solala Vernon, the material for quite other books was in poor Anne's mind. She was then teaching in the family at Thorpe Green, where Branwell joined her as tutor in 1843, and where, owing to events that are still a mystery, she seems to have passed through an ordeal that left her shattered in health and nerve, with nothing gained but those melancholy and repulsive memories that she was afterwards to embody in *Wildfell Hall*. She seems, indeed, to have been partly the victim of Branwell's morbid imagination, the imagination of an opium-eater and a drunkard. That he was neither the conqueror nor the villain that he made his sisters believe, all the evidence that has been gathered since Mrs. Gaskell wrote goes to show. But poor Anne believed his account of himself, and no doubt saw enough evidence of vicious character in Branwell's daily life to make the worst enormities credible. She seems to have passed the last months of her stay at Thorpe Green under a cloud of dread and miserable suspicion, and was thankful to escape from her situation in the summer of 1845. At the same moment Branwell was summarily dismissed from his tutorship, his employer, Mr. Robinson, writing a stern letter of complaint to Branwell's father, concerned no doubt with the young man's disorderly and intemperate habits. Mrs. Gaskell says: 'The premature deaths of two at least of the sisters—all the great possibilities of their earthly lives snapped short—may be dated from Midsummer 1845.' The facts as we now know them hardly bear out so strong a judgment. There is nothing to show that Branwell's conduct was responsible in any way for Emily's illness and death, and Anne, in the contemporary fragment recovered by Mr. Shorter, gives a less tragic account of the matter. 'During my stay (at Thorpe Green),' she writes on July 31, 1845, 'I have had some very unpleasant and undreamt-of experience of human nature. . . . Branwell has . . . been a tutor at Thorpe Green, and had much tribulation and ill-health. . . . We hope he will be better and do better in future.' And at the end of the paper she says, sadly, forecasting the coming years, 'I for my part cannot well be flatter or older in mind than I am now.' This is the language of disappointment and anxiety; but it hardly fits the tragic story that Mrs. Gaskell believed.

That story was, no doubt, the elaboration of Branwell's diseased fancy during the three years which elapsed between his dismissal from Thorpe Green and his death. He imagined a guilty romance with himself and his employer's wife for characters, and he imposed the horrid story upon his sisters. Opium and drink are the sufficient explanations; and no time need now be wasted upon unravelling the sordid mystery. But the vices of the brother, real or imaginary, have a certain importance in literature, because of the effect they produced upon his sisters. There can be no question that Branwell's opium madness, his bouts of drunkenness at the Black Bull, his violence at home, his free and coarse talk, and his perpetual boast of guilty secrets, influenced the imagination of his wholly pure and inexperienced sisters. Much of *Wuthering Heights*, and all of *Wildfell Hall*, show Branwell's mark, and there are many passages in Charlotte's books also, where those who know the history of the parsonage can hear the voice of those sharp moral repulsions, those dismal moral questionings, to which Branwell's misconduct and ruin gave rise. Their brother's fate was an element in the genius of Emily and Charlotte which they were strong enough to assimilate, which may have done them some harm, and weakened in them certain delicate or sane perceptions, but was ultimately, by the strange alchemy of talent, far more profitable than hurtful, inasmuch as it troubled the waters of the soul, and brought them near to the more desperate realities of our 'frail, fall'n humankind.'

But Anne was not strong enough, her gift was not vigorous enough, to enable her thus to transmute experience and grief. The probability is that when she left Thorpe Green in 1845 she was already suffering from that religious melancholy of which Charlotte discovered such piteous evidence among her papers after death. It did not much affect the writing of *Agnes Grey*, which was completed in 1846, and reflected the minor pains and discomforts of her teaching experience, but it combined with the spectacle of Branwell's increasing moral and physical decay to produce that bitter mandate of conscience under which she wrote *The Tenant of Wildfell Hall*.

'Hers was naturally a sensitive, reserved, and dejected nature. She hated her work, but would pursue it. It was written as a warning,'—so said Charlotte when, in the pathetic Preface of 1850, she was endeavouring to explain to the public how a creature so gentle and so good as Acton Bell should have written such a book as *Wildfell Hall*. And in the second edition of *Wildfell Hall* which appeared in 1848 Anne Brontë herself justified her novel in a Preface which is reprinted in this volume for the first time. The little preface is a curious document. It has the same determined didactic tone which pervades the book itself, the same narrowness of view, and inflation of expression, an inflation which is really due not to any personal egotism in the writer, but rather to that very gentleness and inexperience which must yet nerve itself under the stimulus of religion to its disagreeable and repulsive task. 'I knew that such characters'—as Huntingdon and his companions—'do exist, and if I have warned one rash youth from following in their steps the book has not been written in vain.'

If the story has given more pain than pleasure to 'any honest reader,' the writer 'craves his pardon, for such was far from my intention.' But at the same time she cannot promise to limit her ambition to the giving of innocent pleasure, or to the production of 'a perfect work of art.' 'Time and talent so spent I should consider wasted and misapplied.' God has given her unpalatable truths to speak and she must speak them.

The measure of misconstruction and abuse therefore which her book brought upon her she bore, says her sister, 'as it was her custom to bear whatever was unpleasant, with mild, steady patience. She was a very sincere and practical Christian, but the tinge of religious melancholy communicated a sad shade to her brief, blameless life.'

In spite of misconstruction and abuse, however, *Wildfell Hall* seems to have attained more immediate success than anything else written by the sisters before 1848, except *Jane Eyre*. It went into a second edition within a very short time of its publication, and Messrs. Newby informed the American publishers with whom they were negotiating that it was the work of the same hand which had produced *Jane Eyre*, and superior to either *Jane Eyre* or *Wuthering Heights*! It was, indeed, the sharp practice connected with this astonishing judgment which led to the sisters' hurried journey to London in 1848—the famous journey when the two little ladies in black revealed themselves to Mr. Smith, and proved to him that they were not one Currer Bell, but two Miss Brontës. It was Anne's sole journey to London—her only contact with a world that was not Haworth, except that supplied by her school-life at Roehead and her two teaching engagements.

And there was and is a considerable narrative ability, a sheer moral energy in *Wildfell Hall*, which would not be enough, indeed, to keep it alive if it were not the work of a Brontë, but still betray it kinship and source. The scenes of Huntingdon's wickedness are less interesting but less improbable than the country-house scenes of *Jane Eyre*; the story of his death has many true and touching passages; the last lovescene is well, even in parts admirably written. But the book's truth, so far as it is true, is scarcely the truth of imagination; it is rather the truth of a tract or a report. There can be little doubt that many of the pages are close transcripts from Branwell's conduct and language,—so far as Anne's slighter personality enabled her to render her brother's temperament, which was more akin to Emily's than to her own. The same material might have been used by Emily or Charlotte; Emily, as we know, did make use of it in *Wuthering Heights*; but only after it had passed through that ineffable transformation, that mysterious, incommunicable heightening which makes and gives rank in literature. Some subtle, innate correspondence between eye and brain, between brain and hand, was present in Emily and Charlotte, and absent in Anne. There is no other account to be given of this or any other case of difference between serviceable talent and the high gifts of 'Delos' and Patara's own 'Apollo.'

The same world of difference appears between her poems and those of her playfellow and comrade Emily. If ever our descendants should establish the schools for writers which are even now threatened or attempted, they will hardly know perhaps any better than we what genius is, nor how it can be produced. But if they try to teach by example, then Anne and Emily Brontë are ready to their hand. Take the verses written by Emily at Roehead which contain the lovely lines which I have already quoted in an earlier 'Introduction.'[1] Just before those lines there are two or three verses which it is worth while to compare with a poem of Anne's called 'Home.' Emily was sixteen at the time of writing; Anne about twenty-one or twenty-two. Both sisters take for their motive the exile's longing thought of home. Emily's lines are full of faults, but they have the indefinable quality—here, no doubt, only in the bud, only as a matter of promise—which Anne's are entirely without. From the twilight schoolroom at Roehead, Emily turns in thought to the distant upland of Haworth and the little stone-built house upon its crest:—

> There is a spot, 'mid barren hills,
>   Where winter howls, and driving rain;
> But, if the dreary tempest chills,
>   There is a light that warms again.
>
> The house is old, the trees are bare,
>   Moonless above bends twilight's dome,
> But what on earth is half so dear—
>   So longed for—as the hearth of home?
>
> The mute bird sitting on the stone,
>   The dank moss dripping from the wall,
> The thorn-trees gaunt, the walks o'ergrown,
>   I love them—how I love them all!

Anne's verses, written from one of the houses where she was a governess, expresses precisely the same feeling, and movement of mind. But notice the instinctive rightness and swiftness of Emily's, the blurred weakness of Anne's!—

> For yonder garden, fair and wide,
>   With groves of evergreen,
> Long winding walks, and borders trim,
>   And velvet lawns between—
>
> Restore to me that little spot,
>   With gray walls compassed round,
> Where knotted grass neglected lies,
>   And weeds usurp the ground,
>
> Though all around this mansion high
>   Invites the foot to roam,
> And though its halls are fair within—
>   Oh, give me back my Home!

A similar parallel lies between Anne's lines 'Domestic Peace,'—a sad and true reflection of the terrible times with Branwell in 1846, and Emily's 'Wanderer from the Fold'; while in Emily's 'Last Lines,' the daring spirit of the sister to whom the magic gift was granted separates itself for ever from the gentle and accustomed piety of the sister to whom it was denied. Yet Anne's 'Last Lines'—'I hoped that with the brave

and strong'—have sweetness and sincerity; they have gained and kept a place in English religious verse, and they must always appeal to those who love the Brontës because, in the language of Christian faith and submission, they record the death of Emily and the passionate affection which her sisters bore her.

And so we are brought back to the point from which we started. It is not as the writer of *Wildfell Hall*, but as the sister of Charlotte and Emily Brontë that Anne Brontë escapes oblivion—as the frail 'little one,' upon whom the other two lavished a tender and protecting care, who was a witness of Emily's death, and herself, within a few minutes of her own farewell to life, bade Charlotte 'take courage.'

'When my thoughts turn to Anne,' said Charlotte many years earlier, 'they always see her as a patient, persecuted stranger,—more lonely, less gifted with the power of making friends even than I am.' Later on, however, this power of making friends seems to have belonged to Anne in greater measure than to the others. Her gentleness conquered; she was not set apart, as they were, by the lonely and self-sufficing activities of great powers; her Christianity, though sad and timid, was of a kind which those around her could understand; she made no grim fight with suffering and death as did Emily. Emily was 'torn' from life 'conscious, panting, reluctant,' to use Charlotte's own words; Anne's 'sufferings were mild,' her mind 'generally serene,' and at the last 'she thanked God that death was come, and come so gently.' When Charlotte returned to the desolate house at Haworth, Emily's large house-dog and Anne's little spaniel welcomed her in 'a strange, heart-touching way,' she writes to Mr. Williams. She alone was left, heir to all the memories and tragedies of the house. She took up again the task of life and labour. She cared for her father; she returned to the writing of *Shirley*; and when she herself passed away, four years later, she had so turned those years to account that not only all she did but all she loved had passed silently into the keeping of fame. Mrs. Gaskell's touching and delightful task was ready for her, and Anne, no less than Charlotte and Emily, was sure of England's remembrance.

Notes

1. Introduction to *Wuthering Heights*, p. xxxix. 'Still, as I mused, the naked room,' &c.

WILLIAM LISLE BOWLES

1762–1850

William Lisle Bowles was born at King's Sutton, Northamptonshire, on September 25, 1762. Educated at Winchester and at Trinity College, Oxford, he was later ordained and served several parishes in Wiltshire.

In 1789 Bowles published two collections of poetry, *Fourteen Sonnets* and *Verses to John Howard*, which attracted favorable attention from Coleridge and established Bowles early on as a Romantic poet. Bowles was later praised by Coleridge in the *Biographia Literaria* along with Cowper as the first poet to combine "natural thoughts with natural diction," and to reconcile "the heart with the head."

A controversy that was to occupy Bowles over two decades was touched off in 1806 when he published an edition of Pope's works that included a personal attack on the neoclassical poet. Byron then leapt to the defense of Pope in *English Bards and Scotch Reviewers*, and was later joined in his attack on Bowles by Thomas Campbell. A "war of pamphlets" ensued, led by Byron, and continued until 1826. At the heart of the controversy was Bowles's belief that naturally occurring objects and emotions were more suitable for poetic expression than the products of art. Despite the fervor of the arguments on both sides, however, little appears to have been resolved.

Bowles published other volumes of verse during his lifetime, including *The Spirit of Discovery* (1804), *The Missionary of the Andes* (1815), *The Grave of the Last Saxon* (1822), and *St. John in Patmos* (1833). A collected edition, *Poetical Works*, appeared posthumously in 1855.

Bowles died in Salisbury on April 7, 1850.

Personal

My Sheridan task in the morning.—interrupted by Bowles, who, however, never comes amiss, the mixture of talent and simplicity in him delightful—His (Bowles's) parsonage-house at Bremhill is beautifully situated, but he has a good deal frittered away its beauty with grottos, hermitages & Shenstonian inscriptions—When company is coming, he cries "here, John, run with the crucifix & missal to the Hermitage & set the fountain going."—His sheep-bells are tuned in thirds & fifths—but he is an excellent fellow notwithstanding, and if the waters of his inspiration be not those of Helicon, they are at least very-sweet waters, and to my taste pleasanter than some that are more strongly impregnated.—THOMAS MOORE, *Journal*, Sept. 1, 1818

When Madame de Staël was here Mr. Bowles the poet or as Lord Byron calls him the sonneteer was invited to dine here. She admired his *Sonnets* and his *Spirit of Maritime Discovery* and ranked him high as an English genius. In riding to Bowood that day he fell from his horse and sprained his shoulder but still came on. Lord Lansdowne willing to shew him to advantage alluded to this in presenting him before dinner to Madame de Staël. He is a simple country curate-looking man and rather blunt and when Madame de Staël in the midst of the listening circle in the drawing room began to compliment him and herself upon the effort he had made to come to see her he replied 'Oh Ma'am say no more about it for I would have done a great deal more to see so great a *curiosity*'. Lord Lansdowne says it is impossible to describe the shock in Madame de Staël's face—the breathless astonishment—and the total change produced in her opinion of the man and her manner towards him. She said afterwards to Lord Lansdowne 'Je vois bien que ce n'est qu'un curé qui n'a pas le sens commun—quoique grand poète.' She never forgot it. Two years afterwards she spoke of it to Lord Lansdowne at Geneva and wondered how it was possible that un tel homme could exist. ⟨. . .⟩

Mr. Bowles dined here the other day and perhaps thought me a *curiosity* but did not tell me so. He is a simple—not curate but rector—full of his poems and his church music and his house at *Bremhill*. Now there is a village of Bromham also in the neighborhood which Lady Lansdowne had taken me to see the morning of the day he dined here and all dinner time he and I and Lord Lansdowne and Dumont were making confusion in French and English between these two names and two places, both of which had pretty churches &c. Mr. Bowles was puzzled almost out of his wits and temper because Lady Lansdowne had promised to take me to *Bremhill* when he was at home and he suspected we had gone that morning. Still he could not believe Lady Lansdowne would use him so and he could not possibly make her hear or venture to put a question to her from one end of the table to the other encompassed too as she was by Grenvilles. He colored and fretted and questioned me and at every one of my blundering answers changed his opinion backwards and forwards. The moment he was released from the dining room and could get to Lady Lansdowne he went to complain that for the life of him he could not make out whether Miss E had been at Brem Hill or

Bromham and that very morning he had received a letter from a Member of parliament a member of a committee reprimanding him as vicar of *Bromham* for something of which he was innocent and ignorant he being vicar or rector of Bremhill you know. ⟨. . .⟩

Mr. Bowles is not like the clergyman that read prayers and preached that day at Ross. Mr. Bowles tho simple has no dignity and is too full of himself. He preached extempore and kept one in painful sympathy lest he should never get through it. After church went to his very pretty old parsonage newly *done up*—with good taste—walked over his little shrubbery—stuck full of inscriptions and grottoes and bowers and came at last to the weary hermitage where apropos to a hermits inscription the question came plump upon me '*Have you read my poem of the Missionary?*' 'No.' The good natured author helped me out by saying 'No. It was published at first without my name.' He gave me a copy and all's well that ends well. So ended our visit to Brem Hill. A happier man in a house and place more suited to him I never saw. Lord Lansdowne made him the happy creature he is. His wife is a plain woman something like Mrs. Alison, who has the good sense understands the affairs of this world and is just the wife necessary for a poet. He was desperately in love with her sister—a most beautiful creature who died of a consumption. This sister comforted him and he married her and has never repented.

Now there is a trait of this man's character which from all that you have heard you would never guess. He is one of the greatest cowards existing—afraid in a carriage—afraid in a room by himself—afraid in a large room—afraid of a large bed—afraid like a child of 4 years old. One night at Bowood when he was to return home in his carriage in the dark he fell into agonies exclaiming that he should certainly die of it if he got into the carriage. Lady Lansdowne asked him to stay all night. So he did—but in the morning he came down all pale to breakfast. He had been so *frightened* when he wakened and found himself in so large a room—so large a bed. He would never sleep at Bowood again.—MARIA EDGEWORTH, Letter to Mrs. Edgeworth (c. Sept. 1818)

I have met Mr. B. occasionally, in the best Society in London; he appeared to me an amiable, well-informed, and extremely able man. I desire nothing better than to dine in company with such a mannered man every day in the week; but of 'his character' I know nothing personally; I can only speak to his manners, and these have my warmest approbation. But I never judge from manners, for I once had my pocket picked by the civilest gentleman I ever met with; and one of the mildest persons I ever saw was Ali Pacha. Of Mr. B.'s '*character*' I will not do him the *injustice* to judge from the Edition of Pope, if he prepared it heedlessly; nor the *justice*, should it be otherwise, because I would neither become a literary executioner nor a personal one. Mr. Bowles the individual, and Mr. Bowles the editor, appear the two most opposite things imaginable.

'And he himself one —— antithesis.'

I won't say 'vile,' because it is harsh; nor 'mistaken,' because it has two syllables too many: but every one must fill up the blank as he pleases.—GEORGE GORDON, LORD BYRON, "Letter to

—— ——, Esqre, on the Rev. W. L. Bowles's Strictures on the Life and Writings of Pope," 1821

Odd he unquestionably was, and Moore, who knew and loved him, described him well when he exclaimed: "How marvelously, by being a genius, he has escaped being a fool!" In absence of mind La Fontaine could scarcely have surpassed him.

He was in the habit of daily riding through a country turnpike-gate, and one day he presented as usual his twopence to the gatekeeper. "What is that for, sir?" he asked. "For my horse, of course." "But, sir, you have no horse." "Dear me!" exclaimed the astonished poet, "am I walking?"

Mrs. Moore told me that anecdote. She also told me that Bowles on one occasion gave her a Bible as a birthday present. She asked him to write her name in it. He did so, inscribing the sacred volume to her as a gift—"From the Author."

I had the following story from a gentleman-farmer, one of Bowles's parishioners, who cherished an affectionate remembrance of the good parson. One day there was a dinner party at the parsonage. The guests and the dinner were both kept waiting by the non-appearance of the host. At last his wife went up-stairs to see what mischance had delayed him. She found him in a terrible "taking," hunting everywhere for a silk stocking that he could not find. After due and careful search, Mrs. Bowles at last discovered the reason of the "loss." He had put both stockings on one leg.

But all the anecdotes of his eccentricities are pleasant, simple, and harmless; and Bowles the man was the faithful counterpart of Bowles the poet—pure in spirit, sweet of nature, and tender of heart—good rather than great.—S. C. HALL, *Retrospect of a Long Life*, 1883, pp. 314–15

General

My heart has thank'd thee, BOWLES! for those soft strains,
  That, on the still air floating, tremblingly
  Wak'd in me Fancy, Love, and Sympathy!
For hence, not callous to a Brother's pains

Thro' Youth's gay prime and thornless paths I went;
  And, when the *darker* day of life began,
  And I did roam, a thought-bewilder'd man!
Thy kindred Lays an healing solace lent,

Each lonely pang with dreamy joys combin'd,
  And stole from vain REGRET her scorpion stings;
  While shadowy PLEASURE, with mysterious wings,
Brooded the wavy and tumultuous mind,

Like that great Spirit, who with plastic sweep
Mov'd on the darkness of the formless Deep!
      —SAMUEL TAYLOR COLERIDGE, "To the Rev.
      W. L. Bowles" (1794), *Sonnets on Eminent
      Characters*, 1794–95

Hail, Sympathy! thy soft idea brings
A thousand visions of a thousand things,
And shows, still whimpering through threescore of years,
The maudlin prince of mournful sonneteers.
And art thou not their prince, harmonious Bowles!
Thou first, great oracle of tender souls?
Whether thou sing'st with equal ease, and grief,
The fall of empires, or a yellow leaf;
Whether thy muse most lamentably tells
What merry sounds proceed from Oxford bells,
Or, still in bells delighting, finds a friend
In every chime that jingled from Ostend;
Ah! how much juster were thy muse's hap,
If to thy bells thou wouldst but add a cap!
Delightful Bowles! still blessing and still blest,

All love thy strain, but children like it best.
'Tis thine, with gentle Little's moral song,
To soothe the mania of the amorous throng!
With thee our nursery damsels shed their tears,
Ere miss as yet completes her infant years:
But in her teens thy whining powers are vain;
She quits poor Bowles for Little's purer strain.
Now to soft themes thou scornest to confine
The lofty numbers of a harp like thine;
'Awake a louder and a loftier strain,'
Such as none heard before, or will again!
Where all Discoveries jumbled from the flood,
Since first the leaky ark reposed in mud,
By more or less, are sung in every book,
From Captain Noah down to Captain Cook.
Nor this alone; but, pausing on the road,
The bard sighs forth a gentle episode;
And gravely tells—attend, each beauteous miss!—
When first Madeira trembled to a kiss.
Bowles! in thy memory let this precept dwell,
Stick to thy sonnets, man!—at least they sell.
But if some new-born whim, or larger bribe,
Prompt thy crude brain, and claim thee for a scribe;
If chance some bard, though once by dunces fear'd,
Now, prone in dust, can only be revered;
If Pope, whose fame and genius, from the first,
Have foil'd the best of critics, needs the worst,
Do thou essay: each fault, each failing scan;
The first of poets was, alas! but man.
Rake from each ancient dunghill every pearl,
Consult Lord Fanny, and confide in Curll;
Let all the scandals of a former age
Perch on thy pen, and flutter o'er thy page;
Affect a candour which thou canst not feel,
Clothe envy in the garb of honest zeal;
Write, as if St. John's soul could still inspire,
And do from hate what Mallet did for hire.
Oh! hadst thou lived in that congenial time,
to rave with Dennis, and with Ralph to rhyme;
Throng'd with the rest around his living head,
Not raised thy hoof against the lion dead;
A meet reward had crown'd thy glorious gains,
And link'd thee to the *Dunciad* for thy pains.
      —GEORGE GORDON, LORD BYRON, *English Bards
      and Scotch Reviewers*, 1809, ll. 327–84

I had just entered on my seventeenth year when the sonnets of Mr Bowles, twenty in number, and just then published in a quarto pamphlet, were first made known and presented to me by a schoolfellow who had quitted us for the University and who, during the whole time that he was in our first form (or in our school language a Grecian), had been my patron and protector. I refer to Dr Middleton, the truly learned and every way excellent Bishop of Calcutta:

Qui laudibus amplis
Ingenium celebrare meum, calamumque solebat,
Calcar agens animo validum. Non omnia terrae
Obruta! Vivit amor, vivit dolor! Ora negatur
Dulcia conspicere; at flere et meminisse relictum est.
      (Petr. *Ep.*, Lib. I, Ep. I)

It was a double pleasure to me, and still remains a tender recollection, that I should have received from a friend so revered the first knowledge of a poet by whose works, year after year, I was so enthusiastically delighted and inspired. My earliest acquaintances will not have forgotten the undisciplined eagerness and impetuous zeal with which I laboured to make proselytes, not only of my companions, but of all with whom

I conversed, of whatever rank and in whatever place. As my school finances did not permit me to purchase copies I made, within less than a year and a half, more than forty transcriptions, as the best presents I could offer to those who had in any way won my regard. And with almost equal delight did I receive the three or four following publications of the same author.

Though I have seen and known enough of mankind to be well aware that I shall perhaps stand alone in my creed, and that it will be well if I subject myself to no worse charge than that of singularity; I am not therefore deterred from avowing that I regard and ever have regarded the obligations of intellect among the most sacred of the claims of gratitude. A valuable thought, or a particular train of thoughts, gives me additional pleasure when I can safely refer and attribute it to the conversation or correspondence of another. My obligations to Mr Bowles were indeed important and for radical good. At a very premature age, even before my fifteenth year, I had bewildered myself in metaphysicks and in theological controversy. Nothing else pleased me. History and particular facts lost all interest in my mind. Poetry (though for a school-boy of that age I was above par in English versification and had already produced two or three compositions which, I may venture to say without reference to my age, were somewhat above mediocrity, and which had gained me more credit than the sound good sense of my old master was at all pleased with), poetry itself, yea novels and romances, became insipid to me. In my friendless wanderings on our leave-days (for I was an orphan, and had scarce any connections in London), highly was I delighted if any passenger, especially if he were dressed in black, would enter into conversation with me. For I soon found the means of directing it to my favorite subjects

> Of providence, fore-knowledge, will, and fate,
> Fixed fate, free will, fore-knowledge absolute,
> And found no end in wandring mazes lost.

This preposterous pursuit was, beyond doubt, injurious both to my natural powers and to the progress of my education. It would perhaps have been destructive had it been continued; but from this I was auspiciously withdrawn, partly indeed by an accidental introduction to an amiable family, chiefly however by the genial influence of a style of poetry so tender and yet so manly, so natural and real, and yet so dignified and harmonious, as the sonnets, etc., of Mr Bowles! Well were it for me, perhaps, had I never relapsed into the same mental disease; if I had continued to pluck the flower and reap the harvest from the cultivated surface, instead of delving in the unwholesome quicksilver mines of metaphysic depths. But if in after time I have sought a refuge from bodily pain and mismanaged sensibility in abstruse researches which exercised the strength and subtlety of the understanding without awakening the feelings of the heart; still there was a long and blessed interval, during which my natural faculties were allowed to expand and my original tendencies to develop themselves; my fancy, and the love of nature, and the sense of beauty in forms and sounds.—SAMUEL TAYLOR COLERIDGE, *Biographia Literaria*, 1817, Ch. 1

Breathes not the man with a more poetical temperament than Bowles. No wonder that his eyes "love all they look on," for they possess the sacred gift of beautifying creation, by shedding over it the charm of melancholy. "Pleasant but mournful to the soul is the memory of joys that are past"—is the text we should choose were we about to preach on his genius. No vain repinings, no idle regrets, does his spirit ever breathe over the still receding Past. But time-sanctified are all the shews that

arise before his pensive imagination—and the common light of day, once gone, in his poetry seems to shine as if it had all been dying sunset or moonlight, or the new-born dawn. His human sensibilities are so fine as to be in themselves poetical; and his poetical aspirations so delicate as to be felt always human. Hence his Sonnets have been dear to poets—having in them "more than meets the ear"—spiritual breathings that hang around the words like light around fair flowers; and hence, too, have they been beloved by all natural hearts who, having not the "faculty divine," have yet the "vision"—that is, the power of seeing and of hearing the sights and the sounds which genius alone can awaken, bringing them from afar, out of the dust and dimness of evanishment. But has Bowles written a Great Poem? If he has, then, as he loves us, let him forthwith publish it in Maga.—JOHN WILSON, "An Hour's Talk about Poetry," *Blackwood's Edinburgh Magazine*, Sept. 1831, pp. 475–76

This morning I received your *St. John in Patmos*, two months after the date of the note which accompanied it: this is mentioned, that you may not think I have been slow in acknowledging and thanking you for it. I have just read the poem through, and with much pleasure. Yours I should have known it to have been by the sweet and unsophisticated style; upon which I endeavoured, now almost forty years ago, to form my own. You have so blended the episodical parts, that they do not in any degree disturb the solemn and mysterious character of the whole.—ROBERT SOUTHEY, Letter to William Lisle Bowles (July 30, 1832)

Bowles was an inferior artist to Rogers, although taste and elegance are also the chief features of his poetry. His early reputation was founded on his sentimental and reflective verses; and these may still be ranked among his happier efforts. Probably, from old associations, I have a sort of lurking fondness for his "Grave of Howard," his "Abba Thule," and "The Elegy at Matlock," which their intrinsic merits may not quite entitle them to; but more certain I am that "St Michael's Mount" and "Coombe Ellen" are two descriptive poems of high merit, whether regarded as the genial outpourings of youthful enthusiasm, or as elegant and tasteful specimens of versification. The "Sonnets," through many years, however, were the sheet-anchors of Bowles's fame; and fine though some of them must be admitted to be, it is yet difficult to account for the impression which assuredly—because we have it from spontaneous personal confession—they made on minds much more lofty and vigorous in imagination than his own. Coleridge had them by heart; and not only made forty autograph copies of them for his particular friends, but declared himself "enthusiastically delighted and inspired by them:" while in the recently published *Life of Robert Southey*, by his son Cuthbert, we find him also saying, in a letter to their author, that "there are three contemporaries, the influence of whose poetry on my own I can distinctly trace—Sayers, yourself, and Savage Landor. I owe you something, therefore, on the score of gratitude." Bowles requires no higher credentials for the legitimacy of his mission; for no uninspired poet ever inspired others. That the flames from a small, rude Indian wigwam may carry conflagration to a whole district-embowering prairie, is quite another matter; the kindling spark alone is wanted—and in poetry genius is that sole desiderated spark. Southey and Coleridge acknowledge having borrowed fire from Bowles to ignite their tinder—*ergo*, Bowles must have been a poet.

The latter and more ambitious efforts of Lisle Bowles—for he wrote at least four long poems—could not be said to have been thoroughly, that is, eminently successful. In all, passages of tender sentiment and fine description abound; but, on the whole, they were more the pumpings up, than the pourings out, of genius. His mind possessed more elegance than vigour; was rather reflective than imaginative. He is deficient in variety; and he ventured not, like Crabbe, to paint things exactly as he saw them; hence there is a sameness about his outlines that savours of mannerism. His familiar walk was amid the gentler affections of our nature; but his tenderness seldom rises into passion; or it is merely the anger of the dove,

Pecking the hand that hovers o'er its mate.

The Attic taste of his scholarship seemed to trammel that enthusiasm, essential for the creation of high lyric poetry; and in this he resembles Thomas Warton—to whom, in his descriptive sketches, as well as in his chivalresque tendencies, he bore a greater resemblance than to any other author.

The first of Bowles's larger poems, *The Spirit of Discovery by Sea*—which comprehends all navigators from Noah downwards—was a daring subject, but treated with distinguished ability; and, taken as a whole, is perhaps the best. *The Missionary*, founded on a romantic incident in South American history, is principally valuable from its many admirable pictures of that varied and gorgeous region. *The Grave of the Last Saxon*, a historico-romantic poem, relating to the times of William the Conqueror and the sons of Harold, is more ambitious in design, is pervaded throughout by a fine antique tone—for Bowles was somewhat of an antiquarian of the Sylvanus Urban school—and is full of chivalrous "renown and knightly worth." His last laborious effort was *Banwell Hill, or Days Departed*—principally to be regarded as a loco-descriptive poem, redolent of fine English scenery, which a Gainsborough might have painted; and of rural manners, which in gentle beauty contrast brightly with the sterner and more rugged portraitures of Crabbe. The striking Cornish legend of *The Spectre and the Prayer-Book*, originally published under the fictitious name of Dr Macleod, was afterwards incorporated with the work of which it now forms the conclusion.

Sixty years ago—*Eheu fugaces, Posthume, labuntur anni!*—many of the shorter productions of Bowles were great favourites with the young and the sentimental, ere supplanted by the more spirit-stirring lays of Scott and Byron. His *Villager's Verse-Book* had for its admirable object the connecting the most obvious images of country life with the earliest impressions of humanity and piety. Several of these little effusions are very beautiful, and are quite equal in poetical merit to the *Hymns for Childhood* by Mrs Hemans; although it must be confessed that neither Bowles nor Mrs Hemans quite understood the mode of writing merely for children. Both are continually shooting beyond the mark, and seem loth to sacrifice a good idea, simply because it is incompatible with the purpose in hand; and they are consequently, in that department, much inferior in success alike to Mrs Barbauld in her *Hymns in Prose*, and to Anne and Jane Taylor, in their appropriately titled *Hymns for Infant Minds*.

Bowles was deficient in the passion and imagination which command great things; but he was, notwithstanding, a true poet. He had a fine eye for the beautiful and the true; and, although his enthusiasm was tempered, we never miss a cordial sympathy with whatever is pure, noble, and generous—for his heart was in the right place. Writers of ephemeral reputation fall with the circumstances to which they owed their rise; but no man who has been giving some measure of delight to thousands, through two or three generations—and Bowles has done so—can be altogether a deception. Casual topics may insure present success; but poetical fame is not, cannot be,

founded on these, however a few apparent exceptions may seem to favour such a supposition—as those of Butler, of Churchill, and of Anstey—for all these were true poets. Grand principles alone insure permanency. The human heart and its sympathies being the same from age to age, it requires only the "touch of nature to make all flesh kin;" but passing purposes are accomplished by passing means. Ere a century has elapsed, the gigantic reputation of Swift is dwarfed by that distance which extinguishes court ladies, ribanded senators, political clubs; and personal squabbles about coin and currency; and Dr Wolcot—the Peter Pindar whose dread satires are said to have caused his being pensioned off in the reign of George the Third—is now as utterly forgotten (although scarcely deservedly so, for he wrote a few good things in quite another and higher vein) as if he had flourished in the reign of Hardicanute.—DAVID MACBETH MOIR, *Sketches of the Poetical Literature of the Past Half-Century*, 1851, pp. 54–57

How diligently he worked, the number and weight of his productions sufficiently prove. Imagination and romance had in his person effectually superseded the wit, and what was called "sense," of a former age. Sententious, sarcastic, and clever verse-making was not his forte; he could do little more than express what he saw and felt. He could not take a theme, and deal with it as an advocate; it must have associated itself with his own heart, with his own hopes, and with his own prejudices (and some of these were very narrow ones indeed), before it could command a single chord of his harp. He mused upon his poems long before he wrote them; carried them about with him in his mind, and moulded them to his mental ear, for some time before he trusted them to ink and paper. The real character of the man was stamped upon his writings; and that character was, like the age in which he began poetising, of the transitional type. Revolutionary in his poetical practice, he had not yet surrendered himself to revolutionary opinions either in religion or politics; but stood on the ancient ways, even while premeditating a new route. Classical in spirit, he yet aimed at, and attained, a popular style. He wrote, indeed, a verse-book for villagers and children, in which the topics were treated with the utmost simplicity and brevity. Some of these were little gems of poetic art. There are many as good, and some better, than the following:

THE SWAN

Look at the swan, how still he goes!
    His neck and breast like silver gleam;
He seems majestic as he rows;
    The glory of the lonely stream.

There is a glory in the war,
    A glory when the warrior wears
(His visage marked with many a scar)
    The laurel wet with human tears.

Such scenes no glory can impart,
    With trumps and drums and noises rude,
Like that which fills his silent heart
    Who walks with God in quietude.

This sort of simplicity was, however, too evidently a condescension. The poet's instincts were to paint the grander features of nature in an ornate style. His diction at the beginning of his career, both in verse and prose, was cumbrous and awkward; but he gradually acquired ease, directness, and elegance. His ear was always correct, and inclined to melodious composition. Yet in his greater blank-verse poems he shows himself acquainted with the intricacies and elaborate subtleties that enter into the production of harmony, and encounters and subdues difficulties with the courage and confidence that imply conscious skill and practised power. To the right-hearted and earnest student of poetry they will always be welcome, and not only be carefully perused, but sedulously studied, as examples of the art in which he would excel.—JOHN A. HERAUD, "William Lisle Bowles," *Temple Bar*, June 1863, p. 446

Those who to-day turn to the much-praised verses will scarcely find in their pensive amenity that enduring charm which they presented to the hungry and restless soul of Coleridge, seeking its fitting food in unpropitious places. They exhibit a grace of expression, a delicate sensibility, and above all a 'musical sweet melancholy' that is especially grateful in certain moods of mind; but with lapse of time and change of fashion they have grown a little thin and faint and colourless. Of Bowles's remaining works it is not necessary to speak. He was overmatched in his controversy with Byron as to Pope, and the blunt

> Stick to thy sonnets, Bowles,—at least they pay

of the former must be accepted as the final word upon the poetical efforts of the cultivated and amiable Canon of Salisbury.—AUSTIN DOBSON, "William Lisle Bowles," *The English Poets*, ed. Thomas Humphry Ward, 1880, Vol. 4, p. 99

WILLIAM TIREBUCK
From "Introduction"
The Poetical Works of Bowles, Lamb, and Hartley Coleridge
1887, pp. vii–xiv

William Lisle Bowles is very little known beyond the special circle of students of poetry; but it is only just to extend his reputation, for his was the first significant note of conscious transition from the formalism and the affected classicism of the epoch of Johnson and Pope to the lyric freedom of Wordsworth, Shelley, and Keats. Even Bowles was rather an indication than a fulfilment. Though he revolved freely on his own individuality, he was not absolutely free from the conventionalities of poetry of his time. Nor did he fully indicate the breadth of the change that was to arise in his own later days. There were depths deeper and flights higher than his to follow; nevertheless, the significant fact is that he had the impulse and the courage to advance according to his light. Compared with his brilliant successors his light was doubtless dim, but on that very account is his case the more interesting, his attitude the more touching. Wordsworth, Coleridge the elder, Shelley, Keats, and Byron, were illumed by the light of a new day; there was a rush of revelation, events were more urgent, democracy was moving, electricity and steam, that were soon to do so much in the world of mechanics, seemed to declare themselves also in the world of poetry. On the other hand, Bowles was groping in that dim twilight when spiritual and material changes are hovering, when the sense of impending change darkens rather than lights the way, and when men have to follow a vague instinct rather than a determining impulse. Some lives are experiments, and others are the demonstrations of success. Bowles' was an experiment, and he survived to witness his experiment become demonstrations of success in others. We must remember that he was born as early as 1762, and that he died as late as 1850. In his last preface he wrote, with the resignation of a poet—"I have lived to hear the sounds of other harps whose masters have struck far more sublime chords, and died. I have lived to see among them females of the highest poetical rank and many illustrious

masters of the lyre, whose names I need not specify, crowned with younger and more verdant laurels which they yet gracefully wear. Some who now rank high in the poet's art have acknowledged that their feelings were first excited by these youthful strains, which I have now, with melancholy feelings, revised for the last time." These delicate but frank allusions are first to Shelley, Keats, and Byron; then to Joanna Baillie, Mrs. Hemans, L. E. Landon, and his own namesake—"no otherwise related than by love of kindred music"—Caroline Bowles; and finally to Wordsworth, Southey, and perhaps more especially to S. T. Coleridge.

⟨. . .⟩ Bowles' influence is an admitted fact in the history both of Coleridge and of poetry. His was a sweet influence, a benign presence, with a melodious utterance of ever-ready emotion for the good, the pathetic, and the beautiful. Not so set in his pictures of nature as Thomson, not so moralising as Cowper, or so probing with his pathos as Crabbe, more free in his form than Collins or Warton, he yet had something of each passing through his own individuality. In him the new tendency of the poetry of his time took form. The effort to express something new became expression. Consciousness, in short, became conscience—a question of right, a question of revolt against the conventional artificialities of song. As already indicated, he protested against the metrical formalism, the stereotyped classicism both in matter and manner, and the artificial mood of the school of Pope. He perceived the effeminacy resulting from one art resorting too much to another for the inspiration it ought to seek from the source of all art, Nature. He disliked the thraldom of poetical work that was wonderful as mosaics are wonderful, brilliant as jewels are brilliant, but lacking glow unless seen in the light of special culture. He disliked the spirit of the period. It was stagnant; and the poets, the putative seers, had perception for little else but peevish complaint. Poet set on poet, and couplets degenerated into rhythmic snaps and sneers. Even with modifications in such men as Gray, Thomson, and Cowper, these degenerating characteristics still lingered about literature when Bowles began to reflect. He felt that the haunting traditions were not only false but shackling, and in an edition of Pope's Works which he edited, Bowles attacked Pope somewhat warmly both as poet and man, pronouncing against his principles of art and the spirit of his life. Discussion upon discussion followed, in which Roscoe, Byron, Campbell, Southey, and Hazlitt took part, and so heated was the conflict, that Jeffrey, the critic, declared that Bowles would only be remembered by his Pope controversy with Lord Byron—a prophecy which has to be accompanied in these days with an explanation of what the controversy was. Bowles, however, stood his ground. He continued to ignore the traditions of the school he attacked, and throwing off the incumbrances of an over-conscious art, he answered the quiet dictates of his intuition, and returned to the freedom of Nature. In that meditative, hopeful, and humble resort to Nature, Bowles anticipated the mood that was deepened and broadened in Wordsworth, some of the sonnets of Bowles coming, historically, as premonitory notes of the strains of the poet of Rydal; coming also as cuckoo-calls prior to the thrush-like warbling of Coleridge, Shelley, and Keats. There were, however, certain acquired influences under which Bowles went to Nature. He admitted the early influence of Warton; but more effectual and more abiding, and certainly more desirable, were the influences of Shakespeare and Milton. There is internal evidence of the shaping power of both on the imagination and style of Bowles. In the main body of his verse Shakespeare's own phrases occur, like the leading *motif* in modern music, and what Bowles attributed to Milton he without doubt emulated. He tried to attain in verse something beyond "the tuneless couplets' weak control"—namely, a "long continuing diapason roll in varied sweetness;" and he did not try in vain. There is a full and melodious flow in his lines tending towards what may be denominated the grand style. Indeed, the diapason roll is sometimes too dominant, too apparent, like the grandiloquent roundness of a Johnsonian period. But this endeavour for full musical expression was perfectly natural in Bowles, because in a modest way he was a composer and set some of his own verse to music. He was an artist, too, confessing, as he does, to "dipping the brush" in addition to "touching the tuneful string." This confession is a key to another phase, the descriptive phase, of his work. Some of his passages would paint. They are like an artist's notes both of detail and general effect. Bowles, in fact, was a many-sided

man, practical as well as poetical. His varied acquirements and labours were remarkable. He was not only poet, musician, and artist, but a country vicar, a preacher, a dignitary in connection with Salisbury Cathedral, a magistrate, an archæologist, a local historian, a biographer, an editor, and a spirited controversialist—"a happy blending," wrote S. C. Hall, who knew him personally, "of the country farmer with the country clergyman of the old times, and recalled the portraitures of 'parsons' of the days of Fielding and Smollett;" and so attached was he to his country life that he described himself, when once in London, as being as much out of place as a daisy in a conservatory. He must have been a lovable man as well as a man of character, for he drew to his quiet vicarage at Bremhill, in Wiltshire, Sir Samuel Romilly, Sir Humphrey Davey, Sir George Beaumont, Madame de Staël, and the poets Rogers, Moore, Crabbe, and Southey.

WILLIAM WORDSWORTH

1770–1850

William Wordsworth was born on April 7, 1770, at Cockermouth, Cumberland, to John Wordsworth, an attorney, and Anne Cookson Wordsworth; he had three brothers and one sister, Dorothy. Wordsworth grew up in the Lake District and lost both his mother (1778) and his father (1783) in early youth. He was educated at Hawkshead Grammar School (1779–83) and at St. John's College, Cambridge (1787–91). Wordsworth went on a European tour in 1790, and after graduating from Cambridge spent a year (1791–92) in France. While in France Wordsworth became an enthusiastic republican, although later developments gradually turned him against the Revolution. He became friendly with some of the Girondists and had an affair with Annette Vallon, the daughter of a French surgeon. Vallon gave birth to Wordsworth's daughter, Caroline, in December 1792, but Wordsworth returned alone to England when war broke out between his country and France in 1793.

In that year Wordsworth published two highly descriptive and relatively conventional poems, *An Evening Walk* and *Descriptive Sketches*, both in heroic couplets. In 1794 he inherited £900, which temporarily freed him of financial worries and allowed him to settle at Racedown in Dorset, where he was joined by his sister Dorothy; she was to be his close companion and an influence on his poetry for the rest of his life. In 1797 the two moved to Alforden, Somerset, to be nearer Samuel Taylor Coleridge, whom Wordsworth had first met in 1795 and with whom he now entered into an artistic partnership. Under Coleridge's influence Wordsworth's poetry became more metaphysical, and for both poets the next several years were to be a period of intense creativity. A selection of their poetry was published as *Lyrical Ballads*, which included Wordsworth's "Tintern Abbey" and "The Idiot Boy"; the first edition appeared in 1798, and a second, with the addition of new poems and the famous "Preface," on January 1, 1801 (although it is known as the 1800 edition). Between 1798 and 1805 Wordsworth worked on his long autobiographical poem *The Prelude; or, Growth of a Poet's Mind*, which he frequently revised and which was not published until 1850, shortly after his death. Together with *The Excursion* (1814), it was to have been part of a long, never-completed philosophical poem, *The Recluse*.

In 1799 Wordsworth and Dorothy returned to the Lake District, where they settled permanently at Grasmere, living first at Dove Cottage, then at nearby Rydal Mount. In 1802 Wordsworth married Mary Hutchinson, by whom he had five children between 1803 and 1810. *Poems in Two Volumes*, containing many of his most celebrated lyrics, such as "Resolution and Independence" and "Intimations of Immortality from Recollections of Early Childhood," was published in 1807, but received poor reviews. In 1813 Wordsworth was appointed stamp distributor, a sinecure which until 1842 brought him some £400 a year. Although his productivity continued and his popularity as one of the so-called Lake Poets gradually increased, Wordsworth wrote little of value, in the opinion of modern critics, after the publication of his *Collected Works* in 1815. His later works include *The White Doe of Rylstone* (1815), *Peter Bell* (1819), and *The Waggoner* (1819). In 1842 Wordsworth was awarded a pension of £300 a year, and in 1843 he succeeded Southey as poet laureate. By this point the young radical of the 1790s had long since become a politically conservative patriot, and had received over the years a great deal of criticism from Byron, Shelley,

Keats, Hazlitt, and others. Wordsworth lived out his last years at Grasmere and died at Rydal Mount on April 23, 1850.

Wordsworth's *Poetical and Prose Works*, together with Dorothy Wordsworth's *Journals*, edited by W. Knight, appeared in 1896, and in the twentieth century several volumes of letters have been published, including *Letters of the Wordsworth Family 1787–1855* (1907; ed. William Knight), *Letters of William and Dorothy Wordsworth* (1935–39; ed. Ernest de Selincourt), and *The Love Letters of William and Mary Wordsworth* (1982; ed. Beth Darlington).

Personal

Wm. was very unwell. Worn out with his bad night's rest. He went to bed—I read to him, to endeavour to make him sleep. Then I came into the other room, and read the first book of *Paradise Lost*. After dinner we walked to Ambleside—found Lloyds at Luff's—we stayed and drank tea by ourselves. A heart-rending letter from Coleridge—we were sad as we could be. Wm. wrote to him. We talked about Wm.'s going to London. It was a mild afternoon—there was an unusual softness in the prospects as we went, a rich yellow upon the fields, and a soft grave purple on the waters. When we returned many stars were out, the clouds were moveless, in the sky soft purple, the Lake of Rydale calm; Jupiter behind, Jupiter at least *we* call him, but William says we always call the largest star Jupiter. When we came home we both wrote to C. I was stupefied.—DOROTHY WORDSWORTH, *Journal*, Jan. 29, 1802

A visit from Wordsworth, who stayed with me from between twelve and one till past three. I then walked with him to Newman Street. His conversation was long and interesting. He spoke of his own poems with the just feeling of confidence which a sense of his own excellence gives him. He is now convinced that he never can derive emolument from them; but, being independent, he willingly gives up all idea of doing so. He is persuaded that if men are to become better and wiser, the poems will sooner or later make their way. But if we are to perish, and society is not to advance in civilization, "it would be," said he, "wretched selfishness to deplore the want of any personal reputation." The approbation he has met with from some superior persons compensates for the loss of popularity, though no man has completely understood him, not excepting Coleridge, who is not happy enough to enter into his feelings. "I am myself," said Wordsworth, "one of the happiest of men; and no man who does not partake of that happiness, who lives a life of constant bustle, and whose felicity depends on the opinions of others, can possibly comprehend the best of my poems." I urged an excuse for those who can really enjoy the better pieces, and who yet are offended by a language they have by early instruction been taught to consider unpoetical; and Wordsworth seemed to tolerate this class, and to allow that his admirers should undergo a sort of education to his works. —HENRY CRABB ROBINSON, *Diary*, May 8, 1812

Wordsworth's residence and mine are fifteen miles asunder, a sufficient distance to preclude any frequent interchange of visits. I have known him nearly twenty years, and, for about half that time, intimately. The strength and the character of his mind you see in the *Excursion*, and his life does not belie his writings, for, in every relation of life, and every point of view, he is a truly exemplary and admirable man. In conversation he is powerful beyond any of his contemporaries; and, as a poet,— I speak not from the partiality of friendship, nor because we have been so absurdly held up as both writing upon one concerted system of poetry, but with the most deliberate exercise of impartial judgment whereof I am capable, when I declare my full conviction that posterity will rank him with Milton.—ROBERT SOUTHEY, Letter to Bernard Barton (Dec. 19, 1814)

I soon entered the house, and was shewn into the parlour, where Mr Wordsworth and his family were assembled to breakfast. The name of Southey acted like a talisman in my favour, and I also found that my name was not unknown to the family as that of a foreigner resident in Ambleside. Their kind and affable reception of me soon relieved me from any temporary embarrassment, and when I told the circuit I had made, they seemed pleased that a foreigner should feel so enthusiastically the beauties of their country. I soon found that even the ladies well knew every step I had taken, and that the poet's wife and sister had trodden with him the mountains and cliffs I had just traversed. Our conversation became every moment more kind and animated, and the room was filled with gentle voices and bright smiles. I know not how to describe to you the great Poet himself. They who have formed to themselves, as many have foolishly done, the idea of a simple pastoral poet, who writes sweet and touching verses, would be somewhat astounded to find themselves in the presence of William Wordsworth. There seemed to me, in his first appearance, something grave almost to austerity, and the deep tones of his voice added strength to that impression of him. There was not visible about him the same easy and disengaged air that so immediately charmed me in Southey— his mind seemed to require an effort to awaken itself thoroughly from some brooding train of thought, and his manner, as I felt at least, at first reluctantly relaxed into blandness and urbanity. There was, however, nothing of vulgar pride in all this, although perhaps it might have seemed so, in an ordinary person. It was the dignity of a mind habitually conversant with high and abstracted thoughts—and unable to divest itself wholly, even in common hours, of the stateliness inspired by the loftiest studies of humanity. No wonder if at first I felt somewhat abashed before such a man—especially when the solemnity of his manner was rendered more striking by the mild simplicity of his wife, and the affectionate earnestness of his sister. But I soon saw how finely characteristic all this was of the man. By degrees he became more lively and careless— and he shewed his politeness towards me his guest and a stranger, by a number of familiar and playful remarks addressed to the members of his own family. I could not help feeling that there was something extremely delicate in this. Often have I been oppressed and almost disgusted with the attention heaped and forced upon me because a stranger, to the utter neglect and seeming forgetfulness of the master of the house towards his own family. But here the kind affections continued in full play—I did not act as a dam to stop the current of domestic enjoyment—and when I saw Mr Wordsworth so kind, so attentive, and so affectionate, to his own happy family, I felt assured that the sunshine of his heart would not fail also to visit me, and that he was disposed to think well of a man before whom he thus freely indulged the best feelings of his human nature.

The features of Wordsworth's face are strong and high, almost harsh and severe—and his eyes have, when he is silent, a dim, thoughtful, I had nearly said melancholy expression— so that when a smile takes possession of his countenance, it is indeed the most powerful smile I ever saw—gives a new character to the whole man, and renders him, who before seemed rather a being for us to respect and venerate, an object to win our love and affection. Smiles are, assuredly, not the abiding light on that grand countenance; but at times they pass finely over it, like playful sunbeams chasing each other over the features of some stern and solemn scene of external nature, that seems willingly to yield itself for a while to the illumination. Never saw I a countenance in which CONTEMPLATION so reigns. His brow is very lofty—and his dark brown hair seems worn away, as it were, by thought, so thinly is it spread over his temples. The colour of his face is almost sallow; but it is not the sallowness of confinement or ill health, it speaks rather of the rude and boisterous greeting of the mountain-weather. He does not seem a recluse philosopher, who pores over the midnight oil in his study; but rather a hermit who converses with nature in his silent cell, whose food is roots and herbs, and whose drink is from

> Wherever fountain or fresh current flowed
> Against the eastern ray, translucent pure,
> With touch ethereal of Heaven's fiery rod.

I at once beheld, in his calm and confident voice—his stedfast and untroubled eyes—the serene expansion of his forehead—and the settled dignity of his demeanour—that original poet, who, in an age of poetry, has walked alone through a world almost exclusively his own, and who has cleared out for himself, by his own labour, a wide and magnificent path through the solitary forests of the human imagination.—JOHN GIBSON LOCKHART, "Letters from the Lakes," *Blackwood's Edinburgh Magazine*, March 1819, pp. 739–40

An extremely pleasant drive of sixteen miles . . . brought me to Wordsworth's door, on a little elevation, commanding a view of Rydal water. . . . It is claimed to be the most beautiful spot and the finest prospect in the lake country, and, even if there be finer, it would be an ungrateful thing to remember them here, where, if anywhere, the eye and the heart ought to be satisfied. Wordsworth knew from Southey that I was coming, and therefore met me at the door and received me heartily. He is about fifty three or four, with a tall, ample, well-proportioned frame, a grave and tranquil manner, a Roman cast of appearance, and Roman dignity and simplicity. He presented me to his wife, a good, very plain woman, who seems to regard him with reverence and affection, and to his sister, not much younger than himself, with a good deal of spirit and, I should think, more than common talent and knowledge. I was at home with them at once, and we went out like friends together to scramble up the mountains, and enjoy the prospects and scenery. . . . We returned to dinner, which was very simple, for, though he has an office under the government and a patrimony besides, yet each is inconsiderable. . . .

His conversation surprised me by being so different from all I had anticipated. It was exceedingly simple, strictly confined to subjects he understood familiarly, and more marked by plain good-sense than by anything else. When, however, he came upon poetry and reviews, he was the Khan of Tartary again, and talked as metaphysically and extravagantly as ever Coleridge wrote; but, excepting this, it was really a consolation to hear him. It was best of all, though, to see how he is loved and respected in his family and neighborhood. . . . The peasantry treated him with marked respect, the children took off their hats to him, and a poor widow in the neighborhood sent to him to come and talk to her son, who had been behaving ill.—GEORGE TICKNOR, *Journal* (March 21, 1819),

Life, Letters, and Journals of George Ticknor, ed. Anna Ticknor, 1876, Vol. 1, p. 287

I observed that, as a rule, Wordsworth allowed Coleridge to have all the talk to himself; but once or twice Coleridge would succeed in entangling Wordsworth in a discussion on some abstract metaphysical question: when I would sit by, reverently attending, and trying hard to look intelligent, though I did not feel so; for at such times a leaden stupor weighed down my faculties. I seemed as if I had been transported by two malignant genii into an atmosphere too rarefied for me to live in. I was soaring, as it were, against my will, 'twixt heaven and the lower parts of the earth. Sometimes I was in pure æther—much oftener *in the clouds*. When, however, these potent spirits descended to a lower level, and deigned to treat of history or politics, theology or belles lettres, I breathed again; and, imbibing fresh ideas from them, felt invigorated.

I must say I never saw any manifestation of small jealousy between Coleridge and Wordsworth; which, considering the vanity possessed by each, I thought uncommonly to the credit of both. I am sure they entertained a thorough respect for each other's intellectual endowments.

Coleridge appeared to me a living refutation of Bacon's axiom, 'that a full man is never a ready man, nor the ready man the full one:' for he was both a full man and a ready man.

Wordsworth was a single-minded man; with less imagination than Coleridge, but with a more harmonious judgment, and better balanced principles. Coleridge, conscious of his transcendant powers, rioted in a license of tongue which no man could tame.

Wordsworth, though he could discourse most eloquent music, was never unwilling to sit still in Coleridge's presence, yet could be as happy in prattling with a child as in communing with a sage.

If Wordsworth condescended to converse with me, he spoke to me as if I were his equal in mind, and made me pleased and proud in consequence. If Coleridge held me by the button, for lack of fitter audience, he had a talent for making me feel *his* wisdom and my own stupidity: so that I was miserable and humiliated by the sense of it. ⟨. . .⟩

Idolatry of nature seemed with Wordsworth both a passion and a principle. She seemed a deity enshrined within his heart. Coleridge studied her rather as a mighty storehouse for poetical imagery than from innate love of her, for her own sweet sake. If once embarked in lecturing, no landscape, however grand, detained his notice for a second: whereas, let Wordsworth have been ever so absorbed in argument, he would drop it without hesitation to feast his eyes on some combination of new scenery. The union of the great and the small, so wonderfully ordered by the Creator, and so wondrously exemplified on the banks of the great German river, had little attraction for the author of *The Ancient Mariner*. The grander features of a landscape he took in at a glance; and he would, with signal power of adaptation, dispose them into a magic world of his own. The rolling mist, as it hung suspended over the valley, and partially revealed the jagged tower and crag of Drachenfels, the river shooting out of sight the burden on its bosom with the velocity and force of an arrow; the presence of elemental power, as exhibited in the thunderstorm, the waterfall, or the avalanche, were stimulus enough to stir the pulses of his teeming brain, and set his imagination afloat with colossal speculations of hereafter. With him terrestrial objects soon expanded into immensity, and were quickly elevated above the stars. The more Rasselas-like mind of the recluse of the Lakes, on the other hand, who 'loved the life removed,' would direct itself to the painstaking investigation of nature's smallest secrets, prompt him to halt by the wayside bank, and dilate with exquisite sensibility and microscopic power of analysis on the construction of the humblest grasses, or on the modest seclusion of some virgin wild-flower nestling in the bosom, or diffidently peering from out the privacy of a shady nook composed of plumes of verdant ferns. In that same stroll to Heisterbach, he pointed out to me such beauty of design in objects I had used to trample under foot, that I felt as if almost every spot on which I trod was holy ground, and that I had rudely desecrated it. His eyes would fill with tears and his voice falter as he dwelt on the benevolent adaptation of means to ends discernible by reverential observation. Nor did his reflections die out in mawkish sentiment; they lay 'two deep for tears,' and, as they crowded thickly on him, his gentle spirit, subdued by the sense of the Divine goodness towards his creature, became attuned to better thoughts; the love of nature inspired his heart with a gratitude to nature's God, and found its most suitable expression in numbers.—CHARLES MAYNE YOUNG, *Journal* (July 6, 1828), cited in Julian Charles Young, *A Memoir of Charles Mayne Young*, 1871, pp. 112–15

Tickler: Ha! what worthies have we got here over the chimney-piece?

North (smiling): Who do you think?

Tickler (with a peculiar face): Wordsworth, with Jeffrey on the one side, and Brougham on the other!

North: How placid and profound the expression of the whole Bard! The face is Miltonic—even to the very eyes; for though, thank Heaven, they are not blind, there is a dimness about the orbs. The temples I remember shaded with thin hair of an indescribable colour, that in the sunlight seemed a kind of mild auburn—but now they are bare—and—nothing to break it—the height is majestic. No furrows—no wrinkles on that contemplative forehead—the sky is without a cloud—

> The image of a Poet's soul,
> How calm! how tranquil! how serene!

It faintly smiles. There is light and motion round the lips, as if they were about to "discourse most eloquent music." In my imagination, that mouth is never mute—I hear it

> Murmuring by the living brooks,
> A music sweeter than their own.

Tickler: Is he wont so to sit with folded arms?

North: 'Twas not his habit of old, but it may be now—there seems to my mind much dignity in that repose. He is privileged to sit with folded arms, for all life long those hands have ministered religiously at the shrine of nature and nature's God, and the Priest, as age advances, may take his rest in the sanctuary, a voiceless worshipper. There is goodness in the great man's aspect—and while I look, love blends with reverence. How bland! The features in themselves are almost stern—but most humane the spirit of the grand assemblage—

> Not harsh, nor greeting, but of amplest power
> To soften and subdue!
> —JOHN WILSON (as "Christopher North"), *Noctes Ambrosianae* (Nov. 1832), 1854

He was, upon the whole, not a well-made man. His legs were pointedly condemned by all female connoisseurs in legs; not that they were bad in any way which *would* force itself upon your notice—there was no absolute deformity about them; and undoubtedly they had been serviceable legs beyond the average standard of human requisition; for I calculate, upon good data, that with these identical legs Wordsworth must have traversed a distance of 175,000 to 180,000 English miles—a mode of exertion which, to him, stood in the stead of alcohol and all other stimulants whatsoever to the animal spirits; to which, indeed, he was indebted for a life of unclouded happiness, and we for much of what is most excellent in his writings. But, useful as they have proved themselves, the Wordsworthian legs were certainly not ornamental; and it was really a pity, as I agreed with a lady in thinking, that he had not another pair for evening dress parties—when no boots lend their friendly aid to mask our imperfections from the eyes of female rigorists—those *elegantes formarum spectatrices*. A sculptor would certainly have disapproved of their contour. But the worst part of Wordsworth's person was the bust; there was a narrowness and a droop about the shoulders which became striking, and had an effect of meanness, when brought into close juxtaposition with a figure of a more statuesque build. Once on a summer evening, walking in the Vale of Langdale with Wordsworth, his sister, and Mr. J——, a native Westmoreland clergyman, I remember that Miss Wordsworth was positively mortified by the peculiar illustration which settled upon this defective conformation. Mr. J——, a fine towering figure, six feet high, massy and columnar in his proportions, happened to be walking, a little in advance, with Wordsworth; Miss Wordsworth and myself being in the rear; and from the nature of the conversation which then prevailed in our front rank, something or other about money, devises, buying and selling, we of the rear-guard thought it requisite to preserve this arrangement for a space of three miles or more; during which time, at intervals, Miss Wordsworth would exclaim, in a tone of vexation, "Is it possible,—can that be William? How very mean he looks!" And she did not conceal a mortification that seemed really painful, until I, for my part, could not forbear laughing outright at the serious interest which she carried into this trifle. She was, however, right, as regarded the mere visual judgment. Wordsworth's figure, with all its defects, was brought into powerful relief by one which had been cast in a more square and massy mould; and in such a case it impressed a spectator with a sense of absolute meanness, more especially when viewed from behind and not counteracted by his countenance; and yet Wordsworth was of a good height (five feet ten), and not a slender man; on the contrary, by the side of Southey, his limbs looked thick, almost in a disproportionate degree. But the total effect of Wordsworth's person was always worst in a state of motion. Meantime, his face—that was one which would have made amends for greater defects of figure. Many such, and finer, I have seen amongst the portraits of Titian, and, in a later period, amongst those of Vandyke, from the great era of Charles I, as also from the court of Elizabeth and of Charles II, but none which has more impressed me in my own time.—THOMAS DE QUINCEY, "The Lake Poets: William Wordsworth" (1839), *Collected Writings*, ed. David Masson, Vol. 2, pp. 242–43

> Just for a handful of silver he left us,
>   Just for a riband to stick in his coat—
> Found the one gift of which fortune bereft us,
>   Lost all the others she lets us devote;
> They, with the gold to give, doled him out silver,
>   So much was theirs who so little allowed:
> How all our copper had gone for his service!
>   Rags—were they purple, his heart had been proud!
> We that had loved him so, followed him, honoured him,
>   Lived in his mild and magnificent eye,
> Learned his great language, caught his clear accents,
>   Made him our pattern to live and to die!

Shakespeare was of us, Milton was for us,
  Burns, Shelley, were with us,—they watch from their
    graves!
He alone breaks from the van and the freemen,
  —He alone sinks to the rear and the slaves!
        —ROBERT BROWNING, "The Lost Leader," *Dramatic Romances and Lyrics*, 1845

Mr. Wordsworth, whom Mr. Hazlitt designated as one that would have had the wide circle of his humanities made still wider, and a good deal more pleasant, by dividing a little more of his time between his lakes in Westmoreland and the hotels of the metropolis, had a dignified manner, with a deep and roughish but not unpleasing voice, and an exalted mode of speaking. He had a habit of keeping his left hand in the bosom of his waistcoat; and in this attitude, except when he turned round to take one of the subjects of his criticism from the shelves (for his contemporaries were there also), he sat dealing forth his eloquent but hardly catholic judgments. In his "father's house" there were not "many mansions". He was as sceptical on the merits of all kinds of poetry but one, as Richardson was on those of the novels of Fielding.

Under the study in which my visitor and I were sitting was an archway, leading to a nursery ground; a cart happened to go through it while I was inquiring whether he would take any refreshment; and he uttered, in so lofty a voice, the words, "Anything which is *going forward*," that I felt inclined to ask him whether he would take a piece of the cart. Lamb would certainly have done it. But this was a levity which would neither have been so proper on my part, after so short an acquaintance, nor very intelligible, perhaps, in any sense of the word, to the serious poet. There are good-humoured warrants for smiling, which lie deeper even than Mr. Wordsworth's thoughts for tears.

I did not see this distinguished person again till thirty years afterwards; when, I should venture to say, his manner was greatly superior to what it was in the former instance; indeed, quite natural and noble, with a cheerful air of animal as well as spiritual confidence; a gallant bearing, curiously reminding me of the Duke of Wellington, as I saw him walking some eighteen years ago by a lady's side, with no unbecoming oblivion of his time of life. I observed, also, that the poet no longer committed himself in scornful criticisms, or, indeed, in any criticisms whatever, at least as far as I knew. He had found out that he could, at least, afford to be silent. Indeed, he spoke very little of anything. The conversation turned upon Milton, and I fancied I had opened a subject that would have "brought him out", by remarking, that the most diabolical thing in all *Paradise Lost* was a feeling attributed to the angels. "Ay!" said Mr. Wordsworth, and inquired what it was. I said it was the passage in which the angels, when they observed Satan journeying through the empyrean, let down a set of steps out of heaven, on purpose to add to his misery—to his despair of ever being able to re-ascend them; they being angels in a state of bliss, and he a fallen spirit doomed to eternal punishment. The passage is as follows:

Each stair was meant mysteriously, nor stood
There always, but, drawn up to heaven, sometimes
Viewless; and underneath a bright sea flow'd
Of jasper, or of liquid pearl, whereon
Who after came from earth sailing arriv'd
Wafted by angels, or flew o'er the lake
Rapt in a chariot drawn by fiery steeds.
The stairs were then let down, whether to dare
The fiend by easy ascent, *or aggravate*
His sad exclusion from the doors of bliss.

Mr. Wordsworth pondered, and said nothing. I thought to myself, what pity for the poor devil would not good Uncle Toby have expressed! Into what indignation would not Burns have exploded! What knowledge of themselves would not have been forced upon those same coxcombical and malignant angels by Fielding or Shakspeare!

Walter Scott said, that the eyes of Burns were the finest he ever saw. I cannot say the same of Mr. Wordsworth's; that is, not in the sense of the beautiful, or even of the profound. But certainly I never beheld eyes that looked so inspired or supernatural. They were like fires half burning, half smouldering, with a sort of acrid fixture of regard, and seated at the further end of two caverns. One might imagine Ezekiel or Isaiah to have had such eyes. The finest eyes, in every sense of the word, which I have ever seen in a man's head (and I have seen many fine ones) are those of Thomas Carlyle.—LEIGH HUNT, *Autobiography*, 1850, Ch. 15

On the 28th August I went to Rydal Mount, to pay my respects to Mr. Wordsworth. His daughters called in their father, a plain, elderly, white-haired man, not prepossessing, and disfigured by green goggles. He sat down, and talked with great simplicity. He had just returned from a journey. His health was good, but he had broken a tooth by a fall, when walking with two lawyers, and had said that he was glad it did not happen forty years ago; whereupon they had praised his philosophy.

He had much to say of America, the more that it gave occasion for his favorite topic,—that society is being enlightened by a superficial tuition, out of all proportion to its being restrained by moral culture. Schools do no good. Tuition is not education. He thinks more of the education of circumstances than of tuition. 'T is not question whether there are offences of which the law takes cognizance, but whether there are offences of which the law does not take cognizance. Sin is what he fears,—and how society is to escape without gravest mischiefs from this source. He has even said, what seemed a paradox, that they needed a civil war in America, to teach the necessity of knitting the social ties stronger. "There may be," he said, "in America some vulgarity in manner, but that's not important. That comes of the pioneer state of things. But I fear they are too much given to the making of money; and secondly, to politics; that they make political distinction the end and not the means. And I fear they lack a class of men of leisure,—in short, of gentlemen,—to give a tone of honor to the community. I am told that things are boasted of in the second class of society there, which, in England,—God knows, are done in England every day, but would never be spoken of. In America I wish to know not how many churches or schools, but what newspapers? My friend Colonel Hamilton, at the foot of the hill, who was a year in America, assures me that the newspapers are atrocious, and accuse members of Congress of stealing spoons!" He was against taking off the tax on newspapers in England,—which the reformers represent as a tax upon knowledge,—for this reason, that they would be inundated with base prints. He said he talked on political aspects, for he wished to impress on me and all good Americans to cultivate the moral, the conservative, etc., etc., and never to call into action the physical strength of the people, as had just now been done in England in the Reform Bill,—a thing prophesied by Delolme. He alluded once or twice to his conversation with Dr. Channing, who had recently visited him (laying his hand on a particular chair in which the Doctor had sat).

The conversation turned on books. Lucretius he esteems a far higher poet than Virgil; not in his system, which is nothing, but in his power of illustration. Faith is necessary to explain anything and to reconcile the foreknowledge of God with human evil. Of Cousin (whose lectures we had all been reading in Boston), he knew only the name.

I inquired if he had read Carlyle's critical articles and translations. He said he thought him sometimes insane. He proceeded to abuse Goethe's *Wilhelm Meister* heartily. It was full of all manner of fornication. It was like the crossing of flies in the air. He had never gone farther than the first part; so disgusted was he that he threw the book across the room. I deprecated this wrath, and said what I could for the better parts of the book, and he courteously promised to look at it again. Carlyle he said wrote most obscurely. He was clever and deep, but he defied the sympathies of every body. Even Mr. Coleridge wrote more clearly, though he had always wished Coleridge would write more to be understood. He led me out into his garden, and showed me the gravel walk in which thousands of his lines were composed. His eyes are much inflamed. This is no loss except for reading, because he never writes prose, and of poetry he carries even hundreds of lines in his head before writing them. He had just returned from a visit to Staffa, and within three days he had made three sonnets on Fingal's Cave, and was composing a fourth when he was called in to see me. He said, "If you are interested in my verses perhaps you will like to hear these lines." I gladly assented, and he recollected himself for a few moments and then stood forth and repeated, one after the other, the three entire sonnets with great animation. I fancied the second and third more beautiful than his poems are wont to be. The third is addressed to the flowers, which, he said, especially the ox-eye daisy, are very abundant on the top of the rock. The second alludes to the name of the cave, which is "Cave of Music;" the first to the circumstance of its being visited by the promiscuous company of the steamboat.

This recitation was so unlooked for and surprising,—he, the old Wordsworth, standing apart, and reciting to me in a garden-walk, like a school-boy declaiming,—that I at first was near to laugh; but recollecting myself, that I had come thus far to see a poet and he was chanting poems to me, I saw that he was right and I was wrong, and gladly gave myself up to hear. I told him how much the few printed extracts had quickened the desire to possess his unpublished poems. He replied he never was in haste to publish; partly because he corrected a good deal, and every alteration is ungraciously received after printing; but what he had written would be printed, whether he lived or died. I said "Tintern Abbey" appeared to be the favorite poem with the public, but more contemplative readers preferred the first books of the *Excursion*, and the Sonnets. He said, "Yes, they are better." He preferred such of his poems as touched the affections, to any others; for whatever is didactic— what theories of society, and so on—might perish quickly; but whatever combined a truth with an affection was κτῆμα ἐς ἀεί, good to-day and good forever. He cited the sonnet, "On the Feelings of a Highminded Spaniard," which he preferred to any other (I so understood him), and the "Two Voices;" and quoted, with evident pleasure, the verses addressed "To the Skylark." In this connection he said of the Newtonian theory that it might yet be superseded and forgotten; and Dalton's atomic theory.

When I prepared to depart he said he wished to show me what a common person in England could do, and he led me into the enclosure of his clerk, a young man to whom he had given this slip of ground, which was laid out, or its natural capabilities shown, with much taste. He then said he would show me a better way towards the inn; and he walked a good part of a mile, talking and ever and anon stopping short to impress the word or the verse, and finally parted from me with great kindness and returned across the fields.

Wordsworth honored himself by his simple adherence to truth, and was very willing not to shine; but he surprised by the hard limits of his thought. To judge from a single conversation, he made the impression of a narrow and very English mind; of one who paid for his rare elevation by general tameness and conformity. Off his own beat, his opinions were of no value. It is not very rare to find persons loving sympathy and ease, who expiate their departure from the common in one direction, by their conformity in every other.—RALPH WALDO EMERSON, "First Visit to England," *English Traits*, 1856

During the last seven or ten years of his life, Wordsworth felt himself to be a recognised lion, in certain considerable London circles, and was in the habit of coming up to town with his wife for a month or two every season, to enjoy his quiet triumph and collect his bits of tribute *tales quales*. The places where I met him oftenest, were Marshall's (the great Leeds linen manufacturer, an excellent and very opulent man), Spring-Rice's (i.e. Lord Monteagle's, who and whose house was strangely intermarried with this Marshall's), and the first Lord Stanley's of Alderley (who then, perhaps, was still Sir Thomas Stanley). Wordsworth took his bit of lionism very quietly, with a smile sardonic rather than triumphant, and certainly got no harm by it, if he got or expected little good. His wife, a small, withered, puckered, winking lady, who never spoke, seemed to be more in earnest about the affair, and was visibly and sometimes ridiculously assiduous to secure her proper place of precedence at table. One evening at Lord Monteagle's—Ah! who was it that then made me laugh as we went home together: Ah me! Wordsworth generally spoke a little with me on those occasions; sometimes, perhaps, we sat by one another; but there came from him nothing considerable, and happily at least nothing with an effort. 'If you think me dull, be it just so!'— this seemed to a most respectable extent to be his inspiring humour. Hardly above once (perhaps at the Stanleys') do I faintly recollect something of the contrary on his part for a little while, which was not pleasant or successful while it lasted. The light was always afflictive to his eyes; he carried in his pocket something like a skeleton brass candlestick, in which, setting it on the dinner-table, between him and the most afflictive or nearest of the chief lights, he touched a little spring, and there flirted out, at the top of his brass implement, a small vertical green circle which prettily enough threw his eyes into shade, and screened him from that sorrow. In proof of his equanimity as lion I remember, in connection with this green shade, one little glimpse which shall be given presently as finis. But first let me say that all these Wordsworth phenomena appear to have been indifferent to me, and have melted to steamy oblivion in a singular degree. Of his talk to others in my hearing I remember simply nothing, not even a word or gesture. To myself it seemed once or twice as if he bore suspicions, thinking I was not a real worshipper, which threw him into something of embarrassment, till I hastened to get them laid, by frank discourse on some suitable thing; nor, when we did talk, was there on his side or on mine the least utterance worth noting. The tone of his voice when I got him afloat on some Cumberland or other matter germane to him, had a braced rustic vivacity, willingness, and solid precision, which alone rings in my ear when all else is gone. Of some Druid circle, for example, he prolonged his response to me with the addition, 'And there is another some miles off, which the country people call Long Meg and her Daughters'; as to the now ownership of which 'It' etc.; 'and then it came into the hands of a Mr. Crackenthorpe;' the sound of those two phrases is still lively and present with me; meaning or sound of absolutely nothing more. Still more memorable is an ocular glimpse I had in one of these Wordsworthian lion-dinners, very symbolic to me of his general deportment there, and far clearer than the little feature of opposite sort, ambiguously given above (recollection of that viz. of unsuccessful exertion at a Stanley dinner being dubious and all but extinct, while this is still vivid to me as of yesternight). Dinner was large, luminous, sumptuous; I sat a long way from Wordsworth; dessert I think had come in, and certainly there reigned in all quarters a cackle as of Babel (only politer perhaps), which far up in Wordsworth's quarter (who was leftward on my side of the table) seemed to have taken a sententious, rather louder, logical and quasi-scientific turn, heartily unimportant to gods and men, so far as I could judge of it and of the other babble reigning. I looked upwards, leftwards, the coast being luckily for a moment clear; there, far off, beautifully screened in the shadow of his vertical green circle, which was on the farther side of him, sate Wordsworth, silent, slowly but steadily gnawing some portion of what I judged to be raisins, with his eye and attention placidly fixed on these and these alone. The sight of whom, and of his rock-like indifference to the babble, quasi-scientific and other, with attention turned on the small practical alone, was comfortable and amusing to me, who felt like him but could not eat raisins. This little glimpse I could still paint, so clear and bright is it, and this shall be symbolical of all.

In a few years, I forget in how many and when, these Wordsworth appearances in London ceased; we heard, not of ill-health perhaps, but of increasing love of rest; at length of the long sleep's coming; and never saw Wordsworth more. One felt his death as the extinction of a public light, but not otherwise. The public itself found not much to say of him, and staggered on to meaner but more pressing objects.—THOMAS CARLYLE, "Appendix" (1867), *Reminiscences*, ed. James Anthony Froude, 1881, Vol. 2, pp. 338–41

General

The reflections (in "Tintern Abbey" are) of no common mind; poetical, beautiful, and philosophical: but somewhat tinctured with gloomy, narrow, and unsociable ideas of seclusion from the commerce of the world: as if men were born to live in woods and wilds, unconnected with each other! Is it not to education and the culture of the mind that we owe the raptures which the author so well describes, as arising from the view of beautiful scenery, and sublime objects of nature enjoyed in tranquillity, when contrasted with the artificial machinery and "busy hum of men" in a city? The savage sees none of the beauties which this author describes. The convenience of food and shelter, which vegetation affords him, is all his concern; he thinks not of its picturesque beauties, the course of rivers, the height of mountains, &c. He has no *dizzy raptures* in youth; nor does he listen in maturer age "to the still sad music of humanity." —CHARLES BURNEY, *Monthly Review*, June 1799, p. 210

Wordsworth will do better, and leave behind him a name, unique in his way; he will rank among the very first poets, and probably possesses a mass of merits superior to all, except only Shakspeare. This is doing much, yet would he be a happier man if he did more.—ROBERT SOUTHEY, Letter to John Rickman (March 30, 1804)

Next comes the dull disciple of thy school,
That mild apostate from poetic rule,
The simple Wordsworth, framer of a lay

As soft as evening in his favourite May,
Who warns his friend 'to shake off toil and trouble,
And quit his books, for fear of growing double;'
Who, both by precept and example, shows
That prose is verse, and verse is merely prose;
Convincing all, by demonstration plain,
Poetic souls delight in prose insane;
And Christmas stories tortured into rhyme
Contain the essence of the true sublime.
Thus, when he tells the tale of Betty Foy,
The idiot mother of 'an idiot boy';
A moon-struck, silly lad, who lost his way,
And, like his bard, confounded night with day;
So close on each pathetic part he dwells,
And each adventure so sublimely tells,
That all who view the 'idiot in his glory'
Conceive the bard the hero of the story.
　　　—GEORGE GORDON, LORD BYRON, *English Bards and Scotch Reviewers*, 1809, ll. 235–54

The causes which have prevented the poetry of Mr. Wordsworth from attaining its full share of popularity are to be found in the boldness and originality of his genius. The times are past when a poet could securely follow the direction of his own mind into whatever tracts it might lead. A writer, who would be popular, must timidly coast the shore of prescribed sentiment and sympathy. He must have just as much more of the imaginative faculty than his readers, as will serve to keep their apprehensions from stagnating, but not so much as to alarm their jealousy. He must not think or feel too deeply.

If he has had the fortune to be bred in the midst of the most magnificent objects of creation, he must not have given away his heart to them; or if he have, he must conceal his love, or not carry his expressions of it beyond that point of rapture, which the occasional tourist thinks it not overstepping decorum to betray, or the limit which that gentlemanly spy upon Nature, the picturesque traveller, has vouchsafed to countenance. He must do this, or be content to be thought an enthusiast.

If from living among simple mountaineers, from a daily intercourse with them, not upon the footing of a patron, but in the character of an equal, he has detected, or imagines that he has detected, through the cloudy medium of their unlettered discourse, thoughts and apprehensions not vulgar; traits of patience and constancy, love unwearied, and heroic endurance, not unfit (as he may judge) to be made the subject of verse, he will be deemed a man of perverted genius by the philanthropist who, conceiving of the peasantry of his country only as objects of a pecuniary sympathy, starts at finding them elevated to a level of humanity with himself, having their own loves, enmities, cravings, aspirations, &c., as much beyond his faculty to believe, as his beneficence to supply.

If from a familiar observation of the ways of children, and much more from a retrospect of his own mind when a child, he has gathered more reverential notions of that state than fall to the lot of ordinary observers, and, escaping from the dissonant wranglings of men, has tuned his lyre, though but for occasional harmonies, to the milder utterance of that soft age,—his verses shall be censured as infantile by critics who confound poetry 'having children for its subject' with poetry that is 'childish,' and who, having themselves perhaps never been *children*, never having possessed the tenderness and docility of that age, know not what the soul of a child is—how apprehensive! how imaginative! how religious!—CHARLES LAMB, WILLIAM GIFFORD, "Wordsworth's *Excursion*," *Quarterly Review*, Oct. 1814, pp. 110–11

I am much obliged to you for the ⟨*Edinburgh*⟩ *Review*, and shall exercise the privilege of an old friend in making some observations upon it. I have not read the review of Wordsworth, because the subject is to me so very uninteresting; but may I ask was it worth while to take any more notice of a man respecting whom the public opinion is completely made up? and do not such repeated attacks upon the man wear in some little degree the shape of persecution?—SYDNEY SMITH, Letter to Francis, Lord Jeffrey (Dec. 30, 1814)

> He of the cloud, the cataract, the lake,
> Who on Helvellyn's summit, wide awake,
> Catches his freshness from Archangel's wing.
> —JOHN KEATS, "Addressed to Haydon," 1816

Mr. Wordsworth is the most original poet now living. He is the reverse of Walter Scott in his defects and excellences. He has nearly all that the other wants, and wants all that the other possesses. His poetry is not external, but internal; it does not depend upon tradition, or story, or old song; he furnishes it from his own mind, and is his own subject. He is the poet of mere sentiment. Of many of the *Lyrical Ballads*, it is not possible to speak in terms of too high praise, such as 'Hart-Leap Well,' the 'Banks of the Wye,' 'Poor Susan,' parts of the 'Leech-Gatherer,' the lines 'To a Cuckoo,' 'To a Daisy,' the 'Complaint,' several of the Sonnets, and a hundred others of inconceivable beauty, of perfect originality and pathos. They open a finer and deeper vein of thought and feeling than any poet in modern times has done, or attempted. He has produced a deeper impression, and on a smaller circle, than any other of his contemporaries. His powers have been mistaken by the age, nor does he exactly understand them himself. He cannot form a whole. He has not the constructive faculty. He can give only the fine tones of thought, drawn from his mind by accident or nature, like the sounds drawn from the Æolian harp by the wandering gale.— He is totally deficient in all the machinery of poetry. His *Excursion*, taken as a whole, notwithstanding the noble materials thrown away in it, is a proof of this. The line labours, the sentiment moves slow, but the poem stands stock-still. The reader makes no way from the first line to the last. It is more than any thing in the world like Robinson Crusoe's boat, which would have been an excellent good boat, and would have carried him to the other side of the globe, but that he could not get it out of the sand where it stuck fast. I did what little I could to help to launch it at the time, but it would not do. I am not, however, one of those who laugh at the attempts or failures of men of genius. It is not my way to cry 'Long life to the conqueror.' Success and desert are not with me synonymous terms; and the less Mr. Wordsworth's general merits have been understood, the more necessary is it to insist upon them.—WILLIAM HAZLITT, *Lectures on the English Poets*, 1818

> He had a mind which was somehow
>   At once circumference and centre
> Of all he might or feel or know;
> Nothing went ever out, although
>   Something did ever enter.
> He had as much imagination
>   As a pint-pot;—he never could
> Fancy another situation,
> From which to dart his contemplation,
>   Than that wherein he stood.
> Yet his was individual mind,
>   And new created all he saw
> In a new manner, and refined
> Those new creations, and combined
>   Them, by a master-spirit's law.

> Thus—though unimaginative—
>   An apprehension clear, intense,
> Of his mind's work, had made alive
> The things it wrought on; I believe
>   Wakening a sort of thought in sense.
> —PERCY BYSSHE SHELLEY, *Peter Bell the Third*, 1819, Pt. 4, Stanzas 7–10

The descriptive poetry of the present day has been called by its cultivators a return to nature. Nothing is more impertinent than this pretension. Poetry cannot travel out of the regions of its birth, the uncultivated lands of semi-civilized men. Mr. Wordsworth, the great leader of the returners to nature, cannot describe a scene under his own eyes without putting into it the shadow of a Danish boy or the living ghost of Lucy Gray, or some similar phantastical parturition of the moods of his own mind.—THOMAS LOVE PEACOCK, "The Four Ages of Poetry," 1820

I do not know a man more to be venerated for uprightness of heart and loftiness of genius. Why he will sometimes choose to crawl upon all-fours, when God has given him so noble a countenance to lift to heaven, I am as little able to account for, as for his quarrelling (as you tell me) with the wrinkles which time and meditation have stamped his brow withal.—SIR WALTER SCOTT, Letter to Allan Cunningham (c. Dec. 1820)

Next to Byron, there is no poet whose writings have had so much influence on the taste of the age as Wordsworth. Byron drove on through the upper air till the thunder of his wheels died on the ear. Wordsworth drove to Parnassus by the lower road, got sometimes lost in bushes and lowland fogs, and was much molested by mosquito critics. In our own country the Wordsworth school has evidently the upper hand. His simple austerity and republican principle in poetry were in unison with our moral and political creed. Our modes of thought are sober and practical. So, in most instances, were his.—HENRY WADSWORTH LONGFELLOW, *Notebook* (1829), cited in Samuel Longfellow, *Life of Henry Wadsworth Longfellow*, 1891, Vol. 1, p. 172

In the *Lyrical Ballads* and the *Excursion* Mr. Wordsworth appeared as the high priest of a worship, of which nature was the idol. No poems have ever indicated a more exquisite perception of the beauty of the outer world, or a more passionate love and reverence for that beauty. Yet they were not popular; and it is not likely that they ever will be popular as the poetry of Sir Walter Scott is popular. The feeling which pervaded them was too deep for general sympathy. Their style was often too mysterious for general comprehension. They made a few esoteric disciples, and many scoffers.—THOMAS BABINGTON MACAULAY, "Moore's Life of Lord Byron" (1831), *Critical, Historical, and Miscellaneous Essays*, 1860, Vol. 2, p. 356

Mr. Wordsworth ⟨. . .⟩, in our estimation, is a philosophic writer in the sense in which any man must be so, who writes from the impulses of a capacious and powerful mind, habituated to observe, to analyse, and to generalise. So far forth was Shakspeare likewise a philosopher. But it does not follow from this that he should be supposed to have invented any peculiar ethical or metaphysical system, or to have discovered any new principles upon which such a system could be built. What is new and peculiar in him as a philosophic thinker is not his view of the primary principles of psychological philosophy, nor the trains of ratiocination by which he descends to those which are secondary and derivative: it consists not so much in reasoning as in judgment; not so much in the exposition of abstract truths, as in his manner of regarding the particulars of life as they arise, and of generalising them into one truth or another, according as the one or the other harmonises with his moral temperament and habitual and cherished states of feeling.

If a poet have any peculiar philosophy of his own, it must be mainly through this modification of the judgment by individual temperament; the affinities of such temperament drawing round him and giving predominant influence to some truths, whilst others are merely not rejected in deference to the reason. Nor is it to be supposed that a judgment so modified, and a philosophy into which sensibility thus enters, are therefore fallacious. Such a supposition will be entertained, we are aware, by those who have imagined to themselves such a mere fiction as the contemporaneous discernment of all moral truth. The real state of the case being, however, that truth can only be shown piecemeal in its component parts, and that poetry, at all events, can do no more than cast partial lights upon it, it is saying nothing in derogation of any man's philosophy, still less of his poetical philosophy, to affirm, that, in so far as it is peculiar to himself, it is so by dealing with that *portion of truth* of which his temperament gives him the most lively consciousness. By his individual temperament it is that Mr. Wordsworth's philosophic perceptions of truth, various and composite as they are, come to have a certain unity of drift, which has given to his writings the character of embodying a peculiar system of philosophy. We shall best explain our view of what that philosophy is, by a commentary upon some of the passages in which it comes to light.

The lines left upon a yew-tree seat, after describing the life of mortification led by a neglected man of genius—

> Who with the food of pride sustained his soul
> In solitude—

conclude with the following moral:—

> If thou be one whose heart the holy forms
> Of young imagination have kept pure,
> Stranger! henceforth be warned; and know that
>   pride,
> Howe'er disguised in its own majesty,
> Is littleness; that he who feels contempt
> For any living thing, hath faculties
> Which he has never used; that thought with him
> Is in its infancy. The man whose eye
> Is ever on himself, doth look on one,
> The least of Nature's works, one who might move
> The wise man to that scorn which wisdom holds
> Unlawful ever. Oh be wiser, thou!
> Instructed that true knowledge leads to love,
> True dignity abides with him alone
> Who, in the silent hour of inward thought,
> Can still suspect, and still revere himself,
> In lowliness of heart.

Let the stranger who is addressed in this passage be supposed to be another Wordsworth, another philosophic poet, or rather a pupil apt for becoming such, and then the injunctions which it contains are admirably calculated to train him in the way that *he* should go, although it may be possible to represent them as requiring to be received with some qualification by others. The nature of these qualifications will present a key to some of the peculiarities of Mr. Wordsworth's moral views.

It is undoubtedly essential not only to the philosophic character, but to the moral elevation of any man, that he should regard every atom of pride which he may detect in his nature as something which detracts from his dignity, inasmuch

as it evinces some want of independence and of natural strength. When Burns breaks out into fiery expressions of contempt for the rich and the great, we recognise the man of genius, but not the man of an independent nature. If in his real feelings he had been independent of the rich and the great, they might have gone their way and he would have gone his, and we should have heard nothing of his scorn or disdain. These were dictated, not as they professed to be, by a spirit of independence, but by that which, wheresoever it exists, comes in abatement of independence—by pride. A keen desire of aggrandisement in the eyes of others, a sensitive apprehension of humiliation in their eyes, are the constituents of pride, and though it may manifest itself in divers forms, leading a man, perhaps, to avoid *a practical* dependence upon others, and even leading him, as in the case which is the subject of Mr. Wordsworth's poem, to terminate, as far as possible, his intercourse with mankind—yet these very courses would be evidences of a weakness of nature; for one who was not unduly dependent upon the opinion of others for his peace of mind would not be driven to seek this shelter; on the contrary, he would go through the world, giving and taking, in the freedom of the feeling, that so long as he should satisfy his own conscience in his dealings with his fellow-creatures, he would always be sure to receive from them as much respect as he had occasion for. It is then this servility and cowardice of the inmost spirit, together with the artifices or the escapes naturally resorted to in such a state of slavery, that Mr. Wordsworth detects—when he bids us

> know that pride,
> Howe'er disguised in its own majesty,
> Is littleness.

So far, however, the sentiment expressed by Mr. Wordsworth, though largely contributing to his system of opinions, may not, perhaps, constitute a peculiarity of them; and in contrasting the sentiments of Burns with those of Wordsworth, we have not intended to represent the one poet any more than the other, as standing alone in his way of thinking; but only to contra-distinguish from the philosophic poet the mere man of genius who writes from the impulses of an ardent mind, and throws light upon human nature, less by the depth of his investigations, than by the liveliness of his sympathies; exhibiting, in truth, a subject for a philosopher to contemplate, rather than the spirit of philosophical contemplation. But proceeding with the passage, the next step takes us into Mr. Wordsworth's peculiar domain. We are told that

> He who feels contempt
> For any living thing, hath faculties
> That he has never used; that thought with him
> Is in its infancy.

It is here that, were we to understand the doctrine as delivered for acceptation by mankind at large, we should, as we have already intimated, take some exceptions. The moral government of the world appears to us to require, that in the every-day intercourse of ordinary man with man, room should be given to the operation of the harsher sentiments of our nature—anger, resentment, contempt. They were planted in us for a purpose, and are not essentially and necessarily wrong in themselves, although they may easily be wrong in their direction. What we have to do is not to subdue such feelings; and we are to control them, not with a view to their suppression, but only with a view to their just application. Let the sentiment of justice be paramount, and it will lead to such serious consideration of the grounds of our hostile feelings as will, in itself and of necessity, temper them; but neither need nor ought to suppress them, nor even to abate their vivacity further than is necessary to admit of clear perceptions and a just judgment of their objects. Anger, resentment, and contempt, are instruments of the penal law of nature and private society, which, as long as evil exists, must require to be administered; and the best interests of mankind demand that they should be tempered with justice much more than with mercy. The public laws of a community, and the penalties they denounce, have their chief importance by giving countenance and operation to the private penalties of society, the judgments of the street and the marketplace, searching and pervasive, by which alone evil inchoate can be contended with and destroyed. That Man, so far as he is liable to evil inclinations, should fear his neighbour, is as requisite for the good of society as that he should love his neighbour, and that which he will commonly stand most in fear of is his neighbour's just contempt.

Do we then, in so far as the doctrine in question is concerned, attribute to Mr. Wordsworth a *false* philosophy? We are by no means so presumptuous, nor (let us hope) so incapable of comprehending Mr. Wordsworth's views. In the first place, we conceive that Mr. Wordsworth adverted more especially to that species of contempt which is immediately connected with the pride denounced previously in the same passage, and the self-love denounced subsequently—the undue contempt which a man conjures up in himself through the workings of self-love, for the ends of self-aggrandisement, or perhaps more frequently to stave off a feeling of humiliation and self-reproach. But without insisting upon a qualification which the language employed may seem to some to refuse, we find in the proposition, taken even in all the absoluteness of its terms, no error, but, we should say, a peculiarity of sentiment, proceeding from a rare constitution of mind, adapted to that constitution, and when enjoined upon men whose minds are similarly constituted, not enjoined amiss.—SIR HENRY TAYLOR, "Wordsworth's *Poetical Works*," *Quarterly Review*, Nov. 1834, pp. 325–29

I have been so self-indulgent as to possess myself of Wordsworth at full length, and I thoroughly like much of the contents of the first three volumes which I fancy are only the low vestibule to the three remaining ones. What I could wish to have added to many of my favorite morceaux is an indication of less satisfaction in terrene objects, a more frequent upturning of the soul's eye. I never before met with so many of my own feelings, expressed just as I could like them.—GEORGE ELIOT, Letter to Maria Lewis (Nov. 22, 1839)

He is scarcely, perhaps, of a passionate temperament, although still less is he cold; rather quiet in his love, as the stockdove, and brooding over it as constantly, and with as soft an inward song lapsing outwardly—serene through deepness—saying himself of his thoughts, that they "do often lie too deep for tears;" which does not mean that their painfulness will not suffer them to be wept for, but that their closeness to the supreme Truth hallows them, like the cheek of an archangel, from tears. Call him the very opposite of Byron, who, with narrower sympathies for the crowd, yet stood nearer to the crowd, because everybody understands passion. Byron was a poet through pain. Wordsworth is a feeling man because he is a thoughtful man; he knows grief itself by a reflex emotion; by sympathy rather than by suffering. He is eminently and humanly expansive; and, spreading his infinite egotism over all the objects of his contemplation, reiterates the love, life, and poetry of his peculiar being in transcribing and chanting the material universe, and so sinks a broad gulf between his descriptive poetry and that of the Darwinian painter-poet school. Darwin

was, as we have intimated, all optic nerve. Wordsworth's eye is his soul. He does not see that which he does not intellectually discern, and he beholds his own cloud-capped Helvellyn under the same conditions with which he would contemplate a grand spiritual abstraction. In his view of the exterior world,—as in a human Spinozism,—mountains and men's hearts share in a sublime unity of humanity; yet his Spinozism is in nowise affront God, for he is eminently a religious poet, if not, indeed, altogether as generous and capacious in his Christianity as in his poetry; and, being a true Christian poet, he is scarcely least so when he is not writing directly upon the subject of religion; just as we learn sometimes without looking up, and by the mere colour of the grass, that the sky is cloudless. But what is most remarkable in this great writer is his poetical consistency. There is a wonderful unity in these multiform poems of one man: they are "bound each to each in natural piety," even as his days are: and why? because they *are* his days—all his days, work days and Sabbath days—his life, in fact, and not the unconnected works of his life, as vulgar men do opine of poetry and do rightly opine of vulgar poems, but the sign, seal, and representation of his life—nay, the actual audible breathing of his inward spirit's life. When Milton said that a poet's life should be a poem, he spoke a high moral truth; if he had added a reversion of the saying, that a poet's poetry should be his life,—he would have spoken a critical truth, not low.—ELIZABETH BARRETT BROWNING, *The Book of the Poets* (1842), *Life, Letters and Essays of Elizabeth Barrett Browning*, 1863

Wordsworth! Beloved friend and venerated teacher; it is more easy and perhaps as profitable to speak of thee. It is less difficult to interpret thee, since no *acquired nature* but merely a theory severs thee from my mind.

Classification on such a subject is rarely satisfactory, yet I will attempt to define in that way the impressions produced by Wordsworth on myself. I esteem his characteristics to be—of spirit,

> Perfect simplicity,
> Perfect truth,
> Perfect love.

Of mind or talent,

> Calmness,
> Penetration,
> Power of Analysis.

Of manner,

> Energetic greatness,
> Pathetic tenderness,
> Mild, persuasive eloquence.

The time has gone by when groundlings could laugh with impunity at *Peter Bell* and the "Idiot Mother." Almost every line of Wordsworth has been quoted and requoted; every feeling echoed back, and every drop of that "cup of still and serious thought" drunk up by some "spirit profound"; enough to satisfy the giver.

Wordsworth is emphatically the friend and teacher of mature years. Youth, in whose bosom "the stately passions burn," is little disposed to drink with him from the

> urn
> Of lowly pleasure.

He has not an idealizing tendency, if by this be meant the desire of creating from materials supplied by our minds, and by the world in which they abide for a season, a new and more beautiful world. It is the aspiration of a noble nature animated by genius, it is allied with the resolve for self-perfection; and few without some of its influence can bring to blossom the bud of any virtue. It is fruitful in illusions, but those illusions have heavenly truth interwoven with their temporary errors. But the mind of Wordsworth, like that of the man of science, finds enough of beauty in the real present world. He delights in penetrating the designs of God rather than in sketching designs of his own. Generally speaking, minds in which the faculty of observation is so prominent have little enthusiasm, little dignity of sentiment. That is indeed an intellect of the first order which can see the great in the little, and dignify the petty operations of Nature by tracing through them her most sublime principles. Wordsworth scrutinizes man and nature with the exact and searching eye of a Cervantes, a Fielding, or a Richter, but without any love for that humorous wit which cannot obtain its needful food unaided by such scrutiny; while dissection merely for curiosity's sake is his horror. He has the delicacy of perception, the universality of feeling which distinguish Shakespeare and the three or four other poets of the first class, and might have taken rank with them had he been equally gifted with versatility of talent. Many might reply, "in wanting this last he wants the better half." To this I cannot agree. Talent, or facility in making use of thought, is dependent in a great measure on education and circumstance; while thought itself is immortal as the soul from which it radiates. Wherever we perceive a profound thought, however imperfectly expressed, we offer a higher homage than we can to commonplace thoughts, however beautiful, or if expressed with all that grace of art which it is often most easy for ordinary minds to acquire. There is a suggestive and stimulating power in original thought which cannot be gauged by the first sensation or temporary effect it produces. The circles grow wider and wider as the impulse is propagated through the deep waters of eternity. An exhibition of talent causes immediate delight; almost all of us can enjoy seeing a thing well done; not all of us can enjoy being roused to do and dare for ourselves. Yet when the mind *is* roused to penetrate the secret meaning of each human effort, a higher pleasure and a greater benefit may be derived from the rude but masterly sketch than from the elaborately finished miniature. In the former case our creative powers are taxed to supply what is wanting, while in the latter our tastes are refined by admiring what another has created. Now since I esteem Wordsworth as superior in originality and philosophic unity of thought to the other poets I have been discussing, I give him the highest place, though they may be superior to *him* either in melody, brilliancy of fancy, dramatic power, or general versatility of talent. Yet I do not place him on a par with those who combine those minor excellencies with originality and philosophic unity of thought. He is not a Shakespeare, but he is the greatest poet of the day; and this is more remarkable, as he is *par excellence* a didactic poet.

I have paid him the most flattering tribute in saying that there is not a line of his which has not been quoted and requoted. Men have found such a response in their lightest as well as their deepest feelings, such beautiful morality with such lucid philosophy, that every thinking mind has consciously or unconsciously appropriated something from Wordsworth. Those who have never read his poems have imbibed some part of their spirit from the public or private discourse of his happy pupils; and it is as yet impossible to estimate duly the effect which the balm of his meditations has had in allaying the fever of the public heart, as exhibited in the writings of Byron and Shelley.—MARGARET FULLER, "Modern British Poets," *Papers on Literature and Art*, 1846

Wordsworth, I am told, does not care for music! And it is very likely, for music (to judge from his verses) does not seem to care

for him. I was astonished the other day, on looking in his works for the first time after a long interval, to find how deficient he was in all that may be called the musical side of a poet's nature,—the genial, the animal-spirited or bird-like,—the happily accordant. Indeed he does not appear to me, now, more than half the man I once took him for, when I was among those who came to the "rescue" for him, and exaggerated his works in the heat of "reaction."—LEIGH HUNT, Letter to "J. F." (July 8, 1848)

> A breath of the mountains, fresh born in the regions majestic,
> That look with their eye-daring summits deep into the sky.
> The voice of great Nature; sublime with her lofty conceptions,
> Yet earnest and simple as any sweet child of the green lowly vale.
> 　　　　—GEORGE MEREDITH, "The Poetry of Wordsworth," 1851

I took up the collection of his poems from curiosity, with no expectation of mental relief from it, though I had before resorted to poetry with that hope. In the worst period of my depression, I had read through the whole of Byron (then new to me), to try whether a poet, whose peculiar department was supposed to be that of the intenser feelings, could rouse any feeling in me. As might be expected, I got no good from this reading, but the reverse. The poet's state of mind was too like my own. His was the lament of a man who had worn out all pleasures, and who seemed to think that life, to all who possess the good things of it, must necessarily be the vapid, uninteresting thing which I found it. His Harold and Manfred had the same burthen on them which I had; and I was not in a frame of mind to derive any comfort from the vehement sensual passion of his Giaours, or the sullenness of his Laras. But while Byron was exactly what did not suit my condition, Wordsworth was exactly what did. I had looked into the *Excursion* two or three years before, and found little in it; and I should probably have found as little, had I read it at this time. But the miscellaneous poems, in the two-volume edition of 1815 (to which little of value was added in the latter part of the author's life), proved to be the precise thing for my mental wants at that particular juncture.

In the first place, these poems addressed themselves powerfully to one of the strongest of my pleasurable susceptibilities, the love of rural objects and natural scenery; to which I had been indebted not only for much of the pleasure of my life, but quite recently for relief from one of my longest relapses into depression. In this power of rural beauty over me, there was a foundation laid for taking pleasure in Wordsworth's poetry; the more so, as his scenery lies mostly among mountains, which, owing to my early Pyrenean excursion, were my ideal of natural beauty. But Wordsworth would never have had any great effect on me, if he had merely placed before me beautiful pictures of natural scenery. Scott does this still better than Wordsworth, and a very second-rate landscape does it more effectually than any poet. What made Wordsworth's poems a medicine for my state of mind, was that they expressed, not mere outward beauty, but states of feeling, and of thought coloured by feeling, under the excitement of beauty. They seemed to be the very culture of the feelings, which I was in quest of. In them I seemed to draw from a source of inward joy, of sympathetic and imaginative pleasure, which could be shared in by all human beings; which had no connexion with struggle or imperfection, but would be made richer by every improvement in the physical or social condition of mankind. From them I seemed to learn what would be the perennial sources of happiness, when all the greater evils of life shall have been removed. And I felt myself at once better and happier as I came under their influence. There have certainly been, even in our own age, greater poets than Wordsworth; but poetry of deeper and loftier feeling could not have done for me at that time what his did. I needed to be made to feel that there was real, permanent happiness in tranquil contemplation. Wordsworth taught me this, not only without turning away from, but with a greatly increased interest in the common feelings and common destiny of human beings. And the delight which these poems gave me, proved that with culture of this sort, there was nothing to dread from the most confirmed habit of analysis. At the conclusion of the Poems came the famous Ode, falsely called Platonic, "Intimations of Immortality:" in which, along with more than his usual sweetness of melody and rhythm, and along with the two passages of grand imagery but bad philosophy so often quoted, I found that he too had had similar experience to mine; that he also had felt that the first freshness of youthful enjoyment of life was not lasting; but that he had sought for compensation, and found it, in the way in which he now was teaching me to find it. The result was that I gradually, but completely, emerged from my habitual depression, and was never again subject to it. I long continued to value Wordsworth less according to his intrinsic merits, than by the measure of what he had done for me. Compared with the greatest poets, he may be said to be the poet of unpoetical natures, possessed of quiet and contemplative tastes. But unpoetical natures are precisely those which require poetic cultivation. This cultivation Wordsworth is much more fitted to give, than poets who are intrinsically far more poets than he.—John Stuart Mill, *Autobiography*, 1873, Ch. 5

There had been a period of a few years, in my youth, when I worshipped Wordsworth. I pinned up his likeness in my room; and I could repeat his poetry by the hour. He had been of great service to me at a very important time of my life. By degrees, and especially for ten or twelve years before I saw him, I found more disappointment than pleasure when I turned again to his works,—feeling at once the absence of sound, accurate, weighty thought, and of genuine poetic inspiration. It is still an increasing wonder with me that he should ever have been considered a *philosophical* poet,—so remarkably as the very basis of philosophy is absent in him, and so thoroughly self-derived, self-conscious and subjective is what he himself mistook for philosophy. As to his poetic genius, it needs but to open Shelley, Tennyson, or even poor Keats, and any of our best classic English poets, to feel at once that, with all their truth and all their charm, few of Wordsworth's pieces are poems. As eloquence, some of them are very beautiful; and others are didactic or metaphysical meditations or speculations poetically rendered: but, to my mind, this is not enough to constitute a man a poet. A benefactor, to poetry and to society, Wordsworth undoubtedly was. He brought us back out of a wrong track into a right one;—out of a fashion of pedantry, antithesis and bombast, in which thought was sacrificed to sound, and common sense was degraded, where it existed, by being made to pass for something else. He taught us to say what we had to say in a way,—not only the more rational but the more beautiful; and, as we have grown more simple in expression, we have become more unsophisticated and clear-seeing and far-seeing in our observation of the scene of life, if not of life itself. These are vast services to have rendered, if no more can be claimed for the poet. In proportion to our need was the early unpopularity of the reform proposed; and in proportion to our gratitude, when we recognized our benefac-

tor, was the temporary exaggeration of his merits as a poet. His fame seems to have now settled in its proper level.—Harriet Martineau, *Autobiography*, ed. Maria Weston Chapman, 1877, Vol. 1, pp. 507–8

The *Excursion* and the *Prelude*, his poems of greatest bulk, are by no means Wordsworth's best work. His best work is in his shorter pieces, and many indeed are there of these which are of first-rate excellence. But in his seven volumes the pieces of high merit are mingled with a mass of pieces very inferior to them; so inferior to them that it seems wonderful how the same poet should have produced both. Shakespeare frequently has lines and passages in a strain quite false, and which are entirely unworthy of him. But one can imagine his smiling if one could meet him in the Elysian Fields and tell him so; smiling and replying that he knew it perfectly well himself, and what did it matter? But with Wordsworth the case is different. Work altogether inferior, work quite uninspired, flat and dull, is produced by him with evident unconsciousness of its defects, and he presents it to us with the same faith and seriousness as his best work. Now a drama or an epic fill the mind, and one does not look beyond them; but in a collection of short pieces the impression made by one piece requires to be continued and sustained by the piece following. In reading Wordsworth the impression made by one of his fine pieces is too often dulled and spoiled by a very inferior piece coming after it.

Wordsworth composed verses during a space of some sixty years; and it is no exaggeration to say that within one single decade of those years, between 1798 and 1808, almost all his really first-rate work was produced. A mass of inferior work remains, work done before and after this golden prime, imbedding the first-rate work and clogging it, obstructing our approach to it, chilling, not unfrequently, the high-wrought mood with which we leave it. To be recognised far and wide as a great poet, to be possible and receivable as a classic, Wordsworth needs to be relieved of a great deal of the poetical baggage which now encumbers him. To administer this relief is indispensable, unless he is to continue to be a poet for the few only,—a poet valued far below his real worth by the world.

There is another thing. Wordsworth classified his poems not according to any commonly received plan of arrangement, but according to a scheme of mental physiology. He has poems of the fancy, poems of the imagination, poems of sentiment and reflection, and so on. His categories are ingenious but farfetched, and the result of his employment of them is unsatisfactory. Poems are separated one from another which possess a kinship of subject or of treatment far more vital and deep than the supposed unity of mental origin which was Wordsworth's reason for joining them with others.

The tact of the Greeks in matters of this kind was infallible. We may rely upon it that we shall not improve upon the classification adopted by the Greeks for kinds of poetry; that their categories of epic, dramatic, lyric, and so forth, have a natural propriety, and should be adhered to. It may sometimes seem doubtful to which of two categories a poem belongs; whether this or that poem is to be called, for instance, narrative or lyric, lyric or elegiac. But there is to be found in every good poem a strain, a predominant note, which determines the poem as belonging to one of these kinds rather than the other; and here is the best proof of value of the classification, and of the advantage of adhering to it. Wordsworth's poems will never produce their due effect until they are freed from their present artificial arrangement, and grouped more naturally.

Disengaged from the quantity of inferior work which now obscures them, the best poems of Wordsworth, I hear many people say, would indeed stand out in great beauty, but they would prove to be very few in number, scarcely more than half a dozen. I maintain, on the other hand, that what strikes me with admiration, what establishes in my opinion Wordsworth's superiority, is the great and ample body of powerful work which remains to him, even after all his inferior work has been cleared away. He gives us so much to rest upon, so much which communicates his spirit and engages ours!

This is of very great importance. If it were a comparison of single pieces, or of three or four pieces, by each poet, I do not say that Wordsworth would stand decisively above Gray, or Burns, or Coleridge, or Keats, or Manzoni, or Heine. It is in his ampler body of powerful work that I find his superiority. His good work itself, his work which counts, is not all of it, of course, of equal value. Some kinds of poetry are in themselves lower kinds than others. The ballad kind is a lower kind; the didactic kind, still more, is a lower kind. Poetry of this latter sort counts, too, sometimes, by its biographical interest partly, not by its poetical interest pure and simple; but then this can only be when the poet producing it has the power and importance of Wordsworth, a power and importance which he assuredly did not establish by such didactic poetry alone. Altogether, it is, I say, by the great body of powerful and significant work which remains to him, after every reduction and deduction has been made, that Wordsworth's superiority is proved.—MATTHEW ARNOLD, "Preface" to *The Poems of Wordsworth*, 1879

I shall point out at once what is wanting and what is faulty in Wordsworth, the qualities which he lacks, and the imperfections which disfigure his poetry. Let us begin with the qualities lacking. No one acknowledges more fully than I do the injustice, not to say the absurdity, of asking a man for something else than he has chosen to give, or, worse still, reproaching him with not being somebody else, and not what nature has made him. Therefore, it is not as a reproach, nor even as a regret, that I examine what is wanting in Wordsworth; it is merely to characterize his genius better, to set his poetical physiognomy in stronger relief.

To great troubles of mind he was a stranger, and his nearest approaches to tender sentiment are the pieces to the memory of that Lucy whom he has himself described. As for political emotions, he had, like many others, hailed in the French Revolution the dawn of a new era for humanity. His sonnets bear witness to his wrath against the conqueror who dispelled his dreams, who put an end to the Venetian Republic and the independence of Switzerland, and who menaced England with invasion. There is nothing in all this which goes beyond respectable Liberalism and patriotism.

Let us then make up our minds not to expect from Wordsworth either that knowledge of the human heart which is given by life in the world, or that inner and dramatic working of passion which no man describes well unless he has been its victim, or those general views on history and society which are formed partly by study, partly by experience in public affairs. Our poet was as much a stranger to the harassings of thought as to those of ambition, to the pangs of love and of hatred as to the resignation at which men arrive when they have seen how small are the great things of this world. He has nothing of the sublime melancholy, the ardent inquiry, the audacious revolt in which the poetry of half a century ago delighted. Still less has he the mocking scepticism, the raillery now gay now bitter, which followed the "songs of despair." He will never rank with those who like Byron, disturb the soul; who like Heine, arm it with irony; or who like Goethe, calm it with the virtues of knowledge. Wordsworth is simply a hermit who has studied

nature much, and has constantly analyzed his own feelings. We could hardly call him a philosopher; his mind is too devoid of the element of reasoning and speculation. Even the name of thinker but half suits him: he is the contemplative man. —EDMOND SCHERER, "Wordsworth and Modern Poetry in England" (1882), *Essays on English Literature*, tr. George Saintsbury, 1891, pp. 199–201

It is easier to feel the strong personality of Wordsworth's poetry than to define critically in what it consists. I have suggested an approximate answer to this question, viz. that it consists—1st, in the unusually large number of qualities, intellectual and moral—qualities often not only remote from each other, but apparently opposed to each other—which are represented by his higher poetry; 2dly, in the absolute unity in which these various qualities are blended; and, 3dly, in the masterful moral strength which results from their *united* expression. This measureless strength was so deeply felt by Coleridge that in his *Friend* he describes Wordsworth's poetry as 'non verba sed tonitrua,' and elsewhere spoke of him as 'the Giant;' while admirers of a very different sort were but beginning to babble about the 'sweet simplicity' of his verse. Wordsworth did a signal injustice to his own poems when he classified them as poems of the 'Affections,' of the 'Fancy,' of the 'Imagination,' of 'Sentiment and Reflection.' There exist no poems which could less equitably be subjected to a classification so arbitrary. It but points to a partial truth, while it conceals one of primary importance. All of these faculties are doubtless found, though with diversities of proportion, in Wordsworth's poems; but they are commonly found in union, and they are found marshalled under the control of the highest poetic faculty, viz. the Imagination. *The Brothers*, 'A Farewell,' 'She dwelt among the untrodden ways,' 'Ruth,' nay, even 'Laodamia,' were classed among the 'Poems of the Affections;' but there was no reason why they should not have been equally classed among those of the 'Imagination,' to which, in his later editions, many poems were transferred. On the other hand, 'She was a phantom of delight,' 'Three years she grew in sun and shower,' 'A slumber did my spirit seal,' and 'Tintern Abbey,' were placed under the title, 'Poems of the Imagination:' but they might with equal justice have been referred to the category of the 'Affections;' while the 'Lines left upon a Seat in a Yew-Tree,' 'The Happy Warrior,' 'A Poet's Epitaph,' 'I heard a thousand blended notes,' and the 'Ode to Duty,' might as fitly have been classed with the poems of the 'Imagination' as with those of 'Sentiment and Reflection.' It is but in a few of Wordsworth's inferior poems, such as might have been written by his imitators, that the higher faculties and impulses are found in separation. In his best poetry the diverse elements of the human intellect and of the human heart are found, not only in a greater variety, but in a closer and more spiritual union, than in any other poetry of his time; and, from that union, rose the extraordinary largeness of character which belonged to it. That characteristic was felt by the discerning, even in his earlier day, when other poets were travelling over the world in search of sensational incidents or picturesque costume, while he seldom sought a theme except among the primary relations of humanity, and those influences of exterior nature by which human nature is moulded.—AUBREY DE VERE, "Remarks on the Personal Character of Wordsworth's Poetry" (1883), *Wordsworthiana*, ed. William Knight, 1889, pp. 148–50

Poet who sleepest by this wandering wave!
  When thou wast born, what birth-gift hadst thou then?
To thee what wealth was that the Immortals gave,
  The wealth thou gavest in thy turn to men?

Not Milton's keen, translunar music thine;
    Not Shakespeare's cloudless, boundless human view;
Not Shelley's flush of rose on peaks divine;
    Nor yet the wizard twilight Coleridge knew.

What hadst thou that could make so large amends
    For all thou hadst not and thy peers possessed,
Motion and fire, swift means to radiant ends?—
    Thou hadst, for weary feet, the gift of rest.

From Shelley's dazzling glow or thunderous haze,
    From Byron's tempest-anger, tempest-mirth,
Men turned to thee and found—not blast and blaze,
    Tumult of tottering heavens, but peace on earth.

Nor peace that grows by Lethe, scentless flower,
    There in white languors to decline and cease;
But peace whose names are also rapture, power,
    Clear sight, and love: for these are parts of peace.
            —WILLIAM WATSON, "Wordsworth's Grave,"
                1890

No one among his contemporaries was more deeply moved than was Wordsworth by the great events in France. The character of his mind fitted him in a peculiar degree for receiving the full influence of the French Revolution; the circumstances of his early life brought him near the vortex of the maelstrom; and that truth to his highest self, which it was a part of his very existence to retain,—that natural piety which bound his days each to each,—made it impossible that he should ever fling away from him as a worthless illusion the hopes and aspirations of his youth. Some readers of Wordsworth are misled in their judgment of the poet by the vulgar error that he was before all else tranquil, mild, gentle, an amiable pastoral spirit. He sang of the daisy and the celandine, the linnet and the lamb; and therefore he must have been always a serene, tender, benign contemplator of things that make for peace. There can be no greater mistake; at the heart of his peace was passion; his benignity was like the greensward upon a rocky hillside. As a boy, Wordsworth was violent and moody; in his early manhood he was stern, bold, worn by exhausting ardors. De Quincey observed that "the secret fire of a temperament too fervid" caused him to look older than his years. Above all, he was strong; and what disguises this fact from careless eyes is that Wordsworth's strength did not lie in a single part or province of his nature, that he brought his several powers into harmonious action, and that each power served to balance the others. Senses, intellect, emotions, imagination, conscience, will, were all of unusual vigor; but each helped the other, each controlled the other, each was to the other an impulse and a law. And thus an equilibrium was gained, resulting from a massive harmony of powers too commonly found among men of genius arrayed against one another in dangerous conflict. His senses were of unusual keenness; his eye lived on forms and colors, on light and shadow; his ear caught the finest differences of all homeless, wandering sounds; but the senses did not war against the spirit; they were auxiliar to higher powers, serving as scouts and intelligencers of the soul. His passions were of ample volume and of persistent force; indignation, wrath, stern joy, deep fears, boundless hopes, possessed him; but these were brought into the bondage of conscience, and became the ministers of love. His imaginative fervor again and again exhausted his physical strength; but the creative mood was balanced by a mood of wise passiveness; it was not the way with his imagination to start forth, as Shelley's imagination did, to create a world of its own upon some swift suggestion of beauty or delight; it rested on reality, brooded upon reality, coalesced with it, interpreted it. His visions and his desires were captured by his intellect, and were made substantial by a moral wisdom infused into them. His intellect did not operate singly and apart, but was vitalized by his passions. If he loved freedom with all the ardor of his soul, he loved order as well. If he hoped for the future with an indefatigable hope, he also reverenced the past. His will applied itself consciously and deliberately to the task of organizing his various faculties and supporting them in their allotted task during all the years of his self-dedication to the life poetic. Each power of his nature lived in and through every other power, and in the massive equilibrium which was the result, strength was masked by strength. And thus, having first effected an inward conciliation of the jarring elements of our humanity, he was enabled to become a reconciler for his age.—EDWARD DOWDEN, *The French Revolution and English Literature*, 1897, pp. 197–200

Works

LYRICAL BALLADS

The principal object ⟨. . .⟩ proposed in these Poems was to choose incidents and situations from common life, and to relate or describe them, throughout, as far as was possible in a selection of language really used by men, and, at the same time, to throw over them a certain colouring of imagination, whereby ordinary things should be presented to the mind in an unusual aspect; and, further, and above all, to make these incidents and situations interesting by tracing in them, truly though not ostentatiously, the primary laws of our nature: chiefly, as far as regards the manner in which we associate ideas in a state of excitement. Humble and rustic life was generally chosen, because, in that condition, the essential passions of the heart find a better soil in which they can attain their maturity, are less under restraint, and speak a plainer and more emphatic language; because in that condition of life our elementary feelings coexist in a state of greater simplicity, and, consequently, may be more accurately contemplated, and more forcibly communicated; because the manners of rural life germinate from those elementary feelings, and, from the necessary character of rural occupations, are more easily comprehended, and are more durable; and, lastly, because in that condition the passions of men are incorporated with the beautiful and permanent forms of nature. The language, too, of these men has been adopted (purified indeed from what appear to be its real defects, from all lasting and rational causes of dislike or disgust) because such men hourly communicate with the best objects from which the best part of language is originally derived; and because, from their rank in society and the sameness and narrow circle of their intercourse, being less under the influence of social vanity, they convey their feelings and notions in simple and unelaborated expressions. Accordingly, such a language, arising out of repeated experience and regular feelings, is a more permanent, and a far more philosophical language, than that which is frequently substituted for it by Poets, who think that they are conferring honour upon themselves and their art, in proportion as they separate themselves from the sympathies of men, and indulge in arbitrary and capricious habits of expression, in order to furnish food for fickle tastes, and fickle appetites, of their own creation.

I cannot, however, be insensible to the present outcry against the triviality and meanness, both of thought and language, which some of my contemporaries have occasionally introduced into their metrical compositions; and I acknowledge that this defect, where it exists, is more dishonourable to the Writer's own character than false refinement or arbitrary innovation, though I should contend at the same time, that it is far less pernicious in the sum of its consequences. From such verses the Poems in these volumes will be found distinguished at least by one mark of difference, that each of them has a worthy *purpose*. Not that I always began to write with a distinct purpose formally conceived; but habits of meditation have, I trust, so prompted and regulated my feelings, that my descriptions of such objects as strongly excite those feelings, will be found to carry along with them a *purpose*. If this opinion be erroneous, I can have little right to the name of a Poet. For all good poetry is the spontaneous overflow of powerful feelings: and though this be true, Poems to which any value can be attached were never produced on any variety of subjects but by a man who, being possessed of more than usual organic sensibility, had also thought long and deeply. For our continued influxes of feeling are modified and directed by our thoughts, which are indeed the representatives of all our past feelings; and, as by contemplating the relation of these general representatives to each other, we discover what is really important to men, so, by the repetition and continuance of this act, our feelings will be connected with important subjects, till at length, if we be originally possessed of much sensibility, such habits of mind will be produced, that, by obeying blindly and mechanically the impulses of those habits, we shall describe objects, and utter sentiments, of such a nature, and in such connection with each other, that the understanding of the Reader must necessarily be in some degree enlightened, and his affections strengthened and purified.—WILLIAM WORDS-WORTH, "Preface" to *Lyrical Ballads* (1798), 1800

It is always worth while to linger over the starting-point of a poet's work. This comes, with Wordsworth, just at the end of the eighteenth century. In 1798, he and Coleridge published the tiny volume of *Lyrical Ballads*.

This little book was to the poetic revolution what the taking of the Bastille was to the historic movement: shock, challenge, manifesto. It was far more than this: it was the prophecy of the poetic achievement of an epoch. In that sad and obscure decade, as in a dark night, shrouded by storm-cloud, the poems shine like a pure, faint line of distant sky, holding the promise of the coming day. All the phases of modern poetry are suggested by them,—romanticism, alike external and spiritual, raised to the highest power in *The Ancient Mariner*; unflinching studies of bare fact in "Animal Tranquillity and Decay," and the little peasant-poems; poetry of mystical and philosophical contemplation in "Tintern Abbey." Romantic verse, realistic verse, reflective verse,— these were the three chief forms which our modern poetry was to develop. Much of Wordsworth's most exquisite work is in this little volume, work supreme in exalted simplicity, instinct with the buoyant, delicate vigor of a youth intensely sensitive yet ascetically pure.

Lyrical Ballads distills youthfulness; yet its authors were not very young. Keats at twenty-four had flung his passionate life away in song and love, Shelley at twenty-eight had but two more years to live, and Shelley and Keats alike take the world into their boyish confidence and grow up in public. Not so their more reticent elder brother. Wordsworth was twenty-eight when he published *Lyrical Ballads*. "Tintern Abbey" alone is enough to show us that the book is no outcome of earliest youth.

Traces of a present struggle are indeed to be found in these pages. In the poem, "The Female Vagrant," still more in that curious drama, *The Borderers*, an attempt now read only from literary interest, we have a glimpse of a strange Wordsworth

morbid and depressed, weighed down by the sorrows of life, drawn towards a diseased introspection and a study of psychological anomalies. In place of simplicity and serenity we have subtlety and unanswered questioning. The poems are still in the shadow of the agnosticism of disillusion. It is curious to read them, and to remember that many years later a Victorian poet was to resume the effort early abandoned by Wordsworth, to dwell with almost pathological interest upon the abnormal manifestations of character, and to adopt the dramatic rather than the contemplative method. But the century had a great deal to say before it was ready for a Browning. Wordsworth's false start was soon forgotten, even by himself, and he first gained the ear of the public and found his own soul in poetry simple as eternal childhood is simple, wise with the deep wisdom of utter peace.

But it is the peace of conquest, gravely pure. The light of spiritual victory, hardly won, rests upon it. All the early poems of Wordsworth shine with the radiance of a faith which has passed through death to victory and knows the glory of the Resurrection. It is impossible to describe the atmosphere of these brief, limpid, perfect poems—poems where a purely spiritual lustre seems to blend with the quiet light of common dawn. They are the expression of emotion recollected or better re-collected, in tranquillity. Their very simplicity, deeply sympathetic with the heart of childhood, is not of the natural child. It belongs to the new birth, the childhood of the Kingdom of Heaven. The contrast is evident, if we put beside Blake's "Infant Joy,"—the pure stammer of a natural baby,— Wordsworth's "We Are Seven,"—the tender bending of a soul that has suffered over the innocence of a child soul outside the ken of loss or pain. A chastened spirit; austere though youthful still, here speaks to us; and the buoyancy and living joy of the poetry are all the clearer because they shine through the limpid purity of lingering tears.

It is the faith in the new democracy that gives to the book its deepest pathos and fullest power. Symbolically rendered as a universal principle in *The Ancient Mariner*, this faith appears simple, earnest, and concrete in Wordsworth's studies of human life. Such brooding love of primal humanity is of an order never known before. The earlier dramatic method, the satiric method of the last century, are both as strange to the young Wordsworth as our own method of peering self-analysis. His attitude is all his own, a tender, reverent, direct contemplation of essential man. The old beggar and the child are his chosen subjects; creatures in whom not only interest of situation but interest of character have vanished or are reduced to lowest terms. Wordsworth watches from a distance which softens all that is distinctive into one common type, and blends the figure into unity with the wide world around. For it is man stripped more utterly than even Carlyle's Teufelsdröckh of all vesture of circumstance, who is dear to his spirit; man in whom the simple fact of absolute humanity shines forth in sacredness naked and supreme.

No boy could thus have written of human life. Wordsworth, when he wrote these poems, had known a great and definite experience. The passion, the tumult, the struggle of his life lay behind him and not before.—VIDA D. SCUDDER, "Wordsworth and New Democracy," *The Life of the Spirit in the Modern English Poets*, 1895, pp. 60–64

THE WHITE DOE OF RYLSTONE

The *White Doe* is not in season; venison is not liked in Edinburgh. It wants flavor; a good Ettrick wether is preferable. Wordsworth has more of the poetical character than any living writer, but he is not a man of first-rate intellect; his genius oversets him.—JOHN WILSON, Letter to James Hogg (1815), cited in Mary Gordon, *"Christopher North": A Memoir of John Wilson*, 1863, p. 130

This, we think, has the merit of being the very worst poem we ever saw imprinted in a quarto volume; and though it was scarcely to be expected, we confess, that Mr Wordsworth, with all his ambition, should so soon have attained to that distinction, the wonder may perhaps be diminished, when we state, that it seems to us to consist of a happy union of all the faults, without any of the beauties, which belong to his school of poetry. It is just such a work, in short, as some wicked enemy of that school might be supposed to have devised, on purpose to make it ridiculous; and when we first took it up, we could not help fancying that some ill-natured critic had taken this harsh method of instructing Mr Wordsworth, by example, in the nature of those errors, against which our precepts had been so often directed in vain. We had not gone far, however, till we felt intimately, that nothing in the nature of a joke could be so insupportably dull;—and that this must be the work of one who honestly believed it to be a pattern of pathetic simplicity, and gave it out as such to the admiration of all intelligent readers. In this point of view, the work may be regarded as curious at least, if not in some degree interesting; and, at all events, it must be instructive to be made aware of the excesses into which superior understandings may be betrayed, by long self-indulgence, and the strange extravagances into which they may run, when under the influence of that intoxication which is produced by unrestrained admiration of themselves. This poetical intoxication, indeed, to pursue the figure a little farther, seems capable of assuming as many forms as the vulgar one which arises from wine; and it appears to require as delicate a management to make a man a good poet by the help of the one, as to make him a good companion by means of the other. In both cases, a little mistake as to the dose or the quality of the inspiring fluid may make him absolutely outrageous, or lull him over into the most profound stupidity, instead of brightening up the hidden stores of his genius: And truly we are concerned to say, that Mr Wordsworth seems hitherto to have been unlucky in the choice of his liquor—or of his bottle holder. In some of his odes and ethic exhortations, he was exposed to the public in a state of incoherent rapture and glorious delirium, to which we think we have seen a parallel among the humbler lovers of jollity. In the *Lyrical Ballads*, he was exhibited, on the whole, in a vein of very pretty deliration; but in the poem before us, he appears in a state of low and maudlin imbecility, which would not have misbecome Master Silence himself, in the close of a social day. Whether this unhappy result is to be ascribed to any adulteration of his Castalian cups, or to the unlucky choice of his company over them, we cannot presume to say. It may be, that he has dashed his Hippocrene with too large an infusion of lake water, or assisted its operation too exclusively by the study of the ancient historical ballads of 'the north countrie.' That there are palpable imitations of the style and manner of those venerable compositions in the work before us, is indeed undeniable; but it unfortunately happens, that while the hobbling versification, the mean diction, and flat stupidity of these models are very exactly copied, and even improved upon, in this imitation, their rude energy, manly simplicity, and occasional felicity of expression, have totally disappeared; and, instead of them, a large allowance of the author's own metaphysical sensibility, and mystical wordiness, is forced into an unnatural combination with the borrowed beauties which have just been mentioned.—FRANCIS, LORD JEFFREY, "Wordsworth's *White Doe*," *Edinburgh Review*, Oct. 1815, pp. 355–56

What is it that gives to it its chief power and charm? Is it not the imaginative use which the poet has made of the White Doe? With her appearance the poem opens, with her reappearance it closes. And the passages in which she is introduced are radiant with the purest light of poetry. A mere floating tradition she was, which the historian of Craven had preserved. How much does the poet bring out of how little! It was a high stroke of genius to seize on this slight traditionary incident, and make it the organ of so much. What were the objects which he had to describe and blend into one harmonious whole? They were these:

1. The last expiring gleam of feudal chivalry, ending in the ruin of an ancient race, and the desolation of an ancestral home.

2. The sole survivor, purified and exalted by the sufferings she had to undergo.

3. The pathos of the decaying sanctities of Bolton, after wrong and outrage, abandoned to the healing of nature and time.

4. Lastly, the beautiful scenery of pastoral Wharfdale, and of the fells around Bolton, which blends so well with these affecting memories.

All these were before him—they had melted into his imagination, and waited to be woven into one harmonious creation. He takes the White Doe, and makes her the exponent, the symbol, the embodiment of them all. The one central aim—to represent the beatification of the heroine—how was this to be attained? Had it been a drama, the poet would have made the heroine give forth in speeches her hidden mind and character. But this was a romantic narrative. Was the poet to make her soliloquize, analyze her own feelings, lay bare her heart in metaphysical monologue? This might have been done by some modern poets, but it was not Wordsworth's way of exhibiting character, reflective though he was. When he analyzes feelings they are generally his own, not those of his characters. To shadow forth that which is invisible, the sanctity of Emily's chastened soul, he lays hold of this sensible image—a creature, the purest, most innocent, most beautiful in the whole realm of nature—and makes her the vehicle in which he embodies the saintliness, which is a thing invisible. It is the hardest of all tasks to make spiritual things sensuous, without degrading them. I know not where this difficulty has been more happily met; for we are made to feel that, before the poem closes, the doe has ceased to be a mere animal, or a physical creature at all, but in the light of the poet's imagination has been transfigured into a heavenly apparition—a type of all that is pure, and affecting, and saintly. And not only the chastened soul of her mistress, but the beautiful Priory of Bolton, the whole vale of Wharf, and all the surrounding scenery, are illumined by the glory which she makes; her presence irradiates them all with a beauty and an interest more than the eye discovers. Seen through her as an imaginative transparency, they become spiritualized; in fact, she and they alike become the symbols and expression of the sentiment which pervades the poem—a sentiment broad and deep as the world. And yet, any one who visits these scenes in a mellow autumnal day, will feel that she is no alien or adventitious image, imported by the caprice of the poet, but one altogether native to the place, one which gathers up and concentrates all the undefined spirit and sentiment which lie spread around it. She both glorifies the scenery by her presence, and herself seems to be a natural growth of the scenery, so that it finds in

her its most appropriate utterance. This power of imagination to divine and project the very corporeal image, which suits and expresses the spirit of a scene, Wordsworth has many times shown. Notably, for instance, do those ghostly shapes, which might meet at noontide under the dark dome of the fraternal yews of Borrowdale, embody the feeling awakened when one stands there. But never perhaps has he shown this embodying power of imagination more felicitously than when he made the White Doe the ideal exponent of the scenery, the memories, and the sympathies which cluster around Bolton Priory.
—John Campbell Shairp, *"The White Doe of Rylstone,"* *Aspects of Poetry*, 1881, pp. 319–21

THE EXCURSION

The poem of The *Excursion* resembles that part of the country in which the scene is laid. It has the same vastness and magnificence, with the same nakedness and confusion. It has the same overwhelming, oppressive power. It excites or recalls the same sensations which those who have traversed that wonderful scenery must have felt. We are surrounded with the constant sense and superstitious awe of the collective power of matter, of the gigantic and eternal forms of nature, on which, from the beginning of time, the hand of man has made no impression. Here are no dotted lines, no hedge-row beauties, no box-tree borders, no gravel walks, no square mechanic inclosures; all is left loose and irregular in the rude chaos of aboriginal nature. The boundaries of hill and valley are the poet's only geography, where we wander with him incessantly over deep beds of moss and waving fern, amidst the troops of red-deer and wild animals. Such is the severe simplicity of Mr. Wordsworth's taste, that we doubt whether he would not reject a druidical temple, or time-hallowed ruin as too modern and artificial for his purpose. He only familiarises himself or his readers with a stone, covered with lichens, which has slept in the same spot of ground from the creation of the world, or with the rocky fissure between two mountains caused by thunder, or with a cavern scooped out by the sea. His mind is, as it were, coëval with the primary forms of things; his imagination holds immediately from nature, and 'owes no allegiance' but 'to the elements.'

The *Excursion* may be considered as a philosophical pastoral poem,—as a scholastic romance. It is less a poem on the country, than on the love of the country. It is not so much a description of natural objects, as of the feelings associated with them; not an account of the manners of rural life, but the result of the poet's reflections on it. He does not present the reader with a lively succession of images or incidents, but paints the outgoings of his own heart, the shapings of his own fancy. He may be said to create his own materials; his thoughts are his real subject. His understanding broods over that which is 'without form and void,' and 'makes it pregnant.' He sees all things in himself. He hardly ever avails himself of remarkable objects or situations, but, in general, rejects them as interfering with the workings of his own mind, as disturbing the smooth, deep, majestic current of his own feelings. Thus his descriptions of natural scenery are not brought home distinctly to the naked eye by forms and circumstances, but every object is seen through the medium of innumerable recollections, is clothed with the haze of imagination like a glittering vapour, is obscured with the excess of glory, has the shadowy brightness of a waking dream. The image is lost in the sentiment, as sound in the multiplication of echoes.

> And visions, as prophetic eyes avow,
> Hang on each leaf, and cling to every bough.

In describing human nature, Mr. Wordsworth equally shuns the common 'vantage-grounds of popular story, of striking incident, or fatal catastrophe, as cheap and vulgar modes of producing an effect. He scans the human race as the naturalist measures the earth's zone, without attending to the picturesque points of view, the abrupt inequalities of surface. He contemplates the passions and habits of men, not in their extremes, but in their first elements; their follies and vices, not at their height, with all their embossed evils upon their heads, but as lurking in embryo,—the seeds of the disorder inwoven with our very constitution. He only sympathises with those simple forms of feeling, which mingle at once with his own identity, or with the stream of general humanity. To him the great and the small are the same; the near and the remote; what appears, and what only is. The general and the permanent, like the Platonic ideas, are his only realities. All accidental varieties and individual contrasts are lost in an endless continuity of feeling, like drops of water in the ocean-stream! An intense intellectual egotism swallows up every thing. Even the dialogues introduced in the present volume are soliloquies of the same character, taking different views of the subject. The recluse, the pastor, and the pedlar, are three persons in one poet. We ourselves disapprove of these 'interlocutions between Lucius and Caius' as impertinent babbling, where there is no dramatic distinction of character. But the evident scope and tendency of Mr. Wordsworth's mind is the reverse of dramatic. It resists all change of character, all variety of scenery, all the bustle, machinery, and pantomime of the stage, or of real life,—whatever might relieve, or relax, or change the direction of its own activity, jealous of all competition. The power of his mind preys upon itself. It is as if there were nothing but himself and the universe. He lives in the busy solitude of his own heart; in the deep silence of thought. His imagination lends life and feeling only to 'the bare trees and mountains bare'; peoples the viewless tracts of air, and converses with the silent clouds!
—William Hazlitt, "Observations on Mr. Wordsworth's Poem the *Excursion*" (1814), *The Round Table*, 1817

November 21st.—In the evening I stepped over to Lamb, and sat with him from ten to eleven. He was very chatty and pleasant. Pictures and poetry were the subjects of our talk. He thinks no description in *The Excursion* so good as the history of the country parson who had been a courtier. In this I agree with him. But he dislikes *The Magdalen*, which he says would be as good in prose; in which I do *not* agree with him.

November 23rd.—This week I finished Wordsworth's poem. It has afforded me less intense pleasure on the whole, perhaps, than I had expected, but it will be a source of frequent gratification. The wisdom and high moral character of the work are beyond anything of the same kind with which I am acquainted, and the spirit of the poetry flags much less frequently than might be expected. There are passages which run heavily, tales which are prolix, and reasonings which are spun out, but in general the narratives are exquisitely tender. That of the courtier parson, who retains in solitude the feelings of high society, whose vigour of mind is unconquerable, and who, even after the death of his wife, appears able for a short time to bear up against desolation and wretchedness, by the powers of his native temperament, is most delightful. Among the discussions, that on Manufactories, in the eighth book, is admirably managed, and forms, in due subordination to the incomparable fourth book, one of the chief excellences of the poem. Wordsworth has succeeded better in light and elegant painting in this poem than in any other. His Hanoverian and

Jacobite are very sweet pictures.—HENRY CRABB ROBINSON, *Diary*, Nov. 21–23, 1814

Jeffrey I hear has written what his admirers call a *crushing* review of the *Excursion*. He might as well seat himself upon Skiddaw and fancy that he crushed the mountain. I heartily wish Wordsworth may one day meet with him, and lay him alongside, yard-arm and yard-arm in argument.—ROBERT SOUTHEY, Letter to Sir Walter Scott (Dec. 24, 1814)

> And Wordsworth, in a rather long 'Excursion'
>   (I think the quarto holds five hundred pages),
> Has given a sample from the vasty version
>   Of his new system to perplex the sages;
> 'Tis poetry—at least by his assertion,
>   And may appear so when the dog-star rages—
> And he who understands it would be able
> To add a story to the Tower of Babel.
> —GEORGE GORDON, LORD BYRON, "Dedication"
>   to *Don Juan*, 1819

⟨. . .⟩ he is the High Priest of Nature—or, to use his own words, or nearly so, he is the High Priest "in the metropolitan temple built by Nature in the heart of mighty poets." But has he—even he—ever written a Great Poem? If he has—it is not the *Excursion*. Nay—the *Excursion* is not a Poem. It is a series of Poems, all swimming in the light of poetry, some of them sweet and simple, some elegant and graceful, some beautiful and most lovely, some of "strength and state," some majestic, some magnificent, some sublime. But though it has an opening, it has no beginning; you can discover the middle only by the numerals on the page; and the most serious apprehensions have been very generally entertained that it has no end. While Pedlar, Poet, and Solitary breathe the vital air, may the *Excursion*, stop where it will, be renewed; and as in its present shape it comprehends but a Three Days' Walk, we have but to think of an Excursion of three weeks, three months, or three years, to feel the difference between a Great and a Long Poem. Then the life of man is not always limited to the term of threescore and ten years! What a Journal might it prove at last! Poetry in profusion till the land overflowed; but whether in one volume, as now, or in fifty, in future, not a Great Poem—nay, not a Poem at all—nor ever to be so esteemed, till the principles on which Great Poets build the lofty rhyme are exploded, and the very names of Art and Science smothered and lost in the bosom of Nature, from which they arose. —JOHN WILSON, "An Hour's Talk about Poetry," *Blackwood's Edinburgh Magazine*, Sept. 1831, pp. 477–78

I have just read *The Excursion*. In book viii, I think, occurs the celebrated line—

> Goes sounding on his dim and perilous way.

Surely I have read somewhere that that line was Coleridge's. Puzzled, I had recourse to Milton, but it was not there, however worthy of him. In *The Excursion* it is quite *in situ*, and there are no marks of quotation. Isn't this all terribly sciolistic? I ought to know these things, but I don't. By-the-bye, in reading *The Excursion* after a long interval, I feel so much how good it would have been for Wordsworth to have gone to Oxford. He is a thorough Cantab, has no philosophical vocabulary, and really rather bores one with his constant philosophizing, which is under difficulties and often only half intelligible. Some periods, all involved and crude of phrase, I can't construe.—T. E. BROWN, Letter to S. T. Irwin (Dec. 11, 1894)

THE PRELUDE

Friend of the wise! and Teacher of the Good!
Into my heart have I received that Lay

More than historic, that prophetic Lay
Wherein (high theme by thee first sung aright)
Of the foundations and the building up
Of a Human Spirit thou hast dared to tell
What may be told, to the understanding mind
Revealable; and what within the mind
By vital breathings secret as the soul
Of vernal growth, oft quickens in the heart
Thoughts all too deep for words!—

        Theme hard as high!
Of smiles spontaneous, and mysterious fears
(The first-born they of Reason and twin-birth),
Of tides obedient to external force,
And currents self-determined, as might seem,
Or by some inner Power; of moments awful,
Now in thy inner life, and now abroad,
When power streamed from thee, and thy soul received
The light reflected, as a light bestowed—
Of fancies fair, and milder hours of youth,
Hyblean murmurs of poetic thought
Industrious in its joy, in vales and glens
Native or outland, lakes and famous hills!
Or on the lonely high-road, when the stars
Were rising; or by secret mountain-streams,
The guides and the companions of thy way!

Of more than Fancy, of the Social Sense
Distending wide, and man beloved as man,
Where France in all her towns lay vibrating
Like some becalméd bark beneath the burst
Of Heaven's immediate thunder, when no cloud
Is visible, or shadow on the main.
For thou wert there, thine own brows garlanded,
Amid the tremor of a realm aglow,
Amid a mighty nation jubilant,
When from the general heart of human kind
Hope sprang forth like a full-born Deity!
—Of that dear Hope afflicted and struck down,
So summoned homeward, thenceforth calm and sure
From the dread watch-tower of man's absolute self,
With light unwaning on her eyes, to look
Far on—herself a glory to behold,
The Angel of the vision! Then (last strain)
Of Duty, chosen Laws controlling choice,
Action and joy!—An Orphic song indeed,
A song divine of high and passionate thoughts
To their own music chaunted!

        O great Bard!
Ere yet that last strain dying awed the air,
With stedfast eye I viewed thee in the choir
Of ever-enduring men. The truly great
Have all one age, and from one visible space
Shed influence! They, both in power and act,
Are permanent, and Time is not with them,
Save as it worketh for them, they in it.
Nor less a sacred Roll, than those of old,
And to be placed, as they, with gradual fame
Among the archives of mankind, thy work
Makes audible, a linkéd lay of Truth,
Of Truth profound a sweet continuous lay,
Not learnt, but native, her own natural notes!
Ah! as I listened with a heart forlorn,
The pulses of my being beat anew:
And even as Life returns upon the drowned,
Life's joy rekindling roused a throng of pains—
Keen pangs of Love, awakening as a babe
Turbulent, with an outcry in the heart;
And fears self-willed, that shunned the eye of Hope;

And Hope that scarce would know itself from Fear;
Sense of past Youth, and Manhood come in vain,
And Genius given, and Knowledge won in vain;
And all which I had culled in wood-walks wild,
And all which patient toil had reared, and all,
Commune with thee had opened out—but flowers
Strewed on my corse, and borne upon my bier
In the same coffin, for the self-same grave!

That way no more! and ill beseems it me,
Who came a welcomer in herald's guise,
Singing of Glory, and Futurity,
To wander back on such unhealthful road,
Plucking the poisons of self-harm! And ill
Such intertwine beseems triumphal wreaths
Strew'd before thy advancing!

Nor do thou,
Sage Bard! impair the memory of that hour
Of thy communion with my nobler mind
By pity or grief, already felt too long!
Nor let my words import more blame than needs.
The tumult rose and ceased: for Peace is nigh
Where Wisdom's voice has found a listening heart.
Amid the howl of more than wintry storms,
The Halcyon hears the voice of vernal hours
Already on the wing.

Eve following eve,
Dear tranquil time, when the sweet sense of Home
Is sweetest! moments for their own sake hailed
And more desired, more precious, for thy song,
In silence listening, like a devout child,
My soul lay passive, by thy various strain
Driven as in surges now beneath the stars,
With momentary stars of my own birth,
Fair constellated foam, still darting off
Into the darkness; now a tranquil sea,
Outspread and bright, yet swelling to the moon.

And when—O Friend! my comforter and guide!
Strong in thyself, and powerful to give strength!—
Thy long sustainéd Song finally closed,
And thy deep voice had ceased—yet thou thyself
Wert still before my eyes, and round us both
That happy vision of belovéd faces—
Scarce conscious, and yet conscious of its close
I sate, my being blended in one thought
(Thought was it? or aspiration? or resolve?)
Absorbed, yet hanging still upon the sound—
And when I rose, I found myself in prayer.
    —SAMUEL TAYLOR COLERIDGE, "To William
        Wordsworth, Composed on the Night after His
        Recitation of a Poem on the Growth of an
        Individual Mind," 1807

I brought home, and read, the *Prelude*. It is a poorer *Excursion*;
the same sort of faults and beauties; but the faults greater and
the beauties fainter, both in themselves and because faults are
always made more offensive, and beauties less pleasing, by
repetition. The story is the old story. There are the old raptures
about mountains and cataracts; the old flimsy philosophy
about the effect of scenery on the mind; the old crazy, mystical
metaphysics; the endless wildernesses of dull, flat, prosaic
twaddle; and here and there fine descriptions and energetic
declamations interspersed. The story of the French Revolution, and of its influence on the character of a young
enthusiast, is told again at greater length, and with less force
and pathos, than in the *Excursion*. The poem is to the last
degree Jacobinical, indeed Socialist. I understand perfectly
why Wordsworth did not choose to publish it in his life-time.

—THOMAS BABINGTON MACAULAY, *Journal* (July 28, 1850),
cited in G. Otto Trevelyan, *The Life and Letters of Lord
Macaulay*, 1876, Vol. 2, pp. 238–39

Already Wordsworth's minor poems had dealt almost entirely
with his own feelings, and with the objects actually before his
eyes; and it was at Goslar that he planned, and on the day of his
quitting Goslar that he began, a much longer poem, whose
subject was to be still more intimately personal, being the
development of his own mind. This poem, dedicated to
Coleridge, and written in the form of a confidence bestowed on
an intimate friend, was finished in 1805, but was not published
till after the poet's death. Mrs. Wordsworth then named it *The
Prelude*, indicating thus the relation which it bears to the
Excursion—or, rather, to the projected poem of the *Recluse*, of
which the *Excursion* was to form only the Second out of three
Divisions. One Book of the First Division of the *Recluse* was
written, but is yet unpublished; the Third Division was never
even begun, and "the materials," we are told, "of which it
would have been formed have been incorporated, for the most
part, in the author's other publications." Nor need this change
of plan be regretted: didactic poems admit easily of mutilation;
and all that can be called plot in this series of works is
contained in the *Prelude*, in which we see Wordsworth arriving
at those convictions which in the *Excursion* he pauses to
expound.

It would be too much to say that Wordsworth has been
wholly successful in the attempt—for such the *Prelude* virtually
is—to write an epic poem on his own education. Such a poem
must almost necessarily appear tedious and egoistic, and
Wordsworth's manner has not tact enough to prevent these
defects from being felt to the full. On the contrary, in his
constant desire frugally to extract, as it were, its full teaching
from the minutest event which has befallen him, he supplements the self-complacency of the autobiographer with the
conscientious exactness of the moralist, and is apt to insist on
trifles such as lodge in the corners of every man's memory, as
if they were unique lessons vouchsafed to himself alone.

Yet it follows from this very temper of mind that there is
scarcely any autobiography which we can read with such
implicit confidence as the *Prelude*. In the case of this, as of so
many of Wordsworth's productions, our first dissatisfaction at
the form which the poem assumes yields to a recognition of its
fitness to express precisely what the poet intends. Nor are there
many men who, in recounting the story of their own lives,
could combine a candour so absolute with so much dignity;
who could treat their personal history so impartially as a means
of conveying lessons of general truth; or who, while chronicling such small things, could remain so great. The *Prelude* is
a book of good augury for human nature. We feel in reading it
as if the stock of mankind were sound. The soul seems going on
from strength to strength by the mere development of her
inborn power. And the scene with which the poem at once
opens and concludes—the return to the Lake country as to a
permanent and satisfying home—places the poet at last amid
his true surroundings, and leaves us to contemplate him as
completed by a harmony without him, which he of all men
most needed to evoke the harmony within.—F. W. H. MYERS,
Wordsworth, 1881, pp. 36–37

WILLIAM WORDSWORTH
Letter to Lady Beaumont
May 21, 1807

Though I am to see you so soon I cannot but write a word or two, to thank you for the interest you take in my Poems as evinced by your solicitude about their immediate reception. I write partly to thank you for this and to express the pleasure it has given me, and partly to remove any uneasiness from your mind which the disappointments you sometimes meet with in this labour of love may occasion. I see that you have many battles to fight for me; more than in the ardour and confidence of your pure and elevated mind you had ever thought of being summoned to; but be assured that this opposition is nothing more than what I distinctly foresaw that you and my other Friends would have to encounter. I say this, not to give myself credit for an eye of prophecy, but to allay any vexatious thoughts on my account which this opposition may have produced in you. It is impossible that any expectations can be lower than mine concerning the immediate effect of this little work upon what is called the Public. I do not here take into consideration the envy and malevolence, and all the bad passions which always stand in the way of a work of any merit from a living Poet; but merely think of the pure absolute honest ignorance, in which all worldlings of every rank and situation must be enveloped, with respect to the thoughts, feelings, and images, on which the life of my Poems depends. The things which I have taken, whether from within or without,—what have they to do with routs, dinners, morning calls, hurry from door to door, from street to street, on foot or in Carriage; with Mr. Pitt or Mr. Fox, Mr. Paul or Sir Francis Burdett, the Westminster Election or the Borough of Honiton; in a word, for I cannot stop to make my way through the hurry of images that present themselves to me, what have they to do with endless talking about things nobody cares anything for except as far as their own vanity is concerned, and this with persons they care nothing for but as their vanity or *selfishness* is concerned; what have they to do (to say all at once) with a life without love? in such a life there can be no thought; for we have no thought (save thoughts of pain) but as far as we have love and admiration. It is an awful truth, that there neither is, nor can be, any genuine enjoyment of Poetry among nineteen out of twenty of those persons who live, or wish to live, in the broad light of the world—among those who either are, or are striving to make themselves, people of consideration in society. This is a truth, and an awful one, because to be incapable of a feeling of Poetry in my sense of the word is to be without love of human nature and reverence for God.

Upon this I shall insist elsewhere; at present let me confine myself to my object, which is to make you, my dear Friend, as easy-hearted as myself with respect to these Poems. Trouble not yourself upon their present reception; of what moment is that compared with what I trust is their destiny, to console the afflicted, to add sunshine to daylight by making the happy happier, to teach the young and the gracious of every age, to see, to think and feel, and therefore to become more actively and securely virtuous; this is their office, which I trust they will faithfully perform long after we (that is, all that is mortal of us) are mouldered in our graves. I am well aware how far it would seem to many I overrate my own exertions when I speak in this way, in direct connection with the Volumes I have just made public.

I am not, however, afraid of such censure, insignificant as probably the majority of those poems would appear to very respectable persons; I do not mean London wits and witlings, for these have too many bad passions about them to be respectable even if they had more intellect than the benign laws of providence will allow to such a heartless existence as theirs is; but grave, kindly-natured, worthy persons, who would be pleased if they could. I hope that these Volumes are not without some recommendations, even for Readers of this class, but their imagination has slept; and the voice which is the voice of my Poetry without Imagination cannot be heard.

Leaving these, I was going to say a word to such Readers as Mr. Rogers. Such!—how would he be offended if he knew I considered him only as a representative of a class, and not as unique! 'Pity,' says Mr. R., 'that so many trifling things should be admitted to obstruct the view of those that have merit;' now, let this candid judge take, by way of example, the sonnets, which, probably, with the exception of two or three other Poems for which I will not contend appear to him the most trifling, as they are the shortest, I would say to him, omitting things of higher consideration, there is one thing which must strike you at once if you will only read these poems,—that those to Liberty, at least, have a connection with, or a bearing upon, each other, and therefore, if individually they want weight, perhaps, as a Body, they may not be so deficient, at least this ought to induce you to suspend your judgement, and qualify it so far as to allow that the writer aims at least at comprehensiveness. But dropping this, I would boldly say at once, that these Sonnets, while they each fix the attention upon some important sentiment separately considered, do at the same time collectively make a Poem on the subject of Civil Liberty and national independence, which, either for simplicity of style or grandeur of moral sentiment, is, alas! likely to have few parallels in the Poetry of the present day. Again, turn to the 'Moods of my own Mind'. There is scarcely a Poem here of above thirty Lines, and very trifling these poems will appear to many; but, omitting to speak of them individually, do they not, taken collectively, fix the attention upon a subject eminently poetical, viz., the interest which objects in nature derive from the predominance of certain affections more or less permanent, more or less capable of salutary renewal in the mind of the being contemplating these objects? This is poetic, and essentially poetic, and why? because it is creative.

But I am wasting words, for it is nothing more than you know, and if said to those for whom it is intended, it would not be understood.

I see by your last Letter that Mrs. Fermor has entered into the spirit of these 'Moods of my own Mind.' Your transcript from her Letter gave me the greatest pleasure; but I must say that even she has something yet to receive from me. I say this with confidence, from her thinking that I have fallen below myself in the Sonnet beginning—'With ships the sea was sprinkled far and nigh.' As to the other which she objects to, I will only observe that there is a misprint in the last line but two, 'And *though* this wilderness' for 'And *through* this wilderness'—that makes it unintelligible. This latter Sonnet for many reasons, though I do not abandon it, I will not now speak of; but upon the other, I could say something important in conversation, and will attempt now to illustrate it by a comment which I feel will be very inadequate to convey my meaning. There is scarcely one of my Poems which does not aim to direct the attention to some moral sentiment, or to some general principle, or law of thought, or of our intellectual constitution. For instance in the present case, who is there that has not felt that the mind can have no rest among a multitude of objects, of which it either cannot make one whole, or from which it cannot single out one individual, whereupon may be concentrated the attention divided among or distracted by a multitude? After a certain time we must either select one image or object, which must put out of view the rest wholly, or must subordinate them to itself while it stands forth as a Head:

> Now glowed the firmament
> With living sapphires! Hesperus, that *led*
> The starry host, rode brightest; till the Moon,
> Rising in clouded majesty, at length,
> Apparent *Queen*, unveiled *her peerless* light,
> And o'er the dark her silver mantle threw.

Having laid this down as a general principle, take the case before us. I am represented in the Sonnet as casting my eyes over the sea, sprinkled with a multitude of Ships, like the heavens with stars, my mind may be supposed to float up and down among them in a kind of dreamy indifference with respect either to this or that one, only in a pleasurable state of feeling with respect to the whole prospect. 'Joyously it showed,' this continued till that feeling may be supposed to have passed away, and a kind of comparative listlessness or apathy to have succeeded, as at this line, 'Some veering up and down, one knew not why.' All at once, while I am in this state, comes forth an object, an individual, and my mind, sleepy and unfixed, is awakened and fastened in a moment. 'Hesperus, that *led* The starry host,' is a poetical object, because the glory of his own Nature gives him the pre-eminence the moment he appears; he calls forth the poetic faculty, receiving its exertions as a tribute; but this Ship in the Sonnet may, in a manner still more appropriate, be said to come upon a mission of the poetic Spirit, because in its own appearance and attributes it is barely sufficiently distinguished to rouse the creative faculty of the human mind; to exertions at all times welcome, but doubly so when they come upon us when in a state of remissness. The mind being once fixed and rouzed, all the rest comes from itself; it is merely a lordly Ship, nothing more:

> This ship was nought to me, nor I to her,
> Yet I pursued her with a lover's look.

My mind wantons with grateful joy in the exercise of its own powers, and, loving its own creation,

> This ship to all the rest I did prefer,

making her a sovereign or a regent, and thus giving body and life to all the rest; mingling up this idea with fondness and praise—

> where she comes the winds must stir;

and concluding the whole with

> On went She, and due north her journey took.

Thus taking up again the Reader with whom I began, letting him know how long I must have watched this favorite Vessel, and inviting him to rest his mind as mine is resting.

Having said so much upon a mere 14 lines, which Mrs. Fermor did not approve, I cannot but add a word or two upon my satisfaction in finding that my mind has so much in common with hers, and that we participate so many of each other's pleasures. I collect this from her having singled out the two little Poems, the Daffodils, and the Rock crowned with snowdrops. I am sure that whoever is much pleased with either of these quiet and tender delineations must be fitted to walk through the recesses of my poetry with delight, and will there recognise, at every turn, something or other in which, and over which, it has that property and right which knowledge and love confer. The line, 'Come, blessed barrier, etc.,' in the sonnet upon Sleep, which Mrs. F. points out, had before been mentioned to me by Coleridge, and indeed by almost everybody who had heard it, as eminently beautiful. My letter (as this 2nd sheet, which I am obliged to take, admonishes me) is growing to an enormous length; and yet, saving that I have expressed my calm confidence that these Poems will live, I have said nothing which has a particular application to the object of it, which was to remove all disquiet from your mind on account of the condemnation they may at present incur from that portion of my contemporaries who are called the Public. I am sure, my dear Lady Beaumont, if you attach any importance it can only be from an apprehension that it may affect me, upon which I have already set you at ease, or from a fear that this present blame is ominous of their future or final destiny. If this be the case, your tenderness for me betrays you; be assured that the decision of these persons has nothing to do with the Question; they are altogether incompetent judges. These people in the senseless hurry of their idle lives do not *read* books, they merely snatch a glance at them that they may talk about them. And even if this were not so, never forget what I believe was observed to you by Coleridge, that every great and original writer, in proportion as he is great or original, must himself create the taste by which he is to be relished; he must teach the art by which he is to be seen; this, in a certain degree, even to all persons, however wise and pure may be their lives, and however unvitiated their taste; but for those who dip into books in order to give an opinion of them, or talk about them to take up an opinion—for this multitude of unhappy, and misguided, and misguiding beings, an entire regeneration must be produced; and if this be possible, it must be a work *of time*. To conclude, my ears are stone-dead to this idle buzz, and my flesh as insensible as iron to these petty stings; and after what I have said I am sure yours will be the same. I doubt not that you will share with me an invincible confidence that my writings (and among them these little Poems) will co-operate with the benign tendencies in human nature and society, wherever found; and that they will, in their degree, be efficacious in making men wiser, better, and happier. Farewell; I will not apologise for this Letter, though its length demands an apology. Believe me, eagerly wishing for the happy day when I shall see you and Sir George here, most affectionately yours,

Wm Wordsworth.

FRANCIS, LORD JEFFREY
From "Wordsworth's *Excursion*"
Edinburgh Review, November 1814, pp. 1–6, 29–30

This will never do. ⟨*The Excursion*⟩ bears no doubt the stamp of the author's heart and fancy; but unfortunately not half so visibly as that of his peculiar system. His former poems were intended to recommend that system, and to bespeak favour for it by their individual merit;—but this, we suspect, must be recommended by the system—and can only expect to succeed where it has been previously established. It is longer, weaker, and tamer, than any of Mr Wordsworth's other productions; with less boldness of originality, and less even of that extreme simplicity and lowliness of tone which wavered so prettily, in the *Lyrical Ballads*, between silliness and pathos. We have imitations of Cowper, and even of Milton here, engrafted on the natural drawl of the Lakers—and all diluted into harmony by that profuse and irrepressible wordiness which deluges all the blank verse of this school of poetry, and lubricates and weakens the whole structure of their style.

Though it fairly fills four hundred and twenty good quarto pages, without note, vignette, or any sort of extraneous assistance, it is stated in the title—with something of an imprudent candour—to be but 'a portion' of a larger work; and in the preface, where an attempt is rather unsuccessfully made to explain the whole design, it is still more rashly disclosed, that it is but 'a part of the second part of a *long* and laborious work'—which is to consist of three parts.

What Mr Wordsworth's ideas of length are, we have no means of accurately judging; but we cannot help suspecting that they are liberal, to a degree that will alarm the weakness of most modern readers. As far as we can gather from the preface, the entire poem—or one of them, for we really are not sure whether there is to be one or two—is of a biographical nature; and is to contain the history of the author's mind, and of the origin and progress of his poetical powers, up to the period when they were sufficiently matured to qualify him for the great work on which he has been so long employed. Now, the quarto before us contains an account of one of his youthful rambles in the vales of Cumberland, and occupies precisely the period of three days; so that, by the use of a very powerful *calculus*, some estimate may be formed of the probable extent of the entire biography.

This small specimen, however, and the statements with which it is prefaced, have been sufficient to set our minds at rest in one particular. The case of Mr Wordsworth, we perceive, is now manifestly hopeless; and we give him up as altogether incurable, and beyond the power of criticism. We cannot indeed altogether omit taking precautions now and then against the spreading of the malady;—but for himself, though we shall watch the progress of his symptoms as a matter of professional curiosity and instruction, we really think it right not to harass him any longer with nauseous remedies,—but rather to throw in cordials and lenitives, and wait in patience for the natural termination of the disorder. In order to justify this desertion of our patient, however, it is proper to state why we despair of the success of a more active practice.

A man who has been for twenty years at work on such matter as is now before us, and who comes complacently forward with a whole quarto of it after all the admonitions he has received, cannot reasonably be expected to 'change his hand, or check his pride,' upon the suggestion of far weightier monitors than we can pretend to be. Inveterate habit must now have given a kind of sanctity to the errors of early taste; and the very powers of which we lament the perversion, have probably become incapable of any other application. The very quantity, too, that he has written, and is at this moment working up for publication upon the old pattern, makes it almost hopeless to look for any change of it. All this is so much capital already sunk in the concern; which must be sacrificed if it be abandoned: and no man likes to give up for lost the time and talent and labour which he has embodied in any permanent production. We were not previously aware of these obstacles to Mr Wordsworth's conversion; and, considering the peculiarities of his former writings merely as the result of certain wanton and capricious experiments on public taste and indulgence, conceived it to be our duty to discourage their repetition by all the means in our power. We now see clearly, however, how the case stands;—and, making up our minds, though with the most sincere pain and reluctance, to consider him as finally lost to the good cause of poetry, shall endeavour to be thankful for the occasional gleams of tenderness and beauty which the natural force of his imagination and affections must still shed over all his productions,—and to which we shall ever turn with delight, in spite of the affectation and mysticism and prolixity, with which they are so abundantly contrasted.

Long habits of seclusion, and an excessive ambition of originality, can alone account for the disproportion which seems to exist between this author's taste and his genius; or for the devotion with which he has sacrificed so many precious gifts at the shrine of those paltry idols which he has set up for himself among his lakes and his mountains. Solitary musings, amidst such scenes, might no doubt be expected to nurse up the mind to the majesty of poetical conception,—(though it is remarkable, that all the greater poets lived, or had lived, in the full current of society):—But the collision of equal minds,—the admonition of prevailing impressions—seems necessary to reduce its redundancies, and repress that tendency to extravagance or puerility, into which the self-indulgence and self-admiration of genius is so apt to be betrayed, when it is allowed to wanton, without awe or restraint, in the triumph and delight of its own intoxication. That its flights should be graceful and glorious in the eyes of men, it seems almost to be necessary that they should be made in the consciousness that mens' eyes are to behold them,—and that the inward transport and vigour by which they are inspired, should be tempered by an occasional reference to what will be thought of them by those ultimate dispensers of glory. An habitual and general knowledge of the few settled and permanent maxims, which form the canon of general taste in all large and polished societies—a certain tact, which informs us at once that many things, which we still love and are moved by in secret, must necessarily be despised as childish, or derided as absurd, in all such societies—though it will not stand in the place of genius, seems necessary to the success of its exertions; and though it will never enable any one to produce the higher beauties of art, can alone secure the talent which does produce them, from errors that must render it useless. Those who have most of the talent, however, commonly acquire this knowledge with the greatest facility;—and if Mr Wordsworth, instead of confining himself almost entirely to the society of the dalesmen and cottagers, and little children, who form the subjects of his book, had condescended to mingle a little more with the people that were to read and judge of it, we cannot help thinking, that its texture would have been considerably improved: At least it appears to us to be absolutely impossible, that any one who had lived or mixed familiarly with men of literature and ordinary judgment in poetry, (of course we exclude the coadjutors and disciples of his own school), could ever have fallen into such gross faults, or so long mistaken them for beauties. His first essays we looked upon in a good degree as poetical paradoxes,—maintained experimentally, in order to display talent, and court notoriety;—and so maintained, with no more serious belief in their truth, than is usually generated by an ingenious and animated defence of other paradoxes. But when we find, that he has been for twenty years exclusively employed upon articles of this very fabric, and that he has still enough of raw material on hand to keep him so employed for twenty years to come, we cannot refuse him the justice of believing that he is a sincere convert to his own system, and must ascribe the peculiarities of his composition, not to any transient affectation, or accidental caprice of imagination, but to a settled perversity of taste or understanding, which has been fostered, if not altogether created, by the circumstances to which we have already alluded.

The volume before us, if we were to describe it very shortly, we should characterize as a tissue of moral and devotional ravings, in which innumerable changes are rung upon a few very simple and familiar ideas:—but with such an accompaniment of long words, long sentences, and unwieldy phrases—and such a hubbub of strained raptures and fantastical sublimities, that it is often extremely difficult for the most skilful and attentive student to obtain a glimpse of the author's meaning—and altogether impossible for an ordinary reader to conjecture what he is about. Moral and religious enthusiasm, though undoubtedly poetical emotions, are at the same time but dangerous inspirers of poetry; nothing being so apt to run into interminable dulness or mellifluous extravagance, without giving the unfortunate author the slightest intimation of his danger. His laudable zeal for the efficacy of his preachments, he very naturally mistakes for the ardour of poetical inspiration;—and, while dealing out the high words and glowing phrases which are so readily supplied by themes of this description, can scarcely avoid believing that he is eminently original and impressive:—All sorts of commonplace notions and expressions are sanctified in his eyes, by the sublime ends for which they are employed; and the mystical verbiage of the methodist pulpit is repeated, till the speaker entertains no doubt that he is the elected organ of divine truth and persuasion. But if such be the common hazards of seeking inspiration from those potent fountains, it may easily be conceived what chance Mr Wordsworth had of escaping their enchantment,—with his natural propensities to wordiness, and his unlucky habit of debasing pathos with vulgarity. The fact accordingly is, that in this production he is more obscure than a Pindaric poet of the seventeenth century; and more verbose 'than even himself of yore;' while the wilfulness with which he persists in choosing his examples of intellectual dignity and tenderness exclusively from the lowest ranks of society, will be sufficiently apparent, from the circumstance of his having thought fit to make his chief prolocutor in this poetical dialogue, and chief advocate of Providence and Virtue, *an old Scotch Pedlar*—retired indeed from business—but still rambling about in his former haunts, and gossiping among his old customers, without his pack on his shoulders. The other persons of the drama are, a retired military chaplain, who has grown half an atheist and half a misanthrope—the wife of an unprosperous weaver—a servant girl with her infant—a parish pauper, and one or two other personages of equal rank and dignity.

The character of the work is decidedly didactic; and more than nine tenths of it are occupied with a species of dialogue, or rather a series of long sermons or harangues which pass between the pedlar, the author, the old chaplain, and a worthy vicar, who entertains the whole party at dinner on the last day of their excursion. The incidents which occur in the course of it are as few and trifling as can be imagined;—and those which the different speakers narrate in the course of their discourses, are introduced rather to illustrate their arguments or opinions, than for any interest they are supposed to possess of their own.—The doctrine which the work is intended to enforce, we are by no means certain that we have discovered. In so far as we can collect, however, it seems to be neither more nor less than the old familiar one, that a firm belief in the providence of a wise and beneficent Being must be our great stay and support under all afflictions and perplexities upon earth—and that there are indications of his power and goodness in all the aspects of the visible universe, whether living or inanimate—every part of which should therefore be regarded with love and reverence, as exponents of those great attributes. We can testify, at least, that these salutary and important truths are inculcated at far greater length, and with more repetitions, than in any ten volumes of sermons that we ever perused. It is also maintained, with equal conciseness and originality, that there is frequently much good sense, as well as much enjoyment, in the humbler conditions of life; and that, in spite of great vices and abuses, there is a reasonable allowance both of happiness and goodness in society at large. If there be any

deeper or more recondite doctrines in Mr Wordsworth's book, we must confess that they have escaped us;—and, convinced as we are of the truth and soundness of those to which we have alluded, we cannot help thinking that they might have been better enforced with less parade and prolixity. His effusions on what may be called the physiognomy of external nature, or its moral and theological expression, are eminently fantastic, obscure, and affected.

⟨. . .⟩ Nobody can be more disposed to do justice to the great powers of Mr Wordsworth than we are; and, from the first time that he came before us, down to the present moment, we have uniformly testified in their favour, and assigned indeed our high sense of their value as the chief ground of the bitterness with which we resented their perversion. That perversion, however, is now far more visible than their original dignity; and while we collect the fragments, it is impossible not to lament the ruins from which we are condemned to pick them. If any one should doubt of the existence of such a perversion, or be disposed to dispute about the instances we have hastily brought forward, we would just beg leave to refer him to the general plan and the characters of the poem now before us.—Why should Mr Wordsworth have made his hero a superannuated Pedlar? What but the most wretched and provoking perversity of taste and judgment, could induce any one to place his chosen advocate of wisdom and virtue in so absurd and fantastic a condition? Did Mr Wordsworth really imagine, that his favourite doctrines were likely to gain any thing in point of effect or authority by being put into the mouth of a person accustomed to higgle about tape, or brass sleeve-buttons? Or is it not plain that, independent of the ridicule and disgust which such a personification must give to many of his readers, its adoption exposes his work throughout to the charge of revolting incongruity, and utter disregard of probability or nature? For, after he has thus wilfully debased his moral teacher by a low occupation, is there one word that he puts into his mouth, or one sentiment of which he makes him the organ, that has the most remote reference to that occupation? Is there any thing in his learned, abstracted, and logical harangues, that savours of the calling that is ascribed to him? Are any of their materials such as a pedlar could possibly have dealt in? Are the manners, the diction, the sentiments, in any, the very smallest degree, accommodated to a person in that condition? or are they not eminently and conspicuously such as could not by possibility belong to it? A man who went about selling flannel and pocket-handkerchiefs in this lofty diction, would soon frighten away all his customers; and would infallibly pass either for a madman, or for some learned and affected gentleman, who, in a frolic, had taken up a character which he was peculiarly ill qualified for supporting.

The absurdity in this case, we think, is palpable and glaring; but it is exactly of the same nature with that which infects the whole substance of the work—a puerile ambition of singularity engrafted on an unlucky predilection for truisms; and an affected passion for simplicity and humble life, most awkwardly combined with a taste for mystical refinements, and all the gorgeousness of obscure phraseology. His taste for simplicity is evinced, by sprinkling up and down his interminable declamations, a few descriptions of baby-houses, and of old hats with wet brims; and his amiable partiality for humble life, by assuring us, that a wordy rhetorician, who talks about Thebes, and allegorizes all the heathen mythology, was once a pedlar—and making him break in upon his magnificent orations with two or three awkward notices of something that he had seen when selling winter raiment about the country—or of the changes in the state of society, which had almost annihilated his former calling.

SAMUEL TAYLOR COLERIDGE
From Chapter 22
Biographia Literaria
1817

If Mr Wordsworth has set forth principles of poetry which his arguments are insufficient to support, let him and those who have adopted his sentiments be set right by the confutation of those arguments and by the substitution of more philosophical principles. And still let the due credit be given to the portion and importance of the truths which are blended with his theory: truths, the too exclusive attention to which had occasioned its errors by tempting him to carry those truths beyond their proper limits. If his mistaken theory has at all influenced his poetic compositions, let the effects be pointed out and the instances given. But let it likewise be shown how far the influence has acted; whether diffusively, or only by starts; whether the number and importance of the poems and passages thus infected be great or trifling compared with the sound portion; and lastly, whether they are inwoven into the texture of his works, or are loose and separable. The result of such a trial would evince beyond a doubt what it is high time to announce decisively and aloud, that the supposed characteristics of Mr Wordsworth's poetry, whether admired or reprobated; whether they are simplicity or simpleness; faithful adherence to essential nature or wilful selections from human nature of its meanest forms and under the least attractive associations: are as little the real characteristics of his poetry at large as of his genius and the constitution of his mind.

In a comparatively small number of poems he chose to try an experiment; and this experiment we will suppose to have failed. Yet even in these poems it is impossible not to perceive that the natural tendency of the poet's mind is to great objects and elevated conceptions. The poem entitled 'Fidelity' is for the greater part written in language as unraised and naked as any perhaps in the two volumes. Yet take the following stanza and compare it with the preceding stanzas of the same poem:

> There sometimes does a leaping fish
> Send through the tarn a lonely cheer;
> The crags repeat the raven's croak
> In symphony austere;
> Thither the rainbow comes—the cloud,
> And mists that spread the flying shroud;
> And sunbeams; and the sounding blast,
> That if it could would hurry past,
> But that enormous barrier holds it fast.

Or compare the four last lines of the concluding stanza with the former half:

> Yes, proof was plain that since the day
> On which the traveller thus had died,
> The dog had watched about the spot,
> Or by his master's side:
> *How nourished here for such long time*
> *He knows who gave that love sublime,*
> *And gave that strength of feeling, great*
> *Above all human estimate.*

Can any candid and intelligent mind hesitate in determining which of these best represents the tendency and native character of the poet's genius? Will he not decide that the one was written because the poet *would* so write, and the other because he could not so entirely repress the force and grandeur of his mind, but that he must in some part or other of every composition write otherwise? In short, that his only disease is

the being out of his element; like the swan, that having amused himself for a while with crushing the weeds on the river's bank soon returns to his own majestic movements on its reflecting and sustaining surface. Let it be observed that I am here supposing the imagined judge to whom I appeal to have already decided against the poet's theory, as far as it is different from the principles of the art generally acknowledged.

I cannot here enter into a detailed examination of Mr Wordsworth's works; but I will attempt to give the main results of my own judgement after an acquaintance of many years and repeated perusals. And though to appreciate the defects of a great mind it is necessary to understand previously its characteristic excellences, yet I have already expressed myself with sufficient fulness to preclude most of the ill effects that might arise from my pursuing a contrary arrangement. I will therefore commence with what I deem the prominent defects of his poems hitherto published.

The first characteristic, though only occasional defect, which I appear to myself to find in these poems is the inconstancy of the style. Under this name I refer to the sudden and unprepared transitions from lines or sentences of peculiar felicity (at all events striking and original) to a style not only unimpassioned but undistinguished. He sinks too often and too abruptly to that style which I should place in the second division of language, dividing it into the three species: first, that which is peculiar to poetry; second, that which is only proper in prose; and third, the neutral or common to both. There have been works, such as Cowley's essay on Cromwell, in which prose and verse are intermixed (not as in the Consolation of Boetius, or the Argenis of Barclay, by the insertion of poems supposed to have been spoken or composed on occasions previously related in prose, but) the poet passing from one to the other as the nature of the thoughts or his own feelings dictated. Yet this mode of composition does not satisfy a cultivated taste. There is something unpleasant in the being thus obliged to alternate states of feeling so dissimilar, and this too in a species of writing the pleasure from which is in part derived from the preparation and previous expectation of the reader. A portion of that awkwardness is felt which hangs upon the introduction of songs in our modern comic operas; and to prevent which the judicious Metastasio (as to whose exquisite taste there can be no hesitation, whatever doubts may be entertained as to his poetic genius) uniformly placed the aria at the end of the scene, at the same time that he almost always raises and impassions the style of the recitative immediately preceding. Even in real life the difference is great and evident between words used as the arbitrary marks of thought, our smooth market-coin of intercourse with the image and superscription worn out by currency, and those which convey pictures either borrowed from one outward object to enliven and particularize some other; or used allegorically to body forth the inward state of the person speaking; or such as are at least the exponents of his peculiar turn and unusual extent of faculty. So much so indeed, that in the social circles of private life we often find a striking use of the latter put a stop to the general flow of conversation, and by the excitement arising from concentered attention produce a sort of damp and interruption for some minutes after. But in the perusal of works of literary art we *prepare* ourselves for such language; and the business of the writer, like that of a painter whose subject requires unusual splendor and prominence, is so to raise the lower and neutral tints, that what in a different style would be the commanding colors are here used as the means of that gentle degradation requisite in order to produce the effect of a whole. Where this is not atchieved in a poem, the metre merely reminds the reader of his claims in order to disappoint them; and where this defect occurs frequently, his feelings are alternately started by anti-climax and hyperclimax. ⟨. . .⟩

The second defect I could generalize with tolerable accuracy if the reader will pardon an uncouth and new coined word. There is, I should say, not seldom a *matter-of-factness* in certain poems. This may be divided into, first, a laborious minuteness and fidelity in the representation of objects and their positions as they appeared to the poet himself; secondly, the insertion of accidental circumstances, in order to the full explanation of his living characters, their dispositions and actions: which circumstances might be necessary to establish the probability of a statement in real life, where nothing is taken for granted by the hearer, but appear superfluous in poetry, where the reader is willing to believe for his own sake. To this accidentality I object, as contravening the essence of poetry, which Aristotle pronounces to be σπουδαιότατον καὶ φιλοσοφώτατον γένος, the most intense, weighty and philo-sophical product of human art; adding, as the reason, that it is the most catholic and abstract. The following passage from Davenant's prefatory letter to Hobbes well expresses this truth: 'When I considered the actions which I meant to describe (those inferring the persons) I was again persuaded rather to choose those of a former age than the present; and in a century so far removed as might preserve me from their improper examinations who know not the requisites of a poem, nor how much pleasure they lose (and even the pleasures of heroic poesy are not unprofitable) who take away the liberty of a poet, and fetter his feet in the shackles of an historian. For why should a poet doubt in story to mend the intrigues of fortune by more delightful conveyances of probable fictions, because austere historians have entered into bond to truth; an obligation which were in poets as foolish and unnecessary as is the bondage of false martyrs, who lie in chains for a mistaken opinion. *But by this I would imply, that truth, narrative and past is the idol of historians (who worship a dead thing), and truth operative, and by effects continually alive, is the mistress of poets, who hath not her existence in matter, but in reason.*'

For this minute accuracy in the painting of local imagery, the lines in the *Excursion*, pp. 96, 97 and 98 may be taken, if not as a striking instance, yet as an illustration of my meaning. It must be some strong motive (as, for instance, that the description was necessary to the intelligibility of the tale) which could induce me to describe in a number of verses what a draftsman could present to the eye with incomparably greater satisfaction by half a dozen strokes of his pencil, or the painter with as many touches of his brush. Such descriptions too often occasion in the mind of a reader who is determined to understand his author a feeling of labour, not very dissimilar to that with which he would construct a diagram, line by line, for a long geometrical proposition. It seems to be like taking the pieces of a dissected map out of its box. We first look at one part, and then at another, then join and dove-tail them; and when the successive acts of attention have been completed, there is a retrogressive effort of mind to behold it as a whole. The poet should paint to the imagination, not to the fancy; and I know no happier case to exemplify the distinction between these two faculties. Masterpieces of the former mode of poetic painting abound in the writings of Milton, ex. gr.

> The fig-tree, not that kind for fruit renown'd,
> But such as at this day to Indians known
> In Malabar or Decan spreads her arms
> Branching so broad and long, that in the ground
> The bended twigs take root, *and daughters grow
> About the mother-tree, a pillar'd shade
> High over-arched, and* ECHOING WALKS BETWEEN:

> *There oft the Indian Herdsman shunning heat
> Shelters in cool, and tends his pasturing herds
> At loopholes cut through thickest shade.*
> 　　　　　　(Milton, *P.L.* 9, 1100.)

This is creation rather than painting, or if painting, yet such, and with such co-presence of the whole picture flash'd at once upon the eye, as the sun paints in a camera obscura. But the poet must likewise understand and command what Bacon calls the *vestigia communia* of the senses, the latency of all in each, and more especially as by a magical *penna duplex*, the excitement of vision by sound and the exponents of sound. Thus, 'the echoing walks between' may be almost said to reverse the fable in tradition of the head of Memnon in the Egyptian statue. Such may be deservedly entitled the *creative words* in the world of imagination.

The second division respects an apparent minute adher-ence to matter-of-fact in character and incidents; a biographi-cal attention to probability, and an anxiety of explanation and retrospect. Under this head I shall deliver, with no feigned diffidence, the results of my best reflection on the great point of controversy between Mr Wordsworth and his objectors; namely, on the choice of his characters. I have already declared, and I trust justified, my utter dissent from the mode of argument which his critics have hitherto employed. To their question, why did you chuse such a character, or a character from such a rank of life? the poet might, in my opinion, fairly retort: why with the conception of my character did you make wilful choice of mean or ludicrous associations not furnished by me but supplied from your own sickly and fastidious feelings? How was it indeed probable that such arguments could have any weight with an author whose plan, whose guiding principle and main object it was to attack and subdue that state of association which leads us to place the chief value on those things on which man differs from man, and to forget or disregard the high dignities which belong to human nature, the sense and the feeling which may be, and ought to be, found in all ranks? The feelings with which, as Christians, we contemplate a mixed congregation rising or kneeling before their common maker, Mr Wordsworth would have us entertain at all times, as men and as readers; and by the excitement of this lofty yet prideless impartiality in poetry, he might hope to have encouraged its continuance in real life. The praise of good men be his! In real life and, I trust, even in my imagination, I honor a virtuous and wise man, without reference to the presence or absence of artificial advantages. Whether in the person of an armed baron, a laurel'd bard, etc., or of an old pedlar, or still older leach-gatherer, the same qualities of head and heart must claim the same reverence. And even in poetry I am not conscious that I have ever suffered my feelings to be disturbed or offended by any thoughts or images which the poet himself has not presented.

But yet I object nevertheless, and for the following reasons. First, because the object in view, as an immediate object, belongs to the moral philosopher, and would be pursued not only more appropriately, but in my opinion with far greater probability of success, in sermons or moral essays than in an elevated poem. It seems, indeed, to destroy the main fundamental distinction, not only between a poem and prose, but even between philosophy and works of fiction, inasmuch as it proposes truth for its immediate object instead of pleasure. Now till the blessed time shall come when truth itself shall be pleasure, and both shall be so united as to be distinguishable in words only, not in feeling, it will remain the poet's office to proceed upon that state of association which actually exists as general; instead of attempting first to make it what it ought to be, and then to let the pleasure follow. But here is unfortunately a small *hysteron-proteron*. For the communication of pleasure is the introductory means by which alone the poet must expect to moralize his readers. Secondly: though I were to admit, for a moment, this argument to be groundless; yet how is the moral effect to be produced by merely attaching the name of some low profession to powers which are least likely, and to qualities which are assuredly not more likely, to be found in it? The poet, speaking in his own person, may at once delight and improve us by sentiments which teach us the independence of goodness, of wisdom, and even of genius, on the favors of fortune. And having made a due reverence before the throne of Antonine, he may bow with equal awe before Epictetus among his fellow-slaves—

> and rejoice
> In the plain presence of his dignity.

Who is not at once delighted and improved, when the *poet* Wordsworth himself exclaims,

> O many are the poets that are sown
> By Nature; men endowed with highest gifts,
> The vision and the faculty divine,
> Yet wanting the accomplishment of verse,
> Nor having e'er, as life advanced, been led
> By circumstance to take unto the height
> The measure of themselves, these favoured beings,
> All but a scattered few, live out their time,
> Husbanding that which they possess within,
> And go to the grave unthought of. Strongest minds
> Are often those of whom the noisy world
> Hears least.
>
> (*Excursion*, B.I.)

To use a colloquial phrase, such sentiments, in such language, do one's heart good; though I for my part have not the fullest faith in the *truth* of the observation. On the contrary I believe the instances to be exceedingly rare; and should feel almost as strong an objection to introduce such a character in a poetic fiction as a pair of black swans on a lake, in a fancy-landscape. When I think how many and how much better books than Homer, or even than Herodotus, Pindar or Eschylus, could have read, are in the power of almost every man, in a country where almost every man is instructed to read and write; and how restless, how difficulty hidden, the powers of genius are, and yet find even in situations the most favorable, according to Mr Wordsworth, for the formation of a pure and poetic language, in situations which ensure familiarity with the grandest objects of the imagination, but one Burns among the shepherds of Scotland, and not a single poet of humble life among those of *English* lakes and mountains; I conclude that Poetic Genius is not only a very delicate but a very rare plant.

But be this as it may, the feelings with which

> I think of Chatterton, the marvellous boy,
> The sleepless soul that perish'd in his pride:
> Of Burns, that walk'd in glory and in joy
> Behind his plough upon the mountain-side,

are widely different from those with which I should read a poem where the author, having occasion for the character of a poet and a philosopher in the fable of his narration, had chosen to make him a chimney-sweeper; and then, in order to remove all doubts on the subject, had invented an account of his birth, parentage and education, with all the strange and fortunate accidents which had concurred in making him at once poet, philosopher and sweep! Nothing but biography can justify this. If it be admissible even in a novel, it must be one in the manner of De Foe's, that were meant to pass for histories, not in the manner of Fielding's: in the life of Moll Flanders, or Colonel Jack, not in a Tom Jones or even a Joseph Andrews. Much less then can it be legitimately introduced in a poem, the characters of which, amid the strongest individualization, must still remain representative. The precepts of Horace, on this point, are grounded on the nature both of poetry and of the human mind. They are not more peremptory than wise and prudent. For in the first place a deviation from them perplexes the reader's feelings, and all the circumstances which are feigned in order to make such accidents less improbable divide and disquiet his faith, rather than aid and support it. Spite of all attempts, the fiction will appear, and unfortunately not as fictitious but as false. The reader not only knows that the sentiments and the language are the poet's own, and his own too in his artificial character, as poet; but by the fruitless endeavours to make him think the contrary he is not even suffered to forget it. The effect is similar to that produced by an epic poet when the fable and characters are derived from Scripture history, as in the *Messiah* of Klopstock, or in Cumberland's *Calvary*: and not merely suggested by it as in the *Paradise Lost* of Milton. That illusion, contradistinguished from delusion, that *negative* faith which simply permits the images presented to work by their own force, without either denial or affirmation of their real existence by the judgement, is rendered impossible by their immediate neighbourhood to words and facts of known and absolute truth. A faith which transcends even historic belief must absolutely put out this mere poetic analogon of faith, as the summer sun is said to extinguish our household fires when it shines full upon them. What would otherwise have been yielded to as pleasing fiction is repelled as revolting falsehood. The effect produced in this latter case by the solemn belief of the reader is in a less degree brought about in the instances to which I have been objecting, by the baffled attempts of the author to *make* him believe.

Add to all the foregoing the seeming uselessness both of the project and of the anecdotes from which it is to derive support. Is there one word, for instance, attributed to the pedlar in the *Excursion* characteristic of a pedlar? One sentiment that might not more plausibly, even without the aid of any previous explanation, have proceeded from any wise and beneficent old man of a rank or profession in which the language of learning and refinement are natural and to be expected? Need the rank have been at all particularized, where nothing follows which the knowledge of that rank is to explain or illustrate? When on the contrary this information renders the man's language, feelings, sentiments and information a riddle which must itself be solved by episodes of anecdote? Finally when this, and this alone, could have induced a genuine poet to inweave in a poem of the loftiest style, and on subjects the loftiest and of the most universal interest such minute matters of fact, not unlike those furnished for the obituary of a magazine by the friends of some obscure *ornament of society lately deceased* in some obscure town, as

> Among the hills of Athol he was born.
> There on a small hereditary farm,
> An unproductive slip of rugged ground,
> His father dwelt; and died in poverty:
> While he, whose lowly fortune I retrace,
> The youngest of three sons, was yet a babe,
> A little one—unconscious of their loss.
> But ere he had outgrown his infant days
> His widowed mother, for a second mate,
> Espoused the teacher of the village school;
> Who on her offspring zealously bestowed
> Needful instruction.

From his sixth year, the boy of whom I speak,
In summer tended cattle on the hills;
But through the inclement and the perilous days
Of long-continuing winter, he repaired
To his step-father's school, etc.

For all the admirable passages interposed in this narration might, with trifling alterations, have been far more appropriately and with far greater verisimilitude told of a poet in the character of a poet; and without incurring another defect which I shall now mention, and a sufficient illustration of which will have been here anticipated.

Third: an undue predilection for the dramatic form in certain poems, from which one or other of two evils result. Either the thoughts and diction are different from that of the poet, and then there arises an incongruity of style; or they are the same and indistinguishable, and then it presents a species of ventriloquism, where two are represented as talking while in truth one man only speaks.

The fourth class of defects is closely connected with the former; but yet are such as arise likewise from an intensity of feeling disproportionate to such knowledge and value of the objects described as can be fairly anticipated of men in general, even of the most cultivated classes; and with which therefore few only, and those few particularly circumstanced, can be supposed to sympathize: in this class I comprize occasional prolixity, repetition and an eddying instead of progression of thought. As instances, see pages 27, 28 and 62 of the *Poems*, vol. i, and the first eighty lines of the Sixth Book of the *Excursion*.

Fifth and last: thoughts and images too great for the subject. This is an approximation to what might be called *mental* bombast, as distinguished from verbal; for as in the latter there is a disproportion of the expressions to the thoughts, so in this there is a disproportion of thought to the circumstance and occasion. This, by the bye, is a fault of which none but a man of genius is capable. It is the awkwardness and strength of Hercules with the distaff of Omphale.

It is a well-known fact that bright colours in motion both make and leave the strongest impressions on the eye. Nothing is more likely too than that a vivid image or visual spectrum thus originated may become the link of association in recalling the feelings and images that had accompanied the original impression. But if we describe this in such lines, as

They flash upon that inward eye,
Which is the bliss of solitude!

in what words shall we describe the joy of retrospection when the images and virtuous actions of a whole well-spent life pass before that conscience which is indeed the inward eye: which is indeed 'the bliss of solitude'? Assuredly we seem to sink most abruptly, not to say burlesquely and almost as in a medley, from this couplet to

And then my heart with pleasure fills,
And dances with the *daffodils*.
(Vol. i. p. 320)

The second instance is from vol. ii., page 12, where the poet having gone out for a day's tour of pleasure meets early in the morning with a knot of gipsies, who had pitched their blanket-tents and straw beds, together with their children and asses, in some field by the road-side. At the close of the day on his return our tourist found them in the same place. 'Twelve hours,' says he,

Twelve hours, twelve bounteous hours are gone, while I
Have been a traveller under open sky,

Much witnessing of change and cheer,
Yet as I left I find them here!

Whereat the poet, without seeming to reflect that the poor tawny wanderers might probably have been tramping for weeks together through road and lane, over moor and mountain, and consequently must have been right glad to rest themselves, their children and cattle for one whole day; and overlooking the obvious truth that such repose might be quite as necessary for them as a walk of the same continuance was pleasing or healthful for the more fortunate poet; expresses his indignation in a series of lines, the diction and imagery of which would have been rather above than below the mark, had they been applied to the immense empire of China improgressive for thirty centuries:

The weary Sun betook himself to rest,—
Then issued Vesper from the fulgent west,
Outshining like a visible God,
The glorious path in which he trod!
And now ascending, after one dark hour,
And one night's diminution of her power,
Behold the mighty Moon! this way
She looks as if at them—but they
Regard not her:—oh, better wrong and strife,
Better vain deed or evil than such life!
The silent Heavens have goings-on:
The stars have tasks!—but these have none!

The last instance of this defect (for I know no other than these already cited), is from the 'Ode,' page 351, vol. ii, where, speaking of a child, 'a six years' darling of a pigmy size,' he thus addresses him:

Thou best philosopher, who yet dost keep
Thy heritage! Thou eye among the blind,
That, deaf and silent, read'st the eternal deep—
Haunted for ever by the eternal mind—
Mighty Prophet! Seer blest!
On whom those truths do rest,
Which we are toiling all our lives to find!
Thou, over whom thy immortality
Broods like the day, a master o'er the slave,
A presence which is not to be put by!

Now here, not to stop at the daring spirit of metaphor which connects the epithets 'deaf and silent' with the apostrophized eye: or (if we are to refer it to the preceding word *philosopher*) the faulty and equivocal syntax of the passage; and without examining the propriety of making a 'master *brood* o'er a slave,' or the day brood at all; we will merely ask, what does all this mean? In what sense is a child of that age a philosopher? In what sense does he read 'the eternal deep'? In what sense is he declared to be 'for ever haunted' by the Supreme Being? or so inspired as to deserve the splendid titles of a mighty prophet, a blessed seer? By reflection? by knowledge? by conscious intuition? or by any form or modification of consciousness? These would be tidings indeed; but such as would pre-suppose an immediate revelation to the inspired communicator and require miracles to authenticate his inspiration. Children at this age give us no such information of themselves; and at what time were we dipt in the Lethe, which has produced such utter oblivion of a state so godlike? There are many of us that still possess some remembrances, more or less distinct, respecting themselves at six years old; pity that the worthless straws only should float while treasures, compared with which all the mines of Golconda and Mexico were but straws, should be absorbed by some unknown gulf into some unknown abyss.

But if this be too wild and exorbitant to be suspected as having been the poet's meaning; if these mysterious gifts, faculties and operations are not accompanied with consciousness; who else is conscious of them? or how can it be called the child, if it be no part of the child's conscious being? For aught I know, the thinking spirit within me may be substantially one with the principle of life and of vital operation. For aught I know, it may be employed as a secondary agent in the marvellous organization and organic movements of my body. But surely it would be strange language to say that I construct my heart! or that I propel the finer influences through my nerves! or that I compress my brain, and draw the curtains of sleep round my own eyes! Spinoza and Behmen were on different systems both Pantheists; and among the ancients there were philosophers, teachers of the EN KAI ΠAN, who not only taught that God was All, but that this All constituted God. Yet not even these would confound the part, as a part, with the Whole, as the whole. Nay, in no system is the distinction between the individual and God, between the modification and the one only substance, more sharply drawn than in that of Spinoza. Jacobi indeed relates of Lessing that after a conversation with him at the house of the poet Gleim (the Tyrtaeus and Anacreon of the German Parnassus) in which conversation L. had avowed privately to Jacobi his reluctance to admit any personal existence of the Supreme Being, or the possibility of personality except in a finite Intellect, and while they were sitting at table a shower of rain came on unexpectedly. Gleim expressed his regret at the circumstance, because they had meant to drink their wine in the garden: upon which Lessing, in one of his half-earnest, half-joking moods, nodded to Jacobi and said, 'It is I, perhaps, that am doing that,' i.e. raining! and J. answered, 'Or perhaps I'; Gleim contented himself with staring at them both, without asking for any explanation.

So with regard to this passage. In what sense can the magnificent attributes above quoted be appropriated to a child, which would not make them equally suitable to a bee, or a dog, or a field of corn; or even to a ship, or to the wind and waves that propel it? The omnipresent Spirit works equally in them as in the child; and the child is equally unconscious of it as they. It cannot surely be that the four lines immediately following are to contain the explanation?

> To whom the grave
> Is but a lonely bed without the sense or sight
> Of day or the warm light,
> A place of thought where we in waiting lie.

Surely, it cannot be that this wonder-rousing apostrophe is but a comment on the little poem of 'We Are Seven'? that the whole meaning of the passage is reducible to the assertion that a child, who by the bye at six years old would have been better instructed in most Christian families, has no other notion of death than that of lying in a dark, cold place? And still, I hope, not as in a place of thought! not the frightful notion of lying awake in his grave! The analogy between death and sleep is too simple, too natural, to render so horrible a belief possible for children; even had they not been in the habit, as all Christian children are, of hearing the latter term used to express the former. But if the child's belief be only that 'he is not dead, but sleepeth,' wherein does it differ from that of his father and mother, or any other adult and instructed person? To form an idea of a thing's becoming nothing, or of nothing becoming a thing, is impossible to all finite beings alike, of whatever age and however educated or uneducated. Thus it is with splendid paradoxes in general. If the words are taken in the common sense, they convey an absurdity; and if, in contempt of dictionaries and custom, they are so interpreted as to avoid the absurdity, the meaning dwindles into some bald truism. Thus you must at once understand the words contrary to their common import, in order to arrive at any sense; and according to their common import, if you are to receive from them any feeling of sublimity or admiration.

Though the instances of this defect in Mr Wordsworth's poems are so few that for themselves it would have been scarcely just to attract the reader's attention toward them, yet I have dwelt on it, and perhaps the more for this very reason. For being so very few, they cannot sensibly detract from the reputation of an author who is even characterized by the number of profound truths in his writings which will stand the severest analysis; and yet few as they are, they are exactly those passages which his blind admirers would be most likely, and best able, to imitate. But Wordsworth, where he is indeed Wordsworth, may be mimicked by copyists, he may be plundered by plagiarists; but he cannot be imitated except by those who are not born to be imitators. For without his depth of feeling and his imaginative power his sense would want its vital warmth and peculiarity; and without his strong sense, his mysticism would become sickly— mere fog and dimness!

WILLIAM HAZLITT
From "Mr. Wordsworth"
The Spirit of the Age
1825

Mr. Wordsworth's genius is a pure emanation of the Spirit of the Age. Had he lived in any other period of the world, he would never have been heard of. As it is, he has some difficulty to contend with the hebetude of his intellect, and the meanness of his subject. With him 'lowliness is young ambition's ladder': but he finds it a toil to climb in this way the steep of Fame. His homely Muse can hardly raise her wing from the ground, nor spread her hidden glories to the sun. He has 'no figures nor no fantasies, which busy *passion* draws in the brains of men': neither the gorgeous machinery of mythologic lore, nor the splendid colours of poetic diction. His style is vernacular: he delivers household truths. He sees nothing loftier than human hopes; nothing deeper than the human heart. This he probes, this he tampers with, this he poises, with all its incalculable weight of thought and feeling, in his hands; and at the same time calms the throbbing pulses of his own heart, by keeping his eye ever fixed on the face of nature. If he can make the lifeblood flow from the wounded breast, this is the living colouring with which he paints his verse: if he can assuage the pain or close up the wound with the balm of solitary musing, or the healing power of plants and herbs and 'skyey influences,' this is the sole triumph of his art. He takes the simplest elements of nature and of the human mind, the mere abstract conditions inseparable from our being, and tries to compound a new system of poetry from them; and has perhaps succeeded as well as any one could. 'Nihil humani a me alienum puto'—is the motto of his works. He thinks nothing low or indifferent of which this can be affirmed: every thing that professes to be more than this, that is not an absolute essence of truth and feeling, he holds to be vitiated, false, and spurious. In a word, his poetry is founded on setting up an opposition (and pushing it to the utmost length) between the natural and the artificial; between the spirit of humanity, and the spirit of fashion and of the world!

It is one of the innovations of the time. It partakes of, and is carried along with, the revolutionary movement of our age:

the political changes of the day were the model on which he formed and conducted his poetical experiments. His Muse (it cannot be denied, and without this we cannot explain its character at all) is a levelling one. It proceeds on a principle of equality, and strives to reduce all things to the same standard. It is distinguished by a proud humility. It relies upon its own resources, and disdains external show and relief. It takes the commonest events and objects, as a test to prove that nature is always interesting from its inherent truth and beauty, without any of the ornaments of dress or pomp of circumstances to set it off. Hence the unaccountable mixture of seeming simplicity and real abstruseness in the *Lyrical Ballads*. Fools have laughed at, wise men scarcely understand them. He takes a subject or a story merely as pegs or loops to hang thought and feeling on; the incidents are trifling, in proportion to his contempt for imposing appearances; the reflections are profound, according to the gravity and the aspiring pretensions of his mind.

His popular, inartificial style gets rid (at a blow) of all the trappings of verse, of all the high places of poetry: 'the cloud-capt towers, the solemn temples, the gorgeous palaces,' are swept to the ground, and 'like the baseless fabric of a vision, leave not a wreck behind.' All the traditions of learning, all the superstitions of age, are obliterated and effaced. We begin *de novo*, on a *tabula rasa* of poetry. The purple pall, the nodding plume of tragedy are exploded as mere pantomime and trick, to return to the simplicity of truth and nature. Kings, queens, priests, nobles, the altar and the throne, the distinctions of rank, birth, wealth, power, 'the judge's robe, the marshal's truncheon, the ceremony that to great ones 'longs,' are not to be found here. The author tramples on the pride of art with greater pride. The Ode and Epode, the Strophe and the Antistrophe, he laughs to scorn. The harp of Homer, the trump of Pindar and of Alcæus are still. The decencies of costume, the decorations of vanity are stripped off without mercy as barbarous, idle, and Gothic. The jewels in the crisped hair, the diadem on the polished brow are thought meretricious, theatrical, vulgar; and nothing contents his fastidious taste beyond a simple garland of flowers. Neither does he avail himself of the advantages which nature or accident holds out to him. He chooses to have his subject a foil to his invention, to owe nothing but to himself. He gathers manna in the wilderness, he strikes the barren rock for the gushing moisture. He elevates the mean by the strength of his own aspirations; he clothes the naked with beauty and grandeur from the stores of his own recollections. No cypress grove loads his verse with funeral pomp: but his imagination lends 'a sense of joy

> To the bare trees and mountains bare,
> And grass in the green field.'

No storm, no shipwreck startles us by its horrors: but the rainbow lifts its head in the cloud, and the breeze sighs through the withered fern. No sad vicissitude of fate, no overwhelming catastrophe in nature deforms his page: but the dew-drop glitters on the bending flower, the tear collects in the glistening eye.

> Beneath the hills, along the flowery vales,
> The generations are prepared; the pangs,
> The internal pangs are ready; the dread strife
> Of poor humanity's afflicted will,
> Struggling in vain with ruthless destiny.

As the lark ascends from its low bed on fluttering wing, and salutes the morning skies; so Mr. Wordsworth's unpretending Muse, in russet guise, scales the summits of reflection, while it makes the round earth its footstool, and its home!

Possibly a good deal of this may be regarded as the effect of disappointed views and an inverted ambition. Prevented by native pride and indolence from climbing the ascent of learning or greatness, taught by political opinions to say to the vain pomp and glory of the world, 'I hate ye,' seeing the path of classical and artificial poetry blocked up by the cumbrous ornaments of style and turgid *commonplaces*, so that nothing more could be achieved in that direction but by the most ridiculous bombast or the tamest servility; he has turned back partly from the bias of his mind, partly perhaps from a judicious policy—has struck into the sequestered vale of humble life, sought out the Muse among sheep-cotes and hamlets and the peasant's mountain-haunts, has discarded all the tinsel pageantry of verse, and endeavoured (not in vain) to aggrandise the trivial and add the charm of novelty to the familiar. No one has shown the same imagination in raising trifles into importance: no one has displayed the same pathos in treating of the simplest feelings of the heart. Reserved, yet haughty, having no unruly or violent passions, (or those passions having been early suppressed,) Mr. Wordsworth has passed his life in solitary musing, or in daily converse with the face of nature. He exemplifies in an eminent degree the power of *association*; for his poetry has no other source or character. He has dwelt among pastoral scenes, till each object has become connected with a thousand feelings, a link in the chain of thought, a fibre of his own heart. Every one is by habit and familiarity strongly attached to the place of his birth, or to objects that recal the most pleasing and eventful circumstances of his life. But to the author of the *Lyrical Ballads*, nature is a kind of home; and he may be said to take a personal interest in the universe. There is no image so insignificant that it has not in some mood or other found the way into his heart: no sound that does not awaken the memory of other years.—

> To him the meanest flower that blows can give
> Thoughts that do often lie too deep for tears.

The daisy looks up to him with sparkling eye as an old acquaintance: the cuckoo haunts him with sounds of early youth not to be expressed: a linnet's nest startles him with boyish delight: an old withered thorn is weighed down with a heap of recollections: a grey cloak, seen on some wild moor, torn by the wind, or drenched in the rain, afterwards becomes an object of imagination to him: even the lichens on the rock have a life and being in his thoughts. He has described all these objects in a way and with an intensity of feeling that no one else had done before him, and has given a new view or aspect of nature. He is in this sense the most original poet now living, and the one whose writings could the least be spared: for they have no substitute elsewhere. The vulgar do not read them, the learned, who see all things through books, do not understand them, the great despise, the fashionable may ridicule them: but the author has created himself an interest in the heart of the retired and lonely student of nature, which can never die. Persons of this class will still continue to feel what he has felt: he has expressed what they might in vain wish to express, except with glistening eye and faultering tongue! There is a lofty philosophic tone, a thoughtful humanity, infused into his pastoral vein. Remote from the passions and events of the great world, he has communicated interest and dignity to the primal movements of the heart of man, and ingrafted his own conscious reflections on the casual thoughts of hinds and shepherds. Nursed amidst the grandeur of mountain scenery, he has stooped to have a nearer view of the daisy under his feet, or plucked a branch of white-thorn from the spray: but in describing it, his mind seems imbued with the majesty and solemnity of the objects around him—the tall rock lifts its head in the erectness of his spirit; the cataract roars in the sound of his verse; and in its dim and mysterious meaning, the mists seem to gather in the hollows of Helvellyn, and the forked Skiddaw hovers in the distance. There is little mention of mountainous scenery in Mr. Wordsworth's poetry; but by internal evidence one might be almost sure that it was written in a mountainous country, from its bareness, its simplicity, its loftiness and its depth!

His later philosophic productions have a somewhat different character. They are a departure from, a dereliction of his first principles. They are classical and courtly. They are polished in style, without being gaudy; dignified in subject, without affectation. They seem to have been composed not in a cottage at Grasmere, but among the half-inspired groves and stately recollections of Cole-Orton. We might allude in particular, for examples of what we mean, to the lines on a Picture by Claude Lorraine, and to the exquisite poem, entitled 'Laodamia.' The last of these breathes the pure spirit of the finest fragments of antiquity—the sweetness, the gravity, the strength, the beauty and the languor of death—

> Calm contemplation and majestic pains.

Its glossy brilliancy arises from the perfection of the finishing, like that of careful sculpture, not from gaudy colouring—the texture of the thoughts has the smoothness and solidity of marble. It is a poem that might be read aloud in Elysium, and the spirits of departed heroes and sages would gather round to listen to it! Mr. Wordsworth's philosophic poetry, with a less glowing aspect and less tumult in the veins than Lord Byron's on similar occasions, bends a calmer and keener eye on mortality; the impression, if less vivid, is more pleasing and permanent; and we confess it (perhaps it is a want of taste and proper feeling) that there are lines and poems of our author's, that we think of ten times for once that we recur to any of Lord Byron's. Or if there are any of the latter's writings, that we can dwell upon in the same way, that is, as lasting and heart-felt sentiments, it is when laying aside his usual pomp and pretension, he descends with Mr. Wordsworth to the common ground of a disinterested humanity. It may be considered as characteristic of our poet's writings, that they either make no impression on the mind at all, seem mere *nonsense-verses*, or that they leave a mark behind them that never wears out. They either

> Fall blunted from the indurated breast—

without any perceptible result, or they absorb it like a passion. To one class of readers he appears sublime, to another (and we fear the largest) ridiculous. He has probably realised Milton's wish,—'and fit audience found, though few'; but we suspect he is not reconciled to the alternative. There are delightful passages in the *Excursion*, both of natural description and of inspired reflection (passages of the latter kind that in the sound of the thoughts and of the swelling language resemble heavenly symphonies, mournful *requiems* over the grave of human hopes); but we must add, in justice and in sincerity, that we think it impossible that this work should ever become popular, even in the same degree as the *Lyrical Ballads*. It affects a system without having any intelligible clue to one; and instead of unfolding a principle in various and striking lights, repeats the same conclusions till they become flat and insipid. Mr. Wordsworth's mind is obtuse, except as it is the organ and the receptacle of accumulated feelings: it is not analytic, but synthetic; it is reflecting, rather than theoretical. The *Excursion*, we believe, fell still-born from the press. There was something abortive, and clumsy, and ill-judged in the attempt.

It was long and laboured. The personages, for the most part, were low, the fare rustic: the plan raised expectations which were not fulfilled, and the effect was like being ushered into a stately hall and invited to sit down to a splendid banquet in the company of clowns, and with nothing but successive courses of apple-dumplings served up. It was not even *toujours perdrix!*

Mr. Wordsworth, in his person, is above the middle size, with marked features, and an air somewhat stately and Quixotic. He reminds one of some of Holbein's heads, grave, saturnine, with a slight indication of sly humour, kept under by the manners of the age or by the pretensions of the person. He has a peculiar sweetness in his smile, and great depth and manliness and a rugged harmony, in the tones of his voice. His manner of reading his own poetry is particularly imposing; and in his favourite passages his eye beams with preternatural lustre, and the meaning labours slowly up from his swelling breast. No one who has seen him at these moments could go away with an impression that he was a 'man of no mark or likelihood.' Perhaps the comment of his face and voice is necessary to convey a full idea of his poetry. His language may not be intelligible, but his manner is not to be mistaken. It is clear that he is either mad or inspired. In company, even in a *tête-à-tête*, Mr. Wordsworth is often silent, indolent, and reserved. If he is become verbose and oracular of late years, he was not so in his better days. He threw out a bold or an indifferent remark without either effort or pretension, and relapsed into musing again. He shone most (because he seemed most roused and animated) in reciting his own poetry, or in talking about it. He sometimes gave striking views of his feelings and trains of association in composing certain passages; or if one did not always understand his distinctions, still there was no want of interest—there was a latent meaning worth inquiring into, like a vein of ore that one cannot exactly hit upon at the moment, but of which there are sure indications. His standard of poetry is high and severe, almost to exclusiveness. He admits of nothing below, scarcely of any thing above himself. It is fine to hear him talk of the way in which certain subjects should have been treated by eminent poets, according to his notions of the art. Thus he finds fault with Dryden's description of Bacchus in the 'Alexander's Feast,' as if he were a mere good-looking youth, or boon companion—

> Flushed with a purple grace,
> He shows his honest face—

instead of representing the God returning from the conquest of India, crowned with vine-leaves, and drawn by panthers, and followed by troops of satyrs, of wild men and animals that he had tamed. You would think, in hearing him speak on this subject, that you saw Titian's picture of the meeting of *Bacchus and Ariadne*—so classic were his conceptions, so glowing his style. Milton is his great idol, and he sometimes dares to compare himself with him. His Sonnets, indeed, have something of the same high-raised tone and prophetic spirit. Chaucer is another prime favourite of his, and he has been at the pains to modernize some of the *Canterbury Tales*. Those persons who look upon Mr. Wordsworth as a merely puerile writer, must be rather at a loss to account for his strong predilection for such geniuses as Dante and Michael Angelo. We do not think our author has any very cordial sympathy with Shakespear. How should he? Shakespear was the least of an egotist of any body in the world. He does not much relish the variety and scope of dramatic composition. 'He hates those interlocutions between Lucius and Caius.' Yet Mr. Wordsworth himself wrote a tragedy when he was young; and we have heard the following energetic lines quoted from it, as put into the mouth of a person smit with remorse for some rash crime:

> Action is momentary,
> The motion of a muscle this way or that;
> Suffering is long, obscure, and infinite!

Perhaps for want of light and shade, and the unshackled spirit of the drama, this performance was never brought forward. Our critic has a great dislike to Gray, and a fondness for Thomson and Collins. It is mortifying to hear him speak of Pope and Dryden, whom, because they have been supposed to have all the possible excellences of poetry, he will allow to have none. Nothing, however, can be fairer, or more amusing, than the way in which he sometimes exposes the unmeaning verbiage of modern poetry. Thus, in the beginning of Dr. Johnson's *Vanity of Human Wishes*—

> Let observation with extensive view
> Survey mankind from China to Peru—

he says there is a total want of imagination accompanying the words, the same idea is repeated three times under the disguise of a different phraseology: it comes to this—'let *observation*, with extensive *observation*, *observe* mankind'; or take away the first line, and the second,

> Survey mankind from China to Peru,

literally conveys the whole. Mr. Wordsworth is, we must say, a perfect Drawcansir as to prose writers. He complains of the dry reasoners and matter-of-fact people for their want of *passion*; and he is jealous of the rhetorical declaimers and rhapsodists as trenching on the province of poetry. He condemns all French writers (as well of poetry as prose) in the lump. His list in this way is indeed small. He approves of Walton's *Angler*, Paley, and some other writers of an inoffensive modesty of pretension. He also likes books of voyages and travels, and *Robinson Crusoe*. In art, he greatly esteems Bewick's woodcuts, and Waterloo's sylvan etchings. But he sometimes takes a higher tone, and gives his mind fair play. We have known him enlarge with a noble intelligence and enthusiasm on Nicolas Poussin's fine landscape-compositions, pointing out the unity of design that pervades them, the superintending mind, the imaginative principle that brings all to bear on the same end; and declaring he would not give a rush for any landscape that did not express the time of day, the climate, the period of the world it was meant to illustrate, or had not this character of *wholeness* in it. His eye also does justice to Rembrandt's fine and masterly effects. In the way in which that artist works something out of nothing, and transforms the stump of a tree, a common figure into an *ideal* object, by the gorgeous light and shade thrown upon it, he perceives an analogy to his own mode of investing the minute details of nature with an atmosphere of sentiment; and in pronouncing Rembrandt to be a man of genius, feels that he strengthens his own claim to the title. It has been said of Mr. Wordsworth, that 'he hates conchology, that he hates the Venus of Medicis.' But these, we hope, are mere epigrams and *jeux-d'esprit*, as far from truth as they are free from malice; a sort of running satire or critical clenches—

> Where one for sense and one for rhyme
> Is quite sufficient at one time.

We think, however, that if Mr. Wordsworth had been a more liberal and candid critic, he would have been a more sterling writer. If a greater number of sources of pleasure had been open to him, he would have communicated pleasure to the world more frequently. Had he been less fastidious in pronouncing sentence on the works of others, his own would have

been received more favourably, and treated more leniently. The current of his feelings is deep, but narrow; the range of his understanding is lofty and aspiring rather than discursive. The force, the originality, the absolute truth and identity with which he feels some things, makes him indifferent to so many others. The simplicity and enthusiasm of his feelings, with respect to nature, renders him bigotted and intolerant in his judgments of men and things. But it happens to him, as to others, that his strength lies in his weakness; and perhaps we have no right to complain. We might get rid of the cynic and the egotist, and find in his stead a commonplace man. We should 'take the good the Gods provide us': a fine and original vein of poetry is not one of their most contemptible gifts, and the rest is scarcely worth thinking of, except as it may be a mortification to those who expect perfection from human nature; or who have been idle enough at some period of their lives, to deify men of genius as possessing claims above it. But this is a chord that jars, and we shall not dwell upon it.

Lord Byron we have called, according to the old proverb, 'the spoiled child of fortune': Mr. Wordsworth might plead, in mitigation of some peculiarities, that he is 'the spoiled child of disappointment.' We are convinced, if he had been early a popular poet, he would have borne his honours meekly, and would have been a person of great *bonhommie* and frankness of disposition. But the sense of injustice and of undeserved ridicule sours the temper and narrows the views. To have produced works of genius, and to find them neglected or treated with scorn, is one of the heaviest trials of human patience. We exaggerate our own merits when they are denied by others, and are apt to grudge and cavil at every particle of praise bestowed on those to whom we feel a conscious superiority. In mere self-defence we turn against the world, when it turns against us; brood over the undeserved slights we receive; and thus the genial current of the soul is stopped, or vents itself in effusions of petulance and self-conceit. Mr. Wordsworth has thought too much of contemporary critics and criticism; and less than he ought of the award of posterity, and of the opinion, we do not say of private friends, but of those who were made so by their admiration of his genius. He did not court popularity by a conformity to established models, and he ought not to have been surprised that his originality was not understood as a matter of course. He has *gnawed too much on the bridle*; and has often thrown out crusts to the critics, in mere defiance or as a point of honour when he was challenged, which otherwise his own good sense would have withheld. We suspect that Mr. Wordsworth's feelings are a little morbid in this respect, or that he resents censure more than he is gratified by praise. Otherwise, the tide has turned much in his favour of late years—he has a large body of determined partisans—and is at present sufficiently in request with the public to save or relieve him from the last necessity to which a man of genius can be reduced—that of becoming the God of his own idolatry!

WALTER PATER
"Wordsworth" (1874)
Appreciations
1889

Some English critics at the beginning of the present century had a great deal to say concerning a distinction, of much importance, as they thought, in the true estimate of poetry, between the *Fancy*, and another more powerful faculty—the

Imagination. This metaphysical distinction, borrowed originally from the writings of German philosophers, and perhaps not always clearly apprehended by those who talked of it, involved a far deeper and more vital distinction, with which indeed all true criticism more or less directly has to do, the distinction, namely, between higher and lower degrees of intensity in the poet's perception of his subject, and in his concentration of himself upon his work. Of those who dwelt upon the metaphysical distinction between the Fancy and the Imagination, it was Wordsworth who made the most of it, assuming it as the basis for the final classification of his poetical writings; and it is in these writings that the deeper and more vital distinction, which, as I have said, underlies the metaphysical distinction, is most needed, and may best be illustrated.

For nowhere is there so perplexed a mixture as in Wordsworth's own poetry, of work touched with intense and individual power, with work of almost no character at all. He has much conventional sentiment, and some of that insincere poetic diction, against which his most serious critical efforts were directed: the reaction in his political ideas, consequent on the excesses of 1795, makes him, at times, a mere declaimer on moral and social topics; and he seems, sometimes, to force an unwilling pen, and write by rule. By making the most of these blemishes it is possible to obscure the true æsthetic value of his work, just as his life also, a life of much quiet delicacy and independence, might easily be placed in a false focus, and made to appear a somewhat tame theme in illustration of the more obvious parochial virtues. And those who wish to understand his influence, and experience his peculiar savour, must bear with patience the presence of an alien element in Wordsworth's work, which never coalesced with what is really delightful in it, nor underwent his special power. Who that values his writings most has not felt the intrusion there, from time to time, of something tedious and prosaic? Of all poets equally great, he would gain most by a skilfully made anthology. Such a selection would show, in truth, not so much what he was, or to himself or others seemed to be, as what, by the more energetic and fertile quality in his writings, he was ever tending to become. And the mixture in his work, as it actually stands, is so perplexed, that one fears to miss the least promising composition even, lest some precious morsel should be lying hidden within—the few perfect lines, the phrase, the single word perhaps, to which he often works up mechanically through a poem, almost the whole of which may be tame enough. He who thought that in all creative work the larger part was *given* passively, to the recipient mind, who waited so dutifully upon the gift, to whom so large a measure was sometimes given, had his times also of desertion and relapse; and he has permitted the impress of these too to remain in his work. And this duality there—the fitfulness with which the higher qualities manifest themselves in it, gives the effect in his poetry of a power not altogether his own, or under his control, which comes and goes when it will, lifting or lowering a matter, poor in itself; so that that old fancy which made the poet's art an enthusiasm, a form of divine possession, seems almost literally true of him.

This constant suggestion of an absolute duality between higher and lower moods, and the work done in them, stimulating one always to look below the surface, makes the reading of Wordsworth an excellent sort of training towards the things of art and poetry. It begets in those, who, coming across him in youth, can bear him at all, a habit of reading between the lines, a faith in the effect of concentration and collectedness of mind in the right appreciation of poetry, an expectation of things, in this order, coming to one by means of a right discipline of the temper as well as of the intellect. He meets us with the promise that he has much, and something very peculiar, to give us, if we will follow a certain difficult way, and seems to have the secret of a special and privileged state of mind. And those who have undergone his influence, and followed this difficult way, are like people who have passed through some initiation, a *disciplina arcani*, by submitting to which they become able constantly to distinguish in art, speech, feeling, manners, that which is organic, animated, expressive, from that which is only conventional, derivative, inexpressive.

But although the necessity of selecting these precious morsels for oneself is an opportunity for the exercise of Wordsworth's peculiar influence, and induces a kind of just criticism and true estimate of it, yet the purely literary product would have been more excellent, had the writer himself purged away that alien element. How perfect would have been the little treasury, shut between the covers of how thin a book! Let us suppose the desired separation made, the electric thread untwined, the golden pieces, great and small, lying apart together.[1] What are the peculiarities of this residue? What special sense does Wordsworth exercise, and what instincts does he satisfy? What are the subjects and the motives which in him excite the imaginative faculty? What are the qualities in things and persons which he values, the impression and sense of which he can convey to others, in an extraordinary way?

An intimate consciousness of the expression of natural things, which weighs, listens, penetrates, where the earlier mind passed roughly by, is a large element in the complexion of modern poetry. It has been remarked as a fact in mental history again and again. It reveals itself in many forms; but is strongest and most attractive in what is strongest and most attractive in modern literature. It is exemplified, almost equally, by writers as unlike each other as Senancour and Théophile Gautier: as a singular chapter in the history of the human mind, its growth might be traced from Rousseau to Chateaubriand, from Chateaubriand to Victor Hugo: it has doubtless some latent connexion with those pantheistic theories which locate an intelligent soul in material things, and have largely exercised men's minds in some modern systems of philosophy: it is traceable even in the graver writings of historians: it makes as much difference between ancient and modern landscape art, as there is between the rough masks of an early mosaic and a portrait by Reynolds or Gainsborough. Of this new sense, the writings of Wordsworth are the central and elementary expression: he is more simply and entirely occupied with it than any other poet, though there are fine expressions of precisely the same thing in so different a poet as Shelley. There was in his own character a certain contentment, a sort of inborn religious placidity, seldom found united with a sensibility so mobile as his, which was favourable to the quiet, habitual observation of inanimate, or imperfectly animate, existence. His life of eighty years is divided by no very profoundly felt incidents: its changes are almost wholly inward, and it falls into broad, untroubled, perhaps somewhat monotonous spaces. What it most resembles is the life of one of those early Italian or Flemish painters, who, just because their minds were full of heavenly visions, passed, some of them, the better part of sixty years in quiet, systematic industry. This placid life matured a quite unusual sensibility, really innate in him, to the sights and sounds of the natural world—the flower and its shadow on the stone, the cuckoo and its echo. The poem of "Resolution and Independence" is a storehouse of such records: for its fulness of imagery it may be compared to Keats's *Saint Agnes' Eve.* To read one of his longer pastoral poems for the first time, is like a day spent in a new country: the memory is crowded for a while with its precise and vivid incidents—

> The pliant harebell swinging in the breeze
> On some grey rock;—
> The single sheep and the one blasted tree
> And the bleak music from that old stone wall;—
> In the meadows and the lower ground
> Was all the sweetness of a common dawn;—
> And that green corn all day is rustling in thine ears.

Clear and delicate at once, as he is in the outlining of visible imagery, he is more clear and delicate still, and finely scrupulous, in the noting of sounds; so that he conceives of noble sound as even moulding the human countenance to nobler types, and as something actually "profaned" by colour, by visible form, or image. He has a power likewise of realising, and conveying to the consciousness of the reader, abstract and elementary impressions—silence, darkness, absolute motionlessness: or, again, the whole complex sentiment of a particular place, the abstract expression of desolation in the long white road, of peacefulness in a particular folding of the hills. In the airy building of the brain, a special day or hour even, comes to have for him a sort of personal identity, a spirit or angel given to it, by which, for its exceptional insight, or the happy light upon it, it has a presence in one's history, and acts there, as a separate power or accomplishment; and he has celebrated in many of his poems the "efficacious spirit," which, as he says, resides in these "particular spots" of time.

It is to such a world, and to a world of congruous meditation thereon, that we see him retiring in his but lately published poem of *The Recluse*—taking leave, without much count of costs, of the world of business, of action and ambition, as also of all that for the majority of mankind counts as sensuous enjoyment. [2]

And so it came about that this sense of a life in natural objects, which in most poetry is but a rhetorical artifice, is with Wordsworth the assertion of what for him is almost literal fact. To him every natural object seemed to possess more or less of a moral or spiritual life, to be capable of a companionship with man, full of expression, of inexplicable affinities and delicacies of intercourse. An emanation, a particular spirit, belonged, not to the moving leaves or water only, but to the distant peak of the hills arising suddenly, by some change of perspective, above the nearer horizon, to the passing space of light across the plain, to the lichened Druidic stone even, for a certain weird fellowship in it with the moods of men. It was like a "survival," in the peculiar intellectual temperament of a man of letters at the end of the eighteenth century, of that primitive condition, which some philosophers have traced in the general history of human culture, wherein all outward objects alike, including even the works of men's hands, were believed to be endowed with animation, and the world was "full of souls"— that mood in which the old Greek gods were first begotten, and which had many strange aftergrowths.

In the early ages, this belief, delightful as its effects on poetry often are, was but the result of a crude intelligence. But, in Wordsworth, such power of seeing life, such perception of a soul, in inanimate things, came of an exceptional susceptibility to the impressions of eye and ear, and was, in its essence, a kind of sensuousness. At least, it is only in a temperament exceptionally susceptible on the sensuous side, that this sense of the expressiveness of outward things comes to be so large a part of life. That he awakened "a sort of thought in sense," is Shelley's just estimate of this element in Wordsworth's poetry.

And it was through nature, thus ennobled by a semblance of passion and thought, that he approached the spectacle of human life. Human life, indeed, is for him, at first, only an additional, accidental grace on an expressive landscape. When he thought of man, it was of man as in the presence and under the influence of these effective natural objects, and linked to them by many associations. The close connexion of man with natural objects, the habitual association of his thoughts and feelings with a particular spot of earth, has sometimes seemed to degrade those who are subject to its influence, as if it did but reinforce that physical connexion of our nature with the actual lime and clay of the soil, which is always drawing us nearer to our end. But for Wordsworth, these influences tended to the dignity of human nature, because they tended to tranquillise it. By raising nature to the level of human thought he gives it power and expression: he subdues man to the level of nature, and gives him thereby a certain breadth and coolness and solemnity. The leech-gatherer on the moor, the woman "stepping westward," are for him natural objects, almost in the same sense as the aged thorn, or the lichened rock on the heath. In this sense the leader of the "Lake School," in spite of an earnest preoccupation with man, his thoughts, his destiny, is the poet of nature. And of nature, after all, in its modesty. The English lake country has, of course, its grandeurs. But the peculiar function of Wordsworth's genius, as carrying in it a power to open out the soul of apparently little or familiar things, would have found its true test had he become the poet of Surrey, say! and the prophet of its life. The glories of Italy and Switzerland, though he did write a little about them, had too potent a material life of their own to serve greatly his poetic purpose.

Religious sentiment, consecrating the affections and natural regrets of the human heart, above all, that pitiful awe and care for the perishing human clay, of which relic-worship is but the corruption, has always had much to do with localities, with the thoughts which attach themselves to actual scenes and places. Now what is true of it everywhere, is truest of it in those secluded valleys where one generation after another maintains the same abiding-place; and it was on this side, that Wordsworth apprehended religion most strongly. Consisting, as it did so much, in the recognition of local sanctities, in the habit of connecting the stones and trees of a particular spot of earth with the great events of life, till the low walls, the green mounds, the half-obliterated epitaphs seemed full of voices, and a sort of natural oracles, the very religion of these people of the dales appeared but as another link between them and the earth, and was literally a religion of nature. It tranquillised them by bringing them under the placid rule of traditional and narrowly localised observances. "Grave livers," they seemed to him, under this aspect, with stately speech, and something of that natural dignity of manners, which underlies the highest courtesy.

And, seeing man thus as a part of nature, elevated and solemnised in proportion as his daily life and occupations brought him into companionship with permanent natural objects, his very religion forming new links for him with the narrow limits of the valley, the low vaults of his church, the rough stones of his home, made intense for him now with profound sentiment, Wordsworth was able to appreciate passion in the lowly. He chooses to depict people from humble life, because, being nearer to nature than others, they are on the whole more impassioned, certainly more direct in their expression of passion, than other men: it is for this direct expression of passion, that he values their humble words. In much that he said in exaltation of rural life, he was but pleading indirectly for that sincerity, that perfect fidelity to one's own inward presentations, to the precise features of the picture within, without which any profound poetry is impossible. It was not for their tameness, but for this passionate sincerity, that he chose incidents and situations from common life, "related in a selection of language really used by men." He constantly endeavours to bring his language near to the real language of men: to the real language of men, however, not on the dead level of their ordinary intercourse, but in select moments of vivid sensation, when this language is winnowed and ennobled by excitement. There are poets who have chosen rural life as their subject, for the sake of its passionless repose, and times when Wordsworth himself extols the mere calm and dispassionate survey of things as the highest aim of poetical culture. But it was not for such passionless calm that he preferred the scenes of pastoral life; and the meditative poet, sheltering himself, as it might seem, from the agitations of the outward world, is in reality only clearing the scene for the great exhibitions of emotion, and what he values most is the almost elementary expression of elementary feelings.

And so he has much for those who value highly the concentrated presentment of passion, who appraise men and women by their susceptibility to it, and art and poetry as they afford the spectacle of it. Breaking from time to time into the pensive spectacle of their daily toil, their occupations near to nature, come those great elementary feelings, lifting and solemnising their language and giving it a natural music. The great, distinguishing passion came to Michael by the sheepfold, to Ruth by the wayside, adding these humble children of the furrow to the true aristocracy of passionate souls. In this respect, Wordsworth's work resembles most that of George Sand, in those of her novels which depict country life. With a penetrative pathos, which puts him in the same rank with the masters of the sentiment of pity in literature, with Meinhold and Victor Hugo, he collects all the traces of vivid excitement which were to be found in that pastoral world—the girl who rung her father's knell; the unborn infant feeling about its mother's heart; the instinctive touches of children; the sorrows of the wild creatures, even—their home-sickness, their strange yearnings; the tales of passionate regret that hang by a ruined farm-building, a heap of stones, a deserted sheepfold; that gay, false, adventurous, outer world, which breaks in from time to time to bewilder and deflower these quiet homes; not "passionate sorrow" only, for the overthrow of the soul's beauty, but the loss of, or carelessness for personal beauty even, in those whom men have wronged—their pathetic wanness; the sailor "who, in his heart, was half a shepherd on the stormy seas"; the wild woman teaching her child to pray for her betrayer; incidents like the making of the shepherd's staff, or that of the young boy laying the first stone of the sheepfold;— all the pathetic episodes of their humble existence, their longing, their wonder at fortune, their poor pathetic pleasures, like the pleasures of children, won so hardly in the struggle for bare existence; their yearning towards each other, in their darkened houses, or at their early toil. A sort of biblical depth and solemnity hangs over this strange, new, passionate, pastoral world, of which he first raised the image, and the reflection of which some of our best modern fiction has caught from him.

He pondered much over the philosophy of his poetry, and reading deeply in the history of his own mind, seems at times to have passed the borders of a world of strange speculations, inconsistent enough, had he cared to note such inconsistencies, with those traditional beliefs, which were otherwise the object of his devout acceptance. Thinking of the high value he set upon customariness, upon all that is habitual, local, rooted

in the ground, in matters of religious sentiment, you might sometimes regard him as one tethered down to a world, refined and peaceful indeed, but with no broad outlook, a world protected, but somewhat narrowed, by the influence of received ideas. But he is at times also something very different from this, and something much bolder. A chance expression is overheard and placed in a new connexion, the sudden memory of a thing long past occurs to him, a distant object is relieved for a while by a random gleam of light—accidents turning up for a moment what lies below the surface of our immediate experience—and he passes from the humble graves and lowly arches of "the little rock-like pile" of a Westmoreland church, on bold trains of speculative thought, and comes, from point to point, into strange contact with thoughts which have visited, from time to time, far more venturesome, perhaps errant, spirits.

He had pondered deeply, for instance, on those strange reminiscences and forebodings, which seem to make our lives stretch before and behind us, beyond where we can see or touch anything, or trace the lines of connexion. Following the soul, backwards and forwards, on these endless ways, his sense of man's dim, potential powers became a pledge to him, indeed, of a future life, but carried him back also to that mysterious notion of an earlier state of existence—the fancy of the Platonists—the old heresy of Origen. It was in this mood that he conceived those oft-reiterated regrets for a half-ideal childhood, when the relics of Paradise still clung about the soul—a childhood, as it seemed, full of the fruits of old age, lost for all, in a degree, in the passing away of the youth of the world, lost for each one, over again, in the passing away of actual youth. It is this ideal childhood which he celebrates in his famous "Ode on the Recollections of Childhood," and some other poems which may be grouped around it, such as the lines on "Tintern Abbey," and something like what he describes was actually truer of himself than he seems to have understood; for his own most delightful poems were really the instinctive productions of earlier life, and most surely for him, "the first diviner influence of this world" passed away, more and more completely, in his contact with experience.

Sometimes as he dwelt upon those moments of profound, imaginative power, in which the outward object appears to take colour and expression, a new nature almost, from the prompting of the observant mind, the actual world would, as it were, dissolve and detach itself, flake by flake, and he himself seemed to be the creator, and when he would the destroyer, of the world in which he lived—that old isolating thought of many a brain-sick mystic of ancient and modern times.

At other times, again, in those periods of intense susceptibility, in which he appeared to himself as but the passive recipient of external influences, he was attracted by the thought of a spirit of life in outward things, a single, all-pervading mind in them, of which man, and even the poet's imaginative energy, are but moments—the old dream of the *anima mundi*, the mother of all things and their grave, in which some had desired to lose themselves, and others had become indifferent to the distinctions of good and evil. It would come, sometimes, like the sign of the *macrocosm* to Faust in his cell: the network of man and nature was seen to be pervaded by a common, universal life: a new, bold thought lifted him above the furrow, above the green turf of the Westmoreland churchyard, to a world altogether different in its vagueness and vastness, and the narrow glen was full of the brooding power of one universal spirit.

And so he has something, also, for those who feel the fascination of bold speculative ideas, who are really capable of rising upon them to conditions of poetical thought. He uses them, indeed, always with a very fine apprehension of the limits within which alone philosophical imaginings have any place in true poetry; and using them only for poetical purposes, is not too careful even to make them consistent with each other. To him, theories which for other men bring a world of technical diction, brought perfect form and expression, as in those two lofty books of *The Prelude*, which describe the decay and the restoration of Imagination and Taste. Skirting the borders of this world of bewildering heights and depths, he got but the first exciting influence of it, that joyful enthusiasm which great imaginative theories prompt, when the mind first comes to have an understanding of them; and it is not under the influence of these thoughts that his poetry becomes tedious or loses its blitheness. He keeps them, too, always within certain ethical bounds, so that no word of his could offend the simplest of those simple souls which are always the largest portion of mankind. But it is, nevertheless, the contact of these thoughts, the speculative boldness in them, which constitutes, at least for some minds, the secret attraction of much of his best poetry—the sudden passage from lowly thoughts and places to the majestic forms of philosophical imagination, the play of these forms over a world so different, enlarging so strangely the bounds of its humble churchyards, and breaking such a wild light on the graves of christened children.

And these moods always brought with them faultless expression. In regard to expression, as with feeling and thought, the duality of the higher and lower moods was absolute. It belonged to the higher, the imaginative mood, and was the pledge of its reality, to bring the appropriate language with it. In him, when the really poetical motive worked at all, it united, with absolute justice, the word and the idea; each, in the imaginative flame, becoming inseparably one with the other, by that fusion of matter and form, which is the characteristic of the highest poetical expression. His words are themselves thought and feeling; not eloquent, or musical words merely, but that sort of creative language which carries the reality of what it depicts, directly, to the consciousness.

The music of mere metre performs but a limited, yet a very peculiar and subtly ascertained function, in Wordsworth's poetry. With him, metre is but an additional grace, accessory to that deeper music of words and sounds, that moving power, which they exercise in the nobler prose no less than in formal poetry. It is a sedative to that excitement, an excitement sometimes almost painful, under which the language, alike of poetry and prose, attains a rhythmical power, independent of metrical combination, and dependent rather on some subtle adjustment of the elementary sounds of words themselves to the image or feeling they convey. Yet some of his pieces, pieces prompted by a sort of half-playful mysticism, like the "Daffodils" and "The Two April Mornings," are distinguished by a certain quaint gaiety of metre, and rival by their perfect execution, in this respect, similar pieces among our own Elizabethan, or contemporary French poetry. And those who take up these poems after an interval of months, or years perhaps, may be surprised at finding how well old favourites wear, how their strange, inventive turns of diction or thought still send through them the old feeling of surprise. Those who lived about Wordsworth were all great lovers of the older English literature, and oftentimes there came out in him a noticeable likeness to our earlier poets. He quotes unconsciously, but with new power of meaning, a clause from one of Shakespeare's sonnets; and, as with some other men's most famous work, the "Ode on the Recollections of Childhood" had its anticipator.[3] He drew something too from the uncon-

scious mysticism of the old English language itself, drawing out the inward significance of its racy idiom, and the not wholly unconscious poetry of the language used by the simplest people under strong excitement—language, therefore, at its origin.

The office of the poet is not that of the moralist, and the first aim of Wordsworth's poetry is to give the reader a peculiar kind of pleasure. But through his poetry, and through this pleasure in it, he does actually convey to the reader an extraordinary wisdom in the things of practice. One lesson, if men must have lessons, he conveys more clearly than all, the supreme importance of contemplation in the conduct of life.

Contemplation—impassioned contemplation—that, is with Wordsworth the end-in-itself, the perfect end. We see the majority of mankind going most often to definite ends, lower or higher ends, as their own instincts may determine; but the end may never be attained, and the means not be quite the right means, great ends and little ones alike being, for the most part, distant, and the ways to them, in this dim world, somewhat vague. Meantime, to higher or lower ends, they move too often with something of a sad countenance, with hurried and ignoble gait, becoming, unconsciously, something like thorns, in their anxiety to bear grapes; it being possible for people, in the pursuit of even great ends, to become themselves thin and impoverished in spirit and temper, thus diminishing the sum of perfection in the world, at its very sources. We understand this when it is a question of mean, or of intensely selfish ends—of Grandet, or Javert. We think it bad morality to say that the end justifies the means, and we know how false to all higher conceptions of the religious life is the type of one who is ready to do evil that good may come. We contrast with such dark, mistaken eagerness, a type like that of Saint Catherine of Siena, who made the means to her ends so attractive, that she has won for herself an undying place in the *House Beautiful*, not by her rectitude of soul only, but by its "fairness"—by those quite different qualities which commend themselves to the poet and the artist.

Yet, for most of us, the conception of means and ends covers the whole of life, and is the exclusive type or figure under which we represent our lives to ourselves. Such a figure, reducing all things to machinery, though it has on its side the authority of that old Greek moralist who has fixed for succeeding generations the outline of the theory of right living, is too like a mere picture or description of men's lives as we actually find them, to be the basis of the higher ethics. It covers the meanness of men's daily lives, and much of the dexterity and the vigour with which they pursue what may seem to them the good of themselves or of others; but not the intangible perfection of those whose ideal is rather in *being* than in *doing*—not those *manners* which are, in the deepest as in the simplest sense, *morals*, and without which one cannot so much as offer a cup of water to a poor man without offence—not the part of "antique Rachel," sitting in the company of Beatrice; and even the moralist might well endeavour rather to withdraw men from the too exclusive consideration of means and ends, in life.

Against this predominance of machinery in our existence, Wordsworth's poetry, like all great art and poetry, is a continual protest. Justify rather the end by the means, it seems to say: whatever may become of the fruit, make sure of the flowers and the leaves. It was justly said, therefore, by one who had meditated very profoundly on the true relation of means to ends in life, and on the distinction between what is desirable in itself and what is desirable only as machinery, that when the battle which he and his friends were waging had been won, the world would need more than ever those qualities which Wordsworth was keeping alive and nourishing.[4]

That the end of life is not action but contemplation—*being* as distinct from *doing*—a certain disposition of the mind: is, in some shape or other, the principle of all the higher morality. In poetry, in art, if you enter into their true spirit at all, you touch this principle, in a measure: these, by their very sterility, are a type of beholding for the mere joy of beholding. To treat life in the spirit of art, is to make life a thing in which means and ends are identified: to encourage such treatment, the true moral significance of art and poetry. Wordsworth, and other poets who have been like him in ancient or more recent times, are the masters, the experts, in this art of impassioned contemplation. Their work is, not to teach lessons, or enforce rules, or even to stimulate us to noble ends; but to withdraw the thoughts for a little while from the mere machinery of life, to fix them, with appropriate emotions, on the spectacle of those great facts in man's existence which no machinery affects, "on the great and universal passions of men, the most general and interesting of their occupations, and the entire world of nature,"—on "the operations of the elements and the appearances of the visible universe, on storm and sunshine, on the revolutions of the seasons, on cold and heat, on loss of friends and kindred, on injuries and resentments, on gratitude and hope, on fear and sorrow." To witness this spectacle with appropriate emotions is the aim of all culture; and of these emotions poetry like Wordsworth's is a great nourisher and stimulant. He sees nature full of sentiment and excitement; he sees men and women as parts of nature, passionate, excited, in strange grouping and connexion with the grandeur and beauty of the natural world:—images, in his own words, "of man suffering, amid awful forms and powers."

Such is the figure of the more powerful and original poet, hidden away, in part, under those weaker elements in Wordsworth's poetry, which for some minds determine their entire character; a poet somewhat bolder and more passionate than might at first sight be supposed, but not too bold for true poetical taste; an unimpassioned writer, you might sometimes fancy, yet thinking the chief aim, in life and art alike, to be a certain deep emotion; seeking most often the great elementary passions in lowly places; having at least this condition of all impassioned work, that he aims always at an absolute sincerity of feeling and diction, so that he is the true forerunner of the deepest and most passionate poetry of our own day; yet going back also, with something of a protest against the conventional fervour of much of the poetry popular in his own time, to those older English poets, whose unconscious likeness often comes out in him.

Notes

1. Since this essay was written, such selections have been made, with excellent taste, by Matthew Arnold and Professor Knight.
2. In Wordsworth's prefatory advertisement to the first edition of *The Prelude*, published in 1850, it is stated that that work was intended to be introductory to *The Recluse*; and that *The Recluse*, if completed, would have consisted of three parts. The second part is *The Excursion*. The third part was only planned; but the first book of the first part was left in manuscript by Wordsworth—though in manuscript, it is said, in no great condition of forwardness for the printers. This book, now for the first time printed *in extenso* (a very noble passage from it found place in that prose advertisement to *The Excursion*), is included in the latest edition of Wordsworth by Mr. John Morley. It was well worth adding to the poet's great bequest to English literature. A true student of his work, who has formulated for himself what he supposes to be the leading characteristics of Wordsworth's genius, will feel, we think, lively interest in testing them by the various fine passages in what is here presented for the first time. Let the following serve for a sample:—

> Thickets full of songsters, and the voice
> Of lordly birds, an unexpected sound

Heard now and then from morn to latest eve,
Admonishing the man who walks below
Of solitude and silence in the sky:—
These have we, and a thousand nooks of earth
Have also these, but nowhere else is found,
Nowhere (or is it fancy?) can be found
The one sensation that is here; 'tis here,
Here as it found its way into my heart
In childhood, here as it abides by day,
By night, here only; or in chosen minds
That take it with them hence, where'er they go.
—'Tis, but I cannot name it, 'tis the sense
Of majesty, and beauty, and repose,
A blended holiness of earth and sky,
Something that makes this individual spot,
This small abiding-place of many men,
A termination, and a last retreat,
A centre, come from wheresoe'er you will,
A whole without dependence or defect,
Made for itself, and happy in itself,
Perfect contentment, Unity entire.

3. Henry Vaughan, in "The Retreat."
4. See an interesting paper, by Mr. John Morley, on "The Death of Mr. Mill," *Fortnightly Review*, June 1873.

SIR LESLIE STEPHEN
From "Wordsworth's Ethics" (1876)
Hours in a Library (1874–79)
1904, Volume 3, pp. 139–78

The great aim of moral philosophy is to unite the disjoined elements, to end the divorce between reason and experience, and to escape from the alternative of dealing with empty but symmetrical formulæ or concrete and chaotic facts. No hint can be given here as to the direction in which a final solution must be sought. Whatever the true method, Wordsworth's mode of conceiving the problem shows how powerfully he grasped the questions at issue. If his doctrines are not symmetrically expounded, they all have a direct bearing upon the real difficulties involved. [1] They are stated so forcibly in his noblest poems that we might almost express a complete theory in his own language. But, without seeking to make a collection of aphorisms from his poetry, we may indicate the cardinal points of his teaching.

The most characteristic of all his doctrines is that which is embodied in the great ode upon the "Intimations of Immortality." The doctrine itself—the theory that the instincts of childhood testify to the pre-existence of the soul—sounds fanciful enough; and Wordsworth took rather unnecessary pains to say that he did not hold it as a serious dogma. We certainly need not ask whether it is reasonable or orthodox to believe that "our birth is but a sleep and a forgetting." The fact symbolised by the poetic fancy—the glory and freshness of our childish instincts—is equally noteworthy, whatever its cause. Some modern reasoners would explain its significance by reference to a very different kind of pre-existence. The instincts, they would say, are valuable, because they register the accumulated and inherited experience of past generations. Wordsworth's delight in wild scenery is regarded by them as due to the "combination of states that were organised in the race during barbarous times, when its pleasurable activities were amongst the mountains, woods, and waters." In childhood we are most completely under the dominion of these inherited impulses. The correlation between the organism and its medium is then most perfect, and hence the peculiar theme of childish communion with nature.

Wordsworth would have repudiated the doctrine with disgust. He would have been "on the side of the angels." No memories of the savage and the monkey, but the reminiscences of the once-glorious soul could explain his emotions. Yet there is this much in common between him and the men of science whom he denounced with too little discrimination. The fact of the value of these primitive instincts is admitted, and admitted for the same purpose. Man, it is agreed, is furnished with sentiments which cannot be explained as the result of his individual experience. They may be intelligible, according to the evolutionist, when regarded as embodying the past experience of the race; or, according to Wordsworth, as implying a certain mysterious faculty imprinted upon the soul. The scientific doctrine, whether sound or not, has modified the whole mode of approaching ethical problems; and Wordsworth, though with a very different purpose, gives a new emphasis to the facts, upon a recognition of which, according to some theorists, must be based the reconciliation of the great rival schools—the intuitionists and the utilitarians. The parallel may at first sight seem fanciful; and it would be too daring to claim for Wordsworth the discovery of the most remarkable phenomenon which modern psychology must take into account. There is, however, a real connection between the two doctrines, though in one sense they are almost antithetical. Meanwhile we observe that the same sensibility which gives poetical power is necessary to the scientific observer. The magic of the Ode, and of many other passages in Wordsworth's poetry, is due to his recognition of this mysterious efficacy of our childish instincts. He gives emphasis to one of the most striking facts of our spiritual experience, which had passed with little notice from professed psychologists. He feels what they afterwards tried to explain.

The full meaning of the doctrine comes out as we study Wordsworth more thoroughly. Other poets—almost all poets—have dwelt fondly upon recollections of childhood. But not feeling so strongly, and therefore not expressing so forcibly, the peculiar character of the emotion, they have not derived the same lessons from their observation. The Epicurean poets are content with Herrick's simple moral—

> Gather ye rosebuds while ye may—

and with this simple explanation—

> That age is best which is the first,
> When youth and blood are warmer.

Others more thoughtful look back upon the early days with the passionate regret of Byron's verses:

> There's not a joy the world can give like that it takes
>   away,
> When the glow of early thought declines in feeling's
>   dull decay;
> 'T is not on youth's smooth cheek the blush alone
>   which fades so fast,
> But the tender bloom of heart is gone, ere youth itself
>   be past.

Such painful longings for the "tender grace of a day that is dead" are spontaneous and natural. Every healthy mind feels the pang in proportion to the strength of its affections. But it is also true that the regret resembles too often the maudlin meditation of a fast young man over his morning's soda-water. It implies, that is, a non-recognition of the higher uses to which the fading memories may still be put. A different tone breathes in Shelley's pathetic but rather hectic moralisings, and his lamentations over the departure of the "spirit of delight." Nowhere has it found more exquisite expression than in the marvellous "Ode to the West Wind." These magical verses—

his best, as it seems to me—describe the reflection of the poet's own mind in the strange stir and commotion of a dying winter's day. They represent, we may say, the fitful melancholy which oppresses a noble spirit when it has recognised the difficulty of forcing facts into conformity with the ideal. He still clings to the hope that his "dead thoughts" may be driven over the universe,

> Like withered leaves to quicken a new birth.

But he bows before the inexorable fate which has cramped his energies:

> A heavy weight of years has chained and bowed
> One too like thee; tameless and swift and proud.

Neither Byron nor Shelley can see any satisfactory solution, and therefore neither can reach a perfect harmony of feeling. The world seems to them to be out of joint, because they have not known how to accept the inevitable, nor to conform to the discipline of facts. And, therefore, however intense the emotion, and however exquisite its expression, we are left in a state of intellectual and emotional discontent. Such utterances may suit us in youth, when we can afford to play with sorrow. As we grow older we feel a certain emptiness in them. A true man ought not to sit down and weep with an exhausted debauchee. He cannot afford to confess himself beaten with the idealist who has discovered that Rome was not built in a day, nor revolutions made with rose-water. He has to work as long as he has strength; to work in spite of, even by strength of, sorrow, disappointment, wounded vanity, and blunted sensibilities; and therefore he must search for some profounder solution for the dark riddle of life.

This solution it is Wordsworth's chief aim to supply. In the familiar verses which stand as a motto to his poems—

> The child is father to the man,
> And I could wish my days to be
> Bound each to each by natural piety—

the great problem of life, that is, as he conceives it, is to secure a continuity between the period at which we are guided by half-conscious instincts, and that in which a man is able to supply the place of these primitive impulses by reasoned convictions. This is the thought which comes over and over again in his deepest poems, and round which all his teaching centred. It supplies the great moral, for example, of "The Leech-Gatherer":

> My whole life I have lived in pleasant thought,
>   As if life's business were a summer mood:
> As if all needful things would come unsought
>   To genial faith still rich in genial good.

When his faith is tried by harsh experience, the leech-gatherer comes,

> Like a man from some far region sent
> To give me human strength by apt admonishment;

for he shows how the "genial faith" may be converted into permanent strength by resolution and independence. The verses most commonly quoted, such as—

> We poets in our youth begin in gladness,
> But thereof come in the end despondency and
>   sadness,

give the ordinary view of the sickly school. Wordsworth's aim is to supply an answer worthy not only of a poet, but a man. The same sentiment again is expressed in the grand "Ode to Duty," where the

> Stern daughter of the voice of God

is invoked to supply that "genial sense of youth" which has hitherto been a sufficient guidance; or in the majestic morality of "The Happy Warrior"; or in the noble verses of "Tintern Abbey"; or, finally, in the great ode which gives most completely the whole theory of that process by which our early intuitions are to be transformed into settled principles of feeling and action.

Wordsworth's philosophical theory, in short, depends upon the asserted identity between our childish instincts and our enlightened reason. The doctrine of a state of pre-existence as it appears in other writers—as, for example, in the Cambridge Platonists[2]—was connected with an obsolete metaphysical system, and the doctrine—exploded in its old form—of innate ideas. Wordsworth does not attribute any such preternatural character to the "blank misgivings" and "shadowy recollections" of which he speaks. They are invaluable data of our spiritual experience; but they do not entitle us to lay down dogmatic propositions independently of experience. They are spontaneous products of a nature in harmony with the universe in which it is placed, and inestimable as a clear indication that such a harmony exists. To interpret and regulate them belongs to the reasoning faculty and the higher imagination of later years. If he does not quite distinguish between the province of reason and emotion—the most difficult of philosophical problems—he keeps clear of the cruder mysticism, because he does not seek to elicit any definite formulæ from those admittedly vague forebodings which lie on the border-land between the two sides of our nature. With his invariable sanity of mind, he more than once notices the difficulty of distinguishing between that which nature teaches us and the interpretations which we impose upon nature.[3] He carefully refrains from pressing the inference too far.

The teaching, indeed, assumes that view of the universe which is implied in his pantheistic language. The Divinity really reveals Himself in the lonely mountains and the starry heavens. By contemplating them we are able to rise into that "blessed mood" in which for a time the burden of the mystery is rolled off our souls, and we can "see into the life of things." And here we must admit that Wordsworth is not entirely free from the weakness which generally besets thinkers of this tendency. Like Shaftesbury in the previous century, who speaks of the universal harmony as emphatically though not as poetically as Wordsworth, he is tempted to adopt a too facile optimism. He seems at times to have overlooked that dark side of nature which is recognised in theological doctrines of corruption, or in the scientific theories about the fierce struggle for existence. Can we in fact say that these early instincts prove more than the happy constitution of the individual who feels them? Is there not a teaching of nature very apt to suggest horror and despair rather than a complacent brooding over soothing thoughts? Do not the mountains which Wordsworth loved so well, speak of decay and catastrophe in every line of their slopes? Do they not suggest the helplessness and narrow limitations of man, as forcibly as his possible exaltation? The awe which they strike into our souls has its terrible as well as its amiable side; and in moods of depression the darker aspect becomes more conspicious than the brighter. Nay, if we admit that we have instincts which are the very substance of all that afterwards becomes ennobling, have we not also instincts which suggest a close alliance with the brutes? If the child amidst his newborn blisses suggests a heavenly origin, does he not also show sensual and cruel instincts which imply at least an admixture of baser elements? If man is responsive to all natural influences, how is he to distinguish between the good and the bad, and, in short, to frame a conscience out of the vague instincts which contain the germs of all the possible developments of the future?

To say that Wordsworth has not given a complete answer to such difficulties, is to say that he has not explained the origin of evil. It may be admitted, however, that he does to a certain extent show a narrowness of conception. The voice of nature, as he says, resembles an echo; but we "unthinking creatures" listen to "voices of two different natures." We do not always distinguish between the echo of our lower passions and the "echoes from beyond the grave." Wordsworth sometimes fails to recognise the ambiguity of the oracle to which he appeals. The "blessed mood" in which we get rid of the burden of the world, is too easily confused with the mood in which we simply refuse to attend to it. He finds lonely meditation so inspiring that he is too indifferent to the troubles of less self-sufficing or clear-sighted human beings. The ambiguity makes itself felt in the sphere of morality. The ethical doctrine that virtue consists in conformity to nature becomes ambiguous with him, as with all its advocates, when we ask for a precise definition of nature. How are we to know which natural forces make for us and which fight against us?

The doctrine of the love of nature, generally regarded as Wordsworth's great lesson to mankind, means, as interpreted by himself and others, a love of the wilder and grander objects of natural scenery; a passion for the "sounding cataract," the rock, the mountain, and the forest; a preference, therefore, of the country to the town, and of the simpler to the more complex forms of social life. But what is the true value of this sentiment? The unfortunate Solitary in the *Excursion* is beset by three Wordsworths; for the Wanderer and the Pastor are little more (as Wordsworth indeed intimates) than reflections of himself, seen in different mirrors. The Solitary represents the anti-social lessons to be derived from communion with nature. He has become a misanthrope, and has learnt from *Candide* the lesson that we clearly do not live in the best of all possible worlds. Instead of learning the true lesson from nature by penetrating its deeper meanings, he manages to feed

> Pity and scorn and melancholy pride

by accidental and fanciful analogies, and sees in rock pyramids or obelisks a rude mockery of human toils. To confute this sentiment, to upset *Candide*,

> This dull product of a scoffer's pen,

is the purpose of the lofty poetry and versified prose of the long dialogues which ensue. That Wordsworth should call Voltaire dull is a curious example of the proverbial blindness of controversalists; but the moral may be equally good. It is given most pithily in the lines—

> We live by admiration, hope, and love;
> And even as these are well and wisely fused,
> The dignity of being we ascend.

"But what is Error?" continues the preacher; and the Solitary replies by saying, "somewhat haughtily," that love, admiration, and hope are "mad fancy's favourite vassals." The distinction between fancy and imagination is, in brief, that fancy deals with the superficial resemblances, and imagination with the deeper truths which underlie them. The purpose, then, of *The Excursion*, and of Wordsworth's poetry in general, is to show how the higher faculty reveals a harmony which we overlook when, with the Solitary, we

> Skim along the surfaces of things.

The rightly prepared mind can recognise the divine harmony which underlies all apparent disorder. The universe is to its perceptions like the shell whose murmur in a child's ear seems to express a mysterious union with the sea. But the mind must be rightly prepared. Everything depends upon the point of view. One man, as he says in an elaborate figure, looking upon a series of ridges in spring from their northern side, sees a waste of snow, and from the south a continuous expanse of green. That view, we must take it, is the right one which is illuminated by the "ray divine." But we must train our eyes to recognise its splendour; and the final answer to the Solitary is therefore embodied in a series of narratives, showing by example how our spiritual vision may be purified or obscured. Our philosophy must be finally based, not upon abstract speculation and metaphysical arguments, but on the diffused consciousness of the healthy mind. As Butler sees the universe by the light of conscience, Wordsworth sees it through the wider emotions of awe, reverence, and love, produced in a sound nature.

The pantheistic conception, in short, leads to an unsatisfactory optimism in the general view of nature, and to an equal tolerance of all passions as equally "natural." To escape from this difficulty we must establish some more discriminative mode of interpreting nature. Man is the instrument played upon by all impulses, good or bad. The music which results may be harmonious or discordant. When the instrument is in tune, the music will be perfect; but when is it in tune, and how are we to know that it is in tune? That problem once solved, we can tell which are the authentic utterances and which are the accidental discords. And by solving it, or by saying what is the right constitution of human beings, we shall discover which is the true philosophy of the universe, and what are the dictates of a sound moral sense. Wordsworth implicitly answers the question by explaining, in his favourite phrase, how we are to build up our moral being.

The voice of nature speaks at first in vague emotions, scarcely distinguishable from mere animal bouyancy. The boy, hooting in mimicry of the owls, receives in his heart the voice of mountain torrents and the solemn imagery of rocks, and woods, and stars. The sportive girl is unconsciously moulded into stateliness and grace by the floating clouds, the bending willow, and even by silent sympathy with the motions of the storm. Nobody has ever shown, with such exquisite power as Wordsworth, how much of the charm of natural objects in later life is due to early associations, thus formed in a mind not yet capable of contemplating its own processes. As old Matthew says in the lines which, however familiar, can never be read with out emotion—

My eyes are dim with childish tears,
  My heart is idly stirred;
For the same sound is in my ears
  Which in those days I heard.

And the strangely beautiful address to the cuckoo might be made into a text for a prolonged commentary by an æsthetic philosopher upon the power of early association. It curiously illustrates, for example, the reason for Wordsworth's delight in recalling sounds. The croak of the distant raven, the bleat of the mountain lamb, the splash of the leaping fish in the lonely tarn, are specially delightful to him, because the hearing is the most spiritual of our senses; and these sounds, like the cuckoo's cry, seem to convert the earth into an "unsubstantial fairy place." The phrase "association" indeed implies a certain arbitrariness in the images suggested, which is not quite in accordance with Wordsworth's feeling. Though the echo depends partly upon the hearer, the mountain voices are specially adapted for certain moods. They have, we may say, a spontaneous affinity for the nobler affections. If some early passage in our childhood is associated with a particular spot, a house or a street will bring back the petty and accidental details:

a mountain or a lake will revive the deeper and more permanent elements of feeling. If you have made love in a palace, according to Mr. Disraeli's prescription, the sight of it will recall the splendour of the object's dress or jewellery; if, as Wordsworth would prefer, with a background of mountains, it will appear in later days as if they had absorbed, and were always ready again to radiate forth, the tender and hallowing influences which then for the first time entered your life. The elementary and deepest passions are most easily associated with the sublime and beautiful in nature.

The primal duties shine aloft like stars;
The charities that soothe, and heal, and bless,
Are scattered at the feet of man like flowers.

And therefore if you have been happy enough to take delight in these natural and universal objects in the early days, when the most permanent associations are formed, the sight of them in later days will bring back by preordained and divine symbolism whatever was most ennobling in your early feelings. The vulgarising associations will drop off of themselves, and what was pure and lofty will remain.

From this natural law follows another of Wordsworth's favourite precepts. The mountains are not with him a symbol of anti-social feelings. On the contrary, they are in their proper place as the background of the simple domestic affections. He loves his native hills, not in the Byronic fashion, as a savage wilderness, but as the appropriate framework in which a healthy social order can permanently maintain itself. That, for example, is, as he tells us, the thought which inspired *The Brothers*, a poem which excels all modern idylls in weight of meaning and depth of feeling, by virtue of the idea thus embodied. The retired valley of Ennerdale, with its grand background of hills, precipitous enough to be fairly called mountains, forces the two lads into closer affection. Shut in by these "enormous barriers," and undistracted by the ebb and flow of the outside world, the mutual love becomes concentrated. A tie like that of family blood is involuntarily imposed upon the little community of dalesmen. The image of sheep-tracks and shepherds clad in country grey is stamped upon the elder brother's mind, and comes back to him in tropical calms; he hears the tones of his waterfalls in the piping shrouds; and when he returns, recognises every fresh scar made by winter storms on the mountain sides, and knows by sight every unmarked grave in the little churchyard. The fraternal affection sanctifies the scenery, and the sight of the scenery brings back the affection with overpowering force upon his return. This is everywhere the sentiment inspired in Wordsworth by his beloved hills. It is not so much the love of nature pure and simple, as of nature seen through the deepest human feelings. The light glimmering in a lonely cottage, the one rude house in the deep valley, with its "small lot of life-supporting fields and guardian rocks," are necessary to point the moral and to draw to a definite focus the various forces of sentiment. The two veins of feeling are inseparably blended. The peasant noble, in the "Song at the Feast of Brougham Castle," learns equally from men and nature:—

Love had he found in huts where poor men lie;
  His daily teachers had been woods and hills,
The silence that is in the starry skies,
  The sleep that is among the lonely hills.

Without the love, the silence and the sleep would have had no spiritual meaning. They are valuable as giving intensity and solemnity to the positive emotion.

The same remark is to be made upon Wordsworth's favourite teaching of the advantages of the contemplative life.

He is fond of enforcing the doctrine of the familiar lines, that we can feed our minds "in a wise passiveness," and that

> One impulse from the vernal wood
> Can teach you more of man,
> Of moral evil and of good,
> Than all the sages can.

And, according to some commentators, this would seem to express the doctrine that the ultimate end of life is the cultivation of tender emotions without reference to action. The doctrine, thus absolutely stated, would be immoral and illogical. To recommend contemplation in preference to action is like preferring sleeping to waking; or saying, as a full expression of the truth, that silence is golden and speech silvern. Like that familiar phrase, Wordsworth's teaching is not to be interpreted literally. The essence of such maxims is to be one-sided. They are paradoxical in order to be emphatic. To have seasons of contemplation, of withdrawal from the world and from books, of calm surrendering of ourselves to the influences of nature, is a practice commended in one form or other by all moral teachers. It is a sanitary rule, resting upon obvious principles. The mind which is always occupied in a multiplicity of small observations, or the regulation of practical details, loses the power of seeing general principles and of associating all objects with the central emotions of "admiration, hope, and love." The philosophic mind is that which habitually sees the general in the particular, and finds food for the deepest thought in the simplest objects. It requires, therefore, periods of repose, in which the fragmentary and complex atoms of distracted feeling which make up the incessant whirl of daily life may have time to crystallise round the central thoughts. But it must feed in order to assimilate; and each process implies the other as its correlative. A constant interest, therefore, in the joys and sorrows of our neighbours is as essential as quiet, self-centred rumination. It is when the eye "has kept watch o'er man's mortality," and by virtue of the tender sympathies of "the human heart by which we live," that to us

> The meanest flower which blows can give
> Thoughts that do often lie too deep for tears.

The solitude which implies severance from natural sympathies and affections is poisonous. The happiness of the heart which lives alone,

> Housed in a dream, an outcast from the kind,
> . . .
> Is to be pitied, for 'tis surely blind.

Wordsworth's meditations upon flowers or animal life are impressive because they have been touched by this constant sympathy. The sermon is always in his mind, and therefore every stone may serve for a text. His contemplation enables him to see the pathetic side of the small pains and pleasures which we are generally in too great a hurry to notice. There are times, of course, when this moralising tendency leads him to the regions of the namby-pamby or sheer prosaic platitude. On the other hand, no one approaches him in the power of touching some rich chord of feeling by help of the pettiest incident. The old man going to the fox-hunt with a tear on his cheek, and saying to himself,

> The key I must take, for my Helen is dead;

or the mother carrying home her dead sailor's bird; the village schoolmaster, in whom a rift in the clouds revives the memory of his little daughter; the old huntsman unable to cut through the stump of rotten wood—touch our hearts at once and for ever. The secret is given in the rather prosaic apology for not relating a tale about poor Simon Lee:

> O reader! had you in your mind
> Such stores as silent thought can bring,
> O gentle reader! you would find
> A tale in everything.

The value of silent thought is so to cultivate the primitive emotions that they may flow spontaneously upon every common incident, and that every familiar object becomes symbolic of them. It is a familiar remark that a philosopher or man of science who has devoted himself to meditation upon some principle or law of nature, is always finding new illustrations in the most unexpected quarters. He cannot take up a novel or walk across the street without hitting upon appropriate instances. Wordsworth would apply the principle to the building up of our "moral being." Admiration, hope, and love should be so constantly in our thoughts, that innumerable sights and sounds which are meaningless to the world should become to us a lan- guage incessantly suggestive of the deepest topics of thought.

This explains his dislike to science, as he understood the word, and his denunciations of the "world." The man of science is one who cuts up nature into fragments, and not only neglects their possible significance for our higher feelings, but refrains on principle from taking it into account. The primrose suggests to him some new device in classification, and he would be worried by the suggestion of any spiritual significance as an annoying distraction. Viewing all objects "in disconnection, dead and spiritless," we are thus really waging

> An impious warfare with the very life
> Of our own souls.

We are putting the letter in place of the spirit, and dealing with nature as a mere grammarian deals with a poem. When we have learnt to associate every object with some lesson

> Of human suffering or of human joy;

when we have thus obtained the "glorious habit,"

> By which sense is made
> Subservient still to moral purposes,
> Auxiliar to divine;

the "dull eye" of science will light up; for, in observing natural processes, it will carry with it an incessant reference to the spiritual processes to which they are allied. Science, in short, requires to be brought into intimate connection with morality and religion. If we are forced for our immediate purpose to pursue truth for itself, regardless of consequences, we must remember all the more carefully that truth is a whole, and that fragmentary bits of knowledge become valuable as they are incorporated into a general system. The tendency of modern times to specialism brings with it a characteristic danger. It requires to be supplemented by a correlative process of integration. We must study details to increase our knowledge; we must accustom ourselves to look at the detail in the light of the general principles in order to make it fruitful.

The influence of that world which "is too much with us late and soon" is of the same kind. The man of science loves barren facts for their own sake. The man of the world becomes devoted to some petty pursuit without reference to ultimate ends. He becomes a slave to money, or power, or praise, without caring for their effect upon his moral character. As social organisation becomes more complete, the social unit becomes a mere fragment instead of being a complete whole in himself. Man becomes

> The senseless member of a vast machine,
> Serving as doth a spindle or a wheel.

The division of labour, celebrated with such enthusiasm by Adam Smith,[4] tends to crush all real life out of its victims. The soul of the political economist may rejoice when he sees a human being devoting his whole faculties to the performance of one subsidiary operation in the manufacture of a pin. The poet and the moralist must notice with anxiety the contrast between the old-fashioned peasant who, if he discharged each particular function clumsily, discharged at least many functions, and found exercise for all the intellectual and moral faculties of his nature, and the modern artisan doomed to the incessant repetition of one petty set of muscular expansions and contractions, and whose soul, if he has one, is therefore rather an encumbrance than otherwise. This is the evil which is constantly before Wordsworth's eyes, as it has certainly not become less prominent since his time. The danger of crushing the individual is a serious one according to his view; not because it implies the neglect of some abstract political rights, but from the impoverishment of character which is implied in the process. Give every man a vote, and abolish all interference with each man's private tastes, and the danger may still be as great as ever. The tendency to "differentiation"—as we call it in modern phraseology—the social pulverisation, the lowering and narrowing of the individual's sphere of action and feeling to the pettiest details, depends upon processes underlying all political changes. It cannot therefore, be cured by any nostrum of constitution-mongers, or by the negative remedy of removing old barriers. It requires to be met by profounder moral and religious teaching. Men must be taught what is the really valuable part of their natures, and what is the purest happiness to be extracted from life, as well as allowed to gratify fully their own tastes; for who can say that men encouraged by all their surroundings and appeals to the most obvious motives to turn themselves into machines, will not deliberately choose to be machines? Many powerful thinkers have illustrated Wordsworth's doctrine more elaborately, but nobody has gone more decisively to the root of the matter.

One other side of Wordsworth's teaching is still more significant and original. Our vague instincts are consolidated into reason by meditation, sympathy with our fellows, communion with nature, and a constant devotion to "high endeavours." If life run smoothly, the transformation may be easy, and our primitive optimism turn imperceptibly into general complacency. The trial comes when we make personal acquaintance with sorrow, and our early bouyancy begins to fail. We are tempted to become querulous or to lap ourselves in indifference. Most poets are content to bewail our lot melodiously, and admit that there is no remedy unless a remedy be found in "the luxury of grief." Prosaic people become selfish though not sentimental. They laugh at their old illusions, and turn to the solid consolations of comfort. Nothing is more melancholy than to study many biographies, and note—not the failure of early promise which may mean merely an aiming above the mark—but the progressive deterioration of character which so often follows grief and disappointment. If it be not true that most men grow worse as they grow old, it is surely true that few men pass through the world without being corrupted as much as purified.

Now Wordsworth's favourite lesson is the possibility of turning grief and disappointment into account. He teaches in many forms the necessity of "transmuting" sorrow into strength. One of the great evils is a lack of power

An agonising sorrow to transmute.

The Happy Warrior is, above all, the man who in face of all human miseries can

Exercise a power
Which is our human nature's highest dower;
Controls them, and subdues, transmutes, bereaves
Of their bad influence, and their good receives;

who is made more compassionate by familiarity with sorrow, more placable by contest, purer by temptation, and more enduring by distress.[5] It is owing to the constant presence of this thought, to his sensibility to the refining influence of sorrow, that Wordsworth is the only poet who will bear reading in times of distress. Other poets mock us by an impossible optimism, or merely reflect the feelings which, however we may play with them in times of cheerfulness, have now become an intolerable burden. Wordsworth suggests the single topic which, so far at least as this world is concerned, can really be called consolatory. None of the ordinary commonplaces will serve, or serve at most as indications of human sympathy. But there is some consolation in the thought that even death may bind the survivors closer, and leave as a legacy enduring motives to noble action. It is easy to say this; but Wordsworth has the merit of feeling the truth in all its force, and expressing it by the most forcible images. In one shape or another the sentiment is embodied in most of his really powerful poetry. It is intended, for example, to be the moral of *The White Doe of Rylstone*. There, as Wordsworth says, everything fails so far as its object is external and unsubstantial; everything succeeds so far as it is moral and spiritual. Success grows out of failure; and the mode in which it grows is indicated by the lines which give the keynote of the poem. Emily, the heroine, is to become a soul

By force of sorrows high
Uplifted to the purest sky
Of undisturbed serenity.

The White Doe is one of those poems which make many readers inclined to feel a certain tenderness for Jeffrey's dogged insensibility; and I confess that I am not one of its warm admirers. The sentiment seems to be unduly relaxed throughout; there is a want of sympathy with heroism of the rough and active type, which is, after all, at least as worthy of admiration as the more passive variety of the virtue; and the defect is made more palpable by the position of the chief actors. These rough borderers, who recall William of Deloraine and Dandie Dinmont, are somehow out of their element when preaching the doctrines of quietism and submission to circumstances. But, whatever our judgment of this particular embodiment of Wordsworth's moral philosophy, the inculcation of the same lesson gives force to many of his finest poems. It is enough to mention "The Leech-Gatherer," the "Stanzas on Peele Castle," *Michael*, and, as expressing the inverse view of the futility of idle grief, "Laodamia," where he has succeeded in combining his morality with more than his ordinary beauty of poetical form. The teaching of all these poems falls in with the doctrine already set forth. All moral teaching, I have sometimes fancied, might be summed up in the one formula, "Waste not." Every element of which our nature is composed may be said to be good in its proper place; and therefore every vicious habit springs out of the misapplication of forces which might be turned to account by judicious training. The waste of sorrow is one of the most lamentable forms of waste. Sorrow too often tends to produce bitterness or effeminacy of character. But it may, if rightly used, serve only to detach us from the lower motives, and give sanctity to the higher. That is what Wordsworth sees with unequalled clearness, and he therefore sees also the condition of profiting. The mind in which the most valuable elements have been systematically strengthened by meditation, by association of deep thought with the most universal presences, by constant sympathy with the joys and sorrows of its fellows, will be prepared to convert sorrow into a medicine instead of a poison. Sorrow is deteriorating so far as it is selfish. The man who is occupied with his own interests makes grief an excuse for effeminate indulgence in self-pity. He becomes weaker and more fretful. The man who has learnt habitually to think of himself as part of a greater whole, whose conduct has been habitually directed to noble ends, is purified and strengthened by the spiritual convulsion. His disappointment, or his loss of some beloved object, makes him more anxious to fix the bases of his happiness widely and deeply, and to be content with the consciousness of honest work, instead of looking for what is called success.

But I must not take to preaching in the place of Wordsworth. The whole theory is most nobly summed up in the grand lines already noticed on "The Character of the Happy Warrior." There Wordsworth has explained in the most forcible and direct language the mode in which a grand character can be formed; how youthful impulses may change into manly purpose; how pain and sorrow may be transmuted into new forces; how the mind may be fixed upon lofty purposes; how the domestic affections—which give the truest happiness—may also be the greatest source of strength to the man who is

> More brave for this, that he has much to lose;

and how, finally, he becomes indifferent to all petty ambition—

> Finds comfort in himself and in his cause;
> And, while the mortal mist is gathering, draws
> His breath in confidence of Heaven's applause.
> This is the Happy Warrior, this is he
> Whom every man in arms should wish to be.

We may now see what ethical theory underlies Wordsworth's teaching of the transformation of instinct into reason. We must start from the postulate that there is in fact a Divine order in the universe; and that conformity to this order produces beauty as embodied in the external world, and is the condition of virtue as regulating our character. It is by obedience to the "stern lawgiver," Duty, that flowers gain their fragrance, and that "the most ancient heavens" preserve their freshness and strength. But this postulate does not seek for justification in abstract metaphysical reasoning. The "Intimations of Immortality" are precisely intimations, not intellectual intuitions. They are vague and emotional, not distinct and logical. They are a feeling of harmony, not a perception of innate ideas. And, on the other hand, our instincts are not a mere chaotic mass of passions, to be gratified without considering their place and function in a certain definite scheme. They have been implanted by the Divine hand, and the harmony which we feel corresponds to a real order. To justify them we must appeal to experience, but to experience interrogated by a certain definite procedure. Acting upon the assumption that the Divine order exists, we shall come to recognise it, though we could not deduce it by an *à priori* method.

The instrument, in fact, finds itself originally tuned by its Maker, and may preserve its original condition by careful obedience to the stern teaching of life. The bouyancy common to all youthful and healthy natures then changes into a deeper and more solemn mood. The great primary emotions retain the original impulse, but increase their volume. Grief and disap-

pointment are transmuted into tenderness, sympathy, and endurance. The reason, as it develops, regulates, without weakening, the primitive instincts. All the greatest, and therefore most common, sights of nature are indelibly associated with "admiration, hope, and love;" and all increase of knowledge and power is regarded as a means for furthering the gratification of our nobler emotions. Under the opposite treatment, the character loses its freshness, and we regard the early happiness as an illusion. The old emotions dry up at their source. Grief produces fretfulness, misanthropy, or effeminacy. Power is wasted on petty ends and frivolous excitement, and knowledge becomes barren and pedantic. In this way the postulate justifies itself by producing the noblest type of character. When the "moral being" is thus built up, its instincts become its convictions, we recognise the true voice of nature, and distinguish it from the echo of our passions. Thus we come to know how the Divine order and the laws by which the character is harmonised are the laws of morality.

To possible objections it might be answered by Wordsworth that this mode of assuming in order to prove is the normal method of philosophy. "You must love him," as he says of the poet,

> Ere to you
> He will seem worthy of your love.

The doctrine corresponds to the *crede ut intelligas* of the divine; or to the philosophic theory that we must start from the knowledge already constructed within us by instincts which have not yet learnt to reason. And, finally, if a persistent reasoner should ask why—even admitting the facts—the higher type should be preferred to the lower, Wordsworth may ask, Why is bodily health preferable to disease? If a man likes weak lungs and a bad digestion, reason cannot convince him of his error. The physician has done enough when he has pointed out the sanitary laws obedience to which generates strength, long life, and power of enjoyment. The moralist is in the same position when he has shown how certain habits conduce to the development of a type superior to its rivals in all the faculties which imply permanent peace of mind and power of resisting the shocks of the world without disintegration. Much undoubtedly remains to be said. Wordsworth's teaching, profound and admirable as it may be, has not the potency to silence the scepticism which has gathered strength since his day, and assailed fundamental—or what to him seemed fundamental—tenets of his system. No one can yet say what transformation may pass upon the thoughts and emotions for which he found utterance in speaking of the divinity and sanctity of nature. Some people vehemently maintain that the words will be emptied of all meaning if the old theological conceptions to which he was so firmly attached should disappear with the development of new modes of thought. Nature, as regarded by the light of modern science, will be the name of a cruel and wasteful, or at least of a purely neutral and indifferent power, or perhaps as merely an equivalent for the Unknowable, to which the conditions of our intellect prevent us from ever attaching any intelligible predicate. Others would say that in whatever terms we choose to speak of the mysterious darkness which surrounds our little island of comparative light, the emotion generated in a thoughtful mind by the contemplation of the universe will remain unaltered or strengthen with clearer knowledge; and that we shall express ourselves in a new dialect without altering the essence of our thought. The emotions to which Wordsworth has given utterance will remain, though the system in which he believed should sink into oblivion; as, indeed, all human systems have found different modes of symbolising the same fundamental feelings. But it is enough vaguely to indicate considerations not here to be developed.

It only remains to be added once more that Wordsworth's poetry derives its power from the same source as his philosophy. It speaks to our strongest feelings because his speculation rests upon our deepest thoughts. His singular capacity for investing all objects with a glow derived from early associations; his keen sympathy with natural and simple emotions; his sense of the sanctifying influences which can be extracted from sorrow, are of equal value to his power over our intellects and our imaginations. His psychology, stated systematically, is rational; and, when expressed passionately, turns into poetry. To be sensitive to the most important phenomena is the first step equally towards a poetical or a scientific exposition. To see these truly is the condition of making the poetry harmonious and the philosophy logical. And it is often difficult to say which power is most remarkable in Wordsworth. It would be easy to illustrate the truth by other than moral topics. His sonnet, noticed by De Quincey, in which he speaks of the abstracting power of darkness, and observes that as the hills pass into twilight we see the same sight as the ancient Britons, is impressive as it stands, but would be equally good as an illustration in a metaphysical treatise. Again, the sonnet beginning

With ships the sea was sprinkled far and wide,

is at once, as he has shown in a commentary of his own, an illustration of a curious psychological law—of our tendency, that is, to introduce an arbitrary principle of order into a random collection of objects—and, for the same reason, a striking embodiment of the corresponding mood of feeling. The little poem called "Stepping Westward" is in the same way at once a delicate expression of a specific sentiment and an acute critical analysis of the subtle associations suggested by a single phrase. But such illustrations might be multiplied indefinitely. As he has himself said, there is scarcely one of his poems which does not call attention to some moral sentiment, or to a general principle or law of thought, of our intellectual constitution.

Finally, we might look at the reverse side of the picture, and endeavour to show how the narrow limits of Wordsworth's power are connected with certain moral defects; with the want of quick sympathy which shows itself in his dramatic feebleness, and the austerity of character which caused him to lose his special gifts too early and become a rather commonplace defender of conservatism; and that curious diffidence (he assures us that it was "diffidence") which induced him to write many thousand lines of blank verse entirely about himself. But the task would be superfluous as well as ungrateful. It was his aim, he tells us, "to console the afflicted; to add sunshine to daylight by making the happy happier; to teach the young and the gracious of every age to see, to think, and therefore to become more actively and securely virtuous;" and, high as was the aim he did much towards its accomplishment.

Notes

1. J. S. Mill and Whewell were, for their generation, the ablest exponents of two opposite systems of thought upon such matters. Mill has expressed his obligations to Wordsworth in his *Autobiography*, and Whewell dedicated to Wordsworth his *Elements of Morality* in acknowledgment of his influence as a moralist.
2. The poem of Henry Vaughan, to which reference is often made in this connection, scarcely contains more than a pregnant hint.
3. As, for example, in the "Lines on Tintern Abbey": "If this be but a vain belief."
4. See Wordsworth's reference to the *Wealth of Nations*, in *The Prelude*, Book xiii.
5. So, too, in *The Prelude:*—

> Then was the truth received into my heart,
> That, under heaviest sorrow earth can bring,
> If from the affliction somewhere do not grow
> Honour which could not else have been, a faith,
> An elevation, and a sanctity;
> If new strength be not given, nor old restored,
> The fault is ours, not Nature's.

FRANCIS, LORD JEFFREY

1773–1850

Francis Jeffrey was born in Edinburgh on October 23, 1773. He was educated at Glasgow and Edinburgh universities, and at Queen's College, Oxford. Jeffrey was admitted to the Scottish bar in 1794 but soon realized that his Whig politics would hinder his professional advancement. Joining with Sydney Smith and several other friends, Jeffrey founded the *Edinburgh Review*, a periodical that became one of the most distinguished and influential of the nineteenth century.

The first issue of the *Review* appeared in October 1802 and, along with the next two, was edited by Smith. In 1803 Jeffrey assumed the editorship, a post he was to hold until 1829. Jeffrey's skill as an editor was especially evidenced in his hiring of distinguished contributors: Book reviews had heretofore been the work of hacks; it is Jeffrey and his periodical that are credited with establishing high standards for literary journalism.

Jeffrey himself wrote many influential essays for the *Review* and was known for his blistering criticism, particularly of Wordsworth. He came to be regarded by later literary scholars as something of a reactionary whose devotion to the eighteenth century prevented him from truly appreciating the significance of work by his contemporaries. Today scholars value his essays for their historical significance, and the achievements and distinction of the *Edinburgh Review* itself have never been questioned.

In addition to his literary career, Jeffrey also remained in the legal profession and, despite early misgivings, earned an enviable reputation as an advocate. In 1820 he was made rector of Glasgow

University, and in 1829 became dean of the faculty of advocates. The following year the Whigs came into power and Jeffrey was appointed Lord Advocate. As a member of the House of Commons he introduced the Scottish Reform Bill of 1831. In 1834 he was made a judge and assumed the title Lord Jeffrey. A selection of his *Contributions to the* Edinburgh Review appeared in four volumes in 1844.

Jeffrey died in Edinburgh on January 26, 1850.

Personal

His manner is not at first pleasing; what is worse, it is of that cast, which almost irresistibly impresses upon strangers the idea of levity and superficial talents. Yet there is not any man, whose real character is so much the reverse; he has indeed a very sportive and playful fancy, but it is accompanied with very extensive and varied information, with a readiness of apprehension almost intuitive, with judicious and calm discernment, with a profound and penetrating understanding. Indeed, both in point of candour and of vigour in the reasoning powers, I have never personally known a finer intellect than Jeffrey's, unless I were to except Allen's.—FRANCIS HORNER, *Journal* (Nov. 20, 1802), *Memoirs and Correspondence*, ed. Leonard Horner, 1843, Vol. 1, pp. 205–6

He was within when I called, and in a second I found myself in the presence of this bugbear of authors. He received me so kindly, (although, from the appearance of his room, he seemed to be immersed in occupation,) and asked so many questions, and said and looked so much, in so short a time, that I had some difficulty in collecting my inquisitorial powers to examine the person of the man. I know not how, there is a kind of atmosphere of activity about him; and my eyes caught so much of the prevailing spirit, that they darted for some minutes from object to object, and refused, for the first time, to settle themselves even upon the features of a man of genius—to them, of all human things, the most potent attractions.

I find that the common prints give a very inadequate notion of his appearance. The artists of this day are such a set of cowardly fellows, that they never dare to give the truth as it is in nature; and the consequence is, after all, that they rather take from, than add to, the impressiveness of the faces they would flatter. What a small matter is smoothness of skin, or even regularity of feature, in the countenance that Nature has formed to be the index of a powerful intellect? Perhaps I am too much of a connoisseur to be a fair judge of such matters; but I am very sure, that the mere handsomeness of a great man is one of the last things about him that fixes my attention. I do not wish, neither, to deny, that, when I first saw Goethe, the sublime simplicity of his Homeric beauty—the awful pile of forehead—the large deep eyes, with their melancholy lightnings—the whole countenance, so radiant with divinity, would have lost much of its power, had it not been, at the same time, the finest specimen of humanity I had ever beheld; neither would I conceal the immeasurable softness of delight which mingled with my reverence, when I detected, as if by intuition, in the midst of the whole artists of St. Luke's, the Hyperion curls, and calm majestic lineaments, which could be nobody's but Canova's. But although beauty never exists in vain, there is nothing more certain than that its absence is scarcely perceived by those who are capable of discovering and enjoying the marks of things more precious than beauty. Could all our countrymen of the present time, of very great reputation for talents or genius, be brought together into a single room, their physiognomies would, I doubt not, form as impressive a group as can well be imagined; but among the whole, there would scarcely be more than one face which any sculptor might be ambitious of imitating on marble. J——'s counte-

nance could not stand such a test. To catch the minutest elements of its eloquent power, would I think be a hard enough task for any painter, and indeed, as I have already told you, it has proved too hard a task for such as have yet attempted it.

It is a face which any man would pass without observation in a crowd, because it is small and swarthy, and entirely devoid of lofty or commanding outlines—and besides, his stature is so low, that he might walk close under your chin or mine without ever catching the eye even for a moment. However, he is scarcely shorter than Campbell; and some inches taller than Tom Moore, or the late Monk Lewis. I remember Lord Clarendon somewhere takes notice, that in his age, (the prime manhood of English intellect, as Coleridge calls it,) a very large proportion of the remarkable men were very short in stature. Such, if my memory serves me, were Hales, and Chillingworth, and Sidney Godolphin, and Lord Falkland himself, who used, I think, to say, that it was a great ingredient into his friendship for Mr. Godolphin, that he was pleased to be in *his* company, where he was the properer man. In our own time, we have more than one striking instance of the "*Mens magna in corpore parvo;*"—Buonaparte himself for one; and, by the way, he is the only little man I ever saw, who seemed to be unconscious, or careless, or disdainful of the circumstance. Almost all other persons of that description appear to labour under a continual and distressing feeling that nature has done them injustice, and not a few of them strive to make up for her defects, by holding their heads as high as possible, and even giving an uncomfortable elevation or projection to the chin, all which has a very mean effect upon their air and attitude—and is particularly hurtful to the features of the face, moreover,— because it tends to reverse the arrangement of Nature, and to throw all those parts into light which she has meant to be in shade. It is exactly the same sort of thing that we all remark on the stage, where the absurd manner in which the lamps are placed, under the feet of the performers, has such a destructive effect, that few actors, except those of the Kemble blood, appear to have any better than snub noses. Now, Napoleon has not the least of this trick; but, on the contrary, carries his head almost constantly in a stooping posture, and so preserves and even increases the natural effect of his grand formation about the eyebrows, and the beautiful classical cut of his mouth and chin—though to be sure, his features are so fine that nothing could take much from their power.—But, to come back to our own small men, J—— has a good deal of this unhappy manner, and so loses much of what his features, such as they are, might be made to convey.—JOHN GIBSON LOCKHART, *Peter's Letters to His Kinsfolk*, 1819, Letter 6

I dined with Walter Scott, and was delighted with the unaffected simplicity of his family. Jeffrey has a singular expression, poignant, bitter, piercing—as if his countenance never lighted up but at the perception of some weakness in human nature. Whatever you praise to Jeffrey, he directly chuckles out some error that you did not perceive. Whatever you praise to Scott, he joins heartily with yourself, and directs your attention to some additional beauty. Scott throws a light on life by the beaming geniality of his soul, and so dazzles you that you have no time or perception for anything but its beauties: while

Jeffrey seems to revel in holding up his hand before the light in order that he may spy out its deformities. The face of Scott is the expression of a man whose great pleasure has been to shake Nature by the hand, while to point at her with his finger has certainly, from the expression of his face, been the chief enjoyment of Jeffrey.—BENJAMIN ROBERT HAYDON, Letter to Mary Russell Mitford (Dec. 5, 1820), *Life, Letters and Table Talk*, ed. Richard Henry Stoddard, 1876, p. 203

Mr. Francis Jeffrey, then Lord Advocate of Scotland, was first returned to Parliament in 1831 for the burgh of Malton; afterwards he was twice elected for the city of Edinburgh. I never knew a parliamentary *debût* which was regarded with greater or more general interest, or respecting the success of which more confident expectations were entertained. He had, by means of the *Edinburgh Review*, which he had conducted from its commencement, not only brought about a complete revolution in periodical criticism, but had given a tone to the literature of the nineteenth century. He was called the Prince of Critics, and his critical supremacy was universally acknowledged. Some of his compositions—his articles on Taste, for example, which were written in reply to the Rev. Archibald Allison, were admitted by every competent judge to be the most beautiful specimens of writing which had appeared in the English language. The parliamentary *debût*, therefore, of a man who had formed so distinguished a part on the literary stage, and who was still regarded as unrivalled in periodical criticism, could not fail to excite very deep and general interest; but that interest was greatly increased by the reputation he had acquired as a lawyer and a speaker. At the Scottish bar, and at public meetings in Edinburgh, he knew no competitor as a speaker. When it was known that he was to speak at a public meeting on any important question, persons would flock from a circuit of twenty miles to hear him. The Scottish Press, knowing Mr. Jeffrey's distinguished reputation in his own country, as a public speaker, never dreamed that he might fail in the House of Commons, where the scene would not only be new to him, but where he would have to compete with persons possessing first-rate talents as public speakers, which he had never had to do in his own country. Hence the Scotch papers increased the interest with which his maiden effort in St. Stephen's was looked forward to, by paragraphs without number, in which they confidently predicted that he would not only gratify, but electrify the House, by the brilliancy of his eloquence. It was expected that he would speak on some important question which stood for discussion the second or third night, I do not recollect which, after he took the oaths and his seat. The house was consequently filled in every part, and an unusual number of literary characters were in and under the gallery. In so far as their expectations relative to the mere circumstance of the Lord Advocate's speaking on that particular night were concerned, honourable members and strangers were not disappointed; as regarded the character and effect of his oratory, they were grievously so. He spoke for about an hour and twenty mintues; but the effort was a complete failure. His matter was refined and philosophical in the highest degree. It was nearly as unintelligible to the majority of his auditory, as if he had spoken some most abstruse article, intended for the *Edinburgh Review*, in answer to Kant, or some of the other German metaphysicians. Of course, it made no impression, and produced no effect. Then, the amazing rapidity of his delivery operated much against the speech. I think I never heard a person, either in or out of the house, speak so fast as he did on that occasion. The most experienced short-hand reporters were unable to follow him; they mentioned the circumstance in the papers of the following morning, as a reason for

not giving his speech at greater length. Members usually speak at the rate of two columns and a half of the *Times* newspaper in an hour. Had a *verbatim* report of what Mr. Jeffrey spoke in an hour been given in that journal, it would have filled four of its columns. Yet notwithstanding the rapidity with which Mr. Jeffrey spoke on this occasion, he never so much as faltered once, nor recalled a word which he uttered, to substitute one more suitable for it. His language indeed was fluent and elegant in the extreme. His manner too, was graceful, but it wanted variety. His voice was clear and pleasant; but it had no flexibility in its intonations. He continued and ended in much the same tones as he began. The same monotony characterised his gesticulation. He was cheered to some extent; but the applause was not so general, nor cordial, nor frequent, as to indicate a successful *debût*. In fact, he himself saw his maiden effort was a failure, and that there was all the difference in the world between the House of Commons, and the Waterloo Hotel, or Law-courts of Edinburgh. He never after volunteered a speech of any length. When he spoke, it was only when forced to do it by his office, and then always as briefly as possible. Latterly, he excited no more interest in the house than the least talented member. It was a great pity for his oratorical fame that he ever entered the house at all.—JAMES GRANT, *Random Recollections of the House of Commons*, 1836, pp. 183–87

Jeffrey is gone. Dear fellow! I loved him as much as it is easy to love a man who belongs to an older generation. And how good, and kind, and generous he was to me! His goodness, too, was the more precious because his perspicacity was so great. He saw through and through you. He marked every fault of taste, every weakness, every ridicule; and yet he loved you as if he had been the dullest fellow in England. He had a much better heart than Sydney Smith. I do not mean that Sydney was in that respect below par. In ability I should say that Jeffrey was higher, but Sydney rarer. I would rather have been Jeffrey; but there will be several Jeffreys, before there is a Sydney. After all, dear Jeffrey's death is hardly matter for mourning. God grant that I may die so! Full of years; full of honors; faculties bright, and affections warm, to the last; lamented by the public, and by many valuable private friends. This is the euthanasia. —THOMAS BABINGTON MACAULAY, *Journal* (Jan. 28, 1850), cited in G. Otto Trevelyan, *The Life and Letters of Lord Macaulay*, 1876, Vol. 2, pp. 234–35

Poor dear Jeffrey! I bought a *Times* at the station yesterday morning, and was so stunned by the announcement, that I felt it in that wounded part of me, almost directly; and the bad symptoms (modified) returned within a few hours. I had a letter from him in extraordinary good spirits within this week or two—he was better, he said, than he had been for a long time—and I sent him proof-sheets of the number only last Wednesday. I say nothing of his wonderful abilities and great career, but he was a most affectionate and devoted friend to me; and though no man could wish to live and die more happily, so old in years and yet so young in faculties and sympathies, I am very deeply grieved for his loss.—CHARLES DICKENS, Letter to John Forster (Jan. 29, 1850)

General

As to Mr. Jeffrey I have great personal regard for him and high estimation of his talents. I have seldom known a man with equal readiness of ideas or power of expressing them. But I had no reason to be so very much gratified by his review of *Marmion* as to propitiate him by a dedication of any work of mine. I have no fault to find with his expressing his sentiments frankly and freely upon the poem yet I think he might without derogation to his impartiality have couched them in language rather more civil to a personal friend and I believe he would have thought twice before he had given himself that air of superiority in a case where I had any chance of defending myself. Besides I really have often told him that I think he wants the taste for poetry which is essentially necessary to enjoy and of course to criticize it with justice. He is learned with the most learned in its canons and laws skilled in its modulation and an excellent judge of the justice of the sentiments which it conveys but he wants that enthusiastic feeling which like sun-shine upon a landscape lights up every beauty and palliates if it cannot hide every defect. To offer a poem of imagination to a man whose whole life and study has been to acquire a stoical indifference towards enthusiasm of every kind would be the last as it would surely be the silliest action of my life. This is really my opinion of Jeffrey not formed yesterday nor upon any coldness between us for there has been none. He has been possessed of it these several years and it certainly never made the least difference between us; but I neither owe him nor have the least inclination to offer him such a mark of regard as the dedication of any work past present or to come.—SIR WALTER SCOTT, Letter to Joanna Baillie (Oct. 31, 1808)

> Health to immortal Jeffrey! once, in name,
> England could boast a judge almost the same;
> In soul so like, so merciful, yet just,
> Some think that Satan has resign'd his trust,
> And given the spirit to the world again,
> To sentence letters, as he sentenced men.
> With hand less mighty, but with heart as black,
> With voice as willing to decree the rack;
> Bred in the courts betimes, though all that law
> As yet hath taught him is to find a flaw;
> Since well instructed in the patriot school
> To rail at party, though a party tool,
> Who knows, if chance his patrons should restore
> Back to the sway they forfeited before,
> His scribbling toils some recompense may meet,
> And raise this Daniel to the judgment-seat?
> Let Jeffreys' shade indulge the pious hope,
> And greeting thus, present him with a rope:
> 'Heir to my virtues! man of equal mind!
> Skill'd to condemn as to traduce mankind,
> This cord receive, for thee reserved with care,
> To wield in judgment, and at length to wear.'
> . . .
> Then prosper, Jeffrey! pertest of the train
> Whom Scotland pampers with her fiery grain!
> Whatever blessing waits a genuine Scot,
> In double portion swells thy glorious lot;
> For thee Edina culls her evening sweets,
> And showers their odours on thy candid sheets,
> Whose hue and fragrance to thy work adhere—
> This scents its pages, and that gilds its rear.
> Lo! blushing Itch, coy nymph, enamour'd grown,
> Forsakes the rest, and cleaves to thee alone;
> And, too unjust to other Pictish men,
> Enjoys thy person, and inspires thy pen!
> —GEORGE GORDON, LORD BYRON, *English Bards and Scotch Reviewers*, 1809, ll. 438–59, 528–39

> Alas for Jeffrey!—if my fancy dreams,
> Let not that dream's delusion pass away—
> For still 'midst all his poverty it seems
> As if a spark of some ethereal ray,

> Some fragment of the true Promethean beams,
> Had been commingled with his infant clay;
> As if for better things he had been born
> Than transient flatteries and eternal scorn.
> Alas for Jeffrey!—for he might have clombe
> To some high niche in glory's marble fane;
> But he, vain man! preferred a lowlier home,
> An easier triumph and a paltrier reign;
> Therefore his name is blotted from the Tome
> Of Fame's enduring record, and his gain
> Hath in his life been given him, and the wreath
> That his youth won scarce waits the wintry breath
> Of the Destroyer, to shed all its bloom
> And dissipate its fragrance in the air,
> Whereof shall nought remain to deck his tomb
> Or please his Manes. No memorial fair
> Of earthly greatness, but one saddening gloom
> Of funeral desolation shall be there.
> And they hereafter on his grave that tread,
> Shall class the Sleeper with the Vulgar Dead.
> —JOHN GIBSON LOCKHART, "The Mad Banker of Amsterdam," *Blackwood's Edinburgh Magazine*, Feb. 1819, p. 565

Tickler: Jeffrey has a fine face. Mere animation is common; but those large dark eyes beam with intellect and sensibility—*naturally* finest both—alive perpetually and at work—yet never weary—as if that work were play—and needed not the restoration of sleep. Wit, in its full acceptation, is a weighty word—and by it I designate the mind of the Man! Taste in him is exalted into Imagination—Ingenuity brightens into Genius. He hath also Wisdom. But *nemo omnibus horis sapit;* and he made an unfortunate stumble over the Lyrical Ballads. He has had the magnanimity, however, I am told, to repent that great mistake, which to his fame was a misfortune—and, knowing the error of his ways, has returned to the broad path of Nature and Truth. How nobly has he written of Crabbe and Campbell, and Scott and Byron! Incomprehensible contradiction—the worst critic of the age is also the best—but the weeds of his mind are dead—the flowers are immortal. He is no orator, they say, in St Stephen's; but that mouth, even on the silent paper, gives them the lie; and I have heard him a hundred times the most eloquent of speakers. His is a brilliant name in the literature of Scotland.—JOHN WILSON, (as "Christopher North"), *Noctes Ambrosianae* (Nov. 1832), 1854

What do you hear of Jeffrey's book? Longman speaks well of the sale. The criticisms in the London papers, of which I think little indeed, are coldly civil. My own general impression is this, that the selection is ill made, and that a certain want of finish which in a periodical work is readily excused and has sometimes even the effect of a grace, is rather too perceptible in many passages. On the other hand the variety and fertility of Jeffrey's mind seem to me more extraordinary than ever. I think that there are few things in the four volumes which one or two other men could not have done as well. But I do not think that any one man, except Jeffrey, nay that any three men could have produced such diversified excellence. When I compare him with Sydney and myself, I feel, with humility perfectly sincere, that his range is immeasurably wider than ours. And this is only as a writer. But he is not only a writer. He has been a great advocate, and he is a great judge. Take him all in all, I think him more nearly an universal genius than any man of our time; certainly far more nearly than Brougham, much as Brougham affects the character.—THOMAS BABINGTON MACAULAY, Letter to Macvey Napier (Dec. 13, 1843)

A prominent defect of Jeffrey's literary criticism arose from his lack of earnestness,—that earnestness which comes, not merely from the assent of the understanding to a proposition, but from the deep convictions of a man's whole nature. He is consequently ingenious and plausible, rather than profound,—a man of expedients rather than of ideas and principles. In too many of his articles, he appears like an advocate, careless of the truth, or sceptical as to its existence or possibility of being reached, and only desirous to make out as good a case for his own assumed position as will puzzle or unsettle the understandings of his hearers. His logical capacity is shown in acute special pleading, in sophistical glosses, more than in fair argument. He is almost always a reasoner on the surface; and the moment he begins to argue, the reader instinctively puts his understanding on guard, with the expectation of the ingenious fallacies that are to come. He cannot handle universal principles, founded in the nature of things, and he would not, if he could; for his object is victory rather than truth. When a proposition is presented to his mind, his inquiry is not whether it be true or false, but what can be said in its favor or against it. The sceptical and refining character of his understanding, leading him to look at things merely as subjects for argument, and the mockery and *persiflage* of manner which such a habit of mind induces, made him a most provoking adversary to a man who viewed things in a more profound and earnest manner.

As an effect of this absence of earnestness, and of the consequent devotion of his faculties to the mere attainment of immediate objects, we may mention this subordination of principle to tact, both in his own writings and in his management of the *Review*. There is no critic more slippery, none who can shift his position so nimbly, or who avoids the consequences of a blunder with such brilliant dexterity. He understood to perfection the art of so mingling praise and blame, that, while the spirit and effect of the *critique* was to represent its object as little better than a dunce, its mere letter was consistent with a more favorable view. Thus, while it was the fashion to underrate and ridicule any class of poets, there was none who could do it with more consummate skill than Jeffrey,—none who could gain more reputation for sense and acumen in the position he assumed; but whenever public feeling changed, he could still refer confidently to his course, and prove that he had always acknowledged the extraordinary gifts of his victims, and only ridiculed or mourned their misdirection. He thus made his writings oracular among all talkers about taste and letters, among all who felt and thought superficially. He was popular with them, not because he gave them deeper principles by which to judge of merit, but because he reconciled them to their own shallowness. The lazy and the superficial, who consider everything as nonsense which they have not the sense to perceive, are especially gratified with the writer who confirms their own impressions by plausible arguments, and expresses them in brilliant language. Profound and earnest feeling, sentiments of awe, wonder, and reverence, a mind trained to habits of contemplation on man and the universe, were needed in the critic who should do justice to Wordsworth and Coleridge. These Jeffrey did not possess; but instead, he had a subtle understanding, considerable quickness of apprehension, sensibility, and fancy, a great deal of wit, a most remarkable fluency of expression, and, with little insight beyond the surface of things, an acute perception of their practical and conventional relations. In the exercise of these powers on their appropriate subjects, he appears to great advantage. No one could demolish a dunce more effectively, or represent in clearer light the follies and crimes of knavish politicians. But when he came to discuss the merits of works of high and refined imagination, or to criticize sentiments lying deeper than those which usually appear in actual life, he did little more than express brilliant absurdities. It is here that we discover his lack of power to perceive the thing he ridicules; and accordingly his wit only beats the air.—EDWIN P. WHIPPLE, "British Critics" (1845), *Essays and Reviews*, 1850, Vol. 2, pp. 100–102

The truth is, that Lord Jeffrey was something of a Whig critic. We have hinted, that among the peculiarities of that character, an excessive partiality for new, arduous, overwhelming, original excellence, was by no means to be numbered. Their tendency inclining to the quiet footsteps of custom, they like to trace the exact fulfilment of admitted rules, a just accordance with the familiar features of ancient merit. But they are most averse to mysticism. A clear, precise, discriminating intellect shrinks at once from the symbolic, the unbounded, the indefinite. The misfortune is that mysticism is true. There certainly are kinds of truth, borne in as it were instinctively on the human intellect, most influential on the character and the heart, yet hardly capable of stringent statement, difficult to limit by an elaborate definition. Their course is shadowy; the mind seems rather to have seen than to see them, more to feel after than definitely apprehend them. They commonly involve an infinite element, which of course cannot be stated precisely, or else a first principle—an original tendency—of our intellectual constitution, which it is impossible not to feel, and yet which it is hard to extricate in terms and words. Of this latter kind is what has been called the religion of nature, or more exactly, perhaps, the religion of the imagination. This is an interpretation of the world. According to it the beauty of the universe has a meaning, its grandeur a soul, its sublimity an expression. As we gaze on the faces of those whom we love; as we watch the light of life in the dawning of their eyes, and the play of their features, and the wildness of their animation; as we trace in changing lineaments a varying sign; as a charm and a thrill seem to run along the tone of a voice, to haunt the mind with a mere word; as a tone seems to roam in the ear; as a trembling fancy hears words that are unspoken; so in nature the mystical sense finds a motion in the mountain, and a power in the waves, and a meaning in the long white line of the shore, and a thought in the blue of heaven, and a gushing soul in the buoyant light, an unbounded being in the vast void air, and

Wakeful watchings in the pointed stars.

There is a philosophy in this which might be explained, if explaining were to our purpose. It might be advanced that there are original sources of expression in the essential grandeur and sublimity of nature, of an analogous though fainter kind, to those familiar, inexplicable signs by which we trace in the very face and outward lineaments of man the existence and working of the mind within. But be this as it may, it is certain that Mr. Wordsworth preached this kind of religion, and that Lord Jeffrey did not believe a word of it. His cool, sharp, collected mind revolted from its mystery; his detective intelligence was absorbed in its apparent fallaciousness; his light humour made sport with the sublimities of the preacher. His love of perspicuity was vexed by its indefiniteness; the precise philosopher was amazed at its mystic unintelligibility. Finding a little fault was doubtless not unpleasant to him. The reviewer's pen— φόνος ἥρωεσσιν—has seldom been more poignantly wielded. 'If,' he was told, 'you could be alarmed into the semblance of modesty, you would charm everybody; but remember my joke against you' (Sydney Smith *loquitur*) 'about the moon. D—n the solar system—bad light—planets too distant—pestered with comets: feeble contrivance; could make a better with great ease.' Yet we do not mean that in this great literary feud either of the combatants had all the right, or gained all the victory. The world has given judgment. Both Mr. Wordsworth and Lord Jeffrey have received their reward. The one had his own generation ; the laughter of men, the applause of drawing-rooms, the concurrence of the crowd: the other a succeeding age, the fond enthusiasm of secret students, the lonely rapture of lonely minds. And each has received according to his kind. If all cultivated men speak differently because of the existence of Wordsworth and Coleridge; if not a thoughtful English book has appeared for forty years, without some trace for good or evil of their influence; if sermon-writers subsist upon their thoughts; if 'sacred poets' thrive by translating their weaker portion into the speech of women; if, when all this is over, some sufficient part of their writing will ever be fitting food for wild musing and solitary meditation, surely this is because they possessed the inner nature—'an intense and glowing mind,' 'the vision and the faculty divine.' But if, perchance, in their weaker moments, the great authors of the *Lyrical Ballads* did ever imagine that the world was to pause because of their verses; that *Peter Bell* would be popular in drawing rooms; that *Christabel* would be perused in the City; that people of fashion would make a hand-book of the *Excursion*,—it was well for them to be told at once that this was not so. Nature ingeniously prepared a shrill artificial voice, which spoke in season and out of season, enough and more than enough, what will ever be the idea of the cities of the plain concerning those who live alone among the mountains; of the frivolous concerning the grave; of the gregarious concerning the recluse; of those who laugh concerning those who laugh not; of the common concerning the uncommon; of those who lend on usury concerning those who lend not; the notion of the world of those whom it will not reckon among the righteous—it said, 'This won't do!' And so in all time will the lovers of polished Liberalism speak, concerning the intense and lonely prophet.

Yet, if Lord Jeffrey had the natural infirmities of a Whig critic, he certainly had also its extrinsic and political advantages. Especially at Edinburgh the Whigs wanted a literary man. The Liberal party in Scotland had long groaned under political exclusion; they had suffered, with acute mortification, the heavy sway of Henry Dundas, but they had been compensated by a literary supremacy; in the book-world they enjoyed a domination. On a sudden this was rudely threatened. The fame of Sir Walter Scott was echoed from the southern world, and appealed to every national sentiment—to the inmost heart of every Scotchman. And what a ruler! A lame Tory, a jocose Jacobite, a laugher at liberalism, a scoffer at metaphysics, an unbeliever in political economy! What a gothic ruler for the modern Athens!—was this man to reign over them? It would not have been like human nature, if a strong and intellectual party had not soon found a clever and noticeable rival. Poets, indeed, are not made 'to order;' but Byron, speaking the sentiment of his time and circle, counted reviewers their equals. If a Tory produced *Marmion*, a Whig wrote the best article upon it; Scott might, so ran Liberal speech, be the best living writer of fiction; Jeffrey, clearly, was the most shrewd and accomplished of literary critics.

And though this was an absurd delusion, Lord Jeffrey was no every-day man. He invented the trade of editorship. Before him an editor was a bookseller's drudge; he is now a distinguished functionary. If Jeffrey was not a great critic, he had, what very great critics have wanted, the art of writing what most people would think good criticism. He might not know his subject, but he knew his readers. People like to read ideas which they can imagine to have been their own. 'Why does Scarlett always persuade the jury?' asked a rustic gentleman. 'Because there are twelve Scarletts in the jury-box,' replied an envious advocate. What Scarlett was in law, Jeffrey was in criticism; he could become that which his readers could not avoid being. He was neither a pathetic writer nor a profound writer; but he was a quick-eyed, bustling, black-haired, sagacious, agreeable, man of the world. He had his day, and was entitled to his day; but a gentle oblivion must now cover his already subsiding reputation.—WALTER BAGEHOT, "The First Edinburgh Reviewers" (1855), *Collected Works*, ed. Norman St. John-Stevas, 1965, Vol. 1, pp. 329–33

He was not so much distinguished by the predominance of any one great quality, as by the union of several of the finest. Rapidity of intellect, instead of misleading, as it often does, was combined in him with great soundness; and a high condition of the reasoning powers with an active and delightful fancy. Though not what is termed learned, his knowledge was various; and on literature, politics, and the philosophy of life, it was deep. A taste exquisitely delicate and largely exercised was one of the great sources of his enjoyment, and of his unmatched critical skill. But the peculiar charm of his character lay in the junction of intellectual power with moral worth. His honour was superior to every temptation by which the world could assail it. The pleasures of the heart were necessary for his existence, and were preferred by him to every other gratification, except the pleasures of conscience. Passing much of his time in literary and political contention, he was never once chilled by an unkind feeling, even toward those he was trying to overcome. An habitual gayety never allowed its thoughtlessness, nor an habitual prudence its caution, to interfere with any claim of charity or duty. Nor was this merely the passive amiableness of a gentle disposition. It was the positive humanity of a resolute man, glowing in the conflicts of the world.

He prepared himself for what he did by judicious early industry. He then chose the most difficult spheres in which talent can be exerted, and excelled in them all; rising from obscurity and dependence to affluence and renown. His splendour as an advocate was exceeded by his eminence as a judge. He was the founder of a new system of criticism, and this a higher one than had ever existed. As an editor, and as a writer, he did as much to improve his country and the world, as can almost ever be done, by discussion, by a single man. He was the last of four pre-eminent Scotchmen, who, living in their own country, raised its character and extended its reputation, during the period of his career. The other three were Dugald Stewart, Walter Scott, and Thomas Chalmers; each of whom, in literature, philosophy, or policy, caused great changes; and each left upon his age the impression of the mind that produced them. Jeffrey, though surpassed in genius certainly by Scott, and perhaps by Chalmers, was inferior to none of them in public usefulness, or in the beauty of the means by which he achieved it, or in its probable duration. The elevation of the public mind was his peculiar glory. In one respect alone he was unfortunate. The assaults which he led against error were efforts in which the value of his personal services can never be duly seen. His position required him to dissipate, in detached and nameless exertions, as much philosophy and beautiful composition as would have sustained avowed and important original works. He has raised a great monument, but it is one on which his own name is too faintly engraved.—HENRY, LORD COCKBURN, *Life of Lord Jeffrey*, 1857, Vol. 1, pp. 319–20

Jeffrey was perhaps at the height of his reputation about 1816; his *Edinburgh Review* a kind of Delphic oracle and voice of the inspired for great majorities of what is called the 'intelligent public,' and himself regarded universally as a man of consummate penetration and the *facile princeps* in the department he had chosen to cultivate and practise. In the half-century that has followed, what a change in all this! the fine gold become dim to such a degree, and the Trismegistus hardly now regarded as a *Megas* by anyone, or by the generality remembered at all. He may be said to have begun the rash reckless style of criticising everything in heaven and earth by appeal to *Molière's maid*; 'Do *you* like it?' '*Don't* you like it?' a style which in hands more and more inferior to that sound-hearted old lady and him, has since grown gradually to such immeasurable length among us; and he himself is one of the first that suffers by it. If praise and blame are to be perfected, not in the mouth of Molière's maid only but in that of mischievous precocious babes and sucklings, you will arrive at singular judgments by degrees! Jeffrey was by no means the supreme in criticism or in anything else; but it is certain there has no critic appeared among us since who was worth naming beside him; and his influence for good and for evil in literature and otherwise has been very great. Democracy, the gradual uprise and rule in all things of roaring million-headed unreflecting, darkly suffering darkly sinning 'Demos,' come to call its old superiors to account at its maddest of tribunals; nothing in my time has so forwarded all this as Jeffrey and his once famous *Edinburgh Review*.

He was not deep enough, pious or reverent enough, to have been great in literature; but he was a man intrinsically of veracity; said nothing without meaning it to some considerable degree, had the quickest perceptions, excellent practical discernment of what lay before him; was in earnest too, though not 'dreadfully in earnest;' in short was well fitted to set forth that *Edinburgh Review* (at the dull opening of our now so tumultuous century), and become coryphæus of his generation in the waste, wide-spreading and incalculable course appointed *it* among the centuries! I used to find in him a finer talent than any he has evidenced in writing. This was chiefly when he got to speak Scotch, and gave me anecdotes of old Scotch Braxfields and vernacular (often enough but not always cynical) curiosities of that type; which he did with a greatness of gusto quite peculiar to the topic, with a fine and deep sense of humour, of real comic mirth, much beyond what was noticeable in him otherwise; not to speak of the perfection of the mimicry, which itself was something. I used to think to myself, 'Here is a man whom they have kneaded into the shape of an Edinburgh reviewer, and clothed the soul of in Whig formulas and blue and yellow; but he might have been a beautiful Goldoni too, or some thing better in that kind, and have given us *comedies* and aerial pictures true and poetic of human life in a far other way!' There was something of Voltaire in him, something even in bodily features; those bright-beaming, swift and piercing hazel eyes, with their accompaniment of rapid keen expression in the other lineaments of face, resembled one's notion of Voltaire; and in the voice too there was a fine half-plangent kind of metallic ringing tone which used to remind me of what I fancied Voltaire's voice might have been: 'voix sombre et majestueuse,' Duvernet calls it. The culture and respective natal scenery of the two men had been very different; nor was their *magnitude* of faculty anthing like the same, had their respective kinds of it been much more identical than they were. You could not define Jeffrey to have been more than a potential Voltaire; say 'Scotch Voltaire'; with about as much reason (which was not very much) as they used in

Edinburgh to call old Playfair the 'Scotch D'Alembert.' Our Voltaire too, whatever else might be said of him, was at least worth a large multiple of our D'Alembert! A beautiful little man the former of these, and a bright island to me and to mine in the sea of things, of whom it is now again mournful and painful to take farewell.—THOMAS CARLYLE, "Lord Jeffrey" (1867), *Reminiscences*, ed. James Anthony Froude, 1881, Vol. 2, pp. 63–66

Though his works no longer delight the general public, Lord Jeffrey will always occupy a respectable position in English letters as the founder, to all intents and purposes, of reviewing. His intellect was nimble rather than penetrating, and his knowledge miscellaneous rather than profound; while his sensibility at times was too strong for his sense. Indeed, his characteristic admission to Macvey Napier that he had read Macaulay's essay on Bacon "not only with delight but with emotion, with throbbings of the heart and tears in the eye," seems to afford a hint at once of the measure of his attainments in philosophy and of his extreme susceptibility to any form of excitation. Yet his brisk and dapper habit of mind was no bad qualification for the literary work of his life; and perhaps the best proof of his success is the long existence which his convention has enjoyed. Every sentence of Macaulay attests his statement that he had read and re-read Jeffrey's old articles till he knew them by heart; and for close upon a hundred years critic after critic, consciously or unconsciously, has copied his methods, has imitated his tone and bearing, has aped his omniscience, and has endeavoured to assume his awful air of authority. The penalty attached to this good fortune has been the obloquy of all who have learned "the cant of an author," and "begun to treat critics with contempt"; who find a singular consolation for the sense of their own incompetence in Jeffrey's declaration that *The Excursion* would "never do"; and who feel their immortality assured by the fact that Jeffrey preferred Rogers and Campbell to Shelley and Byron. Whatever lack of perception such notorious judgments may argue, Lord Jeffrey has at all events made good a substantial claim to applause, if not upon the dubiously relevant ground of having "made the Moral tendencies of the works under consideration a leading subject of discussion," and "neglected no opportunity of elucidating the true constituents of human happiness and virtue," at all events for having succeeded in "permanently raising the standard, and increasing the influence of all such Occasional writings" as his own.

An overflowing vocabulary and an unhesitating fluency are apt to be bad masters; to Jeffrey they were ever the best of servants; for he never suffered them to impair the lucidity which is the outstanding merit of his writing. The thought he desires to express may be little worth expressing, but it is always clothed in language of which the meaning is impossible to mistake. In spite of occasional grammatical errors, he never becomes slipshod, and his style is so clean, so finished, and so scrupulously precise as to partake in some degree of the peculiar charm of good French prose. He had measured his own powers, it may be assumed, with tolerable accuracy, and seldom attempted flights for which he was naturally unfitted. But his imagination was a lively one, and the similes in which from time to time he indulges possess the merits of being neither trite nor far-fetched, of being exactly appropriate, and of never breaking down. Finally, the want of more substantial and impressive excellences is felt to be almost atoned for by the irresistible sprightliness and vivacity which animate all his pieces.

Of Jeffrey in his capacity of critic, something has been

already hinted, and little more need be said. He is charged with a lack of humour, and he was doubtless unable to see the joke of being attacked as he himself had attacked others. But the *Edinburgh* reviewer who spoke of "the deliberate and indulgent criticism which *we* exercise rather for the encouragement of talent than its warning" can scarcely have been destitute of the saving quality. His campaign against the Lake school was vigorous and persistent; yet the worst that he said against Wordsworth is perhaps more excusable than the faint praise with which he welcomed the poetry of Sir Walter Scott. For this, however, he made ample amends when he reviewed the works of the author of *Waverley*; and, indeed, he could turn a compliment with at least as good a grace as he could direct a sarcasm. His powers of detraction and depreciation have probably been overestimated; and though he could sneer and banter with unflagging spirit, his genius was of too restless and pert an order ever to attain to that sublime of insolence which Lockhart scaled. Nevertheless, he dispensed his chastisements with all his heart; and if the blows sometimes fell upon the wrong back, it must be remembered that they were prompted, not by malice nor stupidity, but by attachment to the cardinal principle that literature is an art, that its practice not only requires the utmost care, diligence, and preparation, but also involves a *convention*, and that, therefore, the haphazard use of the common unsifted vocabulary of everyday life can never consist with poetry. Against the indiscriminate censure bestowed by Jeffrey upon Wordsworth may fairly be set off his generous, yet judicious, eulogy of Keats.—J. H. MILLAR, "Francis Jeffrey," *English Prose*, ed. Henry Craik, 1896, Vol. 5, pp. 143–45

Jeffrey profited from the conspiracy of a great many fortunate circumstances, and for a series of years enjoyed, as dictator of the policy of the *Edinburgh Review*, a reputation as critic that was really far beyond what his intrinsic merit justified. Leigh Hunt and Lamb were much more delicate and imaginative appreciators of literature than Jeffrey; Hazlitt, despite his waywardness and arrogance, was a subtler and more stimulating literary interpreter. Coleridge was incomparably Jeffrey's superior in penetrating insight, in learning and scholarship, in philosophic scope, and in refinement and sureness of taste. Yet Jeffrey, by dint of his cleverness, versatility, brilliancy, readiness of resource, and, above all, because of his commanding position as the director of the new Whig *Review*, outstripped all these competitors and imposed himself on public opinion as the typically infallible critic of his day and generation. His personal charm, too, worked in his favour; his Whig following was enthusiastically loyal. Everything tended to increase, for the time being, his fame as a literary autocrat.

The later reaction, which has so nearly consigned Jeffrey to the region of unread authors, was in its turn extreme, and yet followed naturally. Wordsworth and Coleridge, whom Jeffrey had assailed persistently till he had become in the public mind the representative foe of Romanticism, had won their cause, and had been received by wider and wider circles of the most cultivated and discerning readers as among the foremost poets of their age. Jeffrey, their arch-enemy, suffered correspondingly in public esteem. Time seemed to have proved him wrong in one of his most strenuously asserted prejudices. Moreover, this particular defeat was merely one special instance of the evil effect that far-reaching influences were having upon Jeffrey's reputation. His modes of conceiving life were being outgrown. His genial, man-of-the-world wisdom and somewhat narrow range of feeling seemed more and more unsatisfactory, as the public gradually made their own the

deeper spiritual experience of idealistic poets, like Shelley, and of transcendental prose-writers, like Carlyle. Jeffrey's dry intellectuality and his shallow associational psychology seemed unequal to the vital problems in art and in ethics that the new age was canvassing. Moreover, his autocratic style and omniscient air had been caught up by all the quarterly Reviews, and no longer served to distinguish him; the methods and the tone of the *Edinburgh* were copied far and wide, and the critics of the new generation were quite a match for Jeffrey in gay, domineering assurance and in easy, swift omniscience. Jeffrey had trained many followers into his own likeness; or, at any rate, the methods and the tone that he had hit upon "survived" and had been universally received as fit.

Finally, Jeffrey's essays, even at their best, had many of the qualities of "occasional" writing, and too often seemed merely meant for the moment; the trail of the periodical was over them all. Their very rapidity, sparkle, and plausibility gave them an air of perishableness; they seemed clever and entertaining improvisations. Work of this sort could hardly hope to maintain itself permanently in public favour. Nor was the collection of his essays, that Jeffrey saw fit to publish in 1843, of a sort to make a stand against the general indifference that was clouding his fame. Two thousand pages of improvised comments on all manner of topics, from the *Memoirs of Baber* to Dugald Stewart's *Philosophical Essays*, could scarcely be expected to secure a fixed place for themselves in the affections of large masses of readers. A far smaller volume, that should have included only the essays, or portions of essays, that were best wrought in style, most vigorously thought out, and contained the most characteristic and final of Jeffrey's opinions, would have been more likely—except in so far as Jeffrey based his claims on his versatility—to have insured him permanent remembrance as critic and prose-writer.

The reaction, then, against Jeffrey was necessary and, in some degree, just. Yet, now that the air is cleared of Romantic prejudices, Jeffrey's real services to the causes both of criticism and of sound literature may be more accurately perceived and defined. Not for a moment can the student who aims at genuine insight into the history of literature and of literary opinion during the first quarter of our century afford to disregard Jeffrey and his *Edinburgh Review* Essays, or to pass him by with a phrase as a mere unsuccessful opponent of Wordsworth and Coleridge. Jeffrey influenced public opinion decisively and beneficially on a vast range of subjects. He broadened the methods of literary criticism and won for it new points of view and new fields. He put the relations between critic and public on a sounder basis, and raised the profession of literary criticism into an honourable calling. Finally, he developed English style, added to its swiftness of play and brilliant serviceableness, and prepared the way for the dazzlingly effective, if somewhat mechanical, technique of Macaulay. All these good works are nowadays too often forgotten; and on the injustice of such neglect one cannot comment more aptly than through the quotation of Jeffrey's own famous phrase—"This will never do."—LEWIS E. GATES, "Francis Jeffrey," *Three Studies in Literature*, 1899, pp. 59–63

WILLIAM HAZLITT
From "Mr. Jeffrey"
The Spirit of the Age
1825

Mr. Jeffrey is the Editor of the *Edinburgh Review*, and is understood to have contributed nearly a fourth part of the articles from its commencement. No man is better qualified for this situation; nor indeed so much so. He is certainly a person in advance of the age, and yet perfectly fitted both from knowledge and habits of mind to put a curb upon its rash and headlong spirit. He is thoroughly acquainted with the progress and pretensions of modern literature and philosophy; and to this he adds the natural acuteness and discrimination of the logician with the habitual caution and coolness of his profession. If the *Edinburgh Review* may be considered as the organ of or at all pledged to a party, that party is at least a respectable one, and is placed in the middle between two extremes. The Editor is bound to lend a patient hearing to the most paradoxical opinions and extravagant theories which have resulted in our times from the 'infinite agitation of wit,' but he is disposed to qualify them by a number of practical objections, of speculative doubts, of checks and drawbacks, arising out of actual circumstances and prevailing opinions, or the frailties of human nature. He has a great range of knowledge, an incessant activity of mind; but the suspension of his judgment, the well-balanced moderation of his sentiments, is the consequence of the very discursiveness of his reason. What may be considered as a *common-place* conclusion is often the result of a comprehensive view of all the circumstances of a case. Paradox, violence, nay even originality of conception is not seldom owing to our dwelling long and pertinaciously on some one part of a subject, instead of attending to the whole. Mr. Jeffrey is neither a bigot nor an enthusiast. He is not the dupe of the prejudices of others, nor of his own. He is not wedded to any dogma, he is not long the sport of any whim; before he can settle in any fond or fantastic opinion, another starts up to match it, like beads on sparkling wine. A too restless display of talent, a too undisguised statement of all that can be said for and against a question, is perhaps the great fault that is to be attributed to him. Where there is so much power and prejudice to contend with in the opposite scale, it may be thought that the balance of truth can hardly be held with a slack or an even hand; and that the infusion of a little more visionary speculation, of a little more popular indignation into the great Whig Review would be an advantage both to itself and to the cause of freedom. Much of this effect is chargeable less on an Epicurean levity of feeling or on party-trammels, than on real sanguineness of disposition, and a certain fineness of professional tact. Our sprightly Scotchman is not of a desponding and gloomy turn of mind. He argues well for the future hopes of mankind from the smallest beginnings, watches the slow, gradual, reluctant growth of liberal views, and smiling sees the aloe of Reform blossom at the end of a hundred years; while the habitual subtlety of his mind makes him perceive decided advantages where vulgar innocence or passion sees only doubts and difficulty; and a flaw in an adversary's argument stands him instead of the shout of a mob, the votes of a majority, or the fate of a pitched battle. The Editor is satisfied with his own conclusions, and does not make himself uneasy about the fate of mankind. The issue, he thinks, will verify his moderate and well-founded expectations.—We believe also that late events have given a more decided turn to Mr. Jeffrey's mind, and that

he feels that as in the struggle between liberty and slavery, the views of the one party have been laid bare with their success, so the exertions on the other side should become more strenuous, and a more positive stand be made against the avowed and appalling encroachments of priestcraft and arbitrary power.

The characteristics of Mr. Jeffrey's general style as a writer correspond, we think, with what we have here stated as the characteristics of his mind. He is a master of the foils; he makes an exulting display of the dazzling fence of wit and argument. His strength consists in great range of knowledge, an equal familiarity with the principles and the details of a subject, and in a glancing brilliancy and rapidity of style. Indeed, we doubt whether the brilliancy of his manner does not resolve itself into the rapidity, the variety and aptness of his illustrations. His pen is never at a loss, never stands still; and would dazzle for this reason alone, like an eye that is ever in motion. Mr. Jeffrey is far from a flowery or affected writer; he has few tropes or figures, still less any odd startling thoughts or quaint innovations in expression:—but he has a constant supply of ingenious solutions and pertinent examples; he never proses, never grows dull, never wears an argument to tatters; and by the number, the liveliness and facility of his transitions, keeps up that appearance of vivacity, of novel and sparkling effect, for which others are too often indebted to singularity of combinations or tinsel ornaments.

It may be discovered, by a nice observer, that Mr. Jeffrey's style of composition is that of a person accustomed to public speaking. There is no pause, no meagreness, no inanimateness, but a flow, a redundance and volubility like that of a stream or of a rolling-stone. The language is more copious than select, and sometimes two or three words perform the office of one. This copiousness and facility is perhaps an advantage in *extempore* speaking, where no stop or break is allowed in the discourse, and where any word or any number of words almost is better than coming to a dead stand; but in written compositions it gives an air of either too much carelessness or too much labour. Mr. Jeffrey's excellence, as a public speaker, has betrayed him into this peculiarity. He makes fewer *blots* in addressing an audience than any one we remember to have heard. There is not a hair's-breadth space between any two of his words, nor is there a single expression either ill-chosen or out of its place. He speaks without stopping to take breath, with ease, with point, with elegance, and without 'spinning the thread of his verbosity finer than the staple of his argument.' He may be said to weave words into any shapes he pleases for use or ornament, as the glass-blower moulds the vitreous fluid with his breath; and his sentences shine like glass from their polished smoothness, and are equally transparent. His style of eloquence, indeed, is remarkable for neatness, for correctness, and epigrammatic point; and he has applied this as a standard to his written compositions, where the very same degree of correctness and precision produces, from the contrast between writing and speaking, an agreeable diffuseness, freedom and animation. Whenever the Scotch advocate has appeared at the bar of the English House of Lords, he has been admired by those who were in the habit of attending to speeches there, as having the greatest fluency of language and the greatest subtlety of distinction of any one of the profession. The law-reporters were as little able to follow him from the extreme rapidity of his utterance as from the tenuity and evanescent nature of his reasoning.

Mr. Jeffrey's conversation is equally lively, various, and instructive. There is no subject on which he is not *au fait*: no company in which he is not ready to scatter his pearls for sport.

Whether it be politics, or poetry, or science, or anecdote, or wit, or raillery, he takes up his cue without effort, without preparation, and appears equally incapable of tiring himself or his hearers. His only difficulty seems to be, not to speak, but to be silent. There is a constitutional buoyancy and elasticity of mind about him that cannot subside into repose, much less sink into dulness. There may be more original talkers, persons who occasionally surprise or interest you more; few, if any, with a more uninterrupted flow of cheerfulness and animal spirits, with a greater fund of information, and with fewer specimens of the *bathos* in their conversation. He is never absurd, nor has he any favourite points which he is always bringing forward. It cannot be denied that there is something bordering on petulance of manner, but it is of that least offensive kind which may be accounted for from merit and from success, and implies no exclusive pretensions nor the least particle of ill-will to others. On the contrary, Mr. Jeffrey is profuse of his encomiums and admiration of others, but still with a certain reservation of a right to differ or to blame. He cannot rest on one side of a question: he is obliged by a mercurial habit and disposition to vary his point of view. If he is ever tedious, it is from an excess of liveliness: he oppresses from a sense of airy lightness. He is always setting out on a fresh scent: there are always *relays* of topics; the harness is put to, and he rattles away as delightfully and as briskly as ever. New causes are called; he holds a brief in his hand for every possible question. This is a fault. Mr. Jeffrey is not obtrusive, is not impatient of opposition, is not unwilling to be interrupted; but what is said by another, seems to make no impression on him; he is bound to dispute, to answer it, as if he was in Court, or as if it were in a paltry Debating Society, where young beginners were trying their hands. This is not to maintain a character, or for want of good nature—it is a thoughtless habit. He cannot help cross-examining a witness, or stating the adverse view of the question. He listens not to judge, but to reply. In consequence of this, you can as little tell the impression your observations make on him as what weight to assign to his. Mr. Jeffrey shines in mixed company; he is not good in a *tête-à-tête*. You can only show your wisdom or your wit in general society: but in private your follies or your weaknesses are not the least interesting topics; and our critic has neither any of his own to confess, nor does he take delight in hearing those of others. Indeed in Scotland generally, the display of personal character, the indulging your whims and humours in the presence of a friend, is not much encouraged—every one there is looked upon in the light of a machine or a collection of topics. They turn you round like a cylinder to see what use they can make of you, and drag you into a dispute with as little ceremony as they would drag out an article from an Encyclopedia. They criticise every thing, analyse every thing, argue upon every thing, dogmatise upon every thing; and the bundle of your habits, feelings, humours, follies and pursuits is regarded by them no more than a bundle of old clothes. They stop you in a sentiment by a question or a stare, and cut you short in a narrative by the time of night. The accomplished and ingenious person of whom we speak, has been a little infected by the tone of his countrymen—he is too didactic, too pugnacious, too full of electrical shocks, too much like a voltaic battery, and reposes too little on his own excellent good sense, his own love of ease, his cordial frankness of temper and unaffected candour. He ought to have belonged to us!

The severest of critics (as he has been sometimes termed) is the best-natured of men. Whatever there may be of wavering or indecision in Mr. Jeffrey's reasoning, or of harshness in his critical decisions, in his disposition there is nothing but simplicity and kindness. He is a person that no one knows without esteeming, and who both in his public connections and private friendships, shows the same manly uprightness and unbiassed independence of spirit. At a distance, in his writings, or even in his manner, there may be something to excite a little uneasiness and apprehension: in his conduct there is nothing to except against. He is a person of strict integrity himself, without pretence or affectation; and knows how to respect this quality in others, without prudery or intolerance. He can censure a friend or a stranger, and serve him effectually at the same time. He expresses his disapprobation, but not as an excuse for closing up the avenues of his liberality. He is a Scotchman without one particle of hypocrisy, of cant, of servility, or selfishness in his composition. He has not been spoiled by fortune—has not been tempted by power—is firm without violence, friendly without weakness—a critic and even-tempered, a casuist and an honest man—and amidst the toils of his profession and the distractions of the world, retains the gaiety, the unpretending carelessness and simplicity of youth. Mr. Jeffrey in his person is slight, with a countenance of much expression, and a voice of great flexibility and acuteness of tone.

GEORGE GILFILLAN
From "Jeffrey and Coleridge"
A *Third Gallery of Portraits*
1854, pp. 215–22

Lord Jeffrey had, unquestionably, many of the elements which unite to form a genuine critic. He had a subtle perception of a certain class of intellectual and literary beauties. He had a generous sympathy with many forms of genius. He had a keen logic with which to defend his views—a lively wit, a fine fancy, and a rapid, varied eloquence with which to expound and illustrate them. There was about his writing, too, a certain inimitable ease, which looked at first like carelessness, but which on closer inspection turned out to be the compounded result of high culture, much intercourse with the best society, and much practice in public speaking. His knowledge of law, too, had whetted his natural acuteness to a razor-like sharpness. His learning was not, perhaps, massive or profound; but his reading had been very extensive, and, retained in its entireness, became exceedingly serviceable to him in all his mental efforts. His genius possessed great versatility, and had been fed with very various provision, so that he was equally fitted to grapple with certain kinds of philosophy, and to discourse on certain schools of poetry, and was familiar alike with law, literature, metaphysics, and history. The moral spirit of his writings was that of a gentleman and man of the world, who was at all times ready to trample on meanness, and to resent every injury done to the common codes of honour, decency, generosity, and external morality.

Such is, we think, a somewhat comprehensive list of the good properties of Jeffrey as a critic. But he laboured not less certainly under various important defects, which we proceed now with all candour to notice. He was not, in the first place, although a subtle and acute, a profound or comprehensive thinker. He saw the edges of a thought, but not a thought in its length, depth, breadth, and in its relation to any great scheme of principles. Hence, with all his logical fence, and clear, rapid induction of particulars, he is often a shallow, and seldom a

satisfactory thinker. He seems constantly, by a tentative process, seeking for his theories, seldom coming down upon them
from the high summit of philosophical views. He has very few
deep glimpses of truth, and scarcely any aphoristic sentences.
His language, rhetoric, and fancy, are often felt to be rich; his
vein of thought seldom if ever—it is diffused in long strata, not
concentrated into solid masses. He had no nuggets in his
mines! Hence he is far from being a suggestive writer. Compare
him in this respect with Burke, with Coleridge, with Foster!
We are not blaming him for not having *been* one of these men;
we are merely thus severely defining what we think the exact
limits, and measuring the proper proportions, of his mind.

Although possessed of much and brilliant fancy, he had
no high imagination, and therefore little true sympathy with it.
The critic of the first poets must be himself potentially a poet.
To *see* the sun, implies only eyes; but to *sing* the sun aright,
implies a spark of his fire in the singer's soul. Jeffrey saw
Milton, Homer, Dante, Shakspere, and the writers of the
Bible, but he could not sing their glories. Indeed, in reference
to the first three and the last of these mighty poets, he has
never, so far as we remember, uttered one word, or at least
shown any thorough or profound appreciation of their power.
Who quotes his panegyrics on Milton and Dante, if such
things there be? Where has he spoken of Isaiah, David, or Job?
Shakspere, indeed, he has often and gracefully praised; but it is
the myriad-minded in undress that he loves, and not as he is
bound up to the full pitch of his transcendent genius—he likes
him better as the Shakspere of *Romeo*, and the *Midsummer
Night's Dream*, than as the Shakspere of *Macbeth*, *Lear*, and
Hamlet; and his remarks, eloquent though they are, show no
such knowledge of him as is manifested by Hazlitt, Coleridge,
and Lamb. Almost all the great original poets of his own time
he has either underrated, or attacked, or passed over in silence.
Think of Wordsworth, Southey, Coleridge, Shelley! Many of
the best English writers of the past are treated with indifference
or neglect. Burke he only mentions once or twice. Johnson he
sometimes sneers at, and sometimes patronises. To Swift as a
writer he has done gross injustice. Sir Thomas Browne seems
unknown to him. Young of the *Night Thoughts*, Thomson,
and Cowper, are all underrated. To Jeremy Taylor, indeed, he
has given his due meed of praise, and to the early English
dramatists much more than their due. And who, on the other
hand, are his special favourites? Pope he admired for his
brilliant wit and polish; Crabbe for his terseness and truth;
Moore for his light and airy fancy; Campbell for his classic
energy and national spirit; and Byron, not for the awful horn of
blasphemy and creative power which rose late on his forehead
in *Cain*, *Heaven and Earth*, and the *Vision of Judgment*, but
for his *Giaours* and *Corsairs*, and the other clever centos of that
imitative period of his poetical life. In praising these writers he
was so far right, but he was not right in exalting them above
their greater contemporaries; and the fact that he did so, simply
shows that there was in his own mind a certain vital imaginative deficiency, disqualifying him from criticising the highest
specimens of the art of poetry. What would we think of a critic
on the fine arts, who should prefer Flaxman to Angelo, or
Reynolds to Raphael, or Danby to Leonardo da Vinci?

In connection with this want of high imagination, there
was in Jeffrey a want of abandonment and enthusiasm: of false
enthusiasm he was incapable, although he was sometimes deceived by it in others. But the genuine child-like ardour which
leads a man to clap his hands or to weep aloud as he sees some
beautiful landscape, or reads some noble passage of poetry or
prose, if it ever was in him, was early frozen up by the influences
of the society with which he mingled in his early days. We

disagree with Thomas Carlyle in many, and these very momentous, things—but we thoroughly agree with him in his
judgment of the mischief which logic and speculation wrought
upon the brains and hearts of the Scottish lawyers and literati
about the end of the last century and the beginning of this. We
have heard of him saying, "that when in Edinburgh, if he had
not thought there were some better people somewhere in the
world than those he met with there, he would have gone away
and hanged himself. The *best* he met were Whig lawyers, and
they believed in *nothing* except what they saw!" Among this class
Jeffrey was reared, and it was no wonder that the wings of his
enthusiasm, which were never of eagle breadth, were sadly
curtailed. Indeed the marvel is, that they were not torn away by
the roots, and that he *has* indited certain panegyrics on certain
favourite authors, which, if cold, resemble at least cold cast, as
we see sometimes in frost-work, into the form of fire.

What a propensity to sneer there was, especially in his
earlier writings! Stab he could not—at least, in the dark. He left
that Italian task to another and a more malignant spirit, of whom
THIS "world is not worthy," and who, maugre Jeffrey's kind
interference to prevent him, often dipped his stiletto in poison—
the poison of his own fierce passions. But Jeffrey's sneers were
nearly as formidable as his coadjutor's stabs. They were so light,
and apparently gentle! The sneer at a distance might almost have
been mistaken for an infant smile; and yet how thoroughly it did
its work! It was as though the shadow of poison could kill. It was
fortunate that alike good sense and generosity taught him in
general to reserve his power of sarcasm for those whom it might
annoy and even check in popularity, but could not harm in
person or in purse. Jeffrey flew at noble game—at Scott, and
Southey, and Wordsworth. This doubtless was done in part from
the levity and persiflage characteristic of an aspiring Edinburgh
youth. Truly does the writer quoted in the last paragraph say,
that there is "a certain age when all young men should be
clapped into barrels, and so kept till they come to years of
discretion"—so intolerable is their conceit, and so absurd their
projects and hopes—especially when to a large quantum of
impudence and a minimum of true enthusiasm they add only
that "little learning" which is so common and so dangerous a
thing in this our day. Jeffrey, although rising ineffably above the
wretched young prigs and pretenders of his own or the present
time, was seldom entirely free from the spirit of intellectual
puppyism. There was a pertness about his general manner of
writing. Amazingly clever, adroit, subtle—he always gave you
the impression of smallness; and you fancied that you saw
Wordsworth, while still smarting under his arrows, lifting him
up in his hand, as did Gulliver a Lilliputian, and admiring the
finished proportions of his tiny antagonist. And yet how, with
his needle-like missiles, did he shed round pain and conster-
nation upon the mightiest of the land! How did James Montgomery, and William Godwin, and Coleridge, and Lamb, and
Southey, and a hundred more of mark and likelihood, groan like
the wounded Cyclops—and how they reeled and staggered
when they felt themselves blinded by weapons which they despised, and victimised by an enemy they previously could hardly
see!

Latterly, indeed, we notice in Jeffrey's style less of the
mannikin, and more of the man—less of the captious critic-
aster, and more of the large-minded judge. His paper on
Byron's Tragedies is a specimen of his better manner, being
bold and masculine; and it does not seem, like many of his
articles, as if it should have been written on a watch-paper. In
treating Warburton, too, he gets up on tiptoe, in sympathy with
the bulky bishop; nor does he lose either his dignity or balance
in the effort. But his attack on Swift is by far his most powerful

review. We demur to his estimate of his talents as a writer. Swift could have swallowed a hundred Jeffreys. *His* power was simple and strong, as one of the energies of Nature. He did by the moving of his finger what others could not by the straining and agitation of their whole frame. It was a stripped, concentred, irresistible force which dwelt in him—fed, too, by unutterable misery; and hence his power, and hence his pollution. He was strong, naked, coarse, savage, and mud-loving, as one of the huge primeval creatures of chaos. Jeffrey's sense of polish, feeling of elegance and propriety, consciousness of inferiority in most things, and consciousness of superiority in some, all contributed to rouse his ire at Swift; and, unequal as on the whole the match was, the clever Scotchman beat the monster Paddy. One is reminded of Gulliver's contest with some of the gigantic reptiles and wasps of Brobdignag. Armed with his hanger, that redoubtable traveller made them resile, or sent them wounded away. And thus the memory of Swift bears Jeffrey's steel-mark on it, and shall bear it for ever.

And yet, although Jeffrey was capable of high moral indignation, he appears to have had very little religious susceptibility. He was one of those who seem never either to have heartily hated or heartily loved religion. He had thought on the subject; but only as he had thought on the guilt of Mary Queen of Scots—as an interesting historical puzzle, and not as a question deeply affecting his own heart and personal interests. We find in his writings no sympathy with the high heroic faith, the dauntless resistance, and the long-continued sufferings of the religious confessors and Covenanters of his own country. He could lay indeed a withering touch on their enemies; but them he passed by in silence, or acknowledged only by sneers. In this respect, however, as well as in his literary tone and temper, we notice a decided improvement in his latter days. He who, in an early number of the *Edinburgh Review*, applied a dancing-master standard to brawny Burns, and would have shorn and scented him down to the standard of Edinburgh modish life, in a diary written a little before his death, calls him a "glorious being," and wishes he had been contemporary with him, that he might have called at his Dumfries hovel, and comforted his unhappy spirit. And he who had sneered, times and ways without number, at Scottish Presbyterian religion, actually shed tears when he saw the Free Church party leaving the General Assembly to cast themselves on the Voluntary Principle; and said that no country but Scotland could have exhibited a spectacle so morally sublime. In both these respects, indeed, latterly, the re-action becomes so complete as to be rather ludicrous than edifying. Think of how, in his letters, he deals with Dickens; how he kisses and fondles him as a lady does her lap-dog; how he weeps instead of laughing over those miserable Christmas tales of his; how he seems to believe a pug of genius to be a very lion! How different had Dickens's worse productions appeared in the earlier part of Jeffrey's critical career! As to religion, his tone becomes that of childish sentimentalism; and, unable to the last to give either to the Bible or to the existence of God the homage of a manly belief, he can yet shed over them floods of silly and senile tears.

Yet let him have his praise, as one of the acutest, most fluent, lively, and on the whole amiable, of our modern Scottish celebrities; although not, as Cockburn calls him in that lamentable life of his, at which the public have scarcely yet ceased to laugh, "the first of British critics!!!" His fame, except in Edinburgh, is fast dwindling away; and although some passages in his writings may long be quoted, his memory is sure of preservation, chiefly from the connection of his name with that of the *Edinburgh Review*, and with those powerful but

uncertain influences in literature, politics, philosophy, and religion which that review once wielded.

GEORGE SAINTSBURY
From "Jeffrey" (1887)
Collected Essays and Papers
1923, Volume 1, pp. 90–105

In reading Jeffrey's work nowadays, the critical reader finds it considerably more difficult to gain and keep the author's own point of view than in the case of any other great English critic. With Hazlitt, with Coleridge, with Wilson, with Carlyle, with Macaulay, we very soon fall into step, so to speak, with our author. If we cannot exactly prophesy what he will say on any given subject, we can make a pretty shrewd guess at it; and when, as it seems to us, he stumbles and shies, we have a sort of feeling beforehand that he is going to do it, and a decided inkling of the reason. But my own experience is, that a modern reader of Jeffrey, who takes him systematically, and endeavours to trace cause and effect in him, is liable to be constantly thrown out before he finds the secret. For Jeffrey, in the most puzzling way, lies between the ancients and the moderns in matter of criticism, and we never quite know where to have him. It is ten to one, for instance, that the novice approaches him with the idea that he is a "classic" of the old rock. Imagine the said novice's confusion, when he finds Jeffrey not merely exalting Shakespeare to the skies, but warmly praising Elizabethan poetry in general, anticipating Mr Matthew Arnold almost literally, in the estimate of Dryden and Pope as classics of our prose, and hailing with tears of joy the herald of the emancipation in Cowper. Surely our novice may be excused if, despite certain misgiving memories of such reviews as that of *The Lay of the Last Minstrel*, he concludes that Jeffrey has been maligned, and that he was really a Romantic before Romanticism. Unhappy novice! he will find his new conclusion not less rapidly and more completely staggered than his old. Indeed, until the clue is once gained, Jeffrey must appear to be one of the most incomprehensibly inconsistent of writers and of critics. On one page he declares that Campbell's extracts from Chamberlayne's *Pharonnida* have made him "quite impatient for an opportunity of perusing the whole poem,"—Romantic surely, quite Romantic. "The tameness and poorness of the serious style of Addison and Swift,"—Romantic again, quite Romantic. Yet when we come to Jeffrey's own contemporaries, he constantly appears as much bewigged and befogged with pseudo-classicism as M. de Jouy himself. He commits himself, in the year of grace 1829, to the statement that "the rich melodies of Keats and Shelley, and the fantastical emphasis of Wordsworth are melting fast from the field of our vision," while he contrasts with this "rapid withering of the laurel" the "comparative absence of marks of decay" on Rogers and Campbell. The poets of his own time whom he praises most heartily, and with least reserve, are Campbell and Crabbe; and he is quite as enthusiastic over *Theodric* and *Gertrude* as over the two great war-pieces of the same author, which are worth a hundred *Gertrudes* and about ten thousand *Theodrics*. Reviewing Scott, not merely when they were personal friends (they were always that), but when Scott was a contributor to the *Edinburgh*, and giving general praise to *The Lay*, he glances with an unmistakable meaning at the "dignity of the subject," regrets the "imitation and antiquarian researches," and criticises the versification in a way which shows that he had not in the least grasped its scheme. It is hardly necessary to quote his well-known attacks on Wordsworth; but, though I am myself anything but a Wordsworthian, and would willingly give up to chaos and old night nineteen-twentieths of the "extremely valooable chains of thought" which the good man used to forge, it is in the first place quite clear that the twentieth ought to have saved him from Jeffrey's claws; in the second, that the critic constantly selects the wrong things as well as the right for condemnation and ridicule; and in the third, that he would have praised, or at any rate not blamed, in another, the very things which he blames in Wordsworth. Even his praise of Crabbe, excessive as it may now appear, is diversified by curious patches of blame which seem to me at any rate, singularly uncritical. There are, for instance, a very great many worse jests in poetry than,

Oh, had he learnt to make the wig he wears!

—which Jeffrey pronounces a misplaced piece of buffoonery. I cannot help thinking that if Campbell instead of Southey had written the lines,

To see brute nature scorn him and renounce
Its homage to the human form divine,

Jeffrey would, to say the least, not have hinted that they were "little better than drivelling." But I do not think that when Jeffrey wrote these things, or when he actually perpetrated such almost unforgivable phrases as "stuff about dancing daffodils," he was speaking away from his sincere conviction. On the contrary, though partisanship may frequently have determined the suppression or the utterance, the emphasising or the softening, of his opinions, I do not think that he ever said anything but what he sincerely thought. The problem, therefore, is to discover and define, if possible, the critical standpoint of a man whose judgment was at once so acute and so purblind; who could write the admirable surveys of English poetry contained in the essays on Mme de Staël and Campbell, and yet be guilty of the stuff (we thank him for the word) about the dancing daffodils; who could talk of "the splendid strains of Moore" (though I have myself a relatively high opinion of Moore) and pronounce *The White Doe of Rylstone* (though I am not very fond of that animal as a whole) "the very worst poem he ever saw printed in a quarto volume"; who could really appreciate parts even of Wordsworth himself, and yet sneer at the very finest passages of the poems he partly admired. It is unnecessary to multiply inconsistencies, because the reader who does not want the trouble of reading Jeffrey must be content to take them for granted, and the reader who does read Jeffrey will discover them in plenty for himself. But they are not limited, it should be said, to purely literary criticism; and they appear, if not quite so strongly, in his estimates of personal character, and even in his purely political arguments.

The explanation, as far as there is any (and perhaps such explanations, as Hume says of another matter, only push ignorance a stage farther back), seems to me to lie in which I can only call the Gallicanism of Jeffrey's mind and character. As Horace Walpole has been pronounced the most French of Englishmen, so may Francis Jeffrey be pronounced the most French of Scotchmen. The reader of his letters, no less than the reader of his essays, constantly comes across the most curious and multiform instances of this Frenchness. The early priggishness is French; the effusive domestic affection is French; the antipathy to dogmatic theology, combined with general recognition of the Supreme Being, is French; the talk (I had almost said the chatter) about virtue and sympathy, and so forth, is French; the Whig recognition of the rights of man, joined to a kind of bureaucratical distrust and terror of the common people (a combination almost unknown in England), is French. Everybody remembers the ingenious argument in *Peter Simple* that the French were quite as brave as the English, indeed more so, but that they were extraordinarily ticklish. Jeffrey, we have seen, was very far from being a coward, but he was very ticklish indeed. His private letters throw the most curious light possible on the secret, as far as he was concerned, of the earlier Whig opposition to the war, and of the later Whig advocacy of reform. Jeffrey by no means thought the cause of the Revolution divine, like the Friends of Liberty, or admired Napoleon like Hazlitt, or believed in the inherent right of Manchester and Birmingham to representation like the zealots of 1830. But he was always dreadfully afraid of invasion in the first place, and of popular insurrection in the second; and he wanted peace and reform to calm his fears. As a young man he was, with a lack of confidence in his countrymen probably unparalleled in a Scotchman, sure that a French corporal's guard might march from end to end of Scotland, and a French privateer's boat's crew carry off "the fattest cattle and the fairest women" (these are his very words) "of any Scotch seaboard county." The famous, or infamous, Cevallos article—an ungenerous and pusillanimous attack on the Spanish patriots, which practically founded the *Quarterly Review*, by finally disgusting all Tories and many Whigs with the *Edinburgh*—was, it seems, prompted merely by the conviction that the Spanish cause was hopeless, and that maintaining it, or assisting it, must lead to mere useless bloodshed. He felt profoundly the crime of Napoleon's rule; but he thought Napoleon unconquerable, and so did his best to prevent him from being conquered. He was sure that the multitude would revolt if reform was not granted; and he was, therefore, eager for reform. Later, he got into his head the oddest crotchet of all his life, which was that a Conservative government, with a sort of approval from the people generally, and especially from the English peasantry, would scheme for a *coup d'état*, and (his own words again) "make mincemeat of their opponents in a single year." He may be said almost to have left the world in a state of despair over the probable results of the Revolutions of 1848–49; and it is impossible to guess what would have happened to him if he had survived to witness the Second of December. Never was there such a case, at least among Englishmen, of timorous pugnacity and plucky pessimism. But it would be by no means difficult to parallel the temperament in France; and, indeed, the comparative frequency of it there, may be thought to be no small cause of the political and military disasters of the country.

In literature, and especially in criticism, Jeffrey's characteristics were still more decidedly and unquestionably French. He came into the world almost too soon to feel the German impulse, even if he had been disposed to feel it. But, as a matter of fact, he was not at all disposed. The faults of taste of the German Romantic School, its alternate homeliness and extravagance, its abuse of the supernatural, its undoubted offences against order and proportion, scandalised him only a little less than they would have scandalised Voltaire and did scandalise the later Voltairians. Jeffrey was perfectly prepared to be Romantic up to a certain point,—the point which he had himself reached in his early course of independent reading and criticism. He was even a little inclined to sympathise with the Reverend Mr Bowles on the great question whether Pope was a poet; and, as I have said, he uses, about the older English literature, phrases which might almost satisfy a fanatic of the school of Hazlitt or of Lamb. He is, if anything, rather too severe on French as compared with English drama. Yet, when he comes to his own contemporaries, and sometimes even in reference to earlier writers, we find him slipping into those purely arbitrary severities of condemnation, those capricious stigmatisings of this as improper, and that as vulgar, and the other as unbecoming, which are the characteristics of the pseudo-correct and pseudo-classical school of criticism. He was a great admirer of Cowper, and yet he is shocked by Cowper's use, in his translation of Homer, of the phrases, "to entreat Achilles to a calm" (evidently he had forgotten Shakespeare's "pursue him and entreat him to a peace"), "this wrangler here," "like a fellow of no worth." He was certainly not likely to be unjust to Charles James Fox. So he is unhappy, rather than contemptuous, over such excellent phrases as "swearing away the lives," "crying injustice," "fond of ill-treating." These appear to Mr Aristarchus Jeffrey too "homely and familiar," too "low and vapid"; while a harmless and rather agreeable Shakespearian parallel of Fox's seems to him downright impropriety. The fun of the thing is that the passage turns on the well-known misuse of "flat burglary"; and if Jeffrey had had a little more sense of humour (his deficiency in which, for all his keen wit, is another Gallic note in him), he must have seen that the words were ludicrously applicable to his own condemnation and his own frame of mind. These settings-up of a wholly arbitrary canon of mere taste, these excommunicatings of such and such a thing as "low" and "improper," without assigned or assignable reason, are eminently Gallic. They may be found not merely in the older school before 1830, but in almost all French critics up to the present day: there is perhaps not one, with the single exception of Sainte-Beuve, who is habitually free from them. The critic may be quite unable to say why *tarte à la crème* is such a shocking expression, or even to produce any important authority for the shockingness of it. But he is quite certain that it is shocking. Jeffrey is but too much given to protesting against *tarte à la crème*; and the reasons for his error are almost exactly the same as in the case of the usual Frenchman; that is to say, a very just and wholesome preference for order, proportion, literary orthodoxy, freedom from will-worship and eccentric divagations, unfortunately distorted by a certain absence of catholicity, by a tendency to regard novelty as bad, merely because it is novelty, and by a curious reluctance, as Lamb has it of another great man of the same generation, to go shares with any newcomer in literary commerce.

But when these reservations have been made, when his standpoint has been clearly discovered and marked out, and when some little tricks, such as the affectation of delivering judgments without appeal, which is still kept up by a few, though very few, reviewers, have been further allowed for, Jeffrey is a most admirable essayist and critic. As an essayist, a writer of *causeries*, I do not think he has been surpassed among Englishmen in the art of interweaving quotation, abstract, and comment. The best proof of his felicity in this respect is that in almost all the books which he has reviewed (and he has reviewed many of the most interesting books in literature) the passages and traits, the anecdotes and phrases, which have made most mark in the general memory, and which are often remembered with very indistinct consciousness of their origin, are to be found in his reviews. Sometimes the very perfection of his skill in this respect makes it rather difficult to know where he is abstracting or paraphrasing, and where he is speaking outright and for himself; but that is a very small fault. Yet his merits as an essayist, though considerable, are not to be compared, even to the extent to which Hazlitt's are to be compared, with his merits as a critic, and especially as a literary critic. It would be interesting to criticise his political criticism; but it is always best to keep politics out where it can be

managed. Besides, Jeffrey as a political critic is a subject of almost exclusively historical interest, while as a literary critic he is important at this very day, and perhaps more important than he was in his own. For the spirit of merely æsthetic criticism, which was in his day only in its infancy, has long been full grown and rampant; so that, good work as it has done in its time, it decidedly needs chastening by an admixture of the dogmatic criticism, which at least tries to keep its impressions together and in order, and to connect them into some coherent doctrine and creed.

Of this dogmatic criticism Jeffrey, with all his shortcomings, is perhaps the very best example that we have in English. He had addressed himself more directly and theoretically to literary criticism than Lockhart. Prejudiced as he often was, he was not affected by the wild gusts of personal and political passion which frequently blew Hazlitt a thousand miles off the course of true criticism. He keeps his eye on the object, which De Quincey seldom does. He is not affected by that desire to preach on certain pet subjects which affects the admirable critical faculty of Carlyle. He never blusters and splashes at random like Wilson. And he never indulges in the mannered and rather superfluous graces which marred, to some tastes, the work of his successor in critical authority, if there has been any such, the author of *Essays in Criticism*.

Let us, as we just now looked through Jeffrey's work to pick out the less favourable characteristics which distinguish his position, look through it again to see those qualities which he shares, but in greater measure than most, with all good critics. The literary essay which stands first in his collected works is on Madame de Staël. Now that good lady, of whom some judges in these days do not think very much, was a kind of goddess on earth in literature, however much she might bore them in life, to the English Whig party in general; while Jeffrey's French tastes must have made her, or at least her books, specially attractive to him. Accordingly he has written a great deal about her, no less than three essays appearing in the collected works. Writing at least partly in her lifetime and under the influences just glanced at, he is of course profuse in compliments. But it is very amusing and highly instructive to observe how, in the intervals of these compliments, he contrives to take the good Corinne to pieces, to smash up her ingenious Perfectibilism, and to put in order her rather rash literary judgments. It is in connection also with her, that he gives one of the best of not a few general sketches of the history of literature which his work contains. Of course there are here, as always, isolated expressions as to which, however much we admit that Jeffrey was a clever man, we cannot agree with Jeffrey. He thinks Aristophanes "coarse" and "vulgar" while (though nobody of course can deny the coarseness) Aristophanes and vulgarity are certainly miles asunder. We may protest against the chronological, even more than against the critical, blunder which couples Cowley and Donne, putting Donne, moreover, who wrote long before Cowley was born, and differs from him in genius almost as the author of the *Iliad* does from the author of the *Henriade*, second. But hardly anything in English criticism is better than Jeffrey's discussion of the general French imputation of "want of taste and politeness" to English and German writers, especially English. It is a very general, and a very mistaken, notion that the Romantic movement in France has done away with this imputation to a great extent. On the contrary, though it has long been a kind of fashion in France to admire Shakespeare, and though since the labours of MM. Taine and Montégut, the study of English literature generally has grown and flourished, it is, I believe, the very rarest thing to find a Frenchman who, in his heart of hearts, does not cling to the old "pearls in the dung-heap" idea, not merely in reference to Shakespeare, but to English writers, and especially English humorists, generally. Nothing can be more admirable than Jeffrey's comments on this matter. They are especially admirable because they are not made from the point of view of a *Romantique à tous crins*; because, as has been already pointed out, he himself is largely penetrated by the very preference for order and proportion which is at the bottom of the French mistake; and because he is, therefore, arguing in a tongue understood of those whom he censures. Another essay which may be read with especial advantage is that on Scott's edition of Swift. Here, again, there was a kind of test subject, and perhaps Jeffrey does not come quite scatheless out of the trial: to me, at any rate, his account of Swift's political and moral conduct and character seems both uncritical and unfair. But here, too, the value of his literary criticism shows itself. He might very easily have been tempted to extend his injustice from the writer to the writings, especially since, as has been elsewhere shown, he was by no means a fanatical admirer of the Augustan age, and thought the serious style of Addison and Swift tame and poor. It is possible of course, here also, to find things that seem to be errors, both in the general sketch which Jeffrey, according to his custom, prefixes and in the particular remarks on Swift himself. For instance, to deny fancy to the author of the *Tale of a Tub*, of *Gulliver*, and of the *Polite Conversation*, is very odd indeed. But there are few instances of a greater triumph of sound literary judgment over political and personal prejudice than Jeffrey's description, not merely of the great works just mentioned (it is curious, and illustrates his defective appreciation of humour, that he likes the greatest least, and is positively unjust to the *Tale of a Tub*), but also of those wonderful pamphlets, articles, lampoons, skits (libels if any one likes), which proved too strong for the generalship of Marlborough and the administrative talents of Godolphin; and which are perhaps the only literary works that ever really changed, for a not inconsiderable period, the government of England. "Considered," he says, "with a view to the purposes for which they were intended, they have probably never been equalled in any period of the world." They certainly have not; but to find a Whig, and a Whig writing in the very moment of Tory triumph after Waterloo, ready to admit the fact, is not a trivial thing. Another excellent example of Jeffrey's strength, by no means unmixed with examples of his weakness, is to be found in his essays on Cowper. I have already given some of the weakness: the strength is to be found in his general description of Cowper's revolt, thought so daring at the time, now so apparently moderate, against poetic diction. These instances are to be found under miscellaneous sections, biographical, historical, and so forth; but the reader will naturally turn to the considerable divisions headed Poetry and Fiction. Here are the chief rocks of offence already indicated, and here also are many excellent things which deserve reading. Here is the remarkable essay, quoted above, on Campbell's *Specimens*. Here is the criticism of Weber's edition of Ford, and another of those critical surveys of the course of English literature which Jeffrey was so fond of doing, and which he did so well, together with some remarks on the magnificently spendthrift style of our Elizabethan dramatists which would deserve almost the first place in an anthology of his critical beauties. The paper on Hazlitt's *Characters of Shakespeare* (Hazlitt was an *Edinburgh* reviewer, and his biographer, not Jeffrey's, has chronicled a remarkable piece of generosity on Jeffrey's part towards his wayward contributor) is a little defaced by a patronising spirit, not, indeed, of that memorably mistaken kind which induced

the famous and unlucky sentence to Macvey Napier about Carlyle, but something in the spirit of the schoolmaster who observes, "See this clever boy of mine, and only think how much better I could do it myself." Yet it contains some admirable passages on Shakespeare, if not on Hazlitt; and it would be impossible to deny that its hinted condemnation of Hazlitt's "desultory and capricious acuteness" is just enough. On the other hand, how significant is it of Jeffrey's own limitations that he should protest against Hazlitt's sympathy with such "conceits and puerilities" as the immortal and unmatchable

> Take him and cut him out in little stars,

with the rest of the passage. But there you have the French spirit. I do not believe that there ever was a Frenchman since the seventeenth century (unless perchance it was Gérard de Nerval, and he was not quite sane), who could put his hand on his heart and deny that the little stars seemed to him puerile and conceited.

Jeffrey's dealings with Byron (I do not now speak of the article on *Hours of Idleness*, which was simply a just rebuke of really puerile and conceited rubbish) are not, to me, very satisfactory. The critic seems, in the rather numerous articles which he has devoted to the "noble Poet," as they used to call him, to have felt his genius unduly rebuked by that of his subject. He spends a great deal, and surely an unnecessarily great deal, of time in solemnly, and no doubt quite sincerely, rebuking Byron's morality; and in doing so he is sometimes almost absurd. He calls him "not more obscene perhaps than Dryden or Prior," which is simply ludicrous, because it is very rare that this particular word can be applied to Byron at all, while even the staunchest champion must admit that it applies to glorious John and to dear Mat Prior. He helps, unconsciously no doubt, to spread the very contagion which he denounces, by talking about Byron's demoniacal power, going so far as actually to contrast *Manfred* with Marlowe to the advantage of the former. And he is so completely overcome by what he calls the "dreadful tone of sincerity" of this "puissant spirit," that he never seems to have had leisure or courage to apply the critical tests and solvents of which few men have had a greater command. Had he done so, it is impossible not to believe that, whether he did or did not pronounce Byron's sentiment to be as theatrical, as vulgar, and as false as it seems to some later critics, he would at any rate have substituted for his edifying but rather irrelevant moral denunciations some exposure of those gross faults in style and metre, in phrase and form, which now disgust us.

There are many essays remaining on which I should like to comment if there were room enough. But I have only space for a few more general remarks on his general characteristics, and especially those which, as Sainte-Beuve said to the altered Jeffrey of our altered days, are "important to us." Let me repeat then that the peculiar value of Jeffrey is not, as is that of Coleridge, of Hazlitt, or of Lamb, in very subtle, very profound, or very original views of his subjects. He is neither a critical Columbus nor a critical Socrates; he neither opens up undiscovered countries, nor provokes and stimulates to the discovery of them. His strength lies in the combination of a fairly wide range of sympathy with an extraordinary shrewdness and good sense in applying that sympathy. Tested for range alone, or for subtlety alone, he will frequently be found wanting; but he almost invariably catches up those who have thus outstripped him, when the subject of the trial is shifted to soundness of estimate, intelligent connection of view, and absence of eccentricity. And it must be again and again repeated that Jeffrey is by no means justly chargeable with the Dryasdust failings so often attributed to academic criticism. They said that on the actual Bench he worried counsel a little too much, but that his decisions were almost invariably sound. Not quite so much perhaps can be said for his other exercise of the judicial function. But however much he may sometimes seem to carp and complain, however much we may sometimes wish for a little more equity and a little less law, it is astonishing how weighty Jeffrey's critical judgments are after three-quarters of a century which has seen so many seeming heavy things grow light. There may be much that he does not see; there may be some things which he is physically unable to see; but what he does see, he sees with a clearness, and co-ordinates in its bearings on other things seen with a precision, which are hardly to be matched among the fluctuating and diverse race of critics.

MARGARET FULLER

1810–1850

Sarah Margaret Fuller was born in Cambridgeport, Massachusetts, on May 23, 1810, the eldest in a family of nine children. Except for a brief period in 1823–24, she was entirely educated at home by her father, Timothy Fuller, a lawyer and politician. In 1835 Timothy Fuller died and it became necessary for Margaret to support the family, which she did by working as a teacher, both privately and at Bronson Alcott's Temple School in Boston (1836–37) and Hiram Fuller's Green Street School in Providence, Rhode Island (1837–39).

In 1836 Fuller began a lifetime correspondence and friendship with Ralph Waldo Emerson. With Emerson she helped to found the *Dial*, which she edited from July 1840 to July 1842. During the same period (1839–44) she conducted a series of conversation classes or seminars for educated women in Boston and Cambridge. In 1844 Fuller published *Summer on the Lakes*, an account of her 1843 trip to the American West. This book attracted the attention of Horace Greeley and was partially responsible for his offering her the job of literary critic for the New York *Daily Tribune*. Fuller accepted this offer and in December 1844 moved to New York. In 1845 she published her influential feminist tract *Woman in the Nineteenth Century*, an expanded version of the July 1843 article in the *Dial*, "The Great Lawsuit: Man vs. Men, Woman vs. Women." This was followed in 1846 by the publication of *Papers on Literature and Art*, a miscellany of critical articles.

In August 1846 Fuller sailed for Europe. After traveling in England, Scotland, and France as foreign correspondent for Greeley's *Tribune*, she settled in Italy. There in 1847 she married one of Mazzini's followers, the Marchese Ossoli, and in 1848 their only son, Angelo, was born. During the seige of Rome by the French in 1849, Fuller worked as director of a hospital, and in 1850, after the fall of the Republic, she and her family went first to Florence, then set sail for America. Just as they had almost reached their destination their ship was wrecked, and all three drowned off Fire Island on July 19, 1850. The *Memoirs of Margaret Fuller Ossoli*, edited by her friends Emerson, W. H. Channing, and J. F. Clarke, was published in 1852.

Personal

Here Miranda came up, and said, "Phœbus! you know
That the infinite Soul has its infinite woe,
As I ought to know, having lived cheek by jowl,
Since the day I was born, with the Infinite Soul;
I myself introduced, I myself, I alone,
To my Land's better life authors solely my own,
Who the sad heart of earth on their shoulders have taken,
Whose works sound a depth by Life's quiet unshaken,
Such as Shakespeare, for instance, the Bible, and Bacon,
Not to mention my own works; Time's nadir is fleet,
And, as for myself, I'm quite out of conceit—"

"Quite out of conceit! I'm enchanted to hear it,"
Cried Apollo aside. "Who'd have thought she was near it?
To be sure, one is apt to exhaust those commodities
He uses too fast, yet in this case as odd it is
As if Neptune should say to his turbots and whitings,
'I'm as much out of salt as Miranda's own writings'
(Which, as she in her own happy manner has said,
Sound a depth, for 't is one of the functions of lead).
She often has asked me if I could not find
A place somewhere near me that suited her mind;
I know but a single one vacant, which she

With her rare talent that way, would fit to a T.
And it would not imply any pause or cessation
In the work she esteems her peculiar vocation,—
She may enter on duty to-day, if she chooses,
And remain Tiring-woman for life to the Muses."

(Miranda meanwhile has succeeded in driving
Up into a corner, in spite of their striving,
A small flock of terrified victims, and there,
With an I-turn-the-crank-of-the-Universe air
And a tone which, at least to *my* fancy, appears
Not so much to be entering as boxing your ears,
Is unfolding a tale (of herself, I surmise),
For 't is dotted as thick as a peacock's with I's).
—JAMES RUSSELL LOWELL, A *Fable for Critics*,
1848

She was the centre of a group very different from each other, and whose only affinity consisted in their all being polarized by the strong attraction of her mind,—all drawn toward herself. Some of her friends were young, gay and beautiful; some old, sick or studious. Some were children of the world, others pale scholars. Some were witty, others slightly dull. But all, in order to be Margaret's friends, must be capable of seeking something,—capable of some aspiration for the better. And how did she glorify life to all! all that was tame and common vanishing away in the picturesque light thrown over the most familiar things by her rapid fancy, her brilliant wit, her sharp insight, her creative imagination, by the inexhaustible resources of her knowledge, and the copious rhetoric which found words and images always apt and always ready. Even then she displayed almost the same marvellous gift of conversation which afterwards dazzled all who knew her,—with more perhaps of freedom, since she floated on the flood of our warm sympathies. Those who know Margaret only by her published writings know her least; her notes and letters contain more of her mind; but it was only in conversation that she was perfectly free and at home.—JAMES FREEMAN CLARKE, *Memoirs of Margaret Fuller Ossoli*, 1852, Vol. 1, p. 78

I still remember the first half-hour of Margaret's conversation. She was then twenty-six years old. She had a face and frame that would indicate fulness and tenacity of life. She was rather under the middle height; her complexion was fair, with strong fair hair. She was then, as always, carefully and becomingly dressed, and of ladylike self-possession. For the rest, her appearance had nothing prepossessing. Her extreme plainness,—a trick of incessantly opening and shutting her eyelids,—the nasal tone of her voice,—all repelled; and I said to myself, we shall never get far. It is to be said, that Margaret made a disagreeable first impression on most persons, including those who became afterwards her best friends, to such an extreme that they did not wish to be in the same room with her. This was partly the effect of her manners, which expressed an overweening sense of power, and slight esteem of others, and partly the prejudice of her fame. She had a dangerous reputation for satire, in addition to her great scholarship. The men thought she carried too many guns, and the women did not like one who despised them. I believe I fancied her too much interested in personal history; and her talk was a comedy in which dramatic justice was done to everybody's foibles. I remember that she made me laugh more than I liked; for I was, at that time, an eager scholar of ethics, and had tasted the sweets of solitude and stoicism, and I found something profane in the hours of amusing gossip into which she drew me, and, when I returned to my library, had much to think of the crackling of thorns under a pot. Margaret, who had stuffed me out as a philosopher, in her own fancy, was too intent on establishing a good footing between us, to omit any art of winning. She studied my tastes, piqued and amused me, challenged frankness by frankness, and did not conceal the good opinion of me she brought with her, nor her wish to please. She was curious to know my opinions and experiences. Of course, it was impossible long to hold out against such urgent assault. She had an incredible variety of anecdotes, and the readiest wit to give an absurd turn to whatever passed; and the eyes, which were so plain at first, soon swam with fun and drolleries, and the very tides of joy and superabundant life.

This rumor was much spread abroad, that she was sneering, scoffing, critical, disdainful of humble people, and of all but the intellectual. I had heard it whenever she was named. It was a superficial judgment. Her satire was only the pastime and necessity of her talent, the play of superabundant animal spirits.—RALPH WALDO EMERSON, *Memoirs of Margaret Fuller Ossoli*, 1852, Vol. 1, pp. 202–3

From first to last she was a woman of noble aims, and, with all her egotism, unselfish in action. The longer I live, the more presumptuous and futile it seems to me to attempt judgment of character, and Miss Fuller's was exceptional. Her self-esteem was so inordinate as to be almost insane, but it appears (and it is, I think, so stated) to have been a constitutional and inherited defect, and certainly without moral taint. Her truth was exemplary, and all her conduct after she had left off theorizing and began the action of life in the accustomed channels was admirable, her Italian life beautiful. The close had the solemnity of a fulfilled prophecy, and, with all its apparent horrors, was it not merciful? Had she come safely to our shores, she must have encountered harassing struggles for the mere means of existence, anxiety, and all the petty cares that perplex and obstruct a noble nature, and, worse than all, disappointment!—CATHARINE M. SEDGWICK, Letter to Mrs. Channing (1852) cited in Mary E. Dewey, *Life and Letters of Catharine M. Sedgwick*, 1871, p. 340

> Over his millions Death has lawful power,
> But over thee, brave D'Ossoli! none, none.
> After a longer struggle, in a fight
> Worthy of Italy to youth restored,
> Thou, far from home, art sunk beneath the surge
> Of the Atlantic; on its shore; in reach
> Of help; in trust of refuge; sunk with all
> Precious on earth to thee . . . a child, a wife!
> Proud as thou wert of her, America
> Is prouder, showing to her sons how high
> Swells woman's courage in a virtuous breast.
> She would not leave behind her those she loved:
> Such solitary safety might become
> Others; not her; not her who stood beside
> The pallet of the wounded, when the worst
> Of France and Perfidy assail'd the walls
> Of unsuspicious Rome. Rest, glorious soul,
> Renowned for strength of genius, Margaret!
> Rest with the twain too dear! My words are few,
> And shortly none will hear my failing voice,
> But the same language with more full appeal
> Shall hail thee. Many are the sons of song
> Whom thou has heard upon thy native plains
> Worthy to sing of thee: the hour is come;
> Take we our seats and let the dirge begin.
> —WALTER SAVAGE LANDOR, "On the Death of M. D'Ossoli and His Wife Margaret Fuller," 1853

He ⟨her husband⟩ could not possibly have had the least appreciation of Margaret; and the wonder is, what attraction she found in this boor, this hymen without the intellectual spark—she that had always shown such a cruel and bitter scorn of intellectual deficiency. As from her towards him, I do not understand what feeling there could have been, except it were purely sensual; as from him towards her, there could hardly have been even this, for she had not the charm of womanhood. But she was a woman anxious to try all things, and fill up her experience in all directions; she had a strong and coarse nature, too, which she had done her utmost to refine, with infinite pains, but which of course could only be superficially changed. The solution of the riddle lies in this direction; nor does one's conscience revolt at the idea of thus solving it; for—at least, this is my own experience—Margaret has not left, in the hearts and minds of those who knew her, any deep witness for her integrity and purity. She was a great humbug; of course with much talent, and much moral reality, or else she could not have been so great a humbug. But she had stuck herself full of borrowed qualities, which she chose to provide herself with, but which had no root in her.

Mr. Mozier added, that Margaret had quite lost all power of literary production, before she left Rome, though occasionally the charm and power of her conversation would re-appear. To his certain knowledge, she had no important manuscripts with her when she sailed, (she having shown him all she had, with a view to his procuring their publication in America;) and the History of the Roman Revolution, about which there was so much lamentation, in the belief that it had been lost with her, never had existence. Thus there appears to have been a total collapse in poor Margaret, morally and intellectually; and tragic as her catastrophe was, Providence was, after all, kind in putting her, and her clownish husband, and their child, on board that fated ship. There never was such a tragedy as her whole story; the sadder and sterner, because so much of the ridiculous was mixed up with it, and because she could bear anything better than to be ridiculous. It was such an awful joke, that she should have resolved—in all sincerity, no doubt—to make herself the greatest, wisest, best woman of the age; and, to that end, she set to work on her strong, heavy, unpliable, and, in many respects, defective and evil nature, and adorned it with a mosaic of admirable qualities, such as she chose to possess; putting in here a splendid talent, and there a moral excellence, and polishing each separate piece, and the whole together, till it seemed to shine afar and dazzle all who saw it. She took credit to herself for having been her own Redeemer, if not her own Creator; and, indeed, she was far more a work of art than any of Mr. Mozier's statues. But she was not working on an inanimate substance, like marble or clay; there was something within her that she could not possibly come at, to re-create and refine it; and, by and by, this rude old potency bestirred itself, and undid all her labor in the twinkling of an eye. On the whole, I do not know but I like her the better for it;—the better, because she proved herself a very woman, after all, and fell as the weakest of her sisters might. —NATHANIEL HAWTHORNE, *The French and Italian Notebooks*, April 3, 1858

> She with wise intuition raised
>   Her image of ideal womanhood,
> The incarnate True and Fair and Good,
> Set in a light but seldom seen before.
> While, with the early watchers in the dawn
> Of intellectual faith, her hopeful eyes,
> Patiently waiting, from the crowd withdrawn,
>   She saw a newer morning rise,
>   And flame from cloud to cloud, and climb
>   Across the dreary tracts of time.
> The garnered wisdom of the past she drew
> Into her life, as flowers the sun and dew;
>   Yet valued all her varied lore
>   But as the avenue and door
>   That opened to the Primal Beam,
>   And sense of Truth supreme.
> And so, beyond her earlier bounds she grew;
>   All the quaint essences from study gained,
> Fused in a human fellowship anew,
> While that too conscious life, in early years o'erstrained,
>   Of long, deep, lonely introversion born,
>   Distilled like dews of morn,
> And dropped on high and low the blessing it contained.
>   Her glowing pen through many a thoughtful page,
>   Discoursed in subtle questions of the age,
>   Or glanced in lighter mood at themes less grave,—
>   The brilliant glitter of a summer wave.
> Her sweet persuasive voice we still can hear,
>   Ruling her charméd circle like a queen;
> While wit and fancy sparkled ever clear
>   Her graver moods between.
>   The pure perennial heat
> Of youth's ideal love forever glowed
> Through all her thoughts and words, and overflowed
>   The listeners round her seat.

> So, like some fine-strung golden harp,
> Tuned by many a twist and warp
> Of discipline and patient toil,
> And oft disheartening recoil,—
> Attuned to highest and to humblest use,—
>   All her large heroic nature
>   Grew to its harmonious stature,
> Nor any allotted service did refuse;
> While those around her but half understood
>   How wise she was, how good,
> How nobly self-denying, as she tasked
> Heart, mind, and strength for truth, nor nobler office asked.
>   —C. P. CRANCH, "Ode," *Atlantic*, Aug. 1870,
>   pp. 232–33

The difference between us was that while she was living and moving in an ideal world, talking in private and discoursing in public about the most fanciful and shallow conceits which the transcendentalists of Boston took for philosophy, she looked down upon persons who acted instead of talking finely, and devoted their fortunes, their peace, their repose, and their very lives to the preservation of the principles of the republic. While Margaret Fuller and her adult pupils sat "gorgeously dressed," talking about Mars and Venus, Plato and Göthe, and fancying themselves the elect of the earth in intellect and refinement, the liberties of the republic were running out as fast as they could go, at a breach which another sort of elect persons were devoting themselves to repair: and my complaint against the "gorgeous" pedants was that they regarded their preservers as hewers of wood and drawers of water, and their work as a less vital one than the pedantic orations which were spoiling a set of well-meaning women in a pitiable way.—HARRIET MARTINEAU, *Autobiography*, ed. Maria Weston Chapman, 1877, Vol. 1, p. 381

> Thou, Sibyl rapt! whose sympathetic soul
> Infused the myst'ries thy tongue failed to tell;
> Though from thy lips the marvellous accents fell,
> And weird wise meanings o'er the senses stole,
> Through those rare cadences, with winsome spell;
> Yet, even in such refrainings of thy voice,
> There struggled up a wailing undertone,
> That spoke thee victim of the Sisters' choice,—
> Charming all others, dwelling still alone.
> They left thee thus disconsolate to roam,
> And scorned thy dear, devoted life to spare.
> Around the storm-tost vessel sinking there
> The wild waves chant thy dirge and welcome home;
> Survives alone thy sex's valiant plea,
> And the great heart that loved the brave and free.
>   —A. BRONSON ALCOTT, *Sonnets and Canzonets*,
>   1882, p. 113

Those who think of this accomplished woman as a mere *bas bleu*, a pedant, a solemn Minerva, should have heard the peals of laughter which her profuse and racy humor drew from old and young. The Easy Chair remembers stepping into Noah Gerrish's West Roxbury omnibus one afternoon in Cornhill, in Boston, to drive out the nine miles to Brook Farm. The only other passenger was Miss Fuller, then freshly returned from her "summer on the lakes," and never was a long, jolting journey more lightened and shortened than by her witty and vivid sketches of life and character. Her quick and shrewd observation is shown in the book, but the book has none of the comedy of the *croquis* of persons which her sparkling humor threw off, and which she too enjoyed with the utmost hilarity, joining heartily in the laughter, which was only increased by her sympathy with the amusement of her auditor.—GEORGE WILLIAM CURTIS, "Editor's Easy Chair," *Harper's New Monthly Magazine*, March 1882, p. 627

Margaret Fuller, who had always struck me as a very plain woman, was the oracle. She had a very long neck, which Dr. Holmes described "as either being swan-like or suggesting the great ophidian who betrayed our Mother Eve." She had a habit of craning her head forward as if her hearing were defective; but she had a set of woman-worshippers who said that the flowers faded when she did not appear.

She was the Aspasia of this great council. She seemed to have a special relationship to each of the intellectual men about her, discerning and reading them better than they did themselves. Some one said of her that she was a kind of spiritual fortune-teller, and that her eyes were at times visible in the dark. Their devotion to her was akin to fanaticism, and they would talk of the magic play of her voice as the singing of a fountain. She had a very kind way to the colored stage-driver, who was the Mr. Weller of Concord, and he distinguished her by his respect. The "chambermaid would confide to her her homely romance." The better class of young Cambridge students believed in her as though she had been a learned professor. Her all-seeing eye could shoot through the problems which engaged them. Many distinguished men kept this opinion of her to their deaths. With such wonderful imagination and a genius like that of George Eliot, there was much that was morbid and unhealthy and strange in Margaret Fuller. She was a victim of dreadful headaches all her life, but she said that "pain acted like a girdle to her powers," and between laughing and crying she would utter her most witty words.

There was a singular mixture of faculties in this gifted woman. She was fully conscious of the male intellect in which was incarnate her truly sensitive feminine heart. She had a tendency to dally with stories of spells and charms, and really thought she had (if she turned her head one side) the power of second-sight.—M. E. W. SHERWOOD, *An Epistle to Posterity*, 1897, pp. 37–38

General

Miss Fuller was at one time editor, or one of the editors of *The Dial*, to which she contributed many of the most forcible, and certainly some of the most peculiar papers. She is known, too, by *Summer on the Lakes*, a remarkable assemblage of sketches, issued in 1844 by Little & Brown, of Boston. More lately she has published *Woman in the Nineteenth Century*, a work which has occasioned much discussion, having had the good fortune to be warmly abused and chivalrously defended. At present, she is assistant editor of *The New York Tribune*, or rather a salaried contributor to that journal, for which she has furnished a great variety of matter, chiefly critical notices of new books, etc. etc., her articles being designated by an asterisk. Two of the best of them were a review of Professor Longfellow's late magnificent edition of his own works, (with a portrait,) and an appeal to the public in behalf of her friend Harro Harring. The review did her infinite credit; it was frank, candid, independent—in even ludicrous contrast to the usual mere glorifications of the day, giving honor *only* where honor was due, yet evincing the most thorough capacity to appreciate and the most sincere intention to place in the fairest light the real and idiosyncratic merits of the poet.

In my opinion it is one of the very few reviews of Longfellow's poems, ever published in America, of which the critics have not had abundant reason to be ashamed. Mr. Longfellow is entitled to a certain and very distinguished rank

among the poets of his country, but that country is disgraced by the evident toadyism which would award to his social position and influence, to his fine paper and large type, to his morocco binding and gilt edges, to his flattering portrait of himself, and to the illustrations of his poems by Huntingdon, that amount of indiscriminate approbation which neither could nor would have been given to the poems themselves.

The defence of Harro Harring, or rather the Philippic against those who were doing him wrong, was one of the most eloquent and well-*put* articles I have ever yet seen in a newspaper.

Woman in the Nineteenth Century is a book which few women in the country could have written, and no woman in the country would have published, with the exception of Miss Fuller. In the way of independence, of unmitigated radicalism, it is one of the *Curiosities of American Literature*, and Doctor Griswold should include it in his book. I need scarcely say that the essay is nervous, forcible, thoughtful, suggestive, brilliant, and to a certain extent scholar-like—for all that Miss Fuller produces is entitled to those epithets—but I must say that the conclusions reached are only in part my own. Not that they are too bold, by any means—too novel, too startling, or too dangerous in their consequences, but that in their attainment too many premises have been distorted and too many analogical inferences left altogether out of sight. I mean to say that the intention of the Deity as regards sexual differences—an intention which can be distinctly comprehended only by throwing the exterior (more sensitive) portions of the mental retina *casually* over the wide field of universal *analogy*—I mean to say that this *intention* has not been sufficiently considered. Miss Fuller has erred, too, through her own excessive objectiveness. She judges *woman* by the heart and intellect of Miss Fuller, but there are not more than one or two dozen Miss Fullers on the whole face of the earth. Holding these opinions in regard to *Woman in the Nineteenth Century*, I still feel myself called upon to disavow the silly, condemnatory criticism on the work which appeared in one of the earlier numbers of *The Broadway Journal*. That article was *not* written by myself, and *was* written by my associate Mr. Briggs.

The most favorable estimate of Miss Fuller's genius (for high genius she unquestionably possesses) is to be obtained, perhaps, from her contributions to *The Dial*, and from her *Summer on the Lakes*. Many of the *descriptions* in this volume are unrivaled for *graphicality*, (why is there not such a word?) for the force with which they convey the true by the novel or unexpected, by the introduction of touches which other artists would be sure to omit as irrelevant to the subject. This faculty, too, springs from her subjectiveness, which leads her to paint a scene less by its features than by its effects.

⟨. . .⟩ She uses, too, the word "ignore," a vulgarity adopted only of late days (and to no good purpose, since there is no necessity for it) from the barbarisms of the law, and makes no scruple of giving the Yankee interpretation to the verbs "witness" and "realize," to say nothing of "use," as in the sentence, "I used to read a short time at night." It will not do to say, in defence of such words, that in such senses they may be found in certain dictionaries—in that of Bolles', for instance;—*some* kind of "authority" may be found for *any* kind of vulgarity under the sun.

In spite of these things, however, and of her frequent unjustifiable Carlyleisms, (such as that of writing sentences which are no sentences, since, to be parsed, reference must be had to sentences preceding,) the style of Miss Fuller is one of the very best with which I am acquainted. In general effect, I know no style which surpasses it. It is singularly piquant, vivid, terse, bold, luminous—leaving details out of sight, it is everything that a style need be.

I believe that Miss Fuller has written much poetry, although she has published little. That little is tainted with the affectation of the *transcendentalists*, (I use this term, of course, in the sense which the public of late days seem resolved to give it,) but is brimful of the poetic *sentiment*.—EDGAR ALLAN POE, "Sarah Margaret Fuller" (1846), *Essays and Reviews*, ed. G. R. Thompson, 1984, pp. 1172–77

The good Miss Fuller has painted us all *en beau*, and your smiling imagination has added new colors. We have not a triumphant life here; very far indeed from that, *ach Gott!*—as you shall see. But Margaret is an excellent soul: in real regard with both of us here. Since she went, I have been reading some of her Papers in a new Book we have got: greatly superior to all I knew before; in fact the undeniable utterances (now first undeniable to me) of a true heroic mind;—altogether unique, so far as I know, among the Writing Women of this generation; rare enough too, God knows, among the writing Men. She is very narrow, sometimes; but she is truly high: honor to Margaret, and more and more good-speed to her.—THOMAS CARLYLE, Letter to Ralph Waldo Emerson (March 2, 1847)

Miss Margaret Fuller is best known as a prose writer. Her *Woman in the Nineteenth Century, Papers on Literature and Art, Summer on the Lakes,* etc., entitle her undoubtedly to be ranked among the first authors of her sex. I have recently re-read these works, incited to do so by the apparent candor and decided sagacity displayed in the Letters she has written to *The Tribune* during her residence in Europe; and I confess some change of opinion in her favor since writing the article upon her in *The Prose Writers of America.* Few can boast so wide a range of literary culture; perhaps none write so well with as much facility; and there is marked individuality in all her productions. As a poet, we have few illustrations of her abilities; but what we have are equal to her reputation. She is said to have written much more poetry than she has published.—RUFUS W. GRISWOLD, "S. Margaret Fuller," *The Female Poets of America*, 1848, p. 251

⟨. . .⟩ she is one of those few authors who have written too little. We hope to read more of her prose, so thoughtful and vigorous; and of her poetry, at once so graceful, yet so strong and simple.—THOMAS POWELL, "S. Margaret Fuller," *The Living Authors of America*, 1850, p. 318

Margaret Fuller—what do you think of her? I have given, after some hesitation, half a guinea for the three volumes concerning her—partly moved by the low price partly by interest about that partly brazen female. I incline to think that the meeting with her would have made me return all the contents of my spiritual stomach but through the screen of a book I willingly look at her and allow her her exquisite intelligence and fineness of aperçus. But my G—d what rot did she and the other female dogs of Boston talk about the Greek mythology! The absence of men of any culture in America, where everybody knows that the Earth is an oblate speroid and nobody knows anything worth knowing, must have made her run riot so wildly, and for many years made her insufferable.—MATTHEW ARNOLD, Letter to Arthur Hugh Clough (March 21, 1853)

Those who knew her in early youth, who witnessed her extraordinary intellectual developments, who experienced her wonderful power in conversation, and who cast the horoscope of the woman from the brilliant promise of the girl, predicted for her a distinguished literary career. They saw in her a future D'Arblay or De Stael. The death of her father, leaving a large family with small means, and the consequent necessity of exertion in ways more profitable than authorship, together with the loss of her health, postponed indefinitely the fulfilment of this hope. But perhaps the hope itself was without foundation. For ourselves, we incline to the belief that in no circumstances, by no favor of fortune, would Margaret have produced a work which should have worthily expressed her genius. With all her mental wealth and rare faculty, we doubt whether she possessed the organic power, the concentration and singleness of purpose, necessary for such an undertaking. Her mind was critical, not constructive; impulsive, not laborious. Her strength lay rather in oracular judgments, in felicitous statements and improvisations, than in patient elaboration. True, she has written much and well. Her critical essays, and especially her papers on Goethe, in the *Dial*, are unsurpassed in their kind. But all that she has written is fragmentary; nothing epic, nothing that possesses formal excellence, no one complete work.—FREDERICK HENRY HEDGE, "Madame Ossoli's *At Home and Abroad*," *North American Review*, July 1856, pp. 261–62

In the third volume of the present series is published *Woman in the Nineteenth Century*; several papers concerning woman and her interests; and some letters from and concerning Margaret, which would more properly have been included in the *Memoirs*. Some of these last show her religious feeling and her sweet womanliness in so bright an aspect, that we would gladly quote them. *Woman in the Nineteenth Century* is, perhaps, more widely known than any of her works. We shall avoid any lengthened criticism of it, because it must open a discussion of the still unfolding "Woman Question," for which we have neither space nor time. It is doubtless the most complete, brilliant, and scholarly statement ever made upon this subject. Its terse epigrammatic sentences have furnished more than one watchword to the reformers with whom the author herself was never associated. The book is interesting as the strongest expression of the aggressive and reformatory element in her. She was interested in the social pioneers of whom she often spoke lightly, and it was reserved for Italy to teach her the practical value of an abstract idea. In the Preface to this volume, the editor bears touching testimony to her domestic virtues.

The fourth volume contains *Summer on the Lakes,*—her *Letters from Europe to the Tribune*, giving the details of Italian politics,—some letters to friends, portions of which had been already incorporated into her *Memoirs*,—and details of the fatal shipwreck. *Summer on the Lakes* has long been one of our favorite summer classics. It first won us, not more by the vital individuality and grace of the style, in which it stands alone among her lighter works, than by the beauty of the little brown etchings with which her friend Miss Clarke adorned the first edition. In the matter of style, it was Margaret's peculiarity to have none when she spoke from her memory. The narrative portions of her *Letters from Abroad*, for example, might just as well have been written by any one else. But once arouse her heart and mind, and out flowed the personality! Let her speak of Mazzini, or describe a fringed flower in the moonbeams, and no one could mistake the author. This volume is especially interesting, as containing all that remains of her Italian experience, her complete work on *Italy* having shared, to our bitter regret, her own fate.

Art, Literature, and the Drama, is a reprint of the volume which she published on the eve of her departure for Europe. A friendly gift to those she was leaving, it proved, in many respects, the most popular thing she had printed,—and deservedly, for her mind was eminently critical. She was often misled in her first judgment, as in one well-known instance, by the strength of her affection and her sympathy; but let the merit be real, and of a kind which she was glad to recognize, and no one ever did more exquisite justice to thought and to its form. Every word which she ever wrote of Goethe was admirable, and yet what we possess was only *her preparation* for better work. Nothing was ever more tender and true than her sketch of "The Two Herberts" in this volume. Let the reader dwell also on what she has to say of "American Literature," and the "Lives of the Great Composers."

The closing volume of this series, entitled, *Life Without and Life Within*, strikes us as the most interesting portion of her miscellaneous writings, and its contents are almost entirely new to the public. Here we have the best of what remained about Goethe,—pleasant criticisms, and ideal sketches of various kinds,—appeals for the unhappy also, and words which, if the fault-finders will but read them, will show, not merely her spiritual capacity, but, in some respects, the measure of her attainment.

It is impossible, in closing, to criticise these works as they deserve. We repeat what is well known, and has been often said, that their *suggestiveness* is their chief and perpetual charm. No one can read attentively what she wrote, without learning to think for himself. The difference between her written works and her marvellous conversation was well indicated by a compliment paid by the Comte de Ségur to Madame de Staël. "Tell me, Count," she asked in a vivacious moment, "which do you like best, my conversation or my printed works?" "Your conversation, Madame," was the immediate reply, "for it does not give you leisure to become obscure." —CAROLINE H. DALL, "Margaret Fuller Ossoli," *North American Review*, July 1860, pp. 126–28

Margaret so lived in the life of her own day and generation, so keenly felt its good and ill, that many remember her as a woman whose spoken word and presence had in them a power which is but faintly imaged in her writings. Nor is this impression wholly a mistaken one. Certain it is that those who recall the enchantment of her conversation always maintain that the same charm is not to be found in the productions of her pen. Yet if we attentively read what she has left us, without this disparagement, we shall find that it entitles her to a position of honour among the prose writers of her time.

The defects of her style are easily seen. They are in some degree the result of her assiduous study of foreign languages, in which the pure and severe idioms of the English tongue were sometimes lost sight of. Among them may be mentioned a want of measure in expression, and also something akin to the fault which is called on the stage "anti-climax," by which some saying of weight and significance loses its point by being followed by another of equal emphasis. With all this, the high quality of her mind has left its stamp upon all that she gave to the reading public. Much of this first appeared in the form of contributions to the *Tribune*, the *Dial*, and other journals and magazines. Some of these papers are brief and even fragmentary; but the shortest of them show careful study and conscientious judgment. All of them are valuable for the admirable view which they present of the time in which Margaret wrote, of its difficulties and limitations, and of the hopes and convictions which, cherished then in the hearts of the few, were destined to make themselves a law to the conscience of the whole community.

The most important of the more elaborate essays is undoubtedly that entitled *Woman in the Nineteenth Century*,

of which some account has already been given in the preceding pages. Of the four volumes published in 1875, one bears this title. A second, entitled *Art, Literature, and the Drama*, contains many of the papers to which reference has been made in our brief account of Margaret and her contemporaries. From a third volume, entitled *Abroad and at Home*, we have quoted some of her most interesting statements concerning the Liberal movement in Europe, of which she was so ardent a friend and promoter. A last volume was collected and published in 1859, by her brother, the Rev. Arthur B. Fuller, who served as an army chaplain in the War of the Southern Rebellion, and met his death on one of its battle-fields. This volume is called *Life Without and Life Within*, and is spoken of in Mr. Fuller's preface as containing, for the most part, matter never before given to the world in book form, and also poems and prose fragments never before published.—JULIA WARD HOWE, *Margaret Fuller*, 1883, pp. 219–21

Even in her printed essays ⟨. . .⟩ she suffered from an exuberance of mental activity, which she had not yet learned to control. Trained early to be methodical in her use of time, she had neither the leisure nor the health nor perhaps the impulse to be methodical in thought. In that teeming period when she lived, method was not the strong point, nor did her friend Emerson set her, in this respect, a controlling example. The habit of conversation was perhaps bad for her, in this way, and may have tended, as does all extemporaneous speaking, toward a desultory habit of mind. Journalism, which was her next resource, leads in the same way; that is, the single editorial demands concentration, but two successive editorials are rarely linked together, and still more rarely give room for what she calls "the third thought." Accordingly her *Tribune* articles had more symmetry than her previous writings, but it was symmetry within the restricted field of the newspaper column, which often unfits the best journalist for a more sustained flight. How far the maturer experience in Italy may have remedied this, in her case, we never shall know, since her book was lost with her; and her record as a writer remains therefore unfinished. Still it is something to know that on the whole she tended more and more to completeness of form, and to the proper control of her own abundant thoughts.

The evidence of this is not to be found in her *Woman in the Nineteenth Century*,—which, while full of thoughts and suggestions, is yet discursive and unmethodical,—but in her *Papers on Literature and Art*. The most satisfactory of these is the essay on Sir James Mackintosh, which still seems to me, as it has seemed for many years, one of the very best critical essays yet written in America. Sir James was a peculiarly good subject to test her powers, because his temperament was wholly alien from hers. He stood to her in a clear light, as the man who by the consent of all contemporaries was best equipped for great deeds, yet never accomplished them; who must be judged by his results as against his promise; *omnium consensu capax imperii, nisi imperâsset*. This has often since been pointed out, but no one stated it so early, or at least so clearly as Margaret Fuller. I know nobody else in American literature who could have handled the theme so well; Lowell would not have done the work so simply, or Whipple so profoundly, while Emerson would not have done it at all. If any reader of this book wishes to be satisfied that Margaret Fuller had her own place and a very high place among American prose-writers, they may turn to that essay.

There were two points in which no one exceeded her at the time and place in which she lived. First, she excelled in "lyric glimpses," or the power of putting a high thought into a sentence. If few of her sentences have passed into the common repertory of quotation, that is not a final test. The greatest poet is not necessarily the most quoted or quotable poet. Pope fills twenty-four pages in Bartlett's *Dictionary of Quotations*, Moore eight, Burns but six, Keats but two, and the Brownings taken together less than half a page. The test of an author is not to be found merely in the number of his phrases that pass current in the corners of newspapers—else would *Josh Billings* be at the head of literature;—but in the number of passages that have really taken root in younger minds. Tried by this standard, Margaret Fuller ranks high, and, if I were to judge strictly by my own personal experience, I should say very high indeed. ⟨. . .⟩

She seems to me to have been, in the second place, the best literary critic whom America has yet seen. Her friend Ripley, who succeeded her in the *Tribune* and held such sway for many years, was not, in the finer aspects of the art, to be compared with Margaret Fuller. Passing from her single phrases and *obiter dicta* to her continuous criticisms, I should name her second paper on Goethe in the *Dial*; as ranking next to that on Mackintosh; and should add, also, her essay on "Modern British Poets" in *Papers on Literature and Art*; and the "dialogue" between Aglauron and Laurie in the same volume. In this last there are criticisms on Wordsworth which go deeper, I venture to think, than anything Lowell has written on the same subject. I do not recall any other critic on this poet who has linked together the poems "A Complaint" and the sonnet beginning

There is a change and I am poor,

and has pointed out that these two give us a glimpse of a profounder personal emotion and a deeper possibility of sadness in Wordsworth than all else that he has written put together.—THOMAS WENTWORTH HIGGINSON, *Margaret Fuller Ossoli*, 1884, pp. 286–91

It not infrequently happens, in these days of widely diffused knowledge, and of multiplied opportunities for intellectual labor, that a potent influence upon thought is exercised by men and women who produce no volumes of importance. Such influences, as a rule, should not be noted, or at any rate described at length, in a history of literature. Yet, in tracing the development of a thing so recent as the literature of the United States, we would go astray did we refuse to recognize and study some influences which affected the intellectual growth of the nation, though not taking permanent form within the covers of bound volumes of the highest class. Of the influence exerted by Dr. Ripley, who did not write a single book of high rank, I have just spoken. Equally notable, though less prolonged, was that exerted by Margaret Fuller, like Ripley first a Transcendentalist, then a worker for the *New York Tribune*. From *The Dial* to a daily newspaper seems a long step; but the work of Ripley and Miss Fuller was aided by their willingness to earn a living in an honorable employment, and therein to spread more widely some of the principles they had advocated in a circle of the Transcendental elect. Few, nowadays, read the "works" of Margaret Fuller: her translation of Eckermann's *Conversations with Goethe*, her unimportant *Summer on the Lakes*, her more ambitious papers on *Art and Literature*, or her principal book, *Woman in the Nineteenth Century*. We cannot say that these papers have fallen out of public notice because they were collected from the pages of periodicals; surely a previous publication did not deter the public of book-readers from the writings of Emerson or Lowell, Carlyle or Macaulay. Nor can it be said that Miss Fuller's writing was of inferior merit, for some of it surpassed

in value the essays and criticisms of Poe, for instance, and equalled a part of Channing's literary product. Friendly eulogists have striven to keep her character and work before the public eye; not many have been so fortunate as to be commemorated by the pen of Emerson, not to enumerate all her lesser and later biographers. In addition to this, readers of Hawthorne cannot fail to see that certain elements in the character of Zenobia, in *The Blithedale Romance*, correspond with some of Miss Fuller's, though, of course, it would be careless to aver that Zenobia was Margaret Fuller. Great romancers are not so clumsy as to introduce real personages into their pages, without many touches and idealizing changes.

Yet, after all that has been said of Miss Fuller by her many earnest friends, after the zealous and sometimes unseemly criticisms and defences of which she has been the subject, and after the fullest recognition of her merits, faults, and foibles, her personality and the memory of her influence are the things that interest us, not the present value of her printed pages. Her learned girlhood, her solitary ways, and her burning zeal, remind us of Mrs. Browning. As Mrs. Browning's name is first among women who have contributed to English literature, so the name of Margaret Fuller is practically the first to show the position woman has already begun to take, and must make more and more conspicuous, in the literature of America. She could understand, share, and spread the philosophical, religious, and literary opinions of Emerson; she could edit *The Dial*, the magazine in which the Transcendental spirit took form; she could rival Alcott as a leader of conversation; she could aid in the excellent movement for the popularization of German literature in America; she could prove "woman's right to labor" in the exacting toils of newspaper writing; and at last she could throw herself, heart and soul, into the early struggles toward Italian unity and freedom, in 1848 and the following years. The parallel between Margaret Fuller and Mrs. Browning, begun in school-girl days, was continued on Italian soil; but not in the tragic water-death of the brave and wayward American. Margaret Fuller had married in Italy, late in 1847, a Marquis Giovanni Angelo Ossoli, of whose character the conflicting accounts need not be discussed here; she had worked for his country with pen and hand, at the desk and in the hospital; she had been a trusted associate of Mazzini in his labor and ambition; and she had written a chronicle of some of the scenes she had beheld and shared. Her life ended, with that of her family, in a shipwreck on the American coast, within a day's sail of home, in 1850. She had done and she had been; what she did and was we cannot forget, though we read not her books, but those of women who followed her, and who were helped toward intellectual freedom and toward the fields of literature by her pioneer toils.—CHARLES F. RICHARDSON, *American Literature, 1607–1885*, 1887, Vol. 1, pp. 431–34

Margaret Fuller never appeared as a candidate for popular favor. On the polishing of furniture she was absolutely silent; nor, though she professed "high respect for those who 'cook something good,' and create and preserve fair order in houses," did she ever fulfil the understood duty of woman by publishing a cookery book. On the education of daughters she had, however, a vital word to say; demanding for them "a far wider and more generous culture." Her own education had been of an exceptional character; she was fortunate in its depth and solidity, though unfortunate in the forcing process that had made her a hard student at six years old. Her equipment was superior to that of any American woman who had previously entered the field of literature; and hers was a powerful genius, but, by the irony of fate, a genius not prompt to clothe itself in the written word. As to the inspiration of her speech all seem to agree; but one who knew her well has spoken of the "singular embarrassment and hesitation induced by the attempt to commit her thoughts to paper." The reader of the sibylline leaves she scattered about her in her strange career receives the constant impression of hampered power, of force that has never found its proper outlet. In *Woman in the Nineteenth Century* there is certainly something of that "shoreless Asiatic dreaminess" complained of by Carlyle; but there are also to be found rich words, fit, like those of Emerson, for "gold nails in temples to hang trophies on." The critical Scotchman himself subsequently owned that "some of her Papers are the undeniable utterances of a true heroic mind; altogether unique, so far as I know, among the Writing Women of this generation; rare enough, too, God knows, among the Writing Men." She accomplished comparatively little that can be shown or reckoned. Her mission was "to free, arouse, dilate." Those who immediately responded were few; and as the circle of her influence has widened through their lives the source of the original impulse has been unnamed and forgotten. But if we are disposed to rank a fragmentary greatness above a narrow perfection, to value loftiness of aim more than the complete attainment of an inferior object, we must set Margaret Fuller, despite all errors of judgment, all faults of style, very high among the "Writing Women" of America. It is time that, ceasing to discuss her personal traits, we dwell only upon the permanent and essential in her whose mind was fixed upon the permanent, the essential. Her place in our literature is her own; it has not been filled, nor does it seem likely to be. The particular kind of force which she exhibited—in so far as it was not individual—stands a chance in our own day of being drawn into the educational field, now that the "wider and more generous culture" which she claimed has been accorded to women.—HELEN GRAY CONE, "Woman in American Literature," *Century Magazine*, Oct. 1890, pp. 924–25

In many respects Margaret Fuller stands, like Poe, solitary in our literature. Her strong, masculine personality which placed her alone among American women, and her keen, peculiar intellect which made her a powerful influence on the intellectual men of her generation, defy classification. If judged alone by her actual literary product, she would deserve but a passing notice, yet she is ranked with the great builders of American literature. Concerning few American writers, save Poe and Whitman, can one find such extremes of opinion. Some of her contemporaries characterized her as superficially learned, disagreeable, warped by intense personal likes and dislikes, domineering, oracular, inordinately fond of monologue; while others, like Emerson, Carlyle, Channing, and Higginson, declared her a rare genius, a profound thinker and scholar, a fountain of "wit, anecdote, love stories, tragedies, oracles"; "the queen of some parliament of love, who carried the key to all confidences and to whom every question had been finally referred." To these she seemed to breathe out constantly "an ineffably sweet, benign, tenderly humane, and serenely high spirit." She is almost the only American author who, like a great singer or actor, keeps a place in our memories chiefly through the testimony of contemporaries.

Before criticizing Margaret Fuller's life and character, one must take into consideration her early education. Her father, a scholarly man, spared no efforts to make her a youthful prodigy. Her brain was terribly stimulated. At the age of six she was poring over Latin verbs; at eight she was eagerly reading

Shakespeare, Cervantes, and Molière, and before she was twelve she had become familiar with the leading masterpieces of the Greek, Latin, French, Italian, and English. She was, consequently, in a few years a phenomenon of learning, "but was paying the penalty for undue application in nearsightedness, awkward manners, extravagant tendencies of thought, and a pedantic style of talk."

In 1840, when she became editor of *The Dial*, Margaret Fuller was regarded as the most intellectual woman of America. She had read deeply in the literature of Germany, and the German philosophy was at her tongue's end. The year before she had translated Eckermann's *Conversations with Goethe*, and the following year she completed a translation of *The Letters of Günderode and Bettine*. In every way she was fitted to become the oracle of the Transcendentalist movement. Her literary life, which now began, may be divided into three periods. The first may be termed the Transcendental period, during which time she published two books: *Summer on the Lakes*, the journal of an excursion to Lake Superior in 1843, and *Woman in the Nineteenth Century*, which had originally appeared in *The Dial* under the title, "The Great Lawsuit." The first, which is in many respects her most literary work, excels in descriptive power. Her condensed and graphic pictures of Niagara, of the wild regions about the Great Lakes, which were then on the borders of civilization, of frontier life in its summer dress, of the boundless prairies, of the rapidly advancing tide of civilization, abound in life and beauty. Her *Woman in the Nineteenth Century* is full of force and earnestness. She was, in the words of Greeley's introduction to the work, "one of the earliest as well as ablest among American women to demand for her sex equality before the law with her titular lord and master." The book is bold and strenuous, and is still readable.

The second period in Margaret Fuller's career opened in 1844, when she removed to New York City to become literary editor of Greeley's *Tribune*. During the twenty months of her connection with this paper she produced her strongest work. As a critic she had rare powers, and her *Papers on Literature and Art*, collected from *The Tribune* and published in 1846, furnish the best basis that we have for an estimate of her powers. "She could appreciate, but not create."

In 1846 she went to Europe and after travelling extensively in England and on the Continent found herself, in 1847, in Rome. Six months later she became the wife of the Italian Marquis Ossoli, a near friend of Mazzini the patriot. She was present in Rome during the Revolution of 1848 and a year later during the French siege of the city, when she rendered invaluable assistance in the hospitals. In 1850 she sailed for America with her husband and child, but the ship was wrecked in sight of the American coast and all were lost. The literary result of this last period of her life, a history of Rome, perished with its author.

The place which Margaret Fuller will ultimately occupy in the history of American letters can only be conjectured. "Her genius was not quick to clothe itself in the written word," and it seems but fair to judge that any literary fame that rests largely upon tradition must ultimately be lost. Her genius lay in her personal influence. She held frequent "Conversations," during which her admirers listened with bated breath as to a goddess. She drew about her with scarcely an effort a circle of the purest and most spiritual men and women of New England and she ruled it with singular power. And after her death the noblest and best minds of both hemispheres united to do honor to her memory.—FRED LEWIS PATTEE, *A History of American Literature*, 1896, pp. 231–34

Her temperament was stormy, her egotism pronounced, her attitude often aggressive, and when she determined to make a personal friend of Emerson, all the resources of his courtesy were taxed to meet the invasion. But by gracious habit of patience and of high expectation he learned her nobleness and, later, took his place at the head of her illustrious biographers, whose judgment of her has become the judgment of time. It is no part of Lowell's greatness to-day that he showered with sneering witticisms the "Miranda" of his *Fable for Critics*, and Hawthorne's harsh detractions have redounded to his discredit rather than to hers; but it is permanently to the praise of Emerson, Higginson, and James Freeman Clarke that, beyond plain face and repellent bearing, they discerned what the English poet Landor was to hail as a "glorious soul." The literary women of America, before the day of Margaret Fuller, pursued their quest for truth or beauty with all feminine timidity. The craven air of Hannah Adams, who had toiled over bookmaking all her apologetic days and, with eyes grown dim, was looking wistfully toward heaven as a place where she might find her "thirst for knowledge fully gratified," is an extreme viewed from which the arrogance of her young contemporary is almost welcome. "Such a predetermination," said Carlyle, "to eat this big Universe as her oyster or her egg, and to be absolute empress of all height and glory in it that her heart could conceive, I have not before seen in any human soul."

Margaret Fuller's literary significance does not chiefly depend upon the actual writings that her busy hand turned off. As the underpaid, overworked editor of the "aëriform" *Dial* and, later, as stated contributor of critical articles to the *New York Tribune*, whose famous chief, Horace Greeley, found her "a most fearless and unselfish champion of truth and human good at all hazards," she accomplished a fair amount of creditable work, suggestive rather than symmetrical, but her inspiring personality counted for more than her best paragraphs. Curious reading now is the record of those Boston "Conversations," where Margaret Fuller discussed, in the heart of the Transcendental camp, the spiritual significance of Greek mythology. There were the enthusiast, George Ripley, and his martyr-wife; Hedge, the German scholar; Wheeler, the Greek scholar; Story, the poet-sculptor; Jones Very, the lyric mystic; the Peabody sisters, the lovely Elizabeth Hoar, James Freeman Clarke, Alcott, and, now and then, Emerson, who remembered these "as a fair, commanding troop, every one of them adorned by some splendor of beauty, of grace, of talent, or of character." With her pen, as with the spoken word, Margaret, as they all called her, was serious, strenuous, but neither soundly learned nor essentially æsthetic. She was not an artist born, and her education, though pursued at high pressure, had been solitary and partial. With all her courage, the years had weighed heavily. "Her face is full of the marks of pain," wrote a girlish worshipper when Margaret was thirty-one. "Young as I am, I feel old when I look at her." Youth and sweetness of life came to that craving nature in far Italy, where, like Mrs. Browning, she made the cause of Italian liberty her own. Efficiently and tenderly she nursed the wounded patriots in hospital during the siege of Rome and wrote a history of the short-lived republic. This manuscript was lost in that tragic shipwreck which, in sight of the American coast, overwhelmed her brave young Italian husband, the Marquis Ossoli, their little son, and Margaret herself. Her principal contribution remaining to our literature is an essay on *Woman in the Nineteenth Century*, claiming for women that larger life which her own career has in no small measure furthered.—KATHARINE LEE BATES, *American Literature*, 1897, pp. 221–24

Works

WOMAN IN THE NINETEENTH CENTURY

Margaret was always a most earnest, devoted champion of the Emancipation of Women, from their past and present condition of inferiority, to an independence on Men. She demanded for them the fullest recognition of Social and Political Equality with the rougher sex; the freest access to all stations, professions, employments, which are open to any. To this demand I heartily acceded. It seemed to me, however, that her clear perceptions of abstract right were often overborne, in practice, by the influence of education and habit; that while she demanded absolute equality for Woman, she exacted a deference and courtesy from men to women, *as* women, which was entirely inconsistent with that requirement. In my view, the equalizing theory can be enforced only by ignoring the habitual discrimination of men and women, as forming separate *classes*, and regarding all alike as simply *persons*,—as human beings. So long as a lady shall deem herself in need of some gentleman's arm to conduct her properly out of a dining or ball-room,—so long as she shall consider it dangerous or unbecoming to walk half a mile alone by night,—I cannot see how the 'Woman's Rights' theory is ever to be anything more than a logically defensible abstraction. In this view Margaret did not at all concur, and the diversity was the incitement to much perfectly good-natured, but nevertheless sharpish sparring between us. Whenever she said or did anything implying the usual demand of Woman on the courtesy and protection of Manhood, I was apt, before complying, to look her in the face and exclaim with marked emphasis,—quoting from her *Woman in the Nineteenth Century*,—'LET THEM BE SEA-CAPTAINS IF THEY WILL!' Of course, this was given and received as raillery, but it did not tend to ripen our intimacy or quicken my esteem into admiration. Though no unkind word ever passed between us, nor any approach to one, yet we two dwelt for months under the same roof, as scarcely more than acquaintants, meeting once a day at a common board, and having certain business relations with each other. Personally, I regarded her rather as my wife's cherished friend than as my own, possessing many lofty qualities and some prominent weaknesses, and a good deal spoiled by the unmeasured flattery of her little circle of inordinate admirers. For myself, burning no incense on any human shrine, I half-consciously resolved to 'keep my eye-beam clear,' and escape the fascination which she seemed to exert over the eminent and cultivated persons, mainly women, who came to our out-of-the-way dwelling to visit her, and who seemed generally to regard her with a strangely Oriental adoration.

But as time wore on, and I became inevitably better and better acquainted with her, I found myself drawn, almost irresistibly, into the general current. I found that her faults and weaknesses were all superficial and obvious to the most casual, if undazzled, observer. They rather dwindled than expanded upon a fuller knowledge; or rather, took on new and brighter aspects in the light of her radiant and lofty soul. I learned to know her as a most fearless and unselfish champion of Truth and Human Good at all hazards, ready to be their standard-bearer through danger and obloquy, and, if need be, their martyr. I think few have more keenly appreciated the material goods of life,—Rank, Riches, Power, Luxury, Enjoyment; but I know none who would have more cheerfully surrendered them all, if the well-being of our Race could thereby have been promoted. I have never met another in whom the inspiring hope of Immortality was so strengthened into profoundest conviction. She did not *believe* in our future and unending existence,—she *knew* it, and lived ever in the broad glare of its morning twilight.—HORACE GREELEY, *Memoirs of Margaret Fuller Ossoli*, 1852, Vol. 2, pp. 155–57

No true word on the themes treated of in this volume can fail to awaken a deep interest. It comes to every home with its voice of counsel, perhaps of warning. The treatise which occupies the first half of the volume whose title is given above, was published by Margaret Fuller, shortly before her departure for Europe, and at that time was widely read and much valued by thoughtful persons, many of whom did not agree with its solution of one of the great problems of the age, but sympathized with its noble and pure spirit, and admired its unmistakable genius. The first edition, we learn, was soon exhausted, but the author's absence from the country prevented another edition at that time, and her tragical death by shipwreck, which is so well remembered by the public, still further postponed its republication. We are now indebted to her brother, Rev. Arthur B. Fuller, for a new edition, carefully prepared, and enriched by papers, previously unpublished, on the same general theme. Every page is loaded, we had almost said overloaded, with thought, and the subject is one which the writer had so near her heart that it commanded her best powers and warmest sympathies, and cannot fail to instruct and interest the reader, even when there is not perfect agreement with the views advanced. There was much in the social position of Margaret Fuller to qualify her to speak wisely on this subject. Her *Memoirs* show her to have been surrounded by a very large circle of female friends, married and unmarried, with whom she occupied the most confidential relations. She had, too, a quick sympathy and a generous heart, which made her feel as her own the experience of others.

The general aim of the book is to elevate the standard of female excellence and usefulness, and to point out the means by which these may be promoted and their obstacles removed. While the writer clearly distinguishes the diversity of the sphere and characteristics of woman from those of the other sex, she would open for her every mode of activity for which she finds herself adapted, widening much her present range of avocations. The gross and selfish sentiment, seldom avowed in theory, but too often exhibited in practice, that woman is made solely for the advantage and service of man, is indignantly and justly rebuked, and woman is exhorted to live *first* for God, ever remembering herself to be an immortal spirit, travelling with man on the same pilgrimage to eternity, and preparing for that state where "they neither marry nor are given in marriage, but are as the angels." The marriage relation, like every other, is one of those positions which, to be filled worthily, requires one to be ever noble and holy, and should never be lightly viewed; but its duties are not all that requires the earnest activity of woman, nor can even these be fulfilled without culture of both mind and heart. Viewing marriage and the relation of mother growing out of it as of the most sacred consequence, the writer impresses us with the importance of preparing for and fulfilling these relations with the most elevated motives. And here she finds enough to reprehend in the general customs of society. Parents are too apt to shape the whole education of the daughter so as to make her attractive to the other sex, and this by the conferment of showy and

superficial accomplishments, as if it were the last of all misfortunes for a female to fail of being married, and as if her fate after that event were of comparative insignificance.

Wherever society is unjust to woman, the author is eloquent in her indignation. She severely deals with that social unfairness, which makes of woman, as soon as she falls, a hopeless outcast beyond the pale of sympathy or reformation, while the serpent who has been her ruin is hospitably received and permitted the opportunity to do more of the work of destruction, and even to make his boast of the evil he has done. At the same time, she attributes this state of things to the want of a proper public opinion among women, who ought to make the seducer aware that he has fallen with his victim, and to exclude him, no less than her, from respectability.

The views of the writer are illustrated by many shining examples, from both ancient and modern times, of true women. The author, while acknowledging the sphere of woman not to be identical with that of man, does not yield to the common notion, that woman is without equal intellect, or that it is improper to cultivate it. She holds that woman has a mind as noble as that of man, and is entitled to every fair opportunity to store it with useful knowledge, and to develop it in a legitimate exercise of its powers. In short, woman is, in her view, a *soul* preparing for eternity, and while on earth her position should be so noble, and the employment of all her powers so definite and earnest, as to call forth what is highest in her nature, and to fit her for a sphere yet wider and nobler in eternity.

The "Kindred Papers," which the Editor has judiciously selected, and which occupy some two hundred pages of this interesting volume, afford not merely a varied and enlarged expression of intellectual endowment and culture, but—exhibiting as they do the author herself as a daughter and sister, then as a wife and mother, and in all other relations as a faithful and true woman—furnish a valuable illustration of her principles, and give additional interest to what she has written.—EDWARD EVERETT HALE, *"Woman in the Nineteenth Century," North American Review*, Oct. 1855, pp. 557–59

The writer of the following pages was one of the earliest as well as ablest among American women, to demand for her sex equality before the law with her titular lord and master. Her writings on this subject have the force which springs from the ripening of profound reflection into assured conviction. She wrote as one who had observed, and who deeply felt what she deliberately uttered. Others have since spoken more fluently, more variously, with a greater affluence of illustration; but none, it is believed, more earnestly or more forcibly. It is due to her memory, as well as to the great and living cause of which she was so eminent and so fearless an advocate, that what she thought and said with regard to the position of her sex and its limitations, should be fully and fairly placed before the public. For several years past her principal essay on "Woman," here given, has not been purchasable at any price, and has only with great difficulty been accessible to the general reader. To place it within the reach of those who need and require it, is the main impulse to the publication of this volume; but the accompanying essays and papers will be found equally worthy of thoughtful consideration.—HORACE GREELEY, "Introduction" to *Woman in the Nineteenth Century*, 1874, p. x

WILLIAM LISLE BOWLES

ANNE BRONTË

WILLIAM WORDSWORTH

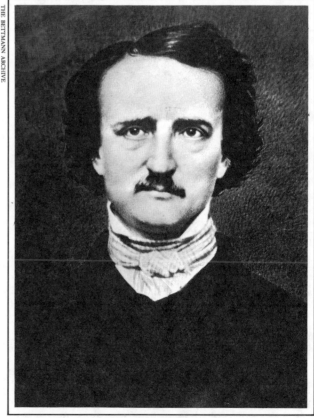

EDGAR ALLAN POE

Francis, Lord Jeffrey

Joanna Baillie

Margaret Fuller

John James Audubon

JOANNA BAILLIE

1762–1851

Joanna Baillie was born at Bothwell, Lanarkshire, Scotland, on September 11, 1762, the younger sister of Matthew Baillie, who became a distinguished pathologist. She began writing verse at an early age and was educated privately. In 1784 she left Scotland and eventually settled permanently in Hampstead with her sister Agnes.

Baillie published her first book, *Fugitive Verses*, in 1790. In 1798 the first volume of *Plays on the Passions* appeared; a second was published in 1802 and a third in 1812. The plays, in the words of the author, presented "the stronger passions of the mind, each passion being the subject of a tragedy and a comedy." Her play *De Montfort*, first produced in 1800 at the Drury Lane theatre, was a great success, and in various revivals over the years featured some of the leading actors of the nineteenth century, including John Kemble, Sara Siddons, and Edmund Kean.

Sir Walter Scott took an early interest in Baillie's work and became her lifelong friend; he contributed the prologue to her play *The Family Legend*, first presented in Edinburgh in 1810. Baillie's collection *Miscellaneous Plays* was published in 1804; a complete edition of her plays and poetry appeared in 1851. Besides being a poet and dramatist, Baillie also wrote songs, many of them adaptations of traditional Scottish folk songs.

Joanna Baillie died at Hampstead on February 23, 1851.

Personal

We met Miss Joanna Baillie, and accompanied her home. She is small in figure, and her gait is mean and shuffling, but her manners are those of a well-bred woman. She has none of the unpleasant airs too common to literary ladies. Her conversation is sensible. She possesses apparently considerable information, is prompt without being forward, and has a fixed judgment of her own, without any disposition to force it on others. Wordsworth said of her with warmth: "If I had to present any one to a foreigner as a model of an English gentlewoman, it would be Joanna Baillie."—HENRY CRABB ROBINSON, *Diary*, May 24, 1812

I saw Mrs. Joanna Baillie before dinner. She wore a delicate lavender satin bonnet; and Mrs. J—— says she is fond of dress, and knows what every one has on. Her taste is certainly exquisite in dress, though (strange to say) not, in my opinion, in poetry. I more than ever admired the harmony of expression and tint, the silver hair and silvery gray eye, the pale skin, and the look which speaks of a mind that has had much communing with high imagination, though such intercourse is only perceptible now by the absence of every thing which that lofty spirit would not set his seal upon. Sir John Herschel says that Mrs. Agnes Baillie is "by far the cleverer woman of the two;" but this is the speech of a *clever* man, a man whose acute mind can pierce some of the mysteries of the world of fact, but which does not sympathize with all the beings of the world of imagination. And then, in Mrs. Joanna Baillie, age has slackened the active part of genius, and yet is in some sort a substitute for it. There is a declining of mental exercitation. She has had enough of that; and now for a calm decline, and thoughts of Heaven.—SARA COLERIDGE, Letter to Samuel Taylor Coleridge (Sept. 4, 1834), *Memoir and Letters of Sara Coleridge*, ed. Edith Coleridge, 1873, Vol. 1, pp. 92–93

We made a most delightful visit to Miss Joanna Baillie. . . . She talked of Scott with a tender enthusiasm that was contagious, and of Lockhart with a kindness that is uncommon when coupled with his name, and which seemed only characteristic of her benevolence. It is very rare that old age, or, indeed, any age, is found so winning and agreeable. I do not

wonder that Scott in his letters treats her with more deference, and writes to her with more care and beauty, than to any other of his correspondents, however high or titled.—GEORGE TICKNOR, *Journal* (Apr. 7, 1838), *Life, Letters, and Journals of George Ticknor*, ed. Anna Ticknor, 1876, Vol. 2, p. 153

She was past fifty when I first saw her, and appeared an old lady to me, then in my teens. She dressed like an aged person, and with scrupulous neatness. She lived with a sister who looked older still, because she had not the vivacity of Joanna, and was only distinguished for the amiability with which she bore being outshone by her more gifted relative.

Miss Baillie, according to the English custom, took the title of Mrs. Joanna Baillie, on passing her fiftieth birthday. She gave the prettiest and the pleasantest dinners, and presided at them with peculiar grace and tact, always attentive to the wants of her guests, and yet keeping up a lively conversation the while. She took such pleasure in writing poetry, and especially in her plays on the Passions, that she said, "If no one ever read them, I should find my happiness in writing them."

Though she was young when she left her native land, she never lost her Scotch accent. I thought it made her conversation only the more piquant. She was full of anecdote and curious facts about remarkable people. I only recollect her telling one of Lord Byron being obliged, by politeness, to escort her and her sister to the opera, and her perceiving that he was provoked beyond measure at being there with them, and that he made faces as he sat behind them.—ELIZA FARRAR, *Recollections of Seventy Years*, 1866, pp. 74–75

Of Joanna Baillie too I saw much both as a friend and patient. Her gentle simplicity, with a Scotch tinge colouring it to the end of life, won the admiration even of those who knew nothing of her power of dramatic poetry. It was pleasant to visit her in the quiet house at Hampstead, in which she lived with her sister Agnes. She reached, I think, her ninety-second year. Agnes lived to a hundred.—SIR HENRY HOLLAND, *Recollections of Past Life*, 1871, p. 246

And there was Joanna Baillie, whose serene and cheerful life was never troubled by the pains and penalties of vanity;—what a charming spectacle was she! Mrs. Barbauld's published correspondence tells of her, in 1800, as "a young lady of Hampstead whom I visited, and who came to Mr. Barbauld's meeting, all the while, with as innocent a face as if she had never written a line." That was two years before I was born. When I met her, about thirty years afterwards, there she was "with as innocent a face as if she had never written a line!" And this was after an experience which would have been a bitter trial to an author with a particle of vanity. She had enjoyed a fame almost without parallel, and had outlived it. She had been told every day for years, through every possible channel, that she was second only to Shakspere,—if second; and then she had seen her works drop out of notice so that, of the generation who grew up before her eyes, not one in a thousand had read a line of her plays:—yet was her serenity never disturbed, nor her merry humour in the least dimmed. I have never lost the impression of the trying circumstances of my first interview with her, nor of the grace, simplicity and sweetness with which she bore them. She was old; and she declined dinner-parties; but she wished to meet me,—having known, I believe, some of my connexions or friends of the past generation;—and therefore she came to Miss Berry's to tea, one day when I was dining there. Miss Berry, her contemporary, put her feelings, it seemed to me, to a most unwarrantable trial, by describing to me, as we three sat together, the celebrity of the *Plays on the Passions* in their day. She told me how she found on her table, on her return from a ball, a volume of plays; and how she kneeled on a chair to look at it, and how she read on till the servant opened the shutters, and let in the daylight of a winter morning. She told me how all the world raved about the plays; and she held on so long that I was in pain for the noble creature to whom it must have been irksome on the one hand to hear her own praises and fame so dwelt upon, and, on the other, to feel that we all knew how long that had been quite over. But, when I looked up at her sweet face, with its composed smile amidst the becoming mob cap, I saw that she was above pain of either kind. We met frequently afterwards, at her house or ours; and I retained my happy impression, till the last call I made on her. She was then over-affectionate, and uttered a good deal of flattery; and I was uneasy at symptoms so unlike her good taste and sincerity. It was a token of approaching departure. She was declining, and she sank and softened for some months more, and then died, revered and beloved as she deserved. Amidst all pedantry, vanity, coquetry, and manners ruined by celebrity which I have seen, for these twenty years past, I have solaced and strengthened myself with the image of Joanna Baillie, and with remembering the invulnerable justification which she set up for intellectual superiority in women, while we may hope that the injury done to that cause by blue-stockings and coquettes will be scarcely more enduring than their own trumpery notoriety.—HARRIET MARTINEAU, *Autobiography*, ed. Maria Weston Chapman, 1877, Vol. 1, pp. 270–71

General

Do you remember my speaking to you in high terms of a series of plays upon the passions of the human mind, which had been sent to me last winter by the author? I talked to everybody else in the same terms of them at the time, anxiously enquiring for the author; but nobody knew them, nobody cared for them, nobody would listen to me; and at last I unwillingly held my tongue, for fear it should be supposed that I thought highly of them only because they had been sent to me. This winter the first question upon everybody's lips is, 'Have you read the series of plays?' Everybody talks in the raptures (I always thought they

deserved) of the tragedies and of the introduction as of a new and admirable piece of criticism. Sir G. Beaumont, who was with us yesterday morning, says he never expected to see such tragedies in his days; and C. Fox, to whom he had sent them, is in such raptures with them, that he has written a critique of 5 pages upon the subject to Sir George. I mention these two as persons of whose taste I, and I believe you too, have a very *decided* opinion. I own my little *amour-propre* is mortified that, having been honoured with a copy of the work, my humble tribute of unfeigned admiration and undictated praise had not reached the author before it is drowned in the general voice. But, whoever that author is, they still persist in preserving a strict incognito, for which I honour their honest pride, which scorns to be indebted to *any* name for the success of such a work, and, with the patient sense of real merit, has quietly waited a whole twelvemonth for the impression it has at last made on an obdurate public. I fancy one of them will be acted—the least good one, in my opinion—but there are two fine characters for Kemble and Mrs. Siddons.—MARY BERRY, *Journal* (March 12, 1799)

The peculiarity of Miss Baillie's plan ⟨. . .⟩ does not consist so much in reducing any play to the exhibition of a single passion, as in attempting to comprehend within it a complete view of the origin, growth, and consummation of this passion, under all its aspects of progress and maturity. This plan seems to us almost as unpoetical as that of the bard who began the tale of the Trojan war from the egg of Leda; and really does not appear very well calculated for a species of composition, in which the time of the action represented has usually been more circumscribed than in any other. Miss Baillie, however, is of opinion, that it will turn out to be a very valuable discovery; and insists much upon the advantage that will be gained by adhering to it, both in the developement of character, the increase of interest, and the promotion of moral improvement. We are afraid that these expectations are more sanguine than reasonable.

To delineate a man's character, by tracing the progress of his ruling passion, is like describing his person by the yearly admeasurement of his foot, or rather by a termly report of the increase of a wen, by which his health and his beauty are ultimately destroyed. A ruling passion distorts and deforms the character; and its growth, instead of developing that character more fully, constantly withdraws more and more of it from our view. The growth of the passion is not the growth of the mind; and its progress and symptoms are pretty conform, in whatever subject it may have originated. *Amor omnibus idem*, at least, says the poet; and it may fairly be admitted, that men become assimilated, by their common subjection to some master passion, who had previously been distinguished by very opposite characters. To delineate character, therefore, by the progress of such a passion, is like following a cloud of smoke, in order to discriminate more clearly the objects that it envelopes.

⟨. . .⟩ We are pretty decidedly of opinion, that Miss Baillie's plan of composing separate plays upon the passions, is, in so far as it is at all new or original, in all respects extremely injudicious; and we have been induced to express this opinion more fully and strongly, from the anxiety that we feel to deliver her pleasing and powerful genius from the trammels that have been imposed upon it by this unfortunate system. It is paying no great compliment, perhaps, to her talents, to say, that they are superior to those of any of her contemporaries among the English writers of tragedy; and that, with proper management, they bid fair to produce something that posterity will not allow to be forgotten. Without perplexing herself with the observances of an arbitrary system, she will find that all tragical subjects imply the agency of the greater passions; and that she will have occasion for all her skill, in the delineation of character, and all her knowledge of the human heart, although she should only aim (as Shakespeare and Otway have done before her) at the excitation of virtuous sympathy, and the production of a high pathetic effect. Her readers, and her critics, will then discover those moral lessons, which she is now a little too eager to obtrude upon their notice; and will admire, more freely, the productions of a genius, that seems less incumbered with its talk, and less conscious of its exertions. ⟨. . .⟩

Upon the whole, we think there is no want of genius in this book, although there are many errors of judgement; and are persuaded, that if Miss Baillie will relinquish her plan of producing twin dramas on each of the passions, and consent to write tragedies without any deeper design than that of interesting her readers, we shall soon have the satisfaction of addressing her with more unqualified praise, than we have yet bestowed upon any poetical adventurer.—FRANCIS, LORD JEFFREY, "Miss Baillie's *Plays on the Passions,*" *Edinburgh Review,* July 1803, pp. 272–86

⟨. . .⟩ if to touch such chord be thine,
Restore the ancient tragic line,
And emulate the notes that rung
From the wild harp which silent hung,
By silver Avon's holy shore,
Till twice an hundred years rolled o'er;
When she, the bold Enchantress, came,
With fearless hand and heart on flame!
From the pale willow snatched the treasure,
And swept it with a kindred measure,
Till Avon's swans, while rung the grove
With Montfort's hate and Basil's love,
Awakening at the inspired strain,
Deemed their own Shakespeare lived again.
—SIR WALTER SCOTT, *Marmion,* 1808, Canto 3, Introduction

Her tragedies and comedies, one of each to illustrate each of the passions, separately from the rest, are heresies in the dramatic art. She is a Unitarian in poetry. With her the passions are, like the French republic, one and indivisible: they are not so in nature, or in Shakspeare. Mr. Southey has, I believe, somewhere expressed an opinion, that the *Basil* of Miss Baillie is superior to *Romeo and Juliet.* I shall not stay to contradict him. On the other hand, I prefer her *De Montfort,* which was condemned on the stage, to some later tragedies, which have been more fortunate—to the *Remorse, Bertram,* and lastly, *Fazio.* There is in the chief character of that play a nerve, a continued unity of interest, a setness of purpose and precision of outline which John Kemble alone was capable of giving; and there is all the grace which women have in writing. In saying that De Montfort was a character which just suited Mr. Kemble, I mean to pay a compliment to both. He was not 'a man of no mark or likelihood': and what he could be supposed to do particularly well, must have a meaning in it. As to the other tragedies just mentioned, there is no reason why any common actor should not 'make mouths in them at the invisible event,'—one as well as another. Having thus expressed my sense of the merits of the authoress, I must add, that her comedy of the *Election,* performed last summer at the Lyceum with indifferent success, appears to me the perfection of baby-house theatricals. Every thing in it has such a *do-me-good* air, is so insipid and amiable. Virtue seems such a pretty playing at make-believe, and vice is such a naughty word. It is

a theory of some French author, that little girls ought not to be suffered to have dolls to play with, to call them *pretty dears,* to admire their black eyes and cherry cheeks, to lament and bewail over them if they fall down and hurt their faces, to praise them when they are good, and scold them when they are naughty. It is a school of affectation: Miss Baillie has profited of it. She treats her grown men and women as little girls treat their dolls—makes moral puppets of them, pulls the wires, and they talk virtue and act vice, according to their cue and the title prefixed to each comedy or tragedy, not from any real passions of their own, or love either of virtue or vice.—WILLIAM HAZLITT, *Lectures on the English Poets,* 1818

I well remember when her plays upon the *Passions* first came out, with a metaphysical preface. All the world wondered and stared at me, who pronounced them the work of a woman, although the remark was made every day and everywhere that it was a masculine performance. No sooner, however, did an unknown girl own the work, than the value so fell, her booksellers complained they could not get themselves paid for what they did, nor did their merits ever again swell the throat of public applause. So fares it with *nous autres,* who expose ourselves to the shifts of malice or the breath of caprice. —HESTER LYNCH PIOZZI, Letter to Sir James Fellowes (March 28, 1819)

And tragic Baillie stole, from nature's side,
The mantle left by Shakspeare when he died?
—EBENEZER ELLIOTT, *Love,* 1823, Bk. 1

She has created tragedies which Sophocles—or Euripides— nay, even Æschylus himself, might have feared, in competition for the crown. She is our Tragic Queen; but she belongs to all places as to all times; and Sir Walter truly said—let them who dare deny it—that he saw her Genius in a sister shape sailing by the side of the Swan of Avon. Yet Joanna loves to pace the pastoral mead; and then we are made to think of the tender dawn, the clear noon, and the bright meridian of her life, past among the tall cliffs of the silver Calder, and in the lonesome heart of the dark Strathaven Muirs.

Plays on the Passions! "How absurd!" said one philosophical writer. "This will never do." It has done—perfectly. What, pray, is the aim of all tragedy? The Stagyrite has told us—to purify the passions by pity and terror. They ventilate and cleanse the soul—till its atmosphere is like that of a calm, bright summer day. All plays, therefore, must be on the Passions. And all that Joanna intended—and it was a great intention greatly effected—was in her Series of Dramas to steady her purposes by ever keeping one great end in view, of which the perpetual perception could not fail to make all the means harmonious, and therefore majestic. One passion was, therefore, constituted sovereign of the soul in each glorious tragedy—sovereign sometimes by divine right—sometimes an usurper—generally a tyrant. In De Monfort we behold the horrid reign of Hate. But in his sister—the seraphic sway of Love. Darkness and light sometimes opposed in sublime contrast—and sometimes the light swallowing up the darkness—or "smoothing its raven down till it smiles." Finally, all is black as night and the grave—for the light, unextinguished, glides away into some far-off world of peace. Count Basil! A woman only could have imagined that divine drama. How different the love Basil feels for Victoria from Anthony's for Cleopatra! Pure, deep, high as the heaven and the sea. Yet on it we see him borne away to shame, destruction, and death. It is indeed his ruling passion. But up to the day he first saw her face his ruling passion had been the love of glory. And the hour he died by his own hand was troubled into madness by many passions; for are they not all mysteriously linked together, sometimes a dreadful brotherhood?—JOHN WILSON, "An Hour's Talk about Poetry" (1831), *The Recreations of Christopher North*, 1842, p. 79

During this season of general poetic fecundity, the drama has, on the whole, been less prolific of excellence than in any preceding age. Few of the great contemporary poets have ventured on this field at all, still fewer have reaped any laurels from it. Miss Baillie is, perhaps, the only writer who has made the attempt on an extended scale, and her pieces are rather addressed to the closet than the stage. She has unfortunately written on a theory; for every body works on a theory in this philosophic age. The principal purpose of her's, was to make each play subservient to the development of some one particular passion. In this way, she excluded herself from the legitimate range of character, which belongs to the drama; nor, indeed, was it possible, with any degree of skill, to adhere to her plan, since the *rôles* of the subordinate agents must often be at variance, and obviously require a different play of passion from that of the principal character.—WILLIAM H. PRESCOTT, "English Literature of the Nineteenth Century," *North American Review*, July 1832, p. 179

On the 29th of April, Mrs. Siddons performed a new part, as the Lady Jane, in Joanna Baillie's tragedy of *De Montfort*. I have already adverted to the surprising fact, that dramas, which we peruse in our libraries with little interest, have sometimes been made, by fine acting, most attractive on the stage. The works of Joanna Baillie afford at least one instance of a perfectly converse nature. They will be read with pleasure as long as our language lasts, and yet they have never acquired popularity in the theatre.

To account for this fact, an indiscreet admirer of this poetess would probably resort to the plausible topics of a degenerate public taste, as well as of the enormous size of our theatres, and the pageantry required for filling the stage, which, undoubtedly, diverts the mind from attention to more spiritual charms; but I have too much respect for Joanna Baillie's genius, to form any estimate of it on questionable grounds. She brought to the drama a wonderful union of many precious requisites for a perfect tragic writer;—deep feeling, a picturesque imagination, and, except where theory and system misled her, a correct taste, that made her diction equally remote from the stiffness of the French, and the flaccid flatness of the German school: a better stage style than any that we have heard since the time of Shakspeare, or, at least, since that of his immediate disciples.

But, to compose a tragedy that shall at once delight the lovers of poetry and the populace, is a prize in the lottery of Fame, which has literally been only once drawn during the whole of the last century, and that was by the author of *Douglas*. He, too, wrote several tragedies that were sheer blanks. Scott and Byron themselves both failed in dramatic composition. It is evident, therefore, that Melpomene demands on the stage something, and a good deal more, than even poetical talent, rare as that is. She requires a potent and peculiar faculty for the invention of incident adapted to theatric effect;—a faculty which may often exist in those who have not been bred to the stage, but which, generally speaking, has seldom been shown by any poets who were not professional players. There are exceptions to the remark, I know, but there are not many. If Shakspeare had not been a player, he would not have been the dramatist that he is.

If Joanna Baillie had known the stage practically, she would never have attached the importance which she does to the development of single passions in single tragedies; and she would have invented more stirring incidents to justify the passion of her characters, and to give them that air of fatality which, though peculiarly predominant in the Greek drama, will also be found, to a certain extent, in all successful tragedies. Instead of this, she contrives to make all the passions of her main characters proceed from the wilful natures of the beings themselves. Their feelings are not precipitated by circumstances, like a stream down a declivity, that leaps from rock to rock; but, for want of incident, they seem often like water on a level, without a propelling impulse.

If, in speaking thus freely of a much regarded contemporary, I should seem indelicate, let it be remembered that Mrs. Siddons's performance of Jane de Montfort is no uninteresting part of the great actress's history; and that, having to deal with the subject, I could not but speak candidly: for, if I took sincerity out of these pages, what value would be in them?

Joanna Baillie's two first tragedies were regarded by the reading world as the sweetest strains that hailed the close of the eighteenth century. John Kemble thought that *De Montfort* would suit the stage; and his acting in the piece, as well as Mrs. Siddons's, was amazingly powerful. Every care was taken that it should receive scenic decoration. Capon painted a very unusual pile of scenery, representing a church of the fourteenth century, with its nave, choir, and side aisles, magnificently decorated, and consisting of seven planes in succession. In width this extraordinary elevation was about 56 feet, 52 in depth, and 37 in height. It was positively a building.

De Montfort had a run of eleven nights. The accounts of its reception are discrepant; but its representation has been, at all events, infrequent. It was brought out again in 1821, when Kean played the part of De Montfort very ably. I shall never forget that performance. There was a vast audience; among whom, I dare say, not threescore persons were personally acquainted with the author of the play. But the poetical character of her who had painted the loves of Count Basil and Victoria was not forgotten; and there was a deep and placid attention paid to *De Montfort*, that might have led you to imagine every one present was the poetess's friend. There was so much silence, and so much applause, that, though I had had misgivings to the contrary, I was impressed, at the end, with a belief that the play had now acquired, and would henceforth for ever retain, stage popularity. But when I congratulated Kean on having rescued *De Montfort*, he told me that, though a fine poem, it would never be an acting play.—THOMAS CAMPBELL, *Life of Mrs. Siddons*, 1834, Ch. 17

Read Joanna Baillie's play of *Basil*, which I think can scarcely be made pathetic enough for representation; there is a stiffness in her style, a want of appropriateness and peculiarity of expression distinguishing each person, that I cannot overcome in reading her plays: it is a sort of brocaded style, a thick kind of silk, that has no fall or play—it is not the flexibility of nature.—WILLIAM CHARLES MACREADY, *Diary*, Feb. 17, 1836

The brightest stars in the poetical firmament, with very few exceptions, have risen and set since then; the greatest revolutions in empire and in opinion have taken place; but she has lived on as if no echo of the upturnings and overthrows which filled the world reached the quiet of her home; the freshness of her inspirations untarnished; writing from the fulness of a true heart of themes belonging equally to all the ages. Personally she is scarcely known in literary society; but from her first appearance as an author, no woman has commanded more respect and admiration by her works; and the most celebrated of her contemporaries have vied with each other in doing her honour. Scott calls her the Shakspeare of her sex. ⟨. . .⟩

The most remarkable of her works are her *Plays of the Passions*, a series in which each passion is made the subject of a tragedy and a comedy. In the comedies she failed completely; they are pointless tales in dialogue. Her tragedies, however, have great merit, though possessing a singular quality for works of such an aim, in being without the earnestness and abruptness of actual and powerful feeling. By refinement and elaboration she makes the passions sentiments. She fears to distract attention by multiplying incidents; her catastrophes are approached by the most gentle gradations; her dramas are therefore slow in action and deficient in interest. Her characters possess little individuality; they are mere generalizations of intellectual attributes, theories personified. The very system of her plays has been the subject of critical censure. The chief object of every dramatic work is to please and interest, and this object may be arrived at as well by situation as by character. Character distinguishes one person from another, while by passion nearly all men are alike. A controlling passion perverts character, rather than developes it; and it is therefore in vain to attempt the delineation of a character by unfolding the progress of a passion. It has been well observed too, that unity of passion is impossible, since to give a just relief and energy to any particular passion, it should be presented in opposition to one of a different sort, so as to produce a powerful conflict in the heart.

In dignity and purity of style, Miss Baillie has not been surpassed by any of the poets of her sex. Her dialogue is formed on the Shaksperean model, and she has succeeded perhaps better than any other dramatist in imitating the manner of the greatest poet of the world.

De Montfort we believe is the only one of Miss Baillie's tragedies which has been successfully presented in the theatres. It was performed in London by John Kemble, and in New York and Philadelphia by Edmund Kean; but no actors of inferior genius have ventured to attempt it, and it will probably never again be brought upon the stage.

Besides her plays Miss Baillie has written *A View of the General Tenor of the New Testament regarding the Nature and Dignity of Jesus Christ, Metrical Legends of Eminent Characters, Fugitive Verses,* and some less important publications. In 1827 she gave the world a new volume of *Plays on the Passions,* and in 1842 Moxon published her *Fugitive Verses.*—RUFUS W. GRISWOLD, "Joanna Baillie," *The Poets and Poetry of England in the Nineteenth Century,* 1844, p. 40

> Long ere my pulse with nascent life had beat,
> The ripe spring of thy early Paradise
> With many a flower, and fruit, and hallow'd spice,
> Was fair to fancy and to feeling sweet.
> Time, that is aye reproach'd to be so fleet,
> Because dear follies vanish in a trice,
> Shall now be clean absolved by judgment nice,
> Since his good speed made thee so soon complete.
> But less I praise the bounty of old Time,
> Lady revered, our Island's Tragic Queen,
> For all achievements of thy hope and prime,
> Than for the beauty of thine age serene,
> That yet delights to weave the moral rhyme,
> Nor fears what is, should dim what thou hast been.
> —HARTLEY COLERIDGE, "To Joanna Baillie,"
> c. 1849

Her tragedies have a boldness and grasp of mind, a firmness of hand, and a resonance of cadence, that scarcely seem within the reach of a female writer; while the tenderness and sweet-

ness of her heroines—the grace of the love-scenes—and the trembling outgushings of sensibility, as in *Orra,* for instance, in the fine tragedy on Fear—would seem exclusively feminine, if we did not know that a true dramatist—as Shakspeare or Fletcher—has the wonderful power of throwing himself, mind and body, into the character that he portrays. That Mrs. Joanna *is* a true dramatist, as well as a great poet, I, for one, can never doubt, although it has been the fashion to say that her plays do not act.—MARY RUSSELL MITFORD, *Recollections of a Literary Life,* 1851, p. 152

Her first dramatic efforts were published in 1798, under the title of A *Series of Plays: in which it is attempted to Delineate the Stronger Passions of the Mind, each Passion being the subject of a Tragedy and a Comedy.* To the volume was prefixed a long and interesting "Introductory Discourse," in which the authoress discusses the subject of the drama in all its bearings, and asserts the supremacy of simple nature over all decoration and refinement. "Let one simple trait of the human heart," says she, "one expression of passion, genuine and true to nature, be introduced, and it will stand forth alone in the boldness of reality, whilst the false and unnatural around it fades away upon every side, like the rising exhalations of the morning." This theory the accomplished dramatist illustrated in her plays, the merits of which were so quickly recognized that a second edition was called for in a few months. Miss Baillie was then in her thirty-fourth year. A second volume was published in 1802, and a third in 1812. During the interval, she gave the world a volume of miscellaneous dramas in 1804, and the *Family Legend* in 1810, a tragedy founded on Highland tradition, and which, principally through the efforts of Sir Walter Scott, was brought out at the Edinbrugh Theatre. The only *Play of the Passions* ever represented on the stage was *De Montfort,* which was brought out by the celebrated actor John Kemble, and played for eleven nights. In fact, like all the dramatic efforts of our authoress, it was a poem—a poem full of genius and the true spirit of poetry—but not a play. Though the best of her dramatic productions, it is deficient in those lifelike, stirring scenes, and in that variety and fullness of passion, the "form and pressure" of everyday life, which are so essential to success on the stage.

In 1823, our authoress published a long-promised collection of *Poetic Miscellanies,* and in 1836 three more volumes of plays. Besides these poetic productions, she is the author of A *View of the General Tenor of the New Testament regarding the Nature and Dignity of Jesus Christ.* She also published *Metrical Legends of Eminent Characters, Fugitive Verses,* and some less important publications. She died on the 22d of February, 1851, retaining her faculties till the last. Gentle and unassuming to all, with an unchangeable simplicity of manner and character, she counted among her friends many of the most celebrated for talent and genius; nor were those who resorted to her modest home confined to the natives of her own country, but many from various parts of Europe, and especially from our own land, sought introduction to one whose fame is commensurate with the knowledge of English Literature.

But a short time before her death, Miss Baillie completed an entire edition of her dramatic works. Upon these she laid out her chief strength. In their general character, they are marked by great originality and invention. Her knowledge of the human heart, of its wide range for good or evil, of its multifarious, changeful, and wayward nature, was great, and her power of portraying character has rarely been excelled. Her female portraits are especially beautiful, and possess an unusual degree of elevation and purity. But though distinguished chiefly for her dramatic writings, her lyric and miscellaneous poetry takes a very high rank among similar productions of the present century. To great simplicity and womanly tenderness of feeling, she unites at times a conciseness and vigor of expression which are not often surpassed.—CHARLES D. CLEVE-LAND, *English Literature of the Nineteenth Century*, 1853, pp. 545–47

Joanna Baillie's dramas are "nice," and rather dull; now and then she can write a song with the ease and sweetness that suggest Shakespearian echoes. But Scott's judgment was obviously blinded by his just and warm regard for Joanna Baillie herself.—RICHARD HOLT HUTTON, *Sir Walter Scott*, 1879, p. 91

In reading Joanna Baillie's poetry we find her to possess a quickness of observation that nearly supplies the place of insight; a strongly moralised temperament delighting in natural things; a vigorous, simple style. These are not especially dramatic qualities, and although she won her reputation through her plays, the poetry by which she is remembered is chiefly of a pastoral kind. She described herself, with justice, as 'a poet of a simple and homely character,' and her truest poems deal with simple and homely things: had she not persuaded herself that she possessed a more ambitious vocation she could have taken an honourable place among idyllic poets. About the year 1790 Miss Baillie published her first little book of poems. It met with little notice, being, as she said, too rustic for those times when Mr. Hayley and Miss Seward were the chief poets south of the Tweed. Before the publication of her next work the great wave of German romanticism had burst on our literature, an impulse inspiring Scott and Southey with the spirit of heroic chivalry, and moving even this quiet singer of woods and fields to tell of supernatural horrors and of 'the great explosions of Passion.'

   In 1798 appeared the earliest volume of a *Series of Plays, in which it is attempted to delineate the stronger passions of the mind—each passion being the subject of a tragedy and a comedy*. These dramas are noticeable for the sustained vigour of their style and for the beautiful lyrics with which they are interspersed, but they have neither passion, interest, nor character. Few women possess the faculty of construction, and Joanna Baillie was not one of these; nor had she qualities rare enough to cover the sins of a wandering story. Even in the revelation of a passion she is more occupied with the moral to be inferred than with the feeling itself, and few of her *dramatis personæ* are more than the means to bring the moral to its conclusion. Late in life Miss Baillie produced a book of *Metrical Legends* in the style of Scott, but without his fine romance and fervour, and quite at the end of her career she republished her earliest poems with the addition of some Scottish songs under the title of *Fugitive Verses*. The little book, with its modest name and prefaced apology, is nevertheless the most enduring of her works. Her country songs, written in the language of her early home, have the best qualities of Scottish national poetry; their simplicity, their cautious humour, endeared them at once to the national heart; they have the shrewdness and the freshness of the morning airs, the homeliness of unsophisticated feeling. Such songs as 'Woo'd and Married and a,' 'The Weary Pund o' Tow,' 'My Nanny O,' and the lovely trysting song beginning 'The gowan glitters on the sward' are among the treasures of Scottish minstrelsy. Only less delightful than these are her earlier sketches of country life, of cottage homes on summer and on winter days, of husbandman and housewife, of lovers happy and unhappy, of idle little village girls and boys—sketches touched with a certain homely

grace whose greatest charm is its sincerity. Among these poems are a series of Farewells—the melancholy, the cheerful-tempered, the proud lover, each bids in turn an adieu to his mistress. Last of all comes the 'poetical or sound-hearted' lover, and even while we smile at the unusual synonym we remember how natural a truth it must have been to her that used it. —A. MARY F. ROBINSON, "Joanna Baillie," *The English Poets*, ed. Thomas Humphry Ward, 1880, Vol. 4, pp. 221–22

As a song-writer, Joanna Baillie is rarely impassioned, but she is always hearty and sympathetic. Her humour is full-flavoured, and her pathos is natural if it is not deep.—ERIC S. ROBERTSON, *English Poetesses*, 1883, p. 174

Joanna Baillie produced the first volume of her *Plays in which it is attempted to delineate the stronger passions of the mind* in 1798; a second followed in 1802, a third in 1812. She prefixed a Discourse urging the need in drama of progressive passion, of natural language, ordinary situations, simple construction. Much of this recalls the contemporary discussions of the Stowey poets, as reported by both; but Miss Baillie neither pushed her principles so far nor fused them in so fine a fire of genius. Her 'natural' language is often as insipid as Wordsworth's, but not so crude, her passion has an air of being rather forced upon her characters in compliance with her program than elicited from their circumstances. She had talent, grace, eloquence; and generous fellow-countrymen, like Scott and Wilson, hailed a new Shakespeare in 'our Joanna,' while more cautious ones, like Jeffrey and Campbell, pointed out her lack of the fundamental nerve and sinew of tragedy. Only one of her plays, *De Montfort*, for a time held the stage. Her comedies, composed with the laudable design of substituting 'character' for satire, sentiment, and intrigue, had too little of the essential *vis comica* to hold their ground against the lively perversities of the Mortons and Reynolds'.—C. H. HERFORD, *The Age of Wordsworth*, 1897, pp. 141–42

MARGARET OLIPHANT
From *The Literary History of England, 1790–1825*
1882, Volume 2, pp. 324–34

We cannot feel that, great as her reputation was, and high as was the opinion expressed of her by many of her most distinguished contemporaries, we should be justified in ⟨. . .⟩ ranking her boldly among the poets, without distinction of sex. That she was superior to many men of her time is no reason for claiming for her an approach to the circle of the greatest: and to name her with Wordsworth or with Coleridge would be folly, although there is now and then a Shakspearian melody in her blank verse which pleased the general ear more than the stronger strain of the *Excursion*, and stood no unfavourable comparison with the diction of Coleridge's dramas. It is evident that she herself aimed at a reputation not inferior to theirs, and that the consciousness of a lofty purpose, and the applause of "those qualified to judge," which she received in no stinted measure, and indeed the favour of the public, which demanded several editions of the first volume of her *Plays on the Passions*, gave her a certain dignified sense of merit, such as of itself impresses the reader, and disposes him to grant the claim so gravely and modestly put forth. Personally no one could be less disposed to plume herself upon her genius, or claim the applause of society; but that she seriously believed herself to have produced great works, which the world would not let die, is we think very clear. And so thought Scott, whose opinion has so much right to be received and honoured. A woman might well think much of her work, of whom he had said that "the harp" had been silent "by silver Avon's holy shore" for two hundred years, until—

—She, the bold enchantress, came
With fearless hand and heart on flame,
From the pale willow snatched the treasure
And swept it with a kindred measure;
Till Avon's Swan, while rang the grove
With Montfort's hate and Basil's love,
Awakening at the inspirèd strain,
Dreamed their own Shakspeare lived again!

This praise, out of all proportion to its object, and which we would not now apply to the greatest of recent poets, was given in all good faith; and Joanna Baillie received it with a sober composure which has nothing of vanity or self-consciousness in it. There is no instance indeed in literature of a self-estimation so lofty, yet so completely modest and untinctured with elation or self-applause. Her ambition reached to the very highest heights of fame, and she believed that she had attained an elevation near them. This of itself is always impressive to contemporaries, who never can be entirely certain how posterity is to receive their estimate of excellence, and who are indeed so continually proved to be wrong in it. Not only from her own generation, however, but to the present time, respect and a kindly veneration have ever attended her name. We honour her fine purpose and intention, if we forget the works in which she believed she had carried them out, and would still meet with almost indignation any attempt at unkindly criticism upon a poet so pure and high-toned, a woman so worthy of all respect. Her gentle and lovely life had no incident in it. She was one of those maiden princesses about whom there always breathes a soft and exquisite perfume, too delicate for common appreciation, of that reserved and high virginity, which, never reaching to any second chapter of life, involves an endless youth. This is not what we mean when we speak, vulgarly and meanly, of an old maid—and yet an old maid, worthy of the name, with all the strange experiences by proxy which life brings, yet with the first awe of imagination still undeparted, and the bloom never banished from her aged cheek, is one of the most delicate objects in nature. Perhaps, however, we must add, such a one is very inadequately qualified for the composition of tragedies, especially those that deal with the passions.

In the preface to her first volume, Joanna Baillie sets forth her theory of the extreme interest of "mankind to man," by way of accounting for the choice of her subjects. Her illustration of the manner in which that interest works is very bold and ingenious; we do not venture to assert that it was altogether original, but it has certainly been often repeated. Not only does she assert this to be "the proper study" of the enlightened mind, but she claims it as the origin even of those hideous curiosities, which move the multitude to the enjoyment of executions and murders, and, indeed, as in the following example, the excuse of absolute cruelty.

Revenge, no doubt, first began among the savages of America that dreadful custom of sacrificing their prisoners of war. But the perpetration of such hideous cruelty could never have become a permanent national custom but for the universal desire in the human mind to behold man in every situation, putting forth his strength against the current of adversity, scorning all bodily anguish, or struggling with those feelings of nature which, like a beating stream, will ofttimes burst through the barriers of pride. Before they begin those terrible rites

they treat their prisoners kindly; and it cannot be supposed that men, alternately enemies and friends to so many neighbouring tribes, in manners and appearance like themselves, should so strongly be actuated by a spirit of public revenge. This custom, therefore, must be considered as a grand and terrible game which every tribe plays against another; where they try, not the strength of the arm, the swiftness of the feet, nor the acuteness of the eye, but the fortitude of the soul. Considered in this light, the excess of cruelty exercised upon their miserable victim, in which every hand is described as ready to inflict its portion of pain, and every head ingenious in the contrivance of it, is no longer to be wondered at. To put into his measure of misery one agony less, would be doing a species of injustice to every hero of their own tribe who had already sustained it, and to those who might be called upon to do so—among whom each of these savage tormentors has his chance of being one, and has prepared himself for it from his childhood. Nay, it would be a species of injustice to the haughty victim himself, who would scorn to purchase his place among the heroes of his nation at an easier price than his undaunted predecessors.

By this startling yet fine example does the author declare her conviction that human character and action are of all things in the world the most interesting to men, a truth which scarcely requires so daring an illustration. It is on this ground that she chooses the action of the passions as her special theme. But the limitation of her powers, and the absence of the broader genius which can conceive life as a whole, is apparent in her parcelling out of the great motives, generally so strangely intertwined, of human action; and a treatment so artificial deprives us of the very sympathy she claims, since, to see a man struggling, for instance, with the passion of hatred is a different thing from seeing him contend in "the grand and terrible game," as she finely calls it, where not strength of arm, nor swiftness of foot, nor keenness of eye, but the fortitude of the soul is concerned. This pedantic separation of one mental force from another turns the men of her tragedies into puppets so helpless in the grip of the formal passion, which is supposed to sway them, that we accompany their mock struggle with impatience rather than sympathy. The most popular of the tragedies, and the one which the author had the gratification of seeing performed by no less actors than John Kemble and Mrs. Siddons, the play of *De Monfort*, affords us at once an instance of this. It is, perhaps, the best of Joanna Baillie's tragedies; but there is no trace in it of "the grand and terrible game." From the moment when the hero presents himself to us he is not struggling against his master-passion, but nursing it in long soliloquies and musings, and seizing every opportunity to secure its ascendency over him. None of that wonderful play of suggestion with which Shakspeare leads us to the inevitable end is possible in so straightforward an exhibition. Nor is there any cause given, anything to justify the victim of passion or to call forth our sympathy. His enemy has done him no harm, his hatred is entirely without reason, his wrath wordy and weak. Artifices of the simplest description suffice to drive him to madness, his revenge is cowardly, and his remorse womanish. He is introduced in gloomy self-absorption, impatient alike of kindness and service, brooding over his passion. "I loathed thee when a boy" is all the excuse he attempts to make for himself: and it is not only when his enemy crosses his path that the ecstasy of rage is on him. It possesses him continually as love does, but with even more constant force. It has

Driven me forth from kindred peace,
From social pleasure, from my native home,
To be a sullen wanderer upon earth,
Avoiding all men, cursing and accursed.

The forced character of the hero's attitude is all the more evident from the fact that the object of this concentrated wrath has no special connection with the hater, and does not force himself upon him in any way, the only direct act of intercourse between them, of which we are informed, being that Rezenvelt has spared the life of De Monfort in an encounter of arms when he was at his enemy's mercy. Nor does Rezenvelt's demeanour, when he is introduced, revolt us as it ought to do, to keep us in sympathy with Monfort, for his light-heartedness is of an innocent kind, and his wit not pungent enough to hurt a fly.

⟨. . .⟩ Besides the absence of any possible sympathy with the hero, the play is without incident or movement. Hatred holds the stage alone, unreasoning and extreme. The play of human life is all suspended, and the central figure has room for no sentiment, no idea, but one. In *Basil* the construction of the play is better, for it is not so entirely monotonous. Besides the love of the hero, there is the desire to conquer on the part of the heroine, mingled with a wavering beginning of affection: and the double intrigue of the Duke and his counsellors to detain the unlucky general and excite against him his mutinous soldiers, relieves the pressure of the one sole passion. It is unnecessary to enter into the whole series in detail. They are all marked with the same faults, and in none is the workmanship so fine as to dazzle the reader. Potent and great poetry will triumph over any fault of construction, but it is marvellous to contemplate the acres of respectable verse, in which an unnatural and formal pose of the soul can be kept up, scene after scene and act after act, with rarely a gleam of nature shining through. The tragedy of *Ethwald* is a double one, two long plays to exemplify the well-worn dangers of ambition, which are only not so trite as they are bloody. But all these tragedies, without exception, are bloody. When there is not a hecatomb of slaughtered victims, the one invariable "corse" is pierced with a dozen wounds at least.

All this is in very strange contrast with the character and position of a woman so womanly and genuine: but stranger still is her sober certainty of the dignity and importance of her work. This conviction shone through every line of her elaborate prefaces, and enshrined her name and her dwelling in the quiet modesty of private life. For many years her house at Hampstead was an object of pilgrimage to many, and the best of the age resorted to it with a respect which was almost allegiance. Not that she they sought had any wealth of instruction or witchery of words to charm them withal, such as were possessed by the greater poet so near her on the other suburban hill at Highgate. It would be hard, indeed, to say what was and has been since the secret of Joanna Baillie's power; perhaps it was at bottom that profound and most modest, yet unwavering faith in herself, which is visible in all

she says. A conviction so serious and so entirely unmingled with vanity, is very impressive, and her generation would seem, respectfully and devoutly, though not without here and there an occasional scepticism, to have taken her at her word. Jeffrey, in his early boldness, in one of the first numbers of the *Edinburgh*, assailed her in his usual frank manner, being no respecter of persons. Some years after, when she and her sister were in Edinburgh, the dauntless critic, who evidently had so little malice in his assaults that he never considered them a reason for keeping aloof from the victims, sought her acquaintance; but, as her biographer says, "Joanna was inexorable." She would have nothing to say, in his own empire and capital, to the Rover-chief, the Arch-critic, as his townsfolk called him. No other author we know of was so stern or determined. Southey sneered in his sleeve, but did not refuse to meet his literary enemy—but Joanna was inexorable. At a later period, however, the poet forgave—and little Lord Jeffrey, in his visits to London, found his way as often as another to Hampstead, where Scott hastened whenever he had a chance, and many a visitor besides, whose visits were well worth remembering. Joanna was not eloquent in talk, nor in any way remarkable to a stranger: her sister Agnes, who was her constant companion, was the first of the two in society: but Sir Walter Scott declared that if he wanted to give an intelligent stranger the best idea possible of an English (he should have said Scots) gentlewoman, he would send him to Joanna Baillie, and it would be hard to find higher praise.

Her first publication was a little volume of *Fugitive Verses*, and this, a reprint of the juvenile collection, was also her last. She dedicated the last edition to Samuel Rogers, who had advised its republication, "a poet," she says, "who, from his own refined genius, classical elegance, and high estimation with the public, is well qualified to judge," and to whom she was indebted for "very great and useful service" in criticism. But at the same time, with a half pathetic apology, through which there tingles an ironical note, Joanna explains that "Modern Poetry, within these last thirty years, has become so imaginative, impassioned, and sentimental, that more homely subjects in simple diction are held in comparatively small estimation." This was long after Wordsworth's defiance of fine words and high poetic language had resounded to all the winds; but contemporaries are oblivious of each other. And Joanna still stood upon the pre-Wordsworth ground, at a time when Byron and Shelley were raising new standards of poetic advancement. "When these poems were written," she adds, "of all our eminent poets of modern times not one was known. Mr. Hayley and Miss Seward, and a few other cultivated poetical writers, were the poets spoken of in literary circles. Burns, read and appreciated as he deserved by his own countrymen, was known to few readers south of the Tweed." What a revolution to have occurred in one woman's life! Joanna Baillie died in the serenest and most beautiful age so short a time ago as 1851, after a long, gentle, and tranquil life.

JOHN JAMES AUDUBON

1785–1851

John James Audubon was born at Les Cayes, Santo Domingo (now Haiti), on April 26, 1785, the son of a French naval officer and planter. He was raised in comfortable surroundings in France by a devoted foster mother and as a child showed a marked aptitude for drawing birds. He did not, however, like school, and at the age of eighteen he was sent to the United States to embark on a business career.

Audubon's various business ventures were never very successful and he devoted more and more attention to drawing birds. Finally, in 1820, he gave up business entirely and embarked upon what was to become his life's work, the illustrating of all the birds of North America. Supported by his wife's teaching—he had married in 1808—and by giving drawing lessons and painting portraits, he traveled over the next six years in the eastern and southern United States, collecting and painting birds.

In 1826 Audubon took a collection of his bird illustrations to Europe, searching for a publisher. In London his genius was immediately recognized by scientists and artists alike and the publisher Robert Havell agreed to issue his work in a series of volumes as *The Birds of America*. Over the next thirteen years Audubon divided his time between England and the United States, assisted by his sons Victor and John, gathering additional material, writing texts (assisted by William MacGillivray), and overseeing the publication of each volume. *The Birds of America*—435 hand-colored folio plates—was issued in four volumes over an eleven-year period beginning in 1827. An accompanying text, *Ornithological Biography*, was published separately in five volumes (1831–39). A separate index, *A Synopsis of the Birds of North America*, appeared in 1839.

Audubon returned permanently to the United States in 1839 and settled in New York. He prepared for American publication a smaller edition of *The Birds of America* (7 vols., 1840–44), then turned his attention to a new work, *Viviparous Quadrupeds of North America*; his sons, together with John Bachman, assisted him with the accompanying text. The color plates of *Viviparous Quadrupeds* were published in two volumes (1845–46); a three-volume text was issued separately (1846–54).

Audubon died on January 27, 1851.

Personal

I cannot help thinking Mr. Audubon a dishonest man. Why did he make you believe that he was a man of property? How is it that his circumstances have altered so suddenly? In truth, I do not believe you fit to deal with the world, or at least the American world.—JOHN KEATS, Letter to George and Georgiana Keats (Sept. 17, 1819)

In private life his virtues endeared him to a large circle of devoted admirers; his sprightly conversation, with a slight French accent; his soft and gentle voice; his frank and fine face, "aye gat him friends in ilka place." With those whose privilege it was to know the Naturalist, so full of fine enthusiasm and intelligence; with so much simplicity of character, frankness and genius, he will continue to live in their memories, though "with the buried gone;" while to the artistic, literary, and scientific world, he has left an imperishable name that is not in the keeping of history alone. Long after the bronze statue of the naturalist that we hope soon to see erected in the Central Park, shall have been wasted and worn beyond recognition, by the winds and rains of Heaven; while the towering and snow-covered peak of the Rocky Mountains known as Mount Audubon, shall rear its lofty head among the clouds; while the little wren chirps about our homes, and the robin and reed-bird sing in the green meadows; while the melody of the mocking-bird is heard in the cypress swamps of Louisiana, or the shrill scream of the eagle on the frozen shores of the Northern seas, the name of John James Audubon, the gifted Artist, the ardent lover of Nature, and the admirable writer, will live in the hearts of his grateful countrymen.—JAMES GRANT WILSON, "Intro-duction" to *The Life of John James Audubon* by Lucy Green Audubon, 1869, p. v

His enthusiasm had in it something absolutely infectious. It was not possible to be in his company, and hear him converse on his favorite theme, without being strongly moved by it. Even they who before meeting with him had been all unconscious of feeling any interest in natural history, under his inspiring influence became for the moment almost equally enthusiastic. His vivid and ever active imagination, united with his ardent and enthusiastic temperament, was constantly stimulating him to renewed adventures in the search for new discoveries, and also was occasionally the means of leading him to too hastily assume as facts clearly established what were in reality only probable but imperfect conclusions. A striking example of this may be cited in his own account of his first finding the nest of the black-poll warbler. Meeting, for the first time, with the nest and eggs of this species during his explorations in Labrador, his joy seems to have known no bounds at securing what seemed to him so great a prize. His expression of delight was unaffectedly sincere and truthful, but we now know that the nest of this bird is by no means so rare, and its breeding-places are not so remote, as Mr. Audubon so enthusiastically yet honestly assumed.

Added to his ardent enthusiasm, and exerting a no less powerful influence over his life, his labors, and his success, must not be forgotten an untiring perseverance that nothing could discourage, a moral courage which no hindrances could daunt, and an unyielding determination to complete whatever he had resolved upon to do. Sea-voyages were to him interminable seasons of misery, discomfort, and wretchedness. Yet his sufferings were never permitted to deter or delay his movements. Loss of property, the destruction of his drawings, involving years of research and toil, with various other disappointments and disasters that would have overwhelmed any one else with despair, or driven him from his purpose, were all met by Audubon with a serenity that knew no defeat, and with only an added desire and determination to persevere, and to overcome all obstacles, and to make all these losses good. The calm and uncomplaining fortitude with which Audubon received and endured the disastrous results of the panic of 1837, when nearly one-half of all the subscribers to his great work, having become either bankrupt or impoverished, withdrew their subscriptions, exhibited all the attributes of the most sublime heroism.

Whatever others may have believed, or professed to believe, in regard to Mr. Audubon's accuracy as a narrator of facts, no one, in the judgment of the writer, was ever more sincerely truthful and honest in presenting his convictions, and in the expression of his own belief. And to this conviction of his truthfulness all unprejudiced parties must have finally reached. Of course Mr. Audubon has made many mistakes, has stated many things as facts that can not be accepted as such, and has often been misled by the inaccurate statements of others. But what pioneer explorer in the untrodden domains of nature has there ever been, or can there ever be, without exhibiting the same evidences of the common proneness of humanity to fall into error? The time has surely come when the unworthy detractions, the false judgments, and the unjust misconceptions of Audubon should give place to a more charitable, a more just, appreciation of his truthful, manly, and honest character and purpose.—THOMAS M. BREWER, "Reminiscences of John James Audubon," *Harper's New Monthly Magazine*, Oct. 1880, pp. 667–68

General

North: What a pity, James, that you were not in Edinburgh in time to see my friend Audubon's Exhibition!

Shepherd: An Exhibition o' what?

North: Of birds painted to the life. Almost the whole American Ornithology, true to nature, as if the creatures were in their native haunts in the forests, or on the sea-shores. Not stiff and staring like stuffed specimens—but in every imaginable characteristic attitude, perched, wading, or a-wing,—not a feather, smooth or ruffled, out of its place,—every song, chirp, chatter, or cry, made audible by the power of genius.

Shepherd: Whare got he sae weel acquaint wi' a the tribes—for do they not herd in swamps and woods whare man's foot intrudes not—and the wilderness is guarded by the Rattlesnake, fearsome Watchman, wi' nae ither bouets than his ain fiery eyne?

North: For upwards of twenty years the enthusiastic Audubon lived in the remotest woods, journeying to and fro on foot thousands of miles—or sailing on great rivers, "great as any seas," with his unerring rifle, slaughtering only to embalm his prey by an art of his own, in form and hue unchanged, unchangeable—and now, for the sum of one shilling, may anybody that chooses it, behold the images of almost all the splendid and gorgeous birds of that Continent.

Shepherd: Whare's the Exhibition now?

North: At Glasgow, I believe—where I have no doubt it will attract thousands of delighted spectators. I must get the friend who gave "A Glance over Selby's Ornithology," to tell the world at large more of Audubon. He is the greatest artist in

his own walk that ever lived, and cannot fail to reap the reward of his genius and perseverance and adventurous zeal in his own beautiful branch of natural history, both in fame and fortune. The man himself—whom I have had the pleasure of frequently meeting—is just what you would expect from his works,—full of fine enthusiasm and intelligence—most interesting in looks and manners—a perfect gentleman—and esteemed by all who know him for the simplicity and frankness of his nature.—JOHN WILSON (as "Christopher North"), *Noctes Ambrosianae* (Jan. 1827), 1854

Soon after his arrival in Edinburgh, where he soon found many friends, he opened his Exhibition. Four hundred drawings—paintings in water-colours—of about two thousand birds, covered the walls of the Institution-Hall, in the Royal Society Buildings, and the effect was like magic. The spectator imagined himself in the forest. All were of the size of life, from the wren and the humming-bird to the wild turkey and the bird of Washington. But what signified the mere size? The colours were all of life too—bright as when borne in beaming beauty through the woods. There too were their attitudes and postures, infinite as they are assumed by the restless creatures, in motion or rest, in their glee and their gambols, their loves and their wars, singing, or caressing, or brooding, or preying, or tearing one another into pieces. The trees, too, on which they sat or sported all true to Nature, in bole, branch, spray, and leaf; the flowering-shrubs and the ground-flowers, the weeds and the very grass, all American—so too the atmosphere and the skies—all Transatlantic. 'Twas a wild and poetical vision of the heart of the New World, inhabited as yet almost wholly by the lovely or noble creatures that "own not man's dominion." There we beheld them all; there was a picture of their various life. How different from stuffed feathers in glass cases—though they too "shine well where they stand" in our College Museum! There many a fantastic tumbler played his strange vagaries in the air—there many a cloud-cleaver swept the skies—there living gleams glanced through the forest glades—there meteor-like plumage shone in the wood-gloom—there strange shapes stalked stately along the shell-bright shores—and there, halcyons all, fair floaters hung in the sunshine on waveless seas. That all this wonderful creation should have been the unassisted work of one man—in his own country almost unknown, and by his own country wholly unbefriended, was a thought that awoke towards "the American woodsman" feelings of more than admiration, of the deepest personal interest; and the hearts of all warmed towards Audubon, who were capable of conceiving the difficulties, and dangers, and sacrifices, that must have been encountered, endured, and overcome, before genius had thus embodied these the glory of its innumerable triumphs.

The impression produced on all minds, learned and unlearned, by this exhibition, was such as to encourage Audubon to venture on the dangerous design of having the whole engraved. Dangerous it might well be called, seeing that the work was to contain Four Hundred Plates and Two Thousand Figures. "A work," says Cuvier, "conceived and executed on so vast a plan has but one fault, that its expense must render it inaccessible to the greatest number of those to whom it will be the most necessary. Yet is the price far from being exorbitant. One *livraison* of five plates costs two guineas; and thus the five *livraisons* can be had at no very great annual expense. Most desirable at least it is, as well for the interests of art as of science, that all the great public bodies, and all persons of wealth who love to enrich their libraries with works of splendour, should provide themselves with that of Audubon."

"It will depend," says Swainson, in the same spirit, "on the powerful and the wealthy, whether Britain shall have the honour of fostering such a magnificent undertaking. It will be a lasting monument, not only to the memory of its author, but to those who employ their wealth in patronising genius, and in supporting the national credit. If any publication deserves such a distinction, it is surely this; inasmuch as it exhibits a perfection in the higher attributes of zoological painting, never before attempted. To represent the passions and the feelings of birds, might, until now, have been well deemed chimerical. Rarely, indeed, do we see their outward forms represented with any thing like nature. In my estimation, *not more than three painters ever lived who could draw a bird*. Of these, the lamented Barrabaud, of whom France may be justly proud, was the chief. He has long passed away; but his mantle has, at length, been recovered in the forests of America."

Generous and eloquent—but, in the line printed in italics, obscure as an oracle. Barrabaud and Audubon are two—why not have told us who is the third? Can Mr Swainson mean *himself*. We have heard as much hinted; if so we cannot but admire his modesty in thus remaining the anonymous hero of his own panegyric. If not so, then has he done himself great injustice, for he is a beautiful bird-painter and drawer, as all the world knows, though assuredly in genius far inferior to Audubon. Is the third Bewick? If so, why shun to name "the genius that dwelt on the banks of the Tyne?" If not so, Mr Swainson may live and die assured, in spite of this sentence of exclusion from the trio, that Bewick will *in sœcula sœculorum* sit on the top of the tree of fame, on the same branch with the most illustrious, nor is there any fear of its breaking, for it is strong, and the company destined to bestride it, *select*.

Audubon speaks modestly of his great work, but with the enthusiasm and confidence, natural and becoming, in a man of such extraordinary genius. We cannot do better than employ, when they come to us, his own words. Not only, then, is every object, as a whole, of the natural size, but also every portion of each object. The compass aided him in its delineation, regulated and corrected each part, even to the very fore-shortening. The bill, feet, legs, and claws, the very feathers as they project one beyond another, have been accurately measured. The birds, almost all of them, were killed by himself, and were regularly drawn on or near the spot. The positions, he observes, may perhaps, in some instances, appear *outré*; but such supposed exaggerations can afford subjects of criticism only to persons unacquainted with the feathered tribes, for nothing can be more transient or varied than the attitudes of birds. For example, the heron, when warming itself in the sun, will sometimes drop its wings several inches, as if they were dislocated; the swan may often be seen floating with one foot extended from the body; and some pigeons turn quite over when playing in the air. The flowers, plants, or portions of the trees which are attached to the principal objects, have always been chosen from amongst those in the vicinity of which the birds were found, and are not, as some persons have thought, the trees or plants on which they always feed or perch. We may mention, too, that Audubon invented ways of placing birds, dead or alive, before him while he was drawing them, so that he saw them still in the very attitudes he had admired when they were free in the air, or on the bough; and, indeed, without such most ingenious apparatus of wires and threads as he employs, it was not in mortal man to have caught as he has done, and fixed them on paper, all the characteristic but evanescent varieties of their motion and their repose. His ingenuity is equal to his genius.—JOHN WILSON, "Audubon's *Ornithological Biography*," *Blackwood's Edinburgh Magazine*, July 1831, pp. 14–16

I take pleasure in introducing to you our distinguished and most meritorious countryman, J. J. Audubon, whose splendid work on American ornithology must of course be well known to you. That work, while it reflects such great credit on our country, and contributes so largely to the advancement of one of the most delightful departments of science, is likely, from the extreme expense attendant upon it, to repay but poorly the indefatigable labor of a lifetime. The high price necessarily put on the copies of Mr. Audubon's magnificent work places it beyond the means of the generality of private individuals. It is entitled therefore to the especial countenance of our libraries and various other public institutions. It appears to me, that the different departments in Washington ought each to have a copy deposited in their libraries or archives. Should you be of the same opinion you might be of great advantage in promoting such a measure.—WASHINGTON IRVING, Letter to Martin Van Buren (Oct. 19, 1836), cited in Lucy Green Audubon, *The Life of John James Audubon*, 1869, pp. 394–95

John James Audubon was a worthy successor of Wilson, in the walk of Ornithology. Audubon's work, *The Birds of America*, equalled Wilson's in the poetical beauty of the descriptions, and surpassed it in the splendor of the engraving and coloring.

Audubon was a resident of Louisiana, of French descent, the son of an admiral in the French navy. He engaged at first in commercial pursuits, but finding himself strongly drawn towards the study of birds, he concluded to follow the bent of his mind, and gave himself up entirely to his favorite pursuit, travelling in every direction in the collection of materials.

After nearly half a lifetime spent in this manner, Audubon visited Europe to obtain subscribers to his great work, *The Birds of America*. He was everywhere received with applause. The most distinguished men of the time, Brewster, Cuvier, Humboldt, Herschel, Sir Walter Scott, Jeffrey, Wilson, and others of that stamp, shared a warm interest both in him and his work, and he proceeded at once with the publication. ⟨. . .⟩

The subscription price of the work was $1000. It contained 448 plates of birds of the natural size, engraved from his original drawings and beautifully colored. The engravings filled 5 folio volumes, and the descriptions filled 5 volumes more, 8vo.

Audubon published also, in connection with his sons, *Quadrupeds of North America*, in 3 vols., folio, 150 plates, with 3 vols., 8vo, of descriptions.

Audubon's work not only won for himself universal renown but gave to the study of ornithology a new impulse, under which it has since made prodigious advances. It is difficult to say which is most fascinating, his pictures of the birds, which were manifestly drawn with a loving hand, or his description of their habits and of his solitary rambles in studying them.—JOHN SEELY HART, A *Manual of American Literature*, 1872, pp. 120–21

After encountering difficulties, and meeting with accidents enough to have checked the enthusiasm of ordinary men, his great work was accomplished. His *Birds of America* is a monument of genius and industry; the designs are exquisite, every bird appearing with its native surroundings. Nor are they merely correct in form and color; on the contrary, they are shown in characteristic attitudes or in natural motion, and every figure is instinct with life. The letter-press descriptions mostly concern us. They are simply perfect, equally removed from the insipidity of a so-called "popular" style and from the scientific dryness that usually marks the mere naturalist. His own personal adventures are modestly told, and give a rare charm to the work. It will readily be imagined that it is very difficult to make selections that will do justice to such an author. Scattered through his volumes are many touches of nature, and hints of scenery that are inimitable—especially because they are the unconscious utterances of a soul highly susceptible to beauty, and without the least vain desire of parading its emotions.—FRANCIS H. UNDERWOOD, *A Hand-Book of English Literature*, 1872, p. 68

⟨. . .⟩ all the great ornithologists—original namers and biographers of the birds—have been poets in deed if not in word. Audubon is a notable case in point, who, if he had not the tongue or pen of the poet, certainly had the eye and ear and heart—"the fluid and attaching character"—and the singleness of purpose, the enthusiasm, the unworldliness, the love, that characterizes the true and divine race of bards.—JOHN BURROUGHS, "The Birds of the Poets," *Scribner's Monthly*, Sept. 1873, p. 565

Audubon, the ornithologist, who seems to have been a born naturalist, tells us that

> no roof seemed so secure to him as that formed of the dense foliage under which the feathered tribes were seen to resort, or the caves and fissures of the massy rocks to which the dark-winged cormorant and the curlew retired to rest, or to protect themselves from the fury of the tempest.

To advance his skill as a draughtsman he went to Paris, and studied under the celebrated artist David. Returning again to the New World, he revisited the woods and fields with increased ardour and enthusiasm; he ransacked the prairies and mountains as well as streams and rivers to learn the habits and retreats of the feathered minstrels of the wilderness. His object at first was not to become a writer, but simply to indulge a passion, to enjoy the study of these beautiful creatures of the air. It was Prince Lucien Bonaparte, an accomplished naturalist, who first incited him to arrange his beautiful drawings in a form for publication. With this object in view he revisited prairies, lakes, rivers, and sea shore, and enriched his portfolio with a mass of information and a large number of drawings, when an accident occurred to his collection. The story is thus briefly given. Leaving his home in Kentucky, he went to Philadelphia, and placing his drawings carefully in a box he gave them for safe keeping into the charge of a relative. After an absence of several months he returned, and on opening the box to his dismay he discovered, instead of his thousand sketches and portraits, nothing remained to him but a pair of Norway rats with their progeny nestled among innumerable bits of paper. The poor artist was overwhelmed; he slept not for a few nights, but his courage returned, and with a new resolution he again sallied forth with notebook, pencil, and gun into the woods as gaily as if nothing had happened. He said he might make better drawings after all than those which had been destroyed, and this he accomplished within an interval of three years. In reading Audubon's books you feel the fresh air blowing in your face, scent the odour of the prairie flowers and autumn woods, or hear the surging of the sea. He takes you into the squatter's hut, in the lowly swamp, where he tells the story of the woodcutter's pioneer life; or he sallies out in the night to hunt the conger, and when daylight returns he invokes the fairy singers of the woods to your listening ear. Audubon's life was full of romantic adventure, and after encountering and surmounting difficulties that would have discouraged other adventurous spirits, he took his splendid collection of drawings to Europe. There he met with the cordial friendship and aid of such men as Herschel, Cuvier, Humboldt, Brewster, Wilson, and Sir Walter Scott. His grand work forms four large folio

volumes, comprising four hundred and forty-eight coloured pictures of the birds of America, life-size; each is so faithfully portrayed that you catch an idea of the bird's habits and nature as well as its plumage. As a monument of American devotion to ornithological science this stately work is unrivalled.—FREDERICK SAUNDERS, *The Story of Some Famous Books*, 1887, pp. 141–44

His great literary and artistic work is *The Birds of America*, consisting of five volumes of Ornithological Biographies and four volumes of exquisite portraits of birds, life-size, in natural colors, and surrounded by the plants which each one most likes. *Quadrupeds of America* was prepared mainly by his sons and Rev. John Bachman of South Carolina. These works gave him a European reputation. He died at Minniesland, now Audubon Park, New York City.

His style in writing is pure, vivid, and so clear as to place before us the very thing or event described. The accounts of his travels and of the adventures he met with in his search for his birds and animals are very natural and picturesque; and they show also his own fine nature and attractive character.—LOUISE MANLY, *Southern Literature*, 1895, pp. 155

Audubon was born in Louisiana some time between 1772 and 1783—the exact date is unknown—and died in New York in January, 1851. His boyhood was spent in France, after which his father, then a retired Admiral in the French navy, sent him to an estate he owned on Perkiomen Creek, in eastern Pennsylvania. On an adjacent estate lived William Bakewell, an Englishman, whose daughter, Lucy, Audubon married in April, 1808. As a young man Audubon was gay and fond of dress, but the sober business of earning a living for his growing family changed all this, and in later years he spoke of his early vanity as "an absurd spectacle." While still in France he had learned to paint birds, and on coming to America he continued painting them at intervals, as a pastime and in a desultory sort of way, until the habit grew to be the ruling passion of his life. But he was not merely a great painter; he had the instincts and tastes of a naturalist. The purely technical details of the science were distasteful to him, and in this part of his work he secured the assistance of others. At the same time, few specialists are better acquainted with the characters of their species than was Audubon. His physical strength and powers of endurance were phenomenal. He habitually rose before daylight and worked continuously until night; and then, apparently, attended to his correspondence and wrote up his copious notes and journals. Four hours is said to have been his allowance for sleep; and when painting birds and mammals in England, he mentions the surprise expressed at his habit of working fourteen hours a day without fatigue. He combined the grace, culture, and pleasing manners of the French with the candor, patience, and earnestness of purpose of the American, and there was something about his personality which appears to have been irresistibly charming. His friend Dr. Bachman of Charleston tells us that people considered it a privilege to give to him what no one else could buy.

Considering the times in which he lived and the facilities for getting about, Audubon was a famous traveller. He visited Texas, Florida, and Canada, conducted special expeditions to the rugged shores of Labrador and the then distant Yellowstone, and crossed the ocean a number of times; and in the eastern United States, from Maine to Louisiana, he travelled thousands of miles on foot. In the daily journals of his expeditions to Labrador, the upper Missouri River, and the Old World, we are permitted to feel his presence and enthusiasm from day to day as he traversed distant and little known lands and saw for the first time new birds and other animals. In his European journals we have entertaining accounts of his experiences and emotions among the naturalists and savants of England, with glimpses of their lives which in several instances throw light on contemporary events in the field of natural science. The Labrador trip, made in 1833, was for the sole purpose of obtaining additional material for the *Birds of America*, then in course of publication. The elephant-folio plates of this magnificent work, described by a well-known bibliographer as "by far the most sumptuous ornithological work ever published," originally appeared in eighty-seven parts running from 1827 to 1838. The text, entitled *Ornithological Biography*, was not begun until 1830, and appeared in five volumes between 1831 and 1839.

In his old age, having completed and published his *magnum opus*, Audubon became interested in mammals, and, in conjunction with Dr. Bachman, undertook the preparation of the splendid work entitled the *Quadrupeds of North America*. Renowned the world over as a painter of birds, he was enabled, by means of his long training and skill with the brush and the versatility of his genius, to achieve if possible even greater distinction as a painter of animals. But he felt the need of personal acquaintance with the quadrupeds of our Western plains, which it was necessary for him to study and paint from living and freshly killed specimens. In order to do this he planned, and in 1843, when nearly seventy, carried out, an expedition to Fort Union, later known as Fort Buford, near the junction of the Missouri and Yellowstone Rivers. He was accompanied by his friend Edward Harris of Philadelphia, and took with him as assistants John G. Bell, the famous New York taxidermist, Isaac Sprague, the botanical artist, and a young man named Lewis Squires.

The journals of this trip are of surpassing interest. To the historian and student of Americana they furnish glimpses of early frontier life, and notes, interspersed with prophetic visions, of commerce and conditions along the Missouri River; to the ethnologist they give truthful pictures of the appearance, dress, and character of the Indians; to the naturalist they offer entertaining accounts of the discovery and habits of new or little known species, of the abundance and manner of hunting wolves, buffaloes, and other big game, and observations concerning the former ranges of animals no longer found in the region. ⟨. . .⟩

The book is attractive and well made. Some of the illustrations are from unpublished drawings by Audubon himself; of the others, no less than twelve are portraits of him at different periods of his life. In addition to the biography and journals, the work contains his famous *Episodes*. These, no less than fifty-eight in number and filling more than three hundred pages, cover a wide range of topics, such as "The Prairie," "The Earthquake," "Colonel Boone," "Natchez in 1820," "A Tough Walk for a Youth," "Niagara," "The Burning of the Forest," "A Long Calm at Sea," "Death of a Pirate," "Wreckers of Florida," "A Moose Hunt," "The Eggers of Labrador," "A Ball in Newfoundland," "Scipio and the Bear," "A Kentucky Barbecue." They show, perhaps better than his more formal writings, the keenness of his appreciation of human nature, the kindness of his heart, the power of his imagination, and the vigor and versatility of his pen.—C. H. MERRIAM, "Audubon," *Nation*, Feb. 24, 1898, pp. 151–52

PARKE GODWIN
From "John James Audubon" (1853)
Commemorative Addresses
1895, pp. 149–51, 182–87

Mr. Carlyle, in his famous book on *Heroes and Hero Worship*, has told us of the hero in the several aspects of Divinity, Prophet, Priest, Poet, King, and Man of Letters, but he overlooked one phase of the character, which human history knows: the Hero as Man of Science. A little before he was writing his volume there roamed in the primeval forests of America a simple naturalist, whose life had exhibited every quality of prowess and endurance, every trait of manly and heroic endeavor, that is to be found in the most illustrious of his Great Men. If we may believe what his fast friend Emerson has said of heroism, that it was "a contempt for safety and ease," "a self-trust which slights the restraints of prudence in the plentitude of its energy and power," "a mind of such a balance that no disturbance can shake its will, which pleasantly, and as it were merrily, advances to its own music," the "extreme of individual nature," "obedience to the impulses of individual character," "undaunted boldness and a fortitude not to be wearied out," then was John James Audubon one of the truest of the world's heroes, worthy to be ranked and recorded on the same page with the most distinguished of human celebrities.

For more than half a century he followed with almost religious devotion a beautiful and elevated pursuit, enlarging its boundaries by his discoveries, and illustrating its objects by his art. In all climates and in all weathers, scorched by tropic suns and frozen by arctic colds; now diving fearlessly into the densest forests and now wandering alone over desolate prairies, far beyond the haunts of civilization, and frequented only by savage beasts or more savage men; in perils, in difficulties and in doubt; listening only to the music of the birds and the lofty inspirations of his own thoughts, he kept for a lifetime on an original path, which to some seemed chimerical and to others utterly useless, until in the later years and fading twilight of his days his efforts were crowned with success. The records of man's endeavor contain few nobler examples of strength of purpose and indefatigable zeal.

⟨. . .⟩ It was not, however, a parlor, or an ordinary reception-room that I entered, but evidently a room for work. In one corner stood a painter's easel, with a half-finished sketch of a beaver on the paper; in the other lay the skin of an American panther. The antlers of elks hung upon the walls; stuffed birds of every description of gay plumage ornamented the mantelpiece; and exquisite drawings of field-mice, orioles, and woodpeckers were scattered promiscuously in other parts of the room, across one end of which a long rude table was stretched to hold artist materials, scraps of drawing-paper, and immense folio volumes, filled with delicious paintings of birds taken in their native haunts.

This, said I to myself, is the studio of the naturalist, but hardly had the thought escaped me when the master himself made his appearance. He was a tall, thin man, with a high, arched and serene forehead, and a bright penetrating gray eye; his white locks fell in clusters upon his shoulders, but were the only signs of age, for his form was erect, and his step as light as that of a deer. The expression of his face was sharp but, noble and commanding, and there was something in it, partly derived from the aquiline nose and partly from the shutting of the mouth, which made you think of the imperial eagle.

His greeting, as he entered, was at once frank and cordial,

and showed you the sincere, true man. "How kind it is," he said, with a slight French accent, and in a pensive tone, "to come to see me; and how wise, too, to leave that crazy city!" He then shook me warmly by the hand. "Do you know," he continued, "how I wonder that men can consent to swelter and fret their lives away amid those hot bricks and pestilent vapors, when the woods and fields are all so near? It would kill me soon to be confined in such a prison-house; and when I am forced to make an occasional visit there, it fills me with loathing and sadness. Ah! how often, when I have been abroad on the mountains, has my heart risen in grateful praise to God that it was not my destiny to waste and pine among these noisome congregations of the city."

It was curious to observe the influence which his life had exerted upon the mind and character of Audubon. Withdrawing him from the conventionalities and cares of a more social condition, he always retained the fresh, spontaneous, elastic manner of a child, yet his constant and deep converse with the thoughtful mysteries of nature had imparted to him also the reflective wisdom of the sage. Whatever came into his mind he uttered with delightful unreserve and naiveté; but those utterances at the same time bore marks of keen, original insight and of the deepest knowledge. Thus, he knew nothing of the theology of the schools, and cared as little for it, because the untaught theology of the woods had filled his mind with a nobler sense of God than the schoolmen had ever dreamed; he knew, too, nothing of our politics, and cared nothing for them, because to his simple integrity they seemed only frivolous and vain debates about rights that none disputed and duties that all fulfilled; and his reading, confined, I suspect, mainly to the necessary literature of his profession, was neither extensive nor choice, because he found in his own activity, earnestness and invention a fountainhead of literature abundantly able to supply all his intellectual and spiritual wants. The heroism and poetry of his own life gave him no occasion to learn the heroism and poetry of others; yet his apparent neglect of the "humanities" had wrought no hardening or vulgarizing effect upon his nature, for his sympathies were always the most delicate, and his manners soft, gentle and refined.

It was impossible, in turning over the leaves of his large book, or in looking at the collection which he exhibited at the Lyceum Hall, not to imbibe some of his own enthusiasm for birds. One was made to feel that they were in some way nearer to our affections than any of the other animal tribes. Other animals are either indifferent or inimical to us, or else mere "servile ministers," while birds are, for the most part, objects of admiration. Nobody but a born specialist ever likes insects or reptiles; fishes have always an unutterably stupid or un-sentimental look, and deserve to be caught out of the dull element in which they live, to die in ecstacies in the oxygen of air; wild beasts, though sometimes savagely grand and majestic, excite terror, while tame beasts, which we subjugate, we are apt to despise; but birds win their way to our hearts and imaginations by a thousand charms. They are mostly lovely in form, brilliant in color, and seductively pleasing in their motions. They have such canny and knowing eyes, and they lead such free, joyous, melodious lives of love. Their swift and graceful evolutions, whether alone or in flocks; now darting like arrows to the very gates of heaven, or outspeeding the wind as it curls the white caps of the sea, or anon gathering for their far-off flights to unknown lands—awaken our aspirations as well as our thoughts, and beget a profound interest in their mysterious destinies; while their varied songs, profuse, sparkling, sympathetic, and glorious, are the richest and tenderest of nature's voices. Among the recollections of our childhood, those of the birds we have fed and cherished are often the dearest; and in maturer years the memory of the country home in which we were reared, the woods in which we wandered, the fields and forests where we weekly worshiped, is the greener and sweeter for the birds. Thus they are associated with the most charming features of the external world, and breathe a spell over the interior world of thought. They are the poetry of nature, and a pervading presence in poetry; and it is no wonder that since the time Aristophanes made them the vehicle for his immortal pen, the poets-laureate—Shakespeare, Burns, Keats, Shelley, Bryant, and Wordsworth—have found in them the sources of their liveliest inspirations.

JAMES FENIMORE COOPER

1789–1851

James Fenimore Cooper was born in Burlington, New Jersey, on September 15, 1789, the son of William Cooper, who in 1790 moved his family to Cooperstown, New York, a frontier village he had founded near Lake Otsego. In 1803 James Cooper entered Yale College but was expelled two years later for misconduct. He then spent three years (1806–08) at sea, first in the merchant marine and then in the U.S. Navy. Following the death of his father, James Cooper married Susan Augusta De Lancey in 1811, and started living the life of a gentleman farmer in Cooperstown and Westchester, New York. In 1820 he began both his political and his literary careers, becoming secretary to the Westchester County Clintonian Republicans and publishing his first book, *Precaution*.

Cooper's next book, *The Spy* (1821), an adventure story set in Revolutionary America, first brought him into prominence. In 1822 he moved to New York City to become a professional writer and in 1823 published *The Pioneers*. This was the first of a group of novels called the Leatherstocking Tales, for which Cooper is best known; the others are *The Last of the Mohicans* (1826), *The Prairie* (1827), *The Pathfinder* (1840), and *The Deerslayer* (1841). In addition to these stories of life on the American frontier, Cooper, an extremely prolific writer, also published ten sea tales, including *The Pilot* (1824) and *The Red Rover* (1827). Beginning in 1826, Cooper lived abroad for seven years and published several novels with a European setting, including *The Bravo* (1831) and *The Headsman* (1833).

After returning to New York City in 1833, Cooper became a vocal critic of American democracy. Although he was a strong believer in equality, Cooper expressed concern that traditional standards of good taste and artistic excellence be preserved. These sentiments he expressed in his long essay, *The American Democrat* (1838), as well as in the novels *Homeward Bound* and *Home as Found* (both 1838). In 1839 Cooper published a *History of the Navy of the United States*, and throughout the 1840s he involved himself in a number of political issues, generally taking a conservative position. Cooper died at his estate in Cooperstown on September 14, 1851.

Personal

Visited Princess Galitzin, and also Cooper, the American novelist. This man, who has shown so much genius, has a good deal of the manner, or want of manner, peculiar to his countrymen.—SIR WALTER SCOTT, *Journal*, November 3, 1826

Mr. Cooper's MS. ⟨signature⟩ is very bad—*unformed*, with little of distinctive character about it, and varying greatly in different epistles. In most of those before us a steel pen has been employed, the lines are crooked, and the whole chirography has a constrained and school-boyish air. The paper is fine, and of a blueish tint. A wafer is always used. Without appearing ill-natured, we could scarcely draw any inferences from such a MS. Mr. Cooper has seen many vicissitudes, and it is probable that he has not always written thus. Whatever are his faults, his genius cannot be doubted.—EDGAR ALLAN POE, "A Chapter on Autography" (1841), *Complete Works*, ed. James A. Harrison, 1902, Vol. 15, p. 205

Mr. Cooper was in person solid, robust, athletic: in voice, manly; in manner, earnest, emphatic, almost dictatorial—with something of self-assertion, bordering on egotism. The first effect was unpleasant, indeed repulsive, but there shone through all this a heartiness, a frankness, which excited confidence, respect, and at last affection.—SAMUEL GRISWOLD GOODRICH, *Recollections of a Lifetime*, 1856, Letter 36

A man of unquestioned talent,—almost genius,—he was aristocratic in feeling and arrogant in bearing, altogether combining in his manners what a Yankee once characterized as "winning ways to make people hate him."—HORACE GREELEY, *Recollections of a Busy Life*, 1868, p. 261

I had known Mr. Cooper during the later years of his life, and used to see him occasionally when he visited New York. He was an amazingly fluent talker as well as speaker and writer; and he affected an intense bitterness against the institutions of his native country in his conversation as well as in his writings. I can see him now, in my mind's eye, standing with his back to the fire-place in my office, with his legs apart and his coat-tails under his arms, pouring out diatribes which did not seem half in earnest.—MAUNSELL B. FIELD, *Memories of Many Men and of Some Women*, 1873, p. 178

He "stalked" about the *salon*—a tall, stalwart man, with the unmistakable air of self-confidence I have noticed in many Americans; as if it were a prime thought that independence was to be maintained by a seeming indifference to the opinions of on-lookers—a sensation that vanishes, however, when the demeanor that has given rise to it is found but the rough shell of a sweet kernel; for Americans are among the most socially generous of humankind. I had other and better opportunities of seeing Fenimore Cooper afterward: but in that *salon*, jostled by *petits maîtres*, he was out of place—as much so as an Indian cross-bow would have been among a collection of Minié rifles.

Proctor, in 1828, wrote of him: "He has a dogged, discontented look, and seems ready to affront or be affronted. His eye is rather deep-set, dull, and with little motion." He describes Cooper as rude even to coarseness in English society. That is not my experience of the author of *The Spy*—the originator of the class of sea-fictions—to whom the reading world owes a large debt. He was certainly the opposite of "genial," and seemed to think it good taste and sound judgment to be condescending to his equals.—S. C. HALL, *Retrospect of a Long Life*, 1883, pp. 227–28

General

Mr Cooper describes things to the life, but he puts no motion into them. While he is insisting on the minutest details, and explaining all the accompaniments of an incident, the story stands still. The elaborate accumulation of particulars serves not to embody his imagery, but to distract and impede the mind. He is not so much the master of his materials as their drudge: He labours under an epilepsy of the fancy. He thinks himself bound in his character of novelist to tell the truth, the whole truth, and nothing but the truth. Thus, if two men are struggling on the edge of a precipice for life or death, he goes not merely into the vicissitudes of action and passion as the chances of the combat vary; but stops to take an inventory of the geography of the place, the shape of the rock, the precise attitude and display of the limbs and muscles, with the eye and habits of a sculptor. Mr Cooper does not seem to be aware of the infinite divisibility of mind and matter; and that an 'abridgment' is all that is possible or desirable in the most individual representation. A person who is so determined, may write volumes on a grain of sand or an insect's wing. Why describe the dress and appearance of an Indian chief, down to his tobacco-stopper and button-holes? It is mistaking the province of the artist for that of the historian; and it is this very obligation of painting and statuary to fill up all the details, that renders them incapable of telling a story, or of expressing more than a single moment, group, or figure. Poetry or romance does not descend into the particulars, but attones for it by a more rapid march and an intuitive glance at the more striking results. By considering truth or matter-of-fact as the sole element of popular fiction, our author fails in massing and in impulse. In the midst of great vividness and fidelity of description, both of nature and manners, there is a sense of jejuneness,—for half of what is described is insignificant and indifferent; there is a hard outline,—a little manner; and his most striking situations do not tell as they might and ought, from his seeming more anxious about the mode and circumstances than the catastrophe. In short, he anatomizes his subjects; and his characters bear the same relation to living beings that the botanic specimens collected in a portfolio do to the living plant or tree. The sap does not circulate kindly; nor does the breath of heaven visit, or its dews moisten them. Or, if Mr Cooper gets hold of an appalling circumstance, he, from the same tenacity and thraldom to outward impressions, never lets it go: He repeats it without end. Thus, if he once hits upon the supposition of a wild Indian's eyes glaring through a thicket, every bush is from that time forward furnished with a pair; the page is studded with them, and you can no longer look about you at ease or in safety. The high finishing we have spoken of is particularly at variance with the rudeness of the materials. In Richardson it was excusable, where all was studied and artificial; but a few dashes of red ochre are sufficient to paint the body of a savage chieftain; nor should his sudden and frantic stride on his prey be treated with the precision and punctiliousness of a piece of *still life*. There are other American writers, (such as the historiographer of *Brother Jonathan*,) who carry this love of veracity to a pitch of the marvellous. They run riot in an account of the dishes at a boarding-house, as if it were a banquet of the Gods; and recount the overturning of a travelling stage-waggon with as much impetuosity, turbulence, and exaggerated enthusiasm, as if it were the fall of Phaeton. In the absence of subjects of real interest, men make themselves an interest out of nothing, and magnify mole-hills into mountains. This is not the fault of Mr Cooper: He is always true, though sometimes tedious; and correct, at the expense of being insipid. His *Pilot* is the best of his works; and truth to say, we think it a master-piece in its kind. It has great unity of purpose and feeling. Every thing in it may be said

To suffer a *sea-change*
Into something new and strange.

His Pilot never appears but when the occasion is worthy of him; and when he appears, the result is sure. The description of his guiding the vessel through the narrow strait left for her escape, the sea-fight, and the incident of the white topsail of the English man-of-war appearing above the fog, where it is first mistaken for a cloud, are of the first order of graphic composition; to say nothing of the admirable episode of Tom Coffin, and his long figure coiled up like a rope in the bottom of the boat. The rest is *common-place*; but then it is American common-place. We thank Mr Cooper he does not take every thing from us, and therefore we can learn something from him. He has the saving grace of originality. We wish we could impress it, 'line upon line, and precept upon precept,' especially upon our American brethren, how precious, how invaluable *that* is. In art, in literature, in science, the least bit of nature is worth all the plagiarism in the world. The great secret of Sir Walter Scott's enviable, but unenvied success, lies in his transcribing from nature instead of transcribing from books. —WILLIAM HAZLITT, "American Literature—Dr. Channing," *Edinburgh Review*, Oct. 1829, pp. 128–29

One main and predominant feature, however, distinguishes itself in Mr. Cooper's work—that to which we have already alluded—his endeavour to make his *personal* distastes *national* grievances, and to enlist his countrymen in general as partners in imaginary slights and visionary insults—which, whatever they may have been, were incurred by Mr. Cooper, not *because*, but *although* he was American—not *parceque*, but *quoique*, as Mr. President Dupin would say:—for it is clear, from his own account, that he received much attention in his national character, which he forfeited when he became personally known.—JOHN GIBSON LOCKHART, "Cooper's England," *Quarterly Review*, Oct. 1837, p. 330

Do not hasten to write; you cannot be too slow about it. Give no ear to any man's praise or censure; know that that is *not* it: on the one side is as Heaven if you have strength to keep silent, and climb unseen; yet on the other side, yawning always at

one's right-hand and one's left, is the frightfullest Abyss and Pandimonium! See Fenimore Cooper,—poor Cooper, he is *down in it*; and had a climbing faculty too.—THOMAS CARLYLE, Letter to Ralph Waldo Emerson (Dec. 8, 1837)

That which renders Cooper inferior to Walter Scott is his profound and radical impotence for the comic, and his perpetual intention to divert you, in which he never succeeds. I feel, in reading Cooper, a singular sensation, as if while listening to beautiful music there was near me some horrible village fiddler scraping his violin and harrowing me by playing the same air. To produce what he thinks to be comic he puts into the mouth of one of his personages a silly joke, invented a *priori*, some notion, a mental vice, a deformity of mind, which is shown in the first chapters and reappears, page after page, to the last. This joke and this personage form the village fiddler I speak of. To this system we owe David in *The Mohicans*, the English sailor and Lieutenant Muir in *The Pathfinder*; in short, all the so-called comic figures in Cooper's works.

⟨. . .⟩ Certainly, Cooper does not owe his fame to his fellow-citizens, neither does he owe it to England; he owes it in a great measure to the passionate admiration of France, to our fine and noble country, more considerate of foreign men of genius than she is of her own poets. Cooper has been understood and, above all, appreciated in France. I am therefore surprised to see him ridicule the French officers who were in Canada in 1750. Those officers were gentlemen, and history tells us that their conduct was noble. Is it for an American, whose position demands of him lofty ideas, to give a gratuitously odious character to one of those officers when the sole succour that America received during her War of Independence came from France? My observation is, I think, the more just because in reading over all Cooper's works I find it impossible to discover even a trace of good-will to France.

The difference that exists between Walter Scott and Cooper is derived essentially from the nature of the subjects towards which their genius led them. From Cooper's scenes nothing philosophical or impressive to the intellect issues when, the work once read, the soul looks back to take in a sense of the whole. Yet both are great historians; both have cold hearts; neither will admit passion, that divine emanation, superior to the virtue that man has constructed for the preservation of society; they have suppressed it, they have offered it as a holocaust to the blue-stockings of their country; but the one initiates you into great human evolutions, the other into the mighty heart of Nature herself. One has brought literature to grasp the earth and ocean, the other makes it grapple body to body with humanity. Read Cooper, and this will strike you, especially in the *Pathfinder*. You will not find a portrait which makes you think, which brings you back into yourself by some subtle or ingenious reflection, which explains to you facts, persons, or actions. He seems, on the contrary, to wish to plunge you into solitude and leave you to dream there. Whereas Scott gives you, wherever you are, a brilliant company of human beings. Cooper's work isolates; Scott weds you to his drama as he paints with broad strokes the features of his country at all epochs. The grandeur of Cooper is a reflection of the Nature he depicts; that of Walter Scott is more peculiarly his own. The Scotchman procreates his work; the American is the son of his. Walter Scott has a hundred aspects; Cooper is a painter of sea and landscape, admirably aided by two academies—the Savage and the Sailor. His noble creation of Leather-Stocking is a work apart. Not understanding English I cannot judge of the style of these two great geniuses, happily for us so different, but I should suppose the Scotchman to be superior to the American in the expression of his thought and in the mechanism of his style. Cooper is illogical; he proceeds by sentences which, taken one by one, are confused, the succeeding phrase not allied to the preceding, though the whole presents an imposing substance. To understand this criticism read the first two pages of the *Pathfinder* and examine each proposition. You will find a muddle of ideas which would bring *pensums* upon any rhetoric pupil in France. But the moment the majesty of his Nature lays hold of you, you forget the clumsy lurching of the vessel, you think only of the ocean or the lake. To sum up once more: one is the historian of Nature, the other of humanity; one attains to the glorious ideal by imagery, the other by action, though without neglecting poesy, the high-priestess of art.—HONORÉ DE BALZAC (1840), *The Personal Opinions of Honoré de Balzac*, tr. Katharine Prescott Wormeley, 1899, pp. 117–20

The first enthusiasm about Cooper having subsided, we remember more his faults than his merits. His ready resentment and way of showing it in cases which it is the wont of gentlemen to pass by in silence or meet with a good-humored smile have caused unpleasant associations with his name, and his fellow-citizens, in danger of being tormented by suits for libel if they spoke freely of him, have ceased to speak of him at all. But neither these causes, nor the baldness of his plots, shallowness of thought, and poverty in the presentation of character, should make us forget the grandeur and originality of his sea-sketches, nor the redemption from oblivion of our forest-scenery, and the noble romance of the hunter-pioneer's life. Already, but for him, this fine page of life's romance would be almost forgotten. He has done much to redeem these irrevocable beauties from the corrosive acid of a semi-civilized invasion.—MARGARET FULLER, "American Literature," *Papers on Literature and Art*, 1846

Here's Cooper, who's written six volumes to show
He's as good as a lord: well, let's grant that he's so;
If a person prefer that description of praise,
Why, a coronet's certainly cheaper than bays;
But he need take no pains to convince us he's not
(As his enemies say) the American Scott.
Choose any twelve men, and let C. read aloud
That one of his novels of which he's most proud,
And I'd lay any bet that, without ever quitting
Their box, they'd be all, to a man, for acquitting.
He has drawn you one character, though, that is new,
One wildflower he's plucked that is wet with the dew
Of this fresh Western world, and, the thing not to mince,
He has done naught but copy it ill ever since;
His Indians, with proper respect be it said,
Are just Natty Bumpo, daubed over with red,
And his very Long Toms are the same useful Nat,
Rigged up in duck pants and a sou'-wester hat
(Though once in a Coffin, a good chance was found
To have slipped the old fellow away underground).
All his other men-figures are clothes upon sticks,
The *dernière chemise* of a man in a fix
(As a captain besieged, when his garrison's small,
Sets up caps upon poles to be seen o'er the wall);
And the women he draws from one model don't vary,
All sappy as maples and flat as a prairie.
When a character's wanted, he goes to the task
As a cooper would do in composing a cask;
He picks out the staves, of their qualities heedful,
Just hoops them together as tight as is needful,

And, if the best fortune should crown the attempt, he
Has made at the most something wooden and empty.
Don't suppose I would underrate Cooper's abilities;
If I thought you'd do that, I should feel very ill at ease;
The men who have given to *one* character life
And objective existence are not very rife;
You may number them all, both prosewriters and singers,
Without overrunning the bounds of your fingers,
And Natty won't go to oblivion quicker
Than Adams the parson or Primrose the vicar.
There is one thing in Cooper I like, too, and that is
That on manners he lectures his countrymen gratis;
Not precisely so either, because, for a rarity,
He is paid for his tickets in unpopularity.
—JAMES RUSSELL LOWELL, *A Fable for Critics*, 1848

He is colonel of the literary regiment; Irving, lieutenant-colonel; Bryant, the major; while Longfellow, Whittier, Holmes, Dana, and myself may be considered captains. . . . Two or three of Cooper's characters I consider the first in American fiction. Which are they? Why, Leatherstocking, Long Tom Coffin, and Uncas. Why this noble creation has been so neglected by painters and sculptors I am at a loss to understand. Certainly there is no nobler Indian character depicted in our literature. Thackeray calls the first of these immortal creations—and he was certainly a competent judge—one of "the great prize-men" of fiction, better perhaps than any of Scott's men, and ranks dear old Natty Bumppo with Uncle Toby, Sir Roger de Coverley, and Falstaff—heroic figures all. If anything from the pen of the writer of these romances is at all to outlive himself, it is unquestionably the series of *The Leatherstocking Tales*. To say this is not to predict a very lasting reputation for the series itself, but simply to express the belief that it will outlast any or all of the works from the same hand.—FITZ-GREENE HALLECK (c. 1850), cited in James Grant Wilson, *Bryant and His Friends*, 1885, pp. 238–39

Of his literary character I have spoken largely in the narrative of his life, but there are yet one or two remarks which must be made to do it justice. In that way of writing in which he excelled, it seems to me that he united, in a preeminent degree, those qualities which enabled him to interest the largest number of readers. He wrote not for the fastidious, the over-refined, the morbidly delicate; for these find in his genius something too robust for their liking—something by which their sensibilities are too rudely shaken; but he wrote for mankind at large—for men and women in the ordinary healthful state of feeling—and in their admiration he found his reward. It is for this class that public libraries are obliged to provide themselves with an extraordinary number of copies of his works: the number in the Mercantile Library in this city, I am told, is forty. Hence it is that he has earned a fame wider, I think, than any author of modern times—wider, certainly, than any author of any age ever enjoyed in his lifetime. All his excellences are translatable—they pass readily into languages the least allied in their genius to that in which he wrote, and in them he touches the heart and kindles the imagination with the same power as in the original English.

Cooper was not wholly without humor; it is sometimes found lurking in the dialogue of Harvey Birch and of Leatherstocking; but it forms no considerable element in his works; and, if it did, it would have stood in the way of his universal popularity, since, of all qualities, it is the most difficult to transfuse into a foreign language. Nor did the effect he produced upon the reader depend on any grace of style which would escape a translator of ordinary skill. With his style, it is true, he took great pains, and in his earlier works, I am told, sometimes altered the proofs sent from the printer so largely that they might be said to be written over. Yet he attained no special felicity, variety, or compass of expression. His style, however, answered his purpose; it has defects, but it is manly and clear, and stamps on the mind of the reader the impression he intended to convey. I am not sure that some of the very defects of Cooper's novels do not add, by a certain force of contrast, to their power over the mind. He is long in getting at the interest of his narrative. The progress of the plot, at first, is like that of one of his own vessels of war, slowly, heavily, and even awkwardly working out of a harbor. We are impatient and weary, but when the vessel is once in the open sea, and feels the free breath of heaven in her full sheets, our delight and admiration are all the greater at the grace, the majesty, and power with which she divides and bears down the waves, and pursues her course at will over the great waste of waters.—WILLIAM CULLEN BRYANT, "James Fenimore Cooper" (1852), *Prose Writings*, ed. Parke Godwin, 1884, Vol. 1, pp. 328–29

I never had the honour of knowing, or even seeing, Mr. Cooper personally; so that, through my past ignorance of his person, the man, though dead, is still as living to me as ever. And this is much; for his works are among the earliest I can remember, as in my boyhood producing a vivid and awakening power upon my mind.

It always much pained me, that for any reason, in his latter years, his fame at home should have apparently received a slight, temporary clouding, from some very paltry accidents, incidents more or less to the general career of letters. But whatever possible things in Mr. Cooper may have seemed to have in some degree provoked the occasional treatment he received, it is certain that he possessed not the slightest weaknesses but those which are only noticeable as the almost infallible indices of pervading greatness. He was a great, robust-souled man, all whose merits are not even, yet fully appreciated. But a grateful posterity will take the best care of Fenimore Cooper.—HERMAN MELVILLE, Letter to the Cooper Memorial Committee (1852), cited in *Memorial of James Fenimore Cooper*, ed. George Palmer Putnam, 1852

With the appearance of Cooper we began to hold up our heads among the romancers of the world. In literary form and workmanship he was far inferior to his great contemporaries abroad. He was utterly deficient in psychological analysis. Of broad humor he had only enough to hold his own in the second rank of his native State. Though he could draw very well a sailor's sweetheart, like Mary Pratt, or a soldier's daughter, like Mabel Dunham, yet of *fine* women he had only a chivalrous notion, and painted them from a respectful distance. They were delicate creatures, to be handled like porcelain. Dressed out and beautified, they were to be protected and worshiped. They walk through the halls of his heroes, and take seats at the upper end to distribute the prizes after the tournament. But in Paulding's Catalina there is more of the sprightly, lovely, living woman than in all the Frances Whartons, Elizabeth Temples, and Gertrude Greysons of Cooper's entire catalogue. The novelist's six years in the navy had made him a complete Jack Tar. He learned there to handle not only the ropes but the "yarn," and whatever he told, he told as "to the marines"; but he told it with such incredible confidence, and, withal, in such a chivalrous spirit, that he made us shut the eye of criticism and open the ear of faith. He never hesitated for a trick. On a pinch, he could extricate a

hero or a heroine twenty times a day, each time by a different device. His *dramatis personæ* were as extravagant in their heroism or in their devotion as Dickens's persons were in their eccentricities. Yet, with all these limitations, he possessed a fine, robust sympathy and manliness, and a creative power equal to the best of men abroad.

Easily superior to all our novelists in sea-tales, which required technical knowledge, and on the frontier, where his imagination had full play, he was in the delineation of the passions probably surpassed by Simms. There is a delightful transmissibility of blood in all his heroes. For instance, though there is no Long Tom Coffin anywhere else so admirably set forth as in *The Pilot*, yet we have him cut up into parcels and distributed everywhere, under a white and under a black skin. He is at once the protector and servant of his master, delicate in his sensibilities and rough in his fists, quite competent to carry a cannon under his arm or a maiden on his shoulder— the ideal sailor, in short, combining strength, dogged faithfulness, and noble self-sacrifice with the most rugged and sometimes deformed exterior.

Two other persons, Chingachcook and the Pathfinder, Cooper created outright. The former, with Uncas to supplement him, is the ideal Indian—grave, silent, acute, self-contained, sufficiently lofty-minded to take in the greatness of the Indian's past, and sufficiently far-sighted to see the hopelessness of his future,—with nobility of soul enough to grasp the white man's virtues, and with inherited wildness enough to keep him true to the instincts of his own race. Probably at his first appearance, in *The Pioneers*, this hero was a study from life. Afterward, when Cooper began to present him in youth and manhood, the character was idealized; but the ideal is a noble one, worthy to stand for the heights of the savage nature—a god-send to the later romancers, who have never been able to escape from him. Chingachcook appears at his best, perhaps, but under another name, in *The Last of the Mohicans*; Natty Bumpo, in *The Pathfinder*, where, with all his excellence as a representative frontiersman and scout, he unites in a most delicious and manly way the tender qualities of a lover. The scenes with Mable Dunham, where he finally merges the lover in the paternal element, present the best range of sentiment that Cooper attained.

In the sea-tales, what strikes us as best is the management of *The Two Admirals*. *The Red Rover* may do for the "marines"; the *Sea Lions* may come closer home to a sailor's experience and please us with its homespun and sensible Mary and its vigorously drawn Vineyard skipper, but the interplay of manly affection in the two admirals, and their reciprocity of self-sacrifice, indicate the largeness of Cooper's nature; while the handling of the two fleets, whatever the nautical critic may say of it, holds the interest of the landsman best. Again, Harvey Birch, in *The Spy*, is perhaps a new creation from the actual; but the combination of the spy and the gentleman is so rare, and is put together in so dry an atmosphere of other incident, that it fails to satisfy. The social life in the old mansion of the Whartons is bare beside the social life which Mrs. Stowe, for example, depicts; while the autumnal glow of the Hudson River scenery never reaches the mellow beauty of autumn days on that noble stream, as painted by Irving and Paulding. Cooper's scenery everywhere, in fact, is indefinite, though often large and effective. Less real in *The Spy*, he is marvelously successful in *The Prairie* and *The Pathfinder* in producing a sense of the primeval prairie and forest grandeur.

Cooper did not,

In years that bring the philosophic mind,

become a philosopher, and one hardly likes to follow him through those rasping times when the spirit of patriotism led him to back up his countrymen abroad, only to back down upon them at home. There is no irritation so uncertain in its results as that of patriotism acting on a thin skin. The patriot who is without a cool philosophy becomes a public scold—abroad, for his country, and against her at home. Yet, however much the critical literary or patriotic spirit may attack Cooper for short-comings, he deepened the sentiment for America among the middle classes of the Old World, and created a genial atmosphere for us there, in which we may thriftily sun ourselves.—JAMES HERBERT MORSE, "The Native Element in American Fiction," *Century Magazine*, June 1883, pp. 290–91

A consideration of Cooper's place in English literature involves a comparison with Scott. In the first place, the Scotchman was the earlier of the two; it was he who widened the field of the romance; it was he who pushed the novel to the front and made fiction the successful rival of poetry and the drama; it was he who showed all men how an historical novel might be written. Cooper is the foremost of Scott's followers, no doubt, and in skill of narration, in the story-telling faculty, in the gift of imparting interest to the incidents of a tale, Cooper at his best is not inferior to Scott at his best. But Scott had far more humor and far more insight into human nature.

Like Scott, Cooper was a writer of romance; that is to say, he was an optimist, an idealizer—one who seeks to see only the best, and who refuses to see what is bad. Scott chose to present only the bright side of chivalry, and to make the Middle Ages far pleasanter than they could have been in reality. Probably Scott knew that the picture he gave of England under Richard the Lion-Hearted was misleading; certainly he knew that he was not telling the whole truth. Cooper's red Indians are quite as real as Scott's black knights, to say the least. Cooper's Indians are true to life, absolutely true to life—so far as they go. Cooper told the truth about them—but he did not tell the whole truth. He put forward the exception as the type, sometimes; and he always suppressed some of the red man's ugliest traits. Cooper tells us that the Indian is cruel as Scott tells us that a tournament was often fatal; but he does not convey to us any realization of the ingrained barbarity and cruelty which was perhaps the chief characteristic of the Indian warrior. This side of the red man is kept in the shadow, while his bravery, his manliness, his skill, his many noble qualities, are dwelt on at length.—BRANDER MATTHEWS, *An Introduction to the Study of American Literature*, 1896, pp. 66–67

Like Scott and most other novelists, Cooper was rarely successful with his main characters, but was saved by his subordinate ones. These were strong, fresh, characteristic, human; and they lay, as has been said, in several different directions, all equally marked. If he did not create permanent types in Harvey Birch the spy, Leather-Stocking the woodsman, Long Tom Coffin the sailor, Chingachgook the Indian, then there is no such thing as the creation of characters in literature. Scott was far more profuse and varied, but he gave no more of life to individual personages and perhaps created no types so universally recognized. What is most remarkable is that, in the case of the Indian especially, Cooper was not only in advance of the knowledge of his own time, but of that of the authors who immediately followed him. In Parkman and Palfrey, for instance, the Indian of Cooper vanishes and seems wholly extinguished, but under the closer inspection of Alice Fletcher and Horatio Hale, the lost figure reappears, and becomes more

picturesque, more poetic, more thoughtful than even Cooper dared to make him.—THOMAS WENTWORTH HIGGINSON, "James Fenimore Cooper," *American Prose*, ed. George Rice Carpenter, 1898, p. 150

In description of nature, afloat and ashore, the good qualities of his style almost invariably predominate. His volumes of travel are so picturesque and entertaining as to lead a discriminating critic to pronounce them "among the best of their kind." His familiar letters of friendship or affection have colloquial ease and graphic lightness. The words of a few of his characters—Harvey Birch, Tom Coffin, Leather-Stocking—are life-like. In short, where he feels at home with his subject, the style responds without apparent effort to a natural impulse. On the other hand, when he tries to produce an effect with thankless or uncongenial material, the style is inert; for he wrote precipitately, and spurned revision.

The gist of the matter is that Cooper was not a verbal artist, and that his endowment of what we are pleased to call literary conscience was scant. With no special training as a writer, when, at thirty or thereabout, it accidentally came into his head to try his hand at a novel, he struck boldly out, not particularly considering whither. Some of his early books, written for his own pleasure, brought him popularity which surprised no one more than himself. The art of writing engaged his attention far less than the panorama and the story. Robust and impetuous, he disdained details of style and academic standards. To apply to him academic standards is as if one should inquire whether Hard-Heart's horsemanship conforms to the rules of the riding-school; for nobody cares. It is to miss the point that, heaven knows how or why, he struck—Heaven be praised!—a new trail which, admitting all the shortcomings in style that any one may choose to allege, the world is not yet weary of following. The indisputable, the essential fact is that, entering unheralded and possessing the land, he founded a realm, and became by divine right king of American fiction. Scott, with whom he is often idly, though perhaps inevitably, compared, had behind him generations of literary association in a country which teemed with thronging suggestion of romance, and which was peopled by an eager audience. The American writers of that early time were, as Bayard Taylor said, "even in advance of their welcome, and created their own audiences." To no such heritage as Scott's was Cooper born. Alone he penetrated and permeated the literary wilderness, blazing paths for those who should come after. To disparage his work on the score of lack of technical finish is to subordinate primary considerations to secondary, and to prove one's self dull to that rarest of endowments, that precious literary prize—originality.—W. B. SHUBRICK CLYMER, *James Fenimore Cooper*, 1900, pp. 58–61

Works

SEA NOVELS

Next week another book will be there for you—an American novel Mrs. Griffith sent to me, *The Spy*; quite new scenes and characters, humor and pathos, a picture of America in Washington's time; a surgeon worthy of Smollett or Moore, and quite different from any of their various surgeons; and an Irishwoman, Betty Flanagan, incomparable.—MARIA EDGEWORTH, Letter to Sophy Ruxton (July 8, 1821)

In regard to the style of execution, the work ⟨*The Pilot*⟩ has one fault which was mentioned in our notice of the *Spy*; it is in some instances, and more especially where the author speaks in his own person, overloaded with epithets, and the detail of particular circumstances. The author leaves too little to his readers, and from his solicitude to omit nothing of the quality, degree, and manner of everything related or described, he impairs the vivacity and force of the expression. Some few passages are perhaps a little too harsh, as, in the battle, one 'buries his weapon in the heart of one of the enemy;' so long Tom 'pinned the English captain to the mast with his harpoon.' We do not think that the agonies of Dillon, in drowning, are too palpably given, the reader being reconciled to the exhibition of them, by the hatred and loathing he had before conceived towards the creature. But without some good reason of this sort, a vivid display of extreme physical suffering, ghastly objects, or horrid cruelty, are more shocking than interesting. Such descriptions do not require great skill in a writer; they may, however, be introduced with great effect, where the reader is fully prepared for them.—W. Phillip, *"The Pilot, A Tale of the Sea," North American Review*, April 1824, p. 328

I read Cooper's new novel work, the *Red Rover;* the current of the novel rolls entirely upon the Ocean. Something there is too much of nautical language; in fact it overpowers every thing else. But so people once take an interest in a description they will swallow a great deal which they do not understand. The sweet word Mesopotamia has its charm in other compositions as well as in sermons. He has much genius, a powerful conception of character and force of execution. The same ideas I see recur upon him that haunt other folks. The graceful form of the spars and the tracery of the ropes and cordage against the sky is too often dwelt upon.—Sir Walter Scott, *Journal*, Jan. 14, 1828

Yet it was during this period, between the years 1815 and 1861, that we began to have a literature of our own, and one which any people could take pride in. Cooper himself was the pioneer. In his second novel, *The Spy*, he threw off the wretched spirit of the colonist, and the story, which at once gained a popularity that broke down all barriers, was read everywhere with delight and approbation. The chief cause of the difference between the fate of this novel and that of its predecessor lies in the fact that *The Spy* was of genuine native origin. Cooper knew and loved American scenery and life. He understood certain phases of American character on the prairie and the ocean, and his genius was no longer smothered by the dead colonialism of the past. *The Spy*, and those of Cooper's novels which belong to the same class, have lived and will live, and certain American characters which he drew will likewise endure. He might have struggled all his life in the limbo of intellectual servitude to which Moore's friends consigned themselves, and no one would have cared for him then or remembered him now. But, with all his foibles, Cooper was inspired by an intense patriotism, and he had a bold, vigorous, aggressive nature. He freed his talents at a stroke, and giving them full play attained at once a world-wide reputation, which no man of colonial mind could ever have dreamed of reaching. Yet his countrymen, long before his days of strife and unpopularity, seem to have taken singularly little patriotic pride in his achievements, and the well bred and well educated shuddered to hear him called the "American Scott;" not because they thought the epithet inappropriate and misapplied, but because it was a piece of irreverent audacity toward a great light of English literature.—Henry Cabot Lodge, *Studies in History*, 1884, pp. 353–54

He is not invincibly young and heroic; he is mature and human, though for him also the stress of adventure and endeavor must end fatally in inheritance and marriage. For James Fenimore Cooper nature was not the framework, it was an essential part of existence. He could hear its voice, he could understand its silence, and he could interpret both for us in his prose with all that felicity and sureness of effect that belong to a poetical conception alone. His fame, as wide but less brilliant than that of his contemporary, rests mostly on a novel which is not of the sea. But he loved the sea and looked at it with consummate understanding. In his sea tales the sea interpenetrates with life; it is in a subtle way a factor in the problem of existence, and, for all its greatness, it is always in touch with the men, who, bound on errands of war or gain, traverse its immense solitudes. His descriptions have the magistral ampleness of a gesture indicating the sweep of a vast horizon. They embrace the colours of sunset, the peace of starlight, the aspects of calm and storm, the great loneliness of the waters, the stillness of watchful coasts, and the alert readiness which marks men who live face to face with the promise and the menace of the sea.

He knows the men and he knows the sea. His method may be often faulty, but his art is genuine. The truth is within him. The road to legitimate realism is through poetical feeling, and he possesses that—only it is expressed in the leisurely manner of his time. He has the knowledge of simple hearts. Long Tom Coffin is a monumental seaman with the individuality of life and the significance of a type. It is hard to believe that Manual and Borroughcliffe, Mr. Marble of Marble-Head, Captain Tuck of the packet-ship *Montauk*, or Daggett, the tenacious commander of the *Sea Lion* of Martha's Vineyard, must pass away some day and be utterly forgotten. His sympathy is large, and his humour is as genuine—and as perfectly unaffected—as is his art. In certain passages he reaches, very simply, the heights of inspired vision.

He wrote before the great American language was born, and he wrote as well as any novelist of his time. If he pitches upon episodes redounding to the glory of the young republic, surely England has glory enough to forgive him, for the sake of his excellence, the patriotic bias at her expense. The interest of his tales is convincing and unflagging; and there runs through his work a steady vein of friendliness for the old country which the succeeding generations of his compatriots have replaced by a less definite sentiment.—Joseph Conrad, "Tales of the Sea" (1898), *Notes on Life and Letters*, 1921, pp. 55–56

THE LEATHERSTOCKING TALES

I have read Cooper's *Prairie*, better I think than his *Red Rover* in which you never get foot on shore and to understand entirely the incidents of the story it requires too much nautical language. It is very clever though.—Sir Walter Scott, *Journal*, Jan. 28, 1828

Mr. Cooper has some little spice of our artist's weakness, and is somewhat too fond of Red Indians, diversifying them by occasionally painting some much *redder* than others.

There is likewise too great a similarity in his plots; we have the same scenes over and over again, until at length we seem to have lost our path in a primeval forest of novels, out of which it is almost impossible to read our way.

The greatest charm about Cooper's novels is the perfect truthfulness of their forest scenery; there is nothing artificial in a single word—the very trees seem to grow around you: it is not scene painting, it is nature. In many of Bulwer's novels we cannot shake off the feeling that the whole is theatrical: we acknowledge the picture, but we see it by the light of the footlamps. It is very good, certainly, but it is not life. We cannot do better than illustrate this by an anecdote we once heard of a very acute critic. A party of friends one evening were discussing the acting of the elder Kean and his son; all agreed in praising the felicity with which the son imitated the father: one went so far as to declare he saw little difference between them. This called up our critic, who said he would endeavor to describe the difference. "Let us select," said he, "the celebrated tent scene of Richard the Third: it is, of all others, that in which the younger is the most successful in imitating the elder one. When I saw old Edmund lying on the couch, writhing as it were beneath all the horrors of a guilty conscience, his restless and disturbed action told me more than words: when, finally, under the paroxysm of the terrible dream, he starts up, and staggers to the very brink of the orchestra, my attention was riveted on the terrible picture before me—that was nature: I saw the remorseful conscience-stung tyrant, and him alone. But in the case of his son 'twas very different; true, he did it physically precisely as his father had done: nothing panto-mimic was omitted, but the soul was wanting, and as he came reeling towards the audience, I said to myself, By heaven he will cut his knees upon the footlights." Thus differ Bulwer and Cooper.

With regard to his Indians, we have heard some Americans declare that they are not natural, but, as they termed them, Mr. Cooper's Indians: we can only speak as they impressed us. It must always be borne in mind that a novelist labors under a disadvantage when he is drawing human nature, which he does not when he is painting nature's scenery; as a matter of necessity, he must *exaggerate*, or, as they term it, *idealize* the living characters in his works. But it is not so with the scene he chooses to describe; he may be as literal as he pleases in the one case—then he is pronounced graphic, and wonderfully true to nature; but if he portrays with equal fidelity the beings he brings forth upon his canvas, he is condemned as tame and common-place. It thus requires a double power to produce a successful romance; and it is in this twofold capacity that we consider Mr. Cooper so admirable a writer.

Even in the very worst of his novels, there are glimpses of nature so exquisitely painted as to justify the highest praise it is possible to bestow. ⟨. . .⟩

The result of a long and attentive consideration of Mr. Cooper's work is, that he is without doubt a man of a shrewd and vigorous intellect, self-willed and opinionated, quick and vindictive in his feelings, but with a kind and generous heart; somewhat too fond, perhaps, of brooding over wrongs which, after all, may be only imaginary, and requiring more deference from the world than it is apt to pay to a Living Author.

But, with regard to the character of his productions, he is deficient in imagination and fancy, and humor.

Invention he certainly possesses, but it is not of the highest kind; his powers of observation are strong, but not universal, and this gives an air of monotony to many of his works.

He also takes an undue advantage of certain opportunities to give lectures, and hence the didactic tone of many dialogues interspersed in the novels. This is a serious defect, in an artistic view; a novelist should instruct by implication, and argue by insinuation. When he becomes didactic he ceases to be romantic, and the effect is neutralized.—THOMAS POWELL, "James Fenimore Cooper," *The Living Authors of America*, 1850, pp. 12–13, 47–48

Cooper's best and most comprehensive picture of border-life is of course to be found in his famous *Leatherstocking Tales*, so called from one of the many names given to the hero. These

books, *The Deerslayer* (1841), *The Last of the Mohicans* (1826), *The Pathfinder* (1840), *The Pioneers* (1823), and *The Prairie* (1827), to name them in the order in which they should be read, are, taken together, Cooper's greatest contribution to literature. Cooper styled them "a drama in five acts:" it would probably be more accurate to call them a rough prose epic of the deeds of a New-World hero, nobler intrinsically than Achilles or Æneas. The stories show us this simple-hearted hunter and scout, Natty Bumppo or Leatherstocking, at five successive stages of his long and hazardous life. We see him on his first war-path, humble as one who has not been proved; we see him in the fulness of his marvellous skill and sagacity; and we see him finally when age has come upon him, his friends dead, his very dog feeble and toothless, his famous rifle, Killdeer, out-of-date, and ready, like its owner, to be laid aside. To thus show the life and development of a single character in five successive novels is a memorable achievement, and the success with which this has been accomplished is one of Cooper's highest claims to distinction. Pure-minded, simple-hearted, ignorant of books, but skilled in every sign of the forest; with a deep sense of religion, half primeval, half Christian, with an aboriginal nearness to nature and an inveterate hatred of towns,—Leatherstocking has rightfully taken his place among the noblest and most original of the great characters of fiction. And Leatherstocking is more than interesting to us as an individual; like most of the great characters which the human imagination has created, he interests us partly for himself and partly because of what he represents. He is as distinctly a typical product of our border life as Rob Roy is of the forays of the Scottish Highlands or Achilles of the heroic age of Greece. He is a national hero: young as we are, he is ours. Living beyond the fringe of civilization and moving in front of the wave of settlement, his life is indirectly associated with that subduing of the West which is perhaps the most wonderful and heroic achievement of the American people. The greatness of this national movement, while it enters into the Leatherstocking stories only as a kind of secondary motive, yet gives to the whole a certain dimly recognized breadth and epic largeness of tone. In 1740–45, when in the *Deerslayer* its hero begins his career, Otsego Lake is yet unmapped by the king's surveyors; in the *Pioneers*, some sixty years later, the country about it has been taken up by the settlers, and the old hunter, compelled to retreat before them, grumbles that he loses himself in the clearings; finally, in *The Prairie*, which carries us to a period just after the Louisiana purchase of 1803, we are shown the emigrant train of the indefatigable settler pushing into the treeless plains of the far West. Leatherstocking's part in this advance is not that of the settler but the pioneer; he even grumbles to find the settler following at his heels; yet, like Daniel Boone, he is a heroic figure in one of the heroic episodes of our history.—HENRY S. PANCOAST, *An Introduction to American Literature*, 1898, pp. 136–38

Cooper's noble Indians ⟨. . .⟩ are rather more like the dreams of eighteenth-century France concerning aboriginal human nature than anything critically observed by ethnology; and Natty Bumppo himself is a creature rather of romantic fancy than of creative sympathy with human nature. The woods and the inland waters, on the other hand, amid which the scenes of these stories unroll themselves, are true American forests and lakes and streams. It is hardly too much to say that Cooper introduced to human recognition certain aspects of Nature unknown to literature before his time, and of a kind which could have been perceived and set forth only by an enthusiastic native of that newest of nations to which he was so devotedly attached.—BARRETT WENDELL, *A Literary History of America,* 1900, p. 186

WILLIAM GILMORE SIMMS
From "The Writings of
James Fenimore Cooper" (1842)
*Views and Reviews in American
Literature, History, and Fiction*
1845

We are among those who regard Mr. Cooper as a wronged and persecuted man. We conceive that his countrymen have done him gross injustice—that they have not only shown themselves ungenerous but ungrateful, and that, in lending a greedy ear to the numerous malicious aspersions which have assailed his person and his reputation, they have only given confirmation and strength to the proverbial reproach, of irreverence and ingratitude, to which countries, distinguished by popular governments, have usually been thought obnoxious. We do not mean to regard him as wholly faultless—on the contrary, we look upon Mr. Cooper as a very imprudent person; one whose determined will, impetuous temperament, and great self-esteem, continually hurry forward into acts and expressions of error and impatience. We propose to compare sides in this question:—to put the case fairly between himself and countrymen, and show where the balance of justice lies.

Of Mr. Cooper, little or nothing was known, by the American people at large, until the publication of *The Spy.* To a few, perhaps, the novel of *Precaution* had brought him acquainted. That was a very feeble work—coldly correct, elaborately tame—a second or third rate imitation of a very inferior school of writings, known as the social life novel. In works of this class, the imagination can have little play. The exercise of the creative faculty is almost entirely denied. The field of speculation is limited; and the analysis of minute shades of character, is all the privilege which taste and philosophy possess, for lifting the narrative above the province of mere lively dialogue, and sweet and fanciful sentiment. The ordinary events of the household, or of the snug family circle, suggest the only materials; and a large gathering of the set, at ball or dinner, affords incident of which the novelist is required to make the highest use. Writers of much earnestness of mood, originality of thought, or intensity of imagination, seldom engage in this class of writing. Scott attempted it in *St. Ronan's Well,* and failed;—rising only into the rank of Scott, in such portions of the story as, by a very violent transition, brought him once more into the bolder displays of wild and stirring romance. He consoled himself with the reflection that male writers were not good at these things. His conclusion, that such writings were best handled by the other sex, may be, or not, construed into a sarcasm.

Mr. Cooper failed egregiously in *Precaution.* So far as we know, and as we believe, that work fell still-born from the press. But for the success of *The Spy,* and the succeeding works, it never would have been heard of. But *The Spy* was an event. It was the boldest and best attempt at the historical romance which had ever been made in America. It is somewhat the practice, at this day, to disparage that story. This is in very bad taste. The book is a good one,—full of faults, perhaps,

and blunders; but full also of decided merits, and marked by a boldness of conception, and a courage in progress, which clearly showed the confidence of genius in its own resources. The conception of the Spy, as a character, was a very noble one. A patriot in the humblest condition of life,—almost wholly motiveless unless for his country—enduring the persecutions of friends, the hate of enemies—the doomed by both parties to the gallows—enduring all in secret, without a murmur,—without a word, when a word might have saved him,—all for his country; and all, under the palsying conviction, not only that his country never could reward him, but that, in all probability, the secret of his patriotism must perish with him, and nothing survive but that obloquy under which he was still content to live and labour.

It does not lessen the value of such a novel, nor the ideal truth of such a conception, that such a character is not often to be found. It is sufficiently true if it wins our sympathies and commands our respect. This is always the purpose of the ideal, which, if it can effect such results, becomes at once a model and a reality. The character of the Spy was not the only good one of the book. Lawton and Sitgreaves were both good conceptions, though rather exaggerated ones. Lawton was a somewhat too burly Virginian; and his appetite was too strong an ingredient in his chivalry. But, as his origin was British, this may have been due to the truthfulness of portraiture.

The defect of the story was rather in its action than its characters. This is the usual and grand defect in all Mr. Cooper's stories. In truth, there is very little story. He seems to exercise none of his genius in the invention of his fable. There is none of that careful grouping of means to ends, and all, to the one end of the dénouement, which so remarkably distinguished the genius of Scott, and made all the parts of his story fit as compactly as the work of the joiner,—but he seems to hurry forward in the delineation of scene after scene, as if wholly indifferent to the catastrophe. The consequence is, that his catastrophe is usually forced and unsatisfactory. He is, for this reason, compelled frequently, at the close, to begin the work of invention;—to bring out some latent matter,—to make unlooked for discoveries, and prove his hero, be he hunter or pirate, to have been the son of somebody of unexpected importance;—a discovery which, it is fancied, will secure him a greater degree of the reader's favour, than he could have before commanded. Mr. Cooper seems to rely wholly on the spirit and success of certain scenes. Take, for example, the work before us. Analyze the parts of the *Two Admirals.* The action of the several fleets in the several progresses of the sea, is, in truth, the only portion of the work on which Mr. Cooper has exercised himself. We may see, also, in the purposeless career of young Wychecombe, the true, and Wychecombe, the pretender, how little pains the author has taken, either in determining, from the first, what they shall severally be and do, or by what performances their conduct, respectively, shall be distinguished. It is very evident, from the first introduction of the American Wychecombe, that he was to become a person of some importance—the hero, in fact; and, for this, the mind of the reader is insensibly prepared by the first chapters of the story. Had Mr. Cooper planned any story at all, this young man must have been the hero—must have maintained throughout, and concentrated within himself, the chief interest of the performance. So, on the other hand, the false Wychecombe, the bastard, was to be his foil—the villain of the piece—and the conflict between the two for mastery, is the great issue for which the reader of the book prepares himself. But, unwilling to give himself the trouble of inventing situations, by which this issue could be made up or carried on, Mr.

Cooper surrenders himself to the progress of events. He leaves to one to beget and occasion the other. Hence the desultory character of his writings; the violence of transition; the strange neglect to which certain of his characters are destined, in whom he at first strives to interest us; and the hard scramble, which the persons of the drama are compelled to make, each to get into his proper place, for the *tableau vivant*, at the falling of the curtain. This young man, Wychecombe, the American, is nothing, and does nothing; and what a poor devil is his foil or shadow, Tom, the *nullus*—"*nullus*" indeed. These persons, brought in with much care, and elaborately portrayed to the reader, are yet—so far as the valuable portions of the story are concerned—left entirely unemployed. The despatching of Wycherley Wychecombe in the Druid, by Admiral Bluewater, to Admiral Oakes, was one of those simple schemes by which the author still endeavoured to maintain an interest in the youth, in whom he felt that he had, at the beginning, too greatly awakened the interest of the readers. The whole machinery here is feeble, and a writer of romance cannot more greatly err than when he subjects his hero to the continual influence of events. We have no respect for heroes placed always in subordinate positions—sent hither and thither—baffled by every breath of circumstance—creatures without will, and constantly governed by the caprices of other persons. This was the enfeebling characteristic in Scott's heroes. Hence it was that the true interest seldom settled on the person whom he chose to be his hero. Look, for example, at his Waverly,—who, contrasted with Claverhouse, or the brother of Flora MacIvor, shrunk into a very petty person. How small a person is his Wilfrid of *Ivanhoe*, in comparison with Brian de Bois Guilbert;—his Morton with his Burley; his Roland Græme, his Quentin Durward, and, indeed, most of his chosen heroes, in comparison with numerous other characters employed as their companions and opposites. This defect, which would be fatal always to purely dramatic composition, must be equally injurious to works of romance, in which, to a certain extent, all the standards are dramatic, and from the somewhat dramatic development of which, by continual action, the chief interest and anxiety of the reader are maintained. Availing ourselves of the dramatic *aside*, we may remark *en-passant*, that the conception of situation in which the two admirals are placed, in the progress of this story, is particularly admirable and touching.—Their respective characteristics are fairly drawn and nicely elaborated, and whenever they have anything to do with the action, they appear to advantage, and operate in a manner equally characteristic and effective. It is, perhaps, the great fault of Mr. Cooper, that, conceiving some few scenes, or even a single one, with great beauty and boldness, he discards from his mind all serious concern for the rest—for all those by which they are introduced and finished. These scenes, in consequence, rise up abruptly—and so far imposingly—like an isolated mountain wall from the dead level of a plain. We are astonished when we see them,—we wonder and admire,—but our feet have grown weary in the search for them,—we have had a long journey,—and the querulous will be apt to ask, as now they do—"fine sight, indeed, very lofty and imposing, but, was it worth while to come so far in search of it?" An equal care in the invention of the fable, at the beginning, would obviate this question. The traveller would start, as it were, in the morning of the day—a cheering sunshine above him—the green woods around him, and some merry songbirds, inviting his forward progress with the most seductive notes. Watchful when he is about to grow weary, his conductor (the novelist) suddenly points his eye to a sweet stream, which glides, like a silvery serpent, through the forest,—seen only at moments, and stealing from sight with a slow sounding but musical murmur which insensibly invites to follow. Easily beguiled, the wayfarer turns aside for an instant, and makes other discoveries. Step by step he is won along—now ravished by flowers, now startled by dreary caverns, wild precipices, and mysterious shadows of rock and forest: Now he passes rivers, and anon the cultivated fields; now he looks on lake or prairie, and now he starts with the sudden rush and tumble of the cataract. At length, towards the close of the day, he arrives at the object of his quest. The desired spectacle, whether grand and terrible, or simply beautiful and sweet, unfolds itself before him. The awful mountain, towering in forbidding grandeur before his eye, or the snow white cottage, smiling in imploring sweetness, at his feet. Around him are the companions of the day—the persons of his story—those who have joyed and those who have wept—the noble hero who led, and the envious rival who would have destroyed—the venerable form that counselled wisdom, or the dear woman that, with greater success, counselled only love. The dénouëment, whether grave or gay, has taken place, and we rejoice in a progress which has warmed our sentiments, inspired just and generous thoughts, informed our affections, and raised our minds in the contemplation of the noblest images of intellect and feelings. Such were Scott's stories. In the gradual progress of the reader, as of a traveller through a new country, the tale carried us on, step by step, from beauty to beauty, from event to event, each beauty becoming brighter and dearer, each event more exciting and interesting, until we reach the crowning event of all; completing, in a fitting manner, and with appropriate superiority, the whole continuous and marvellous history. There was no violence done to the reader's judgment—his sense of propriety or of justice. So insensible was the progress, so natural the transitions, that we gave ready faith to all his wonders; and the eyes became filled with tears, and the breathing suspended, as the events thickened and strove together; generating in our souls, hope and fear, anxious apprehensions, and those emotions, equally exciting and honourable to our nature, which awaken, in unavoidable testimony, to the skill of the consummate artist. This is the harmonious achievement. It is a tolerably easy thing to write a spirited sketch—a startling event—a hurried and passionate delineation of an action, which, in itself, involves, necessarily, strife and hate, and the wilder phrenzies of the human heart and feeling. But the perfecting of the wondrous whole—the admirable adaptation of means to ends—the fitness of parts,—the propriety of the action—the employment of the right materials,—and the fine architectural proportions of the fabric,—these are the essentials which determine the claim of the writer to be the BUILDER!—by whose standard other artists are to model,—by whose labours other labourers are to learn.

The success of *The Spy* was very great, and it at once gave Mr. Cooper reputation in Europe. It may be said to have occasioned a greater sensation in Europe than at home;—and there were good reasons for this. At that period America had no literature. Just before this time, or about this time, it was the favourite sarcasm of the British Reviewers that such a thing as an American book was never read. Mr. Irving, it is true, was writing his sweet and delicate essays; but he was not accounted in England an American writer, and he himself,—no doubt with a sufficient policy—his own fortunes alone being the subject of consideration—took no pains to assert his paternity. The publication of *The Spy* may be assumed to have been the first practical reply to a sarcasm, which, since that day, has found its ample refutation. It was immediately republished in England, and soon after, we believe, found its way into half the languages of Europe. Its farther and more important effect was upon the intellect of our own country. It at once opened the eyes of our people to their own resources. It was something of a wonder, to ourselves, that we should be able—(strange, self-destroying humility in a people springing directly from the Anglo-Norman stock)—to produce a writer who should so suddenly, and in his very first work (*Precaution* was not known and scarcely named in that day) rise to such an eminence—equalling most, excelling most, and second to but one, of the great historical romance writers of Britain. This itself was an important achievement—a step gained, without which, no other step could possibly have been taken. It need scarcely be said, that the efforts of a nation at performance,—particularly in letters and the arts,—must first be preceded by a certain consciousness of the necessary resources. This consciousness, in the case of America, was wanting. Our colonial relation to Great Britain had filled us with a feeling of intellectual dependence, of which our success in shaking off her political dominion had in no respect relieved us. We had not then, and, indeed, have not entirely to this day, arrived at any just idea of the inevitable connexion between an ability to maintain ourselves in arts as well as in arms—the ability in both cases arising only from our intellectual resources, and a manly reliance upon the just origin of national strength,—Self-dependence! To Mr. Cooper the merit is due, of having first awakened us to this self-reference,—to this consciousness of mental resources, of which our provincialism dealt, not only in constant doubts, but in constant denials. The first step is half the march, as in ordinary cases, the first blow is half the battle. With what rapidity after that did the American press operate. How many new writers rose up suddenly, the moment that their neighbours had made the discovery that there were such writers—that such writers should be. Every form of fiction, the legend, tale, novel and romance—the poem, narrative and dramatic—were poured out with a prolific abundance, which proved the possession, not only of large resources of thought, but of fancy, and of an imagination equal to every department of creative fiction. It will not matter to show that a great deal of this was crude, faulty, undigested—contracted and narrow in design, and spasmodic in execution. The demand of the country called for no more. The wonder was that, so suddenly, and at such short notice, such resources could be found as had not before been imagined. The sudden rise and progress of German literature seems to have been equally surprising and sudden—equally the result of a national impulse, newly moved in a novel and unexpected direction. The wonderful birth and progress of American letters in the last twenty years—and in every department of thought, art and science, so far from discouraging, because of its imperfections, holds forth the most signal encouragement to industry and hope—showing most clearly, that the deficiency was not in the resource but in the demand, not in the inferior quality, or limited quantity, but in the utter indifference of our people to the possession of the material.

Having struck the vein, and convinced the people not only that there was gold in the land, but that the gold of the land was good, Mr. Cooper proceeded with proper industry to supply the demand which his own genius had occasioned in the markets, as well of Europe as his own country, for his productions. *The Spy* was followed by *Lionel Lincoln, The Pioneers, The Last of the Mohicans, The Pilot, Red Rover, Prairie, Water Witch*, &c. We speak from memory—we are not so sure that we name these writings in their proper order, not is this important to us in the plan of this paper, which does not contemplate their examination in detail. All these works were

more or less interesting. In most of them, the improvement in style, continuity of narrative, propriety of incident, &c., was obvious. In all of them were obvious, in greater or less degree, the characteristics of the author. The plots were generally simple, not always coherent, and proving either an incapacity for, or an indifference to the exercise of much invention. The reader was led through long and dead levels of dialogue—sensible enough,—sometimes smart, sarcastic or playful,—occasionally marked by depth or originality of thought, and occasionally exhibiting resources of study and reflection in the departments of law and morals, which are not common to the ordinary novel writer. But these things kept us from the story,—to which they were sometimes foreign, and always in some degree, unnecessary. His characters were not often felicitous, and, as in the case of most writers, Mr. Cooper had hobbies on which he rode too often, to the great disquiet of his friends and companions. He rang the changes on words, as Scott once suffered himself to do, in the "Prodigious" of Dominie Sampson, until readers sickened of the stupidity; and occasionally, as in the case of David Gamut, mistaking his own powers of the humorous, he afflicted us with the dispensation of a bore, which qualified seriously the really meritorious in his performance. But, to compensate us for these trials of our tastes and tempers, he gave us the most exquisite scenes of minute artifice, as in his Indian stories,—in which the events were elaborated with a nicety and patience, reminding us of the spider at his web, that curious and complicated spinner, which may well be employed to illustrate by his own labours and ingenuity the subtle frame-work of Indian cunning—the labyrinth of his artifice,—his wily traps and pitfalls, and indomitable perseverance. In these details of Indian art and resource, Mr. Cooper was inimitable. In his pursuits, flights, captures,—in his encounters,—cunning opposed to cunning,—man to man—the trapper and the hunter, against the red man whose life he envies and emulates,—Mr. Cooper has no superior as he has had no master. His conception of the frontier white man, if less true than picturesque, is also not less happy as an artistical conception of great originality and effect. In him, the author embodied his ideal of the philosopher of the foremast—Hawkeye is a sailor in a hunting shirt—and in this respect he committed no error in propriety. The sailor and the forester both derive their philosophies and character from the same sources,—though the one disdains the land, and the other trembles at the sight of the sea. They both think and feel, with a highly individual nature, that has been taught, by constant contemplation, in scenes of solitude. The vast unbroken ranges of forest, to its one lonely occupant, press upon the mind with the same sort of solemnity which one feels condemned to a life of partial isolation upon the ocean. Both are permitted that degree of commerce with their fellow beings, which suffice to maintain in strength the sweet and sacred sources of their humanity. It is through these that they are commended to our sympathies, and it is through the same medium that they acquire that habit of moral musing and meditation which expresses itself finely in the most delightful of all human philosophies. The very isolation to which, in the most successful of his stories, Mr. Cooper subjects his favourite personages, is, alone, a proof of his strength and genius. While the ordinary writer, the man of mere talent, is compelled to look around him among masses for his material, he contents himself with one man, and flings him upon the wilderness. The picture then, which follows, must be one of intense individuality. Out of this one man's nature, his moods and fortunes, he spins his story. The agencies and dependencies are few. With the self-reliance which is only found in true genius, he goes forward into the wilderness, whether of land or ocean; and the vicissitudes of either region, acting upon the natural resources of one man's mind, furnish the whole material of his work-shop. This mode of performance is highly dramatic, and thus it is that his scout, his trapper, his hunter, his pilot, all live to our eyes and thoughts, the perfect ideals of moral individuality. For this we admire them—love them we do not—they are objects not made to love—they do not appeal to our affections so much as to our minds. We admire their progress through sea and forest—their strange ingenuity, the skill with which they provide against human and savage enemies, against cold and hunger, with the same sort of admiration which we feel at watching any novel progress in arts or arms—a noble ship darting like a bird over the deep, unshivering, though the storm threatens to shiver every thing else around it—a splendid piece of machinery which works to the most consummate ends by a *modus operandi*, which we yet fail to detect—any curious and complex invention which dazzles our eyes, confounds our judgment, and mocks the search which would discover its secret principles. Take, for example, the character of the Pilot, in the rapid and exciting story of that name. Here is a remarkable instance of the sort of interest which Mr. Cooper's writings are chiefly calculated to inspire. Marble could not be more inflexible than this cold, immovable, pulseless personage. He says nothing, shows nothing, promises nothing. Yet we are interested in his very first appearance. Why and how? Naturally enough by the anxiety with which he is sought and looked for;—by the fact that he promises nothing, yet goes to work, without a word, in a manner that promises every thing. We feel, at a glance, that if any mortal man can save the ship, he is the man. Why is this? Simply because he goes to work, without a word, as if it was in him to do so;—as if a calm consciousness of power was his possession; as if he knew just where to lay his hands, and in what direction to expend his strength. He shows *the capacity for work*, and this constitutes the sort of manhood upon which all men rely in moments of doubt or danger. Yet he gives you no process of reasoning—he has no word save that which commands obedience,—he neither storms, implores, nor threatens—he has no books,—he deals in no declamation. He is the ideal of an abstract but innate power, which we acknowledge and perhaps fear, but cannot fathom. All is hidden within himself, and, except when at work, he is nothing—he might as well be stone. Yet, around him,—such a man—a wonderful interest gathers like a halo—bright and inscrutable,—which fills us with equal curiosity and reverence. With him, a man of whom we know nothing,—whom we see now for the first time,—whom we may never see again,—whom we cannot love—whom we should never seek; and with his ship,—timbers, tackle, ropes, spars and cordage,—a frail fabric, such as goes to and fro along our shores, in our daily sight, without awakening a single thought or feeling;—with ship and man we grow fascinated beyond all measure of ordinary attraction. In his hands the ship becomes a being, instinct with life, beauty, sentiment—in danger, and to be saved;—and our interest in her fate, grows from our anxiety to behold the issue, in which human skill, courage and ingenuity, are to contend with storm and sea, rocks and tempest—as it were, man against omnipotence. Our interest springs from our curiosity rather than from our affections. We do not care a straw for the inmates of the vessel. They are very ordinary persons, that one man excepted—and *he* will not suffer us to love him. But *manhood*, true manhood, is a sight, always, of wondrous beauty and magnificence. The courage that looks steadily on the danger, however terrible; the

composure that never swerves from its centre under the pressure of unexpected misfortune;—the knowledge that can properly apply its strength, and the adroitness and energy, which, feeling the force of a manly will, flies to their task, in instant and hearty obedience;—these form a picture of singular beauty, and must always rivet the admiration of the spectator. We regard Mr. Cooper's Pilot—breasting the storm, tried by, and finally baffling all its powers, as the Prometheus in action—inflexible, ready to endure,—isolated, but still human in a fond loyalty to all the great hopes and interests of humanity.

Hawkeye, the land sailor of Mr. Cooper, is, with certain suitable modifications, the same personage. We see and admire, in him, the qualities of hardihood and endurance, coolness, readiness of resource, keen, clear sighted observation, just reflection, and a sincere, direct, honest heart. He is more human than the other, since, naturally of gentler temperament, the life-conflict has not left upon his mind so many traces of its volcanic fires. He has had more patience, been more easily persuaded; has endured with less struggle if not more fortitude, and, in his greater pliancy, has escaped the greater force of the tempest. But he is, in all substantial respects, the same personage, and inspires us with like feelings. In the hour of danger,—at midnight,—in the green camp of the hunter,—trembling women, timid men, and weeping children, grouped together in doubt,—all eyes turn to him, as, on the sea, in storm, all eyes address themselves to the Pilot. If any one can save them he is the man. Meanwhile, the shouts of savages are heard on every side,—the fearful whoop of slaughter;—as, on the sea, the wind howls through the ship's cordage, and the storm shrieks a requiem, in anticipation of ultimate triumph, around the shivering inmates. It is only upon true manhood that man can rely, and these are genuine men—not blocks, not feathers—neither dull, nor light of brain,—neither the stubbornly stupid, nor the frothily shallow. Now, as nothing in nature is more noble than a noble-minded, whole-souled man,—however ignorant, however poor, however deficient in imposing costume or imposing person,—so nothing, in nature, is better calculated to win the homage and command the obedience of men, than the presence of such a person in their moments of doubt and danger. It is inevitable, most usually, that such a man will save them, if they are to be saved by human agency. To Mr. Cooper we owe several specimens of this sort of moral manhood. It does not qualify our obligation to him, that they have their little defects,—that he has sometimes failed to hit the true line that divides the simplicity of nature, from the puerility of ignorance or childhood. His pictures are as perfect, of their kind, as the artist of fiction has ever given us. We say this after due reflection.

FRANCIS PARKMAN
From "James Fenimore Cooper"
North American Review, January 1852, pp. 147–58

No American writer has been so extensively read as James Fenimore Cooper. His novels have been translated into nearly every European tongue. Nay, we are told—but hardly know how to believe it—that they may be had duly rendered into Persian at the bazaars of Ispahan. We have seen some of them, well thumbed and worn, at a little village in a remote mountainous district of Sicily; and in Naples and Milan, the bookstalls bear witness that *L'Ultimo dei Mohecanni* is still a popular work. In England, these American novels have been eagerly read and transformed into popular dramas; while cheap and often stupidly mutilated editions of them have been circulated through all her colonies, garrisons, and naval stations, from New Zealand to Canada.

Nor is this widely spread popularity undeserved. Of all American writers, Cooper is the most original, the most thoroughly national. His genius drew aliment from the soil where God had planted it, and rose to a vigorous growth, rough and gnarled, but strong as a mountain cedar. His volumes are a faithful mirror of that rude transatlantic nature, which to European eyes appears so strange and new. The sea and the forest have been the scenes of his countrymen's most conspicuous achievements; and it is on the sea and in the forest that Cooper is most at home. Their spirit inspired him, their images were graven on his heart; and the men whom their embrace has nurtured, the sailor, the hunter, the pioneer, move and act upon his pages with all the truth and energy of real life.

There is one great writer with whom Cooper has been often compared, and the comparison is not void of justice; for though, on the whole, far inferior, there are certain high points of literary excellence in regard to which he may contest the palm with Sir Walter Scott. It is true, that he has no claim to share the humor and pathos, the fine perception of beauty and delicacy in character, which adds such charms to the romances of Scott. Nor can he boast that compass and variety of power, which could deal alike with forms of humanity so diverse; which could portray with equal mastery the Templar Bois Guilbert, and the Jewess Rebecca; the manly heart of Henry Morton, and the gentle heroism of Jeanie Deans. But notwithstanding this unquestioned inferiority on the part of Cooper, there were marked affinities between him and his great contemporary. Both were practical men, able and willing to grapple with the hard realities of the world. Either might have learned with ease to lead a regiment, or command a line-of-battle ship. Their conceptions of character were no mere abstract ideas, or unsubstantial images, but solid embodiments in living flesh and blood. Bulwer and Hawthorne—the conjunction may excite a smile—are writers of a different stamp. Their conceptions are often exhibited with consummate skill, and, in one of these examples at least, with admirable truthfulness; but they never cheat us into a belief of their reality. We may marvel at the skill of the artist, but we are prone to regard his creations rather as figments of art than as reproductions of nature,—as a series of vivified and animate pictures, rather than as breathing men and women. With Scott and with Cooper it is far otherwise. Dominie Sampson and the Antiquary are as distinct and familiar to our minds as some eccentric acquaintance of our childhood. If we met Long Tom Coffin on the wharf at New Bedford, we should wonder where we had before seen that familiar face and figure. The tall, gaunt form of Leatherstocking, the weather-beaten face, the bony hand, the cap of fox-skin, and the old hunting frock, polished with long service, seem so palpable and real, that, in some moods of mind, one may easily confound them with the memories of his own experiences. Others have been gifted to conceive the elements of far loftier character, and even to combine these elements in a manner equally truthful; but few have rivalled Cooper in the power of breathing into his creations the breath of life, and turning the phantoms of his brain into seeming realities. It is to this, in no small measure, that he owes his widely spread popularity. His most successful portraitures are drawn, it is true, from humble walks and rude associations; yet they are instinct with life, and stamped with the impress of a masculine and original genius.

The descriptions of external nature with which Cooper's

works abound bear a certain analogy to his portraitures of character. There is no glow upon his pictures, no warm and varied coloring, no studied contrast of light and shade. Their virtue consists in their fidelity, in the strength with which they impress themselves upon the mind, and the strange tenacity with which they cling to the memory. For our own part, it was many years since we had turned the pages of Cooper, but still we were haunted by the images which his spell had evoked;—the dark gleaming of hill-embosomed lakes, the tracery of forest boughs against the red evening sky, and the raven flapping his black wings above the carnage field near the Horican. These descriptions have often, it must be confessed, the grave fault of being overloaded with detail; but they are utterly mistaken who affirm, as some have done, that they are but a catalogue of commonplaces,—mountains and woods, rivers and torrents, thrown together as a matter of course. A genuine love of nature inspired the artist's pen; and they who cannot feel the efficacy of its strong picturing have neither heart nor mind for the grandeur of the outer world.

Before proceeding, however, we must observe that, in speaking of Cooper's writings, we have reference only to those happier offspring of his genius which form the basis of his reputation; for, of that numerous progeny which of late years have swarmed from his pen, we have never read one, and therefore, notwithstanding the ancient usage of reviewers, do not think ourselves entitled to comment upon them.

The style of Cooper is, as style must always be, in no small measure the exponent of the author's mind. It is not elastic or varied, and is certainly far from elegant. Its best characteristics are a manly directness, and a freedom from those prettinesses, studied turns of expression, and petty tricks of rhetoric, which are the pride of less masculine writers. Cooper is no favorite with *dilettanti* critics. In truth, such criticism does not suit his case. He should be measured on deeper principles, not by his manner, but by his pith and substance. A rough diamond, and he is one of the roughest, is worth more than a jewel of paste, though its facets may not shine so clearly.

And yet, try Cooper by what test we may, we shall discover in him grave defects. The field of his success is, after all, a narrow one, and even in his best works he often oversteps its limits. His attempts at sentiment are notoriously unsuccessful. Above all, when he aspires to portray a heroine, no words can express the remarkable character of the product. With simple country girls he succeeds somewhat better; but when he essays a higher flight, his failure is calamitous. The most rabid asserter of the rights of woman is scarcely more ignorant of woman's true power and dignity. This is the more singular, as his novels are very far from being void of feeling. They seldom, however—and who can wonder at it?—find much favor with women, who for the most part can see little in them but ghastly stories of shipwrecks, ambuscades, and bush fights, mingled with prolix descriptions and stupid dialogues. Their most appreciating readers may perhaps be found, not among persons of sedentary and studious habits, but among those of a more active turn, military officers and the like, whose tastes have not been trained into fastidiousness, and who are often better qualified than literary men to feel the freshness and truth of the author's descriptions.

The merit of a novelist is usually measured less by his mere power of description than by his skill in delineating character. The permanency of Cooper's reputation must, as it seems to us, rest upon three or four finely conceived and admirably executed portraits. We do not allude to his Indian characters, which it must be granted, are for the most part either superficially or falsely drawn; while the long conversations which he puts into their mouths, are as truthless as they are tiresome. Such as they are, however, they have been eagerly copied by a legion of the smaller poets and novel writers; so that, jointly with Thomas Campbell, Cooper is responsible for the fathering of those aboriginal heroes, lovers, and sages, who have long formed a petty nuisance in our literature. The portraits of which we have spoken are all those of white men, from humble ranks of society, yet not of a mean or vulgar stamp. Conspicuous before them all stands the well known figure of Leatherstocking. The life and character of this personage are contained in a series of five independent novels, entitled, in honor of him, *The Leatherstocking Tales*. Cooper has been censured, and even ridiculed, for this frequent reproduction of his favorite hero, which, it is affirmed, argues poverty of invention; and yet there is not one of the tales in question with which we would willingly part. To have drawn such a character is in itself sufficient honor; and had Cooper achieved nothing else, this alone must have insured him a wide and merited renown. There is something admirably felicitous in the conception of this hybrid offspring of civilization and barbarism, in whom uprightness, kindliness, innate philosophy, and the truest moral perceptions are joined with the wandering instincts and hatred of restraint which stamp the Indian or the Bedouin. Nor is the character in the least unnatural. The white denizens of the forest and the prairie are often among the worst, though never among the meanest, of mankind; but it is equally true, that where the moral instincts are originally strong, they may find nutriment and growth among the rude scenes and grand associations of the wilderness. Men as true, generous, and kindly as Leatherstocking may still be found among the perilous solitudes of the West. The quiet, unostentatious courage of Cooper's hero had its counterpart in the character of Daniel Boone; and the latter had the same unaffected love of nature which forms so pleasing a feature in the mind of Leatherstocking.

Civilization has a destroying as well as a creating power. It is exterminating the buffalo and the Indian, over whose fate too many lamentations, real or affected, have been sounded for us to renew them here. It must, moreover, eventually sweep from before it a class of men, its own precursors and pioneers, so remarkable both in their virtues and their faults, that few will see their extinction without regret. Of these men Leatherstocking is the representative; and though in him the traits of the individual are quite as prominent as those of the class, yet his character is not on this account less interesting, or less worthy of permanent remembrance. His life conveys in some sort an epitome of American history, during one of its most busy and decisive periods. At first, we find him a lonely young hunter in what was then the wilderness of New York. Ten or twelve years later, he is playing his part manfully in the Old French War. After the close of the Revolution, we meet him again on the same spot where he was first introduced to us; but now every thing is changed. The solitary margin of the Otsego lake is transformed into the seat of a growing settlement, and the hunter, oppressed by the restraints of society, turns his aged footsteps westward in search of his congenial solitudes. At length, we discover him for the last time, an octogenarian trapper, far out on the prairies of the West. It is clear that the successive stages of his retreat from society could not well be presented in a single story, and that the repetition which has been charged against Cooper as a fault was indispensable to the development of his design.

The Deerslayer, the first novel in the series of the *Leatherstocking Tales*, seems to us one of the most interesting of Coo-

per's productions. He has chosen for the scene of his story the Otsego lake, on whose banks he lived and died, and whose scenery he has introduced into three, if not more, of his novels. The Deerslayer, or Leatherstocking, here makes his first appearance as a young man, in fact scarcely emerged from boyhood, yet with all the simplicity, candor, feeling, and penetration, which mark his riper years. The old buccaneer in his aquatic habitation, and the contrasted characters of his two daughters, add a human interest to the scene, for the want of which the highest skill in mere landscape painting cannot compensate. The character of Judith seems to us the best drawn, and by far the most interesting, female portrait in any of Cooper's novels with which we are acquainted. The story, however, is not free from the characteristic faults of its author. Above all, it contains, in one instance at least, a glaring exhibition of his aptitude for describing horrors. When he compels his marvellously graphic pen to depict scenes which would disgrace the shambles or the dissecting table, none can wonder that ladies and young clergymen regard his pages with abhorrence. These, however, are but casual defects in a work which bears the unmistakable impress of genius.

The Pathfinder forms the second volume of the series, and is remarkable, even among its companions, for the force and distinctness of its pictures. For ourselves—though we diligently perused the despatches—the battle of Palo Alto and the storming of Monterey are not more real and present to our mind than some of the scenes and characters of *The Pathfinder*, though we have not read it for nine years;—the little fort on the margin of Lake Ontario, the surrounding woods and waters, the veteran major in command, the treacherous Scotchman, the dogmatic old sailor, and the Pathfinder himself. Several of these scenes are borrowed in part from Mrs. Grant's *Memoirs of an American Lady*; but in borrowing, Cooper has transmuted shadows into substance. Mrs. Grant's facts—for as such we are to take them—have an air of fiction; while Cooper's fiction wears the aspect of solid fact. His peculiar powers could not be better illustrated than by a comparison of the passages alluded to in the two books.

One of the most widely known of Cooper's novels is *The Last of the Mohicans*, which forms the third volume of the series, and which, with all the elements of a vulgar popularity, combines excellences of a far higher order. It has, nevertheless, its great and obtrusive faults. It takes needless liberties with history; and though it would be folly to demand that an historical novelist should always conform to received authorities, yet it is certainly desirable that he should not unnecessarily set them at defiance; since the incidents of the novel are apt to remain longer in the memory than those of the less palatable history. But whatever may be the extent of the novelist's license, it is, at all events, essential that his story should have some semblance of probability, and not run counter to nature and common sense. In *The Last of the Mohicans*, the machinery of the plot falls little short of absurdity. Why a veteran officer, pent up in a little fort, and hourly expecting to be beleaguered by a vastly superior force, consisting in great part of bloodthirsty savages, should at that particular time desire or permit a visit from his two daughters, is a question not easy to answer. Nor is the difficulty lessened when it is remembered, that the young ladies are to make the journey through a wilderness full of Indian scalping parties. It is equally difficult to see why the lover of Alice should choose, merely for the sake of a romantic ride, to conduct her and her sister by a circuitous and most perilous by-path through the forests, when they might more easily have gone by a good road under the safe escort of a column of troops who marched for the fort that very morning. The story founded on these gross inventions is sustained by various minor improbabilities, which cannot escape the reader unless his attention is absorbed by the powerful interest of the narrative.

It seems to us a defect in a novel or a poem, when the heroine is compelled to undergo bodily hardship, to sleep out at night in the woods, drenched by rain, stung by mosquitos and scratched by briars,—to forego all appliances of the toilet, and above all, to lodge in an Indian wigwam. Women have sometimes endured such privation, and endured it with fortitude; but it may be safely affirmed, that for the time, all grace and romance were banished from their presence. We read Longfellow's *Evangeline* with much sympathy in the fortunes of the errant heroine, until, as we approached the end of the poem, every other sentiment was lost in admiration at the unparalleled extent of her wanderings, at the dexterity with which she contrived to elude at least a dozen tribes of savages at that time in a state of war, at the strength of her constitution, and at her marvellous proficiency in woodcraft. When, however, we had followed her for about two thousand miles on her forest pilgrimage, and reflected on the figure she must have made, so tattered and bepatched, bedrenched and bedraggled, we could not but esteem it a happy circumstance that she failed, as she did, to meet her lover; since, had he seen her in such plight, every spark of sentiment must have vanished from his breast, and all the romance of the poem have been ingloriously extinguished. With Cooper's heroines, Cora and Alice, the case is not so hard. Yet, as it does not appear that, on a journey of several weeks, they were permitted to carry so much as a valise or a carpet bag, and as we are expressly told, that on several occasions, they dropped by the wayside their gloves, veils, and other useful articles of apparel, it is certain, that at the journey's end, they must have presented an appearance more adapted to call forth a Christian sympathy than any emotion of a more romantic nature.

In respect to the delineation of character, *The Last of the Mohicans* is surpassed by several other works of the author. Its distinguishing merit lies in its descriptions of scenery and action. Of the personages who figure in it, one of the most interesting is the young Mohican, Uncas, who, however, does not at all resemble a genuine Indian. Magua, the villain of the story, is a less untruthful portrait. Cooper has been criticized for having represented him as falling in love with Cora; and the criticism is based on the alleged ground that passions of this kind are not characteristic of the Indian. This may, in some qualified sense, be true; but it is well known that Indians, in real life as well as in novels, display a peculiar partiality for white women, on the same principle by which Italians are prone to admire a light complexion, while Swedes regard a brunette with highest esteem. Cora was the very person to fascinate an Indian. The coldest warrior would gladly have received her into his lodge, and promoted her to be his favorite wife, wholly dispensing, in honor of her charms, with flagellation or any of the severer marks of conjugal displeasure.

The character of Hawkeye or Leatherstocking is, in the *Mohicans* as elsewhere, clearly and admirably drawn. He often displays, however, a weakness which excites the impatience of the reader,—an excessive and ill-timed loquacity. When, for example, in the fight at Glenn's Falls, he and Major Heywood are crouching in the thicket, watching the motions of four Indians, whose heads are visible above a log at a little distance, and who, in the expression of Hawkeye himself, are gathering for a rush, the scout employs the time in dilating upon the properties of the "long-barrelled, soft-metalled rifle." The design is, no doubt, to convey an impression of his coolness in

moments of extreme danger; but under such circumstances, the bravest man would judge it the part of good sense to use his eyes rather than his tongue. Men of Hawkeye's class, however talkative they may be at the camp-fire, are remarkable for preserving a close silence while engaged in the active labors of their calling.

It is easy to find fault with *The Last of the Mohicans*; but it is far from easy to rival or even approach its excellences. The book has the genuine game flavor; it exhales the odors of the pine woods and the freshness of the mountain wind. Its dark and rugged scenery rises as distinctly on the eye as the images of the painter's canvas, or rather as the reflection of nature herself. But it is not as the mere rendering of material forms, that these wood paintings are most highly to be esteemed. They are instinct with life, with the very spirit of the wilderness; they breathe the sombre poetry of solitude and danger. In these achievements of his art, Cooper, we think, has no equal, unless it may be the author of that striking romance, Wacousta or the Prophecy, whose fine powers of imagination are, however, even less under the guidance of a just taste than those of the American novelist.

The most obvious merit of *The Last of the Mohicans* consists in its descriptions of action, in the power with which the author absorbs the reader's sympathies, and leads him, as it were, to play a part in the scene. One reads the accounts of a great battle—aside from any cause or principle at issue—with the same kind of interest with which he beholds the grand destructive phenomena of nature, a tempest at sea, or a tornado in the tropics; yet with a feeling far more intense, since the conflict is not a mere striving of insensate elements, but of living tides of human wrath and valor. With descriptions of petty skirmishes or single combats, the feeling is of a different kind. The reader is enlisted in the fray, a partaker, as it were, in every thought and movement of the combatants, in the alternations of fear and triumph, the prompt expedient, the desperate resort, the palpitations of human weakness, or the courage that faces death. Of this species of description, the scene of the conflict at Glenn's Falls is an admirable example, unsurpassed, we think, even by the combat of Balfour and Bothwell, or by any other passage of the kind in the novels of Scott. The scenery of the fight, the foaming cataract, the little islet with its stout-hearted defenders, the precipices and the dark pine woods, add greatly to the effect. The scene is conjured before the reader's eye, not as a vision or a picture, but like the tangible presence of rock, river, and forest. His very senses seem conspiring to deceive him. He seems to feel against his cheek the wind and spray of the cataract, and hear its sullen roar, amid the yells of the assailants and the sharp crack of the answering rifle. The scene of the strife is pointed out to travellers as if this fictitious combat were a real event of history. Mills, factories, and bridges have marred the native wildness of the spot, and a village has usurped the domain of the forest; yet still those foaming waters and black sheets of limestone rock are clothed with all the interest of an historic memory; and the cicerone of the place can show the caves where the affrighted sisters took refuge, the point where the Indians landed, and the rock whence the despairing Huron was flung into the abyss. Nay, if the lapse of a few years has not enlightened his understanding, the guide would as soon doubt the reality of the battle of Saratoga, as that of Hawkeye's fight with the Mingoes.

The Pioneers, the fourth volume of the series, is, in several respects, the best of Cooper's works. Unlike some of its companions, it bears every mark of having been written from the results of personal experience; and indeed, Cooper is well known to have drawn largely on the recollections of his earlier years in the composition of this novel. The characters are full of vitality and truth, though, in one or two instances, the excellence of delineation is impaired by a certain taint of vulgarity. Leatherstocking, as he appears in *The Pioneers*, must certainly have had his living original in some gaunt, gray-haired old woodsman, to whose stories of hunts and Indian fights the author may perhaps have listened in his boyhood with rapt ears, unconsciously garnering up in memory the germs which time was to develop into a rich harvest. The scenes of the Christmas turkey-shooting, the fish-spearing by firelight on Otsego lake, the rescue from the panther, and the burning of the woods, are all inimitable in their way. Of all Cooper's works, *The Pioneers* seems to us most likely to hold a permanent place in literature, for it preserves a vivid reflection of scenes and characters which will soon have passed away.

The Prairie, the last of the *Leatherstocking Tales*, is a novel of far inferior merit. The story is very improbable, and not very interesting. The pictures of scenery are less true to nature than in the previous volumes, and seem to indicate that Cooper had little or no personal acquaintance with the remoter parts of the West. The book, however, has several passages of much interest, one of the best of which is the scene in which the aged trapper discovers, in the person of a young officer, the grandson of Duncan Heywood and Alice Munro, whom, half a century before, he had protected when in such imminent jeopardy on the rocks of Glenn's Falls and among the mountains of Lake George. The death of Abiram White is very striking, though reminding the reader too much of a similar scene in the *Spy*. The grand deformity of the story is the wretched attempt at humor in the person of Dr. Obed Battius. David Gamut, in *The Mohicans*, is bad enough; but Battius outherods Herod, and great must be the merit of the book which one such incubus can not sink beyond redemption.

The novel, which first brought the name of Cooper into distinguished notice, was *The Spy*; and this book, which gave him his earliest reputation, will contribute largely to preserve it. The story is full of interest, and the character of Harvey Birch is drawn with singular skill.

The Pilot is usually considered the best of Cooper's sea tales. It is in truth a masterpiece of his genius; and although the reader is apt to pass with impatience over the long conversations among the ladies at St. Ruth's, and between Alice Dunscombe and the disguised Paul Jones, yet he is amply repaid when he follows the author to his congenial element. The description of the wreck of the Ariel, and the death of Long Tom Coffin, can scarcely be spoken of in terms of too much admiration. Long Tom is to Cooper's sea tales what Leatherstocking is to the novels of the forest,—a conception so original and forcible, that posterity will hardly suffer it to escape from remembrance. *The Red Rover, The Water-Witch*, and the remainder of the sea tales, are marked with the same excellences and defects with the novels already mentioned, and further comments would therefore be useless.

MARK TWAIN

"Fenimore Cooper's Literary Offences"

North American Review, July 1895, pp. 1–12

The Pathfinder and *The Deerslayer* stand at the head of Cooper's novels as artistic creations. There are others of his works which contain parts as perfect as are to be found in these, and scenes even more

thrilling. Not one can be compared with either of them as a finished whole.

The defects in both of these tales are comparatively slight. They were pure works of art.—*Prof. Lounsbury*.

The five tales reveal an extraordinary fulness of invention.

. . . One of the very greatest characters in fiction, Natty Bumppo. . . .

The craft of the woodsman, the tricks of the trapper, all the delicate art of the forest, were familiar to Cooper from his youth up.—*Prof. Brander Matthews*.

Cooper is the greatest artist in the domain of romantic fiction yet produced by America.—*Wilkie Collins*.

It seems to me that it was far from right for the Professor of English Literature in Yale, the Professor of English Literature in Columbia, and Wilkie Collins to deliver opinions on Cooper's literature without having read some of it. It would have been much more decorous to keep silent and let persons talk who have read Cooper.

Cooper's art has some defects. In once place in *Deerslayer*, and in the restricted space of two-thirds of a page, Cooper has scored 114 offences against literary art out of a possible 115. It breaks the record.

There are nineteen rules governing literary art in the domain of romantic fiction—some say twenty-two. In *Deerslayer* Cooper violated eighteen of them. These eighteen require:

1. That a tale shall accomplish something and arrive somewhere. But the *Deerslayer* tale accomplishes nothing and arrives in the air.

2. They require that the episodes of a tale shall be necessary parts of the tale, and shall help to develop it. But as the *Deerslayer* tale is not a tale, and accomplishes nothing and arrives nowhere, the episodes have no rightful place in the work, since there was nothing for them to develop.

3. They require that the personages in a tale shall be alive, except in the case of corpses, and that always the reader shall be able to tell the corpses from the others. But this detail has often been overlooked in the *Deerslayer* tale.

4. They require that the personages in a tale, both dead and alive, shall exhibit a sufficient excuse for being there. But this detail also has been overlooked in the *Deerslayer* tale.

5. They require that when the personages of a tale deal in conversation, the talk shall sound like human talk, and be talk such as human beings would be likely to talk in the given circumstances, and have a discoverable meaning, also a discoverable purpose, and a show of relevancy, and remain in the neighborhood of the subject in hand, and be interesting to the reader, and help out the tale, and stop when the people cannot think of anything more to say. But this requirement has been ignored from the beginning of the *Deerslayer* tale to the end of it.

6. They require that when the author describes the character of a personage in his tale, the conduct and conversation of that personage shall justify said description. But this law gets little or no attention in the *Deerslayer* tale, as Natty Bumppo's case will amply prove.

7. They require that when a personage talks like an illustrated, gilt-edged, tree-calf, hand-tooled, seven-dollar Friendship's Offering in the beginning of a paragraph, he shall not talk like a negro minstrel in the end of it. But this rule is flung down and danced upon in the *Deerslayer* tale.

8. They require that crass stupidities shall not be played upon the reader as "the craft of the woodsman, the delicate art of the forest," by either the author or the people in the tale. But this rule is persistently violated in the *Deerslayer* tale.

9. They require that the personages of a tale shall confine themselves to possibilities and let miracles alone; or, if they venture a miracle, the author must so plausibly set it forth as to make it look possible and reasonable. But these rules are not respected in the *Deerslayer* tale.

10. They require that the author shall make the reader feel a deep interest in the personages of his tale and in their fate; and that he shall make the reader love the good people in the tale and hate the bad ones. But the reader of the *Deerslayer* tale dislikes the good people in it, is indifferent to the others, and wishes they would all get drowned together.

11. They require that the characters in a tale shall be so clearly defined that the reader can tell beforehand what each will do in a given emergency. But in the *Deerslayer* tale this rule is vacated.

In addition to these large rules there are some little ones. These require that the author shall

12. *Say* what he is proposing to say, not merely come near it.

13. Use the right word, not its second cousin.

14. Eschew surplusage.

15. Not omit necessary details.

16. Avoid slovenliness of form.

17. Use good grammar.

18. Employ a simple and straightforward style.

Even these seven are coldly and persistently violated in the *Deerslayer* tale.

Cooper's gift in the way of invention was not a rich endowment; but such as it was he liked to work it, he was pleased with the effects, and indeed he did some quite sweet things with it. In his little box of stage properties he kept six or eight cunning devices, tricks, artifices of his savages and woodsmen to deceive and circumvent each other with, and he was never so happy as when he was working these innocent things and seeing them go. A favorite one was to make a moccasined person tread in the tracks of the moccasined enemy, and thus hide his own trail. Cooper wore out barrels and barrels of moccasins in working that trick. Another stage-property that he pulled out of his box pretty frequently was his broken twig. He prized his broken twig above all the rest of his effects, and worked it the hardest. It is a restful chapter in any book of his when somebody doesn't step on a dry twig and alarm all the reds and whites for two hundred yards around. Every time a Cooper person is in peril, and absolute silence is worth four dollars a minute, he is sure to step on a dry twig. There may be a hundred handier things to step on, but that wouldn't satisfy Cooper. Cooper requires him to turn out and find a dry twig; and if he can't do it, go and borrow one. In fact, the Leather Stocking Series ought to have been called the Broken Twig Series.

I am sorry there is not room to put in a few dozen instances of the delicate art of the forest, as practised by Natty Bumppo and some of the other Cooperian experts. Perhaps we may venture two or three samples. Cooper was a sailor—a naval officer; yet he gravely tells us how a vessel, driving towards a lee shore in a gale, is steered for a particular spot by her skipper because he knows of an *undertow* there which will hold her back against the gale and save her. For just pure woodcraft, or sailorcraft, or whatever it is, isn't that neat? For several years Cooper was daily in the society of artillery, and he ought to have noticed that when a cannon-ball strikes the

ground it either buries itself or skips a hundred feet or so; skips again a hundred feet or so—and so on, till finally it gets tired and rolls. Now in one place he loses some "females"—as he always calls women—in the edge of a wood near a plain at night in a fog, on purpose to give Bumppo a chance to show off the delicate art of the forest before the reader. These mislaid people are hunting for a fort. They hear a cannon-blast, and a cannon-ball presently comes rolling into the wood and stops at their feet. To the females this suggests nothing. The case is very different with the admirable Bumppo. I wish I may never know peace again if he doesn't strike out promptly and *follow the track* of that cannon-ball across the plain through the dense fog and find the fort. Isn't it a daisy? If Cooper had any real knowledge of Nature's ways of doing things, he had a most delicate art in concealing the fact. For instance: one of his acute Indian experts, Chingachgook (pronounced Chicago, I think), has lost the trail of a person he is tracking through the forest. Apparently that trail is hopelessly lost. Neither you nor I could ever have guessed out the way to find it. It was very different with Chicago. Chicago was not stumped for long. He turned a running stream out of its course, and there, in the slush in its old bed, were that person's moccasin-tracks. The current did not wash them away, as it would have done in all other like cases—no, even the eternal laws of Nature have to vacate when Cooper wants to put up a delicate job of woodcraft on the reader.

We must be a little wary when Brander Matthews tells us that Cooper's books "reveal an extraordinary fulness of invention." As a rule, I am quite willing to accept Brander Matthews's literary judgments and applaud his lucid and graceful phrasing of them; but that particular statement needs to be taken with a few tons of salt. Bless your heart, Cooper hadn't any more invention than a horse; and I don't mean a high-class horse, either; I mean a clothes-horse. It would be very difficult to find a really clever "situation" in Cooper's books, and still more difficult to find one of any kind which he has failed to render absurd by his handling of it. Look at the episodes of "the caves"; and at the celebrated scuffle between Maqua and those others on the table-land a few days later; and at Hurry Harry's queer water-transit from the castle to the ark; and at Deerslayer's half-hour with his first corpse; and at the quarrel between Hurry Harry and Deerslayer later; and at—but choose for yourself; you can't go amiss.

If Cooper had been an observer his inventive faculty would have worked better; not more interestingly, but more rationally, more plausibly. Cooper's proudest creations in the way of "situations" suffer noticeably from the absence of the observer's protecting gift. Cooper's eye was splendidly inaccurate. Cooper seldom saw anything correctly. He saw nearly all things as through a glass eye, darkly. Of course a man who cannot see the commonest little every-day matters accurately is working at a disadvantage when he is constructing a "situation." In the *Deerslayer* tale Cooper has a stream which is fifty feet wide where it flows out of a lake; it presently narrows to twenty as it meanders along for no given reason, and yet when a stream acts like that it ought to be required to explain itself. Fourteen pages later the width of the brook's outlet from the lake has suddenly shrunk thirty feet, and become "the narrowest part of the stream." This shrinkage is not accounted for. The stream has bends in it, a sure indication that it has alluvial banks and cuts them; yet these bends are only thirty and fifty feet long. If Cooper had been a nice and punctilious observer he would have noticed that the bends were oftener nine hundred feet long than short of it.

Cooper made the exit of that stream fifty feet wide, in the

first place, for no particular reason; in the second place, he narrowed it to less than twenty to accommodate some Indians. He bends a "sapling" to the form of an arch over this narrow passage, and conceals six Indians in its foliage. They are "laying" for a settler's scow or ark which is coming up the stream on its way to the lake; it is being hauled against the stiff current by a rope whose stationary end is anchored in the lake; its rate of progress cannot be more than a mile an hour. Cooper describes the ark, but pretty obscurely. In the matter of dimensions "it was little more than a modern canal-boat." Let us guess, then, that it was about one hundred and forty feet long. It was of "greater breadth than common." Let us guess, then, that it was about sixteen feet wide. This leviathan had been prowling down bends which were but a third as long as itself, and scraping between banks where it had only two feet of space to spare on each side. We cannot too much admire this miracle. A low-roofed log dwelling occupies "two-thirds of the ark's length"—a dwelling ninety feet long and sixteen feet wide, let us say—a kind of vestibule train. The dwelling has two rooms—each forty-five feet long and sixteen feet wide, let us guess. One of them is the bedroom of the Hutter girls, Judith and Hetty; the other is the parlor in the daytime, at night it is papa's bedchamber. The ark is arriving at the stream's exit now, whose width has been reduced to less than twenty feet to accommodate the Indians—say to eighteen. There is a foot to spare on each side of the boat. Did the Indians notice that there was going to be a tight squeeze there? Did they notice that they could make money by climbing down out of that arched sapling and just stepping aboard when the ark scraped by? No, other Indians would have noticed these things, but Cooper's Indians never notice anything. Cooper thinks they are marvelous creatures for noticing, but he was almost always in error about his Indians. There was seldom a sane one among them.

The ark is one hundred and forty feet long; the dwelling is ninety feet long. The idea of the Indians is to drop softly and secretly from the arched sapling to the dwelling as the ark creeps along under it at the rate of a mile an hour, and butcher the family. It will take the ark a minute and a half to pass under. It will take the ninety foot dwelling a minute to pass under. Now, then, what did the six Indians do? It would take you thirty years to guess, and even then you would have to give it up, I believe. Therefore, I will tell you what the Indians did. Their chief, a person of quite extraordinary intellect for a Cooper Indian, warily watched the canal-boat as it squeezed along under him, and when he had got his calculations fined down to exactly the right shade, as he judged, he let go and dropped. And *missed the house!* That is actually what he did. He missed the house, and landed in the stern of the scow. It was not much of a fall, yet it knocked him silly. He lay there unconscious. If the house had been ninety-seven feet long he would have made the trip. The fault was Cooper's, not his. The error lay in the construction of the house. Cooper was no architect.

There still remained in the roost five Indians. The boat has passed under and is now out of their reach. Let me explain what the five did—you would not be able to reason it out for yourself. No. 1 jumped for the boat, but fell in the water astern of it. Then No. 2 jumped for the boat, but fell in the water still farther astern of it. Then No. 3 jumped for the boat, and fell a good way astern of it. Then No. 4 jumped for the boat, and fell in the water *away* astern. Then even No. 5 made a jump for the boat—for he was a Cooper Indian. In the matter of intellect, the difference between a Cooper Indian and the Indian that stands in front of the cigar-shop is not spacious. The scow episode is really a sublime burst of invention; but it

does not thrill, because the inaccuracy of the details throws a sort of air of fictitiousness and general improbability over it. This comes of Cooper's inadequacy as an observer.

The reader will find some examples of Cooper's high talent for inaccurate observation in the account of the shooting-match in *The Pathfinder*.

A common wrought nail was driven lightly into the target, its head having been first touched with paint.

The color of the paint is not stated—an important omission, but Cooper deals freely in important omissions. No, after all, it was not an important omission; for this nail-head is *a hundred yards from* the marksmen, and could not be seen by them at that distance, no matter what its color might be. How far can the best eyes see a common house-fly? A hundred yards? It is quite impossible. Very well; eyes that cannot see a house-fly that is a hundred yards away cannot see an ordinary nail-head at that distance, for the size of the two objects is the same. It takes a keen eye to see a fly or a nailhead at fifty yards—one hundred and fifty feet. Can the reader do it?

The nail was lightly driven, its head painted, and game called. Then the Cooper miracles began. The bullet of the first marksman chipped an edge of the nail-head; the next man's bullet drove the nail a little way into the target—and removed all the paint. Haven't the miracles gone far enough now? Not to suit Cooper; for the purpose of this whole scheme is to show off his prodigy, Deerslayer-Hawkeye-Long-Rifle-Leather-Stocking-Pathfinder-Bumppo before the ladies.

"Be all ready to clench it, boys!" cried out Pathfinder, stepping into his friend's tracks the instant they were vacant. "Never mind a new nail; I can see that, though the paint is gone, and what I can see I can hit at a hundred yards, though it were only a mosquito's eye. Be ready to clench!"

The rifle cracked, the bullet sped its way, and the head of the nail was buried in the wood, covered by the piece of flattened lead.

There, you see, is a man who could hunt flies with a rifle, and command a ducal salary in a Wild West show to-day if we had him back with us.

The recorded feat is certainly surprising just as it stands; but it is not surprising enough for Cooper. Cooper adds a touch. He has made Pathfinder do this miracle with another man's rifle; and not only that, but Pathfinder did not have even the advantage of loading it himself. He had everything against him, and yet he made that impossible shot; and not only made it, but did it with absolute confidence, saying, "Be ready to clench." Now a person like that would have undertaken that same feat with a brickbat, and with Cooper to help he would have achieved it, too.

Pathfinder showed off handsomely that day before the ladies. His very first feat was a thing which no Wild West show can touch. He was standing with the group of marksmen, observing—a hundred yards from the target, mind; one Jasper raised his rifle and drove the centre of the bull's-eye. Then the Quartermaster fired. The target exhibited no result this time. There was a laugh. "It's a dead miss," said Major Lundie. Pathfinder waited an impressive moment or two; then said, in that calm, indifferent, know-it-all way of his, "No, Major, he has covered Jasper's bullet, as will be seen if any one will take the trouble to examine the target."

Wasn't it remarkable! How *could* he see that little pellet fly through the air and enter that distant bullet-hole? Yet that is what he did; for nothing is impossible to a Cooper person. Did any of those people have any deep-seated doubts about this thing? No; for that would imply sanity, and these were all Cooper people.

The respect for Pathfinder's skill and for his *quickness and accuracy of sight* (the italics are mine) was so profound and general, that the instant he made this declaration the spectators began to distrust their own opinions, and a dozen rushed to the target in order to ascertain the fact. There, sure enough, it was found that the Quartermaster's bullet had gone through the hole made by Jasper's, and that, too, so accurately as to require a minute examination to be certain of the circumstance, which, however, was soon clearly established by discovering one bullet over the other in the stump against which the target was placed.

The made a "minute" examination; but never mind, how could they know that there were two bullets in that hole without digging the latest one out? for neither probe nor eyesight could prove the presence of any more than one bullet. Did they dig? No; as we shall see. It is the Pathfinder's turn now; he steps out before the ladies, takes aim, and fires.

But, alas! here is a disappointment; an incredible, an unimaginable disappointment—for the target's aspect is unchanged; there is nothing there but that same old bullet-hole!

"If one dared to hint at such a thing," cried Major Duncan, "I should say that the Pathfinder has also missed the target!"

As nobody had missed it yet, the "also" was not necessary; but never mind about that, for the Pathfinder is going to speak.

"No, no, Major," said he, confidently, "that *would* be a risky declaration. I didn't load the piece, and can't say what was in it; but if it was lead, you will find the bullet driving down those of the Quartermaster and Jasper, else is not my name Pathfinder."

A shout from the target announced the truth of this assertion.

Is the miracle sufficient as it stands? Not for Cooper. The Pathfinder speaks again, as he "now slowly advances towards the stage occupied by the females":

"That's not all, boys, that's not all; if you find the target touched at all, I'll own to a miss. The Quartermaster cut the wood, but you'll find no wood cut by that last messenger."

The miracle is at last complete. He knew—doubtless *saw*—at the distance of a hundred yards—that his bullet had passed into the hole *without fraying the edges*. There were now three bullets in that one hole—three bullets embedded processionally in the body of the stump back of the target. Everybody knew this—somehow or other—and yet nobody had dug any of them out to make sure. Cooper is not a close observer, but he is interesting. He is certainly always that, no matter what happens. And he is more interesting when he is not noticing what he is about than when he is. This is a considerable merit.

The conversations in the Cooper books have a curious sound in our modern ears. To believe that such talk really ever came out of people's mouths would be to believe that there was a time when time was of no value to a person who thought he had something to say; when it was the custom to spread a two-minute remark out to ten; when a man's mouth was a rolling-mill, and busied itself all day long in turning four-foot pigs of thought into thirty-foot bars of conversational railroad iron by attenuation; when subjects were seldom faithfully stuck to, but the talk wandered all around and arrived nowhere;

when conversations consisted mainly of irrelevancies, with here and there a relevancy, a relevancy with an embarrassed look, as not being able to explain how it got there.

Cooper was certainly not a master in the construction of dialogue. Inaccurate observation defeated him here as it defeated him in so many other enterprises of his. He even failed to notice that the man who talks corrupt English six days in the week must and will talk it on the seventh, and can't help himself. In the *Deerslayer* story he lets Deerslayer talk the showiest kind of book-talk sometimes, and at other times the basest of base dialects. For instance, when some one asks him if he has a sweetheart, and if so, where she abides, this is his majestic answer:

"She's in the forest—hanging from the boughs of the trees, in a soft rain—in the dew on the open grass—the clouds that float about in the blue heavens—the birds that sing in the woods—the sweet springs where I slake my thirst—and in all the other glorious gifts that come from God's Providence!"

And he preceded that, a little before, with this:

"It consarns me as all things that touches a fri'nd consarns a fri'nd."

And this is another of his remarks:

"If I was Injin born, now, I might tell of this, or carry in the scalp and boast of the expl'ite afore the whole tribe; or if my inimy had only been a bear"— and so on.

We cannot imagine such a thing as a veteran Scotch Commander-in-Chief comporting himself in the field like a windy melodramatic actor, but Cooper could. On one occasion Alice and Cora were being chased by the French through a fog in the neighborhood of their father's fort:

"*Point de quartier aux coquins!*" cried an eager pursuer, who seemed to direct the operations of the enemy.

"Stand firm and be ready, my gallant 60ths!" suddenly exclaimed a voice above them; "wait to see the enemy; fire low, and sweep the glacis."

"Father! father!" exclaimed a piercing cry from out the mist; "it is I! Alice! thy own Elsie! spare, O! save your daughters!"

"Hold!" shouted the former speaker, in the awful tones of parental agony, the sound reaching even to the woods, and rolling back in solemn echo. "'Tis she! God has restored me my children! Throw open the sally-port; to the field, 60ths, to the field! pull not a trigger, lest ye kill my lambs! Drive off these dogs of France with your steel!"

Cooper's word-sense was singularly dull. When a person has a poor ear for music he will flat and sharp right along without knowing it. He keeps near the tune, but it is *not* the tune. When a person has a poor ear for words, the result is a literary flatting and sharping; you perceive what he is intending to say, but you also perceive that he doesn't *say* it. This is Cooper. He was not a word-musician. His ear was satisfied with the *approximate* word. I will furnish some circumstantial evidence in support of this charge. My instances are gathered from half a dozen pages of the tale called *Deerslayer*. He uses "verbal," for "oral"; "precision," for "facility"; "phenomena," for "marvels"; "necessary," for "predetermined"; "unsophisticated," for "primitive"; "preparation," for "expectancy"; "rebuked," for "subdued"; "dependent on," for "resulting from"; "fact," for "condition"; "fact," for "conjecture"; "precaution," for "caution"; "explain," for "determine"; "mortified," for "disappointed"; "meretricious," for "factitious"; "materially," for "considerably"; "decreasing," for "deepening"; "increasing," for "disappearing"; "embedded," for "enclosed"; "treacherous," for "hostile"; "stood," for "stooped"; "softened," for "replaced"; "rejoined," for "remarked"; "situation," for "condition"; "different," for "differing"; "insensible," for "unsentient"; "brevity," for "celerity"; "distrusted," for "suspicious"; "mental imbecility," for "imbecility"; "eyes," for "sight"; "counteracting," for "opposing"; "funeral obsequies," for "obsequies."

There have been daring people in the world who claimed that Cooper could write English, but they are all dead now—all dead but Lounsbury. I don't remember that Lounsbury makes the claim in so many words, still he makes it, for he says that *Deerslayer* is a "pure work of art." Pure, in that connection, means faultless—faultless in all details—and language is a detail. If Mr. Lounsbury had only compared Cooper's English with the English which he writes himself—but it is plain that he didn't; and so it is likely that he imagines until this day that Cooper's is as clean and compact as his own. Now I feel sure, deep down in my heart, that Cooper wrote about the poorest English that exists in our language, and that the English of *Deerslayer* is the very worst that even Cooper ever wrote.

I may be mistaken, but it does seem to me that *Deerslayer* is not a work of art in any sense; it does seem to me that it is destitute of every detail that goes to the making of a work of art; in truth, it seems to me that *Deerslayer* is just simply a literary *delirium tremens*.

A work of art? It has no invention; it has no order, system, sequence, or result; it has no lifelikeness, no thrill, no stir, no seeming of reality; its characters are confusedly drawn, and by their acts and words they prove that they are not the sort of people the author claims that they are; its humor is pathetic; its pathos is funny; its conversations are—oh! indescribable; its love-scenes odious; its English a crime against the language.

Counting these out, what is left is Art. I think we must all admit that.

T. E. KEBBEL
From "Leather-Stocking"
Macmillan's Magazine, January 1899, pp. 195–97

It will be seen that Cooper troubled himself very little with the construction of his plots. It might be said indeed, with small exaggeration, that he made one do for all. His two girls captured by savages, and rescued in each case by the same hero or heroes, reappear punctually in four out of the five stories; and in the fifth, though the danger is different, the deliverance is the same. Unquestionably this is a defect, and if our interest in the story depended on the machinery, on the means, that is to say, by which the heroines are first entrapped and afterwards extricated from the toils, nobody would read any one of them a second time. But Cooper doubtless knew where his own strength lay, and confident in his powers of description may have relied on them to compensate not only for all want of variety in his situations, but for any other faults which professional critics might discover; and there are some to be mentioned presently which it would seem that he mistook for beauties. But who can think of these things when standing by the side of Deerslayer on the banks of Oswego, and contemplating the lovely scene which even the untutored hunter cannot view without emotion? Who can remember,

when reading the thrilling story of the fight on the river and the siege of the block-house in *The Pathfinder*, that he has practically read it all before in *The Last of the Mohicans?* Does the fact that Judith and Hetty, Alice and Cora have undergone exactly the same sufferings and perils as the heroine of *The Prairie* lessen for one moment the interest which absorbs us in the fortunes of Inez? In what way does Hardheart at the stake differ from the Deerslayer when bound for torture? Yet we watch the fate of the Pawnee warrior with as keen an anxiety as if we saw the scene for the first time. Not only does the vivid reality with which these incidents are depicted engross our attention for the time to the exclusion of all such mental processes as comparison or discrimination, but the exquisite setting in which each is presented to us, the picturesque combination of rock, stream, and waterfall, of hills clothed with virgin forests reaching down to the water's edge, where the oaks fling their untamed branches into the bosom of the lake, or form a natural arch across the narrow bed of the brook as it hurries down the glen, the boundless and unbroken canopy of the forest, on which the traveller looks down from some mountain-top, stretching on every side as far as the eye can reach, and hiding in its recesses the Huron or Iroquois watching like a tiger for his prey,—these wild woodland glories, with all the charm of mystery and danger superadded, effectually prevent us from wishing for one moment that anything in the picture could be different. We rather hug the monotony, than turn away from it. This constant succession of stirring incidents, one very like another, environed with scenery in which there is never any great variety, never palls upon us. They are always fresh, rekindling hope and fear and rousing the imagination to renewed activity as often as we read them.

As the descriptive powers of the *Leather-Stocking Tales* do so much towards redeeming the sameness of the plots, they have been taken next in order, though according to all established rules and forms of criticism the second place should have been reserved for the characters. Let us now glance at these. It will be allowed on the threshold that in stories of savage, or half savage, life we cannot expect to encounter those complex or eccentric characters which seem to be the growth of civilisation, far less those compounds of folly, vanity and meanness which it is the business of the modern novelist to reproduce. But in Leather-Stocking himself, in Ishmael of *The Prairie*, and in Judith of *The Deerslayer* Cooper shows considerable knowledge of human nature, and a skilful touch in the delineation of it. The relations between Judith Hutter, the daughter of Old Tom, and the young hunter himself at the outset of his career, are made extremely interesting; and as a study in psychology they deserve more attention than perhaps has yet been bestowed on them.

Judith is a girl of great beauty, high spirit, and no small mental powers. While living for a time near the settlements, as they were called, she had acquired manners above her station, which would all tend to increase her powers of fascination for a half savage nature. She had been seduced by an English officer at one of the forts, and though nobody knew of the fact, many suspected it. Her whole soul was in revolt against the baseness with which she had been treated, and when she first met the hunter she was in a mood to prize simple honesty and straightfowardness above all other qualities. These she found in Deerslayer, and was seriously prepared to abandon all her former social ambitions and pass her life with him in the wilderness. In a word, she fell passionately in love with him; though the rude young woodsman, dressed in skins and unable to read or write, presented as wide a contrast to the smart uniforms, gallant demeanour, and polished manners which she had met with at the garrison as could well be imagined. The gradual growth of her feelings is well described. At first, no doubt, she is actuated only by coquetry and a desire to prove the power of her charms over this child of Nature; but it ends in her falling into the snare which she had set for another. Instead of making a conquest of Deerslayer, she allows Deerslayer to make a conquest of herself, and has the mortification to find herself rejected when driven to make the first overtures. The hunter's feelings seem to have been of a somewhat blended character. He was a total stranger to the tender passion, and now, just setting out on his first war-path,

> His soul was all on honour bent,
> He could not stoop to love.

But over and above this his own open nature, and love of what was true and genuine, revolts from the somewhat artificial character which Judith represents in his eyes, at all events on their first acquaintance, while it suffers still more from contrast with her sister Hetty, whose simplicity, innocence, and veracity make a deeper impression on the youth than Judith's beauty. He too has heard stories to Judith's disadvantage, but we are not to suppose that it was these alone which makes him reject her proffered hand. Had Deerslayer been a mere inexperienced denizen of the forest, with no knowledge of civilised life or manners, one would have said that his indifference to Judith's charms was not true to human nature. But he had seen towns and camps, and came into the forest with more knowledge of the world than perhaps Judith imagined.

In *The Pathfinder* the position of our hero is exactly reversed. Here he is the disappointed lover, and his behaviour under the circumstances and towards a favoured rival are consistent with his whole career. He had suffered himself as the Deerslayer to be taken captive by the Mingoes in order to facilitate the escape of his bosom friend the Serpent with his betrothed bride, and he now sacrifices his own affections to Mabel Dunham when he sees on whom they are fixed, though had he held her to her promise she would, as he knew, have taken him without a murmur.

Ishmael in *The Prairie*, the other character I have mentioned as displaying those lights and shades which the modern novel-reader expects to find in some at least of the personages introduced to him, is perhaps from one point of view the best drawn in the series. He is the leader of the band of emigrants with whom we find ourselves at the beginning of the story, a rough, vindictive, unscrupulous man, apparently bent only on gain. But gleams of light are occasionally thrown upon his character in the course of the story to prepare us for the better traits which show themselves at the end of it. He appears suddenly awakened to a sense of justice, owns that he was wrong in being a party to the kidnapping of Inez, dismisses all his prisoners freely, and completes his part of the sternly just man by putting to death his brother-in-law, who had been convicted of murdering one of Ishmael's sons. Altogether he is certainly an impressive character, and the skill with which his latent good qualities are gradually revealed to us through the coarser and more savage outside, which is all that we see on our first acquaintance with him, deserves high praise. Nearly as much perhaps may be said of his wife Esther, who till the last moment has appeared only as a scolding termagant. The death of their favourite son seems to have softened both, and the communing together of husband and wife over their great loss and over the necessary punishment of the assassin, the woman's brother, is full of genuine pathos, and touches a deeper key than Cooper generally strikes.

MARY SHELLEY

1797–1851

Mary Wollstonecraft Shelley was born in London on August 30, 1797, the only daughter of the philosopher William Godwin and the writer Mary Wollstonecraft. Her mother died giving birth to her, and in 1801 Godwin took a second wife, whom Mary passionately disliked. In 1812 Godwin sent Mary to live in Dundee, where she remained, except for brief visits, until 1814. During one of these visits, at the end of 1812, Mary met Percy Bysshe Shelley and his wife Harriet. After meeting a second time in 1814, Percy and Mary fell in love and left England together, traveling through France, Switzerland, Germany, and Holland. In 1815, after they had returned to England, Mary gave birth to a daughter, who died less than two weeks later; of their four children only one, Percy (b. 1819), was to survive infancy. Shelley and Mary Godwin were married in 1816, shortly after Harriet Shelley's death by drowning. In 1817 Mary Shelley published anonymously the *History of a Six Week's Tour*. The following year her most famous work—and one of the most famous novels of the nineteenth century—was published: *Frankenstein; or, The Modern Prometheus*. It was the product of a contest among Mary Shelley, Percy Shelley, Lord Byron, and John William Polidori as to who could write the most frightening tale; Mary's was the only one brought to a conclusion, although Polidori produced the able short story "The Vampyre."

Shortly after the publication of *Frankenstein*, Mary and Percy left for Italy, where on July 28, 1822, Shelley was drowned in the Bay of Spezia during a heavy squall. Because Mary did not wish to surrender her only remaining child, Percy, to Shelley's father, Sir Timothy, the latter refused to give any financial support, and it became necessary for Mary to support herself by writing. Between Shelley's death and her own in 1851 she produced four novels: *Valperga* (1823), *The Last Man* (1826), *Perkin Warbeck* (1830), and *Lodore* (1835). She also wrote five volumes of biographical sketches of "eminent literary and scientific men" written for Lardner's *Cabinet Cyclopedia* (1835–38); a two-volume travel book, *Rambles in Germany and Italy during 1840, 1842, and 1843* (1844); and a number of poems, essays, and short stories, mostly published in the periodical *Keepsake*. Mary Shelley edited and published her husband's *Complete Poetical Works* (4 vols., 1839) and his *Essays, Letters from Abroad, Translations and Fragments* (2 vols., 1840). She died in London on February 1, 1851.

Personal

Mrs. Shelley was, I have been told, the intimate friend of my son in the lifetime of his first wife, and to the time of her death, and in no small degree, as I suspect, estranged my son's mind from his family, and all his first duties in life; with that impression on my mind, I cannot agree with your Lordship that, though my son was unfortunate, Mrs. Shelley is innocent; on the contrary, I think that her conduct was the very reverse of what it ought to have been, and I must, therefore, decline all interference in matters in which Mrs. Shelley is interested. As to the child, I am inclined to afford the means of a suitable protection and care of him in this country, if he shall be placed with a person I shall approve; but your Lordship will allow me to say that the means I can furnish will be limited, as I have important duties to perform towards others, which I cannot forget.—SIR TIMOTHY SHELLEY, Letter to Lord Byron (Feb. 6, 1823), cited in Florence Ashton Marshall, *The Life and Letters of Mary Wollstonecraft Shelley*, 1889, Vol. 2, p. 66

It appears to me that the mode in which Sir Timothy Shelley expresses himself about my child plainly shows by what mean principles he would be actuated. He does not offer him an asylum in his own house, but a beggarly provision under the care of a stranger.

Setting aside that, I would not part with him. Something is due to me. I should not live ten days separated from him. If it were necessary for me to die for his benefit the sacrifice would be easy; but his delicate frame requires all a mother's solicitude; nor shall he be deprived of my anxious love and assiduous attention to his happiness while I have it in my power to bestow it on him; not to mention that his future respect for his excellent Father and his moral wellbeing greatly depend upon his being away from the immediate influence of his relations.

This, perhaps, you will think nonsense, and it is inconceivably painful to me to discuss a point which appears to me as clear as noonday; besides I lose all—all honourable station and name—when I admit that I am not a fitting person to take charge of my infant. The insult is keen; the pretence of heaping it upon me too gross; the advantage to them, if the will came to be contested, would be too immense.

As a matter of feeling, I would never consent to it. I am said to have a cold heart; there are feelings, however, so strongly implanted in my nature that, to root them out, life will go with it.—MARY SHELLEY, Letter to Lord Byron (Feb. 1823), cited in Florence Ashton Marshall, *The Life and Letters of Mary Wollstonecraft Shelley*, 1889, Vol. 2, p. 67

Do not, I entreat you, be cast down about your worldly circumstances. You certainly contain within yourself the means of your subsistence. Your talents are truly extraordinary. *Frankenstein* is universally known, and though it can never be a book for vulgar reading, is everywhere respected. It is the most wonderful work to have been written at twenty years of age that I ever heard of. You are now five and twenty, and, most fortunately, you have pursued a course of reading, and cultivated your mind, in a manner the most admirably adapted to make you a great and successful author. If you cannot be independent, who should be?

Your talents, as far as I can at present discern, are turned for the writing of fictitious adventures.

If it shall ever happen to you to be placed in sudden and urgent want of a small sum, I entreat you to let me know immediately; we must see what I can do. We must help one another.—WILLIAM GODWIN, Letter to Mary Shelley (Feb. 18, 1823), cited in Florence Ashton Marshall, *The Life and Letters of Mary Wollstonecraft Shelley*, 1889, Vol. 2, pp. 68–69

Such a rare pedigree of genius was enough to interest me in her, irrespective of her own merits as an authoress. The most striking feature in her face was her calm, grey eyes; she was rather under the English standard of woman's height, very fair and light-haired, witty, social, and animated in the society of friends, though mournful in solitude; like Shelley, though in a minor degree, she had the power of expressing her thoughts in varied and appropriate words, derived from familiarity with the works of our vigorous old writers. Neither of them used obsolete or foreign words. This command of our language struck me the more as contrasted with the scanty vocabulary used by ladies in society, in which a score of poor hackneyed phrases suffice to express all that is felt or considered proper to reveal.—EDWARD JOHN TRELAWNY, *Recollections of the Last Days of Shelley and Byron*, 1858

I expected to find Mrs. Shelley a radical reformer, probably self-asserting, somewhat aggressive, and at war with the world; more decidedly heterodox in religion and morals than I myself was; endorsing and enforcing the extreme opinions of her father and mother, and (as I then understood them) of her husband. I found her very different from my preconceptions.

Genial, gentle, sympathetic, thoughtful and matured in opinion beyond her years, for she was then but twenty-nine; essentially liberal in politics, ethics, and theology, indeed, yet devoid alike of stiff prejudice against the old or ill-considered prepossession in favor of the new; and, above all, womanly, in the best sense, in every sentiment and instinct; she impressed me also as a person with warm social feelings, dependent for happiness on loving encouragement; needing a guiding and sustaining hand.

I felt all this, rather than reasoned it out, during our too brief acquaintance; and few women have ever attracted me so much in so short a time. Had I remained in London I am sure we should have been dear friends. She wrote me several charming letters to America.

In person, she was of middle height and graceful figure. Her face, though not regularly beautiful, was comely and spiritual, of winning expression, and with a look of inborn refinement as well as culture. It had a touch of sadness when at rest; yet when it woke up in animated conversation, one could see that underneath there was a bright, cheerful, even playful nature, at variance, I thought, with depressing circumstances and isolated position.—ROBERT DALE OWEN, *Threading My Way: An Autobiography*, 1874, pp. 322–23

Mary Wolstonecraft Godwin Shelley, with her well-shaped, golden-haired head, almost always a little bent and drooping;

her marble-white shoulders and arms statuesquely visible in the perfectly plain black velvet dress, which the customs of that time allowed to be cut low, and which her own taste adopted (for neither she nor her sister-in-sorrow ever wore the conventional "widow's weeds" and "widow's cap"); her thoughtful, earnest eyes; her short upper lip and intellectually curved mouth, with a certain close-compressed and decisive expression while she listened, and a relaxation into fuller redness and mobility when speaking; her exquisitely-formed, white, dimpled, small hands, with rosy palms, and plumply commencing fingers, that tapered into tips as slender and delicate as those in a Vandyk portrait—all remain palpably present to memory. Another peculiarity in Mrs. Shelley's hand was its singular flexibility, which permitted her bending the fingers back so as almost to approach the portion of her arm above her wrist. She once did this smilingly and repeatedly, to amuse the girl who was noting its whiteness and pliancy, and who now, as an old woman, records its remarkable beauty.—MARY COWDEN CLARKE, *Recollections of Writers*, 1878, pp. 37–38

The true success of Mary Shelley's life was not, therefore, the intellectual triumph of which, during her youth, she had loved to dream, and which at one time seemed to be actually within her grasp, but the moral success of beauty of character. To those people—a daily increasing number in this tired world—who erect the natural grace of animal spirits to the rank of the highest virtue, this success may appear hardly worth the name. Yet it was a very real victory. Her nature was not without faults or tendencies which, if undisciplined, might have developed into faults, but every year she lived seemed to mellow and ripen her finer qualities, while blemishes or weaknesses were suppressed or overcome, and finally disappeared altogether.

As to her theological views, about which the most contradictory opinions have been expressed, it can but be said that nothing in Mrs. Shelley's writings gives other people the right to formulate for her any dogmatic opinions at all. Brought up in a purely rationalistic creed, her education had of course, no tinge of what is known as "personal religion," and it must be repeated here that none of her acts and views were founded, or should be judged as if they were founded on Biblical commands or prohibitions. That the temper of her mind, so to speak, was eminently religious there can be no doubt; that she believed in God and a future state there are many allusions to show. Perhaps no one, having lived with the so-called atheist, Shelley, could have accepted the idea of the limitation, or the extinction of intelligence and goodness. Her liberality of mind, however, was rewarded by abuse from some of her acquaintance, because her toleration was extended even to the orthodox.

Her moral opinions, had they ever been formulated, which they never were, would have approximated closely to those of Mary Wollstonecraft, limited, however, by an inability, like her father's, *not* to see both sides of a question, and also by the severest and most elevated standard of moral purity, of personal faith and loyalty. To be judged by such a standard she would have regarded as a woman's highest privilege. To claim as a "woman's right" any licence, any lowering of the standard of duty in these matters, would have been to her incomprehensible and impossible. But, with all this, she discriminated. Her standard was not that of the conventional world.

At every risk, as she says, she befriended those whom she considered "victims to the social system." It was a difficult course; for, while her acquaintance of the "advanced" type accused her of cowardice and worldliness for not asserting herself as a champion of universal liberty, there were more

who were ready to decry her for her friendly relations with Countess Guiccioli, Lady Mountcashel, and others not named here; to say nothing of Clare, to whom much of her happiness had been sacrificed. She refrained from pronouncing judgment, but reserved her liberty of action, and in all doubtful cases gave others the benefit of the doubt, and this without respect of persons. She would not excommunicate a humble individual for what was passed over in a man or woman of genius; nor condemn a woman for what, in a man, might be excused, or might even add to his social reputation. Least of all would she secure her own position by shunning those whose case had once been hers, and who in their after life had been less fortunate than she. Pure herself, she could be charitable, and she could be just.

The influence of such a wife on Shelley's more vehement, visionary temperament can hardly be over-estimated. Their moods did not always suit or coincide; each, at times, made the other suffer. It could not be otherwise with two natures so young, so strong, and so individual. But, if forbearance may have been sometimes called for on the one hand, and on the other a charity which is kind and thinks no evil, it was only a part of that discipline from which the married life of geniuses is not exempt, and which tests the temper and quality of the metal it tries; an ordeal from which two noble natures come forth the purer and the stronger.

The indirect, unconscious power of elevation of character is great, and not even a Shelley but must be the better for association with it, not even he but must be the nobler, "yea, three times less unworthy" through the love of such a woman as Mary. He would not have been all he was without her sustaining and refining influence; without the constant sense that in loving him she loved his ideals also. We owe him, in part, to her.

Love—the love of Love—was Shelley's life and creed. This, in Mary's creed, was interpreted as love of Shelley. By all the rest she strove to do her duty, but, when the end came, that survived as the one great fact of her life—a fact she might have uttered in words like his—

And where is Truth? On tombs; for such to thee
Has been my heart; and thy dead memory
Has lain from (girlhood), many a changeful year,
Unchangingly preserved, and buried there.
—FLORENCE ASHTON MARSHALL, *The Life and Letters of Mary Wollstonecraft Shelley*, 1889, Vol. 2, pp. 322–25

General

Mrs. Shelley found Italy for the first time, real Italy, at Sorrento, she says. Oh that book (*Rambles in Germany and Italy*)—does one wake or sleep? The "Mary dear" with the brown eyes, and Godwin's daughter and Shelley's wife, and who surely was something better once upon a time—and to go thro' Rome & Florence & the rest, after what I suppose to be Lady Londonderry's fashion: the intrepidity of the commonplace quite astounds me.—ROBERT BROWNING, Letter to Elizabeth Barrett Browning (Sept. 11, 1845)

There can be no doubt that he had profited greatly in his moral condition, as well as in his bodily health, by the greater tranquillity which he enjoyed in the society of Mary, and also by the sympathy which gave full play to his ideas, instead of diverting and disappointing them. She was, indeed, herself a woman of extraordinary power, of heart as well as head. Many circumstances conspired to conceal some of her natural faculties. She lost her mother very young; her father—speaking with great diffidence, from a very slight and imperfect knowledge—appeared to me a harsh and ungenial man. She inherited from him her thin voice, but not the steel-edged sharpness of his own; and she inherited, not from him, but from her mother, a largeness of heart that entered proportionately into the working of her mind. She had a masculine capacity for study; for, though I suspect her early schooling was irregular, she remained a student all her life, and by painstaking industry made herself acquainted with any subject that she had to handle. Her command of history and her imaginative power are shown in such books as *Valperga* and *Castruccio*; but the daring originality of her mind comes out most distinctly in her earliest published work, *Frankenstein*. Its leading idea has been ascribed to her husband, but, I am sure, unduly; and the vividness with which she has brought out the monstrous tale in all its horror, but without coarse or revolting incidents, is a proof of the genius which she inherited alike from both her parents. It is clear, also, that the society of Shelley was to her a great school, which she did not appreciate to the full until most calamitously it was taken away; and yet, of course, she could not fail to learn the greater part of what it had become to her. This again showed itself even in her appearance, after she had spent some years in Italy; for, while she had grown far more comely than she was in her mere youth, she had acquired a deeper insight into many subjects that interested Shelley, and some others; and she had learned to express the force of natural affection, which she was born to feel, but which had somehow been stunted and suppressed in her youth. In the preface to the collected edition of his works, she says: "I have the liveliest recollection of all that was done and said during the period of my knowing him. Every impression is as clear as if stamped yesterday, and I have no apprehension of any mistake in my statements, as far as they go. In other respects I am, indeed, incompetent; but I feel the importance of the task, and regard it as my most sacred duty. I endeavor to fulfil it in a manner he would himself approve; and hope in this publication to lay the first stone of a monument due to Shelley's genius, his sufferings, and his virtues." And in the postscript, written in November, 1839, she says: "At my request, the publisher has restored the omitted passages of *Queen Mab*. I now present this edition as a complete collection of my husband's poetical works, and I do not foresee that I can hereafter add to or take away a word or line." So writes the wife-editor; and then *The Poetical Works of Percy Bysshe Shelley* begin with a dedication to Harriet, restored to its place by Mary. While the biographers of Shelley are chargeable with suppression, the most straightforward and frank of all of them is Mary, who, although not insensible to the passion of jealousy, and carrying with her the painful sense of a life-opportunity not fully used, thus writes the name of Harriet the first on her husband's monument, while she has nobly abstained from telling those things that other persons should have supplied to the narrative. I have heard her accused of an over-anxiety to be admired; and something of the sort was discernible in society: it was a weakness as venial as it was purely superficial. Away from society, she was as truthful and simple a woman as I have ever met,—was as faithful a friend as the world has produced, —using that unreserved directness towards those whom she regarded with affection which is the very crowning glory of friendly intercourse. I suspect that these qualities came out in their greatest force after her calamity; for many things which she said in her regret, and passages in Shelley's own poetry, make me doubt whether little habits of temper, and possibly of a refined and exacting coquettishness, had not prevented him from acquiring so full a knowledge of her as she had of him.

—THORNTON HUNT, "Shelley," *Atlantic*, Feb. 1863, pp. 198–99

Lodore, Mrs. Shelley's fifth novel, came out in 1835. It differs from the others in being a novel of society, and has been stigmatised, rather unjustly, as weak and colourless, although at the time of its publication it had a great success. It is written in a style which is now out of date, and undoubtedly fails to fulfil the promise of power held out by *Frankenstein* and to some extent by *Valperga*, but it bears on every page the impress of the refinement and sensibility of the author, and has, moreover, a special interest of its own, due to the fact that some of the incidents are taken from actual occurrences in her early life, and some of the characters sketched from people she had known.—FLORENCE ASHTON MARSHALL, *The Life and Letters of Mary Wollstonecraft Shelley*, 1889, Vol. 2, p. 264

The wife of Shelley and daughter of Godwin and Mary Wollstonecraft shines a good deal by reflected light, but she has one well-grounded title to literary remembrance in her romance of *Frankenstein*. It originated in the speculative discussions of the memorable summer of 1816, when the Shelleys and Byron were daily companions at the Villa Diodati. Though doubtless a tale of wonder, *Frankenstein* belongs in reality less to the school of Lewis, than to that of Godwin's *St. Leon*. Its invention betrays a vein of eager philosophic and scientific curiosity of which Lewis's purely literary mind was quite innocent. The problem of creating life had fascinated the daring brains of the Revolution as it had done those of the Renascence. To suppose it solved was merely to prolong and expand tendencies already vigorous in experience, while the wonders of Lewis and his tribe were wilful negations of experience, 'shot from a pistol' with a boyish delight in the impossible. The vivid drawing of the discomforts of supernatural or quasi-supernatural knowledge, in particular, shows the influence of *St. Leon*. She subsequently attempted historical romance (*Valperga, or the Life and Adventures of Castruccio, Prince of Lucca*, written at Pisa in 1821, published 1823, the *Perkin Warbeck*, 1830) with estimable success. In spite of much descriptive and analytic talent she shared the inaptitude for history which marked the Godwinian and Radcliffian schools alike. *The Last Man* (1826) which so deeply impressed the not very susceptible Jefferson Hogg, has a pathetic significance as shadowing her own tragic loneliness,—the 'loneliness of Crusoe'—as she herself long afterwards declared it to have been.—C. H. HERFORD, *The Age of Wordsworth*, 1897, pp. 97–98

Works

FRANKENSTEIN

How changed is the taste of verse, prose, and painting! since *le bon vieux temps*, dear Madam! Nothing attracts us but what terrifies, and is within—*if* within—a hair's-breadth of positive disgust. The picture of Death on his Pale Horse, however, is very grand certainly—and some of the strange things they *write* remind me of Squoire Richard's visit to the Tower Menagerie, when he says "They are *pure* grim devils,"—particularly a wild and hideous tale called *Frankenstein*.—HESTER LYNCH PIOZZI, Letter to Fanny Burney (Oct. 20, 1820)

The imaginative romance as distinguished from the historical romance, and the actual or social life fiction, is of very rare occurrence in the literature of the present day. Whether the cause lies with the writers or the public, or the character of events and influence now operating on society, certain it is that the imaginative romance is almost extinct among us.

We had outgrown the curdling horrors and breathless apprehensions of Mrs. Ratcliffe, and the roseate pomps of Miss Jane Porter. But why have we no Frankensteins, for that fine work is in advance of the age?

Perhaps we ought to seek the cause of the scarcity in the difficulty of the production. A mere fruitless, purposeless excitement of the imagination will not do *now*. The imaginative romance is required to be a sort of epic—a power to advance—a something to propel the frame of things. Such is Bulwer's *Zanoni*, a profound and beautiful work of fiction, which has been reviewed in its place, and in which Godwin's *St. Leon* found a worthy successor. With this single exception, the first place among the romances of our day belongs to the *Frankenstein* of Mrs. Shelley.

The solitary student with whom the longing desire to pry into the secrets of nature ends in the discovery of the vital principle itself, and the means of communicating it, thus describes the consummation of his toils. We quote the passage as illustrative of the genius by which the extravagance of the conception is rendered subservient to artistical effect:—

> It was on a dreary night of November, that I beheld the accomplishment of my toils. With an anxiety that almost amounted to agony, I collected the instruments of life around me, that I might infuse a spark of being into the lifeless thing that lay at my feet. It was already one in the morning; the rain pattered dismally against the panes, and my candle was nearly burnt out, when, by the glimmer of the half-extinguished light, I saw the dull yellow eye of the creature open; it breathed hard, and a convulsive motion agitated its limbs.
>
> How can I describe my emotions at this catastrophe, or how delineate the wretch whom with such infinite pains and care I had endeavoured to form? His limbs were in proportion, and I had selected his features as beautiful. Beautiful!—Great God! His yellow skin scarcely covered the work of muscles and arteries beneath; his hair was of a lustrous black, and flowing; his teeth of a pearly whiteness; but these luxuriances only formed a more horrid contrast with his watery eyes, that seemed almost of the same colour as the dun white sockets in which they were set, his shrivelled complexion, and straight black lips.

The Monster in *Frankenstein*, sublime in his ugliness, his simplicity, his passions, his wrongs and his strength, physical and mental, embodies in the wild narrative more than one distinct and important moral theory or proposition. In himself he is the type of a class deeply and cruelly aggrieved by nature—the Deformed or hideous in figure or countenance, whose sympathies and passions are as strong as their bodily deformity renders them repulsive. An amount of human woe, great beyond reckoning, have such experienced. When the Monster pleads his cause against cruel man, and when he finally disappears on his raft on the icy sea to build his own funeral pile, he pleads the cause of all that class who have so strong a claim on the help and sympathy of the world, yet find little else but disgust, or, at best, neglect.

The Monster created by Frankenstein is also an illustration of the embodied consequences of our actions. As he, when formed and endowed with life, became to his imaginary creator an everlasting ever-present curse, so may one single action, nay a word, or it may be a thought, thrown upon the tide of time

become to its originator a curse, never to be recovered, never to be shaken off.

Frankenstein suggests yet another analogy. It teaches the tragic results of attainment when an impetuous irresistible passion hurries on the soul to its doom. Such tragic results are the sacrificial fires out of which humanity rises purified. They constitute one form of the great ministry of Pain. The conception of *Frankenstein* is the converse of that of the delightful German fiction of Peter Schlemil, in which the *loss* of his shadow (reputation or honour) leads on the hero through several griefs and troubles to the great simplicity of nature and truth; while in *Frankenstein* the *attainment* of a gigantic reality leads through crime and desolation to the same goal, but it is only reached in the moment of death.⟨. . .⟩

Mrs. Shelley has published, besides *Frankenstein*, a romance entitled *Valperga*, which is less known than the former, but is of high merit. She exhibits in her hero, a brave and successful warrior, arriving at the height of his ambition, endowed with uncommon beauty and strength, and with many good qualities, yet causes him to excite emotions of reprobation and pity, because he is cruel and a tyrant, and because in the truth of things he is unhappy. This is doing a good work, taking the false glory from the eyes and showing things as they are. There are two female characters of wonderful power and beauty. The heroine is a lovely and noble creation. The work taken as a whole, if below *Frankenstein* in genius, is yet worthy of its author and of her high rank in the aristocracy of genius, as the daughter of Godwin and Mary Wolstonecraft, and the widow of Shelley.—R. H. HORNE, "Mrs. Shelley," *A New Spirit of the Age*, 1844, pp. 317–21

Lewis, popularly known as Monk Lewis, paid Byron a visit at his villa, and became one of the little society, which was often confined within four walls by the rain, and eager after every new excitement, as people imprisoned in a country house so universally are. They told each other ghost stories, and tales of mystery and wonder under the inspiration of the kind little inoffensive romancer, who was then master of that branch of the arts; and he or some one else suggested that they should all write for their mutual diversion tales of this character. The only one who carried out the suggestion was Mary, the youngest of the party, a girl not yet eighteen, notwithstanding the turmoil of life into which she had been plunged. That a young creature of this age should have produced anything at once so horrible and so original as the hideous romance of *Frankenstein*, is one of the most extraordinary accidents in literature; and that she should never, having made such a beginning, have done anything more, is almost equally wonderful. Byron is said to have begun a similar sketch, entitled "The Vampyre," which his physician-attendant, Polidori, afterwards added to and printed; but none of the detailed records of the time inform us what were the feelings of excitement and terror with which the little company, thrilled by the tales of Lewis, listened to the portentous and extraordinary production with which the fair small girl, with her big forehead and her sedate aspect, out-Heroded Herod. Mary Shelley's individual appearances afterwards are only those of a romantically-desolate widow, pouring out her grief and fondness in sentimental gushes, which look somewhat overstrained and ridiculous in print, whatever they may have done in fact; but to hear her read, with her girlish lips, this most extraordinary and terrible of imaginations, must have been a sensation unparalleled. It is one of the books adopted into the universal memory, which everybody alludes to, and thousands who can never have read it understand the main incidents of—which is a wonderful instance of actual fame. That this should be merely stated as a fact in the history, and no one pause to wonder at it, is another odd instance of the insensibility of contemporaries.—MARGARET OLIPHANT, *The Literary History of England, 1790–1825*, 1882, Vol. 3, pp. 69–70

————

PERCY BYSSHE SHELLEY
"Dedication: to Mary —— ——"
The Revolt of Islam
1817

> There is no danger to a man, that knows
> What life and death is: there's not any law
> Exceeds his knowledge; neither is it lawful
> That he should stoop to any other law.
> (Chapman)

So now my summer task is ended, Mary,
  And I return to thee, mine own heart's home;
As to his Queen some victor Knight of Faëry,
  Earning bright spoils for her enchanted dome;
  Nor thou disdain, that ere my fame become
A star among the stars of mortal night,
  If it indeed may cleave its natal gloom,
Its doubtful promise thus I would unite
With thy belovèd name, thou Child of love and light.

The toil which stole from thee so many an hour,
  Is ended,—and the fruit is at thy feet!
No longer where the woods to frame a bower
  With interlacèd branches mix and meet,
  Or where with sound like many voices sweet,
Waterfalls leap among wild islands green,
  Which framed for my lone boat a lone retreat
Of moss-grown trees and weeds, shall I be seen:
But beside thee, where still my heart has even been.

Thoughts of great deeds were mine, dear Friend, when first
  The clouds which wrap this world from youth did pass.
I do remember well the hour which burst
  My spirit's sleep: a fresh May-dawn it was,
  When I walked forth upon the glittering grass,
And wept, I knew not why; until there rose
  From the near schoolroom, voices, that, alas!
Were but one echo from a world of woes—
The harsh and grating strife of tyrants and of foes.

And then I clasped my hands and looked around—
  —But none was near to mock my streaming eyes,
Which poured their warm drops on the sunny ground—
  So, without shame, I spake:—'I will be wise,
  And just, and free, and mild, if in me lies
Such power, for I grow weary to behold
  The selfish and the strong still tyrannise
Without reproach or check.' I then controlled
My tears, my heart grew calm, and I was meek and bold.

And from that hour did I with earnest thought
  Heap knowledge from forbidden mines of lore,
Yet nothing that my tyrants knew or taught
  I cared to learn, but from that secret store
  Wrought linkèd armour for my soul, before
It might walk forth to war among mankind;
  Thus power and hope were strengthened more and more
Within me, till there came upon my mind
A sense of loneliness, a thirst with which I pined.

Alas, that love should be a blight and snare
  To those who seek all sympathies in one!—

Such once I sought in vain; then black despair,
  The shadow of a starless night, was thrown
  Over the world in which I moved alone:—
Yet never found I one not false to me,
  Hard hearts, and cold, like weights of icy stone
Which crushed and withered mine, that could not be
Aught but a lifeless clod, until revived by thee.

Thou Friend, whose presence on my wintry heart
  Fell, like bright Spring upon some herbless plain;
How beautiful and calm and free thou wert
  In thy young wisdom, when the mortal chain
  Of Custom thou didst burst and rend in twain,
And walked as free as light the clouds among,
  Which many an envious slave then breathed in vain
From his dim dungeon, and my spirit sprung
To meet thee from the woes which had begirt it long!

No more alone through the world's wilderness,
  Although I trod the paths of high intent,
I journeyed now: no more companionless,
  Where solitude is like despair, I went.—
  There is the wisdom of a stern content
When Poverty can blight the just and good,
  When Infamy dares mock the innocent,
And cherished friends turn with the multitude
To trample: this was ours, and we unshaken stood!

Now has descended a serener hour,
  And with inconstant fortune, friends return;
Though suffering leaves the knowledge and the power
  Which says:—Let scorn be not repaid with scorn.
  And from thy side two gentle babes are born
To fill our home with smiles, and thus are we
  Most fortunate beneath life's beaming morn;
And these delights, and thou, have been to me
The parents of the Song I consecrate to thee.

Is it, that now my inexperienced fingers
  But strike the prelude of a loftier strain?
Or, must the lyre on which my spirit lingers
  Soon pause in silence, ne'er to sound again,
  Though it might shake the Anarch Custom's reign,
And charm the minds of men to Truth's own sway
  Holier than was Amphion's? I would fain
Reply in hope—but I am worn away,
And Death and Love are yet contending for their prey.

And what art thou? I know, but dare not speak:
  Time may interpret to his silent years.
Yet in the paleness of thy thoughtful cheek,
  And in the light thine ample forehead wears,
  And in thy sweetest smiles, and in thy tears,
And in thy gentle speech, a prophecy
  Is whispered, to subdue my fondest fears:
And through thine eyes, even in thy soul I see
A lamp of vestal fire burning internally.

They say that thou wert lovely from thy birth,
  Of glorious parents, thou aspiring Child.
I wonder not—for One then left this earth
  Whose life was like a setting planet mild,
  Which clothed thee in the radiance undefiled
Of its departing glory; still her fame
  Shines on thee, through the tempests dark and wild
Which shake these latter days; and thou canst claim
The shelter, from thy Sire, of an immortal name.

One voice came forth from many a mighty spirit,
  Which was the echo of three thousand years;
And the tumultuous world stood mute to hear it,
  As some lone man who in a desert hears
  The music of his home:—unwonted fears

Fell on the pale oppressors of our race,
    And Faith, and Custom, and low-thoughted cares,
Like thunder-stricken dragons, for a space
Left the torn human heart, their food and dwelling-place.

    Truth's deathless voice pauses among mankind!
        If there must be no response to my cry—
    If men must rise and stamp with fury blind
        On his pure name who loves them,—thou and I,
        Sweet friend! can look from our tranquillity
    Like lamps into the world's tempestuous night,—
        Two tranquil stars, while clouds are passing by
    Which wrap them from the foundering seaman's sight,
That burn from year to year with unextinguished light.

SIR WALTER SCOTT
"Remarks on *Frankenstein*"

Blackwood's Edinburgh Magazine, March 1818, pp. 613–20

    Did I request thee, Maker, from my clay
    To mould me man? Did I solicit thee
    From darkness to promote me?—
                                    (*Paradise Lost*)

This is a novel, or more properly a romantic fiction, of a nature so peculiar, that we ought to describe the species before attempting any account of the individual production.

The first general division of works of fiction, into such as bound the events they narrate by the actual laws of nature, and such as, passing these limits, are managed by marvellous and supernatural machinery, is sufficiently obvious and decided. But the class of marvellous romances admits of several subdivisions. In the earlier productions of imagination, the poet, or tale-teller does not, in his own opinion, transgress the laws of credibility, when he introduces into his narration the witches, goblins, and magicians, in the existence of which he himself, as well as his hearers, is a firm believer. This good faith, however, passes away, and works turning upon the marvellous are written and read merely on account of the exercise which they afford to the imagination of those who, like the poet Collins, love to riot in the luxuriance of oriental fiction, to rove through the meanders of enchantment, to gaze on the magnificence of golden palaces, and to repose by the water-falls of Elysian gardens. In this species of composition, the marvellous is itself the principal and most important object both to the author and reader. To describe its effect upon the mind of the human personages engaged in its wonders, and dragged along by its machinery, is comparatively an inferior object. The hero and heroine, partakers of the supernatural character which belongs to their adventures, walk the maze of enchantment with a firm and undaunted step, and appear as much at their ease, amid the wonders around them, as the young fellow described by the Spectator, who was discovered taking a snuff with great composure in the midst of a stormy ocean, represented on the stage of the Opera.

A more philosophical and refined use of the supernatural in works of fiction, is proper to that class in which the laws of nature are represented as altered, not for the purpose of pampering the imagination with wonders, but in order to shew the probable effect which the supposed miracles would produce on those who witnessed them. In this case, the pleasure ordinarily derived from the marvellous incidents is secondary to that which we extract from observing how mortals like ourselves would be affected,

By scenes like these which, daring to depart
From sober truth, are still to nature true.

Even in the description of his marvels, however, the author who manages this stile of composition with address, gives them an indirect importance with the reader, when he is able to describe with nature, and with truth, the effects which they are calculated to produce upon his dramatis personæ. It will be remembered, that the sapient Partridge was too wise to be terrified at the mere appearance of the ghost of Hamlet, whom he knew to be a man dressed up in pasteboard armour for the nonce—it was when he saw the "little man," as he called Garrick, so frightened, that a sympathetic horror took hold of him. Of this we shall presently produce some examples from the narrative before us. But success in this point is still subordinate to the author's principal object, which is less to produce an effect by means of the marvels of the narrations, than to open new trains and channels of thought, by placing men in supposed situations of an extraordinary and preternatural character, and then describing the mode of feeling and conduct which they are most likely to adopt.

To make more clear the distinction we have endeavoured to draw between the marvellous and the effects of the marvellous, considered as separate objects, we may briefly invite our readers to compare the common tale of Tom Thumb with Gulliver's Voyage to Brobdingnag; one of the most childish fictions, with one which is pregnant with wit and satire, yet both turning upon the same assumed possibility of the existence of a pigmy among a race of giants. In the former case, when the imagination of the story-teller has exhausted itself in every species of hyperbole, in order to describe the diminutive size of his hero, the interest of the tale is at an end; but in the romance of the Dean of St Patrick's, the exquisite humour with which the natural consequences of so strange and unusual a situation is detailed, has a canvass on which to expand itself, as broad as the luxuriance even of the author's talents could desire. Gulliver stuck into a marrow bone, and Master Thomas Thumb's disastrous fall into the bowl of hasty-pudding, are, in the general outline, kindred incidents; but the jest is exhausted in the latter case, when the accident is told; whereas in the former, it lies not so much in the comparatively pigmy size which subjected Gulliver to such a ludicrous misfortune, as in the tone of grave and dignified feeling with which he resents the disgrace of the incident.

In the class of fictitious narrations to which we allude, the author opens a sort of account-current with the reader; drawing upon him, in the first place, for credit to that degree of the marvellous which he proposes to employ; and becoming virtually bound, in consequence of this indulgence, that his personages shall conduct themselves, in the extraordinary circumstances in which they are placed, according to the rules of probability, and the nature of the human heart. In this view, the *probable* is far from being laid out of sight even amid the wildest freaks of imagination; on the contrary, we grant the extraordinary postulates which the author demands as the foundation of his narrative, only on condition of his deducing the consequences with logical precision.

We have only to add, that this class of fiction has been sometimes applied to the purposes of political satire, and sometimes to the general illustration of the powers and workings of the human mind. Swift, Bergerac, and others, have employed it for the former purpose, and a good illustration of the latter is the well known *Saint Leon* of William Godwin. In this latter work, assuming the possibility of the transmutation of metals, and of the *elixir vitæ*, the author has deduced, in the course of his narrative, the probable consequences of the possession of such secrets upon the fortunes and mind of him who might enjoy them. *Frankenstein* is a novel upon the same plan with *Saint Leon*; it is said to be written by Mr Percy Bysshe Shelley, who, if we are rightly informed, is son-in-law to Mr Godwin; and it is inscribed to that ingenious author.

In the preface, the author lays claim to rank his work among the class which we have endeavoured to describe.

> The event on which this fiction is founded has been supposed by Dr Darwin, and some of the physiological writers of Germany, as not of impossible occurrence. I shall not be supposed as according the remotest degree of serious faith to such an imagination; yet, in assuming it as the basis of a work of fancy, I have not considered myself as merely weaving a series of supernatural terrors. The event on which the interest of the story depends is exempt from the disadvantages of a mere tale of spectres or enchantment. It was recommended by the novelty of the situations which it developes; and, however impossible as a physical fact, affords a point of view to the imagination for the delineating of human passions more comprehensive and commanding than any which the ordinary relations of existing events can yield.
>
> I have thus endeavoured to preserve the truth of the elementary principles of human nature, while I have not scrupled to innovate upon their combinations. The *Iliad*, the tragic poetry of Greece,— Shakespeare, in the *Tempest* and *Midsummer Night's Dream*,—and most especially Milton, in *Paradise Lost*, conform to this rule; and the most humble novellist, who seeks to confer or receive amusement from his labours, may, without presumption, apply to prose fiction a license, or rather a rule, from the adoption of which so many exquisite combinations of human feeling have resulted in the highest specimens of poetry.

We shall, without farther preface, detail the particulars of the singular story, which is thus introduced.

A vessel, engaged in a voyage of discovery to the North Pole, having become embayed among the ice at a very high latitude, the crew, and particularly the captain or owner of the ship, are surprised at perceiving a gigantic form pass at some distance from them, on a car drawn by dogs, in a place where they conceived no mortal could exist. While they are speculating on this singular apparition, a thaw commences, and disengages them from their precarious situation. On the next morning they pick up, upon a floating fragment of the broken ice, a sledge like that they had before seen, with a human being in the act of perishing. He is with difficulty recalled to life, and proves to be a young man of the most amiable manners and extended acquirements, but, extenuated by fatigue, wrapped in dejection and gloom of the darkest kind. The captain of the ship, a gentleman whose ardent love of science had engaged him on an expedition so dangerous, becomes attached to the stranger, and at length extorts from him the wonderful tale of his misery, which he thus attains the means of preserving from oblivion.

Frankenstein describes himself as a native of Geneva, born and bred up in the bosom of domestic love and affection. His father—his friend Henry Clerval—Elizabeth, an orphan of extreme beauty and talent, bred up in the same house with him, are possessed of all the qualifications which could render him happy as a son, a friend, and a lover. In the course of his

studies he becomes acquainted with the works of Cornelius Agrippa, and other authors treating of occult philosophy, on whose venerable tomes modern neglect has scattered no slight portion of dust. Frankenstein remains ignorant of the contempt in which his favourites are held, until he is separated from his family to pursue his studies at the university of Ingolstadt. Here he is introduced to the wonders of modern chemistry, as well as of natural philosophy in all its branches. Prosecuting these sciences into their innermost and most abstruse recesses, with unusual talent and unexampled success, he at length makes that discovery on which the marvellous part of the work is grounded. His attention had been especially bound to the structure of the human frame and of the principle of life. He engaged in physiological researches of the most recondite and abstruse nature, searching among charnel vaults and in dissection rooms, and the objects most insupportable to the delicacy of human feelings, in order to trace the minute chain of causation which takes place in the change from life to death, and from death to life. In the midst of this darkness a light broke in upon him.

> "Remember," says his narrative, "I am not recording the vision of a madman. The sun does not more certainly shine in the heavens than that which I now affirm is true. Some miracle might have produced it, yet the stages of the discovery were distinct and probable. After days and nights of incredible labour and fatigue, I succeeded in discovering the cause of generation and life; nay, more, I became my self capable of bestowing animation upon lifeless matter."

This wonderful discovery impelled Frankenstein to avail himself of his art by the creation (if we dare to call it so), or formation of a living and sentient being. As the minuteness of the parts formed a great difficulty, he constructed the figure which he proposed to animate of a gigantic size, that is, about eight feet high, and strong and large in proportion. The feverish anxiety with which the young philosopher toils through the horrors of his secret task, now dabbling among the unhallowed reliques of the grave, and now torturing the living animal to animate the lifeless clay, are described generally, but with great vigour of language. Although supported by the hope of producing a new species that should bless him as his creator and source, he nearly sinks under the protracted labour, and loathsome details, of the work he had undertaken, and scarcely is his fatal enthusiasm sufficient to support his nerves, or animate his resolution. The result of this extraordinary discovery it would be unjust to give in any words save those of the author. We shall give it at length as an excellent specimen of the style and manner of the work.

> It was on a dreary night of November that I beheld the accomplishment of my toils. With an anxiety that almost amounted to agony, I collected the instruments of life around me, that I might infuse a spark of being into the lifeless thing that lay at my feet. It was already one in the morning; the rain pattered dismally against the panes, and my candle was nearly burnt out, when, by the glimmer of the half-extinguished light, I saw the dull yellow eye of the creature open; it breathed hard, and a convulsive motion agitated its limbs.
>
> How can I describe my emotions at this catastrophe, or how delineate the wretch whom with such infinite pains and care I had endeavoured to form? His limbs were in proportion, and I had selected his features as beautiful. Beautiful!—Great God! His

yellow skin scarcely covered the work of muscles and arteries beneath; his hair was of a lustrous black, and flowing; his teeth of a pearly whiteness; but these luxuriances only formed a more horrid contrast with his watery eyes, that seemed almost of the same colour as the dun white sockets in which they were set—his shrivelled complexion, and straight black lips.

The different accidents of life are not so changeable as the feelings of human nature. I had worked hard for nearly two years, for the sole purpose of infusing life into an inanimate body. For this I had deprived myself of rest and health. I had desired it with an ardour that far exceeded moderation; but now that I had finished, the beauty of the dream vanished, and breathless horror and disgust filled my heart. Unable to endure the aspect of the being I had created, I rushed out of the room, and continued a long time traversing my bedchamber, unable to compose my mind to sleep. At length lassitude succeeded to the tumult I had before endured; and I threw myself on the bed in my clothes, endeavouring to seek a few moments of forgetfulness. But it was in vain: I slept indeed, but I was disturbed by the wildest dreams. I thought I saw Elizabeth, in the bloom of health, walking in the streets of Ingolstadt. Delighted and surprised, I embraced her; but as I imprinted the first kiss on her lips, they became livid with the hue of death; her features appeared to change, and I thought that I held the corpse of my dead mother in my arms; a shroud enveloped her form, and I saw the grave-worms crawling in the folds of the flannel. I started from my sleep with horror; a cold dew covered my forehead, my teeth chattered, and every limb became convulsed; when, by the dim and yellow light of the moon, as it forced its way through the window-shutters, I beheld the wretch—the miserable monster whom I had created. He held up the curtain of the bed; and his eyes, if eyes they may be called, were fixed on me. His jaws opened, and he muttered some inarticulate sounds, while a grin wrinkled his cheeks. He might have spoken, but I did not hear; one hand was stretched out, seemingly to detain me, but I escaped, and rushed down stairs. I took refuge in the court-yard belonging to the house which I inhabited; where I remained during the rest of the night, walking up and down in the greatest agitation, listening attentively, catching and fearing each sound as if it were to announce the approach of the demoniacal corpse to which I had so miserably given life.

Oh! no mortal could support the horror of that countenance. A mummy again endued with animation could not be so hideous as that wretch. I had gazed on him while unfinished; he was ugly then; but when those muscles and joints were rendered capable of motion, it became a thing such as even Dante could not have conceived.

I passed the night wretchedly. Sometimes my pulse beat so quickly and hardly, that I felt the palpitation of every artery; at others, I nearly sank to the ground through languor and extreme weakness. Mingled with this horror, I felt the bitterness of disappointment: dreams, that had been my food and pleasant rest for so long a space, were now become a hell to me; and the change was so rapid, the overthrow so complete!

Morning, dismal and wet, at length dawned,

and discovered, to my sleepless and aching eyes, the church of Ingolstadt, its white steeple and clock, which indicated the sixth hour. The porter opened the gates of the court, which had that night been my asylum, and I issued into the streets, pacing them with quick steps, as if I sought to avoid the wretch whom I feared every turning of the street would present to my view. I did not dare return to the apartment which I inhabited, but felt impelled to hurry on, although wetted by the rain, which poured from a black and comfortless sky.

I continued walking in this manner for some time, endeavouring, by bodily exercise, to ease the load that weighed upon my mind. I traversed the streets without any clear conception of where I was or what I was doing. My heart palpitated in the sickness of fear; and I hurried on with irregular steps, not daring to look about me:

Like one who, on a lonely road
    Doth walk in fear and dread,
And, having once turn'd round, walks on,
    And turns no more his head;
Because he knows a frightful fiend
    Doth close behind him tread. [1]

He is relieved by the arrival of the diligence from Geneva, out of which jumps his friend Henry Clerval, who had come to spend a season at the college. Compelled to carry Clerval to his lodgings, which, he supposed, must still contain the prodigious and hideous specimen of his Promethean art, his feelings are again admirably described, allowing always for the extraordinary cause supposed to give them birth.

I trembled excessively; I could not endure to think of, and far less to allude to, the occurrences of the preceding night. I walked with a quick pace, and we soon arrived at my college. I then reflected, and the thought made me shiver, that the creature whom I had left in my apartment might still be there, alive, and walking about. I dreaded to behold this monster; but I feared still more that Henry should see him. Entreating him therefore to remain a few minutes at the bottom of the stairs, I darted up towards my own room. My hand was already on the lock of the door before I recollected myself. I then paused; and a cold shivering came over me. I threw the door forcibly open, as children are accustomed to do when they expect a spectre to stand in waiting for them on the other side; but nothing appeared. I stepped fearfully in: the apartment was empty; and my bed-room was also freed from its hideous guest. I could hardly believe that so great a good fortune could have befallen me; but when I became assured that my enemy had indeed fled, I clapped my hands for joy, and ran down to Clerval.

The animated monster is heard of no more for a season. Frankenstein pays the penalty of his rash researches into the *arcana* of human nature, in a long illness, after which the two friends prosecute their studies for two years in uninterrupted quiet. Frankenstein, as may be supposed, abstaining, with a sort of abhorrence, from those in which he had once so greatly delighted. At the lapse of this period, he is made acquainted with a dreadful misfortune which has befallen his family, by the violent death of his youngest brother, an interesting child, who, while straying from his keeper, had been murdered by some villain in the walks of Plainpalais. The marks of strangling were distinct on the neck of the unfortunate infant, and a gold ornament which it wore, and which was amissing, was supposed to have been the murderer's motive for perpetrating the crime.

At this dismal intelligence Frankenstein flies to Geneva, and impelled by fraternal affection, visits the spot where this horrid accident had happened. In the midst of a thunderstorm, with which the evening had closed, and just as he had attained the fatal spot on which Victor had been murdered, a flash of lightning displays to him the hideous demon to which he had given life, gliding towards a neighbouring precipice. Another flash shews him hanging among the cliffs, up which he scrambles with far more than mortal agility, and is seen no more. The inference, that this being was the murderer of his brother, flashed on Frankenstein's mind as irresistibly as the lightning itself, and he was tempted to consider the creature whom he had cast among mankind to work, it would seem, acts of horror and depravity, nearly in the light of his own vampire let loose from the grave, and destined to destroy all that was dear to him.

Frankenstein was right in his apprehensions. Justine, the maid to whom the youthful Victor had been intrusted, is found to be in possession of the golden trinket which had been taken from the child's person; and by a variety of combining circumstances of combined evidence, she is concluded to be the murtheress, and, as such, condemned to death and executed. It does not appear that Frankenstein attempted to avert her fate, by communicating his horrible secret; but, indeed, who would have given him credit, or in what manner could he have supported his tale?

In a solitary expedition to the top of Mount Aveyron, undertaken to dispel the melancholy which clouded his mind, Frankenstein unexpectedly meets with the monster he had animated, who compels him to a conference and a parley. The material demon gives an account, at great length, of his history since his animation, of the mode in which he acquired various points of knowledge, and of the disasters which befell him, when, full of benevolence and philanthropy, he endeavoured to introduce himself into human society. The most material part of his education was acquired in a ruinous pig-stye—a Lyceum which this strange student occupied, he assures us, for a good many months undiscovered, and in constant observance of the motions of an amiable family, from imitating whom he learns the use of language, and other accomplishments, much more successfully than Caliban, though the latter had a conjuror to his tutor. This detail is not only highly improbable, but it is injudicious, as its unnecessary minuteness tends rather too much to familiarize us with the being whom it regards, and who loses, by this *lengthy* oration, some part of the mysterious sublimity annexed to his first appearance. The result is, this monster, who was at first, according to his own account, but a harmless monster, becomes ferocious and malignant, in consequence of finding all his approaches to human society repelled with injurious violence and offensive marks of disgust. Some papers concealed in his dress acquainted him with the circumstances and person to whom he owed his origin; and the hate which he felt towards the whole human race was now concentrated in resentment against Frankenstein. In this humour he murdered the child, and disposed the picture so as to induce a belief of Justine's guilt. The last is an inartificial circumstance: this indirect mode of mischief was not likely to occur to the being the narrative presents to us. The conclusion of this strange narrative is a peremptory demand on the part of the demon, as he is usually termed, that Frankenstein should renew his fearful experiment, and create for him an helpmate hideous as himself, who should have no pretence for shunning his society. On this condition he promises to withdraw to some

distant desert, and shun the human race for ever. If his creator shall refuse him this consolation, he vows the prosecution of the most frightful vengeance. Frankenstein, after a long pause of reflection, imagines he sees that the justice due to the miserable being, as well as to mankind, who might be exposed to so much misery, from the power and evil dispositions of a creature who could climb perpendicular cliffs and exist among glaciers, demanded that he should comply with the request; and granted his promise accordingly.

Frankenstein retreats to one of the distant islands of the Orcades, that in secrecy and solitude he might resume his detestable and ill-omened labours, which now were doubly hideous, since he was deprived of the enthusiasm with which he formerly prosecuted them. As he is sitting one night in his laboratory, and recollecting the consequences of his first essay in the Promethean art, he begins to hesitate concerning the right he had to form another being as malignant and bloodthirsty as that he had unfortunately already animated. It is evident that he would thereby give the demon the means of propagating a hideous race, superior to mankind in strength and hardihood, who might render the very existence of the present human race a condition precarious and full of terror. Just as these reflections lead him to the conclusion that his promise was criminal, and ought not to be kept, he looks up, and sees, by the light of the moon, the demon at the casement.

> A ghastly grin wrinkled his lips as he gazed on me, where I sat fulfilling the task which he allotted to me. Yes, he had followed me in my travels; he had loitered in forests, hid himself in caves, or taken refuge in wide and desert heaths; and he now came to mark my progress, and claim the fulfilment of my promise.
>
> As I looked on him, his countenance expressed the utmost extent of malice and treachery. I thought with a sensation of madness on my promise of creating another like to him, and, trembling with passion, tore to pieces the thing on which I was engaged. The wretch saw me destroy the creature on whose future existence he depended for happiness, and, with a howl of devilish despair and revenge, withdrew.

At a subsequent interview, described with the same wild energy, all treaty is broken off betwixt Frankenstein and the work of his hands, and they part on terms of open and declared hatred and defiance. Our limits do not allow us to trace in detail the progress of the demon's vengeance. Clerval falls its first victim, and under circumstances which had very nearly conducted the new Prometheus to the gallows as his supposed murderer. Elizabeth, his bride, is next strangled on her wedding-night; his father dies of grief; and at length Frankenstein, driven to despair and distraction, sees nothing left for him in life but vengeance on the singular cause of his misery. With this purpose he pursues the monster from clime to clime, receiving only such intimations of his being on the right scent, as served to shew that the demon delighted in thus protracting his fury and his sufferings. At length, after the flight and pursuit had terminated among the frost-fogs, and icy islands of the northern ocean, and just when he had a glimpse of his adversary, the ground sea was heard, the ice gave way, and Frankenstein was placed in the perilous situation in which he is first introduced to the reader.

Exhausted by his sufferings, but still breathing vengeance against the being which was at once his creature and his persecutor, this unhappy victim to physiological discovery expires just as the clearing away of the ice permits Captain

Walton's vessel to hoist sail for their return to Britain. At midnight, the dæmon, who had been his destroyer, is discovered in the cabin, lamenting over the corpse of the person who gave him being. To Walton he attempts to justify his resentment towards the human race, while, at the same time, he acknowledges himself a wretch who had murdered the lovely and the helpless, and pursued to irremediable ruin his creator, the select specimen of all that was worthy of love and admiration.

"Fear not," he continues, addressing the astonished Walton, "that I shall be the instrument of future mischief. My work is nearly complete. Neither yours nor any man's death is needed to consummate the series of my being, and accomplish that which must be done; but it requires my own. Do not think that I shall be slow to perform this sacrifice. I shall quit your vessel on the ice-raft which brought me hither, and shall seek the most northern extremity of the globe; I shall collect my funeral pile, and consume to ashes this miserable frame, that its remains may afford no light to any curious and unhallowed wretch, who would create such another as I have been.—"

He sprung from the cabin-window, as he said this, upon the ice-raft which lay close to the vessel. He was soon borne away by the waves, and lost in darkness and distance.

Whether this singular being executed his purpose or no must necessarily remain an uncertainty, unless the voyage of discovery to the north pole should throw any light on the subject.

So concludes this extraordinary tale, in which the author seems to us to disclose uncommon powers of poetic imagination. The feeling with which we perused the unexpected and fearful, yet, allowing the possibility of the event, very natural conclusion of Frankenstein's experiment, shook a little even our firm nerves; although such and so numerous have been the expedients for exciting terror employed by the romantic writers of the age, that the reader may adopt Macbeth's words with a slight alteration:

We have supp'd full with horrors:
Direness, familiar to our "callous" thoughts,
Cannot once startle us.

It is no slight merit in our eyes, that the tale, though wild in incident, is written in plain and forcible English, without exhibiting that mixture of hyperbolical Germanisms with which tales of wonder are usually told, as if it were necessary that the language should be as extravagant as the fiction. The ideas of the author are always clearly as well as forcibly expressed; and his descriptions of landscape have in them the choice requisites of truth, freshness, precision, and beauty. The self-education of the monster, considering the slender opportunities of acquiring knowledge that he possessed, we have already noticed as improbable and overstrained. That he should have not only learned to speak, but to read, and, for aught we know, to write—that he should have become acquainted with Werter, with Plutarch's *Lives*, and with *Paradise Lost*, by listening through a hole in a wall, seems as unlikely as that he should have acquired, in the same way, the problems of Euclid, or the art of book-keeping by single and double entry. The author has however two apologies—the first, the necessity that his monster should acquire those endowments, and the other, that his neighbours were engaged in teaching the language of the country to a young foreigner. His progress in self-knowledge, and the acquisition of information, is, after

all, more wonderful than that of Hai Eben Yokhdan, or Automathes, or the hero of the little romance called *The Child of Nature*, one of which works might perhaps suggest the train of ideas followed by the author of *Frankenstein*. We should also be disposed, in support of the principles with which we set out, to question whether the monster, how tall, agile, and strong however, could have perpetrated so much mischief undiscovered, or passed through so many countries without being secured, either on account of his crimes, or for the benefit of some such speculator as Mr Polito, who would have been happy to have added to his museum so curious a specimen of natural history. But as we have consented to admit the leading incident of the work, perhaps some of our readers may be of opinion, that to stickle upon lesser improbabilities, is to incur the censure bestowed by the Scottish proverb on those who start at straws after swallowing *windlings*.

The following lines, which occur in the second volume, mark, we think, that the author possesses the same facility in expressing himself in verse as in prose.

We rest; a dream has power to poison sleep.
We rise; one wand'ring thought pollutes the
day.
We feel, conceive, or reason; laugh, or weep,
Embrace fond woe, or cast our cares away;
It is the same: for, be it joy or sorrow,
The path of its departure still is free.
Man's yesterday may ne'er belike his morrow;
Nought may endure but mutability!

Upon the whole, the work impresses us with a high idea of the author's original genius and happy power of expression. We shall be delighted to hear that he has aspired to the *paullo majora*; and in the meantime, congratulate our readers upon a novel which excites new reflections and untried sources of emotion. If Gray's definition of Paradise, to lie on a couch, namely, and read new novels, come any thing near truth, no small praise is due to him, who, like the author of Frankenstein, has enlarged the sphere of that fascinating enjoyment.

Notes
1. Coleridge's *Ancient Mariner*.

HELEN MOORE
From "*Frankenstein*, and Other Writings"
Mary Wollstonecraft Shelley
1886, pp. 244–64

The published books of an author bear no necessary relation to his literary work, still less are they a gauge of his intellectual life. The faculty for literary production is something apart, often possessed by those who have little worth producing, denied to those who die—as galleons sink—carrying their golden wealth with them. Of no one is this more true than of Mrs. Shelley. Her literary productions were few and disproportionate to her intellectual force; disappointing when viewed side by side with her peculiar gift of evoking the most artistic literary work in others. Her published writings comprise, *Frankenstein*, in 1818; *Valperga*, 1823; *The Last Man*, 1824; *Perkin Warbeck*, 1830; *Lodore*, 1835; and *Falkner*, 1837; the Italian and Spanish lives in *Lardner's Encyclopedia*, with the exception of "Tasso" and "Galileo." She published also Shelley's prose works, his poems, with valuable notes, two volumes of travels, *Rambles in Germany and Italy*, besides contributing to the magazines.

Of Mrs. Shelley's writings, *Frankenstein* is without question the most noteworthy. From the day of its first appearance in print down to the present, it has had accorded to it a position as a unique and remarkable production. This reputation, gained equally from two classes who rarely agree in reading the same book, still less in praising it—thoughtful *littérateurs* and mere readers of stories,—it has steadily maintained. This fact of itself is doubtless due to, and in a measure significant of, the dual character of the romance. It is one of the few books that can be called *sui generis*. The advent of such books into the literary world is always a subject of interest. And the wonder is not lessened when we are told that this book was the production of a girl of eighteen, and her first attempt at sustained literary work. Allusion has already been made to the period of Mrs. Shelley's life in which *Frankenstein* was written, but in order to gain a critical comprehension of the work, the details of its production are of the highest interest.

During the summer of 1816, while the Shelleys were neighbors of Lord Byron, on the borders of Lake Geneva, the intercourse between the two poets and their households was daily and intimate. Byron was at that time composing the third canto of "Childe Harold," and as each successive scene was finished he brought his work to his poet neighbor, who thus partook of the first fruits of a genius he was so well adapted to recognize and value. Moreover, the prolonged rains keeping them in-doors, they chanced to find some volumes of fiction,—principally ghost stories and fantastic fairy tales translated from the French and German. The drift of much of their talk tended into the atmosphere of the supernatural and horrible.

It is worthy of passing note that many of these stories were of a strictly allegorical type. Thus one was the history of the inconstant lover, who having deserted his betrothed when most he should have befriended her, chose a bride, and clasped her to his arms only to find himself embracing the pale ghost of his deserted. Another story was of a parent who by crime bestowed life upon a race and was doomed to give the kiss of death to all the sons of his ill-fated house, just as they in turn reached the age of promise.

While under the influence of these fantastic tales and the impromptu ones which they told each other, the agreement was made that each should write a ghost story. The proposition was Byron's; it was accorded to and entered upon by all. The poets themselves failed, and it is more than probable that the persistence of Mrs. Shelley was due rather to the wishes and urgency of Shelley than to any innate energy or will of her own in the matter. He, from the time of their first acquaintance, had been anxious that she should attempt literary work of some kind, partly because of his faith in the theory of heredity, and partly from a confidence in his own estimate of her mental qualities. He believed that the daughter of William Godwin and Mary Wollstonecraft, the woman whose mental brightness and spirit had for himself a never-failing endurance, could not but be remarkable in any literary work to which she might turn her mind.

Mrs. Shelley herself, in the preface of the last London edition of *Frankenstein*, published during her life, has told how she tried day after day to think of a plot; to invent something uncanny or horribly fantastic, and how each morning, to the question, "Have you thought of a story?" she was obliged to answer "No," until a train of thought supplied by conversation of a metaphysical tone which she had listened to between Shelley and Byron, entered into her state of reverie in semi-sleep, and suggested the essential outlines of the plot of *Frankenstein*.

What was thus suggested was probably nothing more than the central figures of the weird conception. Nothing could be simpler than the plot, nothing more horrible than the situations and the details. Frankenstein is a student who, by the study of occult sciences, acquires the power of imparting life to a figure which he had made. Graves and charnel-house had furnished the needed material from which he had constructed this colossal human form. To the thing thus prepared he is able to impart life. It lives and possesses human attributes. The rest of the tale is occupied in depicting the nameless horrors which visited Frankenstein as the result of his creation. The thing becomes the bane of his life. He tries to fly from it, but there is no final escape. One by one, the monster that he had created slays the brother, friend, sister, and bride of the luckless student, who himself finally falls a victim to his own wretched and untoward creation. The monster, upon its part, strives to adapt itself to life, but fails; finds no possibility of companionship, no admission into any human fellowship.

Such in brief outline is the plot, if it can be so called, of the tale which, with eager hands, the youthful romancer penned before the first horror of the idea had faded from her brain. At Shelley's suggestion the story was amplified. The introductory letters were inserted and the pastoral episode and other incidents were added to the later part of the narrative. As originally written the story began with the words, "It was on a dreary night of November that I beheld the accomplishment of my toils." In the work as published these words introduce Chapter IV.

Regarded as a mere tale, it is difficult to account for the hold this story has always had upon the minds of the reading world. As a story it does not justify its own success. To say that it is remarkable as a work of imagination does not meet the difficulty. By a work of the imagination, as used in the current criticism of *Frankenstein*, is simply meant that it is a fantastic romance, such as we find in the *Arabian Nights*, or in the prose tales of Poe. But a position utterly different from these is accorded to *Frankenstein*.

We have intimated that there was a dual quality in it, to which it owed its singular power and place in literature. One element is doubtless the horror of the tale and the weird fancy of the author's imagination in the ordinary acceptation of the word. But it is to an entirely different department of mental conception that we must look for the secret of its peculiar influence. The faculty of imagination is something more than the recalling and rearrangements of past impressions. Profoundly considered, it is that function of the mind which formulates, as though real, a state of things which if present would so appear. It is the power of projecting the mind into unhappened realities. It is the faculty of picturing unseen verities. There is thus in it a prophetic element, not at all miraculous, but dependent upon subtle laws of association and suggestion. It is to this element that *Frankenstein* owes its power over thoughtful minds. It is by virtue of the allegorical element in it that it holds its high position as a work of the imagination. Yet so unobtrusively is the allegory woven through the thread of the romance, that, while always felt, it can scarcely be said to have been detected. Certain it is that no one has directed attention to this phase, or carefully attempted an analysis of the work, with the view of deducing the meaning thus legible between the lines.

That Mrs. Shelley herself was conscious of this element is certain, by the double title she gave it,—*Frankenstein, or the Modern Prometheus*. Furthermore, that she should thus embody, under the apparent guise of a weird story, suggestions of moral truths, development of mental traits,—normal and abnormal,—and hints at, and solutions of, social questions, was in strict accord both with her own intellectual state and with the circumstances under which *Frankenstein* was produced. And yet nothing is more improbable than that it was written with such design, or that the youthful author was fully aware or even conscious of the extent to which the allegorical overlies largely the narrative in her work. This very unconsciousness of result, this obliviousness to hidden truths, is a distinguishing mark of genius. To take daily account of stock proclaims the small trader, not the merchant prince. Placed in a congenial atmosphere, genius in breathing the breath of life will exhale truths. The very gist of genius is embodied in this hidden relation to truth. That mind has genius which, detecting germs of truth under forms where the common eye sees them not, affords in itself the place and pabulum for their growth.

We know the circumstance under which the book was written; the stories which suggested it were all weird in form and allegorical in type; the minds of those by whom Mrs. Shelley was at that time surrounded were minds to whom the mystical was the natural mode of thought and speech. Her own inherited and acquired mental traits were markedly of this same character. Furthermore, at this time the influence of Shelley was strongest upon her. Not that of one nature mastering and overpowering a weaker, but that yet stronger bond of one mind fitted by nature and oneness of motive to gain insight into, and be in unison with, the other.

Such, in a remarkable degree, was her relation at this time to Shelley; to her his nature was revealed. They had spoken and dwelt upon his past until it was an open book to her. His aims and his failures, his aspirations and fears, his nature and philosophy were familiar and ever present to her mind. Moreover, from him she had learned much about the great world of men and things, broadening her nature and conceptions beyond the ordinary limit of feminine knowledge; indeed, with the result of attaching her own peculiar insight to the facts and ideas thus included within her extending horizon. In both of their minds the tendency to dwell on social and ethical problems was strong, and to such natures union means cubic strength. What wonder that, if, underlying her story thus produced, should lie partly concealed or vaguely hinted, social and moral ideas, awaiting but recognition, to become in turn the suggestors of their own redevelopment in the minds of us who read.

That some, nay, many, of these have an almost direct bearing upon Shelley himself, either as proceeding from him or pointing to him, is to be expected; to say that they all thus have would be perhaps straining a theory otherwise tenable. What we can safely affirm is that he who, with this idea of the allegorical substratum, will reread the story, will be richly repaid in the suggestions the mind cannot fail to receive, and which, according to the mind of each, will attach to the nature of Shelley himself, or, more widely taken, will stand as general truths, applicable alike to all.

Such a general truth is that pictured in the character and pursuit of the student Frankenstein himself. He exhibits to us the man of one idea, absorbed in but one department of science, not only abandoning other studies, but rejecting the ordinary avocations of life. Family, friend, even the voice of her who loved him, fails to recall him to action or to a sense of the proper proportion of things. We see the result not only in the loss of symmetry and balance in his character, but find it having its legitimate effect in making him the slave of his own

too concentrated studies. So that finally he becomes possessed by the ruling idea he had so dearly cherished, and the reward of his infatuation is the delusion that he can accomplish that which a healthful mind would have avoided,—a delusion which had grown up in the very seclusion and isolation of life that the unhappy student had adopted; to which the fitting antidote would have been the diversion of the commonplace interests which he had carefully excluded. The power to produce the horrible creature, as the fruit of this delusion, is but the poetic justice of his sentence. The terrible result of his creation furnishes the morale and teaching of the allegory. Into this part of the story is interposed the train of thought which is suggested by the construction of the human form by Frankenstein. In its preparation the student selects the most beautiful models for each limb and feature. He spares no pains, and each separate anatomical part is, taken by itself, perfect in symmetry and adaptation. But when once the breath of life is breathed into the creation, and life quickens its being and gleams from its eyes, and function succeeds in the hitherto inanimate parts, all beauty disappears; the separate excellence of each several part is lost in the general incongruity and lack of harmony of the whole.

Can art see no suggestiveness in this? Can society, in its attempt to manufacture conglomerate masses out of dissimilar elements, learn nothing from the teaching here inculcated?

Once become a living being, Frankenstein and this monster that he had made bear to one another the sustained relation of creator and creature. Throughout the entire narrative this relationship is one long allegory with phases as diverse as a prism. Most prominent is the total failure to create that which should find place in life only by growth. In the sad, lone, utter incompatibility which environed the creature,—in the inability of others to accept or tolerate it,—in its own desperate, heart-sickening attempts to educate and train itself into harmony and communion with those who should have been its fellow-beings, and in its final despair and terrible outlawry and revenge, is shown the futility of the attempt to regulate human beings, or their concerns, except under the laws of growth and development. And *Frankenstein* contains no deeper teaching than that we cannot legislate happiness into this world; that such attempt at last, after affording a maximum of misery, returns to plague the inventor.

Another phase of this relationship between the creator and his creature is so strongly suggestive of a certain period of Shelley's religious life that the mind hesitates before denying the likeness. The creature of Frankenstein, finding itself in a world in which all happiness is denied it; to which its powers of strengthfulness, however exercised, bring it no good, but serve only to increase its misery and sense of loneliness, turns to its creator and, with alternate curses and prayers, beseeches him to either slay it or fit the world for its companionship. In this dilemma the creator does neither. He merely admits either his unwillingness or his inability to do that which simple justice to his creature, to say nothing of his love and duty, would prompt. Thus the creator is made to figure as lacking either justice or omnipotence.

How Shelleyan this idea, the closest student of him will best judge.

But the chief allegorical interest in the narrative concerns itself about that tendency in the human being to discard the established order of things and to create for itself a new and independent existence. In the simple story, Frankenstein made a being responsible to him alone for its creation,—a being not produced by the ordinary course of life, not amenable or even adaptable to the existing world of men. Right or wrong, better or worse, the creature may be, but different certainly, and this irreconcilable disparity points back ever to its origin, which had been anomalous and strange.

The whole story is but the elaboration of the embarrassment and dangers which flow from departure from the ordinary course of nature; this forced attempt to invade society from within. What strong existence in real life of this same tendency Mary Shelley had seen in those nearest and dearest to her! She has not failed to learn the lesson of her mother's history; time analyzes rather than destroys. And the life of Mary Wollstonecraft was doubtless seen by the clear-minded daughter in stronger contrast of light and shade than it had been by its contemporaries. Who knew so well the glories of that life? Its successes as well as its miseries had sprung from the self-same causes as those of Frankenstein,—from the breach of the conventional; from overstepping the limits; from creating an individuality and a sphere of existence denied it by Nomos, and consequently sure of the hostility of society.

To this same cause Shelley himself attributed justly the events and moral struggle of his own life. From earliest childhood revolt against convention, and rebellion against authority, had characterized him. His perpetual tendency, like that of Mary Wollstonecraft, like that typified in *Frankenstein*, was ever to create for himself an existence not conforming to the ways of the world.

As we read the story of the modern Prometheus, and page by page trace the evolution of this idea, the ethical aspect is oppressive in its prophetic truth. Each must do this for himself. One thing, however, we may note. The visitation of judgment, the terrible results of the exercise of the power of creation, do not begin, do not recoil upon Frankenstein, until he has actually launched his creature into the world of men about him. So long as he kept the scheme within himself; so long as the influence of the thought and work was confined to him alone, no evil came; on the contrary, after a certain point the struggle after this ideal was a stimulation and an incentive of the highest order. It was only when the overt act of introducing his new existence into the world was accomplished, that misery began to flow from it to all concerned, and even to those apparently not concerned in it. This is the saving clause in the prophetic allegory. Without this it would fail to square with the truth.

See how far-reaching are the ideas which this allegory evokes, how subtle its suggestions are. Mind after mind has felt the power of this story, so simple in its apparent construction, and has again and again returned to it, not asking itself why; feeling a power it did not recognize, much less analyze; hovering, in fact, around it as birds do when charmed, because of an attraction which was persistent and real, although unknown, even unsuspected. All attraction implies some sort of a magnet. Nothing attracts so powerfully as the true.

The world, by its acknowledgment of the coercive quality of *Frankenstein*, has given silent acceptance of its genius. The other works, novels, critiques, biographies, while they have had literary merit, feeling, even power, have not shown genius. *Frankenstein* alone was personal, it alone reflected Mrs. Shelley's true self. Her other books contain simply what she wrote in them; this alone contains what was written in her. Being, as she was, stronger in her personality than as a literary artist, the book that alone partook of that personality would alone partake of her peculiar genius. This, considered in its fullest light, *Frankenstein* does.

It is a thankless task to sit in judgment upon a novel like *Valperga*, and only the difficulty of obtaining the work and the curiosity to know Mrs. Shelley's most serious endeavor at romance, justify the extended extracts which follow. Formed upon the old-fashioned models, it, like them, essentially lacks action, incident, and dramatic expression. It is unrelieved by nicely-drawn character sketches. It so abounds in long and learned speeches, dull descriptions, lifeless records of events, that to our highly exacting modern mind, as a novel, it is a complete failure. But it is not as a novel that the book ought to be judged. As an illustration of its author's mental and moral development it has a place and a purpose. For although she has a certain sympathetic insight into the imaginative, the emotional; although she delights in the deeply tragical,—page follows page of unmitigated melancholy—it is totally without the light and shade which would make us feel the pathos of the story intensely. Indeed, one could not call it pathetic; it is simply tragical.

Not an emotion of pity visits you while you read; not a spark of enthusiasm, not an impulse of sympathy. Its people are as dead to you as they have been these hundreds of years to the world. One reads the three volumes stolidly, unmoved; interested only because of the insight which one gains of its author.

Castruccio, Prince of Lucca, the tyrant, the caustic wit of history, the first soldier and satirist of his age, moves laboriously through the book. His ambitions do not penetrate, his villanies do not touch one. He is a thing without life, without passion; the events of his career are dull-recorded facts. Mrs. Shelley has not done justice to his keen and crafty generalship, to his trenchant and powerful satire. You do not get a glimpse of the man of history, who, when he was dying in the zenith of his glory, said, "Lay me on my face in the coffin, for everything will be reversed ere long after my departure;" or who rebuked a young man whom he met coming out of a house of ill repute, and who blushed at seeing Castruccio,—"It was when you went in that you should have colored, not when you come out." Again, when in a storm Castruccio was alarmed, a stupid fool derided, saying he had no fear, as he did not value his own life at a farthing. "Everybody," said Castruccio, "makes the best estimate of his own wares." When a sage rebuked Castruccio for some extravagances at an evening revelry, he replied, "He who is held as a wise man by day, will not be taken to be a fool by night." And again, on remarking the radiant countenance of an envious man, he exclaimed, "Is it that some good hath befallen thee, or that some evil hath befallen another?"

What Mrs. Shelley tried to do—and this, I take it, to be the motive of the book—was to show how from a generous, deep-souled, guileless youth, Castruccio became a cruel, ambitious tyrant, a being deaf to all the appeals of mercy or justice. She has given us an account of his exiled youth, its innocent occupations, its gentle and ennobling influences, its dreams of power and glory for his oppressed native city, Lucca. She has told how, after an apprenticeship spent in the English Court of Edward the Second, in the wars of Flanders, and in the atmosphere of intriguing European countries, he appears as the liberator of his native city; how, after destroying the Guelphic rule by banishing three hundred Guelph families, his idea of liberty was to reinstate the Ghibellines, of which he, the last heir of the noble Antiminelli family, was the head; how, moderate in all his habits and wants, he was yet insatiable in his ambition. Liberty for his country being only the ruse to conceal his greed for power and autocracy.

She has shown how the pure and elevated nature of Euthanasia, his betrothed bride, whose ideal love for him was only equalled by her desire for peace and freedom for her distracted Italy, was as naught to hinder the evil development of his own mind; how the terrible misfortunes of the inspired and misled Beatrice brought no serious regret to him, the careless cause of her misery. It is true that she has shown us all this, but we stand as upon the outer wall, viewing the conflict through the obscurations of the dust and confusion. We fail to discern there the great soldier, the real Castruccio.

The characters of the two women, Euthanasia, Countess of Valperga, and Beatrice, Prophetess of Ferrara, are drawn with more vigor. The intimate workings of their souls are laid bare to us; the deep melancholy of their lives is portrayed with all the detail of one gifted in such analysis. We are reminded of Romola in the story of Euthanasia's life. Nearly two hundred years earlier, in an old library in the same city of Florence, Euthanasia, like Romola, spent her young life reading dull, musty parchments to her blind father, and her after life was not unlike Romola's in its moral conflicts.

In the young Euthanasia, as she sat at her father's feet and drank eagerly his eloquent rhapsodies on the Latin poets, Mrs. Shelley unconsciously describes herself. She says of her heroine, "Her soul was adapted for the reception of all good." Her own education under Shelley's guidance was not unlike that of the child Euthanasia, who from love mastered with amazing skill the difficult Latin transcriptions on the old parchments, that she might read them to her father, for Shelley writes of Mary's progress in Latin shortly after their marriage,—"She has satisfied my best expectations." Many qualities of heart and mind attributed to Euthanasia or Beatrice, one recognizes as but the unconscious portrayal of her own nature. Euthanasia grows up as a Guelph and a Florentine, holding sacred the friendship of the noble-hearted Castruccio, who had been her knight and playmate before his exile. One by one, her father, mother, brothers die, and she is left the last survivor of her family. After Castruccio's return to Italy they renew their vows and are betrothed; but it is now that she sees with despair the seeds of evil in her lover's character which finally divide them. The conflict between Euthanasia's love for Castruccio and her hatred of tyranny and bloodshed is perhaps the chief interest of the romance.

But it is the character of Beatrice—a character fraught with passion and madness—which displays the peculiar power of Mrs. Shelley's imagination; the power of realizing and dealing with the terrible. Like Frankenstein, Beatrice is the result of an abnormal and one-sided development. Like him, she creates for herself a strange and unnatural state of existence. Like him, she suffers the fatal consequence of an intense absorption to one idea,—the idea of her divine inspiration. Here again does the dual tendency of Mrs. Shelley's mind show itself. Beatrice is the outgrowth of all the religious frenzies and persecutions of the age; her prophetic dreams and enthusiasms are the wild and morbid development of a highly overstrung and unbalanced mind, encouraged by the superstitious reverence of her countrymen and friends and her own credulous belief in her divine inspirations. Her final awakening, her realization of the deception under which she has lived, her love for Castruccio, her pilgrimage to Rome, her abhorrence of the religion in which she had been nurtured, and which had made her fanaticism possible, her despair of truth or humanity, her final madness, are all highly dramatic possibilities, had Mrs. Shelley but let the simple truths speak for themselves; but she so dissipates the strength of her situations by long and tedious sentences and dull narrations that you feel like one who, walking over endless stretch of plain, longs for broken country.

The tone of the book is pure and high. There is in it the intense earnestness that actuated Mary Shelley throughout her life. There are careful and laborious details of manners and customs; long and erudite speeches, religious and political; a conscientious study of Italy and her internal strife. The flowing eloquence and rhapsodies of the imaginative Beatrice are well sustained; the unswerving truth and nobility of Euthanasia's character are drawn with tenderness and appreciation. But the book will not stand the test of a good novel; its characters do not remain in your mind like the memories of real people. They are passionless and lifeless.

LUCY MADOX ROSSETTI
From "Literary Work"
Mrs. Shelley
1890, pp. 186–204

This highly imaginative work of Mary Shelley's twenty-sixth year ⟨*Valperga*⟩ contains some of the author's most powerful ideas; but is marred in the commencement by some of her most stilted writing.

The account of the events recorded professes to be found in the cave of the Cumæan Sibyl, near Naples, where they had remained for centuries, outlasting the changes of nature and, when found, being still two hundred and fifty years in advance of the time foretold. The accounts are all written on the sibylline leaves; they are in all languages, ancient and modern; and those concerning this story are in English.

We find ourselves in England, in 2073, in the midst of a Republic, the last king of England having abdicated at the quietly expressed wish of his subjects. This book, like all Mrs. Shelley's, is full of biographical reminiscences; the introduction gives the date of her own visit to Naples with Shelley, in 1818; the places they visited are there indicated; the poetry, romance, the pleasures and pains of her own existence, are worked into her subjects; while her imagination carries her out of her own surroundings. We clearly recognise in the ideal character of the son of the abdicated king an imaginary portrait of Shelley as Mary would have him known, not as she knew him as a living person. To give an adequate idea of genius with all its charm, and yet with its human imperfections, was beyond Mary's power. Adrian, the son of kings, the aristocratic republican, is the weakest part, and one cannot help being struck by Mary Shelley's preference for the aristocrat over the plebeian. In fact, Mary's idea of a republic still needed kings' sons by their good manners to grace it, while, at the same time, the king's son had to be transmuted into an ideal Shelley. This strange confusion of ideas allowed for, and the fact that over half a century of perhaps the earth's most rapid period of progress has passed, the imaginative qualities are still remarkable in Mary. Balloons, then dreamed of, were attained; but naturally the steam-engine and other wonders of science, now achieved, were unknown to Mary. When the plague breaks out she has scope for her fancy, and she certainly adds vivid pictures of horror and pathos to a subject which has been handled by masters of thought at different periods. In this time of horror it is amusing to note how the people's candidate, Ryland, represented as a vulgar specimen of humanity, succumbs to abject fear. The description of the deserted towns and grass-grown streets of London is impressive. The fortunes of the family, to whom the last man, Lionel Verney, belongs, are traced through their varying phases, as one by one the dire plague assails them, and Verney, the only man who recovers from the disease, becomes the leader of the remnant of the English nation. This small handful of humanity leaves England, and wanders through France on its way to the favoured southern countries where human aid, now so scarce, was less needed. On this journey Mrs. Shelley avails herself of reminiscences of her own travelling with Shelley some few years before; and we pass the places noted in her diary; but strange grotesque figures cross the path of the wanderers, who are decimated each day. At one moment a dying acrobat, deserted by his companions, is seen bounding in the air behind a hedge in the dusk of evening. At another, a black figure mounted on a horse, which only shows itself after dark, to cause apprehensions soon calmed by the death of the poor wanderer, who wished only for distant companionship through dread of contagion. Dijon is reached and passed, and here the old Countess of Windsor, the ex-Queen of England, dies: she had only been reconciled to her changed position by the destruction of humanity. Once, near Geneva, they come upon the sound of divine music in a church, and find a dying girl playing to her blind father to keep up the delusion to the last. The small party, reduced by this time to five, reach Chamouni, and the grand scenes so familiar to Mary contrast with the final tragedy of the human race; yet one more dies, and only four of one family remain; they bury the dead man in an ice cavern, and with this last victim find the pestilence has ended, after a seven years' reign over the earth. A weight is lifted from the atmosphere, and the world is before them; but now alone they must visit her ruins; and the beauty of the earth and the love of each other, bear them up till none but the last man remains to complete the Cumæan Sibyl's prophecy.

Various stories of minor importance followed from Mrs. Shelley's pen, and preparations were made for the lives of eminent literary men. But it was not till the year preceding her father's death that we have *Lodore*, published in 1835. Of this novel we have already spoken in relation to the separation of Shelley and Harriet.

Mary had too much feeling of art in her work to make an imaginary character a mere portrait, and we are constantly reminded in her novels of the different wonderful and interesting personages whom she knew intimately, though most of their characters were far too subtle and complex to be unravelled by her, even with her intimate knowledge. Indeed, the very fact of having known some of the greatest people of her age, or of almost any age, gives an appearance of affectation to her novels, as it fills them with characters so far from the common run that their place in life cannot be reduced to an ordinary fashionable level. Romantic episodes there may be, but their true place is in the theatre of time of which they are the movers, not the Lilliputians of life who are slowly worked on and moulder by them, and whose small doings are the material of most novels. We know of few novelists who have touched at all successfully on the less known characters. This accomplishment seems to need the great poet himself.

The manner in which Lady Lodore is influenced seems to point to Harriet; but the unyielding and revengeful side of her character has certainly more of Lady Byron. She is charmingly described, and shows a great deal of insight on Mary's part into the life of fashionable people of her time, which then, perhaps more than now, was the favourite theme with novelists. This must be owing to a certain innate Tory propensity in the English classes or masses for whom Mary Shelley had to work hard, and for whose tendencies in this respect she certainly had a sympathy. Mary's own life, at the point we have now reached, is also here touched on in the character of Ethel, Lord and Lady Lodore's daughter, who is brought up in America by her father, and on his death entrusted to an aunt, with injunctions in his will that she is not to be allowed to be brought in contact with her mother. Her character is sweetly feminine and trusting, and in her fortunate love and marriage (in all but early money matters) might be considered quite unlike Mary's own less fortunate experiences; but in her perfect love and confidence in her husband, her devotion and unselfishness through the trials of poverty in London, the descriptions of which were evidently taken from Mary's own experiences, there is no doubt of the resemblance, as also in her love and reverence for all connected with her father. There are also passages undoubtedly expressive of her own inner feelings—such as this when describing the young husband and wife at a *tête-à-tête* supper:—

> Mutual esteem and gratitude sanctified the unreserved sympathy which made each so happy in the other. Did they love the less for not loving "in sin and fear"? Far from it. The certainty of being the cause of good to each other tended to foster the most delicate of all passions, more than the rough ministrations of terror and the knowledge that each was the occasion of injury. A woman's heart is peculiarly unfitted to sustain this conflict. Her sensibility gives keenness to her imagination and she magnifies every peril, and writhes beneath every sacrifice which tends to humiliate her in her own eyes. The natural pride of her sex struggles with her desire to confer happiness, and her peace is wrecked.

What stronger expression of feeling could be needed than this, of a woman speaking from her heart and her own experiences? Does it not remind one of the moral on this subject in all George Eliot's writing, where she shows that the outcome of what by some might be considered minor transgressions against morality leads even in modern times to the Nemesis of the most terrible Greek Dramas?

The complicated money transactions carried on with the aid of lawyers were clearly a reminiscence of Shelley's troubles, and of her own incapacity to feel all the distress contingent so long as she was with him, and there was evidently money somewhere in the family, and it would come some time. In this novel we also perceive that Mary works off her pent-up feelings with regard to Emilia Viviani. It cannot be supposed that the corporeal part of Shelley's creation of *Epipsychidion* (so exquisite in appearance and touching in manner and story as to give rise, when transmitted through the poet's brain, to the most perfect of love ideals) really ultimately became the fiery-tempered worldly-minded virago that Mary Shelley indulges herself in depicting, after first, in spite of altering some relations and circumstances, clearly showing whom the character was intended for. It is true that Shelley himself, after investing her with divinity to serve the purposes of art, speaks later of her as a very commonplace worldly-minded woman; but poets, like artists, seem at times to need lay figures to attire with their thoughts. Enough has been shown to prove that there is genuine subject of interest in this work of Mary's thirty-seventh year.

The next work, *Falkner*, published in 1837, is the last novel we have by Mary Shelley; and as we see from her letter she had been passing through a period of ill-health and depression while writing it, this may account for less spontaneity in the style, which is decidedly more stilted; but, here again, we feel that we are admitted to some of the circle which Mary had encountered in the stirring times of her life, and there is undoubted imagination with some fine descriptive passages.

The opening chapter introduces a little deserted child in a picturesque Cornish village. Her parents had died there in apartments, one after the other, the husband having married a governess against the wishes of his relations; consequently, the wife was first neglected on her husband's death; and on her own sudden death, a few months later, the child was simply left to the care of the poor people of the village—a dreamy, poetic little thing, whose one pleasure was to stroll in the twilight to the village churchyard and be with her mamma. Here she was found by Falkner, the principal character of the romance, who had selected this very spot to end a ruined existence; in which attempt he was frustrated by the child jogging his arm to move him from her mother's grave. His life being thus saved by the child's instrumentality, he naturally became interested in her. He is allowed to look through the few remaining papers of the parents. Among these he finds an unfinished letter of the wife, evidently addressed to a lady he had known, and also indications who the parents were. He was much moved, and offered to relieve the poor people of the child and to restore her to her relations.

The mother's unfinished letter to her friend contains the following passage, surely autobiographical:—

> When I lost Edwin (the husband), I wrote to Mr. Raby (the husband's father) acquainting him with the sad intelligence, and asking for a maintenance for myself and my child. The family solicitor answered my letter. Edwin's conduct had, I was told, estranged his family from him, and they could only regard me as one encouraging his disobedience and apostasy. I had no claim on them. If my child were sent to them, and I would promise to abstain from all intercourse with her, she should be brought up with her cousins, and treated in all respects like one of the family. I declined their barbarous offer, and haughtily and in few words relinquished every claim on their bounty, declaring my intention to support and bring up my child myself. This was foolishly done, I fear; but I cannot regret it, even now.
>
> I cannot regret the impulse that made me disdain these unnatural and cruel relatives, or that led me to take my poor orphan to my heart with pride as being all my own. What had they done to merit such a treasure? And did they show themselves capable of replacing a fond and anxious mother?

This reminds the reader of the correspondence between Mary and her father on Shelley's death.

It suffices to say that Falkner became so attached to the small child, that by the time he discovered her relations he had not the heart to confide her to their hard guardianship, and as he was compelled to leave England shortly, he took her with him, and through all difficulties he contrived that she should be well guarded and brought up. There is much in the character of Falkner that reminds the reader of Trelawny, the gallant and generous friend of Byron and Shelley in their last years, the brave and romantic traveller. The description of Falkner's face and figure must have much resembled that of Trelawny when young, though, of course, the incidents of the story have no connection with him. In the meantime the little girl is growing up, and the nurses are replaced by an English governess, whom Falkner engages abroad, and whose praises and qualifications he hears from everyone at Odessa. The story progresses through various incidents foreshadowing the cause of Falkner's mystery. Elizabeth, the child, now grown up, passes under his surname. While travelling in Germany they come across a youth of great personal attraction, who appears, however, to be of a singularly reckless and misanthropical disposition for one so young. Elizabeth seeming attracted by his daring and beauty, Falkner suddenly finds it necessary to

return to England. Shortly afterwards, he is moved to go to Greece during the War of Independence, and wishes to leave Elizabeth with her relations in England; but this she strenuously opposes so far as to induce Falkner to let her accompany him to Greece, where he places her with a family while he rushes into the thick of the danger, only hoping to end his life in a good cause. In this he nearly succeeds, but Elizabeth, hearing of his danger, hastens to his side, and nurses him assiduously through the fever brought on from his wounds and the malarious climate. By short stages and the utmost care, she succeeds in reaching Malta on their homeward journey, and Falkner, a second time rescued from death by his beloved adopted child, determines not again to endanger recklessly the life more dear to her than that of many fathers. Again, at Malta, during a fortnight's quarantine, the smallness of the world of fashionable people brings them in contact with an English party, a Lord and Lady Cecil, who are travelling with their family. Falkner is too ill to see anyone, and when Elizabeth finally gets him on board a vessel to proceed to Genoa, he seems rapidly sinking. In his despair and loneliness, feeling unable to cope with all the difficulties of burning sun and cold winds, help unexpectedly comes: a gentleman whom Elizabeth has not before perceived, and whom now she is too much preoccupied to observe, quietly arranges the sail to shelter the dying man from sun and wind, places pillows, and does all that is possible; he even induces the poor girl to go below and rest on a couch for a time while he watches. Falkner becomes easier in the course of the night; he sleeps and gains in strength, and from this he progresses till, while at Marseilles, he hears the name, Neville, of the unknown friend who had helped to restore him to life. He becomes extremely agitated and faints. On being restored to consciousness he begs Elizabeth to continue the journey with him alone, as he can bear no one but her near him. The mystery of Falkner's life seems to be forcing itself to the surface.

The travellers reach England, and Elizabeth is sought out by Lady Cecil, who had been much struck by her devotion to her father. Elizabeth is invited to stay with Lady Cecil, as she much needs rest in her turn. During a pleasant time of repose near Hastings, Elizabeth hears Lady Cecil talk much of her brother Gerard; but it is not till he, too, arrives on a visit, that she acknowledges to herself that he is really the same Mr. Neville whom she had met, and from whom she had received such kindness. Nor had Gerard spoken of Elizabeth; he had been too much drawn towards her, as his life also is darkened by a mystery. They spend a short tranquil time together, when a letter announces the approaching arrival of Sir Boyvill Neville, the young man's father (although Lady Cecil called Gerard her brother, they were not really related; Sir Boyvill had married the mother of Lady Cecil, who was the offspring of a previous marriage).

Gerard Neville at once determines to leave the house, but before going refers Elizabeth to his sister, Lady Cecil, to hear the particulars of the tragedy which surrounds him. The story told is this. Sir Boyvill Neville was a man of the world with all the too frequent disbelief in women and selfishness. This led to his becoming very tyrannical when he married, at the age of 45, Alethea, a charming young woman who had recently lost her mother, and whose father, a retired naval officer of limited means, would not hear of her refusing so good an offer as Sir Boyvill's. After their marriage Sir Boyvill, feeling himself too fortunate in having secured so charming and beautiful a wife, kept out of all society, and after living abroad for some years took her to an estate he possessed in Cumberland. They lived there shut out from all the world, except for trips which he took himself to London, or elsewhere, whenever *ennui* assailed him. They had, at the time we are approaching, two charming children, a beautiful boy of some ten years and a little girl of two. At this time while Alethea was perfectly happy with her children, and quite contended with her retirement, which she perceived took away the jealous tortures of her husband, he left home for a week, drawn out to two months, on one of his periodical visits to the capital. Lady Neville's frequent letters concerning her home and her children were always cheerful and placid, and the time for her husband's return was fixed. He arrived at the appointed hour in the evening. The servants were at the door to receive him, but in an instant alarm prevailed; Lady Neville and her son Gerard were not with him. They had left the house some hours before to walk in the park, and had not since been seen or heard of, an unprecedented occurrence. The alarm was raised; the country searched in all directions, but ineffectually, during a fearful tempest. Ultimately the poor boy was found unconscious on the ground, drenched to the skin. On his being taken home, and his father questioning him, all that could be heard were his cries "Come back, mamma; stop, stop for me!" Nothing else but the tossings of fever. Once again, "Then she has come back," he cried, "that man did not take her quite away; the carriage drove here at last." The story slowly elicited from the child on his gaining strength was this. On his going for a walk with his mother in the park, she took the key of a gate which led into a lane. A gentleman was waiting outside. Gerard had never seen him before, but he heard his mother call him Rupert. They walked together through the lane accompanied by the child, and talked earnestly. She wept, and the boy was indignant. When they reached a cross-road, a carriage was waiting. On approaching it the gentleman pulled the child's hands from hers, lifted her in, sprang in after, and the coachman drove like the wind, leaving the child to hear his mother shriek in agony, "My child—my son!" Nothing more could be discovered; the country was ransacked in vain. The servants only stated that ten days ago a gentleman called, asked for Lady Neville and was shown in to her; he remained some two hours, and on his leaving it was remarked that she had been weeping. He had called again but was not admitted. One letter was found, signed "Rupert," begging for one more meeting, and if that were granted he would leave her and his just revenge for ever; otherwise, he could not tell what the consequences might be on her husband's return that night. In answer to this letter she went, but with her child, which clearly proved her innocent intention. Months passed with no fresh result, till her husband, beside himself with wounded pride, determined to be avenged by obtaining a Bill of Divorce in the House of Lords, and producing his son Gerard as evidence against his lost mother, whom he so dearly loved. The poor child by this time, by dint of thinking and weighing every word he could remember, such as "I grieve deeply for you, Rupert: my good wishes are all I have to give you," became more and more convinced that his mother was taken forcibly away, and would return at any moment if she were able. He only longed for the time when he should be old enough to go and seek her through the world. His father was relentless, and the child was brought before the House of Lords to repeat the evidence he had innocently given against her; but when called on to speak in that awful position, no word could be drawn from him except "She is innocent." The House was moved by the brave child's agony, and resolved to carry on the case without him, from the witnesses whom he had spoken to, and finally they pronounced a decree of divorce in Sir Boyvill's favour. The struggle and agony of the poor child are admirably described, as also his subsequent flight from his father's house, and wanderings round his old home in Cumberland. In his fruitless search for his mother he reached a deserted sea-coast. After wandering about for two months barefoot, and almost starving but for the ewe's milk and bread given him by the cottagers, he was recognized. His father, being informed, had him seized and brought home, where he was confined and treated as a criminal. His state became so helpless that even his father was at length moved to some feeling of self-restraint, and finally took Gerard with him abroad, where he was first seen at Baden by Elizabeth and Falkner. There also he first met his sister by affinity, Lady Cecil. With her he lost somewhat his defiant tone, and felt that for his mother's sake he must not appear to others as lost in sullenness and despair. He now talked of his mother, and reasoned about her; but although he much interested Lady Cecil, he did not convince her really of his mother's innocence, so much did all circumstances weigh against her. But now, during Elizabeth's visit to Lady Cecil, a letter is received by Gerard and his father informing them that one Gregory Hoskins believed he could give some information; he was at Lancaster. Sir Boyvill, only anxious to hush up the matter by which his pride had suffered, hastened to prevent his son from taking steps to re-open the subject. This Hoskins was originally a native of the district round Dromoor, Neville's home, and had emigrated to America at the time of Sir Boyvill's marriage. At one time—years ago—he met a man named Osborne, who confided to him how he had gained money before coming to America by helping a gentleman to carry off a lady, and how terribly the affair ended, as the lady got drowned in a river near which they had placed her while nearly dead from fright, on the dangerous coast of Cumberland. On returning to England, and hearing the talk about the Nevilles in his native village, this old story came to his mind, and he wrote his letter. Neville, on hearing this, instantly determined to proceed to Mexico, trace out Osborne, and bring him to accuse his mother's murderer.

All these details were written by Elizabeth to her beloved father. After some delay, one line entreated her to come to him instantly for one day.

Falkner could not ignore the present state of things—the mutual attraction of his Elizabeth and of Gerard. Yet how, with all he knew, could that be suffered to proceed? Never, except by eternal separation from his adored child; but this should be done. He would now tell her his story. He could not speak, but he wrote it, and now she must come and receive it from him. He told of all his solitary, unloved youth, the miseries and tyranny of school to the unprotected—a reminiscence of Shelley; how, on emerging from childhood, one gleam of happiness entered his life in the friendship of a lady, an old friend of his mother's, who had one lovely daughter; of the happy, innocent time spent in their cottage during holidays; of the dear lady's death; of her daughter's despair; then how he was sent off to India; of letters he wrote to the daughter Alethea, letters unanswered, as the father, the naval officer, intercepted all; of his return, after years, to England, his one hope that which had buoyed him up through years of constancy, to meet and marry his only love, for that he felt she was and must remain. He recounted his return, and the news he received; his one rash visit to her to judge for himself whether she was happy—this, from her manner, he could not feel, in spite of her delight in her children; his mad request to see her; mad plot, and still madder execution of it, till he had her in his arms, dashing through the country, through storm and thunder, unable to tell whether she lived or died; the first moment of pause; the efforts to save the ebbing life in a ruined hut; the few minutes' absence to seek materials for fire; the return, to find her a floating corpse in the wild little river flowing to the sea; the rescue of her body from the waves; her burial on the sea-shore; and his own subsequent life of despair, saved twice by Elizabeth. All this was told to the son, to whom Falkner denounced himself as his mother's destroyer. He named the spot where the remains would be found. And now what was left to be done? Only to wait a little, while Sir Boyvill and Gerard Neville proved his words, and traced out the grave. An inquest was held, and Falkner apprehended. A few days passed, and then Elizabeth found her father gone; and by degrees it was broken to her that he was in Carlisle gaol on the charge of murder. She, who had not feared the dangers in Greece of war and fever, was not to be deterred now; she, who believed in his innocence. No minutes were needed to decide her to go straight to Carlisle, and remain as near as she could to the dear father who had rescued and cared for her when deserted. Gerard, who was with his father when the bones were exhumed at the spot indicated, soon realised the new situation. His passion for justice to his mother did not deaden his feeling for others. He felt that Falkner's story was true, and though nothing could restore his mother's life, her honour was intact. Sir Boyvill would leave no stone unturned to be revenged, rightly or wrongly, on the man who had assailed his domestic peace; but Gerard saw Elizabeth, gave what consolation he could, and determined to set off at once to America to seek Osborne, as the only witness who could exculpate Falkner from the charge of murder. After various difficulties Osborne was found in England, where he had returned in terror of being taken in America as accomplice in the murder. With great difficulty he is brought to give evidence, for all his thoughts and fears are for himself; but at length, when all hopes seem failing, he is induced by Elizabeth to give his evidence, which fully confirms Falkner's statement.

At length the day of trial came. The news of liberty arrived. "Not Guilty!" Who can imagine the effect but those who have passed innocently through the ordeal? Once more all are united. Gerard has to remain for the funeral of his father, who had died affirming his belief, which in fact he had always entertained, in Falkner's innocence. Lady Cecil had secured for Elizabeth the companionship of Mrs. Raby, her relation on the father's side. She takes Falkner and Elizabeth home to the beautiful ancestral Belleforest. Here a time of rest and happiness ensues. Those so much tried by adversity would not let real happiness escape for a chimera; honour being restored, love and friendship remained, and Gerard, Elizabeth, and Falkner felt that now they ought to remain together, death not having disunited them.

Too much space may appear to be here given to one romance; but it seems just to show the scope of Mary's imaginative conception. There are certainly both imagination and power in carrying it out. It is true that the idea seems founded, to some extent, on Godwin's *Caleb Williams*, the man passing through life with a mystery; the similar names of Falkner and Falkland may even be meant to call attention to this fact. The three-volume form, in this as in many novels, seems to detract from the strength of the work in parts, the second volume being noticeably drawn out here and there. It may be questioned, also, whether the form adopted in this as in many romances of giving the early history by way of narrative told by one of the *dramatis personæ* to another, is the desirable one—a point to which we have already adverted in relation to *Frankenstein*. Can it be true to nature to make one character give a description, over a hundred pages long, repeating at length, word for word, long conversations which he has never

heard, marking the changes of colour which he has not seen—and all this with a minuteness which even the firmest memory and the most loquacious tongue could not recall? Does not this give an unreality to the style incompatible with art, which ought to be the mainspring of all imaginative work? This, however, is not Mrs. Shelley's error alone, but is traceable through many masterpieces. The author, the creator, who sees the workings of the souls of his characters, has, naturally, memory and perception for all. Yet Mary Shelley, in this as in most of her work, has great insight into character. Elizabeth's grandfather in his dotage is quite a photograph from life; old Oswig Raby, who was more shrivelled with narrowness of mind than with age, but who felt himself and his house, the oldest in England, of more importance than aught else he knew of. His daughter-in-law, the widow of his eldest son, is also well drawn; a woman of upright nature who can acknowledge the faults of the family, and try to retrieve them, and who finally does her best to atone for the past.

RICHARD GARNETT
"Introduction"
Tales and Stories of Mary Wollstonecraft Shelley
1891, pp. v–xii

It is customary to regard Mary Shelley's claims to literary distinction as so entirely rooted and grounded in her husband's as to constitute a merely parasitic growth upon his fame. It may be unreservedly admitted that her association with Shelley, and her care of his writings and memory after his death, are the strongest of her titles to remembrance. It is further undeniable that the most original of her works is also that which betrays the strongest traces of his influence. *Frankenstein* was written when her brain, magnetized by his companionship, was capable of an effort never to be repeated. But if the frame of mind which engendered and sustained the work was created by Shelley, the conception was not his, and the diction is dissimilar to his. Both derive from Godwin, but neither is Godwin's. The same observation, except for an occasional phrase caught from Shelley, applies to all her subsequent work. The frequent exaltation of spirit, the ideality and romance, may well have been Shelley's—the general style of execution neither repeats nor resembles him.

Mary Shelley's voice, then, is not to die away as a mere echo of her illustrious husband's. She has the *prima facie* claim to a hearing due to every writer who can assert the possession of a distinctive individuality; and if originality be once conceded to *Frankenstein*, as in all equity it must, none will dispute the validity of a title to fame grounded on such a work. It has solved the question itself—it *is* famous. It is full of faults venial in an author of nineteen; but, apart from the wild grandeur of the conception, it has that which even the maturity of mere talent never attains—the insight of genius which looks below the appearances of things, and perhaps even reverses its own first conception by the discovery of some underlying truth. Mary Shelley's original intention was probably that which would alone have occurred to most writers in her place. She meant to paint Frankenstein's monstrous creation as an object of unmitigated horror. The perception that he was an object of intense compassion as well imparted a moral value to what otherwise would have remained a daring flight of imagination. It has done more: it has helped to create, if it did not itself beget, a type of personage unknown to ancient fiction. The conception of a character at once justly execrable and truly pitiable is altogether modern. Richard the Third and Caliban make some approach towards it; but the former is too self-sufficing in his valour and his villainy to be deeply pitied, and the latter too senseless and brutal. Victor Hugo has made himself the laureate of pathetic deformity, but much of his work is a conscious or unconscious variation on the original theme of *Frankenstein*.

None of Mary Shelley's subsequent romances approached *Frankenstein* in power and popularity. The reason may be summed up in a word—Languor. After the death of her infant son in 1819, she could never again command the energy which had carried her so vigorously through *Frankenstein*. Except in one instance, her work did not really interest her. Her heart is not in it. *Valperga* contains many passages of exquisite beauty; but it was, as the authoress herself says, "a child of mighty slow growth;" "laboriously dug," Shelley adds, "out of a hundred old chronicles," and wants the fire of imagination which alone could have interpenetrated the mass and fused its diverse ingredients into a satisfying whole. Of the later novels, *The Last Man* excepted, it is needless to speak, save for the autobiographic interest with which Professor Dowden's fortunate discovery has informed the hitherto slighted pages of *Lodore*. But *The Last Man* demands great attention, for it is not only a work of far higher merit than commonly admitted, but of all her works the most characteristic of the authoress, the most representative of Mary Shelley in the character of pining widowhood which it was her destiny to support for the remainder of her life. It is an idealized version of her sorrows and sufferings, made to contribute a note to the strain which celebrates the final dissolution of the world. The languor which mars her other writings is a beauty here, harmonizing with the general tone of sublime melancholy. Most pictures of the end of the world, painted or penned, have an apocalyptic character. Men's imaginations are powerfully impressed by great convulsions of nature; fire, tempest, and earthquake are summoned to effect the dissolution of the expiring earth. In *The Last Man* pestilence is the sole agent, and the tragedy is purely human. The tale consequently lacks the magnificence which the subject might have seemed to invite, but, on the other hand, gains in pathos—a pathos greatly increased when the authoress's identity is recollected, and it is observed how vividly actual experience traverses her web of fiction. None can have been affected by Mary Shelley's work so deeply as Mary Shelley herself; for the scenery is that of her familiar haunts, the personages are her intimates under thin disguises, the universal catastrophe is but the magnified image of the overthrow of her own fortunes; and there are pages on pages where every word must have come to her fraught with some unutterably sweet or bitter association. Yet, though her romance could never be to the public what it was to the author, it is surprising that criticism should have hitherto done so little justice either to its pervading nobility of thought or to the eloquence and beauty of very many inspired passages.

When *The Last Man* is reprinted it will come before the world as a new work. The same is the case with the short tales in this collection, the very existence of which is probably unknown to those most deeply interested in Mary Shelley. The entire class of literature to which they belong has long ago gone into Time's wallet as "alms for oblivion." They are exclusively contributions to a form of publication utterly superseded in this hasty age—the Annual, whose very name seemed to prophesy that it would not be perennial. For the creations of the intellect, however, there *is* a way back from Avernus. Every new generation convicts the last of undue precipitation in

discarding the work of its own immediate predecessor. The special literary form may be incapable of revival; but the substance of that which has pleased or profited its age, be it Crashaw's verse, or Etherege's comedies, or Hoadly's pamphlets, or what it may, always repays a fresh examination, and is always found to contribute some element useful or acceptable to the literature of a later day. The day of the "splendid annual" was certainly not a vigorous or healthy one in the history of English *belles-lettres*. It came in at the ebb of the great tide of poetry which followed on the French Revolution, and before the insetting of the great tide of Victorian prose. A pretentious feebleness characterizes the majority of its productions, half of which are hardly above the level of the album. Yet it had its good points, worthy to be taken into account. The necessary brevity of contributions to an annual operated as a powerful check on the loquacity so unfortunately encouraged by the three-volume novel. There was no room for tiresome descriptions of minutiæ, or interminable talk about uninteresting people. Being, moreover, largely intended for the perusal of high-born maidens in palace towers, the annuals frequently affected an exalted order of sentiment, which, if intolerable in insincere or merely mechanical hands, encouraged the emotion of a really passionate writer as much as the present taste for minute delineation represses it. This perfectly suited Mary Shelley. No writer felt less call to reproduce the society around her. It did not interest her in the smallest degree. The bent of her soul was entirely towards the ideal. This ideal was by no means buried in the grave of Shelley. She aspired passionately towards an imaginary perfection all her life, and solaced disappointment with what, in actual existence, too often proved the parent of fresh disillusion. In fiction it was otherwise; the fashionable style of publication, with all its faults, encouraged the enthusiasm, rapturous or melancholy, with which she adored the present or lamented the lost. She could fully indulge her taste for exalted sentiment in the Annual, and the necessary limitations of space afforded less scope for that creeping languor which relaxed the nerve of her more ambitious productions. In these little tales she is her perfect self, and the reader will find not only the entertainment of interesting fiction, but a fair picture of the mind, repressed in its energies by circumstances, but naturally enthusiastic and aspiring, of a lonely, thwarted, misunderstood woman, who could seldom do herself justice, and whose precise place in the contemporary constellation of genius remains to be determined.

The merit of a collection of stories, casually written at different periods and under different influences, must necessarily be various. As a rule, it may be said that Mary Shelley is best when most ideal, and excels in proportion to the exaltation of the sentiment embodied in her tale. Virtue, patriotism, disinterested affection, are very real things to her; and her heroes and heroines, if generally above the ordinary plane of humanity, never transgress the limits of humanity itself. Her fault is the other way, and arises from a positive incapacity for painting the ugly and the commonplace. She does her best, but her villains do not impress us. Minute delineation of character is never attempted; it lay entirely out of her sphere. Her tales are consequently executed in the free, broad style of the eighteenth century, towards which a reaction is now fortunately observable. As stories, they are very good. The theme is always interesting, and the sequence of events natural. No person and no incident, perhaps, takes a very strong hold upon the imagination; but the general impression is one of a sphere of exalted feeling into which it is good to enter, and which ennobles as much as the photography of ugliness degrades. The diction, as usual in the imaginative literature of the period, is frequently too ornate, and could spare a good many adjectives. But its native strength is revealed in passages of impassioned feeling; and remarkable command over the resources of the language is displayed in descriptions of scenes of natural beauty. The microscopic touch of a Browning or a Meredith, bringing the scene vividly before the mind's eye, is indeed absolutely wanting; but the landscape is suffused with the poetical atmosphere of a Claude or a Danby. The description at the beginning of "The Sisters of Albano" is a characteristic and beautiful instance.

The biographical element is deeply interwoven with these as with all Mary Shelley's writings. It is of especial interest to search out the traces of her own history, and the sources from which her descriptions and ideas may have been derived. "The Mourner" has evident vestiges of her residence near Windsor when *Alastor* was written, and probably reflects the general impression derived from Shelley's recollections of Eton. The

visit to Pæstum in "The Pole" recalls one of the most beautiful of Shelley's letters, which Mary, however, probably never saw. Claire Clairmont's fortunes seem glanced at in one or two places; and the story of "The Pole" may be partly founded on some experience of hers in Russia. Trelawny probably suggested the subjects of the two Greek tales, "The Evil Eye," and "Euphrasia." "The Mortal Immortal" is a variation on the theme of *St. Leon*, and "Transformation" on that of *Frankenstein*. These are the only tales in the collection which betray the influence of Godwin, and neither is so fully worked out as it might have been. Mary Shelley was evidently more at home with a human than with a superhuman ideal; her enthusiasm soars high, but does not transcend the possibilities of human nature. The artistic merit of her tales will be diversely estimated, but no reader will refuse the authoress facility of invention, or command of language, or elevation of soul.

THOMAS MOORE

1779–1852

Thomas Moore was born in Dublin on May 28, 1779. The son of a grocer, he was educated at Trinity College, Dublin (1795–99), and for three months during 1799 read law at London's Middle Temple, though he was never admitted to the bar. In 1800 Moore brought attention to himself with the publication of his translations of the *Odes of Anacreon*. In the following year he increased his reputation and popularity when he brought out the pseudonymous *Poetical Works of Thomas Little, Esq.* (1801), which was widely recognized as his work.

In 1803 Moore was appointed registrar of the admiralty prize-court in Bermuda, a post which he quickly transferred to a deputy. In 1806 he published *Epistles, Odes, and Other Poems*, which was denounced in the pages of the *Edinburgh Review* by Francis, Lord Jeffrey, whom Moore challenged to a duel; the duel was stopped by police and the two later became close friends. The first and second volumes of *Irish Melodies* appeared in 1808; this series, which eventually ran to ten volumes (1808–34), contained patriotic verses set to Irish melodies, mainly of the eighteenth century. Among the more famous songs are "The Harp That Once through Tara's Halls," "The Minstrel Boy," and "The Last Rose of Summer." In 1813 Moore published *Intercepted Letters, or The Two-Penny Post-Bag*, a collection of satires directed against the prince regent. This was followed in 1817 by *Lalla Rookh*, a series of Oriental tales in verse connected by a story in prose, with which Moore achieved his greatest success. In 1818 appeared the satirical *Fudge Family in Paris*, in which the English tourist was lampooned.

In 1819 Moore's deputy absconded with £6000, for which Moore was responsible. To avoid arrest for debt, Moore left for the Continent, where he remained until 1822, by which time his debts had been settled. In 1823 he published the controversial *The Loves of the Angels*, based on the Oriental tale of Harût and Marût and certain rabbinical legends. Moore became the center of another controversy when in 1824 he permitted the burning of Byron's memoirs, which Byron (a close friend) had given to him. In 1825 he published *Memoirs of the Life of the Right Honourable Richard Brinsley Sheridan*, followed by among other works: *The Epicurean* (1827), a novel based on his long poem *Alciphron*; *Letters and Journals of Lord Byron, with Notices of His Life* (1830); and *The Life and Death of Lord Fitzgerald* (1831). Moore was awarded a civil list pension in 1835, the same year in which he published *The Fudges in England*, and the first volume of his *History of Ireland* (4 vols., 1835–46). The ten-volume *Poetical Works of Thomas Moore* appeared in 1841. Moore's health began to fail in 1846, and by 1849 he had lapsed into senile dementia. He died on February 25, 1852. *The Memoirs, Journal and Correspondence of Thomas Moore*, edited by Lord John Russell, appeared in eight volumes between 1853 and 1856.

Personal

Moore has a peculiarity of talent, or rather talents,—poetry, music, voice, all his own; and an expression in each, which never was, nor will be, possessed by another. But he is capable of still higher flights in poetry. By the by, what humour, what—every thing, in the *Post-Bag!* There is nothing Moore may not do, if he will but seriously set about it. In society, he is gentlemanly, gentle, and, altogether more pleasing than any individual with whom I am acquainted. For his honour, principle, and independence, his conduct to **** speaks "trumpet-tongued." He has but one fault—and that one I daily regret—he is not *here*.—GEORGE GORDON, LORD BYRON, *Journal*, Nov. 22, 1813

I saw Moore (for the first time I may say) this season. We had indeed met in public twenty years ago. There is a manly frankness and perfect ease and good breeding about him which is delightful. Not the least touch of the poet or the pedant. A little—very little man—less I think than Lewis and somewhat like him in person, God knows not in conversation, for Matt though a clever fellow was a bore of the first description. Moreover he looked always like a school boy. I remember a picture of him being handed about at Dalkeith House. It was a miniature I think by Saunders who had contrived to mufle Lewis's person in a cloak and placed some poniard or dark-lanthorn appurtenance (I think) in his hand so as to give the picture the cast of a Bravo. 'That like Matt Lewis,' said Duke Henry to whom it had passed in turn. 'Why that is like a MAN.' Imagine the effect. Lewis was at his elbow. Now Moore has none of this insignificance. To be sure his person is much stouter than that of M. G. L. His countenance is decidedly plain but the expression is so very animated especially in speaking or singing that it is far more interesting than the finest features could have renderd.

I was aware that Byron had often spoken both in private society and in his journal of Moore and myself in the same breath and with the same sort of regard. So I was curious to see what there could be in common betwixt us, Moore having lived so much in the gay world I in the country and with people of business and sometimes with politicians, Moore a scholar—I none—He a musician and artist—I without knowledge of a note—He a democrat—I an aristocrat—with many other points of difference besides his being an Irishman, I a Scotchman, and both tolerably national. Yet there is a point of resemblance and a strong one. We are both goodhumoured fellows who rather seek to enjoy what is going forward than to maintain our dignity as Lions. And we have both seen the world too widely and too well not to contemn in our souls the imaginary consequence of literary people who walk with their noses in the air and remind me always of the fellow whom Johnson met in an ale-house and who calld himself 'the great Twalmly, Inventor of the flood-gate iron for smoothing linen.' He also enjoys the *Mot pour rire* and so do I. Moore has I think been ill treated about Byron's Memoirs. He surrendered them to the family (Ld. Byron's exors) and thus lost £2000 which he had raised upon them at a most distressing moment of his life. It is true they offerd and pressd the money on him afterwards but they ought to have settled it with the Booksellers and not put poor Tom's spirit in arms against his interest. I think at least it might have been so managed. At any rate there must be an authentic life of Byron by somebody. Why should they not give the benefit of their materials to Tom Moore whom Byron had made the depositary of his own Memoirs? But T. M. thinks that Cam Hobhouse has the purpose of writing Byron's life himself. He and Moore were at sharp words during the negotiation and there was some explanation necessary before the affair ended. It was a pity that nothing save the total destruction of Byron's Memoirs would satisfy his Exors—But there was a reason— *Premet Nox alta*.

It would be a delightful addition to life if T. M. had a cottage within two miles of one. We went to the theatre together and the House being luckily a good one received T. M. with rapture. I could have huggd them for it paid back the debt of the kind reception I met with in Ireland.—SIR WALTER SCOTT, *Journal*, Nov. 22, 1825

I thought Thomas Moore, when I first knew him, as delightful a person as one could imagine. He could not help being an interesting one; and his sort of talent has this advantage in it, that being of a description intelligible to all, the possessor is equally sure of present future fame. I never received a visit from him, but I felt as if I had been talking with Prior or Sir Charles Sedley. His acquaintance with Lord Byron began by talking of a duel. With me it commenced in as gallant a way, though of a different sort. I had cut up an opera of his, (the *Blue Stocking*,) as unworthy of so great a wit. He came to see me, saying I was very much in the right; and an intercourse took place, which I might have enjoyed to this day, had he valued his real fame as much as I did. I mean to assume nothing in saying this, either as a dispenser of reputation, or as a man of undisputed reputation myself. I live too much out of the world, and differ too plainly with what is in it, to pretend to be either one or the other. But Mr. Moore, in his serious as well as gayer verses, talked a great deal of independence and openness, and the contempt of commonplaces; and on this account he owed it to his admirers not to disappoint them. He was bound to them the more especially, when they put hearty faith in him, and when they thought they paid him a compliment in being independent themselves. The reader has seen to what I allude. At the time I am speaking of, my acquaintance, perhaps, was of some little service to Mr. Moore; at least, he thought so. I am sure I never valued myself on any service which a very hearty admiration of his wit and independence could render him. It was involuntary on my part; I could not have helped it; and at all times, the advantage of personal intercourse would have been on my side.—LEIGH HUNT, *Lord Byron and Some of His Contemporaries*, 1828, pp. 165–66

"I never spent an hour with Moore (said Byron) without being ready to apply to him the expression attributed to Aristophanes, 'You have spoken roses;' his thoughts and expressions have all the beauty and freshness of those flowers, but the piquancy of his wit, and the readiness of his repartees, prevent one's ear being cloyed by too much sweets, and one cannot 'die of a rose in aromatic pain' with Moore, though he does speak roses, there is such an endless variety in his conversation. Moore is the only poet I know (continued Byron) whose conversation equals his writings; he comes into society with a mind as fresh and buoyant as if he had not expended such a multiplicity of thoughts on paper; and leaves behind him an impression that he possesses an inexhaustible mine equally brilliant as the specimens he has given us. Will you, after this frank confession of my opinion of your countryman, ever accuse me of injustice again? ⟨. . .⟩

"No one writes songs like Moore (said Byron). Sentiment and imagination are joined to the most harmonious versification, and I know no greater treat than to hear him sing his own compositions; the powerful expression he gives to them, and the pathos of the tones of his voice, tend to produce an effect on my feelings that no other songs, or singer, ever could."—MARGUERITE, COUNTESS OF BLESSINGTON, *Conversations of Lord Byron*, 1834

General

You may remember the reign of Darwinian poetry, and the fopperies of Della Crusca. To these succeeded the school of *simplicity*, in which Wordsworth, Southey, and Coleridge are so deservedly eminent. I think that the new tribe of poets endeavour to combine these two opposite sects, and to unite richness of language and warmth of colouring with simplicity and pathos. They have certainly succeeded; but Moore unhappily wished to be a Catullus, and from him has sprung the licentiousness of the new school. Moore's poems and his translations will, I think, have more influence on the female society of this kingdom, than the stage has had in its *worst period*, the reign of Charles II.—HENRY KIRKE WHITE, Letter to P. Thompson (April 8, 1806), *The Remains of Henry Kirke White*, ed. Robert Southey, 1807, Vol. 1, p. 219

A singular sweetness and melody of versification,—smooth, copious, and familiar diction,—with some brilliancy of fancy, and some show of classical erudition, might have raised Mr Moore to an innocent distinction among the song-writers and occasional poets of his day; but he is indebted, we fear, for the celebrity he actually enjoys to accomplishments of a different description; and may boast, if the boast can please him, of being the most licentious of modern versifiers, and the most poetical of those who, in our times, have devoted their talents to the propagation of immorality. We regard his book ⟨*Epistles, Odes, and Other Poems*⟩, indeed, as a public nuisance; and would willingly trample it down by one short movement of contempt and indignation, had we not reason to apprehend, that it was abetted by patrons who are entitled to a more respectful remonstrance, and by admirers who may require a more extended exposition of their dangers.

⟨. . .⟩ It seems to be his aim to impose corruption upon his readers, by concealing it under the mask of refinement; to reconcile them imperceptibly to the most vile and vulgar sensuality, by blending its language with that of exalted feeling and tender emotion; and to steal impurity into their hearts, by gently perverting the most simple and generous of their affections. In the execution of this unworthy task, he labours with a perseverance at once ludicrous and detestable. He may be seen in every page running round the paltry circle of his seductions with incredible zeal and anxiety, and stimulating his jaded fancy for new images of impurity, with as much melancholy industry as ever outcast of the muses hunted for epithets or metre.

It is needless, we hope, to go deep into the inquiry, why certain compositions have been reprobated as licentious, and their authors ranked among the worst enemies of morality. The criterion by which their delinquency may be determined, is fortunately very obvious: no scene can be tolerated in description, which could not be contemplated in reality, without a gross violation of propriety; no expression can be pardoned in poetry to which delicacy could not listen in the prose of real life.

No writer can transgress those limits, and be held guiltless; but there are degrees of guiltiness, and circumstances of aggravation or apology, which ought not to be disregarded. A poet of a luxuriant imagination may give too warm a colouring to the representation of innocent endearments, or be betrayed into indelicacies in delineating the allurements of some fair seducer, while it is obviously his general intention to give attraction to the picture of virtue, and to put the reader on his guard against the assault of temptation. Mr Moore has no such apology;—he takes to intimate to us, in every page, that the raptures which he celebrates do not spring from the excesses of an innocent love, or the extravagance of a romantic attachment; but are the unhallowed fruits of cheap and vulgar prostitution, the inspiration of casual amours, and the chorus of habitual debauchery. He is at pains to let the world know

that he is still fonder of roving, than of loving; and that all the Caras and the Fannys, with whom he holds dalliance in these pages, have had each a long series of preceding lovers, as highly favoured as their present poetical paramour: that they meet without any purpose of constancy, and do not think it necessary to grace their connexion with any professions of esteem or permanent attachment. The greater part of the book is filled with serious and elaborate descriptions of the ecstacies of such an intercourse, and with passionate exhortations to snatch the joys, which are thus abundantly poured forth from 'the fertile fount of sense.' ⟨. . .⟩

There is one other consideration which has helped to excite our apprehension on occasion of this particular performance. Many of the pieces are dedicated to persons of the first consideration in the country, both for rank and accomplishments; and the author appears to consider the greater part of them as his intimate friends, and undoubted patrons and admirers. Now, this we confess is to us a very alarming consideration. By these channels, the book will easily pass into circulation in those classes of society, which it is of most consequence to keep free of contamination; and from which its reputation and its influence will descend with the greatest effect to the great body of the community. In this reading and opulent country, there are no fashions which diffuse themselves so fast, as those of literature and immorality: there is no palpable boundary between the *noblesse* and the *bourgeoisie*, as in old France, by which the corruption and intelligence of the former can be prevented from spreading to the latter. All the parts of the mass, act and react upon each other with a powerful and unintermitted agency; and if the head be once infected, the corruption will spread irresistibly through the whole body. It is doubly necessary, therefore, to put the law in force against this delinquent, since he has not only indicated a disposition to do mischief, but seems unfortunately to have found an opportunity.—FRANCIS, LORD JEFFREY, "Moore's Poems," *Edinburgh Review*, July 1806, pp. 456–60

> Who in soft guise, surrounded by a choir
> Of virgins melting, not to Vesta's fire,
> With sparkling eyes, and cheek by passion flush'd,
> Strikes his wild lyre, whilst listening dames are hush'd?
> 'Tis Little! young Catullus of his day,
> As sweet, but as immortal, in his lay!
> Grieved to condemn, the muse must still be just,
> Nor spare melodious advocates of lust.
> Pure is the flame which o'er her altar burns;
> From grosser incense with disgust she turns;
> Yet kind to youth, this expiation o'er,
> She bids thee 'mend thy line and sin no more.'
> —GEORGE GORDON, LORD BYRON, *English Bards and Scotch Reviewers*, 1809, ll. 283–94

Tom Moore ⟨. . .⟩ is as heedless, gay, and prodigal of his poetical wealth, as ⟨Thomas Campbell⟩ is careful, reserved, and parsimonious. The genius of both is national. Mr. Moore's Muse is another Ariel, as light, as tricksy, as indefatigable, and as humane a spirit. His fancy is for ever on the wing, flutters in the gale, glitters in the sun. Every thing lives, moves, and sparkles in his poetry, while over all love waves his purple light. His thoughts are as restless, as many, and as bright as the insects that people the sun's beam. 'So work the honey-bees,' extracting liquid sweets from opening buds; so the butterfly expands its wings to the idle air; so the thistle's silver down is wafted over summer seas. An airy voyager on life's stream, his mind inhales the fragrance of a thousand shores, and drinks of endless pleasures under halcyon skies. Wherever his footsteps tend over the enamelled ground of fairy fiction—

Around him the bees in play flutter and cluster,
And gaudy butterflies frolic around.

The fault of Mr. Moore is an exuberance of involuntary power. His facility of production lessens the effect of, and hangs as a dead weight upon, what he produces. His levity at last oppresses. The infinite delight he takes in such an infinite number of things, creates indifference in minds less susceptible of pleasure than his own. He exhausts attention by being inexhaustible. His variety cloys; his rapidity dazzles and distracts the sight. The graceful ease with which he lends himself to every subject, the genial spirit with which he indulges in every sentiment, prevents him from giving their full force to the masses of things, from connecting them into a whole. He wants intensity, strength, and grandeur. His mind does not brood over the great and permanent; it glances over the surfaces, the first impressions of things, instead of grappling with the deep-rooted prejudices of the mind, its inveterate habits, and that 'perilous stuff that weighs upon the heart.' His pen, as it is rapid and fanciful, wants momentum and passion. It requires the same principle to make us thoroughly like poetry, that makes us like ourselves so well, the feeling of continued identity. The impressions of Mr. Moore's poetry are detached, desultory, and physical. Its gorgeous colours brighten and fade like the rainbow's. Its sweetness evaporates like the effluvia exhaled from beds of flowers! His gay laughing style, which relates to the immediate pleasures of love or wine, is better than his sentimental and romantic vein. His Irish melodies are not free from affectation and a certain sickliness of pretension. His serious descriptions are apt to run into flowery tenderness. His pathos sometimes melts into a mawkish sensibility, or crystallizes into all the prettinesses of allegorical language, and glittering hardness of external imagery. But he has wit at will, and of the first quality. His satirical and burlesque poetry is his best: it is first-rate. His *Twopenny Post-Bag* is a perfect 'nest of spicery'; where the Cayenne is not spared. The politician there sharpens the poet's pen. In this too, our bard resembles the bee—he has its honey and its sting.

Mr. Moore ought not to have written *Lalla Rookh*, even for three thousand guineas. His fame is worth more than that. He should have minded the advice of Fadladeen. It is not, however, a failure, so much as an evasion and a consequent disappointment of public expectation. He should have left it to others to break conventions with nations, and faith with the world. He should, at any rate, have kept his with the public. *Lalla Rookh* is not what people wanted to see whether Mr. Moore could do; namely, whether he could write a long epic poem. The interest, however, is four short tales. The interest, however, is often high-wrought and tragic, but the execution still turns to the effeminate and voluptuous side. Fortitude of mind is the first requisite of a tragic or epic writer. Happiness of nature and felicity of genius are the pre-eminent characteristics of the bard of Erin. If he is not perfectly contented with what he is, all the world beside is. He had no temptation to risk any thing in adding to the love and admiration of his age, and more than one country.

> Therefore to be possessed with double pomp,
> To guard a title that was rich before,
> To gild refined gold, to paint the lily,
> To throw a perfume on the violet,
> To smooth the ice, or add another hue
> Unto the rainbow, or with taper light
> To seek the beauteous eye of heav'n to garnish,
> Is wasteful and ridiculous excess.

The same might be said of Mr. Moore's seeking to bind an epic crown, or the shadow of one, round his other laurels.
—WILLIAM HAZLITT, *Lectures on the English Poets*, 1818

> 'Twas on the sixth of June, about the hour
>   Of half-past six—perhaps still nearer seven—
> When Julia sate within as pretty a bower
>   As e'er held houri in that heathenish heaven
> Described by Mahomet, and Anacreon Moore,
>   To whom the lyre and laurels have been given,
> With all the trophies of triumphant song—
> He won them well, and may he wear them long!
>   —GEORGE GORDON, LORD BYRON, "Dedication"
>   to *Don Juan*, 1819, Stanza 104

The Loves of the Angels is an invaluable gem, which will rank, not with the *Elegy in a Country Churchyard*, but with the *Rape of the Lock*. Sometimes, indeed, we cannot help thinking that the author might have perriwigged his angels with advantage. But I beg pardon—it is no longer fashionable for young coxcombs to wear wigs.—EBENEZER ELLIOTT, "Preface" to *Spirits and Men*, 1833

Blank verse, as far as we are aware, he has never attempted. But ⟨. . .⟩ he has presented himself to the public as a voluminous writer of prose, having entered the domain of fiction in the *Epicurean*—of biography, in the lives of Sheridan, and Lord Byron, and Lord Edward Fitzgerald—of political and religious controversy, in the *Memoirs of Captain Rock*, and *The Travels of an Irish Gentleman*—and of history, in the recent volumes on Ireland, contributed to Dr. Lardner's Cyclopedia. None of these works, in right of their execution, can rank as high as Mr. Moore's poems. The *Epicurean* contains elaborate descriptions, in which the antique knowledge mentioned awhile since is turned carefully to account; and the contrast between the gorgeous mysteries of Egyptian idolatry and the simple heart-influencing faith of the Christians, is happily sustained: but the book, save to very young readers, is a cloying one. In the *Life of Sheridan* the biographer had a subject of no ordinary impracticability; to write the adventures of a wit, is the next difficult task to painting a rainbow; and there is no small danger of such a work, if confided to one who bears in character and temperament a certain similarity with his subject, coming from the hands of the latter over-charged and over-laboured. Such, at least, seems the case with the *Life of Sheridan*. Again, in the *Byron Memoirs*, the author's difficulties were an hundred-fold greater. Having incurred suspicion and misconstruction from the sacrifice of the auto-biography committed to his care by his friend, he placed himself in the position of one who knows more than he will or ought to tell—and has still to justify and maintain his reader's interest in a character, which, by its inconsistencies, is placed upon the list of eccentric prodigies, with whom the general world can have little consistent sympathy. But apart from all this inherent difficulty, there were small defences and subtle distinctions attempted, which were felt to be useless to the subject of the biography, and unworthy of his biographer; there was every where visible the disposition, born of personal affection, to tamper with the faults of "the wandering Childe"—whereas, it would have been wiser, with a judicious daring, to have stated them without apology—drawing out and dwelling upon those brilliant lights which so largely redeemed the tremendous shadows of Byron's character. In Lord Edward Fitzgerald Mr. Moore had his simplest subject; and the work is, accordingly, his best; and it is written throughout with heart and feeling, without either the effort at brilliancy, or the uneasy constraint and misgiving discernible in the other two biographies. We feel in every page that the author loved his task, and that the tale of the fortunes of the amiable and highly-gifted and ill-starred young nobleman, who was wrecked in the convulsions of a disastrous and terrible time, could not have been better confided, than to him who sung in the war song of "Brien the Brave,"

> Forget not our wounded companions who stood
>   In the day of distress by our side;
> While the moss of the valley grew red with their
>   blood
> They stirred not, but conquered and died!
> —HENRY F. CHORLEY, "Thomas Moore," *The Authors of England*, 1838, p. 69

Moore has always been renowned for the number and appositeness, as well as novelty, of his similes; and the renown thus acquired is strongly indicial of his deficiency in that nobler merit—the noblest of them all. No poet thus distinguished was ever richly ideal. Pope and Cowper are remarkable instances in point. Similes (so much insisted upon by the critics of the reign of Queen Anne) are never, in our opinion, strictly in good taste, whatever may be said to the contrary, and certainly can never be made to accord with other high qualities, except when naturally arising from the subject in the way of illustration—and, when thus arising, they have seldom the merit of novelty. To be novel, they must fail in essential particulars. The higher minds will avoid their frequent use. They form no portion of the ideal, and appertain to the fancy alone.

We proceed with a few random observations upon *Alciphron*. The poem is distinguished throughout by a very happy facility which has never been mentioned in connection with its author, but which has much to do with the reputation he has obtained. We allude to the facility with which he recounts a poetical story in a *prosaic* way. By this is meant that he preserves the tone and method of arrangement of a prose relation, and thus obtains great advantages over his more stilted compeers. His is no poetical *style*, (such, for example, as the French have—a distinct style for a distinct purpose,) but an easy and ordinary prose manner, *ornamented into poetry*. By means of this he is enabled to enter, with ease, into details which would baffle any other versifier of the age, and at which La Martine would stand aghast. For any thing that we see to the contrary, Moore might solve a cubic equation in verse, or go through with the three several demonstrations of the binomial theorem, one after the other, or indeed all at the same time. His facility in this respect is truly admirable, and is, no doubt, the result of long practice after mature deliberation. We refer the reader to page 50, of the pamphlet now reviewed; where the minute and conflicting incidents of the descent into the pyramid are detailed with absolutely *more* precision than we have ever known a similar relation detailed with in prose.

⟨. . .⟩ In truth, the exceeding beauty of *Alciphron* has bewildered and detained us. We could not point out a poem in any language which, as a whole, greatly excels it. It is far superior to *Lalla Rookh*. While Moore does not reach, except in rare snatches, the height of the loftiest qualities of some whom we have named, yet he has written finer poems than any, of equal length, by the greatest of his rivals. His radiance, not always as bright as some flashes from other pens, is yet a radiance of equable glow, whose total amount of light exceeds, by very much, we think, that total amount in the case of any cotemporary writer whatsoever. A vivid fancy; an epigrammatic spirit; a fine taste; vivacity, dexterity and a musical ear; have made him very easily what he is, the most popular poet now living—if not the most popular that ever lived—and, perhaps, a slight modification at birth of that which phrenol-

ogists have agreed to term *temperament*, might have made him the truest and noblest votary of the muse of any age or clime. As it is, we have only casual glimpses of that *mens divinior* which is assuredly enshrined within him.—EDGAR ALLAN POE, "Thomas Moore" (1840), *Essays and Reviews*, ed. G. R. Thompson, 1984, pp. 339–41

Thomas Moore began his career with singing, not the *Loves of the Angels*, but the loves of the roués. His early poems are probably the most disgraceful legacies of licentious thought ever bequeathed by prurient youth to a half-penitent age. They are exceedingly clever, unprincipled, and pernicious. We never read any verses, produced by one at the same tender years, so utterly deficient in moral sense. Their gilded vulgarity is not even redeemed by any depth of passion. They are the mere children of fancy and sensation, having no law higher than appetite. They constitute the libertine's text-book of pleasant sins, full of nice morsels of wickedness, and choice tit-bits of dissoluteness. What there is poetical in them is like the reflection of a star in a mud-puddle, or the shining of rotten wood in the dark.

The taint of this youthful voluptuousness infects much of Moore's more matured composition. His mind never wholly became emancipated from the dominion of his senses. His notion of Paradise comes from the Koran, not the New Testament. His works are pictorial representations of Epicureanism. Pathos, passion, sentiment, fancy, wit, are poured melodiously forth in seemingly inexhaustible abundance, and glitter along his page as though written down with sunbeams; but they are still more or less referable to sensation, and the "trail of the serpent is over them all." He is the most superficial and empirical of all the prominent poets of his day; and, with all his acknowledged fertility of mind, with all his artistical skill and brilliancy, with all his popularity, he never makes a profound impression on the soul, and few ever think of calling him a great poet, even in the sense in which Byron is great. He is the most magnificent trifler that ever versified. Nothing can be finer than his sarcasm, nothing more brilliant than his fancy, nothing more softly voluptuous than his sentiment. But he possesses no depth of imagination, no grandeur of thought, no clear vision of purity and holiness. He has neither loftiness nor comprehension. Those who claim for him a place among the immortals are most generally young people, who are conquered by the "dazzling fence" of his rhetoric, and the lightning-like rapidity with which he scatters fancies one upon another. He blinds the eye with diamond dust, and lulls the ear with the singing sweetness of his versification. Much of his sentiment, which fair throats warble so melodiously, is merely idealized lust. The pitch of his thought and feeling is not high. The impression gained from his works is most assuredly that of a man variously gifted by nature, adroit, ingenious, keen, versatile, "forgetive,"—a most remarkable man, but not a great poet. Nothing about his works "wears the aspect of eternity."

As a lyrical poet, he has written many exquisite songs, and no bad ones. His power of expression is always equal to the thought or emotion to be expressed. As far as he has conception, he has language. His lyrics are numerous and various, and relatively excellent. But even here, his strongest ground, he is not great. According to the character and capacities of a poet, will be the merit of his lyrics. Moore, in all his celebrations of patriotism and love, has never reached the elevation of his great contemporaries. To be a great lyrist, a poet must have great elements of character. These Moore does not possess. He has written nothing equal to the best songs and odes of Campbell, though the latter has no claim to his versatility and fluency of feeling and fancy.—EDWIN P. WHIPPLE, "English Poets of the Nineteenth Century" (1845), *Essays and Reviews*, 1850, Vol. 1, pp. 335–37

> Idol of youths and virgins, Moore!
> Thy days, the bright, the calm, are o'er!
> No gentler mortal ever prest
> His parent Earth's benignant breast.
> What of the powerful can be said
> They did for thee? They *edited*.
> What of that royal gourd? Thy verse
> Excites our scorn and spares our curse.
> Each truant wife, each trusting maid,
> All loves, all friendships, he betraid.
> Despised in life by those he fed,
> By his last mistress left ere dead,
> Hearing her only wrench the locks
> Of every latent jewel-box.
> There spouse and husband strove alike,
> Fearing lest Death too soon should strike,
> But fixt no plunder to forego
> Til the gross spirit sank below.
>   Thy closing days I envied most,
> When all worth losing had been lost.
> Alone I spent my earlier hour
> While thou wert in the roseate bower,
> And raised to thee was every eye,
> And every song won every sigh.
> One servant and one chest of books
> Follow'd me into mountain nooks,
> Where shelter'd from the sun and breeze
> Lay Pindar and Thucydides.
> There antient days came back again,
> And British kings renew'd their reign;
> There Arthur and his knights sat round
> Cups far too busy to be crown'd;
> There Alfred's glorious shade appear'd,
> Of higher mien than Greece e'er rear'd.
> I never sought in prime or age
> The smile of Fortune to engage,
> Nor rais'd nor lower'd the telescope
> Erected on the tower of Hope.
> From Pindus and Parnassus far
> Blinks cold and dim the Georgian star.
>   —WALTER SAVAGE LANDOR, "On Moore's
>   Death," 1853

Moore had a very fair share of learning, as well as steady application, greatly as he sacrificed to the graces of life, and especially of "good society." His face was not perhaps much more impressive in its contour than his diminutive figure. His eyes, however, were dark and fine; his forehead bony, and with what a phrenologist would recognize as large bumps of wit; the mouth pleasingly dimpled. His manner and talk were bright, abounding rather in lively anecdote and point than in wit and humour, strictly so called. To term him amiable according to any standard, and estimable too as men of an unheroic fibre go, is no more than his due.

No doubt the world has already seen the most brilliant days of Moore's poetry. Its fascinations are manifestly of the more temporary sort: partly through fleetingness of subject-matter and evanescence of allusion (as in the clever and still readable satirical poems); partly through the aroma of sentimental patriotism, hardly strong enough in stamina to make the compositions national, or to maintain their high level of popularity after the lyrist himself has long been at rest; partly through the essentially commonplace sources and forms of inspiration which belong to his more elaborate and ambitious

works. No poetical reader of the present day is the poorer for knowing absolutely nothing of *Lalla Rookh* or the *Loves of the Angels*. What then will be the hold or the claim of these writings upon a reader of the twenty-first century? If we except the satirical compositions, choice in a different way, the best things of Moore are to be sought in the *Irish Melodies*, to which a considerable share of merit, and of apposite merit, is not to be denied: yet even here what deserts around the oases, and the oases themselves how soon exhaustible and forgetable! There are but few thoroughly beautiful and touching lines in the whole of Moore's poetry: here is one—

Come rest in this bosom, mine own stricken deer.

A great deal has been said upon the overpowering "lusciousness" of his poetry, and the magical "melody" of his verse: most of this is futile. There is in the former as much of *fadeur* as of lusciousness; and a certain tripping or trotting exactitude, not less fully reducible to the test of scansion than of a well-attuned ear, is but a rudimentary form of melody—while of harmony or rhythmic volume of sound Moore is as decisively destitute as any correct versifier can well be. No clearer proof of the incapacity of the mass of critics and readers to appreciate the *calibre* of poetical work in point of musical and general execution could be given than the fact that Moore has always with them passed, and still passes, for an eminently melodious poet. What then remains? Chiefly this. In one class of writing, liveliness of witty banter, along with neatness; and, in the other and ostensibly more permanent class, elegance, also along with neatness. Reduce these qualities to one denomination, and we come to something that may be called "Propriety": a sufficiently disastrous "raw material" for the purposes of a poet, and by no means loftily to be praised or admired even when regarded as the outer investiture of a nobler poetic something within. But let desert of every kind have its place, and welcome. In the cosmical diapason and august orchestra of poetry, Tom Moore's little Pan's-pipe can at odd moments be heard, and interjects an appreciable and right-combined twiddle or two. To be gratified with these at the instant is no more than the instrument justifies, and the executant claims: to think much about them when the organ is pealing or the violin plaining (with a Shelley performing on the first, or a Mrs. Browning on the second), or to be on the watch for their recurrences, would be equally superfluous and weak-minded.
—WILLIAM MICHAEL ROSSETTI, "Thomas Moore," *Lives of Famous Poets*, 1878, pp. 282–84

When Moore wrote his *Life of Byron* in 1830 and casually spoke of Mr. Shelley as a finer poet than himself, the world admired his generous modesty, but smiled at the exaggerated instance of it. Yet, even then, close observers like Leigh Hunt noticed that the dazzling reputation of the Irish lyrist was on the wane, and that his supremacy as a singer was by no means likely to remain long unchallenged. A few years earlier Christopher North had said, in his autocratical manner, 'of all the song-writers that ever warbled, the best is Thomas Moore.' A few years later, as Keats and Tennyson came before the world with a richer and more artistic growth of verse, the author of *The Loves of the Angels* passed more and more into the background, until at last in our own day critics have dared to deny him all merit, and even to treat him as a kind of lyrical Pariah, an outcast at whom every one is welcome to cast a stone.

As usual in the case of such vicissitudes of taste, the truth seems to lie midway between the extremes, and as in 1830 it would have been salutary to point out how limited in interest, poor in execution, and tawdry in ornament much of Moore's work was, it is now quite as necessary to recall to the minds of readers of poetry the great claims that he possesses to our respect and allegiance. When Moore began to publish,—and it must be remembered that his earliest printed verses show much of his peculiar individuality,—the genius of Burns alone reminded the public of that day of the existence of a singing element in literature. Neither Crabbe nor Rogers, the two poets then most prominently before the world, knew what it was to write a song, and it was into an atmosphere of refined and frigid reflection that Tom Moore brought the fervour of his Irish heart and the liquid numbers of his Irish tongue. He heralded a new age of poetic song, for although the *Lyrical Ballads* two years before had, in a far truer sense, announced a fresh epoch, yet their voice had been heard only by one or two. The easy muse of Moore conquered the town; he popularised the use of bright and varied measures, sparkling rhymes, and all the bewitching panoply of artistic form in which Shelley, the true song-writer, was to array himself. In a larger sense than he himself was conscious of, he was a pioneer in letters. He boasted, with no more gaiety than truth, that he originated modern Irish poetry:

> Dear Harp of my Country! in darkness I found thee,
>   The cold chain of silence had hung o'er thee long,
> When proudly, my own Island Harp, I unbound
>   thee,
>   And gave all thy chords to light, freedom, and
>   song.

He might have applied these words to the harp of England also, for if he was not destined to strike from it the noblest music, he it was at least who took it down from the wall, and tuned it for the service of greater poets than himself.

It is still possible to read *Lalla Rookh* with pleasure, and even with a sort of indulgent enthusiasm. Rococo prettiness could hardly reach a higher point of accomplishment, and the sham-oriental is perhaps not more hopelessly antiquated than our own sham-mediæval will be sixty years hence. The brilliance of Moore's voluptuous scenes has faded; he gilded them too much with the gold of Mrs. Tighe's *Psyche*, a preparation that was expressly made to tarnish. But underneath the smooth and faded surface lie much tenderness and pathos in the story of the Peri, much genuine patriotism in the fate of the Fire-Worshippers, much tropical sweetness in the adventures of the 'Light of the Haram.' These narratives possess more worth, for instance, than all but the very best of Byron's tales, and would be read with more pleasure than those, were they not overburdened by sensuous richness of style. This quality, which Moore considered his chief claim to immortality, was in point of fact a great snare to him. His idealism, so far from allowing the presence of coarse and passionate touches, expunges them with incessant care, so that throughout the gush and glow of his descriptive scenes the eye and ear alike are conscious of no salient point, no break or discord by which the beauty of the whole can be tested. The reader sympathises with the French gentleman who said that he admired the pastorals of M. de Florian very much, but that he considered a wolf would improve them. In the *Loves of the Angels* this honeyed elegance degenerates into a tiresome mannerism; in *Lalla Rookh* it is still tempered by the vigour of the narrative, the freshness of the scenes, and the skill of the artist. The latter poem, indeed, is constructed with consummate cleverness; the prose story, in which the poetical episodes are enshrined, is both interesting and amusing, so that the whole work leaves on the mind of the reader a greater sense of completeness than any other of Moore's books. In versification it displays him at his

best and at his worst, it shows his mellifluous charm, his ardent flow of verse, and his weak, uncertain wing.

In one only of his writings Moore attained a positive perfection of style. Those homely and sentimental lyrics which have endeared themselves to thousands of hearts under the name of the *Irish Melodies* form a part and parcel of our literature the extinction of which would leave a sad blank behind it. When they were first produced, in slender instalments spread over a period of more than twenty-five years, they seemed universally brilliant and fascinating to the ears on whom their fresh tunes and dulcet numbers fell in a most amiable union. Here for once, it seemed, music and sweet poetry agreed in complete harmony, the one not brighter or more dainty than the other. Exposed to the wear and tear of sixty years, all the jewels in the casket do not now, any longer, look equally brilliant. Some have wholly faded, others have become weak or crude in colouring, while a few, perhaps one eighth of the whole, are as glowing and exquisite as ever, and shine like real stones in a heap of false jewellery. It is upon these fifteen or sixteen songs, amatory, patriotic and jocose, that Moore's fame mainly rests, but though the support has become slender, it is lifted beyond all further fear of disintegration. The *Irish Melodies* belong preeminently to that minor and less ambitious school of lyrics which of set purpose dedicates itself to vocal singing. The highest lyrical poetry, of course, appeals to the inner ear alone, in that silent singing which is a sweeter thing than any triumph of the vocalist. No tune of the most transcendent aptness could throw fresh charm into the finest stanzas of Shelley, while the most clear-voiced and sympathetic singer would probably fail to make so subtle a scheme of words intelligible to any audience previously ignorant of them. But Moore is a master in that ritual of which Burns is the high priest, in which words of a commonplace character are so strung together as to form poetry easily grasped and enjoyed by the ear, while sometimes the *Melodies* reach a higher pitch, and may be judged by a more severe standard than the improvisatore ever knows. When his genuine and burning love of Irish liberty inspires him, the little amatory bard rises for a moment to the level of Tyrtæus and Campbell.

It is difficult at the present day to revive an interest in Moore's satirical and humourous collections of verse, yet their gaiety was hailed with great enjoyment by a generation accustomed to Wolcot's sturdy fun and the heavy hand of Gifford. In fact the public was excessively entertained by these brisk, smart epistles, in which the Horatian manner was carried to its last excess of levity, and in which witty personalities against public individuals were as thick as plums in a pudding. The *Fables for the Holy Alliance* were more serious and more trenchant than the rest, and perhaps just because their effect was greater at the time, it is less now. It is precisely the lightness of *The Twopenny Post-Bag* that supports it still on the stream of literature. In *Rhymes on the Road* Moore seems to be emulating Byron in his rapid interchange of cynical with romantic reflection, but he has not the muscular strength needed to draw the bow of Byron, and when he describes the view of Lake Leman from the Jura we miss almost painfully the note of the master. He is infinitely more at home in describing the gay world of Florence, and sentimentally regretting the domestic pleasures of an English home. Nor is the modern reader much scandalised, but only very much amused, to find little Mr. Moore inditing a long poem at Les Charmettes merely to insist upon the fact that he was *not* roused by reminiscences of Rousseau.—EDMUND GOSSE, "Thomas Moore," *The English Poets*, ed. Thomas Humphry Ward, 1880, Vol. 4, pp. 309–12

I have granted the merit of Moore's verses and the amusing nature of his personality; but I must protest in the name of justice against his acceptance as the national poet of Ireland. If Irishmen accept him and honour him as such, so much the worse for Irishmen, since his falsehood of poetical touch must respond to something false and unpoetical in their own natures. I have said that a national poet must be simple—Moore was always ornate in the bad sense. Listen to him when he is "patriotic:"

> Forget not the field where they perished;
>   The truest—the last of the brave!
> All gone—and the bright hope we cherished
>   Gone with them, and quenched in their grave!

Or elsewhere when he cries in more ringing cadence:

> Let Erin remember the days of old,
>   Ere her faithless sons betrayed her;
> When Malachi wore the collar of gold
>   Which he won from the proud invader;
> When her Kings, with standards of green unfurled,
>   Led the Red Cross Knights to danger;
> Ere the emerald gem of the western world
>   Was set in the crown of a stranger!

Compare any of this fustian with "Scots wha hae," or the "Marseillaise," or "Les Gaulois et les Francs;" compare it even, which is more to the point, with Curran's "Wearing of the Green," or Thomas Davis's "Green above the Red." Another characteristic of a truly national poet is what is termed "local colour." Beyond making a tautological parade of the shamrock (the only trefoil he appears to have ever seen), Moore never even attempts to depict the common objects of the landscape of his country. Even when he sings of Arranmore he can only tell us of "breezy cliffs," "flowery mazes," "skiffs that dance along the flood," "daylight's parting wing," and all the stock phenomena of the albums. His "Vale of Avoca" might be situated anywhere between Ireland and Japan; there are a thousand "sweet valleys" where "dark waters meet," but surely an Irish poet might have conveyed by some felicitous touch or image that the waters in question met in the Wicklow Mountains? As in his pictures of nature, so in his renderings of the transports of love. Who that has read Burns' "Highland Mary," or Tannahill's "Jessie, the Flower o' Dunblane," or Béranger's "Lisette," can tolerate the affectations of "Come rest in this bosom, my own stricken deer," or "Lesbia has a beaming eye"? Again, a national poet should be pathetic. The high-water mark of Moore's pathos is to be found in such lyrics as "She is far from the land," which is the mere twaddle of a keepsake compared with "Ye banks and braes," or "Adieu, charmant pays de France," or (to come back to Ireland again) with Clarence Mangan's "Dark Rosaleen," or Banim's "Soggarth Aroon." Lastly, a national poet should have humour. The humour of Thomas Moore is not even good wholesome "blarney"—it is the mere fluent *persiflage* of a diner-out.

The question which occurs to me, apropos of the present centenary, is not a merely literary one. Criticism has long ago settled the poetical rank of Thomas Moore, and no amount of local enthusiasm, no association of that delightful melody to which his falsest songs are set, will alter the supreme fiat of the critical world. But I cannot help asking myself again whether or not the choice of so shallow and insincere a poet is an indication of shallowness and insincerity in the Irish character itself? I am very unwilling to think so. I would rather believe that the apotheosis of Thomas Moore is the work of an over-zealous minority, and that the great strong heart of the people has no real response for such a singer. A national poet represents his nation, as Burns represents Scotland, as Béranger represents France. I should be sorry to believe that Moore represents Ireland—sorry, I mean, for Ireland's sake. I have heard Irishmen, quite alive to Moore's defects, defend his fame by saying that he is, if not a great poet, at any rate the greatest Ireland has produced. That is a matter of opinion. Judged by the voluminousness of his works, he is perhaps paramount. But do not let us forget that Ireland can boast of such poets as Thomas Davis, John Banim, Gerald Griffin, Callanan, Curran, Samuel Lover, Wolfe, Samuel Ferguson, Edward Walsh, and Clarence Mangan. Where in Moore's tinsel poems shall we find such a piece of wondrous workmanship as Mangan's "Vision of Connaught in the Thirteenth Century," such a heart-rending ballad as Banim's "Soggarth Aroon," such a torrent of native strength as Ferguson's "Welshmen of Tirawley," such a bit of rollicking vigour as Lysaght's "Sprig of Shillelah," or such a thrill of simple pathos as Gerald Griffin's "The tie is broke, my Irish girl"? John Banim sleeps unhonoured, Clarence Mangan lies forgotten, Gerald Griffin is best remembered for his masterly piece of prose fiction. Yet these men were truly national poets; every word they wrote had an Irish ring, and their simple and noble efforts in Irish minstrelsy have gone right home to the spirits of the people. I am sorry indeed for Ireland, if, with such men for singers, she can persist in crowning as her laureate the ghost of a parvenu gentleman in tights and pumps, who spent his days and nights among the Whigs in London, whose patriotism was an amusing farce, and who, merely to make himself look interesting, pinned a shamrock to the buttonhole of his dress-coat, and warbled cheerful little dirges about the sorrows of the country he had left behind him.—ROBERT BUCHANAN, "The Irish 'National' Poet," *A Look round Literature*, 1887, pp. 206–9

Works

LALLA ROOKH

I have read two pages of *Lalla Rook* or whatever it is called. Merciful Heaven! I dare read no more—that I may be able to answer at once to any questions—'I have but just looked at the work.'—O, Robinson! if I could, or if I dared, act and feel as Moore & his Set do—what havock could I not make amongst their crockery ware! Why, there are not 3 lines together without some adulteration of common English—and the ever recurring blunder of using the possessive Case '*compassion's* tears' &c—for the preposition 'of'—a blunder of which I have found no instances earlier than Dryden's slovenly verses written for the Trade.—The rule is—that the case 's is always *personal*—either it marks a person, or a personification, or the relique of some proverbial personification, as 'who for their Belly's sake' in 'Lycidas'—Belly-Gods. Worshippers of their Belly—the Belly will make himself heard &c—. But for A. to weep the Tears of B. is just as modest and rational as if A. were to request B. to be so good as to make water for him—It puts one in mind of the exquisite passage in Rabelais where Pantagruel gives the Page his Cup & begs him to go down into the Court yard, and curse and swear for him, about half an hour or so.—SAMUEL TAYLOR COLERIDGE, Letter to Henry Crabb Robinson (June 15, 1817)

There is something very extraordinary, we think, in the work before us—and something which indicates in the author, not only a great exuberance of talent, but a very singular constitution of genius. While it is more splendid in imagery—and for the most part in very good taste—more rich in sparkling thoughts and original conceptions, and more full indeed of exquisite pictures, both of all sorts of beauties and virtues, and all sorts of sufferings and crimes, than any other poem that has yet come before us; we rather think we speak the sense of all classes of readers when we add, that the effect of the whole is to mingle a certain feeling of disappointment with that of admiration—to excite admiration rather than any warmer sentiment of delight—to dazzle, more than to enchant—and, in the end, more frequently to startle the fancy, and fatigue the attention, with the constant succession of glittering images and high-strained emotions, than to maintain a rising interest, or win a growing sympathy, by a less profuse or more systematic display of attractions.

The style is, on the whole, rather diffuse, and too unvaried in its character. But its greatest fault, in our eyes, is the uniformity of its brilliancy—the want of plainness, simplicity and repose. We have heard it observed, by some very zealous admirers of Mr. Moore's genius, that you cannot open this book without finding a cluster of beauties in every page. Now, this is only another way of expressing what we think its greatest defect. No work, consisting of many pages, should have detached and distinguishable beauties in every one of them. No great work, indeed, should have *many* beauties: If it were perfect, it would have but *one*, and that but faintly perceptible, except on a view of the whole. Look, for example, at what is perhaps the most finished and exquisite production of human art—the design and elevation of a Grecian temple, in its old severe simplicity. What penury of ornament—what neglect of beauties of detail—what masses of plain surface— what rigid economical limitation to the useful and the necessary! The cottage of a peasant is scarcely more simple in its structure, and has not fewer parts that are superfluous. Yet what grandeur—what elegance—what grace and completeness in the effect! The whole is beautiful—because the beauty is in the whole; but there is little merit in any of the parts, except that of fitness and careful finishing. Contrast this, now, with a Dutch pleasure-house, or a Chinese—where every part is meant to be beautiful, and the result is deformity,—where there is not an inch of the surface that is not brilliant with colour, and rough with curves and angles,—and where the effect of the whole is monstrous and offensive. We are as far as possible from meaning to insinuate that Mr. Moore's poetry is of this description; on the contrary, we think his ornaments are, for the most part, truly and exquisitely beautiful; and the general design of his pieces very elegant and ingenious: All that we mean to say is, that there is too much ornament—too many insulated and independent beauties—and that the notice, and the very admiration they excite, hurt the interest of the general design; and not only withdraw our attention too importunately from it, but at last weary it out with their perpetual recurrence.

It seems to be a law of our intellectual constitution, that the powers of taste cannot be permanently gratified, except by some *sustained* or continuous emotion; and that a series, even of the most agreeable excitements, soon ceases, if broken and disconnected to give any pleasure. No conversation fatigues so soon as that which is made up of points and epigrams; and the accomplished rhetorician, who

> could not ope
> His mouth, but out there flew a trope,

must have been a most intolerable companion. There are some things, too, that seem so plainly intended for ornaments and seasonings only, that they are only agreeable, when sprinkled in moderation over a plainer medium. No one would like to make an entire meal on *sauce piquante*; or to appear in a coat

crusted thick over with diamonds; or to pass a day in a steam of rich distilled perfumes. It is the same with the glittering ornaments of poetry—with splendid metaphors and ingenious allusions, and all the figures of speech and of thought that constitute its outward pomp and glory. Now, Mr. Moore, it appears to us, is decidedly too lavish of his gems and sweets;— he labours under a plethora of wit and imagination—impairs his credit by the palpable exuberance of his possessions, and would be richer with half his wealth. His works are not only of rich materials and graceful design, but they are everywhere glistening with small beauties and transitory inspirations— sudden flashes of fancy, that blaze out and perish; like earth-born meteors that crackle in the lower sky, and unseasonably divert our eyes from the great and lofty bodies which pursue their harmonious courses in a serener region.

We have spoken of these as faults of style,—but they could scarcely have existed without going deeper; and though they first strike us as qualities of the composition only, we find, upon a little reflection, that the same general character belongs to the fable, the characters, and the sentiments,—that they all sin alike in the excess of their means of attraction,—and fail to interest, chiefly by being too interesting.

In order to avoid the debasement of ordinary or familiar life, the author has soared to a region beyond the comprehension of most of his readers. All his personages are so very beautiful, and brave, and agonizing—so totally wrapt up in the exaltation of their vehement emotions, and withal so lofty in rank, and so sumptuous and magnificent in all that relates to their external condition, that the herd of ordinary mortals can scarcely venture to conceive of their proceedings, or to sympathize freely with their fortunes. The disasters to which they are exposed, and the designs in which they are engaged, are of the same ambitious and exaggerated character; and all are involved in so much pomp, and splendour, and luxury, and the description of their extreme grandeur and elegance forms so considerable a part of the whole work, that the less sublime portion of the species can with difficulty presume to judge of them, or to enter into the concernments of such very exquisite persons. The incidents, in like manner, are so prodigiously moving, so excessively improbable, and so terribly critical, that we have the same difficulty of raising our sentiments to the proper pitch for them;—and, finding it impossible to sympathize as we ought to do with such portentous occurrences, are sometimes tempted to withhold our sympathy altogether, and to seek for its objects among more familiar adventures. Scenes of voluptuous splendour and ecstasy alternate suddenly with agonizing separations, atrocious crimes, and tremendous sufferings;—battles, incredibly fierce and sanguinary, follow close on entertainments incredibly sumptuous and elegant;—terrific tempests are succeeded by delicious calms at sea; and the land scenes are divided between horrible chasms and precipices, and vales and gardens rich in eternal blooms, and glittering with palaces and temples—while the interest of the story is maintained by instruments and agents of no less potency than insanity, blasphemy, poisonings, religious hatred, national antipathy, demoniacal misanthropy, and devoted love. —FRANCIS, LORD JEFFREY, "Moore's *Lalla Rookh*," *Edinburgh Review*, Nov. 1817, pp. 2–4

Moore's *Lalla Rookh* & Byron's *Childe Harold* canto fourth formed an odd mixture with these speculations. It was foolish, you may think, to exchange the truths of philosophy, for the airy nothings of these sweet singers: but I could not help it. Do not fear that I will spend time in criticising the *tulip-cheek*. Moore is but a sort of refined Mahometan, and (with immense deference) I think that his character in a later *Edinr Review* is somewhat too high. His imagination seldom quits material even sexual objects—he describes them admirably—and intermingles here & there some beautiful traits of natural pathos; but he seems to have failed (excepting partially the fire-worshippers) in his attempts to pourtray the fierce or lofty features of human character. Mokannah, in particular, insensible to pain or pity or any earthly feelings, might as well, at least for all poetical purposes, have been made of clock-work as of flesh & blood.—I grieve to say that the catastrophe excited laughter rather than horror. The poisoned believers sitting round the table, with their black swoln jobbernowls reclining on their breasts, and saucer-eyes fixed upon the ill-favoured prophet—appeared so like the concluding scene of an election-dinner, when all are dead-drunk but the Provost, a man of five bottles, with a carbuncled face & an amorphous nose, that, I was forced to exclaim *du sublime au ridicule il n'y a qu'un pas.*—THOMAS CARLYLE, Letter to Robert Mitchell (May 25, 1818)

WILLIAM HAZLITT

From "Mr. T. Moore—Mr. Leigh Hunt"

The Spirit of the Age

1825

Or winglet of the fairy humming-bird,
Like atoms of the rainbow fluttering round.
(Campbell)

The lines placed at the head of this sketch, from a contemporary writer, appear to us very descriptive of Mr. Moore's poetry. His verse is like a shower of beauty; a dance of images; a stream of music; or like the spray of the water-fall, tinged by the morning-beam with rosy light. The characteristic distinction of our author's style is this continuous and incessant flow of voluptuous thoughts and shining allusions. He ought to write with a crystal pen on silver paper. His subject is set off by a dazzling veil of poetic diction, like a wreath of flowers gemmed with innumerous dew-drops, that weep, tremble, and glitter in liquid softness and pearly light, while the song of birds ravishes the ear, and languid odours breathe around, and Aurora opens Heaven's smiling portals, Peris and nymphs peep through the golden glades, and an Angel's wing glances over the glossy scene.

> No dainty flower or herb that grows on ground,
> No arboret with painted blossoms drest,
> And smelling sweet, but there it might be found
> To bud out fair, and its sweet smells throw all
>   around.
> No tree, whose branches did not bravely spring;
> No branch, whereon a fine bird did not sit;
> No bird, but did her shrill notes sweetly sing;
> No song, but did contain a lovely dit:
> Trees, branches, birds, and songs were framed fit
> For to allure frail minds to careless ease. . . .

Mr. Campbell's imagination is fastidious and select; and hence, though we meet with more exquisite beauties in his writings, we meet with them more rarely: there is comparatively a dearth of ornament. But Mr. Moore's strictest economy is 'wasteful and superfluous excess': he is always liberal, and never at a loss; for sooner than not stimulate and delight the reader, he is willing to be tawdry, or superficial, or common-place. His Muse must be fine at any rate, though she should paint, and wear cast-off decorations. Rather than have any lack of excitement, he repeats himself; and 'Eden, and

Eblis, and cherub-smiles' fill up the pauses of the sentiment with a sickly monotony.—It has been too much our author's object to pander to the artificial taste of the age; and his productions, however, brilliant and agreeable, are in consequence somewhat meretricious and effeminate. It was thought formerly enough to have an occasionally fine passage in the progress of a story or a poem, and an occasionally striking image or expression in a fine passage or description. But this style, it seems, was to be exploded as rude, Gothic, meagre, and dry. Now all must be raised to the same tantalising and preposterous level. There must be no pause, no interval, no repose, no gradation. Simplicity and truth yield up the palm to affectation and grimace. The craving of the public mind after novelty and effect is a false and uneasy appetite that must be pampered with fine words at every step—we must be tickled with sound, startled with show, and relieved by the importunate, uninterrupted display of fancy and verbal tinsel as much as possible from the fatigue of thought or shock of feeling. A poem is to resemble an exhibition of fire-works, with a continual explosion of quaint figures and devices, flash after flash, that surprise for the moment, and leave no trace of light or warmth behind them. Or modern poetry in its retrograde progress comes at last to be constructed on the principles of the modern OPERA, where an attempt is made to gratify every sense at every instant, and where the understanding alone is insulted and the heart mocked. It is in this view only that we can discover that Mr. Moore's poetry is vitiated or immoral,—it seduces the taste and enervates the imagination. It creates a false standard of reference, and inverts or decompounds the natural order of association, in which objects strike the thoughts and feelings. His is the poetry of the bath, of the toilette, of the saloon, of the fashionable world; not the poetry of nature, of the heart, or of human life. He stunts and enfeebles equally the growth of the imagination and the affections, by not taking the seed of poetry and sowing it in the ground of truth, and letting it expand in the dew and rain, and shoot up to heaven,

> And spread its sweet leaves to the air,
> Or dedicate its beauty to the sun,—

instead of which he anticipates and defeats his own object, by plucking flowers and blossoms from the stem, and setting them in the ground of idleness and folly—or in the cap of his own vanity, where they soon wither and disappear, 'dying or ere they sicken!' This is but a sort of child's play, a short-sighted ambition. In Milton we meet with many prosaic lines, either because the subject does not require raising or because they are necessary to connect the story, or serve as a relief to other passages—there is not such a thing to be found in all Mr. Moore's writings. His volumes present us with 'a perpetual feast of nectar'd sweets'—but we cannot add—'where no crude surfeit reigns.' He indeed cloys with sweetness; he obscures with splendour; he fatigues with gaiety. We are stifled on beds of roses—we literally lie 'on the rack of restless ecstacy.' His flowery fancy 'looks so fair and smells so sweet, that the sense aches at it.' His verse droops and languishes under a load of beauty, like a bough laden with fruit. His gorgeous style is like 'another morn risen on mid-noon.' There is no passage that is not made up of blushing lines, no line that is not enriched with a sparkling metaphor, no image that is left unadorned with a double epithet—all his verbs, nouns, adjectives, are equally glossy, smooth, and beautiful. Every stanza is transparent with light, perfumed with odours, floating in liquid harmony, melting in luxurious, evanescent delights. His Muse is never contented with an offering from one sense alone, but brings another rifled charm to match it, and revels in a fairy round of pleasure. The interest is not dramatic, but melodramatic—it is a mixture of painting, poetry, and music, of the natural and preternatural, of obvious sentiment and romantic costume. A rose is a *Gul*, a nightingale a *Bulbul*. We might fancy ourselves in an eastern harem, amidst Ottomans, and otto of roses, and veils and spangles, and marble pillars, and cool fountains, and Arab maids and Genii, and magicians, and Peris, and cherubs, and what not? Mr. Moore has a little mistaken the art of poetry for the *cosmetic art*. He does not compose an historic group, or work out a single figure; but throws a variety of elementary sensations, of vivid impressions together, and calls it a description. He makes out an inventory of beauty—the smile on the lips, the dimple on the cheeks, *item*, golden locks, *item*, a pair of blue wings, *item*, a silver sound, with a breathing fragrance and radiant light, and thinks it a character or a story. He gets together a number of fine things and fine names, and thinks that, flung on heaps, they make up a fine poem. This dissipated, fulsome, painted, patch-work style may succeed in the levity and languor of the *boudoir*, or might have been adapted to the Pavilions of royalty, but it is not the style of Parnassus, nor a passport to Immortality. It is not the taste of the ancients, ''tis not classical lore'—nor the fashion of Tibullus, or Theocritus, or Anacreon, or Virgil, or Ariosto, or Pope, or Byron, or any great writer among the living or the dead, but it is the style of our English Anacreon, and it is (or was) the fashion of the day! ⟨. . .⟩

Mr. Moore ought not to contend with serious difficulties or with entire subjects. He can write verses, not a poem. There is no principle of massing or of continuity in his productions—neither height nor breadth nor depth of capacity. There is no truth of representation, no strong internal feeling—but a continual flutter and display of affected airs and graces, like a finished coquette, who hides the want of symmetry by extravagance of dress, and the want of passion by flippant forwardness and unmeaning sentimentality. All is flimsy, all is florid to excess. His imagination may dally with insect beauties, with Rosicrucian spells; may describe a butterfly's wing, a flower-pot, a fan: but it should not attempt to span the great outlines of nature, or keep pace with the sounding march of events, or grapple with the strong fibres of the human heart. The great becomes turgid in his hands, the pathetic insipid. If Mr. Moore were to describe the heights of Chimboraco, instead of the loneliness, the vastness and the shadowy might, he would only think of adorning it with roseate tints, like a strawberry-ice, and would transform a magician's fortress in the Himmalaya (stripped of its mysterious gloom and frowning horrors) into a jeweller's toy, to be set upon a lady's toilette. In proof of this, see above 'the diamond turrets of Shadukiam,' &c. The description of Mokanna in the fight, though it has spirit and grandeur of effect, has still a great alloy of the mock-heroic in it. The route of blood and death, which is otherwise well marked, is infested with a swarm of 'fire-fly' fancies.

> In vain Mokanna, 'midst the general flight,
> Stands, like the red moon, in some stormy night,
> Among the fugitive clouds, that hurrying by,
> Leave only her unshaken in the sky.

This simile is fine, and would have been perfect, but that the moon is not red, and that she seems to hurry by the clouds, not they by her.

The description of the warrior's youthful adversary,

> Whose coming seems
> A light, a glory, such as breaks in dreams—

is fantastic and enervated—a field of battle has nothing to do with dreams:—and again, the two lines immediately after,

> And every sword, true as o'er billows dim
> The needle tracks the load-star, following him—

are a mere piece of enigmatical ingenuity and scientific *mimminee-pimminee*.

We cannot except the *Irish Melodies* from the same censure. If these national airs do indeed express the soul of impassioned feeling in his countrymen, the case of Ireland is hopeless. If these prettinesses pass for patriotism, if a country can heave from its heart's core only these vapid, varnished sentiments, lip-deep, and let its tears of blood evaporate in an empty conceit, let it be governed as it has been. There are here no tones to waken Liberty, to console Humanity. Mr. Moore converts the wild harp of Erin into a musical snuff-box![1]—We *do* except from this censure the author's political squibs, and the *Twopenny Post-bag*. These are essences, are 'nests of spicery,' bitter and sweet, honey and gall together. No one can so well describe the set speech of a dull formalist,[2] or the flowing locks of a Dowager,

> In the manner of Ackermann's dresses for May.

His light, agreeable, polished style pierces through the body of the court—hits off the faded graces of 'an Adonis of fifty,' weighs the vanity of fashion in tremulous scales, mimics the grimace of affectation and folly, shows up the littleness of the great, and spears a phalanx of statesmen with its glittering point as with a diamond broach.

> In choosing songs the Regent named,
> 'Had I a heart for falsehood fram'd:'
> While gentle Hertford begg'd and pray'd
> For 'Young I am, and sore afraid.'

Nothing in Pope or Prior ever surpassed the delicate insinuation and adroit satire of these lines, and hundreds more of our author's composition. We wish he would not take pains to make us think of them with less pleasure than formerly.—The *Fudge Family* is in the same spirit, but with a little falling-off. There is too great a mixture of undisguised Jacobinism and fashionable *slang*. The 'divine Fanny Bias' and 'the mountains *à la Russe*' figure in somewhat quaintly with Buonaparte and the Bourbons. The poet also launches the lightning of political indignation; but it rather plays round and illumines his own pen than reaches the devoted heads at which it is aimed!

Notes
1. Compare his songs with Burns's.
2.

> There was a little man, and he had a little soul,
>   And he said, Little soul, let us try, &c.

Parody on

> There was a little man, and he had a little gun.—

One should think this exquisite ridicule of a pedantic effusion might have silenced for ever the automaton that delivered it: but the official personage in question at the close of the Session addressed an extra-official congratulation to the Prince Regent on a bill that had *not* passed—as if to repeat and insist upon our errors were to justify them.

GEORGE SAINTSBURY
From "Moore" (1886)
Collected Essays and Papers
1923, Volume 1, pp. 134–57

It would be interesting, though perhaps a little impertinent, to put to any given number of well-informed persons under the age of forty or fifty the sudden query, who was Thomas Brown the Younger? And it is very possible that a majority of them would answer that he had something to do with Rugby. It is certain that with respect to that part of his work in which he was pleased so to call himself, Moore is but little known. The considerable mass of his hack-work has gone whither all hack-work goes, fortunately enough for those of us who have to do it. The vast monument erected to him by his pupil, friend, and literary executor, Lord Russell, or rather Lord John Russell, is a monument of such a Cyclopean order of architecture, both in respect of bulk and in respect of style, that most honest biographers and critics acknowledge themselves to have explored its recesses but cursorily. Less of him, even as a poet proper, is now read than of any of the brilliant group of poets of which he was one, with the possible exceptions of Crabbe and Rogers; while, more unfortunate than Crabbe, he has had no Mr Courthope to come to his rescue. But he has recently had what is an unusual thing for an English poet, a French biographer[1]. I shall not have very much to say of the details of M. Vallat's very creditable and useful monograph. It would be possible, if I were merely reviewing it, to pick out some of the curious errors of hasty deduction which are rarely wanting in a book of its nationality. If (and no shame to him) Moore's father sold cheese and whisky, *le whisky d'Irlande* was no doubt his staple commodity in the one branch, but scarcely *le fromage de Stilton* in the other. An English lawyer's studies are not even now, except at the universities and for purposes of perfunctory examination, very much in "Justinian," and in Moore's time they were still less so. And if Bromham Church is near Sloperton, then it will follow as the night the day that it is not *dans le Bedfordshire*. But these things matter very little. They are found, in their different kinds, in all books; and if we English bookmakers (at least some of us) are not likely to make a Bordeaux wine merchant sell Burgundy as his chief commodity, or say that a village near Amiens is *dans le Béarn*, we no doubt do other things quite as bad. On the whole, M. Vallat's sketch, though of moderate length, is quite the soberest and most trustworthy sketch of Moore's life and of his books, as books merely, that I know. In matters of pure criticism M. Vallat is less blameless. He quotes authorities with that apparent indifference to, or even ignorance of, their relative value which is so yawning a pit for the feet of the foreigner in all cases; and perhaps a wider knowledge of English poetry in general would have been a better preparation for the study of Moore's in particular. "Never," says M. Renan very wisely, "never does a foreigner satisfy the nation whose history he writes"; and this is as true of literary history as of history proper. But M. Vallat satisfies us in a very considerable degree; and even putting aside the question whether he is satisfactory altogether, he has given us quite sufficient text in the mere fact that he has bestowed upon Moore an amount of attention and competence which no compatriot of the author of *Lalla Rookh* has cared to bestow for many years.

I shall also here take the liberty of neglecting a very great—as far as bulk goes, by far the greatest—part of Moore's own performance. He has inserted so many interesting autobiographical particulars in the prefaces to his complete works, that visits to the great mausoleum of the Russell memoirs are rarely necessary, and still more rarely profitable. His work for the booksellers was done at a time when the best class of such work was much better done than the best class of it is now; but it was after all work for the booksellers. His *History of Ireland*, his *Life of Lord Edward Fitzgerald*, etc., may be pretty exactly gauged by saying that they are a good deal better than Scott's work of a merely similar kind (in which it is hardly necessary to say that I do not include the *Tales of a Grandfather* or the introductions to the Dryden, the Swift, and the Ballantyne novels), not nearly so good as Southey's, and not quite so good as Campbell's. The *Life of Byron* holds a different place. With the poems, or some of them, it forms the only part of Moore's literary work which is still read; and though it is read much more for its substance than for its execution, it is still a masterly performance of a very difficult task. The circumstances which brought it about are well known, and no discussion of them would be possible without plunging into the Byron controversy generally, which the present writer most distinctly declines to do. But these circumstances, with other things among which Moore's own comparative faculty for the business may be not unjustly mentioned, prevent it from taking rank at all approaching that of Boswell's or Lockhart's inimitable biographies. The chief thing to note in it as regards Moore himself, is the help it gives in a matter to which we shall have to refer again, his attitude towards those whom his time still called "the great."

And so we are left with the poems—not an inconsiderable companion seeing that its stature is some seven hundred small quarto pages closely packed with verses in double columns. Part of this volume is, however, devoted to the *Epicurean*, a not unremarkable example of ornate prose in many respects resembling the author's verse. Indeed, as close readers of Moore know, there exists an unfinished verse form of it which, in style and general character, is not unlike a more serious *Lalla Rookh*. As far as poetry goes, almost everything that will be said of *Lalla Rookh* might be said of *Alciphron*: this latter, however, is a little more Byronic than its more famous sister, and in that respect not quite so successful. ⟨. . .⟩

Of Moore's character not much need be said, nor need what is said be otherwise than favourable. Not only to modern tastes, but to the sturdier tastes of his own day, and even of the days immediately before his, there was a little too much of the parasite and the hanger-on about him. It is easy to say that a man of his talents, when he had once obtained a start, might surely have gone his own way and lived his own life, without taking up the position of a kind of superior gamekeeper or steward at rich men's gates. But race, fashion, and a good many other things have to be taken into account; and it is fair to Moore to remember that he was, as it were from the first, bound to the chariot-wheels of "the great," and could hardly liberate himself from them without churlishness and violence. Moreover, it cannot possibly be denied by any fair critic that if he accepted to some extent the awkward position of led-poet, he showed in it as much independence as was compatible with the function. Both in money matters, in his language to his patrons, and in a certain general but indefinable tone of behaviour, he contrasts not less favourably than remarkably, both with the ultra-Tory Hook, to whom we have already compared him, and with the ultra-Radical Leigh Hunt. Moore had as little of Wagg as he had of Skimpole about him; though he allowed his way of life to compare in some respects perilously with theirs. It is only necessary to look at his letters to Byron—always ready enough to treat as spaniels those of his inferiors in station who appeared to be of the spaniel kind—to appreciate his general attitude, and his behaviour in this instance is by no means different from his behaviour in others. As a politician there is no doubt that he at least thought himself to be quite sincere. It may be that, if he had been, his political satires would have galled Tories more than they did then, and could hardly be read by persons of that persuasion with such complete enjoyment as they can now. But the insincerity was quite unconscious, and indeed can hardly be said to have been insincerity at all. Moore had not a political head, and in English as in Irish politics his beliefs were probably not founded on any clearly comprehended principles. But such as they were he held to them firmly. Against his domestic character nobody has ever said anything; and it is sufficient to observe that not a few of the best as well as of the greatest men of his time, Scott as well as Byron, Lord John Russell as well as Lord Moira, appear not only to have admired his abilities and liked his social qualities, but to have sincerely respected his character. And so we may at last find ourselves alone with the plump volume of poems in which we shall hardly discover with the amiable M. Vallat "the greatest lyric poet of England," but in which we shall find a poet certainly, and if not a very great poet, at any rate a poet who has done many things well, and one particular thing better than anybody else.

The volume opens with *Lalla Rookh*, a proceeding which, if not justified by chronology, is completely justified by the facts that Moore was to his contemporaries the author of that poem chiefly, and that it is by far the most considerable thing not only in mere bulk, but in arrangement, plan, and style, that he ever did. Perhaps I am not quite a fair judge of *Lalla Rookh*. I was brought up in what is called a strict household where, though the rule was not, as far as I can remember, enforced by any penalties, it was a point of honour that in the nursery and schoolroom none but "Sunday books" should be read on Sunday. But this severity was tempered by one of the easements often occurring in a world which, if not the best, is certainly not the worst of all possible worlds. For the convenience of servants, or for some other reason, the children were much more in the drawing-room on Sundays than on any other day, and it was an unwritten rule that any book that lived in the drawing-room was fit Sunday-reading. The consequence was that from the time I could read, till childish things were put away, I used to spend a considerable part of the first day of the week in reading and re-reading a collection of books, four of which were Scott's poems, *Lalla Rookh*, *The Essays of Elia* (First Edition,—I have got it now), and Southey's *Doctor*. Therefore it may be that I rank *Lalla Rookh* rather too high. At the same time I confess that it still seems to me a very respectable poem indeed of the second rank. Of course it is artificial. The parade of second, or third, or twentieth-hand learning in the notes makes one smile, and the whole reminds one (as I daresay it has reminded many others before) of a harp of the period with the gilt a little tarnished, the ribbons more than a little faded, and the silk stool on which the young woman in ringlets used to sit much worn. All this is easy metaphorical criticism, if it is criticism at all. For I am not sure that, when the last age has got a little farther off from our descendants, they will see anything more ludicrous in such a harp than we see in the faded spinets of a generation earlier still. But much remains to Lalla if not to Feramorz. The prose interludes have lost none of their airy grace. Even Mr Burnand has not been able to make Mokanna ridiculous, nor have the recent accounts of the actual waste of

desert and felt huts banished at least the poetical beauty of "Merou's bright palaces and groves." There are those who laugh at the bower of roses by Bendemeer's stream: I do not. "Paradise and the Peri" is perhaps the prettiest purely sentimental poem that English or any other language can show. "The Fire Worshippers" are rather long, but there is a famous fight—more than one indeed—in them to relieve the monotony. For "The Light of the Harem" alone I have never been able to get up much enthusiasm; but even "The Light of the Harem" is a great deal better than Moore's subsequent attempt in the style of *Lalla Rookh*, or something like it, *The Loves of the Angels*. There is only one good thing that I can find to say of that: it is not so bad as the poem which similarity of title makes one think of in connection with it—Lamartine's disastrous *Chute d'un ange*.

As *Lalla Rookh* is far the most important of Moore's serious poems, so *The Fudge Family at Paris* is far the best of his humorous poems. I do not forget *The Two-penny Postbag*, nor many capital later verses of the same kind, the best of which perhaps is the Epistle from Henry of Exeter to John of Tchume. But *The Fudge Family* has all the merits of these, with a scheme and framework of dramatic character which they lack. Miss Biddy and her vanities, Master Bob and his guttling, the eminent turncoat Phil Fudge, Esq. himself and his politics, are all excellent. But I avow that Phelim Connor is to me the most delightful, though he has always been rather a puzzle. If he is intended to be a satire on the class now represented by the O'Briens and the McCarthys he is exquisite, and it is small wonder that Young Ireland has never loved Moore much. But I do not think that Thomas Brown the Younger meant it, or at least wholly meant it, as satire, and this is perhaps the best proof of his unpractical way of looking at politics. For Phelim Connor is a much more damning sketch than any of the Fudges. Vanity, gluttony, the scheming intrigues of eld, may not be nice things, but they are common to the whole human race. The hollow rant which enjoys the advantages of liberty and declaims against the excesses of tyranny is in its perfection Irish alone. However this may be, these lighter poems of Moore are great fun, and it is no small misfortune that the younger generation of readers pays so little attention to them. For they are full of acute observation of manners, politics, and society by an accomplished man of the world, put into pointed and notable form by an accomplished man of letters. Our fathers knew them well, and many a quotation familiar enough at second hand is due originally to the Fudge Family in their second appearance (not so good, but still good) many years later, to *The Two-penny Postbag* and to the long list of miscellaneous satires and skits. The last sentence is, however, to be taken as most strictly excluding "Corruption," "Intolerance," and "The Sceptic." *Rhymes on the Road*, travel-pieces out of Moore's line, may also be mercifully left aside: and "Evenings in Greece"; and "The Summer Fête" (any universal provider would have supplied as good a poem with the supper and the rout-seats) need not delay the critic and will not extraordinarily delight the reader. Not here is Moore's spur of Parnassus to be found.

For that domain of his we must go to the songs which, in extraordinary numbers, make up the whole of the divisions headed Irish Melodies, National Airs, Sacred Songs, Ballads and Songs, and some of the finest of which are found outside these divisions in the longer poems from *Lalla Rookh* downwards. The singular musical melody of these pieces has never been seriously denied by any one, but it seems to be thought, especially nowadays, that because they are musically melodious they are not poetical. It is probably useless to protest against a prejudice which, where it is not due to simple thoughtlessness or to blind following of fashion, argues a certain constitutional defect of the understanding powers. But it may be just necessary to repeat pretty firmly that any one who regards, even with a tincture of contempt, such work (to take various characteristic examples) as Dryden's lyrics, as Shenstone's, as Moore's, as Macaulay's Lays, because he thinks that, if he did not contemn them, his worship of Shakespeare, of Shelley, of Wordsworth would be suspect, is most emphatically not a critic of poetry and not even a catholic lover of it. Which said, let us betake ourselves to seeing what Moore's special virtue is. It is acknowledged that it consists partly in marrying music most happily to verse; but what is not so fully acknowledged as it ought to be is, that it also consists in marrying music not merely to verse, but to poetry. Among the more abstract questions of poetical criticism few are more interesting than this, the connection of what may be called musical music with poetical music; and it is one which has not been much discussed. Let us take the two greatest of Moore's own contemporaries in lyric, the two greatest lyrists as some think (I give no opinion on this) in English, and compare their work with his. Shelley has the poetical music in an unsurpassable and sometimes in an almost unapproached degree, but his verse is admittedly very difficult to set to music. I should myself go farther and say that it has in it some indefinable quality antagonistic to such setting. Except the famous Indian Serenade, I do not know any poem of Shelley's that has been set with anything approaching to success, and in the best setting that I know of this the honeymoon of the marriage turns into a "red moon" before long. That this is not merely due to the fact that Shelley likes intricate metres any one who examines Moore can see. That it is due merely to the fact that Shelley, as we know from Peacock, was almost destitute of any ear for music is the obvious and common explanation. But neither will this serve, for we happen also to know that Burns, whose lyric, of a higher quality than Moore's, assorts with music as naturally as Moore's own, was quite as deficient as Shelley in this respect. So was Scott, who could yet write admirable songs to be sung. It seems therefore almost impossible, on the comparison of these three instances, to deny the existence of some peculiar musical music in poetry, which is distinct from poetical music, though it may coexist with it or may be separated from it, and which is independent both of technical musical training and even of what is commonly called "ear" in the poet. That Moore possessed it in probably the highest degree will, I think, hardly be denied. It never seems to have mattered to him whether he wrote the words for the air or altered the air to suit the words. The two fit like a glove, and if, as is sometimes the case, the same or a similar poetical measure is heard set to another air than Moore's, this other always seems intrusive and wrong. He draws attention in one case to the extraordinary irregularity of his own metre (an irregularity to which the average pindaric is a mere jog-trot), yet the air fits it exactly[2]. Of course the two feet which most naturally go to music, the anapæst and the trochee, are commonest with him; but the point is that he seems to find no more difficulty, if he does not take so much pleasure, in setting combinations of a very different kind. Nor is this peculiar gift by any means unimportant from the purely poetical side, the side on which the verse is looked at without any regard to air or accompaniment. For the great drawback to "songs to be sung" in general since Elizabethan days (when, as Mr Arber and Mr Bullen have shown, it was very different) has

been the constant tendency of the verse-writer to sacrifice to his musical necessities either meaning or poetic sound or both. The climax of this is of course reached in the ineffable balderdash which usually does duty for the libretto of an opera, but it is quite as noticeable in the ordinary songs of the drawing-room. Now Moore is quite free from this blame. He may not have the highest and rarest strokes of poetic expression; but at any rate he seldom or never sins against either reason or poetry for the sake of rhythm and rhyme. He is always the master not the servant, the artist not the clumsy craftsman. And this I say not by any means as one likely to pardon poetical shortcomings in consideration of musical merit, for, shameful as the confession may be, a little music goes a long way with me; and what music I do like, is rather of the kind opposite to Moore's facile styles. Yet it is easy, even from the musical view, to exaggerate his facility. Berlioz is not generally thought a barrel-organ composer, and he bestowed early and particular pains on Moore.

To many persons, however, the results are more interesting than the analysis of their qualities and principles; so let us go to the songs themselves. To my fancy the three best of Moore's songs, and three of the finest songs in any language, are "Oft in the stilly Night," "When in Death I shall calm recline," and "I saw from the Beach." They all exemplify what has been pointed out above, the complete adaptation of words to music and music to words, coupled with a decidedly high quality of poetical merit in the verse, quite apart from the mere music. It can hardly be necessary to quote them, for they are or ought to be familiar to everybody; but in selecting these three I have no intention of distinguishing them in point of general excellence from scores, nay hundreds of others. "Go where Glory waits thee" is the first of the Irish Melodies, and one of those most hackneyed by the enthusiasm of bygone Pogsons. But its merit ought in no way to suffer on that account with persons who are not Pogsons. It ought to be possible for the reader, it is certainly possible for the critic, to dismiss Pogson altogether, to wave Pogson off, and to read anything as if it had never been read before. If this be done we shall hardly wonder at the delight which our fathers, who will not compare altogether badly with ourselves, took in Thomas Moore. "When he who adores thee" is supposed on pretty good evidence to have been inspired by the most hollow and senseless of all pseudo-patriotic delusions, a delusion of which the best thing that can be said is that "the pride of thus dying for" it has been about the last thing that it ever did inspire, and that most persons who have suffered from it have usually had the good sense to take lucrative places from the tyrant as soon as they could get them, and to live happily ever after. But the basest, the most brutal, and the bloodiest of Saxons may recognise in Moore's poem the expression of a possible, if not a real, feeling given with infinite grace and pathos. The same string reverberates even in the thrice and thousand times hackneyed Harp of Tara. "Rich and rare were the Gems she wore" is chiefly comic opera, but it is very pretty comic opera; and the two pieces, "There is not in the wide world" and "How dear to me" exemplify, for the first but by no means for the last time, Moore's extraordinary command of the last phase of that curious thing called by the century that gave him birth Sensibility. We have turned Sensibility out of doors; but he would be a rash man who would say that we have not let in seven worse devils of the gushing kind in her comparatively innocent room.

Then we may skip not a few pieces, only referring once more to "The Legacy" ("When in Death I shall calm recline"), an anacreontic quite unsurpassable in its own kind.

We need dwell but briefly on such pieces as "Believe me if all those endearing young Charms," which is typical of much that Moore wrote, but does not reach the true devil-may-care note of Suckling, or as "By the Hope within us springing," for Moore's warlike pieces are seldom or never good. But with "Love's Young Dream" we come back to the style of which it is impossible to say less than that it is quite admirable in its kind. Then after a page or two we come to the chief *cruces* of Moore's pathetic and of his comic manner, "The Last Rose of Summer," "The Young May Moon," and "The Minstrel Boy." I cannot say very much for the last, which is tainted with the unreality of all Moore's Tyrtean efforts; but "The Young May Moon" could not be better, and I am not going to abandon the Rose, for all her perfume be something musty— a *pot-pourri* rose rather than a fresh one. The song of O'Ruark with its altogether fatal climax—

> On our side is virtue and Erin,
> On theirs is the Saxon and guilt—

(which carries with it the delightful reflection that it was an Irishman running away with an Irish woman that occasioned this sweeping moral contrast) must be given up; but surely not so "Oh had we some bright little Isle of our own." For indeed if one only had some bright little isle of that kind, some *rive fidèle où l'on aime toujours*, and where things in general are adjusted to such a state, then would Thomas Moore be the Laureate of that bright and tight little island.

But it is alarming to find that we have not yet got through twenty-five pages out of some hundred or two, and that the Irish Melodies are not yet nearly exhausted. Not a few of the best known of Moore's songs, including "Oft in the stilly Night," are to be found in the division of National Airs, which is as a whole a triumph of that extraordinary genius for setting which has been already noticed. Here is "Flow on thou shining River," here the capital "When I touch the String," on which Thackeray loved to make variations. But "Oft in the stilly Night" itself is far above the others. We do not say "stilly" now: we have been taught by Coleridge (who used to use it freely himself before he laughed at it) to laugh at "stilly" and "paly" and so forth. But the most acrimonious critic may be challenged to point out another weakness of the same kind, and on the whole the straightforward simplicity of the phrase equals the melody of the rhythm.

The Sacred Songs need not delay us long; for they are not better than sacred songs in general, which is saying remarkably little. Perhaps the most interesting thing in them is the well-known couplet,

> This world is but a fleeting show
> For man's illusion given—

which, as has justly been observed, contains one of the most singular estimates of the divine purpose anywhere to be found. But Moore might, like Mr Midshipman Easy, have excused himself by remarking, "Ah! well, I don't understand these things." The miscellaneous division of Ballads, Songs, etc., is much more fruitful. "The Leaf and the Fountain," beginning "Tell me, kind seer, I pray thee," though rather long, is singularly good of its kind—the kind of half-narrative ballad. So in a lighter strain is "The Indian Bark." Nor is Moore less at home after his own fashion in the songs from the Anthology. It is true that the same fault which has been found with his *Anacreon* may be found here, and that it is all the more sensible because at least in some cases the originals are much higher poetry than the pseudo-Teian. To the form and style of Meleager Moore could not pretend; but as these are rather songs on Greek motives than translations from the Greek, the

slackness and dilution matter less. But the strictly miscellaneous division holds some of the best work. We could no doubt dispense with the well-known ditty (for once very nearly the "rubbish" with which Moore is so often and so unjustly charged) where Posada rhymes of necessity to Granada, and where, quite against the author's habit, the ridiculous term "Sultana" is fished out to do similar duty in reference to the Dulcinea, or rather to the Maritornes, of a muleteer. But this is quite an exception, and as a rule the facile verse is as felicitous as it is facile. Perhaps no one stands out very far above the rest; perhaps all have more or less the mark of easy variations on a few well-known themes. The old comparison that they are as numerous as motes, as bright, as fleeting, and as individually insignificant, comes naturally enough to the mind. But then they are very numerous, they are very bright, and if they are fleeting, their number provides plenty more to take the place of that which passes away. Nor is it by any means true that they lack individual significance.

This enumeration of a few out of many ornaments of Moore's muse will of course irritate those who object to the "brick-of-the-house" mode of criticism; while it may not be minute enough, or sufficiently bolstered by actual quotation, to please those who hold that simple extract is the best, if not the only tolerable form of criticism. But the critic is not alone in finding that, whether he carry his ass or ride upon it, he cannot please all his public. What has been said is probably enough, in the case of a writer whose work, though as a whole rather unjustly forgotten, survives in parts more securely even than the work of greater men, to remind readers of at least the outlines and bases of his claim to esteem. And the more those outlines are followed up, and the structure founded on those bases is examined, the more certain, I think, is Moore of recovering, not the position which M. Vallat would assign to him of the greatest lyrist of England (a position which he never held and never could hold except with very prejudiced or very incompetent judges), not that of the equal of Scott or Byron or Shelley or Wordsworth, but still a position high enough and singularly isolated at its height. Viewed from the point of strictly poetical criticism, he no doubt ranks only with those poets who have expressed easily and acceptably the likings and passions and thoughts and fancies of the average man, and who have expressed these with no extraordinary cunning or witchery. To go further in limitation, the average man, of whom he is thus the bard, is a rather sophisticated average man, without very deep thoughts or feelings, without a very fertile or fresh imagination or fancy, with even a touch—a little touch—of cant and "gush" and other defects incident to average and sophisticated humanity. But this humanity is at any time and every time no small portion of humanity at large, and it is to Moore's credit that he sings its feelings and its thoughts so as always to get the human and durable element in them visible and audible through the "trappings of convention." Again, he has that all-saving touch of humour which enables him, sentimentalist as he is, to be an admirable comedian as well. Yet again, he has at least something of the two qualities which one must demand of a poet who is a poet, and not a mere maker of rhymes. His note of feeling, if not full or deep, is true and real. His faculty of expression is not only considerable, but it is also distinguished; it is a faculty which in the same measure and degree nobody else has possessed. On one side he had the gift of singing those admirable songs of which we have been talking. On the other, he had the gift of right satiric verse to a degree which only three others of the great dead men of the century in England—Canning, Praed, and Thackeray—have reached. Besides all this, he was a "considerable man of letters." But your considerable men of letters, after flourishing, turn to dust in their season, and other considerable or inconsiderable men of letters spring out of it. The true poets and even the true satirists abide, and both as a poet and a satirist Thomas Moore abides and will abide with them.

Notes

1. *Etude sur la vie et les œuvres de Thomas Moore*; by Gustave Vallat. Paris: Rousseau. London: Asher and Co. Dublin: Hodges, Figgis, and Co. 1887.
2. I do not wish to multiply references to other books of my own. But the treatment of Moore in my *History of Prosody*, vol. III. completes this Essay in a rather unusual degree.

SARA COLERIDGE

1802–1852

Sara Coleridge was born on December 22, 1802, at Keswick, Cumberland, the only daughter of Samuel Taylor Coleridge. She rarely saw her father as a young child, however, because of the estrangement between her parents, and her early development was mainly overseen by her uncle Robert Southey. A lengthy period of total separation between father and daughter, beginning in 1812, finally ended a decade later when she went with her mother to visit him at Highgate in 1822, and from that time on Sara and her father developed a close relationship. Encouraged by her father, Sara translated from the Latin Martin Dobrizhöffer's *An Account of the Abipones* (1822); she later translated from the French the *Memoirs of the Chevalier Bayard* (1825).

In 1829 Sara married her cousin Henry Nelson Coleridge, who undertook the editing of her father's works. For her children Sara wrote a collection of poetry, *Pretty Lessons in Verse for Good Children* (1834), and a fairy story, *Phantasmion* (1837). Upon her husband's death in 1843 she took over the editing of her father's works and achieved a certain eminence as a Coleridge scholar. Her "Essay on Rationalism" was included in the fifth edition of *Aids to Reflection* (1843), and she contributed a supplement and extensive notes to the second edition of the *Biographia Literaria* (1847).

Sara Coleridge died in London on May 3, 1852. *Memoir and Letters of Sara Coleridge*, which includes many reminiscences about her literary friendships, was edited by her daughter Edith and published in 1873.

'Last of the Three, though eldest born,
Reveal thyself, like pensive Morn
Touched by the skylark's earliest note,
Ere humbler gladness be afloat.
But whether in the semblance drest
Of Dawn—or Eve, fair vision of the west,
Come with each anxious hope subdued
By woman's gentle fortitude,
Each grief, through meekness, settling into rest.
—Or I would hail thee when some high-wrought page
Of a closed volume lingering in thy hand
Has raised thy spirit to a peaceful stand
Among the glories of a happier age.'

Her brow hath opened on me—see it there,
Brightening the umbrage of her hair;
So gleams the crescent moon, that loves
To be descried through shady groves.
Tenderest bloom is on her cheek;
Wish not for a richer streak;
Nor dread the depth of meditative eye;
But let thy love, upon that azure field
Of thoughtfulness and beauty, yield
Its homage offered up in purity.
What wouldst thou more? In sunny glade,
Or under leaves of thickest shade,
Was such a stillness e'er diffused
Since earth grew calm while angels mused?
Softly she treads, as if her foot were loth
To crush the mountain dew-drops—soon to melt
On the flower's breast; as if she felt
That flowers themselves, whate'er their hue,

With all their fragrance, all their glistening,
Call to the heart for inward listening—
And though for bridal wreaths and tokens true
Welcomed wisely; though a growth
Which the careless shepherd sleeps on,
As fitly spring from turf the mourner weeps on—
And without wrong are cropped the marble tomb to strew.
The Charm is over; the mute Phantoms gone,
Nor will return—but droop not, favoured Youth;
The apparition that before thee shone
Obeyed a summons covetous of truth.
From these wild rocks thy footsteps I will guide
To bowers in which thy fortune may be tried,
And one of the bright Three become thy happy Bride.
  —WILLIAM WORDSWORTH, "The Triad," 1828,
    ll. 174–218

Sara Coleridge is writing a defence of her father's theology, proving how very orthodox he was and how well he deserved to be the pet son of the Church. Sterling remarked that she shows the limited nature of a woman's mind in her *Phantasmion*: she does not make Ariel an element, but the whole thing is Ariel, and therefore very wearisome and unsubstantial.—CAROLINE FOX, *Journal* (Oct. 30, 1843), *Memories of Old Friends*, ed. Horace N. Pym, 1882, p. 204

Mrs. Sarah Henry Coleridge, in some fugitive pieces, but especially in her exquisite prose tale *Phantasmion* (1837), has evinced poetical talent of no common order. With an imagination like a prism shedding rainbow changes on her thoughts, she shows study without the affectation of it, and a Greek-like closeness of expression.—GEORGE WASHINGTON BETHUNE, *The British Female Poets*, 1848, p. 430

To those who knew her she remains an image of grace and intellectual beauty that time can never tarnish. A larger circle will now know, in part at least, what she was. Her correspondence will, to thoughtful readers, convey a clearer impression than aught beside could convey of one who of course could only be fully understood by those who had known her personally and known her long.

In their memories she will ever possess a place apart from all others. With all her high literary powers she was utterly unlike the mass of those who are called 'literary persons.' Few have possessed such learning; and when one calls to mind the arduous character of those studies, which seemed but a refreshment to her clear intellect, like a walk in mountain air, it seems a marvel how a woman's faculties could have grappled with those Greek philosophers and Greek fathers, just as no doubt it seemed a marvel when her father, at the age of fourteen, woke the echoes of that famous old cloister with declamations from Plato and Plotinus. But in the daughter, as in the father, the real marvel was neither the accumulated knowledge nor the literary power. It was the spiritual mind.

The rapt one of the Godlike forehead,
The heaven-eyed creature,

was Wordsworth's description of Coleridge, the most spiritual perhaps of England's poets, certainly of her modern poets. Of her some one said, 'Her father had looked down into her eyes, and left in them the light of his own.' Her great characteristic was the radiant spirituality of her intellectual and imaginative being. This it was that looked forth from her countenance.

Great and various as were your mother's talents, it was not from them that she derived what was special to her. It was from the degree in which she had inherited the feminine portion of genius. She had a keener appreciation of what was highest and most original in thought than of subjects nearer the range of ordinary intellects. She moved with the lightest step when she moved over the loftiest ground. Her 'feet were beautiful on the mountain-tops' of ideal thought. They were her native land; for her they were not barren; honey came up from the stony rock. In this respect I should suppose she must have differed from almost all women whom we associate with literature. I remember hearing her say that she hardly considered herself to be a woman 'of letters.' She felt herself more at east when musing on the mysteries of the soul, or discussing the most arduous speculations of philosophy and theology, than when dealing with the humbler topics of literature.

As might have been expected, the department of literature which interested her most was that of poetry—that is, poetry of the loftiest and most spiritual order, for to much of what is now popular she would have refused the name. How well I remember our discussions about Wordsworth! She was jealous of my admiration for his poems, because it extended to *too many* of them. No one could be a true Wordsworthian, she maintained, who admired so much of his later poems, his poems of accomplishment, such as the 'Triad.' It implied a disparagement of his earlier poems, such as 'Resolution and Independence,' in which the genuine Wordsworthian inspiration, and that alone, uttered itself! I suspect, however, that she must have taken a yet more vivid delight in some of her father's poems. Beside their music and their spirituality, they have another quality, in which they stand almost without a rival,— their subtle sweetness. I remember Leigh Hunt once remarking to me on this characteristic of them, and observing that in this respect they were unapproached. It is like distant music, when

the tone comes to you pure, without any coarser sound of wood or of wire; or like odour on the air, when you smell the flower, without detecting in it the stalk or the earth. As regards this characteristic of her father's genius, as well as its spirituality, there was something in hers that resembled it. One is reminded of it by the fairy-like music of the songs in *Phantasmion*.

There is a certain gentleness and a modesty which belong to real genius, and which are in striking contrast with the self-confidence and self-assertion, so often found in persons possessed of vigorous talents, but to whom literature is but a rough sport or a coarse profession. It was these qualities that gave to her manners their charm of feminine grace, self-possession, and sweetness. She was one of those whose thoughts are growing while they speak, and who never speak to surprise. Her intellectual fervour was not that which runs over in excitement; a quietude belonged to it, and it was ever modulated by a womanly instinct of reserve and dignity. She never 'thought for effect,' or cared to have the last word in discussion, or found it difficult to conceive how others should differ from her conclusions. She was more a woman than those who had not a tenth part of her intellectual energy. The seriousness and the softness of her nature raised her above vanity and its contortions. Her mind could move at once and be at rest.

I fear that the type of character and intellect to which your mother belonged must be expected to grow rarer in these days of 'fast' intellect. Talents rush to the market, the theatre, or the arena, and genius itself becomes vulgarized for want of that 'hermit heart' which ought to belong to it, whether it be genius of the creative or the susceptive order. There will always, however, be those whose discernment can trace in your mother's correspondence and in her works the impress of what once was so fair. But, alas! how little will be known of her even by such. Something they will guess of her mind, but it is only a more fortunate few who can know her yet higher gifts, those that belong to the heart and moral being. If they have a loss which is theirs only, they too have remembrances which none can share with them. They remember the wide sympathies and the high aspirations, the courageous love of knowledge, and the devout submission to Revealed Truth; the domestic affections so tender, so dutiful, and so self-sacrificing, the friendships so faithful and so unexacting. For her great things and little lived on together through the fidelity of a heart that seemed never to forget. I never walk beside the Greta or the Derwent without hearing her describe the flowers she had gathered on their margin in her early girlhood. For her they seemed to preserve their fragrance, amid the din and the smoke of the great metropolis.—AUBREY DE VERE, Letter to Edith Coleridge (c. 1873), cited in Sara Coleridge, *Memoir and Letters of Sara Coleridge*, ed. Edith Coleridge, 1873, Vol. 1, pp. 48–53

Phantasmion was at first intended (though it soon outgrew its original limits) as a mere child's story for the amusement of her little boy. A series of educational rhymes, written for her children, was afterward published under the title of *Pretty Lessons for Good Children*. It proved a popular work, and passed through five editions. These things were, however, merely the amusements of her literary career; its serious work, first pursued in conjunction with her husband, and after his death, in 1843, alone, was that of collecting and arranging for publication the scattered literary remains of her father. The task was left incomplete at her own death ten years later, when it was taken up by her brother, the Rev. Derwent Coleridge. The helpful, loving, and unselfish spirit which made her a willing and affectionate partner in her husband's labors, after his death took a more commanding form, and led her to dedicate the whole of her intellectual existence to the great object of carrying out a husband's wishes, of doing justice to a father's name. In the fulfillment of this sacred trust she found occasion to illustrate and adorn the works which fell under her editorship with several compositions of no inconsiderable extent, and displaying powers of critical analysis, and of doctrinal, political, and historical research and discussion, of no common order. The most important of these are the "Essay on Rationalism, with a special Application to the Doctrine of Baptismal Regeneration," appended to Vol. II. of the *Aids to Reflection*, the "Introduction" to the *Biographia Literaria*, and a preface to the collection of her father's political writings, entitled *Essays on his Own Times, by S. T. Coleridge*, which contains, according to a high authority, the most judicious and impartial comparison between British and American civilization, and the social and intellectual conditions of the two countries, that has yet been written. In the desultory form of notes, appendices, and prefaces were thus expended an amount of original thought and an affluence of learning which, differently and more prominently presented, would have made her famous. It has been well said that there is not one woman in a thousand, not one man in ten thousand, who would have been thus prodigal of the means of celebrity. Her own feeling lines, from an unpublished poem, reveal the depth and strength of her affection for her father's memory:

> Father! no amaranths e'er shall wreathe my brow;
> Enough that round thy grave they flourish now!
> But Love his roses 'mid my young locks braided,
> And what cared I for flowers of richer bloom?
> Those too seemed deathless—here they never faded,
> But, drenched and shattered, dropped into the tomb.

These affectionate labors continued for about seven years after her husband's death, when failing health compelled the relinquishment of the task to other hands. ⟨. . .⟩

There are many pleasant touches and bits of personal history in ⟨her⟩ letters, which, for the most part, can only be appreciated in connection with the text. Some of the most interesting portions of her correspondence are those in which she writes familiarly, but often profoundly, of literature and art. Her letters on Keats and Shelley betray a clear and independent judgment, while her criticisms on Wordsworth, whom as a man she almost worshiped, are very striking from her clear appreciation of the falling off in his later productions, to which neither affection nor reverence for his great genius could blind her. Her critique on his *Laodamia* may be cited as an illustration of her clear intellectual perception. She was before Ruskin in appreciating Turner's veracity in landscape painting. In religious philosophy she was a consistent and intelligent disciple of her father; but though holding firmly to her own opinions on points of faith and doctrine, she was never illiberal. She could be just to the heart and mind of poor Blanco White, and protested against the bigotry which classed Shelley's poems under the sixth vial of the Apocalypse.—S. S. Conant, "The Last of the Three," *Harper's New Monthly Magazine*, Nov. 1873, pp. 898–99

Sara Coleridge's chief claim to remembrance in connection with literature lies in the essays and notes, mainly on controverted topics of theology and metaphysics, with which she illustrated the editions of her father's works that she superintended. They display learning rare in a woman, as well as a considerable power of speculation and of skill in dealing with the terms and propositions of metaphysics. But she had inherited from her father the tendency to over-refinement and subtlety rather than clearness of thought, and she had adopted

from him his mode of speculation, in which baseless assumptions are often made to do the duty of sound arguments, and to serve as substructure for the most lofty but unsubstantial edifices of fancy. Coleridge had the faculty of deceiving himself with the notion that he was thinking, when in truth he was dissipating his intellectual energies in the practice of the mere form without the substance of thought. This faculty was helped by his tendency to mysticism, and by his adoption of an unintelligible scheme of theology. Nothing impresses a certain class of minds more effectively than the self-confidence of an inaccurate thinker, especially if it be united, as in Coleridge's case, with great powers of expression, gleams of true insight, and a highly poetic genius. His daughter became one of his most thorough disciples. Her affection, which had found little opportunity for expression in personal relations with her neglectful parent, her pride in his repute, and her inheritance of intellectual tendencies and sympathies, seem gradually to have shaped her mind upon the model of his. But it was the speculative, more than the imaginative and poetic, side of his nature that was reflected by hers. And that portion of his speculations was specially attractive to her in which he attempted to build up a system of evangelical theology upon a curiously ingenious and complex metaphysical basis. The more important letters in the volume before us are metaphysico-theological discussions, in which the cut-and-dry formulas of the evangelical school have a large place. The letters show an admirable temper and spirit, reveal a very pure and pious soul, but are dreary expositions of a scheme which, in the effort to reconcile philosophy with the creed of a narrow party of a single church, resulted in an unsatisfactory and lifeless compound of formalism and mysticism.

The chief impression left by the letters is that Sara Coleridge's existence was far too much intellectualized. The sweet feminine soul was starved by the claims of the restless and dissatisfied intelligence. Her letters, even those to her husband, take the form of essays; they want the grace of easy friendly communication. She is always a little conscious of being seated in the lecturer's chair, and what she has to say must, to our regret, turn out at times, if not tedious, at least commonplace. Her notion of letter-writing is given by herself in a letter to a friend, and the passage is characteristic of her manner. "Letter-writing," she says, "is a method of visiting our friends in their absence, and one which has some advantages peculiar to itself; for persons who have any seriousness of character at all endeavor to put the better part of their mind upon paper; and letter-writing is one of the many calls which life affords to put our minds in order, the salutary effect of which is obvious" (p. 159).

What memories of delightful letters of women who were not always putting their minds in order, however salutary might be the process, rise to the thought—letters in which the heart, the fancy, the playful wit, the delicate observation, the exquisite expression, all have share! It is with a smile, but with a smile that does not exclude a tender, pathetic sense of the incomplete life of a woman who could write in this fashion to her husband, that we read such a passage as the following: "We ought, indeed, my beloved husband, to be conscious of our blessings, for we are better off than all below us, perhaps than almost all above us. The great art of life, especially for persons of our age, who are leaving the vale of youth behind us, just lingering still perhaps in the latter stage of it, and seeing the bright golden fields at the entrance of it more distinctly than those nearer to our present station, is to cultivate the love of doing good and promoting the interests of others, avoiding at the same time," etc., etc. (p. 179). We cannot quote more. It is too hard to see the ideal Sara Coleridge of the "Triad" thus changing into a figure as stiff and unattractive as one of Mrs. Jarley's wax-works.

A touch, a look, a single brief expression, may afford the measure of a character more truly than long speech or usual habit. The gesture, the glance, betray the inner recesses of the soul. The following sentences are extraordinary revelations of the writer's character. We will not qualify them with the epithet they deserve. She is writing to Mr. De Vere, concerning Dante:

> Don't you observe how much less of sturdy, independent pride and reserve there is in Italians, and in all foreigners, than in us Englishmen? An English poet would not have written this of himself—he would have thought it babyish; and still more much of Dante's behavior with Beatrice, which I have always thought has a touch of Jerry Sneak in it. Indeed, he actually compares himself to a baby fixing its eyes on its ma (p. 457).

Failure of perception, blankness of mind, absence of feeling, could hardly find more absolute expression than in these words. There are happily better things than this in the book: some pleasing reflections, some natural feeling, some fair criticism. But the general effect of the volume is one of disappointment. Sara Coleridge is no longer a creature for the imagination to delight in. She will remain of interest as the daughter of the poet, more than by her own right. These letters show her to us as a serious-minded, good woman, with

unusual intellectual powers, and with personal graces that attracted a narrow circle of friends. But of the woman complete in all sweet feminine gifts and charms, free from self-consciousness, free from dogmatism and vanity, with feelings unformalized by creed or theory, with a deep and simple heart, of such a woman the traces are slight in the *Memoir and Letters of Sara Coleridge.*—CHARLES ELIOT NORTON, "Sara Coleridge," *Nation*, Dec. 25, 1873, p. 426

After George Eliot's, we should pronounce Sara Coleridge's the most powerful female mind which has yet addressed itself to English literature. While deficient in no feminine grace, she is intellectually distinguished by a quality for which we can find no better name than manliness. She displays the strongest, massiest common sense, goes direct to the root of a matter, sweeps antagonism from her path in a twinkling, and exhibits a refreshing liberality, despite a burden of hereditary and conventional prejudice. Circumstances forced her learning and her reasoning faculty into prominence, her pious labours as her father's editor and annotator leaving her but little opportunity for the exercise of the imaginative gift which she had equally inherited from him. *Phantasmion*, though too unsubstantial a work to create a permanent impression, shows that she possessed this endowment in rich measure, and the little lyrics scattered through its pages confer upon her a secure though a modest place among English poetesses.—RICHARD GARNETT, "Sara Coleridge," *The Poets and the Poetry of the Century*, ed. Alfred H. Miles, 1892, Vol. 8, p. 127

AMELIA OPIE

1769–1853

Amelia Opie was born Amelia Alderson on November 12, 1769, in Norwich, the daughter of a physician. Although she had no formal schooling, her interest in literature led her to move in intellectual circles with such figures as William Godwin, Mary Shelley, and John Horne Tooke. In 1798 she married John Opie, a self-educated man who became a prominent painter.

Beginning in 1790 Mrs. Opie embarked on a literary career that was to continue for more than forty years. She was the author of thirteen volumes of prose, including *Adeline Mowbray* (1804) and *Simple Tales* (1806), and of five volumes of verse. She achieved her greatest fame with the novel *Father and Daughter* (1801), a moralistic tale of seduction and insanity that had a significant influence on later popular fiction of the nineteenth century.

A devout Quaker, Mrs. Opie preached asceticism and moral earnestness in her works; in real life she was, however, far from dour, and led a strenuous social life. The conflict between her religious beliefs and her natural inclinations caused her much distress in her later years and may have been responsible for the termination of her literary career in 1834. She died in Norwich on December 2, 1853.

Personal

Dined with Amelia Opie: she was in great force and really jolly. Exhibited her gallery containing some fine portraits by her husband, one being of her old French master, which she insisted on Opie painting before she would accept him. She is enthusiastic about Father Mathew, reads Dickens voraciously, takes to Carlyle, but thinks his appearance against him; talks much and with great spirit of people, but never ill-naturedly. —CAROLINE FOX, *Journal* (Oct. 22, 1843), *Memories of Old Friends*, ed. Horace N. Pym, 1882, p. 203

She was of about the standard height of woman; her hair was worn in waving folds in front, and behind, it was seen through

the cap, gathered into a braid; its colour was peculiar—'twixt flaxen and gray; it was unusually fine and delicate, and had a natural bend or wave. Her Quaker cap was of beautiful lawn, and fastened beneath the chin with whimpers, which had small crimped frills: her dress was usually of rich silk or satin, often of a fawn or grey colour; and over the bust was drawn a muslin or net handkerchief in thick folds, fastening into the waist, round which was worn a band of the same material as the dress; an apron, usually of net or muslin, protected (or *adorned*) the front of the gown. Her feet, which were small and well formed, peeped out beneath the dress. On her hands she wore small, black, netted muffatees, (she sometimes repaired them while talking to her friends,) and the cuffs of her gown were secured by a small loop at one corner, which she wore passed over the thumb, so as to prevent them from turning back or rucking upon the arm; her figure was stout, the throat short; her carriage was invariably erect, and she bore her head rather thrown back, and with an air of dignity. Her countenance, in her later years, lost much of that fire which once irradiated it; but the expression was more pleasing, softer, more tender, and loving. Her eyes were especially charming; there was in them an ardour mingled with gentleness that bespoke her true nature, and occasionally they were raised upwards with a look most peculiar and expressive, when her sympathy was more than usually excited. Her complexion was fair, and the kindling blush mantled in her cheek, betraying any passing emotion; for, like her friend Lafayette, she "blushed like a girl to hear her own praises." Altogether she attracted you, and you drew near to her, and liked to look into her face, and felt that old age, in her, was beautiful and comely.

Often, very often, has the writer, while listening to her lively anecdotes, and watching her animated countenance, drawn her chair closer and yet closer, and at length, slipping down, rested on one knee, in order the better to see her; and after bidding her farewell again and again, returned to the same position and "staid a little longer."

How lively were her narratives; and with what minute touches she gave the details of the scene she was describing. What spirit and life did she breathe into the portraits of those whom she admired! Certainly her conversation was superior to her writing; perhaps the charm of manner aided to enhance the effect of her words.—CECILIA LUCY BRIGHTWELL, *Memorials of the Life of Amelia Opie*, 1854, pp. 407–8

Mrs. Opie, another author and poet, as different as possible from Mrs. Barbauld, was an acquaintance of my mother. Her novels were at this time very popular, and her husband was equally famous as an historical painter. He had many admirers, but his works were not of a high order. He made all his male faces with large, ugly noses, so that one could always know his pictures by that feature. My mother had such an instinctive appreciation of painting, that Mr. West made a point of going with her to the annual exhibition of the works of living artists, that he might hear her natural remarks on the principal pictures. She criticised all Opie's so severely that Mr. West feared she might be overheard by him and hastened to tell her whose they were. Mr. West's pictures did not wholly escape her criticism, but she generally knew beforehand which were his.

When Mrs. Opie became a gay widow, we often met her at the house of a mutual friend, where her eccentric conduct amused some, and disgusted others. I have seen her astonish a grave circle of elderly people by jumping up and dancing a shawl-dance then in vogue on the stage, flourishing away to a tune of her own singing, apparently unconscious of the effect she was producing. She used to carry about with her in all her visits a pretty little stringed instrument, in the classic form of a lyre, and sing her own songs, with great expression, to that accompaniment. She said she could always find out the secrets of a young girl's heart, if she could sing to her alone. She tried her experiment on me and proved right.

Mrs. Opie was fair, with delicate features and a form of symmetrical beauty. The well-formed hands and arms were always on exhibition, and short and scanty skirts disclosed the prettiest feet and ankles. Her talents and accomplishments, her novels, her poetry, and her singing, made her, for a time, a favorite with the fashionables of London, and she highly enjoyed her popularity; but it did not last long, and when it

failed, she took refuge from the gay world in a circle of wealthy and highly cultivated Quakers. The Gurneys, Barclays, Hoares, Woods, and Frys, were her intimate friends, and after several years passed among them, she joined the Society of Friends and adopted their dress and language. I saw her once after her metamorphosis, and could but remark the discrepancy between her costume and her manners, which still savored of the wicked world. The pretty foot was still seen, though the dress was long and ample, and the glove was unnecessarily taken off to show the beautiful hand. Amelia Opie was not changed, only acting a new part.—ELIZA FARRAR, *Recollections of Seventy Years*, 1866, pp. 24–26

We suddenly heard a whisper, of which the words *Sœur de charité* were distinct, and saw walking up the room with stately step, leaning on the arm of a tall Irishman—who had made himself conspicuous by a large shirt-front and absence of waistcoat—a lady, stout and short, clad in a dress which, though very strange in that assembly, was familiar to us, for it was the simple habit of a Quakeress—bonnet and all. To our astonishment, we recognized Amelia Opie. Her cavalier was O'Gorman Mahon, who looked what he really was—a wild Irishman. A bird-of-paradise suddenly descending to pick up crumbs in an English farmyard could scarcely have created more astonishment among Dame Partlet's brood than did this pea-hen among the superbly dressed and jeweled dames of the Parisian *salon*. The good General seemed to know her well, and rose and greeted her with the grace of the days he had so largely helped to spoil—when a French gentleman was understood to be the gentleman *par excellence*. Dear Mrs. Opie: she seemed utterly indifferent to the murmurs of inquiry and surprise that would have confounded any one less self-possessed, and turned to us with that sweet *naïveté* which was at all periods of her life her especial charm.—S. C. HALL, *Retrospect of a Long Life*, 1883, p. 228

General

Mrs Opie has no great share of invention, either in incident or in character. We often see through the whole story from its first opening; and few of her personages can be said to be original, or even uncommon, when compared either with the inventions of dramatists, or the variety of common life. They have a merit, however, which in our eyes is incomparably superior: they are strictly true to general nature, and are rarely exhibited, except in interesting situations. ⟨. . .⟩

There is something delightfully feminine in all Mrs Opie's writings; an apparent artlessness in the composition of her narrative, and something which looks like want of skill or of practice in writing for the public, that gives a powerful effect to the occasional beauties and successes of her genius. There is nothing like an ambitious or even a sustained tone in her stories; we often think she is going to be tedious or silly; and immediately, without effort or apparent consciousness of improvement, she slides into some graceful and interesting dialogue, or charms us with some fine and delicate analysis of the subtler feelings, which would have done honour to the genius of Marivaux. She does not reason well; but she has, like most accomplished women, the talent of perceiving truth, without the process of reasoning, and of bringing it out with the facility and the effect of an an obvious and natural sentiment. Her language is often inaccurate, but is almost always graceful and harmonious. She can do nothing well that requires to be done with formality; and, therefore, has not succeeded in copying either the concentrated force of weighty and deliberate reason, or the severe and solemn dignity of majestic virtue. To make amends, however, she represents admirably every thing that is amiable, generous, and gentle.

These tales are of very unequal merit; and we do not propose to give any detailed account of them. Those in the third volume, we think, are clearly the best. 'The Soldier's Return,' and the 'Brother and Sister,' though the scene is laid, in both, in humble life, and the incidents by no means new either in real or fictitious story, are pathetic to a painful and distressing degree. The latter in particular is written with great delicacy and beauty. ⟨. . .⟩

The story of 'The Orphan' is pretty, and very interesting. It contains the following verses, supposed to be written by a gentle and timid young woman, pining under the oppression of a romantic and concealed passion for a man who entertained no suspicion of her attachment. We think they have great tenderness and beauty. ⟨. . .⟩

'The Uncle and Nephew' is amiable and well managed.— 'The Death-Bed'—'The Robber'—and 'Murder will out,' are not very natural. 'The Fashionable Wife' is still worse; and, though many of the particular scenes are well drawn, we cannot help withholding our sympathy from distresses, deduced from a source so inadequate and fantastic. In the other tales, there is occasionally something frivolous, and something too obvious and inartificial; but in all, there is much just representation of manners and character, and much pleasing composition.

We cannot place Mrs Opie so high in the scale of intellect as Miss Edgeworth; nor are her *Tales*, though perfectly unobjectionable on the score of morality, calculated to do so much good. They are too fine for common use; and do not aim at the correction of errors and follies of so extensive and fundamental a nature. She does not reason so powerfully; and she is not sufficiently cheerful: indeed she is too pathetic, to be read with much advantage to practical morality. Her writings, however, are very amiable and very beautiful; and exhibit virtuous emotions under a very graceful aspect. They would do very well to form a woman that a gentleman should fall in love with; but can be of no great use in training ordinary mortals to ordinary duties.—FRANCIS, LORD JEFFREY, "Mrs. Opie's *Simple Tales*," *Edinburgh Review*, July 1806, pp. 465–71

Amelia Opie, the daughter of Dr. Alderson, an eminent physician of Norwich, was born in that city, in 1771. At a very early period, she evinced talents of a very superior order; composing, whilst still a child, poems, descriptive pieces, and novels; though none of them, with the exception of some poetical pieces in the *Monthly Magazine*, were published before her marriage, which took place in May, 1798, with Mr. Opie, the celebrated painter. Her first publication, *The Father and Daughter, a Tale*, with other pieces, appeared in 1801, which at once drew upon its author the public attention; and it has always remained a favourite of its class. It was succeeded in 1802 by "An Elegy to the Memory of the late Duke of Bedford," and a volume of other poems; and, in 1804, she gave to the world her Tale of *Adeline Mowbray, or the Mother and Daughter*. This was followed, in 1806, by *Simple Tales*, in four volumes, duodecimo; and, in 1808, appeared, anonymously, in two volumes, duodecimo, her *Dangers of Coquetry*; and an octavo volume, under the title of the *Warrior's Return*, and other poems. Having become a widow in 1807, she published, in 1810, *Memoirs of Mr. Opie*, prefixed to the lectures he had read at the Royal Academy. Her subsequent productions are, a novel entitled *Temper, or Domestic Scenes*; *Tales of Real Life*; *Simple Tales*; *Valentine's Eve*; *New Tales*, in four volumes; *Tales of the Heart*; and, *The Black Man's*

Lament, in advocacy of the abolition of slavery, which appeared in 1826. The most remarkable feature in her life, since this period, is her entrance into the Society of Friends, and her retirement from society, after having been one of its most cheerful votaries. Of all female writers of the present age, Mrs. Opie is the most forcible and affecting; in her power of displaying the workings of the passions, she is very little inferior to Godwin. She falls short of Miss Edgeworth, in her descriptions of real life, and delineation of domestic character; but, in originality, and vigour of conception, and creation of appalling interest, she is infinitely superior. Her *Father and Daughter* is a harmonious piece of domestic tragedy; "though," says a writer in the Edinburgh review, "for a short and convincing proof of her powers, we would refer to a little Tale, entitled, 'Confessions of an Odd-Tempered Man,' contained in a collection called *Tales of Real Life*, and which bears some resemblance to the *Adolphe*, of Benjamin Constant." Mrs. Opie holds no mean rank as a poetess, though her prose writings have procured her the greatest share of approbation. —UNSIGNED, "Biographical Sketch of Amelia Opie," *The Works of Amelia Opie*, 1841, p. v

This estimable lady, who is a member of the Society of Friends, is chiefly known for her admirable prose stories, in which is contained a pure, simple, and sweet morality, not surpassed by any writer in our literature. She, however, published, in 1802, a volume of miscellaneous Poems, and, in 1834, a work entitled *Lays for the Dead*, both of which are characterised by great tenderness and grace of feeling. Her song of "The Orphan Boy" is one of the most touching productions contained in our language. ⟨. . .⟩

It is a fault of the Female Poets of the last century that they expended their strength rather on sentiment than on feeling. This makes most of the verse which they produced, appear tame and unimpassioned; and it is a reason, perhaps the chief reason, why so many of their names have nearly passed into oblivion: for sentiment is, in its very nature, evanescent: and, even when painted in its brightest colours, lasts but a little while. It is a phosphorescent flame, flashing for a moment through the mental atmosphere, but giving neither warmth nor light: whilst true passion is a ray shot from the everlasting sun of the spiritual firmament, shedding a glow and a brightness upon all time. Of this true sterling sort is the pathos of Mrs. Opie. ⟨. . .⟩

Mrs. Opie's poems bear fresh evidence to the truth of an assertion more than once made in this work, that woman's moral sentiments are generally in advance of man's. Those who doubt the fact will do well to remember how continually man's verse celebrates the infernal glories of war, the cruel excitements of the chase, or the selfish pleasures of bacchanalian enjoyment; and, on the other hand, how unceasingly woman's verse exposes the wickedness and folly of such pursuits. Very rarely do we find in the writings of the male sex, passages like the following, though we continually see similar sentiments in the works of our female writers:—

Alas! to think one Christian soul
    At War's red shrine can worship still,
Nor heed, though seas of carnage roll,
    Those awful words—"THOU SHALT NOT KILL!"

O Lord of all, and Prince of Peace,
    Speed, speed the long-predicted day,
When War throughout the world shall cease,
    And Love shall hold eternal sway!

Mrs. Opie's *Lays for the Dead* is a book of truest beauty: and, although the perusal of it resembles (from the mournfulness of its subjects) a visit to a churchyard, the effect it produces upon us is of a most pleasing character. It hushes all unquiet emotion; bids the cares of earth far into the distance; and awakens a calm sweet pensiveness of feeling, which nothing could make us wish to change. We seem to converse with the Past and the Departed, and to stand on the very shore of the great ocean of Eternity.—FREDERIC ROWTON, "Mrs. Amelia Opie," *The Female Poets of Great Britain*, 1848, pp. 280–84

It would be impossible to attempt a serious critique of Mrs. Opie's stories. They are artless, graceful, written with an innocent good faith which disarms criticism. That Southey, Sydney Smith, and Mackintosh should also have read them and praised them may, as I have said, prove as much for the personal charm of the writer, and her warm sunshine of pleasant companionship, as for the books themselves. They seem to have run through many editions, and to have received no little encouragement. Morality and sensation alternate in her pages. Monsters abound there. They hire young men to act base parts, to hold villainous conversations which the husbands are intended to overhear. They plot and scheme to ruin the fair fame and domestic happiness of the charming heroines, but they are justly punished, and their plots are defeated. One villain, on his way to an appointment with a married woman, receives so severe a blow upon the head from her brother, that he dies in agonies of fruitless remorse. Another, who incautiously boasts aloud his deep-laid scheme against Constantia's reputation in the dark recesses of a stage-coach, is unexpectedly seized by the arm. A stranger in the corner, whom he had not noticed, was no other than the baronet whom Constantia has loved all along. The dawn breaks in brightly, shining on the stranger's face: baffled, disgraced, the wicked schemer leaves the coach at the very next stage, and Constantia's happiness is insured by a brilliant marriage with the man she loves. 'Lucy is the dark sky,' cries another lovely heroine, 'but you, my lord, and my smiling children, these are the rainbow that illumines it, and who would look at the gloom that see the many-tinted iris? not I, indeed.' *Valentine's Eve*, from which this is quoted, was published after John Opie's death. So was a novel called *Temper*, and the *Tales of Real Life*. Mrs. Opie, however, gave up writing novels when she joined the Society of Friends. —ANNE THACKERAY RITCHIE, "Mrs. Opie." *Cornhill Magazine*, Oct. 1883, pp. 376–77

Looking back on the record of Mrs. Opie's life, one hesitates to agree with either judgment. There was, indeed, as we have seen, a period during which, with the hyper-sensitiveness of a convert, she felt agonies of contrition for venial faults, and indulged with remorse in very harmless pleasures. But this soon passed, and beyond the renunciation of novel writing (in which it is probable that her best work was done, for her imaginative vein was neither deep nor strong), her creed does not seem to have entailed any sacrifice of dear affection or reasonable enjoyment. On the other hand, it is impossible not to recognise, in comparing her earlier and later years, the increased activity in every form of benevolence and helpfulness to which it impelled her. She had a temperament both excitable and indolent, and essentially pleasure-loving. With a sufficient income, absolute independence and leisure, many flatterers, and no close home ties or duties, she might easily have drifted into aimless self-indulgence in the world *où l'on s'amuse*, had she been without the restraints of deepened religious feeling, and a creed which especially enjoined temperance, moderation, and quietness.—UNSIGNED, "Amelia Opie," *Temple Bar*, Aug. 1893, pp. 512–13

JAMES MONTGOMERY

1771–1854

James Montgomery was born on November 4, 1771, in Ayrshire, Scotland, the son of a Moravian minister. He was educated at a Moravian school at Fulneck, near Leeds, then worked briefly as a shop assistant before becoming a journalist. As editor of the *Sheffield Iris* (1794–1825) he was imprisoned on several occasions for printing allegedly seditious material.

In addition to his newspaper work Montgomery published twenty-two volumes of verse during his lifetime. The best-known among them include *The Wanderer of Switzerland* (1806), an account of exiles from revolutionary France; *The World before the Flood* (1813); *Greenland* (1819); and *The Pelican Island* (1828). His collected *Poetical Works* was published in four volumes in 1841.

Montgomery is remembered today primarily as the author of a number of well-known hymns, including "Angels, from the realms of glory," "O bless the Lord, my soul," and "Hail to the Lord's anointed." He died in Sheffield on April 30, 1854, having subsisted during the last twenty years of his life on a pension from the Crown, procured for him through the intervention of Sir Robert Peel in 1835.

Personal

He was usually in ill health; and as I think, judging by the much I heard and the little I saw, seldom cheerful, yet always (paradoxical as it may seem) happy; but he looked beyond this life, and had the consolation of faith, trust, and hope. Like Leigh Hunt, he suffered fine and imprisonment for libel; but the offense in Montgomery's case was far less grave: indeed, we should be astonished now to find it pronounced an offense at all. But when he conducted the *Sheffield Iris*, a libel was a thing easy to fall into; and so perilous was it for journalists to speak out that the "liberty of the press" was practically a myth.

Montgomery, though usually classed among Scottish poets, was an Irishman. His father, mother, and all his family were Irish; and in the North of Ireland he was reared and educated, although born at Irvine, in Ayrshire, where his father had for a brief while the charge of a small congregation. Father and son were Christians of the sect of the Moravian

Brethren. But Ireland, Scotland, Wales, and England may be proud of a man who did so much that was good and so little that was bad; in whose long life, indeed, we find nothing that was not designed, and calculated, to advance the temporal and spiritual welfare of humanity. He is one of the Band of Immortal Poets, who, while they confer honor on their country are foremost among missionaries sent to do the work of God for man.

In 1830, James Montgomery came to London to deliver lectures on English literature at the Royal Institution. It was then that he visited us in Sloane Street.

Few poets ever suffered more severely at the hands of critics; and, acting on a naturally sensitive nature, the attacks of Jeffrey in the *Edinburgh*, and of lesser Zoiluses in other reviews, probably had the effect they were designed to produce. In a letter I received from him in 1837, Montgomery thus alludes to himself: "The disappointment of my premature poetical hopes brought a blight with it, from which my mind has never recovered. For many years, I was as mute as a molting bird; and when the power of song returned, it was without the energy, self-confidence, and freedom which happier minstrels among my contemporaries manifested."
—S. C. HALL, *Retrospect of a Long Life*, 1883, pp. 412–13

General

We took compassion upon Mr Montgomery on his first appearance; conceiving him to be some slender youth of seventeen, intoxicated with weak tea, and the praises of sentimental Ensigns and other provincial literati, and tempted, in that situation, to commit a feeble outrage on the public, of which the recollection would be a sufficient punishment. A third edition, however, is too alarming to be passed over in silence; and though we are perfectly persuaded, that in less than three years, nobody will know the name of the *Wanderer of Switzerland*, or any of the other poems in this collection, still we think ourselves called on to interfere, to prevent, as far as in us lies, the mischief that may arise from the intermediate prevalence of so distressing an epidemic. It is hard to say what numbers of ingenuous youth may be led to expose themselves in public, by the success of this performance, or what addition may be made in a few months to that great sinking fund of bad taste, which is daily wearing down the debt which we have so long owed to the classical writers of antiquity.

After all, we believe it is scarcely possible to sell three editions of a work absolutely without merit; and Mr Montgomery has the merit of smooth versification, blameless morality, and a sort of sickly affectation of delicacy and fine feelings, which is apt to impose on the amiable part of the young and the illiterate. The wonder, with us, is, how these qualities should still excite any portion of admiration: for there is no mistake more gross or more palpable, than that it requires any extraordinary talents to write tolerable verses upon ordinary subjects. On the contrary, we are persuaded that this is an accomplishment which may be acquired, more certainly and more speedily, than most of those to which the studies of youth are directed, and in which mere industry will always be able to secure a certain degree of excellence. There are few young men who have the slightest tincture of literary ambition, who have not, at some time in their lives, indited middling verses; and, accordingly, in the instructed classes of society, there is nothing more nauseated than middling poetry. The truth is, however, that the diligent readers of poetry, in this country, are by no means instructed. They consist chiefly of young, half-educated women, sickly tradesmen, and enamoured ap-

prentices. To such persons the faculty of composing in rhyme always appears little less than miraculous; and if the verses be tolerably melodious, and contain a sufficient allowance of those exaggerated phrases, with which they have become familiar at the playhouse and the circulating library, they have a fair chance of being extolled with unmeasured praises, till supplanted by some newer or more fashionable object of idolatry. These are the true poetical consumers of a community,—the persons who take off editions,—and create a demand for nonsense, which the improved ingenuity of the times can with difficulty supply. It is in the increasing number and luxury of this class of readers, that we must seek for the solution of such a phenomenon, as a third edition of the *Wanderer of Switzerland*, within six months from the appearance of the first. The perishable nature of the celebrity which is derived from this kind of patronage, may be accounted for as easily, from the character and condition of those who confer it. The girls grow up into women, and occupy themselves in suckling their children, or scolding their servants; the tradesmen take to drinking, or to honest industry; and the lovers, when metamorphosed into husbands, lay aside their poetical favourites, with their thin shoes and perfumed handkerchiefs. All of them grow ashamed of their admiration in a reasonably short time; and no more think of imposing the taste, than the dress of their youth, upon a succeeding generation.

Mr Montgomery is one of the most musical and melancholy fine gentlemen we have lately descried on the lower slopes of Parnassus. He is very weakly, very finical, and very affected. His affectations, too, are the most usual, and the most offensive of those that are commonly met with in the species to which he belongs: they are affectations of extreme tenderness and delicacy, and of great energy and enthusiasm. Whenever he does not whine, he must rant. The scanty stream of his genius is never allowed to steal quietly along its channel; but is either poured out in melodious tears, or thrown up to heaven in all the frothy magnificence of tiny jets and artificial commotions.

The first and the longest poem in the volume is the *Wanderer of Switzerland*, in which the author informs us it was his design to celebrate an *epic* subject in a *lyric* measure and on a *dramatic* plan. It consists, accordingly, of a series of conversations between an old gentleman, who had escaped from the battle of Underwalden with a part of his family, and a hospitable and poetical shepherd, in whose cottage they had sought shelter. Of the richness of this triple essence of ode, epic, and drama, the reader may judge from the opening stanzas.

> *Shep.*: Wanderer! whither dost thou roam?
> Weary Wanderer, old and grey!
> Wherefore hast thou left thine home
> In the sunset of thy day?
> *Wand.*: In the sunset of my day,
> Stranger! I have lost my home:
> Weary, wandering, old and grey,
> Therefore, therefore do I roam.
> (p. 11. 12.)

He then tells him in the same dancing measure, that he has just escaped from the ruin of Switzerland; and the sentimental swain immediately replies—

> *Shep.*: Welcome, Wanderer as thou art,
> All my blessings to partake;
> Yet thrice welcome to my heart,
> For thine injur'd country's sake.
> . . .
> Spouse! I bring a suffering guest,
> With his family of grief;

Bid the weary pilgrims rest,
Yield, O yield them sweet relief!
Shep.'s Wife.: I will yield them sweet relief:
Weary Pilgrims! welcome here;
Welcome, family of grief!
Welcome to my warmest cheer.
(p. 14. 15.)

This, we own, appears to us like the singing of a bad pantomine; and is more inspid and disgusting than any tragic ballad, either antient or modern, that we recollect to have met with.

⟨. . .⟩ When every day is bringing forth some new work from the pen of Scott, Campbell, Rogers, Baillie, Sotheby, Wordsworth, or Southey, it is natural to feel some disgust at the undistinguishing voracity which can swallow down three editions of songs to convivial societies, and verses to a pillow.
—FRANCIS, LORD JEFFREY, "Montgomery's *Poems*," *Edinburgh Review*, Jan. 1807, pp. 347–54

Of all our living poets Mr. Montgomery is the one whose reputation can least be ascribed to temporary and transitory causes. He began by publishing under a fictitious signature in the newspapers: these pieces found their way into the magazines, then into miscellaneous collections, and from those collections they were selected for admiration by the public, and for praise by the majority of the critics. They were moral, they were pious, they were patriotic; but they spoke the language of no sect and of no party; they contained neither panegyric nor satire; the subjects were general, and nothing but an originality in the manner of treating them could have attracted notice. Encouraged by their favourable reception, the author ventured to publish them in a volume, (with a few other pieces,) and to acknowledge them, now that they had thus fairly succeeded. His name could add nothing to his chance of becoming popular; a printer at Sheffield was remote from the world of literature, and beneath that of fashion; the volume however did become exceedingly popular, and second and third editions were speedily called for.

Never did any volume more truly deserve the reception which it found. Faults there were in it; for where is the volume without them? The longest of the poems is an experiment, treating an heroic subject in lyric measure and upon a dramatic plan. It is full of feeling, of beauty, and of power: still the experiment has not succeeded; for if there be any thing radically erroneous in the plan of an edifice, the most exquisite workmanship may be bestowed upon it in vain. There is a radical error in the *Wanderer of Switzerland*. The dialogue is carried on in short and highly polished lines of a stimulating trochaic movement; the first impression which this makes upon the reader is a sense of incongruity, and even if this were not the case, the measure is too brisk for so long a poem. For dialogue it is peculiarly unfit, and especially for impassioned dialogue, for which unquestionably the blank verse of our old dramatic writers is the best conceivable metre. But notwithstanding the inherent and irremediable defect of the poem, no person capable of appreciating poetry could read it without perceiving that it was the production of a rich and powerful mind.

The smaller poems are not without their faults; these, where they occur, are the faults of redundance and effort—weeds which indicate the strength and richness of the soil. Sometimes, too, Mr. Montgomery has used the tinsel and taudry with which our modern poetry has so long abounded. ⟨. . .⟩

It is to the honour of the age that Mr. Montgomery was welcomed with the applause which he deserved. He flattered none of the vices of mankind, nor even any of their opinions; he had no charm of story to win the attention of those who read a poem as they do a novel; he imitated no fashionable style, and he had no friends among the oligarchs of literature to go before him with a trumpet and announce his merits. In spite of these disadvantages, his book was read and admired; the name of Montgomery speedily attained a degree of celebrity, which encouraged and rewarded him; he had struggled through many difficulties and endured many afflictions, and the well deserved applause which he was now receiving came to him like sunshine to a flower which has been bent by the storm.

At this time the master of the new school of criticism ⟨Lord Jeffrey⟩ thought proper to crush the rising poet. ⟨. . .⟩

There stands upon record only one piece of formal criticism as mischievous as this, and that is the criticism upon Kirke White in a *Monthly Journal*, of which the notorious folly and injustice have been reprobated by the thousands who regret and admire that extraordinary and excellent youth. Had Montgomery's poems been in reality as worthless as here represented, the volume, upon the critic's own principle of exclusion, should have been past over in silence as the remains of Kirke White have been, because he has not a heart to praise them, and has had decency enough to abstain from censure.
—ROBERT SOUTHEY, "Montgomery's *Poems*," *Quarterly Review*, Dec. 1811, pp. 407–13

With broken lyre, and cheek serenely pale,
Lo! sad Alcæus wanders down the vale;
Though fair they rose, and might have bloom'd at last,
His hopes have perish'd by the northern blast:
Nipp'd in the bud by Caledonian gales,
His blossoms wither as the blast prevails!
O'er his lost works let *classic* Sheffield weep;
May no rude hand disturb their early sleep!
Yet say! why should the bard at once resign
His claim to favour from the sacred Nine?
For ever startled by the mingled howl
Of northern wolves, that still in darkness prowl;
A coward brood, which mangle as they prey,
By hellish instinct, all that cross their way;
Aged or young, the living or the dead,
No mercy find—these harpies must be fed.
Why do the injured unresisting yield
The calm possession of their native field?
Why tamely thus before their fangs retreat,
Nor hunt the blood-hounds back to Arthur's Seat?
—GEORGE GORDON, LORD BYRON, *English Bards and Scotch Reviewers*, 1809, ll. 418–37

His bursts of sacred poetry, compared with his *Greenland*, remind us of a person singing enchantingly by ear, but becoming languid and powerless the moment he sets down to a note-book.—JOHN KEBLE, "Sacred Poetry," *Quarterly Review*, June 1825, p. 217

It was said many long years ago in the *Edinburgh Review*, that none but maudlin milliners and sentimental ensigns supposed that James Montgomery was a poet. Then is Maga a maudlin milliner—and Christopher North a sentimental ensign. We once called Montgomery a Moravian; and though he assures us that we were mistaken, yet having made an assertion, we always stick to it, and therefore he must remain a Moravian, if not in his own belief, yet in ours. Of all religious sects, the Moravians are the most simple-minded, pure-hearted, and high-souled—and these qualities shine serenely in *The Pelican*

Island. In earnestness and fervour, that poem is by few or none excelled; it is embalmed in sincerity, and therefore shall fade not away; neither shall it moulder—not even although exposed to the air, and blow the air ever so rudely through time's mutations. Not that it is a mummy. Say rather a fair form laid asleep in immortality—its face wearing, day and night, summer and winter, look at it when you will, a saintly—a celestial smile. That is a true image; but is *The Pelican Island* a Great Poem? We pause not for a reply.—JOHN WILSON, "An Hour's Talk about Poetry" (1831), *The Recreations of Christopher North*, 1842, p. 73

It is now about twenty-eight years since we noticed in this Journal, Mr Montgomery's *Wanderer of Switzerland*; and looking back to what we then wrote, we fairly confess, that were the task now to be performed for the first time, our criticism would probably be characterised by a milder spirit. Not that in reference to the particular subject of the article alluded to, our opinions have undergone any material change: we still think that while the poem was characterised by much that was offensive to good taste—much that would now be offensive to the taste of the author himself—it showed little of those higher qualities which Mr Montgomery has since displayed, and which have secured to him a not undistinguished place in modern poetry. On this point we scarcely think that even the warmest admirers of his genius will be materially at issue with us. But the experience of the additional lustres which have since rolled over his head and ours, has convinced us, that as in many cases the anticipations we had been led to form from a brilliant first appearance, have been by no means justified by the future, so on the other, the unfavourable auguries arising from an ill-omened beginning have sometimes been not unpleasantly disappointed by subsequent displays of genius, energy, or good taste. Not unpleasantly, we say; for we can venture to add, that in this latter case, few have been better pleased than ourselves at the failure of our own anticipations; and on the whole the conviction has been growing upon us of the danger of all literary predictions, and of the propriety of leaning to the side of hope and encouragement, rather than that of despondency and censure.

But if there has been some change in this respect in our views, the change in Mr Montgomery has been indeed remarkable. In his earliest production little was discernible beyond a vague admiration of nature, exhibited in language certainly more pompous than picturesque and discriminating;—a sensibility running into wasteful and ridiculous excess, too lively and too incessant to be natural, and a style, in many parts, sicklied over with the pale cast of affectation. The fertility of the soil, in short, was chiefly indicated by the luxuriance of the weeds. Gradually, however, with every successive production, these excrescences have been pruned away. Earnestness has succeeded to affectation; a manly simplicity of thought and reserve of expression, to the flowery exuberance and strained conceits of youth; overcharged and almost whining pathos has softened into a more chastened, natural, and unobtrusive tenderness; and a spirit of religion, profound and awe-inspiring, yet withal cheerful and consolatory, forming a part of the man himself, pervades and informs all his works till the poet who seemed at one time too likely to prolong the absurdities of the Della Crusca School, has taken his place not unworthily among the classics of our nation.

If Mr Montgomery has attained the position of a popular poet, no one has been less indebted for that distinction to the fortunate selection of his subjects; at least, in as far as regards his longer and more elaborate productions. His popularity has

in fact been attained, not in consequence, but in spite of his themes. In general these have been most remote from those stirring questions which agitate the general mind;—borrowing no interest or influence from the fashions and opinions of the time,—simple and limited in their form, almost monotonous in incident,—with little movement in the narrative, and that, too, erratic, and broken by those trains of reflection, in which the individual feelings of the author find a vent, whilst his imaginary creations stand still.—GEORGE MOIR, "Montgomery's *Poems*," *Edinburgh Review*, July 1835, pp. 473–74

James Montgomery is the most popular of the religious poets who have written in England since the time of COWPER, and he is more exclusively the poet of devotion than even the bard of Olney. Probably no writer is less indebted to a felicitous selection of subjects, since the themes of nearly all his longer productions are unpleasing and unpoetical; but for half a century he has been slowly and constantly increasing in reputation, and he has now a name which will not be forgotten, while taste and the religious sentiment exist together.—RUFUS W. GRISWOLD, "James Montgomery," *The Poets and Poetry of England in the Nineteenth Century*, 1844, p. 73

Of all dull, stagnant, unedifying *entourages*, that of middleclass Dissent, which environed Montgomery, seems to me the stupidest.—MATTHEW ARNOLD, Letter to His Mother (Feb. 27, 1855)

With none of the classic richness of Rogers, the weird originality of Coleridge, the introspective sweetness of Wordsworth, or the fascinating romance of Scott, there is a moral earnestness, an unaffected grace, a purity of diction, which penetrate the heart and place his poetry among the permanent literature of England.

The Christian element of his hymns gave them wings. Besides expressing what the renewed soul has felt through all ages, he gave utterance to many of the new forms of Christian life, with their corresponding inspirations, thrilling the spirit and firing it with fresh devotion to the Master's work.

Not as a poet only does Montgomery claim our reverent attention. As a model of the Christian citizen, he stands pre-eminent.

Steadfastly promoting public improvements, and patiently fostering every charitable enterprise, catholic in spirit and loyal to conscience, unselfish in his aims and rich in practical wisdom, prudent in counsel and warm in his affections, he identified himself with all the best interests of Sheffield, and took a high place in the confidence and respect of his towns-fellows.

Nor were his labors of love bounded by Sheffield. Welcoming all the new-born activities, which mark the Church of Christ during the present century, he engaged in their furtherance with singular devotedness. And even when age and infirmities might justly have pleaded exemption from duty, a scrupulous fidelity to its claims kept him to his post even to the end.

Born to stand
A prince among the worthies of the land.
More than a prince—a sinner saved by grace,
Prompt, at his meek and lowly Master's call,
To prove himself the minister of all.

> —HELEN C. KNIGHT, "Preface" to *Life of James Montgomery*, 1857, pp. iii–iv

It is not however by these longer poems that the name of James Montgomery will be perpetrated. It is as a religious poet, and as a writer of sacred lyrics which give expression to the aspirations and reflections of devout hearts, that he will be longest remembered; and it is not too much to say that in this department of poetic work his permanence seems fairly secure. Over a hundred of his hymns are said to be still in use. Among the more successful and popular of these are "Songs of praise the Angels sang," "Hail to the Lord's Anointed," "At home in Heaven," and "Go to dark Gethsemane." "James Montgomery is essentially a religious poet," wrote William Howitt, "and it is what of all things upon earth we can well believe he would most desire to be." His Christian songs are vigorous in thought and feeling, simple and direct in diction, broad in Christian charity, lofty in spiritual aspiration, and entirely free from cant. As such they form a not unworthy opening section for a volume devoted to the sacred poetry of the century.—ALFRED H. MILES, "James Montgomery," *The Poets and the Poetry of the Century*, ed. Alfred H. Miles, 1897, Vol. 11, pp. 3–4

DAVID MACBETH MOIR
From *Sketches of the Poetical Literature
of the Past Half-Century*
1851, pp. 152–57

The Wanderer of Switzerland, Montgomery's earliest performance, could scarcely have attained its popularity, either from its subject, which is local, or its treatment, which verges on common-place, or from its poetical merits, which are not of the rarest; but along with it some fine lyrics were published, high-toned in sentiment and feeling, which bespoke the true touch, and found an echo in many hearts. *The West Indies*, a poem written in commemoration of the abolition of the slave-trade by the British Legislature, was also an unequal although a much superior production; and has a raciness of manner, a beauty of thought, and occasionally an indignant vehemence of expression about it, which, coupled with the nature of its subject, deservedly won for it a wide acceptation. Had it been the work of his later years, Montgomery would have assumed a higher and more exulting tone, and made it a jubilee hymn, instead of its being, what in its least inspired portions it is, an exposition, from local and historical sources, of the horrors of that abominable traffic rendered into elegant verse. What he has done, however, he has done well; and its finest passages and apostrophes—as that on love of country—could only have been written by a genuine poet; for it is but to a certain height in heaven that the vulture can maintain his semblance to the eagle. Somewhat loosely put together as it here and there is, it sparkles throughout with gems of thought, which are appropriately and beautifully set, yet lose little of their lustre when removed from their places, and shine by their own intrinsic light. It is a poem, however, rather of the feelings than of the fancy, and has too much to do with stern facts to be throughout delightful; and in this respect is inferior to the other three larger works which succeeded it—*The World before the Flood*, *Greenland*, and *The Pelican Island*—the two former likewise in the heroic couplet, the last in a peculiar kind of blank verse, which has much less reference to that of Milton, Thomson, Cowper, or Wordsworth, than to our early dramatic writers, and with all their force, freedom, and ease; in many parts more resembling an improvisation than a composition.

Of these three last-mentioned performances, each may be said to be successively in advance of the other in development of poetical power and resources. In the first, the description of the antediluvian patriarchs in their valleys of bliss—the true

Arcadia—allows him a free and full range for his pleasant fancies; and he luxuriates in describing the large happiness they enjoyed ere invaded by the giant descendants of Cain. Among its finer delineations are the innocent loves of Javan and Zillah, the translation of Enoch, and the death-scene of our first parent Adam. The prevailing fault of the poem is a monotony and languor arising from its length, and the deficiency in stirring incident—in short, from the preponderance of description over action: and this notwithstanding its being written throughout with great care, and studded over with passages of uncommon elegance and beauty.

Greenland is shorter, but perhaps still more highly finished. The subject being quite congenial to the taste, feelings, and genius of the author, is written *con amore*, and the composition is pervaded by a noble but subdued enthusiasm. The voyage of the Moravian missionaries to the inhospitable Arctic regions is finely described; and their appearance there, under the touches of his pen, is as if angels of light had been commissioned to walk for a season amid the darkness and desolation of the realms of frost and snow. But by far its finest section is that commemorative of the depopulation of the Norwegian colonies on the east coast of Greenland, and its final abandonment by Europeans, from the increasing inclemency of the winters about the beginning of the fifteenth century. Montgomery here rises above himself in passionate earnestness, and in force of description; and by that canto alone would have distinctly stamped himself a poet of original power.

Essaying a still loftier flight, the whole of his imaginative strength was garnered up to be put forth in *The Pelican Island*; nor was his attempt like that of Icarus. It must be placed at the head of his works, whether we regard it as a whole, or in insulated passages; for it exhibits a richer command of language, and its imagery is collected from a much more extended field of thought and research, than any of its predecessors. It is also more remarkable for careful artistic adaptation of its parts to the general design, while its situations are more varied in their aspects, its suggestions more original, and its speculations more bold and daring. ⟨. . .⟩

Undeniable, however, as are the merits of Montgomery's longer and more ambitious works, and highly creditable as these are to his enterprise and achievement, it is as a lyrical poet that he has won his freshest laurels, and will be best remembered; for on these he has the most unreservedly shed the peculiar beauty of his genius. He is there himself, and can be confounded with no other; and few that have read can readily forget his pieces severally entitled "The Common Lot," "Night," "Prayer," "The Grave," "Aspirations of Youth," "Incognita," "Bolehill Trees," "Make Way for Liberty," "A Walk in Spring," and "The Alps, a Reverie." With the exceptions, perhaps, of Moore, Campbell, and Hemans, I doubt indeed if an equal number of the lyrics of any other modern poet have so completely found their way to the national heart, there to be enshrined in hallowed remembrance. ⟨. . .⟩

One great merit which may be claimed for James Montgomery is, that he has encroached on no man's property as a poet; he has staked off a portion of the great common of literature for himself, and cultivated it according to his own taste and fancy. In his appropriated garden, you find herbs and sweet-smelling flowers—the rosemary, and the thyme, and the marjoram—the lily, the pink, and the pansy—the musk-rose and the gilly-flower; but you have no staring sunflowers, no Brobdignag hollyhocks, no flaunting dahlias—for he clings to a simplicity that disdains ostentatious ornament; and thus many are apt to think the stream of his inspiration shallow, simply because it is pellucid. It is not easy to characterise his poetry, so as to convey any adequate idea of its excellencies—except by saying, in negatives, that it shuns all glare, glitter, and eccentricity; and that it cannot be expected to find admirers among those who bow down at the shrines of exaggeration or false taste.

Some have asserted—truly most idly—that the fame of Montgomery was founded on, and has been supported by, his sectarianism. If so, the Moravians are a much more potent body than they are generally accredited to be. However the applause of a class may have originally given an impetus to his

popularity, from the very first, as his works attest—and they are full of faith, hope, and charity—he wrote not for a section, but for mankind; and well has Professor Wilson remarked, in reference to this very topic, that "had Mr Montgomery not been a true poet, all the religious magazines in the world would not have saved his name from forgetfulness and oblivion. He might have flaunted his day like the melancholy poppy—melancholy in all its ill-scented gaudiness; but, as it is, he is like the rose of Sharon, whose balm and beauty shall not wither, planted on the banks of 'that river whose streams make glad the city of the Lord.'"

JOHN WILSON
"Christopher North"
1785–1854

John Wilson was born at Paisley on May 18, 1785, the son of a wealthy manufacturer. He was educated at Glasgow University and at Magdalen College, Oxford, where he received a B.A. in 1807. Wilson then settled at Elleray, his estate at Windermere, and devoted himself to the pursuit of athletics and literature. In 1812 he published a volume of poems, *The Isle of Palms*, and for several years moved in English literary circles, becoming especially friendly with Wordsworth.

Wilson, who had married in 1811, moved to Edinburgh in 1815 following the loss of his fortune. Two years later he began to write for the newly founded *Blackwood's Edinburgh Magazine* under the pseudonym "Christopher North" and was instrumental in the development of the periodical. After 1825 he was the principal contributor to a famous series of symposia *Noctes Ambrosianae*, that ran for many years in *Blackwood's*.

Through political influence Wilson received an appointment as professor of moral philosophy at Edinburgh University in 1820. In addition to his frequent contributions to *Blackwood's* he wrote several volumes of sentimental, moralistic fiction, relying for guidance on his close friend Alexander Blair, a professor of rhetoric and belles-lettres at the University of London.

Wilson died in Edinburgh on April 3, 1854.

Personal

The author of the elegy upon poor Grahame is John Wilson, a young man of very considerable poetical powers. He is now engaged in a poem called the *Isle of Palms* somewhat in the stile of Southey. He is an eccentric genius and has fixd himself upon the banks of Windermere but occasionally resides in Edinburgh where he now is. Perhaps you have seen him. His father was a Paisley wealthy manufacturer; his mother a sister of Robert Syme. He seems an excellent warm-hearted and enthusiastic young man something too much perhaps of the latter quality places him among the list of originals.—SIR WALTER SCOTT, Letter to Joanna Baillie (Jan. 17, 1812)

He is, I imagine, (but I guess principally from the date of his Oxford prize poem) some ten years your junior and mine—a very robust athletic man, broad across the back—firm set upon his limbs—and having altogether very much of that sort of air which is inseparable from the consciousness of great bodily energies. I suppose in leaping, wrestling, or boxing, he might easily beat any of the poets, his contemporaries—and I rather suspect, that in speaking, he would have as easy a triumph over the whole of them, except Coleridge. In complexion, he is the best specimen I have ever seen of the genuine or ideal *Goth*. His hair is of the true Sicambrian yellow; his eyes are of the lightest, and at the same time of the clearest blue; and the blood glows in his cheek with as firm a fervour as it did,

according to the description of Jornandes, in those of the "Bello gaudentes prælio ridentes Teutones" of Attila. I had never suspected before I saw him, that such extreme fairness and freshness of complexion could be compatible with so much variety and tenderness, but above all, with so much depth of expression. His forehead is finely, but strangely shaped; the regions of pure fancy, and of pure wit being both developed in a very striking manner—which is but seldom the case in any one individual—and the organ of observation having projected the *sinus frontalis* to a degree that is altogether uncommon. I have never seen a physiognomy which could pass with so much rapidity from the serious to the most ludicrous of effects. It is more eloquent, both in its gravity and in its levity, than almost any countenance I am acquainted with is in any one cast of expression; and yet I am not without my suspicions that the versatility of its language may, in the end, take away from its power.

In a convivial meeting—more particularly after the first two hours are over—the beauty to which men are most alive in any piece of eloquence is that which depends on its being impregnated and instinct with feeling. Of this beauty, no eloquence can be more full than that of Mr. J—— Wilson. His declamation is often loose and irregular to an extent that is not quite worthy of a man of his fine education and masculine powers; but all is redeemed, and more than redeemed, by his rich abundance of quick, generous, and expansive feeling. The flashing brightness, and now and then the still more expressive dimness of his eye—and the tremulous music of a voice that is equally at home in the highest and the lowest of notes—and the attitude bent forward with an earnestness to which the graces could make no valuable addition—all together compose an index which they that run may read—a rod of communication to whose electricity no heart is barred. Inaccuracies of language are small matters when the ear is fed with the wild and mysterious cadences of the most natural of all melodies, and the mind filled to overflowing with the bright suggestions of an imagination, whose only fault lies in the uncontrollable profusion with which it scatters forth its fruits. With such gifts as these, and with the noblest of themes to excite and adorn them, I have no doubt, that Mr. Wilson, had he been in the church, would have left all the impassioned preachers I have ever heard, many thousand leagues behind him. Nor do I at all question, that even in some departments of his own profession of the law, had he in good earnest devoted his energies to its service, his success might have been equally brilliant. But his ambition had probably taken too decidedly another turn; nor, perhaps, would it be quite fair, either to him or to ourselves, to wish that the thing had been otherwise.—JOHN GIBSON LOCKHART, *Peter's Letters to His Kinfolk*, 1819, Letter 12

I went to hear a lecture on "Moral Philosophy" from Professor Wilson, the celebrated editor of *Blackwood's Magazine*. He is what some people would think a fine-looking man; but to my eye there appeared to be something excessively low and gross in his countenance. His lecture was, in parts, pretty good. His appearance was that of a man who had been spending the whole night at the shrine of Bacchus, and had just got himself gathered together to discharge what appeared to him a very irksome duty. His papers were all to regulate when he came to his chair; and four times he had to stop in the lecture till he found the right piece of paper, to enable him to go on with his remarks.—ROBERT BLAKEY (1838), *Memoirs*, 1873, p. 113

It was at Mr. Wordsworth's house that I first became acquainted with Professor (then Mr.) Wilson, of Elleray. I have elsewhere described the impression which he made upon me at my first acquaintance; and it is sufficiently known, from other accounts of Mr. Wilson (as, for example, that written by Mr. Lockhart in *Peter's Letters*), that he divided his time and the utmost sincerity of his love between literature and the stormiest pleasures of real life. Cock-fighting, wrestling, pugilistic contests, boat-racing, horse-racing, all enjoyed Mr. Wilson's patronage; all were occasionally honoured by his personal participation. I mention this in no unfriendly spirit toward Professor Wilson; on the contrary, these propensities grew out of his ardent temperament and his constitutional endowments—his strength, speed, and agility: and, being confined to the period of youth—for I am speaking of a period removed by five-and-twenty years—can do him no dishonour amongst the candid and the judicious. "*Non lusisse pudet, sed non incidere ludum.*" The truth was that Professor Wilson had in him, at that period of life, something of the old English chivalric feeling which our old ballad poetry agrees in ascribing to Robin Hood. Several men of genius have expressed to me, at different times, the delight they had in the traditional character of Robin Hood. He has no resemblance to the old heroes of Continental romance in one important feature: they are uniformly victorious: and this gives even a tone of monotony to the Continental poems: for, let them involve their hero in what dangers they may, the reader still feels them to be as illusory as those which menace an enchanter—an Astolpho, for instance, who, by one blast of his horn, can dissipate an army of opponents. But

Robin is frequently beaten: he never declines a challenge; sometimes he courts one; and occasionally he learns a lesson from some proud tinker or masterful beggar, the moral of which teaches him that there are better men in the world than himself. What follows? Is the brave man angry with his stout-hearted antagonist because he is no less brave and a little stronger than himself? Not at all; he insists on making him a present, on giving him a *dejeuner à la fourchette*, and (in case he is disposed to take service in the forest) finally adopts him into his band of archers. Much the same spirit governed, in his earlier years, Professor Wilson. And, though a man of prudence cannot altogether approve of his throwing himself into the convivial society of gipsies, tinkers, potters, strolling players, &c., nevertheless it tells altogether in favour of Professor Wilson's generosity of mind, that he was ever ready to forgo his advantages of station and birth, and to throw himself fearlessly upon his own native powers, as man opposed to man. Even at Oxford he fought an aspiring shoemaker repeatedly— which is creditable to both sides; for the very *prestige* of the gown is already overpowering to the artisan from the beginning, and he is half beaten by terror at his own presumption. Elsewhere he sought out, or, at least, did not avoid the most dreaded of the local heroes; and fought his way through his "most verdant years," taking or giving defiances to the right and the left in perfect carelessness, as chance or occasion offered. No man could well show more generosity in these struggles, nor more magnanimity in reporting their issue, which naturally went many times against him. But Mr. Wilson neither sought to disguise the issue nor showed himself at all displeased with it: even brutal ill-usage did not seem to have left any vindictive remembrance of itself. These features of his character, however, and these propensities, which naturally belonged merely to the transitional state from boyhood to manhood, would have drawn little attention on their own account, had they not been relieved and emphatically contrasted by his passion for literature, and the fluent command which he soon showed over a rich and voluptuous poetic diction. In everything Mr. Wilson showed himself an Athenian. Athenians were all lovers of the cockpit; and, howsoever shocking to the sensibilities of modern refinement, we have no doubt that Plato was a frequent better at cock-fights; and Socrates is known to have bred cocks himself. If he were any Athenian, however, in particular, it was Alcibiades; for he had his marvellous versatility; and to the Windermere neighbourhood, in which he had settled, this versatility came recommended by something of the very same position in society—the same wealth, the same social temper, the same jovial hospitality. No person was better fitted to win or to maintain a high place in social esteem; for he could adapt himself to all companies; and the wish to conciliate and to win his way by flattering the self-love of others was so predominant over all personal self-love and vanity

> That *he* did in the general bosom reign
> Of young and old.

Mr. Wilson and most of his family I had already known for six years. We had projected journeys together through Spain and Greece, all of which had been nipped in the bud by Napoleon's furious and barbarous mode of making war. It was no joke, as it had been in past times, for an Englishman to be found wandering in continental regions; the pretence that he was, or might be, a spy—a charge so easy to make, so impossible to throw off—at once sufficed for the hanging of the unhappy traveller. In one of his Spanish bulletins, Napoleon even boasted of having hanged sixteen Englishmen, "merchants or others of that nation," whom he taxed with no suspicion even of being suspected, beyond the simple fact of being detected in the act of breathing Spanish air. These atrocities had interrupted our continental schemes; and we were thus led the more to roam amongst home scenes. How it happened I know not—for we had wandered together often in England—but, by some accident, it was not until 1814 that we visited Edinburgh together. Then it was that I first saw Scotland.

I remember a singular incident which befell us on the road. Breakfasting together, before starting, at Mr. Wilson's place of Elleray, we had roamed, through a long and delightful day, by way of Ulleswater, &c. Reaching Penrith at night, we slept there; and in the morning, as we were sunning ourselves in the street, we saw, seated in an arm-chair, and dedicating himself to the self-same task of *apricating* his jolly personage, a rosy, jovial, portly man, having something of the air of a Quaker. Good nature was clearly his predominating quality; and, as that happened to be our foible also, we soon fell into talk; and from that into reciprocations of good will; and from those into a direct proposal, on our new friend's part, that we should set out upon our travels together. How—whither—to what end or object—seemed as little to enter into his speculations as the cost of realizing them. Rare it is, in this business world of ours, to find any man in so absolute a state of indifference and neutrality that for him all quarters of the globe, and all points of the compass, are self-balanced by philosophic equilibrium of choice. There seemed to us something amusing and yet monstrous in such a man; and, perhaps, had we been in the same condition of exquisite indetermination, to this hour we might all have been staying together at Penrith. We, however, were previously bound to Edinburgh; and, as soon as this was explained to him, that way he proposed to accompany us. We took a chaise, therefore, jointly, to Carlisle; and, during the whole eighteen miles, he astonished us by the wildest and most frantic displays of erudition, much of it levelled at Sir Isaac Newton. Much philosophical learning also he exhibited; but the grotesque accompaniment of the whole was that, after every bravura, he fell back into his corner in fits of laughter at himself. We began to find out the unhappy solution of his indifference and purposeless condition; he was a lunatic; and, afterwards, we had reason to suppose that he was now a fugitive from his keepers. At Carlisle he became restless and suspicious; and, finally, upon some real or imaginary business, he turned aside to Whitehaven. We were not the objects of his jealousy; for he parted with us reluctantly and anxiously. On our part, we felt our pleasure overcast by sadness; for we had been much amused by his conversation, and could not but respect the philological learning which he had displayed. But one thing was whimsical enough:—Wilson purposely said some startling things—startling in point of decorum, or gay pleasantries *contra bonos mores*; at every sally of which he looked as awfully shocked as though he himself had not been holding the most licentious talk in another key, licentious as respected all truth of history or of science. Another illustration, in fact, he furnished of what I have so often heard Coleridge say—that lunatics, in general, so far from being the brilliant persons they are thought, and having a preternatural brightness of fancy, usually are the very dullest and most uninspired of mortals. The sequel of our poor friend's history—for the apparent goodness of his nature had interested us both in his fortunes, and caused us to inquire after him through all probable channels—was, that he was last seen by a Cambridge man of our acquaintance, but under circumstances which confirmed our worst fears. It was in a stage-coach; and, at first, the Cantab suspected nothing amiss; but, some acci-

dent of conversation having started the topic of La Place's *Mechanique Celeste*, off flew our jolly Penrith friend in a tirade against Sir Isaac Newton; so that at once we recognised him, as the Vicar of Wakefield his "cosmogony friend" in prison; but—and that was melancholy to hear—this tirade was suddenly checked, in the rudest manner, by a brutal fellow in one corner of the carriage, who, as it now appeared, was attending him as a regular keeper, and, according to the custom of such people, always laid an interdict upon every ebullition of fancy or animated thought. He was a man whose mind had got some wheel entangled, or some spring overloaded, but else was a learned and able person; and he was to be silent at the bidding of a low, brutal fellow, incapable of distinguishing between the gaieties of fancy and the wandering of the intellect. Sad fate! and sad inversion of the natural relations between the accomplished scholar and the rude illiterate boor!—THOMAS DE QUINCEY, "Society of the Lakes" (1840), *Collected Writings*, ed. David Masson, Vol. 2, pp. 432–37

Walking up and down the hall of the courts of law (which was full of advocates, writers to the signet, clerks, and idlers) was a tall, burly, handsome man of eight and fifty, with a gait like O'Connell's, the bluest eye you can imagine, and long hair—longer than mine—falling down in a wild way under the broad brim of his hat. He had on a surtout coat, a blue checked shirt; the collar standing up, and kept in its place with a wisp of black neckerchief; no waistcoat; and a large pocket-handkerchief thrust into his breast, which was all broad and open. At his heels followed a wiry, sharp-eyed, shaggy devil of a terrier, dogging his steps as he went slashing up and down, now with one man beside him, now with another, and now quite alone, but always at a fast, rolling pace, with his head in the air, and his eyes as wide open as he could get them. I guessed it was Wilson, and it was. A bright, clear-complexioned, mountain-looking fellow, he looks as though he had just come down from the Highlands, and had never in his life taken pen in hand. But he has had an attack of paralysis in his right arm, within this month. He winced when I shook hands with him; and once or twice when we were walking up and down, slipped as if he had stumbled on a piece of orange-peel. He is a great fellow to look at, and to talk to; and, if you could divest your mind of the actual Scott, is just the figure you would put in his place. —CHARLES DICKENS, Letter to John Forster (June 23, 1841)

General

There is something extremely amiable, at all events, in the character of Mr Wilson's genius:—a constant glow of kind and of pure affection—a great sensibility to the charms of external nature, and the delights of a private, innocent, and contemplative life—a fancy richly stored with images of natural beauty and simple enjoyments—great tenderness and pathos in the representation of sufferings and sorrow, though almost always calmed, and even brightened, by the healing influences of pitying love, confiding piety, and conscious innocence. Almost the only passions with which his poetry is conversant, are the gentler sympathies of our nature—tender compassion—confiding affection, and guiltless sorrow. From all this there results, along with a most touching and tranquillizing sweetness, a certain monotony and languour, which, to those who read poetry for amusement merely, will be apt to appear like dullness, and must be felt as a defect by all who have been used to the variety, rapidity, and energy of the more popular poetry of the day.

⟨. . .⟩ He has undoubtedly both the heart and the fancy of a poet; and, with these great requisites, is almost sure of attaining the higher honours of his art, if he continue to cultivate it with the docility and diligence of which he has already given proof. Though his style is still too diffuse, and his range too limited, the present volume is greatly less objectionable on these grounds than the former. It has also less of the peculiarities of the Lake School; and, in particular, is honourably distinguished from the productions of its founders, by being quite free from the paltry spite and fanatical reprobation with which, like other fierce and narrow-minded sectaries, they think it necessary to abuse all whose tastes or opinions are not exactly conformable to their own.—FRANCIS, LORD JEFFREY, "Wilson's *City of the Plague*," *Edinburgh Review*, June 1816, pp. 460–61, 475–76

Wilson's papers, though not perfect, have a masterly cast about them: a little custom would make him the best periodical writer of the age,—keep hold of him.—JAMES HOGG, Letter to William Blackwood (Aug. 12, 1817), cited in Margaret Oliphant, *Annals of a Publishing House: William Blackwood and His Sons*, 1897, Vol. 1, p. 324

⟨. . .⟩ John Wilson, a man of great powers and acquirements, well known to the public as the author of the *City of the Plague, Isle of Palms*, and other productions.—GEORGE GORDON, LORD BYRON, "Some Observations upon an Article in *Blackwood's Magazine*," 1819

> You did late review my lays,
>   Crusty Christopher;
> You did mingle blame and praise,
>   Rusty Christopher.
> When I learnt from whom it came,
> I forgave you all the blame,
>   Musty Christopher;
> I could *not* forgive the praise,
>   Fusty Christopher.
>   —ALFRED, LORD TENNYSON, "To Christopher North," 1833

The great defect in the earlier poetry of Professor Wilson will be found to result from "the fatal facility" with which he found expression for his exuberant riches of thought and imagery. Life seemed to him a scene of enchantments; earth was a wilderness of sweets; language syllabled itself into music; and his imagining thus spontaneously seemed to arrange themselves in verse. The welling fountain of his mind, instead of requiring to be pumped up, ever superabundantly overflowed; and his poems thus often read more like improvisations than compositions. It is difficult to say, therefore, whether the years of his sojourn beside Windermere were more beneficial or otherwise to his fame as a poet. Most assuredly they determined his tone of thought, and influenced, perhaps, more than he is himself aware of, his habits of looking on and regarding man and nature. This position is rendered less dubious, from his after works, in which he thought and reasoned more decidedly and independently for himself; and who can doubt that he might not have from the first diffused through his poetry what he afterwards did through his prose,—that emphatic vigour, and ever-varying beauty of thought, that boundless amplitude of illustration, and that impassioned torrent-like eloquence— that despotic command alike over our reason and our sympathies, never conspicuous save in minds of the very highest order?—DAVID MACBETH MOIR, *Sketches of the Poetical Literature of the Past Half-Century*, 1851, pp. 133–34

Poor Wilson! I cannot remember ever to have at all much respected his judgment, or depth of sincere insight into anything whatever; and by this time I was abroad in fields quite foreign to him, where his word was of less and less avail to me. In London, indeed, I seldom or never heard any talk of him. I never read his blustering, drunken *Noctes* after Gordon in Edinburgh ceased to bring them to me. We lived apart, as in different centuries; though, to say the truth, I always loved Wilson—really rather loved him, and could have fancied a most strict and very profitable *friendship* between us in different, happier circumstances. But it was not to be. It was not the way of this poor epoch, nor a possibility of the century we lived in. One had to bid adieu to it therefore. Wilson had much nobleness of heart, and many traits of noble genius, but the central *tie-beam* seemed always wanting; very long ago I perceived in him the most irreconcilable contradictions, Toryism with *sansculottism*; Methodism of a sort with total incredulity; a noble, loyal, and religious nature, not *strong* enough to vanquish the perverse element it is born into. Hence a being all split into precipitous chasms and the wildest volcanic tumults; rocks overgrown, indeed, with tropical luxuriance of leaf and flower, but knit together at the bottom—that was my old figure of speech—only by an ocean—of whisky punch. On these terms nothing can be done. Wilson seemed to me always by far the most *gifted* of all our literary men, either then or still; and yet intrinsically he has written nothing that can endure. The central gift was wanting. Adieu! adieu! oh, noble, ill-starred brother! Who shall say I am not myself *farther* wrong, and in a more hopeless course and case, though on the opposite side. . . . Wilson spoke always in a curious dialect, full of humour and ingenuity, but with an uncomfortable wavering between jest and earnest, as if it were his interest and unconscious purpose to *conceal* his real meaning in most things. So far as I can recollect, he was once in my house (Comely Bank, with a testimonial, poor fellow!) and I once in his, De Quincey, &c., a little while one afternoon. One night, at Gordon's, I supped with him, or witnessed *his* supper—ten or twelve tumblers of whisky punch, continued till the daylight shone in on him and us; and such a *firework* of wildly ingenious—I should say volcanically vivid—hearty, humorous, and otherwise remarkable, entertaining, and *not* venerable talk (Wordsworth, Dugald Stewart, many men, as well as things, came in for a lick), as I never listened to before or since. We walked homewards together through the summer sunrise, I remember well. Good Wilson! Poor Wilson! That must be twenty-six years ago. I know not if among all his 'friends' he has left one who feels more recognisingly what he was, and how tragical his life when seemingly most successful, than I now. Adieu to him, good, grand, ruined soul, that never could be great, or, indeed, *be* anything. This present is a ruinous and ruining world.—THOMAS CARLYLE, *Journal* (April 29, 1854), cited in James Anthony Froude, *Thomas Carlyle: A History of His Life in London*, 1884, Vol. 2, pp. 170–71

It is curious that, whereas it is universally agreed that it is by his prose that he won his immortality, he argued with Moore that the inferiority of prose to poetry was proved by the fact that there is no such thing as a school of prose, while literary history consists of a succession of schools of poetry. It may be that his prose is something new in the world. At this moment, under the emotion of parting from him, we are disposed to think it is. Nowhere can we look for such a combination of music, emotion, speculation, comment, wit, and imagination, as in some of his *Noctes Ambrosianæ*, and in hundreds of the pages of *Christopher's Recreations*. In them we rejoice to think the subdued spirit is revived that we have seen fail, and the dumb voice reawakened for the delight of many a future generation.—HARRIET MARTINEAU, "Professor Wilson ('Christopher North')" (1854), *Biographical Sketches*, 1869, pp. 26–27

Blackwood's Magazine was long enlivened by the *Noctes Ambrosianæ*, a series of scenes supposed to have occurred in a tavern in West Register Street kept by one Ambrose. No periodical publication that I know of can boast so extraordinary a series of jovial dramatic fiction. Wilson, I believe, now professes to regret and condemn many things in these papers, and to deny his authorship of them; but substantially they are all his. I have not the slightest doubt that he wrote at least ninety per cent. of them. I wish no man had anything worse to be timid about. There is not so curious and original a work in the English or Scotch languages. It is a most singular and delightful outpouring of criticism, politics, and descriptions of feeling, character, and scenery, of verse and prose, and maudlin eloquence, and especially of wild fun. It breathes the very essence of the Bacchanalian revel of clever men. And its Scotch is the best Scotch that has been written in modern times. I am really sorry for the poor one-tongued Englishman, by whom, because the Ettrick Shepherd uses the sweetest and most expressive of living languages, the homely humour, the sensibility, the descriptive power, the eloquence, and the strong joyous hilarity of that animated rustic can never be felt. The characters are all well drawn, and well sustained, except that of the Opium Eater, who is heavy and prosy: but this is perhaps natural to opium. Few efforts could be more difficult than to keep up the bounding spirit of fresh boyish gaiety which is constantly made to break out amidst the serious discussions of these tavern philosophers and patriots. After all just deductions, these *Noctes* are bright with genius.—HENRY, LORD COCKBURN, *Memorials of His Time*, 1856, Ch. 5

In Wilson's *Lights and Shadows of Scottish Life*, and in his other Scottish stories, we have, unless my impression of them deceives me, a spirit of lyrical pathos, and of poetical Arcadianism, which tinges, without obscuring, the real Scottish colour, and reminds us of the Lake poet and disciple of Wordsworth, as well as of the follower of Scott; while in his *Noctes Ambrosianæ*, he burst away in a riot of Scotticism on which Scott had never ventured—a Scotticism, not only real and humorous, but daringly imaginative and poetic, to the verge of Lakism and beyond—displaying withal an originality of manner natural to a new cast of genius, and a command of resources in the Scottish idiom and dialect unfathomed even by Scott. Wilson's "Ettrick Shepherd" is one of the most extraordinary creations of recent prose fiction.—DAVID MASSON, *British Novelists and Their Styles*, 1859, pp. 216–17

How many diligent readers nowadays know Christopher North? The question "reminds me of a little story." In the last days of the old antislavery agitation, when it was supposed by Boston roughs and their inspirers that a few abolitionists' heads thrown to the South would dissolve the nascent Confederacy, there was a furious mob in the Music Hall. The uproar was continuous, deafening. The saintly face of Garrison beamed on the crowd, but his voice was unheard; the stately form of Phillips uprose, but not a syllable could be caught even by those on the platform. All efforts at gaining silence having failed, all orators having given up, Wendell Phillips espied in a distant nook the serene face of Emerson. The idea struck him that perhaps that calm face might have some effect. Emerson was persuaded, and advanced to the front. The mob did not know him, and the noise very slightly abated, because some were asking who he was. Emerson began his speech with these words: "Christopher North—of course you all know Chris-

topher North—" These were magic words. Whether it was the compliment to their intelligence, or whether the startling wildness of the proposition that they had ever heard of him, the crowd was instantly hushed, and the mob was chilled and foiled. Emerson went on with a capital speech, and he began it with the story of Christopher North, when rebuked for his anger and violence toward two scamps, declaring that he had treated them with the utmost self-restraint—he had "only pitched them out of the window." Emerson based on that his assertion that the abolitionists had exercised even more self-command under more tempting circumstances; they had been peaceful when it might have been expected they would be revolutionists. But the main force of the speech was in its gentle parenthesis, "Of course you all know Christopher North."—MONCURE D. CONWAY, "The English Lakes and Their Genii," *Harper's New Monthly Magazine*, Dec. 1880, p. 18

John Wilson, better known by the name of Professor Wilson, and better still as the Christopher North of *Blackwood's Magazine*, was unquestionably one of the most remarkable men of his age. He was essentially a man of genius: you could not converse with him for five minutes without perceiving it. His very look revealed the fervour of his mind. Blue piercing eyes, thin and flying yellow hair, a fair complexion, and sanguine temperament, bespoke the Danish blood, as much as the dark eyes, black hair, sallow complexion, and bilious disposition of Lockhart revealed a Celtic descent. I never met a man whose conversation evinced so many flashes of genius as that of Wilson. He was greatly superior in originality to either Sir Walter Scott, Byron, Southey, or Jeffrey. If his perseverance had been equal to his conceptions, and he had brought the force of a mind enriched by a thorough acquaintance with the acquisitions of others, to bear on some one work of such dimensions as to form the principal object of his life, he would have been the first literary man after Scott of his age. But the desultory habits of a poet proved the great impediment to his success. He had not the good sense and steady perseverance which in Scott were combined in so marvellous a manner with the fervour of the poetic temperament. He did nothing regularly or consecutively; he was always the poet working, not the worker become a poet. Though educated at Oxford, and a good scholar, he made little use of classical knowledge or allusions in his compositions; and it was in domestic literature, especially that which related to poetry, and by the working out of home images, that he obtained his reputation. He was essentially national in all his ideas; and that, too, in the most catholic of all senses, as embracing every class of the community. Like Burns, he was the poet and novelist of the fireside. Though strongly Conservative in his political views, it was from no preference of the aristocratic to the popular interest, but from a decided conviction that it was by the maintenance of the former that the latter could alone be durably maintained. He never courted the great; while maintaining their cause with strenuous ability, he was never seen at their tables. He was too proud to condescend to the obsequiousness which they require. His heart was essentially bound up in the peasantry of the country; but it was the peasantry as they were, and still are, on the mountain and in the glen, not as they have become in the plain and the workshop. His heart contained many of the purest and noblest sentiments; but with these were combined a strange mixture of humour and drollery, sometimes of not the most refined kind, which strongly appears in his *Miscellaneous Essays*. As a critic he was generally lenient, and always generous, sometimes even to a fault, if that could be called a fault which arose from the high-minded and unenvying sympathy of genius with kindred excellence, wherever it was to be found. No man had a more profound admiration of the beauties of nature, or had sought them out with more fervent devotion.—SIR ARCHIBALD ALISON, *Some Account of My Life and Writings*, 1883, pp. 192–94

⟨. . .⟩ one always thinks of Wilson, as of Kingsley, as a forerunner of muscular Christianity—leaping twenty-three feet on a level; walking over from London to Oxford—fifty-three miles—in a night, six miles an hour heel-and-toe walking (Wilson once made seventy miles in the Highlands in twenty-four hours); jumping tables at Ambrose's, or swallowing monstrous bowls of whisky and milk at Scotch shielings, where he paused for refreshment on his midnight rambles through the bens and glens; swimming Highland lochs, fishing-rod in hand, and arriving late at lonely bothies with basket, pockets, and hat-crown filled with trout; sailing on Windermere, and cock-breeding at Elleray; tramping over the Cumberland hills with the Opium Eater, or hunting bulls on horseback with prick of spear. At Oxford the tradition of his physical prowess lingered long, and even gave rise to legends—as of his joining a band of strolling actors, and abiding in gipsy tents for a season with a gipsy wife. All his contemporaries were impressed by his personal vigor, the size of his chest, his florid complexion, the brightness of his eye, the length of his limbs. His portraits show a certain aquiline cast of countenance, and a leonine air—given him not, as in Landor's case, by the cut of the features, but by the length of tawny mane. De Quincey, however, denies that Christopher was a handsome man: his mouth and chin, he says, were Ciceronian, but his hair was too light, and his blue eye lacked depth—its brightness was superficial.

The little passage at arms between Wilson and Tennyson is an interesting point of contact between Georgian and Victorian literature. Wilson was a member of the generation of Scott and Byron and Moore. He belonged to an "era of expansion," and was himself expansive. The writings of the generation of Tennyson, Thackeray, and Matthew Arnold are in many ways a reaction and a protest against the emotional excesses of the Georgian time. Spontaneity, creative impulse, versatility belonged to the elders, but their art was less fine. The rich perfection of Tennyson's verse, the chastened perfection of Arnold's verse and prose, are rare among Wilson's contemporaries. His own work is profuse and diffuse, without selection and restraint. He was the most brilliant of magazinists, and Carlyle thought that he had the greatest gifts among the writers of his day, but that he had produced nothing that would endure. He compared his *Blackwood* papers to rugged rocks overgrown with luxuriant foliage, but bound together at bottom by "an ocean of whisky punch." Tennyson himself inherits of Keats, who was most purely the artist among the poets of his generation.

Who now reads *The Isle of Palms*, or *The City of the Plague*, or the miscellaneous verse of Wilson, which was thought to resemble Wordsworth's? Do young men nowadays read even the *Noctes*, which their fathers and grandfathers read eagerly, and imitated in countless sanctum dialogues, "coffee clubs," and such like? I trow not. Nevertheless Christopher was a great creature, and there is imperishable stuff in the *Noctes*. That famous series has not the even excellence—the close grain—of Holmes *Breakfast-Table* papers. There is too much of it, and it should be read with judicious skipping. A large part of the dialogue is concerned with matters of temporary interest. The bacchanalian note in it becomes at times rather forced, and the reader wearies of the incessant consumption of

powl-doodies, porter, and Welsh rabbits. But the Ettrick Shepherd is a dramatic creation of a high order, and the vehicle of wit, eloquence, and poetry always racy, if not always fine. The same exuberance, for good and for bad, characterizes the *Recreations* and the other miscellaneous papers, which place their author high, though not among the highest, in the line of British essayists. Christopher was, after all, most at home in his sporting-jacket, and his outdoor papers are the best—"The Moors," "The Stroll to Grasmere," and the rest. His literary criticism, though interesting as the utterance of a rich personality, is seldom wise or sure. But those who should know have said that none ever knew the scenery of the Western Highlands like "Christopher North," or wrote of it so well.—HENRY A. BEERS, "'Crusty Christopher' (John Wilson)," *Century Magazine*, Jan. 1893, p. 362

It happened the other day, in the library of a remote house, that I lighted upon a shelf of old *Blackwoods*, from fifty to sixty years old, and, being confined to the house by wet weather, read largely in them. Christopher North was at his glory then, with his flagrant egotism and stupid bellowings. But what struck me most in the old pages was that, with all his loud Philistinism, he was penetrated with a profound respect for poetry.—A. C. BENSON, "The Poetry of Edmund Gosse" (1894), *Essays*, 1896, p. 292

⟨. . .⟩ the far-famed *Noctes Ambrosianae*, by much the most celebrated of Wilson's writings, though they may still be dipped into with pleasure, will scarcely stand critical examination nowadays. Of course, from their very nature, they have come to labour under the disadvantage of being largely concerned with topics and persons of long since exhausted interest. And, again, their convivial setting, which pleased in its own day, is now probably by many looked upon askance, and that, it must be confessed, not without some show of excuse. If this were all, it would be well. ⟨. . .⟩ Wilson wrote his dialogues hastily and presumably wrote them for the moment, so that to judge them as permanent contributions to literature is to judge them by a standard contemplated not by the author, but by his injudicious critics. Amongst these, Professor Ferrier, in his introductory critique to the authoritative edition of the *Noctes*, published forty years ago, most confidently claims that they possess solid and lasting qualities, and in the front rank of these qualities he places humour and dramatic power. Now to us, except in outward form, the *Noctes* appear almost anything rather than dramatic; they are even less dramatic than the conversation-pieces of Thomas Love Peacock. It is true that of the two principal talkers one speaks Scotch and the other English; but in every other respect they might exchange almost any of their longest and most important speeches without the smallest loss to characterisation. The same authority (I use the word in a purely empirical sense) enthusiastically lauds the creation of The Shepherd; and upon him it is true that, by dint of insistence on two or three superficial mannerisms, a certain shadowy individuality has been conferred. But surely it is needless to point out that a label is not a personality, and that this sort of thing is something quite apart from dramatic creation. The critic then goes on to say that 'in wisdom the Shepherd equals the Socrates of Plato; in humour he surpasses the Falstaff of Shakespeare.' The last part of the sentence strikes us as even more surprising than the first, for had our opinion of the imaginary revellers at Ambrose's been asked we should have had to confess that, though they possess high spirits in abundance and a certain sense of the ludicrous, of humour in the true sense—of the humour, I won't say of a Sterne, but of a Michael Scott—all are alike entirely destitute. And one may even add that with persons of equally high spirits such is almost always the case. Well then, it may be asked, if they lack both humour and dramatic power, in what qualities, pray, do these world-famed dialogues excel? The answer is, of course, that in brilliant intellectual and rhetorical display the *Noctes* are supreme. Yet here, also, there is often about them something too much of deliberate and self-conscious fine-writing. And yet, even to-day, when tastes have changed and fashions altered, the exuberance of their eloquence is hard to withstand, and in reading them we sometimes almost believe that we are touched when in reality we are merely dazzled. This dazzling quality is not one of the highest in literature: with the single possible exception of Victor Hugo, the greater writers have always been without it. But it pervades, floods, overwhelms the *Noctes*. It is a somewhat barren, and unendearing quality at best; yet, after all, it is an undoubted manifestation of intellectual power; and whatever it may be worth, let us give Wilson full credit for having excelled in it.—Sir George Douglas, "John Wilson," *The "Blackwood" Group*, 1897, pp. 43–45

Taking his work as a whole ⟨. . .⟩ he has wonderful sweep of wing, and he always brings with him the atmosphere of the moors, the sense of bleak, shrewd mountain air, richened with the scent of peat and heather. But his manner, as a rule, is rather energetic than fine; at least it is so where he is not dealing with external nature, and it is a certain want of fineness that distinguishes him from the three or four contemporary masters of prose who stand beyond cavil upon a higher plane. He was not, for example, a man of such a rare and exquisite spirit as Lamb; although Lamb was not merely "a cockney," to use Wilson's own favourite term of general reproach, but the very Saint of Cockaigne. There is no single place of which Wilson can give the whole genius as Lamb seems to give the soul of old London, just faintly idealised, so that it seems a more staid and dreamy place than our London, with its concourse of incessant vehicles, and the voices of the evening newspaper venders "prophesying war."

Neither has he like Hazlitt a completely sustained and overmastering style, terse, mordant, cutting, closely woven in texture, and so full of the marrow of idiom and the rude glow of life, that his panegyrics are flushed with the freshest colour and his denunciations written in vitriol and sulphuric acid.

Nor is he like De Quincey the master of a rich, dim, dreamy rhetoric, a processional pomp of clauses, subdued and mellowed to the very finest musical pitch, an emblazoned but not garish pageantry of phrase; although he has certainly not De Quincey's gossiping irresponsibility of temperament. And, as before said, he has—in mere authorship, for it is not a question of social attraction—none of the imperious personality of Landor writing upon tablets of granite and of marble and assiduously burying them in the sands of the desert.

He is not to be named with these; he has not often their consummate felicities and finalities of expression; he does not mint his paragraphs with an unmistakable individuality, nor make an image of himself in language as undeniable and less perishable than his bodily form. One knows instinctively that a misplaced comma or an omitted colon would have caused De Quincey sleepless nights, because it would have defaced the character of a sentence. But, as often as not, a paragraph in Wilson will be punctuated by a flight of ardent dashes, although where it is good his prose is singularly easy and dignified in movement notwithstanding its fervour.

Above all, Wilson has not the solidity of any of these great writers. He is altogether more unsound and unsafe, and can be merely featureless and fatiguing. His best work is rarely so

delicate as theirs and there is far less of it. But distinct disservice was done to Wilson since far too much of his inferior and merely futile work—such as reviews on books dead, or as good as dead, and clumsy failures like 'Christopher on Colonsay'—was originally republished; though more, perhaps, through his own fault than that of Professor Ferrier, who endeavoured in editing him to carry out his known wishes as faithfully as might be. Besides in many cases it would have been impossible to separate the dross in him from the gold.

Still for rapid, daring, vehement, electrifying bursts of straightforward rushing eloquence, as a matter of course defective in the very best kinds of chiselled or intricate beauty, but full of splendour, he is, where really inspired, unrivalled in his own generation; and the last impressions of him left on a reader's mind are those of amazing energy and fire.—Arthur Cecil Hillier, "'Christopher North,'" *Temple Bar*, Jan. 1899, pp. 74–75

GEORGE GILFILLAN
From "Professor Wilson"
A Third Gallery of Portraits
1854, pp. 445–56

As a man, Wilson was much misunderstood. Not only were his personal habits grossly misrepresented, but his whole nature was belied. He was set down by many as a strange compound of wilful oddity, boisterous spirits, swaggering ostentation, and true genius. Let us hear, on the other side, one who knew him intimately, and loved him as a son a father—our friend Thomas Aird. His words, written since Wilson's decease, are identical with all his private statements to us on the same subject:—"He was singularly modest, and even deferential. His estimates of life were severely practical; he was not sanguine; he was not even hopeful enough. Those who approached the author of the *Noctes* in domestic life, expecting exchanges of boisterous glee, soon found out their mistake. No writing for mere money, no 'dabbling in the pettiness of fame,' with this great spirit, in its own negligent grandeur, modest, quiet, negligent, because, amidst all the beauty and joy of the world, it stood *waiting and wondering on vaster shores than lie by the seas of time.*"

These words are not only beautiful, but true, although they represent Wilson only in his higher moods. He could, and often did, indulge in boisterous glee, while, like many humorists, his heart within was serious, if not sad enough. And this leads us to the question as to his faith—what was it? He was unquestionably of a deeply religious temperament; but he had not given it a proper culture. He was not, we think, satisfied with any of the present *forms* of the Christian religion; yet there was something in him far beyond nature-worship. His attitude, indeed, was just that described by Aird. Like the spirits of Foster, Coleridge, Arnold, and many others in our strange era, while accepting Christianity as a whole, Wilson's spirit was "waiting and wondering" till the mighty veil should drop, and show all mysteries made plain in the light of another sphere. Had he more resolutely lived the Christian life in its energetic activities, and approved himself more a servant of duty, his views had perhaps become clearer and more consoling. And yet, what can we say? Arnold was a high heroic worker, nay, seemed a humble, devoted Christian, and yet died with a heart broken by the uncertainties of this transition and twilight age.

Many thought and called Wilson a careless, neglectful man. He was not, indeed, so punctual as the Iron Duke in answering letters, nor could he be always "fashed" with young aspirants. But this arose more from indolence than from indifference. He was to many men a generous and constant friend and patron. Few have had encouraging letters from him, but many have had cheering words, and a word from him went as far as a letter, or many letters from others.

We pass to speak of the constituents of his genius. These were distinguished by their prodigal abundance and variety. He was what the Germans call an "all-sided man." He had, contrary to common opinion, much metaphysical subtlety, which had not indeed been subjected, any more than some of his other faculties, to careful cultivation. But none can read some of his articles, or could have listened to many of his lectures, without the conviction that the metaphysical power was strong within him, and that, had he not by instinct been taught to despise metaphysics, he might have become a metaphysician, as universally wise, as elaborately ingenious, as captiously critical, as wilfully novel, and as plausibly and profoundly wrong, as any of the same class that ever lived. But he *did* despise this science of pretensions, and used to call it "dry as the dust of summer." Of his imagination we need not speak. It was large, rich, ungovernable, fond alike of the Beautiful and the Sublime, of the Pathetic and the Terrible. His wit was less remarkable than his humour, which was one of the most lavish and piquant of his faculties. Add to this, great memory, keen, sharp intellect, wide sympathies, strong passion, and a boundless command of a somewhat loose, but musical and energetic diction, and you have the outline of his gifts and endowments. He was deficient only in that plodding, painstaking sagacity which enables many commonplace men to excel in the physical sciences. If he ever crossed the "Ass' Bridge," it must have been at a flying leap, and with recalcitrating heels, and he was much better acquainted, we suspect, with the "Fluxions" of the Tweed, than with those of Leibnitz and Newton.

His powers have never, we think, found an adequate development. It is only the bust of Wilson we have before us. Yet let us not, because he has not done mightier things, call his achievements small; they are not only very considerable in themselves, but of a very diversified character. He was a critic, humorist, writer of fiction, professor, poet, and periodical writer. And, first, as a critic, criticism with him was not an art or an attainment: it was an insight and an enthusiasm. He loved everything that was beautiful in literature, and abhorred all that was false and affected, and pitied all that was weak and dull; and his criticism was just the frank, fearless, and eloquent expression of that love, that abhorrence, and that pity. Hence his was a catholic criticism; hence his canons were not artificial; hence he abhorred the formal, the mystical, and the pseudo-philosophic schools of criticism; hence the reasons he gave for his verdicts were drawn, not from arbitrary rules, but directly from the great principles of human nature. With what joyous gusto did he approach a favourite author! His praise fell on books like autumn sunshine, and whatever it touched it gilded and glorified. And when, on the other hand, he was disgusted or offended, with what vehement sincerity, with what a noble rage, with what withering sarcasm, or with what tumultuous invective, did he express his wrath. His criticisms are sometimes rambling, sometimes rhapsodical, sometimes overdone in praise or in blame; often you are compelled to differ from his opinions, and sometimes to doubt if they are fully formed in his own mind, and in polish, precision, and depth, they are inferior to a few others; but, in heartiness, eloquence, variety, consummate ease of motion, native insight, and sincerity, they stand alone.

We have alluded to his extraordinary gift of humour. It was not masked and subtle, like Lamb's; it was broad, rich, bordering on farce, and strongly impregnated with imagination. It was this last characteristic which gave it its peculiar power, as Patrick Robertson can testify. This gentleman possesses nearly as much fun as Wilson, but, in their conversational contests, Wilson, whenever he lifted up the daring wing of imagination, left him floundering far behind.

Good old Dr MacIntyre ⟨. . .⟩ thought Wilson's *forte* was fiction. We can hardly concur with the doctor in this opinion, for although many of his tales are fine, they are so principally from the poetry of the descriptions which are sprinkled through them. He does not tell a story well, and this because he is not calm enough. As Cowper says, he prefers John Newton, as a historian, to Gibbon and Robertson; because, while they *sing*, you *say* your story; and history is a thing to be said, not sung. Before we met this remark, we had *made* it in reference to Wilson and Scott. Scott *says* his stories, and Wilson *sings* them. Hence, while Wilson in passages is equal to Scott, as a whole, his works of fiction are greatly less interesting, and seem less natural. Wilson is a northern Scald, not so much narrating as pouring out passionate poetic rhapsodies, thinly threaded with incident; Scott is a Minstrel of the border, who can be poetical when he pleases, but who lays more stress upon the general interest of the tale he tells. Even in description he is not, in general, equal to Scott, and that for a similar reason. Wilson, when describing, rises out of the sphere of prose into a kind of poetic rhythm; Scott never goes beyond the line which separates the style of lofty prose from that of absolute poetry. Wilson is too Ossianic in his style of narration and description; and had he attempted a novel in three or four volumes, it had been absolutely illegible. Even "Margaret Lindsay," his longest tale, rather tires before the close, through its sameness of eloquence and monotony of pathos; only very short letters should be *all* written in tears and blood. And his alternations of gay and grave are not so well managed in his tales as in his *Noctes*. Yet nothing can be finer than some of his individual scenes and pictures. Who has forgotten his Scottish sunset, which seems dipped in fiery gold, or that Rainbow which bridges over one of his most pathetic stories, or the drowning of Henry Needham, or the Elder's Death-bed, or that incomparable Thunderstorm, which seems still to bow its giant wing of gloom over Ben Nevis and the glen below? In no modern, not even Scott, do we find prose passages so gorgeous, so filled with the intensest spirit of poetry, and rising so finely into its language and rhythm as these. ⟨. . .⟩

His poetry proper has been generally thought inferior to his prose, and beneath the level of his powers. Yet, if we admire it less, we at times love it more. It is not great, or intense, or highly impassioned, but it is true, tender, and pastoral. It has been well called the "poetry of peace;" it is from "towns and toils remote." In it the author seems to be exiled from the bustle and conflict of the world, and to inhabit a country of his own, not an entirely "Happy Valley," for tears there fall, and clouds gather, and hearts break, and death enters, but the tears are quiet, the clouds are windless, the hearts break in silence, and the awful Shadow comes in softly, and on tiptoe departs. Sometimes, indeed, the solitude and silence are disturbed by the apparition of a "wild deer," and the poet is surprised into momentary rapture, and a stormy lyric is flung abroad on the winds. But, in general, the region is calm, and the very sounds are all in unison and league with silence. As a poet, however, Wilson was deficient, far more than as a prose writer, in objective interest, as well as in concentration of purpose. His poetry has neither that reflective depth which causes you to recur so frequently to the poetry of Wordsworth, nor that dazzling lightness and brilliance of movement which fascinates you in Scott. It is far, too, from being a full reflection of his multifarious and powerful nature; it represents only a little quiet nook in his heart, a small sweet vein in his genius, as though a lion were to carry somewhere within his broad breast a little bag of honey, like that of the bee. It does not discover him as he is, but as he would wish to have been. His poetry is the Sabbath of his soul. And there are moods of mind—quiet, peaceful, autumnal moments—in which you enjoy it better than the poetry of any one else, and find a metaphor for its calm and holy charm in the words of Coleridge—

> The moonbeams *steep'd in silentness,*
> The *steady weather-cock.*

The revolving, impatient wheel, the boundless versatility of Wilson's genius, quieted and at rest, as we see it in his poetry, could not be better represented than in these lines. In Coleridge, indeed, as in some true poets, we find all characters and varieties of intellect represented *unconsciously and by anticipation,* even as frost, fire, and rock-work—each contains all architecture and all art, silently anticipated in its varied forms and prophetic imitations.

In his periodical writings alone do we find anything like an adequate display of his varied powers. You saw only the half-man in the professor's chair, and only the quarter-man in his poetry; but in the *Noctes,* and the satirico-serious papers he scattered over *Blackwood,* you saw the whole Wilson—the Cyclops now at play, and now manufacturing thunderbolts for Jove; now cachinnating in his cave, now throwing rocks and mountains at his enemies, and now pouring out awful complaints, and asking strange, yet reverent queries in the ear of the gods.

Wilson's relation to his age has been, like Byron's, somewhat uncertain and vacillating. He has been, on the whole, a "lost leader." He has, properly speaking, belonged neither to the old nor new, neither to the conservative nor to the movement, neither to the infidel nor the evangelical sides. Indeed, our grand quarrel with him is, that he was not sufficiently in earnest; that he did not with his might what his hand found to do; that he hid his *ten* talents in a napkin; that he trifled with his inestimable powers, and had not a sufficiently strong sense of stewardship on his conscience. This has been often said, and we thought it generally agreed on, till our attention was turned to a pamphlet, entitled *Professor Wilson—a Memorial and Estimate,* which, amid tolerably good points and thoughts here and there, is written in a style which, for looseness, inaccuracy, verbosity, and affected obscurity, baffles description, besides abounding in flagrant and, we fear, wilful mis-statements, and in efforts at fine writing, which make you blush for Scottish literature. The poor creature who indites this farrago of pretentious nonsense, asserts that the "Life of Wilson seems to have been as truly fruitful as that of any author within the range of English literature," and proves the statement by the following portentous query:—"That *wild air* of the unexpressed poet, the inglorious Milton, the Shakspere that might have been, what was it but a *rich spice* of the fantastic humour of the man, a part of that extraordinary character which so delighted in its sport, that, whether he jested on himself, or from behind a mask might be making some play of you, you knew not, nor were sure if it meant mirth, confidence, or a solemn earnest such as *he* only could appreciate?" What this may mean we cannot tell; but the writer becomes a little more intelligible when he speaks, in some later portion of his production, of the great popularity which Wilson's redacted

and collected works are to obtain, not appearing to know the fact, that the *Recreations of Christopher North,* published some twelve years ago, have never reached a second edition, and that old William Blackwood, one of the acutest bibliopoles that ever lived, refused to re-publish Wilson's principal articles in *Maga;* nor did the *Recreations* appear till after Blackwood's death. Splendid passages and inestimable thoughts, of course, abound in all that Wilson wrote, but the want of pervasive purpose, of genuine artistic instinct, of condensation, and of finish, has denied true unity, and perhaps permanent power, to his writings. He will probably be best remembered for his *Lights and Shadows*—a book which, although not a full discovery of his powers, lies in portable compass, and embalms that fine nationality which so peculiarly distinguished his genius. Probably a wise selection from his *Noctes,* too, might become a popular book.

Wilson had every inducement to have done more than he did. He was a strong healthy nature; he had much leisure; he had great, perhaps too great facility of expression. He was the pet of the public for many years. But he did not, alas! live habitually in his "great Taskmaster's eye." We quarrel not with his unhappy uncertainties of mind; they are but too incident to all imaginative and thoughtful spirits. We quarrel not with his "waiting and wondering" on the brink of the unseen, but his uncertainty should not have paralysed and emasculated a man of his gigantic proportions. If beset by doubts and demons, he ought to have tried at least to fight his way through them, as many a resolute spirit has done before him. What had he to endure, compared to Cowper, who for many years imagined that a being, mightier than the fallen angels—Ahrimanes himself—held him as his property, and yet who, under the pressure of this fearful delusion, wrote and did his best, and has left some works which, while satisfying the severest critics, are manuals and household words everywhere? Wilson, on the other hand, seldom wrote anything except from the compulsion of necessity. Although not a writer for bread, much of his writing arose to the tune of the knock of the printer's "devil;" and his efforts for the advancement of the race, although we believe really sincere, were to the last degree fluctuating, irregular, and uncertain.

It is a proof, we think, of Wilson's weakness, as well as of his power, that he has been claimed as a possible prize on so many and such diverse sides. He might have been, says one, the greatest preacher of the age. He might have been, says another, the greatest actor of the day. He might have been, says a third, the greatest dramatist, next to Shakspere, that ever lived. He might have been, says a fourth, a powerful parliamentary orator. He might have been, says a fifth, a traveller superior to Bruce or Park. Now, while this proves the estimation in which men hold his vast versatility, it proves also, that there was something wrong and shattered in the structure of a mind which, while presenting so many angles to so many objects, never fully embraced any of them, and while displaying powers so universal, has left results so comparatively slender.

Nevertheless, after all these deductions, where shall we look for his like again? A more generous, a more wide-minded, a more courteous, and a more gifted man, probably never lived. By nature he was Scotland's brightest son, not, perhaps, even excepting Burns; and he, Scott, and Burns, must rank everlastingly together as the first Three of her men of genius. A cheerless feeling of desolation creeps across us, as we remember—that majestic form shall press this earth no more; those eyes of fire shall sound human hearts no more; that voice, mellow as that of the summer ocean breaking on a silver strand, shall swell and sink no more; and that large heart shall no more mirror nature and humanity on its stormy, yet sunlit surface. Yet long shall Scotland, ay, and the world, continue to cherish his image, and to bless his memory; and whether or not he obtain a splendid mausoleum, he will not require it, for he can (we heard him once quote the words in reference to Scott, as he only could quote them)

A mightier monument command—
The mountains of his native land.

GEORGE SAINTSBURY
From "Wilson" (1886)
Collected Essays and Papers
1923, Volume 1, pp. 190–98

It must be confessed that the *Noctes Ambrosianæ* are not easy things to commend to the modern reader, if I may use the word "commend" in its proper sense and with no air of patronage. Even Scotchmen (perhaps, indeed, Scotchmen most of all) are wont nowadays to praise them rather apologetically, as may be seen in the case of their editor and abridger Mr Skelton. Like most other very original things they drew after them a flock of imbecile imitations; and up to the present day those who have lived in the remoter parts of Scotland must know, or recently remember, dreary compositions in corrupt following of the *Noctes*, with exaggerated attempts at Christopher's worst mannerisms, and invariably including a ghastly caricature of the Shepherd. Even in themselves they abound in stumbling-blocks, which are perhaps multiplied, at least at the threshold, by the arbitrary separation in Ferrier's edition of Wilson's part, and not all his part, from the whole series; eighteen numbers being excluded bodily to begin with, while many more and parts of more are omitted subsequently. The critical mistake of this is evident, for much of the machinery and all the characters of the *Noctes* were given to, not by, Wilson, and in all probability he accepted them not too willingly. The origin of the fantastic personages, the creation of which was a perfect mania with the early contibutors to *Blackwood*, and who are, it is to be feared, too often a nuisance to modern readers, is rather dubious. Maginn's friends have claimed the origination of the *Noctes* proper, and of its well-known motto paraphrased from Phocylides, for "The Doctor," or, if his chief *Blackwood* designation be preferred, for the Ensign—Ensign O'Doherty. Professor Ferrier, on the other hand, has shown a not unnatural but by no means critical or exact desire to hint that Wilson invented the whole. There is no doubt that the real original is to be found in the actual suppers at "Ambrose's." These Lockhart had described, in *Peter's Letters*, before the appearance of the first *Noctes* (the reader must not be shocked, the false concord is invariable in the book itself) and not long after the establishment of *Maga*. As was the case with the magazine generally, the early numbers were extremely local and extremely personal. Wilson's glory is that he to a great extent, though not wholly, lifted them out of this rut, when he became the chief if not the sole writer after Lockhart's removal to London, and, with rare exceptions, reduced the personages to three strongly marked and very dramatic characters, Christopher North himself, the Ettrick Shepherd, and "Tickler." All these three were in a manner portraits, but no one is a mere photograph from a single person. On the whole, however, I suspect that Christopher North is a much closer likeness, if not of what Wilson himself was, yet at any rate of what he would have liked to be, than

some of his apologists maintain. These charitable souls excuse the egotism, the personality, the violence, the inconsistency, the absurd assumption of omniscience and Admirable-Crichtonism, on the plea that "Christopher" is only the ideal Editor and not the actual Professor. It is quite true that Wilson, who, like all men of humour, must have known his own foibles, not unfrequently satirises them; but it is clear from his other work and from his private letters that they *were* his foibles. The figure of the Shepherd, who is the chief speaker and on the whole the most interesting, is a more debatable one. It is certain that many of Hogg's friends, and, in his touchy moments he himself, considered that great liberty was taken with him, if not that (as the *Quarterly* put it in a phrase which evidently made Wilson very angry) he was represented as a mere "boozing buffoon." On the other hand it is equally certain that the Shepherd never did anything that exhibited half the power over thought and language which is shown in the best passages of his *Noctes* eidolon. Some of the adventures described as having happened to him are historically known as having happened to Wilson himself, and his sentiments are much more the writer's than the speaker's. At the same time the admirably imitated patois and the subtle rendering of Hogg's very well known foibles—his inordinate and stupendous vanity, his proneness to take liberties with his betters, his irritable temper, and the rest—give a false air of identity which is very noteworthy. The third portrait is said to have been the farthest from life, except in some physical peculiarities, of the three. "Tickler," whose original was Wilson's maternal uncle Robert Sym, an Edinburgh "writer," and something of a humorist in the flesh, is very skilfully made to hold the position of common-sense intermediary between the two originals, North and the Shepherd. He has his own peculiarities, but he has also a habit of bringing his friends down from their altitudes in a Voltairian fashion which is of great benefit to the dialogues, and may be compared to Peacock's similar use of some of his characters. The few occasional interlocutors are of little moment, with one exception; and the only female characters, Mrs and Miss Gentle, would have been very much better away. They are not in the least life-like, and usually exhibit the namby-pambiness into which Wilson too often fell when he wished to be refined and pathetic. The "English" or half-English characters, who come in sometimes as foils, are also rather of the stick, sticky. On the other hand, the interruptions of Ambrose, the host, and his household, though a little farcical, are well judged. And of the one exception above mentioned, the live Thomas De Quincey, who is brought in without disguise or excuse in some of the very best of the series, it can only be said that the imitation of his written style is extraordinary, and that men who knew his conversation say that the rendering of that is more extraordinary still.

The same designed exaggeration which some uncritical persons have called Rabelaisian (not noticing that the very fault of the *Noctes* is that, unlike Rabelais, their author mixes up probabilities and improbabilities so that there is a perpetual jarring) is maintained throughout the scenery and etceteras. The comfortable but modest accommodations of Ambrose's hotels in Gabriel's Road and Picardy Place are turned into abodes of not particularly tasteful luxury which put Lord Beaconsfield's famous upholstery to shame, and remind one of what they probably suggested, Edgar Poe's equally famous and much more terrible sketch of a model drawing-room. All the plate is carefully described as "silver"; if it had been gold there might have been some humour in it. The "wax" candles and "silken" curtains (if they had been *Arabian Nights* lamps and oriental drapery the same might be said) are always insisted on.

If there is any joke here it seems to lie in the contrast with Wilson's actual habits, which were very simple. For instance, he gives us a gorgeous description of the apparatus of North's solitary confinement when writing for *Blackwood*; his daughter's unvarnished account of the same process agrees exactly as to time, rate of production, and so forth, but substitutes water for the old hock and "Scots pint" (magnum) of claret, a dirty little terra-cotta inkstand for the silver utensil of the *Noctes*, and a single large tallow candle for Christopher's "floods of light." He carried the whim so far as to construct for himself— his *Noctes* self—an imaginary hall-by-the-sea on the Firth of Forth, which in the same way seems to have had an actual resemblance, half of likeness, half of contrast, to the actual Elleray, and to enlarge his own comfortable town house in Gloucester Place to a sort of fairy palace in Moray Place. But that which has most puzzled and shocked readers are the specially Gargantuan passages relating to eating and drinking. The comments made on this seem (he was anything but patient of criticism) to have annoyed Wilson very much; and in some of the later *Noctes* he drops hints that the whole is mere Barmecide business. Unfortunately the same criticism applies to this as to the upholstery—the exaggeration is "done too natural." The Shepherd's consumption of oysters not by dozens but by fifties, the allowance of "six common kettlesfull of water" for the night's toddy ration of the three, North's above-mentioned bottle of old hock at dinner and magnum of claret after, the dinners and suppers and "whets" which appear so often;—all these stop short of the actually incredible, and are nothing more than extremely convivial men of the time, who were also large eaters, would have actually consumed. Lord Alvanley's three hearty suppers, the exploits of the old member of Parliament in Boz's sketch of Bellamy's (I forget his real name, but he was not a myth), and other things might be quoted to show that there is a fatal verisimilitude in the Ambrosian feasts which may, or may not, make them shocking (they don't shock me), but which certainly takes them out of the category of merely humorous exaggeration. The Shepherd's "jugs" numerous as they are (and by the way the Shepherd propounds two absolutely contradictory theories of toddy-making, one of which, according to the instructions of my preceptors in that art, who lived within sight of the hills that look down on Glenlivet, is a damnable heresy) are not in the least like the *seze muiz, deux bussars, et six tupins* of tripe that Gargamelle so rashly devoured. There are men now living, and honoured members of society in Scotland, who admit the soft impeachment of having drunk in their youth twelve or fourteen "double" tumblers at a sitting. Now a double tumbler, be it known to the Southron, is a jorum of toddy to which there go two wineglasses (of course of the old-fashioned size, not our modern goblets) of whisky. "Indeed," said a humorous and indulgent lady correspondent of Wilson's, "indeed, I really think you eat too many oysters at the *Noctes*"; and any one who believes in distributive justice must admit that they did.

If, therefore, the reader is of the modern cutlet-and-cup-of-coffee school of feeding, he will no doubt find the *Noctes* most grossly and palpably gluttonous. If he be a very superior person he will smile at the upholstery. If he objects to horseplay he will be horrified at finding the characters on one occasion engaging in a regular "mill," on more than one corking each other's faces during slumber, sometimes playing at pyramids like the bounding brothers of acrobatic fame, at others indulg-

ing in leap-frog with the servants, permitting themselves practical jokes of all kinds, affecting to be drowned by an explosive haggis, and so forth. Every now and then he will come to a passage at which, without being superfine at all, he may find his gorge rise; though there is nothing quite so bad in the *Noctes* as the picture of the ravens eating a dead Quaker in the *Recreations*, a picture for which Wilson offers a very lame defence elsewhere. He must put all sorts of prejudice, literary, political, and other, in his pocket. He must be prepared not only for constant and very scurrilous flings at "Cockneys" (Wilson extends the term far beyond the Hunt and Hazlitt school, an extension which to this day seems to give a strange delight to Edinburgh journalists), but for the wildest heterodoxies and inconsistencies of political, literary, and miscellaneous judgment, for much bastard verse-prose, for a good many quite uninteresting local and ephemeral allusions, and, of course, for any quantity of Scotch dialect. If all these allowances and provisos are too many for him to make, it is probably useless for him to attempt the *Noctes* at all. He will pretty certainly, with the *Quarterly* reviewer, set their characters down as boozing buffoons, and decline the honour of an invitation to Ambrose's or The Lodge, to Southside or the tent in Ettrick Forest.

But any one who can accommodate himself to these little matters, much more any one who can enter into the spirit of days merrier, more leisurely, and if not less straitlaced than our own, yet lacing their laces in a different fashion, will find the *Noctes* very delightful indeed. The mere high jinks, when the secret of being in the vein with them has been mastered, are seldom unamusing, and sometimes (notably in the long swim out to sea of Tickler and the Shepherd) are quite admirable fooling. No one who has an eye for the literary-dramatic can help, after a few *Noctes* have been read, admiring the skill with which the characters are at once typified and individualised, the substance which they acquire in the reader's mind, the personal interest in them which is excited. And to all this, peculiarly suited for an alternative in these solemn days, has to be added the abundance of scattered and incomplete but remarkable gems of expression and thought that come at every few pages, sometimes at every page, of the series.

Some of the burlesque narratives (such as the Shepherd's Mazeppa-like ride on the Bonassus) are inimitably good, though they are too often spoilt by Wilson's great faults of prolixity and uncertainty of touch. The criticisms, of which there are many, are also extremely unequal, but not a few very fine passages may be found among them. The politics, it must be owned, are not good for much, even from the Tory point of view. But the greatest attraction of the whole, next to its sunshiny heartiness and humour, is to be found in innumerable and indescribable bits, phrases, sentences, short paragraphs, which have, more than anything out of the dialogues of the very best novels, the character and charm of actual conversation. To read a *Noctes* has, for those who have the happy gift of realising literature, not much less than the effect of actually taking part in one, with no danger of headache or indigestion after, and without the risk of being playfully corked, or required to leap the table for a wager, or forced to extemporise sixteen stanzas standing on the mantelpiece. There must be some peculiar virtue in this, for, as is very well known, the usual dialogue leaves the reader more outside of it than almost any other kind of literature.

JAMES MONTGOMERY

THOMAS MOORE

MARY SHELLEY

JAMES FENIMORE COOPER

JOHN WILSON ("CHRISTOPHER NORTH")

JOHN GIBSON LOCKHART

MARY RUSSELL MITFORD

SAMUEL ROGERS

JOHN GIBSON LOCKHART

1794–1854

John Gibson Lockhart was born in Lanarkshire, Scotland, on July 14, 1794, the son of a Presbyterian minister who was descended from landed gentry. He was educated at Glasgow and Oxford universities and was admitted to the Scottish bar in 1816, but his reserved personality made him unsuitable for the legal profession.

Lockhart began contributing to *Blackwood's Edinburgh Magazine* upon its founding in 1817, helping to write the notorious parody *Chaldee MS.* that appeared in the first issue. His cutting wit earned him the nickname "Scorpion" among fellow staff members of the magazine and is much in evidence in his satirical look at the Scottish scene entitled *Peter's Letters to His Kinsfolk* (1819). A romantic side to his nature is revealed in his verse translations, *Ancient Spanish Ballads* (1823). Lockhart was also the author of four novels, including *Adam Blair* (1822), whose theme of a clergyman's seduction attracted a fairly wide readership.

Early in his literary career Lockhart became friendly with Sir Walter Scott, whose daughter Sophia he married in 1820. Through Scott's influence Lockhart was appointed editor of the Tory publication *Quarterly Review* in 1825, and contributed a number of perceptive essays on the Romantic poets; he was also the author of a damaging attack on Tennyson's *Poems*, published in the *Review* in 1833.

Lockhart published a biography of the poet Robert Burns in 1828; it was well received, praised in particular for its sympathetic understanding of its subject. Lockhart's major work was the *Life of Scott* (1837–38), which is often compared favorably to Boswell's biography of Samuel Johnson. At the time of its publication the *Life* was attacked for its depiction of Scott's faults as well as his virtues, but modern critics view it as an artful combination of adulation tempered wittily by a delineation of Scott's foibles.

In his later years Lockhart suffered from chronic ill-health and resigned the editorship of the *Quarterly* in 1853. He died at Abbotsford on November 25, 1854.

Personal

⟨. . .⟩ a precise, brief, active person of considerable faculty, which, however, had shaped itself *gigmanically* only. Fond of quizzing, yet not *very* maliciously. Has a broad black brow, indicating force and penetration, but a lower half of face diminishing into the character at best of distinctness, almost of triviality. Rather liked the man, and shall like to meet him again.—THOMAS CARLYLE, *Journal* (Jan. 21, 1832), cited in James Anthony Froude, *Thomas Carlyle*, 1882, Vol. 2, p. 188

When it is considered what literary celebrity Lockhart has gained so early in life, and how warm and disinterested a friend he has been to me, it argues but little for my sagacity that I scarcely recollect any thing of our first encounters. He was a mischievous Oxford puppy, for whom I was terrified, dancing after the young ladies, and drawing caricatures of every one who came in contact with him. But then I found him constantly in company with all the better rank of people with whom I associated, and consequently it was impossible for me not to meet with him. I dreaded his eye terribly; and it was not without reason, for he was very fond of playing tricks on me, but always in such a way, that it was impossible to lose temper with him. I never parted company with him that my judgment was not entirely jumbled with regard to characters, books, and literary articles of every description.—JAMES HOGG, *Memoir of the Author's Life*, 1832

Among some other places I went to afterwards was John Murray's,—the publisher's,—where I fell in with Lockhart, with whom I have exchanged cards this week, but whom I had not seen. He is the same man he always was and always will be, with the coldest and most disagreeable manners I have ever seen. I wanted to talk with him about Prescott's *Ferdinand and Isabella*, and by a sort of violence done to myself, as well as to him, I did so. He said he had seen it, but had heard no opinion about it. I gave him one with little ceremony, which I dare say he thought was not worth a button; but I did it in a sort of tone of defiance, to which Lockhart's manners irresistibly impelled me, and which I dare say was as judicious with him as any other tone, though I am sure it quite astonished Murray, who looked . . . as if he did not quite comprehend what I was saying.—GEORGE TICKNOR, *Journal* (March 29, 1838), *Life, Letters, and Journals of George Ticknor*, ed. Anna Ticknor, 1876, Vol. 2, p. 147

He has been spoken of as cold, heartless, incapable of friendship. We have written in vain, and his own letters are vainly displayed, if it be not now recognised that the intensity of his affections rivalled, and partly caused, the intensity of his reserve. Garrulous lax affections and emotions are recognised and praised: ready tears, voluble sorrows, win sympathy,—and may have forsaken the heart they tenanted almost in the hour of their expression. Lockhart felt too strongly for words, and his griefs were "too great for tears," as the Greek says. His silence was not so much the result of a stoical philosophy, as of that constitutional and ineradicable ply of nature which, when he was a child, left his cheeks dry while others wept, and ended in a malady of voiceless grief. He was born to be so, and to be misconstrued.

The loyalty of his friendships, and the loyalty of his friends to him, is not of common example. His great devotion to Sir Walter Scott, so unaffected, so enduring, coloured all his life and thought. To have won the entire trust and love of Scott, the singular affection of Carlyle, who saw him so rarely, yet who remembered and regretted him so keenly,—having "fallen in love with him," as it were,—is no ordinary proof of extraordinary qualities in heart and brain.—ANDREW LANG, *The Life and Letters of John Gibson Lockhart*, 1897, Vol. 2, pp. 408–9

As a man of letters, Lockhart is a fascinating, if not a prominent, figure in the history of the earlier half of our century; but to the majority he will never be more than the biographer of Scott, and for them the one important question concerning him will always be: Whether, when judged with all due candour and modesty, he can be pronounced to have been, on the whole, *a good man*. Thankful for the precious legacy he has bequeathed them, they would fain be assured that he who has thus earned their gratitude deserves no less their esteem.—T. HUTCHINSON, *Academy*, Nov. 7, 1896, p. 344

General

At the close of 1836, appeared the first volume of *Memoirs of the Life of Sir Walter Scott, Bart., by J. G. Lockhart, Esq., his Literary Executor*. This work was completed within two years, and a revised and richly illustrated edition immediately followed. It is not necessary to give particulars respecting a work so widely known and so generally liked. To say that its place is next to, and certainly not lower than, Boswell's *Johnson*, is to say no more than the truth. Boswell devotes himself more particularly to what may be called the personality of his hero; Lockhart includes a variety of particulars relative to Scott's contemporaries. The two biographies, in fact, contain a graphic history of British Literature during the greater part of the Georgian era—from the commencement of Johnson's career, to the close of Scott's.

The defect of Lockhart's book is that he devotes too much space to a discussion of the connection between Scott and the Ballantynes. The tone and temper of this discussion are equally out of keeping with the biography and its author's intention of exhibiting Scott in a favorable light. The executors of James Ballantyne replied, in a voluminous pamphlet, the object of which was to show that Ballantyne was more sinned against than sinning. Lockhart retorted, in a bitter publication called *The Ballantyne Humbug Handled*. It was contemptuous and personal. Then followed a rejoinder, going closely into detail, in which they showed how constantly Scott used to draw on Ballantyne for money, and how improvident he was. To this there was no reply, but the discussion, which was provoked by Lockhart's aspersions, did not tend to exalt Scott in public estimation.—R. SHELTON MACKENZIE, "Memoir of John Gibson Lockhart," *Noctes Ambrosianae*, 1854, Vol. 3, pp. xiii–xiv

In 1820 Mr. Lockhart published his first novel, *Valerius, a Roman Story*, which immediately took its place among the secondary Scottish novels, as those were called which would have been first but for Scott's series. That book was full of interest, and of promise of moral beauty which was not fulfilled. The influences then surrounding the author were eminently favorable. He always said that the happiest years of his life were those spent at Chiefswood. During those few years of domestic peace he seems to have had a stronger hold of reality than either before or after. The inveterate skepticism of his nature was kept down, and he found dearer delights than that of giving pain. Other novels followed,—*Reginald Dalton, Adam Blair*, and *Gilbert Earle*. All are more remarkable for power in the delineation of passion, and for beauty of writing, than for higher qualities. Carlyle has described Lockhart's style as "good, clear, direct, and nervous:" and so it is; and with genuine beauty in it, too, both of music and of pathos. And of

all he ever wrote, nothing is probably so dear to his readers as his accounts, in his Life of his father-in-law, of the pleasures of Chiefswood, when Scott used to sit under the great ash, with all the dogs about him, and help the young people with their hospitable arrangements, cooling the wine in the brook, and proposing to dine out of doors, to get rid of the inconvenience of small rooms and few servants.—HARRIET MARTINEAU, "John Gibson Lockhart" (1854), *Biographical Sketches*, 1869, pp. 30–31

J. G. Lockhart, though Scott's son-in-law, was not his disciple in four novels of a modern and more or less psychological class. *Adam Blair* (1822) is the best of these, and escapes the frigidity of the author's one classical romance, *Valerius* (1821), a highly accomplished attempt to resuscitate domestic society under Trajan.—EDMUND GOSSE, *A Short History of Modern English Literature*, 1897, p. 327

Works

PETER'S LETTERS TO HIS KINSFOLK

Peter's Letters to His Kinsfolk, a worthless book, will give you some idea of the state of literature in Edinr at this time: it was in great vogue three years ago, but is now dead as mutton.—THOMAS CARLYLE, Letter to John A. Carlyle (Nov. 11, 1823)

I have had some hesitation about introducing the next letter—which refers to the then recent publication of a sort of mock-tour in Scotland, entitled *Peter's Letters to His Kinsfolk*. Nobody but a very young and a very thoughtless person could have dreamt of putting forth such a book; yet the Epistles of the imaginary Dr. Morris have been so often denounced as a mere string of libels, that I think it fair to show how much more leniently Scott judged of them at the time. Moreover, his letter is a good specimen of the liberal courtesy with which, on all occasions, he treated the humblest aspirants in literature. Since I have alluded to *Peter's Letters* at all, I may as well take the opportunity of adding that they were not wholly the work of one hand.—JOHN GIBSON LOCKHART, *Memoirs of the Life of Sir Walter Scott*, 1837–38, Ch. 45

What an acquisition it would have been to our general information to have had such a work written, I do not say fifty, but even five-and-twenty years ago; and how much of grave and gay might then have been preserved, as it were, in amber, which have now mouldered away. When I think that at an age not much younger than yours I knew Black, Ferguson, Robertson, Erskine, Adam Smith, John Home, &c. &c., and at least saw Burns, I can appreciate better than any one the value of a work which, like this, would have handed them down to posterity in their living colours.—SIR WALTER SCOTT, Letter to John Gibson Lockhart (July 19, 1819), cited in John Gibson Lockhart, *Memoirs of the Life of Sir Walter Scott*, 1837–38, Ch. 45

A prying criticism may discern a few of those contraband epithets and slipshod sentences, more excusable in *young* Peter's Letters to His Kinsfolk, where, indeed, they are thickly sown, than in the production of a grave Aristarch of British criticism.—WILLIAM H. PRESCOTT, "Sir Walter Scott" (1838), *Biographical and Critical Miscellanies*, 1845, p. 149

In *Blackwood*, for February, 1819, had appeared a review of *Peter's Letters to His Kinsfolk*,—a work professing to be written by Dr. Peter Morris, of Pensharpe Hall, Aberystwith. No such book was then published, or written. It was said to contain the Doctor's letters from Edinburgh and Glasgow, during a visit to both places in the winter of 1818–19, treating most freely indeed of the Whigs of Edinburgh—Scottish University Education—the *Edinburgh* and *Quarterly Reviews*—the state of society in Edinburgh and Glasgow—the bar of Scotland, with sketches of its leading members—the famous Glasgow punch —the state of religion, &c. This review, apparently written by Mordecai Mullion, (one of Lockhart's numerous eidolons of the pen,) excited so much curiosity, that *Peter's Letters* was greatly inquired for. In the following month (March, 1819) a further and fuller review was given, with copious extracts, including descriptions of Clerk, Cranstoun, and Jeffrey, (the leading lawyers of the place and time,) and the sensation thus created and kept up was so considerable that the actual composition and publication of the work was determined on.

Accordingly, *Peter's Letters* was put into type as fast as written, and emanated, in July, 1819, from Blackwood's as the "second edition." It was, and continues to be, a work of great interest. Twenty years afterwards, Lockhart said, "Nobody but a very young and very thoughtless person could have dreamt of putting forth such a book." Scott, after reading the work twice over, expressed his opinion that Dr. Morris had "got over his ground admirably," only that the general turn of the book was perhaps too favorable, both to the state of Scottish public society and of individual character. He added that, every half century, Dr. Morris should revive "to record the fleeting manners of the age, and the interesting features of those who will be known only to posterity by their works."

There was abundant outcry against *Peter's Letters*, at first, for the author had keenly assaulted and ridiculed the Edinburgh Whigs, but the merit of the work was great, and has carried it into repeated editions. The descriptions of Edinburgh and Glasgow are appreciative and racy,—the sketches of Jeffrey and his distinguished contemporaries are forcibly, yet delicately done,—the glance at Henry Mackenzie has produced a sun-portrait, so true is it in all respects,—Wilson, Hogg, Playfair, Brewster, Jameson, and Lord Buchan are portraits. So are the theatrical etchings, and the broad, Raeburn-like full-lengths of the Scottish bar, judges and advocates. Very vivid, too, are the delineations of leading book-makers and booksellers,—the *con amore* criticisms upon the Fine Arts in Scotland,—the faithful account of Abbotsford, and its minstrel lord,—the clerical groupings of the General Assembly of the Scottish Church,—the anatomic dissection of society in Edinburgh and Glasgow,—and, in its strange mixture of serious feeling and subdued fun, the account of a Sacrament Sabbath in the country. In truth, the mélange was very clever, and made its way.

Some of its success was collateral. The work contained several well-engraved portraits, (some, like Hogg's, dashed with caricature,) which gave it great value. Among these were Professor Leslie, Playfair, and Jameson; my venerable relative, Henry Mackenzie, author of *The Man of Feeling*; John Clerk, of Eldin; Jeffrey; Macqueen of Braxfield; Allan, the painter; Walter Scott; Alison, author of the *Essay on the Principles of Taste*, and father of the historian; the Ettrick Shepherd; Dr. Chalmers; and John Wilson. All have departed, but their portraits, as they looked five-and-thirty years ago, flourish greenly and truly in *Peter's Letters*.—R. SHELTON MACKENZIE, "Memoir of John Gibson Lockhart," *Noctes Ambrosianae*, 1854, Vol. 3, pp. v–vi

———

GEORGE SAINTSBURY
"John Gibson Lockhart"
English Prose, ed. Henry Craik
1896, Volume 5, pp. 313–17

Lockhart, one of the most distinguished of that class of men of letters whose career has been determined by the spread of periodical literature during the nineteenth century, stands almost alone as an example of certain disadvantages which attend this kind of literary production. That no complete edition of his work exists is not surprising; it is usual and certainly salutary, that editions of writers who have been journalists should be incomplete. But Lockhart, almost alone of the great journalists of the century, offers to the critic the embarrassing subject of a man whose work in periodicals, though it was admittedly very large indeed, has never been authoritatively collected, and cannot be identified in the papers where it appeared without access to records always confidential, and perhaps now not in all cases existent. The article on Theodore Hook he acknowledged and reprinted. But all the rest of the matter contributed during nearly thirty years to the *Quarterly* is still unacknowledged; it is to this day uncertain whether some of the famous *Blackwood* articles—that on Keats, the "Zeta" attack on the Cockneys, the Baron Lauerwinkel attack on Playfair—were Lockhart's or not; and his contributions to *Fraser* are, I believe, the least traceable of all. It is true that students of his acknowledged and independent work, of his letters, and of the general body of history or fiction about him, will never be at a loss for a pretty strong opinion as to what is and is not Lockhart's. But it is of course impossible to deliver such an opinion with the certainty which attends the judgment of unquestionably authentic work.

The reference just made to the "history or fiction" about Lockhart concerns a matter of no slight importance in the estimate of his work, though one which cannot receive extended treatment here. A legend was early formed—assisted no doubt if not actually started by the youthful description of himself by himself as a "scorpion which delights to sting the faces of men" in the famous *Chaldee Manuscript*—attributing to Lockhart not merely the possession of a biting pen, but the disposition to use it in a manner very aggressive and not too scrupulous. The uproarious Ishmaelism of *Blackwood* and the more sedate carping of the *Quarterly* were successively laid to his charge; and in some cases the matter reached, in others it very nearly reached, the then usual arbitrament of the pistol. Some pains have been taken to show that Lockhart was not to blame in the complicated and unhappy affair that led to the death of John Scott, editor of the *London Magazine*; and still later, the previously unpublished letters of Sir Walter have come to the support of those who take this view by showing that at all events the Duke of Wellington pronounced his conduct unimpeachable, a sentence in a case of honour not easily to be set aside. Charges, not better supported but not so easily refuted, have been brought against him in reference to Keats, to Playfair, and others; while his pamphlet war with the Ballantynes, as a sequel to his *Life of Scott*, has not seemed, even to some well-disposed judges, to have been conducted in a wholly creditable manner.

The point, however, chiefly or rather solely important here, is that—whether Lockhart did or not strain the licence of a time when party and other feeling ran very high, and when the responsibilities of anonymous journalism were not so strictly construed even by men of honour, as by men of honour they are now supposed to be—he was at any rate capable of using the pen for purposes both of offence and defence in a very dangerous manner. And of this there can be no doubt. Young as he was at the time of *Peter's Letters* his formidable powers are clearly perceptible there; the famous Tennyson review more than ten years later (never formally acknowledged, but now attributed on the most certain evidence) is a masterpiece of what has since been termed "slating"; and there are passages in the "Theodore Hook," friendly and apologetic as it is, which would show any intelligent reader what Lockhart's sting would be like when he chose to use it.

He was, however, very much more than a satirist and a snarler. From the first he seems to have had the command of a really excellent style—a style in which a few slight oversights may be noted here and there, but which in the main is one of the very best examples of a class too generally undervalued—the class showing the latest phase of the "classical" style of the eighteenth century, free from over-classicism, slightly suppled and modernised by foreign and vernacular influences, but as yet untouched by the tendencies to lawlessness, to extreme ornament, and to other excesses which were successively illustrated in Landor, in De Quincey, in Carlyle, and in Mr. Ruskin. And he put this style, in his avowed and substantive work, to most excellent use, assisting its operation by the display of good reading, of sound, if sometimes slightly grudging criticism, and above all of a manly and judicial sense with which few have shown themselves better provided.

The minor works above mentioned—the *Napoleon*, the *Burns* (a really admirable book), and the miniature sketch of *Theodore Hook*, first written for the *Quarterly* and then separately printed, display these qualities well enough. The Hook, in particular, is the equal of any essay of Macaulay's in finish, grasp, and ease, superior to most of Macaulay's essays in fairness and freedom from mere advocacy, and certainly not the inferior of any in literary merit for those who can taste sobriety as well as brilliancy of literary manner.

The novels, admitting of more variety of handling, though perhaps not showing their writer to be an absolute master of the novel, increase the estimate of his general literary powers very greatly. *Valerius* is an estimable attempt in a kind where hardly anyone has succeeded; some vivid sketches of a long past Oxford, relieve *Reginald Dalton*; and even the excessive gloom and defective interest of *Matthew Wald* do not obscure what is certainly evident in Lockhart's work, and is one of its most interesting features, the existence of very deep feeling under a cynical exterior. But *Adam Blair* is almost a masterpiece in concentrated power and passion; and though, like most novels, it lends itself ill to excerpt, it will show Lockhart's mastery of that perilous "grand style," the form of which in each generation is more apt to seem tawdry or ludicrous than grand to the next.

But it would be folly to deny that without the *Scott* Lockhart could not pretend to anything like the position which he at present holds; and would have to be left to the appreciation of a few students of literature like-minded with himself. The charm and abundance of the letters and diaries which the book contains, together with the modesty and reticence of the editorial appearance in it, have, perhaps, lowered the general opinion of the credit due to Lockhart himself. But this will certainly not be the case with those who have been accustomed to sift and weigh the constituents of literary excellence. Rather will their admiration for Lockhart be increased, knowing as they do how perilous the handling of such matters as the diaries and letters of a man of genius is, and how rarely the task of marshalling and arranging so vast a

mass of miscellaneous material has been successfully performed. The architectural skill of the arrangement must be patent; and it was no surprise to good judges when the full publication of the *Diary* and the *Letters* the other day showed that Lockhart had been not less judicial in choosing his materials, than skilful in using them. Add the taste, the sense, nay the feeling—little credit as Lockhart has usually received on this last score—which he displayed in the original contributions, the excellence of the writing, the masterly infusion of enough and not too much anecdote and humour, and it will I think be hard to find a greater biography. No doubt the respective partisans of Lockhart and Boswell—pair strangely different in everything but success as biographers, and almost as different in the character of that success—will always award the prize according to their partisanship. The wiser few will say, "Give us both!"

HUGH WALKER
From *The Age of Tennyson*
1897, pp. 136–39

John Gibson Lockhart was a man of many gifts and accomplishments, a good scholar, a keen satirist and critic, a powerful novelist, an excellent translator. He was accomplished with the pencil as well as with the pen, and some of his caricatures are at once irresistibly amusing and profoundly true. His 'Scotch judge' and 'Scotch minister' would make the reputation of a number of *Punch*. His biting wit won for him the *sobriquet* of 'the Scorpion;' but notwithstanding his sting he won and retained through life many warm friends. He was trained for the Scottish bar, but attached himself to the literary set of *Blackwood*, in which Christopher North was the most striking figure. With him and Hogg Lockhart was concerned in an exceedingly amusing skit, the famous *Chaldee Manuscript*; but the joke gave so much offence that this 'promising babe' was strangled in the cradle. A good deal of more serious literary work belongs to the period before 1830, —the novels, a mass of criticism, and the *Spanish Ballads*. Then too was formed the connexion which opened to Lockhart the great work of his life. He was introduced to Scott in 1818. The acquaintance prospered. Scott liked the clever young man, Scott's daughter liked him still better, and in 1820 Lockhart married Sophia Scott. Largely through her father's influence he was appointed editor of the *Quarterly Review*, an office which he held until 1853, and in which he became to a very great degree, both by reason of what he wrote and of what he printed, responsible for the tone of criticism at the time.

Lockhart undoubtedly shared that excessive personality which was the blot of criticism, and especially of the *Blackwood* school, in his generation. He has been charged with the *Blackwood* articles on Keats, and with the *Quarterly* article on *Jane Eyre*, but he may now be acquitted of both these sins. It was however Lockhart who wrote the *Quarterly* article on Tennyson's early poems; but this, though bad in tone and excessively severe, is to a large extent critically sound. So far as they can be traced, Lockhart's criticisms are such as might be expected from his mind,—clear, incisive and vigorous. They are however often unsympathetic and harsh, because criticism was then too apt to be interpreted as fault-finding, and Lockhart could not wholly free himself from the influence of a vicious tradition.

But it is by his *Life of Scott* (1837–1838) that Lockhart will live in literature. He had in an ample measure the first of all requirements in a biographer, personal acquaintance with the man whose life he wrote. Almost from the time of his introduction, and certainly from the date of his marriage, Lockhart's relations with Scott were of the closest; and though he was not personally familiar with the facts of Scott's earlier life, he knew quite enough to understand the springs of the man's character. Moreover, in the autobiographical fragment and in the endless stores of family and friendly anecdotes open to him he had ample means of making good the deficiency. For among Lockhart's advantages is to be reckoned the fact that he had not merely married into the family, but had married, as it were, into the circle of friends. The *Life of Scott* shows that the families of Abbotsford, of Chiefswood and of Huntley Burn (the last Scott's great friends the Fergusons) were for many purposes only one larger family.

There are certain dangers, as well as great advantages, to the biographer even in intimate friendship. Misused in one way, it lowers the biographer's own character; misused in another, it either lowers or unnaturally exalts that of his subject. Boswell, employing his materials with excellent effect for the purposes of his book, degrades himself. Froude, making a mistake of another sort, exaggerates all the less lovable characteristics of Carlyle; while there are multitudes who paint pictures not of flesh and blood, but of impossible saints and heroes. 'A love passing the love of biographers' was Macaulay's phrase for the excess of hero-worship. Lockhart has avoided all these errors. When his book was read the contradictory charges were brought against him, on the one hand of having exaggerated Scott's virtues and concealed his faults, and on the other of ungenerous and derogatory criticism. We may be sure that Lockhart's temptation, if he felt any, was rather to 'extenuate' than to 'set down in malice.' But, with a noble confidence in a noble character, he does not extenuate. To describe Scott as a mere money-lover would be untrue; yet many have felt that there is a fault in his relation to wealth, and Lockhart uses just the right words when he says, 'I dare not deny that he set more of his affections, during great part of his life, upon worldly things, wealth among others, than might have become such an intellect;' and he gives just the right explanation when he goes on to trace this defect to its root in the imagination. In his treatment of the commercial matters in which Scott was involved, Lockhart is equally judicial.

The tact of Lockhart deserves as much praise as his fairness of judgment. As regards part of his work, he was put to the test a few years ago by the publication of Scott's *Journal*. Lockhart had made liberal extracts from this journal, explaining at the same time that passages were necessarily suppressed because of their bearing upon persons then alive. A comparison of his extracts with the journal now accessible *in extenso* shows how skilfully he suppressed what was likely to give pain, while at the same time producing much the same general impression as the whole document leaves.

A biography, like a letter, may be said to have two authors, the man written about and the person who writes. Scott certainly gave Lockhart the greatest assistance, both by what he wrote and by what he was. At the beginning the delightful fragment of autobiography, towards the end the profoundly interesting *Journal*, and all through the free, manly, large-hearted letters, were materials of the choicest sort. Scott himself moreover, genial, cordial, of manifold activity, a centre of racy anecdote, was a person whom it was far more easy to set in an attractive frame than any mere literary recluse. Many could have produced a good life of such a man. Lockhart's special praise is that he has written a great one. Except Johnson, there is no English man of letters so well depicted as Scott. Lockhart's taste and style are excellent. The caustic wit which ran riot in the young *Blackwood* reviewer is restrained by the experience of years and by the necessities of the subject. Lockhart's own part of the narrative is told in grave, temperate English, simple almost to severity, but in a high degree flexible. In the brighter parts there is a pleasant lightness in Lockhart's touch; in the more serious parts he is weighty and powerful; and on occasion, especially towards the end, there is a restrained emotion which proves that part of his wonderful success is due to the fact that his heart was in his work.

SAMUEL ROGERS

1763–1855

Samuel Rogers was born at Stoke Newington, a village that now forms part of London, on July 30, 1763. He was educated at private schools in Hackney and by private tutors, and entered the family bank at an early age at his father's request. The death of his father in 1793 left Rogers with a controlling interest in the bank and an annual income of £5,000. After this a younger brother took over the responsibilities of actually managing the bank, allowing Rogers to devote himself to literary and social pursuits.

Rogers's literary career began with the publication of some short essays in the *Gentleman's Magazine* in 1781. His first volume of poems, *An Ode to Superstition*, was published anonymously in 1786, and in 1792 he published his most successful book, *The Pleasures of Memory*. Set in the villages of his childhood, this poem went into four editions in its first year, and by 1816 more than 23,000 copies had been sold. Among Rogers's later publications are *The Voyage of Columbus* (1810); *Jacqueline* (1814); *Italy* (1822–28; later illustrated by J. M. W. Turner and T. Stothard); and *Poems* (1832).

In 1803 Rogers built a house in St. James's Street, Westminster, where he entertained many leading literary, social, and political figures, including Charles James Fox, Richard Brinsley Sheridan, Thomas Moore, Francis, Lord Jeffrey, Lord Byron, Charles Lamb, William Wordsworth, and Lord Holland. Rogers's friend Alexander Dyce kept a detailed record of the anecdotes he heard at these gatherings and published them in 1856 as *Recollections of the Table-Talk of Samuel Rogers*. Rogers's own notes on these conversations were published by his nephew in 1859 as *Recollections*. In addition to these social activities Rogers was a generous patron, helping to support such authors as Sheridan and Wordsworth. Rogers died on December 18, 1855.

Personal

Rogers is silent,—and, it is said, severe. When he does talk, he talks well; and, on all subjects of taste, his delicacy of expression is pure as his poetry. If you enter his house—his drawing-room—his library—you of yourself say, this is not the dwelling of a common mind. There is not a gem, a coin, a book thrown aside on his chimney-piece, his sofa, his table, that does not bespeak an almost fastidious elegance in the possessor. But this very delicacy must be the misery of his existence. Oh the jarrings his disposition must have encountered through life!—GEORGE GORDON, LORD BYRON, *Journal*, Nov. 22, 1813

I think you very fortunate in having Rogers at Rome. Show me a more kindly and friendly man; 2, one from good manners, knowledge fun taste and observation more agreeable; 3, a man of more strict political integrity, and of better character in private life. If I were to chuse any Englishman in *foreign parts* whom I should chuse to blunder upon, it should be Rogers. —SYDNEY SMITH, Letter to Lady Holland (Feb. 1, 1815)

At parting, Rogers gave me a gold-mounted pair of glasses, which I will not part with in a hurry. I really like S. R., and have always found him most friendly.—SIR WALTER SCOTT, *Journal*, May 25, 1828

⟨. . .⟩ Rogers said that we must have the talk out; so we are to meet at his house again to breakfast. What a delightful house it is! It looks out on the Green Park just at the most pleasant point. The furniture has been selected with a delicacy of taste quite unique. Its value does not depend on fashion, but must be the same while the fine arts are held in any esteem. In the drawing-room, for example, the chimney-pieces are carved by Flaxman into the most beautiful Grecian forms. The book-case is painted by Stothard, in his very best manner, with groups from Chaucer, Shakspeare, and Boccaccio. The pictures are not numerous; but every one is excellent. In the dining-room there are also some beautiful paintings. But the three most remarkable objects in that room are, I think, a cast of Pope taken after death by Roubiliac; a noble model in terra-cotta by Michael Angelo, from which he afterward made one of his finest statues, that of Lorenzo de' Medici; and, lastly, a mahogany table on which stands an antique vase.—THOMAS BABINGTON MACAULAY, Letter to Hannah M. Macaulay (June 25, 1831), cited in G. Otto Trevelyan, *The Life and Letters of Lord Macaulay*, 1876, Vol. 1, p. 206

Rogers (an elegant, politely malignant old lady, I think) is in town and probably I might see him.—THOMAS CARLYLE, *Journal* (Jan. 13, 1832), cited in James Anthony Froude, *Thomas Carlyle*, 1882, Vol. 2, p. 187

I breakfasted with Mr. Rogers *tête-à-tête*, staying with him from ten till one o'clock. A very agreeable morning, and I left him with feelings of enhanced respect. There was very little of that severity of remark for which he is reproached. Candour and good sense marked all he said.—HENRY CRABB ROBINSON, *Diary*, Nov. 29, 1835

Did I tell you, or Mr. Martin, that Rogers the poet, at eighty-three or four years of age, bore the bank robbery with the light-hearted bearing of a man 'young and bold,' went out

to dinner two or three times the same week, and said witty things on his own griefs. One of the other partners went to bed instead, and was not likely, I heard, to 'get over it.' I felt quite glad and proud for Rogers. He was in Germany last year, and this summer in Paris; but he *first* went to see Wordsworth at the Lakes.

It is a fine thing when a light burns so clear down into the socket, isn't it? I, who am not a devout admirer of the *Pleasures of Memory*, do admire this perpetual youth and untired energy; it is a fine thing to my mind. Then, there are other noble characteristics about this Rogers. A common friend said the other day to Mr. Kenyon, 'Rogers hates me, I know. He is always saying bitter speeches in relation to me, and yesterday he said so and so. *But*,' he continued, 'if I were in distress, there is one man in the world to whom I would go without doubt and without hesitation, at once, and as to a brother, and *that* man is Rogers.' Not that I would choose to be obliged to a man who hated me; but it is an illustration of the fact that if Rogers is bitter in his words, which we all know he is, he is always benevolent and generous in his deeds. He makes an epigram on a man, and gives him a thousand pounds; and the deed is the truer expression of his own nature. An uncommon development of character, in any case.—ELIZABETH BARRETT BROWNING, Letter to Mrs. Martin (Dec. 1844)

Forster called, went with him to Rogers. Found the old man very cheerful, thinner than when I last saw him, but in very good spirits. He told all his stories 'over again'. . . . Spoke of Scott, Byron, and Moore, and of his own poetry, quoting us a particularly fine line, 'Their very shadows consecrate the ground.' Took leave of dear old Rogers once more. I think indeed for the last time. I cannot make out his character. He is surely good-natured, with philanthropic and religious feelings, but his fondness for saying a sharp thing shakes one's certainty in him; his apparent desire, too, to produce effect, I think, sometimes awakens doubts of his sincerity in some minds. —WILLIAM CHARLES MACREADY, *Diary*, May 4, 1851

There is something preternatural in the cold, clear, marbly paleness that pervades, and, as it were, penetrates his features to a depth that seems to preclude all change, even that of death itself. Yet there is nothing in the least degree painful or repulsive in the sight, nothing that is suggestive of death, or even of decay—but, on the contrary, something that seems to speak beforehand of that immortality at which this poet has so earnestly aimed, and of which he is entitled to entertain so fair a hope. It is scarcely fanciful to say that the *living* bust of the author of *Human Life*, *The Pleasures of Memory*, &c., can scarcely be looked upon without calling to mind the bust of marble, sculptured by some immortal hand, which he so well deserves to have consecrated to him in the Temple of Fame. —P. G. PATMORE, *My Friends and Acquaintance*, 1854, Vol. 1, p. 160

Rogers never quite got over the feeling of social inequality with which he started. We once heard him exclaim, with a burst of bitterness: 'I hate the aristocracy, but I love their women.' It should be added that he had a morbid aversion for what he called 'dog and horse men.' He had omitted to observe how completely the coarseness and ignorance which was supposed, or at least declared by novelists and dramatists, to mark the country gentlemen of his youth, have been rubbed off and refined away by increased facilities of intercourse and the resulting cultivation of all classes.—ABRAHAM HAYWARD, "Samuel Rogers" (1856), *Selected Essays*, 1879, Vol. 1, pp. 133–34

Whatever place may be assigned to Samuel Rogers among poets, he deserves to hold the highest place among men of taste; not merely taste for this or that, but of general good taste in all things. He was the only man I have ever known (not an artist) who felt the beauties of art like an artist. He was too quiet to exercise the influence he should have maintained among the patrons of art; but, as far as his own patronage extended, it was most useful. He employed, and always spoke his mind in favour of, Flaxman, Stothard, and Turner, when they were little appreciated by their countrymen. The proof of his superior judgment to that of any contemporary collector of art or *vertu* is to be found in the fact that there was nothing in his house that was not valuable. In most other collections with which I am acquainted, however fine the works of art, or however rare the objects of curiosity, I have always found something that betrayed a want of taste—an indifferent picture, a copy passing for an original, or something vulgar in the way of ornament. Then, too, his collection was entirely formed by himself, whereas most of the great collections of pictures of the beginning of the present century were formed under the direction of the most respectable dealers—men whose characters warranted their honesty.

Those who are disposed to think the worst of Mr. Rogers, say that, by the severity of his remarks, he delighted in giving pain. I know that, by the kindliness of his remarks, and still more by the kindliness of his acts, he delighted to give pleasure.—CHARLES ROBERT LESLIE, *Autobiographical Recollections*, ed. Tom Taylor, 1860, pp. 155–56

Spedding (of course) used to deny that R. deserved his ill Reputation: but I never heard any one else deny it. All his little malignities (unless the Epigram on Ward be his) are dead along with his little sentimentalities; while Byron's Scourge hangs over his Memory. The only one who, so far as I have seen, has given any idea of his little cavilling style, is Mrs. Trench in her Letters.—EDWARD FITZGERALD, Letter to W. F. Pollock (Nov. 20, 1872)

"Has Rogers written any thing lately?" asked somebody; to which another replied,—"No, I believe not. Nothing but a couplet."

"Nothing but a couplet!" exclaimed Sydney Smith. "Why, what would you have? When Rogers produces a couplet, he goes to bed:

> And the caudle is made:
> And the knocker is tied:
> And straw is laid down:

And when his friends send to inquire,—'Mr. Rogers is as well as can be expected.'"—HARRIET MARTINEAU, *Autobiography*, ed. Maria Weston Chapman, 1877, Vol. 1, p. 325

Mr. Rogers's inveterate tongue-gall was like an irresistible impulse, and he certainly bestowed it occasionally, without the least provocation, upon persons whom he professed to like. He was habitually kind to me, and declared he was fond of me.

⟨. . .⟩ when I used to go and sit with Mr. Rogers, I never asked him what I should read to him without his putting into my hands his own poems, which always lay by him on his table.—FRANCES ANN KEMBLE, *Records of Later Life*, 1882, p. 66

You could not fancy, when you looked upon him, that you saw a good man. It was a repulsive countenance; to say it was ugly would be to pay it a compliment, and I verily believe it was indicative of a naturally shriveled heart and contracted soul. What we might have done is surely recorded as well as what we have done, and God will call us to account for the good we have omitted to do, as well as the evil we have committed. Such is the teaching of the New Testament. With enormous power to do good, how did Rogers use it? If he lent—and it was seldom he did—to a distressed brother of the pen, he required the return of the loan with interest—when it could be had; if he gave, it was grudgingly and with a shrug. He was prudence personified; some one said of him: "I am sure that as a baby he never fell down unless he was pushed, but walked from chair to chair in the drawing-room, steadily and quietly, till he reached a place where the sunbeams fell on the carpet."

In all I have heard and read concerning him I can not find that he had at any time in his long life "learned the *luxury* of doing good." Yet his means of increasing the happiness, or alleviating the misery, of others were large, and his opportunities immense.—S. C. HALL, *Retrospect of a Long Life*, 1883, pp. 370–71

General

The Pleasures of Memory, by Mr. Rogers, is another effort of the modern muses which calls for admiration; the subject is happily chosen, and its polished flow of verse and tender sentiment have justly made it a favourite with the public.—NATHAN DRAKE, *Literary Hours*, 1798–1820, No. 29

I can visit the justly-admired author of *The Pleasures of Memory*, and find myself with a friend, who together with the brightest genius possesses elegance of manners and excellence of heart. He tells me he remembers the day of our first meeting at Mr. Dilly's; I also remember it, and though his modest unassuming nature held back and shrunk from all appearances of ostentation and display of talents, yet even then I take credit for discovering a promise of good things to come, and suspected him of holding secret commerce with the Muse, before the proof appeared in shape of one of the most beautiful and harmonious poems in our language. I do not say that he has not ornamented the age he lives in, though he were to stop where he is, but I hope he will not so totally deliver himself over to the Arts as to neglect the Muses; and I now publicly call upon Samuel Rogers to answer to his name, and stand forth in the title page of some future work that shall be in substance greater, in dignity of subject more sublime, and in purity of versification not less charming than his poem above-mentioned.—RICHARD CUMBERLAND, *Memoirs*, 1807, Vol. 2, pp. 229–30

> Absent or present, still to thee,
>   My friend, what magic spells belong!
> As all can tell, who share, like me,
>   In turn thy converse, and thy song.
> But when the dreaded hour shall come
>   By Friendship ever deemed too nigh,
> And "MEMORY" o'er her Druid's tomb
>   Shall weep that aught of thee can die,
> How fondly will she then repay
>   Thy homage offered at her shrine,
> And blend, while ages roll away,
>   *Her* name immortally with *thine*!
>   —GEORGE GORDON, LORD BYRON, "Lines
>   Written on a Blank Leaf of *The Pleasures of
>   Memory*," 1812

Question

Nose and chin would shame a knocker;
Wrinkles that would puzzle Cocker;
Mouth which marks the envious Scorner
With a Scorpion in each Corner
Curling its quick tail to sting you
In the place that most may wring you;
Eyes of leadlike hue, and gummy;
Carcass picked out from some Mummy,
Bowels (but they were forgotten
Save the Liver and that's rotten),
Skin all sallow, flesh all sodden,
Form the Devil would frighten G-d in;
Is't a Corpse stuck up for show?
Galvanised at times to go?
With the Scripture in Connection
New proof of the resurrection?
Vampire, Ghost, or Ghoul, what is it?
I would walk ten miles to miss it.

Answer

Many Passengers arrest one
To demand the same free question.
Shorter's my reply and franker,
That's the bard, the beau, and banker.
Yet if you could bring about
Just to turn him inside out,
Satan's self would seem less sooty,
And his present aspect—Beauty.
Mark that—(as he masks the bilious)
Air so softly supercilious—
Chastened bow, and mock humility
Almost sickened to Servility,
Hear his tone (which is to talking
That which creeping is to walking
Now on all fours, now on tiptoe)
Hear the tales he lends his lip to,
Little hints of heavy scandals
Every friend in turn he handles,
All which women or which men do
Glides forth in an innuendo,
Cloathed in odds and ends of humour,
Herald of each paltry rumour,
From divorces down to dresses,
Woman's frailties, Man's excesses,
All which Life presents of evil
Make for him a constant revel.
You're his foe, for that he fears you,
And in absence blasts and sears you!
You're his friend, for that he hates you,
First caresses, and then baits you—
Darting on the opportunity
When to do it with impunity;
You are neither, then he'll flatter,
Till he finds some trait for Satire,
Hunts your weak point out, then shows it
Where it injures to disclose it,
In the mode that's most invidious,
Adding every trait that's hideous—
From the bile whose blackening river
Rushes through his Stygian liver.

Then he thinks himself a lover—
Why? I really can't discover,
In his mind, age, face, or figure;
Viper Broth might give him vigour,—
Let him keep the cauldron steady,
He the venom has already.
For his faults he has but *one*

'Tis but Envy when all's done:
He but pays the pain he suffers
Clipping like a pair of Snuffers
Lights which ought to burn the brighter
For this temporary blighter;
He's the Cancer of his Species
And will eat himself to pieces,
Plague personified and Famine,
Devil, with *such* delight in damning,
That if at the resurrection
Unto him the free selection
Of his future could be given—
'Twould be rather Hell than Heaven.

For his Merits, would you know 'em?
Once he wrote a pretty poem.—
—GEORGE GORDON, LORD BYRON, "Question
and Answer," 1818

⟨. . .⟩ he is a very lady-like poet. He is an elegant, but feeble writer. He wraps up obvious thoughts in a glittering cover of fine words; is full of enigmas with no meaning to them; is studiously inverted, and scrupulously far-fetched; and his verses are poetry, chiefly because no particle, line, or syllable of them reads like prose. He differs from Milton in this respect, who is accused of having inserted a number of prosaic lines in *Paradise Lost*. This kind of poetry, which is a more minute and inoffensive species of the Della Cruscan, is like the game of asking what one's thoughts are like. It is a tortuous, tottering, wriggling, fidgetty translation of every thing from the vulgar tongue, into all the tantalizing, teasing, tripping, lisping *mimminee-pimminee* of the highest brilliancy and fashion of poetical diction. You have nothing like truth of nature or simplicity of expression. The fastidious and languid reader is never shocked by meeting, from the rarest chance in the world, with a single homely phrase or intelligible idea. You cannot see the thought for the ambiguity of the language, the figure for the finery, the picture for the varnish. The whole is refined, and frittered away into an appearance of the most evanescent brilliancy and tremulous imbecility.—There is no other fault to be found with the *Pleasures of Memory*, than a want of taste and genius. The sentiments are amiable, and the notes at the end highly interesting, particularly the one relating to the Countess Pillar (as it is called) between Appleby and Penrith, erected (as the inscription tells the thoughtful traveller) by Anne Countess of Pembroke, in the year 1648, in memory of her last parting with her good and pious mother in the same place in the year 1616.

> To shew that power of love, how great
> Beyond all human estimate.

This story is also told in the poem, but with so many artful innuendos and tinsel words, that it is hardly intelligible; and still less does it reach the heart.—WILLIAM HAZLITT, *Lectures on the English Poets*, 1818

These are very sweet verses ⟨*Human Life*⟩. They do not indeed stir the spirit like the strong lines of Byron, nor make our hearts dance within us, like the inspiring strains of Scott; but they come over us with a bewitching softness that, in certain moods, is still more delightful—and soothe the troubled spirits with a refreshing sense of truth, purity and elegance. They are pensive, rather than passionate; and more full of wisdom and tenderness than of high flights of fancy, or overwhelming bursts of emotion—while they are moulded into grace, at least as much by the effect of the Moral beauties they disclose, as by the taste and judgment with which they are constructed.

—Francis, Lord Jeffrey, "Rogers's *Human Life,*" *Edinburgh Review*, March 1819, p. 325

I have been put into so good a temper with Rogers, that I have paid him, what is as rare with me as with him, a very handsome compliment in my review. It is not undeserved, but I confess that I can not understand the popularity of his poetry. It is pleasant and flowing enough, less monotonous than most of the imitations of Pope and Goldsmith, and calls up many agreeable images and recollections. But that such men as Lord Granville, Lord Holland, Hobhouse, Lord Byron, and others of high rank in intellect, should place Rogers, as they do, above Southey, Moore, and even Scott himself, is what I can not conceive. But this comes of being in the highest society of London. What Lady Jane Granville called the Patronage of Fashion can do as much for a middling poet as for a plain girl like Miss Arabella Falconer.—Thomas Babington Macaulay, Letter to Hannah M. Macaulay (June 3, 1831), cited in G. Otto Trevelyan, *The Life and Letters of Lord Macaulay*, 1876, Vol. 1, p. 198

⟨. . .⟩ one of our greatest poets and finest prose writers; who to this unstable fame adds the more imperishable renown of being also one of the most honourable men, and most uncompromising friends of civil and religious liberty, who have appeared in any age. The rare felicity of our times, in possessing two individuals to whom this description might be applied,—Rogers and Campbell—alone makes it necessary to add that the former is here meant.—Henry, Lord Brougham, "Mr. Grattan," *Historical Sketches of Statesmen Who Flourished in the Time of George III*, 1839, Vol. 1, p. 341

If the *Pleasures of Hope* to the end of time will fascinate the young and the ardent, those of *Memory* will have equal charms for the advanced in years and the reflecting. Rogers has struck a chord which will for ever vibrate in the human heart, and he has touched it with so much delicacy and pathos, that his poetry is felt as the more charming the more that the taste is improved and the mind is filled with the recollections of the past. His verses have not the vehemence of Byron's imagination, nor the ardour of Campbell's soul: "thoughts that breathe and words that burn" will be looked for in vain in his compositions. He was not fitted, therefore, to reach the highest flights of lyric poetry. He never could have written the "Feast of Alexander," like Dryden; nor the *Bard* of Gray, nor the "Stanzas to Painting" of Campbell; but he possessed, perhaps, in a still higher degree than any of them, the power of casting together pleasing and charming images, and pouring them forth in soft and mellifluous language. This is his great charm; and it is one so great, that, in the estimation of many, particularly those with whom the whirl and agitation of life is past, it more than compensates for the absence of every other. To the young, who have the future before them, imagination and hope are the most entrancing powers, for they gild the as yet untrodden path of life with the wished-for flowers. But to the aged, by whom its vicissitudes have been experienced and its enjoyments known, memory and reflection are the faculties which confer the most unmixed pleasure, for they dwell on the past, and recall its most enchanting moments. Campbell had the most sincere admiration for Rogers, and repeatedly said that he was a greater poet than himself. Without going such a length, it may safely be affirmed that there is none more chaste, none more refined; and that some of his verses will bear a comparison with the most perfect in the English language. —Sir Archibald Alison, *History of Europe from 1815 to 1852*, 1852–59, Ch. 5

When a poet has become a poet of the past and in the natural course of things his poetry has ceased to be talked about, it is not easy to ascertain how far it may or may not have ceased to be read. Has it ceased to be bought? The answer to that question might be accepted in most cases as answering the other. But in the case of Rogers an element of ambiguity was introduced long since. When a well-known firm some fifty years ago expressed a doubt whether the public would provide a market for a volume he wished them to publish, Rogers, in a tone half serious, half comic, said—'I will *make* them buy it;' and being a rich man and a great lover of art, he sent for Turner and Stothard, and a volume appeared with such adornments as have never been equalled before or since. It was called by a sarcastic friend of mine 'Turner illustrated.'

The Pleasures of Memory is an excellent specimen of what Wordsworth calls 'the *accomplishment* of verse'; and it was well worthy to attract attention and admiration at the time when it appeared; for at that time poetry, with few exceptions, was to be distinguished from prose by versification and little else. *The Pleasures of Memory* is an essay in verse, not wanting in tender sentiment and just reflection, expressed, gracefully no doubt, but with a formal and elaborate grace, and in studiously pointed and carefully poised diction, such as the heroic couplet had been trained to assume since the days of Pope. In 1793 very different days were approaching—days in which poetry was to break its chains, and formality to be thrown to the winds. The didactic dullness of the eighteenth century was presently to be supplanted by the romantic spirit and easy animation of Scott, the amorous appeals of Moore, and the passion of Byron; whilst mere tenderness, thoughtfulness and grace were to share its fate, and be trampled in the dust.

An author's name will generally continue long to be associated with that of the work which has first made him known to the world, whether or not it be his best. *The Pleasures of Memory* is probably to this day the best known by name of the author's principal poems. They were seven in number—an *Ode to Superstition, The Pleasures of Memory, An Epistle to a Friend, Columbus, Jacqueline, Human Life,* and *Italy*; and they were written, the earliest at twenty-two years of age, the latest at seventy-one.

Human Life is a poem of the same type as *The Pleasures of Memory*, and in the same verse. The fault of such poems is that they are about nothing in particular. Their range and scope is so wide that one theme is almost as apposite as another. The poet sets himself to work to think thoughts and devise episodes, and to give them what coherency he can; the result being, that some are forced and others commonplace. But if such poems are to be written by a poet who is not a philosopher, they could not well be executed by any one with more care and skill than by Rogers.

The subject of *Italy* was better chosen. The poet travels from Geneva to Naples; and his itinerary brings picturesque features, alternately with romantic traditions and memorable facts in history, into a natural sequence of poetic themes. They are described and related always in a way to please, often with striking effect; and any one who travels the same road and desires to see with the eyes of a poet what is best worth seeing, and to be reminded of what is best worth remembering, can have no better companion.

The heroic couplet, moreover, is left behind. For before the first of the fifteen years occupied in the composition of *Italy* (1819–34) Spenserian stanzas, *ottava rima*, octosyllabic verse, blank verse, any verse, had found itself to be more in harmony with the poetic spirit of the time. *Italy* is the longest of the author's poems; and for a poem of such length, blank verse is best. It is a form of verse which, since the Elizabethans, no poet except Milton had hitherto used with what could be called signal success; and the abrupt contrasts and startling significance of which it was capable in their hands, will always find a place more naturally in dramatic than in narrative poetry. But the blank verse written by Rogers, though not very expressive, flows with an easy and gentle melody, sufficiently varied, and almost free from faults.

Of the other poems, the *Epistle to a Friend* will perhaps be read with the most pleasure. It is short, familiar, and graceful. The subject is entirely within his powers, though wholly remote from his experience. 'Every reader,' he says in the preface, 'turns with pleasure to those passages of Horace, Pope, and Boileau, which describe how they lived and where they dwelt; and which, being interspersed among their satirical writings, derive a secret and irresistible grace from the contrast, and are admirable examples of what in painting is the termed repose;' and he proceeds to describe a sort of Sabine Farm in which he supposes himself to pass his days in studious seclusion and absolute repose. His real life was the reverse of all this. His house in St. James's Place did indeed exemplify the classic ideal described in his poem; it was adorned with exquisite works of art, and with these only; rejecting as inconsistent with purity of taste all ornaments which are ornaments and nothing more; and in its interior it might be said to be a work of art in itself. But his life was a life of society; and in the circles which he frequented, including all who were eminent in literature as well as celebrities in every other walk of life, he was more conspicuous by his conversation and by his wit, than admired as a poet. He had kindness of heart, benevolence, and tender emotions: but his wit was a better wit; and it found its way into verse only in the shape of epigrams, too personal and pungent for publication. It may be matter of regret that he did not adopt the converse of the examples he quotes, of Horace, Pope, and Boileau, and intersperse some satirical writings amongst his other works. His poetic gifts were surpassed by half a dozen or more of his contemporaries; his gift of wit equalled by only one or two. His deliberate and quiet manner of speaking made it the more effective. I remember one occasion on which he threw a satire into a sentence:— 'They tell me I say ill-natured things. I have a very weak voice: If I did not say ill-natured things, no one would hear what I said.'

If it is true that he said ill-natured things, it is equally so that he did kind and charitable and generous things, and that he did them in large measure, though, to his credit, with less notoriety.—SIR HENRY TAYLOR, "Samuel Rogers," *The English Poets*, ed. Thomas Humphry Ward, 1880, Vol. 4, pp. 89–91

He had poetic feeling, sociable instincts, a shrewd sharp wit in conversation, and a ready kindness. If he had been born poor, he might have been a poet of considerable power. He made his reputation, in 1792, when he was thirty, with *The Pleasures of Memory*. It was the best of a group of books, *Pleasures of Refinement*, *Pleasures of Charity*, &c., which had been suggested to imitative writers by the success of Akenside's *Pleasures of Imagination*. Akenside's *Pleasures of Imagination* was a rhetorical poem, first published when he was a young man, and in good accordance with the fashion of its time. Rogers's *Pleasures of Memory* was not only better than any other imitation of Akenside, but it was better than Akenside. There was a simpler and a truer grace of style, due partly to change of literary fashion; a theme pleasant to every reader; and the ease of a man of taste who could give and take refined pleasure, but

"whose sails were never to the tempest given." Samuel Rogers might have become an English author of great mark if, at some time before he was forty years old, his bank had broken. His poem of *Italy* was published in an elegant manner, and maintained his credit. The shrewd wit of Rogers's conversation ought to have shown only the social side of an intellectual vigour that stirred in his writing; but as writer, his whole vitality was never shown. In the reign of Victoria it was for many years the principal charm of a social breakfast table. Samuel Rogers's breakfasts were in the reign of Victoria what suppers at the Mermaid had been in Elizabeth's time; no doubt a highly civilized variation from the older fashion. The foremost men in politics, literature and art were among Rogers's guests, and in the wit combats the venerable host could parry and thrust with the nimblest.—HENRY MORLEY, *Of English Literature in the Reign of Victoria*, 1881, pp. 117–18

Nevertheless Rogers as a poet belongs to a school of the past. He may still be popular with many, as Pope, Dryden, Gray, and Goldsmith will ever be popular, but he ranks after these, and stands distinctly apart from the poets of the nineteenth century. "Rogers is the only poet of the old school," was said by W. Schlegel in 1814, and the saying remains true. He was the last of his school, and as such he holds a rank which if not exalted is sufficient to give him a distinct, honourable, and permanent place in the history of English literature.—EDWARD BELL, "Memoir of Samuel Rogers," *The Poetical Works of Samuel Rogers*, 1891, pp. xlv–xlvi

Samuel Rogers, the son of a London banker, was born at Newington Green, July 30th, 1763. He was privately educated, and entered his father's banking house, in which he became a partner.

The poet's ambition was fired by the perusal of Beattie's *Minstrel*, when but nine years old; and he was so far carried away by his literary enthusiasm, that, at the age of fourteen, he twice called at the house of Dr. Johnson, in Bolt Court, in the hope of seeing the great critic and moralist. On the first occasion the doctor was unfortunately not at home, and on the second the young poet's heart misgave him, and, having rung the bell, he ran away. While yet in his teens, he commenced his literary career by contributing a series of essays to the *Gentleman's Magazine*, under the title of "The Scribbler," 1781. These were followed in 1786 by his *Ode to Superstition*, and other poems; and in 1792 by the poem usually associated with his name, *The Pleasures of Memory*. This work, written in English rhymed heroics, and published at a time when poetry was at a very low ebb, attracted great attention, and excited general admiration. In 1798 appeared the *Epistle to a Friend*, deemed by some the poet's best work, as being more within the scope of his powers. It has certainly a brightness and vivacity of movement not so evident in his longer poems, though he touches in it the very reverse of his actual life and experience. ⟨. . .⟩ After a lapse of fourteen years, *The Voyage of Columbus* appeared in 1812, followed by *Jacqueline: a Tale*, published in company with Byron's *Lara* in 1813. *Human Life* followed in 1819, and *Italy*, which was subsequently largely added to, in 1822, the complete edition being issued in 1834.

At the age of thirty, Rogers retired from the active management of the bank, and devoted himself entirely to literature and society. Prior to 1803, he occupied rooms in the Temple, from whence he removed to No. 22, St. James's Place, a house overlooking the Green Park, which became a rendezvous for the illustrious in literature and art. During his long life the poet accumulated such stores of art-treasures, that on his death they realised £50,000; many of them finding their way to the National Gallery and the British Museum. Byron, writing of this house, says:—"If you enter his house—his drawing-room, his library—you of yourself say, This is not the dwelling of a common mind. There is not a gem, a coin, a book thrown aside on his chimney-piece, his sofa, his table, that does not bespeak an almost fastidious elegance in the possessor." Such was the house in which Rogers gathered round him the most brilliant company of his time.

The poet's later years were devoted to the superintendence of the issue of his *Italy* and *Poems*, with illustrations by Stothard and Turner, the originals of which, with the exception of that of "The Hospice of St. Bernard's," are now in the National Gallery. On the death of Wordsworth in 1850, the office of Laureate was offered to Rogers by Prince Albert, but declined upon the ground of age. Shortly after this, a fall in the street injured the poet so much that he was ever afterwards confined to his chair. He died December 18th, 1855.

As a man, Rogers presents the singular contrast of good-natured actions with ill-natured words. His generosity cheered the last hours of Sheridan, and in countless instances relieved the necessities of suffering and neglected talent; while it was probably his ill-natured speech that embittered Byron towards him and drew upon him "the greatest of modern satirical portraits in verse," which, entitled "Question and Answer," appeared in *Fraser's Magazine* after Byron's death. He was a brilliant conversationalist, a genial and accomplished host, and in his best days entertained such gatherings of genius as have probably never since assembled. Scott, Byron, Moore, Crabbe, Campbell, Fox, Canning, Grattan, Porson, and Erskine, were all among the visitors who received from him a poet's welcome and an Englishman's hospitality.

Rogers was a poet of *culture*. His workmanship is artistic in a high degree, his diction as clear and polished as art can make it, and his versification everywhere elegant, refined, and graceful. He paints us finely-finished pictures, suffused with soft and mellow light, and exhibits them in carefully carven frames—pictures that awaken gentle sympathy and stimulate quiet thought—pictures that please without moving us. He is often tender in sentiment and wise in reflection; but he lacks force and originality, and is altogether destitute of passion. He never annoys us with the faults of taste and style which disfigure the writings of some greater poets; but, on the other hand, he never thrills our emotions nor fires our imaginations as they do. He manipulates the heroic couplet with skill and grace in both *The Pleasures of Memory* and *Human Life*, and in the latter poem reaches lower depths of feeling than in the former. His blank verse is smooth, easy, and graceful, and at the same time sufficiently varied to prevent monotony. Wisely adopted for his *Italy*, his longest work, it serves well for the setting of the many cameos of Italian life and legend which he has enshrined therein. Wanting in the higher qualities of a poet he may perhaps, be best described as a scholarly and accomplished writer of polished and refined verse. The poet's estimate of himself, written in 1839, in his farewell to the readers of *Italy*, does honour to his own self-judgment:—

> Nature denied him much,
> But gave him at his birth what most he values,
> A passionate love for music, sculpture, painting,
> For poetry, the language of the gods,
> For all things here, or grand or beautiful,
> A setting sun, a lake among the mountains,
> The light of an ingenuous countenance,
> And what transcends them all, a noble action.
> Nature denied him much, but gave him more;

> And ever, ever grateful should he be,
> Though from his cheek, ere yet the down was there,
> Health fled; for in his heaviest hours would come
> Gleams such as come not now; nor failed he then,
> (Then and through life his happiest privilege)
> Full oft to wander where the Muses haunt,
> Smit with the love of song.
>   'Tis now long since;
> And now, while yet 'tis day, would he withdraw,
> Who, when in youth he strung his lyre, addressed
> A former generation. Many an eye,
> Bright as the brightest now, is closed in night,
> And many a voice, how eloquent, is mute,
> That, when he came, disdained not to receive
> His lays with favour.

—ALFRED H. MILES, "Samuel Rogers," *The Poets and the Poetry of the Century*, ed. Alfred H. Miles, 1891, Vol. 1, pp. 123–28

SIR JAMES MACKINTOSH
From "Rogers's *Poems*"

Edinburgh Review, October 1813, pp. 38–50

It is not uninteresting, even as a matter of speculation, to observe the fortune of a poem which, like the *Pleasures of Memory*, appeared at the commencement of this literary revolution, without paying court to the revolutionary tastes, or seeking distinction by resistance to them. It borrowed no aid either from prejudice or innovation. It neither copied the fashion of the age which was passing away, nor offered any homage to the rising novelties. It resembles, only in measure, the poems of the eighteenth century, which were written in heroic rhyme. Neither the brilliant sententiousness of Pope, nor the frequent languor and negligence perhaps inseparable from the exquisite nature of Goldsmith, could be traced in a poem, from which taste and labour equally banished mannerism and inequality. It was patronized by no sect or faction. It was neither imposed on the public by any literary cabal, nor forced into notice by the noisy anger of conspicuous enemies. Yet, destitute as it was of every foreign help, it acquired a popularity originally very great; and which has not only continued amidst extraordinary fluctuation of general taste, but increased amidst a succession of formidable competitors. No production, so popular, was probably ever so little censured by criticism. It was approved by the critics, as much as read and applauded by the people; and thus seemed to combine the applause of Contemporaries with the suffrage of the representatives of Posterity.

It is needless to make extracts from a poem which is familiar to every reader. In selection, indeed, no two readers would probably agree. But the description of the Gypsies—of the Boy quitting his Father's house—and of the Savoyard recollecting the mountainous scenery of his country—and the descriptive commencement of the Tale in Cumberland, have remained most deeply impressed on our minds. We should be disposed to quote the following verses, as not surpassed, in pure and chaste elegance, by any English lines.

> When Joy's bright sun has shed his evening ray,
> And Hope's delusive meteors cease to play;
> When clouds on clouds the smiling prospect close,
> Still through the gloom thy star serenely glows:
> Like yon fair orb she gilds the brow of Night
> With the mild magic of reflected light.

The conclusion of the fine passage on the Veterans at Greenwich and Chelsea, has a pensive dignity which beautifully corresponds with the scene.

> Long have ye known Reflection's genial ray
> Gild the calm close of Valour's various day.

And we cannot resist the pleasure of quoting the moral, tender, and elegant lines which close the Poems.

> Lighter than air, Hope's summer-visions fly,
> If but a fleeting cloud obscure the sky;
> If but a beam of sober Reason play,
> Lo, Fancy's fairy frost-work melts away!
> But can the wiles of Art, the grasp of Power,
> Snatch the rich relics of a well-spent hour?
> These, when the trembling spirit wings her flight,
> Pour round her path a stream of living light;
> And gild those pure and perfect realms of rest,
> Where Virtue triumphs, and her sons are blest!

The descriptive passages of this classical poem, require indeed a closer inspection, and a more exercised eye, than those of some celebrated contemporaries who sacrifice elegance to effect, and whose figures stand out in bold relief, from the general roughness of their more unfinished compositions. And in the moral parts, there is often discoverable a Virgilian art, which suggests, rather than displays, the various and contrasted scenes of human life,—and adds to the power of language by a certain air of reflection and modesty, in the preference of measured terms over those of more apparent energy.

In the *Epistle to a Friend*, the 'Panegyric on Engraving'— the 'View from the Poet's Country-house'—the 'Bee-hives of the Loire'—and the 'Rustic Bath,' will immediately present themselves to the recollection of most poetical readers.

In the 'View from the House,' the scene is neither delightful from very superior beauty, nor striking by singularity, nor powerful from reminding us of terrible passions or memorable deeds. It consists of the more ordinary of the beautiful features of Nature, neither exaggerated nor represented with curious minuteness, but exhibited with picturesque elegance, in connexion with those tranquil emotions which they call up in the calm order of a virtuous mind, in every condition of society and of life.

The 'Verses on the Torso,' are in a more severe style. The 'Fragment of a Divine Artist,' which awakened the genius of Michael Angelo, seems to disdain ornament.

> And dost thou still, thou mass of breathing stone,
> (Thy giant limbs to Night and Chaos hurl'd)
> Still sit as on the fragment of a World;
> Surviving all, majestic and alone?
> What though the Spirits of the North, that swept
> Rome from the earth, when in her pomp she slept,
> Smote thee with fury, and thy headless trunk
> Deep in the dust 'mid tower and temple sunk;
> Soon to subdue mankind 'twas thine to rise,
> Still, still unquell'd thy glorious energies!
> Aspiring minds, with thee conversing, caught
> Bright revelations of the Good they sought;
> By thee that long-lost spell in secret given,
> To draw down Gods, and lift the soul to Heaven!

If poetical merit bore any proportion to magnitude, 'The Sick Chamber,' and 'The Butterfly,' would deserve no attention: But it would be difficult to name two small poems, by the same writer, in which he has attained such high degrees of kinds of excellence so dissimilar. The first has a truth of detail, which, considered merely as painting, is admirable; but assumes a higher character, when it is felt to be that minute remembrance, with which affection recollects every circum-

stance that could influence a beloved sufferer. Though the morality which concludes the second, be in itself very beautiful, it may be doubted whether the verses would not have left a more unmixed delight, if the address had remained as a mere sport of fancy, without the seriousness of an object, or an application.

The 'Verses, written in Westminster Abbey,' are surrounded by dangerous recollections. They aspire to commemorate Fox—and to copy some of the grandest thoughts in the most sublime work of Boussuet. Nothing can satisfy the expectation awakened by such names. Yet we venture to quote the following lines, with the assurance, that there are some of them which would be most envied by the best writers of this age.

> Friend of the Absent! Guardian of the Dead!
> Who but would here their sacred sorrows shed?
> (Such as He shed on NELSON's closing grave;
> How soon to claim the sympathy He gave!)
> In Him, resentful of another's wrong,
> The dumb were eloquent, the feeble strong.
> Truth from his lips a charm celestial drew—
> Ah, who so mighty and so gentle too?

The scenery of Loch Long is among the grandest in Scotland; and the description of it shows the power of feeling and painting. Perhaps, however, it partly owes its insertion here, to individual recollections, as well as national sentiments. In this island, the taste for Nature has grown with the progress of refinement. It is most alive in those who are most brilliantly distinguished in social and active life. It elevates the mind above the meanness which it might contract in the rivalship for praise; and preserves those habits of reflection and sensibility, which receive so many rude shocks in the coarse contests of the world. Not many summer hours can be passed in the most mountainous solitudes of Scotland, without meeting some who are worthy to be remembered with the sublime objects of Nature which they had travelled so far to admire. ⟨. . .⟩

The most conspicuous of the novelties of this volume, is the poem or poems, entitled, *Fragments of the Voyage of Columbus*. The subject of this poem is, politically, or philosophically, considered among the most important in the annals of mankind. The introduction of Christianity (humanly viewed)—the irruption of the Northern barbarians—the contest between the Christian and Mussulman nations in Syria— the two inventions of Gunpowder and Printing—the emancipation of the human understanding by the Reformation—the discovery of America, and of a maritime passage to Asia in the last ten years of the 15th century—are the events which have produced the greatest and most durable effects, since the establishment of civilization, and the consequent commencement of authentic history. But the poetical capabilities of an event bear no proportion to historical importance. None of the consequences that do not strike the senses or the fancy, can interest the poet. The greatest of the transactions above enumerated, are obviously incapable of entering into poetry. The Crusades were not without permanent effects on the state of men: But their poetical interest does not arise from these effects;—and it immeasurably surpasses them.

Whether the voyage of Columbus be destined to be for ever incapable of becoming the subject of an Epic poem, is a question which we have scarcely the means of answering. The success of great writers has often so little corresponded with the promise of their subject, that we might be almost tempted to think the choice of a subject indifferent. The story of *Hamlet*, or of *Paradise Lost*, would beforehand have been pronounced to be unmanageable. Perhaps the genius of Shakespeare and of Milton has rather compensated for the incorrigible defects of ungrateful subjects, then conquered them. The course of ages may produce the poetical genius—the historical materials and the national feelings, for an American Epic poem. There is yet but one State in America, and that State is hardly become a nation. At some future period, when every part of the continent has been the scene of memorable events, when the discovery and conquest have receded into that legendary dimness which allows fancy to mould them at her pleasure, the early history of America may afford scope for the genius of a thousand national poets; and while some may soften the cruelty which darkens the daring energy of Cortez and Pizarro—while others may, in perhaps new forms of poetry, ennoble the pacific conquests of Penn—and while the genius, the exploits, and the fate of Raleigh, may render his establishments probably the most alluring of American subjects—every inhabitant of the new world will turn his eyes with filial reverence towards Columbus,—and regard, with equal enthusiasm, the voyage which laid the foundation of so many states, and peopled a continent with civilized men.—Most epic subjects, but especially such a subject as Columbus, require either the fire of an actor in the scene, or the religious reverence of a very distant posterity. Homer, as well as Ercilla, and Camoens, show what may be done by an epic poet who himself feels the passions of his heroes. It must not be denied, that Virgil has borrowed a colour of refinement from the Court of Augustus, in painting the age of Priam and of Dido. Evander is a solitary and exquisite model of primitive manners, divested of grossness, without losing their simplicity. But to an European poet, in this age of the world, the Voyage of Columbus is too naked and too exactly defined by history. It has no variety, scarcely any succession of events. It consists of one scene, during which two or three simple passions continue in a state of the highest excitement. It is a voyage with intense anxiety in every bosom, controlled by magnanimous fortitude in the leader, and producing among his followers a fear sometimes submissive, sometimes mutinous, always ignoble. It admits no variety of character—no unexpected revolutions; and even the issue—the sight of undiscovered land, though of unspeakable importance, and admirably adapted to some kinds of poetry, is not an event of such outward dignity and splendour as ought naturally to close the active and brilliant course of an Epic poem.

The author has accordingly not attempted such a poem; he professes only to offer fragments of the Voyage. To prove that these fragments have not the interest of a story, is a mere waste of critical ingenuity. The very title of Fragments, is a disavowal of all pretension to such an interest. Many of them have the appearance of having been originally members of a Lyric poem on the voyage of Columbus; and they still retain that predominant character. They are not so much parts of a narrative, as the sentiments or the visions of the poet. In the progress of insertion and amplification, they seem to have become separate poems—Lyrical, Descriptive and Dramatic—on various events and scenes of the voyage. It cannot be true, that, because the whole is not a favourable subject for Epic poetry, many of the parts should not be well adapted to such poems. Each fragment is to be tried by its separate excellence. Part of that excellence will consist in their relation and allusion to each other, which naturally arises from affinity of subject. If there be any other criterion by which such poems are to be tried, it can only be their fitness to be inserted into an epic poem, if such a poem could be founded upon the event. The title, Fragments, implies also a renunciation of all claim to whatever merit may arise from the artifices of connexion and transition. This will be considered as

matter of very serious reproach, by those who adopt the maxim of French criticism—that, difficulty conquered, is the chief triumph of talent—who, to be consistent with themselves, ought to consider the most minute expedient of art as superior to the noblest exertions of genius.

To examine the general question of epic machinery, on an occasion like the present, would be impertinent. It is natural that the Fragments should give a specimen of the marvellous as well as of the other constituents of epic fiction. We may however observe, that it is neither the intention nor the tendency of poetical machinery, to supersede second causes—to fetter the will—and to make human creatures appear as the mere instruments of Destiny. It is introduced, to satisfy that insatiable demand for a nature more exalted than that which we know by experience—which creates all poetry—and which is most active in its highest species, and in its most perfect productions. It is not to account for the thoughts and feelings, that the superhuman agents are brought down upon earth. It is rather for the contrary purpose, of lifting them into a mysterious dignity beyond the cognizance of reason. There is a material difference between the acts which superior beings perform, and the sentiments which they inspire. It is true, that when a God fights against men, there can be no uncertainty or anxiety, and consequently no interest about the event,—unless indeed in the rude theology of Homer, where Minerva may animate the Greeks, while Mars excites the Trojans. But it is quite otherwise with these divine persons inspiring passion, or represented as agents in the great phenomena of nature. Venus and Mars inspire love or valour. They give a noble origin and a dignified character to these sentiments. But the sentiments themselves act according to the laws of our nature; and their celestial source has no tendency to impair their power over human sympathy. No event, which has not too much modern vulgarity to be susceptible of alliance with poetry, can be incapable of being ennobled by that eminently poetical art which ascribes it either to the supreme will, or to the agency of beings who are greater than human. The wisdom of Columbus is neither less venerable, nor less his own, because it is supposed to flow more directly than that of other wise men, from the inspiration of heaven. The mutiny of his seamen is not less interesting or formidable because the poet traces it to the suggestion of those malignant spirits, in whom the imagination, independent of all theological doctrines, is naturally prone to personify and embody the causes of evil.

Unless, indeed, the marvellous be a part of the popular creed at the period of the action, the reader of a subsequent age will refuse to sympathize with it. His poetical faith is founded in sympathy with the poetical personages. What they believed during their lives, he suffers to enter his imagination during the moment of enthusiasm in which he adopts their feelings. Still more objectionable is a marvellous, neither believed by the reader nor by the hero;—like a great part of the machinery of the Henriade and the Lusiad, which indeed is not only absolutely ineffective, but rather dissennobles heroic fiction, by association with light and frivolous ideas. Allegorical persons (if the expression be allowed) are only in the way to become agents. The abstraction has received a faint outline of form; but it has not yet acquired those individual marks and characteristic peculiarities, which render it a really existing being. Beauty and love gradually form themselves into Venus and Cupid. To employ them in the intermediate stage through which they must pass in the course of their transformation from abstractions into deities, is an inartificial and uninteresting expedient. On the other hand, the more sublime parts of our own religion, and more especially those which are common to all religion, are too awful and too philosophical for poetical effect. If we except *Paradise Lost*, where all is supernatural, and where the ancestors of the human race are not strictly human beings, it must be owned that no successful attempt has been made to ally a human action with the sublimer principles of the Christian theology. Some opinions, which may perhaps, without irreverence, be said to be rather appendages to the Christian system, than essential parts of it, are in that sort of intermediate state which fits them for the purposes of poetry;— sufficiently exalted to ennoble those human actions with which they are blended—and not so exactly defined, nor so deeply revered, as to be inconsistent with the liberty of imagination. The guardian angels, in the project of Dryden, had the inconvenience of having never taken any deep root in popular belief. The agency of evil spirits, firmly believed in the age of Columbus, seems to afford the only species of machinery which can be introduced into his voyage. With the truth of facts poetry can have no concern; but the truth of manners is necessary to its persons—and its marvellous must be such as these persons believed. If the minute investigations of the notes to this poem had related to historical details, they would have been insignificant; but they are intended to justify the human and the supernatural parts of it, by an appeal to the manners and to the opinions of the age. ⟨. . .⟩

The whole vision which concludes the poem, is eminently beautiful. But it is needless to prolong our extracts from a volume, which must long ago have been in the hands of every reader of this Review. The extracts already given will show, that it always has consummate elegance, and often unaffected grandeur. The author is not one of those poets who is flat for a hundred lines, in order to heighten the apparent elevation of one more fortunate verse. He does not conduct his readers over a desert, to betray them into the temper in which they bestow the charms of Paradise on a few trees and a fountain in a green spot.

Perhaps there is no volume in our language of which it can be so truly said, as of the present, that it is equally exempt from the frailties of negligence and the vices of affectation. The exquisite polish of style is indeed more admired by the artist than by the people. The gentle and elegant pleasure which it imparts, can only be felt by a calm reason, an exercised taste, and a mind free from turbulent passions. But these beauties of execution can exist only in combination with much of the primary beauties of thought and feeling. Without a considerable portion of them, the works of the greatest genius must perish; and poets of the first rank depend on them for no small part of the perpetuity of their fame. They are permanent beauties. In poetry, though not in eloquence, it is less to rouse the passions of a moment, than to satisfy the taste of all ages.

In estimating the poetical rank of Mr Rogers, it must not be forgotten that popularity never can arise from elegance alone. The vices of a poem may render it popular; and virtues of a faint character may be sufficient to preserve a languishing and cold reputation. But to be both popular poets and classical writers, is the rare lot of those few who are released from all solicitude about their literary fame. It often happens to successful writers, that the lustre of their first productions throws a temporary cloud over some of those which follow. Of all literary misfortunes, this is the most easily endured, and the most speedily repaired. It is generally no more than a momentary illusion produced by disappointed admiration, which expected more from the talents of the admired writer than any talents could perform.

Mr Rogers has long passed that period of probation, during which it may be excuseable to feel some painful solicitude about the reception of every new work. Whatever may be the rank assigned hereafter to his writings, when compared to each other, the writer has most certainly taken his place among the classical poets of his country.

DAVID MACBETH MOIR
From *Sketches of the Poetical Literature of the Past Half-Century*
1851, pp. 47–53

*T*he *Ode to Superstition* ⟨. . .⟩ not only smacks of his peculiar genius, but is characterised by that elaboration for which all his subsequent writings are noted; but his reputation was not established until he gave to the world *The Pleasures of Memory*, a poem exquisite in conception and execution, combining a fine feeling of nature and a high tone of morality, with elegant scholarship, and a nicety of taste approaching to fastidiousness. Nor was it wonderful that it immediately rose into that popular favour which, after a lapse of sixty years, it still deservedly retains; for it is pervaded by beauty and grace of sentiment, and in versification approaches the perfection of art. Although its highest passages are not so high as the finest in *The Pleasures of Hope*, it is freer from traces of juvenility, and, with less of ardent enthusiasm, may be said to be better sustained throughout. Yet it also has its more prominent passages; and these, as it strikes me, are the twilight landscape with which it opens; the introduction to the tale of Derwent Lake; the allusion to the Savoyard Boy leaving the Alps; the apostrophe to the Bee, as illustrative of the powers of memory; the affecting reference to a deceased brother; and the lines on Greenwich Hospital. The concluding paragraph is also apposite and beautiful:—

> Hail! Memory, hail! in thy exhaustless mine,
> From age to age, unnumbered treasures shine;
> Thought and her shadowy brood thy call obey,
> And Place and Time are subject to thy sway;
> Thy pleasures most we feel when most alone,
> The only pleasures we can call our own.
> Lighter than air Hope's summer visions die,
> If but a fleeting cloud obscure the sky;
> If but a beam of sober reason play,
> Lo! Fancy's fairy frost-work melts away!
> But can the wiles of Art, the grasp of Power,
> Snatch the rich relics of a well-spent hour?
> These, when the trembling spirit wings her flight,
> Pour round her path a stream of living light;
> And gild those pure and perfect realms of rest,
> When Virtue triumphs, and her sons are blest!

The *Epistle to a Friend*, which followed in 1797, was another working out of the same classic vein of thought, imagery, and sentiment—a little inferior, perhaps, in freshness, and a good deal so in interest. Some of its descriptive sketches are elaborately fine, and not only graceful, but exquisite touches of nature sparkle throughout. A general straining after effect, however, is but too apparent; and, in spite of his own anathema against false taste, Rogers here occasionally reminds us of the scholar of Apelles, who, unable to paint his Helen beautiful, was determined to make her fine.

The *Fragments of a Voyage of Columbus* did not appear for a good many years after, and are of a higher cast than any of his former writings. A deep-toned solemnity pervades the whole, and occasionally we have thoughts that verge on the sublime. But it can only be likened to snatches of a fine melody heard by summer sunset on the sea-beach, or transient glimpses of a magnificent landscape caught through clouds of white rolling mist.

The allusion to Columbus entering the vast Atlantic is full of solemn grandeur:—

> 'Twas night. The moon, o'er the wide wave, dis-
> closed
> Her awful face; and Nature's self reposed;
> When slowly rising in the azure sky,
> Three white sails shone—but to no mortal eye,
> Entering a boundless sea. In slumber cast,
> The very ship-boy on the dizzy mast
> Half breathed his orisons! Alone unchanged,
> Calmly beneath, the great Commander ranged
> Thoughtful, not sad.

The work, however, fine as it is in detached portions, is too fragmentary, and rather stimulates curiosity than gratifies expectation.

Jacqueline is pitched on quite another and opposite key. It is far less ambitious, and seems an attempt to catch those natural evanescent domestic graces which lie beyond the reach of art. If so, it cannot be said to be quite successful; for, with some touches of simple beauty, it is, to say the best of it, a faint and feeble performance—and, certes, at antipodes to the *Lara* of Byron, along with which it was originally published. The fastidiousness of Rogers must have ever rendered his success as a narrative writer more than doubtful. "What would offend the eye in a good picture, the painter casts discreetly into shade;" but Rogers would not only have done this, but have blotted out everything save beauties alone, of which, exclusively, no landscape, however fine, can be formed.

Like Dryden, and very unlike the majority of poets, Rogers gradually went on, surpassing himself as he grew older; for his *Human Life* and his *Italy* are his best works. In the former we have, along with much of the same mellow colouring and delicacy of conception which distinguished *The Pleasures of Memory*, the outpourings also of a richer and deeper vein of feeling—a contemplation more grounded on experiences. Even more than its precursor, *The Pleasures of Memory*, it has all the high finish of a cabinet picture. *Italy*, to our mind, however, is the freshest and finest of all the compositions of its author—the one most unequivocally his own; and the one whose passages most frequently recur to mind, from their peculiar graces of style and language. Its blank verse is not that of Milton, or Thomson, or Akenside, or Cowper, or Wordsworth. It is pitched on a less lofty key than any of these—nay, occasionally almost descends to a conversational tone, but without ever being commonplace in thought, or lax in diction. It is full of the easy elegance of the author's mind, and forms an admirable vehicle for those delightful glimpses of Ausonian life and natural scenery, which he has tinted with that exquisite grace inseparable from his pencil. Several of its descriptions, as those of Pæstum, of the Great St. Bernard, and of Venice, are inimitable; and its episode of Ginevra touches on a hidden spring, which finds a response in every heart. ⟨. . .⟩

Whatever portion of the writings of Samuel Rogers may die, this tale cannot. His minor poems are all elaborately graceful and elegant; but, save in one or two instances, possess little originality, and never once rise into lyrical grandeur. The best are "The Alps at Daybreak," "To the Torso," the "Lines Written in the Highlands of Scotland," and the "Verses in Westminster Abbey."

The reader of Rogers ever finds that he is on secure ground,—that his author is in earnest, and that his afflatus is the true inspiration. The feast spread for him has all the marks of cost and care:—it is the result of choice study, of nice observation, of fine feeling, of exquisite fancy, of consummate art; and the exuberances of the mere bard are everywhere toned down by the graceful tact of the scholar. Among great or original minds Rogers scarcely claims a place—nay, his genius may not seldom be said to glow with something of a reflected light; but, in this age of slovenly prolixity, where elaboration is held at a discount, and volume after volume, sparkling with something good, is poured forth in its crudity, only to be sighed over and forgotten, I look upon his example of elegance and correctness as quite invaluable.

MARY RUSSELL MITFORD

1787–1855

Mary Russell Mitford was born at Alresford, Hampshire, on December 16, 1787. Between 1797 and 1802 she was educated in London, but her family's increasing poverty, brought about by her father's extravagance, caused Mitford to leave school in 1802. Financial necessity drove her to publish several long poems in 1810 and 1811; they were followed in 1812 by *Blanche of Castile* which she sent to Coleridge, who encouraged her to continue writing. Mitford's first real triumph came in 1823, when her drama *Julian* was produced successfully at Covent Garden, with William Macready in the title role. This was followed by two even more successful plays, *Foscani* (1826) and *Rienzi* (1828). Mitford wrote several other historical dramas, but it is not for her plays that she is best remembered. Her most lasting work is a series of sketches and stories written between 1824 and 1832 and published in 1832 as *Our Village: Sketches of Rural Life, Character, and Scenery*. This collection was following by *Belford Regis* (1835), a portrait of Reading; *Country Stories* (1837); *Recollections of a Literary Life* (1852); and *Atherton and Other Tales* (1854). Some of Mitford's correspondence with Macready, Felicia Dorothea Hemans, Harriet Martineau, Charles Lamb, Elizabeth Barrett Browning, John Ruskin, Walter Savage Landor, and others was published in A. G. L'Estrange's *Life of Mary Russell Mitford in a Selection from Her Letters to Her Friends* (3 vols., 1870) and in *Letters of Mary Russell Mitford: Second Series*, edited by Henry Chorley (2 vols., 1872). Mitford died at Swallowfield, her last home, on January 10, 1855.

Personal

Our residence is a cottage—no, not a cottage—it does not deserve the name—a messuage or tenement, such as a little farmer who had made twelve or fourteen hundred pounds might retire to when he left off business to live on his means. It consists of a series of closets, the largest of which may be about eight feet square, which they call parlors, and kitchens, and pantries; some of them minus a corner, which has been unnaturally filched for a chimney; others deficient in half a side, which has been truncated by the shelving roof. Behind is a garden about the size of a good drawing-room, with an arbor which is a complete sentry-box of privet. On one side a public house, on the other a village shop, and right opposite a cobbler's stall.

Notwithstanding all this, "the cabin," as Bobadil says, "is convenient." It is within reach of my dear old walks; the banks where I find my violets; the meadows full of cowslips; and the woods where the wood-sorrel blows.—MARY RUSSELL MIT-FORD, Letter to Sir William Elford (April 8, 1820)

You must know I have a great horror about hearing about Miss M., for she once wrote me a letter in which she called me a delightful poet, and no less delightful *proser*; which I did not know whether to take for a panegyric, or a satire; so I never answered the letter, which was horribly unpolite; and I have ever since, when I hear her name mentioned, not known whether to feel remorse or satisfaction. I conclude, upon the whole, the former; so if ever you fall in the way of her or her friend, pray state the case as it really was.—LEIGH HUNT, Letter to Elizabeth Kent (Jan. 4, 1825)

It is long since I have been so pleased with any one, whether for sweetness of voice, kindness and cheerfulness of countenance (with *one* look which reminds me of a look I shall meet no more), or high-bred plainness of manner. I was fascinated. —HENRY F. CHORLEY, *Journal* (May 1836), *Autobiography, Memoir and Letters*, ed. Henry G. Hewlett, 1873, Vol. 1, p. 200

Miss M. is truly "a little body," and dressed a little quaintly, and as unlike as possible to the faces we have seen of her in the magazines, which all have a broad humour bordering on coarseness. She has a pale gray, soul-lit eye, and hair as white as snow: a wintry sign that has come prematurely upon her, as like signs come upon us, while the year is yet fresh and undecayed. Her voice has a sweet, low tone, and her manner a naturalness, frankness, and affectionateness that we have been so long familiar with in their other modes of manifestation, that it would have been indeed a disappointment not to have found them.

She led us directly through her house into her garden, a perfect bouquet of flowers. "I must show you my geraniums while it is light," she said, "for I love them next to my father." And they were indeed treated like petted children, guarded by a very ingenious contrivance from the rough visitation of the elements. They are all, I believe, seedlings. She raises two crops in a year, and may well pride herself on the variety and beauty of her collection. Geraniums are her favourites; but she does not love others less that she loves these more. The garden is filled, matted with flowering shrubs and vines; the trees are wreathed with honeysuckles and roses; and the girls have brought away the most splendid specimens of heart's-ease to press in their journals. Oh, that I could give some of my countrywomen a vision of this little paradise of flowers, that they might learn how *taste and industry*, and an earnest love

and study of the art of garden-culture, might triumph over small space and small means.

Miss Mitford's house is, with the exception of certainly not more than two or three, as small and humble as the smallest and humblest in our village of S——; and such is the difference, in some respects, in the modes of expense in this country from ours; she keeps two men-servants (one a gardner), two or three maid-servants, and two horses. In this very humble home, which she illustrates as much by her unsparing filial devotion as by her genius, she receives on equal terms the best in the land. Her literary reputation might have gained for her this elevation, but she started on vantage ground, being allied by blood to the Duke of Bedford's family.—CATHARINE M. SEDGWICK, Letter (June 13, 1839), *Letters from Abroad to Kindred at Home*, 1841, Vol. 1, pp. 46–48

> The hay is carried; and the Hours
> Snatch, as they pass, the linden-flow'rs;
> And children leap to pluck a spray
> Bent earthward, and then run away.
> Park-keeper! catch me those grave thieves
> About whose frocks the fragrant leaves,
> Sticking and fluttering here and there,
> No false nor faltering witness bear.
>   I never view such scenes as these,
> In grassy meadow girt with trees,
> But comes a thought of her who now
> Sits with serenely patient brow
> Amid deep sufferings: none hath told
> More pleasant tales to young and old.
> Fondest was she of Father Thames,
> But rambled to Hellenic streams;
> Nor even there could any tell
> The country's purer charms so well
> As Mary Mitford.
>   Verse! go forth
> And breathe o'er gentle breasts her worth.
> Needless the task . . . but should she see
> One hearty wish from you and me,
> A moment's pain it may assuage . . .
> A roseleaf on the couch of Age.
>   —WALTER SAVAGE LANDOR, "To Mary Russell
>   Mitford," 1854

It surprised me to hear allusions indicating that Miss Mitford was not the invariably amiable person that her writings would suggest; but the whole drift of what they say tended, nevertheless, towards the idea that she was an excellent and generous person, loved most by those who knew her best.—NATHANIEL HAWTHORNE, *The English Note-Books*, April 6, 1856

On her tenth birthday Dr. Mitford took the child to a lottery-office, and bade her select a ticket. She determined—guided, to all appearance, by one of the unaccountable whims of childhood—that she would have none other than that numbered 2,224. Some difficulty attended the purchase of the coveted number, but the little lottery patroness had her way at last, and on the day of drawing there fell to the lot of the happy holder of ticket No. 2,224 a prize of £20,000. Alas! the holder of the fortunate ticket was happy only in name. By the time his daughter was a woman, there remained to Dr. Mitford, of all his lottery adventure had brought him, a Wedgwood dinner-service with the family crest!—S. C. HALL, *Retrospect of a Long Life*, 1883, p. 405

In the case of Miss Mitford, indeed, it seems quite hopeless to search for even the ghost of a love-story, and, although she certainly did devote her life with touching unselfishness to the comfort and support of a very exacting father, it cannot for a moment be urged that, in so doing, she relinquished any distinct desire or prospect of matrimony. Perhaps the exasperating qualities of her parent inclined her unconsciously to remain single; for, with all her unsparing devotion, she must, in the course of sorely tried years, have grown to regard men very much as Dolly Winthrop regarded them,—"in the light of animals whom it had pleased Heaven to make naturally troublesome." Mr. Mitford, a most genial and handsome old gentleman of the Turveydrop pattern, managed to keep his daughter's hands full of work, and her heart full of love, and left her little chance or disposition for any wandering fancies. All the exuberant affection of her girlhood, all the mature attachment of later years, were concentrated upon him alone. Her youth waned, her freshness faded, her indomitable courage and cheerfulness quailed a little before the ever-increasing burdens of her life; but through it all, in joy and sorrow, no shadow of a suitor stands beckoning by her side. Her serene old age was haunted by no dim voices crying out of the past for the joy which had slipped from her grasp. She wrote love-stories by the score, always approaching the subject from the outside, and treating it with the easy conventionality, the generous yet imperfect sympathy of a warm-hearted woman not prone to analyze motives. They are very pleasant stories for the most part, sensible, healthy, and happy; but they are not convincing. The reader feels that if Polly did not marry Joe she would be just as well satisfied with William, and that if Edwin failed to win Angelina he would soon content himself with Dorothy. This is a comfortable state of affairs, and doubtless true to life; but it is not precisely the element which makes a successful love-tale. The fact is, Miss Mitford described things pretty much as she found them, not seeking to dive below the surface, and always adding a little sunshine of her own. She was a happy woman, save for some sad years of overwork, and her life was full of pleasant detail, of cherished duties, and of felicitous labor; but, from first to last, love had no part in it, and, fancy free, she never reckoned of her loss.—AGNES REPPLIER, "Three Famous Old Maids" (1891), *Essays in Miniature*, 1895, pp. 159–61

General

In our cursory examination of this little volume, we have noticed several unpoetical and ungraceful, and not a few ungrammatical lines. It must be apparent, we think, to every one, that Miss Mitford's taste and judgment are not yet matured; that her poems ought to have been kept back much longer, and revised much oftener, before they were submitted to the public; and, above all, that she wanted some friend who, without wounding her feelings, or damping the fire of her genius, would have led her to corrector models of taste, and taught her more cautious habits of composition. That such instruction would not have been thrown away, we judge from many pleasing passages scattered through her little volume, which do no discredit to the amiableness of her mind, and the cultivation of her talents. When she attempts to describe the higher passions, as in *Sybille*, she fails from want of strength for the flight. But in the description of natural scenery, or the delineation of humbler and calmer feelings, she is more successful.—WILLIAM GIFFORD, "Mary Russell Mitford's Poems," *Quarterly Review*, Nov. 1810, p. 517

Tickler: Master Christopher North, there's Miss Mitford, author of *Our Village*, an admirable person in all respects, of whom you have never, to my recollection, taken any notice in the Magazine. What is the meaning of that? Is it an oversight?

Or have you omitted her name intentionally, from your eulogies on our female worthies?

North: I am waiting for her second volume. Miss Mitford has not, in my opinion, either the pathos or humour of Washington Irvine; but she excels him in vigorous conception of character, and in the truth of her pictures of English life and manners. Her writings breathe a sound, pure, and healthy morality, and are pervaded by a genuine rural spirit—the spirit of merry England. Every line bespeaks the lady.

Shepherd: I admire Miss Mitford just excessively. I dinna wunner at her being able to write sae weel as she does about drawing-rooms wi' sofas and settees, and about the fine folk in them seein' themsells in lookin'-glasses frae tap to tae; but what puzzles the like o' me, is her pictures o' poachers, and tinklers, and pottery-trampers, and ither neer-do-weels, and o' huts and hovels without riggin by the way-side, and the cottages o' honest puir men, and byres, and barns, and stack-yards; and merry-makin's at winter-ingles, and courtship aneath trees, and at the gabel-ends o' farm-houses, atween lads and lasses as laigh in life as the servants in her father's ha'. That's the puzzle, and that's the praise. But ae word explains a'—Genius—Genius—wull a' the metafhizzians in the warld ever expound that mysterious monysyllable?—JOHN WILSON (as "Christopher North"), *Noctes Ambrosianae* (Nov. 1826), 1854

I shall at last see dear Miss Mitford, who wrote to me not long ago to say that she would soon be in London with *Otto*, her new tragedy, which was written at Mr. Forrest's own request, he in the most flattering manner having applied to her a stranger, as the authoress of *Rienzi*, for a dramatic work worthy of his acting—after rejecting many plays offered to him, and among them Mr. Knowles's. . . . She says that her play will be quite opposed, in its execution, to *Ion*, as unlike it 'as a ruined castle overhanging the Rhine, to a Grecian temple.' And I do not doubt that it will be full of ability; although my own opinion is that she stands higher as the authoress of *Our Village* than of *Rienzi*, and writes prose better than poetry, and transcends rather in Dutch minuteness and high finishing, than in Italian ideality and passion.—ELIZABETH BARRETT BROWNING, Letter to Mrs. Martin (Jan. 23, 1837)

Her first publication was a volume of *Miscellaneous Poems*, in 1810; followed in 1811 by *Christine, The Maid of the South Seas* (a nautical tale of Pitcairn's Island); in 1812 by *Wattington Hill* (a descriptive poem), and *Narrative Poems on the Female Characters*. After a studious retirement of nearly twelve years, she reappeared as a dramatist by the production of *Julian*, a tragedy, the success of which, as a reading play, encouraged her to pursue her fame with *Rienzi, The Vespers of Palermo, Foscari,* and *Charles the First*. The first-named three were brought on the stage; but *Rienzi*, certainly the best of them, alone met with much favour. She published the first volume of *Our Village* in 1824, which was carried through four more; the last appearing in 1832. Her *Belford Regis*, a description of a market-town, is characterized by the same graphic talent. Miss Mitford's early poems prove the absence of an ear for rhythm; and her sense of natural beauty, so eloquent in prose, struggles in vain for expression through the difficulties of rhyme. She succeeds better in dramatic verse, and some of her scenes have much tragic power. Her study of the Greek dramatists, especially Euripides, is often distinctly traceable; and in the address of Claudia to Rienzi, as also in that of Annabel to Julian, we find the very thoughts of Iphigenia pleading with Agamemnon. Her prose is simple, natural, and full of frank, kind-judging lovingness. Her autumnal landscape has all the soft brown beauty, with the exquisite finish of a Cuyp; and we almost hear the rustling of the flags in the summer wind, as she leads us to chat with our familiar friend the Basket-maker, by the side of the pool. Her sunny spirit makes beautiful with light the most commonplace scenes, and she has the rare faculty of concealing the coarseness of rustic poverty, while she presents the simple graces of homely good-feeling and sportive childhood. As a proof that we *love her, we love her dog;* Walter Scott's stately Maida is not more an historical character, than her springing spaniel or Italian greyhound. If she began by being prosaic in poetry, she has redeemed herself by being most poetical in pastoral prose.—GEORGE WASHINGTON BETHUNE, "Mary Russell Mitford," *The British Female Poets,* 1848, p. 318

Her first claims on the public were no doubt as a poetess, in her early *Sketches,* and in her *Christina, the Maid of the South Seas*—a six-canto production of the Sir Walter Scott school, of considerable merit; but she is chiefly to be remembered as the author of *Our Village,* so full of truth and raciness and fine English life; and for her three tragedies—*Julian, The Vespers of Palermo,* and *Rienzi*—the last of which was, I believe, eminently successful in representation. Her latter verses are all able and elegant; but she is deficient in that nameless adaptation of expression to thought accomplished by some indescribable, some inexplicable collocation of the best words in their best places, apparently quite necessary for the success of poetical phrase. This power, on the contrary, Mary Howitt possesses in perfection, while she is somewhat wanting in the essential matter—the more solid materials—which Miss Mitford seems to have ever at command. The one is mightiest in facts, the other in fancy.—DAVID MACBETH MOIR, *Sketches of the Poetical Literature of the Past Half-Century,* 1851, pp. 271–72

I agree quite with you that she was stronger and wider in her conversation and letters than in her books. Oh, I have said so a hundred times. The heat of human sympathy seemed to bring out her powerful vitality, rustling all over with laces and flowers. She seemed to think and speak stronger holding a hand—not that she required help or borrowed a word, but that the human magnetism acted on her nature, as it does upon men born to speak. Perhaps if she had been a man with a man's opportunities, she would have spoken rather than written a reputation. Who can say? She hated the act of composition. Did you hear that from her ever?—ELIZABETH BARRETT BROWNING, Letter to John Ruskin (Nov. 5, 1855)

Miss Mitford had not time to be a good letter-writer; her day was taken up, her brain was jaded by work of another kind. "I am now chained to a desk," she says, "eight, ten, twelve hours a day, at mere drudgery; all my thoughts of writing are for hard money." How, then, could she in her correspondence find mental power for the happy expressions, the graceful turns, and the artlessness so full of art, to which, no doubt, Madame de Sévigné's whole mind was given. The letters of Miss Mitford have no pretension to the character of works of art; they are mere medleys, such as one scrawls off in an odd half-hour to an uncritical friend; more, perhaps, because something must be said than because one has anything to say, and rather following one's pen than guiding it. We cannot say, therefore, *materiem superavit opus:* if interesting matter is wanting, the form will not atone for its absence.

To review Miss Mitford's other writings is beyond our present purpose. She had, we repeat, talent and facility, but no genius; she wrote for bread, chained to her desk all day long. She produced, under these adverse circumstances, dramas which had and deserved a temporary success, and one of which

is even yet not dead. She produced, no doubt, a mass of contributions to periodicals, which have perished with the periodicals themselves. The best of her works, as we have said before, is *Our Village,* and the next best is *Belford Regis,* in which she photographs (for she had not imagination enough to paint anything but portraits) the life of a country town. In *Our Village* one finds, among other things, a religious enjoyment of the beauty of nature which, if we do not mistake the general cast of Miss Mitford's character, would scarcely have been expected by her friends, but which has its explanation and the warrant of its sincerity in the history of her devoted life. —GOLDWIN SMITH, "Miss Mitford's Letters," *Nation,* March 31, 1870, p. 212

I was early fond of her tales and descriptions, and have always regarded her as the originator of that new style of "graphic description" to which literature owes a great deal, however weary we may sometimes have felt of the excess into which the practice of detail has run. In my childhood, there was no such thing known, in the works of the day, as "graphic description:" and most people delighted as much as I did in Mrs. Ratcliffe's gorgeous or luscious generalities,—just as we admired in picture galleries landscapes all misty and glowing indefinitely with bright colours,—yellow sunrises and purple and crimson sunsets,—because we had no conception of detail like Miss Austen's in manners, and Miss Mitford's in scenery, or of Millais' and Wilkie's analogous life pictures, or Rosa Bonheur's adventurous Hayfield at noon-tide. Miss Austen had claims to other and greater honours; but she and Miss Mitford deserve no small gratitude for rescuing us from the folly and bad taste of slovenly indefiniteness in delineation. School-girls are now taught to draw from objects: but in my time they merely copied their masters' vague and slovenly drawings: and the case was the same with writers and readers. Miss Mitford's tales appealed to a new sense, as it were, in a multitude of minds,— greatly to the amazement of the whole circle of publishers, who had rejected, in her works, as good a bargain as is often offered to publishers. Miss Mitford showed me at once that she undervalued her tales, and rested her claims on her plays. I suppose every body who writes a tragedy, and certainly every body who writes a successful tragedy, must inevitably do this. Miss Mitford must have possessed some dramatic requisites, or her success could not have been so decided as it was; but my own opinion always was that her mind wanted the breadth, and her character the depth, necessary for genuine achievement in the highest enterprise of literature.—HARRIET MARTINEAU, *Autobiography,* ed. Maria Weston Chapman, 1877, Vol. 1, pp. 315–16

"Of course I shall copy as closely as I can nature and Miss Austen—keeping, like her, to genteel country life; or rather going a little lower, perhaps; and, I am afraid, with more of sentiment and less of humour. I do not *intend* to commit these delinquencies, mind. I *mean* to keep as playful as I can; but I am afraid of their happening in spite of me . . . It will be called—at least, I mean it so to be—*Our Village*; will consist of essays and characters and stories, chiefly of country life, in the manner of *The Sketch Book*; . . . connected by unity of locality, and of purpose. It is exceedingly playful and lively, and I think you will like it. Charles Lamb (the matchless *Elia* of the London Magazine) says nothing so fresh and characteristic has appeared for a long time."

So wrote Miss Mitford in those delightful letters which, by her own account, "are just like so many bottles of ginger-beer, bouncing and frothy, and flying in everybody's face," concerning the work with which her name has since become inseparably connected.

Her own estimate of her powers and their limitations is singularly discerning, though somewhat over modest, for *Our Village* is not entirely imitative. At another time, indeed, she ventured to criticise the authoress whom she thus frankly owns as her model, and she had doubtless some right to desire for Miss Austen "a little more taste, a little more perception of the graceful," since these are the very qualities in which her own writings excel. With an individuality of their own, a charm rather subtle than brilliant, they have the flavour of culture, and were clearly composed by a woman familiar with the world of books and in touch with the best intellects of the day—a professional in comparison with the authoress of *Pride and Prejudice*.

She was not without experience in composition when she began *Our Village*, though at that time, and apparently always, she found much difficulty in writing prose; being more at home in metre, and having accustomed herself by much letter-writing "to a certain careless sauciness, a fluent incorrectness," that she feared would "not do at all for that tremendous correspondent, the public." We are less pedantic, however, than she anticipated, and rather choose to praise her style for the epistolary characteristics, which it exhibits in such perfection.

In her own day Miss Mitford was charged with working in the literal manner of Crabbe or Teniers, and it is certain that she drew entirely from her own experience. But, unlike them, she always sought out the beautiful and, despite her own protests to the contrary, regarded life with the eyes of a sentimentalist. "Are your characters and descriptions true?" asked her friend Sir William Elford, and she replied: "Yes! yes! yes! as true as is well possible. You, as a great landscape painter, know that, in painting a favourite scene, you do a little embellish, and can't help it; you avail yourself of happy accidents of atmosphere, and *if anything be ugly, you strike it out*, or if anything be wanting, you put it in. But still the picture is a likeness."

Mrs. Anne Thackeray Ritchie, has thus recorded, in the new illustrated edition of *Our Village*, her impressions of the little hamlet from which it was named: "I saw two or three commonplace looking houses skirting the dusty road, I saw a comfortable public house with an elm tree, and beside it another gray unpretentious little house, with a slate roof and square walls, and an inscription, 'The Mitford,' painted over the doorway." She who found so much beauty and goodness in this spot, must have been acting on the motto,

> Be to her virtues very kind;
> Be to her faults a little blind.

It may be acknowledged that Miss Mitford's work requires pruning, though the excuse is not far to seek:—"I write for remuneration," she says emphatically, "and I would rather scrub floors, if I could get as much by that healthier, more respectable, and more feminine employment." The urgent necessity for earning money, from which she was never absolved, forced her to use her pen when, to put it plainly, she had nothing to say. The most sprightly writing requires more body than is provided for some of her sketches, and the most charming spots or characters become tiresome when treated at too great length.

Thus it happens that the first series of *Our Village* is on the whole the best, and that her later books are again on a slightly lower level. In *Belford Regis* she touches on the comparatively new material of a small country town (i.e.

Reading), and introduces the same character in several of the stories; features which led her to prefer it above her other works, and gave her some confidence in attempting to comply with "Mr. Bentley's desire for a novel." But, though *Atherton*, her one attempt at the novel proper, contains some charming passages, it is wanting in varied interest, and the progress of the story is too slow. She had not, in fact, enough imagination to construct a plot or create a character. Persons and scenes which were before her, whether in books or in nature, she could describe and even "compose," but more ambitious attempts proved a failure.

Her letters are almost as interesting as *Our Village*, and the attractiveness of both springs from the writer's own personality, her enthusiasm for books and friends, her devotion to animals, and her great love for flowers, so prettily recognised by the gardeners, who "were constantly calling plants after her, and sending her one of the first cuttings as presents." That which she loved, moreover, she observed with unerring attention, and described with a light touch and graphic humour, tempered and refined by a generous loving-kindness for humanity, which long trials could not weaken.—R. BRIMLEY JOHNSON, "Mary Russell Mitford," *English Prose*, ed. Henry Craik, 1896, Vol. 5, pp. 299–301

Coleridge saw some of her dramatic sketches, and praised her work. This encouraged her to write plays for the stage. Macready, Talfourd, Charles Kemble, and others became her friends and helpers, and Miss Edgeworth, Joanna Baillie, and Mrs. Hemans expressed their approval of her work. She made a good deal of money, especially by the performances of *Rienzi*. But everything she gained was soon swallowed in the pit of her father's pocket, and although her industry did not slacken, neither did his expenses cease. After all, it was from the windows of the cottage at "Three-Mile Cross" and from the walks in that vicinity that her true vocation came to her. When Miss Mitford wrote *Our Village*, the reading world recognized a new note, a fresh sympathy, the beginning of a literary epoch. The modern short story was perhaps born to the world straight from Miss Mitford's heart. There never was a kinder nor a larger one, and although the largest room of her cottage, as she says, was only eight feet square, it proved to be more than most palaces in its ability to harbor and to nourish human sympathies.—ANNIE FIELDS, "Mary Russell Mitford," *Critic*, Dec. 1900, p. 512

Works

OUR VILLAGE

We have no passion for 'breaking a butterfly upon the wheel,' and should not notice this little volume, if we were not on the whole pleased with its contents. The sketches of country scenery, in which it abounds, have such a convincing air of locality; the human figures, interspersed among them, are touched in such a laughter-loving, good-humoured spirit of caricature, innocent, and yet often pungent withal, that we scarcely know a more agreeable portfolio of trifles for the amusement of an idle hour. Abundant matter for small criticism, indeed, might be found in the details of the work. In the first place, several of the pieces have too much of the manner of Teniers about them; particularly for the productions of a female pencil. They are too broad and Flemish in the outlines, too low in the situations, and too coarse in the expression, although, doubtless, free from intentional offence or impurity of thought. Miss Mitford is painting rural scenes and often humble life, it is true; and we are not fastidious enough to desire that she should people the tufted hedgerows and green uplands, the wild heaths and the shady lanes of her village, with the costume of the drawing-room; as artists of the last century were wont to adorn their prim landscapes with laced macaronies and furbelowed dames. But she seems to have forgotten, or to have yet to learn, that vulgarity is not nature; and that it is very possible—a truth which the example of several amiable writers of her own sex might have taught her—to seize, and to record with fidelity, the peculiarities of uneducated society, without identifying herself too closely with them; to describe the manners, the occupations, and even the pastimes of her rustic neighbours, without adopting their vulgarisms of language, or descending to clothe her ideas in the phraseology of the dog-kennel and the kitchen.

We notice these defects in Miss Mitford's volume with no uncourteous spirit; and we expose them with the less hesitation because the style of expression of which we complain is quite foreign to the poetical refinement of fancy displayed in some of her earlier productions, and is in a great degree assumed, very injudiciously, for the present occasion. It is really provoking to find a lady, who has evidently been reared in the lap of English country gentility—that pure retreat of simple pretensions, elegant sufficiency, and intellectual tastes, the proudest boast of our island—and who has, moreover, communed much with the chastest part of our literature; it is really provoking to find her studiously labouring to familiarize herself with the use, and to soil her pages by the introduction of such low and provincial corruptions of language as 'transmogrified,' 'betweenity,' 'dumpiness,' 'rolypoly,' 'kickshaws,' 'hurry-scurry,' 'scrap-dinners,' 'pot-luck,' and similar flowers of diction scarcely worthy of Lady Morgan. We should have been better satisfied also, to have found Miss Mitford less ambitious of astonishing us male creatures by her acquaintance with the mysteries of cricketing and coursing: it is very difficult for a lady to descant gracefully upon the athletic qualities of blacksmiths and ploughmen, the merits of batters and bowlers, of long-stops and fielders, and the arithmetic of notches and innings. But it is against the unnatural amalgamation of the craft of the kennel with the light and tasteful pursuits of her sex, that we especially protest. ⟨. . .⟩

We would earnestly recommend our fair friend to leave the qualities of the 'little bitches,' and the gross technicalities of the sports of the field, to her coursing acquaintance, the gentleman farmer.

We have taken the trouble of making these observations, because Miss Mitford is really capable of better things; and we have no doubt that our hints will not be thrown away on her. While we are engaged in this ungracious office of censure, we must say a few words more. We like the conceit of pastoral infantine simplicity as little as the assumption of coarseness; the baby frock and pinafore as little as the russet gown and hunting whip. Miss Mitford's greyhound, May, and her little spoiled favourite Lizzy, the carpenter's daughter, are tedious beyond endurance; and the repetition of her chidings and caresses to the one, and of her colloquies with the other, is sadly puerile and unmeaning. "'Faster, my Lizzy! Oh what a bad runner!" "Faster, faster! Oh what a bad runner," echoed my sauce-box. "You are so fat, Lizzy, you make no way!" "Ah! who else is fat?" retorted the darling. Certainly her mother is right, I do spoil that child.' In the same spirit we have whole pages devoted to the process of making a *cowslip ball* for the child—miserably tiresome—and another paper on '*Violeting*.' There is no greater charm in woman than the enthusiastic admiration of nature; but the feeling should be tempered by discretion, and not evaporate into mere 'babbling o' green

fields.'—WILLIAM GIFFORD, "Village Sketches," *Quarterly Review*, Dec. 1824, pp. 166–69

During my convalescence, I read a considerable part of Miss Mitford's *Village*, perhaps for the third time. Her short sketches, overflowing with life and beauty, refresh me when I am too weak for long stories, and she has often been a cheering friend in my sick room.—WILLIAM ELLERY CHANNING, Letter to Lucy Aikin (Dec. 15, 1841), *Correspondence of William Ellery Channing and Lucy Aikin*, ed. Anna Letitia Le Breton, 1874, p. 410

Mary Russell Mitford, whose name has been pleasantly recalled to our remembrance by the publication of her charming letters, was well known to American readers of thirty years ago as the author of several popular dramas and a series of delightful sketches called *Our Village*. Her dramas have failed, however, to keep possession of the stage, and the sensational fiction of the day has crowded her sketches into the background. Most American readers of this generation are probably unaware even of the existence of this charming book, or at any rate regard it, as most readers regard the *Spectator*, as a classic, to be mentioned always with becoming admiration, but rarely taken down from the library shelves. Yet there is not a more enjoyable book of the kind in the English language than *Our Village*; and readers whose taste is not wholly vitiated by the sensational element in the fiction of the time will always linger with delight over its pages. It is a book that Washington Irving might have been justly proud to claim as his own; nay, it is doubtful whether any work of his exhibits a finer insight into character, more exquisite appreciation of humor, more touching pathos, or a more delicate perception of the beautiful in nature.—SAMUEL STILLMAN CONANT, "Mary Russell Mitford," *Harper's New Monthly Magazine*, Feb. 1870, pp. 409–10

Nearly half a century ago the present writer was taken, at a very early age, to a little tea-party at Chelsea, where all were elderly except herself; and while the seniors, chiefly tired men of letters and their wives, were recreating themselves with a game of whist, there was no happier person than the youngest, who in a sofa corner first made acquaintance with *Our Village*. As long as I read, I was enthralled. I knew little, then, of real country life, but I can truly say of Miss Mitford that then and thereafter

> She gave me eyes, she gave me ears;

in fact, opened a gate into a path leading to pleasures that have been prolonged throughout my life. Her style became my ideal; it was never overweighted with allusion or metaphor, but had a freshness peculiar to itself, and to wilding thickets "such as Hobbima or Ruysdael might have painted," full of violets and funguses, ringdoves and squirrels, yet at some unexpected turn bringing one to a crumbling vase or mouldy statue.

Yes, she taught many of the young to look for interest among the poor, as well as for beauty in their surroundings. Her tragic poetry, too, had its charm for them; though it was in the precincts of *Our Village* that one liked her best. A shadowy vision of her, something like Wordsworth's "Louisa," struggling against a squall of rain and wind, or laughing in the sun, with Lizzy and Mayflower racing beside her, and Joel and Ben touching their hats as they met, was not at all improved by Haydon's picture of her at the Royal Academy, which her father declared he would not admit into his house.—ANNE MANNING, "Mary Russell Mitford," *Macmillan's Magazine*, Feb. 1870, p. 346

The charming country sketches of *Our Village* rank not far below White's *Selborne* in accuracy, and surpass them in variety and ornament.—GEORGE SAINTSBURY, *Specimens of English Prose Style*, 1886, p. 331

HARRIET MARTINEAU
From "Mary Russell Mitford" (1855)
Biographical Sketches
1869, pp. 37–43

The interest which was taken in her state might appear to be disproportionate to her abilities and her achievements; but if so, there must be a reason for it, and the reason is that she was so genial and so cheerful as to command the affection of multitudes who would have given no heed to a much higher order of genius invested with less of moral charm. There is nothing so popular as cheerfulness; and when the cheerfulness is of the unfailing sort which arises from amiability and interior content, it deserves such love as attended Mary Russell Mitford to her grave. Her ability was very considerable. Her power of description was unique. She had a charming humour, and her style was delightful. Yet were her stories read with a relish which exceeded even so fair a justification as this—with a relish which the judgment could hardly account for; and this pleasant, compelled enjoyment was no doubt ascribable to the glow of good spirits and kindliness which lighted up and warmed everything that her mind produced. She may be considered as the representative of household cheerfulness in the humbler range of the literature of fiction.

Her tendencies showed themselves early. She took up the pen almost in childhood, and was an avowed poet, in print, before she was four-and-twenty. However hard was her filial duty when she was herself growing old, she had all her own way in her early years; and her way seems to have been to write an immense quantity of verse as the pleasantest thing she could find to do.

She was born at Alresford, in Hampshire. Her father was a physician, one of the Northumberland family of Mitfords. Her mother was the child of the old age of a Hampshire clergyman, who had seen Pope, and been intimate with Fielding. Her father was, as it is understood, disliked and disapproved, if not despised, by everybody but his devoted daughter, whose infatuation it was to think him something very great and good; whereas there seems to be really nothing to remember him by but his singular and unaccountable extravagance in money matters, and the selfishness with which he went on to the last obtaining, by hook and by crook, costly indulgences, which nobody else in his line of life, however independent of creditors, thought of wishing for. Dr. Mitford ran through half-a-dozen fortunes, shifted about to half-a-dozen grand residences, and passed the last quarter of a century of his life in a cottage, where, humble as seemed his mode of living, he could not keep out of debt, or the shame of perpetual begging from the friends whom his daughter had won. His only child was carried about, before she was old enough for school, from Alresford to Reading; from Reading to Lyme, and thence to London, where, when she was ten years old, her father was making up his mind to retrench and do something at last—a resolution which went the way of all the former ones. It was at that time that the well-known incident happened which Miss Mitford related with so much spirit half a century afterwards.

The little girl chose for a birthday present a lottery ticket of a particular number, to which she stuck, in spite of much persuasion to change it, and which turned up a prize of 20,000*l*. This money soon disappeared, like some 40,000*l*.

which had vanished before. Her father put her to school in London, and there she spent five years, while he was amusing himself with building a very large house, four miles from Reading, to which she returned at the age of fifteen, to write poetry, and dream of becoming an authoress. After 1810 she put forth a volume almost every year. This was all done for pleasure; but she was meanwhile giving up to her selfish father one legacy after another, left to herself by the opulent families on both sides, after her mother's handsome fortune was exhausted; and hence at length arose the necessity of her writing for the sake of the money she could earn.

In their poverty they went to lodge for a summer at a cottage in the village of Three Mile Cross, near Reading, and there they held on for the rest of Dr. Mitford's long life. The poetess looked round her, and described in prose what she saw, sending the papers which, collected, form the celebrated *Our Village*, to Campbell for the *New Monthly Magazine*. Campbell made the mistake of rejecting them—an error in which he was followed by a great number and variety of other editors. It was in *The Lady's Magazine*, of all places, that articles destined to make a literary reputation of no mean order first appeared. They were published in a collected form in 1823; and from that time forward Miss Mitford was sure of the guineas whenever she chose to draw for them in the form of pleasant stories under her well-known and welcome signature. Few of her many readers, however, knew at what cost these pleasant pieces were produced. They seem to flow easily enough; and their sportive style suggests anything but the toil and anxiety amidst which they were spun out. It is observable that each story is as complete and rounded as a sonnet, and provided with a plot which would serve for a novel if expanded. Each has a catastrophe,—generally a surprise, elaborately wrought out in concealment. It was for stories of this kind that Miss Mitford exchanged the earlier and easier sketches from the Nature around her which we find in *Our Village*; and the exchange increased immensely the call upon her energies. But the money must be had, and the Annuals paid handsomely; and thus, therefore, the devoted daughter employed her talents, spoiling her father, and wearing herself out, but delighting an enormous number of readers. After frittering away the whole day, incessantly on foot, or otherwise fatiguing herself, at his beck and call, and receiving his friends, and reading him to sleep in the afternoons till she had no voice left, the hour came when she might put him to bed. But her own day's work still remained to be done. It was not a sort of work which could be done by powers, jaded like hers, without some stimulus or relief; and hence the necessity of doses of laudanum to carry her through her task. When the necessity ceased by the death of her father, her practice of taking laudanum ceased; but her health had become radically impaired, and her nervous system was rendered unfit to meet any such shock as that which overthrew it at last. Miss Mitford so toiling by candlelight, while the hard master who had made her his servant all day was asleep in the next room, is as painful an instance of the struggles of human life as the melancholy of a buffoon, or the heart-break—that "secret known to all"—of a boasting Emperor of All the Russias.

While this was her course of life, however, she was undergoing something of an intellectual training, together with her moral discipline. All this reading to her father, and the impossibility of commanding her time for any other employment than reading by snatches (except gardening), brought her into acquaintance with a wide field of English literature; and some of it of an uncommon kind. The fruits are seen in one of her latest works—her *Notes of a Literary Life*; and in her indomitable inclination to write Tragedies for immediate representation. Several of her plays were acted; and she herself was wont to declare that she should be immortalized by them, if at all; moreover, there are critics who agree with her; yet her case certainly appears to us to be one of that numerous class in which the pursuit of dramatic fame is a delusion and a snare. In no other act or attempt of her life did Miss Mitford manifest any of those qualities of mind which are essential to success in this the highest walk of literature. It does not appear that she had any insight into passion, any conception of the depths of human character, or the scope of human experience. Ability of a certain sort there is in her plays; but no depth, and no compass. Four tragedies and an opera of hers were acted at our first theatres; and we hear no more of *Julian, Foscari, Rienzi,* or *Charles I.* At first the difficulties were imputed to dramatic censors, and the great actors, and injudicious or lukewarm friends; but all that was over long ago. The tragedies were acted, and we hear no more of them. It is true Mr. Colman did refuse his sanction to *Charles I.* when it bore the name *Cromwell* (an amusing incident to have happened in the reign of poor William IV., whose simple head was very safe on his shoulders); and it is true that Young and Macready wrangled so long about the principal characters in her first acted play, that the tantalised authoress began to wonder whether it would ever appear: but the plays have all appeared; and they do not keep the stage, though Miss Mitford's friends were able and willing to do all that interest, literary and dramatic, can do in such a case. All the evidence of her career seems to show that her true line was that in which she obtained an early, decisive, and permanent success—much humbler than the Dramatic, but that in which she has given a great deal of pleasure to a multitude of readers. Her descriptions of scenery, brutes, and human beings have such singular merit that she may be regarded as the founder of a new style; and if the freshness wore off with time, there was much more than a compensation in the fine spirit of resignation and cheerfulness which breathed through everything she wrote, and endeared her as a suffering friend to thousands who formerly regarded her only as a most entertaining stranger.

Dr. Mitford died in 1842, leaving his affairs in such a state, that relief for his daughter had to be obtained by a subscription among her friends and admirers, which was soon followed by a pension from the Crown. The daughter inherited or contracted some of her father's extremely easy feelings about money, and its sources and uses; but the temptation to that sort of laxity was removed or infinitely lessened when she was left alone with a very sufficient provision. She removed to a cottage at Swallowfield, near Reading, in 1851; and there, with her pony-chaise, her kind neighbours, her distant admirers, and the amusement of bringing out a succession of volumes, the materials of which were under her hand, she found resources enough to make her days cheerful, even after the accident which rendered her a suffering prisoner for the last two years of her life. She remained to the end the most sympathising and indulgent friend of the young, and the most good-humoured of comrades to people of all ages and conditions. However helpless, she was still bright; and her vitality of mind and heart was never more striking or more genial than when she was visibly dying by inches, and alluding with a smile to the deep and still bed which she should occupy among the sunshine and flickering shadows of the village churchyard. Finally, the long exhaustion ended in an easy and quiet death.

Though not gifted with lofty genius, or commanding powers of any sort, Miss Mitford has been sufficiently conspicuous in the literary history of her time to claim an expression

of respect and regret on her leaving us. Her talents and her character were essentially womanly; and she was fortunate in living in an age when womanly ability in the department of Letters obtains respect and observance, as sincerely and readily as womanly character commands reverence and affection in every age.

G. F. CHORLEY
From "Miss Austen and Miss Mitford"
Quarterly Review, January 1870, pp. 204–5, 215–18

Passing from Jane Austen to Mary Russell Mitford, we pass from a sunny to a sad story. Whereas the author of *Persuasion* led a happy life, among 'her own people;' beloved and worthy even if they failed sufficiently to value her merit, and to foresee her fame—the author of *Our Village,* and *Rienzi* was driven out into conflict and struggle from almost the earliest moment at which her peculiar genius revealed itself, to support and to maintain the credit of as miserable a creature as ever preyed on, and weighed down, the women of his family.

The sorrow—the disadvantage—the mistake of Miss Mitford's life must be clearly unfolded if only because among her contemporaries, and her survivors, they have caused some misconstruction. Hers was the history of a credulous woman sacrificing herself to an utterly worthless idol—told over again; but with some difference from its usual formula. The heroine, who stakes her all on a love attachment—who braves ill-repute, ill-usage, want, even—for some worthless, showy creature who has first won her heart, then drained her purse, lastly, left her in the mire of disgrace,—is, and ought to be, an object of generous charity; but the woman who perils her delicacy of nature to screen a vicious parent, not being interesting, is confounded in his shame, and meets with less pity than is awarded to a Marion Lescaut, or an Esmeralda. There is no survivor who can be pained by a plain statement of matters as they really stood in the present case.

⟨. . .⟩ *Our Village,* which may be said, without caricature, to have become a classic, and to have set the fashion in literature of a series of sketches of home scenery and natural life—akin to the woodcuts of Bewick, or the etchings of Read of Salisbury—will bear return and reprint, so long as the taste for close observation and miniature painting of scenery and manners shall last. It was probably, like many another creation of the kind, begun by chance; its writer led on from picture to picture, from conceit to conceit, from character to character, as her work proceeded. One quality may be mentioned which recommended Miss Mitford's village sketches from their first appearance—the clearness and purity of the language in which they are written. When we think of the dashes, indications, epithets misapplied, makeshifts in point of grammatical construction which are to-day tolerated, we come to understand, in part, how men of high scholarship and various acquirement at once recognised the contributions, unobtrusive but complete in their finish, which came from a Berkshire village. They may be laid by, but they will not, we predict, be forgotten. *Belford Regis,* a series of country and town sketches, intended to embrace a wider range of characters, is, like most sequels in imaginative literature, a comparative failure.

Miss Mitford's tragedies are less easy to deal with; our present duty not being that of Mr. Curdle, in *Nicholas Nickleby,* who held forth weightily on the unities and disunities of modern tragedy. And yet the female dramatists are a group well worth considering,—the list including such widely differing celebrities as Afra Behn, Margaret Duchess of Newcastle, Susanna Centlivre, Mrs. Cowley, Fanny Burney, Hannah More, Joanna Baillie, Barbarina Lady Dacre, Felicia Hemans;—not to forget Mrs. Gore, with her prize comedy; Miss Landon, the Princess Amalia of Saxony, Mrs. Fanny Kemble, Madame de Girardin (whose *La joie fait peur* contains one of the few stage inventions of modern times), and Madame Dudevant, who has succeeded in planting French country life and peasant manners on the Parisian stage. It would be hard to name one of the sisterhood who planted her foot on the boards so firmly as Miss Mitford, and who gained and maintained her successes in a manner so honourable to herself, and withal so creditable to womanhood. On this a word remains to be said.

Female jealousy is a theme as old as the tongue of male sarcasm. Phillis and Brunetta are, after all, only expressions of the grudging, vieing, uncharitable spirit with which beauties, wits, leaders of fashion, or political intriguers have, since the age of Fair Rosamond, been credited with regard to one another. But a protest of singular and significant force is contained in this book. In no arena of literature are envy and 'all uncharitableness' more notoriously provoked than in the theatre. Personal vanity, immediate triumph, rivalry to be cajoled, animosity to be silenced, defects and excellences of interpretation to be allowed for or encouraged—all come into the amusing, fascinating, and yet rueful history of Drama, and its production. But in the book under notice nothing is more remarkable than the graceful generosity of dramatic authoresses to a dramatic authoress. None of the sisterhood seems to have held back from cordial recognition of certainly the greatest and most continuous success in serious drama won by any English woman. Miss Mitford's four plays—the *Foscari*, produced under the disadvantage of what might have been thought rivalry with Byron; *Julian*, more successful; *Rienzi*, yet more clear, powerful, and sustained (as such gracefully complimented by Lord Lytton, in the preface to his best historical romance); *Charles the First*, in spite of the tremendous difficulties of its subject—all made their mark at the time of their appearance. The best of them, *Rienzi*, may possibly reappear should the Fates resuscitate poetical tragedy, and withal, vouchsafe us actors able to understand and instructed to deliver verse. These tragedies were all warmly greeted, and the greeting came more warmly from none than from female dramatists—Mrs. Joanna Baillie, whose *De Montfort* had the rare advantage of being interpreted by Mrs. Siddons, and her less glorious, but still glorious, brother, John Kemble;—and whose *Henriquez*—a tragedy produced some quarter of a century later—contains one of the strongest and most original situations existing in any play ancient or modern; a woman who loved and who wrought for, the stage,—Mrs. Hemans, whose *Vespers of Palermo* failed—to name the two most distinguished poetesses out of a long list—were one and all eager in their expression of welcome and sympathy. This cannot have been grimace in place of reality; no manifestation having been called for. It tells well for both the givers and the receiver of the praise. One so catholic and cordial as Miss Mitford generally was in admitting the excellences of writers so widely apart one from the other as some of her favourites, was only justly repaid by the kind construction of her rivals and contemporaries.

Let it be added that Miss Mitford was neither egotistic nor arrogant in producing herself and her works, as themes for conversation with her admirers, some of whom (may it not be said?), especially those from America, desired nothing better than to assail her with an incense of compliment, though high-flown, sincere enough to have turned a weaker head than her own. When we think of Madame D'Arblay's diary, which, bright and clever as it is, is in too many of its pages little more than a hymn in her own praise, sung at 'the request of friends'; when we think of the complacent accounts which Hannah More's letters contain of what the success of her *Percy*—so justly styled by Mrs. Piozzi a foolish play—her propriety, 'which' (as Horace Walpole put it) 'is a grace when all other graces have fled,' rises by retrospect and comparison. It is not a genuine love of letters that will save its owner from foolish self-occupation;— but the absence of such spirit in man or woman who has earned distinction makes them endearing no less than admirable. We believe that few who consider such an example as this in conjunction with the sparing revelations of hard and, it might have been assumed, hardening trial to be derived from Miss Mitford's correspondence will fail to value such an abstinence from self-glorification as something not common in the world of letters,—most especially in the quarter of it inhabited by those whom one Jonathan Oldbuck scornfully called 'the women-kind.'

CHARLOTTE BRONTË

1816–1855

Charlotte Brontë was born at Thornton in Yorkshire on April 21, 1816. The elder sister of Emily (1818–1848), Anne (1820–1849), and Branwell (1817–1848) Brontë, Charlotte spent most of her life living with her family in Haworth, Yorkshire, where her father was perpetual curate. Charlotte's mother died in 1821, and in 1823 her mother's sister, Elizabeth Branwell, moved in with the family to take care of the children. In 1824 Charlotte and Emily entered the Clergy Daughters' School at Cowan Bridge, but they were both unhappy there and returned a year later. From then on Charlotte was educated mostly at home, until 1831, when she enrolled at Miss Wooler's School in Roe Head. She returned home to tutor her sisters in 1832, and in 1835 went back to Roe Head as a teacher. Charlotte resigned her position in 1838, came home, and in 1842 went with Emily to study at the Pensionnat Heger in Brussels; they returned later that year after the death of their aunt, Elizabeth Branwell. Charlotte revisited Brussels in 1843 to teach English and to study, and on her return in 1844 she and her sisters attempted unsuccessfully to open a school.

Perhaps because they spent so much time alone together at Haworth, in a remote and isolated part of Yorkshire, Charlotte, Emily, Anne, and Branwell shared an active imaginative life together as children. They began at an early age to collaborate on putting together collections of verse and stories, and Charlotte and Branwell together created the imaginary world of Angria, which figured in many of Charlotte's early tales. In 1845 Charlotte began gathering some of this juvenilia, and in the following year the three sisters published a slim volume of sixty-one poems entitled *Poems by Currer, Ellis and Acton Bell* (the respective pseudonyms of Charlotte, Emily, and Anne). This collection did not sell well, and Charlotte was unsuccessful in finding a publisher for her first novel, *The Professor*, which she had completed in 1846; it did not appear until after her death. Charlotte's second novel, *Jane Eyre*, was published pseudonymously in 1847 and became an immediate success, arousing much speculation as to the identity of its author.

Charlotte was not, however, able to enjoy this new-found success. In 1848 both Branwell and Emily died, and in the following year Anne died also. Despite these tragedies, Charlotte completed another novel, *Shirley*, again published under the name Currer Bell in 1849. Her fourth novel, *Villette*, appeared in 1853, also under the name Currer Bell, despite the fact that her identity was then widely known. In 1854 Charlotte married A. B. Nicholls; less than a year later, on March 31, 1855, she died of complications resulting from a severe cold while in the early stages of pregnancy.

After her death Charlotte Brontë's fame increased with the publication of her friend Elizabeth Gaskell's *Life of Charlotte Brontë* (1857). Her first novel, *The Professor*, was published in 1857, and in the twentieth century several volumes of her juvenilia have appeared, including *The Twelve Adventurers and Other Stories* (1925; ed. C. K. Shorter and C. W. Hatfield), *Legends of Angria* (1933; ed. Fanny Elizabeth Ratchford and W. C. De Vane), and *Five Novelettes* (1971; ed. Winifred Gérin).

Personal

I sent a dose of cooling admonition to the poor girl whose flighty letter reached me at Buckland. It was well taken, and she thanked me for it. It seems she is the eldest daughter of a clergyman, has been expensively educated, and is laudably employed as a governess in some private family. About the same time that she wrote to me, her brother wrote to Wordsworth, who was disgusted with the letter, for it contained gross flattery to him, and plenty of abuse of other poets, including me. I think well of the sister from her second letter, and probably she will think kindly of me as long as she lives.
—ROBERT SOUTHEY, Letter to Caroline Bowles (1837), *The Correspondence of Robert Southey with Caroline Bowles*, ed. Edward Dowden, 1881, p. 348.

We had very early cherished the dream of one day becoming authors. This dream, never relinquished even when distance divided and absorbing tasks occupied us, now suddenly acquired strength and consistency: it took the character of a resolve. We agreed to arrange a small selection of our poems, and, if possible, to get them printed. Averse to personal publicity, we veiled our own names under those of Currer, Ellis, and Acton Bell; the ambiguous choice being dictated by a sort of conscientious scruple at assuming Christian names positively masculine, while we did not like to declare ourselves women, because—without at that time suspecting that our mode of writing and thinking was not what is called "feminine"—we had a vague impression that authoresses are liable to be looked on with prejudice; we had noticed how critics sometimes use for their chastisement the weapon of personality, and for their reward, a flattery, which is not true praise.
—CHARLOTTE BRONTË (as "Currer Bell"), "Biographical Notice of Ellis and Acton Bell," *Wuthering Heights and Agnes Grey*, 1850

Lewes was describing Currer Bell to me yesterday as a little, plain, provincial, sickly-looking old maid. Yet what passion, what fire in her! Quite as much as in George Sand, only the clothing is less voluptuous.—GEORGE ELIOT, Letter to Mr. and Mrs. Charles Bray (March 5, 1853)

—How shall we honour the young,
The ardent, the gifted? how mourn?

Console we cannot, her ear
Is deaf. Far northward from here,
In a churchyard high 'mid the moors
Of Yorkshire, a little earth
Stops it for ever to praise.

Where, behind Keighley, the road
Up to the heart of the moors
Between heath-clad showery hills
Runs, and colliers' carts
Poach the deep ways coming down,
And a rough, grimed race have their homes—
There on its slope is built
The moorland town. But the church
Stands on the crest of the hill,
Lonely and bleak;—at its side
The parsonage-house and the graves.

Strew with laurel the grave
Of the early-dying! Alas,
Early she goes on the path
To the silent country, and leaves
Half her laurels unwon,
Dying too soon!—yet green
Laurels she had, and a course
Short, but redoubled by fame.

And not friendless, and not
Only with strangers to meet,
Faces ungreeting and cold,
Thou, O mourn'd one, to-day
Enterest the house of the grave!
Those of thy blood, whom thou lov'dst,
Have preceded thee—young,
Loving, a sisterly band;
Some in art, some in gift
Inferior—all in fame.
They, like friends, shall receive
This comer, greet her with joy;
Welcome the sister, the friend;
Hear with delight of thy fame!
—MATTHEW ARNOLD, "Haworth Churchyard," 1855

We are reading the *Life of Charlotte Brontë*, a most striking book. Genius as she was, she is beautifully attentive to the smallest practical matters affecting the comforts of others. She is intensely true, and draws from actual life, cost what it may; and in that remote little world of hers—a village, as it seems, of a hundred years back—facts came to light of a frightful unmitigated force; events accompanied them, burning with a lurid glow and setting their very hearts on fire. She is like her books, and her life explains much in them which needs explanation.—CAROLINE FOX, *Journal* (July 9, 1857), *Memories of Old Friends*, ed. Horace N. Pym, 1881, p. 336

Between the appearance of *Shirley* and that of *Villette*, she came to me;—in December, 1850. Our intercourse then confirmed my deep impression of her integrity, her noble conscientiousness about her vocation, and her consequent self-reliance in the moral conduct of her life. I saw at the same time tokens of a morbid condition of mind, in one or two directions;—much less than might have been expected, or than would have been seen in almost any one else under circumstances so unfavourable to health of body and mind as those in which she lived; and the one fault which I pointed out to her in *Villette* was so clearly traceable to these unwholesome influences that I would fain have been spared a task of criticism which could hardly be of much use while the circumstances remained unchanged. ⟨. . .⟩ She might be weak for once; but her permanent temper was one of humility, candour, integrity and conscientiousness. She was not only unspoiled by her sudden and prodigious fame, but obviously unspoilable. She was somewhat amused by her fame, but oftener annoyed;—at least, when obliged to come out into the world to meet it, instead of its reaching her in her secluded home, in the wilds of Yorkshire.—HARRIET MARTINEAU, *Autobiography*, ed. Maria Weston Chapman, 1877, Vol. 2, p. 24

The loving admirers of Charlotte Brontë can never feel much enthusiasm for Mr. Nicholls. Mrs. Gaskell states that he was not attracted by her literary fame, but was rather repelled by it; he appears to have used her up remorselessly, in their short married life, in the routine drudgery of parish work. She did not complain, on the contrary, she seemed more than contented to sacrifice everything for him and his work; but she remarks in one of her letters, "I have less time for thinking." Apparently she had none for writing. Surely the husband of a Charlotte Brontë, just as much as the wife of a Wordsworth or a Tennyson, ought to be attracted by literary fame. To be the life partner of one to whom the most precious of Nature's gifts is confided, and to be unappreciative of it and even repelled by it, shows a littleness of nature and essential meanness of soul. A true wife or husband of one of these gifted beings should rather regard herself or himself as responsible to the world for making the conditions of the daily life of their distinguished partners favourable to the development of their genius. But pearls have before now been cast before swine, and one cannot but regret that Charlotte Brontë was married to a man who did not value her place in literature as he ought.—MILLICENT GARRETT FAWCETT, *Some Eminent Women of Our Times*, 1889, p. 109

One of the most notable persons who ever came into our old bow-windowed drawing-room in Young Street is a guest never to be forgotten by me, a tiny, delicate, little person, whose small hand nevertheless grasped a mighty lever which set all the literary world of that day vibrating. I can still see the scene quite plainly!—the hot summer evening, the open windows, the carriage driving to the door as we all sat silent and expectant; my father ⟨W. M. Thackeray⟩, who rarely waited, waiting with us; our governess and my sister and I all in a row, and prepared for the great event. We saw the carriage stop, and

out of it sprang the active, well-knit figure of young Mr. George Smith, who was bringing Miss Brontë to see our father. My father, who had been walking up and down the room, goes out into the hall to meet his guests, and then after a moment's delay the door opens wide, and the two gentlemen come in, leading a tiny, delicate, serious, little lady, pale, with fair straight hair, and steady eyes. She may be a little over thirty; she is dressed in a little *barège* dress with a pattern of faint green moss. She enters in mittens, in silence, in seriousness; our hearts are beating with wild excitement. This then is the authoress, the unknown power whose books have set all London talking, reading, speculating; some people even say our father wrote the books—the wonderful books. To say that we little girls had been given *Jane Eyre* to read scarcely represents the facts of the case; to say that we had taken it without leave, read bits here and read bits there, been carried away by an undreamed-of and hitherto unimagined whirlwind into things, times, places, all utterly absorbing and at the same time absolutely unintelligible to us, would more accurately describe our states of mind on that summer's evening as we look at Jane Eyre—the great Jane Eyre—the tiny little lady. The moment is so breathless that dinner comes as a relief to the solemnity of the occasion, and we all smile as my father stoops to offer his arm, for, genius though she may be, Miss Brontë can barely reach his elbow.—ANNE THACKERAY RITCHIE, "My Witches Caldron," *Macmillan's Magazine*, Feb. 1891, pp. 251–52

Story-telling, as we shall see, was a hereditary gift in the Brontë family, and Patrick ⟨Charlotte's father⟩ inherited it from his father. Charlotte's friend, Miss Ellen Nussey, has often told me of the marvellous fascination with which the girls would hang on their father's lips as he depicted scene after scene of some tragic story in glowing words and with harrowing details. The breakfast would remain untouched till the story had passed the crisis, and sometimes the narration became so real and vivid and intense that the listeners begged the vicar to proceed no farther. Sleepless nights succeeded story-telling evenings at the vicarage.—WILLIAM WRIGHT, *The Brontës in Ireland*, 1893, pp. 15–16

Taken as a whole, the life of Charlotte Brontë was among the saddest in literature. At a miserable school, where she herself was unhappy, she saw her two elder sisters stricken down and carried home to die. In her home was the narrowest poverty. She had, in the years when that was most essential, no mother's care; and perhaps there was a somewhat too rigid disciplinarian in the aunt who took the mother's place. Her second school brought her, indeed, two kind friends; but her shyness made that school-life in itself a prolonged tragedy. Of the two experiences as a private governess I shall have more to say. They were periods of torture to her sensitive nature. The ambition of the three girls to start a school on their own account failed ignominiously. The suppressed vitality of childhood and early womanhood made Charlotte unable to enter with sympathy and toleration into the life of a foreign city, and Brussels was for her a further disaster. Then within two years, just as literary fame was bringing its consolation for the trials of the past, she saw her two beloved sisters taken from her. And, finally, when at last a good man won her love, there were left to her only nine months of happy married life. "I am not going to die. We have been so happy." These words to her husband on her deathbed are not the least piteously sad in her tragic story.—CLEMENT K. SHORTER, *The Brontës and Their Circle*, 1896, p. 21

General

The style of Currer Bell is one which will reward study for its own sake. Its character is directness, clearness, force. We could point to no style which appears to us more genuinely and nobly English. Prompt and businesslike, perfectly free of obscurity, refining, or involution, it seems the native garment of honest passion and clear thought, the natural dialect of men that can work and will. It reminds one of a good highway among English hills: leading straight to its destination, and turning aside for no rare glimpse of landscape, yet bordered by dewy fields, and woods, and crags, with a mountain stream here rolling beneath it, and a thin cascade here whitening the face of the rock by its side: utility embosomed in beauty. Perhaps its tone is somewhat too uniform, its balance and cadence too unvaried. Perhaps, also, there is too much of the abruptness of passion. We should certainly set it far below many styles in richness, delicacy, calmness, and grace. But there is no writer whose style can be pronounced a universal model; and for simple narrative, for the relation of what one would hear with all speed, yet with a spice of accompanying pleasure, this style is a model as nearly perfect as we can conceive. And its beauty is so genuine and honest! You are at first at a loss to account for the charm which breathes around, filling the air as with the fragrance of roses after showers; but the secret cannot long remain hidden from the poor critic, doomed to know how he is pleased. It lies in the perfect honesty, combined with the perfect accuracy, of the sympathy with nature's beauty which dwelt in the breast of the author; in the fact that she ever loved the dew-drop, the daisy, the mountain bird, the vernal branch. Uncalled for and to her unconsciously, at the smile of sympathy, the flowers and the dew-drops come to soften and adorn her page. ⟨. . .⟩

The peculiar strength of Currer Bell as a novelist can be pointed out in a single word. It is that to which allusion was made in speaking of *Wuthering Heights*; the delineation of one relentless and tyrannizing passion. In hope, in ardor, in joy, with proud, entrancing emotion, such as might have filled the breast of him who bore away the fire of Jove, love is wooed to the breast. But a storm as of fate awakens: the blue sky is broken into lightnings, and hope smitten dead; and now the love which formerly was a dove of Eden is changed into a vulture, to gnaw the heart, retained in its power by bands of adamant. As the victim lies on his rock, the whole aspect of the world changes to his eye. Ordinary pleasures and ordinary pains are impotent to engage the attention, to assuage the torment. No dance of the nymphs of ocean attracts the wan eye, or for a moment turns the vulture aside. Such a passion is the love of Rochester for Jane, perhaps in a somewhat less degree, that of Jane for Rochester; such, slightly changed in aspect, is the passion beneath which Caroline pines away, and that which convulses the brave bosom of Shirley. With steady and daring hand, Currer Bell depicts this agony in all its stages; we may weep and tremble, but we feel that her nerves do not quiver, that her eye is unfilmed. So perfect is the verisimilitude, nay the truth, of the delineation, that you cannot for a moment doubt that living hearts have actually throbbed with like passion. It is matter, we believe, of universal assent, that Currer Bell here stands almost alone among the female novelists of Britain, and we doubt whether, however they surpass her in the variety of their delineations, there is any novelist of the other sex who, in this department, has exhibited greater power. —Peter Bayne, "Currer Bell," *Essays in Biography*, 1857, pp. 409–15

To think of your asking such a question as "Do I care about Charlotte Brontë"! As if I did not care everything I am capable of caring of anything! As if Levi and I had not read her books with rapture, and hadn't looked forward to the publishing of Mrs. Gaskell's books as one of the most interesting things that could happen; as if we didn't lament her loss to the world every year of our lives! Oh, Lizzie! I'm ashamed that you know so little of your friends.—Celia Thaxter, Letter to Elizabeth Hoxie (March 28, 1857)

Say that two foreigners have passed through Staffordshire, leaving us their reports of what they have seen. The first, going by day, will tell us of the hideous blackness of the country, but yet more, no doubt, of that awful, patient struggle of man with fire and darkness, of the grim courage of those unknown lives; and he would see what they toil for, women with little children in their arms; and he would notice the blue sky beyond the smoke, doubly precious for such horrible environment. But the second traveller has journeyed through the night; neither squalor nor ugliness, neither sky nor children, has he seen, only a vast stretch of blackness shot through with flaming fires, or here and there burned to a dull red by heated furnaces; and before these, strange toilers, half naked, scarcely human, and red in the leaping flicker and gleam of the fire. The meaning of their work he could not see, but a fearful and impressive phantasmagoria of flame and blackness and fiery energies at work in the encompassing night.

So differently did the black country of this world appear to Charlotte, clear-seeing and compassionate, and to Emily Brontë, a traveller through the shadows. Each faithfully recorded what she saw, and the place was the same, but how unlike the vision!—A. Mary F. Robinson, *Emily Brontë*, 1883, pp. 5–6

Charlotte Brontë was surely a marvellous woman. If it could be right to judge the work of a novelist from one small portion of one novel, and to say of an author that he is to be accounted as strong as he shows himself to be in his strongest morsel of work, I should be inclined to put Miss Brontë very high indeed. I know no interest more thrilling than that which she has been able to throw into the characters of Rochester and the governess, in the second volume of *Jane Eyre*. She lived with those characters, and felt with every fibre of her heart, the longings of the one and the sufferings of the other. And therefore, though the end of the book is weak, and the beginning not very good, I venture to predict that *Jane Eyre* will be read among English novels when many whose names are now better known shall have been forgotten. *Jane Eyre*, and *Esmond*, and *Adam Bede* will be in the hands of our grandchildren, when *Pickwick*, and *Pelham*, and *Harry Lorrequer* are forgotten; because the men and women depicted are human in their aspirations, human in their sympathies, and human in their actions.

In *Villette*, too, and in *Shirley*, there is to be found human life as natural and as real, though in circumstances not so full of interest as those told in *Jane Eyre*. The character of Paul in the former of the two is a wonderful study. She must herself have been in love with some Paul when she wrote the book, and have been determined to prove to herself that she was capable of loving one whose exterior circumstances were mean and in every way unprepossessing.—Anthony Trollope, *An Autobiography*, 1883, Ch. 13

Miss Brontë's novels are day-dreams and memories rather than stories. In *Jane Eyre* she is dealing with the eternal day-dream of the disinherited; the unfortunate guest at life's banquet. It is a vision that has many shapes: some see it in the form of a buried treasure to make them suddenly wealthy—this was the day-dream of Poe; or of a mine to be discovered, a company to be formed—thus it haunted Balzac. The lodging-house servant straight of foundlings dreams, and behold she is a young countess, changed at nurse, and kept out of her own. The poor author dreams of a "hit," and (in this novel) Miss Brontë dwelt in fantasy on the love and the adventures that might come to a clever governess, who was not beautiful. The love and the adventures—these led her on in that path of story-telling where, perhaps, she might have done more and more fortunate work. *Jane Eyre* is her best story, and far the most secure of life, because it has plenty of good, old-fashioned, foolish, immortal romance. The shrieks, and cries, and nocturnal laughters, the wandering vampire of a mad woman, the shadow of a voice heard clamouring in lonely places, the forlorn child, the demon lover (for Mr. Rochester is a modern Euhemerised version of the demon lover)—these are all parts and parcels of the old romantic treasure, and they never weary us in the proper hands. Mr. Rochester is a mere child of dreams, of visions that sprang out of forty French novels, devoured at Haworth's in one winter! But *Shirley* is a day-dream far less successful. The heroine is Emily Brontë, as she might have been if the great god, Wünsch, who inspires day-dreamers, had given her wealth and health. One might as readily fancy the fortunes of a stormy sea-petrel in a parrot's gilded cage. *Shirley* cannot live with *Jane Eyre*, and *Villette* appears to be a thing of memories rather than of dreams; of bitter memories, too, and of despairing resignations. If people do not read it, one can only say, like the cook in "Ravenshoe," that one "does not wonder at it."

Miss Brontë had few strings to her bow as a novelist. She had not, apparently, the delight in invention, in character, in life, which inspires a writer like Scott, and she never would have been a manufacturer of fiction. She only said what she had to say, and her vitality was so depressed by sorrow and thwarting circumstances, that she could not wander into fresh and happier fields of thought and experience. Perhaps if she had lived longer as a clergyman's wife, she might have become the prose Crabbe of English literature. It is only a guess; almost as probably, like other ladies happy mothers made, she might have ceased to write altogether.

About her poetry, it is not easy to speak, so much has her poetry been overshadowed by her prose. Mr. Birrell calls it "the poetry of commerce," but then this critic detects the commercial element, unless he be venturing some kind of joke, in the author of *Atalanta*. To myself it appears that Miss Brontë often made verses as they ought to be made, that she had an accent of her own. These lines ⟨. . .⟩ have, unless one's ear is quite mistaken, the firm foot of Mr. Matthew Arnold's reflective poetry.—ANDREW LANG, "Charlotte Brontë," *Good Words*, 1889, p. 239

It is quite natural and right that Thackeray, Mrs. Gaskell, indeed all who have spoken of the author of *Jane Eyre*, should insist primarily on the personality of Charlotte Brontë. It is this intense personality which is the distinctive note of her books. They are not so much tales as imaginary autobiographies. They are not objective presentations of men and women in the world. They are subjective sketches of a Brontë under various conditions, and of the few men and women who occasionally cross the narrow circle of the Brontë world. Of the three stories she published, two are autobiographies, and the third is a fancy portrait of her sister Emily. Charlotte Brontë is herself Jane Eyre and Lucy Snowe, and Emily Brontë is Shirley Keeldar. So in *The Professor*, her earliest but posthumous tale, Frances Henri again is simply a little Swiss Brontë. That story also is told as an autobiography, but, though the narrator is supposed to be one William Crimsworth, it is a woman who speaks, sees, and dreams all through the book. The four tales, which together were the work of eight years, are all variations upon a Brontë and the two Brontë worlds in Yorkshire and Belgium. It is most significant (but quite natural) that Mrs. Gaskell in her *Life of Charlotte Brontë* devotes more than half her book to the story of the family before the publication of *Jane Eyre*. The four tales are not so much romances as artistic and imaginative autobiographies.

To say this is by no means to detract from their rare value. The romances of adventure, of incident, of intrigue, of character, of society, or of humor, depend on a great variety of observation and a multiplicity of contrasts. There is not much of Walter Scott in *Ivanhoe* or of Alexandre Dumas in the *Trois Mousquetaires*; and Dickens, Thackeray, Trollope, Bulwer, Miss Edgeworth, Stevenson, and Meredith—even Miss Austen and George Eliot—seek to paint men and women whom they conceive and whom we may see and know, and not themselves and their own home circle. But Charlotte Brontë told us her own life, her own feelings, sufferings, pride, joy, and ambition. She bared for us her own inner soul, and all that it had known and desired, and this she did with a noble, pure, simple, but intense truth. There was neither egoism, nor monotony, nor commonplace in it. It was all coloured with native imagination and a sense of true art. There is ample room in Art for these subjective idealisations of even the narrowest world. Shelley's lyrics are intensely self-centered, but no one can find in them either realism or egoism. The field in prose is far more limited, and the risk of becoming tedious and morbid is greater. But a true artist can now and then in prose produce most precious portraits of self and glowing autobiographic fantasies of a noble kind.

And Charlotte Brontë was a true artist. She was also more than this: a brave, sincere, high-minded woman, with a soul, as the great moralist saw, "of impetuous honesty." She was not seduced, or even moved, by her sudden fame. She put aside the prospect of success, money, and social distinction as things which revolted her. She was quite right. With all her genius it was strictly and narrowly limited; she was ignorant of the world to a degree immeasurably below that of any other known writer of fiction; her world was incredibly scanty and barren. She had to spin everything out of her own brain in that cold, still, gruesome Haworth parsonage. It was impossible for any genius to paint a world of which it was as ignorant as a child. Hence, in eight years she only completed four tales for publication. And she did right. With her strict limits both of brain and of experience she could not go further. Perhaps, as it was, she did more than was needed. *Shirley* and *Villette*, with all their fine scenes, are interesting now mainly because Charlotte Brontë wrote them, and because they throw light upon her brain and nature. *The Professor* is entirely so, and has hardly any other quality. We need not groan that we have no more than we have from her pen. *Jane Eyre* would suffice for many reputations and alone will live. ⟨. . .⟩

It is true that a purely subjective work in prose romance, an autobiographic revelation of a sensitive heart, is not the highest and certainly not the widest art. Scott and Thackeray—even Jane Austen and Maria Edgeworth—paint the world, or part of the world, as it is, crowded with men and women of various characters. Charlotte Brontë painted not the world, hardly a corner of the world, but the very soul of one proud and loving girl. That is enough: we need ask no more. It was done with consummate power. We feel that we know her life, from ill-used childhood to her proud matronhood; we know her home, her school, her professional duties, her loves and hates, her agonies and her joys, with that intense familiarity and certainty of vision with which our own personal memories are graven on our brain. With all its faults, its narrowness of range, its occasional extravagances, *Jane Eyre* will long be remembered as one of the most creative influences of the Victorian literature, one of the most poetic pieces of English romance, and among the most vivid masterpieces in the rare order of literary "Confessions."—FREDERIC HARRISON, "Charlotte Brontë's Place in Literature," *Forum*, March 1895, pp. 30–40.

The author of *Jane Eyre* has had one indisputable reward for the shortness of her brilliant career. She has become a classic; she has been recently reprinted as such with authors the youngest of whom was her senior by nearly half a century; and though it cannot be said that she had ever quite fallen out of even popular knowledge, any one with a tolerably sharp eye for criticism must have perceived that not a few readers come to her, as they come to a classic, with a more or less respectful ignorance. She was protected from that most ungracious stage of depreciation which attacks many of her kind immediately after, if not even before, their death, first by the earliness of that event in her case, and secondly by the fact that it happened at a peculiar period. In 1855 the English world had not yet become literary; and though I do not know that the quality of the best literary criticism was much better or much worse than it is now, the volume of it was infinitely smaller. There were far fewer newspapers; and the young person who, on the strength of a modern education, a comfortable confidence in his own judgment, and a hand-book or two of authorities quotable and pillageable, commences critic, existed in smaller numbers, and had very much fewer openings. Moreover, Currer Bell had held one of those literary positions which expose the holder to more hardships at first than afterwards. She belonged to no school; she was not involved in any literary parties; she rose with few rivals, and she died before she had time to create any. So that, though she had great difficulties in making her way, and was subjected to some unfair and ungenerous comments at first, when she had begun to make that way she had little direct detraction to fear.

I do not think that she was exactly what can be called a great genius, or that she would ever have given us anything much better than she did give; and I do not think that with critical reading *Jane Eyre* improves, or even holds its ground very well. It has strength, or at any rate force; it has sufficient originality of manner; it has some direct observation of life within the due limits of art; and it has the piquancy of an unfashionable unconventionality at a very conventional time. These are good things, but they are not necessarily great; and it is to me a very suspicious point that quite the best parts of Charlotte Brontë's work are admittedly something like transcripts of her personal experience. It is very good to be able to record personal experience in this pointed and vivid way; and perhaps few great creators, if any, have been independent of personal experience. But they have for the most part transcribed it very far off; and they have intermixed the transcription with a far larger amount of direct observation of others, and of direct imagination or creation. Those who have not done so fall into the second or lower place, and do not often rise out of it. This is an experience for confirmation of which I can, I think, confidently appeal to all competent reviewers and most competent editors. A book appears, or an article is sent in, wherein this or that incident, mood, character, what not, is treated with distinct vigour and freshness. The reviewer praises, and looks with languid interest tempered by sad experience for the second book; the editor accepts, and looks

with eagerness tempered by experience still more fatal for the second article. Both come, and lo! there is either a distinct falling off from, or a total absence of, the first fine rapture. I think Charlotte Brontë is the capital example of this familiar fact, in a person who has actually attained to literature.

Not that she never did anything good after *Jane Eyre*. I think better than most people seem to have done of *Shirley*, somewhat less well perhaps of *Villette* and *The Professor*. But in all, from *Jane Eyre* itself downward, there is that rather fatal note of the presence and apparent necessity of the personal experience. It is portrait painting or *genre*, not creative art of the unmistakable kind, and in the one case where there seems to be a certain projection of the ideal, the egregious Mr. Rochester, even contemporary opinion—thankful as it was for a variation of type from the usual hero with the chiselled nose, the impeccable, or, if peccable, amiable character, and the general nullity—recognised at once that the ideal was rather a poor one. It was as much of a schoolgirl's or a governess's hero as any one of Scott's or Byron's. It is quite true that Rochester is not merely ugly and rude, but his ugliness and his rudeness are so much of him! And though Jane herself is much more than an underbred little hussy, I fear there is underbreeding and hussyness in her, where she is not a mere photograph. I used to think, years ago, that the finest touch in all Miss Brontë's work is where the boy in *Shirley* makes up his mind to ask Caroline for a kiss as the price of his services, and does not. I am not much otherwise minded now.—GEORGE SAINTSBURY, "Three Mid-Century Novelists," *Corrected Impressions*, 1895, pp. 157–62

Charlotte Brontë's own art was the antithesis of that of Jane Austen. It was hers to depict love in its deeper, more tragic, more serious moods and aspects. She could give us the ordinary "love scene," and charm us with a spell such as few others can command—witness the passage in *The Professor*, in which Crimsworth claims Frances Henri—but it is the love agony which is her element. The pain of unrequited affection is the feeling she never tires of depicting, and in describing this she has no equal. Her novels may end happily, but not till they have been made the medium of exhibiting the suffering which the master passion brings with it when unaccompanied by hope. Nowhere else are to be found such piercing cries of lonely anguish as may be heard in *Shirley* and *Villette*. They are the very *de profundis* of love sunk in the abyss of despair. And their author insists throughout how much greater this suffering must be for women than for men, both because they are doomed to bear in silence, and because they have not the distraction of an active career.—ANGUS M. MACKAY, *The Brontës: Fact and Fiction*, 1897, pp. 40–42

For several reasons Charlotte Brontë holds a higher place in literature than her sister. She has not to be judged by one work only. *Jane Eyre* was followed by *Shirley* (1849), by *Villette* (1853), by *The Professor* (1857), published posthumously, and by the fragment *Emma* (1860). In none of these did she equal her first novel, but she exhibited different sides and aspects of her genius, she multiplied her creations, and she proved, as long as life was given her, that she had what in the language of sport is called 'staying power.' Moreover, Charlotte was decidedly more of the artist than Emily. She understood better the importance of relief. Her imagination too was prevailingly sombre; yet though *Jane Eyre* is sufficiently gloomy, it is less uniformly so than *Wuthering Heights*. The shadow is flecked here and there with light. Again, Charlotte is more versatile in her imagination and much more pictorial than Emily. All the members of the Brontë family had a love and apparently some talent for art; but it is in the works of Charlotte that this talent leaves the clearest traces. There are few things in *Jane Eyre* more impressive than her description in words of the picture her imagination, if not her brush, drew. More ample scope, greater variety, a more humane tone,—these then are the points in which Charlotte surpasses Emily.

⟨. . .⟩ Probably no English writer of equal rank has transcribed so much from experience as Charlotte Brontë. Many of her characters were so like the originals as to be immediately recognised by themselves or by their neighbours. Shirley Keeldar was her sister Emily, Mr. Helstone was her father, the three curates were real men, and some of Charlotte's school friends were depicted, it is said, with the accuracy of daguerreotypes. This minute fidelity to fact occasionally brought Miss Brontë into trouble; for she was not particularly sagacious in estimating the effect of what she wrote. We may argue from it, moreover, that if she had lived she would soon have exhausted her material.

Charlotte Brontë was likewise deficient in humour. This might be safely inferred from her works, where there are hardly any humorous characters or situations; and the inference would be confirmed by her life. Her letters, often excellent for their common sense and their high standard of duty, and sometimes for their dignity, are almost destitute of playfulness. Neither does she seem to have readily recognised humour in others. She admired Thackeray above almost all men of her time, but she was completely puzzled by him when they met. She lectured him on his faults, and quaintly adds that his excuses made them worse. The humourist was playing with the too serious mind. Had Miss Brontë been as Irish in nature as she was by blood she would not have made this mistake.

In the case of the Brontës it would be peculiarly ungenerous to insist on defects. All life long they fought against odds. With inadequate means and imperfect training, without friends and without advice, they won by their own force and genius alone a position in literature which is higher now than it was forty years ago. Charlotte is one of the half-dozen or so of great English novelists of the present century.—HUGH WALKER, *The Age of Tennyson*, 1897, pp. 103–6

Life was worth living to Charlotte Brontë only when it offered opportunity for such intense attachment as would make her willing to die for the object of her emotion. This intense, personal life went into the novels, and has made Villette and Jane Eyre as distinct and definite personalities as Charlotte Brontë herself. Indeed, perhaps they are more so, for I suspect it would be easier for most of us to draw a picture of the soul-life of the struggling teacher-governess of Haworth from the story of Jane Eyre, or from the story of Villette, than from the records of authentic history. The characters are creations, and their appearance marks an epoch in literature, marks a distinct and definite era in the history of the novel. Before their appearance we had had personages in fiction. In *Jane Eyre*, for the first time in English fiction, the intensity of life-craving which dominates a woman who loves is presented in the pages of the novel; and the voice of the outcry of her longing comes to the world. The story of Jane Eyre is familiar enough to all of us. She is a heroine of the inner life. In the depiction of her every advantage of the external is deliberately, almost defiantly, sacrificed. In our oldest English epic, the hero, Beówulf, fights a dragon, and when going to fight with a foe who cannot wear armor and cannot carry a sword, even though that foe is a fire-breathing dragon, Beówulf chooses to sacrifice every external advantage and fights without his armor and without his sword. In the *Orlando Furioso* of Ariosto, though the hero carries an enchanted ring and wields a magic sword at tournaments, yet when the conflict is for life, he throws away these adventitious and external aids and fights with simpler weapons. So, when Charlotte Brontë sets out to depict a stern struggle of the soul of a woman, she throws aside the external excellences by time-honored custom given to heroines. The heroine of her novel is small, dark, plain, almost insignificant, in person; she is poor; she is a governess serving under orders. How shall one make a heroine out of such as this? And the hero, what shall he be in a novel? Shall he not be beautiful, graceful, courteous, virtuous, and eligible? What say you to a hero who is ugly, who is awkward and brutal, who has been dissipated, and who has a wife? It is as if in the interest of the intenser life that Charlotte Brontë counted all external things but as dross, and would have us also count them as things not worth our care. The influences upon the heroine in *Jane Eyre* are not from the outside. She is moved, stirred, aroused, by the strength of her own emotion solely. The dominance of the external in the novel of personal life was ended when *Jane Eyre* was written. The one thing lacking in *Pride and Prejudice* is intensity of interest. The one thing thrilling through *Jane Eyre* and *Villette* is intensity of interest—interest in a system of life, interest in nature, interest in one's own soul-life, interest in emotion as emotion. When *Jane Eyre* is finished, passion has entered into the novel.—FRANCIS HOVEY STODDARD, *The Evolution of the English Novel*, 1900, pp. 62–65

Works

JANE EYRE

I now send you per rail a MS. entitled *Jane Eyre*, a novel in three volumes, by Currer Bell. I find I cannot prepay the carriage of the parcel, as money for that purpose is not received at the small station-house where it is left. If, when you acknowledge the receipt of the MS., you would have the goodness to mention the amount charged on delivery, I will immediately transmit it in postage-stamps. It is better in future to address Mr. Currer Bell, under cover to Miss Brontë, Haworth, Bradford, Yorkshire, as there is a risk of letters otherwise directed not reaching me at present. To save trouble, I enclose an envelope.—CHARLOTTE BRONTË (as "Currer Bell"), Letter to Messrs. Smith, Elder, & Co. (August 24, 1847)

After breakfast on Sunday morning I took the MS. of *Jane Eyre* to my little study, and began to read it. The story quickly took me captive. Before twelve o'clock my horse came to the door, but I could not put the book down. I scribbled two or three lines to my friend, saying I was very sorry circumstances had arisen to prevent my meeting him, sent the note off by my groom, and went on reading the MS. Presently the servant came to tell me that luncheon was ready; I asked him to bring me a sandwich and a glass of wine, and still went on with *Jane Eyre*. Dinner came; for me the meal was a very hasty one, and before I went to bed that night I had finished reading the manuscript.

The next day we wrote to "Currer Bell" accepting the book for publication. I need say nothing about the success which the book achieved, and the speculations as to whether it was written by a man or a woman. For my own part, I never had much doubt on the subject of the writer's sex; but then I had the advantage over the general public of having the handwriting of the author before me. There were qualities of style, too, and turns of expression, which satisfied me that "Currer Bell" was a woman.—SIR GEORGE MURRAY SMITH, "In the Early Forties," *Critic*, Jan. 1901, p. 52

There is so much power in this novel as to make us overlook certain eccentricities in the invention, which trench in one or two places on what is improbable, if not unpleasant. Jane Eyre is an orphan thrown upon the protection—or, to speak correctly, the cruelty—of relations living in an out-of-the-way corner of England; who neglect, maltreat, chastize, and personally abuse her. She becomes dogged, revengeful, superstitious: and at length, after a scene,—which we hope is out of nature now that "the Iron Rule" is over-ruled and the reign of the tribe Squeers ended,—the child turns upon her persecutors with such precocious power to threaten and alarm, that they condemn her to an *oubliette*—sending her out of the house to a so-called charitable institution. There she has again to prove wretchedness, hard fare, and misconstruction. The trial, however, is this time not unaccompanied by more gracious influences. Jane Eyre is taught, by example, that patience is nobler than passion; and so far as we can gather from her own confessions, grows up into a plain, self-sustained young woman, with a capital of principle sufficient to regulate those more dangerous gifts which the influences of her childhood had so exasperated. Weary of the monotonous life of a teacher, she advertises for the situation of a governess; and is engaged into an establishment—singular, but not without prototype—to take care of the education of the French ward of a country gentleman; which said girl proves, when called by her right name, to be the child of an opera *danseuse*. The pretty, frivolous, little faëry Adele, with her hereditary taste for dress, coquetry, and pantomimic grace, is true to life. Perhaps, too—we dare not speak more positively—there is truth in the abrupt, strange, clever Mr. Rochester; and in the fearless, original way in which the strong man and the young governess travel over each other's minds till, in a puzzled and uncomfortable manner enough, they come to a mutual understanding. Neither is the mystery of Thornfield an exaggeration of reality. We, ourselves, know of a large mansion-house in a distant county where, for many years, a miscreant was kept in close confinement,—and his existence, at best, only darkly hinted in the neighbourhood. Some such tale as this was told in a now-forgotten novel— *Sketches of a Seaport Town*. We do not quarrel with the author of *Jane Eyre* for the manner in which he has made the secret explode at a critical juncture of the story. From that point forward, however, we think the heroine is too outrageously tried, and too romantically assisted in her difficulties:—until arrives the last moment, at which obstacles fall down like the battlements of *Castle Mélodrame*, in the closing scene, when "avenging thunder strikes the towers of Crime, and far above in Heaven's etherial light young Hymen's flower-decked temple shines revealed." No matter, however:—as exciting strong interest of its old-fashioned kind *Jane Eyre* deserves high praise, and commendation to the novel-reader who prefers story to philosophy, pedantry, or Puseyite controversy.—HENRY F. CHORLEY, *Athenaeum*, Oct. 23, 1847, pp. 1100–1101

I have finished the adventures of Miss Jane Eyre, and think her far the cleverest that has written since Austen and Edgeworth were in their prime. Worth fifty Trollopes and Martineaus rolled into one counterpane, with fifty Dickenses and Bulwers to keep them company; but rather a brazen Miss.—JOHN GIBSON LOCKHART, Letter to Mrs. Hope (Dec. 29, 1847), cited in Andrew Lang, *The Life and Letters of John Gibson Lockhart*, 1897, Vol. 2, p. 310

I have read *Jane Eyre*, mon ami, and shall be glad to know what you admire in it. All self-sacrifice is good—but one would like it to be in a somewhat nobler cause than that of a diabolical law which chains a man soul and body to a putrefying carcase.

However the book *is* interesting—only I wish the characters would talk a little less like the heroes and heroines of police reports.—GEORGE ELIOT, Letter to Charles Bray (June 11, 1848)

Not many months ago, the New England States were visited by a distressing mental epidemic, passing under the name of the "Jane Eyre fever," which defied all the usual nostrums of the established doctors of criticism. Its effects varied with different constitutions, in some producing a soft ethical sentimentality, which relaxed all the fibres of conscience, and in others exciting a general fever of moral and religious indignation. It was to no purpose that the public were solemnly assured, through the intelligent press, that the malady was not likely to have any permanent effect either on the intellectual or moral constitution. The book which caused the distemper would probably have been inoffensive, had not some sly manufacturer of mischief hinted that it was a book which no respectable man should bring into his family circle. Of course, every family soon had a copy of it, and one edition after another found eager purchasers. The hero, Mr. Rochester, (not the same person who comes to so edifying an end in the pages of Dr. Gilbert Burnet,) became a great favorite in the boarding-schools and in the worshipful society of governesses. That portion of Young America known as ladies' men began to swagger and swear in the presence of the gentler sex, and to allude darkly to events in their lives which excused impudence and profanity.

The novel of *Jane Eyre*, which caused this great excitement, purports to have been edited by Currer Bell, and the said Currer divides the authorship, if we are not misinformed, with a brother and sister. The work bears the marks of more than one mind and one sex, and has more variety than either of the novels which claim to have been written by Acton Bell. The family mind is strikingly peculiar, giving a strong impression of unity, but it is still male and female. From the masculine tone of *Jane Eyre*, it might pass altogether as the composition of a man, were it not for some unconscious feminine peculiarities, which the strongest-minded woman that ever aspired after manhood cannot suppress. These peculiarities refer not only to elaborate descriptions of dress, and the minutiæ of the sick-chamber, but to various superficial refinements of feeling in regard to the external relations of the sex. It is true that the noblest and best representations of female character have been produced by men; but there are niceties of thought and emotion in a woman's mind which no man can delineate, but which often escape unawares from a female writer. There are numerous examples of these in *Jane Eyre*. The leading characteristic of the novel, however, and the secret of its charm, is the clear, distinct, decisive style of its representation of character, manners, and scenery; and this continually suggests a male mind. In the earlier chapters, there is little, perhaps, to break the impression that we are reading the autobiography of a powerful and peculiar female intellect; but when the admirable Mr. Rochester appears, and the profanity, brutality, and slang of the misanthropic profligate give their torpedo shocks to the nervous system,—and especially when we are favored with more than one scene given to the exhibition of mere animal appetite, and to courtship after the manner of kangaroos and the heroes of Dryden's plays,—we are gallant enough to detect the hand of a gentleman in the composition. There are also scenes of passion, so hot, emphatic, and condensed in expression, and so sternly masculine in feeling, that we are almost sure we observe the mind of the author of *Wuthering Heights* at work in the text.

The popularity of *Jane Eyre* was doubtless due in part to the freshness, raciness, and vigor of mind it evinced; but it was obtained not so much by these qualities as by frequent dealings in moral paradox, and by the hardihood of its assaults upon the prejudices of proper people. Nothing causes more delight, at least to one third of every community, than a successful attempt to wound the delicacy of their scrupulous neighbours, and a daring peep into regions which acknowledge the authority of no conventional rules. The authors of *Jane Eyre* have not accomplished this end without an occasional violation of probability and considerable confusion of plot and character, and they have made the capital mistake of supposing that an artistic representation of character and manners is a literal imitation of individual life. The consequence is, that in dealing with vicious personages they confound vulgarity with truth, and awaken too often a feeling of unmitigated disgust. The writer who colors too warmly the degrading scenes through which his immaculate hero passes is rightly held as an equivocal teacher of purity; it is not by the bold expression of blasphemy and ribaldry that a great novelist conveys the most truthful idea of the misanthropic and the dissolute. The truth is, that the whole firm of Bell & Co. seem to have a sense of the depravity of human nature peculiarly their own. It is the yahoo, not the demon, that they select for representation; their Pandemonium is of mud rather than fire.—EDWIN P. WHIPPLE, "Novels of the Season," *North American Review*, Oct. 1848, pp. 355–57

How well I remember the delight, and wonder, and pleasure with which I read *Jane Eyre*, sent to me by an author whose name and sex were then alike unknown to me; the strange fascinations of the book; and how with my own work pressing upon me, I could not, having taken the volumes up, lay them down until they were read through! Hundreds of those who, like myself, recognized and admired that master-work of a great genius.—WILLIAM MAKEPEACE THACKERAY, "The Last Sketch," *Cornhill Magazine*, April 1860, p. 487

I have been reading novels—*Jane Eyre*, among the rest. It was very pleasant to me for its inexperience. It is a girl's dream of a world not yet known, or only glimpsed from afar. But there is real power in it, and the descriptions of scenery are the best I know, out of Ruskin.—JAMES RUSSELL LOWELL, Letter to Charles Eliot Norton (July 8, 1867)

Take the first work of her genius in its ripe fullness and freshness of new fruit; a twig or two is twisted or blighted of the noble tree, a bud or so has been nipped or cankered by adverse winds or frost; but root and branch and bole are all straight and strong and solid and sound in grain. Whatever in *Jane Eyre* is other than good is also less than important. The accident which brings a famished wanderer to the door of unknown kinsfolk might be a damning flaw in a novel of mere incident; but incident is not the keystone and commonplace is not the touchstone of this. The vulgar insolence and brutish malignity of the well-born guests at Thornfield Hall are grotesque and incredible in speakers of their imputed station; these are the natural properties of that class of persons which then supplied, as it yet supplies, the writers of such articles as one of memorable infamy and imbecility on *Jane Eyre* to the artistic and literary department of the *Quarterly Review*. So gross and grievous a blunder would entail no less than ruin on a mere novel of manners; but accuracy in the distinction and reproduction of social characteristics is not the test of capacity for such work as this. That test is only to be found in the grasp and manipulation of manly and womanly character. And, to

my mind, the figure of Edward Rochester in this book remains, and seems like to remain, one of the only two male figures of wholly truthful workmanship and vitally heroic mould ever carved and coloured by a woman's hand. The other it is superfluous to mention; all possible readers will have uttered before I can transcribe the name of Paul Emanuel.—ALGERNON CHARLES SWINBURNE, *A Note on Charlotte Brontë*, 1877, pp. 26–28

Finished *Jane Eyre*, which is really a wonderful book, very peculiar in parts, but so powerfully and admirably written, such a fine tone in it, such fine religious feeling, and such beautiful writings. The description of the mysterious maniac's nightly appearances awfully thrilling. Mr Rochester's character a very remarkable one, and Jane Eyre's herself a beautiful one. The end is very touching, when Jane Eyre returns to him and finds him blind, with one hand gone from injuries during the fire in his house, which was caused by his mad wife.—QUEEN VICTORIA, *Journal*, Nov. 23, 1880

The crowning merit of *Jane Eyre* is its energy—a delightful quality at any time, but perhaps especially so just now. Some of our novelists make their characters walk through their parts after the languid fashions lately prevailing in the ball-room, and this proving irritating to some others of robuster frame of mind, has caused these latter, out of sheer temper, to make their heroines skip about like so many Kitty Clovers on the village green. But Jane Eyre neither languishes in drawing-rooms nor sits dangling her ankles upon gates, but is always interesting, eloquent, vehement. ⟨. . .⟩

Miss Brontë's errors lie on the surface, and can be easily removed. Half-a-dozen deletions and as many wisely-tempered alterations, and the work of correction would be done in any one of her novels. I am far from saying they would then be faultless, but at least they would be free from those faults which make the fortunes of small critics and jokes for the evening papers.

A novel like *Jane Eyre*, fresh from the hands of its creator—unmistakably alive—speaking a bold, unconventional language, recognizing love even in a woman's heart as something which does not always wait to be asked before springing into being, was sure to disturb those who worship the goddess Propriety. Prim women, living hardly on the interest of "a little hoard of maxims," men judiciously anxious to confine their own female folk to a diet of literary lentils, read *Jane Eyre* with undisguised alarm. There was an outrageous frankness about the book—a brushing away of phrases and formulas calculated to horrify those who, to do them justice, generally recognize an enemy when they see him.—AUGUSTINE BIRRELL, *Life of Charlotte Brontë*, 1887, pp. 105–8

SHIRLEY

I have read *Shirley* lately; it is not equal to *Jane Eyre* in spontaneousness and earnestness. I found it heavy, I confess, though in the mechanical part of the writing—the compositional *savoir faire*—there is an advance.—ELIZABETH BARRETT BROWNING, Letter to Mrs. Jameson (April 2, 1850)

Shirley disgusted me at the opening: and I gave up the writer and her books with the notion that she was a person who liked coarseness. How I misjudged her! and how thankful I am that I never put a word of my misconceptions into print, or recorded my misjudgments of one who is a whole heaven above me. —CHARLES KINGSLEY, Letter to Elizabeth Gaskell (May 14, 1857)

Shirley (1849) is milder in tone ⟨than *Jane Eyre*⟩; in it Charlotte Brontë is not quite herself. Much disturbed by criticism of *Jane Eyre*, she undertook to profit by it, particularly by the advice of George Henry Lewes, who told her to avoid poetry, sentiment, and melodrama, and to read Jane Austen. She now sought to daguerreotype Yorkshire life and scenes; and this is the way she did it. For an enveloping plot of exciting incident, she went back some forty years to the commercial troubles with the United States, and to the contest between mill-owners and operatives over the introduction of labor-saving machinery. She thus made for herself an opportunity to describe the battering of a woollen mill by starlight, and the shooting of the manager. In this setting she placed Yorkshire men and women with whom she was acquainted,—her sister Emily, her father, her school friends, one of her lovers, and the neighboring curates. Incident, too, she reproduced from life, with varying degrees of modification. The novel is thus an historical allegory. It is hardly necessary to observe that it is constructed on false notions of art and on a complete misunderstanding of Jane Austen. It is, however, as a description of externals the most careful and most sympathetic of all Charlotte Brontë's work, and is still the novel of hers most liked by Yorkshiremen, who see themselves there. The portrait which has the most unusual interest is the minute study of Emily Brontë under the name of Shirley Keeldar. In all her moods and loves and changes of feature under excitement, Charlotte represents her,—her indolence, her passion for fierce dogs and the moors; the quivering lip, the trembling voice, the eye flashing dark, the dilating nostrils, the sarcastic laugh, the expansion of the frail body in indignation, and her wild picturesque beauty when visited by one of her rare dreams, such, for example, as the vision of Nature, the Titanic mother.

Shirley failed to please Lewes, who was expecting another *Pride and Prejudice*. To his flippant criticism Charlotte Brontë replied cavalierly ⟨with *Villette*⟩, and became herself once more.—WILBUR L. CROSS, *The Development of the English Novel*, 1899, pp. 231–32

VILLETTE

Everything written by 'Currer Bell' is remarkable. She can touch nothing without leaving on it the stamp of originality. Of her three books, this is perhaps the strangest, the most astonishing, though not the best. The sustained ability is perhaps greater in *Villette* than in its two predecessors, there being no intervals of weakness, except in the form of a few passages, chiefly episodical, of over-wrought writing, which, though evidently a sincere endeavour to express real feeling, are not felt to be congenial, or very intelligible, in the midst of so much that is strong and clear. In regard to interest, we think that this book will be pronounced inferior to *Jane Eyre* and superior to *Shirley*. In point of construction it is superior to both; and this is a vast gain and a great encouragement to hope for future benefits from the same hand which shall surpass any yet given. The whole three volumes are crowded with beauties—with the good things for which we look to the clear sight, deep feeling and singular, though not extensive, experience of life which we associate with the name of 'Currer Bell'. But under all, through all, over all, is felt a drawback, of which we were anxious before, but which is terribly aggravated here—the book is almost intolerably painful. We are wont to say, when we read narratives which are made up of the external woes of life, such as may and do happen every day, but are never congregated in one experience—that the author has no right to make readers so miserable. We do not know whether the right will be admitted in the present case, on the ground of the woes

not being external; but certainly we ourselves have felt inclined to rebel against the pain, and, perhaps on account of protraction, are disposed to deny its necessity and truth. With all her objectivity, 'Currer Bell' here afflicts us with an amount of subjective misery which we may fairly remonstrate against; and she allows us no respite—even while treating us with humour, with charming description and the presence of those whom she herself regards as the good and gay. In truth, there is scarcely anybody that is good—serenely and cheerfully good, and the gaiety has pain in it. An atmosphere of pain hangs about the whole, forbidding that repose which we hold to be essential to the true presentment of any large portion of life and experience. In this pervading pain, the book reminds us of Balzac; and so it does in the prevalence of one tendency, or one idea, throughout the whole conception and action. All the female characters, in all their thoughts and lives, are full of one thing, or are regarded by the reader in the light of that one thought—love. It begins with the child of six years old, at the opening—a charming picture—and it closes with it at the last page; and, so dominant is this idea—so incessant is the writer's tendency to describe the need of being loved, that the heroine, who tells her own story, leaves the reader at last under the uncomfortable impression of her having either entertained a double love, or allowed one to supersede another without notification of the transition. It is not thus in real life. There are substantial, heartfelt interests for women of all ages, and under ordinary circumstances, quite apart from love: there is an absence of introspection, an unconsciousness, a repose in women's lives—unless under peculiarly unfortunate circumstances—of which we find no admission in this book; and to the absence of it, may be attributed some of the criticism which the book will meet from readers who are not prudes, but whose reason and taste will reject the assumption that events and characters are to be regarded through the medium of one passion only.

And here ends all demur. We have thought it right to indicate clearly the two faults in the book, which it is scarcely probable that anyone will deny. Abstractions made of these, all else is power, skill and interest. The freshness will be complete to readers who know none but English novels. Those who are familiar with Balzac may be reminded, by the sharp distinction of the pictured life, place and circumstance, of some of the best of his tales: but there is nothing borrowed; nothing that we might not as well have had if 'Currer Bell' had never read a line of Balzac—which may very likely be the case. As far as we know, the life of a foreign *pension* (Belgian, evidently) and of a third-rate capital, with its half provincial population and proceedings, is new in purely English literature; and most lifelike and spirited it is. The humour which peeps out in the names—the court of Labassecour, with its heir-apparent, the Duc of Dindoneau—the Professors Boissec and Rochemorte—and so forth—is felt throughout, though there is not a touch of lightheartedness from end to end. The presence of the heroine in that capital and *pension* is strangely managed; and so is the gathering of her British friends around her there; but, that strangeness surmounted, the picture of their lives is admirable. The reader must go to the book for it; for it fills two volumes and a half out of the three. The heroine, Lucy Snowe, tells her own story. Every reader of *Jane Eyre* will be glad to see the autobiographical form returned to. Lucy may be thought a younger, feebler sister of Jane. There is just enough resemblance for that—but she has not Jane's charm of mental and moral health, and consequent repose. She is in a state of chronic nervous fever for the most part; is usually silent and suffering; when she speaks, speaks in enigmas or in raillery, and now and then breaks out under the torture of passion; but she acts admirably—with readiness, sense, conscience and kindliness. Still we do not wonder that she loved more than she was beloved, and the love at last would be surprising enough, if love could ever be so. Perhaps Pauline and her father are the best-drawn characters in the book, where all are more or less admirably delineated. We are not aware that there is one failure.

A striking peculiarity comes out in the third volume, striking from one so large and liberal, so removed from ordinary social prejudices as we have been accustomed to think 'Currer Bell'. She goes out of her way to express a passionate hatred of Romanism. It is not the calm disapproval of a ritual religion, such as we should have expected from her, ensuing upon a presentment of her own better faith. The religion she envokes is itself but a dark and doubtful refuge from the pain which impels the invocation; while the Catholicism on which she enlarges is even virulently reprobated. We do not exactly see the moral necessity for this (there is no artistical necessity) and we are rather sorry for it, occurring as it does at a time when catholics and protestants hate each other quite sufficiently; and in a mode which will not affect conversion. A better advocacy of protestantism would have been to show that it can give rest to the weary and heavy laden; whereas it seems to yield no comfort in return for every variety of sorrowful invocation. —Harriet Martineau, *Daily News*, Feb. 3, 1853, p. 2

I am only just returned to a sense of the real world about me for I have been reading *Villette*, a still more wonderful book than *Jane Eyre*. There is something almost preternatural in its power.—George Eliot, Letter to Mrs. Charles Bray (Feb. 15, 1853)

The most striking book which has been recently published here is *Villette*, by the authoress of *Jane Eyre*, who, as you know, is a Miss Brontë. The book does not give one the most pleasing notion of the authoress, perhaps, but it is very clever, graphic, vigorous. It is 'man's meat,' and not the whipped syllabub, which is *all* froth, without any jam at the bottom. The scene of the drama is Brussels.—Bryan Waller Procter, Letter to James T. Fields (Feb. 1853), cited in James T. Fields, "'Barry Cornwall' and Some of His Friends," *Harper's New Monthly Magazine*, Dec. 1875, p. 60

Why is *Villette* disagreeable? Because the writer's mind contains nothing but hunger, rebellion, and rage, and therefore that is all she can, in fact, put into her book. No fine writing can hide this thoroughly, and it will be fatal to her in the long run.—Matthew Arnold, Letter to Mrs. Forster (April 14, 1853)

There is a moral too in *Villette*, or rather many morals, but not so distinctly a *morale en action*. It is a work of astonishing power and passion. From its pages there issues an influence of truth as healthful as a mountain breeze. Contempt of conventions in all things, in style, in thought, even in the art of story-telling, here visibly springs from the independent originality of a strong mind nurtured in solitude. As a novel, in the ordinary sense of the word, *Villette* has few claims; as a *book*, it is one which, having read, you will not easily forget. It is quite true that the episode of Miss Marchmont, early in the first volume, is unnecessary, having no obvious connexion with the plot or the characters; but with what wonderful imagination is it painted! Where shall we find such writing as in that description of her last night, wherein the memories of bygone years come trooping in upon her with a vividness partaking of the last energy of life? It is true also that the visit to London is unnecessary, and has many unreal details. Much of the book seems to be brought in merely that the writer may

express something which is in her mind; but at any rate she *has* something in her mind, and expresses it as no other can.

⟨. . .⟩ In this world, as Goethe tells us, "there are so few voices, and so many echoes;" there are so few books, and so many volumes—so few persons thinking and speaking for themselves, so many reverberating the vague noises of others. Among the few stands *Villette*. In it we read the actual thoughts and feelings of a strong, struggling soul; we hear the cry of pain from one who has loved passionately, and who has sorrowed sorely. Indeed, no more distinct characteristic of Currer Bell's genius can be named, than the depth of her capacity for all passionate emotions.—George Henry Lewes, "*Ruth* and *Villette*," *Westminster Review*, April 1853, pp. 485–90

Have you all read *Villette*? and do you not admire the book, and own it as one of the great books of the time? I confess that I have seldom been more impressed with the genius of the writer, and seldom less drawn to her personally. She has nerves of such delicate fineness of edge that the least touch turns them, or she has had an exasperating experience. Whether she calls herself Jane Eyre, or Lucy Snowe, it does not matter—it is Miss Brontë. She has the intensity of Byron—of our own Fanny Kemble. She unconsciously infuses herself into her heroine. It is an egotism whose fires are fed by the inferior vitality of others; and how well she conceives others! how she daguerreotypes them!—Catharine M. Sedgwick, Letter to Dr. Dewey (April 1853), cited in Mary E. Dewey, *Life and Letters of Catharine M. Sedgwick*, 1871, p. 349

The third of Miss Brontë's works, *Villette*, published 1853, returned in a great measure to the atmosphere of *Jane Eyre*, the scene being chiefly laid in Brussels, and in a school there; and the real hero—after one or two failures—being found in the person of a French master, the fiery, vivacious, undignified and altogether delightful M. Paul Emmanuel, who plays upon the heroine's heart and nerves something after the manner of Rochester, but who is so absolutely real in his fantastic peculiarities and admirable, tender, manly character, that the pranks he plays and the confusion he produces are all forgiven him. Lucy Snowe, the heroine, the cool little proper English-woman with the well-concealed volcano under her primness, is by no means so captivating as Jane Eyre, but every detail is so astonishingly true to life, and the force and vigour of the romance—occasionally reaching to fever-heat, and all the more startling from its contrast with the cold white Brussels house, the school atmosphere, and the chill exterior of Miss Snowe—so absorbing, that the book made a still greater impression than *Jane Eyre*, and the ultimate fate of M. Paul, left uncertain at the conclusion, was debated in a hundred circles with greater vehemence than many a national problem.—Margaret Oliphant, *The Victorian Age of English Literature*, 1892, Vol. 1, pp. 307–8

ELIZABETH RIGBY
From "*Vanity Fair* and *Jane Eyre*"
Quarterly Review, December 1848, pp. 165–76

Jane Eyre, as a work, and one of equal popularity, is, in almost every respect, a total contrast to *Vanity Fair*. The characters and events, though some of them masterly in conception, are coined expressly for the purpose of bringing out great effects. The hero and heroine are beings both so singularly unattractive that the reader feels they can have no vocation in the novel but to be brought together; and they do things which, though not impossible, lie utterly beyond the bounds of probability. On this account a short sketch of the plan seems requisite; not but what it is a plan familiar enough to all readers of novels—especially those of the old school and those of the lowest school of our own day. For Jane Eyre is merely another Pamela, who, by the force of her character and the strength of her principles, is carried victoriously through great trials and temptations from the man she loves. Nor is she even a Pamela adapted and refined to modern notions; for though the story is conducted without those derelictions of decorum which we are to believe had their excuse in the manners of Richardson's time, yet it is stamped with a coarseness of language and laxity of tone which have certainly no excuse in ours. It is a very remarkable book: we have no remembrance of another combining such genuine power with such horrid taste. Both together have equally assisted to gain the great popularity it has enjoyed; for in these days of extravagant adoration of all that bears the stamp of novelty and originality, sheer rudeness and vulgarity have come in for a most mistaken worship.

⟨. . .⟩ This, to our view, is the great and crying mischief of the book. Jane Eyre is throughout the personification of an unregenerate and undisciplined spirit, the more dangerous to exhibit from that prestige of principle and self-control which is liable to dazzle the eye too much for it to observe the inefficient and unsound foundation on which it rests. It is true Jane does right, and exerts great moral strength, but it is the strength of a mere heathen mind which is a law unto itself. No Christian grace is perceptible upon her. She has inherited in fullest measure the worst sin of our fallen nature—the sin of pride. Jane Eyre is proud, and therefore she is ungrateful too. It pleased God to make her an orphan, friendless, and penniless—yet she thanks nobody, and least of all Him, for the food and raiment, the friends, companions, and instructors of her helpless youth—for the care and education vouchsafed to her till she was capable in mind as fitted in years to provide for herself. On the contrary, she looks upon all that has been done for her not only as her undoubted right, but as falling far short of it. The doctrine of humility is not more foreign to her mind than it is repudiated by her heart. It is by her own talents, virtues, and courage, that she is made to attain the summit of human happiness, and, as far as Jane Eyre's own statement is concerned, no one would think that she owed anything either to God above or to man below. She flees from Mr. Rochester, and has not a being to turn to. Why was this? The excellence of the present institution at Casterton, which succeeded that of Cowan Bridge near Kirkby Lonsdale—these being distinctly, as we hear, the original and the reformed Lowoods of the book—is pretty generally known. Jane had lived there for eight years with 110 girls and 15 teachers. Why had she formed no friendships among them? Other orphans have left the same and similar institutions, furnished with friends for life, and puzzled with homes to choose from. How comes it that Jane had acquired neither? Among that number of associates there were surely some exceptions to what she so presumptuously stigmatises as 'the society of inferior minds.' Of course it suited the author's end to represent the heroine as utterly destitute of the common means of assistance, in order to exhibit both her trials and her powers of self-support—the whole book rests on this assumption—but it is one which, under the circumstances, is very unnatural and very unjust.

Altogether the autobiography of Jane Eyre is preeminently an anti-Christian composition. There is throughout it a murmuring against the comforts of the rich and against the privations of the poor, which, as far as each individual is concerned, is a murmuring against God's appointment—there is a proud and perpetual assertion of the rights of man, for which we find no authority either in God's word or in God's providence—there is that pervading tone of ungodly discontent which is at once the most prominent and the most subtle evil which the law and the pulpit, which all civilized society in fact, has at the present day to contend with. We do not hesitate to say that the tone of mind and thought which has overthrown authority and violated every code human and divine abroad, and fostered Chartism and rebellion at home, is the same which has also written *Jane Eyre*.

Still we say again this is a very remarkable book. We are painfully alive to the moral, religious, and literary deficiencies of the picture, and such passages of beauty and power as we have quoted cannot redeem it, but it is impossible not to be spellbound with the freedom of the touch. It would be mere hackneyed courtesy to call it 'fine writing.' It bears no impress of being written at all, but is poured out rather in the heat and hurry of an instinct, which flows ungovernably on to its object, indifferent by what means it reaches it, and unconscious too. As regards the author's chief object, however, it is a failure—that, namely, of making a plain, odd woman, destitute of all the conventional features of feminine attraction, interesting in our sight. We deny that he has succeeded in this. Jane Eyre, in spite of some grand things about her, is a being totally uncongenial to our feelings from beginning to end. We acknowledge her firmness—we respect her determination—we feel for her struggles; but, for all that, and setting aside higher considerations, the impression she leaves on our mind is that of a decidedly vulgar-minded woman—one whom we should not care for as an acquaintance, whom we should not seek as a friend, whom we should not desire for a relation, and whom we should scrupulously avoid for a governess.

There seem to have arisen in the novel-reading world some doubts as to who really wrote this book; and various rumours, more or less romantic, have been current in Mayfair, the metropolis of gossip, as to the authorship. For example, *Jane Eyre* is sentimentally assumed to have proceeded from the pen of Mr. Thackeray's governess, whom he had himself chosen as his model of Becky, and who, in mingled love and revenge, personified him in return as Mr. Rochester. In this case, it is evident that the author of *Vanity Fair*, whose own pencil makes him grey-haired, has had the best of it, though his children may have had the worst, having, at all events, succeeded in hitting that vulnerable point in the Becky bosom, which it is our firm belief no man born of woman, from her Soho to her Ostend days, had ever so much as grazed. To this ingenious rumour the coincidence of the second edition of *Jane Eyre* being dedicated to Mr. Thackeray has probably given rise. For our parts, we see no great interest in the question at all. The first edition of *Jane Eyre* purports to be edited by Currer Bell, one of a trio of brothers, or sisters, or cousins, by names Currer, Acton, and Ellis Bell, already known as the joint-authors of a volume of poems. The second edition the same—dedicated, however, 'by the author,' to Mr. Thackeray; and the dedication (itself an indubitable *chip* of *Jane Eyre*) signed Currer Bell. Author and editor therefore are one, and we are as much satisfied to accept this double individual under the name of 'Currer Bell,' as under any other, more or less euphonious. Whoever it be, it is a person who, with great mental powers, combines a total ignorance of the habits of society, a great coarseness of taste, and a heathenish doctrine of religion. And as these characteristics appear more or less in the writings of all three, Currer, Acton, and Ellis alike, for their poems differ less in degree of power than in kind, we are ready to accept the fact of their identity or of their relationship with equal satisfaction. At all events there can be no interest attached to the writer of *Wuthering Heights*—a novel succeeding *Jane Eyre,* and purporting to be written by Ellis Bell—unless it were for the sake of more individual reprobation. For though there is a decided family likeness between the two, yet the aspect of the Jane and Rochester animals in their native state, as Catherine and Heathfield, is too odiously and abominably pagan to be palatable even to the most vitiated class of English readers. With all the unscrupulousness of the French school of novels it combines that repulsive vulgarity in the choice of its vice which supplies its own antidote. The question of authorship, therefore, can deserve a moment's curiosity only as far as *Jane Eyre* is concerned, and though we cannot pronounce that it appertains to a real Mr. Currer Bell and to no other, yet that it appertains to a man, and not, as many assert, to a woman, we are strongly inclined to affirm. Without entering into the question whether the power of the writing be above her, or the vulgarity below her, there are, we believe, minutiæ of circumstantial evidence which at once acquit the feminine hand. No woman—a lady friend, whom we are always happy to consult, assures us—makes mistakes in her own *metier*—no woman *trusses game* and garnishes dessert-dishes with the same hands, or talks of so doing in the same breath. Above all, no woman attires another in such fancy dresses as Jane's ladies assume—Miss Ingram coming down, irresistible, 'in a *morning* robe of sky-blue crape, a gauze azure scarf twisted in her hair!!' No lady, we understand, when suddenly roused in the night, would think of hurrying on '*a frock.*' They have garments more convenient for such occasions, and more becoming too. This evidence seems incontrovertible. Even granting that these incongruities were purposely assumed, for the sake of disguising the female pen, there is nothing gained; for if we ascribe the book to a woman at all, we have no alternative but to ascribe it to one who has, for some sufficient reason, long forfeited the society of her own sex.

And if by no woman, it is certainly also by no artist. The Thackeray eye has had no part there. There is not more disparity between the art of drawing Jane assumes and her evident total ignorance of its first principles, than between the report she gives of her own character and the conclusions we form for ourselves. Not but what, in another sense, the author may be classed as an artist of very high grade. Let him describe the simplest things in nature—a rainy landscape, a cloudy sky, or a bare moorside, and he shows the hand of a master; but the moment he talks of the art itself, it is obvious that he is a complete ignoramus.

GEORGE HENRY LEWES
From "Currer Bell's *Shirley*"

Edinburgh Review, January 1850, pp. 158–61

We take Currer Bell to be one of the most remarkable of *female* writers; and believe it is now scarcely a secret that Currer Bell is the pseudonyme of a woman. An eminent contemporary, indeed, has employed the sharp vivacity of a female pen to prove 'upon irresistible evidence' that *Jane Eyre must be* the work of a man! But all that 'irresistible evidence' is set aside by the simple fact that Currer Bell *is* a woman. We never, for our own parts, had a moment's doubt on the subject. That Jane herself was drawn by a woman's delicate hand, and that Rochester equally betrayed the sex of the artist, was to our

minds so obvious, as absolutely to shut our ears to all the evidence which could be adduced by the erudition even of a *marchande des modes;* and that simply because we knew that there were women profoundly ignorant of the mysteries of the toilette, and the terminology of fashion (independent of the obvious solution, that such ignorance might be counterfeited, to mislead), and felt that there was no man who *could* so have delineated a woman—or *would* so have delineated a man. The fair and ingenious critic was misled by her own acuteness in the perception of details; and misled also in some other way, and more uncharitably, in concluding that the *author* of *Jane Eyre* was a heathen educated among heathens,—the *fact* being, that the *authoress* is the daughter of a clergyman!

This question of authorship, which was somewhat hotly debated a little while ago, helped to keep up the excitement about *Jane Eyre;* but, independently of that title to notoriety, it is certain that, for many years, there had been no work of such power, piquancy, and originality. Its very faults were faults on the side of vigour; and its beauties were all original. The grand secret of its success, however,—as of all genuine and lasting success,—was its *reality.* From out the depths of a sorrowing experience, here was a voice speaking to the experience of thousands. The aspects of external nature, too, were painted with equal fidelity,—the long cheerless winter days, chilled with rolling mists occasionally gathering into the strength of rains,—the bright spring mornings,—the clear solemn nights,—were all painted to your *soul* as well as to your eye, by a pencil dipped into a soul's experience for its colours. Faults enough the book has undoubtedly: faults of conception, faults of taste, faults of ignorance, but in spite of all, it remains a book of singular fascination. A more masculine book, in the sense of vigour, was never written. Indeed that vigour often amounts to coarseness,—and is certainly the very antipode to 'lady like.'

This same over-masculine vigour is even more prominent in *Shirley,* and does not increase the pleasantness of the book. A pleasant book, indeed, we are not sure that we can style it. Power it has unquestionably, and interest too, of a peculiar sort; but not the agreeableness of a work of art. Through its pages we are carried as over a wild and desolate heath, with a sharp east wind blowing the hair into our eyes, and making the blood tingle in our veins: There is health perhaps in the drive; but not much pleasantness. Nature speaks to us distinctly enough, but she does not speak sweetly. She is in her stern and sombre mood, and we see only her dreary aspects.

Shirley is inferior to *Jane Eyre* in several important points. It is not quite so true; and it is not so fascinating. It does not so rivet the reader's attention, nor hurry him through all obstacles of improbability, with so keen a sympathy in its reality. It is even coarser in texture, too, and not unfrequently flippant; while the characters are almost all disagreeable, and exhibit intolerable rudeness of manner. In *Jane Eyre* life was viewed from the standing point of individual experience; in *Shirley* that standing point is frequently abandoned, and the artist paints only a panorama of which she, as well as you, are but spectators. Hence the unity of *Jane Eyre* in spite of its clumsy and improbable contrivances, was great and effective: the fire of one passion fused the discordant materials into one mould. But in *Shirley* all unity, in consequence of defective art, is wanting. There is no passionate link; nor is there any artistic fusion, or intergrowth, by which one part evolves itself from another. Hence its falling-off in interest, coherent movement, and life. The book may be laid down at any chapter, and almost any chapter might be omitted. The various scenes are gathered up into three volumes,—they have not grown into a work. The characters often need a justification for their introduction; as in the case of the three Curates, who are offensive, uninstructive, and unamusing. That they are not *inventions*, however, we feel persuaded. For nothing but a strong sense of their reality could have seduced the authoress into such a mistake as admitting them at all. We are confident she has seen them, known them, despised them; and *therefore* she paints them! although they have no relation with the story, have no interest in themselves, and cannot be accepted as types of a class,—for they are not *Curates* but *boors:* and although not inventions, we must be permitted to say that they are *not true.* Some such objection the authoress seems indeed to have anticipated; and thus towards the close of her work defends herself against it. 'Note well! wherever you present *the actual simple truth, it is somehow always denounced as a lie*: they disown it, cast it off, throw it on the parish; whereas the product of your imagination, the mere figment, the sheer fiction, is adopted, petted, termed pretty, proper, sweetly natural.' Now Currer Bell, we fear, has here fallen into a vulgar error. It is one, indeed, into which even Miss Edgeworth has also fallen: who conceived that she justified the introduction of an improbable anecdote in her text, by averring in a note that it was a 'fact.' But, the intrusion is not less an error for all that. Truth is never rejected, unless it be truth so exceptional as to stagger our belief; and in that case the artist is wrong to employ it, without so *preparing* our minds that we might receive it unquestioned. The coinage of imagination, on the other hand, is not accepted *because* it departs from the actual truth, but only because it presents the recognised attributes of our nature in new and striking combinations. If it falsify these attributes, or the known laws of their associations, the fiction is at once pronounced to be *monstrous*, and is rejected. Art, in short, deals with the broad principles of human nature, not with idiosyncracies: and, although it requires an experience of life both comprehensive and profound, to enable us to say with confidence, that '*this* motive is unnatural,' or '*that* passion is untrue,' it requires no great experience to say 'this character has not the air of reality; it may be copied from nature, but it does not *look* so.' Were Currer Bell's defence allowable, all criticism must be silenced at once. ·An author has only to say that his characters *are copied from nature*, and the discussion is closed. But though the portraits may be like the oddities from whom they are copied, they are faulty as works of art, if they strike all who never met with these oddities, as unnatural. The curious anomalies of life, which find their proper niches in Southey's *Omniana, or Commonplace Book*, are not suitable to a novel. It is the same with incidents.

Again we say that *Shirley* cannot be received as a work of art. It is not a picture; but a portfolio of random sketches for one or more pictures. The authoress never seems distinctly to have made up her mind as to what she was to do; whether to describe the habits and manners of Yorkshire and its social aspects in the days of King Lud, or to paint character, or to tell a love story. All are by turns attempted and abandoned; and the book consequently moves slowly, and by starts—leaving behind it no distinct or satisfactory impression. Power is stamped on various parts of it; power unmistakeable, but often misapplied. Currer Bell has much yet to learn,—and, especially, the discipline of her own tumultuous energies. She must learn also to sacrifice a little of her Yorkshire roughness to the demands of good taste: neither saturating her writings with such rudeness and offensive harshness, nor suffering her style to wander into such vulgarities as would be inexcusable—even in a man. No good critic will object to the homeliness of natural diction, or to the racy flavour of conversational idiom; but every one must

object to such phrases as 'Miss Mary, *getting up the steam* in her turn, now asked,' &c., or as 'making hard-handed worsted spinners *cash up to the tune of* four or five hundred per cent.,' or as 'Malone much chagrined at hearing him *pipe up in most superior style;*' all which phrases occur within the space of about a dozen pages, and that not in dialogue, but in the authoress's own narrative. And while touching on this minor, yet not trivial point, we may also venture a word of quiet remonstrance against a most inappropriate obtrusion of French phrases. When Gerard Moore and his sister talk in French, *which the authoress translates*, it surely is not allowable to leave scraps of French in the translation. A French word or two may be introduced now and then on account of some peculiar fitness, but Currer Bell's use of the language is little better than that of the 'fashionable' novelists. To speak of a grandmother as *une grand'mère*, and of treacle as *mélasse*, or of a young lady being angry as *courroucée*, gives an air of affectation to the style strangely at variance with the frankness of its general tone.

JOHN SKELTON
From "Charlotte Brontë"
Fraser's Magazine, May 1857, pp. 579–82

Shirley presents a notable contrast to Miss Brontë's other novels. In them there is a profound and frequently overmastering sense of the intense dreariness of existence to certain classes. The creative spirit of poetry and romance breaks at times through the dull and stagnant life; but as a rule it is different; and *Villette*, especially, becomes monotonous from the curb maintained upon the imagination. But *Shirley* is a Holiday of the Heart. It is glad, buoyant, sunshiny. The imagination is liberated, and revels in its liberty. It is the pleasant summer-time, and the worker is idling among the hills. The world of toil and suffering lies behind, but ever so far away. True, it must be again encountered, its problems resolved, its sores probed; the hard and obstinate war again waged manfully; but in the mean time the burn foams and sparkles through the glen; there is sunshine among the purple harebells; and the leaves in the birken glade dance merrily in the summer wind.

> Surely, surely, slumber is more sweet than toil, the shore
> Than labour in the deep mid ocean, wind, and wave, and oar;
> O, rest ye, brother mariners, we will not wander more.

In *Villette* Miss Brontë returns to the realities of life; but with power more conscious and sustained. She is less absorbed, and more comprehensive. There is the same passionate force; but the horizon is wider.

Villette is by no means a cheerful book; on the contrary, it is often very painful, especially where the central figure—the heroine—is involved. *Her* pain—her tearless pain—is intense and protracted. And in this connexion *Villette* may be regarded as an elaborate psychological examination—the anatomy of a powerful but pained intellect—of exuberant emotions watchfully and vigilantly curbed. The character of this woman is peculiar, but drawn with a masterly hand. She *endures* much in a certain Pagan strength, not defiantly, but coldly and without submission. Over her heart and her intellect she exercises an incessant restraint—a restraint whose vigilant activity curbs every feeling, controls every speculation, becomes as it were engrained into her very nature. *She*, at least, will by all means look at the world as it is—a hard, dry, practical world, not wholly devoid of certain compensating elements—and she will not be cajoled into seeing it, or making others see it, under any other light. For herself, she will live honestly upon the earth, and invite or suffer no delusions; strong, composed, self-reliant, sedate in the sustaining sense of independence. But cold and reserved as she may appear, she is not without imagination—rich, even, and affluent as a poet's. This is in a measure, however, the root of her peculiar misery. The dull and cheerless routine of homely life is not in her case relieved and penetrated by the creative intellect, but on the contrary, acquires through its aid a subtle and sensitive energy to hurt, to afflict, and to annoy. Thus she is not always strong; her imagination sometimes becomes loaded and surcharged; but she is always passionately ashamed of weakness. And through all this torture she is very solitary: her heart is very empty; she bears her own burden. There are cheerful hearths, and the pleasant firelight plays on the purple drapery that shuts out the inhospitable night; but none are here who can convey to her the profound sympathy her heart needs pitifully; and so she passes on, pale and unrelenting, into the night. Undoubtedly there is a very subtle, some may say obnoxious, charm in this pale, watchful, lynx-like woman—a charm, certainly, but for our own part we have an ancient prejudice in behalf of 'Shirley's' piquant and charming ferocity.

Miss Brontë always wrote earnestly, and in *Villette* she is peremptorily honest. In it she shows no mercy for any of the engaging *ruses* and artifices of life: with her it is something too real, earnest, and even tragic, to be wantonly trifled with or foolishly disguised. She will therefore tolerate no hypocrisy, however decent or fastidious; and her subdued and direct insight goes at once to the root of the matter. She carries this perhaps too far—it may be she lacks a measure of charity and toleration, not for what is bad—for *that* there must be no toleration—but for what is humanly weak and insufficient. Graham Bretton, for instance, with his light hair and kind heart and pleasant sensitiveness, is ultimately treated with a certain implied contempt; and this solely because he happens to be what God made him, and not something deeper and more devout, the incarnation of another and more vivid kind of goodness, which it is not in his nature to be, and to which he makes no claim. It is the patience, the fortitude, the endurance, the strong love that has been consecrated by Death and the Grave, the spirit that has been tried in fire and mortal pain and temptation,—it is these alone she can utterly admire. We believe she is wrong. But as we recal the lone woman sitting by the desolate hearthstone, and remember all that she lost and suffered, we cannot blame very gravely the occasional harshness and impatience of her language when dealing with men who have been cast in a different mould.

Villette excels Miss Brontë's other fictions in the artistic skill with which the characters are—I use the word advisedly—*developed*. She brings us into contact with certain men and women with whom she wishes to make us acquainted. She writes no formal biography; there is no elaborate introduction; the characters appear incidently during the course of the narrative, and by degrees are worked into the heart of the every-day life with which the story is concerned. But the dissection goes on patiently all the time—so leisurely and yet so ruthlessly—one homely trait accumulated upon another with such steady, untiring pertinacity, that the man grows upon us line by line, feature by feature, until his idiosyncrasy is stamped and branded upon the brain. Probably the most genuine power is manifested in the mode in which the interest is shifted from Graham Bretton to the ill-favoured little despot—Paul Emmanuel. No essential

change takes place in *their* characters, *they* remain the same, the colours in which they were originally painted were quite faithful, perfectly accurate—not by any means exaggerated for subsequent effect and contrast. It is only that a deeper insight has been gained by *us*, and if our original judgment undergoes modification, it is not because any new or inconsistent element has been introduced, but because, the conditions remaining the same, *we* see further. Leaf after leaf has been unfolded with a cold and impartial hand, until we have been let down into the innermost hearts of the men, and taught by the scrutiny a new sense of their relative value and worthiness. And Paul Emmanuel is surely a very rich and genuine conception. 'The Professor' will ever be associated in our memory with a certain soft and breezy laughter; for though the love he inspires in the heroine is very deep and even pathetic after its kind, yet the whole idea of the man is wrought and worked out in a spirit of joyous and mellow ridicule, that is full of affection, however, and perhaps at times closely akin to tears. ⟨. . .⟩

To ourselves, one of the most surprising gifts of the authoress of these volumes is the racy and inimitable English she writes. No other Englishwoman ever commanded such language—terse and compact, and yet fiercely eloquent. We have already had occasion to notice the absence of comparison or metaphor in her poetry; the same is true of her prose. The lava is at white heat; it pours down clear, silent, pitiless; there are no bright bubbles nor gleaming foam. A mind of this order—tempered, and which cuts like steel—uses none of the pretty dexterities of the imagination; for to use these infers a pause of satisfied reflection and conscious enjoyment which it seldom or never experiences. Its rigorous intellect seeks no trappings of pearl or gold. It is content to abide in its white veil of marble—naked and chaste, like 'Death' in the Vatican. Yet, the still severity is more effective than any paint could make it. The chisel has been held by a Greek, the marble hewed from Pentelicus.

T. WEMYSS REID
From *Charlotte Brontë: A Monograph*
1877, pp. 7–13, 219–25
II. *The Story of* Jane Eyre

In the late autumn of 1847 the reading public of London suddenly found itself called to admire and wonder at a novel which, without preliminary puff of any kind, had been placed in its hands. *Jane Eyre*, by Currer Bell, became the theme of every tongue, and society exhausted itself in conjectures as to the identity of the author, and the real meaning of the book. It was no ordinary book, and it produced no ordinary sensation. Disfigured here and there by certain crudities of thought and by a clumsiness of expression which betrayed the hand of a novice, it was nevertheless lit up from the first page to the last by the fire of a genius the depth and power of which none but the dullest could deny. The hand of its author seized upon the public mind whether it would or no, and society was led captive, in the main against its will, by one who had little of the prevailing spirit of the age, and who either knew nothing of conventionalism, or despised it with heart and soul. Fierce was the revolt against the influence of this new-comer in the wide arena of letters, who had stolen in, as it were in the night, and taken the citadel by surprise. But for the moment all opposition was beaten down by sheer force of genius, and *Jane Eyre* made her way, compelling recognition, wherever men and women were capable of seeing and admitting a rare and extraordinary intellectual supremacy. "How well I remember," says Mr. Thackeray, "the delight and wonder and pleasure with which I read *Jane Eyre*, sent to me by an author whose name and sex were then alike unknown to me; and how with my own work pressing upon me, I could not, having taken the volumes up, lay them down until they were read through." It was the same everywhere. Even those who saw nothing to commend in the story, those who revolted against its free employment of great passions and great griefs, and those who were elaborately critical upon its author's ignorance of the ways of polite society, had to confess themselves bound by the spell of the magician. *Jane Eyre* gathered admirers fast; and for every admirer she had a score of readers.

Those who remember that winter of nine-and-twenty years ago know how something like a *Jane Eyre* fever raged among us. The story which had suddenly discovered a glory in uncomeliness, a grandeur in overmastering passion, moulded the fashion of the hour, and "Rochester airs" and "Jane Eyre graces" became the rage. The book, and its fame and influence, travelled beyond the seas with a speed which in those days was marvellous. In sedate New England homes the history of the English governess was read with an avidity which was not surpassed in London itself, and within a few months of the publication of the novel it was famous throughout two continents. No such triumph has been achieved in our time by any other English author; nor can it be said, upon the whole, that many triumphs have been better merited. It happened that this anonymous story, bearing the unmistakable marks of an unpractised hand, was put before the world at the very moment when another great masterpiece of fiction was just beginning to gain the ear of the English public. But at the moment of publication *Jane Eyre* swept past *Vanity Fair* with a marvellous and impetuous speed which left Thackeray's work in the distant background; and its unknown author in a few weeks gained a wider reputation than that which one of the master minds of the century had been engaged for long years in building up.

The reaction from this exaggerated fame, of course, set in, and it was sharp and severe. The blots in the book were easily hit; its author's unfamiliarity with the stage business of the play was evident enough—even to dunces; so it was a simple matter to write smart articles at the expense of a novelist who laid himself open to the whole battery of conventional criticism. In *Jane Eyre* there was much painting of souls in their naked reality; the writer had gauged depths which the plummet of the common story-teller could never have sounded, and conflicting passions were marshalled on the stage with a masterful daring which Shakespeare might have envied; but the costumes, the conventional by-play, the scenery, even the wording of the dialogue, were poor enough in all conscience. The merest playwright or reviewer could have done better in these matters—as the unknown author was soon made to understand. Additional piquancy was given to the attack by the appearance, at the very time when the *Jane Eyre* fever was at its height, of two other novels, written by persons whose sexless names proclaimed them the brothers or the sisters of Currer Bell. Human nature is not so much changed from what it was in 1847 that one need apologise for the readiness with which the reading world in general, and the critical world in particular, adopted the theory that *Wuthering Heights* and *Agnes Grey* were earlier works from the pen which had given them *Jane Eyre*. In *Wuthering Heights* some of the faults of the other book were carried to an extreme, and some of its conspicuous merits were distorted and exaggerated until they became positive blemishes; whilst *Agnes Grey* was a feeble and commonplace tale which it was easy to condemn. So the author of

Jane Eyre was compelled to bear not only her own burden, but that of the two stories which had followed the successful novel; and the reviewers—ignorant of the fact that they were killing three birds at a single shot—rejoiced in the larger scope which was thus afforded to their critical energy.

Here and there, indeed, a manful fight on behalf of Currer Bell was made by writers who knew nothing but the name and the book. "It is soul speaking to soul," cried *Fraser's Magazine* in December, 1847; "it is not a book for prudes," added *Blackwood*, a few months later; "it is not a book for effeminate and tasteless men; it is for the enjoyment of a feeling heart and critical understanding." But in the main the verdict of the critics was adverse. It was discovered that the story was improper and immoral; it was said to be filled with descriptions of "courtship after the manner of kangaroos," and to be impregnated with a "heathenish doctrine of religion;" whilst there went up a perfect chorus of reprobation directed against its "coarseness of language," "laxity of tone," "horrid taste," and "sheer rudeness and vulgarity." From the book to the author was of course an easy transition. London had been bewildered, and its literary quidnuncs utterly puzzled, when such a story first came forth inscribed with an unknown name. Many had been the rumours eagerly passed from mouth to mouth as to the real identity of Currer Bell. Upon one point there had, indeed, been something like unanimity among the critics, and the story of *Jane Eyre* had been accepted as something more than a romance, as a genuine autobiography in which real and sorrowful experiences were related. Even the most hostile critic of the book had acknowledged that "it contained the story of struggles with such intense suffering and sorrow, as it was sufficient misery to know that any one had conceived, far less passed through." Where then was this wonderful governess to be found? In what obscure hiding-place could the forlorn soul, whose cry of agony had stirred the hearts of readers everywhere, be discovered? We may smile now, with more of sadness than of bitterness, at the base calumnies of the hour, put forth in mere wantonness and levity by a people ever seeking to know some new thing, and to taste some new sensation. The favourite theory of the day—a theory duly elaborated and discussed in the most orthodox and respectable of the reviews—was that Jane Eyre and Becky Sharp were merely different portraits of the same character; and that their original was to be found in the person of a discarded mistress of Mr. Thackeray, who had furnished the great author with a model for the heroine of *Vanity Fair*, and had revenged herself upon him by painting him as the Rochester of *Jane Eyre!* It was after dwelling upon this marvellous theory of the authorship of the story that the *Quarterly Review*, with Pecksniffian charity, calmly summed up its conclusions in these memorable words: "If we ascribe the book to a woman at all, we have no alternative but to ascribe it to one who has for some sufficient reason long forfeited the society of her own sex."

The world knows the truth now. It knows that these bitter and shameful words were applied to one of the truest and purest of women; to a woman who from her birth had led a life of self-sacrifice and patient endurance; to a woman whose affections dwelt only in the sacred shelter of her home, or with companions as pure and worthy as herself; to one of those few women who can pour out all their hearts in converse with their friends, happy in the assurance that years hence the stranger into whose hands their frank confessions may pass will find nothing there that is not loyal, true, and blameless. There was wonder among the critics, wonder too in the gay world of London, when the secret was revealed, and men were told that the author of *Jane Eyre* was no passionate light-o'-love who had merely transcribed the sad experiences of her own life; but "an austere little Joan of Arc," pure, gentle, and high-minded, of whom Thackeray himself could say that "a great and holy reverence of right and truth seemed to be with her always." The quidnuncs had searched far and wide for the author of *Jane Eyre*; but we may well doubt whether, when the truth came out at last, they were not more than ever mystified by the discovery that Currer Bell was Charlotte Brontë, the young daughter of a country parson in a remote moorland parish of Yorkshire.

That such a woman should have written such a book was more than a nine days' wonder; and for the key to that which is one of the great marvels and mysteries of English literature we must go to Charlotte Brontë's life itself. ⟨. . .⟩

XIII. The Brontë Novels

⟨. . .⟩ Of Charlotte Brontë's novels, as a whole, I shall say nothing at this point; but something may very properly be said here of the story which she wrote at the time when her sisters were engaged in writing *Wuthering Heights* and *Agnes Grey*. It was not published until after her death, and after the world had learned from Mrs. Gaskell's pages something of the truth about her life. Its interest to the ordinary reader was to a considerable extent discounted by the fact that the author had so largely used the materials in her last great work, *Villette*. But even as a mere novel *The Professor* has striking merits, and would well repay perusal from that point of view alone; whilst as a means of gaining fresh light with regard to the character of the writer, it is not less valuable than *Wuthering Heights* itself. True, *The Professor* is not really a first attempt. "A first attempt it certainly was not," says Charlotte in reference to it, "as the pen which wrote it had previously been worn a good deal in a practice of some years." But the previous writings, of which hardly a trace now remains—those early MSS. having been carefully destroyed, with the exception of the few which Mrs. Gaskell was permitted to see—were in no respect finished productions, nor had they been written with a view to publication. The first occasion on which Charlotte Brontë really began a prose work which she proposed to commit to the press was on that day when, seated by her two sisters, she joined them in penning the first page of a new novel.

To all practical intents, therefore, *The Professor* is entitled to be regarded as a first work; and certainly nothing can show Charlotte's peculiar views on the subject of novel-writing more clearly or strikingly than this book does. The world knows how resolutely in all her writings she strove to be true to life as she saw it. In *Jane Eyre* there are, indeed, romantic incidents and situations, but even in that work there is no trespassing beyond the limits always allowed to the writer of fiction; whilst it must not be forgotten that *Jane Eyre* was in part a response to the direct appeal from the publishers for something different in character from *The Professor*. In that first story she determined that she would write a man's life as men's lives usually are. Her hero was "never to get a shilling he had not earned;" no sudden turns of fortune were "to lift him in a moment to wealth and high station;" and he was not even to marry "a beautiful girl or a lady of rank." "As Adam's son he should share Adam's doom, and drain throughout life a mixed and moderate cup of enjoyment."

Very few novel-readers will share this conception of what a novel ought to be. The writer of fiction is an artist whose accepted duty it is to lift men and women out of the cares of ordinary life, out of the sordid surroundings which belong to every lot in this world, and to show us life under different, perhaps under fantastic, conditions: a life which by its contrast

to that we ourselves are leading shall furnish some relief to our mental vision, wearied and jaded by its constant contemplation of the fevers and disappointments, the crosses and long years of weary monotony, which belong to life as it is. We know how a great living writer has ventured to protest against this theory, and how in her finest works of fiction she has shown us life as it is, under the sad and bitter conditions of pain, sorrow, and hopelessness. But Charlotte Brontë wrote *The Professor* long before "George Eliot" took up her pen; and she must at least receive credit for having been in the field as a reformer of fiction before her fellow-labourer was heard of.

She was true to the conditions she had laid down for herself in writing *The Professor*. Nothing more sober and matter-of-fact than that story is to be found in English literature. And yet, though the landscape one is invited to view is but a vast plain, without even a hillock to give variety to the prospect, it has beauties of its own which commend it to our admiration. The story, as everybody knows, deals with Brussels, from which she had just returned when she began to write it. But it is sad to note the difference between the spirit of *The Professor* and that which is exhibited in *Villette*. Dealing with the same circumstances, and substantially with the same story, the author has nevertheless cast each in a mould of its own. Nor is the cause of this any secret to those who know Charlotte Brontë. When she wrote *The Professor*, disillusioned though she was, she was still young, and still blessed with that fervent belief in a better future which the youthful heart can never quite cast out, even under the heaviest blows of fate. She had come home restless and miserable, feeling Haworth to be far too small and quiet a place for her; and her mind could not take in the reality that under that modest roof the remainder of her life was destined to be spent. Suffering and unhappy as she was, she could not shut out the hope that brighter days lay before her. The fever of life racked her; but in the very fact that it burnt so high there was proof that love and hope, the capacity for a large enjoyment of existence, still lived within her. So *The Professor*, though a sad, monotonous book, has life and hope, and a fair faith in the ultimate blessedness of all sorrowful ones, shining through all its pages; and it closes in a scene of rest and peace.

Very different is the case with *Villette*. It was written years after the period when *The Professor* was composed, when the hard realities of life had ceased to be veiled under tender mists of sentiment or imagination, and when the lonely present, the future, "which often appals me," made the writer too painfully aware that she had drunk the cup of existence almost to the dregs. As a piece of workmanship there is no comparison between it and the earlier story. On every page we see traces of the artist's hand. Genius flashes forth from both works it is true, but in *Villette* it is genius chastened and restrained by a cultivated taste, or working under that high pressure which only the trained writer can bring to bear upon it. Yet, whilst we must admit the immense superiority of the later over the earlier work, we cannot turn from the one to the other without being painfully touched by the sad, strange difference in the spirit which animates them. The stories, as I have said, are nearly the same. With some curious transformations, in fact, they are practically identical. But they are only the same in the sense in which the portrait of the fair and hopeful girl, with life's romance shining before her eyes, is the same as the portrait of the worn and solitary woman for whom the romance is at an end. A whole world of suffering, of sorrow, of patient endurance, lies between the two. I have spoken of the mood in which *The Professor* was written—Hope still lingered at that time in the heart, breathing its merciful though illusory suggestions of something brighter and better in the future. All who have passed through the ordeal of a life's sorrow will be able to understand the distinction between the temperament of the author at that period in her life, and her temperament when she composed *Villette*. For such suffering ones know, how, in the first and bitterest moment of sorrow, the heart cannot shut out the blessed belief that a time of release from the pain will come—a time far off, perhaps, but in which a day bright as that which has suddenly been eclipsed will shine again. It is only as the years go by, and as the first ache of intolerable anguish has been lulled into a dreary rest by habit, that the faith which gave them strength to bear the keenest smart, takes flight, and leaves them to the pale monotony of a twilight which can know no dawn. It was in this later and saddest stage of endurance that *Villette* was written. The sharpest pangs of the heart-experiences at Brussels had vanished. The author, no longer full of the self-consciousness of the girl, could even treat her own story, her own sorrows of that period, with a lighter hand, a more artistic touch, than when she first wrote of them; but through all her work there ran the dreary conviction that in those days of mingled joy and suffering she had tasted life at its best, and that in the future which lay before her there could be nothing which should renew either the strong delights or keen anguish of that time. So the book is pitched, as we know, in a key of almost absolute hopelessness. Nothing but the genius of Charlotte Brontë could have saved such a work from sinking under its own burden of gloom. That this intense and tragic study of a soul should have had power to fascinate, not the psychologist alone, but the vast masses of the reading world, is a triumph which can hardly be paralleled in recent literary efforts. In *The Professor* we move among the same scenes, almost among the same characters and incidents, but the whole atmosphere is a different one. It is a dull, cold atmosphere, if you will, but one feels that behind the clouds the sun is shining, and that sooner or later the hero and heroine will be allowed to bask in his reviving rays. Set the two stories together, and read them in the light of all that passed between the years in which they were written—the death of Branwell, of Emily, and of Anne, the utter shattering of some fair illusions which buoyed up Charlotte's heart in the first years of her literary triumph, the apparent extinction of all hope as to future happiness—and you will get from them a truer knowledge of the author's soul than any critic or biographer could convey to you.

JAMES OLIPHANT
From *Victorian Novelists*
1899, pp. 72–77

She shares with Hawthorne the merit of discovering the possibilities of what has been called the *motif*. She saw that in the relation between two people there lay a capacity for dramatic development which could scarcely be exceeded by the greatest wealth of incident or complexity of plot. It is true that, as we have seen, she had not the courage to throw aside entirely the more conventional properties of the novelist, but we have also seen that her stories lose more than they gain from these theatrical expedients. It is not the mysterious lunatic in *Jane Eyre* that enthralls our attention; it is simply the relation between Rochester and Jane. We are deeply interested in each of these characters by itself, and in close relation they move us many times more strongly. It seems so natural now for a novelist to depend on a situation of this kind, that we find it

difficult to remember how entirely new the idea was when *Jane Eyre* was given to the world. Hawthorne's *motifs* were equally fresh and stimulating, but they were different from Charlotte Brontë's. He dealt mainly with the individual experiences of a human soul struggling with fate, while his English contemporary found her material in the action and reaction of two strongly-marked characters whose interchange of thought and emotion stirs our sympathy to its depths. It is this that constitutes the absorbing interest of her stories, and the discovery that such a firm foundation could be built with such simple materials was of the highest consequence in the development of the art of fiction.

It has been objected, and will no doubt be objected again, that Charlotte Brontë secured this unusually strong interest by attaching an importance to the passion of love which it does not possess, and ought not to possess, in real life, and which it is therefore wrong in a novelist to represent. But in the first place it may be fairly maintained that love, even in this restricted sense, is the most potent factor in human nature, and that if its significance is not realised in actual life as it is in fiction it is because reflection has been so largely and so unfortunately diverted from it. If this all-important element in the evolution of the race were in any adequate sense understood we should not have people marrying and giving in marriage in the hap-hazard and irresponsible and sordid fashion of our undeveloped civilisation. It is Charlotte Brontë's chief claim to greatness that she has ennobled the passion of love by triumphantly proving that it may be independent of physical attraction, and revealing its true basis in the subtle affinities of character. She has idealised love in the truest sense, by interweaving with its self-regarding instincts the golden threads of a spiritual and imaginative sympathy. We have all in some degree experienced, in friendship or in love, the unique delight of meeting a kindred soul whose whole being seems to vibrate in unison with our own. It is then that, in the words of Matthew Arnold:

> A bolt is shot back somewhere in our heart,
> And a lost pulse of feeling stirs again;
> The eye sinks inward, and the heart lies plain,
> And what we mean we say, and what we would we
> 　know.

If this mysterious feeling which reveals us to ourselves in the responsive sympathy of our spiritual counterpart, has in any degree been strengthened by communion with the ideal types held together in such a bond in the realms of poetic fiction, we owe a debt of gratitude for the precious gift to the creator of Rochester and Jane Eyre, of Lucy Snowe and Paul Emanuel, of Louis Moore and Shirley Keeldar.

The discovery of the possibilities of such a *motif* would have been of little avail, however, if there had not been in Charlotte Brontë an unusual power of conceiving and representing characters that are at once entirely lifelike and thoroughly interesting. Her portraiture was not always perfect. We have seen that it sometimes became caricature (as it certainly does in the description of the curates in *Shirley*), that in the case of children it was unreal and unsympathetic, that it was apt to err in a too literal transcript of insignificant peculiarities. Even her successes are not always beyond reproach. Fairfax Rochester has been called a woman's man, and it is perhaps true that there are some traits about him that are not entirely drawn as if from within. But as a whole he forms one of the most striking individualities in fiction. We follow all he says and does with the closest interest, knowing that he will constantly surprise us, but also knowing that every fresh revelation will be consistent with what we have already heard. We can have no deeper impression of reality and strength combined than to find our confidence uniformly justified in such a case. There is scarcely the same absolute success in her other heroes. Paul Emanuel certainly comes very near it, and Robert Moore is also thoroughly good, but his brother Lewis is a little shadowy, and his relation to Shirley Keeldar is not perfectly intelligible. There is indeed one mistake that runs through the relations of all the lovers. The assumption of authority on the part of the man, which the authoress supposed to be a proper attribute of the masculine character, and which she represents all her heroines as expecting and approving, is exaggerated till it approaches brutality. In Rochester it takes a specially ferocious form; in M. Paul it is an ungovernable temper; in Robert Moore it is a condescending superiority; in Lewis it is the privilege of a dominie. These are faults not so much in drawing as in the novelist's theory of the relations between men and women. They are to be regretted, but they can be allowed for without seriously interfering with the reader's enjoyment and appreciation. In her heroines Charlotte Brontë naturally achieves an even greater success. Here she had the knowledge of her own thoughts and feelings to guide her, and in two of her heroines, Jane Eyre and Lucy Snowe, she is understood to have largely reproduced not only her own mental experience but many of the scenes and events of her life. In Pauline and Caroline Helstone she drew partly from herself and partly from her sisters, while Shirley Keeldar is believed to be an idealised portrait of her sister Emily, as she might have been had fortune smiled on her. The two figures that most nearly represent the authoress herself are on the whole the most lifelike that she has drawn, and the interest which the novelist naturally takes in them is communicated to the reader. The two resemble each other rather too closely to attain separate and distinct individualities, but the model from which they are both evidently drawn is a perfectly definite as well as an entirely interesting character. She judged rightly when she put herself, literally as well as figuratively, into her novels. The portrait in each case is that of a girl of acute sensibility, made to be very happy or very miserable, but strong enough to bear either lot with firmness and self-control, in whom the discipline of early neglect or unkindness has caused a repression of feeling that might well have engendered bitterness, but has only intensified a noble pride and a stern sense of duty. It is a sad picture to be drawn from the life, this, for which the rule of conduct was the motto, "If you ever really wish to do anything, you may be sure it is wrong", but as material for imaginative treatment it could not easily have been surpassed. We follow the modest fortunes of this plain-looking girl with an absorbing interest, far greater than is called forth by the thrilling adventures of many a beautiful and romantic heroine. The secret of our sympathy lies in our consciousness of the intense capacity of emotion that underlies the calm face and self-contained manner, but it is a notable achievement of art to impress this consciousness upon us without departing from legitimate means of suggestion. Though in both cases the girl tells her own story, the reader is never bored by the confidences of the narrator, and no impression is left of egotism or undue expansiveness. But the most charming feminine characters are to be found, not in these autobiographical books, but in *Shirley*, in the person of the two friends, Caroline Helstone and Shirley Keeldar. Indeed the love episodes in the book are less interesting than the history of the friendship of the two girls. Caroline is perhaps the most charming of Charlotte Brontë's heroines, and this in spite of the fact that here the novelist has been decidedly less successful

in endowing her characters with vivid natural speech. Some of the conversations between Shirley and Caroline are expressed in phraseology that is wholly out of keeping with the age and culture of the speakers. This must of course be distinguished from the much more serious error in a dramatic artist of making the characters *act* or *feel* in a way that is inconsistent with their general nature. Charlotte Brontë rarely makes that mistake, but in *Shirley* especially she allows them sometimes to talk more as the mouthpieces of the author than in their own proper persons. In spite of this, however, the relation between the two friends is very finely portrayed, and enlists our sympathies in a high degree. But notwithstanding the excellence of the chief characters, the book as a whole is scarcely equal to *Jane Eyre* or *Villette*. It attempts more. The canvas is larger, and the *motif* is wider, embracing not only the personal relations of the main figures, but the conflict of capital and labour in one of its striking phases. But the success is scarcely in proportion to the greater ambition, and there are more faults of detail than in the other novels. Some of the minor characters, such as Mrs. Prior and Mr. Yorke, cannot be believed in. A slight but irritating blemish which runs through all Charlotte Brontë's books may further be mentioned as illustrating curiously the want of taste for which her narrow circumstances were responsible—namely, her constant introduction of French words and phrases where English would have done as well. She had learned French thoroughly during her stay in Brussels, which must have been in many ways the most exciting period of her life, and as her mind was full of it she could not help putting it into her books. It is a mistake to call this affectation; it only proves the absence of a perfectly sure taste.

A study of Charlotte Brontë's novels suggests the judgment that while in all of them there is much that is of high value and interest, there is only one part of one of them that leaves the distinct impression of unmistakable greatness, namely, the relation between Rochester and Jane Eyre. This may seem a small achievement on which to base security of fame, but it is not to be measured by the number of pages in which it is contained. It struck a new note in the history of fiction—a note which has added many grand and subtle harmonies to itself in the works of succeeding writers, and the sweetness and power of which will never die away.

LEWIS E. GATES
From "Charlotte Brontë"
Studies and Appreciations
1900, pp. 129–62

Charlotte Brontë was once reproached by the vivacious and ever-confident George Henry Lewes for not more nearly resembling, in her artistic methods, that favourite novelist of the gently cynical and worldly wise,—Jane Austen. Her answering letter, while in tone very prettily submissive, nevertheless justifies vigorously her own methods of writing and her treatment of life. "If I ever *do* write another book," she says, "I think I will have nothing of what you call 'melodrama'; I *think* so, but I am not sure. I *think*, too, I will endeavour to follow the counsel which shines out of Miss Austen's 'mild eyes,' 'to finish more and be more subdued'; but neither am I sure of that. When authors write best, or, at least, when they write most fluently, an influence seems to waken in them, which becomes their master,—which will have its own way,—putting out of view all behests but its own, dictating certain words, and insisting on their being used, whether vehement or measured in their nature; new-moulding characters, giving unthought-of turns to incidents, rejecting carefully elaborated old ideas, and suddenly creating and adopting new ones."

These words of Miss Brontë's carry with them a flash from eyes very different in quality from "Miss Austen's mild eyes," and they express more than a passing mood of protest. Charlotte Brontë really believed in her dæmon. She had the faith which so many romantic poets from Blake to Shelley have confessed to, that her words and images were, not cleverly devised, but inevitably suggested. Novelists do not often take themselves so seriously, at least in public, particularly novelists who keep so sanely near the world of fact as Charlotte Brontë keeps. Your Poe and your Hoffmann may professedly dream out and set down their wildly fantastic tales with the same visionary glibness with which Coleridge wrote *Kubla Khan*. But the noteworthy fact is that Charlotte Brontë lays claim to much this same sort of inspiration for her narratives of actual Yorkshire life. Her visions of characters and incidents must have mastered her like veritable hallucinations to lead to such a claim; and this visionary eye of hers may well account, at least in part, for the astonishing vividness of her narratives and for their success in again and again imposing themselves for moments on our faith with a thoroughness that the more sophisticated art of to-day rarely attains. Charlotte Brontë has something of the seer's persuasiveness; she captures our faith at unawares.

In the letter already quoted Charlotte Brontë, while commenting on Jane Austen's work, puts to Lewes a very pertinent question. "Can there be a great artist," she asks, "without poetry?" She herself believed not, and her novels are from first to last faithful illustrations of her creed. It was not for nothing that she lived for so many years a lonely, introspective life between an overcrowded graveyard and the desolate expanses of the Yorkshire moors. The world, as she conceived of it, was not the world of conventional intrigue in drawing-rooms or pump-rooms or gossiping country-side towns; and the news of the world that she sent out through her novels was news that had come to her not by hearsay or tittle-tattle, or authenticated by painstaking watchfulness in the midst of tea-drinkers and scandal-mongers, but news that could bear the comment of the sweep of the moors by day and of the host of stars by night. She was a lyrical poet, and in each of her novels she set herself the task, or rather, her whole energy went into the task, of re-creating the world in such guise that it should have something of the intrinsic beauty of poetry conferred upon it.

Her interpretation of life was, first of all, a woman's interpretation. This is, of course, the conventional thing to say of Charlotte Brontë; but here, as so often, the conventional thing is the true thing, merely in need of a little exposition. Her novels are not feminine readings of life simply in the sense of portraying the passion of love from a woman's point of view. This she does, to be sure, with a power and a beauty that George Eliot, for example, with her impersonal point of view and her withering sense of the rights of intellect, never attains to. But vibrant Jane Eyrism is far from being the sole staple out of which Charlotte Brontë's novels are wrought. Intense sympathy with human love in all its myriad forms, together with an audacious belief in its power to bring happiness, or something better than happiness, *is*, one is tempted to assert, that sole staple. She has an obsession of reckless faith in the worth of love, and from first to last her novels are full of the pathos of craving hearts, and of the worth that life gains when their craving is contented. It is in the tenderness and strength

of her loyalty to love in all its guises, and in her delicate perception and brave portrayal of all the fine ministrations of love to life, that the peculiar feminine quality of her novels resides.

For Charlotte Brontë, the struggle for life is the struggle for affection. There is a pathetic uniformity in the development of her stories when one stops to analyze them. In each, some creature striving for happiness is the central controlling character, and the plot of the story is the process by which this needy pensioner of the author is ultimately made heir to unexpected stores of appreciation and sympathy and love. Jane Eyre, at the opening of her history, is a tragically isolated little figure, without a sincere friend in the world, and symbolically busy over a woodcut of the lonely and frigid arctic regions. At the close, she has three excellent cousins—the two girls are as good as sisters; she casually gets, at the same time with her relatives, a very decent fortune; and above all, she falls heir to the vast hoard of passion long secreted in the caverns of Rochester's heart. Lucy Snowe in *Villette* has much the same fate; after long months or years of loneliness, she gets back old friends who are thrice as friendly as before; and the story of *Villette* is simply the history of Lucy's search for sympathy and of her acquisition of Monsieur Paul. The same is true of *Shirley*; the reader's vital interest in the story depends on his wish to see Caroline Helstone, Shirley, and Louis Moore duly fitted out with their fair share of love: Caroline wins a mother and a lover in a month; and Shirley also, as the reader doubtless remembers, fares sumptuously at the last. It is droll to note how little any of Charlotte Brontë's heroines care for literature or art. She herself was apparently hungry for fame as a writer, but all her heroines are lovers of life, and of life only; not one of them so much as coquets with art or literature except as she may write "exercises" for some favourite master. Very un-modern are all these young women, and the young men, too, for that matter, with no subtle dilettante theories, no morbid contempt for life, no erratic veins of enthusiasm or strange kinds of faculty or of genius. They are all simply bent on getting happiness through love of one sort or another.

Dorothea Brooke and her abstract ideal enthusiasm, Charlotte Brontë could not have conceived or created, any more than she could have traced out with relentless sociological and psychological detail the revenge that the "world" took on Dorothea for her fine passion of unconventionality. Not that Charlotte Brontë was less brave in her contempt of cheap worldly standards than George Eliot; but Dorothea's spiritual restlessness and ambition sprang from a complexity of moral and mental life that Charlotte Brontë's culture was too narrow to have suggested to her, and involves a passion for subtler kinds of goodness than Charlotte Brontë's simple, intense nature brought within her ken. Jane Eyre, when waxing discontented with the tameness of her early life at Thornfield Hall, describes her longing to get away in search of "other and more vivid kinds of goodness." *More vivid kinds of goodness* than those that the common run of mortals reach—these Charlotte Brontë ardently believed in and portrayed. Much of the permanent power of her stories comes from the "impetuous honesty" (to quote from Thackeray's characterization of her), and the fiery intensity of imagination with which she puts before even readers of the present day her sense and vision of what life may be made to mean for those who will live sincerely and resolutely. There is something elemental in her. She gives a new zest to life like the encounter with a bit of wild nature,—with a sea-breeze or the tense germinating silence in the depths of a wood. But she is elemental at the cost of being primitive,—primitive in her devotion to a few great interests, and in her lack of refining complexity of thought. Hence one's sense in reading her that one is moving in a world remote from the present. Her heroines indulge in no self-analysis, have no quarrels with their consciences, no torturing doubts about duty, no moral or spiritual struggles. They are curiously definite and resolute little persons, who at every crisis know in a trice just where duty lies and just what they want to do. Their minds are clear, their ideas about what makes life worth while are certain, their wills are intact; their only quarrel is with circumstance. They have no wish to play with life imaginatively, no sense of the cost of committing themselves to a single ideal, no critical fear of the narrowing effects of action. What would Charlotte Brontë have made, one wonders, of Marie Bashkirtzeff?

Life itself, then, not fancies or speculations about life,—life of an almost primitive intensity,—is what Charlotte Brontë's novels still offer to readers of to-day who may be surfeited with intellectual refinements of thought and feeling. Doubtless there is in her work something of the romantic false preference for savagery and barbarism over civilization, and of the romantic inclination to confuse crudeness with strength. She loathes conventional life and commonplace characters, and her art has to pay the penalty through growing now and then melodramatic and absurd. Her heroes, notably Rochester and Monsieur Paul, cannot always get themselves taken seriously. Their grotesqueness is overaccentuated. They seem to study oddity. They drape themselves in extravagance as in a mantle. But although Miss Brontë's romantic bias—her fondness for the strange—may now and then distort the action and the characters of her stories, she never, unless rarely in her last novel, *Villette*, offends in her own style. She never rants; her taste is sure. Even in describing the most exciting scenes, her style has no strut and no stridency. And so it is easy to forgive the occasional grotesqueness of her incident and to yield to the sincerity of her art. Her romances deal with confessedly exceptional states of passion,—with almost such passions as a lyrical poet might deal with. And the imaginative truth and the beauty of phrase with which she realizes the moods of her heroines—moods which have the beat of the heart behind them, and are not mere fancies of brain-sick dilettantes—give to many passages in her stories almost the splendour and power of lyrical poetry.

It used to be said of Dante Gabriel Rossetti that life was, with him, always at a crisis. Much the same thing is true of Charlotte Brontë and of her heroines. Her novels—and this, when one stops to consider, helps largely to give them their peculiar tone—are perpetually busy with emotional crises; they are bent on portraying just the feverish expectation, the poignant grief, the joy, the glow of passion, which some special moment or incident stirs in the heart of the heroine. Very often the moods that colour her fiction are moods of anxiety, of breathless waiting, of nervous suspense. Jane Eyre's moods are continually of this sort. "I shall be called discontented," she says in one place. "I could not help it; the restlessness was in my nature; it agitated me to pain sometimes. Then my sole relief was to walk along the corridor of the third story, backward and forward, safe in the silence and solitude of the spot."

Early and late in *Jane Eyre*, these moments of eager waiting, sometimes for a definite sorrow or joy or excitement, sometimes merely with poignant longing for change, are described fully and vividly. When Jane, still a wee girl, has to make a start by coach before break of day for a distant school, the childish, half-haggard worry of the early morning is not taken for granted, but is put before the reader with almost oppressive truth. Jane's drive, many years later, across the

country to Thornfield Hall, and her tremulous sensitiveness meantime to every new impression,—these also are keenly realized and faithfully reproduced. Throughout the story, wherever she is, Jane is continually aware of the sky-line and half-consciously quarrelling with the horizon. At Thornfield she often climbed to the leads of the Hall and "looked out afar over sequestered field and hill, and along dim sky-line," and "longed for a power of vision which might overpass that limit." And earlier, at Lowood, she speaks of "the hilly horizon," and adds: "My eye passed all other objects to rest on those most remote, the blue peaks; it was those I longed to surmount."

Lucy Snowe, whose fortunes make up the story of *Villette*, is not quite so fiery a young particle as Jane Eyre; but she has almost as many moods of thrilling restlessness to tell about. Her nerves vibrate to the "subtle, searching cry of the wind"; she answers half-superstitiously to all the skyey influences; she watches with a breathless exhilaration the Aurora Borealis,—its "quivering of serried lances," "its swift ascent of messengers from below the north star." And so throughout *Jane Eyre* and *Villette*,—*Shirley*, as will presently be noted, is somewhat differently conceived,—moods of acute and febrile intensity are imaginatively put before us. We are kept perpetually within sound of the heroine's breathing, and are forced to watch from hour to hour the anguished or joyful play of her pulse. The moods are not difficult moods, or subtly reflective moods; they are not the ingenious imitations of feelings which the pseudo-artistic temperament of to-day vamps up to while away the time and in emulation of the woes of special souls. They are the veritable joys and sorrows of eager and keenly sensitive natures that are bent above all upon living, and that never think of posing, or of mitigating the severity of life by artistic watchfulness over their own experiences. They are primitive, elemental, tyrannical emotions, and not to be disbelieved.

Another source of the almost lyrical intensity which runs through Charlotte Brontë's fiction is her sensitiveness to natural beauty. She had all a romantic poet's tremulous awareness of the bright and shadowed world of moor and field and sky. Her nerves knew nature through and through and answered to all its changing moods, and rarely do her stories, even when the scene is laid in a city, leave long out of notice the coursing of the clouds, the sound of the winds, the gay or ominous play of light and shade through the hours of the day, the look of the moon at night. The creativeness of her imagination, its searching inclusiveness, are not to be missed. It is a whole new world she gives us; she is not content with working out for us the acts or thoughts or looks of imaginary folk who may move satisfactorily across any sort of conventional stage. Her imagination is too elemental for this, too vital, includes too much of the universe within its sensitive grasp. Her people are knit by "organic filaments" to the nature they inhabit, and they can be thoroughly and persuasively realized only as their sensitive union with this nature-world which is their home is continually suggested. With the romantic poet, the individual is far more closely dependent on the vast instinctive world of nature for comfort and help and even for the life of the spirit, than on the conventional world of society, to which his relations seem to such a poet more nearly accidental. In her sympathy with this conception of man as intimately communing with the mysterious life of the physical universe, Charlotte Brontë shows once more her romantic bias.

Accordingly, the pages of her novels are full of delicate transcripts of the changing aspects of night and day, as these aspects record themselves on sensitive temperaments—more particularly on the temperaments of her heroines. *Jane Eyre* is perhaps most richly wrought with these half-lyrical impressions of what the earth and the sky have to say to the initiated. Yet, even through the more objective *Shirley*, Charlotte Brontë's love of nature follows her unmistakably,—the hero, Moore, owing his very name to her passion for the wild Yorkshire downs. In *Villette*, the scene is in Brussels; yet Charlotte Brontë's imagination, even when thus circumscribed, will not wholly give up the world of nature, and Lucy Snowe finds in the wind, in the sky, in the moon, companionable presences whose varying aspects and utterances symbolize again and again her joys or griefs or wringing anxieties. "It was a day of winter east winds," she says in one place, "and I had now for some time entered into that dreary fellowship with the winds and their changes, so little known, so incomprehensible, to the healthy. The north and the east owned a terrific influence, making all pain more poignant, all sorrow sadder. The south could calm, the west sometimes cheer; unless indeed, they brought on their wings the burden of thunder-clouds, under the weight and warmth of which all energy died." Of the moon as well as the winds, Lucy is strangely watchful; and often at some crisis in her externally placid but internally stormy life she describes its splendour or its sadness. So in Chapter xii: "A moon was in the sky, not a full moon, but a young crescent. I saw her through a space in the boughs overhead. She and the stars, visible beside her, were no strangers where all else was strange; my childhood knew them. I had seen that golden sign with the dark globe in its curve leaning back on azure, beside an old thorn at the top of an old field, in Old England, in long past days, just as it now leaned back beside a stately spire in this continental capital." Again: "Leaving the radiant park and well-lit Haute-Ville . . . I sought the dim lower quarter. Dim I should not say, for the beauty of the moonlight—forgotten in the park—here once more flowed in upon perception. High she rode, and calm and stainlessly she shone. . . . The rival lamps were dying; she held her course like a white fate." Finally, a single passage may be quoted from *Shirley* because of the way it testifies, through the moon's subjugation of the surly and stormy temperament of old Yorke, to both the dramatic and the romantic power of Charlotte Brontë's imagination. Yorke, the brusque and violent Yorkshire squire, riding in the late evening over the downs with Moore, the hero, has been betrayed into talk about a woman he had long ago loved; suddenly he breaks off. "'The moon is up,' was his first not quite relevant remark, pointing with his whip across the moor. 'There she is, rising into the haze, staring at us in a strange red glower. She is no more silver than old Helstone's brow is ivory. What does she mean by leaning her cheek on Rushedge i' that way, and looking at us wi' a scowl and a menace?'"

Charlotte Brontë's sensitiveness to the sinister or seductive beauty of the moon, illustrated by all these passages, may be taken as typical of her relation to all nature, and of her use of it throughout her stories. She has an almost transcendental faith in the meaning of natural sights and sounds; she reproduces them with a glamour that only a romantic imagination can catch and suggest; and the unmistakable sincerity of her moods and the lyrical intensity of her interpretations help to give to her novels a peculiarly vivid beauty that the modern instructed, scientific, and faithless novelist can rarely attain to. ⟨. . .⟩

The new world, then, into which Charlotte Brontë's imagination inducts the modern reader and of which she makes him free, is a world where casuistry and philosophy are unknown, where they put no mist of abstractions between the reader and the poignant fact. It is a world where love and hate and the few great primary savage passions, of which recent literary folk of the first order fight so shy, are portrayed vigorously and convincingly. It is a world in which the elements, air and earth and water, flash and blossom and ripple, where the clouds and the winds, the sun and the moon, are never quite out of mind, and set the nerves a-tingle and put the imagination in play, even of the folk who are shut indoors.

And yet, though life, as Charlotte Brontë portrays it, is so passionate, and though the world is so primitive and elemental, the life that she puts before us is *actual* life, not a whimsical or fantastic or falsifying counterfeit of life, and the world in which her characters live and move and have their being, is the *actual* world, not a mystical dream-region, beautifully false in its colours and chiaroscuro and artificially filled like Hawthorne's world, for example, with omens and portents and moral symbolism. Her characters, too, are real men and women, not types, not figures in melodrama, not creatures of one idea, or one humour, or one passion. Doubtless they are not studied with the minuteness that modern realists use. Yet they have complex personalities and lead thoroughly individual lives. And they are flashed on the reader's retina with a vividness of colour and a dramatic truthfulness and suggestiveness in act and gesture that modern scientific novels rarely reach. Herein, perhaps, lies Charlotte Brontë's unique power,—in her ability to make her stories seem close to fact and yet strange and almost mystically imaginative. Her hallucinations are sane, and her victims of passion keep, after all, within the bounds of reason.

And indeed this is an aspect of Charlotte Brontë's genius that has not in general been insisted upon sufficiently—her self-control and her loyalty to reason, in all that is essential, whether in art or in morals, a loyalty that is none the less consistent and controlling because it is half-grudging. As a result of this loyalty she escapes in her stories much of the extravagance and absurdity that her sisters were led into. In some respects, Emily Brontë was a greater artist than Charlotte; she had an intenseness of vision, and an occasional beauty of image and phrase, that Charlotte Brontë never quite reaches. The vividness of some of her scenes and the acrid intensity of the counterfeit life in *Wuthering Heights* are beyond anything in *Jane Eyre* or *Shirley*. But the work of Emily Brontë is lacking in the moral and artistic sanity which is characteristic of Charlotte Brontë. *Wuthering Heights* has here and there greater lyrical beauty and power than anything that Charlotte Brontë has written. But Emily Brontë takes us wholly out of ordinary daylight into a region of nightmare horrors. Dante Rossetti used to say of *Wuthering Heights* that its scenes were laid in hell, though oddly enough the places and the people had English names. The story, too, is illogical and structureless, and hence fails to make a lastingly great impression; it spends itself in paroxysms and lacks sustained power and cumulative effect.

Charlotte Brontë, on the other hand, is never completely the victim of her hallucinations. Contemptuous as she may be of "common sense" in conventional matters, she is never really false to reason or careless of its dictates in the regions either of conduct or of art. When all is said, *Jane Eyre*, the wildest of her stories, is a shining example of the infinite importance, both in life and in art, of reason. As a story, it is from beginning to end admirably wrought. It moves forward with an inevitableness, a logic of passion, an undeviating aim, that become more and more impressive, the more familiar one is with the novel, and that mark it as the work of a soundly intellectual artist—of an artist who is instinctively true to the organizing force of reason as well as to the visions of a passionate imagination. In spite of its length and wealth of detail, *Jane Eyre* is an admirably unified work of art. Every moment prepares for, or reenforces, or heightens by way of subsequent contrast, the effect of the tragic complication in the lives of Rochester and Jane Eyre,— the complication in that passion which seeming for the moment about to bring perfect happiness to the dreary existence of the little green-eyed, desolate waif of a woman, finally overwhelms her and seems to have wrecked her life. The steady march of destiny may be heard if one will listen for it; the fate-*motif* sounds almost as plainly as in *Tristan und Isolde*. To give us now and then this sense that we are watching the working out of fate, is the great triumph of the imaginative artist.

To some, this praise of *Jane Eyre* may sound like droll hyperbole, for there are undoubtedly sadly distracting defects in the story which for certain readers, particularly on a first reading, mar irretrievably its essential greatness. The most important of these have already been noted. "The long arm of coincidence" stretches out absurdly in one or two places, and makes all thought of fate for the moment grotesque. The vices and the ugliness of Rochester are dwelt upon with a fervour that suggests an old maid's belated infatuation for a monstrosity. The sempiternally solemn love-making of Jane and Rochester drones its pitilessly slow length along, with no slightest ironical consciousness or comment on the part of the author. These faults and these lapses of taste are undeniably exasperating, but they grow less prominent as one comes to know the story intimately and to feel its strenuous movement and sincerity; and they finally sink, for any reader who has an instinct for essentials, into their true place, as superficial blemishes on a powerfully original work of art.

Of the existence of these defects in *Jane Eyre*, however, Charlotte Brontë was liberally informed by the critics, and in her later stories she guards against them. Both *Shirley* and *Villette* are freer from absurdities than *Jane Eyre*; neither is quite so frankly devout toward the *outré*, and in both a certain insidious humour is cultivated. *Shirley* is a roundabout tribute to Thackeray. The point of view, the method, the tone, are the result of a hero-worshipping study of the novelist to whom *Jane Eyre* was finally dedicated. The story aims to be more a criticism of life than *Jane Eyre*, and less a personal confession; the point of view is that of "the author," and the tone is often whimsical or ironical. From the very first page the style betokens a changed attitude toward life. The novel is not to be a semi-lyrical record of moods of hope and grief and revolt and passion and joy; it is to portray with a certain delicate and at times ironical detachment the fortunes of a small group of characters whom the author lovingly but shrewdly watches. The brisk satire at the expense of the curates is something that lies quite out of the scope of *Jane Eyre*. The gain that *Shirley* shows in conscious breadth of outlook and in confidence of bearing,—in authority,—is noteworthy. *Jane Eyre* is the work of an audacious solitary dreamer; *Shirley* is the work of an author who has "arrived," who has made the world listen, and who feels sure that she has a right to speak. The monotonous poignancy of *Jane Eyre* gives place in *Shirley* to a wide range of moods; the story moves forward with a buoyant sense of the charm of life as well as with a half-indignant sense of its daunting and harrowing difficulty. The author escapes from the tyranny of a single, somewhat morbid, though courageous, temperament, and gives us incidents and characters with more of the checkered light upon them that ordinary mortals are from day to day aware of.

Shirley takes in, too, more of the light miscellaneousness of life than *Jane Eyre*,—more of its variegated surface. *Jane*

Eyre concentrates all the interest on the struggle of two hearts with fate; *Shirley*, while loyal to the fortunes of a few principal characters, suggests the whole little world of the country-side, through conflict and coöperation with which these characters gain their strength and quality. At least it tries to suggest this world,—a world of curates, rectors, squires, and even labourers. Tea-drinkings and church festivals and labour riots are conscientiously set forth, and in the midst of their bustle and confusion the wooings of Robert Moore and Louis Moore go on.

Yet one has after all but to think of *Middlemarch* to feel how superficial in Charlotte Brontë's novels is the treatment of sociological detail. In *Shirley* the labourers and their riotous attacks on the mill are plainly enough simply used to heighten the effect of the plot; the rioters come in almost as perfunctorily as the mob in a melodrama, and they pass out of view the moment they have served the purpose of giving the reader an exciting scene in which Moore may act heroically, and over which Shirley and Charlotte may feel intensely. The genius of Charlotte Brontë lay not in the power to realize minutely and thoroughly the dependence of character on social environment, but in her power to portray with lyrical intensity the fates of a few important characters. *Shirley* isolates its characters far less than *Jane Eyre*,—tries to see them and portray them as more intimately and complexly acted upon by a great many forces. It is therefore a wiser, saner, and more modern book than *Jane Eyre*. But in proportion it loses in intensity, passionate colour, and in subduing singleness of aim. The interest is divided; the dreamlike involvement of the reader in the mist of a single temperament's fancies and feelings disappears; the peculiar, half-hypnotizing effect of *Jane Eyre's* murmurous, monotonous recital vanishes; and in the place of all this we have a brilliant, often powerful, and undeniably picturesque and entertaining criticism of various aspects of Yorkshire life, written somewhat after the method that George Eliot later used much more skilfully.

In *Villette* Charlotte Brontë returns to the personal point of view and the more lyrical tone. Lucy Snowe, who is merely a reincarnation of Jane Eyre, though somewhat less energetic and less ugly, puts upon us in this story, as Jane Eyre had put upon us before, the spell of her dream, and imposes on us the sad or happy hallucinations that made up her life. In some respects, *Villette* is the most of a *tour de force* of Charlotte Brontë's novels. She takes for heroine a plain, shy, colourless school-teacher; she puts her in the midst of a girl's boarding-school, and keeps her there pitilessly from almost the start to the finish of the story; she makes use of hardly any exciting incident—the Spectral Nun is a mere picturesque hoax, though her repeated introduction illustrates the weakness for sensationalism in plots that Charlotte Brontë could never quite rid herself of; there are, however, this time no mad wives, no hollow mysterious laughter, no men or women with suspicious pasts. Yet in spite of the commonplace characters and the seemingly dull situations, the story that results holds the reader's interest firmly with its alternate gayety, pathos, and passion. In places it is as poignant as *Jane Eyre*. After all, we mortals are ridiculously sympathetic creatures; it is the fluttering of the human heart that captures us; and Lucy Snowe's heart finds enough excitement in her Belgian boarding-school to justify a great deal of passionate beating.

Villette suffers, however, from a divided allegiance on the part of the author. Her method in the story is plainly a compromise between the egoistic self-concentration of *Jane Eyre* and the professional detachment of *Shirley*. Lucy Snowe is made more speculative, less acridly self-assertive, than Jane Eyre, to the very end that she may note more of the ordinary happenings of life, and set down a more reflective and inclusive record of what goes on about her than the impassioned Jane would have had patience for. As a consequence, *Villette* gains in range but loses in intensity. The fortunes of the Bassompierres, which, in spite of Lucy's loyalty to the charm of these worthy folk, fail to perturb the reader very deeply, fill far too much space. In a letter written about the time of the publication of the novel, Charlotte Brontë laments the weakness of the character of Paulina, and the apparent *non-sequitur* that results in the story from the early importance of the Bassompierres and of Dr. John, and from their later obscuration by Lucy's love for the Professor. This flickering purpose is perhaps the sign of the difficulty the author met in trying to be objective. The power to portray the world with passionate truth as seen through a woman's temperament,—a narrowly exacting and somewhat morbidly self-centred temperament,—this was the peculiar power of Charlotte Brontë; and in *Jane Eyre* this power found its perfect expression. In her other novels, though she wins a greater range, she sacrifices her peculiar coign of vantage.

It must, then, be admitted with all frankness that life is not for most people the sort of thing that Charlotte Brontë represents. The moods that fill the pages of *Jane Eyre* are no more the common moods with which the ordinary man or woman looks at life than are the lyrics of *In Memoriam* like the daily records of a clubman's thoughts. For most people, life is not perpetually at a crisis; nor are they all the time yearning intensely for love and sympathy. Petty personal rivalries and the pleasure that comes from success in them, silly little vanities that fancy themselves flattered, cheap bodily delights, a pleased ironical sense of the absurdities of other people,—these are the satisfactions that for half the world redeem the monotony of existence and make it no hardship to go on living; and these are precisely the phases of life that such novelists as Jane Austen delight to depict. Of all these frivolous feelings Charlotte Brontë's account of life contains scarcely a hint. *Shirley* now and then has glimpses of the absurd trivialities that the cynic likes to find and sneer at. But for the most part Charlotte Brontë is as oblivious as Shelley or Wordsworth of the possible delights of irony. Perhaps it is still an open question whether the ironical or the passionately sincere relation to life is the worthier in morals and in art. The imaginations that can reconcile the two are doubtless the most penetrating and potent. Miss Brontë showed that she could appreciate the ironical manner through her warm admiration of Thackeray,—an admiration, however, be it noted that expressly insists on the "sentiment, which, jealously hidden, but genuine, extracts the venom from that formidable Thackeray, and converts what might be corrosive poison into purifying elixir." As for her own work, however, she was too contemptuous of conventionality in all its forms to be a fit interpreter of the Spirit of Comedy.

Indeed, she now and then herself becomes in her art fair game for the Spirit of Comedy, because of the dulness of her conventional conscience. She does not always know when the laugh is bound to be against her. Her heroes often wax silly or grotesque. Rochester's smile which "he used but on rare occasions," his "ebon eyebrows," his "precious grimness," his "bursts of maniacal rage," all his extravagances of look and demeanour, are insisted upon absurdly. Paul Emmanuel's tricks of manner, his wilfulness, his self-conceit, his fidgetiness,—these are played upon out of all measure, and described with a fondness that must now and then seem ludicrous. And so, too, with the peculiarities of Louis Moore; his sardonic self-satisfaction, his somewhat pretentious iciness of de-

meanour, his satanic pride and so on, are made abundantly grotesque through overemphasis. Melodramatic incident, too, Miss Brontë shows a perilous fondness for. Not easy is it to take seriously the crazy wife of Rochester, who goes on all fours in an upper chamber, and now and then sallies forth to set fire to something or other. Excesses of this sort both in characterization and in incident are the penalty that Miss Brontë has to pay for her contempt for conventional standards and modes of judgment.

Gradually she doubtless came to recognize the danger involved in her fondness for the abnormal, and in her distrust of everyday virtues and modes of life. In her last novel, *Villette*, she tried to be fair to conventional types of men and women, and to portray worldly success sympathetically. In Dr. John Bretton she aims to draw the character of a well-bred, good-tempered, prosperous gentleman,—a man in no disgrace with fortune and men's eyes. And in Paulina she makes a brave effort to depict sympathetically a pretty and charming young society girl. Both Bretton and Paulina, however, are mere copperplate nonentities. Miss Brontë herself laments in one of her letters her failure with Paulina; and John Graham Bretton, the handsome young doctor at whom Lucy Snowe confesses she dare not look for fear of being dazzled for a half-hour afterward, is also a mere figment. Paul Emmanuel is the real hero of *Villette*,—a hero in his own way as *outré* as Rochester himself. In *Shirley*, the insufferable Sympsons—Shirley's buckram uncle and his faultless daughters—together with Sir Philip Nunnely, the lily-fingered baronet, who writes sentimental verses, are the only really conventional folk portrayed. The daughters "knew by heart a certain young-ladies'-schoolroom code of laws on language, demeanour, etc.; themselves never deviated from its curious little pragmatical provisions; and they regarded with secret, whispered horror all deviations in others." Mr. Sympson's god was "the World," as Shirley tells him in a virago-like speech toward the close of the story. All these devotees of "correctness" Miss Brontë detests; "these things we artists hate," as Blake said of the *Mechanics' Magazine*. And her hatred of them gives a kind of dissenting bitterness to parts of her treatment of life,—a false note of acerbity like that of the professional heretic. This is another of the penalties she pays for that fervid unconventionality which was alike her strength and her weakness.

In morals, her unconventionality will hardly seem nowadays very startling, although in her own day there was much head-wagging among prim persons, male and female, over the vagaries and frank passionateness of Jane Eyre. Miss Brontë never pleaded for a moral revolution. She had no prophetic glimpses of "the modern woman," and she neither preached nor implied a gospel of woman's rights. She makes brisk war on Mrs. Grundy and on her notions of womanly propriety, but beyond this she never ventures. She limits herself expressly in the preface to the second edition of *Jane Eyre*. "Conventionality is not morality. Self-righteousness is not religion. To attack the first is not to assail the last. . . . These things and deeds are diametrically opposed; they are as distinct as is vice from virtue. Men too often confound them; they should not be confounded; appearance should not be mistaken for truth." Never does one of Miss Brontë's heroines actually violate a moral law. Jane Eyre is a signal martyr to the sacredness of received ideas concerning marriage and divorce; and Rochester has to pay dearly for his lax notions about the rights of crazy wives. His Hall is burned and he just misses burning with it; he finally gets off with the loss of an arm and an eye and with several months of parboiled suffering. No; Charlotte Brontë is a relentless little conservative as regards all the essentials of the moral code. Her ideal for woman is the traditional domestic ideal freed from worldliness and hypocrisy,—the domestic ideal purged of non-essentials and carried to the nth degree of potency. All her women are merely fragments till they meet a man they can adore.

Perhaps, however, Shirley may be brought up as premonitory of the modern woman. In the "mutinous" Shirley, "made out of fire and air," frank and wilful and just a bit mannish, who parted her hair over one temple, who was not afraid of a musket, and who managed her own estate with a pretty air of self-sufficiency—surely, in *her*, so one is at first tempted to think, there is a suggestion of the new woman. Yet, after all, the suggestion is very slight. Shirley wears her mannishness merely as a challenging bit of colour. She is not intellectual; she has no theories; in her heart of hearts she longs to be bitted and ruled; in the core of her nature she is very woman of very woman, delighting in bravado, in playing at shrewishness, and then in suddenly obeying orders. She is merely a modern Rosalind masquerading for a summer's day in doublet and hose.

It nevertheless remains true that in one sense Charlotte Brontë prepared the way for the crusade of the modern woman. Her prodigiously vivid portrayal of the endless possibilities of woman's nature in power and passion and devotion inevitably suggests the rights of women to richer fields for the play of their faculties. "Women are supposed to be very calm generally," Jane Eyre exclaims; "but women feel just as men feel; they need exercise for their faculties and a field for their efforts as much as their brothers do; they suffer from too rigid a restraint, too absolute a stagnation, precisely as men would suffer. . . . It is thoughtless to condemn them, or laugh at them, if they seek to do more or to learn more than custom has pronounced necessary for their sex." This passage in *Jane Eyre* is indeed almost revolutionary. And although it cannot readily be paralleled elsewhere in Miss Brontë's writings, the spirit that pervades it, the indignation of its protest against tyrannical and contemptuous limitations of woman's freedom, doubtless runs through all her novels. In this sense she may truly be described as preparing the way for the saner and more generous conceptions of woman and of her relations to man, that are characteristic of our own day.

What is true of Charlotte Brontë's ideas about women is true of her ethics in general. She has no radically new, no really revolutionary, doctrine. The great good in life—she is never weary of praising it and of illustrating its pricelessness—is pure human affection. Jane Eyre's cry, in a childish outbreak of feeling, is typical of all Miss Brontë's heroines: "If others don't love me, I would rather die than live." Each of her novels, as has already been noted, reduces in the last analysis to a pathetic quest after affection.

Callousness of heart, lack of "true generous feeling,"—this is for Miss Brontë the one fatal defect of character. Not even unflinching devotion to an abstract moral code or to a systematic round of religious observances can excuse in her eyes rigidity of nature and dearth of genuine human affection. Jane Eyre's cousin Eliza has her time parcelled out into ten minute intervals, which she spends day after day with splendid regularity on the same round of duties; yet she is to Jane Eyre,

and to Charlotte Brontë as well, *anathema maranatha*, because she is "heartless." St. John Rivers, with whose fate the very last sentences in *Jane Eyre* concern themselves, is a still more striking case in point. He is consumed with religious zeal; he is absolutely sincere in his devotion to the cause of religion. Yet because he sacrifices love to the successful pursuit of his mission, and because he acts from severely conceived principle instead of from warm human feeling, the fiery little author can hardly keep her hand from angry tremulousness while she portrays him. She loathes him because he forgets "the feelings and claims of little people, in pursuing his own large views." Intense imaginative sympathy with life in all its forms,—even with animals and with nature,—this is what Miss Brontë demands of the characters she will approve. There must be no cheap sentiment; her heroes are apt to be stern or even ferocious in manner; but under a wilful exterior there must be a glowing spirit of human affection ready to flash out loyally, though capriciously, whenever there is real need.

And it is because she believes so unswervingly in the worth of life as ministered to by love, and because she sets forth with such manifold truth of detail and such visionary intensity the realities of life and love, that her novels, in spite of their obvious defects, keep their power, and are even in some ways doubly grateful in these latter days of cynical moralizing. She quickens faith in human nature and in human destiny. She gives the reader who will readily lend himself to her spell a new sense of the heights and depths of passion and of the unlimited possibilities of life. The finical reader will find in her much to shock him and bring his hand to his mouth, and the nicely intellectual reader will be sure that her *naïveté* is by no means the finally satisfactory relation to life. The admirers of George Eliot and of Mrs. Ward will carp at her ethics or at her lack of them. Doubtless, her characters love love almost selfishly, and seem to struggle for it with something of the gambler's greed. George Eliot's analyses of the dangers of the self-centred and wilful pursuit even of love may lead to a much more scientifically accurate sense of the unimportance of the individual man or woman, and of the absurdity of hoping that the world will order itself to suit the needs of a single heart. George Eliot asserted the rights of the social order; Charlotte Brontë asserted the individual. And for that very reason her novels are tonic in these days when gently cynical resignation has become so largely a fashionable habit of mind in literature and art. George Eliot never tells of love at first hand, and always puts a mist of philosophizing and a blur of moral suasion between her readers and any passionate experience she recites. Charlotte Brontë tells of the joy and the terror and the tragedy of love and life with the intense directness of the lyric poet, and hence even the direst sufferings her characters undergo do not daunt or depress the reader, but rather quicken his sense of kinship with all forms of human experience and his realization of the dignity and scope of man's nature. The human will is never at a disadvantage with Charlotte Brontë. The struggle with circumstance and with fate is bitter, often exhausting; yet there is a curious constitutional buoyant courage in her work that more than counteracts any sympathetic sadness the story may for the moment carry with it.

Sir William Hamilton

1788–1856

William Hamilton was born on March 8, 1788, in Glasgow, the son of a professor of anatomy and botany at the university. He was educated at Glasgow, Edinburgh, and Oxford universities, and was admitted to the Scottish bar in 1813. He was appointed professor of civil history at the University of Edinburgh in 1821, and fifteen years later was elected to the chair of metaphysics and logic at the university.

Hamilton's reputation as a philosopher was launched in 1829 with the publication of his essay, "Philosophy of the Unconditioned," in the *Edinburgh Review*, and was strengthened by subsequent articles that appeared in the *Review* on German philosophy. His articles were later collected and published as *Discussions on Philosophy, Literature and Education* (1852). Hamilton's other major publications included an incomplete edition of the works of Thomas Reid (1846), A *Letter to Augustus Morgan* (1847), and a nine-volume edition of the works of the philosopher Dugald Stewart (1854–56). Two essays in the *Edinburgh Review* by Hamilton on education—"The State of the English Universities" (1831) and "The Right of Dissenters to Admission into the English Universities" (1834)—led to the formation of the Royal Commission of 1850 and to subsequent educational reforms in Great Britain.

Hamilton was stricken with paralysis in 1844 but despite semi-invalidism continued to write. He died in Edinburgh on May 6, 1856.

Personal

John Wilson's triumph is gratifying, and I greatly rejoice in it. His excellent and amiable rival, Sir William Hamilton, is like a fine miniature picture, which cannot be viewed too near, and could bear to be seen through a microscope. He retires most honourably from a contest which has produced testimonies to his virtues and abilities, a contest which forced them into observation, and has thrown aside the veil of scrupulous modesty that shrouded his fine qualities and attainments.
—ANNE GRANT, Letter to Her Sister (July 26, 1820), *Memoir and Correspondence of Mrs. Grant of Laggan*, ed. J. P. Grant, 1844, Vol. 2, pp. 267–68

Sir William Hamilton, when I first knew him, was not properly a philosopher—nor would *then* have called himself such—but a polyhistor, of a higher class, and with far more combining powers, than Bayle,—having (or taking means to have) a pancyclopædic acquaintance with every section of knowledge that could furnish keys for unlocking man's inner nature. Already, in 1814, I conceive that he must have been studying physiology upon principles of investigation suggested by himself. In 1820, 1827, and the following years, up to 1832, on revisiting Edinburgh, I found him master of all the knowledge that France and Germany had then accumulated upon animal magnetism; which he justly conceived to hide within itself shy secrets as to "the dark foundations" of our human nature, such as cannot *now* be lawfully neglected—secrets which evidently had gleamed and *cropped out* at intervals through past ages of the world in various phenomena that were tarnished or were darkened into apparent doubtfulness only by the superstitions that surrounded them. The immensity of Sir William's attainments was best laid open by consulting him (or by hearing him consulted) upon intellectual difficulties, or upon schemes literary and philosophic. Such applications, come from what point of the compass they would, found him always prepared. Nor did it seem to make any difference whether it were the erudition of words or things that was needed. Amongst the books for which I am indebted to his kindness as memorials of his regard, one which I value most is a copy of the *Scaligerana*, and for this reason, that it is intrinsically a characteristic

memento of himself when first I knew him. In the Scaligers, father and son, who were both astonishing men, I fancied this resemblance to himself, that there was the same equilibrium in all three as to *thing*-knowledge and *word*-knowledge. Again, Scaliger the elder, as is well known, had been a cavalry officer up to his fortieth year; and often, in his controversial writings, one deciphers the *quondam* trooper cutting furiously right and left in a *melée*. There, also, I fancy a resemblance: now and then, in Sir William's polemics, I seem to trace the sword-arm that charged at Drumclog; or is that story all a dream?
—THOMAS DE QUINCEY, "Sir William Hamilton" (1852), *Collected Writings*, ed. David Masson, Vol. 5, pp. 314–15

The name of Sir William Hamilton I had before heard; but this was the first time he appeared definitely before my memory or imagination; in which his place was permanent thenceforth. A man of good birth, I was told, though of small fortune, who had deep faculties and an insatiable appetite for wise knowledge; was titularly an advocate here, but had no practice, nor sought any; had gathered his modest means thriftily together, and sat down here, with his mother and sister (cousin, I believe, it really was), and his ample store of books; frankly renouncing all lower ambitions, and indeed all ambitions together, except what I well recognised to be the highest and one real ambition in this dark ambiguous world. A man honourable to me, a man lovingly enviable; to whom, in silence, I heartily bade good speed. It was also an interesting circumstance, which did not fail of mention, that his ancestor, Hamilton of Preston, was leader of the Cameronians at Bothwell Brig, and had stood by the Covenant and Cause of Scotland in that old time and form. "This baronetcy, if carried forward on those principles, may well enough be poor," thought I; "and beautifully well may it issue in such a Hamilton as this one aims to be, still piously bearing aloft, on the new terms, *his* God's-Banner intrepidly against the World and the Devil!"

It was years after this, perhaps four or five, before I had the honour of any personal acquaintance with Sir William; his figure on the street had become familiar, but I forget, too, when this was first pointed out to me; and cannot recollect even when I first came to speech with him, which must have been by accident and his own voluntary favour, on some slight occasion, probably at *The Advocates' Library*, which was my principal or almost sole literary resource (lasting thanks to *it*, alone of Scottish institutions!) in those obstructed, neglectful, and grimly-forbidding years. Perhaps it was in 1824 or 1825. I recollect right well the bright affable manners of Sir William, radiant with frank kindliness, honest humanity, and intelligence ready to help; and how completely prepossessing they were. A fine firm figure of middle height; one of the finest cheerfully-serious human faces, of square, solid, and yet rather *aquiline* type; a little marked with smallpox—marked, not deformed, but rather the reverse (like a rock rough-hewn, not spoiled by polishing); and a pair of the beautifullest kindly-beaming hazel eyes, well open, and every now and then with a lambency of smiling fire in them, which I always remember as if with trust and gratitude. Our conversation did not amount to much, in those times; mainly about German books, philosophies and persons, it is like; and my usual place of abode was in the country then. Letter to him, or from, I do not recollect there was ever any; though there might well enough have been, had either of us been prone that way.

In the end of 1826 I came to live in Edinburgh under circumstances new and ever memorable to me: from then till the spring of 1828—and, still more, once again in 1832–33, when I had brought my little household to Edinburgh for the winter—must have been the chief times of personal intercourse between us. I recollect hearing much more of him, in 1826 and onward, than formerly: to what depths he had gone in study and philosophy; of his simple, independent, meditative habits, ruggedly athletic modes of exercise, fondness for his big dog, &c. &c.: everybody seemed to speak of him with favour, those of his immediate acquaintance uniformly with affectionate respect.

I did not witness, much less share in, any of his swimming or other athletic prowesses. I have once or twice been on long walks with him in the Edinburgh environs, oftenest with some other companion, or perhaps even two, whom he had found vigorous and worthy: pleasant walks and abundantly enlivened with speech from Sir William. He was willing to talk of any humanly-interesting subject; and threw out sound observations upon any topic started: if left to his own choice, he circled and gravitated, naturally, into subjects that were his own, and were habitually occupying him;—of which, I can still remember animal magnetism and the German revival of it, not yet known of in England, was one that frequently turned up. Mesmer and his "four Academicians," he assured us, had *not* been the finale of that matter; that it was a matter tending into realities far deeper and more intricate than had been supposed;—of which, for the rest, he did not seem to augur much good, but rather folly and mischief. Craniology, too, he had been examining; but freely allowed us to reckon that an extremely ignorant story. On German bibliography and authors, especially of the learned kind—Erasmus, Ruhnken, Ulrich von Hutten—he could descant copiously, and liked to be inquired of. On Kant, Reid, and the metaphysicians, German and other, though there was such abundance to have said, he did not often speak; but politely abstained rather, when not expressly called on.

He was finely social and human, in these walks or interviews. Honesty, frankness, friendly veracity, courageous trust in humanity and in you, were charmingly visible. His talk was forcible, copious, discursive, careless rather than otherwise; and, on abstruse topics, I observed, was apt to become embroiled and revelly, much less perspicuous and elucidative

than with a little deliberation he could have made it. "The fact is," he would often say: and then plunging into new circuitous depths and distinctions, again on a new grand, "The fact is," and still again,—till what the essential "fact" might be was not a little obscure to you. He evidently had not been engaged in *speaking* these things, but only in thinking them, for his own behoof, not yours. By lucid questioning you could get lucidity from him on any topic. Nowhere did he give you the least notion of his not understanding the thing himself; but it lay like an unwinnowed threshing-floor, the corn-grains, the natural chaff, and somewhat even of the straw, still unseparated there. This sometimes would befall, not only when the meaning itself was delicate or abstruse, but also if several were listening, and he doubted whether they could understand. On solid realistic points he was abundantly luminous; promptitude, solid sense, free-flowing intelligibility always the characteristics. The tones of his voice were themselves attractive, physiognomic of the man: a strong, carelessly-melodious, tenor voice, the sound of it betokening seriousness and cheerfulness; occasionally something of slightly remonstrative was in the undertones, indicating, well in the background, possibilities of virtuous wrath and fire; seldom anything of laughter, of levity never anything: thoroughly a serious, cheerful, sincere, and kindly voice, with looks corresponding. In dialogue, face to face, with one he trusted, his speech, both voice and words, was still more engaging; lucid, free, persuasive, with a bell-like harmony, and from time to time, in the bright eyes, a beaming smile, which was the crown and seal of all to you.—THOMAS CARLYLE, Letter to John Veitch (Feb. 19, 1868), cited in John Veitch, *Memoir of Sir William Hamilton*, 1869, pp. 121–25

He was from his early years an ardent student of classical literature, and his subsequent speculations were no doubt largely influenced by this fact, and by his having been sent to complete his education at the University of Oxford, where the writings of Aristotle were then held in high esteem. Hamilton's studies, however, soon extended far beyond the limits of the Oxford curriculum. Not content with the works of the ancient Greek and Roman philosophers, he turned with avidity to those of the Schoolmen, and thence to those of the modern Continental philosophers. The Scottish School had hitherto attached too little importance to the writings of its predecessors and foreign contemporaries. Hamilton undoubtedly went into the opposite extreme. In turning over his pages we might frequently imagine that we were reading some curious volume of antiquarian research, rather than a treatise on a science by a professed expositor. His philosophical erudition has probably never been equalled, but it was far too vast to be accurate. It would be difficult to name a philosophical author whose system he had thoroughly mastered, with two exceptions—Aristotle and Reid. If he erred in any respect in his exposition of these writers, it was not from want of acquaintance with their works, but from his desire to assimilate their systems to his own. But even as regards Stewart, I think he cannot always be acquitted of errors of another kind.

His great erudition had another ill effect. When about to write on any subject, he consulted so many authors, and made so many extracts, that the work soon extended beyond all reasonable dimensions, and unless compelled by the pressure of necessity (as in the case of his lectures) to give the results to the world, he ultimately became disheartened, and abandoned the effort in despair. There can be no doubt that if he had read less he would have produced more, and with his powerful intellect I doubt if his productions would even have been deteriorated in quality. I venture to suggest one more bad consequence arising from the peculiar bent of his studies. His wonderful acquaintance with Formal Logic led him almost invariably to seek for some logical fallacy in an opponent's argument, and when he hit upon a careless expression (arising, perhaps, from a studied disregard of the technicalities of Logic), he imagined he had found it, whereas a more careful examination would have shown him that all appearance of logical irregularity could have been got rid of while leaving the argument intact. The truth is that investigators very seldom really fall into any logical fallacy, though disputants often do so.—W. H. S. MONCK, *Sir William Hamilton*, 1881, pp. 12–13

General

"Cousin" I pronounce, beyond all doubt, the most unreadable thing that ever appeared in the *Review*. The only chance is, that gentle readers may take it to be very profound, and conclude that the fault is in their want of understanding. But I am not disposed to agree with them. It is ten times more *mystical* than anything my friend Carlyle ever wrote, and not half so agreeably written. It is nothing to the purpose that he does not agree with the worst part of the mysticism, for he affects to understand it, and to explain it, and to think it very ingenious and respectable, and it is mere gibberish. He may possibly be a clever man. There are even some indications of that in his paper, but he is not a *very* clever man, nor of much power; and beyond all question he is not a good writer on such subjects.—FRANCIS, LORD JEFFREY, Letter to Macvey Napier (Nov. 23, 1829), *Selection from the Correspondence of Macvey Napier*, ed. Macvey Napier, 1879, p. 70

The various disquisitions of Sir William Hamilton seem to have attracted but little attention on this side of the Atlantic, from the fact that they deal with subjects somewhat removed from popular taste and popular apprehension; yet it would be difficult to name any contributions to a review which display such a despotic command of all the resources of logic and metaphysics as his articles in the *Edinburgh Review* on Cousin, Dr. Brown, and Bishop Whately. Apart from their scientific value, they should be read as specimens of intellectual power. They evince more intense strength of understanding than any other writings of the age; and in the blended merits of their logic, rhetoric, and learning, they may challenge comparison with the best works of any British metaphysicians. He seems to have read every writer, ancient and modern, on logic and metaphysics, and is conversant with every philosophical theory, from the lowest form of materialism to the most abstract development of idealism; and yet his learning is not so remarkable as the thorough manner in which he has digested it, and the perfect command he has of all its stores. Everything that he comprehends, no matter how abstruse, he comprehends with the utmost clearness, and employs with consummate skill. He is altogether the best trained reasoner on abstract subjects of his time. He is a most terrible adversary, because his logic is unalloyed by an atom of passion or prejudice; and nothing is more merciless than the intellect. No fallacy, or sophism, or half-proof, can escape his analysis, and he is pitiless in its exposure. His method is to strike directly at his object, and he accomplishes it in a few stern, brief sentences. His path is over the wreck of opinions, which he demolishes as he goes. After he has decided a question, it seems to be at rest forever, for his rigorous logic leaves no room for controversy. He will not allow his adversary a single loop-hole for escape. He forces him back from one position to another, he trips up his most ingenious reasonings, and leaves him at the end naked

and defenceless, mournfully gathering up the scattered fragments of his once symmetrical system. The article on "Cousin's *Course of Philosophy*," and that on "Reid and Brown," are grand examples of this gladiatorial exercise of intellectual power.

Hamilton is not only a great logician, but a great rhetorician. His matter is arranged with the utmost art; his style is a model of philosophical clearness, conciseness and energy. Every word is in its right place, has a precise scientific meaning, can stand the severest tests of analysis, and bears but one interpretation. He is as impregnable in his terms as in his argument; and with all the hard accuracy of his language, the movement of his style is as rapid, and sometimes as brilliant, as that of Macaulay. It seems to drag on the mind of the student by pure force. The key to a whole philosophical system is often given in a single emphatic sentence, whose stern compression has sometimes the effect of epigram,—as when he condenses the results of the Scotch philosophy into these few words:—"It proved that intelligence *supposed* principles, which, as the *conditions* of its activity, could not be the *results* of its operation; and that the mind contained notions, which, as primitive, necessary, and universal, were not to be explained as generalizations from the contingent and particular, about which alone our external experience was conversant. The phenomena of mind were thus distinguished from the phenomena of matter, and if the impossibility of materialism were not demonstrated, there was, at least, demonstrated the impossibility of its proof." The mastery of his subject, which Hamilton possesses, the perfect order with which his thoughts are arranged, and his exact knowledge of terms, free him altogether from that comparative vassalage to words which so often confuses the understandings of metaphysicians. His style has the hard brilliancy of polished steel; its lustre comes from its strength and compactness.—EDWIN P. WHIPPLE, "British Critics" (1845), *Essays and Reviews*, 1850, Vol. 2, pp. 117–19

⟨. . .⟩ it is the distinction of Sir W. Hamilton that from his scheme of thought national limitations and peculiarities fall away; and that, of all our metaphysical writers, he first has sufficient appreciation of every "school," and sufficient independence of all, to assume a cosmopolitan character, and produce dispositions that may travel without a passport, and be at home in every civilized land. Of whom else among our countrymen could we say,—what surely may be said of him,—that if there were to be a congress of all the philosophies, he would be chosen universal interpreter? In this respect he occupies, in the series of British professors, nearly the same place that we must assign to Aristotle among the Greeks.

⟨. . .⟩ He is the first eminent writer of his class, in our language, over whose imagination Lord Bacon has exercised no tyranny; and who has therefore been able to appreciate the problems regarded in other countries as the very essence of "philosophy," but treated as its delirium in this.—JAMES MARTINEAU, "Sir W. Hamilton's Philosophy" (1853), *Essays, Philosophical and Theological*, 1868, Vol. 2, pp. 233–34

As Mill's is a *sweated* mind, often entangled in the sudorific blankets, when wanting to move, and incapable of walking, though a splendid rider—of hobbies—so Sir William Hamilton's was a swollen mind. The good Sir William was the Daniel Lambert of Philosophy. He had the shark's, the ostrich's enormous appetite, with no more power of discrimination than the ostrich or the shark. Quantity was everything, quality nothing. Blending the shark and the ostrich, he could make a decent meal of bricks, empty barrels, copper bolts, and

THE NEW MOULTON'S LIBRARY

tenpenny nails. He is almost the only learned man that Scotland has had since George Buchanan, and there are no signs that Scotland will ever have a learned man again. But his learning was a pedantic plethora, an apoplectic monstrosity, an asthmatic ventriloquism squeaking and growling through layers and convolutions of fat. It would be difficult to say whether Sir William Hamilton devoured books and systems, or was devoured by them. The result, at all events, was chaotic conglomeration. Little would it have mattered how many books or systems Sir William Hamilton had swallowed, if he had not been tormented by the unhappy yearning to be a creator of systems himself.—WILLIAM MACCALL, *The New Materialism*, 1873

He attempts far too much by logical differentiation and formalization. No man purposes now to proceed in physical investigation by logical dissection, as was done by Aristotle and the schoolmen. I have at times looked into the old compends of physical science which were used in the colleges down even to an age after the time of Newton. Ingenious they were beyond measure, and perfect in form far beyond what Herschel or Faraday have attempted. I am convinced that logical operations can do nearly as little in the mental as they have done in the material sciences. I admit that Sir William Hamilton had deeply observed the operations of the mind, and that his lectures contribute more largely to psychology than any work published in his day. But his induction is too much subordinated to logical arrangement and critical rules. His system will be found, when fully unfolded, to have a completeness such as Reid and Stewart did not pretend to, but it is effected by a logical analysis and synthesis, and much that he has built up will require to be taken down.—JAMES MCCOSH, *The Scottish Philosophy*, 1874, p. 417

It is very handsomely allowed by his posthumous opponent that Sir William Hamilton was a man "of abundant acuteness and more than abundant learning"; that he was the "founder of a school of thought"; and that he was "one of the ablest, the most far-sighted, and the most candid" of his way of thinking. Such compliments may or may not be designed to enhance the triumph of his assailant, but no stronger testimony to Sir William Hamilton's greatness could be brought forward than the mere fact that his system was made the peg upon which Mr. John Mill deliberately chose to hang his vindication of the utilitarian doctrines. By the present generation, which has never beheld the noble features and the commanding presence, which has never been thrilled by the sonorous voice, nor fascinated by the kindling eye, of which his pupils speak with one accord,—some such testimony is certainly required. For Sir William Hamilton's consequence in the realm of philosophy has diminished in proportion as time has necessarily contracted the sphere in which his personality asserted itself; insomuch that to-day the "school of thought" which he founded is almost barren of pupils; while for the present, at all events, the Necessary Laws of Thought, the Quantification of the Predicate, and the Philosophy of the Conditioned have withdrawn into obscurity.

It would be vain to deny that for this result Sir William Hamilton himself is largely to blame. The scope of his reading was immense; his knowledge of the ancient and modern philosophers was well-nigh boundless in extent. But there is some little plausibility in Mr. Mill's criticism that the time he devoted to mere erudition permitted of his giving only the remains of his mind to the real business of thinking; and, at any rate, it is plain that the mass of material he had accumulated was too unwieldy for skilful and workmanlike handling. An insatiable appetite for learning was accompanied by an impaired power of assimilation; and the quotations with which he is so fond of fortifying his propositions can often be compared, in respect of relevance and conclusiveness, to nothing save to some of the Scriptural "proofs" subjoined to the answers in the Shorter Catechism. Moreover, he has left no truly satisfactory and adequate exposition of his views, which have in many cases to be collected from scattered and disjointed *dicta*, and frequently present inconsistencies which a more thorough and systematic treatment might easily have removed. The *Lectures*, written, each series in five months, each lecture the night before it was delivered—and once so written, never altered— are full of the faults which such a method of composition must needs beget; and the most coherent and satisfying statement of his philosophical position must be sought in his elaborate commentary on the writings of another.

Sir William Hamilton's English is bald without simplicity, and severe without impressiveness. The *Lectures*, it is true, contain passages of considerable power and animation when he is making preparations to clinch his argument with an extract from the poets. But, in common with the rest of his writings, they are so interwoven with quotations, and these frequently of great length, that the movement of his prose is arrested before any impetus has been acquired, and the curious reader is hurried away from Hamilton to some one else. It is consequently peculiarly difficult to do justice to Hamilton's style by means of selections. Even at its best, however, it is wholly destitute of the charm which springs from aptly arranged words and nicely balanced sentences. Its supreme merit is clearness. He states his propositions I., II., III., as articulately as though he were drawing the pleadings in an action (indeed, a turn of phrase here and there irresistibly reminds one that he was an advocate before he became a professor), and in the discussion of each separate proposition he invokes the aid even of the printer's art to purge his statement of all possible ambiguity by means of capitals, italics, and inset paragraphs. The worst of all this painful lucidity is that it is often indistinguishable from pedantry. But the philosopher whose task it is to be to win the ear of the world once more for the system of Common Sense (so-called) will do well to imitate Sir William's zeal for accuracy and exactitude, though these excellences are doubtless attainable at a somewhat less serious sacrifice of attractiveness and grace. —J. H. MILLAR, "Sir William Hamilton," *English Prose*, ed. Henry Craik, 1896, Vol. 5, pp. 331–33

JOHN STUART MILL
From "Concluding Remarks"
An Examination of
Sir William Hamilton's Philosophy
1865, Volume 2, pp. 337–54

In the examination which I have now concluded of Sir W. Hamilton's philosophical achievements, I have unavoidably laid stress on points of difference from him rather than on those of agreement; the reason being, that I differ from almost everything in his philosophy on which he particularly valued himself, or which is specially his own. His merits, which, though I do not rate them so high, I feel and admire as sincerely as his most enthusiastic disciples, are rather diffused through his speculations generally, than concentrated on any particular point. They chiefly consist in his clear and distinct mode of bringing before the reader many of the fundamental questions of metaphysics; some good specimens of psychological analysis on a small scale; and the many detached logical and psychological truths which he has separately seized, and which are scattered through his writings, mostly applied to resolve some special difficulty, and again lost sight of. I can hardly point to anything he has done towards helping the more thorough understanding of the greater mental phænomena, unless it be his theory of Attention (including Abstraction), which seems to me the most perfect we have: but the subject, though a highly important, is a comparatively simple one.

With regard to the causes which prevented a thinker of such abundant acuteness, and more than abundant industry, from accomplishing the great things at which he aimed, it would ill become me to speak dogmatically. It would be a very unwarrantable assumption of superiority over a mind like Sir W. Hamilton's, if I attempted to gauge and measure his faculties, or give a complete theory of his successes and failures. The utmost I venture on, is to suggest, as simple possibilities, some of the causes which may have partly contributed to his shortcomings as a philosopher. One of those causes is so common as to be the next thing to universal, but requires all the more to be signalized for its unfortunate consequences; over-anxiety to make safe a foregone conclusion. The whole philosophy of Sir W. Hamilton seems to have had its character determined by the requirements of the doctrine of Free-will; and to that doctrine he clung, because he had persuaded himself that it afforded the only premises from which human reason could deduce the doctrines of natural religion. I believe that in this persuasion he was thoroughly his own dupe, and that his speculations have weakened the philosophical foundation of religion fully as much as they have confirmed it.

A second cause which may help to account for his not having effected more in philosophy, is the enormous amount of time and mental vigor which he expended on mere philosophical erudition, leaving, it may be said, only the remains of his mind for the real business of thinking. While he seems to have known, almost by heart, the voluminous Greek commentators on Aristotle, and to have read all that the most obscure schoolman or fifth-rate German transcendentalist had written on the subjects with which he occupied himself; while, not content with a general knowledge of these authors, he could tell with the greatest precision what each of them thought on any given topic, and in what each differed from every other; while expending his time and energy on all this, he had not enough of them left to complete his *Lectures*. Those on Metaphysics, as already remarked, stopped short on the threshold of what was, especially in his own opinion, the most important part of it, and never reached even the threshold of the third and last of the parts into which, in an early lecture, he divided his subject. Those on Logic he left dependent, for most of the subordinate developments, on extracts strung together from German writers, chiefly Krug and Esser; often not destitute of merit, but generally so vague, as to make all those parts of his exposition in which they predominate, unsatisfactory; sometimes written from points of view different from Sir W. Hamilton's own, but which he never found time or took the trouble to re-express in adaptation to his own mode of thought. In the whole circle of psychological and logical speculation, it is astonishing how few are the topics into which he has thrown any of the powers of his own intellect; and on how small a proportion even of these he has pushed his investigations beyond what seemed necessary for the purposes of some particular controversy. In consequence, philosophical doctrines are taken up, and again laid down, with perfect

unconsciousness, and his philosophy seems made up of scraps from several conflicting metaphysical systems. The Relativity of human knowledge is made a great deal of in opposition to Schelling and Cousin, but drops out or dwindles into nothing in Sir W. Hamilton's own psychology. The validity of our natural beliefs, and the doctrine that the incogitable is not therefore impossible, are strenuously asserted in this place and disregarded in that, according to the question in hand. On the subject of General Notions he is avowedly a Nominalist, but teaches the whole of Logic as if he had never heard of any doctrine but the Conceptualist; what he presents as a reconcilement of the two being never adverted to afterwards, and serving only as an excuse to himself for accepting the one doctrine and invariably using the language of the other. Arriving at his doctrines almost always under the stimulus of some special dispute, he never knows how far to press them: consequently there is a region of haze round the place where opinions of different origin meet. I formerly quoted from him a felicitous illustration drawn from the mechanical operation of tunnelling; that process affords another, justly applicable to himself. The reader must have heard of that gigantic enterprise of the Italian Government, the tunnel through Mont Cenis. This great work is carried on simultaneously from both ends, in well-grounded confidence (such is now the minute accuracy of engineering operations) that the two parties of workmen will correctly meet in the middle. Were they to disappoint this expectation, and work past one another in the dark, they would afford a likeness of Sir W. Hamilton's mode of tunnelling the human mind.

This failure to think out subjects until they had been thoroughly mastered, or until consistency had been attained between the different views which the author took of them from different points of observation, may, like the unfinished state of the *Lectures*, be with great probability ascribed to the excessive absorption of his time and energies by the study of old writers. That absorption did worse; for it left him with neither leisure nor vigor for what was far more important in every sense, and an entirely indispensable qualification for a master in philosophy—the systematic study of the sciences. Except physiology, on some parts of which his mental powers were really employed, he may be said to have known nothing of any physical science. I do not mean that he was ignorant of familiar facts, or that he may not, in the course of his education, have gone through the curriculum. But it must have been as Gibbon did, who says, in his autobiography, "I was content to receive the passive impressions of my professor's lectures, without any active exercise of my own powers." For any trace the study had left in Sir W. Hamilton's mind, he might as well never have heard of it.

⟨. . .⟩ Sir W. Hamilton studied the eminent thinkers of old, only from the outside. He did not throw his own mind into their manner of thought; he did not survey the field of philosophic speculation from their standing point, and see each object as it would be seen with their lights, and with their modes of looking. The opinion of an author stands an isolated fact in Sir W. Hamilton's pages, without foundation in the author's individuality, or connection with his other doctrines. For want of this elucidation one by another, even the opinions themselves are ⟨. . .⟩ very liable to be misunderstood. Yet, such as his expositions of the opinions of philosophers are, it is greatly to be regretted that we have not more of them; and that his unrivalled knowledge of all the antecedents of Philosophy, has enriched the world with nothing but a few selections of passages on topics on which circumstances had led Sir W. Hamilton to write. He is known to have left copious common-place books, without which indeed it would have been hardly possible that such stores of knowledge could be kept within easy reference. Let us hope that they are carefully preserved; that they will, in some form or other, be made accessible to students, and will yet do good service to the future historian of philosophy. Should this hope be fulfilled, future ages will have greater cause than, I think, Sir W. Hamilton's published philosophical speculations will ever give them, to rejoice in the fruits of his labors, and to celebrate his name.

JOHN WILSON CROKER

1780–1857

John Wilson Croker was born at Galway, Ireland, on December 20, 1780. He was educated at Trinity College, Dublin, and spent some time at Lincoln's Inn before being called to the Irish bar in 1802.

In 1804 Croker published anonymously his verse satire *Familiar Epistles to Frederick E. Jones, Esquire, on the Present State of the Irish Stage*; it was an enormous success. Equally successful were a number of pamphlets on Irish society and affairs written by Croker, among them the satirical *Intercepted Letter from Canton* (1804) and a more serious essay, *Sketch of the State of Ireland, Past and Present* (1808), which advocated Catholic emancipation.

In 1807 Croker entered Parliament as the member for Downpatrick and soon achieved prominence as a Tory politician, aided by his friend Sir Arthur Wellesley, chief secretary for Ireland who later became the Duke of Wellington. Croker played a leading role in the opposition to the Reform Bill and later refused to sit in the Reform Parliament, although he continued his personal association with Tory leaders. From 1831 until 1854 Croker was the chief political writer for the *Quarterly Review*, a publication with which he had been associated since its founding in 1809. Over a nearly fifty-year period Croker contributed hundreds of articles on a variety of subjects to the *Review*, often instigating controversy; his rigid Toryism often made him the subject of attack in other journals by his political opponents, in particular Macaulay. Neither Croker nor Macaulay seems to have missed an opportunity to attack the other, often with damaging consequences: Croker's edition of Boswell's *Life of Johnson* (1831) received a harsh review from Macaulay, and Croker reciprocated some years later with a devastating critique of the first two volumes of Macaulay's *History of England* (1849).

Croker was a man of wide-ranging interests. His preference for eighteenth-century literature led him to begin work on an annotated edition of Pope's poetry (later completed by W. J. Courthope) and, not unexpectedly, to severe criticism of Keats and Tennyson. He was an authority on the French Revolution and at his death left his collection of related documents to the British Museum. In and out of Parliament Croker was an outspoken advocate of public support for the arts and sciences, in particular encouraging nautical science and exploration, and played a leading role in the purchase of the Elgin Marbles. His strong interest in contemporary history led to his editing several volumes of letters and reminiscences, including *Memoirs of the Reign of George II* (1848). He was as well a founder of the Athenaeum Club.

Croker died at Hampton, Middlesex, on August 10, 1857.

Personal

While Macaulay is thus ascending to the House of Peers, his old enemy and rival Croker has descended to the grave, very noiselessly and almost without observation, for he had been for some time so withdrawn from the world that he was nearly forgotten. He had lived to see all his predictions of ruin and disaster to the country completely falsified. He continued till the last year or two to exhale his bitterness and spite in the columns of the *Quarterly Review*, but at last the Editor (who had long been sick of his contributions) contrived to get rid of him. He was particularly disliked by Macaulay, who never lost an opportunity of venting his antipathy by attacks upon him.
—CHARLES CAVENDISH FULKE GREVILLE, *Diary*, Sept. 6, 1857

Few men whose names are known to the public have received harder usage than John Wilson Croker. All whom he offended by his articles, or by articles which they thought proper to attribute to him, took care, sooner or later, to exact vengeance.

In his lifetime he never replied to any of these attacks, although he could not have been insensible to their injustice. After his death their bitterness was redoubled. He was exhibited to the view of the world as "the wickedest of reviewers," with a "malignant ulcer" in his mind; a man who employed his faculties "for the gratification of his own morbid inclination to give pain." These were the softest words which Miss Martineau could find to say of him while the grave was still open to receive his remains. She thought that Mr. Croker had done her a wrong. In 1839 a severe article upon her *Illustrations of Political Economy* appeared in the *Quarterly Review*, and in 1852 there was a notice in the same pages—not altogether complimentary, although not severe—of her *History of England*. Smarting under these criticisms, Miss Martineau struck back at Mr. Croker, and yet he was not the offender. He had nothing whatever to do with either article. In like manner Lord Macaulay, who almost avowedly wrote from motives of revenge, placed it upon record, though the record was not published till after his death, that he was a "bad, a very bad man: a scandal to politics and to letters." These are examples of the portraits which have been drawn by his political and personal adversaries.

On the other hand, when we get fairly behind the scenes of his life, we find that Mr. Croker was the close and intimate friend of many of the most eminent men of his day, and not only their friend, but their adviser in every great emergency which befell them. They attached an extraordinary value to his opinions, and trusted in him to a degree which is rare either in public or in private life. Never was he known to betray this confidence. His discretion and his sturdy common sense could be depended on to the last extremity. Political differences sometimes cost him the loss of a friend; no man can take an active part in public affairs without being required, sooner or later, to pay that penalty. But his sincerity was never called in question by those who were compelled to part company with him. He was severed from most of his acquaintances only by the hand of death. "Our friendship," wrote one of them—the Earl of Lonsdale—"has lasted fifty years without a cloud." He had the cordial respect of Mr. Canning, of the Duke of Wellington, of Sir Robert Peel, and of every Conservative leader, from Mr. Perceval down to the late Lord Derby; and he enjoyed the confidence and esteem of many who were habitually opposed to him in politics,—as Sir Robert Peel himself became in the latter part of his career. In private life we find him free from blame or reproach, devoted to his home, overshadowed as it was by the loss of his only son; deeply attached to his kinsfolk, and never turning a deaf ear either to friends or strangers who came to him for help, and who could prove that they deserved it.

Such is the man who is presented to us when we see him as he really was. The immense correspondence of all kinds which he left strips away disguises. If he had been the unjust, selfish, and bad man described by his foes, this correspondence would have told the tale. That his character was not without defects, assuredly he would have been the last to pretend. He sometimes held extreme opinions, and was extreme in his way of advocating them. He was of a combative disposition, ever ready for a fray, and seldom happier than when the cry of battle rung in his ears. He was a redoubtable opponent, as his enemies found out to their cost; and a man who struck so hard, and so often, was sure to make many enemies. But any fair-minded reader who dispassionately considers his life and work, with the aid of the materials which are now produced for the formation of a right conclusion, will speedily be convinced that, so far from being wholly "bad," the vehement controversialist had, after all, a kindly heart and a generous nature; and that in everything he undertook he was animated by a lofty sense of duty, which alone would entitle him to respectful recollection.—LOUIS J. JENNINGS, *The Croker Papers*, 1884, Vol. 1, pp. 1–4

General

North: ⟨. . .⟩ the *Thoughts on Ireland* ⟨. . .⟩ , to be sure, were written when he was very young, and the style has the faults of youth, inexperience, and over imitation of Tacitus; but still one may see the pace of the man's mind there; and a very fiery pace it is.—JOHN WILSON (as "Christopher North"), *Noctes Ambrosianae* (March 1823), 1854

The letters and diaries of Mr. Croker will not disappoint the expectations which were raised by Mr. Murray's advertisement. They fully deserve the description given of them by the editor as "a correspondence which presents a contribution to the history of our times not surpassed in general interest or in

historical importance by any similar records which have been brought to light during the present century," and the editor himself deserves our best thanks for the skill with which he has arranged them. From May, 1807, when he first took his seat in the House of Commons as member for Downpatrick, down to the repeal of the Corn Laws some forty years afterwards, Mr. Croker was in constant communication with all the most distinguished public men belonging to the Tory party, and seems to have enjoyed their full confidence and esteem. As the principal political writer in the *Quarterly Review* for nearly a quarter of a century, he was necessarily admitted to their most secret counsels, was constantly engaged in the defence and explanation of their policy, and in setting it before the public eye in the light in which they wished it to appear. The ability which he displayed in the fulfilment of this difficult duty caused men such as the Duke of Wellington, Mr. Canning, Sir Robert Peel, Lord Lyndhurst, and Lord Stanley to form a high opinion of his judgment, to receive his suggestions with respect, and endure his monitions with good humour. With these statesmen he preserved an unbroken intimacy down to 1846, when he forfeited the friendship of Sir Robert Peel by his protectionist articles in the *Quarterly*. The break-up of the Tory party at the same time brought new men to the front, who either knew not Croker, or knew him only to dislike him; so that for some years before his death the number of his political informants had been greatly thinned, and his papers bear traces of a less intimate acquaintance than of old with the conduct of public affairs and the course of Parliamentary campaigns. But as the evidence of a combatant in the greatest constitutional struggle which has been fought in this country since the Long Parliament, who enjoyed at the same time unrivalled opportunities of observing the characters and motives of that brilliant group of statesmen whose individual genius stands in such marked contrast to their collective failure, the political value of the volumes now before us reaches a higher level than has been attained by any contemporary publication with which we are acquainted. They are rich as well both in military and literary interest: for Croker's conversations with the Duke of Wellington bring out more that is new than even his political memoranda; while his correspondence with authors, editors, and publishers is sometimes an agreeable relief from the mingled morosity and despondency with which, for many years together, he never fails to speak of public affairs.—T. E. KEBBEL, "John Wilson Croker," *Fortnightly Review*, Nov. 1884, pp. 688–89

And what delirious aberration of tasteless caprice can possibly have suggested the admission of a doggerel epithalamium by Croker—of all scribblers on record!—into the very last niche of this radiant and harmonious gallery of song? "You have a very great name of your own"—"But I may be allowed to confess"—here is proper lyric stuff to wind up with! There is a due conformity of cadence and of style in these twenty villainous lines which should have sufficed to exclude them from any collection above the literary level of an old annual— *Gem, Keepsake*, or *Souvenir*. O Sminthian Apollo! what a malodorous mouse to nail up on the hinder door of such a gracious little chapel, under the very nose as it were of the departing choir! Were but this utterly miserable rubbish once duly struck out and swept away, the close of a beautiful volume would be beautiful and appropriate beyond all praise or thanks.—ALGERNON CHARLES SWINBURNE, "Social Verse" (1891), *Studies in Prose and Poetry*, 1894, p. 108

The life of a writer has been said to be a warfare upon earth, and Croker's experience was largely in support of the proposition. From his first appearance in literature to his last he was the object of unjust and unsparing attack. Political differences largely accounted for this, as did also the fact that he was frequently on the winning side. "His sarcastic sallies," said the *Quarterly Review*, writing of him some years after his death, "and pungent wit made him many enemies . . . but it is not to be endured that the authority of Macaulay should be evoked in order to support false and railing accusations against the private life of a writer who for fifty years rendered important services to letters and to literary men."

His alleged sins of criticism in the *Quarterly* were not more grievous than those of the "Blue and Yellow," many of the criticisms in which have been food for the mirth of a later generation. As a critic, Croker was perhaps somewhat *borné*, but as an active political life hardly conduces to the soundest judgment on literary subjects, this would be his misfortune, and not his fault. He reviewed *Waverley* in the *Quarterly* for July 1814, and *Guy Mannering* the following January, and also *The Antiquary* when it appeared a year later; and each of these reviews was full of warm yet judicious praise. This may seem little at this late day, but it must be borne in mind that these immortal works appeared anonymously, and had to be judged solely on their merits, to which not all critics were equally alive. "When the reputation of authors is made," says Sainte-Beuve, "it is easy to speak of them *convenablement*: we have only to guide ourselves by the common opinion. But at the start, at the moment when they are trying their first flight, and are in part ignorant of themselves, then to judge them with tact, with precision, not to exaggerate their scope, to predict their flight, or divine their limits, to put the reasonable objections in the midst of all due respect—this is the quality of a critic who is born to be a critic."

In criticising a poet he would

> Insist on knowing what he means—a hard
> And hapless situation for a bard;

and although, as has been shown, he was not the writer of the article on Keats, the poetry of the school to which Keats belonged was especially distasteful to him. The fondness which he had shown when a boy for the poetry of Pope grew into admiration as his judgment ripened, and the task which he set himself in his old age was a collected edition of this poet's works, the notes for which he was engaged upon up to the day of his death.

His judgments on literary and political matters, even after his retirement from parliament and public life, had great influence. As a politician he was always at least consistent, and Irishmen especially should remember that he advocated the Catholic claims nearly a quarter of a century before the passing of the Emancipation Act by a Government of which he was a member. He sometimes held extreme views, and supported them with vigour, and occasionally with bitterness. Had he imparted less of a certain arrogance of tone into his speeches, he might have made fewer enemies; and his manner towards strangers or those who did not know him certainly savoured of harshness; but, as was said of Dr. Johnson, there was "nothing of the bear about him except the skin."

As depicted by Maclise in *Fraser's Magazine*, he is shown to have had a fine, intellectual head of the type of Canning, with a kindly and slightly melancholy expression of face. The same impression is conveyed by the fine portrait of him painted by Sir Thomas Lawrence, and when we add that he was slightly under the middle height, slender, and well knit, the reader has a faithful presentation of the outward appearance of this most remarkable and much maligned man. Forty years have passed

away since he died, on August 10, 1857. Let us hope that we may not have to wait many more years for that complete biography which all who love justice will be glad to see; for calumny need only fear the truth. Let us also hope that his biographer, whoever he may be, will approach his subject in the right spirit, and will "nothing extenuate, nor set down aught in malice."—P. A. SILLARD, "John Wilson Croker," *Gentleman's Magazine*, Aug. 1898, pp. 157–58

Works

EDITION OF BOSWELL

This work has greatly disappointed us. Whatever faults we may have been prepared to find in it, we fully expected that it would be a valuable addition to English literature; that it would contain many curious facts, and many judicious remarks; that the style of the notes would be neat, clear, and precise; and that the typographical execution would be, as in new editions of classical works it ought to be, almost faultless. We are sorry to be obliged to say that the merits of Mr. Croker's performance are on a par with those of a certain leg of mutton on which Dr. Johnson dined, while travelling from London to Oxford, and which he, with characteristic energy, pronounced to be "as bad as bad could be, ill fed, ill killed, ill kept, and ill dressed." This edition is ill compiled, ill arranged, ill written, and ill printed.

Nothing in the work has astonished us so much as the ignorance or carelessness of Mr. Croker with respect to facts and dates. Many of his blunders are such as we should be surprised to hear any well educated gentleman commit, even in conversation. The notes absolutely swarm with misstatements into which the editor never would have fallen, if he had taken the slightest pains to investigate the truth of his assertions, or if he had even been well acquainted with the book on which he undertook to comment.—THOMAS BABINGTON MACAULAY, "Samuel Johnson" (1831), *Critical, Historical, and Miscellaneous Essays*, 1860, Vol. 2, pp. 368–69

I should be wanting in justice were I not to acknowledge that I owe much to the labours of Mr. Croker. No one can know better than I do his great failings as an editor. His remarks and criticisms far too often deserve the contempt that Macaulay so liberally poured on them. Without being deeply versed in books, he was shallow in himself. Johnson's strong character was never known to him. Its breadth and length, and depth and height were far beyond his measure. With his writings even he shows few signs of being familiar. Boswell's genius, a genius which even to Lord Macaulay was foolishness, was altogether hidden from his dull eye. No one surely but a 'blockhead,' a 'barren rascal,' could with scissors and paste-pot have mangled the biography which of all others is the delight and the boast of the English-speaking world. He is careless in small matters, and his blunders are numerous. These I have only noticed in the more important cases, remembering what Johnson somewhere points out, that the triumphs of one critic over another only fatigue and disgust the reader. Yet he has added considerably to our knowledge of Johnson. He knew men who had intimately known both the hero and his biographer, and he gathered much that but for his care would have been lost for ever. He was diligent and successful in his search after Johnson's letters, of so many of which Boswell with all his persevering and pushing diligence had not been able to get a sight. The editor of Mr. Croker's *Correspondence and Diaries* goes, however, much too far when, in writing of Macaulay's criticism, he says: 'The attack defeated itself by its very violence, and therefore it did the book no harm whatever.

Between forty and fifty thousand copies have been sold, although Macaulay boasted with great glee that he had smashed it.' The book that Macaulay attacked was withdrawn. That monstrous medley reached no second edition. In its new form all the worst excrescences had been cleared away, and though what was left was not Boswell, still less was it unchastened Croker. His repentance, however, was not thorough. He never restored the text to its old state; wanton transpositions of passages still remain, and numerous insertions break the narrative. It was my good fortune to become a sound Boswellian before I even looked at his edition. It was not indeed till I came to write out my notes for the press that I examined his with any thoroughness.—GEORGE BIRKBECK HILL, "Preface" to *Boswell's Life of Johnson*, 1887, Vol. 1, pp. xxii–xxiii

It has been Boswell's fate to be universally read and almost as universally despised. What he suffered at the hands of Croker and Macaulay is typical of his fortune. In character, in politics, in attainments, in capacity, the two were poles apart; but they were agreed in this: that Boswell must be castigated and contemned, and that they were the men to do it. Croker's achievement, consider it how you will, remains the most preposterous in literary history. He could see nothing in the *Life* but a highly entertaining compilation greatly in need of annotation and correction. Accordingly he took up Boswell's text and interlarded it with scraps of his own and other people's; he pegged into it a sophisticated version of the *Tour*; and he overwhelmed his amazing compound with notes and commentaries in which he took occasion to snub, scold, 'improve,' and insult his author at every turn. What came of it one knows. Macaulay, in the combined interests of Whiggism and good literature, made Boswell's quarrel his own, and the expiation was as bitter as the offence was wanton and scandalous. —W. E. HENLEY, "Boswell," *Views and Reviews*, 1890, p. 194

A. V. DICEY
From "John Wilson Croker"
Nation, February 5, 1885, pp. 122–23

The permanent interest of Croker's letters and diaries lies in circumstances independent of the rumors or slanders which still cast a dubious hue over his private character. Croker was a moral and political survivor. He died in 1857; he was intimately known to many men still living, and was seen and spoken to by persons who are now not far past middle age, but he remained essentially the man of 1800. Amid a changing world, in the age of Cobden, of Bright, and of Louis Napoleon, he retained unaltered the sentiments natural to a stanch Tory official who remembered Pitt, and who had served under Perceval and Liverpool. He was the incarnation of official Toryism as it flourished during the Great War and the Regency. Some gift or defect of nature made his mind armor-proof against influences which moulded and transformed the policy, if not the character, of Peel, and which told upon the conduct of the Iron Duke himself. In Croker one can see, not indeed the heroism—for of everything heroic he was absolutely devoid—but the strength and the virtues, no less than the weaknesses and the faults, of the Tories who resisted with unequal success the attacks of Napoleonic France and the advance of social and political reform. It is well worth while to take Croker as the representative of a class, and to note his typical excellences and his typical faults, as far as may be, with equal impartiality.

The Toryism of Croker was something much more than a political doctrine. It may almost be described as a political, a social, and a religious faith. To men who remembered the Reign of Terror, and who saw it much in the light in which it is again revealed for the present age by Taine, the Revolution was little else than the outburst of the powers of hell, and Napoleon was the devil who ruled the new pandemonium. Grant, as every rational person now must, that this view of a world-wide movement was partial and distorted; grant, as, even with the pages of Lanfrey before them, most calm judges will concede, that Napoleon, and still more the work of Napoleon, presented a good as well as a bad side, yet the fact remains that the Tories of the Revolutionary and the Napoleonic era did in very truth regard the Revolution as the work of the devil, and had far more cause for so regarding it than a generation who know the "Terror" only as a matter of history are apt to think. The conviction, further—which was ultimately held by Whigs like Lord John Russell and Sydney Smith as firmly as by Tories like Perceval or Liverpool—that French aggression would, unless resisted, be fatal to the national independence of England, and in fact menaced the independence of every state throughout Europe, gave to the Toryism which flourished during the Great War, not only an impress of patriotism, but a good deal of sympathy (in the case, at any rate, of Spain and Germany) with what a later generation called "the cause of nationalities." Under the inspiration of political zeal and patriotic fervor, Croker, and hundreds better or worse than he, did a great work. They manned the ship of state, and carried it through a storm which wrecked vessels as noble and apparently as strong as that which carried the fortunes of England.

The best trait about Croker was his strenuous work at the Admiralty. That he got fair day's wages for the day's labors may well be admitted; but it must also be borne in mind that he threw his whole heart into the task before him, and gave to the country a kind of unremitting toil which cannot be bought for mere money. What is true of Croker was, we may be sure, equally true of hundreds whose names are now forgotten. A party which holds power for nearly half a century is certain, in Anglo-Saxon countries at least, to become corrupted by its own success. But it is not in virtue, but in spite, of vileness and corruption that a great party controls for more than a generation the destinies of a great state. It were curious to trace the mode in which "character," which has always told for more in England than talent, has passed at different times from one party to another. For our present purpose it is enough to note that between 1784 and 1820 the Tories possessed a repute for moral worth which did not belong to their opponents. There were hundreds of Tories whose public and private character did not deserve any special respect; there were scores of men among the Whigs who represented the highest moral feeling of their age. But no candid reader of history can deny that during the earlier part of the century the Tories were, on the whole, the moral and religious party. Most good men were Tories, and this fact gave currency to the utterly erroneous notion that all Tories were good men, and that persons who were not Tories were bad men. This was the undoubted creed of Croker and of far better men than Croker, such as Walter Scott. And one cannot doubt that the identification of political prejudices or principles with the cause of morality did lend to the Tory party an amount of force and of earnestness which both caused, and, within certain limits, justified, the success and triumph of Toryism.

With parties, however, as with men, their strength is also their weakness. Toryism displayed the bigotry, narrowness, and blindness no less than the fervor of a religious creed. The tacit assumption that a Tory was a good man, accounts for the tolerance or favor with which Scott and Peel regarded Croker.

That anyone endowed with Scott's nobility of nature could have failed to be shocked by the mean side of Croker's character, and the odiousness of what one may call Crokerism, is inexplicable, unless one allows for the fact that Croker was, in Scott's eyes, a soldier fighting manfully for the cause of virtue; and according to a Tory standard, Croker was, it must be admitted, the stanchest of fighters. He never missed giving a blow, fair or unfair, at a Whig; he never, like Lyndhurst, dallied, to say the least, with Liberalism; he never, like Canning, was carried away from his Tory standing-point by rhetorical enthusiasm for freedom; he never, like Peel, was shaken by the force of argument; he never, like Wellington, acknowledged the necessity of yielding to the logic of facts. He was one of those blind leaders of the blind who step out with all the boldness of a guide gifted with the clearest foresight, who, when kept by wiser heads from irreparable disaster, turn round and swear at the friends by whom they are saved, and who, when they and their followers fall into a ditch, lay the blame of their mishap on everything except their own blindness. Croker, who never failed to mistake the patent signs of the time, asseverated with such good faith the dogma of his own infallibility that he persuaded a generation of Tories to believe that he never was wrong. Yet every fact showed him to be gifted with neither insight nor foresight. He knew Peel with intimacy for years; he had watched him closely and had studied every turn of Sir Robert's sinuous, not to say tortuous career. He would, one would have thought, have soon perceived that the essential difference between his own and Peel's views of statesmanship must at last lead Peel away from the path of rigid Toryism. Yet Croker, at a time when every Liberal perceived that Peel was tending, and rapidly tending, toward free trade, made himself the political surety for the Prime Minister's steadfast adherence to protection. Let us grant, as we are afraid must be granted, that Croker was the dupe of his hero, and concede that Sir Robert set an example of political casuistry which has done so much harm to the public life of England as to constitute an immense set-off to the services which he rendered to the country. But when every concession is made, Croker's tremendous blunder can be explained only by the fact that Croker was, as a judge of character, the dullest of men. ⟨. . .⟩

Mr. Croker as a literary critic is only less out of place than Mr. Croker as a writer on matters which concern the Church and, to a certain extent, religion itself. One can in a measure pardon the political pugilist for taking a part in ecclesiastical controversy when one finds that Samuel Wilberforce (who, by the way, found old Lord Lyndhurst an agreeable and impressive supporter of orthodoxy) used to correspond with Croker on Tractarianism, on Newman's sermons, on the Hampden controversy. No doubt the Bishop addressed himself rather to the editor or guide of the *Quarterly Review* than to the hardened political controversialist. Still, the friendly communication between the two men on matters of religion is not a very pleasant trait in the character either of Wilberforce or of his correspondent. Here, however, we touch upon one of the points on which Croker was, as on so many others, the representative of his party. The Tories to whom he belonged were, as part of their political creed, guardians and protectors of the Church. They stood toward the Church of England much as French Conservatives now stand toward Roman Catholicism; they looked upon religion (when it assumed a respectable form) as an ally of the State, and treated the cause of the Church as part of the general cause of social order. To suppose that men like Croker professed to be religious men in the sense in which the term might be applied to Newman, or Maurice, or Arnold, or Zachary Macaulay, would be to impute to Croker and his associates a kind of hypocrisy of which he was entirely guiltless. But unfortunately Croker, who admired George the Fourth, and who served Lord Hertford, was, like other men of his type, the official defender, so to speak, of religion and of the Establishment. This was, take it all in all, the worst side of the Toryism which flourished during the Regency. It was this official connection with religion which roused the moral indignation of men who themselves made no pretension to fervent religious convictions, but who hated cant. "I might add," says Macaulay with reference to Croker, "a hundred other charges. These are things done by a Privy Councillor, by a man who has a pension from the country of £2,000 a year, by a man who affects to be a champion of order and religion." When we weigh the full meaning of this language we can well understand why, in 1830, all that was youthful and generous in the spirit of England condemned ruthlessly the whole régime of which Croker was the representative.

Douglas Jerrold

1803–1857

Douglas William Jerrold was born on January 3, 1803, in London, the son of a theatre manager. While still a child (1813–15) he served in the navy during the Napoleonic Wars; his experiences during those years later found their way into his plays. The first, *Black-Eyed Susan*, was based on a ballad by John Gay; its successful opening on June 8, 1829, at the Surrey Theatre followed years of drudgery on the stage in a variety of occupations, including resident dramatist at the Coburg Theatre. Jerrold went on to write other plays, including *The Mutiny at the Nore* (1830), *The Rent Day* (1832), *Bubbles of the Day* (1842), and *Time Works Wonders* (1845), but none achieved the success of *Black-Eyed Susan*.

In addition to his work in the theatre Jerrold was a journalist, frequently contributing to a variety of periodicals, including *Blackwood's Edinburgh Magazine*. He also founded several short-lived journals and edited *Lloyd's Weekly Newspaper*. From 1841 until his death sixteen years later Jerrold achieved celebrity as a contributor of satirical sketches to *Punch*. His series "Mrs. Caudle's Curtain Lectures," which ran in *Punch* in 1845, was especially popular. It was later collected in book form and frequently reprinted.

Jerrold died at his home, Kilburn Priory, London, on June 8, 1857.

Personal

Douglas Jerrold talked of Thackeray and his success in America, and said that he himself purposed going and had been invited thither to lecture. I asked him whether it was pleasant to a writer of plays to see them performed; and he said it was intolerable, the presentation of the author's idea being so imperfect; and Dr. —— observed that it was excruciating to hear one of his own songs sung. Jerrold spoke of the Duke of Devonshire with great warmth, as a true, honest, simple, most kind-hearted man, from whom he himself had received great courtesies and kindnesses (not, as I understood, in the way of patronage or essential favors); and I (Heaven forgive me!) queried within myself whether this English reforming author would have been quite so sensible of the Duke's excellence if his Grace had not been a duke. But, indeed, a nobleman, who is at the same time a true and whole-hearted man, feeling his brotherhood with men, does really deserve some credit for it.

In the course of the evening Jerrold spoke with high appreciation of Emerson; and of Longfellow, whose *Hiawatha* he considered a wonderful performance; and of Lowell, whose *Fable for Critics* he especially admired. I mentioned Thoreau, and proposed to send his works to Dr. ——, who, being connected with the *Illustrated News*, and otherwise a writer, might be inclined to draw attention to them. Douglas Jerrold asked why he should not have them too. I hesitated a little, but as he pressed me, and would have an answer, I said that I did not feel quite so sure of his kindly judgment on Thoreau's books; and it so chanced that I used the word "acrid" for lack of a better, in endeavoring to express my idea of Jerrold's way of looking at men and books. It was not quite what I meant; but, in fact, he often *is* acrid, and has written pages and volumes of acridity, though, no doubt, with an honest purpose, and from a manly disgust at the cant and humbug of the world. Jerrold said no more, and I went on talking with Dr. ——; but, in a minute or two, I became aware that something had gone wrong, and, looking at Douglas Jerrold, there was an expression of pain and emotion on his face. By this time a second bottle of Burgundy had been opened (Clos Vougeot, the best the Club could produce, and far richer than the Chambertin), and that warm and potent wine may have had something to do with the depth and vivacity of Mr. Jerrold's feelings. But he was indeed greatly hurt by that little word "acrid." "He knew," he said, "that the world considered him a sour, bitter, ill-natured man; but that such a man as I should have the same opinion was almost more than he could bear." As he spoke, he threw out his arms, sank back in his seat, and I was really a little apprehensive of his actual dissolution into tears. Hereupon I spoke, as was good need, and though, as usual, I have forgotten everything I said, I am quite sure it was to the purpose, and went to this good fellow's heart, as it came warmly from my own. I do remember saying that I felt him to be as genial as the glass of Burgundy which I held in my hand; and I think that touched the very right spot; for he smiled and said he was afraid the Burgundy was better than he, but yet he was comforted. Dr. —— said that he likewise had a reputation for bitterness; and I assured him, if I might venture to join myself to the brotherhood of two such men, that I was considered a very ill-natured person by many people in my own country. Douglas Jerrold said he was glad of it.

We were now in sweetest harmony, and Jerrold spoke more than it would become me to repeat in praise of my own books, which he said he admired, and he found the man more admirable than his books! I hope so, certainly.

We now went to the Haymarket Theatre, where Douglas

Jerrold is on the free list; and after seeing a ballet by some Spanish dancers, we separated, and betook ourselves to our several homes. I like Douglas Jerrold very much.—NATHANIEL HAWTHORNE, *The English Note-Books*, April 5, 1856

Jerrold in his little study, with a cigar, a flask of Rhine wine on the table, a cedar log on the fire, and half-a-dozen literary youngsters round the board listening to his bright wit and his wisdom that was brighter even than his wit,—this is, we think, the image of the good friend and singular humourist that will live most brightly and permanently in the minds of those who knew him. Warmth and generosity, haste in giving and forgiving, a passionate desire to see every one cheery, prosperous, and content, went with him from cradle to tomb. His mound of flowers was nobly earned. Men who linger wistfully on the memory of that tiny frame, on that eager, radiant face, on those infantine ways, with their wonderfully subtle and elaborate guilelessness, on that ailing constitution and fiery blood, on that joyous, tender, teasing, frolicsome, thoughtful heart, must always think of him, less as of the flashing wit and scathing satirist,—than as of some marvellously gifted, noble, and wayward child, the sport of nature and the delight of man. He will be recalled to those who knew and loved him, not by any big and sounding appellation, but by some affectionate and soft diminutive:—not as brilliant Douglas or magnificent Douglas, but simply and fondly as *dear* Douglas.—HEPWORTH DIXON, *Athenaeum*, Dec. 25, 1858, pp. 830–31

It was in June, 1857; the place was Norwood Cemetery. A multitude had gathered there to bury a man known to both of them ⟨Dickens and Thackeray⟩, and who had known both of them well—a man whom we have had incidentally to name as holding a place, in some respects peculiar, in the class of writers to which *they* belong, though his most effective place was in a kindred department of literature; a man, too, of whom I will say that, let the judgment on his remaining writings be permanently what it may, and let tongues have spoken of him this or that awry, there breathed not, to my knowledge, within the unwholesome bounds of what is specially London, any one in whose actual person there was more of the pith of energy at its tensest, of that which in a given myriad anywhere distinguishes the one. How like a little Nelson he stood, dashing back his hair, and quivering for the verbal combat! The flash of his wit, in which one quality the island had not his match, was but the manifestation easiest to be observed of a mind compact of sense and information, and of a soul generous and on fire. And now all that remained of Jerrold was enclosed within the leaden coffin which entered the cemetery gates. As it passed, one saw Dickens among the bearers of the pall, his uncovered head of genius stooped, and the wind blowing his hair. Close behind came Thackeray; and, as the slow procession wound up the hill to the chapel, the crowd falling into it in twos and threes and increasing its length, his head was to be seen by the later ranks, towering far in the front above all the others, like that of a marching Saul. And so up to the little chapel they moved; and, after the service for the dead, down again to another slope of the hill, where, by the side of one of the walks, and opposite to the tombstone of Blanchard, Jerrold's grave was open. There the last words were read; the coffin was lowered; and the two, among hundreds of others, looked down their farewell. And so, dead at the age of fifty-four, Jerrold was left in his solitary place, where the rains were to fall, and the nights were to roll overhead, and but now and then, on a summer's day, a chance stroller would linger in curiosity; and back into the roar of London dispersed the funeral crowd.—DAVID MASSON, *British Novelists and Their Styles*, 1859, pp. 235–37

Few of his friends, I think, can have had more favourable opportunities of knowing him in his gentlest and most affectionate aspect than I have had. He was one of the gentlest and most affectionate of men. I remember very well that when I first saw him, in about the year 1835, when I went into his sick room in Thistle Grove, Brompton, and found him propped up in a great chair, bright-eyed, and quick, and eager in spirit, but very lame in body, he gave me an impression of tenderness. It never became dissociated from him. There was nothing cynical or sour in his heart, as I knew it. In the company of children and young people he was particularly happy, and showed to extraordinary advantage. He never was so gay, so sweet-tempered, so pleasing, and so pleased as then. Among my own children I have observed this many and many a time. When they and I came home from Italy, in 1845, your father went to Brussels to meet us, in company with our friends, Mr. Forster and Mr. Maclise. We all travelled together about Belgium for a little while, and all came home together. He was the delight of the children all the time, and they were his delight. He was in his most brilliant spirits, and I doubt if he were ever more humorous in his life. But the most enduring impression that he left upon us, who are grown up—and we have all often spoken of it since—was, that Jerrold, in his amiable capacity of being easily pleased, in his freshness, in his good nature, in his cordiality, and in the unrestrained openness of his heart, had quite captivated us.

Of his generosity I had a proof within these two or three years, which it saddens me to think of now. There had been an estrangement between us—not on any personal subject, and not involving an angry word—and a good many months had passed without my even seeing him in the street, when it fell out that we dined each with his own separate party, in the STRANGER'S ROOM of a club. Our chairs were almost back to back, and I took mine after he was seated and at dinner. I said not a word (I am sorry to remember), and did not look that way. Before we had sat so long, he openly wheeled his chair round, stretched out both his hands in a most engaging manner, and said aloud, with a bright and loving face that I can see as I write to you, "For God's sake let us be friends again! A life's not long enough for this."—CHARLES DICKENS, Letter to Blanchard Jerrold (c. 1859), cited in Blanchard Jerrold, *The Life and Remains of Douglas Jerrold*, 1859, pp. 356–57

I owed the pleasure of Mr. Jerrold's acquaintance to Mr. ⟨Charles⟩ Knight; and I wish I had known him more. My first impression was one of surprise,—not at his remarkable appearance, of which I was aware;—the eyes and the mobile countenance, the stoop and the small figure, reminding one of Coleridge, without being like him,—but at the gentle and thoughtful kindness which set its mark on all he said and did. Somehow, all his good things were so dropped as to fall into my trumpet, without any trouble or ostentation. This was the dreaded and unpopular man who must have been hated (for he *was* hated) as *Punch* and not as Jerrold,—through fear, and not through reason or feeling. His wit always appeared to me as gentle as it was honest,—as innocent as it was sound. I could say of him as of Sydney Smith, that I never heard him say, in the way of raillery, any thing of others that I should mind his saying of me. I never feared him in the least, nor saw reason why any but knaves or fools should fear him.—HARRIET MARTINEAU, *Autobiography*, ed. Maria Weston Chapman, 1877, Vol. 2, p. 32

General

Let me thank you, most cordially, for your books—not only for their own sakes (and I have read them with perfect delight) but also for this hearty and most welcome mark of your recollection of the friendship we have established; in which light I know I may regard and prize them.

I am greatly pleased with your opening paper in the *Illuminated*. It is very wise, and capital; written with the finest end of that iron pen of yours; witty, much needed, and full of Truth. I vow to God that I think the Parrots of Society are more intolerable and mischievous than its Birds of Prey.—CHARLES DICKENS, Letter to Douglas Jerrold (May 3, 1843)

Jerrold's first papers of mark in *Punch* were those signed "Q." His style was now formed, as his mind was, and these papers bear the stamp of his peculiar way of thinking and writing. Assuredly, his is a *peculiar* style in the strict sense; and as marked as that of Carlyle or Dickens. You see the self-made man in it,—a something *sui generis*,—not formed on the "classical models," but which has grown up with a kind of twist in it, like a tree that has had to force its way up surrounded by awkward environments. Fundamentally, the man is a thinking humorist; but his mode of expression is strange. The perpetual inversions, the habitual irony, the mingled tenderness and mockery, give a kind of gnarled surface to the style, which is pleasant when you get familiar with it, but which repels the stranger, and to some people even remains permanently disagreeable. I think it was his continual irony which at last brought him to writings as if under a mask; whereas it would have been better to write out flowingly, musically, and lucidly. His mixture of satire and kindliness always reminds me of those lanes near Beyrout in which you ride with the prickly-pear bristling alongside of you, and yet can pluck the grapes which force themselves among it from the fields. Inveterately satirical as Jerrold is, he is even "spoonily" tender at the same time; and it lay deep in his character; for this wit and *bon-vivant*, the merriest and wittiest man of the company, would cry like a child, as the night drew on, and the talk grew serious. No theory could be more false than that he was a cold-blooded satirist,—sharp as steel is sharp, from being hard. The basis of his nature was sensitiveness and impulsiveness. His wit is not of the head only, but of the heart,—often sentimental, and constantly *fanciful*, that is, dependent on a quality which imperatively requires a sympathetic nature to give it full play. Take those *Punch* papers which soon helped to make *Punch* famous, and Jerrold himself better known. Take the "Story of a Feather," as a good expression of his more earnest and tender mood. How delicately all the part about the poor actress is worked up! How moral, how stoical, the feeling that pervades it! The bitterness is healthy,—healthy as bark. We cannot always be

> Seeing only what is fair,
> Sipping only what is sweet,

in the presence of such phenomena as are to be seen in London alongside of our civilization. If any feeling of Jerrold's was intense, it was his feeling of sympathy with the poor. I shall not soon forget the energy and tenderness with which he would quote these lines of his favorite Hood:—

> Poor Peggy sells flowers from street to street,
> And—think of that, ye who find life sweet!—
> She hates the smell of roses.

He was, therefore, to be pardoned when he looked with extreme suspicion and severity on the failings of the rich. *They* at least, he knew, were free from those terrible temptations which beset the unfortunate. They could protect themselves. They needed to be reminded of their duties. Such was his view, though I don't think he ever carried it so far as he was accused of doing. Nay, I think he sometimes had to prick up his zeal before assuming the *flagellum*. For a successful, brilliant man like himself,—full of humor and wit,—eminently convivial, and sensitive to pleasure,—the temptation rather was to adopt the easy philosophy that every thing was all right,—that the rich were wise to enjoy themselves with as little trouble as possible,—and that the poor (good fellows, no doubt) must help themselves on according as they got a chance. It was to Douglas's credit that he always felt the want of a deeper and holier theory, and that, with all his gaiety, he felt it incumbent on him to use his pen as an implement of what he thought reform. Indeed, it was a well-known characteristic of his, that he disliked being talked of as "a wit." He thought (with justice) that he had something better in him than most wits, and he sacredly cherished high aspirations. To him buffoonery was pollution. He attached to *salt* something of the sacredness which it bears in the East. He was fuller of repartee than any man in England, and yet was about the last man that would have condescended to be what is called a "diner-out." It is a fact which illustrates his mind, his character, and biography. —JAMES HANNAY, "Douglas Jerrold," *Atlantic*, Nov. 1857, pp. 5–7

Douglas Jerrold was accused of setting class against class by his writings, and it cannot be denied that the most moving passages in his works are those in which he depicts the sufferings of the poor and the harshness of the world towards them. It is these passages which explain the charge of bitterness so frequently brought against him. How keenly he resented that charge is known to all who have read his works. It evidently wounded him deeply and filled his sensitive nature with acute pain, whether directed against himself or his writings. But in the latter case can it be altogether dismissed? People who speak bitterly speak in most cases from mere excess of feeling. It is much the same with Douglas Jerrold. In his indignation he spares no sarcasm to give effect to his invectives; he strives to the utmost to make each sentence as pointed as possible, nay, as one of his critics remarked, every word seems to have been specially sharpened before being used. He wrote, as Hawthorne says, with an honest and a manly purpose; he was thoroughly sincere; he earnestly desired to make the world better, to lighten its suffering, and give a nobler dignity to life. But like Carlyle he lacked the higher qualities of the teacher: gentleness, forbearance, patience. He was too impulsive, too eager, too desirous of enforcing his views with peremptory sternness. An author who sees scarcely anything but the imperfections of human nature and the injustice of the world, who is so severe upon our faults, and who shows so little indulgence for our weakness, seems to take up a position outside the range of our sympathies, and thus alienates himself from his fellow men. There can be no doubt that Douglas Jerrold's writings fail of their full effect from this cause. We feel that we are not so black as we are painted; that the world is not so selfish, so mean, and so cruel as the satirist represents.

Douglas Jerrold was never as widely popular as Dickens, but during his lifetime his reputation had spread so far that he had many readers and many ardent admirers. When he died it was felt that there was a public loss. Since then his influence as a writer seems to have passed away year by year. Edition after edition of the works of his two contemporaries, Dickens and Thackeray, has been issued since the death of those authors, and the reputation of Thackeray has certainly risen higher and

seems to rest on a broader basis than before. Of Douglas Jerrold the same cannot be said. Some of his writings reappear from time to time, and quite recently an early satire, *The Handbook of Swindling*, was reprinted in the Camelot Series, with an introduction by Mr. Walter Jerrold. But no complete edition of his works has appeared since his death, more than thirty years ago. It is impossible to resist the inference that they are no longer generally read. They have secured a place in our literature; but it is not the place their author strove to reach. —EDWARD COPPING, "Douglas Jerrold," *New Review*, Sept. 1892, pp. 363–64

G. S. PHILLIPS
From "Douglas Jerrold"

North American Review, October 1859, pp. 431–39

Douglas Jerrold has passed away forever from the earth; but he has left behind him such memorials of his wit, genius, and intellectual ability, as the world will not willingly let die. Nor are these his only triumphs. Time and death have their separate, inalienable sovereignties, and exercise with remorseless despotism their conscriptive rights over individuals, and all personal and historic achievements,—often diminishing what seemed great in human character, and enlarging what at first sight, and in the common estimation, was regarded as mean and insignificant; but neither time, death, nor eternity can change that which is essentially true in the soul of man, nor rob it of its moral grandeur and sublimity. For, as Cicero devoutly urges, "Truth is unchanged, and unchangeable; not one thing to-day, and another to-morrow, but the same great, eternal, and immutable thing forever."

In truth, in stern loyalty to his principles and convictions lies the crowning glory of Jerrold. Higher trophy can no man have laid upon his tomb than this; higher legacy can no man leave, and none more sacred and vitalizing. We have had many wits in the world, from and before Rabelais, to Swift and Sheridan; but if we except the Frenchman, and can pardon his continents of mud for the sake of his sincerity, his work as a reformer, and those seams of light and truth which burn and flash amidst the torpid corruption, the rotting sensual imagery of his mind, who among these naked and unnamed worthies can lay claim to the moral title of Jerrold? Swift assuredly can make no such pretensions; for he was at the bottom a man-hater, having the intellect and also the heart of Satan, to whom virtue and morality were an idle dream. Neither can Sheridan—welcome as he was and is to all Champagne circles, and, for his wit and talent, to cultivated men in all time—put in credentials high enough to win this highest of all the noble styles of heraldry. Sydney Smith alone among moderns is worthy to compare with Jerrold, not only in the sudden promptness and keen edge of his retort, but in the fine morality of his humor and sarcasm. Jerrold exceeds him, however, in fancy, in the symbolism of truth, and in those grand attributes of intellect and imagination which render this wit equally a man of genius and of profound practical wisdom. It is true that the jovial and learned divine is also a man of genius, and that he possesses faculties and acquirements which cannot be claimed for Jerrold,—elaborate humour, for example, and scholarship; but, large and liberal as he was in mind and character, and ever ready, like his great compeer, to lend his lance for the succor of the oppressed and the punishment of the oppressor, he was necessarily, from his position and profession, walled round by many obstructions to the free play of his intellect, and lacked, as we think, that keen, instinctive recognition and appreciation of truth in its absolute nature, which are so characteristic of Jerrold, in his graver and professedly artistic writings.

Be this as it may, however, one thing is certain; that the obscure player's son has stamped the impress of his genius upon the literature and character of his age and country, with an authentic and royal seal. Like most men who have achieved permanent fame, and won for themselves a definite *status* in the republic of letters, in science, or in art, he had to struggle through long years of toil, poverty, and neglect, before he could command a platform high enough to compel the public to listen to him, and acknowledge the supremacy of his intellect. But bitter and cruel as oftentimes were his disappointments and wrongs, through the mercenary nature of theatrical lessees, and London publishers, with whom he had continual dealings, we nowhere find the record of any complaint from his brave and manly heart. He battled and struggled onward and upward against them all, in the full consciousness of his own power, and the assurance of final triumph. ⟨. . .⟩

The truth is, that Jerrold was an earnest and sincere man, having solid foundations within him, which reached far below the brilliant surface of his character. He had learned many dreadful lessons in the hard school of the world, which, happily for him, he wisely digested, so that he suffered no harm by them; and he stored them up as experience not too dearly purchased, because of the strength and wisdom which they brought him. This experience empowered and commissioned him to speak, not as a wit only, but as a moral teacher, when the time had come for the people of England to listen to him. For he was not merely a wit; nothing pained him more than to be so regarded and estimated. The central fires of a great Sinai of passion burned within him, and what are called his "bitter sarcasms" and "scathing utterances," so far from being the splenetic offspring of a sour, angry, and mocking nature, were the genuine expressions of a soul surcharged with the sense of human wrong and misery. These were the intellectual weapons wherewith he fought so long and so bravely the social and moral battle of the people against their rulers and oppressors. And it should be remembered to his honor that this savage Berserker "cynic," without "love or pity in his heart," was always to be found in the front rank on the side of virtue and freedom. All his writings in *Punch*, in the *Illuminated Magazine*, in his books, and in his innumerable plays, prove the truth of this beyond doubt or question. Like a knight of the old chivalry, he kept his eye ever upon the broad field of the world, for a just occasion of combat. Let Lord Palmerston, who has been chargeable with so many and such atrocious crimes and treasons in England during the last forty years, or Sir Robert Peel, or Lord John Russell, or any other statesman, commit himself by speech or action, compromise the interests of the people at home, or the liberties of Europe abroad, Jerrold nails him to a shameful cross, and pierces him with wounds, whose gaping mouths no emollient can readily close. Let even so small a man as Sir Peter Laurie send a starving tailor to the treadmill for a month as a rogue and vagabond, for having attempted to commit suicide, and he cannot escape the lash of the avenger. "I shall look after such cases in future," quoth Sir Peter. And Jerrold, under the signature of Q. in *Punch*, ventures to contrast life as seen by the sleek alderman with life as regarded by the "famine-stricken multitudes of Bolton."

"Let Comfort," Q. concludes, "paint a portrait of life, and now Penury take the pencil. 'Pooh, pooh!' cry the sage Lauries of the world, looking at the two pictures; 'that scoundrel Penury has drawn an infamous libel. *That* life! with that withered face, sunken eye, and shrivelled lip; and what is worse, with a suicidal scar in its throat! *That* life! The painter Penury is committed for a month as a rogue and vagabond. We shall look very narrowly into these cases.' We agree with the profound Sir Peter Laurie that it is a most wicked, a most foolish act of the poor man, to end his misery by suicide. But we think there is a better remedy for such desperation than the treadmill. The surest way for the rich and powerful of the world to make the poor man more careful of his life is to render it of greater value to him."

It is curious to observe how the critics become themselves perplexed, while attempting to unravel the character of Jerrold. There is as little agreement about him anywhere, as if he were some incarnate rune or hieroglyph. And yet there is nothing difficult in his case, which, indeed, is one of the simplest in biographical history. Notoriously, he "wore his heart on his sleeve," and any competent person could read his last secret. For he had nothing to hide, and there was no guile nor disguise in him. A great, free, impulsive nature, hating restraints and the bondage of conventional life, he was never so happy as when he had gathered his choice troops of friends around him at his own table. He was a man also of thorough, uncompromising independence, and, although he received daily invitations to the palaces of the aristocracy in London, he very rarely availed himself of the courtesy, looking upon them with feelings almost of suspicion, as if, perhaps, neither he nor they were to be trusted. Lord John Russell gave one of his sons a government appointment, and, although Jerrold was an admirer and supporter of his Lordship and of most of his public measures, he accepted it with compunction, fearing that the time might one day come when he should half unconsciously spare the rod for the sake of this personal benevolence. He had no contempt for the aristocracy, nor did he undervalue the advantages of position and influence which spring from a long background of ancestry and good family connections. He was a radical, it is true, but not in the low Chartist sense. No one ever heard him, even in times of the most stormy political excitement, advocate any measures, save those of a peaceful reform, to be won gradually by the diffusion of intelligence and morality among the people.

Indeed, he can scarcely be called a politician, though he wrote many political articles, some of which made Wellington, who stood firm amidst the flashings of Vittoria and the thunders of Waterloo, tremble in his white waistcoat in the House of Lords. He had his political theories, it is true, but he wrote on politics like a moral censor and a man of letters, not as an editor of the Times newspaper, or a leader in the House of Commons. Nor could he, by any possibility, have been converted into a politician. The drudgery would have repelled and disgusted him, and the bonds of party would have chafed his soul so painfully, that he would have cast them from him in open and defiant rebellion.

Although a hard-working, laborious writer, Jerrold was a fragmentary man, and expressed himself best in fragments. Those short, piquant pieces in *Punch*, how admirable they are! How he adapts himself to the space he has to occupy, and how well he fills it! Some of his magazine articles,—those contributed to *Blackwood*,—tales, the incidents and machinery of which we feel, while we read, to be but secondary, and care only for the fine fancies and philosophical speculations, in the midst of which they rather clumsily move; and those in his own magazines appear to us to outweigh in value, as idiomatic and genuine performances, all his printed books, except *The Man Made of Money*, and *The Chronicles of Clovernook*. "The Story of a Feather," so gentle and tender, so sincere and earnest, which appeared in *Punch*, is one of his highest achievements, although it is easy to see how rapidly it fell from his pen.

A catalogue of his printed performances, including his plays, magazine articles, pamphlets, *Punch* contributions, and books, would be a startlingly voluminous affair, and we dare not attempt it in these pages. Nor indeed would it be worth the trouble, so far as the literary merit of many of them is concerned; but it would illustrate better than many sounding sentences could the indomitable energy and industry of the author. Jerrold himself set small value upon his plays, although he naturally enough loved the salt-water smack of *Black-Eyed Susan*, the flavor of which so well suited the popular taste, and established him, while yet a very young man, as a solid power in the realm. *Time Works Wonders* is one of his most mature plays; but we doubt if it will survive the present century.

His prose writings are far better than his plays. There are whole poems of great beauty in his *Chronicles of Clovernook*,— a book in which is revealed, we think, more of his real nature than in any other of his works. It sparkles with poetic genius,— contains much profound thinking, imaginative suggestion, and wise practical teaching. The style,too, is more artistic than his usual method, which, while it possesses sufficient originality, is sometimes crooked, distorted, and unmusical.

He hated cant and humbug, and hunted that kind of game straight down to death. He was merciless in all such cases, sparing neither high nor low, rich nor poor, when they were brought within the range of his vision. Perhaps he was the most sarcastic man of his time, and, as was said of Pope, men who feared not God, feared him and trembled.

WILKIE COLLINS
From "Douglas Jerrold" (1863)
My Miscellanies
1875, pp. 393–96

Judged from the literary point of view, these comedies were all original and striking contributions to the library of the stage. From the dramatic point of view, however, it must not be concealed that they were less satisfactory; and that some of them were scarcely so successful with audiences as their author's earlier and humbler efforts. The one solid critical reason which it is possible to assign for this, implies in itself a compliment which could be paid to no other dramatist of modern times. The perpetual glitter of Jerrold's wit seems to have blinded him to some of the more sober requirements of the Dramatic art. When Charles Kemble said, and said truly, that there was wit enough for three comedies in *Bubbles of the Day*, he implied that this brilliant overflow left little or no room for the indispensable resources of story and situation to display themselves fairly on the stage. The comedies themselves, examined with reference to their success in representation, as well as to their intrinsic merits, help to support this view. *Time Works Wonders* was the most prosperous of all, and it is that comedy precisely which has the most story and the most situation in it. The idea and the management of the charming love-tale out of which the events of this play spring, show what Jerrold might have achieved in the construction of other plots, if his own superabundant wit had not dazzled him

and led him astray. As it is, the readers of these comedies who can appreciate the rich fancy, the delicate subtleties of thought, the masterly terseness of expression, and the exquisite play and sparkle of wit scattered over every page, may rest assured that they rather gain than lose—especially in the present condition of theatrical companies—by not seeing the last dramatic works of Douglas Jerrold represented on the stage.

The next, and, sad to say, the final achievement of his life, connected him most honourably and profitably with the newspaper press. Many readers will remember the starting of *Douglas Jerrold's Weekly Newspaper*—its great temporary success—and then its sudden decline, through defects in management, to which it is not now necessary to refer at length. The signal ability with which the editorial articles in the paper were written, the remarkable aptitude which they displayed in striking straight at the sympathies of large masses of readers, did not escape the notice of men who were well fitted to judge of the more solid qualifications which go to the production of a popular journalist. In the spring of the year eighteen hundred and fifty-two, the proprietor of *Lloyd's Weekly Newspaper* proposed the editorship to Jerrold, on terms of such wise liberality as to ensure the ready acceptance of his offer. From the spring of eighteen hundred and fifty-two, to the spring of eighteen hundred and fifty-seven—the last he was ever to see— Jerrold conducted the paper, with such extraordinary success as is rare in the history of journalism. Under his supervision, and with the regular assistance of his pen, Lloyd's newspaper rose, by thousands and thousands a week, to the great circulation which it now enjoys. Of the many successful labours of Jerrold's life, none had been so substantially prosperous as the labour that was destined to close it.

His health had shown signs of breaking, and his heart was known to be affected, for some little time before his last brief illness; but the unconquerable energy and spirit of the man upheld him through all bodily trials, until the first day of June, eighteen hundred and fifty-seven. Even his medical attendant did not abandon all hope when his strength first gave way. But he sank rapidly—so rapidly, that in one short week the struggle was over. On the eighth day of June, surrounded by his family and his friends, preserving all his faculties to the last, passing away calmly, resignedly, affectionately, Douglas Jerrold closed his eyes on the world which it had been the long and noble purpose of his life to inform and to improve.

It is too early yet to attempt any estimate of the place which his writings will ultimately occupy in English literature. So long as honesty, energy, and variety are held to be among the prominent qualities which should distinguish a genuine writer, there can be no doubt of the vitality of Douglas Jerrold's reputation. The one objection urged against the works, which, feeble and ignorant though it was, often went to the heart of the writer, was the objection of bitterness. Calling to mind many of the passages in his books in which this bitterness most sharply appears, and seeing plainly in those passages what the cause was that provoked it, we venture to speak out our own opinion boldly, and to acknowledge at once, that we admire this so-called bitterness as one of the great and valuable qualities of Douglas Jerrold's writings; because we can see for ourselves that it springs from the uncompromising earnestness and honesty of the author. In an age when it is becoming unfashionable to have a positive opinion about anything; when the modern invasion of burlesque scatters its profanation with impunity on all beautiful and all serious things; when much, far too much, of the current literature of the day vibrates contemptibly between unbelieving banter and unblushing clap-trap, that element of bitterness in Jerrold's writings—

which never stands alone in them; which is never disassociated from the kind word that goes before, or the generous thought that comes after—is in our opinion an essentially wholesome element, breathing that admiration of truth, and that hatred of falsehood, which is the chiefest and brightest jewel in the crown of any writer, living or dead.

This same cry of bitterness, which assailed him in his literary character, assailed him in his social character also. Absurd as the bare idea of bitterness must appear in connection with such a nature as his, to those who really knew him, the reason why strangers so often and so ridiculously misunderstood him is not difficult to discover. That marvellous brightness and quickness of perception which has distinguished him far and wide as the sayer of some of the wittiest, and often some of the wisest things also, in the English language, expressed itself almost with the suddenness of lightning. This absence of all appearance of artifice or preparation, this flash and readiness which made the great charm of his wit, rendered him, at the same time, quite incapable of suppressing a good thing from prudential considerations. It sparkled off his tongue before he was aware of it. It was always a bright surprise to himself; and it never occurred to him that it could be anything but a bright surprise to others. All his so-called bitter things were said with a burst of hearty schoolboy laughter, which showed how far he was himself from attaching a serious importance to them. Strangers apparently failed to draw this inference, plain as it was; and often mistook him accordingly. If they had seen him in the society of children; if they had surprised him in the house of any one of his literary brethren who was in difficulty and distress; if they had met him by the bedside of a sick friend—how simply and how irresistibly the gentle, generous, affectionate nature of the man would then have disclosed itself to the most careless chance acquaintance who ever misunderstood him! Very few men have won the loving regard of so many friends so rapidly, and have kept that regard so enduringly to the last day of their lives, as Douglas Jerrold.

RUFUS WILMOT GRISWOLD

1815–1857

Rufus Wilmot Griswold was born on February 15, 1815, in Rutland County, Vermont, one of fourteen children of a poor farmer. At the age of fifteen he began what was to become a lifelong career as a journalist, working in a newspaper office in Albany, New York. Although little is known about the next few years of his life, it is generally believed that he worked as an itinerant printer in New York state and later was a sailor. In 1837 he married Caroline Searles in New York City and about this time also obtained a license as a Baptist minister. Although he was never apparently given a regular church assignment, he preached often and was generally addressed as a clergyman.

For several years Griswold worked for newspapers in Vermont, New York City, and Philadelphia, espousing in particular his opposition to imprisonment for debt and to capital punishment. In New York he helped establish a library in the city prison.

Griswold appears to have discovered his life's cause following his introduction to Edgar Allan Poe in 1842. For the next fifteen years he devoted himself tirelessly to increasing public recognition of and esteem for American authors. His anthology, *The Poets and Poetry of America* (1842), was issued in numerous editions during the nineteenth century. For a time he was assistant editor of *Graham's Magazine*, succeeding Poe in that post. His numerous publications included *The Poets and Poetry of England in the Nineteenth Century* (1844); *The Prose Works of John Milton* (2 vols.; 1845, 1847), the first American edition of Milton's prose; *The Prose Writers of America* (1847); and *The Female Poets of America* (1848).

Griswold's increasing wealth and prestige led him to be courted by a host of minor writers, many of whom became his protégés. Over the years he had several encounters with Poe and apparently treated him kindly. Upon Poe's death, however, in 1849, Griswold wrote a harsh obituary for the New York *Daily Tribune*, signing it "Ludwig." Poe's friends were outraged, and even more so when they discovered that Poe had appointed Griswold as his literary executor. In an attempt to justify himself, the proud Griswold collected as much scandal about Poe as he could, much of it erroneous, and published it as a memoir in the *International Monthly Magazine* for October 1850; it was later included in Volume III of Griswold's edition of *The Works of the Late Edgar Allan Poe*. Griswold further outraged Poe's defenders by inserting in two of Poe's letters that he published false passages that complimented his own work.

Griswold's last years were undoubtedly miserable. He was plagued by illness and domestic troubles—married twice following the death of his first wife, he was hounded by his enemies, who tried to have his divorce from his second wife declared invalid—but he continued to write. He served as editor of the *International Monthly Magazine* and the *Illustrated News*, and during a recurrence of chronic tuberculosis produced his most substantial work, *The Republican Court, or American Society in the Days of Washington* (1855; rev. 1864). One of his last publications was his notorious, damaging review in the February 13, 1856, edition of the *New York Herald* of the Duyckincks' *Cyclopaedia of American Literature*, in which he attempted to gain revenge on his enemies for a final time.

Griswold died at his home in New York on August 27, 1857.

General

But stay, here comes Tityrus Griswold, and leads on
The flocks whom he first plucks alive, and then feeds on,—
A loud-cackling swarm, in whose feathers warm-drest,
He goes for as perfect a—swan as the rest.
—JAMES RUSSELL LOWELL, A *Fable for Critics*,
1848

If any one deserves a place and an honorable mention in these pages, it is Rufus Wilmot Griswold, not only for his learning and literary achievements, which will place him on the level of many of our best authors, but because he has done more than any other man to make American writers known and honored both at home and abroad.—CHARLES D. CLEVELAND, "Rufus Wilmot Griswold," A *Compendium of American Literature*, 1859, p. 690

Works

THE POETS AND POETRY OF AMERICA

The work before us is indeed so vast an improvement upon those of a similar character which have preceded it, that we do its author some wrong in classing all together. Having explained, somewhat minutely, our views of the proper mode of compilation, and of the general aims of the species of book in question, it but remains to say that these views have been very nearly fulfilled in the *Poets and Poetry of America*, while altogether unsatisfied by the earlier publications.

The volume opens with a preface, which, with some little supererogation, is addressed "To the Reader;" inducing very naturally the query, whether the whole book is not addressed to the same individual. In this preface, which is remarkably well written and strictly to the purpose, the author thus evinces a just comprehension of the nature and objects of true poesy:

"He who looks on Lake George, or sees the sun rise on Mackinaw, or listens to the grand music of a storm, is divested, certainly for a time, of a portion of the alloy of his nature. The elements of power in all sublime sights and heavenly harmonies, should live in the poet's song, to which they can be transferred only by him who possesses the creative faculty. The sense of beauty, next to the miraculous divine suasion, is the means through which the human character is purified and elevated. *The creation of beauty, the manifestation of the real by the ideal, 'in words that move in metrical array,' is poetry.*"

The italics are our own; and we quote the passage because it embodies the *sole true* definition of what has been a thousand times erroneously defined.

The earliest specimens of poetry presented in the body of the work, are from the writings of Philip Freneau, "one of those worthies who, both with lyre and sword, aided in the achievement of our independence." But, in a volume professing to treat, generally, of the *Poets and Poetry of America*, some mention of those who versified before Freneau, would of course, be considered desirable. Mr. Griswold has included, therefore, most of our earlier votaries of the Muse, with many specimens of their powers, in an exceedingly valuable "Historical Introduction;" his design being to exhibit as well "*the progress* as the condition of poetry in the United States." ⟨. . .⟩

Of the general plan and execution of the work we have already expressed the fullest approbation. We know no one in America who could, or *who would*, have performed the task here undertaken, at once so well in accordance with the judgment of the critical, and so much to the satisfaction of the public. The labors, the embarrassments, the great difficulties of the achievement are not easily estimated by those before the scenes.

The writer of this article, in saying that, individually, he disagrees with many of the opinions expressed by Mr. Griswold, is merely suggesting what, in itself, would have been obvious without the suggestion. It rarely happens that any two persons thoroughly agree upon any one point. It would be mere madness to imagine that any two could coincide in every point of a case where exists a multiplicity of opinions upon a multiplicity of points. There is no one who, reading the volume before us, will not in a thousand instances, be tempted to throw it aside, because its prejudices and partialities are, in a thousand instances, altogether at war with his own. But when so tempted, he should bear in mind, that had the work been that of Aristarchus himself, the discrepancies of opinion would still have startled him and vexed him as now.

We disagree then, with Mr. Griswold in *many* of his critical estimates; although in general, we are proud to find his decisions our own. He has omitted from the body of his book, some one or two whom we should have been tempted to introduce. On the other hand, he has scarcely made us amends by introducing some one or two dozen whom we should have treated with contempt. We might complain too of a prepossession, evidently unperceived by himself, for the writers of New England. We might hint also, that in two or three cases, he has rendered himself liable to the charge of personal partiality; it is often so *very* difficult a thing to keep separate in the mind's eye, our conceptions of the poetry of a friend, from our impressions of his good fellowship and our recollections of the flavor of his wine.

But having said thus much in the way of fault-finding, we have said all. The book should be regarded as *the most important addition which our literature has for many years received*. It fills a void which should have been long ago supplied. It is written with judgment, with dignity and candor. Steering with a dexterity not to be sufficiently admired, between the Scylla of Prejudice on the one hand, and the Charybdis of Conscience on the other, Mr. Griswold in the *Poets and Poetry of America*, has entitled himself to the thanks of his countrymen, while showing himself a man of taste, talent, *and tact*.—EDGAR ALLAN POE, "Rufus W. Griswold" (1842), *Essays and Reviews*, ed. G. R. Thompson, 1984, pp. 553–56

This large and well-printed volume has been domesticated on our table for a long time, and although not publicly noticed, has not been forgotten. A review of it has held, for many months, a prominent place among our deferred projects and virtuous intentions. The book, however, has not thought proper to await our judgment before it commenced its tour of the country, but has quietly travelled through many States and four editions, and now returns our glance with all the careless impertinence inspired by success. That fickle-minded monster, called "the reading public," which sometimes buys and praises before it receives its cue from the reviewer, has taken the work under its own patronage, and spread before it the broad shield of its favor, as a protection against the critical knife. We hope, nevertheless, to be able to give it a sly thrust, here and there, in places where it is still vulnerable.

Mr. Griswold has prefixed to his book an eloquent, hopeful, and extenuating preface. This is followed by a lively and learned historical introduction, displaying much research, devoted to a consideration of the defects and meagreness of American poetry during the Colonial period. He has disturbed the dust which had mercifully gathered around antiquated doggerel and venerable bathos, with no reverential fingers; and his good taste has not been choked or blinded by the cloud he has raised. The common fault of antiquaries, that of deeming puerility and meanness invaluable because they happen to be scarce and old, and of attempting to link some deep meaning to what is simply bombast, affectation, or nonsense, he has avoided with commendable diligence. He makes no demand on our charity, in favor of some poetaster, for whom he may have imbibed a strange affection. He does not estimate the value of his antiquarian spoils by the labor and money expended in their acquisition. He has emerged from his resurrectionist delvings in the grave-yards of rhyme, without confounding moral distinctions, vitiating his taste, or becoming imbued with any malevolent designs against good composition or public patience.

The series of selections and biographies begins with Freneau, and ends with the Davidsons. Between these, Mr. Griswold has contrived to press into the nominal service of the Muses no less than eighty-eight persons, all of whom, it can be proved by indisputable evidence, did, at various periods, and inspired by different motives, exhibit their ideas, or their lack of ideas, in a metrical form. The editor is well aware, that a strict definition of poetry would shut out many whom he has admitted. Much of the verse in his collection is not "the creation of new beauty, the manifestation of the real by the ideal, in 'words that move in metrical array.'" It is rather commonplace, jingling its bells at certain fixed pauses in its smooth or rugged march. To versify sermons is not to create beauty; nor can good morality be taken in apology for bad poetry. A morbid and uneasy sensibility may give a certain swell and grandness to diction without the aid of imagination. A young gentleman, while groaning beneath some fancied woes, may ask for public commiseration in the husky utterance of grating rhyme, and yet display no depth and intensity of feeling. We think, therefore, that Mr. Griswold has "been too liberal of his aqueous mixture" in his selections. Some of the authors whom he has included in the list are unworthy of the honor of having their feebleness thrust into notice. From others of more pretensions he has copied too unsparingly. A few of his critical notices reflect more credit upon his benevolence than his taste. He seems to have fixed the price of admittance low, in order, as the show-bills say, that the public might be more generally accommodated. King James the First debased the ancient order of knighthood, by laying his sword on the shoulder of every pander or buffoon who recommended himself by the fulness of his purse, the readiness of his jests, or the pliancy of his conscience. Editors should keep this fact in mind, and extract from it the warning and admonition it is so eminently calculated to suggest.

Although we deem Mr. Griswold deserving of a little gentle correction for his literary beneficence, we are not insensible to his merits. The work before us must have demanded the labor of years. Those portions which are intrinsically the least valuable undoubtedly cost the editor the most toil, and afforded him the least gratification. To hunt out mediocrity and feebleness, and append correct dates to their forgotten effusions, is an exercise of philanthropy which is likely to be little appreciated; and yet, in many instances, it was necessary, in order to give a fair reflection of the poetical spirit of the country and the time. In the editor's wanderings in some of the secluded lanes of letters, he has rescued from oblivion many poems of considerable value. He has been compelled to search for most of his facts in places only accessible by great exertion and perseverance. Many of the poets from whom he has made selections have never published editions of their writings, and had never before been honored with biographies.

He might easily have written better poems than some which he must have expended much time and labor in obtaining. The vanities and jealousies of his band of authors he was compelled to take into consideration, and to forbear giving them unnecessary offence. Among all the fierce enmities which a person may provoke by sincerely expressing his opinions, we know of none more dangerous than that which follows from informing a rhyming scribbler, that his fame will not equal his ambition, or from omitting to notice him at all out of commiseration for his well-meaning stupidities. We think, therefore, that Mr. Griswold has succeeded as well in his book, as the nature of the case admitted; that his patient research and general correctness of taste are worthy of praise; that his difficulties and temptations would have extenuated far graver errors than he has committed; and that his volume well deserves the approbation it has received.—EDWIN P. WHIPPLE, "Griswold's *Poets and Poetry of America*," *North American Review*, Jan. 1844, pp. 1–3

Of each of these ⟨poets⟩ we have a biographical sketch,—brief and skeleton-wise for the recent and still living, sufficiently minute to satisfy curiosity for the earlier names on the list. In these sketches we find reason to admire the author's impartiality and kindness. We have been unable to find a single instance in which he has suffered any of the usual grounds of prejudice to warp his judgment or to scant his eulogy, and where it has been his duty to refer to obliquities of temper and conduct, he has done so with singular delicacy and gentleness.—ANDREW P. PEABODY, "American Poetry," *North American Review*, Jan. 1856, pp. 236–37

Rufus Wilmot Griswold, when he was thus publicly announced as the new editor of *Graham's* in May, 1842, was a young man of twenty-seven years, who had some time before left the Baptist ministry for the more attractive walks of literature. He had published both sermons and songs, and had served on several newspapers in Boston, New York, and Philadelphia; latterly he had been engaged in compiling his popular volume, *The Poets and Poetry of America*,—that *Hic Jacet* of American mediocrities of the first generation.—GEORGE E. WOODBERRY, *Edgar Allan Poe*, 1885, p. 172

I have just been looking over the headstones in Mr. Griswold's cemetery, entitled *The Poets and Poetry of America*. In that venerable receptacle, just completing its half century of existence—for the date of the edition before me is 1842—I find the names of John Greenleaf Whittier and Oliver Wendell Holmes next each other, in their due order, as they should be. All around are the names of the dead—too often of forgotten dead.—OLIVER WENDELL HOLMES, Letter to John Greenleaf Whittier (1891), cited in Samuel T. Pickard, *Life and Letters of John Greenleaf Whittier*, 1895, Vol. 2, p. 756

PROSE WRITERS OF AMERICA

No man is more deserving of the public gratitude than he who teaches a nation to respect itself. A proper confidence in one's own standards, in one's own judgment, and in one's own abilities, is so important for the full development of intellectual capacity, and social dignity and happiness, and moral power, that it ought to be considered a duty of every one who holds the place of a guide or teacher to implant and cultivate it in the subjects of his care, whether communities or individuals. Personal or national vanity, indeed, may become even bloated upon the contempt and ridicule of the rest of the world; but an honorable self-dependence, a manly self-reliance, can be inspired only by contemplating, as external, the monuments of one's own character and ability, or by seeing that others regard them with esteem and deference and admiration. For either purpose, of enabling the literary genius of the country to know itself, objectively, or of causing other countries to receive the complete impression of its power, we hold such efforts as have been made by Mr. Griswold to be of great value. He has done a useful work, and he has done it well. The book now before us is more than respectable; it is executed ably, and in many parts brilliantly. In some respects it is an extraordinary work; such as few men in America, perhaps, besides its author, could have produced, and he only after years of sedulous investigation, and under many advantages of circumstance or accident. He has long shown himself to be of Cicero's mind: "*Mihi quidem nulli satis erudito videntur, quibus nostra ignota sunt.*" The distribution of the various writers into their classes, and the selection of representatives of each class or type, exhibit much skill. Many passages present fine specimens of acute, original and just criticism, eloquently delivered. We differ from Mr. Griswold sometimes, but never without a respect for his judgment, and never without feeling that we owe it to the public in all cases to give a reason why we do not assent to the conclusions of so candid and discriminating a judge. We acknowledge Mr. Griswold to be a good critic; and if his personal friends or others claim for him the title of a writer of first-rate merit, we make no other hesitation than that we have not yet seen quite enough of original matter from his pen. "The strength of the eagle," says Mr. Hallam, "is to be measured, not only by the height of his place, but by the time that he continues on the wing." If the editor of *The Prose Writers* will produce an entire volume on some continuous subject, in the same style of fearless and acute discussion, and of graceful and elegant composition, which is displayed in some of the paragraphs here—which we do not question his ability to do—we shall readily admit his right to take a place among the foremost authors of the country. The present volume we have read with constant interest and frequent admiration. We have derived more instruction from it than it would be becoming in a reviewer to admit. The reader is here brought for a time into society with the greatest and most accomplished of the minds of this country:

> Et varias audit voces fruiturque deorum
> Colloquio.

It is much to admit that we pass to the comments of the author without any very sensible diminution of interest or respect. —HORACE BINNEY WALLACE, "Literary Criticisms," *Literary Criticisms and Other Papers*, 1846, pp. 3–4

MEMOIR OF POE

In September 1850, the third volume of Poe's works when published was found to be prefaced by the anxiously looked-for *Memoir*—the "labour of love" of Rufus Griswold. The secret of the man's disinterested aid was soon manifest; never before had so slanderous a collection of falsehoods and libels—so calumnious a product of envy, hatred, and malice—been offered to the public as this *Memoir* of an ill-fated child of genius. The distress and indignation of Mrs. Clemm were intense, and she continually, when alluding to Griswold, writes of him as "that villain." Poe's literary friends gathered round her and promised to expose and refute the slanderous fabrications. "I have received a kind letter from that noble fellow, Graham," she writes at this period, "telling me to *remain quiet*, that he had a host of my Eddie's friends prepared to do him justice, and that he intends to devote nearly half of the December number to the memory and defence of my injured Eddie."

Mr. Graham, and many others who had been personally acquainted with Poe, took up cudgels in his defence, but, as Griswold's *Memoir* prefaced the poet's works, and all refutations and objections were published in the ephemeral pages of periodicals, until 1874 this veritable *scandalum magnatum* remained unexpunged.—JOHN H. INGRAM, *Edgar Allan Poe: His Life, Letters and Opinions*, 1880, Vol. 2, pp. 242–43

Griswold never received a cent for his labors. Poe named him as his literary executor, shortly before he died, although they had quarreled not long before. Griswold's labor was no joke. Few men would have undertaken it with no hope of reward. It is fashionable now-a-days to throw mud at him. Knowing as I did, both of the men, and knowing also how assiduously Griswold labored to say everything he could in the biography in Poe's favor, it is very annoying to read these things. The matter of the biography was all read over to me, talked and discussed before printing, and I *know* he did his best to 'set down naught in malice.' He was obliged, as he thought, to state the facts in all cases, and he did state them, favorably as he could to Poe. I *know* he tried to do so. Now he is accused everywhere by people who know nothing about it, of vilely slandering Poe. I had a better opportunity than anyone else to know all about it, and I know he did not. If I had not entirely rusted out of the use of the pen, I should like to write a magazine article on Griswold and Poe, and would give these young scribblers 'Jesse,' who are so fond of throwing mud at Griswold and lauding Poe.—J. S. REDFIELD, cited in James Cephas Derby, *Fifty Years among Authors, Books and Publishers*, 1884, pp. 587–88

Dr. Griswold was always a little "queer," and I used to scold and reprove him for it. He had got himself into great trouble by his remarks on Edgar A. Poe. Mr. Kimball and others, who knew the Doctor, believed, as I do, that there was no deliberate evil or envy in those remarks. Poe's best friends told severe stories of him in those days—*me ipso teste*—and Griswold, naught extenuating and setting down naught in malice, wrote incautiously more than he should. These are the words of another than I. But when Griswold was attacked, then he became savage. One day I found in his desk, which he had committed to me, a great number of further material collected to Poe's discredit. I burnt it all up at once, and told the Doctor what I had done, and scolded him well into the bargain. He took it all very amiably. There was also much more matter to other men's discredit—*ascensionem expectans*—awaiting publication, all of which I burned. It was the result of long research, and evidently formed the material for a book. Had it ever been published, it would have made Rome howl! But, as I said, I was angry, and I knew it would injure Dr. Griswold more than anybody. It is a pity that I had not always had the Doctor in hand—though I must here again repeat that, as regards Poe, he is, in my opinion, not so much to blame as a score of writers have made out. The tales, which were certainly most authentic, or at least apparently so, during the life of the latter, among his best friends regarding him, were, to say the least, discreditable, albeit that is no excuse whatever for publishing them.—CHARLES GODFREY LELAND, *Memoirs*, 1893, pp. 201–2

No piece of biography in the annals of literature has so unenviable a reputation as that memoir which Dr. Rufus W. Griswold, acting as Poe's literary executor, prefixed to the first complete edition of his works. Its authenticity has been attacked from the time of its appearance, and no words of objurgation have been too harsh to characterize the man who penned it; at the same time very little of its substance has ever been invalidated. The papers on which it was based passed into the hands of Griswold's own executor, and have never been seen by any of Poe's later biographers. They have recently come, by inheritance, into the possession of Griswold's son, William M. Griswold of Cambridge, Mass., by whose permission the following account of them, with extracts, is given, in anticipation of their publication in full under his own editorship.

⟨. . .⟩ In writing a biography of Poe some years ago, the present writer had occasion to investigate the charges made against Griswold. The result was a conviction that the documents he quoted were genuine, and that the impression he gave of Poe's character and career was just, while his errors were due to Poe's own falsehoods. The question of Griswold's discretion in his memoir is governed by the fact that Poe's defects and troubles were notorious at the time, and could not be concealed; the question of Griswold's motives is more difficult, but is now more easily to be judged. It is also fair to Griswold to add that the characterization he gave is that which has uniformly prevailed in tradition in the best informed literary circles in this country.

As will be seen, these papers fully vindicate Griswold's veracity in essentials.—GEORGE E. WOODBERRY, "Poe in the South," *Century Magazine*, Aug. 1894, pp. 572–73

HENRY HALLAM

1777–1859

Henry Hallam was born at Windsor, Berkshire, on July 9, 1777. Educated at Eton and at Christ Church, Oxford, he was called to the bar in 1799. He inherited an estate in Lincolnshire in 1812 and, after securing a sinecure as commissioner of stamps, was able to devote the remainder of his life to historical writing.

Hallam's first important work was *The View of the State of Europe during the Middle Ages* (1818), in which he traces the history of France, Italy, Spain, Germany, and the Greek and Saracen empires, and describes in detail the feudal and ecclesiastical systems and the free political system of England. His *Constitutional History of England* (1827) describes the period from Henry VII's accession up to the rule of George III. Hallam's other major work is *Introduction to the Literature of Europe during the 15th, 16th and 17th Centuries* (1837–39).

Throughout his life Hallam was an ardent Whig and an outspoken advocate of the abolition of the slave trade. His son, Arthur Henry Hallam, who died in 1833, was a close friend of Tennyson and the subject of his *In Memoriam*.

Henry Hallam died at Penshurst, Kent, on January 21, 1859.

Personal

I had a long visit this morning from Hallam, whom I never saw before, because he was not in London, either in 1819 or 1835, when I was here. It gratified me very much. He is such a man as I should have desired to find him; a little sensitive and nervous, perhaps, but dignified, quiet, and wishing to please. Before he came, he had taken pains to ascertain that there was a vacant place at the Athenæum Club, where only twelve strangers are permitted at a time, and offered it to me; but though this was quite an agreeable distinction, I declined it, since, being here with my family, I care nothing about the club houses. But this is good English hospitality, and a fair specimen of it.

Mr. Hallam is, I suppose, about sixty years old, gray-headed, hesitates a little in his speech, is lame, and has a shy manner, which makes him blush, frequently, when he expresses as decided an opinion as his temperament constantly leads him to entertain. Except his lameness, he has a fine, dignified person, and talked pleasantly, with that air of kindness which is always so welcome to a stranger.—GEORGE TICKNOR, *Journal* (March 24, 1838), *Life, Letters, and Journals of George Ticknor*, ed. Anna Ticknor, 1876, Vol. 2, pp. 144–45

The same forenoon Mackintosh came to me by appointment to go with me to Mr. Hallam's, who had previously expressed a wish that I should call. The great historian is long past the "middle ages" now. He is paralysed in the right leg, the right arm, and slightly in the tongue. His face is large, regularly handsome, ruddy, fresh, and very good-humoured. He received me with great cordiality, and we had half an hour's talk. He begged me to leave my address, and I suppose he means to invite me to something or other, for I believe he occasionally entertains his friends. His mind does not seem essentially dimmed, and there is nothing senile in his aspect, crippled as he is. He is a wreck, but he has not sunk head downwards, as you sometimes see, which is the most melancholy termination to the voyage. His mind seems bright and his spirits seem light.—JOHN LOTHROP MOTLEY, Letter to His Wife (June 6, 1858), *Correspondence*, ed. George William Curtis, 1889, Vol. 1, pp. 251–52

He was the representative, in a time of much crudeness, of the old scholar-like race of authors, while keeping up with the foremost men and interests of his time. He was an honorable gentleman, disinterested alike in regard to money and to fame, with a youthful innocence and earnestness unimpaired in old age, and a manly spirit of justice and independence, which made him an object of respect as much in his weakest as in his highest moments. It will not be pretended anywhere that he was not a gossip; but his coterie was the most gossiping perhaps in London; and in Hallam's gossip there was no ill-nature, though sometimes a good deal of imprudence, which came curiously from a man who was always testifying on behalf of prudence. It would be amusing to know what he was as a courtier. He was one of the two or three literary persons who were invited to the Palace in the early days of the reign; and the question was whether that remarkable notice was owing, like the royal notice of Rogers, to Mr. Hallam's knowledge of Art; or to his intimacy with the Queen's earliest and most favored advisers; or to his being a man of large fortune—independent of literature while illustrated by it. However that may be, we know what he was to us—a man who represented a fine phase of the Literary Life, and who was faithful to Literature, its champion, its worshipper, and its ornament, throughout a half-century whose peculiar influences justified an apprehension that such a man and mode of life might appear among us no more. His name is thus fraught with associations which will last as long as his books; and that they will be long-lived was years ago settled by the acclamation of the wise.—HARRIET MARTINEAU, "Henry Hallam" (1859), *Biographical Sketches*, 1869, pp. 84–85

General

"Do you know Hallam? (said Byron.) Of course I need not ask you if you have read his *Middle Ages*. it is an admirable work, full of research, and does Hallam honour. I know no one capable of having written it except him; for, admitting that a writer could be found who could bring to the task his knowledge and talents, it would be difficult to find one who united to these his research, patience, and perspicuity of style. The reflections of Hallam are at once just and profound—his language well chosen and impressive. I remember (continued Byron) being struck by a passage, where, touching on the Venetians, he writes—'Too blind to avert danger, too cowardly to withstand it, the most ancient government of Europe made not an instant's resistance: the peasants of Underwald died upon their mountains—the nobles of Venice clung only to their lives.' This is the style in which history ought to be written, if it is wished to impress it on the memory; and I found myself, on my first perusal of the *Middle Ages*, repeating aloud many such passages as the one I have cited, they struck my fancy so much."—MARGUERITE, COUNTESS OF BLESSINGTON, *Conversations of Lord Byron*, 1834

⟨. . .⟩ the extreme austerity of Mr. Hallam takes away something from the pleasure of reading his learned, eloquent, and judicious writings. He is a judge, but a hanging judge, the Page or Buller of the High Court of Literary Justice. His black cap is in constant requisition. In the long calendar of those whom he has tried, there is hardly one who has not, in spite of evidence to character and recommendations to mercy, been sentenced and left for execution.—THOMAS BABINGTON MACAULAY, "Sir James Mackintosh" (1835), *Critical, Historical, and Miscellaneous Essays*, 1860, Vol. 3, p. 259

In point of learning, culture, calmness, and the command of the powers he has, Hallam, of course, excels Hazlitt, even as a bust is much smoother than a man's head; but he is altogether destitute of that fine instinctive sense of poetic beauty which was in Hazlitt's mind, and of that eloquent, fervid, and fearless expression of it which came, like inspiration, into Hazlitt's pen. The "gods have not made him poetical;" and when he talks about poetry, you are reminded of a blind man discoursing on the rainbow. He has far too much tact and knowledge to commit any gross blunder—nay, the bust seems often half-alive, but it never becomes more. You never feel that this man, who talks so ably about politics, and evidence, and international law, has a "native and indefeasible right" to speak to you about poetry. The power of criticising it is as completely

denied him as is a sixth sense; and worst, he is not conscious of the want.—GEORGE GILFILLAN, "Hazlitt and Hallam," *A Third Gallery of Portraits*, 1854, p. 182

The truth about Hallam seems to have been that books were more to him than men, and literature than life. The pulse of human feeling beats faintly in his writings, through which the reader moves as in a shadowy intellectual world inhabited by the departed actors of a real, indeed, but unresuscitated past. We feel that this is the land of shades, and the ghost of history, which needs to be clothed upon with flesh and blood. Hallam's works are a capital demonstration of the thesis that imagination is indispensable to the writing of history, whether social or political. It was the intellectual framework of things that interested him: action, passion, the busy world of moving humanity, for these he had no eye, or no reconstructive talent. The warmth, colour, and animation of the brisk humorous drama of life are not suggested on his canvas, and it would be difficult, perhaps, to recall a single scene or single character of which he speaks in words that betray a keen personal pleasure, sympathy, or aversion. With one he deals as with another, much as the geometrician deals with his cubes and squares. Impartial, let it be freely granted, the historian must be, but there are occasions upon which, as the representative of universal human feeling, it is possible, nay, fitting, that he speak his mind, and with the unmistakable emphasis of emotion. Hallam never loses his measured accent, never frees his soul in a passionate outburst, and the note of inspired conviction that rings in poetry, that rings at times also in great history, is missing. The unwearying self-suppression of the writer becomes a source of weariness to the reader. Yet, it must be said, the rigidity of his method, the colourlessness of his style, are in great measure justified by his choice of subjects, and may even be counted to him for virtues. Calm, strictly judicial in temper, accurately and widely learned, dignified, almost stately, and that despite occasional harshness in his diction, Hallam pronounces judgments in perhaps the most convincing tones of any English author.

Though a Whig, his range of political speculation was narrow, nor beyond his words do we discern the open heavens and their free horizons of thought; but as an exponent of political principles he never forfeits our respect, and if he cannot inspire, may be trusted not to mislead us.

Probably the *Constitutional History* is Hallam's greatest work; yet in the *Introduction to the Literature of Europe*, we may occasionally enjoy a singular and refreshing spectacle—gleams of real enthusiasm struck by the steel of poetic genius from the flint of the critic's coldly impartial mind.

Writing, as he did, before it was thought necessary to combine entertainment with instruction, Hallam addressed himself exclusively to the student, and the student comes in time to entertain an affection for an author who is always sanely master of himself and of his subject. Among the critics of to-day are some light-armed skirmishers who may win and keep the public favour for an hour; but when one has learned how infinitely, inexpressibly easier it is to be clever than to be wise, one is more than compensated for the absence of superficial brilliance of conceit or phrase by sureness of step, reasonableness of estimate, and grave simplicity of style. Far indeed from being a born master of language, far below the great in almost all the distinctive qualities of greatness, he has fairly earned a place among enduring names; he is, and will remain, our judicious Hallam.—W. MACNEILE DIXON, "Henry Hallam," *English Prose*, ed. Henry Craik, 1896, Vol. 5, pp. 185–87

Works

THE CONSTITUTIONAL HISTORY OF ENGLAND

To pursue this *Constitutional History* through all its misrepresentations, and the whole sophistry of its special pleading, would require a work of equal bulk. Enough has been done to exhibit its design and character; *ex pede;*—Mr. Hallam is no Hercules,—and the foot is a cloven one.

It is not necessary for us to dwell upon the hostility to the principle of hereditary succession, which is, on every occasion, displayed by this historian; nor to adduce further proofs of the ill-will with which he regards the ecclesiastical part of our constitution; and which he manifests with so much animosity, and so little prudence, that he must have calculated very largely upon the malevolence and the ignorance of his readers. Nor need we bring forward more examples of the disposition which seems to delight in detracting from the Good and the Great; nor of opinions which tend to the subversion of all legitimate authority, and which in their consequences would place all government upon Hobbes's foundation, leaving it no other support than military force. The disagreeable temper of the book would alone subtract much from the pleasure to be derived from the general ability which it displays, and the even tenour of its plain, strong, perspicuous style. Well, indeed, would it be if the spirit were as English as the language: well, even, if want of generosity, want of candour, and want of feeling were its worst faults. But in no English writer who makes the slightest pretensions to morality and religion, have we seen the abominable doctrine so openly maintained, that the end justifies the means, and that conspiracy, treason, and rebellion, are to be treated as questions of expediency, laudable if they succeed, and only imprudent if they are undertaken without a sufficient likelihood of success!—

Unto thee,
Let thine own times like an old story be,

is the advice which Donne gives to him who would derive wisdom from the course of passing events. A writer of contemporary history could take no better motto. Mr. Hallam has proceeded upon a system precisely the reverse of this; and carried into the history of the past, not merely the maxims of his own age, as infallible laws by which all former actions are to be tried, but the spirit and the feeling of the party to which he has attached himself, its acrimony and its arrogance, its injustice and its ill-temper.—ROBERT SOUTHEY, "Hallam's *Constitutional History of England*," *Quarterly Review*, Jan. 1828, pp. 259–60

Mr. Hallam is, on the whole, far better qualified than any other writer of our time for the office which he has undertaken. He has great industry and great acuteness. His knowledge is extensive, various, and profound. His mind is equally distinguished by the amplitude of its grasp, and by the delicacy of its tact. His speculations have none of that vagueness which is the common fault of political philosophy. On the contrary, they are strikingly practical, and teach us not only the general rule, but the mode of applying it to solve particular cases. In this respect they often remind us of the *Discourses* of Machiavelli.

The style is sometimes open to the charge of harshness. We have also here and there remarked a little of that unpleasant trick, which Gibbon brought into fashion, the trick, we mean, of telling a story by implication and allusion. Mr. Hallam, however, has an excuse which Gibbon had not. His work is designed for readers who are already acquainted with the ordinary books on English history, and who can therefore unriddle these little enigmas without difficulty. The manner of

the book is, on the whole, not unworthy of the matter. The language, even where most faulty, is weighty and massive, and indicates strong sense in every line. It often rises to an eloquence, not florid or impassioned, but high, grave, and sober; such as would become a state paper, or a judgment delivered by a great magistrate, a Somers or a D'Aguesseau.

In this respect the character of Mr. Hallam's mind corresponds strikingly with that of his style. His work is eminently judicial. Its whole spirit is that of the bench, not that of the bar. He sums up with a calm, steady impartiality, turning neither to the right nor to the left, glossing over nothing, exaggerating nothing, while the advocates on both sides are alternately biting their lips to hear their conflicting misstatements and sophisms exposed. On a general survey, we do not scruple to pronounce the *Constitutional History* the most impartial book that we ever read.—THOMAS BABINGTON MACAULAY, "Hallam" (1828), *Critical, Historical, and Miscellaneous Essays*, 1860, Vol. 1, pp. 435–36

Mr. Hallam's *Constitutional History of England* I must earnestly recommend, for it is a work of great research, great ability, great impartiality, often of very manly eloquence; the work of an enlightened lawyer, an accomplished scholar, and a steady assertor of the best interests of mankind. It is a source of great satisfaction to me, that such a work exists, for every page is full of statements and opinions on every topic and character of consequence since the reign of Henry the Seventh; and these sentiments and opinions are so learned and well reasoned, that I am quite gratified to think, that the student can now never want a guide and an instructor, worthy to conduct and counsel him in his constitutional inquiries. Mr. Hallam is indeed a stern and severe critic, and the student may be allowed to love and honor many of our patriots, statesmen, and divines, in a more warm and unqualified manner, than does Mr. Hallam; but the perfect calmness of Mr. Hallam's temperament, makes his standard of moral and political virtue high, and the fitter on that account to be presented to youthful minds.

There are objectionable passages and even strange passages, more particularly in the notes; but they are of no consequence in a work of so vast a range, and of so much merit; and Mr. Hallam may have given offence, which could never have been his intention, to some good men, to whom their establishments are naturally so dear; but I see not how this was to be avoided, if he was to render equal justice to all persons and parties, all sects and churches in their turn; and if he was to do his duty, as he has nobly done, to the civil and religious liberties of his country.—WILLIAM SMYTH, *Lectures on Modern History*, 1840, Note to Lecture 6

INTRODUCTION TO THE LITERATURE OF EUROPE

I have read Hallam's book, which is dry, meagre, and ill written, with a few misplaced patches of laboured rhetoric. So far from understanding any one *subject* well, he does not seem to understand any one book well. His text is a mere digest of compilations and biographical dictionaries. I believe that he knows a little German, for a governess who lived in his family went afterwards to Lady ——, who told me that Hallam had learnt of her. Probably he spells through a book by the help of a dictionary with about the same success that he translates 'das Bücherwesen,' 'the being of books.' It must be confessed that charlatanerie is marvellously successful. I do not think Hallam had seen my essay on the Romance languages till after his lucubrations on the subject had been printed; for he spoke to me about it at the end of last London season, when, I believe, most of his book was through the press.—SIR GEORGE CORNE-WALL LEWIS, Letter to E. W. Head (June 2, 1837), *Letters*, ed. Sir Gilbert Frankland Lewis, 1870, p. 80

I have been good for nothing for a week, and have been looking for amusement to a book which deserves serious study, Hallam's *Literature of the Middle Ages*. I am glad to find in it more unction than in his former writings—more to please as well as instruct. I am much pleased with his view of Luther, the hardest character, perhaps, to be understood in modern time, not from any inherent difficulty, but from the prejudices and passions awakened by his name.—WILLIAM ELLERY CHANNING, Letter to Lucy Aikin (April 28, 1839), *Correspondence of William Ellery Channing and Lucy Aikin*, ed. Anna Letitia Le Breton, 1874, p. 338

The literary criticism contained in these volumes is of great merit. It is neither commonplace nor affectedly profound. So much has been written upon the poets of the sixteenth and seventeenth centuries, that it was difficult to offer any thing further, which should bear even the semblance of novelty and truth. But Mr. Hallam's remarks, even here, have all the air of freshness, which naturally invests a virgin subject, and his disquisitions upon the great Italian poets, and even upon Shakspeare and Milton, are among the most ingenious and interesting portions of the work. This task had been an easy one, if his taste had allowed him to indulge in the misty speculations and fine-spun theories, which too often form the staple of German criticism. An endless thread of this sort may be spun by any one of an ingenious and fanciful turn of mind, but it will not sustain the lightest touch of scrutiny. Naturally averse to this dreamy kind of writing, Mr. Hallam's remarks bear a strong impress of good sense and correct taste, and are adapted rather to please and convince, than to bewilder or astonish the reader. It may not appear the highest praise to say, that the criticism is sound and judicious; but so much *æsthetical* cant, formed upon foreign models, is in vogue at the present day, that it is truly refreshing to find a subdued, temperate, and unambitious tone once more adopted in the school of taste. Paying the tribute of hearty admiration to his favorite authors, our historian is still not carried away so far by his enthusiasm, as to indulge in the rash and extravagant assertions, in which some writers labor to display their sensibility, but which lead one to doubt the sincerity of the very feeling which they are designed to prove. He ventures to point out faults even in Shakspeare, and in nearly every instance to qualify praise with some censure. His carefully regulated judgment appears as much in his notices of individuals, as of books. The Boswellian disease of inordinate admiration never fastens upon him, nor, on the other hand, does he ever appear ambitious of Johnson's favorite character of "a good hater." With such characteristics, it appears, that, if Mr. Hallam is not always a brilliant companion, he is at least a safe guide. —FRANCIS BOWEN, "Hallam's *Introduction to the Literature of Europe*," *North American Review*, Jan. 1843, pp. 47–48

Mr. Hallam, a learned and elegant scholar, has written the history of European literature for three centuries,—a performance of great ambition, inasmuch as a judgment was to be attempted on every book. But his eye does not reach to the ideal standards: the verdicts are all dated from London; all new thought must be cast into the old moulds. The expansive element which creates literature is steadily denied. Plato is resisted, and his school. Hallam is uniformly polite, but with deficient sympathy; writes with resolute generosity, but is unconscious of the deep worth which lies in the mystics, and which often outvalues as a seed of power and a source of revolution all the correct writers and shining reputations of their day. He passes in silence, or dismisses with a kind of contempt, the profounder masters: a lover of ideas is not only uncongenial, but unintelligible. Hallam inspires respect by his knowledge and fidelity, by his manifest love of good books, and he lifts himself to own better than almost any the greatness of Shakspeare, and better than Johnson he appreciates Milton. But in Hallam, or in the firmer intellectual nerve of Mackintosh, one still finds the same type of English genius. It is wise and rich, but it lives on its capital. It is retrospective. How can it discern and hail the new forms that are looming up on the horizon, new and gigantic thoughts which cannot dress themselves out of any old wardrobe of the past?—RALPH WALDO EMERSON, "Literature," *English Traits*, 1856

There is Hallam's *Introduction to the Literature of Europe during the Fifteenth, Sixteenth, and Seventeenth Centuries*, a sober, sensible, learned work, but not effervescent. It is falling into disrepute, and if you ask why, you will probably be told by some young exquisite, who has never read it, that its author must have been a blockhead because he did not sufficiently admire Shakespeare's sonnets, and calls them remarkable productions, and goes so far as to wish Shakespeare had never written them. To display temper on such a subject is ridiculous. Replace Hallam, if you can, by a writer of equal learning and better judgment; but, till you have done so, the English student who wishes to get a general acquaintance with the course of European literature, will not do wrong to devote a few hours a week to the careful reading of this book, even though it does not bubble or sparkle.—AUGUSTINE BIRRELL, "Good Taste," *Scribner's Magazine*, Jan. 1895, p. 119

C. C. SMITH
From "Hallam as an Historian"

North American Review, January 1861, pp. 166–77

In the breadth and accuracy of his knowledge, indeed, which must always be regarded as the most important qualification of an historian, Mr. Hallam is scarcely surpassed by Gibbon, while in this respect he is much superior to Hume and Robertson. His text offers to us only the ripened fruits of a thoroughly cultivated mind; and his notes are immense store houses of curious and minute learning, often drawn from recondite sources, and indicating a range of previous reading seldom attempted in England, except by some laborious drudge. "I have quoted to my recollection," he says in the Preface to his latest work, and we suppose the remark is not less true of his other books, "no passage which I have not seen in its own place; though I may possibly have transcribed in some instances, for the sake of convenience, from a secondary authority." The plan of each of his works included the discussion of a great variety of topics, and though he is much better informed as to some of them than he is as to others, there are very few which he has not investigated with conscientious fidelity, or on which he has not shed much light. It is true, that some parts of his *View of the Middle Ages* have been pronounced superficial; but this is the judgment of those writers alone who were disappointed or aggrieved that greater prominence is not assigned to the topics in which they were most interested. Indeed, the extent of his researches and the copiousness of his information on these very topics have been frequently attested by writers who had made them a specialty; and since Mr. Hallam's death, a distinguished mathematician, Mr. De Morgan, has publicly borne witness to the fulness and accuracy of his history of mathematical studies during the Middle Age,—one of the subjects as to which it has sometimes been alleged that his knowledge was insufficient. On this point no higher authority could be cited; nor could a more explicit declaration be desired. "Were I to write the History of Mathematics," says Mr. De Morgan, in a letter to the London *Athenæum*, "I should certainly look on Hallam as one of the writers of authoritative opinion whom I should be glad to cite in my favor, and bound to oppose with reason when I differed from him."

This thorough and accurate acquaintance with every fact relating to the subject before him is, perhaps, the most noteworthy element in Mr. Hallam's character as an historian, though the greatest prominence is not usually assigned to it in speaking of his works. Without it he could not have secured the place among English historians which he has long maintained by universal consent; for his writings exhibit few graces of style when compared with the productions of other historians of the same rank. In this respect there can scarcely be a greater contrast than that which exists between Mr. Hallam's books and Hume's *History of England*. The latter work is marked by a notorious carelessness and by frequent misrepresentations; but it has secured a permanent place in English literature by its simple beauty of style, scarcely less than by its happy blending of general observations and philosophical reflections with the narrative. In reading Mr. Hallam's works, on the other hand, we feel entire confidence that we are under the guidance of a writer whose knowledge of his subject is ample, and who bases his statements on a personal examination of the authorities cited, while we constantly miss the transparent simplicity of Hume's unambitious style. This amplitude of knowledge, however, would be insufficient, and indeed worthless, if it were not accompanied by equal acuteness in determining the real worth of any authority, and in deciding between conflicting accounts of the same transaction; and this quality Mr. Hallam also possesses in large measure. Though he had a firm belief in the truths of religion, his mind was naturally sceptical; and he brought to the examination of all historical questions a disposition to investigate them thoroughly for himself, and a determination to take as little as possible on trust. His discussion of them shows the effect of his legal training, and is uniformly marked by great logical skill. Many of his notes afford striking illustrations of his acuteness in detecting mistakes and misrepresentations, and in settling disputed points. At the same time his mind was not by nature analytical; and while he was acute in investigating facts, his literary criticisms, though for the most part judicious, often fail to lay bare the heart of the subject. Of this defect he seems to have been fully aware; and in the Preface to his *Introduction to the Literature of Europe*, he expressly says, that he does not wish the work "to be considered as a book of reference on particular topics, in which point of view it must often appear to disadvantage,"—adding, that, "if it proves of any value, it will be as an entire and synoptical work." In one word, Mr. Hallam is to be regarded as a philosophical historian, rather than as a philosophical critic.

Closely connected with these fundamental qualities of knowledge and discrimination is a third characteristic not less obvious in any analysis of Mr. Hallam's character,—his extreme caution. We have already referred to his disinclination to quote anything at second hand, and to state any fact without reference to the original sources of information. But his caution is even more apparent when it becomes necessary for him to express an opinion on any doubtful point. Numerous illustrations of this characteristic will occur to every one who is familiar with his writings. They are found in all his works; but

we are inclined to think they are most numerous in the eighth chapter of his *View of the Middle Ages*, which treats of the early Constitutional History of England. Thus, in speaking of the origin of county representation in Parliament, he says: "Since there is no sufficient proof whereon to decide, we can only say with hesitation, that there *may* have been an instance of county representation in the fifteenth year of John." Such passages show at once the cautiousness and the candor of a writer, and are among the most convincing proofs that he is entitled to confidence when his language assumes a more positive tone.

Passing now from these qualities, which are exhibited in an equal degree perhaps by many other historians, we have to consider another class of moral and intellectual traits in respect to which Mr. Hallam has fewer rivals, and no superior. Of these the most conspicuous is his impartiality; and here his preeminence is at present undisputed. "On a general survey," says Lord Macaulay, "we do not scruple to pronounce the *Constitutional History* the most impartial book that we ever read." This strong commendation is almost equally applicable to his other works, and has been sanctioned by the concurrent testimony of nearly an entire generation of readers, though at the time of its publication the book referred to was fiercely attacked by some of the party journals. With the blindness of partisan malice, they denied that Mr. Hallam possessed even this merit; and one writer, Mr. Southey, went so far as to assert, that the author "carried into the history of the past, not merely the maxims of his own age, as infallible laws by which all former actions are to be tried, but the spirit and the feeling of the party to which he has attached himself, its acrimony and its arrogance, its injustice and its ill-temper." But this grave charge is utterly unfounded. There is not a page in either of Mr. Hallam's works which is acrimonious, arrogant, or ill-tempered; and few writers have endeavored more sedulously, or more successfully, to avoid even the appearance of injustice. His path often lies across the battlefields on which rival biographers, historians, and critics have contended with characteristic bitterness; but he never suffers himself to be drawn aside by either faction, or to become the advocate and apologist of any party. Yet he never exhibits that weak and timeserving spirit which regards with an indifferent eye virtue and vice, liberality and bigotry, the cause of popular rights and the cause of irresponsible power. "Tyranny, indeed, and injustice," he says, "will by all historians, not absolutely servile, be noted with moral reprobation"; and it is in the spirit of this declaration that all his writings are composed.

Mr. Hallam's impartiality does not proceed, therefore, from indifference as to the topics which he discusses, but from the moderation of his views, and the calmness of his judgment. Extreme opinions find little favor in his eyes. He was a Whig; but he was a Whig educated at Oxford, and this circumstance doubtless exerted a very fortunate influence on the character of his writings. Even when he expresses the strongest disapprobation of any system of policy, or pronounces the most unfavorable opinion as to the character of any individual, or any body of men, he never suffers himself to lapse into partisanship, and his language has the calmness and dignity of a judicial opinion. Unlike Mr. Carlyle, he never attempts to make a man odious by personal abuse, and in his delineation of character he uses other colors beside black and white. It is this moderation in his views—this inflexible determination to follow the narrow path between the mountain and the sea—which, as we conceive, constitutes Mr. Hallam's least questionable title to a place among the greatest historians who have written in our language. It is very easy to be a partisan: it is very hard to hold moderate opinions.

Akin to this important element in the character of a great

historian, is a modesty unfortunately as rare as it is praiseworthy. Though Mr. Hallam's information on nearly every topic is so copious, his whole tone is singularly free from pedantry and dogmatism; and, as we have already intimated, his language is never positive unless he is perfectly sure of his ground. He does not disparage other writers; nor does he boast of his own labors. He makes no pretension to a knowledge which he does not possess, and if he has occasion to cite any authority which he has not personally examined, or to refer to any fact beyond his personal observation, he never fails to mention the circumstance. Thus, when speaking of the controversy respecting the authorship of the treatise *De Imitatione Christi*, he commences an elaborate note with the declaration, "I am not prepared to state the external evidence upon this keenly debated question with sufficient precision." In quoting some observations of Mr. Panizzi on Pulci's *Morgante Maggiore*, he introduces them with the modest confession, "The following remarks on Pulci's style come from a more competent judge than myself." Of Lord Stuart of Rothsay's collection of ancient Portuguese songs, he says: "I have been favored by my noble friend the editor with the loan of a copy, though my ignorance of the language prevented me from forming an exact judgment of its contents." At the same time, it is certain from other passages that he had a sufficient knowledge of Portuguese to read portions of this very book with some degree of ease. Many other

passages of a similar character might be cited in illustration of this honorable trait; but it is needless to multiply instances of the direct manifestation of a quality which underlies all of Mr. Hallam's writings.

Only one other prominent characteristic of his works remains to be noticed. We mean their clearness of statement. On every subject which Mr. Hallam examines, either cursorily or at length, his views are free from obscurity, and are stated with precision. His materials are judiciously arranged, according to a definite and well-considered plan; his narrative is luminous; and his judgments are expressed in no ambiguous terms. In his own mind he had a clear view of his subject under all its relations; and therefore he had no difficulty in conveying a clear view of it to other minds. Occasionally, indeed, he presupposes in his readers a degree of familiarity with his subject which many of them perhaps do not possess, especially in his first two works; and in his *Introduction to the Literature of Europe* his plan is faulty in not combining in a single view all that is said of each writer under different heads. With the qualification implied in this remark, his writings cannot be justly charged with obscurity of thought or ambiguity of expression; and these defects, if they are to be regarded as such, do not affect the substantial excellence of his works. In distinctness of purpose and general clearness of statement, his books leave little to be desired.

WASHINGTON IRVING

1783–1859

Washington Irving was born in New York City on April 3, 1783, the son of a wealthy British merchant who had sided with the Americans during the Revolution. He was educated at Josiah Henderson's seminary, and in 1801 began to study law, which he was later to practice for a number of years as his brother John's partner. From 1802 until 1805 he wrote for his brother Peter's paper, *The Morning Chronicle*, and in 1804 he also made many submissions to the *Corrector*, which have been collected and published as *Washington Irving's Contributions to* The Corrector (1968; ed. Martin Roth). Between 1807 and 1808 Irving, his brother William, and his friend J. K. Paulding published, under assumed names, a series of satirical essays and poems about life in New York, collected in book form as *Salmagundi; or, The Whim-Whams and Opinions of Launcelot Langstaff, Esq. and Others* (1808). This was followed in 1809 by Irving's highly successful burlesque, *A History of New York from the Beginning of the World to the End of the Dutch Dynasty*, published under the name "Diedrich Knickerbocker."

In 1815 Irving sailed for Europe, where he was to remain until 1832. His first five years abroad were spent in Great Britain, where he became acquainted with Sir Walter Scott, Thomas Moore, Thomas Campbell, and John Murray. His experiences during this period led to a number of books containing humorous accounts of English life, beginning with *The Sketch Book*, published serially in the United States (1819–20) and in book form in England (1820). Attributed to "Geoffrey Crayon, Gent.," this volume contains most of Irving's best-known stories, including "The Christmas Dinner," "Westminster Abbey," "The Spectre Bridegroom," and two adaptations of German folk tales, "Rip Van Winkle" and "The Legend of Sleepy Hollow." It was followed in 1822 by *Bracebridge Hall*, and in 1824 by *Tales of a Traveller*.

Irving left England for France and Germany in 1820, and in 1826 went on to Spain, where he served as a diplomatic attaché between 1826 and 1829. His contact with Spanish culture inspired Irving to write one serious historical study, *The Life and Voyages of Christopher Columbus* (1828), and three anecdotal, semi-fictionalized collections of satirical sketches, *A Chronicle of the Conquest of Granada* (1829), *Voyages and Discoveries of the Companions of Columbus* (1831), and *Legends of the Alhambra* (1832). Irving moved to London in 1829, and served as a secretary to the U. S. legation (1829–32). In 1832 he returned to New York, where he was enthusiastically received as the first American author to have achieved an international reputation.

In 1835 Irving published *The Crayon Miscellany*, consisting of three volumes of sketches and stories: A *Tour on the Prairies, Abbotsford and Newstead Abbey*, and *Legends of the Conquest of Spain*. This was followed by *Astoria* (1836), an historical account of John Jacob Astor's establishment of the Pacific Fur Company, and by *The Adventures of Captain Bonneville* (1837; also known as *The Rocky Mountains*), a partially fictionalized biography of a famous fur trapper. Next came two literary biographies, of Margaret Miller Davidson (1841) and of Oliver Goldsmith (1849), and also a popularized account of the life of Mahomet (1849), as well as a chronicle of the Moslem empire, *Mahomet and His Successors* (1850). During this period Irving also served for four years as U.S. ambassador to Spain (1842–46). *Wolfert's Roost*, Irving's last collection of sketches and tales, appeared in 1855, and was followed by his last book, a five-volume *Life of George Washington* (1855–59). He spent the last years of his life at his home, Sunnyside, on the banks of the Hudson River. Irving died on November 28, 1859, and was buried at the Sleepy Hollow cemetery near his home.

Personal

He is so sensible, sound, and straightforward in his way of seeing everything, and at the same time so full of hopefulness, so simple, unaffected, true, and good, that it is a privilege to converse with him, for which one is the wiser, the happier and the better.—FRANCES ANN KEMBLE, Letter (April 10, 1833), *Records of a Girlhood*, 1878, p. 572

There is no man in the world who could have given me the heartfelt pleasure you have, by your kind note of the 13th of last month. There is no living writer, and there are very few among the dead, whose approbation I should feel so proud to earn. And with everything you have written upon my shelves, and in my thoughts, and in my heart of hearts, I may honestly and truly say so. If you could know how earnestly I write this, you would be glad to read it—as I hope you will be, faintly guessing at the warmth of the hand I autobiographically hold out to you over the broad Atlantic.

I wish I could find in your welcome letter some hint of an intention to visit England. I can't. I have held it at arm's length, and taken a bird's-eye view of it, after reading it a great many times, but there is no greater encouragement in it this way than on a microscopic inspection. I should love to go with you—as I have gone, God knows how often—into Little Britain, and Eastcheap, and Green Arbor Court, and Westminster Abbey. I should like to travel with you, outside the last of the coaches, down to Bracebridge Hall. It would make my heart glad to compare notes with you about that shabby gentleman in the oilcloth hat and red nose, who sat in the nine-cornered back parlor of the Masons' Arms; and about Robert Preston, and the tallow chandler's widow, whose sitting room is second nature to me; and about all those delightful places and people that I used to talk about and dream of in the daytime, when a very small and not over-particularly-taken-care-of boy. I have a good deal to say, too, about that dashing Alonzo de Ojeda, that you can't help being fonder of than you ought to be; and much to hear concerning Moorish legend, and poor, unhappy Boabdil. Diedrich Knickerbocker I have worn to death in my pocket, and yet I should show you his mutilated carcass with a joy past all expression.

I have been so accustomed to associate you with my pleasantest and happiest thoughts, and with my leisure hours, that I rush at once into full confidence with you, and fall, as it were naturally, and by the very laws of gravity, into your open arms. Questions come thronging to my pen as to the lips of people who meet after long hoping to do so. I don't know what to say first, or what to leave unsaid, and am constantly disposed to break off and tell you again how glad I am this moment has arrived.

My dear Washington Irving, I cannot thank you enough for your cordial and generous praise, or tell you what deep and lasting gratification it has given me. I hope to have many letters from you, and to exchange a frequent correspondence. I send this to say so. After the first two or three, I shall settle down into a connected style, and become gradually rational.

You know what the feeling is, after having written a letter, sealed it, and sent it off. I shall picture you reading this, and answering it before it has lain one night in the post office. Ten to one that before the fastest packet could reach New York I shall be writing again.—CHARLES DICKENS, Letter to Washington Irving (1841), cited in Pierre M. Irving, *The Life and Letters of Washington Irving*, 1862–63, Vol. 3, pp. 164–65

He was slighter, and more delicately organized, than I had supposed; of less than average stature, I should think; looking feeble, but with kindness beaming from every feature. He spoke almost in a whisper, with effort, his voice muffled by some obstruction. Age had treated him like a friend; borrowing somewhat, as is his wont, but lending also those gentle graces which give an inexpressible charm to the converse of wise and good old men, whose sympathies keep their hearts young and their minds open.

I could not repeat the half-hour's talk I enjoyed with him, if I would. It would be pardonable in any of us, whose boyhood had breathed the atmosphere of his delicious daydreams, to speak of the pleasure we had received from a writer whom we had so long loved unseen. It was not unnatural that he should speak with indulgent good nature to a visitor from a distant place, almost a generation younger than himself; since he was born in the same year which saw the advent in the literary world of the renowned Diedrich Knickerbocker. But it was painful to see the labor which it cost Mr. Irving to talk; and I could not forget, that, however warm my welcome, I was calling upon an invalid, and that my visit must be short.—OLIVER WENDELL HOLMES, *Proceedings of the Massachusetts Historical Society*, Dec. 1859, p. 420

Was Irving not good, and, of his works, was not his life the best part? In his family, gentle, generous, good-humored, affectionate, self-denying: in society, a delightful example of complete gentlemanhood; quite unspoiled by prosperity; never obsequious to the great (or, worse still, to the base and mean, as some public men are forced to be in his and other countries); eager to acknowledge every contemporary's merit; always kind and affable to the young members of his calling; in his professional bargains and mercantile dealings delicately honest and grateful; one of the most charming masters of our lighter language; the constant friend to us and our nation; to men of letters doubly dear, not for his wit and genius merely, but as an examplar of goodness, probity, and pure life.—WILLIAM MAKEPEACE THACKERAY, "Nil Nisi Bonum" (1860), *Roundabout Papers*, 1863.

Washington Irving, when I knew him, was past the zenith both of his life and his fame. He was inclined to rest and be thankful, to wear placidly the crown of bays that his intellectual activity had woven for him in earlier years; and so I found him, as others had found him, sleepy in a double sense—physically and mentally.—S. C. HALL, *Retrospect of a Long Life*, 1883, p. 421

General

Mr. Irving is by birth an American, and has, as it were, *skimmed the cream*, and taken off patterns with great skill and cleverness, from our best-known and happiest writers, so that their thoughts and almost their reputation are indirectly transferred to his page, and smile upon us from another hemisphere, like 'the pale reflex of Cynthia's brow.' He succeeds to our admiration and our sympathy by a sort of prescriptive title and traditional privilege. ⟨. . .⟩

Mr. Washington Irving's acquaintance with English literature begins almost where Mr. Lamb's ends,—with the *Spectator*, Tom Brown's works and the wits of Queen Anne. He is not bottomed in our elder writers, nor do we think he has tasked his own faculties much, at least on English ground. Of the merit of his *Knickerbocker* and New York stories we cannot pretend to judge. But in his *Sketch-book* and *Bracebridge-Hall* he gives us very good American copies of our British Essayists and Novelists, which may be very well on the other side of the water, or as proofs of the capabilities of the national genius, but which might be dispensed with here, where we have to boast of the originals. Not only Mr. Irving's language is with great taste and felicity modelled on that of Addison, Goldsmith, Sterne, or Mackenzie: but the thoughts and sentiments are taken at the rebound, and, as they are brought forward at the present period, want both freshness and probability.

Mr. Irving's writings are literary *anachronisms*. He comes to England for the first time, and being on the spot, fancies himself in the midst of those characters and manners which he had read of in the *Spectator* and other approved authors, and which were the only idea he had hitherto formed of the parent country. Instead of looking round to see what *we are*, he sets to work to describe us as *we were*—at second hand. He has Parson Adams or Sir Roger de Coverley in his '*mind's eye*'; and he makes a village curate or a country 'squire in Yorkshire or Hampshire sit to these admired models for their portraits in the beginning of the nineteenth century. Whatever the ingenious author has been most delighted with in the representations of books he transfers to his port-folio, and swears that he has found it actually existing in the course of his observation and travels through Great Britain. Instead of tracing the changes that have taken place in society since Addison or Fielding wrote, he transcribes their account in a different handwriting, and thus keeps us stationary, at least in our most attractive and praise-worthy qualities of simplicity, honesty, hospitality, modesty, and good-nature. This is a very flattering mode of turning fiction into history or history into fiction; and we should scarcely know ourselves again in the softened and altered likeness, but that it bears the date of 1820, and issues from the press in Albemarle-street.

This is one way of complimenting our national and Tory prejudices, and, coupled with literal or exaggerated portraits of *Yankee* peculiarities, could hardly fail to please. The first Essay in the *Sketch-book*, that on National Antipathies, is the best; but, after that, the sterling ore of wit or feeling is gradually spun thinner and thinner, till it fades to the shadow of a shade. Mr. Irving is himself, we believe, a most agreeable and deserving man, and has been led into the natural and pardonable error we speak of by the tempting bait of European popularity, in which he thought there was no more likely method of succeeding than by imitating the style of our standard authors, and giving us credit for the virtues of our forefathers.—WILLIAM HAZLITT, "Elia, and Geoffrey Crayon," *The Spirit of the Age*, 1825

If we examine the works of Mr Irving, with reference to the usual division of manner and substance, we may remark, in the first place, that his style is undoubtedly one of the most finished and agreeable forms, in which the English language has ever been presented. Lord Byron has somewhere spoken of him, as the second prose writer of the day, considering Sir Walter Scott as the first; but with due deference to his lordship's judgment, which was far from being infallible in criticism or anything else, we cannot but consider Mr Irving, as respects mere style, decidedly superior to Sir Walter. The latter, no doubt, has exhibited a greater vigor and fertility of imagination, which, with his talent for versification, entitle him to a higher rank in the world of letters; but viewing him merely as a prose writer, his style, when not sustained by the interest of a connected narrative, will be found to possess no particular merit, and in some of his later writings is negligent and incorrect to an extent, that places it below mediocrity. That of Mr Irving, on the contrary, is, in all his works, uniformly of the first order. Its peculiar characteristic is a continual and sustained elegance, the result of the union of a naturally fine taste, with conscientious and unwearied industry. His language is not remarkable for energy, nor have we often noticed in it any extraordinary happiness or brilliancy of mere expression. Though generally pure and correct, it is not uniformly so; and there are one or two unauthorized forms, which will be found by a nice observer to recur pretty often. Its attraction lies, as we have said, in the charm of finished elegance, which it never loses. The most harmonious and poetical words are carefully selected. Every period is measured and harmonized with nice precision. The length of the sentences is judiciously varied; and the *tout ensemble* produces on the ear an effect very little, if at all, inferior to that of the finest versification. Indeed such prose, while it is from the nature of the topics substantially poetry, does not appear to us, when viewed merely as a form of language, to differ essentially from verse. The distinction between verse and prose evidently does not lie in *rhyme*, taking the word in its modern sense, or in any particular species of *rhythm*, as it was understood by the ancients. *Rhyme*, however pleasing to accustomed ears (and we 'own the soft impeachment' of relishing it as much as others), is, we fear, but too evidently a remnant of the false taste of a barbarous age; and of *rhythm* there are a thousand varieties in the poetry of every cultivated language, which agree in nothing, but that they are all harmonious arrangements of words. If then we mean by rhythm or verse merely the form of poetry, and not any particular measure or set of measures to which we are accustomed, it seems to imply nothing but such a disposition of words and sentences, as shall strike the ear with a regular melodious flow; and elegant prose, like that of Mr Irving, for instance, comes clearly within the definition. Nor are we quite sure that this delicate species of rhythm ought to be regarded as inferior in beauty to the more artificial ones. The latter, which are obvious and, as it were, coarse methods of arrangement, are perhaps natural to the ruder periods of language, and are absolutely necessary in poems intended for music; but for every other purpose it would seem, that the most perfect melody is that, which is most completely unfettered, and in which the traces of art are best concealed. There is something more exquisitely sweet in the natural strains of the Eolian harp, as they swell and fall upon the ear, under the inspiration of a gentle breeze, on a fine moonlight evening, than in the measured flow of any artificial music. But we must leave these considerations, which would admit of some development, and return to our author.

If the elegant prose of Mr Irving be, as we think it is, but little inferior in beauty to the finest verse, and at all events one of the most finished forms of the English language, the character and the substance of his writings is also entirely and exclusively poetical. It is evident enough that 'divine Philosophy' has no part nor lot in his affections. Shakspeare, though he was willing to 'hang up philosophy,' out of compliment to the charming Juliet, when he chose to take it down again, could put the Seven Sages of Greece to the blush. But such is not the taste of Mr Irving. His aim is always to please; and never to instruct, at least by general truths. If he ever teaches, he confines himself to plain matter of fact. He even goes farther, and with the partiality of a true lover, who can see no beauty except in the eyes of his own mistress, he at times deals rather rudely with philosophy, and more than insinuates that she is a sort of prosing mad-cap, who babbles eternally without ever knowing what she is talking of. Now we hold this doctrine to be clearly heretical. We conceive that the universe is not less worthy of being studied as an expression of the pure and glorious *ideas* or images that dwell eternally in the Supreme mind, than when viewed merely as a pleasing and varied panorama, or moving picture; and that it even acquires, in the former case, a sublimity and beauty, of which it is not susceptible in the latter, and which, in all ages, have exalted and ravished the souls of the best and greatest men, the Platos and Ciceros of the olden time, and the Miltons and Newtons of the modern. But though we think Mr Irving heretical on this head, we can hardly say that we like him the less for it, being always pleased to see a man put his heart and soul into his business, whatever it may be, even though he may, by so doing, (as often happens) generate in himself a sort of hatred and contempt for every other. Within the domain of poetry, taking this word in its large sense, to which he religiously confines himself, Mr Irving's range is somewhat extensive. He does not attempt the sublime, but he is often successful in the tender, and disports himself, at his ease, in the comic. Humor is obviously his *forte*, and his best touches of pathos are those, which are thrown in casually, to break the continuity of a train of melancholy thoughts, when they sparkle in part by the effect of contrast, like diamonds on a black mantle. But it is when employed on humorous subjects, that he puts forth the vigor of a really inventive genius, and proves himself substantially a poet. *Knickerbocker*, for example, is a true original creation. His purely pathetic essays, though occasionally pleasing, are more generally somewhat tame and spiritless. As a writer of serious biography and history he possesses the merit of plain and elegant narrative, but does not aspire to the higher palm of just and deep thought in the investigation of causes and effects, that constitutes the distinction of the real historian, and supposes the taste for philosophical research, which, as we have said before, is foreign to the temper of our author.—ALEXANDER HILL EVERETT, "Irving's *Life of Columbus*," *North American Review*, Jan. 1829, pp. 113–15

The MS. of Mr. Irving has little about it indicative of his genius. Certainly, no one could suspect from it any nice *finish* in the writer's compositions; nor is this nice finish to be found. The letters now before us vary remarkably in appearance; and those of late date are not nearly so well written as the more

antique. Mr. Irving has travelled much, has seen many vicissitudes, and has been so thoroughly satiated with fame as to grow slovenly in the performance of his literary tasks. This slovenliness has affected his hand-writing. But even from his earlier MSS. there is little to be gleaned, except the ideas of simplicity and precision. It must be admitted, however, that this fact, in itself, is characteristic of the literary manner, which, however excellent, has no prominent or very remarkable features.—EDGAR ALLAN POE, "Autography" (1841), *Complete Works*, ed. James A. Harrison, 1902, Vol. 15, p. 182

I do not go to bed two nights out of seven without taking Washington Irving under my arm upstairs to bed with me; and when I don't take him I take his next of kin—his own brother—Oliver Goldsmith.—CHARLES DICKENS, Speech at Banquet in His Honour, New York (Feb. 18, 1842)

The *Spectator*, Mr. Irving, and Mr. Hawthorne have in common that tranquil and subdued manner which we have chosen to denominate *repose*; but, in the case of the two former, this repose is attained rather by the absence of novel combination, or of originality, than otherwise, and consists chiefly in the calm, quiet, unostentatious expression of commonplace thoughts, in an unambitious unadulterated Saxon. In them, by strong effort, we are made to conceive the absence of all.—EDGAR ALLAN POE, "Nathaniel Hawthorne" (1842), *Essays and Reviews*, ed. G. R. Thompson, 1984, pp. 570–71

What! Irving? thrice welcome, warm heart and fine brain,
You bring back the happiest spirit from Spain,
And the gravest sweet humor, that ever were there
Since Cervantes met death in his gentle despair;
Nay, don't be embarrassed, nor look so beseeching,—
I sha' n't run directly against my own preaching,
And, having just laughed at their Raphaels and Dantes,
Go to setting you up beside matchless Cervantes;
But allow me to speak what I honestly feel,—
To a true poet-heart add the fun of Dick Steele,
Throw in all of Addison, *minus* the chill,
With the whole of that partnership's stock and good-will,
Mix well, and while stirring, hum o'er, as a spell,
The fine *old* English Gentleman, simmer it well,
Sweeten just to your own private liking, then strain,
That only the finest and clearest remain,
Let it stand out of doors till a soul it receives
From the warm lazy sun loitering down through green leaves,
And you'll find a choice nature, not wholly deserving
A name either English or Yankee,—just Irving.
　　　　—JAMES RUSSELL LOWELL, A *Fable for Critics*,
　　　　1848

Few, very few, can show a long succession of volumes, so pure, so graceful, and so varied as Mr. Irving. To my poor cottage, rich only in printed paper, people often come to borrow books for themselves or their children. Sometimes they make their own selection; sometimes, much against my will, they leave the choice to me; and in either case I know no works that are oftener lent than those that bear the pseudonym of Geoffrey Crayon.—MARY RUSSELL MITFORD, *Recollections of a Literary Life*, 1851, p. 516

Every reader has his first book: I mean to say, one book, among all others, which, in early youth, first fascinates his imagination, and at once excites and satisfies the desires of his mind. To me, this first book was the *Sketch-Book* of Washington Irving. I was a schoolboy when it was published, and read each succeeding number with ever-increasing wonder and delight,—spell-bound by its pleasant humor, its melancholy tenderness, its atmosphere of revery; nay, even by its gray-brown covers, the shaded letters of the titles, and the fair, clear type,—which seemed an outward symbol of the style.

How many delightful books the same author has given us, written before and since,—volumes of history and of fiction, most of which illustrate his native land, and some of which illuminate it, and make the Hudson, I will not say as classic, but as romantic, as the Rhine! Yet still the charm of the *Sketch-Book* remains unbroken; the old fascination still lingers about it; and, whenever I open its pages, I open also that mysterious door which leads back into the haunted chambers of youth.

Many years afterward, I had the pleasure of meeting Mr. Irving in Spain; and found the author, whom I had loved, repeated in the man,—the same playful humor, the same touches of sentiment, the same poetic atmosphere, and, what I admired still more, the entire absence of all literary jealousy, of all that mean avarice of fame, which counts what is given to another as so much taken from one's self,—

> And, rustling, hears in every breeze
> The laurels of Miltiades.

At this time, Mr. Irving was at Madrid, engaged upon his *Life of Columbus*; and, if the work itself did not bear ample testimony to his zealous and conscientious labor, I could do so from personal observation. He seemed to be always at work. "Sit down," he would say: "I will talk with you in a moment; but I must first finish this sentence."

One summer morning, passing his house at the early hour of six, I saw his study-window already wide open. On my mentioning it to him afterwards, he said, "Yes: I am always at my work as early as six." Since then, I have often remembered that sunny morning and that open window, so suggestive of his sunny temperament and his open heart, and equally so of his patient and persistent toil; and have recalled those striking words of Dante:—

> Seggendo in piuma,
> In fama non si vien, nè sotto coltre;
> Senza la qual, chi sua vita consuma,
> Cotal vestigio in terra, di sè lascia
> Qual fummo in aere ed in acqua la schiuma.

> Seated upon down,
> Or in his bed, man cometh not to fame;
> Withouten which, whose his life consumes,
> Such vestige of himself on earth shall leave
> As smoke in air and in the water foam.
>
> —HENRY WADSWORTH LONGFELLOW, *Proceedings of the Massachusetts Historical Society*, Dec. 1859, pp. 393–94

Mr. Irving's manner is often compared with Addison's; though, closely examined, there is no great resemblance between them, except that they both write in a simple, unaffected style, remote from the tiresome stateliness of Johnson and Gibbon. It was one of the witty but rather ill-natured sayings of Mr. Samuel Rogers, whose epigrams sometimes did as much injustice to his own kind and generous nature as they did to the victims of his pleasantry, that Washington Irving was Addison and Water,—a judgment which, if seriously dealt with, is altogether aside from the merits of the two writers, who have very little in common. Addison had received a finished classical education at the Charter-House and at Oxford; was eminently a man of books, and had a decided taste for literary criticism. Mr. Irving, for a man of letters, was not a great reader; and, if he possessed the critical faculty, never exercised it. Addison quoted the Latin poets freely, and wrote correct Latin verses himself. Mr. Irving made no pretensions to a

familiar acquaintance with the classics, and probably never made a hexameter in his life. Addison wrote some smooth English poetry, which Mr. Irving, I believe, never attempted; but, with the exception of two or three exquisite hymns (which will last as long as the English language does), one brilliant simile of six lines in the *Campaign*, and one or two sententious but not very brilliant passages from *Cato*, not a line of Addison's poetry has been quoted for a hundred years. But Mr. Irving's peculiar vein of humor is not inferior in playful raciness to Addison's; his nicety of characterization is quite equal; his judgment upon all moral relations as sound and true; his human sympathies more comprehensive, tenderer and chaster; and his poetical faculty, though never developed in verse, vastly above Addison's. One chord in the human heart,—the pathetic,—for whose sweet music Addison had no ear, Irving touched with the hand of a master. He learned that skill in the school of early disappointment.

In this respect, the writer was, in both cases, reflected in the man. Addison, after a protracted suit, made an "ambitious match" with a termagant peeress. Irving, who would as soon have married Hecate as a woman like the Countess of Warwick, buried a blighted hope, never to be rekindled, in the grave of a youthful sorrow.

As miscellaneous essayists, in which capacity only they can be compared, Irving exceeds Addison in versatility and range, quite as much as Addison exceeds Irving in the far less important quality of classical tincture; while, as a great national historian, our countryman reaped laurels in a field which Addison never entered.—EDWARD EVERETT, *Proceedings of the Massachusetts Historical Society*, Dec. 1859, pp. 399–400

That amiable character which makes itself so manifest in the writings of Irving was seen in all his daily actions. He was ever ready to do kind offices; tender of the feelings of others; carefully just, but ever leaning to the merciful side of justice; averse to strife; and so modest that the world never ceased to wonder how it should have happened that one so much praised should have gained so little assurance. He envied no man's success, he sought to detract from no man's merits, but he was acutely sensitive both to praise and to blame—sensitive to such a degree that an unfavorable criticism of any of his works would almost persuade him that they were as worthless as the critic represented them. He thought so little of himself that he could never comprehend why it was that he should be the object of curiosity or reverence.

From the time that he began the composition of his *Sketch Book* his whole life was the life of an author. His habits of composition were, however, by no means regular. When he was in the vein, the periods would literally stream from his pen; at other times he would scarcely write anything. For two years after the failure of his brothers at Liverpool he found it almost impossible to write a line. He was throughout life an early riser, and, when in the mood, would write all the morning and till late in the day, wholly engrossed with his subject. In the evening he was ready for any cheerful pastime, in which he took part with an animation almost amounting to high spirits. These intervals of excitement and intense labor, sometimes lasting for weeks, were succeeded by languor, and at times by depression of spirits, and for months the pen would lie untouched; even to answer a letter at these times was an irksome task.

He wrote but rarely in the evening, knowing—so at least I infer—that no habit makes severer demands upon the nervous system than this. It was owing, I doubt not, to this prudent husbanding of his powers, along with his somewhat abstinent habits and the exercise which he took every day, that he was able to preserve unimpaired to so late a period the faculties employed in original composition. He had been a vigorous walker and a fearless rider, and in his declining years he drove out daily, not only for the sake of the open air and motion, but to refresh his mind with the aspect of nature. One of his favorite recreations was listening to music, of which he was an indulgent critic, and he contrived to be pleased and soothed by strains less artfully modulated than fastidious ears are apt to require.

His facility in writing and the charm of his style were owing to very early practice, the reading of good authors, and the native elegance of his mind; and not, in my opinion, to any special study of the graces of manner or any anxious care in the use of terms and phrases. Words and combinations of words are sometimes found in his writings to which a fastidious taste might object; but these do not prevent his style from being one of the most agreeable in the whole range of our literature. It is transparent as the light, sweetly modulated, unaffected, the native expression of a fertile fancy, a benignant temper, and a mind which, delighting in the noble and the beautiful, turned involuntarily away from their opposites. His peculiar humor was, in a great measure, the offspring of this constitution of his mind. This "fanciful playing with common things," as Mr. Dana calls it, is never coarse, never tainted with grossness, and always in harmony with our better sympathies. It not only tinged his writings, but overflowed in his delightful conversation.—WILLIAM CULLEN BRYANT, "Washington Irving" (1860), *Prose Writings*, ed. Parke Godwin, 1884, Vol. 1, pp. 364–66

> Chaucer I fancied had been dead
>   Some centuries, some four or five;
> By fancy I have been misled
>   Like many: he is yet alive.
> *The Widow's Ordeal* who beside
>   Could thus relate? Yes, there is one,
> He bears beyond the Atlantic wide
>   The glorious name of Washington.
>   —WALTER SAVAGE LANDOR, *"On the Widow's Ordeal* by Washington Irving," 1863

The books I have lately been reading are the works of Washington Irving. None of our present writers write such pure English; he reminds me of Addison, but has more genius and a richer invention. Perhaps on the whole he is more like Goldsmith.—WALTER SAVAGE LANDOR, Letter to Rose Graves-Sawle (Jan. 19, 1863)

Longfellow's fellow-countryman, Irving, might have walked arm-in-arm with Addison, and Addison would have run no risk of being discomposed by a trans-Atlantic twang in his companion's accent. Irving, if he betrays his origin at all, betrays it somewhat in the same way as Longfellow, by his tender, satisfied repose in the venerable, chiefly the venerable in English society and manners, by his quiet delight in the implicit tradition of English civility, the scarcely-felt yet everywhere influential presence of a beautiful and grave Past, and the company of unseen beneficent associations.—EDWARD DOWDEN, "The Poetry of Democracy: Walt Whitman," *Studies in Literature*, 1878, p. 470

It is in the *Sketch-Book* that Irving first appeals to us as a torchbearer in the great procession of English prose-writers. In *Knickerbocker* he had been dancing or skipping in the lightness of his heart to a delicious measure of his own; in *Salmagundi* he had waked up to a sense of literary responsibility, without quite knowing in what direction his new-found sense of style

would lead him. In the *Sketch-Book* he is a finished and classic writer, bowing to the great tradition of English prose, and knowing precisely what it is that he would do, and how to do it. He sustains this easy mastery of manner through his next book, *Bracebridge Hall*, and then, if he wrote no less well in future, the voice at least had become familiar, and the peculiar wonder and delight with which his age received him faded into a common pleasure. The *Sketch-Book* and *Bracebridge Hall*, then, remain the bright original stars in this gracious constellation.

⟨. . .⟩ It scarcely occurs to the modern reader, perhaps, that the text of the chapters in the *Sketch-Book*, taken as they are from writers such as Lyly, Churchyard, Herrick, and Middleton, were in the highest degree unusual in 1820, though almost commonplace in 1830. They showed Irving's instinctive adherence to the new romantic principles which had begun to spread over every country of Europe from Germany. He is, indeed, more distinctly romantic than either of the other three essayists. He is more susceptible than they to picturesque, as distinguished from literary, antiquity. Neither Lamb nor Hunt would have been able to sustain the high romantic pitch of the noble essay on 'Westminister Abbey;' they would have stolen round to Poet's Corner, or have loitered among the modern busts. In this Irving was more closely related to Sir Walter Scott than they, and when we consider the fascination which the Waverley novels must have exercised over the imagination of this fervid and pensive young man, we may be surprised to find so little trace of Scott's direct influence upon the *Sketch-Book*.

If the mark of any modern writer is to be found on the early style of Washington Irving, it appears to me to be rather that of Cobbett than of any other. I do not know whether there is any record of such influence in the *Life or Letters of Irving*, but it is certainly to be traced in his style. The author of *The Political Register* was not always foaming with malevolence, and when he was engaged in describing English scenery, his periods have sometimes the very ring of the *Sketch-Book*. It is partly to Cobbett that Irving owes the one blemish of his style,—a determination to be arch and rustic at all hazards, and old-fashioned when the fashion was a bad one. If it were possible to be irritated with so suave and sympathetic a companion, it would be when he lavishes his sentiment on 'the elegant and interesting young female.' In such essays as 'The Wife' and 'The Pride of the Village' a whole half-century seems to divide us, not merely from De Quincey, but from Irving himself when he attains the true modern note in that master-piece of refined humor, 'The Boar's Head Tavern.' In truth, there have been few writers of Irving's eminence who have been so little anxious for a novel delivery. The affectation of strangeness is absolutely foreign to him, and he is never so happy as when he is setting the old themes to new tunes upon his pastoral pipe. And, as an example of his simplicity, when he is trying, in 'Westminster Abbey,' to repeat in a new form the reflections of Sir Thomas Browne, he is artless enough to quote twice from the *Urn Burial* itself.—EDMUND GOSSE, "Irving's *Sketch-Book*," *Critic*, March 31, 1883, pp. 140–41

Irving's centenary has produced few attempts to estimate critically the strength of the foundations on which his literary fame rests. That he was in his day a very popular writer is a fact that cannot be disputed, any more than can the fact that interest in him has greatly waned since his death. But this change of itself proves little. The same thing may be said of the reputation of Scott, of Cooper, of Byron, even of so recently famous a writer as Dickens. In Byron's case, the generation now on the stage has witnessed two changes of opinion—one to his disadvantage, and a second, within a few years, toward the rehabilitation of his fame. It is impossible to say how long a period the world will take, in the case of any given writer, to make up its mind as to the permanent position it is willing to accord him; but a hundred years is probably too short a time, and neither in Irving's case nor in that of his rivals or successors is it safe to assume that our present estimate of them will be confirmed by those who come after us.

There is no doubt that the feeling about Irving in this country is still, to a certain extent, affected by considerations which will, as time goes on, lose their influence altogether. He was one of the first of a little band of writers who redeemed this country from the reproach of being without a literature. When he appeared on the scene there was not only no literary class in America, but hardly a belief that the country could produce any. The United States had emancipated itself from English control in politics, but mentally it was still provincial. Cooper, when he began to write, was considered to have done a very sensible thing in taking the materials of his first novel from English society, of which he knew absolutely nothing, and his subsequent innovation of drawing upon America was viewed at first with alarm and distrust by his friends. At the same time it was certain that, could a literature be produced, it would, as the politicians say, be "hailed with delight" by the nascent patriotism of the country. This was Irving's opportunity. His success, when it came, was immense, because he proved to everybody's satisfaction that there really could be American authors.

But Irving did something more than this. He showed, in a certain sense, that there could be such a thing as a New York author—that the local legends and traditions could be used in literature. There were not many of them, but certainly Irving turned them to good account. The history of New York has been for the most part the prosaic and material history of a commercial capital. In our own day we are fond of reproaching it for its materialism; but at the beginning of this century it was far more open to the charge than it is now. Irving himself could do nothing with its history but make a burlesque of it; but in the Hudson and its half-mythical, half-historical associations he found material for the exercise of his imagination and fancy. If the Hudson is to us something more than a mere waterway and convenient natural agency for "moving the crops to tide-water"; if the Catskills are something more than a good place for establishing summer hotels, it is to Irving that the fact is due. If there is a touch of poetry, or romance, or human interest, about the background of New York, a mellow sugges-tion of myth and superstition, a legendary halo that soothes the sight tortured by the flaring, garish noon of our materialism, it is Irving who put it there. To the world at large, it may make very little difference whether the sketches of which Rip Van Winkle and the legend of Sleepy Hollow are the best remem-bered, were or were not added to literature; but to a community as scantily supplied with literature as ours, it ought to make a good deal.

Irving's reputation, so far as it rests on this, ought to be entirely discriminated from his repute as an essayist and historical writer. In the latter fields it is quite clear that he had no originality, and that his friends and admirers, had they desired to make sure that oblivion should overtake his fame, could not have set about it in a better way than by holding him up as an American Addison. Irving lived at a time when the old imitative theory of style prevailed, and led young writers to "form" themselves upon acknowledged masters. Franklin, if we remember right, mentions in his autobiography that he

prepared himself to communicate with the public in this way. In Irving's case it is difficult to make out how much his similarity to Addison is the result of conscious imitation and how much of inborn literary sympathy. In our day we have pushed the natural theory of style—the theory that it must be a growth, and not a manufactured product—to the opposite extreme, so that our grandfathers' and grandmothers' habit of praising new writers as they appeared for their resemblance to classics strikes us as little less than ludicrous. Possibly we have gone too far. Perhaps we have fostered originality in expression to an excess, as they fostered imitation, until we have confused the grotesque with the original, and given vogue to writers whose chief claim to attention is not what they say, but their saying things in such a queer way.

Irving offended his neighbors and friends by turning into burlesque the Dutch annals of New York; but for this, too, New York owes him a debt of gratitude, for if the city was to redeem itself from the provincialism of its early days and become a great capital, it was absolutely necessary that it should learn to get a proper perspective for its past. Ridicule is the only test by which we get the true measure of the unimportance to the world at large of local celebrity. We are accustomed now to a humorous view of New York, of its society, of its government, of its literature, of its art. It does not offend us, because we are so secure in our position. The Knickerbocker tradition is fair game for all the world. But Irving was a pioneer in this field. The New York of his day was a small provincial town, which thought itself a city, and to make fun of it was a bold thing to do. Irving perceived that the thin stream of provincial history was very slender capital for self-glorification, and refused to connive at the attempt to make grand historical figures out of the phlegmatic, hard-fisted Dutch founders. In this respect he may be regarded as the father of a long line of American humorists who have persisted in exhibiting the reverse of the heroic view of American history and tradition to our generation.—A. G. SEDGWICK, "Wash-ington Irving," *Nation*, April 5, 1883, pp. 291–92

The "revival" of American literature in New York differed much in character from its revival in New England. In New York it was purely human in tone; in New England it was a little superhuman in tone. In New England they feared the devil; in New York they dared the devil; and the greatest and most original literary dare-devil in New York was a young gentleman of good family, whose "schooling" ended with his sixteenth year, who had rambled much about the island of Manhattan, who had in his saunterings gleaned and brooded over many Dutch legends of an elder time, who had read much but had studied little, who possessed fine observation, quick intelligence, a genial disposition, and an indolently original genius in detecting the ludicrous side of things, and whose name was Washington Irving. After some preliminary essays in humorous literature his genius arrived at the age of *indiscre-tion*, and he produced at the age of twenty-six the most deliciously audacious work of humor in our literature, namely, *The History of New York, by Diedrich Knickerbocker*. It is said of some reformers that they have not only opinions, but the courage of their opinions. It may be said of Irving that he not only caricatured, but had the courage of his caricatures. The persons whom he covered with ridicule were the ancestors of the leading families of New York, and these families prided themselves on their descent. After the publication of such a book he could hardly enter the "best society" of New York, to which he naturally belonged, without running the risk of being insulted, especially by the elderly women of fashion; but he conquered their prejudices by the same grace and geniality of manner, by the same unmistakable tokens that he was an inborn gentleman, through which he afterward won his way into the first society of England, France, Germany, Italy, and Spain. Still, the promise of Knickerbocker was not fulfilled. That book, if considered as an imitation at all, was an imitation of Rabelais, or Swift, or of any author in any language who had shown an independence of all convention, who did not hesitate to commit indecorums, and who laughed at all the regalities of the world. The author lived long enough to be called a timid imitator of Addison and Goldsmith. In fact, he imitated nobody. His genius, at first riotous and unrestrained, became tamed and regulated by a larger intercourse with the world, by the saddening experience of life, and by the gradual development of some deep sentiments which held in check the audacities of his wit and humor. But even in the portions of *The Sketch-Book* relating to England it will be seen that his favorite authors belonged rather to the age of Elizabeth than to the age of Anne. In *Bracebridge Hall* there is one chapter called "The Rookery," which in exquisitely poetic humor is hardly equalled by the best productions of the authors he is said to have made his models. That he possessed essential humor and pathos, is proved by the warm admiration he excited in such masters of humor and pathos as Scott and Dickens; and style is but a secondary consideration when it expresses vital qualities of genius. If he subordinated energy to elegance, he did it, not because he had the ignoble ambition to be ranked as "a fine writer," but because he was free from the ambition, equally ignoble, of simulating a passion which he did not feel. The period which elapsed between the publication of Knickerbocker's history and *The Sketch-Book* was ten years. During this time his mind acquired the habit of tranquilly contemplating the objects which filled his imagination, and what it lost in spontaneous vigor it gained in sureness of insight and completeness of representation. "Rip Van Winkle" and "The Legend of Sleepy Hollow" have not the humorous inspiration of some passages in Knickerbocker, but perhaps they give more permanent delight, for the scenes and characters are so harmonized that they have the effect of a picture, in which all the parts combine to produce one charming whole. Besides, Irving is one of those exceptional authors who are regarded by their readers as personal friends, and the felicity of nature by which he obtained this distinction was expressed in that amenity, that amiability of tone, which some of his austere critics have called elegant feebleness. As a biographer and historian, his *Life of Columbus* and his *Life of Washington* have indissolubly connected his name with the discoverer of the American continent and the champion of the liberties of his country. In *The Chronicle of the Conquest of Granada* and *The Alhambra* he occupies a unique position among those writers of fiction who have based fiction on a laborious investigation into the facts of history. His reputation is not local, but is recognized by all cultivated people who speak the English language. If Great Britain established an English intellectual colony in the United States, such men as Irving and Cooper may be said to have retorted by establishing an American intellectual colony in England.—EDWIN P. WHIPPLE, "American Literature" (1886), *American Literature and Other Papers*, 1887, pp. 42–45

I did my poor best to be amused by his *Knickerbocker History of New York*, because my father liked it so much, but secretly I found it heavy; and a few years ago when I went carefully through it again I could not laugh. Even as a boy I found some other things of his uphill work. There was the beautiful

manner, but the thought seemed thin; and I do not remember having been much amused by *Bracebridge Hall*, though I read it devoutly, and with a full sense that it would be very *comme il faut* to like it. But I did like the *Life of Goldsmith*; I liked it a great deal better than the more authoritative *Life* by Forster, and I think there is a deeper and sweeter sense of Goldsmith in it. Better than all, except the *Conquest of Granada*, I liked the "Legend of Sleepy Hollow" and the story of Rip Van Winkle, with their humorous and affectionate caricatures of life that was once of our own soil and air; and the *Tales of the Alhambra*, which transported me again to the scenes of my youth beside the Xenil. It was long after my acquaintance with his work that I came to a due sense of Irving as an artist, and perhaps I have come to feel a full sense of it only now, when I perceive that he worked willingly only when he worked inventively. At last I can do justice to the exquisite conception of his *Conquest of Granada*, a study of history which, in unique measure, conveys not only the pathos, but the humor of one of the most splendid and impressive situations in the experience of the race. Very possibly something of the severer truth might have been sacrificed to the effect of the pleasing and touching tale, but I do not understand that this was really done. Upon the whole I am very well content with my first three loves in literature, and if I were to choose for any other boy I do not see how I could choose better than Goldsmith and Cervantes and Irving, kindred spirits, and each not a master only, but a sweet and gentle friend, whose kindness could not fail to profit him.—WILLIAM DEAN HOWELLS, "Irving," *My Literary Passions*, 1895

"There are few writers," wrote Washington Irving, "for whom the reader feels such personal kindness as for Oliver Goldsmith, for few have so eminently possessed the magic gift of identifying themselves with their writings." The remark is equally applicable to Goldsmith's biographer. His every page overflows with benevolence and geniality. A refined and highly trained intellect, a delicate and discriminating taste, an unaffected love of letters, and a truly amiable disposition are everywhere manifest. His notes of a visit paid to Sir Walter Scott at Abbotsford, are a model of tact, reticence, and good feeling. Moreover, a strong and refreshing vein of common-sense runs through all the opinions he expresses. No American, before or since, has given utterance to views more manly, more clear-headed, or more just, on the relations of the old country to the new. In short, all his writings conspire to present the portrait of a man whose mental and moral qualities would command the highest esteem in private life.

Unluckily, something more than extreme amiability, even when combined with the soundest sense, is necessary to the attainment of greatness in literature; and it is a fact that Washington Irving went far to blast the rich promise of his natural parts, and to render his admirable equipment of no avail by his blind and obstinate devotion to an obsolete and exploded convention. He did well to study Addison, Goldsmith, and Sterne with profound attention. He did very ill to imitate them with a fidelity as servile as it is ridiculous. No excellence was too great, no mannerism too trivial for him to mimic. Types of character and tricks of style, modes of thought and turns of phrase, all are appropriated and reproduced with the most painful exactitude. And they suffer sadly in the process. Pleasing and pertinent reflections become chilly and colourless platitudes; while exquisite humour is transformed into a laboured archness. A favourite and highly effective artifice of the novelists and essayists of the eighteenth century was the apparently grave and ingenuous collocation of two absolutely incongruous ideas. This whimsical device Washington Irving employs with a persistency of reiteration almost maddening to a mind already fatigued by his cumbrous and unnecessary apparatus of story within story. The "rich spirit of pensive eloquence" which a former generation detected in his works, is as poor an atonement for such wilful artistic blunders as are the "singular sweetness of the composition and the mildness of the sentiments." The accuracy of the last phrase is beyond question. Washington Irving assuredly does not "over-stimulate." He is too often content to appeal to the ear by "mechanic echoes" of what has been said before; he is too apt to tempt the literary appetite with a dish of "cauld kail het again"; though the kail is never uneatable, and performances like the *Life of Goldsmith* may be read without effort, if without the keen pleasure afforded by Lockhart's biography of Burns, or Southey's of Nelson.

In view of what has been said it is not surprising that Washington Irving's style should be signally deficient in two respects: it lacks life, and it lacks distinction. One crowded hour of Sir Walter Scott's careless and often slovenly prose is worth an age of Washington Irving's insipidities; and a single "tow-row" of Mr. Stevenson's thunder is infinitely more alarming than all the storms in which the clouds "roll in volumes over the mountain tops," the rain "begins to patter down in broad and scattered drops," the wind "freshens," the lightning "leaps from cloud to cloud," the peals "are echoed from mountain to mountain," and, in short, all the elements go through their appropriate and stereotyped evolutions with the punctuality, precision, and tameness of clock-work. The bones of the skeleton, to employ a familiar metaphor, are adjusted with the utmost nicety and correctness, but they have lost the potentiality of life. On the other hand, it is to be said, that the close study of such writers as Washington Irving selected for his models could scarce be barren of all good result; that if he never rises to animation he never sinks below a tolerably high standard of elegance; and that he everywhere preserves a spotless purity of idiom. Nor must it be forgotten that from the foregoing strictures a portion—though not a large one—of his compositions fails to be excluded. When he writes in the character of Diedrich Knickerbocker, and deals with the early Dutch settlers in America, their manners and superstitions, their traditions and customs, he contrives for the moment to shake off many of his accustomed fetters. The *History of New York*, indeed, is extremely tedious because it is extremely long. But the tale of "Rip van Winkle," for example, is a little masterpiece of its kind, and several other stories display an almost equally firm command of material, and an almost equally happy adaptation of means to end. A comparison of "The Student of Salamanca" with "Dolph Heyliger" will demonstrate more clearly, perhaps, than aught else, the difference between Washington Irving trudging along the beaten track, and Washington Irving following the true bent of his genius. It can hardly fail to inspire sincere regret that he turned his natural gifts to so little purpose, and refused to strive for that position among English prose writers to which he might, without presumption, have aspired.—J. H. MILLAR, "Washington Irving," *English Prose*, ed. Henry Craik, 1896, Vol. 5, pp. 233–35

Works

A HISTORY OF NEW YORK

I beg you to accept my best thanks for the uncommon degree of entertainment which I have received from the most excellently jocose history of New York. I am sensible that as a stranger to American parties and politics I must lose much of the conceald satire of the piece but I must own that looking at the simple and obvious meaning only I have never read anything so closely resembling the stile of Dean Swift as the annals of Diedrich Knickerbocker. I have been employed these few evenings in reading them aloud to Mrs. S. and two ladies who are our guests and our sides have been absolutely tense with laughing. I think too, there are passages which indicate that the author possesses powers of a different kind & has some touches which remind me much of Sterne. I beg you will have the kindness to let me know when Mr. Irvine take pen in hand again for assuredly I shall expect a very great treat which I may chance never to hear of but through your kindness.—SIR WALTER SCOTT, Letter to Henry Brevoort (April 23, 1813)

The following work, in which, at the outset, nothing more was contemplated than a temporary *jeu d'esprit*, was commenced in company with my brother, the late Peter Irving, Esq. Our idea was to parody a small hand-book which had recently appeared, entitled A *Picture of New York*. Like that, our work was to begin with an historical sketch; to be followed by notices of the customs, manners, and institutions of the city; written in a serio-comic vein, and treating local errors, follies, and abuses with good-humored satire.

To burlesque the pedantic lore displayed in certain American works, our historical sketch was to commence with the creation of the world; and we laid all kinds of works under contribution for trite citations, relevant or irrelevant, to give it the proper air of learned research. Before this crude mass of mock erudition could be digested into form, my brother departed for Europe, and I was left to prosecute the enterprise alone.

I now altered the plan of the work. Discarding all idea of a parody on the *Picture of New York*, I determined that what had been originally intended as an introductory sketch, should comprise the whole work, and form a comic history of the city. I accordingly moulded the mass of citations and disquisitions into introductory chapters forming the first book; but it soon became evident to me that, like Robinson Crusoe with his boat, I had begun on too large a scale, and that, to launch my history successfully, I must reduce its proportions. I accordingly resolved to confine it to the period of the Dutch domination, which, in its rise, progress, and decline, presented that unity of subject required by classic rule. It was a period, also, at that time almost a *terra incognita* in history. In fact, I was surprised to find how few of my fellow-citizens were aware that New York had ever been called New Amsterdam, or had heard of the names of its early Dutch governors, or cared a straw about their ancient Dutch progenitors.

This, then, broke upon me as the poetic age of our city; poetic from its very obscurity; and open, like the early and obscure days of ancient Rome, to all the embellishments of heroic fiction. I hailed my native city, as fortunate above all other American cities, in having an antiquity thus extending back into the regions of doubt and fable; neither did I conceive I was committing any grievous historical sin in helping out the few facts I could collect in this remote and forgotten region with figments of my own brain, or in giving characteristic attributes to the few names connected with it which I might dig up from oblivion.

In this, doubtless, I reasoned like a young and inexperienced writer, besotted with his own fancies; and my presumptuous trespasses into this sacred, though neglected, region of history have met with deserved rebuke from men of soberer minds. It is too late, however, to recall the shaft thus rashly launched. To any one whose sense of fitness it may wound, I can only say with Hamlet,

> Let my disclaiming from a purposed evil
> Free me so far in your most generous thoughts,
> That I have shot my arrow o'er the house,
> And hurt my brother.

I will say this in further apology for my work: that if it has taken an unwarrantable liberty with our early provincial history, it has at least turned attention to that history and provoked research. It is only since this work appeared that the forgotten archives of the province have been rummaged, and the facts and personages of the olden time rescued from the dust of oblivion and elevated into whatever importance they may actually possess.

The main object of my work, in fact, had a bearing wide from the sober aim of history; but one which, I trust, will meet with some indulgence from poetic minds. It was to embody the traditions of our city in an amusing form; to illustrate its local humors, customs, and peculiarities; to clothe home scenes and places and familiar names with those imaginative and whimsical associations so seldom met with in our new country, but which live like charms and spells about the cities of the old world, binding the heart of the native inhabitant to his home.

In this I have reason to believe I have in some measure succeeded. Before the appearance of my work the popular traditions of our city were unrecorded; the peculiar and racy customs and usages derived from our Dutch progenitors were unnoticed, or regarded with indifference, or adverted to with a sneer. Now they form a convivial currency, and are brought forward on all occasions; they link our whole community together in good humor and good fellowship; they are the rallying points of home feeling; the seasoning of our civic festivities; the staple of local tales and local pleasantries; and are so harped upon by our writers of popular fiction, that I find myself almost crowded off the legendary ground which I was the first to explore, by the host who have followed in my footsteps.

I dwell on this head because, at the first appearance of my work, its aim and drift were misapprehended by some of the descendants of the Dutch worthies; and because I understand that now and then one may still be found to regard it with a captious eye. The far greater part, however, I have reason to flatter myself, receive my good-humored picturings in the same temper with which they were executed; and when I find, after a lapse of forty years, this hap-hazard production of my youth still cherished among them; when I find its very name become a "household word," and used to give the home stamp to everything recommended for popular acceptation, such as Knickerbocker societies; Knickerbocker insurance companies; Knickerbocker steamboats; Knickerbocker omnibuses; Knickerbocker bread, and Knickerbocker ice; and when I find New Yorkers of Dutch descent priding themselves upon being "genuine Knickerbockers," I please myself with the persuasion that I have struck the right chord; that my dealings with the good old Dutch times, and the customs and usages derived from them, are in harmony with the feelings and humors of my townsmen; that I have opened a vein of pleasant associations and quaint characteristics peculiar to my native place, and which its inhabitants will not willingly suffer to pass away; and that, though other histories of New York may appear of higher claims to learned acceptation, and may take their dignified and appropriate rank in the family library, Knickerbocker's history will still be received with good-humored indulgence, and be thumbed and chuckled over by the family fireside.—WASHING-TON IRVING, "The Author's Apology," A *History of New York*, 1848

In fact, it is quite possible that no one of his mature and sober pieces of writing had as much real effect on the progress of American historiography as the admirable humorous composition with which he began, as far back as 1809,—the *History of New York* by Dietrich Knickerbocker. Aside from its striking success as a literary production, the book had a great effect in awakening interest in the early or Dutch period of New York history. Descendants rushed with sober indignation to the defense of ancestors at whom the genial humorist poked his fun, and very likely the great amount of work which the state government in the next generation did for the historical illustration of the Dutch period, through the researches of Mr. Brodhead in foreign archives, had this unhistorical little book for one of its principal causes. But, on the other hand, he made it permanently difficult for the American public to take a serious view of those early Dutch days. Oloffe the Dreamer and Walter the Doubter, Abraham with the ten breeches and Stuyvesant with the wooden leg, have become too thoroughly domesticated among us to admit of that.—J. FRANKLIN JAMESON, *The History of Historical Writing in America*, 1891, pp. 97–98

THE SKETCH BOOK

It will be needless to inform any who have read the book, that it is from the pen of Mr. Irving. His rich, and sometimes extravagant humour, his gay and graceful fancy, his peculiar choice and felicity of original expression, as well as the pure and fine moral feelings which imperceptibly pervades every thought and image, without being any where ostentatious or dogmatic, betray the author in every page; even without the aid of those minor peculiarities of style, taste, and local allusions, which at once identify the travelled Geoffrey Crayon with the venerable Knickerbocker.

The plan of the work is that of a series of extracts from the common-place book of an American, residing or travelling in Europe, sometimes describing the scenes and manners around him, and the various emotions and reflections which they call forth, and sometimes wandering back to the recollections of his native country and filling up the vivid pictures of its grand and beautiful scenery, which are still fresh in his memory, by imaginary creations of humour or of fancy. These he proposes to communicate to his countrymen in a series of numbers from time to time as leisure, health, and other circumstances may admit.

We are exceedingly tempted to enrich our pages with such extracts as might convey some idea of the manner in which this plan is executed, but we fear that we cannot do it without committing an act of injustice towards the author as well as to our readers. We must therefore content ourselves with a short notice of the several articles it contains. A brief and unpretending prospectus is followed by the 'author's account of himself,' not written in the common plan of describing a fictitious assumed character, but vividly painting his own youthful feelings and that stirring instinct of curiosity which forced him to become a traveller. 'The voyage' to Europe, and the mental employments of the traveller during his passage, are then described with admirable truth and deep feeling, generally in a tone of pensive morality, but occasionally rising into highly poetical feeling and expression.

The third article is headed Roscoe, and is devoted to the eulogy of that elegant writer and most liberal, benevolent, and learned merchant, the chief benefactor and ornament of

Liverpool. The writer enters into the praises of his favourite with that warmth and cordiality which indicate the strong sympathies of a congenial and kindred mind.

The next piece is a tale, 'The Wife;' it is peculiarly appropriate to the present state of the commercial world, and though drawn from domestic life, is full of very elevated—we may almost say—of sublime, moral sentiment. Its object is to paint the fortitude with which women of well constituted minds and strong affections can sustain the most overwhelming calamities and reverses of fortune, and to show how those disasters which humble the spirit of the lords of creation to the very dust, serve only to call forth the energies of the weaker sex, and give to their character a self-concentrated intrepidity which bears them buoyant through the storm.

The last article is 'Rips Van Winkle,' 'a tale found among the papers of the late Diedrich Knickerbocker,' in which the writer seems to have aspired to unite the Dutch painting of Crabbe and Smollet with the wild frolic and fancy of an Arabian tale.

We have now we think said enough on the subject to stimulate the curiosity of our readers, and we will not take off from this effect by any heavy and common-place criticism. —GULIAN C. VERPLANCK, "Sketch Book of Geoffrey Crayon," *Analectic Magazine*, July 1819, pp. 78–79

Everywhere I find in it the marks of a mind of the utmost elegance and refinement, a thing as you know that I was not exactly prepared to look for in an American. Each of the essays is entitled to its appropriate praise, and the whole is such as I scarcely know an Englishman that could have written. The author powerfully conciliates to himself our kindness and affection. But the "Essay on Rural Life in England" is incomparably the best. It is, I believe, all true; and one wonders, while reading, that nobody every said this before. There is wonderful sweetness in it.—WILLIAM GODWIN, Letter to James Ogilvie (Sept. 15, 1819), cited in Pierre M. Irving, *The Life and Letters of Washington Irving*, 1862–63, Vol. 1, p. 422

Though this is a very pleasing book in itself, and displays no ordinary reach of thought and elegance of fancy, it is not exactly on that account that we are now tempted to notice it as a very remarkable publication,—and to predict that it will form an era in the literature of the nation to which it belongs. It is the work of an American, entirely bred and trained in that country—originally published within its territory—and, as we understand, very extensively circulated, and very much admired among its natives. Now, the most remarkable thing in a work so circumstanced certainly is, that it should be written throughout with the greatest care and accuracy, and worked up to great purity and beauty of diction, on the model of the most elegant and polished of our native writers. It is the first American work, we rather think, of any description, but certainly the first purely literary production, to which we could give this praise; and we hope and trust that we may hail it as the harbinger of a purer and juster taste—the foundation of a chaster and better school, for the writers of that great and intelligent country. ⟨. . .⟩

But though it is primarily for its style and composition that we are induced to notice this book, it would be quite unjust to the author not to add, that he deserves very high commendation for its more substantial qualities; and that we have seldom seen a work that gave us a more pleasing impression of the writer's character, or a more favourable one of his judgment and taste. There is a tone of fairness and indulgence—and of gentleness and philanthropy so unaffectedly diffused through the whole work, and tempering and harmonizing so gracefully, both with its pensive and its gayer humours, as to disarm all ordinarily good-natured critics of their asperity, and to secure to the author, from all worthy readers, the same candour and kindness of which he sets so laudable an example. The want is of force and originality in the reasoning, and speculative parts, and of boldness and incident in the inventive:—though the place of these more commanding qualities is not ill supplied by great liberality and sound sense, and by a very considerable vein of humour, and no ordinary grace and tenderness of fancy. The manner perhaps throughout is more attended to than the matter; and the care necessary to maintain the rythm and polish of the sentences, has sometimes interfered with the force of the reasoning, or limited and impoverished the illustrations they might otherwise have supplied.

We have forgotten all this time to inform our readers, that the publication consists of a series or collection of detached essays and tales of various descriptions—originally published apart, in the form of a periodical miscellany, for the instruction and delight of America—and now collected into two volumes for the refreshment of the English public. The English writers whom the author has chiefly copied, are Addison and Goldsmith, in the humorous and discursive parts—and our own excellent Mackenzie, in the more soft and pathetic. In their highest and most characteristic merits, we do not mean to say that he has equalled any of his originals, or even to deny that he has occasionally caricatured their defects. But the resemblance is near enough to be highly creditable to any living author; and there is sometimes a compass of reasoning which his originals have but rarely attained.—FRANCIS, LORD JEFFREY, "The Sketch Book," *Edinburgh Review*, Aug. 1820, pp. 160–62

BRACEBRIDGE HALL

We have no hesitation in pronouncing *Bracebridge* quite equal to any thing, which the present age of English literature has produced in this department. In saying this, we class it in the branch of essay writing. It may, perhaps, be called a novel in disguise; since a series of personages are made the subject or authors of the sketches of life and manners, which it contains, and it is conducted to a wedding, the regular *denouement* of a novel. The plot, however, is quite subordinate; not exceeding in intricacy or amount of incident the history of those various respectable personages, with whom the *Spectator*, the *Tatler*, and other ancient humorists had to do. In fact it is the first observation, which the perusal of *Bracebridge* excites, that the Squire is a kind of extended Sir Roger de Coverley; and could Addison have foreseen that the worthy knight would be so honorably supported, we think he would not have been in haste 'to kill him.' Looking on this work then as a series of essays and sketches on English rural life and manners, we may venture to put it in comparison with any thing else of the kind in English literature, for accuracy and fidelity of observation, for spirit of description, for a certain peculiar sly pleasantry, like the very happiest touches of the Addisonian school, and for uncommon simplicity and purity of style. In this last respect, however, we do not know that it is any way superior to the former writings of its author. It was therefore not learned by him in England, and must accordingly constitute a problem curious to be solved by the philologers, who have written on the American language.—EDWARD EVERETT, "Bracebridge Hall," *North American Review*, July 1822, pp. 209–10

⟨. . .⟩ an author who is admitted by the public not to have fallen off in a second work, has in reality improved upon his first, and has truly deserved a higher place, by merely maintaining that which he had formerly earned. We would not have Mr Crayon, however, plume himself too much upon this sage observation; for though *we*, and other great lights of public judgment, have decided that his former level has been maintained in this work with the most marvellous precision, we must whisper in his ear that the million are not exactly of that opinion; and that the common buz among the idle and impatient critics of the drawingroom is, that, in comparison with the *Sketch Book*, it is rather monotonous and languid; that there is too little variety of characters for two thick volumes; and that the said few characters come on so often, and stay so long, that the gentlest reader at last detects himself in rejoicing at being done with them. The premises of this enthymem we do not much dispute; but the conclusion, for all that, is wrong: for, in spite of these defects, *Bracebridge Hall* is quite as good as the *Sketch Book*; and Mr C. may take comfort,—if he is humble enough to be comforted with such an assurance—and trust to us, that it will be quite as popular, and that he still holds his own with the efficient body of his English readers.

The great charm and peculiarity of his work consists now, as on former occasions, in the singular sweetness of the composition, and the mildness of the sentiments,—sicklied over perhaps a little, now and then, with that cloying heaviness into which unvaried sweetness is so apt to subside. The rythm and melody of the sentences is certainly excessive: As it not only gives an air of mannerism from its uniformity, but raises too strong an impression of the labour that must have been bestowed, and the importance which must have been attached to that which is, after all, but a secondary attribute to good writing. It is very ill-natured in us, however, to object to what has given us so much pleasure; for we happen to be very intense and sensitive admirers of those soft harmonies of studied speech in which this author is so apt to indulge himself; and have caught ourselves, oftener than we shall confess, neglecting his excellent matter, to lap ourselves in the liquid music of his periods—and letting ourselves float passively down the mellow falls and windings of his soft flowing sentences, with a delight, not inferior to that which we derive from fine versification.—FRANCIS, LORD JEFFREY, "Bracebridge Hall," *Edinburgh Review*, Nov. 1822, pp. 338–39

LIFE OF COLUMBUS

This, on the whole, is an excellent book; and we venture to anticipate that it will be an enduring one. Neither do we hazard this prediction lightly, or without a full consciousness of all that it implies. We are perfectly aware that there are but few modern works that are likely to verify it; and that it probably could not be extended with safety to so many as one in a hundred even of those which we praise. For we mean, not merely that the book will be familiarly known and referred to some twenty or thirty years hence, and will pass in solid binding into every considerable collection; but that it will supersede all former works on the same subject, and never be itself superseded.—FRANCIS, LORD JEFFREY, "Life and Voyages of Christopher Columbus," *Edinburgh Review*, Sept. 1828, p. 1

I am just reading Irving's *Columbus* for the first time, with much pleasure. I esteem it the first of American classics, and can never be affected enough to join in the clamour against his crystal flow of purest English.—JAMES W. ALEXANDER, Letter (Feb. 17, 1829), *Forty Years' Familiar Letters*, ed. John Hall, 1860, Vol. 1, p. 122

Since I have been here, I have contrived (by reading a half hour in the night and a half hour in the morning) to peruse the whole of Irving's *Life of Columbus*, in three volumes. It is quite an interesting work, though I think too much spread out by repetition of the same thoughts and descriptions. It is, in all respects, however, reputable to the literature of our country. —JOSEPH STORY, Letter to William W. Story (Feb. 21, 1836), cited in William W. Story, *Life and Letters of Joseph Story*, 1851, Vol. 2, p. 229

The *Life and Voyages of Christopher Columbus* placed Irving among the historians, for the biography of that great discoverer is a part, and a remarkable part, of the history of the world. Of what was strictly and simply personal in his adventures, much, of course, has passed into irremediable oblivion; what was both personal and historical is yet outstanding above the shadow that has settled upon the rest. The work of Irving was at once in everybody's hands and eagerly read. Navarrete vouched for its historical accuracy and completeness. Jeffrey declared that no work could ever take its place. It was written with a strong love of the subject, and to this it owes much of its power over the reader. Columbus was one of those who, with all their faculties occupied by one great idea, and bent on making it a practical reality, are looked upon as crazed, and pitied and forgotten if they fail; but, if they succeed, are venerated as the glory of their age. The poetic elements of his character and history, the grandeur and mystery of his design, his prophetic sagacity, his hopeful and devout courage, and his disregard of the ridicule of meaner intellects took a strong hold on the mind of Irving, and formed the inspiration of the work.

Mr. Duyckinck gives, on the authority of one who knew Irving intimately, an instructive anecdote relating to the *Life of Columbus*. When the work was nearly finished, it was put into the hands of Lieutenant Slidell Mackenzie, himself an agreeable writer, then on a visit to Spain, who read it with a view of giving a critical opinion of its merits. "It is quite perfect," said he, on returning the manuscript, "except the style, and that is unequal." The remark made such an impression on the mind of the author that he wrote over the whole narrative with a view of making the style more uniform but he afterward thought that he had not improved it.

In this I have no doubt that Irving was quite right, and that it would have been better if he had never touched the work after he had brought it to the state which satisfied his individual judgment. An author can scarcely commit a greater error than to alter what he writes, except when he has a clear perception that the alteration is for the better, and can make it with as hearty a confidence in himself as he felt in giving the work its first shape. What strikes me as an occasional defect in the *Life of Columbus* is this elaborate uniformity of style—a certain prismatic coloring in passages where absolute simplicity would have satisfied us better. It may well be supposed that Irving originally wrote some parts of the work with the quiet plainness of a calm relater of facts, and others with the spirit and fire of one who had become warmed with his subject, and this probably gave occasion to what was said of the inequality of the style. The attempt to elevate the diction of the simpler portions, we may suppose, marred what Irving afterward perceived had really been one of the merits of the work. —WILLIAM CULLEN BRYANT, "Washington Irving" (1860), *Prose Writings*, ed. Parke Godwin, 1884, Vol. 1, pp. 352–54

ALHAMBRA AND THE CONQUEST OF GRANADA

Mr. Irving has seldom selected a subject better suited to his peculiar powers than the conquest of Granada. Indeed, it would hardly have been possible for one of his warm sensibilities to linger so long among the remains of Moorish magnificence with which Spain is covered, without being interested in the fortunes of a people whose memory has almost passed into oblivion, but who once preserved the "sacred flame" when it had become extinct in every corner of Christendom, and whose influence is still visible on the intellectual culture of Modern Europe.—WILLIAM H. PRESCOTT, "Irving's *Conquest of Granada*" (1829), *Biographical and Critical Miscellanies*, 1845

The tales, though not to us, as we have said, the most agreeable portion of the work ⟨*Alhambra*⟩, and though, in fact, not distinguished by any particular power or point, are written in the correct and graceful style peculiar to the author, and will be read with pleasure, were it only for the beauty of the language, which is in fact their principal merit. "The Moor's Legacy" and "Governor Manco" are perhaps the best. "Prince Ahmed, or the Pilgrim of Love," though evidently among the more elaborate, appears to us somewhat less successful than the others, which is rather remarkable, considering the attractive character of the subject, and the profusion of machinery which the author has brought into action. It would give us pleasure to adorn our pages with one of these narratives, but we deem it unnecessary for the purpose of making them known, as they are doubtless already familiar to our readers. On the whole, we consider the work before us as equal in literary value to any of the others of the same class, with the exception of the *Sketch Book*, and we should not be surprised, if it were read as extensively as even that very popular production. We hope to have it in our power, at no remote period, to announce a continuation of the series, which we are satisfied will bear, in the bookseller's phrase, several more volumes.—EDWARD EVERETT, "Irving's *Alhambra*," *North American Review*, Oct. 1832, p. 281

LIFE OF WASHINGTON

Your volume, of which I gained a copy last night, and this morning have received one made still more precious by your own hand, shortened my sleep last night at both ends. I was up late and early, and could not rest until I had finished the last page. Candor, good judgment that knows no bias, the felicity of selection, these are yours in common with the best historians. But, in addition, you have the peculiarity of writing from the heart, enchaining sympathy as well as commanding confidence; the happy magic that makes scenes, events, and personal anecdotes present themselves to you at your bidding, and fall into their natural places, and take color and warmth from your own nature. The style, too, is masterly, clear, easy, and graceful; picturesque without mannerism, and ornamented without losing simplicity. Among men of letters, who do well, you must above all take the name of Felix, which so few of the great Roman generals could claim. You do everything rightly, as if by grace; and I am in no fear of offending your modesty, for I think you were elected and foreordained to excel your contemporaries.—GEORGE BANCROFT, Letter to Washington Irving (May 30, 1855), cited in Pierre M. Irving, *The Life and Letters of Washington Irving*, 1862–63, Vol. 4, p. 194

The crowning work of Mr. Irving's literary life—connecting his literary fame, as his baptismal name had from his infancy connected him, with the Father of his country—was, of course, the *Life of Washington*. Every American must have hailed with no common delight a work on such a subject, from such a pen. I have read but few books in my life with so deep an interest as I read the successive volumes of that most faithful yet brilliant and picturesque biography. The genius of the author and the character of the man seemed to me to shine with peculiar brightness from its enchanting pages. In the description of life in Virginia, during Washington's youth, Irving's power of word-painting is beautifully shown. In the sketches of the frontier wars, in which the youthful hero bore so conspicuous a part; in the tragedy of Braddock's rash expedition; in the military narratives of the Revolution; in the presentation of Washington as the Chief Magistrate of the Republic; in the picture of his retirement, and his peaceful death,—everywhere we feel the inspiration of genius working upon a congenial theme; everywhere we discern a profound and loving appreciation of Washington's peerless character. —CORNELIUS CONWAY FELTON, *Proceedings of the Massachusetts Historical Society*, Dec. 1859, pp. 413–14

In his retirement at Sunnyside, Irving planned and executed his last great work, the *Life of Washington*, to which he says he had long looked forward as his crowning literary effort. Constable, the Edinburgh bookseller, had proposed it to him thirty years before, and he then resolved to undertake it as soon as he should return to the United States. It was postponed in favor of other projects, but never abandoned. At length the expected time seemed to have arrived; his other tasks had been successfully performed; the world was waiting for new works from his pen; his mind and body were yet in their vigor; the habit and the love of literary production yet remained, and he addressed himself to this greatest of his labors.

Yet he had his misgivings, though they could not divert him from his purpose. "They expect too much—too much," he said to a friend of mine, to whom he was speaking of the magnitude of the task and the difficulty of satisfying the public. We cannot wonder at these doubts. At the time when he began to employ himself steadily on this work, he was near the age of threescore and ten, when with most men the season of hope and confidence is past. He was like one who should begin the great labor of the day when the sun was shedding his latest beams, and what if the shadows of night should descend upon him before his task was ended! A vast labor had been thrown upon him by the almost numberless documents and papers recently brought to light relating to the events in which Washington was concerned—such as were amassed and digested by the research of Sparks, and accompanied by the commentary of his excellent biography. These were all to be carefully examined and their spirit extracted. Historians had in the mean time arisen in our country, of a world-wide fame, with whose works his own must be compared, and he was to be judged by a public whom he, more than almost any other man, had taught to be impatient of mediocrity.

I do not believe, however, that Irving's task would have been performed so ably if it had been undertaken when it was suggested by Constable; the narrative could not have been so complete in its facts; it might not have been written with the same becoming simplicity. It was fortunate that the work was delayed till it could be written from the largest store of materials, till its plan was fully matured in all its fair proportions, and till the author's mind had become filled with the profoundest veneration for his subject.

The simplicity already mentioned is the first quality of this work which impresses the reader. Here is a man of genius, a poet by temperament, writing the life of a man of transcendent wisdom and virtue—a life passed amid great events, and marked by inestimable public services. There is a constant temptation to eulogy, but the temptation is resisted; the actions of his hero are left to speak their own praise. He records events reverently, as one might have recorded them before the art of rhetoric was invented, with no exaggeration, with no parade of reflection; the lessons of the narrative are made to impress themselves on the mind by the earnest and conscientious relation of facts. Meantime, the narrator keeps himself in the background, solely occupied with the due presentation of his subject. Our eyes are upon the actors whom he sets before us—we never think of Mr. Irving.

A closer examination reveals another great merit of the work, the admirable proportion in which the author keeps the characters and events of his story. I suppose he could hardly have been conscious of this merit, and that it was attained without a direct effort. Long meditation had probably so shaped and matured the plan in his mind, and so arranged its parts in their just symmetry, that, executing it conscientiously as he did, he could not have made it a different thing from what we have it. There is nothing distorted, nothing placed in too broad a light or thrown too far in the shade. The incidents of our Revolutionary War, the great event of Washington's life, pass before us as they passed before the eyes of the commander-in-chief himself, and from time to time varied his designs. Washington is kept always in sight, and the office of the biographer is never allowed to become merged in that of the historian.

The men who were the companions of Washington in the field or in civil life are shown only in their association with him, yet are their characters drawn, not only with skill and spirit, but with a hand that delighted to do them justice. Nothing, I believe, could be more abhorrent to Irving's ideas of the province of a biographer than the slightest detraction from the merits of others, that his hero might appear the more eminent. So remarkable is his work in this respect that an accomplished member of the Historical Society, who has analyzed the merits of the *Life of Washington* with a critical skill which makes me ashamed to speak of the work after him, has declared that no writer, within the circle of his reading, "has so successfully established his claim to the rare and difficult virtue of impartiality."

I confess my admiration of this work becomes the greater the more I examine it. In the other writings of Irving are beauties which strike the reader at once. In this I recognize qualities which lie deeper, and which I was not sure of finding—a rare equity of judgment; a large grasp of the subject; a profound philosophy, independent of philosophical forms, and even instinctively rejecting them; the power of reducing an immense crowd of loose materials to clear and orderly arrangement, and forming them into one grand whole, as a skilful commander, from a rabble of raw recruits, forms a disciplined army, animated and moved by a single will.

The greater part of this last work of Irving was composed while he was in the enjoyment of what might be called a happy old age. This period of his life was not without its infirmities, but his frame was yet unwasted, his intellect bright and active, and the hour of decay seemed distant. He had become more than ever the object of public veneration, and in his beautiful retreat enjoyed all the advantages with few of the molestations of acknowledged greatness; a little too much visited, perhaps, but submitting to the intrusion of his admirers with his characteristic patience and kindness. That retreat had now become more charming than ever, and the domestic life within was as beautiful as the nature without. A surviving brother, older than himself, shared it with him, and several affectionate nephews and nieces stood to him in the relation of sons and daughters. He was surrounded by neighbors who saw him daily, and honored and loved him the more for knowing him so well.—WILLIAM CULLEN BRYANT, "Washington Irving"

(1860), *Prose Writings*, ed. Parke Godwin, 1884, Vol. 1, pp. 360–63

There are those who have objected that the last subject of his labor—the *Life of Washington*—was little suited to his imaginative tone of mind, and should have been worked up with a larger and more philosophic grasp of thought. It may well be that at some future time we shall have a more profound estimate of the relations which our great Leader held to his cause and to his time; but, however profound and just such a work may be, we feel quite safe in predicting that it will never supplant the graceful labor of Mr. Irving in the hearts of the American people. Precisely what was wanted Mr. Irving has given: such charming, faithful, truthful picture of the great hero of our Revolution as should carry knowledge of him, of the battles he fought, of his large, self-denying, unswerving patriotism, of the purity of his life, into every household. No man could have done this work better; nor do we think any other will ever do it as well.—DONALD G. MITCHELL, "Washington Irving," *Atlantic*, June 1864, pp. 700–701

GEORGE WASHINGTON GREENE
From "Irving's Works"
Biographical Studies
1860, pp. 163–76

His style possesses that exquisite charm which nothing but the study of books, combined with that of nature, can give. You feel that he has drunk deep at the pure wells of literature, and looked on men and nature with a loving heart. If style be a reflection of the mind, Mr. Irving's must be a beautiful one. And yet, clearly marked as the characteristics of his style are, we are at a loss to seize upon the secret of its power. It is natural, for you feel all the while you are reading him as if you ought to have written just so yourself. It is simple, for there is not an overstrained expression or a cumbrous epithet in it. It is elegant, for it has all the richness which imagery and language can give. It is picturesque, for it paints to the eye like poetry. It is harmonious, for it falls on the ear like music. It is transparent—the meadow-brook is not more so. And yet of these and of all the qualities which it possesses in so eminent a degree, which are those that mark him out as a writer by himself, and make it impossible for you to confound him with any other?

One of them doubtless is his peculiar felicity in the choice of epithets. This is, as every writer knows, one of the greatest difficulties in the art of writing. It is one thing to describe a scene accurately, another to throw into your description some happy expression which shall imprint it on the memory and become permanently associated with it. It is the poet's gift, requiring quick sensibilities and a lively fancy. Mr. Irving has it in an eminent degree. He never plucks a flower without seeing something in it that you never saw there before,—some connection between the visible and the invisible world, some new alliance betwixt thought and feeling, which embalms it in odors richer than its own. His landscapes show with what a thoughtful and confiding spirit he has looked upon nature, drawing in cheering inspirations and a soothing trust for the hour of gloom. Did you ever look, kind reader, upon an Italian landscape in October? We will suppose it to be a mountain scene,—Florence, if you choose, for there the mountains are drawn in a semicircle around you, and the sweet valley of the

Arno lies like a sunbeam between. Look upon that valley and those mountains. They are the same that you saw a few months ago,—the same sharp outline on the clear blue sky, the same mingling of olive and vineyard below. But there is something there unseen before, something which softens down every rougher feature, and gives a deeper yet a calmer glow to the sunlight that rests upon it like a smile of love. It is nothing but a thin veil of unsubstantial mist, which the first rough breeze will scatter, or which may rise up to float away with the clouds, and fall back to earth or ocean again in rain; and yet with that veil over it with what a new and magic power does the spell of the landscape steal into your soul.

Now this is just the effect of Mr. Irving's epithets. You knew the object before, its form and history, and could tell, as you thought, all about it; and yet how different it appears when you look at it through the magic of his words. ⟨. . .⟩

Mr. Irving's style has neither the point of Macaulay nor the earnestness of Arnold, but there is a gentle persuasiveness about it which carries you forward with an imperceptible, but at the same time an irresistible, force. It is like floating down some broad stream, with towers and old castles, and groves, and vineyards, and green meadows scattered all along its banks. You can look at them all as you glide gently by, and catch the sweet odors of the blossoms and the flowers; and it is only when you pause to look backwards that you feel that the greatest wonder of all is the stream on whose bosom you have floated so sweetly.

Another charm of Mr. Irving's writings is the skill with which he winds into his subject. His introductions always seem to rise from it naturally, and prepare the way for what follows, just as a well arranged prelude prepares the ear for the music. There is generally a certain amount of common-place in an introduction, whether it be grave or gay; and the utmost that can be asked of a writer is that he should give it a new turn. There is great danger, too, of promising too much, of starting upon a high key which you cannot get down from without a discord. It is seldom that there is any such jar in Mr. Irving. He has none of the listlessness either, with which you sometimes take up your pen, and which hangs over you till you are fairly started. He always seems to come well prepared, and to know where he means to begin. If he does gnaw his pen, the reader never finds it out. ⟨. . .⟩

It would be easy to go on and speak of Irving's humor and pathos, of the pure tone of his writings, and his true American spirit. We must say one word about the last, for some exacting critics have seen fit to charge him with a lack of it, and lay it to his door as a fault that he has written so much about Europe. We have never counted the purely American pages in his works, but there is not one of them in which the subject admitted of it, which does not contain some illustration of American scenery or tradition. King Philip, and the chapter on the Indians, in the *Sketch Book*, are certainly not European, any more than "Rip Van Winkle" and "Sleepy Hollow." "Dolph Heyliger" is one of the best things in *Bracebridge Hall*. A volume has been made out of what he has written about the Hudson,[1] and Columbus is all American. But those who accuse Irving of writing too much about Europe forget that he was writing for Americans who wanted to be told something about that Old World which so few of them, when he first began to write, had ever seen. Circumstances had put it in his power to meet one of the great wants of our public, and he did it. Some crusty European may perhaps blame him, but the ten thousand copies which have already been sold of this last edition of the *Sketch Book*, tell clearly enough what his own countrymen think of it.

We must add, too, a few words about the *Life of Goldsmith*. Mahomet belongs to the Spanish series, of which we hope to speak at length on some future occasion. But the Goldsmith is complete.

If there is anybody of whom it could be said that it was his duty to write a life of Goldsmith, it is Washington Irving; and often as we have had occasion to thank him for happy hours, we do not know that we ever felt so grateful to him for anything as for this. We have always loved Goldsmith, his poetry and his prose, and everything about him. There is not a poem in the language that we can go back to with the same zest with which we open the *Traveller* or the *Deserted Village* for the five hundredth time; and we can never get through a ten minutes' speech without quoting the *Vicar of Wakefield*. And yet we must say frankly that we never understood Goldsmith's character until now. We have been vexed at his weakness and have blushed at his blunders. We had always wished he could have thrown off his brogue and had never put on his bloom-colored coat. That he should not have known how to keep his money was not very wonderful,—it is a professional weakness; but he might at any rate have thrown it away in better company. We have been more than once sorely troubled too by sundry little slips that savored somewhat of moral obliquity; and never been able to reconcile the elevation of his intellect with acts that far less rigorous judges than we have characterized as mean and degrading. In short, with all our contempt for Boswell, we had been fairly Boswellised, and much as we loved Goldsmith, loved him somewhat in despite of what we thought our better judgment.

Thanks to Mr. Irving, our doubts have all been solved, and we can love the kind, simple-hearted, genial man with as much confidence as we admire his writings. This overflowing of the heart, this true philosophy so interwoven with his whole nature that whether he acts or speaks you find it as strongly marked in his actions as in his language; that quick sensibility which makes him so keenly alive to all the petty annoyances of his dependent position, and that buoyancy of spirit which raises him above them, and bears him up on the wave while many a stouter heart is sinking around him; those ready sympathies, that self-forgetfulness, that innate, unprompted, spontaneous philanthropy which, in the days of his prosperity as well as in his days of trial, was never belied by word or by deed,—all these we understand as we never understood them before, and feel how rare and beautiful they are. He was not wise in his own concerns, and yet what treasures of wisdom has he bequeathed to the world. Artless as an infant, yet how deeply read in human nature; with all his feelings upon the surface, ruffled by every breeze and glowing in every sunbeam, and yet how skilled in all the secret windings of the heart. None but a man of genial nature should ever attempt to write the life of Goldsmith: one who knows how much wisdom can be extracted from folly; how much better for the heart it is to trust than to doubt; how much nobler is a generous impulse than a cautious reserve; how much truer a wisdom there is in benevolence than in all the shrewd devices of worldly craft.

Now Mr. Irving is just the man to feel all this and to make you feel it too. He sees how weak Goldsmith is in many things, how wise in others, and he sees how closely his wisdom and his weakness are allied. There is no condescension in his pity, none of that parade which often makes pity tenfold more bitter than the sufferings which call it forth. He tells you the story of his hero's errors as freely as he does that of his virtues, and in a way to make you feel that a man may have many a human weakness lie heavy at his door, and yet be worthy of our love and admiration still. He has no desire to conceal, makes no attempt to palliate. He understands his hero's character thoroughly, and feels that if he can only make you understand it, you will love him as much as he does. Therefore he draws him just as he is, lights and shadows, virtues and foibles,—vices you cannot call them, be you never so unkind. At his blunders he laughs just as Goldsmith himself used to laugh in recounting them, and he feels the secret of his virtues too justly to attempt to gild them over with useless embellishments.

We have always fancied that there was a strong resemblance between Goldsmith and Irving. They both look at human nature from the same generous point of view, with the same kindly sympathies and the same tolerant philosophy. They have the same quick perception of the ludicrous, and the same tender simplicity in the pathetic. There is the same quiet vein of humor in both, and the same cheerful spirit of hopefulness. You are at a loss to conceive how either of them can ever have had an enemy; and as for jealousy and malice, and all that brood of evil passions which beset the path of fame so thickly, you feel that there can be no resting-place for them in bosoms like theirs. Yet each preserves his individuality as distinctly as if there were no points of resemblance between them. Irving's style is as much his own as though Goldsmith had never written, and his pictures have that freshness about them which nothing but life-studies can give. He has written no poem, no *Traveller*, no *Deserted Village*, no exquisite ballad like *The Hermit*, no touching little stanzas of unapproachable pathos, like "Woman." But how much real poetry and how much real pathos has he not written. We do not believe that there was ever such a description of the song of a bird as his description of the soaring of a lark in "Buckthorn;" and the poor old widow in the *Sketch Book* who, the first Sunday after her son's burial, comes to church with a few bits of black silk and ribbon about her, the only external emblem of mourning which her poverty allowed her to make, is a picture that we can never look at through his simple and graphic periods without sobbing like a child. Poet he is, and that too of the best and noblest kind, for he stores our memories with lovely images and our hearts with humane affections. If you would learn to be kinder and truer, if you would learn to bear life's burden manfully, and make for yourself sunshine where half your fellow-men see nothing but shadows and gloom,—read and meditate Goldsmith and Irving. And if you too are an author, at the first gentle acclivity or far upwards on the heights of fame, learn to turn backwards to your teacher with the same generous and fervent gratitude with which Irving at the close of his preface addresses himself to Goldsmith in the noble language of Dante:—

> Tu se' lo mio maestro, e 'l mio autore;
> Tu se' solo colui da cui io tolsi
> Lo bello stile che m' ba fatto onore.

> Thou art my master, and my teacher thou;
> It was from thee, and thee alone, I took
> That noble style for which men honor me.

Notes
1. *Book of the Hudson, &c.*

CHARLES DUDLEY WARNER
From *Washington Irving*
1881, pp. 285–303

I do not know any other author whose writings so perfectly reproduce his character, or whose character may be more certainly measured by his writings. His character is perfectly transparent: his predominant traits were humor and sentiment;

his temperament was gay with a dash of melancholy; his inner life and his mental operations were the reverse of complex, and his literary method is simple. He *felt* his subject, and he expressed his conception not so much by direct statement or description as by almost imperceptible touches and shadings here and there, by a diffused tone and color, with very little show of analysis. Perhaps it is a sufficient definition to say that his method was the sympathetic. In the end the reader is put in possession of the luminous and complete idea upon which the author has been brooding, though he may not be able to say exactly how the impression has been conveyed to him; and I doubt if the author could have explained his sympathetic process. He certainly would have lacked precision in any philosophical or metaphysical theme, and when, in his letters, he touches upon politics there is a little vagueness of definition that indicates want of mental grip in that direction. But in the region of feeling his genius is sufficient to his purpose; either when that purpose is a highly creative one, as in the character and achievements of his Dutch heroes, or merely that of portraiture, as in the *Columbus* and the *Washington*. The analysis of a nature so simple and a character so transparent as Irving's, who lived in the sunlight and had no envelope of mystery, has not the fascination that attaches to Hawthorne.

Although the direction of his work as a man of letters was largely determined by his early surroundings,—that is, by his birth in a land void of traditions, and into a society without much literary life, so that his intellectual food was of necessity a foreign literature that was at the moment becoming a little antiquated in the land of its birth, and his warm imagination was forced to revert to the past for that nourishment which his crude environment did not offer,—yet he was by nature a retrospective man. His face was set towards the past, not towards the future. He never caught the restlessness of this century, nor the prophetic light that shone in the faces of Coleridge, Shelley, and Keats; if he apprehended the stir of the new spirit he still, by mental affiliation, belonged rather to the age of Addison than to that of Macaulay. And his placid, retrospective, optimistic strain pleased a public that were excited and harrowed by the mocking and lamenting of Lord Byron, and, singularly enough, pleased even the great pessimist himself.

His writings induce to reflection, to quiet musing, to tenderness for tradition; they amuse, they entertain, they call a check to the feverishness of modern life; but they are rarely stimulating or suggestive. They are better adapted, it must be owned, to please the many than the critical few, who demand more incisive treatment and a deeper consideration of the problems of life. And it is very fortunate that a writer who can reach the great public and entertain it can also elevate and refine its tastes, set before it high ideas, instruct it agreeably, and all this in a style that belongs to the best literature. It is a safe model for young readers; and for young readers there is very little in the overwhelming flood of to-day that is comparable to Irving's books, and, especially, it seems to me, because they were not written for children.

Irving's position in American literature, or in that of the English tongue, will only be determined by the slow settling of opinion, which no critic can foretell, and the operation of which no criticism seems able to explain. I venture to believe, however, that the verdict will not be in accord with much of the present prevalent criticism. The service that he rendered to American letters no critic disputes; nor is there any question of our national indebtedness to him for investing a crude and new land with the enduring charms of romance and tradition. In this respect, our obligation to him is that of Scotland to Scott and Burns; and it is an obligation due only, in all history, to here and there a fortunate creator to whose genius opportunity is kind. The Knickerbocker Legend and the romance with which Irving has invested the Hudson are a priceless legacy; and this would remain an imperishable possession in popular tradition if the literature creating it were destroyed. This sort of creation is unique in modern times. New York is the Knicker-bocker city; its whole social life remains colored by his fiction; and the romantic background it owes to him in some measure supplies to it what great age has given to European cities. This creation is sufficient to secure for him an immortality, a length of earthly remembrance that all the rest of his writings together might not give.

Irving was always the literary man; he had the habits, the idiosyncrasies, of his small genus. I mean that he regarded life not from the philanthropic, the economic, the political, the philosophic, the metaphysic, the scientific, or the theologic, but purely from the literary point of view. He belongs to that small class of which Johnson and Goldsmith are perhaps as good types as any, and to which America has added very few. The literary point of view is taken by few in any generation; it may seem to the world of very little consequence in the pressure of all the complex interests of life, and it may even seem trivial amid the tremendous energies applied to immedi-ate affairs; but it is the point of view that endures; if its creations do not mould human life, like the Roman law, they remain to charm and civilize, like the poems of Horace. You must not ask more of them than that. This attitude toward life is defensible on the highest grounds. A man with Irving's gifts has the right to take the position of an observer and describer, and not to be called on for a more active participation in affairs than he chooses to take. He is doing the world the highest service of which he is capable, and the most enduring it can receive from any man. It is not a question whether the work of the literary man is higher than that of the reformer or the statesman; it is a distinct work, and is justified by the result, even when the work is that of the humorist only. We recognize this in the case of the poet. Although Goethe has been reproached for his lack of sympathy with the liberalizing movement of his day (as if his novels were quieting social influences), it is felt by this generation that the author of *Faust* needs no apology that he did not spend his energies in the effervescing politics of the German states. I mean, that while we may like or dislike the man for his sympathy or want of sympathy, we concede to the author the right of his attitude; if Goethe had not assumed freedom from moral responsibility, I suppose that criticism of his aloofness would long ago have ceased. Irving did not lack sympathy with humanity in the concrete; it colored whatever he wrote. But he regarded the politics of his own country, the revolutions in France, the long struggle in Spain, without heat; and he held aloof from projects of agitation and reform, and maintained the attitude of an observer, regarding the life about him from the point of view of the literary artist, as he was justified in doing.

Irving had the defects of his peculiar genius, and these have no doubt helped to fix upon him the complimentary disparagement of "genial." He was not aggressive; in his nature he was wholly unpartisan, and full of lenient charity; and I suspect that his kindly regard of the world, although returned with kindly liking, cost him something of that respect for sturdiness and force which men feel for writers who flout them as fools in the main. Like Scott, he belonged to the idealists, and not to the realists, whom our generation affects. Both writers stimulate the longing for something better. Their creed was short: "Love God and honor the King." It is a very good

one for a literary man, and might do for a Christian. The supernatural was still a reality in the age in which they wrote. Irving's faith in God and his love of humanity were very simple; I do not suppose he was much disturbed by the deep problems that have set us all adrift. In every age, whatever is astir, literature, theology, all intellectual activity, takes one and the same drift, and approximates in color. The bent of Irving's spirit was fixed in his youth, and he escaped the desperate realism of this generation, which has no outcome, and is likely to produce little that is noble.

I do not know how to account, on principles of culture which we recognize, for our author's style. His education was exceedingly defective, nor was his want of discipline supplied by subsequent desultory application. He seems to have been born with a rare sense of literary proportion and form; into this, as into a mould, were run his apparently lazy and really acute observations of life. That he thoroughly mastered such litera-ture as he fancied there is abundant evidence; that his style was influenced by the purest English models is also apparent. But there remains a large margin for wonder how, with his want of training, he could have elaborated a style which is distinctively his own, and is as copious, felicitous in the choice of words, flowing, spontaneous, flexible, engaging, clear, and as little wearisome when read continuously in quantity as any in the English tongue. This is saying a great deal, though it is not claiming for him the compactness, nor the robust vigor, nor the depth of thought, of many others masters in it. It is sometimes praised for its simplicity. It is certainly lucid, but its simplicity is not that of Benjamin Franklin's style; it is often ornate, not seldom somewhat diffuse, and always exceedingly melodious. It is noticeable for its metaphorical felicity. But it was not in the sympathetic nature of the author, to which I just referred, to come sharply to the point. It is much to have merited the eulogy of Campbell that he had "added clarity to the English tongue." This elegance and finish of style (which seems to have been as natural to the man as his amiable manner) is sometimes made his reproach, as if it were his sole merit, and as if he had concealed under this charming form a want of substance. In literature form is vital. But his case does not rest upon that. As an illustration his *Life of Washington* may be put in evidence. Probably this work lost something in incisiveness and brilliancy by being postponed till the writer's old age. But whatever this loss, it is impossible for any biography to be less pretentious in style, or less ambitious in proclamation. The only pretension of matter is in the early chapters, in which a more than doubtful genealogy is elabo-rated, and in which it is thought necessary to Washington's dignity to give a fictitious importance to his family and his childhood, and to accept the southern estimate of the hut in which he was born as a "mansion." In much of this false estimate Irving was doubtless misled by the fables of Weems. But while he has given us a dignified portrait of Washington, it is as far as possible removed from that of the smileless prig which has begun to weary even the popular fancy. The man he paints is flesh and blood, presented, I believe, with substantial faithfulness to his character; with a recognition of the defects of his education and the deliberation of his mental operations; with at least a hint of that want of breadth of culture and knowledge of the past, the possession of which characterized many of his great associates; and with no concealment that he had a dower of passions and a temper which only vigorous self-watchfulness kept under. But he portrays, with an admi-ration not too highly colored, the magnificent patience, the courage to bear misconstruction, the unfailing patriotism, the practical sagacity, the level balance of judgment combined with the wisest toleration, the dignity of mind, and the lofty moral nature which made him the great man of his epoch. Irving's grasp of this character; his lucid marshaling of the scattered, often wearisome and uninteresting details of our dragging, unpicturesque Revolutionary War; his just judgment of men; his even almost judicial, moderation of tone; and his admirable proportion of space to events, render the discussion of style in reference to this work superfluous. Another writer might have made a more brilliant performance: descriptions sparkling with antitheses, characters projected into startling attitudes by the use of epithets; a work more exciting and more piquant, that would have started a thousand controversies, and engaged the attention by daring conjectures and attempts to make a dramatic spectacle; a book interesting and notable, but false in philosophy and untrue in fact.

When the *Sketch-Book* appeared, an English critic said it should have been first published in England, for Irving was an English writer. The idea has been more than once echoed here. The truth is that while Irving was intensely American in feeling he was first of all a man of letters, and in that capacity he was cosmopolitan; he certainly was not insular. He had a rare accommodation of tone to his theme. Of England, whose traditions kindled his susceptible fancy, he wrote as Englishmen would like to write about it. In Spain he was saturated with the romantic story of the people and the fascination of the clime; and he was so true an interpreter of both as to earn from the Spaniards the title of "the poet Irving." I chanced once, in an inn at Frascati, to take up *The Tales of a Traveller*, which I had not seen for many years. I expected to revive the somewhat faded humor and fancy of the past generation. But I found not only a sprightly humor and vivacity which are modern, but a truth to Italian local color that is very rare in any writer foreign to the soil. As to America, I do not know what can be more characteristically American than the Knickerbocker, the Hudson River tales, the sketches of life and adventure in the far West. But underneath all this diversity there is one constant quality,—the flavor of the author. Open by chance and read almost anywhere in his score of books,—it may be the *Tour on the Prairies*, the familiar dream of the Alhambra, or the narratives of the brilliant exploits of New World explorers; surrender yourself to the flowing current of his transparent style, and you are conscious of a beguilement which is the crowning excellence of all lighter literature, for which we have no word but "charm."

The consensus of opinion about Irving in England and America for thirty years was very remarkable. He had a universal popularity rarely enjoyed by any writer. England returned him to America medalled by the king, honored by the university which is chary of its favors, followed by the applause of the whole English people. In English households, in drawing-rooms of the metropolis in political circles no less than among the literary coteries, in the best reviews, and in the popular newspapers the opinion of him was pretty much the same. And even in the lapse of time and the change of literary fashion authors so unlike as Byron and Dickens were equally warm in admiration of him. To the English indorsement America added her own enthusiasm, which was as universal. His readers were the million, and all his readers were admirers. Even American statesmen, who feed their minds on food we know not of, read Irving. It is true that the uncritical opinion of New York was never exactly re-echoed in the cool recesses of Boston culture; but the magnates of the *North American Review* gave him their meed of cordial praise. The country at large put him on a pinnacle. If you attempt to account for the position he occupied by his character, which won the love of all men, it must be remembered that the quality which won this, whatever its value, pervades his books also.

And yet it must be said that the total impression left upon the mind by the man and his works is not that of the greatest intellectual force. I have no doubt that this was the impression he made upon his ablest contemporaries. And this fact, when I consider the effect the man produced, makes the study of him all the more interesting. As an intellectual personality he makes no such impression, for instance, as Carlyle, or a dozen other writers now living who could be named. The incisive critical faculty was almost entirely wanting in him. He had neither the power nor the disposition to cut his way transversely across popular opinion and prejudice that Ruskin has, nor to draw around him disciples equally well pleased to see him fiercely demolish today what they had delighted to see him set up yesterday as eternal. He evoked neither violent partisanship nor violent opposition. He was an extremely sensitive man, and if he had been capable of creating a conflict he would only have been miserable in it. The play of his mind depended upon the sunshine of approval. And all this shows a certain want of intellectual virility.

A recent anonymous writer has said that most of the writing of our day is characterized by an intellectual strain. I have no doubt that this will appear to be the case to the next generation. It is a strain to say something new even at the risk of paradox, or to say something in a new way at the risk of obscurity. From this Irving was entirely free. There is no visible straining to attract attention. His mood is calm and unexaggerated. Even in some of his pathos, which is open to the suspicion of being "literary," there is no literary exaggeration. He seems always writing from an internal calm, which is the necessary condition of his production. If he wins at all by his style, by his humor, by his portraiture of scenes or of character, it is by a gentle force, like that of the sun in spring. There are many men now living, or recently dead, intellectual prodigies, who have stimulated thought, upset opinions, created mental eras, to whom Irving stands hardly in as fair a relation as Goldsmith to Johnson. What verdict the next generation will put upon their achievements I do not know; but it is safe to say that their position and that of Irving as well will depend largely upon the affirmation or the reversal of their views of life and their judgments of character. I think the calm work of Irving will stand when much of the more startling and perhaps more brilliant intellectual achievement of this age has passed away.

And this leads me to speak of Irving's moral quality, which I cannot bring myself to exclude from a literary estimate, even in the face of the current gospel of art for art's sake. There is something that made Scott and Irving personally loved by the millions of their readers, who had only the dimmest ideas of their personality. This was some quality perceived in what they wrote. Each one can define it for himself; there it is, and I do not see why it is not as integral a part of the authors—an element in the estimate of their future position—as what we term their intellect, their knowledge, their skill, or their art. However you rate it, you cannot account for Irving's influence in the world without it. In his tender tribute to Irving, the great-hearted Thackeray, who saw as clearly as anybody the place of mere literary art in the sum total of life, quoted the dying words of Scott to Lockhart,—"Be a good man, my dear." We know well enough that the great author of *The Newcomes* and the great author of *The Heart of Midlothian* recognized the abiding value in literature of integrity, sincerity, purity, charity, faith. These are beneficences; and Irving's literature, walk round it and measure it by whatever critical instruments you will, is a beneficient literature. The author loved good women and little children and a pure life; he had faith in his fellow-men, a kindly sympathy with the lowest, without any subservience to the highest; he retained a belief in the possibility of chivalrous actions, and did not care to envelop them in a cynical suspicion; he was an author still capable of an enthusiasm. His books are wholesome, full of sweetness and charm, of humor without any sting, of amusement without any stain; and their more solid qualities are marred by neither pedantry nor pretension.

BARRETT WENDELL
From A *Literary History of America*
1900, pp. 171–80

Irving was the first American man of letters to attract wide attention abroad. The *Knickerbocker History* was favourably received by contemporary England; and the *Sketch Book* and *Bracebridge Hall*, which followed it, were from the beginning what they have remained,—as popular in England as they have been in his native country. The same, on the whole, is true of his writings about Spain; and, to somewhat slighter degree, of his *Life of Goldsmith* and his *Life of Washington*. The four general classes of work here mentioned followed one another in fairly distinct succession through his half-century of literary life. We may perhaps get our clearest notion of him by considering them in turn.

The *Knickerbocker History of New York* has properly lasted. The origin of this book resembles that of Fielding's *Joseph Andrews* some seventy years before, and of Dickens's *Pickwick Papers* some twenty-five years later. All three began as burlesques and ended as independent works of fiction, retaining of their origin little more trace than occasional extravagance. In 1807 one Dr. Samuel Latham Mitchill had published *A Picture of New York*, said to be ridiculous, even among works of its time, for ponderous pretentiousness. The book had such success, however, that Irving and his brother were moved to write a parody of it. Before long Irving's brother tired of the work, which was left to Irving himself. As he wrote on, his style and purpose underwent a change. Instead of burlesquing Mitchill, he found himself composing a comic history of old New York, and incidentally introducing a good deal of personal and political satire, now as forgotten as that which lies neglected in *Gulliver's Travels*. His style, which began in deliberately ponderous imitation of Dr. Mitchill's, passed almost insensibly into one of considerable freedom, evidently modelled on that of eighteenth-century England. Most of the book, then, reads like some skilful bit of English writing during the generation which preceded the American Revolution. The substance of the book, however, is distinctly different from what was then usual in England.

Assuming throughout the character of Diedrich Knickerbocker, an eccentric old bachelor who typifies the decaying Dutch families of New York, Irving mingles with many actual facts of colonial history all manner of unbridled extravagance. The governors and certain other of his personages are historical; the wars with New Englanders are historical wars; and historical, too, is the profound distaste for Yankee character which Washington Irving needed no assumed personality to feel. But throughout the book there mingles with these historical facts the wildest sort of sportive nonsense. Wouter Van Twiller, to take a casual example, was an authentic Dutch

governor of New Amsterdam; and here is the way in which Irving writes about him:—

> In his council he presided with great state and solemnity. He sat in a huge chair of solid oak, hewn in the celebrated forest of the Hague, fabricated by an experienced timmerman of Amsterdam, and curiously carved about the arms and feet, into exact imitations of gigantic eagle's claws. Instead of a sceptre he swayed a long Turkish pipe, wrought with jasmin and amber, which had been presented to a stadtholder of Holland, at the conclusion of a treaty with one of the petty Barbary powers. In this stately chair would he sit, and this magnificent pipe would he smoke, shaking his right knee with constant motion, and fixing his eye for hours together upon a little print of Amsterdam, which hung in a black frame against the opposite wall of the council chamber. Nay, it has even been said that when any deliberation of extraordinary length and intricacy was on the carpet, the renowned Wouter would shut his eyes for full two hours at a time, that he might not be disturbed by external objects—and at such times the internal commotion of his mind was evinced by certain regular guttural sounds, which his admirers declared were merely the noise of conflict, made by his contending doubts and opinions.

More than possibly the chair here mentioned was some real chair which Irving had seen and in which an old Dutch governor might have sat. Conceivably the Turkish pipe may have been at least legendarily true. The rest of the passage is utter extravagance; yet you will be at a little pains to say just where fact passes nonsense.

Though this kind of humour is not unprecedented, one thing about it is worth attention. When we were considering the work of Franklin, we found in his letter to a London newspaper concerning the state of the American colonies a grave mixture of fact and nonsense, remarkably like the American humour of our later days. In Irving's *Knickerbocker History* one finds something very similar. The fun of the thing lies in frequent and often imperceptible lapses from sense to nonsense and back again. Something of the same kind, expressed in a far less gracious manner than Irving's, underlies Mark Twain's comic work and that of our latest journalistic humourist, Mr. Dooley. This deliberate confusion of sense and nonsense, in short, proves generally characteristic of American humour; and although the formal amenity of Irving's style often makes him seem rather an imitator of the eighteenth-century English writers than a native American, one can feel that if the *Knickerbocker History* and Franklin's letter could be reduced to algebraic formulæ, these formulæ would pretty nearly coincide both with one another and with that of the *Innocents Abroad*. The temper of the *Knickerbocker History*, may, accordingly, be regarded as freshly American. The style, meanwhile, is rather like that of Goldsmith. When the *Knickerbocker History* was published, Goldsmith had been dead for thirty-five years. In Irving, then, we find a man who used the traditional style of eighteenth-century England for a purpose foreign at once to the century and the country of its origin.

It was ten years before Irving again appeared as a serious man of letters. Then came the *Sketch Book*, which contains his best-known stories,—"Rip Van Winkle" and "The Legend of Sleepy Hollow." The book is a collection of essays and short stories, written in a style more like Goldsmith's than ever. The year in which it appeared was that which gave to England the first two cantos of *Don Juan*, Hazlitt's *Lectures on the Comic Writers*, Leigh Hunt's *Indicator*, Scott's *Bride of Lammermoor* and *Legend of Montrose*, Shelley's *Cenci*, and Wordsworth's *Peter Bell*. There can be little doubt that in formal style the *Sketch Book* is more conscientious than any of these. Its prose, in fact, has hardly been surpassed, if indeed it has been equalled, in nineteenth-century England. This prose, however, is of that balanced, cool, rhythmical sort which in England flourished most during the mid years of the eighteenth century.

In the *Sketch Book*, too, there are many papers and passages which might have come straight from some of the later eighteenth-century essayists. On the other hand, there are many passages, such as "Rip Van Winkle," which could hardly have appeared in Goldsmith's England. Though Goldsmith's England, of course, was becoming sentimental, it never got to that delight in a romantic past which characterised the period of which the dominant writer was Sir Walter Scott. By 1819, however, Scott had attained his highest development. In his work there was far more passion and meaning than in the romantic stories of Irving; in technical form, on the other hand, it is comparatively careless, nor on the whole is it more genuinely permeated with the romantic sentiment of the nineteenth century. The story of Rip Van Winkle, for example, is a legend which exists in various European forms. Whether Irving adopted it from such old German tales as that of the sleeping Barbarossa, or from some Spanish story such as he later told when he described the sleep of enchanted Moors, or whether in his time the legend itself had migrated to the Hudson Valley, makes no difference. He assumed that it belonged in the Catskills. He placed it, as a little earlier Brockden Brown placed his less significant romances, in a real background; and he infused into it the romantic spirit which was already characteristic of European letters, and soon to be almost more so of American. He enlivened the tale, meanwhile, with a subdued form of such humour as runs riot in the *Knickerbocker History*; and all this modern sentiment, he phrased as he had phrased his first book, in terms modelled on the traditional style of a generation or two before. The peculiar trait of the *Sketch Book*, in short, is its combination of fresh romantic feeling with traditional Augustan style.

The passages of the *Sketch Book* which deal with England reveal so sympathetic a sense of old English tradition that some of them, like those concerning Stratford and Westminster Abbey, have become almost classical; just as Irving's later work, *Bracebridge Hall*, is now generally admitted to typify a pleasant phase of country life in England almost as well as Sir Roger de Coverley typified another, a century earlier. There are papers in the *Sketch Book*, however, which from our point of view are more significant. Take those, for example, on "John Bull" and on "English Writers concerning America." Like the writing of Hopkinson at the time of the American Revolution, these reveal a distinct sense on the part of an able and cultivated American that the contemporary English differ from our countrymen. The eye which observed John Bull in the aspect which follows, is foreign to England:—

> Though really a good-hearted, good-tempered old fellow at bottom, yet he is singularly fond of being in the midst of contention. It is one of his peculiarities, however, that he only relishes the beginning of an affray; he always goes into a fight with alacrity, but comes out of it grumbling even when victorious; and though no one fights with more obstinacy to carry a contested point, yet, when the battle is over, and he comes to the reconciliation, he

is so much taken up with the mere shaking of hands, that he is apt to let his antagonist pocket all that they have been quarrelling about. It is not, therefore, fighting that he ought so much to be on his guard against, as making friends. It is difficult to cudgel him out of a farthing; but put him in a good humour, and you may bargain him out of all the money in his pocket. He is like a stout ship, which will weather the roughest storm uninjured, but roll its masts overboard in the succeeding calm.

He is a little fond of playing the magnifico abroad; of pulling out a long purse; flinging his money bravely about at boxing matches, horse races, cock fights, and carrying a high head among 'gentlemen of the fancy;' but immediately after one of these fits of extravagance, he will be taken with violent qualms of economy; talk desperately of being ruined and brought upon the parish; and, in such moods, will not pay the smallest tradesman's bill, without violent altercation. He is in fact the most punctual and discontented paymaster in the world; drawing his coin out of his breeches pocket with infinite reluctance; paying to the uttermost farthing, but accompanying every guinea with a growl.

With all his talk of economy, however, he is a bountiful provider, and a hospitable housekeeper. His economy is of a whimsical kind, its chief object being to devise how he may afford to be extravagant; for he will begrudge himself a beef-steak and pint of port one day, that he may roast an ox whole, broach a hogshead of ale, and treat all his neighbours on the next.

In *Bracebridge Hall* and the *Tales of a Traveller*, works which followed the *Sketch Book*, Irving did little more than continue the sort of thing which he had done in the first. Perhaps his most noteworthy feat in all three books is that he made prominent in English literature a literary form in which for a long time to come Americans excelled native Englishmen,—the short story. During our century, of course, England has produced a great school of fiction; and except for Cooper and one or two living writers, America can hardly show full-grown novels so good even as those of Anthony Trollope, not to speak of the masterpieces of Dickens, Thackeray, and George Eliot. Certainly until the time of Robert Louis Stevenson, however, no English-speaking writer out of America had produced many short stories of such merit as anybody can recognise in the work of Hawthorne and Poe and Irving. In this fact there is something akin to that other fact which we have just remarked,—the formal superiority of Irving's style to that of contemporary Englishmen. The English novel, whatever its merits, runs to interminable length, with a disregard of form unprecedented in other civilised literature. A good short story, on the other hand, must generally have complete and finished form. Now, during the nineteenth century American men of letters have usually had a more conscious sense of form than their English contemporaries. The American conscience, in fact, always a bit overdeveloped, has sometimes seemed evident in our attempts at literary art. No one who lacks artistic conscience can write an effective short story; and it is doubtful whether any one troubled with much artistic conscience can write in less than a lifetime a three-volume novel. The artistic conscience revealed in the finish of Irving's style and in his mastery of the short story, then, may be called characteristic of his country.

Equally characteristic of America, in the somewhat different manner foreshadowed by *Bracebridge Hall* and the *Tales of a Traveller*, are the series of Irving's writings, between 1828 and 1832, which deal with Spain. He was first attracted thither by a proposition that he should translate a Spanish book concerning Columbus. Instead of so doing, he ended by writing his *Life of Columbus*, which was followed by his *Conquest of Granada* and his *Tales of the Alhambra*. For Americans, Spain has sometimes had more romantic charm than all the rest of Europe put together. In the first place, as the very name of Columbus should remind us, its history is inextricably connected with our own. In the second place, at the very moment when this lasting connection between Spain and the New World declared itself, the eight hundred years' struggle between Moors and Spaniards had at length ended in the triumph of the Christians; and no other conflict to the whole European past involved a contrast of life and of ideals more vivid, more complete, more varied, or more prolonged. In the third place, the decline of Spain began almost immediately; so in the early nineteenth century Spain had altered less since the middle ages than any other part of Europe. Elsewhere an American traveller could find traces of the picturesque, romantic, vanished past. In Spain he could find a state of life so little changed from olden time that he seemed almost to travel into that vanished past itself.

Now, as the American character of the nineteenth century has declared itself, few of its æsthetic traits are more marked than eager delight in olden splendours. Such delight, of course, has characterised the nineteenth century in Europe as well as among ourselves. A modern Londoner, however, who can walk in a forenoon from Westminster Abbey to the Temple Church and so to the Tower, can never dream of what such monuments mean to an imagination which has grown up amid no grander relics of antiquity than King's Chapel or Independence Hall, than gray New England farmhouses and the moss-grown gravestones of Yankee burying-grounds. To any sensitive nature, brought up in nineteenth-century America, the mere sight of anything so immemorially human as a European landscape must have in it some touch of that stimulating power which the Europe of the Renaissance found in the fresh discovery of classical literature and art. Americans can still feel the romance even of modern London or Paris; and to this day there is no spot where our starved craving for human antiquity can be more profusely satisfied than amid the decaying but not vanished monuments of Christian and of Moorish Spain. No words have ever expressed this satisfaction more sincerely or more spontaneously than the fantastic stories of old Spain which Irving has left us.

His later work was chiefly biographical. His *Life of Goldsmith* and his *Life of Washington* alike are written with all his charm and with vivid imagination. Irving, however was no trained scholar. He was far even from the critical habit of the New England historians, and further still from such learning as is now apt to make history something like exact science. It may be doubted whether Irving's Goldsmith or his Washington can be accepted as the Goldsmith or the Washington who once trod the earth; yet his Goldsmith and Washington, and the other personages whom he introduced into their stories, are at least living human beings. His work is perhaps halfway between history and fiction; imaginative history is perhaps the best name for it. As usual, he was preoccupied almost as much with a desire to write charmingly as with a purpose to write truly; but in itself this desire was beautifully true. Throughout, one feels, Irving wrote as well as he could, and he knew how to write better than almost any contemporary Englishman.

No doubt a great deal of English work contemporary with Irving's is of deeper value. Our hasty glance at his literary career has perhaps shown what this first of our recognised men of letters—the first American who in his own lifetime established a lasting European reputation—really accomplished. His greatest merits, which nothing can abate, are pervasive artistic conscience, admirable and persistent sense of form, and constant devotion to his literary ideals. If we ask ourselves, however, what he used his admirable style to express, we find in the first place a quaintly extravagant sort of humour growing more delicate with the years; next we find romantic sentiment set forth in the beautifully polished phrases of a past English generation whose native temper had been rather classical than romantic; then we find a deeply lasting delight in the splendours of an unfathomably romantic past; and finally we come to pleasantly vivid romantic biographies. One thing here is pretty clear: the man had no message. From beginning to end he was animated by no profound sense of the mystery of existence. Neither the solemn eternities which stir philosophers and theologians, nor the actual lessons as distinguished from the superficial circumstances of human experience, ever much engaged his thought. Delicate, refined, romantic sentiment he set forth in delicate, refined classic style. One may often wonder whether he had much to say; one can never question that he wrote beautifully.

This was the first recognised literary revelation of the New World to the Old. In a previous generation, Edwards had made American theology a fact for all Calvinists to reckon with. The political philosophers of the Revolution had made our political and legal thought matters which even the Old World could hardly neglect. When we come to pure literature, however, in which America should at last express to Europe what life meant to men of artistic sensitiveness living under the conditions of our new and emancipated society, what we find is little more than greater delicacy of form than existed in contemporary England. Irving is certainly a permanent literary figure. What makes him so is not novelty or power, but charming refinement.

CHARLOTTE BRONTË

JOHN WILSON CROKER

RUFUS WILMOT GRISWOLD

SIR WILLIAM HAMILTON

HENRY HALLAM

SYDNEY OWENSON, LADY MORGAN

LEIGH HUNT

WASHINGTON IRVING

SYDNEY OWENSON

Lady Morgan

c. 1783–1859

Sydney Owenson was born in Dublin on Christmas Day; the year of her birth has never been firmly established, as she herself gave different dates at different times, but is generally assumed to have been 1783. The daughter of an actor, she attended various schools around Dublin but was brought up for the most part backstage by her father's fellow actors. From 1798 until 1800 she worked as a governess. In 1801 she published her first work, a volume of verse. In 1804 her first novel, *St. Clair; or, The Heiress of Desmond*, appeared, and many more works of sentimental fiction followed over the next thirty-five years. Her best-known work is *The Wild Irish Girl* (1806), which caused a sensation and gave its author thereafter the nickname of "Glorvina," after its heroine.

Despite attacks by the *Quarterly Review* and other Tory publications, Owenson and her fiction were both extremely popular, and even her severest critics acknowledged that she had literary talent, particularly when she wrote about Irish nationalism or the local peasantry. Through the Marquis of Abercorn, who became her patron, she met and married Sir Thomas Charles Morgan in 1812. The marriage lasted for more than thirty years, until his death in 1843, but was childless and apparently unhappy.

In addition to her many novels, Sydney Owenson wrote several travel books (*France*, 1817; *Italy*, 1821) and an opera (*The First Attempt*, 1807). In 1837 she received a pension of £300 (the first ever granted a woman) and two years later moved permanently to London, where she devoted the remainder of her life to social activities, occasionally revising her earlier works for new editions. She died on April 14, 1859.

Personal

I dined with Storks, to meet Lady and Sir Charles Morgan, and I was much amused by the visit. Before I went, I was satisfied that I should recognize in the lady one who had attracted my attention at Pistrucci's, and my guess was a hit. Lady Morgan did not displease me till I reflected on her conversation. She seems good-natured as well as lively. She talked like one conscious of her importance and superiority.—HENRY CRABB ROBINSON, *Diary*, July 1, 1824

The success of my first Irish national novel, *The Wild Irish Girl*, my attempts to advocate liberal opinions in my works on France and Italy, when I stood forth in the cause of civil and religious liberty, dipped many a pen in gall against me which would otherwise have more gently scanned my faults. However, here I am once more, and to you, dear, kind, fair-judging public, who are always for giving a fair field and no favour, and who are always willing to take the odds for those who "show pluck" and who "hit out," to you I dedicate these pages, in which I have entered the circumstances of my life, *sans peur et sans tache. Memoires pour servir* generally mean either "serving out" one's friends and enemies, or feeding a morbid appetite for secret slander. I can promise no scandal, neither can I open a biographical ledger, after the fashion of Miss Betsy Thoughtless and others, with an "I was born, &c., &c.," or "the villain who deceived me was quartered in the town where my father lived;" nor yet can I pretend to give a description of the "scene of rural innocence where first I saw the light."

The sum of my long experience in society leaves in its total a large balance in favour of what is good. I have no reason to complain of memory; I find in my efforts to track its records, guided by the fond feelings of my life, and warmed by the fancifulness of my Celtic temperament, bright hues come forward like the colours of the tesselated pavement of antiquity when the renovating water is flung upon them. I pause here for a moment to mention as a curious physiological fact, that this memory is much preserved to me through musical association. My father died singing an Irish cronan; and when in the confusion of illness I have spent weariful hours in the visions of the night, I have cheered gloom and lightened pain by humming a song of other times, which embodied dear remembrances and sustained memory by music. The songs taught me on my father's knee, have lost nothing of their power even to the present day. I have other links connecting me with the past; of the many kind and illustrious friends whom I have made through life, I have never lost one except by death; and I am now enjoying in the second and third generation of those who are gone, the distinction conferred upon me by the personal kindness of their grandsires. One of the chief temptations to present the principal facts of my life to the public, has been to prove the readiness with which society is willing to help those who are honestly and fervently ready to help themselves. I would wish to impress on young people who are beginning life as I did, dependent on their own exertions, the absolute need of concentrated industry; a definite purpose, and above all, conduct dictated by common sense, as absolutely essential to give genius its value and its success. No woman, from Sappho downwards, ever fell out of the ranks without finding that her "self-sacrifice" was only another name for indulged selfishness. "The light that leads astray" is *not*, and never will be, "light from Heaven."—SYDNEY OWENSON, LADY MORGAN, "Prefatory Address" (1857) to *Lady Morgan's Memoir: Autobiography, Diaries and Correspondence*, eds. William Hepworth Dixon, Geraldine Endsor Jewsbury, 1862, Vol. 1, pp. 2–3

Lady Morgan's house was the resort of all who were the best worth knowing in London society, and she had the art of drawing out all the best faculties of those who came to her. She herself had become a name connected with the past—a tradition of times, and manners, and events, which had been historical. Her own conversation was to the last hour brilliant and fascinating as it ever had been, not a shadow had fallen over the sparkling wit and grace of her stories and *bon mots*. The sarcastic severity of tongue, which had made her formidable to friends and foes in early life, softened greatly during the later years of her life. She used to say, that it was only the *young* who were pitiless in their judgment of others, and when she heard any one saying bitter things against another, she would say, "Ah ma chère ne vous chargez pas des haines." At the severest, her sarcasm had been always light and airy—it shared the harmlessness of hard words, in that "it broke no bones,"—it glanced off the object, and did not burn into the feelings or rest upon the memory. Lady Morgan was always a true, steady, and zealous friend to those she cared for, and had a singular faculty for attaching her servants to her; she interested herself in their welfare, and treated them with invariable courtesy and respect; during her illness, their affectionate attentions had been those of attached relatives rather than servants; they had all lived many years in her service. She had the courage to tell her friends the truth when it was needful; she was essentially sincere, though not always consistent, for she never troubled herself to reconcile the opinion she might have expressed one year with that which she held another; she said what she thought and felt at the moment, and left discrepancies to take care of themselves. With all her frank vanity she had shrewd good sense, and she valued herself much more on her *industry* than on her genius, because the one she said "she owed to her organisation, but the other was a virtue of her own rearing."

Perhaps no other woman ever received so much flattery, or had such brilliant and tangible success; both as a woman and an author, she seems to have had a larger portion of the good things of this life than generally falls to the lot of the daughters of Eve. Her prosperity was almost unclouded during her long life. The death of her husband, her sister, and her favourite niece, within a short period of each other, was her share of affliction, and she felt it deeply.

She was not afraid of death; but she disliked the idea of dying very much. Often when looking round her pretty room, she would say, "I shall be very sorry to leave all these things and the friends who have been so kind to me—the world has been a good world to me.

Lady Morgan was not a woman to be judged by ordinary rules. She was the last type of a class long passed away; she belonged to another time and mode of thought altogether; she was like the French women of the old *régime* to whom society was the only condition in which they could exist, who would go to a ball or a hunting party when in the last stage of mortal sickness; who would insist on being attired in full dress on the day of their death, and who would not die except surrounded by their circle and doing the honours of a *salon* to the last. Oddly enough, clergymen were very fond of her society, and she used to tell, with great fun a whimsical incident, *à propos* to this. She had written a note to a dignitary of the Church, a very old friend, addressing him as her "dear father confessor," saying, to pique his curiosity, "come to me—I want to have a talk with you." He was from home and the note went to his curate, who took it *au serieux*, thinking his rector could only be sent for professionally. He went to her house, and gravely said "that as his rector was out of town, he came to see her ladyship, and if she had any thing upon her mind, he would be happy to give her his best advice." Of course he was soon disabused of his mistake; but the drollest part of the story was the indignation of her maid, who, when she was told what had passed, drew herself up and said with scorn, "As if your ladyship had wished to confess, you would open your mind to a *curate!*"

Lady Morgan kept her faculty of enjoyment to the last; she had as much pleasure in her books, music, and society, as in her youth. She loved the young, and was always charming with them. She said that, "living with the young kept her young." —WILLIAM HEPWORTH DIXON, GERALDINE ENDSOR JEWSBURY, *Lady Morgan's Memoir: Autobiography, Diaries and Correspondence*, 1862, Vol. 2, pp. 549–52

Vain, gay, and charming to the last, Lady Morgan lived and reigned; and the society in which such a reign as hers was possible, and over which she exercised a fascination more potent than that of beauty, like the brilliant Glorvina herself, has passed away.—S. C. HALL, *Retrospect of a Long Life*, 1883, pp. 346–47

⟨. . .⟩ a little old woman of such pungent wit, that Mr. Fonblanque, then the editor of the *Examiner*, used to say of her, "She is just a spark of hell-fire, and is soon going back to her native element."—AUGUSTUS J. C. HARE, "Mrs. Duncan Stewart," *Biographical Sketches*, 1895, p. 145

General

I have just read your *Wild Irish Girl*, a title which will attract by its novelty, but which does not well suit the charming character of Glorvina.

As a sincere and warm friend to Ireland, I return you my thanks for the just character which you have given to the lower Irish, and for the sound and judicious observations which you have attributed to the priest. The notices of Irish history are ingeniously introduced, and are related in such a manner as to induce belief amongst infidels.

It is with much self-complacency that I recollect our meeting, and my having in a few minutes' conversation at a literary dinner in London, discovered that I was talking to a young lady of uncommon genius and talents.—RICHARD LOVELL EDGEWORTH, Letter to Sydney Owenson (Dec. 23, 1806), *Lady Morgan's Memoir: Autobiography, Diaries and Correspondence*, eds. William Hepworth Dixon, Geraldine Endsor Jewsbury, 1862, Vol. 1, p. 293

Literary fiction, whether directed to the purpose of transient amusement, or adopted as an indirect medium of instruction, should exhibit a mirror of the times in which it was composed,—reflecting morals, customs, manners, peculiarity of character, and prevalence of opinion.

But, though such be its primary character, we find it, in its progress, producing arbitrary models, derived from conventional modes of thinking amongst writers, and influenced by the doctrines of the learned, and the opinions of the refined. Ideal beauties and ideal perfection take the place of nature, and approbation is sought rather by a description of *what is not*, than a faithful portraiture of *what is*. He, however, who soars beyond the line of general knowledge and common feelings, must be content to remain within the exclusive pale of particular approbation. It is the interest, therefore, of the novelist, who is, *par état*, the servant of the many, not the minister of the few, to abandon pure abstractions, and "thick-coming fancies," to philosophers and to poets; to adopt, rather than create; to combine, rather than invent; and to take nature and manners for the grounds and groupings of works, which are professedly addressed to popular feelings and ideas.

Influenced by this impression, I have for the first time ventured on that style of novel, which simply bears upon the "flat realities of life." Having determined upon taking Ireland as my theme, I had sought in its records and chronicles for the ground-work of a story, and the character of a hero. The romantic adventures and unsubdued valour of O'Donnel *the Red*, Chief of Tirconnel, in the reign of Elizabeth, promised at the first glance all I wished, and seemed happily adapted to my purpose. I had already advanced as far as the second volume of my MS., and had expended much time and labour, when I found it necessary to forego my original plan. In touching those parts of Irish history, which were connected with my tale, it would have been desirable to turn them to purposes of conciliation, and to incorporate the leaven of favourable opinion with that heavy mass of bitter prejudice, which writers, both grave and trifling, have delighted to raise against my country. But when I fondly thought to send forth a dove bearing the olive of peace, I found I was on the point of flinging an arrow winged with discord. I had hoped, as far as my feeble efforts could go, to extenuate the errors attributed to Ireland, by an exposition of their causes, drawn from historic facts; but I found that, like the spirit in *Macbeth*, I should at the same moment hold up a glass to my countrymen, reflecting but *too* many fearful images. I discovered, far beyond my expectation, that I had fallen upon "evil men and evil days;" and that in proceeding, I must raise a veil which ought never to be drawn, and should renew the memory of events, which the interests of humanity require to be for ever buried in oblivion.

I abandoned therefore my original plan, took up a happier view of things, advanced my story to more modern and more liberal times, and exchanged the rude chief of the days of old, for his polished descendant in a more refined age: and I trust the various branches of the ancient house with whose name I have honoured him, will not find reason to disown their newly discovered kinsman.—SYDNEY OWENSON, LADY MORGAN, "Preface" to *O'Donnel: A National Tale*, 1814

France! Lady Morgan appears to have gone to Paris by the high road of Calais and returned by that of Dieppe. In that capital she seems to have resided about four months, and thence to have made one or two short excursions; and with this extent of ocular inspection of that immense country, she returns and boldly affixes to her travelling memoranda diluted into a quarto volume, the title of *France!* One merit, however, the title has—it is appropriate to the volume which it introduces, for to falsehood it adds the other qualities of the work,—vagueness, bombast, and affectation. This does not surprize us, and will not surprize our readers when they are told that Lady Morgan is no other than the ci-devant Miss Owenson, the author of those tomes of absurdity—those puzzles in three volumes, called *Ida of Athens*, the *Missionary*, the *Wild Irish Girl*, and that still wilder rhapsody of nonsense, *O'Donnell*—which served Miss Plumptre, kindred soul! in her famous tour through Ireland, as an introduction to society, a history of the country, and a book of the post-roads.

⟨. . .⟩ We trust our readers will excuse us for paying so much attention to what they will find to be so worthless a publication; but the subject of that publication is important, and the manner in which Lady Morgan treats it deserves the severest reprehension.

Our charges (to omit minor faults) fall readily under the heads of—Bad taste—Bombast and Nonsense—Blunders—Ignorance of the French Language and Manners—General Ignorance—Jacobinism—Falsehood—Licentiousness, and Impiety. ⟨. . .⟩

We must now have done:—to confess the truth we have long since been weary of Lady Morgan, and shall not therefore offend our readers by any further exposure of the wickedness and folly of her book; of both of which we have given an idea less perfect, we readily admit, than we had materials for, but

one which will, we hope, prevent, in some degree, the circulation of trash which under the name of a *Lady* author might otherwise find its way into the hands of young persons of both sexes, for whose perusal it is utterly, on the score both of morals and politics, unfit.—JOHN WILSON CROKER, "*France*, by Lady Morgan," *Quarterly Review*, April 1817, pp. 260–64, 286

Thank you for your information about Lady Morgan. She, it seems, is resolved to make me read one of her novels. I hope I shall feel interested enough to be able to learn the language. I wrote the main part of the article in the *Quarterly*, but, as you know, was called away to Ireland when it was in the press; and I am sorry to say that some blunders crept in accidentally, and one or two were premeditatedly added, which, however, I do not think Lady Morgan knows enough either of English, French, or Italian to find out. If she goes on we shall have sport.—JOHN WILSON CROKER, Letter to Robert Peel (Nov. 26, 1817), *The Croker Papers*, ed. Louis J. Jennings, 1885, Vol. 1, pp. 111–12

Though by no means approving of some of the opinions in her later publications, yet I admired the ability shown in *O'Donnel*, the only work of hers that I have ever read through.—ANNE GRANT, Letter to Mrs. Gorman (March 23, 1825), *Memoir and Correspondence of Mrs. Grant of Laggan*, ed. J. P. Grant, 1844, Vol. 3, p. 581

I have amused myself occasionally very pleasantly during the last few days, by reading over Lady Morgan's novel of *O'Donnel*, which has some striking and beautiful passages of situation and description, and in the comic part is very rich and entertaining. I do not remember being so much pleased with it at first. There is a want of story, always fatal to a book the first reading—and it is well if it gets a chance of a second. Alas! poor novel!—SIR WALTER SCOTT, *Journal*, March 14, 1826

Though a fiction, not free from numerous inaccuracies inappropriate dialogue, and forced incident, it is impossible to peruse the *Wild Irish Girl*, of Lady Morgan without deep interest, or to dispute its claims as a production of true national feeling as well as literary talent.

The tale was the first and is perhaps the best of all her writings. Compared with her *Ida of Athens*, it strikingly exhibits the author's *falling off* from the unsophisticated dictates of nature to the less-refined conceptions induced by what she herself styles fashionable society.

To persons unacquainted with Ireland, the *Wild Irish Girl* may appear an ordinary tale of romance and fancy: but to such as understand the ancient history of that people, it may be considered as a delightful legend. The authoress might perhaps have had somewhat in view the last descendant of the Irish princes, who did not altogether forget the station of his forefathers.—SIR JONAH BARRINGTON, "Lady Morgan and Miss Edgeworth," *Personal Sketches of His Own Times*, 1830, pp. 373–74

Lady Morgan took ⟨in *Princess*⟩ such an unfair advantage of the masculine portion of the public, in chusing the moment when European freedom might say with the apostle 'no man stood by me,' to brave the alliance of despots abroad and monopolize the honours of the *Quarterly* at home,—that she cannot wonder at any quantity of spleen she may have since encountered. As the time however has come, when the accused before the ancient Nero frowns over Rome in marble from the loftiest of its palaces; so a shorter lapse of years has turned the tables on the modern autocrats in politics and in literature, and reversed the opinion of the world upon the merits of the opposing parties. ⟨. . .⟩

The powerful and great have never wanted story-tellers to be pathetic on their magnanimity when they either abstain from evil, or consent to do any good like ordinary men. A kick from their loftiness is to be held most gracious; and the rudest insult is to be set store by, as if their Highnesses rheum were amber. It is in human nature; and as long as the temptation is there, there is no help for it. But this only makes the obligation greater, to such as will put forward and adorn the working of those homely affections and familiar interests, which crush the pageantry of power whenever the two are brought into fair collision. A people may be kicked for a season, and their mouth-pieces, if they have no better, call it gracious. But the hope of mankind is in the kick too much; and when that comes, it needs no curious research in history to tell the issue.

One of these outbreaks, the Belgian one, forms a principal part of the groundwork of the present story. It is true that the boiling over of the Belgian pot, was in point of time the consequence of the ebullition of the Gallic; but the boiling materials were there, or the phenomenon could not have taken place. Many lights are thrown by the novelist's true fiction or feigned truth, on the reasons why the people beat kings, when kings give the last blow too many to the people. ⟨. . .⟩

Whatever the novelist may be elsewhere, it is clear that as long as to have propped rising states can give a claim to the title, she must be a 'stateswoman' in Belgium.—T. P. THOMP-SON, "Lady Morgan's *Princess*," *Westminster Review*, April 1835, pp. 281–82, 304

And dear Lady Morgan! Look, look how she comes,
With her pulses all beating for freedom, like drums,—
So Irish, so modish, so *mixtish*, so wild,
So committing herself, as she talks, like a child,
So trim yet so easy, polite yet big-hearted,
That truth and she, try all she can, won't be parted.
She'll put on your fashions, your latest new air,
And then talk so frankly, she'll make you all stare:—
Mrs. Hall may say 'Oh', and Miss Edgeworth say 'Fie',
But my lady will know all the what and the why.
Her books, a like mixture, are so very clever,
The god himself swore he could read them for ever;
Plot, character, freakishness, all are so good;
And the heroine's herself, playing tricks in a hood.
So he kissed her, and called her 'eternal good wench';
But asked, why the devil she spoke so much French?
        —LEIGH HUNT, *Blue-Stocking Revels; or, The Feast of the Violets*, 1837, ll. 162–77

In our day she finds no readers. Her books, if now first produced, would assuredly excite no commotion at Mudie's; for her talents are by no means above the line. Is the reason of her being neglected to be sought in the fact of our public having reached a higher stage of culture? Against such a supposition there is the undoubted popularity of many worthless works. Moreover, we may remember that Lady Morgan was a celebrated writer in days when Scott, Byron, Moore, Campbell, Wordsworth, Coleridge, Shelley, Keats, Leigh Hunt, Godwin, Wilson, and others were claiming attention—names certainly equal to the leading names of our own day; yet, among the writers of our own day, she would not hold eminent rank. What then gave her eminence? Opportunity. *Habent sua fata libelli.* Reputation—as distinguished from fame—is determined by opportunity. Lady Morgan wrote Irish novels at a time when Irish questions were of supreme interest; she was a partisan, and gained the partisan's reward. She wrote about France at a time when France was newly reopened to

Englishmen, and about Italy before Italy was overrun by tourists. If she were now in her prime, and could write such a book about South America, the success would be the same. It was the temporal, not the intrinsic value of her books, which gave them success. Compare her novels with those of her predecessor Jane Austen, then scarcely heard of, but now recognized as secure of immortality, and the difference between works which reflect the passing moods of the hour, and works which reflect the eternal truths of life and character, will be conspicuous.—GERALDINE ENDSOR JEWSBURY, "Our Survey of Literature and Science," *Cornhill Magazine*, Jan. 1863, p. 132

It is true that her writings were not the result of study, but rather of a vivid fancy. In fact all her works were of the latter character, or else they were descriptive of passing scenes at home and objects abroad, that chanced to come before her. She had not read to any extent, and she stated as much, and that she painted only what she saw. I had been at a party in town, of which she made one. I left at half-past eleven P.M. On calling on her the next day, she told me she did not leave until three. I rallied her on being out so late night after night, and she replied that she came to town so seldom, and remained so short a time, that she must needs supply herself with materials from fashionable life in London to work upon at home. She was not an adept in the circle of her own walk in literature. Thus she invented most of what she wrote, and coloured from life. She read, too, works easily accessible when she intended to write upon any particular topic, but upon that alone, and often hurriedly and without digestion of the materials; but, then, her style and her writings, as I have observed before, made no pretence to any thing profound. They were lively sketches, more especially those touching upon Irish manners; but they had the merit of being faithfully drawn, and not without humour. ⟨. . .⟩

When Lady Morgan began her novel-writing, it was one of those lucky accidents which happen sometimes at an outset in life. Haunted houses and spirits, old castles and robbers through trap-doors, daggers and prison-bolts were going out of fashion; and she selected, without any consideration of that kind, the romantic scenery and unknown incidents characteristic of Irish life. It was almost a new field. Her affections were eminently those of her country; and in her *Wild Irish Girl*—if I mistake not, her third publication, in 1806 or the following year—she touched a chord which could not but arouse the affections of her countrymen, of which the appliances and story were new to the people of England. She had early in life been accustomed from her father's profession to the wild and melancholy notes of her country's music, and she was not of a nature to resist their effect. Several of the native airs she published in London with English words.—CYRUS REDDING, "Lady Morgan," *Personal Reminiscences of Eminent Men*, 1867, Vol. 3, pp. 7–8, 24

There is no need to dwell on Lady Morgan's first attempts at fiction; *Ida of Athens*, *The Novice of St. Dominick*, *The Wild Irish Girl*, the last probably the least imitative, the one which gave to its writer her own pet name of Glorvina, after its heroine. All are as much forgotten as the tale *St. Irvyne*, by which Shelley began his literary career. A collection of Irish Melodies, long preceding those of Bunting and Moore, was of better promise. One of these, "Kate Kearney," still lives in cheap editions of popular songs.

It is as little my business to offer any judgment here on Lady Morgan's National Tales; neither on her travels in France and Italy, her *Life of Salvator Rosa*, and the most serious and best of her works, *Woman and Her Master*. Whatever be their real merit, it is past doubt that they established for her a brilliant reputation in France and Italy, and this expressed in forms which were not calculated to give ballast to one of the most feather-brained, restless creatures who ever glittered in the world of female authorship. After her first book on *France*

was published she became the *rage* in Paris; and I have been told, on good authority, that on one occasion, at some grand reception, she had a raised seat on the *dais*, only a little lower than that provided for the Duchesse de Berri.—HENRY F. CHORLEY, *Autobiography, Memoir, and Letters*, ed. Henry G. Hewlett, 1873, Vol. 1, pp. 234–35

LEIGH HUNT

1784–1859

James Henry Leigh Hunt was born in Southgate, Middlesex, on October 19, 1784. The son of an Anglican minister, he was educated in London at Christ's Hospital School (1791–99). His first collection of verse, *Juvenilia*, appeared in 1801, and was followed in 1808 by a collection of theatre reviews, *Critical Essays on the Performers of the London Theatres* (dated 1807). Also in 1808 Hunt and his brother John founded the *Examiner*, which Hunt edited for twenty years. During this time he used his journal to campaign actively for liberal reform, and also did much to support the writing of his friends Shelley, Keats, Hazlitt, and Lamb. Lamb was also published in Hunt's short-lived paper, the *Reflector* (1810–11), a quarterly which lasted only four issues.

In 1813 Hunt and his brother were fined £500 and sentenced to two years' imprisonment for libelling the Prince Regent in the *Examiner*. Although he served his sentence, Hunt was able to continue writing and editing his paper from prison. In 1816, after his release, Hunt published his influential poem *The Story of Rimini*, based on Dante's story of Paolo and Francesca and written while he was in prison. This was followed in 1818 by *Foliage*, a collection of his verses, and in 1819 by his poems *Hero and Leander* and *Bacchus and Ariadne*. Also in 1819 Hunt founded the *Indicator*, a purely literary paper, which folded in 1821; with Byron he then started another journal, the *Liberal* (1822–24), in which appeared works by Byron, Shelley, Hazlitt, Hunt, Hogg, and others. The *Companion*, a magazine which contains some of Hunt's best work, appeared in 1828; his *Tatler* in 1830–32; and his *London Journal* in 1834–35.

In 1835 Hunt published his long anti-war poem *Captain Sword and Captain Pen*, followed in 1838 by the *Book of Gems*, an anthology containing one of his best-known poems, "Abou Ben Adhem." In 1840 Hunt's play *A Legend of Florence* was successfully produced at Covent Garden; he subsequently wrote many other plays, but none were well received. In 1844 appeared his *Poetical Works* and *Imagination and Fancy*, a critical study in which poetry and painting are compared. His later works include an anthology *Wit and Humour* (1846); *Stories from Italian Poets* (1846); *Men, Women, and Books* (1847); *A Jar of Honey from Mount Hybla* (1848); *The Town* (1848), about London; Hunt's *Autobiography* (1850); *Table Talk* (1851); *The Religion of the Heart* (1853); and *The Old Court Suburb* (1855), a collection of essays on Kensington.

Hunt, who married Marianne Kent in 1809, had seven children, and died in Putney on August 28, 1859. While his greatest desire was to be known as a poet, today he is best remembered as an essayist and an associate of other writers.

Personal

Had I known a person more highly endowed than yourself with all that it becomes a man to possess, I had solicited for this work the ornament of his name. One more gentle, honourable, innocent and brave; one of more exalted toleration for all who do and think evil, and yet himself more free from evil; one who knows better how to receive, and how to confer a benefit, though he must ever confer far more than he can receive; one of simpler, and, in the highest sense of the word, of purer life and manners I never knew: and I had already been fortunate in friendships when your name was added to the list.

In that patient and irreconcilable enmity with domestic and political tyranny and imposture which the tenor of your life has illustrated, and which, had I health and talents, should illustrate mine, let us, comforting each other in our task, live and die.

All happiness attend you!—PERCY BYSSHE SHELLEY, "Dedication to Leigh Hunt, Esq.," *The Cenci*, 1819

You will see Hunt—one of those happy souls
Which are the salt of the earth, and without whom
This world would smell like what it is—a tomb;
Who is, what others seem;—his room no doubt
Is still adorned by many a cast from Shout,
With graceful flowers tastefully placed about;
And coronals of bay from ribbons hung,
And brighter wreaths in neat disorder flung;
The gifts of the most learn'd among some dozens
Of female friends, sisters-in-law and cousins.
And there is he with his eternal puns,
Which beat the dullest brain for smiles, like duns
Thundering for money at a poet's door;
Alas! it is no use to say, "I'm poor!"
Or oft in graver mood, when he will look
Things wiser than were ever read in book,
Except in Shakspeare's wisest tenderness.
—PERCY BYSSHE SHELLEY, *Letter to Maria Gisborne*, 1820, ll. 209–25

I have no quarrel with you, nor can I have. You are one of those people that I like, do what they will; there are others that I do not like, do what they may. I have always spoken well of you to friend or foe, viz. I have said you were one of the pleasantest and cleverest persons I ever knew; but that you teazed any one you had to deal with out of their lives.
—WILLIAM HAZLITT, Letter to Leigh Hunt (April 21, 1821), cited in William Carew Hazlitt, *Four Generations of a Literary Family*, 1897, Vol. 1, p. 133

Accident introduced me to the acquaintance of Mr. L. H.—and the experience of his many friendly qualities confirmed a friendship between us. You, who have been misrepresented yourself, I should hope, have not lent an idle ear to the calumnies which have been spread abroad respecting this gentleman. I was admitted to his household for some years, and do most solemnly aver that I believe him to be in his domestic relations as correct as any man. He chose an ill-judged subject for a poem; the peccant humours of which have been visited on him tenfold by the artful use, which his adversaries have made, of an *equivocal term*. The subject itself was started by Dante, but better because brietlier treated of. But the crime of the Lovers, in the Italian and the English poet, with its aggravated enormity of circumstance, is not of a kind (as the critics of the latter well knew) with those conjunctions, for which Nature herself has provided no excuse, because no temptation.—It has nothing in common with the black horrors, sung by Ford and Massinger. The familiarising of it in tale or fable may be for that reason incidentally more contagious. In spite of *Rimini*, I must look upon its author as a man of taste, and a poet. He is better than so, he is one of the most cordial-minded men I ever knew, and matchless as a fire-side companion. I mean not to affront or wound your feelings when I say that, in his more genial moods, he has often reminded me of you. There is the same air of mild dogmatism—the same condescending to a boyish sportiveness—in both your conversations. His hand-writing is so much the same with your own, that I have opened more than one letter of his, hoping, nay, not doubting, but it was from you, and have been disappointed (he will bear with my saying so) at the discovery of my error. L. H. is unfortunate in holding some loose and not very definite speculations (for at times I think he hardly knows whither his premises would carry him) on marriage—the tenets, I conceive, of the *Political Justice*, carried a little further. For any thing I could discover in his practice, they have reference, like those, to some future possible condition of society, and not to the present times. But neither for these obliquities of thinking (upon which my own conclusions are as distant as the poles asunder)—nor for his political asperities and petulancies, which are wearing out with the heats and vanities of youth—did I select him for a friend; but for qualities which fitted him for that relation.—CHARLES LAMB, *Letter of Elia to Robert Southey*, 1823

Hunt and the Hunts, as you have heard, live only in the next street from us. Hunt is always ready to go and walk with me, or sit and talk with me to all lengths if I want him. He comes in once a week (when invited, for he is very modest), takes a cup of tea, and sits discoursing in his brisk, fanciful way till supper time, and then cheerfully eats a cup of porridge (to sugar only), which he praises to the skies, and vows he will make his supper of at home. He is a man of thoroughly London make, such as you could not find elsewhere, and I think about the *best* possible to be made of his sort: an airy, crotchety, most copious clever talker, with an honest undercurrent of reason too, but unfortunately not the deepest, not the most practical—or

rather it is the most *un*practical ever man dealt in. His hair is grizzled, eyes black-hazel, complexion of the clearest dusky brown; a thin glimmer of a smile plays over a face of cast-iron gravity. He never laughs—can only titter, which I think indicates his worst deficiency. His house excels all you have ever read of—a *poetical Tinkerdom*, without parallel even in literature. In his family room, where are a sickly large wife and a whole shoal of well-conditioned wild children, you will find half a dozen old rickety chairs gathered from half a dozen different hucksters, and all seemingly engaged, and just pausing, in a violent *hornpipe*. On these and around them and over the dusty table and ragged carpet lie all kinds of litter—books, papers, egg-shells, scissors, and last night when I was there the torn heart of a half-quartern loaf. His own room above stairs, into which alone I strive to enter, he keeps cleaner. It has only two chairs, a bookcase, and a writing-table; yet the noble Hunt receives you in his Tinkerdom in the spirit of a king, apologises for nothing, places you in the best seat, takes a window-sill himself if there is no other, and there folding closer his loose-flowing 'muslin cloud' of a printed nightgown in which he always writes, commences the liveliest dialogue on philosophy and the prospects of man (who is to be beyond measure 'happy' yet); which again he will courteously terminate the moment you are bound to go: a most interesting, pitiable, lovable man, to be used kindly but with discretion. After all, it is perhaps rather a comfort to be near honest, friendly people—at least, an honest, friendly man of that sort. We stand sharp but mannerly for his sake and for ours, and endeavour to get and do what good we can, and avoid the evil.—THOMAS CARLYLE, Letter to Alexander Carlyle (June 27, 1834)

An odd declaration by Dickens, that he did not mean Leigh Hunt by Harold Skimpole. Yet he owns that he took the light externals of the character from Leigh Hunt, and surely it is by those light externals that the bulk of mankind will always recognize character. Besides, it is to be observed that the vices of Harold Skimpole are vices to which Leigh Hunt had, to say the least, some little leaning, and which the world generally imputed to him most unsparingly. That he had loose notions of *meum* and *tuum*, that he had no high feeling of independence, that he had no sense of obligation, that he took money wherever he could get it, that he felt no gratitude for it, that he was just as ready to defame a person who had relieved his distress as a person who had refused him relief—these were things which, as Dickens must have known, were said, truly or falsely, about Leigh Hunt, and had made a deep impression on the public mind. Indeed, Leigh Hunt had said himself: "I have some peculiar notions about money. They will be found to involve considerable difference of opinion with the community, particularly in a commercial country. I have not that horror of being under obligation which is thought an essential refinement in money matters." This is Harold Skimpole all over. How, then, could D. doubt that H. S. would be supposed to be a portrait of L. H.?—THOMAS BABINGTON MACAULAY, *Journal* (Dec. 23, 1859), cited in G. Otto Trevelyan, *The Life and Letters of Lord Macaulay*, 1876, Vol. 2, p. 403

His whole life was one of pecuniary anxiety. His father was a refugee from America, the representative of a Barbados family, whose fortunes had declined; and although Isaac Hunt was a man who could at dangerous junctures put forth resolution and energy, it seems evident that he was inclined to repose on the traditions of his family, and on a vague general hopefulness, rather than active endeavour. Emerging from the Bluecoat School, Leigh Hunt found himself placed in the hereditary condition of an impoverished relative; and the employment sought for him was such as could be found, rather than such as suited either his natural disposition or his training, which had been exclusively scholastic. By the force of accidental circumstances, he became, as we have seen, a writer for the periodical press, in itself not a very certain mode of livelihood, and one not calculated to develop regular business habits. In addition to these untoward circumstances, there was a peculiarity of his character—it was no affectation when he declared himself entirely incompetent to deal with the simplest question of arithmetic. The very commonest sum was a bewilderment to him. He learned addition in order that he might be fitted for his place in a public office. It was a born incapacity, similar to that of people who cannot distinguish the notes of music or the colours of the prism. Perpetually reproached with it, very conscious of his mistakes, he took his deficiency to heart, and, with the emphatic turn of his temperament, increased it by exaggerating his own estimate of it. Thus he regarded himself as a sort of idiot in the handling of figures; and he was consequently incapacitated for many subjects which he could handle very well when they were explained to him in another form. A secondary consequence was the habit, acquired very early, of trusting to others. His wife was clever in the special handling of arithmetic, a fact which he knew and admired. She had been brought up by a mother who was a thrifty housewife, and thus became, in all domestic matters, a business agent for a man who trusted her less like a husband than like a child. —THORNTON HUNT, *The Correspondence of Leigh Hunt*, 1862, Vol. 1, pp. 110–11

Leigh Hunt was there, with his cheery face, bright, acute, and full of sensibility; and his thick grizzled hair combed down smooth, and his homely figure;—black handkerchief, grey stockings and stout shoes, while he was full of gratitude to ladies who dress in winter in velvet, and in rich colours; and to old dames in the streets or the country who still wear scarlet cloaks. His conversation was lively, rapid, highly illustrative, and perfectly natural.—HARRIET MARTINEAU, *Autobiography*, ed. Maria Weston Chapman, 1877, Vol. 1, p. 287

As to Leigh Hunt's friendship for Keats, I think the points you mention look equivocal; but Hunt was a many-laboured and much belaboured man, and as much allowance as may be made on this score is perhaps due to him—no more than that much. His own powers stand high in various ways—poetically higher perhaps than is at present admitted, despite his detestable flutter and airiness for the most part. But assuredly by no means could he have stood so high in the long-run, as by a loud and earnest defence of Keats. Perhaps the best excuse for him is the remaining possibility of an idea on his part, that any defence coming from one who had himself so many powerful enemies might seem to Keats rather to damage than improve his position.—DANTE GABRIEL ROSSETTI, cited in Hall Caine, *Recollections of Dante Gabriel Rossetti*, 1882, p. 179

Though Leigh Hunt's character was simple and his gifts distinct, he is not easy to class either as an author or a man. His literary pretensions were well summed up by Charles Lamb in the couplet—

> Wit, poet, proseman, party man, translator,
> Hunt, thy best title yet is *Indicator*.

With a nature filled with poetry, but yet most faulty as a poet; learned beyond the average, but hardly a scholar; full of sweet thoughts, but no thinker; vivacious and sportive to an extraordinary degree, yet falling short of supreme qualities as a humourist, Leigh Hunt scarcely attained to the first rank of writers, except as a sentimentalist, an anthologist, and a gossip,

yet he so nearly touched it at so many points, and there is such a special quality in almost everything he wrote, that one hesitates to set him in a duller circle.

When we consider his character similar difficulties beset us. Not quite a martyr, for his sufferings were too self-provoked; far too self-indulgent to be worshipped as a saint; with too little backbone for a hero, yet, when seen in a kindly light, he had some touches of them all.

At least it can be said, as James Hannay said, that he was the finest belles-lettrist of his day. Few writers have given more pleasure or worked harder in the cause of humanity, few men have shown such an example of truthfulness and cheerfulness under the most trying circumstances. For these reasons alone Leigh Hunt deserves to be honoured much and loved still more.—COSMO MONKHOUSE, *Life of Leigh Hunt*, 1893, pp. 238–39

Mr. Hunt was most amiable: he discoursed about poetry as exhilaratingly as Ruskin does about art. He spoke of his own writings, and quite unaffectedly. It appeared to give him pleasure to do so. Perhaps if he had talked less about them it would have been because he thought the more.

He seemed proud of his old age, speaking with a smile of his *soixante et mille ans*. He gave me the impression of being rich in the milk of amiability and optimism. I do not think this was feigned, for I often heard of him as a benevolently minded man.

I could hardly realise that this was the Mr. Hunt who had written that underbred book about *Byron and his Contemporaries*. I suppose age and experience had mellowed him.—FREDERICK LOCKER-LAMPSON, *My Confidences*, 1896, p. 338

⟨. . .⟩ there was another respect in which the accomplished essayist suffered injustice. I refer to the report which spread abroad after the appearance of Dickens's *Bleak House*, that the creation of *Harold Skimpole* was borrowed from Hunt. The prevalence of this impression naturally afforded much pain to the individual most concerned, and his feelings were communicated to the author, who came down to Hammersmith in order to tender Hunt his solemn assurance that he had not designed anything of the kind, and that he would do anything in his power to make reparation for the unintentional wrong. Hunt told my informant that Dickens was affected almost to tears; but I never heard of any public or direct disavowal. —WILLIAM CAREW HAZLITT, *Four Generations of a Literary Family*, 1897, Vol. 1, p. 292

Business was by no means Leigh Hunt's strong point. In this respect, but not otherwise, he may have suggested Skimpole to Charles Dickens. On one of my visits I found him trying to puzzle out the abstruse question of how he should deduct some such sum as thirteen shillings and ninepence from a sovereign. On another occasion I had to pay him a sum of money, £100 or £200, and I wrote him a check for the amount. "Well," he said, "what am I to do with this little bit of paper?" I told him that if he presented it at the bank they would pay him cash for it, but I added, "I will save you that trouble." I sent to the bank and cashed the check for him. He took the notes away carefully enclosed in an envelope. Two days afterwards Leigh Hunt came in a state of great agitation to tell me that his wife had burned them. He had thrown the envelope, with the banknotes inside, carelessly down, and his wife had flung it into the fire. Leigh Hunt's agitation while on his way to bring this news had not prevented him from purchasing on the road a little statuette of Psyche which he carried, without any paper round it, in his hand. I told him I thought something might be done in the matter; I sent to the bankers and got the numbers of the notes, and then in company with Leigh Hunt went off to the Bank of England. I explained our business and we were shown into a room where three old gentlemen were sitting at tables. They kept us waiting some time, and Leigh Hunt, who had meantime been staring all round the room, at last got up, walked up to one of the staid officials, and addressing him said in wondering tones, "And this is the Bank of England! And do you sit here all day, and never see the green woods and the trees and flowers and the charming country?" Then in tones of remonstrance he demanded, "Are you contented with such a life?" All this time he was holding the little naked Psyche in one hand, and with his long hair and flashing eyes made a surprising figure. I fancy I can still see the astonished faces of the three officials; they would have made a most delightful picture. I said, "Come away, Mr. Hunt, these gentlemen are very busy." I succeeded in carrying Leigh Hunt off, and after entering into certain formalities, we were told that the value of the notes would be paid in twelve months. I gave Leigh Hunt the money at once, and he went away rejoicing.—SIR GEORGE MURRAY SMITH, "In the Early Forties," *Critic*, Jan. 1901, p. 49

General

What though, for showing truth to flattered state,
    Kind Hunt was shut in prison, yet has he,
    In his immortal spirit, been as free
As the sky-searching lark, and as elate.
Minion of grandeur! think you he did wait?
    Think you he naught but prison walls did see,
    Till, so unwilling, thou unturned'st the key?
Ah, no! far happier, nobler was his fate!
In Spenser's halls he strayed, and bowers fair,
    Culling enchanted flowers; and he flew
With daring Milton through the fields of air:
    To regions of his own his genius true
Took happy flights. Who shall his fame impair
    When thou art dead, and all thy wretched crew?
       —JOHN KEATS, "Written on the Day that Mr.
        Leigh Hunt Left Prison," 1815

Who loves to peer up at the morning sun,
    With half-shut eyes and comfortable cheek,
    Let him, with this sweet tale, full often seek
For meadows where the little rivers run;
Who loves to linger with that brightest one
    Of Heaven—Hesperus—let him lowly speak
    These numbers to the night, and starlight meek,
Or moon, if that her hunting be begun.
He who knows these delights, and too is prone
    To moralise upon a smile or tear,
Will find at once a region of his own,
    A bower for his spirit, and will steer
To alleys, where the fir-tree drops its cone,
    Where robins hop, and fallen leaves are sear.
       —JOHN KEATS, "On *The Story of Rimini*," 1816

He of the rose, the violet, the spring,
    The social smile, the chain for Freedom's sake:
    And lo!—whose steadfastness would never take
A meaner sound than Raphael's whispering.
       —JOHN KEATS, "Addressed to Haydon," 1817

I wrote to Hunt yesterday—scarcely know what I said in it—I could not talk about Poetry in the way I should have liked for I was not in humor with either his or mine. His self delusions are very lamentable they have inticed him into a Situation which I should be less eager after than that of a galley Slave—

what you observe thereon is very true must be in time. Perhaps it is a self delusion to say so—but I think I could not be deceived in the Manner that Hunt is—may I die tomorrow if I am to be. There is no greater Sin after the 7 deadly than to flatter oneself into an idea of being a great Poet—or one of those beings who are privileged to wear out their Lives in the pursuit of Honor—how comfortable a feel it is that such a Crime must bring its heavy Penalty? That if one be a Selfdeluder accounts will be balanced?—JOHN KEATS, Letter to Benjamin Robert Haydon (May 11, 1817)

He is a good man, with some poetical elements in his chaos; but spoilt by the Christ-Church Hospital and a Sunday newspaper,—to say nothing of the Surry Jail, which conceited him into a martyr. But he is a good man. When I saw *Rimini* in MSS., I told him that I deemed it good poetry at bottom, disfigured only by a strange style. His answer was, that his style was a system, or *upon system*, or some such cant; and, when a man talks of system, his case is hopeless: so I said no more to him, and very little to any one else.

    He believes his trash of vulgar phrases tortured into compound barbarisms to be *old* English; and we may say of it as Aimwell says of Captain Gibbet's regiment, when the Captain calls it an "old corps."—"the *oldest* in Europe, if I may judge by your uniform," He sent out his *Foliage* by Percy Shelley, and, of all the ineffable Centaurs that were ever begotten by Selflove upon a Night-mare, I think this monstrous Sagittary the most prodigious. *He* (Leigh H.) is an honest Charlatan, who has persuaded himself into a belief of his own impostures, and talks Punch in pure simplicity of heart, taking himself (as poor Fitzgerald said of *him*self in the Morning Post) for *Vates* in both senses, or nonsenses, of the word. ⟨. . .⟩

    But Leigh Hunt is a good man, and a good father—see his Odes to all the Masters Hunt;—a good husband—see his Sonnet to Mrs. Hunt;—a good friend—see his Epistles to different people;—and a great coxcomb and a very vulgar person in every thing about him. But that's not his fault, but of circumstances.—GEORGE GORDON, LORD BYRON, Letter to Thomas Moore (June 1, 1818)

I then walked in the rain to Clapton, reading by the way the *Indicator*. There is a spirit of enjoyment in this little work which gives a charm to it. Leigh Hunt seems the very opposite of Hazlitt. He loves everything, he catches the sunny side of everything, and, excepting that he has a few polemical antipathies, finds everything beautiful.—HENRY CRABB ROBINSON, *Diary*, Oct. 29, 1820

The most rural of these gentlemen is my friend Leigh Hunt, who lives at Hampstead. I believe that I need not disclaim any personal or poetical hostility against that gentleman. A more amiable man in society I know not; nor (when he will allow his sense to prevail over his sectarian principles) a better writer. When he was writing his *Rimini*, I was not the last to discover its beauties, long before it was published. Even then I remonstrated against its vulgarisms; which are the more extraordinary, because the author is any thing but a vulgar man. Mr. Hunt's answer was, that he wrote them upon principle; they made part of his *system!!* I then said no more. When a man talks of his system, it is like a woman's talking of her *virtue*. I let them talk on. Whether there are writers who could have written *Rimini*, as it might have been written, I know not; but Mr. Hunt is, probably, the only poet who could have had the heart to spoil his own Capo d'Opera.

    ⟨. . .⟩ I would also observe to my friend Hunt, that I shall be very glad to see him at *Ravenna*, not only for my sincere pleasure in his company, and the advantage which a thousand miles or so of travel might produce to a 'natural' poet, but also to point out one or two little things in *Rimini*, which he probably would not have placed in his opening to that poem, if he had ever *seen Ravenna;*—unless, indeed, it made 'part of his system!!'—GEORGE GORDON, LORD BYRON, "A Second Letter to John Murray, Esq., on the Rev. W. L. Bowles's Strictures on the Life and Writings of Pope," 1821

To my taste, the Author of *Rimini*, and Editor of the *Examiner*, is among the best and least corrupted of our poetical prose-writers. In his light but well supported columns we find the raciness, the sharpness, and sparkling effect of poetry, with little that is extravagant or far-fetched, and no turgidity or pompous pretension. Perhaps there is too much the appearance of relaxation and trifling (as if he had escaped the shackles of rhyme), a caprice, a levity, and a disposition to innovate in words and ideas. Still the genuine master-spirit of the prose-writer is there; the tone of lively, sensible conversation; and this may in part arise from the author's being himself an animated talker. Mr. Hunt wants something of the heat and earnestness of the political partisan; but his familiar and miscellaneous papers have all the ease, grace, and point of the best style of Essay-writing. Many of his effusions in the *Indicator* show, that if he had devoted himself exclusively to that mode of writing, he inherits more of the spirit of Steele than any man since his time.—WILLIAM HAZLITT, "Of the Prose-Style of Poets" (1822), *The Plain Speaker*, 1826

We shall conclude the present article with a short notice of an individual who, in the cast of his mind and in political principle, bears no very remote resemblance to the patriot and wit just spoken of ⟨Thomas Moore⟩, and on whose merits we should descant at greater length, but that personal intimacy might be supposed to render us partial. It is well when personal intimacy produces this effect; and when the light, that dazzled us at a distance, does not on a closer inspection turn out an opaque substance.

This is a charge that none of his friends will bring against Mr. Leigh Hunt. He improves upon acquaintance. The author translates admirably into the man. Indeed, the very faults of his style are virtues in the individual. His natural gaiety and sprightliness of manner, his high animal spirits, and the *vinous* quality of his mind, produce an immediate fascination and intoxication in those who come in contact with him, and carry off in society whatever in his writings may to some seem flat and impertinent. From great sanguineness of temper, from great quickness and unsuspecting simplicity, he runs on to the public as he does at his own fire-side, and talks about himself, forgetting that he is not always among friends. His look, his tone are required to point many things that he says: his frank, cordial manner reconciles you instantly to a little over-bearing, over-weening self-complacency. 'To be admired, he needs but to be seen': but perhaps he ought to be seen to be fully appreciated. No one ever sought his society who did not come away with a more favourable opinion of him: no one was ever disappointed, except those who had entertained idle prejudices against him. He sometimes trifles with his readers, or tires of a subject (from not being urged on by the stimulus of immediate sympathy); but in conversation he is all life and animation, combining the vivacity of the school-boy with the resources of the wit and the taste of the scholar. The personal character, the spontaneous impulses, do not appear to excuse the author, unless you are acquainted with his situation and habits: like some great beauty who gives herself what we think strange airs and graces under a mask, but who is instantly forgiven when she shews her face.

We have said that Lord Byron is a sublime coxcomb: why should we not say that Mr. Hunt is a delightful one? There is certainly an exuberance of satisfaction in his manner which is more than the strict logical premises warrant, and which dull and phlegmatic constitutions know nothing of, and cannot understand till they see it. He is the only poet or literary man we ever knew, who puts us in mind of Sir John Suckling or Killigrew, or Carew; or who united rare intellectual acquirements with outward grace and natural gentility. Mr. Hunt ought to have been a gentleman born, and to have patronised men of letters. He might then have played, and sung, and laughed, and talked his life away; have written manly prose, elegant verse: and his *Story of Rimini* would have been praised by Mr. Blackwood. As it is, there is no man now living who at the same time writes prose and verse so well, with the exception of Mr. Southey (an exception, we fear, that will be little palatable to either of these gentlemen). His prose writings, however, display more consistency of princple than the Laureate's, his verses more taste. We will venture to oppose his Third Canto of the *Story of Rimini* for classic elegance and natural feeling to any equal number of lines from Mr. Southey's Epics or from Mr. Moore's *Lalla Rookh*. In a more gay and conversational style of writing, we think his *Epistle to Lord Byron* on his going abroad is a masterpiece; and the *Feast of the Poets* has run through several editions. A light, familiar grace, and mild unpretending pathos, are the characteristics of his more sportive or serious writings, whether in poetry or prose. A smile plays round the sparkling features of the one; a tear is ready to start from the thoughtful gaze of the other. He perhaps takes too little pains, and indulges in too much wayward caprice in both.

A wit and a poet, Mr. Hunt is also distinguished by fineness of tact and sterling sense: he has only been a visionary in humanity, the fool of virtue. What then is the drawback to so many shining qualities, that has made them useless, or even hurtful to their owner? His crime is, to have been Editor of the *Examiner* ten years ago, when some allusion was made in it to the age of the present king, and though his Majesty has grown older, our luckless politician is no wiser than he was then!—WILLIAM HAZLITT, "Mr. T. Moore—Mr. Leigh Hunt," *The Spirit of the Age*, 1825

What is this periodical of Leigh Hunt's, and have you seen that wondrous *Life of Byron*? Was it not a thousand pities Hunt had borrowed money of the man he was to disinhume and behead in the course of *duty* afterwards? But for love or money I cannot see Hunt's Book; or anything but extracts of it, and so must hold my tongue. Poor Hunt! He has a strain of music in him too, but poverty and vanity have smote too rudely over the strings.—THOMAS CARLYLE, Letter to Bryan Waller Procter (Jan. 17, 1828)

We have a kindness for Mr. Leigh Hunt. We form our judgment of him, indeed, only from events of universal notoriety, from his own works and from the works of other writers, who have generally abused him in the most rancorous manner. But, unless we are greatly mistaken, he is a very clever, a very honest, and a very good-natured man. We can clearly discern, together with many merits, many faults both in his writings and in his conduct. But we really think that there is hardly a man living whose merits have been so grudgingly allowed, and whose faults have been so cruelly expiated.

In some respects Mr. Leigh Hunt is excellently qualified for the task which he has now undertaken. His style, in spite of its mannerism, nay, partly by reason of its mannerism, is well suited for light garrulous, desultory *ana*, half critical, half biographical. We do not always agree with his literary judgments; but we find in him what is very rare in our time, the power of justly appreciating and heartily enjoying good things of very different kinds.—THOMAS BABINGTON MACAULAY, "Leigh Hunt" (1841), *Critical, Historical, and Miscellaneous Essays*, 1860, Vol. 4, p. 350

Do you know Leigh Hunt's exquisite essays called *The Indicator and Companion* &c., published by Moxon? I hold them at once in delight and reverence.—ELIZABETH BARRETT BROWNING, Letter to Mrs. Martin (Nov. 16, 1844)

One of Hunt's most apparent characteristics is his cheerfulness. His temperament is obviously mercurial. His fondness for the gayer class of Italian writers indicates a sympathy with southern buoyancy not often encountered in English poetry. His versification is easy and playful; too much so, indeed, for imposing effect. He seems to have written generally under the inspiration of high animal spirits. His sentiment is lively and tender, rather than serious and impressive. The reviewers have censured him with rather too much severity for occasional affectations. With a few exceptions on this score his *Story of Rimini* is a charming poem. *The Legend of Florence*, written at a later period, is one of the most original and captivating of modern plays. Many of his Epistles glow with a genial humour and spirit of fellowship which betray fine social qualities. He lives obviously in his affections, and cultivates literature with refined taste rather than with lukewarm assiduity.—RUFUS W. GRISWOLD, "Leigh Hunt," *The Poets and Poetry of England in the Nineteenth Century*, 1844, p. 194

On a survey of the ordinary experiences of poets, we are apt to come hastily to a conclusion, that a true poet may have quite enough tribulation by his poetry, for all good purposes of adversity, without finding it necessary to break any fresh ground of vexation:—but Leigh Hunt, imprudent in his generation, was a gallant politician, as well as a genuine poet; and, by his connection with the *Examiner* newspaper, did, in all the superfluity of a youth full of animal spirits, sow the whirlwind and reap the tornado. We have also heard of some other literary offences of thirty or forty years ago, but nobody cares to recollect them. In religious feeling, however, he has been misrepresented. It is certain that no man was ever more capable of the spirit of reverence; for God gifted him with a loving genius—with a genius to love and bless. He looks full tenderly into the face of every man, and woman, and child, and living creature; and the beautiful exterior world, even when it is in angry mood, he smoothes down softly, as in recognition of its sentiency, with a gentle caressing of the fancy—Chaucer's irrepressible "Ah, benedicite," falling for ever from his lips! There is another point of resemblance between him and several of the elder poets, who have a social joyous full-heartedness; a pathetic sweetness; a love of old stories, and of sauntering about green places; and a liking for gardens and drest nature, as well as fields and forests; though he is not always so simple as they, in his mode of describing, but is apt to elaborate his admiration, while his elder brothers described the thing—and left it so. He presses into association with the old Elizabethan singing choir, just as the purple light from Italy and Marini had flushed their foreheads; and he is an Italian scholar himself, besides having read the Greek idyls. He has drunken deep from "the beaker full of the warm South," and loves to sit in the sun, indolently turning and shaping a fancy "light as air," or—and here he has never had

justice done him—in brooding deeply over the welfare, the struggles, and hopes of humanity. Traces of this high companionship and these pleasant dispositions are to be found like lavender between the leaves of his books; while a fragrance native to the ground—which would be enough for the reader's pleasure, though the lavender were shaken out—diffuses itself fresh and peculiar over all. He is an original writer: his individuality extending into mannerism, which is individuality prominent in the mode. When he says new things, he puts them strikingly; when he says old things, he puts them newly—and no intellectual and good-tempered reader will complain of this freshness, on account of a certain "knack at trifling," in which he sometimes chooses to indulge. He does, in fact, constrain such a reader into sympathy with him—constrain him to be glad "with the spirit of joy" of which he, the poet, is possessed—and no living poet has that obvious and overflowing delight in the bare act of composition, of which this poet gives sign. 'Composition' is not a word for him—we might as well use it of a bird—such is the ease with which it seems to flow! Yet he is an artist and constructor also, and is known to work very hard at times before it comes out so bright, and graceful, and pretending to have cost no pains at all. He spins golden lines round and round and round, as a silk-worm in its cocoon. He is not without consciousness of art—only he is conscious less of design in it, than of pleasure and beauty. His excessive consciousness of grace in the turning of a line, and of richness in the perfecting of an image, is what some people have called "coxcombry;" and the manner of it approaches to that conscious, sidelong, swimming gait, balancing between the beautiful and the witty, which is remarkable in some elder poets. His versification is sweet and various, running into Chaucer's cadences. His blank verse is the most successfully original in its freedom, of any that has appeared since the time of Beaumont and Fletcher. His images are commonly beautiful, if often fantastic—clustering like bees, or like grapes—sometimes too many for the vines— a good fault in these bare modern days. His gatherings from nature are true to nature; and we might quote passages which would disprove the old bygone charge of 'Cockneyism,' by showing that he had brought to bear an exceeding niceness of actual observation upon the exterior world. His nature, however, is seldom moor-land and mountain land; nor is it, for the most part, English nature—we have hints of fauns and the nymphs lying hidden in the shadow of the old Italian woods; and the sky overhead is several tints too blue for home experiences. It is nature, not by tradition, like Pope's nature, nor quite by sensation and reflection, like Wordsworth's: it is nature by memory and phantasy; true, but touched with an exotic purple. His sympathies with men are wide as the distance between joy and grief: and while his laughter is audible and resistless, in pathos and depth of tender passionateness, he is no less sufficient. The tragic power of the *Story of Rimini*, has scarcely been exceeded by any English poet, alive or dead; and his *Legend of Florence*, is full of the 'purification of pity,' and the power of the most Christian-like manhood and sympathy. We might have fancied that the consciousness of pleasure in composition, which has been attributed to this poet, and the sense of individuality which it implies, would have interfered with the right exercise of the dramatic faculty—but the reason of tears is probably stronger in him than the consciousness of beauty. He has in him, and has displayed it occasionally, an exaltation and a sense of the divine, under a general aspect: a very noble dramatic lyric on the liberation of the soul from the body, published within the last seven years, has both those qualities, in the highest degree.—R. H. HORNE, "William Wordsworth and Leigh Hunt," A *New Spirit of the Age*, 1844, pp. 183–85

He is, in truth, one of the pleasantest writers of his time,—easy, colloquial, genial, humane, full of fine fancies and verbal niceties, possessing a loving if not a "learned spirit," with hardly a spice of bitterness in his composition. He is an excellent commentator on the minute beauties of poetry. He has little grasp of acuteness of understanding, and his opinions are valueless where those qualities should be called into play; but he has a natural taste, which detects with nice accuracy what is beautiful, and a power of jaunty expression, which conveys its intuitive decisions directly to other minds. He surveys poetry almost always from a luxurious point of view, and his criticism therefore is merely a transcript of the fine and warm sensations it has awakened in himself. He is a sympathizing critic of words, sentences, and images, but has little success in explaining the grounds of his instinctive judgments, and is feeble and jejune in generalization. He broods over a dainty bit of fancy or feeling, until he overflows with affection for it. He dandles a poetic image on his knee as though it were a child, pats it lovingly on the back, and addresses to it all manner of dainty phrases; and, consequently, he has much of the baby-talk, as well as the warm appreciation, which comes from affection. This billing and cooing is often distasteful, especially if it be employed on some passages which the reader desires to keep sacred from such handling; and we cannot see him approaching a poet like Shelley without a gesture of impatience; but generally it is far from unpleasant. His *Imagination and Fancy* is a delightful book.

The *Indicator* and *Seer* are filled with essays of peculiar excellence. Hunt's faults of style and thinking are ingrained, and cannot be weeded out by criticism, and to get at what is really valuable in his writings, considerable toleration must be exercised towards his effeminacy of manner and daintiness of sentiment. That, with all his faults, he has a mind of great delicacy and fulness, a fluent fancy, unrivalled good-will to the whole world, a pervading sweetness of feeling, and that he occasionally displays remarkable clearness of perception, must be cheerfully acknowledged by every reader of his essays. —EDWIN P. WHIPPLE, "British Critics" (1845), *Essays and Reviews*, 1850, Vol. 2, pp. 127–29

Mr Hunt's ablest production in verse, is the *Story of Rimini*. It is an attempt to convey an affecting narrative through the medium of more idiomatic cast of language and freer versification, than is common to English poetry. Thus regarded, it may justly be pronounced a highly successful poem. Open to criticism, as it unquestionably is considered abstractly, when viewed with reference to the author's theories, and judged by its own law, no reader of taste and sensibility can hesitate to approve as well as admire its execution. The poet seems to have caught the very spirit of his scene. The tale is presented, as we might imagine it to have flowed from an *improvisatore*. Its tone is singularly familiar and fanciful. It is precisely such a poem as we love to read under the trees on a summer afternoon, or in a garden by moonlight. All appearance of effort in the construction is concealed. Some of the descriptive passages are perfect pictures, and the sentiment is portrayed by a feeling hand. We can easily imagine the cool contempt with which a certain class of critics would regard this little work. They would rank it with the music of unfledged warblers, and, from the absence of certain very formal and decided traits, confidently assign it "an immortality of near a week." But there are some rare felicities in this unpretending poem which will always be appreciated. It will touch and please many a young heart yet;

and have its due influence in letting down the stilted style of more assuming rhymers. The description of the procession in the first canto is very spirited and true to life. We can almost see the gaily-adorned knights and prancing horses, and hear

> Their golden bits keep wrangling as they go.

We can almost behold the expectant princess, as

> with an impulse and affection free
> She lays her hand upon her father's knee,
> Who looks upon her with a laboured smile,
> Gathering it up into his own the while.

And we mentally join in the greetings of the multitude, when Paulo

> on a milk-white courser, like the air,
> A glorious figure, springs into the square.

The appearance of the hero is painted most vividly to the eye, as is the bride's journey to Rimini; and throughout, there is a zest and beauty of imagery, that is redolent of the "sweet south." The consummation of the "fatal passion," is admirably and poetically traced. The author acknowledges his obligations to Dante for the last touch to the picture. ⟨. . .⟩

Whatever may be deemed the success, as that term is popularly used, of Leigh Hunt, in literature, he may claim the happy distinction of interesting his readers in himself. Let critics pick as many flaws as they will, the pervading good-nature and poetic feeling of the author of *Rimini*, will ever be recognized. In an age like our own, it is no small triumph for a writer to feel, that, both in practice and precept, he has advocated a cheerful philosophy; that he has celebrated the charms of refined friendship, the unworn attractiveness of fields and flowers, the true amenities of social life, and the delights of imaginative literature. The spirit of our author's life and writings, like that of his friend Lamb, is cheering and beautiful. He manifests a liberal and candid heart. His influence is benign and genial; and the thought of him, even to the strangers to his person on this side of the ocean, is kindly and refreshing.—HENRY T. TUCKERMAN, "Leigh Hunt," *Thoughts on the Poets*, 1846, pp. 125–28

I took up Leigh Hunt's book *The Town* with the impression that it would be interesting only to Londoners, and I was surprised, ere I had read many pages, to find myself enchained by his pleasant, graceful, easy style, varied knowledge, just views, and kindly spirit. There is something peculiarly anti-melancholic in Leigh Hunt's writings, and yet they are never boisterous. They resemble sunshine, being at once bright and tranquil. —CHARLOTTE BRONTË, Letter to W. S. Williams (April 16, 1849)

Four or five years ago, the writer of these lines was much pained by accidentally encountering a printed statement, 'that Mr. Leigh Hunt was the original of Harold Skimpole in *Bleak House*.' The writer of these lines, is the author of that book. The statement came from America. It is no disrespect to that country, in which the writer has, perhaps, as many friends and as true an interest as any man that lives, good-humouredly to state the fact, that he has, now and then, been the subject of paragraphs in Transatlantic newspapers, more surprisingly destitute of all foundation in truth than the wildest delusions of the wildest lunatics. For reasons born of this experience, he let the thing go by.

But, since Mr. Leigh Hunt's death, the statement has been revived in England. The delicacy and generosity evinced in its revival, are for the rather late consideration of its revivers. The fact is this:

Exactly those graces and charms of manner which are remembered in the words we have quoted, were remembered by the author of the work of fiction in question, when he drew the character in question. Above all other things, that 'sort of gay and ostentatious wilfulness' in the humouring of a subject, which had many a time delighted him, and impressed him as being unspeakably whimsical and attractive, was the airy quality he wanted for the man he invented. Partly for this reason, and partly (he has since often grieved to think) for the pleasure it afforded him to find that delightful manner reproducing itself under his hand, he yielded to the temptation of too often making the character *speak* like his old friend. He no more thought, God forgive him! that the admired original would ever be charged with the imaginary vices of the fictitious creature, than he has himself ever thought of charging the blood of Desdemona and Othello, on the innocent Academy model who sat for Iago's leg in the picture. Even as to the mere occasional manner, he meant to be so cautious and conscientious, that he privately referred the proof sheets of the first number of that book to two intimate literary friends of Leigh Hunt (both still living), and altered the whole of that part of the text on their discovering too strong a resemblance to his 'way.'—CHARLES DICKENS, "Leigh Hunt: A Remonstrance" (1859), *Works*, 1908, Vol. 36, pp. 209–10

His *Story of Rimini*, published in 1816, being, as it was, indisputably the finest inspiration of Italian song that had yet been heard in our modern English literature, had given him a place of his own as distinct as that of any other poetical writer of the day. Whatever may be thought of some peculiarities in his manner of writing, nobody will now be found to dispute either the originality of his genius, or his claim to the title of a true poet. Into whatever he has written he has put a living soul; and much of what he has produced is brilliant either with wit and humor, or with tenderness and beauty. In some of the best of his pieces too there is scarcely to be found a trace of anything illegitimate or doubtful in the matter of diction or versification.—GEORGE L. CRAIK, *A Compendious History of English Literature*, 1861, Vol. 2, p. 531

Leigh Hunt, for example, would be pleased, even now, if he could learn that his bust had been reposited in the midst of the old poets whom he admired and loved; though there is hardly a man among the authors of to-day and yesterday, whom the judgment of Englishmen would be less likely to place there. He deserves it, however, if not for his verse, (the value of which I do not estimate, never having been able to read it,) yet for his delightful prose, his unmeasured poetry, the inscrutable happiness of his touch, working soft miracles by a life-process like the growth of grass and flowers. As with all such gentle writers, his page sometimes betrayed a vestige of affectation, but, the next moment, a rich natural luxuriance overgrew and buried it out of sight.—NATHANIEL HAWTHORNE, "Up the Thames," *Our Old Home*, 1863

In Leigh Hunt's poem of *Rimini* there is not the least resemblance to any of his views in the youthful volumes of which I have spoken. The latter is in style and subject much in the mode of other works of the kind, written by young men just coming out into the world, and it is marked by no peculiar excellences or novelties. His poem of *Rimini* was the work of more advanced years. In that poem it may be supposed his style was fixed. Bearing no resemblance at all to his youthful efforts, it may be said to carry out the peculiar feeling of the writer. He completed it at Hampstead in 1816. The year before, about midsummer, I had frequently visited him there in the Vale of

Health, as he styled it. I have said before that while Lamb deemed the Temple and its vicinity his world, and proclaimed his evening symposium almost the boundary of all possible local enjoyment, Hunt placed himself in the centre of a larger web, and expatiated over a more considerable superfices. He had not then been abroad, and his ideas were connected with what he visited in his own neighbourhood almost wholly at intervals when he put by his books. ⟨. . .⟩

He inscribed his poem of *Rimini* to Byron. The tale, as all the world knows, is founded on Dante, in the episode of Paulo and Francesca—the substance of which everybody knows. It is sufficiently explanatory, both of the design and of the source whence the tale is derived. The style is marked by the author's peculiarities to a considerable extent.

The poem has many pleasing, and some very sweet lines, but by endeavouring to be singular, or to exhibit somewhat of a novelty in his verse, he has introduced expressions and phrases that do not fall harmoniously upon the English ear. I mean they want that natural flow and those verbal combinations which are most pleasing. Some one, I remember, attacked his use of the word "swirl,"—

Swirl into the bay.

If this were the only objection to the structure and language of a poem that contains many fine lines, with what may be called here and there a concetto, it would be indeed hypercritical to notice them. Whoever has seen a vessel with a gentle breeze and strong tide in her favour run into a bay and anchor, will feel how very descriptive of the actual fact the word he thus used.

There are fine lines, too, intermingled with some that do not harmonise with them, and others too minutely descriptive, instead of being struck off by the delineation of the principal and more striking features alone of the object designated. Yet whoever says that the poem wants power, and that it is not faithfully descriptive, greatly errs. Some delineations are not natural—for example,—

And in the midst, fresh whistling through the scene,
A lightsome fountain starts from out the green.

The "whistling" of a fountain seems an odd expression, and a thing itself not quite natural.—CYRUS REDDING, "James Henry Leigh Hunt," *Personal Reminiscences of Eminent Men*, 1867, Vol. 2, pp. 200–203

⟨. . .⟩ as pure-minded a man as ever lived, and a critic whose subtlety of discrimination and whose soundness of judgment, supported as it was on a broad base of truly liberal scholarship, have hardly yet won fitting appreciation.—JAMES RUSSELL LOWELL, "Address on Unveiling the Bust of Fielding" (1883), *Works*, Riverside ed., Vol. 6, p. 57

Charming as his *Story of Rimini* is, long as it will maintain for him a place among the poets of his time, notable as its influence has been on the use of the heroic couplet, it is as a critic that Hunt takes his highest place in the literature of the century. In truth, he was well equipped for the critic's office. He had a keen eye, an open mind, an even judgment, a warm but intrepid heart, and a light incisive utterance. There were few of his illustrious contemporaries who were not indebted to him for vindication or exposition. He was one of the earliest champions of "The Lake Poets," and did much to awaken interest in the true charm of their work; later, he gave similar service for Keats and Shelley, and in each case did honour alike to literature and to his own generous and penetrating judgment.—THOMAS ARCHER, "Leigh Hunt," *The Poets and the*

Poetry of the Century, ed. Alfred H. Miles, 1892, Vol. 2, p. 306

⟨. . .⟩ it would not be too harsh to say that Leigh Hunt's character was chiefly influenced by feebleness of mind and body. His faults and his good qualities alike were those of a weaker organisation; the petty meannesses, the enduring spite, the unwillingness or incapacity to take a high view even of friends and benefactors, as much as the light-heartedness and frivolity, the almost feminine grace and charm, belong alike to one who looked upon his stronger fellow-creatures as in some sort his natural protectors, endued with a special mission to watch over his delicate existence, deserving only casual thanks when they did what was but their manifest duty, and of bitter and spiteful satire when they attended to their own affairs instead. ⟨. . .⟩

It is not easy to decide what place in literature should be assigned to Leigh Hunt, but we certainly think that he has generally been ranked much too high, owing in great part to the factitious importance attaching to him as the friend of Byron and Shelley. The great bulk of his work is merely that of an agreeable *littérateur*, possessed of much fluency and ease in writing and a peculiarly graceful turn of expression. Of his poems, the *Story of Rimini*, which we should rank among the highest, is full of charming poetical conceits, such as the picture of that scene where—

> April with his white hands wet with flowers,
> Dazzles the bridesmaids looking from the towers:
> Green vineyards and fair orchards, far and near,
> Glitter with drops; and heaven is sapphire clear,
> And the lark rings it, and the pine-trees glow,
> And odours from the citrons come and go;
> And all the landscape—earth and sky and sea—
> Breathes like a bright-eyed face that laughs out
> openly.

But the whole composition lacks depth; it is charming upon the surface, but there is nothing to be found below. This quality of shallowness, which we regard as attaching more or less to almost all of Leigh Hunt's work, is naturally most observable in his poetry; yet that there was something deeper and higher in the strange little man, with his half-childish, half-womanish charm, is shown by one or two gems which would make up for a great deal of lightness and superficiality. The well-known verses to his child during a sickness are sufficient evidence of what he could write when deeply moved, but a more perfect specimen of the true, poetic sympathy with noble thoughts not necessarily brought home to him by actual experience is given in the little poem of "Abou Ben Adhem," which we quote, well known as it is, to demonstrate the potential greatness of a man who, in our judgment, achieved but little.

> Abou Ben Adhem—may his tribe increase—
> Awoke one night from a deep dream of peace,
> And saw within the moonlight in his room,
> Making it rich and like a lily in bloom,
> An angel writing in a book of gold.
> Exceeding peace had made Ben Adhem bold,
> And to the presence in the room he said,
> "What writest thou?" The vision raised his head,
> And with a voice made of all sweet accord,
> Answered, "The names of those who love the Lord."
> "And is mine one?" said Adhem. "Nay, not so,"
> Replied the Angel. Abou spoke more low,
> But cheerly still and said, "I pray thee then
> Write me as one who loves his fellow-men."
> The Angel wrote and vanished. The next night
> He came again with a great wakening light,

> And showed the names whom love of God had blest,
> And lo! Ben Adhem's name led all the rest.

Before these noble lines the voice of criticism is silent. This is not the poetry that a man can make out of his own head, but that which can only come from the true spirit working within him. Doubtless there was much good in Leigh Hunt; he was the close friend of Carlyle and of many others whose friendship was in itself a mark of honour and of merit. His life was in many ways a hard one; debt, deception and disappointment were the companions of many a time when he kept a contented, smiling face to the outer world. His faults, at least, he made no attempt to hide, and the love that he gained was in spite of the knowledge of them. We may hope that his name too may be found in the angel's list, for surely no unloving heart could have given birth to so lofty a conception.
—MARGARET OLIPHANT, *The Victorian Age of English Literature*, 1892, Vol. 1, pp. 94–101

We need not go the absurd lengths to which Leigh Hunt's enthusiasm carried that genial, and only too impressionable critic, as when, in his *Imagination and Fancy*, a sort of poetic *Baedeker* or Tourist's Guide to Parnassus, he discovered the prototype of Milton's passages of glorified nomenclature.
—WILLIAM WATSON, "Some Literary Idolatries," *Excursions in Criticism*, 1893, p. 6

Much of Leigh Hunt's prose was written for the day, and meant to be forgotten to-morrow. His *Men, Women and Books*, the transcriptions from Italian romances, the *Jar of Honey from Mount Hybla* (set off by Doyle's delightful illustrations), and the *Wit and Humour*, served the purpose for which they were written, and may now be left on the shelf. The *Essays* remain, and have much of the felicity of the *Autobiography*. As an essayist, Hunt will bear comparison with Hazlitt, if not with Lamb himself; though, indeed, it is only fair to remember that Hunt, Hazlitt, and Lamb did not copy one another, but used a common language.

It seems strange, nowadays, that Leigh Hunt, as a poet, should have been reckoned as the rival, if not the equal, of Wordsworth, Keats, and Shelley. We would rather rank him, as a poet, with Lamb and Barry Cornwall. But he was one of the leaders of the natural school—a literary pre-Raphaelite or pre-Popeite, taking his starting-point from Dryden. He and his school were poets of fancy—neither romanticists nor classicists; realists in a sense, but not students of the facts at their feet, like Crabbe or Wordsworth; and their departure from the well-worn ways of poetry brought them praise and blame, rather on account of their common principles than in proportion to their comparative merits as poets. It is so in the case of every new movement; the final verdict—if there be such a thing—is given by a later generation, which is not affected by the jealousies and friendships of to-day.

Leigh Hunt had good authority for thinking himself a poet. His detractors in the *Quarterly* called him the "hierophant of the new school of Cockney poetry," and spoke of Keats as his "simple neophyte and copyist." The Whig reviewers, while they lectured him for affectation, negligence, and vulgar diction, awarded him the praise of "genuine poetry," "grace and spirit," and "infinite beauty and delicacy." The *Story of Rimini* was much admired at the time; Byron commended it warmly; and Scott, gossiping in Murray's shop, put the volume into his pocket. Shelley praised "The Nymphs," one of the pieces in *Foliage*, as "truly poetical, in the intense and emphatic sense of the word." Robert Browning many years later wrote: "I have always venerated you as a poet. I believe your poetry to be sure of its eventual reward." ⟨. . .⟩

When all is said, it may be admitted that his poetry will not survive. His reputation was won, as he himself confessed, too early and too easily; and our age has been taught by Tennyson and Browning to disparage fluency and admire fulness of thought or perfection of manner. The generation of Byron, Scott and Rogers allowed a larger dilution of sense and style, and was more tolerant of commonplace; and when the turn of fluency comes again, it will not be worth while to disinter Leigh Hunt's flowing numbers and breezy sentiment. It is enough for his credit if a few poems be remembered to show what a fine poetical sense was his, tinctured with Keats and Shelley, Spenser and Ariosto, as his prose was tinctured with Lamb, Addison and Steele. His verse, though neither deep nor strong, is delicate, fresh, sunshiny and original. He could, as Professor Dowden says, "have passed his whole life writing eternal new stories in verse, part grave, part gay, of no great length, but 'just sufficient,' as he himself writes, 'to vent the pleasure with which I am stung on meeting some touching adventure, and which haunts me till I can speak of it somehow.'"

He turned the thoughts of English poets towards Chaucer, Spenser and Dryden, and in so doing purified his native tongue, whilst he enriched it with echoes of Italy. He was an important element in shaping the course of Keats and Shelley. To him, more than to anyone else, is due that modern study of Italian literature which was caught up and carried on by Landor, Tennyson and the Brownings, and has borne other fruit in the study of Dante, and the poets whom Rossetti taught us to know. And indeed it is not far-fetched to put down to his score something of that international feeling which took shape in Mr. Gladstone's attack upon the Bourbon misgovernment at Naples, and the sympathy of this Government and nation with Italy in the War of Independence in 1859 and 1860. Italy to Leigh Hunt was a poetical expression; but his latest thoughts were of her redemption, and he would have rejoiced, had he lived so long, to follow the career of Cavour and Garibaldi, and welcome Victor Emmanuel as liberator and king.

Leigh Hunt was a true poet, if a small one, which is more than can be said of many of the craft who nowadays are so numerous and so unnecessary. In verse and in prose he spoke to his contemporaries, anticipating and answering their thought; and poetry which does this, though it may perish, has sweetened and elevated the life of its own time and increased "the gladness of the world," like the plays, the pictures, the conversations, the loves and friendships of those whose eyes have long since sunk into their orbits. Poor Yorick did not live in vain, though his lips can charm no more. The greatest, perhaps the best, part of our lives is made up of perishing trifles; and Leigh Hunt, whose self-conceit was always bounded by modesty, would never have claimed or desired for himself the immortality of the half-dozen great wits with whom he was privileged to consort.—F. CORNISH WARRE, "Leigh Hunt," *Temple Bar*, Jan. 1896, pp. 199–202

When Leigh Hunt commenced to write essays, he was plainly under the spell of a past age, and the *Connoisseur* was admittedly his model. Nor did he ever wholly succeed in throwing off the faded garments of the eighteenth century, and there is always present in his style a touch of archaism which makes one rank him with the earlier essayists rather than with his own vigorous contemporaries. In 1812 he was known only as an unusually capable dramatic critic, and it was not till seven years later that he began in the *Indicator* to revive the essay on the lines of Addison and Goldsmith. He cannot, however, be placed in the first rank of English essayists. In all

his work there is a lack of virility, and he had no special endowment of pathos or of humour. When it is said that he could write commonplace gracefully, his merits and defects are summarized. His essays bear nowhere the impress of a strong personality, they contain no fresh creations, and they scarcely ever deviate from one level of unemotional calm. Yet he had indubitable skill in writing on familiar subjects, and he wielded a simple style that on rare occasions became even eloquent. The essays "On Sleep," and "On the Deaths of Little Children" are his finest pieces of word-painting. The former, if disfigured by some patches of cheap moralizing, concludes with two paragraphs of singular beauty, while the other, though not displaying Steele's pathos, nor Lamb's April blending of tears and smiles, is a masterpiece of tender imagery and artistic restraint. Leigh Hunt was a genuine man of letters, with no very strong feelings and with but little imagination, loving books and flowers, and able to treat any subject in a pleasant and cultured style. The indisputable decline of his reputation is to be accounted for by his want of any striking originality, and by his being overshadowed by his greater contemporaries. —J. H. LOBBAN, "Introduction" to *English Essays*, 1896, pp. liv–lv

The fame of Leigh Hunt, like that of most writers of the second or lower ranks who have not come to the period when their works are finally classed, has probably on the whole sunk a good deal since his death, though there has been a recent revival of interest in him. But though, as has been said above, there is no complete collection of his works, certain parts of it appear to be kept steadily in print by the booksellers, while of others reprints in different forms still appear from time to time. With the exception of a novel of no great merit, of one or two religious or quasi-religious books, and of a little nondescript matter, the whole of his work in prose belongs to what is called occasional writing. Even where his books were issued with titles intimating a certain unity, such as *The Town, The Old Court Suburb, A Jar of Honey from Mount Hybla*, and so forth, they are not in reality anything more than collections or strings of separate articles, and though an exception has been sought by some for the *Autobiography*, I am not myself much inclined to grant it.

Leigh Hunt was in fact a born article-writer, if not a born journalist. For the occupations of journalism proper, though he had a good deal of practice in them, he was, I suspect, both too original in fancy and too desultory in temper. He could write on an immense variety of subjects, but they must be subjects which hit his own taste and caprice at the moment, not subjects dictated by the events of the day or the needs of an editor. At the same time, he was not very capable of conceiving, or, having conceived, of working out any large and orderly scheme. Accordingly, the great mass of his work, though it has qualities which raise it far above ordinary journalism, still has some of the defects of journalism upon it. It consists of hundreds—it might hardly be an exaggeration to say thousands—of articles, essays, sketches, reviews, short stories, sometimes mere paragraphs which touch on the widest diversity of subject. Hunt busied himself with literary history and criticism, art, politics, topography, social life, religion as he conceived it—a very vague and formless religion, which epithets will also apply to his politics—almost everything except the more serious subjects of science and scholarship. Even these, though with uniformly disastrous results, he now and then attempted to touch. To this multifarious and miscellaneous industry he brought a fair amount of rather desultory reading, a very fine taste in some departments (especially the poetical) of literary criticism, some knowledge of art, especially of the drama, a peculiar loving affection for the monuments and the memories of old London (which, with Italy, was almost his sole place of residence), a great deal of interest in the ordinary concerns of humanity, and above all a distinct style. This style, with a certain tendency to the careless and slipshod, has a very remarkable vividness, no small share of grace, and a peculiar attractive quality which contrives to surmount and survive occasional shocks to refined taste in matter of manners, and contempts of logical exigences in point of ethics and of thought.

Except in this quality of manner Leigh Hunt is not, in prose, a very original writer. He is most original in literary criticism where, chiefly by dint of intense affection for and sympathy with the writers, especially the poets, whom he handles, he holds a position quite by himself. He was the contemporary and the more or less intimate associate of Coleridge, Lamb, Hazlitt, and Carlyle; the contemporary if not the associate of Jeffrey, Wilson, Lockhart, De Quincey, and Macaulay. All these men were of much robuster intelligence, most of them were of far greater erudition, and some of them had a finer critical originality than Hunt could boast. Yet if it should happen (as it very well may) that all of them have written on some one literary subject, especially if that subject be poetry, the reading of the whole will not make it superfluous to see what Leigh Hunt has to say. His criticism is the reverse of methodical; it rarely attempts to grasp and never succeeds in grasping the whole of the subject; it is the last criticism to go to if what one wants is the latitude and longitude of the writer or the book in the great chart of literature. It may almost be said of Hunt's criticism of poetry in the late Laureate's words that "it cannot understand, it loves"; and by virtue of love it frequently detects and reveals peculiarities of the subject which more strictly intelligent treatment has missed. For this irregular desultory "impressionist" criticism, as well as for his topographical narratives and descriptions, his sketches of manners, his stories and anecdotes, his eighteenth-century essay-writing adjusted to a looser nineteenth-century standard—Leigh Hunt's style is excellently suited. Save now and then when his poetic fit comes on while he is wielding the pen of prose, it cannot be said to be a very dignified or distinguished style; it is even, as has been hinted, sometimes slipshod and out-at-elbows, suggestive of the peculiar and rather slovenly ease and *bonhomie* which characterised its author's whole life and conversation. But at its best it can be almost beautiful; and except when it is at its very worst (which is very seldom) it is always agreeable. As a style it has no very salient characteristics, and is almost devoid of mannerisms; such as it shows being chiefly vestiges of the old eighteenth-century essay habit of imitating the mannerisms of the *Tatler* and the *Spectator*. Indeed, one of Hunt's chief charms is his extreme naturalness, which steers quite clear of the excessively artificial nature too common in literature, and makes any idea of affectation impossible. His writing thus has the great and rare merit of being perfectly adapted to his thought and subject—to his easy but by no means always trivial humour, to his wide if not very scholarly reading, to his still wider and for the most part perfectly genuine range of human interests, and above all to his intense love of some of the sides of poetry, and most of the gentler emotions of life.—GEORGE SAINTSBURY, "Leigh Hunt," *English Prose*, ed. Henry Craik, 1896, Vol. 5, pp. 247–50

Leigh Hunt had a certain bright chivalry on behalf of whatever assumed to itself the cherished name or the aspect of Liberty; at times he could present a gallant front to her foes. But Hunt's

shafts, if occasionally keen, were always light-timbered, and rather annoyed the enemy than achieved their ruin. He was framed less for the rough tumble of English radical politics than for "dance and Provençal song and sunburnt mirth."—EDWARD DOWDEN, *The French Revolution and English Literature*, 1897, p. 249

Leigh Hunt was, with Hazlitt, in 1820, among the best-hated men in England. They, almost alone among men of letters who were primarily such, represented uncompromising Radicalism. But while Hazlitt was a genuine critical force in politics as well as in literature, Hunt was a man of letters playing the politician. Henry James Leigh Hunt, born in 1784, near London, the son of a West Indian, followed Coleridge and Lamb at Christ's Hospital. At twenty-one he began his long career of journalism by writing theatrical critiques for his brother's paper the *News*. In 1808 the two started *The Examiner*, which at once took rank among the boldest and liveliest journals on the Opposition side. Hunt's trenchant and powerful dramatic criticism broke down the venal collusion between the stage and the press, and attracted general attention. The zest of battle wrought its full effect upon Hunt's sensitive brain. His famous so-called 'libel' upon the Prince Regent (1811) made him the hero of the Liberal world, and provided him with many valuable and some perilous friendships. Condemned to two years of imprisonment, which the votive offerings of his friends and his own buoyant spirits made a pleasant retreat, he reaped the advantages of martyrdom without its inconveniences. Embowered in the pleasant greenery of his rose-trellised cell he read the Italian poets, meditated metrical reforms, and applied both studies in his *Story of Rimini*, a daring expansion of the great Francesca scene in the *Inferno*. The *Story of Rimini* (1816) is the starting-point of that free or Chaucerian treatment of the heroic couplet, and of the colloquial style, eschewing epigram and full of familiar turns, which Shelley in *Julian and Maddalo*, and Keats in *Lamia*, made classical. But Hunt's freedom is controlled by no such subtle art as theirs. His familiarity inclines to be vulgar. His bits of banal dialogue jar upon an atmosphere often full of the perfume of romance. This atmosphere is a principal charm in all his verse. The luscious richness of Keats he in some degree anticipated as he in some degree provoked it. But of the riper and austerer Keats of *Hyperion* and *The Odes* he has hardly a trace.

The years succeeding his imprisonment were Hunt's golden time. *Foliage* followed *Rimini* (1818); and into his literary journal, the *Indicator*, he poured, week by week, a stream of bright, warm-hearted, voluble prose, interspersed with dainty renderings from his Italian poets; and Hunt had but one or two equals among his contemporaries as a verse translator.

His journey to Italy in 1821, to edit the *Liberal*, was the beginning of misfortune. The *Liberal*, after a momentary glory, was ruined by Shelley's death and Byron's withdrawal; and Hunt, mortified by failure, and humiliated by his dependence on Byron's contemptuous generosity, returned home to write his volumes of malignant gossip, *Lord Byron and His Contemporaries* (1827), and to resume his old career of literary journalism, with tarnished honour. He lived through another generation, till 1859, struggling for some years with actual want, and only more deeply immersed by the successive literary enterprises with which he strove to meet it. Most of his shorter lyrics appeared in his *Poetical Works*, 1832; *A Legend of Florence* in 1840; *The Palfrey* in 1842. It is chiefly by some of the briefer pieces that he lives. His jocund and joyous spirit 'sings its own natural song' in the sonnet to the cricket and grasshopper, his quaint humour in *The Man and the Fish*. And he had moments of lofty inspiration in which he was capable of "Abou ben Adhem" and the Nile Sonnet. An essayist, poet, and translator, full (at his best) of grace and charm in a kind quite his own, he lacked both the stamina and the piercing imaginative vision which make Hazlitt so great. In temperament he was more akin to Lamb, but he equally lacked Lamb's rarer qualities both as a man and as a writer; and his chief function in literature was to further the ease, vivacity, and grace of which, though in a far choicer kind, Lamb was a master in prose, and Chaucer and Ariosto in verse.—C. H. HERFORD, *The Age of Wordsworth*, 1897, pp. 82–84

GEORGE GILFILLAN
From "Leigh Hunt"
A Second Gallery of Literary Portraits
1850, pp. 348–52

It is pleasant, in some moods, to pass from these poets (Tennyson and the Brownings), with their passionate, or fierce, or heroic attitudes, to the blended ease and earnestness of Leigh Hunt. He stands among them like an oak amidst the surrounding pines, or birches, or sensitive plants, less tremulous, dark, drooping, or defiant, to every breath of heaven, but greener, ampler, calmer, albeit ready always to resist strong aggression, as well as to shade unassuming merit. If they aspire to the rank of prophets, he is a patriarch, seated and uttering gentle yet profound responses at his tent-door.

The highest compliment ever paid to Hunt is, perhaps, that of Byron, who, after a furious and vulgar diatribe against him, owns him to be a "good man." This may seem poor praise, but a cold shower-bath from Hecla were less astonishing than the acknowledgment of any human virtue from the mouth of a man who had set himself elaborately to erase each vestige of goodness from his own character, and had well nigh succeeded—who had nearly completed an exchange between his heart and the "nether millstone,"—and whose praises of all but his personal friends came forth rare and reluctant, as do the audible groans of his proud spirit. Hunt's goodness and talent he always admitted—and with regard to the charge of vulgarity, which now, at this distance of time, is the vulgar person of the two? Hunt's vulgarity is that of circumstances and education, Byron's was ingrained in his nature—and neither the Highlands, with their grandeur, nor Holland House, with its varied and brilliant converse, nor Italy, with the *recherché* society of its better classes, were able to erase the original stamp of the degraded and blackguard lord, which had been transmitted from generations downwards, till it was fortunate in his countenance to meet and contend with the blaze of genius and the pale impress of coming death.

In our notion, Thomas Macaulay is an infinitely more vulgar person than Leigh Hunt or even Lord Byron—if vulgarity mean the want of all those qualities which go to constitute a gentleman. Our readers, in illustration of this, may take the following anecdote, which we know to be correct. A writer who had, some year or two ago, rather severely, although with a friendly feeling, criticised Macaulay in one of our leading periodicals, chanced to read Croker's assault upon his *History of England* in the *Quarterly*. Struck with its unfairness and with the *animus* which pervaded it, he wrote Mr Macaulay a note, couched in the most respectful terms,

not retracting his former statements, but expressing a manly sympathy with him under an unjust attack. He was not a little surprised to receive an extremely harsh and contemptuous reply, in which the Edinburgh ex-member told his correspondent that he cared neither for his blame nor his praise. Had the writer been a clamorous petitioner for his pelf or his praise—had he approached him in an unfriendly guise, and with unfriendly language, or had he been base enough to have flattered the man whom he had criticised, he could have accounted for such treatment; as it was he was forced to regard it as a breach of the laws of common courtesy, as a specimen of the wretched airs of aristocracy which upstarts often assume—as the action of a coxcomb, not a gentleman—and we understand told the historian so in language which he is not likely soon to forget or to forgive. Leigh Hunt is incapable, both from geniality and gentlemanly feeling, of such conduct as this. He always dips his pen in a reservoir compounded of warm blood and of the milk of human kindness. This element, indeed, bathes his whole being and person. It swims in his restless eye—it throbs in his hot hand—it, and not age's winter, seems to have whitened his locks—it gushes out in the jets and sparkles of his conversation, which is yet evidently only the relic of what it was in earlier times—and it is the mild or mirthful inspiration of his various writings.

Had Hunt been a less sincere and simple-minded person than he has been, he might, we think, have been quite as popular a writer as Thomas Moore. He has the *champagne* qualities of that writer, without, indeed, so many or such brilliant bubbles of wit and fancy upon the top—and has a world more of body, solidity, and truth. It is his assuming the fairy shape, that has made some (ourselves at one time included) to underrate his powers. But why did he assume it? Why did he, like the devils in Milton, shrink his stature to gain admission to the halls of Pandemonium? Why did he not rather, in dignified humility, wait without as he was till the great main door was opened, and till in full size and panoply he entered in, and sat down a giant among giants, a god amidst gods? In such figured language we convey our notion at once of Hunt's strength and weakness. He has been, partly owing to circumstances and partly to himself, little other than a glorious trifler. He has smiled, or lounged, or teased, or translated, away faculties which, with proper concentration and a perpetual view toward one single object, had been incalculably beneficial to the general progress of literature and of man.

Moore again seems made for trifling. It is his element. The window pane being his world, may we not call him the fly? His love is skin-deep; his anger, too, is a mere itch on the surface; his patriotism is easy, beginning and ending at the piano; his friendship all oozes out in a memoir of his departed friend; his hatred is exhausted in a single satire; and even his melody, while suiting the ivory keys of Lady Blessington's harpsichord, shrinks from the full diapason of the organ or the terrible unity of the fife; he has no powers which earnestness would much care to challenge as her own. Hunt, on the contrary, has put martial faculties upon perpetual parade—they have walked to and fro to beautiful music, but they have rarely mounted the breach, or even seen the enemy. This has not sprung either from the want of power or of courage, but from a kind of amiable ease of temperament, and, perhaps, also from a defect of constitutional stamina. A soul of fire has been yoked to a nervous and feeble constitution.

We can hardly charge the author of forty volumes with having written little, but, perhaps, there is not one among all those volumes to which you can point as entirely worthy, and fully reflective, of the powers which are visible in all. Throughout them all you have a beautiful diffusion—over many of them hangs a certain weary langour—in some you are saluted with an explosion of wit like the crackers of a birth-night—and the others are full of a pensive poetry, tremulous with sentiment, and starred with the strangest and most expressive *epithets*. Heart, geniality, humanity, and genius pervade the whole.

Altogether, we cannot but look upon Hunt's present position as an enviable and fortunate one. He is in the evening of his days, but at evening time it is light with him; he has outlived many a struggle; he has survived a storm in which many larger ships were wrecked; he has not now a single enemy; his name is a household word throughout the world; his fame is dear to every lover of poetry and of liberty; the government of his country has appreciated and rewarded his services. Whatever of the fierce or bitter circumstances had infused into his mind has now been extracted. Above all, milder and juster views of Christianity, its claims and character, seem entering his mind. We will not, therefore, close by wishing him happiness—it is his, we trust, already—but by wishing him long life to enjoy the meek and bright sunset of his chequered and troublous day.

ARMINE T. KENT
From "Leigh Hunt as a Poet"
Fortnightly Review, August 1881, pp. 227–36

The *Story of Rimini*, Leigh Hunt's first serious poem of importance, and written in the ten-syllable couplet, was published in 1816, with a preface advocating the still unpopular theories of poetry upheld by Wordsworth sixteen years before in his famous *Preface to the Lyrical Ballads*. But it is observable that Leigh Hunt's instinctive critical insight kept him clear of the mistake into which his great predecessor had fallen, in looking to an unlettered peasantry for poetical language. "The proper language of poetry is in fact nothing different from that of real life, and depends for its dignity on the strength and sentiment of what it speaks." Thus far they are agreed. But Leigh Hunt goes on, "It is only adding *musical modulation* to what a *fine understanding* might naturally utter in the midst of its griefs or enjoyments." We have here just the two vital points on which Wordsworth, in his capacity of critic, had failed to insist. A quotation from the *Story of Rimini* will exemplify what has been said with respect to versification, and present to those who may be unfamiliar with Leigh Hunt's poetry some slight notion of its distinctive character. Literary criticism without quotation is indeed "vescum papaver"—at once innutritious and soporific. An adequate idea cannot, however, be conveyed, without more copious citation than will here be possible, since much of the beauty of the poem consists in the unembarrassed vivacity of transition with which the story is made to move before the reader—the affluent vigour of invention with which picture after picture is touched in before his eyes. This art of telling a story is rare in English poetry. Even considerable poets will seem at times, when occupied with narrative, to flag and loiter, to dwell, as it were, in their stride; their notion, to vary the metaphor, is not so much a triumphal progress as a series of bivouacks. In the *Story of Rimini* succession seems to be reconciled with continuity, and every new surprise of fancy comes upon the reader with the satisfying force of an iteration. ⟨. . .⟩

There is here an *abandon*, an hilarity, a glad acceptance of the pleasure and beauty to be found in trifles, to parallel which in England we have to go back to the poets more immediately under Italian influence, and to express one aspect of which we have been forced to borrow an Italian word—gusto. This spirit has now become so alien to our literature, the poetry of pure high spirits without any "undercurrent woe" is a thing so rare, that it is perhaps not surprising if it fails to meet with ready recognition. Leigh Hunt himself was fond of attributing his cheerfulness to the West Indian blood in his veins, and accounted in this way for the more cordial reception his poems met with in America. In England his "animal spirits" were set down in many or most critical quarters to mere affectation, especially when they manifested themselves in any verbal eccentricities. Gifford in the *Quarterly* fell with rabid violence on such expressions as "scattery light." Gifford, it is true, was one of the "critics who themselves are sore," having been made ridiculous in the *Feast of the Poets*; but other judges, who had less reason to be biassed, concurred in his strictures. Leigh Hunt accordingly altered this and other offending phrases in subsequent editions. Unfortunately, he further allowed himself to be criticized out of such expressions as "freaks and snatches," to which no one would now think of demurring. And yet more unfortunately, he was induced to give up a considerable number of dissyllabic rhymes. The first couplet in the passage quoted he altered as follows:—

Tis nature, full of spirits, waked and loved,—
E'en sloth to-day goes quick and unreproved—

lines pleasant in themselves, but how inferior to those which they supplant!

'Tis nature, full of spirits, waked and springing,
The birds to the delicious time are singing,—

The hypermetric syllables here are like the first hurried notes of the birds themselves, impatient to get into the thick of their own music.

The excellently realistic lines—

Callings, and clapping doors, and curs unite,
And shouts from mere exuberance of delight—

he also sacrificed to I know not what stilted folly of censorship. Over-diffidence in self-criticism was perhaps natural to one who occupied himself so much with the study of masterpieces; but it is none the less lamentable to find him making such concessions as these to the requirements of a theory even then obsolescent. To those who are tempted to think that diffidence in a poet is its own justification, it may be sufficient to recall the preface to *Endymion*. Most of the quotations here made I have ventured to give as they stood in the earlier editions. ⟨. . .⟩

Leigh Hunt felt and expressed the commonest sights and sounds in this minute and forcible fashion, as when he speaks in his *Autobiography* of the "mud-shine" on the pavement in front of a theatre at night, or describes how—

Childhood I saw, glad-faced, that squeezeth tight
One's hand, *while the rapt curtain soars away.*

There is a theory propounded in *Rasselas* to the effect that the business of the poet is to remark only "general properties and large appearances. He does not number the streaks of the tulip, or describe the different shades in the verdure of the forest." He must "neglect the minuter discriminations for those characteristics which are alike obvious to vigilance and carelessness." The statement, as might have been expected from its authorship, goes somewhat too far, but the theory itself is perhaps not altogether unsound. The difficulty of course is to determine what may be considered to amount to vigilance or carelessness in observation. There are, however, undoubted instances in poetry of a tendency to mistake the discursive knowledge of the naturalist for the unifying emotion of the poet, and to adopt a theory which would make the admirable author of the *Gamekeeper at Home* potentially as great a poet as Keats. Leigh Hunt is never obnoxious to criticism of this kind. To be aware, for instance, of the truth of the following passage, it is enough to have walked in the streets; to feel it thus intensely, to utter it thus felicitously, was assuredly to be no inconsiderable poet.

> His haughty steed, that seems by turns to be
> Vexed and made proud by that cool mastery,
> Shakes at his bit, and rolls his eyes with care,
> Reaching with stately step at the fine air;
> And now and then, sideling his restless pace,
> *Drops with his hinder legs, and shifts his place,*
> And feels through all his frame a fiery thrill;
> The princely rider on his back sits still,
> And looks where'er he likes, and sways him at his
>   will.

The last three lines are a fine example of Leigh Hunt's remark that the triplet "enables a poet to finish his impulse with triumph." He characteristically adds: "I confess I like the very bracket that marks out the triplet to the reader's eye, and prepares him for the music of it. It has a look like the bridge of a lute."

There are other lines descriptive of horses in the *Story of Rimini* to the full as good as those quoted; but enough perhaps has been said of Leigh Hunt's mastery of the picturesque. Word-painting is an art not always looked upon with favour by the austere votaries of form. To those who have a keen sense of niceties of language, it must, however, be always a source of the intensest pleasure. A certain measure of attraction it will retain, even when it borders on mere ingenuity, but when it rises upon the wings of its own self-delight into the higher levels of emotion, theories can touch it no longer. "The general consent and delight of poetic readers" is, after all, the only true touch-stone of poetry. It seems a deplorably indefinite standard, but a better has yet to be found. ⟨. . .⟩

Leigh Hunt's own estimate of his poetical status was the reverse of overweening, but shows his usual discrimination. "I please myself with thinking, that had the circumstances of my life permitted it, I might have done something a little worthier of acceptance in the way of a mixed kind of narrative poetry, part lively and part serious, somewhere between the longer poems of the Italians, and the fabliaux of the old French. My propensity would have been (and oh! had my duties permitted, how willingly would I have passed my life in it! how willingly now pass it!) to write 'eternal new stories' in verse, of no great length, but just sufficient to vent the pleasure with which I am stung on meeting with some touching adventure, and which haunts me till I can speak of it somehow. I would have dared to pretend to be a servant in the train of Ariosto, nay, of Chaucer,

> 'and far off his skirts adore.'

As it is, his best poetical work is limited in quantity, and he must be included in the long list of poets whose infertility is a stock grievance. As he makes Apollo lament—

> There's Collins, it's true, had a good deal to say,
> But the dog had no industry, neither had Gray,

and the same might be said even more truly of Coleridge and others. On Leigh Hunt's part there was no lack of industry; but his amiable eagerness to leave the world better than he found it, beguiled him into the then dangerous path of political journalism, brought him into collision with the law of libel, and was every way unfavourable to free poetical activity. It would be hasty and ungrateful to affirm that the world is none the better for his struggles and sufferings. It may be believed, for instance, that every ill-judged prosecution for libel must have forwarded the legitimate freedom of the press. And if the good that a man does may in any degree be measured by the abuse that he gets for doing it, Leigh Hunt must be ranked very high amongst reformers. "He will live and die," wrote Gifford, in reviewing his poems, "unhonoured in his own generation; and for his own sake it is to be hoped, moulder unknown in those which are to follow." One cannot but feel that "a very clever, a very honest, and a very good-natured man," to quote Macaulay's description of Leigh Hunt, must have done good to an extent very considerable indeed, to be written of in this fashion.

His occupations as a critic further contributed to withdraw Leigh Hunt from poetry, but this was a distraction scarcely to be regretted. The pleasure of hearing the judgments of a poet on fine specimens of his own art is rare enough to reconcile us to the loss of a certain proportion of his own poetical work, especially when the criticism is not of that barren sort which disdains to dwell upon minutiæ of style. In order to be fully alive to the improvement brought about in popular taste by Leigh Hunt's criticism, it should be remembered that it appeared in days when the criticism in vogue was of the following sort. "The very essence of versification is uniformity; and while anything like versification is preserved, it is evident that uniformity continues to be aimed at. What pleasure is to be derived from an occasional failure in this aim, we cannot exactly understand. It must afford the same gratification, we should imagine, to have one of the buttons on a coat a little larger than the rest, or one or two of the pillars of a colonnade a little out of the perpendicular."

It was against facetious incompetence of this kind that Leigh Hunt defended Keats; in the words of the criticism of the day, "it was he who first puffed the youth into notice in his newspaper."

JAMES ASHCROFT NOBLE
From "Leigh Hunt: The Man and the Writer" (1886)
The Sonnet in England and Other Essays
1893, pp. 93–94, 128–33

He was not, like Gibbon or Wordsworth or Dickens, pre-eminent in any one province of the republic of letters, but he was a free citizen of the whole domain. Loving literature with a passionate ardour, the work of his life was an expression of his love; and he is best described by a vague but large phrase of his friend Carlyle as a 'writer of books.' ⟨. . .⟩

Of the many charms of Hunt's writings, perhaps the most powerful is the personal accent which brings the writer near to us. It seems strange at first sight that we should feel this with regard to a man whose work was so largely critical, for the traditional view of criticism is that it is something essentially abstract and *un*human—not to say *in*human—but the very thing which makes Leigh Hunt a memorable worker in this field of literature is that in his hands criticism became vascular and alive, a thing of flesh and blood. Professor Dowden, in a sentence which would have, in itself, endeared him to Hunt, has said that 'the best criticism . . . is not that which comes out of profound cogitation, but out of immense enjoyment; and the most valuable critic is the critic who communicates sympathy by an exquisite record of his own delights, not the critic who attempts to communicate thought.' This is a penetratively truthful utterance, but long before the truth had been formulated by Mr Dowden, it had been vindicated by the practice of Leigh Hunt. His criticism was, indeed, the outcome of an immense enjoyment, and we feel that this enjoyment has been at once the primary and the most powerful impulse to expression. It is because he enjoys, and because he expresses his enjoyment with such naïveté, that he almost compels us, by a gracious compulsion, to enjoy with him; and our debt to Hunt is the debt we owe to one who has multiplied indefinitely our purest and most super-sensuous delights, and, while multiplying them, has given to each of them a new and peculiar poignancy.

There are no doubt many portions of Hunt's work which lack what one may call the classical note. It was inevitable that it should be thus. He often had to write hastily, under pressure not of the spirit within but of the necessity without; and even when the pressure was of the true kind—the pressure of inspiration—this very fact engendered a certain impulsive, uncalculating eagerness of utterance hardly compatible with that nice perfectness of phrase which Hunt valued so much in others, but which he may have felt in his heart might be won at too great a sacrifice of something better. We may smile—indeed many of us have often smiled—at the utterly prosaic and fatuous criticisms, by Mr Macvey Napier, of Hunt's contributions to the *Edinburgh Review*; but, as the common phrase has it, there was 'something in them,' by which we mean that there was *this* in them—that Hunt's style would at times be found irritating by one to whom the mint, anise, and cummin of expression were everything, the weightier matter of adequacy nothing. For Hunt *is* adequate: he does say what he had to say, not hint at it blunderingly; his rendering of his thought and emotion may at times be careless, but it is always complete.

Still it is to be doubted whether it is as a critic that Hunt would have best cared to be remembered. Poetry was his first, his last, his most constant love; and if by prose he had to win the meat and the raiment of life it was poetry that to him was life itself. In one respect—and sufficient note has hardly been taken of it—Hunt's place is a singularly high one, for he is among the originators. Readers who have studied these poems of Hunt which had been published before the appearance of *Endymion* can hardly fail to recognise that to him Keats owed much of what has often been regarded as most distinctly his own; and a man of whom it can be truly said that he influenced Keats is a man of whom it can be said as truly that he has influenced the whole course of English poetry since Keats was laid in his Italian grave. But, however this may be, those who admire and love the poetry of Hunt need not be afraid of allowing him to be judged by his own achievement without thought of any such side issue. Even among poets who are poets beyond all doubt, we recognise some as specially poetical poets, and Hunt is one of these. He is never supreme in the way that some poets are supreme, and even on his own level, he is at one time less felicitous than at another; but there is one thing in which he never fails—that imaginative glow and warmth which takes us into another world than the prosaic life of every day, and enables us to forget the dulnesses and the meannesses of the actual. Whatever else it may lack, his work never lacks gusto—the sense and expression of quick keen delight in all things naturally and wholesomely delightful. To us who are familiar with the heated tones of some contemporary verse it may seem almost ludicrous that such an instinctively stainless poem as *The Story of Rimini* should have been considered to be in some way an offence against the ordered

proprieties of life; but the fact is that Hunt had a singular healthfulness, and therefore a singular purity, which enabled him to handle worthily and with a sweet wholesome simplicity of touch themes which in the hands of coarser or more self-conscious men would inevitably catch some glow of unwholesome voluptuousness or hint of subtle pruriency. We know what the age of the Regency was, and we can imagine how difficult it was for the average man of the world in that age to conceive the possibility of treating with absolute purity—purity that was instinctive and unconscious of itself—a subject which in any way lent itself to grossness or suggestiveness of expatiation. Hunt, however, though in the age was not of it. The companions of his spirit were Petrarch, Chaucer, Spenser; and in the Una of the last named poet who rode upon the lion we have an imaginative type of the passionately pure genius of Hunt. No most solicitous mother of any carefully nurtured English girl need look with even a momentary glance of suspicion upon any line written by this stainless soul; and the guarantee for her confidence is not to be found in any of Hunt's opinions or convictions, but in the fact that his nature was not one in which anything but the sweet and the innocent could live.

Hunt's mission among English poets was to be a celebrator of the beauty and gladness of nature and of human life, and to the Puritan element, which has as yet hardly worn out of the English character, beauty is a temptation and gladness a snare. But this feeling is a result of intellectual action—of considering too curiously—and Hunt's was a nature framed for fine emotion and keen sensation rather than for ethical or other considering. He simply turned instinctively to the sun in whatever region of sky or home the sun might be, and it is little wonder that the sunlight is reflected in his verse. A sunny spirit—that is the true name for Leigh Hunt. His sky indeed was often clouded, but he waited cheerfully and hopefully for the clouds to pass away; and when now and then he touches some sad theme he dwells most insistently, not upon the sadness itself, but upon that element of beauty which adheres in all sadness which is not ignoble. He was a good man: he was also, in spite of troubles which would have crushed the heart out of most of us, a happy man; and it is impossible for any spirit who has been 'finely touched' to be long in his company without being consciously both better and happier. It is difficult to leave him, but the parting must come. Let it be brief. Beloved Leigh Hunt, *Ave atque vale!*

ARTHUR SYMONS
From "Introduction"
Essays of Leigh Hunt
1889, pp. xiii–xix

The position of Leigh Hunt in our literature might easily be exaggerated, and still more easily under-estimated. Born in the year of Johnson's death, he died only two years earlier than Mrs. Browning; and during the whole of an exceptionally long career he was, both in prose and in poetry, exceptionally prominent without ever attaining quite the first rank. In poetry, his influence can be traced in Keats, and he had the honour of being assaulted by *Blackwood* and the *Quarterly* as the leader of the "Cockney" school. In prose he belonged to the generation of Lamb, Coleridge, Landor, De Quincey, Hazlitt. From the earliest years of the century down to to-day, or at least yesterday, his name has been a household word; yet he has left us little, perhaps nothing, of a secured immortality, and before the name of any of the comrades beside whom he worked and wrought on equal terms, his own name pales and flickers. He himself perhaps expected nothing more; he made no extravagant claims on his day or its morrow. Of his books he said, "They never pretended to be anything greater than birds singing among the trees:" nor are they. But to be that only is to be something delightful.

It has to be remembered, in passing judgment on Leigh Hunt, that nearly the whole of his work was produced rapidly, to meet temporary requirements; that he had not always the choice of work; and that he never had leisure to polish, to correct, to eliminate. He had a ready and most genuine inspiration, an immense diligence, and the necessity to write for his living. As a consequence, he has left us a mass of work which is much of it still pleasant to read, but of very varying and very uncertain value as literature. No single achievement, with the possible exception of the *Autobiography*, stands out boldly from its fellows, firm enough to build a reputation on. Every book, almost every essay, has its charming and admirable qualities, side by side with others less charming and less admirable; so that to find work of Leigh Hunt with which we can be definitely and completely satisfied, work practically flawless and rounded, is rare, more so, I think, than in almost any other writer of at all equal eminence. How far this is due to the circumstances under which it was composed, and how far to inherent limitations, it would be difficult, I suppose impossible, to decide. I can only say that, while I think much, very much, must be allowed in Hunt's favour, on the score of external pressure, we have no reason to suppose him capable, under more favourable circumstances, of any work of altogether sustained elevation. He certainly did not possess the secret of that alchemy by which Charles Lamb distilled the very essence of his quality into each small essay and every little note or fragment. Hunt's quality, as it is, is diluted through hundreds of essays and over thousands of pages; and it is, to say the least, unlikely that he could ever have manifested himself altogether differently—could ever have stamped quite finally his image and superscription on any conceivable circle of currency.

Hunt's best work is to be found in his most spontaneous and casual writings—in his periodical essays, written for the most part rapidly, and at the beck of any chance suggestion, but on a plan and in a manner perfectly suited to his capacity. He had a model after his own heart in the *Spectator* of Addison and Steele, the two essayists with whom, of all his predecessors, he had most in common. To something of eighteenth century humour and sobriety he added a certain modern sparkle and informal lightness of touch; with a bookish intelligence, acutely cognisant of men and things through a medium of reminiscence and reflection, quite peculiar to himself. With the essays we must join the *Autobiography*,—"a pious, ingenious, altogether *human* and worthy book," as Carlyle rightly styled it—in which a congenial subject, lending itself, turn by turn, to the exhibition of his finest characteristics, is so graphically and delicately treated that we can claim for it something of permanent value, of abiding interest. Many of Hunt's books are little more than compilations; compilations made, as a rule, with lively skill, and pleasant enough to read; but still, compilations. The volume of essays most easily accessible, the excellently-named *Men, Women, and Books*, does him great injustice. A *Jar of Honey from Mount Hybla* comes midway between the better and the lesser work; the two volumes of annotated selections from the English poets, *Imagination and Fancy*, and *Wit and Humour*, lean more

definitely to the former. Hunt's literary notes and jottings are always good in substance or in form, often in both. His reading was unusually wide, and his sympathies, vivid and ready as they were, were held in check, balanced and directed, by an excellent and impartial judgment. He is usually safe, little likely to be hurried into an excess of enthusiasm or flung upon a raid of vituperation. His notes are not, like those of Lamb, actual revelations; he had not the profound and subtle insight of Coleridge; but as a careful and accurate appraiser of values, his hand and eye are exceptionally sure. Nor is he without flashes of the rarer sort of insight, as the recognition of the now famous character of De Flores in Middleton's *Changeling*—a recognition which he was the first to give—sufficiently proves. He was beyond almost any writer a lover of books, and everything he wrote was written, as it were, under their shadow.

A single one of his works stands quite apart and by itself— *The Religion of the Heart*. This book, and the feelings which prompted it, must be taken into account in any consideration of Leigh Hunt, for it represents very fully the religious side of an essentially pious nature. "A natural piety, no less than cheerfulness, has," he remarks in the Preface, and he never said a truer thing, "ever pervaded my writings; the cheerfulness, indeed, was a part of the piety, flowing from the same tendency to love and admire." *The Religion of the Heart* is a sort of devotional manual, curiously minute and ceremonial in some of its arrangements, but breathing a spirit of large humanity and most serious and genial piety. The latter and later portion of it is mainly a compilation, and it deals with controversial matters on which opinions must always be very much divided; but the earlier half, without ever being profound, or opening new highroads of thought, is exquisitely just, pious and reasonable—the voice of a good heart on the lips of a beautiful speaker. It is Hunt's only work of the kind, but it is the manifestation, as I have intimated, of a pervading principle. Hunt's literary merits are singularly dependent on his moral qualities; his essential peculiarity, his special originality, being the offspring of two ideas—the idea of Happiness, and the idea of Duty. In the Seventeenth of the "Rules of Life and Manners" contained in *The Religion of the Heart*, we find the following maxim:—

> To consider the healthy, and therefore, as far as mortality permits, happy exercise of all the faculties with which we have been gifted, as the self-evident final purpose of our being, so far as existence in this world is concerned; and as constituting therefore the right of every individual human creature, and the main earthly object of all social endeavour.

In these words Leigh Hunt expresses his firmest conviction and touches the very spring of his literary method. He wrote to make men happy, and to advocate their making themselves happy. He assures us that he wrestled with dark problems, that he grappled with the powers of evil and of doubt. If so, it was as the angel in Raphael's picture grapples with the Fiend— easily, gracefully, without noise or dust or disarray of conflict. He tells us nothing of the sterner realities of life, the blacker depths of thought; but he calls out our minds to see the beauty making for happiness in the common things around us. He brings poetry to our breakfast-table, and strikes light out of the pebble at our feet. But his delight in the beauty of the visible world is not a delight purely æsthetic; he does not see with the eye of the painter, to whom the beautiful is supremely interesting for and in itself. He presses beauty into the service of man, and constitutes it an auxiliary and helpmate of happiness. He would have a world of happy and good men and women, pleasing one another and themselves, and delighting to read Spenser, to look at pictures, to wander in the fields, to see plays—their life being all the time a sort of gentle and moral play. He is a lounger in the gardens of literature; a plucker of fruits from the trees of unfallen Edens. In his company we are travellers in enchanted countries, not indeed on the high-roads, not in the cities, but among the meadows, in the villages and pastoral places, with our face to the sunlight and our feet in the long grass. His choicest essays give us the very sense of golden summer afternoons—an innocent entire voluptuousness of mind and body. This is conceivably less mighty a rôle to play than that rôle of Elijah on Carmel enacted so impressively by Leigh Hunt's neighbour and friend at Chelsea; it is not less useful in its way.

Leigh Hunt does not distinctly brace the moral fibre; but he does not relax it. That idea of Happiness, of which I have spoken, was closely connected with its twin-born idea of Duty—a strain, we might say, of his mother's Puritan blood mingling with and tempering the warm Barbadian blood of his father. His sensuous nature, his tropical temperament, his Italianised imagination, are kept in check—kept sweet and clean and pure—by a delicately English sense of the abidingness and the authority of moral sanctions, of Duty—not the Pagan nor the Puritan, but Wordsworth's "stern Daughter of the voice of God," who makes the perfume of the flowers and the light and colour of the stars. Thus it is that the Edens of his fancy have no snake, the enchanted gardens no Armida. It is amusing to hear him apologising for the "vivacity—I will not call it levity" of his writings: as if apology were needed! Wholesome air and sweet sunshine are not too common to be less than the most precious of our possessions; and in literature the pleasantness of air and sunshine, such as we meet in the pages of Leigh Hunt, is not common at all.

Leigh Hunt's range, in his essays, is wide; but his topics may all be classed under the two heads of Books and Nature. Under the second head I would include *genre* pictures such as Hunt defined when, in the introduction to just such a sketch as he was describing, he said, "Writers, we think, might oftener indulge themselves in direct picture-making—that is to say, in detached sketches of men and things, which should be to *manners* what those of Theophrastus are to *character*." The country essays, and the lessons and pictures from common things, are among the most delightful and the most characteristic of his writings; a few of rare pensiveness and serious imagination touch our deeper feelings most finely; the bookish papers have the constant charm of the book-lover, and run frequently into the highest reaches of fancy and of style; but the *genre* pictures have a peculiar attractiveness of their own, not exceeded, in its kind, by the qualities of any of the others. The fancy, the homely and remote knowledge, the quiet enjoyable humour contained in these unpretentious little sketches, are of such fine and yet simple and taking quality, that they hold a distinct place in literature—a place not of the highest, but pleasant, and one to be frequented.

That word "pleasant" seems to have a peculiar appropriateness to Leigh Hunt, and comes first to the lips and last in speaking of him. He is the *pleasantest* writer we have; to him belongs that "sweet temperature of thought" which Landor observed in Addison, and that "attractive countenance, with which he meets us upon every occasion." I cannot think that Leigh Hunt was of the build and stature to "wrestle with and conquer Time;" his flight was the swallow's—short, uneven, uncertain—and, like the swallow, his day may be over with the summer. But he is specially eminent among the lesser men,

and to neglect him is to lose a pleasure which we can get only from him. He is never quite without attractiveness; but his best writings are those in which a congenial subject carries him away, in which he finds scope for an often felicitous fancy, and a frequently charming grace of style.

REGINALD BRIMLEY JOHNSON
From "Introduction"
Essays of Leigh Hunt
1891, pp. xxiii–xxviii

In a critical estimate of Hunt's writings, allowance must be made for two adverse influences—the models that his contemporaries admired, and the pressure under which he worked.

At the time he began to write, the fatal habit of imitating Dr. Johnson's pomposity was in vogue, while "in poetry the Della Cruscan manner prevailed, with its false simplicity and real tinsel, its lachrymose tenderness and sham romance." He first imitated this artificiality, and then, by his very detestation of it, was led to adopt a freedom of style that sometimes degenerated into incorrectness. If he seems to dwell upon trifles, or to affect too much simplicity, the impulse may probably be traced to an impatience of false ideals of dignity in writing, as the occasionally involved and parenthetic construction of his sentences seems to arise from an intense desire for truth.

In the case of his prose work, the Herculean journalistic responsibilities that he undertook may have stood in the way of his recognition of these defects, while they must obviously have encouraged the tendency to express any idea as fully and from as many points of view as possible. When it is remembered that he had to produce copy almost daily for more than fifty years, the wonder is that so much should be worth reprinting. An explanation may be found in the great care with which he invariably wrote, in the extraordinary width of his acquaintance with the best literature, and in the fact that "he was a man of genius in a very strict sense of that word."[1]

It is a difficult matter indeed to postulate the unique beauties of his writings. They defy definition. "Versatility, clearness, lovingness, truthfulness," and absolute healthfulness are there. The touch is light and rapid, yet the deepest and widest sympathies are evinced. His pages are illuminated with passages of delicate wit and unexpected poetry, and enriched by the most happily chosen quotations.

He is most charming when writing of his friends,— Shelley, his mother, and many others that live before us in the fascinating pages of his *Autobiography*. His imaginary character-sketches are scarcely less sympathetic, and, though the publication of Professor Knight's *Tales from Leigh Hunt* has perhaps shown that he was not himself a master of pure fiction, it has reminded us that he can inspire fresh interest in an old story by his manner of reproducing it. The familiar narrative assumes an added significance in his hands; reflections, morals, side issues are suggested; and the forgotten heroes live again before another generation, clothed in a new garb, and displaying new charms. Nor is this all, for he can breathe life into the dry bones of an obscure chronicle, and fascinate his readers with the gossip of the past.

But the most popular of his writings have always been his purely miscellaneous essays, which depend for their subject and treatment on the suggestion of the moment:[2] as he said, in the *Wishing Cap*,—"I will take up in this paper any subject to which I feel an impulse." And the subjects are often commonplace enough, but "he brings poetry to our breakfast-table, and strikes light out of the pebble at our feet," finding—

> Sermons in stones, and good in everything.

In these miscellaneous essays we meet with some occasional literary criticism in which "a sentence does the work of a chapter;" thus he writes of Charles Lamb that "his essays will take their place among the daintiest productions of English wit-melancholy," and of O'Keefe that "his muse was as fresh as a dairy-maid." His longer criticisms are seldom less happy. They are nearly always *appreciations*, and yet discriminating. He delighted to consider himself a taster in literature, the *Indicator*, or honey-hunter, among the flowers of the past. He does not construct theories of composition, but gives utterance to his delight in an author, and makes his reader share it. He seems to have no prejudices,[3] though he does not praise blindly.

His more strictly journalistic work may be estimated by a brief *résumé* of the main characteristics of the *Examiner*, which are fully set forth in its prospectus (see vol ii.). The independent theatrical criticism, which he had originated in the *News*, was here maintained, and his carefully written miscellaneous articles gave it a literary tone, which was unusual in newspapers of that time. Here also he bore witness to his admiration for the men of real genius among his contemporaries, welcoming contributions from Lamb, Hazlitt, Keats, and Shelley, at a time when the last three were almost entirely unknown or despised. The same judgment was shown later in the *London Journal*, where the writings of Bentham and Hugh Miller received some of their earliest recognitions, and where Carlyle's translations of Goethe were enthusiastically noticed. In the *Tatler*, we find him working with Barry Cornwall, and, in the *Monthly Repository*, with W. S. Landor.

The attitude of the *Examiner* with regard to political matters was equally advanced. "It began by being of no party, but reform gave it one;" and although it was against the grain that Hunt ever wrote on politics, there can be no doubt that the energy and fearlessness of his editorial utterances and the consistent vigour of his paper did no little service to the cause of Liberalism in one of its darkest periods.

Turning to the consideration of his poetry, we can see the same obvious faults in it as in his prose. It is often trivial in subject, always slight in treatment, and pet ideas are sometimes allowed to run to seed. He was too much inclined to use words in unusual connections and with a meaning of his own, though without producing obscurity. It may also perhaps be criticised with less compunction than his prose, because it was his chosen work, written in times of comparative leisure, and by which he hoped to live.

But "his poetry never fails in that imaginative glow and glamour which takes us into another world than the prosaic life of every day, and enables us to forget the dullness and meanness of the actual. . . . Whatever else it may lack, it never lacks gusto,—the sense of the expression of quick, keen delight in all things naturally and wholesomely delightful."[4] His nature was essentially romantic. His thoughts kept company with brave knights and fair ladies, wandering in beautiful gardens and exchanging tender compliments. The ceremonies and customs that had grown archaic in the world of action retained their full significance in his imagination, and it was upon them that he delighted to dwell.

It is largely because he was so much at home in the fields of imagination that his poetry possesses its peculiar faults and its peculiar merits. His most perfect poems are the short

Eastern tales and some of the translations, while the *Story of Rimini* well represents his genius as a whole, and is of supreme interest on account of the admiration it excited in some of the master-minds of his day.

And finally his writings are the expression of his moral nature. They are genial, sympathetic, and chivalrous like himself; revealing the main motive of his life—the desire to increase the happiness of mankind. They seem to echo the ever-memorable petition of Abou Ben Adhem:—

> Write me as one that loves his fellow-men.

Notes

1. Carlyle.
2. Yet those who knew him best agree in testifying that even these casual writings "were the result of very considerable labour and painstaking, of the most conscientious investigation of facts, where facts were needed; and of a complete devotion of his faculties towards the objects to be accomplished."
3. This impartiality, however, cannot be claimed for the criticism in the early numbers of the *Examiner*, while he retained two prejudices throughout life: against Dante, for his belief in hell, and against Southey, for his complacent Toryism.
4. From a most interesting article on "Leigh Hunt, His Life, Character, and Work," in the *London Quarterly Review*, written, I believe, by Mr. J. A. Noble, author of *The Pelican Papers*.

REGINALD BRIMLEY JOHNSON
From *Leigh Hunt*
1896, pp. 93–106

In the following year ⟨1816⟩ appeared *The Story of Rimini*, which led a reform in English poetry, and remains, in spite of patent defects, the most solid monument of Hunt's poetical achievements. There is a passage in the *Autobiography* that accounts for the form in which it was written, and estimates, not unwisely, its merits and defects:—

> Dryden, at that time, in spite of my sense of Milton's superiority, and my early love of Spenser, was the most delightful name to me in English literature. I had found in him more vigour, and music too, than in Pope, who had been my closest poetical acquaintance, and I could not rest till I had played upon his instrument. I brought, however, to my task a sympathy with the tender and the pathetic which I did not find in my master, and there was also an impulsive difference now and then in the style, and a greater tendency to simplicity of words. My versification was not so vigorous as his. There were many weak lines in it. It succeeded best in catching the variety of his cadences; at least, so far as they broke up the monotony of Pope. But I had a greater love for the beauties of external nature; I think also I partook of a more southern insight into the beauties of colour, of which I made abundant use in the procession which is described in the first canto;[1] and if I invested my story with too many circumstances of description, especially on points not essential to its progress, and thus took leave *in toto* of the brevity, as well as the force of Dante, still the enjoyment which led me into the superfluity was manifest, and so far became its warrant.

The Story of Rimini, then, was a protest against the polished couplet of Pope—a call to revive the freer manner of Dryden— a protest and a call expressed already to some extent in *The Lyrical Ballads*, but, through Hunt's influence, guiding the pens of Keats, Shelley, and some of their noblest successors. The poem to which we indirectly owe so much was itself a failure. In the first place, as Hunt himself points out, the whole conception was an act of bad taste—"to enlarge upon a subject which had been treated with exquisite sufficiency, and to his immortal renown, by a great master"—and the passions with which it deals are not naturally introduced or vigorously depicted. The digressions and descriptions, indeed, are the only parts of the poem which can be read with pleasure. They contain that *evidence of his own enjoyment* which Leigh Hunt, as we see from the above quotation, regarded as a warrant for their existence, and which does, in fact, form one of the principal charms of his work in poetry and prose.

The Story of Rimini elicited many expressions of enthusiasm from those who afterwards profited by its influence and from others of Hunt's own circle; but it was met by his political enemies with a storm of virulent and personal abuse almost unparalleled in the history of journalism. It was treated by *Blackwood* and the *Quarterly* as an indecent manifesto of the so-called Cockney school in whose dishonour they were eager to triumph. The fact that the Cockney king had written a poem (although he was not responsible for the plot) about an intrigue between an Italian princess and her brother-in-law afforded them an opportunity—it cannot be called an excuse—for perpetually whispering insinuations against his own private moral character, and implying that all his friends were equally disreputable.

Leigh Hunt himself found a moral lesson in the story, that deceit is vicious and impolitic. He throws the blame of Francesca's sin on her father, who, in order to force her marriage, directed the surly Giovanni to woo her by deputy in the person of his brother Paolo, and told her that she should find the former as charming as the latter was universally admitted to be. The defence is not very effectively conducted, perhaps. The mere attempt may serve to illustrate the kind of attitude always adopted by Leigh Hunt on similar questions, unconventional but *not* lax.

The versification was also abused, and here Hunt's principles were far superior to his practice. He never realised the proper dignity of poetry, and in discarding monotony, became slipshod. Hard polish was replaced by limp jerkiness, and the couplet in his hands grew pert and garrulous. There are beautiful passages in the poem worthy of the great reform to be inaugurated, but they are few and far between. In the matter of language, again, he could not *maintain* a high standard. His very simplicity was in part artificial, and he had a singular taste for giving ordinary words on original significance which ruined his phrases, though it never made him obscure. The poem was considerably revised, but the changes relate principally to the final development of the plot, and are not all improvements.

In old age Leigh Hunt referred to *Rimini* as the work of a "tyro," but it does not contain any signs of youth from which he was afterwards exempt, and reaches as high a level as any of his longer pieces. It proves conclusively that he was not, in the highest sense, a poet. ⟨. . .⟩

His strength lies, as he himself suspected, in the brief narrative poems of which "Abou Ben Adhem" is the highest example. Here the impulse is from without, the lines are prompted by the enjoyment of a "tale that is told," and by the desire to express and impart that pleasure. The critical powers guide the creative, and lend them a vigour not their own. His manner at such times is simple and lucid, playful or tender according to circumstances, but always sincere and glowing. His ear, so keen for judgment, directs the rhythm, and makes the verse flowing and easy. His many admirable translations are composed in the same spirit. A loyal enthusiasm for the originals prompts him to a rare fidelity in language and style, often achieved with marked success.

Could Hunt have *maintained* these qualities of taste and self-control for any considerable period, he might have taken high rank as a poet. But, in spite of evidence concerning the labour he actually expended on the polishing process, we cannot refute the charge of carelessness against almost everything he wrote. Whether from the blindness of partiality, or the incapacity of sustained concentration, he permitted flaws in his own work which he would have been the first to detect in that of others. Thus it is that in any longer pieces he is certain to offend the critical reader, and weaken his own claims to consideration.

The qualities of grace, delicate fancy, and tender sentiment have enabled him, however, to produce some more strictly original poems of undoubted merit, in the lyrical form; while the limitations of the sonnet have sometimes checked his animal vivacity and lent an unwonted firmness of touch to the expression of thoughts, themselves worthy of a poetical dress.

He lacks passion, dignity, and restraint, his imagination is almost entirely fanciful; but by the winning charm of his own fresh and cultured personality he attracts and even occasionally subdues. Part of the secret may be told in his own words. After relating the nervous excitement caused by serious composition, he proceeds:—

"The reader may be surprised to hear, after these remarks, that what I write with the greatest composure is verses. He may smile, and say that he does not wonder, since the more art the less nature, the more artificiality the less earnestness. But it is not that; it is that I write verses only when I most like to write; that I write them slowly, with loving recurrence, and that the musical form is a perpetual solace and refreshment. The earnestness is not less. In one respect it is greater, for it is more concentrated. It is forced, by a sweet necessity, to say more things in less compass. But the necessity *is* sweet. The mode, and the sense of being able to meet its requirements, in however comparative a degree, are more than a sustainment: they are a charm. *This is the reason why poetry, not of the highest order, is sometimes found so acceptable. The author feels so much happiness in his task, that he cannot but convey happiness to his reader.*"

Notes

1. Perhaps the most really poetical passage in the book.

THOMAS DE QUINCEY

1785–1859

Thomas De Quincey was born in Manchester on August 15, 1785. The son of a linen merchant, he attended schools in Bath and Winkfield, and in 1800 entered the Manchester Grammar School. In 1802 De Quincey ran away from school, spending eight months wandering homelessly in Wales and London. In December 1803 he entered Worcester College, Oxford. While visiting London in 1804 De Quincey first took opium to alleviate severe rheumatic pains in his head and face; his experiments with the drug were to continue intermittently and secretly until he became thoroughly addicted.

In 1806 De Quincey reached his majority and received the inheritance left to him by his father, who had died in 1793. In 1807 he first met Coleridge, Wordsworth, and Southey, and in the following year he abruptly left Oxford before completing his examinations. From November 1808 until February 1809 De Quincey lived with the Wordsworths at Allen Bank, and then leased their former home, Dove Cottage in Grasmere. By 1813 De Quincey's confirmed addiction to opium had led to his gradual estrangement from the Wordsworths and to the depletion of his fortune. After the birth of a son, William, in 1816, De Quincey in 1817 married a local farmer's daughter, Margaret Simpson, who bore him seven more children. Deeply in debt and with a family to provide for, he soon began to try to support himself through journalism.

In 1821 De Quincey published *The Confessions of an English Opium Eater* in the *London Magazine*; the most famous of his works, it first appeared in book form in 1822. Still suffering from his drug addiction, De Quincey in 1826 went to Edinburgh, where he began writing for *Blackwood's*; he would continue contributing to it until 1849. In 1830 he settled permanently in Edinburgh with his wife and children. In 1832 he published a novel, *Klosterheim*, and began publishing articles in *Tait's*, to which he contributed until 1851. Despite his voluminous writing, De Quincey was perpetually hounded by serious financial difficulties through most of the 1830s and 1840s, and also suffered the deaths of his wife and several of his children. By 1847 his earnings, combined with a modest inheritance from his mother, were finally large enough to bring an end to his financial worries, and in 1848 De Quincey at last overcame his opium addiction. The publications that had brought him these earnings included *Recollections of the Lake Poets* (1834–39), *Sketches from the Autobiography of an English Opium Eater* (1834–41; later entitled *Autobiographic Sketches*), *Suspiria de Profundis*, and *The English Mail-Coach* (1849). In 1853 a collected edition of De Quincey's works was begun under his supervision as *Selections Grave and Gay*. Before it could be completed De Quincey died in Edinburgh on December 8, 1859.

Although he is also remembered for a number of shorter pieces, including "On the Knocking on the Gate in *Macbeth*," "On Murder Considered as One of the Fine Arts," and "The Revolt of the Tartars," De Quincey's most widely read work today is his *Confessions*. This is also the work which has had the widest influence on other writers, including Edgar Allan Poe and Charles Baudelaire. His *Collected Writings* were edited by David Masson in 1889–90.

Personal

De Quincey is a singular man, but better informed than any person almost that I ever met at his age.—ROBERT SOUTHEY, Letter to John Rickman (Jan. 21, 1810)

At four o'clock dined in the Hall with De Quincey, who was very civil to me, and cordially invited me to visit his cottage in Cumberland. Like myself, he is an enthusiast for Wordsworth. His person is small, his complexion fair, and his air and manner are those of a sickly and enfeebled man. From this circumstance his sensibility, which I have no doubt is genuine, is in danger of being mistaken for effeminateness. At least coarser and more robustly healthful persons may fall into this mistake.—HENRY CRABB ROBINSON, *Diary* (June 17, 1812)

Today too I saw Dequincey: alas poor Yorick!—THOMAS CARLYLE, Letter to Bryan Waller Procter (Jan. 17, 1828)

You will doubtless read the last *Tait's Magazine*. It contains the first of a series of articles by De Quincey on Wordsworth. Poor De Quincey had a small fortune of eight or nine thousand pounds, which he has lost or spent; and now he lets his pen for

hire. You know his article on Coleridge: Wordsworth's turn has now come. At the close of his article, he alludes to a killing neglect which he once received from the poet, and which embittered his peace. I know the facts, which are not given. De Quincey married some humble country-girl in the neighborhood of Wordsworth; she was of good character, but not of that rank in which W. moved. The family of the latter never made her acquaintance or showed her any civilities, though living comparatively in the same neighborhood. "Hinc illæ lacrymæ." When you now read De Quincey's lamentations you may better understand them.—CHARLES SUMNER, Letter to George S. Hillard (Jan. 23, 1839), cited in Edward L. Pierce, *Memoir and Letters of Charles Sumner*, 1877, Vol. 2, pp. 45–46

De Quincey is a small old man of 70 years, with a very handsome face, and a face too expressing the highest refinement, a very gentle old man, speaking with the greatest deliberation & softness, and so refined in speech & manners as to make quite indifferent his extremely plain & poor dress. For the old man summoned by message on Saturday by Mrs Crowe to this dinner had walked on this stormy muddy Sunday ten miles from Lass Wade, where his cottage is, and was not yet dry, and though Mrs Crowe's hospitality is comprehensive & minute, yet she had no pantaloons in her house. Here De Quincey is very serene & happy among just these friends where I found him, for he has suffered in all ways & lived the life of a wretch for many years; but Samuel Brown & Mrs C. & one or two more have saved him from himself & defended him from bailiffs & a certain fury of a Mrs Macbold, (I think it is, whom he yet shudders to remember,) and from opium, and he is now clean, clothed, & in his right mind.—RALPH WALDO EMERSON, Letter to Lidian Emerson (Feb. 21, 1848)

During the winter of 1815–16 (or the next) Mr. De Quincey accompanied his friend, the author of the *Isle of Palms*, from Westmoreland to Edinburgh. I had then an opportunity of observing the literary character in an entirely new phasis, for up to that time, De Quincey, though he had spent long years in assiduous study, and by his friends was regarded as a powerful author, had not, so far as I know, published a single line. He seemed, indeed, to live for the sake of the labour alone, and to fling overboard all considerations either of the *palma* or *pecunia*. His various literary compositions, written in his exemplary hand (the best I ever saw, except Southey's) on little scraps of paper, must have reached to a great extent, but in his own estimation they were by no means "ready for the press;" like an over-cautious general, he withheld his fire, and remained "*multa et pulchra minans.*" Not only for this reason, but in other respects Mr. De Quincey seemed to me to bring out the literary character in a new light. Very decisively he realized my plan of moving in a separate world (having no doubt realities of its own); moreover, he neither spoke nor acted in the every-day world like any one else, for which, of course, I greatly honoured him. He was then in the habit of taking opium daily as an article of food, and the drug, though used for years, had scarcely *begun* to tell on his constitution, by those effects which, sooner or later, overtake every one of its persevering votaries; and which, when they once appear, make quick work in demolishing together the man physical and the man intellectual; the latter being reduced to the pitiable plight of a musician who essays to play by means of a harp unstrung and broken. But in his case, it had not worked any such evils as yet, and in after years, though not without a long and tough battle, Mr. De Quincey succeeded in vanquishing the narcotic devil.

His voice was extraordinary; it came as if from dream-land; but it was the most musical and impressive of voices. In convivial life, what then seemed to me the most remarkable trait of De Quincey's character was the power he possessed of easily changing the tone of ordinary thought and conversation into that of his own dream-land, till his auditors, with wonder, found themselves moving pleasantly along with him in a sphere of which they might have heard and read, perhaps, but which had ever appeared to them inaccessible, and far, far away! Seeing that he was always good-natured and social, he would take part, at commencement, in any sort of tattle or twaddle. The talk might be of "beeves," and he could grapple with them if expected to do so, but his musical cadences were not in keeping with such work, and in a few minutes (not without some strictly logical sequence) he could escape at will from beeves to butterflies, and thence to the soul's immortality, to Plato, and Kant, and Schelling, and Fichte, to Milton's early years and Shakspeare's sonnets, to Wordsworth and Coleridge, to Homer and Eschylus, to St. Thomas of Aquin, St. Basil, and St. Chrysostom. But he by no means excluded

themes from real life, according to his own views of that life, but would recount profound mysteries from his own experiences—visions that had come over him in his loneliest walks among the mountains, and passages within his own personal knowledge, illustrating, if not proving, the doctrines of dreams, of warnings, of second-sight, and mesmerism. And whatsoever the subject might be, every one of his sentences (or of his chapters I might say) was woven into the most perfect logical texture, and uttered in a tone of sustained melody.

Such powers and acquirements could not fail to excite wonder at Edinburgh. He had, indeed, studied "all such books as are never read" in that enlightened capital, and was the first friend I had ever met who could profess to have a command over the German language, and who consequently was able *(ex cathedrâ)* to corroborate my notions of the great stores that were contained therein. I flatter myself that he found our house not altogether uncongenial, as he was kind enough to visit there more frequently than in any other.—R. P. GILLIES, *Memoirs of a Literary Veteran*, 1851, Vol. 2, pp. 219–21

Let this strange commentator on individual character meet with more mercy and a wiser interpretation than he was himself capable of. He was not made like other men; and he did not live, think, or feel like them. A singular organization was singularly and fatally deranged in its action before it could show its best quality. Marvellous analytical faculty he had; but it all oozed out in barren words. Charming eloquence he had; but it degenerated into egotistical garrulity, rendered tempting by the gilding of his genius. It is questionable whether, if he had never touched opium or wine, his real achievements would have been substantial—for he had no conception of a veritable standpoint of philosophical investigation; but the actual effect of his intemperance was to aggravate to excess his introspective tendencies, and to remove him incessantly further from the needful discipline of true science. His conditions of body and mind were abnormal, and his study of the one thing he knew anything about—the human mind—was radically imperfect. His powers, noble and charming as they might have been, were at once wasted and weakened through their own partial excess. His moral nature relaxed and sank, as must always be the case where sensibility is stimulated and action paralyzed; and the man of genius who, forty years before, administered a moral warning to all England, and commanded the sympathy and admiration of a nation, has lived on, to achieve nothing but the delivery of some confidences of questionable value and beauty, and to command from us nothing more than a compassionate sorrow that an intellect so subtle and an eloquence so charming in its pathos, its humor, its insight, and its music, should have left the world in no way the better for such gifts—unless by the warning afforded in *Confessions* first, and then by example, against the curse which neutralized their influence and corrupted its source.—HARRIET MARTINEAU, "Thomas De Quincey" (1859), *Biographical Sketches*, 1869, pp. 100–101

I recollect, too, how in Edinburgh a year or two after, poor De Quincey, whom I wished to know, was reported to tremble at the thought of such a thing; and did fly pale as ashes, poor little soul, the first time we actually met. He was a pretty little creature, full of wire-drawn ingenuities, bankrupt enthusiasms, bankrupt pride, with the finest silver-toned low voice, and most elaborate gently-winding courtesies and ingenuities in conversation. 'What wouldn't one give to have him in a box, and take him out to talk!' That was Her criticism of him, and it was right good. A bright, ready, and melodious talker, but in the end an inconclusive and long-winded. One of the smallest man figures

I ever saw; shaped like a pair of tongs, and hardly above five feet in all. When he sate, you would have taken him, by candle-light, for the beautifullest little child; blue-eyed, sparkling face, had there not been a something, too, which said '*Eccovi*—this child has been in hell.' After leaving Edinburgh I never saw him, hardly ever heard of him. His fate, owing to opium etc., was hard and sore, poor fine-strung weak creature, launched *so* into the literary career of ambition and mother of dead dogs. —THOMAS CARLYLE, "Edward Irving" (1866), *Reminiscences*, ed. James Anthony Froude, 1881, Vol. 1, pp. 256–57

In the ensuing summer, after the publication of another volume of poems, I visited Edinburgh and called upon De Quincey, to whom I had a letter of introduction from Miss Mitford. He was at that time residing in Lasswade, a few miles from the town, and I went thither by coach. He lived a secluded life, and even at that date had become to the world a name rather than a real personage; but it was a great name. Considerable alarm agitated my youthful heart as I drew near the house; I felt like Burns on the occasion when he was first about "to dinner wi' a Lord:" it was a great honor, but something rather to be talked about afterwards than to be enjoyed in itself. There were passages in De Quincey's writings which showed that the English opium-eater was not always in a dreamy state, but could be severe and satirical. My apprehensions, however, proved to be utterly groundless, for a more gracious and genial personage I never met. Picture to yourself a very diminutive man, carelessly—very carelessly—dressed; a face lined, careworn, and so expressionless that it reminded one of "that chill, changeless brow, where cold Obstruction's apathy appals the gazing mourner's heart"—a face like death in life. The instant he began to speak, however, it lit up as though by electric light; this came from his marvellous eyes, brighter and more intelligent (though by fits) than I have ever seen in any other mortal. They seemed to me to glow with eloquence. He spoke of my introducer, of Cambridge, of the Lake Country, and of English poets. Each theme was interesting to me, but made infinitely more so by some apt personal reminiscence. As for the last-named subject, it was like talking of the Olympian gods to one not only cradled in their creed, but who had mingled with them, himself half an immortal.

The announcement of luncheon was perhaps for the first time in my young life unwelcome to me. Miss De Quincey did the honors with gracious hospitality, pleased, I think, to find that her father had so rapt a listener. I was asked what wine I would take, and not caring which it was, I was about to pour myself out a glass from the decanter that stood next to me. "You must not take that," whispered my hostess, "it is not port-wine, as you think." It was in fact laudanum, to which De Quincey presently helped himself with the greatest *sang-froid*. I regarded him aghast, with much the same feelings as those with which he himself had watched the Malay at Grasmere eat the cake of opium, and with the same harmless result. The liquor seemed to stimulate rather than dull his eloquence. —JAMES PAYN, *Some Literary Recollections*, 1884, pp. 48–49

During his last illness he sent for me, and I saw him several times. On the last occasion I remained only a few minutes, as he was extremely feeble; yet in all his weakness his wonted courtesy prompted him, on my rising to leave, to deplore that, from inability to rise, or even to turn fully in bed, he was unable to ring, and that so I was left to show myself out. His youngest and only unmarried daughter, Emily, was with him at this time, and she promised to let me know if I, or any of our family, could be of any service. We did not therefore risk disturbing them by sending or calling often, and, indeed,

having had experience of his surprising recoveries from previous illnesses, we were not fully alive to the gravity of this one. Most unfortunately, two notes which Miss De Quincey posted to me failed, through being imperfectly addressed, to reach me in time. On the afternoon of the 8th December 1859 a rumour reached me that De Quincey was dead, and I hastened to Lothian Street, in some hope, however faint, that rumour lied. "Is what I hear true?" I said to the kind landlady, Mrs. Wilson, who opened the door. Without answering she ushered me at once into the chamber of death. On the simple uncurtained pallet, whence in that last interview he had smilingly, with all those delicately polite regrets, said goodbye, the tiny frame of this great dreamer lay stretched in his last long dreamless sleep. Attenuated to an extreme degree, the body looked infantile in size—a very slender stem for the shapely and massive head that crowned it. The face was little changed; its delicate bloom indeed was gone, but the sweet expression lingered, and the finely-chiselled features were unaltered. I was profoundly impressed; the more so, perhaps, that, as it so happened, I had never seen a dead person since I was a child of seven years old. In the next room I found his tearful and agitated daughters— Mrs. Craig, who had arrived a day or two before, and Miss Emily. They spoke much of the patience and resignation with which he suffered; of his gentleness and considerateness to the last. He grudged giving them the slightest trouble, even when he most required attendance. On one occasion when they were moving him in bed, and lifting his feet, he, using a grand generalisation in a spirit of the most profound humility, and snatching, as it were, at a sacred sanction for his exacting the care he needed, said, "Be gentle, be tender; remember that those are the feet that Christ washed."—JOHN RITCHIE FIND-LAY, *Personal Recollections of Thomas De Quincey*, 1885, pp. 66–68

General

Taylor has lately refused a paper of Procter's & one of Reynolds's, & kept back Darley's reply to Terentius Secundus, for the purpose of introducing that thrice-double demoniac the aeconomical opium-eater.—THOMAS LOVELL BEDDOES, Letter to Thomas Forbes Kelsall (April 17, 1824)

There was a luckless wight of an *Opium-eater* here, one Dequincey, for instance, who wrote a very vulgar and brutish Review of *Meister* in the *London Magazine*: I read three pages of it one *sick* day at Birmingham; and said: "Here is a man who writes of things which he does not rightly understand; I see clean over the top of *him*, and his vulgar spite, and his common-place philosophy; and I will away and have a ride on (Badams') Taffy, and leave *him* to cry in the ears of the simple." So I went out, and had my ride accordingly; and if Dequincey, poor little fellow, *made* any thing by his review, he can put it in his waistcoat pocket, and thank the god Mercurius. —THOMAS CARLYLE, Letter to John A. Carlyle (Jan. 22, 1825)

Did you read *Blackwood*? and in that case have you had deep delight in an exquisite paper by the Opium-eater, which my heart trembled through from end to end? What a poet that man is! how he vivifies words, or deepens them, and gives them profound significance.—ELIZABETH BARRETT BROWNING, Letter to Mr. Westwood (Dec. 31, 1843)

His general character as a periodical writer may be summed up in a few words. He is remarkable, first of all, for the most decided and dogmatical assertion of his opinions. Were it not for the stores of learning by which he is manifestly backed, and for the visible and constant play of a strong intellect, you would charge him with extreme and offensive arrogance. As it is, you know not sometimes whether more to admire the acuteness, or to wonder at the acerbity of his strictures. He throws a paradox at you like a sledge-hammer,—he pulls down a favourite idol with as little ceremony or remorse, as you would snap a poppy which had shed its flowers. Witness his onset, in "The Old London," at Grotius, or as he perversely persisted in calling him, Groot, from which, we fear, the fame of that greatly overrated personage never can recover. Witness his perpetual sneers at Parr, and all that class of mere scholars! Witness the abating process he so dexterously applied to Watson, and with less success to Roscoe, and with least of all to Goethe! Nor does this habit spring from any feeling like envy, or the desire to detract. De Quincey is altogether above such feelings; but the truth is, the current of his literary sympathies, though strong as a cataract, and profound as an abyss, is narrow as a footpath. He is too much engrossed in the admiration of two or three models of supreme excellence, to have much to spare for aught inferior. And for mere notoriety, and mere popularity, he has the most absolute contempt. He has studied Kant too closely to care much for Paley, and appreciated Wordsworth too intensely to admire the poetry of Moore. Another characteristic of his criticism, is its conversational cast; and hence its endless digressions, and its imperfect and unfinished character; and yet hence, too, its interest and its ease. His philosophy may be called a sublime gossip; and finely doth she chirp over her cups, and garnish the most abstruse speculations with tid-bits of literary scandal, and with a rich anecdotage, teeming from the stores of a most circumstantial memory. In all his writings, we find a lavish display of learning. You see it bursting out, whether he will or no; never dragged in as by cart ropes. And his allusions, glancing in all directions, show, even more than his direct quotations, that his knowledge is encyclopædic. His book of reference is the brain. A friend of ours found him writing some most elaborate articles, and not a book beside him, but an odd volume of the *Casquet of Literary Gems!* Nor must we forget his style. It is massive, masculine, and energetic; ponderous in its construction, slow in its motion, thoroughly English, yet thickly sprinkled with archaisms and "big words," peppered to just the proper degree with the condiments of simile, metaphor, and poetical quotation; select without being fastidious; strong, without being harsh; elaborate, without being starched into formal and false precision. Its great faults are an air of effort, and a frequent use of scholastic terms, and the forms of logic. It is, as nearly as may be, the pure vehicle of his strong, subtle, fiery, and learned nature. Nor does it disdain frequently to express an elephantine humour, more rich and racy, however, than choice or delicate. It is a style, in short, adapted well for pure metaphysical discussion,—better still for philosophical criticism or biography, and perhaps, best of all, for the sublime yet shifting purposes of some large national history. We refer those who doubt his capacity for this last undertaking, to a description he has written of the Exodus of a Tartar tribe from their native land to the paternal sway of the Emperor of China, which they will find in *Blackwood* for July 1837, and which, for broad and massive grandeur of historical depiction, we have never seen surpassed. In fact, the man has hitherto done comparatively nothing with his powers. In common with all who know him, we deem him to have been capable of the loftiest things, whether in the field of psychology, or in more verdant and popular regions. Especially was he qualified by his superb classical learning, by the taste and tendency of his mind, by the graver graces of his diction, by his intimacy with the spirit and philosophy of Roman story, and by his belief in the Christian

faith, for the proud task of writing the history of the Fourth Monarchy. Gibbon, no one knows better than De Quincey, has not nearly exhausted the magnificent theme. He is, no doubt, a great, strutting, splendid writer, rolling on his huge periods, scattering his fiery sneers, mouthing out his oracular dogmatism, spreading forth the riches of his ostentatious learning, and, as with gorgeous colours, red, green, orange, and yellow, surrounding the great sinking sun of the Roman power. But his work is not only disfigured by the blue and blistering venom of infidelity; not only does it keep up a bitter, running fire against the blessed faith of Christ, from every corner and point, in the great guns of the celebrated two chapters, in the glancing side-fire of the text, and in the base bush-fighting of the notes, but it has other important blemishes; stupendous as it is, it is incomplete; it abounds with inaccuracies and indelicate allusions; it wants a true and profound insight into the causes of Roman decline; as a narrative, it is indirect, cumbrous, and frequently obscure; as a composition, its colours are often false, barbaric, and overlaid, and though sparkling with sudden brilliances, it has no sustained power or splendour. What a different, and, in many respects, what a superior and monumental work of it might De Quincey have made, had he, ten or twenty years ago, set himself resolutely to the task! In the year 1839, after long absence from the arena of *Blackwood's Magazine*, he leaped down upon it again, as with a thunder-tramp. He is the author of that series of scholarly articles which appeared since then, on "Milton," "The Philosophy of Roman History," "Dinner, Real and Reputed," "The Essenes," "Style," "The Opium Question," "Ricardo Made Easy," &c., &c. And a marvellous series it is, when you take it in connexion with his advanced age and shattered system. We were particularly interested by his paper on the "Essenes." It is in the style of the best of Horsley's sermons. He begins, as that prelate was wont, by the statement of what seems a hopeless paradox; but, ere he be done, he has surrounded it with such plausible analogies, he has darted upon it such a glare of learning, he has so fenced it in with bristling dilemmas, he has so cut the difficulties, and strangled the objections started against it, that you lay down the paper, believing, or, at least, wishing to believe, that the Essenes and the Christians were identical.—GEORGE GILFILLAN, "Thomas De Quincey," *A Gallery of Literary Portraits*, 1845, Vol. 1, pp. 183–86

⟨. . .⟩ will our readers be prepared to estimate the difficulty which attends a decision of the question, whether, on the whole, it is to be regretted that De Quincey fell under the influence of opium? ⟨. . .⟩ We think De Quincey was naturally fitted to take his station among the great systematic thinkers of the olden time, and something unique in literature might have been achieved by the combined operation of such a piercing intellect and so imperial an imagination on the pedestal of the nineteenth century. When his arms, in the strength of manhood, and with all their gigantic powers untrammeled, might have been piling mountain upon mountain, he had still to wrestle in mortal agony with a serpent of deadlier venom and more overwhelming power than ever coiled around an ancient hero. No man has more than a certain force allotted him by nature; it may be greater or less, but it is measured; and it cannot be expended twice. Consider the intellectual might necessary to vanquish opium in the three fearful assaults of which De Quincey informs us, and then decide concerning the powers of him whose works, wondrous as they are, were all accomplished in the breathing spaces between paroxysms of convulsive warfare. It may, of course, be alleged, that without the opium we never should have had those writings which are most closely associated with the name of De Quincey. But it is our decided opinion that the dreams produced by opium were but the occasion of the visions wherewith the opium eater has amazed the world. These are strictly works of imagination, and may be tried by the same tests as the dreams of Richter and Novalis. We concede that much of their terrific coloring is traceable to opium; but De Quincey's imagination, we are assured, would have worked under any conditions.—PETER BAYNE, "Thomas De Quincey and His Works," *Essays in Biography and Criticism*, 1857, pp. 45–46

De Quincey was the prince of hierophants, or of pontifical hierarchs, as regards all those profound mysteries which from the beginning have swayed the human heart, sometimes through the light of angelic smiles lifting it upwards to an altitude just beneath the heavens, and sometimes shattering it, with the shock of quaking anguish, down to earth. As it was the function of the hierophant, in the Grecian mysteries, to show the sacred symbols as concrete incarnations of faith, so was it De Quincey's to reveal in open light the everlasting symbols, universally intelligible when once disclosed, which are folded in the involutions of dreams and of those meditations which most resemble dreams; and as to the manner of these revelations, no Roman *pontifex maximus*, were it even Cæsar himself, could have rivalled their magisterial pomp.—HENRY M. ALDEN, "Thomas De Quincey," *Atlantic*, Sept. 1863, pp. 345–46

We might divide his mind into two hemispheres—the mathematical or abstractive, the imaginative or poetical, which are the opposite poles of the sphere of thought. Whether his subjects are logic, political economy, or criticisms upon the higher forms of poetry, he brings to bear upon them the keen analytic faculty of his brain, piercing into the hidden combination of things; at the same time he illuminates and pours into their depths the light of a vivid imagination, clothing them with beauty and poetic sympathy. As examples of his powers of discernment and discrimination, we would refer to his papers upon Plato, Socrates, and Kant, which are of the highest order of philosophical criticism, and also to his articles upon political economy, pronounced by Mr. M'Culloch to be "unequalled for their brevity, pungency, and force." Now, there is not a more difficult study than the science of Political Economy, requiring as it does the greatest tension of the mind, for it embraces all the multifarious social problems of the time, dealing with the abstract calculations of the mathematician and the ideal laws of the socialist on the one hand, and the concrete facts of the moralist, statesman, and philanthropist on the other; and we think it is a proof of the great powers of De Quincey's mind, that he has mastered this subject, and made it intelligible to the ordinary mind. At times, a soft and almost ethereal light gleams through the surface of his writings, tempering his philosophy and connecting it with the subtle mysteries of the universe and of Divine revelation. In reading his autobiographic sketches, we find that even when a boy he was haunted by shadows, and much given to thought and speculation, especially upon religious matters; building castles in the air, ofttimes the abode of giants, such as good old Bunyan saw in his dreams—huge incarnations of doubt and fear. And no enemies are so hard to conquer as invisible ones. The phantoms of the mind cannot be dispatched with knife or sword; and many men, who have stood firm before cannon and steel, and others also who have defied the contradiction of the world, have trembled like children before the creatures of their imagination. These shadowy recollections and dim visions of

life, death, and immortality, which flitted across the golden brain of his childhood, were in after-life transfigured before him in his dreams, with all their awe-inspiring associations of grandeur and terror, and in some of his retrospective glances into his childhood—

> When the breeze of a joyful dawn blew free
> In the silken sail of infancy.

He makes us feel—

> The truth the poet sings,
> That a sorrow's crown of sorrow is remembering
> happier things.

But the crowning glory of De Quincey's writings is the overmastering power and splendour of his imaginative faculty which is manifested in its full strength in his dreams. The world has always had its dreamers. Plato, of old, had his dreams, and strange dreams too; the mystics of the middle ages walked in the cloudland and dreamland of their poetic philosophy. Shakespeare's spirit held its carnival in his *Midsummer Night's Dream*; and Milton's sightless orbs, with that vision and faculty divine, saw "beyond the compass of sea and land." Of De Quincey's dreams we might say that they are unique in our literature; to find anything like unto them we must go to the writings of the Germans, who have a dream-literature of their own. But, we think, few have dreamed so vividly and magnificently as De Quincey has done. None, we think, have so dipped their pens in the varied hues of sunshine and gloom, or been able to fix that which is fleeting and transient, so as to record the effects produced by that drug which had such a fascinating influence over him.—SAMUEL DAVEY, "Thomas De Quincey," *Darwin, Carlyle, and Dickens, with Other Essays*, 1876, pp. 163–65

In one of his many footnotes De Quincey has given an excellent definition of genius as distinguished from talent. "Talent," he asserts, "is intellectual power of every kind, which acts and manifests itself by and through the will and the active forces. Genius, as the verbal origin implies, is that much rarer species of intellectual power which is derived from the *genial* nature—from the spirit of suffering and enjoyment, from the spirit of pleasure and pain, as organised more or less perfectly; and this is independent of will. It is a function of the *passive* nature." Judged by this distinction—and it would be difficult to find a sounder one—De Quincey must always be classed with men of genius rather than with men of talent, for the spontaneity of his writings is fully as apparent as their power. Though he was largely indebted to the accession of learning and literary taste, and to the external embellishments of his brilliant rhetorical fancy, yet his success was primarily due to his imaginative subtlety, to the inspiration that is inborn, rather than to the culture that can be acquired. Thus it was that though his life was cast in an age of mighty intellects, with some of whom he was himself closely associated, he preserved to the end his own individuality and independence, setting the stamp of his peculiar genius clearly and unmistakably upon every page of his works. The only writer of this century, or indeed of any century, to whom he bears much affinity, is Coleridge; and even here the similarity, though very striking as regards the general disposition and mode of life, does not extend to the manner of thought and expression. A reader of De Quincey's biographical essay on Coleridge must be struck by the fact that much of what he says of Coleridge's dreamy nature and dilatory habits would apply equally well to himself; and in both cases the use of opium brought an aggravation of the evil. The same resemblance may be traced in the prodigious memory, great conversational powers, and general literary scope of the two authors. De Quincey has himself remarked that he "read for thirty years in the same track as Coleridge—that track in which few of any age will ever follow us, such as German metaphysicians, Latin schoolmen, thaumaturgic Platonists, religious mystics." Finally, the same reproach has been commonly urged against both, of having wasted their fine powers in trivial and desultory occupations, and of having left no great monumental work. It has been my endeavour to show that this assertion, as regards De Quincey at any rate, is only true in the very limited sense that he instinctively preferred to throw his writings into the form of short papers, rather than bulky volumes. Those who condemn him on this account should remember Addison's satire on the tendency to estimate the value of books by their quantity rather than their quality. "I have observed," he says, "that the author of a *folio*, in all companies and conversations, sets himself above the author of a *quarto*; the author of a *quarto* above the author of an *octavo*, and so on, by a gradual descent and subordination to an author in *twenty-fours*. In a word, authors are usually ranged in company after the same manner as their works are upon a shelf." It is only by the adoption of some such criterion as this, that De Quincey's masterpieces can be ruled out of the category of great works.—H. S. SALT, "Some Thoughts on De Quincey" (1877), *Literary Sketches*, 1888, pp. 232–35

A great deal of De Quincey's best and most characteristic writing is in the stately and elaborate style here described, the style of sustained splendour, of prolonged wheeling and soaring, as distinct from the style of crackle and brief glitter, of chirp and short flight. This is precisely on account of the exalted and intricate nature of his meaning and feeling in those cases; and, if some readers there fall off from him or dislike him, it is because they themselves are deficient in wing and sinew. For those who do adhere to him and follow him in his passages of more involved and sustained eloquence, there are few greater pleasures possible in modern English prose. However magnificent the wording, there is always such an exact fit between it and the amount and shape of the under-fluctuating thought that suspicion of inflation or bombast anywhere never occurs to one. The same presence everywhere of a vigilant intellect appears in the perfect logical articulation of sentence with sentence and of clause with clause; while the taste of the technical artist appears equally in the study of minute optical coherence in the imagery and in the fastidious care for fine sound. In this last quality of style,—to which, in its lowest degree, Bentham gave the name of *pronunciability*, insisting most strenuously on its importance in all writing,—De Quincey is a master. Such was the delicacy of his ear, however, that mere *pronunciability* was not enough for him, and *musical beauty* had to be superadded. Once, writing of Father Newman, and having described him as "originally the ablest son of Puseyism, but now a powerful architect of religious philosophy on his own account," he interrupts himself to explain that he might have ended the sentence more briefly by substituting for the last nine words the single phrase "master-builder," but that his ear could not endure "a sentence ending with two consecutive trochees, and each of those trochees ending with the same syllable *er*." He adds, "Ah, reader! I would the gods had made thee rhythmical, that thou mightest comprehend the thousandth part of my labours in the evasion of cacophony." The last phrase, "the evasion of cacophony," is an instance of another of De Quincey's verbal habits in his more elaborate writing,—his deliberate choice now and then of an unusually learned combination of Latin or Greek or other polysyllabic words. Often, as in the present instance, it is a whim of mere

humour or self-irony. Often, however, it is from a desire to be exact to his meaning and to leave that meaning indissolubly associated with the word or phrase that does most closely express it. Occasionally, as when he speaks of "the crepuscular antelucan worship" of the Essenes, or of a sentence as being liable to "a whole nosology of malconformations," or of the importance attached to the mystery of baptism among our forefathers as "shown by the multiplied *ricochets* through which it impressed itself upon their vocabulary," it will depend on the temper and the intellectual alertness of the reader at the moment whether the phrase is accepted or voted needlessly quaint and abstruse; but most of his Latinisms or other neologisms do recommend themselves as at once luminous and tasteful, and it is hardly to them that exception is taken by his most severe critics. They object rather to certain faults to which he is liable in those portions of his writings where he affects the brisk and popular. By a kind of reaction from his other extreme of stateliness, he is then apt to be too familiar and colloquial, and to help himself to slang and kitchen-rhetoric. He will speak of a thing as "smashed,"—which is too violent for the nerves of those who cannot bear to see a thing "smashed," but prefer that it should be "broken in pieces" or "reduced to fragments"; he will interject such an exclamation as "O crimini!",—which is unpardonable in sedate society; he will take the Jewish historian Josephus by the button, address him as "Joe" through a whole article, and give him a black eye into the bargain,—which is positively profane. In most such cases one does not see why De Quincey should not have the same liberty as Swift or Thackeray; but it must be admitted that sometimes the joke is feeble and the slang unpleasant. In excuse one has to remember that a magazine-writer is often driven to shifts. And, slips of taste in the vocabulary discounted, how many magazine-writers will compete with De Quincey in the accuracy, the disciplined accuracy, of his grammar? His pointing in itself is a testimony to the logical clearness of his intellect; and I have found no single recurring fault of syntax in his style, unless it be in his sanction of a very questionable use of the English participle. "No Christian state could be much in advance of another, *supposing* that Popery opposed no barriers to free communication," is an example of a frequent construction with De Quincey, which I wish he had avoided. As he has not, the benefit of his authority may be claimed for that apparent slovenliness of an unrelated or misrelated participle which, by some fiction of an elliptical case-absolute, or of transmutation of the participial form into a conjunction or adverb, passes as consistent with the free genius of our uninflected language. But it jars on a classic sense of grammar, and is wholly unnecessary.—DAVID MASSON, *De Quincey*, 1888, pp. 155–58

In the narrow range of that fascinating section of literature which deals with the intimate self-disclosure of the soul, the *Confessions of an English Opium-Eater* holds conspicuous place. Marcus Aurelius, Rousseau, Amiel,—the most diverse personalities have an abiding claim upon our imaginative sympathy. We come face to face with the moral, the intellectual, the spiritual emotions of men who pass before us with the inmost secrets of their hearts laid bare to curious eyes—and we are electrified by what we see. The natural sounds of earth—wind in the branches, a wave falling on the sea-shore—appeal to all, but not in the same way as does some subtle chord struck by a great musician, some string with its pathetic *vox humana*, thrilling from the touch of the master violinist. The inner lives of our kind are to us as these natural sounds—to be interpreted but by very few—while like these revealing passages of lyric passion are the rare individuals whose "souls and bodies are one, for their spirit is not hidden, but, as their body is, visible." To this rare band De Quincey, by virtue of his *Confessions*, belongs.

Landor utters a fine and true saying when in one of his *Imaginary Conversations* he makes Vittoria Colonna remark that "the human heart is a world of poetry; the imagination is only its atmosphere." It is because so much of De Quincey's finest work is so essentially human that he has taken and is likely to retain the high place in the realm of literature which is undeniably his. Universal human interest—herein lies the sole secret of literary immortality: the revelation of the individual heart, its struggles and sorrows, its keen human sympathies in contact with a difficult world, finding an unrestful ease in that "power of dreaming" which is so familiar and yet so mysterious, and whose visionary emanations have never ceased to interest since waking and sleeping first were. Given these things, and for their interpretation the magic of a style like De Quincey's at its best, and the result is one of the rarest in literature—a work whose appeal "out of space, out of time," is perennial, unaffected by the changing fashions and periods of the literary world. ⟨. . .⟩

As a great master in that "other harmony of prose," to quote Dryden's fine phrase, De Quincey cannot fail to be considered by all who read the *Confessions* or the marvellous fragment *Our Ladies of Sorrow*. It is undeniable that much of his work has, not unnaturally, lost all attractiveness for latter-day readers—that there are indeed large portions of it which have not even the most ordinary charm of style to recommend them—mere hack-work indifferently written. At its poorest, however, there is always an intellectual basis: De Quincey might at times write without style, even in bad style, but he never spun verbal webs out of nothing. Working with his heart in his labour, with his poetic imagination fired, he became a master-architect of words—a power playing in unrivalled fashion with the subtleties and splendours of our language. In sombre imagination, in what may be called passionate pathos, he is supreme among masters of English prose. At times, indeed, his art is too conspicuous—with a corresponding lessening of effect upon the reader; but even in the most artificial of those marvellous visionary passages, dream-fugues as he called them, what magnificence of speech there is, what overwhelming music! Is there in the prose literature of imagination a more thrilling passage than that last "Dream," cited in *The Pains of Opium*, that dream opening with its "music of preparation and of awakening suspense," and ending with "darkness and lights; tempest and human faces, clasped hands, and heart-breaking partings, and then—everlasting farewells!" De Quincey's highest reach, however, is not in the *Confessions*, but in *Suspiria de Profundis*, in the most important of the sections, *Levana: And Our Ladies of Sorrow*. This magnificent fragment—if that can be called a fragment which though brief is so complete, which in conception is so epically grand—would alone suffice to prove the justness of the claim for De Quincey's being one of the greatest masters of English prose. The best word that has been said upon *Our Ladies of Sorrow* has been uttered by Professor Masson, with whose eloquent summary of *Levana* this introduction may fittingly close. "[It] is prose-poetry; but it is more. It is a permanent addition to the mythology of the human race. As the Graces are three, as the Fates are three, as the Furies are three, as the Muses were originally three, so many the varieties and degrees of misery that there are in the world, and the proportions of their distribution among mankind, be represented to the human imagination for ever by De Quincey's

Three Ladies of Sorrow, and his sketch of their figures and kingdoms.*"*—WILLIAM SHARP, "Introduction" to *Confessions of an English Opium-Eater*, 1888, pp. v–vi, xxi–xxii

I don't know De Quincey well enough to write anything about him. I have not read a line of him these thirty years. I never write about anybody without reading him through so as to get a total impression, and I have not time enough to do that in his case now. The only feeling I find in my memory concerning him is, that he was a kind of inspired *cad*, and an amplification of that with critical rose-water wouldn't answer your purpose.—JAMES RUSSELL LOWELL, Letter to R. W. Gilder (Oct. 9, 1890)

Narrative with De Quincey is seldom merely narrative. He imagines situations, which create sublime contrasts for the emotions, or which suggest prolonged psychological analyses, analyses conducted with a view to presenting all the sources and elements of great passion, and this partly for the sake of philosophic directness, partly for the sake of rhetorical effect. Where the mere narrator abbreviates in order that the sequence of events may become swift and clear, De Quincey elaborates, in order that all the inner relations, all the remote yet thrilling associations of feeling, may be exposed and imaginatively heightened. But sometimes the discursive tendency of his mind, and sometimes his studious, intellectual pursuit of the humorous led him astray, and on reconsideration he struck his pen through entire paragraphs with a courage which the reader must applaud. And yet passages, admirable and characteristic in themselves, may be recovered by one who will revert from the collected essays to their original sources in the various magazines to which De Quincey contributed. A diver here might bring up sunken treasure, for which we should be grateful, ducats—shall we say?—from a lost galleon of the Spanish main, which bear the impress of the regal mint. —EDWARD DOWDEN, "How De Quincey Worked," *Saturday Review* (London), Feb. 23, 1895, pp. 246–47

Another author who was a prime favorite with me about this time was De Quincey, whose books I took out of the State Library, one after another, until I had read them all. We who were young people of that day thought his style something wonderful, and so indeed it was, especially in those passages, abundant everywhere in his work, relating to his own life with an intimacy which was always more rather than less. His rhetoric there, and in certain of his historical studies, had a sort of luminous richness, without losing its colloquial ease. I keenly enjoyed this subtle spirit, and the play of that brilliant intelligence which lighted up so many ways of literature with its lambent glow or its tricky glimmer, and I had a deep sympathy with certain morbid moods and experiences so like my own, as I was pleased to fancy. I have not looked at his *Twelve Cæsars* for twice as many years, but I should be greatly surprised to find it other than one of the greatest historical monographs ever written. His literary criticisms seemed to me not only exquisitely humorous, but perfectly sane and just; and it delighted me to have him personally present, with the warmth of his own temperament in regions of cold abstraction; I am not sure that I should like that so much now. De Quincey was hardly less autobiographical when he wrote of Kant, or the Flight of the Crim-Tartars, than when he wrote of his own boyhood or the miseries of the opium habit. He had the hospitable gift of making you at home with him, and appealing to your sense of comradery with something of the flattering confidentiality of Thackeray, but with a wholly different effect.

In fact, although De Quincey was from time to time

perfunctorily Tory, and always a good and faithful British subject, he was so eliminated from his time and place by his single love for books, that one could be in his company through the whole vast range of his writings, and come away without a touch of snobbishness; and that is saying a great deal for an English writer. He was a great little creature, and through his intense personality he achieved a sort of impersonality, so that you loved the man, who was forever talking of himself, for his modesty and reticence. He left you feeling intimate with him but by no means familiar; with all his frailties, and with all those freedoms he permitted himself with the lives of his contemporaries, he is to me a figure of delicate dignity, and winning kindness. I think it a misfortune for the present generation that his books have fallen into a kind of neglect, and I believe that they will emerge from it again to the advantage of literature.—W. D. HOWELLS, *My Literary Passions*, 1895

He was before all things a student who, though supremely interested in his fellow-creatures, both individually and in masses, was entirely without a sense of responsibility towards his generation. His writings are pre-eminently exegetical, lacking in the imperative mood. He analyses, interprets, or expounds after his subtle, philosophic, though somewhat eccentric and paradoxical manner; taking nothing for granted, probing into everything he touches, and illuminating it by some flash of originality. Though not always a sound thinker, he marshals his arguments with an orderly precision, which is invaluable in a good cause. Exactness, carried to the verge of pedantry, is the conspicuous merit of his style; which is further strengthened by a scrupulous attention to the conditions of effective comparison, and by the explicitness with which his statements and clauses are connected. Even his grammar and punctuation are singularly clear and careful.

Beneath this vigorous intellectuality lurks a curiously deliberate and "dæmonic" kind of humour, which largely consists in the sudden introduction of an unexpected point of view, the use of dignified language for the discussion of trivialities, and the application of artistic or professional terms to records of crime and passion. On such occasions he may be said to parody his own manner with conspicuous success. Unfortunately he sometimes descends to a style of "buttonhole" facetiousness, caught perhaps from his boisterous friend Wilson, which is entirely out of place in his writings, and seems, for the time being, to destroy his usually fine sense of artistic propriety.

Composition, indeed, with De Quincey was in the highest sense of the word an art. He had what he called "an electric aptitude for seizing analogies," or "a logical instinct for feeling in a moment the secret analogies or parallelisms that connect things else apparently remote," and his erudition furnished a plentiful supply of recondite metaphors, personifications, and figures of speech. His vocabulary was copious, and he had a marked fondness for the Latin portion of it, which assisted his precision, his humour, and the stately rhythm in which he delighted.

His style is essentially decorative, and he aims consciously at sublimity of thought and diction. He does not shrink from daring appeals to the infinite, and risks bewildering his reader by dizzy flights to the uttermost limits of time and space. He builds up his sentences and his paragraphs with a sensitive ear for the music of words. One phrase seems like the echo of another, and even the impression of distance in sound is cunningly produced. His finest passages are distinguished by the crowded richness of fancy, the greater range and arbitrari-

ness of combination, which are the peculiar attributes of poetry.

At times, indeed, he becomes obscure from over-elaboration; and there can be no doubt that his digressions are too frequent and too lengthy. The tendency towards verbosity, however, is considerably checked by his intellectual alertness, and by his preference for miniatures, narrative and philosophic.

De Quincey of course was not the first writer of "impassioned prose." He shared the reaction of his day against the severer classicism of the eighteenth century, preferring rather the ornate manner of Jeremy Taylor, Sir Thomas Browne, and their contemporaries; and following somewhat closely in the steps of Jean Paul Richter. He claimed only to be the author of a "mode of impassioned prose ranging under no precedents that he was aware of in any literature," of which, as Professor Minto has pointed out, "the speciality consists in describing incidents of purely personal interest in language suited to their magnitude as they appear in the eyes of the writer." The splendour of his style prepares the reader to be attracted, and he has moreover the wisdom to avoid comparing his experiences to those of others, or suggesting that they are in themselves extraordinary.

Such are the characteristics of *The Confessions of an English Opium Eater*, by which De Quincey introduced himself to the public, the *Suspiria de Profundis*, the opium dreams of *The English Mail Coach*, and many of the "autobiographic sketches." The first-named, considered merely as "confessions," are not so remarkable as those, for instance, of Rousseau. The story is comparatively commonplace, the attitude is less morbidly frank, and the author is in no sense the emotional mouthpiece of his generation.

While writing of himself, he naturally spoke also of his friends and contemporaries, and the frankness with which he did so has earned for him the reputation of spitefulness. But he lived so entirely out of the world, that he probably did not realise the wisdom and kindness of reticence, while for posterity his acute "revelations" are both interesting and valuable. He wrote able biographies, moreover, of a number of classical, historical, and literary personages; though these are somewhat marred by a tendency to dwell too much on disputed "points." His most ambitious attempt, *The Cæsars*, is very unequal.

Indeed, historical speculation and research seem to have had a fascination for him, and in this region his wide reading and acuteness enabled him to question received theories, and support paradoxes with ingenuity and vigour; while his treatment of some passages of history is romantic and imaginative. The character of "The Spanish Military Nun," for instance, is drawn with delicate sympathy, and the paper on "Joan of Arc" is almost perfect.

His biographical and historical essays contain a good deal of the criticism which he has elsewhere expounded in a more connected form. As a critic, he is illuminating, erudite, and thoughtful; but decidedly untrustworthy. He is childishly prejudiced, especially with regard to anything French; and his mental solitariness, which stood in the way of improvement in this matter, led him at other times into the most astounding critical blunders. His essays on the science and principles of literature are original and penetrating, though a little digressive. He asserts that many of his ideas came from Wordsworth. His most noted contributions to the subject are: the distinctions between the literature of knowledge and of power, between the organic and the mechanic aspects of style, and the development of Wordsworth's utterance that language is the incarnation rather than the dress of thoughts.

De Quincey is further known for his excursions into German literature. Explanations have been offered of his treatment of Kant and Goethe, which are assuredly required; but, these questions apart, he shared with Coleridge the honour of opening English eyes to the treasures of German thought and genius. His various tales from the German are permeated with the weird, romantic spirit of their originals, and his own novels, *The Avenger* and *Klosterheim*, were evidently written under the same influence, though the latter is also curiously reminiscent of Mrs. Radcliffe.

His contributions to philosophy, in which he was largely an interpreter of the Germans, are somewhat difficult to estimate. "My proper vocation," he remarks pathetically, "was the exercise of the analytic understanding. Now, for the most part, analytic studies are continuous, not to be pursued by fits and starts, or fragmentary efforts;" and it was of these alone that he was capable during the greater part of his life. However, his "System of the Heavens" and "The Palimpsest of the Human Brain" are suggestive; and, though his interpretations may be questioned, it remains a fact that he was one of the first to recognise Kant's greatness, and did much to make him known in England. His translation of the *Idea of a Universal History* was an important service to the philosophy of the subject.

Again, his papers on ethics, though concerned mainly with the exposition of "cases," are instructive and vigorous. In theology he was a staunch Churchman, and in politics a prejudiced John Bull.

The "Logic of Political Economy" and the "Templar's Dialogues" contain his most strictly scientific work, in which he appears chiefly as an exponent of Ricardo. His lucidity of style is here particularly helpful, and Mill, though differing from him on certain principles, adopts some of his illustrations, and treats his work with respect.

The genius of De Quincey, like all genuine manifestations, cannot be dismissed with a label or crowded into a pigeon-hole. He was associated with the Lake School, and sympathised with many of their aims; but as a scholar in many fields, and a master of English prose, he stands alone. —R. Brimley Johnson, "Thomas De Quincey," *English Prose*, ed. Henry Craik, 1896, Vol. 5, pp. 260–63

He added to literature several branches or provinces which had up to his day scarcely been cultivated in English; among these, impassioned autobiography, distinguished by an exquisite minuteness in the analysis of recollected sensations, is pre-eminent. He revelled in presenting impressions of intellectual self-consciousness in phrases of what he might have called sequacious splendour. De Quincey was but little enamoured of the naked truth, and a suspicion of the fabulous hangs, like a mist, over all his narrations. The most elaborate of them, the "Revolt of the Tartars," a large canvas covered with groups of hurrying figures in sustained and painful flight, is now understood to be pure romance. The first example of his direct criticism is "Whiggism in Its Relations to Literature," which might be called the Anatomy of a Pedant.

De Quincey is sometimes noisy and flatulent, sometimes trivial, sometimes unpardonably discursive. But when he is at his best, the rapidity of his mind, its lucidity, its humour and good sense, the writer's passionate loyalty to letters, and his organ-melody of style command our deep respect. He does not, like the majority of his critical colleagues, approach literature for purposes of research, but to obtain moral effects. De Quincey, a dreamer of beautiful dreams, disdained an obstinate vassalage to mere matters of fact, but sought with intense concentration of effort after a conscientious and profound psychology of letters.—Edmund Gosse, *A Short History of Modern English Literature*, 1897, p. 323

The work of De Quincey must be read tolerantly, rarely, and in fragments. Not even Coleridge is so uneven as De Quincey, for with Coleridge there is always an alert intellectual subtlety, troubling itself very little about the words in which it is to express itself; an unsteady, but incessant, inner illumination. De Quincey, always experimentalising with his form, forgetting and remembering it with equal persistence, has no fixed mind underneath the swaying surface of his digressions, and holds our interest, when he has once captured it, in a kind of unquiet expectancy. He will write about anything, making what he chooses of his subject, as in the fantasias around the mail-coach; he writes, certainly, for the sake of writing, and also to rid himself of all the cobwebs that are darkening his brain. His mind is subtle, yet without direction; his nerves are morbidly sensitive, and they speak through all his work; he is a scholar outside life, to whom his own mind is interesting, not in the least because it is his own; and he has the scholar's ideal of a style which is a separate thing from the thing which it expresses.

"My mother," he says in a significant passage, "was predisposed to think ill of all causes that required many words: I, predisposed to subtleties of all sorts and degrees, had naturally become acquainted with cases that could not unrobe their apparellings down to that degree of simplicity. . . . I sank away in a hopelessness that was immeasurable from all effort at explanation." And he defines "the one misery having no relief," as "the burden of the incommunicable." That burden, thus desperately realised, was always his, and the whole of his work is a tangled attempt to communicate the incommunicable. He has a morbid kind of conscience, an abstract, almost literary conscience, which drives him to the very edge and last gulf of language, in his endeavour to express every fine shade of fact and sensation. At times this search is rewarded with miraculous findings, and all the colours seem to fade down to him out of the sunset when he would put purple into speech, words turn into solemn music when he would have them chant, and sensations become embodied fear or pain or wonder when he evokes them upon the page. But, in its restlessness, its discontent with the best service that words can render, it heaps parenthesis on parenthesis, drags down paragraphs with leaden foot-notes, and pulls up the reader at every other moment to remind him of something which he has forgotten or does not wish to know. De Quincey never knows when to stop, because his own mind never stops. He turns upon himself, like a nervous man trying to get out of a room full of people; apologises, interrupts his own apologies, leaving you at last a sharer of his own fluster. And in all this search for exactitude there is a certain pedantry, and also a certain mental haze. His imagination was pictorial, but it was not always precise enough in its outlines. Rhetoric comes into even the finest of his "dream-scenery," and rhetoric, in a picture, is colour making up for absence of form. He believed in words too much and too little.

De Quincey's *Confessions* are among the most fascinating of autobiographies, but they have an air of unreality because they are written round such experiences as only a very unreal kind of man could have known. However sincere he may mean to be, De Quincey must always make a deliberate arrangement of what he has to tell us; things fall into attitudes as he looks at them; he hears them in long and winding sentences. To an opium-smoker time and space lose even that sort of reality which normal people are accustomed to assign to them. Under the influence of such a drug it is somewhat perilous to cross the street, for it is impossible to realise the distance between oneself and the hansom which is coming towards one, or the length of time which it will require to get from pavement to pavement. It is this disturbed sense of proportion, this broken equilibrium of the mind, which gave De Quincey so faint and variable a hold on fact, even mental fact. He saw everything on the same plane, one thing not more important than another; at the moment when it engaged his interest anything was of supreme importance. But interest drove out interest, or came and went, with the disturbance of an obsession. In writing he wants to tell us everything about everything; he takes up first one subject, handling it elaborately; then handles another subject elaborately; then goes back to the first; and so the narrative moves onward, like a worm, turning back upon itself as it moves.

When people praise the style of De Quincey, they praise isolated outbursts, and there are outbursts in his work which have almost every quality of external splendour. But it was De Quincey's error to seek splendour for its own sake, to cultivate eloquence in rhetoric, to write prose loudly, as if it were to be delivered from a pulpit. Listen to the first sentence of his famous "dream-fugue": "Passion of sudden death! that once in youth I read and interpreted by the shadows of thy averted signs!—rapture of panic taking the shape (which amongst tombs in churches I have seen) of woman bursting her sepulchral bonds—of woman's Ionic form bending forward from the ruins of her grave with arching foot, with eyes upraised, with clasped adoring hands—waiting, watching, trembling, praying for the trumpet's call to rise from dust for ever." Now if prose is something said, as poetry is something sung, that is not good prose, any more than it is even bad poetry. It is oratory, and oratory has qualities quite different from literature; qualities which fit it to impress a multitude when spoken aloud, in a voice artificially heightened in order to be heard by that multitude. De Quincey's prose is artificially heightened; it cannot be spoken naturally, but must be spoken with an emphasis quite unlike that of even the most emotional speech. Perhaps the most perfect prose in the English language is the prose of Shakespeare: take a single sentence from *Love's Labour's Lost:* "The sweet war-man is dead and rotten; sweet chucks, beat not the bones of the buried: when he breathed, he was a man!" There you have every merit of prose, in form and substance, and it may be spoken as easily as the expression of one's own thought. Hamlet's "What a piece of work is man!" with its elaborate splendour, can be spoken on the conversational level of the voice. Now De Quincey thinks it a mean thing to write as if he were but talking, and, whenever he rises with his subject, seems to get on a platform. It is a wonderful thing, undoubtedly, that he gives us, but a thing structurally unsatisfactory. Carried further, used with less imagination but with a finer sense for the colour of words, it becomes the style of Ruskin, and is what is frankly called prose poetry, a lucky bastard, glorying in the illegitimacy of its origin.—ARTHUR SYMONS, "A Word on De Quincey" (1901), *Studies in Prose and Verse*, 1904, pp. 47–51

SIR LESLIE STEPHEN
From "De Quincey" (1871)
Hours in a Library (1874–79)
1904, Volume 1, pp. 325–51

De Quincey implicitly puts forward a claim which has been accepted by all competent critics. They declare, and he tacitly assumes, that he is a master of the English language. He claims a sort of infallibility in deciding upon the precise use of words and the merits of various styles. But he explicitly claims something more. He declares that he has used language for purposes to which it has hardly been applied by any prose writer. The *Confessions of an Opium-eater* and the *Suspiria de Profundis* are, he tells us, "modes of impassioned prose, ranging under no precedents that I am aware of in any literature." The only confessions that have previously made any great impression upon the world are those of St. Augustine and of Rousseau; but, with one short exception in St. Augustine, neither of those compositions contains any passion, and, therefore, De Quincey stands absolutely alone as the inventor and sole performer on a new musical instrument—for such an instrument is the English language in his hands. He belongs to a genius in which he is the only individual. The novelty and the difficulty of the task must be his apology if he fails, and causes of additional glory if he succeeds. He alone of all human beings who have written since the world began, has entered a path, which the absence of rivals proves to be encumbered with some unusual obstacles. The accuracy and value of so bold a claim require a short examination. After all, every writer, however obscure, may contrive by a judicious definition to put himself into a solitary class. He has some peculiarities which distinguish him from all other mortals. He is the only journalist who writes at a given epoch from a particular garret in Grub Street, or the only poet who is exactly six feet high and measures precisely forty-two inches round the chest. Any difference whatever may be applied to purposes of classification, and the question is whether the difference is, or is not, of much importance. By examining, therefore, the propriety of De Quincey's view of his own place in literature, we shall be naturally led to some valuation of his distinctive merits. In deciding whether a bat should be classed with birds or beasts, we have to determine the nature of the beast and the true theory of his wings. And De Quincey, if the comparison be not too quaint, is like the bat, an ambiguous character, rising on the wings of prose to the borders of the true poetical region.

De Quincey, then, announces himself as an impassioned writer, as a writer in impassioned prose, and, finally, as applying impassioned prose to confessions. The first question suggested by this assertion concerns the sense of the word "impassioned." There is very little of what one ordinarily means by passion in the *Confessions* or elsewhere. There are no explosions of political wrath, such as animate the *Letters on a Regicide Peace*, or of a deep religious emotion, which breathes through many of our greatest prose-writers. The language is undoubtedly a vehicle for sentiments of a certain kind, but hardly of that burning and impetuous order which we generally indicate by impassioned. It is deep, melancholy reverie, not concentrated essence of emotion; and the epithet fails to indicate any specific difference between himself and many other writers. The real peculiarity is not in the passion expressed, but in the mode of expressing it. De Quincey resembles the story-tellers mentioned by some Eastern travellers. So extraordinary is their power of face, and so skilfully modulated are the inflections of their voices, that even a European, ignorant of the language, can follow the narrative with absorbing interest. One may fancy that if De Quincey's language were emptied of all meaning whatever, the mere sound of the words would move us, as the lovely word Mesopotamia moved Whitefield's hearer. The sentences are so delicately balanced, and so skilfully constructed, that his finer passages fix themselves in the memory without the aid of metre. Humbler writers are content if they can get through a single phrase without producing a decided jar. They aim at keeping up a steady jog-trot, which shall not give actual pain to the jaws of the reader. They no more think of weaving whole paragraphs or chapters into complex harmonies, than an ordinary pedestrian of "going to church in a galliard and coming home in a coranto." Even our great writers generally settle down to a stately but monotonous gait, after the fashion of Johnson or Gibbon, or are content with adopting a style as transparent and inconspicuous as possible. Language, according to the common phrase, is the dress of thought; and that dress is the best, according to modern canons of taste, which attracts least attention from its wearer. De Quincey scorns this sneaking maxim of prudence, and boldly challenges our admiration by indulgence in what he often calls "bravura." His language deserves a commendation sometimes bestowed by ladies upon rich garments, that it is capable of standing up by itself. The form is so admirable that, for purposes of criticism, we must consider it as something apart from the substance. The most exquisite passages in De Quincey's writing are all more or less attempts to carry out the idea expressed in the title of the dream fugue. They are intended to be musical compositions, in which words have to play the part of notes. They are impassioned, not in the sense of expressing any definite sentiment, but because, from the structure and combination of the sentences, they harmonise with certain phases of emotion.

Briefly, De Quincey is doing in prose what every great poet does in verse. The specific mark thus indicated is still insufficient to give him a solitary position among writers. All great rhetoricians, as De Quincey defines and explains the term, rise to the borders of poetry, and the art which has recently been cultivated among us under the name of word-painting may be more fitly described as an attempt to produce poetical effects without the aid of metre. From most of the writers described under this rather unpleasant phrase he differs by the circumstance, that his art is more nearly allied to music than to painting. Or, if compared to any painters, it must be to those who care comparatively little for distinct portraiture or dramatic interest. He resembles rather the school which is satisfied by contemplating gorgeous draperies, and graceful limbs and long processions of imposing figures, without caring to interpret the meaning of their works, or to seek for more than the harmonious arrangement of form and colour. In other words, his prose-poems should be compared to the paintings which aim at an effect analogous to that of stately pieces of music. Milton is the poet whom he seems to regard with the sincerest admiration; and he apparently wishes to emulate the majestic rhythm of the "God-gifted organ-voice of England." Or we may, perhaps, admit some analogy between his prose and the poetry of Keats, though it is remarkable that he speaks with very scant appreciation of his contemporary. The "Ode to a Nightingale," with its marvellous beauty of versification and the dim associations half-consciously suggested by its language, surpasses, though it resembles, some of De Quincey's finest passages; and the *Hyperion* might have been translated into prose as a fitting companion for some of the opium dreams. It

is in the success with which he produces such effects as these that De Quincey may fairly claim to be unsurpassed in our language. Pompous (if that word may be used in a good sense) declamation in prose, where the beauty of the thought is lost in the splendour of the style, is certainly a rare literary product. Of the great rhetoricians whom De Quincey quotes in the Essay on "Rhetoric" ⟨. . .⟩, such men as Burke and Jeremy Taylor lead us to forget the means in the end. They sound the trumpet as a warning, not for the mere delight in its volume of sound. Perhaps his affinity to Sir Thomas Browne is more obvious; and one can understand the admiration which he bestows upon the opening bar of a passage in the *Urn-Burial*:

> Now since these bones have rested quietly in the grave under the drums and tramplings of three conquests [etc.]. What a melodious ascent [he exclaims], as of a prelude to some impassioned requiem breathing from the pomps of earth and from the sanctities of the grave! What a *fluctus decumanus* of rhetoric! Time expounded, not by generations or centuries, but by vast periods of conquests and dynasties; by cycles of Pharaohs and Ptolemies, Antiochi and Arsacides! And these vast successions of time distinguished and figured by the uproars which revolve at their inaugurations; by the drums and tramplings rolling overhead upon the chambers of forgotten dead—the trepidations of time and mortality vexing, at secular intervals, the everlasting sabbaths of the grave!

The commentator is seeking to eclipse the text, and his words are at once a description and an example of his own most characteristic rhetoric. Wordsworth once uttered an aphorism which De Quincey repeats with great admiration: that language is not, as I have just said, the dress, but "the incarnation of thought." But though accepting and enforcing the doctrine by showing that the "mixture is too subtle, the intertexture too ineffable" to admit of expression, he condemns the style which is the best illustration of its truth. He is very angry with the admirers of Swift; De Foe and "many hundreds" of others wrote something quite as good; it only wanted "plain good sense, natural feeling, unpretendingness, some little scholarly practice in putting together the clockwork of sentences, and, above all, the advantage of an appropriate subject." Could Swift, he asks, have written a pendant to passages in Sir W. Raleigh, or Sir Thomas Browne, or Jeremy Taylor? He would have cut the same figure as "a forlorn scullion from a greasy eating-house at Rotterdam, if suddenly called away in vision to act as seneschal to the festival of Belshazzar the King, before a thousand of his lords." And what, we may retort, would Taylor, or Browne, or De Quincey himself, have done, had one of them been wanted to write down the project of Wood's half-pence in Ireland? He would have resembled a king in his coronation robes compelled to lead a forlorn hope up the scaling ladders. The fact is, that Swift required for his style not only the plain good sense and other rare qualities enumerated, but pungent humour, quick insight, deep passion, and general power of mind, such as is given to few men in a century. But, as in his case the thought is really incarnated in the language we cannot criticise the style separately from the thoughts, or we can only assign, as its highest merit, its admirable fitness for producing the desired effect. It would be wrong to invert De Quincey's censure, and blame him because his gorgeous robes are not fitted for more practical purposes. To everything there is a time; for plain English, and for De Quincey's highly-wrought passages.

It would be difficult or impossible, and certainly it would be superfluous, to define with any precision the peculiar flavour of De Quincey's style. A few specimens would do more than any description; and De Quincey is too well known to justify quotation. It may be enough to notice that most of his brilliant performances are variations on the same theme. He appeals to our terror of the infinite, to the shrinking of the human mind before astronomical distances and geological periods of time. He paints vast perspectives, opening in long succession, till we grow dizzy in the contemplation. The cadence of his style suggests sounds echoing each other, and growing gradually fainter, till they die away into infinite distance. Two great characteristics, he tells us, of his opium dreams were a deep-seated melancholy and an exaggeration of the things of space and time. Nightly he descended "into chasms and sunless abysses, depths below depths, from which it seemed hopeless that he could ever reascend." He saw buildings and landscapes "in proportion so vast as the human eye is not fitted to receive." He seemed to live ninety or a hundred years in a night, and even to pass through periods far beyond the limits of human existence. Melancholy and an awe-stricken sense of the vast and vague are the emotions which he communicates with the greatest power; though the melancholy is too dreamy to deserve the name of passion, and the terror of the infinite is not explicitly connected with any religious emotion. It is a proof of the fineness of his taste, that he scarcely ever falls into bombast; we tremble at his audacity in accumulating gorgeous phrases; but we confess that he is justified by the result. The only exception that I can remember is the passage in "The English Mail-Coach," where his exaggerated patriotism leads him into what strikes me at least as a rather vulgar bit of claptrap. If any reader will take the trouble to compare De Quincey's account of a kind of anticipation of the Balaclava charge at the battle of Talavera, with Napier's description of the same facts, he will be amused at the distortion of history; but whatever the accuracy of the statements, one is a little shocked at finding "the inspiration of God" attributed to the gallant dragoons who were cut to pieces on that occasion, as other gallant men have been before and since. The phrase is overcharged, and inevitably suggests a cynical reaction of mind. The ideas of dragoons and inspiration do not coalesce so easily as might be wished; but, with this exception, I think that his purple patches are almost irreproachable, and may be read and re-read with increasing delight. I know of no other modern writer who has soared into the same regions with so uniform and easy a flight.

The question is often raised how far the attempt to produce by one art effects specially characteristic of another can be considered as legitimate; whether, for example, a sculptor, when encroaching upon the province of the painter, or a prose writer attempting to rival poets, may not be summarily condemned. The answer probably would be that a critic who lays down such rules is erecting himself into a legislator, when he should be a simple observer. Success justifies itself; and when De Quincey obtains, without the aid of metre, graces which few other writers have won by the same means, it is all the more creditable to De Quincey. A certain presumption, however, remains in such cases, that the failure to adopt the ordinary methods implies a certain deficiency of power. If we ask why De Quincey, who trenched so boldly upon the peculiar province of the poet, yet failed to use the poetical form, there is one very obvious answer. He has one intolerable fault, a fault which has probably done more than any other to diminish his popularity, and which is, of all faults, most diametrically opposed to poetical excellence. He is utterly incapable of concentration. He is, from the very principles on which his style is constructed, the most diffuse of writers. Other men will pack half-a-dozen distinct propositions into a sentence, and care little if they are somewhat crushed and distorted in the process. De Quincey insists upon putting each of them separately, smoothing them out elaborately, till not a wrinkle disturbs their uniform surface, and then presenting each of them for our acceptance with a placid smile. His commendable desire for lucidity of expression makes him nervously anxious to avoid any complexity of thought. Each step of his argument, each shade of meaning, and each fact in his narrative, must have its own separate embodiment; and every joint and connecting link must be carefully and accurately defined. The clearness is won at a price. There is some advantage in this elaborate method of dissecting out every distinct fibre and ramification of an argument. But, on the whole, one is apt to remember that life is limited, and that there are some things in this world which must be taken for granted. If a man's boyhood fill two volumes, and if one of these (though under unfavourable circumstances) took six months to revise, it seems probable that in later years he would have taken longer to record events than to live them. No autobiography written on such principles could ever reach even the middle life of the author. Take up, for example, the first volume of his collected works. Why, on the very first page, having occasion to mention Christendom in the fifteenth century, should he provide against some eccentric misconception by telling us that it did not, at that time, include any part of America? Why should it take considerably more than a page to explain that when a schoolmaster begins lessons punctually, and leaves off too late, there will be an encroachment on the hours of play? Or two pages to describe how a porter dropped a portmanteau on a flight of stairs, and didn't waken a schoolmaster? Or two more to account for the fact that he asked a woman the meaning of the noise produced by the "bore" in the Dee, instead of waiting till she spoke to him? Impassioned prose may be a very good thing; but when its current is arrested by such incessant stoppages, and the beauty of the English language displayed by showing how many faultless sentences may be expended on an exhaustive description of irrelevant trifles, the human mind becomes recalcitrant. A man may become prolix from the fulness or fervency of his mind; but prolixity produced by this finical minuteness of language, ends by distressing one's nerves. It is the same sense of irritation as is produced by waiting for the tedious completion of an elaborate toilette, and one is rather tempted to remember Artemus Ward's description of the Fourth of July oration, which took four hours "to pass a given point."

This peculiarity of his style is connected with other qualities upon which a great deal of eulogy has been bestowed. There are two faculties in which, so far as my experience goes, no man, woman, or child ever admits his or her own deficiency. The driest of human beings will boast of their sense of humour; and the most perplexed, of their logical acuteness. De Quincey has been highly praised, both as a humourist and as a logician. He believed in his own powers, and exhibits them rather ostentatiously. He says, pleasantly enough, but not without a substratum of real conviction, that he is "a *doctor seraphicus*, and also *inexpugnabilis* upon quillets of logic." I confess that I am generally sceptical as to the merits of infallible dialecticians, because I have observed that a man's reputation for inexorable logic is generally in proportion to the error of his conclusions. A logician, in popular estimation, seems to be one who never shrinks from a *reductio ad absurdum*. His merits are measured, not by the accuracy of his conclusions, but by the distance which separates them from his premises. The explanation doubtless lies in the general impression that logic is concerned with words and not with things. There is a vague belief that by skilfully linking syllogisms you can form a chain sufficiently strong to cross the profoundest abyss, and which will need no test of observation and verification. A dexterous performer, it is supposed, might pass from one extremity of the universe to the other without ever touching ground; and people do not observe that the refusal to draw an inference may be just as great a proof of logical skill as ingenuity in drawing it. Now De Quincey's claim to infallibility would be plausible, if we still believed that to define words accurately is the same thing as to discover facts, and that binding them skilfully together is equivalent to reasoning securely. He is a kind of rhetorical Euclid. He makes such a flourish with his apparatus of axioms and definitions that you do not suspect any lurking fallacy. He is careful to show you the minutest details of his argumentative mechanism. Each step in the process is elaborately and separately set forth; you are not assumed to know anything, or to be capable of supplying any links for yourself; it shall not even be taken for granted without due notice that things which are equal to a third thing are equal to each other; and the consequence is, that few people venture to question processes which seem to be so plainly set forth, and to advance by such a careful development.

When, indeed, De Quincey has a safe guide, he can put an argument with admirable clearness. The expositions of political economy, for example, are clear and ingenious, though even here I may quote Mr. Mill's remark, that he should have imagined a certain principle—obvious enough when once stated—to have been familiar to all economists, "if the instance of Mr. De Quincey did not prove that the complete non-recognition and implied denial of it are compatible with great intellectual ingenuity and close intimacy with the subject matter."[1] Upon this question, Mr. Shadworth Hodgson has maintained that De Quincey was in the right as against Mill, and I cannot here argue the point. I think, however, that all economists would admit that De Quincey's merits were confined to an admirable exposition of another man's reasoning, and included no substantial addition to the inquiry. Certainly he does not count as one of those whose writings marked any epoch in the development of the science—if it be a science. Admirable skill of expression is, indeed, no real safeguard against logical blunders; and I will venture to say that De Quincey rarely indulges in this ostentatious logical precision without plunging into downright fallacies. I will take two instances. The first is trifling, but characteristic. Poor Dr. Johnson used to reproach himself, as De Quincey puts it, "with lying too long in bed." How absurd! is the comment.

The doctor got up at eleven because he went to bed at three. If he had gone to bed at twelve, could he not easily have got up at eight? The remark would have been sound in form, though a quibble in substance, if Johnson had complained of lying in bed "too late;" but as De Quincey himself speaks of "too long" instead of "too late," it is an obvious reply that eight hours are the same length at every period of the day. The great logician falls into another characteristic error in the same paragraph. Dr. Johnson, he says, was not "indolent;" but he adds that Johnson "had a morbid predisposition to decline labour from his scrofulous habit of body," which was increased by over-eating and want of exercise. It is a cruel mode of vindication to say that you are not indolent, but only predisposed by a bad constitution and bad habits to decline labour;

but the advantage of accurate definition is, that you can knock a man down with one hand, and pick him up with the other.

To take a more serious case. De Quincey undertakes to refute Hume's memorable argument against miracles. There are few better arenas for intellectual combats, and De Quincey has in it an unusual opportunity for display. He is obviously on his mettle. He comes forward with a whole battery of propositions, carefully marshalled in strategical order, and supported by appropriate "lemmas." One of his arguments, whether cogent or not, is that Hume's objection will not apply to the evidence of a multitude of witnesses. Now, a conspicuous miracle, he says, can be produced resting on such evidence, to wit, that of the thousands fed by a few loaves and fishes. The simplest infidel will, of course, reply that as these thousands of witnesses cannot be produced, the evidence open to us reduces itself to that of the Evangelists. De Quincey recollects this, and replies to it in a note. "Yes," he says, "the Evangelists certainly; and, let us add, all those contemporaries to whom the Evangelists silently appealed. These make up the 'multitude' contemplated in the case" under consideration. That is, to make up the multitude, you have to reckon as witnesses all those persons who did not contradict the "silent appeal," or whose contradiction has not reached us. With such canons of criticism it is hard to say what might not be proved. When a man with a great reputation for learning and logical ability tries to put us off with these wretched quibbles, one is fairly bewildered. He shows an ignorance of the real strength and weakness of the position, which, but for his reputation, one would summarily explain by incapacity for reasoning. As it is, we must suppose that, living apart from the daily battle of life, he had lost that quick instinct possessed by all genuine logicians for recognising the vital points of an argument. A day in a court of justice would have taught him more about evidence than a month spent over Aristotle. He had become fitter for the parade of the fencing-room than for the real thrust and parry of a duel in earnest. The mere rhetorical flourish pleases him as much as a blow at his antagonist's heart. Another glaring instance in the same paper is his apparent failure to perceive that there is a difference between proving that such a prophecy as that announcing the fall of Babylon was fulfilled, and proving that it was supernaturally inspired. Hume, without a tenth part of the logical apparatus, would have exposed the fallacy in a sentence. Paley, whom he never tires of treating to contemptuous abuse, was incapable of such feeble sophistry. De Quincey, in short, was a very able expositor; but he was not, though under better discipline he might probably have become, a sound original thinker. He is an interpreter, not an originator of thought. His skill in setting forth an argument blinds him to its most palpable defects. If language is a powerful weapon in his hands, it is only when the direction of the blow is dictated by some more manly, if less ingenious, understanding.

Let us inquire, and it is a more delicate question, whether he is better qualified to use it as a plaything. He has a reputation as a humourist. The Essay on "Murder Considered as One of the Fine Arts" is probably the most popular of his writings. The conception is undoubtedly meritorious, and De Quincey returns to it more than once in his other works. The description of the Williams murders is inimitable, and the execution even in the humorous passages is frequently good. We may praise particular sentences: such as the well-known remark that "if a man once indulges himself in murder, he comes to think little of robbing; and from robbing he comes next to drinking and Sabbath-breaking; and from that to incivility and procrastination." One laughs at this whimsical inversion; but I don't think one laughs very heartily; and certainly one does not find, as in really deep humour, that the paradox is pregnant with further meaning, and the laugh a prelude to a more melancholy smile. Many of the best things ever said are couched in a similar form: the old remark that the use of language is the concealment of thought; the saying that the half is greater than the whole, and that two and two don't always make four, are familiar instances; but each of them really contains a profound truth expressed in a paradoxical form, which is a sufficient justification of their extraordinary popularity. But if every inversion of a commonplace were humorous, we should be able to make jokes by machinery. There is no humour that I can see in the statement that honesty is the worst policy, or that procrastination saves time; and De Quincey's phrase, though I admit that it is amusing as a kind of summary of his essay, seems to me to rank little higher than an ingenious pun. It is a clever trick of language, but does not lead any further.

Here, too, and elsewhere, the humour gives us a certain impression of thinness. It is pressed too far, and spun out too long. Compare De Quincey's mode of beating out his one joke through pages of laboured facetiousness, with Swift's concentrated and pungent irony, as in the proposal for eating babies, or the argument to prove that the abolition of Christianity may be attended with some inconveniences. It is the difference between the stiffest of nautical grogs and the negus provided by thoughtful parents for a child's evening party. In some parts of the essay De Quincey sinks far lower. I do not believe that in any English author of reputation there is a more feeble piece of forced fun, than in the description of the fight of the amateur in murder with the baker at Munich. One knows by a process of reasoning that the man is joking; but one feels inclined to blush, through sympathy with a very clear man so exposing himself. A blemish of the same kind makes itself unpleasantly obvious at many points of his writings. He seems to fear that we shall find his stately and elaborate style rather too much for our nerves. He is conscious that, as a great master of language, he can play what tricks he pleases, without danger of remonstrance. And therefore, he every now and then plunges into slang, not irreverently, as a vulgar writer might do, but of malice prepense. The shock is almost as great as if an organist performing a solemn tune should suddenly introduce an imitation of the mewing of a cat. Now, he seems to say, you can't accuse me of being dull and pompous. Let me quote an instance or two from his graver writings. He wishes to argue, in defence of Christianity, that the ancients were insensible to ordinary duties of humanity:

> Our wicked friend Kikero, for instance, who *was* so bad, but *wrote* so well, who *did* such naughty things, but *said* such pretty things, has himself noticed in one of his letters, with petrifying coolness, that he knew of destitute old women in Rome who went without tasting food for one, two, or even three days. After making such a statement, did Kikero not tumble downstairs and break at least three of his legs in his hurry to call a public meeting [etc., etc.].

What delicate humour! The grave apologist of Christianity actually calls Cicero, Kikero, and talks about "three of his legs!" Do we not all explode with laughter? A parallel case occurs in his argument about the Essenes; where he grows so irrepressibly funny as to call Josephus "Mr. Joe," and addresses him as follows:

> Wicked Joseph, listen to me: you've been telling us a fairy tale; and for my part, I've no objection to a fairy tale in any situation, because if one can make no use of it oneself, always one knows that a child will be thankful for it. But this tale, Mr. Joseph, happens also to be a lie; secondly, a fraudulent lie; thirdly, a malicious lie.

I have seen this stuff described as "scholarlike badinage;" but the only effect of such exquisite foolery, within my mind, is to persuade one that a writer assailed by such weapons, and those weapons used by a man who has the whole resources of the English language at his command, must probably have been encountering an inconvenient truth. I will simply refer to the story of Sir Isaac Newton sitting all day with one stocking on and one off, in the *Casuistry of Roman Meals*, as an illustration of the way in which a story ought not to be told. Its most conspicuous, though not its worst fault, its extreme length, protects it from quotation.

It is strange to find that a writer, pre-eminently endowed with delicacy of ear, and boasting of the complex harmonies of his style, should condescend to such an irritating defect. De Quincey says of one of the greatest masters of the humorous:

> The gyration within which his (Lamb's) sentiment wheels, no matter of what kind it may be, is always the shortest possible. It does not prolong itself, it does not repeat itself, it does not propagate itself.

And he goes on to connect the failing with Lamb's utter insensibility to music, and indifference to "the rhythmical in prose composition." The criticism is a fine one in its way, but it may perhaps explain some of De Quincey's shortcomings in Lamb's particular sphere. De Quincey's jokes are apt to repeat and prolong and propagate themselves, till they become tiresome; and the delicate touch of the true humourist, just indicating a half-comic, half-pathetic thought, is alien to De Quincey's more elaborate style. Yet he had a true and peculiar sense of humour. That faculty may be predominant or latent; it may form the substance of a whole book, as in the case of Sterne; or it may permeate every sentence, as in Carlyle's writings; or it may simply give a faint tinge, rather perceived by subsequent analysis than consciously felt at the time; and in this lowest degree it frequently gives a certain charm to De Quincey's writing. When he tries overt acts of wit, he becomes simply vulgar; when he directly aims at the humorous, we feel his hand to be rather heavy; but he is occasionally very happy in that ironical method, of which the Essay on "Murder" is the most notorious specimen. The best example, in my opinion, is the description of his elder brother in the *Autobiographical Sketches*. The account of the rival kingdoms of Gombroon and Tigrasylvania; of poor De Quincey's troubles in getting rid of his subjects' tails; of his despair at the suggestion that by making them sit down for six hours a day they might rub them off in the course of several centuries; of his ingenious plan of placing his unlucky island at a distance of 75 degrees of latitude from his brother's capital; and of his dismay at hearing of the "vast horns and promontories" which run down from all parts of the hostile dominions towards his unoffending little territory, are touched with admirable skill. The grave, elaborate detail of the perplexities of his childish imagination is pleasant, and at the same time pathetic. When, in short, by simply applying his usual stateliness of manner to a subject a little beneath it in dignity, he can produce the desired effect, he is eminently successful. The same rhetoric which would be appropriate (to use his favourite illustration) in treating the theme of "Belshazzar the King giving a great feast to a thousand of his lords," has a certain piquancy, when for Belshazzar we substitute a schoolboy playing at monarchy. He is indulging in a whimsical masquerade, and the pomp is assumed in sport instead of in earnest. Nobody can do a little mock majesty so well as he who on occasion can be seriously majestic. Yet when he altogether abandons his strong ground, and chooses to tumble and make grimaces before us, like an ordinary clown, he becomes simply offensive. The great tragedian is capable on due occasion of pleasant burlesque; but sheer unadulterated comedy is beyond his powers. De Quincey, in short, can parody his own serious writing better than anybody, and the capacity is a proof that he had the faculty of humour; but for a genuine substantive joke—a joke which, resting on its own merits, instead of being the shadow of his serious writing, is to be independently humorous—he seems, to me at least, to be generally insufferable.

Notes

1. It is curious that De Quincey, in his "Essay on Style," explains that political economy, and especially the doctrine of value, is one of those subjects which cannot be satisfactorily treated in dialogue—the very form which he chose to adopt for that particular purpose.

GEORGE PARSONS LATHROP
From "Some Aspects of De Quincey"
Atlantic, November 1877, pp. 577–84

Originality, in many kinds of writing, is the maintenance of the child's freshness of vision along with the man's ripened perception. We know something about the peculiar value of their childhood in the later activity of some imaginative authors, but we no doubt often fail to estimate rightly the full extent of the reserved originality thus carried over from one period to the other. De Quincey is an exceptionally strong instance in point. He seems never to have altered. His own account of himself tends to show that in boyhood the same kind of questions occupied him as in subsequent years, and he had even then the same subtle way of thinking about them. Everything that happened to him in boyhood seems to have produced an impression of wonderful depth. At four years of age, seeing the house-maid about to raise her broom to destroy a spider, his sense of "the holiness of all life" caused him to devise instantly a piece of strategy for drawing her off: he showed her a picture, and thus attracted her attention long enough to allow of the spider's escaping. He expressly maintains that "into all the *elementary* feelings of man, children look with more searching gaze than adults;" but he was a child who also faced the most perplexing problems, and never rested satisfied with elementary feelings or superficial aspects. The house-maid, finally detecting his stratagem for saving spiders, explained to him that they deserved death in punishment for the many murders they had committed and would again commit. "This staggered me," he proceeds. "I could gladly have forgiven the past, but it *did* seem a false mercy to spare one spider in order to scatter death amongst fifty flies. The difficulty which the house-maid had suggested did not depart; it troubled my musing mind to perceive that the welfare of one creature might stand upon the ruin of another, and the case of the spider remained still more perplexing to my understanding than it was painful to my heart." With like meditativeness but also profound emotion he endured the loss of a favorite kitten, killed by a dog. In another place he says: "The earliest incidents in my life which left stings in my memory so as to be remembered at this day [more than sixty years after] were two,

and both before I could have completed my second year: namely, first, a remarkable dream of terrific grandeur about a favorite nurse; . . . and secondly, the fact of having connected a profound sense of pathos with the reappearance, very early in the spring, of some crocuses. This I mention as inexplicable; for such annual resurrections of plants and flowers affect us only as memorials, or suggestions of some higher change, and therefore in connection with the idea of death; yet of death I could, at that time, have had no experience whatever." These things all point to an extraordinary internal life in his earliest years; and it is significant to note that in his twelfth year he was removed from the Bath Grammar School on account of an accident to his head, by which it was at first supposed that his skull had been fractured. Upon this he makes the comment: "At present I doubt whether in reality anything very serious had happened. In fact, *I was always under a nervous panic for my head.*" That is a curious apprehension for a boy of twelve, and shows a half-conscious knowledge of the great delicacy of his brain. Two well-known passages from the *Suspiria de Profundis* open still wider the gates of this "marvelous boy's" strange world of self-communion: "O burthen of solitude, that cleavest to man through every stage of his being! in his birth, which *has* been—in his life, which *is*—in his death, which *shall* be—mighty and essential solitude! that wast, and art, and art to be;—thou broodest, like the spirit of God moving upon the surface of the deeps, over every heart that sleeps in the nurseries of Christendom. Like the vast laboratory of the air, which, seeming to be nothing, or less than the shadow of a shade, hides within itself the principles of all things, solitude for the child is the Agrippa's mirror of the unseen universe. Deep is the solitude in life of millions upon millions, who, with hearts welling forth love, have none to love them. Deep is the solitude of those who, with secret griefs, have none to pity them. Deep is the solitude of those who, fighting with doubts or darkness, have none to counsel them. But deeper than the deepest of these solitudes is that which broods over childhood." The other passage begins that part of the *Suspiria* entitled "The Vision of Life": "Upon me, as upon others scattered thinly by tens and twenties over every thousand years, fell too powerfully and too early the vision of life. The horror of life mixed itself already in earliest youth with the heavenly sweetness of life; that grief, which one in a hundred has sensibility enough to gather from the sad retrospect of life in its closing stage, for me shed its dews as a prelibation upon the fountains of life whilst yet sparkling to the morning sun. I saw from afar and from before what I was to see from behind. Is this the description of an early youth passed in the shades of gloom? No; but of a youth passed in the divinest happiness."

The solitude to which he felt that he owed so much—afterwards expressing his conviction in the general formula, "How much solitude, so much power"—was the loneliness in which genius is born and abides that it may be sheltered from the sophistication which too often obscures the insight into truth so soon as childhood is over. De Quincey's inner life in boyhood was always intense, full of intricate reasoning, and charged with emotions that are constantly mounting to fever heat, precipitating crises. At fourteen, he has so far matured that "everything connected with schools and the business of schools" has become hateful to him. At fifteen, he visits Lady Carberry, meeting her as an equal,—nay, a superior, for he is teaching her Greek and imparting to her subtle distinctions of his own manufacture respecting Christianity, Greek and English tragedy, and the philosophy of Locke, all of which she receives eagerly; and when she, thinking to compliment him, calls him her "admirable Crichton," the boy demurs, for two carefully selected and discriminated reasons, which he sets forth, pointing out to her that he does not think it a title honorable enough to be desired,—"which made her stare." Within a year and a half later he goes upon that memorable wandering in Wales and to London which is so closely bound up with his opium history. With the exception of the chapter on Oxford, the picture of his boyhood and youth, and of the opium dreams therewith connected, is painted with an impressiveness and richness that elevate the most of it to something like an heroic scale. Notwithstanding that the different parts were written at periods so distant from each other, if we leave out certain garrulities which De Quincey interjected in his old age, the whole possesses a sumptuous unity; it is full of the artistic instinct for composition; and it would be hard to find another autobiographic revelation which relies for its most solemn and unique effects upon incidents the most ordinary and slight, with such stately results. It might be supposed that some of those reminiscences which figure in the dreams had received their colossal quality from the action of opium, but large portions that have nothing to do with the dreams have precisely the same weird magnifying force. The truth is that all throughout this body of writing we meet the atmosphere of a precocious and partially morbid child's mind, the dreams being in accord with it because they resulted from the same mind's being put in action along the same lines of fancy and experience. We have here a disclosure of the condition of a large number of precocious minds that, lacking the force to survive, are never heard from. Strange, to think of that great freight of hidden human existence lost with the early dying, which never finds expression or place in this human world for which it was made, but is diffused among the interstellar glooms and leaves no trace! But still stranger to think that one voice should have been found, one life preserved, to tell us something of it,—enabling us to apprehend the depths of life that lie all around us, unsuspected, in hearts that we could hardly penetrate even were we imaginative enough to attempt doing so!

I think the ultimate cause of De Quincey's half unearthly spell will be found in this relation of his to a class of which he was of course an exceptional example, like all men of genius illustrating a type, yet standing high above any other instance of that type. There are minds, like Shelley's, whose precocity is also accompanied by early production; but I doubt if this could have been so with De Quincey; for the very fact that he was to express a peculiar kind of childhood required that he should get a good distance away from it before beginning to make literature of it. His genius, in all its manifestations, depended largely on accumulation. He did not begin the account of his own early experience until he was thirty-seven years old, and did not finish it till he was sixty-five. His literary and historical essays equally demanded years of preparation, resting as they did on broad expanses of reading. Yet it remains true that he seems to have changed but little from what he was at the very first; and in the few notes of his earliest remembrances, given above, may be found the characteristics of his later career and of all his productions. The impassioned self-absorption of his first boyish griefs comes up again with a sort of volcanic outburst in his anguish at Kate Wordsworth's death. In the pathos that he felt at seeing crocuses in the spring, when less than two years old, and in that mingled dawn of the horror as well as the sweetness of life, even in his childhood of "divinest happiness," we find the germ of that immensely pregnant thought of his concerning the law of antipodal associations,—one thing suggesting its opposite: the luxury and peace of a summer morning, for example, bringing with it the

sense of desolation and death. This thought gives the pattern to almost all De Quincey's most valuable suggestions. They are generally based upon some such opposition to the prevalent and obvious idea, whatever it may be,—an opposition at first striking us as captious or eccentric, but by deft touches made reconcilable with some profounder reasoning than the usual one, and hence filling us with a delighted surprise, a perception of new harmony, when accepted. This is shown in the essay "On the Knocking at the Gate (in *Macbeth*)." At first blush it seems superfluous to explain *why* we should be impressed by the knocking; we know already that it is because we don't want Macbeth to be found out. But why do we wish him to be sheltered? Do we approve what he has done? De Quincey reminds us that murder "is an incident of coarse and vulgar horror," and that up to the moment of the knocking we sympathize with the murdered man; but this sudden alarm throws our sympathy on the murderer, and thus brings home to us an additional horror of the situation which had really been left out before. It is a simple piece of reasoning, but the sudden revelation of so nice a mechanism underlying what we supposed to be an impression needing no explanation pleases the intellect. In a similar way, the presentation of Judas Iscariot as a perfectly conscientious man, who sacrificed Jesus in attempting to force him to what he thought the good of Judæa, and hung himself in remorse for the wholly unforeseen result, is something which so appeals to our sense of mercy—harmonized as it is by De Quincey with the gospel narrative—that we cannot altogether reject it, though probably very few persons have accepted it in full. The essays on the Essenes have the same sort of movement, but are less successful, for the author works himself up to such a pitch of enthusiastic purpose to convince, that he threatens us: he declares that if we do not embrace his theory, we are responsible for leaving at large and rampant an argument entirely destructive to the received tradition of the origin of the Christian church. The truth is, that if we do not accept his theory we have a sufficient shelter in the possibility that the Essenes were not nearly so much like the Christians as he supposes. De Quincey delivers his premises, often, with such a captivating roulade of words that we have to look out sharply not to be misled; for—master of logic as he is, and frequently unanswerable—there is no writer of equal prominence who more readily disarms himself in his haste to rush into discussion, carry everything before him, and sit down to the enjoyment of a triumph afterwards. The essay "On War" is based on a very insufficient assumption that wars are always undertaken for the most trivial reasons; and dozens of instances might be collected from De Quincey's other writings to show how completely he can at times deceive himself, and perhaps his readers, by a faulty argument covered with plausible appeals, by timely and dazzling exhibitions of learning, or by ingenious and attractive side-issues that help him on to some conclusion which he never could have reached if he had pursued fairly the line he began upon. He had a dangerous conviction that he was almost never in the wrong. "I was right, as I usually am," he records, on one occasion; and on another: "In vain I sowed errors in my premises, or planted absurdities in my assumptions. Vainly I tried such blunders as putting four terms into a syllogism, which as all the world knows ought to run on three. . . . With disgust *I* saw, with disgust *he* saw, that too apparently the advantage lay with me in the result; and, whilst I worked like a dragon to place myself in the wrong, some fiend apparently so counterworked me that I" was always in the right. But in his published discussions De Quincey's efforts to be in the wrong are sometimes crowned with the most brilliant success. Conversant at once with the world of affairs and with letters, De Quincey recalls the double interests of Burke, though with a flexible and full-colored beauty of style which the statesman did not possess; but one might apply to him the converse of Macaulay's remark on Burke, that "he chose his side like a philosopher and defended it like a fanatic."

It is perhaps in some of his purely literary criticism that he is seen at his weakest. The article on Goethe, originally published in the *Encyclopædia Britannica*, is a harsh, one-sided condemnation which certainly culminates in a most inadequate inference. The three long essays on Pope seem to have been inspired by what De Quincey himself names the "sympathy of disgust." In them the writer raises, twice or thrice, a needless outcry about the "correctness" of Pope, and the "French school" in English literature. It cannot carry conviction when De Quincey says that even if an English author *should* have had his genius turned in a particular direction by happening to look into a French book, the mere fact that the French nation had gone in that direction first does not matter, because every nation has to pass through different periods in its literature, and the English would have come to this style sooner or later. Literary history would be a very simple thing if it could be disposed of in this way, and we should hardly need to discuss at all the relative influence of literary schools in different countries. But our opium-eater is still more unreasonable about Keats. Half of the short paper devoted to that poet is given up to disputing with Mr. Gilfillan the comparative laziness of authors, and the only part relating to Keats is a sharp expression of De Quincey's own distaste for *Endymion* and his equally decided admiration of *Hyperion*. He thinks it mysterious that one man should have written in two styles so unlike; but this does not move him to any respect for the mind that could master them both.

Yet, whatever his foibles, De Quincey possessed in a high degree that skill for finding a new point of view which establishes new conclusions on the same ground occupied by those he opposed. This faculty for running counter to received opinions is clearly traceable in his lighter passages. If humor is the perception of incongruous resemblances, and wit the discernment of amusing differences, then De Quincey would seem to be witty rather than humorous. But it is not his wit that we feel most. Take the clever inversion in "Murder as One of the Fine Arts": "For, if once a man indulges himself in murder, very soon he comes to think little of robbing; and from robbing he comes next to drink on the Sabbath, and from that to incivility and procrastination." In this and a hundred like instances the comic element is more humorous than witty; but fantastic exaggeration takes the lead in it. De Quincey is almost never broadly funny; the fantastic and grotesque cast of his humor gives it an echo that turns into solemnity. Now, this genius for taking a fresh start, for opposition and correction, which shows even through his humor, insured him originality; but it was originality depending immediately on something which had been prepared for him to restate. The story of Apelles and Protogenes seems to apply: given a very fine line by Protogenes, De Quincey as Apelles could draw one still better on the panel. He had such a taste for making distinctions that he sometimes took those of other men and set them forth as his own, with all that paraphernalia of impressiveness he so well knew how to use; though it is not to be supposed that he did so with any deceptive intent. As, in his own right, he may be called a *corrector* of views, so—as a delegate for others who had not given their ideas the best setting—he may be looked upon as a valuable *developer* of views. These are his two chief functions, aside from his interpretation of precocious child-life

and his magnificent narration of dreams. But this correcting tendency, united with a grim humor often taking the tone of whimsical irritation, with an arrogant sense of infallibility and with a love of displaying erudition, excites a natural opposition in some readers, and perhaps in all readers at some moments. "I do not know any instance in the writings of an author of note," writes Bryan Procter, "comprehending so much pedantry, pretension, and impertinence" as the *Reminiscences* and *Biographical Essays* of De Quincey. "They are all divergence." Procter was evidently annoyed at De Quincey's attempting to write Recollections of Charles Lamb, and intimates strongly that De Quincey pretended to an acquaintance with Lamb much beyond what he really had. But, though there is no doubt that Procter held the better authority to write of Lamb, and though the pompousness, the garrulity, and the querulousness that evidently troubled him are undeniable, I own to finding in De Quincey's fragmentary glimpses of Elia a charm entirely superior to that of the song-writer's somewhat cold and stiff biography. It is mainly a question of literary art: Procter was hampered by his indigent prose style, while De Quincey's sketch is full of delicious modulations of light and shade; and in it you feel the personality of Lamb reflected as his own quaint visage might be seen glimmering out from some half-dimmed mirror in the halls of memory. This power of bringing us so close,—as if we had met and described the men whom *he* describes,—gives a value to De Quincey's recollections of his literary acquaintance which will be even better appreciated by another generation than by our own.

The claim which De Quincey took the precaution to set up, that he had carried the composition of impassioned prose farther than any other man, may not be accepted by everybody, although Professor Masson has shown clearly how much foundation there is for it. The counter-claim of Jean Paul Richter can hardly be set aside merely on the ground that he did not understand "the law of the *too much*." But granting the undeniable achievements of De Quincey in majestically sonorous prose,—rolling with long cadences full of a profound music like that of the sea-rote,—we must also admit that these impassioned bursts are of brief duration, and that there are wide intervals in which none of this preeminent power is found. The essay on "Style," by an unhappy coincidence, does not contain in all its hundred and fifty pages a single piece of signally good writing, and is full of clumsy passages, the best conceivable examples of some of those faults which the essay itself condemns; and De Quincey's use of slang has been justly criticised. In many of the compositions, of course, there is no occasion for the highest flight of eloquence; but in the *Essays in Philosophy*, in the *Christianity and Paganism in the Eighteenth Century*, and in the *Literary Criticism*, there is often a tedious diffuseness. If De Quincey can burnish words until they shine like gold, and chafe his page until it breaks into fire, he is equally apt to obliterate all sense and beauty with an emmollescent gush of foolishness, erroneously supposed to be humor. But we could probably not have had De Quincey's uniquely splendid or amusing triumphs in writing, without those failings which at other times make his productions so empty of everything we should like them to contain. The impulsiveness and sensibility that give him wings for exceptional flights seem at unfavorable times to hold him down and cause him to wander this way and that, until his mind, though always making for a single objective point, has run off into a maze of subdivisions and correlated thoughts intricate as the channels at the Delta of the Ganges.

It is partly these defects that have caused De Quincey to be underrated and looked upon too much as an opium-dreamer and an entertaining but somewhat superfluous essayist. Still other facts have prevented his acquiring an influence or following like those of Carlyle or Macaulay; namely, that he heads no great tendency and does not concentrate himself sufficiently upon any one subject to become a popular authority; that he always speaks with exacting positiveness, yet in some things flatly contradicts himself; and that—although a wide reader and well-furnished scholar—he has an unfortunate way of parading his accomplishments which gives him an appearance of something like quackery. He indulges also in vagaries that detract from his character for solidity. The papers on "Murder" and the account of "Three Memorable Murders" do not supply an excuse for their being as plausible as that of Carlyle's equally extravagant though symbolic *Sartor Resartus*; they are morbid. *Klosterheim* and "The Household Wreck" have probably weakened rather than helped De Quincey's reputation, though they are stories that must be read to the end, and in their unrelieved gloom are very impressive as well as oppressive. There is a difficulty about this group among his compositions, that in distracting his attention from graver themes he appears to be letting himself down to a sort of elaborate trifling, merely to secure popularity. "The Spanish Nun" has always seemed to me an intolerably prolonged exhibition of over-conscious skill and excessive mannerism, though perhaps not more so than Carlyle's account of Cagliostro; and the discovery by somebody that "The Flight of a Tartar Tribe" was derived largely from a German writer throws discredit on all these foreign concoctions. Peter Bayne appears to have had full faith that had De Quincey carried out his proposed philosophic work, *De Emendatione Humani Intellectûs*,—observe, even here he was going to correct and emend,—the result would have been of great permanent value. But the *Essays in Philosophy* actually prepared by De Quincey amount to almost nothing in the way of thinking. They are for the most part made up of rambling talk about Sir William Hamilton as De Quincey had seen and known him, a condensation from a Life of Kant, and "Letters to a Young Man," on education, with very slight bearings on philosophy. The best of these essays is that "On Suicide," in which it is proposed to measure degrees in self-murder, as we distinguish between manslaughter and murder.

English literature, in its remarkable succession of essayists from Cowley to Addison and from Addison to Johnson, Goldsmith, Macaulay, and Carlyle, continually presents to us instances of the union of literary and intellectual exercise with a striving towards the plane of imaginative production. In some instances this has been much more than a striving, as in Goldsmith's *Deserted Village* and *Vicar*, or in Macaulay's vigorous *Lays of Ancient Rome*. Carlyle, like Macaulay, comes under the head both of essayist and of historian, and his non-literary essays, his translations from the German, and *Sartor Resartus* establish a strong and sympathetic connection with the creative order of writing. The relative calibres of Macaulay and Carlyle can be gauged very well in their essays on history. Macaulay, accepting conveniently the definition that "history is philosophy teaching by experience," enters at once into a brilliant review of the different kinds of history, or rather the different modes of presenting it. Carlyle, wanting the clear, cool, levigate phraseology of his lordship, takes up the very same definition with which Macaulay began, pulls it loftily to pieces, and—with oracular obscurity yet unsurpassable depth and comprehension—shows us what *really are* the different kinds of history, and that they by no means depend for their virtue on the mere manner or crust with which Macaulay was so busy. From the historical studies which De Quincey

left,—the *Cæsars*, "Greece under the Romans," and so forth, —we can guess that if *he* had begun an essay on history in general with a quotation of the phrase "philosophy teaching by experience," his whole paper would have been devoted to a discussion of that one thing, with copious illustrations, long reaches backwards and forwards, amusing digressions, learned allusions, and subtilizing foot-notes. We might not, in reading it, have advanced very perceptibly; but we should have been entertained, brightened, should have received many hints, each of some value, and have found ourselves at the close much encouraged and assisted to think further. The very fact that De Quincey often calls forth his reader's opposition gives his rambling reflections a tonic efficacy.

All three of these essayists have copious and special learning, but vary amazingly among themselves in style and trend. Macaulay is the polished master of the superficial and the becoming, Carlyle the stern seeker of truthful outlines, and De Quincey the Apelles, again, who can put a line between those of the other two, which often for some nicety of æsthetic instinct will in that way be finer and more skillful than theirs. He possesses, besides, a style by many degrees more pliant than either Macaulay's or Carlyle's; and no other author has put the best qualities of conversation into printed form on so vast a scale as De Quincey. In this he altogether surpasses, for variety, agreeableness, and insight, the conversationist of that older trio composed of Johnson, Addison, and Goldsmith. He has sounded so many depths of feeling, risen to so many heights of perception, and explored so many wide areas and dim by-paths of knowledge that he is surely entitled to a place with Carlyle and Macaulay in a modern trio of great essayists, which will probably in due time be universally held to include the name of Thomas De Quincey.

GEORGE SAINTSBURY
From "De Quincey" (1890)
Collected Essays and Papers
1923, Volume 1, pp. 210–35

In not a few respects the literary lot of Thomas De Quincey, both during his life and after it, has been exceedingly peculiar. In one respect it has been unique. I do not know that any other author of anything like his merit, during our time, has had a piece of work published for fully twenty years as his, only for it to be excluded as somebody else's at the end of that time. Certainly *The Traditions of the Rabbins* was very De Quinceyish; indeed, it was so De Quinceyish that the discovery, after such a length of time, that it was not De Quincey's at all, but "Salathiel" Croly's, must have given unpleasant qualms to more than one critic accustomed to be positive on internal evidence. But if De Quincey had thus attributed to him work that was not his, he has also had the utmost difficulty in getting attributed to him, in any accessible form, work that was his own. Three, or nominally four, editions—one in the decade of his death, superintended for the most part by himself; another in 1862, whose blue coat and white labels dwell in the fond memory; and another in 1878 (reprinted in 1880) a little altered and enlarged, with the *Rabbins* turned out and more soberly clad, but identical in the main—put before the British public for some thirty-five years a certain portion of his strange, long-delayed, but voluminous work. This work had occupied him for about the same period, that is to say for the last and shorter half of his extraordinary and yet uneventful life. Now, after much praying of readers, and grumbling of critics, we have a fifth and definitive edition from the English critic who has given most attention to De Quincey, Professor Masson[1].

Will readers of it form a different estimate from that which those of us who have known the older editions for a quarter of a century have formed, and will that estimate, if it is different, be higher or lower? To answer such questions is always difficult; but it is especially difficult here, for a certain reason which I had chiefly in mind when I said just now that De Quincey's literary lot has been very peculiar. I believe that I am not speaking for myself only; I am quite sure that I am speaking my own deliberate opinion when I say that on scarcely any English writer is it so hard to strike a critical balance—to get a clear definite opinion that you can put on the shelf and need merely take down now and then to be dusted and polished up by a fresh reading—as on De Quincey. This is partly due to the fact that his merits are of the class that appeals to, while his faults are of the class that is excused by, the average boy who has some interest in literature. To read the "Essay on Murder," the *English Mail Coach*, "The Spanish Nun," *The Cæsars*, and half a score other things at the age of about fifteen or sixteen is, or ought to be, to fall in love with them. And there is nothing more unpleasant for *les âmes bien nées*, as the famous distich has it, than to find fault in after life with that with which you have fallen in love at fifteen or sixteen. Yet most unfortunately, just as De Quincey's merits, or some of them, appeal specially to youth, and his defects specially escape the notice of youth, so age with stealing steps especially claws those merits into his clutch and leaves the defects exposed to derision. The most gracious state of authors is that they shall charm at all ages those whom they do charm. There are others—Dante, Cervantes, Goethe are instances—as to whom you may even begin with a little aversion, and go on to love them more and more. De Quincey, I fear, belongs to a third class, with whom it is difficult to keep up the first love, or rather whose defects begin before long to urge themselves upon the critical lover (some would say there are no critical lovers, but that I deny) with an even less happy result than is recorded in one of Catullus's finest lines. This kind of discovery

> Cogit amare *minus, nec* bene velle *magis.*

How and to what extent this is the case, it must be the business of this paper to attempt to show. ⟨. . .⟩

For pure rigmarole, for stories, as Mr Chadband has it, "of a cock and of a bull, and of a lady and of a half-crown," few things, even in De Quincey, can exceed, and nothing out of De Quincey can approach, the passages about the woman he met on the "cop" at Chester, and about the Greek letter that he did not send to the Bishop of Bangor, in the preliminary part of the *Confessions*. The first is the more teasing, because with a quite elvish superfluity of naughtiness he has here indulged in a kind of double rigmarole about the woman and the "bore" in the river, and flits from one to the other, and from the other to the one (his main story standing still the while), for half a dozen pages, till the reader feels as Coleridge's auditors must have felt when he talked about "Ball and Bell, Bell and Ball." But the Greek letter episode, or rather, the episode about the Greek letter which never was written, is, if possible, more flagrantly rigmarolish. The-cop-and-bore-and-woman digres-sion contains some remarkable description as a kind of solace to the Puck-led traveller; the other is bare of any such comfort. The Bishop's old housekeeper, who was De Quincey's land-lady, told him, it seems, that the Bishop had cautioned her against taking in lodgers whom she did not know, and De Quincey was very angry. As he thought he could write Greek

much better than the Bishop, he meditated expostulation in that language. He did not expostulate, but he proceeds instead to consider the possible effect on the Bishop if he had. There was a contemporary writer whom we can imagine struck by a similar whimsy: but Charles Lamb would have given us the Bishop and himself "quite natural and distinct" in a dozen lines, and then have dropped the subject, leaving our sides aching with laughter, and our appetites longing for more. De Quincey tells us at great length who the Bishop was, and how he was the Head of Brasenose, with some remarks on the relative status of Oxford Colleges. Then he debates the pros and cons on the question whether the Bishop would have answered the letter or not, with some remarks on the difference between strict scholarship and the power of composing in a dead language. He rises to real humour in the remark, that as "Methodists swarmed in Carnarvonshire," he "could in no case have found pleasure in causing mortification" to the Bishop, even if he had vanquished him. By this time we have had some three pages of it, and could well, especially with this lively touch to finish, accept them, though they be something tedious, supposing the incident to be closed. The treacherous author leads us to suppose that it is closed; telling us how he left Bangor, and went to Carnarvon, which change gradually drew his thoughts away from the Bishop. So far is this from being the case, that he goes back to that Reverend Father, and for two mortal pages more, speculates further what would happen if he had written to the Bishop, what the Bishop would have said, whether he would not have asked him (De Quincey) to the Palace, whether, in his capacity of Head of a House, he would not have welcomed him to that seat of learning, and finally smoothed his way to a fellowship. By which time, one is perfectly sick of the Bishop, and of these speculations on the might-have-been, which are indeed by no means unnatural, being exactly what every man indulges in now and then in his own case, which, in conversation, would not be unpleasant, but which, gradually and diffusedly set down in a book, and interrupting a narrative, are most certainly "rigmarole."

Rigmarole, however, can be a very agreeable thing in its way, and De Quincey has carried it to a point of perfection never reached by any other rigmaroler. Despite his undoubted possession of a kind of humour, it is a very remarkable thing that he rigmaroles, so far as can be made out by the application of the most sensitive tests, quite seriously, and almost, if not quite, unconsciously. These digressions or deviations are studded with quips and jests, good, bad, and indifferent. But the writer never seems to suspect that his own general attitude is at least susceptible of being made fun of. It is said, and we can very well believe it, that he was excessively annoyed at Lamb's delightful parody of his *Letters to a Young Man Whose Education Has Been Neglected*; and, on the whole, I should say that no great man of letters in the century, except Balzac and Victor Hugo, was so insensible to the ludicrous aspect of his own performances. This in the author of the "Essay on Murder" may seem surprising, but, in fact, there are few things of which there are so many subdivisions, or in which the subdivisions are marked off from each other by such apparently impermeable lines, as humour. If I may refine a little I should say that there was very frequently, if not generally, a humorous basis for these divagations of De Quincey's; but that he almost invariably lost sight of that basis, and proceeded to reason quite gravely away from it, in what is (not entirely with justice) called the scholastic manner. How much of this was due to the influence of Jean Paul and the other German humorists of the last century, with whom he became acquainted very early, I should not like to say. I confess that my own enjoyment of

Richter, which has nevertheless been considerable, has always been lessened by the presence in him, to a still greater degree, of this same habit of quasi-serious divagation. To appreciate the mistake of it, it is only necessary to compare the manner of Swift. The *Tale of a Tub* is in appearance as daringly discursive as anything can be, but the author in the first place never loses his way, and in the second never fails to keep a watchful eye on himself, lest he should be getting too serious or too tedious. That is what Richter and De Quincey fail to do.

Yet though these drawbacks are grave, and though they are (to judge from my own experience) felt more seriously at each successive reading, most assuredly no man who loves English literature could spare De Quincey from it; most assuredly all who love English literature would sooner spare some much more faultless writers. Even that quality of his which has been already noted, his extraordinary attraction for youth, is a singular and priceless one. The Master of the Court of the Gentiles, or the Instructor of the Sons of the Prophets, he might be called in a fantastic nomenclature, which he would have himself appreciated, if it had been applied to any one but himself. What he somewhere calls his "extraordinary ignorance of daily life" does not revolt youth. His little pedantries, which to the day of his death were like those of a clever schoolboy, appeal directly to it. His best fun is quite intelligible; his worst not wholly uncongenial. His habit (a certain most respected professor[2] in a northern university may recognise the words) of "getting into logical coaches and letting himself be carried on without minding where he is going" is anything but repugnant to brisk minds of seventeen. They are quite able to comprehend the great if mannered beauty of his finest style—the style, to quote his own words once more, as of "an elaborate and pompous sunset." Such a schoolmaster to bring youths of promise, not merely to good literature but to the best, nowhere else exists. But he is much more than a mere schoolmaster, and in order that we may see what he is, it is desirable first of all to despatch two other objections made to him from different quarters, and on different lines of thought. The one objection (I should say that I do not fully espouse either of them) is that he is an untrustworthy critic of books; the other is that he is a very spiteful commentator on men.

This latter charge has found wide acceptance and has been practically corroborated and endorsed by persons as different as Southey and Carlyle. It would not in any case concern us much, for when a man is once dead it matters uncommonly little whether he was personally unamiable or not. But I think that De Quincey has in this respect been hardly treated. He led such a wholly unnatural life, he was at all times and in all places so thoroughly excluded from the natural contact and friction of society, that his utterances hardly partake of the ordinary character of men's speech. In the "vacant interlunar caves" where he hid himself, he could hardly feel the restraints that press on those who move within ear-shot and jostle of their fellows on this actual earth. This is not a triumphant defence, no doubt; but I think it is a defence. And further, it has yet to be proved that De Quincey set down anything in malice. He called his literary idol, Wordsworth, "inhumanly arrogant." (Does anybody—not being a Wordsworthian and therefore out of reach of reason—doubt that Wordsworth's arrogance was inhuman?) He, not unprovoked by scant gratitude on Coleridge's part for very solid services, and by a doubtless sincere but rather unctuous protest of his brother in opium-eating against the *Confessions*, told some home truths against that magnificent genius but most unsatisfactory man. A sort of foolish folk has recently arisen which tells us that because Coleridge wrote *The Ancient Mariner* and

Kubla Khan, he was quite entitled to leave his wife and children to be looked after by anybody who chose, to take stipends from casual benefactors, and to scold, by himself or by his next friend Mr Wordsworth, other benefactors, like Thomas Poole, who were not prepared at a moment's notice to give him a hundred pounds for a trip to the Azores. The rest of us, though we may feel no call to denounce Coleridge for these proceedings, may surely hold that *The Ancient Mariner* and *Kubla Khan* are no defence to the particular charges. I do not see that De Quincey said anything worse of Coleridge than any man who knew the then little, but now well-known facts of Coleridge's life, was entitled to say if he chose. And so in other cases. That he was what is called a thoughtful person—that is to say that he ever said to himself, "Will what I am writing give pain, and ought I to give that pain?"—I do not allege. In fact, the very excuse which has been made for him above is inconsistent with it. He always wrote far too much as one in another planet for anything of the kind to occur to him, and he was perhaps for a very similar reason rather too fond of the "personal talk" which Wordsworth wisely disdained. But that he was in any proper sense spiteful, that is to say that he ever wrote either with a deliberate intention to wound or with a deliberate indifference whether he wounded or not, I do not believe.

The other charge, that he was a bad or rather a very untrustworthy critic of books, cannot be met quite so directly. He is indeed responsible for a singularly large number of singularly grave critical blunders—by which I mean of course not critical opinions disagreeing with my own, but critical opinions which the general consent of competent critics, on the whole, negatives. The minor classical writers are not much read now, but there must be a sufficient jury to whom I can appeal to know what is to be done with a professed critic of style—at least asserting himself to be no mean classical scholar—who declares that "Paganism had no more brilliant master of composition to show than"—Velleius Paterculus! Suppose this to be a mere fling or freak, what is to be thought of a man who evidently sets Cicero, as a writer, if not as a thinker, above Plato? It would be not only possible but easy to follow this up with a long list of critical enormities on De Quincey's part, enormities due not to accidental and casual crotchet or prejudice, as in Hazlitt's case, but apparently to some perverse idiosyncrasy. I doubt very much, though the doubt may seem horribly heretical to some people, whether De Quincey really cared much for poetry as poetry. He liked philosophical poets:—Milton, Wordsworth, Shakespeare (inasmuch as he perceived Shakespeare to be the greatest of philosophical poets), Pope even in a certain way. But read the interesting paper which late in life he devoted to Shelley. He treats Shelley as a man admirably, with freedom alike from the maudlin sentiment of our modern chatterers and from Puritanical preciseness. He is not too hard on him in any way, he thinks him a pleasing personality and a thinker distorted but interesting. Of Shelley's strictly poetical quality he says nothing, if he knew or felt anything. In fact, of lyrical poetry generally, that is to say of poetry in its most purely poetical condition, he speaks very little in all his extensive critical dissertations. His want of appreciation of it may supply explanation of his unpardonable treatment of Goethe. That he should have maltreated *Wilhelm Meister* is quite excusable. There are fervent admirers of Goethe at his best who acknowledge most fully the presence in *Wilhelm* of the two worst characteristics of German life and literature, bad taste and tediousness. But it is not excusable that much later, and indeed at the very height of his literary powers and practice, he should have written the article in the *Encyclopædia Britannica* on the author of *Faust*, of *Egmont*, and above all of the shorter poems. Here he deliberately assents to the opinion that *Werther* is "superior to everything that came after it, and for mere power, Goethe's paramount work," dismisses *Faust* as something that "no two people have ever agreed about," sentences *Egmont* as "violating the historic truth of character," and mentions not a single one of those lyrics, unmatched, or rather only matched by Heine, in the language, by which Goethe first gave German rank with the great poetic tongues. His severity on Swift is connected with his special "will-worship" of ornate style, of which more presently, and in general it may be said that De Quincey's extremely logical disposition of mind was rather a snare to him in his criticism. He was constantly constructing general principles and then arguing downwards from them; in which case woe to any individual fact or person that happened to get in the way. Where Wilson, the "only intimate male friend I have had" (as he somewhere says with a half-pathetic touch of self-illumination more instructive than reams of imaginative autobiography), went wrong from not having enough of general principle, where Hazlitt went wrong from letting prejudices unconnected with the literary side of the matter blind his otherwise piercing literary sight, De Quincey fell through an unswervingness of deduction more French than English. Your ornate writer must be better than your plain one, *ergo*, let us say, Cicero must be better than Swift.

One other curious weakness of his (which has been glanced at already) remains to be noticed. This is the altogether deplorable notion of jocularity which he only too often exhibits. Mr Masson, trying to propitiate the enemy, admits that "to address the historian Josephus as 'Joe,' through a whole article, and give him a black eye into the bargain, is positively profane." I am not sure as to the profanity, knowing nothing particularly sacred about Josephus. But if Mr Masson had called it excessively silly, I should have agreed heartily; and if any one else denounced it as a breach of good literary manners, I do not know that I should protest. The habit is the more curious in that all authorities agree as to the exceptional combination of scholarliness and courtliness which marked De Quincey's colloquial style and expression. Wilson's daughter, Mrs Gordon, says that he used to address her father's cook "as if she had been a duchess"; and that the cook, though much flattered, was somewhat aghast at his *punctilio*. That a man of this kind should think it both allowable and funny to talk of Josephus as "Joe," and of Magliabecchi as "Mag," may be only a new example of that odd law of human nature which constantly prompts people in various relations of life, and not least in literature, to assume most the particular qualities (not always virtues or graces) that they have not. Yet it is fair to remember that Wilson and the *Blackwood* set, together with not a few writers in the *London Magazine*—the two literary coteries in connection with whom De Quincey started as a writer—had deliberately imported this element of horse-play into literature, that it at least did not seem to interfere with their popularity, and that De Quincey himself, after 1830, lived too little in touch with actual life to be aware that the style was becoming as unfashionable as it had always, save on very exceptional subjects, been ungraceful. Even on Wilson, who was to the manner born of riotous spirits, it often sits awkwardly; in De Quincey's case it is, to borrow Sir Walter's admirable simile in another case, like "the forced impudence of a bashful man." Grim humour he can manage admirably, and he also—as in the passage about the fate which waited upon all who possessed anything which might be convenient to

Wordsworth, if they died—can manage a certain kind of sly humour not much less admirably. But "Joe" and "Mag," and, to take another example, the stuff about Catalina's "crocodile papa" in "The Spanish Nun," are neither grim nor sly, they are only puerile. His staunchest defender asks, "why De Quincey should not have the same license as Swift and Thackeray?" The answer is quick and crushing. Swift and Thackeray justify their license by their use of it; De Quincey does not. After which it is hardly necessary to add, though this is almost final in itself, that neither Swift nor Thackeray interlards perfectly and unaffectedly serious work with mere fooling of the "Joe" and "Mag" kind. Swift did not put *mollis abuti* in the "Four Last Years of Queen Anne," nor Thackeray his *Punch* jokes in the death-scene of Colonel Newcome. I can quite conceive De Quincey doing both.

And now I have done enough in the fault-finding way, and nothing shall induce me to say another word of De Quincey in this article save in praise. For praise he himself gives the amplest occasion; he might almost remain unblamed altogether if his praisers had not been frequently unwise, and if his *exemplar* were not specially *vitiis imitabile*. Few English writers have touched so large a number of subjects with such competence both in information and in power of handling. Still fewer have exhibited such remarkable logical faculty. One main reason why one is sometimes tempted to quarrel with him is that his play of fence is so excellent that one longs to cross swords. For this and for other reasons no writer has a more stimulating effect, or is more likely to lead his readers on to explore and to think for themselves. In none is that incurable curiosity, that infinite variety of desire for knowledge and for argument which age cannot quench, more observable. Few if any have the indefinable quality of freshness in so large a measure. You never quite know, though you may have a shrewd suspicion, what De Quincey will say on any subject; his gift of sighting and approaching new facets of it is so immense. Whether he was in truth as accomplished a classical scholar as he claimed to be I do not know; he has left few positive documents to tell us. But I should think that he was, for he has all the characteristics of a scholar of the best and rarest kind—the scholar who is exact as to language without failing to comprehend literature, and competent in literature without being slipshod as to language. His historical insight, of which the famous *Cæsars* is the best example, was, though sometimes coloured by his fancy, and at other times distorted by a slight tendency to *supercherie* as in "The Tartars" and "The Spanish Nun," wonderfully powerful and acute. He was not exactly as Southey was, "omnilegent"; but in his own departments, and they were numerous, he went farther below the surface and connected his readings together better than Southey did. Of the two classes of severer study to which he specially addicted himself, his political economy suffered perhaps a little, acute as his views in it often are, from the fact that in his time it was practically a new study, and that he had neither sufficient facts nor sufficient literature to go upon. In metaphysics, to which he gave himself up for years, and in which he seems really to have known whatever there was to know, I fear that the opium fiend cheated the world of something like masterpieces. Only three men during De Quincey's lifetime had anything like his powers in this department. Of these three men, Sir William Hamilton either could not or would not write English. Ferrier could and did write English; but he could not, as De Quincey could, throw upon philosophy the play of literary and miscellaneous illustration which of all the sciences it most requires, and which all its really supreme exponents have been able to give it. Mansel could do both these things; but he was somewhat indolent, and had many avocations. De Quincey could write perfect English, he had every resource of illustration and relief at command, he was in his way as "brazen-bowelled" at work as he was "golden-mouthed" at expression, and he had ample leisure. But the inability to undertake sustained labour, which he himself recognises as the one unquestionable curse of opium, deprived us of an English philosopher who would have stood as far above Kant in exoteric graces, as he would have stood above Bacon in esoteric value. It was not entirely De Quincey's fault. It seems to be generally recognised now that whatever occasional excesses he may have committed, opium was really required in his case, and gave us what we have as much as it took away what we have not. But if any one chose to write in the antique style a debate between Philosophy, Tar-water, and Laudanum, it would be almost enough to put in the mouth of Philosophy, "This gave me Berkeley and that deprived me of De Quincey."

De Quincey is, however, first of all a writer of ornate English, which was never, with him, a mere cover to bare thought. Overpraise and mispraise him as anybody may, he cannot be overpraised for this. Mistake as he chose to do, and as others have chosen to do, the relative value of his gift, the absolute value of it is unmistakable. What other Englishman, from Sir Thomas Browne downwards, has written a sentence surpassing in melody that on Our Lady of Sighs: "And her eyes, if they were ever seen, would be neither sweet nor subtle; no man could read their story; they would be found filled with perishing dreams and with wrecks of forgotten delirium"? Compare that with the masterpieces of some later practitioners. There are no out-of-the-way words; there is no needless expense of adjectives; the sense is quite adequate to the sound; the sound is only what is required as accompaniment to the sense. And though I do not know that in a single instance of equal length—even in the still more famous, and as a whole justly more famous, *tour de force* on Our Lady of Darkness— De Quincey ever quite equalled the combined simplicity and majesty of this phrase, he has constantly come close to it. The *Suspiria* are full of such passages—there are even some who prefer *Savannah la Mar* to the *Ladies of Sorrow*. Beautiful as it is I do not, because the accursed superfluous adjective appears there. The famous passages of the *Confessions* are in every one's memory; and so I suppose is the "Vision of Sudden Death." Many passages in *The Cæsars*, though somewhat less florid, are hardly less good; and the close of "Joan of Arc" is as famous as the most ambitious attempts of the *Confessions* and the *Mail Coach*. Moreover, in all the sixteen volumes, specimens of the same kind may be found here and there, alternating with very different matter; so much so, that it has no doubt often occurred to readers that the author's occasional divergence into questionable quips and cranks is a deliberate attempt to set off his rhetoric, as dramatists of the noblest school have often set off their tragedy, with comedy, if not with farce. That such a principle would imply confusion of the study and the stage is arguable enough, but it does not follow that it was not present. At any rate the contrast, deliberate or not, is very strong indeed in De Quincey—stronger than in any other prose author except his friend, and pupil rather than master, Wilson.

The great advantage that De Quincey has, not only over this friend of his but over all practitioners of the ornate style in the century, lies in his sureness of hand in the first place, and secondly in the comparative frugality of means which perhaps is an inseparable accompaniment of sureness of hand. To mention living persons would be invidious; but Wilson and Landor are within the most scrupulous critic's right of comparison. All three were contemporaries; all three were Oxford men—Landor about ten years senior to the other two—and all three in their different ways set themselves deliberately to reverse the practice of English prose for nearly a century and a half. They did great things, but De Quincey did, I think, the greatest and certainly the most classical in the proper sense, for all Landor's superior air of Hellenism. Voluble as De Quincey often is, he seems always to have felt that when you are in your altitudes it is well not to stay there too long. And his flights, while they are far more uniformly high than Wilson's, which alternately soar and drag, are much more merciful in regard of length than Landor's, as well as for the most part much more closely connected with the sense of his subjects. There is scarcely one of the *Imaginary Conversations* which would not be the better for very considerable thinning, while, with the exception perhaps of *The English Mail Coach*, De Quincey's surplusage, obvious enough in many cases, is scarcely ever found in his most elaborate and ornate passages. The total amount of such passages in the *Confessions* is by no means large, and the more ambitious parts of the *Suspiria* do not much exceed a dozen pages. De Quincey was certainly justified by his own practice in adopting and urging as he did the distinction, due, he says, to Wordsworth, between the common and erroneous idea of style as the *dress* of thought, and the true definition of it as the *incarnation* of thought. The most wizened of coxcombs may spend days and years in dressing up his meagre and ugly carcass; but few are the sons of men who have sufficient thought to provide the soul of any considerable series of avatars. De Quincey had; and therefore, though the manner (with certain exceptions heretofore taken) in him is always worth attention, it never need or should divert attention from the matter. And thus he was not driven to make a little thought do tyrannous duty as lay-figure for an infinite amount of dress, or to hang out frippery on a clothes-line with not so much as a lay-figure inside it. Even when he is most conspicuously "fighting a prize," there is always solid stuff in him.

Few indeed are the writers of whom so much can be said, and fewer still the miscellaneous writers, among whom De Quincey must be classed. On almost any subject that interested him—and the number of such subjects was astonishing, curious as are the gaps between the different groups of them— what he has to say is pretty sure, even if it be the wildest paradox in appearance, to be worth attending to. And in regard to most things that he has to say, the reader may be pretty sure also that he will not find them better said elsewhere. It has sometimes been complained by students, both of De Quincey the man and of De Quincey the writer, that there is something not exactly human in him. There is certainly much in him of the dæmonic, to use a word which was a very good word and really required in the language, and which ought not to be exiled because it has been foolishly abused. Sometimes, as has also been complained, the demon is a mere familiar with the tricksiness of Puck rather than the lightness of Ariel. But far oftener he is a more potent spirit than any Robin Goodfellow, and as powerful as Ariel and Ariel's master. Trust him wholly you may not; a characteristic often noted in intelligences that are neither exactly human, nor exactly diabolic, nor exactly divine. But he will do great things for you, and a little wit and courage on your part will prevent his doing anything serious against you. To him, with much greater justice than to Hogg, might Wilson have applied the nickname of Brownie, which he was so fond of bestowing upon the author of *Kilmeny*. He will do solid work, conjure up a concert of aerial music, play a shrewd trick now and then, and all this with a curious air of irresponsibility and of remoteness of nature. In ancient days when kings played experiments to ascertain the universal or original language, some monarch might have been tempted to take a very clever child, interest him so far as possible in nothing but books and opium, and see whether he would turn out anything like De Quincey. But it is in the highest degree improbable that he would. Therefore let us rejoice, though

according to the precepts of wisdom and not too indiscriminately, in our De Quincey as we once, and probably once for all, received him.

Notes
1. *The Collected Writings of Thomas de Quincey*; edited by David Masson. In fourteen volumes; Edinburgh, 1889–90.
2. Edward Caird, afterwards Master of Balliol.

WILLIAM H. PRESCOTT

1796–1859

William Hickling Prescott was born in Salem, Massachusetts, on May 4, 1796, into a distinguished family prominent in Colonial history. Shortly after he entered Harvard in 1811, an injury caused the loss of sight in his left eye; an infection later weakened his other eye and he was left virtually blind. He nevertheless excelled in his studies and determined at an early age to pursue a literary career.

Prescott's intensive study of Spanish history led to the publication in 1837 of the *History of the Reign of Ferdinand and Isabella, the Catholic*, a three-volume work. His major work, *The History of the Conquest of Mexico*, appeared in 1843; it continues to be one of the most distinguished historical accounts written in English. His *History of the Conquest of Peru* was published in 1847. Prescott's last major work was the *History of the Reign of Philip the Second, King of Spain*, but he died before its completion, on January 28, 1859.

Prescott's storytelling ability combined with his devotion to historical truth gave his books a wide readership. Later historians have noted several minor errors in his accounts of Mexico and Peru, but he is nevertheless still highly regarded. A twenty-two volume edition of Prescott's works, edited by W. H. Munro, was published in 1904.

Personal

This morning, as I was sitting at breakfast, a gentleman on horseback sent up word that I should come down to him. It was Prescott, author of *Ferdinand and Isabella*. He is an early riser and rides about the country. There on his horse sat the *great author*. He is one of the best fellows in the world, and much my friend; handsome, gay, and forty; a great diner-out; gentle, companionable, and modest; quite astonished to find himself so famous.—HENRY WADSWORTH LONGFELLOW, Letter to George W. Greene (Oct. 22, 1838), cited in Samuel Longfellow, *Life of Henry Wadsworth Longfellow*, 1891, Vol. 1, p. 300

The *Niagara* steamer arrived this morning from Liverpool. In her came passenger William H. Prescott, our eminent historian, and excellent good fellow. I had a visit from him this morning at my office. He returns in good health and excellent spirits, after an absence of five months, during which time the greatest respect and attention were paid to him by the distinguished people of England, from the Queen down; as an evidence of which he told me (but without any vainglorious boasting) that he had, during his sojourn in London, twelve dinner invitations for one day. These highly merited compliments reflect equal honor on both parties.—PHILIP HONE, *Diary*, Sept. 27, 1850

Yes, it was your letter which first told me of Prescott's death. The next day I read it in the Paris papers. Taillandier announced it at the opening of his lecture. The current of grief and praise is everywhere unbroken. Perhaps no man, so much in people's mouths, was ever the subject of so little unkindness. How different his fate from that of others! Something of that

immunity which he enjoyed in life must be referred to his beautiful nature, in which enmity could not live. This death touches me much. You remember that my relations with him had for years been of peculiar intimacy. Every return to Boston has always been consecrated by an evening with him. I am sad to think of my own personal loss. There is a charm taken from Boston.—CHARLES SUMNER, Letter to Henry Wadsworth Longfellow (March 4, 1859), cited in Edward L. Pierce, *Memoir and Letters of Charles Sumner*, 1893, Vol. 3, p. 597

Mr. Prescott was a true son of Boston; well-born, well-bred, of extremely dignified and agreeable manners, and with a delicate and nobly chiselled face. He was a perfect man of the world, fond of society, and with not the slightest touch of the pedant about him. I saw him frequently and intimately at his Nahant house and at the neighboring villa of his daughter, Mrs. Lawrence, who was an admirable hostess as well as a beautiful woman. Although he was past sixty when I first met him, he was still as attractive as a man of thirty in dress and manner, and with the added delight of his extremely cultivated mind. His infirmity of sight did not prevent his getting about alone and eating his dinner with the grace of a diplomatist. If he asked any one for the toast or the cream at one of his daughter's delicious country teas, it was really a pleasantry and a compliment, and he could make his infirmity of sight a joke. If the cream-pitcher turned up under his hand, he would thank the finder and say, "If it had been a bear it would have bit me." He asked my husband and myself to his "workshop," as he called his library, and showed us the apparatus which is used by the blind—a wire-ruled machine for guiding the hand.—M. E. W. SHERWOOD, *An Epistle to Posterity*, 1897, pp. 117–18

General

Mr. Prescott is not a mannerist in his style, and does not deal in elaborate, antithetical, nicely balanced periods. His sentences are not cast in the same artificial mould, nor is there a perpetual recurrence of the same turns of expression, as in the writings of Johnson or Gibbon; nor have they that satin-like smoothness and gloss, for which Robertson is so remarkable. The dignified simplicity of his style is still further removed from any thing like pertness, smartness, or affectation; from tawdry gum-flowers of rhetoric, and brass-gilt ornaments; from those fantastic tricks with language, which bear the same relation to good writing that vaulting and tumbling do to walking. It is perspicuous, flexible, and natural; sometimes betraying a want of high finish, but always manly, always correct, never feeble, and never inflated. He does not darkly insinuate statements, or leave his reader to infer facts. Indeed, it may be said of his style, that it has no marked character at all. Without ever offending the mind or the ear, it has nothing that attracts observation to it, simply as a style. It is a transparent medium, through which we see the form and movement of the writer's mind. In this respect, we may compare it with the manners of a well-bred gentleman, which have nothing so peculiar as to awaken attention, and which, from their very ease and simplicity, enable the essential qualities of the understanding and character to be more clearly discerned. —GEORGE S. HILLARD, "Prescott's *History of the Conquest of Mexico*," *North American Review*, Jan. 1844, pp. 208–9

In history there has been nothing done to which the world at large has not been eager to award the full meed of its deserts. Mr. Prescott, for instance, has been greeted with as much warmth abroad as here. We are not disposed to undervalue his industry and power of clear and elegant arrangement. The richness and freshness of his materials is such that a sense of enchantment must be felt in their contemplation. We must regret, however, that they should have been first presented to the public by one who possesses nothing of the higher powers of the historian, great leading views, or discernment as to the motives of action and the spirit of an era. Considering the splendour of the materials the books are wonderfully tame, and every one must feel that having once passed through them and got the sketch in the mind, there is nothing else to which it will recur. The absence of thought, as to that great picture of Mexican life, with its heroisms, its terrible but deeply significant superstitions, its admirable civic refinement, seems to be quite unbroken.—MARGARET FULLER, "American Literature," *Papers on Literature and Art*, 1846

Mr. Prescott is undoubtedly entitled to a prominent place in the first rank of historians. With extraordinary industry he explores every source of information relating to his subjects, and with sagacity as remarkable decides between conflicting authorities and rejects improbable relations. His judgment of character is calm, comprehensive, and profoundly just. He enters into the midst of an age, and with all its influences about him, estimates its actors and its deeds. His arrangement of facts is always effective, and his style flowing, familiar, singularly transparent, and marked throughout with the most felicitous expressions.

Whatever may be the comparative merits of the two great histories he has already published, as intellectual efforts, there is little room to doubt that *The Conquest of Mexico* will continue to be the most popular. It is justly remarked in the *Edinburgh Review*, that, considered merely as a work of amusement, it will bear a favourable comparison with the best romances in the language. The careful, judicious, and comprehensive essay on the Aztec civilization, with which it opens, is not inferior in interest to the wonderful drama to which it is an epilogue. The scenery, which is sketched with remarkable vividness and accuracy, is wonderful, beautiful, and peculiar. The characters are various, strongly marked, and not more numerous than is necessary for the purposes of art. Cortez himself is a knight errant, "filled with the spirit of romantic enterprise," yet a skilful general, fruitful of resources, and of almost superhuman energies; of extraordinary cunning, but without any rectitude of judgment; a bigoted churchman, yet having no sympathy with virtue; of kind manners, but remorseless in his cruelties. His associates, Valasquez, Ordaz, Sandoval, Alvarado, the priest Olmedo, the heroine Doña Marina, and others of whom we have glimpses more or less distinct, seem to have been formed as well to fill their places in the written history, as to act their parts in the crusade. And the philosophical king of Tezcuco, and Montezuma, whose character and misfortunes are reflected in his mild and melancholy face, and Guatemozin, the last of the emperors, and other Aztecs, in many of the higher qualities of civilization superior to their invaders, and inferior in scarcely any thing but a knowledge of the art of war, are grouped and contrasted most effectively with such characters as are more familiar in the scenes of history.

The biographical and bibliographical information and criticism contained in notes and addenda to the different books of *Ferdinand and Isabella* and *The Conquest of Mexico*, form one of the most attractive of their features, and would alone sustain a high reputation for learning and judgment.

Mr. Prescott perhaps excels most in description and narration, but his histories combine in a high degree almost every merit that can belong to such works. They are pervaded by a truly and profoundly philosophical spirit, the more deserving of recognition because it is natural and unobtrusive, and are distinguished above all others for their uniform candour, a quality which might reasonably be demanded of an American writing of early European policy and adventure. —RUFUS W. GRISWOLD, "William H. Prescott," *The Prose Writers of America*, 1847, p. 373

Hardly nine years have passed since the publication of the *History of Ferdinand and Isabella* placed Mr. Prescott at once, by universal consent both in England and America, in the front rank of English historians. And what a golden account he has rendered of his labors during this brief period! Taking up the theme of Spanish discovery and conquest nearly where he had left it in his first work, passing by an easy transition from the story of Columbus to that of Cortés and the Pizarros, he has followed their track amid the virgin forests and gorgeous mountain scenery of the tropical regions of this continent, till he has reached the close of what may be called the heroic period of Spanish adventure in the settlement of America, and has left as little to be done by his successors as he had found accomplished by those who had preceded him in the enterprise. The subject of his last two histories, the conquest of Mexico and Peru, does not equal his earliest topic in splendor and variety, but is superior to it in freshness and abundance of romantic incident. It has the absorbing interest of a chivalrous legend or an Oriental tale, while it lacks the dignity and complexity of the vast subjects treated by Gibbon and Hume. The picturesque style of the old chroniclers is better adapted to it than the thoughtful manner and sharp analysis of the philosophical historian. It could not have fallen into better hands, therefore; for Mr. Prescott's temperament is more that of a poet than a philosopher. Seldom and unwillingly does he interrupt the clear and brilliant flow of the narrative, or the imposing trains of vivid description, to moralize or speculate upon the succession of events, or upon the characters of the personages who were concerned in them. He has skilfully preserved the romantic coloring which the old Spanish story-tellers gave to the incidents and scenes they described, and which is the more glowing as many of them are led to speak of their personal adventures, or of what their own eyes had witnessed.—FRANCIS BOWEN, "Prescott's *Conquest of Peru*," *North American Review*, Oct. 1847, pp. 366–67

We consider Prescott the most unobjectionable representative of that school of history, the ideal of which is correct and tasteful narrative. In other respects, he seems to us vastly overrated. We look in vain for that earnestness of purpose, that high and uncompromising tone of sentiment, that genuine love of humanity, which should distinguish the historian of the nineteenth century. Prescott is a kind of elegant trimmer in literature.—HENRY T. TUCKERMAN, *Characteristics of Literature*, 1849, p. 190

He has selected portions of history of great intrinsic attractiveness, and, by confining himself within their boundaries, has had ample room and verge enough to do them full justice,— has produced thoroughly elaborated and perfect pictures, that will hang for ever on the walls of the great temple of time. So true are they to fact, and so thoroughly wrought and finished, that subsequent artists will never attempt to improve upon them, but only aspire to rival them by executing equally faithful and beautiful portraitures of other great characters and events. In this way the history of nations, the careers of illustrious actors on the world's stage, and the decisive movements of society, will be preserved and delineated by innumerable writers, whose productions, taken together, will constitute an aggregate result far nobler and better than any one author could possibly achieve in a single comprehensive and extended work.—C. W. UPHAM, "Prescott as an Historian," *North American Review*, July 1856, p. 101

It has, I believe, been generally thought that Mr. Prescott's style reached its happiest development in his *Conquest of Mexico*. No doubt, a more exact finish prevails in many parts of the *Ferdinand and Isabella*, and a high authority has said that there are portions of *Philip the Second* written with a vigor as great as its author has anywhere shown. But the freshness and freedom of his descriptions in the *Mexico*, especially the descriptions of scenery, battles, and marches, are, I think, not found to the same degree in either of his other histories, and have rendered the style of that work singularly attractive. Certainly, it is a style well fitted to its romantic subject, although it may be one which it would have been adventurous or unwise to apply, in the same degree, to subjects from their nature more grave and philosophical.—GEORGE TICKNOR, *Life of William Hickling Prescott*, 1864, pp. 217–18

I have a notion that no one can reach the finest harmonies of style who has not a musical ear. Prescott had no music.—ROBERT C. WINTHROP, *Journal* (Nov. 17, 1880), cited in Robert C. Winthrop, Jr., *A Memoir of Robert C. Winthrop*, 1897, p. 303

The works of William H. Prescott, the most artistic historian to whom the United States have hitherto given birth, are remarkable from the difficulties under which they were produced, and for the well-deserved success which they have achieved. This success is due in part to the genius and indomitable industry of the writer, in part to the steady concentration of his powers on

the arduous undertaking of which he had, at an early age, formed a just estimate. In a diary of 1819 (that is in his twenty-fifth year), he allows ten years for preliminary studies, and ten more for the execution of his task, a notable example to his countrymen, nine-tenths of whose literary performances will prove ephemeral, less from lack of ability in the writers than from an utterly inadequate sense of the time and toil that the Muses demand of their votaries. *Ferdinand and Isabella*, given to the world in 1838, was written while Mr. Prescott was, owing to an accident at college, almost wholly deprived of his sight. His authorities in a foreign tongue were read to him by an assistant, and by aid of a writing-case for the blind he scrawled the pages of his great work. It soon attained a European as well as an American fame, and superseded all other records of the period of which it treats. No such comprehensive view of Spain at the zenith of her greatness has ever appeared in English. The proportion of its parts and the justice of its estimates are universally acknowledged, while hypercriticism of the style—graceful, correct, and sufficiently varied—can only point to the occasional possibility of greater condensation. Among the most notable of the descriptions, which can seldom be detached from the whole into which they are woven, we may refer to the return of Columbus, and the contrasted characters of Queens Isabella and Elizabeth. The *Conquest of Mexico* (written with somewhat improved sight) followed in 1843, that of Peru in 1847. These have attained an even wider popularity than their precursor, owing to the more condensed romance and greater novelty of their themes: they are "open sesames" to an old world of wonders—real, and yet, from its strangeness, invested with half the charms of Fairyland. Few passages of fiction are so enthralling to the youthful reader as the first sight of the Spanish adventurers of the plain and city of the Aztecs—the story of Nezahualcoyotl King of Tezcuco; the whole life, exploits, and tragic end of Montezuma; the night retreat from the Aztec capital; the account of the sun-worshippers in the golden city. ⟨. . .⟩

Both these later works are dramas, in which our sympathy is divided between the chivalry of Spain in her prime and the poetical traditions and patriotism of a vanished race. But their author has never, in the midst of his "Claude-like descriptions" and charmingly-vivid narratives, allowed himself to forget that he is writing history. Boys read his *Mexico* and *Peru* as they read the *Arabian Nights*; critics can point to few flaws in the accuracy of his judgment. *Philip II.*, Mr. Prescott's latest and unfinished work—with less brilliancy of colouring, as becomes the more sombre theme—is rendered even more weighty by the solidity of its judgments. For an example of his disenchanting view of the fables of history, we may refer to his refutation of the romantic story—made famous by Schiller—of Don Carlos and Queen Isabella.—JOHN NICHOL, *American Literature*, 1882, pp. 147–50

In his field Prescott has been equalled only by Cooper and surpassed only by Parkman. The defects of his style are chiefly those of excess. The writer of graphic pictorial description must ever career upon the verge of a precipice, and Prescott, like Cooper, sometimes fell into the depths of bombast and fine writing. He delighted in battles and scenes of action, but he never, like Macaulay, sacrificed truth to rhetoric nor dragged in useless scenes to exhibit his mastery over them. His power was chiefly that of a skilful narrator. Stripped of their pictorial effects, his histories would still be valuable, but they would lose the greater part of their charm.

From the first publication of *Ferdinand and Isabella* until long after its author's death, Prescott was ranked both at home and abroad as the leader of American historians. In later days, however, this position has been sharply questioned. Much of Prescott's early popularity was won by the brilliancy of his themes and of his rhetoric. It is now evident that his works lack the broad horizon and the critical insight which characterize the histories of Bancroft and Motley. He has been surpassed, too, by Parkman in his own field of graphic delineation. Yet Prescott's place is still an enviable one. He was wise in his choice of subjects, and exhaustive in his accumulation of materials. He had the tireless patience and the mania for exactness which are the distinctive marks of the modern historian, and his judgment as to the genuineness and value of authorities was seldom at fault. He was lacking in analytical power and philosophical insight, and lacking this, his histories can never gain a place beside the great histories that are for all time; yet with their accuracy and thoroughness and brilliancy it will indeed be long before they will be rewritten or forgotten. —FRED LEWIS PATTEE, A *History of American Literature,* 1896, pp. 309–10

Prescott, like Irving, had come under the fascination of Spain in the days of her greatest power, when she was laying the foundations of her empire beyond the seas. His selection of the Spanish conquest in South America as a subject was a particularly happy one; for, in addition to the fact that this great era of discovery possesses an especial interest for Americans, it was a theme which afforded a fine opportunity for graphic description. Few novels move us more deeply than Prescott's vivid story of the perilous escapes, the trials, the hardships, and the daring of this band of romantic adventurers, discovering and conquering a new world, gorgeous with the rich and brilliant coloring of tropical life, and filled with a fabulous wealth and treasure long dreamed of by Old-World explorers. Prescott's work as a whole maintains a high order of excellence, but in this fascinating book the nature of his subject has enabled him to give us a peculiarly poetic and rounded production. The daring exploits of Cortes and his little band; the extraordinary richness of the kingdom they subdued, and the tragic fate of its unhappy ruler,—all these combine to give the story the unity and poetic quality of a great epic. Although, in the light of recent knowledge, critics have questioned some of Prescott's statements, his histories are, in nearly all essential points, to be relied upon as correct, and we may still take pleasure in the thought that, in the wonderful pictures he has given us, truth has not been sacrificed to effect.—HENRY S. PANCOAST, *An Introduction to American Literature,* 1898, pp. 229–30

Since Prescott's time, the tendency has been more and more to regard history as a matter rather of science than of literature; the fashion of style, too, has greatly changed from that which prevailed when New England found the model of rhetorical excellence in its formal oratory. Prescott's work, then, is often mentioned as rather romantic than scholarly. In this view there is some justice. The scholarship of his day had not collected anything like the material now at the disposal of students; and Prescott's infirmity of sight could not help limiting the range of his investigation. His style, too, always clear and readable, and often vivid, is somewhat florid and generally coloured by what seems a conviction that historical writers should maintain the dignity of history. For all this, his works so admirably combine substantial truth with literary spirit that they are more useful than many which are respected as more authoritative. What he tells us is the result of thoughtful study; and he tells it in a manner so clear, and for all its formality so agreeable, that when you have read one of

his chapters you remember without effort what it is about. With a spirit as modern as George Ticknor's, and with much of the systematic scholarship of Jared Sparks, Prescott combined unusual literary power.

For our purposes, however, the most notable phase of his work is to be found in the subjects to which he turned. At first his aspirations to historical writing took a general form. At last, after hesitation whether to write of antiquity, of Italy, or of what not, he was most attracted by the same romantic Spain which a few years before had captivated Irving. Sitting blind in his New England of the early Renaissance, whose outward aspect was so staidly decorous, he found his imagination most stirred by those phases of modern history which were most splendidly unlike his ancestral inexperience. He chose first that climax of Spanish history when in the same year, 1492, native Spaniards triumphantly closed their eight hundred years of conflict against the Moorish invaders, and the voyage of Columbus opened to Spain those new empires of which for a while our own New England had seemed likely to be a part. Then he found deeply stirring the fatal conflict between Spanish invaders and the civilisations of prehistoric America. Finally, having written of Spanish power at its zenith, he began to record the tale of its stormy sunset in the cloudy reign of Philip II. So the impulse of this first of our literary historians seems very like that of Irving. Irving's books on Spain, however, are rather historical romances than scholarly histories. Instead of being a serious narrative, for example, duly referred to authority, Irving's *Conquest of Granada* takes the form of a make-believe chronicle similar to that in which Mark Twain lately told the story of Joan of Arc. Prescott, a little later, treated Irving's subjects in the spirit of a scholarly historian. In Irving and Prescott alike, however, the inexperienced American imagination, starved at home of all traces of antique splendour, found itself most strongly stimulated by the most brilliant pageant of the romantic European past.—BARRETT WENDELL, A *Literary History of America,* 1900, pp. 269–71

Works

HISTORY OF THE CONQUEST OF MEXICO

Mr. Prescott possesses high qualifications, and some peculiar advantages for the execution of such a work. He has a high sense of the obligation of an historian to explore every source of information relating to his subject; to spare neither industry, nor, we may add, expense, in the collection of materials; and his extensive acquaintance with Spanish literature, and the name which he has already established in connexion with Spanish history, have, perhaps, enabled him to command sources of knowledge unattainable by an unknown author. In his disquisitions on the political state and the civilization of the Aztec kingdoms, he is full and copious, without being prolix and wearisome; his narrative is flowing and spirited, sometimes very picturesque; his style has dropped the few Americanisms which still jarred on our fastidious ear in his former work, and is in general pure and sound English. Above all, his judgments are unaffectedly candid and impartial; he never loses sight of the immutable principles of justice and humanity, yet allows to the Spanish conquerors the palliation for their enormities, to be drawn from those deeply-rooted and miscalled Christian principles, which authorised and even sanctified all acts of ambition and violence committed by Europeans and Christians against barbarians and infidels.—H. H. MILMAN, "Prescott's *History of the Conquest of Mexico," Quarterly Review,* Dec. 1843, p. 188

I wrote to Prescott about his book, with which I was perfectly charmed. I think his descriptions, Masterly; his style, brilliant; his purpose, manly and gallant always. The introductory account of Aztec civilisation impressed me, exactly as it impressed you. From beginning to end, the whole History is enchanting and full of Genius.—CHARLES DICKENS, Letter to C. C. Felton (Jan. 2, 1844)

I doubt whether Mr. Prescott was aware of the extent of the sacrifice I made. This was a favorite subject, which had delighted my imagination ever since I was a boy. I had brought home books from Spain to aid me in it, and looked upon it as the pendent to my Columbus. When I gave it up to him, I in a manner gave him up my bread, for I depended upon the profit of it to recruit my waning finances. I had no other subject at hand to supply its place. I was dismounted from my *cheval de bataille*, and have never been completely mounted since. Had I accomplished that work, my whole pecuniary situation would have been altered. When I made the sacrifice, it was not with a view to compliments or thanks, but from a warm and sudden impulse. I am not sorry for having made it. Mr. Prescott has justified the opinion I expressed at the time, that he would treat the subject with more close and ample research than I should probably do, and would produce a work more thoroughly worthy of the theme. He has produced a work that does honor to himself and his country, and I wish him the full enjoyment of his laurels.—WASHINGTON IRVING, Letter to Pierre M. Irving (March 24, 1844), cited in Pierre M. Irving, *The Life and Letters of Washington Irving*, 1863, Vol. 3, pp. 143–44

We shall not pretend to have examined a narrative which has given us so much pleasure, with the keen scrutiny of a severe criticism; but we can conscientiously affirm, that we remember little or nothing in the manner of its execution which we could have wished otherwise. Mr Prescott appears to us to possess almost every qualification for his task. He has a pure, simple, and eloquent style—a keen relish for the picturesque—a quick and discerning judgment of character—and a calm, generous, and enlightened spirit of philanthropy. There is no exaggeration in asserting, that his *Conquest of Mexico* combines—some allowance, where that is necessary, being made for the inferior extent and importance of its subject—most of the valuable qualities which distinguish the most popular historical writers, in our own language, of the present day.—CHARLES PHILLIPPS, "Prescott's *Conquest of Mexico*," *Edinburgh Review*, April 1845, pp. 434–35

HISTORY OF THE REIGN OF PHILIP THE SECOND

I finished Prescott's *Philip the Second*. What strikes me most about him is, that, though he has had new materials, and tells his story well, he does not put any thing in a light very different from that in which I had before seen it; and I have never studied that part of history deeply.—THOMAS BABINGTON MACAULAY, *Journal* (Nov. 27, 1855), cited in G. Otto Trevelyan, *The Life and Letters of Lord Macaulay*, 1876, Vol. 2, p. 323

To this merit of a well-arranged history Mr. Prescott adds that of an easy, unaffected, though somewhat frigid, power of narration. He belongs to the historical school of Robertson, judicious rather than profound in its general views, and more remarkable for simplicity than for descriptive power. The pictures Mr. Prescott has given us are never wanting in truth, but they are sometimes wanting in life. History only becomes dramatic on two conditions; it must have either the passion of

the politician or the imagination of the poet. Mr. Prescott has neither one nor the other; he is a calm and enlightened philosopher, an accomplished man of letters; he is well read in the history of Philip II., and he relates it with fidelity; but he has studied it after the lapse of three centuries in all the serenity of his own reflections and the tranquillity of a New England study,—faithfully, therefore, as these events and these personages are described by him, he leaves them where he finds them, in their tombs.—FRANÇOIS PIERRE GUILLAUME GUIZOT, "Philip II and His Times: Prescott and Motley," *Edinburgh Review*, Jan. 1857, p. 44

Two volumes of *Philip II.* were published in 1855, and the third appeared only a few months ago. To the grace and vivacity of the narratives of the rebellion of the Moriscos, and of the battle of Lepanto, and to the undiminished fire and power displayed in this last instalment of the work, our current magazines and reviews have borne, and are still bearing, testimony. It will be long indeed ere a historian is found worthy to take up the thread where it has been so suddenly and so unhappily broken.—SIR WILLIAM STIRLING-MAXWELL, "William Hickling Prescott" (1859), *Miscellaneous Essays and Addresses*, 1891, p. 73

EDWIN P. WHIPPLE
From "Prescott's Histories" (1848)
Essays and Reviews
1850, Volume 2, pp. 154–67

The distinguishing merit of Mr. Prescott is his power of vividly representing characters and events in their just relations, and applying to them their proper principles. He thus presents a true exhibition of the period of time he has chosen for his subject, enabling the reader to comprehend its peculiar character, to realize its passions and prejudices, and at once to observe it with the eye of a contemporary, and judge it with the calmness of a philosopher. To succeed in this difficult object of historical art, requires not only mental powers of a high order, but a general healthiness of moral and intellectual constitution, which is uncommon, even among historians who evince no lack of forcible thought and intense conception. History is false, not only when the historian wilfully lies, but also when facts, true in themselves, are forced out of their proper relations through the unconscious operation of the historian's feelings, prejudices, or modes of thought. He thus represents, not his subject, but his subject as modified by his own character. Certain facts and persons are exaggerated into undue importance, while others are unduly depressed, in order that they may more readily fall within the range of his generalizations, or harmonize with his preconceived opinions. He may have a system so fixed in his mind, or a passion so lodged in his heart, as to see facts in relation to it, instead of seeing them in relation to each other. An honest sectarian or partisan, an admirable moralist or philanthropist, might make his history a tissue of fallacies and falsehoods, without being justly chargeable with intentional untruth. This is done by confounding individual impressions with objective facts and principles.

Now, Mr. Prescott's narrative of events and delineations of character are characterized by singular objectiveness. By a fine felicity of his nature, he is content to consider his subject as everything, and himself as nothing. Objects stand out on his page in clear light, undiscolored by the hues of his own passions, unmixed with any peculiarities of his own character. This disposition and power to see things as they are in themselves, when joined to a corresponding capacity to convey them to other minds in their true proportions, indicates a finely balanced as well as largely endowed nature, and implies moral as well as intellectual strength. The moral qualities evinced in Mr. Prescott's histories, though they are seen in no ostentation of conscience and parade of noble sentiments, are still of a fine and rare order, and constitute no inconsiderable portion of his excellence as a historian. These are modesty, conscientiousness, candor, toleration,—a hatred of wrong, modified by charity for the wrong-doer,—a love of truth, expressed not in resounding commonplaces, but in diligence in seeking it out,—and a comprehension of heart which noiselessly embraces all degrees of the human family, just and merciful to all, looking at motives as well as actions, and finding its fit expression in a certain indescribable sweetness of tone pervading his style like an invisible essence. It is one of the greatest charms of his compositions, that these qualities are so unostentatiously displayed that they can be best described in negatives. Thus we speak of his absence of egotism, of intolerance, of narrowness, of rancor, of exaggeration, rather than of the positive qualities through which such faults are avoided.

The intellectual power displayed in Mr. Prescott's works has a similar character of unobtrusiveness and reserve. It would, doubtless, appear to many readers much greater were it asserted with more emphasis, and occasionally allowed to disport itself in the snapping contrasts of antithesis, or the cunning contortions of disputation. A writer may easily gain the reputation of a strong and striking thinker, by sacrificing artistical effect to momentary surprises, or by exhibiting his thoughts in their making, before they have attained precision and definiteness, and taken their place in the general plan of his work. To the generality of readers, depth of thought is confounded with confusion of thoughts. Events and ideas, heaped and huddled together, and lit up here and there with flashes of wit and imagination, are often received in their chaotic state as indications of greater mental power than they would be if reduced to order and connection by the stringent exercise of a patient, penetrating, and comprehensive intellect. Now, pure force of understanding is principally shown in so grappling with the subject as to educe simplicity from complexity, and order from confusion. According to the perfection with which this is done will be the apparent ease of the achievement; and a thinker who follows this method rarely parades its processes. His mind, like that of Mr. Prescott, operates to the reader softly and without noise. Any strain or contortion in thought or expression would indicate imperfect comprehension of his subject, and exhibit the pains of labor instead of its results. Far from desiring to tickle attention by giving undue prominence to single thoughts or incidents, such a thinker would be chiefly solicitous to keep them in subjection to his general purpose; for it is violating the first principle of art to break up the unity of a subject into a series of exaggerated individual parts.

The moment we consider the materials which form the foundation of Mr. Prescott's elaborate histories, we perceive the high degree of intellect they imply in the writer, and are able to estimate that healthiness of mind by which he shunned the numerous temptations to brilliant faults which beset his path. In the collection of these materials he has displayed all the industry and diligence of an antiquary. With the utmost indifference to labor and expense, he has gathered from every quarter all books and MSS. which could elucidate or illustrate his subjects, and nothing which could cast the minutest thread of light into any unexplored corner of history seems to have escaped his terrible vigilance. With all his taste for large views, which comprehend years in sentences, the most mole-eyed analyst has not a keener sight for the small curiosities of history. No chronicle or personal history, happy in the consciousness of its insignificance, can hide itself from his quick eye, if it chance to contain a single fact which he needs. He has shown more industry and acuteness than almost any other contemporary resurrectionist in the grave-yards of deceased books. Yet he has not one of the faults which cling so obstinately to most antiquaries. He does not estimate the importance of a fact or date by the trouble he experienced in hunting it out. He does not plume himself on the acquisition of what has baffled others. None of the dust of antiquity creeps into his soul. His style glides along with the same unassuming ease in the narration of discoveries as of common facts.

Indeed, it is not so much in the collection as in the use of his materials that Mr. Prescott claims our regard as a historical artist. These materials are, it is true, original and valuable beyond any which have fallen into the hands of any contemporary historian; but to analyze them, and to compose accurate histories from their conflicting statements, required judgment in its most comprehensive sense. They are the productions of men who looked at persons and events from different points of view. They are vitiated with the worst faults of bad historians. They all reflect their age in its common passions and prejudices, and each is disfigured by some unconscious or wilful misrepresentations, springing from personal bias or imperfect comprehension. They are full of credulity and bigotry, of individual and national prejudices,—sometimes the mere vehicles of private malice, almost always characterized by a bad arrangement of facts and confusion of principles. Together they present so strange a medley of shrewdness and fanaticism, of fact and fiction, and throw over the subject they are intended to illustrate such a variety of cross lights, and entangle it in such perplexing contradictions, that to sift out the truth requires the most cautious consideration and comparison of authorities. The testimony of kings, statesmen, scholars, priests, soldiers, philanthropists, each inaccurate after a fashion of his own, Mr. Prescott was compelled to estimate at its exact worth, disregarding all the exaggerations of pride, interest, and sensibility. To do this, he was necessarily obliged to study the personal history of his authorities, to examine the construction of their minds, and to consider all inducements to false coloring which would result from their position and character. Those who have carefully read the critical notes of his authorities, subjoined to each division of his histories, must admit that Mr. Prescott has shown himself abundantly capable of performing this difficult and delicate task. He analyzes the mental and moral constitution of his veterans with singular acuteness, laying open to the eye their subtlest excellences and defects, and showing in every sentence that in receiving their statements of facts he has allowed much for the medium through which they have passed. This portion of his duty, as a historian, demanded a judgment as nice in its tact as it was broad in its grasp. The scales must have been large enough to take in the weightiest masses of details, and perfect enough to show the slightest variation of the balance.

Mr. Prescott's understanding is thus judicial in its character, uniting to a love for truth diligence in its search and judgment in its detection. But this does not comprehend all his merits as a historian of the past; and, indeed, might be compatible with an absence of life in his narrative, and vitality in his conceptions. Among those historians who combine rectitude of purpose with strength of understanding, Mr. Hallam stands preëminent. All his histories have a judicial character. He is almost unexcelled in sifting testimony, in detecting inaccuracies, in reducing swollen reputations to their proper dimensions, in placing facts and principles in their natural order. He has no prepossessions, no preferences, no prejudices, no theories. He passes over a tract of history sacred to partisan fraud and theological rancor, where every event and character is considered in relation to some system still acrimoniously debated, without adopting any of the passions with which he comes in contact. No sophistical apology for convenient crime, no hypocrite or oppressor pranked out in the colors of religion or loyalty, can deceive his cold, calm, austere, remorseless intellect. He sums up each case which comes before him for judgment with a surly impartiality, applying to external events or acts two or three rigid rules and then fixing on them the brand of his condemnation. The shrieks of their partisans he deems the most flattering tribute to the justice of his judgment. This method of writing history has, doubtless, its advantages; and, in regard to Mr. Hallam, it must be admitted that he has corrected many pernicious errors of fact, and overthrown many absurd estimates of character. But, valuable as his histories are in many important respects, they generally want grace, lightness, sympathy, picturesqueness, glow. From his deficiency of sensibility and imagination, and from his habit of bringing everything to the tribunal of the understanding, he rarely grasps character or incidents in the concrete. Both are interesting to him only as they illustrate certain practical or abstract principles. He looks at external acts without being able to discern inward motives. He cannot see things with the same eyes, and from the same position, as did the persons whom he judges; and, consequently, all those extenuations and explanations of conduct which are revealed in an insight into character are of little account with him. He does not realize a past age to his imagination, and will not come down from his pinnacle of judgment to mingle with its living realities. As he coldly dissects some statesman, warrior, or patriot, who at least had a living heart and brain, we are inclined to exclaim with Hamlet, "Has this fellow no feeling of his business?" It is the same in his literary criticisms. He gives the truth as it is *about* the author, not as it is *in* the author. He describes his genius in general terms, not in characteristic epithets. Everything that is peculiar to a particular writer slips through his analysis. That mysterious interpenetration of personality with feelings and powers which distinguishes one man's genius from another's escapes the processes of his understanding. Persons, in Mr. Hallam's hands, commonly subside into general ideas, events into generalizations. He does not appear to think that persons and events have any value in themselves, apart from the principles they illustrate; and, consequently, he conceives neither with sufficient intensity to bring out always the principles they really contain. ⟨. . .⟩

The style of Mr. Prescott's works, as might be expected from his character, is manly, perspicuous, picturesque, lucid, equally removed from stateliness and levity, disdaining all tawdry ornaments and simulated energy, and combining clearness and simplicity with glow. In the composition of a long work, it is a delicate matter to fix upon a proper form. The style which would delight in an essay might grow intolerably tedious in a volume. When brilliancy or dignity, intensity or melody, become monotonous, they tire nearly as much as dulness or discord. The only safe style for a long history is one without peculiarities which call attention to itself, apart from what it conveys. It must be sufficiently elevated to be on a level with the matter, or its meagre simplicity and plainness would distract attention as much as luxuriant ornament, while it must vigorously resist all temptations to display for the mere sake of display. Mr. Prescott has been compared with Robertson in

respect to style. The comparison holds as far as regards luminous arrangement of matter and clearness of narration; but, with the exception, perhaps, of passages in *America*, not in the graces of expression. The manner of Robertson is a fair representation of his patient, passionless, elegant mind. Its simplicity is often too prim, its elegance too nice. The smooth-rubbed mind of the Scotchman risks nothing; is fearful of natural graces, fearful of English verbal criticism, fearful of violating the dignity of history. His diction loses sweetness and raciness in its effort after correctness, and, as a general thing, is colorless, characterless, without glow or pictorial effect. The water is clear and mirrors facts in beautiful distinctness, but it neither sparkles nor flows. His diction, however, has the rare quality of never being tedious, and fixes the pleased attention of the reader when the labored splendor of Gibbon would fatigue from its monotony. Mr. Prescott has the characteristic merits of Robertson, with other merits superadded. His style is flowing, plastic, all alive with the life of his mind. It varies with the objects it describes, and is cautious or vehement, concise or luxuriant, plain or pictorial, as the occasion demands. It glides from object to object with unforced ease, passing from discussion to description, from the council-chamber to the battle-field, without any preliminary flourishes, without any break in that unity which declares it the natural action of one mind readily accommodating itself to events as they rise. Such a style is to be judged not from the sparkle or splendor of separate sentences or paragraphs, but from its effect as a whole. A person can only appreciate it by following its windings through a long work. Of course, we speak of Mr. Prescott's style, in this connection, in its general character, after his powers of composition had been well trained by exercise. The diction of the earlier chapters of *Ferdinand and Isabella* displays an effort after elegance, and an occasional timidity of movement, natural to a man who had not learned to dare, and mistook elegant composition for a living style. He soon worked himself free from such shackles, and left off writing sentences. With the exceptions we have mentioned, there is no fine writing— no writing for the sake of words instead of things—in Mr. Prescott's works. His mind is too large and healthy for such vanities. Perhaps the perfection of his style, in its flowing movement, is seen in *The Conquest of Peru*. There are passages in that which seem to have run out of his mind, clear as rills of rock water. They are like beautiful improvisations, where passions and objects so fill the mind that the words in which they are expressed are at once perfect and unpremeditated.

EDWARD EVERETT HALE, JR.
"William Hickling Prescott"
American Prose, ed. George Rice Carpenter
1898, pp. 172–75

The chief merits of Prescott as a historian are breadth and accuracy of information and impartiality of judgment. As a writer he has qualities which harmonize well with such characteristics: he has the classic excellencies of style. He is not so very suggestive, animated, sympathetic: his virtues are strength, outline, form.

And these excellencies Prescott has to a very considerable degree. He was passionate for knowledge of his subject, for power. Sparks had already shown American students the necessity of exhaustive material. History was no longer a matter for any honest gentleman who felt impelled to write, as Gibbon remarked, and had the needful paper and ink. Bancroft, Prescott, Motley, Parkman, were, first and foremost, investigators. They not only accumulated in their libraries everything in print which bore on their subjects, but they had their copyists at work in the archives of all Europe. They wrote from contemporary authorities, when they could get them, and always wrote as original students. Prescott was the great champion of footnotes. Almost one-third of his good-sized volumes was made up of titles and quotations, which, as they were in Spanish, were entirely unintelligible to the greater number of those who admired his romance and his style.

Prescott was master of his voluminous material. But not only that, he had also in mind a very definite conception of what form that material was to take. He was no Barante, to write as his own authorities would have written. Nor did he imagine, like Carlyle, that he was part and parcel of that which he was describing. He saw how things had gone, even if sometimes from a considerable distance, and his idea was to put them as he saw them, with a firm, clear outline, which would bring them rightly to the mind of one who had not had his opportunities. But not only did he see everything clearly, he saw everything in relation; he conceived his subjects as wholes, saw each part as a part, not for itself. He had not only a sense of outline, but a sense of form.

It is true that in presenting the conception as it took shape in his mind, Prescott was not, we think, very happy. He lived toward the beginning of an effort in the writing of English prose which he may not have understood, may not have appreciated, for he continued the traditions to which he had been accustomed. Thus he calmly uses the most general word, and shuns anything that might possibly be striking, and so interfere with a becoming dignity. Had he really had an original sense of style, he would have expressed himself with some originality. As it was, he continued to write as it had been the habit of historians to write, and he achieved a very striking success.

Prescott has been called a romantic historian, and so in a certain sense he was, though not, as we have seen, so far as style is concerned. His time was a romantic time, and historians felt romantic, as much as anybody else. Macaulay announced that the "truly great historian would reclaim those materials which the novelist had appropriated." Carlyle said that any one who read "the inscrutable Book of Nature as if it were a merchant's Ledger, is justly suspected of having never seen that Book." Thierry composed his *Merovingians* with occasional shouts of "Pharamond, Pharamond, we have battled with the sword!" Barante, out of the Burgundian chronicles, wove eleven volumes of mediæval tapestry, and concealed himself behind it. In Germany the learned Niebuhr was dazzled by the fascination of his lays of ancient Rome. In America (or, more correctly, in Spain) Washington Irving could not write his *Conquest of Granada* without imagining a Fray Agapida, to whom it might be attributed. Prescott, too, felt the influence, although he was a different man from any of these, with aims different from theirs.

Prescott's ideal was not romantic: it was the more serene, more severe, classic ideal. Still there is no doubt that he liked to think of his subjects as being romantic in themselves; he thought of Spaniards and Moors, *adelantados* and conquerors, Aztecs and Peruvians, as being naturally romantic, as may be seen from the prefaces to *Ferdinand and Isabella* and *The Conquest of Peru*. So they doubtless were at that time; they were, in fact, a part of the undoubted possession of the romancer of Prescott's day. But with plenty of local color in his subjects, Prescott had not more than a general feeling for romantic quality. M. de Heredia's "ivres d'un rêve héroïque et brutal" has a romantic idealism which cannot be found in the whole *Conquest of Mexico*. Kingsley's "Fat Carbajal charged our cannon like an elephant" has a romantic realism which cannot be found in all the *Peru*. A romantic mind loses much, but it is apt to get the play of real life. This Prescott generally missed: he was always viewing the matter as a whole, and rarely got down to particulars.

If, then, we turn to Prescott nowadays for romance, or if we study him for his technique, we shall find only what long since had its day. If we come to him from the post-Darwinian historians, we may think him superficial and inattentive to matters of importance. But even from these mistaken standpoints we shall hardly be able to read one of his histories without the feeling that he is a man of letters of distinguished power. He stood between great traditions and a great future; he certainly had some of the weaknesses of those who had gone before as well as some of their merits; and certainly, too, he missed some of the merits of those who were to come. On the other hand, he avoided the great faults of romanticism, and presents to us a singularly attractive combination of classic excellencies.

THOMAS BABINGTON MACAULAY

1800–1859

Thomas Babington Macaulay was born on October 24, 1800, at Rothley Temple, Leicestershire, but grew up in London, where he spent most of his life. His father, Zachary Macaulay, was a noted evangelical reformer and editor of the *Christian Observer*. Thomas Macaulay, a precocious student, entered Trinity College, Cambridge, in 1818, and in 1824 became a fellow. He was called to the bar in 1826 but never practiced. Meanwhile, in 1823, he had begun his literary career with several essays printed in *Knight's Quarterly*; by 1825 he had made his first submissions to the *Edinburgh Review*, for which he was to write numerous articles over the next twenty years.

Macaulay's essays for the *Edinburgh Review*, on literature, politics, and history, made him an immediate celebrity and led to his being elected to the House of Commons for Calne in 1830. He soon became known for his speeches in support of the Reform Bill, and in 1832 was elected M.P. for Leeds. In 1834, in order to achieve financial independence, Macaulay went to India as a member of the Supreme Council, and there increased his fame by writing two highly celebrated accounts of Indian education and the Indian penal code. After returning from India in 1838 he was elected M.P. for Edinburgh (1839) and made secretary of war in Melbourne's cabinet (1839–41).

In 1842 Macaulay published *Lays of Ancient Rome*, a collection of poems that boldly attempted to imitate the lost ballads of the ancient Romans; it was the first of several books which were to make Macaulay one of the most widely read authors of the nineteenth century. The first edition of *Critical and Historical Essays* followed in 1843. In 1846 Macaulay was re-elected M.P. for Edinburgh, and in that year was appointed paymaster general in Russell's cabinet (1846–47). Macaulay lost his parliamentary seat in 1847, but in the following year published the first two volumes of what was to become his most celebrated work, the *History of England*. Begun in 1839 and never completed, it was intended to cover the period from the beginning of James II's reign (1685) to the end of the eighteenth century or even later, but in fact ended with the death of William III in 1702. In 1852 Macaulay was re-elected M.P. for Edinburgh, but in that year suffered a heart attack from which he never recovered, leading him to resign his seat in 1856. Macaulay began a series of five biographical articles for the *Encyclopaedia Britannica* in 1853 (completed in 1858 and published as a volume in 1860), and in 1854 twenty-nine of his most famous speeches appeared in a collected edition. The third and fourth volumes of the *History of England* appeared in 1855, and in 1857 he became Lord Macaulay (Baron Macaulay of Rothley).

Macaulay, who never married, died on December 28, 1859. A more complete edition of the *Critical, Historical, and Miscellaneous Essays* was published in 1860, and in 1861 the fifth volume of the *History* appeared. In 1876 *The Life and Letters of Lord Macaulay*, by his nephew Sir. G. Otto Trevelyan, was published; it became one of the best-known biographies in English. Macaulay's essays and, in particular, his *History of England* were immensely influential during the nineteenth century, in no small part because of the liveliness of his style, which helped to create a new market for historical writing. In the twentieth century Macaulay has been widely attacked for fostering the so-called "Whig" interpretation of history, which glorified the Revolution of 1688 and saw the whole of England's past as leading inexorably to the liberal reforms of the nineteenth century.

Personal

I hope that Mrs. M. has quite recovered her strength. Remember us kindly to her, and give my particular love to Tom. I am glad to perceive that his classicality has not extinguished his piety. His hymns were really extraordinary for such a baby. —HANNAH MORE, Letter to Zachary Macaulay (June 28, 1808), *Letters of Hannah More to Zachary Macaulay*, ed. Arthur Roberts, 1860, pp. 26–27

At home over books. An hour at the Temple Library helping Gordon in lettering some German books. At four I went to James Stephen, and drove down with him to his house at Hendon. A dinner-party. I had a most interesting companion in young Macaulay, one of the most promising of the rising generation I have seen for a long time. He is the author of several much admired articles in the *Edinburgh Review*. A review of Milton's lately discovered work on Christian Doctrine, and of his political and poetical character, is by him. I prefer the political to the critical remarks. In a paper of his on the new London University, his low estimate of the advantages of our University education, i.e. at Oxford and Cambridge, is remarkable in one who is himself so much indebted to University training. He has a good face,—not the delicate features of a man of genius and sensibility, but the strong lines and well-knit limbs of a man sturdy in body and mind. Very eloquent and cheerful. Overflowing with words, and not poor in thought. Liberal in opinion, but no radical. He seems a correct as well as a full man. He showed a minute knowledge of subjects not introduced by himself.—HENRY CRABB ROBINSON, *Diary*, Nov. 29, 1826

The strongest young man, one Macaulay (now in Parliament, as I from the first predicted), an emphatic, hottish, really forcible person, but unhappily without divine idea.—THOMAS CARLYLE, *Journal* (Jan. 13, 1832), cited in James Anthony Froude, *Thomas Carlyle*, 1882, Vol. 2, pp. 186–87

Dined yesterday with Lord Holland; came very late, and found a vacant place between Sir George Robinson and a common-looking man in black. As soon as I had time to look at my neighbour, I began to speculate (as one usually does) as to who he might be, and as he did not for some time open his lips except to eat, I settled that he was some obscure man of letters or of medicine, perhaps a cholera doctor. In a short time the conversation turned upon early and late education, and Lord Holland said he had always remarked that self-educated men were peculiarly conceited and arrogant, and apt to look down upon the generality of mankind, from their being ignorant of how much other people knew; not having been at public schools, they are uninformed of the course of general education. My neighbour observed that he thought the most remarkable example of self-education was that of Alfieri, who had reached the age of thirty without having acquired any accomplishment save that of driving, and who was so ignorant of his own language that he had to learn it like a child, beginning with elementary books. Lord Holland quoted Julius Cæsar Scaliger as an example of late education, saying that he had been married and commenced learning Greek the same day, when my neighbour remarked "that he supposed his learning Greek was not an instantaneous act like his marriage." This remark, and the manner of it, gave me the notion that he was a dull fellow, for it came out in a way which bordered on the ridiculous, so as to excite something like a sneer. I was a little surprised to hear him continue the thread of conversation (from Scaliger's wound) and talk of Loyola having been wounded at Pampeluna. I wondered how he happened to know anything about Loyola's wound. Having thus settled my opinion, I went on eating my dinner, when Auckland, who was sitting opposite to me, addressed my neighbour, "Mr. Macaulay, will you drink a glass of wine?" I thought I should have dropped off my chair. It was MACAULAY, the man I had been so long most curious to see and to hear, whose genius, eloquence, astonishing knowledge, and diversified talents have excited my wonder and admiration for such a length of time, and here I had been sitting next to him, hearing him talk, and setting him down for a dull fellow. I felt as if he could have read my thoughts, and the perspiration burst from every pore of my face, and yet it was impossible not to be amused at the idea. It was not till Macaulay stood up that I was aware of all the vulgarity and ungainliness of his appearance; not a ray of intellect beams from his countenance; a lump of more ordinary clay never enclosed a powerful mind and lively imagination. He had a cold and sore throat, the latter of which occasioned a constant contraction of the muscles of the thorax, making him appear as if in momentary danger of a fit. His manner struck me as not pleasing, but it was not assuming, unembarrassed, yet not easy, unpolished, yet not coarse; there was no kind of usurpation of the conversation, no tenacity as to opinion or facts, no assumption of superiority but the variety and extent of his information were soon apparent, for whatever subject was touched upon he evinced the utmost familiarity with it; quotation, illustration, anecdote, seemed ready in his hands for every topic. Primogeniture in this country, in others, and particularly in ancient Rome, was the principal topic, I think, but Macaulay was not certain what was the law of Rome, except that when a man died intestate his estate was divided between his children. After dinner Talleyrand and Madame de Dino came in. Macaulay was introduced to Talleyrand, who told him that he meant to go to the House of Commons on Tuesday, and that he hoped he would speak, "qu'il avait entendu tous les grands orateurs, et il désirait à présent entendre Monsieur Macaulay."—CHARLES CAVENDISH FULKE GREVILLE, *Diary*, Feb. 6, 1832

Went to Bowood to dinner. Found, besides those Lady L. had mentioned (Lady Cunliffe, Lady Morley, and Rogers), Lord John and his children, Lady Macdonald and Macaulay. The dinner and evening very agreeable. Macaulay wonderful; never, perhaps, was there combined so much talent with so marvellous a memory. To attempt to record his conversation one must be as wonderfully gifted with memory as himself. —THOMAS MOORE, *Journal*, Oct. 21, 1840

It is very provoking, when a man has such extraordinary abilities, and really some powers of a first-rate order, and see the result of it all. He is absolutely renowned in society as the greatest bore that ever yet appeared. I have seen people come in from Holland House, breathless and knocked up, and able to say nothing but "Oh dear, oh mercy." What's the matter? being asked. "Oh, Macaulay." Then every one said, "That accounts for it—you're lucky to be alive," etc. Edinburgh is now celebrated for having given us the two most perfect bores that have ever yet been known in London, for Jack Campbell in the House of Lords is just what poor Tom is in private society.—HENRY, LORD BROUGHAM, Letter to Macvey Napier (Aug. 14, 1842), *Selection from the Correspondence of the Late Macvey Napier*, ed. Macvey Napier, 1879, p. 403

I was too much engaged with these personal talks to attend much to what was going on elsewhere; but all through breakfast I had been more and more impressed by the aspect of one of the guests, sitting next to Milnes. He was a man of large presence,—a portly personage, gray-haired, but scarcely as yet aged; and his face had a remarkable intelligence, not vivid nor sparkling, but conjoined with great quietude,—and if it gleamed or brightened at one time more than another, it was like the sheen over a broad surface of sea. There was a somewhat careless self-possession, large and broad enough to

be called dignity; and the more I looked at him, the more I knew that he was a distinguished person, and wondered who. He might have been a minister of state; only there is not one of them who has any right to such a face and presence. At last,— I do not know how the conviction came,—but I became aware that it was Macaulay, and began to see some slight resemblance to his portraits. But I have never seen any that is not wretchedly unworthy of the original. As soon as I knew him, I began to listen to his conversation, but he did not talk a great deal,— contrary to his usual custom; for I am told he is apt to engross all the talk to himself. Probably he may have been restrained by the presence of Ticknor, and Mr. Palfrey, who were among his auditors and interlocutors; and as the conversation seemed to turn much on American subjects, he could not well have assumed to talk them down. I am glad to have seen him,—a face fit for a scholar, a man of the world, a cultivated intelligence.—NATHANIEL HAWTHORNE, *The English Note-Books*, July 13, 1856

On Monday I dined with the Mackintoshes. Macaulay, Dean Milman, and Mr. and Mrs. Farrar composed the party. Of course you would like a photograph of Macaulay, as faithfully as I can give it. He impressed me on the whole agreeably. To me, personally, he spoke courteously, respectfully, showed by allusion to the subject in various ways that he was quite aware of my book and its subject, although I doubt whether he had read it. He may have done so, but he manifested no special interest in me. I believe that he is troubled about his health (having a kind of bronchial or asthmatic cough), and that herarely dines out now-a-days, so that it is perhaps a good deal of a compliment that he came on this occasion on purpose to meet me. His general appearance is singularly common-place. I cannot describe him better than by saying he has exactly that kind of face and figure which by no possibility would be selected, out of even a very small number of persons, as those of a remarkable personage. He is of the middle height, neither above nor below it. The outline of his face in profile is rather good. The nose, very slightly aquiline, is well cut, and the expression of the mouth and chin agreeable. His hair is thin and silvery, and he looks a good deal older than many men of his years—for, if I am not mistaken, he is just as old as his century, like Cromwell, Balzac, Charles V., and other notorious individuals. Now those two imposters, so far as appearances go, Prescott and Mignet, who are sixty-two, look young enough, in comparison, to be Macaulay's sons. The face, to resume my description, seen in front, is blank, and as it were badly lighted. There is nothing luminous in the eye, nothing impressive in the brow. The forehead is spacious, but it is scooped entirely away in the region where benevolence ought to be, while beyond rise reverence, firmness and self-esteem, like Alps on Alps. The under eyelids are so swollen as almost to close the eyes, and it would be quite impossible to tell the colour of those orbs, and equally so, from the neutral tint of his hair and face, to say of what complexion he had originally been. His voice is agreeable, and its intonations delightful, although that is so common a gift with Englishmen as to be almost a national characteristic.

As usual, he took up the ribands of the conversation, and kept them in his own hand, driving wherever it suited him. I believe he is thought by many people a bore, and you remember that Sydney Smith spoke of him as "our Tom, the greatest engine of social oppression in England." I should think he might be to those who wanted to talk also. I can imagine no better fun than to have Carlyle and himself meet accidentally at the same dinner-table with a small company. It would be like two locomotives, each with a long train, coming against each other at express speed. Both, I have no doubt, could be smashed into silence at the first collision. Macaulay, however, is not so dogmatic, or so outrageously absurd as Carlyle often is, neither is he half so grotesque or amusing. His whole manner has the smoothness and polished surface of the man of the world, the politician, and the new peer, spread over the man of letters within. I do not know that I can repeat any of his conversation, for there was nothing to excite very particular attention in its even flow. There was not a touch of Holmes's ever bubbling wit, imagination, enthusiasm, and arabesqueness. It is the perfection of the commonplace, without sparkle or flash, but at the same time always interesting and agreeable. I could listen to him with pleasure for an hour or two every day, and I have no doubt I should thence grow wiser every day, for his brain is full, as hardly any man's ever was, and his way of delivering himself is easy and fluent.—JOHN LOTHROP MOTLEY, Letter to His Wife (May 30, 1858), *The Correspondence of John Lothrop Motley*, ed. George William Curtis, 1889, Vol. 1, pp. 236–37

I sympathised with you when I read of Macaulay's death in the *Times*. He was, was he not, your next-door neighbour? I can easily conceive what a loss you must have had in the want of his brilliant conversation. I hardly knew him: met him once, I remember, when Hallam and Guizot were in his company: Hallam was showing Guizot the Houses of Parliament then building, and Macaulay went on like a cataract for an hour or so to those two great men, and, when they had gone, turned to me and said, "Good morning, I am happy to have had the pleasure of making your acquaintance," and strode away. Had I been a piquable man I should have been piqued, but I don't think I was, for the movement after all was amicable. —ALFRED, LORD TENNYSON, Letter to the Duke of Argyll (1860), cited in Hallam Tennyson, *Alfred Lord Tennyson: A Memoir*, 1897, Vol. 1, p. 458

Bulwer and Talfourd were hardly thought of as Members of Parliament at that time, except in connexion with the international copyright treaty which authors were endeavouring to procure, and with the Copyright Act, which was obtained a few years after. Mr. Macaulay was another Member of Parliament who associated his name very discreditably at first with the copyright bill, which was thrown out one session in consequence of a speech of his which has always remained a puzzle to me. What could have been the inducement to such a man to talk such nonsense as he did, and to set at naught every principle of justice in regard to authors' earnings, it is impossible, to me and others, to conceive. Nothing that he could propose,—nothing that he could do, could ever compensate to him for the forfeiture of good fame and public confidence which he seems to have actually volunteered in that speech. He changed his mind or his tactics afterwards; but he could not change people's feelings in regard to himself, or make any body believe that he was a man to be relied upon. He never appeared to me to be so. When I went to London he was a new Member of Parliament, and the object of unbounded hope and expectation to the Whig statesmen, who, according to their curious practice of considering all of the generation below their own as chicks, spoke rapturously of this promising young man. They went on doing so till his return from India, five years afterwards, by which time the world began to inquire when the promise was to begin to fructify,—this young fellow being by that time seven-and-thirty. To impartial observers, the true quality of Macaulay's mind was as clear then as now.

In Parliament, he was no more than a most brilliant speaker; and in his speeches there was the same fundamental weakness which pervades his writings,—unsoundness in the presentment of his case. Some one element was sure to be left out, which falsified his statement, and vitiated his conclusions; and there never was perhaps a speaker or writer of eminence, so prone to presentments of cases, who so rarely offered one which was complete and true. My own impression is, and always was, that the cause of the defect is constitutional in Macaulay. The evidence seems to indicate that he wants heart. He appears to be wholly unaware of this deficiency; and the superficial fervour which suns over his disclosures probably deceives himself, as it deceives a good many other people; and he may really believe that he has a heart. To those who do not hold this key to the interpretaton of his career, it must be a very mysterious thing that a man of such imposing and real ability, with every circumstance and influence in his favour, should never have achieved any complete success. As a politician, his failure has been signal, notwithstanding his irresistible power as a speaker, and his possession of every possible facility. As a practical legislator, his failure was unsurpassed, when he brought home his Code from India. I was witness to the amazement and grief of some able lawyers, in studying that Code,—of which they could scarcely lay their finger on a provision through which you could not drive a coach and six.—HARRIET MARTINEAU, *Autobiography*, ed. Maria Weston Chapman, 1877, Vol. 1, pp. 261–62

General

Macaulay has obtained a reputation which, although deservedly great, is yet in a remarkable measure undeserved. The few who regard him merely as a terse, forcible and logical writer, full of thought, and abounding in original views often sagacious and never otherwise than admirably expressed—appear to us precisely in the right. The many who look upon him as not only all this, but as a comprehensive and profound thinker, little prone to error, err essentially themselves. The source of the general mistake lies in a very singular consideration—yet in one upon which we do not remember ever to have heard a word of comment. We allude to a tendency in the public mind towards logic for logic's sake—a liability to confound the vehicle with the conveyed—an aptitude to be so dazzled by the luminousness with which an idea is set forth, as to mistake it for the luminousness of the idea itself. The error is one exactly analogous with that which leads the immature poet to think himself sublime wherever he is obscure, because obscurity is a source of the sublime—thus confounding obscurity of expression with the expression of obscurity. In the case of Macaulay—and we may say, *en passant*, of our own Channing—we assent to what he says, too often because we so very clearly understand what it is that he intends to say. Comprehending vividly the points and the sequence of his argument, we fancy that we are concurring in the argument itself. It is not every mind which is at once able to analyze the satisfaction it receives from such Essays as we see here. If it were merely *beauty* of style for which they were distinguished—if they were remarkable only for rhetorical flourishes—we would not be apt to estimate these flourishes at more than their due value. We would not agree with the doctrines of the essayist on account of the elegance with which they were urged. On the contrary, we would be inclined to disbelief. But when all ornament save that of simplicity is disclaimed—when we are attacked by precision of language, by perfect accuracy of expression, by directness and singleness of thought, and above all by a logic the most rigorously close and consequential—it is hardly a matter for wonder that nine of us out of ten are content to rest in the gratification thus received as in the gratification of absolute truth.

Of the terseness and simple vigor of Macaulay's style it is unnecessary to point out instances. Every one will acknowledge his merits on this score. His exceeding *closeness* of logic, however, is more especially remarkable. With this he suffers nothing to interfere. Here, for example, is a sentence in which, to preserve entire the chain of his argument—*to leave no minute gap which the reader might have to fill up with thought*—he runs into most unusual tautology.

"The books and traditions of a sect may contain, mingled with propositions strictly theological, other propositions, purporting to rest on the same authority, which relate to physics. If new discoveries should throw discredit on the physical propositions, the theological propositions, unless they can be separated from the physical propositions, will share in their discredit."

These things are very well in their way; but it is indeed questionable whether they do not appertain rather to the trickery of thought's vehicle, than to thought itself—rather to reason's shadow than to reason. Truth, for truth's sake, is seldom so enforced. It is scarcely too much to say that the style of the profound thinker is never closely logical. Here we might instance George Combe—than whom a more candid reasoner never, perhaps, wrote or spoke—than whom a more complete antipodes to Babington Macaulay there certainly never existed. The former *reasons* to discover the true. The latter *argues* to convince the world, and, in arguing, not unfrequently surprises himself into conviction. What Combe appears to Macaulay it would be a difficult thing to say. What Macaulay is thought of by Combe we can understand very well. The man who looks at an argument in its details alone, will not fail to be misled by the one; while he who keeps steadily in view the *generality* of a thesis will always at least approximate the truth under guidance of the other.

Macaulay's tendency—and the tendency of mere logic in general—to concentrate force upon minutiæ, at the expense of a subject as a whole, is well instanced in an article (in the volume now before us) on Ranke's *History of the Popes*. This article is called a review—possibly because it is anything else—as *lucus* is *lucus a non lucendo*. In fact it is nothing more than a beautifully written treatise on the main theme of Ranke himself; the whole matter of the treatise being deduced from the *History*. In the way of criticism there is nothing worth the name. The strength of the essayist is put forth to account for the progress of Romanism by maintaining that divinity is not a progressive science. The enigmas, says he in substance, which perplex the natural theologian are the same in all ages, while the Bible, where alone we are to seek revealed truth, has always been what it is.

The manner in which these two propositions are set forth, is a model for the logician and for the student of *belles lettres*—yet the error into which the essayist has rushed headlong, is egregious. He attempts to deceive his readers, or has deceived himself, by confounding the nature of that proof from which we reason of the concerns of earth, considered as man's habitation, and the nature of that evidence from which we reason of the same earth regarded as a unit of that vast whole, the universe. In the former case the *data* being palpable, the proof is direct: in the latter it is purely *analogical*. Were the indications we derive from science, of the nature and designs of Deity, and thence, by inference, of man's destiny—were these indications proof direct, no advance in science would strength-

en them—for, as our author truly observes, "nothing could be added to the force of the argument which the mind finds in every beast, bird, or flower"—but as these indications are rigidly analogical, every step in human knowledge—every astronomical discovery, for instance—throws additional light upon the august subject, *by extending the range of analogy*. That we know no more to-day of the nature of Deity—of its purposes—and thus of man himself—than we did even a dozen years ago—is a proposition disgracefully absurd; and of this any astronomer could assure Mr. Macaulay. Indeed, to our own mind, the *only* irrefutable argument in support of the soul's immortality—or, rather, the only conclusive proof of man's alternate dissolution and re-juvenescence *ad infinitum*—is to be found in analogies deduced from the modern established theory of the nebular cosmogony. Mr. Macaulay, in short, has forgotten what he frequently forgets, or neglects,—the very gist of his subject. He has forgotten that analogical evidence cannot, at all times, be discoursed of as if identical with proof direct. Throughout the whole of his treatise he has made no distinction whatever.—EDGAR ALLAN POE, "Thomas Babington Macaulay" (1841), *Essays and Reviews*, ed. G.R. Thompson, 1984, pp. 321–24

The brilliant Macaulay, who expresses the tone of the English governing classes of the day, explicitly teaches that *good* means good to eat, good to wear, material commodity; that the glory of modern philosophy is its direction on "fruit;" to yield economical inventions; and that its merit is to avoid ideas and avoid morals. He thinks it the distinctive merit of the Baconian philosophy in its triumph over the old Platonic, its disentangling the intellect from theories of the all-Fair and all-Good, and pinning it down to the making a better sick chair and a better wine-whey for an invalid;—this not ironically, but in good faith;—that, "solid advantage," as he calls it, meaning always sensual benefit, is the only good. The eminent benefit of astronomy is the better navigation it creates to enable the fruit-ships to bring home their lemons and wine to the London grocer. It was a curious result, in which the civility and religion of England for a thousand years ends in denying morals and reducing the intellect to a sauce-pan.—RALPH WALDO EMERSON, "Literature," *English Traits*, 1856

It has long been settled that literature alone remains open to him; and in that he has, with all his brillancy and captivating accomplishment destroyed the ground of confidence on which his adorers met him when, in his mature years, he published the first two volumes of his *History*. His review articles, and especially the one on Bacon, ought to have abolished all confidence in his honesty, as well as in his capacity for philosophy. Not only did he show himself to be disqualified for any appreciation of Bacon's philosophy, but his plagiarisms from the very author (Basil Montagu) whom he was pretending to demolish, (one instance of plagiarism among many) might have shown any conscientious reader how little he was to be trusted in regard to mere integrity of statement. But, as he announced a History, the public received as a *bona fide* History the work on which he proposes to build his fame. If it had been announced as a historical romance, it might have been read with almost unmixed delight, though exception might have been taken to his presentment of several characters and facts. He has been abundantly punished, for instance, for his slanderous exhibition of William Penn. But he has fatally manifested his loose and unscrupulous method of narrating, and, in his first edition, gave no clue whatever to his authorities, and no information in regard to dates which he could possibly suppress. Public opinion compelled, in future editions, some appearance of furnishing references to authorities, such as every conscientious historian finds it indispensable to his peace of mind to afford; but it is done by Macaulay in the most ineffectual and baffling way possible,—by clubbing together the mere names of his authorities at the bottom of the page, so that reference is all but impracticable. Where it is made, by painstaking readers, the inaccuracies and misrepresentations of the historian are found to multiply as the work of verification proceeds. In fact, the only way to accept his *History* is to take it as a brilliant fancypiece,—wanting not only the truth but the repose of history,—but stimulating, and even, to a degree, suggestive. While I write, announcement is made of two more volumes to appear in the course of the year. If the radical faults of the former ones are remedied, there may yet be before this gifted man something like the "career," so proudly anticipated for him a quarter of a century ago. If not, all is over; and his powers, once believed adequate to the construction of eternal monuments of statesmanship and noble edifices for intellectual worship, will be found capable of nothing better than rearing gay kiosks in the flower gardens of literature, to be soon swept away by the caprices of a new taste, as superficial as his own.—HARRIET MARTINEAU, *Autobiography*, ed. Maria Weston Chapman, 1877, Vol. 1, pp. 262–64

Macaulay's position never admitted of doubt. We know what to expect, and we always get it. It is like the old days of W. G. Grace's cricket. We went to see the leviathan slog for six, and we saw it. We expected him to do it, and he did it. So with Macaulay—the good Whig, as he takes up the *History*, settles himself down in his chair, and knows it is going to be a bad time for the Tories. Macaulay's style—his much-praised style —is ineffectual for the purpose of telling the truth about anything. It is splendid, but *splendide mendax*, and in Macaulay's case the style was the man. He had enormous knowledge, and a noble spirit; his knowledge enriched his style and his spirit consecrated it to the service of Liberty. We do well to be proud of Macaulay; but we must add that, great as was his knowledge, great also was his ignorance, which was none the less ignorance because it was wilful; noble as was his spirit, the range of subject over which it energized was painfully restricted. He looked out upon the world, but, behold, only the Whigs were good. Luther and Loyola, Cromwell and Claverhouse, Carlyle and Newman—they moved him not; their enthusiasms were delusions, and their politics demonstrable errors. Whereas, of Lord Somers and Charles first Earl Grey it is impossible to speak without emotion. But the world does not belong to the Whigs; and a great historian must be capable of sympathizing both with delusions and demonstrable errors. Mr. Gladstone has commented with force upon what he calls Macaulay's invincible ignorance, and further says that to certain aspects of a case (particularly those aspects most pleasing to Mr. Gladstone) Macaulay's mind was hermetically sealed. It is difficult to resist these conclusions; and it would appear no rash inference from them, that a man in a state of invincible ignorance and with a mind hermetically sealed, whatever else he may be—orator, advocate, statesman, journalist, man of letters—can never be a great historian. But, indeed, when one remembers Macaulay's limited range of ideas: the commonplaceness of his morality, and of his descriptions; his absence of humour, and of pathos—for though Miss Martineau says she found one pathetic passage in the *History*, I have often searched for it in vain; and then turns to Carlyle—to his almost bewildering affluence of thought, fancy, feeling, humour, pathos—his biting pen, his scorching criticism, his world-wide sympathy (save in certain moods)

with everything but the smug commonplace—to prefer Macaulay to him, is like giving the preference to Birket Foster over Salvator Rosa.—AUGUSTINE BIRRELL, "Carlyle," *Obiter Dicta*, 1885, pp. 29–32

The variety and brilliance of details in Macaulay's writing make one of the chief distinctions between his manner and that of the preceding century. He kept the old standards of taste in many things. His fondness for abrupt short sentences does not always conceal the old model on which they are formed. His short sentences are generally clauses in an old-fashioned antithetic period. Instead of the roll and volume of the periods of Gibbon, there is a succession of short waves; but these are carried forward generally on the top of a swell, the rhythm of which is the rhythm of the older period, while this older periodic cadence reappears undisguised whenever Macaulay chooses to keep his sentences long. Though he had escaped with his contemporaries from the old dogmas of criticism, he had no hatred of the eighteenth century and its respectability, such as moved the more vehement spirits in his day. He had, however, in common with men as unlike him as Carlyle, an aversion to the colourless and abstract graces of the old polite literature. In the plan of his work he seldom chooses to vary much from the old conventions of literary architecture; he does not envy the craft of Teufelsdröckh; his building is ruled by the simplest principles of proportion. But while the outlines are thus conformable to the old fashions, there is a very much greater amount of picturesque detail than would have been admitted by the old masters. The outlines are filled up with crowds of particulars. That fondness for particulars in description which distinguished the poems and novels of the new age from the more generalised and abstract compositions of the old school was hardly less strong in Macaulay than in Carlyle or in Browning. Though even in this respect, where Macaulay seems to come nearest in his prose to the flamboyant varieties of romance and poetry, he invents no new procedure or method of handling, but keeps the old tools of illustrative rhetoric. Johnson could write that "no man can reasonably be thought a lover of his country for roasting an ox, or burning a boot, or attending the meeting at Mile-End, or registering his name in the lumber-troop." Macaulay's illustrations are introduced by the same familiar method of satirical elaboration. He goes to greater expense in this way than his predecessors had done, but he does not go out of his way to invent new devices like those of *Sartor Resartus* or the *Opium Eater*. Though he may be more extravagant and profuse in his variety of details than is consistent with the old "dignity of history," this variety is all supported by a structure of great plainness. Some of his decorations appear to have surprised "the judicious" almost as much as Carlyle's *French Revolution*, but there was nothing in Macaulay's general plan of writing that was at all in sympathy with that new model. ⟨. . .⟩

Macaulay's weak places are those in which his memory fails to make up for the want of a philosophy. He did not feel the want of a theory of the universe, when he had his retentive and quick memory to supply him with images and ideas. There was no need for him to go burrowing and mining under the surface of phenomena; that painful work might be left to men who had not his range of vision on the whole field of history. He was not tempted to look for metaphysical explanations: he saw things framed in a large historical picture, and the picture was generally enough for him. His style was the style of a man singularly at ease in his own mind and in the command of his knowledge. He shows little trace of the sordid business of study, of the mechanical and laborious part of literary work. The picture of the world comes of itself before his mind, and flashes into vividness in this corner and in that, showing the relations of things to one another before he has had time to grow weary in puzzling them out. He can look down from his point of vantage on the crowd of antiquarian sappers and miners, creeping from fact to fact. His style reflects the cheerfulness of the mind that has secured itself in a specular tower, and has no need to vex itself about its point of view, or its principles of criticism. His view is its own justification, because it is a view full of light and variety, and different from that of the historical pioneer in his gallery underground.

A mind of this sort, relying on extent of view, without special science, is not out of danger of fallacies. The wide view and the long memory are wonderful and glorious; but if ever a mist comes over them, or the telescopic sight is accidentally blurred or hindered, then the failure is more hopeless and absolute than the errors of duller men who without genius rely on their training and scientific instruments. In his discussion of Bacon's theory of knowledge, Macaulay had neglected to provide himself with any other than his ordinary methods of work, and unhappily in this case his ordinary methods failed him.

Wherever Macaulay's view is restricted or prejudiced, it loses all light: there is no spiritual zeal in his argument, such as enlivens the judgment of Carlyle, even when its historical soundness is questionable. No writer is placed at such a disadvantage as Macaulay, when his worst passages are taken up and criticised minutely. With no writer is criticism so apt to be unjust, simply because it is impossible to represent in detail a genius which was great by the extent of its empire, rather than by any mystery of its inner shrines. To remember particular bits of Macaulay's prose is not always as satisfactory as to remember his heroic ballads. But in the variegated mass of his writings, and in the impression of life and zest in all that he wrote, the particular faults and fallacies may easily and rightly pass out of notice. In the works that he wrote, as in his courageous and fortunate life, there is little claim to any deeper source or higher standard of knowledge than is recognised in the market place. For all that, his works and his life command the respect that is only paid to clearer sight and stronger wills than those of the general multitude.—W. P. KER, "Thomas Babington Macaulay," *English Prose*, ed. Henry Craik, 1896, Vol. 5, pp. 411–18

Works

SPEECHES

Tickler: ⟨. . .⟩ do you know it is a plain simple fact, that this Tom Macaulay put me much more in mind of the Jeffrey of ten years ago, than did the Jeffrey *ipsissimus* of *hodie.*

North: You pay Mr. Macaulay a high compliment—the highest, I think, he has ever met with.

Tickler: Not quite—for it is the fashion, among a certain small coterie at least, to talk of him as "the Burke of our age."—However, he is certainly a very clever fellow, the cleverest declaimer by far on that side of the House, and, had he happened to be a *somebody*, we should, no doubt, have seen Tom in high places ere now.

North: A son of old Zachary, I believe? Is he like the papa?

Tickler: So I have heard—but I never saw the senior, of whom some poetical planter has so unjustifiably sung—

How smooth, persuasive, plausible, and glib
From holy lips is dropp'd the specious fib.

The son is an ugly, cross-made, splay-footed, shapeless little dumpling of a fellow, with a featureless face too—except

indeed a good expansive forehead—sleek puritanical sandy hair—large glimmering eyes—and a mouth from ear to ear. He has a lisp and a burr, moreover, and speaks thickly and huskily for several minutes before he gets into the swing of his discourse; but after that, nothing can be more dazzling than his whole execution. What he says is substantially, of course, mere stuff and nonsense; but it is so well worded, and so volubly and forcibly delivered—there is such an endless string of epigram and antithesis—such a flashing of epithets—such an accumulation of images—and the voice is so trumpetlike, and the action so grotesquely emphatic, that you might hear a pin drop in the House. Manners Sutton himself listens. It is obvious that he has got the main parts at least by heart—but for this I gave him the more praise and glory. Altogether, the impression on my mind was very much beyond what I had been prepared for—so much so, that I can honestly and sincerely say I felt for his situation most deeply, when Peel was skinning him alive the next evening, and the sweat of agony kept pouring down his well-bronzed cheeks under the merciless infliction.—JOHN WILSON (as "Christopher North"), *Noctes Ambrosianae* (Aug. 1831), 1854

I say, Sir, that I admit the learned gentleman's eloquence, and feel it peculiarly, not only from the admiration it excites, but from the difficulty it imposes upon the humble individual whose fortune it is—*haud passibus æquis*—to follow him. But I am relieved, in some degree, by the reflection that, as from the highest flights men are liable to the heaviest falls, and in the swiftest courses to the most serious disasters, so, I will say, is the most brilliant eloquence sometimes interrupted by intervals of the greatest obscurity, and the most impassioned declamation defeated by the most fatal contradictions; and I must assert that the speech of the learned gentleman had points of weakness which no imprudence or want of judgment ever surpassed, and carried within itself its own refutation beyond any other speech I almost ever heard. The learned gentleman seemed, sometimes, to forget that he was addressing the House of Commons; or, aware that a voice so eloquent was not to be confined within these walls, he took the opportunity of the debate here, of addressing himself also to another branch of the Legislature, in, as he no doubt thought, the words of wisdom taught by experience. Not satisfied with those vague generalities, which he handled with that brilliant declamation which tickles the ear and amuses the imagination, without satisfying the reason, he unluckily, I think, for the force of his appeal, thought proper to descend to argumentative illustration and historical precedents. But whence has he drawn his experience? Sir, he drew his weapon from the very armoury to which, if I had been aware of his attack, I should myself have resorted for the means of repelling it.—JOHN WILSON CROKER, Speech in the House of Commons on the Reform Bill (Sept. 22, 1831), *The Croker Papers*, ed. Louis J. Jennings, 1885, Vol. 2, pp. 130–31

Mr. Thomas Macaulay, late member for Leeds, and now a member of Council in India, could boast of a brilliant, if not a very long parliamentary career. He was one of those men who at once raised himself to the first rank in the Senate. His maiden speech electrified the house, and called forth the highest compliments to the speaker from men of all parties. He was careful to preserve the laurels he had thus so easily and suddenly won. He was a man of shrewd mind, and knew that if he spoke often, the probability was, he could not speak so well; and that consequently there could be no more likely means of lowering him from the elevated station to which he had raised himself, than frequently addressing the House. In this he was quite right, for he had no talents for extempore speaking. I have seen him attempt it—only, however, when forced to it by the situation he held under Government—on several occasions; but in every such instance he acquitted himself very indifferently. He never made above three or four speeches in the course of a Session—sometimes not so many,—and these were always on questions involving some great principle of politics or justice, and which commanded deep and universal attention at the time. His speeches were always most carefully studied, and committed to memory, exactly as he delivered them, beforehand. He bestowed a world of labour on their preparation; and, certainly, never was labour bestowed to more purpose. In every sentence you saw the man of genius—the profound scholar—the deep thinker—the close and powerful reasoner. You scarcely knew which most to admire—the beauty of his ideas, or of the language in which they were clothed. His diction was faultless; his matter was strongly imbued with the spirit of what, for want of a better expression, I would call the poetry of philosophy. He was, in this respect, the same man in the house as he was when penning such articles for the *Edinburgh Review* as his celebrated one on the genius and writings of Milton. He was an excellent speaker withal—not forcible or vehement, carrying you away, as it were, by force; but seducing you, taking you a willing captive, if I may so speak, by his dulcet tones and engaging manner, wherever he chose to go. Time after time has the House listened to him as if entranced.

His personal appearance is prepossessing. In stature he is about the middle size, and well formed. His eyes are of a deep blue, and have a very intelligent expression. His complexion is dark, and his hair of a dark brown colour. His face is rather inclined to the oval form. His features are small and regular. He is now in the thirty-eighth year of his age.—JAMES GRANT, *Random Recollections of the House of Commons*, 1836, pp. 176–78

Macaulay had no thought of resting his fame on his parliamentary speeches; he would willingly have left them to the rarely visited cemetery of the parliamentary history. He was placed under compulsion by the act of a piratical bookseller, who printed many of them (insinuating that he did so by authority) bristling with blunders, bad English, loose argument, errors and mistakes about events and persons, everything most abhorrent to Macaulay's taste and judgement. He was under the necessity of publishing a more trustworthy edition. We confess some gratitude for this bad act of the unprincipled Curll of our days, for some of these speeches appear to us oratorical compositions of the highest order. By all accounts Macaulay's delivery was far too rapid to be impressive; it wanted also variety and flexibility of intonation. Even the most practised reporters panted after him in vain; how much more the slower intellects of country gentlemen and the mass of the House! This, however, only heightens our astonishment that speeches so full, so profoundly meditated, yet with so much freedom, with no appearance of being got by heart, with such prodigality of illustration and allusion, should be poured forth with such unhesitating flow, with such bewildering quickness of utterance. To read them with delight and profit, we read them rather slowly; we can hardly conceive that they were spoken less deliberately. It may be questioned, and has been questioned, whether Macaulay was, or could have become, a masterly debater. This accomplishment, except in rare examples, is acquired only by long use and practice. When Macaulay entered the House, the first places were filled by men of established influence and much parliamentary train-

ing. Even if he had felt called upon to make himself more prominent, it may be doubted whether he could have sufficiently curbed his impetuous energy, or checked his torrent of words. He would have found it difficult to assume the stately, prudent, reserved, compressed reply; he might have torn his adversaries' arguments to shreds, but he would not have been content without a host of other arguments, and so would have destroyed the effect of his own confutation. Still it is remarkable that on two occasions a speech of Macaulay's actually turned the vote of the house, and carried the question (a very rare event) in his own way,—the debate on the Copyright Act, and the question of Judges holding seats in the House of Commons. Though he took his seat, Lord Macaulay never spoke in the House of Peers; he went down, we believe, more than once, with the intention of speaking, but some unexpected turn in the debate deprived him of his opportunity; his friends, who knew the feeble state of his health at that time, were almost rejoiced at their disappointment in not hearing him in that which would have been so congenial a field for his studied and matured eloquence.—H. H. MILMAN, *Proceedings of the Royal Society of London*, 1860–62, Vol. 11, pp. xix–xx

ESSAYS

Edinburgh Review came last night. A smart, vigorous paper by Macaulay on Horace Walpole. Ambitious; too antithetic; the heart of the matter not struck. What will that man become? He has more force and emphasis in him than any other of my British contemporaries (coevals). Wants the root of belief, however. May fail to accomplish much. Let us hope better things.—THOMAS CARLYLE, *Journal* (Nov. 1, 1833), cited in James Anthony Froude, *Thomas Carlyle*, 1882, Vol. 2, p. 301

At last I send you an article of interminable length about Lord Bacon. I hardly know whether it is not too long for an article in a Review; but the subject is of such vast extent that I could easily have made the paper twice as long as it is.

About the historical and political part there is no great probability that we shall differ in opinion. But what I have said about Bacon's philosophy is widely at variance with what Dugald Stewart and Mackintosh have said on the same subject. I have not your essay, nor have ever read it since I read it at Cambridge with very great pleasure, but without any knowledge of the subject. I have at present only a very faint and general recollection of its contents, and have in vain tried to procure a copy of it here. I fear, however, that, differing widely as I do from Stewart and Mackintosh, I shall hardly agree with you. My opinion is formed, not at second-hand, like those of nine-tenths of the people who talk about Bacon, but after several very attentive perusals of his greatest works, and after a good deal of thought. If I am in the wrong, my errors may set the minds of others at work, and may be the means of bringing both them and me to a knowledge of the truth. I never bestowed so much care on anything that I have written. There is not a sentence in the latter half of the article which has not been repeatedly re-cast. I have no expectation that the popularity of the article will bear any proportion to the trouble which I have expended on it. But the trouble has been so great a pleasure to me that I have already been very greatly overpaid.—THOMAS BABINGTON MACAULAY, Letter to Macvey Napier (Nov. 26, 1836), *Selection from the Correspondence of Macvey Napier*, ed. Macvey Napier, 1879, pp. 180–81

I received the Review [July 1837], and have read most of it, and with great pleasure. There is more variety and more good matter in it than there has been for a long time. The *Bacon* is, as you say, very striking, and no doubt is the work of an extremely clever man. It is so very long that I think you might have cut it in two, there being an obvious divison. But (not to trouble you with the superfluous enumeration of its good qualities), it has two grievous defects,—a redundancy, an over-crowding of every one thing that is touched upon, that almost turns one's head; for it is out of one digression into another, and each thought in each is illustrated by twenty different cases and anecdotes, all of which follow from the first without any effort. This is a sad defect in Macaulay, and it really seems to get worse instead of better. I need not say that it is the defect of a very clever person—it is indeed exuberance. But it is a defect also that *old age* is liable to. The other fault you have alluded to, but I will expose it after Macaulay's own manner of writing. "You might as well say that all men balance themselves in order to walk, and, therefore, there is no science of mechanics, or that every child learns to suck, and, therefore, the Torricellian experiment was of no use to science, or that the dullest of human beings goes to his point by one straight line and not by the two other sides of a triangle, and, therefore, there is no Geometry, or that the most ordinary workman, be he mason building an arch, or cooper making a cask, forms a curve by joining straight lines short in proportion to the whole length, and, therefore, the fluxional calculus was no discovery;" through two or three pages as easy to fill with such trash as it would be unprofitable. In fact, this way of treating a subject is somewhat mistaking garrulity for copiousness, but I am now complaining much more of the matter than the manner. Greater blunder never was committed than the one Macaulay has made on the Inductive Philosophy. He is quite ignorant of the subject. He may garnish his pages as he pleases with references: it only shows he has read Bacon for the *flowers* and not the *fruit*, and this is indeed the fact. He has no science at all, and cannot reason. His contemporaries at Cambridge always said he had not the conception of what an argument was; and surely it was not right for a person who never had heard of Gilbert's treatise, to discuss Bacon's originality, nay, to descant on Bacon at all, who seems never to have read the *Sylva Sylvarum* (for see p. 83 about ointments for broken bones); and who goes through the whole of his speculation (or whatever you choose to term it) without making any allusion to Bacon's notorious failure when he came to put his own rules in practice, and without seeming to be at all aware that Sir I. Newton was an experimental philosopher.—HENRY, LORD BROUGHAM, Letter to Macvey Napier (July 28, 1837), *Selection from the Correspondence of Macvey Napier*, ed. Macvey Napier, 1879, pp. 196–97

With the "Essay on Milton" began Macaulay's literary career, and, brilliant as the career was, it had few points more brilliant than its beginning.

⟨. . .⟩ already, in the "Essay on Milton," the style of Macaulay is, indeed, that which we know so well. A style to dazzle, to gain admirers everywhere, to attract imitators in multitude! A style brilliant, metallic, exterior; making strong points, alternating invective with eulogy, wrapping in a robe of rhetoric the thing it represents; not, with the soft play of life, following and rendering the thing's very form and pressure. For, indeed, in rendering things in this fashion, Macaulay's gift did not lie. Mr. Trevelyan reminds us that in the preface to his collected Essays, Lord Macaulay himself "unsparingly condemns the redundance of youthful enthusiasm" of the "Essay on Milton." But the unsoundness of the essay does not spring from its "redundance of youthful enthusiasm." It springs from this: that the writer has not for his aim to see and to utter the real truth about his object. Whoever comes to the "Essay

on Milton" with the desire to get at the real truth about Milton, whether as a man or as a poet, will feel that the essay in nowise helps him. A reader who only wants rhetoric, a reader who wants a panegyric on Milton, a panegyric on the Puritans, will find what he wants. A reader who wants criticism will be disappointed.

This would be palpable to all the world, and every one would feel, not pleased, but disappointed, by the "Essay on Milton," were it not that the readers who seek for rhetoric, or who seek for praise and blame to suit their own already established likes and dislikes, are extremely many. A man who is fond of rhetoric may find pleasure in hearing that in *Paradise Lost* "Milton's conception of love unites all the voluptuousness of the Oriental haram, and all the gallantry of the chivalric tournament, with all the pure and quiet affection of an English fireside." He may glow at being told that "Milton's thoughts resemble those celestial fruits and flowers which the Virgin Martyr of Massinger sent down from the gardens of Paradise to the earth, and which were distinguished from the productions of other soils not only by superior bloom and sweetness, but by miraculous efficacy to invigorate and to heal." He may imagine that he has got something profound when he reads that, if we compare Milton and Dante in their management of the agency of supernatural beings,—"the exact details of Dante with the dim intimations of Milton,"—the right conclusion of the whole matter is this:—

> Milton wrote in an age of philosophers and theologians. It was necessary, therefore, for him to abstain from giving such a shock to their understandings as might break the charm which it was his object to throw over their imaginations. It was impossible for him to adopt altogether the material or the immaterial system. He therefore took his stand on the debateable ground. He left the whole in ambiguity. He has doubtless, by so doing, laid himself open to the charge of inconsistency. But though philosophically in the wrong he was poetically in the right.

Poor Robert Hall, "well-nigh worn out with that long disease, his life," and, in the last precious days of it, "discovered lying on the floor, employed in learning, by aid of grammar and dictionary, enough Italian to enable him to verify" this ingenious criticism! Alas! even had his life been prolonged like Hezekiah's, he could not have verified it, for it is unverifiable. A poet who, writing "in an age of philosophers and theologians," finds it "impossible for him to adopt altogether the material or the immaterial system," who, therefore, "takes his stand on the debateable ground," who "leaves the whole in ambiguity," and who, in doing so, "though philosophically in the wrong, was poetically in the right!" Substantial meaning such lucubrations have none. And in like manner, a distinct and substantial meaning can never be got out of the fine phrases about "Milton's conception of love uniting all the voluptuousness of the Oriental haram, and all the gallantry of the chivalric tournament, with all the pure and quiet affection of an English fireside;" or about "Milton's thoughts resembling those celestial fruits and flowers which the Virgin Martyr of Massinger sent down from the gardens of Paradise to the earth;" the phrases are mere rhetoric. Macaulay's writing passes for being admirably clear, and so externally it is; but often it is really obscure, if one takes his deliverances seriously, and seeks to find in them a definite meaning. However, there is a multitude of readers, doubtless, for whom it is sufficient to have their ears tickled with fine rhetoric; but the tickling makes a serious reader impatient.—MATTHEW

ARNOLD, "A French Critic on Milton" (1877), *Mixed Essays*, 1879

LAYS OF ANCIENT ROME

What! Poetry from Macaulay? Ay—and why not? The House hushes itself to hear him, even when "Stanley is the cry." If he be not the first of critics, (spare our blushes,) who is? Name the Young Poet who could have written *The Armada*, and kindled, as if by electricity, beacons on all the brows of England till night grew day?

The Young Poets, we said, all want fire. Macaulay, then, is not one of the set; for he is full of fire. The Young Poets, too, are somewhat weakly; he is strong. The Young Poets are rather ignorant; his knowledge is great. The Young Poets mumble books; he devours them. The Young Poets dally with their subject; he strikes its heart. The Young Poets twiddle on the Jew's harp; he sounds the trumpet. The Young Poets are arrayed in long singing-robes, and look like women; he chants succinct—if need be—for a charge. The Young Poets are still their own heroes; he sees but the chiefs he celebrates. The Young Poets weave dreams with shadows transitory as clouds; with substances he builds realities lasting as rocks. The Young Poets are imitators all; he is original. The Young Poets steal from all and sundry, and deny their thefts. He robs in the face of day. Whom? Homer. ⟨. . .⟩

All scholars know that Niebuhr speaks of the *lays and legends* out of which grew the fabulous history of old Rome. He calls Livy's account of the battle at the Lake Regillus, "a rich and beautiful epical narrative;" and says, "the gigantic battle, in which the gods openly take part, and determine the result, closes the *Lay of the Tarquins*; and I am convinced that I am not mistaken in conjecturing, that, in the old poem, the whole generations who had been warring with one another ever since the crime of Sextus, were swept away in this *Mort of heroes*." *Lays of Ancient Rome*, then, is not a thought of Macaulay's; but the thought, though suggested before, would not have appeared capable and worthy of execution except to a man of genius and a scholar, one who had a strong power of placing himself under the full influence of an imagined situation, and whose elaborate and accurate study of antiquity furnished him with an ample and authentic store of names and incidents, dress and drapery, manners and feelings. The seed scattered abroad found here a fit and fertile soil to receive it. ⟨. . .⟩

It is a great merit of these poems, that they are free from ambition or exaggeration. Nothing seems overdone—no tawdry piece of finery disfigures the simplicity of the plan that has been chosen. They seem to have been framed with great artistical skill—with much self-denial, and abstinence from any thing incongruous—and with a very successful imitation of the effects intended to be represented. Yet every here and there images of beauty, and expressions of feeling, are thrown out that are wholly independent of Rome or the Romans, and that appeal to the widest sensibilities of the human heart. In point of homeliness of thought and language, there is often a boldness which none but a man conscious of great powers of writing would have ventured to show.

In these rare qualities, *Lays of Ancient Rome* resemble Lockhart's *Spanish Ballads*, which must have been often ringing in Macaulay's ears, since first he caught their inspiring music more than twenty years ago—when, "like a burnished fly in pride of May," he bounced through the open windows of *Knight's Quarterly Magazine*. Two such volumes all a summer's day you may seek without finding among the *works!* of "our Young Poets." People do not call Lockhart and Macaulay poets at all—for both have acquired an inveterate habit of writing prose in preference to verse, and first-rate prose too; but then the genius of the one man is as different as may be from that of the other—agreeing, however, in this, that each exhibits bone and muscle sufficient, if equitably distributed among ten "Young Poets," to set them up among the "rural villages" as strong men, who might even occasionally exhibit in booths as giants.—JOHN WILSON, *"Lays of Ancient Rome," Blackwood's Edinburgh Magazine*, Dec. 1842, pp. 805–7, 823–24

The *Lays*, in point of form, are not in the least like the genuine productions of a primitive age or people, and it is no blame to Mr Macaulay that they are not. He professes imitation of Homer, but we really see no resemblance, except in the nature of some of the incidents, and the animation and vigour of the narrative; and the *Iliad*, after all, is not the original ballads of the Trojan war, but those ballads moulded together, and wrought into the forms of a more civilized and cultivated age. It is difficult to conjecture what the forms of the old Roman ballad may have been, and certain, that whatever they were, they could no more satisfy the æsthetic requirements of modern culture, than an ear accustomed to the great organ of Freyburg or Harlem could relish Orpheus's hurdy-gurdy; although the airs which Orpheus played, if they could be recovered, might perhaps be executed with great effect on the more perfect instrument.

The forms of Mr Macaulay's ballad poetry are essentially modern; they are those of the romantic and chivalrous, not the classical ages, and even in those they are a reproduction, not of the originals, but of the imitations of Scott. In this we think he has done well, for Scott's style is as near to that of the ancient ballad as we conceive to be at all compatible with real popular effect on the modern mind. The difference between the two may be seen by the most cursory comparison of any real old ballad, 'Chevy Chase' for instance, with the last canto of *Marmion*, or with any of these Lays. Conciseness is the characteristic of the real ballad—diffuseness, of the modern adaptation. The old bard did everything by single touches; Scott and Mr Macaulay by repetition and accumulation of particulars. They produce all their effect by what they *say*; he by what he *suggested*; by what he stimulated the imagination to paint for itself. But then the old ballads were not written for the light reading of tired readers. To do the work in *their* way, they required to be brooded over, or had at least the aid of tune and of impassioned recitation. Stories which are to be told to children in the age of eagerness and excitability, or sung in banquet halls to assembled warriors, whose daily ideas and feelings supply a flood of comment ready to gush forth on the slightest hint of the poet, cannot fly too swift and straight to the mark. But Mr Macaulay wrote to be only read, and by readers for whom it was necessary to do all.

These poems, therefore, are not the worse for being un-Roman in their form; and in their substance they are Roman to a degree which deserves great admiration. Mr Macaulay's prose writings had not prepared us for the power which he has here manifested of identifying himself easily and completely with states of feeling and modes of life alien to modern experience. Nobody could have previously doubted that he possessed fancy, but he has here added to it the higher faculty of Imagination. We have not been able to detect, in the four poems, one idea or feeling which was not, or might not have been, Roman; while the externals of Roman life, and the feelings characteristic of Rome and of that particular age, are reproduced with great felicity, and without being made unduly predominant over the universal features of human nature and human life.—JOHN STUART MILL, "Macaulay's *Lays of Ancient Rome,*" *Westminster Review,* Feb. 1843, pp. 105–6

> The dreamy rhymer's measured snore
> Falls heavy on our ears no more;
> And by long strides are left behind
> The dear delights of woman-kind,
> Who win their battles like their loves,
> In satin waistcoats and kid gloves,
> And have achieved the crowning work
> When they have truss'd and skewer'd a Turk.
> Another comes wtih stouter tread,
> And stalks among the statelier dead.
> He rushes on, and hails by turns
> High-crested Scott, broad-breasted Burns,
> And shows the British youth, who ne'er
> Will lag behind, what Romans were,
> When all the Tuscans and their Lars
> Shouted, and shook the towers of Mars.
> —WALTER SAVAGE LANDOR, "To Macaulay,"
> 1846

As to Lord Macaulay—the *History of England* did not come out till I had left Oxford, and I doubt if I read the *Essays* till about the same time; but of the *Lays of Ancient Rome*—I believe the critics of the grand style call them "pinchbeck," which I fancy is meant to be scornful—I can only say that they are still ringing in my ears with a note as fresh as they had fifty years back. I have said them over on their own ground; I have proved the truth of every epithet; and now, with the Sicilian deeds of Pyrrhus as my day's work, it is the notes of the "Prophecy of Capys" which comes first home to me at the thought of the "Red King" and his bold Epirotes. Still, the *Lays* are play-work beside the *History.*—EDWARD A. FREEMAN, "A Review of My Opinions," *Forum,* April 1892, pp. 152–53

HISTORY OF ENGLAND

My dear Macaulay, the mother that bore you, had she been yet alive, could scarcely have felt prouder or happier than I do at this outburst of your graver fame. I have long had a sort of parental interest in your glory; and it is now mingled with a feeling of deference to your intellectual superiority which can only consort, I take it, with the character of a female parent. —FRANCIS, LORD JEFFREY, Letter to Thomas Babington Macaulay (1848), cited in G. Otto Trevelyan, *The Life and Letters of Lord Macaulay,* 1876, Vol. 2, pp. 205–6

If you could do it pure justice, nothing more is wanted to give the author sufficient pain. He has written some very brilliant essays—very transparent in artifice, and I suspect not over honest in scope and management, but he has written *no history*; and he has, I believe, committed himself ingeniously in two or three points, which, fitly exposed, would confound him a good deal, and check his breeze from El Dorado. Chiefly, his bitter hatred of the Church of England all through is evident; it is, I think, the only very strong feeling in the book; and his depreciation of the station and character of the clergy of Charles II and James II to-day is but a symptom.

Then his treatment of the Whig criminals Sidney and Russell, is very shabby, and might be awfully shown up by merely a few quotations from the State trials and Barillon.

You will tell me by-and-bye what you think of this. I own that I read the book with breathless interest, in spite of occasional indignations, but I am now reading Grote's new volume of his *History of Greece,* and, upon my word, I find the contrast of his calm, stately, tranquil narrative very soothing. In short, I doubt if Macaulay's book will go down as a standard addition to our *historical* library, though it must always keep a high place among the specimens of English rhetoric.—JOHN GIBSON LOCKHART, Letter to John Wilson Croker (Jan. 12, 1849), *The Croker Papers,* ed. Louis J. Jennings, 1885, Vol. 3, pp. 194–95

The sect of Quakers has been in high dudgeon with Macaulay, for what they consider an unjust attack upon Penn in his *History.* They demanded an interview, which he at once granted, and they remonstrated with him upon what they considered his aspersions on their fame, particularly as referring to the transaction of the money which was extorted from the girls who went out to meet Monmouth for the use of the maids of honour, and which was carried on by Penn. The Quakers denied the facts, but Macaulay produced all the official documents on which he had founded his statement, and they were entirely *floored.* Macaulay offered to print the documents from which he had gathered his facts, but they were in no hurry to accept this proposal, and said they would confer further before they gave their answer.

Macaulay was much amused by this incident, and contrived to please the Quakers by his courtesy. Two editions of 3,000 each of his *History* were sold in two weeks. A third edition of 10,000 is about to be issued, of which 4,000 copies are already ordered.—HENRY GREVILLE, *Diary,* Feb. 7, 1849

Macaulay's style, like other original things, has already produced a school of imitators. Its influence may distinctly be traced, both in the periodical and daily literature of the day. Its great characteristic is the shortness of the sentences, which often equals that of Tacitus himself, and the rapidity with which new and distinct ideas or facts succeed each other in his richly-stored pages. He is the Pope of English prose: he often gives two sentiments and facts in a single line. No preceding writer in prose, in any modern language with which we are acquainted, has carried this art of abbreviation, or rather cramming of ideas, to such a length; and to its felicitous use much of the celebrity which he has acquired is to be ascribed. There is no doubt that it is a most powerful engine for the stirring of the mind, and when not repeated too often, or carried too far, has a surprising effect. Its introduction forms an era in historical composition. ⟨. . .⟩

This style does admirably well for short biographies, such as those of Warren Hastings, or Clive, in the *Edinburgh Review,* in which the object is to condense the important events of a whole lifetime into comparatively few pages, and fascinate the reader by as condensed and brilliant a picture as it is possible to present, of the most striking features of their character and story. But how will it answer for a lengthened history, such as Macaulay's great work promises to be, extending to twelve or fifteen volumes? How will it do to make the "extreme medicine of the constitution its daily bread?" Ragouts and French dishes are admirable at a feast, or on particular occasions, but what should we say to a diet prescribed of such highly seasoned food every day? ⟨. . .⟩ The subject, of course, would not admit of, the mind of the reader would sink under, the frequent repetition of such powerful emotion. But the style is generally the same. It almost always indicates a crowd of separate ideas, facts, or assertions, in such close juxtaposition, that they literally seem wedged together. Such is the extent of the magazine of reading and information from which they are drawn, that they come tumbling out, often without much order or arrangement, and generally so close together that it is difficult for a person not previously acquainted with the subject to tell which are of importance and which are immaterial.

This tendency, when as confirmed and general as it has

now become, we consider by far the most serious fault in Mr Macaulay's style; and it is not less conspicuous in his general history than in his detached biographies. Indeed, its continuance in the former species of composition is mainly owing to the brilliant success with which it has been attended in the latter. In historical essays it is not a blemish, it is rather a beauty; because, in such miniature portraits or cabinet pieces, minuteness of finishing and crowding of incidents in a small space are among the principal requisites we desire, the chief charm we admire. But the style of painting which we justly admire in Albano and Vanderwerf, would be misplaced in the ceiling of the Sistine Chapel, or even the extended canvass of the Transfiguration. We do not object to such elaborate finishing, such brevity of sentences, such crowding of facts and ideas, in the delineation of the striking incidents or principal characters of the work; what we object to is its continuance on ordinary occasions, in the drawing of inconsiderable characters, and in what should be the simple thread of the story. Look how easy Hume is in his ordinary narrative—how unambitious Livy, in the greater part of his history. We desiderate such periods of relaxation and repose in Macaulay. We there always discover learning, genius, power; but the prodigal display of these powers often mars their effect. We see it not only in delineating the immortal deeds of heroes, or the virtues of princesses, but in portraying the habits of serving-women or the frailties of maids of honour. With all its elevated and poetical qualities, the mind of Macaulay occasionally gives token of its descent from our common ancestress, Eve, in an evident fondness for gossip. It would perhaps be well for him to remember that the scandal of our great great-grandmothers is not generally interesting, or permanently edifying; and that he is not to measure the gratification it will give to the world in general, by the avidity with which it is devoured among the titled descendants of the fair sinners in the Whig coteries. There is often a want of breadth and keeping in his pictures. To resume our pictorial metaphor, Macaulay's pages often remind us of the paintings of Bassano, in which warriors and pilgrims, horses and mules, dromedaries and camels, sheep and lambs, Arabs and Ethiopians, shining armour and glistening pans, spears and pruning-hooks, scimitars and shepherds' crooks, baskets, tents, and precious stuffs, are crammed together without mercy, and with an equal light thrown on the most insignificant as the most important parts of the piece. —SIR ARCHIBALD ALISON, "Macaulay's *History of England*," *Blackwood's Edinburgh Magazine*, April 1849, pp. 387–90

I have just finished Macaulay's two volumes of the *History of England* with the same feeling that you expressed—regret at coming to the end, and longing for another volume—the most uncommon feeling, I suppose, that readers of two thick octavo volumes of the history of England and of times so well known, or whose story has been so often written, ever experienced. In truth, in the whole course of reading or hearing it read I was sorry to stop and glad to go on. It bears peculiarly well that severe test of being read aloud; it never wearies the ear by the long resounding line, but keeps the attention alive by the energy shown. It is the perfection of style so varied, and yet the same in fitness, in propriety, in perspicuity, in grace, in dignity and eloquence, and, whenever naturally called forth, in that just indignation which makes the historian as well as the poet. If Voltaire says true that "the style is the man," what a man must Macaulay be! But the man is in fact as much more than the style, as the matter is more than the manner. It is astonishing with what ease Macaulay wields, manages, arranges his vast materials collected far and near, and knows their

value and proportions so as to give the utmost strength and force and light and life to the whole, and sustains the whole. Such new lights are thrown upon historic facts and historic characters that the old appear new, and that which had been dull becomes bright and entertaining and interesting. Exceedingly interesting he has made history by the happy use and aid of biography and anecdote. A word brings the individual before us, and shows not only his character, but the character of the times, and at once illustrates or condemns to everlasting fame. Macaulay has proved by example how false Madame de Staël's principle was that biography and biographical anecdotes were altogether inadmissible in history—below the dignity or breaking the proportion or unity, I suppose she thought. But whatever might be her reasons, she gave this opinion to Dumont, who told it to me. Much good it did her! How much more interesting historical *précis* in painting or in writing, which is painting in word, are made by the introduction of portraits of celebrated individuals! Either as actors or even as spectators, the bold figures live, and merely by their life further the action and impress the sense of truth and reality. I have pleasure, my dear Dr. Holland, in pointing out to you, warm as it first comes, the admiration which this work has raised to this height in my mind. I know this will give you a sympathetic pleasure.—MARIA EDGEWORTH, Letter to Dr. Holland (April 2, 1849), cited in Helen Zimmern, *Maria Edgeworth*, 1884, pp. 299–300

It may be thought that the successful work of that great master in the art of descriptive history would have deterred me from my attempt; but, on the contrary, it acted as an incentive, since it breaks off just at the point where the great difficulties of the new government began, and the new system finally consolidated itself. I should not have been contented with my work had I not (to keep up the simile) attempted the ascent of this last height, from which I might hope to survey the past and the future, the whence and the whither of the history.—LEOPOLD VON RANKE, *History of England*, 1875, Vol. 6, p. 144

What Macaulay does well he does incomparably. Who else can mass the details as he does, and yet not mar or obscure, but only heighten, the effect of the picture as a whole? Who else can bring so amazing a profusion of knowledge within the strait limits of a simple plan, nowhere encumbered, everywhere free and obvious in its movement? How sure the strokes, and how bold and vivid the result! Yet when we have laid the book aside, when the charm and the excitement of the telling narrative have worn off, when we have lost step with the swinging gait at which the style goes, when the details have faded from our recollection, and we sit removed and thoughtful, with only the greater outlines of the story sharp upon our minds, a deep misgiving and dissatisfaction take possession of us. We are no longer young, and we are chagrined that we should have been so pleased and taken with the glitter and color and mere life of the picture. Let boys be cajoled by rhetoric, we cry; men must look deeper. What of the judgment of this facile and eloquent man? Can we agree with him, when he is not talking and the charm is gone? What shall we say of his assessment of men and measures? Is he just? Is he himself in possession of the whole truth? Does he open the matter to us as it was? Does he not, rather, rule us like an advocate, and make himself master of our judgments?

Then it is that we become aware that there were two Macaulays: Macaulay the artist, with an exquisite gift for telling a story, filling his pages with little vignettes it is impossible to forget, fixing these with an inimitable art upon the surface of a narrative that did not need the ornament they gave it, so strong and large and adequate was it; and Macaulay the Whig, subtly turning narrative into argument, and making history the vindication of a party. The mighty narrative is a great engine of proof. It is not told for its own sake. It is evidence summed up in order to justify a judgment. We detect the tone of the advocate, and though if we are just we must deem him honest, we cannot deem him safe. The great story-teller is discredited; and, willingly or unwillingly, we reject the guide who takes it upon himself to determine for us what we shall see. That, we feel sure, cannot be true which makes of so complex a history so simple a thesis for the judgment. There is art here; but it is the art of special pleading, misleading even to the pleader.—WOODROW WILSON, *Mere Literature and Other Essays*, 1896, pp. 167–69

JOHN WILSON CROKER
From "Mr. Macaulay's *History of England*"
Quarterly Review, October 1849, pp. 549–53, 629–30

The reading world will not need our testimony, though we willingly give it, that Mr. Macaulay possesses great talents and extraordinary acquirements. He unites powers and has achieved successes, not only various, but different in their character, and seldom indeed conjoined in one individual. He was while in Parliament, though not quite an orator, and still less a debater, the most brilliant rhetorician of the House. His Roman ballads (as we said in an article on their first appearance) exhibit a novel idea worked out with a rare felicity, so as to combine the spirit of the ancient minstrels with the regularity of construction and sweetness of versification which modern taste requires, and his critical Essays exhibit a wide variety of knowledge with a great fertility of illustration, and enough of the salt of pleasantry and sarcasm to flavour and in some degree disguise a somewhat declamatory and pretentious dogmatism. It may seem too epigrammatic, but it is, in our serious judgment, strictly true, to say that his *History* seems to be a kind of combination and exaggeration of the peculiarities of all his former efforts. It is as full of political prejudice and partisan advocacy as any of his parliamentary speeches. It makes the facts of English History as fabulous as his Lays do those of Roman tradition; and it is written with as captious, as dogmatical, and as cynical a spirit as the bitterest of his Reviews. That upon so serious an undertaking he has lavished uncommon exertion, is not to be doubted; nor can any one during the first reading escape the *entraînement* of his picturesque, vivid, and pregnant execution: but we have fairly stated the impression left on ourselves by a more calm and leisurely perusal. We have been so long the opponents of the political party to which Mr. Macaulay belongs that we welcomed the prospect of again meeting him on the neutral ground of literature. We are of that class of Tories—Protestant Tories, as they were called—that have no sympathy with the Jacobites. We are as strongly convinced as Mr. Macaulay can be of the necessity of the Revolution of 1688—of the general prudence and expediency of the steps taken by our Whig and Tory ancestors, of the Convention Parliament, and of the happiness, for a century and a half, of the constitutional results. We were, therefore, not without hope that at least in these two volumes, almost entirely occupied with the progress and accomplishment of that Revolution, we might without any sacrifice of our political feelings enjoy unalloyed the pleasures reasonably to be expected from Mr. Macaulay's high powers both of research and illustration. That hope has been deceived: Mr. Macaulay's

historical narrative is poisoned with a rancour more violent than even the passions of the time; and the literary qualities of the work, though in some respects very remarkable, are far from redeeming its substantial defects. There is hardly a page— we speak literally, hardly a page—that does not contain something objectionable either in substance or in colour: and the whole of the brilliant and at first captivating narrative is perceived on examination to be impregnated to a really marvellous degree with bad taste, bad feeling, and, we are under the painful necessity of adding—bad faith.

These are grave charges: but we make them in sincerity, and we think that we shall be able to prove them; and if, here or hereafter, we should seem to our readers to use harsher terms than good taste might approve, we beg in excuse to plead that it is impossible to fix one's attention on, and to transcribe large portions of a work, without being in some degree infected with its spirit; and Mr. Macaulay's pages, whatever may be their other characteristics, are as copious a repertorium of vituperative eloquence as, we believe, our language can produce, and especially against everything in which he chooses (whether right or wrong) to recognise the shiboleth of Toryism. We shall endeavour, however, in the expression of our opinions, to remember the respect we owe to our readers and to Mr. Macaulay's general character and standing in the world of letters, rather than the provocations and example of the volumes immediately before us.

Mr. Macaulay announces his intention of bringing down the history of England almost to our own times; but these two volumes are complete in themselves, and we may fairly consider them as a history of the Revolution; and in that light the first question that presents itself to us is why Mr. Macaulay has been induced to re-write what had already been so often and even so recently written—among others, by Dalrymple, a strenuous but honest Whig, and by Mr. Macaulay's own oracles, Fox and Mackintosh? It may be answered that both Fox and Mackintosh left their works imperfect. Fox got no farther than Monmouth's death; but Mackintosh came down to the Orange invasion, and covered full nine-tenths of the period as yet occupied by Mr. Macaulay. Why then did Mr. Macaulay not content himself with beginning where Mackintosh left off—that is, with the Revolution? and it would have been the more natural, because, as our readers know, it is there that Hume's history terminates.

What reason does he give for this work of supererogation? None. He does not (as we shall see more fully by and by) take the slightest notice of Mackintosh's history, no more than if it had never existed. Had he produced a new fact? Not one. Has he discovered any new materials? None, as far as we can judge, but the collections of Fox and Mackintosh, confided to him by their families.[1] It seems to us a novelty in literary practice that a writer raised far by fame and fortune above the vulgar temptations of the craft should undertake to tell a story already frequently and recently told by masters of the highest authority and most extensive information, without having, or even professing to have, any additional means or special motive to account for the attempt.

We suspect, however, that we can trace Mr. Macaulay's design to its true source—the example and success of the author of *Waverley*. The Historical Novel, if not invented, at least first developed and illustrated by the happy genius of Scott, took a sudden and extensive hold of the public taste; he himself, in most of his subsequent novels, availed himself largely of the historical element which had contributed so much to the popularity of *Waverley*. The press has since that time groaned with his imitators. We have had historical novels of all classes and grades. We have had served up in this form the Norman Conquest and the Wars of the Roses, the Gunpowder Plot and the Fire of London, Darnley and Richelieu—and almost at the same moment with Mr. Macaulay's appeared a professed romance of Mr. Ainsworth's on the same subject—James II. Nay, on a novelist of this popular order has been conferred the office of *Historiographer* to the Queen.

Mr. Macaulay, too mature not to have well measured his own peculiar capacities, not rich in invention, but ingenious in application, saw the use that might be made of this principle, and that history itself would be much more popular with a large embroidery of personal, social, and even topographical anecdote and illustration, instead of the sober garb in which we had been in the habit of seeing it. Few histories indeed ever were or could be written without some admixture of this sort. The father of the art himself, old Herodotus, vivified his text with a greater share of what we may call personal anecdote than any of his classical followers. Modern historians, as they happened to have more or less of what we may call *artistic* feeling, admitted more or less of this decoration into their text, but always with an eye (which Mr. Macaulay never exercises) to the appropriateness and value of the illustration. Generally, however, such matters have been thrown into notes, or, in a few instances—as by Dr. Henry and in Mr. Knight's interesting and instructive *Pictorial History*—into separate chapters. The large class of memoir-writers may also be fairly considered as anecdotical historians—and they are in fact the sources from which the novelists of the new school extract their principal characters and main incidents.

Mr. Macaulay deals with history, evidently, as we think, in imitation of the novelists—his first object being always picturesque effect—his constant endeavour to give from all the repositories of gossip that have reached us a kind of circumstantial reality to his incidents, and a sort of dramatic life to his personages. For this purpose he would not be very solicitous about contributing any substantial addition to history, strictly so called; on the contrary, indeed, he seems to have willingly taken it as he found it, adding to it such lace and trimmings as he could collect from the Monmouth-street of literature, seldom it may be safely presumed of very delicate quality. It is, as Johnson drolly said, 'an old coat with a new facing—the old dog in a new doublet.' The conception was bold, and—so far as availing himself, like other novelists, of the fashion of the day to produce a popular and profitable effect—the experiment has been eminently successful.

But besides the obvious incentives just noticed, Mr. Macaulay had also the stimulus of what we may compendiously call a strong party spirit. One would have thought that the Whigs might have been satisfied with their share in the historical library of the Revolution:—besides Rapin, Echard, and Jones, who, though of moderate politics in general, were stout friends to the Revolution, they have had of professed and zealous Whigs, Burnet, the foundation of all, Kennett, Oldmixon, Dalrymple, Laing, Brodie, Fox, and finally Mackintosh and his continuator, besides innumerable writers of less note, who naturally adopted the successful side; and we should not have supposed that the reader of any of those historians, and particularly the later ones, could complain that they had been too sparing of imputation, or even vituperation, to the opposite party. But not so Mr. Macaulay. The most distincitve feature on the face of his pages is personal virulence—if he has at all succeeded in throwing an air of fresh life into his characters, it is mainly due, as any impartial and collected reader will soon discover, to the simple circumstance of his

hating the individuals of the opposite party as bitterly, as passionately, as if they were his own personal enemies—more so, indeed, we hope than he would a mere political antagonist of his own day. When some one suggested to the angry O'Neil that one of the Anglo-Irish families whom he was reviling as strangers had been four hunderd years settled in Ireland, the Milesian replied, '*I hate the churls as if they had come but yesterday.*' Mr. Macaulay seems largely endowed with this (as with a more enviable) species of memory, and he hates, for example, King Charles I. as if he had been murdered only yesterday. Let us not be understood as wishing to abridge an historian's full liberty of censure—but he should not be a satirist, still less a libeller. We do not say nor think that Mr. Macaulay's censures were always unmerited—far from it—but they are always, we think without exception, immoderate. Nay, it would scarcely be too much to say that this massacre of character is the point on which Mr. Macaulay must chiefly rest any claims he can advance to the praise of impartiality, for while he paints everything that looks like a Tory in the blackest colours, he does not altogether spare any of the Whigs against whom he takes a spite, though he always visits them with a gentler correction. In fact, except Oliver Cromwell, King William, a few gentlemen who had the misfortune to be executed or exiled for high treason, and every dissenting minister that he has or can find occasion to notice, there are hardly any persons mentioned who are not stigmatized as knaves or fools, differing only in degrees of 'turpitude' and 'imbecility.' Mr. Macaulay has almost realized the work that Alexander Chalmer's playful imagination had fancied, a *Biographia Flagitiosa*, or *The Lives of Eminent Scoundrels*. This is also an imitation of the Historical Novel, though rather in the track of *Eugene Aram* and *Jack Sheppard* than of *Waverley* or *Woodstock*; but what would you have? To attain the picturesque—the chief object of our artist—he adopts the ready process of dark colours and a rough brush. Nature, even at the worst, is never gloomy enough for a Spagnoletto, and Judge Jeffries himself, for the first time, excites a kind of pity when we find him (like one to whom he was nearly akin) not so black as he is painted.

⟨. . .⟩ He takes much pains to parade—perhaps he really believes in—his impartiality, with what justice we appeal to the foregoing pages; but he is guilty of a prejudice as injurious in its consequences to truth as any political bias. He abhors whatever is not in itself picturesque, while he clings with the tenacity of a Novelist to the *piquant* and the startling. Whether it be the boudoir of a strumpet or the deathbed of a monarch—the strong character of a statesman-warrior abounding in contrasts and rich in mystery, or the personal history of a judge trained in the Old Bailey to vulgarize and ensanguine the King's Bench—he luxuriates with a vigour and variety of language and illustration which renders his *History* an attractive and absorbing story-book. And so spontaneously redundant are these errors—so inwoven in the very texture of Mr. Macaulay's mind—that he seems never able to escape from them. Even after the reader is led to believe that all that can be said either of praise or vituperation as to character, of voluptuous description and minute delineation as to fact and circumstance, has been passed in review before him—when a new subject, indeed, seems to have been started—all at once the old theme is renewed, and the old ideas are redressed in all the affluent imagery and profuse eloquence of which Mr. Macaulay is so eminent a master. Now of the fancy and fashion of this we should not complain—quite the contrary—in a professed novel: there is a theatre in which it would be exquisitely appropriate and attractive; but the Temple of

History is not the floor for a morris-dance—the Muse Clio is not to be worshipped in the halls of Terpsichore. We protest against this species of *carnival* history; no more like the reality than the Eglintoun Tournament or the Costume Quadrilles of Buckingham Palace; and we deplore the squandering of so much melodramatic talent on a subject which we have hitherto reverenced as the figure of Truth arrayed in the simple garments of Philosophy. We are ready to admit an hundred times over Mr. Macaulay's literary powers—brilliant even under the affectation with which he too frequently disfigures them. He is a great painter, but a suspicious narrator; a grand proficient in the picturesque, but a very poor professor of the historic. These volumes have been and his future volumes as they appear will be, devoured with the same eagerness that *Oliver Twist* or *Vanity Fair* excite—with the same quality of zest, though perhaps with a higher degree of it;—but his pages will seldom, we think, receive a second perusal—and the work, we apprehend, will hardly find a permanent place on the historic shelf—nor ever assuredly, if continued in the spirit of the first two volumes, be quoted as authority on any question or point of the History of England.

Notes

1. It appears from two notes of acknowledgments to M. Guizot and the keepers of the archives at the Hague, that Mr. Macaulay obtained some additions to the copies which Mackintosh already had of the letters of Ronquillo the Spanish and Citters the Dutch minister at the court of James. We may conjecture that these additions were insignificant, since Mr. Macaulay has nowhere, that we have observed, specially noticed them; but except these, whatever they may be, we find no trace of anything that Fox and Mackintosh had not already examined and classed.

WALTER BAGEHOT
From "Mr. Macaulay" (1856)
Collected Works, ed. Norman St. John-Stevas
1965, Volume 1, pp. 421–28

Macaulay's peculiarities of character and mind may be very conspicuously traced through the *History of England,* and in the *Essays.* Their first and most striking quality is the *intellectual entertainment* which they afford. This, as practical readers know, is a kind of sensation which is not very common, and which is very productive of great and healthy enjoyment. It is quite distinct from the amusement which is derived from common light works. The latter is very great; but it is passive. The mind of the reader is not awakened to any independent action: you see the farce, but you see it without effort; not simply without painful effort, but without any perceptible mental activity whatever. Again, entertainment of intellect is contrasted with the high enjoyment of consciously following pure and difficult reasoning; such a sensation is a sort of sublimated pain. The highest and most intense action of the intellectual powers is like the most intense action of the bodily on a high mountain. We climb and climb: we have a thrill of pleasure, but we have also a sense of effort and anguish. Nor is the sensation to be confounded with that which we experience from the best and purest works of art. The pleasure of high tragedy is also painful: the whole soul is stretched; the spirit pants; the passions scarcely breathe: it is a rapt and eager moment, too intense for continuance—so overpowering, that we scarcely know whether it be joy or pain. The sensation of intellectual entertainment is altogether distinguished from

these by not being accompanied by any pain, and yet being consequent on, or being contemporaneous with, a high and constant exercise of mind. While we read works which so delight us, we are conscious that we are delighted, and are conscious that we are not idle. The opposite pleasures of indolence and exertion seem for a moment combined. A sort of elasticity pervades us; thoughts come easily and quickly; we seem capable of many ideas; we follow cleverness till we fancy that we are clever. This feeling is only given by writers who stimulate the mind just to the degree which is pleasant, and who do not stimulate it more; who exact a moderate exercise of mind, and who seduce us to it insensibly. This can only be, of course, by a charm of style; by the inexplicable *je ne sais quoi* which attracts our attention; by constantly raising and constantly satisfying our curiosity. And there seems to be a further condition. A writer who wishes to produce this constant effect must not appeal to any single separate faculty of mind, but to the whole mind at once. The fancy tires, if you appeal only to the fancy: the understanding is aware of its dullness, if you appeal only to the understanding; the curiosity is soon satiated unless you pique it with variety. This is the very opportunity for Macaulay. He has fancy, sense, abundance; he appeals to both fancy and understanding. There is no sense of effort. His books read like an elastic dream. There is a continual sense of instruction; for who had an idea of the transactions before? The emotions, too, which he appeals to are the easy admiration, the cool disapprobation, the gentle worldly curiosity, which quietly excite us, never fatigue us,—which we could bear for ever. To read Macaulay for a day, would be to pass a day of easy thought, of pleasant placid emotion.

Nor is this a small matter. In a state of high civilisation it is no simple matter to give multitudes a large and healthy enjoyment. The old bodily enjoyments are dying out; there is no room for them any more; the complex apparatus of civilisation cumbers the ground. We are thrown back upon the mind, and the mind is a barren thing. It can spin little from itself: few that describe what they see are in the way to discern much. Exaggerated emotions, violent incidents, monstrous characters, crowd our canvas; they are the resource of a weakness which would obtain the fame of strength. Reading is about to become a series of collisions against aggravated breakers, of beatings with imaginary surf. In such times a book of sensible attraction is a public benefit; it diffuses a sensation of vigour through the multitude. Perhaps there is a danger that the extreme popularity of the manner may make many persons fancy they understand the matter more perfectly than they do: some readers may become conceited; several boys believe that they too are Macaulays. Yet, duly allowing for this defect, it is a great good that so many people should learn so much on such topics so agreeably; that they should feel that they *can* understand them; that their minds should be stimulated by a consciousness of health and power.

The same peculiarities influence the style of the narrative. The art of narration is the art of writing in hooks-and-eyes. The principle consists in making the appropriate thought follow the appropriate thought, the proper fact the proper fact; in first preparing the mind for what is to come, and then letting it come. This can only be achieved by keeping continually and insensibly before the mind of the reader some one object, character, or image, whose variations are the events of the story, whose unity is the unity of it. Scott, for example, keeps before you the mind of some one person,—that of Morton in *Old Mortality,* of Rebecca in *Ivanhoe,* of Love in *The Antiquary,*—whose fortunes and mental changes are the central incidents, whose personality is the string of unity. It is the defect of the great Scotch novels that their central figure is frequently not their most interesting topic,—that their interest is often rather in the accessories than in the essential principle—in that which surrounds the centre of narration rather than in the centre itself. Scott tries to meet this objection by varying the mind which he selects for his unit; in one of his chapters it is one character, in the next a different; he shifts the scene from the hero to the heroine, from the 'Protector of the settlement' of the story to the evil being who mars it perpetually: but when narrowly examined, the principle of his narration will be found nearly always the same,—the changes in the position—external or mental—of some one human being. The most curiously opposite sort of narration is that of Hume. He seems to carry a *view*, as the moderns call it, through everything. He forms to himself a metaphysical—that perhaps is a harsh word—an intellectual conception of the time and character before him; and the gradual working out or development of that view is the principle of his narration. He tells the story of the conception. You rise from his pages without much remembrance of or regard for the mere people, but with a clear notion of an elaborated view, skilfully abstracted and perpetually impressed upon you. A critic of detail should scarcely require a better task than to show how insensibly and artfully the subtle historian infuses his doctrine among the facts, indicates somehow—you can scarcely say how—their relation to it; strings them, as it were, upon it, concealing it in seeming beneath them, while in fact it altogether determines their form, their grouping, and their consistency. The style of Macaulay is very different from either of these. It is a diorama of political pictures. You seem to begin with a brilliant picture,—its colours are distinct, its lines are firm; on a sudden it changes, at first gradually, you can scarcely tell how or in what, but truly and unmistakably,—a slightly different picture is before you; then the second vision seems to change,—it too is another and yet the same; then the third shines forth and fades; and so without end. The unity of this delineation is the identity—the apparent identity—of the picture; on no two moments does it seem quite different, on no two is it identically the same. It grows and alters as our bodies would appear to alter and grow, if you could fancy any one watching them, and being conscious of their daily little changes. The events are picturesque variations; the unity is a unity of political painting, of represented external form. It is evident how suitable this is to a writer whose understanding is solid, whose sense is political, whose fancy is fine and delineative.

To this merit of Macaulay is to be added another. No one describes so well what we may call the *spectacle* of a character. The art of delineating character by protracted description is one which grows in spite of the critics. In vain is it alleged that the character should be shown dramatically; that it should be illustrated by events; that it should be exhibited in its actions. The truth is, that these homilies are excellent, but incomplete; true, but out of season. There is a utility in verbal portrait, as Lord Stanhope says there is in painted. Goethe use to observe, that in society—in a tête-à-tête, rather—you often thought of your companion as if he was his protrait; you were silent; you did not care what he said; but you considered him as a picture, as a whole, especially as regards yourself and your relations towards him. You require something of the same kind in literature: *some* description of a man is clearly necessary as an introduction to the story of his life and actions. But more than this is wanted; you require to have the object placed before you as a whole, to have the characteristic traits mentioned, the delicate qualities drawn out, the firm features gently depicted. As the practice which Goethe hints at is, of all others, the most

favourable to a just and calm judgment of character, so the literary substitute is essential as a steadying element, as a summary, to bring together and give a unity to our views. We must see the man's face. Without it, we seem to have heard a great deal about the person, but not to have known him; to be aware that he had done a good deal, but to have no settled, ineradicable notion what manner of man he was. This is the reason why critics like Macaulay, who sneer at the practice when estimating the works of others, yet make use of it at great length, and, in his case, with great skill, when they come to be historians themselves. The kind of characters whom Macaulay can describe is limited—at least we think so—by the bounds which we indicated just now. There are some men whom he is too impassive to comprehend; but he can always tell us of such as he does comprehend, what they looked like, and what they were.

A great deal of this vividness Macaulay of course owes to his style. Of its effectiveness there can be no doubt; its agreeability no one who has just been reading it is likely to deny. Yet it has a defect. It is not, as Bishop Butler would have expressed it, such a style as 'is suitable to such a being as man, in such a world as the present one.' It is too omniscient. Everything is too plain. All is clear; nothing is doubtful. Instead of probability being, as the great thinker expressed it, 'the very guide of life,' it has become a rare exception—an uncommon phenomenon. You rarely come across anything which is not decided; and when you do come across it, you seem to wonder that the positiveness, which has accomplished so much, should have been unwilling to decide everything. This is hardly the style for history. The data of historical narratives, especially of modern histories, are a heap of confusion. No one can tell where they lie, or where they do not lie; what is in them, or what is not in them. Literature is called the 'fragment of fragments;' little has been written, and but little of that little has been preserved. So history is a vestige of vestiges; few facts leave any trace of themselves, any witness of their occurrence; of fewer still is that witness preserved; a slight track is all any thing leaves, and the confusion of life, the tumult of change sweep even that away in a moment. It is not possible that these data can be very fertile in certainties. Few people would make any thing of them: a memoir here, a MS. there—two letters in a magazine—an assertion by a person whose veracity is denied,—these are the sort of evidence out of which a flowing narrative is to be educed—of course it ought not to be too flowing. 'If you please, sir, to tell me what you do *not* know,' was the inquiry of a humble pupil addressed to a great man of science. It would have been a relief to the readers of Macaulay if he had shown a little the outside of uncertainties, which there must be—the gradations of doubt, which there ought to be—the singular accumulation of difficulties, which must beset the extraction of a very easy narrative from very confused materials.

This defect in style is, indeed, indicative of a defect in understanding. Mr. Macaulay's mind is eminently gifted, but there is a want of graduation in it. He has a fine eye for probabilities, a clear perception of evidence, a shrewd guess at missing links of fact; but each probability seems to him a certainty, each piece of evidence conclusive, each analogy exact. The heavy Scotch intellect is a little prone to this: one figures it as a heap of formulæ, and if fact *b* is reducible to formula B, that is all which it regards; the mathematical mill grinds with equal energy at flour perfect and imperfect—at matter which is quite certain, and at matter which is only a little probable. But the great cause of this error is, an abstinence from practical action. Life is a school of probability.

In the writings of every man of patient practicality, in the midst of whatever other defects, you will find a careful appreciation of the degrees of likelihood; a steady balancing of them one against another; a disinclination to make things too clear, to overlook the debit side of the account in mere contemplation of the enormousness of the credit. The reason is obvious: action is a business of risk; the real question is the magnitude of that risk. Failure is ever impending; success is ever uncertain; there is always, in the very best of affairs, a slight probability of the former, a contingent possibility of the non-occurrence of the latter. For practical men, the problem ever is to test the amount of these inevitable probabilities; to make sure that no one increases too far; that by a well-varied choice the number of risks may in itself be a protection—be an insurance to you, as it were, against the capricious result of any one. A man like Macaulay, who stands aloof from life, is not so instructed; he sits secure: nothing happens in his study: he does not care to test probabilities; he loses the detective sensation.

Mr. Macaulay's so-called inaccuracy is likewise a phase of this defect. Considering the enormous advantages which a picturesque style gives to ill-disposed critics; the number of points of investigation which it suggests; the number of assertions it makes, sentence by sentence; the number of ill-disposed critics that there are in the world; remembering Mr. Macaulay's position,—set on a hill to be spied at by them,—he can scarcely be thought an inaccurate historian. Considering all things, they have found few certain blunders, hardly any direct mistakes. Every sentence of his style requires minute knowledge; the vivid picture has a hundred details; each of those details must have an evidence, an authority, a proof. An historian like Hume passes easily over a period; his chart is large; if he gets the conspicuous headlands, the large harbours, duly marked, he does not care. Macaulay puts in the depth of each wave, every remarkable rock, every tree on the shore. Nothing gives a critic so great an advantage. It is difficult to do this for a volume; simple for a page. It is easy to select a particular event, and learn all which any one can know about it; examine Macaulay's descriptions, say he is wrong, that X is not buried where he asserts, that a little boy was one year older than he states. But how would the critic manage, if he had to work out all this for a million facts, for a whole period? Few men, we suspect, would be able to make so few errors of simple and provable fact. On the other hand, few men would arouse a sleepy critic by such startling assertion. If Macaulay finds a new theory, he states it as a fact. Very likely it really is the most probable theory; at any rate, we know of no case in which his theory is not one among the most plausible. If it had only been so stated, it would have been well received. His view of Marlborough's character, for instance, is a specious one; it has a good deal of evidence, a large amount of real probability, but it has scarcely more. Marlborough *may* have been as bad as is said, but we can hardly be *sure* of it at this time.

Macaulay's 'party-spirit' is another consequence of his positiveness. When he inclines to a side, he inclines to it too much. His opinions are a shade too strong; his predilections some degrees at least too warm. William is too perfect, James too imperfect. The Whigs are a trifle like angels; the Tories like, let us say, 'our inferiors.' Yet this is evidently an honest party-spirit. It does not lurk in the corners of sentences, it is not insinuated without being alleged; it does not, like the unfairness of Hume, secrete itself so subtly in the turns of the words, that when you look to prove it, it is gone. On the contrary, it rushes into broad day. William is loaded with panegyric; James is always spoken evil of. Hume's is the artful pleading of a hired advocate; Macaulay's the bold eulogy of a sincere friend. As far

as effect goes, this is an error. The very earnestness of the affection leads to a reaction; we are tired of having William called the 'just;' we cannot believe so many pages; 'all that' can scarcely be correct. As we said, if the historian's preference for persons and parties had been duly tempered and mitigated, if the probably good were only said to be probably good, if the rather bad were only alleged to be rather bad, the reader would have been convinced, and the historian escaped the savage censure of envious critics.

The one thing which detracts from the pleasure of reading these volumes, is the doubt whether they should have been written. Should not these great powers be reserved for great periods? Is this abounding, picturesque style, suited for continuous history? Are small men to be so largely described? Should not admirable delineation be kept for admirable people? We think so. You do not want Raphael to paint sign-posts, or Palladio to build dirt-pies. Much of history is necessarily of little value,—the superficies of circumstance, the scum of events. It is very well to have it described, indeed you must have it described; the chain must be kept complete; the narrative of a country's fortunes will not allow of breaks or gaps. Yet all things need not be done equally well. The life of a great painter is short. Even the industry of Macaulay will not complete this history. It is a pity to spend such powers on such events. It would have been better to have some new volumes of essays solely on great men and great things. The diffuseness of the style would have been then in place; we could have borne to hear the smallest minutiæ of magnificent epochs. If an inferior hand had executed the connecting-links, our notions would have acquired an insensible perspective; the works of the great artist, the best themes, would have stood out from the canvas. They are now confused by the equal brilliancy of the adjacent inferiorities.

Much more might be said on this narrative. As it will be read for very many years, it will employ the critics for very many years. It would be unkind to make all the best observations. Something, as Mr. Disraeli said in a budget-speech, something should be left for 'future statements of this nature.' There will be an opportunity. Whatever those who come after may say against this book, it will be, and remain, the 'Pictorial History of England.'

SIR LESLIE STEPHEN
From "Macaulay"
Hours in a Library (1874–79)
1904, Volume 3, pp. 237–71

The first and most obvious power in which Macaulay excelled his neighbours was his portentous memory. He could assimilate printed pages, says his nephew, more quickly than others could glance over them. Whatever he read was stamped upon his mind instantaneously and permanently, and he read everything. In the midst of severe labours in India, he read enough classical authors to stock the mind of an ordinary professor. At the same time he framed a criminal code and devoured masses of trashy novels. From the works of the ancient Fathers of the Church to English political pamphlets and to modern street ballads, no printed matter came amiss to his omnivorous appetite. All that he had read could be reproduced at a moment's notice. Every fool, he said, can repeat his Archbishops of Canterbury backwards; and he was as familiar with the Cambridge Calendar as the most devout Protestant with the Bible. He could have re-written *Sir Charles*

Grandison from memory if every copy had been lost. Now it might perhaps be plausibly maintained that the possession of such a memory is unfavourable to a high development of the reasoning powers. The case of Pascal, indeed, who is said never to have forgotten anything, shows that the two powers may co-exist; and other cases might of course be mentioned. But it is true that a powerful memory may enable a man to save himself the trouble of reasoning. It encourages the indolent propensity of deciding difficulties by precedent instead of principles. Macaulay, for example, was once required to argue the point of political casuistry as to the degree of independent action permissible to members of a Cabinet. An ordinary mind would have to answer by striking a rough balance between the conveniences and inconveniences likely to arise. It would be forced, that is to say, to reason from the nature of the case. But Macaulay had at his fingers' end every instance from the days of Walpole to his own in which Ministers had been allowed to vote against the general policy of the Government. By quoting them, he seemed to decide the point by authority, instead of taking the troublesome and dangerous road of abstract reasoning. Thus to appeal to experience is with him to appeal to the stores of a gigantic memory; and is generally the same thing as to deny the value of all general rules. This is the true Whig doctrine of referring to precedent rather than to theory. Our popular leaders were always glad to quote Hampden and Sidney instead of venturing upon the dangerous ground of abstract rights.

Macaulay's love of deciding all points by an accumulation of appropriate instances is indeed characteristic of his mind. It is connected with a curious defect of analytical power. It appears in his literary criticism as much as in his political speculations. In an interesting letter to Mr. Napier, he states the case himself as an excuse for not writing upon Scott.

> Hazlitt used to say, "I am nothing if not critical." The case with me [says Macaulay] is precisely the reverse. I have a strong and acute enjoyment of works of the imagination, but I have never habituated myself to dissect them. Perhaps I enjoy them the more keenly for that very reason. Such books as Lessing's *Laocoön*, such passages as the criticism on *Hamlet* in *Wilhelm Meister*, fill me with wonder and despair.

If we take any of Macaulay's criticisms, we shall see how truly he had gauged his own capacity. They are either random discharges of superlatives or vigorous assertions of sound moral principles. He compliments some favourite author with an emphatic repetition of the ordinary eulogies, or shows conclusively that Montgomery was a sham poet, and Wycherley a corrupt ribald. Nobody can hit a haystack with more certainty, but he is not so good at a difficult mark. He never makes a fine suggestion as to the secrets of the art whose products he admires or describes. His mode, for example, of criticising Bunyan is to give a list of the passages which he remembers, and of course he remembers everything. He observes, what is tolerably clear, that Bunyan's allegory is as vivid as a concrete history, through strangely comparing him in this respect to Shelley—the least concrete of poets; and he makes the discovery, which did not require his vast stores of historical knowledge, "that it is impossible to doubt that" Bunyan's trial of Christian and Faithful is meant to satirise the judges of the time of Charles II. That is as plain as the intention of the last cartoon in *Punch*. Macaulay can draw a most vivid portrait, so far as that can be done by a picturesque accumulation of characteristic facts, but he never gets below the surface, or details the principles whose embodiment he describes from without.

The defect is connected with further peculiarities, in which Macaulay is the genuine representative of the true Whig type. The practical value of adherence to precedent is obvious. It may be justified by the assertion that all sound political philosophy must be based upon experience: and no one will deny that assertion to contain a most important truth. But in Macaulay's mind this sound doctrine seems to be confused with the very questionable doctrine that in political questions there is no philosophy at all. To appeal to experience may mean either to appeal to facts so classified and systematically arranged as to illustrate general truths, or to appeal to a mere mass of observations, wtihout taking the trouble to elicit their true significance, or even to believe that they can be resolved into particular cases of a general truth. This is the difference between an experimental philosophy and a crude empiricism. Macaulay takes the lower alternative. The vigorous attack upon James Mill, which he very promptly suppressed during his life on account of its juvenile arrogance, curiously illustrates his mode of thought. No one can deny, I think, that he makes some very good points against a very questionable system of political dogmatism. But when we ask what are Macaulay's own principles, we are left at a stand. He ought, by all his intellectual sympathies, to be a utilitarian. Yet he treats utilitarianism with the utmost contempt, though he has no alternative theory to suggest. He ends his first Essay against Mill by one of his customary purple patches about Baconian induction. He tells us, in the second, how to apply it. Bacon proposed to discover the principle of heat by observing in what qualities all hot bodies agreed, and in what qualities all cold bodies. Similarly, we are to make a list of all constitutions which have produced good or bad government, and to investigate their points of agreement and difference. This sounds plausible to the uninstructed, but is a mere rhetorical flourish. Bacon's method is admittedly inadequate, for reasons which I leave to men of science to explain, and Macaulay's method is equally hopeless in politics. It is hopeless for the simple reason that the complexity of the phenomena makes it impracticable. We cannot find out what constitution is best after this fashion, simply because the goodness or badness of a constitution depends upon a thousand conditions of social, moral, and intellectual development. When stripped of its pretentious phraseology, Macaulay's teaching comes simply to this: the only rule in politics is the rule of thumb. All general principles are wrong or futile. We have found out in England that our constitution, constructed in absolute defiance of all *à priori* reasoning, is the best in the world: it is the best for providing us with the maximum of bread, beef, beer, and means of buying bread, beer, and beef: and we have got it because we have never—like those publicans the French—trusted to fine sayings about truth and justice and human rights, but blundered on, adding a patch here and knocking a hole there, as our humour prompted us.

This sovereign contempt of all speculation—simply as speculation—reaches its acme in the Essay on Bacon. The curious naïveté with which Macaulay denounces all philosophy in that vigorous production excites a kind of perverse admiration. How can one refuse to admire the audacity which enables a man explicitly to identify philosophy with humbug? It is what ninety-nine men out of a hundred think, but not one in a thousand dares to say. Goethe says somewhere that he likes Englishmen because English fools are the most thoroughgoing of fools. English "Philistines," as represented by Macaulay, the prince of Philistines, according to Matthew Arnold, carry their contempt of the higher intellectual interests to a pitch of real sublimity. Bacon's theory of induction, says Macaulay, in so many words, was valueless. Everybody could reason before it as well as after. But Bacon really performed a service of inestimable value to mankind; and it consisted precisely in this, that he called their attention from philosophy to the pursuit of material advantages. The old philosophers had gone on bothering about theology, ethics, and the true and beautiful, and such other nonsense. Bacon taught us to work at chemistry and mechanics, to invent diving-bells and steam-engines and spinning-jennies. We could never, it seems, have found out the advantages of this direction of our energies without a philosopher, and so far philosophy is negatively good. It has written up upon all the supposed avenues to inquiry, "No admission except on business;" that is, upon the business of direct practical discovery. We English have taken the hint, and we have therefore lived to see when a man can breakfast in London and dine in Edinburgh, and may look forward to a day when the tops of Ben Nevis and Helvellyn will be cultivated like flower-gardens, and when machines constructed on principles yet to be discovered will be in every house.

The theory which underlies this conclusion is often explicitly stated. All philosophy has produced mere futile logomachy. Greek sages and Roman moralists and mediæval schoolmen have amassed words, and amassed nothing else. One distinct discovery of a solid truth, however humble, is worth all their labours. This condemnation applies not only to philosophy, but to the religious embodiment of philosophy. No satisfactory conclusion ever has been reached or ever will be reached in theological disputes. On all such topics, he tells Mr. Gladstone, there has always been the widest divergence of opinion. Nor are there better hopes for the future. The ablest minds, he says in the Essay upon Ranke, have believed in transubstantiation; that is, according to him, in the most ineffable nonsense. There is no certainty that men will not believe to the end of time the doctrines which imposed upon so able a man as Sir Thomas More. Not only, that is, have men been hitherto wandering in a labyrinth without a clue, but there is no chance that any clue will ever be found. The doctrine, so familiar to our generation, of laws of intellectual development, never even occurs to him. The collective thought of generations marks time without advancing. A guess of Sir Thomas More is as good or as bad as the guess of the last philosopher. This theory, if true, implies utter scepticism. And yet Macaulay was clearly not a sceptic. His creed was hidden under a systematic reticence, and he resisted every attempt to raise the veil with rather superfluous indignation. When a constituent dared to ask about his religious views, he denounced the rash inquirer in terms applicable to an agent of the Inquisition. He vouchsafed, indeed, the information that he was a Christian. We may accept the phrase, not only on the strength of his invariable sincerity, but because it falls in with the general turn of his arguments. He denounces the futility of the ancient moralists, but he asserts the enormous social value of Christianity.

His attitude, in fact, is equally characteristic of the man and his surroundings. The old Clapham teaching had faded in his mind: it had not produced a revolt. He retained the old hatred for slavery; and he retained, with the whole force of his affectionate nature, reverence for the school of Wilberforce, Thornton, and his own father. He estimated most highly, not perhaps more highly than they deserved, the value of the services rendered by them in awakening the conscience of the nation. In their persistent and disinterested labours he recognised a manifestation of the great social force of Christianity. But a belief that Christianity is useful, and even that it is true, may consist with a profound conviction of the futility of the

philosophy with which it has been associated. Here again Macaulay is a true Whig. The Whig love of precedent, the Whig hatred for abstract theories, may consist with a Tory application. But the true Whig differed from the Tory in adding to these views and invincible suspicion of parsons. The first Whig battles were fought against the Church as much as against the King. From the struggle with Sacheverell down to the struggle for Catholic emancipation, Toryism and High-Church principles were associated against Whigs and Dissenters. By that kind of dumb instinct which outruns reason, the Whig had learnt that there was some occult bond of union between the claims of a priesthood and the claims of a monarchy. The old maxim, "No bishop, no king," suggested the opposite principle that you must keep down the clergy if you would limit the monarchy. The natural interpretation of this prejudice into political theory, is that the Church is extremely useful as an ally of the constable, but possesses a most dangerous explosive power if allowed to claim independent authority. In practice we must resist all claims of the Church to dictate to the State. In theory we must deny the foundation upon which such claims can alone be founded. Dogmatism must be pronounced to be fundamentally irrational. Nobody knows anything about theology; or, what is the same thing, no two people agree. As they don't agree, they cannot claim to impose their beliefs upon others.

This sentiment comes out curiously in the characteristic Essay just mentioned. Macaulay says, in reply to Mr. Gladstone, that there is no more reason for the introduction of religious questions into State affairs than for introducing them into the affairs of a Canal Company. He puts his argument with an admirable vigour and clearness which blinds many readers to the fact that he is begging the question by evading the real difficulty. If, in fact, Government had as little to do as a Canal Company with religious opinion, we should have long ago learnt the great lesson of toleration. But that is just the very *crux*. Can we draw the line between the spiritual and the secular? Nothing, replies Macaulay, is easier; and his method has been already indicated. We all agree that we don't want to be robbed or murdered: we are by no means all agreed about the doctrine of Trinity. But, says a churchman, a certain creed is necessary to men's moral and spiritual welfare, and therefore of the utmost importance even for the prevention of robbery and murder. This is what Macaulay implicitly denies. The whole of dogmatic theology belongs to that region of philosophy, metaphysics, or whatever you please to call it, in which men are doomed to dispute for ever without coming any nearer to a decision. All that the statesman has to do with such matters is to see that if men are fools enough to speculate, they shall not be allowed to cut each other's throats when they reach, as they always must reach, contradictory results. If you raise a difficult point—such, for example, as the education question—Macaulay replies, as so many people have replied before and since, Teach the people "those principles of morality which are common to all the forms of Christianity." That is easier said than done! The plausibility of the solution in Macaulay's mouth is due to the fundamental assumption that everything except morality is hopeless ground of inquiry. Once get beyond the Ten Commandments and you will sink to a bottomless morass of argument, counter-argument, quibble, logomachy, superstition, and confusion worse confounded.

In Macaulay's teaching, as in that of his party, there is doubtless much that is noble. He has a righteous hatred of oppression in all shapes and disguises. He can tear to pieces with great logical power many of the fallacies alleged by his opponents. Our sympathies are certainly with him as against men who advocate persecution on any grounds, and he is fully qualified to crush his ordinary opponents. But it is plain that his whole political and (if we may use the word) philosophical teaching rests on something like a downright aversion to the higher order of speculation. He despises it. He wants something tangible and concrete—something in favour of which he may appeal to the immediate testimony of the senses. He must feel his feet planted on the solid earth. The pain of attempting to soar into higher regions is not compensated to him by the increased width of horizon. And in this respect he is but the type of most of his countrymen, and reflects what has been (as I should say) erroneously called their "unimaginative" view of things in general.

Macaulay, at any rate, distinctly belongs to the imaginative class of minds, if only in virtue of his instinctive preference of the concrete to the abstract, and his dislike, already noticed, to analysis. He has a thirst for distinct and vivid images. He reasons by examples instead of appealing to formulæ. There is a characteristic account in Mr. Trevelyan's volumes of his habit of rambling amongst the older parts of London, his fancy teeming with stories attached to the picturesque fragments of antiquity, and carrying on dialogues between imaginary persons as vivid, if not as forcible, as those of Scott's novels. To this habit—rather inverting the order of cause and effect—he attributes his accuracy of detail. We should rather say that the intensity of the impressions generated both the accuracy and the day-dreams. A philosopher would be arguing in his daily rambles where an imaginative mind is creating a series of pictures. But Macaulay's imagination is as definitely limited as his speculation. The genuine poet is also a philosopher. He sees intuitively what the reasoner evolves by argument. The greatest minds in both classes are equally marked by their naturalisation in the lofty regions of thought, inaccessible or uncongenial to men of inferior stamp. It is tempting in some ways to compare Macaulay to Burke. Burke's superiority is marked by this, that he is primarily a philosopher, and therefore instinctively sees the illustration of a general law in every particular fact. Macaulay, on the contrary, gets away from theory as fast as possible, and tries to conceal his poverty of thought under masses of ingenious illustration.

His imaginative narrowness would come out still more clearly by a comparison with Carlyle. One significant fact must be enough. Every one must have observed how powerfully Carlyle expresses the emotion suggested by the brief appearance of some little waif from past history. We may remember, for example, how the usher, De Brézé, appears for a moment to utter the last shriek of the old monarchical etiquette, and then vanishes into the dim abysses of the past. The imagination is excited by the little glimpse of light flashing for a moment upon some special point in the cloudy phantasmagoria of human history. The image of a past existence is projected for a moment upon our eyes, to make us feel how transitory is life, and how rapidly one visionary existence expels another. We are such stuff as dreams are made of:

> None other than a moving row
> Of visionary shapes that come and go
> Around the sun-illumined lantern held
> In midnight by the master of the show.

Every object is seen against the background of eternal mystery. In Macaulay's pages this element is altogether absent. We see a figure from the past as vividly as if he were present. We observe the details of his dress, the odd oaths with which his discourse is interlarded, the minute peculiarities of his features

or manner. We laugh or admire as we should do at a living man; and we rightly admire the force of the illusion. But the thought never suggests itself that we too are passing into oblivion, that our little island of daylight will soon be shrouded in the gathering mist, and that we tread at every instant on the dust of forgotten continents. We treat the men of past ages quite at our ease. We applaud and criticise Hampden or Chatham as we should applaud Peel or Cobden. There is no atmospheric effect—no sense of the dim march of ages, or of the vast procession of human life. It is doubtless a great feat to make the past present. It is a greater to emancipate us from the tyranny of the present, and to raise us to a point at which we feel that we too are almost as dreamlike as the men of old time. To gain clearness and definition Macaulay has dropped the element of mystery. He sees perfectly whatever can be seen by the ordinary lawyer, or politician, or merchant; he is insensible to the visions which reveal themselves only to minds haunted by thoughts of eternity, and delighting to dwell in the borderland where dreams blend with realities. Mysticism is to him hateful, and historical figures form groups of individuals, not symbols of forces working behind the veil.

Macaulay, therefore, can be no more a poet in the sense in which the word is applied to Spenser, or to Wordsworth, both of whom he holds to be simply intolerable bores, than he can be a metaphysician or a scientific thinker. In common phraseology, he is a Philistine—a word which I understand properly to denote indifference to the higher intellectual interests. The word may also be defined, however, as the name applied by prigs to the rest of their species. And I hold that the modern fashion of using it as a common term of abuse amounts to a literary nuisance. It enables intellectual coxcombs to brand men with an offensive epithet for being a degree more manly than themselves. There is much that is good in your Philistine; and when we ask what Macaulay was, instead of showing what he was not, we shall perhaps find that the popular estimate is not altogether wrong.

Macaulay was not only a typical Whig, but the prophet of Whiggism to his generation. Though not a poet or a philosopher, he was a born rhetorician. His parliamentary career proves his capacity sufficiently, though want of the physical qualifications, and of exclusive devotion to political success, prevented him, as perhaps a want of subtlety or flexibility of mind would have always prevented him, from attaining excellence as a debater. In everything that he wrote, however, we see the true rhetorician. He tells us that Fox wrote debates, whilst Mackintosh spoke essays. Macaulay did both. His compositions are a series of orations on behalf of sound Whig views, whatever their external form. Given a certain audience—and every orator supposes a particular audience—their effectiveness is undeniable. Macaulay's may be composed of ordinary Englishmen, with a moderate standard of education. His arguments are adapted to the ordinary Cabinet Minister, or, what is much the same, to the person who is willing to pay a shilling to hear an evening lecture. He can hit an audience composed of such materials—to quote Burke's phrase about George Grenville—"between wind and water." He uses the language, the logic, and the images which they can fully understand; and though his hearer, like his schoolboy, is ostensibly credited at times with a portentous memory, Macaulay always takes excellent care to put him in mind of the facts which he is assumed to remember. The faults and the merits of his style follow from his resolute determination to be understood of the people. He was specially delighted, as his nephew tells us, by a reader at Messrs. Spottiswoode's, who said that in all the *History* there was only one sentence the meaning of which was not obvious to him at first sight. We are more surprised that there was one such sentence. Clearness is the first of the cardinal virtues of style; and nobody ever wrote more clearly than Macaulay. He sacrifices much, it is true, to obtain it. He proves that two and two make four with a pertinacity which would make him dull, if it were not for his abundance of brilliant illustration. He always remembers the principle which should guide a barrister in addressing a jury. He has not merely to exhibit his proofs, but to hammer them into the heads of his audience by incessant repetition. It is no small proof of artistic skill that a writer who systematically adopts this method should yet be invariably lively. He goes on blacking the chimney with a persistency which somehow amuses us because he puts so much heart into his work. He proves the most obvious truths again and again; but his vivacity never flags. This tendency undoubtedly leads to great defects of style. His sentences are monotonous and mechanical. He has a perfect hatred of pronouns, and for fear of a possible entanglement between "hims" and "hers" and "its," he will repeat not merely a substantive, but a whole group of substantives. Sometimes, to make his sense unmistakable, he will repeat a whole formula, with only a change in the copula. For the same reason, he hates all qualifications and parentheses. Each thought must be resolved into its constituent parts; each argument must be expressed as a simple proposition: and his paragraphs are rather aggregates of independent atoms than possessed of a continuous unity. His writing—to use a favourite formula of his own—bears the same relation to a style of graceful modulation that a bit of mosaic work bears to a picture. Each phrase has its distinct hue, instead of melting into its neighbors. Here we have a black patch and there a white. There are no half tones, no subtle interblending of different currents of thought. It is partly for this reason that his descriptions of character are often so unsatisfactory. He likes to represent a man as a bundle of contradictions, because it enables him to obtain startling contrasts. He heightens a vice in one place, a virtue in another, and piles them together in a heap, wtihout troubling himself to ask whether nature can make such monsters, or preserve them if made. To any one given to analysis, these contrasts are actually painful. There is a story of the Duke of Wellington having once stated that the rats got into his bottles in Spain. "They must have been very large bottles or very small rats," said somebody. "On the contrary," replied the Duke, "the rats were very large and the bottles very small." Macaulay delights in leaving us face to face with such contrasts in more important matters. Boswell must, we would say, have been a clever man or his biography cannot have been so good as you say. On the contrary, says Macaulay, he was the greatest of fools and the best of biographers. He strikes a discord and purposely fails to resolve it. To men of more delicate sensibility the result is an intolerable jar.

For the same reason, Macaulay's genuine eloquence is marred by the symptoms of malice prepense. When he sews on a purple patch, he is resolved that there shall be no mistake about it; it must stand out from a radical contrast of colours. The emotion is not to swell by degrees, till you find yourself carried away in the torrent which set out as a tranquil stream. The transition is deliberately emphasised. On one side of a full stop you are listening to a matter-of-fact statement; on the other, there is all at once a blare of trumpets and a beating of drums, till the crash almost deafens you. He regrets in one of his letters that he has used up the celebrated, and, it must be confessed, really forcible passage about the impeachment scene in Westminster Hall. It might have come in usefully in the *History*, which, as he then hoped, would reach the time of

Warren Hastings. The regret is unpleasantly suggestive of that deliberation in the manufacture of eloquence which stamps it as artificial.

Such faults may annoy critics, even of no very sensitive fibre. What is it that redeems them? The first answer is, that the work is impressive because it is thoroughly genuine. The stream, it is true, comes forth by spasmodic gushes, when it ought to flow in a continuous current; but it flows from a full reservoir instead of being pumped from a shallow cistern. The knowledge and, what is more, the thoroughly assimilated knowledge, is enormous. Mr. Trevelyan has shown in detail what we had all divined for ourselves, how much patient labour is often employed in a paragraph or the turn of a phrase. To accuse Macaulay of superficiality is, in this sense, altogether absurd. His speculation may be meagre, but his store of information is simply inexhaustible. Mill's writing was impressive, because one often felt that a single argument condensed the result of a long process of reflection. Macaulay has the lower but similar merit that a single picturesque touch implies incalculable masses of knowledge. It is but an insignificant part of the building which appears above ground. Compare a passage with the assigned authority, and you are inclined to accuse him—sometimes it may be rightfully—of amplifying and modifying. But more often the particular authority is merely the nucleus round which a whole volume of other knowledge has crystallised. A single hint is significant to a properly prepared mind of a thousand facts not explicitly contained in it. Nobody, he said, could judge of the accuracy of one part of his *History* who had not "soaked his mind with the transitory literature of the day." His real authority was not this or that particular passage, but a literature. And for this reason alone, Macaulay's historical writings have a permanent value which will prevent them from being superseded even by more philosophical thinkers whose minds have not undergone the "soaking" process.

It is significant again that imitations of Macaulay are almost as offensive as imitations of Carlyle. Every great writer has his parasites. Macaulay's false glitter and jingle, his frequent flippancy and superficiality of thought, are more easily caught than his virtues; but so are all faults. Would-be followers of Carlyle catch the strained gestures without the rapture of his inspiration. Would-be followers of Mill fancied themselves to be logical when they were only hopelessly unsympathetic and unimaginative; and would-be followers of some other writers can be effeminate and foppish without being subtle or graceful. Macaulay's thoroughness of work has, perhaps, been less contagious than we could wish. Something of the modern raising of the standard of accuracy in historical inquiry may be set down to his influence. The misfortune is that, if some writers have learnt from him to be flippant without learning to be laborious, others have caught the accuracy without the liveliness. In the later volumes of his *History*, his vigour began to be a little clogged by the fulness of his knowledge; and we can observe symptoms of the tendency of modern historians to grudge the sacrifice of sifting their knowledge. They read enough, but instead of giving us the results, they tumble out the accumulated mass of raw materials upon our devoted heads, til they make us long for a fire in the State Paper Office.

Fortunately, Macaulay did not yield to this temptation in his earlier writings, and the result is that he is, for the ordinary reader, one of the two authorities for English history, the other being Shakespeare. Without comparing their merits, we must admit that the compression of so much into a few short narratives shows intensity as well as compass of mind. He could digest as well as devour, and he tried his digestion pretty severely. It is fashionable to say that part of his practical force is due to the training of parliamentary life. Familiarity with the course of affarirs doubtless strengthened his insight into history, and taught him the value of downright common-sense in teaching an average audience. Speaking purely from the literary point of view, I cannot agree further in the opinion suggested. I suspect the *History* would have been better if Macaulay had not been so deeply immersed in all the business of legislation and electioneering. I do not profoundly reverence the House of Commons' tone—even in the House of Commons; and in literature it easily becomes a nuisance. Familiarity with the actual machinery of politics tends to strengthen the contempt for general principles, of which Macaulay had an ample share. It encourages the illusion of the fly upon the wheel, the doctrine that the dust and din of debate and the worry of lobbies and committee-rooms are not the effect but the cause of the great social movement. The historian of the Roman Empire, as we know, owed something to the captain of Hampshire Militia; but years of life absorbed in parliamentary wrangling and in sitting at the feet of philosophers of Holland House were not likely to widen a mind already disposed to narrow views of the world.

For Macaulay's immediate success, indeed, the training was undoubtedly valuable. As he carried into Parliament the authority of a great writer, so he wrote books with the authority of the practical politician. He has the true instinct of affairs. He knows what are the immediate motives which move masses of men; and is never misled by fanciful analogies or blindfolded by the pedantry of official language. He has seen flesh-and-blood statesmen—at any rate, English statesmen—and understands the nature of the animal. Nobody can be freer from the dominion of crotchets. All his reasoning is made of the soundest common-sense, and represents, if not the ultimate forces, yet forces with which we have to reckon. And he knows, too, how to stir the blood of the average Englishman. He understands most thoroughly the value of concentration, unity, and simplicity. Every speech or essay forms an artistic whole, in which some distinct moral is vigorously driven home by a succession of downright blows. This strong rhetorical instinct is shown conspicuously in the *Lays of Ancient Rome*, which, whatever we might say of them as poetry, are an admirable specimen of rhymed rhetoric. We know how good they are when we see how incapable are modern ballad-writers in general of putting the same swing and fire into their verses. Compare, for example, Aytoun's *Lays of the Cavaliers*, as the most obvious parallel:

> Not swifter pours the avalanche
> Adown the steep incline,
> That rises o'er the parent springs
> Of rough and rapid Rhine,

than certain Scotch heroes over an entrenchment. Place this mouthing by any parallel passage in Macaulay:

> Now, by our sire Quirinus,
> It was a goodly sight
> To see the thirty standards
> Swept down the tide of flight.
> So flies the spray in Adria
> When the black squall doth blow.
> So corn-sheaves in the flood time
> Spin down the whirling Po.

And so on in verses which innumerable schoolboys of inferior pretensions of Macaulay's know by heart. And in such cases the verdict of the schoolboy is perhaps more valuable than that of

the literary connoisseur. There are, of course, many living poets who can do tolerably something of far higher quality, which Macaulay could not do at all. But I don't know who, since Scott, could have done this particular thing. Possibly Mr. Kingsley might have approached it, or the poet, if he would have condescended so far, who sang the bearing of the good news from Ghent to Aix. In any case, the feat is significant of Macaulay's true power. It looks easy; it involves no demands upon the higher reasoning or imaginative powers: but nobody will believe it to be easy who observes the extreme rarity of a success in a feat so often attempted.

A similar remark is suggested by Macaulay's *Essays*. Read such an essay as that upon Clive, or Warren Hastings, or Chatham. The story seems to tell itself. The characters are so strongly marked, the events fall so easily into their places, that we fancy that the narrator's business has been done to his hand. It wants little critical experience to discover that this massive simplicity is really indicative of an art not, it may be, of the highest order, but truly admirable for its purpose. It indicates not only a gigantic memory, but a glowing mind, which has fused a crude mass of materials into unity. If we do not find the sudden touches which reveal the philosophical sagacity or the imaginative insight of the highest order of intellects, we recognise the true rhetorical instinct. The outlines may be harsh, and the colours too glaring; but the general effect has been carefully studied. The details are wrought in with consummate skill. We indulge in an intercalary pish! here and there; but we are fascinated and we remember. The actual amount of intellectual force which goes to the composition of such written archives is immense, though the quality may leave something to be desired. Shrewd common-sense may be an inferior substitute for philosophy, and the faculty which brings remote objects close to the eye of an ordinary observer for the loftier faculty which tinges everyday life with the hues of mystic contemplation. But when the common faculties are present in so abnormal a degree, they begin to have a dignity of their own.

It is impossible in such matters to establish any measure of comparison. No analysis will enable us to say how much pedestrian capacity may be fairly regarded as equivalent to a small capacity for soaring above the solid earth, and therefore the question as to the relative value of Macaulay's work and that of some men of loftier aims and less perfect execution must be left to individual taste. We can only say that it is something so to have written the history of many national heroes as to make their faded glories revive to active life in the memory of their countrymen. So long as Englishmen are what they are—and they don't seem to change as rapidly as might be wished—they will turn to Macaulay's pages to gain a vivid impression of our greatest achievements during an important period.

Nor is this all. The fire which glows in Macaulay's history, the intense patriotic feeling, the love of certain moral qualities, is not altogether of the highest kind. His ideal of national and individual greatness might easily be criticised. But the sentiment, as far as it goes, is altogether sound and manly. He is too fond, it has been said, of incessant moralising. From a scientific point of view the moralising is irrelevant. We want to study the causes and the nature of great social movements; and when we are stopped in order to inquire how far the prominent actors in them were hurried beyond ordinary rules, we are transported to a different order of thought. It would be as much to the purpose if we approved an earthquake for upsetting a fort, and blamed it for moving the foundations of a church. Macaulay can never understand this point of view.

With him, history is nothing more than a sum of biographies. And even from a biographical point of view his moralising is often troublesome. He not only insists upon transporting party prejudice into his estimates, and mauls poor James II. as he mauled the Tories in 1832; but he applies obviously inadequate tests. It is absurd to call upon men engaged in a life-and-death wrestle to pay scrupulous attention to the ordinary rules of politeness. There are times when judgments guided by constitutional precedent become ludicrously out of place, and when the best man is he who aims straightest at the heart of his antagonist. But, in spite of such drawbacks, Macaulay's genuine sympathy for manliness and force of character generally enables him to strike pretty nearly the true note. To learn the true secret of Cromwell's character we must go to Carlyle, who can sympathise with deep currents of religious enthusiasm. Macaulay retains too much of the old Whig distrust for all that it calls fanaticism fully to recognise the grandeur beneath the grotesque outside of the Puritan. But Macaulay tells us most distinctly why Englishmen warm at the name of the great Protector. We, like the banished Cavaliers, "glow with an emotion of national pride" at his animated picture of the unconquerable Ironsides. One phrase may be sufficiently illustrative. After quoting Clarendon's story of the Scotch nobleman who forced Charles to leave the field of Naseby by seizing his horse's bridle, "no man," says Macaulay, "who had much value for his life would have tried to perform the same friendly office on that day for Oliver Cromwell."

Macaulay, in short, always feels, and therefore communicates, a hearty admiration for sheer manliness. And some of his portraits of great men have therefore a genuine power, and show the deeper insight which comes from true sympathy. He estimates the respectable observer of constitutional proprieties too highly; he is unduly repelled by the external oddities of the truly masculine and noble Johnson; but his enthusiasm for his pet hero, William, or for Chatham or Clive, carries us along with him. And at moments when he is narrating their exploits, and can forget his elaborate argumentations and refrain from bits of deliberate bombast, the style becomes graphic in the higher sense of a much-abused word, and we confess that we are listening to genuine eloquence. Putting aside for the moment recollection of foibles, almost too obvious to deserve the careful demonstration which they have sometimes received, we are glad to surrender ourselves to the charm of his straightforward, clear-headed, hard-hitting declamation. There is no writer with whom it is easier to find fault, or the limits of whose power may be more distinctly defined; but within his own sphere he goes forward, as he went through life, with a kind of grand confidence in himself and his cause, which is attractive, and at times even provocative of sympathetic enthusiasm.

Macaulay said, in his Diary, that he wrote his *History* with an eye to a remote past and a remote future. He meant to erect a monument more enduring than brass, and the ambition at least stimulated him to admirable thoroughness of workmanship. How far his aim was secured must be left to the decision of a posterity which will not trouble itself about the susceptibilities of candidates for its favour. In one sense, however, Macaulay must be interesting so long as the type which he so fully represents continues to exist. Whig has become an old-fashioned phrase, and is repudiated by modern Liberals and Radicals, who think themselves wiser than their fathers. The decay of the old name implies a remarkable political change; but I doubt whether it implies more than a very superficial change in the national character. New classes and new ideas have come upon the stage; but they have a curious family likeness to the old. The Whiggism whose peculiarities Macaulay reflected so faithfully represents some of the most deeply seated tendencies of the national character. It has, therefore, both its ugly and its honourable side. Its disregard, or rather its hatred, for pure reason, its exaltation of expediency above truth and precedent above principle, its instinctive dread of strong religious or political faiths, are of course questionable qualities. Yet even they have their nobler side. There is something almost sublime about the grand unreasonableness of the average Englishman. His dogged contempt for all foreigners and philosophers, his intense resolution to have his own way and use his own eyes, to see nothing that does not come within his narrow sphere of vision, and to see it quite clearly before he acts upon it, are of course abhorrent to thinkers of a different order. But they are great qualities in the struggle for existence which must determine the future of the world. The Englishman, armed in his panoply of self-content, and grasping facts with unequalled tenacity, goes on trampling upon acuter sensibilities, but somehow shouldering his way successfully through the troubles of the universe. Strength may be combined with stupidity, but even then it is not to be trifled with. Macaulay's sympathy with these qualities led to some annoying peculiarities, to a certain brutal insularity, and to a commonness, sometimes a vulgarity, of style which is easily criticised. But, at least, we must confess that, to use an epithet which always comes up in speaking of him, he is a thoroughly manly writer. There is nothing silly or finical about him. He sticks to his colours resolutely and honourably. If he flatters his countrymen, it is the unconscious and spontaneous effect of his participation in their weaknesses. He never knowingly calls black white, or panders to an ungenerous sentiment. He is combative to a fault, but his combativeness is allied to a genuine love of fair-play. When he hates a man, he calls him knave or fool with unflinching frankness, but he never uses a base weapon. The wounds which he inflicts may hurt, but they do not fester. His patriotism may be narrow, but it implies faith in the really good qualities, the manliness, the spirit of justice, and the strong moral sense of his countrymen. He is proud of the healthy, vigorous stock from which he springs; and the fervour of his enthusiasm, though it may shock a delicate taste, has embodied itself in writings which will long continue to be the typical illustration of qualities of which we are all proud at bottom—indeed, be it said in passing, a good deal too proud.

WILLIAM EWART GLADSTONE
From "Lord Macaulay"
Quarterly Review, July 1876, pp. 15–24

It has been felt and pointed out in many quarters that Macaulay, as a writer, was the child, and became the type, of his country and his age. As, fifty years ago, the inscription 'Bath' used to be carried on our letter-paper, so the word 'English' is as it were in the water-mark of every leaf of Macaulay's writing. His country was not the Empire, nor was it the United Kingdom. It was not even Great Britain, though he was descended in the higher, that is the paternal, half from Scottish ancestry, and was linked specially with that country through the signal virtues, the victorious labours, and the considerable reputation of his father Zachary. His country was England. On this little spot he concentrated a force of admiration and of worship, which might have covered all the world. But as in space, so in time, it was limited. It was the England of his own age. The higher energies of his life were as completely summed up in the present, as those of Walter Scott were projected upon the past. He would not have filled an Abbotsford with armour and relics of the middle ages. He judges the men and institutions and events of other times by the instruments and measures of the present. The characters whom he admires are those who would have conformed to the type that was before his eyes, who would have moved with effect in the court, the camp, the senate, the drawing-room of to-day. He contemplates the past with no *desiderium*, no regretful longing, no sense of things admirable, which are also lost and irrecoverable. Upon this limitation of his retrospects it follows in natural sequence that of the future he has no glowing anticipations, and even the present he is not apt to contemplate in its mysterious and ideal side. As in respect to his personal capacity of loving, so in regard to the corresponding literary power. The faculty was singularly intense, and yet it was spent within a narrow circle. There is a marked sign of this narrowness in his disinclination even to look at the works of contemporaries whose tone or manner he disliked. It appears that this dislike, and the ignorance consequent upon it, applied to the works of Carlyle. Now we may have little faith in Carlyle as a philosopher or as an historian. Half-lights and half-truths may be the utmost which in these departments his works will be found to yield. But the total want of sympathy is the more noteworthy, because the resemblances, though partial, are both numerous and substantial between these two remarkable men and powerful writers, as well in their strength as in their weakness. Both are honest, and both, notwithstanding honesty, are partisans. Each is vastly, though diversely, powerful in expression; and each is more powerful in expression than in thought. Both are, though variously, poets in prose. Both have the power of portraitures, extraordinary for vividness and strength. For comprehensive disquisition, for balanced and impartial judgments, the world will probably resort to neither; and if Carlyle gains on the comparison in this strong sense of the inward and the idea, he loses in the absolute and violent character of his onesidedness. Without doubt, Carlyle's licentious, though striking, peculiarities of style have been of a nature allowably to repel, so far as they go, one who was so rigid as Macaulay in his literary orthodoxy, and who so highly appreciated, and with such expenditure of labour, all that relates to the exterior or body of a book. Still if there be resemblances so strong, the want of appreciation, which has possibly been reciprocal, seems to be of that nature which Aristotle would have explained by his favourite proverb: κερα-μεὺς κεραμεῖ. The discrepancy is like the discrepancy of colours that are too near. Carlyle is at least a great fact in the literature of his time, and has contributed largely, in some respects too largely, towards forming its characteristic habits of thought. But on these very grounds he should not have been excluded from the horizon of a mind like Macaulay's, with all its large, and varied, and most active interests.

His early training, and consequently the cast of his early opinions, was Conservative. But these views did not survive his career at Cambridge as an undergraduate. No details are given, but we hear that, during that period, Mr. Charles Austin effected, it would seem with facility, the work of his conversion. He supplied an example rather rare of one who, not having been a Whig by birth, became one, and thereafter constantly presented the aspect of that well-marked class of politicians. *Poeta nascitur, orator fit*; and so as a rule a man not born a Liberal, may become a Liberal; but to be a Whig, he must be born Whig. At any rate Macaulay offers to our view one of the most enviable qualities characteristic of that 'variety' of the Liberal 'species'—a singularly large measure of consis-

tency. In this he will bear comparison with Lord Lansdowne or Lord Grey; but in proportion as the pressure of events is sharper on a Commoner than on a Peer, so the phenomenon of consistency is more remarkable. And the feature belongs to his mental character at large. It would be difficult to point out any great and signal change of views on any important subject between the beginning of his full manhood, and the close of his career. His life is like a great volume; the sheets are of one size, type, and paper. Here again Macaulay becomes for us a typical man, and suggests the question whether the conditions of our nature will permit so close and sustained an unity to be had without some sacrifice of expansion? The feature is rendered in his case more noteworthy by the fact that all his life long, with an insatiable avidity, he was taking in whole cargoes of knowledge, and that nothing which he imported into his mind remained there barren and inert. On the other hand, he was perhaps assisted, or, as a censor might call it, manacled, by the perpetual and always living presence in his consciousness, through the enormous tenacity of his memory, of whatever he had himself thought, said, or written, at an earlier time. It may even be, as he himself said, that of the whole of this huge mass he had forgotten nothing. It cannot be doubted that he remembered a far larger proportion, than did other men who had ten or twenty times less to remember. And there was this peculiarity in his recollections; they were not, like those of ordinary men, attended at times with difficulty, elicited from the recesses of the brain by effort. He was alike favoured in the quantity of what he possessed, and in the free and immediate command of his possessions. The effect was most singular. He was (as has been variously shown) often inaccurate: he was seldom, perhaps never, inconsistent. He remembered his own knowledge, in the modern phrase his own concepts, better than he retained, if indeed he ever had embraced, the true sense of the authorities on which these 'concepts' were originally framed. In the initial work of collection, he was often misled by fancy or by prejudice; but in the after work of recollection, he kept faithfully, and never failed to grasp at a moment's notice, the images which the tablets of his brain, so susceptible and so tenacious, had once received. *Diù servavit odorem*. Among Macaulay's mental gifts and habits, it was perhaps this vast memory by which he was most conspicuously known. There was here even a waste of power. His mind, like a dredging-net at the bottom of the sea, took up all that it encountered, both bad and good, nor even seemed to feel the burden. Peerless treasures lay there, mixed, yet never confounded, with worthless trash. This was not the only peculiarity of the wondrous organ.

There have been other men of our own generation, though very few, who, without equalling, have approached Macaulay in power of memory, and who have certainly exceeded him in the unfailing accuracy of their recollections. And yet not in accuracy as to dates, or names, or quotations, or other matters of hard fact, when the question was one simply between aye and no. In these he may have been without a rival. In a list of Kings, or Popes, or Senior Wranglers, or Prime Ministers, or battles, or palaces, or as to the houses in Pall Mall, or about Leicester Square, he might be followed with implicit confidence. But a large and important class of human recollections are not of this order; recollections for example of characters, of feelings, of opinions; of the intrinsic nature, details, and bearings of occurrences. And here it was that Macaulay's wealth 'was unto him an occasion of falling.' And that in two ways. First the possessor of such a vehicle as his memory could not but have something of an overweening confidence in what it told him; and quite apart from any tendency to be vain or overbearing, he could hardly enjoy the benefits of that caution which arises from self-interest, and the sad experience of frequent falls. But what is more, the possessor of so powerful a fancy could not but illuminate with the colours it supplied the matters which he gathered into his great magazine, wherever the definiteness of their outline was not so rigid as to defy or disarm the action of the intruding and falsifying faculty. Imagination could not alter the date of the battle of Marathon, or the Council of Nice, or the crowning of Pepin. But it might seriously or even fundamentally disturb the balance of light and dark in his account of the opinions of Milton or of Laud, or his estimate of the effects of the Protectorate or the Restoration, or of the character, and even the adulteries, of William III. He could detect justly this want of dry light in others: he probably suspected it in himself: but it was hardly possible for him to be enough upon his guard against the distracting action of a faculty at once so vigorous, so crafty, and so pleasurable in its intense activity.

Hence arose, it seems reasonable to believe, that charge of partisanship against Macaulay as an historian, on which much has been, and probably much more will be, said. He may not have possessed that scrupulously tender sense of obligation, that nice tact of exact justice, which is among the very rarest, as well as the most precious, of human virtues. But there never was a writer less capable of intentional unfairness. This during his lifetime was the belief of his friends, but was hardly admitted by opponents. His biographer has really lifted the question out of the range of controversy. He wrote for truth; but, of course, for truth such as he saw it; and his sight was coloured from within. This colour, once attached, was what in manufacture is called a mordent; it was a fast colour; he could not distinguish between what his mind had received and what his mind had imparted. Hence when he was wrong, he could not see that he was wrong; and of those calamities which are due to the intellect only, and not the heart, there can hardly be a greater. The hope of amending is, after all, our very best and brightest hope; of amending our works as well as ourselves. Without it, we are forbidden *revocare gradum, superasque evadere ad auras*, when we have accidentally, as is the way with men, slipped into Avernus. While, as to his authorship, Macaulay was incessantly labouring to improve, in the substance of what he had written he could neither himself detect his errors, nor could he perceive them when they were pointed out. There was a strange contrast between his own confidence in what he said, and his misgivings about his manner of saying it. Woe to him, he says of his History, if some one should review him as he could review another man. He had, and could not but have, the sense of his own scarifying and tomahawking power, and would, we firmly believe, not have resented its use against himself. 'I see every day more and more clearly how far my performance is below excellence.' 'When I compare my book with what I imagine history ought to be, I feel dejected and ashamed.' It was only on comparing it with concrete examples that he felt reassured. He never so conclusively proved himself to be a true artist, as in this dissatisfaction with the products of his art because they fell below his ideal; that Will-o'-the-wisp who, like the fabled sprite, ever stirs pursuit, and ever baffles it, but who, unlike that imp, rewards with large, even if unsatisfying, results every step of real progress. But it is quite plain that all this dissatisfaction had reference to the form, not the matter, of his works. Unhappily, he never so much as glances at any general or serious fear lest he should have mistaken the nature or proportions of events, or, what is, perhaps, still more serious, lest he should have done injustice to characters; although he must have well

known that injustice from his χεὶρ παχεια, his great, massive hand, was a thing so crushing and so terrible. Hence what is at first sight a strange contrast—his insensibility to censure in the forum, his uneasiness in the study; his constant repulsion of the censure of others; his not less constant misgiving, nay censure on himself. In a debased form this phenomenon is, indeed, common, nay the commonest of all. But he was no Sir Fretful Plagiary, to press for criticism, and then, in wrath and agony, to damn the critic. The explanation is simple. He criticised what men approved; he approved what they criticised. His style, unless when in some very rare cases it was wrought up to palpable excess, [1] no one attempted to criticise. It was felt to be a thing above the heads of common mortals. But this it was which he watched with an incessant, a passionate, and a jealous care, the care of a fond parent, if not of a lover; of a parent fond, but not doting, who never spared the rod, that he might not spoil the child. Of his matter, his mode of dealing with the substance of men and things, by the constitution of his mind he was blind to the defects. As other men do in yet higher and more inward regions of their being, he missed the view of his own besetting sin.

However true it may be that Macaulay was a far more consummate workman in the manner than in the matter of his works, we do not doubt that the works contain, in multitudes, passages of high emotion and ennobling sentiment, just awards of praise and blame, and solid expositions of principle, social, moral, and constitutional. They are pervaded by a generous love of liberty, and their atmosphere is pure and bracing, their general aim and basis morally sound. Of the qualifications of this eulogy we have spoken, and have yet to speak. But we can speak of the style of the works with little qualification. We do not, indeed, venture to assert that his style ought to be imitated. Yet this is not because it was vicious, but because it was individual and incommunicable. It was one of those gifts, of which, when it had been conferred, Nature broke the mould. That it is the head of all literary styles we do not allege; but it is different from them all, and perhaps more different from them all than they are usually different from one another. We speak only of natural styles, of styles where the manner waits upon the matter, and not where an artificial structure has been reared either to hide or to make up for poverty of substance. It is paramount in the union of ease in movement with perspicuity of matter, of both with real splendour, and of all with immense rapidity, and striking force. From any other pen, such masses of ornament would be tawdry; with him they are only rich. As a model of art concealing art, the finest cabinet pictures of Holland are almost his only rivals. Like Pascal, he makes the heaviest subject light; like Burke, he embellishes the barrenest. When he walks over arid plains, the springs of milk and honey, as in a march of Bacchus, seem to rise beneath his tread. The repast he serves is always sumptuous, but it seems to create an appetite proportioned to its abundance; for who has ever heard of the reader that was cloyed with Macaulay? In none, perhaps, of our prose writers are lessons, such as he gives, of truth and beauty, of virtue and of freedom, so vividly associated with delight. Could some magician but do for the career of life what he has done for the arm-chair and the study, what a change would pass on the face (at least) of the world we live in, what an accession of recruits would there be to the professing followers of virtue!

As the serious flaw in Macaulay's mind was want of depth, so the central defect with which his productions appear to be chargeable is a pervading strain of exaggeration. He belonged to that class of minds, whose views of single objects are singularly and almost preternaturally luminous. But Nature sows her bounty wide; and those, who possess this precious and fascinating gift as to things in themselves, are very commonly deficient beyond ordinary men in discerning and measuring their relations to one another. For them all things are either absolutely transparent, or else unapproachable from dense and utter darkness. Hence, amidst a blaze of glory, there is a want of perspective, of balance, and of breadth. Themselves knowing nothing of difficulty, or of obscurity, or mental struggle to work out of it, they are liable to be intolerant of those who stumble at the impediments they have overleapt; and even the kindest hearts may be led not merely by the abundance, but by the peculiarities, of their powers, into the most precipitate and partial judgments. From this result Macaulay has not been preserved; and we are convinced that the charges against him would have been multiplied tenfold, had not the exuberant kindness of his heart oftentimes done for him the office of a cautious and self-denying intellect.

Minds of the class to which we refer are like the bodies in the outer world fashioned without gaps or flaws or angles; the whole outline of their formation is continuous, the whole surface is smooth. They are, in this sense, complete men, and they do not readily comprehend those who are incomplete. They do not readily understand either the inferiority, or the superiority, of opponents; the inferiority of their slower sight, or the superiority of their deeper insight; their at once seeing less, and seeing more. In Macaulay's case this defect could not but be enhanced by his living habitually with men of congenial mind, and his comparatively limited acquaintance with that contentious world of practical politics which, like the heaviest wrestling-match for the body, exhibits the unlimited diversities in the attitudes of the human mind, and helps to show how subtle and manifold a thing, is the nature that we bear. Parliament could not but have opened out in one direction a new avenue of knowledge for Macaulay; but we do not agree with Mr. Trevelyan in thinking that the comparatively few hours he spent there, most commonly with his thoughts ranging far abroad, could have largely entered into, or perceptibly modified, the habits of his mind.

The very common association between seeing clearly and seeing narrowly is a law or a frailty of our nature not enough understood. Paley was perhaps the most notable instance of it among our writers. Among living politicians, it would be easy to point to very conspicuous instances. This habit of mind is extremely attractive in that it makes incisive speakers and pellucid writers, who respectively save their hearers and their readers trouble. Its natural tendency is towards hopeless intolerance; it makes all hesitation, all misgiving, all suspense, an infirmity, or a treachery to truth; it generates an appetite for intellectual butchery. There was no man in whom the fault would have been more excusable than in Macaulay; for while with him the clearness was almost preterhuman, the narrowness was, after all, but qualified and relative. The tendency was almost uniformly controlled by the kindly nature and genuine chivalry of the man; so that even, in some of his scathing criticisms, he seems to have a real delight in such countervailing compliments as he bestows: while in conversation, where he was always copious, sometimes redundant, more overbearing, the mischief was effectually neutralised by the strength and abundance of his social sympathies. Yet he exhibited on some occasions a more than ordinary defect in the mental faculty of appreciating opponents. He did not fully take the measure of those from whom he differed, in the things wherein he differed. There is, for example, a parliamentary tradition sufficiently well established[2] that Croker assailed, and assailed

on the instant, some of Macaulay's celebrated speeches on Reform with signal talent, and with no inconsiderable effect. But he never mentions Croker except with an aversion which may be partially understood, and also with a contempt which it is not so easy to account for. It is common to misunderstand the acts of an adversary, and even to depreciate his motives; but Macaulay cannot even acknowledge the strength of his arm. It is yet more to be lamented that, in this instance, he carried the passions of politics into the Elysian fields of literature; and that the scales in which he tried the merits of Croker's edition of Boswell seem to have been weighted, on the descending side, with his recollections of parliamentary collision. But the controversy relating to this work is too important to be dismissed with a passing notice; for what touches Boswell touches Johnson, and what touches Johnson touches a large and an immortal chapter of our English tradition. This is the most glaring instance. There are many others. His estimate of Lord Derby is absurdly low. He hardly mentions Peel during his lifetime except with an extreme severity; and even on the sad occasion of his death, although he speaks kindly of the 'poor fellow,' and cries for his death, he does not supply a single touch of appreciation of his great qualities. Yet Sir Robert Peel, if on rare occasions he possibly fell short in considerateness to friends, was eagerly generous to an opponent like Macaulay, during the struggle on Reform, and again in 1841. Peel moreover had for four years before his decease, from his dread of a possible struggle for the revival of protective duties, been the main prop of the Government which had all the sympathies of Macaulay. There is something yet more marked in the case of Brougham, who is said to have shown towards him in early life a jealousy not generous or worthy. In 1858, at a period when Brougham's character was greatly mellowed and softened, and he had discharged almost all his antipathies, Macaulay writes of him, 'Strange fellow! His powers gone. His spite immortal. A dead nettle!' At this point only, in the wide circuit of Macaulay's recorded words or acts, do we seem to find evidence of a moral defect. Under the semblance of a homage to justice, he seems to have been occasionally seduced into the indulgence of a measure of vindictive feeling.

The combination of great knowledge, great diligence, great powers of appreciation, and great uprightness and kindliness of mind with a constant tendency to exaggerate, with unjust and hasty judgments, and with a nearly uniform refusal to accept correction, offers a riddle not unknown on a smaller scale in smaller men, but here of peculiar interest, because, though Macaulay's kind may not have been the greatest, he was, in his kind, so singularly great. The solution of it seems to lie in this: that, with a breathless rapidity, he filled in his picture before his outline was complete, and then with an extreme of confidence he supplied the colour from his own mind and prepossessions, instead of submitting to take them from his theme. Thus each subject that he treated of became, as has been observed, a mirror which reflected the image of himself. The worshipping estimate, which Mr. John Stuart Mill formed of his wife's powers, was unintelligible to those who had known her, until it was remembered that she was simply the echo of his own voice. She repeated to him his own thoughts and his own conclusions; and he took them, when they proceeded from her lips, for the independent oracles of truth. The echo of himself, which Mill found in his wife, was provided for Macaulay in his own literary creations; and what he thought was loyal adhesion to the true and right was only the more and more close embrace of the image he himself had fashioned and adored.

Notes

1. We may take the liberty, after the lapse of more than eight years, of pointing to a successful parody in the number of this *Review* for April 1868, p. 290.

2. In the valuable Biography of Lord Althorp which has just appeared, it is said that Croker attempted a reply to Macaulay, on the second reading of the second Bill, in a speech of two hours and a half, which utterly failed (p. 383). It is not common to make (apparently off-hand) a reply of two hours and a half upon historical details without the possession of rather remarkable faculties. But this volume, though from the opposite camp, bears witness to Croker's powers: it mentions at p. 400 'a most able and argumentative speech of Croker,' and other living witnesses, of Liberal opinions, might be cited to a like effect. This subject is discussed more fully on pages 83–126 of our present number.

A. V. DICEY
"Macaulay and His Critics"
Nation, May 15, 1902, pp. 388–89

How does it happen that Macaulay, who, to judge from the extent to which his works are read, has been and is the idol of the English people on both sides the Atlantic, has, for the last thirty or forty years, aroused the censure, not to say the aversion, of critics who claim to represent education and culture? The time has come for attempting a reply to a question of considerable curiosity, and, to persons interested in the flow and ebb of opinion, of a certain importance. The period of indiscriminating admiration and the period (certain to follow it) of exaggerated censure have passed away. Sir Richard Jebb's exquisite and impartial apology is a sign that a master of style and a scholar of the highest culture can, while admitting the limits, also recognize the rareness and brilliancy of Macaulay's genius. Mr. Macgregor's painstaking study of Macaulay's writings is a proof that, at Cambridge at any rate, young men just entering into life have no wish to detract from the reputation of the most popular among English historians, but desire to understand what is the permanent rank to be assigned him in the world of English letters. Under the guidance of a critic so skilful, so fair, and so subtle as the Regius Professor of Greek in the University of Cambridge, it is possible to answer with some confidence the question which we have propounded, and to show that the quarrel between Macaulay and his critics is due in the main to two causes.

First, Macaulay's tone and the very texture of his genius were antipathetic to the men who, in the main, guided the educated opinion of England during the latter part of the nineteenth century. Nor need this fact excite surprise. Macaulay, born in 1800, belonged in character to the eighteenth century. There is profound truth in the paradox to be found somewhere in the writings of Mr. Leslie Stephen, that in England the eighteenth century lasted on till 1830; and Macaulay was heart and soul the man of 1830. In this he resembled the Whigs and the Edinburgh Reviewers. In virtue, indeed, of his genius, of his youth, and of his historical enthusiasm, he saw truths and sympathized with feelings unrevealed to and unshared by Jeffrey or Sydney Smith. His onslaught on the *à priori* and unhistorical method of political reasoning characteristic of the Benthamites not only exhibits a dialectical power to which even Sir George Trevelyan hardly does justice, but also breaks with the intellectual tradition of the eighteenth century, and anticipates the historical view of political science; his keen appreciation of the revival of civic and even democratic life due to the rise of Christianity is

foreign to the ideas of Hume and of Gibbon, and generally Macaulay's youthful article on the study of history teems with notions usually placed to the credit of later writers, such, for example, as the suggestion made with much less moderation and force by Merivale and by Mommsen, that Cicero's or Sallust's account of the Catilinian conspiracy deserved no more trust than other official proclamations or party pamphlets that tell the story of a revolutionary movement which has been condemned by failure. And though Macaulay's strength did not lie in the criticism of art or of poetry, his fervent admiration for Lessing's *Laocoön* and for Goethe's analysis of Hamlet's character shows that Macaulay as a critic had progressed far beyond the ideas of Jeffrey and his school. But though Macaulay shared to some extent the ideas of the coming age, he was at bottom a man of the eighteenth century; his optimism, his manly vigor, his decisive outspokenness, his admiration for material progress—which, however, as Sir Richard Jebb well points out, was to Macaulay and to Macaulay's contemporaries chiefly valuable as the sign of moral and intellectual improvement—the very tone of satisfaction and triumph which runs through his resounding sentences, all express the very spirit of 1832, and all jar upon the taste of the writers and critics who, in one form or another, represent the reaction of the nineteenth century against the rationalism of the eighteenth.

With the reaction, in any case, Macaulay had throughout his life nothing to do. One can hardly imagine thinkers with whose tone he had less in common than Carlyle, Froude, Newman, or Matthew Arnold. These men, who are more samples of a whole body of writers, were in many points—and these points of vital importance—as opposed to one another as it was possible for one writer to be opposed to a writer of a different school. Yet, if you look at the sentiment of the nineteenth century as a whole, you may easily perceive that they all and each of them represent a reaction, if not of opinion, yet of feeling, and a reaction in which Macaulay had no share; and the same thing is true of thinkers of a different class from those already mentioned. John Mill and Mr. John Morley no doubt have carried on from some points of view the ideas of the eighteenth century. Yet it is palpable to any one who has studied their writings that Mill and Mr. John Morley (who would not, we imagine, repudiate the name of Mr. Mill's disciple) keenly sympathize with the feeling, if not with the creeds, of the nineteenth century. The attacks then, made upon Macaulay by later critics are from one point of view simply part of the conflict between the intellectual revolution of the eighteenth and the reactionary movement of the nineteenth century.

Secondly, Macaulay maintained a conception of the proper function of an historian which is opposed to the ideals formed by a later generation of historical writers. To Macaulay, as to the greatest historians whom the world has seen, history was primarily narration; the perfect historian was in his eyes the writer who, having obtained knowledge of past events, placed them in due order and proportion before the eyes of his readers. The object of history is, on this view, to give a true picture of the past, or, in other words, to make the men of one generation see past events as they were seen by their contemporaries. To historical inquirers, on the other hand, of to-day, the function of the historian seems to be primarily either what is called scientific—that is, the classificaiton of details under principles and the references of effects to causes—or else discovery; that is, the revealing of facts, whether small or great, hitherto unknown. On the one view, history is a branch, and, as Macaulay certainly deemed it, the noblest branch, of literature. On the other view, history, or rather historical inquiry, is, as far as may be, assimilated to, if not made a branch of, physical science. The two conceptions, be it noted, are not in reality antagonistic. The ideal historian—if such a person should ever exist—could be at once a narrator, an analyzer, and a discoverer of the past. No one, again, will dispute—Macaulay certainly did not forget—that the basis of historical narrative must be knowledge of the past, and that the foundation of knowledge is study and investigation. Nor, may it be supposed, does the most scientific of historical investigators in reality doubt, thought their practice does not always show full appreciation of this truth, that to narrate—that is, to set forth in due order and proportion the results of discovery and investigation—is no small achievement and no mean contribution to the knowledge and to the instruction of mankind. But, though this is true, it is none the less true that there is, as things now stand, practically a marked contrast or even opposition between the author who regards history as primarily narrative, and the author who regards history as primarily a branch either of science or of discovery. This difference deserves attention in itself, and certainly goes far to account for the feud between Macaulay and his critics.

Macaulay was the most effective or narrators. This, be it remarked, is a merit independent of his "style," if that word be used in a narrow sense, as meaning merely his language and mode of expression. His narrative power consisted not in a command of words, but in the capacity for grasping a large body of complicated events as a whole, and then so narrating them that every part of a complex transaction should become perfectly clear, because every fact is put in its right place. The power to do this is not given to some historians whose work is otherwise above praise. That Mr. Gardiner, for instance, might have cultivated this gift may be safely inferred from his short but admirable sketch of the Thirty Years' War; but it would be untrue to assert that he exhibits any remarkable capacity for narration in his otherwise admirable history of the Stuarts, which, especially in his later volumes, becomes more and more of an *Annual Register*. That Macaulay's achievement as a narrator was extraordinarily successful no one would dream of denying; the essential matter is to recognize the importance of his success. This may to a certain extent be measured by one consideration: the few volumes of his English History have made one bit of the annals of England better known to the English people than the events of their own day. True of course it is that the labor bestowed by Macaulay on narration is not balanced, as in the case of an absolutely perfect historian it would be, by the assiduous attempt to connect results with general causes. Yet to make this a serious charge against our author savors of that futile criticism which belittles one man of genius simply because he has not the special qualities of another man of equal though different genius. To complain of Macaulay because he had not the analytical subtlety of Tocqueville is hardly wiser than to attack Tocqueville's

L'Ancien Régime because it does not give such a picture of pre-Revolutionary France as Macaulay's *History of England* affords of the age of Charles II.

It may further be urged that the attempt to establish a science of history is premature. The grandiloquent generalizations of Buckle, the laws of Comte, and even the theories of Tocqueville, to many critics will seem of dubious truth in this matter. Thucydides affords us a warning. Thucydides came as near as any man could to the perfect historian; in him the capacity for historical narration is blended with and balanced by a genius for scientific analysis. He narrates, he inquires, he refers effects to causes; but though the man appeared, the hour for creating scientific history has not arrived—the attempt to do so was premature. The science of Thucydides is of less importance than his narrative. It is at least arguable that the miscellaneous information collected by the restless and unscientific curiosity of Herodotus has been of more value to the world than the historical or political theories of Thucydides.

But Macaulay, it will be said, has not discovered new facts, and the very essence of historical inquiry of discovery. It is at this point that the defenders and critics of Macaulay must in reality join issue. No doubt if it once be granted that the main function of an historian is to discover, then it will follow that Macaulay, while making every effort to ascertain the truth of the facts which he narrated, did not devote himself to what Carlyle has somewhere called "navvy-work"; but then, this admission is exactly what Macaulay and those who try to do him justice will deny. Every kind of praise is due to men whose turn of mind leads them to ascertain new facts concerning the past, even though the facts may be in themselves of no great importance; the writer, for example, who finally determines the question whether Dr. Johnson was three years or six months at Oxford; or ascertains, if it be ascertainable, who was the man who wore the iron mask; or proves conclusively that the Girondins did not, the night before their execution, partake of a good supper, has done something for the promotion of truth that is worth doing, and no sensible man ought to grudge the credit due to even the minor laborers in the field of research. But, so high is the value placed by modern critics on research which may or may not be the result of great intellectual powers, that the time has come to remind the world that the laborers who collect the materials for history are not, of necessity, themselves historians; an honest brickmaker deserves credit for the goodness of his bricks, but he has no right to claim the admiration due to an architect of genius. On the recognition of this principle is based the verdict of popular admiration which gives to Macaulay his deservedly high place among England's men of letters. To the neglect of this principle is due at least one-half of the attacks on Macaulay by men of culture and refinement who fail to perceive that, deep as is the respect due to research, the capacity for historical exposition will always be held the mark of a great historian.

G. P. R. JAMES

1799–1860

George Payne Rainsford James was born on August 9, 1799, in London, the son of a physician. He was educated at a school in Putney, where he became proficient in Italian and French. He later traveled extensively on the Continent, participating in the Napoleonic Wars (he was briefly imprisoned in France) and reading deeply in French history. During his years abroad he killed an opponent in a duel, and the incident was a source of grief to him for the remainder of his life.

Failing to receive an expected political appointment upon his return to England, James turned to literature, contributing anonymous pieces to magazines. His work impressed Washington Irving, who encouraged the young writer to embark on a more ambitious project; the historical novel *Richelieu* (1829) was the result. Praised by Sir Walter Scott, *Richelieu* launched its author on a successful writing career that included the composition of more than one hundred novels, most on historical themes. In addition, he wrote nonfictional histories as well as a number of biographies of prominent figures, including Charlemagne, Louis the XIV, and Henry of Navarre, and prepared an edition of the letters of William III. His historical writing led to his appointment as Historiographer Royal to William IV.

Despite his apparent literary successes James appears always to have been concerned about his finances; thus when political appointments were at last made available to him, he eagerly accepted them. Around 1850 he was named consul to Massachusetts; two years later he was sent to serve in Virginia in a similar post. In 1856 he was appointed consul-general of the Austrian ports on the Adriatic. James, who was married and had four children, died of apoplexy in Venice on June 9, 1860.

North: Mr. Colburn has lately given us two books of a very different character, *Richelieu* and *Darnley*—by Mr. James. *Richelieu* is one of the most spirited, amusing, and interesting romances I ever read; characters well drawn—incidents well managed—story perpetually progressive—catastrophe at once natural and unexpected—moral good, but not goody—and the whole felt, in every chapter, to be the work of a—Gentleman.—JOHN WILSON (as "Christopher North"), *Noctes Ambrosianae* (April 1830), 1854

Mr. James ⟨. . .⟩ may be regarded as not less fortunate in the choice of his subject than meritorious in its treatment; indeed, his work is not so much the best as the only History of Charlemagne which will hereafter be cited. For it reposes upon a far greater body of research and collation than has hitherto been applied even in France to this interesting theme; and in effect it is the first account of the great emperor and his times which can, with a due valuation of the term, be complimented with the title of a *critical* memoir.—THOMAS DE QUINCEY, "Charlemagne" (1832), *Collected Writings*, ed. David Masson, Vol. 5, p. 362

The voluminousness—we choose the word advisedly for the occasion—of Mr. James's writings is the idea instantly suggested to the mind upon the bare mention of his name. The first thing you think of is the enormous quantity of books he has written. You fancy a man seated at a table in the centre of a commodious library, with the gift of perpetual motion in his wrist, as incapable of fatigue in brains or fingers as the steam-apparatus that hatches eggs, and possessed with a terrible determination of blood to the head—relieving itself instinctively by a fearful resolution to write on—on—on—during *secula seculorum*, at all hazards to gods, men and columns, "till the great globe itself," &c. Fifty other strange notions of a like bewildering kind rise up and surround this image of an inexhaustible author; and the more you attempt to close with the phenomenon, the more incomprehensible it becomes, like a dim perplexing figure in a dream. ⟨. . .⟩

It is not entirely ⟨. . .⟩ because Mr. James has written so much, that we think he might have done better had he written less. The manner of composition has had something to do with it, and is mainly answerable for that uniformity of style, that smooth onward flat over which the narrative rolls with such regularity, and that want of compactness in details, which, with all our admiration of the versatile talents of the author, we constantly feel in these very clever and very numerous novels. If he had not drawn so extensively upon history, and availed himself so largely of characters whose lineaments were already familiar to the reader, these deficiencies would have been still more apparent. But, fortunately, the reader is enabled by his previous knowledge to fill up many of the faint and hasty outlines of the author, an involuntary process which frequently atones for the short-comings of the fiction.

The "fatal facility" of these novels must be apparent to the most superficial critic. It is impossible not to see that they have been hurried out pell-mell, with wonderful self-reliance and an almost constitutional contempt of system and responsibility. The fluency of the manner is not more palpable than the diffusiveness of the matter. The figures are in eternal motion; the dialogue seems everlasting; the descriptions have the breadth and incoherency and joyous flush of a stage diorama. The flurry of the incidents, the number of the characters, and the mass of subordinate details that stifle the main action, leave upon the memory a very confused sense of the particular merits or final aim of the story. Looking back upon the whole series, one is apt, from the homogeneity, or family-likeness, which pervades them, to mistake one for another, to run Darnley into Richelieu, or jumble up De L'Orme with De Leon. This indistinctness arises from want of care and reflection in the preliminary settlement of a definite design. The novel seems to be begun and finished at a single heat, while the first thought was still fresh, and before time had been allowed to examine its capabilities, or shape it to an end. The consequences of this indiscretion rise up in judgment against the author in every page. There is no repose in the action, the portraiture, the embroidery, the scenery, to give leisure for the reader to take in the vital elements of the subject, or for the prominent person- ages to grow out into their full and natural proportions, and fix themselves calmly, but forcibly, upon his attention.—R. H. HORNE, "G. P. R. James, Mrs. Gore, Capt. Marryatt, and Mrs. Trollope," A New Spirit of the Age, 1844, pp. 130–34

He is a picturesque writer, and paints his canvas-deep figures in bright costume, and in the midst of excellent landscape. Often when I have been very unwell, I have been able to read his books with advantage, when I could not read better ones. You may read him from end to end without a superfluous beat of the heart,—and they are just the sort of intellectual diet fitted for persons "ordered to be kept quiet" by their physicians. Do not mistake, I am writing quite gravely, and not, I hope, ungratefully. I am grateful to Mr. James for many a still, serene hour. I have every respect for him as a sensible level writer— a very agreeable writer—pure-minded, and with talents in his own province. But to give him place as a romance writer over Bulwer, the prose-poet of the day, and over Banim, the prose-dramatist, is, must be, a monstrous exaggeration of his actual claim.—ELIZABETH BARRETT BROWNING, Letter to Richard Henry Horne (Jan. 5, 1844), Letters of Elizabeth Barrett Browning Addressed to Richard Hengist Horne, ed. S. R. Townshend Mayer, 1877, Vol. 1, pp. 215–16

James ⟨is⟩ the most industrious, if not always most successful, imitator of Scott, in revival of chivalric and middle-age scenes. The number of James's works is immense, but they bear among themselves a family likeness so strong, and even oppressive, that it is impossible to consider this author otherwise than as an ingenious imitator and copyist—first of Scott, and secondly of himself. The spirit of repetition is, indeed, carried so far, that it is possible to guess beforehand, and with perfect certainty, the principal contents, and even the chief persons, of one of James's historical novels. His heroes and heroines, whose features are almost always gracefully and elegantly sketched in, have more of the English than continental character. We are sure to have a nondescript grotesque as a secondary person- age—a half-crazy jester, ever hovering between the hare- brained villain and the faithful retainer: we may count upon abundance of woodland scenery (often described with singular delicacy and tenderness of language) and moonlight rendez- vous of robbers and conspirators. But whereas Scott has all these things, it must be remembered how much more he has beside. He looks through all things "with a learned spirit:" James stops short here, unless we notice his innumerable pictures of battles, tournaments, hunting-scenes, and old castles, where we find much more of the forced and artificial accuracy of the antiquary, than of the poet's all-embracing, all-imagining eye. James is particularly versed in the history of France, and some of his most successful novels have reference to that country, among which we may mention Richelieu. His great deficiency is want of real, direct, powerful human passion, and consequently of life and movement in his in- trigues. There is thrown over his fictions a general air of good-natured, frank, and well-bred refinement, which, how- ever laudable, cannot fail to be found rather tiresome and monotonous.—THOMAS B. SHAW, Outlines of English Litera- ture, 1847

James's multitudinous novels seem to be written upon the plan of "the songs of the Bard of Schiraz," in which, we are assured by Fadladeen, "the same beautiful thought occurs again and again in every possible variety of phrase."—EDGAR ALLAN POE,

"Fifty Suggestions" (1849), Essays and Reviews, ed. G. R. Thompson, 1984, p. 1297

I read everything that was readable, old and new ⟨. . .⟩ and hailed every fresh publication of James, though I knew half what he was going to do with his lady, and his gentleman, and his landscape, and his mystery, and his orthodoxy, and his criminal trial. But I was charmed with the new amusement which he brought out of old materials. I looked on him as I should look upon a musician, famous for "variations". I was grateful for his vein of cheerfulness, for his singularly varied and vivid landscapes, for his power of painting women at once ladylike and loving (a rare talent), for his making lovers to match, at once beautiful and well bred, and for the solace which all this has afforded me, sometimes over and over again, in illness and in convalescence, when I required interest without violence, and entertainment at once animated and mild.—LEIGH HUNT, Autobiography, 1850, Ch. 25

If he was sometimes a tedious writer, he was always the best story-teller that I ever listened to. He had known almost every body in his own country, and he never forgot any thing. The literary anecdotes alone which I have heard him relate would suffice to fill an ordinary volume. He was a big-hearted man, too—tender, merciful, and full of religious sentiment; a good husband, a devoted father, and a fast friend. If I dwell longer upon him than upon some others who occupy a higher niche in the temple of fame, it is because I knew him so well, and there always existed so affectionate a regard between us. —MAUNSELL B. FIELD, Memoirs of Many Men and Some Women, 1873, p. 206

James wrote better than Ainsworth: his historical knowledge was of a much wider and more accurate kind, and he was not unimbued with the spirit of romance. But the sameness of his situations (it became a stock joke to speak of the "two horsemen" who so often appeared in his opening scenes), the exceedingly conventional character of his handling, and the theatrical feebleness of his dialogue, were always reprehended and open to reprehension.—GEORGE SAINTSBURY, A History of Nineteenth Century Literature, 1896, p. 139

George Paine Rainsford James was even more prolific than Ainsworth. He is said to have written more than one hundred novels, besides historical books and poetry. No wonder there- fore that the name of James became a by-word for convention- ality of opening and for diffuse weakness of style. More perhaps than Ainsworth he has suffered from time, because he remains more constantly on a dead level of mediocrity. James trusted, and in his own day trusted not in vain, to adventure; but unless there is some saving virtue of style, or of thought, or of character, each generation insists on making its own adven- tures. James has sunk under the operation of this law, and he is not likely to be revived.—HUGH WALKER, The Age of Tennyson, 1897, pp. 78–79

EDWIN P. WHIPPLE
From "James's Novels" (1844)
Essays and Reviews
1850, Volume 1, pp. 116–37

The author of *Sartor Resartus*, in a petition to the House of Commons, on the copyright question, signs himself "Thomas Carlyle, a Maker of Books." This phrase, which applies to Herr Teufelsdröckh only in a quaint sense, is applicable to Mr. G. P. R. James in its literal meaning. He is, indeed, no "maker" in the old significance of that term, for he creates nothing; but he is emphatically a literary mechanic. The organs of his brain are the tools of his trade. He manufactures novels, as other people manufacture shoes, shirts, and sheetings; he continually works up the same raw material into very nearly the same shapes. The success he has met with in his literary speculations should be chronicled in the *Merchants'* or *Mechanics' Magazine*. He is a most scientific expositor of the fact, that a man may be a maker of books without being a maker of thoughts; that he may be the reputed author of a hundred volumes, and flood the market with his literary wares, and yet have very few ideas and principles for his stock in trade. For the last ten years, he has been repeating his own repetitions, and echoing his own echoes. His first novel was a shot that went through the target, and he has ever since been assiduously firing through the hole. To protect his person from critical assault, he might pile up a bulwark of books many volumes thick and many feet high; yet the essence of all that he has written, if subjected to a refining process, might be compressed into a small space, and even then would hardly bear the test of time, and journey safely down to posterity. When we reflect upon the character and construction of his works, and apply to them certain searching tests, they dwindle quickly into very moderate dimensions. We find that the enormous helmet encloses only a small nut, that the nut is an amplified exponent of the kernel, and that the kernel itself is neither very rich nor very rare. As space has no limits, and as large portions of it are still unoccupied by tangible bodies, it seems not very philosophical to quarrel with any person who endeavors to fill up its wide chasms; yet, in the case of Mr. James, we grudge the portion of infinite space which his writings occupy, and dispute his right to pile up matter which is the type or symbol of so small an amount of spirit. We sigh for the old vacuum, and think, that though nature may have abhorred it in the days of Aristotle, her feelings must have changed since modern mediocrity has filled it with such weak apologies for substance and form. ⟨. . .⟩

Now, Mr. James, in some of the most important qualifications as a novelist, is remarkably deficient. He has little objectivity. He is chained to his own consciousness. His insight into character and life is feeble. He cannot go out of his own little world of thought and emotion, and sympathize with other grades and modes of being. Everything he writes is "sicklied o'er" with his own feelings. There is no spontaneous exercise of his faculties,—none of that yielding of the will and reason to the impulses of imagination and passion,—none of that running over of the heart in the worship of the mind's creations,—none of that forgetfulness of self in sympathy with other beings,—which we observe in the masters of his art. His plots, his characters, his emotions, his outbreaks of feeling, are all deliberated and forced. He places a moral reflection, or a feeble speculation, at due pauses in the march of his story, with a sort of mathematical precision. The reader who desires not to have his principles corrupted by unconscious sympathy with any act or utterances of the characters in the novel which may not square with the moral code, is soon relieved from any apprehension of the kind, by noticing that Mr. James follows the progress of the plot, catechism in hand, and reads a homily from it whenever the necessities of morality require. If he had written the tragedy of *Othello*, and had put into Iago's mouth the words which Shakespeare uses, he would have filled half of the page with notes, stating his reasons for such an outrage upon morality, carefully distinguishing between his own opinions and those of the character, and adding copious truisms on

the wickedness of malice and revenge. Mothers, therefore, think they can trust their children to the care of Mr. James, and are willing that they should journey through the land of romance under his guidance. As soon as one of his novels is issued, the newspapers devote a column to his "beautiful" moral reflections and rose-colored sentiments. Readers who have a right to demand that the journal should be filled with news and advertisements, find themselves cheated and bored, by being compelled to admire the old speculations of Mr. James on destiny, fatalism, the affections, the will, and such other topics as form the staple of his colloquies with the reader.

Now, this is "from the purpose" of novel-writing. To a person accustomed to the manner of greater and more artistical novelists, it is an unendurable infliction. If the thoughts were valuable in themselves, bore any marks of originality and freshness, seemed to be called forth naturally by the incidents related, or were woven with any skill into the texture of the narrative, they might be pleasing; but the understanding of Mr. James never succeeds in the attempt to clutch an original idea, or to speculate on any subject which requires dialectical powers; and, consequently, he doses the reader with truisms, or perplexes him with reveries. He gives dim hints of his opinions on any question of metaphysics which crosses the path of his narrative, but he does not grasp and attempt to settle it. The most striking instances of "catching at ideas by the tail," of which we have any knowledge, are seen in his reveries on destiny, which reäppear in each successive work that comes from his fertile pen and unfruitful intellect. It seems astonishing, that a man could have this subject so often in his mind, for a period of twenty years, and not blunder upon some opinion about it, correct or erroneous. He does not appear to know, that his unformed notions on this point, so far as they can be reduced to formulas, lead directly to fatalism.

But the great defect of Mr. James as a novelist is his lack of skill in the creation or accurate delineation of individual character. If the novel be intended as a mirror of actual life, either past or present, it should contain not only events, but men and women. Character should be exhibited, not didactically, but dramatically. We demand human beings,—not embodied antitheses, or personified qualities, thoughts or passions. The author has no right to project himself into his characters, and give different proper names to one personality. We want a forcible conception and consistent development of individual minds, with traits and peculiarities which constitute their distinction from other minds. They should be drawn with sufficient distinctness to enable the reader to give them a place in his memory, and to detect all departures, either in language or action, from the original types. We desire beings, not ideas; something concrete, not abstract. ⟨. . .⟩

The incidents in his novels are brought together with much cunning skill. Every person who begins one of his books desires to get through it as quickly as possible. To many this may appear the highest praise, and to settle the question at once. To us it appears to do no such thing. Although the power of creating incident, and of skilfully linking one event to another, is an important element of a good novel, yet it is not the most important, nor is it one in which Mr. James enjoys preëminence. When we discover the secret of his method of story-building, our admiration decreases greatly. We acknowledge that his novels are interesting, that they awaken and fix attention; but we discriminate between the kind of interest they excite, and the interest of *Tom Jones* or *Ivanhoe*. We perceive that his plots are pieces of machinery, constructed according to the laws of mathematics. Their intricacy, and not their naturalness, is the source of their hold upon our minds. The characters seem not to have free play. They are puppets, moved by the scheming brain of the author. We know that the hero and the heroine will enjoy no felicity or peace until the conclusion of the third volume, and we hasten to the consummation as fast as our eyes can carry us. The world to which we are introduced is not a free, common world, where there are chances in favor both of vice and virtue, but a fenced park, full of man-traps and spring-guns. A sort of iron necessity conducts everything. We do not feel ourselves safe, until we have come to the conclusion. A sort of feverish, unhealthy excitement is the feeling we experience as we read. There is always some murder, forgery, or other dark crime, in the past or the future, which we have a natural desire to expose and punish. The good characters are entangled in such a web of evil; there is such a provoking succession of premeditated accidents which seem untoward; they are walking so long on the verge of a deep gulf, into which the slightest false step may precipitate them; that our feelings of philanthropy are enlisted in their behalf, and the common axioms which forbid cruelty to animals impel us to wish them speedy death or happiness.

Mr. James is also a spendthrift of human life. When he has done with a character, or thinks it necessary to enhance the interest of his story by something awful, he strikes his pen into one of his *dramatis personæ*, without the slightest mercy, and literally blots him from existence. He knows well that murder and violence are popular in romance, and he is desirous, like a sagacious book merchant, to make the supply equal to the demand. Whether he has any compunctious visitings of conscience, after gratifying, in this manner, his murderous thoughts, we are unable to determine; but we think the carelessness with which he slays evinces the feebleness with which he conceives. If his personages were real to his own heart or imagination, if they were anything more than clothed ideas and passions, we doubt if he would part with them so easily, or kill them with such *nonchalance*. His hero, of course, is preserved amidst the general slaughter, but not without many wounds both of the body and spirit.

We have heard the style of Mr. James praised, but on what principle of taste we could never discover. To us it seems but ill adapted to narrative. It has little flow and perspicuity, and no variety. It is usually heavy, lumbering, and monotonous. His sentences seem constructed painfully, yet doggedly, and not to spring spontaneously from his brain, inspired by the thought or feeling they are intended to convey. Half of the words seem in the way of the idea, and the latter appears not to have strength enough to clear the passage. Occasionally a swift, sharp sentence comes, like a flash of lightning, from the cloud of his verbiage, and relieves the twilight of his diction; but generally the reader must plod laboriously through one of his volumes, and, if he can overlook the style in the incidents, it is all the better for his patience. James has none of that wonderful power of clear narration which we observe in Scott; that ductile style, which changes with each change in the story, and seems insensibly to mould itself into the shape of the thought and emotion which are uppermost at the time. Nor has he any of that quiet, demure humor, which Scott often infuses into the very heart of his diction, as in the first hundred pages of *Redgauntlet*. There is a strait-laced gravity in Mr. James's manner which is often ridiculous, because wholly inappropriate. In all those higher qualities of style, which do not relate to the mere rhetorical arrangement of words and sentences, but spring directly from passion, fancy, or imagination, and bear the impress of the writer's nature, he is very deficient. There are but few felicitous passages in his manifold volumes. He has

hardly any of those happy combinations of words, which stick fast to the memory, and do more than pages to express the author's meaning. With all his command of a certain kind of elegant language, he has little command of expression. His imagination, as a shaping power, has either no existence, or he writes too rapidly to allow it time to perform its office. His imagery is common; and his manner of arraying a trite figure in a rich suit of verbiage, only makes its essential commonness and poverty more evident. His style is not dotted over with any of those shining points, either of imagery or epigram, which illumine works of less popularity and pretension. To us his temperament seems sluggish, and is only kindled into energy by the most fiery stimulants. "A slow, rolling grandiloquence" seems his rhetorical ideal, and he does not always succeed in attaining even that humble height of expression. As his object, however, seems to be to fill out three volumes with a narration of incidents which will please, rather than to cultivate any of those qualities of condensation and picturesqueness which would compress them into one, we may not be justified in interfering between him and his bookseller.

In these remarks we do not intend to say that our novelist has no passages which clash with this opinion of his style. It would be a monstrous supposition, that a human being could possibly write a hundred volumes, without being betrayed at times into eloquence and beauty of expression. We refer in our strictures, to general traits, not to individual exceptions; to the desert, and not to the oases in it. Mr. James evidently possesses talent sufficiently great to enable him to write well, if he could only learn to "labor and to wait;" but he is cursed with the mania of book-making, and seems to look more to the number of his pages than to the quality of his rhetoric.

In these remarks on Mr. James, as a novelist, we have intended to do him no injustice. We are willing to grant him the praise of talents and learning, and to do fit honor to the moral purpose he seems to have in his writings. But we dispute his claim to those qualities which constitute the chief excellence of a novelist; we doubt his possession of that fecundity of mind which can produce a series of novels without constant repetition of old types of character, and old machinery of plot. If the severity of our criticism has ever run into fanciful exaggeration, it has been owing to the petulant humor engendered by exposing unfounded pretension.

Indeed, Mr. James does not appear like a man who could be wounded or hurt by severe criticism. The abstract character of the personages of his novels affects our own view of himself. We oppose him as we would oppose an idea or a principle. We do not consider him as an individual. Our imagination refuses to shape the idea suggested by his name into a palpable person. Whenever an author appears to our mind in a concrete form, the quality of mercy we extend to his compositions is never "strained." We feel for his pardonable vanity, and we would launch at him no sarcasm calculated to lacerate his delicate sensibilities. He is a human being, a brother, or, at least, a cousin. If he be a dunce, we pat him on the shoulder, and tell him to try again. If he be a man of talents, with some absurd or pernicious principles, we regret that the latter should weaken the respect we bear to the former. But not so is it with Mr. James. We no more think of hurting his feelings by sharp criticism, than of wounding the sensibility of Babbage's calculating machine by detecting it in a mathematical error. To us he is a thin essence, impenetrable to the weapons of earthly combat, and unmoved by any hail-storm of satire which might seem to beat on his frame. He is an abstraction, and, therefore, the last person to expect that a reviewer will hide the thorns of analysis in the flowers of panegyric.

THE BETTMANN ARCHIVE

THOMAS DE QUINCEY

THE BETTMANN ARCHIVE

THOMAS BABINGTON MACAULAY

THE BETTMANN ARCHIVE

ELIZABETH BARRETT BROWNING

THE BETTMANN ARCHIVE

WILLIAM H. PRESCOTT

JAMES SHERIDAN KNOWLES

HENRY THOMAS BUCKLE

HENRY DAVID THOREAU

ELIZABETH BARRETT BROWNING

1806–1861

Elizabeth Barrett Browning was born Elizabeth Barrett Moulton Barrett at Coxhoe Hall, County Durham, on March 6, 1806; she was the eldest of the twelve children of Edward Barrett Moulton Barrett, whose wealth was derived from Jamaican plantations. Her childhood was spent at Hope End in Herefordshire, where she was largely self-educated, though she learned much from her correspondence with her neighbors Uvedale Price and Hugh Stuart Boyd. In 1832 the Barrett family moved to Sidmouth, and in 1835 to London; in 1838 Elizabeth was sent to Torquay, after suffering a broken blood vessel which led to a serious illness. It was at Torquay, two years later, that Elizabeth's favorite brother was drowned, a shock from which she never fully recovered.

In September 1841 Elizabeth left Torquay for London, where she rejoined her family. In 1845 she first met the poet Robert Browning, to whom she was secretly married in 1846. They left for Italy and made their permanent home at Casa Guidi in Florence. Throughout her married life Elizabeth Barrett Browning was passionately interested in Italian and French politics, and was a strong supporter of Italian unity. She also had a great interest in spiritualism, although this is not reflected in her poetry. The Brownings' only child, Robert Wiedemann (known as Penini), was born in 1849. After a year of deteriorating health Elizabeth died in Florence on June 29, 1861.

Elizabeth Barrett Browning began writing poetry at a very early age. Her juvenilia, *The Battle of Marathon* (1820), *An Essay on Mind* (1826), and a translation of *Prometheus Bound*, with other poems (1833), appeared anonymously, and the first two were privately printed at her father's expense. The first work to achieve any real recognition was *The Seraphim and Other Poems* published in 1838. Her next collection, *Poems*, appeared in two volumes in 1844, and was so highly regarded that, when Wordsworth died in 1850, there were many who considered her his most appropriate successor as poet laureate. Indeed, during the years of her married life Elizabeth's reputation was greater than that of her husband. The famous *Sonnets from the Portuguese* first appeared in a collected edition of her poems in 1850, followed in 1851 by *Casa Guidi Windows*, a poem on the theme of Italian liberation. *Aurora Leigh*, an 11,000-line life-story of a woman poet, described by its author as a "novel in verse," was published in 1856, and was followed in 1860 by the highly political *Poems before Congress*. *Last Poems*, containing some of Elizabeth Barrett Browning's best-known lyrics, including "De Profundis," was published posthumously in 1862, and since that time many volumes of her correspondence with Robert Browning, Benjamin Robert Haydon, Mary Russell Mitford, and others have appeared.

Personal

My true initials are *E.B.M.B.*—my long name, as opposed to my short one, being: . . . Elizabeth Barrett Moulton Barrett!—there's a full length to take away one's breath!—Christian name . . . Elizabeth Barrett:—surname, Moulton Barrett. So long it is, that to make it portable, I fell into the habit of doubling it up & packing it closely, . . . & of forgetting that I was a *Moulton*, altogether. One might as well write the alphabet as all four initials. Yet our family-name is *Moulton Barrett*, & my brothers reproach me sometimes for sacrificing the governorship of an old town in Norfolk with a little honorable verdigris from the Heralds' Office.—ELIZABETH BARRETT BROWNING, Letter to Robert Browning (Dec. 20, 1845)

Dined at home, and at eight dressed to go to Kenyon. With him I found an interesting person I had never seen before, Mrs. Browning, late Miss Barrett—not the invalid I expected; she has a handsome oval face, a fine eye, and altogether a pleasing person. She had no opportunity of display, and apparently no desire.—HENRY CRABB ROBINSON, *Diary*, Oct. 6, 1852

Mrs. Browning seems to be a vegetarian; at least, she ate nothing but an egg. We talked a good deal during breakfast; for she is of that quickly appreciative and responsive order of women, with whom I can talk more freely than with any men; and she has, besides, her own originality wherewith to help on conversation; though, I should say, not of a loquacious tendency. She introduced the subject of spiritualism, which, she says, interests her very much; indeed, she seems to be a believer. Her husband, she told me, utterly rejects the subject, and will not believe even in the outer manifestations, of which there is such overwhelming evidence. We also talked of Miss Bacon; and I developed something of that lady's theory respecting Shakspeare, greatly to the horror of Mrs. Browning and that of her next neighbor—some nobleman, whose name I did not know. On the whole, I like her the better for loving the man Shakspeare with a personal love. We talked, too, of Margaret Fuller, who spent her last night in Italy with the Brownings; and of William Story, with whom they have been intimate, and who, Mrs. Browning says, is much stirred up about Spiritualism. Really, I cannot help wondering that so fine a spirit as hers should not reject the matter, till, at least, it is forced upon her. But I like her very much—a great deal better than her poetry, which I could hardly suppose to have been written by such a quiet little person as she.—NATHANIEL HAWTHORNE, *The English Note-Books*, July 13, 1856

Mrs. Browning met us at the door of the drawing-room and greeted us most kindly; a pale little woman, scarcely embodied at all; at any rate, only substantial enough to put forth her slender fingers to be grasped, and to speak with a shrill, yet sweet, tenuity of voice. Really, I do not see how Mr. Browning can suppose that he has an earthly wife, any more than an earthly child; both are of the elfin-breed, and will flit away from him, some day, when he least thinks of it. She is a good and kind fairy, however, and sweetly disposed towards the human race, although only remotely akin to it. It is wonderful to see how small she is; how diminutive, and peaked, as it were, her face, without being ugly; how pale her cheek; how bright and dark her eyes. There is not such another figure in this world; and her black ringlets cluster down into her neck and make her face look the whiter by their sable profusion. I could not form any judgement about her age; it may range any where within the limits of human life, or elfin-life. When I met her in London, at Mr. Milnes's breakfast-table, she did not impress me so strangely; for the morning light is more prosaic than the dim illumination of their great, tapestried drawing-room; and besides, sitting next to her, she did not then have occasion to raise her voice in speaking, and I was not sensible what a slender pipe she has. It is as if a grasshopper should speak. It is marvellous to me how so extraordinary, so acute, so sensitive a creature, can impress us, as she does, with the certainty of her benevolence. It seems to me there were a million chances to one that she would have been a miracle of acidity and bitterness.—NATHANIEL HAWTHORNE, *The French and Italian Note-Books*, June 9, 1858

The main comfort is that she suffered very little pain, none beside that ordinarily attending the simple attacks of cold and cough she was subject to, had no presentiment of the result whatever, and was consequently spared the misery of knowing she was about to leave us: she was smilingly assuring me she was "better," "quite comfortable—if I would but come to bed—" to within a few minutes of the last. ⟨. . .⟩ Thro' the night she slept heavily, and brokenly—that was the bad sign. But then she would sit up, take her medicine, say unrepeatable things to me and sleep again. At four o'clock there were symptoms that alarmed me,—I called the maid and sent for the Doctor.—She smiled as I proposed to bathe her feet "Well, you *are* making an exaggerated case of it!" Then came what my heart will keep till I see her and longer—the most perfect expression of her love to me within my whole knowledge of her—always smilingly, happily, and with a face like a girl's—and in a few minutes she died in my arms, her head on my cheek. These incidents so sustain me that I tell them to her beloved ones as their right: there was no lingering, nor acute pain, nor consciousness of separation, but God took her to himself as you would lift a sleeping child from a dark, uneasy bed into your arms and the light. Thank God. Annunziata thought by her earnest ways with me, happy and smiling as they were, that she must have been aware of our parting's approach—but she was quite conscious, had words at command, and yet did not even speak of Peni who was in the next room. Her last word was—when I asked "How do you feel?"— "*Beautiful.*"—ROBERT BROWNING, Letter to Euphrasia Fanny Haworth (July 20, 1861)

> The white-rose garland at her feet,
>   The crown of laurel at her head,
> Her noble life on earth complete,
>   Lay her in the last low bed
> For the slumber calm and deep:
> "He giveth His belovèd sleep."
>
> Soldiers find their fittest grave
>   In the field whereon they died;
> So her spirit pure and brave
>   Leaves the clay it glorified
> To the land for which she fought
> With such grand impassioned thought.

> Keats and Shelley sleep at Rome,
>   She in well-loved Tuscan earth;
> Finding all their death's long home
>   Far from their old home of birth.
> Italy, you hold in trust
> Very sacred English dust.
>
> Therefore this one prayer I breathe,—
>   That you yet may worthy prove
> Of the heirlooms they bequeath
>   Who have loved you with such love:
> Fairest land while land of slaves
> Yields their free souls no fit graves.
> —JAMES THOMSON, "E. B. B.," 1861

General

> A young lady then, whom to miss were a *caret*
> In any verse-history, named, I think, Barrett,
> (I took her at first for a sister of Tennyson)
> Knelt, and received the god's kindliest benison.
> —'Truly,' said he, 'dost thou share the blest power
> Poetic, the fragrance as well as the flower;
> The gift of conveying impressions unseen,
> And making the vaguest thoughts know what they mean.'
>   —LEIGH HUNT, *Blue-Stocking Revels; or, The Feast of the Violets*, 1837, Canto 2, ll. 36–43

But if my dream be true that Æschylus might have turned to the subject before us, in poetic instinct; and if in such a case—and here is no dream—its terror and its pathos would have shattered into weakness the strong Greek tongue, and caused the conscious chorus to tremble round the thymele,—how much more may *I* turn from it, in the instinct of incompetence! In a manner I have done so. I have worn no shoes upon this holy ground: I have stood there, but have not walked. I have drawn no copy of the statue of this GREAT PAN,—but have caught its shadow,—shortened in the dawn of my imperfect knowledge, and distorted and broken by the unevenness of our earthly ground. I have written no work, but a suggestion. Nor has even so little been attempted, without as deep a consciousness of weakness as the severest critic and the humblest Christian could desire to impress upon me. I have felt in the midst of my own thoughts upon my own theme, like Homer's 'children in a battle.'

The agents in this poem of imperfect form—a dramatic lyric, rather than a lyrical drama—are those mystic beings who are designated in Scripture the Seraphim. The subject has thus assumed a character of exaggerated difficulty, the full sense of which I have tried to express in my Epilogue. But my desire was, to gather some vision of the supreme spectacle under a less usual aspect,—to glance at it, as dilated in seraphic eyes, and darkened and deepened by the near association with blessedness and Heaven. Are we not too apt to measure the depth of the Saviour's humiliation from the common estate of man, instead of from his own peculiar and primæval one? To avoid which error, I have endeavored to count some steps of the ladder at Bethel,—a very few steps, and as seen between the clouds.

And thus I have endeavored to mark in my two Seraphic personages, distinctly and predominantly, that shrinking from, and repugnance to, evil, which, in my weaker Seraph, is expressed by *fear*, and in my stronger one, by a more complex passion; in order to contrast with such, the voluntary debasement of Him who became lower than the angels, and touched in his own sinless being, sin and sorrow and death. In my attempted production of such a contrast, I have been true to at least my own idea of angelic excellence, as well as to that of His perfection. For one holiness differs from another holiness in glory. To recoil from evil, is according to the stature of an angel: to subdue it, is according to the infinitude of a God.

Of the poems which succeed *The Seraphim*, two ballads have been published in the *New Monthly Magazine*; one, the "Romance of the Ganges," was written for the illustration of *Finden's Tableaux*, edited by Miss Mitford; and a few miscellaneous verses have appeared in the *Athenæum*.

Lest in any of these poems a dreaminess be observed upon, while a lawlessness is imputed to their writer, she is anxious to assure whatever reader may think it worth while to listen to her defence, that none of them were written with a lawless purpose. For instance, *The Poet's Vow*, was intended to enforce a truth—that the creature cannot be *isolated* from the creature; and the *Romaunt of Margret*, a corresponding one, that the creature cannot be *sustained* by the creature. And if, indeed, the faintest character of poetry be granted to these compositions, it must be granted to them besides, that they contain a certain verity. For there is no greater fiction, than that poetry is fiction. Poetry is essentially truthfulness; and the very incoherences of poetic dreaming are but the struggle and the strife to reach the True in the Unknown. "If you please to call it but a dream," says Cowley, "I shall not take it ill; because the father of poets tells us, even dreams, too, are from God."

It was subsequent to my writing the poem called "The Virgin Mary to the Child Jesus," that I read in a selection of religious poetry, made by Mr. James Montgomery, a lyric of the sixteenth century upon the same subject, together with an observation of the editor, that no living poet would be daring enough to approach it. As it has here been approached and attempted by the "weak'st of many," I would prove by this explanation, that consciously to impugn an opinion of Mr. Montgomery's, and enter into rivalship with the bold simplicity of an ancient ballad, made no part of the daringness of which I confess myself guilty.

Nothing more is left to me to explain in relation to any particular poem of this collection. I need not defend them for being religious in their general character. The generation of such as held the doctrine of that critic who was *not* Longinus, and believed in the inadmissibility of religion into poetry, may have seen the end of vanity. That "contemplative piety, or the intercourse between God and the human soul, cannot be poetical," is true, *if* it be true that the human soul having such intercourse is parted from its humanity, or *if* it be true that poetry is not expressive of that humanity's most exalted state. The first supposition is contradicted by man's own experience, and the latter by the testimony of Him who knoweth what is in man. For otherwise, David's 'glory' would have awakened with no 'harp and lute;' and Isaiah's poetry of diction would have fallen in ashes from his lips, beneath the fire which cleansed them.—ELIZABETH BARRETT BROWNING, "Preface" to *Poems*, 1838

⟨Miss Barrett⟩ is not known personally, to anybody, we had almost said; but her poetry is known to a highly intellectual class, and she "lives" in constant correspondence with many of the most eminent persons of the time. When, however, we consider the many strange and ingenious conjectures that are made in after years, concerning authors who appeared but little among their contemporaries, or of whose biography little is actually known, we should not be in the least surprised, could we lift up our ear out of our grave a century hence, to hear some learned Thebans expressing shrewd doubts as to whether such an individual as Miss E. B. Barrett had ever really existed. Letters and notes, and exquisite English lyrics, and perhaps

a few elegant Latin verses, and spirited translations from Æschylus, might all be discovered under that name; but this would not prove that such a lady had ever dwelt among us. Certain admirable and erudite prose articles on the "Greek Christian Poets," might likewise be ascertained by the exhumation of sundry private letters and documents, touching periodical literature, to have been from the hand of that same "Valerian;" but neither the poetry, nor the prose, nor the delightfully gossipping notes to fair friends, nor the frank correspondence with scholars, such as Lady Jane Grey might have written to Roger Ascham—no, not even if the great-grandson of some learned Jewish doctor could show a note in Hebrew (quite a likely thing really to be extant) with the same signature, darkly translated by four letters—nay, though he should display as a relic treasured in his family, the very pen, with its oblique Hebraic nib, that wrote it—not any one, nor all of those things could be sufficient to demonstrate the fact, that such a lady had really adorned the present century.

In such *chiaroscuro*, therefore, as circumstances permit, we will endeavour to offer sufficient grounds for our readers' belief, to the end that posterity may at least have the best authorities and precedents we can furnish. Confined entirely to her own apartment, and almost hermetically sealed, in consequence of some extremely delicate state of health, the poetess of whom we write is scarcely seen by any but her own family. But though thus separated from the world—and often, during many weeks at a time, in darkness almost equal to that of night, Miss Barrett has yet found means by extraordinary inherent energies to develope her inward nature; to give vent to the soul in a successful struggle with its destiny while on earth; and to attain and master more knowledge and accomplishments than are usually within the power of those of either sex who possess every adventitious opportunity, as well as health and industry. Six or seven years of this imprisonment she has now endured, not with vain repinings, though deeply conscious of the loss of external nature's beauty; but with resignation, with patience, with cheerfulness, and generous sympathies towards the world without;—with indefatigable "work" by thought, by book, by the pen, and with devout faith, and adoration, and a high and hopeful waiting for the time when this mortal frame "putteth on immortality."

The period when a strong prejudice existed against learned ladies and "blues" has gone by, some time since; yet in case any elderly objections may still exist on this score, or that some even of the most liberal-minded readers may entertain a degree of doubt as to whether a certain austere exclusiveness and ungenial pedantry might infuse a slight tinge into the character of ladies possessing Miss Barrett's attainments, a few words may be added to prevent erroneous impressions on this score. Probably no living individual has a more extensive and diffuse acquaintance with literature—that of the present day inclusive—than Miss Barrett. Although she has read Plato, in the original, from beginning to end, and the Hebrew Bible from Genesis to Malachi (nor suffered her course to be stopped by the Chaldean), yet there is probably not a single good romance of the most romantic kind in whose marvellous and impossible scenes she has not delighted, over the fortunes of whose immaculate or incredible heroes and heroines she has not wept; nor a clever novel or fanciful sketch of our own day, over the brightest pages of which she has not smiled inwardly, or laughed outright, just as their authors themselves would have desired. All of this, our readers may be assured that we believe to be as strictly authentic as the very existence of the lady in question, although, as we have already confessed, we have no absolute knowledge of this fact. But lest the reader should exclaim, "Then, *after all*, there really may be no such person!" we should bear witness to having been shown a letter of Miss Mitford's to a friend, from which it was plainly to be inferred that she had actually seen and conversed with her. The date has unfortunately escaped us.—R. H. HORNE, "Miss E. B. Barrett and Mrs. Norton," *A New Spirit of the Age*, 1844, pp. 266–68

A poem should tell its own story, without need of preface; but if ever there were excuse for a formal explanation of the motive, plan, and intention of an author, it is in the instance of Miss Barrett's introductory remarks to her *Drama of Exile*. From the internal evidence in her books—at all times of more value than outward report—Miss Barrett is herself an exile;— one secluded from society by long-continued ill health. This, while an excuse for some garrulity of pen, also accounts for faults which, under different circumstances, might have substantiated against her a charge of pedantry; her style, not unfrequently, wanting the ease of colloquial expression. Books her only companions, she has been led to adopt their language, and hence many of the terms she has employed, more erudite than familiar, may seem to some critics the result of affectation, while they have weakened instead of assisting the development of real power.—S. F. ADAMS, "Poems by Elizabeth Barrett," *Westminster Review*, Dec. 1844, pp. 381–82

She is a woman of vigorous thought, but not very poetical thought, and throwing herself into verse involuntarily becomes honied and ornate, so that her verse cloys.—GEORGE WILLIAM CURTIS, Letter to John S. Dwight (Jan. 12, 1845), *Early Letters of George William Curtis*, ed. George Willis Cooke, 1898, p. 200

But probably the greatest female poet that England has ever produced, and one of the most unreadable, is Elizabeth B. Barrett. In the works of no woman have we ever observed so much grandeur of imagination, disguised, as it is in an elaborately infelicitous style. She has a large heart and a large brain; but many of her thoughts are hooded eagles. That a woman of such varied acquirements, of so much delicacy of sentiment and depth of feeling, of so much holiness and elevation of thought, possessing, too, an imagination of such shaping power and piercing vision, should not consent always to write English, should often consent to manufacture a barbarous jargon compounded of all languages, is a public calamity. "The Cry of the Human," to her, is, "Be more intelligible." The scholar who was in the custom of "unbending himself over the lighter mathematics" might find an agreeable recreation in Miss Barrett's abstruse windings of thought, and terrible phalanxes of Greek and German expressions. A number of her poems are absolutely good for nothing, from their harshness and obscurity of language. Her mind has taken its tone and character from the study of Æschylus, Milton, and the Hebrew poets; and she is more familiar with them than with the world. Vast and vague imaginations, excited by such high communion, float duskily before her mind, and she mutters mysteriously of their majestic presence; but she does not always run them into intelligible form. We could understand this, if she displayed any lack, on other occasions, of high imagination; but her frequent inexpressiveness is a voluntary offering on the altar of obscurity. "We understand a fury in the words, but not the words." In one of her sonnets, "The Soul's Expression," we are made acquainted with her condition of mind, when she wishes to utter her deep imaginings. Nothing could better represent a heart possessed

by the mightiest poetic feeling yet awed before its own mystical emotions. It is the soul "falling away from the imagination."

THE SOUL'S EXPRESSION

With stammering lips, and insufficient sound,
I strive and struggle to deliver right
That music of my nature, day and night
Both dream, and thought, and feeling interwound,
And inly answering all the senses round
With octaves of a mystic depth and height,
Which step out grandly to the infinite
From the dark edges of the sensual ground!
This song of soul I struggle to outbear
Through portals of the sense, sublime and whole
And utter all myself into the air—
But if I did it,—as the thunder-roll
Breaks its own cloud—my flesh would perish there,
Before that dread apocalypse of soul.

Miss Barrett's genius, though subjective in its general character, is of considerable range. She is especially powerful in dealing with the affections. Her religious poetry is characterized by a most intense and solemn reverence for divine things, and often swells into magnificent bursts of rapture and adoration. Her feeling for humanity is deep and tender, and she has a warm sympathy with its wants and immunities. Her sonnets, though of various degrees of merit, and some of them crabbed in their versification, have generally a rough grandeur which is very imposing. *The Drama of Exile*, though teeming with faults, has noble traits of intellect and passion, which no faults can conceal. Many of her minor pieces show a most delicate perception of beauty and sentiment, expressed with much simplicity and melody of style.—EDWIN P. WHIPPLE, "English Poets of the Nineteenth Century" (1845), *Essays and Reviews*, 1850, Vol. 1, pp. 361–63

In the *Drama of Exile* and the *Vision of Poets*, where she aims at a Miltonic flight or Dantesque grasp—not in any spirit of rivalry or imitation, but because she is really possessed of a similar mental scope—her success is far below what we find in the poems of feeling and experience; for she has the vision of a great poet, but little in proportion of his plastic power. She is at home in the Universe; she sees its laws; she sympathises with its motions. She has the imagination all compact—the healthy archetypal plant from which all forms may be divined, and, so far as now existent, understood. Like Milton, she sees the angelic hosts in real presence; like Dante, she hears the spheral concords and shares the planetary motions. But she cannot, like Milton, marshal the angels so near the earth as to impart the presence other than by sympathy. He who is near her level of mind may, through the magnetic sympathy, see the angels with her. Others will feel only the grandeur and sweetness she expresses in these forms. Still less can she, like Dante, give, by a touch, the key which enables ourselves to play on the same instrument. She is singularly deficient in the power of compression. There are always far more words and verses than are needed to convey the meaning, and it is a great proof of her strength, that the thought still seems strong, when arrayed in a form so Briarean clumsy and many-handed. ⟨. . .⟩

We have seen women use with skill and grace, the practical goose-quill, the sentimental crow-quill, and even the lyrical, the consecrated feathers of the swan. But we have never seen one to whom the white eagle would have descended; and, for a while, were inclined to think that the hour had now, for the first time, arrived. But, upon full deliberation, we will award to Miss Barrett one from the wing of the sea-gull. That is also a white bird, rapid, soaring, majestic, and which can alight with ease, and poise itself upon the stormiest wave. —MARGARET FULLER, "Miss Barrett's Poems," *Papers on Literature and Art*, 1846

"My poems," says Mrs. Browning, "while full of faults, as I go forward to my critics and confess, have my soul and life in them." We gather from other hints in the preface and especially from her poetry itself, that the life of which it is "the completest expression" attainable, has been one of unusual physical suffering, frequent loneliness and great study. As a natural result there is a remarkable predominance of thought and learning, even in the most inartificial overflow of her muse. Continually we are met by allusions which indicate familiarity with classic lore. Her reveries are imbued with the spirit of antique models. The scholar is everywhere co-evident with the poet. In this respect Mrs. Browning differs from Mrs. Hemans and Mrs. Norton, in whose effusions enthusiasm gives the tone and color. In each we perceive a sense of beauty and the pathos born of grief, but in the former these have a statuesque, and in the two latter a glowing development. The cheerfulness of Mrs. Browning appears the fruit of philosophy and faith. She labors to reconcile herself to life through wisdom and her religious creed, and justifies tenderness by reason. This is a rather masculine process. The intellect is the main agent in realizing such an end. Yet discipline and isolation explain it readily; and the poetess doubtless speaks from consciousness when she declares the object of her art "to vindicate the necessary relation of genius to suffering and self-sacrifice." The defect of poetry thus conceived is the absence of spontaneous, artless and exuberant feeling. There is a certain hardness and formality, a want of *abandon* of manner, a lack of gushing melody, such as takes the sympathies captive at once. We are conscious, indeed—painfully conscious—that strong feeling is here at work, but it is restrained, high-strung and profound. The human seems to find no natural repose, and strives, with a tragic vigor that excites admiration, to anticipate its spiritual destiny even while arrayed in mortal habiliments. Without subscribing to her theology we respect her piety. "Angelic patience" is the lesson she teaches with skill and eloquence. She would have the soul ever "*nobler than its mood.*" In her isolation and pain she communed with bards and sages, and found in their noble features, encouragement such as petty joys failed to give. She learned to delight in the ideals of humanity, and gaze with awe and love on their

> Sublime significance of mouth,
> Dilated nostrils full of youth,
> *And forehead royal with the truth.*

In her view,

> Life treads on life and heart on heart—
> We press too close in church and mart,
> To keep a dream or grave apart.

And from all this she turns to herself, and cherishes her individuality with a kind of holy pride. She seeks in the ardent cultivation of her intellectual resources a solace for the wounds and privations of life. She reflects intensely—traces the footsteps of heroes—endeavors to make the wisdom of the Past and the truths of God her own—and finds a high consolation in embodying the fruits of this experience in verse:

> In my large joy of sight and touch,
> Beyond what others count as such,
> I am content to suffer much.

It would argue a strange insensibility not to recognize a redeeming beauty in such an example. Mrs. Browning is an

honor to her sex, and no member thereof can fail to derive advantage from the spirit of her muse. It speaks words of "heroic cheer," and suggests thoughtful courage, sublime resignation, and exalted hope. At the same time, we cannot but feel her incompleteness. We incline to, and have faith in less systematic phases of woman's character. There is a native tenderness and grace, a child-like play of emotion, a simple utterance, that brings more genial refreshment. We do not deprecate Mrs. Browning's lofty spirit and brave scholarship. They are alike honorable and efficient; but sometimes they over-lay nature and formalize emotion, making the pathway to the heart rather too long and coldly elegant for quick and entire sympathy. Yet this very blending of sense and sensibility, learning and love, reason and emotion, will do much, and has already done much, (as we can perceive by recent criticisms,) to vindicate true sentiment and a genuine devotion to the beautiful. These glorious instincts are sternly rebuked every day under the name of enthusiasm, imagination and romance, as vain and absurd, by those who have intelligent but wholly practical minds. The sound and vigorous thought visible in Mrs. Browning's poetry, and the self-dependence she inculcates, will command the respect and win the attention of a class who sneer at Tennyson as fantastic, and Keats as lack-a-daisical. They may thus come to realize how the most kindling fancies and earnest love, ay, the very gentleness and idealism which they deem so false and weak, may co-exist with firm will, rare judgment, conscientiousness and truth, lending them both fire and grace, and educing from actual and inevitable ill, thoughts of comfort.—HENRY T. TUCKERMAN, "The Poetry of Elizabeth Barrett Browning" (1846), *Poems*, 1850, Vol. 1, pp. ix–xii

Even Miss Barrett, whom we take to be the most imaginative poetess that has appeared in England, perhaps in Europe, and who will attain to great eminence if the fineness of her vein can outgrow a certain morbidity, reminds our readers of the peculiarities of contemporary genius. She is like an ultra-sensitive sister of Alfred Tennyson.—LEIGH HUNT, "Specimens of British Poetesses," *Men, Women, and Books*, 1847, pp. 257–58

The poems of this lady are marked with strength of beauty and beauty of strength. She is deeply read, being familiar with the original of the great ancients (the Greek dramatists having been her particular study), and with the more attractive of the Christian fathers. Her translation of the untranslatable *Prometheus Bound* of Æschylus received high praise as a worthy attempt; and her various writings show that she has drunk true inspiration from the fountain to which she has so often resorted with the graceful vase of her natural genius. Miss Barrett is singularly bold and adventurous. Her wing carries her, without faltering at their obscurity, into the cloud and the mist, where not seldom we fail to follow her, but are tempted, while we admire the honesty of her enthusiasm, to believe that she utters what she herself has but dimly perceived. Much of this, however, arises from her disdain of carefulness. Her lines are often rude, her rhymes forced, from impatience rather than affectation; and for the same reason, she falls into the kindred fault of verboseness, which is always obscure. She forgets the advice which Aspasia gave a young poet, "to sow with the hand, and not with the bag." Her Greek studies should have taught her more sculptor-like finish and dignity; but the glowing, generous impulses of her woman's heart are too much for the discipline of the classics. Hence it is that we like her less as a scholar than as a woman; for then she compels our sympathy with her high religious faith, her love of children, her delight in the graceful and beautiful, her revelations of feminine feeling, her sorrow over the suffering, and her indignation against the oppressor. It is easy to see, from the melody of rhythm in "Cowper's Grave," and a few shorter pieces, that her faults spring not from inability to avoid them, if she would. Her ear, like that of Tennyson (whom she resembles more than any other poet), thirsts for a *refrain*; and like him, she indulges it to the weariness of her reader. Her sonnets, though complete in measure, are more like fragments, or unfinished outlines; but not a few of them are full of vigour. Her verses must be recited; none of them could be sung. There is scarcely anything in the language more exquisitely natural than the ballad of *The Swan's Nest among the Reeds*, which she playfully calls a "romance;" and we may regret that she has not written more in the same delicious strain. As it is, we would scarcely take the bays from her muse-like head, but love her better when she herself is content to replace it by the "simple myrtle," or the wild-flower garland from the meadows and hedge-rows of her native England. The thyme of Hymettus is not so sweet in her fair hands, as the daisy, the cowslip, the violet, or the porch-encircling brier, no unfit emblem of love shedding sweetness amidst the thorns of daily life.—GEORGE WASHINGTON BETHUNE, "Elizabeth B. Barrett," *The British Female Poets*, 1848, pp. 452–53

I think it may be said that she is chief amongst the learned poetesses of our land: at least, I know of no British female writer who exhibits so intimate an acquaintance with the *spirit* of both antique and modern philosophy, or so refined a perception of intellectual purity and beauty. Her poetry is the poetry of pure reason.

It may be a question, however, whether an intense devotion to scholastic learning is not rather injurious than beneficial to the female mind. It cannot be pretended, of course, that school-craft, and the philosophy of art, science, and reason, ought to be altogether overlooked and unstudied by woman:—the proposition would be monstrous. But it may perhaps be fairly argued that, as woman's faculties are rather perceptive than investigative, and as her knowledge of truth is rather intuitive than acquired, there is a possibility of her understanding being injured by over-cultivation. Just as some flowers lose their native beauty when forced by horticultural art, may the female mind be spoiled by excess of intellectual culture.

⟨. . .⟩ I scruple not to say that she is certainly most effective in her least laboured compositions. Her genius, it is impossible not to see, is of the highest order—strong, deep-seeing, enthusiastic and loving; but although all her compositions prove this, I find the greatest evidences of her powers in her most unpretending works. Where there is effort, there is often obscurity; but where she gives her soul free unconscious vent, she writes with a truth and force of touch which none of the poetic sisterhood surpass.

In justification of the opinion which I have here expressed, I would particularly instance the poem called *A Drama of Exile*. The intellect displayed in this noble production is stupendous. The conception is massive: the treatment of the prominent idea truly consistent and powerful: the pathos such as only a woman could have written: and the moral tone of the work most lofty and pure. But, in spite of all these excellencies, the poem often fatigues us. It keeps the mind too much on the stretch; requires an unceasing exercise of our deepest thoughts; and while we never fail at last to see the extreme beauty of the writer's ideas, we grow tired in studying them.—FREDERIC ROWTON, "Elizabeth Barrett Browning," *The Female Poets of Great Britain*, 1848, pp. 500–502

My daughter and I lately met at the house of my excellent old friend, Mr. Kenyon, that poetical pair, Mr. and Mrs. Browning. You probably know her as Elizabeth Barrett, author of the *Seraphim*, *Drama of Exile*, and many ballads and minor poems, among which "Cowper's Grave" is of special excellence. She has lately published *Casa Guidi Windows*, a meditative political poem of considerable merit; Mazzini admires it, and it has been translated into Italian. Mrs. Browning is in weak health, and can not remain in this foggy clime; they are to reside in Paris. She is little, hard-featured, with long, dark ringlets, a pale face, and plaintive voice—something very impressive in her dark eyes and her brow. Her general aspect puts me in mind of Mignon—what Mignon might be in maturity and maternity. She has more poetic genius than any other woman living—perhaps more than any woman ever showed before, except Sappho. Still there is an imperfectness in what she produces; in many passages the expressions are very faulty, the images forced and untrue, the sentiments exaggerated, and the situations unnatural and unpleasant. Another pervading fault of Mrs. Browning's poetry is rugged, harsh versification, with imperfect rhymes, and altogether that want of art in the department of metre which prevents the language from being an unobstructive medium for the thought.—SARA COLERIDGE, Letter to Ellis Yarnall (Aug. 28, 1851), *Memoir and Letters of Sara Coleridge*, ed. Edith Coleridge, 1873, Vol. 2, pp. 446–47

In the poems of Mrs. Browning are qualities which admit of their being compared with those of the greatest men; touches which *only* the mightiest give. With the few sovereigns of literature, the Homers, Shakspeares, Miltons, she will not rank. But in full recollection of Scott's magical versatility and bright, cheerful glow, of Byron's fervid passion and magnificent description, of Wordsworth's majesty, of Shelley's million-colored fancy, of Coleridge's occasional flights right into the sun-glare, of Bailey's marvellous exuberance, and of Tennyson's golden calm, I yet hold her worthy of being mentioned with any poet of this century. She has the breadth and versatility of a man, no sameliness, no one idea, no type character: our single Shaksperian woman.—PETER BAYNE, "Mrs. Barrett Browning," *Essays in Biography and Criticism*, 1857, p. 209

Mrs. Browning's Death is rather a relief to me, I must say: no more Aurora Leighs, thank God! A Woman of real Genius, I know: but what is the upshot of it all? She and her Sex had better mind the Kitchen and their Children; and perhaps the Poor: except in such things as little Novels, they only devote themselves to what Men do much better, leaving that which Men do worse or not at all.—EDWARD FITZGERALD, Letter to W. H. Thompson (July 15, 1861)

I have written only the two first chapters of my novel besides the Proem, and I have an oppressive sense of the far-stretching task before me, health being feeble just now. I have lately read again with great delight Mrs. Browning's *Casa Guidi Windows*. It contains, amongst other admirable things, a very noble expression of what I believe to be the true relation of the religious mind to the past.—GEORGE ELIOT, *Journal* (Feb. 17, 1862), cited in John W. Cross, *George Eliot's Life as Related in Her Letters and Journals*, 1884, Vol. 2, p. 263

The long study of her sick-bed (and her constant chafing against the common estimate of the talents and genius of her sex) overcharged her works with allusions and thoughts relating to books, and made her style rugged with pedantry. She was often intoxicated, too, with her own vehemence. *Aurora Leigh* sets out determined to walk the world with the great Shakespearian stride, whence desperate entanglement of feminine draperies and blinding swirls of dust. The sonnets entitled *From the Portuguese* reveal better her inmost simple nature. —JAMES THOMSON, "The Poems of William Blake" (1864), *Biographical and Critical Sketches*, 1896, p. 267

Her poems were to me, in my sick-room, marvellously beautiful: and, now that from the atmosphere of the sick-room, my life has been transferred to the free open air of real, practical existence, I still think her poetry wonderfully beautiful in its way, while wishing that she was more familiar with the external realities which are needed to balance her ideal conceptions.—HARRIET MARTINEAU, *Autobiography*, ed. Maria Weston Chapman, 1877, Vol. 1, p. 315

No more impassioned soul ever found expression in rhythmical speech than Elizabeth Barrett Browning, and there is nothing in her poetry which is finer than that famous love-record, the so-called *Sonnets from the Portuguese*. Impetuous as was her genius, hasty and frequently careless as she is in production, she never found the archetypal sonnet too circumscribed for her. The pathetic beauty, the fascinating personality, the pure poetry displayed in these sonnets, have touched many and many a heart since the tired singer was laid to rest under the cypresses not far from that beloved river whose flow she had so often followed in thought down to the far-off Pisan sea. Only those who have thoroughly studied contemporary poetry, and not only the poetry which is familiar to many but that also which is quite unknown, and by minor writers of no reputation or likelihood of reputation, can realise the potency of Mrs. Browning's influence, especially among women.—WILLIAM SHARP, "Introduction" to *Sonnets of This Century*, 1886, pp. lxx–lxxi

The theme of the *Drama of Exile* is so daring, and the execution, despite innumerable faults, so excellent, that either condemnation or praise is hard to award. The great defect in what the poetess intended should be her masterpiece is that, notwithstanding the introduction of Adam and Eve, and the self-sacrificing love of the latter for her partner in sorrow, it is almost entirely devoid of human interest. Admiration is frequently compelled by bursts of true lyrical beauty; but the heart never throbs with hope nor thrills with terror for the poetic phantasmata whose weeping and wailing fill so many pages of the drama. There are, it is true, some magnificent passages of poetry in the work, notably Lucifer's description of the effect of the curse upon animal creation. Reminding Adam of "when the curse took us in Eden," he says:—

> On a mountain-peak,
> Half-sheathed in primal woods, and glittering
> In spasms of awful sunshine, at that hour
> A lion couched—part raised upon his paws,
> With his calm, massive face turned full on thine,
> And his mane listening. When the ended curse
> Left silence in the world, right suddenly
> He sprang up rampant, and stood straight and stiff
> As if the new reality of death
> Were dashed against his eyes, and roared so fierce
> (Such thick carnivorous passion in his throat
> Tearing a passage through the wrath and fear),
> And roared so wild, and smote from all the hills
> Such fast, keen echoes crumbling down the vales
> Precipitately, that the forest beasts,
> One after one, did mutter a response

> In savage and in sorrowful complaint,
> Which trailed along the gorges. Then, at once,
> He fell back, and rolled crashing from the height.

This is a magnificent picture most grandiloquently portrayed, but it is the finest passage in the *Drama*. Its author appears to have felt that there was something wanting in her work, and therefore strives to explain away what might be objected to, and to deprecate criticism, by a lengthy Preface.

⟨. . .⟩ The *Drama of Exile*, evidently the author's favorite, her most ambitious performance, and the work on which she had relied for fame, is a failure; a grand failure it is true, but from the very nature of its theme bound to be more or less a failure, notwithstanding the fact that it contains passages of extraordinary grandeur and is replete with others of lyrical sweetness.

Lady Geraldine's Courtship is, deservedly, one of the most popular poems of the age. The best-known legend connected with its composition was doubtless originally promulgated by Miss Mitford to account for its wonderful rush of glowing language, and to enhance the mystery of its authoress, of whose personality so few people knew anything. The poem, making forty-two octavo pages, was averred to have been written within the space of twelve hours,—written off at electric speed in order to make up the number of sheets required by the American publisher of the poems. How much of truth may be contained in this myth is hard to say; but that Miss Barrett composed at times with great rapidity is a fact. Much of the rugged rhythm and apparent carelessness of construction which characterize so many of her poems is doubtless due to the speed at which they were evolved, and to the same cause may be ascribed their occasional obscurity and other defects; but that their defective or affected rhyming was not due to this cause we have her own words to prove.

Of *Lady Geraldine's Courtship* Edgar Poe, no careless critic, said that, with the exception of Tennyson's "Locksley Hall," he had never perused a poem "containing so much of the fiercest passion with so much of the most ethereal fancy." *Lady Geraldine's Courtship* he somewhat too dogmatically pronounced to be "the only poem of its author which is not deficient, considered as an artistic whole. Her constructive ability," he added, "is either not very remarkable, or has never been properly brought into play. In truth, her genius is too impetuous for the minuter technicalities of that elaborate *art* so needful in the building up of pyramids for immortality." ⟨. . .⟩

The poverty of the plot, the improbability of the whole story, the author's frequent ignorance of worldly matters, the faulty and too long deferred rhymes, lapses in the rhythm, and occasional commonplaces, all vanish in the passionate glow of thought, in the rush of burning words, and the magnificent flood of imaginative poetry, bearing everything along with it in a resistless torrent of glory and grandeur that fairly overpowers and conquers the most critical reader's judgment.—JOHN H. INGRAM, *Elizabeth Barrett Browning*, 1888, pp. 115–27

Mrs. Browning, with all her noble idealism and her profound sense of responsibility, was most depressingly indifferent about form, and was quite a law to herself in the matter of rhymes. —AGNES REPPLIER, "English Love-Songs," *Points of View*, 1891, p. 38

In the spirituality of life that characterised Elizabeth Barrett Browning genius assumes its highest form; and it is in this spiritualisation of human life that Mrs. Browning is seen apart from all other great modern poets. In her expression she has embodied a potency of influence which the world is only beginning to recognise and estimate aright. Among women poets she easily stands supreme, and there are passages in her work which surpass anything that has been given to the world since Shakespeare. Nor is this assertion a mere trick of phrasing that should shrink abashed before so lofty a presence. It is but a simple expression of truth. Spirituality of life is the condition of being more alive, of possessing swifter sympathy and finer insight, of holding a truer relation to progress. "I am come that ye might have life more abundant," said the Christ, and spirituality might fitly be defined as the condition of higher sensibility and responsiveness.

Kant tells us that the other world is not another place, but another view. Accepting this, it is evident that Elizabeth Barrett lived, even as a child, in the other world. The picture of the delicate little girl sitting on the floor of her large, oriel-windowed chamber leaning against the wall, her dark, clustering hair falling over her shoulders, and the prismatic light from the pictured window enveloping her in its glory as she held with one hand her doll, with the other a Greek book, haunts the imagination. What manner of spirit was thus embodied?

I lived with visions for my company.

From the time we catch the first glimpse of the child in her earliest home, Hope End, in Herefordshire, till she fades from mortal vision in the blue shadows of the Arno hills, we see her only as a spirit passing. Her form of greatness was that which touched only the enduring realities, never the superficial aspects of life. ⟨. . .⟩

The poetry of Mrs. Browning is not only that of the poet's inspiration, but it has the influence of exquisite and extended culture. Her genius was of that highest order—the spiritualisation of intellect. She is the first woman who has expressed the pathos of struggling and repressed life in poetry, as Millet has expressed it in painting. She felt, as did Hood, that the lover's song, and even that the intimations of nature, are less appealing than the grinding toil that submerges the uncomforted poor. To her was given the task to arouse England and the modern world, indeed, to a sense of the child suffering in factory life. Her poem "The Cry of the Children" appeared almost simultaneously with Lord Shaftesbury's great speech in Parliament on child labour. The poem and the eloquence together aroused England, nor has the echo lessened with the years.—LILIAN WHITING, "Elizabeth Barrett Browning," *Bookman* (New York), March 1896, pp. 35–38

Her best poetry is that which is most full of her personal emotions. The *Sonnets from the Portuguese*, the 'Cry of the Children,' 'Cowper's Grave,' the *Dead Pan*, *Aurora Leigh*, and the Italian poems, owe their value to the pure and earnest character, the strong love of truth and right, the enthusiasm on behalf of what is oppressed and the indignation against all kinds of oppression and wrong, which were prominent elements in a personality of exceptional worth and beauty.—FREDERIC G. KENYON, "Preface" to *The Letters of Elizabeth Barrett Browning*, 1898, Vol. 1, p. x

Mrs. Browning's intuitive spiritual perception discerned this future of which we are now on the threshold, and it was this that gave to her life the serenity and equipoise which perpetuates its influence and renders her a living power in the life of to-day.

Mrs. Browning's married life covered but fifteen out of her fifty-five years. All through her maidenhood she might, indeed, well have said, "the best is yet to be;" and although the curiously unreasonable attitude of her father regarding her marriage never relaxed, yet with this exception those fifteen years were to the wedded poets a dream of bliss which even death itself could not break. The genius of each was perfected by this union. His art gained in clearness; hers in strength.

The poetry of Elizabeth Barrett Browning is singularly calculated to communicate to the reader an exaltation of purpose and of spiritual energy. Like Emerson, she must be judged by something larger than the mere literary standard. One turns from her pages to the problems of life and destiny to feel anew that sublime significance thrilling through her words:—

> I can live,
> At least, my soul's life without alms from men;
> And if it be in heaven instead of earth,
> Let heaven look to it,—I am not afraid!

Not only as literary art, but as the expression of consecrated genius, the poems of Elizabeth Barrett Browning will stand immortal in their influence. For this is the secret of her life and power,—that she recognized the inter-blending of the two worlds of the Seen and the Unseen; that she held her art as a sacred gift intrusted to her for divine purposes; that she recognized the nobler self in each person whom she met and thus stimulated him to realize his truer ideal; that her mind was generously hospitable to all the intellectual movements of her time; and that, above all, it may truly be said of Elizabeth Barrett Browning that she lived in conscious relations with those in the Unseen and in perpetual communion with the Heavenly Vision!—LILIAN WHITING, *A Study of Elizabeth Barrett Browning*, 1899, pp. 182–84

"The daughter of Shakespeare" forever crowns the wearer as with a glory of filial tenderness; and we are aware of no incongruity, no disparity in its application. Is it that we feel the verity goes deeper than any mere attribution of intellectual gifts—any inheritance in quality of thought, or of Elizabethan-freighted diction conveying that thought? It is even more than this, we believe—a truth of comparison that finds its *raison d'être* in temperament itself. Elizabeth Barrett Browning is a "daughter of Shakespeare" in the sense that she is own sister, in the spirit, to all those exquisite creations we think of in the naming of "Shakespeare's heroines"; or rather say she is in herself identical with the dearest of those oft-doubted types of quintessential womanhood: Portia for the subtility and adroitness of her reasoning; Rosalind for nimblest wit on the lips of woman; Juliet for the all-adorning idolatry of love; Imogen for most constant tenderness; and an Isabella for worship! And it should not be forgotten that, above all other gifts and qualities, it is the fact of her intense womanhood which sets her apart from all other women-artists whatsoever (shall we, perhaps, except the author of *Jane Eyre*?). Even her dear faults as an artist are those of a woman, and not such as surely befall to the woman who fails to write out of the depths of her womanly consciousness and experience. What these faults are, the author of *Aurora Leigh* knows full well; and knows, also, that the woman-artist shall not escape them even by the knowing of them! It has, of late years, been urged that this poem, by reason of its length, transcends the good reader's patience. I do not agree with this lazy consensus.—EDITH M. THOMAS, "Elizabeth Barrett Browning," *Critic*, Dec. 1900, p. 516

Works

AURORA LEIGH

The most successful book of the season has been Mrs. Browning's *Aurora Leigh*. I could wish some things altered, I confess; but as it is, it is by far (a hundred times over) the finest poem ever written by a woman. We know little or nothing of Sappho—nothing to induce comparison—and all other wearers of petticoats must courtesy to the ground.—BRYAN WALLER PROCTER, Letter to James T. Fields (1856), cited in James T. Fields, "'Barry Cornwall' and Some of His Friends," *Harper's New Monthly Magazine*, Dec. 1875, p. 63

I am greatly delighted with Mrs. Browning's *Aurora Leigh*. It is full of strong things, and brilliant things, and beautiful things. And how glad I am to see modern literature tending so much toward the breaking down of social distinctions!—LYDIA MARIA CHILD, Letter to Mrs. S. B. Shaw (Dec. 8, 1856)

The piece of news freshest in my mind is *Aurora Leigh*,—an astounding work, surely. You said nothing of it. I know that St. Francis and Poverty do not wed in these days of St. James' Church, with rows of portrait figures on either side, and the corners neatly finished with angels. I know that if a blind man were to enter the room this evening and talk to me for some hours, I should, with the best intentions, be in danger of twigging his blindness before the right moment came, if such there were, for the chord in the orchestra and the proper theatrical start; yet with all my knowledge, I have felt something like a bug ever since reading *Aurora Leigh*. O the wonder of it!—and O the bore of writing about it.—DANTE GABRIEL ROSSETTI, Letter to William Allingham (Dec. 17, 1856)

We are reading *Aurora Leigh* for the third time with more enjoyment than ever. I know no book that gives me a deeper sense of communion with a large as well as beautiful mind. It is in process of appearing in a third edition, and no wonder. —GEORGE ELIOT, Letter to Sophia Hennell (June 5, 1857)

I am reading a poem full of thought and fascinating with fancy,—Mrs. Browning's *Aurora Leigh*. In many pages, and particularly 126 and 127, there is the wild imagination of Shakespeare. I have not yet read much further. I had no idea that any one in this age was capable of so much poetry. I am half drunk with it. Never did I think I should have a good hearty draught of poetry again: the distemper had got into the vineyard that produced it. Here are indeed, even here, some flies upon the surface, as there always will be upon what is sweet and strong. I know not yet what the story is. Few possess the power of construction.—WALTER SAVAGE LANDOR, Letter to John Forster (1857), cited in John Forster, *Walter Savage Landor: A Biography*, 1869, Bk. 2, Note

⟨. . .⟩ worst school of modern poetry,—the physically intense school, as I should be inclined to call it, of which Mrs. Browning's *Aurora Leigh* is the worst example, whose muse is a *fast* young woman with the lavish ornament and somewhat overpowering perfume of the *demimonde*, and which pushes expression to the last gasp of sensuous exhaustion.—JAMES RUSSELL LOWELL, "Swinburne's Tragedies" (1866), *Works*, Riverside ed., Vol. 2, p. 122

She was at once forbearing and dogmatic, willing to accept differences, resolute to admit no argument; without any more practical knowledge of social life than a nun might have, when, after long years, she emerged from her cloister and her shroud. How she used her experiences as a great poetess, is to be felt and is evidenced in her *Aurora Leigh*, after every allowance has been made for an extreme fearlessness in certain passages of the story and forms of expression, and that want of finish in execution with which almost all her efforts are chargeable.

The success of *Aurora Leigh* (with all its drawbacks) was immediate, wide, and, I conceive, is one likely to last. The

noble and impassioned passages which printed themselves on memory as I hurried through the tale, carried along by its deep interest, the brilliancy of allusion, the felicity of description, separate it from any effort of the kind which I could name. Those who care for comparison may come to something like a right appreciation of this poem, on comparing it with efforts in the same form by M. de Lamartine, or an English novel in verse which followed it, by the accomplished but imitative author of *Lucille*.—HENRY F. CHORLEY, *Autobiography, Memoir, and Letters*, ed. Henry G. Hewlett, 1873, Vol. 2, pp. 36–37

EDGAR ALLAN POE
From "Elizabeth Barrett Browning" (1845)
Essays and Reviews, ed. G. R. Thompson
1984, pp. 139–41

That Miss Barrett has done more, in poetry, than any woman, living or dead, will scarcely be questioned:—that she has surpassed all her poetical contemporaries of either sex (with a single exception) is our deliberate opinion—not idly entertained, we think, nor founded on any visionary basis. It may not be uninteresting, therefore, in closing this examination of her claims, to determine in what manner she holds poetical relation with these contemporaries, or with her immediate predecessors, and especially with the great exception to which we have alluded,—if at all.

If ever mortal "wreaked his thoughts upon expression" it was Shelley. If ever poet sang (as a bird sings)—impulsively—earnestly—with utter abandonment—to himself solely—and for the mere joy of his own song—that poet was the author of the *Sensitive Plant*. Of Art—beyond that which is the inalienable instinct of Genius—he either had little or disdained all. He *really* disdained that Rule which is the emanation from Law, because his own soul was law in itself. His rhapsodies are but the rough notes—the stenographic memoranda of poems—memoranda which, because they were all-sufficient for his own intelligence, he cared not to be at the trouble of transcribing in full for mankind. In his whole life he wrought not thoroughly out a single conception. For this reason it is that he is the most fatiguing of poets. Yet he wearies in having done too little, rather than too much; what seems in him the diffuseness of one idea, is the conglomerate concision of many;—and this concision it is which renders him obscure. With such a man, to imitate was out of the question; it would have answered no purpose—for he spoke to his own spirit alone, which would have comprehended no alien tongue;—he was, therefore, profoundly original. His quaintness arose from intuitive perception of that truth to which Lord Verulam alone has given distinct voice:—"There is no exquisite beauty which has not some strangeness in its proportion." But whether obscure, original, or quaint, he was at all times sincere. He had no *affectations*.

From the ruins of Shelley there sprang into existence, affronting the Heavens, a tottering and fantastic pagoda, in which the salient angles, tipped with mad jangling bells, were the idiosyncratic *faults* of the great original—faults which cannot be called such in view of his purposes, but which are monstrous when we regard his works as addressed to mankind. A "school" arose—if that absurd term must still be employed—a school—a system of rules—upon the basis of the Shelley who had none. Young men innumerable, dazzled with the glare and bewildered with the *bizarrerie* of the divine lightning that flickered through the clouds of the Prometheus, had no trouble whatever in heaping up imitative vapors, but, for the lightning, were content, perforce, with its *spectrum*, in which the *bizarrerie* appeared without the fire. Nor were great and mature minds unimpressed by the contemplation of a greater and more mature; and thus gradually were interwoven into this school of all Lawlessness—of obscurity, quaintness, exaggeration—the misplaced didacticism of Wordsworth, and the even more preposterously anomalous metaphysicianism of Coleridge. Matters were now fast verging to their worst, and at length, in Tennyson, poetic inconsistency attained its extreme. But it was precisely this extreme (for the greatest error and the greatest truth are scarcely two points in a circle)—it was this extreme which, following the law of all extremes, wrought in him—in Tennyson—a natural and inevitable revulsion, leading him first to contemn and secondly to investigate his early manner, and, finally, to winnow from its magnificent elements the truest and purest of all poetical styles. But not even yet is the process complete; and for this reason in part, but chiefly on account of the mere fortuitousness of that mental and moral combination which shall unite in one person (if *ever* it shall) the Shelleyan *abandon*, the Tennysonian poetic sense, the most profound instinct of Art, and the sternest Will properly to blend and vigorously to control all;—chiefly, we say, because such combination of antagonisms must be purely fortuitous, has the world never yet seen the noblest of the poems of which it is *possible* that it may be put in possession.

And yet Miss Barrett has narrowly missed the fulfilment of these conditions. Her poetic inspiration is the highest—we can conceive nothing more august. Her sense of Art is pure in itself, but has been contaminated by pedantic study of false models—a study which has the more easily led her astray, because she placed an undue value upon it as rare—as alien to her character of woman. The accident of having been long secluded by ill health from the world has effected, moreover, in her behalf, what an innate recklessness did for Shelley—has imparted to her, if not precisely that *abandon* to which I have referred, at least a something that stands well in its stead—a comparative independence of men and opinions with which she did not come personally in contact—a happy audacity of thought and expression never before known in one of her sex. It is, however, this same accident of ill health, perhaps, which has invalidated her original Will—diverted her from proper individuality of purpose—and seduced her into the sin of imitation. Thus, what she might have done we cannot altogether determine. What she has actually accomplished is before us. With Tennyson's works beside her, and a keen appreciation of them in her soul—appreciation too keen to be discriminative;—with an imagination even more vigorous than his, although somewhat less ethereally delicate; with inferior art and more feeble volition; she has written poems such as he *could not write*, but such as he, under *her* conditions of ill health and seclusion, *would have written* during the epoch of his pupildom in that school which arose out of Shelley, and from which, over a disgustful gulf of utter incongruity and absurdity, lit only by miasmatic flashes, into the broad open meadows of Natural Art and Divine Genius, he—Tennyson—is at once the bridge and the transition.

GEORGE GILFILLAN
From "Mrs. Elizabeth Barrett Browning" (1847)
A Second Gallery of Literary Portraits
1850, pp. 269–81

In selecting Mrs Hemans as our first specimen of Female Authors, we did so avowedly, because she seemed to us the most feminine writer of the day. We now select Mrs Browning for the opposite reason, that she is, or at least is said by many to be, the most masculine of our female writers. ⟨. . .⟩

To say that Mrs Browning has more of the man than any female writer of the period, may appear rather an equivocal compliment; and its truth even may be questioned. We may, however, be permitted to say, that she has more of the *heroine* than her compeers. Hers is a high, heroic nature, which adopts for the motto at once of its life and of its poetry, "Perfect through suffering." Shelley says:—

> Most wretched men
> Are cradled into poetry by wrong;
> They learn in suffering what they teach in song.

But wrong is not always the stern schoolmistress of song. There are sufferings springing from other sources—from intense sensibility—from bodily ailment—from the loss of cherished objects, which also find in poetry their natural vent. And we do think that such poetry, if not so powerful, is infinitely more pleasing and more instructive than that which is inspired by real or imaginary grievance. The turbid torrent is not the proper mirror for reflecting the face of nature; and none but the moody and the discontented will seek to see in it an aggravated and distorted edition of their own gloomy brows. The poetry of wrong is not the best and most permanent. It was not wrong alone that excited, though it unquestionably directed, the course of Dante's and Milton's vein. The poetry of Shakspere's wrong is condensed in his sonnets—the poetry of his forbearance and forgiveness, of his gratitude and his happiness, is in his dramas. The poetry of Pope's wrong (a scratch from a thorn hedge!) is in his *Dunciad*, not in his *Rape of the Lock*. The poetry of Wordsworth's wrong is in his *Prefaces*, not in his *Excursion*. The poetry of Byron's wrong is in those deep curses which sometimes disturb the harmony of his poems; and that of Shelley's in the maniacal scream which occasionally interrupts the pæans of his song. But all these had probably been as great, or greater poets, had no wrong befallen them, or had it taught them another lesson, than either peevishly to proclaim or furiously to resent it.

Mrs Browning has suffered, so far as we are aware, no wrong from the age. She might, indeed, for some time have spoken of neglect. But people of genius should now learn the truth, that *neglect* is not *wrong*; or if it be, it is a wrong in which they often set the example. Neglecting the tastes of the majority, the majority avenges itself by neglecting them. Standing and singing in a congregation of the deaf, they are senseless enough to complain that they are not heard. Or should they address the multitude, and should the multitude not listen, it never strikes them that the fault is their own; they ought to have compelled attention. Orpheus was listened to: the thunder is: even the gentlest spring shower commands its audience. If neglect means wilful winking at claims which are *felt*, it is indeed a wrong; but a wrong seldom if ever committed, and which complaint will not cure—if it means, merely, ignorance of claims which have never been presented or enforced, where and whose is the criminality?

To do Mrs Browning justice, she has not complained of

neglect nor injury at all. But she has acknowledged herself inspired by the genius of suffering. And this seems to have exerted divers influences upon her poetry. It has, in the first place, taught her to rear for herself a spot of transcendental retreat, a city of refuge in the clouds. Scared away from her own heart, she has soared upwards, and found a rest elsewhere. To those flights of idealism in which she indulges, to those distant and daring themes which she selects, she is urged less, we think, through native tendency of mind, than to fill the vacuity of a sick and craving spirit. This is not peculiar to her. It may be called, indeed, the "Retreat of the Ten Thousand;" though strong and daring must be those that can successfully accomplish it. Only the steps of sorrow—we had almost said only the steps of despair—can climb such dizzy heights. The healthy and the happy mind selects subjects of a healthy and a happy sort, and which lie within the sphere of every-day life and every-day thought. But for minds which have been wrung and riven, there is a similar attraction in gloomy themes, as that which leads them to the side of dark rivers, to the heart of deep forests, or into the centre of waste glens. Step forth, ye giant children of Sorrow and Genius, that we may tell your names, and compute your multitudes. First, there is the proud thundershod Æschylean family, all conceived in the "eclipse" of that most powerful of Grecian spirits. Then follows Lucretius—

> Who cast his plummet down the broad
> Deep universe, and said, No God;
> Finding no bottom, he denied
> Divinely the divine, and died,
> Chief poet upon Tiber side.
> —(Mrs Browning)

There stalk forward, next in the procession, the kings, priests, popes, prelates, and the yet guiltier and mightier shapes of Dante's Hell. Next, the Satan of Milton advances, champing the curb, and regarding even Prometheus as no mate for his proud and lonely misery. Then comes, cowering and shivering on, the timid Castaway of Cowper. He is followed by Byron's heroes, a haughty yet melancholy troop, with *conscious madness* animating their gestures and glaring in their eyes. The Anciente Marinere succeeds, now fearfully reverting his looks, and now fixing his glittering eye forward on a peopled and terrible vacancy. And, lastly, a frail shadowy and shifting shape, looking now Laon, now like Lionel, and now like Prometheus, proclaims that Alastor himself is here, the Benjamin in this family of tears.

"Whither shall I wander," seems Mrs Browning to have said to herself, "to-day to escape from my own sad thoughts, and to lose, to noble purpose, the sense of my own identity? I will go eastward to Eden, where perfection and happiness once dwelt. I will pass, secure in virtue, the far-flashing sword of the cherubim; I will knock at the door and enter. I will lie down in the forsaken garden; I will pillow my head where Milton pillowed his, on the grass cool with the shadow of the Tree of Life; and I will dream a vision of my own, of what this place once was, and of what it was to leave it for the wilderness." And she has passed the waving sword, and she has entered the awful garden, and she has dreamed a dream, and she has, awaking, told it as a *Drama of Exile*. It were vain to deny that the dream is one full of genius—that it is entirely original; and that it never once, except by antithesis, suggests a thought of Milton's more massive and palpable vision. Her Paradise is not a garden, it is a flush on a summer evening sky. Her Adam is not the fair large-fronted man, with all manlike qualities meeting unconsciously in his full clear nature—he is a German metaphysician.

Her Eve is *herself*, an amiable and gifted blue-stocking, not the mere meek motherly woman, with what Aird beautifully calls the "broad, ripe, serene, and gracious composure of love about her." Her spirits are neither cherubim nor seraphim—neither knowing nor burning ones—they are fairies, not, however, of the Puck or Ariel species, but of a new metaphysical breed; they do not ride on, but split hairs; they do not dance, but reason; or if they dance, it is on the point of a needle, in cycles and epicycles of mystic and mazy motion. There is much beauty and power in passages of the poem, and a sweet inarticulate melody, like the fabled cry of mandrakes, in the lyrics. Still we do not see the taste of turning the sweet open garden of Eden into a maze—we do not approve of the daring precedent of trying conclusions with Milton on his own high field of victory—and we are, we must say, jealous of all encroachments upon that fair Paradise which has so long painted itself upon our imaginations—where all the luxuries of earth mingled in the feast with all the dainties of the heavens—where celestial plants grew under the same sun with terrestrial blossoms, and where the cadences of seraphic music filled up the pauses in the voice of God. Far different, indeed, is Mrs Browning's from Dryden's digusting inroad into Eden—as different, almost, as the advent of Raphael from the encroachment of Satan. But the poem professed to stand in the lustre of the fiery sword, and this should have burnt up some of its conceits, and silenced some of its meaner minstrelsies. And all such attempts we regard precisely as we do the beauties of the Apocrypha, when compared to the beauties of the Bible. They are as certainly beauties, but beauties of an inferior order—they are flowers, but not the roses which grew along the banks of the Four Rivers, or caught in their crimson cups the "first sad drops wept at committing of the mortal sin." "One blossom of Eden outblooms them all."

Having accepted from Mrs Browning's own hand sadness, or at least seriousness, as the key to her nature and genius, let us continue to apply it in our future remarks. This at once impels her to, and fits her for, the high position she has assumed, uttering the "Cry of the Human." And whom would the human race prefer as their earthly advocate, to a high-souled and gifted woman? What voice but the female voice could so softly and strongly, so eloquently and meltingly, interpret to the ear of him whose name is Love, the deep woes and deeper wants of "poor humanity's afflicted will, struggling in vain with ruthless destiny?" Some may quarrel with the title, "The Human," as an affectation; but, in the first place, if so, it is a very small one, and a small affectation can never furnish matter for a great quarrel; secondly, we are not disposed to make a man, and still less a woman, an offender for a word; and thirdly, we fancy we can discern a good reason for her use of the term. What is it that is crying aloud through her voice to Heaven? It is not the feral or fiendish element in human nature? That has found an organ in Byron—an echo in his bellowing verse. It is the human element in man—bruised, bleeding, all but dead under the pressure of evil circumstances, under the ten thousand tyrannies, mistakes, and delusions of the world, that has here ceased any longer to be silent, and is speaking in a sister's voice to Time and to Eternity—to Earth and Heaven. The poem may truly be called a prayer for the times, and no collect in the English liturgy surpasses it in truth and tenderness, though some may think its tone daring to the brink of blasphemy, and piercing almost to anguish.

Gracefully from this proud and giddy pinnacle, where she had stood as the conscious and commissioned representative of the human race, she descends to the door of the factory, and pleads for the children enclosed in that crowded and busy hell. The "Cry of the Factory Children" moves you, because it is no poem at all—it is just a long sob, veiled and stifled as it ascends through the hoarse voices of the poor beings themselves. Since we read it we can scarcely pass a factory without seeming to hear this psalm issuing from the machinery, as if it were protesting against its own abused powers. But, to use the language of a writer quoted a little before, "The Fairy Queen is dead, shrouded in a yard of cotton stuff made by the spinning-jenny, and by that other piece of new improved machinery, *the souls and bodies of British children*, for which death alone holds the patent." From Mrs Browning, perhaps the most imaginative and intellectual of British females, down to a pale-faced, thick-voiced, degraded, hardly human, factory girl, what a long and precipitous descent! But though hardly, she is human; and availing herself of the small, trembling, but eternally indestructible link of connection implied in a common nature, our author can identify herself with the cause, and incarnate her genius in the person of the poor perishing child. How unspeakably more affecting is a pleading in behalf of a particular portion of the race, than in behalf of the entire family! Mrs Browning might have uttered a hundred "cries of the human," and proved herself only a sentimental artist, and awakened little save an echo dying away in distant elfin laughter; but the cry of a factory child, coming through a woman's, has gone to a nation's heart.

Although occupied thus with the sterner wants and sorrows of society, she is not devoid of interest in its minor miseries and disappointments. She can sit down beside little Ella (the miniature of Alnaschar) and watch the history of her day-dream beside the swan's nest among the reeds, and see in her disappointment a type of human hopes in general, even when towering and radiant as summer clouds. Ella's dream among the reeds! What else was Godwin's Political Justice? What else was St Simonianism? What else is Young Englandism. And what else are the hopes built by many now upon *certain* perfected schemes of education, which, freely translated, just mean the farther sharpening and furnishing of knaves and fools; and now upon a "Coming Man," who is to supply every deficiency, reconcile every contradiction, and right every wrong. Yes, he will come mounted on the red-roan horse of sweet Ella's vision!

Shadowed by the same uniform seriousness are the only two poems of hers which we shall farther at present mention— we mean her *Vision of Poets*, and her *Geraldine's Courtship*. The aim of the first is to present, in short compass, and almost in single lines, the characteristics of the greater poets of past and present times. This undertaking involved in it very considerable difficulties. For, in the first place, most great poets possess more than one distinguishing peculiarity. To select a single differential point is always hazardous, and often deceptive. 2dly, After you have selected the prominent characteristic of your author, it is no easy task to express it in a word, or in a line. To compress thus an Iliad in a nutshell, to imprison a giant geni in an iron pot, is more a feat of magic than an act of criticism. 3dly, It is especially difficult to express the differentia of a writer in a manner at once easy and natural, picturesque and poetical. In the very terms of such an attempt as Mrs Browning makes, it is implied that she not only defines, but describes the particular writer. But to curdle up a character into one noble word, to describe Shakspere, for instance, in such compass, what sun-syllable shall suffice; or must we renew Byron's wish?—

Could I unbosom and embody now
That which is most within me; could I wreak
My thought upon expression!

. . .

And that *one word were Lightning*, I would speak;
But as it is, I live and die unheard,
With a most voiceless thought, sheathing it as a
      sword.

Accordingly, this style of portraiture (shall we call it, as generally pursued, the thumb-nail style?) has seldom been prosecuted with much success. Ebenezer Elliot has a copy of verses after this fashion, not quite worthy of him. What for example, does the following line tell us of Shelley?

Ill-fated Shelley, vainly great and brave.

The same words might have been used about Sir John Moore, or Pompey. Mrs Browning's verses are far superior. Sometimes, indeed, we see her clipping at a character, in order to fit it better into the place she has prepared for it. Sometimes she crams the half of an author into a verse, and has to leave out the rest for want of room. Sometimes over a familiar face she throws a veil of words and darkness. But often her one glance sees, and her one word shows, the very heart of an author's genius and character. Our readers may recur to the lines already quoted in reference to Lucretius, as one of her best portraitures. Altogether this style, as generally prosecuted, is a small one, not much better than anagrams and acrostics— ranks, indeed, not much higher than the ingenuity of the persons who transcribe the *Pleasures of Hope* on the breadth of a crown-piece, and should be resigned to such praiseworthy personages. By far the best specimen of it we remember, is the very clever list involving a running commentary of the works of Lord Byron, by Dr M'Ginn; unless, indeed, it be Gay's *Catalogue Raisonné* of the portentous poems of Sir Richard Blackmore. Who shall embalm, in a similar way, the endless writings of James, Cooper, and Dickens?

Lady Geraldine's Courtship, as a transcript from the "red-leaved tablets of the heart"—as a tale of love, set to the richest music—as a picture of the subtle workings, the stern reasonings, and the terrible bursts of passion—is above praise. How like a volcano does the poet's heart at length explode! How first all power is given him in the dreadful trance of silence, and then in the loosened tempest of speech! What a wild, fierce logic flows forth from his lips, in which, as in that of Lear's madness, the foundations of society seem to quiver like reeds, and the mountains of conventionalism are no longer found; and in the lull of that tempest, and in the returning sunshine, how beautiful, how almost superhuman, seem the figures of the two lovers, seen now and magnified through the mist of the reader's fast-flowing tears. It is a tale of successful love, and yet it melts you like a tragedy, and most melts you in the crisis of the triumph. On Geraldine we had gazed as on a star, with dry-eyed and distant admiration; but when that star dissolves in showers at the feet of her poet lover, we weep for very joy. Truly a tear is a sad yet beautiful thing; it constitutes a link connecting us with distant countries, nay, connecting us with distant worlds. Gravitation has, amid all her immensity, wrought no such lovely work as when she rounded a tear.

From this beautiful poem alone, we might argue Mrs Browning's capacity for producing a great domestic tragedy. We might argue it, also, from the various peculiarities of her genius—her far vision into the springs of human conduct— into those viewless veins of fire, or of poison, which wind within the human heart—her sympathy with dark bosoms— the passion for truth, which pierces often the mist of her dimmer thought, like a flash of irrepressible lightning—her fervid temperament, always glowing round her intellectual sight—and her queen-like dominion over imagery and language. We think, meanwhile, that she has mistaken her sphere. In that rare atmosphere of transcendentalism which she has reached, she respires with difficulty, and with pain. She is not "native and endued" into that element. We would warn her off the giddy region, where tempests may blow as well as clouds gather. Her recent sonnets in "Blackwood" are sad failures—the very light in them is darkness—thoughts, in themselves as untangible as the films upon the window pane, are concealed in a woof of words, till their thin and shadowy meaning fades utterly away. Morbid weakness, she should remember, is not masculine strength. But can she not, through the rents in her cloudy tabernacle, discern, far below in the vale, fields of deep though homely beauty, where she might more gracefully and successfully exercise her exquisite genius? She has only to stoop to conquer. By and by we may—using unprofanely an expression originally profane—be tempted to say, as we look up the darkened mountain, with its flashes of fire hourly waxing fewer and feebler, "As for this poetess, we wot not what has become of her."

CHARLES CARROLL EVERETT
From "Elizabeth Barrett Browning"
North American Review, October 1857, pp. 418–41

When we transfer Mrs. Browning from the ranks of the female poets to those of the poets of England, we would not be understood to separate her from the first class. Mrs. Browning's poems are, in all respects, the utterances of a woman,—of a woman of great learning, rich experience, and powerful genius, uniting to her woman's nature the strength which is sometimes thought peculiar to man. She is like the Amazon in the midst of battle, hiding not her sex, but demanding no favor for her beardless lip.

The fact that Mrs. Browning has attained to such a height of poetic excellence, not in spite of her woman's nature, but by means of it, shows that the difference which has been hitherto supposed to exist between poets and poetesses is not, so far as relates to the matter of power, founded upon the nature of things. It explains also, in some degree, the ardor of admiration with which she is regarded by many of the most cultivated of her sex. She speaks what is struggling for utterance in their own hearts, and they find in her poems the revelation of themselves. ⟨. . .⟩

Such is the substance of Mrs. Browning's earlier poems,—sorrow and longing, mediated by faith; her sorrows becoming, through faith, the stepping-stones to that joy for which she longs. In the series entitled *Casa Guidi Windows*, we find ourselves at a very different stage of experience. In the leading poems of this series, we have no more the utterances of sorrow and longing, nor even the clear voice of faith giving assurance of future joy. The joy is no longer future, but has become present; instead of struggle, there is attainment. This difference is especially marked in the sonnets *From the Portuguese*. There are, indeed, in the same series other poems which belong to the earlier period. Such is the one entitled "Human Life's Misery." These, if not all written during the earlier period, yet are the results of it; as the ocean casts up fragments of wrecks for days after the storm has ended. From the *Aurora Leigh* we learn indirectly that much of the restlessness and sadness expressed in the earlier poems was the result of that loneliness, which a woman feels when she has to meet unaided the storms of life. Her spirit needs some stronger

spirit upon which to lean. A prose version of this we have in the life of Margaret Fuller Ossoli. The greater her genius, the more does she feel this need; for her very genius separates her from the common relations of life, and the more intense, therefore, is the demand for some one to walk with her through her lonely path, and the less is the likelihood that it will be satisfied. She must have one loftier and stronger than herself. A companion without companionship only increases the feeling of loneliness. If she have to stoop to the level of him who should aid her upward flight, the craving remains unfilled. She must have a spirit strong-winged as her own, that shall soar with her towards the sun, and support her when she is ready to sink back again to the earth. Such a feeling, as we may gather from Mrs. Browning's self-revelations, was, perhaps unconsciously, coloring her earlier poems, and, from the characteristics of her genius, it might have been supposed, that it would remain unsatisfied. With her strength of intellect, her soaring imagination, her delicate spiritual perceptions, where could she find one whose strength should be greater, whose imagination loftier, and whose spirituality, if less delicate, should yet be no less strongly marked, and sturdier than her own? We know of but one poet of the present age whose character would correspond to the ideal which we have sketched, and that poet it was her good fortune to meet and to become united with. The genius of Robert and that of Elizabeth Barrett Browning stand, we might almost say, in the contrast of male and female to each other. His is the stronger, the sterner, the more comprehensive; hers the more delicate, the more tender. Thus did Mrs. Browning's life become rounded to its completion. The sorrows had given way to gladness; the future joys for which she longed had become present; earth no longer served merely as a sad and dark passage to heaven, but was itself radiant with heaven's glorious light, and penetrated with the sweetness of its love. Thus she sings:

> I lived with visions for my company
> Instead of men and women, years ago,
> And found them gentle mates, nor thought to know
> A sweeter music than they played to me.
> But soon their trailing purple was not free
> Of this world's dust,—their lutes did silent grow,
> And I myself grew faint and blind below
> Their vanishing eyes. Then THOU didst come . . to
>   be,
> Beloved, what they *seemed*. Their shining fronts,
> Their songs, their splendors . . (better, yet the
>   same,. .
> As river-water hallowed into fonts . .)
> Met in thee, and from out thee overcame
> My soul with satisfaction of all wants,—
> Because God's gifts put man's best dreams to shame.

And again:

> As brighter ladies do not count it strange
> For love to give up acres and degree,
> I yield the grave for thy sake, and exchange
> My near, sweet view of heaven for earth with thee.

Having thus escaped from the struggles and darkness by which she had been surrounded, she looks upon the world as it really is. She sings of Italy as it lies before her, and describes in clear, ringing rhymes her hopes for it, and their disappointment.

Mrs. Browning has, however, not yet attained in these poems to her complete artistic development. Thus far she has sung of sorrow when she was sad, and of joy in her hours of happiness. She has not yet acquired that command of her material, by which, these emotions already passed, the days of weeping over, and the flush of joy faded into the common daylight, they may still be represented by her as truthfully as ever;—no longer in their antagonism to each other, but united in a single work of art. As yet she

> Cannot teach
> Her hand to hold her spirit so far off
> From herself.

This is accomplished in the *Aurora Leigh*. Here her whole past life, with its many griefs and disappointments, with its aspirations and its failures, and with its final crown of love and joy, is placed before us. In it we have the substance of the earlier and that of the later poems, each of which had been before incomplete without the other, made the elements of a new and more perfect work, their union mediated by deeper views of art and of life than she had before expressed. We do not mean that it is, in the common sense of the word, an autobiography, like the earlier and the later sonnets. That which before had gushed directly from her heart is now treated as something entirely outside of herself. Yet so far as the spiritual development is concerned, it may be called an autobiography. It appears to express the complete development of the life of a woman and of an artist.

⟨. . .⟩ Thus far we have studied the development of the external and internal elements of these poems, as if they were entirely distinct from each other. By uniting them, it will be seen how perfectly the three stages just described are exhibited in them. In the first period we found that the subject-matter was for the most part made up of sorrow, longing, and faith. The highest truths of religion and of the spiritual consciousness gathered about her, and these she strove to express. A yearning filled her soul to penetrate into those shadowy regions, which she felt were stretching around her. This very yearning implied that she had not yet reached the true centre of things,—the height from which one

> Sees the world as one vast plain,
> And one boundless reach of sky.

These undefined longings, this restless yearning for something as yet unrealized, and consequently not yet understood, and this striving to image forth the spiritual phantasms which loom up dimly and loftily about her, mould the outward form of her poems. She has power enough over language to exhibit her thought clearly and gracefully; but so far as this thought is vague and shadowy, so far do her expressions become harsh and obscure. As the Egyptians reared the mighty Pyramids, or hewed in rude proportions the gigantic Sphinx, with its twofold nature, so she piles together Greek and Hebrew, Grecisms, Hebraisms, and Germanisms, and the lore of all ages, to utter that which she feels the common modes of speech would fail to express. As the Hindoo twisted the ordinary forms of things into strange and uncouth shapes, to make them body forth that for which he and they had no adequate utterance, so she twists the forms of speech into unwonted expressions, and new relations, to satisfy a similar need. But in addition to this she adopts sometimes, for the same purpose, a wild and lofty symbolism, in whose mazes we are almost lost. Examples of this may be found in the *Drama of Exile* and in the *Vision of Poets*. Even in her sonnets, which we have classed among her most nearly perfect works, she is careful to state how imperfectly that which she would say is uttered:—

> With stammering lips and insufficient sound,
> I strive and struggle to deliver right
> That music of my nature, day and night,
> With dream and thought and feeling, interwound
> And inly answering all the senses round

> With octaves of a mystic depth and height,
> Which step out grandly to the infinite
> From the dark edges of the sensual ground!
> This song of soul I struggle to outbear
> Through portals of the sense, sublime and whole,
> And utter all myself into the air:
> But if I did it,—as the thunder-roll
> Breaks its own cloud,—my flesh would perish there,
> Before that dread apocalypse of soul.

And again:—

> O, the world is weak—
> The effluence of each is false to all;
> And what we best conceive, we fail to speak.
> Wait, soul, until thine ashen garments fall!
> And then resume thy broken strains, and seek
> Fit peroration, without let or thrall.

At last the "ashen garments" do fall; these vague yearnings become satisfied; the sorrow that had striven for utterance passes away; the realities of earth replace the "visions" in which she has thus far lived; the inward conflict has become changed to a joyous peace. Her poems exhibit this change in their outward form. What she has to say is distinctly before her, and is clearly and gracefully spoken. She has learned

> The whole of life
> In a new rhythm,

as she herself informs us. She sings her song of love. She gazes from the Windows of Casa Guidi, and describes the world as it is. At this period she seems herself to feel that she is nearer the Grecian stand-point than she has been before or is to be afterward; and she gives us a translation of the Prometheus of Æschylus full of strength and beauty.

Her spiritual growth, however, is not yet completed. Under genial influences it advances rapidly and healthfully. She has acquired a command of her own resources; her thought arises before her, grand and clear. She demands only a medium for its representation. She does not wander, as before, among symbols and types. She does not seek, on the other hand, that beauty of expression which marks her later sonnets and her *Casa Guidi*. It is enough for her that her thought is understood. If a figure suits her turn, no matter how often she may have used it before, it will serve just as well again. If an expression means just what she wants to say, no matter how revolting it may be. She cares as little about mere outward beauty, as did the early Christian painters. We thus understand the carelessness and the realism which we found to mark the *Aurora Leigh*.

We have considered the poems of Mrs. Browning as forming a connected whole. In our citations we have confined ourselves to those passages which have a bearing upon this general result. Had we stopped to gather flowers, we know not when our journey would have been ended. We have therefore hurried past much that is beautiful. Above all, the large eyes of Marian Earle, at once Madonna and Magdalene, look back sadly and half reproachfully upon us.

It remains to inquire what we have still to expect from a writer whose development has been hitherto so regular. Mrs. Browning's genius is lyric rather than dramatic. Her material is gathered principally from within. She tells us, in the Preface to *Aurora Leigh*, that the work contains her "highest convictions upon Life and Art." She has passed through the three periods which represent those of the development of Art. She has embodied the results of this process in a noble work which we think will continue to be her finest. That she will still refresh and inspire us with her song, we cannot doubt. As the art of the present age can at will make use of all the forms which originally answered to a particular epoch of history; so Mrs. Browning can reproduce for us, to a certain degree, the various stages through which she has thus far passed. These results will, however, probably stand in the same relation to the *Aurora Leigh*, which Tennyson's *Maud* bears to his *In Memoriam*.

Although, as we have said, Mrs. Browning's *Aurora Leigh* is her finest work, there are many among her admirers whom her earlier poems will still move the most deeply. Comparatively few can follow, with full sympathy, her entire course. Perhaps most of those whose spiritual life has actually begun, stand yet upon the stage of sorrow and longing. While such gaze with admiration on the shining path of their poet, they will yet feel the deepest sympathy with her, as she is still walking among the shadows, and cheering them with her songs. It appears to us, also, that the *Aurora Leigh* is not to be reckoned among the works destined for immortality. The universal element in it is too much mingled with the peculiarities of our time, to admit of its becoming naturalized in another age. This need not, however, lessen our enjoyment of it; as we should not find the blossom of the century-plant less beautiful for the thought that the entire age had been needed for its production, and that it yet would wither, very shortly, before our eyes.

JAMES ASHCROFT NOBLE
From "Elizabeth Barrett Browning"
The Poets and the Poetry of the Century
ed. Alfred H. Miles
1892, Volume 8, pp. 159–64

Perhaps the first and the last, the strongest and most enduring impression stamped upon the mind by the poetry of Elizabeth Barrett Browning is that it is the poetry of instinct, or—to use a word which has of late become somewhat unfashionable—of inspiration. We feel that to her the measured but incalculable music of verse was what the common prose of the street or the drawing-room is to most of us, a natural and inevitable vehicle of expression,—that she saw and felt herself truly when she wrote in *Aurora Leigh*—

> My joy and pain,
> My thought and aspiration, like the stops
> Of flute or pipe, are absolutely dumb
> Unless melodious.

The word "inspiration" I have said has become unfashionable, it has given place to that much smaller word *technique*; and it may frankly be admitted that in those qualities of exquisite and flawless rendering which contribute to technical literary perfection Mrs. Browning's work is frequently deficient. It may indeed be said that she is more obviously faulty than any poet who is equally distinguished; but, after all, faultiness in every kind of work is too common to stand in need of being laboriously pointed out, while distinction in any kind of work is somewhat rare; and where the latter is present the added presence of the former is of comparatively little moment. In any brief estimate it would indeed be foolish to waste space in dwelling upon the heresies of rhyme, the fantastic epithets, the incoherencies of phrase which are to be found by all who care to seek them in the books of the poet to whom we owe "The Sleep," "The Cry of the Children," *Aurora Leigh*, and the *Sonnets from the Portuguese*.

If, as it is sometimes contended, the highest art must be art in which distinctively masculine and feminine characteristics disappear in some transcendental human synthesis which knows no sex, then assuredly the place of Mrs. Browning is below the highest, for she was pre-eminently a great woman poet, and not simply a woman who wrote great poetry. Though her work was in external form, sometimes narrative and sometimes dramatic, it was always in essence the poetry of self-expression—the poetry in which the treatment of external things, howsoever admirable in itself, is always subsidiary to the imaginative utterance of personal thought and emotion. In poetry of this kind typical masculine work and typical feminine work are distinguished from each other by the fact that in the former the thought comes first and inspires the emotion, while in the latter the emotion comes first and suggests the thought. "As I was musing the fire burned";—that is an adequate description of the genesis of masculine poetry. In the poetry of womanhood the fire burns first and the musings, the thoughts, are generated by the warmth. It is thus in the work of Mrs. Browning. It has no lack of intellectual substance; on the contrary, it has been held by some that in *Aurora Leigh*, and elsewhere this intellectual substance is inartistically obtrusive; but the thought is always the child and vassal of emotion:—the brain is as alert as the pulse is strong, yet everywhere, in *Aurora Leigh*, in *Casa Guidi Windows*, and in the *Poems before Congress*, not less than in such intimately personal utterances as "A Denial," "Inclusions," and the Portuguese Sonnets "the heart still overrules the head."

This last wonderful, indeed unique series of poems—the noblest anthology for noble lovers which any literature has to show—provides striking illustrations both of the close combination of the passionate and the reflective element in Mrs. Browning's verse, and of the dominance of the former over the latter. Take for example the well-known fourteenth number of the sequence,—a poem born of the strongest emotion in the heart of one beloved—the all-powerful desire to be loved for her very self, for what she *is*, not for what she *has*. "If thou must love me, let it be for love's sake only,"—the fiery heart of the sonnet is in that first line: love me because I am I, not for my smile, my look, my way of gentle speech, my thought in accord with yours. And then as the fire burns the musing begins, the thought is born, the intellect supplies a justification for the emotion. These things are transient, and the love that is fixed upon them may not survive them; but the soul, the self, endures, and the love which is bound to it—to the essential not to the accidental—is therefore the love which lives on "through love's eternity."

This method, if any habit so instinctive can be called a method, may be traced through the greater part of Mrs. Browning's work; and it gives to that work an immediate charm for that majority of poetry-lovers who are one with the poet in reaching thought through feeling rather than feeling through thought. And this majority will respond with not less ready sympathy and appreciation to the special tone of the emotion,—the prevalent pensiveness and sadness which are all the more impressive because so obviously spontaneous, so entirely free from a suspicion of affectation. The domination of the mood of melancholy, manifests itself both in the choice of themes which lend themselves readily to its expression, and by the sombre treatment of other themes which are in themselves devoid of sombre suggestions. Many of the best known and most deservedly popular of Mrs. Browning's shorter poems—"Confessions," "The Mask," *The Lay of the Brown Rosary*, "Bertha in the Lane," and "The Cry of the Children"—are poems of unrelieved sadness; the hero and heroine of *Aurora*

Leigh, have to be taught life's lesson by the anguish of failure; and even when, as in "The Sea-Mew," she lights upon a theme which seems full of suggestions of the free joyousness of vivid life, the music is still in the minor key, for even the bright wild bird is drawn into the human shadow.

> He lay down in his grief to die,
> (First looking to the sea-like sky
> That hath no waves) because, alas!
> Our human touch did on him pass,
> And with our touch, our agony.

In spite, however, of its uniformity of emotional tone there is in Mrs. Browning's work a variety of matter and form which render detailed comment altogether impossible here. The finest of her pure lyrics have the richness and the rapture of the song of the nightingale, with now and again a certain unearthliness in the melody, as if the singer were indeed what she was declared to be by the one who knew her best, "half-angel and half-bird." Her narrative ballads have a swift directness and an impressive pictorialism which hold the imagination and stir the blood. In her sonnets, especially in the marvellous sequence purporting to be "from the Portuguese" the poet is seen at her loftiest altitude for here art is as victorious as inspiration. The irresistibly winning individuality is as distinct as ever; but the style has cleared itself of its dross its occasional ruggedness, and grating grotesqueness, and has, without losing force, gained ease, clearness, balance, and all the qualities which in the mass we call classical. Many a great poet has his own peculiar honour: it was given to Mrs. Browning to render in perfect verse the very apotheosis of love. Concerning *Aurora Leigh* there will always be differences of opinion and feeling, for it exhibits the poet's weakness not less manifestly than her strength. Its form is defective, its inspiration intermittent, its style unequal; it is greater in parts than as a whole; but if we regard its finest details of description and characterisation, if we weigh the nuggets of imaginative thought which we turn over on nearly every page, we may fairly pronounce it, with all its faults, one of the fullest and most opulent poems produced in this century by an English poet.

The work of Mrs. Browning appeals to us by its fervidly eloquent rendering of imaginative vision, ethical fervour, and profound passion, employing the last word not in the special sense to which usage has confined it, but as comprehending all outgoings of strong emotion towards God, or country, or human fellows, or those aspects of nature which rouse within us love or awe, wonder or hushed delight. The sadness which utters itself in so much of her verse is the sadness of that keen sensation which brings exquisite sympathy, not the sadness of the dimmed faith which brings despair; and when the song which comes from her lips is most mournful the eye of the singer is fixed upon the far horizon with a look of hope. She lived in the shadow of human weakness, human sorrow, human disquietude, but she never failed in her witness to the light behind the cloud; and we discern the constant attitude of her nature in the tender and triumphant utterance which closes *The Rhyme of the Duchess May*:—

> Oh, the little birds sang east, and the little birds sang west,
> And I said in underbreath,—All our life is mixed with death,
>   And who knoweth which is best?
> Oh, the little birds sang east, and the little birds sang west,
> And I smiled to think God's greatness flowed around our incompleteness,—
>   Round our restlessness, His rest.

MARGARET OLIPHANT
From *The Victorian Age of English Literature*
1892, Volume 1, pp. 228–33

A wonderful girl, educated as few girls are, with all the classic inspirations that come from the poetry of the Greeks, she began to write at an extraordinarily early age, translating the *Prometheus* of Eschylus and even venturing into philosophy with a youthful "Essay on Mind," while still so young that Miss Mitford had "some difficulty in persuading a friend," that the young author "was old enough to be introduced into company, in technical language was *out*"—Elizabeth Barrett, this miraculous child, was early stricken down by illness and sorrow, and for many years had all the appearance of a confirmed invalid shut up in her room for life. It was from her sickroom that her first collection of poems, including many of her finest productions, came forth in 1844. In these, among many reminiscences and inspirations of her then singular education—poems of which *Pan is Dead* is much the most remarkable—there burst forth also the voice of her time, the voice of the enthusiast and philanthropist, which scarcely had become before one of the highest voices of poetry. "The Cry of the Children," which was included in these first volumes, has a passion and pathos with which the soul of England was wrung, and formed at once the highest expression and stimulus of a great wave of popular feeling, very curious to find side by side with the half-triumphant, half-regretful proclamation of the Gods of Hellas, whose doom had gone forth from among the spheres.

One of the longest of Miss Barrett's poems, a poetical narrative hurriedly written, but full of picturesque life and power, has a curious and interesting reference to the other poet, unknown to her as yet, in whose name her own was to be merged, the future companion of her life. Browning's *Bell and Pomegranates*, were in course of publication when this young lady rushed with flying pen through the tale of *Lady Geraldine's Courtship*, describing her, the highborn lady in her old hereditary home, surrounded by everything that was best and most beautiful, enjoying all the highest luxuries of life, sometimes ancient, sometimes modern, the old poets and the new—among which latter class there might be for her refreshment,

> Of Browning one pomegranate which, when cut
>   down through the middle,
> Showed a heart within blood-tinctured with a veined
>   humanity.

Not so much this touch of anticipated acquaintance, but the possession of a mutual friend anxious to secure a moment's pleasure for the invalid, brought these two together. She was on the sofa from which she could scarcely rise, from whence she apostrophises so prettily and touchingly the spaniel Flush, who was her devoted attendant, and herself not unlike that wistful, affectionate creature, with long curls half veiling her face, after the romantic fashion of the time—when the robust young poet, in the full flush of his manhood and strength, was introduced into her darkened room. He brought romance and all the glories of awakening life with him into that retirement, from whence a little while after he stole his wife, restoring her almost by a miracle to comparative health, and the open-air world, and a young woman's natural capacity for enjoyment. The marriage was not only opposed but forbidden by her family, notwithstanding that residence abroad had been announced to be her only chance of life and restoration. Love, which thus came unexpected, a little tardy, but all the more wonderful and sweet, into her seclusion, awakened in her a fountain of poetry more personal than anything that had gone before. The Gods of Hellas gave place to a more potent influence, and the course of her own singular courtship pushed aside all the Lady Geraldines of so much more commonplace an inspiration. Nothing prettier can be than the little glimpse into the tremulous newly-awakened hopes of the invalid which is afforded to us, when she describes herself as stepping breathlessly and furtively out of the carriage in which she is taking the daily drive of routine, to stand for a moment on the grass, and feel herself upon her feet, in a tremulous ecstasy of new being. In a higher sense we have the same sensation in those *Sonnets from the Portuguese*, tenderly veiled in the transparent mist of supposed translation where this awakening to life and love is shadowed forth. These Sonnets reach the highest poetic tide of her genius—the modest *abandon* of a heart overflowing with tenderness, and that surprise of delight as of the primal creation, which the true poet finds in each new thing that meets his sight and experience, but still more strongly in what was almost, in this particular case, a resurrection from the dead.

Mrs. Browning's poems after her marriage were longer and of more importance so far as purpose and intention went. *Casa Guidi Windows* is an expression of her interest in the advancing course of Italian independence, for which she had the most passionate sympathy. The force of contemporary feeling which is poured forth in this poem, and also in the *Poems before Congress*, which made them especially striking at the moment, is naturally rather to their disadvantage now, when all those agitations are happily overpast, and the inexperienced observer begins to wonder whether it can be possible that Italian Unity is so new as to have been the object of such warm, impassioned, almost unhoping desires, so short a time ago. That it should have been only the Austrian uniform which was visible from Casa Guidi windows where now the lively Bersaglieri pass daily at their running trot, so familiar, so completely a part of the scene, is all but incredible; or that the heart of an English lady there should have swelled so full of alarm and indignation and fear lest some disastrous compromise should cut the wings of her beloved adopted country. These poems must ever have an interest for the historical student, as showing what that period of agitation, fear, and hope, really was.

The last great work of Mrs. Browning's life was the poem of *Aurora Leigh*, published in 1856, the most complete monument perhaps of her genius. The remarkable thing in this work is its energy and strong poetical vitality, the rush and spring of life which is in a narrative, often lengthy, and of which the subject and story are not sufficient for the fervour and power of utterance. The development of the woman-poet, brought from a wild no-training among the Italian hills into a prim English feminine household, and inevitably assuming there that attitude of superiority to everything about her which is so contrary to that of true genius, and so melancholy a mistake in art—gives the reader at first a strong prepossession against, instead of in favour of, the young Aurora, so conscious as she is of her qualities among the limited persons and things about her. The story, however, soon plunges, in the person of its hero, into those wild depths of philanthropy and sublime intention towards the poor and miserable, which to all sober eyes turn the way of madness. Romney's conclusion that it is his duty to marry the unfortunate Marian Erle, who has been the victim of brutal passion, thus showing how divine pity transcends all other forces, and that the innocent in will and

intention can never be sullied—notwithstanding the fact that he does not love her, that indeed he loves another woman, conventionally suitable to him in every respect—is the climax of the tale;—in which something of that perverse sense of duty in plunging into the most horrible depths, which is the natural balance of those limitations which the world imposes or endeavours to impose on women, is apparent through the indignant denunciations of too prevalent evil, and recognition of much belied and unacknowledged good. There are really admirable pieces of description and bursts of feeling in this poem, but it is throughout a little rhetorical, and its great quality, is as we have said, the remarkable sustained energy and vitality of the long volume of verse.

ARTHUR CHRISTOPHER BENSON
From "Elizabeth Barrett Browning"
Essays
1896, pp. 212–29

Mrs. Browning's best lyrical work was all done before her marriage; but the stirring of the truest depths of her emotional nature took voice in the collection of sonnets entitled *From the Portuguese*—strung, in Omar's words, like pearls upon the string of circumstance. In these sonnets (which it is hardly necessary to say are not translations) she speaks the universal language; to her other graces had now been added that which she had somewhat lacked before, the grace of content; and for these probably she will be longest and most gratefully admired. Any one who steps for the first time through the door into which he has seen so many enter, and finds that poets and lovers and married folk, in their well-worn commonplaces, have exaggerated nothing, will love these sonnets as one of the sweetest and most natural records of a thing which will never lose its absorbing fascination for humanity. To those that are without, except for the sustained melody of expression, the poetess almost seems to have passed on to a lower level, to have lost originality—like the celebrated lady whose friends said that till she wrote to announce her engagement she had never written a commonplace letter. Their fervour indeed rises from the resolute virginity of a heart to whom love had been scarcely a dream, never a hope. We must think of the isolation, sublime it may have been, but yet desolate, from which her marriage was to rescue her—coming not as only the satisfaction of imperious human needs, but to meet and crown her whole nature with a fulness of which few can dream. As she was afterwards to write:

> How dreary 'tis for women to sit still
> On winter nights by *solitary* fires
> And hear the nations praising them far off.

And again:

> To sit alone
> And think, for comfort, how that very night
> Affianced lovers, leaning face to face,
> With sweet half-listenings for each other's breath
> Are reading haply from some page of ours
> To pause with a thrill, as if their cheeks had touched
> When such a stanza level to their mood
> Seems floating their own thoughts out—"So I feel
> For thee"—"And I for thee: this poet knows
> What everlasting love is."

> To have our books
> Appraised by love, associated with love
> While we sit loveless.

Such a heart deserved all the love it could get.

The latter years of Mrs. Browning's life have a certain shadowiness for English readers. The *Casa Guidi*, if we were not painfully haunted by the English in which interviewers have given their impressions of it, is a memory to linger over. The high dusty passage that gave access to the tall, gloomy house; the huge cool rooms, with little Pennini, so called in contrast to the colossal statue Apennino, "slender, fragile, spirit-like" flitting about from stair to stair: the faint sounds of music breathing about the huge corridors; the scent, the stillness,—such a home as only two poets could create, and two lovers inhabit. ⟨. . .⟩

To secure an audience a poet must be diplomatic; he must know whose ear he intends to catch. It is mere cant to say that the best poetry cannot be popular; that it should be read is its first requisite. When Gray wrote φωνᾶντα συνετοῖσιν on his Odes he meant that there would be many people to whom they would not appeal; but it is ridiculous to say that the merit of poetry is in proportion to the paucity of its admirers. If Mrs. Browning aimed at any particular class it was perhaps at intellectual sentimentalists. As the two characteristics are rarely found united, in fact are liable to exclude one another, it may perhaps be the reason why she is so little appreciated in her entirety: she is perhaps too learned for women and too emotional for men.

Let us consider for a moment where her intellectual training came from. Roughly speaking, the basis of it was Greek from first to last; at nine years old she measured her life by the years of the siege of Troy, and carved a figure out of the turf in her garden to represent a recumbent warrior, naming it Hector. Then came her version of the *Prometheus Vinctus*; her long studious mornings over Plato and Theocritus with the blind scholar, Mr. Boyd, whom she commemorates in "Wine of Cyprus," when she read, as she writes, "the Greek poets, with Plato, from end to end"; her dolorous excursion with the Fathers; and at last, in the *Casa Guidi*, the little row of miniature classics, annotated in her own hand, standing within easy reach of her couch. Of course she was an omnivorous reader besides. She speaks of reading the Hebrew Bible, "from Genesis to Malachi,—never stopped by the Chaldean,—and the flood of all possible and impossible British and foreign novels and romances, with slices of metaphysics laid thick between the sorrows of the multitudinous Celestinas." But it was evidently in Greek, in the philosophical poetry of Euripides and the poetical philosophy of Plato, that she found her deepest satisfaction.

At the same time she was not in the true sense learned, though possessing learning far greater than commonly falls to a woman's lot to possess. Her education in Greek must have been unsystematic and unscholarly; her classical allusions, which fall so thick in letters and poems have seldom quite the genuine ring; we do not mean that she did not get nearer the heart of the Greek writers and appreciate their spirit more intimately than many a far more erudite scholar; that was to be expected, for she brought enthusiasm and insight and genius to the task; but her learning is not an animated part of her; it is sometimes almost an incubus. The character of her allusions too is often remote and fanciful. They fall, it is true, from a teeming brain, but they are not the simple direct comparisons which would occur to a man who had made Greek literature his own, but rather the unexpected, modern turns which so often surprise a student, like the red bunches of valerian which thrust out of the sand-stone frieze of a Sicilian temple—such comparisons, for instance, as the celebrated one in *Aurora*

Leigh of the peasant who might have been gathering brushwood in the ear of a colossus had Xerxes carried out his design of carving Athos into the likeness of a man. Her characterization of the classical poets in *The Poet's Vow* will also illustrate this; now so extraordinarily felicitous and clear-sighted, as for instance in the case of Shakespeare and Ossian, and now so alien to the true spirit of the men described.

> Sophocles
> With that king's-look which down the trees
> Followed the dark effigies
> Of the lost Theban. Hesiod old,
> Who, somewhat blind and deaf and cold,
> Cared most for gods and bulls.

The fact was that she read the Greeks as a woman of genius was sure to do; she passed by their majestic grace, amazed at their solemn profundity, and yet unaware that she was projecting into them a feeling, a sentimental outlook which they did not possess, attributing directly to them a deliberate power which was merely the effect of their unconscious, antique, and limited vision upon the emotional child of a later age.

The strangest thing is that a woman of such complex and sensitive faculties should have given in her allegiance to such models. Never was there a writer in whom the best characteristics of the Greeks were more conspicuously absent. Their balance, their solidity, their calm, their gloomy acquiescence in the bitter side of life, have surely little in common with the passionate spirit that beat so wildly against the bars, and asked the stars and hills so eagerly for their secrets. Such a passage as the following, grand as is the central idea, is surely enough to show the utter incompatibility which existed between them: "I thought that had Æschylus lived after the incarnation and crucifixion of our Lord Jesus Christ, he might have turned, if not in moral and intellectual, yet in poetic faith, from the solitude of Caucasus to the deeper desertness of that crowded Jerusalem, where none had any pity,—from the faded white flower of a Titanic brow to the withered grass of a heart trampled on by its own beloved—from the glorying of him who gloried that he could not die, to the sublime meekness of the Taster of death for every man: from the taunt stung into being by the torment, to his more awful silence, when the agony stood dumb before the love." . . . It was characteristic of a woman to bring the two personalities together, to dwell on what might have been; but this is not Greek.

The two poems which are the best instances of the classical mood, are the two of which Pan, the spirit of the solitary country, half beast, half god, is the hero. In these Mrs. Browning appears in her strength and in her weakness. In *The Dead Pan*, in spite of its solemn refrain, the lengthy disordered mode of thought is seen to the worst advantage: the progression of ideas is obscure, the workmanship is not hurried, but deliberately distressing; the rhymes, owing to that unfortunate fancy for double rhyming, being positively terrific; the brief fury of the lyric mood passing into the utterances of a digressive moralist. But when we turn to the other, "A Musical Instrument," what a relief we experience. "What was he doing, the great god Pan, down in the reeds by the river?" The splendid shock of the rhythm, like the solid plunge of a cataract into a mountain-pool, captivates, for all its roughness, the metrical ear. There is not a word or a thought too much: the scene shapes itself, striking straight out into the thought; the waste and horror that encircle the birth of the poet in the man; the brutish elements out of which such divinity is compounded— these are flung down in simple, delicate outlines: such a lyric is an eternal possession of the English language.

As a natural result of a certain discursiveness of mind, there is hardly any kind of writing unrepresented in Mrs. Browning's poems. She had at one time a fancy for pure romantic writing, since developed to such perfection by Rossetti. There is a peculiar charm about such composition. In such works we seem to breathe a freer air, separated as we are from special limitations of time and place; the play of passion is more simple and direct, and the passion itself is of a less complex and restrained character. Besides, there is a certain element of horror and mystery, which the modern spirit excludes, while it still hungers for it, but is not unnatural when mediævalized. Nothing in Mrs. Browning can bear comparison with "Sister Helen" or "The Beryl Stone"; but *The Romaunt of the Page* and the *Rhyme of the Duchess May* stand among her most successful pieces.

The latter opens with a simple solemnity:

> To the belfry, one by one, went the ringers from the
>   sun,
>   *Toll slowly.*
> And the oldest ringer said, "Ours is music for the
>   dead,
>   When the rebecks are all done."
> Six abeles i' the churchyard grow on the north side in
>   a row,
>   *Toll slowly.*
> And the shadow of their tops rock across the little
>   slopes
>   Of the grassy graves below.
> On the south side and the west a small river runs in
>   haste,
>   *Toll slowly.*
> And between the river flowing and the fair green trees
>   a-growing,
>   Do the dead lie at their rest.
> On the east I sat that day, up against a willow grey:
>   *Toll slowly.*
> Through the rain of willow-branches I could see the
>   low hill ranges,
>   And the river on its way.

This is like the direct opening notes of the overture of a dirge. Whatever may be said about such writing we feel at once that it comes from a master's hand. So the poem opens, but alas for the close! Some chord seems to snap; it is no longer the spirit of the ancient rhymer, but Miss Mitford's friend who catches up the lyre and will have her last word. The poem passes, still in the same metre, out of the definite materialism, the ghastly excitements of the story into a species of pious churchyard meditation; and the pity of it is that we cannot say that this is not characteristic.

Then closely connected with the last comes a class of poems, of so-called modern life, of which *Lady Geraldine's Courtship* shall stand for an example. This is a poem of nineteenth-century adventure, which is as impossible in design and as fantastic in detail as a poem may well be. The reader does not know whether to be most amazed at the fire and glow of the whole story, or at the hopeless ignorance of the world betrayed by it. The impossible Earls with their immeasurable pride and intolerable pomposities; the fashionable ladies with their delicate exteriors and callous hearts,—these are like the creations of Charlotte Brontë, and recall Blanche and Baroness Ingram of Ingram Park. And at the same time, when we have said all this, we read the poem and we can forgive all or nearly all—the spirit is so high, the passion is so fierce and glowing, the poetry that bursts out, stanza after stanza, contrives to involve even these dolorous mistakes in such a glamour, that

we can only admire the genius that could contend against such visionary errors.

But we must turn to what after all is Mrs. Browning's most important and most characteristic work, *Aurora Leigh*. Unfortunately its length alone, were there not any other reasons, would prevent its ever being popular. Ten thousand lines of blank verse is a serious thing. The fact that the poem is to a great extent autobiographical, combined with the comparative mystery in which the authoress was shrouded and the romance belonging to a marriage of poets—these elements are enough to account for the general enthusiasm with which the poem was received. Landor said that it made him drunk with poetry,—that was the kind of expression that its admirers allowed themselves to make use of with respect to it. And yet in spite of these credentials, the fact remains that it is a difficult volume to work through. It is the kind of book that one begins to read for the first time with intense enjoyment, congratulating oneself after the first hundred pages that there are still three-hundred to come. Then the mood gradually changes; it becomes difficult to read without a marker; and at last it goes back to the shelf with the marker about three-fourths of the way through. As she herself wrote,

> The prospects were too far and indistinct.
> 'Tis true my critics said "A fine view that."
> The public scarcely cared to climb my book
> For even the finest;—and the public's right.

Now what is the reason of this? In the first place it is a romance with a rather intricate plot, and a romance requires continuous reading and cannot be laid aside for a few days with impunity. Secondly, it requires hard and continuous study; there is hardly a page without two or three splendid thoughts, and several weighty expressions; it is a perfect mine of felicitous though somewhat lengthy quotations upon almost every question of art and life, yet it is sententious without being exactly epigrammatic. Thirdly, it is very digressive, distressingly so when you are once interested in the story. Lastly, it is not dramatic; whoever is speaking, Lord Howe, Aurora, Romney Leigh, Marian Earle, they all express themselves in a precisely similar way; it is even sometimes necessary to reckon back the speeches in a dialogue to see who has got the ball. In fact it is not they who speak, but Mrs. Browning. To sum up, it is the attempted union of the dramatic and meditative elements that is fatal to the work from an artistic point of view.

Perhaps, if we are to try and disentangle the motive of the whole piece, to lay our finger on the main idea, we may say that it lies in the contrast between the solidity and unity of the artistic life, as opposed to the tinkering philanthropy of the Sociologist. *Aurora Leigh* is an attempt from an artistic point of view to realise in concrete form the truth that the way to attack the bewildering problem of the nineteenth century, the moral elevation of the democracy, is not by attempting to cure in detail the material evils, which are after all nothing but the symptoms of a huge moral disease expressing itself in concrete fact, but by infusing a spirit which shall raise them from within. To attack it from its material side is like picking off the outer covering of a bud to assist it to blow, rather than by watering the plant to increase its vitality and its own power of internal action; in fact, as our clergy are so fond of saying, a spiritual solution is the only possible one, with this difference, that in *Aurora Leigh* this attempt is made not so much from the side of dogmatic religion as of pure and more general enthusiasms. The insoluble enigma is unfortunately, whether, under the pressure of the present material surroundings, there is any hope of eliciting such an instinct at all; whether it is not actually annihilated by want and woe and the diseased transmission of hereditary sin.

ARTHUR HUGH CLOUGH

1819–1861

Arthur Hugh Clough was born in Liverpool on January 1, 1819, the son of a Liverpool cotton merchant. In 1829 he entered Rugby, where he was one of Thomas Arnold's most devoted and brilliant pupils. In 1837 he went on to Balliol College, Oxford, where he received his degree in 1841. Clough became a Fellow of Oriel in 1842, and in 1847 led a series of student reading parties to Scotland. This latter experience provided the inspiration for his first important poem, *The Bothie of Toper-na-Fuosich* (1848; later published as *The Bothie of Tober-na-Vuolick*). Clough, who had intended to prepare for the clergy while at Oriel, resigned his fellowship in 1848 after religious introspection led him to reject the dogma of the Church of England.

In 1849 Clough published *Ambarvalia*, a poem written with Thomas Burbridge. Later that same year, after visiting Rome during the French siege of Mazzini's Republic, he composed *Amours de Voyage* (published 1858), a long poem inspired by those experiences. After returning to England at the end of 1849, Clough spent three years as the principal of University Hall, a students' hostel in London. While vacationing in Venice during 1850 he began *Dipsychus* (published posthumously in 1865), a Faustian dialogue set in Venice. In 1852 he resigned as principal of University Hall and sailed for America, where he spent eight months tutoring students and enjoying the friendship of writers such as Emerson, Lowell, Longfellow, and Charles Eliot Norton. Upon returning to England in 1853 Clough became an examiner in the London Education Office. In 1854 he married Blanche Smith, and in 1857 began acting as an editor for Florence Nightingale, his wife's cousin. Clough's health began to fail after he was stricken with scarlet fever in December 1859, and he died in Florence on November 13, 1861, shortly after beginning the partly autobiographical poem *Mari Magnus*. His passing was commemorated by his friend Matthew Arnold in the poem "Thyrsis," published in 1866.

In 1862 appeared *Poems of Arthur Hugh Clough*, edited by Blanche Clough and with a memoir by F. T. Palgrave; this collection contained Clough's two best-known shorter poems, "Say not the struggle nought availeth" and the satirical "The Latest Decalogue." A new edition of Clough's poems (edited by H. F. Lowry, A. L. P. Norrington, and F. L. Milhauser), containing material never before published, appeared in 1951 and helped to revive interest in Clough's verse, which was little read during the first half of the twentieth century.

Personal

Clough came in the afternoon. I like him exceedingly; with his gentleness, and his bewildered look, and his half-closed eyes. —HENRY WADSWORTH LONGFELLOW, *Journal* (Dec. 30, 1852), cited in Samuel Longfellow, *Life of Henry Wadsworth Longfellow*, 1891, Vol. 2, p. 230

⟨. . .⟩ I was glad to see Clough here, with whom I had established some kind of robust working-friendship, & who had some great permanent values for me. Had he not taken me by surprise & fled in a night, I should have done what I could to block his way. I am too sure he will not return. The first months comprise all the shocks of disappointment that are likely to disgust a newcomer. The sphere of opportunities opens slowly, but to a man of his abilities & culture,—rare enough here—with the sureness of chemistry. The giraffe entering Paris wore the label, "Eh bien, messieurs, il n'y a qu'une bete de plus!" And Oxonians are cheap in London; but here, the eternal economy of sending things where they are wanted makes a commanding claim. Do not suffer him to relapse into London. He had made himself already cordially welcome to many good people, & would have soon made his own place. He had just established his valise at my house, & was to come,—the gay deceiver—once a fortnight, for his Sunday; & his individualities & his nationalities are alike valuable to me. I beseech you not to commend his unheroic retreat.—RALPH WALDO EMERSON, Letter to Thomas Carlyle (Aug. 10, 1853)

A man more vivid, ingenious, veracious, mildly radiant, I have seldom met with, and in a character so honest, modest, kindly. I expected very considerable things of him.—THOMAS CARLYLE, Letter to James Anthony Froude (1860), cited in James Anthony Froude, *Thomas Carlyle: A History of His Life in London*, 1884, Vol. 2, p. 207

First of all, you will expect me to say something about poor Clough. That is a loss which I shall feel more and more as time goes on, for he is one of the few people who ever made a deep impression upon me, and as time goes on, and one finds no one else who makes such an impression, one's feeling about those who did make it gets to be something more and more distinct and unique. Besides, the object of it no longer survives to wear it out himself by becoming ordinary and different from what he was. People were beginning to say about Clough that he never would do anything now, and, in short, to pass him over. I foresee that there will now be a change, and attention will be fixed on what there was of extraordinary promise and interest in him when young, and of unique and imposing even as he grew older without fulfilling people's expectations. I have been asked to write a Memoir of him for the *Daily News*, but that I cannot do. I could not write about him in a newspaper now, nor can, I think, at length in a review, but I shall some day in some way or other relieve myself of what I think about him.—MATTHEW ARNOLD, Letter to His Mother (Nov. 20, 1861)

It irk'd him to be here, he could not rest.
He loved each simple joy the country yields,
He loved his mates; but yet he could not keep,

For that a shadow lour'd on the fields,
　Here with the shepherds and the silly sheep.
　　Some life of men unblest
He knew, which made him droop, and fill'd his head.
　He went; his piping took a troubled sound
　　Of storms that rage outside our happy ground;
He could not wait their passing, he is dead.
　　　　—MATTHEW ARNOLD, "Thyrsis," 1866, ll. 41–50

The memory of Arthur Clough will be safe in the hearts of his friends. Few beyond his friends have known him at all; his writings may not reach beyond a small circle; but those who have received his image into their hearts know that something has been given them which no time can take away, and to them we think no words will seem fitter than those of the poet, happily also his friend, which have cherished the memory of another beautiful soul:—

　　So, dearest, now thy brows are cold,
　　　We see thee as thou art, and know
　　　Thy likeness to the wise below,
　Thy kindred with the great of old.
　　　　—BLANCHE CLOUGH, "Life of Arthur Hugh
　　　　Clough," *Prose Remains of Arthur Hugh
　　　　Clough*, 1869, p. 56

　　　And he our passing guest,
Shy nature, too, and stung with life's unrest,
Whom we too briefly had but could not hold,
Who brought ripe Oxford's culture to our board,
　　The Past's incalculable hoard,
Mellowed by scutcheoned panes in cloisters old,
Seclusions ivy-hushed, and pavements sweet
With immemorial lisp of musing feet;
Young head time-tonsured smoother than a friar's,
Boy face, but grave with answerless desires,
Poet in all that poets have of best,
But foiled with riddles dark and cloudy aims,
　　Who now hath found sure rest,
Not by still Isis or historic Thames,
Nor by the Charles he tried to love with me,
But, not misplaced, by Arno's hallowed brim,
Nor scorned by Santa Croce's neighboring frames,
　　Haply not mindless, wheresoe'er he be,
Of violets that to-day I scattered over him;
　　　　—JAMES RUSSELL LOWELL, *Agassiz*, 1874

Apart from the gifts of imagination and mental analysis, Clough was of a noble, pure, and self-controlling nature. His friends felt certain that the temptations to excess which assail young men, at Universities and elsewhere, had by him been resolutely and victoriously resisted. His clear black eyes, under a broad, full, and lofty forehead, were often partly closed, as if through the pressure of thought; but when the problem occupying him was solved, a glorious flash would break from the eyes, expressive of an inner joy and sudden illumination, which fascinated any who were present. For though his sense of humour was keen, the spirit of satire was absent; benevolence in his kindly heart never finding a difficulty in quelling ill-nature. It will be said that there are many satirical strokes in *Dipsychus*, and this is true; but they are aimed at classes—their follies and hypocrisies—never at any individual, except himself. His mouth was beautifully formed, but both it and the chin were characterised by some lack of determination and firmness. This deficiency, however, so far as it existed, was harmful only to himself; those who sought his counsel or help found in him the wisest of advisers, the steadiest and kindest of friends.—THOMAS ARNOLD, "Arthur Hugh Clough," *Nineteenth Century*, Jan. 1898, pp. 105–6

In appearance I thought him rather striking. He was tall, tending a little to stoutness, with a beautifully ruddy complexion and dark eyes which twinkled with suppressed humor. His sweet, cheery manner at once attracted my young children to him, and I was amused, on passing near the open door of his room, to see him engaged in conversation with my little son, then some five or six years of age.—JULIA WARD HOWE, *Reminiscences, 1819–1899*, 1899, p. 185

General

⟨. . .⟩ I write to you now merely to thank you for having given me a great and unexpected pleasure, by leaving with me *The Bothie of Tober-na-Vuolich*, which Mrs. Arnold, too, had recommended me to read. I was very unwilling to commence it, for I detest English hexameters, from Surrey's to Southey's; and Mr. Clough's spondaic lines are, to my ear, detestable too—that is to begin with. Yet I am really charmed with his poem. There is a great deal of mere prose in it, and the worse, to my taste, for being prose upon stilts; but, take it for all in all, there is more freshness of heart and soul and sense in it than it has been my chance to find and feel in any poem of recent date—perhaps I ought to say than in any recent poem of which the author is not yet much known; for I have no mind to depreciate Alfred Tennyson, nor any other man who has fairly won his laurel.—EDWARD QUILLINAN, Letter to Henry Crabb Robinson (Jan. 12, 1849), cited in *Diary, Reminiscences, and Correspondence of Henry Crabb Robinson*, ed. Thomas Sadler, 1872, Vol. 2, p. 303

Why did you not send me word of Clough's hexameter poem ⟨*Bothie of Toper-na-fuosich*⟩, which I have now received and read with much joy. But no, you will never forgive him his metres. He is a stout, solid, reliable man and friend,—I knew well; but this fine poem has taken me by surprise. I cannot find that your journals have yet discovered its existence.—RALPH WALDO EMERSON, Letter to Thomas Carlyle (Jan. 23, 1849)

His *Bothie* is a rare and original poem, quite Homeric in treatment and modern to the full in spirit. I do not know a poem more impregnated with the nineteenth century or fuller of tender force and shy, delicate humor. Is it within the possibilities of human nature that I like it all the better, and feel more inclined to stand by it, because it was unsuccessful? At any rate, I formed my opinion of it when I did not know whether it were popular or not.—JAMES RUSSELL LOWELL, Letter to C. F. Briggs (June 10, 1853)

Most of you, probably, have some knowledge of a poem by Mr. Clough, *The Bothie of Toper-na-fuosich*, a long-vacation pastoral, in hexameters. The general merits of that poem I am not going to discuss: it is a serio-comic poem, and, therefore, of essentially different nature from the *Iliad*. Still in two things it is, more than any other English poem which I can call to mind, like the *Iliad*: in the rapidity of its movement, and the plainness and directness of its style. The thought in this poem is often curious and subtle, and that is not Homeric; the diction is often grotesque, and that is not Homeric. Still, by its rapidity of movement, and plain and direct manner of presenting the thought however curious in itself, this poem, which, being as I say a serio-comic poem, has a right to be grotesque, is grotesque *truly*, not, like Mr. Newman's version of the *Iliad*, *falsely*. Mr. Clough's odd epithets, 'The grave man nicknamed Adam,' 'The hairy Aldrich,' and so on, grow vitally and appear naturally in their place; while Mr. Newman's 'dapper-greaved Achaians,' and 'motley-helmed Hector,' have all the air of being mechanically elaborated and artificially stuck in. Mr.

Clough's hexameters are excessively, needlessly rough; still, owing to the native rapidity of this measure, and to the directness of style which so well allies itself with it, his composition produces a sense in the reader which Homer's composition also produces, and which Homer's translator ought to reproduce,—the sense of having, within short limits of time, a large portion of human life presented to him, instead of a small portion.

Mr. Clough's hexameters are, as I have just said, too rough and irregular; and indeed a good model, on any considerable scale, of this metre, the English translator will nowhere find. He must not follow the model offered by Mr. Longfellow in his pleasing and popular poem of *Evangeline*; for the merit of the manner and movement of *Evangeline*, when they are at their best, is to be tenderly elegant; and their fault, when they are at their worst, is to be lumbering; but Homer's defect is not lumberingness, neither is tender elegance his excellence. The lumbering effect of most English hexameters is caused by their being much too dactylic; the translator must learn to use spondees freely. Mr. Clough has done this, but he has not sufficiently observed another rule which the translator cannot follow too strictly; and that is, to have no lines which will not, as it is familiarly said, *read themselves.*
—MATTHEW ARNOLD, *On Translating Homer*, 1861

He, too, was busy with Homer; but it is not on that account that I now speak of him. Nor do I speak of him in order to call attention to his qualities and powers in general, admirable as these were. I mention him because, in so eminent a degree, he possessed these two invaluable literary qualities,—a true sense for his object of study, and a single-hearted care for it. He had both; but he had the second even more eminently than the first. He greatly developed the first through means of the second. In the study of art, poetry, or philosophy, he had the most undivided and disinterested love for his object in itself, the greatest aversion to mixing up with it anything accidental or personal. His interest was in literature itself; and it was this which gave so rare a stamp to his character, which kept him so free from all taint of littleness. In the saturnalia of ignoble personal passions, of which the struggle for literary success, in old and crowded communities, offers so sad a spectacle, he never mingled. He had not yet traduced his friends, nor flattered his enemies, nor disparaged what he admired, nor praised what he despised. Those who knew him well had the conviction that, even with time, these literary arts would never be his. His poem, of which I before spoke, has some admirable Homeric qualities;—out-of-doors freshness, life, naturalness, buoyant rapidity. Some of the expressions in that poem,— '*Dangerous Corrievreckan . . . Where roads are unknown to Loch Nevish,*'—come back now to my ear with the true Homeric ring. But that in him of which I think oftenest is the Homeric simplicity of his literary life.—MATTHEW ARNOLD, *On Translating Homer: Last Words*, 1862

The remarkable poem ⟨*Bothie of Toper-na-fuosich*⟩, published by Clough, as if his farewell to the University, in the autumn of 1848, might be said to close the first period of his life, and to sum up the features in his character hitherto indicated:—the deep interest in that ancient literature which, more than anywhere else, survives in Oxford; the deep sympathy with those who live by the labours we too slightingly call mechanical, and with minds which owe more to nature than to society or study; the delight in friendship and in solitude; the love of wild wandering, and intense—not appreciation of, say rather 'acceptance in,' the natural landscape, in which Arthur Clough, more than any man known to the writer, seemed to

have inherited a double portion of the spirit of William Wordsworth. With the great early works of that glorious poet, to whom, beyond all others of this century, Clough looked up as a teacher, it would be childish to compare his own imperfect art; yet it will be felt by those who know the *Bothie of Toper-na-fuosich*, that we have here a stronger grasp of feeling, a simpler and less self-conscious apprehension of the primal sympathies of humanity, a more personal and passionate sense of 'the mystery of all this unintelligible world;' and all blended with a spirit of humour and genial life, which finds little expression in Wordsworth's poetry. Nor would qualities less rare and sterling than these have reconciled readers to the uncouth verse, the inequality and unfinish of the poem, to the many more questions raised than answered, to the minute local touches, which make this truly a 'Long Vacation Pastoral;' to what, in one word, we may call the intense Oxonianism in style and thought. Another characteristic of the writer appears in the curious political reflections which the events of 1848 cast over the story, as the 'Tityrus' and the 'Pollio' of Virgil are coloured by the war-scathed aspect of Italy, and the religious unrest of the Augustan age. But to compare this Pastoral with the Latin, even by suggestion, would be incorrect; for Clough's work, in tone, more resembles the great masters of simplicity and majesty to whom he always turned with increasing reverence—Homer, or Sophocles, or Milton, or that earlier Englishman who in the *Tales* renewed, or seemed to renew, the very genius of the *Odyssey*. Nor, however vast the difference in realized poetry, is his poem unworthy these splendid models. A sense of fresh, healthy manliness; a scorn of base and selfish motives; a beauty and tenderness of nature; a frank acceptance of common life; a love of earth, not 'only for its earthly sake,' but for the divine and the eternal interfused in it—such, and other such, are the impressions left. These noble qualities are rare in any literature; they have a charm so great that, like Beauty before the Areopagus, they almost disarm the judgment. Viewed in that aspect, Clough's work is wanting in art; the language and the thought are often unequal and incomplete; the poetical fusion into a harmonious whole, imperfect. Here, and in his other writings, one feels a doubt whether in verse he chose the right vehicle, the truly natural mode of utterance. His poetry, in a word, belongs to that uncommon class in which the matter everywhere far outruns the workmanship.

Such writing, it might be thought, from its merits equally with its faults, addresses itself to no numerous audience; yet the *Bothie* was quickly known and valued; and as a true man, from whom much might be hoped, the author was henceforth spoken of, not only in the sphere of friendship and of Oxford, but in many places where the life around them, from different circumstances, rendered men sensitive to his tone of thought:—in Northern England especially, in America, and in those wide regions overseas to which Englishmen have carried endurance of toil and energy of intellect. It is not an autobiography in disguise; but it will readily be felt that so honest a nature could not do otherwise than utter itself in its work. And truly much of Clough is there, and better than any friend could describe him—in the Tutor, in Lindsay, in Hobbes, in the athletic delights of Arthur, in the reveries, equally poetical and practical, of the democratic hero. He is there, too, in that strangely blended passion, so ideal and so sensuous at once, I know not whether homelier or holier, with which girlhood and womanhood are often glorified by those who have 'passed by the ambush of young days' with unstained purity. And Clough is there, lastly, to turn to characteristics more distinctively mental, in a certain caprice or over-fantasy of taste, in a subtle and far-fetched mode of reasoning which returns to plain conclusions through almost paradoxical premises, in a singular toleration and largeness towards views opposed to his own; it may be added, in an honesty of mind which confesses itself not only perplexed with the 'riddle of the universe,' but indignant at those complacent explanations which those who proclaim it insoluble enforce on all comers.—FRANCIS TURNER PALGRAVE, "Arthur Hugh Clough," *Fraser's Magazine*, April 1862, pp. 529–30

As a man, he was doubtless loveable and loved; as a writer, he can claim but a very modest place. He was thoughtful and cultivated, and all thoughtful, cultivated minds will recognize this in his poems. They will also recognize a sincere and sensitive nature, shrinking from the rough and ready acquiescences of conventional beliefs, and withdrawing from the conflicts of life, conscious of being unfitted for them. But as to poetry, there is little or none. ⟨. . .⟩

We shall have misled the reader if he have understood us to say that this volume is only interesting as an example of the actual work achieved by a man who greatly impressed his friends. It is interesting, though less so, for its own sake. The verses are not good, but they are far from commonplace. They express real thoughts and real feelings, and in the *Bothie of Tober na Vuolich* there is considerable promise; for, in spite of its being exclusively a bit of Oxford-student life, in spite of its intentional imitations of Homer and Goethe, and its classical allusions, there is enough humour and fancy, and enough originality, to make it popular in a wider circle, and suggest that the writer, in ripening years, might have produced a remarkable work in prose. His later writings, however, are inferior to it.—GEORGE HENRY LEWES, "Our Survey of Literature, Science, and Art," *Cornhill Magazine*, Sept. 1862, pp. 399–400

This almost morbid craving for a firm base on the absolute realities of life was very wearying to a mind so self-conscious as Clough's, and tended to paralyse the expression of a certainly great genius. As a rule, his lyrical poems fall short of complete success in delineating the mood which they are really meant to delineate, owing to this chronic state of introspective criticism on himself in which he is apt to write, and which, characteristic as it is, necessarily diminishes the linearity and directness of the feeling expressed, refracting it, as it were, through media of very variable density. As he himself,—no doubt in this stanza delineating himself,—says of one of his heroes in "The Clergyman's first tale":—

> With all his eager motions still there went
> A self-correcting and ascetic bent,
> That from the obvious good still led astray,
> And set him travelling on the longest way.

And in the same poem there are descriptive touches which very skilfully portray the nature of those dispersive influences, as I may call them, in his character, which, while they may injure his lyrical, add a great wealth of criticism to his speculative and disquisitional poems:—

> Beside the wishing-gate, which so they name
> 'Mid Northern hills, to me this fancy came;
> A wish I formed, my wish I thus expressed:
> 'Would I could wish my wishes all to rest,
> And know to wish the wish that were the best!
> Oh, for some winnowing wind to th' empty air
> This chaff of easy sympathies to bear
> Far off, and leave me of myself aware!'

That is clearly self-portraiture, and it describes an element in Clough's nature which, no doubt, contributed greatly to

diminish the number of his few but exquisite lyrical poems, and sometimes to confine even those to the delineation of feelings of a certain vagueness of drift. Yet there was, besides this most subtle and almost over-perfect intellectual culture in Clough, much of a boyish, half-formed nature in him, even to the last; and this, when fully roused, contributed a great deal of the animation, and, when least roused, contributed not a little of the embarrassed, shy, half-articulate tone to some of the most critical passages of his finest poems. He describes this side of boyish feeling admirably in one of his *In Mari Magno* tales:—

> How ill our boyhood understands
> Incipient manhood's strong demands!
> Boys have such trouble of their own
> As none, they fancy, e'er have known,
> Such as to speak of, or to tell
> They hold were unendurable:
> Religious, social, of all kinds,
> That tear and agitate their minds.
> A thousand thoughts within me stirred
> Of which I could not speak a word;
> Strange efforts after something new
> Which I was wretched not to do;
> Passions, ambitions, lay and lurked,
> Wants, counter-wants, obscurely worked
> Without their names, and unexplained.

And even in his latest and most finished poems you see the traces of this half-developed element of Clough's massive and rich but to some extent inert imagination; and you see, too, how powerfully it operated to discontent him with his own productions, to make him underrate vastly their real worth. Rapidly as his genius ripened at an age when, with most men, the first flush of it would have passed over, there was something of conscious inertia, not unlike immaturity, in it to the last, which gives a tone of proud hesitation, a slowness of hand, to the literary style of his finest poems. He calls himself, in his "Long Vacation Pastoral," "the grave man, nicknamed Adam," and there is really something of the flavour of primeval earth, of its unready vigour and crude laboriousness, about his literary nature. Even when he succeeds best, the reader seems to see him 'wipe his honourable brows bedewed with toil." And yet he is impatient with himself for not succeeding better, and despises his own work.—RICHARD HOLT HUTTON, "Arthur Hugh Clough" (1869), *Literary Essays*, 1871, pp. 288–90

The intellectual element of Clough's nature was eventually dominant in all divided counsels, and was the ultimate arbiter in all the casuistries of the heart. But there can be no greater mistake than to fail to recognise the vigour and strength of his feelings. Thoughtless readers, contrasting him with poets who delight to exhibit their passion uncontrolled, will be sure to underrate the power and depth of the emotion which at times we see tiding up and filling to the full every reach of his heart. Clough's is essentially a *strong* character, but strong with the strength of two contending lines of force, limiting and counteracting one another. He feels strongly, but he *knows* as well as feels. And his powerful mind never for a moment loses its grasp of intellectual convictions. One of the highest triumphs of his skill is the manner, exquisitely truthful, in which he portrays the strong strugglings of the heart as circumscribed and restrained by the bonds of mental foresight. It may seem, indeed, a ruthless thing when the whole soul is moving onward, under the force of a simple and beautiful impulse, to take young love and scrutinize it, and look close into its face.

And Clough felt the sacredness of all noble feelings, but truth too was sacred for him.

At this point in our criticism we may notice the fact, that no poet of this century who can justly claim so high a place in literature is so little possessed by *the appetite for beauty*, which is in general a leading note of the poetic temperament. He has a free, spontaneous, healthy enjoyment in external nature, but he is never forced away from thought, or from human interests, to feed upon beauty, and fill himself with its pleasures. His intercourse with nature, when it came, was an exhilarating delight, as of sunshine and fresh breezes; not a brooding lust, as for Keats; not a supersensuous, spiritual communion, as with Shelley; not, as with Wordsworth, a perpetual close friendship, with its most sweet confidences. The joys and sorrows of men possessed for him an overmastering attraction, with which nothing else could compete. He tells himself that he could not sympathize with Wordsworth's repeated poems to the daisy, that he recoiled from the statement that—

> To me the meanest flower that blows doth give
> Thoughts that do often lie too deep for tears.

Without stopping here to point out the injustice done to Wordsworth in suggesting a want on his part of sympathy with human nature, it is quite certain that, after a different sort, Clough was possessed by "the enthusiasm of humanity" as by a fierce passion. Sincere as he was in his appreciation of the pure, elevated calm of Wordsworth's philosophy, and in his admiration of its chief doctrine of self-supervision, Clough's nature was too robust and its fibre tingling with too vigorous a life to allow him to sit long listening to the piping of the linnet, or resting in contemplation of daisies or celandines.

Of course we find in Clough's poems several clever descriptions of natural scenery; but incomparably the best are those, like some in the "Bothie," which smack of the keen relish of the enjoyment imparted by mere healthy physical life, and glow with the brightness of high spirits. The bathing-place, for instance, by the falls of the Highland river, "where over a ledge of granite, into a granite bason, the amber torrent descended," would lose much of its charm were it not for the shock of the delicious plunge which we enjoy as much as "the glory of headers" himself.

> On the ledge, bare-limbed, an Apollo,
>   down gazing,
> Eying one moment the beauty, the life, ere he flung
>   himself in it;
> Eying through eddying green waters the green-tinting
>   floor underneath them;
> Eying the bead on the surface, the bead, like a cloud,
>   rising to it;
> Drinking in, deep in his soul, the beautiful hue and
>   the clearness,—
> Arthur, the shapely, the brave, the unboasting, the
>   glory of headers.

And we ourselves are ready to shriek and to shout in the mere joy of living, as

> There, overbold, great Hobbes from a ten-foot height
>   descended,
> Prone, as a quadruped, prone with hands and feet
>   protending;
> There in the sparkling champagne, ecstatic, they
>   shrieked and shouted.

Clough explicitly sets forth in one place,—with his own acceptance of the principle,—that the object which the phenomena of the external world were made to fulfil by the older and greater poets was to supply analogies and similitudes of the phenomena of human nature. It is for such a purpose he draws the fine picture of the flow and ebb of the strong tide in the narrow loch of the western Highlands; or, with a few facile touches, shows us Claude, in *Amours de Voyage*,

> Standing, uplifted, alone, on the heaving poop of the
>   vessel,
> Looking around on the waste of the rushing incuri-
>   ous billows.

A higher glow of enthusiasm spreads over the passage in *Dipsychus* (Scene II.), commencing—

> Clear stars above, thou roseate westward sky,—

but what we observe as noteworthy is the absence on the whole, not the presence, of a feeling for external nature, at least as shown in its more sensitive forms.

Here too we may observe that, in artistic execution, Clough cannot occupy a high place among English poets. He was too full, and too eager to give expression to all he had to say, to be very careful about the manner in which it was effected, so only he did effect his end. Nor did he belong to that highest order of poetic minds with whom expression is part of thought, inseparable from it, its vital body,—not a garment fitted to it with a measuring-rod. Seldom can we gather from Clough, as we do from the greater poets, a haunting phrase of melodious words, or a memorable sentence, or a thought compacted and close-wrought, that will break off, crystal-like, complete in its own brightness and beauty. There is little of that delicate fastidiousness of form and of diction that marks the poems of Mr. Matthew Arnold, who, in other points, sometimes reminds us of him; and there is a carelessness about the musical modulation of many of his verses, which we feel to be the less excusable when we perceive the fine ear for harmony betrayed in some of his lines.—JOHN DOWDEN, "Arthur Hugh Clough," *Contemporary Review*, Dec. 1869, pp. 522–24

There is no weakness in his longer poems. The *Bothie of Tober-na-Vuolich*, which was the first of these to appear, is an idyl of country-life, as fresh as a breeze in summer, into which is woven a social problem of love-making such as Clough was fond of introducing into his more ambitious poems. With even its decided merits, it is less characteristic of the author than one piece written in the succeeding year, 1849, which first saw light, nine years later, in the earliest pages of *The Atlantic*. The poem we mean is the *Amours de Voyage*. In it, we find drawn with great comprehension a character such as Clough imagined might well be the result of the uncertainty, self-questioning, and wondering indecision consequent on the inactivity of æsthetic enjoyment. The poet saw the danger of our delicate civilization, and in the hero of the *Amours de Voyage*, who certainly is not the usual hero of poetry or of fiction, he draws a very delightful man, cultivated and accomplished, who lacks the energy and enthusiasm requisite for the most urgent of the practical affairs of life, for certainly choice in marriage deserves to be included in this category, at least for the purposes of the writer of novels or poems. In Rome he meets and falls in love with a young girl, sensible and refined, but with a much truer knowledge of the world than that which he possesses. The story is told in a series of letters, in which the hero, Claude, portrays himself at great length as a halting, hesitating creature, looking at both sides of a question and weighing every argument, capable, to be sure, of falling in love with the girl, but meanwhile doubting, as the motto prefixed to the poem says, about love. In short, Clough drew here a picture of one of the dangers of the present day, as truly as Goethe, in his *Sorrows of Werther*, represented one of the follies of his time. To us there is something bordering on the old-fashioned in *Werther*. We read it without being moved to suicide, just as we are able to see Jack Sheppard without taking to the road for a livelihood. But in its day it was a most fatal story. It described what was at the time a common disease, and thereby helped to spread it among its readers, who caught the infection from its pages and suffered like pangs, just as beginners in the study of medicine imagine themselves the prey of every new ailment they come across in their text-books. *Werther* is the greater book because it describes what has been a more widely-spread evil, and because its passionate outbursts take stronger hold of the reader's imagination than do Claude's tepid self-communings. Then the tragic ending of *Werther* outweighs the uneventful termination of the *Amours de Voyage*, if not in truth, at least in dramatic effect. A conclusion of this sort to the poem would have been impossible; the hero, who, as it was, had self-conscious trepidation about the part he was playing in the comedy, would have shrunk from a tragedy as from the most violent breach of decorum. The whole portrayal of Claude's state of mind deserves great praise. Clough very wisely chose for a background to the unenergetic hesitation of his hero's mind the futile activity of the struggle of the Roman republicans against the French in 1849. To tell the story of the poem over again in prose, or by means of brief extracts, would be treating it with but little justice. It may be fairer simply to call the reader's attention to certain passages, as, for instance, to the naturalness with which the brief spasm of energy is introduced into Claude's mind by the consciousness of his folly in letting happiness, or rather the chance of it, slip from between his fingers. His ineffectual efforts to find the heroine, after she had left Rome, are soon followed by a resignation which is in some measure the result of doubt about the reality of the feeling which is urging him on. For a time he had acted instinctively, without analyzing his emotions; but his habits are too strong, and he soon relapses into pondering about the good of everything except his usual uncertain state of mind. What is pathetic in the poem is not his suffering, which is so speedily consoled by reflection, but, rather, the gently indicated disappointment of the heroine, who sees very clearly, being unaccustomed to the sophistication of clever selfishness, how benumbing is the web which the hero spins about himself. In comparison with her straightfowardness his vexatious hair-splitting, which is nowhere exaggerated, stands out in its proper light. It is nowhere contemptible, otherwise she could not have been willing to love him, but it is truly pitiable. With him it is not a crime, it is a disease, and it is a form of disease which is known to those who complacently suffer from it as the spirit of the nineteenth century; for the self-consciousness of the age has reached the height of recognizing and naming its own spirit in this fashion, and of calling a man who represents that spirit a representative man of the nineteenth century. This is a habit which was unknown to those who lived in other centuries. The flattering model of characters like these is Hamlet. Nowhere in literature is there to be found a better picture of a man of this sort than in the *Amours de Voyage*, and hence it is that Clough so well deserves the credit of having understood and drawn one of the people of his time. It is not in this study of character alone that he has been successful. There is a charm in his verses which is very noteworthy. The poem itself, like the *Bothie of Tober-na-Vuolich*, is written in hexameters. In the hands of a master like Clough this metre shows itself adapted to the practical purpose of telling the story in an impressive and artistic way, while at the same time it shows great fitness for poetical expression.—T. S. PERRY, "Arthur Hugh Clough," *Atlantic*, Oct. 1875, pp. 413–15

There was nothing second-rate in his nature, and his *Bothie of Tober-na-Vuolich*, which bears the reader along less easily than the billowy hexameters of Kingsley, is charmingly faithful to its Highland theme, and has a Doric simplicty and strength. His shorter pieces are uneven in merit, but all suggestive and worth a thinker's attention. If he could have remained in the liberal American atmosphere, and have been spared his untimely taking-off, he might have come to greatness; but he is now no more, and with him departed a radical thinker and a living protest against the truckling expedients of the mode.—EDMUND CLARENCE STEDMAN, *Victorian Poets*, 1875, p. 244

Yet in stating that Clough's 'interest was in literature itself,' one would fain observe that this interest in literature was subordinate to the higher, holier interest which he took in the pursuit of truth, and more especially of religious truth. Towards science and the facts which scientific research is slowly but surely adding to the storehouse of human knowledge, he had not so strong, so enthusiastic an inclination. Indeed, it might almost be said that the development of his intellectual nature in this respect was somewhat defective, were it not that the tendency of his mind to seek above all things accuracy and exactness, is especially in unison with the teaching of modern science.

This tendency in Clough was, however, chiefly exhibited, first, in endeavouring to solve the complex problems of the universe, and secondly, in his attempt to find a firm and satisfactory basis for that higher spirituality which shall, in practical everyday life, blossom into noble action. As regards the first of these, it may be that Clough completely failed in his endeavours, but who, after all, is prepared to say that he did?— It may be that, like Goethe, his position was on the borderlands that lie between dogma and denial, and that the lines which Faust addresses to Margaret most adequately express his views, the lines—

> Him who dare name?
> Or who proclaim,
> Him I believe?
> Who feel,
> Yet steel
> Himself to say; Him I do not believe.

But, after all, it does not indeed very much matter whether Clough succeeded or not, so long as he was possessed of what is far more precious than truth itself, namely, the love of truth, and the earnest desire to seek after, and if possible, to obtain it.—SAMUEL WADDINGTON, *Arthur Hugh Clough: A Monograph*, 1882, pp. 322–23

Literary history wlll hardly care to remember or to register the fact that there was a bad poet named Clough, whom his friends found it useless to puff: for the public, if dull, has not quite such a skull as belongs to believers in Clough.—ALGERNON CHARLES SWINBURNE, "Social Verse," *Forum*, Oct. 1891, p. 182

The literary reputation of Arthur Hugh Clough has been largely posthumous. The man himself was known to few outside the circumference of a small private circle, and beyond that circle the few books of verse which he published during his lifetime had little vogue or influence. It was the publication in the year 1863 of the small volume of *Poems*, with a brief introductory memoir by Mr. Francis Turner Palgrave, which first roused the interest of a larger public, such interest being widened and intensified by the subsequent appearance of a complete collection of Clough's work in prose and verse, and of a fuller biographical record edited by the poet's wife. Clough's poetry never has been, and is never likely to be, popular in the ordinary sense of that word; but during the past quarter of a century it has possessed—and, in all probability, will long continue to possess—a peculiar and, in its way, unique fascination for an increasingly large class of men and women who feel that Clough speaks to and for them, and in uttering his own thought and emotion gives also expression to theirs. He was a true literary artist, but his art is mainly valuable not for its own sake but for its transparency as a medium of large self-revelation.

⟨. . .⟩ It may be doubted whether any poet of our century has been at once so sensitive as was Clough, to the conflicting spiritual and intellectual influences of his time, and so unsparingly sincere in his record of his own spiritual and intellectual sensations. We have poets of faith and poets of doubt; and by a skilful arrangement of illustrative quotations, it would not be difficult to range Clough in either category, but so to range him would be to give currency to another of the already too numerous half-truths of criticism. He was really the poet of intellectual suspense, of dubitation, of questioning,—of that unstable equilibrium of the spirit with which all who think and who strive to be honest both to themselves and to their thought are so painfully familiar. His questioning of the self was as keen and searching as his questioning of the not-self: he suspected not merely the dogmas presented to him from without, but the very movements of his own mind which prompted him to welcome or to spurn the waiting guests, demanding from them testimonials of honesty such as are, perhaps, hardly procurable. Concerning the very characteristic lines in which he represents himself as

> Seeking in vain in all my store,
> One feeling based on truth,

Mr. R. H. Hutton has the penetratingly truthful remark that Clough "wanted some guarantee for simplicity deeper than simplicity itself"; and this desire—as vain as that of "the moth for the star"—was undoubtedly a defect, but it was the defect of a very noble quality which gives his poetry the power at once to soothe and to illuminate. He would have none of the hypocrisies of faith, but he would also have none of the hypocrisies of scepticism. What a glow of white light is there in words like these:—

> Old things need not be therefore true,
> O brother men, nor yet the new;
> Ah! still awhile the old thought retain,
> And yet consider it again.

He can listen to the two voices of Easter Day with their conflicting messages of death and resurrection, and while neither fails to move him, neither can altogether vanquish him, for he feels he has that in him which responds to the wail as well as to the cry of jubilation. Were this, however, all, those who class Clough among the poets of scepticism, would not be far wrong. As a matter of fact he was saved from the abyss by a faith so sure and steadfast that it might be called his one certainty,—the fixed assurance of a Harmony in which the discords of phenomena find their resolution, in a divine future which lights up the shadows of the human present. After unavailing struggles to grasp the unattainable true, after manly refusal to be contented with the many counterfeits of present certainty, after all his questionings of the why and wherefore of existence he has always the one conclusion:—

> My child, we still must think, when we
> That ampler life together see,
> Some true result will yet appear
> Of what we are together here.

It "will yet appear" because it exists now, and exists for the sake of revelation to those who are faithful through the darkness.

> The Summum Pulchrum rests in heaven above;
> Do thou, as best thou may'st, thy duty do:
> Amid the things allowed thee live and love;
> Some day thou shalt it view.

In an unavoidably brief survey of Clough's poetical demesne, there must needs be a measure of inadequacy; but an estimate howsoever brief, which left the impression of a subjective brooding poet, spinning cobwebs of metaphysics and spiritual psychology, would be not merely inadequate but misleading. Those who love Clough best because they know him best, are those who find the keenest delight in such a poem as *The Bothie of Tober-na-Vuolich*, or in some of the tales in *Mari Magno*, which are so simply objective, as free from haunting self-consciousness, as is anything in Homer or Chaucer or Crabbe,—poems which tell not of curious questionings, but of the glory of sunshine and fresh air, of the swirl of water in the brook, and the bloom of heather on the moor, of simple, unthinking human delight and love. Clough not only thought but lived; he was a full-blooded man as well as an eager questioner; and it may be that his questions and his answers come home to us the more intimately, because they had behind them not a mere brain, but a healthy and harmoniously developed human nature.—JAMES ASHCROFT NOBLE, "Arthur Hugh Clough," *The Poets and the Poetry of the Century*, ed. Alfred H. Miles, 1894, Vol. 4, pp. 645–52

⟨. . .⟩ among poets, the truest brother in spirit to Arnold is Arthur Hugh Clough. Close friends and companions, the two were in boyhood and early manhood subjected to the same training and influences at Rugby and Oxford. In Clough, as in his friend, the flood of scientific skepticism rushed mercilessly over the ardent religious instincts developed by education. They were both sons of the early Victorian age, when social consciousness had not yet become dominant over the individualism even of the inner life; yet both reacted with vigor and sorrow against the outward materialism of the times. Neither could find a home in the accepted Christian tradition. Poets of the intellectual emotions, the character in each was—shall we say too weak, or too evenly balanced?—to yield itself unfalteringly to any influence, and clearness of vision ended in feebleness of will. Clough, like Arnold, drifted, swayed by the ebb and flow of opposing currents; his poetry also gains its special and intimate power from its revelation of the agony of the spirit; and he, too, succumbed to the disease of inaction, and allowed his poetic impulse to be sterilized by the surrounding chill.

Yet to the close observer, there is a searching difference in the temper of the two men. Far less polished than Arnold's, Clough's poetry yet shows in some respects a freer and broader power. His outlook on modern society is more manly, as more specific in severity; and his pungent gift of mockery is foreign to Arnold's pensive grace and musical despair. But the spiritual attitude of the two is wider apart than their artistic or social temper. We read Arnold's laments over the past, his intense longing for steadfastness and peace, and the conviction grows upon us that his keenest regret is not faith but assurance, less the truth which the world has forfeited than the tranquillity which the truth produced. He craves with an almost querulous desire the unquestioning and serene spirit, which has fled never to return. Passing to the pages of his friend, we find pain of a different order—the agonized desire for a faith that is lost, and for a distant God. Tranquillity is the supreme end of

Arnold's ambition; the Truth alone could satisfy the soul of Clough.

> Resolve to be thyself: and know that he
> Who finds himself loses his misery,

is Arnold's supreme wisdom. Clough reverses the cry. Let sorrow be his heritage, if only God endure:—

> It fortifies my soul to know
> That though I perish, Truth is so.
> That howsoe'er I stray and range,
> Where'er I go, Thou dost not change.
> I steadier step when I recall
> That if I slip, Thou dost not fall.

This is the message not of self-dependence, but of self-abnegation. Intellectually agnostic as Arnold, the poetry of Clough marks a new spiritual stage. Out of the very heart of doubt and self-despair he wrests a religious fervor as deep and reverent, one is almost tempted to say, as that of Thomas à Kempis or Dante.

⟨. . .⟩ Like Arnold, Clough never denies that if religious certainty is over, the joy and freedom of life are gone; unlike Arnold he escapes from knowledge of self to hope of God. Arnold's tranquillity, if attained, would shut away forever all hope of spiritual insight; for so long as the soul suspects the existence of an absolute verity, it may know faith and pain and hope and woe, but it can never know quiescence. His ideal brings to the soul at best the serene and barren calm of subservience to natural law. Better than this the despairing self-abnegation of Clough, the dim hope that there is a Truth though we never attain it, a God though we never find Him. Clough's poetry marks the furthest reach of the devout spirit consistent with entire agnosticism of thought.—VIDA D. SCUDDER, *The Life of the Spirit in the Modern English Poets*, 1895, pp. 265–68

His earliest and most popular considerable work, *The Bothie of Tober-na-Vuolich* (the title of which was originally rather different), is written in hexameters which do not, like Kingsley's, escape the curse of that "pestilent heresy"; and the later *Amours de Voyage* and *Dipsychus*, though there are fine passages in both, bring him very close to the Spasmodic school, of which in fact he was an unattached and more cultivated member, with fancies directed rather to religiousity than to strict literature. *Ambarvalia* had preceded the *Bothie*, and other things followed. On the whole, Clough is one of the most unsatisfactory products of that well-known form of nineteenth century scepticism which has neither the strength to believe nor the courage to disbelieve "and have done with it." He hankers and looks back, his "two souls" are always warring with each other, and though the clash and conflict sometimes bring out fine things (as in the two pieces above cited and the still finer poem at Naples with the refrain "Christ is not risen"), though his "Latest Decalogue" has satirical merit, and some of his country poems, written without undercurrent of thought, are fresh and genial, he is on the whole a failure. But he is a failure of a considerable poet, and some fragments of success chequer him.—GEORGE SAINTSBURY, *A History of Nineteenth Century Literature*, 1896, pp. 308–9

Arthur Hugh Clough was in no respect a "man of letters." Literature was not his business. It does not fall to the lot of those who may have to deal with his life and his work to be compelled to trace out a perhaps sordid and coarse personality beneath the robes of an almost regal success in the world of letters. There is little that Clough has left us that is not transparent and natural. But within this we find so attractive a personality that we may perhaps be in some danger of exaggerating the merely literary importance of the forms through which that personality expressed itself. We find that personality ever most sensitively alive to everything in nature that is gentle and beautiful, ever tenderly tolerant towards every kind of human defect or shortcoming, but at the same time severely and inexorably just towards itself. It is this mixing of tenderness and severity, coupled as it is with the utmost sensitiveness to every beautiful and ennobling impression, that gives the distinctive charm to one of the very few men of the present century who can claim to be studied, not for what they did, but for what they were. ⟨. . .⟩

There is not much in such a life as this to attract those who regard success as the test of worth. Looked at from an ordinary point of view, Clough's life was essentially unsuccessful. He failed to achieve the distinction that was anticipated for him at Oxford; he threw up, on grounds which not a few regarded as Quixotic, an assured academical position; he accepted and then resigned an uncongenial and unsatisfying task in connection with what must have seemed to him, with his Oxford traditions and culture, a second-rate or third-rate university organization; he crossed the Atlantic and did little save make new friends; he returned to England and put himself into the official mill which claimed his energies until his death; he left no great work behind him, only fragmentary glimpses of a literary power which could not be summoned at will, and which refused to apply itself to subjects which failed to touch his higher and inner nature. Yet, in spite of all this, and perhaps in some considerable degree because of all this, the sweetness, the sincerity, the beauty of his nature enabled him to attract the very best minds of his time, and to set up a standard of living and thinking which, if adopted, would be found capable of regenerating and revivifying human society. In a world saturated with the spirit of competition, it might prove difficult to make generally attractive a life which moved apart from the struggle for material success. Nevertheless, whenever the rage of competition exhausts itself, the figure of this man of unquenchable faith—faith in the essential beneficence of all the facts of the universe—and of external failures will assuredly be found among "the one or two immortal lights" that will rise up into the firmament, "to shine there everlastingly." The man who could hold that

> 'Tis better to have fought and lost
> Than never to have fought at all;

who could rally the faint-hearted with the thought that their individual effort might be all that was needed to gain a victory; who could declare that "it fortified his soul to know that though he perished, Truth was so"; who could deny himself every comfortable belief that seemed touched by doubt, and yet be ever conscious of

> The strong current flowing
> Right onward to the eternal shore;

—such a man as this is one to whom the world may well turn in the doubt and turmoil that will inevitably arise when mere success has become discredited, and when once more the cry goes up, "Who will show us any good?" And then the fact will be realized that Arthur Hugh Clough, though not indeed "a man of letters," was something infinitely greater.—F. REGINALD STATHAM, "Arthur Hugh Clough," *National Review*, April 1897, pp. 201, 211–12

Clough was a modern Hamlet, his world, both outer and inner, out of joint, and he powerless to set it right. Its riddle was a knot that he was too weak to cleave. He stands, like patience on her monument, the witness and the martyr of morals divorced from religion. He is a type of conscience just coming short of Christian faith, or better, of conscience falling away from the faith of youth. He represents, that is, a stage through which almost every acutely conscientious temperament must pass in the process from the unreasoning faith of childhood to the reasoned faith of maturity. He is a relatively perfect type of the undogmatic poetic sceptic.

To understand his peculiar mood, it is necessary constantly to refer to his training at Rugby. It is needless, it would be an impertinence, to extol Dr. Arnold and his educational reformation; one may question whether his moral standard, noble as it essentially was, was not too exacting, too Quixotically ideal, for ordinary boy-nature; whether it did not tend to induce, in the finer, more serious spirits, an excessive scrupulousness, a self-conscious virtue, a self-questioning, introspective habit, analysis of motives, and critical morality that hindered healthy, instinctive action. This moral frame is certainly mirrored to the life in Clough's verse. He left Rugby with a conscience morbidly tender, and the oppositions of opinion he encountered at Oxford deprived him of what his state of mind imperatively demanded—definite religious conviction. So he became, pre-eminently, the poet of Doubt. —GREENOUGH WHITE, "Character of A. H. Clough as Revealed in His Poems," *Matthew Arnold and the Spirit of the Age*, 1898, pp. 9–10

Clough had thrown the first freshness of his genius into his best-known tales, the *Bothie* and *Amours de Voyage*—modern idylls, in which the perplexed spirit of the fifties breathes a grave undertone through the amenities of Long Vacation Oxford, or is sharply set off against the gay insouciance of the well-to-do bourgeois travellers. To Goethe's *Hermann und Dorothea*, the first and greatest example of the purely modern idyll, Clough (like Longfellow in *Evangeline*) plainly owed his poetic realism as well as his accentual hexameters; outdaring in both respects 'daring Germany' herself. Goethe's realism affected Clough somewhat as Chaucer's colloquialism had affected Hunt; both felt themselves emancipated by a classic and authoritative example from the bondage of a literary tradition; and both played fantastic tricks in the ardour of recovered liberty. Clough's work is controlled by no prevailing sense of beauty, like Goethe's; he has moments of greatness, and may perhaps still claim to have written three or four of the finest English hexameters; but it is almost as certain that he has to answer for a hundred or more of the worst. In the closing year of his life Clough applied the frank modernity of tone and topic which he had learnt from Goethe to the dramatic scheme of Chaucer. The *Mari Magno* is founded upon a pilgrimage of to-day,—the deck of an Atlantic liner for the Canterbury highway, and the great Republic, big with the destinies of the future, for the gray old medieval shrine. The enforced leisure of a voyage makes the high seas a natural framework for tales. Three centuries before Clough, Cinthio had made the tellers of his *Hecatommithi* fugitives on shipboard from the sack of Rome. So the Elizabethan *Westward for Smelts* already mentioned. But the pilgrims are very slightly drawn. Clough is interested in his speakers only as types of different ways of regarding the particular social problem which all their stories illustrate.—C. H. HERFORD, "Introduction" to *English Tales in Verse*, 1902, pp. liv–lv

---

WALTER BAGEHOT
From "Mr. Clough's Poems" (1862)
Collected Works, ed. Norman St. John-Stevas
1965, Volume 2, pp. 241–60

If we did not believe that Mr. Clough's poems, or at least several of them, had real merit, not as promissory germs, but as completed performances, it would not seem to us to be within our province to notice them. Nor if Mr. Clough were now living among us, would he wish us to do so. The marked peculiarity, and, so to say, the *flavour* of his mind, was a sort of truthful scepticism, which made him anxious never to overstate his own assurance of anything; disinclined him to overrate the doings of his friends; and absolutely compelled him to underrate his own past writings, as well as his capability for future literary succes. He could not have borne to have his poems reviewed with 'nice remarks' and sentimental epithets of insincere praise. He was equal to his precept:

> Where are the great, whom thou would'st wish to
>   praise thee?
> Where are the pure, whom thou would'st choose to
>   love thee?
> Where are the brave, to stand supreme above thee,
> Whose high commands, would cheer, whose chiding raise thee?
>   Seek, seeker, in thyself; submit to find
>   In the stones bread; and life in the blank mind.

To offer petty praise and posthumous compliments to a stoic of this temper is like buying sugar-plums for St. Simon Stylites. We venture to write an article on Mr. Clough, because we believe that his poems depict an intellect in a state which is always natural 'to such a being as man in such a world as the present,' which is peculiarly natural to us just now; and because we believe that many of these poems are very remarkable for true vigour and artistic excellence, although they certainly have several defects and shortcomings, which would have been lessened, if not removed, if their author had lived longer and had written more. ⟨. . .⟩

There are ⟨. . .⟩ some minds (and of these Mr. Clough's was one) which will not accept what appears to be an intellectual destiny. They struggle against the limitations of mortality, and will not condescend to use the natural and needful aids of human thought. They will not *make their image*. They struggle after an 'actual abstract.' They feel, and they rightly feel, that every image, every translation, every mode of conception by which the human mind tries to place before itself the Divine mind, is imperfect, halting, changing. They feel, from their own experience, that there is no one such mode of representation which will suit their own minds at all times, and they smile with bitterness at the notion that they could contrive an image which will suit all other minds. They could not become fanatics or missionaries, or even common preachers, without forfeiting their natural dignity, and foregoing their very essence. To cry in the streets, to uplift their voice in Israel, to be 'pained with hot thoughts,' to be 'preachers of a dream,' would reverse their whole cast of mind. It would metamorphose them into something which omits every striking trait for which they were remarked, and which contains every trait for which they were not remarked. On the other hand, it would be quite as opposite to their whole nature to become followers of Voltaire. No one knows more certainly and feels more surely that there is an invisible world, than those very persons who decline to make an image or representation of it, who shrink with a nervous horror from every such attempt when it is made by any others. All this inevitably leads to what common practical people term a 'curious' sort of mind. You do not know how to describe these 'universal negatives,' as they seem to be. They will not fall into place in the ordinary intellectual world anyhow. If you offer them any known religion, they 'won't have that;' if you offer them no religion, they will not have that either; if you ask them to accept a new and as yet unrecognised religion, they altogether refuse to do so. They seem not only to believe in an 'unknown God,' but in a God whom no man can ever know. Mr. Clough has expressed, in a sort of lyric, what may be called their essential religion:

> O Thou whose image in the shrine
> Of human spirits dwells divine;
> Which from that precinct once conveyed,
> To be to outer day displayed,
> Doth vanish, part, and leave behind
> Mere blank and void of empty mind,
> Which wilful fancy seeks in vain
> With casual shapes to fill again—
>
> O thou that in our bosoms' shrine
> Dost dwell, because unknown divine!
> I thought to speak, I thought to say,
> 'The light is here,' 'behold the way,'
> 'The voice was thus,' and 'thus the word,'
> And 'thus I saw,' and 'that I heard,'—
> But from the lips but half essayed
> The imperfect utterance fell unmade.
>
> O thou, in that mysterious shrine
> Enthroned, as we must say, divine!
> I will not frame one thought of what
> Thou mayest either be or not.
> I will not prate of 'thus' and 'so,'
> And be profane with 'yes' and 'no.'
> Enough that in our soul and heart
> Thou, whatsoe'er thou may'st be, art.

It was exceedingly natural that Mr. Clough should incline to some such creed as this, with his character and in his circumstances. He had by nature, probably, an exceedingly real mind, in the good sense of that expression and the bad sense. The actual visible world, as it was and he saw it, exercised over him a compulsory influence. The hills among which he had wandered, the cities he had visited, the friends whom he knew,—these were his world. Many minds of the poetic sort easily melt down these palpable facts into some impalpable ether of their own. To such a mind as Shelley's the 'solid earth' is an immaterial fact; it is not even a cumbersome difficulty—it is a preposterous imposture. Whatever may exist, all that *clay* does not exist; it would be too absurd to think so. Common persons can make nothing of this dreaminess; and Mr. Clough, though superficial observers set him down as a dreamer, could not make much either. To him, as to the mass of men, the vulgar outward world was a primitive fact. 'Taxes *is* true,' as the miser said. Reconcile what you have to say with green peas, for green peas are certain; such was Mr. Clough's idea. He could not dissolve the world into credible ideas and then believe those ideas, as many poets have done. He could not catch up a creed, as ordinary men do. He had a *straining*, inquisitive, critical mind; he scrutinised every idea before he took it in; he did not allow the moral forces of life to act as they should; he was not content to gain a belief 'by going on living.' He said,

> Action *will furnish belief,* but will that belief be the
>   true one?

This is the point, you know.

He felt the coarse facts of the plain world so thoroughly that he could not readily take in anything which did not seem in accordance with them and like them. And what common idea of the invisible world seems in the least in accordance with them or like them?

A journal-writer, in one of his poems, has expressed this:

> Comfort has come to me here in the dreary streets of
>   the city,
> Comfort—how do you think?—with a barrel-organ
>   to bring it.
> Moping along the streets, and cursing my day, as I
>   wandered,..
> All of a sudden my ear met the sound of an English
>   psalm-tune.
> Comfort me it did, till indeed I was very near crying.
> Ah, there is some great truth, partial, very likely, but
>   needful,
> Lodged, I am strangely sure, in the tones of the
>   English psalm-tune.
> Comfort it was at least; and I must take without
>   question
> Comfort, however it come, in the dreary streets of
>   the city.
> What with trusting myself, and seeking support from
>   within me,
> Almost I could believe I had gained a religious
>   assurance,
> Found in my own poor soul a great moral basis to rest
>   on.
> Ah, but indeed I see, I feel it factitious entirely;
> I refuse, reject, and put it utterly from me;
> I will look straight out, see things, not try to evade
>   them;
> Fact shall be fact for me, and the Truth the Truth as
>   ever,
> Flexible, changeable, vague, and multiform, and
>   doubtful.—
> Off, and depart to the void, thou subtle, fanatical
>   tempter!

Mr. Clough's fate in life had been such as to exaggerate this naturally peculiar temper. He was a pupil of Arnold's; one of his best, most susceptible, and favourite pupils. Some years since, there was much doubt and interest as to the effect of Arnold's teaching. His sudden death, so to say, cut his life in the middle, and opened a tempting discussion as to the effect of his teaching when those taught by him should have become men and not boys. The interest which his own character then awakened, and must always awaken, stimulated the discussion, and there was much doubt about it. But now we need doubt no longer. The Rugby 'men' are *real* men, and the world can pronounce its judgment. Perhaps that part of the world which cares for such things has pronounced it. Dr. Arnold was almost indisputably an admirable master for a common English boy,—the small, apple-eating animal whom we know. He worked, he pounded, if the phrase may be used, into the boy a belief, or at any rate a floating, confused conception, that there are great subjects, that there are strange problems, that knowledge has an indefinite value, that life is a serious and solemn thing. The influence of Arnold's teaching upon the majority of his pupils was probably very vague, but very good. To impress on the ordinary Englishman a general notion of the importance of what is intellectual and the reality of what is supernatural, is the greatest benefit which can be conferred upon him. The common English mind is too coarse, sluggish, and worldly to take such lessons too much to heart. It is improved by them in many ways, and is not harmed by them at all. But there are a few minds which are very likely to think too much of such things. A susceptible, serious, intellectual boy may be injured by the incessant inculcation of the awfulness of life and the magnitude of great problems. It is not desirable to take this world too much *au sérieux*; most persons will not; and the one in a thousand who will, should not. Mr. Clough was one of those who will. He was one of Arnold's favourite pupils, because he gave heed so much to Arnold's teaching; and exactly because he gave heed to it was it bad for him. He required quite another sort of teaching: to be told to take things easily; not to try to be wise overmuch; to be 'something beside critical;' to go on living quietly and obviously, and see what truth would come to him. Mr. Clough had to his latest years what may be noticed in others of Arnold's disciples,—a fatigued way of looking at great subjects. It seemed as if he had been put into them before his time, had seen through them, heard all which could be said about them, had been bored by them, and had come to want something else.

⟨. . .⟩ There was an odd peculiarity in Mr. Clough's mind; you never could tell whether it was that he would not show himself to the best advantage, or whether he *could* not; it is certain that he very often did not, whether in life or in books. His intellect moved with a great difficulty, and it had a larger inertia than any other which we have ever known. Probably there was an awkwardness born with him and his shyness and pride prevented him from curing that awkwardness as most men would have done. He felt he might fail, and he knew that he hated to fail. He neglected, therefore, many of the thousand petty trials which fashion and form the accomplished man of the world. Accordingly, when at last he wanted to do something, or was obliged to attempt something, he had occasionally a singular difficulty. He could not get his matter out of him.

In poetry he had a further difficulty, arising from perhaps an over-cultivated taste. He was so good a disciple of Wordsworth, he hated so thoroughly the common sing-song metres of Moore and Byron, that he was apt to try to write what will seem to many persons to have scarcely a metre at all. It is quite true that the metre of intellectual poetry should not be so pretty as that of songs, or so plain and impressive as that of vigorous passion. The rhythm should pervade it and animate it, but should not protrude itself upon the surface, or intrude itself upon the attention. It should be a latent charm, though a real one. Yet though this doctrine is true, it is nevertheless a dangerous doctrine. Most writers need the strict fetters of familiar metre; as soon as they are emancipated from this, they fancy that *any* words of theirs are metrical. If a man will read any expressive and favourite words of his own often enough, he will come to believe that they are rhythmical; probably they have a rhythm as he reads them; but no notation of pauses and accents could tell the reader how to read them in that manner; and when read in any other mode they may be prose itself. Some of Mr. Clough's early poems, which are placed at the beginning of this volume, are perhaps examples of more or less of this natural self-delusion. Their writer could read them as verse, but that was scarcely his business; and the common reader fails.

Of one metre, however, the hexameter, we believe the most accomplished judges, and also common readers, agree that Mr. Clough possessed a very peculiar mastery. Perhaps he first showed in English its *flexibility*. Whether any consummate poem of great length and sustained dignity can be written in this metre, and in our language, we do not know. Until a great poet has written his poem, there are commonly no lack of

plausible arguments that seem to prove he cannot write it; but Mr. Clough has certainly shown that in the hands of a skilful and animated artist it is capable of adapting itself to varied descriptions of life and manners, to noble sentiments, and to changing thoughts. It is perhaps the most flexible of English metres. Better than any others it changes from grave to gay without desecrating what should be solemn, or disenchanting that which should be graceful. And Mr. Clough was the first to prove this, by writing a noble poem, in which it was done.

In one principal respect Mr. Clough's two poems in hexameters, and especially the Roman one, from which we made so many extracts, are very excellent. Somehow or other he makes you understand what the people of whom he is writing precisely were. You may object to the means, but you cannot deny the result. By fate he was thrown into a vortex of theological and metaphysical speculation, but his genius was better suited to be the spectator of a more active and moving scene. The play of mind upon mind; the contrasted view which contrasted minds take of great subjects; the odd irony of life which so often thrusts into conspicuous places exactly what no one would expect to find in those places,—these were his subjects. Under happy circumstances, he might have produced on such themes something which the mass of readers would have greatly liked; as it is, he has produced a little which meditative readers will much value, and which they will long remember.

Of Mr. Clough's character it would be out of place to say anything, except in so far as it elucidates his poems. The sort of conversation for which he was most remarkable rises again in the *Amours de Voyage*, and gives them, to those who knew him in life, a very peculiar charm. It would not be exact to call its best lines a pleasant cynicism; for cynicism has a bad name, and the ill-nature and other offensive qualities which have given it that name were utterly out of Mr. Clough's way. Though without much fame, he had no envy. But he had a strong realism. He saw what it is considered cynical to see—the absurdities of many persons, the pomposities of many creeds, the splendid zeal with which missionaries rush on to teach what they do not know, the wonderful earnestness with which most incomplete solutions of the universe are thrust upon us as complete and satisfying. 'Le fond de la Providence,' says the French novelist, 'c'est l'ironie.' Mr. Clough would not have said that; but he knew what it meant, and what was the portion of truth contained in it. Undeniably this *is* an *odd* world, whether it should have been so or no; and all our speculations upon it should begin with some admission of its strangeness and singularity. The habit of dwelling on such thoughts as these will not of itself make a man happy, and may make unhappy one who is inclined to be so. Mr. Clough in his time felt more than most men the weight of the unintelligible world; but such thoughts make an instructive man. Several survivors may think they owe much to Mr. Clough's quiet question, 'Ah, then you think—?' Many pretending creeds, and many wonderful demonstrations, passed away before that calm inquiry. He had a habit of putting your own doctrine concisely before you, so that you might see what it came to, and that you did not like it. Even now that he is gone, some may feel the recollection of his society a check on unreal theories and half-mastered thoughts.

THOMAS HUMPHRY WARD
"Arthur Hugh Clough"
The English Poets, ed. Thomas Humphry Ward
1880, Volume 4, pp. 589–92

'We have a foreboding,' says Mr. Lowell in one of his essays, 'that Clough, imperfect as he was in many respects, and dying before he had subdued his sensitive temperament to the sterner requirements of his art, will be thought a hundred years hence to have been the truest expression in verse of the moral and intellectual tendencies, the doubt and struggle towards settled convictions, of the period in which he lived.' If doubt and struggle were the ruling tendencies of Clough's time, this lofty estimate may well be true; for in no writer of that day are they more vividly reflected. They are the very substance of his verse, they give it strength, they impose upon it the limitations from which it suffers. Clough has never been a popular poet, and it may be doubted if he ever will be. His poetry has too much of the element of conflict, too much uncertainty, ever to become what the best of it ought to become, a household word. But from beginning to end it exhibits that devotion to truth which was in a special degree the characteristic of the finer minds of his epoch; a devotion which in his case was fostered by his early training under Arnold at Rugby, and by the atmosphere of theological controversy in which he found himself at Oxford. The warmth of his feelings, the width of his sympathies, the fineness of his physical sensibilities, made him a poet rather than a writer of prose treatises; but the other element, that element of impassioned search for reality, gives his poems their distinctive quality—namely, an air of strenuous mental effort which is almost greater than verse can bear.

'Clough was a philosophic poet in a sense in which no man since Lucretius has been so.'[1] This judgment, the judgment of a very competent critic, is at first unpalatable; one is not used to this matching of the men of our own time, and the men who are not among the most famous, with the giants of antiquity. The comparison however is no mere phrase. 'These two men were philosophers, not from the desire of fame, not from the pleasure of intellectual discovery, not because they hoped that philosophy would suggest thoughts that would soothe some private grief of their own, but because it was to them an overpowering interest to have some key to the universe, because all even of their desires were suspected by them until they could find some central desire on which to link the rest; and love and beauty, and the animation of life, were no pleasure to them, except as testifying to that *something beyond* of which they were in search.' The unlikeness between the two poets is far more apparent than the likeness; for Lucretius has found his solution of the puzzle of existence, and Clough has not; the ancient poet believes that he has reached the point at which all contradictions are harmonised, the modern poet is sure that he has done nothing of the kind. But in this they are one, that both are philosophic, are 'lovers of the knowledge which reveals to them real existence,' are content with nothing less. A reader of Clough's poetry, marked as so much of it is by indecision and manifoldness of view, is startled when he comes upon such passages as these from his American letters—

I think I must have been getting into a little mysticism lately. It won't do: twice two are four, all the world over, and there's no harm in its being so;

'tisn't the devil's doing that it is; il faut s'y soumettre, and all right.

And again—

What I mean by mysticism, is letting feelings run on without thinking of the reality of their object, letting them out merely like water. The plain rule in all matters is, not to think what you are thinking about the question, but to look straight out at the things and let them affect you; otherwise how can you judge at all? look at them at any rate, and judge while looking.

This is not the most obvious feature of Clough's mind, but it is the most real; and it explains much in his work that is otherwise difficult to account for. It explains, for example, the scantiness of his production; as Mrs. Clough says in her memoir of him, 'his absolute sincerity of thought, his intense feeling of reality, rendered it impossible for him to produce anything superficial.' When taken together with his sense of the infinite complexity of human life, it explains the play of conflicting thoughts and feelings which is the very essence of *Dipsychus*, and gives *The Bothie* its truth and charm. These poems, however, present the struggle between opposing views so strongly, that it is only when looked at from close by that we detect the positive element in them. It is otherwise with those short lyrics, than which nothing can be more perfect in form or stronger and surer in matter, those lyrics 'Say not the struggle nought availeth,' and 'As ships becalmed at eve,' and 'O stream descending to the sea,'—they have the note of certainty without which the poet, whatever else he may have, can have no message for mankind.

There will always be a great charm, especially for Oxford men, in the 'Long Vacation pastoral' *The Bothie of Tober-na-Vuolich*. Humour, pathos, clear character-drawing, real delight in nature and a power of rendering her beauties, above all a sense of life, of 'the joy of eventful living'—it has all these, and over the whole is thrown, through the associations of the hexameter, a half-burlesque veil of academic illusion that produces the happiest effect. Yet throughout there runs a current of controversy with the world; the hero 'Philip Hewson, the poet; Hewson, a radical hot,' an idealist who ends by marrying a peasant girl and emigrating with her to New Zealand—this Philip is a type that is always present to Clough's mind, as much in *Dipsychus* and *Amours de Voyage* as in *The Bothie*. Idealism triumphs in him, indeed, whereas in Dipsychus it is finally defeated by the world-spirit, and in Claude it is checked and baffled by the sheer Hamlet-like weakness of the man. But the likeness which the three bear to one another is too strong to be accidental; it springs from the unity of the poet's thought. Clough was in the true sense of the term a sceptic; and his three heroes, whatever the difference of their destinies, are alike sceptics too.

Clough holds a high and permanent place among our poets, not only because, as Mr. Lowell says, he represents an epoch of thought, but because he represents it in a manner so rare, so individual. He is neither singer nor prophet; but he is a poet in virtue of the depth and sincerity with which he felt certain great emotions, and the absolute veracity with which he expressed them. 'His mind seems habitually to have been swayed by large, slow, deep-sea currents,' says one of the best of his critics[2]—currents partly general in their operation on his time, partly special to himself; and his utterances when so swayed are intensely real. But he never was driven by them into a want of sympathy with other natures; and it was this extraordinary union of sincerity and sympathy, of depth and breadth, that so endeared him to his friends, and that make it difficult even now for the critic of his poetry not to be moved by the 'personal estimate.' We find in his poems all sorts of drawbacks; we find a prevailing indecision that injures their moral effect in most cases; we find fragmentariness, inequality, looseness of construction, occasional difficulty of rhythm. Yet what of this? one is tempted to ask. In the presence of that sincerity, that delight in all that is best in the physical and moral world, that humour at once bold and delicate, that moral ardour, often baffled, never extinguished, we feel that the deductions of criticism are unwelcome: we are more than content to take Thyrsis as we find him, though

> the music of his rustic flute
> Kept not for long its happy country tone;
>   Lost it too soon, and learnt a stormy note
> Of men contention-tost, of men who groan,
>   Which tasked his pipe too sore, and tired his
>   throat.

Notes
1. *Quarterly Review*, April 1869.
2. *Westminster Review*, October 1869.

COVENTRY PATMORE
"Arthur Hugh Clough"
Principle in Art
1889, pp. 118–24

Clough worshipped Truth with more than the passion of a lover, and his writings are, for the most part, the tragic records of a life-long devotion to a mistress who steadily refused his embraces; but as it is greatly better to have loved without attaining than to have attained without loving, so Clough's ardent and unrewarded stumblings in the dark towards his adored though unseen divinity are greatly more attractive and edifying to those who have shared, successfully or not, the same passion, than is that complacent fruition of her smiles which she often accords to those who are contented to be no more than her speaking acquaintances. Regarded from a purely intellectual point of view, Clough's utterances on religion, duty, etc., are little better than the commonplaces which in these days pass through the mind and more or less affect the feelings of almost every intelligent and educated youth before he is twenty years of age; but there are commonplaces which cease to be such, and become indefinitely interesting, in proportion as they are animated by moral ardour and passion. Speech may work good by warming as well as by enlightening; and if Clough's writings teach no new truth, they may inflame the love of truth, which is perhaps as great a service. Though he professes that he can nowhere see light where light is most necessary and longed for, his mind is utterly opposed to the negative type; and he exactly exemplifies the class of believer whom Richard Hooker endeavours to comfort, in his great sermon on "the perpetuity of faith in the elect," by the reminder that a longing to believe is implicit faith, and that we cannot sorrow for the lack of that which we interiorly hold to be non-existent. A question that must suggest itself to most readers is, What is the use and justification of these endless and tautological lamentations over the fact—as Clough conceived it to be—that, for such as him at least, "Christ is not risen"? The reply is, that the responsibility of the publication of so much that is profoundly passionate but far from profoundly intellectual scepticism was not his. With the exception of some

not very significant critical essays, his prose consists of letters, which were of course not meant for the public; and the greater part of his poetry remained to the day of Clough's death in his desk, and would probably never have left it, with his consent, unless to be put in the fire.

Those who recognise in the *Bothie* Clough's almost solitary claim to literary eminence must somewhat wonder at the considerable figure he stands for in the estimation of the present generation. The fact is that Clough, like James Spedding, was personally far more impressive than his works; and the singularly strong effect produced among his friends by the extreme simplicity and shy kindliness of his life and manners, and the at once repellent and alluring severity of his truthfulness, gave his character a consequence beyond that of his writings with all who knew him though ever so slightly; and the halo of this sanctity hangs, through the report of his friends, about all that he has done, and renders cold criticism of it almost impossible. No one who knew Clough can so separate his personality from his writings as to be able to criticise them fairly as literature; no one who has not known him can understand their value as the outcome of character.

The impressionable and feminine element, which is manifest in all genius, but which in truly effective genius is always subordinate to power of intellect, had in Clough's mind the preponderance. The masculine power of intellect consists scarcely so much in the ability to see truth, as in the tenacity of spirit which cleaves to and assimilates the truth when it is found, and which steadfastly refuses to be blown about by every wind of doctrine and feeling. The reiterated theme of Clough's poetry is that the only way of forgetting certain problems now, and of securing their solution hereafter, is to do faithfully our nearest duty. This is no new teaching: it is that of every religion and all philosophy. But Clough had no power of trusting patiently to the promise, "Do my commandments, and you shall know of the doctrine." This was the ruin of what might otherwise have been a fine poetic faculty. A "Problem" will not sing even in the process of solution, much less while it is only a hopeless and irritating "Pons." Clough was curiously attracted by Emerson, of whom he spoke as the only great contemporary American. Now Emerson, at his very best, never approached greatness. He was at highest only a brilliant metaphysical epigrammatist. But a religion without a dogma, and with only one commandment, "Thou shalt neither think nor do anything that is customary," had great attractions for Clough; to whom it never seems to have occurred that the vast mass of mankind, for whose moral and religious welfare he felt so keenly, has not and never can have a religion of speechless aspirations and incommunicable feelings, and that to teach men to despise custom is to cut the immense majority of them adrift from all moral restraint. The promise that we shall all be priests and kings seems scarcely to be for this world. At all events we are as far from its fulfilment now as we were two thousand years ago; and we shall not be brought nearer to it by any such outpourings of sarcastic discontent as go to the making of such poems as the tedious Mephistophelian drama called *Dipsychus*, which Clough had the good sense not to publish, though it is included with many others of equally doubtful value in posthumous editions of his works. This class of his poems possesses, indeed, a lively interest for a great many people of our own time, who are in the painful state of moral and religious ferment which these verses represent; but it is a mere accident of the time that there is any considerable audience for such utterances, and in a generation or two it is probable that most men will feel surprise that there could ever have been a public who found poetry in this sort of matter.

The *Bothie of Tober-na-Vuolich* is the only considerable poem of Clough's in which he seems, for a time, to have got out of his slough of introspection and doubt and to have breathed the healthy air of nature and common humanity. In spite of many artistic shortcomings, this poem is so healthy, human, and original, that it can scarcely fail to survive when a good deal of far more fashionable verse shall have disappeared from men's memories. The one infallible note of a true poet—the power of expressing himself in rhythmical movements of subtilty and sweetness which baffle analysis—is also distinctly manifest in passages of the *Bothie*, passages the music of which was, we fancy, lingering in the ear of Tennyson when he wrote certain parts of *Maud*. The originality of this idyl is beyond question. It is not in the least like any other poem, and

an occasionally ostentatious touch of the manner of *Herman and Dorothea* seems to render this originality all the more conspicuous in the main. Another note of poetical power, scarcely less questionable than is that of sweetness and subtilty of rhythm, is the warm and pure breath of womanhood which is exhaled from the love-passages of this poem. Clough seems to have felt, in the presence of a simple and amiable woman, a mystery of life which acted for a time as the rebuke and speechless solution of all doubts and intellectual distresses. These passages in the *Bothie*, and, in a less degree, some others in the *Amours de Voyage*, stand, in the disturbed course of Clough's ordinary verse, like the deep, pure, and sky-reflecting pools which occasionally appear in the course of a restless mountain river.

JAMES SHERIDAN KNOWLES

1784–1862

James Sheridan Knowles was born on May 12, 1784, in Cork. His father, James Knowles, was a prominent lexicographer and a first cousin of the dramatist Richard Brinsley Sheridan. The family moved to London when young Knowles was nine years old, and as a youth he became acquainted with Hazlitt, Lamb, and Coleridge. An early interest in drama was ignored by his family, and Knowles eventually ran away from home, serving briefly in the army. He studied medicine privately and received a medical degree, then decided to pursue a career on the stage, acting in plays that he had either written himself or adapted from earlier versions.

Knowles's career as a dramatist was launched with *Leo* (1810), but despite its success and perhaps concerned about supporting his family—he had married an actress, Maria Charteris, and they eventually had ten children—he turned for several years to teaching, first in Belfast and then in Glasgow. After nearly a decade of only peripheral involvement with the theatre, Knowles returned to the stage with *Virginius* (1820). It was a rousing success, as were his next two plays, *Caius Gracchus* (1823) and *William Tell* (1825), although Knowles continued to require additional financial resources and turned to lecturing for a time.

Knowles continued writing plays until 1843; *The Secretary* was produced in that year. Another Knowles plays, *Alexina; or, True unto Death*, received its first production in 1866, following Knowles's death. During the 1830s he made a successful tour of the United States with his theatrical company. In 1841 his first wife died and the following year he married Emma Elphinstone, another actress. Knowles's abandonment of play-writing coincided with an increasing interest in religion that led to his ordination as a Baptist minister. In his later years he preached against all sorts of frivolities, but the stage was not among them. Always a generous man, he had by this time very little money and gratefully accepted a civil list pension of £200 in 1848. Despite poor health he continued to preach and to lecture, and was briefly considered for the position of poet laureate in 1850.

Knowles died at Torquay on November 30, 1862.

General

When Mr. James Sheridan Knowles shall die, the newspapers will mourn the loss of the best, most successful dramatist of the day; they will discourse pathetically of the many ills, which during life, he suffered at the hands of a public. A goodly number of obituary notices will appear, and in the place of his burial, there will be erected, by the beneficently disposed, a monument, to perpetuate the memory of so popular a dramatist. No matter if the cost of this monument would, while he lived, have relieved his distress; no matter if even then his plays shall be acted, to thin houses, for the benefit of his widow and children.

Mr. Knowles's life, till the appearance of his popular drama, *The Hunchback*, and the passing of Mr. Bulwer's bill,

(which secured to writers of plays a sort of copyright,) was made up of a constant series of struggles against poverty. His efforts, one after another, were directed to the obtaining of bread for his family, and an education for his children. He travelled all over the United Kingdom, lecturing on dramatic literature. His lectures were loudly applauded, but his rewards were small. Favor and patronage were not the pioneers of his way. He labored alone, as an emigrant to the Western wilds, who shoulders his axe, bundles up his household goods, and gods, and goes forth with self-relying firmness—so, on his literary emigration, proceeded, 'The author of *Virginius*.' His labours were manifold and arduous; and were not assisted by the most systematic economy.

Mr. Knowles never received anything like an adequate compensation for his works, until after the very positive, and remarkable success of *The Hunchback*, which redeemed Covent Garden from embarrassment. When *Virginius* was in full possession of the stage, and a source of profit for the manager of the theatre at which it was played, Mr. Knowles was casting about him with feverish anxiety, to find, in the busy thronging world around, means of support for his family,—and wherewithal to purchase the next weeks' food.—PARK BENJAMIN, "Sheridan Knowles," *North American Review*, Jan. 1835, p. 142

The only way in which Mr. Knowles personifies our age, is in his truly domestic feeling. The age is domestic, and so is he. Comfort—not passionate imaginings,—is the aim of every body, and he seeks to aid and gratify this love of comfort. All his dramas are domestic, and strange to say, those that should be most classic, or most chivalric, most above and beyond it, are the most imbued with this spirit. In what consists the interest and force of his popular play of *Virginius*? The domestic feeling. The costume, the setting, the decorations are heroic. We have Roman tunics, but a modern English heart,—the scene is the Forum, but the sentiments those of the *Bedford Arms*. The affection of the father for his daughter—the pride of the daughter in her father, are the main principles of the play, and the pit and galleries and even much of the boxes are only *perplexed* with the lictors and Decemviri, and the strange garments of the actors. These are a part of the shew folks' endeavour to amuse. Is Caius Gracchus not heroic?—are there not very long speeches about Liberty and Rome? Undoubtedly: but still the whole care of Gracchus is for his family: and to the audience the interest is entirely domestic.

It is the same in *William Tell*; though liberty and heroism should be the prevailing subject, the interest is entirely domestic. For the freedom of a country, for the punishment of a petty-minded tyrant the auditor of this play but slenderly cares,—while for the security of Tell's family and the personal success of Tell, every one is anxious. This feeling, in proportion as our author became popular, has only more visibly developed itself; and his later productions have manifested his prevailing quality more powerfully in the pure form of woman's characteristics. Julia,—the Wife—the Countess Eppenstein, are fine impersonations of the affections; elaborated and exfoliated into all the ramifications of womanhood. Is this assertion of his ruling principle stated in a spirit of detraction? By no means: but only to enable us to trace the cause of Mr. Knowles' popularity, as far as it extends, and to show the inevitable connexion the writer's genius must have with the Spirit of the Age. Mr. Knowles is at the head of the acted Dramatists of the age, assuredly not because he has more invention, more wit, more knowledge of human character, or more artistical skill than many other living dramatic writers, but because his genius, for domestic interests, added to his stage influence as an actor, has forced his talents into higher or fuller employment than that of any of his compeers. He has delved into the human breast, and traced the secret windings of the affections. Limited, indeed, to the emotions elicited by modern social intercourse, but still with genuine truth and varied knowledge. For this he is greatest in dialogue scenes that gradually and completely unfold a feeling. And again, this tendency of his genius induces him to delight in delineating the characteristics of woman.

He is entitled to respect inasmuch as he has risen instead of fallen with public approbation. In *Virginius, Caius Gracchus, Tell*, we see the play-wright predominant. Mr. Knowles, when composing these, was struggling for fame, perhaps for existence, and he was compelled to pass through the turnpikes that public taste had erected, and managers maintained.

Consequently, we find all the formula of the received drama,—shows, battles, bustle, antiquated phraseology, vapid imitations of obsolete humours, and altogether a barbarous medley of the traditional and commonplace tricks of the theatre, introduced, first to attract managers and through them to charm the multitude. Gradually, however, as he won his way from servitude to power he used his success manfully. In the *Hunchback*, he emancipated himself greatly from the trammels of the play-wright, and in the character of Julia gave full licence to his genius to develope his intuitions of female nature. The plot of this play is absurd, the construction clumsy, the attempt to delineate human character in many instances feeble—the language often grotesque; but it took hold of the public, it elicited unanimous applause, because in the woman it spoke the language of nature to nature. Herein he vindicated his high calling—herein he was the poet. Situation—sentiment—circumstance—show—processions—groupings—were abandoned, and human emotion finely expressed, won, and subdued all hearts,—chastening, whilst interesting; instructing, while it moved.

As an artist in dramatic composition, Mr. Knowles must be ranked with the least skilful, particularly of late. The comparative failure of his last three or four productions is chiefly attributable to their inefficiency of construction, though they contain more beautiful poetry in detached fragments than can be found in any of his former works.

So much space would not rightly have been given to remarks on Mr. Knowles, but that he speaks the predominating feeling of the age. Were we to estimate him by comparison, or by analysis—by what has been, what is, and what may be, he would not hold a high rank—so great, so vast are the capacities of the Drama. Placed beside Shakspeare, and the powerful-minded men of Elizabeth's day, he dwindles, it is true;" but placed beside the Rowes, the Southerns, the Murphys—he is as a man to mouthing dwarfs. But, whatever he may be by comparison, he is truly a poet, and as such should be honoured.—R. H. HORNE, "Sheridan Knowles and William Macready," *A New Spirit of the Age*, 1844, pp. 239–41

We have seen many a barrister famed for cross-examination unable to comprehend, till the piece was half over, the drift of Sheridan Knowles's dramas.—SIR ARCHIBALD ALISON, "The Romantic Drama," *Blackwood's Edinburgh Magazine*, Aug. 1846, p. 164

Now finish, my song, with one visitor more;
The good old boy's face—how it bloomed at the door!
Hazlitt, painting it during its childhood, turned grim,
Saying, 'D—n your fat cheeks!' then out louder, 'Frown, Jim.'
Those cheeks still adorned the most natural of souls,
Whose style yet was not so—James Sheridan Knowles.
His style had been taught him in those his green days;
His soul was his own, and brought crowds to his plays.
          —LEIGH HUNT, "Postscript" (1860) to *The Feast of the Poets*, 1814

On the 18th of November, 1823, Knowles's tragedy of *Caius Gracchus*, which had been some time in rehearsal, was produced. This play, although not one of the best from the gifted author's pen, abounds in passages of lofty thought, and is marked by the impress of his genius with that truth of character so constantly observable in his writings. But among scenes of striking power, pathetic situations, and bursts of heroic passion, there is great inequality. Whole pages are given to the cavillings of the plebeians, who in their contentions neither sustain the dignity of tragedy nor recall the idea of the Roman people. Indeed the mob, though advancing the action but little, is too prominent an agent, whilst the familiar language of their altercations often descends to vulgarity. But in the poet's conception and draught of Cornelia we see before us the mother of the Gracchi, the ideal of the Roman matron. She gazes on her offspring with all a mother's fondness, but with an unflinching eye looks through the transitory brightness of the present to the darker destiny that awaits the future, and steels her soul to the inevitable sacrifice of her beloved son upon the altar of his country. ⟨. . .⟩

But though instances of power and pathos may be multiplied from the poet's page, yet it must be admitted there is a want of sustained progressive interest in the plot, the fluctuation of party triumph not very actively agitating the hopes and fears of the auditors. The death of Gracchus, stabbing himself with the dagger concealed under the folds of his toga, is nobly conceived, and was startling in its effect. In Caius the passion of the more energetic parts and the tenderness of the domestic interviews laid strong hold on my sympathies, and I gave myself to the study of the part with no ordinary alacrity and ardour.—WILLIAM C. MACREADY, *Reminiscences*, ed. Sir Frederick Pollock, 1873, pp. 220–21

James Sheridan Knowles, an older man, who was born at Cork in 1784 and died in 1862, had been known to Macready since 1820. In that year the MS. of *Virginius* was sent to him by a friend at Glasgow, with account of the success of the play at the Glasgow theatre. The play was then produced at Covent Garden, with Charles Kemble and Miss Foote among its actors, as well as Macready, who delighted in the part of Virginius, and to whom Sheridan Knowles became thenceforth a dramatic poet laureate. Although his style as a poet was but weakly imitative of our elder drama, Sheridan Knowles had skill in the construction of his plots, and that quick sense of stage effect which gratifies an actor who must needs think of the figure he will make upon the stage. Knowles's *William Tell* had been written in 1825. *The Hunchback* was produced in 1832, and another very successful comedy, produced under Victoria, was *The Love Chase*, in the first year of the reign. Talfourd's third play, *Glencoe*, was shown to Macready by Charles Dickens as work of a stranger, accepted on its merits, and acted at the Haymarket Theatre in 1840. The name of the author was withheld also from the public until after the play had succeeded. This was designed as a suggestion to the unacted dramatists, who were then loudly complaining of neglect.—HENRY MORLEY, *Of English Literature in the Reign of Victoria*, 1881, pp. 347–48

Well I remember his acting the part of Master Walter in his play of *The Hunchback* in 1832. It was a great success—the play, I mean, not the impersonation, for an actor Sheridan Knowles was not. He lived a long life, and did not waste it. Up to a good old age he was healthy and hearty. Macready described to me their first interview, when the actor received the dramatist in the green-room. Sheridan Knowles presented himself—a jolly-looking fellow, with red cheeks, a man obviously full of buoyancy and good-humor—and read to the great manager his tragedy of *Virginius*. "What!" cried Macready, half-pleasantly, half-seriously, when the reading was over, "you the author of that tragedy—you? Why you look more like the captain of a Leith smack!"

Nature had endowed Sheridan Knowles with a rare gift, but it was not improved by learning or study, and he owed little, if anything, to his great predecessors in dramatic art.

In his later days, as I have remarked, the celebrated dramatist became a Baptist minister. I regret now that I never heard him preach, although I am told it was a performance that one might have been satisfied to witness only once. But I am sure that, whatever and wherever he was, in the pulpit or on the stage, Sheridan Knowles was in earnest—simple, honest and hearty always. His was a nature that remained thoroughly unspoiled by extraordinary success.—S. C. HALL, *Retrospect of a Long Life*, 1883, pp. 388–89

He was about thirty when he turned dramatist, and though his plays justify the theatrical maxim that no one who has not practical knowledge of the stage can write a good acting play, they also justify the maxim of the study that in his day literary excellence had in some mysterious way obtained or suffered a divorce from dramatic merit. Not that these plays are exactly contemptible as literature, but that as literature they are not in the least remarkable. The most famous of his tragedies is *Virginius*, which dates, as performed in London at least, from 1820. It was preceded and followed by others, of which the best are perhaps *Caius Gracchus* (1815), and *William Tell* (1834). His comedies have worn better, and *The Hunchback* (1832), and the *Love Chase* (1836), are still interesting examples of last-century artificial comedy slightly refreshed. Independently of his technical knowledge, Knowles really had that knowledge of human nature without which drama is impossible, and he could write very respectable English. But the fatal thing about him is that he is content to dwell in decencies for ever. There is no inspiration in him; his style, his verse, his theme, his character, his treatment are all emphatically mediocre, and his technique as a dramatist deserves only a little, though a little, warmer praise. —GEORGE SAINTSBURY, A *History of Nineteenth Century Literature*, 1896, p. 422

As literature, his plays are far from remarkable. His tragedies are of little interest, and his comedies, while ingenious, are pieces of skilful mechanism rather than works inspired by the poetic spirit.—HUGH WALKER, *The Age of Tennyson*, 1897, pp. 46–47

Works

VIRGINIUS

Twelve years ago I knew thee, Knowles, and then
Esteemed you a perfect specimen
Of those fine spirits warm-soul'd Ireland sends,
To teach us colder English how a friend's
Quick pulse should beat. I knew you brave, and plain,
Strong-sensed, rough-witted, above fear or gain;
But nothing further had the gift to espy.
Sudden you re-appear. With wonder I
Hear my old friend (turn'd Shakspeare) read a scene
Only to *his* inferior in the clean
Passes of pathos: with such fence-like art—
Ere we can see the steel, 'tis in our heart.
Almost without the aid language affords,
Your piece seems wrought. That huffing medium, *words,*
(Which in the modern Tamburlaines quite sway
Our shamed souls from their bias) in your play
We scarce attend to. Hastier passion draws
Our tears on credit: and we find the cause
Some two hours after, spelling o'er again
Those strange few words at ease, that wrought the pain.
Proceed, old friend; and, as the year returns,
Still snatch some new old story from the urns
Of long-dead virtue. We, that knew before
Your worth, may admire, we cannot love you more.
　　　　　—CHARLES LAMB, "To R. S. Knowles, Esq., on
　　　　　　His Tragedy of *Virginius*," 1820

We should not feel that we had discharged our obligations to truth or friendship, if we were to let this volume go without introducing into it the name of the author of *Virginius*. This is the more proper, inasmuch as he is a character by himself, and the only poet now living that is a mere poet. If we were asked what sort of man Mr. Knowles is, we could only say, 'he is the writer of *Virginius*.' His most intimate friends see nothing in him, by which they could trace the work to the author. The seeds of dramatic genius are contained and fostered in the warmth of the blood that flows in his veins; his heart dictates to his head. The most unconscious, the most unpretending, the most artless of mortals, he instinctively obeys the impulses of natural feeling, and produces a perfect work of art. He has hardly read a poem or a play or seen any thing of the world, but he hears the anxious beatings of his own heart, and makes others feel them by the force of sympathy. Ignorant alike of rules, regardless of models, he follows the steps of truth and simplicity; and strength, proportion, and delicacy are the infallible results. By thinking of nothing but his subject, he rivets the attention of the audience to it. All his dialogue tends to action, all his situations form classic groups. There is no doubt that *Virginius* is the best acting tragedy that has been produced on the modern stage. Mr. Knowles himself was a player at one time, and this circumstance has probably enabled him to judge of the picturesque and dramatic effect of his lines, as we think it might have assisted Shakespear. There is no impertinent display, no flaunting poetry; the writer immediately conceives how a thought would tell if he had to speak it himself. Mr. Knowles is the first tragic writer of the age; in other respects he is a common man; and divides his time and his affections between his plots and his fishing-tackle, between the Muses' spring, and those mountain-streams which sparkle like his own eye, that gush out like his own voice at the sight of an old friend. We have known him almost from a child, and we must say he appears to us the same boy-poet that he ever was. He has been cradled in song, and rocked in it as in a dream, forgetful of himself and of the world!—WILLIAM HAZLITT, *The Spirit of the Age*, 1825

In the course of the month of April ⟨1820⟩ an application was made to me by my old Glasgow friend, John Tait, on the subject of a tragedy that had been produced at Glasgow with much applause. The author he described as a man of original genius, and one in whose fortunes he and many of his fellow-citizens took a deep interest. It so happened that I had undergone the reading of two or three tragedies when late at Glasgow, and it was with consequent distrust that, to oblige a very good friend, I undertook to read this. Tait was to send the MS. without delay, and I looked forward to my task with no very good-will. It was about three o'clock one day that I was preparing to go out, when a parcel arrived containing a letter from Tait and the MS. of *Virginius*. After some hesitation I thought it best to get the business over, to do at once what I had engaged to do, and I sat down determinedly to my work. The freshness and simplicity of the dialogue fixed my attention; I read on and on, and was soon absorbed in the interest of the story and the passion of its scenes, till at its close I found myself in such a state of excitement that for a time I was undecided what step to take. Impulse was in the ascendant, and snatching up my pen I hurriedly wrote, as my agitated feelings prompted, a letter to the author, to me then a perfect stranger. I was closing my letter as the postman's bell was sounded up the street, when the thought occurred to me, "What have I written? It may seem wild and extravagant; I had better re-consider it." I tore the letter, and, sallying out, hastened

directly to my friend Procter's lodgings, wishing to consult him, and test by his the correctness of my own judgment. He was from home, and I left a card, requesting him to breakfast with me next day, having something very remarkable to show him. After dinner at a coffee-house I returned home, and in more collected mood again read over the impassioned scenes, in which Knowles has given heart and life to the characters of the old Roman story. My first impressions were confirmed by a careful re-perusal, and in sober certainty of its justness I wrote my opinion of the work to Knowles, pointing out some little oversights, and assuring him of my best exertions to procure its acceptance from the managers, and to obtain the highest payment for it.—WILLIAM C. MACREADY, *Reminiscences*, ed. Sir Frederick Pollock, 1873, p. 157

THE HUNCHBACK

After my riding lesson, went and sat in the library to hear Sheridan Knowles's play of *The Hunchback*. Mr. Bartley and my father and mother were his only audience, and he read it himself to us. A real play, with real characters, individuals, human beings, it is a good deal after the fashion of our old playwrights, and does not disgrace its models. I was delighted with it; it is full of life and originality; a little long, but that's a trifle. There is a want of clearness and coherence in the plot, and the comic part has really no necessary connection with the rest of the piece; but none of that will signify much, or, I think, prevent it from succeeding. I like the woman's part exceedingly, but am afraid I shall find it very difficult to act.— FRANCES ANN KEMBLE, *Journal* (April 23, 1831), *Record of a Girlhood*, 1878, p. 390

A man who writes a poem, a history, a novel—in fact, any thing *but a play*—enjoys his right to the proceeds of his labour for twenty-eight years. On the contrary, the dramatist enjoys no such right for twenty-eight hours. The work of his brain is instantly torn from his possession; he produces, and he is pillaged. *The Hunchback*, a play made up of the rarest qualities of literary genius; a production which has shed a golden light on the cold and comfortless gloom of the modern theatre; a mental achievement that places its author in "the forehead of the times," that will embalm his memory with the highest dramatic genius of England, mighty and glorious as she is in that genius—*The Hunchback*, which has acted as a dream, a talisman, on the intellect of this vast metropolis—*The Hunchback* is no more protected by the British legislature than is the meanest fern on the most public common.—DOUGLAS JERROLD (1832), cited in Blanchard Jerrold, *The Life and Remains of Douglas Jerrold*, 1859, p. 423

No wonder the character of Julia is so popular, and so often selected by a débutante. There is an infinite variety in it; there is a double crucial test by which the actress can be judged. In the early acts, opportunities are given for the display of the highest comedy-acting—the country girl, content and happy with her country life; then a change—her head is turned by the gay and novel scenes in which she finds herself placed in that first London season. The whirl of pleasure has turned her into a woman of fashion. All this wants refinement, elegance of carriage, grace in movement; in fact, all the attributes which make your Lady Townleys and your Lady Teazles. A change again: we shift from gay and airy graces to the deep feelings and passionate love of woman. Her pride is stung when Sir Thomas Clifford breaks off his engagement with her, and in a mad moment she accepts another offer. But the old love, the first love, is not dead; it rekindles and burns fiercely when she finds Sir Thomas Clifford bankrupt in fortune, bereft of title, and secretary to the very man to whom she has hastily plighted her troth. Here, then, is the tragic side of the character; here pathos has full play; here those tones, best described by the phrase "larmes dans la voix," tell so admirably. The actress has her chance to hold her audience, to carry them with her, to move them to tears by her despair, and to make them share her joy when, at the last, true love proves triumphant. Yes, an actress who can perfectly realise these varied changes, can play the whole range of leading parts in tragedy and comedy.

The incidents of *The Hunchback* are somewhat confused and difficult to unravel. How Sir Thomas Clifford is not Sir Thomas Clifford, and yet at the end of the play is Sir Thomas Clifford, is a little puzzling and perplexing. The Rochdale Peerage is another mystery which would almost require Sir Bernard Burke to elucidate. Still, with this confusion, which it is said "bothered" even Sheridan Knowles himself to explain, the scenes are well linked together for dramatic purposes, the

interest is progressive and powerfully maintained; there is romance in the story—in fact it is a good love story.

The underplot is separate from the main action—this is a fault in construction—so divided from it that the scenes of Modus and Helen may be acted separately and apart from the play, as they have lately been on the occasion of Mr. Toole's benefit, when Mr. Henry Irving and Miss Ellen Terry played those characters. Helen will run an indifferent Julia very hard; even where Julia is strong, she will make her way. Her scenes are so bright, and they form such a pleasant contrast to the more serious interest that, although not belonging to the plot, the introduction of them may be pardoned. ⟨. . .⟩

That *The Hunchback* will remain as a stock-play and a popular play there can be no manner of doubt; it may be put aside for the newer fancies of the hour, but there is always a time when a new actress will find it a necessity, or an established favourite may seek to add it to her répertoire.—WALTER GORDON, "*The Hunchback*," *Theatre*, March 1882, pp. 146–47

HENRY DAVID THOREAU

1817–1862

Henry David Thoreau was born on July 12, 1817, in Concord, Massachusetts, where he grew up and spent most of his life. He entered Harvard in 1833, and upon graduating in 1837 returned to Concord, where he attempted to support himself by teaching, first for a few weeks in public schools, then in a highly successful private school which he and his brother John maintained from 1838 to 1841. In 1839 Thoreau and his brother made an excursion on the Concord and Merrimack rivers, which Thoreau later recorded as a memorial to his brother, who died in 1842. Sometime before this expedition, in 1836 or 1837, Thoreau first became acquainted with Ralph Waldo Emerson, in whose household he lived from 1841 to 1843. During those two years Thoreau helped Emerson edit his literary periodical, *The Dial*, to which Thoreau had been contributing poems and articles since 1840. He was not, however, able to support himself through these literary activities, and was eventually forced to earn a meager living by carrying on his father's trade as a pencil maker.

On July 4, 1845, Thoreau moved into a cabin he had built near Walden Pond, in a wooded area purchased by Emerson in 1844. Here he hoped finally to be able to compose his memorial tribute to his brother. While he did in fact produce this account, published in 1849 as *A Week on the Concord and Merrimack Rivers*, Thoreau from the very beginning also kept a journal. After two and a half years of living alone in extreme simplicity, Thoreau left Walden Pond in 1847 and began working his journals into what was to become his masterpiece, *Walden* (1854). In 1849 he published the essay "Civil Disobedience" (originally titled "Resistance to Civil Government"), which argued the right of the individual to refuse to pay taxes when his conscience so dictated. In 1846 Thoreau himself had been briefly jailed for non-payment of the Massachusetts poll tax, a gesture of protest against the Mexican War and the institution of slavery. He died in Concord on May 6, 1862.

Both *Walden* and "Civil Disobedience" were largely ignored during Thoreau's lifetime. In the years following his death, however, Thoreau's reputation grew and he is now considered one of America's greatest writers and thinkers. His *Journals* (14 vols.) were first published in 1906, and a new edition of his *Writings* began publication in 1971.

Personal

We, sighing, said, "Our Pan is dead;
  His pipe hangs mute beside the river;—
  Around it wistful sunbeams quiver,
But Music's airy voice is fled.
Spring mourns as for untimely frost;
  The bluebird chants a requiem;
  The willow-blossom waits for him;—
The Genius of the wood is lost."

Then from the flute, untouched by hands,
  There came a low, harmonious breath:
  "For such as he there is no death;—
His life the eternal life commands;
Above man's aims his nature rose:
  The wisdom of a just content
  Made one small spot a continent,
And tuned to poetry Life's prose.

"Haunting the hills, the stream, the wild,
  Swallow and aster, lake and pine,

To him grew human or divine,—
Fit mates for this large-hearted child.
Such homage Nature ne'er forgets,
    And yearly on the coverlid
    'Neath which her darling lieth hid
Will write his name in violets.
"To him no vain regrets belong,
    Whose soul, that finer instrument,
    Gave to the world no poor lament,
But wood-notes ever sweet and strong.
O lonely friend! he still will be
    A potent presence, though unseen,—
    Steadfast, sagacious, and serene:
Seek not for him,—he is with thee."
        —LOUISA MAY ALCOTT, "Thoreau's Flute," *Atlantic*, Sept. 1863, pp. 280–81

He was short of stature, well built, and such a man as I have fancied Julius Cæsar to have been. Every movement was full of courage and repose; the tones of his voice were those of Truth herself; and there was in his eye the pure bright blue of the New England sky, as there was sunshine in his flaxen hair. He had a particularly strong aquiline-Roman nose, which somehow reminded me of the prow of a ship. There was in his face and expression, with all its sincerity, a kind of intellectual furtiveness: no wild thing could escape him more than it could be harmed by him. The grey huntsman's suit which he wore enhanced this expression.

He took the colour of his vest
From rabbit's coat and grouse's breast;
For as the wild kinds lurk and hide,
So walks the huntsman unespied.

The cruellest weapons of attack, however, which this huntsman took with him were a spyglass for birds, a microscope for the game that would hide in smallness, and an old book in which to press plants. His powers of conversation were extraordinary. I remember being surprised and delighted at every step with revelations of laws and significant attributes in common things—as a relation between different kinds of grass and the geological characters beneath them, the variety and grouping of pine-needles and the effect of these differences on the sounds they yield when struck by the wind, and the shades, so to speak, of taste represented by grasses and common herbs when applied to the tongue. The acuteness of his senses was marvellous: no hound could scent better, and he could hear the most faint and distant sounds without even laying his ear to the ground like an Indian. As we penetrated farther and farther into the woods, he seemed to gain a certain transformation, and his face shone with a light that I had not seen in the village. He had a calendar of the plants and flowers of the neighbourhood, and would sometimes go around a quarter of a mile to visit some floral friend, whom he had not seen for a year, who would appear for that day only. We were too early for the *hibiscus*, a rare flower in New England, which I desired to see. He pointed out the spot by the river-side where alone it could be found, and said it would open about the following Monday and not stay long. I went on Tuesday evening and found myself a day too late—the petals were scattered on the ground.—MONCURE DANIEL CONWAY, "Thoreau," *Fraser's Magazine*, April 1866, pp. 461–62

Another peculiar spirit now and then haunted us, usually sad as a pine-tree—Thoreau. His enormous eyes, tame with religious intellect and wild with the loose rein, making a steady flash in this strange unison of forces, frightened me dreadfully at first. The unanswerable argument which he unwittingly made to soften my heart towards him was to fall desperately ill. During his long illness my mother lent him our sweet old music-box, to which she had danced as it warbled at the Old Manse, in the first year of her marriage, and which now softly dreamed forth its tunes in a time-mellowed tone. When he died, it seemed as if an anemone, more lovely than any other, had been carried from the borders of a wood into its silent depths, and dropped, in solitude and shadow, among the recluse ferns and mosses which are so seldom disturbed by passing feet. Son of freedom and opportunity that he was, he touched the heart by going to nature's peacefulness like the saints, and girding upon his American sovereignty the hair-shirt of service to self-denial. He was happy in his intense discipline of the flesh, as all men are when they have once tasted power—if it is the power which awakens perception of the highest concerns. His countenance had an April pensiveness about it; you would never have guessed that he could write of owls so jocosely. His manner was such as to suggest that he could mope and weep *with* them. I never crossed an airy hill or broad field in Concord, without thinking of him who had been the companion of space as well as of delicacy; the lover of the wood-thrush, as well as of the Indian. Walden woods rustled the name of Thoreau whenever we walked in them.—ROSE HAWTHORNE LATHROP, *Memories of Hawthorne*, 1897, p. 420

General

A vigorous Mr. Thoreau,—who has formed himself a good deal upon one Emerson, but does not want abundant fire and stamina of his own;—recognizes us, and various other things, in a most admiring great-hearted manner; for which, as for *part* of the confused voice from the jury-box (not yet summed into a verdict, nor likely to be summed till Doomsday, nor needful to sum), the poor prisoner at the bar may justly express himself thankful! In plain prose, I like Mr. Thoreau very well; and hope yet to hear good and better news of him:—only let him not "turn to foolishness"; which seems to me to be terribly easy, at present, both in New England and Old!—THOMAS CARLYLE, Letter to Ralph Waldo Emerson (May 18, 1847)

My friend and neighbor united these qualities of sylvan and human in a more remarkable manner than any whom it has been my happiness to know. Lover of the wild, he lived a borderer on the confines of civilization, jealous of the least encroachment upon his possessions.

Society were all but rude
In his umbrageous solitude.

I had never thought of knowing a man so thoroughly of the country, and so purely a son of nature. I think he had the profoundest passion for it of any one of his time; and had the human sentiment been as tender and pervading, would have given us pastorals of which Virgil and Theocritus might have envied him the authorship had they chanced to be his contemporaries. As it was, he came nearer the antique spirit than any of our native poets, and touched the fields and groves and streams of his native town with a classic interest that shall not fade. Some of his verses are suffused with an elegiac tenderness, as if the woods and brooks bewailed the absence of their Lycidas, and murmured their griefs meanwhile to one another,—responsive like idyls. Living in close companionship with nature, his muse breathed the spirit and voice of poetry. For when the heart is once divorced from the senses and all sympathy with common things, then poetry has fled and the love that sings.

The most welcome of companions was this plain countryman. One seldom meets with thoughts like his, coming so scented of mountain and field breezes and rippling springs, so like a luxuriant clod from under forest leaves, moist and mossy with earth-spirits. His presence was tonic, like ice-water in dog-days to the parched citizen pent in chambers and under brazen ceilings. Welcome as the gurgle of brooks and dipping of pitchers,—then drink and be cool! He seemed one with things, of nature's essence and core, knit of strong timbers,— like a wood and its inhabitants. There was in him sod and shade, wilds and waters manifold,—the mould and mist of earth and sky. Self-poised and sagacious as any denizen of the elements, he had the key to every animal's brain, every plant; and were an Indian to flower forth and reveal the scents hidden in his cranium, it would not be more surprising than the speech of our Sylvanus. He belonged to the Homeric age,— was older than pastures and gardens, as if he were of the race of heroes and one with the elements. He of all men seemed to be the native New-Englander, as much so as the oak, the granite ledge; our best sample of an indigenous American, untouched by the old country, unless he came down rather from Thor, the Northman, whose name he bore.

A peripatetic philosopher, and out-of-doors for the best part of his days and nights, he had manifold weather and seasons in him; the manners of an animal of probity and virtue unstained. Of all our moralists, he seemed the wholesomest, the busiest, and the best republican citizen in the world; always at home minding his own affairs. A little over-confident by genius, and stiffly individual, dropping society clean out of his theories, while standing friendly in his strict sense of friendship, there was in him an integrity and love of justice that made possible and actual the virtues of Sparta and the Stoics,—all the more welcome in his time of shuffling and pusillanimity. Plutarch would have made him immortal in his pages had he lived before his day. Nor have we any so modern withal, so entirely his own and ours: too purely so to be appreciated at once. A scholar by birthright, and an author, his fame had not, at his decease, travelled far from the banks of the rivers he described in his books; but one hazards only the truth in affirming of his prose, that in substance and pith, it surpasses that of any naturalist of his time; and he is sure of large reading in the future. There are fairer fishes in his pages than any swimming in our streams; some sleep of his on the banks of the Merrimack by moonlight that Egypt never rivalled; a morning of which Memnon might have envied the music, and a greyhound he once had, meant for Adonis; frogs, better than any of Aristophanes; apples wilder than Adam's. His senses seemed double, giving him access to secrets not easily read by others; in sagacity resembling that of the beaver, the bee, the dog, the deer; an instinct for seeing and judging, as by some other, or seventh sense; dealing with objects as if they were shooting forth from his mind mythologically, thus completing the world all round to his senses; a creation of his at the moment. I am sure he knew the animals one by one, as most else knowable in his town; the plants, the geography, as Adam did in his Paradise, if, indeed, he were not that ancestor himself. His works are pieces of exquisite sense, celebrations of Nature's virginity exemplified by rare learning, delicate art, replete with observations as accurate as original; contributions of the unique to the natural history of his country, and without which it were incomplete. Seldom has a head circumscribed so much of the sense and core of Cosmos as this footed intelligence.

If one would learn the wealth of wit there was in this plain man, the information, the poetry, the piety, he should have accompanied him on an afternoon walk to Walden, or elsewhere about the skirts of his village residence. Pagan as he might outwardly appear, yet he was the hearty worshipper of whatsoever is sound and wholesome in nature,—a piece of russet probity and strong sense, that nature delighted to own and honor. His talk was suggestive, subtle, sincere, under as many masks and mimicries as the shows he might pass; as significant, substantial,—nature choosing to speak through his mouth-piece,—cynically, perhaps, and searching into the marrows of men and times he spoke of, to his discomfort mostly and avoidance.

Nature, poetry, life,—not politics, not strict science, not society as it is,—were his preferred themes. The world was holy, the things seen symbolizing the things unseen, and thus worthy of worship, calling men out-of-doors and under the firmament for health and wholesomeness to be insinuated into their souls, not as idolators, but as idealists. His religion was of the most primitive type, inclusive of all natural creatures and things, even to "the sparrow that falls to the ground," though never by shot of his, and for whatsoever was manly in men, his worship was comparable to that of the priests and heroes of all time. I should say he inspired the sentiment of love, if, indeed, the sentiment did not seem to partake of something purer, were that possible, but nameless from its excellency. Certainly he was better poised and more nearly self-reliant than other men.

> The happy man who lived content
> With his own town, his continent,
> Whose chiding streams its banks did curb
> As ocean circumscribes its orb,
> Round which, when he his walk did take,
> Thought he performed far more than Drake;
> For other lands he took less thought
> Than this his muse and mother brought.

More primitive and Homeric than any American, his style of thinking was robust, racy, as if Nature herself had built his sentences and seasoned the sense of his paragraphs with her own vigor and salubrity. Nothing can be spared from them; there is nothing superfluous; all is compact, concrete, as nature is.—A. BRONSON ALCOTT, "Thoreau" (April 5, 1869), *Concord Days*, 1872, pp. 11–16

One of the objects of our poet-naturalist was to acquire the art of writing a good English style. So Goethe, that slow and artful formalist, spent himself in acquiring a good German style. And what Thoreau thought of this matter of writing may be learned from many passages in this sketch, and from this among the rest: "It is the fault of some excellent writers, and De Quincey's first impressions on seeing London suggest it to me, that they express themselves with too great fulness and detail. They give the most faithful, natural, and lifelike account of their sensations, mental and physical, but they lack moderation and sententiousness. They do not affect us as an ineffectual earnest, and a reserve of meaning, like a stutterer: they say all they mean. Their sentences are not concentrated and nutty,— sentences which suggest far more than they say, which have an atmosphere about them, which do not report an old, but make a new impression; sentences which suggest on many things, and are as durable as a Roman aqueduct: to frame these,—that is the *art* of writing. Sentences which are expressive, towards which so many volumes, so much life, went; which lie like boulders on the page up and down, or across; which contain the seed of other sentences, not mere repetition, but creation; and which a man might sell his ground or cattle to build. De Quincey's style is nowhere kinked or knotted up into something hard and significant, which you could swallow like a diamond, without digesting."

As in the story, "And that's Peg Woffington's notion of an actress! Better it, Cibber and Bracegirdle, if you can!" This moderation does, *for the most part*, characterize his works, both of prose and verse. They have their stoical merits, their uncomfortableness! It is one result to be lean and sacrificial; yet a balance of comfort and a house of freestone on the sunny side of Beacon Street can be endured, in a manner, by weak nerves. But the fact that our author lived for a while alone in a shanty near a pond or *stagnum*, and named one of his books after the place where it stood, has led some to say he was a barbarian or a misanthrope. It was a writing-case:—

> This, as an amber drop enwraps a bee,
> Covering discovers your quick soul, that we
> May in your through-shine front your heart's
>   thoughts see.
>
> (Donne)

Here, in this wooden inkstand, he wrote a good part of his famous *Walden*; and this solitary woodland pool was more to his muse than all oceans of the planet, by the force of that faculty on which he was never weary of descanting,—Imagination. Without this, he says, human life, dressed in its Jewish or other gaberdine, would be a kind of lunatic's hospital,—insane with the prose of it, mad with the drouth of society's remainder-biscuits; but add the phantasy, that glorious, that divine gift, and then—

> The earth, the air, and seas I know, and all
> The joys and horrors of their peace and wars;
> And now will view the gods' state and the stars.
>
> (Chapman)

Out of this faculty was his written experience chiefly constructed,—upon this he lived; not upon the cracked wheats and bread-fruits of an outward platter. His essays, those masterful creations, taking up the commonest topics; a sour apple, an autumn leaf, are features of this wondrous imagination of his; and, as it was his very life-blood, he, least of all, sets it forth in labored description. He did not bring forward his means, or unlock the closet of his Maelzel's automaton chess-player. The reader cares not that the writer of a novel, with two lovers in hand, should walk out in the fool's-cap, and begin balancing some peacock's feather on his nose.

> Begin, murderer,—leave thy damnable faces, and
>   begin!

He loved antithesis in verse. It could pass for paradox,—something subtractive and unsatisfactory, as the four herrings provided by Caleb Balderstone for Ravenswood's dinner: come, he says, let us see how miserably uncomfortable we can feel. Hawthorne, too, enjoyed a grave, and a pocket full of miseries to nibble upon.

There was a lurking humor in almost all that he said,—a dry wit, often expressed. He used to laugh heartily and many times in all the interviews I had, when anything in that direction was needed. Certainly he has left some exquisitely humorous pieces, showing his nice discernment; and he has narrated an encounter truly curious and wonderful,—the story of a snapping-turtle swallowing a horn-pout. In the latest pieces on which he worked he showed an anxiety to correct them by leaving out the few innuendoes, sallies, or puns, that formerly luxuriated amid the serious pages. No one more quickly entertained the apprehension of a jest; and his replies often came with a startling promptness, as well as perfection,—as if premeditated. This offhand talent lay in his habit of deep thought and mature reflection; in the great treasury of his wit he had weapons ready furnished for nearly all occasions.

Of his own works, the *Week* was at his death for the most part still in the sheets, unbound; a small edition of *Walden* was sold in some seven years after its publishing. His dealings with publishers (who dealt with him in the most mean and niggardly style) affected him with a shyness of that class. It was with the utmost difficulty he was paid for what he wrote by the persons who bought his wares; for one of his printed articles the note of the publishers was put by him in the bank for collection. Of the non-sale of the *Week* he said, "I believe that this result is more inspiring and better for me than if a thousand had bought my wares. It affects my privacy less, and leaves me freer." Some cultivated minds place *Walden* in the front rank; but both his books are so good they will stand on their own merits. His latest-written work (the *Excursions*—a collection of lectures, mainly) is a great favorite with his friends. His works are household words to those who have long known them; and the larger circle he is sure, with time, to address will follow in our footsteps. Such a treasure as the *Week*,—so filled with images from nature,—such a faithful record of the scenery and the people on the banks,—could not fail to make a deep impression. Its literary merit is also great; as a treasury of citations from other authors, it gives a favorable view of his widely extended reading. Few books in this respect can be found to surpass it.

In his discourse of Friendship, Thoreau starts with the idea of "*underpropping* his love by such pure hate, that it would *end* in sympathy," like sweet butter from sour cream. And in this:—

> Two solitary stars,—
> Unmeasured systems far
> Between us roll;

getting off into the agonies of space, where everything freezes, yet he adds as inducement,—

> But by our conscious light we are
> Determined to one pole.

In other words, there was a pole apiece. He continues the antithesis, and says there is "no more use in friendship than in the tints of flowers" (the chief use in them); "pathless the gulf of feeling yawns," and the reader yawns, too, at the idea of tumbling into it. And so he packs up in his mind "all the clothes which outward nature wears," like a young lady's trunk going to Mount Desert.

We must not expect literature, in such case, to run its hands round the dial-plate of style with cuckoo repetition: the snarls he criticises De Quincey for *not* getting into are the places where *his* bundles of sweetmeats untie. As in the Vendidad, "Hail to thee, O man! who art come from the transitory place to the imperishable":—

> In Nature's nothing, be not nature's toy.

This feature in his style is by no means so much bestowed upon his prose as his poetry. In his verse he more than once attained to beauty, more often to quaintness. He did not court admiration, though he admired fame; and he might have said to his reader,—

> Whoe'er thou beest who read'st this sullen writ,
> Which just so much courts thee as thou dost it.
>
> —WILLIAM ELLERY CHANNING, *Thoreau: The Poet-Naturalist* (1873), ed. F. B. Sanborn, 1902, pp. 229–34

Thoreau has been too absolutely claimed by the transcendentalists and treated as a mere disciple of Emerson. This has led in large measure to his being rejected all too decisively by the purely scientific men, for whom, nevertheless, he has many hints that are equally original and valuable. It must be admitted, however, that if he had been less of a poet, he would have recommended himself better to the scientific class, precisely as he would have been a better Emersonian, if his eye for concrete facts had been less keen. He is impatient of certain forms of analysis—more concerned to gain insight into the inner nature than to anatomize and win knowledge of the mere details of structure.

Both these circumstances have tended to deprive Thoreau of the credit that belongs to him. After you deduct in the most exacting manner all that is due to Emerson and Transcendentalism, and allow that in some points he failed under the most rigid reckonings of science, much remains to establish his claims on our sympathy and deference. His instincts were true; his patience was unbounded; he never flinched from pain or labour when it lay in the way of his object; and complaint he was never known to utter on his own account.

No hard logical line ought to be laid to his utterances in the sphere of personal opinion or liking. He confessedly wrote without regard to abstract consistency. His whole life was determined by sympathy, though he sometimes seemed cynical. We are fain to think, indeed, that under his brusqueness, there lay a suppressed humorous questioning of his reader's capacity and consequent right to understand him and to offer sympathy. If, on this account, he may be said to have sacrificed popularity, he paid the penalty, which people often pay in actual life for too consciously hiding their true feelings under a veil of indifference; and it is much if we find that the cynical manner seldom intruded on the real nature.

The story of Thoreau's life has a value too, inasmuch as we see in him how the tendency of culture, and of theoretic speculation, towards rationalistic indifference, and a general unconcern in the fate of others, may be checked by a genuine love of nature, and by the self-denials she can prompt in the regard that she conveys and enforces for the individual life and for freedom. The practical lesson of a true Transcendentalism, faithfully applied, must issue thus—and it is the same whether we see it in St. Francis, in the saintly Eckhart, in William Law, or in the naturalist Thoreau. All life is sanctified by the relation in which it is seen to the source of life—an idea which lies close to the Christian spirit, however much a fixed and rationalized dogmatic relation to it may tend to dessicate and render bare and arid those spaces of the individual nature, which can bloom and blossom only through sympathy and emotions that ally themselves with what is strictly mystical.

It was through nature, to which he retreated, that Thoreau recovered his philanthropic interests—his love of mankind, which he might have come near to losing through the spirit of culture which can only encourage cynicism and weariness in view of artificial conventions and pretexts. Thoreau would have shrunk with loathing horror from the touch of that savant, who, as Agassiz seriously assures us, said to him that the age of real civilization would have begun when you could go out and shoot a man for scientific purposes. This seems very awful when put baldly on paper: it is but the necessary expression of the last result of culture coldly rationalistic, of science determinately materialistic, since both alike must operate towards loosening the bonds of natural sympathy. Thoreau was saved from the "modern curse of culture" by his innocent delights, and his reverence for all forms of life, so stimulated. His strong faith in the higher destiny of humanity through the triumph of clearer moral aims, and the apprehension of a good beyond the individual or even the national interest, would have linked him practically with the Christian philanthropist rather than with the cultured indifferentist or worshipper of artistic beauty or knowledge for their own sakes.

In this view Thoreau, in spite of his transcendentalism, or, as some would say, professed pantheism, was a missionary. His testimony bears in the direction of showing that the study of nature, when pursued in such a way as to keep alive individual affection and the sentiments of reverence, is one that practically must work in alliance with enlightened Christian conceptions, and that in a moment of real peril, when cruelty and wrong and disorder else would triumph, the true votary of nature will be on the side of the Christian hero, who suffers wrong to redeem the weak. Thoreau thus exhibits to us one way of uplifting science, in relieving her from the false associations which would disconnect her from common humanity, and set her in opposition to its strongest instincts—the science falsely so called, which by baseless assumptions would demoralize, materialize, and brutify, and refuse scope to the exercise of the more ideal and beneficent part of man because it fails to comprehend it or to cover it adequately by its exacting definitions.

It would be ungrateful in us, who are so deeply indebted to Emerson for many benefits, to analyze at length the deteriorating effect which his teachings had, in certain directions, on Thoreau. But they are too outstanding to be wholly passed over without notice. It is patent that Thoreau's peculiar gifts led him to deal with outward things. He was an observer, a quick-eyed and sympathetic recorder of the inner life of nature. Emerson's teaching developed a certain self-conscious and theorising tendency far from natural to Thoreau. He is often too concerned to seek justification for certain facts in purely ideal conceptions which nevertheless have not been reduced to coherency with a general scheme. He is too indifferent to the ordinary scientific order, too much intent on giving us a cosmology in fragments, in which paradox shall startle, if it does not enlighten. Whenever Thoreau proceeds to air abstract statements he is treading on insecure ground; his love of Emersonian philosphy leads him some strange dances. Above all, this foreign element is seen in the effusive egotism which constantly appears when he leaves the ground of facts for general disquisition. He would fain attract us by forced freshness and by the effort to utter paradoxical and startling statements. No man could be more clear, simple, direct, incisive than he is when he has a real nature-object before his eye or his mind; for memory never fails him. But when he is abstract and oracular, he is oftentimes more puzzling than his master. When Thoreau is telling his own story—what he saw, what he heard, what he did,—he is simply delightful. His pantheism, so far as it was a conscious thing with him, is not inviting; and would often be very hard and unattractive, were it not that his instincts were far truer than his mind was exact on the logical side, and saved him from the natural effects of such vagary and paradoxical assertions. But we can dissociate Thoreau's merits from these adhesions. His Emersonian pantheism did not destroy his finer sensibilities and sympathies, which made him, as he certainly was, one of nature's diviners and reconcilers—a pantheist as all true poets have been, as Christ Himself was. Like many others, he brought a double gift; but that which is truest and most available is that of which he made but little account. So it is that we believe we can detach from his writings what will serve to illustrate the better side of his genius. Fitly and fully done, this cannot but prove a service; for we can ill afford wholly to miss the benefit of the record of such a peculiar experience—a discerning and divining instinct, on the whole wisely directed to its true purpose, and revealing rare possibilities in human life, new relationships and sources of deep joy.—ALEXANDER HAY JAPP (as "H. A. Page"), *Thoreau: His Life and Aims*, 1878, pp. 257–64

It will always be an interesting question, how far Thoreau's peculiar genius might have been modified or enriched by society or travel. In his diary he expresses gratitude to Providence, or, as he quaintly puts it, "to those who have had the handling of me," that his life has been so restricted in these directions, and that he has thus been compelled to extract its utmost nutriment from the soil where he was born. Yet in examining these diaries, even more than in reading his books, one is led to doubt, after all, whether this mental asceticism was best for him, just as one suspects that the vegetable diet in which he exulted may possibly have shortened his life. A larger experience might have liberalized some of his judgments, and softened some of his verdicts. He was not as just to men as to woodchucks; and his "simplify, I say, simplify," might well have been relaxed a little for mankind, in view of the boundless affluence of external nature. The world of art might also have deeply influenced him, had the way been opened for its closer study. Emerson speaks of "the raptures of a citizen arrived at his first meadow;" but a deep, ascetic soul like Thoreau's could hardly have failed to be touched to a far profounder emotion by the first sight of a cathedral.

The impression that Thoreau was but a minor Emerson will in time pass away, like the early classification of Emerson as a second-hand Carlyle. All three were the children of their time, and had its family likeness; but Thoreau had the *lumen siccum*, or "dry light," beyond either of the others; indeed, beyond all men of his day. His temperament was like his native air in winter,—clear, frosty, inexpressibly pure and bracing. His power of literary appreciation was something marvellous, and his books might well be read for their quotations, like the sermons of Jeremy Taylor. His daring imagination ventured on the delineation of just those objects in nature which seem most defiant of description, as smoke, mist, haze; and his three poems on these themes have an exquisite felicity of structure such as nothing this side of the Greek anthology can equal. Indeed, the value of the classic languages was never better exemplified than in their influence on his training. They were real "humanities" to him; linking him with the great memories of the race, and with high intellectual standards, so that he could never, like some of his imitators, treat literary art as a thing unmanly and trivial. His selection of points in praising his favorite books shows this discrimination. He loves to speak of "the elaborate beauty and finish, and the lifelong literary labors of the ancients . . . works as refined, as solidly done, and as beautiful almost, as the morning itself." I remember how that fine old classical scholar, the late John Glen King, of Salem, used to delight in Thoreau as being "the only man who thoroughly loved both nature and Greek."—THOMAS WENTWORTH HIGGINSON, "Thoreau" (1879), *Short Studies of American Authors*, 1888, pp. 27–30

I said, a little way back, that the New England Transcendental movement had suffered, in the estimation of the world at large, from not having (putting Emerson aside) produced any superior talents. But any reference to it would be ungenerous which should omit to pay a tribute, in passing, to the author of *Walden*. Whatever question there may be of his talent, there can be none, I think, of his genius. It was a slim and crooked one, but it was eminently personal. He was imperfect, unfinished, inartistic; he was worse than provincial—he was parochial; it is only at his best that he is readable. But at his best he has an extreme natural charm, and he must always be mentioned after those Americans—Emerson, Hawthorne, Longfellow, Lowell, Motley—who have written originally. He was Emerson's independent moral man made flesh—living for the ages, and not for Saturday and Sunday; for the Universe, and not for Concord. In fact, however, Thoreau lived for Concord very effectually; and by his remarkable genius for the observation of the phenomena of woods and streams, of plants and trees, and beasts and fishes, and for flinging a kind of spiritual interest over these things, he did more than he perhaps intended towards consolidating the fame of his accidental human sojourn. He was as shy and ungregarious as Hawthorne; but he and the latter appear to have been sociably disposed towards each other, and there are some charming touches in the preface to the *Mosses* in regard to the hours they spent in boating together on the large, quiet Concord river. Thoreau was a great voyager, in a canoe which he had constructed himself, and which he eventually made over to Hawthorne, and as expert in the use of the paddle as the Red men who had once haunted the same silent stream.—HENRY JAMES, *Hawthorne*, 1879, pp. 93–94

Emerson is primarily and chiefly a poet, and only a philosopher in his second intention; and thus also Thoreau, though a naturalist by habit, and a moralist by constitution, was inwardly a poet by force of that shaping and controlling imagination, which was his strongest faculty. His mind tended naturally to the ideal side. He would have been an idealist in any circumstances; a fluent and glowing poet, had he been born among a people to whom poesy is native, like the Greeks, the Italians, the Irish. As it was, his poetic light illumined every wide prospect and every narrow cranny in which his active, patient spirit pursued its task. It was this inward illumination as well as the star-like beam of Emerson's genius in "Nature," which caused Thoreau to write in his senior year at college, "This curious world which we inhabit is more wonderful than it is convenient; more beautiful than it is useful," and he cherished this belief through life. In youth, too, he said, "The other world is all my art, my pencils will draw no other, my jackknife will cut nothing else; I do not use it as a means." ⟨. . .⟩

It seems to have been the habit of Thoreau, in writing verse, to compose a couplet, a quatrain, or other short metrical expression, copy it in his journal, and afterward, when these verses had grown to a considerable number, to arrange them in the form of a single piece. This gives to his poems the epigrammatic air which most of them have. After he was thirty years old, he wrote scarcely any verse, and he even destroyed much that he had previously written, following in this the judgment of Mr. Emerson, rather than his own, as he told me one day during his last illness. He had read all that was best in English and in Greek poetry, but was more familiar with the English poets of Milton's time and earlier, than with those more recent, except his own townsmen and companions. He valued Milton above Shakespeare, and had a special love for Æschylus, two of whose tragedies he translated. He had read Pindar, Simonides, and the Greek Anthology, and wrote, at his best, as well as the finest of the Greek lyric poets. Even Emerson, who was a severe critic of his verses, says, "His classic poem on 'Smoke' suggests Simonides, but is better than any poem of Simonides." ⟨. . .⟩

His method in writing was peculiarly his own, though it bore some external resemblance to that of his friends, Emerson and Alcott. Like them he early began to keep a journal, which became both diary and commonplace book. But while they noted down the thoughts which occurred to them, without premeditation or consecutive arrangement, Thoreau made studies and observations for his journal as carefully and habitually as he noted the angles and distances in surveying a

Concord farm. In all his daily walks and distant journeys, he took notes on the spot of what occurred to him, and these, often very brief and symbolic, he carefully wrote out, as soon as he could get time, in his diary, not classified by topics, but just as they had come to him. To these he added his daily meditations, sometimes expressed in verse, especially in the years between 1837 and 1850, but generally in close and pertinent prose. Many details are found in his diaries, but not such as are common in the diaries of other men,—not trivial but significant details. From these daily entries he made up his essays, his lectures, and his volumes; all being slowly, and with much deliberation and revision, brought into the form in which he gave them to the public. After that he scarcely changed them at all; they had received the last imprint of his mind, and he allowed them to stand and speak for themselves. But before printing, they underwent constant change, by addition, erasure, transposition, correction, and combination. A given lecture might be two years, or twenty years in preparation; or it might be, like his defense of John Brown, copied with little change from the pages of his diary for the fortnight previous. But that was an exceptional case; and Thoreau was stirred and quickened by the campaign and capture of Brown, as perhaps he had never been before. ⟨. . .⟩

The fact that Thoreau noted down his thoughts by night as well as by day, appears also from an entry in one of his journals, where he is describing the coming on of day, as witnessed by him at the close of a September night in Concord. "Some bird flies over," he writes, "making a noise like the barking of a puppy (it was a cuckoo). It is yet so dark that I have dropped my pencil and cannot find it." No writer of modern times, in fact, was so much awake and abroad at night, or has described better the phenomena of darkness and of moonlight.—F. B. SANBORN, *Henry D. Thoreau*, 1882, pp. 284–87, 301–4

His English, we might judge, was acquired from the poets and prose-writers of its best days. His metaphors and images have the freshness of the soil. His range was narrow, but within his limits he was a master. He needed only a tender and pervading sentiment to have been a Homer. Pure and guileless, and fond of sympathy, he yet was cold and wintry. 'I love Henry,' said one of his friends, 'but I cannot like him; and as for taking his arm, I should as soon think of taking the arm of an elm-tree.' His works are replete with fine observations, finely expressed. One cannot fail to see the resemblance of his style to Emerson's and Alcott's. Nothing that he wrote can be spared.
—ALFRED H. WELSH, *Development of English Literature and Language*, 1883, Vol. 2, p. 413

There are certain writers in American literature who charm by their eccentricity as well as by their genius, who are both original and originals. The most eminent, perhaps, of these was Henry D. Thoreau—a man who may be said to have penetrated nearer to the physical heart of Nature than any other American author. Indeed, he "experienced" nature as others are said to experience religion. Lowell says that in reading him it seems as "if all out-doors had kept a diary, and become its own Montaigne." He was so completely a naturalist that the inhabitants of the woods in which he sojourned forgot their well-founded distrust of man, and voted him the freedom of their city. His descriptions excel even those of Wilson, Audubon, and Wilson Flagg, admirable as these are, for he was in closer relations with the birds than they, and carried no gun in his hand. In respect to human society, he pushed his individuality to individualism; he was never happier than when absent from the abodes of civilization, and the toleration he

would not extend to a Webster or a Calhoun he extended freely to a robin or a woodchuck. With all this peculiarity, he was a poet, a scholar, a humorist,—also, in his way, a philosopher and philanthropist; and those who knew him best, and entered most thoroughly into the spirit of his character and writings, are the warmest of all the admirers of his genius.—EDWIN P. WHIPPLE, "American Literature" (1886), *American Literature and Other Papers*, 1887, pp. 111–12

As a rule, ⟨. . .⟩ Thoreau is a remarkably even writer; his chapters were like his days, merely separate parts of a serene and little-diversified life, free from the restraints and pleasures of a real home, remote from burning human hopes and struggles, and, while caring much for the slave, caring little for country. No one would have thought of turning to this isolated life for personal sympathy, but Thoreau, in his turn, stood in small need of eliciting human help beyond his family, between whose members and himself there was a mild but genuine affection. He seemed to add something to the Emersonian courageous individuality, but in fact he let go from it the strongest part, its helpful humanity. It would not be a pleasant task to cull from Thoreau's writings proofs of an individualism which, to speak plainly, was terribly unlike the individualism of Jesus. After all, we read and praise Thoreau for what he tells us of the things he saw, and not for his records of himself.
—CHARLES F. RICHARDSON, *American Literature, 1607–1885*, 1887, Vol. 1, pp. 388–89

It has been claimed for Thoreau by some of his admirers, never by himself, that he was a man of science, a naturalist. Certainly, in some respects, he had in him the material for an almost ideal naturalist. His peculiar powers of observation, and habits of noting and recording natural facts, his patience, his taste for spending his days and nights in the open air, seem to furnish everything that is required. Nor would his morbid dislike of dissection have been any serious bar, for the least worked but by no means the least important portion of natural history is the study of living forms, and for this Thoreau seems to have been peculiarly adapted; he had acquired one of the rarest of arts, that of approaching birds, beasts and fishes, and exciting no fear. There are all sorts of profoundly interesting investigations which only such a man can profitably undertake. But that right question which is at least the half of knowledge was hidden from Thoreau; he seems to have been absolutely deficient in scientific sense. His bare, impersonal records of observations are always dull and unprofitable reading; occasionally he stumbles on a good observation, but, not realizing its significance, he never verifies it or follows it up. His science is that of a fairly intelligent schoolboy—a counting of birds' eggs and a running after squirrels. Of the vital and organic relationships of facts, or even of the existence of such relationships, he seems to have no perception. Compare any of his books with, for instance, Belt's *Naturalist in Nicaragua*, or any of Wallace's books: for the men of science, in their spirit of illuminating inquisitiveness, all facts are instructive; in Thoreau's hands they are all dead. He was not a naturalist: he was an artist and a moralist.

He was born into an atmosphere of literary culture, and the great art he cultivated was that of framing sentences. He desired to make sentences which would "suggest far more than they say," which would "lie like boulders on the page, up and down or across, not mere repetition, but creation, and which a man might sell his ground or cattle to build," sentences "as durable as a Roman aqueduct." Undoubtedly he succeeded; his sentences frequently have all the massive and elemental qualities that he desired. They have more; if he knew little of the architectonic qualities of style, there is a keen exhilarating breeze blowing about these boulders, and when we look at them they have the grace and audacity, the happy, natural extravagance of fragments of the finest Decorated Gothic on the site of a fourteenth century abbey. He was in love with the things that are wildest and most untamable in Nature, and of these his sentences often seem to be a solid artistic embodiment, the mountain side, "its sublime gray mass, that antique, brownish-gray, Ararat colour," or the "ancient, familiar, immortal cricket sound," the thrush's song, his *ranz des vâches*, or the song that of all seemed to rejoice him most, the clear, exhilarating, braggart, clarion-crow of the cock. Thoreau's favourite reading was among the Greeks, Pindar, Simonides, the Greek Anthology, especially Æschylus, and a later ancient, Milton. There is something of his paganism in all this, his cult of the aboriginal health-bearing forces of Nature. His paganism, however unobtrusive, was radical and genuine. It was a paganism much earlier than Plato, and which had never heard of Christ.

Thoreau was of a piece; he was at harmony with himself, though it may be that the elements that went to make up the harmony were few. The austerity and exhilaration and simple paganism of his art were at one with his morality. He was, at the very core, a preacher; the morality that he preached, interesting in itself, is, for us, the most significant thing about him. Thoreau was, in the noblest sense of the word, a Cynic. The school of Antisthenes is not the least interesting of the Socratic schools, and Thoreau is perhaps the finest flower that that school has ever yielded. He may not have been aware of his affinities, but it will help us if we bear them in mind. The charm that Diogenes exercised over men seems to have consisted in his peculiarly fresh and original intellect, his extravagant independence and self-control, his coarse and effective wit. Thoreau sat in his jar at Walden with the same originality, independence, and sublime contentment; but his wisdom was suave and his wit was never coarse—exalted, rather, into a perennial humour, flashing now and then into divine epigram. A life in harmony with Nature, the culture of joyous simplicity, the subordination of science to ethics—these were the principles of Cynicism, and to these Thoreau was always true. ⟨. . .⟩

Every true Cynic is, above all, a moralist and a preacher. Thoreau could never be anything else; that was, in the end, his greatest weakness. This unfailing ethereality, this perpetual challenge of the acridity and simplicity of Nature, becomes at last hypernatural. Thoreau breakfasts on the dawn: it is well; but he dines on the rainbow and sups on the Aurora borealis. Of Nature's treasure more than half is man. Thoreau, with his noble Cynicism, had, as he thought, driven life into a corner, but he had to confess that of all phenomena his own race was to him the most mysterious and undiscoverable.

⟨. . .⟩ Thoreau has heightened for us the wildness of Nature, and his work—all written, as we need not be told, in the open air—is full of this tonicity; it is a sort of moral quinine, and, like quinine under certain circumstances, it leaves a sweet taste behind.—HAVELOCK ELLIS, "Whitman," *The New Spirit*, 1890, pp. 93–99

He never was out of America, and with the exception of one or two short periods, the whole of his life was spent in and about Concord, yet his reflections might have come from Fleet Street. His railings against the world, his protests against luxury and competition, his fierce condemnation of the aims and labour of his fellow-men are more suggestive of a disappointed cit than of an ingenuous wild man of the woods. At college and at the feet of Emerson he had imbibed a second-hand and discoloured Carlylean philosophy, the effect of which was to spoil him for his obvious life-work. Without it he might have developed into a great naturalist, one to inform that science with new life, and from that pursuit he would assuredly have sucked more pleasure than from hoeing beans and surveying wood lots. The world is not after all so stupid as to refuse a livelihood for a service that his journals prove Thoreau to have been eminently capable of rendering. There was an element of weakness in his character, however, that led him to curb and hamper his inclinations in small things and in great.

Just as he was a born hunter who forswore the gun, scrupled at the angle, and refused to eat flesh, so also he was a most companionable man who chose an artificial solitude. If he made an excursion, he was as careful to look out for a fellow-traveller, as is the ordinary pedestrian tourist. He was 'a man of good fellowship' who loved a 'dish of gossip,' and one who never could stay long away from his fellows; and it was not long before he wearied of the Walden loneliness. Though love of out-of-door life was the predominant feature of his character, he must needs sandwich his descriptions with preaching and moralisation about a world of which he was ignorant. When the editors of the future approach their inevitable duty of separating the dead from the living in the swiftly accumulating literature of our time, the works of Thoreau will be the easiest to deal with; all they require is for every passage with a precept, a teaching or a doctrine to be ruthlessly excised, and the remainder will be his lasting and valuable contribution.

Students of extraordinary phenomena, those who have described the avalanche, the earthquake, and the volcano, great battles by sea and land, plague, famine, and tempest, untrodden mountain tops, unfurrowed seas, and lands virgin to the explorer, may well ask in wonder the secret of that charm by which Thoreau pins the interest of his hearer to things the most trivial and homely—a warfare of emmets, the helve of a lost axe waving at the bottom of a pond, the musical thrum of telegraph wires, an owl's hooting, or a cockerel's cry. When a Pasteur deals with bacteria infinitely smaller, or a Darwin examines the infinitesimal grains of sand borne hither on a migrant's feet, a further interest of science is reflected on the description. It is not so with Thoreau; he aims neither at an exhaustive and orderly examination nor at discovery. He was a correspondent and helper of Agassiz, but not himself a toiler in the field of formal natural history, and he declined to write for the Boston Society, because he could not properly detach the mere external record of observation from the inner associations with which such facts were connected in his mind. To have laboured for the increase of positive knowledge would have been heresy to his doctrine of idleness. No one reads *Walden* for information.—P. ANDERSON GRAHAM, "The Philosophy of Idleness," *Nature in Books*, 1891, pp. 85–87

He was always more poet than naturalist, for his observation, interesting as it ever is, is rarely novel. It is his way of putting what he has seen that takes us rather than any freshness in the observation itself. His sentences have sometimes a Greek perfection; they have the freshness, the sharpness, and the truth which we find so often in the writings of the Greeks who came early into literature, before everything had been seen and said. Thoreau had a Yankee skill with his fingers, and he could whittle the English language in like manner; so he had also a Greek faculty of packing an old truth into an unexpected sentence. He was not afraid of exaggeration and paradox, so long as he could surprise the reader into a startled reception of his thought. He was above all an artist in words, a ruler of the vocabulary, a master phrasemaker. But his phrases were all sincere; he never said what he did not think; he was true to himself always.—BRANDER MATTHEWS, *An Introduction to the Study of American Literature*, 1896, pp. 192–93

Unlike many book-making folk, this swart, bumptious man has grown in literary stature since his death; his drawers have been searched, and cast-away papers brought to day. Why this renewed popularity and access of fame? Not by reason of newly detected graces of style; not for weight of his *dicta* about morals, manners, letters; there are safer guides in all these. But there is a new-kindled welcome for the independence, the tender particularity, and the outspokenness of this journal-maker.

If asked for a first-rate essayist, nobody would name Thoreau; if a poet, not Thoreau; if a scientist, not Thoreau; if a political sage, not Thoreau; if a historian of small socialities and of town affairs, again not Thoreau. Yet we read him—with zest, though he is sometimes prosy, sometimes overlong and tedious; but always—Thoreau.—DONALD G. MITCHELL, *American Lands and Letters (Leather-Stocking to Poe's "Raven")*, 1899, pp. 278–80

His writings cleave so closely to the man that they can hardly be studied wholly apart, nor is it necessary so to consider them at length here. What is most remarkable in them is their wild "tang," the subtlety and the penetrative quality of their imaginative sympathy with the things of field, forest, and stream. The minuteness, accuracy, and delicacy of the observation and feeling are remarkable; while mysticism, fancy, poetic beauty, and a vein of shrewd humor often combine with the other qualities to make a whole whose effect is unique. Thoreau's verse is much like Emerson's on a smaller scale and a lower plane, having the same technical faults and occasionally the same piercing felicity of phrase. On the whole, Thoreau must be classed with the minor American authors; but there is no one just like him, and the flavor of his best work is exceedingly fine.—WALTER C. BRONSON, *A Short History of American Literature*, 1900, p. 213

Of course Thoreau was eccentric, but his eccentricity was not misanthropic. Inclined by temperament and philosophy alike to this life of protestant solitude, he seems to have regarded his course as an experimental example. He was not disposed to quarrel with people who disagreed with him. All he asked was to be let alone. If his life turned out well, others would ultimately imitate him; if it turned out ill, nobody else would be the worse. Though his philosophising often seems unpractically individual, then, it never exhales such unwholesomeness as underlay Alcott's self-esteem. What is more, there can be no question that his speculations have appealed to some very sensible minds. All the same, if he had confined himself to ruminating on the eternities and human nature, with which his sympathy was at best limited, his position in literary history would hardly be important. What gave him lasting power was his unusually sympathetic observation of Nature. A natural vein of indolence, to be sure, prevented him from observing either precociously or systematically; but when, as was more and more the case, he found himself alone with woods and fields and waters, he had true delight in the little sights which met his eyes, in the little sounds which came to his ears, in all the constant, inconspicuous beauties which the prosaic toilsomeness of Yankee life had hitherto failed to perceive.

Nature, as every one knows, had been a favourite theme of that romantic revival in England whose leader was Wordsworth. In one aspect, then, Thoreau's writing often seems little

more than an American evidence of a temper which had declared itself in the old world a generation before. Nothing, however, can alter the fact that the Nature he delighted in was characteristically American. First of all men, Thoreau brought that revolutionary temper which recoils from the artificialities of civilisation face to face with the rugged fields, the pine woods and the apple orchards, the lonely ponds and the crystalline skies of eastern New England. His travels occasionally ranged so far as the Merrimac River, Cape Cod, or even beyond Maine into Canada; but pleasant as the books are in which he recorded these wanderings, as exceptional as were Cotton Mather's infrequent excursions through the bear-haunted wilds to Andover, we could spare them far better than *Walden*, or than the journals in which for years he set down his daily observations in the single town of Concord. Thoreau's individuality is often so assertive as to repel a sympathy which it happens not instantly to attract; but that sympathy must be unwholesomely sluggish which would willingly resist the appeal of his communion with Nature. If your lot be ever cast in some remote region of our simple country, he can do you, when you will, a rare service, stimulating your eye to see, and your ear to hear, in all the little commonplaces about you, those endlessly changing details which make life everywhere so unfathomably, immeasurably wondrous. For Nature is truly a miracle; and he who will regard her lovingly shall never lack that inspiration which miracles breathe into the spirit of mankind.

Nor is Thoreau's vitality in literature a matter only of his observation. Open his works almost anywhere,—there are ten volumes of them now,—and even in the philosophic passages you will find loving precision of touch. He was no immortal maker of phrases. Amid bewildering obscurities, Emerson now and again flashed out utterances which may last as long as our language. Thoreau had no such power; but he did possess in higher degree than Emerson himself the power of making sentences and paragraphs artistically beautiful. Read him aloud, and you will find in his work a trait like that which we remarked in the cadences of Brockden Brown and of Poe; the emphasis of your voice is bound to fall where meaning demands. An effect like this is attainable only through delicate sensitiveness to rhythm. So when you come to Thoreau's pictures of Nature you have an almost inexhaustible series of verbal sketches in which every touch has the grace of precision. On a large scale, to be sure, his composition falls to pieces; he never troubled himself about a systematically made book, or even a systematic chapter. In mere choice of words, too, he is generally so simple as to seem almost commonplace. But his sentences and paragraphs are often models of art so fine as to seem artless. Take, for example, this well-known passage from *Walden*:

> Early in May, the oaks, hickories, maples, and other trees, just putting out amidst the pine woods around the pond, imparted a brightness like sunshine to the landscape, especially in cloudy days, as if the sun were breaking through mists and shining faintly on the hillsides here and there. On the third or fourth of May I saw a loon in the pond, and during the first week of the month I heard the whippoorwill, the brown thrasher, the veery, the wood-pewee, the chewink, and other birds. I had heard the wood-thrush long before. The phebe had already come once more and looked in at my door and window, to see if my house were cavern-like enough for her, sustaining herself on humming wings with clinched talons, as if she held by the air, while she surveyed

the premises. The sulphur-like pollen of the pitch-pine soon covered the pond and the stones and the rotten wood along the shore, so that you could have collected a barrelful. This is the "sulphur showers" we hear of. Even in Calidas' drama of Sacontala, we read of "rills dyed yellow with the golden dust of the lotus." And so the seasons went rolling on into summer, as one rambles into higher and higher grass.

The more you read work like that, the more admirable you will find its artistic form.

With Thoreau's philosophising the case is different. Among Emerson's chief traits was the fact that when he scrutinised the eternities in search of ideal truth, his whole energy was devoted to the act of scrutiny. Vague, then, and bewildering as his phrases may often seem, we are sensible of a feeling that this Emerson is actually contemplating the immensities; and these are so unspeakably vaster than all mankind—not to speak of the single human being who for the moment is striving to point our eyes toward them—that our thoughts again and again concern themselves rather with the truths thus dimly seen than with anything concerning the seer. The glass through which Emerson contemplated the mysteries is achromatic. Now, Thoreau's philosophic speculations so surely appeal to powerful minds who find them sympathetic that we may well admit them to involve more than they instantly reveal to minds not disposed to sympathise. Even their admirers, however, must admit them to be coloured throughout by the unflagging self-consciousness involved in Thoreau's eccentric, harmless life. Perhaps, like Emerson, Thoreau had the true gift of vision; but surely he could never report his visions in terms which may suffer us to forget himself. The glass which he offers to our eyes is always tinctured with his own disturbing individuality. In spite, then, of the fact that Thoreau was a more conscientious artist than Emerson, this constant obstrusion of his personality ranges him in a lower rank, just as surely as his loving sense of nature ranges him far above the half-foolish egotism of Bronson Alcott. More and more the emergence of Emerson from his surroundings grows distinct. Like truly great men, whether he was truly great or not, he possessed the gift of such common-sense as saves men from the perversities of eccentricity. —BARRETT WENDELL, A *Literary History of America*, 1900, pp. 333–37

Works

WALDEN

The economical details and calculations in this book are more curious than useful; for the author's life in the woods was on too narrow a scale to find imitators. But in describing his hermitage and his forest life, he says so many pithy and brilliant things, and offers so many piquant, and, we may add, so many just, comments on society as it is, that his book is well worth the reading, both for its actual contents and its suggestive capacity.—ANDREW PRESTON PEABODY, *North American Review*, Oct. 1854, p. 536

This book, the record of his residence, his thoughts, and observations during the time he lived in the woods upon the shore of Walden Pond, in Concord, Massachusetts, is of the very best of its kind in any literature.—GEORGE WILLIAM CURTIS, "Editor's Easy Chair," *Harper's New Monthly Magazine*, July 1862, p. 270

He is an author who has fallen into that abeyance, awaiting all authors, great or small, at some time or another; but I think

that with him, at least in regard to his most important book, it can be only transitory. I have not read the story of his hermitage beside Walden Pond since the year 1858, but I have a fancy that if I should take it up now, I should think it a wiser and truer conception of the world than I thought it then. It is no solution of the problem; men are not going to answer the riddle of the painful earth by building themselves shanties and living upon beans and watching ant-fights; but I do not believe Tolstoy himself has more clearly shown the hollowness, the hopelessness, the unworthiness of the life of the world than Thoreau did in that book. If it were newly written it could not fail of a far vaster acceptance than it had then, when to those who thought and felt seriously it seemed that if slavery could only be controlled, all things else would come right of themselves with us.—WILLIAM DEAN HOWELLS, "My First Visit to New England" (1894), *Literary Friends and Acquaintance*, 1900

Some one has said, "Thoreau experienced Nature as other men experience religion." Certainly the life at Walden, which he depicted in one of the most fascinating of books, was in all its details—whether he was ecstatically hoeing beans in his field or dreaming on his door-step, floating on the lake or rambling in forest and field—that of an ascetic and devout worshipper of Nature in all her moods.—THEODORE F. WOLFE, "The Concord Pilgrimage," *Literary Shrines*, 1895, p. 71

Walden, which contains a minute account of the two years at Walden Pond, is Thoreau's best book. It is full of the wild aroma of the woods. In no other book can one come so close to Nature's heart. We hear in it the weird cry of the loons over the water; we watch the frolics of the squirrels; we observe the thousand phenomena of the wonderful little lake; we listen to the forest sounds by day and by night; we study the tell-tale snow; we watch, with bated breath, a battle to the death between two armies of ants. For minute and loving descriptions of the woods and fields, *Walden* has had no rival.—FRED LEWIS PATTEE, A *History of American Literature*, 1896, pp. 224–25

RALPH WALDO EMERSON
From "Thoreau"

Atlantic, August 1862, pp. 239–49

Henry David Thoreau was the last male descendant of a French ancestor who came to this country from the Isle of Guernsey. His character exhibited occasional traits drawn from this blood in singular combination with a very strong Saxon genius.

He was born in Concord, Massachusetts, on the 12th of July, 1817. He was graduated at Harvard College in 1837, but without any literary distinction. An iconoclast in literature, he seldom thanked colleges for their service to him, holding them in small esteem, whilst yet his debt to them was important. After leaving the University, he joined his brother in teaching a private school, which he soon renounced. His father was a manufacturer of lead-pencils, and Henry applied himself for a time to this craft, believing he could make a better pencil than was then in use. After completing his experiments, he exhibited his work to chemists and artists in Boston, and having obtained their certificates to its excellence and to its equality with the best London manufacture, he returned home contented. His friends congratulated him that he had now opened his way to fortune. But he replied, that he should never make another pencil. "Why should I? I would not do again what I have done once." He resumed his endless walks and miscellaneous studies, making every day some new acquaintance with Nature, though as yet never speaking of zoölogy or botany, since, though very studious of natural facts, he was incurious of technical and textual science.

At this time, a strong, healthy youth, fresh from college, whilst all his companions were choosing their profession, or eager to begin some lucrative employment, it was inevitable that his thoughts should be exercised on the same question, and it required rare decision to refuse all the accustomed paths, and keep his solitary freedom at the cost of disappointing the natural expectations of his family and friends: all the more difficult that he had a perfect probity, was exact in securing his own independence, and in holding every man to the like duty. But Thoreau never faltered. He was a born protestant. He declined to give up his large ambition of knowledge and action for any narrow craft or profession, aiming at a much more comprehensive calling, the art of living well. If he slighted and defied the opinions of others, it was only that he was more intent to reconcile his practice with his own belief. Never idle or self-indulgent, he preferred, when he wanted money, earning it by some piece of manual labor agreeable to him, as building a boat or a fence, planting, grafting, surveying, or other short work, to any long engagements. With his hardy habits and few wants, his skill in wood-craft, and his powerful arithmetic, he was very competent to live in any part of the world. It would cost him less time to supply his wants than another. He was therefore secure of his leisure.

A natural skill for mensuration, growing out of his mathematical knowledge, and his habit of ascertaining the measures and distances of objects which interested him, the size of trees, the depth and extent of ponds and rivers, the height of mountains, and the air-line distance of his favorite summits,—this, and his intimate knowledge of the territory about Concord, made him drift into the profession of land-surveyor. It had the advantage for him that it led him continually into new and secluded grounds, and helped his studies of Nature. His accuracy and skill in this work were readily appreciated, and he found all the employment he wanted.

He could easily solve the problems of the surveyor, but he was daily beset with graver questions, which he manfully confronted. He interrogated every custom, and wished to settle all his practice on an ideal foundation. He was a protestant *à l'outrance*, and few lives contain so many renunciations. He was bred to no profession; he never married; he lived alone; he never went to church; he never voted; he refused to pay a tax to the State; he ate no flesh, he drank no wine, he never knew the use of tobacco; and, though a naturalist, he used neither trap nor gun. He chose, wisely, no doubt, for himself, to be the bachelor of thought and Nature. He had no talent for wealth, and knew how to be poor without the least hint of squalor or inelegance. Perhaps he fell into his way of living without forecasting it much, but approved it with later wisdom. "I am often reminded," he wrote in his journal, "that, if I had bestowed on me the wealth of Crœsus, my aims must be still the same, and my means essentially the same." He had no temptations to fight against,—no appetites, no passions, no taste for elegant trifles. A fine house, dress, the manners and talk of highly cultivated people were all thrown away on him. He much preferred a good Indian, and considered these refinements as impediments to conversation, wishing to meet his companion on the simplest terms. He declined invitations to dinner-parties, because there each was in every one's way,

and he could not meet the individuals to any purpose. "They make their pride," he said, "in making their dinner cost much; I make my pride in making my dinner cost little." When asked at table what dish he preferred, he answered, "The nearest." He did not like the taste of wine, and never had a vice in his life. He said,—"I have a faint recollection of pleasure derived from smoking dried lily-stems, before I was a man. I had commonly a supply of these. I have never smoked anything more noxious."

He chose to be rich by making his wants few, and supplying them himself. In his travels, he used the railroad only to get over so much country as was unimportant to the present purpose, walking hundreds of miles, avoiding taverns, buying a lodging in farmers' and fishermen's houses, as cheaper, and more agreeable to him, and because there he could better find the men and the information he wanted.

There was somewhat military in his nature not to be subdued, always manly and able, but rarely tender, as if he did not feel himself except in opposition. He wanted a fallacy to expose, a blunder to pillory, I may say required a little sense of victory, a roll of the drum, to call his powers into full exercise. It cost him nothing to say No; indeed, he found it much easier than to say Yes. It seemed as if his first instinct on hearing a proposition was to controvert it, so impatient was he of the limitations of our daily thought. This habit, of course, is a little chilling to the social affections; and though the companion would in the end acquit him of any malice or untruth, yet it mars conversation. Hence, no equal companion stood in affectionate relations with one so pure and guileless. "I love Henry," said one of his friends, "but I cannot like him; and as for taking his arm, I should as soon think of taking the arm of an elm-tree."

Yet, hermit and stoic as he was, he was really fond of sympathy, and threw himself heartily and childlike into the company of young people whom he loved, and whom he delighted to entertain, as he only could, with the varied and endless anecdotes of his experiences by field and river. And he was always ready to lead a huckleberry-party or a search for chestnuts or grapes. Talking, one day, of a public discourse, Henry remarked, that whatever succeeded with the audience was bad. I said, "Who would not like to write something which all can read, like *Robinson Crusoe?* and who does not see with regret that his page is not solid with a right materialistic treatment, which delights everybody?" Henry objected, of course, and vaunted the better lectures which reached only a few persons. But, at supper, a young girl, understanding that he was to lecture at the Lyceum, sharply asked him, "whether his lecture would be a nice, interesting story, such as she wished to hear, or whether it was one of those old philosophical things that she did not care about." Henry turned to her, and bethought himself, and, I saw, was trying to believe that he had matter that might fit her and her brother, who were to sit up and go to the lecture, if it was a good one for them.

He was a speaker and actor of the truth,—born such,— and was ever running into dramatic situations from this cause. In any circumstance, it interested all bystanders to know what part Henry would take, and what he would say; and he did not disappoint expectation, but used an original judgment on each emergency. In 1845 he built himself a small framed house on the shores of Walden Pond, and lived there two years alone, a life of labor and study. This action was quite native and fit for him. No one who knew him would tax him with affectation. He was more unlike his neighbors in his thought than in his action. As soon as he had exhausted the advantages of that solitude, he abandoned it. In 1847, not approving some uses to which the public expenditure was applied, he refused to pay his town tax, and was put in jail. A friend paid the tax for him, and he was released. The like annoyance was threatened the next year. But, as his friends paid the tax, notwithstanding his protest, I believe he ceased to resist. No opposition or ridicule had any weight with him. He coldly and fully stated his opinion without affecting to believe that it was the opinion of the company. It was of no consequence, if every one present held the opposite opinion. On one occasion he went to the University Library to procure some books. The librarian refused to lend them. Mr. Thoreau repaired to the President, who stated to him the rules and usages, which permitted the loan of books to resident graduates, to clergymen who were alumni, and to some others resident within a circle of ten miles' radius from the College. Mr. Thoreau explained to the President that the railroad had destroyed the old scale of distances,—that the library was useless, yes, and President and College useless, on the terms of his rules,—that the one benefit he owed to the College was its library,—that, at this moment, not only his want of books was imperative, but he wanted a large number of books, and assured him that he, Thoreau, and not the librarian, was the proper custodian of these. In short, the President found the petitioner so formidable, and the rules getting to look so ridiculous, that he ended by giving him a privilege which in his hands proved unlimited thereafter.

No truer American existed than Thoreau. His preference of his country and condition was genuine, and his aversation from English and European manners and tastes almost reached contempt. He listened impatiently to news or *bon mots* gleaned from London circles; and though he tried to be civil, these anecdotes fatigued him. The men were all imitating each other, and on a small mould. Why can they not live as far apart as possible, and each be a man by himself? What he sought was the most energetic nature; and he wished to go to Oregon, not to London. "In every part of Great Britain," he wrote in his diary, "are discovered traces of the Romans, their funereal urns, their camps, their roads, their dwellings. But New England, at least, is not based on any Roman ruins. We have not to lay the foundations of our houses on the ashes of a former civilization."

But, idealist as he was, standing for abolition of slavery, abolition of tariffs, almost for abolition of government, it is needless to say he found himself not only unrepresented in actual politics, but almost equally opposed to every class of reformers. Yet he paid the tribute of his uniform respect to the Anti-Slavery party. One man, whose personal acquaintance he had formed, he honored with exceptional regard. Before the first friendly word had been spoken for Captain John Brown, he sent notices to most houses in Concord, that he would speak in a public hall on the condition and character of John Brown, on Sunday evening, and invited all people to come. The Republican Committee, the Abolitionist Committee, sent him word that it was premature and not advisable. He replied,—"I did not send to you for advice, but to announce that I am to speak." The hall was filled at an early hour by people of all parties, and his earnest eulogy of the hero was heard by all respectfully, by many with a sympathy that surprised themselves.

It was said of Plotinus that he was ashamed of his body, and 'tis very likely he had good reason for it,—that his body was a bad servant, and he had not skill in dealing with the material world, as happens often to men of abstract intellect. But Mr. Thoreau was equipped with a most adapted and serviceable body. He was of short stature, firmly built, of light complexion, with strong, serious blue eyes, and a grave aspect,—his face covered in the late years with a becoming beard. His senses were acute, his frame well-knit and hardy, his hands strong and skilful in the use of tools. And there was a wonderful fitness of body and mind. He could pace sixteen rods more accurately than another man could measure them with rod and chain. He could find his path in the woods at night, he said, better by his feet than his eyes. He could estimate the measure of a tree very well by his eye; he could estimate the weight of a calf or a pig, like a dealer. From a box containing a bushel or more of loose pencils, he could take up with his hands fast enough just a dozen pencils at every grasp. He was a good swimmer, runner, skater, boatman, and would probably outwalk most countrymen in a day's journey. And the relation of body to mind was still finer than we have indicated. He said he wanted every stride his legs made. The length of his walk uniformly made the length of his writing. If shut up in the house, he did not write at all.

He had a strong common sense, like that which Rose Flammock, the weaver's daughter, in Scott's romance, commends in her father, as resembling a yardstick, which, whilst it measures dowlas and diaper, can equally well measure tapestry and cloth of gold. He had always a new resource. When I was planting forest-trees, and had procured half a peck of acorns, he said that only a small portion of them would be sound, and proceeded to examine them, and select the sound ones. But finding this took time, he said, "I think, if you put them all into water, the good ones will sink"; which experiment we tried with success. He could plan a garden, or a house, or a barn; would have been competent to lead a "Pacific Exploring Expedition"; could give judicious counsel in the gravest private or public affairs.

He lived for the day, not cumbered and mortified by his memory. If he brought you yesterday a new proposition, he would bring you to-day another not less revolutionary. A very industrious man, and setting, like all highly organized men, a high value on his time, he seemed the only man of leisure in town, always ready for any excursion that promised well, or for conversation prolonged into late hours. His trenchant sense was never stopped by his rules of daily prudence, but was always up to the new occasion. He liked and used the simplest food, yet, when some one urged a vegetable diet, Thoreau thought all diets a very small matter, saying that "the man who shoots the buffalo lives better than the man who boards at the Graham House." He said,—"You can sleep near the railroad, and never be disturbed: Nature knows very well what sounds are worth attending to, and has made up her mind not to hear the railroad-whistle. But things respect the devout mind, and a mental ecstasy was never interrupted." He noted, what repeatedly befell him, that, after receiving from a distance a rare plant, he would presently find the same in his own haunts. And those pieces of luck which happen only to good players happened to him. One day, walking with a stranger, who inquired where Indian arrow-heads could be found, he replied, "Everywhere," and, stooping forward, picked one on the instant from the ground. At Mount Washington, in Tuckerman's Ravine, Thoreau had a bad fall, and sprained his foot. As he was in the act of getting up from his fall, he saw for the first time the leaves of the *Arnica mollis*.

His robust common sense, armed with stout hands, keen perceptions, and strong will, cannot yet account for the superiority which shone in his simple and hidden life. I must add the cardinal fact, that there was an excellent wisdom in him, proper to a rare class of men, which showed him the material world as a means and symbol. This discovery, which sometimes yields to poets a certain casual and interrupted light, serving for the ornament of their writing, was in him an unsleeping insight; and whatever faults or obstructions of temperament might cloud it, he was not disobedient to the heavenly vision. In his youth, he said, one day, "The other world is all my art: my pencils will draw no other; my jack-knife will cut nothing else; I do not use it as a means." This was the muse and genius that rules his opinions, conversation, studies, work, and course of life. This made him a searching judge of men. At first glance he measured his companion, and, though insensible to some fine traits of culture, could very well report his weight and calibre. And this made the impression of genius which his conversation sometimes gave.

He understood the matter in hand at a glance, and saw the limitations and poverty of those he talked with, so that nothing seemed concealed from such terrible eyes. I have repeatedly known young men of sensibility converted in a moment to the belief that this was the man they were in search of, the man of men, who could tell them all they should do. His own dealing with them was never affectionate, but superior, didactic,— scorning their petty ways,—very slowly conceding, or not conceding at all, the promise of his society at their houses, or even at his own. "Would he not walk with them?" "He did not know. There was nothing so important to him as his walk; he had no walks to throw away on company." Visits were offered him from respectful parties, but he declined them. Admiring friends offered to carry him at their own cost to the Yellow-Stone River,—to the West Indies,—to South America. But though nothing could be more grave or considered than his refusals, they remind one in quite new relations of that fop Brummel's reply to the gentleman who offered him his carriage in a shower, "But where will *you* ride, then?"—and what accusing silences, and what searching and irresistible speeches, battering down all defences, his companions can remember!

Mr. Thoreau dedicated his genius with such entire love to the fields, hills, and waters of his native town, that he made them known and interesting to all reading Americans, and to people over the sea. The river on whose banks he was born and died he knew from its springs to its confluence with the Merrimack. He had made summer and winter observations on it for many years, and at every hour of the day and the night. The result of the recent survey of the Water Commissioners appointed by the State of Massachusetts he had reached by his private experiments, several years earlier. Every fact which occurs in the bed, on the banks, or in the air over it; the fishes, and their spawning and nests, their manners, their food; the shad-flies which fill the air on a certain evening once a year, and which are snapped at by the fishes so ravenously that many of these die of repletion; the conical heaps of small stones on the river-shallows, one of which heaps will sometimes overfill a cart,—these heaps the huge nests of small fishes; the birds which frequent the stream, heron, duck, sheldrake, loon, osprey; the snake, muskrat, otter, woodchuck, and fox, on the banks; the turtle, frog, hyla, and cricket, which make the banks vocal,—were all known to him, and, as it were, townsmen and fellow-creatures; so that he felt an absurdity or violence in any narrative of one of these by itself apart, and still more of its dimensions on an inch-rule, or in the exhibition of its skeleton, or the specimen of a squirrel or a bird in brandy. He liked to speak of the manners of the river, as itself a lawful creature, yet with exactness, and always to an observed fact. As he knew the river, so the ponds in this region.

One of the weapons he used, more important than microscope or alcohol-receiver to other investigators, was a whim which grew on him by indulgence, yet appeared in gravest statement, namely, of extolling his own town and neighborhood as the most favored centre for natural observa-

tion. He remarked that the Flora of Massachusetts embraced almost all the important plants of America,—most of the oaks, most of the willows, the best pines, the ash, the maple, the beech, the nuts. He returned Kane's *Arctic Voyage* to a friend of whom he had borrowed it, with the remark, that "most of the phenomena noted might be observed in Concord." He seemed a little envious of the Pole, for the coincident sunrise and sunset, or five minutes' day after six months: a splendid fact, which Annursnuc had never afforded him. He found red snow in one of his walks, and told me that he expected to find yet the *Victoria regia* in Concord. He was the attorney of the indigenous plants, and owned to a preference of the weeds to the imported plants, as of the Indian to the civilized man,— and noticed, with pleasure, that the willow bean-poles of his neighbor had grown more than his beans. "See these weeds," he said, "which have been hoed at by a million farmers all spring and summer, and yet have prevailed, and just now come out triumphant over all lanes, pastures, fields, and gardens, such is their vigor. We have insulted them with low names, too,—as Pigweed, Wormwood, Chickweed, Shad-Blossom." He says, "They have brave names, too,—Ambrosia, Stellaria, Amelanchia, Amaranth, etc."

I think his fancy for referring everything to the meridian of Concord did not grow out of any ignorance or depreciation of other longitudes or latitudes, but was rather a playful expression of his conviction of the indifferency of all places, and that the best place for each is where he stands. He expressed it once in this wise:—"I think nothing is to be hoped from you, if this bit of mould under your feet is not sweeter to you to eat than any other in this world, or in any world."

The other weapon with which he conquered all obstacles in science was patience. He knew how to sit immovable, a part of the rock he rested on, until the bird, the reptile, the fish, which had retired from him, should come back, and resume its habits, nay, moved by curiosity, should come to him and watch him.

It was a pleasure and a privilege to walk with him. He knew the country like a fox or a bird, and passed through it as freely by paths of his own. He knew every track in the snow or on the ground, and what creature had taken this path before him. One must submit abjectly to such a guide, and the reward was great. Under his arm he carried an old music-book to press plants; in his pocket, his diary and pencil, a spy-glass for birds, microscope, jack-knife, and twine. He wore straw hat, stout shoes, strong gray trousers, to brave shrub-oaks and smilax, and to climb a tree for a hawk's or a squirrel's nest. He waded into the pool for the water-plants, and his strong legs were no insignificant part of his armor. On the day I speak of he looked for the Menyanthes, detected it across the wide pool, and, on examination of the florets, decided that it had been in flower five days. He drew out of his breast-pocket his diary, and read the names of all the plants that should bloom on this day, whereof he kept account as a banker when his notes fall due. The Cypripedium not due till to-morrow. He thought, that, if waked up from a trance, in this swamp, he could tell by the plants what time of the year it was within two days. The redstart was flying about, and presently the fine grosbeaks, whose brilliant scarlet makes the rash gazer wipe his eye, and whose fine clear note Thoreau compared to that of a tanager which has got rid of its hoarseness. Presently he heard a note which he called that of the night-warbler, a bird he had never identified, had been in search of twelve years, which always, when he saw it, was in the act of diving down into a tree or bush, and which it was vain to seek; the only bird that sings indifferently by night and by day. I told him he must beware of finding and booking it, lest life should have nothing more to show him. He said, "What you seek in vain for, half your life, one day you come full upon all the family at dinner. You seek it like a dream, and as soon as you find it you become its prey."

His interest in the flower or the bird lay very deep in his mind, was connected with Nature,—and the meaning of Nature was never attempted to be defined by him. He would not offer a memoir of his observations to the Natural History Society. "Why should I? To detach the description from its connections in my mind would make it no longer true or valuable to me: and they do not wish what belongs to it." His power of observation seemed to indicate additional senses. He saw as with microscope, heard as with ear-trumpet, and his memory was a photographic register of all he saw and heard. And yet none knew better than he that it is not the fact that imports, but the impression or effect of the fact on your mind. Every fact lay in glory in his mind, a type of the order and beauty of the whole.

His determination on Natural History was organic. He confessed that he sometimes felt like a hound or a panther, and, if born among Indians, would have been a fell hunter. But, restrained by his Massachusetts culture, he played out the game in this mild form of botany and ichthyology. His intimacy with animals suggested what Thomas Fuller records of Butler the apiologist, that "either he had told the bees things or the bees had told him." Snakes coiled round his leg; the fishes swam into his hand; and he took them out of the water; he pulled the woodchuck out of its hole by the tail, and took the foxes under his protection from the hunters. Our naturalist had perfect magnanimity; he had no secrets: he would carry you to the heron's haunt, or even to his most prized botanical swamp,—possibly knowing that you could never find it again, yet willing to take his risks.

No college ever offered him a diploma, or a professor's chair; no academy made him its corresponding secretary, its discoverer, or even its member. Whether these learned bodies feared the satire of his presence. Yet so much knowledge of Nature's secret and genius few others possessed, none in a more large and religious synthesis. For not a particle of respect had he to the opinions of any man or body of men, but homage solely to the truth itself; and as he discovered everywhere among doctors some leaning of courtesy, it discredited them. He grew to be revered and admired by his townsmen, who had at first known him only as an oddity. The farmers who employed him as a surveyor soon discovered his rare accuracy and skill, his knowledge of their lands, of trees, of birds, of Indian remains, and the like, which enabled him to tell every farmer more than he knew before of his own farm; so that he began to feel a little as if Mr. Thoreau had better rights in his land than he. They felt, too, the superiority of character which addressed all men with a native authority.

Indian relics abound in Concord,—arrow-heads, stone chisels, pestles, and fragments of pottery; and on the river-bank, large heaps of clam-shells and ashes mark spots which the savages frequented. These, and every circumstance touching the Indian, were important in his eyes. His visits to Maine were chiefly for love of the Indian. He had the satisfaction of seeing the manufacture of the bark-canoe, as well as of trying his hand in its management on the rapids. He was inquisitive about the making of the stone arrow-head, and in his last days charged a youth setting out for the Rocky Mountains to find an Indian who could tell him that: "It was well worth a visit to California to learn it." Occasionally, a small party of Penobscot Indians would visit Concord, and pitch their tents for a few weeks in summer on the river-bank. He failed not to make acquaintance with the best of them; though he well knew that asking questions of Indians is like catechizing beavers and rabbits. In his last visit to Maine he had great satisfaction from Joseph Polis, an intelligent Indian of Oldtown, who was his guide for some weeks.

He was equally interested in every natural fact. The depth of his perception found likeness of law throughout Nature, and I know not any genius who so swiftly inferred universal law from the single fact. He was no pedant of a department. His eye was open to beauty, and his ear to music. He found these, not in rare conditions, but wheresoever he went. He thought the best of music was in single strains; and he found poetic suggestion in the humming of the telegraph-wire.

His poetry might be bad or good; he no doubt wanted a lyric facility and technical skill; but he had the source of poetry in his spiritual perception. He was a good reader and critic, and his judgment on poetry was to the ground of it. He could not be deceived as to the presence or absence of the poetic element in any composition, and his thirst for this made him negligent and perhaps scornful of superficial graces. He would pass by many delicate rhythms, but he would have detected every live stanza or line in a volume, and knew very well where to find an equal poetic charm in prose. He was so enamored of the spiritual beauty that he held all actual written poems in very light esteem in the comparison. He admired Æschylus and Pindar; but, when some one was commending them, he said that "Æschylus and the Greeks, in describing Apollo and Orpheus, had given no song, or no good one. They ought not to have moved trees, but to have chanted to the gods such a hymn as would have sung all their old ideas out of their heads, and new ones in." His own verses are often rude and defective. The gold does not yet run pure, is drossy and crude. The thyme and marjoram are not yet honey. But if he want lyric fineness and technical merits, if he have not the poetic temperament, he never lacks the causal thought, showing that his genius was better than his talent. He knew the worth of the Imagination for the uplifting and consolation of human life, and liked to throw every thought into a symbol. The fact you tell is of no value, but only the impression. For this reason his presence was poetic, always piqued the curiosity to know more deeply the secrets of his mind. He had many reserves, an unwillingness to exhibit to profane eyes what was still sacred in his own, and knew well how to throw a poetic veil over his experience. All readers of *Walden* will remember his mythical record of his disappointments:—

> I long ago lost a hound, a bay horse, and a turtle-dove, and am still on their trail. Many are the travellers I have spoken concerning them, describing their tracks, and what calls they answered to. I have met one or two who had heard the hound, and the tramp of the horse, and even seen the dove disappear behind a cloud; and they seemed as anxious to recover them as if they had lost them themselves. [1]

His riddles were worth the reading, and I confide, that, if at any time I do not understand the expression, it is yet just. Such was the wealth of his truth that it was not worth his while to use words in vain. His poem entitled "Sympathy" reveals the tenderness under that triple steel of stoicism, and the intellectual subtilty it could animate. His classic poem on "Smoke" suggests Simonides, but is better than any poem of Simonides. His biography is in his verses. His habitual thought makes all his poetry a hymn to the Cause of causes, the Spirit which vivifies and controls his own.

I hearing get, who had but ears,
And sight, who had but eyes before;
I moments live, who lived but years,
And truth discern, who knew but learning's lore.

And still more in these religious lines:—

Now chiefly is my natal hour,
And only now my prime of life;
I will not doubt the love untold,
Which not my worth or want hath bought,
Which wooed me young, and wooes me old,
And to this evening hath me brought.

Whilst he used in his writings a certain petulance of remark in reference to churches or churchmen, he was a person of a rare, tender, and absolute religion, a person incapable of any profanation, by act or by thought. Of course, the same isolation which belonged to his original thinking and living detached him from the social religious forms. This is neither to be censured nor regretted. Aristotle long ago explained it, when he said, "One who surpasses his fellow-citizens in virtue is no longer a part of the city. Their law is not for him, since he is a law to himself."

Thoreau was sincerity itself, and might fortify the convictions of prophets in the ethical laws by his holy living. It was an affirmative experience which refused to be set aside. A truth-speaker he, capable of the most deep and strict conversation; a physician to the wounds of any soul; a friend, knowing not only the secret of friendship, but almost worshipped by those few persons who resorted to him as their confessor and prophet, and knew the deep value of his mind and great heart. He thought that without religion or devotion of some kind nothing great was ever accomplished: and he thought that the bigoted sectarian had better bear this in mind.

His virtues, of course, sometimes ran into extremes. It was easy to trace to the inexorable demand on all for exact truth that austerity which made this willing hermit more solitary even than he wished. Himself of a perfect probity, he required not less of others. He had a disgust at crime, and no worldly success would cover it. He detected paltering as readily in dignified and prosperous persons as in beggars, and with equal scorn. Such dangerous frankness was in his dealing that his admirers called him "that terrible Thoreau," as if he spoke when silent, and was still present when he had departed. I think the severity of his ideal interfered to deprive him of a healthy sufficiency of human society.

The habit of a realist to find things the reverse of their appearance inclined him to put every statement in a paradox. A certain habit of antagonism defaced his earlier writings,—a trick of rhetoric not quite outgrown in his later, of substituting for the obvious word and thought its diametrical opposite. He praised wild mountains and winter forests for their domestic air, in snow and ice he would find sultriness, and commended the wilderness for resembling Rome and Paris. "It was so dry, that you might call it wet."

The tendency to magnify the moment, to read all the laws of Nature in the one object or one combination under your eye, is of course comic to those who do not share the philosopher's perception of identity. To him there was no such thing as size. The pond was a small ocean; the Atlantic, a large Walden Pond. He referred every minute fact to cosmical laws. Though he meant to be just, he seemed haunted by a certain chronic assumption that the science of the day pretended completeness, and he had just found out that the *savans* had neglected to discriminate a particular botanical variety, had failed to describe the seeds or count the sepals. "That is to say,"

we replied, "the blockheads were not born in Concord; but who said they were? It was their unspeakable misfortune to be born in London, or Paris, or Rome; but, poor fellows, they did what they could, considering that they never saw Bateman's Pond, or Nine-Acre Corner, or Becky-Stow's Swamp. Besides, what were you sent into the world for, but to add this observation?"

Had his genius been only contemplative, he had been fitted to his life, but with his energy and practical ability he seemed born for great enterprise and for command; and I so much regret the loss of his rare powers of action, that I cannot help counting it a fault in him that he had no ambition. Wanting this, instead of engineering for all America, he was the captain of a huckleberry-party. Pounding beans is good to the end of pounding empires one of these days; but if, at the end of years, it is still only beans!

But these foibles, real or apparent, were fast vanishing in the incessant growth of a spirit so robust and wise, and which effaced its defeats with new triumphs. His study of Nature was a perpetual ornament to him, and inspired his friends with curiosity to see the world through his eyes, and to hear his adventures. They possessed every kind of interest.

He had many elegances of his own, whilst he scoffed at conventional elegance. Thus, he could not bear to hear the sound of his own steps, the grit of gravel; and therefore never willingly walked in the road, but in the grass, on mountains and in woods. His senses were acute, and he remarked that by night every dwelling-house gives out bad air, like a slaughter-house. He liked the pure fragrance of melilot. He honored certain plants with special regard, and, over all, the pond-lily,—then, the gentian, and the *Mikania scandens*, and "life-everlasting," and a bass-tree which he visited every year when it bloomed, in the middle of July. He thought the scent a more oracular inquisition than the sight,—more oracular and trustworthy. The scent, of course, reveals what is concealed from the other senses. By it he detected earthiness. He delighted in echoes, and said they were almost the only kind of kindred voices that he heard. He loved Nature so well, was so happy in her solitude, that he became very jealous of cities, and the sad work which their refinements and artifices made with man and his dwelling. The axe was always destroying his forest. "Thank God," he said, "they cannot cut down the clouds!" "All kinds of figures are drawn on the blue ground with this fibrous white paint." ⟨. . .⟩

There is a flower known to botanists, one of the same genus with our summer plant called "Life-Everlasting," a *Gnaphalium* like that, which grows on the most inaccessible cliffs of the Tyrolese mountains, where the chamois dare hardly venture, and which the hunter, tempted by its beauty, and by his love, (for it is immensely valued by the Swiss maidens,) climbs the cliffs to gather, and is sometimes found dead at the foot, with the flower in his hand. It is called by botanists the *Gnaphalium leontopodium*, but by the Swiss *Edelweisse*, which signifies *Noble Purity*. Thoreau seemed to me living in the hope to gather this plant, which belonged to him of right. The scale on which his studies proceeded was so large as to require longevity, and we were the less prepared for his sudden disappearance. The country knows not yet, or in the least part, how great a son it has lost. It seems an injury that he should leave in the midst his broken task, which none else can finish,—a kind of indignity to so noble a soul, that it should depart out of Nature before yet he has been really shown to his peers for what he is. But he, at least, is content. His soul was made for the noblest society; he had in a short life exhausted the capabilities of this world; wherever there is knowledge, wherever there is virtue, wherever there is beauty, he will find a home.

Notes
1. *Walden*, p. 20.

JAMES RUSSELL LOWELL
From "Thoreau" (1865)
Works, Riverside ed.
1890, Volume 1, pp. 368–81

I have just been renewing my recollection of Mr. Thoreau's writings, and have read through his six volumes in the order of their production. I shall try to give an adequate report of their impression upon me both as critic and as mere reader. He seems to me to have been a man with so high a conceit of himself that he accepted without questioning, and insisted on our accepting, his defects and weaknesses of character as virtues and powers peculiar to himself. Was he indolent, he finds none of the activities which attract or employ the rest of mankind worthy of him. Was he wanting in the qualities that make success, it is success that is contemptible, and not himself that lacks persistency and purpose. Was he poor, money was an unmixed evil. Did his life seem a selfish one, he condemns doing good as one of the weakest of superstitions. To be of use was with him the most killing bait of the wily tempter Uselessness. He had no faculty of generalization from outside of himself, or at least no experience which would supply the material of such, and he makes his own whim the law, his own range the horizon of the universe. He condemns a world, the hollowness of whose satisfactions he had never had the means of testing, and we recognize Apemantus behind the mask of Timon. He had little active imagination; of the receptive he had much. His appreciation is of the highest quality; his critical power, from want of continuity of mind, very limited and inadequate. He somewhere cites a simile from Ossian, as an example of the superiority of the old poetry to the new, though, even were the historic evidence less convincing, the sentimental melancholy of those poems should be conclusive of their modernness. He had none of the artistic mastery which controls a great work to the serene balance of completeness, but exquisite mechanical skill in the shaping of sentences and paragraphs, or (more rarely) short bits of verse for the expression of a detached thought, sentiment, or image. His works give one the feeling of a sky full of stars,—something impressive and exhilarating certainly, something high overhead and freckled thickly with spots of isolated brightness; but whether these have any mutual relation with each other, or have any concern with our mundane matters, is for the most part matter of conjecture,—astrology as yet, and not astronomy.

It is curious, considering what Thoreau afterwards became, that he was not by nature an observer. He only saw the things he looked for, and was less poet than naturalist. Till he built his Walden shanty, he did not know that the hickory grew in Concord. Till he went to Maine, he had never seen phosphorescent wood, a phenomenon early familiar to most country boys. At forty he speaks of the seeding of the pine as a new discovery, though one should have thought that its gold-dust of blowing pollen might have earlier drawn his eye. Neither his attention nor his genius was of the spontaneous kind. He discovered nothing. He thought everything a discovery of his own, from moonlight to the planting of acorns and nuts by squirrels. This is a defect in his character, but one of

his chief charms as a writer. Everything grows fresh under his hand. He delved in his mind and nature; he planted them with all manner of native and foreign seeds, and reaped assiduously. He was not merely solitary, he would be isolated, and succeeded at last in almost persuading himself that he was autochtonous. He valued everything in proportion as he fancied it to be exclusively his own. He complains in *Walden* that there is no one in Concord with whom he could talk of Oriental literature, though the man was living within two miles of his hut who had introduced him to it. This intellectual selfishness becomes sometimes almost painful in reading him. He lacked that generosity of "communication" which Johnson admired in Burke. De Quincey tells us that Wordsworth was impatient when any one else spoke of mountains, as if he had a peculiar property in them. And we can readily understand why it should be so: no one is satisfied with another's appreciation of his mistress. But Thoreau seems to have prized a lofty way of thinking (often we should be inclined to call it a remote one) not so much because it was good in itself as because he wished few to share it with him. It seems now and then as if he did not seek to lure others up "above our lower region of turmoil," but to leave his own name cut on the mountain peak as the first climber. This itch of originality infects his thought and style. To be misty is not to be mystic. He turns commonplaces end for end, and fancies it makes something new of them. As we walk down Park Street, our eye is caught by Dr. Winship's dumb-bells, one of which bears an inscription testifying that it is the heaviest ever put up at arm's length by any athlete; and in reading Mr. Thoreau's books we cannot help feeling as if he sometimes invited our attention to a particular sophism or parodox as the biggest yet maintained by any single writer. He seeks, at all risks, for perversity of thought, and revives the age of *concetti* while he fancies himself going back to a pre-classical nature. "A day," he says, "passed in the society of those Greek sages, such as described in the Banquet of Xenophon, would not be comparable with the dry wit of decayed cranberry-vines and the fresh Attic salt of the moss-beds." It is not so much the True that he loves as the Out-of-the-Way. As the Brazen Age shows itself in other men by exaggeration of phrase, so in him by extravagance of statement. He wishes always to trump your suit and to *ruff* when you least expect it. Do you love Nature because she is beautiful? He will find a better argument in her ugliness. Are you tired of the artificial man? He instantly dresses you up an ideal in a Penobscot Indian, and attributes to this creature of his otherwise-mindedness as peculiarities things that are common to all woodsmen, white or red, and this simply because he has not studied the pale-faced variety.

This notion of an absolute originality, as if one could have a patent-right in it, is an absurdity. A man cannot escape in thought, any more than he can in language, from the past and the present. As no one ever invents a word, and yet language somehow grows by general contribution and necessity, so it is with thought. Mr. Thoreau seems to me to insist in public on going back to flint and steel, when there is a match-box in his pocket which he knows very well how to use at a pinch. Originality consists in power of digesting and assimilating thought, so that they become part of our life and substance. Montaigne, for example, is one of the most original of authors, though he helped himself to ideas in every direction. But they turn to blood and coloring in his style, and give a freshness of complexion that is forever charming. In Thoreau much seems yet to be foreign and unassimilated, showing itself in symptoms of indigestion. A preacher-up of Nature, we now and then detect under the surly and stoic garb something of the sophist and the sentimentalizer. I am far from implying that this was conscious on his part. But it is much easier for a man to impose on himself when he measures only with himself. A greater familiarity with ordinary men would have done Thoreau good, by showing him how many fine qualities are common to the race. The radical vice of his theory of life was that he confounded physical with spiritual remoteness from men. A man is far enough withdrawn from his fellows if he keep himself clear of their weaknesses. He is not so truly withdrawn as exiled, if he refuse to share in their strength. "Solitude," says Cowley, "can be well fitted and set right but upon a very few persons. They must have enough knowledge of the world to see the vanity of it, and enough virtue to despise all vanity." It is a morbid self-consciousness that pronounces the world of men empty and worthless before trying it, the instinctive evasion of one who is sensible of some innate weakness, and retorts the accusation of it before any has made it but himself. To a healthy mind, the world is a constant challenge of opportunity. Mr. Thoreau had not a healthy mind, or he would not have been so fond of prescribing. His whole life was a search for the doctor. The old mystics had a wiser sense of what the world was worth. They ordained a severe apprenticeship to law, and even ceremonial, in order to the gaining of freedom and mastery over these. Seven years of service for Rachel were to be rewarded at last with Leah. Seven other years of faithfulness with her were to win them at last the true bride of their souls. Active Life was with them the only path to the Contemplative.

Thoreau had no humor, and this implies that he was a sorry logician. Himself an artist in rhetoric, he confounds thought with style when he undertakes to speak of the latter. He was forever talking of getting away from the world, but he must be always near enough to it, nay, to the Concord corner of it, to feel the impression he makes there. He verifies the shrewd remark of Sainte-Beuve, "On touche encore à son temps et très-fort, même quand on le repousse." This egotism of his is a Stylites pillar after all, a seclusion which keeps him in the public eye. The dignity of man is an excellent thing, but therefore to hold one's self too sacred and precious is the reverse of excellent. There is something delightfully absurd in six volumes addressed to a world of such "vulgar fellows" as Thoreau affirmed his fellowmen to be. I once had a glimpse of a genuine solitary who spent his winters one hundred and fifty miles beyond all human communication, and there dwelt with his rifle as his only confidant. Compared with this, the shanty on Walden Pond has something the air, it must be confessed, of the Hermitage of La Chevrette. I do not believe that the way to a true cosmopolitanism carries one into the woods or the society of musquashes. Perhaps the narrowest provincialism is that of Self; that of Kleinwinkel is nothing to it. The natural man, like the singing birds, comes out of the forest as inevitably as the natural bear and the wildcat stick there. To seek to be natural implies a consciousness that forbids all naturalness forever. It is as easy—and no easier—to be natural in a *salon* as in a swamp, if one do not aim at it, for what we call unnaturalness always has its spring in a man's thinking too much about himself. "It is impossible," said Turgot, "for a vulgar man to be simple."

I look upon a great deal of the modern sentimentalism about Nature as a mark of disease. It is one more symptom of the general liver-complaint. To a man of wholesome constitution the wilderness is well enough for a mood or a vacation, but not for a habit of life. Those who have most loudly advertised their passion for seclusion and their intimacy with nature, from Petrarch down, have been mostly sentimentalists, unreal men, misanthropes on the spindle side, solacing an uneasy suspicion

of themselves by professing contempt for their kind. They make demands on the world in advance proportioned to their inward measure of their own merit, and are angry that the world pays only by the visible measure of performance. It is true of Rousseau, the modern founder of the sect, true of Saint Pierre, his intellectual child, and of Châteaubriand, his grandchild, the inventor, we might almost say, of the primitive forest, and who first was touched by the solemn falling of a tree from natural decay in the windless silence of the woods. It is a very shallow view that affirms trees and rocks to be healthy, and cannot see that men in communities are just as true to the laws of their organization and destiny; that can tolerate the puffin and the fox, but not the fool and the knave; that would shun politics because of its demagogues, and snuff up the stench of the obscene fungus. The divine life of Nature is more wonderful, more various, more sublime in man than in any other of her works, and the wisdom that is gained by commerce with men, as Montaigne and Shakespeare gained it, or with one's own soul among men, as Dante, is the most delightful, as it is the most precious, of all. In outward nature it is still man that interests us, and we care far less for the things seen than the way in which they are seen by poetic eyes like Wordsworth's or Thoreau's, and the reflections they cast there. To hear the to-do that is often made over the simple fact that a man sees the image of himself in the outward world, one is reminded of a savage when he for the first time catches a glimpse of himself in a looking-glass. "Venerable child of Nature," we are tempted to say, "to whose science in the invention of the tobacco-pipe, to whose art in the tattooing of thine undegenerate hide not yet enslaved by tailors, we are slowly striving to climb back, the miracle thou beholdest is sold in my unhappy country for a shilling!" If matters go on as they have done, and everybody must needs blab of all the favors that have been done him by roadside and river-brink and woodland walk, as if to kiss and tell were no longer treachery, it will be a positive refreshment to meet a man who is as superbly indifferent to Nature as she is to him. By and by we shall have John Smith, of No. –12 –12th Street, advertising that he is not the J. S. who saw a cowlily on Thursday last, as he never saw one in his life, would not see one if he could, and is prepared to prove an alibi on the day in question.

Solitary communion with Nature does not seem to have been sanitary or sweetening in its influence on Thoreau's character. On the contrary, his letters show him more cynical as he grew older. While he studied with respectful attention the minks and woodchucks, his neighbors, he looked with utter contempt on the august drama of destiny of which his country was the scene, and on which the curtain had already risen. He was converting us back to a state of nature "so eloquently," as Voltaire said of Rousseau, "that he almost persuaded us to go on all fours," while the wiser fates were making it possible for us to walk erect for the first time. Had he conversed more with his fellows, his sympathies would have widened with the assurance that his peculiar genius had more appreciation, and his writings a larger circle of readers, or at least a warmer one, than he dreamed of. We have the highest testimony[1] to the natural sweetness, sincerity, and nobleness of his temper, and in his books an equally irrefragable one to the rare quality of his mind. He was not a strong thinker, but a sensitive feeler. Yet his mind strikes us as cold and wintry in its purity. A light snow has fallen everywhere in which he seems to come on the track of the shier sensations that would elsewhere leave no trace. We think greater compression would have done more for his fame. A feeling of sameness comes over us as we read so much. Trifles are recorded with an over-minute punctuality and conscientiousness of detail. He registers the state of his personal thermometer thirteen times a day. We cannot help thinking sometimes of the man who

> Watches, starves, freezes, and sweats
> To learn but catechisms and alphabets
> Of unconcerning things, matters of fact,

and sometimes of the saying of the Persian poet, that "when the owl would boast, he boasts of catching mice at the edge of a hole." We could readily part with some of his affectations. It was well enough for Pythagoras to say, once for all, "When I was Euphorbus at the siege of Troy"; not so well for Thoreau to travesty it into "When I was a shepherd on the plains of Assyria." A naïve thing said over again is anything but naïve. But with every exception, there is no writing comparable with Thoreau's in kind, that is comparable with it in degree where it is best; where it disengages itself, that is, from the tangled roots and dead leaves of a second-hand Orientalism, and runs limpid and smooth and broadening as it runs, a mirror for whatever is grand and lovely in both worlds.

George Sand says neatly, that "Art is not a study of positive reality," (*actuality* were the fitter word,) "but a seeking after ideal truth." It would be doing very inadequate justice to Thoreau if we left it to be inferred that this ideal element did not exist in him, and that too in larger proportion, if less obtrusive, than his nature-worship. He took nature as the mountain-path to an ideal world. If the path wind a good deal, if he record too faithfully every trip over a root, if he botanize somewhat wearisomely, he gives us now and then superb outlooks from some jutting crag, and brings us out at last into an illimitable ether, where the breathing is not difficult for those who have any true touch of the climbing spirit. His shanty-life was a mere impossibility, so far as his own conception of it goes, as an entire independency of mankind. The tub of Diogenes had a sounder bottom. Thoreau's experiment actually presupposed all that complicated civilization which it theoretically abjured. He squatted on another man's land; he borrows an axe; his boards, his nails, his bricks, his mortar, his books, his lamp, his fish-hooks, his plough, his hoe, all turn state's evidence against him as an accomplice in the sin of that artificial civilization which rendered it possible that such a person as Henry D. Thoreau should exist at all. *Magnis tamen excidit ausis.* His aim was a noble and a useful one, in the direction of "plain living and high thinking." It was a practical sermon on Emerson's text that "things are in the saddle and ride mankind," an attempt to solve Carlyle's problem (condensed from Johnson) of "lessening your denominator." His whole life was a rebuke of the waste and aimlessness of our American luxury, which is an abject enslavement to tawdry upholstery. He had "fine translunary things" in him. His better style as a writer is in keeping with the simplicity and purity of his life. We have said that his range was narrow, but to be a master is to be a master. He had caught his English at its living source, among the poets and prose-writers of its best days; his literature was extensive and recondite; his quotations are always nuggets of the purest ore: there are sentences of his as perfect as anything in the language, and thoughts as clearly crystallized; his metaphors and images are always fresh from the soil; he had watched Nature like a detective who is to go upon the stand; as we read him, it seems as if all-out-of-doors had kept a diary and become its own Montaigne; we look at the landscape as in a Claude Lorraine glass; compared with his, all other books of similar aim, even White's "Selborne," seem dry as a country clergyman's meteorological journal in an old almanac. He belongs with Donne and Browne and Novalis; if not with the

originally creative men, with the scarcely smaller class who are peculiar, and whose leaves shed their invisible thought-seed like ferns.

Notes

1. Mr. Emerson, in the Biographical Sketch prefixed to the *Excursions.*

ROBERT LOUIS STEVENSON
"Henry David Thoreau:
His Character and Opinions" (1880)
and "Preface, By Way of Criticism" (1882)
Familiar Studies of Men and Books
1882, pp. 137–73, 18–21

I

Thoreau's thin, penetrating, big-nosed face, even in a bad woodcut, conveys some hint of the limitations of his mind and character. With his almost acid sharpness of insight, with his almost animal dexterity in act, there went none of that large, unconscious geniality of the world's heroes. He was not easy, not ample, not urbane, not even kind; his enjoyment was hardly smiling, or the smile was not broad enough to be convincing; he had no waste lands nor kitchen-midden in his nature, but was all improved and sharpened to a point. "He was bred to no profession," says Emerson; "he never married; he lived alone; he never went to church; he never voted; he refused to pay a tax to the State; he ate no flesh, he drank no wine, he never knew the use of tobacco; and, though a naturalist, he used neither trap nor gun. When asked at dinner what dish he preferred, he answered, 'the nearest.'" So many negative superiorities begin to smack a little of the prig. From his later works he was in the habit of cutting out the humorous passages, under the impression that they were beneath the dignity of his moral muse; and there we see the prig stand public and confessed. It was "much easier," says Emerson acutely, much easier for Thoreau to say *no* than *yes*; and that is a characteristic which depicts the man. It is a useful accomplishment to be able to say *no*, but surely it is the essence of amiability to prefer to say *yes* where it is possible. There is something wanting in the man who does not hate himself whenever he is constrained to say no. And there was a great deal wanting in this born dissenter. He was almost shockingly devoid of weaknesses; he had not enough of them to be truly polar with humanity; whether you call him demi-god or demi-man, he was at least not altogether one of us, for he was not touched with a feeling of our infirmities. The world's heroes have room for all positive qualities, even those which are disreputable, in the capacious theatre of their dispositions. Such can live many lives; while a Thoreau can live but one, and that only with perpetual foresight.

He was no ascetic, rather an Epicurean of the nobler sort; and he had this one great merit, that he succeeded so far as to be happy. "I love my fate to the core and rind," he wrote once; and even while he lay dying, here is what he dictated (for it seems he was already too feeble to control the pen): "You ask particularly after my health. I *suppose* that I have not many months to live, but of course know nothing about it. I may say that I am enjoying existence as much as ever, and regret nothing." It is not given to all to bear so clear a testimony to the sweetness of their fate, nor to any without courage and wisdom; for this world in itself is but a painful and uneasy place of residence, and lasting happiness, at least to the self-conscious, comes only from within. Now Thoreau's content and ecstasy in living was, we may say, like a plant that he had watered and tended with womanish solicitude; for there is apt to be something unmanly, something almost dastardly, in a life that does not move with dash and freedom, and that fears the bracing contact of the world. In one word, Thoreau was a skulker. He did not wish virtue to go out of him among his fellow-men, but slunk into a corner to hoard it for himself. He left all for the sake of certain virtuous self-indulgences. It is true that his tastes were noble; that his ruling passion was to keep himself unspotted from the world; and that his luxuries were all of the same healthy order as cold tubs and early rising. But a man may be both coldly cruel in the pursuit of goodness, and morbid even in the pursuit of health. I cannot lay my hands on the passage in which he explains his abstinence from tea and coffee, but I am sure I have the meaning correctly. It is this: He thought it bad economy and worthy of no true virtuoso to spoil the natural rapture of the morning with such muddy stimulants; let him but see the sun rise, and he was already sufficiently inspirited for the labors of the day. That may be reason good enough to abstain from tea; but when we go on to find the same man, on the same or similar grounds, abstain from nearly everything that his neighbors innocently and pleasurably use, and from the rubs and trials of human society itself into the bargain, we recognize that valetudinarian healthfulness which is more delicate than sickness itself. We need have no respect for a state of artificial training. True health is to be able to do without it. Shakespeare, we can imagine, might begin the day upon a quart of ale, and yet enjoy the sunrise to the full as much as Thoreau, and commemorate his enjoyment in vastly better verses. A man who must separate himself from his neighbors' habits in order to be happy, is in much the same case with one who requires to take opium for the same purpose. What we want to see is one who can breast into the world, do a man's work, and still preserve his first and pure enjoyment of existence.

Thoreau's faculties were of a piece with his moral shyness; for they were all delicacies. He could guide himself about the woods on the darkest night by the touch of his feet. He could pick up at once an exact dozen of pencils by the feeling, pace distances with accuracy, and gauge cubic contents by the eye. His smell was so dainty that he could perceive the fœtor of dwelling-houses as he passed them by at night; his palate so unsophisticated that, like a child, he disliked the taste of wine—or perhaps, living in America, had never tasted any that was good; and his knowledge of nature was so complete and curious that he could have told the time of year, within a day or so, by the aspect of the plants. In his dealings with animals, he was the original of Hawthorne's Donatello. He pulled the woodchuck out of its hole by the tail; the hunted fox came to him for protection; wild squirrels have been seen to nestle in his waistcoat; he would thrust his arm into a pool and bring forth a bright, panting fish, lying undismayed in the palm of his hand. There were few things that he could not do. He could make a house, a boat, a pencil, or a book. He was a surveyor, a scholar, a natural historian. He could run, walk, climb, skate, swim, and manage a boat. The smallest occasion served to display his physical accomplishment; and a manufacturer, from merely observing his dexterity with the window of a railway carriage, offered him a situation on the spot. "The only fruit of much living," he observes, "is the ability to do some slight thing better." But such was the exactitude of his senses, so alive was he in every fibre, that it seems as if the maxim should be changed in his case, for he could do most things with unusual perfection. And perhaps he had an approving eye to himself when he wrote: "Though the youth at last grows indifferent, the laws of the universe are not indifferent, *but are forever on the side of the most sensitive.*"

II

Thoreau had decided, it would seem, from the very first to lead a life of self-improvement: the needle did not tremble as with richer natures, but pointed steadily north; and as he saw duty and inclination in one, he turned all his strength in that direction. He was met upon the threshold by a common difficulty. In this world, in spite of its many agreeable features, even the most sensitive must undergo some drudgery to live. It is not possible to devote your time to study and meditation without what are quaintly but happily denominated private means; these absent, a man must contrive to earn his bread by some service to the public such as the public cares to pay him for; or, as Thoreau loved to put it, Apollo must serve Admetus. This was to Thoreau even a sourer necessity than it is to most; there was a love of freedom, a strain of the wild man, in his nature, that rebelled with violence against the yoke of custom; and he was so eager to cultivate himself and to be happy in his own society, that he could consent with difficulty even to the interruptions of friendship. "*Such are my engagements to myself* that I dare not promise," he once wrote in answer to an invitation; and the italics are his own. Marcus Aurelius found time to study virtue, and between whiles to conduct the imperial affairs of Rome; but Thoreau is so busy improving himself, that he must think twice about a morning call. And now imagine him condemned for eight hours a day to some uncongenial and unmeaning business! He shrank from the very look of the mechanical in life; all should, if possible, be sweetly spontaneous and swimmingly progressive. Thus he learned to make leadpencils, and, when he had gained the best certificate and his friends began to congratulate him on his establishment in life, calmly announced that he should never make another. "Why should I?" said he; "I would not do again what I have done once." For when a thing has once been done as well as it wants to be, it is of no further interest to the self-improver. Yet in after years, and when it became needful to support his family, he returned patiently to this mechanical art—a step more than worthy of himself.

The pencils seem to have been Apollo's first experiment in the service of Admetus; but others followed. "I have thoroughly tried school-keeping," he writes, "and found that my expenses were in proportion, or rather out of proportion, to my income; for I was obliged to dress and train, not to say think and believe, accordingly, and I lost my time into the bargain. As I did not teach for the benefit of my fellowmen, but simply for a livelihood, this was a failure. I have tried trade, but I found that it would take ten years to get under way in that, and that then I should probably be on my way to the devil." Nothing, indeed, can surpass his scorn for all so-called business. Upon that subject gall squirts from him at a touch. "The whole enterprise of this nation is not illustrated by a thought," he writes; "it is not warmed by a sentiment; there is nothing in it for which a man should lay down his life, nor even his gloves." And again: "If our merchants did not most of them fail, and the banks too, my faith in the old laws of this world would be staggered. The statement that ninety-six in a hundred doing such business surely break down is perhaps the sweetest fact that statistics have revealed." The wish was probably father to the figures; but there is something enlivening in a hatred of so genuine a brand, hot as Corsican revenge, and sneering like Voltaire.

Pencils, school-keeping, and trade being thus discarded

one after another, Thoreau, with a stroke of strategy, turned the position. He saw his way to get his board and lodging for practically nothing; and Admetus never got less work out of any servant since the world began. It was his ambition to be an oriental philosopher; but he was always a very Yankee sort of oriental. Even in the peculiar attitude in which he stood to money, his system of personal economics, as we may call it, he displayed a vast amount of truly down-East calculation, and he adopted poverty like a piece of business. Yet his system is based on one or two ideas which, I believe, come naturally to all thoughtful youths, and are only pounded out of them by city uncles. Indeed, something essentially youthful distinguishes all Thoreau's knock-down blows at current opinion. Like the posers of a child, they leave the orthodox in a kind of speechless agony. These know the thing is nonsense. They are sure there must be an answer, yet somehow cannot find it. So it is with his system of economy. He cuts through the subject on so new a plane that the accepted arguments apply no longer; he attacks it in a new dialect where there are no catchwords ready made for the defender; after you have been boxing for years on a polite, gladiatorial convention, here is an assailant who does not scruple to hit below the belt.

"The cost of a thing," says he, "is *the amount of what I will call life* which is required to be exchanged for it, immediately or in the long run." I have been accustomed to put it to myself, perhaps more clearly, that the price we have to pay for money is paid in liberty. Between these two ways of it, at least, the reader will probably not fail to find a third definition of his own; and it follows, on one or other, that a man may pay too dearly for his livelihood, by giving, in Thoreau's terms, his whole life for it, or, in mine, bartering for it the whole of his available liberty, and becoming a slave till death. There are two questions to be considered—the quality of what we buy, and the price we have to pay for it. Do you want a thousand a year, a two thousand a year, or a ten thousand a year livelihood? and can you afford the one you want? It is a matter of taste; it is not in the least degree a question of duty, though commonly supposed so. But there is no authority for that view anywhere. It is nowhere in the Bible. It is true that we might do a vast amount of good if we were wealthy, but it is also highly improbable; not many do; and the art of growing rich is not only quite distinct from that of doing good, but the practice of the one does not at all train a man for practising the other. "Money might be of great service to me," writes Thoreau; "but the difficulty now is that I do not improve my opportunities, and therefore I am not prepared to have my opportunities increased." It is a mere illusion that, above a certain income, the personal desires will be satisfied and leave a wider margin for the generous impulse. It is as difficult to be generous, or anything else, except perhaps a member of Parliament, on thirty thousand as on two hundred a year.

Now Thoreau's tastes were well defined. He loved to be free, to be master of his times and seasons, to indulge the mind rather than the body; he preferred long rambles to rich dinners, his own reflections to the consideration of society, and an easy, calm, unfettered, active life among green trees to dull toiling at the counter of a bank. And such being his inclination he determined to gratify it. A poor man must save off something; he determined to save off his livelihood. "When a man has attained those things which are necessary to life," he writes, "there is another alternative than to obtain the superfluities; *he may adventure on life now*, his vacation from humbler toil having commenced." Thoreau would get shelter, some kind of covering for his body, and necessary daily bread; even these he should get as cheaply as possible; and then, his vacation from humbler toil having commenced, devote himself to oriental philosophers, the study of nature, and the work of self-improvement.

Prudence, which bids us all go to the ant for wisdom and hoard against the day of sickness, was not a favorite with Thoreau. He preferred that other, whose name is so much misappropriated: Faith. When he had secured the necessaries of the moment, he would not reckon up possible accidents or torment himself with trouble for the future. He had no toleration for the man "who ventures to live only by the aid of the mutual insurance company, which has promised to bury him decently." He would trust himself a little to the world. "We may safely trust a good deal more than we do," says he. "How much is not done by us! or what if we had been taken sick?" And then, with a stab of satire, he describes contemporary mankind in a phrase: "All the day long on the alert, at night we unwillingly say our prayers and commit ourselves to uncertainties." It is not likely that the public will be much affected by Thoreau, when they blink the direct injunctions of the religion they profess; and yet, whether we will or no, we make the same hazardous ventures; we back our own health and the honesty of our neighbors for all that we are worth; and it is chilling to think how many must lose their wager.

In 1845, twenty-eight years old, an age by which the liveliest have usually declined into some conformity with the world, Thoreau, with a capital of something less than five pounds and a borrowed axe, walked forth into the woods by Walden Pond, and began his new experiment in life. He built himself a dwelling, and returned the axe, he says with characteristic and workman-like pride, sharper than when he borrowed it; he reclaimed a patch, where he cultivated beans, peas, potatoes, and sweet corn; he had his bread to bake, his farm to dig, and for the matter of six weeks in the summer he worked at surveying, carpentry, or some other of his numerous dexterities, for hire. For more than five years, this was all that he required to do for his support, and he had the winter and most of the summer at his entire disposal. For six weeks of occupation, a little cooking and a little gentle hygienic gardening, the man, you may say, had as good as stolen his livelihood. Or we must rather allow that he had done far better; for the thief himself is continually and busily occupied; and even one born to inherit a million will have more calls upon his time than Thoreau. Well might he say, "What old people tell you you cannot do, you try and find you can." And how surprising is his conclusion: "I am convinced that *to maintain oneself on this earth is not a hardship, but a pastime*, if we will live simply and wisely; *as the pursuits of simpler nations are still the sports of the more artificial.*"

When he had enough of that kind of life, he showed the same simplicity in giving it up as in beginning it. There are some who could have done the one, but, vanity forbidding, not the other; and that is perhaps the story of the hermits; but Thoreau made no fetich of his own example, and did what he wanted squarely. And five years is long enough for an experiment and to prove the success of transcendental Yankeeism. It is not his frugality which is worthy of note; for, to begin with, that was inborn, and therefore inimitable by others who are differently constituted; and again, it was no new thing, but has often been equalled by poor Scotch students at the universities. The point is the sanity of his view of life, and the insight with which he recognized the position of money, and thought out for himself the problem of riches and a livelihood. Apart from his eccentricities, he had perceived, and was acting on, a truth of universal application. For money enters in two different characters into the scheme of life. A certain amount, varying with the number and empire of our desires, is a true necessary to each one of us in the present order of society; but beyond that amount, money is a commodity to be bought or not to be bought, a luxury in which we may either indulge or stint ourselves, like any other. And there are many luxuries that we may legitimately prefer to it, such as a grateful conscience, a country life, or the woman of our inclination. Trite, flat, and obvious as this conclusion may appear, we have only to look round us in society to see how scantily it has been recognized; and perhaps even ourselves, after a little reflection, may decide to spend a trifle less for money, and indulge ourselves a trifle more in the article of freedom.

III .

"To have done anything by which you earned money merely," says Thoreau, "is to be" (have been, he means) "idle and worse." There are two passages in his letters, both, oddly enough, relating to firewood, which must be brought together to be rightly understood. So taken, they contain between them the marrow of all good sense on the subject of work in its relation to something broader than mere livelihood. Here is the first: "I suppose I have burned up a good-sized tree to-night— and for what? I settled with Mr. Tarbell for it the other day; but that wasn't the final settlement. I got off cheaply from him. At last one will say: 'Let us see, how much wood did you burn, sir?' And I shall shudder to think that the next question will be, 'What did you do while you were warm?'" Even after we have settled with Admetus in the person of Mr. Tarbell, there comes, you see, a further question. It is not enough to have earned our livelihood. Either the earning itself should have been serviceable to mankind, or something else must follow. To live is sometimes very difficult, but it is never meritorious in itself; and we must have a reason to allege to our own conscience why we should continue to exist upon this crowded earth. If Thoreau had simply dwelt in his house at Walden, a lover of trees, birds, and fishes, and the open air and virtue, a reader of wise books, an idle, selfish self-improver, he would have managed to cheat Admetus, but, to cling to metaphor, the devil would have had him in the end. Those who can avoid toil altogether and dwell in the Arcadia of private means, and even those who can, by abstinence, reduce the necessary amount of it to some six weeks a year, having the more liberty, have only the higher moral obligation to be up and doing in the interest of man.

The second passage is this: "There is a far more important and warming heat, commonly lost, which precedes the burn-ing of the wood. It is the smoke of industry, which is incense. I had been so thoroughly warmed in body and spirit, that when at length my fuel was housed, I came near selling it to the ashman, as if I had extracted all its heat." Industry is, in itself and when properly chosen, delightful and profitable to the worker; and when your toil has been a pleasure, you have not, as Thoreau says, "earned money merely," but money, health, delight, and moral profit, all in one. "We must heap up a great pile of doing for a small diameter of being," he says in another place; and then exclaims, "How admirably the artist is made to accomplish his self-culture by devotion to his art!" We may escape uncongenial toil, only to devote ourselves to that which is congenial. It is only to transact some higher business that even Apollo dare play the truant from Admetus. We must all work for the sake of work; we must all work, as Thoreau says again, in any "absorbing pursuit—it does not much matter what, so it be honest;" but the most profitable work is that which combines into one continued effort the largest propor-tion of the powers and desires of a man's nature; that into

which he will plunge with ardor, and from which he will desist with reluctance; in which he will know the weariness of fatigue, but not that of satiety; and which will be ever fresh, pleasing, and stimulating to his taste. Such work holds a man together, braced at all points; it does not suffer him to doze or wander; it keeps him actively conscious of himself, yet raised among superior interests; it gives him the profit of industry with the pleasures of a pastime. This is what his art should be to the true artist, and that to a degree unknown in other and less intimate pursuits. For other professions stand apart from the human business of life; but an art has its seat at the centre of the artist's doings and sufferings, deals directly with his experi-ences, teaches him the lessons of his own fortunes and mishaps, and becomes a part of his biography. So says Goethe:

Spät erklingt was früh erklang;
Glück und Unglück wird Gesang.

Now Thoreau's art was literature; and it was one of which he had conceived most ambitiously. He loved and believed in good books. He said well, "Life is not habitually seen from any common platform so truly and unexaggerated as in the light of literature." But the literature he loved was of the heroic order. "Books, not which afford us a cowering enjoyment, but in which each thought is of unusual daring; such as an idle man cannot read, and a timid one would not be entertained by, which even make us dangerous to existing institutions—such I call good books." He did not think them easy to be read. "The heroic books," he says, "even if printed in the character of our mother-tongue, will always be in a language dead to degenerate times; and we must laboriously seek the meaning of each word and line, conjecturing a larger sense than common use permits out of what wisdom and valor and generosity we have." Nor does he suppose that such books are easily written. "Great prose, of equal elevation, commands our respect more than great verse," says he, "since it implies a more permanent and level height, a life more pervaded with the grandeur of the thought. The poet often only makes an irruption, like the Parthian, and is off again, shooting while he retreats; but the prose writer has con-quered like a Roman and settled colonies." We may ask our-selves, almost with dismay, whether such works exist at all but in the imagination of the student. For the bulk of the best of books is apt to be made up with ballast; and those in which energy of thought is combined with any stateliness of utterance may be almost counted on the fingers. Looking round in English for a book that should answer Thoreau's two demands of a style like poetry and sense that shall be both original and inspiriting, I come to Milton's *Areopagitica*, and can name no other in-stance for the moment. Two things at least are plain: that if a man will condescend to nothing more commonplace in the way of reading, he must not look to have a large library; and that if he proposes himself to write in a similar vein, he will find his work cut out for him.

Thoreau composed seemingly while he walked, or at least exercise and composition were with him intimately connected; for we are told that "the length of his walk uniformly made the length of his writing." He speaks in one place of "plainness and vigor, the ornaments of style," which is rather too paradoxical to be comprehensively true. In another he remarks: "As for style of writing, if one has anything to say it drops from him simply as a stone falls to the ground." We must conjecture a very large sense indeed for the phrase "if one has anything to say." When truth flows from a man, fittingly clothed in style and without conscious effort, it is because the effort has been made and the work practically completed before he sat down to write. It is only out of fulness of thinking that expression drops perfect like a ripe fruit; and when Thoreau wrote so nonchalantly at his desk, it was because he had been vigorously active during his walk. For neither clearness, compression, nor beauty of language, come to any living creature till after a busy and a prolonged acquaintance with the subject at hand. Easy writers are those who, like Walter Scott, choose to remain contented with a less degree of perfection than is legitimately within the compass of their powers. We hear of Shakespeare and his clean manuscript; but in face of the evidence of the style itself and of the various editions of *Hamlet*, this merely proves that Messrs. Hemming and Condell were unacquainted with the common enough phenomenon called a fair copy. He who would recast a tragedy already given to the world must frequently and earnestly have revised details in the study. Thoreau himself, and in spite of his protestations, is an instance of even extreme research in one direction; and his effort after heroic utterance is proved not only by the occasional finish, but by the determined exaggeration of his style. "I trust you realize what an exaggerator I am—that I lay myself out to exaggerate," he writes. And again, hinting at the explanation: "Who that has heard a strain of music feared lest he should speak extravagantly any more forever?" And yet once more, in his essay on Carlyle, and this time with his meaning well in hand: "No truth, we think, was ever expressed but with this sort of emphasis, that for the time there seemed to be no other." Thus Thoreau was an exaggerative and a parabolical writer, not because he loved the literature of the East, but from a desire that people should understand and realize what he was writing. He was near the truth upon the general question; but in his own particular method, it appears to me, he wandered. Literature is not less a conventional art than painting or sculpture; and it is the least striking, as it is the most comprehensive of the three. To hear a strain of music, to see a beautiful woman, a river, a great city, or a starry night, is to make a man despair of his Lilliputian arts in language. Now, to gain that emphasis which seems denied to us by the very nature of the medium, the proper method of literature is by selection, which is a kind of negative exaggeration. It is the right of the literary artist, as Thoreau was on the point of seeing, to leave out whatever does not suit his purpose. Thus we extract the pure gold; and thus the well-written story of a noble life becomes, by its very omissions, more thrilling to the reader. But to go beyond this, like Thoreau, and to exaggerate directly, is to leave the saner classical tradition, and to put the reader on his guard. And when you write the whole for the half, you do not express your thought more forcibly, but only express a different thought which is not yours.

Thoreau's true subject was the pursuit of self-improvement combined with an unfriendly criticism of life as it goes on in our societies; it is there that he best displays the freshness and surprising trenchancy of his intellect; it is there that his style becomes plain and vigorous, and therefore, according to his own formula, ornamental. Yet he did not care to follow this vein singly, but must drop into it by the way in books of a different purport. *Walden, or Life in the Woods, A Week on the Concord and Merrimack Rivers, The Maine Woods,*—such are the titles he affects. He was probably reminded by his delicate critical perception that the true business of literature is with narrative; in reasoned narrative, and there alone, that art enjoys all its advantages, and suffers least from its defects. Dry precept and disembodied disquisition, as they can only be read with an effort of abstraction, can never convey a perfectly complete or a perfectly natural impression. Truth, even in literature, must be clothed with flesh and blood, or it cannot tell its whole story to the reader.

Hence the effect of anecdote on simple minds; and hence good biographies and works of high, imaginative art, are not only far more entertaining, but far more edifying, than books of theory or precept. Now Thoreau could not clothe his opinions in the garment of art, for that was not his talent; but he sought to gain the same elbow-room for himself, and to afford a similar relief to his readers, by mingling his thoughts with a record of experience.

Again, he was a lover of nature. The quality, which we should call mystery in a painting, and which belongs so particularly to the aspect of the external world and to its influence upon our feelings, was one which he was never weary of attempting to reproduce in his books. The seeming significance of nature's appearances, their unchanging strangeness to the senses, and the thrilling response which they waken in the mind of man, continued to surprise and stimulate his spirits. It appeared to him, I think, that if we could only write near enough to the facts, and yet with no pedestrian calm, but ardently, we might transfer the glamour of reality direct upon our pages; and that, if it were once thus captured and expressed, a new and instructive relation might appear between men's thoughts and the phenomena of nature. This was the eagle that he pursued all his life long, like a schoolboy with a butterfly net. Hear him to a friend: "Let me suggest a theme for you—to state to yourself precisely and completely what that walk over the mountains amounted to for you, returning to this essay again and again until you are satisfied that all that was important in your experience is in it. Don't suppose that you can tell it precisely the first dozen times you try, but at 'em again; especially when, after a sufficient pause, you suspect that you are touching the heart or summit of the matter, reiterate your blows there, and account for the mountain to yourself. Not that the story need be long, but it will take a long while to make it short." Such was the method, not consistent for a man whose meanings were to "drop from him as a stone falls to the ground." Perhaps the most successful work that Thoreau ever accomplished in this direction is to be found in the passages relating to fish in the *Week*. These are remarkable for a vivid truth of impression and a happy suitability of language, not frequently surpassed.

Whatever Thoreau tried to do was tried in fair, square prose, with sentences solidly built, and no help from bastard rhythms. Moreover, there is a progression—I cannot call it a progress—in his work toward a more and more strictly prosaic level, until at last he sinks into the bathos of the prosy. Emerson mentions having once remarked to Thoreau: "Who would not like to write something which all can read, like *Robinson Crusoe?* and who does not see with regret that his page is not solid with a right materialistic treatment which delights everybody?" I must say in passing that it is not the right materialistic treatment which delights the world in *Robinson*, but the romantic and philosophic interest of the fable. The same treatment does quite the reverse of delighting us when it is applied, in *Colonel Jack*, to the management of a plantation. But I cannot help suspecting Thoreau to have been influenced either by this identical remark or by some other closely similar in meaning. He began to fall more and more into a detailed materialistic treatment; he went into the business doggedly, as one who should make a guide-book; he not only chronicled what had been important in his own experience, but whatever might have been important in the experience of anybody else; not only what had affected him, but all that he saw or heard. His ardor had grown less, or perhaps it was inconsistent with a right materialistic treatment to display such emotions as he felt; and, to complete the eventful change, he chose, from a sense of moral dignity, to gut these later works of the saving quality of humor. He was not one of those authors who have learned, in his own words, "to leave out their dulness." He inflicts his full quantity upon the reader in such books as *Cape Cod*, or *The Yankee in Canada*. Of the latter he confessed that he had not managed to get much of himself into it. Heaven knows he had not, nor yet much of Canada, we may hope. "Nothing," he says somewhere, "can shock a brave man but dulness." Well, there are few spots more shocking to the brave than the pages of *The Yankee in Canada*.

There are but three books of his that will be read with much pleasure: the *Week*, *Walden*, and the collected letters. As to his poetry, Emerson's word shall suffice for us, it is so accurate and so prettily said: "The thyme and marjoram are not yet honey." In this, as in his prose, he relied greatly on the goodwill of the reader and wrote throughout in faith. It was an exercise of faith to suppose that many would understand the sense of his best work, or that any could be exhilarated by the dreary chronicling of his worst. "But," as he says, "the gods do not hear any rude or discordant sound, as we learn from the echo; and I know that the nature toward which I launch these sounds is so rich that it will modulate anew and wonderfully improve my rudest strain."

IV

"What means the fact," he cries, "that a soul which has lost all hope for itself can inspire in another listening soul such an infinite confidence in it, even while it is expressing its despair?" The question is an echo and an illustration of the words last quoted; and it forms the key-note of his thoughts on friendship. No one else, to my knowledge, has spoken in so high and just a spirit of the kindly relations; and I doubt whether it be a drawback that these lessons should come from one in many ways so unfitted to be a teacher in this branch. The very coldness and egoism of his own intercourse gave him a clearer insight into the intellectual basis of our warm, mutual tolerations; and testimony to their worth comes with added force from one who was solitary and disobliging, and of whom a friend remarked, with equal wit and wisdom, "I love Henry, but I cannot like him."

He can hardly be persuaded to make any distinction between love and friendship; in such rarefied and freezing air, upon the mountain-tops of meditation, had he taught himself to breathe. He was, indeed, too accurate an observer not to have remarked that "there exists already a natural disinterestedness and liberality" between men and women; yet, he thought, "friendship is no respecter of sex." Perhaps there is a sense in which the words are true; but they were spoken in ignorance; and perhaps we shall have put the matter most correctly, if we call love a foundation for a nearer and freer degree of friendship than can be possible without it. For there are delicacies, eternal between persons of the same sex, which are melted and disappear in the warmth of love.

To both, if they are to be right, he attributes the same nature and condition. "We are not what we are," says he, "nor do we treat or esteem each other for such, but for what we are capable of being." "A friend is one who incessantly pays us the compliment of expecting all the virtues from us, and who can appreciate them in us." "The friend asks no return but that his friend will religiously accept and wear and not disgrace his apotheosis of him." "It is the merit and preservation of friendship that it takes place on a level higher than the actual characters of the parties would seem to warrant." This is to put friendship on a pedestal indeed; and yet the root of the matter is there; and the last sentence, in particular, is like a light in a

dark place, and makes many mysteries plain. We are different with different friends; yet if we look closely we shall find that every such relation reposes on some particular apotheosis of oneself; with each friend, although we could not distinguish it in words from any other, we have at least one special reputation to preserve: and it is thus that we run, when mortified, to our friend or the woman that we love, not to hear ourselves called better, but to be better men in point of fact. We seek this society to flatter ourselves with our own good conduct. And hence any falsehood in the relation, any incomplete or perverted understanding, will spoil even the pleasure of these visits. Thus says Thoreau again: "Only lovers know the value of truth." And yet again: "They ask for words and deeds, when a true relation is word and deed."

But it follows that since they are neither of them so good as the other hopes, and each is, in a very honest manner, playing a part above his powers, such an intercourse must often be disappointing to both. "We may bid farewell sooner than complain," says Thoreau, "for our complaint is too well grounded to be uttered." "We have not so good a right to hate any as our friend."

> It were treason to our love
> And a sin to God above,
> One iota to abate
> Of a pure, impartial hate.

Love is not blind, nor yet forgiving. "O yes, believe me," as the songs says, "Love has eyes!" The nearer the intimacy, the more cuttingly do we feel the unworthiness of those we love; and because you love one, and would die for that love to-morrow, you have not forgiven, and you never will forgive, that friend's misconduct. If you want a person's faults, go to those who love him. They will not tell you, but they know. And herein lies the magnanimous courage of love, that it endures this knowledge without change.

It required a cold, distant personality like that of Thoreau, perhaps, to recognize and certainly to utter this truth; for a more human love makes it a point of honor not to acknowledge those faults of which it is most conscious. But his point of view is both high and dry. He has no illusions; he does not give way to love any more than to hatred, but preserves them both with care like valuable curiosities. A more bald-headed picture of life, if I may so express myself, has seldom been presented. He is an egoist; he does not remember, or does not think it worth while to remark, that, in these near intimacies, we are ninety-nine times disappointed in our beggarly selves for once that we are disappointed in our friend; that it is we who seem most frequently undeserving of the love that unites us; and that it is by our friend's conduct that we are continually rebuked and yet strengthened for a fresh endeavor. Thoreau is dry, priggish, and selfish. It is profit he is after in these intimacies; moral profit, certainly, but still profit to himself. If you will be the sort of friend I want, he remarks naïvely, "my education cannot dispense with your society." His education! as though a friend were a dictionary. And with all this, not one word about pleasure, or laughter, or kisses, or any quality of flesh and blood. It was not inappropriate, surely, that he had such close relations with the fish. We can understand the friend already quoted, when he cried: "As for taking his arm, I would as soon think of taking the arm of an elm-tree!"

As a matter of fact he experienced but a broken enjoyment in his intimacies. He says he has been perpetually on the brink of the sort of intercourse he wanted, and yet never completely attained it. And what else had he to expect when he would not, in a happy phrase of Carlyle's, "nestle down into it"? Truly, so it will be always if you only stroll in upon your friends as you might stroll in to see a cricket match; and even then not simply for the pleasure of the thing, but with some after-thought of self-improvement, as though you had come to the cricket match to bet. It was his theory that people saw each other too frequently, so that their curiosity was not properly whetted, nor had they anything fresh to communicate; but friendship must be something else than a society for mutual improvement—indeed, it must only be that by the way, and to some extent unconsciously; and if Thoreau had been a man instead of a manner of elm-tree, he would have felt that he saw his friends too seldom, and have reaped benefits unknown to his philosophy from a more sustained and easy intercourse. We might remind him of his own words about love: "We should have no reserve; we should give the whole of ourselves to that business. But commonly men have not imagination enough to be thus employed about a human being, but must be coopering a barrel, forsooth." Ay, or reading oriental philosophers. It is not the nature of the rival occupation, it is the fact that you suffer it to be a rival, that renders loving intimacy impossible. Nothing is given for nothing in this world; there can be no true love, even on your own side, without devotion; devotion is the exercise of love, by which it grows; but if you will give enough of that, if you will pay the price in a sufficient "amount of what you call life," why then, indeed, whether with wife or comrade, you may have months and even years of such easy, natural, pleasurable, and yet improving intercourse as shall make time a moment and kindness a delight.

The secret of his retirement lies not in misanthropy, of which he had no tincture, but part in his engrossing design of self-improvement and part in the real deficiencies of social intercourse. He was not so much difficult about his fellow human beings as he could not tolerate the terms of their association. He could take to a man for any genuine qualities, as we see by his admirable sketch of the Canadian woodcutter in *Walden*; but he would not consent, in his own words, to "feebly fabulate and paddle in the social slush." It seemed to him, I think, that society is precisely the reverse of friendship, in that it takes place on a lower level than the characters of any of the parties would warrant us to expect. The society talk of even the most brilliant man is of greatly less account than what you will get from him in (as the French say) a little committee. And Thoreau wanted geniality; he had not enough of the superficial, even at command; he could not swoop into a parlor and, in the naval phrase, "cut out" a human being from that dreary port; nor had he inclination for the task. I suspect he loved books and nature as well and near as warmly as he loved his fellow-creatures,—a melancholy, lean degeneration of the human character.

"As for the dispute about solitude and society," he thus sums up: "Any comparison is impertinent. It is an idling down on the plain at the base of the mountain instead of climbing steadily to its top. Of course you will be glad of all the society you can get to go up with? Will you go to glory with me? is the burden of the song. It is not that we love to be alone, but that we love to soar, and when we do soar the company grows thinner and thinner till there is none at all. It is either the tribune on the plain, a sermon on the mount, or a very private ecstasy still higher up. Use all the society that will abet you." But surely it is no very extravagant opinion that it is better to give than to receive, to serve than to use our companions; and above all, where there is no question of service upon either side, that it is good to enjoy their company like a natural man. It is curious and in some ways dispiriting that a writer may be always best corrected out of his own mouth; and so, to conclude, here is another passage from Thoreau which seems aimed directly at himself: "Do not be too moral: you may cheat yourself out of much life so. . . . *All fables, indeed, have their morals; but the innocent enjoy the story.*"

V

"The only obligation," says he, "which I have a right to assume is to do at any time what I think right." "Why should we ever go abroad, even across the way, to ask a neighbor's advice?" "There is a nearer neighbor within, who is incessantly telling us how we should behave. *But we wait for the neighbor without to tell us of some false, easier way.*" "The greater part of what my neighbors call good I believe in my soul to be bad." To be what we are, and to become what we are capable of becoming, is the only end of life. It is "when we fall behind ourselves" that "we are cursed with duties and the neglect of duties." "I love the wild," he says, "not less than the good." And again: "The life of a good man will hardly improve us more than the life of a freebooter, for the inevitable laws appear as plainly in the infringement as in the observance, and" (mark this) "*our lives are sustained by a nearly equal expense of virtue of some kind.*" Even although he were a prig, it will be owned he could announce a startling doctrine. "As for doing good," he writes elsewhere, "that is one of the professions that are full. Moreover, I have tried it fairly, and, strange as it may seem, am satisfied that it does not agree with my constitution. Probably I should not conscientiously and deliberately forsake my particular calling to do the good which society demands of me, to save the universe from annihilation; and I believe that a like but infinitely greater steadfastness elsewhere is all that now preserves it. If you should ever be betrayed into any of these philanthropies, do not let your left hand know what your right hand does, for it is not worth knowing." Elsewhere he returns upon the subject, and explains his meaning thus: "If I ever *did* a man any good in their sense, of course it was something exceptional and insignificant compared with the good and evil I am constantly doing by being what I am."

There is a rude nobility, like that of a barbarian king, in this unshaken confidence in himself and indifference to the wants, thoughts, or sufferings of others. In his whole works I find no trace of pity. This was partly the result of theory, for he held the world too mysterious to be criticised, and asks conclusively: "What right have I to grieve who have not ceased to wonder?" But it sprang still more from constitutional indifference and superiority; and he grew up healthy, composed, and unconscious from among life's horrors, like a green bay-tree from a field of battle. It was from this lack in himself that he failed to do justice to the spirit of Christ; for while he could glean more meaning from individual precepts than any score of Christians, yet he conceived life in such a different hope, and viewed it with such contrary emotions, that the sense and purport of the doctrine as a whole seems to have passed him by or left him unimpressed. He could understand the idealism of the Christian view, but he was himself so unaffectedly unhuman that he did not recognize the human intention and essence of that teaching. Hence he complained that Christ did not leave us a rule that was proper and sufficient for this world, not having conceived the nature of the rule that was laid down; for things of that character that are sufficiently unacceptable become positively non-existent to the mind. But perhaps we shall best appreciate the defect in Thoreau by seeing it supplied in the case of Whitman. For the one, I feel confident, is the disciple of the other; it is what Thoreau clearly whispered that Whitman so uproariously bawls; it is the same doctrine, but with how immense a difference! the same argument, but used to what a new conclusion! Thoreau had plenty of humor until he tutored himself out of it, and so forfeited that best birthright of a sensible man; Whitman, in that respect, seems to have been sent into the world naked and unashamed; and yet by a strange consummation, it is the theory of the former that is arid, abstract, and claustral. Of these two philosophies so nearly identical at bottom, the one pursues Self-improvement—a churlish, mangy dog; the other is up with the morning, in the best of health, and following the nymph Happiness, buxom, blithe, and debonair. Happiness, at least, is not solitary; it joys to communicate; it loves others, for it depends on them for its existence; it sanctions and encourages to all delights that are not unkind in themselves; if it lived to a thousand, it would not make excision of a single humorous passage; and while the self-improver dwindles toward the prig, and, if he be not of an excellent constitution, may even grow deformed into an Obermann, the very name and appearance of a happy man breathe of good-nature, and help the rest of us to live.

In the case of Thoreau, so great a show of doctrine demands some outcome in the field of action. If nothing were to be done but build a shanty beside Walden Pond, we have heard altogether too much of these declarations of independence. That the man wrote some books is nothing to the purpose, for the same has been done in a suburban villa. That he kept himself happy is perhaps a sufficient excuse, but it is disappointing to the reader. We may be unjust, but when a man despises commerce and philanthropy alike, and has views of good so soaring that he must take himself apart from mankind for their cultivation, we will not be content without some striking act. It was not Thoreau's fault if he were not martyred; had the occasion come, he would have made a noble ending. As it is, he did once seek to interfere in the world's course; he made one practical appearance on the stage of affairs; and a strange one it was, and strangely characteristic of the nobility and the eccentricity of the man. It was forced on him by his calm but radical opposition to negro slavery. "Voting for the right is doing nothing for it," he saw; "it is only expressing to men feebly your desire that it should prevail." For his part, he would not "for an instant recognize that political organization for *his* government which is the *slave's* government also." "I do not hesitate to say," he adds, "that those who call themselves Abolitionists should at once effectually withdraw their support, both in person and property, from the government of Massachusetts." That is what he did: in 1843 he ceased to pay the poll-tax. The highway-tax he paid, for he said he was as desirous to be a good neighbor as to be a bad subject; but no more poll-tax to the State of Massachusetts. Thoreau had now seceded, and was a polity unto himself; or, as he explains it with admirable sense, "In fact, I quietly declare war with the State after my fashion, though I will still make what use and get what advantage of her I can, as is usual in such cases." He was put in prison; but that was a part of his design. "Under a government which imprisons any unjustly, the true place for a just man is also a prison. I know this well, that if one thousand, if one hundred, if ten men whom I could name— ay, if *one* HONEST man, in this State of Massachusetts, *ceasing to hold slaves*, were actually to withdraw from this copartnership, and be locked up in the county jail therefor, it would be the abolition of slavery in America. For it matters not how small the beginning may seem to be; what is once well done is done forever." Such was his theory of civil disobedience.

And the upshot? A friend paid the tax for him; continued year by year to pay it in the sequel; and Thoreau was free to walk the woods unmolested. It was a *fiasco*, but to me it does

not seem laughable; even those who joined in the laughter at the moment would be insensibly affected by this quaint instance of a good man's horror for injustice. We may compute the worth of that one night's imprisonment as outweighing half a hundred voters at some subsequent election: and if Thoreau had possessed as great a power of persuasion as (let us say) Falstaff, if he had counted a party however small, if his example had been followed by a hundred or by thirty of his fellows, I cannot but believe it would have greatly precipitated the era of freedom and justice. We feel the misdeeds of our country with so little fervor, for we are not witnesses to the suffering they cause; but when we see them wake an active horror in our fellowman, when we see a neighbor prefer to lie in prison rather than be so much as passively implicated in their perpetration, even the dullest of us will begin to realize them with a quicker pulse.

Not far from twenty years later, when Captain John Brown was taken at Harper's Ferry, Thoreau was the first to come forward in his defence. The committees wrote to him unanimously that his action was premature. "I did not send to you for advice," said he, "but to announce that I was to speak." I have used the word "defence;" in truth he did not seek to defend him, even declared it would be better for the good cause that he should die; but he praised his action as I think Brown would have liked to hear it praised.

Thus this singularly eccentric and independent mind, wedded to a character of so much strength, singleness, and purity, pursued its own path of self-improvement for more than half a century, part gymnosophist, part backwoodsman; and thus did it come twice, though in a subaltern attitude, into the field of political history. [1]

Preface, By Way of Criticism.

Here is an admirable instance of the "point of view" forced throughout, and of too earnest reflection on imperfect facts. Upon me this pure, narrow, sunnily-ascetic Thoreau had exercised a great charm. I have scarce written ten sentences since I was introduced to him, but his influence might be somewhere detected by a close observer. Still it was as a writer that I had made his acquaintance; I took him on his own explicit terms; and when I learned details of his life, they were, by the nature of the case and my own *parti-pris*, read even with a certain violence in terms of his writings. There could scarce be a perversion more justifiable than that; yet it was still a perversion. The study, indeed, raised so much ire in the breast of Dr. Japp (H. A. Page), Thoreau's sincere and learned disciple, that had either of us been men, I please myself with thinking, of less temper and justice, the difference might have made us enemies instead of making us friends. To him who knew the man from the inside, many of my statements sounded like inversions made on purpose; and yet when we came to talk of them together, and he had understood how I was looking at the man through the books, while he had long since learned to read the books through the man, I believe he understood the spirit in which I had been led astray.

On two most important points, Dr. Japp added to my knowledge, and with the same blow fairly demolished that part of my criticism. First, if Thoreau were content to dwell by Walden Pond, it was not merely with designs of self-improvement, but to serve mankind in the highest sense. Hither came the fleeing slave; thence was he despatched along the road to freedom. That shanty in the woods was a station in the great Underground Railroad; that adroit and philosophic solitary was an ardent worker, soul and body, in that so much more than honorable movement, which, if atonement were possible for nations, should have gone far to wipe away the guilt of slavery. But in history sin always meets with condign punishment; the generation passes, the offence remains, and the innocent must suffer. No underground railroad could atone for slavery, even as no bills in Parliament can redeem the ancient wrongs of Ireland. But here at least is a new light shed on the Walden episode.

Second, it appears, and the point is capital, that Thoreau was once fairly and manfully in love, and, with perhaps too much aping of the angel, relinquished the woman to his brother. Even though the brother were like to die of it, we have not yet heard the last opinion of the woman. But be that as it may, we have here the explanation of the "rarefied and freezing air" in which I complained that he had taught himself to breathe. Reading the man through the books, I took his professions in good faith. He made a dupe of me, even as he was seeking to make a dupe of himself, wresting philosophy to the needs of his own sorrow. But in the light of this new fact, those pages, seemingly so cold, are seen to be alive with feeling. What appeared to be a lack of interest in the philosopher turns out to have been a touching insincerity of the man to his own heart; and that fine-spun airy theory of friendship, so devoid, as I complained, of any quality of flesh and blood, a mere anodyne to lull his pains. The most temperate of living critics once marked a passage of my own with a cross and the words, "This seems nonsense." It not only seemed; it was so. It was a private bravado of my own, which I had so often repeated to keep up my spirits, that I had grown at last wholly to believe it, and had ended by setting it down as a contribution to the theory of life. So with the more icy parts of this philosophy of Thoreau's. He was affecting the Spartanism he had not; and the old sentimental wound still bled afresh, while he deceived himself with reasons.

Thoreau's theory, in short, was one thing and himself another: of the first, the reader will find what I believe to be a pretty faithful statement and a fairly just criticism in the study; of the second he will find but a contorted shadow. So much of the man as fitted nicely with his doctrines, in the photographer's phrase, came out. But that large part which lay outside and beyond, for which he had found or sought no formula, on which perhaps his philosophy even looked askance, is wanting in my study, as it was wanting in the guide I followed. In some ways a less serious writer, in all ways a nobler man, the true Thoreau still remains to be depicted.

Notes

1. For many facts in the above essay, among which I may mention the incident of the squirrel, I am indebted to *Thoreau: His Life and Aims*, by H. A. Page, or, as is well known, Dr. Japp.

HENRY S. SALT
From *Life of Henry David Thoreau*
1890, pp. 170–76

The lack of system which is noticeable in Thoreau's character may be traced in the style of his writings as plainly as in his philosophical views. He was not careful as to the outer form and finish of his works, for he believed that the mere literary contour is of quite secondary importance in comparison with the inner animating spirit; let the worthiness of the latter once be assured, and the former will fall naturally into its proper shape. Furthermore, although, as we have seen, writing was more and more recognised by him as his profession

in his later years, he was at all times conscious of a fuller and higher calling than that of the literary man—as he valued nature before art, so he valued life before literature. He both preached and practised a combination of literary work and manual; of the pen and of the spade; of the study and of the open sky. He protested against that tendency in our civilisation which carries division of labour to such an extent that the student is deprived of healthy out-door work, while the labourer is deprived of opportunity for self-culture. He imagines the case of some literary professor, who sits in his library writing a treatise on the huckleberry, while hired huckleberry-pickers and cooks are engaged in the task of preparing him a pudding of the berries. A book written under such conditions will be worthless. "There will be none of the spirit of the huckleberry in it. I believe in a different kind of division of labour, and that the professor should divide himself between the library and the huckleberry field." His opinions on the subject of literary style are clearly stated in *The Week*, and are no doubt in great measure a record of his own practice:

> Can there be any greater reproach than an idle learning? Learn to split wood at least. The necessity of labour and conversation with many men and things to the scholar is rarely well remembered; steady labour with the hands, which engrosses the attention also, is unquestionably the best method of removing palaver and sentimentality out of one's style, both of speaking and writing. If he has worked hard from morning till night, though he may have grieved that he could not be watching the train of his thoughts during that time, yet the few hasty lines which at evening record his day's experience will be more musical and true than his freest but idle fancy could have furnished. Surely the writer is to address a world of labourers, and such therefore must be his own discipline. He will not idly dance at his work who has wood to cut and cord before nightfall in the short days of winter, but every stroke will be husbanded, and ring soberly through the wood; and so will the strokes of that scholar's pen, which at evening record the story of the day, ring soberly, yet cheerily, on the ear of the reader, long after the echoes of his axe have died away.

Such were, in fact, the conditions under which Thoreau wrote many of the pages of the journal from which his own essays were constructed; and, whatever may be thought of the force of his general principle, there can be no doubt that in his particular case the result was very felicitous. It was his pleasure and his determination that his writing should be redolent of the open-air scenery by which it was primarily inspired. "I trust," he says of *The Week* (and the same may be said of all his volumes), "it does not smell so much of the study and library, even of the poet's attic, as of the fields and woods; that it is a hypæthral or unroofed book, lying open under the ether, and permeated by it, open to all weathers, not easy to be kept on a shelf." In this way Thoreau added a new flavour to literature by the unstudied freshness and wildness of his tone, and succeeded best where he made least effort to be successful. "It is only out of the fulness of thinking," says Mr. R. L. Stevenson, "that expression drops perfect like a ripe fruit; and when Thoreau wrote so nonchalantly at his desk, it was because he had been vigorously active during his walk." Even Mr. Lowell, a far less friendly critic, is compelled, on this point, to express his admiration "With every exception, there is no writing comparable with Thoreau's in kind that is comparable with it in degree, where it is best. His range was narrow, but to be a master is to be a master. There are sentences of his as perfect as anything in the language, and thoughts as clearly crystallised; his metaphors and images are always fresh from the soil."

This success, although naturally and unconsciously attained, had of course been rendered possible in the first instance by an honest course of study; for Thoreau, like every other master of literary expression, had passed through his strict apprenticeship of intellectual labour. Though comparatively indifferent to modern languages, he was familiar with the best classical writers of Greece and Rome, and his style was partly formed on models drawn from one of the great eras in English literature, the post-Elizabethan period. It is a noticeable fact that "mother-tongue" was a word which he loved to use even in his college days; and the homely native vigour of his own writings was largely due to the sympathetic industry with which he had laboured in these quiet but fertile fields. Nor must it be supposed, because he did not elaborate his work according to the usual canons, that he was a careless or indolent writer—on the contrary, it was his habit to correct his manuscripts with unfailing diligence. He deliberately examined and re-examined each sentence of his journal before admitting it into the essays which he sent to the printer, finding that a certain lapse of time was necessary before he could arrive at a satisfactory decision. His absolute sincerity showed itself as clearly in the style of his writing as in the manner of his life. "The one great rule of composition—and if I were a professor of rhetoric I should insist on this—is to *speak the truth*. This first, this second, this third."

In his choice of subjects it was the common that most often enlisted his sympathy and attention. "The theme," he says, "is nothing; the life is everything. Give me simple, cheap, and homely themes. I omit the unusual—the hurricanes and earth-quakes, and describe the common. This has the greatest charm, and is the true theme of poetry. Give me the obscure life, the cottage of the poor and humble, the work-days of the world, the barren fields." But while he took these as the subjects for his pen, he so idealised and transformed them by the power of his imagination as to present them in aspects altogether novel and unsuspected; it being his delight to bring to view the latent harmony and beauty of all existent things, and thus indirectly to demonstrate the unity and perfection of nature.

Numerous passages might be quoted from Thoreau's works which exhibit these picturesque and suggestive qualities. He had a poet's eye for all forms of beauty, moral and material alike, and for the subtle analogies that exist between the one class and the other—in a word, he was possessed of a most vivid and quickening imagination. His images and metaphors are bold, novel, and impressive—as when, to take but a couple of instances, he alludes to the lost anchors of vessels wrecked off the coast of Cape Cod as "the sunken faith and hope of mariners, to which they trusted in vain;" or describes the autumnal warmth on the sheltered side of Walden as "the still glowing embers which the summer, like a departing hunter, had left." And, with all his simplicity and directness of speech, he has an unconscious, almost mystic, eloquence which stamps him unmistakably as an inspired writer, a man of true and rare genius; so that it has been well said of him that "he lived and died to transfuse external nature into human words." In this respect his position among prose-writers is unique; no one, unless it be Richard Jefferies, can be placed in the same category with him.

In so far as he studied the external form of his writings, the aim and object which Thoreau set before him may be summed up in one word—concentration. He avows his delight in sentences which are "concentrated and nutty." The distinctive feature of his own literary style could not have been more accurately described. The brief, barbed, epigrammatic sentences which bristle throughout his writings, pungent with shrewd wisdom and humour, are the appropriate expression of his keen thrifty nature; there is not a superfluous word or syllable, but each passage goes straight to the mark, and tells its tale, as the work of a man who has some more urgent duty to perform than to adorn his pages with artificial tropes and embellishments. He is fond of surprising and challenging his readers by the piquancy and strangeness of his sayings, and his use of paradox is partly due to the same desire to stimulate and awaken curiosity, partly to his wayward and contradictory nature. The dangers and demerits of a paradoxical style are sufficiently obvious; and no writer has ever been less careful than Thoreau to safeguard himself against misunderstandings on this score. He has consequently been much misunderstood, and will always be so, save where the reader brings to his task a certain amount of sympathy and kindred sense of humour.

To those who are not gifted with the same sense of the inner identity which links together many things that are externally unlike, some of Thoreau's thoughts and sayings must necessarily appear to be a fair subject for ridicule. Yet that he should have been charged with possessing no "humour" would be inexplicable, save for the fact that the definitions of that quality are so various and so vague. Broad wit and mirthful genial humour he certainly had not, and he confessedly disliked writings in which there is a conscious and deliberate attempt to be amusing. He found Rabelais, for instance, intolerable; "it may be sport to him," he says, "but it is death to us; a mere humorist, indeed, is a most unhappy man, and his readers are most unhappy also." But though he would not or could not recognise humour as a distinct and independent quality, and even attempted, as we are told, to eliminate what he considered "levity" from some of his essays, he none the less enjoyed keenly—and himself unmistakably exhibited—the quiet, latent, unobtrusive humour which is one of the wholesome and saving principles of human life. Among Thoreau's own writings, *Walden* is especially pervaded by this subtle sense of humour, grave, dry, pithy, sententious, almost saturnine in its tone, yet perhaps for that very reason the more racy and suggestive to those readers who have the faculty for appreciating it.

FREDERICK M. SMITH
"Thoreau"
Critic, July 1900, pp. 60–67

To-day the attempt to write about Henry David Thoreau must be prefaced with an explanation. It cannot be claimed that there is anything new to add; nor can one hope to say the old things in so taking a fashion as to make that a plea for venturing upon ground where such men as Sanborn, Channing, Salt, Burroughs, Lowell, and Stevenson have trodden. There is, however, one excuse. To have been helped by an author is somehow to be put under obligation; and as an acknowledgment of this, it is perhaps pardonable to set down some impressions of the man's character, style, and opinions, with the hope that such impressions may show why Thoreau is to be regarded as a healthful, helpful influence, as well as wherein lies some of the fascination of his work.

It cannot be denied, I think, that Thoreau fascinates. To begin with a minor reason: he is blunt. He attracts a young man because he is an iconoclast. He is no respecter of persons, and he says what he thinks. Often we find that he thinks things we should like to think if we only dared. He is very plain-spoken with his reader. In life such treatment would not be tolerated; in a book it is, on the whole, pleasant. The free-handed way in which he criticises the world and the conventions it has learned to work with is delicious. He has no time to waste upon the things most persons have been taught they have to do. He says those things are unnecessary, and he proceeds to do as he pleases. A man who has found time to do that in this world is to be listened to. It does not matter whether what he pleases is what we please; it does not even matter whether his ways are the best ways or the practical ones; so long as he has the courage of his convictions he is an inspiration. But there are men in plenty who have such a possession and are bankrupt at that. With Thoreau one soon begins to find that the better things lie deeper.

Perhaps his chief trait (and it is a good sign when you find it in a man) was what he called his yearning toward wildness. He felt this, I think, not because he was a rover, but because he had the soul of a poet; and no better appellation can be found for him than that given by his friend Channing. He is above all things the "Poet-Naturalist."

His business seems to have been to get close to Nature. Man somehow failed to interest him, and he tried flowers and bees. As he smelt, tasted, saw, and heard better than most men, he recorded the slightest impressions that animated nature made upon him with as much care as though they were factors in a mathematical proposition. At whatever cost he must get the thing accurately and always get everything,—so that he even "waked in the night to take notes." Yet it is not so much the fact that he is after as the truth behind the fact. Fond as he is of mere measurement, the poet gets the better of him, and though he start in with cold figures he often ends in rhapsody. He is so precise that one feels moved to acknowledge that he has traits of the scientist—and at the same time he is as open-minded and delicate as the poet. The outward look of the world appeals to him,—the shapes of things, the play of light, and the splash of color. There is something almost oriental in his love of sensation. He revels in pure color, and loves to press poke-berries that he may see the red juice stain his fingers. When carried to that extreme, it is a note which seems almost out of place in such an austere character as we fancy him.

In a way, it is out of place, as, for the greater part, Nature is far more to him than beautiful, and he approaches her not only as an admirer, but as a friend and devotee. She is not to be worshipped as a spirit, not to be looked at as though peopled with nymphs and goddesses. True, he very often personifies her and her manifestations (for she is always a real being), and the trick not only makes his descriptions more vivid and colorful, but it shows the strange fellowship that he felt for her. There is that which is friendly and companionable in his intercourse with trees and streams and wild things, as it were between neighbors. And with that, in his rare moments she speaks to him of God, and gives the final word of hope which echoes in all his pages. "He who hears the rippling of rivers in these degenerate days will not utterly despair." The song of the thrush exhilarates him. "It is a medicative draught to my soul, an elixir to my eyes, and a fountain of youth to all my senses." If a man would but drink at these springs, there is abundant reason why he should keep his life simple and healthful.

Thoreau was doubtless considered "queer" during his lifetime, and some of his poses strike us as radical and unusual; but for all that the best parts of his work have the clear, fresh, earthy touch which means health. It could not be otherwise. Any work which has its well-spring in the open, where the

breezes play upon it, and with the blue of heaven and the green of earth reflected in its depths, must partake of the nature of these things and run pure.

It is a healthful thing, too, when he lifts his voice in favor of simplicity and shows himself so capable of celebrating the joys of small things. In the simplest occupation he finds some poetry which gives it dignity. Indeed, he made it his business at all times to chant the beauty of the common. Because a thing was with us every day, it was not therefore cheap; and a single red maple in the autumn time gave him as much pleasure as a glimpse of strange lands, and glorified all sublunary things for him. "Keep your eyes open and see the good about you," is his teaching, and "he found at home what other men went abroad to see."

It is a sign of health again that he hated all sham, and respected genuineness and sincerity wherever he saw it. Gossip and triviality had no place in his scheme, for he believed that they tainted the mind and crowded out better things and higher thoughts. In his ardor he sometimes condemns too widely; for many things which the world has thought necessary he treats with scant respect. Yet it will usually be found that it is not these things in themselves but undue attention to them which occasions his severity.

With all his sourness and sharpness, with all the pleasure he gets in pricking his fellows with a goad, one comes at times, and not rarely, upon reaches where the nature of the man flows sweet and delicate and romantic. Take his description of roses and lilies: "The red rose, with the intense color of many suns concentrated, spreads its tender petals perfectly fair, its flower not to be overlooked, modest, yet queenly, on the edges of shady copses and meadows, against its green leaves, surrounded by blushing buds, of perfect form, not only beautiful, but rightly commanding attention, unspoiled by the admiration of gazers. And the water-lily floats on the surface of slow waters, amid rounded shields of leaves, bucklers, red beneath, which simulate a green field, perfuming the air." And again he says: "I can go out in the morning and gather flowers with which to perfume my chamber where I read and write all day long."

One finds, moreover, a play of fancy which strikes you not so much by its whimsicality as by an airiness and grace which you had not expected. Delightful as he is, he is never, I should say, blithe. True, he says: "Not by constraint or severity shall you have access to true wisdom, but by abandonment to childlike mirthfulness." It was a truth which his intellect had grasped, but which he could not put to practice. Music enchants him because it speaks to him of higher things; an oak leaf delights him and sends him to telling himself stories about it. The laborer, singing, stirs his blood. The hand of romance has apparently touched him and left a mark.

There is, too, a sparkle of kindliness in his nature which makes you warm toward him. He appreciates the generosity of the farmer who feeds him, and is at pains to set down the incident. He seems to have been just on the verge of a full and warm sympathy with mankind, but continually sets it aside for what he believes are the more spiritual and higher virtues. So on the whole we are apt to count him cold.

Toward this higher life he is constantly striving. He lived on the border of a good land, where the wood thrush sang eternally and where the rarest flowers bloomed; a shadowy land on which he forever kept his eyes; and he had an abiding faith that some day he would be an inhabitant thereof. Something of its mystery reached out to him, and his allusions to it are constant. It was not the heaven of the Christian where the streets were more or less suggestive of a lapidary's shop, and where everybody was a musician. It was a place where a mortal should at last get hold of his ideals and make in the end a *man* of himself; a place where he should live up to the best that was in him and have fellowship with Nature and with God.

Thoreau is usually thought of as an advocate of Nature, and we do not remember that he drew from other sources. The mistake is natural, for Nature does seem everything. Looking a little closer one finds that he derived much from books. The sacred literature of many nations was familiar to him, while the Greek and Latin poets were his daily companions. The strength, freshness, and simplicity of the Greeks found in his heart a ready response. Homer got down "close to the bone" of life, and that made his election sure to Thoreau. No other literature does he praise so much as Greek, but he quotes widely—old French writers, and the English poets, Tennyson and Landor. Wordsworth he knew; and one's respect for Thoreau is a trifle increased because he makes record of his appreciation of *Peter Bell*. A list of the English writers he quotes would require pages, would begin before Chaucer, and be fullest, perhaps, at the seventeenth-century men. He knew, too, all the writings of old New England, the town histories, the chronicles of early travellers, and the like. If a writer had in any way touched Nature, Thoreau had the work at his tongue's end. Even obscure and dry treatises on agricultural or horticultural subjects seem to have been read with avidity and treasured against the day when he should have need of them. He loved to read those who, like the Greeks, wrote from the heart; who gave a true account of themselves and of their thoughts, who wrote sincerely and simply.

Sincere I always believe him, and it will perhaps be paradoxical to say that, after all, he is at times something of a *poseur*. But so it is, and the two things can and do exist together. He lays down the law in too dogmatic a fashion not to make one feel that he is straining a point for the effect. He takes pains to impress the fact that he is not a gentleman, but a common man; yet he wants to be different from many common men, and he is careful to make the most of these differences. There is a touch of vanity and affectation in the way he patronizes farmers. He lays a claim to knowing more of their farms than they do. If he dressed simply, he did so partly because it tickled his vanity. He was proud of a patch not because it was a patch, but because he liked to feel that he was above being ashamed of it. He was superior in some things, but we suspect a man who thrusts his superiority upon us. Like the boys on the links at night, he carried a lantern under his jacket. He liked to cast a big shadow, and he sometimes held the lantern so close that the shadow was distorted and not quite like the true man. It was doubtless this trick of posing, this habit of illogical exaggeration, which made Lowell say of him that he had no humor. What he meant was, that Thoreau had not that faculty of turning an amused eye upon himself and of spying out his own faults. To have it saves one much of the worry of the world and sweetens the sour spots mightily. A man who can smile at himself will not be for long in any black humor. Thoreau could not do that. He could smile at his friends and neighbors, and he never loses occasion to. His wit is sharp, and he can be bitterly satirical; it is his delight to prick bubbles. But his smile is always at you, not with you; his humor is not genial and warm; he is a man with a twinkle in his gray eye, but with no laugh in his belly. Sometimes even his eyes do not show it—it is deeper than that. You feel, indeed, from his opinions, that he did not entirely grasp the meaning of humor, for in speaking of Carlyle he appears to think that a man is only at his best when he is too in earnest even to smile. As if a smile would taint the truth!

In talking about his style, one finds himself in the way to repeat many things that were said of his character; for the style, perhaps, is only the character shining through words. "I resolved," he says, in speaking of a certain lecture, "to give them a strong dose of myself." That is what one gets in reading him. First of all you put him down as unequal. At times he is careless in the structure of his sentences. You may have a lingering doubt as to the antecedent of a certain relative; or you come upon long, trailing clauses in which he has tangled himself and you may get him out at your leisure. But this is only occasional. For the greater part his meaning is cut clear.

Precise he always intends to be, and details delight him. He takes great care to tell exactly how everything was done, as in the building of his boat. It is like making a partner of the reader, who feels often that he was there himself and had a hand in the business. Thoreau must even measure the axe before a Maine settler's door that his description may be accurate. Long practice in trying to describe taught him the use of fit words. We find him searching for just the word that will suit his impression, and often in his journal he will put a question-mark after a word or phrase which does not entirely satisfy him.

Sometimes he has a paragraph of brilliant and charming description, overflowing with poetic feeling, full of delicate shading, and soft flower bloom. On the other hand, he will fill pages with paragraphs as hard as steel, full of sharp and pithy sayings, which glitter with satire and slip into the mind like proverbs. Of this oracular manner of delivery he is especially fond, and the serenity with which he lays down the laws of life gives one the sense of reading old philosophers. It is as though the writer had thousands of years at his back and spoke to you out of them. His whole compositions, like Emerson's, hang together rather by weight of the underlying idea rather than by any structural coherence.

The word whimsical fits certain of his turns. He gives unexpected twists to sentences, brings in puns and unlooked-for metaphors. The punning habit was one that he apparently chuckled over. His early works do not show any excess of it, but later it tickled him monstrously to make a bad pun. Then he has fancies which he dresses up for his own amusement, and we find him projecting a tea-party of sixty old women, from Eve to his mother. Lake Champlain looks "like the picture of Lake Lucerne on a music-box." This fancifulness made him speak often in metaphors, so that his sentences are at times riddles or half-riddles. He strove for a certain mystery of expression which should be tantalizing to a reader without completely misleading him. This habit of teasing you with phrases makes you like him all the better, for at least he counts somewhat on your intellect. One of his tricks was to speak of things spiritual and mental in terms of Nature, geography, and history. "Whenever a man fronts a fact there is an unsettled wilderness between him and it. Let him build himself a log-house with the bark on it, and wage an old French war."

The quality of mystery in his style is the mystery got from Nature. The landscape is vague, moving, and shadowy as the living atmosphere. Thoreau put it into his words. His quick feeling for Nature is that which gives his style charm,—that and the habit of tilting at things of which he disapproves. He says of Evelyn that "love of subject teaches him many impressive words." That could be said of his own writings with equal truth. The feel of the air, the color of a leaf, the smell of herbs, touched him, and he sought to put this on paper just as it came to him. It made him a poet. Where will you match for poetic sincerity that description of the old fisherman, his "old experienced coat hanging long and straight and brown as the yellow pine bark, glittering with so much smothered sunlight if you stood near enough." When he speaks thus you feel that he is akin to Ruskin in his great enthusiasm for Nature's wonders in small things.

There is something exhilarant and morning-like in his writing. It is crisp, and suggests the crackling of fire or the pungent odors of autumn. It is a product of outdoors, a thing which has escaped cultivation and grown up in the outlots. It is not so rich and rounded, perhaps, as indoor fruit, but it has a tang; it is like his own wild apples.

"I would have," he says, "my thoughts like wild apples, to be food for walkers, and will not warrant them to be palatable in the house." He had his wish; he can only be truly appreciated by outdoor men. His opinions are too audacious for the fireside. He shocks the steady by the way in which he girds at Christianity and sneers at churches. He is bitter in his denunciation of both priests and physicians. His criticism of Christ was that he taught imperfectly how to live. The sight of a church spire or a clergyman is to Thoreau as a red rag to a turkey cock. It sets him ruffling and crackling. But he is not so fierce as he looks. It was ordinary youthful affectation which made him talk of "his Buddha" as set over against "their Christ." But as you read farther you find that it was the cant and hypocrisy of some of its professors that set him railing at their religion. What he fought against was insincerity, not belief.

He did not wish a creed cut and measured for him, but must blaze his own way, have his own experience, and by favor of God find his own heaven. He wished to be free and open, ready to mind the least change in his spirit. On one side he was wise enough to know that all men cannot fit into the same hole, but on the other he was narrow enough not to credit men with a full measure of sincerity if they differed too widely from him. But perhaps such is the case with all reformers.

Society he claims to have found cheap and unsatisfying. The majority of people, he thought, led lives which stood for nothing; but gave their time over to the race for pleasure or pennies, all the while covering their better natures. He wanted men to work or play, or whatever they would be about, for love of it, and not for low ends. If he complained of his townsmen, it was because he thought they were not true to their best advices. And if he asked them to shun some things and embrace others, it was because he believed that life lay in the latter direction.

The usual criticism of Thoreau is that his ideas are unpractical. It will not do, so his critics say, if one is dissatisfied with one's fellows, to sulk in a corner and call names. I have tried in vain to prove from his writings that these persons are right in their point of view. It is easy to see how they have come to it by a superficial reading of the man, but it is not easy to see why one should persist in supposing that Thoreau ever wanted the world to live in a cottage on a pond's edge. If he chose to try an experiment or two, that was nobody's business,—or else it was everybody's,—and they should have thanked a pioneer. What Thoreau did proclaim

from the housetops was, that the people he knew were chasing false ideals, laying up treasure on earth, intent on a fool's game indoors while all the time a parade was passing in the streets. It does not matter that the remedy he hit upon was a bit radical; it does not matter that there are some happy souls who can keep in the thick of the game and yet listen to the music out of their windows; he told the truth about the foolishness of the many as anybody who has spent a week in trade can testify. All he asked was that people be true to the call of their own genius. Always to keep clear-headed, fresh, and waiting, to be on tiptoe for the glorious facts of life,—that was the burden of his conjuration.

That he was forever calling his fellows to the front is one of the values of his writings. But his chief merit is the cheerful word that he has to say for life. Take it how you will, we are always in debate as to whether this life is, or is not, worth living. We can never come to a decision that we can call stable or that may not see change. But whether we decide one way or another, it is beyond dispute that the happiest way out of the matter is to believe that life is good. Otherwise we are soured at the start and at the last taste. There are too many men who pull long faces. When we find one who stands up and tells us that our little life is only the bud of some great flower, which with work we can make blossom gloriously, we may well hear him.

Thoreau is one of those men. "Every sound," says he, "is fraught with the mysterious assurance of health," and life is a good thing and will yield us something in proportion as we have courage and common-sense to face it. This is no sporadic idea which crops up unexpectedly in the intervals of gloom; it is a sense which pervades his whole work and makes you wonder how Stevenson could have called him a skulker. Passage after passage echoes with his shrill "chanticleer brag."

"It is very rare that you meet with an obstacle in this world which the humblest man has not the faculties to surmount."

"Love your life, poor as it is; meet it and live it; do not shun it and call it hard names."

"Mind your own business and endeavor to be what you were made."

He grumbles, we know, but he does not despair. He seeks to excite in us a "morning joy" which shall wake us to try with our might till the evening time, and the reward shall surely be with us. It is characteristic of him to end hopefully, and for us the thing is a gospel of hope and not of desperation. "The sun is but a morning star."

And so we look upon him as seldom smiling, never melancholy; severe with his neighbors, yet having in his heart the strands of sympathy, following his genius where it led him, and proclaiming his individuality in such strenuous terms that it sometimes becomes a pose; striving for simplicity of life because it gave him more time for living; an intimate of Nature, with an eye trained to catch the slightest nuance of her beauty, and a man's pen to set forth her glory and her sweetness and her strength; and, above everything, a heart to catch the meaning of it all, and a valiant word to say for life and living.

HENRY THOMAS BUCKLE

1821–1862

Henry Thomas Buckle was born at Lee, Kent, on November 24, 1821. Childhood illnesses prevented him from receiving much formal education, but he read widely and as a young man traveled extensively in Europe. He was also a gifted chess player, for which he was widely known in his youth.

From an early age Buckle determined to write an account of the history of civilization; by 1853, after years of work, he decided to restrict his study to England. The first volume of his magnum opus, the *History of Civilization in England*, was published in 1857 and was an immediate success. A second volume was published in 1861. In that year he undertook an extensive trip through the Middle East, beginning in Egypt and traveling through Sinai to Petra, Hebron, Jerusalem, and Nazareth, where he became ill with typhoid fever. He died in Damascus on May 29, 1862, leaving his *History* unfinished. A later edition of Buckle's *History of Civilization in England*, edited by J. M. Robertson, was published in 1904.

Personal

Dined with Grote yesterday to meet Mr Buckle, the literary Lion of the day. He is not prepossessing in appearance, but he talks very well and makes a great display of knowledge and extensive reading, though without pedantry or dogmatism. —CHARLES CAVENDISH FULKE GREVILLE, *Diary*, March 10, 1858

I live merely for literature; my works are my only actions; they are not wholly unknown, and I leave it to them to protect my name. If they cannot do that, they are little worth. I have never written an essay, or even a single line anonymously, and nothing would induce me to do so, because I deem anonymous writing of every kind to be an evasion of responsibility, and consequently unsuited to the citizen of a free country. Therefore it is that I can easily be judged. I have myself supplied the materials, and to them I appeal. So far from despising public opinion, I regard it with great, though not with excessive respect; and I acknowledge in it the principal source of such influence as I have been able to wield. But this respect which I feel for public opinion is only when I consider it as a whole. For the opinion of individuals I care nothing, because, now at least, there is no one whose censure I fear, or whose praise I covet. Once, indeed, it was otherwise, but that is past and gone for ever. Desiring rather to move masses than to influence persons, I am nowise troubled by accusations before which many would shrink. They who dislike my principles, and who dread that boldness of inquiry, and that freedom of expression which this age desires, and which I seek to uphold, have already taken their course, and done what they could to bring me into discredit, and prevent my writings from being read. If I say that they have failed, I am not speaking arrogantly, but am simply stating a notorious fact.—HENRY THOMAS BUCKLE, "Letter to Gentleman Respecting Pooley's Case" (1859), *Miscellaneous and Posthumous Works of Henry Thomas Buckle*, ed. Helen Taylor, 1872, Vol. 1, pp. 71–72

He talked with a velocity and fulness of facts that was wonderful. The rest of us could do little but listen and ask questions. And yet he did not seem to be lecturing us; the stream of his conversation flowed along easily and naturally. Nor was it didactic; Buckle's range of reading has covered everything in elegant literature, as well as the ponderous works whose titles make so formidable a list at the beginning of his History, and, as he remembers everything he has read, he can produce his stores upon the moment for the illustration of whatever subject happens to come up.—CHARLES HALE, "Personal Reminiscences of the Late Henry Thomas Buckle," *Atlantic*, April 1863, p. 489

In whom is there not narrowness? Is there, then, presumption in my saying that there appeared to me to be narrowness in Mr. Buckle? Yet he is not only worthily lamented by personal friends, but will, I believe, by those who clearest see the forces of the age, be most mourned as a national loss. Truth is only to be attained by conflict; and the establishment of true principles is hastened by the vigour, not only of those who proclaim, but of those also who oppose them. Mr. Buckle in this may be an illustration of the error of one of his own views, that, namely, as to the influence of individuals. They, at least, incalculably influence, if not the manner and order, the celerity of human progress. And in the words of Mr. John Stuart Mill, 'Mr. Buckle, with characteristic energy, has flung down the great principle that the course of history is subject to general laws, together with many striking exemplifications of it, into the arena of popular discussion, to be fought over by a sort of combatants in the presence of a sort of spectators, who would never even have been aware that there existed such a principle if they had been left to learn its existence from the speculations of pure science. And hence has arisen a considerable amount of controversy, tending, not only to make the principle rapidly familiar to the majority of cultivated minds, but also to clear it from the confusions and misunderstandings by which it was but natural that it should for a time be clouded, and which impair the worth of the doctrine to those who accept it, and are the stumbling-block of many who do not.'—J. S. S. GLENNIE, "Mr. Buckle in the East," *Fraser's Magazine*, Aug. 1863, pp. 187–88

⟨. . .⟩ a great thinker, a great writer, and a great scholar—whose life, unfortunately for mankind, was cut short.—CHARLES DICKENS, Speech, Jan. 6, 1870

Works

HISTORY OF CIVILIZATION IN ENGLAND

This volume is certainly the most important work of the season; and it is perhaps the most comprehensive contribution to philosophical history that has ever been attempted in the English language. It is full of thought and original observation; but it is no speculative creation of a brilliant theorist. It is learned in the only true sense of the word. A mere glance at the matter accumulated in the notes will show the labour and reading which it has cost to quarry the materials. These are as judiciously selected as they have been widely sought, and make the volume, besides its proper merits, a most instructive repertory of facts. The style of the text is clear, and always easily followed. It is too diffuse, and a little cumbrous; but it is never tedious.—MARK PATTISON, *"History of Civilization in England"* (1857), *Essays*, ed. Henry Nettleship, 1889, Vol. 2, p. 396

I read Buckle's book all day, and got to the end, skipping of course. A man of talent and of a good deal of reading, but paradoxical and incoherent. He is eminently an anticipator, as Bacon would have said. He wants to make a system before he has got the materials; and he has not the excuse which Aristotle had, of having an eminently systematizing mind. The book reminds me perpetually of the *Divine Legation*. I could draw the parallel out far.—THOMAS BABINGTON MACAULAY, *Journal* (March 25, 1858), cited in G. Otto Trevelyan, *The Life and Letters of Lord Macaulay*, 1876, Vol. 2, pp. 388-89, Note

It is a remarkable book, as you say, and shows an astonishing amount of knowledge for a man of his years, and a power of generalization remarkable at any age. His views of what is connected with our spiritual nature are, no doubt, unsound, and his radicalism is always offensive. I have seldom read a book with which I have so often been angry, and yet I have learnt, I think, a great deal from it, and had my mind waked up by it upon many matters, for it has suggested to me a great variety of points for inquiry, of which I might otherwise never have thought.—GEORGE TICKNOR, Letter to Robert H. Gardiner (June 25, 1858), *Life, Letters, and Journals of George Ticknor*, ed. Anna Ticknor, 1876, Vol. 2, p. 410

In two respects, it seems to me, he deserves the honour of real distinction among his literary contemporaries. In the first place, though not a rich thinker—though rather a man of three or four ideas which he uses as a constant and prong-like apparatus than a man of fertile invention from moment to moment—yet he is a thinker, and a thinker of real force. All that he writes is vertebrate, if one may so express it, with some distinct proportion or other, true or false; and there is consequently the same kind of pleasure in reading anything he writes that there is in reading a dissertation by Mr. John Stuart Mill, or Mr. Herbert Spencer, or others of that select class. In the second place, he is characterized, in a singular degree, by moral fearlessness, by a boldness in speaking right out whatever he thinks. This is a quality that has been recently much needed in our literature; and I believe that the present exercise of it in so conspicuous a manner upon Scotland and the Scotch will do much good. In much that he says as to the present state of Scotland, Mr. Buckle is as ludicrously ignorant and as grossly unjust as in his representations of the past history of the country; nevertheless there is a vein of truth in what he says, and Scotland has been in want of some such rousing.—DAVID MASSON, "Mr. Buckle's Doctrine as to the Scotch and Their History," *Macmillan's Magazine*, June 1861, p. 189

With respect to the tendency of Mr. Buckle's work, an unprejudiced mind can have but one opinion. It is calculated to awaken independent thought, and to diffuse a spirit of scientific inquiry. Written in an easy and elegant style, it will be read with pleasure by many who would not otherwise have the patience to go through with the subjects of which it treats. Thus, grand and startling in its views, impressive and charming in its eloquence, it cannot fail to arouse many a slumbering

mind to intellectual effort. Such has its tendency already been, and such it will continue to be. Indeed, with Mr. Buckle's diligence, his honesty, his freedom of thought, his bold outspokenness, his hearty admiration for whatever is good and great in man, the tendency of his work could not well be otherwise. All these are qualities which will be remembered when his inaccuracies and errors, however great, shall be forgotten. And whatever may be thought about the correctness or incorrectness of Mr. Buckle's opinions, the world cannot be long in coming to the conclusion that his *History of Civilization in England* is a great and noble book, written by a great and noble man.—JOHN FISKE, "Mr. Buckle's Fallacies" (1861), *Darwinism and Other Essays*, 1879, pp. 194-95

In truth, the title of the work, as far as it has proceeded, is a misnomer. It is not a history of civilization or of anything else, but the statement of a system of doctrine, borrowed in great part from the Positive Philosophy of Comte, and supported by a series of illustrations drawn at random from the history of all nations and all ages, and from the records of literature and science. Hence the work is eminently discursive and ill-digested, and might be prosecuted through a dozen more thick volumes, filled with the fruits of the author's desultory reading, but having no more connection with the history of England than with that of China, and affording not even a glimpse of the writer's theory respecting the nature of civilization. In point of mere style, the merits of the book are considerable, and even the rambling and desultory nature of its contents is a source of attractiveness and power. The language is clear, animated, and forcible, sometimes rising very nearly to eloquence, and marked with the earnestness of one who thoroughly believes the doctrine which he expounds. Even the cool dogmatism of Mr. Buckle's assertions, and his entire confidence in the truth of his opinions and the force of his arguments, are often as amusing as they are unreasonable. One who has no doubts to express, and no qualifications or exceptions to state, has a great advantage in point of liveliness of manner. Like his great master, Hobbes, he betrays a good deal of egotism also, a quality which adds much to the freshness and raciness of his style.

We have already intimated that there is no novelty in Mr. Buckle's doctrines, however new may be his manner of stating and defending them. He is simply a necessitarian and a sceptic; and he shows all the earnestness of a fanatic in preaching the gospel of fatalism and unbelief. In his view, man is a plant that grows and thinks, the form and place of his growth, and the products of his thought, being as little dependent on his will or effort as the bark, leaves, and fruit of a tree are on its own choice. All alike are subject to the "skyey influences." Food, soil, climate,—these make up the man, and determine what he must be. They make up the whole man,—not merely his animal frame, but his life and soul, if he has any. If these are rich and generous, so will be the man, and his thoughts and actions. His moral nature is nothing; it has no lasting effect upon his character or conduct. And his spiritual nature is a mere fiction. The laws of matter and the laws of intellect,—these govern all, and shape our nature and destiny. And these laws are as permanent and uncontrollable as the laws of gravitation and chemical affinity. If we knew them perfectly, we could tell what the past must have been, and what the future will inevitably be; we could "look into the seeds of time, and see which grain would grow, and which would not." And we *can* learn them; from the statistics of what has been, we can prophesy what will be. As with individuals, so with communities and nations. These are but aggregates of individuals, and their history, also, is shaped by irreversible laws; and the system of averages, which eliminates small disturbing forces and abnormal instances, enables us to predict the result with greater ease and certainty in the case of these aggregates than in that of individuals. The history of human beings, the history of civilization, is like that of the solar and starry systems. When a Kepler, a Newton, and a Laplace shall arise to reduce the complexity of the observed and tabulated results to order, we shall see that all is subject to law; and knowing the law, we shall know all.—FRANCIS BOWEN, "Buckle's *History of Civilization*" (1861), *Gleanings from a Literary Life*, 1880, pp. 249–50

The most effective sketch of the intellectual and social state of France in the last century is given in Buckle's *History of Civilisation*, vol. i; especially in ch. 8, 11, 12, and 14. His narrative only sets forth the dark side of the picture, and the Christian reader frequently feels pained at some of his remarks; but it is generally correct so far as it goes, and the references are copious to the original sources which the author used. I have therefore frequently rested content with quoting this work without indicating further sources.—ADAM STOREY FARRAR, *A Critical History of Free Thought*, 1862, p. 164, Note

Many of you, perhaps, recollect Mr. Buckle as he stood not so long ago in this place. He spoke more than an hour without a note,—never repeating himself, never wasting words; laying out his matter as easily and as pleasantly as if he had been talking to us at his own fireside. We might think what we pleased of Mr. Buckle's views, but it was plain enough that he was a man of uncommon power; and he had qualities also— qualities to which he, perhaps, himself attached little value— as rare as they were admirable.

Most of us, when we have hit on something which we are pleased to think important and original, feel as if we should burst with it. We come out into the book-market with our wares in hand, and ask for thanks and recognition. Mr. Buckle, at an early age, conceived the thought which made him famous, but he took the measure of his abilities. He knew that whenever he pleased he could command personal distinction, but he cared more for his subject than for himself. He was contented to work with patient reticence, unknown and un-heard of, for twenty years; and then, at middle life, he produced a work which was translated at once into French and German, and, of all places in the world, fluttered the dovecotes of the Imperial Academy of St. Petersburg. ⟨. . .⟩

And thus consistently Mr. Buckle cared little for individuals. He did not believe (as some one has said) that the history of mankind is the history of its great men. Great men with him were but larger atoms, obeying the same impulses with the rest, only perhaps a trifle more erratic. With them or without them, the course of things would have been much the same.

As an illustration of the truth of his view, he would point to the new science of Political Economy. Here already was a large area of human activity in which natural laws were found to act unerringly. Men had gone on for centuries trying to regulate trade on moral principles. They would fix wages according to some imaginary rule of fairness; they would fix prices by what they considered things ought to cost; they encouraged one trade or discouraged another, for moral reasons. They might as well have tried to work a steam-engine on moral reasons. The great statesmen whose names were connected with these enterprises might have as well legislated that water should run up-hill. There were natural laws, fixed in the conditions of things; and to contend against them was the old battle of the Titans against the gods.—JAMES ANTHONY

FROUDE, "The Science of History" (1864), *Short Studies on Great Subjects*, 1881, Vol. 1, pp. 7–13

⟨. . .⟩ it may be inferred with tolerable certainty that it was during these eight years—from 1842 to 1850—that his grad-ually amassed knowledge of the great outlines of modern history, together with the experience he was acquiring of the tendencies of his own mind, led him to the choice of his subject. His literary style seems also to have been completely formed by this time, for all its main characteristics are to be found in the fragments on the reign of Elizabeth, written at least as early as 1850. One of its most marked characteristics, and one which principally contributes to its energy and, above all, to its picturesque charm, is his frequent use of those metaphors and of those rhetorical forms of speech to which all the world is accustomed, and which have become common-places in the language.—HELEN TAYLOR, "Biographical No-tice," *Miscellaneous and Posthumous Works of Henry Thomas Buckle*, 1872, Vol. 1, p. 16

Not only did Mr. Buckle's impatient and uncritical habit prevent his vast reading from resulting in sound scholarship, but his lack of subtlety and precision was so marked as to stamp all his thinking with the character of shallowness. He seized readily upon the broader and vaguer distinctions among things, the force of which the ordinary reader feels most strongly and with least mental effort, and of such raw material, without further analysis, and without suspecting the need for further analysis, he constructed his historical theories. To this mode of proceeding, aided by his warmth of temperament and the lavish profusion of his illustrations, he undoubtedly owed the great though ephemeral success which his book attained. The average reader is much sooner stimulated by generalizations that are broad and indistinct than by such as are subtle and precise; and if we stop to consider why Mr. Buckle's name has been sometimes associated with those of men so far beyond his calibre as Mill and Darwin, we may see the reason in the fact that Mr. Buckle could be entirely grasped by many of those very admirers of the latter writers who least appreciate or fathom their finest and deepest mental qualities. But this essentially superficial character of Mr. Buckle's thought is shown not only in his obtuseness to subtle distinctions, but even more conspicuously in his utter failure to seize upon any deeply significant but previously hidden relations among facts, in the work which he put forth as the *Novum Organum* of historical science.—JOHN FISKE, "Postscript on Mr. Buckle" (1875), *Darwinism and Other Essays*, 1879, pp. 202–3

The author's want of systematic training was itself an advantage for the immediate effect of his work; he knew nothing but the prejudices he had escaped, the facts he had accumulated, and the doctrines he had marshalled them to support; he addressed a public as ignorant as he had been, and as acute as his father had been. He had followed the scientific movement of his day, and observed with prophetic insight that the discussion of the transmutation of species was the weak point in Lyell's great work on Geology, but he had not busied himself with the speculative movement then mainly political or theological. If he had done so he would have been in danger of losing himself in side issues. As it was he stated and illustrated clearly and weightily, so that the work will not have to be done again for any section of the Western world, the conception of an orderly movement of human affairs depending upon ascertained facts of all degrees of generality. This is his great service: his special theories were of value chiefly as they furnished headings under which facts could be classified.—GEORGE AUGUSTUS SIMCOX,

"Henry Thomas Buckle," *Fortnightly Review*, Feb. 1880, p. 276

In one respect, too, Buckle was singularly unfortunate in the time in which he appeared. From the days of Bacon and Locke to the days of Condillac and Bentham, it had been the tendency of advanced liberal thinkers to aggrandize as much as possible the power of circumstances and experience over the individual, and to reduce to the narrowest limits every influence that is innate, transmitted, or hereditary. They represented man as essentially the creature of circumstances, and his mind as a sheet of blank paper on which education might write what it pleased. Buckle pushed this habit of thought so far that he even questioned the reality of such an evident and well-known fact as hereditary insanity. But only two years after the appearance of the first volume of the *History of Civilization*, Darwin published his *Origin of Species*, which gradually effected a revolution in speculative philosophy almost as great as it effected in natural science; and from that time the supreme importance of inborn and hereditary tendencies has become the very central fact in English philosophy. It must be added that Buckle had many of the distinctive faults of a young writer; of a writer who had mixed little with men, and had formed his mind almost exclusively by solitary, unguided study. He had a very imperfect appreciation of the extreme complexity of social phenomena, an excessive tendency to sweeping generalizations, and an arrogance of assertion which provoked much hostility. His wide and multifarious knowledge was not always discriminating, and he sometimes mixed good and bad authorities with a strange indifference.

This is a long catalogue of defects, but in spite of them Buckle opened out wider horizons than any previous writer in the field of history. No other English historian had sketched his plan with so bold a hand, or had shown so clearly the transcendent importance of studying not merely the actions of soldiers, politicians, and diplomatists, but also those great connected evolutions of intellectual, social, and industrial life on which the type of each succeeding age mainly depends. To not a few of his contemporaries he imparted an altogether new interest in history, and his admirable literary talent, the vast range of topics which he illuminated with a fresh significance, and the noble enthusiasm for knowledge and for freedom that pervades his work, made its appearance an epoch in the lives of many who have passed far from its definite conclusions. —W. E. H. LECKY, "Formative Influences," *Forum*, June 1890, pp. 388–89

Nothing can be more remarkable or more typical of his inner life than the picture of Buckle as presented to us by his biographer, working in a great room, lighted from the roof, and lined with books, shut out from every influence of real life, reading, reading, making volumes of notes, and tracing the action of laws which he knew by their letter, upon men whom he scarcely knew at all. It was in this closely-shut-up hermit's cell in the midst of London that the *History of Civilisation* was written. A very simple mistake originating in this way, by which he took the institution of the Fast Day in Scotland as meaning an extreme asceticism of actual fasting, upon which idea he founded an entire argument, and added many grave reproaches in respect to the gloomy religion of the country—is a case in point: for had Buckle known anything beyond the words, he would have been aware that religious fasting is in Scotland a habit unknown in practice, and much discountenanced as a relic of Popery. The example is not one of much importance, but it serves to show what was the defect of his mind. Curiously enough, however, this book of limited per-

ceptions and scholastic origin struck the world with that sudden accidental and unreal effect which sometimes makes a man with no particular right to distinction awake to find himself famous. The first volume appeared in 1858, and being merely introductory to the great work, raised a universal expectation. The second appeared in 1861, but even in that he had not as yet begun the history he had planned on so colossal a scale. The third volume was published only after his death in 1862, but before that time the fervour of interest had already abated. ⟨. . .⟩ His unaccomplished work, the immense labour with which it was begun, and its sudden failure and dropping off from the great and sudden reputation it brought him, threw a shade of pathos over the life of one who was nothing if not a student, and to whom books were everything in life.—MARGARET OLIPHANT, *The Victorian Age of English Literature*, 1892, Vol. 2, pp. 119–21

Enough has now been done, perhaps, to set in a reasonably clear light the critical problem represented by the work of Buckle. It has been obscured more than most, I cannot but think, by careless handling; and, rightly or wrongly, I have been impressed by a certain ungenerous wantonness of injustice in the matter, on the part of a number of critics whose position gives them a wide influence over public opinion, but who, as I have attempted to show, are not fully entitled to their authority. I can but ask the reader to note the process of argument by which it has been sought to decide the questions in dispute, giving me credit only for some judicial comparison of pros and cons, and for a certain measure of impartiality; to which last I pretend on the score of sharing opinions that Buckle disliked and denounced.

There has been far too much play of mere "authority" in the discussion of the case hitherto; and the extreme seems to be reached when writers with not a moiety of Buckle's information and orderliness of mind go about to dismiss him as uninstructed, hasty, amateurish. In final opposition to the "amateur" view, I would make this suggestion to the general student of history. Let him read Buckle carefully through (a thing seldom done, I fancy, by his critics), noting not only the narrative and the theory in the text, but the range of erudition and critical judgment in the notes; let him once for all set down the general rhetorical element in the former—to say nothing in particular of the Theism—as a matter of form, and deal with the kernel rather than the husk; let him at the close say whether he knows of any writer of Buckle's time or since who shows a more universal openness of mind to ideas, or a sounder and more independent judgment of writers of all sorts and calibres; and let him say finally whether, on the vexed question of the philosophy of history, he has got any clearer and wider light from any one other writer than he has got from Buckle's series of generalisations, granting these to be not fully co-ordinated and at times mistaken. If he is what I understand by a materialist, I think I can anticipate his judgment; if he is a transcendentalist, I cannot forecast it with any confidence. But I have a general confidence that as time goes on and men look at Buckle with the eyes of dispassionate science, unprepossessed by philosophies "held in solution," they will recognise in him one of the most suggestive and competent of modern writers on sociological questions. They will see, I think, that he had an extraordinarily quick appreciation of every sort of insight among his contemporaries—witness his footnote and other references to the earliest performances of Darwin, Spencer, Grove, and Lewes, not to speak of his praise of Comte, Carlyle, and Macaulay. They will recognise in his work a practical mastery of physical science, combined with a width of historic grasp, such as no other historian of his time can pretend to. They will be incapable of the blunder of setting him down as lacking in adaptability to the conception of evolution, merely because he did not do Darwin's work as well as his own; they will see on the contrary that he had a very large share in preparing men's minds for the full adoption of the evolution principle. And though they may see readily enough the faults of form which arose from the nature of Buckle's training, they will not improbably do as I venture to do now—recommend his book to young students as one the study of which, with all its faults, will widen, clarify, and methodise their notions of general history as no other book of these times can.

It has sometimes occurred to me to ask myself by way of a practical test of Buckle's power and importance, whether there is any living writer who could be trusted, not to carry out his whole scheme—that were too large a demand—but simply to complete his Introduction, handling the proposed problems of the intellectual development of Germany and the United States with such fulness of knowledge and mastery of material as Buckle has shown in his treatment of the intellectual history of France, Spain, and Scotland. It would be absurd to say there is nobody who can do it: something of the kind will certainly be done some day: but what one perceives at once is that the mere doing of either section of that work, no more efficiently than Buckle has done the rest, would be regarded by most qualified men as in itself a *magnum opus*, calling for years of special study and thought. If that can be said without extravagance, it is difficult to evade the conclusion that the man who gave us the existing fragment of the *Introduction to the History of Civilisation in England* was among the strongest of his time. —JOHN MACKINNON ROBERTSON, *Buckle and His Critics: A Study in Sociology*, 1895, pp. 546–48

The book attained at once, and for some time kept, an extraordinary popularity, which has been succeeded by a rather unjust depreciation. Both are to be accounted for by the fact that it is in many ways a book rather of the French than of the English type, and displays in fuller measure than almost any of Buckle's contemporaries in France itself, with the possible exception of Taine, could boast, the frank and fearless, some would say the headlong and headstrong, habit of generalisation—scorning particulars, or merely impressing into service such as are useful to it and drumming the others out—on which Frenchmen pride themselves, and for the lack of which they are apt to pronounce English historians, and indeed English men of letters of all kinds, plodding and unilluminated craftsmen rather than artists. In Buckle's reflections on Spain and Scotland, he accounts for the whole history of both countries and the whole character of both peoples by local conditions in the first place, and by forms of civil and ecclesiastical government. In respect to these last, his views were crude Voltairianism; but perhaps this is the best and most characteristic example of his method. He was extremely prejudiced; his lack of solid disciplinary education made him unapt to understand the true force and relative value of his facts and arguments; and as his premises are for the most part capriciously selected facts cemented together with an untempered mortar of theory, his actual conclusions are rarely of much value. But his style is clear and vigorous; the aggressive *raiding* character of his argument is agreeably stimulating, and excellent to make his readers clear up their minds on the other side; while the dread of over-generalisation, however healthy in itself, has been so long a dominant force in English letters and philosophy that a little excess the other way might

be decidedly useful as an alterative. The worst fault of Buckle was the Voltairianism above referred to, causing or caused by, as is always the case, a deplorable lack of taste, which is not confined to religious matters.—GEORGE SAINTSBURY, *A History of Nineteenth Century Literature*, 1896, pp. 243–44

Buckle was a man of vast reading and tenacious memory; but no knowledge, however extensive, could at that time have sufficed to do what he attempted. He soon discovered this himself, and what he has executed is a mere fragment of his daring design. Even so, it is larger than his materials justified. In accounting for Buckle's failure, stress has often been laid upon the fact that his education was private. This is a little pedantic. ⟨. . .⟩ The real reason, besides the cardinal fact that the attempt was premature, is that Buckle, though he had the daring of the speculator's temperament, had neither its caution nor its breadth. The great speculative geniuses of the world have been prudent as well as bold. No one is bolder than Aristotle, but no one is more careful to lay first a broad foundation for his speculations. Buckle did not use his great knowledge so. His account of the causes of things always rouses suspicion because it is far too simple. He never understood how complex the life of a nation is; and when he came to write he practically rejected the greater part of his knowledge and used only the small remainder. He was moreover a man of strong prejudices. He could not endure the ecclesiastical type of mind or the ecclesiastical view of things; and his account of civilisation in Scotland is completely vitiated by his determination to regard the Church, before the Reformation and after the Reformation alike, as merely a weight on the wheel, not a source of energy and forward movement.

Buckle then illustrates the tendency of the mind, noted by Bacon, to grasp prematurely at unity. This very fact, conjoined with the clearness and vigour of his style, was the reason of his popularity. When the inadequacy of his theories began to be perceived there came a reaction.—HUGH WALKER, *The Age of Tennyson*, 1897, pp. 133–34

GEORGE HENRY LEWES
From "Mr. Buckle's Scientific Errors"

Blackwood's Edinburgh Magazine, November 1861, pp. 582–83

It must be owned that Mr Buckle has given great and often just offence, both by his matter and his manner. On the one hand, a large class of thinking men is offended by certain speculative conclusions which he advocates; and, on the other hand, many of those who are inclined to agree with his conclusions are irritated by the arrogance of his tone. Mr Buckle is not a modest man; but others, equally self-assured, are more amiable in manner. He is not only a man *extrêmement de son avis*, but one whose tone rather ostentatiously implies that all who differ from him are fools. This is not conciliatory. Even the admiration excited by his erudition is qualified by the bad taste of his ostentation. He is wearisome, and even frivolous, in his love of accumulated references—often to books of no value at all. In days when few men think it necessary to read all the books they quote, he seems to think it necessary to quote every book he reads.[1]

Besides these general qualities which excite critical objection, it must be noted that the course of his argument leads him over various fields of inquiry, demanding a knowledge of each seldom possessed, except by the special students of each. Great as his knowledge is, it is too various not to be occasionally imperfect. To special students he often appears superficial or inaccurate; and as his tone is magisterial even where he is least informed, it occasionally excites a contemptuous contradiction from a more instructed reader. This is echoed in many empty pates. There is always a set of men who fancy they raise themselves above a distinguished writer, by citing some error into which he has fallen; such men eagerly parade some blunder as "a specimen of Buckle." We are almost ashamed to reply, that were the blunder ten times as great, it could only form one item in a considerable work, and is not to be taken as a "specimen" of it. Fortunately this kind of cackle, which is heard in society respecting all noticeable works, though it may teaze an author and exasperate his admirers, has no influence on the permanent prosperity of a good book, which is certain to find, and to hold, its public. Even the scornful writers are among the first to gather instruction from the despised author, and would gather more were they competent to more. And it is now pretty well understood that every book which commands attention and respect from serious readers, does so in virtue of sterling qualities: it may have deficiencies and errors, both numerous and great; but it must have excellencies of a positive order, if it gain acceptance. Mr Buckle's book has gained this acceptance; it has notoriously achieved an immense success. We are sorry to say that this very success has been an offence to one class of readers; and it is precisely the class from which he would have received the highest eulogies, had he written in a style sufficiently unattractive to *repel* the general public. But his splendid abilities made it a commonplace to admire him; and some of those who profess to lead opinion were thereby thrown into antagonism by their jealousy of commonplace. They preferred the merit they had themselves discovered. A conspicuous triumph is suspicious to them. Like that ancient cynic who, on being applauded, asked what absurdity he had committed, they conclude that an author who commands general applause must be unworthy of theirs.

To deny that Mr Buckle's *History of Civilisation* has several rare and admirable qualities, seems to us as foolish as to deny that it has numerous faults and deficiencies. We have read the first volume three times, and each time with increasing respect; and yet on many points we are profoundly at variance with him. On several points we see that his knowledge is manifestly deficient and inaccurate: we neither agree with him in his philosophy, nor do we find that novelty in his book, which to so many readers has been a surprise and delight. When, however, we read him, we are both instructed by his

knowledge, and stimulated by his thoughts; and when we think of the immense mass of material which he has assimilated and re-shaped—when we consider the vastness of his undertaking, and the brilliant success with which he has, on the whole, executed it—the vigour of thought, the patience of research, and the power of writing displayed—we silence our objections, and merge them in a feeling of admiration. To use the language of Sir Thomas Browne, "If detraction could invite us, discretion surely would contain us from any derogatory intention, where highest pens and friendliest eloquence must fail in commendation." Remarkable writers are not so common that we can afford to speak grudingly of any. It is a hard thing to write a good book. Critics who do not, by sad experience, know how hard it is, may indulge their cheap scorn by off-hand judgments of successful writers; but we are not at such a lofty height; and if, in the remarks which are to follow, we shall have to apply the scalpel with unhesitating freedom—if our attitude will be purely one of antagonism—it is the more incumbent on us to express here, without stint, our general admiration of the book which contains the errors we point out.

Errors of course there are; it is the fate of mortal books: *aliter non fit, Avite, liber.* In so extensive a work, the calculation of chances must show a large amount of probable error. Mr Buckle, if not omniscient, is multiscient. He has studied Greek, Latin, French, Italian, Spanish, and German, political economy, law, philosophy, all the physical sciences, history, and literature. He is not a book-worm, but a thinker. In his almost unrivalled erudition there will necessarily be deficiencies; but properly to estimate these, there should be a series of criticisms directed to the several subjects. We have chosen one of these for our remarks, and that one is Science, on which his reading is probably more extensive than that of any man who has not directly studied science. If here we find him erring from imperfect information, or from that want of intimate familiarity with details which is inseparable from second-hand knowledge, we must not conceal the fact that his work is greatly enriched by his knowledge of science; and that it would have been less admirable had he, by complete abstinence from any allusion to such topics, exposed no such target for our shots.

Notes

1. "On m'a demandé si j'ai lu moi-même tous les livres que j'ai cités. J'ai repondu que non: certainement il aurait fallu que j'eusse passé une grande partie de ma vie à lire de très-mauvais livres."—Pascal.

FRANCES TROLLOPE

1780–1863

Frances Milton was born on March 10, 1780, near Bristol, the daughter of a clergyman. She was educated privately at home, then went to London to keep house for her brother, who was employed by the War Office. There she met Thomas Anthony Trollope, and they were married in 1809.

Trollope appears to have been a man of much energy and many interests, but he seemed unable to succeed in any field of endeavor. He failed as a lawyer, then tried to farm at Harrow Weald but was unsuccessful. At the suggestion of his friend Frances Wright, the feminist and reformer, he moved his family to America in 1827 and attempted to be a merchant in Cincinnati. Once again he failed and the family returned to England. But out of this experience his wife, Frances, wrote her controversial account, *Domestic Manners of the Americans*, a censorious report on American behavior that made her a sensation in England and caused a furor in the United States.

Mrs. Trollope had turned to writing in a desperate attempt to support her family (she had six children, three of whom reached adulthood). *Domestic Manners* made her a success at the age of fifty-one and led to a prolific—and lucrative—writing career. For a time she concentrated on travel books, going about the Continent gathering material, then turned to fiction. Her other major works include *The Vicar of Wrexhill* (1837), *The Widow Barnaby* (1838), *The Lottery of Marriage* (1846), and *The Life and Adventures of a Clever Woman* (1854).

In her later years, following her husband's death, she settled in Florence with a son and daughter-in-law, establishing a salon that became a center for supporters of the Italian Revolution (although she herself was too busy writing to pay much attention to her guests). She died in Florence on October 6, 1863. Mrs. Trollope's three surviving children were themselves writers; Anthony Trollope (1815–1882), a prolific Victorian novelist, is the best known.

General

I have been reading Bulwer's novels and Mrs. Trollope's libels, and Dr. Parr's works. I am sure *you* are not an admirer of Mrs. Trollope's. She has neither the delicacy nor the candour which constitute true nobility of mind, and her extent of talent forms but a scanty veil to shadow her other defects.—ELIZABETH BARRETT BROWNING, Letter to Mrs. Martin (Dec. 14, 1832)

Speaking of travellers, I have amused myself with looking over Mrs. Trollope's *Paris*. She is certainly clever at observing the surface, but, like other superficial book-makers, leaves you about as wise as she found you. You see through the whole that she is plotting future visits to Paris, and means to be well received. The tone of fearless truth, which cares not for giving offence, is singularly wanting. I was quite amused with her Toryism. It aims to be authoritative and dignified, but cannot rise above scolding. ⟨. . .⟩ Mrs. Trollope's book is an amusing comment on the national vanity, not by her description of it, but by the degree in which she has caught the contagion herself.—WILLIAM ELLERY CHANNING, Letter to Lucy Aikin (May 10, 1836), *Correspondence of William Ellery Channing and Lucy Aikin*, ed. Anna Letitia LeBreton, 1874, pp. 267–68

The class to which she belongs is, fortunately, very small; but it will always be recruited from the ranks of the unscrupulous, so long as a corrupt taste is likely to yield a trifling profit. She owes everything to that audacious contempt of public opinion, which is the distinguishing mark of persons who are said to *stick at nothing*. Nothing but this sticking at nothing could have produced some of the books she has written, in which her wonderful impunity of face is so remarkable. Her constitutional coarseness is the natural element of a low popularity, and is sure to pass for cleverness, shrewdness, and strength, where cultivated judgment and chaste inspiration would be thrown away. Her books of travel are crowded with plebeian criticisms on works of art and the usages of courts, and are doubtless held in great esteem by her admirers, who love to see such things overhauled and dragged down to their own level. The book on America is of a different class. The subject exactly suited her style and her taste, and people looked on at the fun as they would at a scramble of sweeps in the kennel; while the reflecting few thought it a little unfair in Mrs. Trollope to find fault with the manners of the Americans. Happy for her she had such a topic to begin with. Had she commenced her literary career with Austria or France, in all likelihood, she would have ended it there.

But it is to her novels she is chiefly indebted for her current reputation; and it is here her defects are most glaringly exhibited. She cannot adapt herself to the characterization requisite in a work of fiction: she cannot go out of herself: she serves up everything with the same sauce: the predominant flavour is Trollope still. The plot is always preposterous, and the actors in it seem to be eternally bullying each other. She

takes a strange delight in the hideous and revolting, and dwells with gusto upon the sins of vulgarity. Her sensitiveness upon this point is striking. She never omits an opportunity of detailing the faults of low-bred people, and even goes out of her way to fasten the stigma upon others who ought to have been more gently tasselled. Then her low people are sunk deeper than the lowest depths, as if they had been bred in and in, to the last dregs. Nothing can exceed the vulgarity of Mrs. Trollope's mob of characters, except the vulgarity of her select aristocracy. That is transcendent—it caps the climax.

We have heard it urged on behalf of Mrs. Trollope, that her novels are, at all events, drawn from life. So are sign-paintings. It is no great proof of their truth that centaurs and griffins do not run loose through her pages, and that her men and women have neither hoofs nor tails. The tawdriest wax-works, girt up in paste and spangles, are also "drawn from life;" but there ends the resemblance.—R. H. HORNE, "G. P. R. James, Mrs. Gore, Captain Marryatt, and Mrs. Trollope," *A New Spirit of the Age*, 1844, pp. 141–42

A tendency to artificial sentiment was certainly not the fault of Mrs. Frances Trollope as a novelist. There was a practical heartiness in her work that gave pleasure to the readers of her own generation, and her name lives for the next generation of readers also in two sons who maintain its credit. ⟨. . .⟩ In 1829 she went to America, stayed three years, and published in 1832 her experience of the *Domestic Life of the Americans*, to the great discontent of those whose manners she described. Then followed light and cheerful records of Travel in Belgium and Western Germany and a book on *Paris and the Parisians*, before Mrs. Trollope began novel writing, in 1837, with *Jonathan Jefferson Whitlaw*, followed promptly by *The Vicar of Wrexhill*. In 1838 Mrs. Trollope in *The Widow Barnaby* produced a picture of a vulgar woman on her travels, drawn with a rough good humour that pleased many readers. Following the lead of Charles Dickens, who, by his *Oliver Twist*, had, in 1838, quickened attention to the working of the Poor Laws, Mrs. Trollope published in 1839, in monthly parts, a novel upon life in the Factory, *Michael Armstrong, the Factory Boy*; she also continued the adventures of her Widow Barnaby in *The Widow Married*, and published a book on *A Visit to Italy*. Another novel, *Jessie Phillips* followed, and, in 1843, *The Barnabys in America*. From this time until 1856 Mrs. Trollope's novels appeared in rapid succession with an occasional light book founded on travel. Sometimes, as in *The Robertses on Their Travels* (1846) travel and fiction were united in one work. Her last novel, *Gertrude*, appeared in the year 1855. —HENRY MORLEY, *Of English Literature in the Reign of Victoria*, 1881, pp. 181–82

In 1827 she went to America, having been partly instigated by the social and communistic ideas of a lady whom I well remember,—a certain Miss Wright,—who was, I think, the first of the American female lecturers. Her chief desire, however, was to establish my brother Henry; and perhaps joined with that was the additional object of breaking up her English home without pleading broken fortunes to all the world. At Cincinnati, in the State of Ohio, she built a bazaar, and I fancy lost all the money which may have been embarked in that speculation. It could not have been much, and I think that others also must have suffered. But she looked about her, at her American cousins, and resolved to write a book about them. This book she brought back with her in 1831, and published it early in 1832. When she did this she was already fifty. When doing this she was aware that unless she could so succeed in making money, there was no money for any of the family. She had never before earned a shilling. She almost immediately received a considerable sum from the publishers,—if I remember rightly, amounting to two sums of £400 each within a few months; and from that moment till nearly the time of her death, at any rate for more than twenty years, she was in the receipt of a considerable income from her writings. It was a late age at which to begin such a career.

The Domestic Manners of the Americans was the first of a series of books of travels, of which it was probably the best, and was certainly the best known. It will not be too much to say of it that it had a material effect upon the manners of the Americans of the day, and that that effect has been fully appreciated by them. No observer was certainly ever less qualified to judge of the prospects or even of the happiness of a young people. No one could have been worse adapted by nature for the task of learning whether a nation was in a way to thrive. Whatever she saw she judged, as most women do, from her own standing-point. If a thing were ugly to her eyes, it ought to be ugly to all eyes,—and if ugly, it must be bad. What though people had plenty to eat and clothes to wear, if they put their feet upon the tables and did not reverence their betters? The Americans were to her rough, uncouth, and vulgar,—and she told them so. Those communistic and social ideas, which had been so pretty in a drawing-room, were scattered to the winds. Her volumes were very bittter; but they were very clever, and they saved the family from ruin.

Book followed book immediately,—first two novels, and then a book on Belgium and Western Germany. She refurnished the house which I have called Orley Farm, and surrounded us again with moderate comforts. Of the mixture of joviality and industry which formed her character, it is almost impossible to speak with exaggeration. The industry was a thing apart, kept to herself. It was not necessary that any one who lived with her should see it. She was at her table at four in the morning, and had finished her work before the world had begun to be aroused. But the joviality was all for others. She could dance with other people's legs, eat and drink with other people's palates, be proud with the lustre of other people's finery. Every mother can do that for her own daughters; but she could do it for any girl whose look, and voice, and manners pleased her. Even when she was at work, the laughter of those she loved was a pleasure to her. She had much, very much, to suffer. Work sometimes came hard to her, so much being required,—for she was extravagant, and liked to have money to spend; but of all people I have known she was the most joyous, or, at any rate, the most capable of joy.

⟨. . .⟩ She continued writing up to 1856, when she was seventy-six years old,—and had at that time produced 114 volumes, of which the first was not written till she was fifty. Her career offers great encouragement to those who have not begun early in life, but are still ambitious to do something before they depart hence.

She was an unselfish, affectionate, and most industrious woman, with great capacity for enjoyment and high physical gifts. She was endowed, too, with much creative power, with considerable humour, and a genuine feeling for romance. But she was neither clear-sighted nor accurate; and in her attempts to describe morals, manners, and even facts, was unable to avoid the pitfalls of exaggeration.—ANTHONY TROLLOPE, *An Autobiography*, 1883, Ch. 2

The record of Frances Trollope as a writer of fiction, which is in all respects most interesting, is unique in this: that at a time of life when the energies of most persons are on the wane, or are at least so curbed and quieted by household cares and troubles as to render any great change of pursuits and aims all but impossible—in short, at the age of fifty this remarkable woman first entered upon her long and successful literary career. These facts alone are ground for wonder and admiration, and such feelings are intensified when we learn the distressing circumstances under which the novelist prosecuted her almost unending work. ⟨. . .⟩

Frances Trollope never possessed sufficient leisure for the production of perfect work, and so, perhaps, cannot be classed among our great writers. She was something, however, more admirable, more worthy of love and praise—she was, in the highest sense, a good woman.—GEORGE NEWCOMBE, *Academy*, Feb. 29, 1896, pp. 171–72

Works

DOMESTIC MANNERS OF THE AMERICANS

This is exactly the title-page we have long wished to see, and we rejoice to say that, now the subject has been taken up, it is handled by an English *lady* of sense and acuteness, who possesses very considerable power of expression, and enjoyed unusually favourable opportunities for observation. A book of travels in any country, by a person so qualified, might be considered valuable; but assuredly it was most wanted in the case of America, and especially at this moment, when so much trash and falsehood pass current respecting that 'terrestrial paradise of the west.'

⟨. . .⟩ Whatever may be said as to particular points of this lady's description of America, it must be allowed to be a remarkable fact, that almost every English liberal accustomed to the social habits of the upper classes in this country, who has recently travelled in the United States, appears to have come back a convert to the old-fashioned doctrines of Toryism. Captain Hall went out with his head quite exalted as to the ineffable advantages of republican institutions—an ultra-whig in Church and State;—we all know the result of his experiences. We have now before us the story of a lady who also carried with her to the New World the most exaggerated notions of liberalism, and who seems to have returned, if possible, a stouter enemy of all such notions than the gallant captain himself.—JOHN GIBSON LOCKHART, "Domestic Manners of the Americans," *Quarterly Review*, March 1832, pp. 39–40, 80

Some of Mrs. Trollope's strictures are well merited; and would perhaps have done good, and entitled her to our gratitude, had they carried with them the appearance of being well meant. The great defect of the work is, that it is throughout conceived in bitterness and ill-nature, evidently indicative of personal disappointment. We see in almost every page a soured and discouraged woman. Hence what is truly said is ungraciously said; much is said on hearsay, which is not true; much is caricatured and exaggerated. She speaks, for instance, of the want of amusements 'from one end of the Union to the other.' What could she know of that which abounded or was wanting from one end of the Union to another? She passed three days in Louisiana, made a flying visit in Tennessee, (the unsettled part of it,) passed perhaps a day or two in Kentucky at Louisville, a couple of years in Ohio, passed, in a stage coach, through a small part of Virginia and Maryland, resided a short time near the Potomac, travelled northeasterly through Baltimore and Philadelphia to New York, and made a visit to Niagara. It does not appear, that she set foot either in Maine, New Hampshire, Vermont, Massachusetts, Rhode Island, Connecticut, New Jersey, (except to drive thirty miles across it,) Delaware, (with the same exception,) Virginia, North Carolina, South Carolina, Georgia, Alabama, Mississippi, Indiana, Illinois, Missouri, Michigan, Arkansaw or Florida; and yet she affects to make observations 'from one end of the Union to the other.' There are, at least, four pretty strongly discriminated sections of the Union, New England, the Middle States, the Southern States, and the North Western. The latter is the only one which Mrs. Trollope can make any pretensions to have observed; and from the very peculiarity of that section, as the newest settled portion of the country, or rather that, in which the process of settlement is going on most rapidly, it is that which could with least justice be taken as a sample of the whole. At best, the personal experience of single travellers, (with the exception of the impartial and gifted few, who are capable of philosophical generalization,) furnish about as good a specimen of a country, as the single brick which was carried about by the simpleton afforded of the house. But if any person will be at the trouble to look at the map of the United States, and compare the extent of those parts of it which this lady traveller did visit, with those she did not, he will perceive at a glance, how limited were her opportunities of observation. ⟨. . .⟩

In conclusion then, we recommend to all persons in England, who have been 'un-whigged' by reading books like that before us, to get whigged again, as soon as possible. They will be greatly out of fashion even in their own country, with their newly imbibed 'old-fashioned toryism.' Of all the unlucky periods to forswear liberal opinions, this is about the most unlucky that could be hit upon. It is like the man of tardy apprehension in the stage coach, who could not catch a joke, till the conversation had taken a turn and a case of murder was under discussion, and who then interrupted the lugubrious exclamations of the company, by his unseasonable laugh at the jest which every body else had forgotten. Old-fashioned toryism was, in the day of it, excellent sport; that is, for those who did not pay the piper. But it has gone by; the jest has evaporated. An awful seriousness has come on. We are getting too earnest for the old-fashioned 'mummery;' and Europe, if we mistake not, will before long look over to our American gravity, as a mighty cheerful, encouraging, desirable frame of mind.—EDWARD EVERETT, "Prince Pückler Muscau and Mrs. Trollope," *North American Review*, Jan. 1833, pp. 38–48

As I had lately returned from the United States, I was asked what Mrs. Trollope's position was there. My reply was that I had no scruple in saying that Mrs. Trollope had no opportunity of knowing what good society was in America, generally speaking. I added that I intended to say this, as often as I was inquired of; for the simple reason that Mrs. Trollope had thought proper to libel and slander a whole nation. If she had been an ordinary discontented tourist, her adventures in America would not be worth the trouble of discussing; but her slanderous book made such exposures necessary.—HARRIET MARTINEAU, *Autobiography*, ed. Maria Weston Chapman, 1877, Vol. 1, p. 240

The true bent of her talents—a sharp, bold, and somewhat coarse satire—she did not discover until after her visit to the United States (1829–1831). There she conceived an antipathy to American manners and customs, which seems to have awakened her powers of sarcasm, and resulted in her first publication, *Domestic Life of the Americans*. The peculiarities she had found so obnoxious she sketched with a strong, rough hand; and the truth of her drawing was proved by the wrathful feelings which it provoked in the breasts of its victims. Reading it now, we are naturally inclined to think it a caricature and an exaggeration; but it is only fair to remember that, since its appearance half a century ago, a great change has come over the temper of American society. The great fault of Mrs. Trollope is, that she is always a critic and never a judge. She looks at everything through the magnifying lens of a microscope. And, again, it must be admitted that she is often vulgar; whatever the want of refinement in American society, it is almost paralleled by the want of refinement in her lively, but coarsely-coloured pages. For the rest, she is a shrewd observer; has a considerable insight into human nature, especially on its "seamy side"; and if a hard hitter, generally keeps her good temper, and does not resent a fair stroke from an antagonist. As a humorist she takes high rank: there are scenes in her novels, as well as in her records of travel, which are marked by a real and vigorous, if somewhat masculine, fun. Perhaps some of her defects are due to the influences among which she lived—that ultra Toryism of the Castlereagh school which resented each movement of reform, each impulse of progress, as a direct revolutionary conspiracy against everything approved and established by "the wisdom of our ancestors"—that narrowness of thought and shallowness of feeling which resisted all change, even when its necessity was most apparent.

That Mrs. Trollope's prejudices sometimes prevail over her sense of justice is apparent in the ridicule she lavishes upon the rigid observance of the Sabbath by the American people. She forgot that they inherited it from the English Puritans. If her evidence may be accepted, it amounted in her day to a bigotry as implacable as that of the straitest sect of the Scotch Presbyterians a generation ago. She tells an anecdote to the following effect:—A New York tailor sold, on a Sunday, some clothes to a sailor whose ship was on the point of sailing. The Guild of Tailors immediately made their erring brother the object of the most determined persecution, and succeeded in ruining him. A lawyer who had undertaken his defence lost all his clients. The nephew of this lawyer sought admission to the bar. His certificates were perfectly regular; but on his presenting himself he was rejected, with the curt explanation that no man bearing the name of F— (his uncle's name) would be admitted. We need hardly add that such fanaticism as this would not be possible now in the United States.

Mrs. Trollope's animadversions are obsolete on many other subjects. Much of her indignation was necessarily, and very justly bestowed on the then flourishing institution of domestic slavery; but that foul blot on her scutcheon America wiped out in blood, the blood of thousands of her bravest children. Her criticism upon manners and social customs has also, to a great extent, lost its power of application.—W. H. DAVENPORT ADAMS, "Mrs. Trollope," *Celebrated Women Travellers*, 1883, pp. 385–87

The Domestic Manners of the Americans was published, and made an immediate and great success. It was emphatically the book of the season, was talked of everywhere, and read by all sorts and conditions of men and women. It was highly praised by all the Conservative organs of the press, and vehemently abused by all those of the opposite party. Edition after edition was sold, and the pecuniary results were large enough to avert from the family of the successful authoress the results of her husband's ruined fortunes.

The Americans were made very angry by this account of their 'domestic manners'—very naturally, but not very wisely. Of course, it was asserted that many of the statements made were false and many of the descriptions caricatured. Nothing in the book from beginning to end was false; nothing of minutest detail which was asserted to have been seen had not been seen; nor was anything intentionally caricatured or exaggerated for the sake of enhancing literary effect. But the tone of the book was unfriendly, and was throughout the result of offended taste rather than of well-weighed opinion. It was full of universal conclusions drawn from particular premises; and no sufficient weight, or rather no weight at all, was allowed to the fact that the observations on which the recorded judgments were founded had been gathered almost entirely in what was then the Far West, and represented the 'domestic manners' of the Atlantic states hardly at all. Unquestionably the book was a very clever one, and written with infinite *verve* and brightness. But—save for the fact that censure and satire are always more amusing than the reverse—an equally clever and equally truthful book might have been written in a diametrically opposite spirit. —THOMAS ADOLPHUS TROLLOPE, *What I Remember*, 1888

Of all books of travel that have appeared during the twelvemonth, this sixty-year old classic ought to be read with the greatest avidity by Americans, for it is history in its most taking form. The style is that of a bright, cultivated Englishwoman, with a "conscious incapacity for description," but with a very unusual capacity for it, nevertheless. She writes not from memory but from notes made on the spot, and with a manifest desire to be moderate and truthful.—W. P. GARRISON, *Nation*, Nov. 8, 1894, p. 345

Now, although her criticisms and assertions were engendered in disappointment, national animosity, and revenge, they were essentially true, and however chagrined we were, we acknowledged them as such by essaying to correct our manners; as was afterward universally demonstrated whenever one in public fell within the range of her criticisms, as the cry of "Trollope! Trollope! Trollope!" was immediately vociferated. In illustration of the extent to which such action was practised: at the Park Theatre on an evening when the house was exceptionally full, one of a party occupying a front seat in the centre of the auditorium, soon after the close of the first act, leisurely and inconsiderately turned his back to the stage and rested himself on the front enclosure of the box, whereupon "Trollope! Trollope! Trollope!" was shouted from several quarters, in which I joined; but so soon as it was apparent that the party was disposed to ignore the rebuke, the pit arose, some occupants of the boxes followed, and the performance was arrested. When the person, in sporting phrase, finally "threw up the sponge," the house gave three cheers, not in compliment to him who had caused the censure, but to itself for its success; and such for many years was the course in public on all similar occasions of evident impropriety or neglect of the accepted observances of society. So much for Mrs. Trollope's book, much talked of at the time. It gave pleasure to the English, but profit to us, however much we may have been annoyed by it at first.—CHARLES H. HASWELL, *Reminiscences of New York by an Octogenarian, 1816–1860*, 1896, pp. 276–77

HENRY T. TUCKERMAN
From "British Travellers and Writers"
America and Her Commentators
1864, pp. 225–29

Of this class of books ⟨. . .⟩ none made so strong a popular impression as the *Domestic Manners of the Americans*, by Mrs. Trollope—a circumstance that the reader of our own day finds it difficult to explain, until he recalls and reflects upon the facts of the case; for the book is superior to the average of a like scope, in narrative interest. It is written in a lively, confident style, and, before the subjects treated had become so familiar and hackneyed, must have proved quite entertaining. The name of the writer, however, was, for a long period, and still is, to a certain extent, more identified with the unsparing social critics of the country than any other in the long catalogue of modern British travellers in America. Until recently, the sight of a human foot protruding over the gallery of a Western theatre was hailed with the instant and vociferous challenge, apparently undisputed as authoritative, of "Trollope!" whereupon the obnoxious member was withdrawn from sight; and the inference to a stranger's mind became inevitable, that this best-abused writer on America was a beneficent, practical reformer.

The truth is, that Mrs. Trollope's powers of observation are remarkable. What she sees, she describes with vivacity, and often with accurate skill. No one can read her Travels in Austria without acknowledging the vigor and brightness of her mind. Personal disappointment in a pecuniary enterprise vexed her judgment; and, like so many of her nation, she thoroughly disliked the political institutions of the United States, was on the lookout for social anomalies and personal defects, and persistent, like her "unreasoning sex," in attributing all that was offensive or undesirable in her experience to the prejudice she cherished. Moreover, her experience itself was limited and local. She entered the country more than thirty years ago, at New Orleans, and passed most of the time, during her sojourn, amid the new and thriving but crude and confident Western communities, where neither manners nor culture, economy nor character had attained any well-organized or harmonious development. The self-love of these independent but sometimes rough pioneers of civilization, was wounded by the severe comments of a stranger who had shared their hospitality, when she expatiated on their reckless use of tobacco, their too free speech and angular attitudes; but, especially, when all their shortcomings were declared the natural result of republican institutions. Hence the outcry her book occasioned, and the factitious importance attached thereto. Not a single fault is found recorded by her, which our own writers, and every candid citizen, have not often admitted and complained of. The fast eating, boastful talk, transient female beauty, inadequate domestic service, abuse of calomel as a remedy, copious and careless expectoration, free and easy manners, superficial culture, and many other traits, more or less true now as then, here or there, are or have been normal subjects of animadversion. It was not because Mrs. Trollope did not write much truth about the country and the people, that, among classes of the latter, her name was a reproach; but because she reasoned so perversely, and did not take the pains to ascertain the whole truth, and to recognize the compensatory facts of American life. But this objection should have been reconciled by her candor. She frankly declares that her chief object is "to encourage her countrymen to hold fast by the Constitution that insures all the blessings which flow from established habits and solid principles;" and elsewhere remarks that the dogma "that all men are born free and equal has done, is doing, and will do much harm to this fair country." Her sympathies overflow toward an English actor, author, and teacher she encounters, and she feels a pang at André's grave; but she looks with the eye of criticism only on the rude masses who are turning the wilderness into cities, refusing to see any prosperity or progress in the scope and impulse of democratic principles. "Some of the native political economists," she writes, "assert that this rapid conversion of a bearbrake into a prosperous city is the result of free political institutions. Not being very deep in such matters, a more obvious cause suggested itself to me, in the unceasing goad which necessity applies to industry in this country, and in the absence of all resources for the idle." Without discussing the abstract merits of her theory, it is obvious that a preconceived antipathy to the institutions of a country unfits even a sensible and frank writer for social criticism thereon; and, in this instance, the writer seems to have known comparatively few of the more enlightened men, and to have enjoyed the intimacy of a still smaller number of the higher class of American women; so that, with the local and social data she chiefly relied on, her conclusions are only unjust inasmuch as they are too general. She describes well what strikes her as new and curious; but her first impressions, always so influential, were forlorn. The flat shores at the mouth of the Mississippi in winter, the muddy current, pelicans, snags, and bulrushes, were to her a desolate change from the bright blue ocean; but the flowers and fruits of Louisiana, the woods and the rivers, as they opened to her view, brought speedy consolation; which, indeed, was modified by disagreeable cookery, bad roads, illness, thunder storms, and unpleasant manners and customs—the depressing influence of which, however, did not prevent her expatiating with zest and skill upon the camp meetings, snakes, insects, elections, house moving, queer phrases, dress, bugs, lingo, parsons, politicians, figures, faces, and opinions which came within her observation.

With more perspicacity and less prejudice, she would have acknowledged the temporary character of many of the facts of the hour, emphasized by her pen as permanent. The superficial reading she notes, for instance, was but the eager thirst for knowledge that has since expanded into so wide a habit of culture that the statistics of the book trade in the United States have become one of the intellectual marvels of the age. Her investigation as to the talent, sources of discipline, and development, were extremely incurious and slight; hence, what she says of our statesmen and men of letters is too meagre for comment. The only American author she appears to have known well was Flint; and her warm appreciation of his writings and conversation, indicates what a better knowledge of our scholars and eminent professional men would have elicited from so shrewd an observer. The redeeming feature of her book is the love of nature it exhibits. American scenery often reconciles her to the bad food and worse manners; the waterfalls, rivers, and forests are themes of perpetual admiration. "So powerful," she writes of a passage down one of the majestic streams of the West, "was the effect of this sweet scenery, that we ceased to grumble at our dinners and suppers." Strange to say, she was delighted with the city of Washington, extols the Capitol, and recognizes the peculiar merits of Philadelphia. In fact, when she writes of what she sees, apart from prejudice, there are true woman's wit and sense in her descriptions; but she does not discriminate, or patiently inquire. Her book is one of impressions—some very just, and others casual. She was provoked at being often told, in reply to some remark, "That is because you know so little of America;" and yet the observation is one continually suggested by her too hasty conclusions. With all its defects, however, few of the class of books to which it belongs are better worth reading now than this once famous record of Mrs. Trollope. It has a certain freshness and boldness about it that explain its original popularity. Its tone, also, in no small degree explains its unpopularity; for the writer, quoting a remark of Basil Hall's, to the effect that the great difference between Americans and English is the want of loyalty, declares it, in her opinion, is the want of refinement. And it is upon this that she harps continually in her strictures, while the reader is offended by the identical deficiency in herself; and herein we find the secret of the popular protest the book elicited on this side of the water; for those who felt they needed to be lectured on manners, repudiated such a female writer as authoritative, and regarded her assumption of the office as more than gratuitous.

WILLIAM MAKEPEACE THACKERAY

1811–1863

William Makepeace Thackeray was born on July 18, 1811, in Calcutta, where his father worked as a collector for the East India Company. In 1817, after his father's death, he was sent to school in England, where his mother and her new husband joined him in 1819. Thackeray attended the Charterhouse School, where he was not happy, and in 1829 entered Trinity College, Cambridge, where he formed a close friendship with Edward FitzGerald. In 1830 he left Cambridge without a degree and traveled in Germany, where he met the aging Goethe. After returning to London in 1831, Thackeray briefly studied law at the Middle Temple, and in 1834 purchased the *National Standard*, a weekly paper which ceased publication a year later. Thackeray next became an art student, first in London, then in Paris (1834–35). By this time he had lost almost his entire inheritance, probably because of the collapse of the Indian agency-houses, and between 1834 and 1837, while living in Paris, he supported himself by working as a journalist.

In 1836 Thackeray published *Flore et Zephyr*, his first book. In that same year he married Isabella Shawe, who gave birth to a daughter, Anne, after they had returned to London in 1837.

Once in London Thackeray began to write for *Fraser's Magazine* and other journals, including the *Morning Chronicle*, the *New Monthly Magazine*, and the *Times*. To *Fraser's* he contributed *The Yellowplush Correspondence* (1837–38), with which he first gained a large readership; *Catherine* (1839–40); *A Shabby Genteel Story* (1840); *The Great Hoggarty Diamond* (1841); and *The Luck of Barry Lyndon* (1844). His first full-length volume, *The Paris Sketch Book*, appeared in 1840.

In 1840, after having given birth to a second and third daughter, Thackeray's wife suffered a mental breakdown and became permanently insane. Thackeray first placed her in the care of a French doctor, then in a private home in England, and sent his children to his mother's home in Paris, where they remained until 1846. In 1842 Thackeray began contributing to *Punch*, which published not only his essays and humorous sketches, but also his caricatures. *The Irish Sketch Book* (1843), with a preface signed for the first time with Thackeray's name, rather than with one of several humorous pseudonyms he had previously used, was followed by *The Snobs of England* (later republished as *The Book of Snobs*), which had appeared in *Punch* in 1846–47.

Thackeray's first important novel, *Vanity Fair*, appeared in monthly installments in 1847–48, with illustrations by the author. It was followed by *Punch's Prize Novelists* (1847), a collection of parodies of leading contemporary authors, and by several other important novels: *The History of Pendennis* (1848–50), *The History of Henry Esmond* (1852), and *The Newcomes* (1853–55). In 1852–53, and again in 1855–56, Thackeray went on lecture tours of the United States, where his novel *The Virginians* (1857–59) is partly set. His lectures on the *English Humourists of the Eighteenth Century*, first delivered in 1851, were published in 1853, while those on the *Four Georges*, first delivered in 1854–55, appeared in print in 1861.

In 1859 Thackeray became the first editor of the *Cornhill Magazine*, for which he wrote *Lovel the Widower* (1860), a story; the *Roundabout Papers* (1860–63), a series of essays; *The Adventures of Philip* (1861–62), his last complete novel; and *Denis Duval* (1864), an unfinished novel published after his sudden death on Christmas Eve of 1863. Thackeray's daughter, Anne Thackeray Ritchie, published *Chapters from Some Memoirs* in 1894. Thackeray's *Letters and Private Papers*, edited by Gordon Ray, were published in 1945–46.

Personal

Thackeray has very rarely come athwart me since his return: he is a big fellow, soul and body; of many gifts and qualities (particularly in the Hogarth line, with a dash of Sterne superadded), of enormous *appetite* withal, and very uncertain and chaotic in all points except his *outer breeding*, which is fixed enough, and *perfect* according to the modern English style. I rather dread explosions in his history. A *big*, fierce, weeping, hungry man; not a strong one. *Ay de mi!*—THOMAS CARLYLE, Letter to Ralph Waldo Emerson (Sept. 9, 1853)

I breakfasted this morning with Fowler of Lincoln to meet Thackeray (the author) who delivered his lecture on George III in Oxford last night. I was much pleased with what I saw of him—his manner is simple and unaffected: he shows no anxiety to shine in conversation though full of fun and anecdote when drawn out. He seemed delighted with the reception he had met with last night: the undergraduates seem to have behaved with most unusual moderation.—LEWIS CARROLL, *Diary*, May 9, 1857

My conviction was, that beneath an occasional affectation of cynicism, there was a tenderness of heart which he was more eager to repress than to exhibit; that he was no idolater of rank in the sense in which Moore was said dearly to love a lord, but had his best pleasures in the society of those of his own social position—men of letters and artists; and that, however fond of "the full flow of London talk," his own home was the centre of his affections. He was a sensitive man, as I have seen on more than one occasion.—CHARLES KNIGHT, *Passages of a Working Life*, 1863, Pt. 3, Ch. 2

I saw him first, nearly twenty-eight years ago, when he proposed to become the illustrator of my earliest book. I saw him last, shortly before Christmas, at the Athenæum Club, when he told me that he had been in bed three days—that, after these attacks, he was troubled with cold shiverings, "which quite took the power of work out of him"—and that he

had it in his mind to try a new remedy which he laughingly described. He was very cheerful, and looked very bright. In the night of that day week, he died.

The long interval between those two periods is marked in my remembrance of him by many occasions when he was supremely humourous, when he was irresistibly extravagant, when he was softened and serious, when he was charming with children. But, by none do I recall him more tenderly than by two or three that start out of the crowd, when he unexpectedly presented himself in my room, announcing how that some passage in a certain book had made him cry yesterday, and how that he had come to dinner, "because he couldn't help it," and must talk such passage over. No one can ever have seen him more genial, natural, cordial, fresh, and honestly impulsive, than I have seen him at those times. No one can be surer than I, of the greatness and the goodness of the heart that then disclosed itself.—CHARLES DICKENS, "In Memoriam," *Cornhill Magazine*, Feb. 1864, p. 129

General

There is a man in our own days whose words are not framed to tickle delicate ears: who, to my thinking, comes before the great ones of society, much as the son of Imlah came before the throned Kings of Judah and Israel; and who speaks truth as deep, with a power as prophet-like and as vital—a mien as dauntless and as daring. Is the satirist of *Vanity Fair* admired in high places? I cannot tell; but I think if some of those amongst whom he hurls the Greek fire of his sarcasm, and over whom he flashes the levin-brand of his denunciation, were to take his warnings in time—they or their seed might yet escape a fatal Ramoth-Gilead.

Why have I alluded to this man? I have alluded to him, Reader, because I think I see in him an intellect profounder and more unique than his contemporaries have yet recognized; because I regard him as the first social regenerator of the day—as the very master of that working corps who would restore to rectitude the warped system of things; because I think no commentator on his writings has yet found the comparison that suits him, the terms which rightly characterise his talent. They say he is like Fielding: they talk of his wit, humour, comic powers. He resembles Fielding as an eagle does a vulture: Fielding could stoop on carrion, but Thackeray never does. His wit is bright, his humour attractive, but both bear the same relation to his serious genius, that the mere lambent sheet-lightning playing under the edge of the summer-cloud, does to the electric death-spark hid in its womb. Finally; I have alluded to Mr. Thackeray, because to him—if he will accept the tribute of a total stranger—I have dedicated this second edition of *Jane Eyre*.—CHARLOTTE BRONTË, "Preface" to *Jane Eyre*, 1847

In Dickens, the lower part of "the World" is brought into the Police Court, as it were, and there, after cross-examination, discharged or committed, as the case may be. The characters are real and low, but they are facts. That is one way. Thackeray's is another and better. One of his books is like a Dionysius ear, through which you hear the World talking, entirely unconscious of being overheard.—JAMES RUSSELL LOWELL, Letter to C. F. Briggs (Feb. 15, 1854)

Thackeray finds that God has made no allowance for the poor thing in his universe;—more's the pity, he thinks;—but 'tis not for us to be wiser: we must renounce ideals, and accept London.—RALPH WALDO EMERSON, "Literature," *English Traits*, 1856

Mr. Thackeray is, as a novelist, so pointed and unmistakable a contrast to Mr. Dickens, that it is interesting to find them writing at the same time. Thackeray is as little of an idealizer as it seems possible to be, if you write novels at all. He cuts into conventionalism so daringly, that you fear sometimes, as when he gives you a novel without a hero, that he goes too far, and puts in peril the essence of his Art. If he does idealize, it is not in the manner of Dickens, but in one strikingly different. He selects characters as Dickens selects characteristics. But he depends for success not on the power of his personages to evoke sympathy, negative or positive, but on their strict correspondence with fact. It cannot, perhaps, be said that he, any more than Mr. Dickens, reaches the Shakspearian substratum of character. His eye is that of an artist. It has been trained to take in the whole aspect of the outer man, not only in the minutiæ of his dress, but in the whole monotonous circumstance of his every day life. His popularity is the most powerful evidence to which one could easily point, of the capacity residing in the exhibition of bare, or even repulsive fact, to interest mankind. It is said that Thackeray abandoned the career of an artist, because, according to his own avowal, he could only carica-ture. He felt the absence of the higher idealizing power. His novels exhibit the radical qualities which would have distin-guished his pictures. It is not emotionally that we regard them. They call forth no glow of admiration, no warm, loving sympathy, no wonder, no reverence. He makes his appeal to sterner, colder powers, to reflection, to the cynic's philosophy, to contempt. It may be better, higher, more noble and self-denying, in him, to do so; but the fact is patent. And its inevitable consequence has been and will be, a popularity not so wide, a command over the heart not so great, as those of men who permit fancy to lay on color, and imagination to heighten life. ⟨. . .⟩

If it were asked what one aspect of life Mr. Thackeray has distinctively exhibited, the answer could be given in one word,—the trivial aspect. The characters he draws are neither the best of men nor the worst. But the atmosphere of triviality which envelopes them all was never before so plainly perceiv-

able. He paints the world as a great Vanity Fair, and none has done that so well.

The realism of Thackeray can hardly fail to have a good effect in fictitious literature. It represents the extreme point of reaction against the false idealism of the Minerva Press. It is a pre-raphaelite school of novel writing. And as pre-raphaelitism is not to be valued in itself, so much as in being the passage to a new and nobler ideal, the stern realism of Thackeray may lead the way to something better than itself.—PETER BAYNE, "The Modern Novel: Dickens—Bulwer—Thackeray," *Essays in Biography and Criticism*, 1857, pp. 389–92

Thackeray's range is limited. His genius is not opulent, but it is profuse. He does not create many types, but he endlessly illustrates what he does create. In this he reminds a traveler of Ruysdael and Wouvermann, the old painters. There are plenty of their pictures in the German galleries, and there is no mistaking them. This is a Ruysdael, how rich and tranquil! this is a Wouvermann, how open and smiling! are the instinctive words with which you greet them. The scope, the method, almost the figures and the composition are the same in each Ruysdael, in each Wouvermann, but you are not troubled. Ruysdael's heavy tree, Wouvermann's white horse, are not less agreeable in Dresden than in Berlin, or Munich, or Vienna. And shall we not be as tolerant in literature as in painting? Why should we expect simple pastoral nature in Victor Hugo, or electrical bursts of passion in Scott, or the "ideal" in Thackeray?—GEORGE WILLIAM CURTIS, "The Easy Chair," *Harper's New Monthly Magazine*, Aug. 1862, p. 423

Thackeray, like Sterne, looked at every thing—at nature, at life, at art—from a *sensitive* aspect. His mind was, to some considerable extent, like a woman's mind. It could compre-hend abstractions when they were unrolled and explained before it but it never naturally created them; never of itself, and without external obligation, devoted itself to them. The visible scene of life—the streets, the servants, the clubs, the gossip, the West End—fastened on his brain. These were to him reality. They burnt in upon his brain; they pained his nerves; their influence reached him through many avenues which ordinary men do not feel much, or to which they are altogether impervious. He had distinct and rather painful sensations where most men have but confused and blurred ones. Most men have felt the *instructive* headache, during which they are more acutely conscious than usual of all which goes on around them,—during which every thing seems to pain them, and in which they understand it because it pains them, and they cannot get their imagination away from it. Thackeray had a nerve-ache of this sort always. He acutely felt every possible passing fact, every trivial interlude in society. Hazlitt used to say of himself, and used to say truly, that he could not enjoy the society in a drawing-room for thinking of the opinion which the footman formed of his odd appearance as he went upstairs. Thackeray had too healthy and stable a nature to be thrown so wholly off his balance; but the footman's view of life was never out of his head. The obvious facts which suggest it to the footman poured it in upon him; he could not exempt himself from them. As most men say that the earth *may* go round the sun, but in fact, when we look at the sun, we cannot help believing it goes round the earth,—just so this most impressible, susceptible genius could not help half accepting, half believing the common ordinary sensitive view of life, although he perfectly knew in his inner mind and deeper nature that this apparent and superficial view of life was misleading, inadequate, and deceptive. He could not help seeing everything, and what he saw made so near and keen an impression upon him that he could not again exclude it from his understanding; it stayed there, and disturbed his thoughts.

If, he often says, 'people could write about that of which they are really thinking, how interesting books would be!' More than most writers of fiction, he felt the difficulty of abstracting his thoughts and imagination from near facts which *would* make themselves felt. The sick wife in the next room, the unpaid baker's bill, the lodging-house keeper who doubts your solvency; these, and such as these,—the usual accompaniments of an early literary life,—are constantly alluded to in his writings. Perhaps he could never take a grand enough view of literature, or accept the truth of 'high art,' because of his natural tendency to this stern and humble realism. He knew that he was writing a tale which would appear in a green magazine (with others) on the 1st of March, and would be paid for perhaps on the 11th, by which time, probably, 'Mr. Smith' would have to 'make up a sum,' and would again present his *little account*. There are many minds besides his who feel an interest in these realities, though they yawn over 'high art' and elaborate judgments.

A painfulness certainly clings like an atmosphere round Mr. Thackeray's writings, in consequence of his inseparable and ever-present realism. We hardly know where it is, yet we are all conscious of it less or more. A free and bold writer, Sir Walter Scott, throws himself far away into fictitious worlds, and soars there without effort, without pain, and with unceasing enjoyment. You see, as it were, between the lines of Mr. Thackeray's writing, that his thoughts were never long away from the close proximate scene. His writings might be better if it had been otherwise; but they would have been less peculiar, less individual; they would have wanted their character, their flavour, if he had been able, while writing them, to forget for many moments the ever-attending, the ever-painful sense of himself.

Hence have arisen most of the censures upon him, both as he seemed to be in society and as he was in his writings. He was certainly uneasy in the common and general world, and it was natural that he should be so. The world poured in upon him, and *inflicted* upon his delicate sensibility a number of petty pains and impressions which others do not feel at all, or which they feel but very indistinctly. As he sat he seemed to read off the passing thoughts—the base, common, ordinary impressions—of every one else. Could such a man be at ease? Could even a quick intellect be asked to set in order with such velocity so many data? Could any temper, however excellent, be asked to bear the contemporaneous influx of innumerable minute annoyances? Men of ordinary nerves, who feel a little of the pains of society, who perceive what really passes, who are not absorbed in the petty pleasures of sociability, could well observe how keen was Thackeray's *sensation* of common events, could easily understand how difficult it must have been for him to keep mind and temper undisturbed by a miscellaneous tide at once so incessant and so forcible.

He could not emancipate himself from such impressions even in a case where most men hardly feel them. Many people have—it is not difficult to have—some vague sensitive perception of what is passing in the minds of the guests, of the ideas of such as sit at meat; but who remembers that there are also nervous apprehensions, also a latent mental life among those who 'stand and wait'—among the floating figures which pass and carve? But there was no impression to which Mr. Thackeray was more constantly alive, or which he was more apt in his writings to express.—WALTER BAGEHOT, "Sterne and Thackeray" (1864), *Collected Works*, ed. Norman St. John-Stevas, 1965, Vol. 2, pp. 304–6

Let me see—have we exchanged a word about Thackeray since his Death? I am quite surprised to see how I sit moping about him: to be sure, I keep reading his Books. Oh, the *Newcomes* are fine! And now I have got hold of *Pendennis*, and seem to like that much more than when I first read it. I keep hearing him say so much of it; and really think I shall hear his Step up the Stairs to this Lodging as in old Charlotte St. thirty years ago. Really, a great Figure has sunk under Earth.—EDWARD FITZGERALD, Letter to George Crabbe (Jan. 12, 1864)

Now, the great merit of Thackeray I take to be, that he *has* reflected—with lucid beauty, with admirable sense, and taste, and impartiality—the whole range of the characteristic English society of his age. He is not a fashionable novelist, though he introduces persons of fashion; nor a military or clerical novelist, though he introduces soldiers and clergymen. His roll of books, like the Bayeux tapestry, gives us the whole generation—men of wit, business, war, art; women beautiful and plain, loving and hateful, clever and stupid. There are types and occupations, no doubt, which he has not meddled with. But such abundant material exists in his books to show what kind of man is an English gentleman of the nineteenth century, that his omissions are of little importance. By the reality with which he painted, he has taught us to divine for ourselves what he did not paint.

Let it be remarked, too, that this admirable fidelity to nature, enlivened with a humour never grotesque, and tinged with a sentiment never maudlin, is wholly Thackeray's own. Many have imitated him, but he imitated nobody. None of the thousand moods or fashions of our modes of our schools of thinking are repeated in his books—even in the earliest of them. He deals neither in Wertherism, Byronism, nor Carlyleism; the French "literature of despair" rolled harmlessly as passing thunder over his head. He worshipped no side of life or thought exclusively; *Ivanhoe* did not fascinate him with chivalry, nor *Wilhelm Meister* with art; nor did the modern realism of fiction destroy his sympathy with romance. His strong intellect kept its independence from the beginning; his strong moral nature did justice from the beginning. Faithfully, and regardless of all sentimental whimpering, he laid bare the selfishness, meanness, and servility of the age. But with equal truth, he brought on the stage noble and kindly characters like Colonel Newcome, Ethel Newcome, and Henry Esmond. Severe upon society as society, he had the strongest faith in human nature; and his own great heart beat responsive to all that was generous in history, or fiction, or the world of his time.

The independence and originality of Thackeray's character as a writer makes it difficult to indicate the sources of the culture by which his genius was formed. The writers of his own age who got the start of him in popularity taught him nothing; but in his youth the genius of Sir Walter Scott towered over Europe, and it is certain that he was deeply influenced by Sir Walter. They had a good deal in common, especially a sound worldly shrewdness tempered by kindness of a homely character, and by humour of that robust sort which finds food for itself in the daily incidents of life. They both had a strong respect for society even while laughing at its prejudices, and never allowed the literature to which their lives were devoted to usurp superiority over other interest. The resemblance between them, however, was rather moral than intellectual. Sir Walter had a general influence over Thackeray, no doubt, as himself the real father of the truthful and natural novel of the nineteenth century; but he had no special influence, and the character of his genius was very different. Thackeray was without

Scott's feudal sympathies, and had far less romance and historical feeling; neither was his imagination so various as that of Scott—which created such diverse characters as Rebecca and Jeannie Deans—nor his vein of poetry so rich. In one point the late writer had an advantage—he wrote a better style. The prose of Scott is cumbrous, and apt to be verbose; whereas Thackeray's English is one of his greatest merits. It is pure, clear, simple in its power, and harmonious; clean, sinewy, fine and yet strong, like the legs of a racehorse. Style is a gift born with a man, but its character is greatly modified by his education and experience. One sees very distinctly in Thackeray's style, as in his way of thinking and feeling about things, the English public-school and university man—the tone of one born and bred in the condition of a gentleman. The facts of his birth and education coloured his thought and his style, just as Scott's was coloured, even more decidedly, by the family traditions of his ancient border-race. He was never zealous for the classics; but the classics form a man who has been nourished on them, whether he is conscious of it or not. We none of us remember taking in our mother's milk, but we know what it has done for us for all that. Thackeray was saturated with Horace, especially the lyrical part of the Venusian; he was also very fond of Montaigne, and intimate with him. In fact, Latin writers, French writers, and the English writers of the eighteenth century, seem to have constituted his favourite reading. Yet he was always more a man of the world than a man of books; and if we allow much influence over the formation of his style to the sources just indicated, we may also see in it a certain conversational ease and grace, which is not a result only of reading, and which is the direct opposite of the detestable style, formed upon newspapers, of so many inferior men. To hit the right mean between a bookishness which is too stiff and a colloquialism which is too loose, is one of the rarest achievements in literature, and one that more than any other secures to an author the position of a classic. No English novelist approached this standard in Thackeray's time so nearly as he, and perhaps no previous novelist except the incomparable Fielding.—JAMES HANNAY, *Studies on Thackeray*, 1864, pp. 8–14

When the great master of English prose left us suddenly in the maturity of his powers, with his enduring position in literature fairly won and recognized, his death saddened us rather through the sense of our own loss than from the tragic regret which is associated with an unaccomplished destiny. More fortunate than Fielding, he was allowed to take the measure of his permanent fame. The niche wherein he shall henceforth stand was chiselled while he lived. One by one the doubters confessed their reluctant faith, unfriendly critics dropped their blunted steel, and no man dared to deny him the place which was his, and his only, by right of genius.

In one sense, however, he was misunderstood by the world, and he has died before that profounder recognition which he craved had time to mature. All the breadth and certainty of his fame failed to compensate him for the lack of this; the man's heart coveted that justice which was accorded only to the author's brain.—BAYARD TAYLOR, "William Makepeace Thackeray" (1864), *Critical Essays and Literary Notes*, 1880, p. 134

Thackeray was a *master* in every sense, having as it were, in himself, a double quantity of being. Robust humor and lofty sentiment alternated so strangely in him, that sometimes he seemed like the natural son of Rabelais, and at others he rose up a very twin brother of the Stratford Seer. There was nothing in him amorphous and unconsidered. Whatever he chose to do was always perfectly done. There was a genuine Thackeray flavor in everything he was willing to say or to write. He detected with unfailing skill the good or the vile wherever it existed. He had an unerring eye, a firm understanding, and abounding truth.—JAMES T. FIELDS, "Thackeray," *Yesterdays with Authors*, 1871, p. 35

About Mr. Thackeray I had no clear notion in any way, except that he seemed cynical; and my first real interest in him arose from reading M. A. Titmarsh in Ireland, during my Tynemouth illness. I confess to being unable to read *Vanity Fair*, from the moral disgust it occasions; and this was my immediate association with the writer's name when I next met him, during the visit to London in 1851. I could not follow his lead into the subject of the Bullers, (then all dead) so strong was my doubt of his real feeling. I was, I fear, rather rough and hard when we talked of *Vanity Fair*; but a sudden and most genuine change of tone,—of voice, face and feeling,—that occurred on my alluding to Dobbin's admirable turning of the tables on Amelia, won my trust and regard more than any thing he had said yet. *Pendennis* much increased my respect and admiration; and *Esmond* appears to me *the* book of the century, in its department. I have read it three times; and each time with new wonder at its rich ripe wisdom, and at the singular charm of Esmond's own character. The power that astonishes me the most in Thackeray is his fertility, shown in the way in which he opens glimpses into a multitudinous world as he proceeds. The chief moral charm is in the paternal vigilance and sympathy which constitute the spirit of his narration. The first drawback in his books, as in his manners, is the impression conveyed by both that he never can have known a good and sensible woman. I do not believe he has any idea whatever of such women as abound among the matronage of England,—women of excellent capacity and cultivation applied to the natural business of life. It is perhaps not changing the subject to say next what the other drawback is. Mr. Thackeray has said more, and more effectually, about snobs and snobbism than any other man; and yet his frittered life, and his obedience to the call of the great are the observed of all observers. As it is so, so it must be; but "O! the pity of it! the pity of it!" Great and unusual allowance is to be made in his case, I am aware; but this does not lessen the concern occasioned by the spectacle of one after another of the aristocracy of nature making the ko-tow to the aristocracy of accident. If society does not owe all it would be thankful to owe to Mr. Thackeray, yet it is under deep and large obligations to him; and if he should even yet be seen to be as wise and happy in his life and temper as he might be any day, he may do much that would far transcend all his great and rising achievements thus far; and I who shall not see it would fain persuade myself that I foresee it. He who stands before the world as a sage *de jure* must surely have impulses to be a sage *de facto*.—HARRIET MARTINEAU, *Autobiography*, ed. Maria Weston Chapman, 1877, Vol. 2, pp. 60–61

His knowledge of human nature was supreme, and his characters stand out as human beings, with a force and a truth which has not, I think, been within the reach of any other English novelist in any period. I know no character in fiction, unless it be Don Quixote, with whom the reader becomes so intimately acquainted as with Colonel Newcombe. How great a thing it is to be a gentleman at all parts! How we admire the man of whom so much may be said with truth! Is there any one of whom we feel more sure in this respect than of Colonel Newcombe? It is not because Colonel Newcombe is a perfect gentleman that we think Thackeray's work to have been so excellent, but because he has had the power to describe him as such, and to force us to love him, a weak and silly old man, on account of this grace of character.

It is evident from all Thackeray's best work that he lived with the characters he was creating. He had always a story to tell until quite late in life; and he shows us that this was so, not by the interest which he had in his own plots,—for I doubt whether his plots did occupy much of his mind,—but by convincing us that his characters were alive to himself. With Becky Sharpe, with Lady Castlewood and her daughter, and with Esmond, with Warrington, Pendennis, and the Major, with Colonel Newcombe, and with Barry Lyndon, he must have lived in perpetual intercourse. Therefore he has made these personages real to us.

Among all our novelists his style is the purest, as to my ear it is also the most harmonious. Sometimes it is disfigured by a slight touch of affectation, by little conceits which smell of the oil;—but the language is always lucid. The reader, without labour, knows what he means, and knows all that he means. As well as I can remember, he deals with no episodes. I think that any critic, examining his work minutely, would find that every scene, and every part of every scene, adds something to the clearness with which the story is told. Among all his stories there is not one which does not leave on the mind a feeling of distress that women should ever be immodest or men dishonest,—and of joy that women should be so devoted and men so honest. How we hate the idle selfishness of Pendennis, the worldliness of Beatrix, the craft of Becky Sharpe!—how we love the honesty of Colonel Newcombe, the nobility of Esmond, and the devoted affection of Mrs. Pendennis! The hatred of evil and love of good can hardly have come upon so many readers without doing much good.

Late in Thackeray's life,—he never was an old man, but towards the end of his career,—he failed in his power of charming, because he allowed his mind to become idle. In the plots which he conceived, and in the language which he used, I do not know that there is any perceptible change; but in *The Virginians* and in *Philip* the reader is introduced to no character with which he makes a close and undying acquaintance. And this, I have no doubt, is so because Thackeray himself had no such intimacy. His mind had come to be weary of that fictitious life which is always demanding the labour of new creation, and he troubled himself with his two Virginians and his Philip only when he was seated at his desk.—ANTHONY TROLLOPE, *An Autobiography*, 1883, Ch. 13

Thackeray had a quarrel with himself and a quarrel with society; but his was not a temper to push things to extremes. He could not acquiesce in the ways of the world, its shabbiness, its shams, its snobbery, its knavery; he could not acquiesce, and yet it is only for born prophets to break with the world and go forth into the wilderness crying, "Repent!" Why affect to be a prophet, and wear camels' hair and eat locusts and wild honey, adding one more sham to the many, when after all the club is a pleasant lounge, and anthropology is a most attractive study? Better patch up a truce with the world, which will not let one be a hero, but is not wholly evil; the great criminals are few; men in general are rather weak than wicked; vain and selfish, but not malignant. It is infinitely diverting to watch the ways of the petty human animal. One can always preserve a certain independence by that unheroic form of warfare suitable to an unheroic age—satire; one can even in a certain sense stand above one's own pettiness by virtue of irony; and there is always the chance of discovering some angel wandering unrecognised among the snobs and the flunkeys in the form of a brave, simple-hearted man or pure-souled, tender woman. Whether

right or wrong, this compromise with the world is only for a few days. Heigh-ho! everything hastens to the common end— *vanitas vanitatum.* ⟨. . .⟩

Thackeray had not the austerity and lonely strength needful for a prophet; he would not be a pseudo-prophet; therefore he chose his part—to remain in the world, to tolerate the worldlings, and yet to be their adversary and circumventer, or at least a thorn in their sides.—EDWARD DOWDEN, "Victorian Literature," *Transcripts and Studies*, 1888, pp. 168–71

Personally, he scarce appeals to us as the ideal gentleman; if there were nothing else, perpetual nosing after snobbery at least suggests the snob; but about the men he made, there can be no such question of reserve. And whether because he was himself a gentleman in a very high degree, or because his methods were in a very high degree suited to this class of work, or from the common operation of both causes, a gentleman came from his pen by the gift of nature. He could draw him as a character part, full of pettiness, tainted with vulgarity, and yet still a gentleman, in the inimitable Major Pendennis. He could draw him as the full-blown hero in Colonel Esmond. He could draw him—the next thing to the work of God—human and true and noble and frail, in Colonel Newcome. If the art of being a gentleman were forgotten, like the art of staining glass, it might be learned anew from that one character.—ROBERT LOUIS STEVENSON, "Some Gentlemen in Fiction," 1888

It is precisely because Thackeray, discerning so well the abundant misery and hollowness in life, discerns also all that is not miserable and hollow, that he is so great. He has neither the somewhat bestial pessimism of M. Zola, nor the fatuous gaiety of M. Ohnet. Like any classic, he stands the test of experience, of psychology. We have mentioned together Swift, Addison, and Steele; we might take Lucretius, Virgil, and Horace. Each has left a picture of patrician life, glittering and tedious. Lucretius, contrasting the splendour without and the gloom within; Virgil, the restlessness and haste with the placid peace of the country; Horace, content to let it all go by, neither envying nor despising. Something of each, again, is in Thackeray: an English classic not less true and real than the classic Romans.

Most of the disputes about Thackeray's art, in the strict sense of art, are occupied with the personal note in his novels: with the intrusion, as some call it, of his personality. Art, we are told, is impersonal; and we believe it. But if that imply that no novel should reflect its author's spirit, then no artistic novel has yet been written. It is a question of words: each writer has his manner of work and habit of mind; let him follow those faithfully, and the result will be good, if he be an artist. Who wishes away Fielding's enchanting chapters between the books of *Tom Jones*? Or who wishes to find essays by Flaubert between the chapters of *Madame Bovary*? Each follows his own way, and there are many ways in art. Thackeray's reflections and discussions do not spoil his story, because they are not mere moralising, which the reader might do for himself. Whenever a reader stops, and says to himself, that the writer might have credited his readers with wits enough to see such and such a thing, without being shown it, then the writer has been superfluous. A sentence instead of a word, a chapter instead of a page, are unpardonable sins: but who can say, that he could have done Thackeray's reflections for himself? And they do not occur in the course of actual narration: Rawdon Crawley confronts Lord Steyne, Lady Castlewood welcomes Esmond at Winchester, without any dissertation from Thackeray. At least, let us call these passages of personal meditation a wrong thing done exquisitely; beyond that we refuse to go.—LIONEL JOHNSON, *Academy*, March 7, 1891, p. 227

Another great name here somewhat wofully misrepresented is that of Thackeray; whose "White Squall" is now and then rather too provocative of such emotions as nature's might provoke in the digestive economy of a bad sailor. To make the gorge rise at it is hardly the sign or the property of elegance in verse: and if indecency, which means nothing more than unseemliness, is very properly considered as a reason for excluding from elegant society the most brilliant examples of the most illustrious writers ever touched by so much as a passing shade of it, the rule should be applied equally to every variety of the repulsive and the unbecoming—not by any means only to matters of sexual indecorum and erotic indelicacy. To none of the other selections from the lighter work of the same illustrious hand is any such objection or suggestion applicable: but not one of them shows Thackeray at his very best as a comic poet.—ALGERNON CHARLES SWINBURNE, "Social Verse" (1891), *Studies in Prose and Poetry*, 1894, pp. 106–7

It is true that Thackeray did not entirely escape the fate which seems to fall on every satirist of being carried too far in his onslaught upon hypocrisy and attacking some things which are in no way deserving of censure. His detestation of humbug was so intense that he seems to forget that there is some of it which we could scarcely do without. Indeed, were all descriptions of humbug to be swept off the face of the earth at once, the very best Christians would be at each other's throats in half an hour. He blamed the writers of the day for being too mealy-mouthed in their descriptions of character. "Since the author of *Tom Jones* was buried, no writer of fiction among us has been permitted to depict to his utmost power a *Man*." We do not know whether Thackeray had temporarily forgotten that it pleased Fielding to put his hero, in an episode of which Colonel Newcome afterwards spoke with just severity, into a position so disgraceful that no subsequent writer to our knowledge had ventured to reproduce it, until M. Octave Mirabeau presented a still more repulsive picture in his extremely powerful and intensely disagreeable novel, *Le Calvaire*. Thackeray himself did not venture to go so far into the life of his man, but only set himself to lop off all possible heroic attributes. Indeed Pendennis, who was to be the real Man without any unnatural decoration, is in reality a very innocent person, with plenty of faults no doubt, but these chiefly of the kind that arise from weakness of character. We are not, indeed, sure that Thackeray's philosophy might not be reduced to a belief that feebleness is the distinguishing characteristic of the male of the human species: but this is by no means a striking view, especially when it is the central figure of a book, ordinarily distinguished as the hero, who is chiefly marked by the peculiar instability which distinguishes him from the stronger figures around him. If Pendennis is the natural man, to what class does George Warrington or Captain Strong belong? or even Major Pendennis, all of whom have at least sufficient strength and individuality to follow out their own objects as seems good in their eyes? Why should we see anything more characteristic of the real man in the wavering figure to which our attention is chiefly directed?

However, Thackeray's desire to represent an unvarnished picture of man as he really is, did not prevent him, as we have already seen, from giving to his next work a central figure which does not fall below the heroic level. Henry Esmond, with all his virtues, is quite as real as Arthur Pendennis. We will not, however, add to what we have already said about this noble figure save as the centre of a very wonderful production.

Esmond is beyond doubt the first of Thackeray's novels as a work of art. There is something in the exquisite finish and harmony of this book which we can only express by the epithet, artistic; it is a pure combination of perfect taste and perfect workmanship which puts it in a separate class, in which many of the greatest literary works have no claim to rank. The genuine literary artist is not common; Balzac might be cited as a specimen, and George Eliot in her early works: and perhaps, without going quite so high, we might say that we have at present a literary artist of high excellence in Mr. R. L. Stevenson. As a composition *Esmond* is almost without a flaw. The details of the execution are all worked out in the same masterly manner, and the language is perfect. We may take as one instance of the exquisite finish of the minor points the little explanation of Esmond's prejudice against Marlborough. He is, of course, a man with views of his own concerning his contemporaries whom he judges according to the light in which they present themselves to him, and, as it happens, he is the opponent of the great general and a merciless critic of his conduct. This is natural enough, but there is a yet further light of reality communicated by the revelation in the footnote added by Esmond's daughter, which tells us how Marlborough had spoken of him as having "the hang-dog look of his rogue of a father." Esmond, himself, did not know that this was the origin of his prejudice and that these few words which he had possibly forgotten, had an influence on his whole life. It is like some of the stray touches in Shakespeare,—when Stephano wonders how Caliban came to speak his language, or Sir Toby prays that "the spirit of humours intimate reading aloud" to Malvolio,—mere by-strokes of the pencil, which a less perfect workman would have utterly neglected, but which have a wonderful effect in realising the scene in the minds of both author and spectator.—MARGARET OLIPHANT, *The Victorian Age of English Literature*, 1892, Vol. 1, pp. 290–93

Thackeray's readers were and are limited by the limitations of his subjects, by nothing else. He did much that Scott did not attempt and that Dickens could not ever have conceived; but for every million that can understand Scott and Dickens there are probably only a thousand that can understand Thackeray. His minute observation of the upper classes of his day is lost on persons to whom those classes are not familiar, partly because such persons do not recognize what he is dealing with, and partly because they are not interested in the questions with which he is most preoccupied. Indeed, of all great novelists Thackeray is the narrowest, not because the range of his vision is confined to the upper classes, for these viewed comprehensively form a complete microcosm and in many ways exhibit the problems and possibilities of life better than any other class; but because, accepting the upper classes as the world, he views them from one position only, and his view of them is extremely partial. Only a few of his characters he knows from the inside; all the rest he knows from the outside only. Men who were clients of the world or its victims, who were struggling with it or hostile to it—these men Thackeray knew from the inside. But the world itself, which for him meant the aristocratic class as a body—he was familiar with its aspect, but he never understood its spirit. Major Pendennis and his nephew, Rawdon Crawley, George Osborne, and Colonel Newcome—he knew these as if each of them were himself. Lord Steyne, Lord Bareacres, and Sir Pitt Crawley he knew merely as a vigilant witness. Hence the narrowness of his view as compared to Scott and Dickens. Hence he seems such a dwarf when placed beside them. And his narrowness of view finds another expression of itself in the fewness of his types of character. It has been well said, for instance, that he could draw but two women—the bad and the good, Becky Sharp being the prototype of the one and Amelia Sedley of the other.

All this, however, is mentioned merely to show why Thackeray's appeal to the world must have always been comparatively limited, and limited not only *to* the upper classes, but *among* them. Whether in process of time the number of his readers is diminishing, I repeat I am unable to say. A more important question is whether the interest with which he is read now is as fresh and vital as that with which he was read originally. I should say it was not; and I should say so for this reason, that as compared with Scott and Dickens he lacked the qualities by which the vitality of his work could be perpetuated. He lacked their extraordinary breadth and their extraordinary variety; he lacked the qualities that made them so peculiarly and so comprehensively national. They each gave us a nation—a nation which still lives; Thackeray gave us a fragment of a generation, which already is almost past.—W. H. MALLOCK, "Are Scott, Dickens, and Thackeray Obsolete?," *Forum*, Dec. 1892, pp. 512–13

I am distinctly conscious of being indebted to Thackeray for having led me out of the "moon-illumined magic night" of German romanticism (in which I once revelled) and accustomed me, by degrees, to a wholesomer, though less poetic, light. Vividly do I remember the distaste, the resentment, with which as a youth of twenty I flung away *The Virginians* at the chapter where Harry's calf-love for Maria is satirized. Like a sting to the quick was to me the remark about his pressing "the wilted vegetable" with rapture to his lips, or was it his heart? The delicious, good-natured ridicule with which the infatuation of Pen for Miss Fotheringay is treated in *Pendennis* hurt and disgusted me. I felt as if the author were personally abusing me. For I was then at the age when Pen's madness seemed to verge more nearly on sublimity than on foolishness. Accordingly I had a low opinion of Thackeray in those days.

But for all that, I could not help reading him; and, truth to tell, I owe him a debt of gratitude which it would be difficult to over-estimate. He saved me from no end of dangerous follies by kindling in me a spark of sobering self-criticism, which enabled me to catch little side-glimpses of myself, when I was on the verge of committing a *bêtise*. He aroused in me a salutary scepticism as to the worth of much which the world has stamped with its approval. He blew away a good deal of that romantic haze which hid reality from me and prevented me from appraising men and things at their proper value. Though no crude Sunday-school moral is appended to *Pendennis*, *The Newcomes* or *Vanity Fair*, he must be duller than an ox to the subtler sense who does not feel in the pervasive atmosphere of these books a wholesome moral tonic. And who can make the acquaintance of Colonel Newcome without having the character of the man stamped on his very soul and feeling a glow of enthusiasm for his nobleness, uprightness and lofty sense of honor? It is because he is so touchingly human, so pathetically true, that he makes so deep an impression. And as for Clive and Rose and the Campaigner, their fates have an educational worth beyond a hundred sermons. Though Thackeray does not often scold his bad and questionable characters (as does, for instance, Dickens), and though he permits an occasional smile to lurk between the lines at Becky Sharp's reprehensible cleverness, there is nowhere any confusion of moral values; and the voice that speaks has a half paternal cadence of genial wisdom and resignation.—HJALMAR HJORTH BOYESEN, "The Great Realists and the Empty Story-Tellers," *Forum*, Feb. 1895, p. 727

It was of the organ-builder that I had Thackeray's books first. He knew their literary quality, and their rank in the literary world; but I believe he was surprised at the passion I instantly conceived for them. He could not understand it; he deplored it almost as a moral defect in me; though he honored it as a proof of my critical taste. In a certain measure he was right.

What flatters the worldly pride in a young man is what fascinates him with Thackeray. With his air of looking down on the highest, and confidentially inviting you to be of his company in the seat of the scorner he is irresistible; his very confession that he is a snob, too, is balm and solace to the reader who secretly admires the splendors he affects to despise. His sentimentality is also dear to the heart of youth, and the boy who is dazzled by his satire is melted by his easy pathos. Then, if the boy has read a good many other books, he is taken with that abundance of literary turn and allusion in Thackeray; there is hardly a sentence but reminds him that he is in the society of a great literary swell, who has read everything, and can mock or burlesque life right and left from the literature always at his command. At the same time he feels his mastery, and is abjectly grateful to him in his own simple love of the good for his patronage of the unassuming virtues. It is so pleasing to one's vanity, and so safe, to be of the master's side when he assails those vices and foibles which are inherent in the system of things, and which one can contemn with vast applause so long as one does not attempt to undo the conditions they spring from.

I exulted to have Thackeray attack the aristocrats, and expose their wicked pride and meanness, and I never noticed that he did not propose to do away with aristocracy, which is and must always be just what it has been, and which cannot be changed while it exists at all. He appeared to me one of the noblest creatures that ever was when he derided the shams of society; and I was far from seeing that society, as we have it, was necessarily a sham; when he made a mock of snobbishness I did not know but snobbishness was something that might be reached and cured by ridicule. Now I know that so long as we have social inequality we shall have snobs; we shall have men who bully and truckle, and women who snub and crawl. I know that it is futile to spurn them, or lash them for trying to get on in the world, and that the world is what it must be from the selfish motives which underlie our economic life. But I did not know these things then, nor for long afterwards, and so I gave my heart to Thackeray, who seemed to promise me in his contempt of the world a refuge from the shame I felt for my own want of figure in it. He had the effect of taking me into the great world, and making me a party to his splendid indifference to titles, and even to royalties; and I could not see that sham for sham he was unwittingly the greatest sham of all.

I think it was *Pendennis* I began with, and I lived in the book to the very last line of it, and made its alien circumstance mine to the smallest detail. I am still not sure but it is the author's greatest book, and I speak from a thorough acquaintance with every line he has written, except the *Virginians*, which I have never been able to read quite through; most of his work I have read twice, and some of it twenty times.

After reading *Pendennis* I went to *Vanity Fair*, which I now think the poorest of Thackeray's novels—crude, heavy-handed, caricatured. About the same time I revelled in the romanticism of *Henry Esmond*, with its pseudo-eighteenth-century sentiment, and its appeals to an overwrought ideal of gentlemanhood and honor. It was long before I was duly revolted by Esmond's transfer of his passion from the daughter to the mother whom he is successively enamoured of. I believe this unpleasant and preposterous affair is thought one of the fine things in the story; I do not mind owning that I thought it so myself when I was seventeen; and if I could have found a Beatrix to be in love with, and a Lady Castlewood to be in love with me, I should have asked nothing finer of fortune. The glamour of *Henry Esmond* was all the deeper because I was reading the *Spectator* then, and was constantly in the company of Addison, and Steele, and Swift, and Pope, and all the wits at Will's, who are presented evanescently in the romance. The intensely literary keeping, as well as quality, of the story I suppose is what formed its highest fascination for me; but that effect of great world which it imparts to the reader, making him citizen, and, if he will, leading citizen of it, was what helped turn my head.

This is the toxic property of all Thackeray's writing. He is himself forever dominated in imagination by the world, and even while he tells you it is not worth while he makes you feel that it is worth while. It is not the honest man, but the man of honor, who shines in his page; his meek folk are proudly meek, and there is a touch of superiority, a glint of mundane splendor, in his lowliest. He rails at the order of things, but he imagines nothing different, even when he shows that its baseness, and cruelty, and hypocrisy are wellnigh inevitable, and, for most of those who wish to get on in it, quite inevitable. He has a good word for the virtues, he patronizes the Christian graces, he pats humble merit on the head; he has even explosions of indignation against the insolence and pride of birth, and purse-pride. But, after all, he is of the world, worldly, and the highest hope he holds out is that you may be in the world and despise its ambitions while you compass its ends.

I should be far from blaming him for all this. He was of his time; but since his time men have thought beyond him, and seen life with a vision which makes his seem rather purblind. He must have been immensely in advance of most of the thinking and feeling of his day, for people then used to accuse his sentimental pessimism of cynical qualities which we could hardly find in it now. It was the age of intense individualism, when you were to do right because it was becoming to you, say, as a gentleman, and you were to have an eye single to the effect upon your character, if not your reputation; you were not to do a mean thing because it was wrong, but because it was mean. It was romanticism carried into the region of morals. But I had very little concern then as to that sort of error.

I was on a very high æsthetic horse, which I could not have conveniently stooped from if I had wished; it was quite enough for me that Thackeray's novels were prodigious works of art, and I acquired merit, at least with myself, for appreciating them so keenly, for liking them so much. It must be, I felt with far less consciousness than my formulation of the feeling expresses, that I was of some finer sort myself to be able to enjoy such a fine sort. No doubt I should have been a coxcomb of some kind, if not that kind, and I shall not be very strenuous in censuring Thackeray for his effect upon me in this way. No doubt the effect was already in me, and he did not so much produce it as find it.—WILLIAM DEAN HOWELLS, "Thackeray," *My Literary Passions*, 1895

And now to come to Thackeray. Assuredly he is very far inferior to Balzac in genius. Nor has he Balzac's talent. He has not that grasp of principles, that faculty of co-ordination, that power of generalization, which Balzac possessed in such ample measure. But he had naturally a great deal in common with Balzac: originality of intellect, perspicuity of observation, a

warm and potent instinct—if I may so speak—of practical life, of all its conditions, and of all its contrasts. Like Balzac, too, he possessed a certain divinatory power, a sort of gift of moral second sight. Mrs. Ritchie, in her fascinating book, which all the world has just been reading, *Chapters from Some Memoirs*, tells us that, "he sometimes spoke of a curious uncomfortable feeling he had about some people, as if uncomfortable facts in their history were actually revealed to him," a feeling which was afterwards, not unfrequently, justified. It is a curious gift and a note of the highest genius.—WILLIAM SAMUEL LILLY, "The Humourist as Philosopher—Thackeray," *Four English Humourists of the Nineteenth Century*, 1895, p. 51

I admire Thackeray's style, and the pathetic quality in his writings; in this he never faltered. I like his sardonic melancholy. Thackeray, in a passing mood, might quite well have said: 'Who breathes must suffer, and who thinks must mourn, and he alone is blest who ne'er was born.'

He shows knowledge of human nature and much acquaintance with life—not a wide acquaintance, but complete within its limits. The vernacular of his Fokers and his Fred Bayhams is classical, and so is their slang.—FREDERICK LOCKER-LAMPSON, *My Confidences*, 1895, p. 302

But there are two ends, according to the proverb, to some if not all subjects; and it is not seldom asked whether there was not a decline as well as a growth of Thackeray's powers, and whether anything but *Vanity Fair*, *Pendennis*, *The Newcomes*, and *Esmond* can be considered to present that power at its height. It is impossible not to observe, in passing, what a genius that must be as to which it is matter of dispute whether anything has to be *added* to such a literary baggage as that of the four books just enumerated. The least of them would be a passport to and a provision for eternity; and we are inquiring whether the gentleman has any more titles and any more luggage than all four. Let me only say that I am more and more convinced that he has: that he has others even besides *The Four Georges*, *The English Humourists*, and the *Roundabout Papers*, which even his most grudging critics would in the same good-natured manner allow. I have never quite understood the common depreciation of *The Virginians*, which contains things equal, if not superior, to the very finest of its author's other work, and includes the very ripest expression of his philosophy of life. For though indeed I do not approve a novel more because it contains the expression of a philosophy of life, others do. So, too, the irregularity and formlessness of plot which characterised most of Thackeray's work undoubtedly appear in it; but then, according to the views of our briskest and most modern critics, plot is a very subordinate requisite in a novel, and may be very well dispensed with. Here again I do not agree, and I should say that Thackeray's greatest fault was his extreme inattention to construction, which is all the more remarkable inasmuch as he was by no means a very rapid or an extremely prolific writer. But if both these faults were infinitely greater than they are, I should say that the perfect command of character and the extraordinary criticisms of life which *The Virginians* contains save it, and not merely save it, but place it far above almost everything outside its writer's own work. —GEORGE SAINTSBURY, "Thackeray," *Corrected Impressions*, 1895

Barry Lyndon (1840) should have been enough, alone, to prove that an author of the first class had arisen, who was prepared to offer to the sickly taste of the age, to its false optimism, its superficiality, the alterative of a caustic drollery and a scrupulous study of nature. But the fact was that Thackeray had not, in any of those early sketches to which we now turn back with so much delight, mastered the technical art of story-telling. The study of Fielding appeared to reveal to him the sort of evolution, the constructive pertinacity, which had hitherto been lacking. He read *Jonathan Wild* and wrote *Barry Lyndon*; by a still severer act of self-command, he studied *Tom Jones* and composed *Vanity Fair*. The lesson was now learned. Thackeray was a finished novelist; but, alas! he was nearly forty years of age, and he was to die at fifty-two. The brief remainder of his existence was crowded with splendid work; but Thackeray is unquestionably one of those writers who give us the impression of having more in them than accident ever permitted them to produce.

Fielding had escorted the genius of Thackeray to the doors of success, and it became convenient to use the name in contrasting the new novelist with Dickens, who was obviously of the tribe of Smollett. But Thackeray was no consistent disciple of Fielding, and when we reach his masterpieces—*Esmond*, for instance—the resemblance between the two writers has become purely superficial. Thackeray is more difficult to describe in a few words than perhaps any other author of his merit. He is a bundle of contradictions—slipshod in style, and yet exquisitely mannered; a student of reality in conduct, and yet carried away by every romantic mirage of sentiment and prejudice; a cynic with a tear in his eye, a pessimist that believes the best of everybody. The fame of Thackeray largely depends on his palpitating and almost pathetic vitality; he suffers, laughs, reflects, sentimentalises, and meanwhile we run beside the giant figure, and, looking up at the gleam of the great spectacles, we share his emotion. His extraordinary power of entering into the life of the eighteenth century, and reconstructing it before us, is the most definite of his purely intellectual claims to our regard. But it is the character of the man himself—plaintive, affectionate, protean in its moods, like April weather in its changes—that, fused with unusual completeness into his works, preserves for us the human intensity which is Thackeray's perennial charm as a writer.—EDMUND GOSSE, *A Short History of Modern English Literature*, 1897, pp. 352–54

A writer is as great as his finest work—Thackeray takes his place in Literature as the author of *Esmond*, *Vanity Fair*, *Pendennis*, *Barry Lyndon*, *The Newcomes*, *Rebecca and Rowena*, and *The Roundabout Papers*—and I believe his name will stand to future ages as that of the most representative Englishman of Letters of our age, and as that of the greatest master of fiction since Henry Fielding.—LEWIS MELVILLE, *The Life of William Makepeace Thackeray*, 1899, Vol. 2, p. 250

Thackeray took no print from the romantic generation; he passed it over, and went back to Addison, Fielding, Goldsmith, Swift. His masters were the English humourists of the eighteenth century. He planned a literary history of that century, a design which was carried out on other lines by his son-in-law, Leslie Stephen. If he wrote historical novels, their period was that of the Georges, and not of Richard the Lion Heart. It will not do, of course, to lay too much stress on Thackeray, whose profession was satire and whose temper purely anti-romantic.—HENRY A. BEERS, *A History of English Romanticism in the Nineteenth Century*, 1901, pp. 397–98

If, then, we find that in all great walks of life—in the Church, in war, in commerce, and in diplomacy—Mr. Thackeray has nothing but abuse and sneers for success; if we find that he loves to portray the ludicrous and the discreditable only, is it unfair to say that he is the Apostle of Mediocrity? Mediocre ways of life, mediocre thoughts, mediocre inclinations (mis-

called passions), mediocre achievements—these, if not positively enjoined, as they sometimes are, are in effect all that is left to one who takes Mr. Thackeray for his guide. For the rest, never had a mean gospel so doughty an Apostle.—WALTER FREWEN LORD, "The Apostle of Mediocrity," *Nineteenth Century*, March 1902, p. 410

Thackeray possessed in a greater measure than any other English writer the *style coulant*, which Baudelaire ascribed in dispraise to George Sand. His words flow like snow-water upon the mountainside. He could no more restrain the current of his prose than a gentle slope could turn a rivulet back upon its course. His sentences dash one over the other in an often aimless succession, as though impelled by a force independent of their author. The style, as employed by Thackeray, has its obvious qualities and defects. It is so easy that it may be followed by the idlest reader, who willingly applies to literature the test of conversation. The thread of argument or of character is so loosely held that it need not elude a half-awakened attention. On the other hand, the style must needs be at times inaccurate and undistinguished. The solecisms of which he is guilty, and they are not few, may readily be forgiven. It is more difficult to pardon the frequent lack of distinction, especially as in *Esmond* Thackeray proved that he could write, if he would, with perfect artistry. But the method of his more familiar books seems the result less of artifice than of temperament. He seldom gives you the impression that he has studied to produce a certain effect. An effect is there, of course, facile and various, but beyond his management. He is so little conscious of his craft, that he rarely arrives at the right phrase, thus presenting an obvious contrast to Disraeli, who, often careless in composition, yet sowed his pages with pearls of speech which time cannot dim. But how little do we take away from the most of Thackeray beyond a general impression of gentlemanly ease!

From this it follows that he possessed no economy of speech. He never used one word, if a page and a half could adequately express the meaning, and at all save his high moments you miss a controlling hand, a settled purpose. Nor is this remarkable, when you recall the shifts and starts in which he did his work. He was of those who write better anywhere than in their own house. He would carry his unfinished manuscript to Greenwich with him, and write a chapter after dinner, or he would go off to Paris, and compose as he went. "I should never be at home," he told Elwin, "if I could help it. . . . I write less at home than anywhere. I did not write ten pages of *The Newcomes* in that house at Brompton. . . . This"—meaning a hotel—"is the best place to work in."

While Thackeray left the words to look after themselves, he confesses himself the humble slave of his own characters. "Once created," said he, "they lead me, and I follow where they direct." He devised his actors as by instinct, and without realising the full meaning of the drama in which they played their part. "I have no idea where it all comes from," he told Elwin. "I have never seen the people I describe, nor heard the conversations I put down. I am often astonished myself to read it when I have got it on paper." It is not strange, therefore, that he regarded the personages in his own dramas as quite outside himself. "I have been surprised," says he, "at the observations made by some of my characters. It seems as if an occult power was moving the pen." And it was precisely this externality which linked Thackeray and his characters in the bonds of acquaintance. Had they been the deliberate and conscious creations of his brain, they would have been at once more and less familiar to him. He would have remembered precisely where the strings lay which pulled the figures; but he could not have said, "I know the people utterly—I know the sound of their voices." He would not have seen Philip Firmin in a chance visitor; he would not have recognised the drunken swagger of Captain Costigan, when he met him, years after his creation, in a tavern. We may be quite sure that he never encountered Sir Francis or Beatrix Esmond, for these he made himself; but the majority of his characters grew without his knowledge, and even against his will. "That turning back to the old pages," he murmurs in a passage of genuine lament, "produces anything but elation of mind. Would you not pay a pretty fine to be able to cancel some of them? Ah, the sad old pages, the dull old pages!"

It was this fatality, this frank obedience to his own puppets and his own pen, which explains the frequent formlessness of Thackeray's work. But though he permitted most of his books to write themselves, it must not be thought that his style was uniformly hazardous. Despite its occasional inaccuracy, despite its loose texture, it has many shining qualities. It is graphic, various, and at times eloquent. It is easy to recall a hundred passages which would entitle Thackeray to a high place among the writers of English. The Waterloo chapters of *Vanity Fair*, much of *Esmond*, Harry Warrington's first visit to England, Denis Duval's journey to London,—these, to name but a few, are touched by the hand of a master, who need fear comparison with none. Even where Thackeray's prose is least under control, it inspires no more than his own regret that he did not write "a completely good book." For it is always the prose of a man of letters.

Now, in Thackeray's time scholarship was not fashionable. Neither Dickens nor Bulwer (save in his last novels) give you a sense of literary allusion. But Thackeray, in his most careless mood, suggests the classics or hints at the eighteenth century. As he wrote rather as an essayist than as a novelist, as his style was a sincere, untrammelled expression of his mind, he reveals his literary preferences by a thousand light touches. His reading, if not wide, was deep. He was perfectly familiar with both the Augustan ages. Horace he knew best of all, and quoted most constantly. Nothing pleases him better than to allude in a phrase to his favourite poet. "Nuper—in former days—I too have militated," thus he writes in *The Roundabout Papers*, "the years slip away fugacius;" and again, "to-morrow the diffugient snows will give place to Spring." Above all, he loved the Augustan doctrine of an easy life. The contemner of Swift naturally found Juvenal a "truculent brute," but he felt a natural sympathy for the satirist of Venusia, who timidly avoided unpleasant themes, and who, had he lived in the nineteenth century, would have been a man about town, and have haunted the very clubs to which Thackeray himself belonged. And when he chose to express himself in verse, he echoed with skill and fidelity both the manner and the philosophy of Horace.—CHARLES WHIBLEY, *William Makepeace Thackeray*, 1903, pp. 234–38

Works

VANITY FAIR

I brought away the last four numbers of *Vanity Fair*, and read one of them in bed, during the night. Very good, indeed, beats Dickens out of the world.—JANE WELSH CARLYLE, Letter to Thomas Carlyle (Sept. 16, 1847)

In forming our general estimate of this writer, we wish to be understood as referring principally, if not exclusively, to *Vanity Fair* (a novel in monthly parts), though still unfinished; so

immeasurably superior, in our opinion, is this to every other known production of his pen. The great charm of this work is its entire freedom from mannerism and affectation both in style and sentiment,—the confiding frankness with which the reader is addressed,—the thoroughbred carelessness with which the author permits the thoughts and feelings suggested by the situations to flow in their natural channel, as if conscious that nothing mean or unworthy, nothing requiring to be shaded, gilded, or dressed up in company attire, could fall from him. In a word, the book is the work of a gentleman, which is one great merit; and not the work of a fine (or would-be fine) gentleman, which is another. Then, again, he never exhausts, elaborates, or insists too much upon anything; he drops his finest remarks and happiest illustrations as Buckingham dropped his pearls, and leaves them to be picked up and appreciated as chance may bring a discriminating observer to the spot. His effects are uniformly the effects of sound wholesome legitimate art; and we need hardly add that we are never harrowed up with physical horrors of the Eugène Sue school in his writings, or that there are no melodramatic villains to be found in them. One touch of nature makes the whole world kin, and here are touches of nature by the dozen. His pathos (though not so deep as Mr. Dickens') is exquisite; the more so, perhaps, because he seems to struggle against it, and to be half ashamed of being caught in the melting mood: but the attempt to be caustic, satirical, ironical, or philosophical, on such occasions, is uniformly vain; and again and again have we found reason to admire how an originally fine and kind nature remains essentially free from worldliness, and, in the highest pride of intellect, pays homage to the heart.

Vanity Fair was certainly meant for a satire: the follies, foibles and weaknesses (if not vices) of the world we live in, were to be shown up in it, and we can hardly be expected to learn philanthropy from the contemplation of them.—ABRAHAM HAYWARD, "Thackeray's Writings," *Edinburgh Review*, Jan. 1848, p. 50

You mention Thackeray and the last number of *Vanity Fair*. The more I read Thackeray's works the more certain I am that he stands alone—alone in his sagacity, alone in his truth, alone in his feeling (his feeling, though he makes no noise about it, is about the most genuine that ever lived on a printed page), alone in his power, alone in his simplicity, alone in his self-control. Thackeray is a Titan, so strong that he can afford to perform with calm the most herculean feats; there is the charm and majesty of repose in his greatest efforts; *he* borrows nothing from fever, his is never the energy of delirium—his energy is sane energy, deliberate energy, thoughtful energy. The last number of *Vanity Fair* proves this peculiarly. Forcible, exciting in its force, still more impressive than exciting, carrying on the interest of the narrative in a flow, deep, full, resistless, it is still quiet—as quiet as reflection, as quiet as memory; and to me there are parts of it that sound as solemn as an oracle. Thackeray is never borne away by his own ardour—he has it under control. His genius obeys him—it is his servant, it works no fantastic changes at its own wild will, it must still achieve the task which reason and sense assign it, and none other. Thackeray is unique. I *can* say no more, I *will* say no less.—CHARLOTTE BRONTË, Letter to W. S. Williams (March 29, 1848)

Vanity Fair, by W. M. Thackeray, one of the most brilliant of English magazine-writers, is an attempt, somewhat after the manner of Fielding, to represent the world as it is, especially the selfish, heartless, and cunning portion of it. The author has Fielding's cosy manner of talking to his readers in the pauses of his narrative, and, like Fielding, takes his personages mostly from ordinary life. The novel, though it touches often upon topics which have been worn threadbare, and reproduces many commonplace types of character, is still, on the whole, a fresh and vigorous transcript of English life, and has numerous profound touches of humanity and humor. Sir Pitt Crawley, a sort of combination of Sir John Brute, Sir Tunbelly Clumsy, and Squire Western, is a very striking piece of caricature; but though exceedingly ludicrous, is hardly natural. George Osborne, Dobbin, and Amelia are characters almost literally true to nature, and are developed with consummate skill and fidelity. Mr. Osborne, we fear, is too fair a representative of the English man of business of the middle class,—selfish, arrogant, purse-proud, cringing to superiors, and ferocious to inferiors, rejoicing in a most profound ignorance of his own meanness and cruelty, and ever disposed to rise on the ruin of his neighbours. That disposition in English society, of every class, to trample on the one immediately beneath it, and to fawn on the one immediately above it, Thackeray felicitously represents in this portrait and in other characters. Nothing can be more edifying than Mr. Osborne's conversations with his son George, on his intimacy with men of rank who fleece him at cards, and on his duty to break off a match with Amelia after her father has become bankrupt. But the finest character in the whole novel is Miss Rebecca Sharp, an original personage, worthy to be called the author's own, and as true to life as hypocrisy, ability, and cunning can make her. She is altogether the most important person in the work, being the very impersonation of talent, tact, and worldliness, and one who works her way with a graceful and effective impudence unparalleled among managing women.

Of all the novels on our list, *Vanity Fair* is the only one in which the author is content to represent actual life. His page swarms with personages whom we recognize at once as genuine. It is also noticeable, that Thackeray alone preserves himself from the illusions of misanthropy or sentimentality, and though dealing with a host of selfish and malicious characters, his book leaves no impression that the world is past praying for, or that the profligate have it. His novel, as a representation of life, is altogether more comprehensive and satisfying than either of the others. Each may excel him in some particular department of character and passion, but each is confined to a narrow space, and discolors or shuts out the other portions of existence. Thackeray looks at the world from no exclusive position, and his view accordingly includes a superficial, if not a substantial whole; and it is creditable to the healthiness of his mind, that he could make so wide a survey without contracting either of the opposite diseases of misanthropy or worldliness.—EDWIN P. WHIPPLE, "Novels of the Season," *North American Review*, Oct. 1848, pp. 368–69

In this book the artist—and he was an eminently great artist—seemed to have endeavored to drive mankind to their own unaided struggles, taking away from them all good examples and leaving them to conclude that nothing is real but folly and perfidy. ⟨. . .⟩

In the literature of fiction there is not to be found a picture drawn more artistically than Rebecca Sharp. She was of the sort upon whom it suited the author to exert his consummate powers. He painted her to the life, with pretended reluctance to evil, suspected, yet not fully known to be persuasible to consent, demanding risk, high pay, so that the pursuit, of which, if easy, a bold lover would weary, acquired the eagerness which must not be allowed to abate. No woman could better understand the trick, as sung by the shepherd in

Virgil, of casting her apple and then fleeing to the covert of willows:

> Malo me Galatea petit lasciva puella;
> Et fugit ad salices; et se cupit ante videri.

It is a sad commentary on the powerlessness and the hopelessness of a poor young woman without other gift than mere virtue to obtain success that appears to attend upon insidiousness and fraud. It would have been a good sight to see the lifting of such a one, even though slowly and through difficulties, where so many thousands of poor girls do rise through toil and patient waiting. In default of this the next best would have been to drive her to the frustration of every dishonorable purpose that had tempted her from the path of rectitude. Better than both of these, for the highest purposes of instruction, would have been pictures of young women who endured temptation and outrage without expecting and without receiving reward except such as came from the testimony of a good conscience and of suffering for the sake of Him who ennobled suffering and put it above successes, victories, and triumphs. For had there not lived in such a career Agnes and Afra, Rose and Eulalia, Lucy and Blandina? If such as these be outside of the art of the novelist, then surely he may hold up to our view young girls such as Richardson presented with generous sympathy to the public of his day. Alas! the eyes of that public were yet moist with tears when the profligate Fielding made them laugh both at them over whom they had wept and at themselves. It was such a joke to imagine it possible for as poor a girl as Pamela to marry a rich, hardened bachelor and reform him after marriage, or for another like Clarissa to endure such trials and yet continue spotless in her virtue! No, no; Rebecca Sharp must be what she was, have a better time than even Amelia Sedley, and thus be made to exhibit that virtue is worth not even as much as a semblance that is suspected and almost known to be false. Satire, indeed! Satire upon the men in highest society, for of the two from this class whom he exhibited one was a heartless profligate, the other a loathsome brute; satire even upon marriage, for the couple who were truest to each other were the O'Dowds, whose rudeness was sufficient to make all of both sexes feel like keeping away from marriage altogether, if this is to be considered a fair illustration of its most honorable estate.—RICHARD MALCOLM JOHNSTON, "The Extremity of Satire," *Catholic World*, Feb 1886, pp. 688–90

ESMOND

Thackeray I saw for ten minutes: he was just in the agony of finishing a Novel: which has arisen out of the Reading necessary for his Lectures, and relates to those Times—of Queen Anne, I mean. He will get £1000 for his Novel. He was wanting to finish it, and rush off to the Continent, I think, to shake off the fumes of it.—EDWARD FITZGERALD, Letter to Frederick Tennyson (June 8, 1852)

Of our late Editor's works, the best known, and most widely appreciated are, no doubt, *Vanity Fair, Pendennis, The Newcomes,* and *Esmond.* The first on the list has been the most widely popular with the world at large. *Pendennis* has been the best loved by those who have felt and tasted the delicacy of Thackeray's tenderness. *The Newcomes* stands conspicuous for the character of the Colonel, who as an English gentleman has no equal in English fiction. *Esmond,* of all his works, has most completely satisfied the critical tastes of those who profess themselves to read critically. For myself, I own that I regard *Esmond* as the first and finest novel in the English language. Taken as a whole, I think that it is without a peer. There is in it a completeness of historical plot, and an absence of that taint of unnatural life which blemishes, perhaps, all our other historical novels, which places it above its brethren. And, beyond this, it is replete with a tenderness which is almost divine,—a tenderness which no poetry has surpassed. Let those who doubt this go back and study again the life of Lady Castlewood. In *Esmond*, above all his works, Thackeray achieves the great triumph of touching the innermost core of his subject, without ever wounding the taste. We catch all the aroma, but the palpable body of the thing never stays with us till it palls us. Who ever wrote of love with more delicacy than Thackeray has written in *Esmond?* May I quote one passage of three or four lines? Who is there that does not remember the meeting between Lady Castlewood and Harry Esmond after Esmond's return. "'Do you know what day it is?' she continued. 'It is the 29th December; it is your birthday! But last year we did not drink it;—no, no! My lord was cold, and my Harry was like to die; and my brain was in a fever; and we had no wine. But now,—now you are come again, bringing your sheaves with you, my dear.' She burst into a wild flood of weeping as she spoke; she laughed and sobbed on the young man's heart, crying out wildly,—'bringing your sheaves with you,—your sheaves with you!'"

But if *Esmond* be, as a whole, our best English novel, Colonel Newcome is the finest single character in English fiction. That it has been surpassed by Cervantes, in *Don Quixote*, we may, perhaps, allow, though *Don Quixote* has the advantage of that hundred years which is necessary to the perfect mellowing of any great work. When Colonel Newcome shall have lived his hundred years, and the lesser works of Thackeray and his compeers shall have died away, then, and not till then, will the proper rank of this creation in literature be appreciated.—ANTHONY TROLLOPE, "W. M. Thackeray," *Cornhill Magazine*, Feb. 1864, pp. 136–37

If I could possess only *one* of his works, I think I should choose *Henry Esmond*. To my thinking, it is a marvel in literature, and I have read it oftener than any of the other works.—JAMES T. FIELDS, "Thackeray," *Yesterdays with Authors*, 1871, p. 16

Of Thackeray's works certainly the most remarkable and perhaps the best is *Esmond*. Many novelists following in the wake of Scott have attempted to reproduce for us past manners, scenes, and characters; but in *Esmond* Thackeray not only does this—he reproduces for us the style in which men wrote and talked in the days of Queen Anne. To reproduce the forgotten phraseology, to remember always not how his age would express an idea, but how Steele, or Swift, or Addison would have expressed it, might have been pronounced impossible of accomplishment. Yet in *Esmond* Thackeray did accomplish it, and with perfect success. The colouring throughout is exquisite and harmonious, never by a single false note is the melody broken. Of his writings in general perhaps the most noticeable characteristic is the hatred they express for all sorts of false pretences, sham sentiment, and unreal professions. He is never wearied of directing his scathing satire against whited sepulchres of all descriptions. "Call things by their right names; do not gloss over the villany of Lord Steyne because he is a lord; do not condone George Osborne's selfishness because he is handsome; don't pretend to be what you are not, and do not let false shame make you conceal what you are," is the burden of his message. To his scorn and hatred of vice and meanness he added sincere love and admiration of all that is true, and good, and honourable. A large-hearted, thoughtful man, the temptations and trials and sorrows of humanity affected him deeply. His pathos is as touching and sincere as his humour is subtle

and delicate. His numerous "asides" to the reader are full of "that sad wisdom which experience brings," in striking contrast to those of Dickens, who, when he leaves his story to indulge in moralising, is generally trite and feeble. In a characteristic passage Thackeray apologises for the frequency of his casual reflections. "Perhaps of all novel-spinners now extant," he says, "the present writer is the most addicted to preaching. Does he not stop perpetually in his story and begin to preach to you? . . . I say *peccavi* loudly and heartily," he adds, but there was no need of this expression of repentance, whether sincere or not, for none ever wished Thackeray's "asides" fewer or shorter. Thackeray's fame as a novelist has caused his poems, of which he wrote a good many, generally in a half-serious, half-comic vein, to be frequently less noticed than they deserve. His admirable mock-heroic ballads and society verses attain a degree of excellence very rarely reached by such performances.

Was Thackeray a cynic? The question has been often asked and variously answered. If we use "cynic" in the proper sense of the word as defined by Johnson, "a philosopher of the snarling or currish sort; a follower of Diogenes; a rude man; a snarler; a misanthrope," most assuredly it cannot with any propriety be applied to him. But in ordinary *parlance* we use "cynic" in a sense different from any of these, meaning by it a man who is apt to look on life with a glance half sad, half humorous, who is prone to be distrustful of fine appearances and professions, who sees keenly the grains of dust mingled in the gold of the finest character, and who is fully aware of the latent meanness and selfish ambition which often lurk under actions professing to be noble and generous. In this sense of the word, Thackeray was a cynic. *Vanitas vanitatum*: all is vanity, is his often-repeated cry; none knew better than he with what richly gilded coverings we are apt to clothe the evil passions and desires of our nature.—HENRY J. NICOLL, *Landmarks of Literature*, 1882, pp. 389–91

THE NEWCOMES

Mr. S—— is a friend of Thackeray, and, speaking of the last number of *The Newcomes*,—so touching that nobody can read it aloud without breaking down,—he mentioned that Thackeray himself had read it to James Russell Lowell and William Story in a cider-cellar! I read all the preceding numbers of *The Newcomes* to my wife, but happened not to have an opportunity to read this last, and was glad of it,—knowing that my eyes would fill, and my voice quiver.—NATHANIEL HAWTHORNE, *The English Note-Books*, 1855

This is Mr. Thackeray's masterpiece, as it is undoubtedly one of the masterpieces of English fiction, if fiction is the proper term to apply to the most minute and faithful transcript of actual life which is anywhere to be found. The ordinary resource of novelists is to describe characters under exceptional circumstances, to show them influenced by passions which seldom operate in their excess with each individual, and to make them actors in adventures which in their aggregate happen to few or none. It is the picked passages of existence which they represent, and these again are often magnified and coloured beyond the measure of nature. Mr. Thackeray looks at life under its ordinary aspects, and copies it with a fidelity and artistic skill which are surprising. Men, women, and children talk, act, and think in his pages exactly as they are talking, acting, and thinking at every hour of every day. The same thorns, the majority of them self-planted, are festering in myriads of bosoms; the same false ambition and crooked devices are fermenting in a thousand hearts; the same malice, lying, and slandering in all their grades, petty and great, are issuing from legions of mouths, and the same mixture of kindness and generosity are checking and tempering the evil. You find yourself in the saloon where upon gala days you are a guest; in the house you frequent as a familiar friend; in the club of which you are a member; you meet there your acquaintances, you hear again the conversation which you have often heard before, and it is by no means unlikely that among the assembled company you may be startled by coming upon the very image of yourself. Truth is never sacrificed to piquancy. The characters in the *Newcomes* are not more witty, wise, or farcical than their prototypes; the dull, the insipid, and the foolish, speak according to their own fashion and not with the tongue of the author; the events which befall them are nowhere made exciting at the expense of probability. Just as the stream of life runs on through these volumes, so may it be seen to flow in the world itself by whoever takes up the same position on the bank. ⟨. . .⟩

Mr. Thackeray is a humourist, as every writer of fiction must be who takes an extended view of human nature. There are few persons who do not deviate in some particular from common forms or common sense; who are not guilty of some vanity, affectation, whim, or inconsistency, which, however far, perchance, from promoting mirth among those who have to bear with them, are comic in the description. The simple Colonel Newcome, when he fancies himself an adept in the wiles of the world, though, 'if he had lived to be as old as Jahaleel, a boy could still have cheated him;' Mrs. Hobson worshipping rank, and pretending to despise the society she cannot obtain; the airs and cowardice of Barnes; the self-importance and primness of Miss Honeyman, who, instead of feeling ashamed at being a gentlewoman reduced to let lodgings, is proud to be a lodging-house keeper who was once a gentle-woman; the clerical impostures of her bland brother, the French-English of Paul de Florac, and his efforts to personate John Bull; Mr. Gandish insisting upon the indifference to 'igh art' as shown in the neglect of his monster pictures, and talking of the heroic in his vulgar language, afford a hundred examples of the ridiculous. Most of the actors in the *Newcomes* are tinged with it, but the quality is always in subjection to truth. There is none of the farcical extravagance which calls forth peals of laughter, always easy to be provoked by absurdity and caricature. In Frederick Bayham there is a two-fold source of merriment, for besides the smiles produced by unconscious infirmities, there is a fertile vein of fun in his expedients and vivacity. It is a peculiar charm of the light and pleasant wit which sparkles through the narrative that it never has the air of being studied. It shines forth in a name, an epithet, a parenthesis, in numberless undefinable ways, and always as if it sprung out of the subject, and had not been introduced for the sake of being facetious.

The execution of the work is not below the conception. Mr. Thackeray is deeply imbued with all our best literature. Numerous phrases and fragments of sentences attest his familiarity with the classic authors of his country—a familiarity which is not less surely shown by the perennial flow of his easy and graceful language. There is no appearance of effort, no studied artifice of composition, but neither is there any approach to baldness in the simplicity of his phraseology, or to carelessness in the freedom of his style. The narrative runs on in a rich abundance of strong, idiomatic, sterling English, often applied in a novel and felicitous manner, and sufficiently adorned by occasional metaphors of the same masculine stamp. He even manages to give additional raciness by the not unfrequent use of colloquial vulgarisms, which if they were

introduced with less skill would debase his style. It is with reluctance we confess that he has turned language to good account which in all other hands has hitherto revolted every person of cultivated mind, for we fear the evil effects of his example, and are sorry the black patches should heighten the beauty.—WHITWELL ELWIN, *"The Newcomes," Quarterly Review*, Sept. 1855, pp. 350–58

This is by far the best of Thackeray's stories. In his earlier works, the scornful has taken precedence of the humane element. His aim has been to satirize pretension, folly, and fashionable vice rather than to present aught that could challenge admiration or deserve imitation. Here the prominent personages command our entire sympathy, and the leading character our profound reverence; while the baser traits of secondary actors are softened and relieved by the admixture of good which is seldom wanting in actual life. Only this was needed to give Thackeray, as a novelist, the vantage-ground over Dickens; for there can be no difference of opinion as to his superiority in the command of language and in artistical resources and skill.—ANDREW PRESTON PEABODY, *North American Review*, Jan. 1856, p. 284

The *Newcomes* was written in the years that came between my father's first and second journey to America. He began the preface at Baden on the 7th of July 1853, he finished his book at Paris on the 28th of June 1855, and in the autumn of that year he returned to America. The story had been in his mind for a long time. While still writing *Esmond* he speaks of a new novel "opening with something like Fareham and the old people there," and of "a hero who will be born in India, and have a half-brother and sister." And there is also the description to be read of the little wood near to Berne, in Switzerland, into which he strayed one day, and where, as he tells us, "the story was actually revealed to him."—ANNE THACKERAY RITCHIE, "Introduction" to *The Newcomes*, 1898–99, p. xxii

ENGLISH HUMOURISTS AND FOUR GEORGES

Went to Thackeray's lecture on the Humorists at Willis's Rooms. It was a very large assembly, including Mrs. Carlyle, Dickens, Leslie, and innumerable noteworthy people. Thackeray is a much older-looking man than I had expected; a square, powerful face, and most acute and sparkling eyes, grayish hair and eyebrows. He reads in a definite, rather dry manner, but makes you understand thoroughly what he is about. The lecture was full of point, but the subject was not a very interesting one, and he tried to fix our sympathy on his good-natured, volatile, and frivolous hero rather more than was meet. "Poor Dick Steele!" one ends with, as one began; and I cannot see, more than I did before, the element of greatness in him.—CAROLINE FOX, *Journal* (June 12, 1851), *Memories of Old Friends*, ed. Horace N. Pym, 1882, p. 292

⟨. . .⟩ that, as a readable book, this ⟨*English Humourists of the Eighteenth Century*⟩ has seldom been surpassed. Whatever quantity of summer-salmon, *hotch-potch*, veal pie, and asparagus you may have been discussing, and however dreary you may feel after your dinner, Thackeray's amusing anecdotes and conversational style will keep you awake. Next to Macaulay and Hazlitt, he is the most entertaining of critics. You read his lectures with quite as much gusto as you do *Pendennis*, and with infinitely more than you do such dull mimicry of the past as is to be found in *Esmond*. Clever, too, of course, sagacious often, and sometimes powerful, are his criticisms, and a geniality not frequent in his fictions is often here. Sympathy with his subject is also a quality he possesses and parades;

indeed, he appears as one born out of his proper time, and seems, occasionally, to sigh for the age of big-wigs, bagnios, and sponging-houses. Such are, we think, the main merits of this very popular volume.—GEORGE GILFILLAN, "Thackeray," A *Third Gallery of Portraits*, 1854, pp. 261–62

I have heard Thackeray's four lectures on the four Georges, truculent enough in their general satire,—though not much beyond the last half-volume of *Harry Esmond* about Queen Anne,—but full of generous passages about individuals. The sketches of the German princes of the seventeenth century, and down to the middle of the eighteenth, with which he opened, amused me more than anything else. They were capital. The passage most applauded was a beautiful tribute of loyalty to Queen Victoria, and the tone and manners of her Court. It was given, on his part, with much feeling, and brought down the house—always crowded—very fervently.—GEORGE TICKNOR, Letter to Sir Edmund Head (Dec. 23, 1855), *Life, Letters, and Journals of George Ticknor*, ed. Anna Ticknor, 1876, Vol. 2, p. 294

He was a complete success. He was as delightful as his own literary personages are, and so "like his writings" that every one spoke of it. His allusions, his voice, his looks, were all just what we had expected. Never did a long-hoped-for hero fill the bill so thoroughly. His loving and life-giving genius spoke in every word. Wonderful examples of excellence those papers on *The Four Georges*, and delivered in a clear, fine, rich voice. Their simplicity was matchless, and the fun in him came out as he described the fourth George, and then stopped, not smiling himself, while we all laughed. He silently stood, his head tipped back, and then calmly wiped his spectacles and went on. He had a charm as a speaker which no one has since caught: it defies analysis, as does his genius. It was Thackerayian. —M. E. W. SHERWOOD, *An Epistle to Posterity*, 1897, p. 79

MARGARET OLIPHANT
From "Mr Thackeray and His Novels"

Blackwood's Edinburgh Magazine, January 1855, pp. 88–96

Future generations will speak of Dickens and Thackeray as we speak of Pepys and Evelyn, and they are quite as dissimilar; but if aught of evil should befall the regnant sovereign of this realm of fancy, we will have a civil war forthwith to decide which of these pretenders shall mount the vacant throne. In the mean time, it is premature to agitate the question; there is no just ground of comparison between these two whose names are so commonly pronounced together. Perhaps there are no two men among their host of readers who are further apart from each other than Mr Dickens and Mr Thackeray; but instead of unnecessarily enlarging upon the difference, we count it better wisdom to take up this pretty pink volume, patiently waiting the conclusion of a rambling preamble, to remind us, that it has nothing to do with Mr Dickens, but in every page of it is solely Mr Thackeray's own.

And the *Rose and the Ring* is not a political satire, though one of its princes is of Crim Tartary; and we are afraid that those who look for one of Mr Thackeray's wicked and witty comments upon the world in general, will be disappointed in this book. He is not in the vein of teaching either; his Christmas carol does not treat of a magical dream and a wonderful transformation, like some other Christmas carols of our acquaintance. Thanks to Mr Thackeray, this fairy tale is a

pure flash of mirth and laughter, and knows no moral. The little children and the great children may venture for once to enjoy their sport in peace, without being called upon to square up into a row with humility and receive their lesson at the end. There are two princes, and two princesses, and two fairy gifts, endowing the fortunate possessors with unlimited beauty and loveableness; and, like a skilful artist, after a few complications, Mr Thackeray contrives to bestow those fairy tokens upon the two poor souls who require to be attracted to one another, and leaves the true lovers to the inalienable glamour of their love. If Angelica loses her rose, or Bulbo his ring, the domestic happiness of this royal pair is not greatly to be calculated upon; and the public peace of the realms of Paflagonia and Crim Tartary may very possibly be disturbed once more; but magnanimous Giglio deprives *his* queen of the enchanted jewel with his own hand, and finds her quite as lovely without its magical influence;—and so Mr Thackeray, who is by no means apt to rhapsodise on this subject, makes a very seemly obeisance to True Love, the oldest of all the witchcrafts. We will not do our readers the injustice to tell them at second-hand how poor little Betsinda danced before their majesties in her one shoe—or how, by means of this little slipper, the persecuted Rosalba attained to her throne—or of Prince Giglio's infatuation with the grim old Countess Gruffanuff—or the magical bag which supplied him with everything he wanted, from blacking for his boots to armour for his battle;—but we have no doubt that everybody who has not read the *Rose and the Ring*, will be satisfied to know that Mr Thackeray dispenses poetic justice with an unfaltering hand—that the exile has his own again—and that the usurpers are sent upon their travels. We will not pause to point out the catastrophe of Gruffanuff, and the lesson it impresses upon the brethren of that unfortunate servitor; but we will promise the fireside circle, which has the *Rose and the Ring* read aloud for its general edification, one hearty laugh at the great and unlooked-for discomfiture of the Countess Gruffanuff.

We are bound to say, that while Mr Thackeray has been disporting himself among the family of Newcomes, Mr Michael Angelo Titmarsh, in his episodical existence, has made great use of his time since his last appearance before the Christmas-keeping public. Mr Titmarsh may rest assured that no thunder will sour the beer which has so little acid in it by nature. The fairy Blackstick is a much more agreeable presiding genius than Lady Kicklebury; and Mr Titmarsh has never before produced so pleasant a picture-book, nor one whose pictures were so worthy of the text. These illustrations are greatly superior to all their predecessors by the same hand; they are so good that the artist is fairly entitled to rank with the author in this pleasant production; and altogether, amidst our wars and our troubles, in this Christmas which is darkened and shadowed over to so many households, and at a time when common tribulation and anxiety put us in charity with all our neighbours, we are glad that we have to thank Mr Thackeray for the honest laugh which is not at any one's expense.

Mr Thackeray, in his own proper person, has not made less progress in kindness and good humour than has his *alter ego*, if we trace his course from *Vanity Fair* to the *Newcomes*. Everybody praises Becky Sharp, and the history in which she fills so important a place. Does everybody like that clever, unbelieving, disagreeable book? But there is nothing to be said on the subject of *Vanity Fair*, which has not been said already—that all its rogues are clever and amusing, and all its good characters fools—that Amelia is a greater libel upon womankind than Becky herself, and that there is a heated crowded atmosphere in the story which has scarcely any relief, seeing that the good people are by no means a match for the bad, and cannot even pretend to balance the heavy scale of evil. There is no one in the book who has the remotest claim to our affection but Dobbin—good Dobbin, with his faithful heart and his splay feet. Why should the Major have splay feet, Mr Thackeray? Must the man who is not distinguished by moral obliquity have some physical misfortune to make amends? But the splay feet carry their owner into the heart of our regard, despite their unloveliness. The warmest admirer of Miss Rebecca Sharp is not moved to bestow his affection upon that amiable young lady; and though poor, little, silly Amelia may chance to touch a heart for a moment as she watches in Russell Square for a glimpse of her boy, she is quite too insignificant a person to insure any regard for herself. Mr Thackeray made a very clever book; and Mr Thackeray's book made a great sensation and success. There are many admirable things in it—a great sparkle of sayings and happy turns of expression; and the scenes are cut sharp and clear in their outline, and dullness is not within these pages. Nevertheless, we carry but one personage with us in real kindness when we close the volume. Of all its men and women, only Major Dobbin is worth the least morsel of love.

In Mr Thackeray's second grand exposition of his own principles, and of the human panorama of which he is a spectator and historian—in *Pendennis*—we find a little more to commend. There is Warrington, who has no splay feet; there is sweet Mrs Pendennis, whom we consent to accept as an angel. It is a sad thing to think of Warrington, such a man as he is, spending his life in those chambers in Lamb Court, with nothing to do but to write articles, the fate of which he cares nothing for, only the Haunt to solace that great heart of his when the day's work is done, and no particular motive for living except the custom and habit of it. Few can paint a wasted life, and great powers wearing down with the continual dropping of every day, better than Mr Thackeray; but we are glad to think that he has still the means of rescue for this character in the exhaustless resources of fiction. Will not Mr Thackeray take into his gracious consideration ways and means for disposing of the graceless unknown Mrs Warrington, and leave Bluebeard free to make his fortune once more? We will answer for the entire satisfaction of the general population of these British Islands with any proceeding of the kind; and we do not doubt that Mr Warrington, when he is a free man, will find some one more faithful than Laura, and will not be forsaken a second time for such a coxcomb as Pen. Pendennis himself, though he is good-looking and fashionable, and writes a successful novel, is but a very poor fellow after all—not only falling far short of an ideal hero, but not much to brag of for a very ordinary man. Mr Thackeray avowedly scorns the loftiness of common romance, and will not have an exalted personage for the principal figure on his canvass; but Mr Arthur Pendennis does not possess a single feature of the heroic. Unfortunately, when we ought to admire, we are a great deal more likely to despise; and this, though it may be original, is neither true art nor noble; it is not original either; but Mr Pen is a meaner sinner than Tom Jones.

Leaving Pen—and leaving Laura, who is a very doubtful person, and whom we do not profess to make much of—if Pen is not the best husband in the world, popular opinion, we are afraid, will pronounce that popular sentence, "Served her right!"—there is much more satisfaction in meeting with Harry Foker, who is Mr Thackeray's special property, the type of a class which our novelist has brought out of the shadows into the clearest and kindliest illumination. Good Harry Foker, who has no great share of brains—who does not spell very well,

perhaps—whose habits are not what they ought to be, but who is the soul of honour, of unpretending simple courage and kind-heartedness. Some score of Harry Fokers, doing, with simple straightforwardness, what their commander ordered, have ridden with open eyes, and without a moment's faltering, right into the open-mouthed destruction, and made heroes of themselves upon the wintry heights of Sebastopol. Not a refined gentleman by any means, it is only genius that can commend this brave good-hearted simpleton to all our affections. A lesser artist might have been afraid of a character so little intellectual, and felt its defective points a reproach to his invention; but Mr Thackeray has been able to seize upon the genuine sparkle of this uncut jewel, upon the reverence for goodness, the humble self-estimation, the tender-heartedness, and the unsuspected pathos which lie in its depths. It is strange, when he has proved himself so capable of its exercise, that Mr Thackeray should so much overlook this true alchemy of genius. Is it best to drag the veil of decorum from a hidden evil, or to disclose a vein of native excellence—a secret even to its owner? Mr Thackeray, who scares his innocent readers with vague intimation of pitfalls round about them, and shocks mamma with terrific hints of the unmentionable ill-doing familiar to the thoughts of her pretty boy at school, does better service when Harry Foker, and Jack Belsize, and even Rawdon Crawley, show their honest hearts to us, than when he produces Mr Pendennis, with all his gifts, as a specimen of modern education, and the civilisation of the nineteenth century. What a simple noble gentleman is Lord Kew, who rises just above the strata of the Belsize formation! Such a hero as he is would leave us little to desire.

Only in one respect does *Pendennis* sin more grossly than *Vanity Fair*. Blanche Amory is more detestable, because she is less clever than Becky. How much does Mr Thackeray owe to the world of womankind, by way of reparation for foisting into their ranks such a creation as this! Nothing less than a Desdemona can atone for such an insult. Can Mr Thackeray make a Desdemona? He has added some few pleasant people to our acquaintance in his day—Warrington may make amends for Pen, but who is to make amends for Blanche?

And here we touch upon our author's greatest imperfection. Mr Thackeray does not seem acquainted with anything feminine between a nursery-maid and a fine lady—an indiscriminate idolater of little children, and an angler for a rich husband. The "perfect woman, nobly planned," has no place in the sphere of Mr Thackeray's fancy. Perhaps the secret of this may be, that Mr Thackeray's world is a conventional world; and that even while he attacks its weak points, "society," the sphere with which he is best acquainted, represents this many-sided globe in our historian's eyes. The mother and the cousin in the little country-house, weeping and adoring as they read the hero's letters, telling each other of his childhood, those blessed days when Pen was in petticoats, seeing in all this heaven and earth only the bit of consecrated soil under his shadow and the sky over his head, and furious at every other pretender for his gracious favour—that is one side of the picture. On the other is Miss Amory, with that bad leer in her eyes, which we are rejoiced to see has disappeared from the sketches of Mr Michael Angelo Titmarsh, calculating her chances of a husband, amusing Mr Pen into that last resource of idleness—falling in love; weeping "Mes Larmes" in public, and in private cuffing her little brother; and Blanche is the other side of the golden shield, the obverse of the coin, the completion of Mr Thackeray's circle of female character. It is not a flattering estimate of Englishwomen which will be formed from the pages of this author, whom, of all others, we should fancy our neighbours over the Channel most likely to form their judgment from. Though Blanche has expanded into Beatrice, and Beatrice progressed to Ethel, the character is still far from satisfactory. And we must once more assure Mr Thackeray, that he owes his countrywomen an Isabella or a Desdemona to make amends.

In the one other creation of *Pendennis*, Mr Thackeray puts forth all his power. The Major rescues *his* class still more clearly out of the shadows than Harry Foker does; henceforward, instead of wordy descriptions of this old gentleman of the clubs, it will be quite enough to say that he is like Major Pendennis. This impersonation is so broad and clear that there is no mistaking it or its identity. There are certain portraits which convince us that they are admirable likenesses, though we are perfectly unacquainted with the original; and even those to whom "society" is an unknown country, must recognise, as an unmistakable individual, this specimen of the aborigines of "the world." Getting on in "society" is the chief end of man to Major Pendennis—it is the grand vocation and duty of life. You must be moderately good, moderately brave and honourable, because the want of these qualities is apt to endanger your success in life; and with all the perseverance and ardour which wins battles or makes fortunes, the Major devotes himself to securing an invitation to Gaunt House, or a gracious recognition from the Marquis of Steyn. It would be a pure waste of sympathy, in author or readers, to condole with the loveless, joyless condition of this old man of fashion. Loves and joys are out of the Major's way—they would simply embarrass and annoy him, these troublesome emotions; the Major has his pleasures instead; and his place in society, which he fills in a manner perfectly becoming the high end he has in view.

When we leave *Pendennis*, we find that Mr Thackeray takes a great leap out of his ordinary domain. It is no longer the English of the present day, careless and easy, just touched with the slang for which our author has a special gift, but it is English of the Augustan age, English which is balanced with antithesis, and polished into epigram, the English of those dainty people who wore bag-wigs and ruffles, patches and powder. Though we have serious fault to find with the story of Esmond, we are constrained to admit, at the outset, that the execution of this story is exquisite. In comparison with this, almost every other historical work we are acquainted with, except the romances of Scott, is a mere piece of masquerade. The age is not a great age, we confess, in spite of its Blenheim and its Ramilies, its Steele and its Addison; but such as it is, we have it here, a picture which is not merely paint, but is about the best example of absolute reproduction which our literature possesses. Nothing can be more real or touching—more like a veritable page of biography, if biographers were usually endowed with such a style as Mr Thackeray confers upon Harry Esmond—than the story of the solitary boy at Castlewood, his patrons and his teachers. The picture is perfect in its truth to nature, which is universal, and to manners, which are limited and transitory. Harry Esmond is not a boy of Queen Victoria's time, in the little cavalier's suit proper to Queen Anne's—he is not in advance of his age, nor has any consciousness of Waterloo dimming the glory of Blenheim. We never find ourselves deceived in him through all his history—the mask does not slip aside for a moment to show a modern face underneath. This book is a marvellous historical picture; in this point of view it is an unrivalled performance, and worthy of all the plaudits which a work, attended by so many difficulties, has a right to claim.

Nevertheless, with so much in its favour, this admirable production carries failure in it as a story, as a piece of hu-

man life represented for the sympathy of all humanity—our most sacred sentiments are outraged, and our best prejudices shocked by the leading feature of this tale. It is not only that Lady Castlewood is the confidant of the hero's passionate love for her daughter, yet compensates his disappointment in that quarter with her own hand—but it is the intolerable idea that this woman, who is pure as an angel, and as severe in her judgment of the backsliding as a pure woman may be—a wife—and, still more, a mother, defended by the spotless love of little children—nevertheless cherishes for years a secret attachment to the boy to whom she gives the protection of her roof! This error is monstrous and unredeemable. If we do not count it among the affronts which Mr Thackeray puts upon his countrywomen, it is because it is too gross an error to look like truth; but it is not less disagreeable on this score. Mr Thackeray has spent all his pains to make this character a loveable and womanly one, and Rachel, Lady Castlewood, is a very "sweet" person we confess, and would be worthy the idolatry of her historian but for this unaccountable blunder. The Love of the poets is young for a necessity. If it is fashionable to have a hero of discreet years, it requires nothing less than a long, constant, single attachment to make a heroine of middle age in any respect tolerable. A woman who loves two men must always condescend to a little derogation from her primal dignity—and the woman who contracts two marriages must be excused, in romance, by either a forced match, in the first instance, or the saddest and completest disappointment. In any way it is degradation to the heroine of our fancy—but Mr Thackeray must thrust *his* lady still further down. What had Lady Castlewood done that she should be compelled to fall in love with Harry Esmond, her daughter's adorer, her husband's faithful attendant, her own devoted and respectful son?

The hero himself is a hero in the proper acceptation of the word. It is not the faulty modern young gentleman any longer, but the antique ideal which Mr Thackeray has resorted to, in consent, perhaps reluctant, but certainly complete, to the old canons of his art. Harry Esmond has all the generosity, all the unselfishness, all the unrewarded and unappreciated virtues of genuine romance. When your hero is an ordinary sinner, it is possible to make him a more distinct personage than your ideal excellence can be—so that Esmond does not always stand quite clear from his background, and has not perhaps such a crisp sharp outline as Mr Arthur Pendennis. To make up for this, there is rather more distinctness than is desirable in the character of Beatrice. This bold, unscrupulous, and daring beauty, in whom the passion for admiration and the delight of conquest seem to possess the full power of passions more gross in their nature, is another of Mr Thackeray's special belongings. Her triumph in her own dazzling charms, and the mischief they make everywhere—the impetus with which her magnificent vanity carries her on—the trickery to which she stoops, and the intrigues into which she enters—never because her own heart is interested, but solely from an insatiable longing to madden every one about her—are combined with a singular power. This splendid creature not only obeys her natural impulse to destroy, but glories in the havoc she makes, and goes forth to new conquests in exulting power over the graves of her victims. For the good of humanity, we may venture to hope that, except within the pages of *Esmond*, the world knows few Beatrices; but it is impossible to deny the power and strength with which this cruel syren is drawn.

And what shall we say to Ethel Newcome? Ethel is not Beatrice, yet she is little better than a proper nineteenth century development of that all-conquering beauty. For our own part, we confess to being in the most perfect bewilderment as to the conclusion of the loves of these cousins, whose fate Mr Thackeray has yet to seal. Though the Bumbelcund bank confers a fortune on Clive, will it confer upon Ethel suitable dispositions to make the young gentleman happy? or is it consistent with the dignity of Mr Clive Newcome to be accepted as a *pis aller?* or must Clive marry Rosey after all, and sink down into humdrum domestic happiness, and leave the brilliant star for which he sighed to sparkle into a still brighter firmament, or to shoot and fall into the unfathomable darkness which swallowed Beatrice? We flatter ourselves that, in twenty years' experience of novel-reading, we have attained to as clear a prescience of a *denouement* as most people; but Mr Thackeray, with his tantalising interviews, and all his hints of the future, puzzles and outwits our ordinary penetration. While the conclusion is not as yet, and everything is possible, we do not even find ourselves in a position to advise Mr Thackeray; we can but assure him honestly, that we see no outlet for him, though we expect he is to make himself a brilliant one. If Clive marries Ethel, how shall we vindicate the dignity of these young people, who cannot marry each other without a mutual sacrifice of pride and propriety; and if Clive marries Rosey, alas for Clive! Solemnly assuring Mr Thackeray of this dilemma, we leave him to make the best of it, only warning him of a storm of universal dissatisfaction if Clive marries no one at all—a miserable expedient, to which, we fear, *we* should be driven were the conclusion of the *Newcomes* left to our inventive powers.

There is no book of Mr Thackeray which is so worthy of a great reputation as this uncompleted story. As full of character as its predecessors, it redeems their errors gallantly; and we could almost fancy that, in the scorn of genius for that accusation which pronounced him unable to manage the ideal, Mr Thackeray has showered a glory of manliness and goodness upon the inhabitants of this little world. There has never been a nobler sketch than that of the Colonel. The innocent heart and simple honour of this old man, and his horror of all falsehood and impurity, are enough to cover a multitude of Mr Thackeray's sins. We can understand how every individual worth caring for in the story or out of it rejoices to gain the acquaintance of Thomas Newcome. We are grateful to Lady Anne, and like her ever after, for her true apprehension of our Colonel's courtly manners, and old fashioned chivalrous politeness. We are as ready to adopt him into our heart as Mr Pendennis and Mr Warrington can be; and Ethel herself gains an additional attraction when we see her beautiful eyes shining with pride for her noble old uncle. The key-note of the story is struck high and sweet in this character, which is at once so lofty and so childlike; and we cannot pass it by without once more admiring Mr Thackeray's skill in the retrospective story—the record of Thomas Newcome's misfortunes and troubles in his boyhood, which is almost as well done as the corresponding period in the history of Henry Esmond.

It is not easy to thread at a glance the lively maze of Mr Thackeray's story—to tell how pretty Ethel is engaged to Lord Kew by family arrangement, and how the young lady filches a green ticket from the Suffolk Street Gallery, with Sold upon it, and comes down to dinner wearing this label, like a wilful and rebellious young lady as she is; nor how good Colonel Newcome, whose great ambition it was to marry Clive to Ethel, and be a happy man in his old age, is balked by this engagement, and goes away sadly to India, to grow rich, if he can, for his dear boy's sake; how Clive is a painter, and varies between ostentation of his art and the least morsel of shame for being engaged in it; how he makes a brave effort, and tears

himself away from Ethel, and has almost got the better of his passion; how, of a sudden, the spirit of his dream is changed by hearing that Lord Kew and Ethel have broken off their engagement, at the first intimation of which poor young Clive finds out that he has not forgotten her, and comes home post-haste to try his hopeless chance once more; how there is a most noble Marquis of Ferintosh in the field before him; how the hero and the heroine have little sparring-matches of courtship, but never come any nearer a conclusion; and how last month brings us to the climax of a farewell, which we, for our own part, have no faith in. Ethel Newcome, like Beatrice, is sometimes intoxicated with her own beauty, and the applauses it brings—sometimes carried off her balance with the *afflatus* of conquest and victory; but Ethel, we are glad to say, is much improved from her forerunner, and is a much less hopeless character than the beautiful tormentor of Harry Esmond. Is Ethel to consume what remnants are left to her of that fresh girl's heart she had when we first knew her—when she first fell in love with her good uncle—and be a great lady, and blaze her youthful days away in barren splendour? She likes being a great lady, you perceive—such a being was not born for love in a cottage, or for Clive's five hundred a-year, and odd position. Has Mr Thackeray prepared this beautiful victim for Moloch, or is there hope for Ethel still? The oracle preserves inexorable silence, and smiles upon our queries. We are quite as curious as you are, young lady; but we venture to predict that Miss Ethel Newcome, even though Mr Thackeray may have compunctions on her behalf, can never "settle down" to romantic happiness. She will have to fulfil her destiny, and marry a most noble marquis. She is surely not for Clive the painter, whether he is to be made a Crœsus or a beggar, by means of the Bumbelcund Bank.

Clive himself, the handsome, dashing open-hearted young fellow, is an admirable hero. He is not called upon for feats of extraordinary generosity or self-sacrifice. His circumstances do not require Clive to take upon himself other people's burdens, or other people's penalties. He has only to enjoy himself, to paint when he pleases, and when he does not please, to draw his father's remittances, and look handsome, and be as happy as he can. There is no great demand made upon Clive's goodness throughout the story; yet we are quite content with him, and willing to believe that he will be equal to an emergency when it comes. We cannot refrain from making one quotation to illustrate the character of Clive, and the quality which, of all other qualities, Mr Thackeray expounds best. Clive is talking to his father:—

> "At Newcome, when they go on about the Newcomes, and that great ass, Barnes Newcome, gives himself his airs, I am ready to die of laughing. That time I went down to Newcome, I went to see old Aunt Sarah, and she told me everything, and showed me the room where my grandfather—you know; and do you know, I was a little hurt at first, for I thought we were swells till then. And when I came back to school, where, perhaps, I had been giving myself airs, and bragging about Newcome, why, you know, I thought it was right to tell the fellows."
>
> "That's a man," said the Colonel with delight; though, had he said, "That's a boy," he had spoken more correctly.

This is a very delicate touch, and shows the hand of a master. Mr Thackeray's young hero, who is so honest and truthful in his boyish days, does not degenerate as he grows a man.

Lord Kew, too, simple, noble, and manful, is a further

example of Mr Thackeray's most felicitous vein. These young men, who have no great intellectual elevation, and whose rank only makes them perfectly humble, unpretending, and free of all temptations to exaggerate themselves, seem characters on whom our author dwells *con amore*. Then there is the Vicomte de Florac, with his amusing French English, and his middle-aged princess, and that witch and malignant fairy, old Lady Kew, and Barnes Newcome the disagreeable, and the various family circles of this most respectable kindred, with all their nicely-touched gradations of character. There is no mist in this book; every one is an individual, pleasant or otherwise, and detaches himself or herself clearly from the background. The story is not in very good order, broken up as it is by retrospections and anticipations; and it is not good taste of Mr Pendennis to appear so frequently before the curtain, and remind us unpleasantly that it is fiction we are attending to, and not reality; but we think the great mass of his readers will bear us out in our opinion, that the *Newcomes* is not only the most agreeable story, but the cleverest book which Mr Thackeray has yet contributed for the amusement and edification of the admiring public.

When all this is said, there still remains a great deal to say which is less complimentary to our novelist. It is not, perhaps, the most agreeable information in the world to understand that our innocent schoolboys must plunge into a very equivocal abyss of "pleasure," before they can come forth purged and renovated like Lord Kew. We are not very glad to hear that somebody could make revelations to us of our brothers and sons and fathers, such as the Duchesse d'Ivry did to Miss Ethel Newcome. We cannot acknowledge that between the innocence of youth and the goodness of matured life, there lies a land of darkness through which every man must pass; nor do we perceive the advantage of convincing Mr Thackeray's youthful audience that this is a necessity. The religious circles of our community have of late very much devoted themselves to that class of "young men" for whom so many lectures, and sermons, and "means of improvement," are provided. We are not quite sure of the wisdom of thus making into a class the exuberant young life, which is, in fact, the world. When boys have ceased to be boys, they become human creatures of the highest order of existence. It is no compliment to their discernment to prepare for them mental food which is not suitable for their fathers or their teachers. They are men, with a larger inheritance of hope than their seniors; but their pride is not to be piqued into rebellion, by thrusting them into a half-way position between the man and the boy. But Mr Thackeray has a natural vocation in respect to his youthful countrymen. If he should happen, in fact, to be a grandfather, in disposition he is a young man continually—it is the life and pursuits of young men in which he is most skilled. Manliness, truthfulness, honour, and courage, are the qualities which he celebrates; and though Mr Thackeray is a favourite in countless households, it is not to be disputed that his stronghold is among those whose portraits he draws so truthfully, and whose life he describes with so much zest. Now here is scope and verge enough for any amount of genius; but surely it is not advisable that our teacher should lead his pupils to great harm on the way to great good. Is not that the loftiest purity which does not find it needful to fall?

We are afraid Mr Thackeray is beyond the reach of advice in respect to his female characters. Ethel is very attractive, very brilliant; but we would rather not have our daughters resemble this young lady, it must be confessed; and poor pretty Rosey, with all her goodness, is nobody, and Mr Thackeray intends that she should be so. If this is not good morals, it is still less

good art. Providence has exempted woman from the grosser temptations, and romance has gifted her with a more ethereal life. If we do not bid Mr Thackeray create a woman of the highest order, or if we are doubtful of his capacity for this delicate formation, we may still beg him to add a little common-sense to his feminine goodness. When these tender pretty fools are rational creatures, the world of Mr Thackeray's imagination will have a better atmosphere; for besides marrying, and contriving opportunities to give in marriage, besides the nursery and its necessities, there are certain uses for womankind in this world of ours, and we are not so rich in good influences as to forfeit any of them. A coronet is certainly not an idol the worship of which gives much elevation to the spirits of its adorers; but when Lord Kew is so little ostentatious of his decoration, why should Ethel, and her friends for her, compass heaven and earth to obtain such another? Does not Mr Thackeray think this is too hackneyed a subject for his fresh and unexhausted invention? Might not the next Ethel do something better by way of novelty, and leave this field to Mrs Gore and Mrs Trollope, and the host of lesser ladies who devote their talents to the noble art of making matches?

We are not sure how far the English language will be benefited by the dialogues of Mr Thackeray; they are very clever, very entertaining, and their slang is admirable; but it is very doubtful if it will be an advantage to make these Islands no better than a broad margin for the witticisms and the dialect of Cockaigne. Our light literature begins to have a great savour of the Cockney in it. Our noble ally on the other side of the Channel does not seem so much the better of making Paris France, that we should repeat the experiment. London is the greatest town in existence, but it is not England, though the dialect of its many vagabonds seems in a fair way for becoming the classic English of our generation. Mr Thackeray's narrative is so pure and vigorous in its language, and his colloquial freedoms are so lively and entertaining, that there are no real exceptions to be taken to him; but every Thackeray and every Dickens has a host of imitators, and it is not an agreeable prospect to contemplate the English of Shakespeare and Bacon overwhelmed with a flood of Cockneyisms—a consummation which seems to approach more nearly every day.

Mr Thackeray is no poet; for one of the highest of the poet's vocations, and perhaps the noblest work of which genius is capable, is to embody the purest ideal soul in the most life-like human garments; and this is an effort which our author has not yet attempted. Perhaps the title which Mr Thackeray would rather choose for himself would be that of an historian of human nature. In his sphere he is so eminently. Human nature in its company dress, and with all its foibles on, is the subject he delights to treat of; but Mr Thackeray is not great in home scenes, where the conventional dress is off, and the good that is in a man expands under the cheerful glow of the domestic fire. Mr Thackeray does not drape his hero in the purple, or make pictures of him as he walks loftily among suffering men; but takes him to pieces with wicked mirth, calling upon all men to laugh with him at the idol's demolition. We are no advocates for idol or for hero worship; but when we remember that there was once in this world a Man who was at once divine and human, whom we are all encouraged to make our example, and following whose wonderful footsteps some have attained to a life grander than that of common humanity, we feel that the highest ideal of the poets is but a fit and seemly acknowledgment of the excellence which has been made possible to our favoured race; and that the circle of life and manners is not complete, till we have admitted into it the loftiest as well as the lowest example of human existence—the saint no less than the sinner.

DAVID MASSON
From "Thackeray"
Macmillan's Magazine, February 1864, pp. 363–68

Thackeray's special place in British literature is that of a star of the first magnitude, but of a colour and mode of brilliancy peculiarly its own, in the composite cluster known as our Novelists, our Humourists, our Imaginative Prose-writers. As this is, however, a very numerous cluster, including writers of all degrees of importance, from the smallest up to some so great that we rank them among the chiefs of our total literature, and are not afraid to cite them as our British equivalents to such names of a larger world as Cervantes, Rabelais, and Jean Paul, so there are many ways in which, on our examining the cluster, it will resolve itself into groups. More especially, there is one way of looking at this large order of writers, according to which they shall seem to part, not so much into groups as into two great divisions, each including names of all degrees of magnitude. Now, although, if we view the cluster entire, without seeking to resolve it at all, Thackeray will strike us simply by his superior magnitude, and although, on the other hand, however minutely we may analyse the cluster, we shall find none precisely like Thackeray, and he will continue to strike us still by his intense peculiarity of hue, yet, if we do persuade ourselves to attend to such a general subdivision of the cluster into two main classes as has been hinted at, Thackeray will then, on the whole, seem to range himself rather with one of the classes than with the other.

While all writers of fiction make it their business to invent stories, and by the presentation of imaginary scenes, imaginary actions, and imaginary characters, to impart to the minds of their fellows a more prompt, rousing, and impassioned kind of pleasure than attends the reading either of speculative disquisitions or of laborious reproductions of real history, and while most of them, in doing so, strew a thousand incidental opinions and fancies by the way, and deviate into delightful and humorous whimsies, a considerable number of such writers are found to differ from the rest in respect of the constant presence in their fictions of a certain heart of doctrine, the constant ruling of their imaginations by a personal philosophy or mode of thinking. It is not always in the fictions of those novelists respecting whom we may know independently that they were themselves men of substantial and distinct moral configuration, of decided ways of thinking and acting, that we find this characteristic. Scott is an instance. He was a man of very solid and distinct personality; and yet, at the outset of his fictions, we see him always, as it were, putting on a dreaming-cap, which transports him away into realms far removed from his own personal position and experience, and from the direct operation of his own moralities. And so with others. When they begin to invent, they put on the dreaming-cap; and many cases might be cited in which this extraordinary power of the dreaming-cap might appear to have been all that the writers possessed—in which, apart from it, they might seem to have had no substantial personality at all. Whether Shakespeare, the greatest genius of the dreaming-cap that ever lived, had any coequal personality himself, of the features of which a glimpse is now recoverable, is, as all know, one of the vexed questions of literary history. We have an opinion of our own on this matter. In every case,

we hold, there is an unseverable relation between the personality and the poetic genius, between what a man is and what he can imagine. Dreams themselves are fantastic constructions out of the *débris* of all the sensations, thoughts, feelings, and experiences, remembered or not remembered, of the waking-life; all that any power of the dreaming-cap, however extraordinary, can do, is to remove one into remoter wastes of the great plain of forgetfulness whereon this *débris* lies shimmering, and to release one more and more from the rule of the waking will or the waking reason in the fantasies that rise from it, and flit and melt into each other. Yet, just as some dreams are closer in their resemblance to waking tissues of thought, and more regulated by the logic of waking reason, than others, so, though in all cases the imaginations of a writer, the creations of his literary genius, are related by absolute necessity to his personal individuality, there are many cases in which the relation is so much more subtle and occult than in others, that we find it convenient in these cases to suppose it non-existing, and to think of the imagination as a kind of special white-winged faculty that can float off at any moment from its poise on the personality, move to any distance whithersoever it listeth, and return again at its own sweet will. Hence, for example, among our writers of prose-fiction, we distinguish such a writer as Scott from such a writer as Swift. The connexion, in Swift's case, between his fictions and his personal philosophy and mode of thought is direct and obvious. In his inventions and fancies he does not move away from himself; he remains where he is, in his fixed and awful habit of mind—expressing that habit or its successive moods in constructions fantastic in form, but of regulated and calculated meaning, and capable at once of exact interpretation. Even his Islands of Lilliput and Brobdingnag, his Laputa, and his country of the Houynhmns and Yahoos, are not so much visions into which he has been carried by any power of the dreaming-cap, as fell Swiftian allegories of the stationary intellect. And, though Swift is almost unique among British writers in respect of the degree to which he thus made imagination a kind of architect-contractor for fixed moods of the reason, he may yet stand as, in this respect, an exaggerated exemplar of a whole class of our writers of fiction. In other words, as has been already said, there is a class of our writers of prose-fiction, including writers of as great total power as are to be found in the class that arrive at their fancies by means of the dreaming-cap, but differing from that class by the presence in their fictions of a more constant element of doctrine, a more distinct vein of personal philosophy.

Thackeray was, on the whole, of the latter class. That he may be considered as belonging to it is one reason the more for maintaining its co-ordinate importance with the other class, and for not giving that other class, as has sometimes been proposed, a theoretical superiority as being more entitled, in virtue of their power with the dreaming-cap, to the high designation of creative or imaginative writers. One reason the more, we say—for might it not have been recollected that even Goethe, whose range of dream was as wide as that of most men, made his imagination but a kind of architect-contractor for his reason in his great prose-novel, and that, if we rank among our highest British artists a Sir Joshua Reynolds, we do not put our Hogarth beneath him? A creative writer! Who shall say that Thackeray did not give us creations? What reader of these pages, at all events, will say it, after his memory has been refreshed by our contributor with those recollections of a few of the wondrous creations that took flight from the single novel of *Vanity Fair* into that vast population of ideal beings of diverse characters and physiognomies with which the genius of imaginative writers has filled the ether of the real world? Nay, on the question whether Thackeray *should* be so decidedly attached to the class of writers of fiction with which at first sight we associate him, there may be some preliminary hesitation. In his smaller pieces, for example—some of his odd whims and absurdities in prose and verse—did he not break away into a riot of humour, a lawlessness of sheer zanyism, as exquisitely suggestive of genius making faces at its keeper as anything we have seen since Shakespeare's clowns walked the earth and sang those jumbled shreds of sense and nonsense which we love now as so keenly Shakespearian, and would not lose for the world? The dreaming-cap!—why, here we have the dreaming-cap, and bells attached to it. He moves to any distance out of sight, and still, by the tinkle, we can follow him and hear "the fool i' the forest." We are not sure but that in some of these small grotesques of Thackeray we have relics of a wilder variety of pure genius than in his more elaborate fictions. But, again, even in some of these larger and more continuous constructions of his genius in fiction, we have examples of a power which he possessed of going out of himself, and away from the habits and humours of his own time and circumstances, into tracts where the mere act of producing facsimiles or verisimilitudes of what he had directly seen and known was not sufficient, and he had to move with the stealthy step of a necromancer, recalling visions of a vanished life. When we think, for instance, of his *Esmond*, and of passages in his other novels where he gives play to his imagination in the historic, and assumes so easily a certain quaintness of conception and of phraseology to correspond, we seem even to catch a glimpse of what that marvellous dreaming-power of the so-called creative writers may after all in part consist in—to wit, a wide range of really historic interest in their own waking persons, and a habit of following out their trains of historic speculation and enthusiasm, rather than their passing observations and experiences, in their dreams. Thackeray, at all events, had a remarkable historic faculty within a certain range of time, which it was perhaps owing to the more paying nature of fiction than of history in these days that he did not more expressly use and develop. The Life of Talleyrand, which he once had in contemplation, before the days of his universal celebrity as a novelist, would have been, if done as Thackeray could have done it, a masterpiece of peculiar eighteenth-nineteenth-century biography. Nor is the story, jocularly spread by himself some years ago, that he meant to continue Macaulay's unfinished *History of England*, taking it up at the reign of Queen Anne, without a certain significance. One of the many distinctions among men is as to the portion of the past by which their imaginations are most fondly fascinated and with which they feel themselves most competent to deal in recollection. Macaulay's real and native historic range began where he began his History—in the interval between the Civil Wars and the Revolution of 1688. Thackeray's began a little later—at the date of Queen Anne's accession, and the opening of the eighteenth century. And, as within this range he would have been a good and shrewd historian, so within this range his imagination moves easily and gracefully in fiction. A man of the era of the later Georges by his birth and youth, and wholly of the Victorian era by his maturity and literary activity, he can go as far back as to Queen Anne's reign by that kind of imaginative second-sight which depends on delight in transmitted reminiscence.

As a Victorian, however, taking for the matter of most of his fictions life as he saw it around him, or as he could recollect it during his own much-experienced and variously-travelled career from his childhood upwards, Thackeray *was* one of those novelists whose writings are distinguished by a constant heart of doctrine, a permanent vein of personal philosophy. Our long and now hackneyed talk about him as a Realist, and our habit of contrasting him perpetually with Dickens, as more a novelist of the Fantastic or Romantic School, are recognitions of this. It would ill become us here and now to resort again to the full pedantry of this contrast; but, in a certain sense, as none knew better than Thackeray himself, there *was* a kind of polar opposition between his method and Dickens's in their art as humourists and writers of fiction. With extraordinary keenness of perception, with the eye of a lynx for the facts, physiognomies, and humours of real life, and taking the suggestions of real life with marvellous aptness for his hints, Dickens does move away with these suggestions into a kind of vacant ground of pure fancy, where the relations and the mode of exhibition may be ideal, and there shapes such tales of wonder and drollery, and holds such masques and revels of imaginary beings, as (witness how we use them, and how our talk and our current literature are enriched by references to them) no genius but his has produced in our day. In him we do see, after a fashion entirely his own, that particular kind of power which we have called the power of the dreaming-cap, and which is oftenest named ideality. Thackeray, on the other hand, is sternly, ruthlessly real. Men and women as they are, and the relations of life as he has actually seen and known them, or in as near approach to facsimile of reality as the conditions of invention of stories for general reading will permit—these are what Thackeray insists on giving us. Fortunate age to have had two such representatives of styles of art the co-existence of which—let us not call it mutual opposition—is everlastingly possible and everlastingly desirable! Fortunate still in having the one master-artist left; unfortunate now, as we all feel—and that artist more than most of us—in having lost the other! For in Thackeray we have lost not only our great master of reality in the matter of prose-fiction, but also the spokesman of a strong personal philosophy, a bracing personal mode of thought, which pervaded all he wrote. Thackeray, it has been well said, is best thought of, in some respects, as a sage, a man of experienced wisdom, and a conclusive grasp of the world and its worth, expressing himself, partly by accident, through the particular modes of story-writing and humorous extravaganza. And what was his philosophy? To tell that wholly, to throw into systematic phrase one tithe even of the characteristic and recurring trains of thought that passed through that grave brain, is what no man can hope to do. But the essential philosophy of any mind is often a thing of few and simple words, repeating a form of thought that it requires no elaborate array of propositions to express, and that may have been as familiar to an ancient Chaldæan making his camel's neck his pillow in the desert as it is to a sage in modern London. It is that elementary mode of thought which comes and goes oftenest, and into which one always sinks when one is meditative and alone. And so may we not recognise Thackeray's habitual philosophy in a peculiar variation of these words of the Laureate, which he makes to be spoken by the hero of his "Maud"?—

We are puppets, Man in his pride, and Beauty fair in
    her flower:
Do we move ourselves, or are moved by an unseen
    hand at a game
That pushes us off the board, and others ever
    succeed?
Ah yet, we cannot be kind to each other here for an
    hour;

We whisper, and hint, and chuckle, and grin at a
brother's shame;
However we brave it out, we men are a little breed.

A monstrous eft was of old the Lord and Master of
Earth;
For him did his high sun flame, and his river
billowing ran,
And he felt himself in his force to be Nature's
crowning race.
As nine months go to the shaping an infant ripe for
his birth,
So many a million of ages have gone to the making
of man:
He now is the first, but is he the last? is he not too
base?

The man of science himself is fonder of glory, and
vain,
An eye well-practised in nature, a spirit bounded and
poor;
The passionate heart of the poet is whirled into folly
and vice.
I would not marvel at either, but keep a temperate
brain;
For not to desire or admire, if a man could learn it
were more
Than to walk all day like the sultan of old in a garden
of spice.

Such, in some form, though not, perhaps, precisely in this
high-rolled and semi-geologic form, was Thackeray's philosophy, breathed through his writings. That we are a little breed—
poets, philosophers, and all of us—that is what he told us.
Nature's crowning race?—Oh no; too base for that! Many
stages beyond the Eft, certainly; but far yet from even the ideal
of our own talk and our pretensions to each other. And so he
lashed us, and dissected us, and tore off our disguises. He did
it in great matters and he did it in small matters; and, that he
might draw a distinction between the great matters and the
small matters, he generalised the smaller kinds of baseness and
littleness of our time, against which he most persistently
directed his satires, under the mock-heroic title of Snobbism.
Anti-Snobbism was his doctrine as applied to many particulars
of our own and of recent times—Victorian or Georgian. But he
took a wider range than that, and laid bare the deeper black-
nesses and hypocrisies of our fairly-seeming lives. And we
called him a cynic in revenge. A cynic! No more will that word
be heard about Thackeray. How, in these few weeks since he
was laid in Kensal Green, have his secret deeds of goodness,
the instances of his incessant benevolence and kindheartedness
to all around him, leapt into regretful light. A cynic! We might
have known, while we used it, that the word was false. Had he
not an eye for the piety and the magnanimity of real human
life, its actually attained and incalculable superiorities over the
Eft; and did he not exult, to the verge of the sentimental, in
reproductions of these in the midst of his descriptions of
meannesses? And did he not always, at least, include himself
for better or for worse in that breed of men of which the
judgment must be so mixed? Not to desire or admire, but to
walk all day like a sultan in his garden, was a dignity of
isolation to which he had never attained. He did not hold
himself aloof. Ah! how he came among us here in London,
simply, quietly, grandly, the large-framed, massive-headed,
and grey-haired sage that he was—comporting himself as one
of us, though he was weightier than all of us; listening to our
many-voiced clamour, and dropping in his wise occasional

word; nay, not forbidding, but rather joining with a smile, if,
in hilarity, we raised his own song of evening festivity:—

Here let us sport,
Boys as we sit,
Laughter and wit
Flashing so free:
Life is but short;
When we are gone,
Let them sing on
Round the old tree.

Ah! the old tree remains, and the surviving company still sits
round it, and they will raise the song in the coming evenings as
in the evenings gone by. But the chair of the sage is vacant. It
will be long before London, or the nation, or our literature,
shall see a substitute for the noble Thackeray.

HENRY D. SEDGWICK, JR.
From "Some Aspects of Thackeray"
Atlantic, November 1898, pp. 707–19

I

Twenty years ago, at Harvard College, in the rooms of all
students of certain social pretensions who affected books,
you were sure to see on the most conspicuous shelf, in green
and gold or in half calf, the works of William Makepeace
Thackeray. The name, boldly printed, greeted you as you
entered the door, and served, together with sundry red-sealed
certificates and beribboned silver medals, to inform you of the
general respectability and gentility of your host. Of a Sunday
morning, this student was likely to be discovered complacent
over the *Book of Snobs* or serious over *Vanity Fair*.

Public opinion went that Thackeray was the novelist of
gentlemen and for gentlemen; that Dickens was undoubtedly
strong, but he had not had the privilege of knowing and of
delineating the things which were adapted to interest the most
select of Harvard undergraduates. In every fold there are some
to lower the general standard of critical excellence; there were
some partisans of Dickens. They were judged, as minorities
are, found guilty of running counter to accepted opinions, and
outlawed from further literary criticism.

These Harvard critics did not make for themselves this
opinion of Thackeray; they brought it with them from home.

We suppose that parents, what time their son started in the
world on the first path which diverged from theirs, deemed that
they were equipping him with the best master to teach him
concerning the ways of that world. Theirs was the old lack of
faith, so common to the fearful; they sought to guard their son
from the world by pointing out to him its vanity, its folly, its
emptiness. "Oh, if he shall only know what the world is," they
thought, "he will escape its evils to come." So they gave him
Thackeray, and wrote him long letters on idleness and vice.
His bookshelves and his inner pockets thus encumbered, the
youth found Harvard College a miniature of the world of
which he had been warned. There were materials enough for
such a conclusion. A seeker will find what he goes forth to
seek. The youth learned his Thackeray well, spent four years
enjoying his little *Vanity Fair*, and then departed from
Cambridge to help build up the larger world of Vanity which
shows so fine in America to-day.

There is no phenomenon so interesting as the unconscious labor of boys and men over the task of shaping, hewing,
whittling, and moulding the world into accord with their
anticipations. All lend helping hands to the great master

implement, public expectation. A young fellow goes to college, and joins a group of a dozen others. Brown, the rake, thinks, "Here's a Lothario who will sup at Dame Quickly's with me;" Smith, the boxer, says, "A quick eye,—I'll make a boxer of him;" Jones, who translates Homer for the group, sees rhythm and Theocritus in the newcomer's curly hair; Robinson, the philosopher, feels a fellow Hegelian. These rival expectations leap out to meet the stranger; they struggle among themselves. Of the students, some agree with Brown, some with Smith, others with Robinson or Jones. The sturdiest of these expectations chokes out the others and survives. After a short time— our young fellow yet entirely undiscovered—a strong current of unanimous expectation has decided that he shall be a boxer. All obstacles to the execution of this judgment are taken away, and moral earthworks are quickly thrown up, guarding him from Brown, Jones, and Robinson. Expectation seats him beside Smith; expectation turns the conversation upon champions of the ring; expectation draws the gloves upon his fists; it offers him no Eastcheap, no Theocritus, no Hegel. The youth takes boxing lessons; soon he learns the language of the fraternity; he walks, runs, avoids mince pies, eschews books, and with a single eye looks forward to a bout in Hemenway Gymnasium. Thus the tricksy spirit expectation shapes the destinies of common humankind. Thus do parents begin to expect that their son will see the world with their own and Thackeray's beam-troubled eyes; they insist that he shall, and in due time he does.

Once convince a young man that Thackeray's world is the real world, that vulgarity, meanness, trickery, and fraud abound, and you put him in a yoke from which he shall never free himself. This is the yoke of base expectation. This is what is known in Scripture as "the world;" it is the habit of screwing up the eyes and squinting in order to see unworthiness, baseness, vice, and wickedness; it is a creeping blindness to nobler things. The weapon against the world is, as of old, to use a word of great associations, faith. Faith is nothing but noble expectation, and all education should be to supplant base expectation by noble expectation. What is the human world in which we live but a mighty mass of sensitive matter, highly susceptible to the great force of human expectation, which flows about it like an ever shifting Gulf Stream, now warming and prospering noble people, and then wantonly comforting the unworthy?

Feeble folk that we are, we have in this power of creation an element of divinity in us. Our expectations hover about like life-giving agencies. We are conscious that our hopes and our fears are at work all the time helping the oncoming of that which we hope or fear. The future is like a newborn babe stretching out its arms to the stronger. It may be that this power in us is weak, intermittent, often pitiably feeble; but now and again comes a man with a larger measure of divine life, and his great expectations pass into deeds. Before every Trafalgar first comes an expectation that duty will be done.

Thackeray has no faith; he does not entertain high expectations. His characters do shameless things, and Thackeray says to the reader, "Be not surprised, injured-seeming friend; you would have done the like under the like temptation." At first you contradict, you resent; but little by little Thackeray's opinion of you inoculates you; the virus takes; you lose your conviction that you would have acted differently; you concede that such conduct was not impossible, even for you,—no, nor improbable,— and, on the whole, after reflection, that the conduct was excusable, was good enough, was justified, was inevitable, was right, was scrupulously right, and only a Don Quixote would have acted otherwise.

Nothing sickens and dies so quickly as noble expectation. Luxury, comfort, custom, the ennui of hourly exertion, the dint of disappointment, assail it unceasingly: if a man of ten talents, like Thackeray, joins the assailants, is it not just that admiration of him should be confined to those who are willing to admire talents, irrespective of the use to which they are put?

II

⟨. . .⟩ Thackeray was bred when Englishmen were forsaking "swords for ledgers," and deserting "the student's bower for gold." His father died when he was very young. His mother married for her second husband an Indian officer, and Thackeray was sent to school in England.

In a new biographical edition of Thackeray's works which Messrs. Harper & Brothers are publishing, Mrs. Ritchie has written brief memories of her father at the beginning of each volume, with special relation to its contents. These memories are done with filial affection. Thackeray's kindness, his tenderness, his sympathetic nature, are written large on every page. He has many virtues. He dislikes vice, drunkenness, betrayal of women, pettifogging, huckstering, lying, cheating, knavery, the annoyance and tomfoolery of social distinctions. He would like to leave the world better than he found it, but he cannot see. Pettiness, the vulgarity of money, the admiration of mean things, hang before him like a curtain at the theatre. Romeo may be on fire, Hotspur leap for the moon, Othello stab Iago, Lear die in Cordelia's lap; but the sixteenth of an inch of frieze and fustian keeps it all from him.

At nineteen Thackeray spent a winter at Weimar. He soon writes to his mother of Goethe as "the great lion of Weimar." He is not eager to possess the great measures of life. He is not sensitive to Goethe, but to the court of Pumpernickel. He wishes he were a cornet in Sir John Kennaway's yeomanry, that he might wear the yeoman's dress. "A yeomanry dress is always a handsome and respectable one."

In 1838, when in Paris, he writes: "I have just come from seeing *Marion Delorme*, the tragedy of Victor Hugo, and am so sickened and disgusted with the horrid piece that I have hardly heart to write." He did not look through pain and extravagance into the noble passion of the play. He lived in a moral Pumpernickel where the ideal is kept outside the town gates.

Pumpernickel was his home, and he has depicted it in *Vanity Fair*. This book reflects Thackeray's intellectual image in his prime; it is his first great novel, and is filled with the most vivid and enduring of his beliefs and convictions. There are in it a vigor, an independence, and a sense of power that come when a man faces his best opportunity. Into it Thackeray has put what he deemed the truest experiences of his life. He has also written two long sequels to it. *The Newcomes* is the story of his stepfather, Major Carmichael-Smyth in *Vanity Fair*; *Pendennis*, that of Thackeray himself and his mother wandering in its outskirts. There is this one family of nice people, gathered into an ark as it were, floating over the muddy waters. Thackeray was able to see that his immediate family were not rogues; he was also able to draw a most noble gentleman, Henry Esmond, by the help of the idealizing lens of a hundred odd years; but the world he thought he saw about him is the world of *Vanity Fair*.

Thackeray had so many fine qualities that one cannot but feel badly to see him in such a place. Had his virtues—his kindness, his tenderness, his charm, his capacity for affection—been energetic enough to dominate his entire character, he would have lived among far different scenes; his readers would have beheld him potting flowers by some vinecovered house in a village where neighbors were simple, honest, and true,—where round the corner stood a Mermaid Tavern, to which poets and far-voyaging sailors would come, full of stories about a glorious world. Who would not have liked to sit by Thackeray's hearth in such a home, a fire warming his kindly feet, his good cheroot gayly burning, a mug at his elbow, and he reading his last manuscript? Was it Thackeray's fault that this was not to be? Or did he suffer the incidental misfortunes which large causes bring to individuals as they follow their own regardless paths?

III

Thackeray is the poet of respectability. His working time stretches from the Reform Act almost to the death of Lord Palmerston. He chronicles the contemporary life of a rich, money-getting generation of merchants and manufacturers, lifted into sudden importance in the national life by steamboats and railroads, by machinery for spinning, weaving, mining, by Arkwright, Watt, Davy, and Stephenson. His is a positive, matter-of-fact world, of which Peel is the statesman and Macaulay the man of letters. Macaulay, in his essay on Bacon, has given us the measure of its spiritual elevation: "We have sometimes thought that an amusing fiction might be written, in which a disciple of Epictetus and a disciple of Bacon should be introduced as fellow travelers. They come to a village where the smallpox has just begun to rage, and find houses shut-up, intercourse suspended, the sick abandoned, mothers weeping in terror over their children. The Stoic assures the dismayed population that there is nothing bad in the smallpox; and that, to a wise man, disease, deformity, death, the loss of friends, are not evils. The Baconian takes out a lancet and begins to vaccinate. They find a body of miners in great dismay. An explosion of noisome vapors has just killed many of those who were at work; and the survivors are afraid to venture into the cavern. The Stoic assures them that such an accident is nothing but a mere ἀποπροήγμενον. The Baconian, who has no such fine word at his command, contents himself with devising a safety-lamp. They find a shipwrecked merchant wringing his hands on the shore. His vessel, with an inestimable cargo, has just gone down, and he is reduced in a moment from opulence to beggary. The Stoic exhorts him not to seek happiness in things which lie without himself; the Baconian constructs a diving-bell. It would be easy to multiply illustrations of the difference between the philosophy of thorns and the philosophy of fruit, the philosophy of words and the philosophy of works." This is the very nobility of machinery. As we read, we listen to the buzz and whir of wheels, the drip of oil-cans, the creaking and straining of muscle and steel. Such things serve, no doubt, in default of other agencies, to create a great empire, but the England of Thackeray's day was a *nouveau riche*, self-made, proud of its lack of occupation other than money-getting. Thackeray was fallen upon evil times. He was born into this moral estate of Pumpernickel, and he has described it with the vividness and vigor of complete comprehension. He has immense cleverness. He knows whereof he talks. Never has a period had so accomplished an historian. The *bourgeoisie* have their epic in *Vanity Fair*.

During the formative period of Thackeray's life the English nation was passing under the influence of machinery. There was the opportunity of a great man of letters, such as Thackeray, to look to it that literature should respond to the stimulus of added power, and grow so potent that it would determine what direction the national life should take. At such a time of national expansion, literature should have seen England in the flush of coming greatness; it should have roused itself to re-create her in nobler imagination, and have spent itself in making her accept this estimate and expectation, and become an England dominating material advantages and leading the world.

The interest in life is this potentiality and malleability. The alloted task of men and women is to take this potentiality and shape it. Men who have strong intelligence and quick perceptions, like Thackeray, accomplish a great deal in the way of giving a definite form to the material with which life furnishes us. What Michelangelo says of marble is true of life:—

> Non ha l'ottimo artista alcun concetto
> Ch'un marmo solo in se non circoscriva
> Col suo soverchio.

The problem of life is to uncover the figures hiding in this material: shall it be Caliban, Circe, Philip Sidney, Jeanne d'Arc? Thackeray, with what Mrs. Ritchie calls "his great deal of common sense," saw Major Pendennis and Becky Sharp; and he gave more effective cuttings and chiselings and form to the potential life of England than any other man of his time.

The common apology for such a novelist is that he describes what he sees. This is the worst with which we charge him. We charge Thackeray with seeing what he describes; and what justification has a man, in a world like this, to spend his time looking at Barnes Newcome and Sir Pitt Crawley? Thackeray takes the motes and beams floating in his mind's eye for men and women, writes about them, and calls his tale a history.

Thackeray wrote, on finishing *Vanity Fair*, that all the characters were odious except Dobbin. Poor Thackeray, what a world to see all about him, with his tender, affectionate nature! Even Colonel Newcome is so crowded round by a mob of rascally fellows that it is hard to do justice to Thackeray's noblest attempt to be a poet. But why see a world, and train children to see a world, where

> The great man is a vulgar clown?

A world with such an unreal standard must be an unreal world. In the real world vulgar clowns are not great men. Thackeray sees a world all topsy-turvy, and it does not occur to him that he, and not the world, is at fault. This is the curse of faithlessness. He himself says, "The world is a looking-glass, and gives back to every man the reflection of his own face."

Thackeray has been praised as a master of reality. As reality is beyond our ken, the phrase is unfortunate; but the significance of it is that if a man will portray to the mob the world with which the mob is familiar, they will huzza themselves hoarse. Has not the Parisian mob shouted for Zola? Do not the Madrileños cheer Valdés? Do not Ouida and the pale youth of Rome and Paris holla, "d'Annunzio! d'Annunzio!" There is no glory here. The poet, not in fine frenzy, but in sober simplicity, tells the mob, not what they see, but what they cannot of themselves perceive, with such a tone of authority that they stand gaping and likewise see.

Thackeray's love of reality was merely an embodiment of the popular feeling which proposed to be direct, business-like, and not to tolerate any nonsense. People felt that a money-getting country must take itself seriously. The Reform Act had brought political control to the bourgeoisie, men of common sense; no ranters, no will-o'-the-wisp chasers, but "burgomasters and great oneyers,"—men who thought very highly of circumstances under which they were prosperous, and asked for no more beautiful sight than their own virtues. Influenced by the sympathetic touch of this atmosphere, novel-readers found their former favorites old-fashioned. Disraeli, Samuel Warren, Bulwer Lytton, G. P. R. James, seemed false, theatrical, and sentimental. Thackeray was of this opinion, and he studied the art of caricature as the surest means of saving himself from any such fantastic nonsense. He approached life as a city man,—one who was convinced that the factories of London, not the theories of the philosopher, were the real motive force underneath all the busy flow of outward life. He found his talents exactly suited to this point of view. His memory was an enormous wallet, into which his hundred-handed observation was day and night tossing scraps and bits of daily experience. He saw the meetings of men as he passed: lords, merchants, tinsmiths, guardsmen, tailors, cooks, valets, nurses, policemen, boys, applewomen,—everybody whom you meet of a morning between your house and your office in the city. He remarked the gestures, he heard the words, he guessed what had gone before, he divined what would happen thereafter: and each sight, sound, guess, and divination was safely stowed away in his marvelous wallet. England of the forties, as Thackeray saw it, is in *Vanity Fair*, *Pendennis*, and *The Newcomes*. "I ask you to believe," he says in the preface to *Pendennis*, "that this person writing strives to tell the truth."

Where lies the truth? Are men merely outward parts of machinery, exposed to view, while down below in the engine-room steam and electricity determine their movements? Or do men live and carry on their daily routine under the influence of some great thought of which they are half unconscious, but by which they are shaped, moulded, and moved? A French poet says:—

Le vrai Dieu, le Dieu fort, est le Dieu des idées.

But Macaulay says that the philosophy of Plato began with words and ended with words; that an acre in Middlesex is better than a principality in Utopia. The British public applauded Macaulay, and young Thackeray took the hint.

IV

Nobody can question Thackeray's style. His fame is proof of its excellence. Even if a man will flatter the mob by saying that he sees what they see, he cannot succeed without skill of expression. Readers are slow to understand. They need grace, pithy sentences, witty turns of phrase, calculated sweep of periods and paragraphs. They must have no labor of attention; the right adjective alone will catch their eyes; they require their pages plain, clear, perspicuous. In all these qualities Thackeray is very nearly perfect. Hardly anybody would say that there is a novel better written than *Vanity Fair*. The story runs as easily as the hours. Chapter after chapter in the best prose carries the reader comfortably on. Probably this excellence is due to Thackeray's great powers of observation. His eyes saw everything, saving for the blindness of his inward eye, and his memory held it. He was exceedingly sensitive. Page after page is filled with the vividness of well-chosen detail. He cultivated the art of writing most assiduously. From 1830 to 1847, when *Vanity Fair*, the first of his great novels, was published, he was writing all the time, and for almost all of that time as a humorist, drawing caricatures,—a kind of writing perhaps better adapted than any other to cultivate the power of portraying scenes. The caricaturist is restricted to a few lines; his task does not allow him to fill in, to amplify; he must say his say in little. The success of wit is the arrangement of a dozen words. This training for sixteen continuous years taught Thackeray a style which, for his subjects, has no equal in English literature.

To-day we greatly admire Stevenson and Kipling. We applaud Stevenson's style for its cultivation and its charm; we heap praises upon Kipling's for its dash, vigor, and accuracy of detail. All these praises are deserved; but when we take up

Thackeray again, we find pages and pages written in a style more cultivated than Stevenson's and equally charming, and with a dash, vigor, and nicety of detail that Kipling might envy. Descriptions that would constitute the bulk of an essay for the one, or of a story for the other, do hasty service as prologues to Thackeray's chapters. Conversations of a happy theatrical turn, with enough exaggeration to appear wholly natural, which Stevenson and Kipling never rivaled, come crowding together in his long novels.

There are two famous scenes which are good examples of Thackeray's power,—one of his sentiment, one of his humor. The first is Colonel Newcome's death in the Charterhouse. The second is the first scene between Pendennis and the Fotheringay. "Pen tried to engage her in conversation about poetry and about her profession. He asked her what she thought of Ophelia's madness, and whether she was in love with Hamlet or not. 'In love with such a little ojus wretch as that stunted manager of a Bingley?' She bristled with indignation at the thought. Pen explained it was not of her he spoke, but of Ophelia of the play. 'Oh, indeed; if no offense was meant, none was taken: but as for Bingley, indeed, she did not value him,—not that glass of punch.' Pen next tried her on Kotzebue. 'Kotzebue? Who was he?' 'The author of the play in which she had been performing so admirably.' 'She did not know that—the man's name at the beginning of the book was Thompson,' she said. Pen laughed at her adorable simplicity. He told her of the melancholy fate of the author of the play, and how Sand had killed him. . . . 'How beautiful she is!' thought Pen, cantering homewards. 'How simple and how tender! How charming it is to see a woman of her genius busying herself with the humble offices of domestic life, cooking dishes to make her old father comfortable, and brewing him drink! How rude it was of me to begin to talk about professional matters, and how well she turned the conversation! . . . Pendennis, Pendennis,—how she spoke the word! Emily, Emily! how good, how noble, how beautiful, how perfect, she is!'"

This scene is very close upon farce, and it is in that borderland that Thackeray's extraordinary skill shows itself most conspicuous. Difficult, however, as it must be to be a master there,—and the fact that Thackeray has no rival in this respect proves it,—it is easy work compared to drawing a scene of real love, of passion. Perhaps some actions of Lady Castlewood are Thackeray's only attempt thereat. The world of passion is not his world. His ear is not attuned to

Das tiefe, schmerzenvolle Glück
Des Hasses Kraft, die Macht der Liebe.

Charlotte Brontë, Tourgenef, Hawthorne, Hugo, Balzac, all excel him. Thackeray hears the click of custom against custom, the throb of habit, the tick-tick of vulgar life, all the sounds of English social machinery. The different degrees of social efficiency and inefficiency rivet his attention. What interests him is the relation that Henry Foker or Blanche Amory bears to the standard of social excellence accepted by commercial England in the forties. He is never—at least as an artist—disturbed by any scheme of metaphysics. His English common sense is never lured afield by any speculations about the value of a human being uncolored by the shadows of time and space. He is never troubled by doubts of standards, by skepticism as to uses, ends, purposes; he has a hard-and-fast British standard. He draws Colonel Newcome as an object of pity; he surrounds him with tenderness and sympathy. Here is Thackeray at his highest. But he never suggests to the reader that Colonel Newcome is not a man to be pitied, but to be envied; not a failure, but a success; not unhappy, but most fortunate. The great poets of the world have turned the malefactor's cross into the symbol of holiness. Thackeray never departs from the British middle class conceptions of triumph and failure. In all his numerous dissertations and asides to the reader, he wrote like the stalwart Briton he was, good, generous, moral, domestic, stern, and tender. You never forget his Puritan ancestry, you can rely upon his honesty; but he is not pure-minded or humble. He dislikes wrong, but he never has a high enough conception of right to hate wrong. His view is that it is a matter to be cured by policemen, propriety, and satire.

Satire is the weapon of the man at odds with the world and at ease with himself. The dissatisfied man—a Juvenal, a Swift, a youthful Thackeray—belabors the world with vociferous indignation; like the wind on the traveler's back, the beating makes him hug his cloaking sins the tighter. Wrong runs no danger from such chastisement. The fight against wrong is made by the man discontented with himself and careless of the world. Satire is harmless as a moral weapon. It is an old-fashioned fowling piece, fit for a man of wit, intelligence, and a certain limited imagination. It runs no risk of having no quarry; the world to it is one vast covert of lawful game. It goes a-traveling with wit, because both are in search of the unworthy. It is well suited to a brilliant style. It is also a conventional department in literature, and as such is demanded by publishers and accepted by the public.

Thackeray was born with dexterity of observation, nimbleness of wit, and a quick sense of the incongruous and the grotesque. He lost his fortune when a young man. He wrote for a livelihood, and naturally turned to that branch of literature which was best suited to his talents. It was his misfortune that satire is bad for a man's moral development. It intensified his natural disbelief in the worth of humanity, but gave him the schooling that enabled him to use his powers so brilliantly.

Thackeray was often hampered by this habit of looking at the grotesque side of things. It continually dragged him into farce, causing feebleness of effect where there should have been power. Sir Pitt Crawley, Jos Sedley, the struggle over Miss Crawley, Harry Foker, the Chevalier de Florac, Aunt Hoggerty, are all in the realm of farce. This is due partly to Thackeray's training, and partly to his attitude toward life. If life consists of money, clothes, and a bundle of social relations, our daily gravity, determination, and vigor are farcical, because they are so out of place; they are as incongruous as a fish in trousers. But Thackeray forgets that there is something disagreeable in this farce, as there would be in looking into Circe's sty and seeing men groveling over broken meats. To be sure, Thackeray makes believe that he finds it comic to see creatures of great pretensions busy themselves so continually with the pettiest things. But it too often seems as if the comic element consisted in our human pretensions, and as if Thackeray merely kept bringing them to the reader's notice for the sake of heightening the contrast between men and their doings.

V

Thackeray is not an innovator; he follows the traditions of English literature. He is in direct descent from the men of the *Spectator*, Addison, Steele, and their friends, and from Fielding. He has far greater powers of observation, wit, humor, sentiment, and description than the Spectator group. He excels Fielding in everything except as a story-teller, and in a kind of intellectual power that is more easily discerned in Fielding than described,—a kind of imperious understanding that breaks down a path before it, whereas Thackeray's intelligence looks in at a window or peeps through the keyhole. Fielding is

the bigger, coarser man of the two; Thackeray is the cleverer. Each is thoroughly English. Fielding embodies the England of George I.; Thackeray, that same England refined by the revolutionary ideas of 1789, trained by long wars, then materialized by machinery, by a successful bourgeoisie and the quick accession of wealth. Each is a good fellow,—quick in receiving ideas, but slow to learn a new point of view. Fielding is inferior to Thackeray in education, in experience of many men, and in foreign travel. Tom Jones is the begetter of Arthur Pendennis, Jonathan Wild of Barry Lyndon. Some of Fielding's heroines, wandering out of *Tom Jones* and *Amelia*, have strayed into *Pendennis*, *Vanity Fair*, and *The Newcomes*. The fair émigrées change their names, but keep their thoughts and behavior.

It is said that a lady once asked Thackeray why he made all his women fools or knaves. "Madam, I know no others." It may be that living in Paris in his youth hurt his insight into women; it may be that the great sorrow of his wife's insanity instinctively turned his thoughts from the higher types of women; perhaps his life in Bohemia and in clubs limited his knowledge during the years when novel-writing was his chief occupation. The truth seems to be that Thackeray, like Fielding, was a man's man,—he understood one cross-section of a common man, his hopes, aims, fears, wishes, habits, and manners; but he was very ignorant of women. He says: "Desdemona was not angry with Cassio, though there is very little doubt she saw the lieutenant's partiality for her (and I, for my part, believe that many more things took place in that sad affair than the worthy Moorish officer ever knew of); why, Miranda was even very kind to Caliban, and we may be pretty sure for the same reason. Not that she would encourage him in the least, the poor uncouth monster,—of course not." Shakespeare and Thackeray looked differently at women.

Thackeray lacked the poet's eye; he could not see and was not troubled.

> Ahi quanto nella mente mi commossi,
> Quando mi volsi per veder Beatrice,
> Per non poter vedere, ben ch'io fossi
> Presso di lei, e nel mondo felice!

But poor Thackeray was never near the ideal, and never in paradise. Some critic has said of him that because he had Eden in his mind's eye, this world appeared a Vanity Fair. No criticism could be more perverted; he had Vanity Fair in his mind's eye, and therefore could not see paradise.

This treatment of women is half from sheer ignorance, and half from Thackeray's habit of dealing in caricature with subjects of which he is ignorant. He behaves toward foreign countries very much as he does toward women. France, Germany, Italy, appear like geography in an opera bouffe. They are places for English blackguards to go to, and very fit places for them, tenanted as they are by natives clad in outlandish trousers, and bearded and moustachioed like pards. His delineations of Germany, and those pen-and-ink sketches by Richard Doyle in his delightful Brown, Jones and Robinson, made so strong an impression upon an ignorant portion of the public, of which we were, that it was frightened to death in 1871, when it thought of the French armies trampling down poor little Germany. Thackeray looked on Germany, as he did upon the world, with the greedy eye of the caricaturist, and he could not refrain from his grotesque sketches. Of the French he says: "In their aptitude to swallow, to utter, to enact humbugs, these French people, from Majesty downwards, beat all the other nations of this earth. In looking at these men, their manners, dresses, opinions, politics, actions, history, it is impossible to preserve a grave countenance; instead of having Carlyle to write a *History of the French Revolution*, I often think it should be handed over to Dickens or Theodore Hook. . . . I can hardly bring my mind to fancy that anything is serious in France,—it seems to be all rant, tinsel, and stage-play." His attitude toward French literature is distorted by lack of sympathy to an astonishing degree.

Thackeray's fault was not merely a certain narrowness of mind, but also that he allowed himself to see only the grotesque and disagreeable, until habit and nature combined to blind him to other things.

VI

Thackeray is not a democrat. Democracy, like many another great and vague social conception, is based upon a fundamental truth, of which truth adherents to the conception are often ignorant, although they brush against it in the dark and unwittingly draw in strength for their belief. The fundamental truth of democracy is that the real pleasures of life are increased by sharing them,—that exclusiveness renders pleasure insipid. One reason why democracy has prevailed so greatly is that everywhere, patent to everybody, in the simplest family life, there is proof of this truth. A man amuses himself skipping stones: the occupation has a pleasure hardly to be detected; with a wife it is interesting, with children it becomes exciting. Every new sharer adds to the father's stock of delight, so that at last he lies awake on winter nights thinking of the summer's pleasure. With a slight application of logic, democrats have struggled, and continually do struggle, to break down all the bastions, walls, fences, and demilunes that time, prejudice, and ignorance have erected between men. They wish to have a ready channel from man to man, through which the emotional floods of life can pour;

> For they, at least,
> Have dream'd that human hearts might blend
> In one, and were through faith released
> From isolation without end.

What is the meaning of patriotism? Does the patriot think his country wiser, better, more gifted, more generous, than another? Perhaps, and in this he is almost certainly wrong; but the power of patriotism to disregard truth lies in the fact that it is one of the most powerful conductors of human emotion ever discovered. It is part of the old human cry, "Self is so small; make me part of something large." *Esprit de corps*, which

makes people unreasonable and troubles the calculations of the bloodless man, is a like conductor of the emotions in lesser matters; and the fact is familiar that the larger the body, the greater is the emotion generated.

Humanity has had a hard task in civilizing itself; in periods of ignorance, ill humor, and hunger it has built up a most elaborate system, which has been a great factor in material prosperity. This system is the specialization of labor, which serves to double the necessary differences among men, and to make every specialty and every difference a hindrance to the joys that should be in commonalty spread. The age of machinery increased specialization, specialization increased wealth, wealth was popularly supposed to be the panacea for human ills; and the bars and barriers between men were repaired and strengthened. Specialization in Thackeray's time was in the very air; everything was specialized,—trade was specialized, society was specialized, money was specialized; there was money made, money inherited from father, money inherited from grandfather,—money, like blood, growing purer and richer the further back it could be traced. Every act of specialization produced a new batch of social relations.

Thackeray is very sensitive, especially to this elaborate system of specialization, and to its dividing properties, strengthened and repaired by the commercial Briton. Thackeray has no gift for abstraction; he does not take a man and grow absorbed in him as a spiritual being, as a creature in relations with some Absolute; he sees men shut off and shut up in all sorts of little coops. He is all attentive to the coops. The world to him is one vast zoölogical garden, this Vanity Fair of his. He does not care that the creatures are living, growing, eating, sun-needing animals; he is interested in the feathers, the curl of the tail, the divided toe, the pink eye, the different occupations, clothes, habits, which separate them into different groups. A democrat does not care for such classification; on the contrary, he wishes to efface it as much as possible. He wishes to abstract man from his conditions and surroundings, and contemplate him as a certain quantity of human essence. He looks upon the distinctions of rank, of occupation, of customs and habits, as so many barricades upon the great avenues of human emotions; Napoleon-like, he would sweep them away. He regards man as a serious reality, and these accidents of social relations as mere shadows passing over. This is the Christian position. This is the attitude of Victor Hugo, George Eliot, George Sand, Hawthorne, Tourgenef, Tolstoi, Charlotte Brontë.

WALTER SAVAGE LANDOR

1775–1864

Walter Savage Landor was born in Warwick on January 30, 1775. He was educated at Rugby, from which he was expelled, and at Trinity College, Cambridge, from which he was suspended after firing a shot at a Tory undergraduate; throughout his life Landor's volatile temper was to involve him in many difficulties. In 1795 Landor issued his first volume of verse, *The Poems of Walter Savage Landor*, but later suppressed it. This was followed by *Gebir* (1798), an epic poem in seven books, and by his verse collection *Poems by the Author of* Gebir (1802). In 1806 he published another collection of poems, *Simonidea*, which included "Rose Aylmer," an elegy for a close friend who had died in India.

In 1809 Landor went to Spain to fight against Napoleon. Upon returning he bought property on the Welsh border, and in 1811 married Julia Thuillier, who bore him four children. Landor's verse tragedy, *Count Julian*, was published in 1812 but never staged. Also in that year appeared the ill-considered "Commentary on the Memoirs of Mr. Fox," which had to be suppressed. In 1815 Landor moved to Italy, where he remained until 1835, the year he was separated from his wife. The lengthy *Imaginary Conversations of Literary Men and Statesmen* appeared in five volumes from 1824 to 1829, and the *Citation and Examination of William Shakespeare*, an imaginary conversation based on the legend of Shakespeare's deer-stealing, came out in 1834. *Pericles and Aspasia*, a full-length prose work which also grew out of an imaginary conversation, appeared in 1836, and was followed in 1837 by *The Pentameron*, in which Boccaccio and Petrarch discuss the poetry of Dante. *Andrea of Hungary*, *Giovanna of Naples*, and *Fra Rupert*, a trilogy of plays, were published in 1839–40, and *The Hellenics*, a retelling in verse of various Greek myths, was completed in 1847. In 1853 appeared *Imaginary Conversations of Greeks and Romans*.

For the last five years of his life Landor lived near the poet Browning's residence in Florence. Landor died there on September 17, 1864.

Personal

Landor has sent over another volume of *Conversations* to the press. Differing as I do from him in constitutional temper, and in some serious opinions, he is yet of all men living the one with whom I feel the most entire and cordial sympathy in heart and mind; were I a single man, I should think the pleasure of a week's abode with him cheaply purchased by a journey to Florence, though, pilgrim-like, the whole way were to be performed on foot.—ROBERT SOUTHEY, Letter to Caroline Bowles (Nov. 13, 1824)

Mr. Landor, who has long been known to scholars as a Latin poet beyond the elegance of centos, and has lately shown himself one of our most powerful writers of prose, is a man of a vehement nature, with great delicacy of imagination. He is like a stormy mountain pine, that should produce lilies. After indulging the partialities of his friendships and enmities, and trampling on kings and ministers, he shall cool himself, like a Spartan worshipping a moon-beam, in the patient meekness of Lady Jane Grey. I used to think he did wrong in choosing to write Latin verse instead of English. The opinions he has expressed on that subject, in the eloquent treatise appended to his Latin poems, will, I am sure, hardly find a single person to agree with them. But as an individual, working out his own case, I think he was right in giving way to the inspiration of his scholarship. Independent, learned, and leisurely, with a temperament, perhaps, rather than a mind, poetical, he walked among the fields of antiquity, till he beheld the forms of poetry with the eyes of their inhabitants; and it is agreeable, as a variety, among the crowds of ordinary scholars, especially such as affect to think the great modern poets little ones because they are not ancient, to have one who can really fancy and feel with Ovid and Catullus, as well as read them. Mr. Landor has the veneration for all poetry, ancient or modern, that belongs to a scholar who is himself a poet. He loves Chaucer and Spenser, as well as Homer. That he deserves the title, the reader will be convinced on opening his book of *Idyls*, where the first thing he encounters will be the charming duel between Cupid and Pan, full of fancy and archness, with a deeper emotion at the end. His *Lyrics*, with the exception of a pretty vision about Ceres and her poppies, (which is in the spirit of an Idyl,) do not appear to me so good: but upon the whole, though it is a point on which I am bound to speak with diffidence, he seems to me by far the best Latin poet we possess, after Milton; more in good taste than the incorrectness and diffuseness of Cowley; and not to be lowered by a comparison with the mimic elegancies of Addison. Vincent Bourne, I conceive to be a genuine hand; but I know him only in a piece or two.

Mr. Landor was educated at Rugby, and became afterwards the friend and favourite pupil of Dr. Parr. With a library, the smallness of which surprised me, and which he must furnish out, when he writes on English subjects, by the help of a rich memory,—he lives, among his paintings and hospitalities, in a style of unostentatious elegance, very becoming a scholar that can afford it. The exile, in which he chooses to continue at present, is as different from that of his friend Ovid, as his *Tristia* would have been, had he thought proper to write any. Augustus would certainly have found no whining in him, much less any worship. He has some fine children, with whom he plays like a real schoolboy, being, in truth, as ready to complain of an undue knock, as he is to laugh, shout, and scramble; and his wife (I really do not know whether I ought to take these liberties, but the nature of the book into which I have been beguiled must excuse me, and ladies must take the consequence of being agreeable,)—his wife would have made Ovid's loneliness quite another thing, with her face radiant with good-humour. Mr. Landor's conversation is lively and unaffected, as full of scholarship or otherwise as you may desire, and dashed now and then with a little superfluous will and vehemence, when he speaks of his likings and dislikes. His laugh is in peals, and climbing: he seems to fetch every fresh one from a higher story.—LEIGH HUNT, *Lord Byron and Some of His Contemporaries*, 1828, Vol. 2, pp. 377–81

Met to-day the one man living in Florence whom I was anxious to know. This was Walter Savage Landor, a man of unquestionable genius, but very questionable good sense; or, rather, one of those unmanageable men—

> Blest with huge stores of wit,
> Who want as much again to manage it.

Without pretending now to characterize him (rather bold in me to attempt such a thing at any time), I will merely bring together the notes that I think it worth while to preserve concerning him during this summer; postponing an account of my subsequent intercourse with him. I had the good fortune to be introduced to him as the friend of his friends, Southey and Wordsworth. He was, in fact, only Southey's friend. Of Wordsworth he *then* professed warm admiration. I received an immediate invitation to his villa. This villa is within a few roods of that most classic point on the Tuscan Mount, Fiesole, where Boccaccio's hundred tales were told. To Landor's society I owed much of my highest enjoyment during my stay at Florence. He was a man of florid complexion, with large full eyes, and altogether a *leonine* man, and with a fierceness of tone well suited to his name; his decisions being confident, and on all subjects, whether of taste or life, unqualified; each standing for itself, not caring whether it was in harmony with what had gone before or would follow from the same oracular lips. But why should I trouble myself to describe him? He is painted by a master hand in Dickens's novel, *Bleak House*, now in course of publication, where he figures as Mr. Boythorn. The combination of superficial ferocity and inherent tenderness, so admirably portrayed in *Bleak House*, still at first strikes every stranger—for twenty-two years have not materially changed him—no less than his perfect frankness and reckless indifference to what he says.—HENRY CRABB ROBINSON, *Diary*, Aug. 16, 1830

We met first, some four years ago, on Cheyne Walk here: a tall broad burly man, with grey hair, and large fierce-rolling eyes; of the most restless impetuous vivacity not to be held in by the most perfect breeding,—expressing itself in high-coloured superlatives, indeed in reckless exaggeration, now and then in a dry sharp laugh not of sport but of mockery; a wild man, whom no extent of culture had been able to tame! His intellectual faculty seemed to me to be weak in proportion to his violence of temper: the judgement he gives about anything is more apt to be wrong than right,—as the inward whirlwind shows him this side or the other of the object; and *sides* of an object are all that he sees. He is not an original man; in most cases, one but sighs over the spectacle of commonplace torn to rags. I find him painful as a writer; like a soul ever promising to take wing into the Aether, yet never doing it, ever splashing web-footed in the terrene mud, and only splashing the worse the more he strives! Two new tragedies of his that I read lately are the fatallest stuff I have seen for long: not an ingot; ah no, a distracted coil of wire-drawings saleable in no market. Poor Landor has left his Wife (who is said to be fool) in Italy, with his children, who would not quit her; but it seems he has honestly surrendered all his money to her, except a bare annuity for furnished lodgings; and now lives at Bath, a solitary sexagenarian, in that manner. He visits London in May; but says always it would kill him soon: alas, I can well believe that! They say he has a kind heart; nor does it seem unlikely: a perfectly honest heart, free and fearless, dwelling amid such hallucinations, excitations, tempestuous confusions, I can see he has. Enough of him! Me he likes well enough, more thanks to him; but two hours of such speech as his leave me giddy and undone.—THOMAS CARLYLE, Letter to Ralph Waldo Emerson (April 1, 1840)

Greenough brought me, through a common friend, an invitation from Mr. Landor, who lived at San Domenica di Fiesole. On the 15th May I dined with Mr. Landor. I found him noble and courteous, living in a cloud of pictures at his Villa Gherardesca, a fine house commanding a beautiful landscape. I had inferred from his books, or magnified from some anecdotes an impression of Achillean wrath—an untameable petulance. I do not know whether the imputation were just or not, but certainly on this May day his courtesy veiled that haughty mind, and he was the most patient and gentle of hosts. He praised the beautiful cyclamen which grows all about Florence; he admired Washington; talked of Wordsworth, Byron, Massinger, Beaumont and Fletcher. To be sure, he is decided in his opinions, likes to surprise, and is well content to impress, if possible, his English whim upon the immutable past. No great man ever had a great son, if Philip and Alexander be not an exception; and Philip he calls the greater man. In art, he loves the Greeks, and in sculpture, them only. He prefers the Venus to everything else, and, after that, the head of Alexander, in the gallery here. He prefers John of Bologna to Michael Angelo; in painting, Raffaelle; and shares the growing taste for Perugino and the early masters. The Greek histories he thought the only good; and after them, Voltaire's. I could not make him praise Mackintosh, nor my more recent friends: Montaigne very cordially—and Charron also, which seemed indiscriminating. He thought Degerando indebted to "Lucas on Happiness" and "Lucas on Holiness!" He pestered me with Southey; but who is Southey?

He invited me to breakfast on Friday. On Friday I did not fail to go, and this time with Greenough. He entertained us at once with reciting half a dozen hexameter lines of Julius Cæsar's!—from Donatus, he said. He glorified Lord Chesterfield more than was necessary, and undervalued Burke, and undervalued Socrates; designated as three of the greatest of men, Washington, Phocion, and Timoleon; much as our pomologists, in their lists, select the three or the six best pears "for a small orchard;" and did not even omit to remark the similar termination of their names. "A great man," he said, "should make great sacrifices, and kill his hundred oxen, without knowing whether they would be consumed by gods and heroes, or whether the flies would eat them." I had visited Professor Amici, who had shown me his microscopes, magnifying (it was said) two thousand diameters; and I spoke of the uses to which they were applied. Landor despised entomology, yet, in the same breath, said, "the sublime was in a grain of dust." I suppose I teased him about recent writers, but he professed never to have heard of Herschel, *not even by name.* One room was full of pictures, which he likes to show, especially one piece, standing before which, he said "he would give fifty guineas to the man that would swear it was a Domenichino." I was more curious to see his library, but Mr. H——, one of the guests, told me that Mr. Landor gives away his books, and has never more than a dozen at a time in his house.

Mr. Landor carries to its height the love of freak which the English delight to indulge, as if to signalise their commanding freedom. He has a wonderful brain, despotic, violent, and inexhaustible, meant for a soldier, by what chance converted to letters, in which there is not a style nor a tint not known to him, yet with an English appetite for action and heroes. The thing done avails, and not what is said about it. An original sentence, a step forward, is worth more than all the censures. Landor is strangely undervalued in England; usually ignored; and sometimes savagely attacked in the Reviews. The criticism may be right, or wrong, and is quickly forgotten; but year after year the scholar must still go back to Landor for a multitude of elegant sentences—for wisdom, wit, and indignation that are unforgettable.—RALPH WALDO EMERSON, "First Visit to England," *English Traits*, 1856

We left Mr. Landor in great comfort. I went to see his apartment before it was furnished. Rooms small, but with a look out into a little garden; quiet and cheerful; and he doesn't mind a situation rather out of the way. He pays four pound ten (English) the month. Wilson has *thirty* pounds a year for taking care of him, which sounds a good deal; but it *is* a difficult position. He has excellent, generous, affectionate impulses, but the impulses of the tiger every now and then. Nothing coheres in him, either in his opinions, or I fear, affections. It isn't age; he is precisely the man of his youth, I must believe. Still, his genius gives him the right of gratitude on all artists at least, and I must say that my Robert has generously paid the debt. Robert always said that he owed more as a writer to Landor than to any contemporary. At present Landor is very fond of him; but I am quite prepared for his turning against us as he has turned against Forster, who has been so devoted for years and years. Only one isn't kind for what one gets by it, or there wouldn't be much kindness in this world.—ELIZABETH BARRETT BROWNING, Letter to Miss Browning (Dec. 1859)

The spectacle of a vigorous, vivid, undaunted old age, true to the aims and convictions of youth, is always a fine one; and it was warmly felt to be so in Landor's case. His prejudices mattered less, when human affairs went on maturing themselves in spite of them; and many of his complaints were silenced in the best possible way—by the reform of the abuses which he, with some unnecessary violence, denounced. He, for his part, talked less about killing kings; and his steady assertion of the claims of the humble fell in better with the spirit of the time, after years had inaugurated the works of peace. About many matters of political principle and practice he was right, while yet the majority of society were wrong; and it would be too much to require that he should be wholly right in doctrine and fact, or very angelic in his way of enforcing his convictions. Nature did not make him a logician, and if we were ever disappointed at not finding him one, the fault was our own. She made him brave, though wayward; an egotist in his method, but with the good of mankind for his aim. He was passionate and prejudiced, but usually in some great cause, and on the right side of it; though there was a deplorable exception to that general rule in the particular instance of defamation which broke up the repose and dignity of his latter days, and caused his self-exile from England for the remnant of his life. This brief notice of the painful fact is enough for truth and justice. As for the rest, he was of aristocratic birth, fortune, and education, with democracy for his political aim, and poverty and helplessness for his clients. All this would have made Walter Savage Landor a remarkable man in his generation, apart from his services to literature; but when we recall some of his works—such pictures as that of the English officer shot at the Pyramids—such criticism as in his *Pentameron*—and discourses so elevating and so heart-moving as some which he has put into the mouths of heroes, sages, scholarly and noble women, and saintly and knightly men, we feel that our cumulative obligations to him are very great, and that his death is a prominent incident of the time.—HARRIET MARTINEAU, "Walter Savage Landor" (1864), *Biographical Sketches*, 1869, pp. 128–29

I saw Landor but once—when I went down from London, by his invitation, to spend a day with him at Bath in the late summer of 1852. His friend the late Mr. Kenyon went with me,—his friend and that of whoever deserved or needed friendship, the divinely appointed *amicus curiæ* of mankind in general. For me it was and is a memorable day, for Landor was to me an ancient, and it seemed a meeting in Elysium. I had looked forward to it, nevertheless, with a twinge of doubt, for three years before I had written a review of the new edition of his works, in which I had discriminated more than had been altogether pleasing to him. But a guest was as sacred to Landor as to an Arab, and the unaffected heartiness of his greeting at once reassured me. I have little to tell of our few hours' converse, for the stream of memory, when it has been flowing so long as mine, gathers an ooze in its bed like that of Lethe, and in this the weightier things embed themselves past recovery, while the lighter, lying nearer the surface, may be fished up again. What I can recollect, therefore, illustrates rather the manner of the man than his matter. His personal appearance has been sufficiently described by others. I will only add, that the suffused and uniform ruddiness of his face, in which the forehead, already heightened by baldness, shared, and something in the bearing of his head, reminded me vividly of the late President Quincy, as did also a certain hearty resonance of speech. You felt yourself in the presence of one who was emphatically a Man, not the image of a man; so emphatically, indeed, that even Carlyle thought the journey to Bath not too dear a prize to pay for seeing him, and found something royal in him. When I saw him he was in his seventy-eighth year, but erect and vigorous as in middle life. There was something of challenge even in the alertness of his pose, and the head was

often thrown back like that of a boxer who awaits a blow. He had the air of the arena. I do not remember that his head was large, or his eyes in any way remarkable.

After the first greetings were over, I thought it might please him to know that I had made a pilgrimage to his Fiesolan villa. I spoke of the beauty of its site. I could not have been more clumsy, had I tried. "Yes," he almost screamed, "and I might have been there now, but for that in-tol-e-rrr-a-ble woman!" pausing on each syllable of the adjective as one who would leave an imprecation there, and making the *r* grate as if it were grinding its teeth at the disabilities which distance imposes on resentment. I was a little embarrassed by this sudden confidence, which I should not here betray had not Mr. Forster already laid Landor's domestic relations sufficiently bare. I am not sure whether he told me the story of his throwing his cook out of a window of this villa. I think he did, but it may have been Mr. Kenyon who told it me on the way back to London. The legend was, that after he had performed this summary act of justice, Mrs. Landor remonstrated with a "There, Walter! I always told you that one day you would do something to be sorry for in these furies of yours." Few men can be serene under an "I always told you so"—least of all men could Landor. But he saw that here was an occasion where calm is more effective than tempest, and where a soft answer is more provoking than a hard. So he replied mildly: "Well, my dear, I *am* sorry, if that will do you any good. If I had remembered that our best tulip-bed was under that window, I'd have flung the dog out of t'other."—JAMES RUSSELL LOWELL, "Some Letters of Walter Savage Landor," *Century Magazine*, Feb. 1888, p. 513

General

O friends! who have accompanied thus far
My quickening steps, sometimes where sorrow sate
Dejected, and sometimes where valour stood
Resplendent, right before us; here perhaps
We best might part; but one to valour dear
Comes up in wrath and calls me worse than foe,
Reminding me of gifts too ill deserved.
I must not blow away the flowers he gave,
Altho' now faded; I must not efface
The letters his own hand has traced for me.
    Here terminates my park of poetry.
Look out no longer for extensive woods,
For clusters of unlopt and lofty trees,
With stately animals couch't under them,
Or grottoes with deep wells of water pure,
And ancient figures in the solid rock:
Come, with our sunny pasture be content,
Our narrow garden and our homestead croft,
And tillage not neglected. Love breathes round;
Love, the bright atmosphere, the vital air,
Of youth; without it life and death are one.
            —WALTER SAVAGE LANDOR, Untitled poem,
            1846

He is a man of great genius, and, as such, he *ought* to interest the public. More than enough appears of his strong, eccentric nature through every page of his now extensive writings to win, amongst those who have read him, a corresponding interest in all that concerns him personally,—in his social relations, in his biography, in his manners, in his appearance. Out of two conditions for attracting a *personal* interest he has powerfully realized one. His moral nature, shining with coloured light through the crystal shrine of his thoughts, will not allow of your forgetting it. A sunset of Claude, or a dying dolphin *can* be forgotten, and generally *is* forgotten; but not the fiery radiations of a human spirit, built by nature to animate a leader in storms, a martyr, a national reformer, an arch-rebel, as circumstances might dictate, but whom too much wealth, and the accidents of education, have turned aside into a contemplative recluse. Had Mr. Landor, therefore, been read in any extent answering to his merits, he must have become, for the English public, an object of prodigious personal interest. We should have had novels upon him, lampoons upon him, libels upon him; he would have been shown up dramatically on the stage; he would, according to the old joke, have been "traduced" (*traduit*) in French, and also "overset" (*oversat*) in Dutch. Meantime he has *not* been read. It would be an affectation to think it. Many a writer is, by the sycophancy of literature, reputed to be read, whom in all Europe not six eyes settle upon through the revolving year. Literature, with its cowardly falsehoods, exhibits the largest field of conscious Phrygian adulation that human life has ever exposed to the derision of the heavens. Demosthenes, for instance, or Plato, is not read to the extent of twenty pages annually by ten people in Europe. The *sale* of their works would not account for three readers; the other six or seven are generally conceded as possibilities furnished by the great public libraries. But, then, Walter Savage Landor, though writing a little in Latin, and a *very* little in Italian, does not write at all in Greek. So far he has some advantage over Plato; and, if he writes chiefly in dialogue, which few people love to read any more than novels in the shape of letters, *that* is a crime common to both. So that he has the d—— l's luck and his own: all Plato's chances, and one of his own beside, viz. his English. Still, it is no use counting chances; facts are the thing. And printing-presses, whether of Europe or of England, bear witness that neither Plato nor Landor is a marketable commodity. In fact, these two men resemble each other in more particulars than it is at present necessary to say. Especially they were both inclined to be voluptuous; both had a hankering after purple and fine linen; both hated "filthy dowlas" with the hatred of Falstaff, whether in apparelling themselves or their diction; and both bestowed pains as elaborate upon the secret *art* of a dialogue as a lapidary would upon the cutting of a Sultan's rubies. —THOMAS DE QUINCEY, "Notes on Walter Savage Landor" (1847), *Collected Writings*, ed. David Masson, Vol. 11, pp. 396–98

We believe that Landor prided himself on his Latin more than on his English writings. He undoubtedly possessed a command of the Latin language which enabled him to use it for every purpose, and to adapt it to every theme, from the fables of Greek mythology to the incidents and characters of his own day. It is not easy to convey a notion either of the merits or of the faults of his Latin poetry to those who cannot judge of it for themselves. Its character cannot be illustrated by a comparison with any other Latin poetry, ancient or modern. Its style is not that of either the golden or the silver, or of any earlier or later age of Latinity. It is the style of Landor, and it is marked with the stamp not only of his intellect, but of his personal idiosyncrasy. This is the cause of that obscurity which must be felt, even by scholars, to mar to some extent the enjoyment of his Latin poetry. He was perfectly able to write in a style transparent as that of Ovid. But such was not his pleasure. He despised popularity; he disdained imitation; he abhorred all that savoured of mannerism, conventionality, and commonplace. He aimed at independence, originality; at the quality for which Mr. Matthew Arnold has endeavoured to naturalise in English literature—the French word *distinction*;

and thus it happened that when he might have clothed his thoughts in clear, simple, and natural language, he preferred forms of expression in which the stone is often too hard for common readers to get at the kernel. Nevertheless there are in these poems passages of exquisite tenderness and pathos, and others which display an extraordinary power of word-painting. We do not know which of them were Landor's favourites; but if we did, it is possible that we might not share his opinion. No doubt the author's poetical faculty is more largely developed in the longer compositions; but the shorter are more deeply impressed with the signature of the man; not, indeed, always in the most winning aspect, or the gentlest mood of inspiration. Now and then harmlessly playful, but much oftener instinct with the bitterest sarcasm; keen and poisoned shafts, levelled sometimes at the objects of his political animosity, sometimes at persons from whom he believed himself to have suffered a private wrong. If it may be said that he set any model before himself, it must have been Catullus. But neither the *Idyllia Hæroica*, nor *Gebirus*, nor *Ulysses in Argiripa*, approach the *Atys* or the *Epithalamium*. The *Hendecasyllabi* remind us not unfrequently of the poet of Como.—RICHARD MONCKTON MILNES, LORD HOUGHTON, "Forster's Life of Landor," *Edinburgh Review*, July 1869, pp. 252–53

Thought gave his wings the width of time to roam,
  Love gave his thought strength equal to release
From bonds of old forgetful years, like foam
  Vanished, the fame of memories that decrease;
So strongly faith had fledged for flight from home
  The soul's large pinions till her strife should cease:
And through the trumpet of a child of Rome
  Rang the pure music of the flutes of Greece.
      As though some northern hand
      Reft from the Latin land
A spoil more costly than the Colchian fleece
      To clothe with golden sound
      Of old joy newly found
And rapture as of penetrating peace
  The naked north-wind's cloudiest clime,
And give its darkness light of the old Sicilian time.

He saw the brand that fired the towers of Troy
  Fade, and the darkness of Œnone's prayer
Close upon her that closed upon her boy,
  For all the curse of godhead that she bare;
And the Apollonian serpent gleam and toy
  With scathless maiden limbs and shuddering hair;
And his love smitten in their dawn of joy
  Leave Pan the pine-leaf of her change to wear;
      And one in flowery coils
      Caught as in fiery toils
  Smite Calydon with mourning unaware;
      And where her low turf shrine
      Showed Modesty divine
The fairest mother's daughter far more fair
  Hide on her breast the heavenly shame
That kindled once with love should kindle Troy with flame.

Nor less the light of story than of song
  With graver glories girt his godlike head,
Reverted alway from the temporal throng
  Of lives that live not toward the living dead.
The shadows and the splendours of their throng
  Made bright and dark about his board and bed
The lines of life and vision, sweet or strong
  With sound of lutes or trumpets blown, that led
      Forth of the ghostly gate
      Opening in spite of fate

Shapes of majestic or tumultuous tread,
Divine and direful things,
These foul as priests or kings,
Those fair as heaven or love or freedom, red
With blood and green with palms and white
With raiment woven of deeds divine and words of light.

The thunder-fire of Cromwell, and the ray
That keeps the place of Phocion's name serene
And clears the cloud from Kosciusko's day,
Alternate as dark hours with bright between,
Met in the heaven of his high thought, which lay
For all stars open that all eyes had seen
Rise on the night or twilight of the way
Where feet of human hopes and fears had been.
Again the sovereign word
On Milton's lips was heard
Living: again the tender three days' queen
Drew bright and gentle breath
On the sharp edge of death:
And, staged again to show of mortal scene,
Tiberius, ere his name grew dire,
Wept, stainless yet of empire, tears of blood and fire.

Most ardent and most awful and most fond,
The fervour of his Apollonian eye
Yearned upon Hellas, yet enthralled in bond
Of time whose years beheld her and past by
Silent and shameful, till she rose and donned
The casque again of Pallas; for her cry
Forth of the past and future, depths beyond
This where the present and its tyrants lie,
As one great voice of twain
For him had pealed again,
Heard but of hearts high as her own was high,
High as her own and his
And pure as love's heart is,
That lives though hope at once and memory die:
And with her breath his clarion's blast
Was filled as cloud with fire or future souls with past.

As a wave only obsequious to the wind
Leaps to the lifting breeze that bids it leap,
Large-hearted, and its thickening mane be thinned
By the strong god's breath moving on the deep
From utmost Atlas even to extremest Ind
That shakes the plain where no men sow nor reap,
So, moved with wrath toward men that ruled and sinned
And pity toward all tears he saw men weep,
Arose to take man's part
His loving lion heart,
Kind as the sun's that has in charge to keep
Earth and the seed thereof
Safe in his lordly love,
Strong as sheer truth and soft as very sleep;
The mightiest heart since Milton's leapt,
The gentlest since the gentlest heart of Shakespeare slept.

Like the wind's own on her divided sea
His song arose on Corinth, and aloud
Recalled her Isthmian song and strife when she
Was thronged with glories as with gods in crowd
And as the wind's own spirit her breath was free
And as the heaven's own heart her soul was proud,
But freer and prouder stood no son than he
Of all she bare before her heart was bowed;
None higher than he who heard
Medea's keen last word
Transpierce her traitor, and like a rushing cloud
That sundering shows a star
Saw pass her thunderous car

And a face whiter and deadlier than a shroud
That lightened from it, and the brand
Of tender blood that falling seared his suppliant hand.
More fair than all things born and slain of fate,
More glorious than all births of days and nights,
He bade the spirit of man regenerate,
Rekindling, rise and reassume the rights
That in high seasons of his old estate
Clothed him and armed with majesties and mights
Heroic, when the times and hearts were great
And in the depths of ages rose the heights
Radiant of high deeds done
And souls that matched the sun
For splendour with the lightnings of their lights
Whence even their uttered names
Burn like the strong twin flames
Of song that shakes a throne and steel that smites;
As on Thermopylæ when shone
Leonidas, on Syracuse Timoleon.

Or, sweeter than the breathless buds when spring
With smiles and tears and kisses bids them breathe,
Fell with its music from his quiring string
Fragrance of pine-leaves and odorous heath
Twined round the lute whereto he sighed to sing
Of the oak that screened and showed its maid beneath,
Who seeing her bee crawl back with broken wing
Faded, a fairer flower than all her wreath,
And paler, though her oak
Stood scathless of the stroke
More sharp than edge of axe or wolfish teeth,
That mixed with mortals dead
Her own half heavenly head
And life incorporate with a sylvan sheath,
And left the wild rose and the dove
A secret place and sacred from all guests but Love.
—ALGERNON CHARLES SWINBURNE, *Song for the
Centenary of Walter Savage Landor*, 1880,
Stanzas 17–25

The causes of his scant popularity are not difficult to discern. His thoughts were not of a nature especially to stir his own or any one time. He was, indeed, the son of his age in his passion for liberty, and in his spirit of humanity and tenderness for the dumb creation; and his imaginative instinct and imaginative longings in the direction of ancient Hellas were shared by the general European culture of his time. But for the rest he ranged, apart from the passions or the tempests of the hour, among the heroic figures of the past and the permanent facts and experiences of life. He "walked along the far eastern uplands, meditating and remembering;" and to the far eastern uplands those who could walk with him must brace themselves to mount. Even then there are difficulties arising from that want of consideration and sympathy in Landor for his readers of which I have spoken. He sometimes puzzles us for want of explanations, and often fatigues us with intrusive disquisitions. These, however, are the imperfections of a great master, and the way to counteract them is by providing the student with help where help is wanted; by selection, above all, and in the next place by occasional comment or introduction. A selection or golden treasury of Landor's shorter dramatic dialogues, edited with such helps for the reader as I suggest, would be, as was said long ago by Julius Hare, "one of the most beautiful books in the language, that is to say in the world." From the longer, the discursive dialogues, perhaps the only selection possible for popular use would be one on the principle adopted by Mr. Hilliard—a selection, that is, of detached sentences and sayings. These form a kind of literature in which England since the seventeenth century has not been rich; and from the conversations and other prose writings of Landor there is to be gathered such an anthology of them as the literature of France itself could hardly surpass. If, indeed, there is any English writer who can be compared to Pascal for power and compression, for incisive strength and imaginative breadth together, in general reflections, and for the combination of conciseness with splendour in their utterance, it is certainly Landor. Space has failed me to illustrate or do more than name this province of his genius. The true Landorian, no doubt, will prefer to dig these jewels for himself from their surroundings—surroundings sometimes attractive and sometimes the reverse; but true Landorians may at present be counted on the fingers, and I speak of what has to be done in order to extend to wider circles the knowledge of so illustrious a master.—SIDNEY COLVIN, *Landor*, 1881, pp. 219–20

A complete list of Landor's writings, published or privately printed, in English, Latin, and Italian, including pamphlets, fly-sheets, and occasional newspaper correspondence on political or literary questions, it would be difficult to give anywhere and impossible to give here. From nineteen almost to ninety his intellectual and literary activity was indefatigably incessant; but, herein at least like Charles Lamb, whose cordial admiration he so cordially returned, he could not write a note of three lines which did not bear the mark of his 'Roman hand' in its matchless and inimitable command of a style at once the most powerful and the purest of his age. The one charge which can ever seriously be brought and maintained against it is that of such occasional obscurity or difficulty as may arise from excessive strictness in condensation of phrase and expurgation of matter not always superfluous, and sometimes almost indispensable. His English prose and his Latin verse are perhaps more frequently and more gravely liable to this charge than either his English verse or his Latin prose. At times it is wellnigh impossible for an eye less keen and swift, a scholarship less exquisite and ready than his own, to catch the precise direction and follow the perfect course of his rapid thought and radiant utterance. This apparently studious pursuit and preference of the most terse and elliptic expression which could be found for anything he might have to say could not but occasionally make even so sovereign a master of two great languages appear 'dark with excess of light;' but from no former master of either tongue in prose or verse was ever the quality of real obscurity, of loose and nebulous incertitude, more utterly alien or more naturally remote. There is nothing of cloud or fog about the path on which he leads us; but we feel now and then the want of a bridge or a handrail; we have to leap from point to point of narrative or argument without the usual help of a connecting plank. Even in his dramatic works, where least of all it should have been found, this lack of visible connection or sequence in details of thought or action is too often a source of sensible perplexity. In his noble trilogy on the history of Giovanna Queen of Naples it is sometimes actually difficult to realize on a first reading what has happened or is happening, or how, or why, or by what agency—a defect alone sufficient, but unhappily sufficient in itself, to explain the too general ignorance of a work so rich in subtle and noble treatment of character, so sure and strong in its grasp and rendering of 'high actions and high passions,' so rich in humour and in pathos, so royally serene in its commanding power upon the tragic mainsprings of terror and of pity. As a poet, he may be said on the whole to stand midway between Byron and Shelley,—about as far above the former as below the latter. If we except Catullus and Simonides, it might be hard to match and it would be impossible to overmatch the flawless and blameless yet living and breathing beauty of his most perfect elegies, epigrams, or epitaphs. As truly as prettily was he likened by Leigh Hunt 'to a stormy mountain pine which should produce lilies.' His passionate compassion, his bitter and burning pity for all wrongs endured in all the world, found only their natural and inevitable outlet in his lifelong defence or advocacy of tyrannicide as the last resource of baffled justice, the last discharge of heroic duty. His tender and ardent love of children, of animals, and of flowers, makes fragrant alike the pages of his writing and the records of his life. He was as surely the most gentle and generous as the most headstrong and hot-headed of heroes or of men. Nor ever was any man's best work more thoroughly imbued and informed with evidence of his noblest qualities. His loyalty and liberality of heart were as inexhaustible as his bounty and beneficence of hand. Praise and encouragement, deserved or undeserved, came yet more readily to his lips than challenge or defiance. Reviled and ridiculed by Lord Byron, he retorted on the offender living less readily and less warmly than he lamented and extolled him dead. On the noble dramatic works of his brother Robert he lavished a magnificence of sympathetic praise which his utmost self-estimate would never have exacted for his own. Age and the lapse of time could neither heighten nor lessen the fullness of this rich and ready generosity. To the poets of his own and of the next generation he was not readier to do honour than to those of a later growth, and not seldom of deserts far lower and far lesser claims than theirs. That he was not unconscious of his own, and avowed it with the frank simplicity of nobler times, is not more evident or more certain than that in comparison with his friends and fellows he was liable rather to undervalue than to overrate himself. He was a classic, and no formalist; the wide range of his just and loyal admiration had room for a genius so far from classical as Blake's. Nor in his own highest mood or method of creative as of critical work was he a classic only, in any narrow or exclusive sense of the term. On either side, immediately or hardly below his mighty masterpiece of *Pericles and Aspasia*, stand the two scarcely less beautiful and vivid studies of mediæval Italy and Shakespearean England. The very finest flower of his immortal dialogues is probably to be found in the single volume comprising only *Imaginary Conversations of Greeks and Romans*; his utmost command of passion and pathos may be tested by its transcendent success in the distilled and concentrated tragedy of *Tiberius and Vipsania*, where for once he shows a quality more proper to romantic than classical imagination—the subtle and sublime and terrible power to enter the dark vestibule of distraction, to throw the whole force of his fancy, the whole fire of his spirit, into the 'shadowing passion' (as Shakespeare calls it) of gradually imminent insanity. Yet, if this and all other studies from ancient history or legend could be subtracted from the volume of his work, enough would be left whereon to rest the foundation of a fame which time could not sensibly impair.—ALGERNON CHARLES SWINBURNE, "Landor" (1882), *Miscellanies*, 1886, pp. 205–9

To the many, Landor has always been more or less unapproachable, and has always seemed more or less shadowy and unreal. To begin with, he wrote for himself and a few others, and principally for himself. Then, he wrote waywardly and unequally as well as selfishly; he published pretty much at random; the bulk of his work is large; and the majority has passed him by for writers more accessible and work less freakish and more comprehensible. It is probable too that even among those who, inspired by natural temerity or the intemperate curiosity of the general reader, have essayed his conquest and set out upon what has been described as 'the Adventure of the Seven Volumes which are Seven Valleys of Dry Bones,' but few have returned victorious. Of course the Seven Volumes are a world. But (it is objected) the world is peculiar in pattern, abounding in antres vast and desarts idle, in gaps and precipices and 'manifest solutions of continuity,' and enveloped in an atmosphere which ordinary lungs find now too rare and now too dense and too anodyne. Moreover, it is peopled chiefly with abstractions: bearing noble and suggestive names but all surprisingly alike in stature and feature, all more or less incapable of sustained emotion and even of logical argument, all inordinately addicted to superb generalities and a kind of monumental skittishness, all expressing themselves in a style whose principal characteristic is a magnificent monotony, and all apparently the outcome of a theory that to be wayward is to be creative, that human interest is a matter of apophthegms and oracular sentences, and that axiomatic and dramatic are identical qualities and convertible terms. This is the opinion of those adventurers in whom defeat has generated a sense of injury and an instinct of antagonism. Others less fortunate still have found Landor a continent of dulness and futility—have come to consider the Seven Volumes as so many aggregations of tedium. Such experiences are one-sided and partial no doubt; and considered from a certain point of view they seem worthless enough. But they exist, and they are in some sort justified. Landor, when all is said, remains a writers' writer; and for my part I find it impossible not to feel a certain sympathy with them that hesitate to accept him for anything else.

Again, to some of us Landor's imagination is not only inferior in kind but poverty-stricken in degree; his creative faculty is limited by the reflection that its one achievement is Landor; his claim to consideration as a dramatic writer is negatived by the fact that, poignant as are the situations with which he loved to deal, he was apparently incapable of perceiving their capacities: inasmuch as he has failed completely and logically to develop a single one of them; inasmuch, too, as he has never once succeeded in conceiving, much less in picturing, such a train of conflicting emotions as any one of the complications from which he starts might be supposed to generate. To many there is nothing Greek about his dramatic work except the absence of stage directions; and to these that quality of 'Landorian abruptness' which seems to Mr. Sidney Colvin to excuse so many of its shortcomings is identical with a certain sort of what in men of lesser mould is called stupidity.—W. E. HENLEY, "Landor," *Views and Reviews*, 1890, pp. 162–64

Among the chief hindrances to reading Landor are the exactions he makes of a reader; whether these are too great depends largely on the reader. With regard to his alleged excessive condensation, wherein lies one difficulty, it is to be said that we who skim novels and newspapers are so in the way of expecting from writers all kinds of useless help, so-called, are so thoroughly accustomed to diffuseness which professes to be explanatory, that we often do not feel, as we read, with what a dead weight of words we are burdened. Verbal prodigality is generally more injurious to style and more tiresome than verbal parsimony. De Quincey, whose habit in this respect is the direct converse of Landor's, I find at least as hard to read for two or three hours on end. Landor's fault—for he sometimes, though by no means always, carries compression too far—makes for greater alertness of mind and keener discrimination in the reader. If he incline to exercise too often our goat-like

power of leaping over spaces usually bridged for travellers on foot, it is equally true that mountain-climbing from which all difficulties have been cleared loses its charm. That in the region, picturesquely indicated by Mr. Swinburne, through which he asks us to follow, people in general are not mentally agile enough to keep him long in sight, in no degree diminishes the exhilarating effect of the climb on those blessed with legs and wind—rather the reverse.

In a word, Landor needs a trained reader, able to tell the best and the second-best apart, and fully to enjoy the best. Such a reader must know more history and more literature than most people know. For Landor's usual method is to presuppose in the reader a knowledge of everything that concerns his speakers, and to put them on the stage not in any scene recorded of them, but in scenes not inconsistent with what is recorded of their lives and characters. Whereas Shakespeare is apt, in his historical plays, to follow history more or less closely, Landor is apt, as it were, to invent history; where Shakespeare tells what happened, Landor would tell something implying a knowledge of what happened. Thus, a reader ignorant of history misses much of the subtlety of Landor's best work. Again, one unfamiliar with classical literature loses the flavor of a style conformed to classical models. Latin and English were almost equally Landor's mother-tongues; to Latin, which was perhaps his favorite, his English owes, as does Ben Jonson's, both merits and defects. It may be that each of them introduced into an uninflected language too many constructions native to an inflected language; it is certain that one who knows no Latin cannot see in the style of either all that a student of Latin can see.—W. B. SHUBRICK CLYMER, "Landor Once More," *Scribner's Magazine*, July 1891, pp. 124–25

That there are limitations to his genius it were folly to deny. The most damaging one consists in his lack of spiritual insight. Wordsworth's intuitional poetry was always an enigma to Landor, who was wont to affirm, that, as the miner cannot delve far into the earth, so man cannot plunge into the abyss of speculative thought without directly reaching the void and formless, and cheating himself and others into the vain belief that nebulous rings, mere airy nothings, are habitable worlds. Landor might have been a student of Kant, considering the accuracy with which, in a literary way, he conveys the impression that supersensible realities, if perchance they exist, are unknown. Landor had nothing of that Oriental insight which leads the mind to discover the one in the many, and a God in all the affairs of nature and man. "As one diffusive air, passing through the perforations of a flute, is distinguished as the notes of a scale, so the nature of the Great Spirit is single, though its forms be manifold, arising from the consequences of acts." Does such a conception possess meaning and truth? Landor would have answered this question in the negative.

Nevertheless, after making due allowance for limitations, it must be conceded that Landor has offered some permanent contributions to literature. His style alone must insure the preservation of much of his best work. Barring the fact of occasional obscurity, arising from undue condensation and a lack of tact and of sympathy for the reader, and also barring the fact that his sentences are at times too regular for exuberant life and reality, Landor's style is flawless. It is characteristic and at the same time universal.

Passing to subject-matter, one can find no valid reason for supposing that Landor has not enduringly enriched literature by the choicest of his idyls, of his scenes in dramatic poetry, of his imaginary conversations, reflective and dramatic, and by his *Pericles and Aspasia*. Moreover, as the author of separate thoughts, which exhibit their extreme delicacy and beauty all the more clearly after they have been detached from their more or less prosaic surroundings, Landor has a special call upon our admiration. With the exception of Coleridge, English literature is almost devoid of really fine *pensée*-writers—like Pascal and Joubert,—who, though they stand related to the philosopher as gardeners do to the geologist, and though they are more concerned about truths than truth in its unity and at the same time its ramifying multiplicity, yet are stimulating and suggestive, often eminently so. And it is in this capacity, as well as in that of idyllist, dramatic poet, writer of imaginary conversations and letters, that Landor must long maintain a notable place in the minds of those choice spirits who love beautiful conceptions and noble thoughts beautifully and nobly expressed. —EDWARD WATERMAN EVANS, JR., *Walter Savage Landor: A Critical Study*, 1892, pp. 184–87

Landor is the great solitary of English literature. So strangely were the elements mixed in him, that, with many of the qualities that endear men to their fellows, to keep on terms with society was too severe a tax upon his temper. Nor are the friends of the author much more numerous than were those of the man. He was content to keep his way apart in life, and content too that the path he trod as a writer should be little travelled. "I shall dine late," he said, "but the dining-room will be well lighted, the guests few and select." They are few and select, and Landor, who was not a man of his time, will never be the people's man. At an epoch, when the cold fires of the classic ritual of eighteenth-century literature began to pale before the passion and colour and mystery of the mediæval revival, with singular indifference to contemporary fashion he began to speak English with a purer classic accent than had yet been heard in the modern world. And the modern world, with its complex interests, its haste and excitement and widening horizons, could not stay to appreciate the unemphasised attraction of themes of mere abstract intellectual moment, however finely articulated the thought, or linger to admire austere beauty of style or the quiet justice of a perfect phrase. And Landor had no stirring message for his time, no revelation, like Wordsworth's, of neglected or undiscovered truth; nor did he write, as did Byron, to make public confession of the sins and disappointments of his life. Not so much because of the classic severity of his form, as because his attitude, his way of thought belong to the pre-Christian world, because he lacks the spirituality, the ethical fervour and elevation that the modern world demands, is he likely to remain a solitary. His own favourites among the greater writers of the past were not those in whom our later age still finds succour for its spiritual needs. Cicero and Ovid and Plutarch were his close intellectual companions and allies; but for Plato and Dante he had no real affection, and Milton he worshipped not as a Puritan, nor for the Hebraic spirit of his theology, but because he was a hater of tyranny and an artist in the great style. His aloofness from the problems that trouble us, the serene distinction with which he sits apart, this and the fact that his ethical code is the code of the fine gentleman who is also a scholar and philosopher, rather than the Christian, give Landor unique place and audience among the writers of the century. And though where he shines, he shines with a brilliance splendid and unborrowed; though at times the heroic, at times the tender strain of his eloquence wins its way to the heart; one cannot accept him as a guide to life or feel that in his company the human mind takes any step in advance.

For an author who makes such continual demand upon our appreciation, who is so full of fine thoughts, Landor is singularly disconnected, frequently unreasonable; and, since his creed of rebellion against kings and priests is merely passionate and elementary, to take him seriously, as we take Milton, in his disquisitions upon politics or religion is impossible. A search for any underlying unity in his thought would be in vain, the lack of sequence in his ideas is a weariness to the reader, and, if it can be said with truth that his writings present any philosophy, it is an unschematised philosophy that bears no fruit.

But when all this has been said, the rest is admiration. Let it not be claimed for Landor that he is a creative artist of the first order, a sure critic of art or life, that he reaches the sympathies that lie at the roots of our higher spiritual nature. He is a critic of genius, a writer of indisputable originality, who in his best moments mingles a marvellous grace and sweetness with his strength, displays a largeness and sanity in his choice of subject as in the management of his form, and preserves throughout his work a certain royalty of mien, writing as one familiar with great circumstances and great men.

Unlike most poets he preferred his prose to his poetry— "Poetry was always my amusement, prose my study and business"—and he was unlike them in this also that, while the law under which he worked was the law of the severest parsimony, he permitted himself indulgence in a richer vein of fancy and employed a more copious imagery in his prose than in his verse. The *Imaginary Conversations* compel an interest somewhat akin to the interest of Plutarch. We have in English no such storehouse of *epigrammata* weighty with a simple gravity of thought, nor, save in the plays of Shakespeare, an equal body of writing which presents such noble groups of men and women with more natural directness or with purer human feeling. For these reasons the dialogues must remain a part of ever current literature, and for one other reason. The author who is a child of his age and speaks a word to his own time secures success, and with success comes at least a transient glory; to style alone the forgetful fates are kind. Without achieving success Landor by reason of his style takes undisputed place among the masters of English prose. The majestic march, the solemn cadences and sustained harmonies of his Roman period are among the golden joys of the student of literature. Landor's was the art of the statuary. His instinct was for that form of excellence which consists in firmly outlined intellectual drawing, and "words that fit the thing." To achieve distinction in this manner is to be subject to no changes of fashion, and to be numbered among those in whose quiet gardens, as in the courts of some ancient college, the artist loves to linger, to recall and meditate the past, secure from the bustle of the crowd and the faces of anxious men.—W. MACNEILE DIXON, "Walter Savage Landor," *English Prose*, ed. Henry Craik, 1896, Vol. 5, pp. 197–200

Landor's position in politics has been accurately defined by his biographer, Mr. Sidney Colvin. He stood midway between the party of conservation and the party of revolt. He was not a democrat; his sympathies were, indeed, alive to the joys and sorrows of the people; but he was essentially an aristocrat of the intellect. His admiration for the majesty of individual character was unbounded; and he held that a "mob" was not "worth a man." His ideal of government resembled that of Milton, a republic ruled by an oligarchy of virtue and of wisdom. The philosophical dogmas of the Revolution had no interest for one who regarded abstract speculation with a lofty scorn. His indignation against the new despotisms of Europe was deep; but in English politics, while he desired, like his friend

Southey, to correct many things, he would change little. "His chief practical exhortations," writes Mr. Colvin, "were against wars of conquest and annexation; against alliance with the despotic powers for the suppression of insurgent nationalities; against the over-endowment of ecclesiastical dignitaries; in favor of the removal of Catholic disabilities; in favor of factory acts, of the mitigation of the penal laws, and of ecclesiastical and agrarian laws for the relief of the Irish." Three Italian orations of Landor against the Holy Alliance seem to have been rewritten in English, and were sent for publication to London; unhappily, no trace of these has been recovered. Their general spirit may be inferred from certain of the *Imaginary Conversations*; we cannot doubt that they were impetuous pleas against tyranny, or that their impetuosity was moulded into stateliness of form.

The first volume of the *Imaginary Conversations* (1824) was dedicated to Major-General Stopford, adjutant-general in the army of Colombia. Landor was deeply interested in the success of the South American republics,—partly, he says, because he wished every nation under heaven to be independent; partly, because he thought it would be advantageous to England that some counterpoise against the power of the United States should be found on the American continent. Mourning over the feebleness of public spirit in his own country and the rarity of political abilities, he chose to place his noble volume of prose in the hands of an Englishman, who seemed to him to have risen above the selfishness and frivolity of the time, and who had aided one of the republics which sprang into existence at the voice of Bolivar. The second volume is inscribed to General Mina, the famous chief of the Spanish guerillas; and with Mina the writer pleads on behalf of the young republics of the West. He desired to see in South America, not a loose and turbulent democracy, but a confederacy against external tyranny, against dependence and usurpation, against "institutions not founded upon that equable, sound, beneficent system, to which the best energies of man, the sterner virtues, the milder charities, the comforts and satisfactions of life, its regulated and right affections, the useful arts, the ennobling sciences, with whatever is innocent in glory or useful in pleasure, owe their origin, their protection, their progress, and their maturity." Landor's scorn for what may be called the metaphysics of Revolution preserved him from the vacuous rhetoric and the bandying of popular catchwords which are dear to the heart of some prophets of democracy. He was in no sense of the school of the prophets. His conception of a free, adult, proud, and cultivated nation has a grandeur derived from the definite and positive character of his imagination. In his private life Landor was the prey of sudden and violent passions; all the more remarkable are the sanity and virile strength of his political convictions. Their tendency is essentially constructive; if he loved liberty like Milton, he loved it, like Milton also, because he perceived that it is the condition of noble vigor. No loftier word on the evil influence of despotism in dwarfing the passions and the deeds of men has been spoken than that of Landor's poem which in some editions brings his *Hellenics* to a close,—

> We are what suns and winds and waters make us;
> The mountains are our sponsors, and the rills
> Fashion and win their nurseling with their smiles.
> But where the land is dim with tyranny,
> There tiny pleasures occupy the place
> Of glories and of duties; as the feet
> Of fabled faeries when the sun goes down
> Trip o'er the grass where wrestlers strove by day.

The heroic ideals of Landor's imagination, derived in part from communion with the great natural aristocrats of all time, helped to save his verse and his prose from the violence and egoism which often confused his life, and which often cleared away as suddenly, like clouds before the wind and sun. He toiled indeed at his art with an intemperate rage that exhausted him; but it was to produce a form of marmoreal purity and permanence, to discover the laws and the lines of ideal majesty or ideal grace.—EDWARD DOWDEN, *The French Revolution and English Literature*, 1897, pp. 255–59

Works

POETRY

We should have no hesitation in ascribing *Count Julian* to the author of a narrative poem of which the story is strange and unprepossessing, and the diction obscure, but in which the higher requisites of poetry are incidentally displayed in an eminent degree. The same powers are exhibited here so strikingly, and the defects which exist partake so much of the same character, that the internal evidence secures decision; but when an author has not thought proper to affix his name, the critic who gives it publicity assumes an authority to which neither the laws of courtesy nor of his profession entitle him. —ROBERT SOUTHEY, "*Count Julian: A Tragedy*," *Quarterly Review*, Sept. 1812, p. 92

I must read again Landor's *Julian*. I have not read it some time. I think he must have failed in Roderick, for I remember nothing of him, nor of any distinct character as a character—only fine-sounding passages. I remember thinking also he had chosen a point of time after the event, as it were, for Roderick survives to no use; but my memory is weak, and I will not wrong a fine Poem by trusting to it.—CHARLES LAMB, Letter to Robert Southey (May 16, 1815)

What is it that Mr. Landor wants, to make him a poet? His powers are certainly very considerable, but he seems to be totally deficient in that modifying faculty which compresses several units into one whole. The truth is, he does not possess imagination in its highest form,—that of stamping *il più nell' uno*. Hence his poems, taken as wholes, are unintelligible; you have eminences excessively bright, and all the ground around and between them in darkness. Besides which, he has never learned, with all his energy, how to write simple and lucid English.—SAMUEL TAYLOR COLERIDGE, *Table Talk*, Jan. 1, 1834

With many high excellencies, Landor's poetry must ever remain "a sealed book" to the multitude; for whoever prefers to the obviously sublime, beautiful, and true, the grotesque, the visionary, and the involved, must submit to be admired by the capricious select, who can alone relish such elements in composition. In the case of Savage Landor, this waywardness is the more to be regretted, as in his genius there are elements, vigorous, fine, and fresh, which might have enabled his muse to soar with eagle pinion high over Parnassus. He seems, however, all along, to have systematically addressed himself only to the ear of an audience "fit, though few," and even to ignore the competency of a popular tribunal. He moulds exclusively according to the antique, and often with classical severity; but although quite willing to admit his general power, I cannot help thinking that his independence of thought not unfrequently degenerates into a tone something like proud self-sufficiency. We have genius, learning, and knowledge, ever apparently in abundance, but ever of a very peculiar kind; and often, after all, from a sheer love of paradox, he follows, by a side-wind, the very authorities apparently held in contempt. His poetic diction is involved and difficult, obscure from never-ending attempts at compression, and only redeemed by a picturesque power and a word-painting, in which he was subsequently followed by Hunt, Keats, and Tennyson. His imagery is cold and statuesque—"we start, for life is wanting there;" but the habit of composing his pieces first in Latin, and then translating them into his mother tongue—said to be his actual practice—may readily be set down as a main source of their obscurity and apparent affectation. He has nothing like geniality of feeling, or warmth of colouring, in his portraits or pictures. His wit is cumbrous: when he exhibits point, it is rather the poisoned sting than the exciting spur; and his glitter can only be compared to sunshine refracted from an icicle. These remarks apply solely to the verse of Landor. As the author of the *Imaginary Conversations*, and "The Trial of Shakespeare," he is an Antæus on his proper soil.—DAVID MACBETH MOIR, *Sketches of the Poetical Literature of the Past Half-Century*, 1851, pp. 99–100

The consummate grace of many of Landor's smaller pieces will ever recommend them to the general reader, but the bulk of his poetry can only be appreciated by those who possess cognate tastes and something of similar acquisitions. There remains however a just interest in this signal example of the enduring dominion of the old classic forms of thought not only over the young imagination but over the matured and most cultivated intelligence. To Keats they assimilated themselves almost without learning by a certain natural affinity; to the industrious and scholarly Landor they became the lifelong vital forces not only of poetic generation but of moral sustenance. They gave to his character the heroic influences which alone subdued the wilfulness of his temperament, and amid all the confusions of life kept his heart high and his fancy pure.—RICHARD MONCKTON MILNES, LORD HOUGHTON, "Walter Savage Landor," *The English Poets*, ed. Thomas Humphry Ward, 1880, Vol. 4, p. 472

As a poet Landor cannot rank with the greatest men of his time; he cannot, one need hardly say, stand beside Shelley and Keats and Wordsworth and Byron. But he did a kind of work unlike the work of any of these, and he did it almost perfectly. From the writings of greater poets the finest spirits of their day, the deepest lovers of art, will again and again turn for change and refreshment to Landor's idyllic verse. He was himself aware that his greatest work was done in prose. And with all his defects, so towering is the excellence of his noblest passages, that it would be hard to name his superior as a master of style among the English prose writers of the century.—WALTER WHYTE, "Walter Savage Landor," *The Poets and the Poetry of the Century*, ed. Alfred H. Miles, 1892, Vol. 2, p. 96

PROSE

Landor's conversation ⟨of Aesop and Rhodope is⟩ among the most charming, profound, and delicate productions I have ever read.—CHARLES DICKENS, Letter to the Countess of Blessington (May 9, 1845)

I have just finished reading Landor's *Pentameron*. It is full of interest for the critical and poetical mind, but is sullied by some *Landorisms*, which are less like weeds in a fine flower bed, than some evil ingredient in the soil, revealing itself here and there by rankish odours, or stains and blotches on leaf and petal. The remarks on Dante, severe as they are, I cannot but agree with in the main. I believe you expressed some dissent

from them. I think that Dante holds the next rank in poetic power and substance after Homer, Shakespeare, and Milton, perhaps above Virgil, Ariosto, and Spenser, but there is much in his mind and frame of thought which I exceedingly dislike,—and I have ever *felt* much of what Landor expresses on the subject, though without speaking it all out even to myself.—SARA COLERIDGE, Letter to Aubrey De Vere (Aug. 31, 1846), *Memoir and Letters of Sara Coleridge*, 1873, Vol. 2, p. 16

It is needless to eulogize the series of *Imaginary Conversations*,—to which the poet kept adding, as the fancy seized him, until the year of his decease, within the memory of us all. They have passed into literature, and their influence and charm are undying. They are an encyclopædia, a panoramic museum, a perpetual drama, a changeful world of fancy, character, and action. Their learning covers languages, histories, inventions; their thought discerns and analyzes literature, art, poetry, philosophy, manners, life, government, religion,—everything to which human faculties have applied themselves, which eye has seen, ear has heard, or the heart of man conceived. Their personages are as noble as those of Sophocles, as sage and famous as Plutarch's, as varied as those of Shakespeare himself: comprising poets, wits, orators, soldiers, statesmen, monarchs, fair women and brave men. Through them all, among them all, breathes the spirit of Landor, and above them waves his compelling wand. Where his subjectivity becomes apparent, it is in a serene and elevated mood; for he is traversing the realm of the ideal, his better angel rules the hour, and the man is transfigured in the magician and poet.

Paulo majora canamus. From the exhaustless resources of Landor's imagination, he was furthermore enabled to construct a trinity of prose-poems, not fragmentary episodes or dialogues, but round and perfect compositions,—each of them finished and artistic in the extreme degree. The "Citation of Shakespeare," the *Pentameron*, and *Pericles and Aspasia* depict England, Italy, and Greece at their renowned and characteristic periods: the greenwood and castle-halls of England, the villas and cloisters of Italy, the sky and marbles of ancient Greece; the pedantry and poetry of the first, the mysticism of the second, the deathless grace and passion of Athens at her prime. Of "The Citation and Examination of William Shakespeare, etc., etc., Touching Deer-Stealing," I can but repeat what Charles Lamb said, and all that need here be said of it,— that only two men could have written it, he who wrote it, and the man it was written on. It can only be judged by reading, for there is nothing resembling it in any tongue. *The Pentameron* (of Boccaccio and Petrarca) was the last in date of these unique conceptions, and the favorite of Hunt, Crabb Robinson, Disraeli; a mediæval reproduction, the tone of which—while always in keeping with itself—is so different from that of the "Citation," that one would think it done by another hand, if any other hand were capable of doing it. Even to those who differ with its estimation of Dante, its learning, fidelity, and picturesqueness seem admirable beyond comparison. The highest luxury of a sensitive, cultured mind is the perusal of a work like this. Mrs. Browning found some of its pages too delicious to turn over. Yet this study had been preceded by the *Pericles and Aspasia*, which, as an exhibition of intellectual beauty, may be termed the masterpiece of Landor's whole career.

Critics are not wanting who maintain *Pericles and Aspasia* to be the purest creation of sustained art in English prose. It is absolutely devoid of such affectations as mark the romances and treatises of Sidney, Browne, and many famous writers of the early and middle periods; and to *The Vicar of Wakefield*, and other classics of a time nearer our own, it bears the relation of a drama to an eclogue, or that of a symphony to some sweet and favorite air. What flawless English! what vivid scenery and movement! Composed without a reference-book, it is accurate in scholarship, free from inconsistencies as Becker's *Charicles*; nevertheless, the action is modern, as that of every golden era must appear; the personages, whether indicated lightly or at full length, are living human beings before our eyes. As all sculpture is included in the Apollo Belvedere, so all Greek life, sunshine, air, sentiment, contribute to these eloquent epistles. A rare imagination is required for such a work. While comparable with nothing but itself, it leaves behind it the flavor of some *Midsummer Night's Dream* or *Winter's Tale*, maugre the unreality and anachronisms. Landor's dainty madrigals are scattered throughout, coming in like bird-songs upon the sprightly or philosophical Athenian converse: here we find "Artemidora" and "Aglaë"; here, too, is the splendid fragment of *Agamemnon*. How vividly Alcibiades, Anaxagoras, Socrates, Pericles, Aspasia, appear before us: the noonday grace and glory, the indoor banquet and intellectual feast! We exclaim, not only: What rulers! what poets and heroes! but—What children of light! what laurelled heads! what lovers—what passionate hearts! How modern, how intense, how human! what beauty, what delicacy, what fire! We penetrate the love of high-bred men and women: nobles by nature and rank;—surely finer subjects for realistic treatment than the boor and the drudge. Where both are equally natural, I would rather contemplate a horse or a falcon, than the newt and the toad. Thus far, I am sure, one may carry the law of aristocracy in art. The people of this book are brave, wise, and beautiful, or at least fitly adapted: some unhappy,—others, under whatsoever misfortune, enraptured, because loving and beloved. Never were women more tenderly depicted. Aspasia, with all her love of glory, confesses: "You men often talk of glorious death, of death met bravely for your country; I too have been warmed by the bright idea in oratory and poetry: but ah! my dear Pericles! I would rather read it on an ancient tomb than a recent one." Again, in the midst of their splendor and luxury, she exclaims: "When the war is over, as surely it must be in another year, let us sail among the islands Ægean and be as young as ever!" Just before the death of Pericles by the plague, amid thickening calamities, they write tragedies and study letters and art. All is heroic and natural: they turn from grand achievements to the delights of intellect and affection. Where is another picture so elevating as this? Fame, power, luxury, are forgotten in the sympathy and glorious communion of kindred souls. Where is one so fitted to reconcile us with death,—the end of all such communings,—the common lot, from which even these beautiful ideals are not exempt? Ay, their deaths, in the midst of so much that made life peerless and worth living, follow each other in pathetic, yet not inharmonious succession, like the silvery chimings of a timepiece at the close of a summer's day.

Pericles and Aspasia is a Greek temple, with frieze and architrave complete. If it be not Athens, it is what we love to think Athens must have been, in the glory of Pericles' last days. It is a thing of beauty for all places and people; for the deep-read man of thought and experience, for the dreamy youth or maiden in the farthest Western wilds. The form is that of prose, simple and translucent, yet it is a poem from beginning to end. I would test the fabric of a person's temper by his appreciation of such a book. If only one work of an author were given as a companion, many would select this: not alone for its wisdom, eloquence, and beauty, but for its pathos and

affection. You can read it again and again, and ever most delightfully. The "Citation" and the *Pentameron* must be studied with the scholar's anointed eyes, and are sealed to the multitude; but *Pericles and Aspasia* is clear as noonday, a book for thinkers,—but a book for lovers also, and should be as immortal as the currents which flow between young hearts. —EDMUND CLARENCE STEDMAN, "Walter Savage Landor," *Victorian Poets*, 1875, pp. 50–54

Readers who refrain from looking in Landor for what he never purposed to give, will not be likely to complain with Mr. Henley of his poverty of imagination. It was by no means with the great dramatists that Landor would have thought of comparing his *Imaginary Conversations*, but rather with the great writers of dialogue. He makes Barrow say to Newton: "I do not urge you to write in dialogue, although the best writers of every age have done it: the best parts of Homer and Milton are speeches and replies, the best parts of every great historian are the same: the wisest men of Athens and of Rome converse together in this manner, as they are shown to us by Xenophon, by Plato, and by Cicero." Again, in his conversation between the two Ciceros, he makes Tully say "that the conversations of Socrates would have lost their form and force, delivered in any other manner." These remarks are recognized as having a personal reference; without them, however, it is surely obvious to any sympathetic reader that Landor's aim is primarily the lively and dramatic utterance of thought and opinion; only secondarily the creation of character; and that greatly as he cares for the *suggestion* of situation, he cares hardly at all for its development.

Significant for Landor's choice of form is the fact that he was, like Milton, "long choosing and beginning late." It was in 1824, when he was nearly fifty, that his first *Imaginary Conversations* were published. By the time a man is fifty he has had occasion to make himself tolerably familiar with his powers and limitations; and it was plainly by a sort of natural selection that Landor finally hit upon the one literary method suited to his genius. He must have discovered, with or without the help of the critics, that his forte was in concentrated vigor rather than in continuity. By skilful management of the dialogue form, however, this very defect in continuity might be turned to good account; accordingly his conversations are full of the subtle transitions and abrupt turns and returns of real conversation: they are never dissertations in dialogue.

All reservations having been made, he is certainly one of our greatest masters of prose. In sentence form he is perhaps more exemplary than any other: no writer is crisper or clearer. His diction is of the choicest, though for the taste of to-day inclining a trifle too much, perhaps, to Latinism. "During my stay at this inn called Human Life, I would trust anything to the chambermaids rather than my English tongue." Having a full mind, the fruit of wide reading and deep reflection, he could afford to write clearly and concisely. "Clear writers, like clear fountains, do not seem so deep as they are: the turbid look most profound." Writing to please himself, not the clientele of some review,—still less any sect or faction,—he could afford to write carefully and with his eye on the object. "I hate false words, and seek with care, difficulty, and moroseness, those that fit the thing." Not being the slave of an editor or of a publisher, he could dwell upon his work; and, having abundant harvests, he could winnow. No writer has fewer commonplaces: "I have expunged many thoughts for their close resemblance to what others had written, whose works I never saw until after."—MELVILLE B. ANDERSON, "Landor," *Dial*, July 1892, p. 72

I have sometimes wondered whether Walter Savage Landor did not really meditate writing an historical novel at some time during the evolution of the *Imaginary Conversations*. More than one work of the kind, and assuredly of the highest order, must have presented itself to his mind, since he possessed in a supreme degree the power most necessary to the historical novelist, that of seizing the dramatic points in the lives of historical personages and of creating splendid dramatic dialogues without at any time compromising undoubted facts. In other words, he knew how to combine the romantic and the real in such true and just proportions as to demonstrate clearly that they may and should go hand in hand.—F. MARION CRAWFORD, *The Novel: What It Is*, 1893, pp. 74–75

RALPH WALDO EMERSON
From "Walter Savage Landor"

Dial, October 1841

We sometimes meet in a stage coach in New England an erect muscular man, with fresh complexion and a smooth hat, whose nervous speech instantly betrays the English traveller;—a man nowise cautious to conceal his name or that of his native country, or his very slight esteem for the persons and the country that surround him. When Mr. Bull rides in an American coach, he speaks quick and strong, he is very ready to confess his ignorance of everything about him, persons, manners, customs, politics, geography. He wonders that the Americans should build with wood, whilst all this stone is lying in the roadside, and is astonished to learn that a wooden house may last a hundred years; nor will he remember the fact as many minutes after it has been told him; he wonders they do not make elder-wine and cherry-bounce, since here are cherries, and every mile is crammed with elder bushes. He has never seen a good horse in America, nor a good coach, nor a good inn. Here is very good earth and water, and plenty of them,—that he is free to allow,—to all other gifts of nature or man, his eyes are sealed by the inexorable demand for the precise conveniences to which he is accustomed in England. Add to this proud blindness the better quality of great downrightness in speaking the truth, and the love of fair play, on all occasions, and, moreover, the peculiarity which is alleged of the Englishman, that his virtues do not come out until he quarrels. Transfer these traits to a very elegant and accomplished mind, and we shall have no bad picture of Walter Savage Landor, who may stand as a favorable impersonation of the genius of his countrymen at the present day. A sharp dogmatic man with a great deal of knowledge, a great deal of worth, and a great deal of pride, with a profound contempt for all that he does not understand, a master of all elegant learning and capable of the utmost delicacy of sentiment, and yet prone to indulge a sort of ostentation of coarse imagery and language. His partialities and dislikes are by no means calculable, but are often whimsical and amusing; yet they are quite sincere, and, like those of Johnson and Coleridge, are easily separable from the man. What he says of Wordsworth, is true of himself, that he delights to throw a clod of dirt on the table, and cry, "Gentlemen, there is a better man than all of you." Bolivar, Mina, and General Jackson will never be greater soldiers than Napoleon and Alexander, let Mr. Landor think as he will; nor will he persuade us to burn Plato and Xenophon, out of our admiration of Bishop Patrick, or "Lucas on Happiness," or "Lucas on Holiness," or even Barrow's Sermons. Yet a man may love a paradox, without losing either his wit or his

honesty. A less pardonable eccentricity is the cold and gratuitous obtrusion of licentious images, not so much the suggestion of merriment as of bitterness. Montaigne assigns as a reason for his license of speech, that he is tired of seeing his Essays on the work-tables of ladies, and he is determined they shall for the future put them out of sight. In Mr. Landor's coarseness there is a certain air of defiance; and the rude word seems sometimes to arise from a disgust at niceness and over-refinement. Before a well-dressed company he plunges his fingers in a sess-pool, as if to expose the whiteness of his hands and the jewels of his ring. Afterward, he washes them in water, he washes them in wine; but you are never secure from his freaks. A sort of Earl Peterborough in literature, his eccentricity is too decided not to have diminished his greatness. He has capital enough to have furnished the brain of fifty stock authors, yet has written no good book.

But we have spoken all our discontent. Possibly his writings are open to harsher censure; but we love the man from sympathy, as well as for reasons to be assigned; and have no wish, if we were able, to put an argument in the mouth of his critics. Now for twenty years we have still found the *Imaginary Conversations* a sure resource in solitude, and it seems to us as original in its form as in its matter. Nay, when we remember his rich and ample page, wherein we are always sure to find free and sustained thought, a keen and precise understanding, an affluent and ready memory familiar with all chosen books, an industrious observation in every department of life, an experience to which nothing has occurred in vain, honor for every just and generous sentiment, and a scourge like that of the Furies for every oppressor, whether public or private, we feel how dignified is this perpetual Censor in his curule chair, and we wish to thank a benefactor of the reading world. ⟨. . .⟩

But beyond his delight in genius, and his love of individual and civil liberty, Mr. Landor has a perception that is much more rare, the appreciation of character. This is the more remarkable considered with his intense nationality, to which we have already alluded. He is buttoned in English broadcloth to the chin. He hates the Austrians, the Italians, the French, the Scotch, and the Irish. He has the common prejudices of an English landholder; values his pedigree, his acres, and the syllables of his name; loves all his advantages, is not insensible to the beauty of his watchseal, or the Turk's head on his umbrella; yet with all this miscellaneous pride, there is a noble nature within him, which instructs him that he is so rich that he can well spare all his trappings, and, leaving to others the painting of circumstance, aspire to the office of delineating character. He draws his own portrait in the costume of a village schoolmaster, and a sailor, and serenely enjoys the victory of nature over fortune. Not only the elaborated story of Normanby, but the whimsical selection of his heads prove this taste. He draws with evident pleasure the portrait of a man, who never said anything right, and never did anything wrong. But in the character of Pericles, he has found full play for beauty and greatness of behavior, where the circumstances are in harmony with the man. These portraits, though mere sketches, must be valued as attempts in the very highest kind of narrative, which not only has very few examples to exhibit of any success, but very few competitors in the attempt. The word Character is in all mouths; it is a force which we all feel; yet who has analyzed it? What is the nature of that subtle, and majestic principle which attaches us to a few persons, not so much by personal as by the most spiritual ties? What is the quality of the persons who, without being public men, or literary men, or rich men, or active men, or (in the popular sense) religious men, have a certain salutary omnipresence in all our life's history, almost giving their own quality to the atmosphere and the landscape? A moral force, yet wholly unmindful of creed and catechism, intellectual, but scornful of books, it works directly and without means, and though it may be resisted at any time, yet resistance to it is a suicide. For the person who stands in this lofty relation to his fellow men is always the impersonation to them of their conscience. It is a sufficient proof of the extreme delicacy of this element, evanescing before any but the most sympathetic vision, that it has so seldom been employed in the drama and in novels. Mr. Landor, almost alone among living English writers, has indicated his perception of it.

These merits make Mr. Landor's position in the republic of letters one of great mark and dignity. He exercises with a grandeur of spirit the office of writer, and carries it with an air of old and unquestionable nobility. We do not recollect an example of more complete independence in literary history. He has no clanship, no friendships, that warp him. He was one of the first to pronounce Wordsworth the great poet of the age, yet he discriminates his faults with the greater freedom. He loves Pindar, Æschylus, Euripides, Aristophanes, Demosthenes, Virgil, yet with open eyes. His position is by no means the highest in literature; he is not a poet or a philosopher. He is a man full of thoughts, but not, like Coleridge, a man of ideas. Only from a mind conversant with the First Philosophy can definitions be expected. Coleridge has contributed many valuable ones to modern literature. Mr. Landor's definitions are only enumerations of particulars; the generic law is not seized. But as it is not from the highest Alps or Andes, but from less elevated summits, that the most attractive landscape is commanded, so is Mr. Landor the most useful and agreeable of critics. He has commented on a wide variety of writers, with a closeness and an extent of view, which has enhanced the value of those authors to his readers. His Dialogue on the Epicurean philosophy is a theory of the genius of Epicurus. The Dialogue between Barrow and Newton is the best of all criticisms on the Essays of Bacon. His picture of Demosthenes in three several Dialogues is new and adequate. He has illustrated the genius of Homer, Æschylus, Pindar, Euripides, Thucydides. Then he has examined before he expatiated, and the minuteness of his verbal criticism gives a confidence in his fidelity, when he speaks the language of meditation or of passion. His acquaintance with the English tongue is unsurpassed. He "hates false words, and seeks with care, difficulty, and moroseness, those that fit the thing." He knows the value of his own words. "They are not," he says, "written on slate." He never stoops to explanation, nor uses seven words where one will do. He is a master of condensation and suppression, and that in no vulgar way. He knows the wide difference between compression and an obscure elliptical style. The dense writer has yet ample room and choice of phrase, and even a gamesome mood often between his valid words. There is no inadequacy or disagreeable contraction in his sentence, any more than in a human face, where in a square space of a few inches is found room for every possible variety of expression.

Yet it is not as an artist, that Mr. Landor commends himself to us. He is not epic or dramatic, he has not the high, overpowering method, by which the master gives unity and integrity to a work of many parts. He is too wilful, and never abandons himself to his genius. His books are a strange mixture of politics, etymology, allegory, sentiment, and personal history, and what skill of transition he may possess is superficial, not spiritual. His merit must rest at last, not on the spirit of the dialogue, or the symmetry of any of his historical portraits, but on the value of his sentences. Many of these will secure their own immortality in English literature; and this, rightly considered, is no mean merit. These are not plants and animals, but the genetical atoms, of which both are composed. All our great debt to the oriental world is of this kind, not utensils and statues of the precious metal, but bullion and gold dust. Of many of Mr. Landor's sentences we are fain to remember what was said of those of Socrates, that they are cubes, which will stand firm, place them how or where you will.

SIR LESLIE STEPHEN
From "Landor's *Imaginary Conversations*" (1878)
Hours in a Library (1874–79)
1904, Volume 3, pp. 186–226

I ⟨. . .⟩ confess that Landor very frequently bores me. So do a good many writers whom I thoroughly admire. If any courage be wanted for such a confession, it is certainly not when writing upon Landor that one should be reticent for want of example. Nobody ever spoke his mind more freely about great reputations. He is, for example, almost the only poet who ever admitted that he could not read Spenser continuously. Even Milton in Landor's hands, in defiance of his known opinions, is made to speak contemptuously of *The Faerie Queene*. "There is scarcely a poet of the same eminence," says Porson, obviously representing Landor in this case, "whom I have found it so delightful to read in, and so hard to read through." What Landor here says of Spenser, I should venture to say of Landor. There are few books of the kind into which one may dip with so great a certainty of finding much to admire as the *Imaginary Conversations*, and few of any high reputation which are so certain to become wearisome after a time. And yet, upon thinking of the whole five volumes so emphatically extolled by their author, one feels the necessity of some apology for this admission of inadequate sympathy. There is a vigour of feeling, an originality of character, a fineness of style which makes one understand, if not quite agree to, the audacious self-commendation. Part of the effect is due simply to the sheer quantity of good writing. Take any essay separately, and one must admit that—to speak only of his contemporaries—there is a greater charm in passages of equal length by Lamb, De Quincey, or even Hazlitt. None of them gets upon such stilts, or seems so anxious to keep the reader at arm's length. But, on the other hand, there is something imposing in so continuous a flow of stately and generally faultless English, with so many weighty aphorisms rising spontaneously, without splashing or disturbance, to the surface of talk, and such an easy felicity of theme unmarred by the flash and glitter of the modern epigrammatic style. Lamb is both sweeter and more profound, to say nothing of his incomparable humour; but then Lamb's flight is short and uncertain. De Quincey's passages of splendid rhetoric are too often succeeded by dead levels of verbosity and laboured puerilities which make annoyance alternate with enthusiasm. Hazlitt is often spasmodic, and his intrusive egotism is pettish and undignified. But so far at least as his style is concerned, Landor's unruffled abundant stream of continuous harmony excites one's admiration the more the longer one reads. Hardly any one who has written so much has kept so uniformly to a high level, and so seldom descended to empty verbosity or to downright slipshod. It is true that the substance does not always correspond to the perfection of the form. There are frequent discontinuities of thought where the style is smoothest. He reminds one at times of those Alpine glaciers where an exquisitely rounded surface of snow conceals yawning crevasses beneath; and if one stops for a moment to think, one is apt to break through the crust with an abrupt and annoying jerk.

⟨. . .⟩ Landor aims, like Bacon, at rich imagery, at giving to thoughts which appear plain more value by fineness of expression, and at compressing shrewd judgments into weighty aphorisms. He would equally rival Cicero in fulness and perspicuity; whilst a severe rejection of everything slovenly or superfluous would save him from ever deviating into the merely florid. So far as style can be really separated from thought, we may admit unreservedly that he has succeeded in his aim, and has attained a rare harmony of tone and colouring.

There may, indeed, be some doubt as to his perspicuity. Southey said that Landor was obscure, whilst adding that he could not explain the cause of the obscurity. Causes enough may be suggested. Besides his incoherency, his love of figures which sometimes become half detached from the underlying thought, and an over-anxiety to avoid mere smartness which sometimes leads to real vagueness, he expects too much from his readers, or perhaps despises them too much. He will not condescend to explanation if you do not catch his drift at half a word. He is so desirous to round off his transitions gracefully, that he obliterates the necessary indications of the main divisions of the subject. When criticising Milton or Dante, he can hardly keep his hand off the finest passages in his desire to pare away superfluities. Treating himself in the same fashion, he leaves none of those little signs which, like the typographical hand prefixed to a notice, are extremely convenient, though strictly superfluous. It is doubtless unpleasant to have the hard framework of logical divisions showing too distinctly in an argument, or to have a too elaborate statement of dates and places and external relations in a romance. But such aids to the memory may be removed too freely. The building may be injured in taking away the scaffolding. Faults of this kind, however, will not explain Landor's failure to get a real hold upon a large body of readers. Writers of far greater obscurity and much more repellant blemishes of style to set against much lower merits, have gained a far wider popularity. The want of sympathy between so eminent a literary artist and his time must rest upon some deeper divergence of sentiment. Landor's writings present the same kind of problem as his life. We are told, and we can see for ourselves, that he was a man of many very high and many very amiable qualities. He was full of chivalrous feeling; capable of the most flowing and delicate courtesy; easily stirred to righteous indignation against every kind of tyranny and bigotry; capable, too, of a tenderness pleasantly contrasted with his outbursts of passing wrath; passionately fond of children, and a true lover of dogs. But with all this, he could never live long at peace with anybody. He was the most impracticable of men, and every turning-point in his career was decided by some vehement quarrel. He had to leave school in consequence of a quarrel, trifling in itself, but aggravated by "a fierce defiance of all authority and a refusal to ask forgiveness." He got into a preposterous scrape at Oxford, and forced the authorities to rusticate him. This branched out into a quarrel with his father. When he set up as a country gentleman at Llanthony Abbey, he managed to quarrel with his neighbours and his tenants, until the accumulating consequences to his purse forced him to go to Italy. On the road thither he began the first of many quarrels with his wife, which ultimately developed into a chronic quarrel and drove him back to England. From England he was finally dislodged by another quarrel which drove him back to Italy. Intermediate quarrels of minor importance are intercalated between those which provoked decisive crises. The lightheartedness which provoked all these difficulties is not more remarkable than the ease with which he threw them off his mind. Blown hither and thither by his own gusts of passion, he always seems to fall on his feet, and forgets his trouble as a schoolboy forgets yesterday's flogging. On the first transitory separation from his wife, he made himself quite happy by writing Latin verses; and he always seems to have found sufficient consolation in such literary occupation for vexations which would have driven some people out of their mind. He would not, he writes, encounter the rudeness of a certain lawyer to save all his property; but he adds, "I have chastised him in my Latin poetry now in the press." Such a mode of chastisement seems to have been as completely satisfactory to Landor as it doubtless was to the lawyer.

His quarrels do not alienate us, for it is evident that they did not proceed from any malignant passion. If his temper was ungovernable, his passions were not odious, or, in any low sense, selfish. In many, if not all, of his quarrels he seems to have had at least a very strong show of right on his side, and to have put himself in the wrong by an excessive insistence upon his own dignity. He was one of those ingenious people who always contrive to be punctilious in the wrong place. It is amusing to observe how Scott generally bestows upon his heroes so keen a sense of honour that he can hardly save them from running their heads against stone walls; whilst to their followers he gives an abundance of shrewd sense which fully appreciates Falstaff's theory of honour. Scott himself managed to combine the two qualities; but poor Landor seems to have had Hotspur's readiness to quarrel on the tenth part of a hair without the redeeming touch of common-sense. In a slightly different social sphere, he must, one would fancy, have been the mark of a dozen bullets before he had grown up to manhood; it is not quite clear how, even as it was, he avoided duels, unless because he regarded the practice as a Christian barbarism to which the ancients had never condescended.

His position and surroundings tended to aggravate his incoherencies of statement. Like his own Peterborough, he was a man of aristocratic feeling, with a hearty contempt for aristocrats. The expectation that he would one day join the ranks of the country gentlemen unsettled him as a scholar; and when he became a landed proprietor he despised his fellow "barbarians" with a true scholar's contempt. He was not forced into the ordinary professional groove, and yet did not fully imbibe the prejudices of the class who can afford to be idle, and the natural result is an odd mixture of conflicting prejudices. He is classical in taste and cosmopolitan in life, and yet he always retains a certain John-Bull element. His preference of Shakespeare to Racine is associated with, if not partly prompted by, a mere English antipathy to foreigners. He never becomes Italianised so far as to lose his contempt for men whose ideas of sport rank larks with the orthodox partridge. He abuses Castlereagh and poor George III. to his heart's content, and so far flies in the face of British prejudice; but it is by no means as a sympathiser with foreign innovations. His republicanism is strongly dashed with old-fashioned conservatism, and he is proud of a doubtful descent from old worthies of the true English type. Through all his would-be paganism we feel that at bottom he is after all a true-born and wrong-headed Englishman. He never, like Shelley, pushed his quarrel with the old order to the extreme, but remained in a solitary cave of Adullam. "There can be no great genius," says Penn to Peterborough, "where there is not profound and continued reasoning." The remark is too good for Penn; and yet it would be dangerous in Landor's own mouth; for certainly the defect which most strikes us, both in his life and his writings, is just the inconsistency which leaves most people as the reasoning powers develop. His work was marred by the unreasonableness of a nature so impetuous and so absorbed by any momentary gust of passion that he could never bring his thoughts or his plans to a focus, or conform them to a general scheme. His prejudices master him both in speculation and practice. He cannot fairly rise above them, or govern them by reference to general principles or the permanent interests of his life. In the vulgar phrase, he is always ready to cut off his nose to spite his face. He quarrels with his schoolmaster or his wife. In an instant he is all fire and fury, runs amuck at his best friends, and does irreparable mischief. Some men might try to atone for such offences by remorse. Landor, unluckily for himself, could forget the past as easily as he could ignore the future. He lives only in the present, and can throw himself into a favourite author or compose Latin verses or an imaginary conversation as though schoolmasters or wives, or duns or critics, had no existence. With such a temperament, reasoning, which implies patient contemplation and painful liberation from prejudice, has no fair chance; his principles are not the growth of thought, but the translation into dogmas of intense likes and dislikes, which have grown up in his mind he scarcely knows how, and gathered strength by sheer force of repetition instead of deliberate examination.

His writings reflect—and in some ways only too faithfully—these idiosyncrasies. Southey said that his temper was the only explanation of his faults. "Never did man represent himself in his writings so much less generous, less just, less compassionate, less noble in all respects than he really is. I certainly," he adds, "never knew any one of brighter genius or of kinder heart." Southey, no doubt, was in this case resenting certain attacks of Landor's upon his most cherished opinions; and, truly, nothing but continuous separation could have preserved the friendship between two men so peremptorily opposed upon so many essential points. Southey's criticism, though sharpened by such latent antagonisms, has really much force. The *Conversations* give much that Landor's friends would have been glad to ignore; and yet they present such a full-length portrait of the man, that it is better to dwell upon them than upon his poetry, which, moreover, with all its fine qualities, is (I cannot help thinking) of less intrinsic value. The ordinary reader, however, is repelled from the *Conversations* not only by mere inherent difficulties, but by comments which raise a false expectation. An easy-going critic is apt to assume of any book that it exactly fulfils the ostensible aim of the author. So we are told of "Shakespeare's Examination" (and on the high authority of Charles Lamb), that no one could have written it except Landor or Shakespeare himself. When Bacon is introduced, we are assured that the aphorisms introduced are worthy of Bacon himself. What Cicero is made to say is exactly what he would have said, "if he could;" and the dialogue between Walton, Cotton, and Oldways is, of course, as good as a passage from the *Complete Angler*. In the same spirit we are told that the dialogues were to be "one-act dramas;" and we are informed how the great philosophers, statesmen, poets, and artists of all ages did in fact pass across the stage, each represented to the life, and each discoursing in his most admirable style.

All this is easy to say, but unluckily represents what the *Conversations* would have been had they been perfect. To say that they are very far from perfect is only to say that they were the compositions of a man; but Landor was also a man to whom his best friends would hardly attribute a remarkable

immunity from fault. The dialogue, it need hardly be remarked, is one of the most difficult of all forms of composition. One rule, however, would be generally admitted. Landor defends his digressions on the ground that they always occur in real conversations. If we "adhere to one point," he says (in Southey's person), "it is a disquisition, not a conversation." And he adds, with one of his wilful back-handed blows at Plato, that most writers of dialogue plunge into abstruse questions, and "collect a heap of arguments to be blown away by the bloated whiff of some rhetorical charlatan tricked out in a multiplicity of ribbons for the occasion." Possibly! but for all that, the perfect dialogue ought not, we should say, to be really incoherent. It should include digressions, but the digressions ought to return upon the main subject. The art consists in preserving real unity in the midst of the superficial deviations rendered easy by this form of composition. The facility of digression is really a temptation, not a privilege. Anybody can write blank verse of a kind, because it so easily slips into prose; and that is why good blank verse is so rare. And so anybody can write a decent dialogue if you allow him to ramble as we all do in actual talk. The finest philosophical dialogues are those in which a complete logical framework underlies the dramatic structure. They are a perfect fusion of logic and imagination. Instead of harsh divisions and cross divisions of the subject, and a balance of abstract arguments, we have vivid portraits of human beings, each embodying a different line of thought. But the logic is still seen, though the more carefully hidden the more exquisite the skill of the artist. And the purely artistic dialogue which describes passion or the emotions arising from a given situation should in the same way set forth a single idea, and preserve a dramatic unity of conception at least as rigidly as a full-grown play. So far as Landor used his facilities as an excuse for rambling, instead of so skilfully subordinating them to the main purpose as to reproduce new variations on the central theme, he is clearly in error, or is at least aiming at a lower kind of excellence. And this, it may be said at once, seems to be the most radical defect in point of composition of Landor's *Conversations*. They have the fault which his real talk is said to have exemplified. We are told that his temperament "disqualified him for anything like sustained reasoning, and he instinctively backed away from discussion or argument." Many of the written dialogues are a prolonged series of explosions; when one expects a continuous development of a theme, they are monotonous thunder-growls. Landor undoubtedly had a sufficient share of dramatic power to write short dialogues expressing a single situation with most admirable power, delicacy, and firmness of touch. Nor, again, does the criticism just made refer to those longer dialogues which are in reality a mere string of notes upon poems or proposals for reforms in spelling. The slight dramatic form binds together his pencillings from the margins of *Paradise Lost* or Wordsworth's poems very pleasantly, and enables him to give additional effect to vivacious outbursts of praise or censure. But the more elaborate dialogues suffer grievously from this absence of a true unity. There is not that skilful evolution of a central idea without the rigid formality of scientific discussion which we admire in the real masterpieces of the art. We have a conglomerate, not an organic growth; a series of observations set forth with never-failing elegance of style, and often with singular keenness of perception; but they do not take us beyond the starting-point. When Robinson Crusoe crossed the Pyrenees, his guide led him by such dexterous windings and gradual ascents that he found himself across the mountains before he knew where he was. With Landor it is just the opposite. After many digressions and ramblings we find ourselves back on the same side of the original question. We are marking time with admirable gracefulness, but somehow we are not advancing. Naturally flesh and blood grow weary when there is no apparent end to a discussion, except that the author must in time be wearied of performing variations upon a single theme. ⟨. . .⟩

Landor, undoubtedly, may be loved; but I fancy that he can be loved unreservedly only by a very narrow circle. For when we pass from the form to the substance—from the manner in which his message is delivered to the message itself—we find that the superficial defects rise from very deep roots. Whenever we penetrate to the underlying character, we find something harsh and uncongenial mixed with very high qualities. He has pronounced himself upon a wide range of subjects; there is much criticism, some of it of a very rare and admirable order; much theological and political disquisition; and much exposition, in various forms, of the practical philosophy which every man imbibes according to his faculties in his passage through the world. It would be undesirable to discuss seriously his political or religious notions. To say the truth, they are not really worth discussing, for they are little more than vehement explosions of unreasoning prejudice. I do not know whether Landor would have approved the famous aspiration about strangling the last of kings with the entrails of the last priest, but some such sentiment seems to sum up all that he really has to say. His doctrine so far coincides with that of Diderot and other revolutionists, though he has no sympathy with their social aspirations. His utterances, however, remind us too much—in substance, though not in form—of the rhetoric of debating societies. They are as factitious as the old-fashioned appeals to the memory of Brutus. They would doubtless make a sensation at the Union. Diogenes tells us that "all nations, all cities, all communities, should combine in one great hunt, like that of the Scythians at the approach of winter, and follow it" (the kingly power, to wit) "up, unrelentingly to its perdition. The diadem should designate the victim; all who wear it, all who offer it, all who bow to it, should perish." Demosthenes, in less direct language, announces the same plan to Eubulides as the one truth, far more important than any other, and "more conducive to whatever is desirable to the well-educated and free." We laugh, not because the phrase is overstrained, or intended to have a merely dramatic truth, for Landor puts similar sentiments into the mouths of all his favourite speakers, but simply because we feel it to be a mere form of swearing. The language would have been less elegant, but the meaning just the same, if he had rapped out a good mouth-filling oath whenever he heard the name of king. When, in reference to some such utterances, Carlyle said that "Landor's principle is mere rebellion," Landor was much nettled, and declared himself to be in favour of authority. He despised American republicanism and regarded Venice as the pattern State. He sympathised in this, as in much else, with the theorists of Milton's time, and would have been approved by Harrington or Algernon Sidney; but, for all that, Carlyle seems pretty well to have hit the mark. Such republicanism is in reality nothing more than the political expression of intense pride, or, if you prefer the word, self-respect. It is the sentiment of personal dignity, which could not bear the thought that he, Landor, should have to bow the knee to a fool like George III.; or that Milton should have been regarded as the inferior of such a sneak as Charles I. But the same feeling would have been just as much shocked by the claim of a demagogue to override high-spirited gentlemen. Mobs were every whit as vile as kings. He might have stood for Shakespeare's Coriolanus, if Coriolanus had not an unfortunate want of taste in his language. Landor, indeed, being never much troubled as to

consistency, is fond of dilating on the absurdity of any kind of hereditary rank; but he sympathises, to his last fibre, with the spirit fostered by the existence of an aristocratic caste, and producible, so far as our experience has gone, in no other way. He is generous enough to hate all oppression in every form, and therefore to hate the oppression exercised by a noble as heartily as oppression exercised by a king. He is a big boy ready to fight any one who bullies his fag; but with no doubts as to the merits of fagging. But then he never chooses to look at the awkward consequences of his opinion. When talking of politics, an aristocracy full of virtue and talent, ruling on generous principles a people sufficiently educated to obey its natural leaders, is the ideal which is vaguely before his mind. To ask how it is to be produced without hereditary rank, or to be prevented from degenerating into a tyrannical oligarchy, or to be reconciled at all with modern principles, is simply to be impertinent. He answers all such questions by putting himself in imagination into the attitude of a Pericles or Demosthenes or Milton, fulminating against tyrants and keeping the mob in its place by the ascendency of genius. To recommend Venice as a model is simply to say that you have nothing but contempt for all politics. It is as if a lad should be asked whether he preferred to join a cavalry or an infantry regiment, and should reply that he would only serve under Leonidas.

His religious principles are in the same way little more than the assertion that he will not be fettered in mind or body by any priest on earth. The priest is to him what he was to the deists and materialists of the eighteenth century—a juggling impostor who uses superstition as an instrument for creeping into the confidence of women and cowards, and burning brave men; but he has no dreams of the advent of a religion of reason. He ridicules the notion that truth will prevail; it never has and it never will. At bottom he prefers paganism to Christianity because it was tolerant and encouraged art, and allowed philosophers to enjoy as much privilege as they can ever really enjoy—that of living in peace and knowing that their neighbours are harmless fools. After a fashion he likes his own version of Christianity, which is superficially that of many popular preachers; Be tolerant, kindly, and happy, and don't worry your head about dogmas, or become a slave to priests. But then one also feels that humility is generally regarded as an essential part of Christianity, and that in Landor's version it is replaced by something like its antithesis. You should do good, too, as you respect yourself and would be respected by men; but the chief good is the philosophic mind, which can wrap itself in its own consciousness of worth, and enjoy the finest pleasures of life without superstitious asceticism. Let the vulgar amuse themselves with the playthings of their creed, so long as they do not take to playing with faggots. Stand apart and enjoy your own superiority with good-natured contempt.

One of his longest and, in this sense, most characteristic dialogues, is that between Penn and Peterborough. Peterborough is the ideal aristocrat with a contempt for the actual aristocracy; and Penn represents the religion of common-sense. "Teach men to calculate rightly and thou wilt have taught them to live religiously," is Penn's sentiment, and perhaps not too unfaithful to the original. No one could have a more thorough contempt for the mystical element in Quakerism than Landor; but he loves Quakers as sober, industrious, easy-going people, who regard good-humour and comfort as the ultimate aim of religious life, and who manage to do without lawyers or priests. Peterborough, meanwhile, represents his other side—the haughty, energetic, cultivated aristocrat, who, on the ground of their common aversions, can hold out a friendly hand to the quiet Quaker. Landor, of course, is both at once. He is the noble who rather enjoys giving a little scandal at times to his drab-suited companion; but, on the whole, thinks that it would be an excellent world if the common people would adopt this harmless form of religion, which tolerates other opinions and does not give any leverage to kings, insolvent aristocrats, or intriguing bishops.

Landor's critical utterances reveal the same tendencies. Much of the criticism has of course an interest of its own. It is the judgment of a real master of language upon many technical points of style, and the judgment, moreover, of a poet who can look even upon classical poets as one who breathes the same atmosphere at an equal elevation, and who speaks out like a cultivated gentleman, not as a schoolmaster or a specialist. But putting aside this and the crotchets about spelling, which have been dignified with the name of philological theories, the general direction of his sympathies is eminently characteristic. Landor of course pays the inevitable homage to the great names of Plato, Dante, and Shakespeare, and yet it would be scarcely unfair to say that he hates Plato, that Dante gives him far more annoyance than pleasure, and that he really cares little for Shakespeare. The last might be denied on the ground of isolated expressions. "A rib of Shakespeare," he says, "would have made a Milton; the same portion of Milton all poets born ever since." But he speaks of Shakespeare in conventional terms, and seldom quotes or alludes to him. When he touches Milton, his eyes brighten and his voice takes a tone of reverent enthusiasm. His ear is dissatisfied with everything for days and weeks after the harmony of *Paradise Lost*. "Leaving this magnificent temple, I am hardly to be pacified by the fairly-built chambers, the rich cupboards of embossed plate, and the omnigenous images of Shakespeare." That is his genuine impression. Some readers may appeal to that "Examination of Shakespeare" which (as we have seen) was held by Lamb to be beyond the powers of any other writer except its hero. I confess that, in my opinion, Lamb could have himself drawn a far more sympathetic portrait of Shakespeare, and that Scott would have brought out the whole scene with incomparably greater vividness. Call it a morning in an English country-house in the sixteenth century, and it will be full of charming passages along with some laborious failures. But when we are forced to think of Slender and Shallow and Sir Hugh Evans, and the Shakespearian method of portraiture, the personages in Landor's talk seem half asleep and terribly given to twaddle. His view of Dante is less equivocal. In the whole *Inferno*, Petrarca (evidently representing Landor) finds nothing admirable but the famous descriptions of Francesca and Ugolino. They are the "greater and lesser oases" in a vast desert. And he would pare one of these fine passages to the quick, whilst the other provokes the remark ("we must whisper it") that Dante is "the great master of the disgusting." He seems really to prefer Boccaccio and Ovid, to say nothing of Homer and Virgil. Plato is denounced still more unsparingly. From Aristotle and Diogenes down to Lord Chatham, assailants are set on to worry him, and tear to pieces his gorgeous robes with just an occasional perfunctory apology. Even Lady Jane Grey is deprived of her favourite. She consents on Ascham's petition to lay aside books, but she excepts Cicero, Epictetus, Plutarch, and Polybius: the "others I do resign;" they are good for the arbour and garden walk, but not for the fireside or pillow. This is surely to wrong the poor soul; but Landor is intolerant in his enthusiasm for his philosophical favourites. Epicurus is the teacher whom he really delights to honour, and Cicero is forced to confess in his last hours that he has nearly come over to the camp of his old adversary.

It is easy to interpret the meaning of these prejudices.

Landor hates and despises the romantic and the mystic. He has not the least feeling for the art which owes its powers to suggestions of the infinite, or to symbols forced into grotesqueness by the effort to express that for which no thought can be adequate. He refuses to bother himself with allegory or dreamy speculation, and, unlike Sir T. Browne, hates to lose himself in an *O Altitudo!* He cares nothing for Dante's inner thoughts, and sees only a hideous chamber of horrors in the *Inferno*. Plato is a mere compiler of idle sophistries, and contemptible to the common-sense and worldly wisdom of Locke and Bacon. In the same spirit he despised Wordsworth's philosophising as heartily as Jeffrey, and, though he tried to be just, could really see nothing in him except the writer of good rustic idylls, and of one good piece of paganism, the *Laodamia*. [1] From such a point of view he ranks him below Burns, Scott, and Cowper, and makes poor Southey consent—Southey who ranked Wordsworth with Milton!

These tendencies are generally summed up by speaking of Landor's objectivity and Hellenism. I have no particular objection to those words except that they seem rather vague and to leave our problem untouched. A man may be as "objective" as you please in a sense, and as thoroughly imbued with the spirit of Greek art, and yet may manage to fall in with the spirit of our own times. The truth is, I fancy, that a simpler name may be given to Landor's tastes, and that we may find them exemplified nearer home. There is many a good country gentleman who rides well to hounds, and is most heartily "objective" in the sense of hating metaphysics and elaborate allegory and unintelligible art, and preferring a glass of wine and a talk with a charming young lady to mystic communings with the world-spirit; and as for Landor's Hellenism, that surely ought not to be an uncommon phenomenon in the region of English public schools. It is an odd circumstance that we should be so much puzzled by the very man who seems to realise precisely that ideal of culture upon which our most popular system of education is apparently moulded. Here at last is a man who is really simple-minded enough to take the habit of writing Latin verses seriously; making it a consolation in trouble as well as an elegant amusement. He hopes to rest his fame upon it, and even by a marvellous *tour de force* writes a great deal of English poetry which for all the world reads exactly like a first-rate copy of modern Greek iambics. For once we have produced, just what the system ought constantly to produce, and yet we cannot make him out.

The reason for our not producing more Landors is indeed pretty simple. Men of real poetic genius are exceedingly rare at all times, and it is still rarer to find such a man who remains a schoolboy all his life. Landor is precisely a glorified and sublime edition of the model sixth-form lad, only with an unusually strong infusion of schoolboy perversion. Perverse lads, indeed, generally kick over the traces at an earlier point, and refuse to learn anything. Boys who take kindly to the classical system are generally good—that is to say, docile. They develop into prosaic tutors and professors; or, when the cares of life begin to press, they start their cargo of classical lumber and fill the void with law or politics. Landor's peculiar temperament led him to kick against authority, whilst he yet imbibed the spirit of the teaching fully, and in some respects rather too fully. He was a rebel against the outward form, and yet more faithful in spirit than most of the obedient subjects.

The impatient and indomitable temper which made quiet or continuous meditation impossible, and the accidental circumstances of his life, left him in possession of qualities which are in most men subdued or expelled by the hard discipline of life. Brought into impulsive collision with all kinds of authorities, he set up a kind of schoolboy republicanism, and used all his poetic eloquence to give it an air of reality. But he never cared to bring it into harmony with any definite system of thought, or let his outbursts of temper transport him into settled antagonism with accepted principles. He troubled himself just as little about theological as about political theories; he was as utterly impervious as the dullest of squires to the mystic philosophy imported by Coleridge, and found the world quite rich enough in sources of enjoyment without tormenting himself about the unseen, and the ugly superstitions which thrive in mental twilight. But he had quarrelled with parsons as much as with lawyers, and could not stand the thought of a priest interfering with his affairs or limiting his amusements. And so he set up as a tolerant and hearty disciple of Epicurus. Chivalrous sentiment and an exquisite perception of the beautiful saved him from any gross interpretation of his master's principles; although, to say the truth, he shows an occasional laxity on some points which savours of the easygoing pagan, or perhaps of the noble of the old school. As he grew up he drank deep of English literature, and sympathised with the grand republican pride of Milton—as sturdy a rebel as himself, and a still nobler because more serious rhetorician. He went to Italy, and, as he imbibed Italian literature, sympathised with the joyous spirit of Boccaccio and the eternal boyishness of classical art. Mediævalism and all mystic philosophies remained unintelligible to this true-born Englishman. Irritated rather than humbled by his incapacity, he cast them aside, pretty much as a schoolboy might throw a Plato at the head of a pedantic master.

The best and most attractive dialogues are those in which he can give free play to this Epicurean sentiment; forget his political mouthing, and inoculate us for the moment with the spirit of youthful enjoyment. Nothing can be more perfectly charming in its way than Epicurus in his exquisite garden, discoursing on his pleasant knoll, where, with violets, cyclamens, and convolvuluses clustering round, he talks to his lovely girl-disciples upon the true theory of life—temperate enjoyment of all refined pleasures, forgetfulness of all cares, and converse with true chosen spirits far from the noise of the profane vulgar: of the art, in short, by which a man of fine cultivation may make the most of this life, and learn to take death as a calm and happy subsidence into oblivion. Nor far behind is the dialogue in which Lucullus entertains Cæsar in his delightful villa, and illustrates by example, as well as precept, Landor's favourite doctrine of the vast superiority of the literary to the active life. Politics, as he makes even Demosthenes admit, are the "sad refuge of restless minds, averse from business and from study." And certainly there are moods in which we could ask nothing better than to live in a remote villa, in which wealth and art have done everything in their power to give all the pleasures compatible with perfect refinement and contempt of the grosser tastes. Only it must be admitted that this is not quite a gospel for the million. And probably the highest triumph is in the *Pentameron* where the whole scene is so vividly coloured by so many delicate touches, and such charming little episodes of Italian life, that we seem almost to have seen the fat, wheezy poet hoisting himself on to his pampered steed, to have listened to the village gossip, and followed the little flirtations in which the true poets take so kindly an interest; and are quite ready to pardon certain useless digressions and critical vagaries, and to overlook complacently any little laxity of morals.

These, and many of the shorter and more dramatic dialogues, have a rare charm, and the critic will return to analyse, if he can, their technical qualities. But little explana-tion can be needed, after reading them, of Landor's want of popularity. If he had applied one-tenth part of his literary skill to expand commonplace sentiment; if he had talked that kind of gentle twaddle by which some recent essayists edify their readers, he might have succeeded in gaining a wide popularity. Or if he had been really, as some writers seem to fancy, a deep and systematic thinker as well as a most admirable artist, he might have extorted a hearing even while provoking dissent. But his boyish waywardness has disqualified him from reaching the deeper sympathies of either class. We feel that the most superhuman of schoolboys has really a rather shallow view of life. His various outbursts of wrath amuse us at best when they do not bore, even though they take the outward form of philosophy or statesmanship. He has really no answer or vestige of answer for any problems of his, nor indeed of any other time, for he has no basis of serious thought. All he can say is, ultimately, that he feels himself in a very uncongenial atmosphere, from which it is delightful to retire, in imagination, to the society of Epicurus, or the study of a few literary masterpieces. That may be very true, but it can be interesting only to a few men of similar taste; and men of profound insight, whether of the poetic or the philosophic temperament, are apt to be vexed by his hasty dogmatism and irritable rejection of much which deserved his sympathy. His wanton quarrel with the world has been avenged by the world's indifference. We may regret the result when we see what rare qualities have been cruelly wasted, but we cannot fairly shut our eyes to the fact that the world has a very strong case.

Notes

1. De Quincey gets into a curious puzzle about Landor's remarks in his essay on Milton *versus* Southey and Landor. He cannot understand to which of Wordsworth's poems Landor is referring, and makes some oddly erroneous guesses.

GEORGE EDWARD WOODBERRY
From "Landor" (1890)
Literary Essays
1920, pp. 18–34

What first strikes the student of Landor is the lack of any development in his genius. This is one reason why Mr. Leslie Stephen, seizing on the characteristic somewhat rudely, and leaping to an ungracious conclusion, calls him "a glorified and sublime edition of the sixth-form schoolboy." Men whose genius is of this fixed type are rare in English literature, and not of the highest rank. They exhibit no radical change; they are at the beginning what they are at the end; their works do not belong to any particular period of their lives; they seem free from their age, and to live outside of it. Hence, in dealing with them, historical criticism—the criticism whose purpose is to explain rather than to judge—soon finds itself at fault. When the circumstances that determined the original bent of their minds have been set forth, there is nothing more to be said. With Landor, this bent seems to have been given by his classical training. To write Latin verses was the earliest serious employment of his genius, and his efforts were immediately crowned with success. These studies, falling in with natural inclinations and aptitudes, pledged him to a classical manner; they made real for him the myths and history of Greece and Rome; they fed his devotion to the ancient virtues,—love of freedom, aspiration for the calm of wisdom, reverence for the dignity of heroism, delight in beauty for its own sake; they supported him in what was more distinctively his own,—his refinement in material tastes, his burning indignation, his defense of tyrannicide. These characteristics he had in youth; they were neither diminished nor increased in age. In youth, too, he displayed all his literary excellences and defects: the fullness and weight of line; the march of sentences; the obscurity arising from over-condensation of thought and abrupt and elliptical constructions; his command of the grand and impressive as well as the beautiful and charming in imagery; his fondness for heroic situation and for the loveliness of minute objects. This was a high endowment; why, then, do its literary results seem inadequate?

With all his gifts, Landor did not possess unifying power. He observed objects as they passed before him at hap-hazard, took them into his mind, and gave them back, untransformed, in their original disorder. He thought disconnectedly, and expressed his thoughts as they came, detached and separate. This lack of unity did not result simply from his choice of the classical mode of treatment, or from a defect in logical or constructive power, although it was connected with these. The ability to fuse experience, to combine its elements and make them one, to give it back to the world, transformed, and yet essentially true, the real creative faculty, is proportioned very strictly to the self-assertive power of genius, to the energy of the reaction of the mind on nature and life; it springs from a strong personality. To say that Landor's personality was weak would be to stultify one's self; but yet the difference between Landor the man and Landor the author is so great as to make the two almost antithetical; and in his imaginative work, by which he must be judged, it is not too much to say that he denied and forswore his personality, and obliterated himself so far as was possible. He not only eliminated self from his style, and, after the classical manner, defined by Arnold, "relied solely on the weight and force of that which, with entire fidelity, he uttered," but he also eliminated self, so far as one can, from his subject. He did not bind his work together by the laws of his own mind; he did not interpenetrate and permeate it with his own beliefs, as the great masters have always done. His principles were at the best vague, hardly amounting to more than an unapplied enthusiasm for liberty, heroism, and the other great watchwords of social rather than individual life. These illuminate his work, but they do not give it consistency. It is crystalline in structure, beautiful, ordered, perfect in form when taken part by part, but conglomerate as a whole; it is a handful of jewels, many of which are singly of the most transparent and glowing light, but unrelated one to another,—placed in juxtaposition, but not set; and in the crystalline mass is imbedded grosser matter, and mingled with the jewels are stones of dull color and light weight. A lovely object caught his eye, and he set it forth in verse; a fine thought came to him, and he inserted it in his dialogues; but his days were not "bound each to each by natural piety," or by any other of the shaping principles of high genius. He was a spectator of life, not an actor in life. Nature was to him a panorama, wonderful, awful, beautiful, and he described its scenes down to its most minute and evanescent details. History was his theatre, where the personages played great parts; and he recorded their words and gestures, always helping them with the device of the high buskin and something of a histrionic air. He was content to be thus guided from without; to have his intellectual activity determined by the chance of sensation and of reading, rather than by a well-thought-out and enthusiastic purpose of his own soul. And so he became hardly more than a mirror of beauty and an Æolian harp of thought; if the vision came, if the wind breathed, he responded.

This self-effacement, this impersonality, as it is called, in literature, is much praised. It is said to be classical, and there is an impression in some minds that such an abdication of the individual's prerogatives is the distinctive mark of classicism. There is no more misleading and confusing error in criticism. Not impersonality, but universality, is that mark; and this is by no means the same thing, differently stated. In any age, the first, although not the sole, characteristic of classical work is that it deals with universal truth, of interest to all men: and hence the poet is required to keep to himself his idiosyncrasies, hobbies, all that is simply his own; all that is not identical with the common human nature; all that men in large bodies cannot sympathize with, understand, and appreciate. Under these conditions direct self-revelation is exceptional. The poet usually expresses himself by so arranging his plot and developing his characters that they will illustrate the laws of life, as he sees these laws, without any direct statement,—though the Greek chorus is full of didactic sayings; and he may also express himself by such a powerful presentation of the morality intrinsic in beautiful things and noble actions as "to soothe the cares and lift the thoughts of men," without any dogmatic insistence in his own person. In these ways Æschylus obliterated himself from his work just as much as Shakespeare, and no more; Swift just as much as Aristophanes, and no more; but the statement that Shakespeare or Swift obliterated themselves from their works needs only to be made to be laughed at. The faith of Æschylus, the wisdom of Sophocles, are in all their dramas; Anacreon is in all his songs, Horace in all his odes. The lasting significance of their productions to mankind is derived from the clearness, the power, the skill, with which they informed their works with their personality. These men had a philosophy of life, that underlay and unified their work. They rebuilt the world in their imagination, and gave it the laws of their own minds. Their spirits were active, molding, shaping, creating, subduing the whole of nature and life to themselves. It is true that the ancients accomplished their purpose rather by thought, the moderns rather by emotion; but this difference is incidental to the change in civilization. Either instrument is sufficient for its end; but he who would now choose the ancient instead of the modern mode, narrows, postpones, and abbreviates his fame only less than Landor, in his youth, by writing in Latin. Whatever be the mode of its operation, the energy of personality is the very essence of effective genius.

That Landor had no philosophy of life, in the same sense as Shakespeare or Æschylus, is plain to any reader. Those who look on art, including poetry, as removed from ordinary human life, who think that its chief service to men lies in affording delight rather than in that quickening of the spirit of which delight is only the sign and efflorescence, would consider Landor's lack of this philosophy a virtue. It accounts largely for his failure to interest even the best in the larger part of his work, and especially for the discontinuity of his reflections. These reflections are always his own; and this fact may seem to make against the view that he eliminated self from his productions so far as possible. But the presence of personality in literature as a force, ordering a great whole and giving it laws, is a very different thing from its presence as a mere mouthpiece of opinion. The thoughts may be numerous, varied, wise, noble; they may have all the virtues of truth and grace; but if they are disparate and scattered, if they tend nowhither, if they leave the reader where they found him, if they subserve no ulterior purpose and accomplish no end, there is a wide gulf between them and the thoughts of Shakespeare and Æschylus, no less their own than were

Landor's his. In the former, personality is a power; in the latter, it is only a voice. In Landor's eight volumes there are more fine thoughts, more wise apothegms, than in any other discursive author's works in English literature; but they do not tell on the mind. They bloom like flowers in their gardens, but they crown no achievement. At the end, no cause is advanced, no goal is won. This incoherence and inefficiency proceed from the absence of any definite scheme of life, any compacted system of thought, any central principles, any strong, pervading, and ordering personality.

In the same way the objectivity of Landor's work, its naturalism as distinguished from imaginativeness, results from the same cause, but with the difference that, while the faults already mentioned are largely due to an imperfect equipment of the mind, his mode of art seems to have been adopted by conscious choice and of set purpose. The opinion of those who look on naturalism as a virtue in art is deserving of respect. We have been admonished for a long while that men should see things as they are, and present them as they are, and that this was the Greek way. The dictum, when applied with the meaning that men should be free from prejudice and impartial in judgment, no one would contest; but when it is proclaimed with the meaning that poets should express ideas nakedly, and should reproduce objects by portraiture, there is excuse for raising some question. No doubt, this was in general the practice of the ancients. The Athenians were primarily intellectual, the Romans unimaginative. But by the operation of various causes—the chief of which are the importance bestowed on the individual and the impulse given to emotion by the Christian religion—mankind has changed somewhat; and therefore the methods of appeal to men, the ways of touching their hearts and enlightening their minds, have been modified. In literature this change is expressed by saying that the romantic manner has, in general, superseded the classical. The romantic manner aims at truth no less than the classical; it sets forth things as they are no less completely and clearly. The difference is rather one of methods than of aims. The classical poet usually perceives the object by his intellect, and makes his appeal to the mind; the romantic poet seizes on the object with his imagination, and makes his appeal to the heart. Not that classical work is without imagination, or romantic work devoid of intellectuality; but that in one the intellect counts for more, in the other imagination. The classical poet, having once presented ideas and objects, leaves them to make their way; the romantic poet not only presents them, but, by awakening the feelings, predisposes the mood of the mind, makes their reception by the mind easier, wins their way for them. In classical work, consequently, success depends mainly on lucidity of understanding, clearness of vision, skill in verbal expression; in romantic work, the poet must not only possess these qualities, but must superadd, as his prime characteristics, rightness, one might better say sanity, of passion. The classical virtues are more common among authors, the romantic far more rare; and hence error in the romantic manner is more frequent, especially in dealing with ideas. But with all its liability to mistake in weak hands, romantic art, by its higher range, its fiercer intensity, especially by its greater certainty, has, in the hands of a master, a clear increase of power over classical art, and under the changed conditions of civilization its resources are not to be lightly neglected. Indeed, one who voluntarily adopts the classical manner as an exclusive mode seems to choose an instrument of less compass and melody, to prefer Greek to modern music. He sings to a secluded and narrow circle, and loses the ear of the world. Certainly Landor made this choice, and by it he must stand. ⟨. . .⟩

The consequence is that Landor, unclassified in his own age, is now to be ranked among the poets, increasing in number, who appeal rather to the artistic than to the poetic sense. He is to be placed in that group which looks on art as a world removed; which prizes it mainly for the delight it gives; which, caring less for truth, deals chiefly with the beauty that charms the senses; and which therefore weaves poetry like tapestry, and uses the web of speech to bring out a succession of fine pictures. The watchwords of any school, whether in thought or art, seldom awake hostility until their bearing on the details of practice reveals their meaning. Art is, in a sense, a world removed from the actual and present life, and beauty is the sole title that admits any work within its limits. Of this there is no question. But that world, however far from what is peculiar to any one age, has its eternal foundations in universal life; and that beauty has its enduring power because it is the incarnation of universal life. What poem has a better right to admission there than *The Eve of St. Agnes?* and in what poem does the heart of life beat more warmly? *Laodamia* belongs in that world, but it is because it voices abiding human feelings no less than because of its serenity. Nature in itself is savage, sterile, and void; individual life in itself is trifling: each obtains its value through its interest to humanity as a whole, and the office of art is to set forth that value. A lovely object, a noble action, are each of worth to men, but the latter is of the more worth; and, as was long ago pointed out, poetry is by the limitations of language at a considerable disadvantage in treating of formal beauty. But without developing these remarks, of which there is no need, the only point here to be made is that in so far as poetry concerns itself with objects without relation to ideas, it loses influence; in so far as it neglects emotion and thought for the purpose of gaining sensuous effects it loses worth; in both it declines from the higher to the lower levels. Landor, notwithstanding his success in presenting objects of artistic beauty—and his poetry is full of exquisite delineations of them—failed to interest men; nor could his skill in expressing thought, although he was far more intellectual than his successors, save his reputation. Landor mistook a few of the marks of art for all. His work has the serenity, the remoteness, that characterize high art, but it lacks an intimate relation with the general life of men; it sets forth formal beauty, as painting does, but that beauty remains a sensation, and does not pass into thought. This absence of any vital relation between his art and life, between his objects and ideas, denotes his failure. There are so many poets whose works contain as perfect beauty, and in addition truth and passion; so many who instead of mirroring beauty make it the voice of life,—who instead of responding in melodious thought to the wandering winds of reverie strike their lyres in the strophe and antistrophe of continuous song,—that the world is content to let Landor go by. The guests at the famous late dinner-party to which he looked forward will indeed be very few, and they will be men of leisure.

Thus far, in examining the work of Landor as a whole, and endeavoring to understand somewhat the public indifference to it, the answer has been found in its objectivity and its discontinuity, both springing from the effacement of his personality as an active power; or, in other words, in the fact that, by failing to link his images with his thoughts, and his thoughts one with another, so as to make them tell on the mind, and especially by eliminating the romantic element of passion, he failed to bring his work into sympathetic or helpful relations with the general emotional and intellectual life of men.

Why, then, do the most sensitive and discriminating critics, as was said at the beginning, list themselves in Landor's favor? They are, without exception, fellow-workers with him in the craft of literature. They have, by their continued eulogy of him, made it a sign of refinement to be charmed by him, a proof of unusually good taste to praise him. His admirers, by their very divergence in opinion from the crowd, seem to claim uncommon sensibilities; and the coterie is certainly one of the highest order, intellectually: Browning, Lowell, Swinburne, to name no more. They are all literary men. They are loud in their plaudits of his workmanship, but are noticeably guarded in their commendation of his entire contents; the passages for which they express unstinted enthusiasm are few. Landor was, beyond doubt, a master-workman, and skill in workmanship is dear to the craft; others may feel its effects, but none appreciate it with the keen relish of the professional author. The fullness, power, and harmony of Landor's language are clearly evident in his earliest work. He had the gift of literary expression from his youth, and in his mature work it shows as careful and high cultivation as such a gift ever received from its possessor. None could give keener point and smoother polish to a short sentence; none could thread the intricacies of long and involved constructions more unerringly. He had at command all the grammatical resources of lucidity, though he did not always care to employ them. He knew all the devices of prose composition to conceal and to disclose; to bring the commonplace to issue in the unexpected; to lead up, to soften, to hesitate, to declaim; to extort all the supplementary and new suggestions of an old comparison; to frame a new and perfect simile; in short, he was thoroughly trained to his art. Yet his prose is not, by present canons, perfect prose. It is not self-possessed, subdued, and graceful conversation, modulated, making its points without aggressive insistence, yet with certainty, keeping interest alive by a brilliant but natural turn and by the brief and luminous flash of truth through a perfect phrase. His prose is rather the monologue of a seer. In reading his works one feels somewhat as if sitting at the feet of Coleridge. Landor has the presence that abashes companions. His manner of speech is more dignified, more ceremonial, his enunciation is more resonant, his accent more exquisite, than belong to the man of the world. He silences his readers by the mere impossibility of interrupting with a question so noble and smooth-sliding a current of words. The style is a sort of modern Miltonic; it has the suggestion of the pulpit divine in Hooker, the touch of formal artificiality that characterizes the first good English prose. Landor goes far afield for his vocables; his page is a trifle too polysyllabic, has too much of the surface glitter of Latinity. But in the age that produced the styles of De Quincey, Ruskin, and Carlyle, it would be mere folly to find fault because Landor did not write, we will not say after the French fashion, but after the fashion of Swift, at his highest and on his level, the unrivaled master of simple English prose. Landor, at his best, is not so picturesque as De Quincey, nor so eloquent as Ruskin, nor so intense as Carlyle; but he has more self-possession, more serenity, more artistic charm, a wider compass, a more equal harmony, than any of these. ⟨. . .⟩

Landor's influence over his critics is due chiefly to his power as a stylist, and to the perfection of form in his shorter poems and his idyls; but something is also due to the passages which, apart from those mentioned, they commend so unreservedly; such as the study of incipient insanity in the dialogue between Tiberius and Vipsania, and the scenes from "Antony and Octavius" where the boy Cæsarion is an actor. Not to be conquered by these argues one's self "dull of soul;" and scattered through the volumes are other passages of only less mastery, especially in the Greek dialogues, which cannot here be particularized. For this reason no author is more served than

Landor by a book of selections. After all, too, an author should be judged by his best. Nevertheless, when one remembers the extraordinary gifts of Landor, one cannot but regret the defects of nature and judgment that have so seriously interfered with his influence. His work as a whole exhibits a sadder waste of genius than is the case even with Coleridge. There is no reason to suppose that the verdict of the public on his value will be reversed. His failure may well serve as a warning to the artistic school in poetry; it affords one more of the long list of illustrations of that fundamental truth in literature,—the truth that a man's work is of service to mankind in proportion as, by expressing himself in it, by filling it with his own personality, he fills it with human interest.

GEORGE SAINTSBURY
From "Landor" (1893)
Collected Essays and Papers
1923, Volume 2, pp. 115–31

It is not easy, in reading over again Landor's voluminous poetical work, to decide on the exact reasons which have, with the large majority of readers, relegated it to the upper shelf. It is almost never bad; it is at times extremely good. The famous passages which lighten the darkness of *Gebir* and *Count Julian* are unstaled in their attraction by any custom. You may read *Rose Aylmer* for the hundredth time with the certain effect of that "divine despair" which inspires and is inspired by only the greatest poetry. "Dirce," and the companion passage which Aspasia sent to Cleone, are equally sure of their own effect. But Landor is by no means obliged to rely on half a dozen purple passages like these. His enormous total of verse, which if printed with the usual luxury of new poetry (a separate page for even the smallest piece, and not more than twenty lines or so of the longest on any), would fill volumes by the dozen or score, never for long fails to yield something altogether out of the common. From the unequal and motelike crowd of the Ianthe trifles to the long "Hellenic" and dramatic or semi-dramatic pieces, the same rule holds good. With Landor you can never read long before coming to the "flashing words, the words of light"; and the light of the flash is always distinct and not like that of any other poetical star. If he is too "classical," he is not more so than many poets of the seventeenth century, especially Jonson, whom he most resembles, and whom (perhaps from a vague sense of likeness) he rather undervalues and belittles. His quality, from its intense peculiarity, is exactly the quality which bribes the literary student. His passion is not unreal; his sense of beauty is exquisite; his power of expressing it is consummate; and yet he is not, at least to some readers, interesting as a whole. They have to gird themselves up to him; to get into training for him; or else to turn basely to the well-known pieces and re-read (he did not like "re-read," by the way, but I do not remember that he allowed us to "relege") these only.

The reasons of this are probably reasons of combination. Landor has accumulated, in a fashion which might seem to be allowable in one whose quest after unpopularity was so ostentatiously intentional, different and even contradictory claims to the honour of remaining unread. The very scholarly poets are usually rather scant producers; he is enormously voluminous. The dealers in epigrams and short lyrics rarely attempt long-breathed poems; Landor, by turns rains epigram (using that word in its proper sense) with the copiousness of a whole anthology, and pours out a steady stream of narrative or dramatic stuff with the ceaseless flow of Spenser. Those two stout volumes, crammed with poems of all sorts and sizes, are full of delight for the few who really like to read poetry. Let us permit ourselves *Sortes Landorianæ* and open one of the pair without even looking to see which it is. We open on "Dry Sticks," certainly not a promising place to open, and find these verses:

> 'Tis pleasant to behold
> The little leaves unfold
> Day after day, still pouting at the sun,
> Until at last they dare
> Lay their pure bosoms bare—
> Of all these flowers, I know the sweetest one.

Quite trifling verses perhaps, but assuredly not written in a quite trifling style. You may open a hundred volumes of verse as they come fresh from the press and not find one with that style-mark on it. Yet somehow the stoutest devotee of style may be smitten with hideous moments of scepticism when reading Landor. Few men in our days, or in any days at all near them, have had such a faculty of embalming in the self-same amber beautiful things, things presentable, and things absolutely trivial and null. All the defects of the classical and "marmoreal" style are perceived when we come to such a thing as this,

> Better to praise too largely small deserts
> Than censure too severely great defects.

That has most eminently the fault of phrase-making. It is a great question whether even what is true in it is worth saying, and it is a greater question still whether the larger part of it is not false. It is moreover especially liable to the pitiless treatment to which Thackeray subjected another aphorism of the same kind. Why not

> Better to praise too largely great deserts
> Than censure too severely small defects?

or

> Better to praise too scantly great deserts
> Than censure over mildly small defects?

or in short a dozen other truisms or paradoxes or what not of the same easy kind? It is the inevitable penalty of the "classical" form that it adapts itself with the most delusive submissiveness to almost any matter. The opposite style (call it Romantic, rococo, or what you will) is at least saved from this exasperating liability; and when Herrick or Donne is not superlatively good, the one or the other is frankly bad.

If we turn from Landor's shorter poems to his longer we shall find, in different matter and in different measure, the same merits and the same defects. The poet with whom it is perhaps most natural to compare him is Mr William Morris. It is indeed almost impossible for any one who knows the two not to think of the *Hellenics* and the *Acts and Scenes* when he reads the *Life and Death of Jason* and the *Earthly Paradise*. Nor is it a very difficult thing to separate the comparative merits and defects of the two. Mr Morris cannot pretend to Landor's dignity, precision, and lasting certainty of touch. He abounds in surplusage; he is often, if not exactly slipshod, loose and fluid; his singing robe is not girt up quite tight enough, and he tends to the garrulous. But he is always interesting; he has the gift of story, he carries us along with him, and the journey is always easy and sometimes exciting. Landor, though nearly if not quite as voluble as the later poet, has an air of the utmost economy, proportion, and rigour. His phrase, if sometimes rather long, is screwed to concert-pitch; he never apparently babbles; there is an air, however modern his subject, of

classical severity about him. Yet Landor can be exceedingly longwinded, and does not often succeed in being very interesting. Now there are kinds of literature, especially of poetry, in which interest is only a secondary consideration. But I can hardly conceive any one, except in the way of paradox, maintaining that either drama or narrative ranks among the kinds which possess and sometimes abuse this august and dangerous privilege.

The merits and defects of Landor's very different prose, are much the same; especially in the chief division of that prose, the vast aggregate of the *Conversations*, into which he preferred to throw such work of his as was not verse, while as has been seen even his verse-work had a tendency to assume the same guise. He seems indeed never to have been quite at home in any other. Perhaps he cannot in any case be ranked high as a critic, but his exercises in that kind which are couched in conversational form are at any rate much more readable than the so-called criticisms which appear in the eighth volume of his *Works*, and which are either desultory jottings in the nature of annotations, or else worked into a continuous form which is stiff and lifeless. In fact I doubt very much whether Landor could possibly have succeeded in regular history or essay, narrative or disquisition. His egotism (using the word in no unfavourable sense) was so intense that only the egotistic forms of literature, as I think we may without unfairness call the Conversation and the Letter, really suited him. And I am not sure that the Letter did not suit him even better than the Conversation.

He himself, however, preferred the Conversation, and he has probably left us the largest, most varied and elaborate collection of the kind in existence. Lucian surpasses Landor as much in variety of literary excellence as he excels Plato in range and diversity of subject; but the whole bulk of Lucian's dialogues would not, I should think, exceed, if it would equal, a volume and a half of the size whereof Landor's fill five. Fontenelle (who for the last century and perhaps more has been too much undervalued) falls into a lower rank than any of the other three, while Erasmus (the only fifth to be set beside these) is, though a much greater man than Fontenelle and even than Landor, inferior to these two, and still more to Plato and Lucian, in intellectual and literary faculty. In these last and greatest respects Plato of course stands alone; and it is not a favourable symptom of Landor's own capacities in either respect that he evidently did not like him. Plato at any rate is the first of all those who have written or ever will write conversations. The only counter claim which Landor can put in against his superiority in dignity of matter and in mastery of style is the greater variety of his own subjects. There is indeed one other claim which he might urge, though it is an illegitimate one at best, the fuller revelation of personality. We know from the works that go under his name very little, hardly anything, of Plato. From the next, and, as it seems to me next greatest, series of dialogues we know a good deal, though in an indirect way, of Lucian. But from the third we know almost everything of Landor. Given the *Conversations* as the authentic data, with such things as early troubles at college, an unsatisfactory marriage, ample means, uncongenial surroundings, foreign residence, and the like as conjectural assistance, any novelist who knew his business could depict the life of Walter Savage Landor almost exactly as it happened. Nay, he would from the *Conversations* divine most of the circumstances just referred to.

The caution of the author to the reader—"Avoid a mistake in attributing to the writer any opinions in this book but what are spoken under his own name" is interesting but infantile. We always know, we always should know if we knew nothing else about him, from the constant presence of a common and unmistakable form, when Landor is putting Landor's opinions in the mouth of no matter who it may be. If this to some extent communicates a charm to the various and voluminous work concerned, it must be admitted that it also imparts a certain monotony to it. Greek or Roman, mediæval or modern, political or amatory, literary or miscellaneous, the *Conversations* simply convey in stately English, the soon known and not exceedingly fresh or wide-ranging opinions of the author on mundane things, with occasional and not particularly happy excursions into things divine. We know that when any person of the other sex, especially if she be very youthful, appears, she will herself deliver sentiments of an amiable but rather giggling and missish mixture of archness and innocence, while the interlocutor who more particularly represents Landor will address her and speak of her in the style of a more cultivated, gentlemanly, and gifted Mr Tupman. We know that if politics are in question, especially recent politics, the sentiments of a generous but republican school-boy will equally appear. If the subject is literature, woe to any one who speaks ill of Southey or well of Gifford. Woe again to any one who speaks ill of Milton; but let nobody speak good of him except in the particular way which is satisfactory to Walter Savage Landor. We must always speak well of Dr Parr, for he was a friend of ours; and we exchanged scholarship and politeness with him when the Warwickshire Militia would have none of us. But we must not speak ill of Dr Johnson, though he was a Tory and a churchman; for he was a man of the Midlands, and so a very honest fellow. Down with the wretch Pitt (against whom we took a grudge when we knew nothing about politics), with the ribald Canning (who was an Oxford man and a scholar like ourselves, but very successful when we were not quite that), with the villain George the Third (who was a king and whose countenance did not please us). We do not like lords, but if we happen to know any particular lord and he is polite to us, or has pretty daughters with euphonious names, or is related to or connected in some way with our own family, and has not quarrelled with us, let us speak of him and his with a sweet and rotund mouth. If anybody dares to interfere with our comfort whether at Llanthony or Fiesole, in Paternoster Row or elsewhere, let us attend to the sacred duty of literary justice by gibbeting the fellow in as Dantean a manner as we can manage. But when there is nothing of this disturbing kind concerned, and when our heart is full (as it very often is) of the milk of human kindness, and our head (as it generally is when it is not in a state of inordinate heat) of the great wisdom and the stately fame of the ancients, let us write with that pen which is always almost a golden one, as very few Englishmen had written before us, and as hardly one has written since. ⟨. . .⟩

There are however few writers on whom it must be more repugnant to any lover of literature to pass harsh judgments, because there are few, if any, who have themselves combined such an intense love for literature with such noble practice in it. For the two things are by no means always combined, and Wordsworth is far from being the only great writer who may be said to have had a very lukewarm affection for any writings but his own. And the quality of production is in Landor's case of extraordinary strength and peculiarity. On all happy occasions when his hand is in, when the right subject is before him, and when he is not tempted away from it into the indulgence of some fling, into the memory of some petty wrong, into the repetition of some tiresome crotchet, he manages language literally as a great musician manages the human voice or some other organ of sound. The meaning, though it is often noble, is never the first thing in Landor, and in particular it is quite useless to go to him for any profound, any novel, any far-reaching thought. The thought is at best sufficient, and it very frequently is that; but it seldom makes any tax upon even the most moderate understanding, and it never by any chance averts attention from the beauty and the finish of the vesture in which it is clothed.

The famous dreams which close *The Pentameron* are things of which it is almost impossible to tire. Nowhere else perhaps in English does prose style, while never trespassing into that which is not prose, accompany itself with such an exquisite harmony of varied sounds; nowhere is there such a complicated and yet such an easily appreciable scheme of verbal music. The sense is, as has been said, just sufficient; it is no more; it is not in itself peculiarly arresting. Although the sentiment is heartfelt, it is not exactly passionate. But it is perfectly and exactly married to the verbal music, and the verbal music is perfectly and exactly married to it. Again, it is a whole; if not perhaps quite flawless yet with flaws which are comparatively unimportant. It does not consist, as "fine" writing too often does, of a certain number of more or less happy phrases, notes, or passages strung together. It is, as I have called it, a "scheme,"—a thing really deserving those terms from the science of actual music which have been so frequently and tediously abused in literary criticism.

Moreover the qualities which exist pre-eminently in this and other great passages of Landor appear everywhere, on smaller scales, in his prose. It is never safe, except when he attempts the comic, to skip a single page. Anywhere you may come across, in five words or in five hundred, the great Landorian phrase, the sentence cunningly balanced or intentionally and deftly broken, the paragraph built with a full knowledge of the fact that a paragraph is a structure and not a heap, the adjective wedded to its proper substantive, not indulging in unseemly promiscuity, the clause proceeding clearly and steadily to the expression of the thought assigned to it. Whatever deficiencies there may be in Landor (and, as has been and will be seen, they are not few) he is seldom if ever guilty of the worst and the commonest fault of the ornate writer, a superabundance of ornament. Of his two contemporaries who tried styles somewhat similar in point of ornateness, Wilson constantly becomes tawdry, while De Quincey sometimes approaches tawdriness. Of this, nearly the worst of literary vices, Landor was constitutionally almost incapable; and his models and methods had converted his natural inaptitude into a complete and absolute immunity. He is sometimes, especially in his fits of personal dignity and scorn, a little too stately for the subject,—the jokes of our rude forefathers on the Castilian strut may recur to us. He is alas! when he unbends this pride, too often clumsily and even indecently gamesome. But with tawdriness, even with indulgence in literary frippery, he cannot for one moment be charged. In this respect, and perhaps in this respect only, his taste was infallible. His good angel was fatally remiss in its warnings on many points wherein such taste is concerned, but on this never.

If we set ourselves to discover the particular note in Landor which occasions these discords we shall find it, I believe, in a quality which I can only call, as I have already called it, silliness. There are other great men of letters who have as much or even more of the quality of mere childishness; but that is a different thing. Lafontaine and Goldsmith are the two stock examples of childishness in literary history; and childish enough they were, almost inexcusably so in life. But when we find them with pen in hand we never think of them as of anything but very clever men. Landor alone, or almost alone, has written like an angel *and* like poor Poll, and has written like both at once. Hazlitt was quite as wrongheaded as Landor and much more bad-blooded. Peacock was, at any rate in his earlier years, as much the slave of whimsical crazes. Coleridge was as unpractical. His own dear friend Southey had almost as great a difficulty in adjusting the things and estimates of the study to the estimates and the things of the forum. De Quincey was still more bookish and out-of-the-worldly. But even in passages of these men with which we least agree we do not find positive silliness, a positive incapacity to take the standpoint and the view of a full-grown man who has or ought to have mingled with and jostled against the things of the world and of life. We do find this in Landor. His apologists have admitted that he was always more or less of a schoolboy; I should say that he was always more or less of a baby.

The time-honoured Norman definition of a man is "One who fights and counsels." Landor had in almost superabundant measure that part of man which fights; he was abnormally deficient in the part which counsels. In some cases where taste (of certain, not of all kinds), scholarship, poetic inspiration, chivalry (again of certain kinds), and the like could supply the place of judgment and ratiocinative faculty, he has done nobly, even without taking into account that matchless gift of expression which never deserts him for long together. But in any kind of reasoning proper he is as an infant in arms; and in that faculty which (though sometimes it be divorced from it) comes nearest to the ratiocinative—the faculty of humour, he is almost as defective. Here I know there is great difference and discrepancy between those who should agree; but I shall boldly avow that I think Landor's attempts both at humour and at wit for the most part simply deplorable, as deplorable as his idol Milton's. Some persons whom I respect, as well as others whom I do not, have professed to see a masterpiece of humour in "The Examination of William Shakespeare." If by a majority of competent critics it is admitted that it is such, I must be a heretic, yet at least a heretic who can rejoice in Aristophanes (whom Landor did not wholly like), in Lucian (in whom he saw much banter and some wisdom but little wit), in Rabelais (of whom he knew little and whom he evidently did not like even so much as he liked Aristophanes), in Swift (at whom he is always girding and grudging), in Fielding (whom he seldom or never mentions), in Thackeray (of whom, though Landor was his contemporary and survived him, I think as much may be said), and in divers others. The fact is that the entire absence of proportion in matter, so strangely contrasted with his excellent sense of proportion in style, which characterised Landor appears in this matter of the humorous not perhaps more strongly but more eminently than anywhere else. It was not that humorous ideas did not visit him, for they did; but he did not in the least know how to deal with them. He mumbles a jest as a bull-dog worries or attempts to worry a rat when he is set to that alien art. His three sets of models, the classics, the English writers of the seventeenth century, and the Italians (for of French, German, and, if I mistake not, Spanish, as well as of large tracts of English, he knew but little) had each in them certain evil precedent suggestions for a jester. Landor with unerring infelicity seized on these, combined them, worked them fully out, and produced things very terrible, things which range from the concentrated dreariness of the "Examination" and the "Pitt and Canning" conversation to the smaller flashes-in-the-pan of joking dulness which are scattered about his writings *passim.*

Another thing which is extremely noticeable about Landor is the marvellously small difference between his poetry and his prose. Except again Milton (an instance ominous and full of fear) and perhaps Wordsworth, I know no other English writer of the first class of whom this can be said. But Landor has versified, or almost versified, some of his actual conversations, and has left explicit declaration that not a few of his poems are simply conversations in verse. He would have us believe that verse was his amusement, prose his serious business; but it is certain that he began and for years continued to write nothing but verse for publication in any lasting form. And of the vast stores of work (forty or fifty thousand lines of verse and some three thousand large and closely-printed pages of prose) which remain to his credit, the verse might almost always be according to the old trick "unrhymed" and made into prose with but slight alterations: the prose, with certain allowances for greater exuberance and verbosity in parts, might with hardly greater trouble be arranged into Landorian verse. The sententious, intense, rhythmical phrase is the same in both; the poetical intuition of sights and sounds, and other delights of sense, is not more obvious in one than in the other. The absence of continuous logical thought is not greater here than there; the remoteness from what may be called the sense of business is always the same, whether the syllables in a line be limited to ten at most, or may run on to as many as the limits of the page will admit. Although he was conscious of, and generally avoided, the mistake of introducing definitely poetic rhythm into prose, it is astonishing how close is the resemblance of a short stave of his verse to a sentence of his prose. It is owing to this, among other things, that his form of verse is as compared with that of others a rather severe form, while his prose is, compared with that of others, rather florid. It is owing to this that, while some of the very happiest efforts of his verse have the simplicity and directness of the ancient epigram, some of the most agreeable efforts of his prose have in the proper sense an idyllic character.

And so we have in Landor an almost unmatched example of the merits and the defects of style by itself. To attempt once more to narrow down the reasons of both, I should say that they lie in his having had nothing particular to say with a matchless faculty for saying anything. When the latter faculty is exercised sparingly on the former defect, we often get some of the finest things in literature. The writer's idiosyncrasy is not too hardpressed; it has no time to tire us; the freshness and savour of it remain upon our palate; and we appreciate it to the full, perhaps indeed beyond the full. But when the thing is administered in larger and ever larger doses the intensity of the flavour palls and the absence of anything else, besides and behind the flavour, begins to tell. Yet at his very best, and taken in not too large quantities, Landor is the equal of all but the greatest, perhaps of the greatest themselves. And if, according to a natural but rather foolish fashion, we feel at any time inclined to regret that he lived so long and had so much time to accumulate indifferent as well as good work, let us remember on the other hand that his best work is scattered over almost every period of his life, except the very last and the very first, and that the best of it is of a kind worth wading through volumes of inferior work to secure. The true critical question with every writer is, "Could we spare him? Could we do without him?" Most assuredly, if we tried to do without Landor, we should lose something with which no one else could supply us.

JOHN CLARE

1793–1864

John Clare was born on July 13, 1793, in Helpston, Northamptonshire. The son of an agricultural day laborer, he worked from an early age, but also attended a day school at Glinton, a neighboring village, for at least three months a year between the ages of seven and twelve. When forced to seek permanent employment he continued to study by attending night school. In 1820 Clare published *Poems Descriptive of Rural Life and Scenery*, an instant success, going through four editions in that year. Later that year he married Martha (Patty) Turner.

In 1821 Clare became a regular contributor to the *London Magazine*. In the same year he published *The Village Minstrel and Other Poems*, followed by *The Shepherd's Calendar* (1827) and *The Rural Muse* (1835). As early as 1824 Clare had begun to show signs of mental illness, partially manifested by his obsession with Mary Joyce, a woman he had been infatuated with while still in school at Glinton. By 1837 he had become seriously ill, and in that year was committed to Dr. Matthew Allen's asylum for the insane at High Beach, Essex. Clare escaped in 1841, thinking to return to Mary Joyce, to whom he then believed himself married. He was once again declared insane and spent the rest of his life at Northampton General Asylum. Clare died at the asylum on May 20, 1864.

Clare's poetry was little read until this century, but it has now been widely appreciated by such poets as Edmund Blunden, Geoffrey Grigson, and C. Day Lewis. *The Later Poems of John Clare*, including Clare's versions of *Childe Harold* and *Don Juan*, appeared in 1964 in an edition prepared by E. Robinson and G. Summerfield, and Clare's *Letters* and *Prose*, edited by J. W. and Anne Tibble, were both published in 1951.

Personal

In a conversation on literary subjects, during the spring of the present year, with my excellent friend Mr. Taylor, of Fleet Street, he inquired of me if I knew any thing of John Clare, an agricultural labourer in the neighbourhood of Stamford, of whose talent for poetical composition he then possessed a considerable number of specimens, transmitted to him by Mr. Drury, a bookseller at Stamford. The name was wholly unknown to me, and,—to drop the style royal and critical, and speak in the first person,—I cannot account for, nor excuse the indifference, by which the subject was afterwards permitted to escape altogether from my regard. Returning, a few days since, from the North of England, Mr. Taylor became my guest for a day or two; and, the name of Clare being repeated, I expressed a wish to see the person of whose abilities my friend's correct judgment pronounced so favourably. Mr. Taylor had seen Clare, for the first time, in the morning, and he doubted much if our invitation would be accepted by the rustic poet, who had now just returned from his daily labour, shy, and reserved, and disarrayed, as he was. In a few minutes, however, Clare announced his arrival by a hesitating knock at the door,—"between a single and a double rap,"—and immediately upon his introduction he dropped into a chair. Nothing could exceed the meekness, and simplicity, and diffidence with which he answered the various inquiries concerning his life and habits, which we mingled with subjects calculated or designed to put him much at his ease. Nothing, certainly, could less resemble splendour than the room into which Clare was shown; but there was a carpet, upon which it is likely he never previously set foot; and wine, of which assuredly he had never tasted before. Of music he expressed himself passionately fond, and had learned to play a little on the violin, in the humble hope of obtaining a trifle at the annual feasts in the neighbourhood, and at Christmas. The piano-forte he had heard, or supposed it must be *that* he heard, passing the house of a family, whose name I am not authorised to mention, and

for whom, if I did name them, I should feel it difficult to express the affection that I feel. No plaudit could equal the acknowledgment paid to her voice, while the tear stole silently down the cheek of the rustic poet, as one of our little party sung the pathetic ballad of "Auld Robin Gray." His account of his birth is melancholy enough. Nothing can be conceived much humbler than the origin of John Clare, poetry herself does not supply a more lowly descent. His father, who still resides, where the poet was born, at Helpstone (a village in North-amptonshire, seven miles distant from Stamford) while health and strength were his possession, was a daily labourer, but decrepitude has now reduced him to the parish for subsistence. His son, when of sufficient age, assisted his father in thrashing, and other agricultural labours;—at intervals, sometimes of great distance, attending a little school in the adjoining village of Glinton, where he learned to read and to write. Having there, also, attained the rudiments of arithmetic, his attention became riveted to figures, and, without assistance, he mastered the first eight problems of Ward's Algebra, stimulated by the laudable but humble ambition of qualifying himself for the office of usher in a village school. The intricacies of mathematics, however, without a guide, at length subdued the zeal of the youth, while the excitement of fancy seduced him from the study of Bonnycastle and Fenning. But to labour was the destiny of John Clare, and gardening being considered by his parents an occupation better fitted than the plough for a frame of no sturdy structure, he was sent for instruction to work in the gardens of the Marquis of Exeter, at Burghley; and, though the brutal disposition and dissolute habits of his teacher compelled him to relinquish his instructions at the end of nine months, it is to the use of the spade that Clare has ever since been indebted for his precarious and narrow subsistence; and, when the writer of this narrative first saw the poet, he had just quitted an engagement in the vicinity of Stamford, because his employer had reduced his stipend from eighteen to fourteen pence *per diem!* Under the circumstances here disclosed, it will not be supposed that Clare had ever much time for study, or even the means for study, if leisure had not been wanting. Beyond his Bible he had read nothing but a few odd volumes, the very titles of some of which he had forgotten, and others, which he remembered, were so utterly worthless, that I should shame to mention the names. A single volume of Pope, however, with the *Wild Flowers* of Bloomfield, and the writings of Burns, were sufficient to stimulate his innate genius for poetry.—OCTAVIUS GILCHRIST, "Some Account of John Clare, an Agricultural Labourer and Poet," *London Magazine*, Jan. 1820, pp. 8–9

For the last ten or twelve years of his existence the poet suffered much from physical infirmities. Previously he was allowed to go almost daily into the town of Northampton, where he used to sit under the portico of All Saints' Church, watching the gambols of the children around him, and the fleeting clouds high up in the sky. When these excursions came to be forbidden, he retired to his window-recess in the asylum, reading little and speaking little; dreaming unutterable dreams of another world. Sometimes his face would brighten up as if illuminated by an inward sun, overwhelming in its glory and beauty. This life of contemplation, extending over many years, was followed by a singular change in the physical constitution. The head seemed to expand vastly; the bushy eyebrows grew downward until they almost obscured the eyes, and the abundant hair, white as snow, came to fall in long curls over the massive shoulders. In outward appearance the poet became the patriarch.

The inmates of the asylum treated Clare with the greatest respect—far greater than that previously allotted to him by the world without. To his fellow-sufferers he always was John Clare the poet; never Clare the farm-labourer or the lime-burner. An artist among the patients was indefatigable in painting his portrait, in all possible attitudes; others never wearied of waiting upon him, or rendering him some slight service. The poet accepted the homage thus rendered, quietly and unaffectedly, as a king would that of his subjects. He gave little utterance to his thoughts, or dreams, whatever they were, and only smiled upon his companions now and then. When he became very weak and infirm, they put him into a chair, and wheeled him about in the garden. The last day he was thus taken out, and enjoyed the fresh air and the golden sunshine, was on Good Friday, 1864. He was too helpless to be moved afterwards; yet would still creep, now and then, from his bed to the window, looking down upon the ever-beautiful world, which he knew he was leaving now, and which he was not loth to leave, though he loved it so much.

Towards noon on the 20th of May, the poet closed his eyes for ever. His last words were, 'I want to go home.' So gentle was his end that the bystanders scarcely knew when he had ceased to breathe. God took his soul away without a struggle.—FREDERICK MARTIN, *Life of John Clare*, 1865, pp. 294–95

John Clare was, far more truly than Ebenezer Elliott, of the class of uneducated poets. I recall him, poor fellow, with his huge overburthening head, that might have dreamed dreams and seen visions, but obviously was not the throne of productive thought. His life was cheerless, or gladdened only by a brief ray of sunshine that speedily gave way to blacker and blacker clouds of calamity, under the gloomy influence of which his mind sank; and after long years of confinement he died in the Insane Asylum at Northampton, the town with which his name is inseparably associated—though not to its honour. He was not buried in a pauper's grave; a few pounds were kindly subscribed to preserve his body from that indignity;

that, and a small annuity purchased for him by subscription, while he was yet free from the most terrible of maladies, is the sum of what his country did for the poor peasant boy who lived through penury and suffering to leave his mark in the literary annals of his time. I knew him in 1826 or 1827, and printed in the *Amulet* some of the best of his poems, notably "Mary Lee." At a later period a memoir of him in the *Book of Gems*, with some examples of his genius and a reference to the sad story of his life, brought me a letter from the noble Marquis who took his title from Clare's native town; but I never heard that it resulted in substantial aid to the poor poet. Yet he had been guilty of no other crime than poverty, and his errors were only those that are unhappily so frequently found in combination with the highest order of genius. London society, certain coteries of it, at least, made a lion of him for a time, and then consigned him to utter and withering neglect; what had been sport to the lionizers was death to poor Clare, whom flattery and patronage had disgusted with his former life of hopeless poverty, and who found himself suddenly plunged back into it.—S. C. HALL, *Retrospect of a Long Life*, 1883, p. 409

General

It is with heartfelt pleasure that we take up a new volume of Poems by John Clare, the Northamptonshire Peasant. Some fifteen years or thereabouts, we believe, have elapsed since he earned that title which, to our ears, has almost as pleasant a sound as that of the Ettrick Shepherd. We rejoice to find that the Rural Muse has been with him during his long retirement—that his fine sensibilities have suffered no abatement under the influence of time—and that, though he says "ill health has almost rendered me incapable of doing any thing," it has not in any degree weakened his mental powers or dulled his genius. Let us hope that ill health may soon take its departure from "the Poet's Cottage, Northborough," of which, facing the titlepage ⟨of *The Rural Muse*⟩, we have here so pretty an impression—and that as he is yet in the prime of life, he may live to sing many such sweet songs as these—and in domestic peace and comfort long enjoy his fame. Yes—his fame. For England has singled out John Clare from among her humble sons (Ebenezer Elliot belongs altogether to another order)—as the most conspicuous for poetical genius, next to Robert Bloomfield. That is a proud distinction—whatever critics may choose to say; and we cordially sympathize with the beautiful expression of his gratitude to the Rural Muse, when he says—

> Like as the little lark from off its nest,
> Beside the mossy hill, awakes in glee,
> To seek the morning's throne, a merry guest—
> So do I seek thy shrine, if that may be,
> To win by new attempts another smile from thee.

The poems now before us are, we think, at least equal to the best of his former productions, and characterised by the same beauties—among which we may mention as the most delightful—rich and various imagery of nature. England is out of all sight the most beautiful country in the whole world—Scotland alone excepted—and, thank heaven, they two are one kingdom—divided by no line either real or imaginary—united by the Tweed. We forget at this moment—if ever we knew it—the precise number of her counties—but we remember that one and all of them— "alike, but oh! how different"—are fit birth places and abodes for poets. Some of them, we know well, are flat—and we in Scotland, with hills or mountains for ever before our eyes, are sometimes disposed to find fault with them on that ground—as if nature were not at liberty to find her own level. Flat indeed! So is the sea. Wait till you have walked a few miles in among the Fens—and you will be wafted along like a little sail-boat, up and down undulations green and gladsome as waves. Think ye there is no scenery there? Why, you are in the heart of a vast metropolis!—yet have not the sense to see the silent city of molehills sleeping in the sun. Call that pond a lake—and by a word how is it transfigured? Now you discern flowers unfolding on its low banks and braes—and the rustle of the rushes is like that of a tiny forest—how appropriate to the wild! Gaze—and to your gaze what colouring grows! Not in green only—or in russet brown doth nature choose to be apparelled in this her solitude—nor ever again will you call her dreary here—for see how every one of those fifty flying showers lightens up its own line of beauty along the waste—instantaneous as dreams—or stationary as waking thought—till, ere you are aware that all was changing, the variety has all melted away into one harmonious glow attempered by that rainbow. —JOHN WILSON, "Clare's Rural Muse," *Blackwood's Edinburgh Magazine*, Aug. 1835, p. 231

His poems were not the mere reflexes of his reading. He had studied for himself in the fields, and in the woods, and by the side of brooks. I very much doubt if there could be found in his poems a single commonplace image, or a description made up of hackneyed elements. In that respect, his poems are original, and have even a separate value, as a sort of calendar (in extent, of course, a very limited one) of many rural appearances, of incidents in the fields not elsewhere noticed, and of the loveliest flowers most felicitously described. The description is often true even to a botanical eye; and in that, perhaps, lies the chief defect; not properly in the scientific accuracy, but that, in searching after this too earnestly, the feeling is sometimes too much neglected. However, taken as a whole, his poems have a very novel quality of merit, though a quality too little, I fear, in the way of public notice. Messrs. Taylor & Hessey had been very kind to him; and, through them, the late Lord Fitzwilliam had settled an annuity upon him. In reality, the annuity had been so far increased, I believe, by the publishers as to release him from the necessities of daily toil. He had thus his time at his own command; and, in 1824, perhaps upon some literary scheme, he came up to London, where, by a few noble families and by his liberal publishers, he was welcomed in a way that, I fear, from all I heard, would but too much embitter the contrast with his own humble opportunities of enjoyment in the country. The contrast of Lord Radstock's brilliant parties, and the glittering theatres of London, would have but a poor effect in training him to bear that want of excitement which even already, I had heard, made his rural life but too insupportable to his mind. It is singular that what most fascinated his rustic English eye was not the gorgeous display of English beauty, but the French style of beauty, as he saw it amongst the French actresses in Tottenham Court Road. He seemed, however, oppressed by the glare and tumultuous existence of London; and, being ill at the time, from an affection of the liver, which did not, of course, tend to improve his spirits, he threw a weight of languor upon any attempt to draw him out into conversation. One thing, meantime, was very honourable to him,—that even in this season of dejection he would uniformly become animated when anybody spoke to him of Wordsworth—animated with the most hearty and almost rapturous spirit of admiration. As regarded his own poems, this admiration seemed to have an unhappy effect of depressing his confidence in himself. It is unfortunate, indeed, to gaze too closely upon models of colossal excellence. Compared with those of his own class, I feel satisfied that Clare will

always maintain an honourable place.—THOMAS DE QUINCEY, *London Reminiscences* (1840), *Collected Writings*, ed. David Masson, Vol. 4, pp. 144–45

Clare is Bloomfield's successor, and he is very far his superior: dwelling among the ever-varying scenes of Nature, and abounding, as he unquestionably does, with homely images, he is yet not merely a rustic Poet, or a rural Bard. Such poets receive, but do not give; they take passing sensible impressions of the Georgic world, but they do not reflect themselves. From such writers, we scarcely expect reflection; their Bucolics abound in prettinesses and generalities, without the boldness of generalization; but Clare has more fully individualized his scenery than any poet of his class, always excepting Burns: it is the poetry of Rural Life and Taste, but it is Rural Life with the dignity of the man, not with the rudeness or mannerism of the clown. It is worth some inquiry, what makes the evident distinction between the methods of Cowper, and Wordsworth, and Keats, and Tennyson; and between these again and our humbler friend, of whom we are now speaking: all love the country, but few love it as Clare loves it. Yet, it seems indispensable to the proper appreciation of rural scenery, that we should not only take our walks there, but find our work there. Clare writes as Gilbert White would have written had he been a poet. He threads his way through all Nature's scenery with a quiet meditation and reflection; and frequently those reflections, if not the result of profound thought, yet bear the stamp of profound beauty. Clare's life is in the country. There are those who study the country, and read the volume of the town by its side; there are those who bring to the study of the country extensive readings and learning; there are those who make each scene of country life only the key to their own imaginations, and move, indeed, very far from the scene of their original thought; but Clare takes the country literally as it is; he brings to it no learning, no historical suggestions; he seeks in the country none of the monuments of haughty human grandeur; he unfolds no political philosophy; he seeks no high idealization; he takes the lessons lying on the surface, and frequently it is so simple and natural, that it affects us to tears. The fields of Nature are not so much a study to which he retires, or an observatory which he mounts; they are rather a book which he reads, and, as he reads, turns down the page. We should be prepared to expect, after this, what we do actually find—an extreme homeliness of style and thought— we mean homeliness in its highest and best sense—not lowness, nor vulgarity—the very reverse of all these. Clare walks through the whole world around him with the impression, that he cannot go where "universal love smiles not around." His whole soul is a fountain of love and sensibility, and it wells forth in loving verse for all and to all creatures. The lessons of his verses may be described as coming, rather than being sought; for they grow up before him; he does not dig for them, and therefore his poems are rather fancies and feelings than imaginations. He throws his whole mind, with all his sensitiveness, into the country; yet not so much does he hang over its human life as the life of Nature, the love and the loveliness of this beautiful world. Traditional tales he does not narrate. A bird's nest has far more attraction to his eyes than the old manor-house or the castle. The life of the cottage, too, is a holy life for him; his home is there, and every season brings, day by day, its treasures of enjoyment and of peace to him. In a new and noble sense all his poems are pastorals; he sings of rural loves and trystings, hopes and joys. He never, indeed, loses himself, as many have done, in vague generalities, for he has been a keen observer of the ways of Nature; he knows her face in all its moods, and to him that face is always cheerful. Other poets go out into the walks of Nature to spend a holiday; they love her, but to see her is an occasional pleasure; but to Clare it is an every-day existence. He has no holiday with Nature; he walks with her as friend with friend. Other poets select a river, or a mountain, and individualize it; but to Clare all are but parts of the same lovely Home, and as every part of the home is endeared—the chair, the shelf, the lattice, the wreathing flower, the fire-place, the table—so is every object in Nature a beloved object, because the whole is beloved. Other poets entertain, as they enter the avenues of Nature, a most solemn awe and dread: we have said that Clare never forgets himself in low coarseness, so neither does he ever shrink or shiver beneath the dread of an overawing presence; he walks with Nature as an angel walks with goodness—naturally, cheerfully, fraternally.—EDWIN PAXTON HOOD, "The Poetry of John Clare" (1851), *The Peerage of Poverty*, 1870, pp. 207–10

Clare, in his humble way, and without consciously sharing in it, was a helper in that reaction against the conventionality and stiff formalism of the Johnsonian era in English poetry, which was led by such men as Wordsworth and Coleridge and Scott. He was not a mannerist nor an imitator. Perhaps, if he had possessed a wider knowledge of books when he began to write, he might have been less original; as it was, his verses aimed only to describe what a genuine lover of nature saw and felt—not merely her more obvious and general aspects, but many such minute charms as no other poet to this day has thought worthy of embalming. The ant, at its toil; the lady-bug, preening its gay wings on the bending grass-spear; the felled tree, that he would fain have left to "grow old in picturesque decay;" the frog, wetting his speckled sides as he leaped across the dewy meadow; the evening daisies, that "button into buds;" the rain-dripping oaks, that "print crimpling dimples" on the lake; the glow-worm, apostrophized as a

Tasteful illumination of the night,
Bright, scatter'd, twinkling star of spangled earth;

all these, and thousands more of such minor beauties, employed his muse, and attested his close and loving observation. Nor did he fail to give graphic pictures of rural character, like that of "The Woodman," or those in "The Haymaker's Story." The joys and sorrows, the hardships and sports, the grinding toil and comfortless old age of the peasantry, were drawn with all the realism of a Crabbe; to which was added the genuine feeling of one who had experienced it all. Outside of Wordsworth, there is no English poet who shows so much sympathy with the common people as Clare; but while, with Wordsworth, this was to some extent a part of his art, and was done upon a theory—though nobly and honestly done—with Clare, it was part of his life, the unstudied outpouring of his being. Without Wordsworth's imaginative power and philosophic insight (which make him the grandest poet of nature in any tongue), Clare had wonderful truth in little, with a sweetness and refinement which are doubly admirable considering his rude origin and uncongenial surroundings. In "The Village Minstrel," published in his second volume, he describes faithfully both the circumstances which led his mind to poetry, and the life of his uncouth neighbors.—BENJAMIN P. AVERY, "Relics of John Clare," *Overland Monthly*, Feb. 1873, p. 136

The poetry of Clare is what might have been expected from his long familiarity with rural scenery, and his intimate knowledge of country life. Simple as the song of a bird, it is best described by Milton's phrase, "native wood-notes wild," for art it has

none, and only such music as lingered in the memory of Clare from the few poets that he had read. It abounds with picturesque details, which declare the naturalist as well as the poet; it sparkles with happy epithets, and to those who delight in Nature for its own sake, and not for the human quality which the present race of poets are striving to infuse into it, it is winsome and charming. It is not the kind of poetry to criticise, for it is full of faults, but to read generously and tenderly, remembering the lowly life of Clare, his want of education, his temptations, his struggles, his sorrow and suffering, and his melancholy end.—RICHARD HENRY STODDARD, "John Clare," *Under the Evening Lamp*, 1892, pp. 132–33

In Clare's early work, which is more definitely the work of the peasant than perhaps any other peasant poetry, there is more reality than poetry.

I found the poems in the fields,
And only wrote them down,

as he says with truth, and it was with an acute sense of the precise thing he was saying, that Lamb complimented him in 1822 on the 'quantity' of his observation.

No one before him had given such a sense of the village, for Bloomfield does not count, not being really a poet; and no one has done it so well since, until a greater poet, Warner, brought more poetry with him. His danger was to be too deliberate, unconscious that there can be choice in descriptive poetry, or that anything which runs naturally into metre may not be the best material for a particular poem. His words are for the most part chosen only to be exact, and he does not know when he is obvious or original in his epithets. The epithets, as he goes on, strengthen and sharpen; in his earliest period he would not have thought of speaking of 'bright glib ice' or of the almanac's 'wisdom gossiped from the stars.' He educated himself with rapidity, and I am inclined to doubt the stories of the illiterate condition of even his early manuscripts. His handwriting, as early as the time of his first published book, is clear, fluent, and energetic. In 1821 Taylor saw in his cupboard copies of Burns, Cowper, Wordsworth, Coleridge, Keats, and Crabbe. And in a printed letter of 1826, addressed to Montgomery, Clare says that he has 'long had a fondness for the poetry of the time of Elizabeth,' which he knows from Ellis's *Specimens of Early English Poets* and Ritson's *English Songs*. It was doubtless in Ellis that he found some of the metres in which we may well be surprised to find him writing as early as 1821; Villon's ballad metre, for instance, which he uses in a poem in *The Village Minstrel*, and which he might have found in poems of Henryson and other Scottish poets quoted in Ellis. Later on, among some poems which he wrote in deliberate imitation of Elizabethan poets, we shall find one in a Wyatt metre, which reads like an anticipation of Bridges.

Thus it cannot be said that in Clare's very earliest work we have an utterance which literary influences have not modified. The impulse and the subject-matter are alike his own, and are taken directly from what was about him. There is no closer attention to nature than in Clare's poems; but the observation begins by being literal; nature a part of his home, rather than his home a part of nature. The things about him are the whole of his material, he does not choose them by preference out of others equally available; all his poems are made out of the incidents and feelings of humble life and the actual fields and flowers of his particular part of England. He does not make pictures, which would imply aloofness and selection; he enumerates, which means a friendly knowledge. It is enough for him, enough for his success in his own kind of poetry, to say them over, saying, 'Such they were, and I loved them because I had always seen them so.'

Yet his nerves were not the nerves of a peasant. Everything that touched him was a delight or an agony, and we hear continually of his bursting into tears. He was restless and loved wandering, but he came back always to the point from which he had started. He could not endure that anything he had once known should be changed. He writes to tell his publisher that the landlord is going to cut down two elm-trees at the back of his hut, and he says: 'I have been several mornings to bid them farewell.' He kept his reason as long as he was left to starve and suffer in that hut, and when he was taken from it, though to a better dwelling, he lost all hold on himself. He was torn up by the roots, and the flower of his mind withered. What this transplanting did for him is enough to show how native to him was his own soil, and how his songs grew out of it.

In the last book published before he entered the asylum, *The Rural Muse,* he repeated all his familiar notes with a fluency which long practice had given him, and what he gains in ease he loses in directness. All that remains to us of his subsequent work is contained in the *Asylum Poems,* first printed in 1873; and it is to be regretted that the too scrupulous editor, Mr. Cherry, did not print them as they stood. 'Scarcely one poem,' he tells us, 'was found in a state in which it could be submitted to the public without more or less of revision and correction.' It is in these poems that, for the first time, Clare's lyrical quality gets free. Strangely enough, a new joy comes into the verse, as if at last he is at rest. It is only rarely, in this new contentment, this solitude even from himself, that recollection returns. Then he remembers—

I am a sad lonely hind:
Trees tell me so, day after day,
As slowly they wave in the wind.

He seems to accept nature now more easily, because his mind is in a kind of oblivion of everything else; madness being, as it were, his security. He writes love songs that have an airy fancy, a liquid and thrilling note of song. They are mostly exultations of memory, which goes from Mary to Patty, and thence to a gipsy girl and to vague Isabellas and Scotch maids. A new feeling for children comes in, sometimes in songs of childish humour, like 'Little Trotty Wagtail' or 'Clock-a-Clay,' made out of bright, laughing sound; and once in a lovely poem, one of the most nearly perfect he ever wrote, called 'The Dying Child,' which reminds one of beautiful things that have been done since, but of nothing done earlier. As we have them (and so subtle an essence could scarcely be extracted by any editor) there is no insanity; they have only dropped nearly all of the prose. A gentle hallucination comes in from time to time, and, no doubt, helps to make the poetry better.

It must not be assumed that because Clare is a peasant, his poetry is in every sense typically peasant poetry. He was gifted for poetry by those very qualities which made him ineffectual as a peasant. The common error about him is repeated by Mr. Lucas in his life of Lamb: 'He was to have been another Burns, but succeeded only in being a better Bloomfield.' The difference between Clare and Bloomfield is the difference between what is poetry and what is not, and neither is nearer to or farther from being a poet because he was also a peasant. The difference between Burns and Clare is the difference between two kinds and qualities of poetry. Burns was a great poet, filled with ideas, passions, and every sort of intoxication; but he had no such minute local love as Clare, nor, indeed, so deep a love of the earth. He could create by naming, while Clare, who lived on the memory of his heart, had to enumerate, not

leaving out one detail, because he loved every detail. Burns or Hogg, however, we can very well imagine at any period following the plough with skill or keeping cattle with care. But Clare was never a good labourer; he pottered in the fields feebly, he tried fruitless way after way of making his living. What was strangely sensitive in him might well have been hereditary if the wild and unproved story told by his biographer Martin is true: that his father was the illegitimate son of a nameless wanderer, who came to the village with his fiddle, saying he was a Scotchman or an Irishman, and taught in the village school, and disappeared one day as suddenly as he had come. The story is at least symbolic, if not true. That wandering and strange instinct was in his blood, and it spoiled the peasant in him and made the poet.—ARTHUR SYMONS, *The Romantic Movement in English Poetry,* 1909, pp. 289–92

ROBERT SOUTHEY
From "Clare's Poems"

Quarterly Review, May 1820, pp. 166–74

We had nearly overlooked, amidst the bulkier works which incessantly solicit our attention, this interesting little volume ⟨*Poems Descriptive of Rural Life and Scenery*⟩; which bears indubitable evidence of being composed altogether from the impulses of the writer's mind, as excited by external objects and internal sensations. Here are no tawdry and feeble paraphrases of former poets, no attempts at describing what the author *might* have become acquainted with in his limited reading: the woods, the vales, the brooks—

the crimson spots
I' the bottom of a cowslip,—

or the loftier phenomena of the heavens, contemplated through the alternations of hope and despondency, are the principal sources whence the youth, whose adverse circumstances and resignation under them extort our sympathy, drew the faithful and vivid pictures before us.

Examples of minds, highly gifted by nature, struggling with and breaking through the bondage of adversity, are not rare in this country; but privation is not destitution; and the instance before us is, perhaps, one of the most striking, of patient and persevering talent existing and enduring in the most forlorn and seemingly hopeless condition, that literature has at any time exhibited.

Clare, the youth of whom we speak, was born at Helpstone, a village most unpoetically situated where the easternmost point of Northamptonshire indents the Lincolnshire fens. His father and mother are parish-paupers; the former, from constant exposure to the inclemency of the seasons, being prematurely decrepit, the latter, his cheerful companion in youth, has become, as they totter down the hill of life, his natural and constant nurse. If this condition of the parents enabled them to afford small indulgence to the son, the example of conjugal affection, we may hope, will not be lost upon a heart very susceptible of kind impressions. Our author, who is the elder of twins, was born in July, 1793;—the sister, who died immediately after the birth, was, to use his mother's figure of speech, 'a bouncing girl, while John might have gone into a pint pot;' indicating a delicacy of frame under which he has always laboured. His education necessarily squared with the limited means of his parents. Of the dame, who in every village wields the 'twa birchen twigs' to the terror of the surrounding urchins, he learnt to spell and put two syllables together; and before he was six years old, was able, his mother says, to read a chapter in the Bible. As soon, however, as he was able to lead the fore-horse of the harvest team, he was set to work, and returning one evening from the field thus occupied, had the misfortune of seeing the loader fall from the waggon, and break his neck: this fatal accident threw him into fits, from which he did not recover till after a considerable lapse of time, nor without much anxiety and expense to his parents: even at this day he is not wholly free from apprehensions of their return. At the age of twelve, he assisted in the laborious employment of thrashing; the boy, in his father's own words, was weak but willing, and the good old man made a flail for him somewhat suitable to his strength. When his share of the day's toil was over, he eagerly ran to the village school under the belfry, and in this desultory and casual manner gathered his imperfect knowledge of language, and skill in writing. At the early period of which we are speaking, Clare felt the poetic œstrum. He relates, that twice or thrice in the winter weeks it was his office to fetch a bag of flour from the village of Maxey, and darkness often came on before he could return. The state of his nerves corresponded with his slender frame. The tales of terror with which his mother's memory shortened the long nights, returned freshly to his fancy the next day, and to beguile the way and dissipate his fears, he used to walk back with his eyes fixed immoveably on the ground, revolving in his mind some adventure 'without a ghost in it,' which he turned into verse; and thus, he adds, he reached the village of Helpstone often before he was aware of his approach.

'The fate of Amy' is one of those stories with which every village, more especially every secluded village, abounds; and the pool, from her catastrophe named the haunted pool, is still shewn, while the mound at the head of it attests the place of her interment. We do not propose to institute a very rigid criticism on these poems, but we must not omit to notice the delicacy with which the circumstances of this inartificial tale are suggested, rather than disclosed; indeed it may be remarked generally that, though associating necessarily with the meanest and most uneducated of society, the poet's homeliest stories have nothing of coarseness and vulgarity in their construction. Some of his ballad stanzas rival the native simplicity of Tickel or Mallett.

> The flowers the sultry summer kills,
>   Spring's milder suns restore;
> But innocence, that fickle charm,
>   Blooms once, and blooms no more.
> The swains who loved no more admire,
>   Their hearts no beauty warms;
> And maidens triumph in her fall,
>   That envied once her charms.
> Lost was that sweet simplicity,
>   Her eye's bright lustre fled;
> And o'er her cheeks, where roses bloom'd,
>   A sickly paleness spread.
> So fades the flower before its time,
>   Where canker-worms assail,
> So droops the bud upon the stem,
>   Beneath the sickly gale.
>   (p. 26)

For the boisterous sports and amusements which form the usual delight of village youth, Clare had neither strength nor relish; his mother found it necessary to drive him from the chimney corner to exercise and to play, whence he quickly returned, contemplative and silent. His parents—we speak from knowledge—were apprehensive for his mind as well as his health; not knowing how to interpret, or to what cause to refer

these habits so opposite to those of other boys of his condition; and when, a few years later, they found him hourly employed in writing,—and writing verses too,—'the gear was not mended' in their estimation. 'When he was fourteen or fifteen,' says Dame Clare, 'he would shew me a piece of paper, printed sometimes on one side, and scrawled all over on the other, and he would say, Mother, this is worth *so* much; and I used to say to him, Aye, boy, it looks as if it warr!—but I thought he was wasting his time.' Clare's history, for a few succeeding years, is composed in two words, spare diet and hard labour, cheered by visions of fancy which promised him happier days: there is an amusing mixture of earnestness and coquetry in his invocation 'to Hope,' the deceitful sustainer, time immemorial, of poets and lovers.

> Come, flattering Hope! now woes distress me,
>   Thy flattery I desire again;
> Again rely on thee to bless me,
>   To find thy vainness doubly vain.
> Though disappointments vex and fetter,
>   And jeering whisper, thou art vain,
> Still must I rest on thee for better,
>   Still hope—and be deceived again.
>   (p. 122)

The eccentricities of genius, as we gently phrase its most reprehensible excesses, contribute no interest to the biography of Clare. We cannot, however, regret this. Once, it seems, 'visions of glory' crowded on his sight, and, he enlisted at Peterboro' in the local militia. He still speaks of the short period passed in his new character, with evident satisfaction. After a while, he took the bounty for extended service, and marched to Oundle; where, at the conclusion of a bloodless campaign, his corps was disbanded, and he was constrained to return to Helpstone, to the dreary abode of poverty and sickness. His novel occupation does not appear to have excited any martial poetry; we need not therefore 'unsphere the spirit of Plato,' adequately to celebrate the warlike strains of the modern Tyrtæus.

The clouds which had hung so heavily over the youth of Clare, far from dispersing, grew denser and darker as he advanced towards manhood. His father, who had been the constant associate of his labours, became more and more infirm, and he was constrained to toil alone, and far beyond his strength, to obtain a mere subsistence. It was at this cheerless moment, he composed 'What Is Life?' in which he has treated a common subject with an earnestness, a solemnity, and an originality deserving of all praise: some of the lines have a terseness of expression and a nervous freedom of versification not unworthy of Drummond, or of Cowley.

> And what is Life?—An hour-glass on the run,
>   A mist, retreating from the morning sun,
> A busy, bustling, still-repeated dream,—
>   Its length?—A minute's pause, a moment's
>   thought.
> And happiness?—A bubble on the stream,
>   That in the act of seizing shrinks to nought.
> And what is Hope?—the puffing gale of morn,
>   That robs each flowret of its gem,—and dies;
> A cobweb, hiding disappointment's thorn,
>   Which stings more keenly through the thin dis-
>   guise.
> And what is Death?—Is still the cause unfound?
> That dark, mysterious name of horrid sound?
>   A long and lingering sleep, the weary crave.
> And peace?—Where can its happiness abound?
>   No where at all, save Heaven, and the grave.

Then what is Life?—When stripp'd of its disguise,
  A thing to be desir'd it cannot be;
Since every thing that meets our foolish eyes,
  Gives proof sufficient of its vanity.
'Tis but a trial all must undergo;
  To teach unthankful mortal how to prize
That happiness vain man's denied to know,
  Until he's call'd to claim it in the skies.

That the author of such verses (and there are abundance of them) should have continued till the age of twenty-five unfriended and unknown, is less calculated perhaps to excite astonishment, than that devotedness to his art, which could sustain him under the pressure of such evils, and that modesty which shrunk from obtruding his writings on the world. Once, indeed, and once only, he appears to have made an effort to emerge from this cheerless obscurity, by submitting his verses to a neighbour, who, it seems, enjoyed a reputation for knowledge 'in such matters.' Even here his ill-fortune awaited him; and his muse met not only with discouragement but rebuke. The circumstance is however valuable, since it serves to illustrate the natural gentleness of the poet's disposition. Instead of venting his spleen against this rustic Aristarch, he only cleaves to his favourite with greater fondness.

  Still must my rudeness pluck the flower
  That's pluck'd, alas! in evil hour;
  And poor, and vain, and sunk beneath
    Oppression's scorn although I be,
  Still will I bind my simple wreath,
    Still will I love thee, Poesy.

                                          (p. 124)

⟨. . .⟩ Looking back upon what we have written, we find we have not accomplished our intention of interspersing with our narrative such extracts as might convey a general character of Clare's poetry,—we have used only such as assorted with the accidents of the poet's life, and the tone of them has necessarily been somewhat gloomy. The volume, however, offers abundant proofs of the author's possessing a cheerful disposition, a mind delighting in the charms of natural scenery, and a heart not to be subdued by the frowns of fortune; though the advantages which he might have derived from these endowments have been checked by the sad realities which hourly reminded him of his unpromising condition. Misery herself cannot, however, keep incessant watch over her victims; and it must have been in a happy interval of abstraction from troublesome feelings that Clare composed 'the Summer morning,' the result, we believe, of a sabbath-day walk; the lively pictures of rural occupation being introduced from the recollections of yesterday, and the anticipations of the morrow. ⟨. . .⟩

It will have appeared, in some measure, from our specimens, that Clare is rather the creature of feeling than of fancy. He looks abroad with the eye of a poet, and with the minuteness of a naturalist, but the intelligence which he gains is always referred to the heart; it is thus that the falling leaves become admonishers and friends, the idlest weed has its resemblance in his own lowly lot, and the opening primrose of spring suggests the promise that his own long winter of neglect and obscurity will yet be succeeded by a summer's sun of happier fortune. The volume, we believe, scarcely contains a poem in which this process is not adopted; nor one in which imagination is excited without some corresponding tone of tenderness, or morality. When the discouraging circumstances under which the bulk of it was composed are considered, it is really astonishing that so few examples should be found of querulousness and impatience, none of envy or depair.

The humble origin of Clare may suggest a comparison with Burns and Bloomfield, which a closer examination will scarcely warrant. Burns was, indeed, as he expresses it, 'born to the plough,' but when in his riper years he held the plough, it was rather as a master than as a menial. He was neither destitute nor uneducated. Secure from poverty, supported by his kindred, and surrounded by grand and exciting scenery, his lot was lofty and his advantages numerous compared with those of the youth before us. There is almost as little resemblance in their minds. To the pointed wit, the bitter sarcasm, the acute discrimination of character, and the powerful pathos of Burns, Clare cannot make pretension; but he has much of his tender feeling in his serious poetry, and an animation, a vivacity, and a delicacy in describing rural scenery, which the mountain bard has not often surpassed. In all the circumstances of his life, the author of the *Farmer's Boy* was far more fortunate than Clare. Though his father was dead, Bloomfield had brothers who were always at his side to cheer and sustain him, while an early residence in the metropolis contributed largely to the extension of his knowledge. To want and poverty he was ever a stranger. Clare never knew a brother; it was his fortune to continue till his twenty-fifth year without education, without hearing the voice of a friend, constrained to follow the most laborious and revolting occupations to obtain the bare necessaries of life. The poetical compositions of the two have few points of contact. The *Farmer's Boy* is the result of careful observations made on the occupations and habits, with few references to the passions of rural life. Clare writes frequently from the same suggestions; but his subject is always enlivened by picturesque and minute description of the landscape around him, and deepened, as we have said, with a powerful reference to emotions within. The one is descriptive, the other contemplative.

A friend of Clare has expressed a doubt of his capacity for the composition of a long poem:—we have no wish that he should make the experiment; but we have an earnest desire that he should be respectable and happy; that he should support a fair name in poetry, and that his condition in life should be ameliorated. It is with this feeling that we counsel—that we entreat him to continue something of his present occupations;—to attach himself to a few in the sincerity of whose friendship he can confide, and to suffer no temptations of the idle and the dissolute to seduce him from the quiet scenes of his youth—scenes so congenial to his taste,—to the hollow and heartless society of cities; to the haunts of men who would court and flatter him while his name was new, and who, when they had contributed to distract his attention and impair his health, would cast him off unceremoniously to seek some other novelty. Of his again encountering the difficulties and privations he lately experienced, there is no danger. Report speaks of honourable and noble friends already secured: with the aid of these, the cultivation of his own excellent talents, and a meek but firm reliance on that GOOD POWER by whom these were bestowed, he may, without presumption, anticipate a rich reward in the future for the evils endured in the morning of his life.

FRANCES TROLLOPE

JOHN CLARE

WALTER SAVAGE LANDOR

WILLIAM MAKEPEACE THACKERAY

John Keble

Elizabeth Gaskell

Richard Cobden

Nathaniel Hawthorne

NATHANIEL HAWTHORNE

1804–1864

Nathaniel Hawthorne was born in Salem, Massachusetts, on July 4, 1804; he was descended on both sides from prominent New England Puritans. In 1809, after the death of his father, Hawthorne began living, along with his mother and two sisters, at the home of his maternal grandparents. After studying at Samuel Archer's School (1819), Hawthorne attended Bowdoin College in Brunswick, Maine (1821–25), where his classmates included Henry Wadsworth Longfellow. In 1825 Hawthorne returned to Salem to live with his mother.

Rather than entering a trade or profession as was expected of him, Hawthorne spent the next dozen years or so in relative isolation, concentrating on reading and writing. In 1828 he published a novel, *Fanshawe*, which drew heavily on his experiences at Bowdoin. Published anonymously and at his own expense, this book was later withdrawn by Hawthorne, who destroyed every copy he could find. Between 1830 and 1837 Hawthorne wrote tales and sketches for various periodicals (notably S. G. Goodrich's annual *The Token*), and in 1837 a collection was published as *Twice-Told Tales*; an expanded edition appeared in 1842. After becoming engaged to Sophia Peabody in 1839, Hawthorne took a job as a measurer in the Boston custom house (1839–40), and in 1841 he joined the Brook Farm Community in West Roxbury, Massachusetts, from which he withdrew after several months. In 1842 Hawthorne and Sophia were married; they settled in Concord, where Hawthorne became a friend of Emerson, Thoreau, Margaret Fuller, and A. Bronson Alcott.

In 1846, the year in which his son Julian was born, Hawthorne published *Mosses from an Old Manse*, a collection of sketches and tales reprinted from a variety of periodicals, including the *Democratic Review*. Between 1846 and 1849 he worked as a surveyor in the Salem custom house, and in 1850 he published *The Scarlet Letter*, which won him considerable fame. In this novel set in seventeenth-century New England, Hawthorne sought to explore the Puritan conscience through a drama of adultery and revenge. During 1850 and 1851 Hawthorne lived in Lenox, Massachusetts, where he became friendly with Herman Melville. In 1851, the year in which his daughter Rose was born, Hawthorne published his second novel, *The House of the Seven Gables*, a story of ancestral guilt partially based on his own family history. Also in that year appeared a third collection of shorter pieces, *The Snow-Image and Other Twice-Told Tales*. *The Blithedale Romance*, based in large part on Hawthorne's experiences at Brook Farm, appeared in 1852, and was followed by two works for children, *A Wonder-Book for Girls and Boys* (1852) and *Tanglewood Tales* (1853), both based on Greek mythology.

In 1853 Hawthorne was appointed by President Franklin Pierce to serve as United States consul at Liverpool, a position he filled until 1857. He then spent the years 1857 to 1859 living in Rome and Florence, an experience that inspired his third novel, *The Marble Faun* (1860; retitled *Transformation* in England); this was to be his last completed work of fiction. In 1860 Hawthorne returned to Concord, where he spent the rest of his life, and in 1863 published *Our Old Home*, a series of essays on England and Anglo-American relations. In 1864 Hawthorne traveled to New Hampshire in an attempt to improve his failing health. On May 19 of that year he died at Plymouth, leaving unfinished four works; *Dr. Grimshawe's Secret* (first published in 1883), *Septimius Felton; or, The Elixir of Life* (1872), *The Ancestral Footstep* (1883), and *The Dolliver Romance* (1876). After his death Sophia Hawthorne edited his English, American, and European notebooks, and there have also been several collected editions of his letters. A landmark critical edition of his work is being published by Ohio State University Press.

Personal

I have not yet concluded what profession I shall have. The being a minister is of course out of the question. I should not think that even you could desire me to choose so dull a way of life. Oh, no, mother, I was not born to vegetate forever in one place, and to live and die as calm and tranquil as—a puddle of water. As to lawyers, there are so many of them already that one half of them (upon a moderate calculation) are in a state of actual starvation. A physician, then, seems to be "Hobson's choice;" but yet I should not like to live by the diseases and infirmities of my fellow-creatures. And it would weigh very heavily on my conscience, in the course of my practice, if I should chance to send any unlucky patient "ad inferum,"

which being interpreted is, "to the realms below." Oh that I was rich enough to live without a profession! What do you think of my becoming an author, and relying for support upon my pen? Indeed, I think the illegibility of my handwriting is very author-like. How proud you would feel to see my works praised by the reviewers, as equal to the proudest productions of the scribbling sons of John Bull. But authors are always poor devils, and therefore Satan may take them. I am in the same predicament as the honest gentleman in *Espriella's Letters*.

I am an Englishman, and naked I stand here,
A-musing in my mind what garment I shall wear.

But as the mail closes soon, I must stop the career of my pen. I will only inform you that I now write no poetry, or anything else.—NATHANIEL HAWTHORNE, Letter to His Mother (March 13, 1821), cited in Julian Hawthorne, *Nathaniel Hawthorne and His Wife*, 1884, Vol. 1, pp. 107–8

Hawthorne ⟨. . .⟩ was of a rather sturdy form, his hair dark and bushy, his eye steel-gray, his brow thick, his mouth sarcastic, his complexion stony, his whole aspect cold, moody, distrustful. He stood aloof, and surveyed the world from shy and sheltered positions.—S. G. GOODRICH, *Recollections of a Lifetime*, 1856, Vol. 2, pp. 269–70

I sent my letter at once; from all that I had heard of Mr. Hawthorne's shyness, I thought it doubtful if he would call, and I was therefore very much pleased when his card was sent in this morning. Mr. Hawthorne was more chatty than I had expected, but not any more diffident. He remained about five minutes, during which time he took his hat from the table and put it back once a minute, brushing it each time. The engravings in the books are much like him. He is not handsome, but looks as the author of his books should look; a little strange and odd, as if not of this earth. He has large, bluish-gray eyes; his hair stands out on each side, so much so that one's thoughts naturally turn to combs and hair-brushes and toilet ceremonies as one looks at him.—MARIA MITCHELL, *Journal* (Aug. 5, 1857), *Life, Letters, and Journals of Maria Mitchell*, ed. Phebe Mitchell Kendall, 1896, p. 89

You will have seen, with profound sorrow, the announcement of the death of the dearest and most cherished among our early friends.

You will wish to know something more of Hawthorne's last days than the articles in the newspapers furnish. ⟨. . .⟩

We arrived at Plymouth about six o'clock. After taking a little tea and toast in his room, and sleeping for nearly an hour upon the sofa, he retired. A door opened from my room to his, and our beds were not more than five or six feet apart. I remained up an hour or two after he fell asleep. He was apparently less restless than the night before. The light was left burning in my room—the door open—and I could see him without moving from my bed. I went, however, between one and two o'clock to his bedside, and supposed him to be in a profound slumber. His eyes were closed, his position and face perfectly natural. His face was towards my bed. I awoke again between three and four o'clock, and was surprised—as he had generally been restless—to notice that his position was unchanged—exactly the same that it was two hours before. I went to his bedside, placed my hand upon his forehead and temple, and found that he was dead. He evidently had passed from natural sleep to that sleep from which there is no waking, without suffering, and without the slightest movement. ⟨. . .⟩

The funeral is to take place at Concord, Monday, at one o'clock. I wish you could be there. I go to Lowell this afternoon, and shall drive across the country to C. to-morrow evening. I need not tell you how lonely I am, and how full of sorrow.—FRANKLIN PIERCE, Letter to Horatio Bridge (May 21, 1864), cited in Horatio Bridge, *Personal Recollections of Nathaniel Hawthorne*, 1893, pp. 176–79

How beautiful it was, that one bright day
  In the long week of rain!
Though all its splendour could not chase away
  The omnipresent pain.

The lovely town was white with apple-blooms,
  And the great elms o'erhead
Dark shadows wove on their aerial looms
  Shot through with golden thread.

Across the meadows, by the gray old manse,
  The historic river flowed:

I was as one who wanders in a trance,
  Unconscious of his road.

The faces of familiar friends seemed strange;
  Their voices I could hear,
And yet the words they uttered seemed to change
  Their meaning to my ear.

For the one face I looked for was not there,
  The one low voice was mute;
Only an unseen presence filled the air,
  And baffled my pursuit.

Now I look back, and meadow, manse, and stream
  Dimly my thought defines;
I only see—a dream within a dream—
  The hill-top hearsed with pines.

I only hear above his place of rest
  Their tender undertone,
The infinite longings of a troubled breast,
  The voice so like his own.

There in seclusion and remote from men
  The wizard hand lies cold,
Which at its topmost speed let fall the pen,
  And left the tale half told.

Ah! who shall lift that wand of magic power,
  And the lost clew regain?
The unfinished window in Aladdin's tower
  Unfinished must remain!
      —HENRY WADSWORTH LONGFELLOW, "Hawthorne," 1864

Hawthorne was of the darker temperament and tendencies. His sensitiveness and sadness were native, and he cultivated them apparently alike by solitude, the pursuits and studies in which he indulged, till he became almost fated to know gayer hours only by stealth. By disposition friendly, he seemed the victim of his temperament, as if he sought distance, if not his pen, to put himself in communication, and possible sympathy with others,—with his nearest friends, even. His reserve and imprisonment were more distant and close, while the desire for conversation was livelier, than any one I have known. There was something of strangeness even in his cherished intimacies, as if he set himself afar from all and from himself with the rest; the most diffident of men, as coy as a maiden, he could only be won by some cunning artifice, his reserve was so habitual, his isolation so entire, the solitude so vast. How distant people were from him, the world they lived in, how he came to know so much about them, by what stratagem he got into his own house or left it, was a marvel. Fancy fixed, he was not to be jostled from himself for a moment, his mood was so persistent. There he was in the twilight, there he stayed. Was he some damsel imprisoned in that manly form pleading alway for release, sighing for the freedom and companionships denied her? Or was he some Assyrian ill at ease afar from the olives and the East? Had he strayed over with William the Conqueror, and true to his Norman nature, was the baron still in republican America, secure in his castle, secure in his tower, whence he could defy all invasion of curious eyes? What neighbor of his ever caught him on the highway, or ventured to approach his threshold?

His bolted Castle gates, what man should ope,
  Unless the Lord did will
    To prove his skill,
And tempt the fates hid in his horoscope?

Yet if by chance admitted, welcome in a voice that a woman might own for its hesitancy and tenderness; his eyes telling the rest.

For such the noble language of his eye,
That when of words his lips were destitute,
Kind eyebeams spake while yet his tongue was mute.

Your intrusion was worth the courage it cost; it emboldened to future assaults to carry this fort of bashfulness. During all the time he lived near me, our estates being separated only by a gate and shaded avenue, I seldom caught sight of him; and when I did it was but to lose it the moment he suspected he was visible; oftenest seen on his hill-top screened behind the shrubbery and disappearing like a hare into the bush when surprised. I remember of his being in my house but twice, and then he was so ill at ease that he found excuse for leaving politely forthwith,—"the stove was so hot," "the clock ticked so loud." Yet he once complained to me of his wish to meet oftener, and dwelt on the delights of fellowship, regretting he had so little. ⟨. . .⟩

He strove by disposition to be sunny and genial, traits not native to him. Constitutionally shy, recluse, melancholy, only by shafts of wit and flow of humor could he deliver himself. There was a soft sadness in his smile, a reserve in his glance, telling how isolate he was. Was he ever one of his company while in it? There was an aloofness, a *besides*, that refused to affiliate himself with himself, even. His readers must feel this, while unable to account for it, perhaps, or express it adequately. A believer in transmitted traits needs but read his pedigree to find the genesis of what characterized him distinctly, and made him and his writings their inevitable sequel. Everywhere you will find persons of his type and complexion similar in cast of character and opinions.—A. BRONSON ALCOTT, "Hawthorne" (July 1869), *Concord Days*, 1872, pp. 193–97

In him opposite qualities met, and were happily and harmoniously blended; and this was true of him physically as well as intellectually. He was tall and strongly built, with broad shoulders, deep chest, a massive head, black hair, and large dark eyes. Wherever he was he attracted attention by his imposing presence. He looked like a man who might have held the stroke-oar in a university boat. And his genius, as all the world knows, was of masculine force and sweep.

But, on the other hand, no man had more of the feminine element than he. He was feminine in his quick perceptions, his fine insight, his sensibility to beauty, his delicate reserve, his purity of feeling. No man comprehended woman more perfectly; none has painted woman with a more exquisite and ethereal pencil. And his face was as mobile and rapid in its changes of expression as is the face of a young girl. His lip and cheek heralded the word before it was spoken. His eyes would darken visibly under the touch of a passing emotion, like the waters of a fountain ruffled by the breeze of summer. So, too, he was the shyest of men. The claims and courtesies of social life were terrible to him. The thought of making a call would keep him awake in his bed. At breakfast, he could not lay a piece of butter upon a lady's plate without a little trembling of the hand: this is a fact, and not a phrase. He was so shy that in the presence of two intimate friends he would be less easy and free-spoken than in that of only one.

And yet the presence of his kind was cordial, and in some sense necessary to him. If his shyness held him back, his sympathies drew him out with a force nearly as strong. And, unlike most men who are at once intellectual and shy, he was not a lover, or a student, of books. He read books as they came in his way, or for a particular purpose, but he made no claim to the honors of learning or scholarship. A great library had no charms for him. He rarely bought a book, and the larger part of his small collection had come to him by gift. His mind did not feed upon the printed page. It will be noticed that in his writings he very seldom introduces a quotation or makes any allusion to the writings of others. The raptures of the bibliomaniac, fondling his tall copies, his wide margins, his unique specimens, his vellum pages, were as strange to him as are the movements of a violin-player's arm to the deaf man's eye. —GEORGE S. HILLARD, "The English Note-Books of Nathaniel Hawthorne," *Atlantic*, Sept. 1870, pp. 258–59

That most lovable of writers was also—to those who knew him intimately—one of the most lovable of men. My acquaintance with him was slight; but it has left on my mind a vivid impression of his painful shyness in general society, and the retiring—nay, morbid delicacy—with which he shrank from notice.—S. C. HALL, *Retrospect of a Long Life*, 1883, p. 420

The door was opened to my ring by a tall handsome boy whom I suppose to have been Mr. Julian Hawthorne; and the next moment I found myself in the presence of the romancer, who entered from some room beyond. He advanced carrying his head with a heavy forward droop, and with a pace for which I decided that the word would be *pondering*. It was the pace of a bulky man of fifty, and his head was that beautiful head we all know from the many pictures of it. But Hawthorne's *look* was different from that of any picture of him that I have seen. It was sombre and brooding, as the look of such a poet should have been; it was the look of a man who had dealt faithfully and therefore sorrowfully with that problem of evil which forever attracted, forever evaded Hawthorne. It was by no means troubled; it was full of a dark repose. Others who knew him better and saw him oftener were familiar with other aspects, and I remember that one night at Longfellow's table, when one of the guests happened to speak of the photograph of Hawthorne which hung in a corner of the room, Lowell said, after a glance at it, "Yes, it's good; but it hasn't his fine *accipitral* look."

In the face that confronted me, however, there was nothing of keen alertness; but only a sort of quiet, patient intelligence, for which I seek the right word in vain. It was a very regular face, with beautiful eyes; the mustache, still entirely dark, was dense over the fine mouth. Hawthorne was dressed in black, and he had a certain effect which I remember, of seeming to have on a black cravat with no visible collar. He was such a man that if I had ignorantly met him anywhere I should have instantly felt him to be a personage.—WILLIAM DEAN HOWELLS, "My First Visit to New England" (1894), *Literary Friends and Acquaintance*, 1900

General

His style is classical and pure, his imagination exceedingly delicate and fanciful, and through all his writings there runs a vein of sweetest poetry.

Perhaps we have no writer so deeply imbued with the early literature of America; or who can so well portray the times and manners of the Puritans.

Hitherto Mr. Hawthorne has published no work of magnitude; but it is to be hoped that one who has shown such unequivocal evidence of talent will soon give to the world some production which shall place him in a higher rank than can be obtained by one whose efforts are confined to the sphere of magazines and annuals.—HORATIO BRIDGE (1836), *Personal Recollections of Nathaniel Hawthorne*, 1893, p. 71

He is peculiar and *not* original—unless in those detailed fancies and detached thoughts which his want of general originality will deprive of the appreciation due to them, in preventing them forever reaching the *public* eye. He is infinitely too fond of allegory, and can never hope for popularity so long as he persists in it. This he will not do, for allegory is at war with the whole tone of his nature, which disports itself never so well as when escaping from the mysticism of his Goodman Browns and White Old Maids into the hearty, genial, but still Indian-summer sunshine of his Wakefields and Little Annie's Rambles. Indeed, *his* spirit of "metaphor runmad" is clearly imbibed from the phalanx and phalanstery atmosphere in which he has been so long struggling for breath. He has not half the material for the exclusiveness of authorship that he possesses for its universality. He has the purest style, the finest taste, the most available scholarship, the most delicate humor, the most touching pathos, the most radiant imagination, the most consummate ingenuity; and with these varied good qualities he has done *well* as a mystic. But is there any one of these qualities which should prevent his doing doubly as well in a career of honest, upright, sensible, prehensible and comprehensible things? Let him mend his pen, get a bottle of visible ink, come out from the Old Manse, cut Mr. Alcott, hang (if possible) the editor of *The Dial*, and throw out of the window to the pigs all his odd numbers of *The North American Review*.—EDGAR ALLAN POE, "Nathaniel Hawthorne" (1847), *Essays and Reviews*, ed. G. R. Thompson, 1984, pp. 587–88

There is Hawthorne, with genius so shrinking and rare
That you hardly at first see the strength that is there;
A frame so robust, with a nature so sweet,
So earnest, so graceful, so solid, so fleet,
Is worth a descent from Olympus to meet;
'T is as if a rough oak that for ages had stood,
With his gnarled bony branches like ribs of the wood,
Should bloom, after cycles of struggle and scathe,
With a single anemone trembly and rathe;
His strength is so tender, his wildness so meek,
That a suitable parallel sets one to seek,—
He's a John Bunyan Fouqué, a Puritan Tieck;
When Nature was shaping him, clay was not granted
For making so full-sized a man as she wanted,
So, to fill out her model, a little she spared
From some finer-grained stuff for a woman prepared,
And she could not have hit a more excellent plan
For making him fully and perfectly man.
The success of her scheme gave her so much delight,
That she tried it again, shortly after, in Dwight;
Only, while she was kneading and shaping the clay,
She sang to her work in her sweet childish way,
And found, when she'd put the last touch to his soul,
That the music had somehow got mixed with the whole.
          —JAMES RUSSELL LOWELL, *A Fable for Critics*,
          1848

⟨. . .⟩ decidedly the greatest living literary man in this country, greatest, in romance, now writing the English language.—RUFUS W. GRISWOLD, Letter to James T. Fields (Jan. 24, 1850), *Passages from the Correspondence and Other Papers of Rufus W. Griswold*, ed. W. M. Griswold, 1898, p. 258

I think we have no romancer but yourself, nor have had any for this long time. I had become so set in this feeling, that but for your last two stories I should have given up hoping, and believed that all we were to look for in the way of spontaneous growth were such languid, lifeless, sexless creations as in the view of certain people constitute the chief triumphs of a sister art as manifested among us.

But there is rich red blood in Hester, and the flavor of the sweet-fern and the bayberry are not truer to the soil than the native sweetness of our little Phœbe! The Yankee mind has for the most part budded and flowered in pots of English earth, but you have fairly raised yours as a seedling in the natural soil. My criticism has to stop here; the moment a fresh mind takes in the elements of the common life about us and transfigures them, I am contented to enjoy and admire, and let others analyze. Otherwise I should be tempted to display my appreciating sagacity in pointing out a hundred touches, transcriptions of nature, of character, of sentiment, true as the daguerreotype, free as crayon sketching, which arrested me even in the midst of the palpitating story. Only one word, then this: that the solid reality and homely truthfulness of the actual and present part of the story are blended with its weird and ghostly shadows with consummate skill and effect; this was perhaps the special difficulty of the story.—OLIVER WENDELL HOLMES, Letter to Nathaniel Hawthorne (April 9, 1851), cited in George Parsons Lathrop, *A Study of Hawthorne*, 1876, p. 232

Hawthorne is a grand favourite of mine, and I shall be sorry if he do not go on surpassing himself.—GEORGE ELIOT, Letter to Mrs. Taylor (Aug. 19, 1852)

First, then, on this special shelf stands Nathaniel Hawthorne's *Twice-Told Tales*. It is difficult to explain why I like these short sketches and essays, written in the author's early youth, better than his later, more finished, and better-known novels and romances. The world sets greater store by *The Scarlet Letter* and *Transformation* than by this little book—and, in such matters of liking against the judgment of the world, there is no appeal. I think the reason of my liking consists in this—that the novels were written for the world, while the tales seem written for the author; in these he is actor and audience in one. Consequently, one gets nearer him, just as one gets nearer an artist in his first sketch than in his finished picture. And after all, one takes the greatest pleasure in those books in which a peculiar personality is most clearly revealed. A thought may be very commendable *as* a thought, but I value it chiefly as a window through which I can obtain insight on the thinker; and Mr Hawthorne's personality is peculiar, and specially peculiar in a new country like America. He is quiet, fanciful, quaint, and his humour is shaded by a certain meditativeness of spirit. Although a Yankee, he partakes of none of the characteristics of a Yankee. His thinking and his style have an antique air. His roots strike down through the visible mould of the present, and draw sustenance from the generations under ground. The ghosts that haunt the chamber of his mind are the ghosts of dead men and women. He has a strong smack of the Puritan; he wears around him, in the New-England town, something of the darkness and mystery of the aboriginal forest. He is a shy, silent, sensitive, much-ruminating man, with no special overflow of animal spirits. He loves solitude and the things which age has made reverent. There is nothing modern about him. Emerson's writing has a cold cheerless glitter, like the new furniture in a warehouse, which will come of use by and by; Hawthorne's, the rich, subdued colour of furniture in a Tudor mansion-house—which has winked to long-extinguished fires, which has been toned by the usage of departed generations. In many of the *Twice-Told Tales* this peculiar personality is charmingly exhibited. He writes of the street or the sea-shore, his eye takes in every object, however trifling, and on these he hangs comments melancholy and humorous. He does not require to go far for a subject; he will stare on the puddles in the street of a New-England village, and immediately it becomes a Mediterranean Sea with empires lying on its muddy shores. If the sermon be written out fully in your heart, almost any text will be suitable—if you have to find your sermon *in* your text, you may search the Testament, New and Old, and be as poor at the close of Revelation as when you started at the first book of Genesis. Several of the papers which I like best are monologues, fanciful, humorous, or melancholy; and of these, my chief favourites are—"Sunday at Home," "Night Sketches," "Footprints on the Sea-shore," and the "Seven Vagabonds." This last seems to me almost the most exquisite thing which has flowed from its author's pen—a perfect little drama, the place a showman's waggon, the time the falling of a summer shower, full of subtle suggestions, which, if followed, will lead the reader away out of the story altogether; and illuminated by a grave, wistful kind of humour, which plays in turns upon the author's companions, and upon the author himself. Of all Mr Hawthorne's gifts, this gift of humour—which would light up the skull and cross-bones of a village churchyard, which would be silent at a dinner-table—is to me the most delightful.

Then this writer has a strangely weird power. He loves ruins like the ivy, he skims the twilight like the bat, he makes himself a familiar of the phantoms of the heart and brain. He believes in ghosts; perhaps he has seen one burst on him from the impalpable air. He is fascinated by the jarred brain and the ruined heart. Other men collect china, books, pictures, jewels, this writer collects singular human experiences, ancient wrongs and agonies, murders done on unfrequented roads, crimes that seem to have no motive, and all the dreary mysteries of the world of will. To his chamber of horrors Madame Tussaud's is nothing. With proud, prosperous, healthy men, Mr Hawthorne has little sympathy; he prefers a cracked piano to a new one, he likes cobwebs in the corner of his rooms. All this peculiar taste comes out strongly in the little book in whose praise I am writing. I read "The Minister's Black Veil," and find it the first sketch of the *Scarlet Letter*. In "Wakefield"—the story of the man who left his wife, remaining away twenty years, but who yet looked upon her every day to appease his burning curiosity as to her manner of enduring his absence—I find the keenest analysis of an almost incomprehensible act. And then Mr Hawthorne has a skill in constructing allegories which no one of his contemporaries, either English or American, possesses. These allegorical papers may be read with pleasure, for their ingenuity, their grace, their poetical feeling; but just as, gazing on the surface of a stream, admiring the ripples and eddies, and the widening rings made by the butterfly falling into it, you begin to be conscious that there is something at the bottom, and gradually a dead face wavers upwards from the oozy weeds, becoming every moment more clearly defined, so through Mr Hawthorne's graceful sentences, if read attentively, begins to flash the hidden meaning, a meaning, perhaps, the writer did not care to express formally and in set terms, and which he merely suggests and leaves the reader to make out for himself. If you have the book I am writing about, turn up "David Swan," "The Great Carbuncle," "The Fancy Show-box," and after you have read these, you will understand what I mean.—ALEXANDER SMITH, "A Shelf in My Bookcase," *Dreamthorp*, 1863, pp. 190–94

Hawthorne was a genius. As a master of prose, he will come in the first class of all who have written the English language. He had not the grand style, but who has had a delicacy of touch superior to his?—CHARLES SUMNER, Letter to Henry Wadsworth Longfellow (May 21, 1864), cited in Edward L. Pierce, *Memoir and Letters of Charles Sumner*, 1893, Vol. 4, p. 202

In a patch of sunlight, flecked by the shade of tall, murmuring pines, at the summit of a gently swelling mound where the wild-flowers had climbed to find the light and the stirring of fresh breezes, the tired poet was laid beneath the green turf.

Poet let us call him, though his chants were not modulated in the rhythm of verse. The element of poetry is air: we know the poet by his atmospheric effects, by the blue of his distances, by the softening of every hard outline he touches, by the silvery mist in which he veils deformity and clothes what is common so that it changes to awe-inspiring mystery, by the clouds of gold and purple which are the drapery of his dreams. And surely we have had but one prose-writer who could be compared with him in aërial perspective, if we may use the painter's term. If Irving is the Claude of our unrhymed poetry, Hawthorne is its Poussin.—OLIVER WENDELL HOLMES, "Hawthorne," *Atlantic*, July 1864, pp. 100–101

The death of Nathaniel Hawthorne is a national event. In original creative genius no name in our literature is superior to his; and while everybody was asking whether it were impossible to write an American novel, he wrote romances that were hardly possible elsewhere, because they were so purely American. There was never, certainly, an author more utterly independent than Hawthorne of the circumstances that surrounded him. In his style, even, which, for a rich, idiomatic raciness, is unsurpassed, there was no touch of any of the schools of his time. It was as clear and simple as Thackeray's, and as felicitous; but there was a flush of color in it, sometimes, of which Thackeray has no trace. But of the literary influences of his time, and even of his personal association, there is no sign in his writings. The form in which his world was revealed, like that world itself, was entirely his own.

Nor was there any foreign flavor whatever in his genius. It was not a growth of the English, or the German, or the French; nor was it eclectic. It was American. It was almost New England, except for that universality which belongs to such genius, and which made the *Marble Faun* no less a characteristic work of Hawthorne's than the *Scarlet Letter*. Yet in both there is the same general quality, although one is a story of old Puritan days in Boston, and the other of modern life in Rome.

It is remarkable that Hawthorne was an author, and a copious one, long before he was generally recognized. His delight, in former days, was to insist that no writer was so obscure as he; and it is one evidence of the vitality of his power that he still wrote on. He piped, and the world would not sing; he played, and it would not dance. But he was sent to be a piper, and so he piped until the world paused, charmed by the rare melody, and acknowledged the master. His place in our literature he took at once when the *Scarlet Letter* was published, and in that place he was never disturbed, and will always remain. ⟨. . .⟩

The charm of his writings is imperishable. The fresh glow of genius which pervades them, apart from the essential interest of the stories, is indescribable. They have an individual pungency which does not always mark the works of our authors of an equal fame. The sparkle of humor which glitters every where upon his page, often weird but never dull, and a certain steadiness and self-possession of tone, equally free from rhetoric or baldness, certify a manly vigor and character which does not necessarily distinguish so subtle and poetic a nature. —GEORGE WILLIAM CURTIS, "Editor's Easy Chair," *Harper's New Monthly Magazine*, Aug. 1864, p. 405

The Puritanism of the past found its unwilling poet in Hawthorne, the rarest creative imagination of the century, the rarest in some ideal respects since Shakespeare.—JAMES RUSSELL LOWELL, "Thoreau" (1865), *Works*, Riverside ed., Vol. 1, p. 365

The devotee of Hawthorne is unrelenting in certain moody prejudices, Epicurean in his tastes and aspirations, and dreamy and uncertain in his theory of this life and the next.—NOAH PORTER, *Books and Reading*, 1870, p. 230

Hawthorne seems to me the most of a Man of Genius America has produced in the way of Imagination: yet I have never found an Appetite for his Books.—EDWARD FITZGERALD, Letter to W. F. Pollock (Nov. 1872)

Hawthorne, it is true, expanded so constantly, that however many works he might have produced, it seems unlikely that any one of them would have failed to record some large movement in his growth; and therefore it is perhaps to be regretted that his life could not have been made to solely serve his genius, so that we might have had the whole sweep of his imagination clearly exposed. As it is, he has not given us a large variety of characters; and Hester, Zenobia, and Miriam bear a certain general likeness one to another. Phœbe, however, is quite at the opposite pole of womanhood; Hilda is as unlike any of them as it is easy to conceive of her being; and Priscilla, again, is a feminine nature of unique calibre, as weird but not so warm as Goethe's Mignon, and at the same time a distinctly American type, in her nervous yet captivating fragility. In Priscilla and Phœbe are embodied two widely opposed classes of New England women. The male characters, with the exception of Donatello and Hollingsworth, are not so remarkable as the feminine ones: Coverdale and Kenyon come very close together, both being artistic and both reflectors for the persons that surround them; and Dimmesdale is to some extent the same character,—with the artistic escape closed upon his passions, so that they turn within and ravage his heart,—arrested and altered by Puritan influences. Chillingworth is perhaps too devilish a shape of revenge to be discussed as a human individual. Septimius, again, is distinct; and the characterization of Westervelt, in *Blithedale*, slight as it is, is very stimulating. Perhaps, after all, what leads us to pronounce upon the whole fictitious company a stricture of homogeneity is the fact that the author, though presenting us each time with a set of persons sufficiently separate from his previous ones, does not emphasize their differences with the same amount of external description that we habitually depend upon from a novelist. The similarity is more in the author's mode of presentation than in the creations themselves.

This monotone in which all the personages of his dramas share is nearly related with some special distinctions of his genius. He is so fastidious in his desire for perfection, that he can scarcely permit his actors to speak loosely or ungrammatically: though retaining their essential individuality, they are endowed with the author's own delightful power of expression. This outward phasis of his work separates it at once from that of the simple novelist, and leads us to consider the special applicability to it of the term "romance." He had not the realistic tendency, as we usually understand that, but he possessed the power to create a new species of fiction. For the kind of romance that he has left us differs from all compositions previously so called. It is not romance in the sense of D'Urfé's or Scudéri's; it is very far from coming within the scope of Fielding's "romances"; and it is entirely unconnected with the tales of the German Romantic school. It is not the romance of sentiment; nor that of incident, adventure, and character viewed under a worldly coloring: it has not the mystic and melodramatic bent belonging to Tieck and Novalis and Fouqué. There are two things which radically isolate it from all these. The first is its quality of revived belief. Hawthorne, as has been urged already, is a great believer, a man who has faith;

his belief goes out toward what is most beautiful, and this he finds only in moral truth. With him, poetry and moral insight are sacredly and indivisibly wedded, and their progeny is perfect beauty. This unsparingly conscientious pursuit of the highest truth, this metaphysical instinct, found in conjunction with a varied and tender appreciation of all forms of human or other life, is what makes him so decidedly the representative of a wholly new order of novelists. Belief, however, is not what he has usually been credited with, so much as incredulity. But the appearance of doubt is superficial, and arises from his fondness for illuminating fine but only half-perceptible traces of truth with the torch of superstition. Speaking of the supernatural, he says in his English journal: "It is remarkable that Scott should have felt interested in such subjects, being such a worldly and earthly man as he was; but then, indeed, almost all forms of popular superstition do clothe the ethereal with earthly attributes, and so make it grossly perceptible." This observation has a still greater value when applied to Hawthorne himself. And out of this questioning belief and transmutation of superstition into truth—for such is more exactly his method—proceeds also that quality of value and rarity and awe-enriched significance, with which he irradiates real life until it is sublimed to a delicate cloud-image of the eternal verities.

If these things are limitations, they are also foundations of a vast originality. Every greatness must have an outline. So that, although he is removed from the list of novelists proper, although his spiritual inspiration scares away a large class of sympathies, and although his strictly New England atmosphere seems to chill and restrain his dramatic fervor, sometimes to his disadvantage, these facts, on the other hand, are so many trenches dug around him, fortifying his fair eminence. Isolation and a certain degree of limitation, in some such sense as this, belong peculiarly to American originality. But Hawthorne is the embodiment of the youth of this country; and though he will doubtless furnish inspiration to a long line of poets and novelists, it must be hoped that they, likewise, will stand for other phases of its development, to be illustrated in other ways. No tribute to Hawthorne is less in accord with the biddings of his genius than that which would merely make a school of followers.

It is too early to say what position Hawthorne will take in the literature of the world; but as his influence gains the ascendant in America, by prompting new and un-Hawthornesque originalities, it is likely also that it will be made manifest in England, according to some unspecifiable ratio. Not that any period is to be distinctly colored by the peculiar dye in which his own pages are dipped; but the renewed tradition of a highly organized yet simple style, and still more the masculine tenderness and delicacy of thought and the fine adjustment of æsthetic and ethical obligations, the omnipresent truthfulness which he carries with him, may be expected to become a constituent part of very many minds widely opposed among themselves. I believe there is no fictionist who penetrates so far into individual consciences as Hawthorne; that many persons will be found who derive a profoundly religious aid from his unobtrusive but commanding sympathy. In the same way, his sway over the literary mind is destined to be one of no secondary degree. "Deeds are the offspring of words," says Heine; "Goethe's pretty words are childless." Not so with Hawthorne's. Hawthorne's repose is the acme of motion; and though turning on an axis of conservatism, the radicalism of his mind is irresistible; he is one of the most powerful because most unsuspected revolutionists of the world. Therefore, not only is he an incalculable factor in private character, but in addition his unnoticed leverage for the thought of the age is prodigious. These great abilities, subsisting with a temper so modest and unaffected, and never unhumanized by the abstract enthusiasm for art, place him on a plane between Shakespere and Goethe. With the universality of the first only just budding within his mind, he has not so clear a response to all the varying tones of lusty human life, and the individuality in his utterance amounts, at particular instants, to constraint. With less erudition than Goethe, but also less of the freezing pride of art, he is infinitely more humane, sympathetic, holy. His creations are statuesquely moulded like Goethe's, but they have the same quick music of heart-throbs that Shakespere's have. Hawthorne is at the same moment ancient and modern, plastic and picturesque.—GEORGE PARSONS LATHROP, A *Study of Hawthorne*, 1876, pp. 326–31

> But he whose quickened eye
> Saw through New England's life her inmost spirit,—
> Her heart, and all the stays on which it leant,—
> Returns not, since he laid the pencil by
> Whose mystic touch none other shall inherit!
> —EDMUND CLARENCE STEDMAN, "Hawthorne,"
> 1877

Hawthorne appalls—entices.—EMILY DICKINSON, Letter to Thomas Wentworth Higginson (1879)

One of the most characteristic of Hawthorne's literary methods is his habitual use of guarded under-statements and veiled hints. It is not a sign of weakness, but of conscious strength, when he surrounds each delineation with a sort of penumbra, takes you into his counsels, offers hypotheses, as, "May it not have been?" or, "Shall we not rather say?" and sometimes, like a conjurer, urges particularly upon you the card he does not intend you to accept. He seems not quite to know whether Arthur Dimmesdale really had a fiery scar on his breast, or what finally became of Miriam and her lover. He will gladly share with you any information he possesses, and, indeed, has several valuable hints to offer; but that is all. The result is, that you place yourself by his side to look with him at his characters, and gradually share with him the conviction that they must be real. Then, when he has you thus in possession, he calls your attention to the profound ethics involved in the tale, and yet does it so gently that you never think of the moral as being obtrusive.

All this involved a trait which was always supreme in him,—a marvellous self-control. He had by nature that gift which the musical composer Jomelli went to a teacher to seek,—"the art of not being embarrassed by his own ideas." Mrs. Hawthorne told me that her husband grappled alone all winter with *The Scarlet Letter*, and came daily from his study with a knot in his forehead; and yet his self-mastery was so complete that every sentence would seem to have crystallized in an atmosphere of perfect calm. We see the value of this element in his literary execution, when we turn from it to that of an author so great as Lowell, for instance, and see him often entangled and weighed down by his own rich thoughts, his style being overcrowded by the very wealth it bears. Hawthorne never needed Italic letters to distribute his emphasis, never a footnote for assistance. There was no conception so daring that he shrank from attempting it; and none that he could not so master as to state it, if he pleased, in terms of monosyllables. —THOMAS WENTWORTH HIGGINSON, "Hawthorne," *Short Studies of American Authors*, 1880, pp. 8–9

In Hawthorne, whose faculty was developed among scholars and with the finest additaments of scholarship, we have our first true artist in literary expression, as well as the most

completely equipped genius of romance. His subtle insight into the elements of character was marvelous. He was original and purely American,—Puritan, even, in his cast of thought and in all the internal and external conditions of his creation. But art is of no country. All ages temper the steel of the fine workman; all literatures whet the edge of his tools. In his sense of the controlling influence of powers beyond the individual's grasp, Hawthorne was Grecian. *The Scarlet Letter* and *The Blithedale Romance* are as fierce, unrelenting tragedy—controlling not only the actors but the writer—as anything in Æschylus. But Hawthorne's Fate came in the more modern form of "heredity." There were no angry gods; the "Sisters Three" had their origin in the ancestral stock a few generations back. His sense of their power, however, was intense, and was deeply based in the constitution of his own mind. He was too sane a man, of course, to yield credence to the Puritan suspicion of demonic influences, yet he was too much of a seer not to have discovered that, whether demons exist in nature or not, there are demons which are the projections of our own minds; and the struggle of his art was so to materialize these projections as to give them, not the reality which Cotton Mather insisted upon, but a spiritualized reality equally potent over the actions of men. Mr. Henry James, Jr., has pointed out—very justly, it would seem—a use made of the "scarlet letter" wherein Hawthorne overreached himself,—where the spiritual projection becomes labored and artificial. As far as Hawthorne attempts to make this image a potent force in Arthur Dimmesdale's mind, his instinct is unerring; but when he tries to make it visible to little Pearl and Roger Chillingworth, he passes from art into artifice. There is, perhaps, no natural person in *The Scarlet Letter*, just as there is no natural Hamlet in life; but we must accept Arthur Dimmesdale as a marvelous embodiment of the Puritan conscience acting upon the finest human clay,—a clay made sensitive to every emotion, quickened by every intellectual force.

The artistic evolution of the plot is as perfect as that of the *Œdipus Tyrannus*. So, too, in *The House of Seven Gables*, Judge Pyncheon is equally an embodiment of the granitic forces of the Puritan temperament, inheriting, not its finer conscience, but its untempered rigidity as acted upon by the forces of life. The man breaks at last, but he never bends. In the same way each character in Hawthorne's small list is a finished study, at once local in its surroundings and general in its psychological elements. It is a study of man in his special environment,—more scientific than the science of to-day, because it does what science fails to do; it tries to settle the spiritual element in its true place as a factor in man's life. Others have surpassed Hawthorne in the management of external conduct, of dialogue, of home life, of local scenery; but none have reached the depth to which he penetrated in the study of the human heart as the creature of its own creation. In every higher qualification of the artist, he easily excels. His style is masterly in ease, grace, clearness,—the winning, absorbing, entrancing quality. His skill in hinting in ideal and spiritual elements is the most perfect in our day. His mastery of light and shade—the power of deepening gloom by sunshine and intensifying sunshine by means of darkness—is of the finest order, at once the gift of original perception and the result of most assiduous practice. Probably few writers ever made so many successes that were failures, or so many failures that were successes; that is, few ever did so much that was to others artistically perfect in order that they might do something artistically perfect to themselves. Mr. James marvels at the existence of the *Note-Books*; yet their publication has thrown a flood of light not only upon the workings of Hawthorne's mind but on the sources of his artistic effects. They supplement with a sunny external quality the gloom of his psychology. They show us in his own nature a capacity for beauty and sweetness, where his own generation saw only a capacity for morbid analysis; that is, they furnish the biography of the sympathetic side of his mind, while the novels represent what was equally real to his emotional nature. No doubt, while his actual life was simple and pure-minded, capable of absorbing beauty and interest, he had, in imagination, lived through the tortures of the damned. He had given to Hester and Dimmesdale no exaltation or despair of which he was not himself capable, and probably none which he had not, by sheer force of imagination, without any adequate external cause, passed through. Others have been capable of such moods—the moods of "angels and ministers of grace" as well as of demons—without being either sinners or angels; but few have obtained the power of expressing them as he did. He spiritualized everything he touched, with a quality which is felt but cannot be analyzed,—which eludes every attempt to fix it. Little Pearl, standing in front of Governor Bellingham's mansion, looking at the "bright wonder of a house, began to caper and dance, and imperatively required that the whole breadth of sunshine should be stripped off its front and given her to play with." It was no harder to strip off that sunshine for little Pearl than it is to detach and handle the spiritual quality of these romances.

We had never reached such insight, or such grace of style, before Hawthorne, and we have never reached it since. As a writer, he was long in obscurity and had little influence on other authors. Emerging into something like local note when the first series of *Twice-Told Tales* was published, in 1837, he dawned upon a wider field, in 1842, with the addition of the *Second Series*. The intensity of his gloom was lightened in the *Mosses from an Old Manse* in 1846, and he then reached a larger circle of readers. In 1850, '51, and '52, he became national in fame, and soon reached the height.—JAMES HERBERT MORSE, "The Native Element in American Fiction," *Century Magazine*, July 1883, pp. 293–94

Simpler, clearer, more elegant English has never—even by Swift, Addison, or Goldsmith—been made the vehicle of thought and emotion equally profound, delicate, variant, and tortuous. Singularly choice and appropriate in diction; flowing and placid in movement, always sweet and pellucid, giving to objects a subtle ethereal aspect. His pen is a magician's wand, 'creating the semblance of a world out of airy matter, with the impalpable beauty of a soap-bubble.' We have all been exhorted to give days and nights to Addison. Rather, let us give days and nights to Macaulay, Carlyle and Hawthorne.

Standing aloof from common interests, looking at the present with shaded eyes, into the past with a half-wistful gaze, attracted by the remote, strange, and unusual, with a style admirably adapted to produce the effect of weird-like mystery,—Hawthorne is not a novelist. His fictions, in conception and performance, are always and essentially romances. Yet have they a character of fundamental trueness to spiritual laws, of harmony with time, place, and circumstance,—of realism existing in an ideal atmosphere, or invested with the halo of a poetic medium. We have not the worn-out paraphernalia of abbeys, castles, courts, gentry, aristocracy, and sovereigns; but we have types, mental conditions,—beyond the sphere of habitual experience, indeed, yet belonging profoundly to spirit and to man. No civilization has produced a romantic genius at all comparable in power to his. Other writers have been more learned, more dramatic, more versatile, more comprehensive. His stories are generally deficient in converging unity. His

personages seldom reveal themselves; but, as in the *Marble Faun*, we are told what they are, in page upon page of description, keen, minute, finished,—marvellous workmanship. No one ever depended so little upon plot or incident. Facts are subordinated to the influences with which they are charged. He is not a portrait-painter who sets forth a complete individuality. His forte is not in adventure, not in movement; but in the depicture of the rare and the occult, in the operation and results of involved and conflicting motives, feelings, and tendencies. He is here a solitary original in English letters. It may be questioned whether the *Scarlet Letter*, as an example of imaginative writing, has its parallel in any literature.—ALFRED H. WELSH, *Development of English Literature and Language*, 1883, Vol. 2, pp. 512–13

⟨. . .⟩ In New England, the history with which we are most familiar is that according to Nathaniel Hawthorne. Now dark and sombre, now warm and full of sunlight, always picturesque and imaginative, the story of the past, disconnected and uncertain, but yet vivid and real, has been woven by the hand of the enchanter to charm and fascinate all who listen. In Hawthorne's pages the ancient Puritan society, austere and rigid, and the later colonial aristocracy, laced and powdered, live and move, a delight to the present generation. But over all alike, over grave and gay, over the forbidding and the attractive, the delicate and morbid genius of the novelist has cast an air of mystery. In these stories we live in an atmosphere of half-told secrets, which are withal so real that we cannot help believing that somewhere, in some musty records or in letters yellow with time, we shall find answers to the questionings with which they fill our minds. Surely there must have been some one who had peeped beneath the black veil, who had known Maule and the Pyncheons, who had seen the prophetic pictures, who could tell us what the little world of Boston said about Hester Prynne and little Pearl, about Arthur Dimmesdale and Roger Chillingworth. One cannot help looking on every page of New England history for the characters of Hawthorne, and for an explanation of their lives. Disappointment always ensues, but hope is revived with each old manuscript that finds its way into print.—HENRY CABOT LODGE, *Studies in History*, 1884, pp. 21–22

He was a great writer—the greatest writer in prose fiction whom America has produced.—ANDREW LANG, "To Edgar Allan Poe," *Letters to Dead Authors*, 1886, p. 149

The people are gaining upon Nathaniel Hawthorne's works. A century hence, when the most popular authors of to-day are forgotten, he will probably be more widely read than ever. —EDWARD P. ROE, "The Element of Life in Fiction," *Forum*, April 1888, p. 229

It is hardly necessary to add that success, such as Hawthorne's, implies the happiest expression. Not to dwell on Hawthorne's style, simple mention may be made of his power of condensation, his exquisite application of the law of contrast, his repose, his judgment or taste; and, over and above all, his poet's skill in suggestiveness and in the creation of atmosphere, his primal power of pure, bold, sustained imagination— imagination which, for purity and subtilty has been equalled in English literature perhaps not more than once before since the robe fell from the shoulders of the unapproachable Elizabethan.—JOHN VANCE CHENEY, "Hawthorne," *The Golden Guess: Essays on Poetry and the Poets*, 1891, pp. 291–92

The Scarlet Letter is beyond doubt the foremost story yet written on this continent, and the fact that it holds the third place in this long list is both suggestive and encouraging. *The*

Marble Faun follows close upon its greater companion; for, however fascinating the later book in its subtle psychologic insight and however beautiful its art, it remains true that the earlier story surpasses it in closeness of construction and in depth and intensity of human interest. That a book of such quality finds so wide a reading shows that the finest art does not fail to charm when it allies itself with the deepest life. —HAMILTON W. MABIE, "The Most Popular Novels in America," *Forum*, Dec. 1893, p. 512

I suppose there are few English readers of fiction, having a taste for better things than the merely sensational novel, who are not acquainted with *The Scarlet Letter, The House of the Seven Gables,* and other works of Nathaniel Hawthorne, though I am afraid they are now less read—and, may I add, appreciated— than they were thirty years ago. Perhaps there is a reason for this; Hawthorne's works remind us of the laborious, patient, and delicate art of the fine gem-cutter, and to "taste" them thoroughly every detail has to be noticed and dwelt upon, and its suggestiveness remembered. A writer who produces this sort of work cannot be extremely voluminous, and, nowadays, for an author to retain his popularity he must be constantly producing some new thing—constantly, as it were, keeping himself "in evidence."—CAMILLA TOULMIN CROSLAND, *Landmarks of a Literary Life,* 1893, pp. 210–11

To men of our time, beyond doubt, his work seems generally not fantastic but imaginative, and surely not meretricious but in its own way beautiful. Nor is this the whole story: almost alone among our writers, we may say, Hawthorne has a lasting native significance. For this there are surely two good reasons. In the first place, he is almost the solitary American artist who has phrased his meaning in words of which the beauty seems sure to grow with the years. In the second place, what marks him as most impregnably American is this: when we look close to see what his meaning really was, we find it a thing that in the old days, at last finally dead and gone, had been the great motive power of his race. What Hawthorne really voices is that strange, morbid, haunting sense of other things that we see or hear, which underlay the intense idealism of the emigrant Puritans, and which remains perhaps the most inalienable emotional heritage of their children. It is Hawthorne, in brief, who finally phrases the meaning of such a life as Theophilus Eaton lived and Cotton Mather recorded.—BARRETT WENDELL, "American Literature," *Stelligeri and Other Essays concerning America,* 1893, p. 139

Hawthorne was no transcendentalist. He dwelt much in a world of ideas, and he sometimes doubted whether the tree on the bank or its image in the stream were the more real. But this had little in common with the philosophical idealism of his neighbors. He reverenced Emerson, and he held kindly intercourse—albeit a silent man and easily bored—with Thoreau and Ellery Channing, and even with Margaret Fuller. But his sharp eyes saw whatever was whimsical or weak in the apostles of the new faith. He had little enthusiasm for causes or reforms, and among so many abolitionists he remained a Democrat, and even wrote a campaign life of his friend Pierce.—HENRY A. BEERS, *Initial Studies in American Letters,* 1895, p. 123

Of the moderns, Hawthorne possesses in a remarkable degree the power of impressing unity on his creations. His hand is firm. He never wavers in style, stand-point, aim, or subject by a hair's-breadth. His plots are simple, his motives more so; in fact, no people ever were dominated by so few impulses as are the characters in Hawthorne's romances. There is something

Greek in their simplicity, although they are as unlike a Greek conception of humanity as are Caliban or Ariel. But they never waver. Such as the author conceived them in the first chapter, they remain to the end. There is no growth or development of character. This gives his tales an atmosphere which is never blown away by any nineteenth-century wind, and a unity which insures them a place in the literature which endures. There is a certain sameness about his style which might become monotonous in spite of its wonderful charm, and a limited experience of life which might become uninteresting, and an impress of a poverty-stricken and repellent external world which might become disheartening, but the unity is so thoroughly artistic that the pleasure received far outweighs the annoyance which is caused by the depressing and fatalistic atmosphere which envelops some of his romances.—CHARLES F. JOHNSON, *Elements of Literary Criticism,* 1898, pp. 34–35

Nearly all the Gothic machinery of Walpole, Mrs. Radcliffe, and Godwin is to be found in this Puritan: high winds, slamming doors, moonlight and starlight, magic and witchcraft, mysterious portraits, transformations, malignant beings, the elixir of life, the skeleton, the funeral, and the corpse in its shroud. To these sources of excitement were added, as time went on, mesmerism and clairvoyance. The novelty of Hawthorne's work is in his treatment. Like Shakespeare, he offers only a partial explanation of his unusual phemonena or none at all. Most unconventional is his use of witchcraft, as was pointed out by Poe, in 'The Hollow of Three Hills,' where to the imagination of the woman of sin, as she lays her head upon the witch's knees beneath the magic cloak, distant scenes of sorrow for which she is responsible are conveyed, not by viewing them in a magic mirror, but by the subtle sense of sound. And almost equally novel is the use made of the fountain of youth in 'Dr. Heidegger's Experiment.' The persecuting demon of romance, when he appears in Hawthorne's pages under the name of Roger Chillingworth, or the Spectre of the Catacomb, is a personification of the mistakes, misfortunes, and sins of our past life, which will not out of our imagination. The transformations—Pearl from a capricious, elfish being into a sober woman, and Donatello from a thoughtless, voluptuous animal into a man who feels the sad weight of humanity—have their analogies in real life. The supernatural world was with Hawthorne but the inner world of the conscience.

The ethical import of his narrative is always conveyed by means of a fanciful symbolism. The embroidered A that is hung about Hester Prynne's neck, the red stigma over Arthur Dimmesdale's heart, and Pearl in scarlet dress, are obviously symbolical. The black veil with which a Puritan minister conceals his face is the shadow of a dark deed. Donatello's hair-tipped ears are suggestions of his animalism. Moreover, Hawthorne was inclined to interpret figuratively events, nature, and art. Little Pearl runs from her mother and cannot be coaxed to return; that is typical of a moral gulf separating them. The sunless wood in which Hester stands alone images a moral solitude. Light streaming through the painted windows of a Gothic church is a foretaste of the 'glories of the better world.' As Hawthorne views a half-finished bust, and sees the human face struggling to get out of the marble, he remarks: 'As this bust in the block of marble, so does our individual fate exist in the limestone of time.' It has been said that Poe was a myth maker; Hawthorne likewise built up his own myths, and then he allegorized them like Bacon, turning them into apologues. Even the allegorical interpretation sometimes given to *The Marble Faun* is not to be ridiculed, for the allegory is there.

Whatever may have been the origin of language, it has now become, in its common use, a direct representation of things, ideas, and feelings. Hawthorne did not always so treat it, but rather conceived of it as a system of hieroglyphics; a secret he does not call a secret, 'it is a wild venomous thing' imprisoned in the heart. This is the way of Spenser.

The story of Hawthorne is only half told when we say he refined Gothic art and fashioned it to high ethical purposes. As in the case of Poe, one of his great charms is his workmanship in structure and style. In the technique of the short tale, Poe was at least his equal; in the longer tale, where Poe left many loose ends, Hawthorne succeeded twice—in *The Scarlet Letter* (1850) and *The House of the Seven Gables* (1851). Poe modelled his style on Defoe and De Quincey, now suggesting the one and now the other. Hawthorne by laborious practice acquired a more individual style; the good taste of Addison and Irving are visible in it, and the brooding and dreamy fancy of Tieck, disguised however in the fusion.—WILBUR L. CROSS, *The Development of the English Novel*, 1899, pp. 163–66

Hawthorne's work you may read from end to end without the temptation to transfer so much as a line to the commonplace book. The road has taken you through many interesting scenes, and past many a beautiful landscape; you may have felt much and learned much; you might be glad to turn back straightway and travel the course over again; but you will have picked up no coin or jewel to put away in a cabinet. This characteristic of Hawthorne is the more noteworthy because of the moral quality of his work. A mere story-teller may naturally keep his narrative on the go, as we say,—that is one of the chief secrets of his art; but Hawthorne was not a mere story-teller. He was a moralist,—Emerson himself hardly more so; yet he has never a moral sentence. The fact is, he did not make sentences; he made books. The story, not the sentence, nor even the paragraph or the chapter, was the unit. The general truth—the moral—informed the work. Not only was it not affixed as a label; it was not given anywhere a direct and separable verbal expression. If the story does not convey it to you, you will never get it. Hawthorne, in short, was what, for lack of a better word, we may call a literary artist.—BRADFORD TORREY, "Writers That Are Quotable," *Atlantic*, March 1899, p. 407

Works

TWICE-TOLD TALES

When a new star rises in the heavens, people gaze after it for a season with the naked eye, and with such telescopes as they may find. In the stream of thought, which flows so peacefully deep and clear, through the pages of this book, we see the bright reflection of a spiritual star, after which men will be fain to gaze "with the naked eye and with the spy-glasses of criticism." This star is but newly risen; and ere long the observations of numerous star-gazers, perched up on arm-chairs and editors' tables, will inform the world of its magnitude and its place in the heaven of poetry, whether it be in the paw of the Great Bear, or on the forehead of Pegasus, or on the strings of the Lyre, or in the wing of the Eagle. Our own observations are as follows. To this little work we would say, "Live ever, sweet, sweet book." It comes from the hand of a man of genius. Everything about it has the freshness of morning and of May. These flowers and green leaves of poetry have not the dust of the highway upon them. They have been gathered fresh from the secret places of a peaceful and gentle heart. There flow deep waters, silent, calm, and cool; and the green trees look into them, and "God's blue heaven." The

book, though in prose, is written nevertheless by a poet. He looks upon all things in the spirit of love, and with lively sympathies; for to him external form is but the representation of internal being, all things having a life, an end and aim. ⟨. . .⟩

Another characteristic of this writer is the exceeding beauty of his style. It is as clear as running waters are. Indeed he uses words as mere stepping-stones, upon which, with a free and youthful bound, his spirit crosses and recrosses the bright and rushing stream of thought. Some writers of the present day have introduced a kind of Gothic architecture into their style. All is fantastic, vast, and wondrous in the outward form, and within is mysterious twilight, and the swelling sound of an organ, and a voice chanting hymns in Latin, which need a translation for many of the crowd. To this we do not object. Let the priest chant in what language he will, so long as he understands his own mass-book. But if he wishes the world to listen and be edified, he will do well to choose a language that is generally understood.—HENRY WADSWORTH LONGFELLOW, "Hawthorne's *Twice-Told Tales*," *North American Review*, July 1837, pp. 59, 63

Mr. Hawthorne's volumes appear to us misnamed in two respects. In the first place they should not have been called *Twice-Told Tales*—for this is a title which will not bear *repetition*. If in the first collected edition they were twice-told, of course now they are thrice-told.—May we live to hear them told a hundred times! In the second place, these compositions are by no means *all* "Tales." The most of them are essays properly so called. It would have been wise in their author to have modified his title, so as to have had reference to all included. This point could have been easily arranged.

But under whatever titular blunders we receive this book, it is most cordially welcome. We have seen no prose composition by any American which can compare with *some* of these articles in the higher merits, or indeed in the lower; while there is not a single piece which would do dishonor to the best of the British essayists.

"The Rill from the Town Pump" which, through the *ad captandum* nature of its title, has attracted more of public notice than any one other of Mr. Hawthorne's compositions, is perhaps, the *least* meritorious. Among his best, we may briefly mention "The Hollow of the Three Hills;" "The Minister's Black Veil;" "Wakefield;" "Mr. Higginbotham's Catastrophe;" "Fancy's Show-Box;" "Dr. Heidegger's Experiment;" "David Swan;" "The Wedding Knell;" and "The White Old Maid." It is remarkable that all these, with one exception, are from the first volume.

The style of Mr. Hawthorne is purity itself. His *tone* is singularly effective—wild, plaintive, thoughtful, and in full accordance with his themes. We have only to object that there is insufficient diversity in these themes themselves, or rather in their character. His *originality* both of incident and of reflection is very remarkable; and this trait alone would ensure him at least *our* warmest regard and commendation. We speak here chiefly of the tales; the essays are not so markedly novel. Upon the whole we look upon him as one of the few men of indisputable genius to whom our country has as yet given birth.—EDGAR ALLAN POE, "Nathaniel Hawthorne" (1842), *Essays and Reviews*, ed. G. R. Thompson, 1984, pp. 568–69

From the press of Munroe & Co., Boston, in the year 1837, appeared *Twice-Told Tales*. Though not widely successful in their day and generation, they had the effect of making me known in my own immediate vicinity; insomuch that, however reluctantly, I was compelled to come out of my owl's nest and lionize in a small way. Thus I was gradually drawn somewhat into the world, and became pretty much like other people. My long seclusion had not made me melancholy or misanthropic, nor wholly unfitted me for the bustle of life; and perhaps it was the kind of discipline which my idiosyncrasy demanded, and chance and my own instincts, operating together, had caused me to do what was fittest.—NATHANIEL HAWTHORNE, Letter to Richard Henry Stoddard (1853), cited in Julian Hawthorne, *Nathaniel Hawthorne and His Wife*, 1884, Vol. 1, p. 98

THE SCARLET LETTER

We shall entirely mislead our reader if we give him to suppose that *The Scarlet Letter* is coarse in its details, or indecent in its phraseology. This very article of our own, is far less suited to ears polite, than any page of the romance before us; and the reason is, we call things by their right names, while the romance never hints the shocking words that belong to its things, but, like Mephistophiles, insinuates that the arch-fiend himself is a very tolerable sort of person, if nobody would call him Mr. Devil. We have heard of persons who could not bear the reading of some Old Testament Lessons in the service of the Church: such persons would be delighted with our author's story; and damsels who shrink at the reading of the Decalogue, would probably luxuriate in bathing their imagination in the crystal of its delicate sensuality. The langauge of our author, like patent blacking, "would not soil the whitest linen," and yet the composition itself, would suffice, if well laid on, to Ethiopize the snowiest conscience that ever sat like a swan upon that mirror of heaven, a Christian maiden's imagination. We are not sure we speak quite strong enough, when we say, that we would much rather listen to the coarsest scene of Goldsmith's *Vicar*, read aloud by a sister or daughter, than to hear from such lips, the perfectly chaste language of a scene in *The Scarlet Letter*, in which a married wife and her reverend paramour, with their unfortunate offspring, are introduced as the actors, and in which the whole tendency of the conversation is to suggest a sympathy for their sin, and an anxiety that they may be able to accomplish a successful escape beyond the seas, to some country where their shameful commerce may be perpetuated. Now, in Goldsmith's story there are very coarse words, but we do not remember anything that saps the foundations of the moral sense, or that goes to create unavoidable sympathy with unrepenting sorrow, and deliberate, premeditated sin. The *Vicar of Wakefield* is sometimes coarsely virtuous, but *The Scarlet Letter* is delicately immoral. —ARTHUR CLEVELAND COXE, "The Writings of Hawthorne," *Church Review*, Jan. 1851, p. 507

I was reading (rather re-reading) the other evening the introductory chapter to the *Scarlet Letter*. It is admirably written. Not having any great sympathy with a custom-house—nor, indeed, with Salem, except that it seems to be Hawthorne's birth-place—all my attention was concentrated on the *style*, which seems to me excellent.—BRYAN WALLER PROCTER, Letter to James T. Fields (Feb. 1853), cited in James T. Fields, "'Barry Cornwall' and Some of His Friends," *Harper's New Monthly Magazine*, Dec. 1875, pp. 59–60

Speaking of Thackeray, I cannot but wonder at his coolness in respect to his own pathos, and compare it with my emotions, when I read the last scene of *The Scarlet Letter* to my wife, just after writing it,—tried to read it rather, for my voice swelled and heaved, as if I were tossed up and down on an ocean as it subsides after a storm. But I was in a very nervous state then, having gone through a great diversity of emotion, while writing it, for many months. I think I have never overcome my own

adamant in any other instance.—NATHANIEL HAWTHORNE, *The English Note-Books*, 1855

I believe and am sure that *The Scarlet Letter* will endure as long as the language in which it is written; and should that language become dead, the wonderful work will be translated. Mr. S. C. Hall says I am to tell you that your works will live when marble crumbles into dust. I can well understand that even genius stands breathless in silence, watching events; still, master, you must send us forth some fresh enchantment ere-long, though you have done so much.—BERKELEY AIKIN, Letter to Nathaniel Hawthorne (1862), cited in Julian Hawthorne, *Nathaniel Hawthorne and His Wife*, 1884, Vol. 2, p. 305

It is conflict that we have in *Jane Eyre*, an assertion of individual will, a fine capacity of individual emotion, and all this in conflict with the world opposing. But it is struggle, not conflict, the inner, not the outer, warfare, that we have in Hester Prynne. It is the stir and the struggle of the soul afflicted, punished, but growing into larger development, into riper life, through this stress and struggle and affliction. And if I seemed to indicate that the novel was in process of development when I wrote that the vitality of the assertion of life was the essence of individuality, and that because of this vitality *Jane Eyre* was an indication of an advance in the art of fiction beyond the spirit and the method of Jane Austen's day, then I may further claim now that the completed picture of the soul of Hester Prynne is indicative of a step in advance as great as, if less marked than, the step from Jane Austen to Charlotte Brontë. It is a step in advance because the picture of Hester Prynne portrays a human soul not merely as a strong, demanding individuality, but as under stress of such relation to verdict of law and to the rights of fellow-mortals as to compel its development into a completed personality. The novel of the *Scarlet Letter* is one of the links in the development of the novel from a means of portraying single phases of emotion to a vehicle of highest expressional power. It was written by a psychological student of the problems which harass the human soul.

⟨. . .⟩ It is a tragedy—a tragedy sombre, intense, unrelieved. It is almost a fatalistic tragedy; almost as stern as if it had been written by Æschylus. It is not a love story; it is not a story of youth; it is not a story of contemporaneous life; it is not a story of eager hope. Hester Prynne having sinned is doomed for punishment to wear the scarlet letter as the symbol of the seared soul forever on her bosom; made an outcast from social joy forever. And the story is the record of the growth of the thoughtless soul of the girl, Hester Prynne, into the sad, strong soul of a mature woman. As accessories to this record of growth, we have scenery of circumstance and scenery of characters. To get perspective, atmosphere, verisimilitude, Hawthorne goes back to a recognizable era of past history. He paints with steadiness the outward aspects, and makes credible the inner motive, of the Puritan Colony in the Boston of 1658. Yet the book is in no sense an historical novel. To give vividness, concreteness, objectivity, to this story of the inner life, to this record of the growth of the conscience, of the growth of responsibility, of the growth of religion, within the breast of Hester Prynne, Hawthorne uses the symbolism which is the picture language of the infancy of awakening fancy. In the story he carries on the crude symbolism of the Puritan court of justice decreeing a visible A as an objective reminder of the branded heart—carries on this crude symbolism into the most delicate and refined suggestions. The unseen forces, the unseen monitors, the unseen avengers, float before our eyes, are painted on the clouds, are burned upon the flesh, in mystic symbols. These mystic symbols are like the weird sisters in *Macbeth*; they are the objectification of mystery. The revelation of the working of the spirit of regeneration upon the soul of Hester Prynne is embodied for us in the weird child, Pearl. She is a living symbol, at once the incarnation of sin, the personification of the Scarlet Letter, the emblem of hope, and the prophecy of pardon. All this is the poetry of mysticism. Yet the *Scarlet Letter* is no more a mystical romance than it is an historical novel.

But if we have mediæval mysticism in the symbolism of the work, we have something very like Greek simplicity and Greek directness in the development. The novel is a Greek tragedy. Like the Greek, it is synthetic and creative rather than analytic. Like the Greek tragedy, the novel of the *Scarlet Letter* has a single story, few principal characters, largeness, unity of treatment, directness, sternness, relentlessness. As in the Greek tragedy, also, the story begins after the guilt has been incurred, and the motive of the story is the relation of the soul of man to Nemesis and justice. There is Greek suggestion even in the minor detail; Pearl is as a chorus to voice for us the comment of the unseen powers. There is Greek atmosphere. All the characters seem to be being rather than acting. Yet the novel is no more a Greek tragedy than it is an historical tale; it is no more a Greek tragedy than it is a mediæval romance. It is, in one, a Greek tragedy, a mediæval romance, a modern historical tale. It is a master work, limited to no age, belonging to all experiences, to all time.—FRANCIS HOVEY STODDARD, *The Evolution of the English Novel*, 1900, pp. 75–80

THE HOUSE OF THE SEVEN GABLES

The House of the Seven Gables was finished yesterday. Mr. Hawthorne read me the close, last evening. There is unspeakable grace and beauty in the conclusion, throwing back upon the sterner tragedy of the commencement an ethereal light, and a dear home-loveliness and satisfaction. How you will enjoy the book,—its depth of wisdom, its high tone, the flowers of Paradise scattered over all the dark places, the sweet wall-flower scent of Phœbe's character, the wonderful pathos and charm of old Uncle Venner. I only wish you could have heard the Poet sing his own song, as I did; but yet the book needs no adventitious aid,—it makes its own music, for I read it all over again to myself yesterday, except the last three chapters.—SOPHIA HAWTHORNE, Letter (Jan. 27, 1851), cited in Julian Hawthorne, *Nathaniel Hawthorne and His Wife*, 1884, Vol. 1, p. 383

The *House of the Seven Gables*, in my opinion, is better than *The Scarlet Letter*; but I should not wonder if I had refined upon the principal character a little too much for popular appreciation; nor if the romance of the book should be found somewhat at odds with the humble and familiar scenery in which I invest it. But I feel that portions of it are as good as anything I can hope to write, and the publisher speaks encouragingly of its success.—NATHANIEL HAWTHORNE, Letter to Horatio Bridge (March 15, 1851), cited in Horatio Bridge, *Personal Recollections of Nathaniel Hawthorne*, 1893, p. 125

I have been so delighted with *The House of the Seven Gables* that I cannot help sitting down to tell you so. I thought I could not forgive you if you wrote anything better than *The Scarlet Letter*; but I cannot help believing it a great triumph that you should have been able to deepen and widen the impression made by such a book as that. It seems to me that the "House" is the most valuable contribution to New England history that has been made. It is with the highest art that you have typified

(in the revived likeness of Judge Pyncheon to his ancestor the Colonel) that intimate relationship between the Present and the Past in the way of ancestry and descent, which historians so carefully overlook. Yesterday is commonly looked upon and written about as of no kin to To-day, though the one is legitimate child of the other, and has its veins filled with the same blood. And the chapter about Alice and the Carpenter,—Salem, which would not even allow you so much as Scotland gave Burns, will build you a monument yet for having shown that she did not hang her witches for nothing. I suppose the true office of the historian is to reconcile the present with the past.—JAMES RUSSELL LOWELL, Letter to Nathaniel Hawthorne (April 24, 1851), cited in Julian Hawthorne, *Nathaniel Hawthorne and His Wife*, 1884, Vol. 1, pp. 390–91

The contents of this book do not belie its clustering romantic title. With great enjoyment we spent almost an hour in each separate gable. This book is like a fine old chamber, abundantly but still judiciously furnished with precisely that sort of furniture best fitted to furnish it. There are rich hangings, whereon are braided scenes from tragedies. There is old china with rare devices, set about on the carved beaufet; there are long and indolent lounges to throw yourself upon; there is an admirable sideboard, plentifully stored with good viands; there is a smell of old wine in the pantry; and finally, in one corner, there is a dark little black-letter volume in golden clasps, entitled *Hawthorne: A Problem*. . . .

We think the book for pleasantness of running interest surpasses the other work of the author. The curtains are now drawn; the sun comes in more; genialities peep out more. Were we to particularize what has most struck us in the deeper passages, we should point out the scene where Clifford, for a minute, would fain throw himself from the window, to join the procession; or the scene where the Judge is left seated in his ancestral chair.

Clifford is full of an awful truth throughout. He is conceived in the finest, truest spirit. He is no caricature. He is Clifford. And here we would say, that did the circumstances permit, we should like nothing better than to devote an elaborate and careful paper to the full consideration and analysis of the purpose and significance of what so strongly characterizes all of this author's writing. There is a certain tragic phase of humanity, which, in our opinion, was never more powerfully embodied than by Hawthorne: we mean the tragicalness of human thought in its own unbiased, native, and profound workings. We think that into no recorded mind has the intense feeling of the whole truth ever entered more deeply than into this man's. By whole truth, we mean the apprehension of the absolute condition of present things as they strike the eye of the man who fears them not, though they do their worst to him.—HERMAN MELVILLE, Letter to Nathaniel Hawthorne (1851), cited in George Parsons Lathrop, A *Study of Hawthorne*, 1876, pp. 230–31

Accept my most cordial thanks for the little volume you have had the kindness to send me. I prize it as the right hand of fellowship extended to me by one whose friendship I am proud and happy to make, and whose writings I have regarded with admiration as among the very best that have ever issued from the American press.—WASHINGTON IRVING, Letter to Nathaniel Hawthorne (1852), cited in Julian Hawthorne, *Nathaniel Hawthorne and His Wife*, 1884, Vol. 1, p. 440

THE BLITHEDALE ROMANCE

It is enough for me that you have put another rose into your chaplet, and I will not ask whether it outblooms or outswells its sister flowers. Zenobia is a splendid creature, and I wish there were more such rich and ripe women about. I wish, too, you could have wound up your story without killing her, or that at least you had given her a drier and handsomer death. Priscilla is an exquisite sketch. I don't know whether you have quite explained Hollingsworth's power over two such diverse natures. Your views about reform and reformers and spiritual rappings are such as I heartily approve. Reformers need the enchantment of distance. Your sketches of things visible, detached observations, and style generally, are exquisite as ever. May you live a thousand years, and write a book every year!—GEORGE S. HILLARD, Letter to Nathaniel Hawthorne (July 27, 1852), cited in Julian Hawthorne, *Nathaniel Hawthorne and His Wife*, 1884, Vol. 1, p. 448

The Blithedale Romance is no bundle of biographies: it has been more properly described as "a humanitarian ballet danced by four figures, who quarrel and dance out of tune." The central idea is, in this case, almost too obvious: the proposition to be proved is that the exaggeration of right may turn to wrong—*Summum jus, summa injuria*. It is *Measure for Measure* without the treason in Angelo's blood, though Hollingsworth is, in the result, as cruel as Angelo meant to be. Much of the work is a comment on the melancholy truth that "half the work of the wise is to counteract the mischief done by the good;" but the only wise man on the stage is Coverdale, and he is not strong enough: all he has to tell us in the end is, by his own confession, "Nothing, nothing, nothing!" Silas Foster interrupting the regenerators of society with the question, "Which man among you is the best judge of swine?" and the discovery, soon made by the masquerading Arcadians, that "intellectual activity is incompatible with any large amount of bodily exercise," point to the foregone conclusion. The descriptive skill displayed in the book is beyond praise. Nowhere has the author more successfully availed himself of his favourite trick of antithesis. The man whose life is ruined by too much, and the man whose life is an emptiness from too little, purpose; the magnificent Zenobia,—the most Titian-like figure on Hawthorne's canvas,—pulsing in every vein with passionate life, and the veiled lady, the pale "anemone," whose appearance in the drama is like the sigh of a flute in a rich orchestra;—these are not more strikingly contrasted than old Moodie, the frail shadow of Fauntleroy, and Westervelt, charlatan and "salamander"—people who seem to have walked entire out of some unwritten novel of Balzac. The variety in the scenery is similarly enhanced by juxtaposition, as of the Hermitage and the Hotel, Elliot's Pulpit and the Boarding-house; just as the healthy atmosphere of the fields is set off by the miasmas of Mesmerism and Spiritualism, which, in this instance, represent the inevitable element of superstition. *The Blithedale Romance* has attracted an unusual amount of attention from French critics, owing to the interest taken by their countrymen in the social problem—a problem which it, however, suggests and sets aside rather than discusses, the references to Fourierism, etc., being mere interpolations cut short by Hollingsworth's dogmatism. The only point made plain is the baleful and blighting effect of the philanthropy that overrides private personal claims. The book is the tragedy of which Dickens' Mrs. Jellaby is the comedy; and it is the most dismal ever written by the author, the only rays of light being the rustic scenes, and the impressive emancipation of Priscilla in the village hall. The finding of Zenobia's body is, perhaps, the most ghastly description in literature: it is aggravated to a climax by the horrible cynicism of Coverdale's remark, that had she foreseen "how ill it would become her, she would no

more have committed the dreadful act than have exhibited herself in public in a badly-fitting garment." Time passes, and the impartial torturer meets the philanthropic bird of prey with the question, "Up to this moment, how many criminals have you reformed?" "No one," said Hollingsworth, with his eyes still fixed on the ground. "Ever since we parted, I have been busy with a single murderer." It is a fit close to the wreck of idealisms and the holocaust of aspirations, that leaves us with a deeper sense of the mockery of life, of more utter hopelessness than any other English work of fiction, excepting perhaps *Middlemarch*.—JOHN NICHOL, *American Literature*, 1882, pp. 345–47

THE MARBLE FAUN

⟨. . .⟩ I have said a dozen times that nobody can write English but you. With regard to the story, which has been somewhat criticised, I can only say that to me it is quite satisfactory. I like those shadowy, weird, fantastic, Hawthornesque shapes flitting through the golden gloom, which is the atmosphere of the book. I like the misty way in which the story is indicated rather than revealed; the outlines are quite definite enough from the beginning to the end to those who have imagination enough to follow you in your airy flights; and to those who complain, I suppose that nothing less than an illustrated edition, with a large gallows on the last page, with Donatello in the most pensile of attitudes,—his ears revealed through a white night-cap,—would be satisfactory. I beg your pardon for such profanation, but it really moves my spleen that people should wish to bring down the volatile figures of your romance to the level of an every-day romance. . . . The way in which the two victims dance through the Carnival on the last day is very striking. It is like a Greek tragedy in its effect, without being in the least Greek.—JOHN LOTHROP MOTLEY, Letter to Nathaniel Hawthorne (March 29, 1860), cited in George Parsons Lathrop, *A Study of Hawthorne*, 1876, pp. 262–63

I've finished *the* book, and am, I think, more angry at your tantalizing cruelty than either *Athenæum* or *Saturday Review*. I want to know a hundred things you do not tell me,—who Miriam was, what was the crime in which she was concerned and of which all Europe knew, what was in the packet, what became of Hilda, whether Miriam married Donatello, whether Donatello got his head cut off, etc. Of course you'll say I ought to *guess*; well, if I do guess, it is but a guess, and I want to *know*. Yesterday I wrote a review of you in the *Examiner*, and in spite of my natural indignation, I hope you will not altogether dislike what I have said. In other respects I admire *Monte Beni* more than I can tell you; and I suppose no one now will visit Rome without a copy of it in his hand. Nowhere are descriptions to be found so beautiful, so true, and so pathetic. And there are little bits of *you* in the book which are best of all,—half moralizing, half thinking aloud. There is a bit about *women sewing* which Harriet raves about. There are bits about Catholicism and love and sin, which are marvellously thought and gloriously written.—HENRY BRIGHT, Letter to Nathaniel Hawthorne (1860), cited in Julian Hawthorne, *Nathaniel Hawthorne and His Wife*, 1884, Vol. 2, p. 240

Smith and Elder certainly do take strange liberties with the titles of books. I wanted to call it *The Marble Faun*, but they insisted upon *Transformation*, which will lead the reader to anticipate a sort of pantomime. They wrote me some days ago that the edition was nearly all sold, and that they are going to print another; to which I mean to append a few pages, in the shape of a conversation between Kenyon, Hilda, and the author, throwing some further light on matters which seem to have been left too much in the dark. For my own part, however, I should prefer the book as it now stands.—NATHANIEL HAWTHORNE, Letter to Henry Bright (1860), cited in Julian Hawthorne, *Nathaniel Hawthorne and His Wife*, 1884, Vol. 2, p. 241

I was greatly pleased with the success of your last book, *The Marble Faun*. It seemed to me at first, until I got well a-going, a little difficult to seize the thread; but when I once found it, I went rapidly forward unto the end. I always consider the rapidity with which I can read a story the test of its merit, at least for me. Many others have spoken to me of its effect on them. I greatly enjoyed the Italian criticism. As a matter of art, there is possibly always a certain danger in combining didactic and dramatic situations; but if any field is open to this, it should be Italy. "Corinne," I think, deals in character rather than criticism. I should be ashamed to tell you how often I have read *The Marble Faun*.—WILLIAM ELLERY CHANNING, Letter to Nathaniel Hawthorne (Sept. 3, 1860), cited in Julian Hawthorne, *Nathaniel Hawthorne and His Wife*, 1884, Vol. 2, p. 265

Marble Faun, whether consciously or not, illustrates that invasion of the æsthetic by the moral which has confused art by dividing its allegiance, and dethroned the old dynasty without as yet firmly establishing the new in an acknowledged legitimacy.—JAMES RUSSELL LOWELL, "Swinburne's Tragedies" (1866), *Works*, Riverside ed., Vol. 2, pp. 125–26

In all we may find our way to some mystic monument of eternal law, or pluck garlands from some new-budded bough of moral truth. The romance is like a portal of ebony inlaid with ivory,—another gate of dreams,—swinging softly open into regions of illimitable wisdom. But some pause on the threshold, unused to such large liberty; and these cry out, in the words of a well-known critic, "It begins in mystery, and ends in mist."

Though the book was very successful, few readers grasped the profounder portions. It is a vast exemplar of the author's consummate charm as a simple storyteller, however, that he exercised a brilliant fascination over all readers, notwithstanding the heavy burden of uncomprehended truths which they were obliged to carry with them. Some critics complain of the extent to which Roman scenery and the artistic life in Rome have been introduced; but, to my mind, there is scarcely a word wasted in the two volumes. The "vague sense of ponderous remembrances" pressing down and crowding out the present moment till "our individual affairs are but half as real here as elsewhere," is essential to the perspective of the whole; and nothing but this rich picturesqueness and variety could avail to balance the depth of tragedy which has to be encountered; so that the nicety of art is unquestionable. It is strange, indeed, that this great modern religious romance should thus have become also the ideal representative of ruined Rome—the home of ruined religions—in its æsthetic aspects.—GEORGE PARSONS LATHROP, *A Study of Hawthorne*, 1876, pp. 260–61

The shadow of a Miriam's guilt dims the purity of a Hilda's innocence. But in painting life as it is, it is always possible to paint it as it ought to be. When it is said that Hawthorne makes us familiar with sin and suffering, it must be remembered that there is a familiarity which degrades and another which ennobles. Out of this sombre background Hawthorne evokes the greatness of human nature. The radiance of a spiritual sky falls upon his darkest picture. From the standpoint of the philosopher or the theologian, every writer will always be subject to criticism, for the reason that the standpoints are many. An early critic complained that Hawthorne was morbid because he evinced "so little conception of the remedial system which God has provided for the sins and sorrows of mankind." Granting the fact set forth in this narrow arraignment, it remains true that without avowing distinctly any ethical purpose Hawthorne is ever revealing the sublimity of life, the grandeur of human nature. The fire of his crucible is a purifying flame. However realistic the woes or littlenesses he portrays, they neither crush nor disgust. His vision was too all-embracing, his purpose too deep for this. He is the thinker interpreting to us the world of reality, not the mirror reflecting it. Even as the realist he reflected the sky above our heads as well as the mud under our feet. ⟨. . .⟩

I may mention one delicious quality in the melancholy of Hawthorne for which we are always grateful— its impersonality. His eye looks outward. There is analysis, but not self-analysis, no introspection. He shows us suffering humanity, not the suffering Hawthorne. His is no Byronic literature of personal griefs, with its littlenesses, self-infatuations, and idolatry. There is, of course, the melancholy of the temperament, the constitutional tendency of the individual, but no autobiography of a bitter personal experience. He is summing up greater than individual issues. It is infinitely refreshing to be free from this oppressive sense of subjective suffering, the single accidental experience, so insignificant when compared with the general law and so fatal to dispassionate analysis.

I may mention one impression derived from a last re-reading of *The Marble Faun* which is perhaps wholly personal, but which has lessened its first effect as a work of art. The local color and descriptive passages of Hawthorne's earlier works impart the information necessary to the setting of the story, and no more. What may be called the decorative elements are so intimately associated with the constructive plan that each heightens the effect of the other. I cannot recall a writer more successful in this union of ornamental detail and organic structure. It is like the pediment end of the Doric order, whose beauty is not applied but wrought in. Whenever this is true, a style, whether in literature or architecture, painting or sculpture, gains immensely in dignity and unity. I do not say that it is not true of *The Marble Faun*, nor that its local color is less natural than that of Hawthorne's New England novels; but that mingled with what is strictly necessary to the scenic effect is a great deal of information which belongs to the guide-book rather than the work of art. Hawthorne's analysis of a painting or interpretation of a statue is often vital to the story, and has a value apart from its relation to it; but there is much of description and history which belongs rather to a work like Irving's *Alhambra* than to a romance.

For this very reason, however, the illustration of *The Marble Faun* is withdrawn from the realm of imagination. We would have no other Donatello than that of Praxiteles, desire no Hilda's Tower but that of the Via Portoghese. The present edition, glorious in red and gold, yet exquisitely tasteful, with its fifty photogravures, is a gem in bookmaking. Remembering that this work was received with so little favor that Hawthorne used to say of it, "The thing is a failure," it makes one wish he might see this last effort to array it in the beauty it deserves.—ARTHUR SHERBURNE HARDY, "Hawthorne's Italian Romance," *Book Buyer*, Nov. 1889, pp. 427–28

In *The Marble Faun* his pure and tranquil grace of style is at its best. The economy of incident is not so strict as in the statuesque simplicity of the *Scarlet Letter* groupings, nor is the dramatic intensity so keen; but there is Hawthorne's own rich, subdued, autumnal coloring, with the first soft shadows deepening into sable. Emerson, whom Hawthorne's Concord journal once noted as coming to call "with a sunbeam in his face," unwittingly returned the compliment by saying that Hawthorne "rides well his horse of the night." Gloom has its own enchantment, and so has mystery, but the issues of this romance were left in an uncertainty that its readers found hard to bear. Hawthorne would not help them. He was fertile in misleading suggestions and tricksy hypotheses, but perhaps he hardly knew the actual fate of Miriam and Donatello. Such a "cloudy veil" as he found stretched over "the abyss" of his own nature may have been interposed between himself and the innermost secrets of his characters. Supernatural forces, too, entered in, as in life, amid the personages of his tales and played their inscrutable parts beside them. Among the baffling questions is one suggested by Hawthorne's younger daughter, who, with her husband, George Parsons Lathrop, poet and novelist, has embraced the Roman faith. Mrs. Lathrop claims that *The Marble Faun*, if closely studied, shows in the treatment of sin and atonement a significant divergence from the Puritan romances.—KATHARINE LEE BATES, *American Literature*, 1897, pp. 314–15

RICHARD HOLT HUTTON
From "Nathaniel Hawthorne"
Literary Essays
1871, pp. 437–58

Hawthorne has been called a mystic, which he was not,—and a psychological dreamer, which he was in very slight degree. He was really the ghost of New England,—I do not mean the "spirit," nor the "phantom," but the ghost in the older sense in which that term is used, the thin, rarefied essence which is supposed to be found somewhere behind the physical organisation: embodied, indeed, and not at all in a shadowy or diminutive earthly tabernacle, but yet only half embodied in it, endowed with a certain painful sense of the gulf between his nature and its organisation, always recognising the gulf, always trying to bridge it over, and always more or less unsuccessful in the attempt. His writings are not exactly spiritual writings, for there is no dominating spirit in them. They are ghostly writings. Hawthorne was, to my mind, a sort of sign to New England of the divorce that has been going on there (and not less perhaps in old England) between its people's spiritual and earthly nature, and of the difficulty which they will soon feel, if they are to be absorbed more and more in that shrewd hard common sense which is one of their most striking characteristics, in even *communicating* with their former self. Hawthorne, with all his shyness, and tenderness, and literary reticence, shows very distinct traces also of understanding well the cold, inquisitive, and shrewd spirit which besets the Yankees even more than other commercial peoples. His heroes have usually not a little of this hardness in them. Coverdale, for instance, in *The Blithedale Romance*, and Holgrave, in *The House of the Seven Gables*, are of this class of shrewd, cold inquisitive heroes. Indeed there are few of his tales without a character of this type. But though Hawthorne had a deep sympathy with the practical as well as the literary genius of New England, it was always in a ghostly kind of way, as though he were stricken by some spell which half-paralysed him, and so prevented him from communicating with the life around him, as though he saw it only by a reflected light. His spirit haunted rather than ruled his body; his body hampered his spirit.

Yet his external career was not only not romantic, but identified with all the dullest routine of commercial duties. That a man who consciously *telegraphed*, as it were, with the world, transmitting meagre messages through his material organisation, should have been first a custom-house officer in Massachusetts, and then the consul in Liverpool, brings out into the strongest possible relief the curiously representative character in which he stood to New England as its literary or intellectual ghost. There is nothing more ghostly in his writings than his account of the consulship in Liverpool,—how he began by trying to communicate frankly with his fellow-countrymen, how he found the task more and more difficult, and gradually drew back into the twilight of his reserve, how he shrewdly and somewhat coldly watched "the dim shadows as they go and come," speculated idly on their fate, and all the time discharged the regular routine of consular business, witnessing the usual depositions, giving captains to captainless crews, affording meagerly doled-out advice or assistance to Yankees when in need of a friend, listening to them when they were only anxious to offer, not ask, assistance, and generally observing them from that distant and speculative outpost of the universe whence all common things looked strange.

Hawthorne, who was a delicate critic of himself, was well aware of the shadowy character of his own genius, though hardly aware that precisely here lay its curious and thrilling power. In the preface to *Twice-Told Tales* he tells us frankly, "The book, if you would see anything in it, requires to be read in the clear brown twilight atmosphere in which it was written; if opened in the sunshine, it is apt to look exceedingly like a volume of blank pages."

It is one of his favourite theories that there must be a vague, remote, and shadowy element in the subject-matter of any narrative with which his own imagination can successfully deal. Sometimes he apologises for this idealistic limitation to his artistic aims. "It was a folly," he says in his preface to *The Scarlet Letter*, "with the materiality of this daily life pressing so intrusively upon me, to attempt to fling myself back into another age, or to insist on creating the semblance of a world out of airy matter, when at every moment the impalpable beauty of my soap-bubble was broken by the rude contact of some actual circumstance. The wiser effort would have been to diffuse thought and imagination through the opaque substance of to-day, and thus to make it a bright transparency; to spiritualise the burden that began to weigh so heavily; to seek resolutely the true and indestructible value that lay hidden in the petty and wearisome incidents and ordinary characters with which I was now conversant. The fault was mine. The page of life that was spread out before me was so dull and commonplace only because I had not fathomed its deeper import. A better book than I shall ever write was there; leaf after leaf presenting itself to me just as it was written out by the reality of the flitting hour, and vanishing as fast as written, only because my brain wanted the insight and my hand the cunning to transcribe it. At some future day, it may be, I shall remember a few scattered fragments and broken paragraphs and write them down, and find the letters turn to gold upon the page."

And yet that dissatisfaction with his own idealism which Hawthorne here expresses never actually sufficed to divert his efforts into the channel indicated. In *The Blithedale Romance* he tells us that he chose the external scenery of the Socialist community at Brook Farm "merely to establish a theatre, a little removed from the highway of ordinary travel, where the creatures of his brain may play their phantasmagorical antics without exposing them to too close a comparison with the actual events of real lives. In the old countries with which fiction has long been conversant, a certain conventional privilege seems to be awarded to the romancer; his work is not put exactly side by side with nature; and he is allowed a license with regard to every-day probability, in view of the improved effects which he is bound to produce thereby. Among ourselves, on the contrary, there is as yet no such Fairy Land so like the real world that, in a suitable remoteness, one cannot well tell the difference, but with an atmosphere of strange enchantment, beheld through which the inhabitants have a propriety of their own. This atmosphere is what the American romancer wants. In its absence, the beings of imagination are compelled to show themselves in the same category as actually living mortals,—a necessity that generally renders the paint and pasteboard of their composition but too painfully discernible." And once more, in the preface to his last novel, *Transformation*, he reiterates as his excuse for laying the scene in Italy, that "no author without a trial can conceive of the difficulty of writing a romance about a country where there is no shadow, no antiquity, no mystery, no picturesque and gloomy wrong, nor anything but a commonplace prosperity in broad and simple daylight, as is happily the case with my dear native land. It will be very long, I trust, before romance writers may find congenial and easily-handled themes either in the annals of our stalwart republic, or in any characteristic and probable event of our individual lives. Romance and poetry, ivy, lichens, and wall-flowers, need ruin to make them grow." These passages throw much light on the secret affinities of Hawthorne's genius. But it would be a mistake to conclude from them, as he himself would apparently have us, that he is a mere romantic idealist, in the sense in which these words are commonly used,—that he is one all whose dramatic conceptions are but the unreal kaleidoscopic combinations of fancies in his own brain.

I may, perhaps, accept a phrase of which Hawthorne himself was fond,—"the moonlight of romance,"—and compel it to explain something of the secret of his characteristic genius. There are writers—chiefly poets, but also occasionally writers of fanciful romances like Longfellow's *Hyperion*— whose productions are purely ideal, are not only seen by the light of their own imagination but constituted out of it,—made of moonshine,—and rendered vivid and beautiful, so far as they are vivid and beautiful, with the vividness and beauty merely of the poet's own mind. In these cases there is no distinction between the delineating power and the delineated object; the dream is indistinguishable from the mind of the dreamer, and varies wholly with its laws. Again, at the opposite extreme, there is a kind of creative imagination which has its origin in a deep sympathy with, and knowledge of, the real world. That which it deals with is actual life as it has existed, or still exists, in forms so innumerable that it is scarcely possible to assert that its range is more limited than life itself. Of course the only adequate example of such an imagination is Shakespeare's, and this kind of imaginative power resembles sunlight, not only in its brilliancy, but especially in this, that it casts a light so full and equable over the universe it reveals, that we never think of its source at all. We forget altogether, as we do by common daylight, that the light by which we see is not part and parcel of the world which it presents to us. The sunlight is so efficient that we forget the sun. We find so rich and various a world before us, dressed in its own proper colours, that no one is reminded that the medium by which those proper colours are seen is uniform and from a single

source. We merge the delineative magic by which the scene is illuminated, in the details of the scene itself.

Between these two kinds of creative imagination there is another, which also shows a real world, but shows it so dimly in comparison with the last as to keep constantly before our minds the unique character of the light by which we see. The ideal light itself becomes a more prominent element in the picture than even the objects on which it shines; and yet is made so chiefly by the very fact of shining on those objects which we are accustomed to think of as they are seen in their own familiar details in full daylight. If the objects illuminated were not real and familiar, the light would not seem so mysterious; it is the pale uniform tint, the loss of colour and detail, and yet the vivid familiar outline and the strong shadow, which produce what Hawthorne calls the "moonlight of romance." "Moonlight in a familiar room," he says, in his preface to *The Scarlet Letter*, "falling so white upon the carpet, and showing all its figures so distinctly, making every object so minutely visible, yet so unlike a morning or noontide visibility,—is a medium the most suitable for a romance writer to get acquainted with his illusive guests. There is the little domestic scenery of the well-known apartment; the chairs, with each its separate individuality; the centre table, sustaining a workbasket, a volume or two, and an extinguished lamp; the sofa, the bookcase, the picture on the wall;—all these details, so completely seen, are so spiritualised by the unusual light, that they seem to lose their actual substance and become things of intellect. Nothing is too small or too trifling to undergo this change and acquire dignity thereby. A child's shoe, the doll seated in her little wicker carriage, the hobby-horse,—whatever, in a word, has been used or played with during the day, is now invested with a quality of strangeness and remoteness, though still almost as vividly present as by daylight. Thus, therefore, the floor of our familiar room has become a neutral territory, somewhere between the real world and fairyland, where the Actual and the Imaginary may meet, and each imbue itself with the nature of the other." Sir Walter Scott's delineative power partakes both of this moonlight imagination and of the other more powerful, brilliant, and realistic kind. Often it is a wide genial sunshine, of which we quite forget the source in the vividness of the common life which it irradiates. At other times, again, when Scott is in his Black Douglas mood, as I may call it, it has all the uniformity of tint and the exciting pallor of what Hawthorne terms the moonlight of romance.

At all events, there is no writer to whose creations the phrase applies more closely than to Hawthorne's own. His characters are by no means such unreal webs of moonshine as the idealists proper constitute into the figures of their romance. They are real and definitely outlined, but they are all seen in a single light,—the contemplative light of the particular idea which has floated before him in each of his stories,—and they are seen, not fully and in their integrity, as things are seen by daylight, but like things touched by moonlight,—only so far as they are lighted up by the idea of the story. The thread of unity which connects his tales is always some pervading thought of his own; they are not written mainly to display character, still less for the mere narrative interest, but for the illustration they cast on some idea or conviction of their author's. Amongst English writers of fiction, we have many besides Shakespeare whose stories are merely appropriate instruments for the portraiture of character, and who therefore never conceive themselves bound to confine themselves scrupulously to the one aspect most naturally developed by the tale. Once introduced, their characters are given in full,—both that side of them which is, so to say, turned *towards* the story, and others which are not. Other writers, again, make the characters quite subsidiary to the epical interest of the plot, using them only to heighten the colouring of the action it describes. Hawthorne's tales belong to neither of these classes. Their unity is ideal. His characters are often real and distinct, but they are illuminated only from one centre of thought. So strictly is this true of them that he has barely *room* for a novel in the ordinary sense of the word. If he were to take his characters through as many phases of life as are ordinarily comprised in a novel, he could not keep the ideal unity of his tales unbroken; he would be obliged to delineate them from many different points of view. Accordingly his novels are not novels in the ordinary sense; they are ideal situations, expanded by minute study and trains of clear, pale thought into the dimensions of novels. A very small group of figures is presented to the reader in some marked ideal relation; or if it be in consequence of some critical event, then it must be some event which has struck the author as rich in ideal or spiritual suggestion. But it is not usually in his way—though his last complete novel gives us one remarkable exception to this observation—to seize any glowing crisis of action where the passion is lit or the blow is struck that gives a new mould to life, for his delineation; he prefers to assume the crisis past, and to delineate as fully as he can the ideal situation to which it has given rise; when it is beginning to assume a fainter and more chronic character. ⟨. . .⟩

His power over his readers always arises from much the same cause as that of his own fanciful creation,—the minister who wore the black veil as a symbol of the veil which is on all hearts, and who startled men less because he was hidden from their view than because he made them aware of their own solitude. "Why do you tremble at *me alone?*" says the mild old man on his deathbed, from beneath his black veil, and with the glimmering smile on his half-hidden lips; "tremble also at each other! Have men avoided me, and women shown no pity, and children screamed and fled only from my black veil? What but the mystery which it obscurely typifies has made this piece of crape so awful? When the friend shows his inmost heart to his friend, the lover to his best beloved, when man does not vainly shrink from the eye of his Creator, loathsomely treasuring up the secret of his sin, then deem me a monster for the symbol beneath which I have lived and died! I look around me, and lo! on every visage a black veil?" Hawthorne, with the pale melancholy smile that seems to be always on his lips, speaks from a somewhat similar solitude. Indeed I suspect the story was a kind of parable of his own experience.

But, though Hawthorne's imagination was a solitary and twilight one, there was nothing allegorical about his genius. If we want to find his power at the very highest, we must look to his instinctive knowledge of what we may call the laws, not exactly of *discordant* emotions, but of emotions which *ought* to be mutually exclusive, and which combine with the thrill and the shudder of disease. This is almost the antithesis of Allegory. And he makes his delineation of such "unblest unions" the more striking, because it stands out from a background of healthy life, of genial scenes and simple beauties, which renders the contrast the more thrilling. I have often heard the term "cobweby" applied to his romances; and their most marking passages certainly cause the same sense of unwelcome shrinking to the spirit which a line of unexpected cobweb suddenly drawn across the face causes physically when one enters a deserted but familiar room. Edgar Poe, indeed, is much fuller of uncanny terrors; but then there is nothing in his writings of the healthy, simple, and natural background which gives sin and disease all its horror. It is the pure and severe New

England simplicity which Hawthorne paints so delicately that brings out in full relief the adulterous mixture of emotions on which he spends his main strength. I might almost say that he has carried into human affairs the old Calvinistic type of imagination. The same strange combination of clear simplicity, high faith, and reverential realism, with a reluctant, but for that very reason intense and devouring, conviction of the large comprehensiveness of the Divine Damnation which that grim creed taught its most honest believers to consider as the true trust in God's providence, Hawthorne copies into his pictures of human life. He presents us with a scene of pale severe beauty, full of truthful goodness, and then he uncovers in some one point of it a plague-spot, that, half-concealed as he keeps it, yet runs away with the imagination till one is scarcely conscious of anything else. Just as Calvinism, with all its noble features, can never keep its eyes off that one fact, as it thinks it, of God's calm foreknowledge of a widespread damnation; and this gradually encroaches on the attention till the mind is utterly absorbed in the fascinating terror of the problem how to combine the clashing emotions of love and horror which its image of Him inspires;—so Hawthorne's finest tales, with all the simplicity of their general outline, never detain you long from some uneasy mixture of emotions which only disease can combine in the same subject, until at last you ask for nothing but the brushing clean away of the infected web.

SIR LESLIE STEPHEN
From "Nathaniel Hawthorne" (1875)
Hours in a Library (1874–79)
1904, Volume 1, pp. 244–70

The story which perhaps generally passes for his masterpiece is *Transformation*, for most readers assume that a writer's longest book must necessarily be his best. In the present case, I think that this method, which has its conveniences, has not led to a perfectly just conclusion. In *Transformation*, Hawthorne has for once the advantage of placing his characters in a land where "a sort of poetic or fairy precinct," as he calls it, is naturally provided for them. The very stones of the streets are full of romance, and he cannot mention a name that has not a musical ring. Hawthorne, moreover, shows his usual tact in confining his aims to the possible. He does not attempt to paint Italian life and manners; his actors belong by birth, or by a kind of naturalisation, to the colony of the American artists in Rome; and he therefore does not labour under the difficulty of being in imperfect sympathy with his creatures. Rome is a mere background, and surely a most felicitous background, to the little group of persons who are effectually detached from all such vulgarising associations with the mechanism of daily life in less poetical countries. The centre of the group, too, who embodies one of Hawthorne's most delicate fancies, could have breathed no atmosphere less richly perfumed with old romance. In New York he would certainly have been in danger of a Barnum's museum, beside Washington's nurse and the woolly horse. It is a triumph of art that a being whose nature trembles on the very verge of the grotesque should walk through Hawthorne's pages with such undeviating grace. In the Roman dreamland he is in little danger of such prying curiosity, though even there he can only be kept out of harm's way by the admirable skill of his creator. Perhaps it may be thought by some severe critics that, with all his merits, Donatello stands on the very outside verge of the province permitted to the romancer. But without cavilling at what is indisputably charming, and without dwelling upon certain defects of construction which slightly mar the general beauty of the story, it has another weakness which it is impossible quite to overlook. Hawthorne himself remarks that he was surprised, in re-writing his story, to see the extent to which he had introduced descriptions of various Italian objects. "Yet these things," he adds, "fill the mind everywhere in Italy, and especially in Rome, and cannot be kept from flowing out upon the page when one writes freely and with self-enjoyment." The associations which they called up in England were so pleasant that he could not find it in his heart to cancel. Doubtless that is the precise truth, and yet it is equally true that they are artistically out of place. There are passages which recall the guide-book. To take one instance—and, certainly, it is about the worst—the whole party is going to the Coliseum, where a very striking scene takes place. On the way they pass a baker's shop.

> "The baker is drawing his loaves out of the oven," remarked Kenyon. "Do you smell how sour they are? I should fancy that Minerva (in revenge for the desecration of her temples) had slyly poured vinegar into the batch, if I did not know that the modern Romans prefer their bread in the acetous fermentation."

The instance is trivial, but it is characteristic. Hawthorne had doubtless remarked the smell of the sour bread, and to him it called up a vivid recollection of some stroll in Rome; for, of all our senses, the smell is notoriously the most powerful in awakening associations. But then what do we who read him care about the Roman taste for bread "in acetous fermentation"? When the high-spirited girl is on the way to meet her tormenter, and to receive the provocation which leads to his murder, why should we be worried by a gratuitous remark up about Roman baking? It somehow jars upon our taste, and we are certain that, in describing a New England village, Hawthorne would never have admitted a touch which has no conceivable bearing upon the situation. There is almost a superabundance of minute local colour in his American Romances, as, for example, in the *House of the Seven Gables*; but still, every touch, however minute, is steeped in the sentiment and contributes to the general effect. In Rome the smell of a loaf is sacred to his imagination, and intrudes itself upon its own merits, and, so far as we can discover, without reference to the central purpose. If a baker's shop impresses him unduly because it is Roman, the influence of ancient ruins and glorious works of art is of course still more distracting. The mysterious Donatello, and the strange psychological problem which he is destined to illustrate, are put aside for an interval, whilst we are called upon to listen to descriptions and meditations, always graceful, and often of great beauty in themselves, but yet, in a strict sense, irrelevant. Hawthorne's want of familiarity with the scenery is of course responsible for part of this failing. Had he been a native Roman, he would not have been so preoccupied with the wonders of Rome. But it seems that for a romance bearing upon a spiritual problem, the scenery, however tempting, is not really so serviceable as the less prepossessing surroundings of America. The objects have too great an intrinsic interest. A counter-attraction distorts the symmetry of the system. In the shadow of the Coliseum and St. Peter's you cannot pay much attention to the troubles of a young lady whose existence is painfully ephemeral. Those mighty objects will not be relegated to the background, and condescend to act as mere scenery. They are, in fact, too

romantic for a romance. The fountain of Trevi, with all its allegorical marbles, may be a very picturesque object to describe, but for Hawthorne's purposes it is really not equal to the town-pump at Salem; and Hilda's poetical tower, with the perpetual light before the Virgin's image, and the doves floating up to her from the street, and the column of Antoninus looking at her from the heart of the city, somehow appeals less to our sympathies than the quaint garret in the House of the Seven Gables, from which Phœbe Pyncheon watched the singular idiosyncrasies of the superannuated breed of fowls in the garden. The garret and the pump are designed in strict subordination to the human figures: the tower and the fountain have a distinctive purpose of their own. Hawthorne, at any rate, seems to have been mastered by his too powerful auxiliaries. A human soul, even in America, is more interesting to us than all the churches and picture-galleries in the world; and, therefore, it is as well that Hawthorne should not be tempted to the too easy method of putting fine description in place of sentiment.

But how was the task to be performed? How was the imaginative glow to be shed over the American scenery, so provokingly raw and deficient in harmony? A similar problem was successfully solved by a writer whose development, in proportion to her means of cultivation, is about the most remarkable of recent literary phenomena. Miss Brontë's bleak Yorkshire moors, with their uncompromising stone walls, and the valleys invaded by factories, are at first sight as little suited to romance as New England itself, to which, indeed, both the inhabitants and the country have a decided family resemblance. Now that she has discovered for us the fountains of poetic interest, we can all see that the region is not a mere stony wilderness; but it is well worth while to make a pilgrimage to Haworth, if only to discover how little the country corresponds to our preconceived impressions, or, in other words, how much depends upon the eye which sees it, and how little upon its intrinsic merits. Miss Brontë's marvellous effects are obtained by the process which enables an "intense and glowing mind" to see everything through its own atmosphere. The ugliest and most trivial objects seem, like objects heated by the sun, to radiate back the glow of passion with which she has regarded them. Perhaps this singular power is still more conspicuous in *Villette*, where she had even less of the raw material of poetry. An odd parallel may be found between one of the most striking passages in *Villette* and one in *Transformation*. Lucy Snowe in one novel, and Hilda in the other, are left to pass a summer vacation, the one in Brussels and the other in pestiferous Rome. Miss Snowe has no external cause of suffering but the natural effect of solitude upon a homeless and helpless governess. Hilda has to bear about with her the weight of a terrible secret, affecting, it may be, even the life of her dearest friend. Each of them wanders into a Roman Catholic church, and each, though they have both been brought up in a Protestant home, seeks relief at the confessional. So far the cases are alike, though Hilda, one might have fancied, has by far the strongest cause for emotion. And yet, after reading the two descriptions—both excellent in their way—one might fancy that the two young ladies had exchanged burdens. Lucy Snowe is as tragic as the innocent confidante of a murderess; Hilda's feelings never seem to rise above that weary sense of melancholy isolation which besieges us in a deserted city. It is needless to ask which is the best bit of work artistically considered. Hawthorne's style is more graceful and flexible; his descriptions of the Roman Catholic ceremonial and its influence upon an imaginative mind in distress are far more sympathetic, and imply wider range of intellect. But Hilda scarcely moves us like Lucy. There is too much delicate artistic description of picture-galleries and of the glories of St. Peter's to allow the poor little American girl to come prominently to the surface. We have been indulging with her in some sad but charming speculations, and not witnessing the tragedy of a deserted soul. Lucy Snowe has very inferior materials at her command; but somehow we are moved by a sympathetic thrill: we taste the bitterness of the awful cup of despair which, as she tells us, is forced to her lips in the night-watches; and are not startled when so prosaic an object as the row of beds in the dormitory of a French school suggests to her images worthy of rather stately tombs in the aisles of a vast cathedral, and recalls dead dreams of an elder world and a mightier race long frozen in death. Comparisons of this kind are almost inevitably unfair; but the difference between the two illustrates one characteristic—we need not regard it as a defect—of Hawthorne. His idealism does not consist in conferring grandeur upon vulgar objects by tinging them with the reflection of deep emotion. He rather shrinks than otherwise from describing the strongest passions, or shows their working by indirect touches and under a side-light. An excellent example of his peculiar method occurs in what is in some respects the most perfect of his works, the *Scarlet Letter.* There, again, we have the spectacle of a man tortured by a life-long repentance. The Puritan Clergyman, reverenced as a saint by all his flock, conscious of a sin which, once revealed, will crush him to the earth, watched with a malignant purpose by the husband whom he has injured, unable to summon up the moral courage to tear off the veil, and make the only atonement in his power, is a singularly striking figure, powerfully conceived and most delicately described. He yields under terrible pressure to the temptation of escaping from the scene of his prolonged torture with the partner of his guilt. And then, as he is returning homewards after yielding a reluctant consent to the flight, we are invited to contemplate the agony of his soul. The form which it takes is curiously characteristic. No vehement pangs of remorse, or desperate hopes of escape overpower his faculties in any simple and straightforward fashion. The poor minister is seized with a strange hallucination. He meets a venerable deacon, and can scarcely restrain himself from uttering blasphemies about the Communion-supper. Next appears an aged widow, and he longs to assail her with what appears to him to be an unanswerable argument against the immortality of the soul. Then follows an impulse to whisper impure suggestions to a fair young maiden, whom he has recently converted. And, finally, he longs to greet a rough sailor with a "volley of good, round, solid, satisfactory, and heaven-defying oaths." The minister, in short, is in that state of mind which gives birth in its victim to a belief in diabolical possession; and the meaning is pointed by an encounter with an old lady, who, in the popular belief, was one of Satan's miserable slaves and dupes, the witches, and is said—for Hawthorne never introduces the supernatural without toning it down by a supposed legendary transmission—to have invited him to meet her at the blasphemous Sabbath in the forest. The sin of endeavouring to escape from the punishment of his sins had brought him into sympathy with wicked mortals and perverted spirits.

This mode of setting forth the agony of a pure mind tainted by one irremovable blot, is undoubtedly impressive to the imagination in a high degree; far more impressive, we may safely say, than any quantity of such rant as very inferior writers could have poured out with the utmost facility on such an occasion. Yet it might possibly be mentioned that a poet of the highest order would have produced the effect by more direct

means. Remorse overpowering and absorbing does not embody itself in these recondite and, one may almost say, over-ingenious fancies. Hawthorne does not give us so much the pure passion as some of its collateral effects. He is still more interested in the curious psychological problem than moved by sympathy with the torture of the soul. We pity poor Mr. Dimmesdale profoundly, but we are also interested in him as the subject of an experiment in analytical psychology. We do not care so much for his emotions as for the strange phantoms which are raised in his intellect by the disturbance of his natural functions. The man is placed upon the rack, but our compassion is aroused, not by feeling our own nerves and sinews twitching in sympathy, but by remarking the strange confusion of ideas produced in his mind, the singularly distorted aspect of things in general introduced by such an experience, and hence, if we please, inferring the keenest of the pangs which have produced them. This turn of thought explains the real meaning of Hawthorne's antipathy to poor John Bull. That worthy gentleman, we will admit, is in a sense more gross and beefy than his American cousin. His nerves are stronger, for we need not decide whether they should be called coarser or less morbid. He is not, in the proper sense of the word, less imaginative, for a vigorous grasp of realities is rather a proof of a powerful than a defective imagination. But he is less accessible to those delicate impulses which are to the ordinary passions as electricity to heat. His imagination is more intense and less mobile. The devils which haunt the two races partake of the national characteristics. John Bunyan, Dimmesdale's contemporary, suffered under the pangs of a remorse equally acute, though with apparently far less cause. The devils who tormented him whispered blasphemies in his ears; they pulled at his clothes; they persuaded him that he had committed the unpardonable sin. They caused the very stones in the streets and tiles on the houses, as he says, to band themselves together against him. But they had not the refined and humorous ingenuity of the American fiends. They tempted him, as their fellows tempted Dimmesdale, to sell his soul; but they were too much in earnest to insist upon queer breaches of decorum. They did not indulge in that quaint play of fancy which tempts us to believe that the devils in New England had seduced the "tricksy spirit," Ariel, to indulge in practical jokes at the expense of a nobler victim than Stephano or Caliban. They were too terribly diabolical to care whether Bunyan blasphemed in solitude or in the presence of human respectabilities. Bunyan's sufferings were as poetical, but less conducive to refined speculation. His were the fiends that haunt the valley of the shadow of death; whereas Hawthorne's are to be encountered in the dim regions of twilight, where realities blend inextricably with mere phantoms, and the mind confers only a kind of provisional existence upon the "airy nothings" of its creation. Apollyon does not appear armed to the teeth and throwing fiery darts, but comes as an unsubstantial shadow threatening vague and undefined dangers, and only half-detaching himself from the background of darkness. He is as intangible as Milton's Death, not the vivid reality which presented itself to mediæval imaginations.

This special attitude of mind is probably easier to the American than to the English imagination. The craving for something substantial, whether in cookery or in poetry, was that which induced Hawthorne to keep John Bull rather at arm's length. We may trace the working of similar tendencies in other American peculiarities. Spiritualism and its attendant superstitions are the gross and vulgar form of the same phase of thought as it occurs in men of highly-strung nerves but defective cultivation. Hawthorne always speaks of these modern goblins with the contempt they deserve, for they shocked his imagination as much as his reason; but he likes to play with fancies which are not altogether dissimilar, though his refined taste warns him that they become disgusting when grossly translated into tangible symbols. Mesmerism, for example, plays an important part in the *Blithedale Romance* and the *House of the Seven Gables*, though judiciously softened and kept in the background. An example of the danger of such tendencies may be found in those works of Edgar Poe, in which he seems to have had recourse to strong stimulants to rouse a flagging imagination. What is exquisitely fanciful and airy in Hawthorne is too often replaced in his rival by an attempt to overpower us by dabblings in the charnel-house and prurient appeals to our fears of the horribly revolting. After reading some of Poe's stories one feels a kind of shock to one's modesty. We require some kind of spiritual ablution to cleanse our minds of his disgusting images; whereas Hawthorne's pure and delightful fancies, though at times they may have led us too far from the healthy contact of everyday interests, never leave a stain upon the imagination, and generally succeed in throwing a harmonious colouring upon some objects in which we had previously failed to recognise the beautiful. To perform that duty effectually is perhaps the highest of artistic merits; and though we may complain of Hawthorne's colouring as too evanescent, its charm grows upon us the more we study it.

Hawthorne seems to have been slow in discovering the secret of his own power. The *Twice-Told Tales*, he tells us, are only a fragmentary selection from a great number which had an ephemeral existence in long-forgotten magazines, and were sentenced to extinction by their author. Though many of the survivors are very striking, no wise reader will regret that sentence. It could be wished that other authors were as ready to bury their innocents, and that injudicious admirers might always abstain from acting as resurrection-men. The fragments, which remain with all their merits, are chiefly interesting as illustrating the intellectual development of their author. Hawthorne, in his preface to the collected edition (all Hawthorne's prefaces are remarkably instructive) tells us what to think of them. The book, he says, "requires to be read in the clear brown twilight atmosphere in which it was written; if opened in the sunshine it is apt to look exceedingly like a volume of blank pages." The remark, with deductions on the score of modesty, is more or less applicable to all his writings. But he explains, and with perfect truth, that though written in solitude, the book has not the abstruse tone which marks the written communications of a solitary mind with itself. The reason is that the sketches "are not the talk of a secluded man with his own mind and heart, but his attempts . . . to open an intercourse with the world." They may, in fact, be compared to Brummel's failures; and, though they do not display the perfect grace and fitness which would justify him in presenting himself to society, they were well worth taking up to illustrate the skill of the master's manipulation. We see him trying various experiments to hit off that delicate mean between the fanciful and the prosaic, which shall satisfy his taste and be intelligible to the outside world. Sometimes he gives us a fragment of historical romance, as in the story of the stern old regicide who suddenly appears from the woods to head the colonists of Massachusetts in a critical emergency; then he tries his hand at a bit of allegory, and describes the search for the mythical carbuncle which blazes by its inherent splendour on the face of a mysterious cliff in the depths of the untrodden wilderness, and lures old and young, the worldly and the romantic, to waste their lives in the vain effort to discover it—for the carbuncle is the ideal which mocks our pursuit, and may be

our curse or our blessing. Then perhaps we have a domestic piece—a quiet description of a New England country scene, touched with a grace which reminds us of the creators of Sir Roger de Coverley or the Vicar of Wakefield. Occasionally there is a fragment of pure *diablerie*, as in the story of the lady who consults the witch in the hollow of the three hills; and more frequently he tries to work out one of those strange psychological problems which he afterwards treated with more fulness of power. The minister who, for an unexplained reason, puts on a black veil one morning in his youth, and wears it until he is laid with it in his grave—a kind of symbolic prophecy of Dimmesdale; the eccentric Wakefield (whose original, if I remember rightly, is to be found in *King's Anecdotes*), who leaves his house one morning for no particular reason, and though living in the next street, does not reveal his existence to his wife for twenty years; and the hero of the "Wedding Knell" the elderly bridegroom whose early love has jilted him, but agrees to marry him when she is an elderly widow and he an old bachelor, and who appals the marriage party by coming to the church in his shroud, with the bell tolling as for a funeral—all these bear the unmistakable stamp of Hawthorne's mint, and each is a study of his favourite subject, the borderland between reason and insanity. In many of these stories appears the element of interest, to which Hawthorne clung the more closely both from early associations and because it is the one undeniable poetical element in the American character. Shallow-minded people fancy Puritanism to be prosaic, because the laces and ruffles of the Cavaliers are a more picturesque costume at a masked ball than the dress of the Roundheads. The Puritan has become a grim and ugly scarecrow, on whom every buffoon may break his jest. But the genuine old Puritan spirit ceases to be picturesque only because of its sublimity: its poetry is sublimed into religion. The great poet of the Puritans fails, as far as he fails, when he tries to transcend the limits of mortal imagination—

> The living throne, the sapphire blaze,
> Where angels tremble as they gaze,
> He saw: but blasted with excess of light,
> Closed his eyes in endless night.

To represent the Puritan from within was not, indeed, a task suitable to Hawthorne's powers. Carlyle has done that for us with more congenial sentiment than could have been well felt by the gentle romancer. Hawthorne fancies the grey shadow of a stern old forefather wondering at his degenerate son. "A writer of story-books! What kind of business in life, what mode of glorifying God, or being serviceable to mankind in his day and generation, may that be? Why, the degenerate fellow might as well have been a fiddler!" And yet the old strain remains, though strangely modified by time and circumstance. In Hawthorne it would seem that the peddling element of the old Puritans had been reduced to its lowest point; the more spiritual element had been refined till it is probable enough that the ancestral shadow would have refused to recognise the connection. The old dogmatical framework to which he attached such vast importance had dropped out of his descendant's mind, and had been replaced by dreamy speculation, obeying no laws save those imposed by its own sense of artistic propriety. But we may often recognise, even where we cannot express in words, the strange family likeness which exists in characteristics which are superficially antagonistic. The man of action may be bound by subtilties to the speculative metaphysician; and Hawthorne's mind, amidst the most obvious differences, had still an affinity to his remote forefathers. Their bugbears had become his playthings; but the witches, though they have no reality, have still a fascination for him. The interest which he feels in them, even in their now shadowy state, is a proof that he would have believed in them in good earnest a century and a half earlier. The imagination, working in a different intellectual atmosphere, is unable to project its images upon the external world; but it still forms them in the old shape. His solitary musings necessarily employ a modern dialect, but they often turn on the same topics which occurred to Jonathan Edwards in the woods of Connecticut. Instead of the old Puritan speculations about predestination and free-will, he dwells upon the transmission by natural laws of an hereditary curse, and upon the strange blending of good and evil, which may cause sin to be an awakening impulse in a human soul. The change which takes place in Donatello in consequence of his crime is a modern symbol of the fall of man and the eating the fruit of the knowledge of good and evil. As an artist he gives concrete images instead of abstract theories; but his thoughts evidently delight to dwell in the same regions where the daring speculations of his theological ancestors took their origin. Septimius, the rather disagreeable hero of his last romance, is a peculiar example of a similar change. Brought up under the strict discipline of New England, he has retained the love of musing upon insoluble mysteries, though he has abandoned the old dogmatic guide-posts. When such a man finds that the orthodox scheme of the universe provided by his official pastors has somehow broken down with him, he forms some audacious theory of his own, and is perhaps plunged into an unhallowed revolt against the divine order. Septimius, under such circumstances, develops into a kind of morbid and sullen Hawthorne. He considers—as other people have done —that death is a disagreeable fact, but refuses to admit that it is inevitable. The romance tends to show that such a state of mind is unhealthy and dangerous, and Septimius is contrasted unfavourably with the vigorous natures who preserve their moral balance by plunging into the stream of practical life. Yet Hawthorne necessarily sympathises with the abnormal being whom he creates. Septimius illustrates the dangers of the musing temperament, but the dangers are produced by a combination of an essentially selfish nature with the meditative tendency. Hawthorne, like his hero, sought refuge from the hard facts of commonplace life by retiring into a visionary world. He delights in propounding much the same questions as those which tormented poor Septimius, though for obvious reasons, he did not try to compound an elixir of life by means of a recipe handed down from Indian ancestors. The strange mysteries in which the world and our nature are shrouded are always present to his imagination; he catches dim glimpses of the laws which bring out strange harmonies, but, on the whole, tend rather to deepen than to clear the mysteries. He loves the marvellous, not in the vulgar sense of the word, but as a symbol of perplexity which encounters every thoughtful man in his journey through life. Similar tenants at an earlier period might, with almost equal probability, have led him to the stake as a dabbler in forbidden sciences, or have caused him to be revered as one to whom a deep spiritual instinct had been granted.

Meanwhile, as it was his calling to tell stories to readers of the English language in the nineteenth century, his power is exercised in a different sphere. No modern writer has the same skill in so using the marvellous as to interest without unduly exciting our incredulity. He makes, indeed, no positive demands on our credulity. The strange influences which are suggested rather than obtruded upon us are kept in the background, so as not to invite, nor indeed to render possible, the application of scientific tests. We may compare him once

more to Miss Brontë, who introduces, in *Villette*, a haunted garden. She shows us a ghost who is for a moment a very terrible spectre indeed, and then, very much to our annoyance, rationalises him into a flesh-and-blood lover. Hawthorne would neither have allowed the ghost to intrude so forcibly, nor have expelled him so decisively. The garden in his hands would have been haunted by a shadowy terror of which we could render no precise account to ourselves. It would have refrained from actual contact with professors and governesses; and as it would never have taken bodily form, it would never have been quite dispelled. His ghosts are confined to their proper sphere, the twilight of the mind, and never venture into the broad glare of daylight. We can see them so long as we do not gaze directly at them; when we turn to examine them they are gone, and we are left in doubt whether they were realities or an ocular delusion generated in our fancy by some accidental collocation of half-seen objects. So in the *House of the Seven Gables* we may hold what opinion we please as to the reality of the curse which hangs over the Pyncheons and the strange connection between them and their hereditary antagonists; in the *Scarlet Letter* we may, if we like, hold that there was really more truth in the witch legends which colour the imaginations of the actors than we are apt to dream of in our philosophy; and in *Transformation* we are left finally in doubt as to the great question of Donatello's ears, and the mysterious influence which he retains over the animal world so long as he is unstained by bloodshed. In *Septimius* alone, it seems to me that the supernatural is left in rather too obtrusive a shape in spite of the final explanations; though it might possibly have been toned down had the story received the last touches of the author. The artifice, if so it may be called, by which this is effected—and the romance is just sufficiently dipped in the shadow of the marvellous to be heightened without becoming offensive—sounds, like other things, tolerably easy when it is explained; and yet the difficulty is enormous, as may appear on reflection as well as from the extreme rarity of any satisfactory work in the same style by other artists. With the exception of a touch or two in Scott's stories, such as the impressive Bodach Glas, in *Waverley*, and the apparition in the exquisite *Bride of Lammermoor*, it would be difficult to discover any parallel.

In fact Hawthorne was able to tread in that magic circle only by an exquisite refinement of taste, and by a delicate sense of humour, which is the best preservative against all extravagance. Both qualities combine in that tender delineation of character which is, after all, one of his greatest charms. His Puritan blood shows itself in sympathy, not with the stern side of the ancestral creed, but with the feebler characters upon whom it weighed as an oppressive terror. He resembles, in some degree, poor Clifford Pyncheon, whose love of the beautiful makes him suffer under the stronger will of his relatives and the prim stiffness of their home. He exhibits the suffering of such a character all the more effectively because, with his kindly compassion there is mixed a delicate flavour of irony. The more tragic scenes affect us, perhaps, with less sense of power; the playful, though melancholy, fancy seems to be less at home when the more powerful emotions are to be excited; and yet once, at least, he draws one of those pictures which engrave themselves instantaneously on the memory. The grimmest or most passionate of writers could hardly have improved the scene where the body of the magnificent Zenobia is discovered in the river. Every touch goes straight to the mark. The narrator of the story, accompanied by the man whose coolness has caused the suicide, and the shrewd, unimaginative Yankee farmer, who interprets into coarse, downright language the suspicions which they fear to confess to themselves, are sounding the depths of the river by night in a leaky punt with a long pole. Silas Foster represents the brutal, commonplace comments of the outside world, which jar so terribly on the more sensitive and closely intersected actors in the tragedy.

> Heigho! [he soliloquises, with offensive loudness], life and death together make sad work for us all. Then I was a boy, bobbing for fish; and now I'm getting to be an old fellow, and here I be, groping for a dead body! I tell you what lads, if I thought anything had really happened to Zenobia, I should feel kind o' sorrowful.

That is the discordant chorus of the gravediggers in *Hamlet*. At length the body is found, and poor Zenobia is brought to the shore with her knees still bent in the attitude of prayer, and her hands clenched in immitigable defiance. Foster tries in vain to straighten the dead limbs. As the teller of the story gazes at her, the grimly ludicrous reflection occurs to him that if Zenobia had foreseen all "the ugly circumstances of death—how ill it would become her, the altogether unseemly aspect which she must put on, and especially old Silas Foster's efforts to improve the matter—she would no more have committed the dreadful act than have exhibited herself to a public assembly in a badly-fitting garment."

HENRY JAMES
From *Hawthorne*
1879, pp. 106–17

If Hawthorne was in a sombre mood, and if his future was painfully vague, *The Scarlet Letter* contains little enough of gaiety or of hopefulness. It is densely dark, with a single spot of vivid colour in it; and it will probably long remain the most consistently gloomy of English novels of the first order. But I just now called it the author's masterpiece, and I imagine it will continue to be, for other generations than ours, his most substantial title to fame. The subject had probably lain a long time in his mind, as his subjects were apt to do; so that he appears completely to possess it, to know it and feel it. It is simpler and more complete than his other novels; it achieves more perfectly what it attempts, and it has about it that charm, very hard to express, which we find in an artist's work the first time he has touched his highest mark—a sort of straightness and naturalness of execution, an unconsciousness of his public, and freshness of interest in his theme. It was a great success, and he immediately found himself famous. The writer of these lines, who was a child at the time, remembers dimly the sensation the book produced, and the little shudder with which people alluded to it, as if a peculiar horror were mixed with its attractions. He was too young to read it himself; but its title, upon which he fixed his eyes as the book lay upon the table, had a mysterious charm. He had a vague belief, indeed, that the "letter" in question was one of the documents that come by the post, and it was a source of perpetual wonderment to him that it should be of such an unaccustomed hue. Of course it was difficult to explain to a child the significance of poor Hester Prynne's blood-coloured A. But the mystery was at last partly dispelled by his being taken to see a collection of pictures (the annual exhibition of the National Academy), where he encountered a representation of a pale, handsome woman, in a quaint black dress and a white coif, holding between her knees an elfish-looking little girl, fantastically

dressed, and crowned with flowers. Embroidered on the woman's breast was a great crimson A, over which the child's fingers, as she glanced strangely out of the picture, were maliciously playing. I was told that this was Hester Prynne and little Pearl, and that when I grew older I might read their interesting history. But the picture remained vividly imprinted on my mind; I had been vaguely frightened and made uneasy by it; and, when years afterwards, I first read the novel, I seemed to myself to have read it before, and to be familiar with its two strange heroines. I mention this incident simply as an indication of the degree to which the success of *The Scarlet Letter* had made the book what is called an actuality. Hawthorne himself was very modest about it; he wrote to his publisher, when there was a question of his undertaking another novel, that what had given the history of Hester Prynne its "vogue" was simply the introductory chapter. In fact, the publication of *The Scarlet Letter* was in the United States a literary event of the first importance. The book was the finest piece of imaginative writing yet put forth in the country. There was a consciousness of this in the welcome that was given it— a satisfaction in the idea of America having produced a novel that belonged to literature, and to the forefront of it. Something might at last be sent to Europe as exquisite in quality as anything that had been received, and the best of it was that the thing was absolutely American; it belonged to the soil, to the air; it came out of the very heart of New England.

It is beautiful, admirable, extraordinary; it has in the highest degree that merit which I have spoken of as the mark of Hawthorne's best things—an indefinable purity and lightness of conception, a quality which in a work of art affects one in the same way as the absence of grossness does in a human being. His fancy, as I just now said, had evidently brooded over the subject for a long time; the situation to be represented had disclosed itself to him in all its phases. When I say in all its phases, the sentence demands modification; for it is to be remembered that if Hawthorne laid his hand upon the well-worn theme, upon the familiar combination of the wife, the lover, and the husband, it was, after all, but to one period of the history of these three persons that he attached himself. The situation is the situation after the woman's fault has been committed, and the current of expiation and repentance has set in. In spite of the relation between Hester Prynne and Arthur Dimmesdale, no story of love was surely ever less of a "love-story." To Hawthorne's imagination the fact that these two persons had loved each other too well was of an interest comparatively vulgar; what appealed to him was the idea of their moral situation in the long years that were to follow. The story, indeed, is in a secondary degree that of Hester Prynne; she becomes, really, after the first scene, an accessory figure; it is not upon her the *dénoûment* depends. It is upon her guilty lover that the author projects most frequently the cold, thin rays of his fitfully-moving lantern, which makes here and there a little luminous circle, on the edge of which hovers the livid and sinister figure of the injured and retributive husband. The story goes on, for the most part, between the lover and the husband—the tormented young Puritan minister, who carries the secret of his own lapse from pastoral purity locked up beneath an exterior that commends itself to the reverence of his flock, while he sees the softer partner of his guilt standing in the full glare of exposure and humbling herself to the misery of atonement—between this more wretched and pitiable culprit, to whom dishonour would come as a comfort and the pillory as a relief, and the older, keener, wiser man, who, to obtain satisfaction for the wrong he has suffered, devises the infernally ingenious plan of conjoining himself with his wronger, living with him, living upon him; and while he pretends to minister to his hidden ailment and to sympathise with his pain, revels in his unsuspected knowledge of these things, and stimulates them by malignant arts. The attitude of Roger Chillingworth, and the means he takes to compensate himself—these are the highly original elements in the situation that Hawthorne so ingeniously treats. None of his works are so impregnated with that after-sense of the old Puritan consciousness of life to which allusion has so often been made. If, as M. Montégut says, the qualities of his ancestors *filtered* down through generations into his composition, *The Scarlet Letter* was, as it were, the vessel that gathered up the last of the precious drops. And I say this not because the story happens to be of so-called historical cast, to be told of the early days of Massachusetts, and of people in steeple-crowned hats and sad-coloured garments. The historical colouring is rather weak than otherwise; there is little elaboration of detail, of the modern realism of research; and the author has made no great point of causing his figures to speak the English of their period. Nevertheless, the book is full of the moral presence of the race that invented Hester's penance—diluted and complicated with other things, but still perfectly recognisable. Puritanism, in a word, is there, not only objectively, as Hawthorne tried to place it there, but subjectively as well. Not, I mean, in his judgment of his characters in any harshness of prejudice, or in the obtrusion of a moral lesson; but in the very quality of his own vision, in the tone of the picture, in a certain coldness and exclusiveness of treatment.

The faults of the book are, to my sense, a want of reality and an abuse of the fanciful element—of a certain superficial symbolism. The people strike me not as characters, but as representatives, very picturesquely arranged, of a single state of mind; and the interest of the story lies, not in them, but in the situation, which is insistently kept before us, with little progression, though with a great deal, as I have said, of a certain stable variation; and to which they, out of their reality, contribute little that helps it to live and move. I was made to feel this want of reality, this over-ingenuity, of *The Scarlet Letter*, by chancing not long since upon a novel which was read fifty years ago much more than to-day, but which is still worth reading—the story of *Adam Blair*, by John Gibson Lockhart. This interesting and powerful little tale has a great deal of analogy with Hawthorne's novel—quite enough, at least, to suggest a comparison between them; and the comparison is a very interesting one to make, for it speedily leads us to larger considerations than simple resemblances and divergences of plot.

Adam Blair, like Arthur Dimmesdale, is a Calvinistic minister who becomes the lover of a married woman, is overwhelmed with remorse at his misdeed, and makes a public confession of it; then expiates it by resigning his pastoral office and becoming a humble tiller of the soil, as his father had been. The two stories are of about the same length, and each is the masterpiece (putting aside, of course, as far as Lockhart is concerned, the *Life of Scott*) of the author. They deal alike with the manners of a rigidly theological society, and even in certain details they correspond. In each of them, between the guilty pair, there is a charming little girl; though I hasten to say that Sarah Blair (who is not the daughter of the heroine, but the legitimate offspring of the hero, a widower) is far from being as brilliant and graceful an apparition as the admirable little Pearl of *The Scarlet Letter*. The main difference between the two tales is the fact that in the American story the husband plays an all-important part, and in the Scottish plays almost none at all. *Adam Blair* is the history of the passion, and *The*

Scarlet Letter the history of its sequel; but nevertheless, if one has read the two books at a short interval, it is impossible to avoid confronting them. I confess that a large portion of the interest of *Adam Blair*, to my mind, when once I had perceived that it would repeat in a great measure the situation of *The Scarlet Letter*, lay in noting its difference of tone. It threw into relief the passionless quality of Hawthorne's novel, its element of cold and ingenious fantasy, its elaborate imaginative delicacy. These things do not precisely constitute a weakness in *The Scarlet Letter*; indeed, in a certain way they constitute a great strength; but the absence of a certain something warm and straightforward, a trifle more grossly human and vulgarly natural, which one finds in *Adam Blair*, will always make Hawthorne's tale less touching to a large number of even very intelligent readers, than a love-story told with the robust, synthetic pathos which served Lockhart so well. His novel is not of the first rank (I should call it an excellent second-rate one), but it borrows a charm from the fact that his vigorous, but not strongly imaginative, mind was impregnated with the reality of his subject. He did not always succeed in rendering this reality; the expression is sometimes awkward and poor. But the reader feels that his vision was clear, and his feeling about the matter very strong and rich. Hawthorne's imagination, on the other hand, plays with the theme so incessantly, leads it such a dance through the moon-lighted air of his intellect, that the thing cools off, as it were, hardens and stiffens, and, producing effects much more exquisite, leaves the reader with a sense of having handled a splendid piece of silversmith's work. Lockhart, by means much more vulgar, produces at moments a greater illusion, and satisfies our inevitable desire for something, in the people in whom it is sought to interest us, that shall be of the same pitch and the same continuity with ourselves. Above all, it is interesting to see how the same subject appears to two men of a thoroughly different cast of mind and of a different race. Lockhart was struck with the warmth of the subject that offered itself to him, and Hawthorne with its coldness; the one with its glow, its sentimental interest—the other with its shadow, its moral interest. Lockhart's story is as decent, as severely draped, as *The Scarlet Letter*; but the author has a more vivid sense than appears to have imposed itself upon Hawthorne, of some of the incidents of the situation he describes; his tempted man and tempting woman are more actual and personal; his heroine in especial, though not in the least a delicate or a subtle conception, has a sort of credible, visible, palpable property, a vulgar roundness and relief, which are lacking to the dim and chastened image of Hester Prynne. But I am going too far; I am comparing simplicity with subtlety, the usual with the refined. Each man wrote as his turn of mind impelled him, but each expressed something more than himself. Lockhart was a dense, substantial Briton, with a taste for the concrete, and Hawthorne was a thin New Englander, with a miasmatic conscience.

In *The Scarlet Letter* there is a great deal of symbolism; there is, I think, too much. It is overdone at times, and becomes mechanical; it ceases to be impressive, and grazes triviality. The idea of the mystic A which the young minister finds imprinted upon his breast and eating into his flesh, in sympathy with the embroidered badge that Hester is condemned to wear, appears to me to be a case in point. This suggestion should, I think, have been just made and dropped; to insist upon it and return to it, is to exaggerate the weak side of the subject. Hawthorne returns to it constantly, plays with it, and seems charmed by it; until at last the reader feels tempted to declare that his enjoyment of it is puerile. In the admirable scene, so superbly conceived and beautifully executed, in which Mr. Dimmesdale, in the stillness of the night, in the middle of the sleeping town, feels impelled to go and stand upon the scaffold where his mistress had formerly enacted her dreadful penance, and then, seeing Hester pass along the street, from watching at a sick-bed, with little Pearl at her side, calls them both to come and stand there beside him—in this masterly episode the effect is almost spoiled by the introduction of one of these superficial conceits. What leads up to it is very fine—so fine that I cannot do better than quote it as a specimen of one of the striking pages of the book.

> But before Mr. Dimmesdale had done speaking, a light gleamed far and wide over all the muffled sky. It was doubtless caused by one of those meteors which the nightwatcher may so often observe burning out to waste in the vacant regions of the atmosphere. So powerful was its radiance that it thoroughly illuminated the dense medium of cloud betwixt the sky and earth. The great vault brightened, like the dome of an immense lamp. It showed the familiar scene of the street with the distinctness of mid-day, but also with the awfulness that is always imparted to familiar objects by an unaccustomed light. The wooden houses, with their jutting stories and quaint gable-peaks; the doorsteps and thresholds, with the early grass springing up about them; the garden-plots, black with freshly-turned earth; the wheel-track, little worn, and, even in the market-place, margined with green on either side;—all were visible, but with a singularity of aspect that seemed to give another moral interpretation to the things of this world than they had ever borne before. And there stood the minister, with his hand over his heart; and Hester Prynne, with the embroidered letter glimmering on her bosom; and little Pearl, herself a symbol, and the connecting link between these two. They stood in the noon of that strange and solemn splendour, as if it were the light that is to reveal all secrets, and the daybreak that shall unite all that belong to one another.

That is imaginative, impressive, poetic; but when, almost immediately afterwards, the author goes on to say that "the minister looking upward to the zenith, beheld there the appearance of an immense letter—the letter A—marked out in lines of dull red light," we feel that he goes too far, and is in danger of crossing the line that separates the sublime from its intimate neighbour. We are tempted to say that this is not moral tragedy, but physical comedy. In the same way, too much is made of the intimation that Hester's badge had a scorching property, and that if one touched it one would immediately withdraw one's hand. Hawthorne is perpetually looking for images which shall place themselves in picturesque correspondence with the spiritual facts with which he is concerned, and of course the search is of the very essence of poetry. But in such a process discretion is everything, and when the image becomes importunate it is in danger of seeming to stand for nothing more serious than itself. When Hester meets the minister by appointment in the forest, and sits talking with him while little Pearl wanders away and plays by the edge of the brook, the child is represented as at last making her way over to the other side of the woodland stream, and disporting herself there in a manner which makes her mother feel herself, "in some indistinct and tantalising manner, estranged from Pearl; as if the child, in her lonely ramble through the forest, had strayed out of the sphere in which she and her mother dwelt together, and was now vainly seeking to return to it." And Hawthorne devotes a chapter to this idea of

the child's having, by putting the brook between Hester and herself, established a kind of spiritual gulf, on the verge of which her little fantastic person innocently mocks at her mother's sense of bereavement. This conception belongs, one would say, quite to the lighter order of a story-teller's devices, and the reader hardly goes with Hawthorne in the large development he gives to it. He hardly goes with him either, I think, in his extreme predilection for a small number of vague ideas which are represented by such terms as "sphere" and "sympathies." Hawthorne makes too liberal a use of these two substantives; it is the solitary defect of his style; and it counts as a defect partly because the words in question are a sort of specialty with certain writers immeasurably inferior to himself.

I had not meant, however, to expatiate upon his defects, which are of the slenderest and most venial kind. *The Scarlet Letter* has the beauty and harmony of all original and complete conceptions, and its weaker spots, whatever they are, are not of its essence; they are mere light flaws and inequalities of surface. One can often return to it; it supports familiarity, and has the inexhaustible charm and mystery of great works of art. It is admirably written. Hawthorne afterwards polished his style to a still higher degree; but in his later productions—it is almost always the case in a writer's later productions—there is a touch of mannerism. In *The Scarlet Letter* there is a high degree of polish, and at the same time a charming freshness; his phrase is less conscious of itself.

ANTHONY TROLLOPE
From "The Genius of Nathaniel Hawthorne"
North American Review, September 1879, pp. 204–22

There never surely was a powerful, active, continually effective mind less round, more lop-sided, than that of Nathaniel Hawthorne. ⟨. . .⟩

I have been specially driven to think of this by the strong divergence between Hawthorne and myself. It has always been my object to draw my little pictures as like to life as possible, so that my readers should feel that they were dealing with people whom they might probably have known, but so to do it that the every day good to be found among them should allure, and the every-day evil repel; and this I have attempted, believing that such ordinary good and ordinary evil would be more powerful in repelling or alluring than great and glowing incidents which, though they might interest, would not come home to the minds of readers. Hawthorne, on the other hand, has dealt with persons and incidents which were often but barely within the bounds of possibility,—which were sometimes altogether without those bounds,—and has determined that his readers should be carried out of their own little mundane ways, and brought into a world of imagination in which their intelligence might be raised, if only for a time, to something higher than the common needs of common life.

⟨. . .⟩ Hawthorne is severe, but his severity is never of a nature to form laws for life. His is a mixture of romance and austerity, quite as far removed from the realities of Puritanism as it is from the sentimentalism of poetry. He creates a melancholy which amounts almost to remorse in the minds of his readers. There falls upon them a conviction of some unutterable woe which is not altogether dispelled till other books and other incidents have had their effects. The woe is of course fictitious, and therefore endurable,—and therefore alluring. And woe itself has its charm. It is a fact that the really miserable will pity the comfortable insignificance of those who are not unhappy, and that they are apt even to boast of their own sufferings. There is a sublimity in mental and even in corporal torment which will sometimes make the position of Lucifer almost enviable. "All is not lost" with him! Prometheus chained, with the bird at his liver, had wherewithal to console himself in the magnificence of his thoughts. And so in the world of melancholy romance, of agony more realistic than melancholy, to which Hawthorne brings his readers, there is compensation to the reader in the feeling that, in having submitted himself to such sublime affliction, he has proved himself capable of sublimity. The bird that feeds upon your vitals would not have gorged himself with common flesh. You are beyond measure depressed by the weird tale that is told to you, but you become conscious of a certain grandness of nature in being susceptible to such suffering. When you hear what Hawthorne has done to others, you long to search his volumes. When he has operated upon you, you would not for the world have foregone it. You have been ennobled by that familiarity with sorrow. You have been, as it were, sent through the fire and purged of so much of your dross. For a time, at least, you have been free from the mundane touch of that beef and ale with which novelists of a meaner school will certainly bring you in contact. No one will feel himself ennobled at once by having read one of my novels. But Hawthorne, when you have studied him, will be very precious to you. He will have plunged you into melancholy, he will have overshadowed you with black forebodings, he will almost have crushed you with imaginary sorrows; but he will have enabled you to feel yourself an inch taller during the process. Something of the sublimity of the transcendent, something of the mystery of the unfathomable, something of the brightness of the celestial, will have attached itself to you, and you will all but think that you too might live to be sublime, and revel in mingled light and mystery.

The creations of American literature generally are no doubt more given to the speculative,—less given to the realistic,—than are those of English literature. On our side of the water we deal more with beef and ale, and less with dreams. Even with the broad humor of Bret Harte, even with the broader humor of Artemus Ward and Mark Twain, there is generally present an undercurrent of melancholy, in which pathos and satire are intermingled. There was a touch of it even with the simple-going Cooper and the kindly Washington Irving. Melancholy and pathos, without the humor, are the springs on which all Longfellow's lines are set moving. But in no American writer is to be found the same predominance of weird imagination as in Hawthorne. There was something of it in M. G. Lewis—our Monk Lewis as he came to be called, from the name of a tale which he wrote; but with him, as with many others, we feel that they have been weird because they have desired to be so. They have struggled to achieve the tone with which their works are pervaded. With Hawthorne we are made to think that he could not have been anything else if he would. It is as though he could certainly have been nothing else in his own inner life. We know that such was not actually the case. Though a man singularly reticent,—what we generally call shy,—he could, when things went well with him, be argumentative, social, and cheery. I have seen him very happy over canvas-back ducks, and have heard him discuss, almost with violence, the superiority of American vegetables. Indeed, he once withered me with a scorn which was anything but mystic or melancholy because I expressed a patriotic preference for English peas. And yet his imagination was such that the creations of his brain could not have been other than such as I have described. Oliver Wendell Holmes has written a

well-known story, weird and witch-like also, and has displayed much genius in the picture which he has given us of Elsie Venner. But the reader is at once aware that Holmes compelled himself to the construction of *Elsie Venner*, and feels equally sure that Hawthorne wrote "The Marble Faun" because he could not help himself.

I will take a few of his novels,—those which I believe to be the best known,—and will endeavor to illustrate my idea of his genius by describing the manner in which his stories have been told.

The Scarlet Letter is, on the English side of the water, perhaps the best known. It is so terrible in its pictures of diseased human nature as to produce most questionable delight. The reader's interest never flags for a moment. There is nothing of episode or digression. The author is always telling his one story with a concentration of energy which, as we can understand, must have made it impossible for him to deviate. The reader will certainly go on with it to the end very quickly, entranced, excited, shuddering, and at times almost wretched. His consolation will be that he too has been able to see into these black deeps of the human heart. The story is one of jealousy,—of love and jealousy,—in which love is allowed but little scope, but full play is given to the hatred that can spring from injured love. A woman has been taken in adultery,—among the Puritans of Boston some two centuries since,—and is brought upon the stage that she may be punished by a public stigma. She was beautiful and young, and had been married to an old husband who had wandered away from her for a time. Then she has sinned, and the partner of her sin, though not of her punishment, is the young minister of the church to which she is attached. It is her doom to wear the Scarlet Letter, the letter A, always worked on her dress,—always there on her bosom, to be seen by all men. The first hour of her punishment has to be endured, in the middle of the town, on the public scaffold, under the gaze of all men. As she stands there, her husband comes by chance into the town and sees her, and she sees him, and they know each other. But no one else in Boston knows that they are man and wife. Then they meet, and she refuses to tell him who has been her fellow sinner. She makes no excuse for herself. She will bear her doom and acknowledge its justice, but to no one will she tell the name of him who is the father of her baby. For her disgrace has borne its fruit, and she has a child. The injured husband is at once aware that he need deal no further with the woman who has been false to him. Her punishment is sure. But it is necessary for his revenge that the man too shall be punished,—and to punish him he must know him. He goes to work to find him out, and he finds him out. Then he does punish him with a vengeance and brings him to death,—does it by the very stress of mental misery. After a while the woman turns and rebels against the atrocity of fate,—not on her own account, but for the sake of that man the sight of whose sufferings she can not bear. They meet once again, the two sinful lovers, and a hope of escape comes upon them,—and another gleam of love. But fate in the shape of the old man is too strong for them. He finds them out, and, not stopping to hinder their flight, merely declares his purpose of accompanying them! Then the lover succumbs and dies, and the woman is left to her solitude. That is the story.

The personages in it with whom the reader will interest himself are four,—the husband, the minister who has been the sinful lover, the woman, and the child. The reader is expected to sympathize only with the woman,—and will sympathize only with her. The husband, an old man who has knowingly married a young woman who did not love him, is a personification of that feeling of injury which is supposed to fall upon a man when his honor has been stained by the falseness of a wife. He has left her and has wandered away, not even telling her of his whereabout. He comes back to her without a sign. The author tells us that he had looked to find his happiness in her solicitude and care for him. The reader, however, gives him credit for no love. But the woman was his wife, and he comes back and finds that she had gone astray. Her he despises, and is content to leave to the ascetic cruelty of the town magistrates; but to find the man out and bring the man to his grave by slow torture is enough of employment for what is left to him of life and energy.

With the man, the minister, the lover, the reader finds that he can have nothing in common, though he is compelled to pity his sufferings. The woman has held her peace when she was discovered and reviled and exposed. She will never whisper his name, never call on him for any comfort or support in her misery; but he, though the very shame is eating into his soul, lives through the seven years of the story, a witness of her misery and solitude, while he himself is surrounded by the very glory of sanctity. Of the two, indeed, he is the greater sufferer. While shame only deals with her, conscience is at work with him. But there can be no sympathy, because he looks on and holds his peace. Her child says to him,—her child, not knowing that he is her father, not knowing what she says, but in answer to him when he would fain take her little hand in his during the darkness of night,—"Wilt thou stand here with mother and me to-morrow noontide"? He can not bring himself to do that, though he struggles hard to do it, and therefore we despise him. He can not do it till the hand of death is upon him, and then the time is too late for reparation in the reader's judgment. Could we have sympathized with a pair of lovers, the human element would have prevailed too strongly for the author's purpose.

He seems hardly to have wished that we should sympathize even with her; or, at any rate, he has not bid us in so many words to do so, as is common with authors. Of course, he has wished it. He has intended that the reader's heart should run over with ruth for the undeserved fate of that wretched woman. And it does. She is pure as undriven snow. We know that at some time far back she loved and sinned, but it was done when we did not know her. We are not told so, but come to understand, by the wonderful power of the writer in conveying that which he never tells, that there has been no taint of foulness in her love, though there has been deep sin. He never even tells us why that letter A has been used, though the abominable word is burning in our ears from first to last. We merely see her with her child, bearing her lot with patience, seeking no comfort, doing what good she can in her humble solitude by the work of her hands, pointed at from all by the finger of scorn, but the purest, the cleanest, the fairest also among women. She never dreams of supposing that she ought not to be regarded as vile, while the reader's heart glows with a longing to take her soft hand and lead her into some pleasant place where the world shall be pleasant and honest and kind to her. I can fancy a reader so loving the image of Hester Prynne as to find himself on the verge of treachery to the real Hester of flesh and blood who may have a claim upon him. Sympathy can not go beyond that; and yet the author deals with her in a spirit of assumed hardness, almost as though he assented to the judgment and the manner in which it was carried out. In this, however, there is a streak of that satire with which Hawthorne always speaks of the peculiar institutions of his own country. The worthy magistrates of Massachusetts are under his lash throughout the story, and so is the virtue of her citizens and the chastity of her matrons, which can take delight in the open shame of a woman whose sin has been discovered. Indeed, there is never a page written by Hawthorne not tinged by satire.

The fourth character is that of the child, Pearl. Here the author has, I think, given way to a temptation, and in doing so has not increased the power of his story. The temptation was, that Pearl should add a picturesque element by being an elf and also a charming child. Elf she is, but, being so, is incongruous with all else in the story, in which, unhuman as it is, there is nothing of the ghost-like, nothing of the unnatural. The old man becomes a fiend, so to say, during the process of the tale; but he is a man-fiend. And Hester becomes sublimated almost to divine purity; but she is still simply a woman. The minister is tortured beyond the power of human endurance; but neither do his sufferings nor his failure of strength adequate to support them come to him from any miraculous agency. But Pearl is miraculous,—speaking, acting, and thinking like an elf,—and is therefore, I think, a drawback rather than an aid. The desolation of the woman, too, would have been more perfect without the child. It seems as though the author's heart had not been hard enough to make her live alone;—as sometimes when you punish a child you can not drive from your face that gleam of love which shoots across your frown and mars its salutary effect.

Hatred, fear, and shame are the passions which revel through the book. To show how a man may so hate as to be content to sacrifice everything to his hatred; how another may fear so that, even though it be for the rescue of his soul, he can not bring himself to face the reproaches of the world; how a woman may bear her load of infamy openly before the eyes of all men,—this has been Hawthorne's object. And surely no author was ever more successful. The relentless purpose of the man, in which is exhibited no passion, in which there is hardly a touch of anger, is as fixed as the hand of Fate. No one in the town knew that the woman was his wife. She had never loved him. He had left her alone in the world. But she was his wife; and, as the injury had been done to him, the punishment should follow from his hands! When he finds out who the sinner was, he does not proclaim him and hold him up to disgrace; he does not crush the almost adored minister of the gospel by declaring the sinner's trespass. He simply lives with his enemy in the same house, attacking not the man's body,—to which, indeed, he acts as a wise physician,—but his conscience, till we see the wretch writhing beneath the treatment.

Hester sees it too, and her strength, which suffices for the bearing of her own misery, fails her almost to fainting as she understands the condition of the man she has loved. Then there is a scene, the one graceful and pretty scene in the book, in which the two meet,—the two who were lovers,—and dare for a moment to think that they can escape. They come together in a wood, and she flings away, but for a moment, the badge of her shame, and lets down the long hair which has been hidden under her cap, and shines out before the reader for once,—just for that once,—as a lovely woman. She counsels him to fly, to go back across the waters to the old home whence he had come, and seek for rest away from the cruelty of his tyrant. When he pleads that he has no strength left to him for such action, then she declares that she will go with him and protect him and minister to him and watch over him with her strength. Yes; this woman proposes that she will then elope with the partner of her former sin. But no idea comes across the reader's mind of sinful love. The poor wretch can not live without service, and she will serve him. Were it herself that was concerned, she would remain there in her solitude, with the brand of her shame still open upon her bosom. But he can not go alone, and she too will therefore go.

As I have said before, the old man discovers the plot, and crushes their hopes simply by declaring that he will also be their companion. Whether there should have been this gleam of sunshine in the story the critic will doubt. The parent who would be altogether like Solomon should not soften the sternness of his frown by any glimmer of parental softness. The extreme pain of the chronicle is mitigated for a moment. The reader almost fears that he is again about to enjoy the satisfaction of a happy ending. When the blackness and the rumbling thunder-claps and the beating hailstones of a mountain storm have burst with all their fearful glories on the wanderer among the Alps, though he trembles and is awestruck and crouches with the cold, he is disappointed rather than gratified when a little space of blue sky shows itself for a moment through the clouds. But soon a blacker mantle covers the gap, louder and nearer comes the crash, heavier fall the big drops till they seem to strike him to the bone. The storm is awful, majestic, beautiful;—but is it not too pitiless? So it is with the storm which bursts over that minister's head when the little space of blue has vanished from the sky.

But through all this intensity of suffering, through this blackness of narrative, there is ever running a vein of drollery. As Hawthorne himself says, "a lively sense of the humorous again stole in among the solemn phantoms of her thought." He is always laughing at something with his weird, mocking spirit. The very children when they see Hester in the streets are supposed to speak of her in this wise: "Behold, verily, there is the woman of the scarlet letter. Come, therefore, and let us fling mud at her." Of some religious book he says, "It must have been a work of vast ability in the somniferous school of literature." "We must not always talk in the market-place of what happens to us in the forest," says even the sad mother to her child. Through it all there is a touch of burlesque,—not as to the suffering of the sufferers, but as to the great question whether it signifies much in what way we suffer, whether by crushing sorrows or little stings. Who would not sooner be Prometheus than a yesterday's tipsy man with this morning's sick-headache? In this way Hawthorne seems to ridicule the very woes which he expends himself in depicting.

As a novel *The House of the Seven Gables* is very inferior to *The Scarlet Letter*. The cause of this inferiority would, I think, be plain to any one who had himself been concerned in the writing of novels. When Hawthorne proposed to himself to write *The Scarlet Letter*, the plot of his story was clear to his mind. He wrote the book because he had the story strongly, lucidly manifest to his own imagination. In composing the other he was driven to search for a plot, and to make a story. *The Scarlet Letter* was written because he had it to write, and the other because he had to write it. The novelist will often find himself in the latter position. He has characters to draw, lessons to teach, philosophy perhaps which he wishes to expose, satire to express, humor to scatter abroad. These he can employ gracefully and easily if he have a story to tell. If he have none, he must concoct something of a story laboriously, when his lesson, his characters, his philosophy, his satire, and his humor will be less graceful and less easy. All the good things I have named are there in *The House of the Seven Gables*; but they are brought in with less artistic skill, because the author has labored over his plot, and never had it clear to his own mind.

There is a mystery attached to the house. That is a matter of course. A rich man obtained the ground on which it was built by fraud from a poor man, and the poor man's curse falls on the rich man's descendants, and the rich man with his rich descendants are abnormally bad, though very respectable. They not only cheat but murder. The original poor man was hung for witchcraft,—only because he had endeavored to hold his own against the original rich man. The rich men in consequence die when they come to advanced age, without any apparent cause of death, sitting probably upright in their chairs, to the great astonishment of the world at large, and with awful signs of blood about their mouths and shirt-fronts. And each man as he dies is in the act of perpetrating some terrible enormity against some poor member of his own family. The respectable rich man with whom we become personally acquainted in the story,—for as to some of the important characters we hear of them only by the records which are given of past times,—begins by getting a cousin convicted of a murder of which he knew that his kinsman was not guilty, and is preparing to have the same kinsman fraudulently and unnecessarily put into a lunatic asylum, when he succumbs to the fate of his family and dies in his chair, all covered with blood. The unraveling of these mysteries is vague, and, as I think, inartistic. The reader is not carried on by any intense interest in the story itself, and comes at last not much to care whether he does or does not understand the unraveling. He finds that his interest in the book lies elsewhere,—that he must seek it in the characters, lessons, philosophy, satire, and humor, and not in the plot. With *The Scarlet Letter* the plot comes first, and the others follow as accessories.

Two or three of the characters here drawn are very good. The wicked and respectable gentleman who *drees* the doom of his family, and dies in his chair all covered with blood, is one Judge Pyncheon. The persistent, unbending, cruel villainy of this man,—whose heart is as hard as a millstone, who knows not the meaning of conscience, to whom money and respectability are everything,—was dear to Hawthorne's heart. He likes to revel in an excess of impossible wickedness, and has done so with the Judge. Though we do not care much for the mysteries of the Judge's family, we like the Judge himself, and we like to feel that the author is pouring out his scorn on the padded respectables of his New England world. No man had a stronger belief than Hawthorne in the superiority of his own country; no man could be more sarcastic as to the deficiencies of another,—as I had reason to discover in that affair of the peas; but, nevertheless, he is always throwing out some satire as to the assumed virtues of his own immediate countrymen. It comes from him in little touches as to every incident he handles. In truth, he can not write without satire; and, as in these novels he writes of his own country, his shafts fall necessarily on that.

But the personage we like best in the book is certainly Miss Hepzibah Pyncheon. She is a cousin of the Judge, and has become, by some family arrangement, the life-possessor of the house with seven gables. She is sister also of the man who had been wrongly convicted of murder, and who, when released after a thirty-years' term of imprisonment, comes also to live at the house. Miss Hepzibah, under a peculiarly ill-grained exterior, possesses an affectionate heart and high principles. Driven by poverty, she keeps a shop,—a cent-shop, a term which is no doubt familiar enough in New England, and by which it would be presumed that all her articles were to be bought for a cent each, did it not appear by the story that she dealt also in goods of greater value. She is a lady by birth, and can not keep her cent-shop without some feeling of degradation; but that is preferable to the receiving of charity from that odious cousin the Judge. Her timidity, her affection, her true appreciation of herself, her ugliness, her hopelessness, and general incapacity for everything,—cent-shop-keeping includ-ed,—are wonderfully drawn. There are characters in novels who walk about on their feet, who stand upright and move, so that readers can look behind them, as one seems to be able to do in looking at a well-painted figure on the canvas. There are others, again, so wooden that no reader expects to find in them any appearance of movement. They are blocks roughly hewed into some more or less imperfect forms of humanity, which are put into their places and which there lie. Miss Hepzibah is one of the former. The reader sees all round her, and is sure that she is alive,—though she is so incapable.

Then there is her brother Clifford, who was supposed to have committed the murder, and who, in the course of the chronicle, comes home to live with his sister. There are morsels in his story, bits of telling in the description of him, which are charming, but he is not so good as his sister, being less intelligible. Hawthorne himself had not realized the half-fatuous, dreamy, ill-used brother, as he had the sister. In painting a figure it is essential that the artist should himself know the figure he means to paint.

There is yet another Pyncheon,—Phœbe Pyncheon, who comes from a distance, Heaven knows why, to live with her far-away cousin. She is intended as a ray of sunlight,—as was Pearl in *The Scarlet Letter,*—and is more successful. As the old maid Pyncheon is capable of nothing, so is the young maid Pyncheon capable of everything. She is, however, hardly wanted in the story, unless it be that the ray of sunlight was necessary. And there is a young "daguerreotypist,"—as the photographer of the day used to be called,—who falls in love with the ray of sunlight, and marries her at the end; and who is indeed the lineal descendant of the original ill-used poor man who was hung as a witch. There is just one love-scene in the novel, most ghastly in its details; for the young man offers his love, and the girl accepts it, while they are aware that the wicked, respectable old Judge is sitting, all smeared with blood, and dead, in the next room to them. The love-scene, and the hurrying up of the marriage, and all the dollars which they inherit from the wicked Judge, and the "handsome dark-green barouche" prepared for their departure, which is altogether unfitted to the ideas which the reader has formed respecting them, are quite unlike Hawthorne, and would seem almost to have been added by some every-day, beef-and-ale, realistic novelist, into whose hands the unfinished story had unfortu-nately fallen.

But no one should read *The House of the Seven Gables* for the sake of the story, or neglect to read it because of such faults as I have described. It is for the humor, the satire, and what I may perhaps call the philosophy which permeates it, that its pages should be turned. Its pages may be turned on any day, and under any circumstances. To *The Scarlet Letter* you have got to adhere till you have done with it; but you may take this volume by bits, here and there, now and again, just as you like it. There is a description of a few poultry, melancholy, unproductive birds, running over four or five pages, and written as no one but Hawthorne could have written it. There are a dozen pages or more in which the author pretends to ask why the busy Judge does not move from his chair,—the Judge the while having dree'd his doom and died as he sat. There is a ghastly spirit of drollery about this which would put the reader into full communion with Hawthorne if he had not read a page before, and did not intend to read a page after. To those who can make literary food of such passages as these, *The House of the Seven Gables* may be recommended. To others it will be caviare.

Mosses from an Old Manse will be caviare to many. By

this I intend no slight to the intelligence of the many readers who may not find themselves charmed by such narratives. In the true enjoyment of Hawthorne's work there is required a peculiar mood of mind. The reader should take a delight in looking round corners, and in seeing how places and things may be approached by other than the direct and obvious route. No writer impresses himself more strongly on the reader who will submit to him; but the reader must consent to put himself altogether under his author's guidance, and to travel by queer passages, the direction of which he will not perceive till, perhaps, he has got quite to the end of them. In *The Scarlet Letter*, though there are many side paths, there is a direct road, so open that the obstinately straightforward traveler will find his way, though he will not, perhaps, see all that there is to be seen. In *The House of the Seven Gables* a kind of thoroughfare does at last make itself visible, though covered over with many tangles. In the volume of which I am now speaking there is no pathway at all. The reader must go where the writer may choose to take him, and must consent to change not only his ground, but the nature of his ground, every minute. This, as the name implies, is a collection of short stories,—and of course no thread or general plot is expected in such a compilation. But here the short narratives are altogether various in their style, no one of them giving any clew as to what may be expected to follow. They are, rather than tales, the jottings down of the author's own fancies, on matters which have subjected themselves to his brain, one after the other, in that promiscuous disorder in which his manner of thinking permitted him to indulge. He conceives a lovely woman, who has on her cheek a "birth-mark," so trifling as to be no flaw to her beauty. But her husband sees it, and, seeing it, can not rid himself of the remembrance of it. He is a man of science, concerned with the secrets of chemistry, and goes to work to concoct some ichor by which the mark may be eradicated. Just as success is being accomplished, the lady dies under the experiment. "You have aimed loftily," she says to her husband, at her last gasp; "you have done nobly. Do not repent." Whether the husband does repent we are not told; but the idea left is that, seeking something more than mortal perfection, he had thrown away the happiness which, as a mortal, he might have enjoyed. This is transcendental enough; but it is followed, a few pages on, by the record of Mrs. Bullfrog, who had got herself married to Mr. Bullfrog, as the natural possessor of all feminine loveliness, and then turns out to be a hideous virago, with false hair and false teeth, but who is at last accepted graciously by Bullfrog, because her money is real. The satire is intelligible, and is Hawthornean, but why Hawthorne should have brought himself to surround himself with objects so disagreeable the reader does not understand.

"The Select Party" is pleasant enough. It is held in a castle in the air, made magnificent with all architectural details, and there the Man of Fancy, who is its owner, entertains the Oldest Inhabitant, Nobody, M. Ondit, the Clerk of the Weather, Mother Carey, the Master Genius of his Age,—a young American, of course,—and sundry others, who among them have a good deal to say which is worth hearing. The student of Hawthorne will understand what quips and quirks will come from this mottled company.

Then there is an Italian, one Rappacini, and his daughter, weird, ghostlike, and I must own very unintelligible. The young lady, however, has learned under the teaching of her father, who is part doctor, part gardener, and part conjurer, to exist on the essence of a flower which is fatal to everybody else. She becomes very detrimental to her lover, who has no such gifts, and the story ends as a tragedy. There is a very pretty prose pastoral called "Buds and Bird-Voices," which is simply the indulgence of a poetic voice in the expression of its love of nature. "The Hall of Fantasy" is a mansion in which some unfortunates make their whole abode and business, and "contract habits which unfit them for all the real employments of life. Others,—but these are few,—possess the faculty, in their occasional visits, of discovering a purer truth than the world can impart." The reader can imagine to himself those who, under Hawthorne's guidance, would succeed and those who would fail by wandering into this hall. "The Procession of Life" is perhaps the strongest piece in the book,—the one most suggestive and most satisfactory. Hawthorne imagines that, by the blowing of some trumpet such as has never yet been heard, the inhabitants of the world shall be brought together under other circumstances than those which at present combine them. The poor now associate with the poor, the rich with the rich, the learned with the learned, the idle with the idle, the orthodox with the orthodox, and so on. By this new amalgamation the sick shall associate with the sick, the strong-bodied with the strong, the weak-bodied with the weak, the gifted with the gifted, the sorrowful with the sorrowful, the wicked with the wicked, and the good with the good. Here is a specimen of Hawthorne's manner in bringing the wicked together: "The hideous appeal has swept round the globe. Come all ye guilty ones, and rank yourselves in accordance with the brotherhood of crime. This, indeed, is an awful summons. I almost tremble to look at the strange partnerships that begin to be formed, reluctantly, but by the invincible necessity of like to like, in this part of the procession. A forger from the State prison seizes the arm of a distinguished financier. . . . Here comes a murderer with his clanking chain, and pairs himself,—horrible to tell!—with as pure and upright a man, in all observable respects, as ever partook of the consecrated bread and wine. . . . Why do that pair of flaunting girls, with the pert, affected laugh, and the sly leer at the bystander, intrude themselves into the same rank with yonder decorous matron and that somewhat prudish maiden?" The scope for irony and satire which Hawthorne could get from such a marshaling as this was unbounded.

There is a droll story, with a half-hidden meaning, called "Drowne's Wooden Image," in which Copley the painter is brought upon the scene, so that I am led to suppose that there was a Drowne who carved head-pieces for ships in Boston, and who, by some masterpiece in his trade, and by the help of Hawthorne, has achieved a sort of immortality. Here the man, by dint of special energy on this special job,—he is supposed to be making a figure-head for a ship,—hews out of the wood a female Frankenstein, all alone, but lovely as was the other one hideous. The old idea, too, is conveyed that, as within every block of marble, so within every log of wood, there is a perfection of symmetry and beauty, to be reached by any one who may have the gift of properly stripping off the outlying matter.

"P.'s Correspondence" is the last I will mention. P. is a madman, who, in writing to his friend in Boston from his madhouse chamber, imagines himself to have met in London Byron, Burns, Scott, and a score of other literary worthies, still alive as he supposes, but who by the stress of years have been changed in all their peculiarities, as men are changed when they live long. Byron becomes very religious, and professes excessive high-church tendencies,—as certain excellent and over-liberal friends of mine have in their old age become more timid and more conservative than they who were to the manner born. Hawthorne adds to this the joke that all his own American literary contemporaries,—men whom he knew to be alive,

and with whom he probably was intimate,—are, alas! dead and gone. The madman weeps over Bryant, Whittier, and Longfellow, while he has been associating with Keats, Canning, and John Kemble.

Such is the nature of the Mosses from the old Manse each morsel of moss damp, tawny, and soft, as it ought to be, but each with enough of virus to give a sting to the tender hand that touches it.

I have space to mention but one other of our author's works; *The Marble Faun*, as it is called in America, and published in England under the name of *Transformation; or, The Romance of Monte Beni*. The double name, which has given rise to some confusion, was, I think, adopted with the view of avoiding the injustice to which American and English authors are subjected by the want of international copyright. Whether the object was attained, or was in any degree attainable by such means, I do not know.

In speaking of *The Marble Faun*, as I will call the story, I hardly know whether, as a just critic, to speak first of its faults or of its virtues. As one always likes to keep the sweetest bits for the end of the banquet, I will give priority of place to my caviling. The great fault of the book lies in the absence of arranged plot. The author, in giving the form of a novel to the beautiful pictures and images which his fancy has enabled him to draw, and in describing Rome and Italian scenes as few others have described them, has in fact been too idle to carry out his own purpose of constructing a tale. We will grant that a novelist may be natural or supernatural. Let us grant, for the occasion, that the latter manner, if well handled, is the better and the more efficacious. And we must grant also that he who soars into the supernatural need not bind himself by any of the ordinary trammels of life. His men may fly, his birds may speak. His women may make angelic music without instruments. His cherubs may sit at the piano. This wide latitude, while its adequate management is much too difficult for ordinary hands, gives facility for the working of a plot. But there must be some plot, some arrangement of circumstances, with an intelligible conclusion, or the reader will not be satisfied. If, then, a ghost, who,—or shall I say which?—is made on all occasions to act as a *Deus ex machina*, and to create and to solve every interest, we should know something of the ghost's antecedents, something of the causes which have induced him, or it, to meddle in the matter under discussion. The ghost of Hamlet's father had a manifest object, and the ghost of Banquo a recognized cause. In *The Marble Faun* there is no ghost, but the heroine of the story is driven to connive at murder, and the hero to commit murder, by the disagreeable intrusion of a personage whose *raison d'être* is left altogether in the dark. "The gentle reader," says our author as he ends his narrative, "would not thank us for one of those minute elucidations which are so tedious and after all so unsatisfactory in clearing up the romantic mysteries of a story." There our author is, I think, in error. His readers will hardly be so gentle as not to require from him some explanation of the causes which have produced the romantic details to which they have given their attention, and will be inclined to say that it should have been the author's business to give an explanation neither tedious nor unsatisfactory. The critic is disposed to think that Hawthorne, as he continued his narrative, postponed his plot till it was too late, and then escaped from his difficulty by the ingenious excuse above given. As a writer of novels, I am bound to say that the excuse can not be altogether accepted.

But the fault, when once admitted, may be well pardoned on account of the beauty of the narrative. There are four persons,—or five, including the mysterious intruder who is only, I think, seen and never heard, but who is thrown down the Tarpeian rock and murdered. Three of them are artists,— a lady named Miriam, who is haunted by the mysterious one and is an assenting party to his murder; another lady named Hilda, an American from New England, who lives alone in a tower surrounded by doves; and a sculptor, one Kenyon, also from the States, who is in love with Hilda. The fourth person is the Faun, as to whom the reader is left in doubt whether he be man or Satyr,—human, or half god half animal. As to this doubt the critic makes no complaint. The author was within his right in creating a creature partaking of these different attributes, and it has to be acknowledged on his behalf that the mystery which he has thrown over this offspring of his brain has been handled by him, a writer of prose, not only with profound skill but with true poetic feeling. This faun, who is Count of Monte Beni,—be he most god, or man, or beast; let him have come from the hills and the woods and the brooks like a Satyr of old, or as any other count from his noble ancestors and ancestral towers,—attaches himself to Miriam, as a dog does to a man, not with an expressed human love in which there is a longing for kisses and a hope for marriage, but with a devotion half doglike as I have said, but in its other half godlike and heavenly pure. He scampers round her in his joy, and is made happy simply by her presence, her influence, and her breath. He is happy, except when the intruder intrudes, and then his jealousy is that as of a dog against an intruding hound. There comes a moment in which the intrusion of the intruder is unbearable. Then he looks into Miriam's eyes, and, obtaining the assent for which he seeks, he hurls the intruder down the Tarpeian rock into eternity. After that the light-hearted creature, overwhelmed by the weight of his sin, becomes miserable, despondent, and unable to bear the presence of her who had so lately been all the world to him. In the end light-hearted joy returns to him; but the reason for this second change is not so apparent.

The lives of Kenyon and Hilda are more commonplace, but, though they are commonplace between man and woman, the manner in which they are told is very beautiful. She is intended to represent perfect innocence, and he manly honesty. The two characters are well conceived and admirably expressed.

In *The Marble Faun*, as in all Hawthorne's tales written after *The Scarlet Letter*, the reader must look rather for a series of pictures than for a novel. It would, perhaps, almost be well that a fastidious reader should cease to read when he comes within that border, toward the end, in which it might be natural to expect that the strings of a story should be gathered together and tied into an intelligible knot. This would be peculiarly desirable in regard to *The Marble Faun*, in which the delight of that fastidious reader, as derived from pictures of character and scenery, will be so extreme that it should not be marred by a sense of failure in other respects.

In speaking of this work in conjunction with Hawthorne's former tales, I should be wrong not to mention the wonderful change which he effected in his own manner of writing when he had traveled out from Massachusetts into Italy. As every word in his earlier volumes savors of New England, so in *The Marble Faun* is the flavor entirely that of Rome and of Italian scenery. His receptive imagination took an impress from what was around him, and then gave it forth again with that wonderful power of expression which belonged to him. Many modern writers have sought to give an interest to their writings by what is called local coloring; but it will too often happen that the reader is made to see the laying on of the colors. In Hawthorne's Roman chronicle the tone of the telling is just as natural,—seems to belong as peculiarly to the author,—as it does with *The Scarlet Letter* or *The House of the Seven Gables*.

RICHARD COBDEN

1804–1865

Richard Cobden was born on June 3, 1804, on a farm near Midhurst, Sussex, to an impoverished family. He and his ten brothers and sisters were raised by relatives. Young Cobden was sent to a dismal boarding school in Yorkshire, and from there went to work in his uncle's warehouse in London. In 1828 he and two friends were able to establish their own business as calico merchants, and the venture proved successful.

As he grew more prosperous Cobden was able to read and travel widely in an attempt to remedy his lack of a formal education. In the 1830s he traveled extensively on the Continent and in the United States and Middle East, and out of his experiences wrote and published two political pamphlets: *England, Ireland and America* (1835) and *Russia* (1836). In both Cobden emphasized the need for Great Britain to expand its foreign trade, pointing out that such expansion was dependent on free trade rather than on military power. From 1838 until 1846 he was active in the struggle for the repeal of the Corn Laws, arguing that they benefited the rich at the expense of the poor. In the course of this campaign he was elected to Parliament as a member for Stockport. He soon made a name for himself as an orator in the House of Commons and as the chief opponent of Sir Robert Peel.

The fight against the Corn Laws absorbed so much of Cobden's attention that he neglected his business interests, and the substantial fortune he had earned was virtually gone by 1846. A public subscription was raised for him the following year and he was able to buy the family farm, Dunford, which thereafter became his home and that of his wife and six children.

After a period of travel, Cobden was reelected to Parliament in 1847 as M.P. for West Riding, Yorkshire, and represented this constituency for ten years. He continued to advocate free trade along with the reduction of armaments as its necessary complement, and argued as well for non-intervention in Europe, opposed the expansion of the British Empire, and pressed for friendship with Russia. He wrote several political pamphlets during this period, including *1793 and 1853 in Three Letters* (1853), a plea for peace with France, and *What Next—and Next?*, a restatement of his views on encouraging friendship with Russia.

Cobden was defeated for reelection in 1857 but was returned to Parliament in 1859 following another trip to the United States. Declining Palmerston's offer to serve in the cabinet, he instead embarked on what were at first unofficial negotiations with France for a new commercial treaty. Backed by Gladstone, his efforts were a success and a treaty was signed in 1860. It was designed as a model for future commercial agreements, and its most-favored-nation clause was copied in many subsequent treaties. During the American Civil War Cobden sided with the North and continued his decade-long correspondence with Charles Sumner; this contact, although unofficial, was an important link between Britain and the United States during the war years.

Cobden's health was undermined by his intensive work on the Anglo-French treaty and he was ill for much of the time in his last years. He died on April 2, 1865, shortly after summoning the energy to cast his vote in Parliament against defense appropriations. A collected edition of his speeches was published in two volumes in 1870; an anthology, *The Political Writings of Richard Cobden*, with an introduction by Sir L. Mallet, appeared in 1878.

On Saturday week I read in the newspapers the speech Cobden made at Manchester abusing the D. of Wellington, and scouting the national defences. On Wednesday I wrote a letter to him in the *Times*, which has had great success. I have received innumerable compliments and expressions of approbation about it from all quarters, and the Old Duke is pleased. I had no idea of making such a *hit*, but the truth is, everybody was disgusted at Cobden's impertinence and (it may be added) folly. His head is turned by all the flattery he has received, and he has miserably exposed himself since his return to England, showing that he is a man of one idea and no Statesman. —CHARLES CAVENDISH FULKE GREVILLE, *Diary*, Feb. 8, 1848

Went to the House of Commons and heard Cobden bring on his Arbitration Motion to produce Universal Peace. He has a good face, and is a clear, manly speaker.—CAROLINE FOX, *Journal* (June 12, 1849), *Memories of Old Friends*, ed. Horace N. Pym, 1882, p. 265

Not even the tragedy here ⟨Lincoln's assassination⟩ can make me indifferent to the death of Richard Cobden, who was my personal friend and the friend of my country. I felt with you entirely in the touching words which you uttered in Parliament. I wish he could have lived to enjoy our triumph and to continue his counsels. His name will be for him more than Westminster Abbey.—CHARLES SUMNER, Letter to John Bright (April 18, 1865), cited in Edward L. Pierce, *Memoir and Letters of Charles Sumner*, 1893, Vol. 4, p. 239

Few who were living, and of sufficiently matured powers of observation at the time, will ever forget the sad and general impression made by the tidings of Mr. Cobden's peaceful release, throughout the whole land, among all classes of its citizens, and in the great countries of Europe and the New World. Mr. Cobden, with a patriotism as undeniable and unquenchable as ever animated a human breast, had nevertheless been the great apostle of kindliness and conciliation in international relations, and one consequence was, that he was more beloved and popular out of his own land than ever statesman was in the history of the world. Englishmen—even those who had admired him most warmly while living—were astounded when they came, after his death, to realize the beauty of his character, the magnitude of his services, and the amount of what they had lost by his somewhat early departure.—JOHN McGILCHRIST, *Richard Cobden*, 1865, p. 262

I now leave the American reader to the perusal of the writings included in this collection. He will find in them the utterances of a true friend of the human race, whose sole aim was so to modify existing institutions, by proper and equitable methods, that all who live under the same government may be equal partakers in its benefits, and to bring all the blessings of life within the reach of the largest number. This great end he kept steadily in view, never intimidated from pursuing it by the danger of unpopularity, nor seduced to abandon it by the love of distinction and the praises of the great. His indignation at the oppression of the weak and helpless was never disguised, and his whole political life was made up of manly labours in the cause of justice. From the writings of this illustrious teacher the wisest statesman may be instructed in the practical application of the maxims of a comprehensive, humane, and generous political philosophy.—WILLIAM CULLEN BRYANT, "Introduction to the American Edition" to *The Political Writings of Richard Cobden*, 1867

Cobden was an honest, an able, and a useful public man, but not, I think, as his admirers claim for him, either a great politician or a great political philosopher. He was prevented from being the first by the mental peculiarity which made him a serviceable ally only when (as he says himself) he was advancing some 'defined and simple principle;' a limitation which, whatever its compensating advantages may be, is an effectual bar to the highest success in a career which requires in those who pursue it a power of dealing not only with principles, but likewise with an infinity of practical problems which are neither 'defined' nor 'simple.' He was, on the other hand, prevented from being a great political philosopher, if by no other causes, still by the circumstances of his early life. His education, pursued with admirable energy while he was immersed in the business of clerk and commercial traveller, was not, and perhaps could not be, of the kind best suited to counteract the influences which, as I have pointed out, surrounded his early political career. His radicalism from the first was the radicalism of a class, and such in all essentials it remained to the end. His lack of the historic sense was not compensated by any great scientific or speculative power. Much as he saw to disapprove of in the existing condition of England, he never framed a large and consistent theory of the methods by which it was to be improved. Outside the narrow bounds of the economics of trade he had political projects, but no coherent political system; so that if he was too theoretical to make a good minister of state, he was too fragmentary and inconsistent to make a really important theorist.—ARTHUR JAMES BALFOUR, "Morley's *Life of Cobden*," *Nineteenth Century*, Jan. 1882, p. 54

Nothing shows the vigour of Cobden's intellect more than the facility with which he mastered and accomplished all that he undertook. He never had to wait long for success in anything to which he laid his hand. Equipped with only a "mockery of education," in a Dotheboys' Hall of the period, he had such a predisposition for culture that he never seemed to be hampered by the want of it; he made up for deficiencies as he went along. His admirable temper and sweetness of nature no doubt made paths smooth to him which would have been rough to others. —JAMES COTTER MORISON, *"The Life of Richard Cobden* by John Morley," *Macmillan's Magazine*, Jan. 1882, p. 213

Richard Cobden's achievements were great, and even astounding, seeing how new were the ideas and the elements which he introduced into the field of practical politics and statesmanship, and how short was the time given to him in which to labour. But what he accomplished was only the beginning of the splendid enterprise to which his days were devoted. The world had almost slept for two or three generations upon the economic discoveries of Adam Smith, until the *Wealth of Nations* fell into the hands of Richard Cobden; and even the magnificent demonstration of the soundness of the Free Trade doctrine which was given to the world in the conversion of Sir Robert Peel by the "Manchester manufacturer"—and in the Repeal of the Corn Laws and its marvellous results—is not enough, in two or three generations, to remove the mountains of prejudice, of fallacy, and of vested interests in monopoly which stand in the way. Cobden the Worker in the nineteenth century, like Adam Smith the Thinker in the eighteenth, found commerce struggling on against old-world delusions while the relations between nation and nation were very much what we find the relations to be between the tribes and potentates of Central Africa. Political Economy may be said to have begun with Adam Smith; there is a sense in which Modern History may be said to have begun with Richard Cobden. Ever since the revival of learning and the discovery of America men have been found proudly declaring that the world has passed over the line of mediæval into modern history: but there will be great historians—students of the phenomena of the modern spirit in domestic and international politics—who will rise up, by-and-by, to tell the world that the real commencement of modern history was when the foremost of the principalities and states of the world began to work out the principle of "Free Trade, Peace, Goodwill among Nations."—RICHARD GOWING, *Richard Cobden*, 1886, pp. 127–28

One may repudiate Cobdenism without any intention to assail or undervalue the personal character of the leading Cobdenites. Most of them were in many respects highly estimable men; and Cobden himself had a large share of the qualities which Englishmen rightly reverence. He was upright, honourable, and disinterested; kindly and affectionate in his private life; an excellent father, husband, and brother; sedulous in his work, simple in his habits, pleasantly free from ostentation and self-seeking ambition; and no one can question his courage, or the conscientious industry and self-sacrificing energy, with which he served the cause of humanity, according to his lights.—SIDNEY LOW, "The Decline of Cobdenism," *Nineteenth Century*, Aug. 1896, p. 184

WALTER BAGEHOT
From "Mr. Cobden" (1865)
Collected Works, ed. Norman St. John-Stevas
1968, Volume 3, pp. 294–97

Mr. Cobden was very anomalous in two respects. He was a *sensitive* agitator. Generally, an agitator is a rough man of the O'Connell type, who says anything himself, and lets others say anything. You 'peg into me and I will peg into you, and let us see which will win,' is his motto. But Mr. Cobden's habit and feeling was utterly different. He never spoke ill of any one. He arraigned principles, but not persons. We fearlessly say that after a career of agitation of thirty years, not one single individual has—we do not say a valid charge, but a producible charge—a charge which he would wish to bring forward against Mr. Cobden. You can't find the man who says 'Mr. Cobden said this of me, and it was not true.' This may seem trivial praise, and on paper it looks easy. But to those who know the great temptations of actual life it means very much. How would any other great agitator, O'Connell, or Hunt, or Cobbett, look if tried by such a test? Very rarely, if even ever in history, has a man achieved so much by his words—been victor in what was thought at the time to be a class struggle—and yet spoken so little evil as Mr. Cobden. There is hardly a word to be found, perhaps, even now, which the recording angel would wish to blot. We may on other grounds object to an agitator who lacerates no one, but no watchful man of the world will deny that such an agitator has vanquished one of life's most imperious and difficult temptations. ⟨. . .⟩

This sensitive nature is one marked peculiarity in Mr. Cobden's career as an agitator, and another is that he was an agitator *for men of business*. Generally speaking, occupied men charged with the responsibilities and laden with the labour of grave affairs are jealous of agitation. They know how much may be said against any one who is responsible for anything. They know how unanswerable such charges nearly always are, and how false they easily may be. A capitalist can hardly help thinking 'Suppose a man was to make a speech against *my* mode of conducting my own business, how much he would have to say.' Now it is an exact description of Mr. Cobden that by the personal magic of a single-minded practicability, he made men of business abandon this objection. He made them rather like the new form of agitation. He made them say, 'How business like, how wise, just what it would have been right to do.'

Mr. Cobden of course was not the discoverer of the Free-trade principle. He did not first find out that the Corn Laws were bad laws. But he was the most effectual of those who discovered how the Corn Laws were to be repealed—how Free-trade was to change from a doctrine into a doctrine of *The Wealth of Nations*, into a principle of tariffs, and a fact of real life. If a thing was right, to Mr. Cobden's mind it ought to be done, and as Adam Smith's doctrines were admitted on theory, he could not believe that they ought to lie idle, that they ought to be 'bedridden in the dormitory of the understanding.'

Lord Houghton once said, 'In my time political economy books used to begin, Suppose a man upon an island.' Mr. Cobden's speeches never began so. He was altogether a man of business speaking to men of business. Some of us may remember the almost arch smile with which he said the House of Commons 'does not seem quite to understand the difference between a cotton mill and a print work.' It was almost amusing to him to think that the first assembly of the first mercantile nation could be, as they were, and are very dim in their notions of the most material divisions of their largest industry. It was this evident and first hand familiarly with real facts and actual life which enabled Mr. Cobden to inspire a curiously diffused confidence through all commercial—we may say through all matter-of-fact men. He diffused a kind of 'economical faith.' People in these days had only to say 'Mr. Cobden said so,' and other people went and believed it.

Mr. Cobden had nothing in the received sense classical about his oratory, but it is quite certain that Aristotle, the greatest teacher of the classical art of rhetoric, would very keenly have appreciated his oratory. This sort of economical faith is exactly what he would most have valued,—what he most prescribed. He said: 'A speaker should convince his audience that he was a likely person to know.' This was exactly what Mr. Cobden did. And the matter-of-fact philosopher would have much liked Mr. Cobden's habit of coming to the point.' It would have been thoroughly agreeable to his positive mind to see so much of clear, obvious argument. He would not indeed, have been able to conceive a 'League meeting.' There has never, perhaps, been another time in the history of the world when excited masses of men and women hung on the words of one talking political economy. The excitement of these meetings were keener than any political excitement of the last twenty years—keener infinitely than any which there is now. It may be said, and truly, that the interest of the subject was Mr. Cobden's felicity, not his mind; but it may be said with equal truth, that the excitement was much greater when he was speaking than when any one else was speaking. By a kind of keenness of nerve, he said the exact word to touch, not the bare abstract understanding, but the quick individual perception of his hearers.

We do not wish to make this article a mere panegyric. Mr. Cobden was far too manly to wish such folly. His mind was very peculiar, and, like all peculiar minds, had its sharp limits. He had what we may call a *supplementary* understanding— that is a bold, original intellect, acting on a special experience, and striking out views and principles not known to, or neglected by, ordinary men. He did not possess the traditional education of his country, and did not understand it. The solid heritage of transmitted knowledge had more value, we believe, than he would have accorded to it. There was a defect in business not identical, but perhaps not altogether without analogy. The late Mr. Wilson used to say 'Cobden's adminis-trative powers I do not think much of, but he is most valuable in counsel, always original, always shrewd, and not at all extreme.' He was not altogether equal to meaner men in some beaten tracks and pathways of life, though he was far their superior in all matters requiring an original stress of specula-tion, an innate energy of thought.

It may be said, and truly said, that he has been cut off before his time. A youth and manhood so spent as his well deserved a green old age. But so it was not to be. He has left us, quite independently of his positive works, of the repeal of the Corn Laws of the French treaty, a rare gift—the gift of *unique* character. There has been nothing before Richard Cobden like him in English history, and perhaps there will not be anything like it. And his character is of the simple, emphatic, pictur-esque sort which must easily, when opportunities are given as they were to him, go down to posterity. May posterity learn from him. Only last week we hoped to have learned something more ourselves.

But what is before us we know not,
And we know not what shall succeed.

JOHN MORLEY
From *The Life of Richard Cobden*
1881

One obvious criticism on Cobden's work, and it has often been made, is that he was expecting the arrival of a great social reform from the mere increase and more equal distribu-tion of material wealth. He ought to have known, they say, that what our society needs is the diffusion of intellectual light and the fire of a higher morality. It is even said by some that Free Trade has done harm rather than good, because it has flooded the country with wealth which men have never been properly taught how to use. In others words, material progress has been out of all proportion to moral progress.

Now nobody had better reason to know this than Cobden. The perpetual chagrin of his life was the obstinate refusal of those on whom he had helped to shower wealth and plenty to hear what he had to say on the social ideals to which their wealth should lead. At last he was obliged to say to himself, as he wrote to a friend: "Nations have not yet learnt to bear prosperity, liberty, and peace. They will learn it in a higher state of civilization. We think we are the models for posterity, when we are little better than beacons to help it to avoid the rocks and quicksands."

"When I come here," he wrote to Mr. Hargreaves from Dunford, "to ramble alone in the fields and to think, I am impressed with the aspect of our political and social relations. We have the spirit of feudalism rife and rampant in the midst of the antagonistic development of the age of Watt, Arkwright, and Stephenson! Nay, feudalism is every day more and more in the ascendant in political and social life. So great is its power and prestige that it draws to it the support and homage of even those who are the natural leaders of the newer and better civilization. Manufacturers and merchants as a rule seem only to desire riches that they may be enabled to prostrate them-selves at the feet of feudalism. How is this to end? And whither are we tending in both our domestic and foreign relations? Can we hope to avoid collisions at home or wars abroad whilst all the tendencies are to throw power and influence into the wrong scale?" [1]

He had begun life with the idea that the great manu-facturers and merchants of England should aspire to that high directing position which had raised the Medici, the Fuggers, and the De Witts to a level with the sovereign princes of the earth. At the end he still thought that no other class possessed wealth and influence enough to counteract the feudal class. Through all his public course Cobden did his best to moralize this great class; to raise its self-respect and its consciousness of its own dignity and power. Like every one else, he could only work within his own limits. It is too soon yet to say how our feudal society will ultimately be recast. So far, plutocracy shows a very slight gain upon aristocracy, of which it remains, as Cobden so constantly deplored, an imitation, and a very bad imitation. The political exclusiveness of the oligarchy has been thoroughly broken down since Cobden's day. It seems, however, as if the preponderance of power were inevitably destined not for the middle class, as he believed, but for the workmen.

For this future *régime* Cobden's work was the best prepa-ration. He conceived a certain measure of material prosperity, generally diffused, to be an indispensable instrument of social well-being. For England, as with admirable foresight he laid down in his first pamphlet in 1835, the cardinal fact is the existence of the United States—its industrial competition and its democratic example. This has transformed the conditions of policy. This is what warns English statesmen to set their house in order. For a country in our position, to keep the standard of living at its right level, free access to the means of subsistence and the material of industry was the first essential. Thrift in government and wise administration of private capital have become equally momentous in presence of the rising world around us. To abstain from intervention in the affairs of other nations is not only recommended by economic prudence, but is the only condition on which proper attention can be paid to the moral and social necessities at home. Let us not, then, tax Cobden with failing to do the work of the social moralist. It is his policy which gives to the social reformer a foothold. He accepted the task which, from the special requirements of the time, it fell to him to do, and it is both unjust and ungrateful to call him narrow for not performing the tasks of others as well as his own.

It was his view of policy as a whole, connected with the movement of wealth and industry all over the world, that distinguished Cobden and his allies from the Philosophic Radicals, who had been expected to form so great and powerful a school in the reformed Parliament.[2] Hume had anticipated him in attacking expenditure, and Mr. Roebuck in preaching self-government in the colonies. It was not until Retrenchment and Colonial Policy were placed in their true relation to the new and vast expansion of commerce and the growth of population, that any considerable number of people accepted them. The Radical party only became effective when it had connected its principles with economic facts. The different points of view of the Manchester School and of the Philosophic Radicals was illustrated in Mr. Mill's opposition to the alterations which Cobden had advocated in international maritime

law. Mr. Mill argued that the best way of stopping wars is to make them as onerous as possible to the citizens of the country concerned, and therefore that to protect the goods of the merchants of a belligerent country is to give them one motive the less for hindering their Government from making war. With all reverence for the ever admirable author of this argument, it must be pronounced to be abstract and unreal, when compared with Cobden's. You are not likely to prevent the practice of war, he contended, but what you can do is to make it less destructive to the interests and the security of great populations. An argument of this kind rests on a more solid basis, and suggests a wider comprehension of actual facts. In the same way he translated the revolutionary watchword of the Fraternity of Peoples into the language of common sense and practice, and the international sentiment as interpreted by him became an instrument for preserving as well as improving European order. He was justified in regarding his principles as the true Conservatism of modern societies.

Great economic and social forces flow with a tidal sweep over communities that are only half-conscious of that which is befalling them. Wise statesmen are those who foresee what time is thus bringing, and endeavour to shape institutions and to mould men's thought and purpose in accordance with the change that is silently surrounding them. To this type Cobden by his character and his influence belonged. Hence, amid the coarse strife and blind passion of the casual factions of the day, his name will stand conspicuously out as a good servant of the Commonwealth, and be long held in grateful memory.

Notes

1. *To Mr. Hargreaves*, April 10, 1863.
2. See Mr. Mill's *Autobiography*, pp. 194–96.

ELIZABETH GASKELL

1810–1865

Elizabeth Gaskell was born Elizabeth Stevenson on September 29, 1810, in Chelsea, the daughter of William Stevenson, a Unitarian minister who later became editor of the *Scots Magazine*. Her mother died when she was a baby, and Elizabeth was raised by a maternal aunt in Knutsford, Cheshire. She attended boarding school at Stratford-upon-Avon for several years, then went to live with her father and stepmother in London until his death in 1829.

In 1832 Elizabeth Stevenson married the Reverend William Gaskell, a Unitarian minister whom she had met while visiting friends in Manchester. Gaskell brought his bride to his church, the Cross Street Unitarian Chapel, where together they continued the work he had begun among the city's poor. They also found time to collaborate on the verse "Sketches among the Poor," which appeared anonymously in *Blackwood's Magazine* in January 1837. In addition to growing domestic responsibilities—the Gaskells eventually had six children, of whom four survived to adulthood—Mrs. Gaskell published pseudonymously several short stories in *Howitt's Journal* and began working on a novel, eventually published anonymously in 1848 as *Mary Barton: A Tale of Manchester Life*. A sympathetic account of the struggling poor during the Chartist agitation of the 1830s, *Mary Barton* was widely praised and led to its author's admission to intellectual circles outside Manchester.

Mrs. Gaskell met Charles Dickens in 1849 and, encouraged by him, published over the next decade a number of stories and tales in his magazine, *Household Words*, including the eight sketches that were later rewritten and published as the novel *Cranford* (1853). *Cranford* is notable not only for its faithful depiction of small-town life in early Victorian England but also for its controlled sympathetic tone that is neither sentimental nor satiric; it was praised by many eminent Victorians, including John Ruskin.

Her next novel, *Ruth* (1853), deals sympathetically with the problems of a seduced girl and the minister who rescues her, and anticipates Hardy's *Tess of the D'Urbervilles. North and South,* which returns to the Manchester factories of *Mary Barton* for its setting, was first published serially in *Household Words* (1854–55), then revised and enlarged for publication in book form (2 vols., 1855).

Mrs. Gaskell enjoyed a wide circle of friends, among them the novelist Charlotte Brontë. Following Brontë's sudden death in 1855, Mrs. Gaskell was asked by Mr. Brontë to write Charlotte's biography. *The Life of Charlotte Brontë,* published in 1857, was not immediately well received; it did, however, later achieve the stature it enjoys today as one of the outstanding literary biographies in the English language, praised not only for its factual interpretation of its subject but also for its graceful prose style.

Mrs. Gaskell continued to contribute stories on diverse topics, including the supernatural, to various periodicals, including *The Ladies' Companion, Household Words,* and *Cornhill Magazine;* they were later collected and published in several volumes, including *Round the Sofa* (1859) and *Cousin Phillis* (1864), a collection of interrelated stories centering on a love affair among the common folk. The novel *Sylvia's Lovers* (1863), depicting the impact of the Napoleonic Wars on the life of a rural English town and its inhabitants, continues to be regarded as an outstanding example of Victorian fiction. Mrs. Gaskell's last novel, *Wives and Daughters,* was published in serial form in *Cornhill Magazine* between August 1864 and January 1866.

Throughout her life Mrs. Gaskell was closely involved with her husband's ministry. The sufferings of the Manchester poor were particularly acute during the American Civil War, and Mrs. Gaskell's energetic work on their behalf undoubtedly contributed to a sharp decline in her health. She died suddenly at Alton, Hampshire, on November 12, 1865.

A few have borne me honor in my day,
Whether for thinking as themselves have thought
Or for what else I know not, nor inquire.
Among them some there are whose name will live
Not in the memories but the hearts of men,
Because those hearts they comforted and rais'd,
And, where they saw God's images cast down,
Lifted them up again, and blew the dust
From the worn feature and disfigured limb.
Such thou art, pure and mighty! such art thou,
Paraclete of the Bartons! Verse is mute
Or husky in this wintery eve of time,
And they who fain would sing can only cough:
We praise them even for that. Men now have left
The narrow field of well-trimm'd poetry
For fresher air and fuller exercise;
And they do wisely: I might do the same
If strength could gird and youth could garland me.
Imagination flaps her purple wing
Above the ancient laurels, and beyond.
There are brave voices that have never sung
Olympic feats or Isthmian; there are hands
Strong as were his who rein'd the fiery steeds
Of proud Achilles on the Phrygian plain;
There are clear eyes, eyes clear as those that pierced
Thro Paradise and Hell and all between.
The human heart holds more within its cell
Than universal Nature holds without.
This thou hast taught me, standing up erect
Where Avon's Genius and where Arno's meet.
I hear another voice, not thine nor theirs,
But clear, and issuing from the fount of Truth . . .
None can confer God's blessing but the poor,
None but the heavy-laden reach His throne.
—WALTER SAVAGE LANDOR, "To the Author of
Mary Barton," 1849

Of course you have read *Ruth* by this time. Its style was a great refreshment to me, from its finish and fulness. How women have the courage to write and publishers the spirit to buy at a high price the false and feeble representations of life and character that most feminine novels give, is a constant marvel to me. *Ruth,* with all its merits, will not be an enduring or classical fiction—will it? Mrs Gaskell seems to me to be constantly misled by a love of sharp contrasts—of "dramatic"

effects. She is not contented with the subdued colouring—the half tints of real life. Hence she agitates one for the moment, but she does not secure one's lasting sympathy; her scenes and characters do not become typical. But how pretty and graphic are the touches of description! That little attic in the minister's house, for example, which, with its pure white dimity bed-curtains, its bright-green walls, and the rich brown of its stained floor, remind one of a snowdrop springing out of the soil. Then the rich humour of Sally, and the sly satire in the description of Mr Bradshaw. Mrs Gaskell has certainly a charming mind, and one cannot help loving her as one reads her books.—GEORGE ELIOT, Letter to Mrs. Taylor (Feb. 1, 1853)

I am told, to my great astonishment, that you have heard painful speeches on account of *Ruth;* what was told me raised all my indignation and disgust.

Now I have read only a little (though, of course, I know the story) of the book; for the same reason that I cannot read *Uncle Tom's Cabin,* or *Othello,* or *The Bride of Lammermoor.* It is too painfully good, as I found before I had read half a volume.

But this I can tell you, that among all my large acquaintance I never heard, or have heard, but one unanimous opinion of the beauty and righteousness of the book, and that, above all, from real *ladies,* and really good women. If you could have heard the things which I heard spoken of it this evening by a thorough High Church fine lady of the world, and by her daughter, too, as pure and pious a soul as one need see, you would have no more doubt than I have, that whatsoever the 'snobs' and the bigots may think, English people, in general, have but one opinion of *Ruth,* and that is, one of utter satisfaction.

I doubt not you have had this said to you already often. Believe me, you may have it said to you as often as you will by the purest and most refined of English women.—CHARLES KINGSLEY, Letter to Elizabeth Gaskell (July 25, 1853), *Charles Kingsley: His Letters and Memories of His Life,* ed. Fanny E. Kingsley, 1877, pp. 180–81

Tell me if you have read Mrs. Gaskell's *Ruth.* That's a novel which I much admire. It is strong and healthy at once, teaching a moral frightfully wanted in English society. Such an interesting letter I had from Mrs. Gaskell a few days ago—

simple, worthy of *Ruth*. By the way, *Ruth* is a great advance on *Mary Barton*, don't you think so?—ELIZABETH BARRETT BROWNING, Letter to Mrs. Martin (Oct. 5, 1853)

Let me renew our long-interrupted acquaintance by complimenting you on poor Miss Brontë's *Life*. You have had a delicate and a great work to do, and you have done it admirably. Be sure that the book will do good. It will shame literary people into some stronger belief that a simple, virtuous, practical home life is consistent with high imaginative genius; and it will shame, too, the prudery of a not over cleanly, though carefully white-washed age, into believing that purity is now (as in all ages till now) quite compatible with the knowledge of evil. I confess that the book has made me ashamed of myself. *Jane Eyre* I hardly looked into, very seldom reading a work of fiction—yours, indeed, and Thackeray's are the only ones I care to open. *Shirley* disgusted me at the opening: and I gave up the writer and her books with the notion that she was a person who liked coarseness. How I misjudged her! and how thankful I am that I never put a word of my misconceptions into print, or recorded my misjudgments of one who is a whole heaven above me.

Well have you done your work, and given us the picture of a valiant woman made perfect by sufferings. I shall now read carefully and lovingly every word she has written, especially those poems, which ought not to have fallen dead as they did, and which seem to be (from a review in the current *Fraser*), of remarkable strength and purity. I must add that Mrs. Kingsley agrees fully with all I have said, and bids me tell you that she is more intensely interested in the book than in almost any which she has ever read.—CHARLES KINGSLEY, Letter to Elizabeth Gaskell (May 14, 1857), *Charles Kingsley: His Letters and Memories of His Life*, ed. Fanny E. Kingsley, 1877, pp. 269–70

For some years after her marriage Mrs. Gaskell lived a domestic life, busy with her children, and ordering her household and training her maids, for which indeed she had a special gift; then a terrible sorrow fell upon her, and we know how she began to write to divert her mind from brooding upon the loss of her only son.

In 1847 she had finished that noble book, *Mary Barton*, that book with 'a sob in it,' as the French critic says. '*Ah! quelle musique douloureuse dans un sanglot.*'

But there is something far beyond a sob in *Mary Barton*. The writer is writing of what she has lived, not only of what she has read or even looked at as she passed her way. It is true she read *Adam Smith* and studied *Social Politics*, but with that admirable blending of the imaginative and the practical qualities which was her gift, she knows how to stir the dry skeleton to life and reach her readers' hearts. Many books and novels dealing with the poor are touchingly expressed and finely conceived, but somehow this particular gift of the spirit is wanting; we admire the books without being ourselves absorbed by them. It is the difference in short between the light of genius and the rays of the prism analysed, calculated, divided. This power of living in the lives of others and calling others to share the emotion, does not mean, as people sometimes imagine, that a writer *copies* textually from the world before her, I have heard my father say that no author worth anything, deliberately, and as a rule, copies the subject before him. And so with Mrs. Gaskell. Her early impressions were vivid and dear to her, but her world, though coloured by remembrance and sympathy, was peopled by the fresh creations of her vivid imagination, not by stale copies of the people she had known.

Mary Barton made a great and remarkable sensation.

Carlyle, Landor, Miss Edgeworth praised and applauded, and nameless thousands also praised and read the noble outspoken book. 'Individuals may have complained,' so says the biographer, from whom I have so often quoted, 'but the work has unquestionably helped to make the manufacturing world very different from what it was forty years ago.'

The same intuition which guided her along the pleasant country lanes made her at home in the teeming streets and crowded alleys of Manchester.

A very interesting article by Monsieur Emile Montégut, written some thirty years ago, pays a fine tribute to Mrs. Gaskell's striking exposition of the life amidst which so much of her own was passed, to her depth of feeling, to her moderation of statement.

The article also, to my surprise, gives an answer to the little riddle I was trying to solve in my own mind as to the difference between the world of Cranford and that of Miss Austen. Each century possesses a force of its own, says the critic, one particular means of action, to the exclusion of others; it may be intelligence, it may be passion, it may be determination, each rules in turn.

In the sixteenth century *will* prevailed, and the character of the men and the martyrs of that time, were in value far beyond their convictions. In the eighteenth century, on the contrary, the ideas were worth more than the lives. Books and pamphlets were better than the men who wrote them. What is the force, says Mr. Montégut, of the age in which we ourselves are living? it is certainly not will, nor is it brilliant intelligence, as in the days of Voltaire. It is a quality which, for want of a better word, we will call 'the force of sentiment.' . . . 'People,' he continues, 'have little confidence in systems, a man with a hobby is immediately a butt, but a man who is not obliged to be right in order to guard his vanity, has but to describe in a few simple and true sentences some fact, some moral wrong which needs redressing, and see the effect, and the silent help which immediately follows, and for this reason it is that in literature we have seen of late the almost exclusive reign of fiction.' . . .

It is this quality of statement which we find in Mrs. Gaskell's books which distinguishes them from so many which preceded them, and which gives them their influence. It was because she had written *Mary Barton* that some deeper echoes reach us in *Cranford* than are to be found in any of Jane Austen's books, delightful as they are. Young people read books to learn about their lives which are to come, old people read them to forget the present; there is yet another class of readers, old and young, who read to find expression to the indefinite unshaped feelings by which they are haunted,—of all these will not each find response in the books of Elizabeth Gaskell, in *Ruth*, in *Cousin Phyllis*, in *Sylvia's Lovers*, in that last fine work which she never finished?

It must be remembered that Mrs. Gaskell wrote in the great time of literature, in the earlier part of the century. It remains for readers of this later time to see how nobly she held her own among the masters of her craft. 'She has done what we none of us could do,' said George Sand to Lord Houghton; 'she has written novels which excite the deepest interest in men of the world, and yet which every girl will be the better for reading.'

We all know what a friend Mrs. Gaskell proved herself to Charlotte Brontë, and what happiness this friendship brought to the author of *Jane Eyre*. Mrs. Gaskell had the gift of giving out in a very remarkable degree. Miss Brontë, as we all know, was tortured and imprisoned by shyness. 'She does not, and cannot care for me, for she does not know me, how should she,' Miss Brontë says, writing of a child of Mrs. Gaskell, but *that* child's mother did Charlotte Brontë justice, and guessed by happy intuition at the treasure concealed in the unpretending casket.—ANNE THACKERAY RITCHIE, "Preface" to *Cranford*, 1891, pp. xvi–xx

Her first novel, *Mary Barton*, published 1848, was an illustration of a life with which she was thoroughly acquainted, the life of Manchester, not only among its aristocracy of wealth (which she treats somewhat harshly), but among the labouring population of the factories, with all its strongly-marked characteristics. The passionate sense of shame mingled with the still more impassioned parental love which seeks and searches for the lost with the ardour of a primitive nature, even while overwhelmed by the weight of disgrace brought upon it—is always a noble and touching picture, and Mrs. Gaskell's perception of the true poetry and nobleness of this situation was much more elevated in fiction than in the after-portrayal of actual life above referred to. She could understand with the profound intuition of genius how the door should be open night and day for Lizzie's return, and the parent's heart ever intent for the tottering footsteps of the wanderer—although she did not hesitate to betray the secrets of poor Bramwell Brontë when the story was one of her own friends and class: thus proving how much more true is sometimes the instinct of art than the misleading guidance of fact and moral indignation.

Mary Barton at once established Mrs. Gaskell's reputation, which was confirmed by its successors. The story of *Ruth*, published in 1850, raised many criticisms and objections which may seem almost ridiculous in this advanced day. It is the old story of seduction, in which an innocent girl is ruined by over-trust in the immemorial villain of romance, but being taken up by compassionate strangers in a place where she is quite unknown, is introduced by them as a young widow, wins the respect of all around, and brings up her child in an atmosphere of almost excessive honour and purity. The harmless fraud was denounced by the critics with a warmth which it is difficult nowadays to understand. *Nous en avons bien vu d'autres*, and are no longer liable to be shocked by such a very pardonable device; though it entails trouble and sorrow we need not add, or it could scarcely have provided machinery enough for a novel. Among Mrs. Gaskell's other works we may mention *Sylvia's Lovers*, a striking and spirited romance, and the remarkable little record of village life, *Cranford*, with its little feminine genteel community in which a man is a startling intruder, in which the gentle benevolences and dove-like rancours of the little place are set forth with admirable fidelity and tenderness, in the subdued colours natural to such a landscape. Without either the keen vivacity or quiet force of Miss Austen, it is yet a book which may be placed on the same shelf with hers; and there could be no higher praise. It was received with an enthusiasm which has suffered no diminution by the course of years.

Mrs. Gaskell's last work, *Wives and Daughters*, which she left unfinished though very near its completion at her death, was a work of broader effects than any of the others, and was in many respects an almost perfect example of the best English novel of the time, a type much followed, and much weakened since.—MARGARET OLIPHANT, *The Victorian Age of English Literature*, 1892, Vol. 1, pp. 326–28

Mary Barton, her first and nearly her best book, appeared in 1848, and its vivid picture of Manchester life, assisted by its great pathos, naturally attracted attention at that particular time. *Cranford* (1853), in a very different style, something like a blend of Miss Mitford and Miss Austen, has been the most permanently popular of her works. *Ruth*, of the same year,

shocked precisians (which it need not have done), but is of much less literary value than *Mary Barton* or *Cranford*. Mrs. Gaskell, who was the biographer of Charlotte Brontë, produced novels regularly till her death in 1865, and never wrote anything bad, though it may be doubted whether anything but *Cranford* will retain permanent rank.—GEORGE SAINTSBURY, *A History of Nineteenth Century Literature*, 1896, p. 335

In the whole of English biographical literature there is no book that can compare in widespread interest with the *Life of Charlotte Brontë* by Mrs. Gaskell. It has held a position of singular popularity for nearly sixty years; and while biography after biography has come and gone, it still commands a place side by side with Boswell's *Johnson* and Lockhart's *Scott*. As far as mere readers are concerned, it may indeed claim its hundreds as against the tens of intrinsically more important rivals. There are obvious reasons for this success. Mrs. Gaskell was herself a popular novelist, who commanded a very wide audience, and *Cranford*, at least, has taken a place among the classics of our literature. She brought to bear upon the biography of Charlotte Brontë all those literary gifts which made the charm of her seven volumes of romance. And these gifts were employed upon a romance of real life, not less fascinating than anything which imagination could have furnished.

⟨. . .⟩ It is quite certain that Charlotte Brontë would not stand on so splendid a pedestal to-day but for the single-minded devotion of her accomplished biographer.—CLEMENT K. SHORTER, *Charlotte Brontë and Her Circle*, 1896, pp. 1, 20

The time may come, peradventure it is even now with us, when the distinction or difference between authors and authoresses will needs be obliterated from any critical survey of the progress of English prose. Whether or not Mrs. Gaskell would have derived any special joy from witnessing the advent of such an epoch, is a more or less idle inquiry; as a matter of fact, although in her way herself a classic writer of English prose, besides being the standard biographer of another, she lived not in a new literary age, but in a period of transition. Beyond a doubt this helps to explain the remarkable contrasts, as well as developments, observable in her style and manner as a writer; although nothing could be more obvious than that it was a conscious restraint of her powers, rather than the granting of a free hand to them, which enabled her genius to concentrate instead of dissipating the efforts of a maturity that knew no decay. In *Mary Barton*, her first and to this day most famous book, Mrs. Gaskell asserted the right of treating serious social problems sentimentally—a woman's right if ever there was one, although women have not always agreed as to which are really the serious problems of society. She vindicated her claim by means of that kind of pathos which comes straight from the heart and goes straight to it, and which, being in this instance fed by just observation not less than by intense sympathy, was already here and there relieved by touches of the humour so characteristic of her later works. Yet it may, notwithstanding, be said of her that her literary reputation was more than half made before she began fully to form her literary manner. In my judgment, the example of Dickens counted for not a little in the process; and to his art her own, without forfeiting at any time its originality, was more signally indebted than was the craft of his hundred imitators to the mannerisms of the master. It has been little noticed, though the phenomenon is full of interest to the students of style, that Mrs. Gaskell had already with conspicuous success essayed what in the absence of dates would inevitably have been set down as her "later" manner, while she was still following to all appearance her earlier lines of composition. The majority of the *Cranford* papers appeared in *Household Words* before *Ruth* was published; and *North and South*, where no doubt a growth of something beyond form is to be noted, was completed some time later. The charm of *Cranford*, although perhaps a little fainter than of old, now that associations of time and place have lost much of their force, is still very real, and the little book will always be treasured by those for'whom the miniatures of the early part of the century have an irresistible attraction. When, after the strain to which Mrs. Gaskell had been subjected by the publication of her *Life of Charlotte Brontë*, a masterpiece, in spite of all early cavils and later supplements, she returned to fiction, she proved to have finally formed the style which is inalienably her own. Its exquisite delicacy of texture and tender grace, subduing but not concealing an irony which is the secret of the finest of English humorous prose, characterise each of her last three fictions. Of these, *Sylvia's Lovers* probably displays the greatest intensity of feeling, together with the most vivid individual colouring, while the (nominally) incomplete *Wives and Daughters* is enlivened by the most masterly management of the tranquil sidelights of pure and playful humour. But the choicest gem of all is the idyll of *Cousin Phillis*, simply set in surroundings which seem as if designed to reveal mysteries of poetic feeling destined to remain for ever peculiar to English art, whose inspiration is drawn from the life of English homes.

The biography of Mrs. Gaskell, we know, is likely to remain unwritten; and though literary criticism must chafe against conditions which impair its force, the restriction may in this instance not prove wholly disadvantageous. Something may be learnt by guessing, instead of being taught in detail, how a self-control which matured a literary style as strong as it is tender, and as subtle as it is sweet, reflected the wondrously diversified experiences of a pure and disciplined woman's life.—ADOLPHUS WILLIAM WARD, "Mrs. Gaskell," *English Prose*, ed. Henry Craik, 1896, Vol. 5, pp. 523–24

⟨. . .⟩ she has written one or two short books which are technically faultless, and might be taken as types of the novel form. Strange to say, the recognition of her delicate and many-sided genius has never been quite universal, and has endured periods of obscuration. Her work has not the personal interest of Thackeray's, nor the intense unity and compression of Charlotte Brontë's. It may even be said that Mrs Gaskell suffers from having done well too many things. She wrote, perhaps, a purer and a more exquisite English than either of her rivals, but she exercised it in too many fields. Having in *Mary Barton* (1848) treated social problems admirably, she threw off a masterpiece of humorous observation in *Cranford*, returned in a different mood to manufacturing life in *North and South*, conquered the pastoral episode in *Cousin Phillis*, and died, more than rivalling Anthony Trollope, in the social-provincial novel of *Wives and Daughters*. Each of these books might have sustained a reputation; they were so different that they have stood somewhat in one another's way. But the absence of the personal magnetism—emphasised by the fact that all particulars regarding the life and character of Mrs. Gaskell have been sedulously concealed from public knowledge—has determined a persistent undervaluation of this writer's gifts, which were of a very high, although a too miscellaneous order.—EDMUND GOSSE, *A Short History of Modern English Literature*, 1897, pp. 355–56

Senior in years to the Brontës was the biographer of Charlotte, Elizabeth Cleghorn Gaskell. Mrs. Gaskell's fame was won chiefly as a novelist, but, both for its intrinsic merits and as a

memorial of a most interesting literary friendship, her *Life of Charlotte Brontë* deserves mention. If not equal to the best biographies in the language, it is worthy of a place in the class nearest to that small group. It gives a delightful impression both of the subject of the memoir and of her biographer. There was sufficient difference between the two to make Mrs. Gaskell's generous appreciation peculiarly creditable to her. Two contemporaries of the same sex, reared amidst men closely akin in character, and confronted, as *Mary Barton* and *Shirley* prove, by similar social problems, could hardly present a greater contrast than there is between Charlotte Brontë and Mrs. Gaskell; the former austere, intense, prone to exaggeration and deficient in humour; the latter genial, balanced, and among the most successful of female humourists. The contrast extended to the personal appearance of the two women. Charlotte Brontë was plain and diminutive, while in her youth Mrs. Gaskell was strikingly beautiful.

The events of Mrs. Gaskell's life were almost wholly literary. Her first novel, *Mary Barton*, published in 1848, remains to this day probably her best known, though not her most perfect book. It deals with the industrial state of Lancashire during the crisis of 1842, and it won, by its vivid and touching picture of the life of the poor, the admiration of some of the most distinguished literary men of the time. The subject was gradually drawing more attention. The evils which begot the socialism of Robert Owen and drew the protests of Carlyle and of Ebenezer Elliott had been brought into prominence by the Luddite riots and by Chartism. Most of the novelists were awakening to a sense of them. Disraeli had anticipated Mrs. Gaskell; and Kingsley as well as Charlotte Brontë followed her. The treatment varies greatly. Mrs. Gaskell, like Kingsley, has much more sympathy with socialism than Charlotte Brontë has. The social aspects of *Mary Barton* caused it to be admired and praised on the one hand, and to be censured on the other, for reasons outside the domain of art; but on the whole they certainly increased its popularity.

The success of *Mary Barton* won for Mrs. Gaskell an invitation from Dickens to contribute to *Household Words*, and some of her best work, including *Cranford* (1851–1853) and *North and South* (1854–1855), first appeared there. She was also a contributor to the *Cornhill*, where her last story, *Wives and Daughters*, was running when she died, with startling suddenness, in 1865.

'George Sand, only a few months before Mrs. Gaskell's death, observed to Lord Houghton: "Mrs. Gaskell has done what neither I nor other female writers in France can accomplish; she has written novels which excite the deepest interest in men of the world, and yet which every girl will be the better for reading."' This is high praise; and it is deserved. It must not indeed be pressed to mean that Mrs. Gaskell is the equal in genius, far less the superior, of writers like George Sand or George Eliot. Neither is she the equal of her friend, Charlotte Brontë. There is a sweep of imagination and a touch of poetry in *Jane Eyre* quite beyond the reach of Mrs. Gaskell. But her work is at once free from weakness and wholly innocent. She is of all the more remarkable female novelists of this period the most feminine. The traits of sex are numerous in her books, but they never appear unpleasantly. Her women are generally better than her men; yet her men are not such monsters as the Brontës loved to depict. On the contrary, she is fond of painting men of quiet worth, such as the country doctor whose 'virtues walk their narrow round,' who lives unknown, but who is sadly missed when he dies. Her best stories are quiet tales of the life of villages and small towns, and they show the shrewd, kindly, genial observation with which all her life she regarded those around her. She was happy in her own domestic life, and she believed that life in general, though chequered, was happy too. In her picture of human nature the virtues on the whole prevail over the vices.

Mrs. Gaskell saw everything in the light of a sympathetic humour. It is this quality that has served hitherto as salt to her books and has preserved their flavour while that of a great deal of more ambitious literature has been lost. If her humour is not equal to the best specimens of that of George Eliot, it is more diffused; if less powerful, it is gentler and quite as subtle. In style she is easy and flowing; and her later books show more freedom than her first attempt. At the same time, her writing rarely rises to eloquence. She had more talent than genius. She has created many good, but no great characters; and she stands midway between Thackeray and Dickens, who are emphatically men of genius, and writers like Trollope who, with abundant talent and exhaustless industry, have no genius whatever.—HUGH WALKER, *The Age of Tennyson*, 1897, pp. 106–8

Hardly aspiring to the title of novelist, she frequently reminded her public that she was writing only tales. These tales were told in the first person, and for the moral edification of her own sex. In form and aim they are accordingly of the Edgeworth type. Indeed Mrs. Gaskell may be said, in a general way, to have performed in them the same noble service to her contemporaries that Maria Edgeworth did to hers. She entered into the thoughts and wayward moods of children with true insight; she gave us the first English nurses and housekeepers of hard common sense and racy wit, the Nancys and the Sallys. Her style, too, at times is most felicitous, as when she says: 'Edith came down upon her feet a little bit sadder; with a romance blown to pieces'—a sentence which in the natural course of events should have been written by George Meredith. One province she discovered and made her own—feminine society in out-of-the-way towns and villages before the encroachment of railroads and penny postage. Of this life *Cranford* (1853) is the classic. Here is described the old-style etiquette, the genteel poverty, the formal calls, and evening parties, of a village wholly in the possession of the Amazons—widows and spinsters—where no men are tolerated, except the country doctor, who is allowed to stay there occasionally over-night when on his long circuit. Old maids spend their time in tea-drinking and stale gossip, and in chasing sunbeams from their carpets. Before going to bed they peep beneath the white dimity valance or roll a ball under it, to be sure no Iachimo with 'great fierce face' lies concealed there. So ends the day of trivialities and Gothic fears. *The Moorland Cottage* (1850) will always have a special interest, for George Eliot in *The Mill on the Floss* revivified some of its incidents and characters: the water, Maggie, the stubborn 'little brown mouse,' her tyrannical brother Edward, and her fault-finding mother.

Ruth (1853), which probably long ago departed from the imagination of novel readers, occupies a very important position in the history of English fiction, for it follows certain ethical lines more ostensibly than any previous novel—what may be called the doctrine of the act and its train of good or evil. 'All deeds,' says Mrs. Gaskell, 'however hidden and long passed by have their eternal consequences.' The doctrine was not new to literature, for it was not new to observation. Macbeth hesitated to assassinate Duncan, for he feared there might issue from the deed a series of extremely disagreeable events over which he could have no control. This ethical theory, which Carlyle and likewise Comte were popularizing, Mrs. Gaskell employed for unifying her plot. Ruth is an attractive sewing-girl, who at the age of sixteen is betrayed by a young gentleman and abandoned. At the point of suicide, she is rescued by a Dissenting minister, who takes her and the child into his home, where at the suggestion of his spinster sister, she passes for a widow. In the course of time Ruth's offence and the parson's deceit are suddenly and unexpectedly revealed, and then follows the retribution. The respectable part of the parson's congregation deserts him; and Ruth, shunned by the village folk, becomes nurse to patients in typhus fever, from one of whom (who turns out to be her former lover) she is infected, and dies. Mrs. Gaskell works her scenes up to crises, where some one must make a decision as to his course of action, to what she once called 'the pivot on which the fate of years moved'; and then she studies the influence of the act on a small group of characters. The motives and the constraining circumstances that lead to the decision are analyzed in detail: We know precisely why Ruth makes her early mistake and why the parson conceals it; and two pages are devoted to cataloguing the reasons why a country gentleman takes his candidate for Parliament to a luxurious house by the sea to pass Sunday. —WILBUR L. CROSS, *The Development of the English Novel*, 1899, pp. 234–36

GEORGE BARNETT SMITH
From "Mrs. Gaskell and Her Novels"

Cornhill Magazine, February 1874, pp. 194–212

The several stages of our author's career may be said to be marked by three of her works, though the lines of demarcation in her case are not so apparent as in most writers; for she appears in her first widely-known work to have attained a power of expression very rarely witnessed in the maturest efforts of those of her order. Still, were we expected to define clearly the various stages of progress which she has attained —or rather to note the influence of time in ripening her gifts— we should direct attention to the first, the middle, and the final stage of her genius—into each of which divisions we should be able, we imagine, to classify her work. The novel which first fixed public attention, and which belongs to the first stage, was *Mary Barton*; that which marks the second is *Sylvia's Lovers*; and that illustrative of the third is *Wives and Daughters*. Each of these works presents considerable points of difference, while they are all at the same time stamped by the genuine impress of genius. Several others could be cited, which for particular qualities may even be superior to those named; but they do not so decisively show Mrs. Gaskell at her best, or her pen animated by the varied charms which these books individually and indisputably discover. The charge has been made that Mrs. Gaskell was but a member of "that school of novelists which her friend Charlotte Brontë inaugurated;" but after a careful study, and possessing a somewhat intimate acquaintance with all that the two have accomplished, we are bound to say that the charge appears to us to have no foundation. In fact, there is a considerable difference in method, as there was a considerable difference in gifts, between the two. The only grounds for the comparison which has been made are these— that the two have successfully dealt with certain phases of Northern English life, and that both, perhaps, have been most successful in their delineation of female character. These are the ostensible grounds assigned. But note the differences. Charlotte Brontë, while possessing, undoubtedly we think, the greater genius, exhibited a much narrower range than Mrs. Gaskell. Such characters as have established the fame of the former are but few in number, though they stand out from the canvas with a Rembrandt-like effect, compelling one to own that we are conversing with real flesh and blood—heroes and heroines drawn because of the circulation of their own blood, and not for the "circulation" of the libraries alone. This is the quality which made the slight, pale country girl famous almost against her will. Again: her men are as powerful as her women—at least in most cases this is so; so that it is not just to assert that she is principally distinguished for her portraiture of her own sex. But that quality which chiefly marks her off from Mrs. Gaskell is her intensity, and any one reading her various enthralling books will acknowledge that this is unmistakeable. Mrs. Gaskell, too, is realistic and intense to a great degree; but this quality, which seems reserved for almost the very highest kinds of genius in its fullest manifestation, is veiled in her by a general excellence which the other did not possess. The modes of life pursued by the two may have had some influence on the development of their talent. The author of *Jane Eyre*, far away on those melancholy Yorkshire moors, asked for nothing but solitude, save that dozen or score of characters with whom she acquired close fellowship, and whom she has rendered immortal. She individualized even the very stones and the trees about her. Mrs. Gaskell, on the other hand, possessed a much wider vision. Having, indubitably, by nature, a great faculty of reading human character, her canvas was necessarily more crowded than that of her friend, and frequently she was unable to arrest herself and complete her individual sketches with the same minuteness. In individualization, she was confessedly Charlotte Brontë's inferior, as she also was George Eliot's, and for that reason a higher position must be accorded to those writers; but in grouping she was inferior to neither, and there are sketches of life in her books which for fulness and variety of detail are almost unrivalled.

Turning to the works themselves, let us take up for a little while *Mary Barton*, the volume by which our author first became distinguished. It is a picture of Manchester life, as its title-page states, and never, in the whole range of novels founded so closely upon fact as this, has the story been made more realizable to the reader. One would think that it was well nigh impossible for the grinders of the poor to read the opening chapters of this story, and still go on heaping up their gains, while they cared little whether those who were instrumental in their accumulation perished by the roadside. The workman's side of the labour question was never more forcibly depicted than in the following passages, which during the last fifty years have now and again been the inarticulate cry of thousands who lacked the power of uttering definite and appropriate language: "At all times it is a bewildering thing to the poor weaver to see his employer removing from house to house, each one grander than the last, till he ends in building one more magnificent than all, or withdrawing his money from the concern, or sell his mill, to buy an estate in the country, while all the time the weaver, who thinks he and his fellows are the real makers of this wealth, are struggling on for bread for his children, through the vicissitudes of lowered wages, short hours, fewer hands employed, &c. And when he knows trade is bad, and could understand (at least partially) that there are not buyers enough in the market to purchase the goods already made, and consequently that there is no demand for more; when he would bear and endure much without complaining, could he also see that his employers were bearing their share; he is, I say, bewildered, and (to use his own word), aggravated, to see that all goes on just as usual with the mill-owners. Large houses are still occupied, while spinners' and weavers' cottages stand empty, because the families which once filled them are obliged to live in rooms or cellars. Carriages still roll along the streets, concerts are still crowded by subscribers, the shops for expensive luxuries still find daily customers, while the workman loiters away his unemployed time in watching these things, and thinking of the pale, uncomplaining wife at home, and the wailing children asking in vain for enough of food,—of the sinking health, of the dying life of those near and dear to him. The contrast is too great." Of course, while there is much truth in this presentment of the case of the workman, Mrs. Gaskell is too conscientious to hide the fact that the other side might be somewhat less harshly stated. But the arguments she employed were those felt by John Barton; and can we wonder at his querulousness when we follow the story, and learn that his mother died from absolute want of the necessaries of life, and that his only son, the apple of his eye, who could only be kept alive by the very best nourishment, also became a corpse through starvation? It is the position of Barton, and such as he, towards the upper classes, their employers, which Mrs. Gaskell set herself to place before the world in this story to which we are referring. Every page teems with evidence of the close knowledge the author had acquired of her topic; and the tragic history related is almost sufficient to blind us to the merit of the book, when regarded as a purely literary effort. From page to page of the narrative we are hurried on, now getting glimpses of a poverty-stricken hovel, and now being introduced to the mansions of the millionaires; again being treated to a glowing description of a mill on fire. The story is too sad a one to write, except by a noble, large-hearted woman—one in whom the fire of benevolence has been kindled by the Divine. Such a being it is who has penned it, and thereby testified for ever her love for suffering, toiling humanity. And after all that she must have seen of the degradation and loathsomeness attaching to many of those whose life-stories she must have probed, it is cheering to hear her say as she does of those who are frequently termed the "dregs" of society:—"There was faith such as the rich can never imagine on earth; there was love strong as death; and self-denial among rude, coarse men, akin to that of Sir Philip Sidney's most glorious deed. The vices of the poor sometimes astound us here; but when the secrets of all hearts shall be made known, their virtues will astound us in far greater degree." We should not be loth to dwell long amid the lights (of which, however, there are few) and the shadows of this book, which was fraught with an interest rarely paralleled in fiction. The poor have here their interpreter. She stands and pours forth the tale of their sufferings into the ear of the rich. That ear, which had hitherto been almost closed to the story, must perforce open now when one appeals to it who has power to deliver the message with which she is charged. It may be painful to read the record, but it should be done. ⟨. . .⟩

Such is the novel by which Mrs. Gaskell first largely gained the public ear; and whilst from the barest outline of the plot we have no difficulty in apprehending why it should have secured general popularity, so, on a study of the book itself, we shall not be astonished that it has almost passed into a classic. In regarding it as an example of Mrs. Gaskell's first stage, we should say that it exhibits, first, force; secondly, truthfulness; and thirdly, concentrativeness. Yet let it not be understood that these qualities are absent from any other work of the author; the fact being simply that, though they may not be so apparent individually in the later novels, it is because they are attended by other graces of composition. The examples we have already cited from *Mary Barton* will demonstrate the first quality, that of force or power; as regards the second, in her construction of the work the author has not suffered herself to be bound by the canons then in vogue as to the writing of novels. She has dared to throw off the trammels, and challenged the reading world with a story which in the hands of a tyro would have been blurred in many of its incidents, tampered with in some of its characters, and probably made altogether to result in a complete fiasco. Perfection is found neither with the rich or the poor to the exclusion of the other; but wrong is never suffered to appear under false colours. About its true designation, aspect, and final arraignment we are allowed to make no mistake. The way of the world in conniving so that "offence's gilded hand may shove by justice" meets with no approval from her; nor, on the other hand, are the poor allowed to suppose that their poverty or wrongs are to absolve them from the exhibition of those virtues which should be common to humanity. Yet, rigid moralist as she is, the woman's heart of sympathy for aught that is unfortunate or miserable throbs through all the words she has penned. And probably this is another reason why the book cannot be easily laid aside by any who are interested in the psychological dissection of their species. The quality of concentrativeness we have mentioned, though apparently trenching on that of force, is really a different quality altogether when speaking of Mrs. Gaskell as a writer. The force refers more to the qualities of the author herself in the expression of her thoughts; the concentrativeness refers to the absolute imprisonment of emotion in a few pages. In very few writers is there less diffusiveness in this respect than in the author of *Mary Barton*. We read page after page, come upon scene after scene, which excites the emotional nature to a very high degree. What appears to be a laborious effort with many in regard to the enlistment of feeling is a work of comparative ease with her. ⟨. . .⟩

The question of the unequal distribution of pain and pleasure—a question which has agitated every thinking mind at some period of its history since Time began—is dealt with in *Sylvia's Lovers*. But to all questioning and deep searching we are left at the close to say with Tennyson, "Behind the veil, behind the veil!" The confession is once more forced, that none ever meet exactly with their due share of either joy or sorrow. The lots are changed, and the deserving are very frequently apportioned the "severer discipline." Mrs. Gaskell, however, be her beliefs right or wrong, has this advantage, that she is unwavering in her inculcation of the highest principles. Yet again she almost overweights her work with the tragic element. Look at the life of Sylvia Robson, and see what is set against the one great charm of personal beauty which she possesses. Her heart is incessantly probed to its very depths by trouble, and when at last she is represented as almost purified from the dross of mortality, it is only by the loss of all which she had at one period imagined to be necessary for her happiness. Hope springs out of the death of the lower pleasures, the pleasures which delight, but do not really touch the depth of the soul's need. A remarkable contrast is witnessed in this respect between Mrs. Gaskell's treatment of the deepest moral and spiritual questions and that of many other writers. One would think, to read scores of works of fiction which issue from the press, that to eat, drink, and be well clothed and housed were the chief and almost only ends of existence. We generally find, at least, that material riches and a coarse kind of happiness are heaped upon the heroes and heroines who are presented to us. And thus, for the most part, in being robbed of their truth to mortal destiny, these lives present no points of sympathy wherein we can be at one. The only result of the novels themselves is to please the fancy, and give a spice of enjoyment to what is by no means the higher part of our nature. In *Sylvia's Lovers* Mrs. Gaskell has been true to humanity as it has been brought before her. She is perfectly

just. Sylvia is no imaginary portrait. How vividly her life realizes the anguish which rends the heart behind many an exterior which seems to be fair! Her character is beautiful, but it is not perfect—we had almost said it was so beautiful because it was *not* perfect. The idea is that it is not impossible; the touches of human weakness at once make Sylvia a part and parcel of that common race to which we all belong. She is not exalted by a fancied perfection up to a sphere into which so many heroines are translated, but which none of the living women ever attain. Philip, too, her husband, has had his imperfections; and, when, after far journeyings, he returns home at last, it is to die. The two, in their moment of understanding each other, are separated by the icy hand of Death. To the question, "What hope of answer or redress?" there is only, we once more remark, the answer of the Poet Laureate.

We mentioned this story as illustrative of the second stage of Mrs. Gaskell's literary career; and for this reason, that it indicates a superior finish to many of her previous novels. It is evident that the author's powers were maturing. There is a greater grasp not only of character but of actual expression, though, as we have said, all her writings are singular for their strength. Life on the North-eastern coast is delineated with perfect skill, the separate studies of Monkshaven fishermen and others being marked with great *verve* and completeness. The story of the press-gang, that institution flourishing in good King George's time, by which his Majesty's subjects were liable to be seized and carried away to the wars by main force, is graphically told, and the horrors which attend it, if history and recollection are to be relied upon, are drawn without the slightest exaggeration. For touches of pathos, the account of the sailor's funeral, and the proceedings subsequent to the arrest of Sylvia's father, Daniel Robson, for the attack on the King's representatives, leave nothing to be desired, whilst the whole scene between the dying Philip and Sylvia is strikingly emotional. Then there is the disappointment of Hester, who loves Philip Hepburn with an intensity rarely witnessed in women, whilst he, on the contrary, is devoted heart and soul to Sylvia, whose affections have long been centred on the handsome Kinraid, a character which is likewise finished in the author's best style. ⟨. . .⟩

There only remains now one work of this gifted and lamented author upon which to offer some observations. And this is in all respects the completest as a work of fiction (as it is the best) which has proceeded from her pen. *Wives and Daughters* exhibits the rich genius of Mrs. Gaskell in its last stage, when perfection had been attained, or at least a perfection as near as can be pointed to in any author. Unfinished as she left it, it still remains for us the best of all her novels, and one which can be recommended to all of her order as a specimen of purity, strength, and sweetness. It has not the quicksilver vivacity of Dickens, the poetic glow of Bulwer, or the wonderful dissection and penetration of Thackeray; but, in addition to a moderate development of the qualities for which these masters were famous, there is a radiating human affection beaming through all its pages. We are robbed of one scene, which in the hands of the author would have been inimitable, viz. the confession of Roger Hamley's love to Molly after his return, and the manner in which the confession would have been received by that charming heroine. There was much to tell in one chapter, we are informed, had the author but lived to tell it. The two persons who have all along been favourites with the reader are of course to be married; and one little anecdote which Mrs. Gaskell intended to relate of Cynthia Kirkpatrick is very characteristic. After her brother-in-law had become a celebrated traveller, his name was mentioned in certain circles which Cynthia frequented, with surprise, as being connected with her family: but it had never occurred to her to mention the little fact. The reticence of some people is almost as remarkable a phenomenon as the silence of others. We think that, had Mrs. Gaskell lived, she would have given to the world a series of novels scarcely inferior to any which we have received from our best known writers of fiction. *Wives and Daughters* abundantly proves this. Regarded either as a piece of writing, or as a reproduction of character, it will stand a severe scrutiny. The only possible fault which might have a basis or foundation in fact is, that the style is never strong to overwhelming. It does not crush one by its force. The book is told rather with quietness than demonstration of power; but when the pathos comes it is natural and unstrained. It reflects the purity of the author's own mind: we see her lifted away from the grosser pursuits of earth, and beckoning those for whom she is writing to come away also into the purer air. Of course we do not escape the narration of trouble, misunderstanding, and regret; that would be for the writer to miss the highest part of her vocation, which is to teach through the ordinary media of all novelists. The plot of this book is of the most meagre description; it makes no demand on our faculties of wonder; it touches at times the springs of humour, and passes away again to call into action those of emotion. The simplest of human lives, with the most ordinary and peaceful of careers, in the majority of cases, are the groundwork of the narrative. But now see what the author has made of her materials. Where shall we find characters more carefully drawn than those of the two brothers Osborne and Roger Hamley, and Cynthia Kirkpatrick? In her way, the last-named is equal to Maggie Tulliver. It is perfect in finish—there is nothing to be desired, and no flaw to be found in the delineation. The same may be said of Osborne Hamley, a most difficult character to draw, and one which requires the negative power of repression in an author as well as the positive power of protrusion. We see less of this personage than of any other through the novel, and yet, on closing it, the figure of Osborne Hamley is one of the most abiding impressions left upon the memory. But a few touches here and there have given us an insight into the mind of the Squire's heir, and the fuller details we obtain of his brother do not suffice to hide him from the view. The same remark also applies to Cynthia. Although early impregnated with a feeling for her half pity, half abhorrence, there is no person whose fortunes kindle the kind of interest we feel in her to such a pitch, or in whose development and final goal we feel more concerned. At the moment she arrives at Mr. Gibson's from France we discover her disposition, and the full manifestation is only a question of time. The few glimpses of aristocratic life obtained are also true, and the aristocrats themselves are human beings, and not mere eccentricities or monstrosities, as is too often the case with sketches and portraits of beings of the upper classes. The amusing element in the story is supplied mostly through the aid of Mrs. Kirkpatrick (afterwards Gibson), whose character, however, is more contemptible than humorous in itself. Still, it is often individuals of this description who are provocative of considerable mirth in others. Her determined angling for Mr. Gibson as her second husband causes some amusement, not unmingled with a disgust akin to that the unfortunate man himself must have felt when he discovered that he had requested a scheming widow to become his wife, and that the chances of the union had been patronizingly discussed beforehand by Lord and Lady Cumnor. But it is a relief to get away from these people into the company of Molly, Mr. Gibson's daughter, and

a most bewitching heroine, though withal as sensible and staid a young lady as any whose acquaintance we make in our rambles through novels. For a time it seems as though misfortune and scheming were in combination to keep her out of the only position we can conceive possible for her—that of Roger Hamley's wife. Blindly and stupidly, perhaps, this youth is attracted by the superior brilliancy of Cynthia, and the exposed surface of her character. He never troubles himself to ask whether there is anything really worthy beneath the showy exterior, and it is when adversity alone demonstrates as usual the true metal of the real heroine that he awakes to the knowledge of the vast superiority of Molly over her attractive sister. It is only when trouble falls upon others that she appears to the best advantage. Then her woman's nature exhibits itself, and she pours forth the stream of long pent-up tenderness. Stay—one person had all along known her heart—Mr. Gibson could testify that it was as free of guile as it was eager to do good for others. Of all characters which seem to bear upon them the stamp of earthly perfection, this is one of the best. It seems to need no purifying, for there is no period when it appears to be mingled with dross. It is the veritable gold of human nature. ⟨. . .⟩

Finally, in stating the qualities for which, as a novelist, Mrs. Gaskell is most conspicuous, we should enumerate them in the following order:—individuality, force, truthfulness, and purity. As regards the first-named quality no one would be inclined to dispute her possession of it after reading *Mary Barton, Ruth,* or *Wives and Daughters.* The power of detaching a human unit, with all its special thoughts, griefs, hopes, and fears, from the rest of its kind, is in full force in all the works we have named. Indeed, there is scarcely any contemporary author who has excelled her in this respect. But upon that quality, and also upon her force or power, we have sufficiently enlarged already. Concerning the truthfulness of Mrs. Gaskell there is room for genuine approval. Into whatever sphere of life she conveys her readers, they are conscious that there is no exaggeration, no undue exaltation of this person, and no undue depression of the other. Upon this estimable quality we should be inclined to build most fearlessly for her assurance of immortality. Yet while there is no quality which should singly so well ensure it, if any work is to live and have a constant impression upon successive generations it must be combined with qualities which may seem humbler, but which in reality have more vitality in them from the fact that however the world changes their special power remains the same. Let Mrs. Gaskell's novels be read after the lapse of a hundred years, and one feels that the verdict delivered then would be that they were penned by the hand of a true observer—one who not only studied human nature with a desire, but a capacity, to comprehend it. This is one of the great motive powers which will ever keep the name of the author green in the public remembrance. The other principal quality to assist this consummation is purity. We were struck in reading her various volumes with this fact—that there is really less in them than there is in most other authors which she herself could wish to be altered. In fact, there is no purer author in modern times. And what has she lost by being pure? Has she failed to give a fair representation of any class of human beings whom she professes to depict? Not one; and her work stands now as an excellent model for those who would avoid the tendencies of the sensuous school, and would seek another basis upon which to acquire a reputation which should have some chances of durability. The author of *Wives and Daughters* will never cease to hold a high place in our regard. Could she do so we should despair for the future of fiction in England. Hers was one of those spirits which led the way to a purer day. The darkness out of which she assisted to bring us with her healthful work is passing away; and it is well to remember, in the splendour of a superior light, our indebtedness to those luminaries—conspicuous amongst whom is the writer whose works have passed in review—who first lifted the veil of the Cimmerian darkness which at one period threatened to envelop our imaginative literature.

WILLIAM MINTO
From "Mrs. Gaskell's Novels"
Fortnightly Review, September 1878, pp. 355–69

In all probability it was *Sybil* that suggested to Mrs. Gaskell the idea of writing *Mary Barton*. Mrs. Gaskell had acquired without conscious effort all the knowledge that Mr. Disraeli laboured to obtain by hurried special study and daring exercise of the imagination. Mr. Disraeli had thrown himself heartily into his task—had spent days and nights over the reports of select committees and royal commissions, had gone down in person to the manufacturing districts, had seen the mills at work, inspected the work-people in their squalid dens, watched them in their glittering temples of amusement, learnt to talk familiarly of "butties" and "doddies," and to explain the mysteries of the "Wadding Hole." For once he had conquered his repugnance to details. But he would have been more than mortal if he had acquired as intimate a knowledge of the poor nation as Mrs. Gaskell had done. She had lived amongst them; her position as the wife of a dissenting minister gave her a privileged access to their homes, of which she availed herself with all the frankness of a tender-hearted energetic woman; and she so won their confidence by her unaffected kindliness, that they spoke to her and laid bare all the incidents of their struggle for existence as freely as if she had been one of themselves. Mr. Disraeli knew the working classes as a traveller knows the botany of a strange country, which he has examined for the purpose of discovering a new staple of commerce. Mrs. Gaskell knew them as an ardent naturalist knows the flora of his own neighbourhood.

When I say that *Mary Barton* was probably suggested by *Sybil*, I do not of course intend to detract from Mrs. Gaskell's originality, to represent her as an imitator or a plagiarist, or even to imply that she was moved to write by a conscious spirit of emulation. I have tried to follow one line of the literary pedigree of Mrs. Gaskell's novels, only because it is interesting to trace how in the world of literature the vital principles are transmitted, and every plant in any cross-section that we may take of the stream of literary history owes the fact that it lives at all to something which has lived before and has blossomed and borne fruit and launched its fertilising seeds upon the great current. I am aware that such pedigree-hunting is a speculative and precarious amusement, and I do not wish to claim for it either scientific exactness or thrilling interest. To trace the influence of one writing upon another is almost as difficult and uncertain as to follow the course of the erratic thistledown with its life-giving burden, and as an employment is only one degree less idle. It is much simpler and perhaps more profitable to determine the larger influences, the permanent and the ephemeral social conditions, that contribute to the genesis of a literary plant, and supply it with sap and fibre. We could have predicted beforehand that the great wave of reforming aspiration and activity which swept over our community in the second quarter of this century, and had not subsided in the third, though now it would seem to have spent its force, would infallibly make itself felt in every branch of literature as well as in the other incorporate members of the body politic. We could also have predicted that the novel, so quick to catch and reflect the passing moods of society, would in an especial degree feel the force of this influence. We might even have predicted that foremost in the good work to which the reformers were inspired, of averting the threatened national disintegration by conciliating the antagonism of classes, would be found women of genius, breeders of strife in peaceful times, but quite as often in the world's history evangelists of reunion and mediators between inflamed combatants.

Mrs. Gaskell may never have read *Sybil*. It was enough that she had heard of this high political attempt to find a *modus vivendi* between "the two nations—the Poor and the Rich." Even that impulse may not have been wanted. She may have resolved to become an interpreter between the working multitude and their wealthy employers, without thinking of the fact that the office had already been assumed; this at least, we may be sure, was but a small part of her motive. She has herself told us how she was directly stirred to write *Mary Barton* by seeing before her eyes in Manchester so many sad instances of the embittered hostility between employers and employed. She believed that much of this hostility arose from mutual ignorance, and that she would do a service to both classes if she could bring them to a better understanding of each other. More particularly, comparing what she knew of them with what she heard about them from manufacturers and their organs in the press, she was convinced that the workmen were misunderstood by their masters, that due allowance was not made for their sufferings, and that due credit was not given to their virtues. She heard them denounced as miscreants, eager to enjoy what they had not laboured for, and only prevented by the fear of the law from seizing and wastefully consuming the hard-earned accumulations of the rich. She went into their homes and made herself acquainted with all the circumstances of their hard lot; she saw how cheerfully they bore their poverty, how generously they gave out of their small superfluities to neighbours in distress; she listened to their tales of grievance, and carefully noted what things they complained of. She found differences of character among them, of course. There were many discontented spirits who were filled with envy and anger when they contrasted their own squalid life with the signs of luxury among their masters—when they saw strong men enfeebled by privation and children dying of want, while others of the same flesh and blood enriched, as they believed in their bitterness, by the work of their hands, lived in palaces and squandered precious money on the pampered appetites and capricious whims of themselves and their families. Mrs. Gaskell had no difficulty in finding among the working classes the miscreant who might have sat for the ideal of manufacturers as bitter and unreasonable as himself, who was ready to throw all the blame of his own idleness and improvidence upon men who had acquired the means of luxury by hard work and frugal living. But her experience taught her that such miscreants were the exception—as, indeed, they must have been if society was to hold together —and that the mass of the working classes were industrious, mutually helpful, orderly citizens, tolerably satisfied with their lot, and disposed to grumble only when their normal burdens were increased. She could not help seeing that the great wages question, the strife between labour and capital as to their respective shares of the profit upon their joint productions, was rooted in the nature of things and permanent; it might sleep but it would never die outright. Nor did she shut her eyes to the fact that in periods of commercial depression, when the number of hands at the mills were reduced, and there was talk of lowering wages, sullen looks and gaunt faces increased among the workmen, subversive opinions found a readier hearing, and feelings were cherished which accident might fan into a revolutionary blaze. But she felt certain that the most dangerous element in this bitterness might be removed, if only the manufacturers could be brought to sympathize with the great trials of the workmen in such seasons of distress—could be taught to recognise that, though they also suffered, their anxious calculations and reduced expenditure were comparatively slight vexations to those which beset men who had to do battle against hunger and nakedness, and could be persuaded to show that they were aware of the difference. To make masters less wrapt up in their own cares, to lay bare to them the depths of wretchedness with which their workmen had to contend, and so quicken their sympathies, teach them habits of forbearance and consideration, and prevent them from stumbling against galled places and pressing upon sensitive sores, was Mrs. Gaskell's object in writing *Mary Barton*. ⟨. . .⟩

To promote a better understanding between different sections of society, to remove prejudices, to enlarge the limits of tolerance and charity, to dispel that ignorance of ways of life different from our own, which is so fruitful a source of injustice in the smaller as well as the weightier matters of social intercourse, may be said to have been the central purpose of all Mrs. Gaskell's earlier novels. As if afraid lest in *Mary Barton* she had produced too unfavourable an impression of the manufacturers as a class by describing the life of the manufacturing towns too exclusively from the workmen's point of view, she wrote *North and South* from the point of view of the masters. She did not hold a brief for the masters in this novel, any more than she held a brief for the men in *Mary Barton*. Shakespeare himself was not more dramatically impartial in his presentation of character; but by choosing her hero from the manufacturing class she centred the interest of the reader in their life, and enabled us, as it were, to look out upon the world from their windows, and justify their conduct as they were in the habit of justifying it to themselves. Mr. Thornton is not a type of the whole manufacturing class, any more than John Barton is a type of the whole artisan class, but he is a type of many, and his faults are explained and his virtues illustrated with the same penetrating insight into the play of lifelong circumstances upon character, and we are taught in the same way how natural it was that two such men should be in antagonism, and how much more smoothly they might work together for their common interest, if their relations had a little of the oil of mutual understanding. In *North and South* also Mrs. Gaskell had another unprejudicing mission to perform, —to remove from the whole industrial system of the North the coarse and savage aspect which it wore in the eyes of populations among whom the ways of life were smoother and the struggle for existence less strenuous and fierce. She shows that the higher elements in man are not all trodden down and extinguished in the sordid race for wealth, that there is opportunity in the manufacturer's life for loftier sentiments than the mere pride of money-getting; nobler visions than bank notes and stock. As her manner is, she does not undertake this apology in her own person, but puts it into the mouth of one of her characters. She makes Mr. Thornton dilate to Mr. Hale, his Oxford-bred friend and tutor, upon "the magnificent power, yet delicate adjustment, of the steam-hammer," till he recalls to the imaginative scholar some of the wonderful stories of the subservient genii in the *Arabian Nights*, "one moment stretching from earth to sky, and filling all the width of the

horizon, at the next obediently compressed into a vase small enough to be borne in the hand of a child." Thornton speaks enthusiastically of the genius of the man out of whose brains this gigantic thought came, and boldly expresses his conviction that "we have many among us who, if he were gone, could spring into the breach, and carry on the war which compels, and shall compel, all material power to yield to science," and Mr. Hale, catching his enthusiasm, quotes the lines—

> "I've a hundred captains in England," he said,
> "As good as ever was he."

Then, when Mr. Hale's daughter, Margaret, whose love in the end Thornton wins, in spite of his rough and awkward manners, by the force of his manliness and tenderness, looks up to wonder how in the world the conversation had passed from cog-wheels to Chevy Chase, Mr. Thornton says—

> It is no boast of mine, it is plain matter-of-fact. I won't deny that I am proud of belonging to a town—or perhaps I should rather say a district—the necessities of which give birth to such grandeur of conception. I would rather be a man toiling, suffering—nay, failing and successless—here, than lead a dull prosperous life in the old worn grooves of what you call more aristocratic society down in the South, with their slow days of careless ease. One may be clogged with honey and unable to fly.

Mrs. Gaskell, in several of her shorter stories, as well as in *North and South*, seeks favour for the men of the North as hiding warm hearts and bold imaginations under hard, inelegant, unceremonious manners. Everywhere in her novels we come upon traces of this persistent desire to break down prejudices and open the way to harmony. It is very prominent in her tragic story of *Ruth*, where she pleads the cause of a class more in need of intercession with society and more likely to be grateful for it than the sturdy manufacturers of "Milton." Even in *Cranford*, brimming over as it is with humorous satire, we are conscious of a kindly underlying moral. The makeshifts and affectations of decayed gentility have long been a favourite subject for ridicule, but Mrs. Gaskell, while she is not inferior to Miss Austen herself in the power of making us laugh at the foibles of her old ladies, takes care to give emphasis to their good qualities. Miss Jenkyns, with all her "Dragon o' Wantley" notions of dress and genteel discipline, does say, when a certain gentleman is seen sitting in the drawing-room with his arm round Miss Jessie Brown's waist, that "it is the most proper place for his arm to be in;" and the prying, man-hunting, tart Miss Pole takes the lead in the "movement" for contributing the mites of the coterie "in a secret and concealed manner" to impoverished Miss Matty. We are disposed to think more amiably of gossiping old women after reading *Cranford*.

Mrs. Gaskell's novels are still so universally popular, that it is needless to say the moral in them is not tiresomely obtruded. Except in *Mary Barton* and *Ruth*, both of which were avowedly written "with a purpose," she does not seem to have been conscious of any moral intention, but to have simply obeyed her strong descriptive instinct, and drawn characters for us with such an unaffected sympathy for all that was good in them, that we feel the better for reading the story of their lives. There never was a writer so essentially a moralist who had less self-consciousness of a mission to be such, and there have been very few moralists who have combined so much earnestness with so hearty an enjoyment of the sunshine of human existence. There are many moralists who derive their mission rather from hatred of the sinner, than from antipathy to the miserable consequences of the sin. One feels that it would have been a misfortune for them if there had been no scoundrels in the world for them to castigate: their lives would in that case have been disappointed. But with Mrs. Gaskell the removal of the unhappiness caused by wrong-doing is always paramount; reproof is with her a means and not an end—she takes no delight in it for its own sake. No part of the zest of her existence is drawn from moral indignation; she is willing to believe that people do wrong from ignorance of the suffering caused to their victims rather than from inherent malice and cruelty. Her preaching takes the form of depicting lives which might have been happy, had they not been marred by misfortunes for which human agencies were responsible, and so appealing to the better instincts of evil-doers, rather than seeking to dismay them with the thunders of the moral law.

Although pre-eminently a moralist in the sense of being a writer whose works touch the heart rather than the imagination or the philosophical intellect, Mrs. Gaskell is not to be numbered among the preachers. No one, however impatient of reproof and correction, need be frightened away from her novels by the fear of having to listen to didactic homilies. She prefixed a little sermon, pithy and well timed, by way of preface to *Mary Barton*, extracting from it a lesson for the day; but the lesson is not formulated and expounded in the novel, which is, what it professes to be, a tale—a representation of life. It is shaped and coloured by the author's good-natured wisdom, but it is not stiffened and distorted as a work of art by any hard specific moral purpose. Mrs. Gaskell was, indeed, a born story-teller, charged through and through with the story-teller's peculiar element, a something which may be called suppressed gipsiness, a restless instinct which impelled her to be constantly making trial in imagination of various modes of life. Her imagination was perpetually busy with the vicissitudes which days and years brought round to others; she entered into their lives, laughed with them, wept with them, speculated on the cardinal incidents and circumstances, the good qualities and the "vicious moles of nature" which had made them what they were, schemed how they might have been different, and lived through the windings and turnings of their destinies the excitement of looking forward to the un-known. We get, perhaps, the best idea of her wealth as a story-teller by looking through the collections of short tales and social essays which she poured forth with ready rapidity for *Household Words* and other magazines. We see there how abundantly her mind was stored with the facts of human life, how learned she was in all the large features and little traits that distinguish different sorts of men and women, and how quickly and surely she could imagine the effect which would be produced upon a given person by the various surroundings, fixed or active, of his existence. She finds one day a story told of a mysterious disappearance; immediately out of her accu-mulated lore she is ready with half-a-dozen others. Any incident within the range of ordinary experience she could, no doubt, have paralleled with equal facility. In describing one of her characters, old Job Legh, in *Mary Barton*, she makes use of Elliott's lines—

> Learned he was; nor bird nor insect flew,
> But he its leafy home and history knew:
> Nor wild flower decked the rock, nor moss the well,
> But he its name and qualities could tell.

Mrs. Gaskell also was a naturalist, only the subjects of her observations were men and women; and her knowledge was less complete than that of her hero, not because she was less enthusiastic, but because the field was so much more compli-cated and inaccessible.

The slight references to scenery in Mrs. Gaskell's novels show how intensely and exclusively she was occupied with human life. She gives no sign of caring much for nature. There are very few set descriptions in her novels, and I do not remember any that can be said to be taken from the point of view of the painter. She does not seem to care how the landscape looks, but how people contrive to make themselves comfortable in it. When she describes the country round Monkshaven, in *Sylvia's Lovers*, she does not dwell upon the beauty of the moorland hollows, but remarks how, "while on the bare swells of the high lands you shivered at the waste desolation of the scenery, when you dropped into these wooded 'bottoms' you were charmed with the nestling shelter which they gave." She carries us out upon the moors, not to touch our imaginations, as the Brontës would have done, with a sense of their lonely grandeur, but to ask us to look at the distance between the bare farmhouses, "the small stacks of coarse, poor hay, and almost larger stacks of turf for winter fuel," the half-starved cattle, and the little black-faced sheep, whose lean condition "did not promise much for the butcher," and whose wool was not "of a quality fine enough to make them profitable in that way to their owners." She leaves us to guess for ourselves what sort of a place Cranford was; she describes the inhabitants with loving care, so that we seem to know every turn of their thoughts and every trick of their gesture, but we learn the details of the scenery by which their lives were bounded only as they come in contact with it. This, so far as I have observed, is Mrs. Gaskell's invariable method of treating a landscape; she does not stand outside her people to describe it as if it had any independent interest for us. Dr. Johnson himself had not a more complete indifference to the forms and colours of still life. "Sir," she seems to say to the nature-worshipper, "let us take a peep into some English household. Let us watch its inmates in comfort and in distress. I will tell you their history. You shall see how a Lancashire mechanic entertains his friends, how a country doctor gets on with his neighbours, how a coquettish farmer's daughter behaves to her lovers. I have no strange experiences to reveal to you, only the life that lies at your doors; but I will show you its tragedies and its comedies, I will describe the characters of your countrymen to you, and I will tell you things about them that will interest you, some things that will make you weep, and many things that will make you smile."

No one would dream of ranking Mrs. Gaskell as a novelist beside Dickens or Thackeray, but she deserves a very high place among those who are comparatively unambitious in their efforts, and who, having a just measure of their own powers, succeed perfectly in what they undertake. She never attempted high flights, but pursued her way steadily and surely at a moderate elevation. Her style has not the magnificent reach of her friend, Charlotte Brontë; it is homely, as suited her subjects. It was natural that art such as hers, working earnestly within a definite field, without straining to get beyond it, and never wasting its strength against the precipices, should be-come more perfect as she went on. She could not easily have written another novel that would take such a hold of the public mind as *Mary Barton* did, because, as we have seen, it ministered so directly to interests that were uppermost at the moment, and gave body and substance to a spirit then predominant. So deep an impression did she produce by this effort to remove misunderstandings between masters and men, that people were for some time unwilling to listen to her on any other subject; her second novel, *Ruth*, was felt as a disappoint-ment, and thought to be a falling off, and it was not till the appearance of *North and South* that she regained her hold of public favour. To the last she was best known as the authoress of *Mary Barton*, and as long as the strife between labour and capital continues, this novel and its companion are likely to remain her chief distinction, and may be read with advantage by both parties to the dispute. Nor could she easily have surpassed the force and delicacy of the touches by which she made the various persons in these novels live and move in our memories as real men and women. But in her later novels, *Sylvia's Lovers* and *Wives and Daughters*, in which she left the manufacturing towns behind her, and essayed to describe less oppressive and painful conditions of life, though she cannot be said to have improved upon the completeness and vividness of her separate portraits, she shows greater art in the management of her story. It has been said with truth, that the beginnings of her earlier novels, where she is setting forth her characters upon the stage, are the most interesting parts of them; the characters once put in motion, she seems to have become too much absorbed in the incidents of the plot, and to have hurried along in a narrow stream without sufficiently relieving the monotony of its course. But she was not exposed to this danger when the current of her story was not too impetuous for her. Her last novel, *Wives and Daughters*, though she did not live to write the concluding chapters, is in many respects the most mature, as it is, with the exception, perhaps, of *Cranford*, the most delightful of her works.

As I spoke at starting of the literary pedigree of Mrs. Gaskell as a novelist, I may say a word in conclusion about her influence. Her novels have not been childless in literature. I have no wish to institute comparisons between Mrs. Gaskell and George Eliot. No comparison is possible between two writers of genius, interpenetrated as these two are by the spirit of different generations. George Eliot has lived and worked in a different social atmosphere, and has pursued the more purely artistic and philosophical aims to which that atmosphere has been favourable, but no one who reads the *Scenes from Clerical Life* and *Adam Bede*, can fail to see that Mrs. Gaskell has been not the least important of her literary progenitors.

MAT HOMPES
From "Mrs. Gaskell"

Gentleman's Magazine, August 1895, pp. 133–37

*R*uth, her second great work in order of publication, is, as regards style and power, inferior to *Mary Barton*, perhaps to all her sustained effort. But it stands out from the rest, as the handling by a woman of a side of life which is unfortunately too often either ignored in real life and in fiction, or treated in a light, flippant manner. It is the story of an innocent young girl, led into sin by a profligate, who afterwards heartlessly deserts her. She is left in that position where, if a woman once reaches it, nearly all virtuous women seem to consider it their duty to keep her, by treating her with utter contempt, debarring her all respectable society and any decent means of earning a livelihood. We will not say all women: there are a few at least among Christian women who can more truly interpret their Master's words when he said, "Neither do I condemn thee; go and sin no more." Mrs. Gaskell bids us consider this problem. She shows us how this poor, erring girl is brought through the kindness extended to her to lead a good life, bringing up her boy in honour and virtue as any mother might be proud to do. It is a tale of tears, most pathetic and pitiful throughout; but it was given us for a high purpose, and we must admire Mrs. Gaskell's womanly courage as well as her talent. The world

should be careful to distinguish, in its zeal for honour and morality, between those who court sin and those who are sorely tempted, and in their weakness fall. Let us be watchful lest we thrust mere weakness into wickedness, by barring the doors for ever against those who are anxious to return where once they stood.

Cranford appeared originally in *Household Words* and Dickens wrote in reference to it: "If you were not the most suspicious of women, always looking for soft solder in the purest metal of praise, I should call your paper delightful, and touched in the tenderest and most delicate manner. Being what you are, I confine myself to the observation that I have called it, *A Love Affair at Cranford*, and sent it off to the printers." No short tale could be more delightful; the early chapters describe the quiet, aristocratic country life of the female population of the little town, and are full of the richest humour. All is so telling and yet so good-natured, for Mrs. Gaskell is telling us about the worthy people among whom she passed the happy days of her girlhood. She loved and respected them, and though she quietly laughs at some of their ways, she makes them very lovable in spite of their oddities and somewhat stilted dignity. Cranford represents Knutsford as Mrs. Gaskell knew it some seventy years ago; many of the characters she drew were true to life; many of the incidents she relates stand out in their bare reality. That most laughable incident of the cow dressed in a grey flannel suit Mrs. Gaskell declared to be perfectly true. The pathetic story of Peter's disappearance was undoubtedly suggested by the loss of her own brother, who visited her a few times during her childhood and then was heard of no more. Probably that sad chapter in her life was the cause of her keen interest in "Disappearances," under which title she wrote a paper in *Household Words*. That most touching, delicately-written account of the failure of the bank in which Miss Matty's money was invested, and which reduced her almost to poverty, was based on the failure of a bank in Macclesfield, about that time, by which many families were ruined. Cranford will bear reading many times, and the same may be said of some of the other short tales bound in the same volume. "Libbie Marsh's Three Eras," the story of a poor girl living in one of the back courts of Manchester, shows us how in this sphere a woman may lead a noble, unselfish life by keeping a high purpose constantly before her. The story is extremely simple and natural, but it is so lovingly told that it lifts us above the level of everyday life. A writer who can with such simple materials make us feel so much deserves our lasting gratitude, and must ever rank among the highest artists. "Libbie Marsh's Three Eras" is worthy to stand in spirit, though the story is much slighter, beside George Eliot's *Silas Marner*. In "Lois the Witch," a sad but true story, we get some glimpses of Mrs. Gaskell's schooldays at Stratford-on-Avon.

Her next great work, also contributed to *Household Words*, appeared in 1854. The editor writes about it thus: "January 1855. Let me congratulate you on the conclusion of your story, not because it is the end of a task to which you have conceived a dislike (for I imagine you have got the better of that delusion by this time), but because it is the vigorous and powerful accomplishment of anxious labour. It seems to me that you have felt the ground thoroughly firm under your feet, and have strided on it with a force and purpose that *must* now give you pleasure. You will not, I hope, allow that non-lucid interval of dissatisfaction with yourself (and me?) which beset you for a minute or two once upon a time, to linger in the shape of any disagreeable associations with H. W. I shall still look forward to the large sides of paper, and shall soon feel disappointed if they don't begin to reappear." *North and South* may be called a companion book to *Mary Barton*, since, like its predecessor, it deals with the labour question in Lancashire. Here Mrs. Gaskell defends the masters' side. But the interest of the book does not centre there, but rather in Mr. Hale's resignation of the ministry for conscience' sake. This subject would have a peculiar interest for Mrs. Gaskell, for her father's sake. The scene is laid in the South of England, and Mrs. Gaskell takes this opportunity of contrasting Hampshire with Lancashire men, greatly to the advantage of the latter. These she knew with a fuller and truer knowledge, and it is plain to see where her heart lies.

There is one weak point in this book, a blemish for which there surely was no need. Margaret Hale, the heroine, is made to tell a lie in order to screen her brother—save his life, indeed—instead of daring to speak the truth. There is no doubt that most people would have done the same, but I like my heroes to be of sterling metal, to stand head and shoulders above the crowd. Such men and women exist, if only rarely; let us take our heroes from the chosen few. Sir Walter Scott thought so when he gave us his Jeanie Deans, and we all know the effect.

In 1857 Mrs. Gaskell published *The Life of Charlotte Brontë*, a biography which has been compared with Boswell's *Life of Johnson*. It brings the little Yorkshire lady, who possessed such great genius, most vividly before us. No one could have been found so well fitted to write her life, and we feel grateful to Mrs. Gaskell for having undertaken the task. She knew Charlotte Brontë as few could know, and she loved her most truly and tenderly. A tender, loving hand was needed to lay bare the records of that sad, lonely life amid the Yorkshire hills. And yet had they not been told how much we should have lost! Not only should we want the key to the books which, coming from the lonely parsonage at Haworth, took the world by surprise, but we should have missed what is of greater value still—namely, the lesson how this woman bore up against the keenest trials and became thereby not hardened, but only more and more refined to the end. Some later authorities think that Mrs. Gaskell put in the dark lines of the picture rather too thickly; but her book remains on the whole tender and true, and will be prized as one of the best biographies in the English language.

Passing over two short tales, "Round the Sofa" and "Right at Last," we come to *Sylvia's Lovers*, which saw the light, as our French neighbours say, in 1863. Its plot deals with the smugglers of the last century, and is cast in the picturesque little Yorkshire town of Whitby, whose real name is but thinly veiled by Mrs. Gaskell's substitute—Monkshaven. What fitter name could she have found for the quaint fishing town, where the ancient abbey of St. Hilda commands a view from every point? All who have visited this delightful spot, who have looked from those glorious east cliffs on which the abbey is situated on to the roaring sea beyond, and tasted the delicious air born of the ocean and the moorland, will not be slow to recognise the descriptions which are drawn for us in *Sylvia's Lovers*. It is a sad, pathetic story of death, betrayal, and disappointment of the worst order—that of a wife in her husband—and it is all the sadder for being so exceedingly true to life. The men and women become real as we read of their fates.

Next came *Cousin Phillis*, in 1865, a short story remarkable for its grace and delicacy. It has been fitly called an "Idyll in Prose." The fresh country air breathes through its pages, and the reader is introduced to the company of good people, who have neither riches nor power, but who possess what is better far than either—content. Poor Phillis goes through a great sorrow, but her heart remains whole, thanks to the kind help of all her friends. The kind but outspoken words of the old servant, many a one, cast down by grief, might do well to ponder, and be roused to action thereby. "Now, Phillis, we ha' done a' we can for you, and th' doctors has done a' they can for you, and I think th' Lord has done a' He can for you, and more than you deserve, if you don't do something for yourself."

And now we come to the last, but by no means least, of Mrs. Gaskell's books, that which the sudden hand of Death arrested and left unfinished. As an artistic production, *Wives and Daughters* is almost perfect, its scenes move so easily and gracefully; nothing very striking or dramatic is introduced, and yet our interest in the progress of the plot never flags. A story of everyday life it is, to be sure, but the life is high-toned, and the writer's true, womanly heart speaks on every page. It was contributed to the pages of *Cornhill* the editor of which wrote, immediately after Mrs. Gaskell's death, as follows: "In these later books you feel yourself caught up out of an abominably wicked world, crawling with selfishness and reeking with base passion, into an atmosphere where there is much weakness, many mistakes, suffering long and bitter, but where it is possible for people to live calm and wholesome lives; and, what is more, you feel that it is at least as real a world as the other." Georges Sand, who was a great admirer of this novel, said to Lord Houghton: "It is a book which might be put into the hands of an innocent girl, while at the same time it would rivet the attention of the most *blasé* man of the world."

THOMAS LOVE PEACOCK

1785–1866

Thomas Love Peacock was born at Weymouth, Dorsetshire, on October 18, 1785. His father, a London glass merchant, died a few years later, and Peacock was raised by his mother in Chertsey, Surrey. He was educated at Englefield Green from 1791 to 1798, after which he was briefly employed as a clerk in London. Peacock then began writing poetry, probably while living with his mother in London. His earliest published works include *The Monks of St Mark* (1804), a humorous poem published as a pamphlet, and *Palmyra and Other Poems* (1806). For several months in 1808–09 he was a secretary aboard the H.M.S. *Venerable*, then went back to writing verse, including *The Genius of the Thames: A Lyrical Poem* (1810) and *The Philosophy of Melancholy: A Poem in Four Parts* (1812). In 1812 he began a close friendship with Percy

Bysshe Shelley, who became a major influence on Peacock's life and work. After Shelley's death in 1822 Peacock was a co-executor of his estate, and wrote various memoirs of the poet.

In 1815 Peacock published *Headlong Hall*, the first of his prose satires, followed by *Melincourt* (1817) and *Nightmare Abbey* (1818). These books—there is some dispute over whether they can be called novels—consist largely of conversations among characters who argue over assorted intellectual and political issues of the day. There are some elements of conventional romantic comedy in the books, but they owe at least as much to such works as Plato's *Symposium* and Burton's *Anatomy of Melancholy*. In 1818 Peacock also published another long poem, *Rhododaphne; or, The Thessalian Spell*, written in the same mythologizing vein as Keats's *Lamia*. In 1819 Peacock began working at the East India Company, where he remained until his retirement in 1856. In 1820 he married Jane Gryffydh. His next two books, *Maid Marian* (1822) and *The Misfortunes of Elphin* (1829), are comic historical romances, and contain a higher ratio of plot to conversation than his earlier works. Peacock wrote two more satires in the vein of *Headlong Hall: Crotchet Castle* (1831) and *Gryll Grange* (1861).

Peacock also produced a number of critical essays and other miscellaneous nonfiction, including "The Four Ages of Poetry" (1820), "French Comic Romances" (1835), and *Memoirs of Percy Bysshe Shelley* (1858–62). He also co-authored "Gastronomy and Civilization" (1851) with his daughter Mary Ellen Peacock Meredith, the wife of George Meredith. Peacock died of shock on January 23, 1866, after refusing to leave his library during a fire.

Personal

⟨. . .⟩ Peacock—did you ever read *Headlong Hall & Maid Marian?*—a charming lyrical poet and Horatian satirist he was when a writer; now he is a whiteheaded jolly old worldling and Secretary to the E. India House full of information about India and everything else in the world.—WILLIAM MAKEPEACE THACKERAY, Letter to Mrs. Brookfield (Dec. 26, 1850)

I met Peacock; a clever fellow, and a good scholar. I am glad to have an opportunity of being better acquainted with him. We had out Aristophanes, Aeschylus, Sophocles, and several other old fellows, and tried each other's quality pretty well. We are both strong enough in these matters for gentlemen. But he is editing the *Supplices*. Aeschylus is not to be edited by a man whose Greek is only a secondary pursuit.—THOMAS BABINGTON MACAULAY, *Journal* (Dec. 31, 1851), cited in G. Otto Trevelyan, *The Life and Letters of Lord Macaulay*, 1876, Vol. 2, pp. 253–54

Talked at the India House with Mr. Peacock about Taylor the Platonist. I think my good old friend, if he had worshipped anything, would have been inclined to worship Jupiter, as it was said that Taylor did. I saw a good deal of Mr. Peacock about this time, and enjoyed his society extremely. He was utterly unlike anybody I have ever seen before or since, and is best represented, to those who never knew him, by *Gryll Grange*—surely one of the brightest, as well as the most fantastic, books that has appeared in our time.—SIR MOUNTSTUART E. GRANT DUFF, *Diary* (April 1, 1853), *Notes from a Diary 1851–1872*, 1897, Vol. 1, p. 53

While a student in Scotland, I had known him as the friend of Shelley, and had read his delightful works with pleasure and profit; until at last I was prompted to write to him, expecting (I remember) to receive but a cold response from one who, to judge him by his works, was too much of a Timon to care for boy's homage. I was agreeably disappointed. The answer came, not savage like a wrap on the knuckles, but cordial as a hand-shake. Afterwards, when I was weary "climbing up the breaking wave" of London, I thought of my old friend, and determined to seek him out. Mainly with the wish to be near him, I retreated to quiet Chertsey; and thence past Chertsey Bridge, through miles of green fields basking in the summer sun, and through delightful lanes to Lower Halliford, I went on pilgrimage, youth in my limbs, reverence in my heart, a pipe in my mouth, and the tiny Pickering edition of Catullus

(a veritable "lepidum libellum," but, alas, far from "novum!") in my waistcoat pocket. And there, at Lower Halliford, I found him as I had described him, seated on his garden lawn in the sun, with the door of his library open behind him, showing such delicious vistas of shady shelves as would have gladdened his own Dr. Opimian, and the little maiden reading from the book upon his knee. Gray-haired and smiling sat the man of many memories, guiding the utterances of one who was herself a pretty two-fold link between the present and the past, being the granddaughter (on the paternal side) of Leigh Hunt, and also the granddaughter (on the maternal side) of the Williams who was drowned with Shelley. Could a youthful student's eyes see any sight fairer?

> And did you once see Shelley plain,
> And did he stop and speak to you? . . .
> How strange it seems, and new!

And this old man had spoken with Shelley, not once, but a thousand times; and had known well both Harriett Westbrook and Mary Godwin; and had cracked jokes with Hobhouse, and chaffed Proctor's latinity; and had seen, and actually criticised, Malibran; and had bought "the vasty version of a new system to perplex the sages," when it first came out, in a bright, new, uncut quarto; and had dined with Jeremy Bentham; and had smiled at Disraeli, when, resplendently attired, he stood chatting in Hookham's with the Countess of Blessington; and had been face to face with that bland Rhadamanthus, Chief Justice Eldon; and was, in short, such a living chronicle of things past and men dead as filled one's soul with delight and ever-varying wonder. "How strange it seemed, and new!"—ROBERT BUCHANAN, "Thomas Love Peacock: A Personal Reminiscence," *A Look round Literature*, 1887, pp. 164–65

General

Peacock has married a Welsh turtle, and is employed at present in devising inextinguishable lanterns: which he puffs at with a pair of bellows.—THOMAS LOVELL BEDDOES, Letter to Thomas Forbes Kelsall (April 17, 1824)

The stories of Peacock must be read for what they are, and nothing else, or not read at all. To read them as we do novels is to read them to no purpose. They are not novels, and were not meant to be novels. Their plots, if the incidents of which they are composed can be called plots, are of the slightest, and not of a kind that creates interest and awakens sympathy, either through the action they involve, or the characters they present.

They are a succession of scenes and a procession of persons—a succession of scenes in English country houses, such as are described in *Headlong Hall* and *Nightmare Abbey*, a procession of persons such as we may suppose to inhabit them, and visit them, and enjoy their hospitality. United by the ties of good breeding and good fellowship, they have enough in common to like each other heartily, and enough individuality to differ from each other widely. Some of them have very decided views, the discussion of which forms the staple of their conversation. The master of the house in which these discussions are held is usually a doctrinaire, who has no sympathy with other doctrinaires, and who, like Iago, is nothing if not critical.

Peacock's prose is what Matthew Arnold maintained poetry should be—a criticism of life, not life in the abstract, but life in the concrete—the social, political, national life of his own people and period. He was thoroughly English in his conservatism; certain of present, but doubtful of future, good. One of his pet aversions was political economy, another was phrenology, a third was animal magnetism, which was odious because it originated in the United States. Americans were repugnant to him, and Scotchmen, even Scott, whose books were written in all the worst dialects of the English language. Like Wordsworth, he was inimical to railroads, that hurry about people who have nothing to do, and telegraphs, that convey the words of people who have nothing to say. He was prone to prejudice and paradox, or pretended to be in order to show his wit. When we read him we should remember that he was a humorist and a satirist, and that he wrote dramatically, assuming for the moment the personality of his characters, for whose opinions and utterances he was not responsible. He was satirical, but not cynical—a sharp-witted, but good-natured censor. He handled his victims as Izaak Walton handled his worms—as if he loved them, and if they did not condone their impalement, they ought to have done so. Shelley did, for he not only forgave but admired Peacock's caricature as Scythrop in *Nightmare Abbey*.—RICHARD HENRY STODDARD, "Thomas Love Peacock," *Under the Evening Lamp*, 1892, pp. 241–42

Peacock's position in the intellectual world was intended by him to have been expressed by the motto on his seal: "Nec tardum opperior, nec praecedentibus insto"; but the first half of the precept was insufficiently observed by him. Injustice, however, is done to him by those who call him a mere Pagan; he allowed English, French, and Italian a place among the great literatures of the world, and his unreasonable prejudice against German at all events prevented his taking trouble to acquire what would not after all have suited him. His knowledge of the literature he did relish was exceedingly accurate, but his reproductions of antique models have neither the antique form nor the antique spirit, and he cannot escape the reproach, common with exact scholars, of anathematising in a modern what he admired in an ancient. Tennyson he could never appreciate, and of Keats he says in a letter to Shelley, "I should never read *Hyperion* if I lived to the age of Methuselah." His tepidity towards Byron and Shelley arose rather from antipathy in the strict etymological sense than from insensibility: we have seen his deliberate verdict on Shelley, and he says in a letter to him, "*Cain* is fine, *Sardanapalus* finer, *Don Juan* best of all." But the milder beauties of Wordsworth and Coleridge were fairly recognised by him. His own strongest predilections were naturally for the humourists, and rather for the genial extravagance of Aristophanes and Rabelais, or the polished wit of Voltaire and Petronius, than the moody bitterness of writers like Swift. Urbane philosophers like Cicero, or romantic narrators like Boiardo, held, however, an almost

equal place in his esteem. He made a particular study of Tacitus, from whom he learned the pregnant brevity that renders both writers such valuable models to an age whose worst literary fault is diffuseness.

Peacock's own place in literature is pre-eminently that of a satirist. This character is not always a passport to goodwill. Satirists have met with much ignorant and invidious depreciation, as though a talent for ridicule was necessarily the index of an unkindly nature. The truth is just the reverse: as the sources of laughter and tears lie near together, so is the geniality of an intellectual man usually accompanied with a keen perception of the ridiculous. Both exist in ample measure in Peacock, whose hearty and sometimes misplaced laughter at what he deemed absurd is usually accompanied with a kindly feeling towards the exemplars of the absurdity. The only very noticeable instance of the contrary is the undoubtedly illiberal ridicule of the Lake poets in his earlier writings; still there is sufficient evidence elsewhere of his sincere admiration of their works. Brougham he certainly abhorred, and yet the denunciation of him in *Crotchet Castle* has hardly more of invective than the gibes at the "modern Athenians." Add to this geniality a bright fancy, a lively sense of the ludicrous, a passion for natural beauty, strong sense, occasionally warped by prejudice, genuine tenderness on occasion, diction of singular purity, and a style of singular elegance, and it will be allowed that, *prima facie*, Peacock should be popular. That he has nevertheless been only the favourite of the few is owing in a measure to the highly intellectual quality of his work, but chiefly to his lack of the ordinary qualifications of the novelist, all pretension to which he entirely disclaims. He has no plot, little human interest, and no consistent delineation of character. His personages are mere puppets, or, at best, incarnations of abstract qualities, or idealisations of disembodied grace or beauty. He affected to prefer—perhaps really did prefer—the pantomimes of "the enchanter of the south" to the novels of "the enchanter of the north"; and, by a whimsical retribution, his own novels have passed for pantomimes. "A queer mixture!" pronounced the *Saturday Review*, criticising *Gryll Grange*, and such has been the judgment of most. It will not be the judgment of any capable of appreciating the Aristophanic comedy of which, restricted as their scale is in comparison, Peacock's fiction is, perhaps, the best modern representative. Nearly everything that can be urged against him can be urged against Aristophanes too; and save that his invention is far less daring and opulent, his Muse can allege most of "the apologies of Aristophanes." When he is depreciated, comparison with another novelist usually seems to be implied, but it would be as unfair to test him by the standard of Miss Austen or Miss Edgeworth, as to try Aristophanes by the rules of the New Comedy. A master of fiction he is not, and he never claimed to be; a satirist, a humourist, a poet he is most undoubtedly. Were these qualities less eminent than they are, he would still live by the truth of his natural description and the grace and finish of his style: were even these in default, the literary historian would still have to note in him the first appearance of a new type, destined to be frequently imitated, but seldom approached, and never exactly reproduced.—RICHARD GARNETT, "Thomas Love Peacock" (1891), *Essays of an Ex-Librarian*, 1901, pp. 279–82

Works

POETRY

Rhododaphne is a poem of the most remarkable character, and the nature of the subject no less than the spirit in which it is written forbid us to range it under any of the classes of modern literature. It is a Greek and Pagan poem. In sentiment and scenery it is essentially antique. There is a strong *religio loci* throughout which almost compels us to believe that the author wrote from the dictation of a voice heard from some Pythian cavern in the solitudes where Delphi stood. We are transported to the banks of the Peneus and linger under the crags of Tempe, and see the water lilies floating on the stream. We sit with Plato by old Ilissus under the sacred Plane tree among the sweet scent of flowering sallows; and above there is the nightingale of Sophocles in the ivy of the pine, who is watching the sunset so that it may dare to sing; it is the radiant evening of a burning day, and the smooth hollow whirlpools of the river are overflowing with the aërial gold of the level sunlight. We stand in the marble temples of the Gods, and see their sculptured forms gazing and almost breathing around. We are led forth from the frequent pomp of sacrifice into the solitude of mountains and forests where Pan, "the life, the intellectual soul of grove and stream," yet lives and yet is worshipped. We visit the solitudes of Thessalian magic, and tremble with new wonder to hear statues speak and move and to see the shaggy changelings minister to their witch queen with the shape of beasts and the reason of men, and move among the animated statues who people her inchanted palaces and gardens. That wonderful overflowing of fancy the *Syria Dea* of Lucian, and the impassioned and elegant pantomime of Apuleius, have contributed to this portion of the poem. There is here, as in the songs of ancient times, music and dancing and the luxury of voluptuous delight. The Bacchanalians toss on high their leaf-inwoven hair, and the tumult and fervour of the chase is depicted; we hear its clamour gathering among the woods, and she who impels it is so graceful and so fearless that we are charmed—and it needs no feeble spell to see nothing of the agony and blood of that royal sport. This it is to be a scholar; this it is to have read Homer and Sophocles and Plato.

Such is the scenery and the spirit of the tale. The story itself presents a more modern aspect, being made up of combinations of human passion which seem to have been developed since the Pagan system has been outworn. The poem opens in a strain of elegant but less powerful versification than that which follows. It is descriptive of the annual festival of Love at his temple in Thespia. Anthemion is among the crowd of votaries; a youth from the banks of Arcadian Ladon:

> The flower of all Arcadia's youth
> Was he: such form and face, in truth,
> As thoughts of gentlest maidens seek
> In their day-dreams: soft glossy hair
> Shadowed his forehead, snowy-fair,
> With many a hyacinthine cluster:
> Lips, that in silence seemed to speak,
> Were his, and eyes of mild blue lustre:
> And even the paleness of his cheek,
> The passing trace of tender care,
> Still shewed how beautiful it were
> If its own natural bloom were there.
> (CANTO I, p. II)

He comes to offer his vows at the shrine for the recovery of his mistress Calliroë, who is suffering under some strange, and as we are led to infer, magical disease. As he presents his wreath of flowers at the altar they are suddenly withered up. He looks and there is standing near him a woman of exquisite beauty who gives him another wreath which he places on the altar and it does not wither. She turns to him and bids him wear a flower which she presents, saying, with other sweet words—

> Some meet for once and part for aye,
> Like thee and me, and scarce a day

> Shall each by each remembered be:
> But take the flower I give to thee,
> And till it fades remember me.
> (CANTO I, p. 22)

As Anthemion passes from the temple among the sports and dances of the festival "with vacant eye"

> the trains
> Of youthful dancers round him float,
> As the musing bard from his sylvan seat
> Looks on the dance of the noontide heat,
> Or the play of the watery flowers, that quiver
> In the eddies of a lowland river.
> (CANTO II, p. 29)

He there meets an old man who tells him that the flower he wears is the profane laurel-rose which grows in Larissa's unholy gardens, that it is impious to wear it in the temple of Love, and that he, who has suffered evils which he dares not tell from Thessalian inchantments, knows that the gift of this flower is a spell only to be dissolved by invoking his natal genius and casting the flower into some stream with the caution of not looking upon it after he has thrown it away. Anthemion obeys his direction, but so soon as he has . . .

> round his neck
> Are closely twined the silken rings
> Of Rhododaphne's glittering hair,
> And round him her bright arms she flings,
> And cinctured thus in loveliest bands
> The charmed waves in safety bear
> The youth and the enchantress fair
> And leave them on the golden sands.
> (CANTO V, pp. 110–11)

They now find themselves on a lonely moor on which stands a solitary cottage—ruined and waste; this scene is transformed by Thessalian magic to a palace surrounded by magnificent gardens. Anthemion enters the hall of the palace where, surrounded by sculptures of divine workmanship, he sees the earthly image of Uranian Love.

Plato says, with profound allegory, that Love is not itself beautiful, but seeks the possession of beauty; this idea seems embodied in the deformed dwarf who bids, with a voice as from a trumpet, Anthemion enter. After feast and music the natural result of the situation of the lovers is related by the poet to have place.

The last Canto relates the enjoyments and occupations of the lovers; and we are astonished to discover that any thing can be added to the gardens of Armida and Alcina, and the Bower of Bliss: the following description among many of a Bacchanalian dance is a remarkable instance of a fertile and elegant imagination.—PERCY BYSSHE SHELLEY, "On *Rhododaphne; or, The Thessalian Spell*," 1818

> and there
> Is English Peacock, with his mountain Fair,
> Turned into a Flamingo;—that shy bird
> That gleams i' the Indian air—have you not heard
> When a man marries, dies, or turns Hindoo,
> His best friends hear no more of him?—but you
> Will see him, and will like him too, I hope,
> With the milk-white Snowdonian Antelope
> Matched with this cameleopard—his fine wit
> Makes such a wound, the knife is lost in it;
> A strain too learnèd for a shallow age,
> Too wise for selfish bigots; let his page,
> Which charms the chosen spirits of the time,

Fold itself up for the serener clime
Of years to come, and find its recompense
In that just expectation.
—PERCY BYSSHE SHELLEY, *Letter to Maria Gisborne*, 1820, ll. 232–47

The fame of Peacock as a prose humourist of incomparable vivacity has tended to overshadow and stunt his reputation as a poet. It is time, however, that his claims in verse should be vindicated, and a place demanded for him as an independent figure in the crowded Parnassus of his age,—a place a little below the highest, and somewhat isolated, at the extreme right of the composition. He has certain relations, not wholly accidental, with Shelley, who stands above him, and with such minor figures as Horace Smith and Thomas Haynes Bayly, who stand no less obviously below him; but in the main he is chiefly notable for his isolation. His ironical and caustic songs are unique in our literature, illuminated by too much fancy to be savage, but crackling with a kind of ghastly merriment that inspires quite as much terror as amusement. In parody he has produced at least one specimen, 'There is a fever of the spirit,' which does not possess its equal for combined sympathy and malice. When we pass to his serious and sentimental lyrics, our praise cannot be so unmeasured. Peacock possessed too much literary refinement, too little personal sensibility to write with passion or to risk a fall by flying; yet his consummate purity of style seldom fails to give a subdued charm to the quietest of his songs. The snatches and refrains which are poured over the novel of *Maid Marian*, like a shower of seed pearl, are full of the very essence of spontaneous song, as opposed to deliberate lyrical writing; while the corresponding chants and ballads in *The Misfortunes of Elphin* show with equal distinctness Peacock's limitations as a poetical artist. Once or twice he has succeeded in writing a lyric that is almost perfect; 'I dug beneath the cypress shade' would, for instance, be worthy of Landor in Landor's best manner, but for a little stiffness in starting.

Twice in mature life Peacock attempted a long flight in poetry, and each time without attracting any serious attention from the public of his own time or from posterity. In one of these cases I hope to show that this neglect has been deeply unjust; for the other I find an excuse in the extreme languor which it has produced on myself to read once more 'The Genius of the Thames.' This poem, written just before the general revival of poetic style, may almost be called the last production of the eighteenth century. It contains all the wintry charms and hypocritical graces of the school of Collins in its last dissolution; it proceeds with mingled pomp and elegance along the conventional path, in the usual genteel manner, until suddenly the reader, familiar with the temperament of Peacock, starts and rubs his eyes to read an invocation of

Sun-crowned Science! child of heaven!
To wandering man by angels given!
Still, nymph divine! on mortal sight
Diffuse thy intellectual light.

from the man to whom the whole spirit of scientific enquiry was entirely hostile.

Rhododaphne, which Peacock published eight years later, is a performance of a very different kind. While somewhat indebted to Akenside for matter, to Byron for style, to Shelley for phraseology, the essential part of this poem is as original as it is delicate and fascinating. There is little plot or action in the piece. A youth, Anthemion, loves a mortal maiden, Calliroë, but is courted and subdued by a supernatural being named Rhododaphne, who exercises over him the poisonous spell of

the rose-laurel. Calliroë dies and Rhododaphne triumphs, but in the end the doom is reversed, Calliroë returns to life, and the charms of the rose-laurel are evaded. It is curious to compare *Rhododaphne* with *Endymion*, which was published in the same year. Peacock leaves Keats far behind in knowledge of the English language and of Greek manners, in grace and learning of every kind, but Keats, as by a diviner instinct, is led by his very ignorance into a mood more truly antique than Peacock attains by such pedantries as—

The rose and myrtle blend in beauty
Round Thespian Love's *hypœthric fane*.

Still *Rhododaphne* is a poem full of eminent beauties and touches of true art. It would be absolutely and not comparatively great were it not that the whole structure of the work is spoiled by a tone of Georgian sentiment which we should scarcely have expected from so genuine a Pagan as 'Greeky-Peeky.' The ethics of the poem are not merely modern, they are positively provincial. In short, *Rhododaphne* may be best compared to a series of charming friezes in antique story carved by some sculptor of the beginning of the present century, some craftsman less soft than Canova, less breezy than Thorwaldsen. The marble is excellently chosen, the artist's touch sharp and delicate, the design flowing and refined, but the figures have the most provoking resemblance to those in the fashion-books of the last age but one—EDMUND GOSSE, "Thomas Love Peacock," *The English Poets*, ed. Thomas Humphry Ward, 1880, Vol. 4, pp. 417–19

The riper and richer humour of Peacock, as superior to Praed's as dry champagne to sweet, or a Sultana grape to a green gooseberry, is excellently well represented by the masterly and generous satire of "Rich and Poor, or Saint and Sinner," his deeper and sweeter gift of grave and tender song, by the matchless elegiac idyl of "Youth and Age." But how came the editors to throw away for the second time—repeating the unhappy exploit of the diving friar—"the stone of all stones, the philosopher's stone"? And how could they ignore the incomparable raiding song which registers for all time the difference between mountain sheep and valley sheep? And if, in the teeth of a promise given or an engagement implied in the preface, a place was to be found for such mean and pitiful parodies as disfigure two or three of these pages, how on earth did they come to overlook the quintessence of Byron as distilled by Peacock into the two consummate stanzas which utter or exhale the lyric agony of Mr. Cypress?—ALGERNON CHARLES SWINBURNE, "Social Verse," *Forum*, Oct. 1891, p. 180

And at precisely this period, when a vapid elegance pervaded the ditties warbled forth in refined drawing-rooms, and when Moore alone, of all the popular song-writers, held the secret of true music in his heart, Thomas Love Peacock wrote for respectable and sentimental England five of the very best drinking-songs ever given to an ungrateful world. No thought of possible disapprobation vexed his soul's serenity. He lived in the nineteenth century, as completely uncontaminated by nineteenth-century ideals as though Robinson Crusoe's desert island had been his resting-place. The shafts of his good-tempered ridicule were leveled at all that his countrymen were striving to prove sacred and beneficial. His easy laugh rang out just when everybody was most strenuous in the cause of progress. His wit was admirably calculated to make people uncomfortable and dissatisfied. And in addition to these disastrous qualities, he apparently thought it natural and reasonable and right that English gentlemen—sensible, educated, *married* English gentlemen—should sit around their dinner-tables until the midnight hour, drinking wine and singing songs with boyish and scandalous joviality.—AGNES REPPLIER, "Cakes and Ale," *Varia*, 1897, pp. 146–47

NOVELS

The author of *Headlong Hall* is a bitter persecutor of the singularities and excrescences of science. He is a prose Peter Pindar, writing however with a vast deal of knowledge on the topics about which he is occupied, but with the keenest eye upon the absurdities of all who come under his cognizance Dr. Walcot represented sir Joseph Banks as boiling fleas, in order to ascertain whether they turned red like lobsters; and the traveller Bruce as cutting his beefsteaks from a living animal, and then sending the bullock to graze. Who now doubts at this time of day that sir Joseph Banks and Bruce were benefactors of society; there will be as little hesitation on the question, whether the phrenologists, the conchologists, and the political economists, with numerous other tribes of scientific devotees, who are described by the Greek termination ιοτης, of the present day, are to be considered as the patrons of human happiness, and the benefactors of their race by our successors in the next age, and in coming centuries. We do not mean, that all who boast the name of science will be so considered; for, as soon as any science or branch of knowledge has made a certain progress, it necessarily follows, that it will be professed by numerous pretenders, who will probably greatly magnify its importance, and at any rate possibly make an outcry, of which the real originators are heartily ashamed. We believe, sincerely, that it is not the warriors, but the followers of the camp, against which Mr. Peacock levels his shafts; he would probably be himself the first to regret his prowess if he thought he had put the whole army to the rout, and we are quite certain that he would much grieve, did he know, that by his very able sharpshooting upon the stragglers he was mistaken for the advance corps of the enemies of all improvement, whether in science or politics.

It is a pity, that men are most inclined to satirise that of which they know the most. Juvenal, hot from the stews, Petronius Arbiter, fresh from the garden of Epicurus, in the first moments of re-action employed their genius upon the exposers of their partners in vice: it is thus with Mr. Peacock, he does not satirise the boroughmongers, for he is not of their click; he does not attack the money-brokers, for he is not a regarder of pelf; were he of the Stock Exchange he would rail against waddlers and men of straw; were he of the Universities, a fellow of some musty college, he would run down the malappropriation of testamentary funds, and the misdirection of the courses of instruction; the idleness which passes under the name of learned ease, the ignorance which is called erudition. Had he been a lawyer or a police magistrate, the chicaneries of the law, or the absurdities of society would have been his food. We should, perhaps, have laughed as much, but not so wisely. Mr. Peacock happens to be well acquainted with those studies on which men at the present day chiefly pride themselves, he consequently detects more acutely than others the hollowness and emptiness of the pretensions of the train-bearers of these particular sciences. Being himself a master of the art, he can instantly discover the clumsy efforts of a sciolist—having a great susceptibility of the ridiculous, he is forced upon comparisons of the most laughable description. In order to be understood, however, he aims at the most distinguished representatives of the science, where others would have satirized the pretenders.

The most conspicuous personage of *Crotchet Castle* is Mr. Mac Quedy, the economist; he is represented in colours not to be mistaken; and it is very possible that they who are incapable of understanding the writings of the author satirized, are quite equal to the comprehension of the satire. Political Economy has enemies enough in the ranks of those who are ignorant of it; weapons are now supplied from its own arsenal. Under the name of Mr. Skionar, the professor of the transcendental school of poetry is ridiculed, and we have no objection. We can also forgive the vagaries of the antiquary, Mr. Chainmail, who lives in the twelfth and thirteenth century. Dr. Folliot is the representative of Common Sense, according to the author's idea of it. Common Sense, then, is a divinity doctor, of a great wine capacity, a parson of uncommon pugilistic force, as clever at knocking down an antagonist with a classical quotation, as with his cudgel. Mr. Peacock's notion of love is of the same quality as that of his idea of Common Sense. Mr. Chainmail finds a romantic beauty in Wales, hanging over a water-fall; she turns out to be a model of accomplishment and amiability in disguise; a London banker's daughter, in a russet boddice, her name is Touchandgo—the only point about her, which is not well adapted to the meridian of the Minerva Library. ⟨. . .⟩

It is impossible to deny the exquisite humour of ⟨. . .⟩ *Crotchet Castle*: and it is pleasant to laugh without, at the same time feeling the twitchings of reason and conscience, sensations which we do not hesitate to say, have presented very considerable drawbacks on the amusement which we cannot help taking in all the writings of our author. He is learned and he plays with his erudition, he is well acquainted with modern discoveries and he laughs at them, he is liberal in all his political opinions, and he attacks liberals only. The hero of the church and the ring, Dr. Folliott is precisely the jovial and narrow-minded athletic grammarian, whom *Blackwood's Magazine* would deify as the model of men, a pattern for all Christendom in religion, politics, and morals, a gormandizer of sensual things, a wielder of the fist, a knocker-down of arguments. It is true that he is the antipodes of cant, which implies professions of distinterestedness: the model of men despises all generosity, and does not pretend to a virtue which no hypocrisy could procure him credit for. It does not become us to assume the direction of the efforts of a man of Mr. Peacock's genius, more particularly after suffering ourselves to be so greatly entertained by the perusal of one of his works, nevertheless we cannot help beseeching him to apply his most tranchant qualities to the extirpation of the greater nuisances which prey upon the well being of society, and impede the future improvement of mankind.—ALBANY FONBLANQUE, "Crotchet Castle," *Westminster Review*, July 1831, pp. 208–9, 218

We have expressed an opinion of his early poetry, the best bits of which are translations of Greek choruses, evidently found amongst his papers, and probably never designed for publication. The *Paper-Money Lyrics* may have been smart at the time of their issue: their personalities fall flat on ears that have not contemporary events and disasters to sharpen them; and perhaps Peacock's impression on his own age was made less by these than by his prose allusions to the same monetary transactions and troubles in the pages of *Melincourt*. Certainly it is pleasanter to thread the meanderings of the Thames in the prose excursion of *Crotchet Castle*, which might have given a hint for Black's *Story of a Phaeton*, than to unwind the meshes of the "Genius of the Thames," an overelaborated classical, historical, topographical, and ambitious 'Pindaric poem on the subject of the national river. Those who travel past Cirencester Junction by the Great Western Railway, will do well to turn aside and visit Kemble Church and its confines, by way of ascertaining how much of stanza vii. in the second part (iii. 83) is the product of youthful and poetic fancy. There is more merit in *Rhododaphne*, a classical poem published by Hookham in 1818, and involving a spirited tale of the conflict between heavenly and earthly, impure and holy, natural and supernatural, love, told in Pindaric measures, and teeming with classic allusions and imitations. Yet even here a comparison forces itself on the reader of *Crotchet Castle* between the romantic treatment of the Uranian and the Pandemian Venus in this poem, and the comic and satiric dialogue between the Rev. Dr. Folliott and Mr. Crotchet, about nude and undraped Venuses in that novelette; and few will deny that the latter is a far better and livelier pastime than the other. "Sir Hornbook," and "The Round Table" are obvious baits for the ears of the author's grandchildren, otherwise likely to be deaf to English grammar and history. In short, there is simply nothing in the poetry ⟨. . .⟩ that is so calculated to extend Peacock's undoubted gift of pleasant prose to the region of poetry, as the songs, redolent of mirth, wit, gaiety, and pathos, which are spread equally over the pages of those novelettes, that are his best title to fame and remembrance. Not to recur to his *Memoirs of Shelley*, which concern rather Shelley's admirers and biographers, a few last words may be devoted to a reiteration of Peacock's claim to a distinct and distinguished place among English writers in the department of "belles lettres." One would like to say "of fiction," but it is a haunting thought that a fiction involves a plot; and for plots and plot-work Peacock has a glorious contempt. We may learn, indeed, what was Peacock's *métier*, by what means he disguises or compensates this lack—by a constant flow of conversation and dialogues replete with the rarest and raciest jets of humour, ancient and modern. He is less a novelist than a humourist, and his interlocutors dine, dance, drive, ride, sail, or walk for the purpose of ventilating their creator's humour. Herein he differs from a rising and popular modern novelist, whom he resembles in manifest fondness for Greek and Latin poetry; though even the point of resemblance is not exact, for Peacock likes to parade his research and learning at the risk of being called a pedant, while the author of *Lorna Doone* runs on in a well of pure, bright, undefiled, uninterrupted English, beneath which the classically nurtured discern a fine rill suggestive of the "Fons Bandusiæ," and of "Pierii Latices." What is common to both is the bond of a vein of humour; and into this humour Peacock's classicality infuses a grace and flavour peculiar to himself, a scholarly refinement lacking in our typical humourists, whether Sterne, or Swift, or even Fielding. His humour is never coarse or indecent, much less ribald or impious. It is the humour of "a scholar and a poet, and above all a man of letters," who has dug deep into Petronius and Athenæus, caught the trick and attraction of the *contes* of eighteenth century France, and by a style, manner, and creative power of his own produced a species of satiric, humouristic, and in a lesser degree romantic *mélange* quite *sui generis* in this country. If his spirit is indeed, as Lord Houghton describes it, "the spirit of an elder time before all the sherry was dry and all the ale bitter, and when men of thought were not ashamed of being merry." so much the more reason is there that our generation should possess such a memorial as these three volumes of a gayer and less matter-of-fact age of literature, and that space should be found in the most accessible shelf of every English library for the works, wit, and wisdom of Thomas Love Peacock.—JAMES DAVIES, "Thomas Love Peacock," *Contemporary Review*, April 1875, pp. 760–62

GEORGE BARNETT SMITH
From "Thomas Love Peacock"

Fortnightly Review, August 1873, pp. 189–206

One trembles to think what the world would have become without its literary scourges. The soft irony of Montaigne, the withering gaze of Voltaire, the lightning flash of Swift, have now and again made it ashamed of its meanness and its vanity, and have discovered the pigmy concealed beneath the folds of the giant. There is no power touching whose exercise the whole of mankind is so sensitive. Man always has objected, and always will object, to being called a fool: how much greater, then, must his horror be at having the fact demonstrated. Agreeing with the critic in his condemnation of the aphorism attributed to Shaftesbury, that "ridicule is the test of truth," we must still hold that it divides power almost equally with all other correctives of the public taste and morals. Wit dissects and destroys, but it has no creative force, is almost devoid of enthusiasm, and is no respecter of dignities and persons. There is much truth, however, which can in nowise come within its scope; hence it is a fallacy to call it the test of truth. It is rather the discoverer of error. There is something in the mental constitution of the satirist which prevents him from taking an optimist view of things. He is all the more useful on that account. The negative gifts of the satirist, while not lifting him to an equality with the being who originates, still entitle him to a high place in the world's regard. It should be borne in mind, too, that though it will be generally found he lacks enthusiasm, yet he possesses a sensitiveness as real, while differing in quality, as that of the artist and the poet.

Thomas Love Peacock had every opportunity for becoming the calm, contemplative cynic. His life was long but uneventful. His fourscore years did not embrace ten events to be remembered even in an ordinary life. He was born at Weymouth in 1785, and when a little over thirty years of age, obtained a post in a public office, as many others have done who afterwards enriched the national literature by their works. Peacock entered the East India House in 1818, and was Examiner of India correspondence from the death of James Mill in 1836 until March 1856, when he retired on a pension. He died January 23rd, 1866. He was a friend of Charles Lamb and of Shelley, for the latter of whom he acted as executor, and his wrongs doubtless made him still more sympathetic and friendly. His hatred of oppression in every guise is to be gathered in his works, which breathe of liberty of thought, speech, and action. There were few, if any, riper scholars in his time. He was distinguished especially for his love of the Greek, Latin, and Italian classics, in editions of which his library was extraordinarily rich. It is not a little singular to find one whose tastes were those of the recluse taking up in his writings the burning questions of the day and mingling in the fray of politics. His observation, however, was most extensive; like his learning, it seemed to embrace all matters and topics which came to the surface of public life. In his own political views he must have been ardently progressive—Liberal in the highest sense of the word, and to the backbone. He would be as opposed to a Whig job as to a Conservative monopoly. The deep-rooted conviction he had of the rights of man, the individual, caused him to loathe injustice in whatever quarter it was perceived. It is impossible to read his works and not to admire his denunciations of the base, and his scorn of the petty, sins which are sometimes hugged so closely. He had many pagan qualities, and among them a pagan kind of rectitude.

As to his humour, it is exclusively his own; one never meets with its precise flavour either before or after him. Mingled sometimes with a dash of effrontery, it is very searching, attaining its end by a kind of intellectual travesty. To the quack and the mountebank he is a most dangerous person, wielding a power of castigation that is amazing. To his honour, however, it can be said that throughout his whole works there is no demonstration of personal feeling. Considering his endowment and the great temptation to wield the lash which invariably accompanies it, his self-repression was very great. Principles, not men, were the objects of his satire, and if occasionally individuals recoiled from the smart, it only showed how true had been his perceptions of character. Some humorists gently play with their subjects and tease them as a cat does a mouse; others knock them down with a bludgeon; whilst others again make them despise themselves by inverting their natures, and showing them their vanity, hollowness, and pretence. Peacock adopted the last method with all the human excrescences he dealt with. To rebuke incapacity in attempting to deal with things too high for it, and to tear the glazed mask from the hollow cheek of pretence, were the objects to which he devoted himself. His success in doing this warrants some reference to the means by which he accomplished it, and justifies us in attempting to recover his name from the comparative indifference in which it has too long lain.

The chronological order in which his works were issued will not be strictly adhered to in the comments it may be necessary to make upon them; in fact there seems to be some doubt as to their order, if not of issue at least of composition. Undoubtedly, however, the public has been right in this instance in its association of his most widely-known work with the name of the author as being intrinsically equal, if not superior, to any of the rest. Other works may have their own special charm, but that which is richest in the exhibition of the most prominent gift of the author is *Headlong Hall*. Before the publication of this work there had been no writer who so boldly flung himself into the arena against contemporary humbugs. It is infinitely refreshing to read his straightforward scathing denunciations as well as his insinuating facetiousness and inuendo. He seems to revel in a tilt against all that the world praises as proper and respectable. An intellectual and material epicureanism pervades his pages, and when the rollicking wit ceases to flow it is only to give time for the passing of the bottle. We not only get "the feast of reason and flow of soul," but an unswerving devotion to those creature comforts in which the clergy—first in good works—have ever been our leaders. Mr. Headlong, the representative of the ancient Welsh family of the Headlongs, claiming superior antiquity to Cadwallader, contracts a strange taste in a Welsh squire—the taste for books. He next desires to pass for a philosopher and a man of taste, and comes up to Oxford to inquire for other men of taste and philosophers; but "being assured by a learned professor that there were no such things in the University," he proceeds to London, where he makes as extensive acquaintance with philosophers and *dilettanti* as his ambition could desire. Several of these he invites to Headlong Hall, and the staple of the volume is composed of their doings and their discussions. The four leading personages who sustain the brunt of the battle are—Mr. Foster, the perfectibilian, who takes the bright view of everything; Mr. Escot, the deteriorationist, who takes the dark view of everything; Mr. Jenkison, the statu-quo-ite, who has arguments to advance on both sides, but is nearly always in favour of allowing things to remain as they are; and the Rev. Dr. Gaster, a worthy divine who can deliver a learned dissertation on the art of stuffing a turkey, and to whom the consumption of a bottle of port is a very slight matter. It is amusing to note how the various classes of thinkers are trotted out one after another on their respective hobbies, and how impartial the author is in dividing his favours amongst them. Nor is it a little singular that all his specimens of the clergy whom Peacock has drawn are of one type; they are all jolly men of the world. About fifty or sixty years ago, the time at which he wrote, the conventional parson was very frequently of this stamp. His life was passed between fox-hunting, card-playing, and drinking. Since then the muscular Christian and other excellent men have arisen. But there have also sprung up with them men almost of a more mischievous type than the old fox-hunter. There are too many pitiful shepherds left who, in quiet, out-of-the-way villages make the life of the poor a burden to them. These continually enlarge on the duty of the labourers to keep their proper stations, and to revere the clergy and the squirearchy—the former of whom are to provide for them their opinions and their spiritual food, the latter their temporal comforts. Many of the later clergy are in the eyes of sensible men little less contemptible than the old; the venue of our contempt has been changed, that is all. But there is the same difficulty existing now that there was in Peacock's time, and indeed has been in all ages,—the difficulty of persuading the clergy to take one step towards reform in any direction, till nearly all other classes have taken ten. Progress, to them, has generally meant the destruction of their cherished rights. The Rev. Dr. Gaster cared little about questions which caused the thoughtful intellects of his day great concern, but in tossing off a bumper of Burgundy he was equal to the best. Occasionally he had a forcible way with him and said smart things, but he did not profess to be so proficient in knowledge as Mr. Panscope, "the chemical, botanical, geological, astronomical, mathematical, metaphysical, meteorological, anatomical, physiological, galvanistical, musical, pictorial, bibliographical, critical philosopher, who had run through the whole circle of the sciences, and understood them all equally well." The author gives us the portraits of four critics, Mr. Gall, Mr. Treacle, Mr. Nightshade, and Mr. Mac Laurel, with accurate descriptions of their various modes of criticism—the criticism seeming at that period to be about as deficient in *vis* as it generally is now; but the happiest passages in the book are those devoted to the speculations of the various philosophers. Two schools of thought are presented to us in the following few sentences:—

"I conceive," said Mr. Foster, "that men are virtuous in proportion as they are enlightened; and that, as every generation increases in knowledge, it also increases in virtue." "I wish it were so," said Mr. Escot, "but to me the very reverse appears to be the fact. The progress of knowledge is not general: it is confined to a chosen few of every age. How far these are better than their neighbours, we may examine by-and-by . . . Give me the wild man of the woods: the original, unthinking, unscientific, unlogical savage: in him there is at least some good; but, in a civilized, sophisticated, cold-blooded, mechanical, calculating slave of Mammon and the world, there is none—absolutely none. Sir, if I fall into a river, an unsophisticated man will jump in and bring me out; but a philosopher will look on with the utmost calmness, and consider me in the light of a projectile, and making a calculation of the degree of force with which I have impinged the surface, the resistance of the fluid, the velocity of the current, and the depth of the water in that particular place, he will ascertain with the greatest nicety in what part of the mud at the bottom I may probably be found, at any given distance of time from the moment of my first immersion!"

All which is rather hard both on the drowning man and the philosopher. The plot of this novel, if novel it can be called, is very subsidiary to the other purposes of the author, and has nothing whatever in it of a striking sort; but there are scattered here and there through its pages fine descriptions of Welsh scenery, which seems to have possessed a peculiar charm for Peacock. His real strength, nevertheless, lies in another direction—a readiness to grasp instantaneously the views and characters of men, and a singular faculty of reproducing them in dialogue. The entire work, *Headlong Hall*, is a series of portraits painted by means of opinions, some of them carefully executed and filled in, others drawn in a few rough but unmistakeable touches. We have Miss Philomela Poppyseed, the compounder of novels; Mr. Chromatic; Sir Patrick Prism; Mr. Cranium; Miss Tenorina; Lord Littlebrain, &c., whose idiosyncrasies are mostly betrayed by their names. The author also exhibits a remarkable power of assimilation from other writers, being able to enforce his points with the most apposite quotations from all sources, in all classes and all ages.

In *Nightmare Abbey*, another remarkable work, we get the same brilliancy, and again meet with characters whom we have recognised in the world. There is Mr. Scythrop Glowry, heir to the owner of the Abbey, who becomes "troubled with the passion for reforming the world," and meditates on the practicability of reviving a confederation of regenerators. He publishes a book on the subject, of which only seven copies are sold; but that does not deter him. He proposes to his beautiful lady-love, Miss Marionetta O'Carroll, that they should each open a vein in the other's arm, mix their blood in a bowl, and drink it as a sacrament of love—and, in fact, plays transcendental madman to the top of his bent. Then we have Mr. Toobad, who prophesies that "the devil has come among mankind, having great wrath;" the Hon. Mr. Listless, with shattered nerves and a system incapable of exertion; Mr. Flosky, who considers modern literature is a north-east wind—"a blight of the human soul." In the mouth of one of the characters two sentences are put which are a deeper, truer comment upon the French character than whole volumes which have been written since. "A Frenchman," he says, "is born in harness, ready saddled, bitted, and bridled, for any tyrant to ride. He will fawn under his rider one moment, and throw him and kick him to death the next; but another adventurer springs on his back, and by dint of whip and spur, on he goes as before." An epitome of the history of France since the Revolution of 1789. The following comparison between our own "enlightened" age and the past, delivered by Mr. Toobad, has in it many points which might well give us pause:—

> "Forsooth, this is the enlightened age. Marry, how! Did our ancestors go peeping about with dark lanterns, and do we walk at our ease in broad sunshine? What do we see by it which our ancestors saw not, and which, at the same time, is worth seeing? We see a hundred men hanged, where they saw one. We see five hundred transported, where they saw one. We see five thousand in the workhouse, where they saw one. We see scores of Bible Societies, where they saw none. We see paper, where they saw gold. We see men in stays, where they saw men in armour. We see painted faces, where they saw healthy ones. We see children perishing in manufactories, where they saw them flourishing in the fields. We see prisons, where they saw castles.

We see masters, where they saw representatives. In short, they saw true men, where we see false knaves. They saw Milton, and we see Mr. Sackbut."

It is impossible even to enumerate here the vast variety of subjects which the writer touches upon. His range is almost unlimited; in every page there is either an old superstition exploded or a new philosophy criticized.

In *Crotchet Castle* the author still writes with the pen of wormwood and ink of gall. The motto sufficiently indicates in the outset what a pungency of wit may be expected —"Le monde est plein de fous, et qui n'en veut pas voir, doit se tenir tout seul, et casser son miroir." The complacency of many people is effectually destroyed by the way the author himself breaks the mirrors in which they have been wont to survey their own perfections. Possibly there may be those who think that in this work he has overstepped the just bounds of ridicule, and endeavoured to bring into contempt persons who are really useful to their generation. This is the conclusion to which a merely surface-reading of his books would lead, and probably many would rise from their perusal with an impression as unjust to the writer as could well be. Because Peacock ruthlessly condemns the pretenders of science, it is not to be supposed, and will not be by the really candid judge, that he has no sympathy with its true and earnest devotees. A Newton would receive his homage equally with an Æschylus or a Homer. He only wishes to prick the windbag; to show upon what a very little a reputation which the world chooses to honour is sometimes built. It is the bubble which he desires to burst—the unsoundness in our social and political economics he endeavours to expose. Probably there was no one who would have felt it more deeply than he, if he had imagined that what he was writing would be turned from its purpose, either wilfully or ignorantly, and the writer made to appear an enemy of truth. It is hard, at times, to get rid of the idea that he is laughing at all the rest of the world, which, in any, is the surest test of folly, for the mighty wisdom of the cachinnatory great one himself is only a river into which the lesser streams of wisdom in others have flowed. There is no human being who can afford to laugh at and despise the whole race, simply because there is no human being who is not indebted to it. But we absolve our author at once from any such charge as this. Having comprehended in some degree the stand-points from which he has shot his arrows, we are bound to confess, not only that his aim is true, but that he has not chosen his subjects thoughtlessly or unjustifiably. Adam Smith lived long before him, and his principles were well established in the public mind, and acknowledged to be in many respects unassailable. It is not to be imagined for a moment that either he or his true followers were satirised in the person of the Scotch political economist who figures in these pages. Yet, strange to say, there have been critics who have credited him with some such aims, and have employed their acumen in discovering how he has transfixed this and that personage who has hitherto been held as an authority in the branch of literature or science to which he has devoted himself. Nothing could be more fallacious. Peacock was a man who was thoroughly abreast with the intellectual progress of his time; he was deeply interested in it, and capable of sympathizing to the full with all those men whose solid attainments and brilliant talents have been of service to humanity. His satire wants looking at as he wished it to be viewed, and it will be seen clearly of what immense value is the winnowing implement of his ridicule. The principal character in *Crotchet Castle* is Mr. Mac Quedy, the Scotch political economist aforesaid, or Mac Q. E. D., the son of a demonstration—and certainly the way in which he is dealt with allows of no misunderstanding. Then we have the transcendental schools criticized in the person of Mr. Skionar, with more of the broad farce in his delineation than is conspicuous in the economist, the subject affording better scope for it. Mr. Chainmail is an antiquary, devoted to singing the glories of the twelfth and thirteenth centuries, whilst Mr. Crotchet, the proprietor of the Castle, is one who has made his money in the City with neither more nor less conscientiousness than thousands who are now continually occupied on 'Change in the same operation. Perhaps the best character in the book for life-like vigour and reality is the Rev. Dr. Folliott, the exceedingly vigorous Christian, who batters down the theories of Messrs. Mac Quedy and Skionar with the force of a sledge-hammer, and who is not unlike, in his style of conversation, the great Johnson. When asked if he sets no value upon "the right principles of rent, profit, wages, and currency," he answers, "Sir, my principles in these things are to take as much as I can get, and to pay no more than I can help. These are every man's principles, whether they be the right principles or no. There, sir, is political economy in a nutshell." The Doctor is wrong; these are not every man's principles, but they are very largely every man's practice—which, notwithstanding, amounts to very nearly the same thing. ⟨. . .⟩

Amongst other subjects which come under the lash in this volume are the practices of Mr. Puffall, who obtains sketches from Lady Clarinda, and recommends them to the world as the work of a lady of quality, who has made very free with the characters of her acquaintance. The novel appears as "the most popular production of the day," but, as the novelist herself slily remarks to a friend, "the day" is a very convenient phrase; it allows of three hundred and sixty-five 'most popular productions' in a year. And in leap year one more." The purse-proud were always the aversion of Peacock, and in this work he is again scathing in his invective upon the greedy appetite for wealth, and the unscrupulousness which so frequently attends its acquirement. The character of Mr. Touch-and-go, the great banker—who, together with the contents of his till, were reported absent one morning—might do duty for many others before and since, and is one of the "representative men" forgotten by Emerson.

Maid Marian is an investiture of the old story of Robin Hood and Sherwood Forest with new grace and vitality. As with all its author's works, however, it is not destitute of a purpose, though the satire is not so apparent upon the face of the story itself. The narrative is excellently told, and we question whether there was ever a more poetical description penned of the home of the bold outlaw than this. It is put into the mouth of the Friar, who, in answer to the remark of a captured baron that he has fallen into "fine company," replies, "In the very best of company, in the high court of Nature, and in the midst of her own nobility. Is it not so? This goodly grove is our palace: the oak and the beech are its colonnade and its canopy: the sun, and the moon, and the stars are its everlasting lamps: the grass, and the daisy, and the primrose, and the violet are its many-coloured floor of green, white, yellow, and blue: the may-flower, and the woodbine, and the eglantine, and the ivy are its decorations, its curtains, and its tapestry: the lark, and the thrush, and the nightingale are its unhired minstrels and musicians. Robin Hood is king of the forest both by dignity of birth and by virtue of his standing army: to say nothing of the free choice of his people." The author strikes, through the medium of the old history, at the assumed principle in many quarters in our own day, that Might involves Right, a matter in which there is no necessity to follow him with a disquisition at the present moment.

A treatise might be written, with an almost numberless catalogue of instances appended, upon authors who, from various circumstances and considerations, have been hurried into too rapid writing. With many minds the mere fact of publication is a great inducement to commit the unpardonable offence, for such it must be regarded in the interests of the general reader. The time came to Peacock once in his career, and at an early stage, when the polished steel weapon was seen to be blunted. The incisiveness which distinguishes most of his writings is not so apparent in *Melincourt; or, Sir Oran Haut-ton*. Here we have less sarcasm, or rather what we have is so largely diluted that occasionally we doubt whether we are drawing from the same spring which has hitherto given us such delight. The book bears the traces of hasty composition, and altogether we should regard it as much inferior to our author at his best. It partakes more of the form of the ordinary novel, but, just as much as this is the case, does it lose in those other qualities which are actually associated with the name of its writer. Isolated scenes and passages may be good, but there exists a verbosity to which we have been unaccustomed, and which we can ill brook. After the feast of sparkling wines and choice viands which he has again and again placed before us, the palate remains comparatively unexcited and unsatiated with this specimen of intellectual catering. The truth is that Peacock's genius was neither of the novelistic nor the dramatic kind, and his attempt to portray an ordinary heroine in Anthelia Melincourt must be pronounced a failure. Far higher success is achieved in some of the other characters which it is easy to classify amongst the peculiar creations of the author. Sir Telegraph Paxarett, for instance, is a character well conceived and sustained, with a great amount of originality in his development, and so is the Rev. Mr. Portpipe, whose very name is a little idyll upon the course and character of his clerical life. But the best of all the characters is Sir Oran Haut-ton, and the happiest parts are those referring to political anomalies, which are castigated *con amore*. There are the boroughs of Onevote and Threevotes and Fewvotes, with the peculiarities attendant upon each, and all touched upon with uncommon humour. The book is probably palling and even foolish to those who take no pleasure in intellectual discussions and arguments, but to the thinker who has at heart the purification of society from all that corrupts and degrades, it will not be without a special attraction. But it is writing which needs digesting, not skimming. The assumptions of one of the learned writers in a celebrated Quarterly are very severely handled, the reviewer being credited with the idea that he and those who think with him are the only wise—a fallacy by no means confined to persons holding one set of opinions. We part from the volume, nevertheless, with a decided impression of genius veiled.

Reference has already been made to the attachment which Peacock conceived for Welsh scenery, and another proof of it is afforded by a later work of his, and one of the most pleasant which has proceeded from his pen, *The Misfortunes of Elphin*. Here we behold a venerable story clothed by genius with all the reality of actual circumstance. The result of the author's labour is perfectly satisfactory. The style is never involved, though the language is now and then pedantic. The history is fixed in the sixth century, when the nominal sovereignty of Britain was held by Uther Pendragon. Amongst the petty kings was Gwythno Garanhir, King of Caredigion. This monarch was not fond of the sea, and built a palace on the rocky banks of the Mawddach, and also erected watchtowers which were subordinate to a central castle commanding the sea-port of Gwythno. In this castle dwelt Prince Seithenyn, who appears to have been a sort of First Commissioner of

Works to the King. He differs in these considerable respects from our modern First Commissioner, namely, that he drank the profits of his office, "and left the embankment which was to keep out the sea to his deputies, who left it to their assistants, who left it to itself." Elphin, the son of the King, informs the Commissioner, to his momentary discomfort, one day, that the embankment is rotten, and should all be made sound, to which the latter replies:—"So I have heard some people say before, perverse people, blind to venerable antiquity: that very unamiable sort of people, who are in the habit of indulging their reason. . . . There is nothing so dangerous as innovation. See the waves in the equinoctial storms, dashing and clashing, roaring and pouring, spattering and battering, rattling and battling against it. I would not be so presumptuous as to say I would build anything that would stand against them half an hour; and here this immortal old work, which God forbid the finger of modern mason should bring into jeopardy, this immortal work has stood for centuries, and will stand for centuries more, if we let it alone. It is well: it works well: let well alone. Cupbearer, fill. It was half rotten when I was born, and that is a conclusive reason why it should be three parts rotten when I die." Admirable sarcasm! The policy of masterly inaction was very disastrous, as of course it always is in matters social and political. The waves beat high and effected an entrance; the tower fell into the surf, and the entire structure was in danger. The inhabitants fled, whilst Seithenyn swore that an enemy had done the deed. He leaped into the torrent, from which we afterwards discover he was miraculously saved by clinging to a barrel, whose contents had previously cheered his inner organization. Elphin quits the castle, bearing with him Angharad, the lovely daughter of Seithenyn. Then come the lamentations of King Gwythno over his inundated lands, in excellent stanzas, graphic and concentrated in expression. Thus was the kingdom of Caredigion ruined. Prince Elphin, who has married Angharad, is very fond of fishing, and one day he has a miraculous draught (subsequent to a dream on the subject) which proves to be a little child. Its surpassing beauty causes Angharad to make the exclamation, "Taliesin," "Radiant Brow." The foundling is adopted by the couple, and in after years becomes the celebrated bard Taliesin, and marries Melanghel, the daughter of his foster-parents. Taliesin grew up in excellent knowledge, but the science of political economy being then unknown, he knew nothing of "the advantage of growing rich by getting into debt and paying interest." The author further remarks, "they had no steam-engines, with fires as eternal as those of the nether world, wherein the squalid many, from infancy to age, might be turned into component portions of machinery for the benefit of the purple-faced few. They could neither poison the air with gas, nor the waters with its dregs: in short, they made their money of metal, and breathed pure air, and drank pure water, like unscientific barbarians." In all which things there is verily much food for reflection. The multiplication of species in a little kingdom like England must be attended with inconvenience and suffering to the majority. The wholesale system of going to the wall is inevitable: but do we not, as some compensation for using up the vital force of the labouring class, offer them churches and chapels, regiments of the cloth, "intellectual" enjoyments, and the brilliant and splendid spectacle for their admiration of an aristocracy which is kind enough to live on the sweat of their brow, and in numberless cases on their absolute degradation? Far be it from us, then, to say that we have made no progress since the time of the Welsh bard.

But, to proceed with the story, leaving all who may be interested in it, to pursue their investigations of the con-

stitution of society at that happy period. Elphin succeeds his father as king, but for certain indiscreet boastings, as they are held, he falls into bondage to King Maelgon, who has resolved to seize upon his wife. The rival king attempts to take her during the absence of her husband. But his emissaries are entrapped, and the matter afterwards coming before the great King Arthur, together with other vexed questions, he decides according to his far-famed principles of equity, and an exchange of prisoners is effected. Taliesin, who has been chiefly instrumental in procuring this termination of affairs, is rewarded by Elphin with his daughter's hand. We get glimpses of Enid, Queen Gwenyvar, Sir Gawain, Sir Tristram, and other knights and ladies familiar to the reader of Arthurian romance; and the volume closes with a Grand Bardic Congress at Caer Lleon. Undoubtedly one of its greatest charms lies in the beauty of the poems which are scattered through the various divisions. They are imbued with more sublimity and tenderness than other poems of the author which may lay claim to be more entirely original in conception. The modern English seems at any rate to have caught the spirit of the old bards if the form of expression be wanting. We cannot reproduce here the most striking of these poems, but the cultivated mind was never more forcibly exhibited than in their composition.

Although travelling over a portion of the ground already covered in previous novels, *Gryll Grange*, the last work by Peacock, is one perhaps intrinsically superior to all except *Headlong Hall*. Here he bravely combats many abuses which we regret to say have even not yet entirely disappeared. It may be commended to those who would rob us of our national lands and forests, to the poisoners of our atmosphere and our water, to the bores in Parliament, and to the useless livers in the world generally. Hear him on Parliament. "The wisdom of Parliament," says the Rev. Dr. Opimian, another of those clever epicurean divines, of whom we have had something already, "is a wisdom *sui generis*. It is not like any other wisdom. It is not the wisdom of Socrates, nor the wisdom of Solomon. It is the Wisdom of Parliament." The excellent Doctor could not get much farther than this in our day. But pursue the analogy between that time and the present. "The Wisdom of Parliament has ordered the Science to do something. The Wisdom does not know what, nor the Science either. But the Wisdom has empowered the Science to spend some millions of money; and this, no doubt, the Science will do. When the money has been spent, it will be found that the Something has been worse than nothing." The term "honourable" is also objected to, for "Palestine soup is not more remote from the true Jerusalem, than many an honourable friend from public honesty and honour." How much golden advice is compressed into the following words, the spirit lying beneath which would save this most Christian nation from humbling itself in the dust before its Creator for many calamities which might have been prevented!

> "Honesty would materially diminish the number of accidents. High-pressure steam boilers would not scatter death and destruction around them, if the dishonesty of avarice did not tempt their employment where the more costly low-pressure would ensure absolute safety. Honestly-built houses would not come suddenly down and crush their occupants. Ships, faithfully built and efficiently manned, would not so readily strike on a lee-shore, nor go instantly to pieces on the first touch of the ground. Honestly-made sweetmeats would not poison children; honestly-compounded drugs would not poison patients.

In short, the larger portion of what we call accidents are crimes."

Criticism could lend no additional force to such language as this, or more clearly show its appropriateness to our present year of grace. The science of panto-pragmatics, which is described as "a real art of talking about an imaginary art of teaching every man his own business," is one that is tantalisingly gridironed, and our system of competitive examinations was never set in a more ridiculous light than in these pages. We have papers which would have excluded Marlborough from the army and Nelson from the navy: on other matters hear what our author says:—

"Ask the hon. member for Muckborough on what acquisitions in history and mental and moral philosophy he founds his claim of competence to make laws for the nation? He can only tell you that he has been chosen as the most conspicuous Grub among the Money-grubs of his borough to be the representative of all that is sordid, selfish, hard-hearted, unintellectual, and anti-patriotic, which are the distinguishing qualities of the majority among them? Ask a candidate for a clerkship what are his qualifications? He may answer, 'All that are requisite—reading, writing, and arithmetic.' 'Nonsense,' says the questioner; 'do you know the number of miles in direct distance from Timbuctoo to the top of Chimborazo?' 'I do not,' says the candidate. 'Then you will not do for a clerk,' says the competitive examiner. Does the Money-grub of Muckborough know? He does not; nor anything else. The clerk may be able to answer some of the questions put to him. Money-grub could not answer one of them. But he is very fit for a legislator."

With which compliment to the Lower House we will close our extracts from this trenchant book. It exhibits Peacock at his highest, with ripened scholarship, polished style, and a varied and profound experience.

As might be expected, the poetry of our author was deeply impregnated with his classical spirit. The vast weight of his learning, which he seemed to "bear lightly as a flower," was exhibited in numberless erudite allusions, whilst occasionally the foot-notes to his efforts were even more full of a ripe scholarship than the poems themselves. Naturally, his bent of mind led him, in his quest of subjects, into the realms of romance and mythology, with which he was in a remarkable degree familiar. One of his most successful poems is that entitled *Rhododaphne, or the Thessalian Spell*. It is a poem which Coleridge might have written. Founded on the ascription of the power of magic to the being from whom it takes its name, the story is worked out with eminent skill and feeling. Anthemion, the flower of all Arcadia's youth, comes to the festival of Love, which was celebrated in honour of that deity every fifth year in the Temple of Love at Thespia, a town near the foot of Mount Helicon. The flowers he presents at the foot of the altar are suddenly blighted. This fills him with terror. He then hears himself addressed, and, looking up, beholds a maiden before him with more than mortal loveliness. She gives flowers to him, which are accepted at the altar, and so she passes out of sight. In the second canto he is made aware that the flower he has accepted is the fatal laurel-rose, and he is bade to seek the stream that laves the foot of the mountain, and there, calling on his Natal Genius, and with averted face, he is to cast the flower into the stream, looking not upon the running wave again. By this means the magic spell now over him will be dissolved. Immediately he has fulfilled the injunc-

tion he hears the cry of his beloved Callirrhoë, and is not proof against looking back; he does so, but all becomes still. The secret that the bright maiden who has bewitched him is Rhododaphne is revealed in the third canto, where she charges him with having thrown away the flower which she gave him. He pleads its disastrous nature; at least so he was informed by a reverend seer, and he is thus forcibly rebuked in lines which bear a sting (and doubtless were intended to do so) for nineteenth-century sophistry.

> The world, oh youth! deems many wise,
> Who dream at noon with waking eyes,
> While spectral fancy round them flings
> Phantoms of unexisting things;
> Whose truth is lies, whose paths are error,
> Whose gods are fiends, whose heaven is terror.

The spell woven round Anthemion is made stronger by the maiden's kiss, which is to be poison to all lips but hers. He returns to his own Arcadian vale and meets his destined bride. She flies to meet him, her eyes imparting and reflecting pleasure, for, as the author beautifully expresses it,—

> This is love's terrestrial treasure,
>   That in participation lives,
>   And evermore, the more it gives,
> Itself abounds in fuller measure.

But Anthemion's embrace proves, as predicted, the death of Callirrhoë, and maddened with despair the lover flies from the scene. Succeeding cantos are devoted to his wanderings, and to his meeting again with the magic maid of Thessaly. At length, for her impious spells, Rhododaphne is slain by the arrow of Uranian Love, and the marble palace in which she has been reclining with Anthemion is riven asunder. By her death the spell is removed from the latter, and once more he finds himself in his native vale, where he meets the risen Callirrhoë, and the happy pair raise a marble tomb to the dead Rhododaphne.

Such is the outline of this poem, which has many poetic graces: it is not, however, impassioned, as lofty poetry should be, and therefore very high rank cannot be conceded to it. It contrasts favourably, nevertheless, with many modern attempts to render into verse ancient stories which would seem of themselves to suggest the loftiest inspiration. The poetry of Peacock is neither the poetry of sentimental namby-pambyism nor of burning passion. If he does not glow with the fire of Shelley, he does not pall with the sickly maunderings of later nerveless versifiers, whose genius has had some difficulty in crawling through its long-clothes. While our author's verse is liquid and musical, it is never weak and faltering. He is able to endow his creations with some amount of life-breathing power. It can scarcely be said that he was happier in his poetry than his prose; rather, indeed, must the reverse be admitted. His intellectual and dissecting strength was greater than his emotional. He knew, probably, that the general reader would take no delight in his verse; but that mattered not to him; he could give him none other—consequently all his work in this direction betrays rather the thinking than the feeling man. In only one of his volumes of verse has he dealt after the manner of versifiers generally. The effort was not successful. It was his first attempt in the more popular style and scope, which he seems afterwards to have abandoned. The truth is that on ordinary topics he had nothing extraordinary to say. It was when he came to re-illume dead torches that his genius shone to advantage. ⟨. . .⟩

Susceptibility, then, or that extreme sensibility which permeates every avenue of the true poet's being, was deficient in Peacock, and in consequence he came short of the standard.

We know the real singer when we meet with him. He is not one who is compelled to ransack the stores of recondite lore before he gives us the treasure we need. He is a man whose heart is turned out towards humanity—and, whether the king on the throne or the beggar in the street be his theme, he is able to invest it with undying interest. He is a mirror upon which is reflected all the complex passions of human nature. He reads the secrets of humanity and of nature as one would read the pages of a book, without faltering, and with a clear apprehension of their meaning and import. There is no need for him to go back into past ages to discover subjects for his muse: the records of the very lives by which he is surrounded furnish him with material as tragic as the death of Cæsar. The gloom and the glory of his own time strike as deeply into his soul as do those of any past age. The great poet of every period has always been the man who was able to interpret the human life which encompassed him, and to paint it as he beheld it. Realities are what he achieves, and these are always recognised, transcending a thousand failures in attempting to revivify the beings of antiquity. In the sense, then, in which such a man as Burns, for instance, was a poet, Peacock was none at all. Impulsiveness was foreign to him. He had too much of the cynic and the critic in his composition to be possessed of the divine afflatus. His verse is ever correct and musical, not burning and overwhelming: it is like the silver stream which meanders pleasantly through the meadows, and not the roaring mountain cataract, or the tempestuous waves which beat against the rockbound shore.

We have left ourselves no space to speak of Peacock's miscellaneous works,—his *Paper Money Lyrics*, his translation of *Gl' Ingannati*, a comedy performed at Siena, in 1531, his *Reminiscences and Correspondence with Shelley*, &c. This is the less to be regretted, however, as these fugitive pieces are to be shortly collected, and republished with his more important works in a uniform and permanent form.

Sufficient ground has, we trust, been shown for turning back to this too-long neglected author. With a chosen few he has ever been a favourite, but to the admirers of a vapid and invertebrate style he must necessarily remain an abomination. To glance at the mere list of works of fiction at the present day which seem to afford most delight to the general reader is a disheartening operation: it will not have been in vain if these observations on one of the most remarkable writers of several generations should induce, in however small a degree, a reaction. In all those respects in which an author is of permanent benefit to mankind the author of *Headlong Hall* is worthy of occupying an eminent position. His vast learning, his precise style, his great research, his boundless sarcasm, his intense abhorrence of cant, are all so many claims upon our regard. With the ordinary novelists he has little in common, as will have been perceived during the course of this article; in most respects he cannot be put into competition with them; for, whilst he has many virtues which they do not possess, he exhibits few of their vices.

GEORGE SAINTSBURY
From "Peacock" (1886)
Collected Essays and Papers
1923, Volume 2, pp. 101–9

Lord Houghton has defined and explained Peacock's literary idiosyncrasy as that of a man of the eighteenth century belated and strayed in the nineteenth. It is always easy to improve on a given pattern, but I certainly think that this definition of Lord Houghton's (which, it should be said, is not given in his own words) needs a little improvement. For the differences which strike us in Peacock—the easy joviality, the satirical view of life, the contempt of formulas and of science—though they certainly distinguish many chief literary men of the eighteenth century from most chief literary men of the nineteenth, are not specially characteristic of the eighteenth century itself. They are found in the seventeenth, in the Renaissance, in classical antiquity—wherever, in short, the art of letters and the art of life have had comparatively free play. The chief differentia of Peacock is a differentia common among men of letters; that is to say, among men of letters who are accustomed to society, who take no sacerdotal or singing-robe view of literature, who appreciate the distinction which literary cultivation gives them over the herd of mankind, but who by no means take that distinction too seriously. Aristophanes, Horace, Lucian, Rabelais, Montaigne, Saint-Evremond, these are all Peacock's literary ancestors, each, of course, with his own difference in especial and in addition. Aristophanes was more of a politician and a patriot, Lucian more of a freethinker, Horace more of a simple *pococurante*. Rabelais may have had a little inclination to science itself (he would soon have found it out if he had lived a little later), Montaigne may have been more of a pure egotist, Saint-Evremond more of a man of society, and of the verse and prose of society. But they all had the same *ethos*, the same love of letters as letters, the same contempt of mere progress as progress, the same relish for the simpler and more human pleasures, the same good fellowship, the same tendency to escape from the labyrinth of life's riddles by what has been called the humour-gate, the same irreconcilable hatred of stupidity and vulgarity and cant. The eighteenth century has, no doubt, had its claim to be regarded as the special flourishing time of this mental state urged by many others besides Lord Houghton; but I doubt whether the claim can be sustained, at any rate to the detriment of other times, and the men of other times. That century took itself too seriously—a fault fatal to the claim at once. Indeed, the truth is that while this attitude has in some periods been very rare, it cannot be said to be the peculiar, still less the universal, characteristic of any period. It is a personal not a periodic distinction; and there are persons who might make out a fair claim to it even in the depths of the Middle Ages or of the nineteenth century.

However this may be, Peacock certainly held the theory of those who take life easily, who do not love anything very much except old books, old wine, and a few other things, not all of which perhaps need be old, who are rather inclined to see the folly of it than the pity of it, and who have an invincible tendency, if they tilt at anything at all, to tilt at the prevailing cants and arrogances of the time. These cants and arrogances of course vary. The position occupied by monkery at one time may be occupied by physical science at another; and a belief in graven images may supply in the third century the target, which is supplied by a belief in the supreme wisdom of majorities in the nineteenth. But the general principles—the cult of the Muses and the Graces for their own sake, and the practice of satiric archery at the follies of the day—appear in all the elect of this particular election, and they certainly appear in Peacock. The results no doubt are distasteful, not to say shocking, to some excellent people. It is impossible to avoid a slight chuckle when one thinks of the horror with which some such people must read Peacock's calm statement, repeated I think more than once, that one of his most perfect heroes "found, as he had often found before, that the more his mind was troubled, the more madeira he could drink without disordering his head." I have no doubt that the United Kingdom Alliance, if it knew this dreadful sentence (but probably the study of the United Kingdom Alliance is not much in Peacock), would like to burn all the copies of *Gryll Grange* by the hands of Mr Berry, and make the reprinting of it a misdemeanour, if not a felony. But it is not necessary to follow Sir Wilfrid Lawson, or to be a believer in education, or in telegraphs, or in majorities, in order to feel the repulsion which some people evidently feel for the manner of Peacock. With one sense absent and another strongly present it is impossible for any one to like him. The present sense is that which has been rather grandiosely called the sense of moral responsibility in literature. The absent sense is that sixth, seventh, or eighth sense, called a sense of humour, and about this there is no arguing. Those who have it, instead of being quietly and humbly thankful, are perhaps a little too apt to celebrate their joy in the face of the afflicted ones who have it not; the afflicted ones, who have it not, only follow a general law in protesting that the sense of humour is a very worthless thing, if not a complete humbug. But there are others of whom it would be absurd to say that they have no sense of humour, and yet who cannot place themselves at the Peacockian point of view, or at the point of view of those who like Peacock. His humour is not their humour; his wit not their wit. Like one of his own characters (who did not show his usual wisdom in the remark), they "must take pleasure in the thing represented before they can take pleasure in the representation." And in the things that Peacock represents they do not take pleasure. That gentlemen should drink a great deal of burgundy and sing songs during the process, appears to them at the best childish, at the worst horribly wrong. The prince-butler Seithenyn is a reprobate old man, who was unfaithful to his trust and shamelessly given to sensual indulgence. Dr Folliott, as a parish priest, should not have drunk so much wine; and it would have been much more satisfactory to hear more of Dr Opimian's sermons and district visiting, and less of his dinners with Squire Gryll and Mr Falconer. Peacock's irony on social and political arrangements is all sterile, all destructive, and the sentiment that "most opinions that have anything to be said for them are about two thousand years old" is a libel on mankind. They feel, in short, for Peacock the animosity, mingled with contempt, which the late M. Amiel felt for "clever mockers."

It is probably useless to argue with any such. It might, indeed, be urged in all seriousness that the Peacockian attitude is not in the least identical with the Mephistophelian; that it is based simply on the very sober and arguable ground that human nature is always very much the same, liable to the same delusions and the same weaknesses; and that the oldest things are likely to be best, not for any intrinsic or mystical virtue of antiquity, but because they have had most time to be found out in, and have not been found out. It may further be argued, as it has often been argued before, that the use of ridicule as a general criterion can do no harm, and may do much good. If the thing ridiculed be of God, it will stand; if it be not, the sooner it is laughed off the face of the earth the better. But there is probably little good in urging all this. Just as a lover of the greatest of Greek dramatists must recognise at once that it would be perfectly useless to attempt to argue Lord Coleridge out of the idea that Aristophanes, though a genius, was vulgar and base of soul, so to go a good deal lower in the scale of years, and somewhat lower in the scale of genius, everybody who rejoices in the author of *Aristophanes in London* must see that he has no chance of converting any person who does not like Peacock. The middle term is not present, the disputants do not

in fact use the same language. The only thing to do is to recommend this particular pleasure to those who are capable of being pleased by it, and to whom, as no doubt it is to a great number, it is pleasure yet untried.

It is well to go about enjoying it with a certain caution. The reader must not expect always to agree with Peacock, who not only did not always agree with himself, but was also a man of almost ludicrously strong prejudices. He hated paper money; whereas the only feeling that most of us have on that subject is that we have not always as much of it as we should like. He hated Scotchmen, and there are many of his readers who without any claim to Scotch blood, but knowing the place and the people, will say,

> That better wine and better men
> We shall not meet in May,

or for the matter of that in any other month. Partly because he hated Scotchmen, and partly because in his earlier days Sir Walter was a pillar of Toryism, he hated Scott, and has been guilty not merely of an absurd and no doubt partly humorous comparison of the Waverley novels to pantomimes, but of more definite criticisms which will bear the test of examination as badly. His strictures on a famous verse of "A Dream of Fair Women" are indefensible, though there is perhaps more to be said for the accompanying gibe at Sir John Millais's endeavour to carry out the description of Cleopatra in black (chiefly black) and white. The reader of Peacock must never mind his author trampling on his, the reader's, favourite corns; or rather he must lay his account with the agreeable certainty that Peacock will shortly afterwards trample on other corns which are not at all his favourites. For my part I am quite willing to accept these conditions. And I do not find that my admiration for Coleridge, and my sympathy with those who opposed the first Reform Bill, and my inclination to dispute the fact that Oxford is only a place of "unread books," make me like Peacock one whit the less. It is the law of the game, and those who play the game must put up with its laws. And it must be remembered that, at any rate in his later and best books, Peacock never wholly "took a side." He has always provided some personage or other who reduces all the whimsies and prejudices of his characters, even including his own, under a kind of dry light. Such is Lady Clarinda, who regards all the crotcheteers of Crotchet Castle with the same benevolent amusement; such Mr McBorrowdale, who, when he is requested to settle the question of the superiority or inferiority of Greek harmony and perspective to modern, replies, "I think ye may just buz that bottle before you." (Alas! to think that if a man used the word "buz" nowadays some wiseacre would accuse him of vulgarity or of false English.) The general criticism in his work is always sane and vigorous, even though there may be flaws in the particular censures; and it is very seldom that even in his utterances of most flagrant prejudice anything really illiberal can be found. He had read much too widely and with too much discrimination for that. His reading had been corrected by too much of the cheerful give-and-take of social discussion, his dry light was softened and coloured by too frequent rainbows, the Apollonian rays being reflected on Bacchic dew. Anything that might otherwise seem hard and harsh in Peacock's perpetual ridicule is softened and mellowed by this pervading good fellowship which, as it is never pushed to the somewhat extravagant limits of the *Noctes Ambrosianæ*, so it distinguishes Peacock himself from the authors to whom in pure style he is most akin, and to whom Lord Houghton has already compared him—the French tale-tellers from Anthony Hamilton to Voltaire. In these, perfect as their form often is, there is constantly a slight want of geniality, a perpetual clatter and glitter of intellectual rapier and dagger which sometimes becomes rather irritating and teasing to ear and eye. Even the objects of Peacock's severest sarcasm, his Galls and Vamps and Eavesdrops, are allowed to join in the choruses and the bumpers of his easy-going symposia. The sole nexus is not cash payment but something much more agreeable, and it is allowed that even Mr Mystic had "some super-excellent madeira." Yet how far the wine is from getting above the wit in these merry books is not likely to escape even the most unsympathetic reader. The mark may be selected recklessly or unjustly, but the arrows always fly straight to it.

Peacock, in short, has eminently that quality of literature which may be called recreation. It may be that he is not extraordinarily instructive, though there is a good deal of quaint and not despicable erudition wrapped up in his apparently careless pages. It may be that he does not prove much; that he has, in fact, very little concern to prove anything. But in one of the only two modes of refreshment and distraction possible in literature, he is a very great master. The first of these modes is that of creation—that in which the writer spirits his readers away into some scene and manner of life quite different from that with which they are ordinarily conversant. With this Peacock, even in his professed poetical work, has not very much to do; and in his novels, even in *Maid Marian*, he hardly attempts it. The other is the mode of satirical present-ment of well-known and familiar things, and this is all his own. Even his remotest subjects are near enough to be in a manner familiar, and *Gryll Grange*, with a few insignificant changes of names and current follies, might have been written yesterday. He is, therefore, not likely for a long time to lose the freshness and point which, at any rate for the ordinary reader, are required in satirical handlings of ordinary life; while his purely literary merits, especially his grasp of the perennial follies and characters of humanity, of the *ludicrum humani generis* which never varies much in substance under its ever-varying dress, are such as to assure him life even after the immediate peculiarities which he satirised have ceased to be anything but history.

JOHN KEBLE

1792–1866

John Keble was born on April 25, 1792, at Fairford, Gloucestershire, the second son of a high-church clergyman. He excelled in his studies at Corpus Christi College, Oxford, graduating in 1810 with double first-class honors. The following year he was elected a fellow of Oriel College. Ordained a priest in 1816, he remained with the Oxford community for several years, then withdrew from the university in 1823 in order to help his father with parish work.

In 1827 Keble published *The Christian Year*, a collection of poems for Sundays and church festivals. It was circulated widely and disseminated the principles of the high-church movement to a large audience. Keble was appointed professor of poetry at Oxford in 1831, a post he held for a decade. A collection of his academic lectures was published in 1841 and reveals his affinity for the Romantic poets.

In 1833 Keble came into public prominence when he preached a sermon at Oxford denouncing the government for supressing ten Irish bishoprics. In the sermon, entitled "National Apostasy," Keble asserted the divine right of the church and its supernatural origin, thereby launching the Oxford Movement, which led to the renewal of Catholic thought and practice within the Church of England. The movement was led by John Henry Newman and a group of younger men, but Keble provided encouragement and support over the next decade. The movement produced a series of ninety pamphlets called *Tracts of the Times*; nine of them were written by Keble. During the years of the movement, Keble also produced an edition of the works of Richard Hooker (1836) and was instrumental in launching a series, *The Library of the Fathers* (1838). Despite Newman's separation from the Oxford Movement upon his conversion to Roman Catholicism in 1845, it did not collapse, owing in large part to the efforts of Keble.

Following the death of his father in 1835 Keble married. He became vicar of Hursley, near Winchester, the following year, and for the remainder of his life he lived there and worked as a country parson.

Keble died in Bournemouth on March 29, 1866. Three years later, Keble College was established at Oxford in his memory.

General

He ⟨Keble⟩ has himself told us that he owed to Wordsworth the tendency *ad sanctiora*, which is the mark of his own writings; and in fact he has but adapted the tone and habit of reverence, which his master applied to common objects and the course of the seasons, to sacred objects and the course of the ecclesiastical year,—diffusing a mist of sentiment and devotion altogether delicious to a gentle and timid devotee. —WALTER BAGEHOT, "Hartley Coleridge" (1852), *Collected Works*, ed. Norman St. John-Stevas, 1965, Vol. 1, pp. 168–69

Now no religious poet has ever more completely caught this spirit of a passionate love for nature than Keble, and in this sense he was the true child of the nineteenth century. In the whole religious poetry of the previous generation we doubt whether there is a single passage which dwells upon or even alludes to natural beauty, so completely had their writers caught the temper of Pope and Dryden. Keble, like the prince in the fairy tale, was the first who was awakened out of the long slumber by her touch, and, in common with Burns, to whom he was always tenderly drawn by that poetical brotherhood which may be expressed in his own words,—"brothers are brothers evermore,"—he shows in every page that he loves her as a mother, and that she had indeed "tempered his heart, as for a favourite child." It added, moreover, greatly to his power of being, so to speak, her religious interpreter, that he was also a man of first-rate natural ability and cultivation in other respects; although these gifts, like his whole character, were held in check, and subordinated to his religious feeling, by a severe modesty and restraint. Now, very few men who have completely given themselves to religious poetry have brought to it a really cultivated and powerful mind, and Mr. Wordsworth is quite right in saying, in a passage already referred to, that "no great poems were ever produced, except by a man who, being possessed of more than ordinary sensibility, *had also thought long and deeply.*" Mr. Keble's poetry has this last and most perfect charm: it is that of an accomplished scholar, leavened with all the old grace and finish of the great minds of antiquity—a grace never protruded, but seen "alike in what it shows, and what conceals," always the pleasant companion of our way, as the brook playing over its pebbles, which solaced the sorrows of Ruth. ⟨. . .⟩

By thus seizing on a passionate feeling of his time Keble introduced a life and reality into religious poetry, which it was beginning to lose. The religious poets who had spoken to the previous generation were the children of the religious movement of the eighteenth century—the two Wesleys, Toplady, and Cowper. They were, many of them, endowed with a true genius for the expression of religious sentiment and passion, and few nobler hymns can be found in any language than that of Charles Wesley, "Come, O thou traveller unknown, whom still I hold but cannot see," or the spirit-stirring strain of Toplady's "Rock of Ages." But like the movement which gave them birth, they had exclusively harped on the single string, worked out the single vein, of emotion and experience; and this indeed in a very narrow sense of the words. The old English hymn-writers had caught far better the larger and more catholic spirit of the English Church; and Herbert, Donne, and Quarles, like the Andrewses and Taylors of their day—nay, even like Milton himself,—had carried religious feeling into every object of nature, and ransacked all the stores of Pagan antiquity for their illustrations. Keble is, in this respect, distinctly a pupil of Herbert and of Spenser; and by adopting their comparatively quiet and natural tone of religious reflection, he fell in with the feeling of his time, "tired with shadows," wearied with the constant strain of emotion, and glad to be taught how to use religious poetry as the companion of their common thoughts and studies, and of the daily business of their lives.—WILLIAM CHARLES LAKE, "Mr. Keble and the *Christian Year*," *Contemporary Review*, July 1866, pp. 325–27

Mr. Keble, the "sweet singer of Israel," and a true saint, if this generation has seen one, did not reside in Oxford.—WILLIAM EWART GLADSTONE, "A Chapter of Autobiography" (1868), *Gleanings of Past Years*, 1879, Vol. 7, p. 141

It was in these years, from 1826 to 1835, at Fairford, that Keble's pen was the most active. In them the *Christian Year* was finally completed and given to the world; in them his prelections as Professor of Poetry in the University of Oxford were composed and published. In them, too, he edited his edition of the works of Hooker. This edition of Hooker occupied him five years, from 1831 to 1836. Of all his prose

works the introduction to this edition seems to us far the ablest. It shows great critical power both in the minuter questions which concern the authenticity of certain portions of the ecclesiastical policy, and in the broader subject of what Hooker's real opinions were upon the turning points of the long controversy he held with the puritan writers, and what the influences were by which they were shaped. This was a work to which his whole heart was given. For though he would call no man master, not even Richard Hooker, and where they differed stated with all boldness and sincerity the difference and its cause, yet he could not but perceive in Hooker's times of opposition and reproach that which shadowed forth to his inner consciousness the likeness of his own work in his own generation. This consciousness often re-appears in his pages, and adds a most life-like reality to them.—SAMUEL WILBERFORCE, "Keble's *Biography*," *Quarterly Review*, July 1869, p. 119

He was a poet; he was a man of eminent goodness; and he was a great Christian thinker and theologian. Of these characters the first has mainly riveted the attention of the world. The name of the author of *The Christian Year* is known to thousands who know nothing, whatever they may infer, about his life and character. And a scarcely smaller number who are aware that he was a man of singular purity and simplicity of life have no idea that his intellect was one of unusual strength and beauty, and that he wielded decisive influence at a crisis pregnant with consequences to the religious future of his country. "The poet Keble!" The phrase is used, often indeed as a title of honour, but sometimes also to imply that he was only a maker of religious verses, and not properly a leader or guide of men. It is meant to suggest that, while the fitful and turbid stream of passion and thought which we term modern life was rolling impetuously onwards, he sat pensive but helpless on the brink of the torrent, and warbled soft strains of mournful half-intelligible song which could not even catch the ear of those who were battling with the angry waters. It is with a view to correcting this impression that I shall say what little I have to say this evening. His poetry already belongs to the literature of the country; and it has been criticised, and will be criticised yet, by those who may rightly venture upon the task.—HENRY PARRY LIDDON, "John Keble" (1876), *Clerical Life and Works*, 1895, pp. 335–36

Keble was not merely, like Isaac Watts or Charles Wesley, a writer of hymns. He was a real poet. Their works, no doubt, have occasional flashes of poetry, but their main object is didactic, devotional, theological. Not so the *Christian Year*, the *Lyra Innocentium*, or the *Psalter*. Very few of his verses can be used in public worship. His hymns are the exception. His originality lies in the fact that whilst the subjects which he touches are for the most part consecrated by religious usage or Biblical allusion, yet he grasps them not chiefly or exclusively as a theologian, or a Churchman, but as a poet. The *Lyra Innocentium*, whilst its more limited range of subjects, and perhaps its more subtle turn of thought, will always exclude it from the rank occupied by the *Christian Year*, has more of the true fire of genius, more of the true rush of poetic diction. The *Psalter* again differs essentially from Sternhold and Hopkins, Tate and Brady, not merely in execution, but in design. It is the only English example of a rendering of Hebrew poetry by one who was himself a poet, with the full appreciation of the poetical thought as well as of the spiritual life which lies enshrined in the deep places of the *Psalter*. A striking instance of this is the version of the 93rd Psalm. The general subject of that Psalm must be obvious to every one in any translation, however meagre. But it required the magic touch of a kindred spirit to bring out of the rugged Hebrew sentences the splendour and beauty of the dashing and breaking waves, which doubtless was intended, though shrouded in that archaic tongue from less keen observers.

Keble was not a sacred but, in the best sense of the word, a secular poet. It is not David only, but the Sibyl, whose accents we catch in his inspirations. The 'sword in myrtle drest' of Harmodius and Aristogeiton, 'the many-twinkling smile of ocean' from Æschylus, are images as familiar to him as 'Bethlehem's glade,' or 'Carmel's haunted strand.' Not George Herbert, or Cowper, but Wordsworth, Scott, and perhaps more than all, Southey, are the English poets that kindled his flame, and coloured his diction. The beautiful stanza, 'Why so stately, maiden fair?' and the whole poem on 'May Garlands,' might have been written by the least theological of men. The allusions to nature are even superabundantly inwoven with the most sacred subjects. Occasionally a thought of much force and sublimity is lost by its entanglement in some merely passing phase of cloud or shadow. The descriptions of natural scenery display a depth of poetical intuition very rarely vouchsafed to any man.—A. P. STANLEY, "John Keble," *The English Poets*, ed. Thomas Humphry Ward, 1880, Vol. 4, pp. 503–4

Keble is undoubtedly to be looked upon as the flower of the Oxford movement—for in Newman the movement moved beyond itself. Keble's theology, Keble's churchmanship, Keble's rectory and life and character, and the whole constitution of his mind, are the precise fulfillment of the Tractarian ideal. The intimate relation between his thought and character is striking. The character is certainly one of rare beauties; and let the thought have credit for all it can do. In that crowded and exciting time we think of no other whose life was so completely a mirror of his doctrine, and whose doctrine was so completely a mirror of his life, save only Arnold.—EDWIN D. MEAD, "Arnold of Rugby and the Oxford Movement," *Andover Review*, May 1884, p. 508

But there was nothing in him to foreshadow the leader in a bold and wide-reaching movement. He was absolutely without ambition. He hated show and mistrusted excitement. The thought of preferment was steadily put aside both from temper and definite principle. He had no popular aptitudes, and was very suspicious of them. He had no care for the possession of influence; he had deliberately chosen the *fallentis semita vitæ*, and to be what his father had been, a faithful and contented country parson, was all that he desired. But idleness was not in his nature. Born a poet, steeped in all that is noblest and tenderest and most beautiful in Greek and Roman literature, with the keenest sympathy with that new school of poetry which, with Wordsworth as its representative, was searching out the deeper relations between nature and the human soul, he found in poetical composition a vent and relief for feelings stirred by the marvels of glory and of awfulness, and by the sorrows and blessings, amid which human life is passed. But his poetry was for a long time only for himself and his intimate friends; his indulgence in poetical composition was partly playful, and it was not till after much hesitation on his own part and also on theirs, and with a contemptuous undervaluing of his work, which continued to the end of his life, that the anonymous little book of poems was published which has since become familiar wherever English is read, as the *Christian Year*. His serious interests were public ones. Though living in the shade, he followed with anxiety and increasing disquiet the changes which went on so rapidly and so formidably, during the end of the first quarter of this century, in opinion and in the possession of political power.—R. W. CHURCH, *The Oxford Movement*, 1891, pp. 25–26

After 1840, when the craving for spiritual guidance came to be widely felt, many turned to the elderly author of *The Christian Year*. They were met with the most embarrassing condescension, the tenderest sympathy, and sure and ready insight; they were not led to make any great venture or scale any great heights; he did not attempt to impose or inspire the very considerable austerities which he practised; his guidance was often hesitating and never peremptory. Probably most who trusted him enough to persevere in acting on his hints did learn to possess their souls in patience, to expend their emotions in safe ways, and in some measure to purify their hearts.

His self-depreciation did not affect his happiness or the esteem of two generations. He was loved and honoured to the last, though he lived to call himself a testy old clerk. Perhaps he will be remembered, like Shelley, as "a beautiful ineffectual angel"; but Keble's wings were never smirched.—G. A. SIMCOX, *Academy*, March 18, 1893, p. 235

What we have noticed about Lyte in some degree applies to John Keble. With him also thought at times outruns expression; whence it doubtless was that Wordsworth wished he could have rewritten the *Christian Year*. Keble, however, has a deeper strain of thought than Lyte; he is in closer harmony with Wordsworth; and the rare fragments of landscape which his train of subjects has admitted are worthy of the Master—true to Nature, dignified, instinct with serious thought and feeling.—FRANCIS T. PALGRAVE, *Landscape in Poetry*, 1896, p. 250

Keble's very generally granted character as one of the holiest persons of modern times, and even his influence on the Oxford Movement, concern us less here than his literary work, which was of almost the first importance merely as literature. The reaction from an enormous popularity of nearly seventy years' date, and the growth of anti-dogmatic opinions, have brought about a sort of tendency in some quarters to belittle, if not positively to sneer at, *The Christian Year*, which, with the *Lyra Innocentium* and a collection of *Miscellaneous Poems*, contains Keble's poetical work. There never was anything more uncritical. The famous reference which Thackeray—the least ecclesiastically inclined, if by no means the least religious, of English men of letters of genius in this century—makes to its appearance in *Pendennis*, shows what the thoughts of unbiassed contemporaries were. And no very different judgment can be formed by unbiassed posterity. With Herbert and Miss Rossetti, Keble ranks as the greatest of English writers in sacred verse, the irregular and unequal efforts of Vaughan and Crashaw sometimes transcending, oftener sinking below the three. If Keble has not the exquisite poetical mysticism of Christina Rossetti he is more copious and more strictly scholarly, while he escapes the quaint triviality, or the triviality sometimes not even quaint, which mars Herbert. The influence of Wordsworth is strongly shown, but it is rendered and redirected in an entirely original manner. The lack of taste which mars so much religious poetry never shows itself even for a moment in Keble; yet the correctness of his diction, like the orthodoxy of his thought, is never frigid or tame. There are few poets who so well deserve the nickname of a Christian Horace, though the phrase may seem to have something of the parodox of "prose Shakespeare." The careful melody of the versification and the exact felicity of the diction exclude, it may be, those highest flights which create most enthusiasm, at any rate in this century. But for measure, proportion, successful attainment

of the proposed end, Keble has few superiors.—GEORGE
SAINTSBURY, A *History of Nineteenth Century Literature*,
1896, pp. 363–64

Keble's influence was essentially personal, and was due to his
saintly life more than to anything he wrote, even in poetry. The
Tractarian movement took its rise in a longing for saintliness,
of which Keble furnished a living example. He was not to any
considerable extent an originator of theory. Certain germs of
theory about the Church, about its relation to pre-Reformation
times, about authority in religion, were in the air, and they
became absorbed in Keble's system. But his was not a creative
mind, and his position at the head of the Anglo-Catholic movement was little more than an accident. He was like a child who
by a thrust of his hand sends a finely-poised rock thundering
down a hill. In his literary aspects he is disappointing. A brilliant
boy and a most blameless man, he remains throughout too little
of this world. The pale perfection of his life is reflected in his
works. He would have been better had he been less good; he
would have been much better had he been less feminine.
—HUGH WALKER, *The Age of Tennyson*, 1897, p. 145

The charm of Keble's best poetry lies chiefly in its purity, its
serenity, its deep transparency of thought and feeling, its
calmness of expression, its consoling spirit. His theory was that
"the utterance of high or tender feeling, controlled or modified
by a certain reserve, is the very soul of poetry." His imagination
is illuminating rather than creative; in this he differs from
Henry Vaughan, to whom in many things he is so near of kin.
Of fancy, and of that striking, inventive power of expression
which usually goes with fancy, he has little or nothing; in this
he differs from his brother preacher-poet, George Herbert. In
broad, buoyant, vigorous emotion, such as finds an utterance
in the noblest hymns, wherein we hear the sound of many
voices triumphantly praising God, Keble was deficient; he was
too reflective, too secluded in spirit, to be among the great
hymn-writers. Keble's real master in poetry—though he himself gave the highest praise and admiration to Scott among the
moderns—his real master was Wordsworth. That clear and
tranquil vision, that meditative look into the heart of things
which Wordsworth turned upon common life, upon the
characters and stories of peasants, upon the outward shores of
Nature, Keble turned upon the services of the Church, the
ordinances of religion, the narratives of the Bible. He perceived
and revealed in them the poetic meaning and the soul of
beauty. To him the prophets and patriarchs and apostles were
real men, and he translated their stories into the language of
personal experience. Take for illustration his poems on Elijah,
on the Disobedient Prophet, on the Conversion of St. Paul, on
St. Andrew. Sometimes, it must be admitted, his paraphrases
of the Scripture suffer by comparison with the simplicity and
strength of the inspired original. But often he casts a ray into
the story that illuminates it with a new light. How exquisite is
the touch with which he describes Daniel praying in Babylon,

> His lattice open towards his darling west,
> Mourning the ruined home he still must love the
>   best.

How profound is the insight with which he speaks of

> Lazarus wakened from his four days' sleep,
> *Enduring life again*, that Passover to keep.

In the close observation of Nature Keble is not Wordsworth's equal, and yet the two poets have much in common,
both in spirit and in method. Keble takes notice of such slight,
significant things as the power of a breath of cold air to kill the
scent of the violet, of the bright thread of green that marks the

course of a spring trickling down the heath-clad hill, of
the clear note of a solitary bird ringing through the hush that
precedes the thunder-storm in a summer noon. How patient
and loving is the skill with which he paints an autumnal
morning:

> The morning mist is cleared away,
>   Yet still the face of heaven is gray,
> Nor yet the autumnal breeze has stirred the grove;
>   Faded yet full, a paler green
>   Skirts soberly the tranquil scene;
> The redbreast warbles round this leafy cove.

The poem entitled "To a Snow-Drop" (which is assigned to
Tuesday in Easter week) is one that Wordsworth himself might
have written. The delicacy of the opening stanzas is perfect:

> Thou first-born of the year's delight,
>   Pride of the dewy glade,
> In vernal green and virgin white
>   Thy vestal robes arrayed;
> . . .
> 'Tis not for these I love thee dear:
>   Thy shy averted smiles
> To Fancy bode a joyous year,
>   One of Life's fairy isles.

And then the closing stanzas—how deep they go, how they
sink inward to the roots of life!

> O guide us, when our faithless hearts
>   From Thee would start aloof,
> Where Patience her sweet skill imparts
>   Beneath some cottage roof;
> Revive our dying fires, to burn
>   High as her anthems soar,
> *And of our scholars let us learn*
>   *Our own forgotten lore.*

It is true that Keble is more sensitive to the sympathetic
aspect of Nature than to her sublime aspect. He expresses the
sense of her consolations far more frequently and more perfectly
than he expresses the sense of awe in her presence. ⟨. . .⟩

Keble's philosophy of life was very simple. It was in effect
a form of Christian mysticism. Perhaps he would have rejected
that name. But, at all events, his way of thinking and the
results of his thought were at the farthest remove from
rationalism. Newman has stated it, with a slight touch of the
controversial spirit (such as he often gave), in the word which
he puts into quotation marks. "Moral truth is gained by patient
study, by calm reflection, silently as the dew falls—unless
miraculously given—and when gained it is transmitted by faith
and by 'prejudice.' Keble's book is full of such truths which any
Cambridge man might refute with ease."

And what are these truths as they are expressed in the
poetic language of *The Christian Year?* They are such truths as
the certainty and sufficiency of the divine revelation, the duty
of humility and submission to the dealings of Providence, the
sacramental character of Nature in which the invisible things
of God are seen by the pure in heart, the blessedness of
obedience to God's law, the beauty of a self-sacrificing life, and
the certainty of its reward in heaven. Keble's poetry breathes a
soothing, subduing, tranquilizing spirit. Its general effect is like
one of those landscapes in the heart of England where peace
and quietness seem to brood over the green meadows, the
rounded hills, the distant woods, and the homes of men,
clustered, as if for shelter and security, around the gray,
ivy-mantled tower of the ancient house of God. There are
other strains in his poetry, I admit—strains of rebuke, of
warning, of conflict; but still this is the general impression—an

impression of tenderness, of calm, of restfulness and confidence—the impression of a consoling landscape. And above there shines the unfading, undeceiving light of a better world in which all the sorrows and sufferings of the faithful shall be rewarded.

> If thou wouldst reap in love,
> First sow in holy fear;
> So life a winter's morn may prove
> To a bright endless year.

Much of Keble's religious power comes from the intensely personal feeling that he has towards the Lord Jesus, and the directness and tenderness with which he expresses it. In this he is like some of the Latin hymnwriters, for example St. Bernard of Clairvaux, and like some of the earlier English sacred poets. How profoundly does he enter, also, into the consolation of the Cross and the comfort of the Atonement!—HENRY VAN DYKE, "Aids to the Devout Life," *Outlook*, Nov. 13, 1897, pp. 663–64

Works

THE CHRISTIAN YEAR

I have Keble lying open before me. The hymns for the Holy Week are beautiful,—Monday is exquisite: I think that I like it best of them all. The use made of Andromache's farewell is quite filling to the heart, and the theology of the fourth stanza, "Thou art as much his care," etc., is worth, in my mind, the whole Shorter and Longer Catechisms together.—THOMAS ERSKINE, Letter to Rachel Erskine (March 11, 1829), *Letters*, ed. William Hanna, 1878, pp. 111–12

> My Helen, for its golden fraught
> Of prayer and praise, of dream and thought,
> Where Poesy finds fitting voice
> For all who hope, fear, grieve, rejoice,
> Long have I loved, and studied long,
> The pious minstrel's varied song.
>
> Whence is the volume dearer now?
> There gleams a smile upon your brow,
> Wherein, methinks, I read how well
> You guess the reason, ere I tell,
> Which makes to me the simple rhymes
> More prized, more conned, a hundred times.
> —WINTHROP MACKWORTH PRAED, "To Helen: Written in the First Leaf of Keble's *Christian Year*," 1836

The Christian Year made its appearance in 1827. It is not necessary, and scarcely becoming, to praise a book which has already become one of the classics of the language. When the general tone of religious literature was so nerveless and impotent, as it was at that time, Keble struck an original note and woke up in the hearts of thousands a new music, the music of a school, long unknown in England.—JOHN HENRY NEWMAN, *Apologia pro Vita Sua*, 1864, Ch. 1

It cannot be too clearly kept in view that Keble is not a hymn writer, and that *The Christian Year* is not a collection of hymns. Those who have come to it expecting to find genuine hymns, will turn away in disappointment. They will seek in vain for anything of the directness, the fervor, the simplicity, the buoyancy of devotion which have delighted them in Charles Wesley. But to demand this is to mistake the nature and form of Keble's poems. There is all the difference between them and Charles Wesley's, that there is between meditation on the one hand, and prayer, or thanksgiving, or praise on the other. Indeed, so little did Keble's genius fit him for hymn

writing, that in his two poems which are intended to be hymns—those for the morning and the evening—the opening in either case is a description of natural facts, wholly unsuited to hymn purposes. And so when these two poems are adopted into hymn collections, as they often are, a mere selection of certain stanzas from each is all that has been found possible. Besides these two, there is no other poem in the book, any large part of which can be used as a hymn. For they are all lyrical religious meditations, not hymns at all. Yet true though this is, every here and there, out of the midst of the reflections, there does flash a verse of fervid emotion and direct heart-appeal to God, which is quite hymnal in character. These occasional bursts are among the highest beauties of *The Christian Year*. Yet they are neither so frequent nor so long-sustained as to change the prevailingly meditative cast of the whole book. It is owing perhaps to this prevalence of meditation, and that often of a refined and subtle kind, that *The Christian Year* is not, as we have often heard said, so well adapted as some simpler, less poetical collections, to be read by the sick-bed to the faint and weak. Unless long familiarity has made it easy, it requires more thought and mental elasticity to follow it, than the sick for the most part can supply. Yet it contains single verses, many, though not whole poems, which will come home full of consolation to any, even the weakest spirit. On the whole, however, it is not with Charles Wesley, or any of the hymn writers of this or the past century, nor even with Cowper in his hymns or his larger poems, that Keble should be compared. In outward form, and not a little in inward spirit, the religious poets to whom he bears the strongest likeness are Henry Vaughan and George Herbert, both of the seventeenth century. A comparison with these would be interesting, were this the place for it, but at present I must confine myself to the consideration of the special characteristics of *The Christian Year*.

These seem to be, *first*, a tone of religious feeling, fresh, deep, and tender, beyond what was common even among religious men in the author's day, perhaps in any day; *secondly*, great intensity and tenderness of home affection; *thirdly*, a shy and delicate reserve, which loved quiet paths and shunned publicity; *fourthly*, a pure love of nature, and a spiritual eye to read nature's symbolism.—JOHN CAMPBELL SHAIRP, "Keble," *Studies in Poetry and Philosophy*, 1868, pp. 250–51

In 1827, when Mr. Keble was residing with his father at Fairford, *The Christian Year* was published. Though he was a man who habitually shrank from notice, a large number of his intimate friends were taken into his counsel, in spite also of the fact that his after estimate of the work he had given to the world was extremely low. Dr. Pusey, in a letter published soon after Mr. Keble's death, related how he ever spoke in a disparaging tone of "that book," and how careless he was about the correction of what was, in his eyes, a manifest blemish. But before publication, the poems were submitted to critics of most varied tastes and character, and it is curious to find that a man so eminently prosaic as the late Archbishop Whately was among those consulted, and one of the earliest of the many friends who urged their wider circulation. The work would seem only gradually to have taken the shape it assumed in the end, a complete series of verses on the Prayer Book; yet it is now difficult to conceive of it as made up of detached devotional pieces, so entirely has it a character of unity and completeness. It stands alone in literature; for though George Herbert's Poems and Bishop Heber's Hymns each present some points of resemblance, we should be inclined to rate Herbert far higher as poet, and Heber far lower. Herbert's verse can only be read with pleasure when the mind is attuned to feelings of personal devotion in which none others can share; Heber's Hymns can be sung by mixed congregations; while *The Christian Year* fits itself to the closet or the drawing-room, not to singing in church; can be read aloud, when to read Herbert were profanation; can be enjoyed for its poetry by those who object to its theology; while its theology has gained an admission for poetic thoughts into the minds of many wooden-headed people.

Of a book of which in "less than twenty-six years 108,000 copies were issued in forty-three editions," the sale of which never has flagged since,—of which in the nine months following the writer's death seven editions were issued of 11,000 copies,—it may seem absurd to say it is less known than it deserves. Yet this very large sale has mainly been restricted to members of the Church of England, and of one only school in the Church; so that, comparatively speaking, only a few of the more cultivated among Nonconformists are well acquainted with its beauties; nor do they at all realise the power that it has had in attaching its readers to the form of words and form of faith which it was written to accompany and explain. It has not been hitherto, even within the limits of English speech, a book for all creeds in spite of its adherence to one; it has not been, as in its degree it deserves to be, to English religious thought, what the *De Imitatione Christi* has been to the religious thought of Europe.—C. KEGAN PAUL, "John Keble" (1869), *Biographical Sketches*, 1883, pp. 42–44

⟨. . .⟩ I am heretical enough to believe that, although the *Christian Year* will always hold a high place in religious poetry, it owes its extraordinary popularity to temporary and accidental causes.

⟨. . .⟩ We look in vain to him for any insight into the complicated problems of humanity, or for any sympathy with the passions which are the pulses of human life. With the Prayer-book for his guide, he has provided us with a manual of religious sentiment corresponding to the Christian theory as taught by the Church of England Prayer-book, beautifully expressed in language which every one can understand and remember. High Churchmanship had been hitherto dry and formal; Keble carried into it the emotions of Evangelicalism, while he avoided angry collision with Evangelical opinions. Thus all parties could find much to admire in him, and little to suspect. English religious poetry was generally weak—was not, indeed, poetry at all. Here was something which in its kind was excellent; and every one who was really religious, or wished to be religious, or even outwardly and from habit professed himself and believed himself to be a Christian, found Keble's verses chime in his heart like church bells.—JAMES ANTHONY FROUDE, "The Oxford Counter-Reformation" (1881), *Short Studies in Great Subjects*, 1883, Vol. 4, pp. 171–74

At different times Keble had written, and still wrote, religious poems in which devotional and domestic feelings were associated with habitual reverence for ordinances of the Church. A poem had often been written on the occasion of some festival. Then came the suggestion that by adding more he might form a chain of devotional pieces extending over all occasions of church worship throughout the Christian year. Under the name of *The Christian Year* this volume of verse was first published in 1827. From that time to this, no new book of religious verse produced in England has been so widely diffused. Within twenty six years one hundred and eight thousand copies were sold in forty-three editions, and *The Christian Year* is still being reproduced in many forms from the cheap shilling edition to the luxurious and costly illustrated

volume. The force of the book lies in its sincerity. Its music is the music of a well harmonized life; the devotion is real; the quiet sense of nature is real. There are no tricks of style, though there are no flashes of genius. Keble laid stress on the authority and customs of the Church, he was what in the language of party is called a High Churchman; but the true man, whichever his side and whatever his cause, belongs to all and is a help to all.—HENRY MORLEY, *Of English Literature in the Reign of Victoria*, 1881, p. 287

His poetic and gracious gifts are embalmed in the *Christian Year*, which has touched so many hearts. There is an ineffable sweetness in its verse. Christian experience may outgrow the savour, but it lingers like a delightful fragrance in the memory.—JOHN TULLOCH, *Movements of Religious Thought in Britain during the Nineteenth Century*, 1885, p. 66

Its most permanent value lies in this power to soothe; but perhaps at the time its power to stir was of even greater weight. ⟨. . .⟩

The poems awe and stir and soothe alike, because they are so real; they have so vivid a sense of the spiritual world, with all its terrors as well as its beauty and grace. He is the prophet of the fear of God no less than the poet of His love.—WALTER LOCK, *John Keble: A Biography*, 1892, pp. 71–72

We will now take the *Christian Year* and we will say at the outset that we do not propose to consider it, except incidentally, from the doctrinal and hortatory point of view. We must first remember that whatever be its merits and demerits, it is a book that has achieved a popularity of an absolutely phenomenal kind. It is a book that has been bought and read in England as Shakespeare, Bunyan's *Pilgrim's Progress*, and *Robinson Crusoe*, and in America as the works of E. P. Roe. In 1853 it was in its forty-second edition, twenty-five years after its publication. In 1873, when the copyright expired, it had reached the 158th edition, and it is still in demand. For many years it took its place, with High Church people, by the side of the Bible and Prayer Book. It would be incredible, were it not true, that a book of religious poetry, not suitable for public worship, the outcome of a very definite school of thought, should have achieved such a success. It was undoubtedly what the world wanted.

Now, let us first take some of its obvious demerits before we proceed to discuss its merits. In the first place, it is often careless in form and obscure in expression. It was consciously so, and Keble, probably wisely, refused to alter and amend it, imagining that such afterwork often sacrificed some of the freshness of inspiration. It was this carelessness that made Wordsworth, who read it with great admiration, say of it, "It is very good—so good that, if it were mine, I should write it all over again."

The metrical schemes are often complicated and unsatisfactory. Many of the poems are far too long, so as to be hardly lyrical. Such poems as that for Advent Sunday, or the Second Sunday after Trinity, contain between seventy and eighty heroic lines. Then, again, the cyclical instinct which beset Keble, made him provide poems for every event, every service of the Christian year. Thus we have Gunpowder Treason and the Churching of Women celebrated, though it must be owned that, in these cases, the poem has but the slightest connection with the subject.

Next—and this is a more serious point—the poems have been praised for their frequent references to nature and the fidelity of their imagery; after careful study of the *Christian Year* one is compelled to say that this praise is not deserved: the imagery is of a purely conventional character, and the observation employed of the most general kind. Dean Stanley said, in praise of Keble's descriptive passages, that his local and topographical details, whenever he spoke of the Holy Land, were marvellously clear and accurate. But this is not really a compliment. It shows that Keble was content to describe without his eye on the object, and relying on the observation of others; and if the pictures of landscapes that he had not seen are among his most felicitous passages, we may well be excused for

mistrusting his powers of observation when dealing with the features of his own native country. The fact is that he did not seize upon salient features; Matthew Arnold, in such a poem as the "Scholar Gypsy," brings the Oxford atmosphere, the high gravelly hills, the deep water-meadows, before the eye; but Keble's landscape is the conventional English landscape, and has no precise definition, no native air.—A. C. BENSON, "The Poetry of Keble," *Essays*, 1896, pp. 185–87

CATHARINE MARIA SEDGWICK

1789–1867

Catharine Maria Sedgwick was born in Stockbridge, Massachusetts, on December 28, 1789. Her mother was a member of one of the commonwealth's wealthiest families; her father served in the U.S. Senate and House of Representatives and was chief justice of the Massachusetts Supreme Court. Educated at home—all seven Sedgwick children were required to read Hume, Butler, Shakespeare, and Cervantes—and at a local grammar school, she later attended finishing schools in Albany and Boston.

Influenced by her father's shift to a more liberal religious ethic shortly before his death in 1813, Catharine Sedgwick joined the Unitarian Church along with two of her brothers, Theodore and Henry, who both became prominent social reformers. In 1822 she began work on what was to be a small pamphlet protesting religious intolerance. It grew into a full-length novel, *A New England Tale*, and was published anonymously later that year. The book, which tells the story of a virtuous orphan girl and her mistreatment by ostensibly pious relatives, became a best-seller in both England and America, and was later recognized as one of the first novels to use actual American settings and characters.

Sedgwick's second novel, *Redwood*, was published in 1824 and was also a great success, placing her in the ranks of fellow story-tellers Cooper and Irving. Her third novel, *Hope Leslie*, appeared in 1827 and made her the most famous American woman writer of her day. Her later works include *Clarence* (1830), *The Linwoods* (1835), *Home* (1835), *The Poor Rich Man and the Rich Poor Man* (1836), and *Live and Let Live* (1837). Her last novel, *Married or Single?*, was published in 1857. Sedgwick intended for many of her works to be read by children and by working-class people, and emphasized in them her strong belief in the importance of education, democracy, and close-knit family ties as means of social improvement.

Sedgwick, who never married, died on July 31, 1867, in West Roxbury, Massachusetts.

Personal

She is decidedly the pleasantest American woman I have ever seen, with more of a turn for humour, and less American sectarianism. The twang, to be sure, there is in plenty; and the toilette is the dowdiness (not the finery) of the backwoods; but then she is lively, kind, heart-warm; and I feel, somehow or other, almost on friendly terms with her, though I never spoke more than twenty consecutive words to her.—HENRY F. CHORLEY (1839), *Autobiography, Memoir, and Letters*, ed. Henry G. Hewlett, 1873, Vol. 1, pp. 279–80

Admirable as it was, her home life was more so; and beautiful as were the examples set forth in her writings, her own example was, if possible, still more beautiful. Her unerring sense of rectitude, her love of truth, her ready sympathy, her active and cheerful beneficence, her winning and gracious manners, the perfection of high breeding, make up a character, the idea of which, as it rests on my mind, I would not exchange for any thing in her own interesting works of fiction.—WILLIAM CULLEN BRYANT, "Reminiscences of Miss Sedgwick," cited in Mary E. Dewey, *Life and Letters of Catharine M. Sedgwick*, 1871, p. 446

The story of her life is a simple tale as regards outward circumstances. No striking incidents, no remarkable occurrences will be found in it, but the gradual unfolding and ripening amid congenial surroundings of a true and beautiful soul, a clear and refined intellect, and a singularly sympathetic social nature. She was born eighty years ago, when the atmosphere was still electric with the storm in which we took our place among the nations, and passing her childhood in the seclusion of a New England valley, while yet her family was linked to the great world without by ties both political and social, early and deep foundations were laid in her character of patriotism, religious feeling, love of nature, and strong attachment to home, and to those who made it what it was. And when, later in life, she took her place among the acknowledged leaders of literature and society, these remained the central features of her character, and around them gathered all the graceful culture, the active philanthropy, the social accomplishment which made her presence a joy wherever it came. —MARY E. DEWEY, *Life and Letters of Catharine M. Sedgwick*, 1871, p. 10

I had a great admiration of much in Miss Sedgwick's character, though we were too opposite in our natures, in many of our views, and in some of our principles, to be very congenial companions. Her domestic attachments and offices were charming to witness; and no one could be further from all conceit and vanity on account of her high reputation in her own country. Her authorship did not constitute her life; and she led a complete life, according to her measure, apart from it: and this is a spectacle which I always enjoy, and especially in the case of a woman. The insuperable difficulty between us,—that which closed our correspondence, though not our good will, was her habit of flattery;—a national weakness, to which I could have wished that she had been superior. But her nature was a timid and sensitive one; and she was thus predisposed to the national failing;—that is, to one side of it; for she could never fall into the cognate error,—of railing and abuse when the flattery no longer answers. She praised or was silent. The mischief was that she praised people to their faces, to a degree which I have never considered it necessary to permit. I told her that I dreaded receiving her letters because, instead of what I wished to hear, I found praise of myself. She informed me that, on trial, she found it a *gêne* to suppress what she wanted to say; and thus it was natural for us to cease from corresponding. I thought she wanted courage, and shrank from using her great influence on behalf of her own convictions; and she thought me rash and rough.—HARRIET MARTINEAU, *Autobiography*, ed. Maria Weston Chapman, 1877, Vol. 1, p. 377

General

Her delineations of character are generally striking and happy, and the national peculiarities are hit off with great dexterity and effect, though perhaps, in some instances, they are brought out a little too broadly. There is, however, very little overcharging and exaggeration; the actors in the plot do not come upon the scene in their stage dresses, ready, on every occasion that offers, as in duty bound, to display, resolutely, and with all their might, the supposed peculiarities of the personages they represent, but they are made to look and act like people in the world about us. The characters are not only thus chastely drawn, but they are varied with exceeding art and judgment, and this variety is, for the most part, founded on essential differences.—WILLIAM CULLEN BRYANT, "Redwood," *North American Review*, April 1825, p. 256

Though a multitude of attempts have been made, the only really successful novel that we remember, founded on the early history of Massachusetts, is Miss Sedgwick's *Hope Leslie*. Even here, however, the writer has judiciously kept the historical element quite in the background, nearly all the incidents and characters being imaginary. The most interesting personage, Magawisca, though a charming conception, is an Indian maiden only in name. She is the poetical, but not the historical, child of the forest; she is Pocahontas transplanted to the North, and not having a drop of kindred blood with the copper-colored savage of our own primitive woods. In truth, the North American Indian is but a sorry subject for poetry and romance; art has tried in vain to idealize his features, and make a hero of him.—FRANCIS BOWEN, "Merry-Mount, a Romance of the Massachusetts Colony," *North American Review*, Jan. 1849, p. 205

Born the same year as Cooper and publishing her first novel, *A New England Tale*, one year after *The Sketch Book* and *The Spy*, Miss Sedgwick was the first American woman to achieve substantial success as a novelist. ⟨. . .⟩ When, in 1824, *Redwood* appeared, it was immediately translated into four European languages, the French translator even attributing the

novel to Cooper. Of the novels written by Miss Sedgwick, all of them dealing with New England life, *Hope Leslie, or Early Times in Massachusetts* (1827) and *The Linwoods, or Sixty Years Since in America* (1835) are undoubtedly the best. Aside from her six novels, she produced nearly twenty volumes, consisting of collected tales and sketches contributed to magazines and annuals, biographies, letters, sketches of travel, juveniles, and essays critical and moralizing. She contributed "Le Bossu" to the *Tales of the Glauber Spa* (1832), a series edited by Robert C. Sands and contributed to by Bryant, Paulding, and William Legget.

Although the day of the leisurely two-volume novel has nearly passed, Miss Sedgwick's novels are still readable. Her greatest defect is the sermonizing tendency of her day, which filled her novels with diffuse and tedious pages. Her excellencies are the quiet, truthful pictures of her native Massachusetts home life.—FRED LEWIS PATTEE, *A History of American Literature*, 1896, pp. 147–48

What Irving was pleased to designate as "the classic pen of Miss Sedgwick" vied in favor with Cooper's stronger quill. Her *Redwood*, remembered for Debby Lennox, its Yankee spinster, was reprinted in England and translated into French. Her *Hope Leslie*, a story of the early Colonial days, ran through edition after edition, and *The Linwoods*, depicting Revolutionary times, accomplished the feat of wringing copious tears from her publisher, one of the Harper brothers, as he read the proof-sheets.—KATHARINE LEE BATES, *American Literature*, 1897, pp. 104–5

W. HILLARD
From "Clarence"

North American Review, January 1831, pp. 74–79

We know of nothing for which she is more remarkable, than her nice and discriminating habits of observation, and that fine tact, which with the directness of instinct, seizes upon what is important for the description of men and things, and rejects what is superfluous. She has an 'eye practised like a blind man's touch,' and she can distinguish instantly those minute shades which are so imperceptibly blended in nature as to seem but one color to common observers. Her pictures of natural scenery are drawn with the distinct pencil of Cowper, and they rise up and appear to the eye as we read, without any effort of our own to give them shape and presence. Almost every page of *Redwood* and *Hope Leslie* will confirm our remarks, and amidst the multitude of admirable descriptions, we are puzzled to select any one. It is no very easy matter, for instance, to describe a country-seat, though it may seem to be so at first; yet how perfectly has she succeeded in delineating the mansion of Mr. Clarence. We have no confused images of lawns, forest, and shrubbery, but every thing is distinct and defined, and we have no doubt, that if ten or twelve artists were employed each, to make a picture of the scene, their sketches would differ very little. The same remark will apply to her descriptions of artificial life and manners;—such as her account of the Shaker establishment in *Redwood*, and the picture in the second volume of *Clarence*, of the tone, dress, and conversation of the fashionable society of New-York. She is evidently more acquainted with men than books, and has sought truth in the 'light of things,' and not in the 'still air of delightful studies;' and her resources are in the highest degree available, for she has collected their very materials herself. She has kept an observant eye on the masques that make up the world's motley pageant, and drawn thence a living wisdom, far higher than the cold forms of mere learning. She has noted the looks and tones of men, the manner in which they are affected by events, the way in which differing characters display themselves, the things in which all men are alike, and those in which they are most dissimilar. We are disposed to think more highly of this habit of discriminating observation, as a means of intellectual developement, than most persons. He who goes about among men with his eyes open, will learn something better than the lore that is hidden in books. This is a thing in which women excel men; it is a merit almost peculiar to female writers. Hence arises the perfect keeping observable in our author's pictures of still life, and the consistency and individuality of her characters, who are always one and the same in their conversation, their letters, and their actions.

She writes English with uncommon elegance and purity; no small merit in these days of extravagance and caricature, when foamy declamation is called strength, and calmness is another name for feebleness. She has the rare merit of never being common-place, and if she has occasion to express a familiar thought, she contrives by some graceful turn or happy allusion, to give it the air and gloss of novelty. She never descends to that vulgar artifice of dressing up little or old ideas in language so ambitious, that we imagine for a moment that we have something very new and fine, till a second glance shews us that all is but varnish and gilding. Her style is perfectly feminine, full of a certain indescribable gracefulness and ease, arising from a fine perception of beauty and an inborn delicacy of taste, which seem always to select the best words, and to put them in their right places. The letters in *Clarence*, we think, are very fine specimens of epistolary style, easy, graceful, and spirited, equally remote from formal stiffness and slipshod carelessness. Almost the only fault of style we have noticed, is an occasional diffuseness, the easily besetting sin of female writers.

We trust that we may be allowed to speak of another winning charm in these novels, arising not so much from the mind as the moral character of the author. We mean the impress everywhere discoverable, of an unaffected goodness of heart, and a warmth of affection which folds in its embrace every thing that lives. As John Paul has somewhere said, she loves God and every little child. Her sympathies are ready and active, and called forth by every shape of distress, and she never turns aside from suffering virtue, however repulsive the garb it may wear. There is a beautiful tenderness and sensibility breathing out from her writings, like the fragrance from a rose. She delights to accumulate images of peace and happiness and sunshine, to describe all that is noble in man and attractive in woman—the virtue that exalts, the struggle that purifies, the trial that calls forth a seraph's energies, and the sweet affections that strew with flowers life's dusty highway. She does not know how to draw a villain; she has no idea of the spasms and convulsions of the mind, around which guilt and remorse have thrown their serpent-folds. Man in the pride of his imperial beauty, full of truth, and honor and grace, with high thoughts and generous affections, with reason sitting on his brow, and the pulse of joy in his veins,—woman, with her veil of gentle loveliness, her lily-like purity, her loving and trusting heart,—the light of friendship, the soul-exchanging glance of love,—these are the themes which call forth her finest powers, and it is in the delineation of these only, that her genius appears in its proper element. Her descriptions of childhood are full of the dewy freshness of life's morning hour. In this respect we know of no one who equals her, no one who draws in colors so speaking the image of a beautiful and happy child, with his

heart of gladness and voice of silver-toned glee, his brave spirit, his frolic blood, and his winning tricks. Years have not brought to her that cold philosophy which looks with a loveless eye upon life in its silken bud, which recalls with no kindly thrill the days when the world was a garden, and the air a rainbow, when the hours brought roses in their hands, and the wings of time made music as they moved. There is a beauty and a mystery in childhood, and the wisest may learn a lesson from the young pilgrim of life, who bears yet fresh about him the brightness of the Spirit-land, which he has so lately left.

> Not in forgetfulness,
> And not in utter nakedness,
> But trailing clouds of glory do we come
> From God, who is our home.

The love of nature, and a familiar acquaintance with the changeful expressions of the 'mighty mother's' countenance, are among the fine gifts of the author of *Clarence*. Her descriptions of scenery in the western part of Massachusetts in her *New-England Tale*, and in *Redwood*, may challenge a comparison with any in the language. She does not merely draw the features of a landscape, but she gives you the expression, and transfuses into her pages the spirit that hangs over it, like an atmosphere. She looks upon the outward world in the vein of the melancholy Jaques, translating its silence into thoughts and images; but she draws thence the elements of a far more cheerful philosophy. She learns wisdom from the cups of flowers, and the whisper of the pine conveys to her a lesson of truth. Every leaf is pregnant with instruction, and every stream teaches as it brawls. The forms of nature have stamped their own likeness upon the soul of their worshipper, and every mute image without has given birth to a correlative idea within, united by a mysterious affinity, which all may feel, but none can define. In her graphic descriptions of natural scenery, there is no small portion of the fine philosophy of Wordsworth, which regards the fair forms of the outward world as the instruments of a spiritual influence upon the mind of man, as the varied stops through which the myriad tones of a universal harmony are breathed. Woods and mountains are not only enjoyed, but felt and understood,—they are as the face of a long-tried and never-failing friend. This sensibility to natural beauty exerts a most expanding and elevating power upon the spirit of man, and when it is united with that gifted eye, which can read the letters of power and love written all over this goodly universe, nothing short of a religion is capable of exerting a more holy ministration.

But more than all the rest, the author of *Clarence* has that high and pure tone of moral and religious feeling, without which genius is a fatal curse, and fine powers are destructive in the exact ratio of their splendor and superiority. She never makes vice interesting or virtue repulsive; but paints each in its true colors, so that the mind obeying its natural instinct is enamored of the one and abhors the other. She draws no beings, half-gods and half-fiends, with a veil of splendid and romantic qualities, covering but not hiding the darkest and foulest traits of character, and constraining us to admire the actor, though we detest the guilt. She never makes merit ludicrous or contemptible, by connecting it with those low or ridiculous qualities, which are offensive to our taste; or vice attractive by a graceful garb, which engages our interest, though we feel angry with ourselves for permitting it to do so. She never relates a deed of villainy in that cool way, which makes us feel some doubt, whether the author do not rather admire than otherwise, what he treats so much as a matter of course. She does not look only among the cultivated and the intellectual for fine traits of humanity, nor shrink with sickly fastidiousness from virtue in humble life. The same Being who gave the lily its exceeding beauty, and painted the enamelled cheek of the tulip, planted also the wild rose by the way-side, and scattered the seeds of the violet in a thousand fields; and He has shown the same equal benevolence in the human soul, His noblest work. He has caused beautiful affections and high virtues to take root in the heart, and they breathe the fragrance and bear the fruits of good works as often in the peasant as in the prince. The incense of love, and faith, and honor, ascends from the lowliest farm-house no less than the proudest palace. Our author, as we have said before, has been a keen observer of life and manners, and in accordance with the noble sentiment of Terence, has felt herself interested in whatever relates to humanity, and has learned to contemplate man as one of a species, separate from all adventitious distinctions. We regard her sketches of humble life as among the most felicitous portions of her works; strong, but not coarse, and full of sense, feeling, truth, and the nicest observation, reminding us in this last particular, of the minute accuracy of one of Wilkie's inimitable pictures. She depends for the interest of her stories rather upon the lowly and unobtrusive virtues, which are felt in the hours and minutes of life, gentle firmness, noiseless benevolence, and modest self-respect, than upon the more dazzling qualities, which can seldom be displayed in the common run of events, and if often exerted, give to the character an air of theatrical affectation. This healthiness of moral feeling gives to her works that kind of charm, which an amiable expression gives to a fine countenance, heightening the beauty of every agreeable feature, and making us overlook those which nature has less carefully moulded. We feel that we can cordially admire with a good conscience. No shadow of pity or regret for powers misapplied glides by to break the spell that charms us. We have no sublime free-thinkers, who boldly attack every thing that man holds sacred, no selfish misanthropes, who dare to hate the creatures God has made, no elegant ruffians rewarded with a fortune and a mistress instead of a halter, but the good man is honored and the villain punished. Our author never separates the tie that unites virtue and happiness, vice and misery, which succeed each other as invariably as thunder follows lightning or as spring comes after winter. But she deserves more than the praise which a virtuous heathen might have won; she has told us of the beauty and excellency of religion, and spoken to us in the name of Jesus of Nazareth. We venture to say, that there are few books which make better Sunday reading than hers.

EDGAR ALLAN POE
From "Catherine M. Sedgwick"
The Literati of New York City
1846

M iss Sedgwick is not only one of our most celebrated and most meritorious writers, but attained reputation at a period when *American* reputation in letters was regarded as a phenomenon; and thus, like Irving, Cooper, Paulding, Bryant, Halleck, and one or two others, she is indebted, certainly, for *some* portion of the esteem in which she was and is held, to that patriotic pride and gratitude to which I have already alluded, and for which we must make reasonable allowance in estimating the absolute merit of our literary pioneers.

Her earliest published work of any length was A *New*

England Tale, designed in the first place as a religious tract, but expanding itself into a volume of considerable size. Its success—partially owing, perhaps, to the influence of the parties for whom or at whose instigation it was written—encouraged the author to attempt a novel of somewhat greater elaborateness as well as length, and *Redwood* was soon announced, establishing her at once as the first female prose writer of her country. It was reprinted in England, and translated, I believe, into French and Italian. *Hope Leslie* next appeared—also a novel—and was more favorably received even than its predecessors. Afterwards came *Clarence*, not quite so successful, and then *The Linwoods*, which took rank in the public esteem with *Hope Leslie*. These are all of her longer prose fictions, but she has written numerous shorter ones of great merit—such as *The Rich Poor Man and the Poor Rich Man, Live and let Live*, (both in volume form,) with various articles for the magazines and annuals, to which she is still an industrious contributor. About ten years since she published a compilation of several of her fugitive prose pieces, under the title *Tales and Sketches*, and a short time ago a series of *Letters from Abroad*—not the least popular or least meritorious of her compositions.

Miss Sedgwick has now and then been nicknamed "the Miss Edgeworth of America;" but she has done nothing to bring down upon her the vengeance of so equivocal a title. That she has thoroughly studied and profoundly admired Miss Edgeworth may, indeed, be gleaned from her works—but what woman has not? Of imitation there is not the slightest perceptible taint. In both authors we observe the same tone of thoughtful morality, but here all resemblance ceases. In the Englishwoman there is far more of a certain Scotch prudence, in the American more of warmth, tenderness, sympathy for the weaknesses of her sex. Miss Edgeworth is the more acute, the more inventive and the more rigid. Miss Sedgwick is the more womanly.

All her stories are full of interest. The *New England Tale* and *Hope Leslie* are especially so, but upon the whole I am best pleased with *The Linwoods*. Its prevailing features are ease, purity of style, pathos, and verisimilitude. To plot it has little pretension. The scene is in America, and, as the sub-title indicates, "Sixty years since." This, by-the-by, is taken from *Waverley*. The adventures of the family of a Mr. Linwood, a resident of New York, form the principal theme. The character of this gentleman is happily drawn, although there is an antagonism between the initial and concluding touches—the end has forgotten the beginning, like the government of Trinculo. Mr. L. has two children, Herbert and Isabella. Being himself a Tory, the boyish impulses of his son in favor of the revolutionists are watched with anxiety and vexation; and on the breaking out of the war, Herbert, positively refusing to drink the king's health, is expelled from home by his father— an event on which hinges the main interest of the narrative. Isabella is the heroine proper, full of generous impulses, beautiful, intellectual, *spirituelle*—indeed, a most fascinating creature. But the family of a Widow Lee throws quite a charm over all the book—a matronly, pious and devoted mother, yielding up her son to the cause of her country—the son gallant, chivalrous, yet thoughtful; a daughter, gentle, loving, melancholy, and susceptible of light impressions. This daughter, Bessie Lee, is one of the most effective personations to be found in our fictitious literature, and may lay claims to the distinction of originality—no slight distinction where *character* is concerned. It is the old story, to be sure, of a meek and trusting heart broken by treachery and abandonment, but in the narration of Miss Sedgwick it breaks upon us with all the freshness of novel emotion. Deserted by her lover, an accomplished and aristocratical coxcomb, the spirits of the gentle girl sink gradually from trust to simple hope, from hope to anxiety, from anxiety to doubt, from doubt to melancholy, and from melancholy to madness. The gradation is depicted in a masterly manner. She escapes from her home in New England and endeavors to make her way alone to New York, with the object of restoring to him who has abandoned her, some tokens he had given her of his love—an act which her disordered fancy assures her will effect in her own person a disenthralment from passion. Her piety, her madness and her beauty, stand her in stead of the lion of Una, and she reaches the city in safety. In that portion of the narrative which embodies this journey are some passages which no mind unimbued with the purest spirit of poetry could have conceived, and they have often made me wonder why Miss Sedgwick has never written a poem.

I have already alluded to her usual excellence of style; but she has a very peculiar fault—that of discrepancy between the words and character of the speaker—the fault, indeed, more properly belongs to the depicting of character itself. ⟨. . .⟩

As the author of many *books*—of several absolutely bound volumes in the ordinary "novel" form of auld lang syne, Miss Sedgwick has a certain adventitious hold upon the attention of the public, a species of tenure that has nothing to do with literature proper—a very decided advantage, in short, over her more modern rivals whom fashion and the growing influence *of the want* of an international copyright law have condemned to the external insignificance of the yellow-backed pamphleteering.

We must permit, however, neither this advantage nor the more obvious one of her having been one of our *pioneers*, to bias the critical judgment as it makes estimate of her abilities in comparison with those of her *present* contemporaries. She has neither the vigor of Mrs. Stephens nor the vivacious grace of Miss Chubbuck, nor the pure style of Mrs. Embury, nor the classic imagination of Mrs. Child, nor the naturalness of Mrs. Annan, nor the thoughtful and suggestive originality of Miss Fuller; but in many of the qualities mentioned she excels, and in no one of them is she particularly deficient. She is an author of marked talent, but by no means of such decided genius as would entitle her to that precedence among our female writers which, under the circumstances to which I have alluded, *seems* to be yielded her by the voice of the public.

Strictly speaking, Miss Sedgwick is *not* one of the *literati* of New York city, but she passes here about half or rather more than half her time. Her home is Stockbridge, Massachusetts. Her family is one of the first in America. Her father, Theodore Sedgwick the elder, was an eminent jurist and descended from one of Cromwell's major-generals. Many of her relatives have distinguished themselves in various ways.

She is about the medium height, perhaps a little below it. Her forehead is an unusually fine one; nose of a slightly Roman curve; eyes dark and piercing; mouth well-formed and remarkably pleasant in its expression. The portrait in *Graham's Magazine* is by no means a likeness, and, although the hair is represented as curled, (Miss Sedgwick at present wears a cap—at least most usually,) gives her the air of being much older than she is.

Her manners are those of a high-bred woman, but her ordinary *manner* vacillates, in a singular way, between cordiality and a reserve amounting to *hauteur*.

FITZ-GREENE HALLECK

1790–1867

Fitz-Greene Halleck was born in Guilford, Connecticut, on July 8, 1790. As a youth he began a career in banking in New York City and for much of his life was employed by John Jacob Astor. As a member of the so-called Knickerbocker Group, Halleck established a second career as a writer of satiric and romantic verse. *The Croaker*, a series of humorous odes written by Halleck and his friend Joseph Rodman Drake, appeared pseudonymously in 1819 in the New York *Evening Post* and made him immediately popular. A year later Drake died, inspiring Halleck to write the well-known ode "On the Death of Joseph Rodman Drake." Halleck's social satire *Fanny* appeared in 1821. Halleck considered his next three poems to be his best work: "Alnwick Castle" (1822); "Marco Bozzaris" (1823), which became a favorite recitation piece in the nineteenth century; and "Burns" (1827).

Strongly influenced by both Scott and Byron, Halleck went on to write romantic poems using American settings, including "Wyoming" (1827); "Red Chief" (1828), an eulogy for a Tuscarora Indian; and "The Field of Grounded Arms" (1831), an account of the Battle of Saratoga.

Halleck's last completed poem was "Young America" (1865). "Connecticut," left unfinished at his death, was a long tribute to his native state. Halleck died in Guilford on November 19, 1867.

General

I give to my friend Fitz-Greene Halleck an annuity of two hundred dollars, commencing at my decease, and payable half-yearly for his life, to be secured by setting apart so much of my personal estate as may be necessary; which I intend as a mark of regard for Mr. Halleck.—JOHN JACOB ASTOR, Will, 1848

There goes Halleck, whose Fanny's a pseudo Don Juan,
With the wickedness out that gave salt to the true one,

He's a wit, though, I hear, of the very first order,
And once made a pun on the words soft Recorder;
More than this, he's a very great poet, I'm told,
And has had his works published in crimson and gold,
With something they call 'Illustrations,' to wit,
Like those with which Chapman obscured Holy Writ,
Which are said to illustrate, because, as I view it,
Like *lucus a non*, they precisely don't do it;
Let a man who can write what himself understands
Keep clear, if he can, of designing men's hands,

Who bury the sense, if there's any worth having,
And then very honestly call it engraving.
But, to quit *badinage*, which there isn't much wit in,
Halleck's better, I doubt not, than all he has written;
In his verse a clear glimpse you will frequently find,
If not of a great, of a fortunate mind,
Which contrives to be true to its natural loves
In a world of back-offices, ledgers, and stoves.
When his heart breaks away from the brokers and banks,
And kneels in his own private shrine to give thanks,
There's a genial manliness in him that earns
Our sincerest respect (read, for instance, his "Burns"),
And we can't but regret (seek excuse where we may)
That so much of a man has been peddled away.
      —JAMES RUSSELL LOWELL, A *Fable for Critics*,
        1848

   Say not the Poet dies!
     Though in the dust he lies,
He cannot forfeit his melodious breath,
     Unsphered by envious death!
Life drops the voiceless myriads from its roll;
     Their fate he cannot share,
     Who, in the enchanted air
Sweet with the lingering strains that Echo stole,
Has left his dearer self, the music of his soul!

   We o'er his turf may raise
     Our notes of feeble praise,
And carve with pious care for after eyes
     The stone with "Here he lies;"
He for himself has built a nobler shrine,
     Whose walls of stately rhyme
     Roll back the tides of time,
While o'er their gates the gleaming tablets shine
That wear his name inwrought with many a golden line!

   Call not our Poet dead,
     Though on his turf we tread!
Green is the wreath their brows so long have worn,—
     The minstrels of the morn,
Who, while the Orient burned with newborn flame,
     Caught that celestial fire
     And struck a Nation's lyre!
These taught the western winds the poet's name;
Theirs the first opening buds, the maiden flowers of fame!

   Count not our Poet dead!
     The stars shall watch his bed,
The rose of June its fragrant life renew
     His blushing mound to strew,
And all the tuneful throats of summer swell
     With trills as crystal-clear
     As when he wooed the ear
Of the young muse that haunts each wooded dell,
With songs of that "rough land" he loved so long and well!

   He sleeps; he cannot die!
     As evening's long-drawn sigh,
Lifting the rose-leaves on his peaceful mound,
     Spreads all their sweets around,
So, laden with his song, the breezes blow
     From where the rustling sedge
     Frets our rude ocean's edge
To the smooth sea beyond the peaks of snow.
His soul the air enshrines and leaves but dust below!
      —OLIVER WENDELL HOLMES, "Poem at the Ded-
        ication of the Halleck Monument," 1869

With the few whom Fitz-Greene Halleck liked, and with
whom he associated on equal terms, he was genial, graceful,
never wanton of speech, and always full of chat and pleasant
humor; apt always and prompt at reply; with that spirit of
repartee and easy wit which makes so much of the charm and
spirit of the *Croaker* epistles. His geniality, with such a circle,
was always active; and he relished nothing better than a snug
and select party, 'fit though few.' He was both socially and
politically a natural aristocrat, and did not cheapen himself by
any too easy entrance into society. He required to respect men,
mentally, before associating with them, and seemed to me to
revolt from all associations of trade, in spite of all his lifelong
connection with it, and, perhaps, because of that connection.
I may add that he seemed very careless of authorship, and,
though he did not undervalue the credit which he had himself
derived from it, he made no ambitious or feverish struggles
after fame or public favor. He was above all meanness, and
never forgot the gentleman in the poet. You will note that, in
his satire, the weapon he uses is the small sword, not the
bludgeon. It is a polished blade, and, however mortal the
thrust, it did not mangle the victim. The grace and dexterity of
his satire were habitual to him in society, and the wit and
humor of his ordinary conversation are admirably illustrated by
his satirical poetry, such as *Fanny* and the *Croakers*. That he
wrote too little is a subject of popular complaint: had he
esteemed the popular judgment, he would probably have
shown himself more voluminous.—WILLIAM GILMORE SIMMS,
Letter to James Grant Wilson (1869), cited in James Grant
Wilson, *The Life and Letters of Fitz-Greene Halleck*, 1869, pp.
544–45

Mr. Halleck never received any compensation for the poems
he contributed to the *Evening Post*, *National Advocate*, and
other journals and magazines, extending over a period of
nearly twenty years—years during which his most admired
productions were published. Halleck appears to have written
with the most unselfish indifference to fame or pecuniary
reward, for, up to the year 1839, neither on the title-pages of
his published volumes, nor with his single contributions to the
press, did his name appear. For *The Croakers* neither he nor
Dr. Drake ever received the slightest pecuniary reward, nor did
they desire any.—JAMES GRANT WILSON, *The Life and Letters
of Fitz-Greene Halleck*, 1869, pp. 442–43

The vein of poetic genius in Halleck's nature was wholly
genuine, yet it was exceptionally quiet and undemonstrative.
Its activity was less inherent in its substance than dependent
on some external stimulus. For one who wrote so much and
so fairly as a boy, his first flush of manhood and contact with
life are surprisingly barren of verse.—BAYARD TAYLOR, "Fitz-
Greene Halleck," *North American Review*, July 1877, p. 61

   Among their graven shapes to whom
     Thy civic wreaths belong,
  O city of his love, make room
     For one whose gift was song.

   Not his the soldier's sword to wield,
     Nor his the helm of state,
  Nor glory of the stricken field,
     Nor triumph of debate.

   In common ways, with common men,
     He served his race and time
  As well as if his clerkly pen
     Had never danced to rhyme.

   If, in the thronged and noisy mart,
     The Muses found their son,
  Could any say his tuneful art
     A duty left undone?

   He toiled and sang; and year by year
     Men found their homes more sweet,

And through a tenderer atmosphere
　　Looked down the brick-walled street.

The Greek's wild onset Wall Street knew;
　　The Red King walked Broadway;
And Alnwick Castle's roses blew
　　From Palisades to Bay.

Fair City by the Sea! upraise
　　His veil with reverent hands;
And mingle with thy own the praise
　　And pride of other lands.

Let Greece his fiery lyric breathe
　　Above her hero-urns;
And Scotland, with her holly, wreathe
　　The flower he culled for Burns.

Oh, stately stand thy palace walls,
　　Thy tall ships ride the seas;
To-day thy poet's name recalls
　　A prouder thought than these.

Not less thy pulse of trade shall beat,
　　Nor less thy tall fleets swim,
That shaded square and dusty street
　　Are classic ground through him.

Alive, he loved, like all who sing,
　　The echoes of his song;
Too late the tardy meed we bring,
　　The praise delayed so long.

Too late, alas! Of all who knew
　　The living man, to-day
Before his unveiled face, how few
　　Make bare their locks of gray!

Our lips of praise must soon be dumb,
　　Our grateful eyes be dim;
O brothers of the days to come,
　　Take tender charge of him!

New hands the wires of song may sweep,
　　New voices challenge fame;
But let no moss of years o'ercreep
　　The lines of Halleck's name.
　　　　—JOHN GREENLEAF WHITTIER, "Fitz-Greene Hal-
　　　　leck," 1877

He, too, was a natural lyrist, whose pathos and eloquence were inborn, and whose sentiment, though he wrote in the prevailing English mode, was that of his own land. As we read those favorites of our school boy days, "Burns" and "Red Jacket" and "Marco Bozzaris," we feel that Halleck was, within his bounds, a national poet. Circumstances dulled his fire, and he lived to write drivel in his old age. But the early lyrics remain, nor was there anything of their kind in our home-poetry to compete with them until long after their first production.—EDMUND CLARENCE STEDMAN, *Poets of America*, 1885, pp. 40–41

One of the puzzles which arrest the attention of a historian of American literature is to account for the strange indifference of Halleck to exercise often the faculty which on occasions he showed he possessed in superabundance. All the subjects he attempted—the *Croaker Papers*, *Fanny*, "Burns," "Red Jacket," "Alnwick Castle," "Connecticut," the magnificent heroic ode, "Marco Bozzaris"—show a complete artistic mastery of the resources of poetic expression, whether his theme be gay or grave, or compounded of the two. His extravagant admiration of Campbell was founded on Campbell's admirable power of compression. Halleck thought that Byron was a mere rhetorician in comparison with his favorite poet. Yet it is evident to a critical reader that a good deal of Campbell's compactness is due to a studied artifice of rhythm and rhyme, while Halleck

seemingly writes in verse as if he were not trammelled by its laws; and his rhymes naturally recur without suggesting to the reader that his condensation of thought and feeling is at all affected by the necessity of rhyming. Prose has rarely been written with more careless ease and more melodious compactness than Halleck has shown in writing verse. The wonder is, that with this conscious command of bending verse into the brief expression of all the moods of his mind, he should have written so little. The only explanation is to be found in his scepticism as to the vital reality of those profound states of consciousness which inspire poets of less imaginative faculty than he possessed to incessant activity. He was among poets what Thackeray is among novelists. Being the well-paid clerk and man of business of a millionaire, his grand talent was not stung into exertion by necessity. Though he lived to the age of seventy-two, he allowed year after year to pass without any exercise of his genius. "What's the use?"—that was the deadening maxim which struck his poetic faculties with paralysis. Yet what he has written, though very small in amount, belongs to the most precious treasures of our poetical literature. What he might have written, had he so chosen, would have raised him to a rank among our first men of letters, which he does not at present hold.—EDWIN P. WHIPPLE, "American Literature" (1886), *American Literature and Other Papers*, 1887, pp. 51–53

⟨. . .⟩ Fitz-Greene Halleck, was the finest and most typical poet of that day. In collaboration with Drake he printed in 1819, under the title of *The Croakers*, a series of poetical satires upon public characters of the period, a series which achieved an immediate local fame; but Halleck is now better known by "Marco Bozzaris" and "Burns." His own character may still better keep him a lasting name. He lacked, however, the intellectual independence and the creative genius which is unhindered by the wearing and destructive effect of drudgery.—ARTHUR B. SIMONDS, *American Song*, 1894, p. 136

Fitz Greene Halleck, Drake's associate, was for years probably the most popular American poet. His clear, lucid style, easy diction and good-natured raillery, appealed at once to the public sentiment, and gave him a temporary prestige in literary circles hardly equalled in our history. His odes, lyrics, and satires were the most polished of their kind, written in a strain at once to catch the popular fancy. Even those of a transient character, with allusions now for the most part of little interest, show the same graceful, poetic spirit that enlivens the more important works. He had that excellent command of language that enabled him to express his meaning in the most felicitous terms, without the slightest apparent effort. It is certainly no rash prediction to assert that his more familiar lyrics, though few in number, will last as long as any short poems in our literature.—JAMES. L. ONDERDONK, *History of American Verse*, 1901, p. 134

Works

FANNY

To render my solitary hours less irksome, I have spun out the poem which I repeated to you last summer into a book of fifty pages, which was published in New York last month. I had no intention of publishing it, but the bookseller who brought out Irving's *Sketch-Book* offering to publish *Fanny* in a style similar to that work, I consented to his doing so. I have, of course, heard nothing of its fate since I left New York, but, as the publisher seemed very sanguine in his expectation of its popularity, I hope, for his sake, as well as my own pride, though the author is unknown, that he will not be disappointed. He is binding a copy for you, which I shall forward immediately on my return. For my own part, I do not think much of the merits of the work, the plague of correcting the proof-sheets, etc., having put me out of conceit with it, and I fear that its localities will render it almost entirely uninteresting to you. The bookseller stated to me that I was the only writer in America, Irving excepted, whose works he would risk publishing. This opinion was founded, of course, upon the popularity of *The Croakers*. I do not anticipate the same popularity for this work. *The Croakers* cost the public nothing, this costs them fifty cents, which will have, no doubt, an effect in limiting the number of readers. I am anxious, as you may well suppose, to learn how it succeeds, but shall not have it in my power to ascertain it till my return.—FITZ-GREENE HALLECK, Letter to His Sister (Jan. 1, 1820), cited in James Grant Wilson, *The Life and Letters of Fitz-Greene Halleck*, 1869, pp. 231–32.

Your pieces, if, as I suppose, you are the author of those signed *Croaker*, have been read in the newspapers with great interest, but *Fanny* is of a higher order, and for its easy conversational wit, and poetry of descriptions, must go alongside of Lord Byron's and Mr. Rose's productions in the same way. It is the admiration of your poetical talents which has led me to make this communication to you, and to request, if you feel inclined to give your pieces a circulation among your Eastern brethren, you would sometimes select the *Club-Room* as the medium of communication. I find no difficulty as the editor in obtaining compositions in prose, but it is otherwise in poetry, which, as it is not necessary to publish, we feel unwilling to publish unless it is particularly good, and I know of no source from which I could be so likely to obtain this as from the author of *Fanny*.—WILLIAM H. PRESCOTT, Letter to Fitz-Greene Halleck (March 15, 1820), cited in James Grant Wilson, *The Life and Letters of Fitz-Greene Halleck*, 1869, p. 239.

The popularity of *Fanny* was so great, that the publisher offered Halleck five hundred dollars for another canto, an offer which he accepted, and in 1821 a second edition appeared, enlarged by the addition of fifty stanzas. Before its appearance, the poem had become so scarce that it sold for fabulous prices ten dollars having been frequently paid for a copy of the thin pamphlet of forty-nine pages, originally published at fifty cents. Its authorship was attributed to a number of prominent literary men, but, except in a few instances, suspicion never rested upon Mr. Halleck, who quietly enjoyed the bewilderment of the town, only sharing his secret with DeKay, Drake, Langstaff, and a few other faithful friends. Henry Brevoort, the friend of Washington Irving, said that he would feel prouder of being the author of *Fanny* than of any other poetical work ever written in America.—JAMES GRANT WILSON, *The Life and Letters of Fitz-Greene Halleck*, 1869, p. 234.

The mistaken belief that he was, or could be, a humorous writer, led to the production of Halleck's first poem of any length,—*Fanny*. It is possible to read *Fanny*, as it is possible to read *The Croakers*, for I have done both. But it is impossible, at least I find it so, to feel any interest therein; for the analysis which could detect poetry in either would be rarer than the alchemy which was once supposed to extract sunbeams from cucumbers. There is no story in *Fanny*, or none to speak of; and the most that one can say of it is that it is an imaginary sketch of the social experiences of its heroine, the daughter of a shopkeeper in Chatham Street, who, having amassed what

was then considered a comfortable little fortune, proceeded to make a brilliant brief splurge in society, and concluded his career by going where the woodbine twineth.

To depict the mortifying experiences of a parvenu's daughter ought not to have been difficult, but it was more than the unpractised pen of Halleck could accomplish; for, flimsy in intention and feeble in execution, *Fanny* was dreary reading, because the author after writing what he probably considered a poetic passage immediately spoiled it by sticking his tongue in his cheek. A certain amount of antiquarian interest attaches to his pointless verse, and there is a pretty description of Weehawken, which was one of his favorite suburban resorts. What the subject-matter of such a poem as *Fanny* could be in the hands of a true poet was shown at a later period by Thomas Hood in *Miss Kilmansegg*, and at a still later period by Mr. Stedman in his "Diamond Wedding."—RICHARD HENRY STODDARD, "Fitz-Greene Halleck," *Lippincott's Magazine*, June 1889, pp. 892–93.

EDGAR ALLAN POE
From "Fitz-Green Halleck"
The Literati of New York City
1846

The name of *Halleck* is at least as well established in the poetical world as that of any American. Our principal poets are, perhaps, most frequently named in this order—Bryant, Halleck, Dana, Sprague, Longfellow, Willis, and so on—Halleck coming second in the series, but holding, in fact, a rank in the public opinion quite equal to that of Bryant. The accuracy of the arrangement as above made may, indeed, be questioned. For my own part, I should have it thus—Longfellow, Bryant, Halleck, Willis, Sprague, Dana; and, estimating rather the poetic capacity than the poems actually accomplished, there are three or four comparatively unknown writers whom I would place in the series between Bryant and Halleck, while there are about a dozen whom I should assign a position between Willis and Sprague. Two dozen at least might find room between Sprague and Dana—this latter, I fear, owing a very large portion of his reputation to his *quondam* editorial connection with *The North American Review*. One or two poets now in my minds eye I should have no hesitation in posting above even Mr. Longfellow—still not intending this as very extravagant praise.

It is noticeable, however, that, in the arrangement which I attribute to the popular understanding, the order observed is nearly, if not exactly, that of the ages—the poetic ages—of the individual poets. Those rank first who were first known. The priority has established the strength of impression. Nor is this result to be accounted for by mere reference to the old saw—that first impressions are the strongest. Gratitude, surprise, and a species of hyper-patriotic triumph have been blended, and finally confounded with admiration or appreciation in regard to the *pioneers* of American literature, among whom there is not one whose productions have not been grossly overrated by his countrymen. Hitherto we have been in no mood to view with calmness and discuss with discrimination the real claims of the few who were *first* in convincing the mother country that her sons were not all brainless, as at one period she half affected and wholly wished to believe. Is there any one so blind as not to see that Mr. Cooper, for example, owes much, and Mr. Paulding nearly all, of his reputation as a novelist to his early occupation of the field? Is there any one so dull as not to know that fictions which neither of these gentlemen *could* have written are written daily by native authors, without attracting much more of commendation than can be included in a newspaper paragraph? And, again, is there any one so prejudiced as not to acknowledge that all this happens because there is no longer either reason or wit in the query, "Who reads an American book?"

I mean to say, of course, that Mr. Halleck, in the *apparent* public estimate, maintains a somewhat better position than that to which, on absolute grounds, he is entitled. There is something, too, in the *bonhommie* of certain of his compositions—something altogether distinct from poetic merit—which has aided to establish him; and much, also, must be admitted on the score of his personal popularity, which is deservedly great. With all these allowances, however, there will still be found a large amount of poetical fame to which he is *fairly* entitled.

He has written very little, although he began at an early age—when quite a boy, indeed. His "juvenile" works, however, have been kept very judiciously from the public eye. Attention was first called to him by his satires signed "Croaker" and "Croaker & Co.," published in *The New York Evening Post*, in 1819. Of these the pieces with the signature "*Croaker & Co.*" were the joint work of Halleck and his friend Drake. The political and personal features of these *jeux d'esprit* gave them a consequence and a notoriety to which they are entitled on no other account. They are not without a species of drollery, but are loosely and no doubt carelessly written.

Neither was *Fanny*, which closely followed the *Croakers*, constructed with any great deliberation. "It was printed," say the ordinary memoirs, "within three weeks from its commencement;" but the truth is, that a couple of days would have been an ample allowance of time for any such composition. If we except a certain gentlemanly ease and *insouciance*, with some fancy of illustration, there is really very little about this poem to be admired. There is really no positive avowal of its authorship, although there can be no doubt of its having been written by Halleck. He, I presume, does not esteem it very highly. It is a mere extravaganza, in close imitation of *Don Juan*—a vehicle for squibs at cotemporary persons and things.

Our poet, indeed, seems to have been much impressed by *Don Juan*, and attempts to engraft its farcicalities even upon the grace and delicacy of "Alnwick Castle;" as, for example, in—

> Men in the coal and cattle line,
>   From Teviot's bard and hero land,
>   From royal Berwick's beach of sand,
>   From Wooler, Morpeth, Hexham, *and*
> Newcastle upon Tyne.

These things may lay claim to oddity, but no more. They are totally out of keeping with the tone of the sweet poem into which they are thus clumsily introduced, and serve no other purpose than to deprive it of all unity of effect. If a poet *must* be farcical, let him be just that; he can be nothing better at the same moment. To be drolly sentimental, or even sentimentally droll, is intolerable to men and gods and columns.

"Alnwick Castle" is distinguished, in general, by that air of quiet grace, both in thought and expression, which is the prevailing feature of the muse of Halleck. Its second stanza is a good specimen of this manner. The commencement of the fourth belongs to a very high order of poetry.

> Wild roses by the Abbey towers
>   Are gay in their young bud and bloom—
> *They were born of a race of funeral flowers*

> That garlanded, in long-gone hours,
>   A Templar's knightly tomb.

This is gloriously imaginative, and the effect is singularly increased by the sudden transition from iambuses to anapæsts. The passage is, I think, the noblest to be found in Halleck, and I would be at a loss to discover its parallel in all American poetry.

"Marco Bozzaris" has much lyrical, without any great amount of *ideal* beauty. Force is its prevailing feature—force resulting rather from well-ordered metre, vigorous rhythm, and a judicious disposal of the circumstances of the poem, than from any of the truer lyric material. I should do my conscience great wrong were I to speak of "Marco Bozzaris" as it is the fashion to speak of it, at least in print. Even as a lyric or ode it is surpassed by many American and a multitude of foreign compositions of a similar character.

"Burns" has numerous passages exemplifying its author's felicity of *expression*; as, for instance—

> Such graves as his are pilgrim shrines—
>   Shrines to no code or creed confined—
> *The Delphian vales, the Palestines,*
>   *The Meccas of the mind.*

And, again—

> There have been loftier themes than his,
>   *And longer scrolls and louder lyres,*
> *And lays lit up with Poesy's*
>   *Purer and holier fires.*

But to the *sentiment* involved in this last quatrain I feel disposed to yield an assent more thorough than might be expected. Burns, indeed, was the puppet of circumstance. As a poet, no person on the face of the earth has been more extravagantly, more absurdly overrated.

"The Poet's Daughter" is one of the most characteristic works of Halleck, abounding in his most distinctive traits, grace, expression, repose, *insouciance*. The vulgarity of

> I'm busy in the cotton trade
>   And sugar line,

has, I rejoice to see, been omitted in the late editions. The eleventh stanza is certainly not English as it stands, and, besides, is quite unintelligible. What is the meaning of this—

> But her who asks, though first among
> The good, the beautiful, the young,
> The birthright of a spell more strong
>   Than these have brought her.

The "Lines on the Death of Joseph Rodman Drake" is, as a whole, one of the best poems of its author. Its simplicity and delicacy of sentiment will recommend it to all readers. It is, however, carelessly written, and the first quatrain,

> Green be the turf above thee,
>   Friend of my better days—
> None knew thee but to love thee,
>   Nor named thee but to praise,

although beautiful, bears too close a resemblance to the still more beautiful lines of Wordsworth—

> She dwelt among the untrodden ways
>   Beside the springs of Dove,
> A maid whom there were none to praise
>   And very few to love.

In versification Mr. Halleck is much as usual, although in this regard Mr. Bryant has paid him numerous compliments. "Marco Bozzaris" has certainly some vigor of rhythm, but its author, in short, writes carelessly, loosely, and, as a matter of course, seldom effectively, so far as the outworks of literature are concerned.

Of late days he has nearly given up the muses, and we recognize his existence as a poet chiefly by occasional translations from the Spanish or German.

Personally, he is a man to be admired, respected, but more especially beloved. His address has all the captivating *bonhommie* which is the leading feature of his poetry, and, indeed, of his whole moral nature. With his friends he is all ardor, enthusiasm and cordiality, but to the world at large he is reserved, shunning society, into which he is seduced only with difficulty and upon rare occasions. The love of solitude seems to have become with him a passion.

WILLIAM CULLEN BRYANT
From "Fitz-Greene Halleck" (1869)
Prose Writings, ed. Parke Godwin
1884, Volume 1, pp. 381–87

It is now five-and-thirty years, the life of one of the generations of mankind, since I contributed to a weekly periodical, published in this city, an estimate of the poetical genius of Halleck. Of course, nobody now remembers having read it, and, as it was written after his most remarkable poems had been given to the public, and as I could say nothing different of them now, I will, with the leave of the audience, make it a part of this paper. ⟨. . .⟩

"Halleck's humorous poems are marked by an uncommon ease of versification, a natural flow and sweetness of language, and a careless, Horatian playfulness and felicity of jest, not, however, imitated from Horace or any other writer. He finds abundant matter for mirth in the peculiar state of our society, in the heterogeneous population of the city—

Of every race the mingled swarm,

in the affectations of newly assumed gentility, the ostentation of wealth, the pretensions of successful quackery, and the awkward attempt to blend with the habits of trade an imitation of the manners of the most luxurious and fastidious nobility in the world—the nobility of England. Sometimes, in the midst of a strain of harmonious diction, and soft and tender imagery—so soft and tender that you willingly yield yourself up to the feeling of pathos or to the sense of beauty it inspires—he surprises you with an irresistible stroke of ridicule,

As if himself he did disdain,
And mock the form he did but feign;

as if he looked with no regard upon the fair poetical vision he had raised, and took pleasure in showing the reader that it was but a cheat. Sometimes the poet, with that aërial facility which is his peculiar endowment, accumulates graceful and agreeable images in a strain of irony so fine that, did not the subject compel you to receive it as irony, you would take it for a beautiful passage of serious poetry—so beautiful that you are tempted to regret that he is not in earnest, and that phrases so exquisitely chosen, and poetic coloring so brilliant, should be employed to embellish subjects to which they do not properly belong. At other times he produces the effect of wit by dexterous allusions to contemporaneous events, introduced as illustrations of the main subject, with all the unconscious gracefulness of the most animated and familiar conversation. He delights in ludicrous contrasts produced by bringing the nobleness of the ideal world into comparison with the homeliness of the actual; the beauty and grace of nature with the awkwardness of art. He venerates the past and laughs at the present. He looks at them through a medium which lends to the former the charm of romance, and exaggerates the deformity of the latter.

"Halleck's poetry, whether serious or sprightly, is remarkable for the melody of the numbers. It is not the melody of monotonous and strictly regular measurement. His verse is constructed to please an ear naturally fine and accustomed to a wide range of metrical modulation. It is as different from that painfully balanced versification, that uniform succession of iambics, closing the sense with the couplet, which some writers practice, and some critics praise, as the note of the thrush is unlike that of the cuckoo. Halleck is familiar with those general rules and principles which are the basis of metrical harmony; and his own unerring taste has taught him the exceptions which a proper attention to variety demands. He understands that the rivulet is made musical by obstructions in its channel. You will find in no poet passages which flow with a more sweet and liquid smoothness; but he knows very well that to make this smoothness perceived, and to prevent it from degenerating into monotony, occasional roughnesses must be interposed.

"But it is not only in humorous or playful poetry that Halleck excels. He has fire and tenderness and manly vigor, and his serious poems are equally admirable with his satirical. What martial lyric can be finer than the verses on the death of Marco Bozzaris? We are made spectators of the slumbers of the Turkish oppressor, dreaming of 'victory in his guarded tent'; we see the Greek warrior ranging his true-hearted band of Suliotes in the forest shades; we behold them throwing themselves into the camp; we hear the shout, the groan, the sabre stroke, the death shot falling thick and fast, and, in the midst of all, the voice of Bozzaris bidding them to strike boldly for God and their native land. The struggle is long and fierce; the ground is piled with Moslem slain; the Greeks are at length victorious; and as the brave chief falls, bleeding from every vein, he hears the proud huzza of his surviving comrades, announcing that the field is won, and he closes his eyes in death,

Calmly, as to a night's repose.

"This picture of the battle is followed by a dirge over the slain hero—a glorious outpouring of lyrical eloquence, worthy to have been chanted by Pindar or Tyrtæus over one of his ancestors. There is in this poem a freedom, a daring, a fervency, a rapidity, an affluence of thick-coming fancies, that make it seem like an inspired improvisation, as if the thoughts had been divinely breathed into the mind of the poet, and uttered themselves, voluntarily, in poetic numbers. We think, as we read it, of

—the large utterance of the early gods.

"If an example is wanted of Halleck's capacity for subjects of a gentler nature, let the reader turn to the verses written in the album of an unknown lady, entitled 'Woman.' In a few lines he has gathered around the name of woman a crowd of delightful associations—all the graces of her sex, delightful pictures of domestic happiness and domestic virtues, gentle affections, pious cares, smiles and tears, that bless and heal,

And earth's lost paradise restored,
In the green bower of home.

"'Red Jacket' is a poem of a yet different kind; a poem of manly vigor of sentiment, noble versification, strong expression, and great power in the delineation of character—the whole dashed off with a great appearance of freedom, and delightfully tempered with the satirical vein of the author. Some British periodical, lately published, contains a criticism on American literature, in which it is arrogantly asserted that our poets have made nothing of the Indian character, and that Campbell's 'Outalissi' is altogether the best portraiture of the mind and manners of an American savage which is to be found in English verse. The critic must have spoken without much knowledge of his subject. He certainly could never have read Halleck's 'Red Jacket.' Campbell's 'Outalissi' is very well. He is 'a stoic of the woods,' and nothing more; an Epictetus put into a blanket and leggins, and translated to the forests of Pennsylvania; but he is no Indian. 'Red Jacket' is the very savage of our wilderness. 'Outalissi' is a fancy sketch of few lineaments. He is brave, faithful, and affectionate, concealing these qualities under an exterior of insensibility. 'Red Jacket' has the spirit and variety of a portrait from nature. He has all the savage virtues and savage vices, and the rude and strong qualities of mind which belong to a warrior, a chief, and an orator of the aboriginal stock. He is set before us with sinewy limbs, gentle voice, motions graceful as a bird's in air, an air of command inspiring deference; brave, cunning, cruel, vindictive, eloquent, skilful to dissemble, and terrible, when the moment of dissembling is past, as the wild beasts or the tempests of his own wilderness.

"A poem which, without being the best he has written, unites many of the different qualities of Halleck's manner, is that entitled 'Alnwick Castle.' The rich imagery, the airy melody of verse, the graceful language which belong to his serious poems, are to be found in the first half of the poem, which relates to the beautiful scenery and venerable traditions of the old home of the Percys; while the author's vein of gay humor, fertile in mirthful allusion, appears in the conclusion, in which he descends to the homely and peaceful occupations of its present proprietors.

"Whoever undertakes the examination of Halleck's poetical character will naturally wish for a greater number of examples from which to collect an estimate of his powers. He has given us only samples of what he can do. His verses are like passages of some noble choral melody, heard in the brief interval between the opening and shutting of the doors of a temple. Why does he not more frequently employ the powers with which he is so eminently gifted? He should know that such faculties are invigorated and enlarged, and rendered obedient to the will by exercise. He need not be afraid of not equalling what he has already written. He will excel himself if he applies his powers, with an earnest and resolute purpose, to the work which justice to his own fame demands of him. There are heroes of our own history who deserve to be embalmed for immortality in strains as noble as those which celebrate the death of Marco Bozzaris; and Halleck has shown how powerfully he can appeal to our sense of patriotism in his 'Field of the Grounded Arms,' a poem which has only been prevented from being universally popular by the peculiar kind of verse in which it is written."

N. P. WILLIS

1806–1867

Nathaniel Parker Willis was born on January 20, 1806, in Portland, Maine. When he was six the family moved to Boston, where young Willis attended the Boston Latin School. After further study at Andover, Willis entered Yale. He began publishing verses in his father's newspaper, the *Boston Recorder*, signing them "Roy" or "Cassius," and became nationally known while still an undergraduate. Many of his poems were paraphrases in verse of Bible stories; they were included in his first book, *Sketches*, published in 1827, the year of his graduation.

After an interval as the editor of several literary magazines Willis in 1829 founded the *American Monthly Magazine*, a venture that lasted for two and a half years. In 1832 Willis went to New York, where he persuaded George Pope Morris, the editor of the *New-York Mirror*, to send him abroad as a correspondent. For three years Willis roamed the Continent, achieving fame as an American man of letters as he sent back a series of letters for publication; these were later collected and published as *Pencillings by the Way* (1835).

Marrying in England, Willis returned to America with his bride. As a means of supplementing his journalistic income he wrote several plays. *Bianca Visconti* (1839) was a moderate success, as was *Tortesa; or, The Usurer Matched* (1839), which earned the praise of Edgar Allan Poe. Willis continued as well to travel and write for the *Mirror*, sending dispatches from Washington and from Niagara. *A l'Abri; or, The Tent Pitch'd*, a collection of these pieces, appeared in 1839; the following year another collection, *American Scenery* (2 vols.), was published. Also appearing in 1840 was *Loiterings of Travel* (3 vols.). During this period Willis traveled for a time in England, meeting with Thackeray and other literary figures, and upon his return to America was engaged by several periodicals, including *Graham's* and *Godey's*, as a contributor. He also continued his association with the *Mirror*, now a daily paper renamed the *Evening Mirror*, as co-editor with Morris; he was as well a major contributor of poems, stories, and essays. One poem by Willis, "Unseen Spirits," was praised by Poe and led to Poe's employment on the newspaper as a staff member. Willis and Poe became close friends, Willis offering Poe both financial and emotional support.

Following the deaths of both his mother and his wife, Willis sought solace abroad and took his young daughter Imogen to England and the Continent in 1845. Shortly before his departure he published *Dashes at Life with a Free Pencil*, a collection of his essays; his letters from his third trip abroad were later published as *Rural Letters* (1849) and *Famous Persons and Places* (1854). Back in the United States in 1846, Willis began with Morris a new venture, the *Home Journal*, to which he contributed a column of goings-on about New York City.

In 1852 Willis traveled to Bermuda and the West Indies in an attempt to restore his failing health; his travel letters from this journey were later published as *Health Trip to the Tropics* (1853). His later works included several collections of short stories, including *People I Have Met* (1850), *Life Here and There* (1850), and *Fun Jottings* (1853). A novel, *Paul Fane*, appeared in 1857. With his second wife and family Willis established a salon at his country home, Idlewild, on the Hudson near Washington Irving's estate. During the Civil War Willis went to the Capitol as a correspondent for the *Home Journal*; there he became a popular figure in Washington society, and was said to have been a particular favorite of Mrs. Lincoln.

Willis died at Idlewild on January 20, 1867.

Personal

I have just returned from bidding Willis farewell, and feel nearly as much regret as on leaving home; for I never met with one in my life who has won my regard and esteem in so short a time. ⟨. . .⟩ I will talk a little more about Willis. Griswold intended giving me a letter of introduction, but had no time. I called at his house, and on telling my name he knew me instantly. On apologizing for calling without a letter, he said it was unnecessary, as we knew each other already, and began conversing as familiarly as if we had been old friends. He commended my plan of going very highly, and gave me a very flattering letter of recommendation to the New York editors, but they appear to be supplied, and a letter to his brother, Richard S. Willis, in Frankfurt, Germany. He did many other kindnesses for me, which I shall not soon forget. I have been at his house three or four times, and when, this afternoon, he gave me his parting "God bless you," I felt as if I had left a true friend. I have not time now to give you much of his conversation, but it is daguerreotyped on my memory. He looks very much like the portrait in *Graham's Mazagine*, but not quite so young, although at times, when he becomes animated, you would not take him to be more than twenty-four; dresses with neatness and the most perfect taste, and has the very *beau idéal* of a study,—you can conceive of nothing more elegant. In fact, his poetry is visible in everything around him.—BAYARD TAYLOR, Letter to J. B. Phillips (June 30, 1844), *Life and Letters of Bayard Taylor*, eds. Marie Hansen-Taylor, Horace E. Scudder, 1885, Vol. 1, pp. 39–40

I lately made a day's excursion up the Hudson, in company with Mr. and Mrs. M—— G—— and two or three others, to visit Willis in his poetical retreat of Idlewild. It is really a beautiful place, the site well chosen, commanding noble and romantic scenery; the house commodious and picturesque, and furnished with much taste. In a word, it is just such a retreat as a poet would desire. I never saw Willis to such advantage as on this occasion. . . . Willis talks and writes much about his ill health, and is really troubled with an ugly cough; but I do not think his lungs are seriously affected, and I think it likely he will be like a cracked pitcher, which lasts the longer for having a flaw in it, being so much the more taken care of.—WASHINGTON IRVING, Letter to John Pendleton Kennedy (Aug. 31, 1854), cited in Pierre M. Irving, *The Life and Letters of Washington Irving*, 1863, Vol. 4, p. 175

I encountered one specimen of American oddity before I left home which should certainly have lessened my surprise at any that I met afterwards. While I was preparing for my travels, an acquaintance one day brought a buxom gentleman, whom he introduced to me under the name of Willis. There was

something rather engaging in the round face, brisk air and *enjouement* of the young man; but his conscious dandyism and unparalleled self-complacency spoiled the satisfaction, though they increased the inclination to laugh. Mr. N. P. Willis's plea for coming to see me was his gratification that I was going to America: and his real reason was presently apparent;—a desire to increase his consequence in London society by giving apparent proof that he was on intimate terms with every eminent person in America. He placed himself in an attitude of infinite ease, and whipped his little bright boot with a little bright cane while he ran over the names of all his distinguished country-men and country-women, and declared he should send me letters to them all. This offer of intervention went so very far that I said (what I have ever since said in the case of introductions offered by strangers) while thanking him for his intended good offices, that I was sufficiently uncertain in my plans to beg for excuse beforehand, in case I should find myself unable to use the letters. It appeared afterwards that to supply them and not to have them used suited Mr. Willis's convenience exactly. It made him appear to have the friendships he boasted of without putting the boast to the proof. It was immediately before a late dinner that the gentleman called; and I found on the breakfast-table, next morning, a great parcel of Mr. Willis's letters, enclosed in a prodigious one to myself, in which he offered advice. Among other things, he desired me not to use his letter to Dr. Channing if I had others from persons more intimate with him; and he proceeded to warn me against two friends of Dr. and Mrs. Channing's, whose names I had never heard, and whom Mr. Willis represented as bad and dangerous people. This gratuitous defamation of strangers whom I was likely to meet confirmed the suspicions my mother and I had confided to each other about the quality of Mr. Willis's introductions. It seemed ungrateful to be so suspicious: but we could not see any good reason for such prodigious efforts on my behalf, nor for his naming any country-women of his to me in a way so spontaneously slanderous. So I resolved to use that packet of letters very cautiously; and to begin with one which should be well accompanied.—In New York harbour, newspapers were brought on board, in one of which was an extract from an article transmitted by Mr. Willis to the *New York Mirror*, containing a most audacious account of me as an intimate friend of the writer. The friendship was not stated, as a matter of fact, but so conveyed that it cost me much trouble to make it understood and believed, even by Mr. Willis's own family, that I had never seen him but once; and then without having previously heard so much as his name. On my return, the acquaintance who brought him was anxious to ask pardon if he had done mischief,—events having by that time made Mr. Willis's ways pretty well known. His partner in the property and editorship of the *New York Mirror* called on me at West Point, and offered and rendered such extraordinary courtesy that I was at first almost as much perplexed as he and his wife were when they learned that I had never seen Mr. Willis but once. They pondered, they consulted, they cross-questioned me; they inquired whether *I* had any notion what Mr. Willis could have meant by writing of me as in a state of close intimacy with him. In like manner, when, some time after, I was in a carriage with some members of a pic-nic party to Monument Mountain, a little girl seated at my feet clasped my knees fondly, looked up in my face, and said "O! Miss Martineau! you are *such* a friend of my uncle Nathaniel's!" Her father was present; and I tried to get off without explanation. But it was impossible,—they all knew how very intimate I was with "Nathaniel": and there was a renewal of the amazement at my having seen him only once.—I tried three of his letters; and the reception was in each case much the same,—a throwing down of the letter with an air not to be mistaken. In each case the reply was the same, when I subsequently found myself at liberty to ask what this might mean. "Mr. Willis is not entitled to write to me: he is no acquaintance of mine." As for the two ladies of whom I was especially to beware, I became exceedingly well acquainted with them, to my own advantage and pleasure; and, as a natural consequence, I discovered Mr. Willis's reasons for desiring to keep us apart. I hardly need add that I burned the rest of his letters. He had better have spared himself the trouble of so much manœuvring, by which he lost a good deal, and could hardly have gained anything. I have simply stated the facts because, in the first place, I do not wish to be considered one of Mr. Willis's friends; and, in the next, it may be useful, and conducive to justice, to show, by a practical instance, what Mr. Willis's pretensions to intimacy are worth. His countrymen and countrywomen accept; in simplicity, his accounts of our aristocracy as from the pen of one of their own coterie; and they may as well have the opportunity of judging for themselves whether their notorious "Penciller" is qualified to write of Scotch Dukes and English Marquises, and European celebrities of all kinds in the way he has done.—HARRIET MARTINEAU, *Autobiography*, ed. Maria Weston Chapman, 1877, Vol. 1, pp. 384–86

Nathaniel Parker Willis was in full bloom when I opened my first Portfolio. He had made himself known by his religious poetry, published in his father's paper, I think, and signed "Roy." He had started the *American Magazine*, afterwards merged in the *New York Mirror*. He had then left off writing scripture pieces, and taken to lighter forms of verse. He had just written

> I'm twenty-two, I'm twenty-two,—
> They idly give me joy,
> As if I should be glad to know
> That I was less a boy.

He was young, therefore, and already famous. He came very near being very handsome. He was tall; his hair, of light brown color, waved in luxuriant abundance; his cheek was as rosy as if it had been painted to show behind the footlights; he dressed with artistic elegance. He was something between a remembrance of Count D'Orsay and an anticipation of Oscar Wilde. There used to be in the gallery of the Luxembourg a picture of Hippolytus and Phædra, in which the beautiful young man, who had kindled a passion in the heart of his wicked step-mother, always reminded me of Willis, in spite of the shortcomings of the living face as compared with the ideal. The painted youth is still blooming on the canvas, but the fresh-cheeked, jaunty young author of the year 1830 has long faded out of human sight.—OLIVER WENDELL HOLMES, "Introduction" to *A Mortal Antipathy*, 1885

General

Pencillings by the Way is a very spirited book. The letters, out of which it is constructed, were written originally for the New York *Mirror*, and were not intended for distinct publication. From this circumstance, the author indulged in a freedom of personal detail, which we must say is wholly unjustifiable, and we have no wish to defend it. This book does not pretend to contain any profound observations or discussions on national character, political condition, literature, or even art. It would be obviously impossible to carry any one of those topics thoroughly out, without spending vastly more time and labor upon it, than a rambling poet is likely to have the inclination to do. In fact, there are very few men, who are qualified, by the nature of their previous studies, to do this with any degree of edification to their readers. But a man of general intellectual culture, especially if he have the poetical imagination super-added, may give us rapid sketches of other countries, which will both entertain and instruct us. Now this book is precisely such an one as we have here indicated. The author travelled through Europe, mingling largely in society, and visited whatever scenes were interesting to him as an American, a scholar, and a poet. The impressions which these scenes made upon his mind, are described in these volumes; and we must say, we have rarely fallen in with a book of a more sprightly character, a more elegant and graceful style, and full of more lively descriptions. The delineations of manners are executed with great tact; and the shifting pictures of natural scenery pass before us as we read, exciting a never-ceasing interest.—C. C. FELTON, "Willis's Writings," *North American Review*, Oct. 1836, p. 407

It has been the fate of this gentleman to be alternately condemned *ad infinitum*, and lauded *ad nauseam*—a fact which speaks much in his praise. We know of no American writer who has evinced greater versatility of talent; that is to say, of high talent, often amounting to genius, and we know of none who has more narrowly missed placing himself at the head of our letters.—EDGAR ALLAN POE, "A Chapter on Autography" (1841), *Collected Works*, ed. James A. Harrison, 1902, Vol. 15, p. 190

> There is Willis, all *natty* and jaunty and gay,
> Who says his best things in so foppish a way,
> With conceits and pet phrases so thickly o'erlaying 'em,
> That one hardly knows whether to thank him for saying 'em;
> Over-ornament ruins both poem and prose,
> Just conceive of a Muse with a ring in her nose!
> His prose had a natural grace of its own,
> And enough of it, too, if he'd let it alone;
> But he twitches and jerks so, one fairly gets tired,
> And is forced to forgive where he might have admired;
> Yet whenever it slips away free and unlaced,
> It runs like a stream with a musical waste,
> And gurgles along with the liquidest sweep;—
> 'T is not deep as a river, but who'd have it deep?
> In a country where scarcely a village is found
> That has not its author sublime and profound,
> For some one to be slightly shoal is a duty,
> And Willis's shallowness makes half his beauty.
> His prose winds along with a blithe, gurgling error,
> And reflects all of Heaven it can see in its mirror.
> 'T is a narrowish strip, but it is not an artifice,—
> 'T is the true out-of-doors with its genuine hearty phiz;
> It is Nature herself, and there's something in that,
> Since most brains reflect but the crown of a hat.
> No volume I know to read under a tree,
> More truly delicious than his *A l'Abri*,

With the shadows of leaves flowing over your book,
Like ripple-shades netting the bed of a brook;
With June coming softly your shoulder to look over,
Breezes waiting to turn every leaf of your book over,
And Nature to criticise still as you read,—
The page that bears that is a rare one indeed.
—JAMES RUSSELL LOWELL, A *Fable for Critics*,
1848

There is a want of naturalness in Mr. Willis's writings which will inevitably affect their continuance, and we have doubts whether any of his numerous prose works will remain permanent portions of Literature.

There are two descriptions of popularity which are essentially different; the first is founded on the human heart, the other is merely supported by the conventionalities of the present time. Popularity is, therefore, not a sure test; we should then first inquire what kind of popularity an author possesses before we decide upon his relative chance of immortality.

How many great celebrities have passed away? Who was so popular as Churchill in his own day? Yet he is now seldom read or quoted. His popularity was built on a figment of Human Nature, and not based on the breath of the Heart of Man. He was a satirist, and not a poet; the personal dies with the man and his victim, but the universal will live for ever. In like manner, to descend to the present day, we can come pretty near a prophetic glance into the future, by carefully selecting the characteristics of any author, and judging him by that unerring standard. We may give as an instance Mr. Thackeray, whose productions are now so generally read and lauded; the slightest glance at him will convince the critic that when the peculiar phase of society he treats on shall pass away, he will likewise go with it. It is also worthy of observation that the very fact which might in some cases preserve it becomes its destroyer. It might naturally be supposed that it would be prized as a record of the past; but it seems as though the interest died away with the thing described.

On this ground we fear that Mr. Willis will not be an enduring writer. The persiflage and piquancy of his style, which are now so enticing, will in a few years become the obscurers of his fame, just as the pertness and vivacity of the blooming girl become intolerable in the matron. Posterity demands something substantial, condensed, and truthful. It is a very close judging critic, and all personal considerations are lost upon it. Appeals to feeling are unknown; it is the Rhadamanthus of authors. The present race, on the other hand, are too apt to overlook the solid merits of a work, and be taken by the tinsel of the outside garb; they choose beauty, grace, or accomplishment, before virtue or truth. Many honorable, noble natures sit in the judgment-seat and discourse most excellent music, but their audiences grow weary and thin away, till they themselves depart unheeded; while the dancing girl, organ-grinder, tumbler, or Punch and Judy, have a ready and numerous crowd of listeners.

However much this may be deplored, it cannot be helped. The present race is not instructed by its contemporaries, but by its ancestors. The writers of *the day* only amuse; the living man is listened to only as long as he is entertaining or exciting; but the grave sanctifies the voice of the dead, and arrests the traveller's attention. The Siste Viator of the sepulchre is the "open sesame" to the attention of the world.

We have thought it necessary to make these preliminary remarks, lest our estimate of so popular an author as Mr. Willis should be considered harsh or unjust. It will be seen we try our American men of genius by the highest standard. It is no child's plaything that they have to bend, but the Bow of

Ulysses; and we feel sure, upon a little consideration, they will consider it as a compliment rather than a detraction or reproach. We want them to be fellow-laborers with Marlow, Shakspeare, Milton, and Halley, and men of that calibre, and not the playfellows of the minnesinger and the troubadour.

To quote the verse of Watts:—

Were I so tall as reach the pole,
    And grasp the ocean with a span,
I would be measured by my soul,
    That is the standard of the man.

It is not his popularity by which we must measure the author, but the intellect he puts forth. This is a perpetual landmark not washed away by every strong tide of opinion, always ebbing and flowing, but unmoved and visible to all.
—THOMAS POWELL, "Nathaniel Parker Willis," *The Living Authors of America*, 1850, pp. 78–80

The obituary notices which were published after Willis's death made it evident that he had, in a sense, survived his own fame. They were reminiscent in tone, as though addressed to a generation that knew not Joseph. It was forty years since he had come before the public with his maiden book. It was twenty since he had put forth anything entitled to live; and meanwhile a new literature had grown up in America. The bells of morning tinkled faintly and far off, lost in the noise of fife and drum, and the war opened its chasm between the present and the past. For a time even Irving seemed sentimental and Cooper melodramatic. Yet these survive, but whether Willis, whose name has so often been joined with theirs, is destined to find still a hearing, it is for the future alone to say. "He will be remembered," wrote his kinsman, Dr. Richard S. Storrs, "as a man eminently human, with almost unique endowments, devoting rare powers to insignificant purposes, and curiously illustrating the 'fine irony of Nature,' with which she often lavishes one of her choice productions on comparatively inferior ends."

But, laying aside all question of appeal to that formidable tribunal, posterity, the many contemporaries who have owed hours of refined enjoyment to his graceful talent will join heartily with Thackeray in his assertion: "It is comfortable that there should have been a Willis."—HENRY A. BEERS, *Nathaniel Parker Willis*, 1885, pp. 351–52

Nathaniel Parker Willis was, perhaps, the first of our poets to prove that literature could be relied upon as a good business. He certainly enjoyed all those advantages which accompany competence, and the only bank he could draw upon was his brain. He thoroughly understood the art of producing what people desired to read, and for which publishers were willing to pay. His early Scripture sketches, written when he was a student at Yale, gave him the reputation of a promising genius; and though the genius did not afterward take the direction to which its first successes pointed, it gained in strength and breadth with the writer's advancing years. In his best poems he displayed energy both of thought and imagination; but his predominant characteristics were keenness of observation, fertility of fancy, quickness of wit, shrewdness of understanding, a fine perception of beauty, a remarkable felicity in the choice of words, and a subtle sense of harmony in their arrangement, whether his purpose was to produce melodious verse or musical prose. But he doubtless squandered his powers in the attempt to turn them into commodities. To this he was driven by his necessities, and he always frankly acknowledged that he could have done better with his brain had he possessed an income corresponding to that of other eminent American men of letters, who could select their topics without regard to the immediate market value of what they wrote. He became the favorite poet, satirist, and "organ" of the fashionable world. He wrote editorials, letters, essays, novels, which were full of evidences of his rare talent without doing justice to it. He idealized trivialities; he gave a kind of reality to the unreal; and week after week he lifted into importance the unsubstantial matters which for the time occupied the attention of "good society." Some of his phrases, such as "the upper ten thousand," "Fifth-Ave-nudity," are still remembered. The paper which Willis edited, the *Home Journal*, exerted a great deal of influence. However slight might be the subjects, there can be no question that the editor worked hard in bringing the resources of his knowledge, observation, wit, and fancy to place them in their most attractive lights. The trouble was not in the vigor of the faculties, but in the thinness of much of the matter. As an editor, however, Willis had an opportunity to display his grand generosity of heart, and the peculiar power he had of detecting the slightest trace of genius in writers who were the objects of his appreciative eulogy. In the whole history of American literature there is no other example of a prominent man of letters who showed, like Willis, such a passionate desire to make his natural influence effective in dragging into prominence writers who either had no reputation at all, or whose reputation was notoriously less than his.—EDWIN P. WHIPPLE, "American Literature" (1886), *American Literature and Other Papers*, 1887, pp. 83–85

An essential element of dandyism in Willis and almost everything he did was probably the cause of what might be called his personal unpopularity in print. His biographer declares that it was second only to the unpopularity of Cooper among American writers; and it is the less easily understood because Willis's heart was really of the kindest and most human. Furthermore, he was not only prompt with words of praise for promising beginners, but seems to have been almost without literary jealousies. The truth must be that our countrymen were less tolerant fifty years ago than they are to-day of anything that even seemed frivolous or flippant. Willis evidently did not take himself too seriously, and if one should seek high and low for terms to define his work, no words more suggestive of its true character could be found than those which he chose as titles for some of his own books. Besides the *Pencillings by the Way*, there are *Inklings of Adventure, Loiterings of Travel, Hurrygraphs*, and *Dashes at Life with a Free Pencil*. Indeed, he was incessantly dashing at life with a free pencil, and just because this was what he did there is little to show for it fifty years after the best of it was done. With his prose, most of his verse, even the once universally known "Love in a Cottage," has ceased to be read. In a few such poems as "Unseen Spirits" and the "Lines on Leaving Europe," the best of Willis is to be found to-day.—M. A. DE WOLFE HOWE, "Willis, Halleck, and Drake," *American Bookmen*, 1898, pp. 112–13

The judgment which posterity—for as related to Willis's era, the present generation may be considered as posterity—has passed upon his writings is eminently just; many of his poems having been confessedly written "from present feelings or for present gain," Willis himself would have been the last to complain of the indifference of those to whom his personal feelings or personal gains are a matter of no importance whatever. Yet, while it is easy enough to criticise our poet for his daintiness and lack of masculinity, it is unjust to regard him as a mere worldling. He possessed no broad, general culture, indeed slight intellectual force, and still slighter poetic imagination. But he gave us much of the best in his time. Many of his lines have become household phrases, and he unquestion-

ably enriched our literature by contributing some of its best lighter lyrics. When occasion demanded, he could exhibit moral as well as physical courage. When reverses and misfortunes befell him, he showed a manly fortitude that must have surprised those who were constantly denouncing him as a dandy. Similarly in his literary work, he occasionally shows the possession of poetic faculties totally unapparent in his average verse. It is but fair to judge him by his best as well as his worst, and his best was very good. The term "Knickerbocker," as applied to the New York writers, is without any special significance. Irving, the acknowledged leader, had not a drop of "Knickerbocker" blood in his veins, and many of the less distinguished writers of this so-called "school" were of New England birth; but it was Irving's geniality and genius that gave literature a foothold in New York, and made it possible for other and less gifted writers to be appreciated. The *Salmagundi Papers* were the precursors of the *Croaker Papers* of Drake and Halleck. The influence of Irving's lighter prose is plainly traceable in the works of Paulding, Sands, and Clark. He was as much a "society man," in the best sense of the term, as Willis, with the additional merit of not permitting his head to be turned by the marked attentions of distinguished people abroad. The *Knickerbocker Magazine* was not established until 1833, and to its contributors, the term of "Knickerbocker writers" was applied as a matter of description rather than as a mark of literary distinction. But as "Knickerbocker" is inseparably connected with the name of Irving, the personification of what at the time was recognized as the best in our literature, it was only natural that the title should be extended to that class of literature at all suggestive of the charms of the author of *Knickerbocker's New York*.—JAMES L. ONDERDONK, *History of American Verse*, 1901, pp. 147–49

The writings of Willis have fallen into neglect; that was predestined from the nature of them, and in the main this was quite deserved. His prose writings are, I believe, out of print, though his poems still have some sale—about two hundred copies annually. This approaches to something like oblivion. When a volume of selections from his prose writings came out about ten years ago, most readers born since 1850 probably met them for the first time. The volume served some purpose, however, in widening public knowledge of a man who, with all his faults, did some real service to our literature.

Professor Beers affirms that Willis's special gift to literature "was in his instinct for style." There was no style in America when he began to write. Cooper had none whatever, and Irving hardly had one that could be called American. "The bright thought" of Willis's writings "interjected into the muddy stream that flows interminably through the magazines and annuals of the thirties and forties must certainly have seemed a fountain of refreshment." Granting all this, and no more can possibly be granted, it stands a slight residuum indeed. So much success, such unchecked popularity, so many books that every one read,—surely all these promised to exact a stronger tribute from posterity.

On the score of Willis's necessities, it should be said that he was all his days writing, not for fame or for public honours, but for dear life itself, and this in a time when pure literature was paid not better than hod-carrying. If Willis chose to write what he could sell at a good price, than write what he believed would live,—in other words, if he preferred Willis's way to Hawthorne's way,—perhaps it is only the stern moralist who would condemn him. He at any rate had small literary ambition, and scarcely pretended to be more than he was, for which some credit is due to him. He was no rival of the men who have survived him. But surely this was not the fault of Willis: he was incapable of becoming their rival. He had talents, but lacked noble ambition. Therein lies the pathos of his life.—Francis Whiting Halsey, "The Pathos of a Master's Fate," *Our Literary Deluge and Some of Its Deeper Waters*, 1902, pp. 102–3

EDGAR ALLAN POE
From "N. P. Willis"
The Literati of New York City
1846

Whatever may be thought of *Mr. Willis's* talents, there can be no doubt about the fact that, both as an author and as a man, he has made a good deal of noise in the world—at least for an American. His literary life, in especial, has been one continual *émeute*; but then his literary character is modified or impelled in a very remarkable degree by his personal one. His success (for in point of fame, if of nothing else, he has certainly been successful) is to be attributed, one-third to his mental ability and two-thirds to his physical temperament—the latter goading him into the accomplishment of what the former merely gave him the means of accomplishing.

At a very early age Mr. Willis seems to have arrived at an understanding that, in a republic such as ours, the *mere* man of letters must ever be a cipher, and endeavoured, accordingly, to unite the *éclat* of the *littérateur* with that of the man of fashion or of society. He "pushed himself," went much into the world, made friends with the gentler sex, "delivered" poetical addresses, wrote "scriptural" poems, traveled, sought the intimacy of noted women, and got into quarrels with notorious men. All these things served his purpose—if, indeed, I am right in supposing that he had any purpose at all. It is quite probable that, as before hinted, he acted only in accordance with his physical temperament; but be this as it may, his personal greatly advanced, if it did not altogether establish his literary fame. I have often carefully considered whether, without the *physique* of which I speak, there is that in the absolute *morale* of Mr. Willis which would have earned him reputation as a man of letters, and my conclusion is, that he could not have failed to become noted in *some* degree under almost any circumstances, but that about two-thirds (as above stated) of his appreciation by the public should be attributed to those *adventures* which grew immediately out of his animal constitution.

He received what is usually regarded as a "good education"—that is to say, he graduated at college; but his education, in the path he pursued, was worth to him, on account of his extraordinary *savoir fare*, fully twice as much as would have been its value in any common case. No man's knowledge is more available, no man has exhibited greater *tact* in the seemingly casual display of his wares. With *him*, at least, a little learning is *no* dangerous thing. He possessed at one time, I believe, the average quantum of American collegiate lore—"a little Latin and less Greek," a smattering of physical and metaphysical science, and (I should judge) a *very* little of the mathematics—but all this must be considered as mere *guess* on my part. Mr. Willis speaks French with some fluency, and Italian not quite so well.

Within the ordinary range of *belles lettres* authorship, he has evinced much versatility. If called on to designate him by any general literary title, I might term him a magazinist—for his compositions have invariably the species of *effect*, with the

brevity which the magazine demands. We may view him as a paragraphist, an essayist, or rather "sketcher," a tale writer and a poet.

In the first capacity he fails. His points, however good when deliberately wrought, are too *récherchés* to be put hurriedly before the public eye. Mr. W. has by no means the *readiness* which the editing a newspaper demands. He composes (as did Addison, and as do many of the most brilliant and seemingly *dashing* writers of the present day,) with great labour and frequent erasure and interlineation. His MSS., in this regard, present a very singular appearance, and indicate the *vacillation* which is, perhaps, the leading trait of his character. A newspaper, too, in its longer articles—its "leaders"—very frequently demands argumentation, and here Mr. W. is remarkably out of his element. His exuberant *fancy* leads him over hedge and ditch—anywhere from the main road; and, besides, he is far too readily self-dispossessed. With time at command, however, his great *tact* stands him instead of all argumentative power, and enables him to overthrow an antagonist without permitting the latter to see how he is overthrown. A fine example of this "management" is to be found in Mr. W.'s reply to a very inconsiderate attack upon his social standing made by one of the editors of the New York *Courier and Inquirer*. I have always regarded this reply as the highest evidence of its author's ability, as a masterpiece of ingenuity, if not of absolute genius. The skill of the whole lay in this—that, without troubling himself to refute the charges themselves brought against him by Mr. Raymond, he put forth his strength in rendering them null, to all intents and purposes, by obliterating, incidentally and without letting his design be perceived, all *the impression* these charges were calculated to convey. But this reply can be called a newspaper article only on the ground of its having appeared in a newspaper.

As a writer of "sketches," properly so called, Mr. Willis is unequaled. Sketches—especially of society—are his *forte*, and they are so for no other reason than that they afford him the best opportunity of introducing the personal Willis—or, more distinctly, because this species of composition is most susceptible of impression from his personal character. The *degagé* tone of this kind of writing, too, best admits and encourages that *fancy* which Mr. W. possesses in the most extraordinary degree; it is in fancy that he reigns supreme: this, more than any one other quality, and, indeed, more than all his other *literary* qualities combined, has made him what he is. It is this which gives him the originality, the freshness, the point, the piquancy, which appear to be the immediate, but which are, in fact, the mediate sources of his popularity.

In *tales* (written with deliberation for the magazines), he has shown greater *constructiveness* than I should have given him credit for had I not read his compositions of this order—for in this faculty all his other works indicate a singular deficiency. The chief charm even of these tales, however, is still referable to *fancy*.

As a poet, Mr. Willis is not entitled, I think, to so high a rank as he may justly claim through his prose; and this for the reason that, although fancy is not inconsistent with any of the demands of those classes of prose composition which he has attempted, and, indeed, is a vital element of most of them, still it is at war ⟨. . .⟩ with that purity and perfection of *beauty* which are the soul of the poem proper. I wish to be understood as saying this *generally* of our author's poems. In some instances, seeming to *feel* the truth of my proposition, (that fancy should have no place in the loftier poesy,) he has denied it a place, as in "Melanie" and his Scriptural pieces; but, unfortunately, he has been unable to supply the void with the true imagination, and these poems consequently are deficient in vigour, in *stamen*. The Scriptural pieces are quite "correct," as the French have it, and are much admired by a certain set of readers, who judge of a poem, not by its effect on themselves, but by the effect which they imagine it *might* have upon themselves were they not unhappily soulless, and by the effect which they take it for granted it *does* have upon others. It cannot be denied, however, that these pieces are, in general, tame, or indebted for what force they possess to the Scriptural passages of which they are merely paraphrastic. ⟨. . .⟩

In classifying Mr. W.'s writings I did not think it worth while to speak of him as a dramatist, because, although he has written plays, what they have of merit is altogether in their character of poem. Of his *Bianca Visconti* I have little to say;— it deserved to fail, and did, although it abounded in *eloquent* passages. *Tortesa* abounded in the same, but had a great many dramatic *points* well calculated to tell with a conventional audience. Its characters, with the exception of Tomaso, a drunken buffoon, had no character at all, and the *plot* was a tissue of absurdities, inconsequences and inconsistencies; yet I cannot help thinking it, upon the whole, the best play ever written by an American.

Mr. Willis has made very few attempts at criticism, and those few (chiefly newspaper articles) have not impressed me with a high idea of his analytic abilities, although with a *very* high idea of his taste and discrimination.

His *style* proper may be called extravagant, *bizarre*, pointed, epigrammatic without being antithetical, (this is very rarely the case,) but, through all its whimsicalities, graceful, classic and *accurate*. He is very seldom to be caught tripping in the minor morals. His English is *correct*; his most outrageous imagery is, at all events, unmixed.

Mr. Willis's career has naturally made him enemies among the envious host of dunces whom he has outstripped in the race for fame; and these his personal manner (a little tinctured with reserve, *brusquerie*, or even haughtiness) is by no means adapted to conciliate. He has innumerable warm friends, however, and is himself a warm friend. His is impulsive, generous, bold, impetuous, vacillating, irregularly energetic—apt to be hurried into error, but incapable of deliberate wrong.

He is yet young, and, without being handsome, in the ordinary sense, is a remarkably well-looking man. In height he is, perhaps, five feet eleven, and justly proportioned. His figure is put in the best light by the ease and assured grace of his carriage. His whole person and personal demeanour bear about them the traces of "good society." His face is somewhat too full, or rather heavy, in its lower portions. Neither his nose nor his forehead can be defended; the latter would puzzle phrenology. His eyes are a dull bluish gray, and small. His hair is of a rich brown, curling naturally and luxuriantly. His mouth is well cut; the teeth fine; the expression of the smile intellectual and winning. He converses little, *well* rather than fluently, and in a subdued tone. The portrait of him published about three years ago in *Graham's Magazine*, conveys by no means so true an idea of the man as does the sketch (by Lawrence) inserted as frontispiece to a late collection of his poems. He is a widower, and has one child, a daughter.

ARTEMUS WARD
Charles Farrar Browne
1834–1867

Artemus Ward was the pseudonym of Charles Farrar Browne, who was born in Waterford, Maine, on April 26, 1834. As a youth he served locally as a printer's apprentice, then went to Boston where he worked as a compositor for a humor magazine. Browne next moved to Ohio, where he lived and worked for seven years, principally as a local editor for the *Toledo Commercial* and the *Cleveland Plain Dealer*. During these years Browne tried his hand at writing various humorous pieces. In 1858, while at the *Plain Dealer*, he invented the character Artemus Ward, an itinerant showman who commented on the world about him in a series of letters. The writings of "Ward" proved enormously popular, and when Browne moved to New York in 1860 to work for *Vanity Fair*, the letters continued in that publication. As Artemus Ward, Browne also became a contributor to *Punch*.

Browne's humorous writings were published in book form as *Artemus Ward: His Book* (1862); *Artemus Ward: His Travels* (1865); and *Artemus Ward in London* (1867). As Artemus Ward, Browne also appeared as a humorous lecturer and had considerable influence on other humorists, including Mark Twain.

Browne died suddenly, during a British lecture tour, on March 6, 1867, in Southampton.

Personally Charles Farrar Browne was one of the kindest and most affectionate of men, and history does not name a man who was so universally beloved by all who knew him. It was remarked, and truly, that the death of no literary character since Washington Irving caused such general and wide-spread regret.

In stature he was tall and slender. His nose was prominent,—outlined like that of Sir Charles Napier, or Mr. Seward; his eyes brilliant, small, and close together; his mouth large, teeth white and pearly; fingers long and slender; hair soft, straight, and blonde; complexion florid; mustache large, and his voice soft and clear. In bearing, he moved like a natural-born gentleman. In his lectures he never smiled—not even while he was giving utterance to the most delicious absurdities;

but all the while the jokes fell from his lips as if he was unconscious of their meaning. While writing his lectures, he would laugh and chuckle to himself continually.

There was one peculiarity about Charles Browne—*he never made an enemy.* ⟨. . .⟩

The wit of Charles Browne is of the most exalted kind. It is only scholars and those thoroughly acquainted with the *subtilty* of our language who fully appreciate it. His wit is generally about historical personages like Cromwell, Garrick, or Shakspeare, or a burlesque on different styles of writing, like his French novel, when *hifalutin* phrases of tragedy come from the clod-hopper who—"sells soap and thrice—refuses a ducal coronet."—MELVILLE LANDON, "Biography of Charles F. Browne," *Artemus Ward: His Works, Complete,* 1875, pp. 22–23

There is another kind of humor, which Artemus Ward, the showman—shrewd and simple, exaggerative and satirical—originated. It never fails to be copied by the press and read by the million. His visit to the President elect was an overdrawn picture of the gang of ravenous office seekers pressing on the "honest old dispenser." He, like Nasby, Billings, and company, hid under bad orthography and worse grammar the neatest nonsense and the broadest satire. While he had not so keen and critical a sense of the dialect or patois as Russell Lowell shows in the character of Hosea Bigelow—while he had not the pointed wit of Holmes or Saxe, whose verses are a fit frame for their exquisite artistic humor, yet Artemus, next to Mark Twain and Bret Harte, hit the very midriff of American humor. I have no time to recall illustrations. They occur to all. His interview with the Prince of Wales in Canada, his amusing attempt to buy the Tower of London, which so shocked the pompous old warder, are samples. How the world was startled to know that it continued to "revolve around on her axle-tree onst in twenty-four hours, subjick to the Constitution of the United States!" "If you ask me," said he, "how pious the muchly married Brigham Young is, I treat it as a conundrum, and give it up."—S. S. COX, "American Humor," *Harper's New Monthly Magazine,* May 1875, pp. 847–48

The productions of Artemus Ward will always retain a high place in humorous literature. He is even more popular with the English than with the American people. The English traveler generally carries with him but one humorous American work—*The Letters of Artemus Ward.* His wit is irresistible and bubbles up like water from a perennial spring, surprising the reader with the freshness, originality and unfailing quantity of the supply. It never made him an enemy because he never sacrificed a friend for the sake of a witticism. He was in a great measure the founder of the American school of humor which has won for itself a distinctive and national character. Like all successful writers he has been followed by a host of imitators, but not one has been found to fill worthily the place which his untimely death made vacant.—C. C. RUTHRAUFF, "Artemus Ward at Cleveland," *Scribner's Monthly,* Oct. 1878, p. 791

With Mr. Lowell, however, this is a passing freak, like that of Mr. Thackeray, who could with impunity masquerade in *Yellow Plush,* or, as in *The Rose and the Ring,* cry boo to the children about a Christmas Tree, or, as in *Rebecca and Rowena* and the *Prize Novelists,* disport himself in a false face. But a life devoted to such antics, if not wasted, is hardly an object of ambition. We have no wish to detract from the literary merit, or to disparage the memory, of the amiable and generally-regretted "Artemus Ward," the most celebrated of the lighter or broader school of western humorists. There was

nothing in his genius of the tragic element that made almost pathetic the representations of the unapproachable actor Robson; but Mr. BROWNE is affectionately remembered as a man of wit and talent, whose refinement of manner conciliated the severest critics. His work is only the perfection of a spurious art; but he wins our regard by the good-humour that smiles alongside of the satire that scathes; disarms censure by laughing at himself, and eludes all suspicion of vulgarity, by never pretending to be other than he was—the son of an old New-England Jackson democrat of the middle-class, who saw through the braggadocio and corruption of either party, and did good service by exposing them in his vivid caricatures. We have no call to criticise minutely, or frequently to quote from, the often irresistible pages of this popular favourite. ⟨. . .⟩

In vindication of Mr. Browne's broadest burlesque, we must remark that it is always directed against mean or ridiculous things. Unfortunately his example has paved, for those who have caught the trick of his phrase, and who are unrestrained by his good feeling and good sense, an easy descent to the buffoonery of making noble things appear mean or ridiculous.—JOHN NICHOL, *American Literature,* 1882, pp. 417–20

Artemus is usually ⟨. . .⟩ a wit who amuses by his absurd and naïvely quiet surprises. "N.B.—Mr. Ward will pay no debts of his own contracting"—this line, on the show-bill of one of his humorous lectures, may stand as a sample of his whole method. This element of surprise is that which makes us laugh at his war-sayings, his panorama-descriptions, his reflections by the tomb of "William W. Shakespeare," and his kindly assertion that Chaucer was a great poet, but couldn't spell; or even, at times, at his coarse and repulsive lectures on the "Mormons." Artemus Ward anticipated Mark Twain as a representative of calm American irreverence, ready to ridicule every thing not in a high degree sacred or lovable; but, like Mark Twain's, his lampoons were either made for the sake of fun alone, or for the ridicule of solemn pretence and hypocrisy. He is not the "characteristic American humorist," because there is no such thing as characteristic American humor. The English mind in its American home is alert and fond of puns, unexpected turns of thought, and the amusement caused by "a shock of surprise, produced by a falsehood plausibly pretending to be true, or by a truism pretending to be a novelty." That is all.—CHARLES F. RICHARDSON, *American Literature, 1607–1885,* 1887, Vol. 1, pp. 523–24

He was a shrewd, naïf, but at the same time modest and unassuming young man. He was a native of Maine, but familiar with the West. Quiet as he seemed, in three weeks he had found out everything in New York.—CHARLES GODFREY LELAND, *Memoirs,* 1893, p. 235

The last of the whimsical group is the only one of the humorists to whom this chapter is devoted that succeeded in making a foreign reputation. Browne is perhaps better known in England than he is in America—a fact, if fact it be, not altogether creditable to his countrymen. He was borne in Maine, became a compositor, worked on the *Carpet Bag* of Shillaber and Halpine, and contributed articles when not setting type, left Boston for Cleveland, Ohio, where he became a reporter, assumed the character of a showman, and began the writings that brought him fame. A short career on a New York humorous journal followed, and about the same time he gave his series of lectures, *The Babes in the Wood* and the like. In 1862 he crossed the continent, and returned to give his popular comic lectures on Mormonism. He broke down with consumption in 1864, but in 1866 he rallied, and in the summer of that year sailed for England. During the autumn and early winter he really won the hearts of thousands by his oddities of manner and speech and the irresistible quaintness of his wit. But success could not repair his health. He grew weaker and weaker, and began his homeward journey, only to die at Southampton on March 6, 1867. His not voluminous writings, which had been partly collected in 1865, were issued ten years later in a complete form. They are now comparatively little read, and many of the persons who do glance over them confess to being unable to understand how "Artemus" could have so thoroughly delighted two nations. But as much of Browne's success depended on his personality, he is practically in the situation of many a by-gone orator whose fame is kept up by tradition, not by his published works. The men and women who heard Browne are alone competent to judge him, yet when one has read what his admirers have written about him, and has avoided underrating the true wit and the fantastic humour of his writings, one is tempted to play the judge one's self and to declare that, as a whimsical genius, not as a broad, hearty humorist, he has had no equal in America. "I've been lingerin' by the Tomb of the lamented Shakspere. It is a success." Who but an American, nay, who but "Artemus Ward," would have put it just that way?—WILLIAM P. TRENT, *A History of American Literature, 1607–1865*, 1903, pp. 534–35

E. S. NADAL
From "Artemus Ward" (1880)
Essays at Home and Elsewhere
1882, pp. 18–30, 40–41

Artemus Ward's New England origin is very plain in his writings. They represent the rural New England life well. They show the country store, the rude and austere village street, the solemn landscape, the humour, and the sense of the people. But they are even more American than Yankee. The *Complete Works of Artemus Ward* is a book which must be very grateful to the American who is living abroad. When he has been long enough away from home, there comes a time when he finds himself reading American newspapers a great deal; or, when reading the newspapers of the country, his eyes will wander away from a good anecdote, or a paragraph of gossip, or a fresh piece of really important European news, to read over several times a telegram from New York, stating the arrival of so many tons of iron, or the embarkation of so many head of cattle. To any one in this state of mind, Artemus Ward's book will be welcome, for it will bring before him the scenery and society of his country.

The writings of Artemus Ward are most expressive of the society of the United States. His genius is very national. Such a character as Artemus Ward could not have existed in any other than a democratic community. The freedom with which he approaches everybody and everything would be possible only to an American, or to some member of society as democratic as ours. In what he has to say about the leading persons of the day, he does not at all take into account the fact that he is an obscure and uneducated youth; that he has never been at college; that he is only a reporter for a country paper; that he was yesterday a type-setter or a farmer's lad. No, he is an intellect, a judgment, which has arrived at a certain degree of power,—by what means it matters not,—and which looks about it with that freedom from corporeal modifications which

might belong to an immaterial intelligence. Ward's humour has many traits which are national. One of these is humility; he is the object of his own ridicule. Betsy Jane, his wife, scolds him, and sometimes pours hot water on him, and even beats him. But this self-ridicule is an old attribute of the joker. The fool in old times for every jest was threatened with three dozen, and the clown of the modern stage is being continually pommelled and knocked about. Again, Ward is always expressing the difficulty he finds in doing the things which romance-writers say are so easy to do. He says of a man who insulted him, that he, Ward, did not strike him, but that he "withered him with a glance of his eye." He says of another, whom he rebuked, that he "qualed before his gase." Ward means, of course, that he ought to have "quailed," but that he did not. This is, again, an ancient and conventional mode of humour. After the famous tumbler, who is the serious attraction of the show, has turned a double-somersault or leaped over four horses, the clown makes a pretence of trying to do one of these feats, but either shirks it or sprawls upon all-fours. But, though humility is a historic feature of humour, I think that it particularly marks the humour of this country. It is to be seen in many American books of humour. Mark Twain has it. John Phœnix, whom Artemus Ward particularly admired, had much of it. We should expect to find it in a society where very few begin with silver spoons in their mouths; where each man has in some degree to contend with the hard and fundamental conditions of human existence and finds himself ungraceful and unsuccessful on comparing himself with those vaunting heroes to whom fortune has given a long start.

In the circumstances of his life, and in his feelings, Ward was just like any other American young man of the people. He was a poor young man, and his books describe the life which a poor young man leads in America. This is done without the least false shame, and indeed without any consciousness that there is a class of society to whom such a life may seem vulgar. The pictures which he draws of that life are not vulgar, because they are true. He would have become vulgar had he professed to a standard of living which was not his own; but this he did not do.

One sees in Ward that sympathy with both ends of society which characterises Americans of his education. He likes bar-keepers and stage-drivers, and does not feel himself to be a bit better than they. In return, they of course like him. The following story is vouched for by Mr. Hingston as quite true. At Big Creek he delivered a lecture in the bar-room, standing behind the counter. The audience was pleased, and particularly the bar-keeper, who, when any good point was made, would deal the counter a vigorous blow with his fist, and would exclaim, "Good boy from the New England States! Bully for William W. Shakspere!"

But if an aspiring and nice young American like Ward feels a friendly equality with stage-drivers, he has also a great respect for the genteel classes, and a desire to be genteel. Ward soon began to show this ambition strongly. He was at first a very uncouth and ugly youth. His ugliness was such a source of misery to him, that he used to lie awake at night thinking of it. From this experience he may perhaps have evolved his remark about the reporter of a rival paper in Cleveland, whom he charged with being so ugly that he was compelled to get up three times every night to "rest his face." The negligence of his dress was at this time in accordance with the mean opinion which he had of his person. But when he began to find out that he was not so ill-looking as he had supposed, he soon showed a desire to obtain for himself the exterior of a member of the better classes.

Ward's sketches, though caricatures, are extremely live-ly representations of American society. He draws a society strongly marked by alert selfishness and good nature. He describes admirably the civility which is half kindness and half policy, the prudence, and the humbug of such a society. The Americans are a very civil people. I do not mean that they are merely civil in their way of speaking to one another; their civility is deeper than that: it is in the attitude of their minds toward one another. That civility may be selfish in its essence; it no doubt is. The silent teaching of American society causes each man to respect his neighbour, because his neighbour possesses a respectable fraction of the general power. But, whatever may be the reason of the matter, there is no doubt of the fact that Americans are very friendly toward one another. Artemus Ward's pages show this quality. Ward really likes the people he laughs at. I believe he really admires the Latin of the Baldinsville schoolmaster, and ridicules his own ignorance quite as much as the schoolmaster's pedantry.

This American friendliness, of which I have been speak-ing, has its bad as well as its good side. Its bad side is its tolerance of that kind of vice, the motive of which is selfish advantage at the expense of public or private honour. Ward's satire, though mild and playful, was keen and accurate enough in its description of these traits of our society. At a war meeting in Baldinsville, which Artemus Ward had interrupted by one of the outbreaks of his irresponsible humour, he was thus called to order by the editor of the *Baldinsville Bugle*, who presided: "I call the Napoleon of showmen, I call that Napoleonic man, whose life is adorned with so many noble virtues, and whose giant mind lights up this warlike scene,—I call him to order." Mr. Ward here remarks that the editor of the *Bugle* does his job printing. He is sufficiently keen in his exhibition of the disparity between big words and small motives. Thus, he says that he wants "editers" to come to his show "free as the flours of May." But he does object to their coming in crowds, and to their charging him ten cents a line for puffs, solely on the ground, alleged by them, that the press is the "Arkymedian Leaver which moves the wurld."

In his remarks upon social and political subjects, Artemus Ward shows that soundness of judgment and that cool and accurate perception of the actual state of affairs which are the characteristics of our population. Artemus Ward evidently was not educated to a dislike of slavery. The black man is the object of his ridicule rather than of his pity. This may have been because it was easier to joke against negroes and abolitionists than against slaveholders. It is certain that, until within a very few years before the war, the American public hated nothing so much as an abolitionist. As it is only possible to make the crowd laugh on the side of their own opinions, the amusers of the public were compelled to cater to the anti-negro sentiment. The American stage of that period was certainly anti-negro. It is thus possible that Ward, being a joker, may have drifted into this manner of writing about slavery. But I rather think that his education and his disposition were not of the sort to incline him to take a strong part against slavery. One imagines him by disposition sceptical, cautious, perhaps timid and despondent, more likely to fear the dangers of a bold movement than to feel

an ardent and sanguine sympathy with its objects. I should think it likely, moreover, though Mr. Hingston has not informed us on this point, that Ward's father was an old-fashioned Democrat.[1] The men who voted for Jackson were most tenacious of their political sentiment, and rarely failed to communicate it to their children. This sentiment was of a virulent type. To many families in the land the mere name of Democrat had a charm which it required all the shock of revolution and civil war to dissipate. I should guess from the manner of Ward's mind towards the discussions which pre-ceded the rebellion, that he had had a Democratic bringing up. But Ward was very loyal during the war, and did the Union good service. It is true that in his address on "The Crisis," delivered before "a c of upturned faces in the red skoolhouse" of Baldinsville, just previous to the outbreak of the war, he exhibits some of the immoral despair of that period. Likewise in his conversation with Prince Napoleon, the comicality of which but slightly veils the feeling of despondency, astonish-ment, and bitter disappointment which the madness of the quarrel had produced upon his reasonable and thoughtful mind, he said: "It cost Columbus twenty thousand dollars to fit out his explorin' expedition. If he had bin a sensible man, he'd hav put the money in a hoss railroad or a gas company, and left this magnificent continent to intelligent savages, who, when they got hold of a good thing, knew enuff to keep it. . . . Chris meant well, but he put his foot in it when he saled for America." But when the war has once begun, he is in favour of it, and, indeed, raises a company. He resembles somewhat his own Squire Baxter. Squire Baxter, like President Buchan-an, did not believe in coercion. But when he learned that the Flag had been assaulted, he changed his mind. Squire Baxter is a representative figure. Ward's writing will, I think, be useful to the future historian who wishes to form an exact idea of the physiognomy of public opinion of that time. ⟨. . .⟩

I have spoken of Ward's peculiar manner. This manner is in everything he writes, but I think it is more apparent in his less ostensible or demonstrable witticisms. Some of his jokes are so good, have such unmistakable novelty, that you would be ready to make an affidavit before a Justice of the Peace that they are good. Others again have a character which eludes the understanding; their quality is an involuntary play of the spirit, the charm of which you only recognise when you have come into some sympathy with the humourist. Now, it is in this latter sort of humour, I think, that Ward's proper manner especially appears. I have not attempted to describe this ultimate manner; perhaps it is unnecessary, or perhaps impos-sible, to do it. But it is only fair to recognise that he has such a manner, that he is original and singular. I have seen him spoken of as one of a "school" of humorous writers; and there seems to be a notion that one joker is about as good as another. But this is not giving due credit to the literary character of this charming writer. He is no more capable of duplication than any other man of genius.

Notes

1. I have since been informed that the father of Artemus Ward was a Jackson Democrat, and a member of the Maine Legislature.

N. P. WILLIS

ARTEMUS WARD (CHARLES FARRAR BROWNE)

FITZ-GREENE HALLECK

HENRY, LORD BROUGHAM

SAMUEL LOVER

WILLIAM CARLETON

CHARLES DICKENS

WILLIAM GILMORE SIMMS

HENRY, LORD BROUGHAM

1778–1868

Henry Peter Brougham was born in Edinburgh on September 19, 1778. He entered the University of Edinburgh in 1792, distinguishing himself by publishing three papers on mathematics and physics. Upon his graduation in 1795 he read law and was called to the bar in 1800. Although very learned and a powerful orator, Brougham disliked the practice of law and in 1802 turned his attention to literature, helping to found the *Edinburgh Review*. He wrote three articles in its first issue, and thereafter contributed extensively to it, first with scientific articles and then with political and critical pieces. Brougham was largely responsible for making the *Edinburgh Review* a mouthpiece for the Whig party, to the point that the Tories were compelled to found the rival *Quarterly Review* to have their own voice in political and literary issues of the day.

In 1805 Brougham went to London, associating with the political, literary, and social circles there. He became an associate of Lord Holland, who helped him to win a seat in Parliament as M.P. for Camelford in 1810. Brougham's oratory was fiery and sometimes uncontrolled, and inspired hostility from the opposition and distrust from his own party. In later years Brougham was to earn the enmity of his fellow Whig Macaulay, a rival contributor to the *Edinburgh Review*. Nevertheless, Brougham became a close advisor to Caroline, Princess of Wales, and when she became queen in 1820 she appointed Brougham her attorney general. But the queen's estrangement from her husband, King George IV, caused Brougham to lose favor at the court, and upon the queen's death in 1821 he resumed his seat in Parliament. In that year he married Mary Anne Spalding; they had two daughters, one dying in infancy.

Throughout the 1820s Brougham was a prominent parliamentary orator, supporting freedom of the press, education, law reform, and the anti-slavery movement. In 1828 he founded London University, principally as a means of promoting scientific and technical knowledge. By 1830 he had become reconciled with the new king, William IV, and accepted the office of Lord Chancellor, becoming Baron Brougham and Vaux. Brougham vigorously supported the Second Reform Bill in 1832, but again fell out with the king in 1834 and withdrew to the Continent. The next year, however, he returned to Parliament. In 1838 he edited four volumes of his *Speeches*.

Although Brougham continued to speak frequently in Parliament in the 1840s, poor health and his waning political influence caused him gradually to withdraw from politics. In 1850 he resumed scientific interests, and in 1857 he was chosen president of the Social Science Association. In 1859 he was elected chancellor of Edinburgh University. Henry, Lord Brougham died at his chateau in Cannes on May 7, 1868.

Aside from his speeches and periodical essays, Brougham is best remembered as the author of *Historical Sketches of Statesmen Who Flourished in the Time of George III* (1839–43; 3 vols.) and *Lives of Men of Letters and Science Who Flourished in the Time of George III* (1845–46; 2 vols.). Brougham prepared his own *Works* in 11 volumes (1855–61). His autobiography, *The Life and Times of Henry, Lord Brougham*, was published posthumously in three volumes in 1871.

Personal

Brougham is a man of the most splendid talents and the most extensive acquirements, and he has used the ample means which he possesses most usefully for mankind. It would be difficult to overrate the services which he has rendered the cause of the slaves in the West Indies, or that of the friends to the extension of knowledge and education among the poor, or to praise too highly his endeavours to serve the oppressed inhabitants of Poland. How much is it to be lamented that his want of judgment and of prudence should prevent his great talents, and such good intentions, from being as great a blessing to mankind as they ought to be.—SIR SAMUEL ROMILLY, *Diary* (March 20, 1816), *Memoirs of the Life of Sir Samuel Romilly*, 1840, Vol. 3, p. 237

Brougham, whom I knew in society, and from seeing him both at his chambers and at my own lodgings, is now about thirty-eight, tall, thin, and rather awkward, with a plain and not very expressive countenance, and simple or even slovenly manners. He is evidently nervous, and a slight convulsive movement about the muscles of his lips gives him an unpleas-

ant expression now and then. In short, all that is exterior in him, and all that goes to make up the first impression, is unfavorable. The first thing that removes this impression is the heartiness and good-will he shows you, whose motive cannot be mistaken, for such kindness can come only from the heart. This is the first thing, but a stranger presently begins to remark his conversation. On common topics, nobody is more commonplace. He does not feel them, but if the subject excites him, there is an air of originality in his remarks, which, if it convinces you of nothing else, convinces you that you are talking with an extraordinary man. He does not like to join in a general conversation, but prefers to talk apart with only two or three persons, and, though with great interest and zeal, in an undertone. If, however, he does launch into it, all the little, trim, gay pleasure-boats must keep well out of the way of his great black collier, as Gibbon said of Fox. He listens carefully and fairly—and with a kindness that would be provoking, if it were not genuine—to all his adversary has to say, but when his time comes to answer, it is with that bare, bold, bullion talent which either crushes itself or its opponent. . . . Yet I suspect the impression Brougham generally leaves is that of a good-natured friend. At least, that is the impression I have most frequently found, both in England and on the Continent.—GEORGE TICKNOR, *Journal* (1819), *Life, Letters and Journals of George Ticknor*, ed. Anna Ticknor, 1876, Vol. 1, p. 266

You are aware that the only point of exception to Wilson may be that with the fire of genius he has possessd some of its excentricities but did he ever approach to those of Harry Brougham who is the God of Whiggish idolatry.—SIR WALTER SCOTT, Letter to J. G. Lockhart (March 30, 1820)

⟨. . .⟩ Henry Brougham ⟨. . .⟩, though he remains a lawyer, presents the singular spectacle of a lawyer, equally active in his lesser calling and his greater, and consenting, perhaps, to realize the gains of the one, only that he may secure the power of pursuing the noblest of all ambitions in the other. Mr. Brougham was "meant for mankind;" and luckily he has not been prevented, by the minuter demands on his eyesight, from looking abroad and knowing it. His world is the world it ought to be,—the noble planet, capable of being added to the number of other planets which have perhaps worked out their moral beauty;—not a mere little despairing corner of it, entitled a court of justice.—LEIGH HUNT, *Lord Byron and Some of His Contemporaries*, 1828, Vol. 1, p. 319, Note

Brougham ⟨. . .⟩, indeed, I should wonder little to see one day a second Cromwell. He is the cunningest and the strongest man in England now, as I construe him, and with no better principle than a Napoleon has—a worship and self-devotion to power. God be thanked I had nothing to do with his University and its committees.—THOMAS CARLYLE, Letter to John Carlyle (1831), cited in James Anthony Froude, *Thomas Carlyle*, 1882, Vol. 1, p. 116

Tickler: Brougham in his robes! Lord High Chancellor of England! Stern face and stalwart frame—and his mind, people say, is gigantic. They name him with Bacon. Be it so; the minister he and interpreter of Nature! Henry Brougham, in the eyes of his idolaters, is also an Edmund Burke. Be it so; at once the most imaginative and most philosophical of orators that ever sounded lament over the decline and fall of empires, while wisdom, listening to his lips, exclaimed,

> Was ne'er prophetic sound so full of woe!
> —JOHN WILSON (as "Christopher North"), *Noctes Ambrosianae* (Nov. 1832), 1854

He had been, and always was, essentially a middle-class man. He was distasteful to the supercilious, cold-blooded, and aristocratic chiefs of the Whig party. They had not forgiven his reception of their first offer of office, that of Solicitor-General, I believe—when, as the story goes, for all answer to the messenger who brought Lord Grey's letter, he cast it upon the ground and trampled upon it, as you have seen Mr. W. H. Payne, as Guy, Earl of Warwick, wipe his feet upon the petition of his vassals in the pantomime. He was not, and never had been, a low-class demagogue, who could be used as a tool and then flung aside. He was the rather elbowed, "scrouged" to the wall, or his quondam parasites passed by on the other side to avoid noticing him. He was not to be shelved with a patent place or an embassy. An embassy! He would have worn his hat before the King of Candy, and written despatches about the Queen of Spain's legs. What could be done with such a man? He was as yet too flagrant with Liberalism to be accepted as a Conservative. There was then no Cave of Adullam into which to retire and grumble. His foes made a cave for him. They fixed it in Coventry, and embowered it with a plantation of bitter aloes thickly tenanted by mocking birds. They tried to kill

the giant with the petty darts of ridicule. So did the Lilliputians strive to kill Gulliver.—GEORGE AUGUSTUS SALA, "Lord Brougham," *Temple Bar*, June 1868, p. 428

It may truly be said of Lord Brougham, that none more completely represented his age, and no one more contributed to the progress of the times in which he lived. He had two qualities, almost in excess, which are rarely combined in the same person—one was energy, and the other versatility. The influence which creative power gave him, combined with strength of character, alone sustained him in a career which for its duration, as well as for its dazzling feats, has rarely been equalled in Europe.—BENJAMIN DISRAELI, Speech in the House of Commons (July 27, 1868)

The first sight of Brougham, then just seated on the wool-sack, and the object of all manner of expectation which he never fulfilled, was an incident to be remembered. I had not previously shared the general expectation of great national benefits from him. I believed that much of his effort for popular objects, even for education, was for party and personal purposes; and that he had no genuine popular sympathy, or real desire that the citizens at large should have any effectual political education. I distrusted his steadiness, and his disinterestedness, and his knowledge of the men and interests of his own time. I believed him too vain and selfish, and too low in morals and unrestrained in temper, to turn out a really great man when his day of action came. Many a time has my mother said to me, "Harriet, you will have much to answer for for speaking as you do if Brougham turns out what the rest of us expect:" to which my answer was "Yes, Mother, indeed I shall." She was at length very glad that I was not among the disappointed. Yet, there was a strong interest in meeting for the first time, and on the safe ground of substantial business, the man of whom I had heard so much from my childhood, and who now had more power over the popular welfare than perhaps any other man in the world. After two or three interviews, he was so manifestly wild, that the old interest was lost in pity and dislike; but at first I knew nothing of the manifestations of eccentricity which he presently made public enough. Those were the days when he uttered from the platform his laments over his folly in accepting a peerage, and when he made no secret to strangers who called on him on business, of his being "the most wretched man on earth." But I first met him when nothing of the sort had taken place so publicly but that his adorers and toadies could conceal it.

A day or two after my arrival in London, I met him at dinner at the house of the correspondent of his through whom he engaged me to help in poor-law reform. By his desire, no one else was asked. The first thing that struck me was his being not only nervous, but thin-skinned to excess. Our hostess's lap-dog brought out the nervousness immediately, by jumping up at his knee. He pretended to play with Gyp, but was obviously annoyed that Gyp would not be called away. He was not accustomed to lap-dogs, it was clear. Before we went to dinner, I could not but see how thin-skinned he was. The *Examiner* newspaper lay on the table; and it chanced to contain, that week, an impertinent article, warning me against being flattered out of my own aims by my host, who was Brougham's cat's-paw. The situation was sufficiently awkward, it must be owned. Brougham did not read the article now, because he had seen it at home: but I saw by glances and pointings that the gentlemen were talking it over, while my hostess and I were consulting about her embroidery: and Brougham looked, not only very black upon it, but evidently annoyed and stung. He looked black in another sense, I remember,—not a morsel of his dress being anything but black, from the ridge of his stock to the toes of his polished shoes. Not an inch of white was there to relieve the combined gloom of his dress and complexion. He was curiously afraid of my trumpet, and managed generally to make me hear without. He talked excessively fast, and ate fast and prodigiously, stretching out his long arm for any dish he had a mind to, and getting hold of the largest spoons which would dispatch the most work in the shortest time. He watched me intently and incessantly when I was conversing with any body else. For my part, I liked to watch him when he was conversing with gentlemen, and his mind and its manifestations really came out. This was never the case, as far as my observation went, when he talked with ladies. I believe I have never met with more than three men, in the whole course of my experience, who talked with women in a perfectly natural manner; that is, precisely as they talked with men: but the difference in Brougham's case was so great as to be disagreeable. He knew many cultivated and intellectual women; but this seemed to be of no effect. If not able to assume with them his ordinary manner towards silly women, he was awkward and at a loss. This was by no means agreeable, though the sin of his bad manners must be laid at the door of the vain women who discarded their ladyhood for his sake, went miles to see him, were early on platforms where he was to be, and admitted him to very broad flirtations. He had pretty nearly settled his own business, in regard to conversation with ladies, before two more years were over. His swearing became so incessant, and the occasional indecency of his talk so insufferable, that I have seen even coquettes and adorers turn pale, and the lady of the house tell her husband that she could not undergo another dinner party with Lord Brougham for a guest. I, for my part, determined to decline quietly henceforth any small party where he was expected; and this simply because there was no pleasure in a visit where every body was on thorns as to what any one guest might say and do next. My own impression that day was that he was either drunk or insane. Drunk he was not; for he had been publicly engaged in business till the last moment. All manner of protestations have been made by his friends, to this day, that he is, with all his eccentricities, "sane enough:" but my impression remains that no man who conducted himself as he did that summer day in 1834 could be sane and sober.—HARRIET MARTINEAU, *Autobiography*, ed. Maria Weston Chapman, 1877, Vol. 1, pp. 233–36

General

Beware lest blundering Brougham destroy the sale,
Turn beef to bannocks, cauliflowers to kail.
　　　—GEORGE GORDON, LORD BYRON, *English Bards
　　　and Scotch Reviewers*, 1809, ll. 524–25

He does not derive his present greatness from his superiority to other men in any one single line of excellence, whether it be learning, eloquence, a profound acquaintance with jurisprudence, or political sagacity—but from the universality of his genius and talents, and from the felicitous combination of the whole of the afore-mentioned excellencies meeting in his character. That the party to whom he has uniformly been opposed in his political views, should labour to depreciate his talents, and endeavour to sink him to their own level, is all matter of course; but whatever Lord Brougham may be, as compared with the great men who are no more; whatever posterity may decide respecting him, when he has ceased to exist in the eye of the present generation; to us, who now hear him—by the side of those, and some not unworthy rivals, near

whom he stands—he is confessedly, and unequivocally, the master-mind, the superior spirit, whose word animates, awes, soothes, electrifies; to whom no one is ashamed to confess himself unequal in that art which Cicero places next to that of arms; and which, perhaps, holds a still higher rank than military science, in a peaceable, and well-ordered, commonwealth.—WILLIAM JONES, *Biographical Sketches of the Reform Ministers*, 1832, Vol. 1, pp. 68–69

As to Brougham, I understand and feel for your embarrassments. I may perhaps refine too much; but I should say that this strange man, finding himself almost alone in the world, absolutely unconnected with either Whigs or Conservatives, and not having a single vote in either House of Parliament at his command except his own, is desirous to make the *Review* his organ. With this intention, unless I am greatly deceived, after having during several years contributed little or nothing of value, he has determined to exert himself as if he were a young writer struggling into note, and to make himself important to the work by his literary services. And he certainly has succeeded. His late articles, particularly the long one in the April number, have very high merit. They are, indeed, models of magazine writing as distinguished from other sorts of writing. They are not, I think, made for duration. Every thing about them is exaggerated, incorrect, sketchy. All the characters are either too black or too fair. The passions of the writer do not suffer him even to maintain the decent appearance of impartiality. And the style, though striking and animated, will not bear examination through a single paragraph. But the effect of the first perusal is great; and few people read an article in a review twice. A bold, dashing, scene-painting manner is that which always succeeds best in periodical writing; and I have no doubt that these lively and vigorous papers of Lord Brougham will be of more use to you than more highly finished compositions. His wish, I imagine, is to establish in this way such an ascendency as may enable him to drag the *Review* along with him to any party to which his furious passions may lead him; to the Radicals; to the Tories; to any set of men by whose help he may be able to revenge himself on old friends, whose only crime is that they could not help finding him to be an habitual and incurable traitor. Hitherto your caution and firmness have done wonders. Yet already he has begun to use the word "Whig" as an epithet of reproach, exactly as it is used in the lowest writings of the Tories, and of the extreme Radicals; exactly as it is used in *Blackwood*, in *Fraser*, in *The Age*, in *Tait's Magazine*. There are several instances in the article on Lady Charlotte Bury. "The Whig notions of female propriety." "The Whig secret tribunal." I have no doubt that the tone of his papers will become more and more hostile to the Government; and that, in a short time, it will be necessary for you to take one of three courses, to every one of which there are strong objections—to break with him; to admit his papers into the *Review*, while the rest of the *Review* continues to be written in quite a different tone; or to yield to his dictation, and to let him make the *Review* a mere tool of his ambition and revenge.—THOMAS BABINGTON MACAULAY, Letter to Macvey Napier (July 20, 1838)

He began his literary and political life with a scanty store of many small commodities. Long after he set out, the witty and wise Lord Stowell said of him, that he wanted only a little law to fill up the vacancy. His shoulders were not overburdened by the well-padded pack he bore on them; and he found a ready sale, where such articles find the readiest, in the town of Edinburgh. Here he entered into a confederacy (the word *conspiracy* may be libellous) to defend the worst atrocities of the

French, and to cry down every author to whom England was dear and venerable. A better spirit now prevails in the *Edinburgh Review,* from the generosity and genius of Macaulay. But in the days when Brougham and his confederates were writers in it, more falsehood and more malignity marked its pages than any other Journal in the language. ⟨. . .⟩

Wavering as he is by habit, malicious as he is by nature, it is evident that Lord Brougham says and does the greater part of his sayings and doings for no other purpose than to display his ability in defending them. He dazzles us by no lights of eloquence, he attracts us by not even a fictitious flue-warmth; but he perplexes and makes us stare and stumble by his angular intricacies and sudden glares. Not a sentence of his speeches or writings will be deposited in the memory as rich or rare; and even what is strange will be cast out of it for what is stranger, until this goes too. Is there a housewife who keeps a cupboardful of cups without handle or bottom; a selection of brokages and flaws?—WALTER SAVAGE LANDOR, Letter to the Editor of the *Examiner* (Aug. 17, 1843), *Letters Public and Private,* ed. Stephen Wheeler, 1899, pp. 259–61

It is well known that no man has gone beyond Lord Brougham in the patient finish of particular passages of his speeches; he has himself recorded that the ultimate peroration on Queen Caroline's case was written ten times over before he thought it worthy of the occasion; and we have heard from his lips within these last few years several outpourings on the Whigs, which no doubt had been concocted with equal and more delightful elaboration. But with rare exceptions we cannot believe that he spends much time on the detail of any of his productions; nor do we suppose that his oral eloquence would be more effective than it is, if he took more pains in immediate preparation:—the preparation of lifelong study is a far better and here a quite sufficient thing. But it is somewhat different in the case of compositions avowedly and exclusively for the press. In these, we think, the public might reasonably expect more of care and deliberation than can usually be recognized in the authorship of Lord Brougham. Nothing like imbecility need be feared— but when there is such obvious strength, it is a pity that there should often be as obvious rashness. Does he, after all, write in general, or content himself with dictating?—JOHN WILSON CROKER, "Lord Brougham's *Lives of Men of Letters,*" *Quarterly Review,* June 1845, p. 62

There can be no doubt that Lord Brougham, however he may be estimated in future times as a statesman, will figure as one of the most remarkable men of the age in which he lives. He is chiefly distinguished for his restless, impatient, feverish activity of mind, a trait not common among the sons of men, few of whom have any quick spring of action within to drive them to incessant exertion, but generally require external inducements of interest or passion to bring forth all their powers. As an orator, he has appeared preëminent among the great,—exerting a mighty influence in favor of some essential reforms in the government of his country, which, mainly because they were so necessary, were fiercely and bitterly resisted. As a lawyer, he has been popular and successful, though generally allowed to be unsuited to the high judicial station for which he was thought the very man till he had reached it. As a lover of his race, he is ever ready to exert himself in the cause of humanity, and not more savage, perhaps, than is common with the philanthropists of the day. As a man, giving no single impression of his own character, but hurrying on through perpetual changes, where neither praise nor censure can steadily follow, he has been a willing slave to impulses of any kind, and particularly sensitive to slights and

irritations; jealous of his own standing, and needlessly overbearing in defence of it; so insolent and vindictive in his usual tone, that self seems always to enter into his assertion of the right or condemnation of the wrong. It is only by an average of merits and failings that one can arrive at any consistent and satisfactory idea of this great and active, but not amiable man, who will hereafter be remembered with wonder certainly, but, if his latter days shall be cast in resemblance of the former, never with admiration or love.

⟨. . .⟩ He shows a familiarity with the details of science, of the mathematics particularly, which could hardly be expected after the busy and tumultuous life which he has led. This cannot be a mere remnant of early education; he must have given to these pursuits the same sort of attention which English statesmen generally devote to classical studies and recollections. And the effect is seen in his oratory, as reported, where strength and energy abound, while grace and elegance are wanting. His style is bold and manly, though sometimes strangely careless and lounging; but it is always expressive of his mind and heart, and through the most labyrinthian sentence it is always easy to follow the sentiments and reasoning of the writer. These are strong in favor of liberality, truth, and freedom; too strong to be relished always by the blind adorers of the past. It is not to be denied, that there is here and there some slight want of Christian meekness; but his buffets are generally bestowed on those who deserve them. He abounds in *unfriends,* as the Scotch call them, having carried on for years a large and successful manufacture of that article, which few desire to possess. But on the whole, we say, *Serus in cœlum redeat;*—if that be his destination, which the persons last mentioned will be inclined to question;—and whenever he departs, let it be remembered, that he lifted his heavy war-club on the side of liberty and toleration, and struck many a crushing blow at the enemies of truth and virtue, while soundly belaboring his own.—W. B. O. PEABODY, "Brougham's *Lives of Men of Letters and Science,*" *North American Review,* Oct. 1845, pp. 383–84, 421

Few eminent men have paid so heavily in posthumous reputation for any failing as Brougham for a jealous and insatiable vanity. His name—apart from the useful vehicle which bears it—conjures up almost no associations that are not ludicrous and grotesque; and as the fame of his achievements as a legislator—of his services to "liberty," education, and a variety of other "causes"—is tainted by the ever-present recollection of his feverish and overwhelming egotism, so his renown as a man of letters has suffered irretrievable damage from the versatility of his gifts. It were vain to look to this champion of progress for any substantial contribution to political philosophy, to physical science, or to literary criticism. Hasty and ill-considered judgments, rash and superficial generalisations, these, together with the commonplace and high-sounding maxims dear to shallow and confident minds, are the chief legacy of one who, to borrow Rogers's enumeration, combined in his own person the characters of Solon, Lycurgus, Demosthenes, Archimedes, Sir Isaac Newton, Lord Chesterfield, and a great many more.

That Brougham's speeches contain much eloquence of a high order it is impossible to deny. True, they lack delicacy and charm; there are few subtle strokes, few memorable cadences, few surprising effects such as Chalmers, for example, could compass by the artful introduction of a single sonorous epithet. But they are all good "fighting" speeches, admirably adapted to the purpose in hand; eminently copious, animated, and vigorous; their happiest moments being probably those when vigour, still at its highest, has not yet been merged in passion. The peroration of the speech on Law Reform, for example, though it doubtless falls short of the best models, has surely a fine ring: "How much nobler will be the sovereign's boast when he shall have it to say that he found law dear and left it cheap; found it a sealed book, left it a living letter; found it the patrimony of the rich, left it the inheritance of the poor; found it the two-edged sword of craft and oppression, left it the staff of honesty and the shield of innocence." On the other hand, there is often manifest a strong tendency to extravagance, as, for instance, in the passage on the "immortal Pitt" in his speech at the Liverpool election: "Immortal in the miseries of his devoted country! Immortal in the wounds of her bleeding liberties! Immortal in the cruel wars which spring from his cold, miscalculating ambition! Immortal in the triumphs of our enemies and the ruin of our allies, the costly purchase of so much blood and treasure! Immortal in the afflictions of England and the humiliation of her friends," etc. This is the frenzied raving of a maniac, not the inspired utterance of an orator; not hyperbole merely, but hysteria.

The composition of Brougham's written works is less careful and less laboured than that of his speeches. He is fond of employing antithesis; but he never attains to the dignity or impressiveness of his arch-enemy Macaulay, while he falls equally short of the neatness and vivacity of Jeffrey. He was, indeed, capable of writing thus of the charges brought by Junius against Lord Mansfield: "They show upon what kind of grounds the fabric of a great man's professional fame, as well as the purity of his moral character, were assailed by the unprincipled violence of party at the instigation of their ignorance, skulking behind a signature made famous by epigrammatic language and the boldness of being venturesome in the person of a printer who gained by allowing dastardly slander to act through him with a vicarious courage." But such a monstrous sentence is an extreme instance of his slovenliness and prolixity, though in another aspect it is highly characteristic, for Brougham was clearly thinking of another "great man," the fabric of whose "professional fame," if not the purity of whose moral character, he conceived to have been unjustly assailed by "the unprincipled violence of party." Both the writings and the speeches, it should be added, are, from time to time, pleasantly relieved by a sardonic cast of humour, akin to, but much less brutal and more delicate than, Macaulay's. A peculiarly favourable specimen of this quality will be found below, and another may be sought in that passage of the speech for the defendant in the Durham Clergy Libel case which treats of the visit of George IV. to Scotland in 1822.

Upon the whole, if Brougham's style is not marked by any conspicuous excellence, neither is it defaced by any very gross or shocking faults; if it has little to gratify or delight, it has as little to disgust or annoy a correct taste. His best work is probably contained in the *Sketches* of such men as Mansfield, Ellenborough, Pitt, Fox, and Windham, which are a repository of interesting information agreeably and unaffectedly imparted.—J. H. MILLAR, "Lord Brougham," *English Prose*, ed. Henry Craik, 1896, Vol. 5, pp. 213–15

Works

SPEECHES

Brougham's speech was four hours long: the greater part dull, cold, heavy, and tautologous to a *wonder*: insolent to intolerability in the placarding of *characters* on all persons he had or found occasion to mention, false to his party, and basely crawling to the Duke of Wellington—the whole a piece of treason under a splash of bravado. The impostor *knelt* at the end.—J. G. LOCKHART, Letter to William Blackwood (Oct. 8, 1831), cited in Margaret Oliphant, *Annals of a Publishing House: William Blackwood and His Sons*, 1897, Vol. 1, pp. 250–51

We advise all who wish to qualify themselves as public speakers to study the orations of Lord Brougham. They will find them a storehouse of manly thought, of vigorous argument, and lofty eloquence upon all the great questions of his time. Few may hope to rival the orator who defeated the bill of Pains and Penalties against Queen Caroline, and snapped asunder the chain of Slavery; but none can fail to profit by the example. —WILLIAM FORSYTH, "The Speeches of Lord Brougham," *Edinburgh Review*, April 1858, p. 463

Lord Brougham was a man of extraordinary powers of mind. It must be said also that, with many aberrations, those powers of mind were generally directed to great and worthy objects,—to the abolition of the Slave Trade and of slavery, to the improvement of law, to the promotion of education, to the furtherance of civil and religious liberty. His speech on the trial and condemnation of missionary Smith combined the closest and most pressing logic with the most eloquent denunciations of oppression and the most powerful appeal to justice. It contributed, no doubt, in a very marked degree, to the extinction of slavery throughout the dominions of the Crown of England. His speech of six hours on the amendment of the law was large and comprehensive in its general view, searching and elaborate in its details. The institution of the Judicial Committee of Privy Council was a most valuable result of his exertions as a law reformer. His labors regarding the endowed schools and misapplied charities of England destroyed many flagrant abuses, detected the perversion of a large amount of charitable funds, and led the way to those further inquiries, and those remedial measures, of which we have seen the commencement and progress, but of which the consummation is yet to come. It would be taking a narrow view to complain that large sums have been spent upon inquiries, and we have not as yet had an adequate return. Lord Brougham's speeches at the bar of the House of Lords, on the Bill of Pains and Penalties against Queen Caroline, were striking specimens of a powerful understanding; and his great speech in opening the defence was the most wonderful effort of oratory I ever heard. Nor can any one who heard him remember with any other feelings than those of the highest admiration his speech on the second reading of the Reform Bill in the House of Lords. The speech which he made at the assizes, in defence of Ambrose Williams, in 1821, carries satire and sarcasm to a height that may be called sublime. But his speech on the conduct of the continental powers of Europe towards Spain—a country which had been guilty of the offence of endeavoring to dispose of its own destiny, and to establish a free government—was certainly one of his brightest flights. His allusion to the protest of the Russian Minister at Madrid, who had declared, with horror, that blood had been shed in the Royal Palace, was at once a withering invective and a just condemnation of despotism. 'If I had been one of the counsellors of the Emperor of Russia,' he said, 'the last subject I would have advised my master to touch upon would have been that of "bloodshed in the Royal Palace."' The reigning Emperor of Russia was Alexander I. At the epoch of his coronation, a lady, writing from St. Petersburg, had described the ceremony in these terms: 'The Emperor entered the church preceded by the assassins of his grandfather, surrounded by the assassins of his father, and followed by his own.'

The question recurs, if such were the qualities and such the achievements of Lord Brougham, why was the Great Seal not restored to him? After one of his most striking speeches against Lord Melbourne, Lord Melbourne replied in these terms: 'My Lords, you have heard the eloquent speech of the noble and learned Lord—one of the most eloquent he ever delivered in this House—and I leave your Lordships to consider what *must be* the nature and strength of the objections which prevent any Government from availing themselves of the services of such a man.'—LORD JOHN RUSSELL, *Recollections and Suggestions 1813–1873*, 1875, pp. 111–13

He was beyond doubt a great Parliamentary orator. His style was too diffuse and sometimes too uncouth to suit a day like our own, when form counts for more than substance, when passion seems out of place in debate, and not to exaggerate is far more the object than to try to be great. Brougham's action was wild, and sometimes even furious; his gestures were singularly ungraceful; his manners were grotesque; but of his power over his hearers there could be no doubt. That power remained with him until a far later date; and long after the years when men usually continue to take part in political debate, Lord Brougham could be impassioned, impressive, and even overwhelming. He was not an orator of the highest class: his speeches have not stood the test of time. Apart from the circumstances of the hour and the personal power of the speaker, they could hardly arouse any great delight, or even interest; for they are by no means models of English style, and they have little of that profound philosophical interest, that pregnancy of thought and meaning, and that splendor of eloquence, which make the speeches of Burke always classic, and even in a certain sense always popular among us. In truth no man could have done with abiding success all the things which Brougham did successfully for the hour. On law, on politics, on literature, on languages, on science, on art, on industrial and commercial enterprise, he professed to pronounce with the authority of a teacher. "If Brougham knew a little of law," said O'Connell when the former became Lord Chancellor, "he would know a little of everything." The anecdote is told in another way too, which perhaps makes it even more piquant. "The new Lord Chancellor knows a little of everything in the world—even of law."—JUSTIN MC-CARTHY, A *History of Our Own Times*, 1879–80, Ch. 2

WILLIAM HAZLITT
From "Mr. Brougham—Sir F. Burdett"
The Spirit of the Age
1825

Mr. Brougham is from the North of England; but he was educated in Edinburgh, and represents that school of politics and political economy in the House. He differs from Sir James Mackintosh in this, that he deals less in abstract principles, and more in individual details. He makes less use of general topics, and more of immediate facts. Sir James is better acquainted with the balance of an argument in old authors, Mr. Brougham with the balance of power in Europe. If the first is better versed in the progress of history, no man excels the last in a knowledge of the course of exchange. He is apprised of the exact state of our exports and imports, and scarce a ship clears out its cargo at Liverpool or Hull, but he has notice of the bill of lading. Our colonial policy, prison discipline, the state of the Hulks, agricultural distress, commerce and manufactures, the Bullion question, the Catholic question, the Bourbons or

the Inquisition, 'domestic treason, foreign levy'—nothing can come amiss to him. He is at home in the crooked mazes of rotten boroughs, is not baffled by Scotch law, and can follow the meaning of one of Mr. Canning's speeches.

With so many resources, with such variety and solidity of information, Mr. Brougham is rather a powerful and alarming, than an effectual debater. In so many details (which he himself goes through with unwearied and unshrinking resolution) the spirit of the question is lost to others who have not the same voluntary power of attention or the same interest in hearing that he has in speaking; the original impulse that urged him forward is forgotten in so wide a field, in so interminable a career. If he can, others *cannot* carry all he knows in their heads at the same time; a rope of circumstantial evidence does not hold well together, nor drag the unwilling mind along with it (the willing mind hurries on before it, and grows impatient and absent). He moves in an unmanageable procession of facts and proofs, instead of coming to the point at once; and his premises (so anxious is he to proceed on sure and ample grounds) overlay and block up his conclusion, so that you cannot arrive at it, or not till the first fury and shock of the onset is over. The ball, from the too great width of the *calibre* from which it is sent, and from striking against such a number of hard, projecting points, is almost spent before it reaches its destination.

He keeps a ledger or a debtor-and-creditor account between the Government and the Country, posts so much actual crime, corruption and injustice against so much contingent advantage or sluggish prejudice, and at the bottom of the page brings in the balance of indignation and contempt, where it is due. But people are not to be *calculated into* contempt or indignation on abstract grounds; for however they may submit to this process where their own interests are concerned, in what regards the public good we believe they must see and feel instinctively, or not at all. There is (it is to be lamented) a good deal of froth as well as strength in the popular spirit, which will not admit of being *decanted* or served out in formal driblets; nor will spleen (the soul of Opposition) bear to be corked up in square patent bottles, and kept for future use! In a word, Mr. Brougham's is ticketed and labelled eloquence, registered and in numeros (like the successive parts of a Scotch Encyclopedia). It is clever, knowing, imposing, masterly: an extraordinary display of clearness of head, of quickness and energy of thought, of application and industry; but it is not the eloquence of the imagination or the heart, and will never save a nation or an individual from perdition.

Mr. Brougham has one considerable advantage in debate: he is overcome by no false modesty, no deference to others. But then, by a natural consequence or parity of reasoning, he has little sympathy with other people, and is liable to be mistaken in the effect his arguments will have upon them. He relies too much, among other things, on the patience of his hearers, and on his ability to turn everything to his own advantage. He accordingly goes to the full length of *his tether* (in vulgar phrase) and often overshoots the mark. *C'est dommage.* He has no reserve of discretion, no retentiveness of mind or check upon himself. He needs, with so much wit,

> As much again to govern it.

He cannot keep a good thing or a shrewd piece of information in his possession, though the letting it out should mar a cause. It is not that he thinks too much of himself, too little of his cause; but he is absorbed in the pursuit of truth as an abstract inquiry. He is led away by the headstrong and overmastering activity of his own mind. He is borne along almost involuntarily, and not impossibly against his better judgment, by the throng and restlessness of his ideas as by a crowd of people in motion.

His perceptions are literal, tenacious, *epileptic:* his understanding voracious of facts, and equally communicative of them—and he proceeds to

> Pour out all as plain
> As downright Shippen or as old Montaigne—

without either the virulence of the one or the *bonhomie* of the other. The repeated, smart, unforeseen discharges of the truth jar those that are next him. He does not dislike this state of irritation and collision, indulges his curiosity or his triumph, till, by calling for more facts or hazarding some extreme inference, he urges a question to the verge of a precipice, his adversaries urge it *over,* and he himself shrinks back from the consequence—

> Scared at the sound himself has made!

Mr. Brougham has great fearlessness, but not equal firmness; and after going too far on the *forlorn hope,* turns short round without due warning to others or respect for himself. He is adventurous, but easily panic-struck, and sacrifices the vanity of self-opinion to the necessity of self-preservation. He is too improvident for a leader, too petulant for a partisan, and does not sufficently consult those with whom he is supposed to act in concert. He sometimes leaves them in the lurch, and is sometimes left in the lurch by them. He wants the principle of co-operation. He frequently, in a fit of thoughtless levity, gives an unexpected turn to the political machine, which alarms older and more experienced heads. If he was not himself the first to get out of harm's way and escape from the danger, it would be well! We hold indeed, as a general rule, that no man born or bred in Scotland can be a great orator, unless he is a mere quack, or a great statesman, unless he turns plain knave. The national gravity is against the first: the national caution is against the last. ⟨. . .⟩

Mr. Brougham speaks in a loud and unmitigated tone of voice, sometimes almost approaching to a scream. He is fluent, rapid, vehement, full of his subject, with evidently a great deal to say, and very regardless of the manner of saying it. As a lawyer, he has not hitherto been remarkably successful. He is not profound in cases and reports, nor does he take much interest in the peculiar features of a particular cause, or show much adroitness in the management of it. He carries too much weight of metal for ordinary and petty occasions: he must have a pretty large question to discuss, and must make *thorough-stitch* work of it. He, however, had an encounter with Mr. Phillips the other day, and shook all his tender blossoms, so that they fell to the ground, and withered in an hour; but they soon bloomed again! Mr. Brougham writes almost, if not quite, as well as he speaks. In the midst of an Election contest he comes out to address the populace, and goes back to his study to finish an article for the Edinburgh Review, sometimes indeed wedging three or four articles (in the shape of *rifaccimentos* of his own pamphlets or speeches in parliament) into a single number. Such indeed is the activity of his mind that it appears to require neither repose nor any other stimulus than a delight in its own exercise. He can turn his hand to anything, but he cannot be idle.

There are few intellectual accomplishments which he does not possess, and possess in a very high degree. He speaks French (and, we believe, several other modern languages) fluently, is a capital mathematician, and obtained an introduction to the celebrated Carnot in this latter character, when the conversation turned on squaring the circle, and not on the propriety of confining France within the natural boundary of the Rhine. Mr. Brougham is, in fact, a striking instance of the versatility and strength of the human mind, and also in one sense of the length of human life, if we make a good use of our time. There is room enough to crowd almost every art and science into it. If we pass 'no day without a line,' visit no place without the company of a book, we may with ease fill libraries or empty them of their contents. Those who complain of the shortness of life, let it slide by them without wishing to seize and make the most of its golden minutes. The more we do, the more we can do; the more busy we are, the more leisure we have. If any one possesses any advantage in a considerable degree, he may make himself master of nearly as many more as he pleases, by employing his spare time and cultivating the waste faculties of his mind. While one person is determining on the choice of a profession or study, another shall have made a fortune or gained a merited reputation. While one person is dreaming over the meaning of a word, another will have learned several languages.

It is not incapacity, but indolence, indecision, want of imagination, and a proneness to a sort of mental tautology, to repeat the same images and tread the same circle, that leaves us so poor, so dull and inert as we are, so naked of acquirement, so barren of resources! While we are walking backwards and forwards between Charing-Cross and Temple-Bar, and sitting in the same coffee-house every day, we might make the grand tour of Europe, and visit the Vatican and the Louvre. Mr. Brougham, among other means of strengthening and enlarging his views, has visited, we believe, most of the courts, and turned his attention to most of the Constitutions of the continent. He is, no doubt, a very accomplished, active-minded, and admirable person.

WALTER BAGEHOT
From "Lord Brougham" (1857)
Collected Works, ed. Norman St.-John Stevas
1968, Volume 3, pp. 173–93

Lord Brougham's intellectual powers were as fitted for the functions of a miscellaneous agitator as his moral character. The first of these, perhaps, is a singular faculty of conspicuous labour. In general, the work of agitation proceeds in this way: a conspicuous, fascinating popular orator is ever on the surface, ever ready with appropriate argument, making motions, attracting public attention; beneath and out of sight are innumerable workers and students, unfit for the public eye, getting up the facts, elaborating conclusions, supplying the conspicuous orator with the *data* on which he lives. There is a perpetual controversy, when the narrative of the agitation comes to be written, whether the merit of what is achieved belongs to the skilful advocate who makes a subtle use of what is provided for him, or the laborious inferiors and juniors who compose the brief and set in order the evidence. For all that comes before the public, Lord Brougham has a wonderful power; he can make motions, addresses, orations, when you wish and on what you wish. He is like a machine for moving amendments. He can keep at work any number of persons under him. Every agitation has a tendency to have an office; some league, some society, some body of labourers must work regularly at its details. Mr. Brougham was able to rush hither and thither through a hundred such kinds of men, and gather up the whole stock of the most recent information, the extreme decimals of the statistics, and diffuse them immediately with eager comment to a listening world. This may not be, indeed is not, the strictest and most straining kind of labour; the anxious, wearing, verifying, self-imposed scrutiny of scattered and complicated details is a far more exhausting task; it is this which makes the eye dim and the face pale and the mind heavy. The excitement of a multifarious agitation will carry the energies through much; the last touches, and it is these which exhaust, need not be put on any one subject. Yet, after all deductions, such a career requires a quantity far surpassing all that most men have of life and *verve* and mind.

Another advantage of Lord Brougham, is his extreme readiness; what he can do, he can do at a moment's notice. He has always had this power. Lord Holland, in his memoirs referring to transactions which took place many years ago, gives an illustration of it. 'The management of our press,' he is speaking of the question of the general election of 1807, 'fell into the hands of Mr. Brougham. With that active and able individual I had become acquainted through Mr. Allen in 1805. At the formation of Lord Grenville's ministry, he had written, at my suggestion, a pamphlet called the *State of the Nation*. He subsequently accompanied Lord Rosslyn to Lisbon. His early connection with the Abolitionists had familiarised him with the means of circulating political papers, and given him some weight with those best qualified to co-operate in such an undertaking. His extensive knowledge, his extraordinary readiness, his assiduity and habits of composition, enabled him to correct some articles, and to furnish a prodigious number himself. With partial and scanty assistance from Mr. Allen, myself, and one or two more, he in the course of a few days filled every bookseller's shop with pamphlets,—most London newspapers, and all country ones without exception, with paragraphs,—and supplied a large portion of the boroughs throughout the kingdom with handbills adapted to the local interests of the candidates, and all tending to enforce the conduct, elucidate the measures, or expose the adversaries of the Whigs.'

Another power which was early remarked of Brougham, and which is as necessary as any to an important leader in great movements, is a skilful manipulation of men. Sir James Mackintosh noted in his Journal on the 30th of January 1818: 'The address and insinuation of Brougham are so great, that nothing but the bad temper which he cannot always hide could hinder him from mastering every body as he does Romilly. He *leads* others to his opinion; he generally appears at first to concur with theirs, and never more than half opposes it at once. This management is helped by an air of easy frankness that would lay suspicion itself asleep. He will place himself at the head of an opposition among whom he is unpopular; he will conquer the House of Commons, who hate, but now begin to fear him.' An observer of faces would fancy he noted in Lord Brougham this pliant astuteness marred by ill-temper. It has marked his career. ⟨. . .⟩

His oratory also suits the character of the hundred-subject agitator well. It is rough-and-ready. It abounds in sarcasm, in vituperation, in aggression. It does not shrink from detail. It would batter any thing at any moment. We may think as we will on its merits as a work of art, but no one can deny its exact adaptation to a versatile and rushing agitator—to a tribune of detail. ⟨. . .⟩

There is a last quality, which is difficult to describe in the language of books, but which Lord Brougham excels in, and which has perhaps been of more value to him than all his other qualities put together. In the speech of ordinary men it is called 'devil;' persons instructed in the German language call it 'the dæmonic element.' What it is one can hardly express in a single sentence. It is most easily explained by physiognomy. There is a glare in some men's eyes which seems to say, 'Beware, I am dangerous; *noli me tangere*.' Lord Brougham's face has this. A mischievous excitability is the most obvious expression of it. If he were a horse, nobody would buy him; with that eye, no one could answer for his temper. Such men are often not really resolute, but they are not pleasant to be near in a difficulty. They have an aggressive eagerness which is formidable. They would kick against the pricks sooner than not kick at all. A little of the demon is excellent for an agitator. ⟨. . .⟩

Lord Brougham has wished to be known not only as an orator but as a writer on oratory. He has written a 'Discourse' on ancient oratory, recommending, and very deservedly, its study to those who would now excel in the art; and there is no denying that he has rivalled the great Greek orator; at least in one of his characteristic excellencies. There is no more manly book in the world than Brougham's *Speeches*; he always 'calls a spade a spade,' the rough energy strikes; we have none of the tawdry metaphor, or half-real finery of the inferior orators, there is not a simile which a man of sense should not own. Nevertheless, we are inclined to question whether his studies on the ancient oratory, especially on the great public oration of Demosthenes, have been entirely beneficial to him. These masterly productions were, as every one knows, the eager expression of an intense mind on questions of the very best interest; they have accordingly the character of vehemence. Speaking on subjects which he thought involved the very existence of his country, he could not be expected to speak very temperately; he did not, and could not admit, that there was fair ground for difference of opinion; that an equally patriotic person, after proper consideration, could by possibility arrive at an opposite conclusion. The circumstances of the parliamentary orator in this country are quite different; a man cannot discuss the dowry of the princess royal, the conditions of the Bank charter, as if they were questions of existence—all questions arising now present masses of fact, antecedents in blue-books, tabulated statistics, on which it is impossible that there should not be a necessity for an elaborate inquiry—that there should not be discrepancy of judgment after that inquiry. The Demosthenic vehemence is out of place. The calm didactic exposition, almost approaching to that of the lecturer, is more efficacious than the intense appeal of an eager orator. That 'Counsellor Broom was all in a fume,' is a line in one of the best ludicrous poems of a time rather fertile in such things; on points of detail it is ridiculous to be in a passion; on matters of business it is unpersuasive to be enthusiastic; even on topics less technical, the Greek oratory is scarcely a model to be imitated precisely. A certain nonchalant ease pervades our modern world—we affect an indifference we scarcely feel; our talk is light, almost to affectation; our best writing is the same; we suggest rather than elaborate, hint rather than declaim. The spirit of the ancient world was very different —the tendency of its conversation probably was, to a rhetorical formality, an haranguing energy; certainly it is the tendency of its written style. 'With every allowance,' says Colonel Mure, 'for the peculiar genius of the age in which the masterpieces of Attic prose were produced,—a consideration which must always have a certain weight in literary judgments,—still, the impartial modern critic cannot but discern in this pervading rhetorical tone a defect, perhaps the only serious defect, in the classical Greek style. . . . It certainly is not natural for the historian or the popular essayist to address his readers in the same tone in which the defender of a client, or the denouncer of a political opponent, addresses a public assembly.' So great a change in the general world, in the audience to be spoken to, requires a change in the speaker. The light touch of Lord Palmerston is more effective than the most elaborated sentences of a formal rhetorician. Of old, when conversation and writing were half oratorical, oratory might be very oratorical; now that conversation is very conversational, oratory must be a little conversational. In real life, Lord Brougham has too much of the orator's tact not to be half aware of this; but his teaching forgets it.

That Lord Brougham should have adopted a theory enjoining vehemence in oratory, is an instance to be cited by those who hold that a man's creed is a justification for his inclinations. He is by nature over-vehement, and what is worse, it is not vehemence of the best kind; there is something of a scream about it. People rather laughed at his kneeling to beseech the peers. No one quite feels there is real feeling in what he reads and hears, it seems like a machine going. Lord Cockburn has an odd anecdote. An old judge, who loved dawdling, disliked the 'discomposing qualities' of Brougham. His revenge consisted in sneering at Brougham's eloquence, by calling it or him *the Harangue*. 'Well, gentlemen, what did *the Harangue* say next? Why it said this (misstating it); but here, gentlemen, *the Harangue* was wrong and not intelligible.' We have some feeling for the old judge. If you take a speech of Brougham, and read it apart from his voice, you have half a notion that it is a gong going, eloquence by machinery, an incessant talking *thing*.

It is needless to point out how completely an excitable ungenial nature, such as we have so much spoken of, incapacitates Lord Brougham for abstract philosophy. His works on that subject are sufficiently numerous, but we are not aware that even his most ardent admirers have considered them as works of really the first class; it would not be difficult to extract from the *Political Philosophy*, which is probably the best of them, singular instances of inconsistency and of confusion. The error was in his writing them: he who runs may *read*, but it does not seem likely he will think. The brooding disposition, and the still investigating intellect, are necessary for consecutive reasonings on delicate philosophy.

The same qualities, however, fit a man for the acquisition of general information. A man who is always rushing into the street will become familiar with the street. One who is for ever changing from subject to subject will not become painfully acquainted with any one, but he will know the outsides of them all, and the road from each to the other. Accordingly, all the descriptions of Lord Brougham, even in his earliest career, speak of his immense information. Mr. Wilberforce, in perhaps the earliest printed notice of him, recommended Mr. Pitt to employ him in a diplomatic capacity, on account of his familiarity with languages, and the other kinds of necessary knowledge. He began by writing on porisms; only the other day he read a paper on some absurdities imputed to the integral calculus, in French, at Paris. It would be in the highest degree tedious to enumerate all the subjects he knows something of. Of course, an extreme correctness cannot be expected. 'The most *mis*informed man in Europe,' is a phrase of satire; yet, even in its satire, it conveys a compliment to his information.

An especial interest in physical science may be remarked in Brougham, as in most men of impressible minds in his generation. He came into life when the great discoveries in our knowledge of the material world were either just made, or on the eve of being made. These enormous advances, which have been actually made in material civilisation, were half anticipated. There was a vague hope in science. The boundaries of the universe, it was hoped, would move. Active, ardent minds

were drawn with extreme action to the study of new moving power; a smattering of science was immeasurably less common then than now, but it exercised a stronger dominion, and influenced a higher class of genius. It was new, and men were sanguine. In the present day, younger men are perhaps repelled into the opposite extreme. We live among the marvels of science, but we know how little they change us. The essentials of life are what they were. We go by the train, but we are not improved at our journey's end. We have railways, and canals, and manufactures,—excellent things, no doubt, but they do not touch the soul. Somehow, they seem to make life more superficial. With a half-wayward dislike, some in the present generation have turned from physical science and material things. 'We have tried these, and they fail,' is the feeling. 'What is the heart of man the better for galvanic engines and hydraulic presses? Leave us to the old poetry and the old philosophy; there is at least a life and a mind.' It is the day after the feast. We do not care for its delicacies; we are rather angry at its profusion: we are cross to hear it praised. Men who came into active life half a century ago were the guests invited to the banquet; they did not know what was coming, but they heard it was something gorgeous and great; they expected it with hope and longing. The influence of this feeling was curiously seen in the Useful Knowledge Society, the first great product of the educational movement in which Lord Brougham was the most ardent leader. No one can deny that their labours were important, their intentions excellent, the collision of mind which they created most beneficial. Still, looking to their well-known publications, beyond question the knowledge they particularly wished to diffuse is, according to the German phrase, 'factish.' Hazlitt said, 'they confounded a knowledge of useful things with useful knowledge.' An idea, half unconscious, pervades them, that a knowledge of the detail of material knowledge, even too of the dates and shell of outside history, are extremely important to the mass of men; that all will be well when we have a cosmical ploughboy, and a mob that knows hydrostatics. We shall never have it; but even if we could, we should not be much the better. The heart and passions of men are moved by things more within their attainment; the essential nature is stirred by the essential life; by the real actual existence of love, and hope, and character, and by the real literature which takes in its spirit, and which is in some sort its undefecated essence. Thirty years ago the preachers of this now familiar doctrine were unknown; nor was their gospel for a moment the one perhaps most in season. It was good that there should be a more diffused knowledge of the material world; and it was good, therefore, that there should be partisans of matter, believers in particles, zealots for tissue, who were ready to incur any odium and any labour that a few more men might learn a few more things. How a man of incessant activity should pass easily to such a creed is evident. He would see the obvious ignorance. The less obvious argument, which shows that this ignorance, in great measure inevitable, was of far less importance than would be thought at first sight, would never be found by one who moved so rapidly.

We have gone through now, in some hasty way, most of the lights in which Lord Brougham has been regarded by his contemporaries. There is still another character in which posterity will especially think him. He is a great memoirist. His *Statesmen of George III* contains the best sketches of the political men of his generation, one with another, which the world has, or is likely to have. He is a fine painter of the exterior of human nature. Some portion of its essence requires a deeper character; another portion, more delicate sensations; but of the rough appearance of men as they struck him in the law-court and in parliament,—of the great debater struggling with his words,—the stealthy advocate gliding into the confidence of the audience,—the great judge unravelling all controversies, and deciding by a well-weighed word all complicated doubts,—of such men as these, and of men engaged in such tasks as these, there is no greater painter perhaps than Brougham. His eager aggressive disposition brought him into collision with conspicuous men; his skill in the obvious parts of human nature has made him understand them. A man who has knocked his head against a wall,—if such an illustration is to be hazarded,—will learn the nature of the wall. Those who have passed fifty years in managing men of the world, will

know their external nature, and, if they have literary power enough, will describe it. In general, Lord Brougham's excellence as a describer of character is confined to men whom he had thus personally and keenly encountered. The sketches of the philosophers of the eighteenth century, of French statesmen, are poor and meagre. He requires evidently the rough necessities of action to make him observe. There is, however, a remarkable exception. He preserves a singularly vivid recollection of the instructors of his youth; he nowhere appears so amiable as in describing them. He is overpartial, no doubt; but an old man may be permitted to reverence, if he can reverence, his schoolmaster.

H. H. MILMAN

1791–1868

Henry Hart Milman was born on February 10, 1791, in London, the son of Sir Francis Milman, physician to George III. He was educated at Eton and at Oxford, where he had a spectacular academic career, winning the Newdigate Prize for poetry and the Chancellor's Prize for the best English essay, and was made a fellow of Brasenose College. Milman was ordained in 1816; two years later he was named vicar at Reading and in 1821 became professor of poetry at Oxford.

As a young man Milman wrote a number of poems, (*Samor*, 1818; *The Fall of Jerusalem*, 1820) and hymns as well as a play, *Fazio* (1815). Around 1830 he turned to the writing of history. Milman's *History of the Jews*, published in that year, created a sensation, for it was the first work to treat the Jews as an Oriental tribe. This approach did not endear him to his fellow clergymen and delayed his promotion within the church hierarchy. Nevertheless, influential friends acting on his behalf secured his appointment as canon of Westminster in 1835, and in 1849 he became the dean of St. Paul's Cathedral.

Milman is credited with raising the standards of ecclesiastical history, and his work is considered sound, if dull. His other major works include the *Life of Gibbon* (1839), *History of Christianity under the Empire* (1840), and *History of Latin Christianity* (1855). His history of St. Paul's Cathedral was edited and published posthumously by his son.

Milman died on September 24, 1868.

Personal

Just before, I had gone down to the Milmans at Ascot, where they have hired a pleasant villa, very near Windsor Forest. They had invited me and *you* to pass several days, but I popped down, with little warning, to dine and pass the night only. I was agreeably disappointed in his appearance. He had been described to me as very much more bent, stooping to the ground; so he is, but the bend is so circular at his back that it has the appearance of a hump; while the face, with the coal-black eyes and raven eyebrows, surmounted by snow-white hair, is really in a true plumb-line from his feet, and he appears to stand erect like a benignant Anthropophagus, with his head beneath his shoulders, at a height of three feet from the ground. He is a good deal more deaf, so that one must change the whole pitch of one's voice. But he is full of life, interest in all things political, scientific, literary; full of work and of plans. She is as sweet, stately, genial, and gentle as she always was—as silvery voiced; and also her sable hair has turned out its silver lining very completely upon the night. In the main I found them singularly unchanged, and as you know them so well, that is their best eulogy. It is most delightful to see that Time, which has been so effective upon his backbone and his tympanum, has had no effect on his splendid intellect and his genial disposition.—JOHN LOTHROP MOTLEY, Letter to His Wife (Aug. 12, 1867), *Correspondence*, ed. George William Curtis, 1889, Vol. 2, p. 279

You know how I loved the dear old Dean, and how much I valued his long, unvarying kindness. It has been a great pleasure to me that I saw him so lately; as always, with the sense that it might be for the last time; as always, with the hope that the extraordinary vitality which he showed might still battle with the advance of age, and keep him yet awhile amongst us. Bitterly, deeply as I mourn for his loss, publicly and privately, I cannot but feel that so to depart, with his eye not dimmed nor his natural force abated, was a blessing such as one always in prospect and retrospect rejoices to think of for those we love.

How very far back that closed chapter takes us! What a host of famous memories! What a defence and bulwark of all that was just and right! Dear, sacred old sage of other days—sacred with our own dearest recollections—there is no like of him left.—A. P. STANLEY, Letter to Louisa Stanley (Sept. 28, 1868), cited in Rowland E. Prothero, G. G. Bradley, *The Life and Correspondence of Arthur Penrhyn Stanley*, 1894, Vol. 2, p. 365

There is one writer ⟨. . .⟩ whom I must especially mention, for his name occurs continually in the following pages, and his memory has been more frequently, and in these latter months more sadly, present to my mind than any other. Brilliant and numerous as are the works of the late Dean Milman, it was those only who had the great privilege of his friendship, who could fully realise the amazing extent and variety of his knowledge; the calm, luminous, and delicate judgment which he carried into so many spheres; the inimitable grace and tact of his conversation, coruscating with the happiest anecdotes, and the brightest and yet the gentlest humour; and, what was perhaps more remarkable than any single faculty, the admirable harmony and symmetry of his mind and character, so free from all the disproportion, and eccentricity, and exaggeration that sometimes make even genius assume the form of a splendid disease. They can never forget those yet higher attributes, which rendered him so unspeakably reverend to all who knew him well—his fervent love of truth, his wide tolerance, his large, generous, and masculine judgments of men and things; his almost instinctive perception of the good that is latent in each opposing party, his disdain for the noisy triumphs and the fleeting popularity of mere sectarian strife, the fond and touching affection with which he dwelt upon the images of the past, combining, even in extreme old age, with the keenest and most hopeful insight into the progressive movements of his time, and with a rare power of winning the confidence and reading the thoughts of the youngest about him. That such a writer should have devoted himself to the department of history, which more than any other has been distorted by ignorance, puerility, and dishonesty, I conceive to be one of the happiest facts in English literature, and (though sometimes diverging from his views) in many parts of the following work I have largely availed myself of his researches. —W. E. H. LECKY, "Preface" to *History of European Morals*, 1869

He is gone; and it has been said more than once that in him the last of his race expired, that the day for such men is over, and that the Church of England will no longer count among its servants such characters as it has hitherto enrolled, from Chillingworth and Cudworth, through Tillotson and Butler and Berkeley, to Heber, Arnold, and Milman. It is indeed true that this type of character, of which Dean Milman was in one aspect the most remarkable representative—connecting by invisible links society and religion, the world and the Church, literature and theology—is the product in an incalculable degree of that subtle framework of social and religious life which has hitherto afforded scope for the gradual and free development of all the diverse elements of the English Church and nation. Wherein lies the essence of this framework, wherein precisely consists the advantage of what is variously called "the connexion of Church and State," or "an Established Church," or "a national Church," may be difficult to analyse or express; and genius is not confined to any form of civil or ecclesiastical arrangement. But if we wished to indicate the effect produced, the gain to be cherished, the loss to be averted, we might name, in one word, the existence and work of Dean Milman. Let us trust that the fatal hour has not yet struck, and let us remember that the best hope of seeing such men again lies in our power of appreciating them whilst they live and after they are departed.—A. P. STANLEY, "The Late Dean of St. Paul's," *Macmillan's Magazine*, Jan. 1869, pp. 182–83

Works

POETRY

I have just finished Henry Milman's poem ⟨*Samor*⟩, a work of great power. But the story is ill constructed, and the style has a vice analogous to that which prevailed in prose about 170 years ago, when every composition was overlaid with strained thoughts and far-fetched allusions. The faults here are a perpetual stretch and strain of feeling; and the too frequent presence of the narrator, bringing his own fancies and meditations in the foreground, and thereby—as in French landscape-engraving—calling off attention from the main subject, and destroying the effect. With less poetry *Samor* would have been a better poem. Milman has been endeavouring to adapt the moody and thoughtful character of Wordsworth's philosophical poetry to heroic narration: they are altogether incompatible; and Wordsworth himself, when he comes to narrate in his higher strains, throws it aside like a wrestler's garment, and is as severe a writer as Dante, who is the great master in this style. If Milman can perceive or be persuaded of his fault, he has powers enough for any thing; but it is a seductive manner, and I think that as our poetry in Cowley's days was overrun with conceits of thought, it is likely in the next generation to be overflown with this exuberance of feeling.—ROBERT SOUTHEY, Letter to Chauncey Hare Townshend (April 12, 1818)

It is only in an age like the present that such poets as Mr. Milman are produced. Place genius where you will, in an age barbarous or civilized, aided by the discoveries of others or without them, and it will distinguish itself in some form or other; it weaves its web from materials within itself and needs but little external aid to effect its purposes. But it is only when civilization has advanced, the means of education been generally diffused, and a taste for reading cultivated, that a new source of pleasure, from a chaste and classical style, and smooth and flowing versification, is opened; that the labour of the mere scholar is appreciated and his productions valued. Poetry may thus be considered either as the work of genius, self dependent, availing itself of these advantages as auxiliaries, or of taste and learning, using them as principals. The poets of the latter class, it is true, cannot thrill us with horror or make us wild with joy, but they can keep our feelings in gentle and delightful play, can fortify virtuous resolutions and implant holy affections; immortality may be beyond their grasp, but they can gain some reputation and do some good for the age in which they live.

In this class of scholar poets, the author of the work before us ⟨*Samor*⟩ takes his place, and he has laboured diligently to obtain it. One of the greatest faults of his poem arises hence. We see the hard working of powers tasked to their utmost, through the whole of it. There is but little free sporting of fancy or feeling; few light and beautiful sketches, but much cold, hard drawing. He sometimes gives us, it is true, a strikingly beautiful and living description of natural scenery, but when he comes to the emotions of the soul, his language is tame and bombastic, or like them, is perplexed and intricate. To describe the soul tossed by the storm of passion or swelling with the grandeur of its emotions is the province of genius, and poets like Mr. Milman should be careful of intruding. It is his misfortune that he has not rightly estimated his strength and the nature of his talents; that he will not be contented to write well. He has adopted the rule of Tacitus to direct his efforts, but forgets that the faults are equal, of soaring above his subject or grovelling beneath it; and often, after toiling up a long and dizzy height, he vanishes into air, like the Saxon deities he describes, out of our reach and sight.

Another fault, which springs naturally from the difficulty of composing, so evident throughout the whole production, is the want of connexion in the general course of the work and even in single sentences. Parts, which should have been cemented together closely, are tied with a pack-thread or left loose and jarring against each other. Without the least preparation, we are hurried from one passage to another, with which it is entirely unconnected or most inartificially joined. Six or seven lines introduced into sixty or seventy different places would improve the poem wonderfully.

But a charge which falls more heavily than either of these is the paucity of moral remark, of general conclusions, of any thing that we can carry away with us for the regulation of conduct or as food for reflection. We rise from reading the work, as from hearing music, the impression of which lasts only during the performance; there is nothing that remains with us; no enlargement of views or elevation of thought; not one feeling altered or confirmed. If it were not for evidences of something better in another production, (his tragedy of Fazio,) we should say there was something radically wrong in this; a faint perception of moral beauty or a mind which could not turn aside from relating a story to apply its moral.

There is little that any of the personages say or do which lends any light to the development of their characters. The poet says such an one is brave and merciful or cruel, and he seems to consider this as sufficient; and we conceive that there is here another very serious fault. It is impossible that we should feel strongly interested in characters, of whom we know so little. He has, indeed, told us more about Samor than about the others, but he is so far removed from human weakness and above human excellence, that we cannot easily sympathize with him. We should have our hopes and fears excited, there should be something in himself to conquer, some lingering trace of earthly feeling, at least, in the hero of a poem, to excite our sympathy, or to serve any purpose of morality as a model. There is an exception to the above remark in the character of Rowena. It is well conceived and described. Her aspiring and determined spirit forms a fine contrast to the exquisitely beautiful and delicate frame it inhabits. With strong passions and boundless ambition, she is alternately the slave and the mistress of her feelings; and the woman who now 'stoops to be a queen,' at another time stands trembling, weak and irresolute before the object of her love.

⟨. . .⟩ Mr. Milman is not master of his subject, but is constantly obliged to conform to it. He has enough of heart, but not enough of mind for it; this constantly breaks and checks that stream of feeling which would flow so beautifully in a humbler channel. Tameness or extravagance are the faults to which it naturally leads him. His cast is always beyond the mark or short of it; he never 'rings the stake.' He seems to be constantly spurring on his powers to the task; and if they sometimes seem animated, it is rather the plunging of restlessness than the free spring of activity and vigour. There is a great deal of good versification, but very little of good poetry. He seems to have some of the accomplishments of a poet, but to want many of the essentials. This gives such a mixed character to his work, that it is difficult to pass a general opinion upon it. It can easily be proved by extracts, to be very good or singularly ridiculous. Its faults are those which spring of course from the selection of a subject above his powers,—indistinctness, tameness, bombast, evident hard labour, great inequality of execution, and a want of nature throughout. We are not willing to take this poem as a specimen of Mr. Milman's powers. The want of interest, arising from the unskilful direction of talent rather than from the want of it, is the great fault of *Samor*. The subject does not admit of the exercise of those powers which Mr. Milman can exercise to most advantage. A humbler theme would suit him better. The description of natural scenery and domestic character would tame his soaring spirit and bring him to meet us on equal ground. He must meet us, for he has not the all-powerful energy of genius to transport us from the world

of our own thoughts and feelings to one of his creation. —W. Loring, "Milman's *Samor*," *North American Review*, June 1819, pp. 26–35

He has now produced a poem ⟨*The Fall of Jerusalem*⟩ in which the peculiar merits of his earlier efforts are heightened, and their besetting faults, even beyond expectation, corrected;—a poem to which, without extravagant encomium it is not unsafe to promise whatever immortality the English language can bestow, and which may, of itself, entitle its author to a conspicuous and honourable place in our poetical pantheon, among those who had drunk deep at the fountain-head of intellect, and enriched themselves with the spoils, without encumbering themselves with the trammels of antiquity. But he must not stop even here. He has yet something to unlearn; he has yet much to add to his own reputation and that of his country. Remarkably as Britain is now distinguished by its living poetical talent, our time has room for him; and has need of him. For sacred poetry, (a walk which Milton alone has hitherto successfully trodden,) his taste, his peculiar talents, his education, and his profession appear alike to designate him; and, while, by a strange predilection for the worser half of manicheism, one of the mightiest spirits of the age has, apparently, devoted himself and his genius to the adornment and extension of evil, we may be well exhilarated by the accession of a new and potent ally to the cause of human virtue and happiness, whose example may furnish an additional evidence that purity and weakness are not synonymous, and that the torch of genius never burns so bright as when duly kindled at the Altar.—Reginald Heber, "Milman's *Fall of Jerusalem*," *Quarterly Review*, May 1820, p. 225

I cannot conclude without expressing, however inadequately, the delight with which I have just risen from the perusal of the "Martyr of Antioch." It has added another noble proof to those you had already given the world of the power and dignity which genius derives from its consecration to high and sacred purposes. Never were the "gay religions full of pomp and gold" so beautifully contrasted with the deep and internal sublimity of Christianity. I could dwell upon many parts which have made a lasting impression upon my mind, did I not fear that it would appear almost presumptuous to offer a tribute of praise so insignificant as mine to that which must have already received the suffrage of all who are entitled to judge of excellence.—Felicia Dorothea Hemans, Letter to H. H. Milman (March 7, 1822), cited in Arthur Milman, *Henry Hart Milman: A Biographical Sketch*, 1900, p. 122

The late Dean Milman, born in 1791, best known by his very valuable labours in history, may be taken as representing a class of writers in whom the poetic fire is ever on the point, and only on the point, of breaking into a flame. His composition is admirable—refined, scholarly, sometimes rich and even gorgeous in expression—yet lacking that radiance of the unutterable to which the loftiest words owe their grandest power. Perhaps the best representative of his style is the hymn on the Incarnation, in his dramatic poem, *The Fall of Jerusalem*. —George Macdonald, *England's Antiphon*, 1868, p. 312

HISTORIES

⟨. . .⟩ pray tell me whether you have read Milman's *History of Christianity*, and what you think of it. Our High-churchmen are shocked at so free and fearless a book from a dignitary, and judiciously enough, instead of abusing, they try to smother it. Their Reviews do not choose to have heard of the work. It shows immense reading and a storehouse of curious and interesting facts; but I cannot say that it makes upon my mind any single, strong, definite impression; nor perhaps could one well expect this from what may be called a *civil* history of the religion from its origin to the suppression of paganism in the Roman empire.—LUCY AIKIN, Letter to William Ellery Channing (Feb. 7, 1841), *Correspondence of William Ellery Channing and Lucy Aikin*, ed. Anna Letitia Le Breton, 1874, p. 380

It is indeed most painful, independently of all personal feelings which a scholar and poet so early distinguished as Mr. Milman must excite in the minds of his brethren, that a work so elaborate and so important ⟨as the *History of Latin Christianity*⟩ should be composed upon principles which are calculated to turn all kindly feeling into mere antipathy and disgust. Indeed there is so much to shock people, that there is comparatively little to injure. To one set of persons only is he likely to do much mischief, those who just at this moment are so ready to use his main principle for the demolition of Catholic views, without seeing that it applies to the New Testament History and teaching just as well. He will assist such persons in carrying out their principle. We observe that a publication, prominent in this warfare, cautions its readers against Mr. Milman's most *dangerous* and *insidious* work. We beg to join this publication and all other similar ones in its sage and seasonable warning. Let all who carp at the Fathers and deny Tradition, who argue against sacramental influence, who refer celibacy to Gnosticism, and episcopal power to Judaism, who declaim against mysticism, and scoff at the miracles of the Church while at the same time they uphold what is called orthodox Protestantism, steadily abstain from Mr. Milman's volumes. On their controversial principles his reasonings and conclusions are irresistible.—JOHN HENRY NEWMAN, "Milman's View of Christianity" (1841), *Essays Critical and Historical*, 1871, Vol. 2, pp. 247–48

Last night I finished your sixth volume ⟨of *History of Latin Christianity*⟩. What can I say, except that you have written the finest historical work in the English language? The interest grows from, perhaps commences with, the four last volumes. The first two, covering a vast period comparatively little known, are less distinct, and fail so powerfully to hold the attention. But what a labour of intellect to have shifted so often your point of vision—to have looked at every event, at every character, on all sides, before you set yourself to draw it! Calmness, impartiality, a belief, fixed as the creed, that the history of man, judged as a whole, is the history of his better nature struggling against his lower, and struggling not altogether unsuccessfully; that in a divinely governed world no system of faith or policy have taken effective and enduring hold upon mankind unless the truth in them has been greater than the falsehood,—these are the essentials of a great writer; and these, more than any one who as yet has taken such subjects in hand, you possess. The *History of Christianity* did not prepare me for the *History of Latin Christianity*. In the first I seemed to see chiefly the philosopher, in the second the man.—JAMES ANTHONY FROUDE, Letter to H. H. Milman (1855), cited in Arthur Milman, *Henry Hart Milman: A Biographical Sketch*, 1900, p. 224

⟨. . .⟩ Milman's *History of Latin Christianity* ⟨is⟩ one of the remarkable works of the present age, in which the author reviews, with curious erudition, and in a profoundly philosophical spirit, the various changes that have taken place in the Roman hierarchy; and while he fully exposes the manifold errors and corruptions of the system, he shows throughout that enlightened charity which is the most precious of Christian graces, as unhappily it is the rarest.—WILLIAM H. PRESCOTT, *History of the Reign of Philip the Second, King of Spain*, 1855, Vol. 2, p. 580, Note

I began Milman's *Latin Christianity*, and was more impressed than ever by the contrast between the substance and the style. The substance is excellent. The style very much otherwise. —THOMAS BABINGTON MACAULAY, *Journal* (Jan. 1856), cited in G. Otto Trevelyan, *The Life and Letters of Lord Macaulay*, 1876, Vol. 2, p. 332

Dean Milman's great and rare qualities were even perhaps more suited for the later history of the Church than for the earlier; and though we should be sorry to be without much of what he has done for the Middle Ages, we are not sure that we would not exchange it for the same amount of work on the time from the fifteenth to the eighteenth century. An English history of the Reformation, its causes and its consequences, has yet to be written. Reminded as we are daily, and in all kinds of ways, of its good and its evil results, and sensible, as we cannot help being, of its overwhelming eventfulness, we yet fail to rise to the height of the historical phenomenon itself, and we see it treated on every side in ways which, either for eulogy or condemnation, narrow, vulgarise, and impoverish our ideas of it. Dean Milman's imagination and insight, his fearless courage, and his unusual combination of the strongest feelings about right and wrong with the largest equity, would have enabled him to handle this perplexed and difficult history in a manner in which no English writer has yet treated it. We do not say that he could be expected to be entirely successful. He wanted, what many of our most eminent teachers of the present day want, a due appreciation of the reality and depth of those eternal problems of religious thought and feeling which have made theology. Impatient, sometimes unduly so, of the attempted solutions, and keenly alive to the strange and grotesque look which they frequently presented side by side with the visible course and show of the world and life, he contemplated them without interest; and deeply stirred as he was by all that the strife about them brought out in the temper and character of the human agents, all that for the sake of them men did and felt and suffered, yet he instinctively turned away as much as he could from adventuring his thoughts very far into the perplexed debates themselves. Of course a history of religion which inadequately understands and estimates religious belief and doctrine, and the earnestness which desires above all things that it should be complete and true, cannot be a perfect one; an account, however excellent, of what is outward in the fortunes and conduct of a religious body, cannot make up for the neglect or superficial understanding of those inward and spiritual ideas and efforts which are its soul and life. Dean Milman would have been more at home with the men and the events of the Reformation than with the philosophy and theology of its disputes. The German, Italian, and English divines, the Popes and Cardinals and Jesuits, who met them in the "world's debate," would have risen before him as men, with their hopes and fears, their temptations and their policies, their greatness and their crimes, much more easily and much more really than he could have entered into the significance of the battles of their day about Justification or the Sacraments. A man must be able to do both, before the history of that great crisis in the fortunes of the world is duly set forth; but to have done the first as Dean Milman would have done it, so loftily, so intelligently, so fearlessly, so justly, would have given us a book which for the present we want.—R. W. CHURCH, "Dean Milman's Essays" (1871), *Occasional Papers*, 1897, Vol. 1, pp. 156–58

What then is the real character of ⟨The History of the Jews⟩? It is a charming and attractive narrative. Forty years ago it charmed me more than I can well recall and express. For the first time one felt the heroes of the Old Testament, and the institutions and usages of the Hebrew people described with a vividness and reality that made them live before the mind's eye and brought them within the sphere of fact, rather than of pulpit convention. Strange, this was one of the very accusations against the History. It spoke of Abraham as an 'Eastern Sheik' or 'Emir,' of the 'quiet and easy Isaac,' of the 'cautious, observant, subtle, and kind Jacob.' It pointed to the undoubted fact that we do not find even in Abraham 'that nice and lofty sense of veracity which came with a later civilisation.' It explained the overthrow of the cities of Sodom by the inflammable character of the soil on which, and of the materials with which, they were built. It made nothing of the then received chronology of the Bible, which has really no higher authority than Archbishop Ussher in the seventeenth century. It recognised the exaggeration of the Scriptural numbers so obvious to every intelligent reader, and naturally arising out of the circumstances. 'All kinds of numbers,' as the author afterwards explained, 'are uncertain in ancient MSS., and have been subject to much greater corruption than any other part of the text.' And so long ago as the time of Bishop Burnet, the matter was left to the free judgment of the clergy of the Church of England. It explained naturally the passage of the Red Sea, and generally brought the light of criticism to bear upon 'the Eastern veil of Allegory' in which much of the narrative of the Old Testament is invested. Doubtless at the time these were startling features in a History of the Jews, and those who are familiar with the state of the religious world then and long afterwards will not wonder at the violent excitement which it raised. In truth, however, Milman, in the light of such Old Testament criticism as we are now familiar with, must be pronounced a highly conservative historian. Our modern schools would, I fear, judge him 'unscientific.' He repudiated in good faith any anti-supernatural bias, and deliberately separated himself from the extreme school of modern criticism. Its spirit of endless analysis and love for turning everything upside down was thoroughly uncongenial to his mind. He had too much imagination as well as faith and sobriety of temper for such work; and he remained to the end what he was plainly from the first, an historical genius who, while urged by his critical powers to sift everything to the bottom and to take nothing for granted merely because it was connected with traditional theology, was yet no less urged by his poetic and concrete tastes to paint a picture rather than give a mere tableau of critical processes. Erudite as any German, and familiar to the time of his death (1868) with the latest results of German critical speculation, he was yet, in the moulding power of his great intellect and his large knowledge of life and literature—in short, in his gifts as an historic artist,—as unlike as possible to the common type of German theologian. He was thoroughly English in his tastes; and his main distinction, like that of Whately and Arnold and Hampden, was his clear recognition of the difference between a simple and traditional Christianity, between what is essential to religion, and what is temporary and extraneous to it. This thought pervades his earlier History; it is emphasised in the Preface to the new and enlarged edition of 1863. It is the closing thought of his great History of Latin Christianity. Whatever part of our ancient dogmatic systems, he says, may fall into disuse 'as beyond the proper range of human thought and language,' and however far the 'Semitic portions' of the sacred records may have to submit to 'wider interpretation' 'in order to harmonise them with the

irrefutable conclusions of science,' the 'unshadowed essence' of Divine Truth as enshrined in the words of Christ, 'the primal and indefeasible truths of Christianity,' will live for ever. All else is transient and mutable—dogmatic form—sacramental usage—ecclesiastical rite. That which in its very nature is changing, and which the history of the Church shows to have already changed many times, cannot be enduring. But the 'truth as it is in Jesus' 'shall not pass away,' 'clearer, fuller, more comprehensive and balanced' as may become our view of it. Here the very note of the 'Noetic' School is struck, and Milman therefore deserves a place by the side of it. He is greater than most if not all of the School, but it is the same liberal spirit which speaks in it and in him.—JOHN TULLOCH, *Movements of Religious Thought in Britain during the Nineteenth Century*, 1885, pp. 82–85

Dean Milman's *Latin Christianity*, which appeared forty years ago, just misses, it may be, being one of 'the great books of history'—but will long hold its own as an almost necessary complement to Gibbon's *Decline and Fall*. It was avowedly designed as its counterpart, its rival, and in one sense its antidote. And we cannot deny that this aim has been, to a great extent, attained. It covers almost exactly the same epoch; it tells the same story; its chief characters are the same as in the work of Gibbon. But they are all viewed from another point of view and are judged by a different standard. Although the period is the same, the personages the same, and even the incidents are usually common to both histories, the subject is different, and the plot of the drama is abruptly contrasted. Gibbon recounts the dissolution of a vast system: Milman recounts the development of another vast system: first the victim, then the rival, and ultimately the successor of the first. Gibbon tells us of the decline and fall of the Roman empire: Milman narrates the rise and constitution of the Catholic Church—the religious and ecclesiastical, the moral and intellectual movements which sprang into full maturity as the political empire of Rome passed through its long transformation of a thousand years. The scheme and ground-plan of Milman are almost perfect. Had he the prodigious learning, the superhuman accuracy of Gibbon, that infallible good sense, that perennial humour, that sense of artistic proportion, the Dean might have rivalled the portly ex-captain of yeomanry, the erudite recluse in his Swiss retreat. He may not be quite strong enough for his giant's task. But no one else has even essayed to bend the bow which the Ulysses of Lausanne hung up on one memorable night in June 1787 in his garden study; none has attempted to recount the marvellous tale of the consolidation of the Christianity of Rome over the whole face of Western Europe during a clear period of a thousand years.—FREDERIC HARRISON, "Some Great Books of History," *The Meaning of History and Other Historical Pieces*, 1894, pp. 107–8

That literary eminence and theological scholarship, authority in matters ecclesiastical and authority in matters of taste have within her borders gone hand in hand, has been at once the strength and the crowning glory of the English Church. It has been her fortune to be represented in almost every epoch of intellectual enlargement by men whom the whole nation might rightly hold in reverence, by men to whom, though dwellers in the serene light of revealed religion, the wisdom and the culture of the children of this world were as familiar as the sacred writings themselves. With Milman the religious sense neither cramped nor overpowered his mental development; there met in him the reverence for Christian tradition that we look for in the pastor, the shepherd of his people, with the wide vision, the full freedom of conscience, and the intense passion for truth, that distinguish the philosopher. He belongs to the long line of illustrious churchmen who have been the true pillars of the faith, because boldly resolute, in Plato's phrase, to follow whithersoever the argument leads. Among the churchmen of his day, who, in the face of the hostile forces of the new methods of critical enquiry, had a sense of grave personal responsibility, and who felt themselves the guardians of the national traditions no less than of the national conscience, among those who were resolved to see to it, that there should be, to use Milman's own words, "no breach between the thought and the religion of England," he was himself the boldest, the strongest, and the best-equipped thinker. *The History of the Jews* was, as Stanley said, "the first decisive inroad of German theology into England, the first palpable indication that 'the Bible could be studied like another book,' that the characters and events of the sacred history could be treated at once critically and reverently." For a time, as was inevitable, Milman's determined attitude in that work, his unflinching application of the principles of scientific criticism was a stumbling block and a stone of offence to many. The march of the quiet years in whose van is revolution, unheralded, but resistless, made good his cause without controversy, upon which he did not care to enter; and in the evening of life he was invited to fill the University pulpit, from which in middle age he had been denounced as a traitor to his Church and his religion.

Milman has, however, claims to be remembered other than that he was a pioneer of a long-ago victorious critical movement. Without question one of the most accomplished men of letters of the present century, a distinguished editor and translator from the classics and from the Sanskrit, a poet of considerable imaginative range and lyrical sweetness, a far-sighted critic, an historian of ample learning and power, he seems to have his place on that border line where rare and brilliant talent melts into genius. Test him by some searching touchstone of genius, and he may indeed fall short; measure him by any rule of talent, and he satisfies but transcends it with much to spare.

The *History of Latin Christianity* is a work of epic proportions, and, save in its style, approaches epic dignity. A subject hardly less majestic than that of Gibbon, it was less susceptible of historic treatment in the grand style because it lacked an inherent unity. Without Gibbon's marked distinction of manner, Milman possesses many of the virtues of a good writer, and sustains with fluent ease the weight of his great narrative. A notable man, one may say of him, in the best company, the company in which the highest names are those of Hooker, of Taylor, and of Berkeley; at his best comparable, if not superior, to any English historian after Gibbon, and one who in every page of his writing stands revealed as above all else a Christian, a scholar, and a gentleman.—W. MACNEILE DIXON, "Henry Hart Milman," *English Prose*, ed. Henry Craik, 1896, Vol. 5, pp. 345–47

SAMUEL LOVER

1797–1868

Samuel Lover was born on February 24, 1797, in Dublin to a Protestant family; his father was a stockbroker. Young Samuel's love for the arts was evident at an early age. As a child he was sent to the country in an effort to improve his delicate health, and there he came to know and love the Irish peasantry.

At the age of fifteen Lover, at the insistence of his father, tried to become a stockbroker in London, but without success. His artistic pursuits ridiculed by the elder Lover, Samuel nevertheless left the business world two years later and returned home to become a painter. Encouraged by his friend, the Irish bard Thomas Moore, Lover also wrote and published his own songs, ballads, and stories. Well established as both a writer and painter by 1827, he married the daughter of a Dutch architect and in that same year produced his first play, *Grania Vaile*. In 1828 he was elected secretary of the Royal Hibernian Society.

Lover frequently spoke out on behalf of the Irish peasantry. He also found time to collect a number of short pieces he had previously published and issue them in 1831 as *Legends and Stories of Ireland*. His first novel, *Rory O'More*, appeared in 1837; his second and best-known novel, *Handy Andy*, was published in 1849. Lover also published several collections of poetry, including *Songs and Ballads* (1839), *Rival Rhymes* (1859), and *Volunteer Songs* (1859). *Selected Irish Lyrics*, edited by Lover, was issued in 1858.

Lover was a stage performer as well as a writer, presenting a series of entertainments known as "Irish Nights" throughout the British Isles and America in the 1840s. During an American tour his wife died suddenly and shortly thereafter the elder of his two daughters died of tuberculosis. Lover remarried in 1852 and had five more children; one daughter, Fannie, survived to adulthood and became the mother of Victor Herbert, the operetta composer.

Lover died on the Isle of Jersey on July 6, 1868, of tuberculosis.

Lover is a very forcibly effective, and truthful writer of Irish novels, and falls into the ranks after Banim. He has less passion, but more picturesque vivacity. As a writer and composer of songs (not to mention the charming expression with which he sings them) Mr. Lover is perhaps still more popular, and his ballads have a certain singable beauty in them, and a happy occasional fancifulness. His novels, however, are the stuff whereof his fame is made, and they are highly vital, and of great value in the sense of commentary on the national character.

Who ever read *Rory O'More* from beginning to end, without being seized with many a fit of uncontrollable laughter, and also shedding some tears?—or who ever began to read it, and left off without reading to the end? Genuine pathos, and as genuine fun—a true love of nature, and simple true-heartedness—are all there; and the dialogues are exquisite, and full of Irish humour.—R. H. HORNE, "Banim and the Irish Novelists," *A New Spirit of the Age*, 1844, p. 275

Lover is, as you know, the writer of songs equal (in popular effect) to any of Burns's. He is the author of Tales of humor in a vein in which he has no equal. His songs are set to his own music, of a twin genius with the words it uses. His power of narration is peculiar and irresistible. His command of that fickle drawbridge between tears and laughter—that ticklish chasm across which touch Mirth and Pathos—is complete and wonderful. He is, besides, a most successful play-writer, and one of the best miniature painters living. He is a Crichton of the arts of joyance for eye and ear.—N. P. WILLIS, "Samuel Lover," *Hurry-Graphs*, 1851

Mr. Samuel Lover, a most good-natured, pleasant Irishman, with a shining and twinkling visage ⟨. . .⟩ , sang some Irish songs, his own in music and words, with rich humorous effect, to which the comicality of his face contributed almost as much as his voice and words.—NATHANIEL HAWTHORNE, *The English Note-Books*, July 9, 1856

Of Lover's merits as a critic, despite his own modest disclaimers, a fair acknowledgment is due. He was no antiquarian, as he confesses—no Celtic scholar who could compare the claims of ancient and modern Irish song—but he was familiar with its history, knew the causes, and could enlarge instructively on the distinctions of its various classes, and, well acquainted with their leading specimens, was not unqualified to weigh and authenticate them in the duty of selection. His biographical notices are always faithful and compact, and if, in his notes, he has chosen to adopt a rambling pleasantry of tone that is occasionally diffuse, this does not exclude exactness when any point of interest occurs.—BAYLE BERNARD, *The Life of Samuel Lover*, 1874, p. 333

With an honest, frank, noble nature, and much deep, though unostentatious, religious feeling, Lover, as well as his true helpmate, was a sincere and devout member of the Church of England.

Bright, pure, honourable, conscientious, and humble,—to the very last, his kindly, genial spirit tried, in countless ways, to make others happy, and "to scatter bliss around!"

In our own pleasant experience, which was also that of his other friends, time strengthened an affectionate regard which was only interrupted by death.

Such was the bright and happy career of one, who, from the time of his boyhood when he breathed health on the Wicklow mountains, down to his peaceful end at St. Helier's, in his seventy-second year, was fortunate in all he undertook; because, along with a brilliant, versatile genius, he was honest, honourable, and dowered with practical common sense; and he also possessed a force of character, with a rare capacity for persistent work, which enabled him successfully to carry through, and master, whatever he resolved to attempt. Warmhearted and pure-minded, tender and true, joyous and brave, —Samuel Lover, humbly accepted the strengthening and comforting truths of Revelation, reverencing God, and sincerely loving his fellow-men.

If the "steel pen," at a rare time, was taken up instead of his "goose-quill," and dipped in gall, it was only in righteous indignation over some wrong done to others, and always in defence of the right.

Lover's beautiful miniature paintings were exquisite works of art, on which were expended his very highest powers; but these, though his greatest works, are but little known to the world in general. In short, the fact that Lover, the author of *Rory O'More*, was a painter at all, is, in the present day, known by very few.

On the other hand, his Irish peasant songs,—inimitable, piquant and unique, terse and musical, overflowing with tender affection and natural pathos, sparkling with wit, and beaming with kindly humour, innocent fun, and cordial geniality,—are universally appreciated, and sung *con amore*, wherever the English language is known.

His features and expression are faithfully and happily represented in Foley's admirable bust.

Lover amply succeeded, as we have seen, in making good his mark, in various walks of art and literature; finding relief, during a busy manifold life, mainly in change of occupation.

His tastes were simple, and his life pure. Thoroughly unselfish, hopeful himself, and helpful to others, possessing a bright, happy disposition, and a noble nature which was the very soul of honour, he was respected and loved, by all who had the privilege of knowing him.

Cherished thus, Lover continues to live in the hearts of his personal friends; while his name will be handed down to posterity by means of his IRISH SONGS, which, matchless and music-winged, assuredly are treasures

> Not of an age, but for all time!

—ANDREW JAMES SYMINGTON, *Samuel Lover*, 1880, pp. 255–56

Whenever Lover was our guest (which he was very often) he seldom failed to sing some song he had not then sung in public, and frequently it was in our circle it was heard for the first time. To hear him sing one of his songs was the next best thing to hearing Moore sing one of his.

He reminded me much of his great prototype: in voice they were not unlike; in singing both moved restlessly, as if they went with the words; they were both small, yet not ungraceful of form; both now and then affected Irish intonation, and both had round faces of the Irish type.

It was not uncommon to hear Lover described as "a Brummagem Tom Moore." That he certainly was not. Far from it. The one was as original as the other, but each in his own way. He was neither copyist nor imitator, and, if he had less of the inventive faculty than Moore, he had the art of making his own the thoughts for which there was no other owner. But it was as a teller of Irish stories Lover most delighted an audience. Few who heard him will forget the inimitable humor, the rich oily brogue, and the perfect ideal, he conveyed into the character when relating "New Pettaties" and "Will ye lend me the loan of a gridiron?"—S. C. HALL, *Retrospect of a Long Life*, 1883, p. 381

I saw a great deal ⟨. . .⟩ of Samuel Lover when he was in America in 1848. He was advertised to appear at the Broadway Theatre, and when he attempted to play in his own piece, "The White Horse of the Peppers," he was certainly the most frightfully nervous man I ever saw in my life. There was a great house because of the natural curiosity to see the poet in his own play. He was a very intimate friend of my father's. I stood in the wings when he came down as *Gerald Pepper*. The costume was the military dress of a cavalier of the time of James II., the scene of the play being the Revolution,—William III. coming over and turning James II. out of the country,—and *Gerald Pepper* was one of the Irish who remained faithful to the Stuart king. His feathers on this occasion were stuck in the back of his hat, his sword-belt was over the wrong shoulder, one of his boots was pulled up over his knee and the other was down over his foot. He looked as if somebody had pitchforked his clothes on to him, and he was trembling like a leaf. I induced him to put a little more color in his face, took his hat off and adjusted the feathers properly, put his sword on as it ought to go, fixed his boots right, and literally pushed him on to the stage. Of course there is no harm now in saying that it was one of the worst amateur performances I ever saw in my life, and I don't think Lover ever acted after that uncomfortable night.—LESTER WALLACK, *Memories of Fifty Years*, 1889, pp. 187–91

Lover, a poorer Moore, not so prolific, but perhaps more genuine, I once heard sing one of his songs—"What would you do? Love!" to his own accompaniment. He struck me only as a pleasant little man of society, of not much weight.—WILLIAM JAMES LINTON, *Threescore and Ten Years*, 1894, p. 174

My father's first novel was *Rory O'More*, and he appears to have had a great partiality for the song of that name, very likely because it was the first of his songs that attained a great popularity. I do not think that he otherwise had any particular favorites among the works of his pen or brush; but Rory O'More he made the hero of his first novel, and afterward he dramatized the book, thus making a threefold use of the name.—FANNY SCHMID, "The Author of *Rory O'More*," *Century Magazine*, Feb. 1897, p. 583

His *Handy Andy* is a formless book, and the fun of it grows tedious.—HUGH WALKER, *The Age of Tennyson*, 1897, p. 99

The versatility of Lover is one of the stock examples in Irish biography, and it is somewhat difficult to say in which of his various capacities he best succeeded. I am inclined to think that it is as a humorous poet that he ranks highest. He has many competitors in other branches of intellectual activity, but there are very few indeed who can be placed on the same level as a humorist in verse. His work as a miniature painter, as a composer, and as a novelist, excellent as it is, is likely to be forgotten long before such racy songs as 'Widow Machree,' 'Molly Carew,' 'Barney O'Hea,' and 'Rory O'More,' to name but a few of his best-known pieces, have become obsolete. There is an archness, an irresistible gaiety in these effusions to which it is difficult to find a parallel even among Irish writers. When he attempts the serious or sentimental, he generally fails lamentably. Humour is his most legitimate quality—he is the arch-humorist among Irish poets. He was born in Dublin on February 24, 1797, and gave early indication of his literary and musical gifts, to the annoyance of his father, a worthy stockbroker, whose intention it was to train him in business, and who disliked the arts. Finally his scruples were overcome, but the result was a permanent estrangement. The younger Lover began his career as a painter, and obtained very considerable reputation by his admirable miniatures of Paganini, Thalberg, and others, which were declared by competent judges to be worthy of the best professors of the art. Weakness of sight compelled him to turn to another means of livelihood, and he wrote many clever short stories, afterwards collected together in the two volumes of *Legends and Stories of Ireland*. Subsequently he produced the longer stories known to most readers as *Handy Andy*; *Rory O'More*; and *Treasure Trove: or, He Would Be a Gentleman*. These were illustrated by capital comic etchings of his own. Meanwhile his songs, nearly three hundred of which were set to music as well as written by himself, extended his fame far and wide. His more ambitious

poetical efforts are weak, and the same thing may be practically said of his stories. He has never done anything in fiction better than *Barney O'Reardon the Navigator*, and certainly his richly humorous songs are the only tolerable efforts of his Muse. He was granted a Civil List pension of 100*l*. in 1856, and after a long and prosperous life died in Jersey on July 6, 1868. In person he was almost as diminutive as his countrymen, Tom Moore and Crofton Croker; and, like them, he was very popular with all who had the pleasure of meeting him.—D. J. O'DONOGHUE, "Samuel Lover," *A Treasury of Irish Poetry in the English Tongue*, eds. Stopford A. Brooke, T. W. Rolleston, 1900, pp. 64–65

JAMES JEFFREY ROCHE
From "Introduction"
The Collected Writings of Samuel Lover
1903, pp. xxiii–xxxi

His Novels

Handy Andy is unique in literature, as a hero with a matchless genius for blundering and a happy faculty for escaping the worst consequences of his own mistakes; which an Englishman would have accounted for by the proverb, "Fools for luck!" But the Irish language has no exact equivalent for the harsh monosyllable; for "omadhaun" is a mild, soft word signifying an "innocent" or a "natural." Call him by whatever name we may, Andy is a triumph of misdirected originality, even as dirt has been defined as matter out of place. Andy's premises are always right, as when he resolves to punish the postmaster for his apparent extortion in charging double postage on a letter, by stealing two others, so as to give his master "the worth of his money." With similar good motives he slips an additional bullet into the duelling pistols before they are loaded, in order, again, that "the Masther" may have the advantage over his opponent. He is the very incarnation of good intentions, which, as we all know, have their Macadamical uses in another world. His more commonplace blunders, such as the exchanging and mis-sending of parcels, display no especial inspiration. They are within the capacity of any mere fool; Andy alone is the *diabolus ex machina* who could do it at the exact time and place calculated to produce the greatest possible amount of mischief. No, Andy is not a fool. That rôle belongs to the denationalised Dublin puppy, Furlong, whose *faux pas* are unrelieved by the slightest touch of originality.

Among the other strong characters in *Handy Andy*, old Squire O'Grady and his rival, Egan, stand out boldly as representatives of their class, though diametrically opposite to each other in character. Murtough Murphy, Dick the Devil, and Tom Durfy play well their several parts, being ably supported by a corps of supernumeraries who cheerfully and impartially assist at race, duel, election, or scrimmage. The Walking Gentleman of the story, Edward O'Connor, is like his prototype on the stage, or the corresponding character in *Rory O'More*, chiefly useful to fill the part of the sentimental lover of his affinity, the sentimental young lady. Needless to say that they seldom utter anything of interest except to themselves, therein being even as their models in real life. All the world loves a lover, but it is not madly covetous of his society while the fit is on him. The droll or humorous remarks which our author puts into the mouths of his characters are all so naïvely delivered that one forgets that they are generally coinage bright from the mint of imagination. For example, there is the

Widow Flanagan's exhortation to the merry-makers: "Come, begin the dance; there's the piper and the fiddler in the corner, *as idle as a milestone without a number;*" and there is the stinging phrase so casually dropped apparently, when, speaking of the tottering Dublin tenements, each marked with an official slab telling its exact distance from the Castle, he says: "The new stone tablets seemed to mock their misery, and looked like a fresh stab into their poor old sides;—*as if the rapier of a king had killed a beggar.*" But the reader will prefer to select his gems without impertinent assistance.

Andy's mother, though slightly sketched, is drawn from the life, as witness her two memorable visits to the Amazonian Mattie Dwyer and the results thereof; while the mother of The O'Grady is a lunatic of such majestic perfection that we know she must have sat in proper person for the vivid portrait. Mere imagination never invents such flights as hers. Father Phil Blake is one of Lover's many attempts to draw an Irish priest. If he sometimes fails in fidelity to life, it is not through lack of the kindliest intent; for no Irish Protestant writer ever felt or expressed more indignation towards the persecutions heaped upon those faithful leaders of their flocks, standing alone, as they did, between the forlorn serf and a master whose cruelty was equalled only by his besotted folly. But for the priest ministering, with a price on his head, to his scattered people, rebellion or anarchy would have deluged the land with blood. None knew this better than Lover. It is not out of place to recall the fact in any allusion to his life-work; for his life was indeed devoted to the championship of his poor countrymen and especially of those who differed from him in creed and station. "Rulers of Ireland!" he exclaims, "why have you not sooner learned to *lead* that people by love whom all your severity has not been able to *drive?*"

This feeling of intense patriotism finds most frequent and vigorous expression in his last novel, *Treasure Trove*, otherwise known as *L.S.D.* or *He Would Be a Gentleman*, in which he deals with some of the loyal Irish who followed the fortunes of Bonnie Prince Charlie, to their own misfortune. The Irish, like the Scotch, paid dearly for their fealty to a line of princes who exemplified the divine right of monarchs in their contempt for every common right and an ingratitude that was royally superhuman. Captain Lynch is a typical Jacobite soldier, loyal, brave, ready to make every honourable sacrifice, even to that of life, for a prince who was equally ready to accept, and forget it. It was such men who cried out after the disaster of the Boyne Water: "Change kings, and we'll fight the battle over again!" and such men who saved the day for France at Fontenoy and made King George exclaim in bitterness: "Curse on the laws that deprive me of such soldiers!" Lover, who had nothing to gain, and much to lose, in a worldly sense, by taking the part of his oppressed fellow-countrymen, hated tyranny of every kind and could not be silent when the wrongs of his native land were his theme. Not alone the wickedness of persecution, but the incredible folly of it, were clear to his honest vision; and he shows the other side of the picture convincingly,—the peace, loyalty, and contentment which followed so surely on the least concession of justice under an occasional just ruler like Chesterfield or Drummond. When intolerable tyranny drove the nation into desperate revolt, he says, "England would not admit that she had cause for discontent. The phrase of the time was, that 'the discontent on the face of Ireland was coloured by caprice and faction.' How capricious!" The reader who wishes to form a just idea of that capricious country will find some of the impelling causes in *Treasure Trove*.

For the rest, the story is full of life and adventure, with well-drawn pictures of Marshal Saxe, Lord Clare, Dillon, and other historical personages. Ned Corkery, the hero of the tale, is a much more interesting character than either De Lacy, of *Rory O'More*, or Edward O'Connor, of *Handy Andy*. His lady love, like theirs, is rather a lay figure. The story abounds in sufficiently moving adventures by flood and field; in the words of Phil Kearney, "There's beautiful fighting along the whole line." For which, and better, reasons, Lover's novels should find a new popularity in the present revival of "strenuous" fiction, whose heroes, to tell the truth, are a trifle too solemn in making either love or war, and lack the sense of humour which tends to lighten both of those rather over-rated diversions.

Lover's novels are all clean, wholesome works of art, plain stories, with little or no attempt at analysis of character or inculcation of any lesson other than that to be deduced from a picture in black and white. Their predominant quality is their humour, which is seldom strained, always laughter-provoking, and never cruel, except towards snobbishness, cant, and all manner of false pretence. In that and in their keen love of justice, they reflect the gentle manliness of their author.

Lover is at his best and his worst in his very unequal short stories. In the former category stand the inimitable "Barny O'Reirdon, the Navigator," "The Gridiron," "The White Horse of the Peppers," "Paddy the Piper" (of which he disclaims full credit as the author), and several delicious sketches of Irish coachmen, ballad-singers, waiters, and other original characters. "Father Roach," whose story he tells both in prose and verse, is an impossible character, as the dramatic incident upon which the tale hinges, the involuntary self-betrayal, outside of the confessional, of a criminal who had already confessed his crime under that inviolable seal could not have been used by the priest who was his confidant in both cases. The priest's supposed assertion that "the bishop of the diocese forwarded a statement to a higher quarter, which procured for me a dispensation as regarded the confessions of the criminal; and I was handed this instrument, absolving me from further secrecy, a few days before the trial"—is contrary to all the laws and traditions of the Catholic Church, and spoils an otherwise good story.

However, the single tale of the "Gridiron, or Paddy Mullowney's Travels in France," has humour enough to redeem a whole volume of inferior stories. It is his own entirely, in conception and execution. The extremely simple *motif* is sustained throughout, and Paddy insists upon it with such convincing sincerity that the reader is compelled to agree with him that the Frenchmen who failed to lend him a gridiron, on the strength of his three magic words, "Parly voo Frongsay?" were not only ignorant of their own language but shamefully inhospitable as well. He and his compatriot, Barny O'Reirdon, are worthy of Rabelais.

His Songs and Poems

Simplicity was the dominant characteristic of Lover's verse. He chose no complex themes, and nobody will ever achieve fame or fortune by founding "Lover Clubs" for the interpretation of his poems. In his preface to a volume of his poetical works, reproduced in this edition, he demonstrates briefly and clearly his theory of song-writing and explains some apparent literary defects in his own work by showing that poetical had occasionally to give way to musical expression when the first object was to make a song; and that, with him, was always the first object.

Among the songs, numbering nearly three hundred, in that collection are lyrics of love, humour, and pathos, together with a few political and "occasional." The best belong to the first three classes. Those of the others are fair of their kind, which is not a very high kind, being, indeed, no better than if they had been written to order by the average Laureate.

Even the reader fairly familiar with Irish poetry is surprised to find how many songs popular to this day are from the prolific pen of Lover, such as "The Low-Back'd Car," "Molly Bawn," "The Whistling Thief," "Barney O'Hea," "The Four-Leaved Shamrock," and nearly a score of others. It is not unreasonable to infer that their long life proves their high merit. "Rory O'More," of course, is known to all the world, and the beautiful songs, "The Angel's Whisper" and "What Will You Do, Love?" bear an appeal to the human affections that will find response in every heart.

It is not every poet who can blend humour and tenderness so exquisitely that neither shall suffer by the union. The absolute delicacy of Lover's humorous love poems is unparalleled in this or any other language. Percy's *Reliques* reflect the coarseness of their age. Burns smirched his pages with Rabelaisian grossness, and English bards, from Chaucer to Byron, have done the same. Even Moore affected the Anacreontic, happily with little success, in his youthful flights. Irish writers of prose and verse are almost always free from any uncleanness. Their literature is as pure as that of America. Lover's wooer, whether it be Rory O'More, or Barney, or the Dying Soldier, or Lanty Leary, is gay as only an Irish lover can be—the only one, it is said by his rivals, who can meet a woman's wiles with a wit as nimble as her own. Lover has drawn him to the life, with his national heritage of good humour, so much more precious than the belauded Hope in Pandora's box, which must have lost a good deal of its saving salt by association with gloomy company in that ill-omened casket.

WILLIAM CARLETON

1794–1869

William Carleton was born near Clogher, County Tyrone, Ireland, on February 20, 1794. He was educated locally and his family intended him to study for the priesthood. Instead he went to Dublin and, enduring poverty, resolved to become a writer. *Traits and Stories of the Irish Peasantry*, his first book, was published in 1830. This was followed by a number of novels over the next four decades. His best-known are *Fardorougha the Miser* (1839), *Valentine McClutchy, the Irish Agent* (1845), and *The Black Prophet* (1847), a novel about the Great Famine. *Traits and Stories*, which offers sympathetic portraits of Irish peasant life before the famine, is considered his best work.

In addition to his novels Carleton began work on an autobiography, left unfinished at his death. It was later completed by D. J. O'Donoghue and published as *The Life of William Carleton* (1896).

Carleton died in Dublin on January 30, 1869.

If Banim may be characterized as the dramatic historian of his countrymen, Carleton may with equal truth be styled their faithful portrait-painter. He draws from the life. In his manly and unaffected introduction to *Traits and Stories of the Irish Peasantry*, he has given his auto-biography, and explained how it is he can so accurately describe, because he was himself one of them:—A good reason for his knowledge; but in himself is the power to use it with talent and effect.—R. H. HORNE, "Banim and the Irish Novelists," *A New Spirit of the Age*, 1844, p. 275

I have not much to say of Carleton, and very little that is good. Undoubtedly he was a powerful writer, a marvelous delineator of Irish character—seen, however, not from its best side. He was essentially of the people he describes, peasant-born and peasant-bred, and most at home in a mud cabin or shebeen-shop. Of the Irish gentry he knew none beyond the "squireens"; his occasional attempts to picture them are absurdities. To him was accorded one of the Crown pensions—£200. It is to be feared the greater portion was spent in low dissipation. At all events he never obtained, never earned, the applause of his country or the respect of those whose respect was worth having in Dublin, the city where he dwelt. He was a Catholic to-day and a Protestant tomorrow, turning from one religion to the other as occasion served or invited.

It is requisite to name him here, among the many Irish authors I have known; but I did not feel for him while he lived, nor can I feel for him now, any respect.—S. C. HALL, *Retrospect of a Long Life*, 1883, p. 385

A more enduring reputation was earned by William Carleton, whose charming *Traits and Stories of the Irish Peasantry* did perhaps more to acquaint the English public with the real nature and characteristics of his people than any of the writers we have already mentioned. His contributions to Victorian literature include *Fardorougha the Miser* (1839), the alternately humorous and melancholy *Misfortunes of Barney Branagan* (1841), and his most elaborate work, *Valentine McClutchy, the Irish Agent*. Carleton continued to write busily up to his death in 1869.—MARGARET OLIPHANT, *The Victorian Age of English Literature*, 1892, Vol. 1, pp. 295–96

Then there is William Carleton, who in a lighter vein is a very skilful delineator of the special traits of the Irish. Among his novels are the *Black Prophet*, graphically describing the appalling features of the famine of 1846, and *Rody the Rover*, the *Tithe Proctor*, and especially the *Traits and Stories of the Irish Peasantry*. Carleton wrote the *Misfortunes of Barney Branagan*, *Valentine McClutchy*, a defence of the Irish Catholic priests, and a plea for separation from England; and it is certain that under the often transparent guise of fiction Carleton is a faithful and a very sympathetic historian of the Irish people. —PERCY RUSSELL, *A Guide to British and American Novels*, 1894, p. 85

I know of ⟨. . .⟩ no narrative so direct ⟨as the *Autobiography*⟩, so simple of form yet so exuberant; for everything, however small as an incident, is on a big scale of representation. The imagination of the writer was evidently set to work again, in retrospect, exactly as it had fulfilled its functions at the actual time of occurrence, and it reproduced the sentiments and sensations of the past with all their fervour, or pain, or acuteness. The very first mental characteristic of Carleton which strikes us is that he habitually "saw men as trees walking." This tendency of his temperament, confirmed by the deficiencies of his education, has an attractive side, for it implies enthusiasm, and the highest endowments lacking this must fail to command complete sympathy.

Had the Carleton of literature and fame found no chronicler, had his works, with their own history (one of odd, irregular emergence from neglect which sometimes neared the point of oblivion), received no side-light illumination, the readers of to-day, made acquainted only with the Carleton of his wonderful first period, would have suffered grievous loss.

No fragmentary record by himself of a man's experience was ever more calculated to whet curiosity than is the autobiographical volume, with its gusts of feeling, its curiously quick and shrewd judgments, its simple ignorance of men and things on certain lines, its fine intensity, its frank, unapologetic vanity, its Rembrandt-like handling in the actualities it portrays of the shadow that had so little shine. Its unashamed narration of the details of his youthful poverty, in other hands might have shocked and wearied the ordinary well-to-do reader who does not like that sort of thing; but, handled in Carleton's broad manner, and with his humour, its fulness of emotion, its wail of complaint, that affects one as the desperate finality of a child's grief might do, and is sometimes equally unreasonable, are alike fascinating and piteous. There is indeed a great deal of the child, a big sort of child, in Carleton's Carleton, and it remains almost to the end in Mr. O'Donoghue's. ⟨. . .⟩

For the right understanding of the whole of his character and his life, and for the full appraisement of his works, it is necessary always to bear in mind Carleton's peasant origin and all that it meant and comprised in the Ireland of his time, not only for the mere marvel of what the man achieved, but because, while he glorified his origin by interpreting his people to the world, he retained its salient characteristics and its distinctive limitations. This fact, while it was of disadvantage to him in the conduct of affairs, and the contacts of life, was of incalculable value to his work, and furnishes the true explanation of his pre-eminence over other national novelists whose endowments and sympathy equalled, while their skill and culture surpassed his own.—CASHEL HOEY, "Introduction" to *The Life of William Carleton* by David J. O'Donoghue, 1896, pp. xvii–xx

It is an easy task to define Carleton's position in Irish literature. He is unquestionably supreme so far as fiction is concerned. But his position in literature generally is not easy to define. Judging him by his best work only—by his wonderful knowledge of human nature, and not by his style—he should occupy one of the proudest places in the whole gallery of masters who have made a study of the human heart. It is imperative to consider for this purpose only the truest revelations of his genius. Judged otherwise, his average merit is not great. There is hardly another writer between whose best and worst writing there is so wide and deep a distinction. Any writer who has written so much must needs have produced something unworthy of his highest powers; but, to be perfectly candid, no writer

has given to the world work more essentially unfit to live than are Carleton's weakest efforts. ⟨. . .⟩

His style is not remarkable for excellence, but in a painter of manners, one may be permitted to say, style is not everything. It is of comparatively little importance to the readers of one country whether the great writers of another are excellent stylists or otherwise—the thought and the dramatic gift are the essentials. Some of Carleton's shorter sketches are admirably written, others are of much poorer quality in that respect. That he was able to adapt himself to more than one style without losing his individuality, the "Battle of the Factions" in the *Traits and Stories* will prove. It is a *tour de force* of versatility.—DAVID J. O'DONOGHUE, *The Life of William Carleton*, 1896, Vol. 2, pp. 350–52

A group of Irish novelists, rather older than Thackeray and Dickens, may be noticed together for the sake of certain features they have in common. If fineness of literary quality alone were in question, the first place must be assigned to William Carleton, whose *Traits and Stories of the Irish Peasantry* are the most carefully executed of their class. Carleton however had neither the verve nor the copiousness of Lever, who has been fixed upon by popular judgment as the leading Irish novelist of his time.—HUGH WALKER, *The Age of Tennyson*, 1897, pp. 98–99

PATRICK A. MURRAY
From "Mr. Carleton's Sketches"
Edinburgh Review, October 1852, pp. 385–88

Mr. Carleton's works are of very unequal merit. To begin with his defects. Some of his scenes and stories are utterly flat and spiritless from beginning to end; and there are here and there, in the collection of his writings, little deposits of unsavoury rubbish, which remind us of certain adjuncts such as he himself described to be sometimes perceived, by more senses than one, beside the habitations of a particular class of his countrymen. He is now and then coarse and vulgar; even his most happy efforts are not always free from this serious drawback. Nor is the fault palliated, for it could not be excused, by an over rigid adherence to actual nature: it is generally found in those scenes where his caricatures and exaggerations are most excessive. His failures begin on his seeking to come out as a colloquial humourist or describer of outlandish incidents, on his own account; as often as he ceases to copy the real language and manners of the people, and to paint events most likely to occur among them. Of attempts at the smart or facetious not true to the usages of Irish speech, and of adventures not true to Irish life, we do not remember a single occasion in which he does not depart as widely from the common principles of good taste as from the duties of a faithful observer of men and things. Several of his dull passages are open to an opposite objection. They are indeed true copies, but copies of scenes not worth copying.

There is another fault, which a few mere strokes of the pen would cancel from all future editions. He at times breaks in upon the narrative with a little lecture on the relations of landlord and tenant, the importance of education, the duty of forethought and economy, and the like. We do not mean to insinuate that these topics are not of the first importance, or that his strictures are not just and valuable; but they are out of place. We go to the lawyer for sound legal advice, to the doctor for his prescription, and to Mr. Carleton for a capital Irish story 'racy of the soil.' We have had so many dissertations on that crowning 'difficulty'—'the Irish Evil'—so many 'remedies' for it, that we doubt if the subject could be made attractive reading in any book: in *his* books it is the portion we skip. The first rule is—stick to your story; whatever you add that is not a part of it, though ever so valuable in itself, will be an incumbrance, as a man's movements are embarrassed by a weight on the back, though it were a weight of gold. One of the merits of Mr. Carleton's best tales is, that they convey their own lessons, and require no gloss. When he epitomises himself into a lecture, it is like the exquisite singing of a beautiful song followed by a drawling recitation of the words. After all, the faults we have noticed are but occasional, so loosely connected with the structure of the sounder and better parts, that their removal might be easily accomplished without leaving any scar behind.

It is among the peasantry that Mr. Carleton is truly at home. He tries other characters, rarely, however, and not unsuccessfully. But the Irish peasant is his strong point: here he is unrivalled, and writes like one who has had nothing to look out for, to collect by study, to select, to mould; who merely utters what comes spontaneously into his thoughts; from whom the language and sentiments flow as easily and naturally as articulate sounds from the human lips or music from the skylark. Those who have in early life dwelt among the Irish peasantry, and since forgotten that period in other and busier scenes of existence, meet again, in the pages of Carleton, the living personages of long past days, like friends returned from distant lands, after an absence of many years. Upon the whole, he paints them with an impartial hand: their excellent qualities he brings out fully, their general defects and the blacker vices which characterise certain individuals, he neither hides nor softens down. Some of his countrymen have been very angry with him for not representing his peasant as the finest in the world, if not absolutely faultless; while others, on the opposite side—his own countrymen still—have assailed him for bestowing graces and noble feelings and noble virtues where they are not to be found. We believe, however, that he wrote with full knowledge and in good faith. Neither his good nor his evil persons are ideal; but it is in the delineation of the former that he appears to most advantage. In portraying scenes of true and pure affection, of generous self-sacrifice, of tender sympathy, of silent and devout resignation, of humble domestic love and happiness, his heart is poured forth in strains too simple and natural not to impress his readers with the belief that he is but recalling a past reality, and describing what he had once seen and perhaps acted and felt himself. He tells us, in the preface to the last edition of the most successful of his longer stories, *Fardorougha the Miser*, that the individual who sat for the character of Honor O'Donovan, the miser's wife, was his own mother. A beautiful impersonation of the purest domestic virtues she undoubtedly is; but, as the type of a pretty large class, we can assure our readers, by no means overdrawn. It is in the relation of mother or daughter or sister of an erring husband, or son or brother, that the truly devoted heart of the Irish peasant female is best tried and seen. We have known instances,—and for our opportunities of observation, not a few,—to which the portrait of Honor O'Donovan would answer without one trait of exaggeration. We can say the same of all his other more quiet and loveable characters, as well as of most of those which interest us by their drollery, or salient absurdity, or good-humoured rustic 'cuteness.

The primary and essential value of Mr. Carleton's sketches of Irish peasant life and character unquestionably consists in this—that they are true, and *so* true to nature: but it is enhanced by a circumstance similar to that recently recorded and lamented by Lord Cockburn in reference to Scotland. The living originals are disappearing, some of them have already disappeared.

⟨. . .⟩ To Mr. Carleton thus belongs the great merit of perpetuating a true and living image of so much of what is already, or, ere long, will be lost. So far as our acquaintance with this sort of literature extends, no other writer has approached him in the freshness and reality of his pictures. He is not only Irish, but thoroughly Irish, intensely Irish, exclusively Irish. Putting aside the few tales and incidental passages, already alluded to, as of an exotic and distorted character, and, taking his best writings, that is, the great mass of them, he stands alone as the exhibiter of the inward and external, the constitutional and the accidental, the life, the feelings, the ways, the customs, and the language of the Irish peasant. Others have given partial sketches and individual portraits, types of no one else, or of but an insignificant few.

G. BARNETT SMITH
From "A Brilliant Irish Novelist"
Fortnightly Review, January 1897, pp. 104, 114–16

All the characteristics of the Irish race seem to have been blended in William Carleton, who has not inaptly been designated "the Walter Scott of Ireland." He was brilliant and wayward, tearful and whimsical, strong in his affections, and passionately attached to his family and the homeland. If it be true what Shelley says of the poets, that "they learn in suffering what they teach in song," it is equally true of the life and writings of Carleton. The intense and full-veined humanity which permeates his works is in a large measure the outcome of his sympathetic heart. The Irish peasant never had a more tender and compassionate interpreter of his complex nature, with all its moods—moods now jocund and sunny as the spring, and now sombre and pathetic as the autumn.

It is the privilege of genius to be erratic, and Carleton used the privilege to the full. To a great extent he did for the Irish peasantry what Scott did for his own fellow-countrymen, but it would have been well had he resembled Scott in his personal as well as his literary character. The conformation of his head resembled Scott's, a fact of which Carleton was inordinately proud; but those sterling qualities which enabled Scott to wage as manly a struggle with adverse fate as is to be found in the whole annals of literature, were too much wanting in Carleton. He was, in truth, far more akin in nature to Burns than to Scott. He was full of sensitiveness, loving yet erring, as glorious as he was contradictory, now on the heights and now in the deeps. He had no more idea of managing men than he had of managing himself. He was constantly in hot water with his publishers, and then, unhappily—and no doubt in consequence thereof—he made the acquaintance too frequently of poverty and potheen. Sorrow marked him for her own, and yet, in spite of all his faults, he was in many respects a fine fellow, and one full of noble impulses.

It is, however, in his literary aspects that the world is chiefly concerned with him, though we shall also find something in the man to interest us. There was nothing classic in his writings; occasionally, indeed, there was an independence of grammar calculated to disturb the shade of Lindley Murray. But if his language was not always correct, it was *living* to a degree. There was nothing of the Dryasdust element about it. His sentences were warm, vivid, palpitating with energy and emotion. Although he might not be able to turn a period with men like Matthew Arnold or Sainte-Beuve, neither could such wielders of a model diction emulate his Titanic rendering of the passions, or his bursts of rugged and perfervid eloquence. ⟨. . .⟩

As a novelist, Carleton was superior in one respect to either Dickens or Thackeray. He could draw women better. So far as I remember there is not a weak creation among all his female characters. They are living, breathing, loving, creatures— women capable of inspiring a deep affection, and at the same time worthy of it. Where is there a nobler being in fiction than Helen Folliard, the heroine of *Willy Reilly?* The way she cheers her lover in all his difficulties, remains true to him through unexampled trials, and finally testifies in his favour when he is tried for his life, has something truly sublime in it. Similar praise is due for the way in which he draws many other heroines.

I find in all Carleton's writings something of the forceful energy and dramatic intensity which characterize the novels of Charlotte and Emily Brontë. His people palpitate with life. From the moment they appear to the last glimpses we have of them we see real men and women, and not phantoms. Look at *Fardorougha, the Miser,* one of the most powerful works of fiction ever penned. The struggle depicted in the breast of Fardorougha is absolutely Titanic. The passion for gold, and the equally strong passion for his son Connor, the child of his old age, contend for the mastery, and the strength of the conflicting elements is terrible to behold. Even when his son is in danger of his life, avarice withholds the means for his defence, and then when affection gains the upper hand, the old man is pitiably rent by the two passions. In the hour of death the passion of avarice momentarily reasserts its power. The story would be unbearable for its gloomy burden of sorrow were it not for the two women characters in it. The beautiful love passages between Nora O'Brien and Connor are scarcely to be matched anywhere, while the noble devotion of Honor O'Donovan, the wife of the miser, stands almost unique. Yet she was no creature of the imagination, but, as Carleton says, "a likeness faithful and true to the virtues of thousands whose glowing piety, meek endurance, and unexampled fortitude, have risen triumphant over some of the severest trials of domestic life." The novelist is right in claiming the conspicuous virtues of truth, purity, and religious principle for the wives and daughters of the Irish peasantry.

There are noticeable qualities in *The Red Hall,* where the character drawing is again especially strong. The cruel, vulgar baronet, Sir Thomas Gourlay, is a vivid but detestable portraiture. His whole soul is bent on making his daughter Lucy a countess, though he knows that there is not a viler creature in existence than the man to whom he promises her hand. By a series of the most frightful persecutions he forces her to yield assent, but happily before the nuptial knot is tied the supposed earl is discovered to be an impostor. The discovery that all his plans have fallen like a pack of cards stuns and bewilders the baronet, and there is nothing more dramatic in the whole of Carleton's works than the closing scene of this novel. The baronet has had all his scheming in vain, and he has taken poison too soon to learn that his daughter finally married the man of her choice, who is the real nobleman, so that she becomes a countess after all. I cannot agree with Mr. O'Donoghue in somewhat underrating this story. On the contrary, I find it one of the best and most readable of Carleton's works.

Valentine M'Clutchy is another of Carleton's novels which no other man could have written. The sharp contrasts between virtue and vice are very striking, and there are some scenes which are overwhelmingly painful. One would wish, for the credit of human nature, that they had never had their counterpart in real life. The novel must have come as a crushing blow upon the author's Orange friends. The eviction carried out in the cabin of the O'Regans, when the dying husband is besought by his agonized wife to give up his last breath before the myrmidons of the law enter, is, so far as I know, unexampled for its sadness and pathos. In this case, as in many others, Carleton wrote with a purpose, but he always claimed credit for his impartiality in scourging the evils of both the Catholic and Protestant systems. In the Preface to *Valentine M'Clutchy* he fearlessly asserted that all the horrors of Orangeism and landlordism which he described were in no whit exaggerated, any more than were those of the opposing side in his other works, and he added, "I have been so completely sickened by the bigoted on each side, that I have come to the determination, as every honest Irishman ought, of knowing no party but my country, and of devoting such talents as God has given me to the promotion of her general interests and the happiness of her whole people."

Those who have formed erroneous estimates of Carleton may well listen to him for a moment upon himself and his literary labours. While he did not claim the passionate eloquence, "the melancholy but indignant reclamations," of John Banim, he did claim to be moved by less of party spirit and prejudice than Banim. He sought to give fair and just estimates of his countrymen, wheresoever and under whatsoever circumstances he found them. The want of a fixed system of wholesome education was one of his chief complaints. The hedge-schoolmaster was a poor substitute for this. Such a miserable education as he was able to impart was "sufficient almost, in the absence of all other causes, to account for much of the agrarian violence and erroneous principles which regulated the movements and feelings of the peasantry." Then the lower Irish were for a long period treated with apathy and gross neglect by the only class to whom they could rightly look for sympathy and protection. "Hence those deep-rooted prejudices and fearful crimes which stain the history of a people remarkable for their social and domestic virtues." Carleton adds to these observations: "In domestic life there is no man so exquisitely affectionate and humanised as the Irishman. The national imagination is active, and the national heart warm, and it follows very naturally that he should be, and is, tender and strong in all his domestic relations. Unlike the people of other nations his grief is loud, but lasting; vehement, but deep; and whilst its shadow has been chequered by the laughter and mirth of a cheerful disposition, still, in the moments of seclusion, at his bed-side prayer, or over the grave of those he loved, it will put itself forth, after half a life, with a vivid power of recollection which is sometimes almost beyond belief." Such is the being, with all his conflicting emotions and aspirations, whom Carleton set himself to depict, and it is safe to affirm that neither before nor since his time has the task been accomplished with so much success.

Undoubtedly one of Carleton's leading claims to permanent remembrance is that he gave faithful representations of an Irish peasantry which is now fast dying out. The old race is almost extinct and a new one is rapidly taking its place. This makes the novelist's pictures of life all the more valuable. But beyond and above this there is the ineffaceable stamp of genius upon his writings. The Irish peasant appears in his habit as he lived. Every character that he has drawn is strong, distinct, individual. It is this or that man or woman and no other. Not Rembrandt could put in deeper lights or shadows when required, nor Teniers more minute or life-like touches. For this reason the best of his works at least must prove abiding. They deserve to be treasured as a precious memory, not only by all Irishmen, but by the whole of the Anglo-Saxon race.

WILLIAM GILMORE SIMMS

1806–1870

William Gilmore Simms was born on April 17, 1806, in Charleston, South Carolina, the son of a self-made Irish immigrant father and a mother related to the Virginia gentry. After his mother's death in 1808, his father moved to Mississippi, leaving him in the care of his maternal grandmother. At the age of ten he was asked to choose between his father and grandmother as his legal guardian. Simms rejected the possibility of a life of action on the frontier and remained in Charleston. There, as a young man, he studied law, edited magazines, and published several volumes of poetry at his own expense.

As editor of the Charleston *City Gazette* Simms took an unpopular stand against Nullification in the early 1830s, though he always remained loyal to the Southern cause. Following the deaths within a short span of his father, grandmother, and first wife (by whom he had one child), Simms lived for a while in the North. His next work, the book-length poem *Atalantis: A Story of the Sea*, received favorable notice from William Cullen Bryant, who was to become a lifelong friend. Simms became acquainted with many important authors of the day, including John Pendleton Kennedy, James K. Paulding, and, briefly, Edgar Allan Poe. While he sided with his New York friends in their disputes with the New England writers, he was always scrupulously fair in his reviews of his literary opponents.

In 1833 Simms published his first novel, *Martin Faber*, which was followed in the next decade by twelve more novels, including *Guy Rivers* (1834), the first of his border romances; *The Yemassee* (1835); *The Partisan* (1835), the first of his Revolutionary War romances; *Border Beagles* (1840); and *The Kinsmen* (1841). During this period Simms contributed a vast number of stories, articles, reviews, and poems to periodicals, most of it of very low quality. In 1854 he published what some consider his best novel, *The Sword and the Distaff* (later retitled *Woodcraft*). During his lifetime Simms wrote a total of eighty-two volumes of fiction, poetry, and essays.

During the Civil War Simms suffered the loss of his second wife (who bore him fourteen children, only six of whom were to survive him), and his house and library were destroyed by General Sherman's army. For the remaining years of his life he accepted whatever humble literary work he could find in an effort to regain his fortune and support his family.

Simms died in Charleston on June 11, 1870. A popular writer during much of his lifetime, Simms is today considered a central figure in the literary tradition of the Old South. Five volumes of his letters were published between 1952 and 1956 by the University of South Carolina Press, which is issuing a centennial edition of his writings.

Personal

For my part, and for the last six months, I have been literally *hors de combat*, from overwork of the brain—brain sweat—as Ben Jonson called it,—and no body sweat—no physical exercise. In the extremity of my need, I took contracts in N.Y. in the autumn of 1868 for no less than three romances, all to be worked, at the same time. I got advances of money on each of these books, and the sense of obligation pressing upon me, I went rigidly to work, concentrating myself at the desk from 20th. Oct. 1868 to the 1st. July 1869.—nearly 9 months, without walking a mile in a week, riding but twice and absent from work but half a day on each of these occasions. The consequence was that I finished two of the books & broke down on the third, having written during that period some 3000 pages of the measure of these which I now write to you. Dyspepsia, in its most aggravated forms,—Indigestion, Constipation, Nausea, frequent vomitings, occasional vertigo, and, as the safety valve to this, hemorrhoids. From July, when I went North, to the present moment, I have been suffering more or less acutely, and at no time without constant abdominal uneasiness. And so it continues even now, though the symptoms are mitigated. I have been forbidden the studio, & do little beyond my correspondence which, at all times has been very exacting.—WILLIAM GILMORE SIMMS, Letter to Paul Hamilton Hayne (Dec. 22, 1869)

No prim Precisian he! his fluent talk
Roved thro' all topics, vivifying all;
Now deftly ranging level plains of thought,
To sink, anon in metaphysical deeps;
Whence, by caprice of strange transition brought
Outward and upward, the free current sought
Ideal summits, gathering in its course,
Splendid momentum and imperious force,
Till, down it rushed as mighty cataracts fall,
Hurled from gaunt mountain steeps!
Sportive he could be as a gamesome boy!
By Heaven! as 'twere but yesterday, I see
His tall frame quake with throes of jollity;
Hear his rich voice that owned a jovial tone,
Jocund as Falstaff's own;
And catch moist glints of steel-blue eyes o'errun
Sideways, by tiny rivulets of fun!
        —PAUL HAMILTON HAYNE, "In Memoriam, W. Gilmore Simms," 1877

I frequently met Mr. Simms at the houses of New York friends, and in my father's residence. He was a voluble talker and a good letter-writer. There was at the period of my first meeting with Mr. Simms, about 1850, something in his strong, earnest, clean-shaven face, blue eye, and stalwart figure singularly suggestive of Christopher North. When, some sixteen or seventeen years later, I met him for the last time under a friend's roof on the banks of the Hudson, he was much changed in appearance and in spirits—much embittered by his losses, and by the result of the war. Before it came, I had heard from his lips these extravagant words: "If it comes to blows between the North and the South, we will crush you [the North] as I would crush an egg," holding up his clenched hand as if in the act of performing that feat. It must be admitted that few men not in politics did more to bring on hostilities between the two sections than William Gilmore Simms, and few men suffered more from them.—JAMES GRANT WILSON, *Bryant, and His Friends*, 1886, pp. 260–61

General

When twenty-one years old, Mr. Simms was admitted to the bar, and began to practise his profession in his native district; but feeling a deep interest in the political questions which then agitated the country, he soon abandoned the courts, and purchased a daily gazette at Charleston, which he edited for several years, with industry, integrity, and ability. It was, however, unsuccessful, and he lost by it all his property, as well as the prospective earnings of several years. His ardour was not lessened by this failure, and, confident of success, he determined to retrieve his fortune by authorship. He had been married at an early age; his wife, as well as his father, was now dead; and no domestic ties binding him to Charleston, he in the spring of 1832 visited for the first time the northern states. After travelling over the most interesting portions of the country, he paused at the rural village of Hingham, in Massachusetts, and there prepared for the press his principal poetical work, *Atalantis, a Story of the Sea*, which was published at New York in the following winter. This is an imaginative story, in the dramatic form; its plot is exceedingly simple, but effectively managed, and it contains much beautiful imagery, and fine description. While a vessel glides over a summer sea, Leon, one of the principal characters, and his sister Isabel, hear a benevolent spirit of the air warning them of the designs of a sea-god to lure them into peril. ⟨. . .⟩

Soon after the appearance of *Atalantis*, Mr. Simms published, in the *American Quarterly*, a review of Mrs. Trollope's *Domestic Manners of the Americans*, which was reprinted, in several editions, in this country and in England; and in 1833 appeared his first romance, *Martin Faber, the Story of a Criminal*, parts of which had been printed several years before in a magazine conducted by him in Charleston. In the same year he published *The Book of My Lady*, and, in the summer of 1834, *Guy Rivers, a Tale of Georgia*, which was followed by *The Yemassee, The Partisan, Mellichampe, Pelayo, Carl Werner, The Damsel of Darien, The Kinsman, The History of South Carolina, The Blind Heart*, and numerous sketches, reviews, and miscellanies, in the periodicals. Several other works have been generally attributed to him; though the amount of his acknowledged writings seems to be as great as one man could have produced since he commenced his career as an author. His novels have been very popular, particularly in the southern states, the scenery and history of which, several of them are designed to illustrate. They exhibit considerable dramatic power, and some of the characters are drawn with great skill.

His *Southern Passages and Pictures* appeared in New York, in 1839, and he has since published *Florida*, in five cantos, and many shorter poems. They are on a great variety of subjects, and in almost every measure. Among them are several very spirited ballads, founded on Indian traditions and on incidents in the war for independence. His style is free and melodious, his fancy fertile and inventive, and his imagery generally well chosen, though its range is limited; but sometimes his rhymes are imperfect, and his meaning not easily understood. He is strongly attached to his country, but his sympathies seem to me to be too local. The rivers, forests, savannas, and institutions of the south, he regards with feelings similar to those with which Whittier looks upon the mountains, lakes, and social systems of New England.

Mr. Simms is again married, and now resides in the vicinity of Charleston. He is in the meridian of life and energy, and is constantly writing and adding to his reputation. He is retiring in his habits, goes little into society, and keeps aloof from all controversies; finding happiness in the bosom of his family, among his books, and in correspondence and personal intercourse with his literary friends. He is a fine specimen of the true southern gentleman, and combines in himself the high qualities attributed to that character.—RUFUS W. GRISWOLD, William Gilmore Simms," *The Poets and Poetry of America*, 1842, pp. 323–24

The author of *The Yemassee, Guy Rivers, Life of Marion*, and a good many other things of that sort, is a writer of great pretensions and some local reputation. We remember to have read, in some one of the numerous journals which have been illustrated by his genius, an amusing explanation from his pen, addressed to persons who had applied to him for information, of the difference between author and publisher,—the object of it being evidently to tell the public that he was often written to by persons who, being anxious to get his works, very naturally fancied that he was the proper person to obtain them from, and to let the applicants know that the trade part of the book business was in quite different hands. We were struck by the ingenuity of the announcement, and grateful for the information thus condescendingly imparted. We availed ourselves of it to procure some of the volumes, which we proceeded forthwith to read and inwardly digest. Both of these processes were attended with no ordinary difficulties; but we believe we were uncommonly successful at last.

The author of these novels means to be understood as setting up for an original, patriotic, native American writer; but we are convinced that every judicious reader will set him down as uncommonly deficient in the first elements of originality. He has put on the cast-off garments of the British novelists, merely endeavouring to give them an American fit; and, like those fine gentlemen who make up their wardrobes from the second-hand clothing shops, or from the "unparalleled" establishment of Oak Hall, there is in his literary outfits a decided touch of the shabby genteel. The outward form of his novels is that of their English models; the current phrases of sentiment and description, worn threadbare in the circulating libraries, and out at the elbows, are the robes wherewith he covers imperfectly the nakedness of his invention. The *obligato* tone of sentimentality wearisomely drones through the soft passages of the thousand times repeated plot of love. To borrow a metaphor from one of the unhappy experiences of domestic life, the *tender lines* are so old that they are spoiled; they have been kept too long, and the hungriest guest at the "intellectual banquet" finds it nauseating to swallow them.

The style of Mr. Simms—we mean (for, like other great writers, he designates himself by the titles of his chief productions, rarely condescending to the comparative vulgarity of using a proper name), we mean the style of the author of *The Yemassee* and *Guy Rivers*—is deficient in grace, picturesqueness, and point. It shows a mind seldom able to seize the characteristic features of the object he undertakes to describe, and of course his descriptions generally fail of arresting the reader's attention by any beauty or felicity of touch. His characters are vaguely conceived, and either faintly or coarsely drawn. The dramatic parts are but bungling imitations of nature, with little sprightliness or wit, and laboring under a heavy load of words.

This author, as if to carry out more completely the contradiction between his statements of principle and his practice in the matter of originality, published a poem, a few years ago, in palpable imitation of *Don Juan*,—a dull travesty of a most reprehensible model. To read canto after canto of Byron's original, in which vulgar sarcasm and licentiousness were redeemed only here and there by a passage of poetic beauty, was a depressing task in the days of its novelty and freshness; but a pointless revival of its forced wit, its painful grimaces, its affected versification, its stingless satire, without one touch of its poetic beauty or one drop of its poignant wickedness in the stale mixture,—the *heolocrasia* of yesterday's debauch,—was an experiment upon the patience of the much reading and long enduring public which could not possibly be successful. The author of *The Yemassee* has, however, written some well versified short pieces, though we cannot recall a single poem which is likely to survive the occasion which brought it forth.—C. C. FELTON, "Simms's *Stories and Reviews*," *North American Review*, Oct. 1846, pp. 357–59

In that wielding of events, that sacrificing of characters to situations, he stands unsurpassed—to a great extent unapproached. In America, neither Brown nor Cooper is his equal in this regard; though both surpass him far in certain other qualities. Here the contest for first place in general merit, or in the balance of merits (including quantity), lies between our author and Cooper. In characterization and in polish, Cooper has the advantage; while in the energy of action, variety of situations, and perhaps in literal truthfulness of delineation—I mean the absence of fanciful and impossible personages—Mr. Simms has clearly the advantage. In general results—take both for all in all, quantity, versatility, and quality—it may be reasonably questioned whether Mr. Simms has an equal in America. I believe he has not. In general value to his sphere of literature he is *facile princeps* both North and South.—JAMES DAVIDSON, *The Living Writers of the South*, 1869, p. 515

A really *great author* (whether in *prose* or verse) *Simms emphatically was not*, and there is no use in maintaining so fulsome a proposition. But his *talents* were splendid, and his whole life seems to me *noble*, because of the "grit," the perseverance, the indomitable energy which it displayed. I've not the remotest idea that his *works* will endure. They were too carelessly written. They lack the "labor limæ" to an extent which is distressing. Nevertheless Simms is worthy of *all honor*. "God rest his *soul*."—PAUL HAMILTON HAYNE, Letter to Dr. Porcher (Aug. 4, 1870)

No writer of modern times has excelled him in industry; but the rapidity with which his works were produced has had its usual effect. None of them show the matured and symmetrical design which marks a work of art, still less the hand of a master in their execution. There are passages of description in many of his novels that are vivid and picturesque, but the style is often redundant, lacking in repose, and scarcely ever free from provincialisms. The characters are like the lay figures of the studio, useful in exigencies and effective in tableaux, but devoid of interest in themselves. The best of his novels are of the historical kind, in which southern life in early times is painted, such as *The Yemassee* and *Guy Rivers*. The most of

them are irredeemably dull, at least for readers who value their time, and they must surely sink into neglect.—FRANCIS H. UNDERWOOD, A *Hand-Book of English Literature*, 1872, p. 257

Simms, with a downward proclivity toward the Newgate Calendar, began, in 1833, to flood the country with every style of fiction. There was no generation of Southern life which he did not touch upon, and no phase of romantic murder which he did not illustrate. With a feeling for reality, which was unknown to Cooper and Kennedy, a certain cleverness of invention and strong sense of subordination which kept him from the obvious artifices of both these writers, he was a superior student of human nature in the peculiar line which he took, and held his characters more rigidly to the sequence of cause and effect. He reaches the depth of cold horror in *Beauchampe*, while in *The Partisan*, and *Mellichampe* he is at his best as an historical novelist,—making the swamps and swamp-like gloom real, and the play of passions of every shade of wickedness and cunning intensely exciting. The women are something like realities, and act an important part in the drama. The romance is made to seem so much like reality, that one is inclined to accept Simms's pictures as justly characterizing the times. They are pictures of action and the external results of passions, rather than studies in the development of character. If they are not pleasing to the fastidious, yet they have undoubtedly tinted the clear stream of history to the unrefined for a long generation.—JAMES HERBERT MORSE, "The Native Element in American Fiction," *Century Magazine*, June 1883, p. 293

The representative Southern man of letters, after Poe and before Cable, Hayne, and Lanier, was William Gilmore Simms. His brain and pen were never idle, and he essayed nearly every sort of writing. Though far removed, in his South Carolina home, from the greater publishing centres, libraries, colleges, and author-coteries, Simms was poet, dramatist, Shakespearean editor, essayist, aphoristic philosopher, historian, biographer, lecturer, commemorative orator, legislator, pro-slavery apologist, journalist, magazinist, critic, and, above all, novelist. Authors have been hacks, helpers, or wage-earners since the art of writing was invented; but Simms' industry and fertility are remarkable in view of his environment, which was not favorable to such facile and miscellaneous productiveness. The novels, naturally, have survived the other writings, so that the "works" of Simms have come to mean, in publishers' parlance, merely the best of his romantic or historical fictions. The most attractive part of the novels, to tell the truth, is their titles. One rolls from the tongue, with a certain pleasure, the names of Simms' best books: *The Partisan, a Romance of the Revolution; The Yemassee, a Romance of Carolina; Beauchampe, or, The Kentucky Tragedy; Southward Ho! a Spell of Sunshine*. When Southerners took up *The Wigwam and the Cabin* or *Mellichampe, a Legend of the Santee*, the very names made them feel that a literature had sprung from the sod. The whole list of his writings is here and there suggestive of historic men and events in the Carolina belt, or of the romance of adventure and discovery elsewhere in America and abroad; as well as of miscellaneous domestic or cheaply sensational themes. Purely exciting methods—the bowie knife, the struggle, the revenge, the rescue—were often employed by Simms, whose hurried and careless pen would turn from *Eutaw* to *Richard Hurdis, or, The Avenger of Blood*; from *The Damsel of Darien* to *The Kinsmen, or, The Black Riders of the Congaree*; or, again, from far-away *Pelayo, a Story of the Goth* to *The Golden Christmas, a Chronicle of St. John's*,

Berkeley. Simms was a sort of American G. P. R. James, without James' regularity in quality of literary product. His tales highly interested a local audience because of their patriotic and sectional pictures and temper, and they were valued elsewhere as contributions toward the delineation of an important American region in an indigenous fiction. The romantic novelists of the time turned most eagerly toward themes of Indian adventure, pioneer settlement or Revolutionary struggle, and therein they began, at least, to do wisely, according to the limitations of their day. The portrayal of living folk-life was to come later, for in Simms' time a "historic background" was commonly deemed essential. Indeed, the unpolished style, and the constant striving for immediate and striking effects, which characterized his fiction, were unfavorable to the production of novels of society, in the full sense, or of stories recording the characteristic vitality of actual existence in the region best known to the author. This fault was partly incident to the time, which influenced the man unfavorably; for Simms sometimes excelled in spontaneous picturesque description, while his familiar letters or comments on men are couched in excellent and telling phrase. There is no inconsistency in saying that Simms won considerable note because he was so sectional, and has lost it because he was not sectional enough. His stories are Southern and characteristic, but to paint actualities and things present—as do Cable, Miss Murfree, and the interesting group of young Southern writers—was not his chief purpose. The tinge of the past and the imaginary is thrown over most of the plots and descriptions, yet without that full and deliberate idealization which is needed. Hawthorne, in *The Scarlet Letter* or *The Marble Faun,* so describes things far in time or space that the men and women seem of our own spiritual world, and yet are helped or tempted by moral and mental forces from out of the infinite. Cooper, with all his faults, is a novelist of large humanity, and hence a novelist of many lands and of more than one time. We do not ask Simms to be a Hawthorne; but in Cooper's field, at least, he should have been either a romancer of the past or a picturer of the present, if he could not be both. Between the two fields of fiction, as we now insist upon separating them, he has no place. It may be that future fashions in literature will restore to him some part of a lost fame; but such is not likely to be the case. Save for the masters, the world turns its face not backward in the search for stories.—CHARLES F. RICHARDSON, *American Literature, 1607–1885,* 1887, Vol. 2, pp. 398–401

Cooper to-day keeps his place close at the heels of Scott, while Simms is fading into oblivion as fast as G. P. R. James, with whose work his may fairly be compared, although Simms was probably far richer in native gifts.—BRANDER MATTHEWS, "Two Studies of the South" (1892), *Aspects of Fiction,* 1896, p. 38

But the most popular and voluminous of all southern writers of fiction was William Gilmore Simms, a South Carolinian, who died in 1870. He wrote over thirty novels, mostly romances of revolutionary history, southern life, and wild adventure, among the best of which were *The Partisan,* 1835, and *The Yemassee.* Simms was an inferior Cooper with a difference. His novels are good boys' books, but are crude and hasty in composition. He was strongly southern in his sympathies, though his newspaper, the *Charleston City Gazette,* took part against the nullifiers. His miscellaneous writings include several histories and biographies, political tracts, addresses, and critical papers contributed to southern magazines. He also wrote numerous poems, the most ambitious of which was *Atlantis, a Story of the Sea,* 1832. His poems have little value

except as here and there illustrating local scenery and manners, as in *Southern Passages and Pictures,* 1839.—HENRY A. BEERS, *Initial Studies in American Letters,* 1895, p. 175

What Cooper had done for the traditions of the North Simms sought to do in some due measure for those of the South, rich as it was, and is yet, in material for the writer of historical romance. From the days of De Soto's wonderful march until the tribes were removed west of the Mississippi, the Indian had been an ever-present factor in all struggles between his paleface brothers, as well as a romantic actor on his own account. The partisan conflicts in the South during the Revolution, often resulting in brave encounters between a few individuals, made inviting themes for the thrilling narrator. ⟨. . .⟩

Here, let it be remarked parenthetically, that while a few Carolinians never gave Simms due honor, his name will remain one of the brightest on their roll of great names, and will not stand far down the list of pioneer American writers. So rich was his field, so industriously did he labor to overcome early disadvantages, so ample were his talents, and so persistent was his purpose in literature, that something was created which must last. The best will be sifted from the indifferent, and take its place among things of permanent value. The South cannot afford to ignore his work, for, take him all in all, she has produced few greater men—few men who have labored harder to give his section her true place in history and literature.—SAMUEL ALBERT LINK, "William Gilmore Simms," *Pioneers of Southern Literature,* 1896, Vol. 1, pp. 159–60, 193–94

The place of Simms, the veteran in southern letters, is at once honorable and pathetic. Striving against wind and tide, he produced as many stories as Cooper, besides a goodly amount of poetry, biography, and miscellany; but the bulk of his writing was too hasty for immortality. His *Yemassee,* a tale of the great Indian rising in early Carolina, challenged Cooper on his own ground.—KATHARINE LEE BATES, *American Literature,* 1897, p. 277

His works are of value as illustrating the earlier history of the United States, especially in the Carolinas; and to a certain extent the life and manners of the people of those states. He was a very voluminous writer, publishing a good deal of verse, as well as editorial and historical work, and a long series of works of fiction. *The Yemassee,* published in 1835, is thought to be his best work. These romances have spirit and vigor of style, but show the defects of the author's lack of thorough literary training. They will always be of interest, however, as illustrations of the life of the time, and as the only important representative, in the Literature of the period, of the part of the country which was the author's home. Simms' publications number forty-four titles. They include poems, novels, histories, biographies, and critical essays.—CHARLES NOBLE, *Studies in American Literature,* 1898, p. 129

William Gilmore Simms stands apart from the men to whom the writing of books was but a side issue, as the first Southern writer of distinction to follow literature as a profession. This circumstance, involving as it did a long and gallant struggle with adverse conditions, gives him an important place, aside from the intrinsic value of his writings, as the pioneer among the Southern men of letters. Simms was a man of fine physique and vigorous personality, his character was noble and impetuous; he had an instinctive delight in the active and adventurous side of life, and described it in many a stirring romance with a true sympathetic power. He was born in Charleston, and became in after years an important influence in its intellectual and literary life. Simms's life began in struggle and uncertainty, for his father had become financially involved, and moved from place to place in the effort to repair his broken fortunes. The boy's early opportunities for education were scanty. He never went to college, but from the first he was an ardent reader. At eight years of age his lifelong passion for writing had already declared itself. As a youth, he was a druggist's apprentice; then he studied law, and was admitted to the bar in 1827. But before this he had published two volumes of youthful verse, and an irresistible inclination urged him towards literature. After several other ventures in verse Simms published *Martin Faber*, 1833, the first of that long succession of romances of adventure on which his chief claim to be remembered rests. The best of these stories deal with the Colonial life of the South, or with that life during the succeeding period of the Revolution. While far from being a finished writer, Simms had great qualifications for such a task, an enthusiastic love for his State and a close acquaintance with its scenery, a pride in the history of his section, and an intimate knowledge of its past. Behind all this lay the genuine narrative power and vigorous spirit of the man.

Simms is distinctly inferior to Cooper, with whom he inevitably suggests comparison; yet his best stories form a kind of companion study to Cooper's work, depicting as they do the same period of our national growth under Southern instead of under Northern or Western conditions. In his portrayal of the Indian character Simms is probably more truthful than Cooper, whose Indian heroes, if more romantic, are, it is to be feared, more ideal. Among Simms's many books, *The Yemassee* (1835), which deals with an Indian outbreak in Colonial South Carolina, and *The Partisan* (1835), a story of the Revolution and the exploits of Marion and his band, may be mentioned as good examples of his powers. Charleston may be thought of as the nearest approach the South had to a literary center in Simms's time, yet Charleston was slow to recognize him, and he was often forced to look to the North for help and encouragement. Many of his works were published in New York, and once on returning from a trip to that city he declared bitterly that he was surprised to find the North so warm and the South so cold. But Simms was a man of generous, helpful temper, and, although nearly ruined by the Civil War, he did all in his power for the younger literary men who were trying to force their way to the front.—HENRY S. PANCOAST, *An Introduction to American Literature*, 1898, pp. 254–56

EDGAR ALLAN POE
From "William Gilmore Simms" (1846)
Essays and Reviews, ed. G. R. Thompson
1984, pp. 902–5

Mr. Simms, we believe, made his first, or nearly his first, appearance before an American audience with a small volume entitled *Martin Faber*, an amplification of a much shorter fiction. He had some difficulty in getting it published, but the Harpers finally undertook it, and it did credit to their judgment. It was well received both by the public and the more discriminative few, although some of the critics objected that the story was an imitation of *Miserrimus*, a very powerful fiction by the author of *Pickwick Abroad*. The original tale, however—the germ of *Martin Faber*—was written long before the publication of *Miserrimus*. But independently of this fact, there is not the slightest ground for the charge of imitation. The thesis and incidents of the two works are totally dissimi-

lar;—the idea of resemblance arises only from the absolute identity of *effect* wrought by both.

Martin Faber was succeeded, at short intervals, by a great number and variety of fictions, some brief, but many of the ordinary novel size. Among these we may notice *Guy Rivers*, *The Partisan*, *The Yemassee*, *Mellichampe*, *Beauchampe*, and *Richard Hurdis*. The last two were issued anonymously, the author wishing to ascertain whether the success of his books (which was great) had anything to do with his mere name as the writer of previous works. The result proved that popularity, in Mr. Simms' case, arose solely from intrinsic merit, for *Beauchampe* and *Richard Hurdis* were the most popular of his fictions, and excited very general attention and curiosity. *Border Beagles* was another of his anonymous novels, published with the same end in view, and, although disfigured by some instances of bad taste, was even more successful than *Richard Hurdis*.

The "bad taste" of the *Border Beagles* was more particularly apparent in *The Partisan*, *The Yemassee*, and one or two other of the author's earlier works, and displayed itself most offensively in a certain fondness for the purely disgusting or repulsive, where the intention was or should have been merely the horrible. The writer evinced a strange propensity for minute details of human and brute suffering, and even indulged at times in more unequivocal obscenities. His English, too, was, in his efforts, exceedingly objectionable—verbose, involute, and not unfrequently ungrammatical. He was especially given to pet words, of which we remember at present only "*hug*," "*coil*," and the compound "*old-time*," and introduced them upon all occasions. Neither was he at this period particularly dexterous in the conduct of his stories. His improvement, however, was rapid at all these points, although, on the first counts of our indictment, there is still abundant room for improvement. But whatever may have been his early defects, or whatever are his present errors, there can be no doubt that from the very beginning he gave evidence of genius, and that of no common order. His *Martin Faber*, in our opinion, is a more forcible story than its supposed prototype *Miserrimus*. The difference in the American reception of the two is to be referred to the fact (we blush while recording it), that *Miserrimus* was understood to be the work of an Englishman, and *Martin Faber* was known to be the composition of an American as yet unaccredited in our Republic of Letters. The fiction of Mr. Simms gave indication, we repeat, of genius, and that of no common order. Had he been even a Yankee, this genius would have been rendered *immediately* manifest to his countrymen, but unhappily (*perhaps*) he was a southerner, and united the southern pride—the southern dislike to the making of bargains—with the southern supineness and general want of tact in all matters relating to the making of money. His book, therefore, depended entirely upon its own intrinsic value and resources, but with these it made its way in the end. The "intrinsic value" consisted first of a very vigorous imagination in the conception of the story; secondly, in artistic skill manifested in its conduct; thirdly, in general vigour, life, movement—the whole resulting in deep interest on the part of the reader. These high qualities Mr. Simms has carried with him in his subsequent books; and they are qualities which, above all others, the fresh and vigorous intellect of America should and does esteem. It may be said, upon the whole, that while there are several of our native writers who excel the author of *Martin Faber* at particular *points*, there is, nevertheless, not one who surpasses him in the aggregate of the higher excellences of fiction. We confidently expect him to do much for the lighter literature of his country.

The volume now before us has a title which may mislead the reader. *The Wigwam and the Cabin* is merely a generic phrase, intended to designate the subject matter of a series of short tales, most of which have first seen the light in the Annuals. "The material employed," says the author, "will be found to illustrate in large degree, the border history of the south. I can speak with confidence of the general truthfulness of its treatment. The life of the planter, the squatter, the Indian, the negro, the bold and hardy pioneer, and the vigorous yeoman—these are the subjects. In their delineation I have mostly drawn from living portraits, and, in frequent instances, from actual scenes and circumstances within the memories of men."

All the tales in this collection have merit, and the first has merit of a very peculiar kind. "Grayling, or Murder Will Out," is the title. The story was well received in England, but on this fact no opinion can be safely based. *The Athenæum*, we believe, or some other of the London weekly critical journals, having its attention called (no doubt through personal influence) to Carey & Hart's beautiful annual *The Gift*, found it convenient, in the course of its notice, to speak at length of some one particular article, and "Murder Will Out" probably arrested the attention of the sub-sub-editor who was employed in so trivial a task as the patting on the head an American book—arrested his attention first from its title, (murder being a taking theme with a cockney,) and secondly, from its details of southern forest scenery. Large quotations were made, as a matter of course, and very ample commendation bestowed—the whole criticism proving nothing, in our opinion, but that the critic had not read a single syllable of the story. The *critique*, however, had at least the good effect of calling American attention to the fact that an American might possibly do a decent thing, (provided the possibility were first admitted by the British sub-editors,) and the result was first, that many persons read, and secondly, that all persons admired the "excellent story in *The Gift* that had actually been called 'readable' by one of the English newspapers."

Now had "Murder Will Out" been a much worse story than was ever written by Professor Ingraham, still, under the circumstances, we patriotic and independent Americans would have declared it inimitable; but, by some species of odd accident, it happened to deserve all that the British sub-sub had condescended to say of it, on the strength of a guess as to what it was all about. It is really an admirable tale, nobly conceived and skilfully carried into execution—the best ghost story ever written *by an American*—for we presume that this is the ultimate extent of commendation to which we, as an humble American, dare go.

The other stories of the volume do credit to the author's abilities, and display their peculiarities in a strong light, but there is no one of them so good as "Murder Will Out."

WILLIAM P. TRENT
From *William Gilmore Simms*
1892, pp. 327–32

There is little reason to differ from Hayne with regard to the quality of Simms's literary work. "A really great author," he "emphatically was not;" a talented author he undoubtedly was. His failure in poetry was marked because the unfavorable influences of his environment, combined with the unfavorable characteristics of his inherited temperament, naturally showed to their fullest effect in that region of art where individual peculiarities are least tolerable. It has been shown already how impossible it was that the ante-bellum South should produce a great artist in verse; and Simms's failure is rendered all the more conspicuous from the fact that he endeavored to excel in forms of poetry that require the highest artistic skill. But even if he had written poetry, it would still have been *English* poetry, which would not have suited his patriotic American heart. So after all there is no great reason to be sorry for the fate of his verses. Yet it should not be forgotten that his poetry was a great solace to him, and that it lifted him above this earth and its cares, and that as no one need read it who does not wish to, no one is any the worse for it.

With regard to his prose, attention must be confined to his revolutionary and colonial romances. If the quality of permanence is to be found in his work, it is to be found here. His miscellaneous critical, political, and biographical work has served its transitory purpose and is already forgotten. His historical work will be consulted occasionally by special students, but is of little general value. It is of far more value, to the Southerner at least, to know that Simms never ceased to bewail the indifference of his people to their own history, and that he never failed to encourage local students like Pickett and Meek of Alabama to prosecute and publish their researches. When the Southern people get a true history of themselves, they will find that they have many things to learn and to unlearn; and one of the things they will vainly wish to forget will be their utter indifference to the unseconded and uncheered efforts of men like Simms, to rescue the history of their State and section from the dust of oblivion.

To return however to the main question: Will the revolutionary and colonial romances be read, say fifty years hence? The border romances are omitted from consideration for the already expressed reason that they should never have been written, since they have nothing ennobling in them. If the friends of romance are to make any firm stand against the attacks of the realists, they must make it right here, on the essentially ennobling qualities of great romances. That the romance, in its old form at least, will play again a serious part in the history of literature is open to grave doubt. Literary forms, like nations, seem to play their parts and then retire from the stage. But because no Englishman will ever again write a great epic is no reason why *Paradise Lost* should cease to delight us. And so, because we shall see no more Scotts or Coopers is no reason why we should prophesy a day of oblivion for their works. If their works fill any one of the world's various needs, they will be preserved in the world's memory and regard. Yet it would seem that their works ennoble all who read them in the right spirit, and that therefore their works will live; for it is no little thing to ennoble a man's mind and heart, and it is perhaps as useful a thing to ennoble a boy's mind and heart. Hence, if Scott and Cooper become more and more the authors of boyhood, their place will be no less honorable and secure.

But was Poe right when he ranked Simms above the herd of American romancers, just after Cooper and Brockden Brown, and are Simms's best romances ennobling? It would seem that Poe was right. Cooper at his best is superior to Simms at his best, and there is no need to compare them at their worst. Brockden Brown, though a follower of Godwin, had a narrow vein of real genius, which can hardly be asserted of Simms. In versatility and talents Brown was Simms's inferior, and in estimating the work of the two writers one is almost inclined, in balancing quantity with quality of work (a process which most critics neglect), to place the two men upon the same level. Any comparison with Hawthorne is of course out of the question. With regard to romancers like Dr. Bird, Kennedy, and Paulding, to say nothing of writers like Miss Sedgwick or Dr. Mayo or Melville, Poe would appear to have stated Simms's position correctly. Both with regard to quantity as well as quality of work he is their superior. His style at its best is not inferior to theirs, and with none of them is it safe to make much question of style. He was more frequently slipshod than they, but that is all that can be said in their favor. In imaginative vigor, in power of description, in the faculty of giving movement to his stories, he leaves them behind. He strikes one as being a born writer, a professional; their works read like those of amateurs.

To consider now the second question: Are his best romances ennobling? In some respects it would seem that they are. They deal with an eventful period, when a young people was struggling for its rights. They show how high and low, rich and poor, were animated by a common patriotism, how they suffered for the cause they espoused, how they triumphed through their bravery and faith. They make the reader familiar with great characters like Marion, and with historic events of no little importance to a nation destined to greatness. Moreover they are full of the freshness of swamp and forest, of the languorous charm of Southern climate and scenery. Then, too, they are full of the heroic deeds of common, unlettered men, and are thus more stimulating than many of those high-flying romances in which lords and ladies undergo their remarkable adventures. It is true, on the other hand, that they are full of an unregulated patriotism which regards every Tory and Englishman, with a few exceptions, as a brute and a villain; that they deal with bloodshed and crime *ad nauseam*; that they are in many places commonplace and dull. Still, after all is said, it would seem that the balance stands in Simms's favor. He has described with vigor, and sometimes with charm, the events of an interesting epoch; he has reproduced the characteristic features of a life that is gone; he has painted a landscape, which, if it still exists, has nevertheless been subject to many changes. No one will ever do the same work as well, and it was worth doing. Hence I cannot conclude with Hayne that his works will die. They will never be very popular, at least

with older readers, but boys will continue to delight in the daring deeds of scout and partisan, and cultivated and curious persons will turn to them as faithful pictures of interesting epochs in their country's history.

But here, too, it must again be noted that Simms was more English than he thought himself. There was of course more room for originality in his essays in prose fiction than in his poetry,—his excursions into the realms of what Mr. Theodore Watts is fond of denominating "essential art." His methods were, however, those of his English predecessors, and whenever he took his eye off his local subject he wrote like an Englishman. He made constant use of the stock materials of former and contemporary romancers, and the comparison which more than one writer has instituted between him and the English G. P. R. James is in many respects admissible. But Simms had what James had not: a small particular field which he made his own, and that field was essentially American. For this reason he will live longer than James, and for this reason he deserves a place among American men of letters. His place is not a high one; but it should never be forgotten that he was not only a pioneer, but *the* pioneer, of American literature, whose destiny forced him to labor in the least favorable section of all America for successful literary work. When his environment is considered, the work he did will be deemed worthy of admiration rather than of fault-finding.

Yes, Hayne was right. The man Simms "is worthy of all honor." Whether as a literary toiler, working successfully under most harassing conditions; whether as a misguided patriot, striving for what he believed to be his section's good; whether as a defeated, worn-out spirit, laboring to relieve the distresses of his children and his friends, the man Simms ceases to be a mere man and assumes proportions that are truly heroic. His State may still point to her Calhouns and McDuffies, and his section may point to politicians and soldiers, contemporary lights that have cast and still cast him in the shade; but it is doubtful whether South Carolina, or indeed the whole South, has produced in this century a man who will better stand a close scrutiny into his motives and his life-work than William Gilmore Simms.

CHARLES DICKENS

1812–1870

Charles John Huffam Dickens was born in Landport, Portsmouth, on February 7, 1812. The family moved to London in 1814, to Chatham in 1817, and then back to London in 1822. By 1824 increasing financial difficulties led Dickens's parents to put him to work at a shoe-blacking warehouse; later that same year his father was briefly imprisoned for debt. Memories of this painful period in his life were to affect much of Dickens's later writing, in particular the early chapters of *David Copperfield.*

After studying at the Wellington House Academy in London (1824–27), Dickens worked as a solicitor's clerk (1827–28), and then became a reporter for the *Morning Chronicle* (1834–36). In 1836–37 a collection of articles contributed to various periodicals appeared in two volumes as *Sketches by "Boz," Illustrative of Every-Day Life and Every-Day People.* This was followed by the enormously popular *Posthumous Papers of the Pickwick Club,* published in twenty monthly numbers (beginning in April 1836) and appearing in book form, as a loosely constructed novel, in 1837. Also in 1836 Dickens married Catherine Hogarth, by whom he had ten children before their separation in 1858.

Between 1837 and 1839 Dickens published a second novel, *Oliver Twist,* in monthly numbers in *Bentley's Miscellany,* a new periodical of which Dickens was the first editor. This was followed in 1838–39 by *Nicholas Nickelby*, another novel that appeared in monthly installments. In 1840 Dickens founded his own weekly, *Master Humphrey's Clock* (1840–41), in which appeared his novels *The Old Curiosity Shop* (1840–41) and *Barnaby Rudge* (1841). In 1842 he and his wife visited the United States and Canada, and after returning Dickens published *American Notes* (1842), two volumes of impressions which caused much offense in the U.S. He then wrote *Martin Chuzzlewit*, a novel set partly in America, which appeared in monthly installments between 1843 and 1844.

In 1843 Dickens published *A Christmas Carol*, the first in a series of Christmas books, the others being *The Chimes* (1844), *The Cricket on the Hearth* (1845), *The Battle of Life* (1846), and *The Haunted Man* (1848). In 1846 he founded the Radical *Daily News*, which he briefly edited himself, and to which he contributed "Pictures of Italy," after visiting Italy in 1844 and again in 1845. During a visit to Switzerland in 1846 Dickens wrote his novel *Dombey and Son*, which appeared in monthly parts between 1846 and 1848. In 1850 he started the periodical *Household Words*; in 1859 it was incorporated into *All the Year Round*, which Dickens continued to edit until his death. Much of his later work was published in these two periodicals, including *David Copperfield* (1849–50), *Bleak House* (1852–53), *Hard Times* (1854), *Little Dorrit* (1855–57), *A Tale of Two Cities* (1859), *Great Expectations* (1860–61), and *Our Mutual Friend* (1864–65).

During these years of intense productivity Dickens also found time to direct amateur theatrical productions, sometimes of his own plays. He also became involved in a variety of philanthropical activities, gave public readings, and in 1867–68 visited America for a second time. Dickens died suddenly in 1870 on June 9, leaving unfinished his last novel, *The Mystery of Edwin Drood*, which was first published later that same year. Several editions of his collected letters have been published. Despite Dickens's tremendous popularity during and after his own life, it was not until the twentieth century that serious critical studies began to appear. Modern critical opinion has tended to favor the later works, which are more somber and complex, over the earlier ones, which are characterized by boisterous humor and broad caricature.

Personal

He is a fine little fellow, Boz, as I think; clear blue intelligent eyes, eyebrows that he arches amazingly, large protrusive rather loose mouth,—a face of the most extreme *mobility*, which he shuttles about, eyebrows, eyes, mouth and all, in a very singular manner while speaking; surmount this with a loose coil of common-coloured hair, and set it on a small compact figure, very small, and dressed rather *à la d'Orsay* than well: this is Pickwick; for the rest a quiet shrewd-looking little fellow, who seems to guess pretty well what he is, and what others are.—THOMAS CARLYLE, Letter to John A. Carlyle (March 17, 1840)

Arrival of Charles Dickens. Among the passengers in the *Britannia* is Mr. Charles Dickens and his wife. This gentleman is the celebrated "Boz," whose name "rings through the world with loud applause"; the fascinating writer whose fertile imagination and ready pen conceived and sketched the immortal Pickwick, his prince of valets and his bodyguard of choice cronies, who has made us laugh with "Mantalini," and cry with "poor little Nell," caused us to shrink with horror from the effects of lynch law, as administered by the misguided Lord George Gordon, and to listen with unmitigated delight to the ticking of "Master Humphrey's Clock." The visit of this popular writer has been heralded in advance. He was expected by this packet, and I signed three or four days ago, with a number of other persons, a letter to be presented to him on his arrival in this city, giving him a hearty welcome and inviting him to a public dinner, which, from the spirit which appears to prevail on the subject, will be no common affair.—PHILIP HONE, *Diary*, Jan. 24, 1842

Called on Dickens at 10.30 A.M. by appointment, as he leaves at one. He was at breakfast. Sat down with him. He was very agreeable and full of life. He is the *cleverest* man I ever met. I mean he impresses you more with the alertness of his various powers. His forces are all light infantry and light cavalry, and always in marching order. There are not many heavy pieces, but few *sappers and miners*, the scientific corps is deficient, and I fear there is no chaplain in the garrison.—RICHARD HENRY DANA, *Journal* (Feb. 5, 1842), cited in Charles Francis Adams, *Richard Henry Dana: A Biography*, 1890, Vol. 1, p. 33

I admire and love the man exceedingly, for he has a deep warm heart, a noble sympathy with and respect for human nature, and great intellectual gifts wherewith to make these fine moral ones fruitful for the delight and consolation and improvement of his fellow-beings.—FRANCES ANN KEMBLE, Letter (April 22, 1842), *Records of a Later Life*, 1882, p. 318

At a dinner-party at Mr. Holland's last evening, a gentleman, in instance of Charles Dickens's unweariability, said that during some theatrical performances in Liverpool he acted in play and farce, spent the rest of the night making speeches, feasting, and drinking at table, and ended at seven o'clock in the morning by jumping leap-frog over the backs of the whole company.—NATHANIEL HAWTHORNE, *The English Note-Books*, Oct. 22, 1853

Dickens is forty-five years old, cheerful, amiable, noble, and good. However highly I may place him as an author, I must prize him just as highly as an actor in tragedy, as well as in comedy.—HANS CHRISTIAN ANDERSEN, Letter to the Grand Duke of Weimar (Aug. 9, 1857)

Of his attractive points in society and conversation I have particularised little, because in truth they were himself. Such as they were, they were never absent from him. His acute sense of enjoyment gave such relish to his social qualities that probably no man, not a great wit or a professed talker, ever left, in leaving any social gathering, a blank so impossible to fill up. In quick and varied sympathy, in ready adaptation to every whim or humour, in help to any mirth or game, he stood for a dozen men. If one may say such a thing, he seemed to be always the more himself for being somebody else, for continually putting off his personality. His versatility made him unique.—JOHN FORSTER, *The Life of Charles Dickens*, 1872–74, Bk. 11, Ch. 3

In publishing the more private letters, we do so with the view of showing him in his homely, domestic life—of showing how in the midst of his own constant and arduous work, no household matter was considered too trivial to claim his care and attention. He would take as much pains about the hanging of a picture, the choosing of furniture, the superintending any little improvement in the house, as he would about the more serious business of his life; thus carrying out to the very letter his favourite motto of "What is worth doing at all is worth doing well."—MAMIE DICKENS, GEORGINA HOGARTH, "Preface" to *The Letters of Charles Dickens*, 1882, Vol. 1, p. viii

His extraordinary charm of manner, never capriciously changed, the smile and laugh always ready—that sympathy, too, which rises before me, and was really unique—I can call no one to mind that possessed it or possesses it now in the same degree.—PERCY FITZGERALD, "Charles Dickens as an Editor," *Recreations of a Literary Man*, 1882, pp. 31–32

Dickens was only thirty-three when I first saw him, being just two years my junior. I have said what he appeared to me then. As I knew him afterwards, and to the end of his days, he was a strikingly manly man, not only in appearance but in bearing. The lustrous brilliancy of his eyes was very striking. And I do not think that I have ever seen it noticed, that those wonderful eyes which saw so much and so keenly, were appreciably, though to a very slight degree, near sighted eyes. Very few persons, even among those who knew him well, were aware of this, for Dickens never used a glass. But he continually exercised his vision by looking at distant objects, and making them out as well as he could without any artificial assistance. It was an instance of that force of will in him, which compelled a naturally somewhat delicate frame to comport itself like that of an athlete. Mr. Forster somewhere says of him, 'Dickens's habits were robust, but his health was not.' This is entirely true as far as my observation extends.

Of the general charm of his manner I despair of giving any idea to those who have not seen or known him. This was a charm by no means dependent on his genius. He might have been the great writer he was and yet not have warmed the social atmosphere wherever he appeared with that summer glow which seemed to attend him. His laugh was brimful of enjoyment. There was a peculiar humorous protest in it when recounting or hearing anything specially absurd, as who should say ''Pon my soul this is *too* ridiculous! This passes all bounds!' and bursting out afresh as though the sense of the ridiculous overwhelmed him like a tide, which carried all hearers away with it, and which I well remember. His enthusiasm was boundless. It entered into everything he said or did. It belonged doubtless to that amazing fertility and wealth of ideas and feeling that distinguished his genius.—THOMAS ADOLPHUS TROLLOPE, *What I Remember*, 1888

General

His more obvious excellences are of the kind which are easily understood by all classes—by the stable-boy as well as the statesman. His intimate knowledge of character, his familiarity with the language and experience of low life, his genuine humor, his narrative power, and the cheerfulness of his philosophy, are traits that impress themselves on minds of every description. But, besides these, he has many characteristics to interest the higher orders of mind. They are such as to recommend him peculiarly to Americans. His sympathies seek out that class with which American institutions and laws sympathize most strongly. He has found subjects of thrilling interest in the passions, sufferings, and virtues of the mass. As Dr. Channing has said, "he shows that life in its rudest form may wear a tragic grandeur, that, amid follies or excesses provoking laughter or scorn, the moral feelings do not wholly die, and that the haunts of the blackest crime are sometimes lighted up by the presence and influence of the noblest souls." Here we have the secret of the attentions that have been showered upon Mr. Dickens. That they may have been carried too far is possible; yet we are disposed to regard them, even in their excess, with favor. We have so long been accustomed to seeing the homage of the multitude paid to men of mere titles, or military chieftains, that we have grown tired of it. We are glad to see the mind asserting its supremacy, to find its rights more generally recognized. We rejoice that a young man, without birth, wealth, title, or a sword, whose only claims to distinction are in his intellect and heart, is received with a feeling that was formerly rendered only to kings and conquerors. The author, by his genius, has contributed happy moments to the lives of thousands, and it is right that the thousands should recompense him for the gift.—WILLIAM CULLEN BRYANT, *New York Evening Post* (Feb. 18, 1842), cited in Parke Godwin, *A Biography of William Cullen Bryant*, 1883, Vol. 1, pp. 396–97

Do you know that the royal Boz lives close to us, three doors from Mr. Kenyon in Harley Place? The new numbers appear to me admirable, and full of life and blood—whatever we may say to the thick rouging and extravagance of gesture. There is a beauty, a tenderness, too, in the organ scene, which is worthy of the gilliflowers. But my admiration for 'Boz' fell from its 'sticking place,' I confess, a good furlong, when I read Victor Hugo; and my creed is, that, *not* in his tenderness, which is as much his own as his humour, but in his serious powerful Jew-trial scenes, he has followed Hugo closely, and never scarcely looked away from *Les Trois jours d'un condamné.*—ELIZABETH BARRETT BROWNING, Letter to James Martin (Feb. 6, 1843)

The immediate and almost unprecedented popularity he attained was owing not more to his own genius than to the general contempt for the school he supplanted. After ten years of conventional frippery and foppery, it was a relief to have once more a view of the earth and firmament,—to feel once more one of those touches of nature "which make the whole world kin." Here was a man, at last, with none of the daintiness of genteel society in his manner, belonging to no clique or sect, with sympathies embracing widely varying conditions of humanity, and whose warm heart and observant eye had been collecting from boyhood those impressions of man and nature which afterwards gushed out in exquisite descriptions of natural scenery, or took shape in his Pickwicks, Wellers, Vardens, Pecksniffs, and their innumerable brotherhood.

Dickens, as a novelist and prose poet, is to be classed in the front rank of the noble company to which he belongs. He has revived the novel of genuine practical life, as it existed in the works of Fielding, Smollett, and Goldsmith, but at the same time has given to his materials an individual coloring and expression peculiarly his own. His characters, like those of his great exemplars, constitute a world of their own, whose truth to nature every reader instinctively recognized in connection with their truth to Dickens. Fielding delineates with more exquisite art, standing more as the spectator of his personages, and commenting on their actions with an ironical humor, and a seeming innocence of insight, which pierces not only into but through their very nature, laying bare their inmost unconscious springs of action, and in every instance indicating that he understands them better than they understand themselves. It is this perfection of knowledge and insight which gives to his novels their naturalness, their freedom of movement, and their value as lessons in human nature as well as consummate representations of actual life. Dickens's eye for the forms of things is as accurate as Fielding's, and his range of vision more extended; but he does not probe so profoundly into the heart of what he sees, and he is more led away from the simplicity of truth by a tricksy spirit of fantastic exaggeration. Mentally he is indisputably below Fielding; but in tenderness, in pathos, in sweetness and purity of feeling, in that comprehensiveness of sympathy which springs from a sense of brotherhood with mankind, he is as indisputably above him.

The tendency of Dickens's genius, both in delineating the actual and the imaginary, is to personify, to individualize. This makes his page all alive with character. Not only does he never treat of man in the abstract, but he gives personality to the rudest shows of nature, everything he touches becoming symbolic of human sympathies or antipathies. There is no writer more deficient in generalization. His comprehensiveness is altogether of the heart, but that heart, like the intelligence of Bacon's cosmopolite, is not "an island cut off from other men's lands, but a continent which joins to them." His observation of life thus beginning and ending with individuals, it seems strange that those highly sensitive and patriotic Americans who paid him the compliment of flying into a passion with his peevish remarks on our institutions, should have overlooked the fact that his mind was altogether destitute of the generalizing qualities of a statesman, and that an angry humorist might have made equally ludicrous pictures of any existing society. When his work on America was quoted in the French Chamber of Deputies, M. de Tocqueville ridiculed the notion that any opinions of Mr. Dickens should be referred to in that place as authoritative. There is a great difference between the criticism of a statesman and the laughter of a tourist, especially when the tourist laughs not from his heart, but his bile. The statesman passes over individual peculiarities to seize on general principles, while the whole force of the other lies in the description of individual peculiarities. Dickens, detecting with the nicest tact the foibles of men, and capable of setting forth our Bevans, Colonel Tompkinses, and Jefferson Bricks, in all the comic splendor of humorous exaggeration, is still unqualified to abstract a general idea of national character from his observation of persons. A man immeasurably inferior to him in creative genius might easily excel him in that operation of the mind. Indeed, were Dickens's understanding as comprehensive as his heart, and as vigorous as his fancy, he would come near realizing the ideal of a novelist; but, as it is, it is as ridiculous to be angry with any generalizations of his on American institutions and politics, as it would be to inveigh against him for any heresies he might blunder into about innate ideas, the freedom of the will, or original sin. Besides, as Americans, we have a decided advantage over our transatlantic friends, even in the matter of being caricatured by the novelist whom both are rivals in admiring; for certainly, if there be any character in which Dickens has seized on a national trait, that character is Pecksniff, and that national trait is English.

The whole originality and power of Dickens lies in this instinctive insight into individual character, to which we have already referred. He has gleaned all his facts from observation and sympathy, in a diligent scrutiny of actual life, and no contemporary author is less indebted to books. His style is all his own, its quaint texture of fancy and humor being spun altogether from his own mind, with hardly a verbal felicity which bears the mark of being stolen. In painting character he is troubled by no uneasy sense of himself. When he is busy with Sam Weller or Mrs. Nickleby, he forgets Charles Dickens. Not taking his own character as the test of character, but entering with genial warmth into the peculiarities of others, and making their joys and sorrows his own, his perceptions are not bounded by his personality, but continually apprehend and interpret new forms of individual being; and thus his mind, by the readiness with which it genially assimilates other minds, and the constancy with which it is fixed on objects external to itself, grows with every exercise of its powers. By this felicity of nature, the man who began his literary life with a condemned farce, a mediocre opera, and some slight sketches of character, written in a style which but feebly indicated the germs of genius, produced before the expiration of eight years, *The Pickwick Papers*, *Oliver Twist*, *Nicholas Nickleby*, *The Old Curiosity Shop*, and *Martin Chuzzlewit*, in a continually ascending scale of intellectual excellence, and achieved a fame not only gladly recognized wherever the English tongue was spoken, but which extended into France, Germany, Italy, and Holland, and caused the translation of his works into languages of which he hardly understood a word. Had he been an egotist, devoured by a ravenous vanity for personal display, and eager to print the image of himself on the popular imagination, his talents would hardly have made him known beyond the street in which he lived, and his mind by self-admiration would soon have been self-consumed. His fellow-feeling with his race is his genius.—EDWIN P. WHIPPLE, "Novels and Novelists: Charles Dickens" (1844), *Literature and Life*, 1849, pp. 58–63

As when a friend (himself in music's list)
Stands by some rare, full-handed organist,
And glorying as he sees the master roll
The surging sweets through all their depths of soul,
Cannot, encouraged by his smile, forbear
With his own hand to join them here and there;
And so, if little, yet add something more
To the sound's volume and the golden roar;

So I, dear friend, Charles Dickens, though thy hand
Needs but itself, to charm from land to land,
Make bold to join in summoning men's ears
To this thy new-found music of our spheres,
In hopes that by thy Household Words and thee
The world may haste to days of harmony.
                    —LEIGH HUNT, "To Charles Dickens," 1849

The English novels of these days seem to me the more detestable the one than the other—Dickens all cant (Liberal cant, the worst sort) and caricature.—MARY RUSSELL MITFORD, Letter to Mr. Starkey (Jan. 31, 1853)

We have one great novelist who is gifted with the utmost power of rendering the external traits of our town population; and if he could give us their psychological character—their conceptions of life, and their emotions—with the same truth as their idiom and manners, his books would be the greatest contribution Art has ever made to the awakening of social sympathies. But while he can copy Mrs. Plornish's colloquial style with the delicate accuracy of a sun-picture, while there is the same startling inspiration in his description of the gestures and phrases of "Boots," as in the speeches of Shakespeare's mobs or numskulls, he scarcely ever passes from the humorous and external to the emotional and tragic, without becoming as transcendent in his unreality as he was a moment before in his artistic truthfulness. But for the precious salt of his humour, which compels him to reproduce external traits that serve, in some degree, as a corrective to his frequently false psychology, his preternaturally virtuous poor children and artisans, his melodramatic boatmen and courtesans, would be as noxious as Eugène Sue's idealized proletaires in encouraging the miserable fallacy that high morality and refined sentiment can grow out of harsh social relations, ignorance, and want; or that the working classes are in a condition to enter at once into a millennial state of *altruism*, wherein every one is caring for every one else, and no one for himself.—GEORGE ELIOT, "Natural History of German Life: Riehl," 1856

Dickens, with preternatural apprehension of the language of manners and the varieties of street life; with pathos and laughter, with patriotic and still enlarging generosity, writes London tracts. He is a painter of English details, like Hogarth; local and temporary in his tints and style, and local in his aims.—RALPH WALDO EMERSON, "Literature," *English Traits*, 1856

⟨. . .⟩ if we glance over the wit and satire of the popular writers of the day, we shall find that the *manner* of it, so far as it is distinctive, is always owing to Dickens; and that out of his first exquisite ironies branched innumerable other forms of wit, varying with the disposition of the writers; original in the matter and substance of them, yet never to have been expressed as they now are, but for Dickens.—JOHN RUSKIN, *Modern Painters*, 1856, Vol. 3, Pt. 4, App. 3

And his genius is worthy of honor. No writer could be named on whom the indefinable gift has been more manifestly conferred. His early works are all aglow with genius. The supreme potency with which he commands it, is shown in the total absence of effort, in the classic chasteness and limpid flow, of thought, fancy, and diction. You are in a meadow just after dawn; the flowers are fresh as if they had awakened from slumber, and the dew is on them all. A word, an idea, a glimpse of beauty, is always at hand; the writer never tarries a moment; yet there is no display, no profusion, of opulence. You do not see him waving the wand; the tear of the smile is on your cheek before you are aware.

The distinctive power of Dickens lies, we think, in a sympathy of extraordinary range, exquisite delicacy, and marvellous truth. He does not so much look, with steady, unparticipating gaze, until he knows and remembers the exact features of life: he feels. With all human sorrow he could weep; with all human mirth he could laugh; and when he came to write, every emotion he aimed at exciting was made sure, by being first experienced in his own breast. It was not with the individual man, in the wholeness of his life, in the depths of his identity, that he naturally concerned himself. It was kindness, rather than the one kind man, that he saw. It was mirth, rather than the whole character which is modified by humor. Qualities, capacities, characteristics, rather than complete men, glassed themselves in the mirror of his clear and open soul. With all his accuracy in detailed portraiture, it is a superficial perception of the order of his genius, which does not see that its power rested naturally less on realism, than on a peculiar, delicate and most captivating idealization. Pickwick, at least in the whole earlier part of his history, is an impossible personage. He belongs to broad farce. But we laugh at his impossible conversation with the cabman. We laugh at his impossible credulity as he listens to Jingle. We laugh at his impossible simplicity at the review. The far-famed Sam Weller, too, corresponds to no reality. The Londoner born and

bred is apt to be the driest and most uninteresting of beings. All things lost for him the gloss of novelty when he was fifteen years old. He would suit the museum of a *nil admirari* philosopher, as a specimen, shrivelled and adust, of the ultimate result of his principle. But Dickens collected more jokes than all the cabmen in London would utter in a year, and bestowed the whole treasure upon Sam. His eye was far too acute for the comical to let it rest on any one funny man. In the case of those of his characters whom we are simply to admire and love, the same distinctive mode of treatment is exhibited. Rose Maylie and Esther Summerson are breathing epitomes of the tendernesses, the sweetnesses, the beauties, of life. Oliver Twist concentrates the single good qualities of a hundred children. The kind-hearted man, Dickens's stock character, be his name Pickwick, Jarndyce, or Clennam, seems always radically the same, and corresponds well enough with our theory. Perhaps it is essential deficiency in the highest power of individualization, which drives Mr. Dickens, it may be unconsciously, to affix, by way of labels, to the personages of his story, those insignificant peculiarities which all can perceive.

Amid the tumult and distracting blaze of his fame, one is by no means safe from the blunder of overlooking the kernel of genuine and precious humanity, of honest kindliness, of tender yet expansive benignity, which is in the centre of Dickens's being. His nature must originally have been most sweetly tuned. He must from the first have abounded in those qualities, which are so beautiful and winning when combined with manly character and vigorous powers; a cheerful gentleness, a loving hopefulness, a willingness to take all things and men for the best, an eye for the loveable; such a disposition as one finds in Goldsmith, a passionate admiration of happy human faces, a delight in the sports and laughter of children.—PETER BAYNE, "The Modern Novel: Dickens—Bulwer—Thackeray," *Essays in Biography and Criticism*, 1857, pp. 384–86

The true objection to Dickens is, that his idealism tends too much to extravagance and caricature. It would be possible for an ill-natured critic to go through all his works, and to draw out in one long column a list of their chief characters, annexing in a parallel column the phrases or labels by which these characters are distinguished, and of which they are generalizations—the "There's some credit in being jolly here" of Mark Tapley; the "It isn't of the slightest consequence" of Toots; the "Something will turn up" of Mr. Micawber, &c., &c. Even this, however, is a mode of art legitimate, I believe, in principle, as it is certainly most effective in fact. There never was a Mr. Micawber in nature, exactly as he appears in the pages of Dickens; but Micawberism pervades nature through and through; and to have extracted this quality from nature, embodying the full essence of a thousand instances of it in one ideal monstrosity, is a feat of invention. From the incessant repetition by Mr. Dickens of this inventive process openly and without variation, except in the results, the public have caught what is called his mannerism or trick; and hence a certain recoil from his later writings among the cultivated and fastidious. But let any one observe our current table-talk or our current literature, and, despite this profession of dissatisfaction, and in the very circles where it most abounds, let him note how gladly Dickens is used, and how frequently his phrases, his fancies, and the names of his characters come in, as illustration, embellishment, proverb, and seasoning. Take any periodical in which there is a severe criticism of Dickens's last publication; and, ten to one, in the same periodical, and perhaps by the same hand, there will be a leading article, setting out with a quotation from Dickens that flashes on the mind of the reader the thought which the whole article is meant to convey, or containing some allusion to one of Dickens's characters which enriches the text in the middle and floods it an inch round with colour and humour.—DAVID MASSON, *British Novelists and Their Styles*, 1859, pp. 251–52

> You ask me what I see in Dickens . . .
> A game-cock among bantam chickens.
> —WALTER SAVAGE LANDOR, "Dickens," 1863

If Mr. Dickens's characters were gathered together, they would constitute a town populous enough to send a representative to Parliament. Let us enter. The style of architecture is unparalleled. There is an individuality about the buildings. In some obscure way they remind one of human faces. There are houses sly-looking, houses wicked-looking, houses pompous-looking. Heaven bless us! what a rakish pump! what a self-important town-hall! what a hard-hearted prison! The dead walls are covered with advertisements of Mr. Sleary's circus. Newman Noggs comes shambling along. Mr. and the Misses Pecksniff come sailing down the sunny side of the street. Miss Mercy's parasol is gay; papa's neckcloth is white, and terribly starched. Dick Swiveller leans against a wall, his hands in his pockets, a primrose held between his teeth, contemplating the opera of Punch and Judy, which is being conducted under the management of Messrs. Codlings and Short. You turn a corner and you meet the coffin of little Paul Dombey borne along. Who would have thought of encountering a funeral in this place? In the afternoon you hear the rich tones of the organ from Miss La Creevy's first floor, for Tom Pinch has gone to live there now; and as you know all the people as you know your own brothers and sisters, and consequently require no letters of introduction, you go up and talk with the dear old fellow about all his friends and your friends, and towards evening he takes your arm, and you walk out to see poor Nelly's grave—a place which he visits often, and which he dresses with flowers with his own hands.—ALEXANDER SMITH, "On Vagabonds," *Dreamthorp*, 1863, pp. 287–88

To give so much pleasure, to add so much to the happiness of the world, by his writings, as Mr. Dickens has succeeded in doing, is a felicity that has never been attained in such full measure by any other author. For the space of a generation he has done his beneficent work, and there are few English-speaking men or women who do not feel themselves under peculiar obligation to the great novelist, and bound to him, not by any mere cold literary tie, but by the warm and vital cords of personal sympathy. The critic gladly lays down his pen in presence of a genius which has won for itself such a recognition, and willingly adopts the words of Ben Jonson in addressing one of his great contemporaries:—

> I yield, I yield. The matter of your praise
> Flows in upon me, and I cannot raise
> A bank against it: nothing but the round,
> Large clasp of Nature such a wit can bound.

If we reflect what contemporary literature would be without Dickens's works,—how much enjoyment would be taken out of our lives,—how much knowledge of human nature and feeling for it, how much genial humor, how much quickening of sympathy, how much heartiness, would be lost, had this long series of books never appeared, we can better appreciate what we owe to their writer. ⟨. . .⟩

No one thinks first of Mr. Dickens as a writer. He is at once, through his books, a friend. He belongs among the intimates of every pleasant-tempered and large-hearted person. He is not so much the guest as the inmate of our homes. He keeps holidays with us, he helps us to celebrate Christmas with heartier cheer, he shares at every New Year in our good wishes: for, indeed, it is not in his purely literary character that he has done most for us, it is as a man of the largest humanity, who has simply used literature as the means by which to bring himself into relation with his fellow-men, and to inspire them with something of his own sweetness, kindness, charity, and good-will.

He is the great magician of our time. His wand is a book, but his power is in his own heart. It is a rare piece of good fortune for us that we are the contemporaries of this benevolent genius, and that he comes among us in bodily presence, bringing in his company such old and valued friends as Mr. Pickwick, and Sam Weller, and Nicholas Nickleby, and David Copperfield, and Boots at the Swan, and Dr. Marigold. —CHARLES ELIOT NORTON, "Charles Dickens," *North American Review*, April 1868, pp. 671–72

But Mr. Dickens's peculiar gift, and his best gift, was not the accumulation and delineation of such items as paint a past period—costume, antiquarian lexicography, archæology generally. These are transitory, and are already dead. There have been great masters in the art of grouping and painting them, no doubt. But the art of this master was in painting the qualities of humanity, not of its costume—the feelings, sentiments, and passions that are everlasting as man. It might therefore have been expected that this part of the work would usurp upon the other in the composition of historical fiction; and so it was accordingly.—F. B. PERKINS, *Charles Dickens: A Sketch of His Life and Works*, 1870, p. 63

I have been sunning myself in Dickens—even in his later and very inferior *Mutual Friend*, and *Great Expectations*—Very inferior to his best: but with things better than any one else's best, caricature as they may be. I really must go and worship at Gadshill, as I have worshipped at Abbotsford, though with less Reverence, to be sure. But I must look on Dickens as a mighty Benefactor to Mankind.—EDWARD FITZGERALD, Letter to Fanny Kemble (Aug. 24, 1874)

Of Mr. Dickens I have seen but little in face-to-face intercourse; but I am glad to have enjoyed that little. There may be, and I believe there are, many who go beyond me in admiration of his works,—high and strong as is my delight in some of them. Many can more keenly enjoy his peculiar humour,—delightful as it is to me; and few seem to miss as I do the pure plain daylight in the atmosphere of his scenery. So many fine painters have been mannerists as to atmosphere and colour that it may be unreasonable to object to one more: but the very excellence and diversity of Mr. Dickens's powers makes one long that they should exercise their full force under the broad open sky of nature, instead of in the most brilliant palace of art. While he tells us a world of things that are natural and even true, his personages are generally, as I suppose is undeniable, profoundly unreal. It is a curious speculation what effect his universally read works will have on the foreign conception of English character. Washington Irving came here expecting to find the English life of Queen Anne's days, as his *Sketch-Book* shows: and very unlike his preconception was the England he found. And thus it must be with Germans, Americans and French who take Mr. Dickens's books to be pictures of our real life.—Another vexation is his vigorous erroneousness about matters of science, as shown in *Oliver Twist* about the new poor-law (which he confounds with the abrogated old one) and in *Hard Times*, about the controversies of employers. Nobody wants to make Mr. Dickens a Political Economist; but there are many who wish that he would abstain from a set of difficult subjects, on which all true sentiment must be underlain by a sort of knowledge which he has not. The more fervent and inexhaustible his kindliness, (and it is fervent and inexhaustible,) the more important it is that it should be well-informed and well-directed, that no errors of his may mislead his readers on the one hand, nor lessen his own genial influence on the other.

The finest thing in Mr. Dickens's case is that he, from time to time, proves himself capable of progress,—however vast his preceding achievements had been. In humour, he will hardly surpass *Pickwick*, simply because *Pickwick* is scarcely surpassable in humour: but in several crises, as it were, of his fame, when every body was disappointed, and his faults seemed running his graces down, there has appeared some thing so prodigiously fine as to make us all joyfully exclaim that Dickens can never permanently fail. It was so with *Copperfield*: and I hope it may be so again with the new work which my survivors will soon have in their hands.—Meantime, every indication seems to show that the man himself is rising. He is a virtuous and happy family man, in the first place. His glowing and generous heart is kept steady by the best domestic influences: and we may fairly hope now that he will fulfil the natural purpose of his life, and stand by literature to the last; and again, that he will be an honour to the high vocation by prudence as well as by power: so that the graces of genius and generosity may rest on the finest basis of probity and prudence; and that his old age may be honoured as heartily as his youth and manhood have been admired.—Nothing could exceed the frank kindness and consideration shown by him in the correspondence and personal intercourse we have had; and my cordial regard has grown with my knowledge of him.—Harriet Martineau, *Autobiography*, ed. Maria Weston Chapman, 1877, Vol. 2, pp. 61–63

Dickens had little or no knowledge of human character, and evidently cared very little about the study. His stories are fairy tales made credible by the masterly realism with which he described all the surroundings and accessories, the costumes and the ways of his men and women. While we are reading of a man whose odd peculiarities strike us with a sense of reality as if we had observed them for ourselves many a time, while we see him surrounded by streets and houses which seem to us rather more real and a hundred times more interesting than those through which we pass every day, we are not likely to observe very quickly, or to take much heed of the fact when we do observe it, that the man acts on various important occasions of his life as only people in fairy stories ever do act.—Justin McCarthy, *A History of Our Own Times*, 1879–80, Ch. 29

Chief in thy generation born of men
  Whom English praise acclaimed as English-born,
  With eyes that matched the worldwide eyes of morn
For gleam of tears or laughter, tenderest then
When thoughts of children warmed their light, or when
  Reverence of age with love and labour worn,
  Or godlike pity fired with godlike scorn,
Shot through them flame that winged thy swift live pen:
Where stars and suns that we behold not burn,
  Higher even than here, though highest was here thy place,
  Love sees thy spirit laugh and speak and shine
With Shakespeare and the soft bright soul of Sterne
  And Fielding's kindliest might and Goldsmith's grace;
  Scarce one more loved or worthier love than thine.
        —Algernon Charles Swinburne, "Dickens,"
        1882

Dickens was not—and to whom in these latter ages of literature could such a term be applied?—a self-made writer, in the sense that he owed nothing to those who had gone before him. He was most assuredly no classical scholar,—how could he have been? But I should hesitate to call him an ill-read man, though he certainly was neither a great nor a catholic reader, and though he could not help thinking about *Nicholas Nickleby* while he was reading the *Curse of Kehama*. In his own branch of literature his judgment was sound and sure-footed. It was of course a happy accident, that as a boy he imbibed that taste for good fiction which is a thing inconceivable to the illiterate. Sneers have been directed against the poverty of his bookshelves in his earlier days of authorship; but I fancy there were not many popular novelists in 1839 who would have taken down with them into the country for a summer sojourn, as Dickens did to Petersham, not only a couple of Scott's novels, but Goldsmith, Swift, Fielding, Smollett, and the British Essayists; nor is there one of these national classics—unless it be Swift—with whom Dickens' books or letters fail to show him to have been familiar. Of Goldsmith's books, he told Forster, in a letter which the biographer of Goldsmith modestly suppressed, he "had no indifferent perception—to the best of his remembrance—when little more than a child." He discusses with understanding the relative literary merits of the serious and humorous papers in *The Spectator*; and, with regard to another work of unique significance in the history of English fiction, *Robinson Crusoe*, he acutely observed that "one of the most popular books on earth has nothing in it to make anyone laugh or cry." "It is a book," he added, which he "read very much." It may be noted, by the way, that he was an attentive and judicious student of Hogarth; and that thus his criticisms of humorous pictorial art rested upon as broad a basis of comparison as did his judgment of his great predecessors in English humorous fiction.

Among these predecessors it has become usual to assert that Smollett exercised the greatest influence upon Dickens. It is no doubt true that in David Copperfield's library Smollett's books are mentioned first, and in the greatest number, that a vision of Roderick Random and Strap haunted the very wicket-gate at Blunderstone, that the poor little hero's first thought on entering the King's Bench prison was the strange company whom Roderick met in the Marshalsea; and that the references to Smollett and his books are frequent in Dickens' other books and in his letters. Leghorn seemed to him "made illustrious" by Smollett's grave, and in a late period of his life he criticises his chief fictions with admirable justice. "*Humphry Clinker*," he writes, "is certainly Smollett's best. I am rather divided between *Peregrine Pickle* and *Roderick Random*, both extraordinarily good in their way, which is a way without tenderness; but you will have to read them both, and I send the first volume of *Peregrine* as the richer of the two." An odd volume of *Peregrine* was one of the books with which the waiter at the *Holly Tree Inn* endeavoured to beguile the lonely Christmas of the snowed-up traveller, but the latter "knew every word of it already." In the *Lazy Tour*, "Thomas, now just able to grope his way along, in a doubled-up condition, was no bad embodiment of Commodore Trunnion." I have noted, moreover, coincidences of detail which bear witness to Dickens' familiarity with Smollett's works. To Lieutenant Bowling and Commodore Trunnion, as to Captain Cuttle, every man was a "brother," and to the Commodore, as to Mr. Smallweed, the most abusive substantive addressed to a woman admitted of intensification by the epithet "brimstone." I think Dickens had not forgotten the opening of the *Adventures of an Atom* when he wrote a passage in the opening of his own *Christmas Carol*; and that the characters of Tom Pinch and Tommy Traddles— the former more especially— were not conceived without some

thought of honest Strap. Furthermore, it was Smollett's example that probably suggested to Dickens the attractive jingle in the title of his *Nicholas Nickleby*. But these are for the most part mere details. The manner of Dickens as a whole resembles Fielding's more strikingly than Smollett's, as it was only natural that it should. The irony of Smollett is drier than was reconcileable with Dickens' nature; it is only in the occasional extravagances of his humour that the former anticipates anything in the latter, and it is only the coarsest scenes of Dickens' earlier books—such as that between Noah, Charlotte, and Mrs. Sowerberry in *Oliver Twist*—which recall the whole manner of his predecessor. They resemble one another in their descriptive accuracy, and in the accumulation of detail by which they produce instead of obscuring vividness of impression; but it was impossible that Dickens should prefer the general method of the novel of adventure pure and simple, such as Smollett produced after the example of *Gil Blas*, to the less crude form adopted by Fielding, who adhered to earlier and nobler models. With Fielding's, moreover, Dickens' whole nature was congenial; they both had that tenderness which Smollett lacked; and the circumstance that of all English writers of the past, Fielding's name alone was given by Dickens to one of his sons, shows how, like so many of Fielding's readers, he had learnt to love him with an almost personal affection. The very spirit of the author of *Tom Jones*—that gaiety which, to borrow the saying of a recent historian concerning Cervantes, renders even brutality agreeable, and that charm of sympathetic feeling which makes us love those of his characters which he loves himself—seem astir in some of the most delightful passages of Dickens' most delightful books.
—ADOLPHUS WILLIAM WARD, *Dickens*, 1882, pp. 197–200

There can be no doubt that the most popular novelist of my time—probably the most popular English novelist of any time—has been Charles Dickens. He has now been dead nearly six years, and the sale of his books goes on as it did during his life. The certainty with which his novels are found in every house—the familiarity of his name in all English-speaking countries—the popularity of such characters as Mrs. Gamp, Micawber, and Pecksniff, and many others whose names have entered into the English language and become well-known words—the grief of the country at his death, and the honours paid to him at his funeral,—all testify to his popularity. Since the last book he wrote himself, I doubt whether any book has been so popular as his biography by John Forster. There is no withstanding such testimony as this. Such evidence of popular appreciation should go for very much, almost for everything, in criticism on the work of a novelist. The primary object of a novelist is to please; and this man's novels have been found more pleasant than those of any other writer. It might of course be objected to this, that though the books have pleased they have been injurious, that their tendency has been immoral and their teaching vicious; but it is almost needless to say that no such charge has ever been made against Dickens. His teaching has ever been good. From all which, there arises to the critic a question whether, with such evidence against him as to the excellence of this writer, he should not subordinate his own opinion to the collected opinion of the world of readers. To me it almost seems that I must be wrong to place Dickens after Thackeray and George Eliot, knowing as I do that so great a majority put him above those authors.

My own peculiar idiosyncrasy in the matter forbids me to do so: I do acknowledge that Mrs. Gamp, Micawber, Pecksniff, and others have become household words in every house, as

though they were human beings; but to my judgment they are not human beings, nor are any of the characters human which Dickens has portrayed. It has been the peculiarity and the marvel of this man's power, that he has invested his puppets with a charm that has enabled him to dispense with human nature. There is a drollery about them, in my estimation, very much below the humour of Thackeray, but which has reached the intellect of all; while Thackeray's humour has escaped the intellect of many. Nor is the pathos of Dickens human. It is stagey and melodramatic. But it is so expressed that it touches every heart a little. There is no real life in Smike. His misery, his idiotcy, his devotion for Nicholas, his love for Kate, are all overdone and incompatible with each other. But still the reader sheds a tear. Every reader can find a tear for Smike. Dickens's novels are like Boucicault's plays. He has known how to draw his lines broadly, so that all should see the colour.

He, too, in his best days, always lived with his characters;—and he, too, as he gradually ceased to have the power of doing so, ceased to charm. Though they are not human beings, we all remember Mrs. Gamp and Pickwick. The Boffins and Veneerings do not, I think, dwell in the minds of so many.

Of Dickens's style it is impossible to speak in praise. It is jerky, ungrammatical, and created by himself in defiance of rules—almost as completely as that created by Carlyle. To readers who have taught themselves to regard language, it must therefore be unpleasant. But the critic is driven to feel the weakness of his criticism, when he acknowledges to himself—as he is compelled in all honesty to do—that with the language, such as it is, the writer has satisfied the great mass of the readers of his country. Both these great writers have satisfied the readers of their own pages; but both have done infinite harm by creating a school of imitators. No young novelist should ever dare to imitate the style of Dickens. If such a one wants a model for his language, let him take Thackeray.—ANTHONY TROLLOPE, *An Autobiography*, 1883, Ch. 13

Dickens must not only have had exceptional powers of observation and imagination, but *extra*-ordinary intensity of sympathy with *ordinary* feelings and beliefs. His genius in characterization tends to the grotesque and extravagant; his personages, in their names as in their qualities, produce on us the effect of strangeness; the plots of the novels in which they appear would with any other characters seem grossly improbable, and yet his mind is unmistakably rooted in common sense and common humanity. He thus succeeds in giving his readers all the pleasure which comes from contemplating what is strange, odd, and eccentric, without disquieting them by any paradoxes in morals or shocking them by any perversions of homely natural sentiment. The *Christmas Carol*, for example, is as wild in grotesque fancy as a dream of Hoffmann, yet in feeling as solid and sweet and humane as a sermon of Channing. It impresses us somewhat as we are impressed by the sight of the Bible as illustrated by Gustave Doré. Thus held fast to common, homely truths and feelings by his sentiments, he can safely give reins to his imagination in his creations. The keenest of observers, both of things and persons, all that he observes is still taken up and transformed by his imagination—becomes *Dickensized*, in fact—so that, whether he describes a landscape, or a boot-jack, or a building, or a man, we see the object, not as it is in itself, but as it is deliciously bewitched by his method of looking at it. Everything is suggested by his outward experience, but modified by his inward experience. The result is that we do not have in him an exact transcript of life, but an individualized ideal of life from his point of view.

He has, in short, discovered and colonized one of the waste districts of Imagination, which we may call Dickens-land or Dickens-ville; from his own brain he has peopled it with some fourteen hundred persons, and it agrees with the settlements made there by Shakespeare and Scott in being better known than such geographical countries as Canada and Australia, and it agrees with them equally in confirming us in the belief of the *reality* of a population which has no *actual* existence. It is distinguished from all other colonies in Brainland by the ineffaceable peculiarities of its colonizer; its inhabitants don't die like other people, but, alas! they also now can't increase; but whithersoever any of them may wander they are recognized at once, by an unmistakable birthmark, as belonging to the race of Dickens. A man who has done this is not merely one of a thousand, but one of a thousand millions; for he has created an ideal population which is more interesting to human beings than the great body of their own actual friends and neighbors.—EDWIN P. WHIPPLE, "In Dickens-Land," *Scribner's Magazine*, Dec. 1887, pp. 744–45

Here was a man and an artist, the most strenuous, one of the most endowed; and for how many years he laboured in vain to create a gentleman! With all his watchfulness of men and manners, with all his fiery industry, with all his exquisite native gift of characterisation, with his clear knowledge of what he meant to do, there was yet something lacking. In part after part, novel after novel, a whole menagerie of characters, the good, the bad, the droll, and the tragic, came at his beck like slaves about an Oriental despot; there was only one who stayed away: the gentleman. If this ill fortune had persisted it might have shaken man's belief in art and industry. But years were given and courage was continued to the indefatigable artist; and at length, after so many and such lamentable failures, success began to attend upon his arms. David Copperfield scrambled through on hands and knees; it was at least a negative success; and Dickens, keenly alive to all he did, must have heaved a sigh of infinite relief. Then came the evil days, the days of *Dombey* and *Dorrit*, from which the lover of Dickens willingly averts his eyes; and when that temporary blight had passed away, and the artist began with a more resolute arm to reap the aftermath of his genius, we find him able to create a Carton, a Wrayburn, a Twemlow. No mistake about these three; they are all gentlemen: the sottish Carton, the effete Twemlow, the insolent Wrayburn, all have doubled the cape.

There were never in any book three perfect sentences on end; there was never a character in any volume but it somewhere tripped. We are like dancing dogs and preaching women: the wonder is not that we should do it well, but that we should do it at all. And Wrayburn, I am free to admit, comes on one occasion to the dust. I mean, of course, the scene with the old Jew. I will make you a present of the Jew for a card-board figure; but that is neither here nor there: the ineffectuality of the one presentment does not mitigate the grossness, the baseness, the inhumanity of the other. In this scene, and in one other (if I remember aright) where it is echoed, Wrayburn combines the wit of the omnibus-cad with the good feeling of the Andaman Islander: in all the remainder of the book, throughout a thousand perils, playing (you would say) with difficulty, the author swimmingly steers his hero on the true course. The error stands by itself, and it is striking to observe the moment of its introduction. It follows immediately upon one of the most dramatic passages in fiction, that in which Bradley Headstone barks his knuckles on the churchyard wall. To handle Bradley (one of Dickens's superlative achievements) were a thing impossible to almost any man but his

creator; and even to him, we may be sure, the effort was exhausting. Dickens was a weary man when he had barked the schoolmaster's knuckles, a weary man and an excited; but the tale of bricks had to be finished, the monthly number waited; and under the false inspiration of irritated nerves, the scene of Wrayburn and the Jew was written and sent forth; and there it is, a blot upon the book and a buffet to the reader.

I make no more account of his passage than of that other in *Hamlet*: a scene that has broken down, the judicious reader cancels for himself. And the general tenor of Wrayburn, and the whole of Carton and Twemlow, are beyond exception. Here, then, we have a man who found it for years an enterprise beyond his art to draw a gentleman, and who in the end succeeded. Is it because Dickens was not a gentleman himself that he so often failed? and if so, then how did he succeed at last? Is it because he was a gentleman that he succeeded? and if so, what made him fail? I feel inclined to stop this paper here, after the manner of conundrums, and offer a moderate reward for a solution. But the true answer lies probably deeper than did ever plummet sound. And mine (such as it is) will hardly appear to the reader to disturb the surface.

These verbal puppets (so to call them once again) are things of a divided parentage: the breath of life may be an emanation from their maker, but they themselves are only strings of words and parts of books; they dwell in, they belong to, literature; convention, technical artifice, technical gusto, the mechanical necessities of the art, these are the flesh and blood with which they are invested. If we look only at Carton and Wrayburn, both leading parts, it must strike us at once that both are most ambitiously attempted; that Dickens was not content to draw a hero and a gentleman plainly and quietly; that after all his ill-success, he must still handicap himself upon these fresh adventures, and make Carton a sot, and sometimes a cantankerous sot, and Wrayburn insolent to the verge, and sometimes beyond the verge, of what is pardonable. A moment's thought will show us this was in the nature of his genius, and a part of his literary method. His fierce intensity of design was not to be slaked with any academic portraiture; not all the arts of individualisation could perfectly content him; he must still seek something more definite and more express than nature. All artists, it may be properly argued, do the like; it is their method to discard the middling and the insignificant, to disengage the charactered and the precise. But it is only a class of artists that pursue so singly the note of personality; and is it not possible that such a preoccupation may disable men from representing gentlefolk? The gentleman passes in the stream of the day's manners, inconspicuous. The lover of the individual may find him scarce worth drawing. And even if he draw him, on what will his attention centre but just upon those points in which his model exceeds or falls short of his subdued ideal—but just upon those points in which the gentleman is not genteel? Dickens, in an hour of irritated nerves, and under the pressure of the monthly number, defaced his Wrayburn. Observe what he sacrifices. The ruling passion strong in his hour of weakness, he sacrifices dignity, decency, the essential human beauties of his hero; he still preserves the dialect, the shrill note of personality, the mark of identification. Thackeray, under the strain of the same villainous system, would have fallen upon the other side; his gentleman would still have been a gentleman, he would have only ceased to be an individual figure.

There are incompatible ambitions. You cannot paint a Vandyke and keep it a Franz Hals.—ROBERT LOUIS STEVENSON, "Some Gentlemen in Fiction," 1888

Dickens's imagination was diligent from the outset; with him conception was not less deliberate and careful than development; and so much he confesses when he describes himself as 'in the first stage of a new book, which consists in going round and round the idea, as you see a bird in his cage go about and about his sugar before he touches it.' 'I have no means,' he writes to a person wanting advice, 'of knowing whether you are patient in the pursuit of this art; but I am inclined to think that you are not, and that you do not discipline yourself enough. When one is impelled to write this or that, one has still to consider: "How much of this will tell for what I mean? How much of it is my own wild emotion and superfluous energy—how much remains that is truly belonging to this ideal character and these ideal circumstances?" It is in the laborious struggle to make this distinction, and in the determination to try for it, that the road to the correction of faults lies. [Perhaps I may remark, in support of the sincerity with which I write this, that I am an impatient and impulsive person myself, but that it has been for many years the constant effort of my life to practise at my desk what I preach to you.] Such golden words could only have come from one enamoured of his art, and holding the utmost endeavour in its behalf of which his heart and mind were capable for a matter of simple duty. They are a proof that Dickens—in intention at least, and if in intention then surely, the fact of his genius being admitted, to some extent in fact as well—was an artist in the best sense of the term.

In the beginning he often wrote exceeding ill, especially when he was doing his best to write seriously. He developed into an artist in words as he developed into an artist in the construction and the evolution of a story. But his development was his own work, and it is a fact that should redound eternally to his honour that he began in newspaper English, and by the production of an imitation of the *novela picaresca*—a string of adventures as broken and disconnected as the adventures of Lazarillo de Tormes or Peregrine Pickle, and went on to become an exemplar. A man self-made and self-taught, if he knew anything at all about the 'art for art' theory—which is doubtful—he may well have held it cheap enough. But he practised Millet's dogma—*Dans l'art il faut sa peau*—as resolutely as Millet himself, and that, too, under conditions that might have proved utterly demoralising had he been less robust and less sincere. He began as a serious novelist with Ralph Nickleby and Lord Frederick Verisopht; he went on to produce such masterpieces as Jonas Chuzzlewit and Doubledick, and Eugene Wrayburn and the immortal Mrs. Gamp, and Fagin and Sikes and Sydney Carton, and many another. The advance is one from positive weakness to positive strength, from ignorance to knowledge, from incapacity to mastery, from the manufacture of lay figures to the creation of human beings.

His faults were many and grave. He wrote some nonsense; he sinned repeatedly against taste; he could be both noisy and vulgar; he was apt to be a caricaturist where he should have been a painter; he was often mawkish and often extravagant; and he was sometimes more inept than a great writer has ever been. But his work, whether bad or good, has in full measure the quality of sincerity. He meant what he did; and he meant it with his whole heart. He looked upon himself as representative and national—as indeed he was; he regarded his work as a universal possession; and he determined to do nothing that for lack of pains should prove unworthy of his function. If he sinned it was unadvisedly and unconsciously; if he failed it was because he knew no better. You feel that as you read. The freshness and fun of *Pickwick*—a comic middle-class epic, so to

speak—seem mainly due to high spirits; and perhaps that immortal book should be described as a first improvisation by a young man of genius not yet sure of either expression or ambition and with only vague and momentary ideas about the duties and necessities of art. But from *Pickwick* onwards to *Edwin Drood* the effort after improvement is manifest. What are *Dombey* and *Dorrit* themselves but the failures of a great and serious artist? In truth the man's genius did but ripen with years and labour; he spent his life in developing from a popular writer into an artist. He extemporised *Pickwick*, it may be, but into *Copperfield* and *Chuzzlewit* and the *Tale of Two Cities* and *Our Mutual Friend* he put his whole might, working at them with a passion of determination not exceeded by Balzac himself. He had enchanted the public without an effort; he was the best-beloved of modern writers almost from the outset of his career. But he had in him at least as much of the French artist as of the middle-class Englishman; and if all his life he never ceased from self-education but went unswervingly in pursuit of culture, it was out of love for his art and because his conscience as an artist would not let him do otherwise. We have been told so often to train ourselves by studying the practice of workmen like Gautier and Hugo and imitating the virtues of work like *Hernani* and *Quatre-Vingt-Treize* and *L'Education sentimentale*—we have heard so much of the æsthetic impeccability of Young France and the section of Young England that affects its qualities and reproduces its fashions—that it is hard to refrain from asking if, when all is said, we should not do well to look for models nearer home? if in place of such moulds of form as *Mademoiselle de Maupin* we might not take to considering stuff like *Rizpah* and *Our Mutual Friend?*

Yes, he had many and grave faults. But so had Sir Walter and the good Dumas; so, to be candid, had Shakespeare himself—Shakespeare the king of poets. To myself he is always the man of his unrivalled and enchanting letters—is always an incarnation of generous and abounding gaiety, a type of beneficent earnestness, a great expression of intellectual vigour and emotional vivacity. I love to remember that I came into the world contemporaneously with some of his bravest work, and to reflect that even as he was the inspiration of my boyhood so is he a delight of my middle age. I love to think that while English literature endures he will be remembered as one that loved his fellow-men, and did more to make them happy and amiable than any other writer of his time.—W. E. HENLEY, "Dickens," *Views and Reviews*, 1890, pp. 3–9

The might of that great talent no one can gainsay, though in the light of the truer work which has since been done his literary principles seem almost as grotesque as his theories of political economy. In no one direction was his erring force more felt than in the creation of holiday literature as we have known it for the last half-century. Creation, of course, is the wrong word; it says too much; but in default of a better word, it may stand. He did not make something out of nothing; the material was there before him; the mood and even the need of his time contributed immensely to his success, as the volition of the subject helps on the mesmerist; but it is within bounds to say that he was the chief agency in the development of holiday literature as we have known it, as he was the chief agency in universalizing the great Christian holiday as we now have it. Other agencies wrought with him and after him; but it was he who rescued Christmas from Puritan distrust, and humanized it and consecrated it to the hearts and homes of all.—WILLIAM DEAN HOWELLS, *Criticism and Fiction*, 1891, pp. 174–75

He accepted the past; it was the present by which he was consciously fascinated; and the past had no meaning for him except as connected with it. An old building for him was not like a dead man, but like an old man—an old man making faces either grotesque or sinister. For him everything was alive with the life of his own day. Houses, crooked courts, four-post bedsteads, cabs, portmanteaus, chimney-pots, and all inanimate objects winked at him, laughed with him, and spoke to him in the vernacular of the streets, and were forever saying to him something fresh and pungent. He had all the familiarity with the life around him that could be produced by the most close acquaintance with it; and yet he was always watching it with the surprise and expectant freshness which, as a rule, belong only to those to whom it is still a novelty. And this vision of his he communicated to his readers. He made them see not what they had not seen before, but what they had not noticed before. He made them conscious of their own unconscious observations. His genius acted on the surface of English life as spilt water acts on the surface of unpolished marble. It suddenly made visible all its colors and veinings; and in this way he may be said to have revealed England to itself: and he still does so.

It is true that this general statement must be made with one reservation. One part of English life was entirely beyond his grasp. He knew nothing of the highest class. He had no true knowledge even of the upper ranks of the middle class. His lords, his baronets, his majors, his ladies and gentlemen generally are not even like enough to reality to be called caricatures. But if we accept these classes and speak only of the bulk of the nation, no writer ever knew the English nation and represented the English nation so thoroughly and comprehensively as Dickens. His style is full of the faults of a man imperfectly educated. Errors of taste abound in it, and much of his sentiment is mawkish, or constrained, or false; and yet, in spite of this, not only do his writings embody the shrewdest, the truest, the widest, and the most various observations of the life around him, but they show him to be, in a certain sense, one of the greatest of English poets. In saying this I am making no allusion to any passages which sentimental admirers of him may consider poetical, or which he probably thought poetical himself. I am alluding to the manner in which, throughout his works, he not only presents what are commonly called the facts of life, but actually gives us that elusive atmosphere which in life surrounds these facts and imparts to them those changing aspects by which in life we know them; an atmosphere impregnated with wandering thoughts and sentiments and volatile associations—an element whch would seem to defy description. This Dickens has described. It penetrates his works and permeates them.

One example may be given, a single touch. He is describing some lawyer's office with dim, dusty windows, and among other details he notes this: that there was on the floor an enormous faded stain, "as if some by-gone clerk had cut his throat there and had bled ink." The whole past and present of the place is suggested in these few words, and what he felt and described in a lawyer's office he felt and described in nearly every scene he dealt with. He felt and he seized its human and, above all, its national meaning. He did this even in cases where it might be thought he would have failed to do so. I said he knew nothing of the highest upper classes; but in a certain way he understood their life as a factor in the life of the country, through certain of their surroundings. He knew the meaning and the sentiment of old English parks, of lodges, and gray gate-posts, damp and mottled with lichens. He knew the spirit which haunted the whispering avenue and hung above the twisted chimney-stacks and mullioned window of the hall; but his comprehension stopped at the front door. It was never at home inside. With this reservation, Dickens is England; and if he could not describe what the upper class see among themselves, he describes what they see whenever they go out of doors. To move out of the seclusion of polite life in England is to walk with Dickens. It is so still, as it was in his own days; and if any proof is needed in addition to those I have already mentioned, it may be found in the English language as spoken at this moment. Dickens' characters exist not in his books only. They have walked out of his books and taken their places among living people. Their looks and manners are social and not literary facts; their jokes and phrases are the common property of the nation. Of one other novelist only can this be said, and that novelist is Scott.—W. H. MALLOCK, "Are Scott, Dickens, and Thackeray Obsolete?," *Forum*, Dec. 1892, pp. 511–12

He is at his best in his earlier works, where he makes small pretence to art. In my opinion his masterpiece is *Pickwick*—"a comic middle-class epic" it has been called, perhaps not unhappily. It is irresistibly funny; inimitably fresh; incomparably fantastic; a farce, but a farce of a very high order. Dickens himself always thought slightingly of it. He was ambitious, laudably ambitious, to do greater things. And during the whole of his literary life he toiled earnestly, passionately, to attain a higher standard. I think he came nearest to that standard in *David Copperfield*. There is much—very much—there which we could wish away. In fact I, if I take the book up, give effect to my wish, and practically put aside a great deal of it. And no doubt many other readers do the same. But it is informed by a simple power, a sober veracity, a sustained interest, peculiarly its own among its author's works. Dickens's young men are, as a rule, impossible. They are well-nigh all of the same inane type. He seems to have got them out of an Adelphi melodrama. But David Copperfield, who is a transcript from his own troublous and distressed childhood and youth, is, at all events, human. His young women are as inane as his young men. His amatory scenes—good heavens let us not speak of them and their mawkish sentimentalities! What a theme for a poet had he in Steerforth and Little Em'ly! How George Sand would have treated it! How George Eliot has treated a similar theme in *Adam Bede*! But Dickens possessed no words to tell forth that idyll. And if he had possessed them he dared not to have uttered them. He stood in too much awe of Mr. Podsnap's "young person." The history of the love of Steerforth and Little Em'ly was impossible to him. He could not have narrated it if he would; and he would not if he could.

I think he never again wrote so felicitously as in *David Copperfield*. No doubt he did many fine things afterwards in the way of genre painting. We may regard him as a literary Teniers. But as years went on his manner seems to me to grow more unnatural, more stilted, more intolerable. The higher art which he tried to grasp, ever eluded him. There is an absence of composition in his work; there is no play of light and shade; there is no proportion, no perspective. His books cannot be said to be composed, they are improvised.—WILLIAM SAMUEL LILLY, "Dickens," *Four English Humourists of the Nineteenth Century*, 1895, pp. 14–15

Dickens has been called the favourite novelist of the middle classes. If the statement be true, it is creditable to their good taste and freedom from prejudice. He certainly did not flatter them. He disliked Dissenters quite as much as Matthew Arnold, whereas Thackeray gave them the Clapham Sect, to which they are not entitled. But the popularity of Dickens in his lifetime was in fact universal. Everybody read his books, because nobody could help reading them. They required no education except a knowledge of the alphabet, and they amused scholars as much as crossing-sweepers. No man ever made a more thorough conquest of his generation. Indeed he was only too successful. Imitation may be the sincerest form of flattery. It is the most dangerous form of admiration. And if ever there was an *exemplar vitiis imitabile*, it was Dickens. His influence upon literature, apart from his contributions to it, has been disastrous. The school of Dickens, for which he cannot be held responsible, is happily at last dying out. Their dreary mechanical jokes, their hideous unmeaning caricatures, their descriptions that describe nothing, their spasms of false sentiment, their tears of gin and water, have ceased to excite even amusement, and provoke only unmitigated disgust. With their disappearance from the stage, and consignment to oblivion, the reputation of the great man they injured is relieved from a temporary strain. The position of Dickens himself is unassailed and unassailable. In this or that generation he may be less read or more. He must always remain an acknowledged master of fiction and a prince of English humorists.—HERBERT PAUL, "The Apotheosis of the Novel," *Nineteenth Century*, May 1892, p. 773

The question, "Will Dickens last?" has been asked a hundred times in print since Dickens died; and many times, and in various ways, has the question been answered. All men admit that Sir Charles Grandison has become a bore, where he is known at all; that G. P. R. James's solitary horseman has ridden on, entirely out of the sight of the present-day reader; that Cooper's Indians and backwoodsmen no longer scalp the imagination of the boy of the period; that Marryat's midshipmen have been left alone and neglected at the mastheads to which he was so fond of sending them; that no one but the antiquary in literature cares now for Waverley or Rob Roy. But it is too soon yet to say how long it will be before Bleak House will become an uninhabitable ruin, or when the firm of Dombey and Son will go out of business altogether. Don Quixote is as vigorous as he was three centuries ago. Robinson Crusoe, born in 1719, still retains all the freshness of youth; who can prophesy how Mr. Samuel Pickwick, the Don Quixote of 1839, will be regarded in 1998? or how Mr. Samuel Weller, his man Friday, will be looked upon by the readers of a hundred years from to-day?

Dickens certainly wrote for his own time, and generally *of* his own time. And during his own time he achieved a popularity without parallel in the history of fiction. But the fashions of all times change; and although Dickens has been in fashion longer than most of his contemporaries, and is still the fashion among old-fashioned folk, there are acute critics who say that his day is over. The booksellers and the officials of circulating libraries tell a different story, however; and when little children, who never heard the name of Dickens, who knew nothing of his great reputation, turn from *Alice in Wonderland* and *Little Lord Fauntleroy* to the *Cricket on the Hearth*, loving the old as much as they love the new, it would seem as if the sun had not yet set upon Dickens; and that the night which is to leave him in total darkness is still far off. —LAURENCE HUTTON, "Charles Dickens," *Outlook*, Oct. 1898, p. 321

Dickens was from the very first a check to mediævalism. After he began writing, knights and ladies and tournaments became rarer. He awakened the interest of the public in the social condition of England after the Napoleonic wars. The Scott novel had come swollen with prefaces, notes, and appendixes,

to show that it was true to the spirit of history; the Dickens novel came considerably enlarged with personal experiences, anecdotes, stories from friends, and statistics, to show that it was founded upon facts. Instead of the pageant of the Middle Age, we now have, in the novels of those who have learned their art from Dickens, strikes and riots, factories and granaries and barns in blaze, employee shooting employer, underground tenements, sewing-garrets, sweating-establishments, workhouses, truck-stores, the ravages of typhus, enthusiastic descriptions of model factories, model prisons, model cottages, discussions of the new poor law, of trade unions, of Chartism, and of the relations of the rich and the poor. The new characters are operatives in factories, agricultural laborers, miners, tailors, seamstresses, and paupers. Patience, longsuffering, gentleness, in stalwart or angelic form, is oppressed by viragoes, tall and bearded and of flashing eyes, or by gentlemen of bloated red faces. Dickens never advocated in his novels any specific means of reform.—WILBUR L. CROSS, *The Development of the English Novel*, 1899, pp. 192–93

Is there any other maker of story in modern English literature—after all allowances have been made, and not forgetting that some current criticism of the man of Gadshill will have it that he is for a more careless age—who has begun to furnish such a portrait-gallery of worthies and adorable grotesques—a motley crowd whom we all know and enjoy and love? I wot not. The fact that Dickens is at times a trifle inchoate or careless in his English, or allows his exuberance to lead him into exaggeration, or fails to blend perfectly the discordant elements of comedy and tragedy, sinks into insignificance when set over against such a faculty as this.—RICHARD BURTON, "The Fundamentals of Fiction," *Forces in Fiction and Other Essays*, 1902, p. 7

Works

PICKWICK PAPERS

The popularity of this writer is one of the most remarkable literary phenomena of recent times, for it has been fairly earned without resorting to any of the means by which most other writers have succeeded in attracting the attention of their contemporaries. He has flattered no popular prejudice and profited by no passing folly: he has attempted no caricature sketches of the manners or conversation of the aristocracy; and there are very few political or personal allusions in his works. Moreover, his class of subjects are such as to expose him at the outset to the fatal objection of vulgarity; and, with the exception of occasional extracts in the newspapers, he received little or no assistance from the press. Yet, in less than six months from the appearance of the first number of the *Pickwick Papers*, the whole reading public were talking about them—the names of Winkle, Wardell, Weller, Snodgrass, Dodson and Fogg, had become familiar in our mouths as household terms; and Mr. Dickens was the grand object of interest to the whole tribe of 'Leo-hunters,' male and female, of the metropolis. Nay, Pickwick chintzes figured in linendrapers' windows, and Weller corduroys in breeches-makers' advertisements; Boz cabs might be seen rattling through the streets, and the portrait of the author of *Pelham* or *Crichton* was scraped down or pasted over to make room for that of the new popular favourite in the omnibusses. This is only to be accounted for on the supposition that a fresh vein of humour had been opened; that a new and decidedly original genius had sprung up.—JOHN WILSON CROKER, "The Pickwick Papers," *Quarterly Review*, Dec. 1837, p. 484

It has been said that *The Pickwick Papers* was its author's best book; and, in certain respects, this judgment is sound. Humor was Mr. Dickens's great distinctive trait; and for humor, pure and simple, he produced in all his life nothing quite equal to *Pickwick*—nothing so sustained, so varied, so unstrained. He afterwards became more conscious of his humor as he wrote, and showed his consciousness. He let us see the preparation of his fun; he made points like an actor who feels that the points are expected by his audience, and also feels, and shows that he feels, that by the use of certain means he can make them. The spontaneous humor of *Pickwick* was never equalled, even by its author. He afterwards gave to too many of his humorous characters certain peculiarities of person, manner, or speech, on which he rung a limited range of changes; and this degenerated into a trick, like the giving of what in stage cant is called a gag to a comic actor, which he uses deliberately to force a laugh. This was a needless device in Mr. Dickens, whose humor seemed exhaustless.—RICHARD GRANT WHITE, "The Styles of Dickens and Disraeli," *Galaxy*, Aug. 1870, p. 258

I well remember my sensations of astonishment and interest when the first number of *Pickwick* was brought me, and I looked it over. Forster was with me at the time. How, on the introduction of Sam Weller, the work took the town by storm, and its author, who, only a short time before, had been an unnoticed parliamentary reporter, reached at a bound the summit of success, and became the literary lion of the day, I need not here describe.

No man since Walter Scott has so amply and efficiently supplied in fiction the intellectual need of the age; but that great man did not do a tithe of what Dickens has done to quicken its social and moral progress.—S. C. HALL, *Retrospect of a Long Life*, 1883, p. 394

The first numbers of the book—which was issued in twenty monthly parts—at once took the public fancy, laying the foundation of a popularity which has never decreased. There is perhaps no book more widely known in the English language, nor, strangely enough, many which have been received with such favour on the Continent, though it is intensely national in character. It is, indeed, an almost perfect specimen of the strictly English quality of fun—using English in its very narrowest sense as applying only to that part of her Majesty's dominions called England—which differs as greatly from the humour of Scotland and Ireland as from French wit or American extravagance. We could quote instances of more genuinely humorous scenes than that of the trial in *Pickwick*, but we cannot think of anything so irresistibly funny. It is hardly high comedy, but neither is it merely farcical; and it has the great qualities of being always good-humoured and hardly ever grotesque.

Another secret of the success of *Pickwick*, perhaps, is that it is not in the ordinary sense of the word, a novel. There is no continuous story to speak of, only a collection of amusing scenes of high average excellence, though of course containing some that are of inferior merit. Nor do we find in *Pickwick* any real delineation of character, with the exception, perhaps, of the Wellers, who are, however, as little real as they are always amusing.—MARGARET OLIPHANT, *The Victorian Age of English Literature*, 1892, Vol. 1, pp. 251–52

BARNABY RUDGE

His opening chapters assure us that he has at length discovered the secret of his true strength, and that *Barnaby Rudge* will appeal principally to the *imagination*. Of this faculty we have many striking instances in the few numbers already issued. We see it where the belfry man in the lonely church at midnight, about to toll the "passing-bell," is struck with horror at hearing the solitary note of another, and awaits, aghast, a repetition of the sound. We recognise it more fully where this single note is discovered, in the morning, to have been that of an alarm pulled by the hand of one in the death-struggle with a murderer:—also in the expression of countenance which is so strikingly attributed to Mrs. Rudge—"the capacity for expressing terror"—something only dimly seen, but never absent for a moment—"the shadow of some look to which an instant of intense and most unutterable horror only could have given rise." This is a conception admirably adapted to whet curiosity in respect to the character of that event which is hinted at as forming the ground-work of the novel; and so far is well suited to the purposes of a periodical story. But this observation should not fail to be made—that the anticipation must surpass the reality; that no matter how terrific be the circumstances which, in the *dénouement*, shall appear to have occasioned the expression of countenance worn habitually by Mrs. Rudge, still they will not be able to satisfy the mind of the reader. He will surely be disappointed. The skilful intimation of horror held out by the artist produces an effect which will deprive his conclusion, of all. These intimations—these dark hints of some uncertain evil—are often rhetorically praised as effective—but are only justly so praised where there is *no dénouement* whatever—where the reader's imagination is left to clear up the mystery for itself—and this, we suppose, is not the design of Mr. Dickens.

But the chief points in which the ideality of this story is apparent are the creation of the hero Barnaby Rudge, and the commingling with his character, as accessory, that of the human-looking raven. Barnaby we regard as an original idea altogether, so far as novel-writing is concerned. He is peculiar, inasmuch as he is an idiot endowed with the fantastic qualities of the madman, and has been born possessed with a maniacal horror of blood—the result of some terrible spectacle seen by his mother during pregnancy. The design of Mr. Dickens is here two-fold—first that of increasing our anticipation in regard to the deed committed—exaggerating our impression of its atrocity—and, secondly, that of causing this horror of blood on the part of the idiot, to bring about, in consistence with poetical justice, the condemnation of the murderer:—for it is a murder that has been committed. We say in accordance with poetical justice—and, in fact, it will be seen hereafter that Barnaby, the idiot, is the murderer's own son. The horror of blood which he feels is the mediate result of the atrocity, since this atrocity it was which impressed the imagination of the pregnant mother; and poetical justice will therefore be well fulfilled when this horror shall urge on the son to the conviction of the father in the perpetrator of the deed.—EDGAR ALLAN POE, "Charles Dickens" (1841), *Essays and Reviews*, ed. G. R. Thompson, 1984, pp. 218–19

OLD CURIOSITY SHOP

But if the conception of this story deserves praise, its execution is beyond all—and here the subject naturally leads us from the generalisation which is the proper province of the critic, into details among which it is scarcely fitting that he should venture. ⟨. . .⟩

When we speak in this manner of the *Old Curiosity Shop*, we speak with entire deliberation, and know quite well what it is we assert. We do not mean to say that it is perfect, as a whole—this could not well have been the case under the circumstances of its composition. But we know that, in all the higher elements which go to make up literary greatness, it is supremely excellent. We think, for instance, that the introduction of Nelly's brother (and here we address those who have read the work) is supererogatory—that the character of Quilp would have been more in keeping had he been confined to petty and grotesque acts of malice—that his death should have been made the *immediate* consequence of his attempt at revenge upon Kit; and that after matters had been put fairly in train for this poetical justice, he should not have perished by an' accident inconsequential upon his villany. We think, too, that there is an air of *ultra*-accident in the finally discovered relationship between Kit's master and the bachelor of the old church—that the sneering politeness put into the mouth of Quilp, with his manner of commencing a question which he wishes answered in the affirmative, with an affirmative interrogatory, instead of the ordinary negative one—are fashions borrowed from the author's own Fagin—that he has repeated himself in many other instances—that the practical tricks and love of mischief of the dwarf's boy are too nearly consonant with the traits of the master—that so much of the propensities of Swiveller as relate to his inapposite appropriation of odds and ends of verse, is stolen from the generic loafer of our fellow-townsman, Neal—and that the writer has suffered the overflowing kindness of his own bosom to mislead him in a very important point of art, when he endows so many of his *dramatis personæ* with a warmth of feeling so very rare in reality. Above all, we acknowledge that the death of Nelly is excessively painful—that it leaves a most distressing oppression of spirit upon the reader—and should, therefore, have been avoided.

But when we come to speak of the excellences of the tale these defects appear really insignificant. It embodies more *originality* in every point, but in character especially, than any single work within our knowledge. There is the grandfather—a truly profound conception; the gentle and lovely Nelly—we have discoursed of her before; Quilp, with mouth like that of the panting dog—(a bold idea which the engraver has neglected to embody) with his hilarious antics, his cowardice, and his very petty and spoilt-child-like malevolence; Dick Swiveller, that prince of good-hearted, good-for-nothing, lazy, luxurious, poetical, brave, romantically generous, gallant, affectionate, and not over-and-above honest, "glorious Apollos;" the marchioness, his bride; Tom Codlin and his partner; Miss Sally Brass, that "fine fellow;" the pony that had an opinion of its own; the boy that stood upon his head; the sexton; the man at the forge; not forgetting the dancing dogs and baby Nubbles. There are other admirably drawn characters—but we note these for their remarkable originality, as well as for their wonderful keeping, and the glowing colors in which they are painted. We have heard some of them called caricatures—but the charge is grossly ill-founded. No critical principle is more firmly based in reason than that a certain amount of exaggeration is essential to the proper depicting of truth itself. We do not paint an object to be true, but to appear true to the beholder. Were we to copy nature with accuracy the object copied would seem unnatural. The columns of the Greek temples, which convey the idea of absolute proportion, are very considerably thicker just beneath the capital than at the base. We regret that we have not left ourselves space in which to examine this whole question as it deserves. We must content ourselves with saying that caricature seldom exists (unless in so gross a form as to disgust at once) where the component parts are *in keeping*; and that the laugh excited by it, in any case, is radically distinct from that induced by a properly artistical *incongruity*—the source of all mirth. Were these creations of Mr. Dickens' really caricatures they would not

live in public estimation beyond the hour of their first survey. We regard them as *creations*—(that is to say as original combinations of character) only not all of the highest order, because the elements employed are not always of the highest. In the instances of Nelly, the grandfather, the Sexton, and the man of the furnace, the force of the creative intellect could scarcely have been engaged with nobler material, and the result is that these personages belong to the most august regions of the *Ideal*.

In truth, the great feature of the *Curiosity Shop* is its chaste, vigorous, and glorious *imagination*. This is the one charm, all potent, which alone would suffice to compensate for a world more of error than Mr. Dickens ever committed. It is not only seen in the conception, and general handling of the story, or in the invention of character; but it pervades every sentence of the book. We recognise its prodigious influence in every inspired word. It is this which induces the reader who is at all ideal, to pause frequently, to re-read the occasionally quaint phrases, to muse in uncontrollable delight over thoughts which, while he wonders he has never hit upon them before, he yet admits that he never has encountered. In fact it is the wand of the enchanter. ⟨. . .⟩

Upon the whole we think the *Curiosity Shop* very much the best of the works of Mr. Dickens. It is scarcely possible to speak of it too well. It is in all respects a tale which will secure for its author the enthusiastic admiration of every man of genius.—Edgar Allan Poe, "Charles Dickens" (1841), *Essays and Reviews*, ed. G. R. Thompson, 1984, pp. 213–17

Whatever may be the separate beauty of Nell's position as to character and situation in relation to her grandfather, it is dreadfully marred to me by the extravagance and caricature (as so often happens in Dickens) of the gambling insanity in the old man. Dickens, like all novelists anxious only for effect, misunderstands the true impulse in obstinate incorrigible gamesters: it is not faith, unconquerable faith, in their luck; it is the very opposite principle—a despair of their own luck—rage and hatred in consequence, as at a blind enemy working in the dark, and furious desire to affront this dark malignant power; just as in the frenzy of hopeless combat you will see a man without a chance, and knowing that he does but prolong his adversary's triumph, yet still flying again with his fists at the face which he can never reach. Without love on the old man's part to Nell, hers for him would be less interesting; and *with* love of any strength, the old fool could not *but* have paused. The risk was *instant*: it ruined Nell's hopes of a breakfast; it tended to a jail. Now Alnaschar delusions take a different flight—they settle on the future. Extravagance and want of fidelity to nature and the possibilities of life are what everywhere mar Dickens to me; and these faults are fatal, because the *modes* of life amongst which these extravagances intrude are always the absolute realities of vulgarised life as it exists in plebeian ranks amongst our countrymen at this moment. Were the mode of life one more idealised or removed from our own, I might be less sensible of the insupportable extravagances. —Thomas De Quincey, Letter to His Daughter (Sept. 19, 1847), cited in Alexander Hay Japp (as "H. A. Page"), *Thomas De Quincey: His Life and Writings*, 1877, Vol. 1, pp. 348–49

I admire Nell in the *Old Curiosity Shop* exceedingly. No doubt the whole thing is a good deal borrowed from Wilhelm Meister. But little Nell is a far purer, lovelier, more *English* conception than Mignon, treasonable as the saying would seem to some. No doubt it was suggested by Mignon.—Sara Coleridge, Letter to Aubrey De Vere (Oct. 2, 1849), *Memoir and Letters of Sara Coleridge*, ed. Edith Coleridge, 1873, Vol. 2, p. 407

Above the pines the moon was slowly drifting,
  The river sang below;
The dim Sierras, far beyond, uplifting
  Their minarets of snow.

The roaring camp-fire, with rude humor, painted
  The ruddy tints of health
On haggard face and form that drooped and fainted
  In the fierce race for wealth;

Till one arose, and from his pack's scant treasure
  A hoarded volume drew,
And cards were dropped from hands of listless leisure
  To hear the tale anew.

And then, while round them shadows gathered faster,
  And as the firelight fell,
He read aloud the book wherein the Master
  Had writ of "Little Nell."

Perhaps 't was boyish fancy,—for the reader
  Was youngest of them all,—
But, as he read, from clustering pine and cedar
  A silence seemed to fall;

The fir-trees, gathering closer in the shadows,
  Listened in every spray,
While the whole camp with "Nell" on English meadows
  Wandered and lost their way.

And so in mountain solitudes—o'ertaken
  As by some spell divine—
Their cares dropped from them like the needles shaken
  From out the gusty pine.

Lost is that camp and wasted all its fire;
  And he who wrought that spell?
Ah! towering pine and stately Kentish spire,
  Ye have one tale to tell!

Lost is that camp, but let its fragrant story
  Blend with the breath that thrills
With hop-vine's incense all the pensive glory
  That fills the Kentish hills.

And on that grave where English oak and holly
  And laurel wreaths entwine,
Deem it not all a too presumptuous folly,
  This spray of Western pine!
  —BRET HARTE, "Dickens in Camp," 1870

I believe that the first book—the first real, substantial book—I read through was *The Old Curiosity Shop*. At all events, it was the first volume of Dickens which I made my own. And I could not have lighted better in my choice. At ten years old, or so, one is not ready for *Pickwick*. I remember very well the day when I plunged into that sea of mirth; I can hear myself, half choked with laughter, clamoring for the attention of my elders whilst I read aloud this and that passage from the great Trial. But *The Old Curiosity Shop* makes strong appeal to a youthful imagination, and contains little that is beyond its scope. Dickens's sentiment, however it may distress the mature mind of our later day, is not unwholesome, and, at all events in this story, addresses itself naturally enough to feelings unsubdued by criticism. His quality of picturesqueness is here seen at its best, with little or nothing of that melodrama which makes the alloy of *Nicholas Nickleby* and *Oliver Twist*—to speak only of the early books. The opening scene, that dim-lighted storehouse of things old and grotesque, is the best approach to Dickens's world, where sights of every day are transfigured in the service of romance. The kindliness of the author's spirit, his overflowing sympathy with poor and humble folk, set one's mind to a sort of music which it is good

to live with; and no writer of moralities ever showed triumphant virtue in so cheery a light as that which falls upon these honest people when rascality has got its deserts. Notably good, too, whether for young or old, is the atmosphere of rural peace breathed in so many pages of this book; I know that it helped to make conscious in me a love of English field and lane and village, one day to become a solacing passion. In *The Old Curiosity Shop*, town is set before you only for effect of contrast; the aspiration of the story is to the country road winding along under a pure sky. Others have pictured with a closer fidelity the scenes of English rustic life, but who succeeds better than Dickens in throwing a charm upon the wayside inn and the village church? Among his supreme merits is that of having presented in abiding form one of the best of our national ideals—rural homeliness. By the way of happiest emotions, the child reader takes this ideal into mind and heart; and perhaps it is in great part because Dickens's books are still so much read, because one sees edition after edition scattered over town and country homes, that one cannot wholly despair of this new England which tries so hard to be unlike the old.—GEORGE GISSING, "Dickens in Memory," *Critic*, Jan. 1902, pp. 48–49

AMERICAN NOTES

A thousand thanks to you for your charming book! and for all the pleasure, profit, and *relief* it has afforded me. You *have* been very tender to our sensitive friends beyond sea, and really said nothing which should give any serious offence to any moderately rational patriot among them. The *Slavers*, of course, will give you no quarter, and I suppose you did not expect they should. But I do not think you could have said less, and my whole heart goes along with every word you have written. Some people will be angry too, that you have been so strict to observe their *spitting*, and neglect of ablutions, &c. And more, that you should have spoken with so little reverence of their courts of law and state legislature, and even of their grand Congress itself. But all this latter part is done in such a spirit of good-humoured playfulness, and so mixed up with clear intimations that you have quite as little veneration for things of the same sort *at home*, that it will not be easy to represent it as the fruit of *English* insolence and envy. —FRANCIS, LORD JEFFREY, Letter to Charles Dickens (Oct. 16, 1842), cited in Lord Henry Cockburn, *Life of Lord Jeffrey*, 1852, Vol. 2, p. 294

I have read Dickens's book. It is jovial and good-natured, and at times very severe. You will read it with delight and, for the most part, approbation. He has a grand chapter on Slavery. *Spitting* and *politics at Washington* are the other topics of censure. Both you and I would censure them with equal severity, to say the least.—HENRY WADSWORTH LONGFELLOW, Letter to Charles Sumner (Oct. 16, 1842), cited in Samuel Longfellow, *Life of Henry Wadsworth Longfellow*, 1891, Vol. 1, p. 421

This morning I received Dickens's book. I have now read it. It is impossible for me to review it; nor do I think that you would wish me to do so. I can not praise it, and I will not cut it up. I can not praise it, though it contains a few lively dialogues and descriptions; for it seems to me to be, on the whole, a failure. It is written like the worst parts of *Humphrey's Clock*. What is meant to be easy and sprightly is vulgar and flippant, as in the first two pages. What is meant to be fine is a great deal too fine for me, as the description of the Fall of Niagara. A reader who wants an amusing account of the United States had better go to Mrs. Trollope, coarse and malignant as she is. A reader who wants information about American politics, manners, and literature had better go even to so poor a creature as Buckingham. In short, I pronounce the book, in spite of some gleams of genius, at once frivolous and dull.

Therefore I will not praise it. Neither will I attack it; first, because I have eaten salt with Dickens; secondly, because he is a good man, and a man of real talent; thirdly, because he hates slavery as heartily as I do; and, fourthly, because I wish to see him enrolled in our blue-and-yellow corps, where he may do excellent service as a skirmisher and sharpshooter.—THOMAS BABINGTON MACAULAY, Letter to Macvey Napier (Oct. 19, 1842), cited in G. Otto Trevelyan, *The Life and Letters of Lord Macaulay*, 1876, Vol. 2, p. 109

Such being our opinion of Mr. Dickens's faculties and opportunities for observation, we expected from him a book, not without large defects both positive and negative, but containing some substantial and valuable addition to our stock of information with regard to this most interesting country—interesting not only for the indissoluble connexion of its interests with our own, but likewise as the quarter from which we must look for light on the great question of these times,—What is to become of *Democracy*, and how is it to be dealt with? We cannot say that our expectations are justified by the result. Though the book is said to have given great offence on the other side of the Atlantic, we cannot see any sufficient reason for it. To us it appears that Mr. Dickens deserves great praise for the care with which he has avoided all offensive topics, and abstained from amusing his readers at the expense of his entertainers; and if we had an account of the temptations in this kind which he has resisted, we do not doubt that the reserve and self-control which he has exercised would appear scarcely less than heroical. But, on the other hand, we cannot say that his book throws any new light on his subject. He has done little more than confide to the public what should have been a series of letters for the entertainment of his private friends. Very agreeable and amusing letters they would have been; and as such, had they been posthumously published, would have been read with interest and pleasure. As it is, in the middle of our amusement at the graphic sketches of life and manners, the ludicrous incidents, the wayside conversations about nothing, so happily told, and the lively remarks, with which these *Notes* abound—in the middle of our respect for the tone of good sense and good humour which runs through them—and in spite of a high appreciation of the gentlemanly feeling which has induced him to refrain from all personal allusions and criticisms, and for the modesty which has kept him silent on so many subjects, concerning which most persons in the same situation (not being reminded of the worthlessness of their opinions by the general inattention of mankind to what they say) are betrayed into the delivery of oracles—in the middle of all this we cannot help feeling that we should have respected Mr. Dickens more if he had kept his book to himself; if he had been so far dissatisfied with these *American Notes* as to shrink from the "general circulation" of them; if he had felt unwilling to stand by and see his nothings trumpeted to all corners of the earth, quoted and criticised in every newspaper, passing through edition after edition in England, and settling in clouds of sixpenny copies all over the United States. That he had nothing better to say is no reproach to him. He had much to say about international copyright, and that, we doubt not, was well worth hearing; we only wish it had been heard with more favour. But, having nothing better to say, why say anything? Or why, at least, sound a trumpet before him to call men away from their business to listen? To us it seems to imply a want of

respect either for himself or for his subject, that he should be thus prompt to gratify the prurient public appetite for novelty, by bringing the fruits of his mind into the market unripe. This, however, is a matter of taste. In reputation, so easy and abundant a writer will suffer little from an occasional mistake. Though this book should only live till New Year's Day, it will have lived long enough for his fame; for on that day we observe that he is himself to come forth again in a series of monthly numbers, so that none but himself will be his extinguisher. —JAMES SPEDDING, "Dickens's *American Notes*" (1843), *Reviews and Discussions*, 1849, pp. 247–48

A CHRISTMAS CAROL

I do not mean that the *Christmas Carol* is quite as brilliant or self-evident as the sun at noonday; but it is so spread over England by this time, that no sceptic, no *Fraser's Magazine*,—no, not even the godlike and ancient *Quarterly* itself (venerable, Saturnian, bigwigged dynasty!) could review it down. ⟨. . .⟩

In fact, one might as well detail the plot of the *Merry Wives of Windsor*, or *Robinson Crusoe*, as recapitulate here the adventures of Scrooge the miser, and his Christmas conversion. I am not sure that the allegory is a very complete one, and protest, with the classics, against the use of blank verse in prose; but here all objections stop. Who can listen to objections regarding such a book as this? It seems to me a national benefit, and to every man or woman who reads it a personal kindness. The last two people I heard speak of it were women; neither knew the other, or the author, and both said, by way of criticism, "God bless him!" A Scotch philosopher, who nationally does not keep Christmas-day, on reading the book, sent out for a turkey, and asked two friends to dine—this is a fact! Many men were known to sit down after perusing it, and write off letters to their friends, not about business, but out of their fulness of heart, and to wish old acquaintances a happy Christmas. Had the book appeared a fortnight earlier, all the prize cattle would have been gobbled up in pure love and friendship, Epping denuded of sausages, and not a turkey left in Norfolk. His royal highness's fat stock would have fetched unheard-of prices, and Alderman Bannister would have been tired of slaying. But there is a Christmas for 1844, too; the book will be as early then as now, and so let speculators look out.

As for Tiny Tim, there is a certain passage in the book regarding that young gentleman, about which a man should hardly venture to speak in print or in public, any more than he would of any other affections of his private heart. There is not a reader in England but that little creature will be a bond of union between the author and him; and he will say of Charles Dickens, as the woman just now, "God Bless Him!" What a feeling is this for a writer to be able to inspire, and what a reward to reap!—WILLIAM MAKEPEACE THACKERAY, "A Box of Novels," *Fraser's Magazine*, Feb. 1844, pp. 168–69

It is easy, too, to say of Dickens that he makes us acquainted with many unsavory characters—people whom we would hardly care to associate with in real life, or to touch without gloves; and it is easy to ask why one need be so familiar with them and their disreputable haunts on paper. But what a thrill ran through the whole English-speaking race when *A Christmas Carol in Prose* announced to it that Marley was dead, to begin with—as dead as a door-nail! No carol that ever was sung so stirred the deep heart of humanity. The world laughed and cried over it, and Scrooge and Scrooge's nephew, and old Fezziwig, and Bob Cratchit, and Tiny Tim, became household words in a million homes. It was not Scrooge only that the Ghost of Christmas Past led backward over the pathway of the years, showing him the wasted opportunities, the graves of buried loves and hopes, the monuments raised to pride and hatred, the littlenesses, the meannesses, the barrenness that made "the shadows of the things that have been" so terrible. It was not to him only that the Ghost of Christmas Present revealed the things that were, the light struggling with darkness, patience and faith and hope and innocent merrymaking in lowliest homes, the love that sweetens penury, and, side by side with it, the degradation that is unutterable. And not to Scrooge alone, thank God, did Christmas Future show that the past, with all its records of sin and misery, could be blotted out, and a new page written.—JULIA C. R. DORR, "Christmas and Its Literature," *Book Buyer*, Dec. 1868, pp. 284–85

MARTIN CHUZZLEWIT

Dickens, Boz—For Shame. Dickens has just published as one of the chapters of *Martin Chuzzlewit* an account of the arrival of his hero in New York, and what he saw, and heard, and did, and suffered, in this land of pagans, brutes, and infidels. I am sorry to see it. Thinking that Mr. Dickens has been ungenerously treated by my countrymen, I have taken his part on most occasions; but he has now written an exceedingly foolish libel upon us, from which he will not obtain credit as an author, nor as a man of wit, any more than as a man of good taste, good nature, or good manners. It is difficult to believe that such unmitigated trash should have flown from the same pen that drew the portrait of the immortal *Pickwick* and his expressive gaiters, the honest locksmith and his pretty Dolly of Clerkenwell, and poor little Nell, who has caused so many tears to flow. Shame, Mr. Dickens! Considering all that we did for you, if, as some folks say, I and others made fools of ourselves to make much of you, you should not afford them the triumph of saying, "There! We told you so!" "It serves you right!" and such other consolatory phrases. If we were fools you were the cause of it, and should have stood by us. *"Et tu, Brute!"*—PHILIP HONE, *Diary*, July 29, 1843

This last work contains, besides all the fun, some very marked and available morals. I scarce know any book in which the evil and odiousness of selfishness is more forcibly brought out, or in a greater variety of exhibitions. In the midst of the merry quotations, or at least on any fair opportunity, I draw the boys' attention to these points, bid them remark how *unmanly* is the selfishness of young Martin, and I insist upon it that Tom Pinch's character, if it could really exist, would be a very beautiful one. But I doubt, as I do in regard to *Pickwick*, that so much sense, and deep, solid goodness, could coexist with such want of discernment and liability to be gulled. Tigg is very clever, and the boys roar with laughter at the "what's-his-name place whence no thingumbob ever came back;" but this is only a new edition of Jingle and Smangles; Mark Tapley, also, is a second Sam Weller. The new characters are Pecksniff, and the thrice-notable Sairey Gamp, with Betsy Prig to show her off. —SARA COLERIDGE, Letter to Mrs. H. M. Jones (Aug. 17, 1848), *Memoir and Letters of Sara Coleridge*, ed. Edith Coleridge, 1873, Vol. 2, p. 346

I liked *Martin Chuzzlewit*, ⟨. . .⟩ and the other day I read a great part of it again, and found it roughly true in the passages that referred to America, though it was surcharged in the serious moods, and caricatured in the comic. The English are always inadequate observers; they seem too full of themselves to have eyes and ears for any alien people; but as far as an Englishman could, Dickens had caught the look of our life in certain aspects. His report of it was clumsy and farcical; but in a large, loose way it was like enough; at least he had caught the

note of our self-satisfied, intolerant, and hypocritical provinciality, and this was not altogether lost in his mocking horseplay.—WILLIAM DEAN HOWELLS, "Dickens," *My Literary Passions*, 1895

DAVID COPPERFIELD

I have read *David Copperfield*; it seems to me very good— admirable in some parts. You said it had affinity to *Jane Eyre*. It has, now and then—only what an advantage has Dickens in his varied knowledge of men and things!—CHARLOTTE BRONTË, Letter to W. S. Williams (Sept. 13, 1849)

⟨. . .⟩ I did not find it easy to get sufficiently far away from it, in the first sensations of having finished it, to refer to it with the composure which this formal heading would seem to require. My interest in it was so recent and strong, and my mind was so divided between pleasure and regret—pleasure in the achievement of a long design, regret in the separation from many companions—that I was in danger of wearying the reader with personal confidences and private emotions.

Besides which, all that I could have said of the Story to any purpose, I had endeavoured to say in it.

It would concern the reader little, perhaps, to know how sorrowfully the pen is laid down at the close of a two-years' imaginative task; or how an Author feels as if he were dismissing some portion of himself into the shadowy world, when a crowd of the creatures of his brain are going from him for ever. Yet, I had nothing else to tell; unless, indeed, I were to confess (which might be of less moment still), that no one can ever believe this Narrative in the reading more than I believed it in the writing.

So true are these avowals at the present day, that I can now only take the reader into one confidence more. Of all my books, I like this the best. It will be easily believed that I am a fond parent to every child of my fancy, and that no one can ever love that family as dearly as I love them. But, like many fond parents, I have in my heart of hearts a favourite child. And his name is David Copperfield.—CHARLES DICKENS, "Preface" to *David Copperfield*, 1850

Have you read *David Copperfield*, by the way? How beautiful it is—how charmingly fresh and simple! In those admirable touches of tender humour—and I should call humour, Bob, a mixture of love and wit—who can equal this great genius? There are little words and phrases in his books which are like personal benefits to the reader. What a place it is to hold in the affections of men! What an awful responsibility hanging over a writer! What man holding such a place, and knowing that his words go forth to vast congregations of mankind,—to grown folks—to their children, and perhaps to their children's children,—but must think of his calling with a solemn and humble heart! May love and truth guide such a man always! It is an awful prayer; may heaven further its fulfilment!—WILLIAM MAKEPEACE THACKERAY, "Mr. Brown the Elder Takes Mr. Brown the Younger to a Club," *Sketches and Travels in London*, 1850

As I was stepping into the house Dickens came out to meet me, with bright looks and a hearty greeting. He looked a little older than when we said good-bye ten years ago; but that was partly owing to the beard he had grown. His eyes were bright as ever; the smile on his lips was the same; his frank voice was just as friendly,—ay, and if possible, more winning still. He was now in the prime of manhood in his 45th year; full of youth and life and eloquence, and rich in a rare humour that glowed with kindliness. I know not how to describe him better than in the

words of one of my first letters home: "Take the best out of all
Dickens's writings, combine them into the picture of a man,
and there thou hast Charles Dickens." And such as in the first
hour he stood before me, the very same he remained all the
time of my visit; ever genuine, and cheerful, and sympathetic.—HANS CHRISTIAN ANDERSEN, "A Visit to Charles
Dickens," *Temple Bar*, Dec. 1870, p. 29

I have said that in *David Copperfield* Dickens is freer from
defect than in any other of his works. It is rarely that public
opinion has ratified an author's judgment so completely as it
has here. As we all know, this was Dickens's favourite, and the
reason we all know. It may be noted in passing how characteristic of the two men is their choice. To Dickens *David
Copperfield* was, to use his own words, his favourite child,
because in its pages he saw the reflection of his own youth.
Thackeray, though he never spoke out on such matters, is
generally believed to have looked not a little into his own heart
when he wrote *Pendennis*. Yet his favourite was *Esmond*, for
Esmond he rightly felt to be the most complete and perfect of
his works; in that exquisite book his *art* touched its highest
point. With *David Copperfield*, no doubt the secret of the
writer's partiality is in some sense the secret of the reader's.
Though none, perhaps, have been so outspoken as Hogg, every
man takes pleasure in writing about himself, and we are always
pleased to hear what he has to say; egotism, as Macaulay says,
so unpopular in conversation, is always popular in writing. But
not in the charm of autobiography alone lies the fascination
which this delightful book has exercised on every class of
readers. It is not only Dickens's most attractive work, but it is
his best work. And it is his best for this reason, that whereas in
all his others he is continually striving to realise the conception
of his fancy, in this alone his business is to idealise the reality;
in this alone, as it seems to me, his imagination prevails over
his fancy. In this alone he is never grotesque, or for him so
rarely that we hardly care to qualify the adverb. Nowhere else
is his pathos so tender and so sure; nowhere else is his humour,
though often more boisterous and more abundant, so easy and
so fine; nowhere else is his observation so vivid and so deep;
nowhere else has he held with so sure a hand the balance
between the classes. If in the character of Daniel Pegotty more
eloquently and more reasonably than he has ever done elsewhere, even in honest Joe Gargery, he has enlarged on his
favourite abiding-place for virtue, he has also nowhere else
been so ready and so glad to welcome her in those more seemly
places wherein for the most part he can find no resting-place
for her feet. Weak-minded as Doctor Strong is, fatuous, if the
reader pleases, we are never asked to laugh at the kindly,
chivalrous old scholar, as we are at Sir Leicester Dedlock; Clara
Pegotty is no better woman than Agnes Wickfield. And even in
smaller matters, and in the characters of second-rate importance, we may find the same sureness of touch. It has been
made a reproach against him that his characters are too apt to
be forgotten in the externals of their callings, that they never
speak without some allusion to their occupations, and cannot
be separated from them. In the extraordinary number and
variety of characters that he has drawn, no doubt one can find
instances of this. For so many of these characters, nearly all,
indeed, of the comic ones, real as he has made them to us, are
not, when we come to examine them, realities, but rather
conceptions of his fancy, which he has to shape into realities by
the use of certain traits and peculiarities of humanity with
which his extraordinary observation has supplied him. Major
Pendennis, and Costigan, and Becky Sharp *are* realities whom
Thackeray idealises, makes characters of fiction out of. But

Sam Weller and Mrs. Gamp are the children of fancy whom
Dickens makes real, partly by the addition of sundry human
attributes, but even more so by the marvellous skill and
distinctness with which he brings them and keeps them before
us. But in order to do this he is obliged never to lose sight, or
to suffer us to lose sight, of those peculiarities, whether of
speech, or manner, or condition, which make them for us the
realities that they are. And in so doing it cannot but happen
that he seems to thrust those peculiarities at times somewhat
too persistently upon us. In *David Copperfield* this is not so, or
much less so than anywhere else, except, of course, in *The Tale
of Two Cities*, Dickens's only essay at the romance proper,
where the characters are subordinate to the story. We may see
this, for example, by comparing Omer, the undertaker, in
David Copperfield, with Mould, the undertaker, in *Martin
Chuzzlewit*. Mould and all his family live in a perpetual
atmosphere of funerals; his children are represented as solacing
their young existences by "playing at buryin's down in the
shop, and follerin' the order-book to its long home in the iron
safe;" and Mr. Mould's own idea of fellowship is of a person
"one would almost feel disposed to bury for nothing, and do it
neatly, too!" On his first introduction, after old Anthony's
death, he sets the seal on his personality by the remark that
Jonas's liberal orders for the funeral prove "what was so forcibly
observed by the lamented theatrical poet—*buried at Stratford*—that there is good in everything." That touch is very
comical, but also very grotesque; it is a touch of fancy, not of
nature. But when David Copperfield, as a man, recalls himself
to the recollection of the good-hearted Omer, who had known
him as a boy, the undertaker is revealed in a very different
fashion. "To be sure," said Mr. Omer, touching my waistcoat
with his forefinger; "and there was a little child too! *There was
two parties. The little party was laid along with the other party*.
Over at Blunderstone it was, of course. Dear me! And how
have you been since?" Every one must be conscious of the difference here.—MOWBRAY MORRIS, "Charles Dickens," *Fortnightly Review*, Dec. 1882, pp. 776–77

I am trying to get rested by reading Dickens, and am over
David Copperfield now. I had never read it, I find, though Mr.
Micawber has become so proverbial that, finding his name in
it, I thought I had. Dickens says in his preface that David
Copperfield was his "favorite child," and I don't wonder, for it
is amazingly well done so far as I have got.—JAMES RUSSELL
LOWELL, Letter to Charles Eliot Norton (April 8, 1887)

WALTER BAGEHOT
From "Charles Dickens" (1858)
Collected Works, ed. Norman St. John-Stevas

1965, Volume 2, pp. 81–107

His genius is essentially irregular and unsymmetrical.
Hardly any English writer perhaps is much more so. His
style is an example of it. It is descriptive, racy, and flowing; it
is instinct with new imagery and singular illustration; but
it does not indicate that due proportion of the faculties to
one another which is a beauty in itself, and which cannot
help diffusing beauty over every happy word and moulded
clause. ⟨. . .⟩
   The truth is that Mr. Dickens wholly wants the two
elements which we have spoken of as one or other requisite for
a symmetrical genius. He is utterly deficient in the faculty of
reasoning. 'Mamma, what shall I think about?' said the small
girl. 'My dear, don't think,' was the old-fashioned reply. We do

not allege that in the strict theory of education this was a correct reply; modern writers think otherwise; but we wish someone would say it to Mr. Dickens. He is often troubled with the idea that he must reflect, and his reflections are perhaps the worst reading in the world. There is a sentimental confusion about them; we never find the consecutive precision of mature theory, or the cold distinctness of clear thought. Vivid facts stand out in his imagination, and a fresh illustrative style brings them home to the imagination of his readers; but his continuous philosophy utterly fails in the attempt to harmonise them,—to educe a theory or elaborate a precept from them. Of his social thinking we shall have a few words to say in detail; his didactic humour is very unfortunate: no writer is less fitted for an excursion to the imperative mood. At present we only say what is so obvious as scarcely to need saying, that his abstract understanding is so far inferior to his picturesque imagination as to give even to his best works the sense of jar and incompleteness, and to deprive them altogether of the crystalline finish which is characteristic of the clear and cultured understanding.

Nor has Mr. Dickens the easy and various sagacity which, as has been said, gives a unity to all which it touches. He has, indeed, a quality which is near allied to it in appearance. His shrewdness in some things, especially in traits and small things, is wonderful. His works are full of acute remarks on petty doings, and well exemplify the telling power of minute circumstantiality. But the minor species of perceptive sharpness is so different from diffused sagacity, that the two scarcely ever are to be found in the same mind. There is nothing less like the great lawyer, acquainted with broad principles and applying them with distinct deduction, than the attorney's clerk who catches at small points like a dog biting at flies. 'Over-sharpness' in the student is the most unpromising symptom of the logical jurist. You must not ask a horse in blinkers for a large view of a landscape. In the same way, a detective ingenuity in microscopic detail is of all mental qualities most unlike the broad sagacity by which the great painters of human affairs have unintentionally stamped the mark of unity on their productions. They show by their treatment of each case that they understand the whole of life; the special delineator of fragments and points shows that he understands them only. In one respect the defect is more striking in Mr. Dickens than in any other novelist of the present day. The most remarkable deficiency in modern fiction is its omission of the business of life, of all those countless occupations, pursuits, and callings in which most men live and move, and by which they have their being. In most novels money *grows*. You have no idea of the toil, the patience, and the wearing anxiety by which men of action provide for the day, and lay up for the future, and support those that are given into their care. Mr. Dickens is not chargeable with this omission. He perpetually deals with the pecuniary part of life. Almost all his characters have determined occupations, of which he is apt to talk even at too much length. When he rises from the toiling to the luxurious classes, his genius in most cases deserts him. The delicate refinement and discriminating taste of the idling orders are not in his way; he knows the dry arches of London Bridge better than Belgravia. He excels in inventories of poor furniture, and is learned in pawnbrokers' tickets. But, although his creative power lives and works among the middle class and industrial section of English society, he has never painted the highest part of their daily intellectual life. He made, indeed, an attempt to paint specimens of the apt and able man of business in *Nicholas Nickleby*; but the Messrs. Cheeryble are among the stupidest of his characters. He forgot that breadth of platitude is

rather different from breadth of sagacity. His delineations of middle-class life have in consequence a harshness and meanness which do not belong to that life in reality. He omits the relieving element. He describes the figs which are sold, but not the talent which sells figs well. And it is the same want of the diffused sagacity in his own nature which has made his pictures of life so odd and disjointed, and which has deprived them of symmetry and unity. ⟨. . .⟩

Mr. Dickens's humour is indeed very much a result of ⟨. . .⟩ two peculiarities ⟨. . .⟩ His power of detailed observation and his power of idealising individual traits of character—sometimes of one or other of them, sometimes of both of them together. His similes on matters of external observation are so admirable that everybody appreciates them, and it would be absurd to quote specimens of them; nor is it the sort of excellence which best bears to be paraded for the purposes of critical example. Its off-hand air and natural connection with the adjacent circumstances are inherent parts of its peculiar merit. Every reader of Mr. Dickens's works knows well what we mean. And who is not a reader of them?

But his peculiar humour is even more indebted to his habit of vivifying external traits, than to his power of external observation. He, as we have explained, expands traits into people; and it is a source of true humour to place these, when so expanded, in circumstances in which only people—that is, complete human beings—can appropriately act. The humour of Mr. Pickwick's character is entirely of this kind. He is a kind of incarnation of simple-mindedness and what we may call obvious-mindedness. The conclusion which each occurrence or position in life most immediately presents to the unsophisticated mind is that which Mr. Pickwick is sure to accept. The proper accompaniments are given to him. He is a stout gentleman in easy circumstances, who is irritated into originality by no impulse from within, and by no stimulus from without. He is stated to have 'retired from business.' But no one can fancy what he was in business. Such guileless simplicity of heart and easy impressibility of disposition would soon have induced a painful failure amid the harsh struggles and the tempting speculations of pecuniary life. As he is represented in the narrative, however, nobody dreams of such antecedents. Mr. Pickwick moves easily over all the surface of English life from Goswell Street to Dingley Dell, from Dingley Dell to the Ipswich elections, from drinking milk-punch in a wheelbarrow to sleeping in the approximate pound, and no one ever thinks of applying to him the ordinary maxims which we should apply to any common person in life, or to any common personage in a fiction. Nobody thinks it is wrong in Mr. Pickwick to drink too much milk-punch in a wheelbarrow, to introduce worthless people of whom he knows nothing to the families of people for whom he really cares; nobody holds him responsible for the consequences; nobody thinks there is anything wrong in his taking Mr. Bob Sawyer and Mr. Benjamin Allen to visit Mr. Winkle senior, and thereby almost irretrievably offending him with his son's marriage. We do not reject moral remarks such as these, but they never occur to us. Indeed, the indistinct consciousness that such observations are possible, and that they are hovering about our minds, enhances the humour of the narrative. We are in a conventional world, where the mere maxims of common life do not apply, and yet which has all the amusing detail, and picturesque elements, and singular eccentricities of common life. Mr. Pickwick is a personified ideal; a kind of amateur in life, whose course we watch through all the circumstances of ordinary existence, and at whose follies we are amused just as really skilled people are at the mistakes of an amateur in their art. His being in the pound is not wrong; his being the victim of Messrs. Dodson is not foolish. 'Always shout with the mob,' said Mr. Pickwick. 'But suppose there are two mobs,' said Mr. Snodgrass. 'Then shout with the loudest,' said Mr. Pickwick. This is not in him weakness or time-serving or want of principle, as in most even of fictitious people it would be. It is his way. Mr. Pickwick was expected to say something, so he said 'Ah!' in a grave voice. This is not pompous as we might fancy, or clever as it might be if intentionally devised; it is simply his way. Mr. Pickwick gets late at night over the wall behind the back-door of a young-ladies' school, is found in that sequestered place by the schoolmistress and the boarders and the cook, and there is a dialogue between them. There is nothing out of possibility in this; it is his way. The humour essentially consists in treating as a moral agent a being who really is not a moral agent. We treat a vivified accident as a man, and we are surprised at the absurd results. We are reading about an acting thing, and we wonder at its scrapes, and laugh at them as if they were those of the man. There is something of this humour in every sort of farce. Everybody knows these are not real beings acting in real life, though they talk as if they were, and want us to believe that they are. Here, as in Mr. Dickens's books, we have exaggerations pretending to comport themselves as ordinary beings, caricatures acting as if they were characters.

At the same time it is essential to remember, that however great may be and is the charm of such exaggerated personifications, the best specimens of them are immensely less excellent, belong to an altogether lower range of intellectual achievements, than the real depiction of actual living men. It is amusing to read of beings *out of* the laws of morality, but it is more profoundly interesting, as well as more instructive, to read of those whose life in its moral conditions resembles our own. We see this most distinctly when both the representations are given by the genius of the same writer. Falstaff is a sort of sack-holding paunch, an exaggerated over-development which no one thinks of holding down to the commonplace rules of the ten commandments and the statute-law. We do not think of them in connection with him. They belong to a world apart. Accordingly, we are vexed when the king discards him and reproves him. Such a fate was a necessary adherence on Shakespeare's part to the historical tradition; he never probably thought of departing from it, nor would his audience have perhaps endured his doing so. But to those who look at the historical plays as pure works of imaginative art, it seems certainly an artistic misconception to have developed so marvellous an *un*moral impersonation, and then to have subjected it to an ethical and punitive judgment. Still, notwithstanding this error, which was very likely inevitable, Falstaff is probably the most remarkable specimen of caricature-representation to be found in literature. And its very excellence of execution only shows how inferior is the kind of art which creates only such representations. Who could compare the genius, marvellous as must be its fertility, which was needful to create a Falstaff, with that shown in the higher productions of the same mind in Hamlet, Ophelia, and Lear? We feel instantaneously the difference between the aggregating accident which rakes up from the externalities of life other accidents analogous to itself, and the central ideal of a real character which cannot show itself wholly in any accidents, but which exemplifies itself partially in many, which unfolds itself gradually in wide spheres of action, and yet, as with those we know best in life, leaves something hardly to be understood, and after years of familiarity is a problem and a difficulty to the last. In the same way, the embodied characteristics and grotesque exaggerations of Mr. Dickens, notwithstanding all their humour and all their

marvellous abundance, can never be for a moment compared with the great works of the real painters of essential human nature.

There is one class of Mr. Dickens's pictures which may seem to form an exception to this criticism. It is the delineation of the outlaw, we might say the anti-law, world in *Oliver Twist*. In one or two instances Mr. Dickens has been so fortunate as to hit on characteristics which, by his system of idealisation and continual repetition, might really be brought to look like a character. A man's trade or profession in regular life can only exhaust a very small portion of his nature; no approach is made to the essence of humanity by the exaggeration of the traits which typify a beadle or an undertaker. With the outlaw world it is somewhat different. The bare fact of a man belonging to that world is so important to his nature, that if it is artistically developed with coherent accessories, some approximation to a distinctly natural character will be almost inevitably made. In the characters of Bill Sykes and Nancy this is so. The former is the skulking ruffian who may be seen any day at the police-courts, and whom any one may fancy he sees by walking through St. Giles's. You cannot attempt to figure to your imagination the existence of such a person without being thrown into the region of the passions, the will, and the conscience; the mere fact of his maintaining, as a condition of life and by settled profession, a struggle with regular society, necessarily brings these deep parts of his nature into prominence; great crime usually proceeds from abnormal impulses or strange effort. Accordingly, Mr. Sykes is the character most approaching to a coherent man who is to be found in Mr. Dickens's works. We do not say that even here there is not some undue heightening admixture of caricature; but this defect is scarcely thought of amid the general coherence of the picture, the painful subject, and the wonderful command of strange accessories. Miss Nancy is a still more delicate artistic effort. She is an idealisation of the girl who may also be seen at the police-courts and St. Giles's; as bad, according to occupation and common character, as a woman can be, yet retaining a tinge of womanhood, and a certain compassion for interesting suffering, which under favouring circumstances might be the germ of a regenerating influence. We need not stay to prove how much the imaginative development of such a personage must concern itself with our deeper humanity; how strongly, if excellent, it must be contrasted with everything conventional or casual or superficial. Mr. Dickens's delineation is in the highest degree excellent. It possesses not only the more obvious merits belonging to the subject, but also that of a singular delicacy of expression and idea. Nobody fancies for a moment that they are reading about anything beyond the pale of ordinary propriety. We read the account of the life which Miss Nancy leads with Bill Sykes without such an idea occurring to us: yet when we reflect upon it, few things in literary painting are more wonderful than the depiction of a professional life of sin and sorrow, so as not even to startle those to whom the deeper forms of either are but names and shadows. Other writers would have given as vivid a picture: Defoe would have poured out even a more copious measure of telling circumstantiality, but he would have narrated his story with an inhuman distinctness which, if not impure is *un*pure; French writers, whom we need not name, would have enhanced the interest of their narrative by trading on the excitement of stimulating scenes. It would be injustice to Mr. Dickens to say that he has surmounted these temptations; the unconscious evidence of innumerable details proves that, from a certain delicacy of imagination and purity of spirit, he has not even experienced them. Criticism is the more bound to dwell at length on the merits of these delineations, because no artistic merit can make *Oliver Twist* a pleasing work. The squalid detail of crime and misery oppresses us too much. If it is to be read at all, it should be read in the first hardness of the youthful imagination, which no touch can move too deeply, and which is never stirred with tremulous suffering at the 'still sad music of humanity.' The coldest critic in later life may never hope to have again the apathy of his boyhood.

It perhaps follows from what has been said of the characteristics of Mr. Dickens's genius, that he would be little skilled in planning plots for his novels. He certainly is not so skilled. He says in his preface to the *Pickwick Papers*, 'that they were designed for the introduction of diverting characters and incidents; that no ingenuity of plot was attempted, or even at that time considered very feasible by the author in connection with the desultory plan of publication adopted;' and he adds an expression of regret that 'these chapters had not been strung together on a stronger thread of more general interest.' It is extremely fortunate that no such attempt was made. In the cases in which Mr. Dickens has attempted to make a long connected story, or to develop into scenes or incidents a plan in any degree elaborate, the result has been a complete failure. A certain consistency of genius seems necessary for the construction of a consecutive plot. An irregular mind naturally shows itself in incoherency of incident and aberration of character. The method in which Mr. Dickens's mind works, if we are correct in our criticism upon it, tends naturally to these blemishes. Caricatures are necessarily isolated; they are produced by the exaggeration of certain conspicuous traits and features; each being is enlarged on its greatest side; and we laugh at the grotesque grouping and the startling contrast. But the connection between human beings on which a plot depends is rather severed than elucidated by the enhancement of their diversities. Interesting stories are founded on the intimate relations of men and women. These intimate relations are based not on their superficial traits, or common occupations, or most visible externalities, but on the inner life of heart and feeling. You simply divert attention from that secret life by enhancing the perceptible diversities of common human nature, and the strange anomalies into which it may be distorted. The original germ of *Pickwick* was a 'Club of Oddities.' The idea was professedly abandoned; but traces of it are to be found in all Mr. Dickens's books. It illustrates the professed grotesqueness of the characters as well as their slender connection.

The defect of plot is heightened by Mr. Dickens's great, we might say complete, inability to make a love-story. A pair of lovers is by custom a necessity of narrative fiction, and writers who possess a great general range of mundane knowledge, and but little knowledge of the special sentimental subject, are often in amusing difficulties. The watchful reader observes the transition from the hearty description of well-known scenes, of prosaic streets, or journeys by wood and river, to the pale colours of ill-attempted poetry, to such sights as the novelist wishes he need not try to see. But few writers exhibit the difficulty in so aggravated a form as Mr. Dickens. Most men by taking thought can make a lay figure to look not so very unlike a young gentleman, and can compose a telling schedule of ladylike charms. Mr. Dickens has no power of doing either. The heroic character—we do not mean the form of character so-called in life and action, but that which is hereditary in the heroes of novels—is not suited to his style of art. Hazlitt wrote an essay to inquire 'Why the heroes of romances are insipid;' and without going that length, it may safely be said that the character of the agreeable young gentleman who loves and is loved should not be of the most marked sort. Flirtation ought

not to be an exaggerated pursuit. Young ladies and their admirers should not express themselves in the heightened and imaginative phraseology suited to Charley Bates and the Dodger. Humour is of no use, for no one makes love in jokes: a tinge of insidious satire may perhaps be permitted as a rare and occasional relief, but it will not be thought 'a pretty book' if so malicious an element be at all habitually perceptible. The broad farce in which Mr. Dickens indulges is thoroughly out of place. If you caricature a pair of lovers ever so little, by the necessity of their calling you make them ridiculous. One of Sheridan's best comedies is remarkable for having no scene in which the hero and heroine are on the stage together; and Mr. Moore suggests that the shrewd wit distrusted his skill in the light dropping love-talk which would have been necessary. Mr. Dickens would have done well to imitate so astute a policy; but he has none of the managing shrewdness which those who look at Sheridan's career attentively will probably think not the least remarkable feature in his singular character. Mr. Dickens, on the contrary, pours out painful sentiments as if he wished the abundance should make up for the inferior quality. The excruciating writing which is expended on Miss Ruth Pinch passes belief. Mr. Dickens is not only unable to make lovers talk, but to describe heroines in mere narrative. As has been said, most men can make a jumble of blue eyes and fair hair and pearly teeth, that does very well for a young lady, at least for a good while; but Mr. Dickens will not, probably cannot, attain even to this humble measure of descriptive art. He vitiates the repose by broad humour, or disenchants the delicacy by an unctuous admiration.

This deficiency is probably nearly connected with one of Mr. Dickens's most remarkable excellencies. No one can read Mr. Thackeray's writings without feeling that he is perpetually treading as close as he dare to the border-line that separates the world which may be described in books from the world which it is prohibited so to describe. No one knows better than this accomplished artist where that line is, and how curious are its windings and turns. The charge against him is that he knows it but too well; that with an anxious care and a wistful eye he is ever approximating to its edge, and hinting with subtle art how thoroughly he is familiar with, and how interesting he could make the interdicted region on the other side. He never violates a single conventional rule; but at the same time the shadow of the immorality that is not seen is scarcely ever wanting to his delineation of the society that is seen. Everyone may perceive what is passing in his fancy. Mr. Dickens is chargeable with no such defect: he does not seem to feel the temptation. By what we may fairly call an instinctive purity of genius, he not only observes the conventional rules, but makes excursions into topics which no other novelist could safely handle, and, by a felicitous instinct, deprives them of all impropriety. No other writer could have managed the humour of Mrs. Gamp without becoming unendurable. At the same time it is difficult not to believe that this singular insensibility to the temptations to which many of the greatest novelists have succumbed is in some measure connected with his utter inaptitude for delineating the portion of life to which their art is specially inclined. He delineates neither the love-affairs which ought to be, nor those which ought not to be.

Mr. Dickens's indisposition to 'make capital' out of the most commonly tempting part of human sentiment is the more remarkable because he certainly does not show the same indisposition in other cases. He has naturally great powers of pathos; his imagination is familiar with the common sorts of human suffering; and his marvellous conversancy with the detail of existence enables him to describe sick-beds and death-beds with an excellence very rarely seen in literature. A nature far more sympathetic than that of most authors has familiarised him with such subjects. In general, a certain apathy is characteristic of book-writers, and dulls the efficacy of their pathos. Mr. Dickens is quite exempt from this defect; but, on the other hand, is exceedingly prone to a very ostentatious exhibition of the opposite excellence. He dwells on dismal scenes with a kind of fawning fondness; and he seems unwilling to leave them, long after his readers have had more than enough of them. He describes Mr. Dennis the hangman as having a professional fondness for his occupation: he has the same sort of fondness apparently for the profession of death-painter. The painful details he accumulates are a very serious drawback from the agreeableness of his writings. Dismal 'light literature' is the dismallest of reading. The reality of the police-reports is sufficiently bad, but a fictitious police-report would be the most disagreeable of conceivable compositions. Some portions of Mr. Dickens's books are liable to a good many of the same objections. They are squalid from noisome trivialities, and horrid with terrifying crime. In his earlier books this is commonly relieved at frequent intervals by a graphic and original mirth. As—we will not say age, but maturity, has passed over his powers, this counteractive element has been lessened; the humour is not so happy as it was, but the wonderful fertility in painful *minutiæ* still remains.

Mr. Dickens's political opinions have subjected him to a good deal of criticism, and to some ridicule. He has shown, on many occasions, the desire,—which we see so frequent among able and influential men,—to start as a political reformer. Mr. Spurgeon said, with an application to himself, 'If you've got the ear of the public, *of course* you must begin to tell it its faults.' Mr. Dickens has been quite disposed to make this use of his popular influence. Even in *Pickwick* there are many traces of this tendency; and the way in which it shows itself in that book and in others is very characteristic of the time at which they appeared. The most instructive political characteristic of the years from 1825 to 1845 is the growth and influence of the scheme of opinion which we call radicalism. There are several species of creeds which are comprehended under this generic name, but they all evince a marked reaction against the worship of the English constitution and the affection for the English *status quo*, which were then the established creed and sentiment. All radicals are anti-Eldonites. This is equally true of the Benthamite or philosophical radicalism of the early period, and the Manchester or 'definite-grievance' radicalism, among the last vestiges of which we are now living. Mr. Dickens represents a species different from either. His is what we may call the 'sentimental radicalism;' and if we recur to the history of the time, we shall find that there would not originally have been any opprobrium attaching to such a name. The whole course of the legislation, and still more of the administration, of the first twenty years of the nineteenth century were marked by a harsh unfeelingness which is of all faults the most contrary to any with which we are chargeable now. The world of the 'Six Acts,' of the frequent executions, of the Draconic criminal law, is so far removed from us that we cannot comprehend its having ever existed. It is more easy to understand the recoil which has followed. All the social speculation, and much of the social action of the few years succeeding the Reform Bill bear the most marked traces of the reaction. The spirit which animates Mr. Dickens's political reasonings and observations expresses it exactly. The vice of the then existing social authorities and of the then existing public had been the forgetfulness of the pain which their own acts evidently produced,—an unrealising

habit which adhered to official rules and established maxims, and which would not be shocked by the evident consequences, by proximate human suffering. The sure result of this habit was the excitement of the habit precisely opposed to it. Mr. Carlyle, in his *Chartism*, we think, observes of the poor-law reform: 'It was then, above all things, necessary that outdoor relief should cease. But how? What means did great Nature take for accomplishing that most desirable end? She created a race of men who believed the cessation of outdoor relief to be the one thing needful.' In the same way, and by the same propensity to exaggerated opposition which is inherent in human nature, the unfeeling obtuseness of the early part of this century was to be corrected by an extreme, perhaps an excessive, sensibility to human suffering in the years which have followed. There was most adequate reason for the sentiment in its origin, and it had a great task to perform in ameliorating harsh customs and repealing dreadful penalties; but it has continued to repine at such evils long after they ceased to exist, and when the only facts that at all resemble them are the necessary painfulness of due punishment and the necessary rigidity of established law.

Mr. Dickens is an example both of the proper use and of the abuse of the sentiment. His earlier works have many excellent descriptions of the abuses which had descended to the present generation from others whose sympathy with pain was less tender. Nothing can be better than the description of the poor debtor's gaol in *Pickwick*, or of the old parochial authorities in *Oliver Twist*. No doubt these descriptions are caricatures, all his delineations are so; but the beneficial use of such art can hardly be better exemplified. Human nature endures the aggravation of vices and foibles in written description better than that of excellencies. We cannot bear to hear even the hero of a book for ever called 'just;' we detest the recurring praise even of beauty, much more of virtue. The moment you begin to exaggerate a character of true excellence, you spoil it; the traits are too delicate not to be injured by heightening or marred by over-emphasis. But a beadle is made for caricature. The slight measure of pomposity that humanises his unfeelingness introduces the requisite comic element; even the turnkeys of a debtors' prison may by skilful hands be similarly used. The contrast between the destitute condition of Job Trotter and Mr. Jingle and their former swindling triumph, is made comic by a rarer touch of unconscious art. Mr. Pickwick's warm heart takes so eager an interest in the misery of his old enemies, that our colder nature is tempted to smile. We endure the over-intensity, at any rate the unnecessary aggravation, of the surrounding misery; and we endure it willingly, because it brings out better than anything else could have done the half-comic intensity of a sympathetic nature.

It is painful to pass from these happy instances of well-used power to the glaring abuses of the same faculty in Mr. Dickens's later books. He began by describing really removable evils in a style which would induce all persons, however insensible, to remove them if they could; he has ended by describing the natural evils and inevitable pains of the present state of being in such a manner as must tend to excite discontent and repining. The result is aggravated, because Mr. Dickens never ceases to hint that these evils are removable, though he does not say by what means. Nothing is easier than to show the evils of anything. Mr. Dickens has not unfrequently spoken, and what is worse, he has taught a great number of parrot-like imitators to speak, in what really is, if they knew it, a tone of objection to the necessary constitution of human society. If you will only write a description of it, any form of government will seem ridiculous. What is more absurd than a despotism, even at its best? A king of ability or an able minister sits in an orderly room filled with memorials, and returns, and documents, and memoranda. These are his world; among these he of necessity lives and moves. Yet how little of the real life of the nation he governs can be represented in an official form! How much of real suffering is there that statistics can never tell! how much of obvious good is there that no memorandum to a minister will ever mention! how much deception is there in what such documents contain! how monstrous must be the ignorance of the closet statesman, after all his life of labour, of much that a ploughman could tell him of! A free government is almost worse, as it must read in a written delineation. Instead of the real attention of a laborious and anxious statesman, we have now the shifting caprices of a popular assembly—elected for one object, deciding on another; changing with the turn of debate; shifting in its very composition; one set of men coming down to vote to-day, to-morrow another and often unlike set, most of them eager for the dinner-hour, actuated by unseen influences,—by a respect for their constituents, by the dread of an attorney in a far-off borough. What people are these to control a nation's destinies, and wield the power of an empire, and regulate the happiness of millions! Either way we are at fault. Free government seems an absurdity, and despotism is so too. Again, every form of law has a distinct expression, a rigid procedure, customary rules and forms. It is administered by human beings liable to mistake, confusion, and forgetfulness, and in the long run, and on the average, is sure to be tainted with vice and fraud. Nothing can be easier than to make a case, as we may say, against any particular system, by pointing out with emphatic caricature its inevitable miscarriages, and by pointing out nothing else. Those who so address us may assume a tone of philanthropy, and for ever exult that they are not so unfeeling as other men are; but the real tendency of their exhortations is to make men dissatisfied with their inevitable condition, and what is worse, to make them fancy that its irremediable evils can be remedied, and indulge in a succession of vague strivings and restless changes. Such, however,—though in a style of expression somewhat different,—is very much the tone with which Mr. Dickens and his followers have in later years made us familiar. To the second-hand repeaters of a cry so feeble, we can have nothing to say; if silly people cry because they think the world is silly, let them cry; but the founder of the school cannot, we are persuaded, peruse without mirth the lachrymose eloquence which his disciples have perpetrated. The soft moisture of irrelevant sentiment cannot have entirely entered into his soul. A truthful genius must have forbidden it. Let us hope that this pernicious example may incite someone of equal genius to preach with equal efficiency a sterner and a wiser gospel; but there is no need just now for us to preach it without genius.

There has been much controversy about Mr. Dickens's taste. A great many cultivated people will scarcely concede that he has any taste at all; a still larger number of fervent admirers point, on the other hand, to a hundred felicitous descriptions and delineations which abound in apt expressions and skilful turns and happy images,—in which it would be impossible to alter a single word without altering for the worse; and naturally inquire whether such excellences in what is written do not indicate good taste in the writer. The truth is that Mr. Dickens has what we may call creative taste; that is to say, the habit or faculty, whichever we may choose to call it, which at the critical instant of artistic production offers to the mind the right word, and the right word only. If he is engaged on a good subject for caricature, there will be no defect of taste

to preclude the caricature from being excellent. But it is only in moments of imaginative production that he has any taste at all. His works nowhere indicate that he possesses in any degree the passive taste which decides what is good in the writings of other people and what is not, and which performs the same critical duty upon a writer's own efforts when the confusing mists of productive imagination have passed away. Nor has Mr. Dickens the gentlemanly instinct which in many minds supplies the place of purely critical discernment, and which, by constant association with those who know what is best, acquires a second-hand perception of that which is best. He has no tendency to conventionalism for good or for evil; his merits are far removed from the ordinary path of writers, and it was not probably so much effort to him as to other men to step so far out of that path: he scarcely knew how far it was. For the same reason he cannot tell how faulty his writing will often be thought, for he cannot tell what people will think.

A few pedantic critics have regretted that Mr. Dickens had not received what they call a regular education. And if we understand their meaning, we believe they mean to regret that he had not received a course of discipline which would probably have impaired his powers. A regular education should mean that ordinary system of regulation and instruction which experience has shown to fit men best for the ordinary pursuits of life. It applies the requisite discipline to each faculty in the exact proportion in which that faculty is wanted in the pursuits of life; it develops understanding, and memory, and imagination, each in accordance with the scale prescribed. To men of ordinary faculties this is nearly essential; it is the only mode in which they can be fitted for the inevitable competition of existence. To men of regular and symmetrical genius also, such a training will often be beneficial. The world knows pretty well what are the great tasks of the human mind, and has learnt in the course of ages with some accuracy what is the kind of culture likely to promote their exact performance. A man of abilities, extraordinary in degree but harmonious in proportion, will be the better for having submitted to the kind of discipline which has been ascertained to fit a man for the work to which powers in that proportion are best fitted; he will do what he has to do better and more gracefully; culture will add a touch to the finish of nature. But the case is very different with men of irregular and anomalous genius, whose excellences consist in the *aggravation* of some special faculty, or at the most of one or two. The discipline which will fit him for the production of great literary works is that which will most develop the peculiar powers in which he excels; the rest of the mind will be far less important; it will not be likely that the culture which is adapted to promote this special development will also be that which is most fitted for expanding the powers of common men in common directions. The precise problem is to develop the powers of a strange man in a strange direction. In the case of Mr. Dickens, it would have been absurd to have shut up his observant youth within the walls of a college. They would have taught him nothing about Mrs. Gamp there; Sam Weller took no degree. The kind of early life fitted to develop the power of apprehensive observation is a brooding life in stirring scenes; the idler in the streets of life knows the streets; the bystander knows the picturesque effect of life better than the player; and the meditative idler amid the hum of existence is much more likely to know its sound and to take in and comprehend its depths and meanings than the scholastic student intent on books, which if they represent any world, represent one which has long passed away, which commonly try rather to develop the reasoning understanding than the seeing observation, which are written in languages that have long been dead. You will not train by such discipline a cari-caturist of obvious manners.

Perhaps, too, a regular instruction and daily experience of the searching ridicule of critical associates would have de-tracted from the *pluck* which Mr. Dickens shows in all his writings. It requires a great deal of courage to be a humorous writer; you are always afraid that people will laugh at you instead of with you: undoubtedly there is a certain eccentricity about it. You take up the esteemed writers, Thucydides and the *Saturday Review*; after all, they do not make you laugh. It is not the function of really artistic productions to contribute to the mirth of human beings. All sensible men are afraid of it, and it is only with an extreme effort that a printed joke attains to the perusal of the public: the chances are many to one that the anxious producer loses heart in the correction of the press, and that the world never laughs at all. Mr. Dickens is quite exempt from this weakness. He has what a Frenchman might call the courage of his faculty. The real daring which is shown in the *Pickwick Papers*, in the whole character of Mr. Weller senior, as well as in that of his son, is immense, far surpassing any which has been shown by any other contemporary writer. The brooding irregular mind is in its first stage prone to this sort of courage. It perhaps knows that its ideas are 'out of the way;' but with the infantine simplicity of youth it supposes that originality is an advantage. Persons more familiar with the ridicule of their equals in station (and this is to most men the great instructress of the college time) well know that of all qualities this one most requires to be clipped and pared and measured. Posterity, we doubt not, will be entirely perfect in every conceivable element of judgment; but the existing generation like what they have heard before—it is much easier. It required great courage in Mr. Dickens to write what his genius has compelled them to appreciate.

We have throughout spoken of Mr. Dickens as he was, rather than as he is; or, to use a less discourteous phrase, and we hope a truer, of his early works rather than of those which are more recent. We could not do otherwise consistently with the true code of criticism. A man of great genius, who has written great and enduring works, must be judged mainly by them; and not by the inferior productions which, from the necessities of personal position, a fatal facility of composition, or other cause, he may pour forth at moments less favourable to his powers. Those who are called on to review these inferior productions themselves, must speak of them in the terms they may deserve; but those who have the more pleasant task of estimating as a whole the genius of the writer, may confine their attention almost wholly to those happier efforts which illustrate that genius. We should not like to have to speak in detail of Mr. Dickens's later works, and we have not done so. There are, indeed, peculiar reasons why a genius constituted as his is (at least if we are correct in the view which we have taken of it) would not endure without injury during a long life the applause of the many, the temptations of composition, and the general excitement of existence. Even in his earlier works it was impossible not to fancy that there was a weakness of fibre unfavourable to the longevity of excellence. This was the effect of his deficiency in those masculine faculties of which we have said so much,—the reasoning understanding and firm far-seeing sagacity. It is these two component elements which stiffen the mind, and give a consistency to the creed and a coherence to its effects,—which enable it to protect itself from the rush of circumstances. If to a deficiency in these we add an extreme sensibility to circumstances,—a mobility, as Lord Byron used to call it, of emotion, which is easily impressed, and still more easily carried away by impression,—we have the

idea of a character peculiarly unfitted to bear the flux of time and chance. A man of very great determination could hardly bear up against them with such slight aids from within and with such peculiar sensibility to temptation. A man of merely ordinary determination would succumb to it; and Mr. Dickens has succumbed. His position was certainly unfavourable. He has told us that the works of his later years, inferior as all good critics have deemed them, have yet been more read than those of his earlier and healthier years. The most characteristic part of his audience, the lower middle-class, were ready to receive with delight the least favourable productions of his genius. Human nature cannot endure this; it is too much to have to endure a coincident temptation both from within and from without. Mr. Dickens was too much inclined by natural disposition to lachrymose eloquence and exaggerated carica-ture. Such was the kind of writing which he wrote most easily. He found likewise that such was the kind of writing that was read most readily; and of course he wrote that kind. Who would have done otherwise? No critic is entitled to speak very harshly of such degeneracy, if he is not sure that he could have coped with difficulties so peculiar. If that rule is to be observed, who is there that will not be silent? No other Englishman has attained such a hold on the vast populace; it is little, therefore, to say that no other has surmounted its attendant temptations.

GEORGE HENRY LEWES
From "Dickens in Relation to Criticism"
Fortnightly Review, February 1872, pp. 143–49

There probably never was a writer of so vast a popularity whose genius was so little *appreciated* by the critics. The very splendour of his successes so deepened the shadow of his failures that to many eyes the shadows supplanted the splen-dour. Fastidious readers were loath to admit that a writer could be justly called great whose defects were so glaring. They admitted, because it was indisputable, that Dickens delighted thousands, that his admirers were found in all classes, and in all countries; that he stirred the sympathy of masses not easily reached through Literature, and always stirred healthy, gener-ous emotions; that he impressed a new direction on popular writing, and modified the Literature of his age, in its spirit no less than in its form; but they nevertheless insisted on his defects as if these outweighed all positive qualities; and spoke of him either with condescending patronage, or with sneering irritation. Surely this is a fact worthy of investigation? Were the critics wrong, and if so, in what consisted their error? How are we to reconcile this immense popularity with this critical contempt? The private readers and the public critics who were eager to take up each successive number of his works as it appeared, whose very talk was seasoned with quotations from and allusions to these works, who, to my knowledge, were wont to lay aside books of which they could only speak in terms of eulogy, in order to bury themselves in the "new number" when the well-known green cover made its appearance—were nev-ertheless at this very time niggard in their praise, and lavish in their scorn of the popular humorist. It is not long since I heard a very distinguished man express measureless contempt for Dickens, and a few minutes afterwards, in reply to some representations on the other side, admit that Dickens had "entered into his life."

Dickens has proved his power by a popularity almost unexampled, embracing all classes. Surely it is a task for criticism to exhibit the sources of that power? If everything that has ever been alleged against the works be admitted, there still remains an immense success to be accounted for. It was not by their defects that these works were carried over Europe and America. It was not their defects which made them the delight of grey heads on the bench, and the study of youngsters in the counting-house and school-room. Other writers have been exaggerated, untrue, fantastic, and melodramatic; but they have gained so little notice that no one thinks of pointing out their defects. It is clear, therefore, that Dickens had powers which enabled him to triumph in spite of the weaknesses which clogged them; and it is worth inquiring what those powers were, and their relation to his undeniable defects.

I am not about to attempt such an inquiry, but simply to indicate two or three general points of view. It will be enough merely to mention in passing the primary cause of his success, his overflowing fun, because even uncompromising opponents admit it. They may be ashamed of their laughter, but they laugh. A revulsion of feeling at the preposterousness or extravagance of the image may follow the burst of laughter, but the laughter is irresistible, whether rational or not, and there is no arguing away such a fact.

Great as Dickens is in fun, so great that Fielding and Smollett are small in comparison, he would have been only a passing amusement for the world had he not been gifted with an imagination of marvellous vividness, and an emotional, sympathetic nature capable of furnishing that imagination with elements of universal power. Of him it may be said with less exaggeration than of most poets, that he was of "imagination all compact;" if the other higher faculties were singularly deficient in him, this faculty was imperial. He was a seer of visions; and his visions were of objects at once familiar and potent. Psychologists will understand both the extent and the limitation of the remark, when I say that in no other perfectly sane mind (Blake, I believe, was not perfectly sane) have I observed vividness of imagination approaching so closely to hallucination. Many who are not psychologists may have had some experience in themselves, or in others, of that abnormal condition in which a man hears voices, and sees objects, with the distinctness of direct perception, although silence and darkness are without him; these *revived* impressions, revived by an internal cause, have precisely the same force and clearness which the impressions originally had when produced by an external cause. In the same degree of vividness are the images *constructed* by his mind in explanation of the voices heard or objects seen: when he imagines that the voice proceeds from a personal friend, or from Satan tempting him, the friend or Satan stands before him with the distinctness of objective reality; when he imagines that he himself has been transformed into a bear, his hands are seen by him as paws. In vain you represent to him that the voices he hears have no external existence; he will answer, as a patient pertinently answered Lélut: "You believe that I am speaking to you because you hear me, is it not so? Very well, I believe that voices are speaking to me because I hear them." There is no power of effacing such conviction by argument. You may get the patient to assent to any premises you please, he will not swerve from his conclusions. I once argued with a patient who believed he had been transformed into a bear; he was quite willing to admit that the idea of such a transformation was utterly at variance with all experience; but he always returned to his position that God being omnipotent there was no reason to doubt his power of transforming men into bears: what remained fixed in his mind was the image of himself under a bear's form.

The characteristic point in the hallucinations of the insane, that which distinguishes them from hallucinations equally vivid in the sane, is the coercion of the image in *suppressing comparison* and all control of experience. Belief always accompanies a vivid image, for a time; but in the sane this belief will not persist against rational control. If I see a stick partly under water, it is impossible for me not to have the same feeling which would be produced by a bent stick out of the water—if I see two plane images in the stereoscope, it is impossible not to have the feeling of seeing one solid object. But these beliefs are rapidly displaced by reference to experience. I know the stick is not bent, and that it will not appear bent when removed from the water. I know the seeming solid is not an object in relief, but two plane pictures. It is by similar focal adjustment of the mind that sane people know that their hallucinations are unreal. The images may have the vividness of real objects, but they have not the properties of real objects, they do not preserve consistent relations with other facts, they appear in contradiction to other beliefs. Thus if I see a black cat on the chair opposite, yet on my approaching the chair feel no soft object, and if my terrier on the hearthrug looking in the direction of the chair shows none of the well-known agitation which the sight of a cat produces, I conclude, in spite of its distinctness, that the image is an hallucination.

Returning from this digression, let me say that I am very far indeed from wishing to imply any agreement in the common notion that "great wits to madness nearly are allied;" on the contrary, my studies have led to the conviction that nothing is less like genius than insanity, although some men of genius have had occasional attacks; and further, that I have never observed any trace of the insane temperament in Dickens's works, or life, they being indeed singularly free even from the eccentricities which often accompany exceptional powers; nevertheless, with all due limitations, it is true that there is considerable light shed upon his works by the action of the imagination in hallucination. To him also *revived* images have the vividness of sensations; to him also *created* images have the coercive force of realities, excluding all control, all contradiction. What seems preposterous, impossible to us, seemed to him simple fact of observation. When he imagined a street, a house, a room, a figure, he saw it not in the vague schematic way of ordinary imagination, but in the sharp definition of actual perception, all the salient details obtruding themselves on his attention. He, seeing it thus vividly, made us also see it; and believing in its reality however fantastic, he communicated something of his belief to us. He presented it in such relief that we ceased to think of it as a picture. So definite and insistent was the image, that even while knowing it was false we could not help, for a moment, being affected, as it were, by his hallucination.

This glorious energy of imagination is that which Dickens had in common with all great writers. It was this which made him a creator, and made his creations universally intelligible, no matter how fantastic and unreal. His types established themselves in the public mind like personal experiences. Their falsity was unnoticed in the blaze of their illumination. Every humbug seemed a Pecksniff, every nurse a Gamp, every jovial improvident a Micawber, every stinted serving-wench a Marchioness. Universal experiences became individualised in these types; an image and a name were given, and the image was so suggestive that it seemed to *express* all that it was found to *recall*, and Dickens was held to have depicted what his readers supplied. Against such power criticism was almost idle. In vain critical reflection showed these figures to be merely masks,— not characters, but personified characteristics, caricatures and distortions of human nature,—the vividness of their presentation triumphed over reflection: their creator managed to communicate to the public his own unhesitating belief. Unreal and impossible as these types were, speaking a language never heard in life, moving like pieces of simple mechanism always in one way (instead of moving with the infinite fluctuations of organisms, incalculable yet intelligible, surprising yet familiar), these unreal figures affected the uncritical reader with the force of reality; and they did so in virtue of their embodiment of some real characteristic vividly presented. The imagination of the author laid hold of some well-marked physical trait, some peculiarity of aspect, speech, or manner which every one recognised at once; and the force with which this was presented made it occupy the mind to the exclusion of all critical doubts: only reflection could detect the incongruity. Think of what this implies! Think how little the mass of men are given to reflect on their impressions, and how their minds are for the most part occupied with sensations rather than ideas, and you will see why Dickens held an undisputed sway. Give a child a wooden horse, with hair for mane and tail, and wafer spots for colouring, he will never be disturbed by the fact that this horse does not move its legs, but runs on wheels—the general suggestion suffices for his belief; and this wooden horse, which he can handle and draw, is believed in more than a pictured horse by a Wouvermanns or an Ansdell. It may be said of Dickens's human figures that they too are wooden, and run on wheels; but these are details which scarcely disturb the belief of admirers. Just as the wooden horse is brought within the range of the child's emotions, and dramatizing tendencies, when he can handle and draw it, so Dickens's figures are brought within the range of the reader's interests, and receive from these interests a sudden illumination, when they are the puppets of a drama every incident of which appeals to the sympathies. With a fine felicity of instinct he seized upon situations having an irresistible hold over the domestic affections and ordinary sympathies. He spoke in the mother-tongue of the heart, and was always sure of ready listeners. He painted the life he knew, the life every one knew; for if the scenes and manners were unlike those we were familiar with, the feelings and motives, the joys and griefs, the mistakes and efforts of the actors were universal, and therefore universally intelligible; so that even critical spectators who complained that these broadly painted pictures were artistic daubs, could not wholly resist their effective suggestiveness. He set in motion the secret springs of sympathy by touching the domestic affections. He painted nothing ideal, heroic; but all the resources of the bourgeois epic were in his grasp. The world of thought and passion lay beyond his horizon. But the joys and pains of childhood, the petty tyrannies of ignoble natures, the genial pleasantries of happy natures, the life of the poor, the struggles of the street and back parlour, the insolence of office, the sharp social contrasts, east-wind and Christmas jollity, hunger, misery, and hot punch—these he could deal with, so that we laughed and cried, were startled at the revelation of familiar facts hitherto unnoted, and felt our pulses quicken as we were hurried along with him in his fanciful flight.

Such were the sources of his power. To understand how it is that critics quite competent to recognise such power, and even so far amenable to it as to be moved and interested by the works in spite of all their drawbacks, should have forgotten this undenied power, and written or spoken of Dickens with mingled irritation and contempt, we must take into account two natural tendencies—the bias of opposition, and the bias of technical estimate.

The bias of opposition may be illustrated in a parallel case. Let us suppose a scientific book to be attracting the attention of Europe by the boldness, suggestiveness, and theoretic plausibility of its hypotheses; this work falls into the hands of a critic sufficiently grounded in the science treated to be aware that its writer, although gifted with great theoretic power and occasional insight into unexplored relations, is nevertheless pitiably ignorant of the elementary facts and principles of the science; the critic noticing the power, and the talent of lucid exposition, is yet perplexed and irritated at ignorance which is inexcusable, and a reckless twisting of known facts into impossible relations, which seems wilful; will he not pass from marvelling at this inextricable web of sense and nonsense, suggestive insight and mischievous error, so jumbled together that the combination of this sagacity with this glaring inefficiency is a paradox, and be driven by the anger of opposition into an emphatic assertion that the belauded philosopher is a charlatan and an ignoramus? A chorus of admirers proclaims the author to be a great teacher, before whom all contemporaries must bow; and the critic observes this teacher on one page throwing out a striking hypothesis of some geometric relations in the planetary movements, and on another assuming that the hypothenuse is equal to its perpendicular and base, because the square of the hypothenuse is equal to the squares of its sides—in one chapter ridiculing the atomic theory, and in another arguing that carbonic acid is obtained from carbon and nitrogen—can this critic be expected to join in the chorus of admirers? and will he not rather be exasperated into an opposition which will lead him to undervalue the undeniable qualities in his insistence on the undeniable defects?

Something like this is the feeling produced by Dickens's works in many cultivated and critical readers. They see there human character and ordinary events pourtrayed with a mingled verisimilitude and falsity altogether unexampled. The drawing is so vivid yet so incorrect, or else is so blurred and formless, with such excess of *effort* (as of a showman beating on the drum) that the doubt arises how an observer so remarkably keen could make observations so remarkably false, and miss such very obvious facts; how the rapid glance which could swoop down on a peculiarity with hawk-like precision, could overlook all that accompanied and was organically related to that peculiarity; how the eye for characteristics could be so blind to character, and the ear for dramatic idiom be so deaf to dramatic language; finally, how the writer's exquisite susceptibility to the grotesque could be insensible to the occasional grotesqueness of his own attitude. Michael Angelo is intelligible, and Giotto is intelligible; but a critic is nonplussed at finding the invention of Angelo with the drawing of Giotto. It is indeed surprising that Dickens should have observed man, and not been impressed with the fact that man is, in the words of Montaigne, *un être ondoyant et diverse*. And the critic is distressed to observe the substitution of mechanisms for minds, puppets for characters. It is needless to dwell on such monstrous failures as Mantalini, Rosa Dartle, Lady Dedlock, Esther Summerson, Mr. Dick, Arthur Gride, Edith Dombey, Mr. Carker—needless, because if one studies the successful figures one finds even in them only touches of verisimilitude. When one thinks of Micawber always presenting himself in the same situation, moved with the same springs, and uttering the same sounds, always confident on something turning up, always crushed and rebounding, always making punch—and his wife always declaring she will never part from him, always referring to his talents and her family—when one thinks of the "catchwords" personified as characters, one is reminded of the frogs whose brains have been taken out for physiological purposes, and whose actions henceforth want the distinctive peculiarity of organic action, that of fluctuating spontaneity.

Place one of these brainless frogs on his back and he will at once recover the sitting posture; draw a leg from under him, and he will draw it back again; tickle or prick him and he will push away the object, or take *one* hop out of the way; stroke his back, and he will utter *one* croak. All these things resemble the actions of the unmutilated frog, but they differ in being *isolated* actions, and *always the same*: they are as uniform and calculable as the movements of a machine. The uninjured frog may or may not croak, may or may not hop away; the result is never calculable, and is rarely a single croak or a single hop. It is this complexity of the organism which Dickens wholly fails to conceive; his characters have nothing fluctuating and incalculable in them, even when they embody true observations; and very often they are creations so fantastic that one is at a loss to understand how he could, without hallucination, believe them to be like reality. There are dialogues bearing the traces of straining effort at effect, which in their incongruity painfully resemble the absurd and eager expositions which insane patients pour into the listener's ear when detailing their wrongs, or their schemes. Dickens once declared to me that every word said by his characters was distinctly *heard* by him; I was at first not a little puzzled to account for the fact that he could hear language so utterly unlike the language of real feeling, and not be aware of its preposterousness; but the surprise vanished when I thought of the phenomena of hallucination. And here it may be needful to remark in passing that it is not because the characters are badly drawn and their language unreal, that they are to be classed among the excesses of imagination; otherwise all the bad novelists and dramatists would be credited with that which they especially want— powerful imagination. His peculiarity is not the incorrectness of the drawing, but the vividness of the imagination which while rendering that incorrectness insensible to him, also renders it potent with multitudes of his fellowmen. For although his weakness comes from excess in one direction, the force which is in excess must not be overlooked; and it is overlooked or undervalued by critics who, with what I have called the bias of opposition, insist only on the weakness.

ALGERNON CHARLES SWINBURNE
From "Charles Dickens"
Quarterly Review, July 1902, pp. 20–32

It is only when such names as Shakespeare's or Hugo's rise and remain as the supreme witnesses of what was highest in any particular country at any particular time that there can be no question among any but irrational and impudent men as to the supremacy of their greatest. England, under the reign of Dickens, had other great names to boast of which may well be allowed to challenge the sovereignty of his genius. But as there certainly was no Shakespeare and no Hugo to rival and eclipse his glory, he will probably and naturally always be accepted and acclaimed as the greatest Englishman of his generation. His first works or attempts at work gave little more promise of such a future than if he had been a Coleridge or a Shelley. No one could have foreseen what all may now foresee in the *Sketches by Boz*—not only a quick and keen-eyed observer, 'a chiel amang us takin' notes' more notable than Captain Grose's, but a great creative genius. Nor could any one have foreseen it in the early chapters of *Pickwick*—which, at their best, do better the sort of thing which had been done fairly well before. Sam Weller and Charles Dickens came to life together, immortal and twin-born. In *Oliver Twist* the quality of a great

tragic and comic poet or dramatist in prose fiction was for the first time combined with the already famous qualities of a great humorist and a born master in the arts of narrative and dialogue.

Like the early works of all other great writers whose critical contemporaries have failed to elude the kindly chance of beneficent oblivion, the early works of Dickens have been made use of to depreciate his later, with the same enlightened and impartial candour which on the appearance of *Othello* must doubtless have deplored the steady though gradual decline of its author's genius from the unfulfilled promise of excellence held forth by *Two Gentlemen of Verona*. There may possibly be some faint and flickering shadow of excuse for the dullards, if unmalignant, who prefer *Nicholas Nickleby* to the riper and sounder fruits of the same splendid and inexhaustible genius. Admirable as it is, full of life and sap and savour, the strength and the weakness of youth are so singularly mingled in the story and the style that readers who knew nothing of its date might naturally have assumed that it must have been the writer's first attempt at fiction. There is perhaps no question which would more thoroughly test the scholarship of the student than this:—What do you know of Jane Dibabs and Horatio Peltiogrus? At fourscore and ten it might be thought 'too late a week' for a reader to revel with insuppressible delight in a first reading of the chapters which enrol all worthy readers in the company of Mr Vincent Crummles; but I can bear witness to the fact that this effect was produced on a reader of that age who had earned honour and respect in public life, affection and veneration in private. It is not, on the other hand, less curious and significant that Sydney Smith, who had held out against Sam Weller, should have been conquered by Miss Squeers; that her letter, which of all Dickens's really good things is perhaps the most obviously imitative and suggestive of its model, should have converted so great an elder humorist to appreciation of a greater than himself; that the echo of familiar fun, an echo from the grave of Smollett, should have done what finer and more original strokes of comic genius had unaccountably failed to do. But in all criticism of such work the merely personal element of the critic, the natural atmosphere in which his mind or his insight works, and uses its faculties of appreciation, is really the first and last thing to be taken into account.

No mortal man or woman, no human boy or girl, can resist the fascination of Mr and Mrs Quilp, of Mr and Miss Brass, of Mr Swiveller and his Marchioness; but even the charm of Mrs Jarley and her surroundings, the magic which enthrals us in the presence of a Codlin and a Short, cannot mesmerise or hypnotise us into belief that the story of *The Old Curiosity Shop* is in any way a good story. But it is the first book in which the background or setting is often as impressive as the figures which can hardly be detached from it in our remembered impression of the whole design. From Quilp's Wharf to Plashwater Weir Mill Lock, the river belongs to Dickens by right of conquest or creation. The part it plays in more than a few of his books is indivisible from the parts played in them by human actors beside it or upon it. Of such actors in this book, the most famous as an example of her creator's power as a master of pathetic tragedy would thoroughly deserve her fame if she were but a thought more human and more credible. 'The child' has never a touch of childhood about her; she is an impeccable and invariable portent of devotion, without a moment's lapse into the humanity of frailty in temper or in conduct. Dickens might as well have fitted her with a pair of wings at once. A woman might possibly be as patient, as resourceful, as indefatigable in well-doing and as faultless in perception of the right thing to do; it would be difficult to make her deeply interesting, but she might be made more or less of an actual creature. But a child whom nothing can ever irritate, whom nothing can ever baffle, whom nothing can ever misguide, whom nothing can ever delude, and whom nothing can ever dismay, is a monster as inhuman as a baby with two heads.

Outside the class which excludes all but the highest masterpieces of poetry it is difficult to find or to imagine a faultless work of creation—in other words, a faultless work of fiction; but the story of *Barnaby Rudge* can hardly, in common justice, be said to fall short of this crowning praise. And in this book, even if not in any of its precursors, an appreciative reader must recognise a quality of humour which will remind him of Shakespeare, and perhaps of Aristophanes. The impetuous and irrepressible volubility of Miss Miggs, when once her eloquence breaks loose and finds vent like raging water or fire, is powerful enough to overbear for the moment any slight objection which a severe morality might suggest with respect to the rectitude and propriety of her conduct. It is impossible to be rigid in our judgment of

> a toiling, moiling, constant-working, always-being-found-fault-with, never-giving-satisfactions, nor-hav-ing-no-time-to-clean-oneself, potter's wessel,' whose 'only becoming occupations is to help young flaunting pagins to brush and comb and titiwate theirselves into whitening and suppulchres, and leave the young men to think that there an't a bit of padding in it nor no pinching-ins nor fillings-out nor pomatums nor de-ceits nor earthly wanities.

To have made malignity as delightful for an instant as simplicity, and Miss Miggs as enchanting as Mrs Quickly or Mrs Gamp, is an unsurpassable triumph of dramatic humour.

But the advance in tragic power is even more notable and memorable than this. The pathos, indeed, is too cruel; the tortures of the idiot's mother and the murderer's wife are so fearful that interest and sympathy are wellnigh superseded or overbalanced by a sense of horror rather than of pity; mag-nificent as is the power of dramatic invention which animates every scene in every stage of her martyrdom. Dennis is the first of those consummate and wonderful ruffians, with two vile faces under one frowsy hood, whose captain or commander-in-chief is Rogue Riderhood; more fearful by far, though not (one would hope) more natural, than Henriet Cousin, who could hardly breathe when fastening the rope round Esme-ralda's neck, 'tant la chose l'apitoyait'; a divine touch of surviving humanity which would have been impossible to the more horrible hangman whose mortal agony in immediate prospect of the imminent gallows is as terribly memorable as anything in the tragedy of fiction or the poetry of prose. His fellow hangbird is a figure no less admirable throughout all his stormy and fiery career till the last moment; and then he drops into poetry. Nor is it poetry above the reach of Silas Wegg which 'invokes the curse of all its victims on that black tree, of which he is the ripened fruit.' The writer's impulse was noble; but its expression or its effusion is such as indifference may deride and sympathy must deplore. Twice only did the greatest English writer of his day make use of history as a background or a stage for fiction; the use made of it in *Barnaby Rudge* is even more admirable in the lifelike tragedy and the terrible comedy of its presentation than the use made of it in *A Tale of Two Cities*.

Dickens was doubtless right in his preference of 'David Copperfield' to all his other masterpieces; it is only among dunces that it is held improbable or impossible for a great writer

to judge aright of his own work at its best, to select and to prefer the finest and the fullest example of his active genius; but, when all deductions have been made from the acknowledg-ment due to the counter-claim of *Martin Chuzzlewit*, the fact remains that in that unequal and irregular masterpiece his comic and his tragic genius rose now and then to the very highest pitch of all. No son of Adam and no daughter of Eve on this God's earth, as his occasional friend Mr Carlyle might have expressed it, could have imagined it possible—humanly possible—for anything in later comedy to rival the unspeakable perfection of Mrs Quickly's eloquence at its best; at such moments as when her claim to be acknowledged as Lady Falstaff was reinforced, if not by the spiritual authority of Master Dumb, by the correlative evidence of Mrs Keech; but no reader above the level of intelligence which prefers to Shakespeare the Parisian Ibsen and the Norwegian Sardou can dispute the fact that Mrs Gamp has once and again risen even to that unimaginable supremacy of triumph.

At the first interview vouchsafed to us with the adorable Sairey, we feel that no words can express our sense of the divinely altruistic and devoted nature which finds utterance in the sweetly and sublimely simple words—'If I could afford to lay all my feller creeturs out for nothink, I would gladly do it: sich is the love I bear 'em.' We think of little Tommy Harris, and the little red worsted shoe gurgling in his throat; of the previous occasion when his father sought shelter and silence in an empty dog-kennel; of that father's immortally infamous reflection on the advent of his ninth; of religious feelings, of life, and the end of all things; of Mr Gamp, his wooden leg, and their precious boy; of her calculations and her experiences with reference to birth and death; of her views as to the expediency of travel by steam, which anticipated Ruskin's and those of later dissenters from the gospel of hurry and the religion of mechanism; of the contents of Mrs Harris's pocket; of the incredible incredulity of the infidel Mrs Prig; we think of all this, and of more than all this, and acknowledge with infinite thanksgiving of inexhaustible laughter and of rapturous admiration the very greatest comic poet or creator that ever lived to make the life of other men more bright and more glad and more perfect than ever, without his beneficent influence, it possibly or imaginably could have been.

The advance in power of tragic invention, the increased strength in grasp of character and grip of situation, which distinguishes Chuzzlewit from Nickleby, may be tested by comparison of the leading villains. Ralph Nickleby might almost have walked straight off the boards on which the dramatic genius of his nephew was employed to bring into action two tubs and a pump: Jonas Chuzzlewit has his place of eminence for ever among the most memorable types of living and breathing wickedness that ever were stamped and branded with immortality by the indignant genius of a great and unrelenting master. Neither Vautrin nor Thénardier has more of evil and of deathless life in him.

It is not only by his masterpieces, it is also by his inferior works or even by his comparative failures that the greatness of a great writer may be reasonably judged and tested. We can measure in some degree the genius of Thackeray by the fact that *Pendennis*, with all its marvellous wealth of character and humour and living truth, has never been and never will be rated among his very greatest works. *Dombey and Son* cannot be held nearly so much of a success as *Pendennis*. I have known a man of the very highest genius and the most fervent enthusiasm for that of Dickens who never could get through it. There is nothing of a story, and all that nothing (to borrow a phrase from Martial) is bad. The Roman starveling had nothing to lose, and lost it all: the story of Dombey has no plot, and that a very stupid one. The struttingly offensive father and his gushingly submissive daughter are failures of the first magnitude. Little Paul is a more credible child than little Nell; he sometimes forgets that he is foredoomed by a more than Pauline or Calvinistic law of predestination to die in the odour of sentiment, and says or thinks or does something really and quaintly childlike. But we get, to say the least, a good deal of him; and how much too little do we get of Jack Bunsby! Not so very much more than of old Bill Barley; and yet those two ancient mariners are berthed for ever in the inmost shrine of our affections. Another patch of the very brightest purple sewn into the sometimes rather threadbare stuff or groundwork of the story is the scene in which the dissolution of a ruined household is so tragicomically set before us in the breaking up of the servants' hall. And when we think upon the cherished names of Toots and Nipper, Gills and Cuttle, Rob the Grinder and good Mrs Brown, we are tempted to throw conscience to the winds, and affirm that the book is a good book.

But even if we admit that here was an interlude of comparative failure, we cannot but feel moved to acclaim with all the more ardent gratitude the appearance of the next and perhaps the greatest gift bestowed on us by this magnificent and immortal benefactor. *David Copperfield*, from the first chapter to the last, is unmistakable by any eye above the level and beyond the insight of a beetle's as one of the masterpieces to which time can only add a new charm and an unimaginable value. The narrative is as coherent and harmonious as that of *Tom Jones*; and to say this is to try it by the very highest and apparently the most unattainable standard. But I must venture to reaffirm my conviction that even the glorious masterpiece of Fielding's radiant and beneficent genius, if in some points superior, is by no means superior in all. Tom is a far completer and more living type of gallant boyhood and generous young manhood than David; but even the lustre of Partridge is pallid and lunar beside the noontide glory of Micawber. Blifil is a more poisonously plausible villain than Uriah: Sophia Western remains unequalled except by her sister heroine Amelia as a perfectly credible and adorable type of young English woman-hood, naturally 'like one of Shakespeare's women,' socially as fine and true a lady as Congreve's Millamant or Angelica. But even so large-minded and liberal a genius as Fielding's could never have conceived any figure like Miss Trotwood's, any group like that of the Peggottys. As easily could it have imagined and realised the magnificent setting of the story, with its homely foreground of street or wayside and its background of tragic sea.

The perfect excellence of this masterpiece has perhaps done some undeserved injury to the less impeccable works of genius which immediately succeeded it. But in *Bleak House* the daring experiment of combination or alternation which divides a story between narrative in the third person and narrative in the first is justified and vindicated by its singular and fascinating success. 'Esther's narrative' is as good as her creator's; and no enthusiasm of praise could overrate the excellence of them both. For wealth and variety of character none of the master's works can be said to surpass and few can be said to equal it. When all necessary allowance has been made for occasional unlikeliness in detail or questionable methods of exposition, the sustained interest and the terrible pathos of Lady Dedlock's tragedy will remain unaffected and unimpaired. Any reader can object that a lady visiting a slum in the disguise of a servant would not have kept jewelled rings on her fingers for the inspection of a crossing-sweeper, or that a less decorous and plausible way of acquainting her with the

fact that a scandalous episode in her early life was no longer a secret for the family lawyer could hardly have been imagined than the public narrative of her story in her own drawing-room by way of an evening's entertainment for her husband and their guests. To these objections, which any Helot of culture whose brain may have been affected by habitual indulgence in the academic delirium of self-complacent superiority may advance or may suggest with the most exquisite infinity of impertinence, it may be impossible to retort an equally obvious and inconsiderable objection.

But to a far more serious charge, which even now appears to survive the confutation of all serious evidence, it is incomprehensible and inexplicable that Dickens should have returned no better an answer than he did. Harold Skimpole was said to be Leigh Hunt; a rascal after the order of Wainewright, without the poisoner's comparatively and diabolically admirable audacity of frank and fiendish self-esteem, was assumed to be meant for a portrait or a caricature of an honest man and a man of unquestionable genius. To this most serious and most disgraceful charge Dickens merely replied that he never anticipated the identification of the rascal Skimpole with the fascinating Harold—the attribution of imaginary villainy to the original model who suggested or supplied a likeness for the externally amiable and ineffectually accomplished lounger and shuffler through life. The simple and final reply should have been that indolence was the essential quality of the character and conduct and philosophy of Skimpole—'a perfectly idle man: a mere amateur,' as he describes himself to the sympathetic and approving Sir Leicester; that Leigh Hunt was one of the hardest and steadiest workers on record, throughout a long and chequered life, at the toilsome trade of letters; and therefore that to represent him as a heartless and shameless idler would have been about as rational an enterprise, as lifelike a design after the life, as it would have been to represent Shelley as a gluttonous and canting hypocrite or Byron as a loyal and unselfish friend. And no one as yet, I believe, has pretended to recognise in Mr Jarndyce a study from Byron, in Mr Chadband a libel on Shelley.

Of the two shorter novels which would suffice to preserve for ever the fame of Dickens, some readers will as probably always prefer *Hard Times* as other will prefer *A Tale of Two Cities*. The later of these is doubtless the most ingeniously and dramatically invented and constructed of all the master's works; the earlier seems to me the greater in moral and pathetic and humorous effect. The martyr workman, beautiful as is the study of his character and terrible as is the record of his tragedy, is almost too spotless a sufferer and a saint; the lifelong lapidation of this unluckier Stephen is somewhat too consistent and insistent and persistent for any record but that of a martyrology; but the obdurate and histrionic affectation which animates the brutality and stimulates the selfishness of Mr Bounderby is only too lamentably truer and nearer to the unlovely side of life. Mr Ruskin—a name never to be mentioned without reverence—thought otherwise; but in knowledge and insight into character and ethics that nobly minded man of genius was no more comparable to Dickens than in sanity of ardour and rationality of aspiration for progressive and practical reform.

As a social satirist Dickens is usually considered to have shown himself at his weakest; the curious and seemingly incorrigible ignorance which imagined that the proper title of Sir John Smith's wife was Lady John Smith, and that the same noble peer could be known to his friends and parasites alternately as Lord Jones and Lord James Jones, may naturally make us regret the absence from their society of our old

Parisian friend Sir Brown, Esquire; but though such singular designations as these were never rectified or removed from the text of 'Nicholas Nickleby,' and though a Lady Kew was as far outside the range of his genius as a Madame Marneffe, his satire of social pretension and pretence was by no means always 'a swordstroke in the water' or a flourish in the air. Mrs Sparsit is as typical and immortal as any figure of Molière's; and the fact that Mr Sparsit was a Powler is one which can never be forgotten.

There is no surer way of testing the greatness of a really great writer than by consideration of his work at its weakest, and comparison of that comparative weakness with the strength of lesser men at their strongest and their best. The romantic and fanciful comedy of *Love's Labour's Lost* is hardly a perceptible jewel in the sovereign crown of Shakespeare; but a single passage in a single scene of it—the last of the fourth act—is more than sufficient to outweigh, to outshine, to eclipse and efface for ever the dramatic lucubrations or prescriptions of Dr Ibsen—Fracastoro of the drama—and his volubly grateful patients. Among the mature works of Dickens and of Thackeray, I suppose most readers would agree in the opinion that the least satisfactory, if considered as representative of the author's incomparable powers, are *Little Dorrit* and *The Virginians*; yet no one above the intellectual level of an Ibsenite or a Zolaist will doubt or will deny that there is enough merit in either of these books for the stable foundation of an enduring fame.

The conception of *Little Dorrit* was far happier and more promising than that of *Dombey and Son*; which indeed is not much to say for it. Mr Dombey is a doll; Mr Dorrit is an everlasting figure of comedy in its most tragic aspect and tragedy in its most comic phase. Little Dorrit herself might be less untruly than unkindly described as Little Nell grown big, or, in Milton's phrase, 'writ large.' But on that very account she is a more credible and therefore a more really and rationally pathetic figure. The incomparable incoherence of the parts which pretend in vain to compose the incomposite story may be gauged by the collapse of some of them and the vehement hurry of cramped and halting invention which huddles up the close of it without an attempt at the rational and natural evolution of others. It is like a child's dissected map with some of the counties or kingdoms missing. Much, though certainly not all, of the humour is of the poorest kind possible to Dickens; and the reiterated repetition of comic catchwords and tragic illustrations of character is such as to affect the nerves no less than the intelligence of the reader with irrepressible irritation. But this, if he be wise, will be got over and kept under by his sense of admiration and of gratitude for the unsurpassable excellence of the finest passages and chapters. The day after the death of Mr Merdle is one of the most memorable dates in all the record of creative history—or, to use one word in place of two, in all the record of fiction. The fusion of humour and horror in the marvellous chapter which describes it is comparable only with the kindred work of such creators as the authors of *Les Misérables* and *King Lear*. And nothing in the work of Balzac is newer and truer and more terrible than the relentless yet not unmerciful evolution of the central figure in the story. The Father of the Marshalsea is so pitiably worthy of pity as well as of scorn that it would have seemed impossible to heighten or to deepen the contempt or the compassion of the reader; but when he falls from adversity to prosperity he succeeds in soaring down and sinking up to a more tragicomic ignominy of more aspiring degradation. And his end is magnificent.

It must always be interesting as well as curious to observe the natural attitude of mind, the inborn instinct of intelligent antipathy or sympathy, discernible or conjecturable in the greatest writer of any nation at any particular date, with regard to the characteristic merits or demerits of foreigners. Dickens was once most unjustly taxed with injustice to the French, by an evidently loyal and cordial French critic, on the ground that the one Frenchman of any mark in all his books was a murderer. The polypseudonymous ruffian who uses and wears out as many stolen names as ever did even the most cowardly and virulent of literary poisoners is doubtless an unlovely figure: but not even Mr Peggotty and his infant niece are painted with more tender and fervent sympathy than the good Corporal and little Bebelle. Hugo could not—even omnipotence has its limits—have given a more perfect and living picture of a hero and a child. I wish I could think he would have given it as the picture of an English hero and an English child. But I do think that Italian readers of *Little Dorrit* ought to appreciate and to enjoy the delightful and admirable personality of Cavalletto. Mr Baptist in Bleeding Heart Yard is as attractively memorable a figure as his excellent friend Signor Panco.

And how much more might be said—would the gods annihilate but time and space for a worthier purpose than that of making two lovers happy—of the splendid successes to be noted in the least successful book or books of this great and inexhaustible writer! And if the figure or development of the story in *Little Dorrit*, the shapeliness in parts or the proportions of the whole, may seem to have suffered from tight-lacing in this part and from padding in that, the harmony and unity of the masterpiece which followed it made ample and magnificent amends. In *A Tale of Two Cities* Dickens, for the second and last time, did history the honour to enrol it in the service of fiction. This faultless work of tragic and creative art has nothing of the rich and various exuberance which makes of *Barnaby Rudge* so marvellous an example of youthful genius in all the glowing growth of its bright and fiery April; but it has the classic and poetic symmetry of perfect execution and of perfect design. One or two of the figures in the story which immediately preceded it are unusually liable to the usually fatuous objection which dullness has not yet grown decently ashamed of bringing against the characters of Dickens: to the charge of exaggeration and unreality in the posture or the mechanism of puppets and of daubs, which found its final and supremely offensive expression in the chattering duncery and the impudent malignity of so consummate and pseudosophical a quack as George Henry Lewes. Not even such a past-master in the noble science of defamation could plausibly have dared to cite in support of his insolent and idiotic impeachment either the leading or the supplementary characters in *A Tale of Two Cities*. The pathetic and heroic figure of Sydney Carton seems rather to have cast into the shade of comparative neglect the no less living and admirable figures among and over which it stands and towers in our memory. Miss Pross and Mr Lorry, Madame Defarge and her husband, are equally and indisputably to be recognised by the sign of eternal life.

Among the highest landmarks of success ever reared for immortality by the triumphant genius of Dickens, the story of *Great Expectations* must for ever stand eminent beside that of *David Copperfield*. These are his great twin masterpieces. Great as they are, there is nothing in them greater than the very best things in some of his other books: there is certainly no person preferable and there is possibly no person comparable to Samuel Weller or to Sarah Gamp. Of the two childish and boyish autobiographers, David is the better little fellow though not the more lifelike little friend; but of all first chapters is there any comparable for impression and for fusion of humour and terror and pity and fancy and truth to that which confronts the child with the convict on the marshes in the twilight? And the story is incomparably the finer story of the two; there can be none superior, if there be any equal to it, in the whole range of English fiction. And except in *Vanity Fair* and *The Newcomes*, if even they may claim exception, there can surely be found no equal or nearly equal number of living and everliving figures. The tragedy and the comedy, the realism and the dreamery of life, are fused or mingled together with little less than Shakesperean strength and skill of hand. To have created Abel Magwitch is to be a god indeed among the creators of deathless men. Pumblechook is actually better and droller and truer to imaginative life than Pecksniff: Joe Gargery is worthy to have been praised and loved at once by Fielding and by Sterne: Mr Jaggers and his clients, Mr Wemmick and his parent and his bride, are such figures as Shakespeare, when dropping out of poetry, might have created, if his lot had been cast in a later century. Can as much be said for the creatures of any other man or god? The ghastly tragedy of Miss Havisham could only have been made at once credible and endurable by Dickens; he alone could have reconciled the strange and sordid horror with the noble and pathetic survival of possible emotion and repentance. And he alone could have eluded condemnation for so gross an oversight as the escape from retribution of so important a criminal as the 'double murderer and monster' whose baffled or inadequate attempts are enough to make Bill Sikes seem comparatively the gentlest and Jonas Chuzzlewit the most amiable of men. I remember no such flaw in any other story I ever read. But in this story it may well have been allowed to pass unrebuked and unobserved; which yet I think it should not.